Good Beer Guide 2006

Edited by

Roger Protz

Glenfiddich Drink Writer of the Year, 1997 and 2004

Deputy Editor

Jill Adam

Assistant Editor

Ione Brown

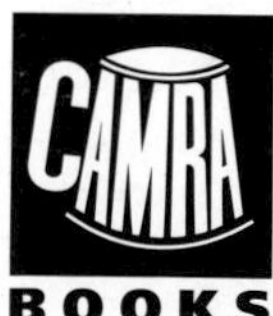

Campaign for Real Ale
230 Hatfield Road, St Albans,
Hertfordshire AL1 4LW

Sponsored by

Contents

CAMRA Books Head of Publications: Joanna Copestick. Emma Lloyd, editorial assistant

Thanks to the following at CAMRA head office: Cressida Feiler, Administration Manager, for research and progress chasing for the Breweries section. Chief Executive Mike Benner. The Campaigns team of Iain Loe, Louise Ashworth, Tony Jerome, Georgina Rudman, Jonathan Mail, and Samantha Jones. The Administration team: John Cottrell, Malcolm Harding, Jean Jones, Gary Fowler, Michael Green, Carwyn Davies, Caroline Clerembeaux, Gillian Dale and Magdalena Madariova. Special thanks to Peter Feiler for crunching the first draft of the Breweries section, and Ted Bruning and Iain Loe for advice on pub companies. Beer Index compiled by Jeff Evans.

Thanks to 77,000 CAMRA members who carried out research for the pubs; Steve Westby for advising on new breweries; Julian Hough and the Campaign's Regional Directors, who co-ordinated the pub entries; Paul Moorhouse for assembling the brewery tasting notes; and CAMRA's National Executive for their support and enthusiasm.

The Good Beer Guide production team: Designed by Rob Howells of Howells Design, London W13. Typeset by Ken Millie, T&O Graphics, Bungay, Suffolk. Maps by David and Morag Perrott, PerroCarto, Machynlleth, Montgomeryshire, Wales. Printed by William Clowes of Beccles, Suffolk.

Front cover photographs: Anne Rippy/Getty Images (above), David Lyons/Alamy (below), Jon Bower/Alamy (spine)

Published by the Campaign for Real Ale Ltd, 230 Hatfield Road, St Albans, Herts, AL1 4LW. Tel 01727 867201. Fax 01727 867670.

Email camra@camra.org.uk Website www.camra.org.uk ISBN 1-85249-211-2

Crisis? What crisis?

A spate of new micros and booming regional brewers prove there is no slump in sales of cask beer. The 'real ale revolution' goes on

THE STAR OF THE 2006 GOOD BEER GUIDE IS THE SIMPLE ASTERISK. More than 80 new breweries carry the * symbol, indicating they have come on stream since the last edition. That figure is almost twice as many new breweries as were listed in the 2005 Guide.

Since 2000, most editions of the Guide have listed some 20 new breweries but with almost as many falling by the wayside. The dramatic increase in the number of new producers in the past two years along with the stability of the independent sector have been fuelled in part by the government's introduction of Progressive Beer Duty (PBD). This enables micros and small regional breweries that produce up to 30,000 barrels of beer a year to pay less duty. PBD has been a considerable boon for the independents, encouraging smaller brewers to invest in new equipment, to promote their brands more effectively and even to buy pubs as shop windows for their wares.

But the main driving force behind the upsurge in new breweries is simply consumer demand. Beer lovers are tired of over-hyped national brands and avoid like the plague the bland apologies for lager and the cold, tasteless keg beers produced by the global giants. Beers with aroma and flavour are back in vogue and smaller brewers are rushing to meet the clamour from consumers. With around 500 micros, 35 family-owned breweries and several bigger regional producers, there is now greater choice than

Double and no quits...Hydes in Manchester has grown its capacity from 100,000 barrels a year to 200,000 – just one of the many success stories from the independent sector

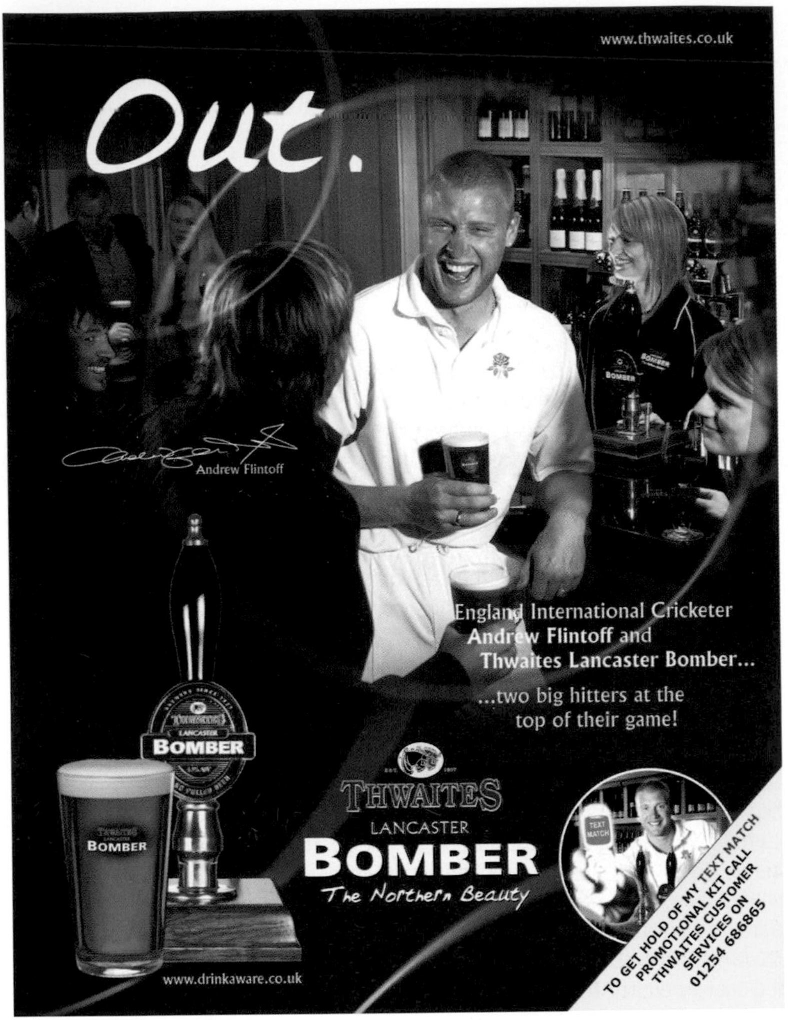

Daniel Thwaites of Blackburn went down the nitro-keg route but has returned to the cask fold with some help from Andrew 'Freddie' Flintoff

at any time since the Campaign for Real Ale was founded in 1971. Britain has more micro brewers per head than any country in the world, including the United States.

Regional and family brewers have estates of tied pubs and it is not difficult to find their beers. But the cosy duopoly of the four global brewers and the giant pub companies, with the former selling heavily discounted beers to the latter, effectively bars most micros from the majority of pubs in the country. Nevertheless, the choice is there: one aim of the Good Beer Guide is to point drinkers in the direction of genuine free houses offering beers from smaller producers. The micros have responded to the hard-faced indifference and even hostility of most of the pubcos by selling beers at farmers' markets, supplying CAMRA beer festivals, and forming co-operatives – notably in East Anglia – to deliver beer from groups of producers to the free trade.

The breweries section in this edition lists familiar reports over and over again: 'Installed new equipment...doubled capacity...never been busier...struggling to cope with demand'. To the cynics who say that micro breweries in total only account for a fraction of total annual production, it is worth pointing out that micros can grow rapidly. Ringwood in Hampshire started in 1978 brewing 10 barrels a week and is now close to 30,000 barrels a year. It built a new brewhouse in 1994 and added new fermenters in 2004. Sharp's in Cornwall is a remarkable success story. It started in 1994 in one unit on an industrial estate, has spread to most of the estate and vies with the long-established St Austell Brewery as the biggest producer of cask beer in the county. In Yorkshire, Copper Dragon in Skipton opened in 2003 but has quadrupled production in just three years. Hogs Back in Surrey has commissioned new coppers and fermenters to cope with demand, a demand that is met not only by selling to pubs but also by e-commerce.

The success of micro brewers is underscored by the 2005 annual report of SIBA, the Society of Independent Brewers. It says that sales among its members have grown by an average of 12 per cent a year compared to 2004, with six out of 10 SIBA members reporting growth in excess of 10 per cent. The micros' share of the cask beer market has grown to more than 20 per cent, up from 14 per cent in 2003. Even the Doubting Thomas of the beer world, the statistical company A C Nielsen, which in recent years has prophesised the virtual obliteration of real ale, reported in July 2005 that the decline in the cask beer sector had bottomed out and there were signs of recovery.

Most significantly, Nielsen now supports what CAMRA and the Good Beer Guide have argued for years: that if the cask beer production figures of the four global brewers are stripped out, the regionals and micros can be seen to be in growth. We would go further and say the so-called decline of real ale is a chimera, masked by the almost total lack of interest in the sector shown by the globals. This is proved by the rude good health of the regional brewing sector. Timothy Taylor in West Yorkshire has invested some £11 million pounds in a decade to enable production to grow from 28,000 barrels a year in 1997 to close to 50,000 barrels today. Fuller's in West London is now a major national force, with London Pride alone accounting for 130,000 barrels a year, making it the biggest-selling premium cask beer in Britain. Adnams in Suffolk has had to add new fermenting capacity three times in recent years to cope with the demand for its beers. Everards of Leicester has invested £20 million in its pub estate and has reaped a rich dividend. Cask beer accounts for 37 per cent of sales in its estate – a high percentage – and between 2004 and 2005 sales of Tiger Best Bitter increased by 40 per cent and Original by 55 per cent.

Charles Wells of Bedford, the biggest family-owned independent in Britain, has turned its Bombardier premium bitter into a national brand that is now in the top ten biggest sellers. Hydes in Manchester has doubled its capacity from 100,000 barrels a year to 200,000, aided by the contract to brew cask Boddingtons. Daniel Thwaites, a regional giant in the North-west, went down the nitro-keg route in the 1990s and early 2000s but has now returned to the cask fold with some enthusiasm, promoting Lancaster Bomber in particular.

The new nationals

The Guide this year marks the emergence of Greene King and Wolverhampton & Dudley as new national groups. Their market penetration is awesome. As well as supplying their own vast pub estates, they have a presence in the free trade that covers most areas of Britain. They offer a fascinating contradiction: flag-wavers for cask beer but pallbearers for choice. In too many parts of the country, the choice in the tied and free trade is their beers and few others. This is especially true of Greene King in its East Anglian heartland.

Unlike the old 'Big Six' national brewers that CAMRA battled with in the 1970s and '80s, Greene King and W&D have a genuine commitment to real ale and leave the keg and lager market to the global producers. But in common with all

Ridley's brewery in Essex was due to close in autumn 2005, taken over and axed by acquisitive Greene King

big companies, they have a lust for growth. Both are massively profitable and in July 2005 W&D remortaged its pub estate in order to give it even more cash for further acquisitions. Earlier in the year, W&D bought Jennings' Brewery in Cumbria for £46 million despite considerable opposition from CAMRA and local beer drinkers. W&D robustly stresses it will keep Jennings open but industry opinion says the plant will close sooner rather than later. A pledge to invest £250,000 in Jenning's amounts to no more than petty cash for the group. Cockermouth is a cramped and remote site, while if the brands move to the Burtonwood Brewery near Warrington they would have easy access to the motorway network in the North-west.

In July 2005, Greene King bought the T D Ridley Brewery in Essex, paying £46 million for the plant and 73 pubs. This was not an aggressive takeover. The chairman of Ridley's, Nicholas of that ilk, from his tax exile in Monaco, is understood to have gone cap in hand to Greene King, Shepherd Neame and Charles Wells, asking them to buy the company. Greene King made the biggest bid, enabling Mr Ridley personally to pocket £11 million. Greene King's chief executive Rooney Anand said the purchase made good sense for his company as it was 'not well represented in that part of Essex'. Greene King, on the other hand, is over-represented in the rest of Essex, Suffolk, Norfolk, Cambridgeshire, Bedfordshire, Hertfordshire and most compass points north, south, east and west. Drinkers in the former Ridley's trading estate will find that the brewery's IPA will disappear, to be replaced by

New pub hours and smoking

The new Licensing Act for England and Wales will come into effect in the autumn of 2005. In spite of media frenzy about '24-hour drinking', only a handful of pubs in the country have applied to open all day and night. Most pubs will either remain with their existing hours or will apply for minor extensions.

Legislation is being considered to ban smoking in pubs. One option could be that pubs that opt not to serve food could allow smoking. CAMRA has called for a return to multi-roomed pubs, with one room set aside for smokers. The legislation will not come into effect until 2008.

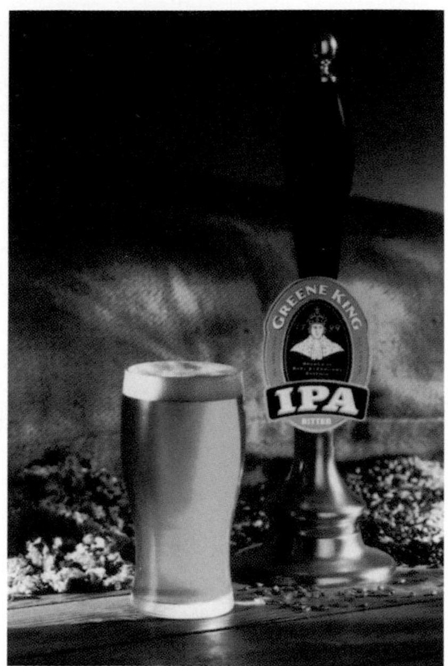

Everywhere but India...Greene King's major brand is a now national one and will replace Ridley's IPA in many Essex pubs

Greene King's own interpretation of the style, just as Jenning's drinkers are likely to find Marston's Burton Bitter and Pedigree propping up their bars.

Pleas to keep Ridley's brewery open fell on deaf ears. The Essex brewery's production, Greene King said, can easily be absorbed at Bury St Edmunds. This misses the point. The brewery at Hartford End near Chelmsford could be viable as both a brewery and a visitor attraction: it is a now rare example of a 19th-century country brewery with many fascinating examples of Victorian equipment and artefacts. As both Scottish & Newcastle and Interbrew proved with their ownerships of Theakston and Hoegaarden respectively, small breweries as visitor attractions can be profitable as well as illuminating.

The trail of destruction of both breweries and consumer choice will go on. Both Greene King and W&D are strongly rumoured to be running their slide rules over Belhaven of Dunbar. Unusually for a Scottish brewer, Belhaven has a large estate of pubs, offering the ideal launch pad for an assault on the beer market north of the border. The Good Beer Guide urges all regional brewers to stand firm against the insidious growth of the two new nationals and maintain their independence.

Global indifference

Little space need be wasted on the four global brewers that dominate the British industry. They run massive factories dedicated to producing plastic beer. Volumes and profits, rather than consumer choice and quality, are their watchwords.

Scottish & Newcastle has closed both its Edinburgh and Newcastle plants in order to concentrate on its 'French' lager brand, Kronenbourg. We can expect a change of name to Kronenbourg UK at any time. Its only major ale brand is John Smith's Bitter, usually found in keg form, while the former Courage brands wither slowly on the bine.

Interbrew's interest in cask can be measured by its decision to have both Boddingtons Bitter and Draught Bass brewed for it by Hydes and Marston's respectively. Coors has followed a similar path: with the exception of Worthington Bitter – scarcely the great taste experience of modern times – all the cask brands it owns are out-sourced to regional producers. Carlsberg, having dropped Tetley from its corporate title, can hardly be bothered to promote the Leeds beer, even in its nitro-keg form.

For readers and users of the Good Beer Guide, our advice is to seek out the craft-brewed beers of the genuine independents listed in this edition. It makes good sense for both your tastebuds and your pockets.

Hit for six

A classic rural pub that marks the birthplace of modern cricket was destroyed by a big brewer and rescued by a family-owned independent. **Roger Protz** visits the Bat & Ball

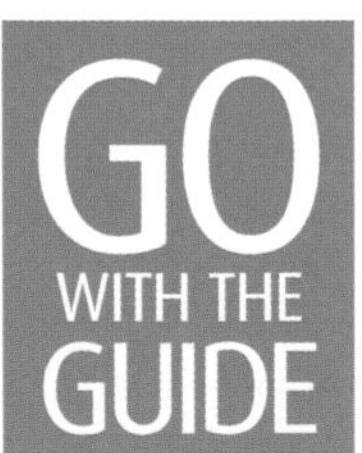

IMAGINE YOU ARE A GIANT BREWING COMPANY that also owns several thousand pubs. You acquire a national treasure, the Bat & Ball at Hambledon in Hampshire, where the modern game of cricket was fashioned in the 18th century and which was later visited by such cricketing luminaries as Dr W G Grace. Would you cherish it, nurture it, give it greater prominence to attract more visitors? Not if you are the marketing department of Allied Breweries. Allied became the owner of the Bat & Ball as a result of taking over and closing down the Guildford brewer, Friary Meux. In the early 1990s Allied, in a fit of cultural vandalism, transformed the ancient inn into a modern eaterie called Natterjacks. A pub that is a shrine to cricket was turned into a pub-restaurant named after a breed of toad. It was painted lime green and customers were not allowed to sit at the bar and enjoy a drink.

All the cricketing memorabilia and artefacts were thrown out. They included ancient scorecards – one records the match in 1777 when Hambledon beat All England by an innings and 168 runs – old cricket bats and a wealth of fascinating prints and photographs that trace the development of the game in the last half of the 18th century.

Natterjacks was not a success. The isolated pub alongside Broadhalfpenny Down did not attract Mr Toad and others more interested in food than ale and cricket.

A sketch of the Bat & Ball in 1978, scarcely changed since the 18th century. Allied Breweries put an end to such sentimental nonsense

Fortunately in 1996 George Gale, the Horndean family-owned brewery, bought the pub and spent the best part of two years restoring it to its old glory as the Bat & Ball. Today you can still dine well in the spacious restaurant but you can also delight, in the Nyren Room and the adjacent bar, in the photos, bats, balls and records that detail the dramatic development of our national summer game that took place in the pub and on the ground opposite.

Cricket had been played for centuries but it was at Hambledon that it took on the rules and appearance of the game we recognise today. It seems remarkable that the changes took place in such a remote locality but Hampshire had a substantial number of talented cricketers with wealthy sponsors who employed them on their land and paid them to play the game. Above all, Hambledon became the driving force for change in the game as a result of the flair, passion and business acumen of the landlord of the Bat & Ball, Richard Nyren, known as 'The General'.

Nyren was an excellent cricketer himself, described as a 'cunning' left-arm bowler and a brave, hard-hitting batsmen. But his greatest skill was to attract to his small ale house the finest cricketers in all England and to get them to face, for wagers of between 500 and 1,000 guineas, a team comprised of farmers and their workers, potters, cobblers, publicans and horse men.

Ferocious games

Enormous crowds somehow found their way to Broadhalfpenny Down to watch the ferocious games played there on a ground described by the peerless cricket writer John Arlott as having turf 'lively and trim as a convict's crop'. Nyren's son, John, vividly described the atmosphere: 'Oh! It was a heart-stirring sight to witness the multitude forming a complete and dense circle round that noble green. Half the county would be present, and all their hearts are with us – Little Hambledon, pitted against All England was a proud thought for the Hampshire men. How those fine, brawn-faced fellows of farmers drink to our success! There would be this company, consisting most likely of some thousands, remain patiently and anxiously

Cricketing memorabilia, trophies and books on display in the bar of the Bat & Ball

watching every turn of fate in the game, as if the event had been the meeting of two armies to decide their liberty.'

When cricket was first played on Broadhalfpenny Down, the ball was bowled along the ground and batsmen clubbed it away with an implement similar to a hockey stick. The wicket consisted of two stumps with a hole in the ground between them where the wicket keeper could deposit the ball and claim a run out. Pads and gloves were unheard of and wicket keepers were supported by specialist long stops. It was said that the deadly fast bowling of a Hambledon man named 'Lumpy' Stevens led to the addition of the third stump.

Round arm bowling was at first banned by the Committee of Hambledon Cricketers. But during the brief period between 1750 and 1791, first round arm and then over arm bowling were introduced, while the familiar straight-bladed bat replaced the curved one. Rudimentary equipment was allowed in order that batsmen and wicket keepers could protect their hands and legs against a hard ball increasingly bowled with fast and venomous accuracy.

The main bar of the Bat & Ball. Note the ancient bat on the wall on the right

Matches were often of two innings per side played over two days. But many lasted just one day, which may come as shock to those of us who endlessly debate the merits of the modern one-day game and 'traditional' three and five day matches. But in an age when players were tied to wealthy, land-owning patrons, there was a limit to how long they could stay away from their gainful employment.

And after the matches, the players would retire to the Bat & Ball. It was here that the Laws of Cricket – other games have rules, only cricket has laws – were drawn up. The laws were devised with copious draughts of wine and ale. The Reverend Reynell Cotton recalled the convivial scene: 'Then fill up your glass, he's the best who drinks most/Here's the Hambledon Club! – who refuses the toast?'

As well as his cricketing and business skills, Richard Nyren was also a fine brewer. John Nyren recalled: 'The ale, too! Barleycorn such as would put the souls of three butchers into one weaver. Ale that would flare like turpentine – genuine Boniface! This immortal viand (for it was more than liquor) was vended at twopence per pint'.

It was the deadly bowling of 'Lumpy' Stevens of Hambledon that led to the addition of the third stump, part of the transformation of the game in the 18th century

Inevitably, with large sums of money to be won and large urban crowds to attract, the game moved away from Hambledon to new grounds in London, including one built by Mr Thomas Lord. Richard Nyren left the Bat & Ball in the 1790s but a century or more later a memorial was erected to the modern game at the ground. W G Grace attended the opening ceremony and one of the many splendid photographs in the pub shows a venerable, grey-bearded Grace speaking to a large crowd on Broadhalfpenny Down.

Cricket continues to be played on the Down while beer drinkers are now encouraged to sit at the bar of the Bat & Ball and sup the full range of Gale's regular and seasonal ales. A national institution has been saved from the desperados of a big brewery's marketing department.

And while the Bat & Ball and George Gale & Co survive and thrive, Allied Breweries no longer exists. Howzat!

Photograph: The Argus, Brighton

Man with a mission

Stuart Ashby has spent 21 years visiting all the pubs in the 1984 Good Beer Guide. And he plans to carry on sampling great beer

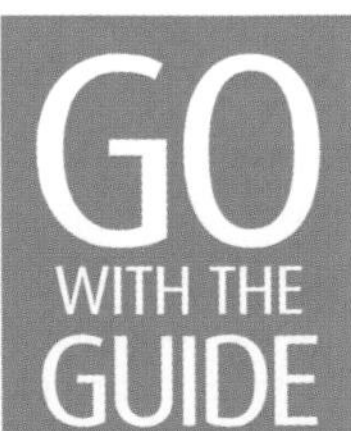

BACK IN 1984 STUART ASHBY took the Good Beer Guide in hand and decided to visit every one of the 5,000 pubs listed inside. In July 2005 he finished the world's greatest pub crawl in the Lamb Inn in Pagham, West Sussex.

Over the years he has been to more than just the pubs in the 1984 Guide. He added the 1987 edition and has since been to additional pubs from further editions along the way. In total he has been to 15,000 pubs, all of them serving real ale because Stuart, from Shoreham-by-Sea, won't touch lager.

His dedication to good beer and travel was sparked by a love of cricket and football. He would go to football matches – he supports Brighton & Hove Albion – and was often disappointed by the pubs near the grounds. So he bought the Guide to find the best pubs and the finest pints. As well as 15,000 pubs he has also been to every one of the 92 Premiership and Football League grounds in the country and all 18 county cricket grounds. He has also seen every county play at home and away.

Stuart, aged 55, does not drive and finds the pubs by public transport and the

One pub Stuart has visited on his travels is the Farriers Arms in St Albans, Hertfordshire, which was listed in the 1984 Good Beer Guide and graces the pages of the current edition. A plaque on the wall of the pub claims it was the meeting place of the first ever branch of CAMRA. This is not strictly true: a branch had been formed in the Midlands in the early 1970s but quickly folded, whereas the South Herts branch was founded in the Farriers and is still going strong, organising the annual St Albans beer festival.

aid of Ordnance Survey maps. If there are no trains or buses to a particular pub then he will walk or hitch-hike. As well as evening and weekend trips, he also plans 'pub holidays', visiting 10 pubs a day in a week and sampling a half pint in every pub.

He photographs all the pubs he visits and makes notes about them, which he keeps cross-referenced in albums. His flat in Shoreham is a shrine to beer and pubs, with cricket and football memorabilia crowding the shelves.

In the course of his travels, he has been to every county in Britain, from Land's End to John O'Groats, with the Isles of Scilly thrown in for good measure. He has taken in just about every village, hamlet, town and city in the country and has made friends in most places. Many of those friends made the trip to the Lamb to help Stuart celebrate his great achievement. Some of his friends stretch back to his first crawls in the early 1980s.

Stuart worked for many years as a clerk on the railways but he was made redundant in 2005. He plans to continue his bibulous travels though he will have to watch his finances.

Even as he prepared to celebrate his first tour of duty round 15,000 pubs, he was planning his next visit to hostelries in Hampshire. He called it his 'Hampshire holiday' and intended to visit 100 pubs in eight days, taking time off to watch a game between Hampshire and his home county, Sussex.

Stuart says he was married 'briefly'. His first love now is clearly cask beer and fine pubs with the aid of the compass called the Good Beer Guide.

If you see him on the road, give him a lift. He might just take you to the best pub you've ever visited.

Designed like a cosy country pub that happens to be based in a city, the Farriers was once a lonely outpost for cask beer in the 1970s, selling McMullen's AK and Country Bitter. Now there is a bountiful choice in St Albans but the Farriers can boast an entry in more than 25 editions of the Guide.

Photograph: Fran Nowak

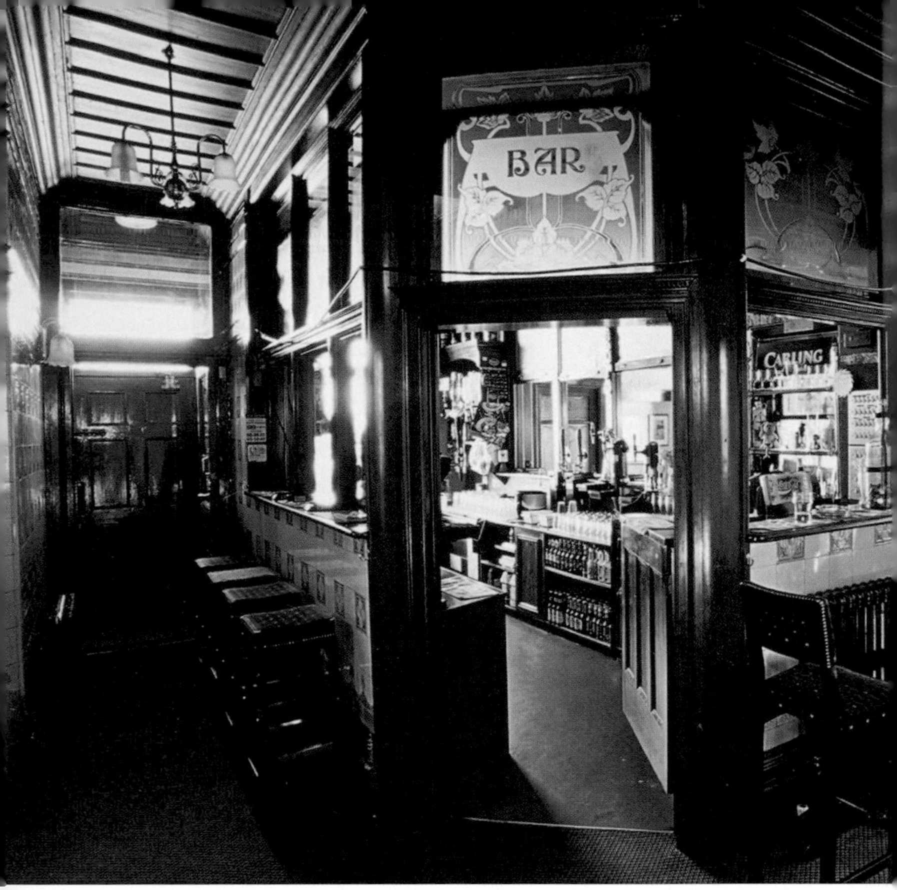

Our pub heritage

Geoff Brandwood traces the pioneering work that created CAMRA's National Inventory of Pubs with interiors of historic importance worthy of saving

GO WITH THE GUIDE

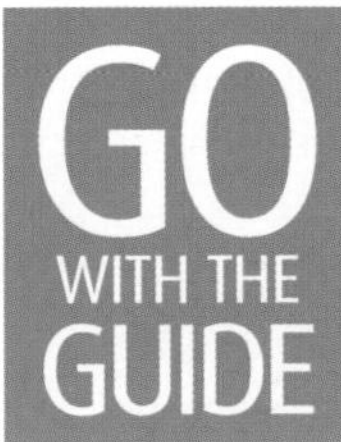

THE NATIONAL INVENTORY IS CAMRA'S PIONEERING INITIATIVE to identify and protect the most important historic pub interiors in this country. The general public knows of CAMRA's work to save and promote real ale and that, of course, was the organisation's initial thrust in the early 1970s when the big brewers seemed hell-bent on consigning our beer heritage to the great cellar in the sky. But, soon, another question emerged. What about our great pub heritage?

The traditional pub was being ravaged too. The 1970s saw a massive increase in the opening up of pubs and the removal of fine fittings, many of which had stood the test of time for nearly a century. Preservation of historic pub interiors was set to become a key issue.

With 60,000 pubs, the aim to identify the nation's best interiors was an ambitious one. Local pilot projects by CAMRA and the Victorian Society in the late 1970s and

Photographs: Michael Slaughter

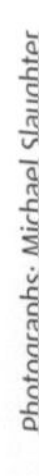

1980s and the escalating loss of traditional pub interiors led to a full national survey using the knowledge of CAMRA's extensive membership. Nothing like it had been done before. Thousands of leads had to be followed up, criteria established, and different pub types and regional variations identified.

The astonishingly ornate and glittering Salisbury in London, N4. Previous page, the Victoria at Great Harwood

The main aim was to list those pub interiors that remained much as they had been before the Second World War. At the outset it was thought the total might be around 500 but it quickly became clear there would be nothing of the sort. After six years' work, the first NI listing appeared in the 1997 Good Beer Guide and totalled just 179, such had been the scale of modern change. Hence it is all the more important to save the best of what's left.

The NI comes in two parts. Part 1 mainly lists pubs whose interiors have not altered significantly since the Second World War. If there have been alterations then these have been done without seriously affecting the character of the historic core. A frequent characteristic is the existence of multiple rooms or at least screens dividing up the drinking areas.

There is invariably a public bar where drink used to cost a little less than the 'better' rooms; these go under various names of which lounge, smoke room and saloon are the most common. Traditional pubs like this were built until the late 1960s but only a tiny handful have escaped major changes. The NI includes two of the best, the March Hare, Ashton-under-Lyne, Greater Manchester, and the Charlie Butler, London SW14.

Part 2 is a new feature of the NI and includes pubs which, although altered, have exceptional rooms or features that CAMRA considers to be of national

importance. These range from, say, an amazing bar-back at the Dun Cow, Sunderland, through spectacular tiling at the Golden Cross, Cardiff, to the rustic bar and stunning Art Deco loos at the Crook Inn, Tweedsmuir. We also list licensed bars in other kinds of establishments such as hotels and railway stations.

Pubs are dynamic commercial enterprises and change is inevitable as customer demand shifts, legislation changes, and the competitive environment alters. But the past three decades have seen an unseemly rush by brewers and pub-owning companies towards homogenisation – giving their pubs the same ambience, often fuelled by the notion that only under-25s use them.

Diversity of pubs

Yet there is a compelling argument for diversity. Just as CAMRA believes in choice for drinkers, it also supports diversity in pub types. Many older drinkers stay away in droves from the modernised, opened-up, and loud music-infested establishments that monopolise many a high street. Market saturation has surely been reached and it is even rumoured that some pub companies consider they now don't have enough community pubs.

Support for traditional pubs was given in March 2005 by the MINTEL 2005 British Lifestyle report which found that 48 per cent of people actually preferred them. Even more interesting food for thought was that no less than 36 per cent of 20-24 year olds favoured an old-style establishment. Traditional, multi-room pubs can cater for the whole community, allowing different rooms to be used by different groups – young, old, those playing games, those eating, those wanting music and those who don't. You can see this in action at many NI pubs.

National Inventory pubs are rare and special places whose very difference from

Ornate tiling, including a tiled mural, at the Cumberland in Carlisle. Previous page, a sweeping staircase at the Barton Arms, Birmingham.

A fireplace and carved wood surround in the Cumberland with a decorative motif, including hops, above. Below, the spacious servery in the Bath, Sheffield

the rest of the field provides a distinctive business opportunity. Two of our finest city drinking palaces from about 1900 are the Bartons Arms in Birmingham and the Salisbury, London N4, both located in unpromising areas and, until recently, depressing, unsuccessful establishments. They have been transformed into thriving businesses by enterprising new owners who have added a range of real ales and good food: both now feature in the Guide. It's been a positive story, too, at the Bath Hotel, Sheffield and, across the Pennines, at the Victoria, Great Harwood, Lancs, where smartening up has enhanced the historic fabric, not destroyed it. The work at the Bath even won the conservation category in the 2002 CAMRA/English Heritage Pub Design Awards. Other NI pubs that have developed successfully in recent years as new Guide entrants are the Cumberland Inn, Carlisle, and the Test Match, West Bridgford, Notts.

CAMRA's next aim is to raise awareness and knowledge about other important historic pub interiors through Regional Inventories. These will include examples that, although not qualifying for the NI, still warrant regional recognition. The first was published for London in 2004, covering 133 pubs: it is available from CAMRA's head office for £4.50 (incl. p&p). It will be followed by East Anglia in 2005 and the North-East in 2006.

The full list of NI pubs in this edition (pages 315 to 317) ranges from tiny rural pubs that are effectively dwelling houses that happen to be licensed to sell drink, to the grandest late Victorian and Edwardian pubs in the land like the Philharmonic in Liverpool and the Garden Gate in Leeds. At the Barley Mow and the Argyll, both London W1, you can see how a century ago drinkers, especially in London, loved tiny, cosy spaces when they popped down the pub. You will find different arrangements in different parts of the country such as drinking lobbies in northern pubs, rows of cubicles in Northern Irish pubs, and single-room bars in Scotland. You will encounter furnishings from simple rustic furniture to spectacular tiling, glass, plaster and woodwork. Enjoy the best of our pub heritage.

The Test Match in Nottingham, a shrine to cricket at Trent Bridge, with some marvellous Art Deco from ceiling to floor

Leeding lights

Let **Barrie Pepper** take you by the hand and show you the best pubs in Leeds listed in this edition of the Good Beer Guide. Join him for a pint

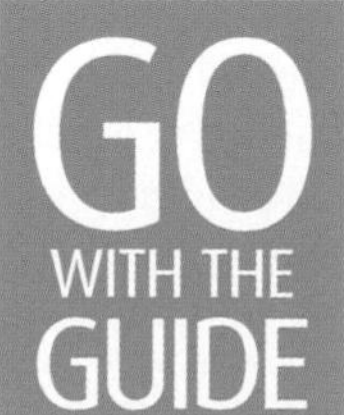

THE WEST END OF LEEDS IS THE POSH END OF THE CITY CENTRE. It's where the Georgian town houses and Victorian villas of the merchants stood in their elegant squares and broad avenues. As the city developed, and the gentry moved to the suburbs, many of these properties became the offices of lawyers, accountants and other professionals. The convenience for the law courts, the town hall and municipal offices was necessary and continues to be so.

A walk around the pubs in this area that are found in the Good Beer Guide should, for convenience, start at Leeds city railway station. Leave by the City Square exit, and cross the square with its statues praising famous Leodiensians and the attractive nymphs depicting night and morn. Go into Infirmary Street and at the major junction with East Parade cross over into St Paul's Street. Take the second right into Park Square East and walk around the leafy square to its opposite corner. Exit

The Victoria, originally built to serve the courts in Leeds, is now enjoyed by musicians and journalists as well as lawyers

by Park Square West into Westgate, turn right and the first stop is on your immediate right.

The Town Hall Tavern was owned for many years by the Musgrave and Sagar company; in business as brewers up to 1958 but continuing as bottlers and owners of a small pub estate until recently. They had a reputation as being the best bottlers of Guinness in the area and were one of the last to use screw-top bottles. The city's main fire station used to stand opposite in Park Street and a lovely old Irish woman who ran the pub for many years kept a mynah bird which, she claimed, started squawking seconds before the fire bells rang. It was a good tale, as was the one that she and her bar cellarman 'sold a head and a half of Tetley Bitter from opening time until all those lawyers went off to the Law Society Ball in the Town Hall'. Reckon that at 648 pints in two hours – one every 10 seconds and believe it if you wish.

Comfortable pub

Today it retains its contacts with all those lawyers in Park Square and the courts across the road. It has been sensitively modernised and displays lots of legal memorabilia along with homage to Leeds United in its mightier days. This is a comfortable pub serving Tetley Bitter as it always did but now alongside two beers from Timothy Taylor's: Golden Best and Landlord. Food is available Monday to Friday lunchtimes and, note, the pub is shut on Sundays.

Go half-left across Westgate and walk up Park Street between the magistrates and crown courts – the fire station is long gone. At the top in Great George Street and facing the Leeds General Infirmary is the George. This is another pub that had contacts with the fire brigade. When the station in Park Street was built in 1883 it was linked to the nearby pub by a bell to tell firemen drinking there that a fire call had been received and to return pretty damn quick. Today in place of the firemen are the staffs of both the hospital and the courts and, of course, the users of both establishments.

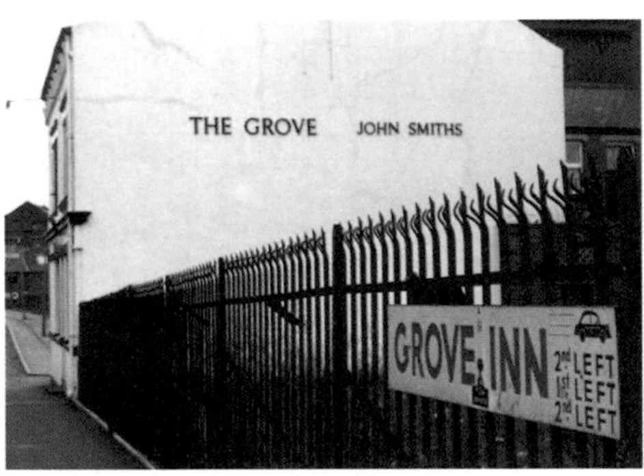

The Grove is a fine traditional Yorkshire pub with cosy lounges and a corridor area

There is a large U-shaped bar serving a large saloon and a snug; it is tastefully decorated with dark mahogany panels, screens with stained glass and a 'city' ambience. The beers include Tetley Bitter, Greene King Abbot and interesting guests. Lunch-time snacks include popular hot beef sandwiches with the meat carved straight from the joint.

Turn right along Great George Street and immediately behind Leeds Town Hall, which was opened by Queen Victoria in 1858, stands the Victoria Family and Commercial Hotel. It went up six years later to serve the courts. It is a superb five-storey building that over the years has been a favourite hostelry for lawyers, politicians, journalists and musicians. Tetley's paid £12,000 for it in 1916. In 1998 it was tastefully restored at a cost of £300,000.

Four years ago speedy action by members of CAMRA with support from the media and local drinkers saved it from conversion to what the then owners, Bass Taverns, called a 'London style' pub. According to the landlord, this meant 'bright

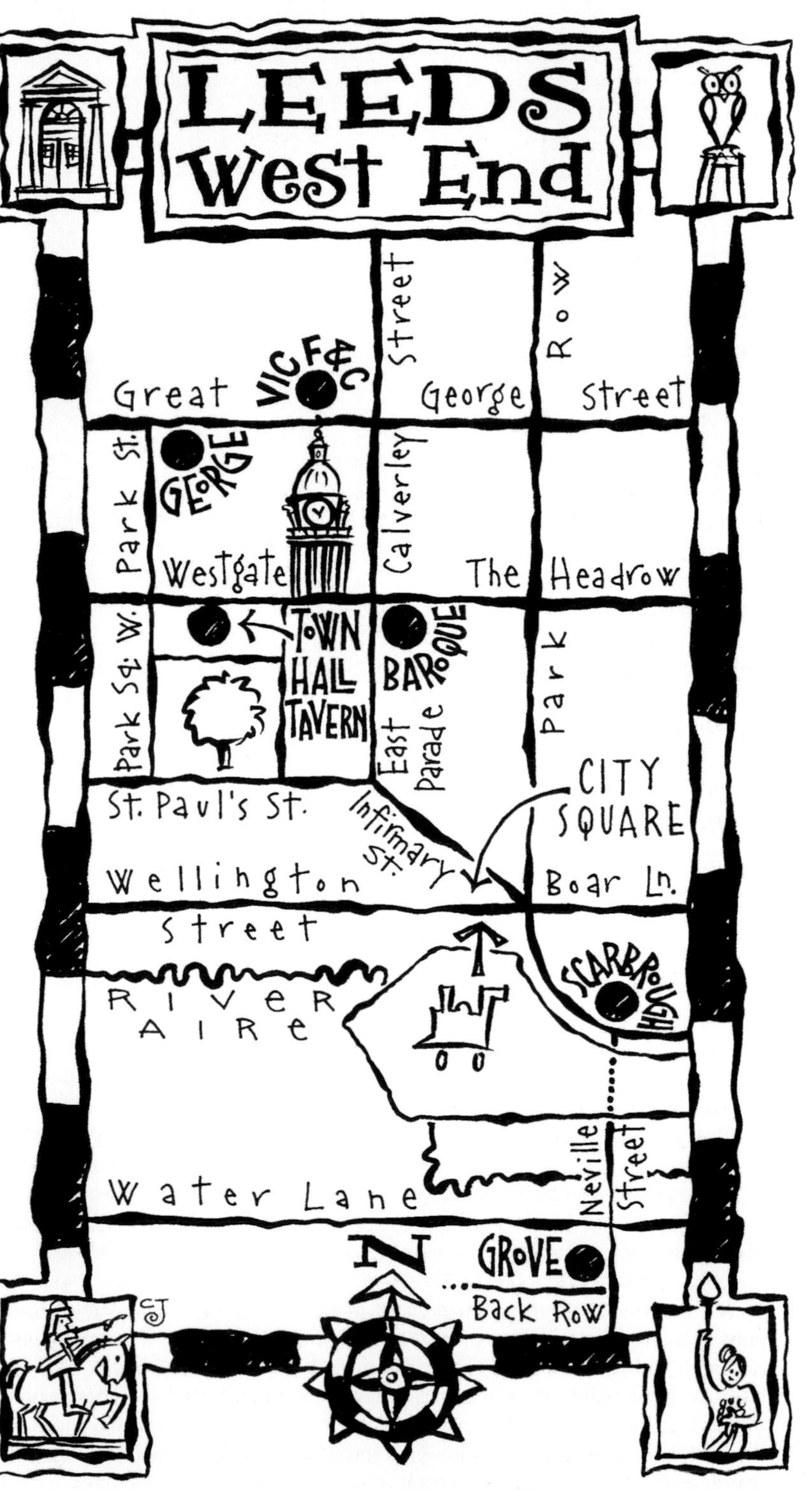
LEEDS
West End
Street
Row
Great
VIC
F&C
George
Street
Park St.
GEORGE
Calverley
Westgate
The
Headrow
Park Sq. W.
TOWN HALL TAVERN
BAROQUE
East Parade
Park
St. Paul's St.
Infirmary St.
CITY SQUARE
Wellington
Boar Ln.
Street
SCARBROUGH
RIVER AIRE
Neville
Street
Water Lane
N
GROVE
Back Row
CJ

The Baroque is a rarity, a pub tied to Okells of the Isle of Man, offering excellent Manx beer and good food

lights, stark wood and a general opening up of the pub to make it another of the large drinking barracks which Leeds has in plenty.' Headlines such as 'Victorian values in peril' and 'Boycott Bass and save The Vic' appeared in the local press. And then, suddenly, Bass Taverns claimed that it was all a misunderstanding, that it had no definite plans, even maintaining, 'We are aware of the sensitivities.' A local CAMRA member said, 'These mealy-mouthed words are merely a damage limitation exercise – they followed a great example of people power, what folk around here might call giving Bass a good kick in the slats. And all within a week!'

So this wonderful, full of character, atmospheric pub was saved, with all its etched glass, polished dark wood in the elegant long bar and its two smaller rooms – Bridget's Bar named after the lovely old lady who presided there for 25 years – and the no-smoking snug at the back. Savour it along with a fine selection of local beers from Tetley, Taylor and Black Sheep as well as three changing guest beers from across the land and good food. This is another pub that closes on Sundays.

On leaving go over to the left of the town hall and walk down Calverley Street to The Headrow and carefully cross to the opposite corner to the splendid turn of the century building that houses a rarity – a tied house belonging to the Isle of Man brewers, Okells – the Baroque.

The company is building a small estate in mainland Britain and has two other pubs in Liverpool. It is facing off the challenge of a number of wine and lager bars and beating them hands down, particularly on price. The building started life as the headquarters of an assurance society and in more recent years has passed through dubious existences as one of the most expensive fish and chip shops in the world and as a Slug and Lettuce wine and cocktail bar where Sex on the Beach was available for a fiver. It's a cocktail.

You enter into a large bar area – a stand-up – with the bar along the left.

Steps lead to three other areas, two overlooking the bar and a no-smoking room at the rear. Three Manx beers are on sale: Bitter, Maclir and Dr Okell's IPA, with usually two guest beers as well as a variety of continental beers on draught and a wide range of bottled ones from all over the world. The food is interesting and reasonably priced.

Go left and left again and head back down East Parade towards the railway station and after crossing City Square take Bishopgate Street, which drops down to the left for the Scarbrough – note the spelling – named after Henry Scarbrough, the man who first ran it as a hotel in 1823, and not as many people imagine after the seaside town of Scarborough. It is on the site of the original Leeds Manor House that dated from before 1560 and was called 'Castyll Hall'. Mr Scarbrough remained there until 1847.

Dr John Simpson, a diarist who visited the place in 1825 called it: '...the best house in Leeds by far.' He went on to detail the dinner his party ate: ' ... salmon and soles; then boiled fowls and ham, roast beef, roast ducks and pastry. We had some most excellent wine. We had Brucellas, Moselle, Sherry, Port and Claret.' In 1857 the Prince of Wales and his entourage stayed the night there on their way to Harewood House. Later when the Wood family owned the hotel it was popular with theatricals and even quite recently its sign showed a Victorian lady bursting into song.

The Scarbrough has one of the most attractive pub facades in Leeds, gently curving, very ornate with glazed tiling and art nouveau lettering, a delight to the eye. It provides a welcome for the treasures inside for, in addition to the ubiquitous Tetley Bitter, there can be up to seven guest beers, often from Yorkshire micros, cider and the rare perry. In summer you can enjoy the vibrancy of city life at the pavement tables. Food is served all day.

You are now back where you started from, but if you have the time you could consider missing a train or two to visit the Grove. There was a time when a sign on the side of the pub read: Grove Inn – second left, first left, second left. Following these instructions brought you back to within 10 yards of where you started from but at least you could park. There is a simpler way these days but it has always been easier to walk the quarter of a mile or so from the railway station. Simply head south under the arches, go over the River Aire and it's on your right.

This is a traditional West Riding corridor pub with two cosy lounges on the right (one is no smoking), an airy tap room and a splendid concert room to the rear. There are also tables outside for balmy days. The Grove is well established as 'the home of acoustic music in Leeds' and it hosts a catholic choice most nights of the week. Everything goes here from blues to rock and jazz to folk and lots between and beyond. Even Mozart's Requiem has been heard on the radio.

The beer selection is excellent with Adnams Broadside, Caledonian Deuchars IPA, Theakston Mild and Wells Bombardier on regular sale along with constantly changing guest ales. Cider is sold during the summer. Recently introduced are Leffe Blonde and Hoegaarden on draught served in the appropriate glasses. The food is generally substantial and Sunday lunches are enormous.

Despite the extensive nature of development going on around it the Grove remains an oasis, a haven of good taste, and it has fought off several attempts to demolish it and build yet another office block. Good luck to it: although it is not strictly part of Leeds's west end it is an ideal pub to end this crawl.

WaverleyTBS

Leading the way in Cask Beer provision

As you will probably be aware, **WaverleyTBS** came to be when cask beer specialists, The Beer Seller, merged with wine and spirit experts, Waverley, to form what is now the leading composite drinks wholesaler in the UK. Combining the knowledge and expertise of the two businesses, and pairing it with a unique localised depot structure, enables us to lead the way in terms of product sourcing and in-outlet support for our customers. It is our cask beer customers in particular, that benefit most from the choice and service we are able to offer.

Building a reputation for cask in your outlet

Cask beer is known to provoke a certain loyalty in regular drinkers, and is a common conversation starter at the bar. A reputation built upon cask will bring in new drinkers for both beer and other drinks, as well as ensuring your regulars keep coming back.

The following components all play a key role in building such a reputation:-

Beer Quality

The quality of your cask beer offering is of paramount importance. Organisations such as Cask Marque are continually helping to raise the standard of cask beer served in the UK, and give publicans a platform on which to publicise the quality of their beers. The Cask Marque logo is highly recognisable to consumers and reassures them of the quality of the beer on offer.

Visibility

Ensuring your cask beer offering is on display to all of your customers will boost sales. Well placed chalkboards or pump clip displays complement the hand pulls on the bar, and ensure that all drinkers in your outlet are able to see your offering at a glance.

Guest Beers

Rotating guest beers is a great way of introducing diversity to your bar and generating an interest in different beer and beer styles. A mix of local beers, well-known brands, award winners and speciality beers can really increase trade.

Beer Festivals

Whether large and comprising dozens of beers, or a simple event run via the hand pulls on the bar, beer festivals are a great way to increase footfall into your pub, and allow you to make the most of key calendar dates.

Education

Ensuring your staff have knowledge of the beers on your bar, and encouraging them to talk to consumers about their beer choice, has a significant impact on repeat sales and enthusiasm for the product.

Why is WaverleyTBS the right choice for you?

WaverleyTBS is proud to be leading the way in the provision of cask beer, and through our committed and knowledgeable sales teams at each of our depots, we are able to offer you unparalleled support in the key areas already mentioned.

Our business is based on 3 things...

- Quality of product
- An excellent range
- Superb service and support

Quality:-

WaverleyTBS is the only wholesaler to be awarded the Cask Marque Distribution Charter for excellence in the handling of cask beer. By way of chilled storage at our depots, strict movement control policies and regular audits, we ensure that beer reaches our customers in optimum condition.

Choice:-

WaverleyTBS has access to an extraordinary range of cask beers from all over the country. Our monthly promotional brochure, TotalCask, offers a wide selection of themed, seasonal, and award winning brands, at varying price points and includes many added value promotions.

Support:-

WaverleyTBS enjoys excellent relationships with Britain's cask beer brewers and can offer in-outlet support for the individual brands you stock. We can also help you with event posters, beer lists, tasting notes and promotional material, as well as give you access to training for you and your staff if required.

For further details on any of the information here, contact your local depot today!

Depot Contacts

Depot	Telephone	Depot	Telephone
Birmingham	0121 505 6228	Glasgow	0141 341 2400
Bodmin	01208 77822	Hailsham	01323 847888
Bristol	01454 413712	Hemel Hempstead	01442 293000
Chandlers Ford	02380 252299	Leeds	0113 231 9125
Chesterfield	01246 453333	London	020 8838 4200
Colchester	01206 577272	Newbury	01635 40136
Cromer	01263 513545	Paignton	01803 559181
Dartford	01323 847888	Peterborough	01733 230167
Edinburgh	0131 528 1500	Warrington	01925 212300
Felling	0191 495 5050	Wincanton	01963 34264

www.waverleytbs.co.uk

The Swan returns to its nest

Villagers in Cheshire raised the cash to buy their GBG-listed local when it was threatened with closure. **Roger Protz** reports from Kettleshulme

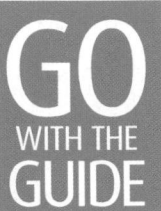

GO WITH THE GUIDE

THE VILLAGE OF KETTLESHULME IN CHESHIRE is in the Peak District National Park, close to the Derbyshire border. It is on a road that was once the salt route from Nantwich to Sheffield and then became an important coaching turnpike.

The green pastures, roads overhanging with foliage, and the green-brown humps of hills and mountains in the background make a pastoral idyll to which visitors flock in their thousands. Along with the 300 folk who live in the village, visitors need refreshment. And since the 15th century, this has been provided by the Swan, a picture-postcard, white-fronted inn with beams, half-panelled walls, open fires, horse brasses and Dutch tiles.

The Swan stands on an ancient salt route and faced closure when the owner put it up for sale

There was consternation in the village in the autumn of 2004 when the owner of the Swan, Ian Edmunds, announced he wanted to sell the inn in order to turn it into a private house. There wasn't a row or any unpleasantness but the villagers were determined to save their local.

Kettleshulme has two pubs but the Bull's Head – also GBG listed – caters for a different clientele and the regulars in the Swan wanted to keep it for its history, its warm welcome for visitors, its reputation for food and its commitment to good beer from small craft breweries.

The villagers have some experience of fighting for local causes. They had waged a vigorous and successful campaign to save the village school when it was threatened with closure and they used their skills to stop the Swan disappearing.

Ian Edmunds knew the value of the inn and he said he would put it on the market for £425,000. It was a daunting sum but the villagers rallied to the cause. Twenty-two shareholders raised the cash by making investments that ranged from small amounts to large chunks of cash. Necessary work on the fabric of the inn, including rewiring it, was carried out on a voluntary basis.

The Swan closed in October 2004, re-opened in March 2005 and has been busy ever since. Seven directors meet monthly while a Beer Committee made up of regulars also meets to plan the breweries it will contact for supplies.

The enterprise qualifies for tax relief but the terms mean the inn can't be handed over to tenants for three years. The directors soon parted company with their first manager and have learnt from the experience. Their plan is to hand over to tenants when the three-year period is up.

The villagers are fortunate to have useful experience to draw on. The operations director at the Swan is John Adamson who has a background in management in pubs and clubs. The directors and the members of the Beer Committee have a passion for the quality of the ales on offer. They include the likes of Martin Kay, a keen home brewer, and Stuart Cafferty, who describes himself as 'a shareholder, a director, a member of the Beer Committee...and divorced'.

Directors and members of the 'Beer Committee' taste the quality of the product in the main bar of the Swan

They choose their beers from their own experience and by using both the Good Beer Guide and beer-related websites. They pick five beers a month: they are restricted by a tiny 'cellar' that is a ground floor room behind the bar.

The only beer from a large brewery is Marston's Burton Bitter, which is a regular and is served from 18-gallon casks. Other beers come in nine-gallon firkins. The villagers are full of praise for Marston's. The brewery has offered help and expertise, and gave the inn 30 days' credit at first to help it get started.

Other beers are drawn from micros, which have to supply direct: no wholesalers are used. On the day of my visit there were beers from Beartown of Congleton and Edale in Derbyshire. Three members of the Edale team were in the pub, sampling the product following a delivery.

At present food is confined to a few simple dishes but this side of the business will develop. Opening hours may also be extended. The most important fact about the Swan is that it is open, saved by its regulars and once again giving pleasure to locals and visitors. It is an important victory for community action to save a key local amenity.

Britain's classic beer styles

You can deepen your appreciation of cask ale and get to grips with all the beers listed in the Breweries section with this run-down on the main styles available

Mild

Mild was once the most popular style of beer but was overtaken by Bitter from the 1950s. It was developed in the 18th and 19th centuries as a less aggressively bitter style of beer than porter and stout. Early Milds were much stronger that modern interpretations, which tend to fall in the 3% to 3.5% category, though there are stronger versions, such as Gale's Festival Mild and Sarah Hughes' Dark Ruby. Mild ale is usually dark brown in colour, due to the use of well-roasted malts or roasted barley, but there are paler versions, such as Banks's Original, Timothy Taylor's Golden Best and McMullen's AK. Look for rich malty aromas and flavours with hints of dark fruit, chocolate, coffee and caramel and a gentle underpinning of hop bitterness.

Old Ale

Old Ale recalls the type of beer brewed before the Industrial Revolution, stored for months or even years in unlined wooden vessels known as tuns. The beer would pick up some lactic sourness as a result of wild yeasts, lactobacilli and tannins in the wood. The result was a beer dubbed 'stale' by drinkers: it was one of the components of the early, blended Porters. The style has re-emerged in recent years, due primarily to the fame of Theakston's Old Peculier, Gale's Prize Old Ale and Thomas Hardy's Ale, the last saved from oblivion by O'Hanlon's Brewery in Devon. Old Ales, contrary to expectation, do not have to be especially strong: they can be no more than 4% alcohol, though the Gale's and O'Hanlon's versions are considerably stronger. Neither do they have to be dark: Old Ale can be pale and burst with lush sappy malt, tart fruit and spicy hop notes. Darker versions will have a more profound malt character with powerful hints of roasted grain, dark fruit, polished leather and fresh tobacco. The hallmark of the style remains a lengthy period of maturation, often in bottle rather than bulk vessels.

Bitter

Towards the end of the 19th century, brewers built large estates of tied pubs. They moved away from vatted beers stored for many months and developed 'running beers' that could be served after a few days' storage in pub cellars. Draught Mild was a 'running beer' along with a new type that was dubbed Bitter by drinkers. Bitter grew out of Pale Ale but was generally deep bronze to copper in colour due to the use of slightly darker malts such as crystal that give the beer fullness of palate. Best is a stronger version of Bitter but there is considerable crossover. Bitter falls into the 3.4% to 3.9% band, with Best Bitter 4% upwards but a number of brewers label their ordinary Bitters 'Best'. A further development of Bitter comes in the shape of Extra or Special Strong Bitters of 5% or more: familiar examples of this style include Fuller's ESB and Greene King Abbot. With ordinary Bitter, look for a spicy, peppery and grassy hop character, a powerful bitterness, tangy fruit and juicy and nutty malt. With Best and Strong Bitters, malt and fruit character will tend to dominate but hop aroma and bitterness are still crucial to the style, often achieved by 'late hopping' in the brewery or adding hops to casks as they leave for pubs.

Golden Ales

This new style of pale, well-hopped and quenching beer developed in the 1980s as independent brewers attempted to win younger drinkers from heavily-promoted lager brands. The first in the field were Exmoor Gold and Hop Back Summer Lightning, though many micros and regionals now make their versions of the style. Strengths will range from 3.5% to 5%. The hallmark will be the biscuity and juicy malt character derived from pale malts, underscored by tart citrus fruit and peppery hops, often with the addition of hints of vanilla and sweetcorn. Above all, such beers are quenching and served cool.

IPA and Pale Ale

India Pale Ale changed the face of brewing early in the 19th century. The new technologies of the Industrial Revolution enabled brewers to use pale malts to fashion beers that were genuinely golden or pale bronze in colour. First brewed in London and Burton-on-Trent for the colonial market, IPAs were strong in alcohol and high in hops: the preservative character of the hops helped keep the beers in good condition during long sea journeys. Beers with less alcohol and hops were developed for the domestic market and were known as Pale Ale. Today Pale Ale is usually a bottled version of Bitter, though historically the styles are different. Marston's Pedigree is an example of Burton Pale Ale, not Bitter, while the same brewery's Old Empire is a fascinating interpretation of a Victorian IPA. So-called IPAs with strengths of around 3.5% are not true to style. Look for juicy malt, citrus fruit and a big spicy, peppery, bitter hop character, with strengths of 4% upwards.

Porter and Stout

Porter was a London style that turned the brewing industry upside down early in the 18th century. It was a dark brown beer – 19th-century versions became jet black – that was originally a blend of brown ale, pale ale and 'stale' or well-matured ale. It acquired the name Porter as a result of its popularity among London's street-market workers. At the time, a generic term for the strongest or stoutest beer in a brewery was stout. The strongest versions of Porter were known as Stout Porter, reduced over the years to simply Stout. Such vast quantities of Porter and Stout flooded into Ireland from London and Bristol that a Dublin brewer named Arthur Guinness decided to fashion his own interpretation of the style. The beers were strong – 6% for Porter, 7% or 8% for Stout. Guinness in Dublin blended some unmalted roasted barley and in so doing produced a style known as Dry Irish Stout. Restrictions on making roasted malts in Britain during World War One led to the demise of Porter and Stout and left the market to the Irish. In recent years, smaller craft brewers in Britain have rekindled an interest in the style, though in keeping with modern drinking habits, strengths have been reduced. Look for profound dark and roasted malt character with raisin and sultana fruit, espresso or cappuccino coffee, liquorice and molasses, all underscored by hefty hop bitterness.

Barley Wine

Barley Wine is a style that dates from the 18th and 19th centuries when England was often at war with France and it was the duty of patriots, usually from the upper classes, to drink ale rather than Claret. Barley Wine had to be strong – often between 10% and 12% – and was stored for prodigious periods of as long at 18 months or two years. When country houses had their own small breweries, it was often the task of the butler to brew ale that was drunk from cut-glass goblets at the dining table. The biggest-selling Barley Wine for years was Whitbread's 10.9% Gold Label, now available only in cans. Bass's No 1 Barley Wine (10.5%) is occasionally brewed in Burton-on-Trent, stored in cask for 12 months and made available to CAMRA beer festivals. Fuller's Vintage Ale (8.5%) is a bottle-conditioned version of its Golden Pride and is brewed with different varieties of malts and hops every year. Many micro-brewers now produce their interpretations of the style. Expect massive sweet malt and ripe fruit of the pear drop, orange and lemon type, with darker fruits, chocolate and coffee if darker malts are used. Hop rates are generous and produce bitterness and peppery, grassy and floral notes.

Scottish Beers

Historically, Scottish beers tend to be darker, sweeter and less heavily hopped than English and Welsh ales: a cold climate demands warming beers. But many of the new craft breweries produce beers lighter in colour and with generous hop rates. The traditional, classic styles are Light, low in strength and so-called even when dark in colour, also known as 60/-, Heavy or 70/-, Export or 80/- and a strong Wee Heavy, similar to a barley wine, and also labelled 90/-. In the 19th century, beers were invoiced according to strength, using the now defunct currency of the shilling.

Compiling the Guide

We start with the beer...

THE GOOD BEER GUIDE is no ordinary pub guide. Our watchwords are beer quality. It has been our belief for thirty-three years that if a pub landlord keeps his beers well and pours perfect pints, then everything else in the pub – welcome, food, other drinks, accommodation and family facilities – will be of a high standard, too. It's the beer that counts first, not roses round the door, turkey carpets, or ciabatta sandwiches filled with sun-dried tomatoes drizzled with olive oil.

The heart of the Guide is the pubs section, offering more than 4,500 pubs in England, Wales, Scotland, Northern Ireland, the Channel Islands and the Isle of Man. They are all full entries. Other guides offer at most 1,000 full entries.

CAMRA members choose the pubs. They visit them on a regular basis to check that beer quality has not declined. The Good Beer Guide does not charge for entry, neither does it make do with questionnaires sent to publicans. Every pub is checked several times a year. Even as the Guide goes to press, we will delete an entry if we receive a report about poor beer quality.

The Guide is unique in several ways. It has an army of 77,000 unpaid CAMRA volunteers who choose the entries, with detailed descriptions of beer, food, history, architecture, facilities and public transport available. There is a considerable turnover of pubs as CAMRA members delete those that have fallen below an acceptable standard or rotate pubs in an area with a substantial number of good outlets.

And it is not a Guide to country pubs alone. CAMRA has fought long and hard to sustain rural pubs and they feature powerfully in these pages. But people also visit urban pubs, too, and all the major towns and cities in Great Britain appear in the Guide with an abundance of choice.

As this is a Guide to beer as well as pubs, we also offer our other unique contribution to beer appreciation: the Breweries section. CAMRA appoints voluntary liaison officers to every brewery in Britain, big and small. As a result of their painstaking work and regular reports, the Breweries section is an annual snapshot of the industry, listing all the beers produced with their strengths and tasting notes. The section is a vade mecum of cask beer, perfectly complementing the pub listings, and stressing the enormous choice and diversity available in Britain.

■ You can keep your Guide up to date by visiting the CAMRA website www.camra.org.uk. Click on Good Beer Guide then Updates to the GBG 2006. You will find information on brewery changes; pubs that CAMRA branches consider should be deleted from the Guide as a result of closure or poor beer quality; and pub entries that have experienced changes to opening hours, beer range and facilities.

England

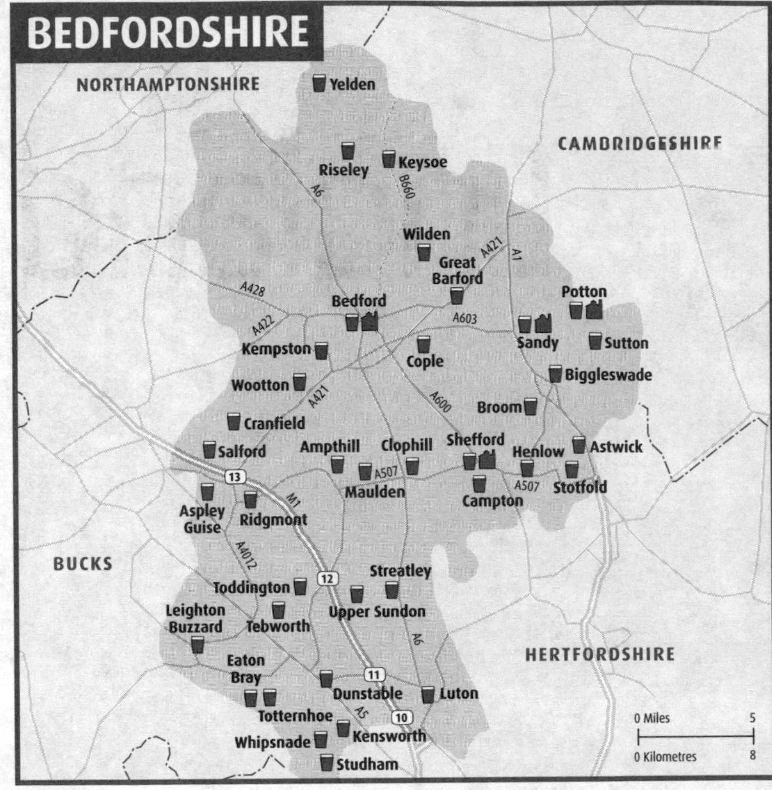

Ampthill

Engine & Tender ✓

11 Dunstable Street, MK45 2NJ

11-2.30, 5-11; 11-11 Fri; 12-2.30, 5-11 Sat; 12-10.30 Sun

☎ (01525) 403319

Greene King IPA, Abbot H

This friendly, jolly one-bar local is on the main road to the south of the town centre. Frequented by pub games players and the local rugby club, it has a large patio area for summer drinking. Bar snacks are served on weekday lunchtimes. The landlord has an unusual 'snuff engine' – if the pub is not too busy ask to try it – an unforgettable experience! Amptill is an attractive Georgian market town, popular for its antique shops and farmers' market.

Aspley Guise

Anchor

10 The Square, MK17 8DF

12-2.30, 5-11; 12-4, 6-11 Sat; 12-4, 7-10.30 Sun

☎ (01908) 582177

Wells Eagle; guest beer H

Charles Wells pub with two bars: the public bar has a TV, darts and an array of board games and the no-smoking lounge bar is often used in the evening by diners. Meals are served at lunchtimes and evenings. A locals' pub, the public bar is busy when there is a big footie match on, and the garden is popular in summer. Visitors are always offered a friendly welcome.

P

Astwick

Tudor Oaks

1 Taylors Road, SG5 4AZ

(on A1 between Letchworth and Biggleswade)

11-11; 12-3.30, 7-10.30 Sun

☎ (01462) 834133

Beer range varies H

A Guide entry for many years, the pub now has seven handpumps with an ever-changing range of beers, mainly from micros and smaller breweries. You may even find some unusual brews such as Williams' Fraoch heather ale, Cains' Raisin beer and two of the landlord's favourites, Nethergate's Umbel Ale and Umbel Magna. Real cider is served cooled. The pub has a reputation for quality food, using fresh ingredients, with seafood and steak particularly recommended. P

Bedford

Castle

17 Newnham Street, MK40 3JR

11.30-2.30, 5.30-11; 11.30-11 Fri & Sat; 12-6 Sun

☎ (01234) 353295

Adnams Broadside; St Austell Tribute; Wells Eagle H

INDEPENDENT BREWERIES

B&T Shefford
Old Stable Sandy
Potton Potton
Wells Bedford

Two-bar pub with a pleasant walled garden on the fringe of the town centre. The beers change occasionally but are always on the Charles Wells guest list. Good value pub food is served (eve meals Mon-Thu). Peacock's auction house is opposite and an interesting place to visit. The Castle is in a good area for real ale pubs, if you are planning a crawl. Limited accommodation is available – ring for details. ❀⇌◐ ⊟♿P

Cricketers Arms ✔
35 Goldington Road, MK40 3LH
(on A428 E of town centre)
✪ 12-3, 5-11; 11-11 Sat; 7-10.30 Sun
☎ (01234) 303958 website: www.cricketersarms.co.uk
Hook Norton Best Bitter; guest beers Ⓗ
Small, one-bar pub opposite the Bedford Blues rugby ground. Popular with fans of the game – live matches are shown on the two small plasma screens at each end of the long wood-panelled bar. New ownership and licensees have revitalised the pub and four real ales are stocked, as well as individually chosen wines. No food is served on Sunday. ❀◐⁄

Phoenix
45 St John's Street, MK42 0AB (on A6 S of town centre)
✪ 11-11; 12-10.30 Sun
☎ (01234) 352862
Wells Eagle, Bombardier Ⓗ
Friendly local overflowing with Irish charm, opposite a large traffic island south of the river. Built in 1900 and extended in the 1960s, there is a fine collection of historic local photographs displayed in the lounge bar. Home-cooked food is served Monday-Saturday, lunchtime and evening. ◐⇌ (St Johns) ♣P

Wellington Arms ✔
40-42 Wellington Street, MK40 2JA (N of town centre)
✪ 12-11; 12-10.30 Sun
☎ (01234) 308033
website: www.wellingtonarms.co.uk
Adnams Bitter; B&T Two Brewers, Shefford Bitter; guest beers Ⓗ
Award-winning B&T pub attracting real ale drinkers from miles around – do not miss it if you are in town. The 13 handpumps offer a wide range of regional and micro-brewery beers, plus real cider and perry. A selection of Belgian and other imported beers is available in bottles and on draught. Five times local CAMRA Pub of the Year, it was regional winner in 2001. ❀♣●⊓

Biggleswade

Wheatsheaf ✔
5 Lawrence Road, SG18 0LS
✪ 11-4, 7-11; 11-11 Fri & Sat; 12-10.30 Sun
☎ (01767) 222220
Greene King XX Mild, IPA Ⓗ
Built in 1873, this end-of-terrace pub is in a time warp. The present licensees have been here since 1989 and the pub has won several CAMRA awards including East Beds Community Pub of the Year in 2005. The XX Mild is as good a pint of Greene King beer as you will get anywhere. A pub not to be missed, as it fields darts, crib and dominoes teams, and holds regular summer barbecues.
❀⇌♣

Broom

White Horse ✔
SG18 9NN
✪ 12-3, 5.30-11; 12-4, 7-10.30 Sun
☎ (01767) 313425
website: www.whitehorsebroom.co.uk
Greene King IPA, Abbot; guest beers Ⓗ
Traditional country pub with an open fire, exposed beams and a true village local atmosphere. Greene King standards are supplemented by two guest beers. The pub boasts an excellent menu with home-cooked food and local produce and 'the best Sunday roast for miles'. Not surprisingly, it is popular and often crowded on Sunday lunchtime and weekend evenings. ♨Q⊳❀P

Campton

White Hart
Mill lane SG17 5NX
✪ 12-3 (not Mon-Thu), 7-11; 12-11 Sat; 12-3, 7-10.30 Sun
☎ (01462) 812567
Beer range varies Ⓗ
This family-run free house has been in the Guide since 1976. A Grade II listed traditional pub, it features quarry-tiled floors, inglenooks and a large garden with a well-equipped play area. The pub runs popular petanque and dominoes teams. No food is available but buffets can be arranged for special occasions. ♨Q❀♣P

Clophill

Stone Jug
10 Back Street, MK45 4BY (off A6 N end of village)
✪ 12-3, 6-11; 12-11 Fri; 11-11 Sat; 12-10.30 Sun
☎ (01525) 860526
B&T Shefford Bitter; Courage Best Bitter; John Smith's Bitter; guest beers Ⓗ
Popular village local close to the Greensand Ridge walk. Converted from a stone cottage in the early 20th century, the single L-shaped bar serves two drinking areas plus a function/children's room. There is a patio garden at the rear and picnic benches at the front. Excellent home-made lunches are served Monday-Saturday. Q⊳❀◐♿♣●P

Cople

Five Bells ✔
1-3 Northill Road, MK44 3TU
✪ 11.30-2.30, 6-11; 12-11 Sat; 12-10.30 Sun
☎ (01234) 838289
Greene King IPA, Abbot Ⓗ
Cosy village pub with low beams and, reputedly, a resident ghost. The pub has three interconnecting rooms, two no-smoking, around a central bar area. A well-deserved reputation for home-cooked food has been achieved by using locally sourced ingredients wherever possible. No evening meals are served on Sunday or Monday. ♨❀◐P⁄

Cranfield

Carpenters Arms
93 High Street, MK43 0DP
✪ 12-3 (not Mon), 6-11; 12-3, 7-10.30 Sun

☎ (01234) 750232
Wells Eagle; guest beers 🄷
Situated in the heart of Cranfield, the 'Carps' is a light and airy modernised pub with wood floors and cladding. Home-cooked meals are served in the popular, no-smoking lounge/restaurant. Traditional pub games are played in the bar. The large car park leads to a secure patio garden.
⛼Q❀◑⊟♿♣P⚟

Dunstable

Victoria
69 West Street, LU6 1ST
⏲ 11-11; 12-10.30 Sun
☎ (01582) 662682
Beer range varies 🄷
Friendly, town-centre local, strong on pub games and TV sport. It has just one bar, but a comfortable function/dining room can be used when not booked. The house beer, Victoria Bitter, is brewed by Tring, while four ever-changing guests come from micros and regional brewers. A paved patio area to the rear hosts summer barbecues. A regular CAMRA local Pub of the Year winner, it stages quarterly beer festivals. ❀◐♣

Eaton Bray

Five Bells
2 Market Square, LU6 2DG
⏲ 12-2.30 (not Mon), 5-11; 12-11 Fri & Sat; 12-10.30 Sun
☎ (01525) 220262
Greene King IPA; Shepherd Neame Spitfire; guest beers 🄷
Village local with a small, no-smoking public bar and a further split-level bar with an inglenook. A large TV in the lower level shows Sky Sports. The function room, with its own bar, can be used as a family room in the daytime and lots of toys are provided. The garden has a children's play area. Food is served at the weekend, including Sunday roasts. Note the Titanic corner next to inglenook. ♉◐♣P⚟

Great Barford

Anchor Inn ✔
High Street, MK44 3LF
⏲ 12-3, 5.30-11; 12-11 Sat; 12-10.30 Sun
☎ (01234) 870364
Wells Eagle; guest beers 🄷
Picturesque village pub next to the church, overlooking the River Ouse. Good, home-cooked food is served in the bar and restaurant. Two guest beers from an extensive range are usually available, as well as a large selection of wines. The pub is popular with boaters in summer.
Q◑⛺P⚟

Henlow

Engineers Arms ✔
68 High Street, SG16 6AA
⏲ 12-11; 12-10.30 Sun
☎ (01462) 812284
website: www.engineersarms.co.uk
Beer range varies 🄷
A genuine, friendly village local where visitors are made to feel more than welcome. Nine handpumps offer around 15-20 different beers each week. Regular beer festivals are held, leading up to the main event in October, when over 60 beers are stocked. Community activities and organised trips at home and abroad make this award-winning pub a hub of local life.
⛼❀⊟♿♣

Kempston

Half Moon ✔
108 High Street, MK42 7BN
⏲ 12-3 (3.30 Sat), 6 (5 Fri; 7 Sat)-11; 12-3.30, 7-10.30 Sun
☎ (01234) 852464
Wells Eagle, Bombardier 🄷
Friendly local, with a cosy, comfortable lounge and a spacious public bar with darts and skittles. A new outdoor drinking area will enhance the existing large garden with a grassed play area. A past Wells Best Pub in Bloom award winner, the pub is situated in the old part of town near the Great Ouse and convenient for country walks by the river. ❀⊟♣P

Kensworth

Farmer's Boy ✔
216 Common Road, LU6 2PJ
⏲ 11-11; 12-10.30 Sun
☎ 01582 872207
Fuller's London Pride, ESB 🄷
Welcoming village pub with a small public bar and a comfortable lounge with a separate dining area where children are welcome. Note the original Mann, Crossman & Pullin brewery leaded windows. The large garden has a fenced off children's play area, and stages a summer beer festival. The pub is renowned for the sport of dwyle flunking – just ask at the bar if you want to know more.
⛼❀◑♣P

Keysoe

White Horse
Kimbolton Road, MK44 2JA
(on B660 at Keysoe Row crossroads)
⏲ 12-3, 5.30 (7 Mon)-11; 12-11 Sat; 12-10.30 Sun
☎ (01234) 376363
Wells Eagle; guest beers 🄷
Traditional single-bar country pub with a thatched roof and low beams, situated in good walking and riding country. It is one of the oldest pubs in the Charles Wells estate and is said to be haunted. Children are welcome in the conservatory and large garden. Two guest beers are always on tap. No food is served Sunday evening or Monday lunchtime. ⛼❀◑♣P

Leighton Buzzard

Hare
10 Southcott Village, Linslade, LU7 2PR
⏲ 12-2.30, 5-11; 12-11 Fri & Sat; 12-10.30 Sun
☎ (01525) 373941
Courage Best Bitter; Fuller's London Pride; Young's Bitter; guest beers 🄷
Popular pub overlooking the village green which attracts a good mix of local drinkers. Over time the village has expanded and it is now part of the town. A collection of historic photographs features in the pub. An annual St George's Day

beer festival is held in a marquee in the large rear garden. Two regularly changing guest beers are always on offer. ⛬❀⇌♣P

Luton

Bramingham ✔

Bramingham Park, Quantock Rise, LU3 4AB

⏲ 11-11; 12-11 Sat; 12-10.30 Sun

☎ (01582) 616767

Wells Eagle, Bombardier; guest beers (occasional) Ⓗ

Friendly bar staff provide a warm welcome at this large pub. Inside is a spacious, open-plan main bar and a smaller bar with TV, pool table and darts. The huge garden makes the pub popular in summer. Although outside the town centre, the pub is well served by local buses. Sunday is quiz night and occasional live music is hosted. A family friendly menu, with Sunday roasts a speciality, is offered in the large, no-smoking dining area (no food Sun eve).

❀◐◗♿P⚟

Bricklayers Arms

16-18 Hightown Road, LU2 0DD

⏲ 12-3, 5-11; 12-11 Fri & Sat; 12-10.30 Sun

☎ (01582) 611017

Everards Beacon, Tiger; guest beers Ⓗ

Very much a locals' pub, especially on match days, when it can get busy, it is somewhat quirky at times. Two TVs show Sky Sports, and on Monday there is a quiz. The house beer is B&T Goalden Hatter. Two guest beers are usually sourced from micro breweries; on average eight a week. Belgian beers are also stocked. Weekday lunchtime snacks are available including a good choice of rolls, toasties and ploughmans. ❀⇌♣P

English Rose

46 Old Bedford Road, LU2 7PA

⏲ 12-11; 12-10.30 Sun

☎ (01582) 723889

Beer range varies Ⓗ

A village local in the town, this friendly corner pub is conveniently situated for the train station. Families are welcome, and there is a large garden and play area. Weekly highlights are Monday's pool league and the quiz on Tuesday. Bar staff have a basic knowledge of British sign language. Three beers are usually on draught, and good food is served, with a take-away service available. It was local CAMRA runner-up Pub of the Year 2005.

❀◐◗⇌♣

Globe

26 Union Street, LU1 3AN

⏲ 11-11; 12-10.30 Sun

☎ (01582) 728681

Caledonian Deuchars IPA; Greene King IPA; guest beer Ⓗ

Popular street-corner pub, just out of the town centre. The one-bar, L-shaped pub offers a frequently changing guest ale, supplied by a micro or regional brewer. Regular beer festivals are hosted. Sport is shown on TVs. Good value lunches are served Monday-Saturday. At the rear of the car park is an enclosed patio area where barbecues are held on summer Sundays. ❀◐♣P

Maulden

George

6 George Street, MK45 2DF

⏲ 11-3, 6-11; 11-11 Sat; 12-10.30 Sun

☎ (01525) 751330

Adnams Bitter; Young's Bitter; guest beer Ⓗ

Heavily beamed, 15th-century country pub. The public bar is used for games, while the lounge has a no-smoking area for diners featuring an extensive menu. Two-course lunches are good value during the week, and there is a special three-course meal deal on a Monday evening. Live music is played on alternate Friday nights. The pub has a good family atmosphere and benefits from a large garden. ❀◐◗⊟♣P

Potton

Old Coach House

12 Market Square, SG19 2NP

⏲ 12-2.30, 5-11; 12-11 Sat; 12-10.30 Sun

☎ (01767) 260221

website: www.pottoncoachhouse.co.uk

Adnams Bitter; Potton Shannon IPA, Shambles; guest beer Ⓗ

Formerly the Rose & Crown Hotel, this 17th-century coaching inn has seen much refurbishment but retains much of its original features and character. As close as you can get to a brewer's tap, the local Potton Brewery beers are always available and much enjoyed by the regulars. An ever-changing guest beer is also on offer. Petanque is played on the patio and a jazz band entertains in the bar on the first Thursday of the month.

⛬Q❀⛟◐◗⊟♿P

Ridgmont

Rose & Crown

89 High Street, MK43 0TT

⏲ 12-3.30, 6-11; 11-11 Sat; 12-10.30 Sun

☎ (01525) 280245

Adnams Broadside; Wells Eagle; guest beer Ⓗ

Attractive pub, built of local brick and dating back some 300 years. The old kitchen has recently been removed, allowing one of the two bars to expand. The other bar is no-smoking and has a raised dining area to the rear. The huge garden has approved camping and caravan facilities. Good food is served at every session except Sunday evening.

⛬❀◐◗⛺P⚟

Riseley

Fox & Hounds ✔

High Street, MK44 1DT

⏲ 11-2.30, 6-11; 12-3, 7-10.30 Sun

☎ (01234) 708240

Wells Eagle, Bombardier; guest beers Ⓗ

This old village inn has a reputation for good food and attracts diners from a wide area. Charcoal-grilled steaks, sold by weight and served with salad, are a speciality (not available Sat lunch). A dining room can be reserved for parties. Booking is not necessary for bar meals – relax and enjoy your pint while your food is cooked. The large, lawned garden has a covered patio with heaters for inclement weather.

Q❀◐◗P

Salford

Red Lion Hotel

Wavendon Road, MK17 8AZ (2 miles N of M1 jct 13)
⏲ 11-2.30, 6-11; 12-2.30, 7-10.30 Sun
☎ (01908) 583117
Wells Eagle, Bombardier Ⓗ
Traditional country hotel serving a fine selection of home-cooked food in the bar and no-smoking dining room. The bar, warmed by an open fire in winter, offers a selection of board games. The large garden includes a covered area and a safe children's playground. The hotel annexe offers well-furnished rooms, some with four-poster beds. ♨Q❀⇄◐◑⊟♿♣P

Sandy

Sir William Peel

39 High Street, SG19 1AG
⏲ 11-11; 12-10.30 Sun
☎ (01767) 680607
Everards Beacon; guest beers Ⓗ
This traditional pub has a single bar with four handpumps, plus a patio garden. The Old Stables Brewery Co is based here, providing a wide range of seasonal ales. Guest beers are supplied by micro-breweries. Friendly staff offer a warm welcome to visitors. There is no food available but a chip shop and Indian restaurant are on either side of the pub. ❀♿≠P

Shefford

Brewery Tap

14 North Bridge Street, SG17 5DH
⏲ 11.30-11; 12-10.30 Sun
☎ (01462) 628448
B&T Shefford Mild, Shefford Bitter, Dragonslayer, seasonal beers; Everards Tiger; guest beers Ⓗ
Basic single-bar drinkers' pub, a short walk from the B&T Brewery. Resurrected by B&T in 1996, the pub features breweriana and a large collection of bottled beers. The single bar serves two areas and a family room. The patio garden is entered through an archway. Bar snacks include hot pies and filled rolls. Occasional live music and entertainment is hosted on Friday evening. ☋❀♣P

Stotfold

Stag Tavern

35 Brook Street, SG5 4LA
⏲ 4 (1 Fri; 12 Sat)-11; 12-10.30 Sun
☎ (01462) 730261
Adnams Bitter, Broadside; guest beers Ⓗ
Friendly village free house with a recently refurbished main bar and separate games area. Adnams Bitter is always on tap, along with two frequently changing guests, often from local Bedfordshire breweries. A real drinkers' pub, no food is served except on occasional themed curry or chilli nights. Live music and quiz nights are also hosted at this regular haunt for local steam traction enthusiasts. ❀♿P

Streatley

Chequers

171 Sharpenhoe Road, LU3 9PS
⏲ 12-11; 12-10.30 Sun
☎ (01582) 882072
Greene King IPA, Morland Original, Abbot, Old Speckled Hen; guest beers Ⓗ
In the centre of the village next to the church, the Chequers is Georgian in origin but has been much extended. Look for the CAMRA board to the right of the bar. A single L-shaped bar offers food all day. Unusually for the area, oversized glasses are used. The pub is popular with walkers from the Chiltern Way nearby. The garden has a play area and hosts monthly Sunday afternoon jazz sessions. Accommodation is available in five guest rooms. ♨❀⇄◐◑♣P⊡

Studham

Red Lion

Church Road, LU6 2QA
⏲ 11.30-11; 12-10.30 Sun
☎ (01582) 872530
Adnams Bitter; Fuller's London Pride; Greene King IPA; Tring Colley's Dog; guest beer Ⓗ
Overlooking the village common, this friendly, welcoming pub has a lounge bar, snug and a no-smoking dining room serving a good and varied menu from bar snacks to substantial meals. The village of Studham is popular with walkers and visitors to Whipsnade Zoo. There is usually at least one beer from a local brewer and real cider has recently been added to the list. Dogs are welcome in the bar. No food is served on Sunday or Monday evenings. ♨☋❀◐◑♣●P

Sutton

John O'Gaunt

30 High Street, SG19 2NG
⏲ 12-3, 7-11; 12-3, 7-10.30 Sun
☎ (01767) 260377
Greene King IPA, Abbot; guest beer Ⓗ
Originally three cottages in the early 1700s, this building became a pub in 1830. The present landlord has been here for 29 years and the pub has featured in this Guide for the last 17 years. Three handpumps serve two Greene King ales plus a guest. The Sutton village quilt hangs in the saloon bar where excellent food is served (not Sun eve). Dogs are welcome in the public bar. ♨Q❀◐◑⊟⛺♣P⊁

Tebworth

Queen's Head

The Lane, LU7 9QB
⏲ 11.30-3 (not Tue), 6-11; 12-3, 7-10.30 Sun
☎ (01525) 874101
Adnams Broadside; Ⓖ **Wells Eagle;** Ⓗ **guest beers** Ⓖ
Two-bar village local built in 1926 following the destruction of the former thatched pub by fire. The public bar is popular for darts and dominoes. The lounge offers a quiz on Thursday and live music on Friday. There is a garden at the rear. No food is served. The pub has featured in this Guide for over 20 years under the present landlord, who also has a career as an actor with innumerable appearances on stage, radio and TV. ♨❀⊟♣P

Toddington

Oddfellows Arms ✔
2 Conger Lane, LU5 6BP
✪ 12-3 (not Mon-Thu), 5-11; 11-11 Sat; 12-10.30 Sun
☎ (01525) 872021
Adnams Broadside; Fuller's London Pride; guest beers [H]
Attractive 15th-century pub facing the village green, with a heavily beamed and brassed L-shaped bar and a no-smoking restaurant. There are over 20 bottled Belgian beers to choose from, all served in their correct glasses. The varied menu offers good food (not served Sun or Mon eve) and beer festivals are held in the spring and autumn. ᗑ❀◑◗♣

Sow & Pigs ✔
14 Church Square, LU5 6AA
✪ 11-11; 12-10.30 Sun
☎ (01525) 873089 website: www.sowandpigs.co.uk
Greene King IPA, Abbot; guest beers [H]
This 19th-century commercial inn has featured in every edition of the Guide. It has one long, narrow bar heated by open fires, decorated with pigs, golf memorabilia and paintings of the pub by local artists. A selection of games is offered. Curries, home-made soup, chilli, cold platters and rolls are served at lunchtime. A well-planted patio garden is to the rear. Comfortable accommodation is available. ᗑQ❀⇌♣P

Totternhoe

Cross Keys
201 Castle Hill Road, LU6 2DA
✪ 11.30-3.30, 5.30-11; 11.30-11 Sat; 12-10.30 Sun
☎ (01525) 220434
Adnams Broadside; Greene King IPA; guest beer [H]
Attractive, Grade II listed, thatched building tastefully restored after a major fire. The fireplace in the saloon dates back to 1433. The quaint, no-smoking restaurant serves lunchtime and early evening meals except Sunday evening. The large garden has extensive views of Aylesbury Vale and Ivinghoe Beacon. It was South Bedfordshire CAMRA Most Improved Pub 2005. ❀◑◗♣P

Old Farm Inn ✔
16 Church Road, LU6 1RE
✪ 12-3, 5-11; 12-11 Fri & Sat; 12-10.30 Sun
☎ (01582) 661294
website: www.theoldfarminn.co.uk
Fuller's London Pride, ESB, seasonal beers; guest beers [H]
Located in the hamlet of Church End under the shadow of Dunstable Downs, this splendid local boast not one but two inglenooks. The bar, with its low, boarded ceiling, is where the locals get together for a good chinwag and play traditional pub games. At the rear is a restaurant serving excellent, good value food. The restaurant has a separate entrance with disabled access. There is a large child-friendly garden. ᗧ❀◑◗ᗺ♿♣P

Upper Sundon

White Hart
56 Streatley Road, LU3 3PQ
✪ 11-11; 12-10.30 Sun
☎ (01525) 872493
Wells Eagle; guest beers [H]
Friendly, mock-Tudor, two-bar village local with low beams and leaded windows. It is tucked away in a side-street in this semi-rural scattered village. The village is on a hill and close by is Sundon Hills country park, a popular walking area. The pub itself has gardens at the front and rear. A large selection of malt whiskies is stocked. ❀ᗺ♣P

Whipsnade

Old Hunter's Lodge
The Cross Roads, LU6 2LN
✪ 11-3, 5-11; 12-3, 7-10.30 Sun
☎ (01582) 872228 website: www.old-hunters.com
Greene King IPA; Abbot; guest beer [H]
Near Whipsnade Zoo, one of Europe's most important centres for breeding and conserving rare animals, the Lodge is a 15th-century thatched inn. Two guest beers are served in the comfortable lounge, usually from micros. There is a large dining area and six guest rooms – the bridal suite has a four-poster. ᗑ❀⇌◑◗ᗺP

Wilden

Victoria
23 High Street, MK44 2PB
✪ 12-2.30, 6.30-11; 12-11 Sat; 12-3.30, 7-10.30 Sun
☎ (01234) 772146
Greene King IPA, Abbot; guest beer [H]
Friendly, one-bar village local with a no-smoking restaurant. Good, home-cooked food includes fish and chips on Tuesday, senior citizens' special deal on Wednesday, pie and a pint on Thursday and curry night on Friday (no eve meals Sun or Mon). Guest beers come from the Greene King range. ᗑᗧ❀◑◗♣P

Wootton

Chequers
Hall End, MK43 9HP OS001458
✪ 11.30-2.30, 5.30-11; 12-10.30 Sun
☎ (01234) 768394
Wells Eagle [H]
Heavy beams and a low ceiling give the lounge bar an intimate atmosphere. The large, lawned garden with its tables and chairs is a popular location on fine weekends in the summer. An interesting range of food is served Wednesday-Sunday lunchtime and Tuesday-Saturday evening. Skittles is played in the public bar. ❀◑◗ᗺ♣P

Yelden

Chequers
High Street, MK44 1AW
✪ 12-2 (not Mon-Thu), 5-11; 12-11 Sat; 12-10.30 Sun
☎ (01933) 356383
Fuller's London Pride; [H] **Greene King Abbot;** [G] **Shepherd Neame Spitfire; guest beers** [H]
Traditional village pub stocking five real ales and two ciders. Families are welcome in the skittles room. Home-cooked pub meals are served in the no-smoking lounge, with occasional ticket-only guest chef days. The large garden has children's play equipment and hosts an annual spring bank holiday beer festival. Yelden is on the Three Shires Way footpath and boasts the impressive earthworks of an abandoned Norman castle. ᗑᗧ❀◑◗▲♣●P⚟

BERKSHIRE

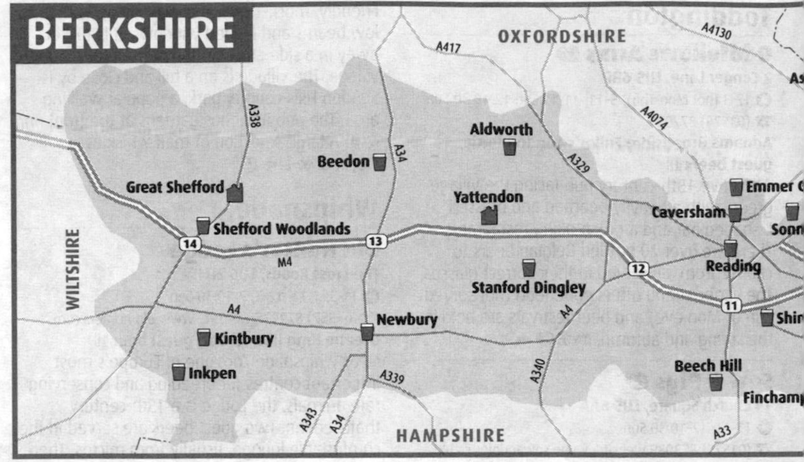

Aldworth

Bell ☆

Bell Lane, RG8 9SE (off B4009) OS555796
11-3, 6-11; closed Mon; 12-3, 7-10.30 Sun
☎ (01635) 578272
Arkells 3B, Kingsdown; West Berkshire Maggs Mild, seasonal beers Ⓗ
Splendid, unspoilt village ale house in a 15th-century hall house near the Ridgeway. Run by the same family for 200 years, it has won many awards including CAMRA West Berkshire Pub of the Year in 2005. The garden is delightful and provides access to the village cricket ground next door. No games machines or piped music intrude here, just friendly conversation. Delicious filled rolls complement the beers and local cider.
ᗑQ❀⊞♣P

Ascot

Swinley

29 Brockenhurst Road, South Ascot, SL5 9DJ (on A330)
11-11; 12-10.30 Sun
☎ (01344) 621743
Greene King IPA, Abbot, Ruddles Best, seasonal beers Ⓗ
This red-brick, street-corner pub with friendly, welcoming staff has no pretensions to be anything other than a genuine down to earth local. It has an unspoilt public bar, a large lounge with a TV and real fire, and a small, well-kept garden/patio. Yvonne, the landlady for over 30 years, has received a special Award of Excellence from the local CAMRA branch.
ᗑ❀◑⊞♿♣P

Aston

Flower Pot

Ferry Lane, RG9 3DG
11-3, 6-11 (11-11 summer Sat); 12-3, 7-10.30 (12-10.30 summer) Sun
☎ (01491) 574721
Brakspear Bitter, Special, seasonal beers; Hook Norton Hooky Dark Ⓗ
Charming red-brick hotel, built around 1890, near the south bank of the Thames, with glorious Chiltern views. The bars and restaurant feature many impressive stuffed fish, while guinea fowl roam the large garden. Children are welcome in the lounge and restaurant. Why not come by boat (tie up at the pub's own landing stage), or walk the three miles along the Thames Path from Henley? A barbecue is held on summer Sunday lunchtimes if the weather is fine.
ᗑQ❀◑⊞P

Beech Hill

Elm Tree ✔

Beech Hill Road, RG7 2AZ (just W of A33)
12-11; 12-10.30 Sun
☎ (0118) 988 3505 website: www.the-elmtree.com
Adnams Bitter; Fuller's London Pride; guest beer Ⓗ
Once a simple, two-room Victorian village pub, the Elm Tree has been extended in recent years, with the barn and conservatory now offering high quality food in a pleasant environment. The Clock Room is packed full of clocks ranging from the antique to the frankly ridiculous. The decked patio has a slightly Mediterranean feel and affords views over the beautiful downland of north Hampshire. National Cycle Route 23 (Reading-Basingstoke) passes nearby. The ladies' toilets are bizarre! ᗑ❀◑P

Beedon

Langley Hall

World's End, RG20 8SA (1 mile S of village) OS484761
11-3, 5.30-11; 11-11 Fri & Sat; 12-6.30 Sun
☎ (01635) 248332
West Berkshire Good Old Boy; guest beers Ⓗ
This well-liked, welcoming roadside pub attracts locals and business people alike. The large single bar is horseshoe shaped with minimalist decor. Board games, including backgammon, are played here. The pub has built up a good reputation for its excellent home-cooked meals, while retaining a friendly, relaxed pub atmosphere. There is a large rear garden and a

INDEPENDENT BREWERIES

Butts Great Shefford
West Berkshire Yattendon

smaller patio at the front for outdoor drinking. Piped music can be loud later in the evening. ♨❀⇌◐◑♣P

Binfield

Victoria Arms

Terrace Road North, RG42 5JA

(N of B3034 at mini roundabout in village centre)

✪ 11.30-11; 12-10.30 Sun

☎ (01344) 483856

Fuller's Chiswick, London Pride, ESB, seasonal beers; guest beer Ⓗ

Popular and friendly village pub with a central bar, exposed brick walls and an enormous bottled beer collection covering every space available on the rafters. A wide range of freshly-made food is served (light snacks only on Sun eve). One small area of the bar is no-smoking. In the winter there is always an open fire blazing and in summer the garden is a great place to spend a summer evening. ♨❀◐◑P⚟

Bracknell

Old Manor ✔

Grenville Place, High Street, RG12 1BP

✪ 11-11; 12-10.30 Sun

☎ (01344) 304490

Marston's Burton Bitter, Pedigree; Greene King Abbot Ⓗ

Dating back to Tudor times, this sympathetically refurbished former manor house is now a Wetherspoon's pub. Full of character throughout, the Monks Room, which can be booked for private functions, features an original priest hole. The main bar, where accompanied children may dine until 8.30pm, offers three changing guest beers, often from the local Loddon Brewery. The lower bar stocks the regular pub range. Smoking is no longer allowed in the pub but it is permitted on the outside patio and garden. Q❀◐◑♿≠●P⚟

Caversham

Baron Cadogan ✔

22-24 Prospect Street, RG4 8JG

✪ 10-11; 12-10.30 Sun

☎ (0118) 947 0626

Courage Directors; Greene King Abbot; Marston's Burton Bitter, Pedigree; guest beers Ⓗ

This Wetherspoon's pub usually has four regular beers and two changing guests, one of which is often from the local Loddon Brewery. It also sometimes stocks the Belgian De Koninck beer, specially brewed in cask condition for Wetherspoon. The pub is open plan but there is a no-smoking area, where children are allowed. The wall decorations include old plates and cooking utensils, and work by local artists is also on display. Q◐◑♿≠P⚟

Crown on the Bridge

3 Bridge Street, RG4 8AA

✪ 12-11; 12-10.30 Sun

☎ (0118) 954 5300

Fuller's London Pride; Young's Bitter; guest beer (occasional) Ⓗ

Lively local where the emphasis is on food during the week. However, visit when there is a big rugby or football match on – shown on all three TVs – and you will find a different atmosphere altogether with a keen sports crowd. The pub has an L-shaped bar with interesting hand-drawn portraits on the walls at the front and a pool table towards the rear. No evening meals are served Friday-Sunday. ◐◑≠P

Prince of Wales

76 Prospect Street, RG4 8JN

✪ 12-3, 6-11; 12-11 Fri & Sat; 12-10.30 Sun

☎ (0118) 947 2267

Brakspear Bitter, Special, seasonal beers; guest beers Ⓗ

This has been a Brakspear house for over 100 years and on the walls are some old pictures of the pub dating back over the years. The bar is wood-panelled and features some attractive fireplaces. The main seating area has a large tank of exotic fish in the corner. Good food is available including Asian and continental favourites. There is a pull-down screen for viewing sporting events and a pool table. No evening meals are served Tuesday-Thursday. ◐◑P

Cookham

Bounty

SL8 5RG (footpath from station car park, across bridge, along towpath) OS893868

✪ 12-10.30 (12-dusk winter Sat; closed winter Mon-Fri); 12-10.30 (12-dusk winter) Sun

☎ (01628) 520056

Rebellion IPA, Mutiny, seasonal beers Ⓗ

There is no road access to this riverside inn – even the beer arrives by boat. The front room has a boat-shaped bar and is decorated with assorted flags and other, mostly nautical, paraphernalia. The back room is no-smoking. A large patio and a garden with children's play area make the pub ideal for families. Food is served until the early evening. Limited free mooring and camping are available – ask at the bar. ♨❀◐⛺≠(Bourne End)⚟

Cookham Dean

Jolly Farmer

Church Road, SL9 9DP

⏲ 11.30-11; 12-10.30 Sun
☎ (01628) 482905
website: www.jollyfarmercookhamdean.co.uk
Brakspear Bitter; Courage Best Bitter; Young's Bitter; guest beer Ⓗ
Brick and flint 18th-century pub opposite the village green and church. In 1987 it was purchased by a consortium of locals to save it from modernisation and it is now free of tie. The intimate main bar has a terracotta tiled floor, a low-beamed ceiling and an open fire. The second bar is more open plan and is used by diners and drinkers alike. For more formal dining there is a small and cosy restaurant. No evening meals are served Sunday or Monday.
⌂Q❀◐◑♣P

Crowthorne

Prince
2 High Street, RG45 7AZ
⏲ 11-11; 12-10.30 Sun
☎ (01344) 772241
Fuller's London Pride; Wells Bombardier; guest beers Ⓗ
Attractive Victorian pub with wooden flooring, stone flags and boasting three log fires. With a mixture of armchairs, sofas and traditional pub furniture, it attracts a wide range of customers – locals and visitors – and has a large, comfortable no-smoking area. Two guest beers are always available, selected by regulars from the landlord's list. Home-cooked food is served from noon every day. Quiz nights are on Tuesday and Sunday and live music is performed on Thursday.
⌂❀◐◑P⊁

Emmer Green

Black Horse ✔
16 Kidmore End Road, RG4 8SE
⏲ 11-11; 12-10.30 Sun
☎ (0118) 947 4111
Caledonian Deuchars IPA; Courage Best Bitter Ⓗ
Unpretentious late Victorian local facing the village green. Two wood-panelled bars are the focal point. Choose from the lively public bar with its pool table or the quieter lounge with a real fire. There is easy access from Reading town centre (No. 45 bus). Do not confuse with the White Horse (Greene King) opposite!
⌂Q⊞

Eton

Waterman's Arms
Brocas Street, SL4 6BW
⏲ 11-11; 12-10.30 Sun
☎ (01753) 861001
Brakspear Bitter; Fuller's London Pride; Hogs Back TEA; guest beer Ⓗ
This 16th-century building has been a workhouse and a mortuary in its time, but a hostelry since the mid-1800s. The restaurant used to be the courtyard, as is evident from the trees remaining in situ. An extensive menu specialises in fish, which is delivered daily from Billingsgate market. Sunday lunch is popular and children are welcome. Real cider is sometimes available.
⌂◐◑⇌(Windsor & Eton Riverside/Central) ●

Finchampstead

Queen's Oak
Church Lane, RG40 4LS
(follow signs to Finchampstead church) OS793639
⏲ 11-11; 12-10.30 Sun
☎ (0118) 973 4855
Brakspear Bitter, Special, seasonal beers Ⓗ
The pub gets its unique name from the oak tree (long gone) on the village green, planted in 1887 to commemorate Victoria's golden jubilee. This pleasant pub has a main bar, no-smoking room and dining area with log fire, where children are permitted until 9pm. The garden has play equipment and an award-winning barbecue. On Wednesday evening in summer Aunt Sally is played in the garden and in winter quiz nights are held. Good food, from snacks to main meals, is available.
⌂Q❀◐◑♣P⊁

Hurley

Dew Drop Inn
Batts Green, Honey Lane, SL6 6RB
(1 mile S of A4130) OS824815
⏲ 12-3, 6-11; 12-3, 7-10.30 Sun
☎ (01628) 824327
Brakspear Bitter, Special; seasonal beers Ⓗ
This fine country pub at the foot of Ashley Hill, between Hurley and Burchetts Green, has deservedly won many local CAMRA awards including Pub of the Year and Publicans of the Year in recent times. The large garden is delightful in summer while log fires make for cosy winter evenings. Home-cooked meals are available, except on Sunday evening. Supervised children and dogs on leads are welcome.
⌂Q❀◐◑♣P

Hurst

Green Man (off A321 between Wokingham and Twyford)
Hinton Road, RG10 0BP
⏲ 11-3, 5.30-11; 12-3.30, 6.30-10.30 Sun
☎ (0118) 934 2599
website: www.thegreenman.uk.com
Brakspear Bitter, Special, seasonal beers Ⓗ
Superb oak-beamed village pub in a rural setting which first became a licensed hostelry in 1602. The emphasis here is on a reasonably-priced range of good quality food with daily specials, but this is also the place to enjoy a fine pint in good company. The attractive garden boasts a delightful array of hanging baskets and floral beds in summer. Children are welcome if dining until 7.30pm. ⌂Q❀◐◑♿P⊁

Inkpen

Crown & Garter
Great Common, RG17 9QR
(follow signs for Inkpen Common from Kintbury) OS378639
⏲ 12-3 (not Mon & Tue), 5.30-11; 12-3, 7-10.30 Sun
☎ (01488) 668325
website: www.crownandgarter.com
Archers Golden; Arkells Moonlight; West Berkshire Mr Chubb's, Good Old Boy Ⓗ
This rural inn is set in an area of outstanding natural beauty and is ideally situated for walking in the surrounding countryside. It offers local

ales from the West Berkshire Brewery, excellent home-cooked food and en-suite accommodation. Families are welcome, with colouring books and crayons provided for children. Dogs are allowed. The large tree-lined garden provides fine views of the nearby Combe Hills.

Swan

Craven Road, RG17 9DX
(follow signs for Inkpen from Hungerford Common) OS359643
11-2.30 (3 Sat), 7-11; 12-3, 7-10.30 Sun
☎ (01488) 668326
website: www.theswaninn-organics.co.uk
Butts Jester, Traditional; guest beers
Large 17th-century inn situated in an area popular with walkers and cyclists. This friendly and spacious pub includes an oak-beamed restaurant, a well-stocked organic farm shop and 10-room accommodation. Local beers come from Butts Brewery and Lambourn Valley cider is available. Good quality organic food is served in the bar and restaurant. No-smoking areas are provided for diners and drinkers. Wheelchair friendly, the pub is ramped throughout. Darts is played in the flagstoned games room.

Kintbury

Dundas Arms

Station Road, RG17 9UT (opp. station) OS386671
11-2.30, 6-11; 12-2.30 (closed eve) Sun
☎ (01488) 658263
website: www.dundasarms.co.uk
Adnams Bitter; West Berkshire Mr Chubb's, Good Old Boy; guest beers
This 18th-century whitewashed building is situated on the bank of the Kennet & Avon Canal and the River Kennet, opposite Kintbury station. It is named after the local dignitary who sponsored the canal's construction. The small single bar has a counter top completely covered with polished old pennies. There is a decked area beside the canal from where you can watch horse-drawn narrowboats in the summer. No food is served on Sunday. Q P

Maidenhead

Ark

20 Ray Street, SL6 8PX (off A4)
12-11; 12-10.30 Sun
☎ (01628) 418707
Courage Best Bitter
The pub gets its name because, situated in the flood plain, it was built above ground level. It is a small, Victorian, back-street local with a tiny patio and grassed area beyond with swings for children. The old pool room has been converted to a quiet lounge area with large sofas. A plasma screen TV is now installed in the main bar. The rear bar is simply decorated in 1930s style with a selection of old Guinness adverts. It has a warm, homely atmosphere, with its own crib team. Bar snacks are served.

Maidenhead Conservative Club

32 York Road, SL6 1SF
10.30-2.30, 5.30-11; 10.30-11 Sat; 12-3, 7-10.30 Sun
☎ (01628) 620579
Fuller's London Pride, seasonal beers; Greene King IPA; guest beers
Friendly real ale outlet close to the station. Show this Guide or a CAMRA membership card to get in. The club steward is a CAMRA member and this is reflected in the beer quality. Two guest ales are always available, as well as bottle-conditioned beers. Monday is crib night, Tuesday and Wednesday darts, and a quiz is held on Sunday. Food is available at lunchtime except Monday. Parking is limited. P

Portland Arms

16 West Street, SL6 1RL
12-3, 5-11; 12-11 Fri & Sat; 12-10.30 Sun
☎ (01628) 634649
Brakspear Bitter; guest beer
One of the few traditional town pubs left in the area, situated in a back road just off the high street. Basic pub food is available at lunchtime and early evening. Visitors can test their shove-ha'penny skills here. A degree of flexibility in opening hours occurs, dependent on how busy the pub is. Street parking is difficult but there is a pay and display car park nearby.

Newbury

Gun

142 Andover Road, Wash Common, RG14 6NE
(on A343)
11-11; 12-10.30 Sun
☎ (01635) 47292
Adnams Broadside; Courage Best Bitter; Greene King Old Speckled Hen; Marston's Pedigree; Wadworth 6X; guest beer
Although the pub is a mile from town it has a large catchment area, helped by the college and rugby club, and possibly the fact that six real ales are stocked. It is one of the few Newbury pubs that remains multi-roomed and the landlord intends to keep it that way. Ask him about the impish ghost who has made his presence felt over the five years he has run the pub. The Gun is situated close to where the first Battle of Newbury was fought during the Civil War. P

Lock Stock & Barrel

104 Northbrook Street, RG14 1AA
11-11; 12-10.30 Sun
☎ (01635) 580550
Fuller's London Pride, ESB, seasonal beers; guest beers (occasional)
A spacious, single room pub situated in the centre of Newbury, in a fine location next to the Kennet & Avon Canal. The outside patio and roof terrace are heated and are used all year round. During the day there is a buffer zone between the smoking and no-smoking areas. Fuller's bottle-conditioned ales are sold. Meals are served all day.

Monument

57 Northbrook Street, RG14 1AN
11-11; 12-10.30 Sun
☎ (01635) 41964
website: www.themonumentonline.co.uk
Butts Traditional, Barbus Barbus; Gale's HSB; Greene King Old Speckled Hen; Theakston Old Peculier

Small, low-beamed, 16th-century pub run by an enterprising New Zealander. It is far from quiet, with a TV, on-line juke box and games machines, all competing for attention with the regular free gigs in the covered, heated courtyard at the back. Traditional games are also available. Simple pub food is served, including Sunday roast, and themed evenings are on Monday and Tuesday. This is the only outlet for Butts beer in town.
❀◑⇌♣●

Reading

Allied Arms

57 St Mary's Butts, RG1 2LG

⏱ 11-11; 12-10.30 Sun

☎ (0118) 959 0865

Fuller's London Pride; Loddon Hullabaloo; guest beer Ⓗ

Dating from 1828, this small two-room pub features a suntrap patio garden at the back and has a real 'country pub in town' feel to it. Enter from the street into the small, no-smoking Yeoman lounge, or via the cobbled side-passageway into the larger Dragoon lounge. The juke box features an eclectic variety of tunes. Popular with rugby fans, major games are shown on TV, and the pub is heaving when locally-based London Irish are playing at home.
❀⇌⚟

Butler

89-91 Chatham Street, RG1 7DS

⏱ 11-11; 12-3, 7-10.30 Sun

☎ (0118) 959 5500

Fuller's London Pride, ESB, seasonal beers Ⓗ

The Butler family ran two businesses from this site for many years – the Baker's Arms pub and Butler's wine merchants – but locals referred to both as 'Butler's'. The nickname was formalised in 1977 when Fuller's bought the pub, looking to expand beyond its native London. The interior features etched glass, plush seating, low lighting and plenty of natural wood. A TV set occupies one corner of the bar but is not intrusive. Food is served Monday-Saturday.
♨❀◑⇌P

Eldon Arms

19 Eldon Terrace, RG1 4DX

⏱ 11-3, 5.30-11; 12-3, 7-10.30 Sun

☎ (0118) 957 3857

Wadworth IPA, 6X; guest beer Ⓗ

Traditional two-room Wadworth's house nestling in the back streets close to the Royal Berkshire Hospital. It is run by the longest serving publicans in the area, who have notched up over 30 years behind the bar. The decor is simple and timeless, with a cosy lounge separated from the larger and livelier public bar by the old 'jug and bottle' hatch. A small patio garden provides outdoor drinking in fine weather. Henry's IPA and 6X are usually served from the wood. Food is available at lunchtime except Sunday.
◐⊟

Hobgoblin

2 Broad Street, RG1 2BH

⏱ 11-11; 12-10.30 Sun

☎ (0118) 950 8119

Beer range varies Ⓗ

The most interesting range of beers in Reading can be found in this oasis in a town centre dominated by circuit bars. Eight beers are available including any three from the West Berkshire Brewery. The rest range from old favourites from regional breweries to the latest micro-brewery offerings. Almost all available wall and ceiling space is used to display pump clips from the thousands of beers sold in the last 12 years. Drinkers in search of a quiet corner can find wood-panelled booths to the rear.
❀⇌●

Hop Leaf

163-165 Southampton Street, RG1 2QZ

⏱ 4 (12 Thu-Sat)-11; 12-10.30 Sun

☎ (0118) 931 4700

website www.thehopleaf.co.uk

Hop Back GFB, Best Bitter, Crop Circle, Entire Stout, Summer Lightning; guest beers Ⓗ

Just outside the town centre stands this welcoming, bustling pub. Friendly staff serve the full range of Hop Back beers plus guests. Pub teams play darts, football, crib and bar billiards, and the quiet back room can be hired for meetings. Regular beer festivals are held including an Oktoberfest; both light and dark Erdinger and a small selection of foreign bottled beers are usually on offer. It was awarded Reading and Mid-Berks CAMRA Pub of the Year 2005. ❀♣●

Outlook

76-78 Kings Road, RG1 3BJ

⏱ 11-11; 12-10.30 Sun

☎ (0118) 958 6549

Beer range varies Ⓗ

Formerly part of the Hogshead chain, this modern, split-level pub is situated on the bank of the River Kennet. Both floors feature wood and flagstone, and lead out to small outdoor terraces overlooking the riverside. The upper level has a no-smoking area with comfortable armchairs. The number of real ales on offer varies from three to eight, usually from regional breweries. Occasional beer festivals are hosted.
❀◑⇌⚟

Retreat

8 St John's Street, RG1 4EH

⏱ 12-3 (not Mon), 5-11; 12-11 Fri & Sat; 12-10.30 Sun

☎ (0118) 957 1593

Caledonian Deuchars IPA; Ringwood Best Bitter; guest beers Ⓗ

This genuine, traditional back-street pub in the middle of a terrace of houses seems to have been little affected by the passing of the years. Five ales are offered, three from an extensive guest list, plus a choice of ciders and perries from interesting sources. There is an unobtrusive juke box but the emphasis here is on conversation with your pint. Music night is Thursday when the pub gets busy. The local Motorcycle Action Group meets here on Monday.
⊟⇌♣●

Roebuck

37 Auckland Road, RG6 1NY

⏱ 11-11; 12-10.30 Sun

☎ (0118) 926 2226

Greene King IPA, Abbot, seasonal beers Ⓗ

A back-street community local just off the

main cross-town No. 17 bus route, used mainly by students and local residents. The long, single room is comfortably furnished with wood-panelled walls. An extensive Thai menu is available at most times. Friendly staff ensure a warm welcome. There is a weekly quiz night.
❀◑

Shefford Woodlands

Pheasant
Ermin Street, RG17 7AA
✪ 11-11; 12-10.30 Sun
☎ (01488) 648284
Butts Jester; Loddon Hoppit; Wadworth 6X; guest beers Ⓗ
Lively, country pub, popular with the local horse racing fraternity. Many unusual sporting cartoons and paintings decorate the walls and dividers around the tables. The busy flagstoned public bar is sadly no longer partitioned from the dining area but those who come just to drink are still made to feel very welcome. The home-cooked food is highly recommended, particularly the fish and chips. The TV is turned on for horse racing. Note the unusual, original glazing around the bar counter. Ring the bull is played here.
♛◑♣P

Shinfield

Magpie & Parrot
Arborfield Road, RG2 9EA (on A327 E of village)
✪ 12-7; 12-3 Sun
☎ (0118) 988 4130
Fuller's London Pride; guest beer Ⓗ
Situated just south of Shinfield roundabout, this tiny pub is easy to miss – even though the ample grounds double as a plant nursery. The single room contains four tables, a comfy sofa and Spencer the pub dog's chair. The beams and walls are cluttered with old beer bottles and other artefacts. A true 'public house' – the living room is visible through the central fireplace. Occasional beer festivals are held in a marquee. Bus No. 144 from Reading stops outside.
♛Q❀P

Slough

Rose & Crown
312 High Street, SL1 1NB
✪ 11-11; 12-10.30 Sun
☎ (01753) 521114
Beer range varies Ⓗ
The oldest pub on Slough High Street, dating back to the late 16th century. Two bars serve a constantly-changing range of three beers on handpumps. Also two real ciders are on offer and sometimes a perry. In July the pub holds a beer festival and stocks a larger range of ales and ciders. Entertainment includes darts, karaoke on a Friday night, and occasional live music on Saturday. There is a large-screen TV in one bar. ❀⇌♣●

Sonning

Bull Hotel ✔
High Street, RG4 6UP (next to St Andrew's church)
✪ 11-3, 5.30-11; 11-11 Sat; 12-10.30 Sun
☎ (0118) 969 3901
Gale's Butser, HSB, seasonal beers; guest beer (occasional) Ⓗ
Full of character, this 16th-century inn was originally called the Church House because it provided accommodation for pilgrims visiting the medieval chapel of St Andrew's church opposite. Meals are served in the main bar and separate no-smoking family dining area, while the pub retains a basic locals' bar for drinkers only. The lounge features an attractive inglenook. The patio is busy in summer when you can admire the award-winning floral display.
♛Q❀⇔◑⊟P

Stanford Dingley

Bull
RG7 6LS (on Yattendon/Burnt Hill road)
✪ 12-3, 6-11; 12-3, 7-10.30 Sun
☎ (0118) 974 4409
website: www.thebullatstanforddingley.co.uk
Brakspear Bitter; West Berkshire Good Old Boy, Dr Hexter's Healer Ⓗ
This 15th-century country pub is situated in

Cask breather

When a pub entry states that some beers are served with the aid of cask breathers, this means that demand valves are connected to cask and cylinders of gas. As beer is drawn off, it is replaced by applied gas (either carbon dioxide or nitrogen, or both) to prevent oxidation. This method is not acceptable to CAMRA as it does not allow beer to condition and mature naturally. The Campaign believes brewers and publicans should use the size of casks best suited to the turnover of beer in order to avoid oxidation. If a pub in the Good Beer Guide uses cask breathers we list only those beers that are free of the device.

the loveliest village in the idyllic Pang Valley. It has a new restaurant to complement the traditional cottage-style, no-smoking saloon and tap room, both of which have low beams and flagstoned floors – note the wattle and daub wall. Visitors are encouraged to try ringing the bull – not easy! Folk music sessions are held monthly and there is a classic car day on the third Saturday of the month April-September.
♨❀⇔◐◑⊟♿⛺♣⚟

Sunningdale

Nag's Head ✔
28 High Street, SL5 0NG
⌚ 11.30-11; 12-10.30 Sun
☎ (01344) 622725
Harveys XX Mild, BB, seasonal beers 🄷
Traditional village two-bar pub. Darts and pool are played in the public bar while the more comfortable lounge has a no-smoking dining area. Children are welcome for lunch and to play in the garden. A short drive from Ascot, this pub is a rare outlet for Mild and other Harveys beers in the area. No food is served on Sunday.
❀◐⊟♣P⚟

Waltham St Lawrence

Bell ✔
The Street, RG10 0JJ (next to church)
⌚ 12-3, 5-11; 12-10.30 Sun
☎ (0118) 934 1788
Beer range varies 🄷
Dating from circa 1400 and an inn since 1723, this genuine free house serves up to five beers, mainly from local independent breweries such as West Berkshire and Loddon. Both the bare-boarded public bar and carpeted lounge have open log fires. There is also a small snug and a larger dining room. Food is served at lunchtime every session except Sunday evening. Outdoor drinking can be enjoyed in the large rear garden or tables at the front.
♨Q♉❀◐◑⊟P

White Waltham

Beehive
Waltham Road, SL6 3SH
⌚ 11-3, 5.30-11; 11-11 Sat; 12-10.30 Sun
☎ (01628) 822877
website: www.thebeehive.co.uk
Fuller's London Pride; Brakspear Bitter; Greene King Abbot; guest beers 🄷
The Beehive stands south-west of White Waltham airfield and close to the historic church. The pub is divided into three: a public bar, a lounge with real fire, and a no-smoking conservatory/restaurant, serving good home-cooked food. The front garden overlooks the village cricket pitch. In the large rear garden bowls, petanque and, in summer, skittles are played. Occasionally morris dancers perform. A plaque in the car park proclaims that the pub burned down in May 1861 but was rebuilt by late June.
♨Q❀◐◑⊟♿♣P⚟

Windsor

Black Horse ✔
290 Dedworth Road, SL4 4JR
⌚ 11-2.30, 5-11; 11-11 Fri & Sat; 12-10.30 Sun
☎ (01753) 861953
Draught Bass; Fuller's London Pride; guest beers 🄷
Community local in Windsor's western suburb, mostly frequented by the over-30s. Guest ales are often from Rebellion. Darts night is Thursday and occasional quizzes and live music are staged. A skittle alley, available to hire, can be set up in the garden in summer. Buses to and from Windsor town centre stop outside. Children are welcome until 6.30pm. Food is served at lunchtime except on Sunday.
♨❀◐♣P

Carpenters Arms
4 Market Street, SL4 1PB
⌚ 11-11; 12-10.30 Sun
☎ (01753) 755961
Beer range varies 🄷
Fifty yards from the castle, in a cobbled street behind the Guildhall, this multi-level pub dates back to around 1518. Tunnels leading from the cellar to the castle were bricked up in the 19th century. Five handpumps serve an ever-changing selection of real ale. Food is available daily until 9pm (8.30 Sun) when children are welcome in the no-smoking area.
♨◐◑⇌(Central)⚟

Swan
9 Mill Lane, Clewer Village, SL4 5JG
⌚ 12-3 (not Mon-Fri), 5.30-11; 12-3, 7-10 Sun
☎ (01753) 862069
Fuller's London Pride; Gale's Best, HSB 🄷
Traditional, friendly, 18th-century back-street pub, cosy in winter with a wood-burning fire. It is mainly frequented by locals but its close proximity to Windsor and the racecourse makes it a good watering hole for visitors. Although the pub has no garden children (and dogs) are welcome in the bar. There is a dartboard in one corner and the pub also holds regular quizzes. Food is not available but the pub has four rooms for B&B accommodation. ♨⇔♣●P

Trooper
37 St Leonards Road, SL4 3BZ
⌚ 11-11; 12-10.30 Sun
☎ (01753) 670123
Gale's Best, HSB, seasonal beers 🄷
Full of character, this 19th-century coaching inn is situated just beyond the end of Windsor's main shopping street and within walking distance of the castle. The main bar is always busy, with office workers at lunchtime, and locals in the evening, particularly when live sport is on TV. A covered garden room serves as a no-smoking area and dining room (no food Sun eve). It is a rare outlet for Gale's in this area.
❀⇔◐◑⇌(Central)⚟

Vansittart Arms ✔
105 Vansittart Road, SL4 5DD
⌚ 12-11; 12-10.30 Sun
☎ (01753) 865988
website: www.chipfreezone.com

Fuller's London Pride, ESB, seasonal beers 🄷
A long-standing regular in the Guide, and deservedly so. This Fuller's pub west of the town centre was once five cottages for castle workers. Its two main bar areas have recesses and cosy real fires. The garden is partly covered and heated for cooler summer evenings. There are occasional beer festivals in summer. Rugby is keenly followed here. Home-cooked food is served (not Sun eve). The website address gives a clue to what is not on the menu!
⚲❀◖◗⇌(Central)♣P

Wokingham

Broad Street Tavern ✔

29 Broad Street, RG40 1AU
⏲ 11-11; 12-3, 7-10.30 Sun
☎ (0118) 977 3706
Wadworth IPA, 6X, JCB, Wells Bombardier, guest beers 🄷
Popular, relaxing, town-centre local with two quiet, wood-panelled rooms facing the street, both no-smoking. A seating area to the rear is the only part of the pub where smoking is permitted. Live music is performed every Thursday evening and rugby and cricket matches are shown on TV. Two changing guest beers are served, and beer festivals are held in February, May, August and November. It was voted local CAMRA Pub of the Year for the last three years.
Q❀◖⇌⚟

Crispin

45 Denmark Street, RG40 2AY
⏲ 12-11; 12-10.30 Sun
☎ (0118) 978 0309
Fuller's London Pride; guest beers 🄷
Cosy, welcoming little hostelry with a real fire. Reputed to be the oldest pub in Wokingham, this timber-beamed building dates back to the 15th century. Good home-made food is served in generous portions every lunchtime and Monday-Thursday evenings. The dartboard and games area to the rear are popular with the friendly regulars. Sport is shown on TV.
⚲❀◖◗⇌♣

Rifle Volunteer ✔

141 Reading Road, RG41 1HD (on A329, W of town centre)
⏲ 11-11; 12-5.30, 7-10.30 Sun
☎ (0118) 978 4484
Courage Best Bitter; Fuller's London Pride; guest beer 🄷
Dating from the 1850s, this welcoming pub has a large, comfortable, single bar and a small, no-smoking family room. Children are also welcome in the garden where there is play equipment. Quiz night is Sunday and occasional live music is played. There is a dartboard and the pub fields its own football team. Major live sporting events are shown on TV. The guest beers usually come from micros. Food is served at lunchtime during the week. It was runner-up CAMRA local Pub of the Year in 2004. ♞❀◖♣P⚟

Woodside

Duke of Edinburgh

Woodside Road, SL4 2DP (off A332)
⏲ 11-11; 12-6 Sun
☎ (01344) 882736
Arkells 2B, 3B, Kingsdown, seasonal beers 🄷
Friendly, comfortable pub, full of character, with two drinking areas and a restaurant offering good food. Exposed beams and wood furnishings add to the traditional feel. The saloon has two TVs which show live sport (the landlord is a Chelsea fanatic!). The lounge has a no-smoking area and there is a garden where children are welcome. The pub is conveniently situated for Ascot racecourse and Windsor's tourist attractions such as the Castle and Legoland.
⚲❀◖◗♣P⚟

Bell, Aldworth

BUCKINGHAMSHIRE

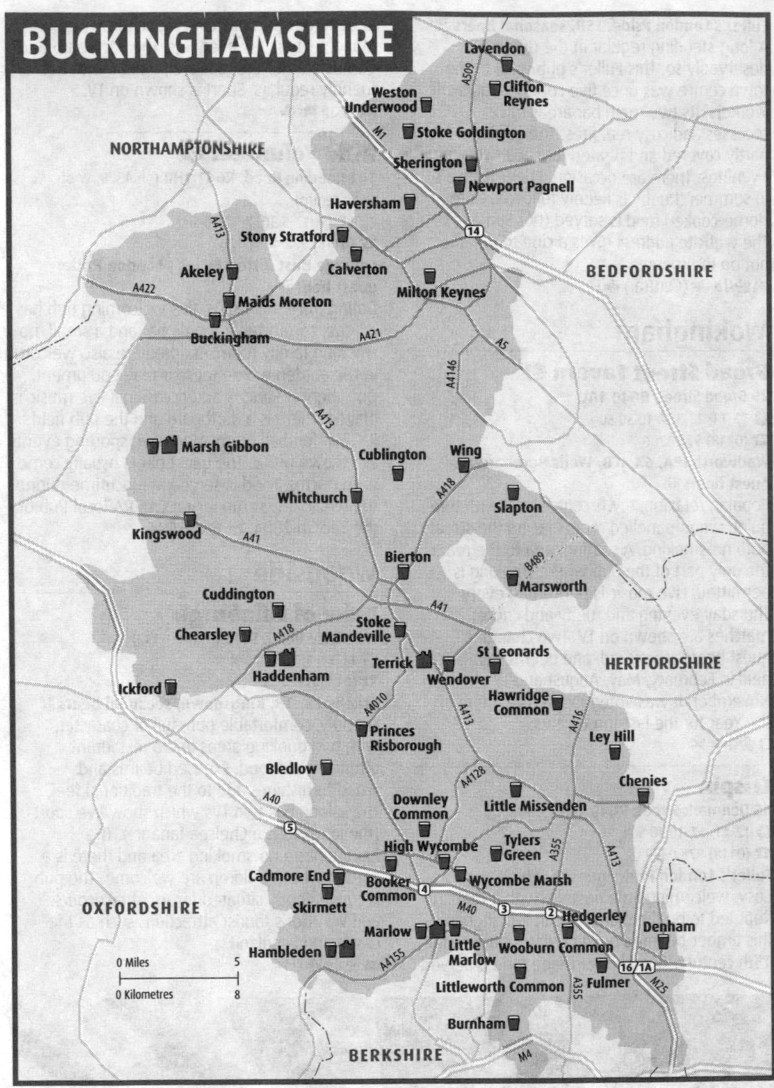

Akeley

Bull & Butcher ✔

The Square, MK18 5HP

(on A413 Buckingham-Towcester road)

⏲ 12-3, 5-11; 12-11 Sat; 12-10.30 Sun

☎ (01280) 860257

Fuller's Chiswick, London Pride; guest beer (occasional) 🄷

Cosy and comfortable Fuller's tied house, a long way from the brewery's Chiswick home. A typical village local, the main bar has a grand fire at one end and the butchered bull's head presides over the fireplace. There is also a dining area. Sunday lunches are excellent (no meals Sun eve). ⛰❀⇌◑▲♣P

Bierton

Bell ✔

191 Aylesbury Road, HP22 5DS (on A418)

⏲ 11-3, 5.30-11; 11-11 Sat; 12-10.30 Sun

☎ (01296) 436055

Fuller's Chiswick, London Pride, ESB, seasonal beers; guest beer 🄷

Village local two miles north of Aylesbury on the main road.There are two rooms: a small traditional public bar and a larger room which doubles as a restaurant. A wide choice of food at affordable prices makes booking advisable at busy times. The pub is open all day Saturday and Sunday and has become a popular venue for watching sporting events on the wide-screen TV. Occasional live music is played on Saturday evening featuring local blues bands.

◑⊟♣P

INDEPENDENT BREWERIES

Chiltern Terrick
Old Luxters Hambleden
Oxfordshire Ales Marsh Gibbon
Rebellion Marlow
Vale Haddenham

Bledlow

Lions of Bledlow

Church End, HP27 9PE (off B4009 between Chinnor and Princes Risborough) OS776020

11.30-3, 6-11; 12-4, 7-10.30 (12-10.30 summer) Sun

☎ (01844) 343345

Wadworth 6X; guest beers H

Rambling, unspoilt, 16th-century inn, complete with beams, inglenooks and a large log fire. Originally three shepherds' cottages, notes and pictures illustrating the pub's earlier days are displayed. There is a games room, restaurant and large bar with wide-ranging blackboard menus. The extensive garden is busy in summer with walkers and families, while tables at the front enjoy a picturesque setting at the junction of footpaths and bridleways. Guest beers are often from local breweries including Vale.

Q P

Booker Common

Live & Let Live

Limmer Lane, HP12 4QZ OS835917

11-11; 12-10.30 Sun

☎ (01494) 520105

Fuller's London Pride; Rebellion IPA H

Modern two-bar pub, popular with walkers on the nearby common and woods. The inn sign shows a cat and mouse existing in harmony against a background of beer barrels. Numerous pictures of local cricket teams linked with the local ground are displayed on the walls. Occasional special food nights are held (booking is essential). Oriental cuisine is a speciality on Tuesday evening. No food is served Sunday and Monday evenings. Barbecues are held in the summer. Wycombe Air Park and museums are close by. Bus Nos. 326 and 339 pass nearby. ♣P

Buckingham

Mitre

2 Mitre Street, MK18 1DW (near university)

7 (12.30 Sat)-11; 12.30-10.30 Sun

☎ (01280) 813080

Beer range varies H

Away from the centre in an old part of town, this pub can be hard to find (via Chandos Road, go left under the railway bridge) and parking is difficult. But it is well worth the effort as the beer is superb, with three ales usually available and a fourth added at weekends. Beers may come from anywhere so a surprise is always in store. The old, disused railway is nearby and the area has some interesting 18th-century properties, so take a look at on your way here.

♣

Burnham

George

20 High Street, SL1 7JH

11-11; 12-10.30 Sun

☎ (01628) 605047

Courage Best Bitter, Directors H

Run by the same licensee for around 40 years, this listed 16th-century coaching inn never seems to change. The single bar has comfy seating on one side and is dominated by the pool table on the other. Directors is known as 'Alice' as it used to be served from a pump in a looking glass. Afternoon access is by the back door, next to the car park. Buses from Slough stop at either end of the High Street.

♣P

Cadmore End

Old Ship

Marlow Road, HP14 3PN

(on B482 between Lane End and Stokenchurch)

11.30-2.30 (not Mon), 5-11; 12-3, 7-10.30 Sun

☎ (01494) 883496

West Berkshire Full Circle; Young's Bitter; guest beers G

This restored, small, country pub is one of the classic gems of the Chilterns. Despite handpumps on the bar, all ales are gravity-dispensed and carried up from the cellar. A free house, it serves a constantly-changing range of guest beers, including ales from local breweries. Meals are available at all times except Sunday evening and Monday lunchtime. The large garden has a covered seating area situated below road level. A pub not to be missed.

Q ♣P

Calverton

Shoulder of Mutton

Lower Weald, MK19 6ED OS801393

12-3, 5-11; 12-11 Fri & Sat; 12-10.30 Sun

☎ (01908) 562183

website: www.shoulder-of-mutton.info

Adnams Broadside; Caledonian Deuchars IPA; Fuller's London Pride; Hook Norton Old Hooky; Vale Edgar's Golden Ale; guest beers H

Lower Weald is one of three villages that comprise Calverton, which is not far from Stony Stratford and Milton Keynes. One guest ale is offered to complement the seven regular fixtures at this genuine free house. Two real fires keep the cold out in winter. A regular, well attended quiz is hosted on Tuesday evening and there is occasional live music. Good value food and accommodation are available.

♣P

Chearsley

Bell

The Green, HP18 0DJ

12-3, 6-11 Sat (12-11 summer); 12-3, 7-10.30 (12-10.30 summer) Sun

☎ (01844) 208077

Fuller's Chiswick, London Pride, seasonal beers H

This thatched country pub on the village green is renowned for its excellent range of food at reasonable prices, from bar snacks to Sunday roasts. Vegetarian and children's options are always available. Evening meals are served Wednesday to Saturday. The 16th-century building has wychert walls and a classic inglenook with open fire. China plates adorn the walls. Outside is a large, secure garden with children's play area. It won local CAMRA Village Pub of the Year award in 1998 and 2000.

Q ♣P

Chenies

Red Lion

WD3 6ED

(off A404 between Chorleywood and Little Chalfont)

11-2.30, 5.30-11; 12.30-3, 7-10.30 Sun

(01923) 282722

Wadworth 6X; guest beer H

Popular free house in a picturesque village close to the River Chess. At the back of the pub is a small snug with four tables and an even snugger room with only one table can be found further back. There is a variety of home-cooked food available every day. The house beer, Lion Pride, is brewed by Rebellion. Ben's Bitter comes from Vale Brewery. Guest beers are usually sourced locally or from micro-breweries. Q❀◐♿P

Clifton Reynes

Robin Hood

MK46 5DR (off Emberton-Turvey road) OS903512

12-3, 6.30-11; closed Mon; 12-3, 7-11 Sun

(01234) 711574 website: www.the-robin-hood.co.uk

Greene King IPA, Abbot; guest beer H

Pleasant pub at the centre of an isolated village close to Olney, which is nearer on foot than by car; the route from Olney was walked by poet William Cowper. Top class, wholesome, home-made food is served here – buffalo sometimes features on the menu. Cosy in winter, it is also delightful in summer when the garden and conservatory can be enjoyed.

⛼Q❀◐♣

Cublington

Unicorn

High Street, LU7 0LQ

12-3, 5-11; 12-11 Sat; 12-10.30 Sun

(01296) 681261

Greene King IPA; Shepherd Neame Spitfire; guest beers H

Despite threats of closure many times during the last decade, this attractive 17th-century village pub has been saved by the determination of the local community not to lose its local. Three village families now run the pub which comprises a long bar with a low ceiling and open fires at each end and a small dining area. Beers from local micros are regularly featured and imaginative food is served at all sessions. Darts and bridge are sometimes played.

⛼Q❀◐♣P

Cuddington

Crown ✔

Spurt Street, HP18 0BB

12-3, 6-11; 12-10.30 Sun

(01844) 292222

Adnams Bitter; Fuller's London Pride, seasonal beers H

Attractive, thatched local in the centre of the village, thought to date from the 13th century. Much care was taken to extend the kitchen and dining area without affecting the main pub. As a result the traditional character dominates, enhanced by two inglenooks and some interesting photographs from yesteryear. A wide range of food is available at lunchtime and evenings throughout the week. ❀◐P

Denham

Falcon ✔

Village Road, UB9 5BE

11-3, 5.30-11; 12-4, 7-10.30 Sun

(01895) 832125

website: www.falconinn.biz

Taylor Landlord; Wells Bombardier; guest beers H

Overlooking the village green, this inn dates from the 16th century. Stone steps rise to the front door five feet above street level. The bar area retains many original features including timber beams and two open hearths. Steps lead down to a back room, where children are permitted, and the garden. A range of food is served, from bar snacks to a full a la carte menu. Three en-suite guest rooms are available.

Q❀◐

Downley Common

Le de Spencer Arms ✔

HP13 5YQ (across the common from the village) OS849959

12-3, 6-11; 12-11 Sat; 12-10.30 Sun

(01494) 535317

Fuller's Chiswick, London Pride, ESB, seasonal beers; guest beers H

Family-oriented brick and flint building remotely situated off Downley Common. It has numerous secluded areas and a small room off the bar. In summer there are barbecues and two mini-beer festivals under canvas. Pub games include mole in the hole. A much-frequented pub for ramblers in the area, food is served every lunchtime and Friday and Saturday evenings. Sunday roasts are popular. Bus No. 31 connects with High Wycombe Station. ⛼Q❀◐♣P

Fulmer

Black Horse ✔

Windmill Road, SL3 6HD

10-3, 5.30-11; 11-11 Sat; 12-10.30 Sun

(01753) 663183

Greene King IPA, Abbot, seasonal beers; guest beers H

The site where the Black Horse now stands was used during the construction of the church next door, completed in 1610, to house workers and materials. By 1650 this building was a court house and ale house. Today there are three bar areas, each retaining its own cosy character. Two are mainly for dining and are no-smoking; booking is necessary for evening meals. In 1672 local magistrate Sir Hugh Hardy-cum-Whittingsall was ambushed here by 'slippery' Dickie Shafto and his horse killed, hence the pub name.

⛼Q❀◐♿♣P

Haddenham

King's Head

52 High Street, HP17 8ET

12-2.30, 5-11; 12-11 Sat; 12-10.30 Sun

(01844) 291391

Fuller's London Pride; Greene King IPA; guest beer H

Somewhat hidden in the centre of this large village, despite having two entrances, this is a traditional, lively pub, parts of which date back to the 16th century. It is well worth the effort to find and is often full of friendly locals. It can be busy, especially in summer when the patio drinking area tends to fill up quickly. The guest beer alternates on a weekly basis. ⌂Q❀◐◑ ≷(Haddenham & Thame Parkway) ♣P

Red Lion
Church End, HP17 8AH
⌚ 11.30-3, 5.30-11; 11-11 Sat; 12-10.30 Sun
☎ (01844) 291606
website: www.theredlion.freeserve.co.uk
Adnams Bitter; Ansells Mild; Brains Rev James; Young's Bitter Ⓗ
Built in 1939, this attractive pub faces the village church and duckpond. It has only had four landlords in its time, the present incumbent having been there for over 30 years. The public bar, with its original oak floor and polished tables, is the place for pub games, with thriving teams in the local crib, darts, pool and dominoes leagues. A function room (the Lion's Den) is available to hire and the outdoor drinking area is popular in summer. ⌂Q❀⇌◐⊟♣P

Hambleden

Stag & Huntsman
RG9 6RP (next to churchyard) OS785866
⌚ 11-2.30 (3 Sat), 6-11; 12-3, 7-10.30 Sun
☎ (01491) 571227
website: www.stagandhuntsman.co.uk
Rebellion IPA; Wadworth 6X; guest beer Ⓗ
Idyllic, unspoilt, rural gem located in a much-filmed, picturesque brick and flint National Trust village. It has three bars: a cosy front bar concealed behind a curtain, a snug public bar, and a larger rear lounge. An extensive menu is on offer, served in all bars as well as the dining room. The frequently-changing guest beer is sourced from independents and micros, often favouring the west country where the landlord hails from. Thatchers dry cider is also stocked at this past local CAMRA Pub of the Year.
⌂❀⇌◐◑⊟♣●P

Haversham

Greyhound
2 High Street, MK19 7DT OS829429
⌚ 12-2.30 (3 Sat), 5.30-11; 12-3, 7-10.30 Sun
☎ (01908) 313487
Greene King IPA, Abbot Ⓗ
A true village local, although close to the sprawl of Milton Keynes. The licensees have created a real community pub and various local clubs are based here. Good, wholesome food is available and Sunday lunches are popular. Families are welcome and the garden is ideal for children. An annual sloe gin competition is held at Christmas. It was awarded local CAMRA Pub of the Year 2005. ⌂Q❀◐◑♣P

Hawridge Common

Full Moon ✔
HP5 2UH
⌚ 12-3, 5.30-11; 12-11 Sat; 12-10.30 Sun
☎ (01494) 758959
Adnams Bitter; Draught Bass; Brakspear Special; Fuller's London Pride; guest beers Ⓗ
Lying in the shadow of a windmill, this 17th-century pub has a Wethereds Brewery lantern over the front door and a large dovecote in the car park. Inside it is divided into several drinking and eating areas, with beamed ceilings, brick bar, log-effect fire and a decorative jug collection, and there is a no-smoking restaurant. The large garden and pergola-covered patio make it a popular pub in summer. It is sited at the starting point for the Iron Age Fort Walk, and children and dogs are welcome. No food is served on Sunday evening. ❀◐◑P

Hedgerley

White Horse
Village Lane, SL2 3UY (off A355)
⌚ 11-2.30, 5.30-11; 11-11 Sat; 12-10.30 Sun
☎ (01753) 643225
Greene King IPA; Rebellion IPA; Ⓗ **guest beers** Ⓖ
Outstanding, 15th-century Grade II listed free house situated next to a RSPB reserve and the 12th-century village church. A constantly changing range of beers is on offer as well as two real ciders and an occasional perry. It offers a varied menu of good home-cooked food. The heated patio and beautiful garden to the rear of the pub are popular in warmer months and host an annual beer festival in May. This is a regular winner of CAMRA local Pub of the Year.
⌂Q❀◐⊟●P

High Wycombe

Bell ✔
Frogmoor, HP13 5DQ
⌚ 11-11; 12-10.30 Sun
☎ (01494) 525588
Fuller's London Pride, ESB, seasonal beer Ⓗ
Traditional town-centre pub; there is no hint of a theme here. Since Fuller's acquired the pub it has been extended to the rear and opened out into one room, although it retains the small frontage of the original 16th-century building. Award-winning Thai cuisine is a speciality (no food served Sun). Accommodation is available in five en-suite rooms. ⌂⇌◐◑≷

Ickford

Rising Sun
36 Worminghall Road, HP18 9JD
⌚ 12-2.30 (not Mon), 5-11; 12-11 Sat; 12-10.30 Sun
☎ (01844) 339238
Adnams Bitter; Flowers IPA; Wadworth 6X; Young's Bitter Ⓗ
This classic thatched local has become the hub of the village. Dating from the 15th century, with many oak beams and a welcoming wood-burning stove, it hosts local events and games, including crib, darts and quizzes. Aunt Sally is played in the garden. Four ales are always available and basic pub food is served most sessions. Close to the Oxfordshire Way, it attracts many ramblers and cyclists. Dogs on leads are welcome. ⌂Q❀◐◑♣P

Kingswood

Plough & Anchor ✔
Bicester Road, HP18 0RD
⌚ 12-3, 6-11; 12-5.30 Sun
☎ (01296) 770251
Fuller's London Pride; guest beer Ⓖ

Comfortable 16th-century roadside pub, catering mainly for diners but drinkers are welcome. The beers are served on gravity by a custom-built dispense and cooling system. The guest beer is sourced from regional or micro-breweries and is usually under 4% ABV. The open fire is fuelled by some of the largest logs you will ever see, and burns continuously from October to April. A patio area is available for outdoor drinking.
⛫Q❀◑◗P

Lavendon

Horseshoe

26 High Street, MK46 4HA (on A428)
✪ 12-3 (not Mon), 5.30-11; 12-3.30, 7.30-10.30 Sun
☎ (01234) 712641
Wells Eagle; guest beer Ⓗ
Popular, main-road village pub with two bars: one is a typical locals' public bar, the other a comfortable lounge for dining. The menu is varied with something for everyone, but fresh fish is the speciality. Watch out for Diesel the dog at lunchtimes. The guest ale is from the Wells list. ⛫Q❀◑◗⊟♣P

Ley Hill

Swan ✔

Ley Hill Common, HP5 1UT
✪ 12-11; 12-10.30 Sun
☎ (01494) 783075
website: www.swanleyhill.com
Adnams Bitter; Brakspear Bitter; Fuller's London Pride; Taylor Landlord; Young's Bitter; guest beer Ⓗ
Built in the 16th and 17th centuries, the Swan was originally three timber-framed cottages, and is one of the county's oldest pubs. It is said to be the place where condemned prisoners, on their way to the nearby gallows, wished to visit for their last request – a final ale. The lounge bar has oak beams, a real fire and an impressive snug. The restaurant has a growing reputation for excellent food; evening meals are served Tuesday-Saturday. ⛫Q❀◑◗🍎

Little Marlow

King's Head

Church Road, SL7 3RZ
(on A4155 between Marlow and Bourne End)
✪ 11-11; 12-10.30 Sun
☎ (01628) 484407
Fuller's London Pride; Taylor Landlord; guest beers Ⓗ
Pleasant 14th-century inn, full of character, in a charming village with a 12th-century church. The four handpumped ales are complemented by an extensive home-cooked food menu. The large, secluded garden attracts many visitors in the summer, and families are welcome. During the winter a large log fire creates a warm atmosphere in the traditional bar with a heavily beamed ceiling. ⛫❀◑◗♿P

Little Missenden

Crown

HP7 0RD (off A413, Amersham end of village)
✪ 12.30-2.30, 6-11; 12-3, 7-10.30 Sun
☎ (01494) 862571
Adnams Bitter; Brakspear Bitter; Fuller's London Pride; guest beer Ⓗ
Timeless, compact, village pub run by the same family for over 90 years. The single-room interior divides into two seating areas – red tiled flooring to the left and oak block parquet to the right, both served by the same small bar and edged with built-in wall seats. Four handpumps dispense two regular beers and two guests. The absence of music and games machines accentuates the traditional atmosphere of this gem of a pub. Pub food is served at lunchtime except Sunday.
⛫Q◑♣P

Littleworth Common

Blackwood Arms

Common Lane, SL1 8PP
✪ 11-3, 6-11 (closed winter Mon); 12-8 Sun
☎ (01753) 642169
Brakspear Bitter, Special; Hook Norton Dark Ⓗ
Charming country pub on the edge of Burnham Beeches, deservedly popular with walkers. It is the only inn in the area that always sells cask mild. The pub is also highly regarded for its food, which is available at all sessions. The large outside seating area makes the pub ideal for families in the summer.
⛫❀◑◗♿⛺P

Jolly Woodman

Littleworth Road, SL1 8PF OS936835
✪ 11-11; 12-10.30 Sun
☎ (01753) 644350
Brakspear Bitter; Caledonian Deuchars IPA; Fuller's London Pride; Shepherd Neame Spitfire; guest beer Ⓗ
Delightful country pub on the northern edge of Burnham Beeches. Different drinking areas are spread around a central atrium, dominated by a rowing scull suspended from the rafters. The bar area features a collection of old beer bottles and agricultural implements. Lively jazz sessions are hosted on Monday evening. Good food, open fires and a fine garden add to the appeal.
⛫❀◑◗♿P⚟

Maids Moreton

Wheatsheaf

Main Street, MK18 1QR
(off A413, Buckingham-Towcester road) OS705355
✪ 12-3, 6-11; 12-3, 6-10.30 Sun
☎ (01280) 815433 website: www.thewheatsheaf.uk.com
Hook Norton Best Bitter; Tring Side Pocket for a Toad; guest beer Ⓗ
A true free house with a village feel, the pub successfully blends the old and new. The rustic bar features old prints on the walls and good food is served in the comfortable restaurant (booking advisable – no meals Sun eve). The location is handy for the National Trust's Stowe Park Gardens and Silverstone race circuit.
⛫🐎❀◑◗P⚟

Marlow

Carpenters Arms

15 Spittal Street, SL7 3HJ (off High St)
✪ 11-11; 12-10.30 Sun
☎ (01628) 473649

Greene King IPA, Abbot, seasonal or guest beer Ⓗ
A genuine working men's town centre local, enjoyed by a wide cross-section of the public who appreciate its traditional values. The buzz of lively banter dominates here, although Sky Sports is popular without being intrusive. The pub does get busy on music jam nights, held on alternate Thursdays. An extension to the rear has allowed more seating and space for a dartboard. A removable ramp, wide rear doors and helpful staff make access simple for wheelchair users.
⚲♿⇌♣

Three Horseshoes
Burroughs Grove Hill, SL7 3RA (1½ miles N of town on Marlow-Wycombe bus route) OS876890
⏲ 11.30-3, 5-11; 11.30-11 Fri & Sat; 12-5, 7-10.30 Sun
☎ (01628) 483109
Rebellion IPA, Smuggler, Mutiny, seasonal beers Ⓗ
The tap for the local Rebellion Brewery, it offers six of its ales, including, exclusively, the mild, plus an extensive menu to marvel at. Popular at all times, the pub gets busy at the weekend. The interior is divided into three areas, catering for drinkers and diners alike. An enclosed rear garden is a safe haven for children to play while parents enjoy a beer in the sunshine. Awarded local CAMRA Pub of the Year 2005, the High Wycombe-Marlow bus stops outside.
⚲Q❀◐◑P⚟

Marsh Gibbon

Greyhound
West Edge, OX27 0HA
⏲ 12-2.30, 6-10 (11 Fri & Sat); closed Mon; 12-4, 7-10.30 Sun
☎ (01869) 277365
Fuller's London Pride; Greene King IPA, Abbot Ⓗ
Country pub in a quiet Domesday village. A listed building with some 17th-century brickwork, it was rebuilt after a fire in 1740. Further refurbishment in 1979 is commemorated by a beech tree planted in front of the pub. The oak-beamed interior includes a restaurant, two drinking areas and an oak-panelled bar. A log fire burns in the main bar. The Greyhound specialises in Thai food, cooked to order (book weekend eves). ⚲Q❀◐◑P▯

Marsworth

Angler's Retreat ✔
Startops End, HP23 4LJ
(on B489, opp. Startops reservoir car park) OS918141
⏲ 11-11; 12-10.30 Sun
☎ (01442) 822250
Fuller's London Pride; Tring Side Pocket for a Toad; guest beers Ⓗ
Country pub opposite two reservoirs and close to the Grand Union Canal and Marsworth flight of locks No. 39. The interior has a fishing theme with displays of fish caught in the reservoirs. Two mini-beer festivals are held in April and September. Mild beers are frequent guests. A no-smoking conservatory, garden and small aviary make the pub popular with families. Home-cooked food is served daily. Dogs are welcome. ⚲Q❀◐◑♣P⚟

Red Lion ✔
90 Vicarage Road, HP23 4LU
(off B489, by canal bridge 130) OS919147
⏲ 11-3, 5 (6 Sat)-11; 12-3, 7-10.30 Sun
☎ (01296) 668366
Fuller's London Pride; Vale Best Bitter; guest beers Ⓗ
Fine, 17th-century pub close to the Grand Union Canal and village church. Fans of traditional games are well catered for here as darts, bar billiards, shove-ha'penny and skittles are all played in the public bar. In contrast, the split-level lounge and restaurant offer a quieter, more comfortable atmosphere. Children are permitted in the games room only. The rear door provides wheelchair access.
⚲Q☋❀◐◑▣♣⚘P

Milton Keynes

Victoria Inn
Vicarage Road, Bradwell Village, MK13 9AQ
⏲ 11-11; 12-10.30 Sun
☎ (01908) 316355
Hook Norton Best Bitter; guest beer Ⓗ
Much-deserved first time entry in the Guide for this pub, which has been run by the same family for many years. The ever-changing guest beer is often from a micro-brewery. Very much a part of the local community, although not far from the city centre, the pub runs quiz, darts and pool teams. The annual beer festival, held over the August bank holiday, is well worth a visit.
❀◐♣⚘P

Newport Pagnell

Cannon
50 High Street, MK16 8AQ
⏲ 11-11; 12-10.30 Sun
☎ (01908) 211495
Banks's Bitter; Marston's Pedigree; guest beers Ⓗ
A Guide regular, this pub sells the cheapest beer for miles around. The landlord not just keeps exemplary ale but speaks fluent Spanish for good measure. Guest ales come from all over the country but are often from the Wolverhampton & Dudley stable or sometimes Frog Island. There was once a brewery on this site as the can be seen from the outbuilding that remains in the car park. ⚲♿♣P

Princes Risborough

Bird in Hand
47 Station Road, HP27 9DE
⏲ 12-3, 5-11; 12-3, 7-10.30 Sun
☎ (01844) 345602
Greene King IPA, Abbot, seasonal beers Ⓗ
Genuine, terraced local on the outskirts of the town centre, popular with all ages, regulars and visitors. The L-shaped interior with traditional furnishings has a cosy feel. Its pub games players are successful, judging by the silverware in the trophy cabinet. This is the fourth year running the pub has featured in the Guide, and deservedly so for its three tied ales. It is convenient for the railway station, but parking can be a chore.
❀◐◑⇌♣

St Leonards

White Lion

Jenkins Lane, HP23 6NW OS918069
⌚ 11.30-11; 12-10.30 Sun
☎ (01494) 758387
Greene King IPA; guest beers Ⓗ
The friendly landlord and landlady offer a warm welcome to all at this classic country pub. It is one of the highest in the Chilterns and close to the Ridgeway and Chiltern path, making it popular with walkers. A mini-beer festival is held in May and a mild is generally included in the guest beers. The popular food is home cooked and the pub can get busy, particularly at Sunday lunchtime. No evening meals are served on Sunday. Dogs are welcome.
♛Q♉❀◐◑♿▲♣P⊬

Sherington

White Hart

1 Gun Lane, MK16 9PE OS892468
⌚ 12-3, 5-11; 12-11 Sat; 12-4, 7-10.30 Sun
☎ (01908) 611953
website: www.whitehartsherington.com
Fuller's London Pride; Young's Bitter; guest beers Ⓗ
A past local CAMRA Pub of the Year, this pub came close to extinction at one time but is now very much at the heart of village life. Superb food is a feature here, and booking a table is essential. Do not miss the annual beer and sausage festival held over the early May bank holiday. No food is served on Sunday evening.
♛Q❀⇄◐◑♣●P

Skirmett

Frog ✔

RG9 6TG (off M40 jct 5, through Ibstone to Skirmett)
OS775903
⌚ 11.30 (11 Sat)-3, 6.30 (6 Fri & Sat)-11; 12-4 (10.30 summer) Sun
☎ (01491) 638996
website: www.thefrog.tablesir.com
Fuller's London Pride; Rebellion IPA; guest beers Ⓗ
With fine views across the countryside, this 300-year-old free house lies in the beautiful Hambleden Valley. The Frog is a family-owned pub, exuding warmth and tranquillity. It offers a fine restaurant and high quality accommodation. Guest beers often come from local breweries. Snacks are available in the bar where an inviting log fire burns in winter. Food is cooked to order; specials are available daily.
♛Q♉❀⇄◐◑♣P⊬

Slapton

Carpenters Arms

1 Horton Road, LU7 9DB
⌚ 12-3 (not Sat), 7-11; 12-4 Sun
☎ (01525) 220563
Vale Notley Ale, Wychert Ale; guest beer Ⓗ
Reputedly haunted, 13th-century thatched pub in the centre of the village on the edge of the Chilterns, just yards from the Bedfordshire border. There is a small bar at the lower end of the pub serving three seating areas on different levels, one set aside for diners and one with a large open fireplace. Benches and scrubbed wooden tables provide seating for drinkers. The adjacent former maltings has recently been converted into houses. ♛❀◐◑♣P

Stoke Goldington

Lamb

16-20 High Street, MK16 8NR (on B526)
⌚ 12-3, 5-11; 12-11 Sat; 12-10.30 Sun
☎ (01908) 551233
Nethergate IPA; guest beers Ⓗ
An important part of the local community, this village pub has one daft dog (there used to be two until old age caught up with the other) and an interesting range of ever-changing guest ales. Often chosen from local micros, the landlord strives to surprise and delight. Bottled Duvel is also available for Belgian beer lovers, and Westons Old Rosie for real cider fans. The pub serves food of the highest quality and booking is advisable for the sumptuous Sunday lunches. No food is served on Tuesday or Sunday evenings. ♛❀◐◑♣●P⊬

Stoke Mandeville

Bull

5 Risborough Road, HP22 5UP
⌚ 12-3, 5.30-11; 12-11 Fri & Sat; 12-10.30 Sun
☎ (01296) 613632
Fuller's London Pride; Tetley Bitter; Wells Bombardier Ⓗ
Small pub situated on a main road which is well served by public transport. The front bar is popular with locals, especially sports fans who gather to watch football and horse racing on TV. The comfortable lounge bar tends to be quieter and leads out to a large, secure garden. Frequented by families in summer, the garden has plenty to entertain children.
Q❀▭⇌♣P

Stony Stratford

Fox & Hounds

87 High Street, MK11 1AT (on old A5)
⌚ 12-11; 12-10.30 Sun
☎ (01908) 563307
Beer range varies Ⓗ
A much deserved return to the Guide for the Fox, now with a new landlord. The beer is always the main attraction here, with constantly changing guests. The pub is at the heart of the local music scene with regular live bands and an open acoustic session on the first Tuesday of the month. It is also a venue for the village's annual music festival. ♛❀◐◑♣P

Tylers Green

Horse & Jockey ✔

Church Road, HP10 8EG
⌚ 11.30-3, 5-11; 11.30-11 Fri & Sat; 12-10.30 Sun
☎ (01494) 815963
website: www.the-horseandjockey.co.uk
Adnams Bitter, Broadside; Greene King Abbot; Tetley Bitter; guest beer Ⓗ
Situated near Tylers Green church, the building was converted into a pub in 1821. The interior has a single U-shaped room with a food counter to one side and the dartboard area to the right.

Food is available all week, lunchtime and evenings. The main car parking area is on the opposite side of the road. P

Wendover

Packhorse

29 Tring Road, HP22 6NR

12-11; 12-10.30 Sun

(01296) 622075

Fuller's Chiswick, London Pride, seasonal beers; guest beer H

Small, friendly village pub situated at the end of a terrace of thatched cottages known as the Anne Boleyn cottages. The pub, a free house, dates from 1769 and has been owned by the same family for 42 years. It is on the Ridgeway path and the wall above the bar is decorated with RAF squadron badges denoting connections with nearby RAF Halton. The pub runs men and women's darts teams, dominoes and crib.

Weston Underwood

Cowpers Oak

High Street, MK46 5JS

(on Olney-Stoke Goldington road) OS865507

12-3, 5.30 (5 Fri)-11; 12-11 Sat; 12-10.30 Sun

(01234) 711382 website: www.cowpersoak.co.uk

Fuller's London Pride; Greene King IPA; guest beers H

This delightful country pub, although not far from urban sprawl, retains a local village feel. A wide range of excellent food is available as the chalkboard testifies. With cosy log fires in winter and ample outdoor space in summer, the pub is popular all year round. Guest ales are usually from local micros, although a semi-permanent winter beer, Theakston's Old Peculier, gives way to Greene King Abbot in the warmer months. P

Whitchurch

White Swan

10 High Street, HP22 4JT

11-11; 12-3, 7-10.30 Sun

(01296) 641228

Fuller's Chiswick, London Pride, ESB, seasonal beers H

Attractive, part-thatched, 16th-century pub with an intimate atmosphere. It boasts a huge, mature garden and distinctive wood panelling in the lounge bar. Good value food is available (not Sun eve), with daily specials and occasional themed food nights. Food is served in both bars and the small, no-smoking dining room. The landlord is Fuller's Master Cellarman No. 22, and has several appearances in this Guide to his credit. Q P

Wing

Cock

26 High Street, LU7 0NR

11.30-3, 6-11; 12-3, 7-10.30 Sun

(01296) 688214

Draught Bass; Fuller's London Pride; Greene King IPA; guest beers H

Former coaching inn that appeals to diners, drinkers and families. Up to six real ales mostly come from independent or micro-breweries, often brews that are unusual for the area. Cottage, Rebellion and Vale beers are popular choices. There are three main drinking areas, one with a dartboard. Food is served in all bars and the spacious restaurant, which can get busy at weekends. A narrow entrance way leads to a large car park. Q P

Wooburn Common

Royal Standard

Wooburn Common Road, HP10 0JS

(follow signs to Odds Farm) OS923876

12-11; 12-10.30 Sun

(01628) 521121

Caledonian Deuchars IPA; H **Hop Back Summer Lightning;** G **guest beers** G/H

Semi-rural roadside pub, a short detour from the A40, and well worth it. Ten frequently-changing real ales, five on handpump, five gravity dispensed, greet the discerning drinker. A large chimney breast acts as an informal divide for drinkers and diners; the real fire is welcome in winter months. The pub's growing popularity is well-deserved, with its excellent range of beers and a cosy, congenial atmosphere.
Q P

Wycombe Marsh

General Havelock

114 Kingsmead Road, Loudwater, HP11 1HZ

(S of A40)

12-2.30, 5.30-11; 11-11 Fri & Sat; 12-10.30 Sun

(01494) 520391

Fuller's Chiswick, London Pride, ESB, seasonal beers H

An old favourite, with 14 consecutive appearances in the Guide, this imposing family-run pub lies between the playing fields and the ski slope. It has been run by the same licensee since it became a Fuller's house. The atmosphere is noisy but friendly – and attracts all ages. The garden is pleasant in summer. Evening meals are only available on Friday. Lunchtime food is served daily except Saturday.
P

Hold the beef

Beer has come to be acknowledged as the national beverage of England. At a recent conference, Lord Burton claimed that this country owed its high and proud position among the nations of the earth simply on account of its characteristic diet, Beef and Beer. Whereupon someone made the waggish comment, 'Why drag in the beef?'

F W Hackwood, 1910.

CAMBRIDGESHIRE

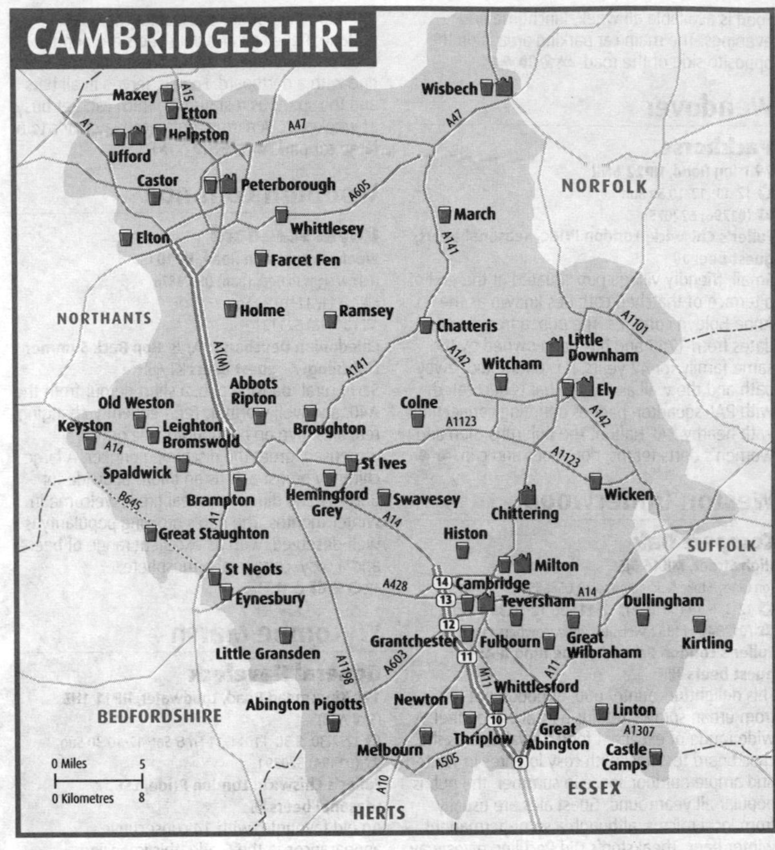

Abbots Ripton

Three Horseshoes

Moat Lane, PE28 2PA (on B1090)
11.30-3, 6-11; closed Mon; 12-5 Sun
(01487) 773440
Adnams Bitter, Broadside, seasonal beers; guest beers H
Picturesque pub in a village of thatched cottages, part of the De Ramsey estate. This small, listed thatched pub has recently been carefully refurbished and extended. The original quarry tiled and oak-beamed bar area has been sensitively retained as a family and no-smoking area. The extensions include a comfortable lounge bar, a restaurant and accommodation with five rooms. The a la carte and set Sunday lunch menus offer a range of cuisine, and typically two guest beers are available.
₼Q❀⇔◑♿P⊬

Abington Pigotts

Pig & Abbot

High Street, SG80 0SD
(off A505 through Litlington) OS306444
12-3, 6-11; 12-11 Sat; 12-10.30 Sun
(01763) 853515
website: www.pigandabbot.co.uk
Adnams Bitter; Fuller's London Pride; guest beers H
Deceptively large pub in a small village. Run by a mother and daughter team, it has a comfortable restaurant and a well-appointed lounge bar where a large inglenook holds a wood-burning stove, creating a cosy atmosphere. An imaginative menu makes the pub a popular choice for food. Various guest beers are offered, often from Woodforde's or Timothy Taylor.
₼Q❀◑P⊬

Brampton

Grange

115 High Street, PE28 4RA
11-11; 12-10.30 Sun
(01480) 459516
website: www.grangehotelbrampton.co.uk
Greene King IPA; guest beers H
Imposing Georgian building with a varied past; it has been a private girls' school, a residence and, during WWII, the HQ of the American Eighth Air Force and later the RAF Air Training Corps. Since

INDEPENDENT BREWERIES

Cambridge Moonshine Cambridge
City of Cambridge Chittering
Elgood's Wisbech
Fenland Little Downham
Hereward Ely
Milton Milton
Oakham Peterborough
Ufford Ufford

1981 it has been a private hotel and now boasts gourmet food (not served Sun eve) and interesting guest ales, usually from local breweries. The house beer is brewed by Potton. The decor is subdued, bearing photographs of its military past.
⩩Q❀⇌◑◗♿P

Broughton

Crown
Bridge Road, PE28 3AY
⊙ 12-3, 6-11; closed Mon & Tue; 12-3, 7-10.30 Sun
☎ (01487) 824428
website: www.thecrownbroughton.co.uk
Adams Broadside; Greene King IPA; guest beer Ⓗ
An idyllic pub next to the village church, in a conservation area. When the pub was under threat of permanent closure around five years ago village residents raised the money to purchase and renovate it. It can now seat up to 40 diners but retains a sociable drinking area with an expanded range of real ales. The decor is modern yet comfortable, with scrubbed pine tables and a stone floor.
Q❀◑◗⊟P

Cambridge

Cambridge Blue ✔
85-87 Gwydir Street, CB1 2LG
⊙ 12-2.30 (3 Sat), 5.30-11; 12-3, 6-10.30 Sun
☎ (01223) 361382
City of Cambridge Hobson's Choice; Elgood's Black Dog; Oakham JHB; Woodforde's Wherry; guest beers Ⓗ
Welcoming Victorian pub with a no-smoking and no-mobile phones policy. Seven handpumps feature a wide range of regular and guest beers. Cassels cider is also stocked in summer. Well-behaved children are welcome in the conservatory and large garden, and dogs too. Healthy, home-cooked food is served at every session.
⩩Q♉❀◑◗⇶♣●⍻

Carlton Arms
Carlton Way, Arbury, CB4 2BY
⊙ 11-11 (closed 3-5 Mon-Thu winter); 12-10.30 Sun
☎ (01223) 355717
website: www.thecarltonarms.co.uk
Adnams Bitter; Taylor Landlord; guest beers Ⓖ
Spacious, two-bar community pub on the northern outskirts of the city, which has been transformed from what was a dire previous incarnation to local CAMRA Pub of the Year in 2004. The lounge is no-smoking and the public bar offers TV, darts, pool and skittles. A dining area to the rear leads to a patio with secluded outside seating. Three beer festivals are held in September, February and June, plus a weekly quiz on Sunday. The food is good value and served every day except Sunday evening.
⩩Q❀◑◗⊟♿♣P⍻

Castle Inn
38 Castle Street, CB3 0AJ
⊙ 11.30-3, 5 (6 Sat)-11; 12-3, 6-10.30 Sun
☎ (01223) 353194
Adnams Bitter, Broadside, seasonal beers; Fuller's London Pride; Wells Bombardier; guest beers Ⓗ
Adnams' western flagship is a textbook example of sensitive pub restoration, run by a one-time rock drummer landlord. The ground floor offers five drinking areas and there are three more upstairs. The suntrap patio garden is bordered by the mound of the long-gone Cambridge Castle. Nine real ales are usually on tap, with beers from regional brewers complementing Adnams' own products. Excellent food is served at every session. ⩩❀◑◗⍻

Champion of the Thames ✔
68 King Street, CB1 1LN
⊙ 11-11; 12-10.30 Sun
☎ (01223) 352043
Greene King IPA, Abbot; guest beer Ⓗ
One of the few remaining traditional pubs in the city centre. The two wood-panelled bars have low ceilings and fine etched windows; the more salubrious bar boasts green leather upholstery and green-topped tables. Air-conditioning and improved ventilation make for a pleasant atmosphere. Charismatic pub-goers are depicted in bold sketches, but unfortunately many have since died and consequently the current regulars are reluctant to be added to the array!
⩩Q♣

Empress
72 Thoday Street, CB1 3AX
⊙ 11-2.30, 6.30-11; 12-2.30, 7-10.30 Sun
☎ (01223) 247236
Adnams Bitter, Broadside; Marston's Pedigree; Taylor Landlord; guest beers Ⓗ
Still a back-street local but with a more upmarket clientele reflecting the changing nature of area. The public bar is a place for quiet drinking and contemplation. Westons Old Rosie cider is also stocked along with the range of real ales. The 'no smoking at the bar' sign is a step in the right direction for bar staff and drinkers propping up the bar, but the rest of the pub can get smoky. The enclosed garden is a suntrap and a popular retreat on warm summer days.
❀⊟♣●

Free Press ✔
Prospect Row, CB1 1DU (behind police station)
⊙ 12-2.30 (3 Sat), 6-11; 12-3, 7-10.30 Sun
☎ (01223) 368337
Greene King XX Mild, IPA, Abbot; guest beer Ⓗ
It is hard to believe that this pub has only been around for 30 years when, then a shell, it was saved from demolition. The small rooms ooze character, especially the snug, where the current record for cramming in people is 61. The menu offers a healthy selection including home-made soups and pasta (no meals Sun eve). A no-smoking and no-mobile phones policy is in place. The tiny walled garden is a delight at this rare outlet for the delicious mild from Greene King.
⩩Q❀◑◗♣⍻⊓

Green Dragon
5 Water Street, Chesterton, CB4 1NZ
⊙ 11-11; 12-10.30 Sun
☎ (01223) 505035
Greene King XX Mild, IPA, Abbot; Taylor Landlord; Bateman XXXB Ⓗ
Originally a row of 16th-century houses, this

bustling pub attracts a wide mix of people. Its garden is across the road overlooking the river. The walls are decorated with historical memorabilia and a TV shows live sport. The excellent beer and cooked-to-order food ensure the pub's continued popularity. No meals are served on Sunday evening. ᗰ❀◐◗♣

Kingston Arms ✔
33 Kingston Road, CB1 2NU
⏲ 12-2.30, 5-11; 12-11 Fri & Sat; 12-10.30 Sun
☎ (01223) 319414
website: www.kingston-arms.co.uk
Crouch Vale Brewers Gold; Elgood's Black Dog; Hop Back Summer Lightning; Oakham JHB; Taylor Landlord; guest beers [H]
Ten handpumps dispensing regular and guest beers, an excellent wine list and award-winning food make this a bustling, lively pub. Evening booking is advisable if you wish to dine. There is a special lunchtime menu. No keg beer or cider is stocked. The sheltered garden has canopies and heaters for cooler evenings in summer. Free wireless Internet access is an added bonus. ᗰQ❀◐◗≋♣

Live & Let Live
40 Mawson Road, CB1 2EA
⏲ 11.30-2.30, 5.30 (6 Sat)-11; 12-3, 7-10.30 Sun
☎ (01223) 460261
Adnams Bitter; Everards Tiger; Nethergate Umbel Ale; guest beers [H]
Friendly back-street local dating from the 19th century. Modern wood panelling, exposed brickwork, beams and bare floorboards contribute to the homely feel. Eight handpumps offer a wide variety of ales from all over the country, always including a dark beer, plus local cider from Cassels. A fine selection of bottled Belgian beer and single malt whiskies is also stocked. Excellent home-cooked food is available at all sessions. Live acoustic music is played on Saturday evening. Q◐◗♿≋♣●⚟

St Radegund
129 King Street, CB1 1LD
⏲ 5 (12 Sat)-11; 6.30-10.30 Sun
☎ (01223) 311794
Fuller's London Pride; Shepherd Neame Spitfire; guest beer [H]
This true free house packs much into a small space. It is named after a 5th-century Frankish queen, founder of a nearby priory. Reference books and ties abound behind the bar; in front plaques commemorate past regulars, while sporting and railway photographs fill the walls. The ceiling has smoked etchings of college society names. Elsewhere are invitations to join Friday night's Vera Lynn Club or Wednesday's Cuban Cocktail night. Background jazz does not intrude – nor should your mobile phone. House brew Habit is from the local Milton Brewery.

Castle Camps

Cock
High Street, CB1 6SN
⏲ 7 (12 Sat)-11; 12-3, 7-10.30 Sun
☎ (01799) 584207
Greene King IPA, Abbot; guest beer [H]
A fine example of a well-kept, well-run village local. The main bar houses a plate collection in the unusual roof arrangement while the public bar is the venue for a regular monthly sing-around-the-room (last Mon). Home-cooked food is available on Thursday-Sunday evenings and Sunday lunch is served in the dining room, bar or outside in summer. The secluded patio and garden lie beyond the chalet accommodation. ᗰ❀⛟◐◗P

Castor

Prince of Wales Feathers
38 Peterborough Road, PE5 7AL
⏲ 12-2.30 (not Tue-Thu), 5-11; 12-3, 5-11 Sat; 12-3, 7-10.30 Sun
☎ (01733) 380936
Adnams Bitter; Greene King Ruddles County; John Smith's Bitter; guest beers [H]
This sympathetically refurbished village pub retains its original leaded, stained-glass windows. A popular local that caters for all ages, it has up to five real ales on tap and an extensive menu as well as freshly-made sandwiches on Friday and Saturday lunchtimes. Monthly live music is hosted and a quiz night is held every other Sunday. Pool, darts, dominoes and crib are all played here. A small, sunny patio attracts drinkers in fine weather. ᗰ◐♣⛉

Royal Oak Inn ✔
24 Peterborough Road, PE5 7AX
⏲ 12-2 (not Mon; 12-3 Sat), 6 (5 Thu-Sat)-11 (12-11 summer Sat); 12-3, 6-10.30 (12-10.30 summer) Sun
☎ (01733) 380217
Draught Bass; Tetley Bitter; guest beers [H]
Attractive, stone-built thatched pub with three drinking areas, each with its own bar and real fire. The pub is popular with groups of cyclists and ramblers. Good lunches are served Tuesday-Saturday. The south-facing patio is popular with drinkers in summer. There is a floodlit petanque court and ring the bull is also played in summer. A quiz night is held every Wednesday. ᗰQ❀◐♣P

Chatteris

Walk the Dog
34 Bridge Street, PE16 6RN
⏲ 12-2.30, 6.30-11; 12-3.30, 7-10.30 Sun
☎ (01354) 693695
Adnams Bitter; Fuller's London Pride; guest beers [H]
Real ale drinkers are especially welcome at this family-owned single room community pub. This free house always serves a selection of frequently changing guest ales and bottle-conditioned beers. A variety of pub games includes Scrabble, chess, dominoes, darts, crib and petanque. There is a sailing group and a golf society. Regular themed evenings include a cheese night on Friday and a Sunday quiz. Four large benches at the front of the pub are popular in summer. Food is served Monday-Saturday lunchtime. ᗰQ❀◐♣P

Colne

Green Man ✔
East Street, PE28 3LZ
⏲ 12-3, 6-11; 12-11 Sat; 12-10.30 Sun
☎ (01487) 840368

Greene King IPA, Abbot; guest beers 🄷
Picturesque village local in an old Fenland fruit-growing area. This busy, friendly pub has a public bar, a warm, sociable lounge and a popular dining area. Trade has steadily grown under the current licensees, who organise occasional special events including a real ale festival on May Day weekend and an annual German Oktoberfest. There is an ever-changing selection of guest beers including many unusual choices. Q❀◖◗⛺♣P⚟

Dullingham

Boot

18 Brinkley Road, CB8 9UW
⏲ 11-2.30, 5-11; 11-11 Sat; 12-2.30, 7-10.30 Sun
☎ (01638) 507327
Adnams Bitter, Broadside; guest beer 🄷
Splendid village pub truly at the hub of the community. The single L-shaped bar, open-plan and with a low ceiling, is decorated in shades of brown and cream. A locals' pub but welcoming to visitors, children are permitted until 8pm. Food is served at lunchtime except Sunday at Cambridge CAMRA's Pub of the Year 2005.
♨❀◖⇌♣P

Elton

Crown

8 Duck Street, PE8 6RQ
⏲ 11.30-2.30 (not Mon), 6-11 (10.30 Mon); 12-3, 7-10.30 Sun
☎ (01832) 280232
Greene King IPA; guest beers 🄷
Listed stone building with a thatched roof overlooking the village green. The pub was rebuilt in 1985 after a major fire. In the large bar shove-ha'penny, Pope Joan and mini-skittles are played. Up to six real ales are available, all from handpumps. Traditional fare is served in the bar or the restaurant (no meals Mon eve). The patio area is popular in summer.
♨Q❀◖◗⊟♿♣P

Ely

Prince Albert

62 Silver Street, CB7 4JF
⏲ 11-3.30 (not Tue; 11.30-3 Mon & Wed), 6.30 (7 Mon & Tue)-11; 12-3.30, 7-10.30 Sun
☎ (01353) 663494
Greene King XX Mild, IPA, Abbot; guest beers 🄷
Excellent back-street local in the shadow of Ely Cathedral, a genuinely quiet pub with no gaming machines or music. Good home-cooked lunches are served Monday-Saturday and you are welcome to bring your own picnic to eat in the attractive garden. It is a rare outlet for mild, and two guest beers are usually available at CAMRA local Pub of the Year 2004.
Q❀◖♣

Town House

60-64 Market Street, CB7 4LS
⏲ 11-11; 11-1am Fri & Sat; 12-10.30 Sun
☎ (01353) 664338
Oakham JHB; guest beers 🄷
Recently refurbished, city-centre pub near the cathedral with friendly, efficient staff. Guest ales change weekly, sometimes chosen from micro-breweries. On Friday and Saturday there is a DJ from 9pm until late closing at 1am and the pub can be busy. A beer festival is held annually during July in the garden and there is a weekly quiz on Sunday evening. ❀◖◗

West End House

16 West End, CB6 3AY
⏲ 12-3, 6-11; 12-11 Fri & Sat; 12-4, 7-10.30 Sun
☎ (01353) 662907
Adnams Bitter; Greene King IPA; guest beers 🄷
Interesting, traditional old pub with plenty of wooden beams, small windows and low ceilings, divided into four drinking areas. Just out of the city centre, it is well worth the effort to find. A small marquee can be erected on the outside patio for special events and private parties. Guest beers often come from the local Fenland Brewery. ♨❀◖♣

Etton

Golden Pheasant

1 Main Road, PE6 7DA
⏲ 12-3, 5.30-11 Wed-Sat; closed Mon & Tue; 12-7 Sun
☎ (01733) 252387
Fuller's ESB; Hop Back Summer Lightning; Oakham JHB; guest beers 🄷
This imposing building is a former Georgian rectory set in grounds of more than an acre. There are rumours of a ghost called Caspar. The grounds contain a play area for children and a petanque court. A marquee with its own bar is used for summer functions. No evening meals are served on Sunday.
Q♉❀◖◗⊟♿P⚟

Eynesbury

Chequers

St Mary's Street, PE19 2TA
⏲ 10.30-2.30, 7-11; 12-2 (closed eve) Sun
☎ (01480) 472116
website: www.thechequers.co.uk
Beer range varies 🄷
This 16th-century inn may be the oldest house in Eynesbury. It has seen many additions and much restoration over the years to extend and enlarge it. Manor courts were held here in the 18th century and a wealth of beams and wood panelling give it olde-worlde charm. There is a comfortable lounge bar with areas set aside for dining; the food is excellent.
♨❀◖◗P

Farcet Fen

Plough

Milk & Water Drove, Ramsey Road, PE7 3DR
(on B1095, S of A605)
⏲ 12-11; 12-10.30 Sun
☎ (01733) 844307
website: www.theploughfarcet.co.uk
Elgood's Black Dog; Oakham JHB; guest beers 🄷
This pub, reputed to be haunted, has had to be refurbished for structural reasons and has lost its real fire, but does now have a separate dining area. Smoking is permitted only in the public bar, where there is a bar billiards table. Live music features on Friday and the local archery group meets on Sunday. Children are welcome.
❀◖◗⊟♿⛺♣P⚟

Fulbourn

Six Bells

9 High Street, CB1 5DH

⏲ 11.30-2.30, 6-11; 11.30-11 Fri & Sat; 12-10.30 Sun

☎ (01223) 880244

Adnams Bitter; Greene King IPA; Young's Special; guest beers 🄷

Friendly, cosy former coaching inn with a welcoming, comfortable atmosphere. The landlord has a policy of trying guest beers from further afield than you might expect in a village local. Good home-cooked food is available in the restaurant and bar (and a take-away service is offered); evening meals are served Tuesday-Saturday. Popular with villagers and business people in the area, there is a regular quiz night and live jazz twice a month. The large, pleasant garden is popular in summer.

⛫☕❀◖◗⊟♿♣P

Grantchester

Blue Ball Inn

57 Broadway, CB3 9NQ

⏲ 11-3, 6-11; 12-5, 7-10.30 Sun

(01223) 840679

Adnams Bitter; guest beer 🄷

Tiny Victorian gem comprising just two small rooms. Photographs of the pub and the village are displayed, along with a list of previous landlords. Good food is available but meals must be booked in advance. Ring the bull, shove-ha'penny and cards are all played here. Children are not permitted.

⛫❀⛟◖◗♣

Great Abington

Three Tuns

75 High Street, CB1 6AB

⏲ 12-2.30, 6-11; 12-11 Sat; 12-10.30 Sun

☎ (01223) 891467

Greene King IPA; Nethergate seasonal beers; guest beers 🄷

Revitalised, refurbished, two-bar free house opposite the village cricket green, popular with a wide range of customers. The small dining room is no-smoking and there is a slightly larger main bar. An excellent, authentic Thai menu is available Monday-Saturday plus a traditional roast on Sunday. Booking is advisable at peak times. The frequently changing beer range includes two guests from Adnams, City of Cambridge, Taylor or Woodforde's. Folk musicians visit on the last Sunday of the month, plus occasional morris dancers. ⛫❀◖◗ΔP⚟

Great Staughton

White Hart ✔

56 The Highway, PE19 5DA

⏲ 12-2 (not Mon-Thu), 5-11; 12-3, 7-11 Sat; 12-3, 7-10.30 Sun

☎ (01480) 860345

Bateman XB, XXXB, seasonal beers 🄷

Fine example of a small coaching inn, dating from the 16th century; driving through the narrow entrance takes you back to the days of horse drawn carriages. Although it has been extended and altered since Cromwell's days it still warrants a Grade II listing and an interior staircase is Grade I listed. Reputedly haunted, the main bar was once several rooms. There is a small dining room and a games room with darts, pool and table skittles. It is an excellent outlet for Bateman beers.

⛫Q❀◖◗♣P⚟

Great Wilbraham

Carpenters Arms

10 High Street, CB1 5JD

⏲ 12-2.30, 7-11; 12-3, 7-10.30 Sun

☎ (01223) 880202

Greene King XX Mild, IPA, Abbot; guest beers 🄷

Whimsical little hostelry, haunt of morris men and mild-seekers, on the main Fulbourn to Bottisham road. The substance of the building has remained unaltered for many years and if you spot an ill-defined figure lurking about, this may be one of the ghosts that inhabit the pub. The main bar hosts lively debates around the large fireplace. The no-smoking lounge/dining room is equally cosy. Good value food is enjoyed here with Sunday lunch particularly popular. The chef's special is always good.

⛫Q❀◖◗⊟♣P

Helpston

Blue Bell ✔

10 Woodgate, PE6 7ED

⏲ 11.30-2.30, 5-11; 11.30-3, 6-11 Sat; 12-10.30 Sun

☎ (01733) 252394

Adnams Bitter; Everards Tiger, Original; guest beer 🄷

Stone-built, 17th-century village pub with traditional values. The wood-panelled bar is popular with locals and a new extension has provided a dining area and a cosy snug, both created from the old cellar. The 18th-century English poet John Clare, known as the peasant poet, was a potboy here. Evening meals are served Tuesday-Saturday.

⛫Q❀◖◗⊟♿♣P⚟

Hemingford Grey

Cock

47 High Street, PE28 9BJ

⏲ 11.30-3, 6-11; 12-4, 6.30-10.30 Sun

☎ (01480) 463609

Elgood's Black Dog; Wolf Golden Jackal; Woodforde's Wherry; guest beers 🄷

An exceptional combination of outstanding real ale in a convivial bar and excellent cuisine in a stylish restaurant. The bar offers modest furnishings, a solid fuel stove and a quiet, sociable environment. The beer range features a selection of distinctive East Anglian ales. The widely-acclaimed food is popular, with a daily fresh fish board, meat and game dishes, and a range of superb sausages. Booking is essential.

⛫Q❀◖◗P

Histon

Red Lion

27 High Street, CB4 4JD

⏲ 10.30-3, 5 (4 Fri)-11; 10.30-11 Sat; 12-6, 7-10.30 Sun

☎ (01223) 564437

Elgood's Black Dog; Everards Beacon, Tiger; Oakham Bishops Farewell; guest beers 🄷

Two-bar free house with a quiet(ish) lounge where food is served and a more boisterous public bar where a fine collection of bottled beers is displayed. Breweriana features throughout including old pub signs and water jugs plus old village photographs and more recent ones of the pub's cricket team. Two beer festivals are hosted annually: an Easter 'aperitif' and the main event in September with a marquee in the garden and live entertainment. Speciality food nights are always popular, especially the monthly curry night.

♨Q❀◐⊟♣P

Holme

Admiral Wells

41 Station Road, PE7 3PH

✪ 12-2.30, 5-11; 12-11 Sat; 12-10.30 Sun

☎ (01487) 831214

Everards Tiger; Woodforde's Wherry; guest beers 🄷

Recently refurbished Victorian inn, said to be the lowest pub in England. Situated next to the East Coast mainline railway, it is named after one of the pall bearers at Nelson's funeral. Up to six beers and a draught cider are available in the two drinking areas, the no-smoking lounge and dining area. Booking is recommended for the popular restaurant, especially at weekends. There is a large, shady garden to one side.

♨❀◐◑♣●P⚟

Keyston

Pheasant

Village Loop, PE28 0RE (on B663, 1 mile S of A14)

✪ 12-3, 6-11; 12-3, 7-10.30 Sun

☎ (01832) 710241

Adnams Bitter; guest beers 🄷

Part of the small Huntsbridge group of pubs, offering high quality food, fine wines and well-kept cask ales. The Pheasant was once a row of thatched cottages and is in an idyllic setting. The village is named after Ketil's Stone, probably an Anglo-Saxon boundary marker. There is a splendid lounge bar and three dining areas (two no-smoking), including the Red Room restaurant in a rear extension. Guest beers usually come from local micro-breweries.

♨Q❀◐◑P

Kirtling

Red Lion

214 The Street, CB8 9PD

✪ 12-3, 7-11; closed Mon; 12-3, 7-10.30 Sun

☎ (01638) 731976

Beer range varies 🄷

The last remaining pub in this country backwater. The bar room is functional but comfortable, uncluttered by superficial tat. An old bread oven features as a display area and the walls are covered with paintings by local artists which are for sale. Internet access is available courtesy of a partnership with the local and district council. Meals can be eaten in the bar or the dining room. The varied menu offers food every day except Sunday evening. Families are welcome.

♨❀◐◑P

Leighton Bromswold

Green Man ✔

37 The Avenue, PE28 5AW OS113754

✪ 12-3 (not Mon-Thu), 7-11 (not Mon); 12-3, 7-10.30 Sun

☎ (01480) 890238

Nethergate IPA; guest beers 🄷

Delightful local in a charming village on a high ridge (the Bromswold) not far from the Northamptonshire border. The Green Man provides a congenial focus for a small village community and attracts visitors from a wide area for good food and an interesting, frequently-changing beer range. Typically three guest ales and Belgian and British bottled ales are stocked. Hood skittles is a popular game here. No food is served on Sunday evening.

♨❀◐◑♣P⚟

Linton

Crown Inn

11 High Street, CB1 6HS

✪ 12-2.30, 5.30-11; 12-11 Fri & Sat; 12-8 Sun

☎ (01223) 891759

Greene King IPA; guest beers 🄷

Situated at the north end of Linton High Street, one of the most varied, interesting and picturesque streets in the area, the Crown is a long, thin pub divided into drinking areas and a no-smoking restaurant. The space is imaginatively used in the narrow but cosy main bar, with various attractive window seats. Note the Watneys Red Barrel lantern hanging in one of the bay windows. Excellent home-cooked food is available in the bar and restaurant at all sessions except Sunday evening.

♨❀⇄◐◑P

Little Gransden

Chequers

71 Main Street, SG19 3DW (on B1046)

✪ 12-2.30, 5-11; 11-11 Sat; 12-3, 7-10.30 Sun

☎ (017687) 677348

Beer range varies 🄷/🄶

A local in the true sense of the word at the heart of this small village, run by the same family for 55 years. A well-researched and documented history of the pub around the walls makes interesting reading. The excellent, unspoilt public bar with wooden bench seating and a roaring fire has been complemented by a comfortable lounge. There is always an interesting guest beer to try here. Check out the collection of beer festival glasses.

♨☋❀⊟♣P

March

Hammer & Anvil

61 Dartford Road, PE15 8BB

✪ 11.30-3 (not Mon), 6-11; 11-11 Sat; 12-3, 7-10.30 Sun

☎ (01354) 658968

Adnams Bitter, Broadside; guest beers 🄷

A short distance west of the town centre, this split-level pub has a large bar at the front and a no-smoking lounge and dining area to the rear. Traditional home-cooked food is available Wednesday-Sunday lunchtimes and Thursday-Saturday evenings. There is a large patio at the rear. Occasional live music is played on Friday evening. The pub runs men's and women's darts teams. Disabled access is via a purpose-built ramp from the car park.

Maxey

Blue Bell
37-39 High Street, PE6 9EE
5.30 (11 Sat)-11; 12-4.30, 7.30-10.30 Sun
☎ (01788) 348182
Abbeydale Absolution; Fuller's London Pride; guest beers [H]
A superb village pub dating from 1645 and built of local limestone. There was no real ale sold here until it became a free house in 1997. Sympathetically modernised with low beams and flagstones, there are always six beers to choose from. The atmosphere can be smoky – an attempted ban on smoking in one room has had to be repealed due to lack of demand.

Melbourn

Star
29 High Street, SG8 6EB
11-11; 12-10.30 Sun
☎ (01763) 260396
website: www.thestarpub.co.uk
Adnams Bitter; Fuller's London Pride; Greene King IPA, Abbot; guest beers [H]
Large and friendly village local which has undergone a recent refurbishment. A consistently good range of ales and an excellent restaurant make the pub popular with local residents and business people. Food is served to diners throughout the pub and those who just want to drink are equally welcome.

Milton

Waggon & Horses
39 High Street, CB4 6DF
12-2.30, 5-11; 12-3, 6-11 Sat; 12-3, 7-10.30 Sun
☎ (01223) 860313
Elgood's Black Dog, Cambridge, Pageant Ale, seasonal beers; guest beers [H]
This imposing mock-Tudor one-room pub, featuring a large hat collection, is Elgood's most southerly house. The large garden is safe for children and has a slide, swings and a petanque terrain. A challenging quiz is held on Wednesday and baltis are the meal speciality on Thursday. All meals are good value and recommended. Bar billiards is still popular here. The real cider comes from local producer Cassels.

Newton

Queen's Head
Fowlmere Road, CB2 5PG
11.30-2.30, 6-11; 12-2.30, 7-10.30 Sun
☎ (01223) 870436
Adnams Bitter, Broadside, seasonal beers [G]
Classic, timeless pub that has had only 18 licensees since 1729 and has featured in every edition of this Guide. In the achingly traditional public bar you will find a high-backed settle, tiled floor and the comforting tick of a large clock. The games annexe offers devil among the tailors and shove-ha'penny. Simple, satisfying food is freshly cooked to order. King George and the Kaiser stopped here for a drink before the Great War.

Old Weston

Swan
Main Street, PE28 5LL (on B660)
12-2.30 (not Mon-Fri), 6.30 (7 Sat)-11; 12-3.30, 7-10.30 Sun
☎ (01832) 293400
Adnams Bitter, Broadside; Greene King Abbot; guest beers [H]
Oak beamed village pub dating from the 16th century which started life as two private houses and has evolved and grown over the years. At the turn of 19th/20th century the pub had its own brewery. The interior has a central bar with a large inglenook, a dining area and a games section offering hood skittles, darts and pool. On Saturday and Sunday a varied menu of traditional pub food is available, including delicious home-made puddings.

Peterborough

Bogarts
17 North Street, PE1 2RA
11-11; 12-10.30 Sun
☎ (01733) 890939
Everards Beacon, Tiger, Original; guest beers [H]
A welcome return to the Guide for this former home-brew shop. The small city-centre bar is now linked to the Italian restaurant next door. A refurbishment last year did away with the pub's kitchen and lunches are now prepared in the Melillos kitchen. An enclosed garden/patio is popular for summer drinking. The regular beers are from Everards with up to four guests available.

Brewery Tap
80 Westgate, PE1 2AA
12-11 (1.30am Fri & Sat); 12-10.30 Sun
☎ (01733) 358500
Elgoods Black Dog; Oakham JHB, White Dwarf, Bishops Farewell; guest beers [H]
This former employment exchange has been converted into a spacious, airy pub. Home to award-winning Oakham Ales, its future is now under threat from plans to redevelop this part of the city. A mix of comfortable leather sofas and low tables combined with tables and chairs for diners suits all tastes. Excellent Thai food is served. The dress code here is smart casual. A late licence until 1.30am allows live music or a DJ on Friday and Saturday nights.

Charters
Town Bridge, PE1 1DG
(moored on S side of riverbank by Town Bridge)
12-11 (1.30am Fri & Sat); 12-10.30 Sun
☎ (01733) 315700
Draught Bass; Oakham JHB, White Dwarf; guest beers [H]

Large Dutch barge, owned by the Oakham Ales group, converted to a café-pub 14 years ago. Up to 12 ales are usually available as well as Belgian bottled beers. Live blues bands perform on Friday and Saturday nights, which means a door charge after 11pm. Popular with locals on football match days, it also gets busy in summer with the large garden and landing stage for boats added attractions. The upper deck has an excellent oriental restaurant and you can also dine in the bar. ❀◑◗≈⅟

Coalheavers Arms

5 Park Street, Woodston, PE2 9BH (off A15)
❂ 12-2 (not Mon-Wed), 5-11; 12-11 Fri & Sat; 12-10.30 Sun
☎ (01733) 565664
Milton Minotaur, Pegasus; guest beers Ⓗ

Small, one-room back-street gem, revived and refurbished by a group of business partners including Milton Brewery. A mild ale is always available, with three guests supplementing the regular brews. A real cider and Belgian bottled beers are also stocked. The large, popular garden holds two beer festival in spring and autumn. Local CAMRA Pub of the Year 2004, the pub is within easy walking distance of the city centre and is one of the busiest pubs south of the river. Q❀≈●▯

College Arms ✔

40 Broadway, PE1 1RS
❂ 10-11; 12-10.30 Sun
☎ (01733) 319745
De Koninck Ambrée; Greene King Abbot; Marston's Pedigree, Burton Bitter; guest beers Ⓗ

The city's first Wetherspoon pub, this is a conversion of an old house with a modern extension. One large bar has different areas for diners, family eating and drinkers. It is decorated with traditional wood panels and subtle shades of paint on the walls, complemented with high ceilings. Up to nine ales are available and beer festivals are frequent events. A wide range of good value food is served; Thursday is curry night. Q❀◑◗♿≈⅟

Goodbarns Yard

64 St Johns Street, PE1 5DD (near Passport office)
❂ 1 (12 Sat)-11; 12-10.30 Sun
☎ (01733) 551830
Caledonian Deuchars IPA; Adnams Broadside; guest beers Ⓖ

Close to the cathedral, this former CAMRA local Pub of the Year continues to serve a good range of beers on gravity dispense from the cellar. Old artefacts and signs adorn the walls of this modern pub. Big on all sports, speedway is well supported here and features in the decor. A large-screen TV in the lounge shows live football matches and bar football is popular. The conservatory is no-smoking and children are welcome. Regular live music is played at the weekend. ❀◑⊟♿♣P⅟

Hand & Heart ☆

12 Highbury Street, Millfield, PE1 3BE
❂ 11-11; 12-10.30 Sun
☎ (01733) 564653
Caledonian Deuchars IPA; John Smith's Bitter; Wychwood Hobgoblin; guest beers Ⓗ

Wonderful 1930s community local with a rare unchanged interior. Two rooms have leatherette seating; the smoke room has no bar – just a serving hatch. Both rooms are accessed by a black and white tiled drinking corridor with its own servery. A lovingly restored garden is an added attraction on warmer days and children are also welcome in the back room. Crib, darts and dominoes are played and a cheese club meets on the last Thursday of the month. Do not miss this gem.
⚠❀⊟♣⅟

Palmerston Arms

82 Oundle Road, Woodston, PE2 9PA (on A605)
❂ 12-11; 12-10.30 Sun
☎ (01733) 565865
Bateman Mild, XXXB; Hop Back Summer Lightning; guest beers Ⓖ

Stone corner pub dating back to the 17th century. Acquired by Bateman in 2003, it continues to offer up to 14 guest ales, all served directly from the cask. Bottled Belgian beer and an extensive malt whisky range are also stocked. Mirrors, jugs and other breweriana adorn the walls. Busy on Friday and Saturday nights, the pub was awarded CAMRA local branch Pub of the Year for 2005.
Q⊟♣●

Royal Oak

1099 Lincoln Road, Walton, PE4 6AX
❂ 12-4, 7-11; 11-11 Fri & Sat; 11-10.30 Sun
☎ (01733) 571032
Beer range varies Ⓗ

This no-frills traditional two-bar pub was built from local brick in the 1930s; the interior bears a sporting theme. Three real ales are available on handpump; one usually from the Newby Wyke Brewery and two varying guests. A function room is available to hire.
⚠🐢❀⊟♿♣P

Ramsey

Jolly Sailor

43 Great Whyte, PE26 1HH
❂ 11-2, 5.30-11; 11-3, 6-11 Sat; 12-3, 7-10.30 Sun
☎ (01487) 813388
Bateman XB; Jennings Cumberland Ale; Wells Bombardier; guest beers Ⓗ

This Grade II listed building has been a pub for over 400 years. The interior has three separate but linked rooms. Welcoming and friendly, it attracts an older clientele who enjoy the fine beer and good conversation. There is no music and no food here, just frequently changing guest beers and a Sunday night quiz.
⚠Q❀⊟♣P

St Ives

Floods Tavern

27 The Broadway, PE27 5BX
❂ 11.30-11 (11.30 Thu; 11.45 Fri & Sat); 12-10.30 Sun
☎ (01480) 467773
Elgood's Cambridge, Greyhound Strong, seasonal beer Ⓗ

Lively town bar in a former bank. Dramatic, large photographs of the historic local floods that gave the pub its name adorn the walls. The Great Ouse flows behind the pub and there is an idyllic garden overlooking the river and its water meadow. Jam sessions are held on Tuesday evening, karaoke on Thursday and live bands on Friday and Saturday evenings. Wednesday is steak night, the only evening when food is served. ❀◑♣

Oliver Cromwell

13 Wellington Street, PE27 5AZ
✪ 11-11; 12-10.30 Sun
☎ (01480) 465601
Adnams Bitter; Oakham JHB; Woodforde's Wherry; guest beers [H]
Warm, congenial and popular wood-panelled bar close to the old town river quay. Built as a cottage in the 18th century, it became a beer house in the 1840s. A glass floor gives a view of an old well, revealed during recent renovation work, and possibly once used for the brewery that operated here from the 1860s to 1919. There is a monthly quiz night on Tuesdays and live music on some Sunday afternoons. ❀◑⊁

St Neots

Woolpack

35 Church Street, PE19 2BU
✪ 12-11; 12-10.30 Sun
☎ (01480) 212030
Wells Eagle, Bombardier; guest beers [H]
Classic Tudor-style pub dating from the 1930s. It has an open-plan public bar and games section, with a small lounge area to one side. There are usually two or three constantly changing guest beers on offer. Traditional home-cooked pub food is available all day. A pub quiz is held on Sunday evening. ❀◐◑⊟♣P

Spaldwick

George

5 High Street, PE28 0TD (off A14)
✪ 11-11; 12-10.30 Sun
☎ (01480) 890293
Adnams Broadside; Fuller's London Pride; Theakston Old Peculier [H]
Follwing a complete refurbishment in 2003, this 16th-century inn is now an airy, smart pub/bistro with large comfortable sofas and a warm fire in winter months. An old barn has been converted into a stylish dining room. The menu is varied with a changing blackboard, and focuses on fresh and local ingredients.
♨Q❀◐◑P

Swavesey

White Horse

1 Market Street, CB4 5QG
✪ 12-2.30, 6-11; 11.30-11 Sat; 12-10.30 Sun
☎ (01945) 232470
Caledonian Deuchars IPA; guest beers [H]
Large pub in the centre of the village. The lounge is comfortable and food-oriented, while the public bar is full of character with a tiled floor and roaring fire in winter. Children are welcome in the pool/family room and spacious garden where there is a play area and barbecues in summer. The beers normally include one from a micro. A beer festival is held on May Day bank holiday weekend. Sunday roasts are renowned; no meals are served on Sunday evening. ♨⛭❀◐◑⊟♣⊁

Teversham

Rose & Crown

1 High Street, CB1 5AF
✪ 11.30-2.30, 6 (5 Fri)-11; 12-11 Sat; 12-3, 7-10.30 Sun
☎ (01223) 292245
Greene King IPA; guest beer [H]
Friendly village pub with an extensive garden including a children's play area. The bar is Z-shaped with a pool table at one end. The guest ale changes with each new cask. Westons Old Rosie scrumpy is now a regular. Live music is played occasionally on Saturday evening. The two-course lunchtime Sunday roast and Monday specials are excellent value – advance booking is recommended. ♨Q❀◐♿♣P

Thriplow

Green Man

2 Lower Street, SG8 7RJ
✪ 12-3, 6-11; closed Mon; 12-3 (closed eve) Sun
☎ (01763) 208855
website: www.greenmanthriplow.co.uk
Beer range varies [H]
Victorian-style pub in a village famous for its daffodil weekend in March. Inside are two drinking areas: one with bench seats and scrubbed tables, the other with comfortable armchairs and a couch. High quality food is served in the dining room. Beers come from Milton, Woodforde's and Oakham, with more unusual offerings also available. There is a choice of outdoor drinking areas: either tables on the green or a courtyard garden.
♨❀◐◑⊟♿P⊁

Ufford

White Hart

Main Street, PE9 3BH
✪ 12-11; 12-10.30 Sun
☎ (01780) 740250
Adnams Bitter; Oakham JHB; guest beer [H]
Recently restored old stone farmhouse with two bars. The public bar has been extended and in the lounge high quality traditional pub food is served all day. The new Ufford Ales Brewery is across the car park, with its beers on sale here. The back of the pub looks out on to a patio and large gardens. Accommodation is now available.
♨Q❀⇌◐◑⊟♿♣P⊁

Whittlesey

Bricklayers Arms

9 Station Road, PE7 1UA
✪ 11-5, 7-11; 11-11 Fri & Sat; 12-5, 7-10.30 Sun
☎ (01733) 262593
John Smith's Bitter; guest beers [H]
Excellent local with a long, plainly furnished public bar and a cosy no-smoking lounge. The large garden is popular in summer. The regulars include a mixed clientele of all ages. Close to the railway station, buses and boat moorings, the pub is HQ for the Whittlesey Straw Bear Festival. A good range of guest beers always includes a mild on offer at a discounted price.
❀⊟♿≹♣P⊁⊡

Whittlesford

Bees in the Wall

36 North Road, CB2 4NZ

12-3, 6-11; 12-11 Sat; 12-10.30 Sun

(01223) 834289

Shepherd Neame Spitfire; Taylor Landlord; guest beers H

There really are bees in the wall in this two-bar pub on the village's northern edge. The public bar oozes atmosphere, especially when the fire is blazing. The long split-level lounge opens on to huge, paddock-style gardens, with plenty of seating. A focal point for village activities, the pub is convenient for visitors to the magnificent Imperial War Museum at Duxford. Two guest beers change weekly. Good value lunches are served and the evening specials are not to be missed, particularly fish and chip night on Thursday.

Q P

Wicken

Maid's Head

12 High Street, CB7 5XR

11.30-3, 6.30-11; 12-3, 7-10.30 Sun

(01353) 720727

Greene King IPA; guest beer H

Family-friendly thatched village local with two bars and a restaurant. One guest beer is available, which changes frequently. Meals can be served in all bars, but most customers opt for the quiet lounge or restaurant. The varied, high quality menu caters for all tastes. A large lawned garden and ample parking add to the appeal. Q P

Wisbech

Rose Tavern

53 North Brink, PE13 1JX

12-3, 6-11; 12-3, 7-10.30 Sun

(01945) 588335

Fuller's London Pride; Kelham Island Pale Rider; Oakham JHB; Shepherd Neame Spitfire; Taylor Landlord; Woodforde's Wherry; guest beers H

Close to Elgood's Brewery, this is one of the town's best kept secrets. A warm, friendly, single-room bar, the frontage dates back over 200 years. Two or three guest beers from local breweries supplement the regular beers. There are no gaming machines or juke box, although live music is played regularly, especially folk and blues. A beer festival takes place on the last weekend in June in the back barn, a former abattoir where the 'plague of Wisbech' began almost 200 years ago.

Witcham

White Horse

7 Silver Street, CB6 2LF (off A142)

12-3 (not Mon & Tue), 6.30-11; 12-3, 7-10.30 Sun

(01353) 778298

Adnams Bitter; guest beers H

Village pub in quiet surroundings with many changing guest beers and excellent home-cooked food. The bar features a mural of Southwold. There is a dining area with a small, comfortable lounge. The garden and patio to the side of the pub are popular in summer. The pub is still visited by veterans from the local World War II airfield nearby.

Q P

Hand & Heart, Peterborough

CHESHIRE

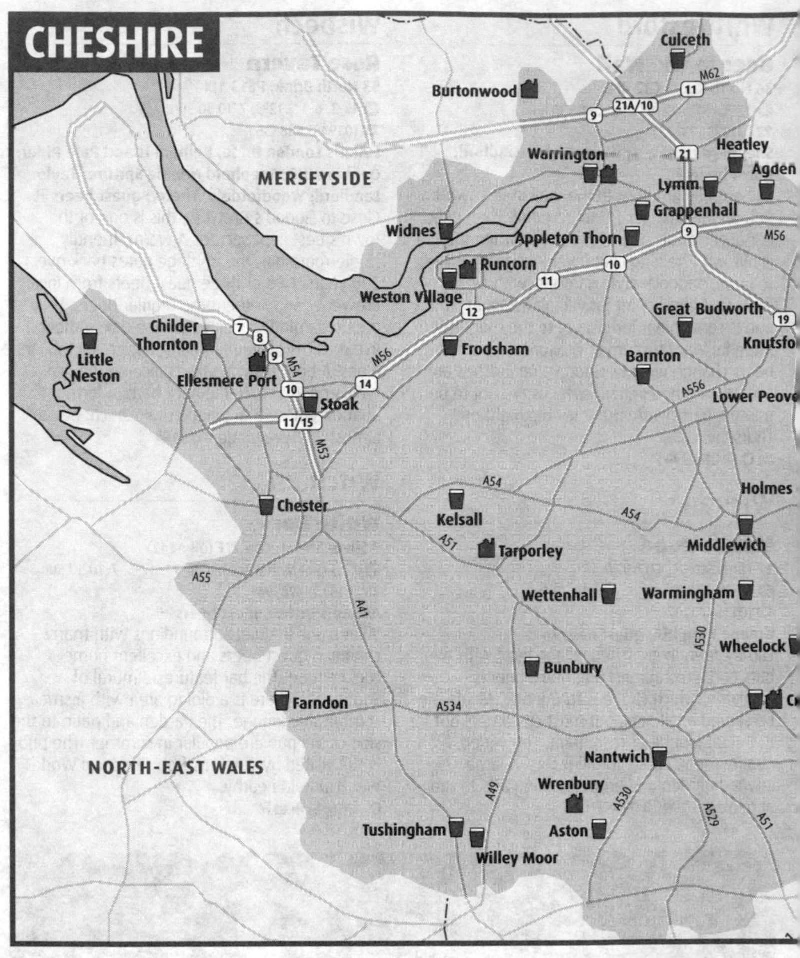

Agden Wharf

Barn Owl ✓

Warrington Lane, WA13 0SW (off A56) OS707872
11-11; 12-10.30 Sun
☎ (01925) 752020 website: www.thebarnowlinn.co.uk
Marston's Burton Bitter, Pedigree; guest beers Ⓗ
Special ingredients are needed to entice both regular drinkers and hungry families to this remote, converted canalside building. Superb farmland vistas, fascinating Bridgewater narrow boat activity, the thrill of the Little Owl ferry to the opposite towpath, duck feeding and a welcoming reception in the pub itself, make this popular pub well worth seeking out. One large room with a conservatory accommodates individuals and club functions. The occasional live music programme is ever changing at this frequent local CAMRA award winner. ❀◐◑ ♿P

Appleton Thorn

Appleton Thorn Village Hall

Stretton Road, WA4 4RT (on B5356)
7.30-11 Thu-Sat; closed Mon-Wed; 1-4, 7.30-11.30 Sun
☎ (01925) 261187
Beer range varies Ⓗ
This ex-school, a former national CAMRA Club of the Year, is now a thriving village hall offering an ever-changing range of six beers from regional and micro-breweries. The attractive sandstone building houses a small, comfortable, lounge and large hall, which acts as a bar area. There is a small pool room attached. To the rear is a garden and bowling green. The club holds regular events in the hall including live music.
Q❀♿P⊁

Ashley

Greyhound

Cow Lane, WA15 0QR
11.30-11; 12-10.30 Sun
☎ (0161) 941 2246
Boddingtons Bitter; Jennings Cumberland Ale; Marston's Pedigree; guest beer Ⓗ
Near the Cheshire-Trafford border, this former farmhouse is the epitome of a good country inn. The pub has been opened out to give separate areas, two of which are primarily, but not exclusively, for diners. This includes an elevated no-smoking section; meals are served all day. A family friendly pub, it has a large garden. The Altrincham to Chester railway line passes through the village and there is an hourly

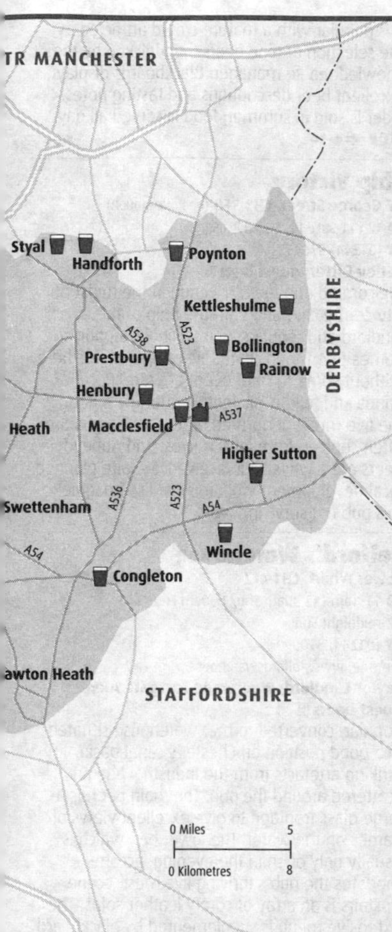

service, although the station is now a request stop. 🏠Q ❀◑◐ ♿ ⇌ P

Aston

Bhurtpore Inn

Wrenbury Road, CW5 8DQ

(¼ mile W of A530 5 miles S of Nantwich)

⏲ 12-2.30 (3 Sat), 6.30-11; 12-10.30 Sun

☎ (01270) 780917

Beer range varies 🄷

This large free house has been run by the same family for many years. Eleven real ales are normally on tap. The range changes regularly and includes the beer of the month. A mild ale is always served as well as a choice of 100 Belgian beers bottled and on tap. The imaginative food menu includes vegetarian options. A beer festival is held in summer at South Cheshire CAMRA Pub of the Year 2005.

🏠Q ❀◑◐ 🛏 ♿ ⛺ ⇌(Wrenbury) ♣ 🍎 P ⛔

Barnton

Barnton Cricket Club

Broomsedge, Townfield Lane, CW8 4PP

(400yds from A533 via Stonehayes Lane)

⏲ 6.30 (12 Sat)-11; 12-10.30 Sun

☎ (01606) 77702 website: www.barntoncc.co.uk

Boddingtons Bitter; Highgate Special Bitter; Hydes Mild; guest beers 🄷

National finalist in CAMRA Club of the Year 2004, this 125-year-old club offers views of the cricket pitch from a large function room which also has a large-screen TV and pool table. A smaller, quieter lounge is to the side of bar. The kitchen has been recently extended and now serves evening meals Tuesday-Friday and food all day at the weekend. A popular annual beer festival is held in mid-November. Show your CAMRA membership card for entry.

❀◐ ♿ ♣ P

Bollington

Poachers Inn ✔

95 Ingersley Road, SK10 5RE

⏲ 12-2 (not Mon), 5.30 (7 Sat)-11; 12-2.30, 7-10.30 Sun

☎ (01625) 572086

website: www.thepoachers.org

Boddingtons Bitter; Taylor Landlord; guest beers 🄷

Single-room pub fashioned from local stone, with an inviting ambience, a real coal fire in winter and a delightful suntrap garden in summer. Near the Peak District national park, there are pleasant walks nearby. The no-smoking restaurant provides a good quality, reasonably priced menu of home-prepared meals (no food on Mon). Meals are also served in the bar. A choice of guest beers is available, one often from local brewery Storm. The pub runs social and golf societies for its regulars.

🏠 ❀◑◐ P

Bunbury

Dysart Arms

Bowes Gate Road, CW6 9PH

⏲ 11.30-11; 12-10.30 Sun

☎ (01829) 260183

website: www.dysartarms-bunbury.co.uk

Thwaites Original; guest beers 🄷

Dating back to the mid-1700s and an inn since the late 1800s, the Dysart Arms was for some time simultaneously a pub, farm and abattoir. It was named after local landowners the Tollemache family, who were the Earls of Dysart. The layout is open plan, but with six distinct areas surrounding a central bar. Although very much meal oriented, as a Brunning and Price pub it is committed to cask beer, particularly from independent micros; Weetwood beers are often on tap here.

🏠Q ❀◑◐ P ⛔

INDEPENDENT BREWERIES

Beartown Congleton
Borough Arms Crewe
Burtonwood Burtonwood
Coach House Warrington
Northern Runcorn
Paradise Wrenbury
Station House Ellesmere Port
Storm Macclesfield
Weetwood Tarporley
Woodlands Wrenbury

Chester

Albion Inn

Park Street, CH1 1RN

12-3, 5 (6 Sat)-11; 11-11 Fri; 12-3, 7-10.30 Sun

(01244) 340345

Banks's Original; Caledonian Deuchars IPA; Jennings Cumberland Ale; Taylor Landlord; guest beer H

The landlord of over 30 years standing has retained the classic Victorian layout of lounge, snug and vault in this unchanging street-corner local facing the city walls. A sign outside proclaims the pub as 'family hostile', but adults venturing inside will find a welcoming ambience. The interior is decorated with William Morris wallpaper, and WWI memorabilia is much in evidence. Good value, home-cooked meals are available and there is an impressive selection of malt whiskies.

Duttons

10-12 Godsall Lane, CH1 1LN

(alley between St Werburgh St and Eastgate Row)

10-11 (1am Fri & Sat); 12-10.30 Sun

(01244) 401869

Lees Bitter, seasonal beers H

Tucked away down a historic side alley, this lively city-centre bar's contemporary interior features an eclectic mix of wood, glass and steel. A predominantly food-oriented establishment with meals served all day, it comprises a recently extended lounge area with comfy chairs and sofas towards the rear and tables filling the remaining space. An area at the front on this pedestrian-only lane allows for outside drinking and eating during good weather. A popular venue, it gets busy at the weekends when a dress code may apply.

Mill Hotel

Milton Street, CH1 3NF (by canal, off inner ring road)

11-11; 12-10.30 Sun

(01244) 350035 website: www.millhotel.com

Cains Bitter; Theakston Cool Cask; Weetwood Best Bitter; guest beers H

City-centre hotel, housed in a former corn mill dating from 1830. The bar is a beer drinkers' paradise with up to 16 real ales on handpump at any time, including two house beers. Large screens show TV sport. The Mill boasts five separate dining areas serving simple bar snacks to full restaurant fare all day. The hotel also offers dining cruises on the adjacent Shropshire Union Canal. Participants may take their beer aboard from the bar. Or you can simply sit on the patio and watch the narrowboats pass by.

P

Old Harkers Arms

1 Russell Street, CH3 5AL

(down steps off City Rd to canal towpath)

12-11; 12-10.30 Sun

(01244) 344525

website: www.harkersarms-chester.co.uk

Cains IPA; Weetwood Best Bitter; guest beers H

Located on the edge of the Shropshire Union Canal, this converted warehouse bears the unmistakable hallmark of the Brunning & Price pub group, but like all its pubs it retains its own style. Invariably busy (especially at weekends), it is popular with a mature crowd attracted by the selection of nine beers, handpicked by the knowledgeable manager. Blackboards display excellent beer descriptions and tasting notes. Cider is sold in summer; food is served all day.

Q

Ship Victory

47 George Street, CH1 3EQ (near fire station)

12 (11 Sat)-11; 12-10.30 Sun

(01244) 376453

Tetley Bitter; guest beer H

Welcoming and friendly venue in the midst of a city-centre car park. With the help of the landlord and regulars who willingly support the games teams and charitable causes, nights here without some form of event are rare. Rock bands and folk music feature strongly among the live music performed here. Guest beers are often sourced from local micros, and Abbeydale beers are always well received. Despite planned local development work it is hard to imagine this pub not surviving.

Telford's Warehouse

Tower Wharf, CH1 4EZ

11-1am (12.30am Thu; 1.30am Fri & Sat); 12-midnight Sun

(01244) 390090

website: www.telfordswarehouse.com

Taylor Landlord; Weetwood Eastgate Ale; guest beers H

Popular, converted former warehouse situated in a good position on Chester's canal basin. Striking artefacts from the Industrial age are scattered around the pub. The main bar has a large glass frontage to give excellent views of barges on the water. The lower bar, which is usually only open in the evening, accommodates the pub's thriving live music scene. Upstairs is an array of comfy leather sofas. The extensive menu is supplemented by blackboard specials. Note: there may be an admission charge after 9pm some evenings. P

Union Vaults

44 Egerton Street, CH1 3ND

11-11; 12-10.30 Sun

(01244) 400556

Caledonian Deuchars IPA; Phoenix Arizona; guest beer H

Small, hard-drinking, street-corner local situated halfway between the city centre and railway station. A split-level pub, the lower level houses a popular billiards table as well as a bagatelle board. Sky TV is normally shown. Upstairs is a quieter lounge area where you can admire some interesting old prints of Chester. Lunchtime snacks are available. Parking is difficult.

Childer Thornton

White Lion

New Road, CH66 5PU (off A41)

11.30-11; 12-10.30 Sun

(0151) 339 3402

Thwaites Mild, Original, Lancaster Bomber H

Small, friendly country pub on the outskirts of Ellesmere Port. It retains some original features such as the brick fireplace, while a new, small room has been created from part of the kitchen.

The snug is popular with families at lunchtimes. Conveniently situated for those travelling to football matches and for the boat museums and Cheshire Oaks outlet village, it offers good value meals – try the excellent home-made chicken tikka (no food on Sun). A former CAMRA Regional Pub of the Year. ⌂Q❀◑P

Congleton

Beartown Tap

18 Willow Street, CW12 1RL (on A54 Buxton road)
12-2, 4-11; 12-11 Fri & Sat; 12-10.30 Sun
☎ (01260) 270990
website: www.beartownbrewery.co.uk
Beartown Kodiak Gold, Bearskinful, Polar Eclipse, Black Bear; guest beer H
Welcoming local just yards from the Beartown Brewery. Opened in 1999, this was the brewery's first pub and such is the beer quality that it has won Regional CAMRA Pub Of The Year in 2003 and 2004. Guest beers are usually sourced from other micros and there is generally another Beartown beer available. Real cider is also stocked and a good selection of Belgian bottled beers. Street parking can be found immediately outside the pub. ⌂Q≉♣●⊬

Congleton Leisure Centre

Worral Street, CW12 1DT
10-1 (not Mon), 7-11 (7-9.30 Sat); 8-10.30 Sun
☎ (01260) 271552
Beer range varies H
Unusually, a municipal leisure centre that sells an ever-changing choice of three real ales. One is from the Woodlands range and the others often from micros. Efforts have been made to create a pub environment in the bar: the walls are adorned with brewery posters and pump clips from the beers sold. The bar has a snug feel but the no-smoking family room is a little bland. The bar is open to everyone – there is no entrance fee and no need to use the sporting facilities. Q♿≉P⊬

Queen's Head

Park Lane, CW12 3DE
(opp station, at bridge 75 of Macclesfield Canal)
11-11; 12-10.30 Sun
☎ (01260) 272546
Greene King Abbot; Tetley Bitter; Wells Bombardier; guest beers H
Canalside pub with its own moorings, popular with locals and canal users. Originally built for the railway trade, the pub has enjoyed something of a revival in recent years under the current landlord. One room has a pool table, while food is served in a dining area at the back; it is mostly home-cooked and there is a changing specials board. Guest beers change frequently and often come from local breweries. The huge garden has a children's play area and stages occasional events in summer.
❀◑●≉♣P⊬

Crewe

Angel

Victoria Street, CW1 2PU
10-7 (10 Thu-Sat); 12-3 Sun
Oakwell Old Tom Mild, Barnsley Bitter, guest beers H
Welcoming, town-centre pub, situated below street level in the Victoria Centre. Two minutes' walk from Crewe bus station, the entrance is snuggled between the Cheshire Building Society and Partners. It is open plan but divided into a number of discrete areas, some for dining and others for drinking. The food and beer are competitively priced. ◑

Borough Arms

33 Earle Street, CW1 2BG
7 (3 Fri)-11; 12-4, 7-11 Sat; 12-3, 7-10.30 Sun
☎ (01270) 254999
Beer range varies H
Comfortable, town-centre pub renowned locally for a choice of up to eight regularly-changing real ales. In addition the range of Belgian beers includes eight on tap and over 100 bottles. There is a TV for occasional major sporting events, but this is a pub where conversation dominates. The landlord installed a two-and-a-half barrel brewing plant in 2005 and intends to produce a variety of beers including some in the Belgian style. Q❀≉

British Lion

58 Nantwich Road, CW2 6AL (¼ mile from station)
12-4, 7-11 Mon & Thu; 3.30-11 Tue & Wed; 12-11 Fri; 12-3 Sat; 12-10.30 Sun
☎ (01270) 214379
Tetley Dark Mild, Bitter; guest beers H
Friendly one-room pub, with a rear alcove, close to Crewe Alexandra football ground in Gresty Road. The pub closes at 3pm on Saturday afternoon – a police requirement. The only real ale pub on this section of Nantwich Road, two guest beers are served from an extensive list of micro and regional breweries. Known locally as the Pig, its nickname probably recalls the escape of a pig from the nearby livestock market many years ago. It is home to thriving darts and dominoes teams. ≉♣

Crown Hotel

25 Earle Street, CW1 2BH
11-11, 12-10.30 Sun
☎ (01270) 257295
Robinson's Hatters, Unicorn, Old Tom (winter), **seasonal beers** H
Town-centre pub with a central bar to serve the surrounding tables and chairs. A former hotel, it is of red brick construction, dating from the late 1900s. A sympathetic updating did not cause any loss in character. Popular with cast members from the nearby Lyceum Theatre, it is a no-nonsense pub, yet welcoming. ≉♣

Culceth

New Inn ✓

474 Warrington Road, WA3 5QX (on A574)
12-11; 12-10.30 Sun
☎ (01925) 763391
Caledonian Deuchars IPA; Greene King Old Speckled Hen; Tetley Bitter; guest beers H
Located on the south side of the village towards Risley, this pub features two rooms: one a smart lounge with an entrance to a large, seated decking area outside, the other a small bar to the side with Sky TV. Quiz night is on Thursday, karaoke on Saturday. Food is served throughout

the week; cider is sold in summer. The village is served by Warrington-Leigh buses.
❀◑⊟♿♣●P

Farndon

Farndon Arms

High Street, CH3 6PU

⏲ 11-3, 5-11; 12-3, 7-10.30 Sun

☎ (01829) 270570

website: www.farndonarms.com

Adnams Bitter; John Smith's Bitter; guest beers Ⓗ

Formerly known as the Raven, with ground-floor etched windows still showing the original name, this black and white half-timbered pub is situated centrally in this picturesque village, just 200 yards from the river bordering Wales. Although now one-roomed, there are three distinct areas including a dining section and an upstairs restaurant serving a good range of dishes as well as traditional pub food. Unobtrusive Sky TV and occasional live music provide the entertainment.

Frodsham

Helter Skelter

31 Church Street, WA6 6PN

⏲ 11-11; 12-10.30 Sun

☎ (01928) 733361

Weetwood Best Bitter; guest beers Ⓗ

Commonly called the Slide by locals, this one-room pub can get busy on weekend evenings. The bar occupies the right-hand wall and is fronted by a standing area. Seating is arranged around the remaining walls, including a raised section to the rear. A bar snack menu is available together with interesting blackboard specials (no food Sun eve). Six handpumps dispense a range of reasonably priced ales, usually from micro-breweries. One handpump dispenses a cider or perry. ◑≋●▯

Grappenhall

Grappenhall Community Centre

Bellhouse Farm, WA4 2SG (off A50) OS642862

⏲ 7.30 (3 Sat)-11, 3-10.30 Sun

☎ (01925) 268633

website: www.grappenhall.com

Greene King Ruddles Best; guest beers Ⓗ

Large private club and social centre, located a short distance from the Bridgewater Canal, supporting a wide range of groups and activities. Converted from an old farm, the bar, lounge and games room were refurbished in summer 2004 and a central bar serves all areas. The lounge has a no-smoking section. The games room is the venue for the Wednesday quiz. An old barn houses the function room, where the spring beer festival is held. Your CAMRA membership card gains admission. ❀♿♣P⊭

Great Budworth

George & Dragon

High Street, CW9 6HG (off A559)

⏲ 11.30-3, 6-11; 12-10.30 Sun

☎ (01606) 891317

Taylor Landlord; guest beers Ⓗ

Great Budworth is rural Cheshire at its best and the George is at the heart of this picturesque village. There are two downstairs rooms – a cosy lounge and a bar – upstairs is the restaurant. Food can be served wherever suits you best and is available at all times. The menu is varied and good value. There are off peak specials and a children's menu. ⌂Q☕◑⊟♣P⊭

Handforth

Railway

Station Road, SK9 3AB (opp. station)

⏲ 12-11; 12-3, 7-10.30 Sun

☎ (01625) 523472

Robinson's Hatters, Unicorn, Old Tom (winter) Ⓗ

The Railway is a friendly pub with a good local following. It has several rooms, one of which is no-smoking. The main bar is also equipped with a large air filter machine. In close proximity to the station, this is an excellent place to wait for your train. It is also on the bus route from Macclesfield to Manchester. Lunches are served Tuesday-Friday. Q❀◐⊟≋♣P

Heatley

Railway ✔

42 Mill Lane, WA13 9SQ

⏲ 12-11; 12-10.30 Sun

☎ (01925) 752742

Boddingtons Bitter; Taylor Landlord; guest beer Ⓗ

They don't make pubs like this any more, run by the same licensee for over two decades. Many different-sized rooms provide diverse facilities to accommodate varying local needs. Folk is the most regular of the many different types of live music hosted here. A large, open, grassed play area is ideal for children, allowing parents to enjoy an outdoor pint in peace. The pub is ideally located for walkers on the Trans-Pennine trail in the green belt of the River Bollin.
❀◐⊟♣P⊭

Henbury

Cock Inn

Chelford Road, SK10 3LH

⏲ 11-3, 4.30-11; 11-11 Fri & Sat; 12-10.30 Sun

☎ (01625) 425659

Robinson's Hatters, XB, Unicorn, Double Hop, Old Tom (winter), **seasonal beers** Ⓗ

Village pub on the main road two miles west of Macclesfield. This is a genuine local with a public bar and darts team. The lounge and dining room can be busy with diners as meals are popular. There is a children's playground at the rear. Robinson's seasonal beers are stocked. ◑⊟⊭

Higher Sutton

Hanging Gate ✔

Meg Lane, SK11 0NG

(follow Ridge Hill Rd from village centre for 1½ miles)

⏲ 12-3, 7 (5.30 Fri)-11; 12-11 Sat; 12-10.30 Sun

☎ (01260) 252238

Hydes Bitter, Jekyll's Gold, seasonal beers Ⓗ

Unusual building, dating from 1621, built on the edge of the hill, with an extensive view across the Cheshire Plain to the Welsh mountains. It has small, cosy rooms and a large dining area down two levels. Warm and welcoming, the

family-run pub is popular with walkers and diners, and has a well-deserved reputation for its home-cooked food (booking recommended). The pub can become busy on summer weekends and weekend evenings.
♨Q⛀❀◐◑⊟P⊬

Holmes Chapel

Victoria Sports & Social Club

Victoria Avenue, London Road, CW4 7BE
(S of village centre, just off A50)
✪ 6-11; 12-10.30 Sun
☎ (01477) 535858
Hydes Bitter; Marston's Pedigree; Worthington's Bitter 🄷
The Victoria Club is situated off London Road, south of the village centre at the end of a cul-de-sac. It has tennis courts and a cricket pitch to the rear. Inside there are snooker tables and a large entertainment hall. The lounge bar looks out onto the bowling green while the cosy main bar has a real fire in winter.
♨Q⛀❀♿⇌♣P⊬

Kelsall

Olive Tree

Chester Road, CW6 0RS (off A54)
✪ 12-11; 12-10.30 Sun
☎ (01829) 751291
Weetwood Best Bitter, Eastgate Ale 🄷
There is a distinct split in this pub between the restaurant and drinking areas. Diners can still enjoy real ale with their meals but the arrangement allows drinkers to escape the hustle and bustle of the all day food service. A central bar serves both the lounge and public bar. The lounge has wooden flooring and many original features, while the livelier bar houses the TV. The annual Chester Folk Festival is held next to the pub at the end of May.
♨❀◐◑⊟♿⛺P

Kettleshulme

Bull's Head

Macclesfield Road, SK23 7QU (on B5470)
✪ 3 (5 Mon)-11; 12-11 Fri & Sat; 12-10.30 Sun
☎ (01663) 733225
Boddingtons Bitter; guest beers 🄷
Stone, end-of-terrace pub, in the village centre. Two rooms: the smaller is cottage style with pine seating, the larger has a farmhouse feel and features a natural stone floor, open fires and a darts area. Background blues music is often playing and live bands perform several times a year on a Sunday evening. The pub is surrounded by good walking country as it is close to Windgather Rocks. ♨❀⛺♣P

Swan

Macclesfield Road, SK23 7QU (on B5470)
✪ 12-3 (not Mon), 5.30-11; 12-11 Sat; 12-10.30 Sun
☎ (01663) 732943
website: www.the-swan-inn-kettleshulme.co.uk
Marston's Burton Bitter; guest beers 🄷
A 15th-century village pub that was saved from closure in 2005 when it was bought by a group of locals and reopened. The quaint interior features timber beams, stone fireplaces and log fires in the two small, cosy rooms. Two changing guest beers from micro-breweries supplement the regular Marston's Bitter. Families and hikers are welcome at this excellent inn in a picturesque Peak District National Park village surrounded by good walking country.
♨❀◐⛺♣P

Knutsford

Cross Keys ✔

52 King Street, WA16 6DT
✪ 11.30-3, 5.30-11; 12-3, 7-10.30 Sun
☎ (01565) 750404
website: www.knutsfordcrosskeys.co.uk
Boddingtons Bitter; Taylor Landlord; Tetley Bitter; guest beers 🄷
Set on an attractive shopping street, this former 18th-century coaching inn was largely rebuilt in 1909. A glass and timber screen separates the lounge from the vault with its pool table and TV. Bar meals are served at lunchtime, while the restaurant, reached by a barrel-vaulted tunnel, opens Tuesday-Saturday evenings. The fine choice of cask ales sets the Cross Keys apart: a gleaming bank of polished brass handpumps dispenses three constantly-changing guest beers. ⇄◐◑⊟⇌●P⊬

Lawton Heath

Horseshoe

Sandbach Road, ST7 3RA
✪ 12-11; 12-10.30 Sun
☎ (01270) 876070
Draught Bass; guest beers 🄷
In a semi-rural location between the A50 and the A533, the Horseshoe has a large open-plan interior with a distinct public bar area. The regularly-changing guest beers include brews from regional and micro-breweries. A blackboard lists the daily beers. Live jazz is a regular feature. A TV in the bar shows sporting events. There is a large car park and a children's play area. Food is served 12-6pm. ❀◐♣P

Little Neston

Harp Inn ✔

19 Quayside, CH64 0TB
(from Burton Rd, down Marshlands Rd to bottom, turn left)
✪ 11-11; 12-10.30 Sun
☎ (0151) 336 6980
Holt Bitter; Taylor Landlord; guest beers 🄷
Former coalminers' pub, converted from two cottages, comprising a public bar and a lounge/family room. Set in a glorious location overlooking the Dee Estuary (a popular location for twitchers), it can be cut off at high tide. The outside drinking area is a superb spot for watching the often breathtaking sunsets. A regular guide entry, it welcomes children (and dogs) and is a popular meeting point for the Mersey morris men. Difficult to find, but worth the effort; meals are served Tuesday-Saturday.
♨Q⛀❀◐⊟P

Lower Peover

Crown

Crown Lane, WA16 9QB
✪ 11.30-3, 5.30-11; 12-10.30 Sun
☎ (01565) 722074

Boddingtons Bitter; Flowers IPA; Greene King Old Speckled Hen; Taylor Landlord; Tetley Dark Mild; guest beer ⊞
A cobbled frontage tempts the passer-by into this homely, 17th-century country inn. Low ceilings and beams enhance the cosy atmosphere of a welcoming village pub. The stone-flagged bar has a well-used dartboard, while the smart front room is used mainly by diners enjoying home-cooked meals made with locally-sourced ingredients (Sun meals are served 12-7). Thursday is quiz night, and a gooseberry competition is held in July. Pleasingly, cask mild is usually available, and the guest beer is often from one of Cheshire's independent brewers. ⛫❀◐◑♣P

Lymm

Spread Eagle

47 Eagle Brow, WA13 0AG
✪ 11-11; 12-10.30 Sun
☎ (01925) 757467
Lees GB Mild, Bitter, seasonal beers ⊞
Situated by the lower dam and a short stroll from the Bridgewater Canal, this large, traditional pub is an integral part of the old village centre. A small public bar and a cosy snug, complete with real fire, complement the lounge and large restaurant area, serving a variety of meals, including Sunday lunches. The pub is popular with the local community and passing trade from the canal. A function room occupies part of the first floor.
⛫Q❀◐◑⊟♿

Macclesfield

Brewers Arms

139 Bridge Street, SK11 6QE
✪ 4 (12 Sat)-11; 12-10.30 Sun
Caledonian Deuchars IPA; guest beers ⊞
Situated on a corner in the narrow streets of the older part of Macclesfield, surrounded by traditional terraced weavers cottages, until recently a keg-only pub, it serves the local community well. Although the pub has been opened out, the seating is divided into small, friendly drinking corners, traditionally decorated, served by a central circular bar. The long room at the rear provides a lively games area, with a large space for pool, a separate dartboard, and a big screen.
♉❀♣

British Flag

42 Coare Street, SK10 1DW
✪ 5.30 (5 Sat)-11; 12-3, 7-10.30 Sun
Robinson's Hatters, Unicorn, ⊞ Old Tom (winter), **Ⓖ seasonal beers ⊞**
This is an old-fashioned and friendly town local where four rooms surround a central bar. Pub games are popular, including table skittles, and one room is dedicated to pool. The tap room, apart from darts and dominoes, is home to the landlord's trophy cabinet of Macclesfield Town FC memorabilia. There is also a large-screen TV for sport. In the 1860s the pub was a ginger beer brewery; it now serves as the local for the staff and old boys of the neighbouring King's School. ≹♣

Dolphin

76 Windmill Street, SK11 4HS
✪ 12-2.30, 5.30-11; 12-11 Sat; 12-10.30 Sun
☎ (01625) 616179
Robinson's Hatters, Unicorn, ⊞ Old Tom (winter), **Ⓖ seasonal beers ⊞**
This traditional, friendly pub, situated on a street corner opposite playing fields, is very much a local pub but also welcoming to visitors. A central bar separates the two drinking areas; a further room provides an ideal venue for meetings. The original glass door is a distinctive feature. Robinson's award-winning Old Tom is always available during the winter; home cooked food is served Monday-Saturday at this former local CAMRA Pub of the Season award winner. ⛫♉◐⊟≹♣

Prince of Wales

33 Roe Street, SK11 6UT
✪ 11.30-11; 12-10.30 Sun
☎ (01625) 424796
website: www.portersprinceofwales.co.uk
Caledonian Deuchars IPA; Theakston Best Bitter; guest beers ⊞
Comfortable and friendly town-centre pub attracting a varied clientele. Look out for the mosaics made by the landlady at the front entrance and in the small back yard, and also for the unusual fish tank separating the gents' toilets from the bar area. One roomed but with quieter corners, it has a real fire in winter. The pub has close links with Macclesfield Rugby Club and supports teams in local leagues. Two constantly-changing guest beers usually come from independent breweries. ⛫❀≹♣

Waters Green Tavern

98 Waters Green, SK11 6LH
✪ 11.30-3, 5.30-11; 11-3, 7-11 Sat; 12-3, 7-10.30 Sun
☎ (01625) 422653
Greene King IPA; Taylor Landlord; guest beers ⊞
Handy for both the train and bus stations, this popular town pub, although unassuming from the outside, provides a warm welcome from staff and regulars alike. It has won numerous awards from the local branch of CAMRA. Seven beers are normally available, often from more unusual breweries. Traditional, home-cooked food is served at lunchtime except Sunday. There are three distinct drinking areas offering plenty of corners for a quiet pint, as well as crib and dominoes, and there is a pool room at the rear. ⛫◐≹♣●

Middlewich

Big Lock Inn

Webbs Lane, CW10 9DN
✪ 11-11; 12-10.30 Sun
Black Sheep Best Bitter; Phoenix Wobbly Bob; Tetley Bitter; guest beers ⊞
Located next to, and named after, lock number 75 on the Trent & Mersey Canal, the inn's balcony and patio overlooking the canal are particularly popular. Multi-roomed, the pub caters for all tastes. The large-screen TV in the pool room shows mostly football, while the peaceful restaurant serves a good range of quality food. The house beer, when it is on tap, is from Phoenix. ❀◐◑⊟♿P

Royal British Legion Club ✔

100 Lewin Street, CW10 9AS

12-3, 7-11; 12-11 Sat; 12-3, 7-10.30 Sun

☎ (01606) 833286

Hydes Dark, Bitter; guest beers Ⓗ

This well-supported club has become a bastion of real ale in the town, with one and sometimes two guest beers as well as Hydes ales. There is a quiet no-smoking room as well as a lounge bar with snooker tables and a back room featuring televised sport. The club has won several CAMRA awards, most recently South Cheshire Club of the Year 2004. Show a valid CAMRA membership card or a copy of this Guide for entry. ❀ ♣ P ⅟

Mobberley

Bull's Head

Mill Lane, WA16 7HX (off Town Lane, signed from B5085)

11.30-11; 12-10.30 Sun

☎ (01565) 873134

Boddingtons Bitter; Taylor Landlord; Tetley Bitter; guest beers Ⓗ

This traditional country local is an integral part of the community, supporting all manner of social and charitable activities. It hosts quiz nights, occasional beer festivals, traction engine rallies, brass band concerts and folk music. Down a quiet lane, it has a cobbled frontage and a bowling green to the rear. Formerly three cottages, it has an unusual through fireplace dividing the main room. With an excellent reputation for food and a good range of real ale including two guest beers, the pub is always popular. ❀ ♣ P

Nantwich

Black Lion

29 Welsh Row, CW5 5ED

(just outside town centre over river bridge)

4 (1 Fri & Sat)-11; 1-10.30 Sun

☎ (01270) 628711

Titanic White Star; Weetwood Best Bitter, Eastgate Ale, Old Dog Ⓗ

The date 1664 appears above the door of this old black and white half-timbered pub with candelit tables in three adjoining rooms downstairs. There is a paved garden at the side for outdoor drinking and a heated conservatory. A friendly pub where the locals regularly play chess, it hosts a quiz night on Wednesday and live music at the weekend. The Shropshire Union Canal is nearby. ❀ ♣

Oddfellows Arms

97 Welsh Row, CW2 5ET

12-3 (not Mon), 6-11; 12-11 Sat; 12-3, 7-10.30 Sun

☎ (01270) 624758

Burtonwood Bitter, Top Hat; Marston's Pedigree; guest beers Ⓗ

Nicknamed the Oddies, this recently extensively refurbished pub retains its original character. It is frequented by a wide cross section of people, especially during the summer due to its proximity to the Shropshire Union Canal. The pub is on the oldest thoroughfare in town (the main Roman road to Wales) and is appropriately decorated with pictures of old Nantwich. The landlord is rightly proud of the absence of TV or a juke box. Q ❀ ♣ ⅟

Nomansheath

Wheatsheaf

Chester Road, SY14 8DY (signed off A41)

12-3, 6-11; 12-3, 6-10.30 Sun

☎ (01948) 820337

Thwaites Original; Weetwood Eastgate Ale; guest beer Ⓗ

Welcoming, cosy 18th-century former coaching inn with a lounge, snug and no-smoking dining room. A rare, genuine free house, it often features locally-sourced guest ales including those from Woodlands Brewery at Wrenbury. Fine home-cooked food makes the pub an ideal refuelling point after healthy exercise on the nearby Cheshire Cycleway or Sandstone Trail. For the less energetic make use of the No. 41 Chester-Whitchurch bus which runs through the village. ❀ ♣ P ⅟

Peover Heath

Dog Inn

Wellbank Lane, WA16 8UP

(off A50 at Whipping Stocks Inn and continue for 2 miles)

11.30-3, 4.30-11; 11.30-11 Sat; 12-10.30 Sun

☎ (01625) 861421

website: www.doginn-overpeover.co.uk

Copper Dragon Scotts 1816; Hydes Bitter; Moorhouses Black Cat; Weetwood Best Bitter Ⓗ

The comfortable bar area provides plenty of seating around a real fire, while pub games including pool, darts and dominoes are played in the public bar. Two dining rooms, one no-smoking, offer a full and varied menu (booking is advisable at weekends). Food is served all day on Sunday. A front patio and garden are available for outdoor drinking. Popular quizzes are held on Thursday and Sunday; live entertainment is hosted usually once a month on Friday. Q ❀ ♣ P

Poynton

Royal British Legion Club

Georges Road West, SK12 1JY

12-11; 12-10.30 Sun

☎ (01605) 873120

Boddingtons Bitter; guest beers Ⓗ

Extensive, comfortable and welcoming club that brings a much-needed variety of real ale to Poynton. The changing guest beers are invariably from micro-breweries. A beer festival is held twice a year in spring and autumn and the club features regular social evenings and live entertainment. This club shows what can be done with real ale and enterprising management. Non-members can be signed in in the usual fashion. ♣ P

Prestbury

Admiral Rodney

New Road, SK10 4HT

11-3, 5.30-11; 11-11 Fri & Sat; 12-3, 7-10.30 Sun

☎ (01625) 829484

Robinson's Hatters, Unicorn Ⓗ

Named after a British naval officer in the Napoleonic Wars, this Grade II listed building dating from 1730 has low ceilings and is divided into small cosy rooms with a central bar area. In keeping with the traditional feel, there are no intrusive noisy games or music to spoil the atmosphere, and good home-cooked food is served. Despite the limitations of a tiny cellar, the landlord frequently features highly in Robinson's Cellarmanship awards. Q❀◖⇌P

Rainow

Highwayman

Macclesfield Road, SK10 5UU (on B5470)
✪ 12-3, 5-11; 12-11 Thu-Sat; 12-10.30 Sun
☎ (01625) 573245
Thwaites Original, Lancaster Bomber, seasonal beers Ⓗ
Known locally as the Patch, this pub is a welcome haven in a remote area, enjoying idyllic views over Cheshire to the Welsh hills. Its name recalls a local highwayman who could spot unwary travellers on the old salt trail a mile off from a nearby vantage point. A maze of connecting rooms, with three log fires, it serves daily specials and traditional home-cooked food. Live music is played on Wednesday and quizzes are held every other Friday. Families are welcome.
♨Q❀◖◗♣P

Stoak

Bunbury Arms

Little Stanney Lane, CH2 4HW (signed off A5117)
✪ 12-11; 12-10.30 Sun
☎ (01244) 301665
Robinson's Best Bitter; guest beers Ⓗ
This attractive red-brick pub with white-latticed windows is an ideal refuge for those wishing to escape the bedlam of the Cheshire Oaks retail outlet. Guest ales are regularly sourced from the Weetwood range. It has a smart open-plan lounge and tiny snug; the garden is a surprising oasis of calm considering the nearby maelstrom of the M53/M56 interchange. Look out for the pipistrelle colony emerging from the chimney! Moorings on the Shropshire Union Canal are close by. ❀◖◗⊟▲♣P⊬

Styal

Ship

Altrincham Road, SK9 4JE (off B5166, 2½ miles N of Wilmslow)
✪ 11.30-11; 12-10.30 Sun
☎ (01625) 523818
Boddingtons Bitter; Theakston Best Bitter; Wells Bombardier; guest beers Ⓗ
Located close to Styal Country Park, Quarry Bank Mill and Manchester Airport, this old, multi-roomed pub started serving beer when it was a farm outhouse or shippon (shortened to ship). The oak-panelled snug, named the Pilot's Room, contains a model ship and a grandfather clock, and is furnished with settles. It hosts a chess club on Tuesday. There are normally four guest ales, food is served all day, and there is live music on Saturday evening. ❀⇔◖◗⇌♣P⊬

Swettenham

Swettenham Arms ✔

CW12 2LF (off A535) OS800672
✪ 11.30-3, 6-11; 12-10.30 Sun
☎ (01477) 571284
website: www.swettenhamarms.co.uk
Beartown Kodiak Gold; Hydes Bitter; Moorhouses Pride of Pendle; guest beers Ⓗ
This picturesque, award-winning free house is situated between the church and an arboretum in a small village. The comfortable bar, which features relaxing live music on Wednesday, includes easy chairs and an open fire, while the adjoining restaurant is always popular for its high quality meals. There is a front patio, garden and large function room named after Sir Bernard Lovell of nearby Jodrell Bank fame. The guest beers usually consist of one or two brews from local micros. ♨Q❀◖◗P⊬

Tushingham

Blue Bell Inn

SY13 4QS (signed Bell o' t'Hill from A41)
✪ 12-3, 6-11; 12-3, 7-10.30 Sun
☎ (01948) 662172
Hanby Drawwell; Olde Swan Original; guest beers Ⓗ
Ancient, 14th-century, timber-framed pub with plenty of atmosphere just off the A41 main road. A cobbled front leads to an ancient, heavy entrance door. The main bar is popular with regulars and their entertaining conversation is enjoyed by visitors as well. A further bar is used for food. Note the amusing collection of lettered brass plates on the wall near the main bar. The pub is dog-friendly. ♨Q☕❀◖◗▲♣P⊬

Warmingham

Bear's Paw

School Lane, CW11 3QN
✪ 5 (12 Sat)-11; 12-10.30 Sun
☎ (01270) 526317
website: www.thebearspaw.co.uk
Tetley Bitter; guest beers Ⓗ
Imposing hotel built in the 1870s by the Earl of Crewe in a small village four miles north of the town that was named after him. It boasts 12 en-suite bedrooms and a restaurant offering an eclectic mix of gourmet dishes. Bar snacks are also available. Meals are served all day Saturday and Sunday. Changing guest beers are often from local brewers. It was voted Rural Pub of the Year in 2005 by local CAMRA members.
❀⇔◗♿P

Warrington

Bluebell

27 Horsemarket Street, WA1 1TS
✪ 11.30 (11 Sat)-11 (midnight Fri & Sat); 7-10.30 Sun
☎ (01925) 637361
Greene King Ruddles Best; guest beers Ⓗ
Typical Greenalls pub conversion from many rooms to an open-plan interior featuring several discrete areas. It retains some of its original features in one area, with wood beams and pillars, and has a raised section to the rear. The pub can be busy at lunchtime and weekend evenings and is popular with all age groups. A disco is held every Saturday evening. Food is served from lunchtime to early evening (not Sun), with special meal deals for senior citizens.
◖◗⇌(Central)⊬

Bull's Head
37-39 Church Street, WA1 2SX
(from town centre cross A49 dual carriageway to Church St)
12-11; 12-10.30 Sun
☎ (01925) 635680
website: www.bullsheadwarrington.co.uk
Cains Bitter; Tetley Bitter; Wells Bombardier; guest beers H
Behind the white walls, bedecked with hanging baskets, lies a welcoming, traditional neighbourhood pub a stone's throw from the town centre. The 17th-century building has been added to and altered over the years but retains its olde-worlde charm; stone flags, polished boards and carpets now grace the open-plan bar areas. A popular pub, it can be crowded at times, however quieter rooms lie to the rear. A function room (Sports Bar lounge) caters for special events. Q ❀ ♿ ⇌ (Central) ♣

Ferry Tavern
Station Road, Penketh, WA5 2UJ (off A562)
12-3, 5.30-11; 12-11 Sat; 12-10.30 Sun
☎ (01925) 791117
Boddingtons Bitter; Courage Directors; Greene King Old Speckled Hen; guest beers H
The Ferry is situated between the Sankey Canal and the River Mersey on the Trans Pennine Trail. Popular with walkers and cyclists as well as locals, the pub has a large garden drinking area which is well used in the summer months. Three guest ales and traditional ciders are served, plus a large range of Scotch and Irish whiskies. There is a regular bus service from Warrington bus station to Station Road-Tannery Lane junction. ♨ ❀ P

Fiddle i'th Bag
Alder Lane, Burtonwood, WA5 4BJ (halfway between Burtonwood and Winwick villages) OS584930
12-11; 12-10.30 Sun
☎ (01925) 225442
Beer range varies H
Locals and visitors alike love this mildly eccentric pub packed with an ever-increasing collection of exotica. The centrally-located bar serves drinking areas on either side and there is a small no-smoking area to the right of the entrance. The extensive food menu offers lunchtime and evening meals, complemented by three regularly-changing cask ales. ♨ Q ❀ ♿ P

Lower Angel
27 Buttermarket Street, WA1 2LY
11-11; 12-4 Sun
☎ (01925) 633299
Tetley Mild, Bitter, Burton Ale; guest beers H
Traditional, unspoilt, two-room, town-centre pub, where the emphasis is on beer rather than food. The windows in the public bar and more comfortable lounge bear the name of the former owners, Walkers of Warrington. Note the music selection on the juke box. The pub has won many CAMRA local and regional awards over the years. ⇌ (Central)

Ring o' Bells
Northwich Road, Lower Stretton, WA4 4NZ
(on A559 just off M56 jct 10)
12-4, 5.30 (7 Sat)-11; 12-4, 7-10.30 Sun
☎ (01925) 730556
Fuller's London Pride; Tetley Bitter; guest beer H
Small, traditional country pub on the south side of Warrington. There is no juke box or fruit machine to drown the conversation in this unspoilt pub. It has three rooms: one a long narrow room with bar and brasses, one small back room and a side room with tall chairs. There is a terraced garden and boules pitch. It was voted CAMRA local Pub of the Year runner-up in 2005. ♨ Q ❀ ♣ P

Tavern
25 Church Street, WA1 2SS
2 (12 Fri & Sat)-11; 12-10.30 Sun
☎ (01925) 577990
Beer range varies H
Formerly known as Wilkies Tavern, this genuine free house serves a changing range of up to six cask beers featuring small and micro-breweries. Belgian bottled beers and a range of Scotch and Irish whiskies are also available. Regular, frequent, themed festivals using the pub handpumps have now replaced the twice-yearly beer festivals. The covered courtyard at the back of this single room pub houses a pool table. It was local CAMRA Pub of the Year 2005.
❀ ⇌ (Central)

Warrington Sports Club ✔
Walton Lea Road, Higher Walton, WA4 6SJ (off A56)
5.30 (11.30 Sat)-11; 12-10.30 Sun
☎ (01925) 263210
Taylor Golden Best; Theakston Best Bitter; guest beers H
Large club on the south side of town yet in the heart of Cheshire countryside, near Walton Gardens. It has large playing areas for cricket, rugby and hockey, plus squash courts inside. The spacious lounge has a large-screen TV and the function room has a stage for live entertainment. Up to six real ales are on handpump. A beer festival is held around Easter. There are regular bus services to Stockton Heath or Walton from Warrington, then you are just a brisk 10-minute walk away (well it is a sports club!) ❀ ♿ ♣ P ⚟

Weston Village

Prospect Inn
Weston Road, WA7 4LD
12-11; 12-10.30 Sun
☎ (01928) 651280
Boddingtons Bitter; Cains Bitter; Tetley Dark Mild; guest beer H
This out of the way pub is well worth a visit for the best selection of real ale in Halton. The public bar houses a pool table and dartboard. The main lounge is a comfortable room where food is served; Sunday lunch is popular and booking is essential. Regular folk nights are held on Monday and a quiz on Tuesday. A free buffet is laid on every Friday and Saturday evening.
Q ❀ ♿ P

Wettenhall

Little Man
Winsford Road, CW7 4DL (½ mile S of village) OS628601
12.30-4, 7.30-11; 12.30-4, 7-10.30 Sun
Beer range varies H

Intimate and cosy country pub with a small public bar opening into a larger lounge/dining room bedecked with fresh flowers in summer. Generous food portions are excellent value, complemented by a choice of up to four different beers from breweries nationwide. Blow lamps and potties dangle from the ceiling, taxidermy and teapots combine with numerous other artefacts to create a fascinating interior. Welcoming all generations, this pub is a gem. ⛼❀◑◗♣P⍌

Wheelock

Commercial ☆

2 Game Street, CW11 3RR
(off Crewe Rd, near canal bridge)
✪ 12-11; 12-10.30 Sun
☎ (01270) 760122
Boddington's Bitter; Thwaites Original; guest beers Ⓗ
Welcoming, family-run free house close to bridge No. 154 on the Trent and Mersey. It is popular with locals and visitors alike, particularly cyclists and boaters. The spacious interior, with three rooms and a public bar, reflects the pub's Birkenhead Brewery origins. Once known as the New Inn, this listed building dates back to the completion of the Trent and Mersey Canal in 1777. Dogs are welcome here. ⛼❀⊟♣●

Nag's Head

504 Crewe Road, CW11 3RL (at A534/Mill Lane jct)
✪ 12-11; 12-10.30 Sun
☎ (01270) 762457
Boddingtons Bitter; guest beers Ⓗ
This friendly black-and-white pub stands back from the main road through the village. It has a cosy dining area at one end with a real fire and a large lounge surrounding the bar. At the rear is a public bar where televised sport draws a younger crowd. The pub has developed a reputation for quality real ale and features two guest beers from small breweries. A children's play area has been added to the garden. ⛼❀◑◗⊟♣

Widnes

Church View

Lunts Heath Road, WA8 9RY
✪ 12-11; 12-10.30 Sun
☎ (0151) 424 3296
Theakston Mild; Tetley Bitter Ⓗ
Warm and friendly pub on the edge of town with a large, single-room, split-level interior. The decor features dark wood and stained glass, and there are two interesting ceiling lights inside the main entrance. A quiet pub, there is no juke box, pool table, dartboard or other distraction from conversation and a peaceful drink. Food is served from noon until 8pm and children are welcome if dining. Sunday lunch is a favourite with locals. There are small outside seating areas at the front and rear. Q❀◑◗♿P⊬

Horse & Jockey ✔

18 Birchfield Road, WA8 7SU (300 yds S of station)
✪ 11-11; 12-10.30 Sun
☎ (0151) 420 2966
John Smith's Bitter; Tetley Bitter; guest beer Ⓗ
Dating back to 1880, this friendly, single-room pub is situated next to Victoria Park and minutes away from both the station and town centre. The pub is frequently busy and alive with banter – there is no juke box. Dominoes and quiz evenings are hosted. The garden is fully-enclosed and family friendly. A regularly-changing guest beer is always available. ❀⇌P

Willey Moor

Willey Moor Lock Tavern

Tarporley Road, SY13 4HF (300 yds off A49) OS534452
✪ 12-2.30 (3 summer), 6-11; 12-2.30 (3 summer), 7-10.30 Sun
☎ (01948) 663274
Theakston Best Bitter; guest beers Ⓗ
Accessed by a footbridge over the Llangollen Canal, the Willey Moor was a former lock keeper's cottage. This genuine free house always has an esoteric range of guest beers. It is popular with canal boaters and walkers on the nearby Sandstone trail. The pub is comfortably furnished with padded wall seats, dimpled copper tables, long-case clocks, local watercolour paintings and a collection of teapots. There are cosy real fires in the winter months or a terrace with an enclosed garden for the summer. ⛼❀◑◗P

Wincle

Ship

SK11 0QE (off A64 near Danebridge) OS652962
✪ 12-3, 7 (5.30 Fri)-11; 12-11 Sat; 12-10.30 Sun
☎ (01260) 227217
Fuller's London Pride; Moorhouses Premier; guest beers Ⓗ
One of the rare regular Fuller's outlets in the area, this attractive 16th-century sandstone village inn is popular with locals, walkers and diners and can become busy on summer weekends. On the edge of the Dane Valley, the pub is divided into two bars, plus a small dining area and a further raised section where families can drink or dine. The pub has a good reputation for its imaginative menu. It stages a beer festival on August Bank Holiday.
⛼Q⛄❀◑◗●P

Your shout

We would like to hear from you. If you think a pub not listed in the Guide is worthy of consideration, please let us know. Send us the name, full address and phone number (if known). If a pub in the Guide has given you poor service, we would also like to know. Write to Good Beer Guide, CAMRA, 230 Hatfield Road, St Albans, Herts, AL1 4LW or email **camra@camra.org.uk**

Transport to pubs

BUSES
Bus Traveline

Most bus timetable enquiries are now dealt with through the National Traveline which is operated under a standard call number by local authorities across the UK for countrywide information
Telephone: 0870 608 2608
Textphone: 0870 241 2216

Information & Journey Planner Websites – some may cover other transport modes.
www.internet.xephos.com
www.pti.org.uk   www.traveline.org.uk

Timetable directory & most websites:
info@barrydoe.co.uk

BUSES, TRAMS & TRAINS
Other sources of information can be found through your local County, District or Unitary Council or Passenger Transport Executive (see Websites below) to ascertain correct contact details. Details of train operating company telephone numbers together with Network Rail, Rail Regulator and Association of Train Operating Companies appear in full in the National Rail Timetable (from some main stations and W H Smith shops). Some tram operators are shown in this, too. Other operators appear in the **www.ukbus.co.uk website**.

www.ukbus.co.uk Station Master Bus & Train Information & Journey Planners with telephone numbers

www.arriva.co.uk Arriva Buses, Trams & Trains

www.firstgroup.com First Group Buses, Trams & Trains

www.stagecoachplc.com Stagecoach Buses, Trams & Trains

www.go-ahead.com Go Ahead Group

www.londontransport.co.uk for all London

www.lothianbuses.co.uk for Edinburgh & Lothian area

www.translink.co.uk Northern Ireland Ulsterbus and Rail

Other large Bus Groups include Blazefield Holdings (Blackburn, Burnley, Harrogate, Keighley & Malton), East Yorkshire Motor Services (Hull & Scarborough), Glenvale (Liverpool), Preston Bus, Solent Blue Line (Southampton), Wellglade Trent (Derby & Nottingham) and Yorkshire Traction (Barnsley, Lincolnshire & Strathtay), often with websites for their local operating companies. Council owned bus companies include Blackburn, Blackpool, Bournemouth, Cardiff, Eastbourne, Halton, Ipswich, Isle of Man, Islwyn, Lothian Buses (Edinburgh), Newport, Nottingham, Plymouth, Reading, Rossendale, Thamesdown (Swindon), and Warrington.

OTHER INFORMATION WEBSITES
Other important local authority public transport websites often give information – the main ones in urban areas are as follows:-

www.gmpte.gov.uk Greater Manchester

www.merseytravel.gov.uk Merseyside

www.nexus.org.uk Tyne & Wear

www.centro.org.uk West Midlands

www.southyorks.org.uk South Yorkshire

www.wymetro.com West Yorkshire

www.spt.co.uk Glasgow & Strathclyde

www.edinburgh.gov.uk Edinburgh & Lothian

www.cardiff.gov.uk Cardiff area

www.londontransport.co.uk London

Many of the other Shire Counties & UAs have a website, often www. ending in .gov.uk

COACHES
National Express · Scottish City Link

For longer distance coach service timetables and planners contact National Express:
08705 808080   www.nationalexpress.co.uk

Scottish Citylink
08705 505050   www.citylink.co.uk

TRAINS
National Train Information Line

The national hotline for all train information
08457 484950   Minicom: 0845 60 50 600

Other Rail Timetable & Fare Information and Journey Planning Websites

www.networkrail.co.uk Enquiries

www.travelinfosystems.com Planning

www.nationalrail.co.uk Current state of rail services:

www.thetrainline.com Booking services

www.londontransport.co.uk London (Covers Buses, Trams, Underground, River, Docklands Rail and Victoria Coach Station)

www.raileurope.co.uk Europe & Foreign
www.railchoice.co.uk

Many of the above websites often refer to a further local site for additional detailed information, and most of the train operating companies also have websites. The lists shown are not exhaustive due to space limitations but many smaller operators have websites too.

For other information about transport websites, activities and other contacts, but NOT timetable or service enquiries, please contact the CAMRA Public Transport Task Group on e-mail: pttgcamra@aol.com or by post or email via CAMRA Headquarters.

Important Note: Don't rely on information from websites being 100% accurate and up-to-date – check before travelling by phone.

CORNWALL

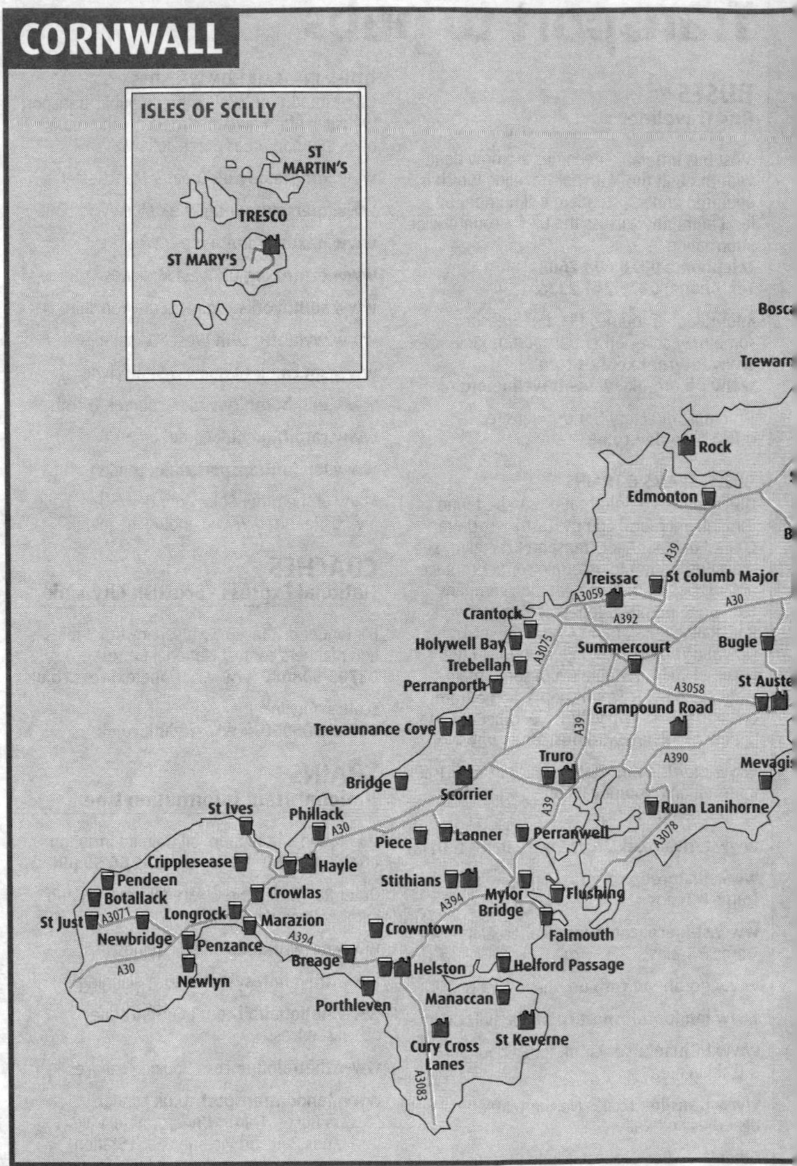

Altarnun

Rising Sun Inn

PL15 7SN (off A30) OS217825

11-3, 6-11; 11-11 Sat & summer; 12-10.30 Sun

(01566) 86636

Beer range varies H

Originally a 16th-century farmhouse, this family and dog-friendly pub retains many original features. There are two small rooms off the main bar area catering for diners and pool players. Four real ales are usually available, with five at weekends and up to six in summer. Legend has it that the front wall collapsed when a former landlord dug out the pub cellar. Camping is available in the pub grounds. The Inny Valley Recreational Walk lies nearby.

Blisland

Blisland Inn

The Green, PL30 4JF

11.30-11; 12-10.30 Sun

(01208) 850739

Beer range varies H

Still CAMRA's premier pub in Cornwall, the Blisland continues to offer an eclectic choice of real ales, with over 2,000 different brews passing over the bar to date. A former national Pub of the Year and four times local winner, the inn strongly supports Cornish breweries which are featured heavily in the line-up of up to seven beers and ciders on offer. The pub has a strong community focus and good food is served, prepared with locally-sourced fresh produce.

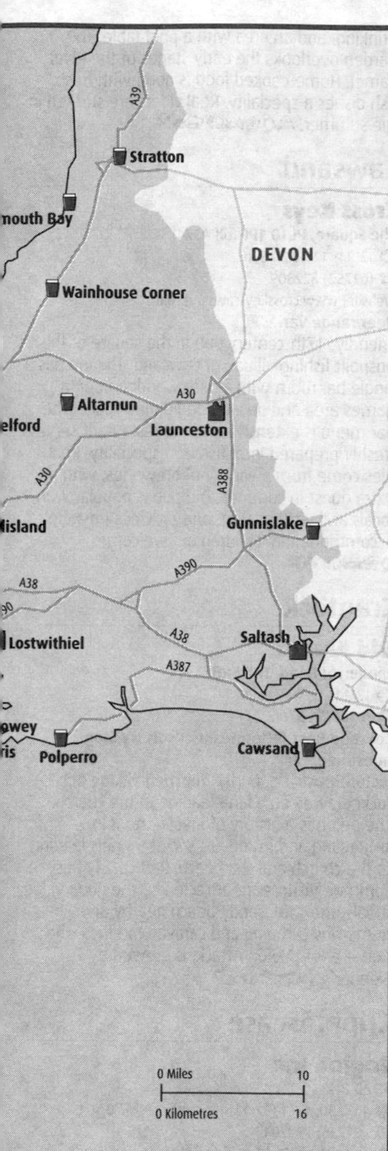

Bodmin

Hole in the Wall

16 Crockwell Street, PL31 2DS

⏲ 12-11, 12-10.30 Sun

☎ (01208) 72397

Draught Bass; Sharp's Doom Bar; guest beers 🄷

Formerly the town debtors' prison, this pub dates from the 18th century. It is entered through a leafy garden with a stream and tropical plants, presided over by a stuffed lion. The single bar, which is subdivided by archways, contains a unique and eclectic collection of antique bric-a-brac and military memorabilia. The clientele is a friendly mix of locals and visitors. Upstairs, the Lion's Den restaurant offers a good menu prepared with local produce (no food on Mon). ♨Q❀◑

Mason's Arms

5-9 Higher Bore Street, PL31 2JS

⏲ 11-11; 12-10.30 Sun

☎ (01208) 72607

Sharp's Cornish Coaster; guest beers 🄷

Dating from Napoleonic times, this pub is thought to be the oldest in town. The lively public bar with slate floor provides games, music and occasional live entertainment. The lounge is a quieter area where locals drink and chat. Autumn brings the conker championship and beer festival. On the edge of town, the Mason's draws a good local trade as well as visitors who come for the new restaurant, with its fine menu and food produced to a high standard, served by friendly staff. ♨Q❀◑⊟●P

Boscastle

Cobweb Inn

The Bridge, PL35 0HE

⏲ 11-11 (midnight Sat); 12-10.30 Sun

☎ (01840) 250278

website: www.cobwebinn.co.uk

Greene King Abbot; St Austell Tinners; Sharp's Doom Bar; guest beers 🄷

Typical Cornish granite pub with a chequered 350 year history, having previously been a corn mill, grain store and bottling plant until becoming a pub in 1947 – reputedly taking its name from the state it was then in. It has two main bars, a sheltered outdoor drinking area and a restaurant upstairs. There are usually two Cornish guest beers and a minimum of four real ales. Draught cider arrives in summer. Regular live music is performed on Saturday night. ♨Q☎❀◑⊟♣●P

Botallack

Queen's Arms

TR19 7QG (off B3306)

⏲ 4 (12 summer)-11; 12-11 Sat; 12-10.30 Sun

☎ (01736) 788318

Sharp's Doom Bar; guest beers 🄷

A typical Cornish granite pub offering a warm welcome and excellent ales. The cosy bar has a real fire and adjoins a no-smoking dining area. A large extension at the rear serves as a family room. The beer range varies with ales usually selected from Cornish micro-breweries. The

INDEPENDENT BREWERIES

Ales of Scilly St Mary's
Atlantic Treisaac
Bathtub Stithians
Blackawton Saltash
Blue Anchor Helston
Doghouse Scorrier
Driftwood Trevaunance Cove
Keltek Lostwithiel
Lizard St Keverne
Organic Cury Cross Lanes
Ring O'Bells Launceston
St Austell St Austell
Sharp's Rock
Skinner's Truro
Wheal Ale Hayle
Wooden Hand Grampound Road

house beer, Tallack Tipple, is from Skinner's. With a reputation for imaginative menus and most ingredients sourced locally, the pub is popular with hungry coastal path walkers. For the less energetic the bus stop is outside the front door. ⛫Q♨❀◐⛺P⚟

Breage

Queen's Arms

TR13 9PD (off A394 Helston-Penzance road)

✪ 11.30-2.30, 6.30-11; 12-10.30 Sun

☎ (01326) 573485

website: www.thequeensarmsinn.co.uk

Caledonian Deuchars IPA; Greene King Abbot; Sharp's Doom Bar; guest beers Ⓗ

Comfortable, friendly, thriving country inn enjoying a strong local trade all year round. It is regularly in the running for CAMRA Cornwall Pub of the Year. The long bar boasts six real ales, including three guests, and real cider. Log fires are a feature at both ends of the bar with a separate games area and no-smoking dining room. With a walled garden and large car park, the Queen's offers a warm welcome to all, including children. Dogs are also permitted. ⛫❀◐♿⛺●P

Bridge

Bridge Inn

TR16 4QW (off B3300 Redruth-Portreath road)

✪ 12-3, 6-11; 12-3, 7-10.30 (12-10.30 summer) Sun

☎ (01209) 842532

Sharp's Doom Bar; guest beers Ⓗ

Once a hunting lodge, this 18th-century granite building is now a traditional Cornish inn. The atmosphere in the L-shaped bar is warm and friendly. Two guest beers (usually at least one Cornish brew) provide variety for the regulars. The riverside garden has a dovecote and boules piste, while the nearby old Portreath tram road offers a coast-to-coast walk through Cornish mining history. Daytime buses to Truro and Redruth stop outside. Q❀◐⛺♣P

Bugle

Bugle Inn

57 Fore Street, PL26 8PB (on A391)

✪ 11-11; 12-10.30 Sun

☎ (01726) 850307

St Austell IPA, Tinners, Dartmoor Best, Tribute Ⓗ

Friendly local in the centre of the village, named after the sound of the horn as the stagecoach passed through. This comfortable pub has a large Z-shaped bar, a pool table and an interesting collection of knives on the wall. It fields its own euchre and darts teams. Meals are served all day. Accommodation is available in five en-suite rooms. ⛫❀⇌◐⇶♣P

Camelford

Mason's Arms

Market Place, PL32 9PB

✪ 12-11; 12-10.30 Sun

☎ (01840) 213309

St Austell Tinners, Tribute, HSD, seasonal beers Ⓗ

Typical basic and unpretentious Cornish market town local with exposed beams and slate walls. Inside is a public bar, a lounge bar for dining and drinking, and an area with a pool table. The garden overlooks the early stages of the River Camel. Home-cooked food is good with fresh fish dishes a speciality. Real ciders are stocked in the summer. ⛫Q❀⇌◐⊟●⚟

Cawsand

Cross Keys

The Square, PL10 1PF (off A374)

✪ 12-11; 12-10.30 Sun

☎ (01752) 822309

website: www.crosskeyscawsand.co.uk

Beer range varies Ⓗ

Friendly, 17th-century pub in the square of the unspoilt fishing village of Cawsand. The inn has a single bar room with a bare wooden floor, a games area and an elevated dining space. The bar menu is extensive and the restaurant serves freshly prepared local fish as a speciality. Real ales come from a variety of breweries, with an extra guest in summer. The pub is popular with locals and visitors alike, and provides en-suite accommodation. Children are welcome. Q❀⇌◐♣⚟

Crantock

Old Albion

Langurroc Road, TR8 5RB

✪ 12-11; 12-10.30 Sun

☎ (01637) 830243

Courage Best Bitter; Skinner's Betty Stogs; guest beers Ⓗ

Picture-postcard, partly-thatched village pub tucked away on a lane leading to the church. The pub has a history of involvement in smuggling and inside are secret tunnels leading to the church and the beach. Particularly busy in summer, visitors are attracted by the good value meals, the safe, sandy beach nearby and numerous camping and caravan facilities. The house beer, Albion Attack, is brewed by Skinner's. ⛫♨❀◐⛺P

Cripplesease

Engine Inn

TR20 8NF

✪ 11-2.30, 6-11 (11-11 summer); 12-10.30 Sun

☎ (01736) 740204

Greene King Old Speckled Hen (summer); **Marston's Pedigree; Sharp's Doom Bar** Ⓗ

This 17th-century cottage-style inn on the edge of the wild Penwith moorland was once a counthouse for the nearby tin mine, whose engine room still stands. Families and dogs are welcome and food is available most of the time. Live entertainment is hosted occasionally in the evening, otherwise this is a quiet pub. Outside drinking on the patio offers impressive views across the moor and children will enjoy the small menagerie in the garden. ⛫Q♨❀◐⛺♣P

Crowlas

Star Inn

TR20 8DX (on A30)

✪ 11.30-11; 12-10.30 Sun

☎ (01736) 740375

Beer range varies Ⓗ

Friendly roadhouse on the A30 near Penzance and a mecca for real ale drinkers in the area. One long bar sports several handpumps dispensing frequently changing beers. This is a beer drinkers' local where conversation is the main entertainment, although meals are served, 12-6, from Thursday to Sunday. A small boat hanging from the ceiling was used in the Crowlas floods of 2003. The B&B is good value, offering an excellent base for local pub crawls.
Q⇄◑ÅP

Crowntown

Crown Inn

TR13 0AD (on B3303)
✪ 6-11; 12-3, 7-10.30 Sun
☎ (01326) 565538
website: www.crownlodges.co.uk
Beer range varies Ⓖ
Large, roadside, Cornish granite pub around 250 years old and once a hunting lodge. The single bar sports handpumps with pump clips, but the four real ales, always from Cornish breweries, are dispensed by gravity from the cellar. Despite limited opening hours, this is a lively local where conversation dominates but there is also a pool table and a popular weekly quiz on Tuesday evening. Note the interesting fish tank. Accommodation is in lodges to the rear.
❀⇄◑♿●P

Edmonton

Quarryman Inn ✔

PL27 7JA (off A39 near Wadebridge)
✪ 12-11; 12-10.30 Sun
☎ (01208) 816444
Beer range varies Ⓗ
Popular, family-friendly free house exuding character and bonhomie, attracts drinkers from town and country. The cosy single room inside divides into public and lounge bars as well as a dining area. The open fire and eclectic decor add to the convivial atmosphere. A varying beer menu, mainly from Skinner's and Sharp's, is complemented by excellent food using local produce. The unusual garden was once the 19th-century quarrymen's cottages and courtyard.
♨Q❀⇄◑Å●P

Falmouth

Oddfellows Arms

Quay Hill, TR11 3HG
✪ 12-11; 12-10.30 Sun
☎ (01326) 318530
website: www.theoddfellowsarms.co.uk
Flowers Original; Sharp's Special Ⓗ
Small but perfectly formed – the pub consists of a tiny main bar and a pool room. Breathtakingly good Sharp's Special provides excellent fuel for the lively and highly entertaining exploits of the regulars, many of whom can be found arguing over recipes way in advance of the pub's annual 'cakefest' – a jolly affair held in June each year. A true gem of a back street local. ⇌ (Town) ♣

Seven Stars ☆

1 The Moor, TR11 3QA
✪ 11-3, 6-11; 12-3, 7-10.30 Sun
☎ (01326) 312111
Draught Bass; Sharp's Special or Skinner's Cornish Knocker; guest beers Ⓖ
A timeless classic, Cornwall's only entry in CAMRA's Inventory of Pubs with Interiors of Outstanding Historic Interest. Tear your gaze away from the dizzying collection of key fobs and you will spot the bespoke and eccentric stillage which supports 18 gallon casks of Bass below, and firkins of guest ales a-top. The pub, with regulars providing a hubbub of lively bar banter, has been carefully watched over for more than 50 years by landlord and parish priest Rev Barrington Bennetts.
Q❀⇌(Penmere) ●

Flushing

Royal Standard

St Peter's Hill, TR11 5TP (off A393 at Penryn)
✪ 11-2.30 (3 Fri & Sat), 6.30-11; 12-3, 7-10.30 Sun; (varies winter)
☎ (01326) 374250
Draught Bass; Sharp's Doom Bar, Eden Ale Ⓗ
Friendly local run by a landlord with more than 30 years' experience. The front patio offers fine views of the Penryn River and Falmouth. Look out for swans in the road when approaching. Parking in the road is limited especially in summer; access by foot using the ferry from Falmouth is a great way to get here. Home-made pasties and apple pies are specialities.
♨❀◑♣

Seven Stars

3 Trefusis Road, TR11 5TY (off A393 at Penryn)
✪ 11-11; 12-10.30 Sun
☎ (01326) 374373
Skinner's Betty Stogs, Cornish Knocker, seasonal beer Ⓗ
Central village pub with tables outside overlooking the Penryn River. Inside is a large, well-furnished L-shaped bar and a restaurant serving good, reasonably-priced food – fish is a speciality. The pub is popular with locals and visitors; access is possible via the passenger ferry from Falmouth.
♨Q❀◑

Fowey

Lugger Inn ✔

5 Fore Street, PL23 1AQ
✪ 11-11; 12-10.30 Sun
☎ (01726) 833435
St Austell Tinners, Tribute, HSD Ⓗ
Small, friendly, one-bar, town-centre pub with a large no-smoking area, popular with locals and visitors. The building is dated 1633 but the front is more recent, with small leaded windows. The interior is decorated with ship memorabilia and a large mural depicting Cornish luggers on the river. In the summer, outdoor tables on the main street are always in demand. An extensive menu of excellent home-cooked food includes fresh local seafood. Q❀⇄◑♿Å⚟

Gunnislake

Rising Sun Inn

Calstock Road, PL18 9BX
✪ 12-2.30, 5-11; 12-3, 7-10.30 Sun
☎ (01822) 832201 website: www.risingsuninn.co.uk

Draught Bass; Sharp's Cornish Coaster, Will's Resolve; Skinner's Betty Stogs ⊞
Welcoming 17th century inn, slightly off the beaten track, with stone walls and a slate roof. It has a warm, cosy interior with real fire, stone floor, low wooden beams and an extensive chinaware collection. The well-kept gardens and patio offer views of the Tamar Valley. Four real ales and locally brewed Countryman cider are all available on handpump. Good food, from snacks to full meals, are served. There is even a small lending library.
⛬Q❀◐▶⇌♣●P

Hayle

Cornish Arms ✔
86 Commercial Road, TR27 4DJ (on B3301)
⚙ 11.30-2.30, 5.30-11; 11-11 Sat & summer; 12-10.30 Sun
☎ (01736) 753237
St Austell IPA, Tinners, Dartmoor Best, Tribute, HSD ⊞
Convivial two-bar locals' pub, popular with a broad mix of the community. The public bar contains a pool table and the roomier lounge a dartboard. A recent extension at the back serves as a restaurant area and there is a garden beyond. It is one of the few pubs to feature most of St Austell's real ales. The pub fields teams in local euchre and darts leagues.
⛬❀◐▶⊟♿▲⇌♣P

Helford Passage

Ferryboat Inn ✔
TR11 5LB
⚙ 11-11; 12-10.30 Sun
☎ (01326) 250625
St Austell Tribute, HSD, seasonal beers ⊞
In an idyllic creek-side position overlooking the Helford River, this large pub has a single open-plan bar room with a more intimate annex for eating and drinking. The walls and beamed ceilings are festooned with an eclectic mix of nautical bric-a-brac including a whole ship's mast, while the wooden furniture is supplemented with comfortable sofas. The patio is a great place to enjoy the river views while supping a pint in the sunshine. Children are welcome. It is handy for nearby Trebah and Glendurgan Gardens.
⛬❀⇄◐▶●P

Helston

Blue Anchor
50 Coinagehall Street, TR13 8EU
⚙ 10-midnight; 12-10.30 Sun
☎ (01326) 562821
Blue Anchor Spingo IPA, Middle, Special, seasonal beer ⊞
Known locally as 'The Blue', this pub is steeped in hundreds of years of tradition. Customers sit at plain wooden tables and chat over a pint of beer brewed on the premises, just as their fathers and forefathers have always done. Local bands provide live entertainment. The garden and skittle alley are popular with regulars. Accommodation is in the pub's B&B next door.
⛬Q☋❀⇄◐▶⊟♣

Holywell Bay

St Piran's Inn
TR8 5PP
⚙ 5-11; 11-11 Fri, Sat & summer; 12-3.30 (10.30 summer) Sun
☎ (01637) 830205
St Austell Tribute; Shepherd Neame Spitfire; guest beers ⊞
Close by a scenic bay, this beach-side free house was originally two coastguards' cottages. The beamed, single bar interior is spacious but homely, with wood furnishings, bric-a-brac and an open fire. The range of beer stocked varies with the season and a good value, high quality food menu is offered. A quiet, family-friendly pub, it also has a large conservatory and children's play area.
⛬Q☋❀◐▶♿▲P

Lanner

Lanner Inn
The Square, TR16 6EH (on A393)
⚙ 12-3 (not Mon), 4.30-11; 12-11 Fri & Sat; 12-3, 7-10.30 Sun
☎ (01209) 215611
Sharp's Doom Bar; guest beer ⊞
Small and busy community pub where the emphasis is on ale – no food is served. The guest beers vary frequently at the recommendation or request of the pub's regulars. Customers enjoy lively conversation and games including darts, euchre, pool, dominoes and quizzes. A delightful orchard doubles as the garden and children's play area in summer. Good value B&B accommodation is available. Buses run to Truro and Camborne.
⛬Q❀⇄⊟P

Longrock

Mexico Inn
Gladstone Terrace, TR20 8JB (off A30)
⚙ 11.30-3, 5-11; 12-10.30 Sun
☎ (01736) 710625
Sharp's Doom Bar, Eden Ale; guest beer ⊞
Once part of a mine, this local free house has a single L-shaped, beamed bar and bare granite walls. The guest beer is often from Skinner's or another Cornish brewery. The pub is particularly popular in summer because of its location close to the beach. Good quality food is available from light bar snacks to full meals served in the no-smoking restaurant. Car parking is limited but a regular bus service passes the door.
⛬Q☋❀◐▶P⚟

Lostwithiel

Globe Inn
3 North Street, PL22 0EG
⚙ 12-2.30, 6-11; 12-2.30, 7-10.30 Sun
☎ (01208) 872501
website: www.globeinn.com
Sharp's Doom Bar; Skinner's Betty Stogs; guest beers ⊞
Cosy and friendly 13th-century pub in the narrow streets of this ancient Cornish capital, close to the station and next to a medieval stone bridge. Inside the rambling old building is a main bar with several drinking areas and a

restaurant at the rear. Two guest ales, usually from local breweries, are always available. The pub gets its name from the ship on which a member of the family of the one-time owners was killed in a sea battle in 1813.
Q❀⇌◑▲≠♣

Royal Oak Hotel

Duke Street, PL22 0AG (off A390)
✪ 11-11; 12.30-10.30 Sun
☎ (01208) 872552
Draught Bass; Fuller's London Pride; Marston's Pedigree; guest beers Ⓗ
Busy, 13th-century inn just off the highway through the ancient capital of Cornwall. A stone-floored traditional public bar contrasts with the carpeted lounge and restaurant. Guest ales come from small independent brewers and unusual bottled beers are stocked too. The nearby Keltek Brewery makes the house beer Royal Oak Special. Award-winning food is produced using local ingredients where possible. The pub is reputed to have a smugglers' tunnel running from the cellar to the dungeons in nearby Restormel Castle.
Q♉❀⇌◑⊟▲≠♣P

Manaccan

New Inn

TR12 6HA (off B3293 Culdrose-St Keverne road, 4 miles beyond Mawgan) OS763249
✪ 12-3, 6-11; 12-3, 7-10.30 Sun
☎ (01326) 231 323
Sharp's Doom Bar; guest beer Ⓗ
Although hard to find down the lanes of the Lizard Peninsula, this traditional thatched village pub is well worth the effort. Families are welcome in the single, small, cosy bar, which also serves home-cooked food from an imaginative menu. The bar is decorated with old prints on the walls and even squeezes a table into the massive inglenook. The pub can often be crowded – phone first to reserve a table if you want to eat here. ♨Q❀◑▲P

Marazion

King's Arms ✔

The Square, TR17 0AP
✪ 11-2.30, 6-11; 11-11 Fri & Sat; 12-10.30 Sun
☎ (01736) 710291
St Austell Tribute, HSD Ⓗ
Old market corner pub opposite the ferry quay for St Michael's Mount, popular with tourists in the summer. Seating is increased at the small, comfortable family-friendly single bar by adding several tables outside on the paved area at the front. Tuesday is quiz night and on the first Thursday of the month there is a live folk music session. An extra ale from the St Austell range may be added in summer. No food is served in January or February. ♨Q❀◑▲♣

Mevagissey

Fountain Inn ✔

3 Cliff Street, PL26 6QH
✪ 11.30-11; 12-10.30 Sun
☎ (01726) 842320
St Austell Tinners, HSD Ⓗ
Friendly, two-bar, 15th-century inn with a slate floor, stone walls, historic photographs and low beams; the passage to the side door is particularly low. The Smugglers' Bar bears signs of the pilchard press which was once housed there. A glass plate in the floor covers the pit where the fish oil was stored which doubled as a hold for contraband. Regular buses run to and from St Austell and Fowey, and the Lost Gardens of Heligan. ♨Q⇌◑⊟♿▲♣

Mylor Bridge

Lemon Arms ✔

Lemon Hill, TR11 5NA (off A393 at Penryn)
✪ 11-3, 6-11; 12-3, 7-10.30 Sun
☎ (01326) 373666
St Austell Tinners, Tribute, HSD Ⓗ
One-bar, friendly, village-centre pub popular with local sports teams. Families with children are made most welcome here and there is a patio/garden for summer use. Good home-cooked food is available. The beers stocked from the St Austell range may vary from time to time. Buses run from Falmouth during the week.
♨❀◑♣P

Newbridge

Fountain Inn ✔

TR20 8QH (on A3071 Penzance-St Just road)
✪ 12-2 (not Mon), 6-11; 11-11 Fri, Sat & summer; 12-10.30 Sun
☎ (01736) 364075
St Austell IPA, Tinners, Tribute, HSD, seasonal beers Ⓗ
A former Cornwall CAMRA Pub of the Year, this Grade II listed building has solid stone walls and a flagstone floor, while the carpeted lounge area has a real fire in an enormous granite fireplace. Note the tables made from old wooden casks with redundant dartboards as tops. This once-failing community pub was rescued from closure by the present owners and now has a reputation for good beer and food. Families are welcome; a regular bus service passes the door.
♨Q♉❀⇌◑♿▲P

Newlyn

Tolcarne Inn

Tolcarne Place, TR18 5PR
✪ 10.30-3, 6.30-11; 12-3, 6.30-10.30 Sun
☎ (01736) 363074
Courage Best Bitter; Sharp's Special; guest beer Ⓗ
Set back from the main road close to the fish market, this 300-year-old beamed inn lies on the Cornish cycle route. With a long bar, restaurant area and patio with barbecue, it is particularly popular in summer. Home-cooked food is prepared with locally-sourced ingredients, including freshly-caught fish. The guest beer changes regularly. Parking is limited – you need a ticket from the bar staff at busy times. ♨Q◑♣P

Pendeen

North Inn ✔

TR19 7DN (on B3306)
✪ 11-11; 12-10.30 Sun
☎ (01736) 788417

St Austell IPA, Tinners, Tribute, HSD 🄷
Welcoming locals' pub in an old mining village; the bar is decorated with mining pictures and artefacts from nearby Geevor Tin Mine, now a mining museum. The inn is in an area of outstanding natural beauty, with nearby cliffs and the coastal path offering good walking country. The pub offers B&B as well as camping facilities. A small upstairs restaurant affords impressive views of the sea. It was voted Cornwall CAMRA Pub of the Year in 2003.
♨Q❀⇌◑⛺♣P

Penzance

Alexandra Inn
Alexandra Road, TR18 4LY (off Promenade)
✪ 11.30-2.30, 5-11; 11.30-11 Sat & summer; 12-3.30, 6-10.30 (12-10.30 summer) Sun
☎ (01736) 365165
Beer range varies 🄷
Near the seafront and 'Pirates' rugby ground, this modernised pub has two bars, attractively decorated, with carpeting and exposed beams. The friendly landlord keeps up to six real ales, with the emphasis on Cornish brews and a distinct bias towards Sharp's and Skinner's offerings. The latter produces Pirate's Pride, the house beer. A beer festival is usually hosted in March. Q❀⇌◑♣🍎

Pirate Inn
Alverton Road, TR18 4PS
✪ 10.30-11, 12-10.30 Sun
☎ (01736) 366094
Beer range varies 🄷
Typical two-bar Cornish country pub in an old granite building dating back to 1624. Up to six ales are offered in an ever-changing mix of national and local brews, including one from Scilly whenever possible. The public bar houses the pool table and TV for watching sport; the lounge is the place for quiet drinking, conversation and dining. The capacious garden includes a children's play area.
♨Q❀⇌◑⊟♣🍎P

Perranporth

Watering Hole
TR6 0BH (on Perranporth beach)
✪ 10 (11 winter, may vary)-11; 12-10.30 Sun
☎ (01872) 572888
website: www.the-wateringhole.co.uk
Skinner's Spriggan Ale, Heligan Honey; guest beer 🄷
Claiming to be the only bar on a beach in this country, the Watering Hole offers three real ales, usually from local breweries. The excellent value food is made with local produce. Cider is stocked in the summer. The bar charges an entrance fee for the live music sessions at the weekend but card-carrying CAMRA members are admitted free of charge. The pub is family friendly but children are not permitted in the bar area.
❀◑⛺🍎

Perranwell

Royal Oak
Perranwell Station, TR3 7PX
✪ 11-3, 6-11; 12-3, 7-10.30 Sun (hours vary in summer)
☎ (01872) 863175
Draught Bass; Flowers IPA; Sharp's Special 🄷
Small, friendly cottage pub dating from the 18th century. This free house has a deserved reputation for good beer and food; tapas are available at the bar which has a cosy drinking area. Good public transport links connect not only to Truro but also to both coasts; the pub is a 10-minute walk from the station despite the address. Q❀◑⇌P

Phillack

Bucket of Blood ✔
14 Churchtown Road, TR27 5AE
✪ 11.30 (12.30 Mon)-2.30, 6-11; 11-3, 6-11 Sat; 12-3, 7-10.30 Sun
☎ (01736) 752378
St Austell Dartmoor Best, HSD 🄷
Friendly old pub near the dunes of Hayle Towans, whose name derives from a gory legend involving the pub's well. Tall people beware: the notice 'familiarity breeds contempt' attached to one of the low beams serves as a warning rather than a proverb! The single bar room has a pool table at one end and a cosy drinking and eating area at the other, with settles and a recently-exposed old fireplace.
♨☋❀◑⛺P

Piece

Countryman Inn
TR16 6SG (on Four Lanes-Pool road)
✪ 11-11; 12-10.30 Sun
☎ (01209) 215960
Beer range varies 🄷
Lively roadside pub, once a shop for miners, in old copper mining territory near the distinctive landmark of Carn Brea. The pub has two bars, the larger hosting some form of entertainment every night, and at Sunday lunchtime there is a local charity raffle every week. The range of up to 10 ales includes some national names, but there are always brews from Skinner's and Sharp's; the house beer from the latter is called No-Name! Food is available all day.
♨☋❀◑⊟⛺P

Polkerris

Rashleigh Inn
PL24 2TL
✪ 11-11; 12-10.30 Sun
☎ (01726) 813991
Sharp's Doom Bar; Taylor Landlord; guest beers (summer) 🄷
Near the Saints' Way coastal path, this excellent free house is on the edge of a secluded beach. The main bar in the 18th-century stone building was a former pilchard boathouse. Exposed stone work, beamed ceilings, open fires and attractive furnishings provide character and comfort. The weather-proofed terrace gives panoramic bay views – the perfect place to watch the sun go down. The house beer, Rashleigh Bitter, is provided by Sharp's. Good food ranges from snacks in the bar to an a la carte menu in the restaurant.
♨Q❀◑⛺🍎P

Polperro

Blue Peter

Quay Road, PL13 2QZ

✪ 11-11; 12-10.30 Sun

☎ (01503) 272743

Sharp's Doom Bar; guest beers Ⓗ

The only pub in Polperro with a sea view, locals, fishermen, coastal path walkers and visitors are all made welcome at this friendly, traditional inn. Inside are low timbered ceilings, brewery memorabilia, and exhibitions of local artists' work. Up to five real ales, mainly from south-west independents, are stocked, plus cider in summer. Live music is performed on Saturday evening and Sunday afternoon, with extra sessions in summer. An excellent, varied menu with vegetarian options is available at lunchtime. ♛♉❀◐●

Porthleven

Harbour Inn ✔

Commercial Road, TR13 9JB

✪ 11-11, 12-10.30 Sun

☎ (01326) 573876

St Austell IPA, Tribute, HSD Ⓗ

Harbourside hotel, known to locals as 'The Commercial', with pleasant views over the harbour of this small old fishing port. One large open-plan bar room leads to a restaurant in an extension to the side where families are welcome. Recently refurbished in a somewhat nautical style, the bar has TV sets for viewing sporting events. The outside tables are on the edge of the harbour. Regular live entertainment is hosted at weekends.

❀⇄◐◑P

Ruan Lanihorne

King's Head Inn

TR2 5NX

✪ 12-2.30 (closed Mon winter), 6-11; 12-2.30, 6.45-10.30 Sun

☎ (01872) 501263

Skinner's Betty Stogs, Cornish Knocker; guest beer Ⓗ

Within the Roseland Peninsula, on the far estuary, lies this delightful family-run free house. Quiet, traditional and full of character, it is renowned for its superb food and drink. The interior is homely with a single bar and two dining areas; log fires add winter warmth and charm. The decor reflects village history. Forecourt seating and a quaint sunken garden provide space for outdoor drinking. The house beer, King's Ruan, is brewed by Skinner's.

♛Q♉❀◐◑♿⛺♣P

St Austell

Western Inn ✔

West Hill, PL25 5EY

✪ 12-11; 12-10.30 Sun

☎ (01726) 72797

St Austell Tinners, Tribute, seasonal beer Ⓗ

One of six pubs bought by the St Austell Brewery from the Treluswell Brewing Company of Penryn in 1943. Until the late 1960s it was a traditional pub with many back rooms and a snug but now it has been modernised into a single bar with a dining area at one end and a raised platform at the other for games, including pool and darts. The bar counter and pews were obtained from a chapel in Lostwithiel.

♛❀◐◑♿⛺⇌♣

St Columb Major

Ring O' Bells

3 Bank Street, TR9 6AT

✪ 12-2 (not winter Mon-Thu), 5-11; 12-2, 5-10.30 Sun

☎ (01637) 880259

Sharp's Doom Bar, Eden Ale; guest beer (summer) Ⓗ

The narrow frontage of this charming 15th-century free house belies the capacious beamed, slate-floored, three-bar interior. Each bar has its own character and is favoured by a different clientele. Wood-burning stoves and wood furnishings give a traditional feel. A former brew-pub established to commemorate the parish church tower, it is the oldest in town. A cosmopolitan menu is available in the comfortable no-smoking restaurant sited in the former brewery.

♛Q♉❀◐◑⊟♿⛺●

St Ives

Golden Lion

High Street, TR26 1RS

✪ 11-11; 12-10.30 Sun

☎ (01736) 793679

Courage Best Bitter; Sharp's Own; guest beer Ⓗ

Situated by the parish church and market place, there is evidence of a hostelry on this site since 1700 when it was a coaching inn with stabling at the rear. There are two bars: the rear 'games' bar which attracts younger drinkers and families, and the front bar for those who like a quiet pint. Note the impressive display of teapots. High quality, good value food is available made with local produce – fish is a speciality.

Q❀◐◑⊟♿⛺⇌♣

St Just

King's Arms ✔

5 Market Square, TR19 7HF

✪ 11-11; 12-10.30 Sun

☎ (01736) 788545

St Austell Tinners, Tribute Ⓗ

Originally three 14th-century cottages, this granite building was converted to an inn then acquired by the St Austell Brewery in 1935. The flagstoned entrance leads to a rambling interior with low ceilings and exposed beams. A real fire adds warmth in winter while outside seating at the front facing the square is popular in summer. Food is home-cooked using local produce. A third ale is added to the two regulars in summer.

♛Q❀⇄◐◑♿♣

Star Inn

1 Fore Street, TR19 7LL

✪ 11-11; 12-10.30 Sun

☎ (01736) 788767

St Austell Tinners, Dartmoor Best, Tribute, HSD Ⓗ

Popular 18th-century inn, reputedly the oldest in St Just. The single bar has a homely atmosphere with its open fire, assorted furnishings and

mining-related artefacts. It is essentially a drinkers' pub where convivial conversation is enjoyed by locals and visitors alike. However, substantial snacks made with locally sourced ingredients are available. A sample of each ale stands in front of its handpump. The 'snuggery' provides a small, cosy family room.
♨Q☋❀⇌◑♿♣●

St Tudy

Cornish Arms

PL30 3NN
⊙ 12-3, 6.30-11; 12-4, 7-10.30 Sun
☎ (01208) 850656
Draught Bass; St Austell Black Prince; guest beer (occasional) [H]
On the edge of Bodmin Moor, this classic 16th-century village local has wooden beams and a slate floor in the main bar. There is a choice of rooms to drink in, including a games room and children's room. The plush dining area offers a varied menu using locally-sourced produce. The guest beer appears only occasionally and may be restricted to the odd pint. Q☋❀◑P

Stithians

Seven Stars Inn

Church Road, TR3 7DH
⊙ 12-2.30, 7 (6 Fri)-11; 12-11 Sat; 12-10.30 Sun
☎ (01209) 860003
Beer range varies [H]
Home to the tiny Bathtub Brewery, this is a typical Cornish granite cottage-style village local. A thriving free house, it is popular with a mix of locals and visitors, who appreciate the ever-changing selection of up to four real ales. The larger Cornish breweries are usually represented, with other beers either brewed on the premises or 'imported' from across the Tamar. Good pub fare is available (no food on Tue), made with local produce. Families are welcome. ♨❀◑♣●⊘

Stratton

King's Arms

EX23 9BX
⊙ 12-2.30, 6.30-11; 12-11 Fri & Sat; 12-10.30 Sun
☎ (01288) 352396
Exmoor Ale; Ring O' Bells Dreckly; Sharp's Doom Bar; guest beer [H]
Just off the A39 near Bude, this is a warm, friendly pub in the heart of the village. Dating from the 17th century, it retains many original features including a fine floor of Delabole slate. In the bar is a small bread oven, discovered while renovating the large fireplace. Stratton is famous for the battle of Stamford Hill where in 1643 the forces of Parliament were defeated by the Royalists. Local cider is sold in summer.
♨Q❀⇌◑⊟♿⛺♣●P

Summercourt

London Inn

School Road, TR8 5EA (off A30)
⊙ 12-2.30 (not Mon-Wed), 6-11; 12-2.30, 7-10.30 Sun
☎ (01872) 510281
Beer range varies [H]
Friendly village pub on the original A30 with a large single bar room divided by wooden screens to provide areas for drinking and dining. Excellent meals are popular with locals and visitors. Once tied to a local brewery, the pub is now a free house and regularly varies the ales dispensed from the two handpumps, with Cornish brews favoured.
❀◑⛺P

Trebellan

Smugglers' Den Inn

TR8 5PY (off A3075)
⊙ 12-2.30 (not winter Mon-Wed), 6-11 (11-11 summer); 12-2.30, 6-10.30 (12-10.30 summer) Sun
☎ (01637) 830209
website: www.thesmugglersden.co.uk
Beer range varies [H]
A drinker's treasure trove awaits in this quaint thatched free house. A former 16th-century farmhouse, frequented by smugglers, the original oak beams, stonehouse walls and paved courtyard remain. Roaring log fires and cosy corners, decorated with curios and artefacts, add to the olde-worlde feel. Superior pub food is served, so popular that booking is essential. Addlestones cider is served in summer. As well as games, the pub hosts jazz and folk evenings and regular beer festivals.
♨Q☋❀◑♿⛺♣●P⊘

Trevaunance Cove

Driftwood Spars Hotel

TR5 0RT
⊙ 11-11 (midnight Fri & Sat); 12-10.30 Sun
☎ (01872) 552428
website: www.driftwoodspars.com
Driftwood Cuckoo Ale; St Austell HSD; Sharp's Doom Bar, Own; Tetley Bitter; guest beer [H]
Outstanding family-run free house, popular with cliff walkers and surfers, with its own flourishing micro-brewery. A former mine warehouse and sail loft, it is built from granite, slate and enormous ships' spars. There is a nautical theme to the interior with beamed ceilings, leaded windows and granite fireplaces featuring within the three comfy bars. A lift provides access to the sun terrace and excellent restaurant specialising in fish and game. Live music and theatre are both frequently staged.
♨Q☋❀⇌◑⛺●P

Trewarmett

Trewarmett Inn

PL34 0ET
⊙ 12-2.30, 7-11; 12-2.30, 7-10.30 Sun
☎ (01840) 770460
Sharp's Doom Bar; [H] **guest beers** [H]/[G]
Welcoming village pub, parts of which date back 300 years. A traditional Cornish local, it features low beams, slate floors and stone walls in its two bars and dining area, where home-cooked food is served. Folk music sessions attract locals and visitors on Wednesday and Saturday evenings. Further events are hosted throughout the year, including the Folk and Cask Ale Festival on the first weekend of September. The house beer Folk 'n' Ale is brewed by Skinner's.
♨Q❀⇌◑●P

Truro

City Inn

Pydar Street, TR1 3SP
11-11; 12-10.30 Sun
(01872) 272623
Courage Best Bitter; Sharp's Doom Bar; Skinner's Betty Stogs; guest beers H
Originally established to serve custom from the old cattle market, this is now a vibrant pub with a spacious single bar and 'sport' room. A 'village pub' in the city, it is comfortable and cosy, decorated with an enormous collection of jugs. Good pub food is served daily. The landlord's motto is 'Let the beer do the talking', and with up to four first class guest ales, often from micro-breweries, customers are getting the message loud and clear.

Wainhouse Corner

Old Wainhouse Inn

EX23 0BA
11.30-11; 12-10.30 Sun
(01840) 230711
Draught Bass; St Austell HSD; guest beers H
Large, friendly two-bar roadside pub with Delabole slate floors, built on the original site of a coaching inn and dating from 1785. Once known as the Hundred of Stratton (despite being eight miles south of that town), the pub remains a focus for the local rural community. It has a games and children's room, and a varied food menu available in both bars. The guest ales (two in summer) are usually from local breweries; the house beer is from Sharp's.
Q P

Widemouth Bay

Bay View Inn

Marine Drive, EX23 0AW
11-11; 12-10.30 Sun
(01288) 361273
website: www.bayviewinn.co.uk
Sharp's Doom Bar, Own; guest beer H
Small, welcoming hotel ideally situated near the coastal path with unrivalled views over the popular surfing beach and bay. Inside is a bar, dining room, family room and conservatory. The decor includes an eclectic collection of beer mats, bar towels and pump clips. The house beer, Bay View Sunset, is brewed by Skinner's. Up to two guest ales are available during the summer.
P

Blue Anchor, Helston

CUMBRIA

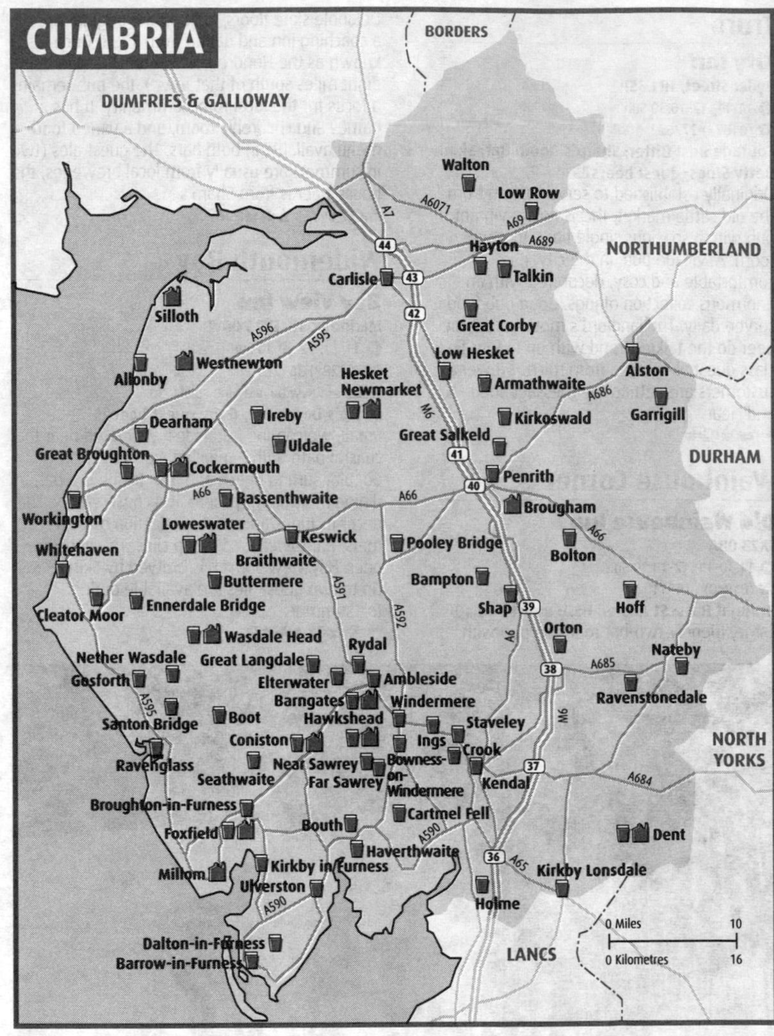

Allonby

Ship Inn

Main Road, CA15 6QF (on B5300)

12-3 (not Mon), 6 (7 winter)-11; 12-3 (not winter), 7-10.30 Sun

☎ (01900) 881017

Yates Bitter, Fever Pitch; guest beer Ⓗ

Overlooking the Solway Firth with its glorious sunsets, this 17th-century coaching inn offers the rare opportunity to sample up to three Yates' beers. The focal point of this peaceful village, fielding darts, pool and quiz teams, it is also the HQ for the village cricket eleven. Good local support ensures success for charity events, which often raise funds for the extensive children's playground, located alongside the beach. The pub offers attractive accommodation in oak-beamed rooms.

Alston

Cumberland Hotel

Townfoot, CA9 3HX

11-11; 12-10.30 Sun

☎ (01434) 381875 website: www.cumberlandalston.co.uk

Jennings Cumberland Ale; guest beers Ⓗ

With four handpumps on the bar, at least one of them will provide a beer from a Cumbrian brewery as well as other micro-breweries' products. A real cider also makes a regular appearance. Ideally situated at the bottom of the town, the hotel is close to the narrow gauge steam railway and other attractions, including mines and museums, and is handy for the start (or end) of one of the world's 'top ten drives', the A686 from Penrith. The food and accommodation at local CAMRA Pub of the Season 2005 are recommended.

Q P

Ambleside

Golden Rule

Smithy Brow, LA22 9AS (100 yds off A591, up hill towards Kirkstone Pass)

11-11; 12-10.30 Sun

☎ (015394) 32257

Robinsons Hatters, Old Stockport, Hartleys XB, Cumbria Way, Unicorn, Double Hop 🄷
Long-standing Guide entry, popular with locals and visitors of all ages. Eschewing meals and most modern contraptions, the pub majors on beer (no smooth to be seen) and conversation. The bar area has bench seating, stools and iron-framed tables. There are three other rooms – one to the left with darts, another, down a couple of steps, has an Internet cubicle and the third is a small no-smoking back room with a TV.
⛰Q❀♿♣⅟

Armathwaite

Fox & Pheasant ✔

CA4 9PY (2 miles E of A6 between Carlisle and Penrith)
⏲ 12-3, 6-11; 12-11 Sat; 12-10.30 Sun
☎ (016974) 72400
Robinson's Cumbria Way, Unicorn, Double Hop, seasonal beers 🄷
Robinson's Brewery bought this former free house in 2003 and their commitment to real ale is apparent in the selection available. Situated on the fringe of a thriving village on the bank of the River Eden, the stable bar, with its subdued lighting, brassware and local photographs, is the largest room, supplemented by a stone-flagged bar, adjacent dining area, restaurant and a small, comfortable, quiet room. Food and accommodation are recommended here.
⛰Q❀🛏◐▶⊟≠♣P⅟

Bampton

Mardale Inn

CA10 2RQ
⏲ 12-3 (not winter Mon-Fri), 6-11; 12-3, 6-10.30 Sun
☎ (01931) 713244 website: www.mardaleinn.co.uk
Beer range varies 🄷
Formerly the St Patrick's Well Inn, this is now a free house, rescued from the brink of closure by sheer enthusiasm. Both handpumps are dedicated to changing local micro-brewery beers, while local produce is used for the freshly cooked meals. No-smoking throughout, lots of wooden puzzles and local newspapers are provided. Haweswater nearby, abounds with wildlife – look out for the golden eagle.
⛰Q❀🛏◐▶▲♣⅟

Barngates

Drunken Duck ✔

LA22 0NG (off B5286 road to Hawkshead, right up Duck Hill) OS351031
⏲ 11.30-11; 12-10.30 Sun
☎ (015394) 36347 website: www.drunkenduckinn.co.uk
Barngates Cat Nap, Cracker Ale, Tag Lag, Chester's Strong & Ugly 🄷
Isolated pub, affording fell views, free from juke box, TV or gaming machines. It is busy all year round, especially with walkers and mountain bikers. The bar area has recently been refurbished to give a more modern look, which may not appeal to previous visitors who enjoyed its olde-worlde feel, although this still applies in the restaurant area. Home to the popular Barngates beers, the brewery is situated in the pub grounds. Food and accommodation are high quality (with prices to match).
⛰Q❀🛏◐▶⊟▲♣P⅟▯

Barrow-in-Furness

Furness Railway

Abbey Road, LA14 1HX (400 yds from railway station)
⏲ 10-11; 12-10.30 Sun
☎ (01229) 820818
Courage Directors; De Koninck Ambrée; Greene King Abbot; Marston's Burton Bitter, Pedigree 🄷
On the ground floor of the old central Co-op building, divided into four distinct drinking areas. A long, narrow place, it mirrors the original layout of the building, which is a fine example of early 20th-century commercial architecture. It can be busy throughout the day but particularly at weekends, when it is a popular starting point on the town-centre circuit. ♿

King's Arms

Quarry Brow, Hawcoat, LA14 4HY
⏲ 7-11; 12-4, 7-10.30 Sun
☎ (01229) 871303
Robinson's Hatters, Hartleys XB, Old Stockport, Unicorn 🄷
Under the direction of the same licensees for 15 years, this traditional, back-street local is the only real ale outlet in this part of town. Divided into two distinct areas, the bar has darts and naval memorabilia, while the lounge displays pictures of the locality dating back to the late 19th century. 'Bullshit corner' is possibly for those who over-indulge. The slate floor in the bar is a notable feature. ⊟▯

Bassenthwaite

Pheasant Inn ✔

CA13 9YE (S off A66, W end of lake)
⏲ 11-2.30, 5.30-10.30 (11 Fri & Sat); 12-2.30, 6-10.30 Sun
☎ (017687) 76234 website: www.the-pheasant.co.uk
Draught Bass; Jennings Cumberland Ale; Theakston Best Bitter 🄷
500-year-old coaching inn, now an upmarket hotel, where non-residents and non-diners are welcome. The walls of the bar are dark and varnished, with antique chairs and settles; the ales are dispensed in heavy mugs. The restaurant boasts superb cuisine and an excellent wine list. In summer, a family of ospreys nests nearby and can be seen fishing on the lake.
⛰Q🐎❀🛏◐▶⊟♿▲P

INDEPENDENT BREWERIES

Barngates Barngates
Beckstones Millom
Bitter End Cockermouth
Coniston Coniston
Dent Dent
Derwent Silloth
Foxfield Foxfield
Great Gable Wasdale Head
Hawkshead Hawkshead
Hesket Newmarket Hesket Newmarket
Jennings Cockermouth
Loweswater Loweswater
Abraham Thompson Barrow-in-Furness
Tirril Brougham
Yates Westnewton

Bolton

Eden Vale Inn

Chapel Street, CA16 6AL

12-3, 6-11; 11-11 Sat; 12-10.30 Sun

(01768) 361428

Black Sheep Best Bitter; guest beers

Formerly the Old Crown, this sympathetically refurbished village local is steadily regaining its place at the centre of the community. Divided into three distinct areas, it caters for all needs – especially those customers seeking out a different micro-brewery beer and a good value, home-cooked meal based on local produce. The River Eden and the historic county town of former Westmorland are nearby. P

Boot

Boot Inn

CA19 1TG (short walk from Dalegarth Station, R&ER)

11-11; 12-10.30 Sun

(019467) 23224 website: www.bootinn.co.uk

Black Sheep Best Bitter; Jennings Cumberland Ale; guest beers

Walkers' pub with great atmosphere, serving a superb range of beers and an entertaining menu. In a superb location, surrounded by the highest fells in Lakeland, it is handy for Dalegarth Station on the famous La'al Ratty. Ideally placed for scenic walks, children (and dogs) are welcome. The inn participates in the annual Boot beer festival.

Q (Dalegarth R&ER) P

Brook House Inn

CA19 1TG (short walk from Dalegarth Station, R&ER)

11-11; 12-10.30 Sun

(019467) 23288 website: www.brookhouseinn.co.uk

Taylor Landlord; Theakston Best Bitter; guest beers

A short walk from Dalegarth Station on the famous La'al Ratty railway, this superbly positioned inn offers four guest beers – usually one is Cumbrian. For walkers, it is surrounded by some of the highest fells in Lakeland and some magnificent scenery. Close by are the remains of the Roman fort at Hardnott. The inn comprises a comfortable bar, adorned with hunting and farming memorabilia, and a no-smoking room. It is a participant in the annual Boot beer festival.

Q (Dalegarth R&ER) P

Bouth

White Hart Inn

LA12 8JB (off A590, 6 miles NE of Ulverston)

12-2, 6-11; 12-11 Sat; 12-10.30 Sun

(01229) 861229 website: www.whitehartbouth.co.uk

Black Sheep Best Bitter; Jennings Cumberland Ale; Tetley Bitter; guest beers

This traditional, central village pub became entirely no-smoking in 2004. The slate floors and real fires give a typical Lakeland atmosphere. A heated terrace is popular with tourists visiting nearby Grizedale Forest, and affords outstanding views. A variety of meals is served in the pub, and there is an upstairs restaurant (booking recommended). Beef from nearby Abbots Reading Farm is a speciality; children's portions are available.

P

Bowness-on-Windermere

Royal Oak

Brantfell Road, LA23 3DB

11-11; 12-10.30 Sun

(015394) 43970 website: www.royaloakwindermere.co.uk

Coniston Bluebird; Greene King Old Speckled Hen; Jennings Cumberland Ale; Marston's Pedigree; Tetley Bitter

Popular local, just away from the main tourist thoroughfare with its shops and visitor attractions. The split-level bar area, reached up a few steps, is complemented by a no-smoking lounge to the left and a raised games section to the right. A good range of meals is available. The patio is a suntrap. A certificate confirms the pub as the official start/finish of the Dalesway long distance walk.

Braithwaite

Coledale Inn

CA12 5TN (top of village, off Whinlatter Rd)

11-11; 12-10.30 Sun

(017687) 78272 website: www.coledaleinn.co.uk

Jennings Bitter; Theakston Black Bull Bitter; Yates Bitter

Historic building dating back to 1824, originally a woollen mill, then a pencil factory, using locally mined graphite. Two bars: note the typical Lakeland carved oak bar, and deep window seat. Decorated with engravings of Lake District scenes, it is well placed for exploring the Northern Fells. Dogs are welcome in one bar. The Royal Oak near the campsite is also worth a visit. P

Broughton-in-Furness

Manor Arms

The Square, LA20 6HY

12-11; 12-10.30 Sun

(01229) 716286

Coniston Bluebird; Yates Bitter; guest beers

If you wanted somebody to try real ale for the first time, the Manor would be the place to take them. Run by father and son, their commitment to real ale ensures the beers are varied and in tip-top condition. A Timothy Taylor beer is usually stocked. It has deservedly won numerous awards over the years, reaching the last 16 in CAMRA's National Pub of the Year. The pub has a no-smoking area.

Q P

Buttermere

Bridge Hotel

CA13 9UZ (off B5289 from Keswick)

10.30-11; 10.30-10.30 Sun

(017687) 70252 website: www.bridge-hotel.co.uk

Black Sheep Best Bitter; Theakston Old Peculier; guest beer

This 18th-century hotel nestles between Buttermere and Crummock Water and is an ideal spot for exploring the Lorton and Buttermere valleys, with their walking and climbing opportunities. First licensed as a coaching inn in 1735, it affords stunning views from the two comfortable bars of the surrounding fells. The bar meals represent excellent quality and value.

The hotel has a restaurant and offers a range of accommodation. The house beer is brewed by Hawkshead. Q❀⇄◐◑ ⅄P

Fish Hotel ✔

CA13 9XA (off B5289 from Keswick)
11.30-3, 6-11; 10.30-10.30 Sun
☎ (017687) 70253 website: www.fish-hotel.co.uk
Hesket Newmarket Catbells Pale Ale; Jennings Bitter, Sneck Lifter; guest beer ⊞
Family-owned, typical Lakeland stone-built hotel, in a lovely setting 'twixt Buttermere and Crummock Water. The spacious, comfortable bar area benefits from views out to the Buttermere Valley. It is ideally located for outdoor pursuits, be it walking around the lake, exploring the valleys or climbing on the surrounding fells. Good value meals offer a wide choice, including vegetarian options and children's meals.
Q❀⇄◐◑♿⅄P

Carlisle

Carlisle Rugby Club

Warwick Road, CA1 1CW (off A69, by Carlisle United FC)
7 (5.30 Fri; 6 Sat)-11 (1-11 Sat in rugby season); 12-3, 7-10.30 Sun
☎ (01228) 521800
Tetley Bitter; Yates Bitter; guest beer ⊞
Having undergone a major refurbishment after suffering in Carlisle's worst flood for 100 years, this club is a winner in Cumbria CAMRA's annual awards. A guest ale is always put on on a Friday during the rugby season; it can get crowded when Carlisle United play at home. Show this Guide to be signed in. Q❀♿⇌P

Crown Inn

Scotland Road, Stanwix, CA3 9HS
11-11; 12-10.30 Sun
☎ (01228) 512789
Theakston Best Bitter; guest beer ⊞
Busy local that serves food all day, every day. The greater part of the large lounge has been made no-smoking following a recent refurbishment; it houses a big screen for major sports events. The bar is divided into two distinct areas, with a pool table and juke box in the rear half. The Crown is renowned in the city for hosting the best pub quiz (Tue eve) when the winning team gets a gallon of beer.
❀◐◑⊟♿⇌♣⚡

Cumberland Inn ☆

22 Botchergate, CA1 1QS (right out of station)
11-11; 12-10.30 Sun
☎ (01228) 536900
Caledonian Deuchars IPA; guest beers ⊞
CAMRA National Inventory pub, retaining fine wood panelling from its past as a Redfern-designed Carlisle State Management scheme house. It has a welcoming fire in the main bar area, and a pool room at the rear. Busy at various times during the day, it is frequented by all age groups. The closest real ale pub to Carlisle Citadel railway station, it is popular with rail trip visitors. ⚲⇌♣

Howard Arms

107 Lowther Street, CA3 8ED (next to the Lanes shopping centre)
11-11; 12-10.30 Sun
☎ (01228) 532926
Theakston Best Bitter, XB ⊞
Popular pub, boasting a superb tiled exterior, with several small rooms, a regular Guide entry. Like all Carlisle's pubs over 30 years old, the Howard Arms is an ex-State Management scheme pub, and has changed little since those days. The city's late-lamented theatre which stood opposite the pub presented Charlie Chaplin, Laurel and Hardy and other notable music hall artists. Old photos and posters are a reminder of the pub's theatrical links. ❀◐⇌

King's Head

Fisher Street, CA3 8RF (behind old town hall)
10-11; 12-10.30 Sun
☎ (01228) 533797
Yates Bitter; guest beers ⊞
The King's Head is one of the older pubs in town, where many pictures of Carlisle through the ages are on display. A plaque outside explains why Carlisle is not in the Domesday Book. The pub is close to the tourist area of Carlisle, with the castle and cathedral, and also the Lanes shopping centre, built on the site of the old lanes that connected the two main roads to the north. ◐⇌⚡

Jovial Sailor

40 Caldecoates, LA2 7AA
(follow signs to hospital, W of city)
12 (11 Sat)-11; 12-10.30 Sun
☎ (01228) 532761
Theakston Best Bitter; guest beer ⊞
Recently reopened after being damaged in Carlisle's worst flood in living memory, it has a traditional bar with possibly the narrowest toilet door into the gents. The lounge is divided into three areas for pool, darts and general seating. There are seats, too, in the rear yard where the smell of baking biscuits from the factory next door is a wonderful accompaniment to a pint of real ale. ⚲❀⊟⇌♣P

Cartmel Fell

Masons Arms

Strawberry Bank, LA11 6NW (4 miles from Newby Bridge on Crosthwaite Road) OS413895
11-3, 6-11; 11-11 Fri, Sat & summer; 12-10.30 Sun
☎ (015395) 68486 website: www.strawberrybank.com
Black Sheep Best Bitter; Hawkshead Bitter; Taylor Landlord; guest beers ⊞
Charming olde-worlde inn set in an isolated position overlooking the Lyth Valley. It is characterised by an eclectic mix of comfortable furniture, flagged floors and beamed ceilings. Large open ranges heat the bars in winter. An extensive outside seating area is heated for prolonged summer use. ⚲☕❀⇄◐◑P⚡

Cleator Moor

Crown

Bowthorn, CA25 5JH
(on B5294, Cleator Moor-Frizington road)
12.30-5.30, 7-11; 12-10.30 Sun
☎ (01946) 810136
Robinson's Hartleys XB, Unicorn ⊞
Well-supported traditional Cumbrian local, with a strong games and sports flavour. With two bars, one small and cosy, the other larger and

spacious, it is worthy of a detour for a visit. A drinkers' pub, serving no food, the two regular beers are supplemented by two changing ales from Robinson's stable.

Cockermouth

Bitter End ✔

15 Kirkgate, CA13 9PJ (off Market Place)
❂ 12-2.30 (11.30-3 Fri & Sat); 6-11; 12-3, 6-10.30 Sun
☎ (01900) 828993 website: www.bitterend.co.uk
Bitter End Farmers Ale, Cuddy Lugs; Jennings Bitter, Cumberland Ale; guest beers Ⓗ
Site of Bitter End Brewery, which can be seen through a glass screen behind the back bar area. This award-winning brew-pub comprises three areas, one no-smoking; the front bar has a welcoming open fire. Note the collection of old Cockermouth photographs and memorabilia. Popular for dining, particularly weekends and evenings, a noisy, free quiz takes place on Tuesday evenings. Local CAMRA Pub of the Year 1999-2002. ⌂◐◑▲⊬

Black Bull

17 Main Street, CA13 9LE (just off town centre)
❂ 11.30-midnight (6-11 Mon; 11.30-11 Tue & Wed); 12-10.30 Sun
☎ (01900) 824071
Theakston Cool Cask; guest beers Ⓗ
Old, low, beamed pub opened up into a large L-shaped, stone-flagged room with a single bar. Cosy and welcoming, it is popular with the younger set and therefore lively, particularly in the evenings and at weekends. Represented in local karaoke as well as pool and darts leagues, it stages occasional live entertainment. The garden is to the rear; limited parking. ❀◐▲♣P

Swan Inn

56 Kirkgate, CA13 9PH (off Market Place)
❂ 12-2 (not Mon or Tue), 6.30 (7 Mon & Tue)-11; 12-2, 6.30-10.30 Sun
☎ (01900) 822425
Jennings Dark Mild, Bitter Ⓗ
This welcoming, edge-of-town pub, is one of the oldest in Cockermouth, and retains much of its earlier character. Cosy, with flagged floors and low beams, it is warmed by an open fire in the front bar area in winter. The horseshoe bar opens on to three areas, one no-smoking. It attracts a good local following, and is home to teams competing in the quiz league. It is also the watering-hole for the Cockermouth Mechanics Band. ⌂Q▲♣⊬

Coniston

Sun

LA21 8HQ (up hill from town)
❂ 12-11; 12-10.30 Sun
☎ (015394) 41248
Coniston Bluebird; guest beers Ⓗ
Pub and hotel situated up the hill from Coniston Village, this typical Lakeland inn boasts a slate floor and large coal-fired range. Five handpumps serve real ale. Bar food is available and the hotel has a spacious restaurant with a large conservatory giving wonderful views of Coniston and the fells. Lakeland and hunting paraphernalia is displayed. The hotel provides good quality accommodation. ⌂Q❀⇌◐◑▲P

Crook

Sun Inn

LA8 8LA
❂ 12-2.30, 6-11; 12-11 Sat; 12-10.30 Sun
☎ (01539) 821351
Coniston Bluebird; Courage Directors; Theakston Best Bitter; guest beer Ⓗ
The spacious bar area has flag flooring and is used both by drinkers and diners studying the extensive menu and specials board. The well-appointed dining areas are separated from the bar by a wall containing an unusual two-way fireplace. Booking for meals is recommended (essential at weekends). Good woodland and low-level walking routes run nearby.
⌂Q❀⇌◐◑▲P⊬

Dalton-in-Furness

Brown Cow

10 Goose Green, LA15 8LP
(below St Mary's Church, on road to Barrow)
❂ 12-11; 12-10.30 Sun
☎ (01229) 462553
Beer range varies Ⓗ
Possibly 900 years old, this family-run pub, with a 70-seater restaurant upstairs (open 12-9pm) provides a cosy place for sampling good food and drink. One central bar serves three distinct areas, one of which is warmed by a coal fire. Nestling below the tower of the parish church, on the western edge of town, it has a patio and garden for the warmer months. It keeps five real ales that change frequently.
⌂❀⇌◐♿⇶♣P⊬

Dearham

Ploughman

Maryport Road, CA15 9EG (on A594, Cockermouth road)
❂ 11-3 (not Mon), 7-11; 12-10.30 Sun
☎ (01900) 814748
Robinson's Unicorn; guest beer Ⓗ
Small country pub, the oldest in Dearham with a main bar, plus an annexe and an upstairs function room, used widely by local groups as their meeting place. It has won the local Village in Bloom competition for commercial premises on a number of occasions. The Ploughman serves a range of meals, including vegetarian options. The guest beer is supplied by Robinson's. ◐◑

Dent

Sun Inn

Main Street, LA10 5QL
❂ 11-11; 12-10.30 Sun
☎ (015396) 25208
Beer range varies Ⓗ
This 16th-century pub stands at the centre of an attractive Dales village. A cosy and unpretentious bar in an L-shape is supplemented by a smaller, no-smoking side room where children are welcome. Local photographs adorn the walls; spot the coins studded into the beams. It is still seen as the Dent Brewery tap, despite the brewery being located a couple of miles along the Dale and now under separate ownership.
⌂Q☕❀⇌◐◑▲♣P⊬

Elterwater

Britannia Inn

LA22 9HP

11-11; 12-10.30 Sun

☎ (015394) 37210 website: www.britinn.co.uk

Coniston Bluebird; Jennings Bitter; Taylor Landlord; guest beers Ⓗ

Pub facing the village green that often acts as an overflow to the patio on a busy summer's day. Inside, the compact bar is on the right of the entrance hall, to the rear under the stairs is the stone-flagged back room. A champion of champions beer festival is held each November. Buses to and from Ambleside stop across the road. ♛Q❀⇌◐◑ĀP⊬

Ennerdale Bridge

Shepherds Arms Hotel

CA23 3AR

12-2.30, 6-11; 12-10.30 Sun

☎ (019467) 23224 website: www.shepherdsarmshotel.co.uk

Coniston Bluebird; Jennings Bitter, seasonal beers; guest beer Ⓗ

Large, welcoming hotel featuring a bar, restaurant and conservatory. A popular staging point on the Coast-to-Coast Walk, a boot rack is provided at the door and rucksacks can be transported to your next stop. The hotel supplies a daily weather forecast for walkers. Meals are based on locally-sourced produce, including fish and game. A great selection of books, pictures, antiques, pottery and artefacts adds interest at this local CAMRA Pub of the Season winner. ♛ᘔ❀⇌◐◑P⊬

Far Sawrey

Claife Crier Bar

LA22 0LQ

11-11; 12-10.30 Sun

☎ (015394) 43425

Black Sheep Best Bitter; Hawkshead Bitter, Red; Jennings Cumberland Ale; Theakston Best Bitter Ⓗ

Pleasant bar, attached to the Far Sawrey Hotel, split into small drinking areas – some were previously used as animal stalls. Parts of the hotel date back to the 1700s and there have only been 10 landlords in 144 years. This typical Lakeland pub stands at the heart of Beatrix Potter country; Lake Windermere is just a mile away. Food is available in the bar and hotel. The large wood-burning stove is lovely to relax by in winter. ♛Q❀⇌◐◑⊟♿P

Foxfield

Prince of Wales

LA20 6BX (opp. station)

5 (12 Fri & Sat)-11; closed Mon & Tue; 12-10.30 Sun

☎ (01229) 716238

website: www.princeofwalesfoxfield.co.uk

Beer range varies Ⓗ

Two house breweries, Foxfield and Tigertops, service this traditional pub, providing beers from all over England, always including a mild. Continental beers are also sold on draught and in bottles. Themed mini-beer festivals occur each year. This pub is next to a rural station and a bus stop. ♛Q❀⇌⊟⇌♣●P⊡

Garrigill

George & Dragon Inn

CA9 3DS (4 miles S of Alston, off B6277)

12-3 (not winter Mon-Fri), 7-11; 12-11 Sat; 12-4, 7-10.30 Sun

☎ (01434) 381293 website: www.garrigill-pub.co.uk

Black Sheep Best Bitter; guest beers Ⓗ

High in the Pennines, this 17th-century inn is well supported as the social centre of its village community. It also extends a warm welcome to visitors, walking or cycling the Pennine Way or Coast-to-Coast routes. Guest ales often include a northern micro-brewery product. At the bar look up to appreciate the decorated glass panels on the hinged bar cover at this former local CAMRA Pub of the Season. Lunches are served Saturday and Sunday (no eve meals Mon or Wed). ♛Q❀⇌◐◑♣

Gosforth

Gosforth Hall Hotel

CA20 1AZ

12-3 (not Mon or Tue), 6-11; 12-11 Sat; 12.2.30, 7-10.30 Sun

☎ (019467) 25322

website: www.gosforthhallhotel.co.uk

Theakston Best Bitter; Yates Fever Pitch; guest beer Ⓗ

Listed building, circa 1658, originally a pele tower and fortified farmhouse. It boasts the largest sandstone arch fireplace surviving in England and a 1673 crest can be seen in the bar. Comprising three rooms, one serving as a dining area, it oozes history and character, while retaining a feeling of cosy comfort. An interesting place to spend time enjoying a pint or two. ♛Q❀⇌◐◑P

Great Broughton

Punchbowl Inn

19 Main Street, CA13 0YJ

11 (2 Mon & Tue)-11; 12-10.30 Sun

☎ (01900) 824708

Jennings Bitter; guest beer Ⓗ

Traditional village pub, originally a 17th-century coaching inn. Rugby League memorabilia cover the walls and water jugs hang from the low ceiling. This friendly pub is HQ for the West Cumbrian Woodcarvers, supports quiz and darts teams and is the centre for village charity fundraising activites. A local CAMRA Pub of the Season winner, it has limited car parking. ♛♣

Great Corby

Corby Bridge Inn

CA4 8LL (off A69, E of Carlisle))

12-11; 12-10.30 Sun

☎ (01228) 560221

Thwaites Original; Lancaster Bomber; guest beer Ⓗ

Friendly, CAMRA award-winning local, situated about a quarter of a mile east of Wetheral Station on the Carlisle–Newcastle line. The walk from the station provides impressive views of the Eden Valley from the viaduct that spans it. The Grade II Listed pub has a three-room, open-plan layout; games and a dining area are

provided (no food Mon). Beer festivals have been held annually in May since 2002, showcasing up to eight local beers.
♨Q❀⇌◑ ⇶♣●P⚟

Great Langdale

Old Dungeon Ghyll Hotel ✔

LA22 9JY

⚙ 11-11; 12-10.30 Sun

☎ (015394) 37272 website: www.odg.co.uk

Black Sheep Special; Jennings Cumberland Ale; Theakston XB, Old Peculier; Yates Bitter; guest beers Ⓗ

The hikers bar adjoining the hotel is geared up for outdoor folk, with a hard floor and wood bench seating, plus a kitchen range often used for drying soaked clothing. The patio area offers mountain views on a spectacular scale. The hotel bar, next to the dining room (where booked meals are served at 7.30pm) is more formal. A bus service to Ambleside starts from across the bridge. ♨Q❀⇌◑ ⛺P⚟

Great Salkeld

Highland Drove Inn

CA11 9NA (off B6412, Edenhall-Lazonby road)

⚙ 12-2 (not Mon), 6-11; 12-11 Sat; 12-3, 6-10.30 Sun

☎ (01768) 898349 website: www.highland-drove.co.uk

John Smith's Bitter; Theakston Black Bull Bitter; guest beers Ⓗ

This popular 18th-century inn, once a stop-over for drovers taking cattle south from Scotland, offers a warm welcome to locals, diners and residents. Carefully refurbished over recent years, and with the addition of an award-winning restaurant, all the work has used old bricks, reclaimed timbers and local sandstone. It was local CAMRA's Pub of the Year 2005. The restaurant menu changes daily; residents may take advantage of trout and salmon fishing rights. ♨❀⇌◑ ⊟⛺♣P

Haverthwaite

Anglers Arms

LA12 8AJ (off A590, on X35 bus route)

⚙ 11.30-11; 12-10.30 Sun

☎ (015395) 31216

Beer range varies Ⓗ

Opposite the Lakeside & Haverthwaite steam railway, the pub's dining area continues the theme with a miniature railway running along the wall. The main bar contains a collection of witches (watch out for Alice!), autographed sports memorabilia, and a sunken games area. The menu places an emphasis on quality seafood and game. An upper function room helps to house the frequent beer festivals, augmenting the usual selection of up to 10 real ales, which includes regulars from Moorhouses and Hawkshead. ❀◑ ⊟♣●⚟

Hawkshead

King's Arms

The Square, LA22 0NZ

⚙ 11-11; 12-10.30 Sun

☎ (015394) 36372

website: www.kingsarmshawkshead.co.uk

Black Sheep Best Bitter; Coniston Bluebird; Hawkshead Bitter, Red Ⓗ

One of four pubs in the village, this 500-year-old inn stands on the north side of the square. Its proximity to the hills and fells makes it an ideal location for visitors and tourists. An unusual aspect of the comfortable bar is the roof support – a sculpture by local artist John Whitworth disguising the Acrow prop. Local Hawkshead beers are always available. A guest ale occasionally replaces one of the regulars. Packed lunches can be provided for residents.
♨Q❀⇌◑ ⛺

Hayton

Stone Inn

Bracken How, CA8 9HR

(½ mile S of A69, two miles W of Brampton)

⚙ 10-3, 5.30-11; 10-11 Sat; 12-3, 7-10.30 Sun

☎ (01228) 670498

Thwaites Mild, Original; guest beer Ⓗ

'The pub is the hub' certainly applies to the Stone, which is very much at the heart of its village community, with a mainly local clientele. Strong naval connections are in evidence, but other artefacts are worthy of closer inspection. The bar and fireplace are built of local sandstone, hence the name (it was formerly the White Lion). Coffee and toasties are available in the bar and private parties can be catered for in an interesting upstairs room. ♨Q⊟♣P

Hesket Newmarket

Old Crown ✔

CA7 8JG

⚙ 12-3 (not Mon & Tue), 5.30-11; 12-3, 7-10.30 Sun

☎ (016974) 78288 website: www.theoldcrownpub.co.uk

Hesket Newmarket Great Cockup Porter, Blencathra Bitter, Skiddaw Special, Hellvelyn Gold, Doris's 90th Birthday Ale, Old Carrock Strong Ale Ⓗ

Winner of various awards from CAMRA and others, this co-operative owned pub and micro-brewery has seen visits from Prince Charles and TV's Two Fat Ladies. Nestled on the boundary of the Lake District, it is a popular pop-in for walkers and tourists. Brewery tours (by arrangement) start and finish in the pub where a meal, usually a curry, can be enjoyed while trying more of the brewery produce. This is a fine example of a community ensuring the survival of a local amenity. ♨Q❀◑ ⛺♣

Hoff

New Inn

CA16 6TA (on B6260)

⚙ 11 (6.30 Mon)-11; 12-10.30 Sun

☎ (017683) 51317

Tirril Bewsher's Best Bitter; guest beers Ⓗ

There are records of licensees here going back to 1823, although the building is considerably older. Converted into a private dwelling in 1999, it made a welcome return as a village local in 2001. Stone-flag flooring and oak furniture predominate, but the array of pump clips affixed to the black ceiling beams gives a clue to the main action. The cider is Westons Old Rosie. Good pub grub (not Mon or Tue) and occasional live music complete the picture.
♨Q❀⇌◑ ♿⛺♣●P⚟

Holme

Smithy Inn

Milnthorpe Road, LA6 1PS

⏲ 11.45-3, 6-11; 11.45-11 Sat; 12-10.30 Sun

☎ (01524) 781302

Thwaites Original, Lancaster Bomber or seasonal beer 🄷

Neat and tidy inn with a spacious bar area that combines plenty of standing as well as seated accommodation. There is a no-smoking dining room with a small bar, where drinkers are welcome. Good value lunches are popular with long-standing regulars while a wider age range is catered for in the evening. Buses running between Lancaster and Kendal stop almost outside the door. 🔥❀◐◑♿♣P⊬

Ings

Watermill Inn ✔

LA8 9PY (off A591, turn by the church)

⏲ 12-11; 12-10.30 Sun

☎ (01539) 821309 website: www.watermillinn.co.uk

Black Sheep Special Bitter; Coniston Bluebird; Hawkshead Best Bitter; Lees Moonraker; Theakston Old Peculier; guest beers 🄷

The pub attracts custom both for the wide range of regular and guest beers and the good value meals on offer. The dog/drinker-friendly bar and the family/drinker-friendly lounge have no-smoking areas. Neither has TV, juke box, pool, machines or other interruptions to civilised conversation. The building to house an on-site micro-brewery was nearing completion as the Guide went to press – look out for house beers. 🔥Q🚼❀🛏◐◑♿♣🍎P⊬

Ireby

Lion

The Square, CA7 1EA

⏲ 6-11; 12-3, 7-10.30 Sun

☎ (016973) 71460 website: www.irebythelion.co.uk

Derwent Carlisle State Bitter; guest beers 🄷

The market cross in the square, opposite the pub, bears testimony to the fact that what is really a large, quiet village has by charter, the right to call itself a town. With a bar from an old pub in Leeds, and wood panelling and seats from a local church, this small pub is at the heart of its community. The four handpumps offer a changing range of beers, with at least one local brew from Hesket Newmarket, Yates, Derwent or Jennings. 🔥Q❀◐◑♣

Kendal

Burgundy's Wine Bar

19 Lowther Street, LA9 4DH

⏲ 11.30-3.30 (not Mon-Wed), 6.30-11 (not Mon); 7-10.30 Sun

☎ (01539) 733803 website: www.burgundyswinebar.com

Yates Fever Pitch; guest beers 🄷

Bistro-style bar on three levels. In the middle is the tile-roofed bar from which you can choose from up to five micro or regional beers; an above-average range of draught and bottled continental lagers is also stocked. The lower level has games machines, and the upper one is set out with tables and seating. In spring it hosts a Cumbria micros beer challenge and St George's Day celebrations. Food is generally provided by arrangement. Bus and train connections are nearby. ≠🍎

Ring o'Bells ✔

37 Kirkland, LA9 5AF

⏲ 12 (6 Tue)-11; 12-10.30 Sun

☎ (01539) 720326

Greene King Old Speckled Hen; Tetley Bitter; guest beers 🄷

This is believed to be the only pub in England standing on consecrated ground. The front bar, popular with locals, and the rear lounge are separated by a tiny snug, which is the subject of a preservation order. No juke box or machines disturb the peace, but it is reputed to be haunted. It has a dining room and offers reasonably-priced accommodation. 🔥Q🛏◐◑🍴≠♣

Keswick

Dog & Gun ✔

2 Lake Road, CA12 5BT (off Market Place)

⏲ 12-11; 12-10.30 Sun

☎ (017687) 73463

Theakston Best Bitter, Old Peculier; Yates Bitter; guest beers 🄷

Busiest of the Keswick pubs, with the best selection of real ales. Full of character with flagged floors, low, oak-beamed ceilings and an open fire, it is famed for its Hungarian goulash, served with a garlic baguette, and Old Peculier stew. Popular quiz nights (Thu) raise funds for the Keswick Mountain Rescue Team. It is handy for the Theatre by the Lake and the town-centre Moot Hall. 🔥◐◑⛺

Kirkby in Furness

Ship

Askewgate, LA17 7TE (50 yds from the station)

⏲ 12-3, 4-11; 12-11 Sat; 12-10.30 Sun

☎ (01229) 889454

Beer range varies 🄷

Free house dating back to 1691, the Ship boasts exposed beams, a slate floor, local oak furniture and a wood-burning stove. This is a no-smoking pub, where the family room has a plasma screen TV for Sky sports fans. Well cooked local produce is backed up by specials, such as Thai curry and vegetarian dishes, a children's menu and lunchtime takeaways. The quiz on Thursday evening can be quite crowded. A bunk house for cyclists and walkers opened in summer 2005. 🔥Q🚼❀🛏◑≠P⊬

Kirkby Lonsdale

Snooty Fox Tavern ✔

Main Street, LA6 2AH

⏲ 11-11; 12-10.30 Sun

☎ (015242) 71308

Black Sheep Best Bitter; Theakston Best Bitter; guest beer 🄷

Standing in the centre of this pleasant market town, it boasts an imposing Georgian façade and rear entrance arch. The elegant front lounge, with unusual memorabilia, is complemented by a plain rear bar. Two inter-connecting dining rooms offer above-average quality meals. Devils

Bridge over the River Lune, a magnet for motorcyclists, is a short walk away.
♨Q✿⇔◑◐⊞♣P

Kirkoswald

Crown Inn ✔

CA10 1DQ (on B6413, 6½ miles NE of Penrith)
✪ 12-3.30 (not Wed), 6.30-11; 12-3, 6.30-10.30 Sun
☎ (01768) 898435
Jennings Dark Mild, Cumberland Ale ⊞
This popular, 17th-century pub with its low ceilings and warm atmosphere stands at the heart of a historic and attractive Eden Valley village. Apart from locals it is well patronised by tourists keeping off the main routes, who can enjoy excellent food based on local produce in either the bar or a no-smoking ante-room (booking advised at weekends). Stairs lead to a pool room in the old hayloft, a remnant of its coaching inn days. ♨Q✿◑◐▲♣

Loweswater

Kirkstile Inn

CA13 0RU (off B5289, S from Cockermouth through Lorton)
✪ 11-11; 11-10.30 Sun
☎ (01900) 85219 website: www.kirkstile.com
Coniston Bluebird; Loweswater Melbreak Bitter, Grasmoor Dark; guest beer ⊞
Home of Loweswater Brewery, this classic Lakeland inn sits below Melbreak in a stunning setting 'twixt Loweswater and Crummock Water. Low ceilings and stone walls add character. An extensive outdooor seated area affords views across to the Buttermere valley. Totally no-smoking, it comprises a single bar with three seated areas, two given over primarily to bar meals, plus a restaurant. Local CAMRA's Pub of the Year 2003 to 2005 offers excellent accommodation. The guest beer comes from Loweswater or another Cumbrian brewery.
♨Q✿⇔◑◐♿P⚡

Low Hesket

Rose & Crown

CA4 0HG
✪ 12-3, 6-11; 12-3, 6.30-10.30 Sun
☎ (016974) 73348
Jennings Mild, Bitter, Cumberland Ale ⊞
Transport is the theme in this pub, situated on the A6 (formerly the main route to Scotland). Old bus seats to sit on and pictures of vintage transport, both road and rail, are featured. Enjoy a good meal (no food Mon) and a pint of rare Jennings mild or one of its other beers. The pub does not accept credit or debit cards.
♨✿◑◐♣P

Low Row

Railway Inn

CA8 2LE (3 miles E of Brampton, N off A9)
✪ 6-11 (12-3, 6-11 summer Mon-Fri); 12-3, 7-10.30 Sun
☎ (016977) 46222
Thwaites Original, Lancaster Bomber ⊞
Drive slowly through the village to ensure you do not miss the right turn, as the pub is tucked away by itself overlooking the Newcastle-Carlisle railway. The views on a clear day across the Pennines are superb. Close to the Hadrian's Wall walk, the pub is an ideal place to relax with a good pint and take in the scenery.
♨Q✿◑◐⊞▲♣P

Nateby

Black Bull

CA17 4JP
✪ 12-2, 6-11 (12-11 summer); 12-2, 6-10.30 (12-10.30 summer) Sun
☎ (017683) 71588
Tetley Bitter; guest beer ⊞
Village local with a split-level, stone-flagged bar area. The lower section has pew seating, the ground floor level has a no-smoking upper area, complete with a jigsaw table. The dining room is to the rear and can be hired for functions. Note the yellow AA mileage indicator set into the front wall. The Cumbria cycleway passes the door. The rear entrance is accessible for wheelchairs. ♨Q☕✿⇔◑◐♿P⚡

Near Sawrey

Tower Bank Arms

LA22 0LF (on B5285, 6 miles S of Ambleside) OS371956
✪ 11-3, 5.30 (6 winter)-11; 12-3, 5.30 (6 winter)-10.30 Sun
☎ (015394) 36334 website: www.towerbankarms.co.uk
Theakston Best Bitter, Old Peculier; guest beer ⊞
Popular little country pub that features in Beatrix Potter's Jemima Puddleduck and stands next door to Hill Top, the author's former home. The bar has a stone-flagged floor, comfortable chairs and photographs of celebrities who have stayed here. It is free from juke box, pool or games machines. The guest beers are often from local breweries, of which there are a growing number; bottled beers are also stocked. Well situated for walking and sailing, the small car park is for residents only. ♨Q✿⇔◑◐P

Nether Wasdale

Screes Inn

CA20 1ET (E off A595, follow signs for 4 miles) OS125040
✪ 11-11; 12-10.30 Sun
☎ (019467) 26262 website: www.thescreesinnwasdale.com
Black Sheep Best Bitter; Coniston Bluebird; Yates Bitter; guest beer ⊞
Multi-level, multi-roomed country pub with a dining room. It hosts occasional live music – folk or jazz. Popular with walkers and therefore busy at times, it is one of two first-class sources of real ale in this tiny hamlet, hidden deep in the heart of Lakeland, close to Wastwater, Great Gable and Scafell Pike. With the Strands (opposite) it jointly hosts the annual Wasdale Real Ale festival. Some food is available all day.
♨Q✿⇔◑◐⊞▲P⚡

Orton

George Hotel ✔

Front Street, CA10 3RJ
✪ 12-3, 6-11; 11-11 Sat; 12-10.30 Sun
☎ (015396) 24229 website: www.georgehotel.net
Greene King IPA; guest beers ⊞
Large, attractive village hotel, an ideal place for Coast-to-Coast walkers to rest their weary legs. It is handy for the chocolate factory shop (opposite) and the local farmers' market on the

second Saturday of the month. The extensive garden and a pool table in the function room are added attractions. Dent Brewery provides the guest ales. ♔Q❀⇔◑⅄♣⅍

Penrith

Gloucester Arms

Great Dockray, CA11 7DE
☉ 11-11; 12-10.30 Sun
☎ (01768) 863745 website: www.gloucesterarms.co.uk
Black Sheep Best Bitter; Greene King Old Speckled Hen; guest beer ⊞
Allegedly visited by Richard III, this 16th-century listed building retains some original features. The lively pub, on the market square, has several rooms including a pool room. At the time of survey it had no chef but hopefully a new one will be in place soon, which should ensure that the massive Gloucester Grill makes a comeback. ♔❀⇌♣P

Lowther Arms

3 Queen Street, CA11 7XD
☉ 11-3, 6-11; 11.30-2.30, 6-10.30 Sun
☎ (01768) 862792
Theakston Best Bitter, seasonal beers; guest beers ⊞
Coaching inn off the old A6 route, it has recently been extended, but without compromising the building; this gives a slight step between the levels. A past winner of various awards from CAMRA and In Bloom competitions, it can be busy at mealtimes, but is always welcoming. Drinkers are spoilt for choice, with a range of up to eight real ales usually available. ♔Q◑⇌

Pooley Bridge

Sun Inn ✔

CA10 2NN
☉ 12-11; 12-10.30 Sun
☎ (017684) 86205
Jennings Bitter, Cumberland Ale, Cocker Hoop, Sneck Lifter, seasonal beers ⊞
Located in the less-frequented north-eastern corner of the Lake District, this popular village pub offers a panelled top lounge and a lower bar with pool (in winter) and sports TV. The large, safe garden is well used in summer by ball-playing dogs and children. The River Eamont and Ullswater steamer pier are nearby.
♔Q❀⇔◑⊟⅄♣P⅍

Ravenglass

Ratty Arms

CA18 1SN (at main line station)
☉ 11-11; 12-10.30 Sun
☎ (01229) 717676
Greene King Ruddles Best; Jennings Bitter; Theakston Best Bitter; guest beers ⊞
Converted railway building, boasting lots of railway memorabilia, wrought iron and glass. This is also the terminus for the Cumbria Coast line and the famous Ravenglass & Eskdale Railway (La'al Ratty), once a narrow gauge mineral line, but now a major tourist attraction. The no-smoking area is an old platform, now covered over. The excellent range of real ales is complemented by the food.
♔Q❀◑♿⅄⇌♣P⅍

Ravenstonedale

King's Head ✔

CA17 4NH (signed off A685)
☉ 11-11; 12-10.30 Sun
☎ (015396) 23284 website: www.kings-head.net
Black Sheep Best Bitter; guest beers ⊞
Now recovered from serious flood damage in early 2005, the full range of guest beers (see regularly updated list/display of pump clips) is flowing again. The cosy bar area is augmented by a games room, a no-smoking lounge and a dining room. Note the huge collection of water jugs. The stream, which (usually) runs just across the road, passes the (usually) lawned garden. This is a red squirrel sanctuary.
♔Q❀⇔◑⅄♣●P⅍

Rydal

Glen Rothay Hotel (Badger Bar) ✔

LA22 9LR
☉ 11-11; 12-10.30 Sun
☎ (015394) 34500
Beer range varies ⊞
Roadside inn bearing a date stone of 1624. The Badger bar offers a range of local beers as well as brews from further afield. Pictures and models of badgers predominate inside, and the real thing can often be seen in the grounds at night. The oak-panelled room to the left boasts an ornate mantelpiece. Meals can be taken in the dining room. Rydal Mount – the last home of William Wordsworth – is a short walk away.
♔Q❀⇔◑P

Santon Bridge

Bridge Inn ✔

CA19 1UX (from A595, turn E at Holmrook, follow signs)
OS111016
☉ 11-11; 12-10.30 Sun
☎ (019467) 26221 website: www.santonbridgeinn.com
Jennings Bitter, Cumberland Ale, Cocker Hoop, Sneck Lifter, seasonal beers ⊞
A treasure, located near some of the most secluded and attractive parts of the Lake District. Once a modest mail coach halt, it is now a comfortable inn with superb food; it is also licensed for weddings. Full of history, with low beams and creaking floors, it comprises one large, open bar area with comfortable alcoves by the windows. The popular Sunday lunch carvery attracts diners from far afield. This is the home of the annual World's Biggest Liar competition, held each November.
♔Q❀⇔◑⅄P

Seathwaite

Newfield Inn

LA20 6ED
☉ 11-11; 12-10.30 Sun
☎ (01229) 716208 website: www.newfieldinn.co.uk
Caledonian Deuchars IPA; Theakston Old Peculier; guest beer ⊞
A fell walkers' oasis, this free house in the tiny hamlet of Seathwaite prides itself on serving both good food and quality ales. A Jennings beer is always available. Situated in Wordsworth's

favourite valley, the Duddon, this unspoilt pub has welcomed travellers since the pack horse days of the 17th century; a joy to find.
Q❀⇌◐◑⊟Å♣P⊬

Shap

Greyhound Hotel

Main Street, CA10 3PW
⚙ 11-11; 12-10.30 Sun
☎ (01931) 716474 website: www.greyhoundhotel.co.uk
Hesket Newmarket Doris's 90th Birthday Ale; Jennings Bitter, Cumberland Ale; Tetley Bitter; guest beers 🄷
Spacious, former coaching inn dating from 1684 that keeps up to four guest beers. Enter the bar through a revolving door to find an open fire on the left and the counter straight ahead. Meals are served in both the bar and the restaurant. Bunkhouse accommodation is available for those on a budget. The Coast-to-Coast walk and Shap Abbey are close by. It was voted Pub of the Year 2004/5 by Westmorland CAMRA.
♨Q❀⇌◐◑♿Å♣P

Staveley

Eagle & Child Hotel

Kendal Road, LA8 9LP
⚙ 11-11; 12-10.30 Sun
☎ (01539) 821320 website: www.eaglechildinn.co.uk
Beer range varies 🄷
Micro-brewery beers (often local) dominate here. The U-shaped bar area displays an abundance of memorabilia on shelves around the walls. The upstairs function room, in the style of a medieval banqueting hall, can be hired. There are two gardens, one to the rear and the other next to the River Kent across the road. Buses to Ambleside and Kendal stop outside. ♨❀⇌◐◑●P

Talkin

Blacksmith's Arms

CA8 1LE (3 miles S of Brampton, left off B6413)
⚙ 12-3, 6-11; 12-3, 6-10.30 Sun
☎ (016977) 3452 website: www.blacksmithsarmstalkin.co.uk
Black Sheep Best Bitter; Coniston Bluebird; Hawkshead Bitter 🄷
In a small, quiet village, the well-appointed Blacksmith's Arms is one of the larger pubs in north Cumbria and recently received a local CAMRA Pub of the Season award. Well supported by locals, it also attracts regular visitors because of its convivial atmosphere and the high quality food served in the bars and restaurant. Local amenities include Brampton golf course and Talking Tarn country park; Hadrian's Wall is just a few miles away.
♨Q❀⇌◐◑ÅP⊬

Uldale

Snooty Fox

CA7 1HA
⚙ 6.30 (6 Fri)-11; 12-2, 6.30-10.30 Sun
☎ (016973) 71479
Beer range varies 🄷
Spacious pub at the centre of a small hamlet. Excellent meals based on local produce are served in the dining room (not Wed). Accommodation is available for those who want to explore this quiet, unspoilt area, known locally as 'Back o'Skiddaw', with easy access to the Caldbeck Fells and Solway Plain. On a clear day the views are stunning. The house beer Old Ale is brewed by the famous Hesket Newmarket Brewery. Jennings Cumberland Ale and Derwent beers are also regularly on tap at local CAMRA's Pub of the Season spring 2005.
♨❀⇌◐◑⊟♣P

Ulverston

Farmers Arms

Market Place, LA12 7BA
⚙ 10-11; 11-10.30 Sun
☎ (01229) 584469
website: www.farmersrestaurant-thelakes.co.uk
Hawkshead Bitter; guest beers 🄷
Busy pub with an excellent front garden overlooking the central hub of this market town. Outdoor heaters and a canopy make it a year-round people-watching spot. Good quality meals, served in the restaurant or bar, pull in diners as well as drinkers. The pub opens at 10am to provide coffee, breakfast and newspapers; it makes a very relaxing start to the day. ❀◐◑Å⇌

King's Head ✔

14 Queen Street, LA12 7AF
⚙ 11.30-11; 12-10.30 Sun
☎ (01229) 588064
Jennings Bitter, Cumberland Ale, Cocker Hoop, Sneck Lifter, seasonal beers 🄷
Well-supported, 17th-century coaching inn located in the town centre with its own crown bowling green at the rear. Several years ago it extended into the undertakers next door, which may explain the two resident ghosts. More recent renovations have revealed a sunken well that now forms a feature in the dining area. Good value meals and good conversation are assured. ♨❀⇌◐◑Å⇌

Walton

Centurion Inn

CA8 2DH (1½ miles N of A6071, W of Brampton)
⚙ 11.30 (5.30 winter Mon-Fri)-11; 12-10.30 Sun
☎ (016977) 2438 website: www.centurion-hadrianswall.com
Jennings Cumberland Ale; guest beers 🄷
Benefiting from its position on the site of milecastle 56 on Hadrian's Wall, the Centurion is a handy watering-hole or overnight stop for hikers on the recently-opened walk stretching from Bowness-on-Solway to Wallsend. The original range is still intact, although much of the 150-year-old building has been altered. Home-made food is served in the conservatory (Fellview Restaurant) or the bar, featuring local produce, including game in season. One of the two guest beers is supplied by Jennings.
♨❀⇌◐◑Å♣P⊬

Wasdale Head

Wasdale Head Inn

CA20 1EX (E off A595 at Gosforth, follow signs) OS187087
⚙ 11-11; 12-10.30 Sun
☎ (019467) 26229 website: www.wasdale.com

Great Gable Great Gable, Burnmoor Pale Ale, Wasd'ale, Scawfell, Illgill IPA, Yewbarrow Ⓗ
Home of the Great Gable Brewery, this famous inn is surrounded by England's highest mountain range. Well off the main roads, deep in Wasdale, past Wastwater the area is the birthplace of mountaineering, but is now also enjoyed by walkers. The full range of Great Gable beers is on offer as available, complemented by the excellent home cooking using local produce. Will Ritson, raconteur and World's Biggest Liar was a former landlord.
Q❀⇆◑♿⛺P⚟🗑

Whitehaven

Bransty Arch ✔

Bransty Row, CA28 7XE (N of town centre, opp. Tesco)
⏲ 11-11; 12-10.30 Sun
☎ (01946) 517640
Greene King Abbot; Marston's Burton Bitter, Pedigree; Shepherd Neame Spitfire; guest beers Ⓗ
Typical Wetherspoon's 'barn', with a committed licensee and staff. It offers a good range of ales and excellent value food. An old bus depot, turned into a single bar, it has a large no-smoking section and a family area. Close to the town centre and the attractive redeveloped harbour, it draws a lively clientele, which makes this a busy place in the evenings and particularly at weekends, when it can be packed.
◑♿⇌⚟

Windermere

Greys Inn

Elleray Road, LA23 1AG
⏲ 11-11; 12-10.30 Sun
☎ (015394) 43741 website: www.greywalls-hotel.co.uk
Black Sheep Best Bitter; Jennings Cumberland Ale; Theakston Best Bitter, Old Peculier Ⓗ
Town-centre pub, handy for the shops, buses and trains. To the right of the main entrance is a small games area with a pool table. To the rear is a raised no-smoking area. Pictures of old Windermere adorn the walls. A small suntrap of a patio is reached down some steps from the back of the bar. ♨❀⇆◑⇌P⚟

Workington

Henry Bessemer ✔

New Oxford Street, CA14 2NA (edge of shopping area)
⏲ 11-11; 12-10.30 Sun
☎ (01900) 734650
Greene King Abbot; Marston's Burton Bitter, Pedigree; Shepherd Neame Spitfire; guest beers Ⓗ
Large Wetherspoon's which was previously a cinema; a single, high-ceilinged bar with separated seated areas, one no-smoking. Seating is plentiful, with a couple of discrete alcoves. The decor has a 1930s feel and many pictures demonstrate the building's previous existence. Noisy when busy, particularly at weekends when it can be packed, it offers a wide range of inexpensive, good quality meals, including many vegetarian options. ◑♿⇌⚟

Pheasant, Bassenthwaite

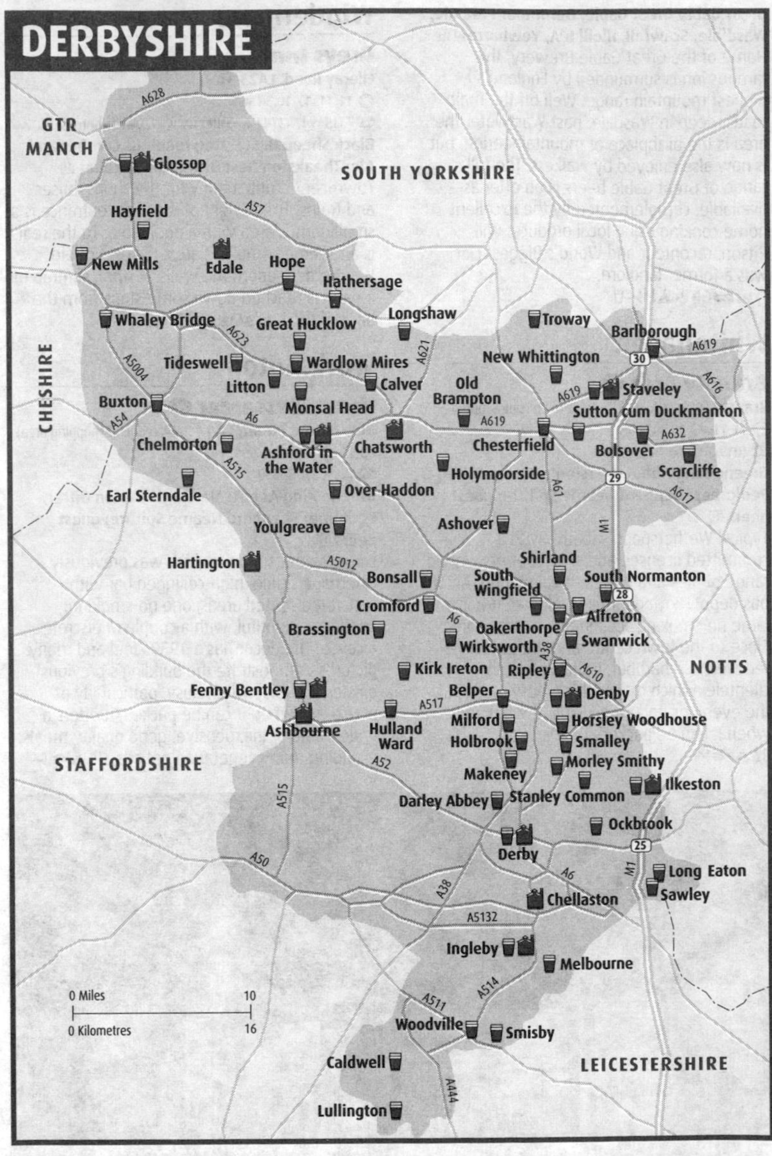

Alfreton

Victoria Inn

80 Nottingham Road, DE55 7EL (on B600)

1 (12 Sat)-11; 12-10.30 Sun

(01773) 520156

Beer range varies Ⓗ

Extensively refurbished, busy but friendly two-roomed local served by a central bar. The lounge features an illuminated aquarium, while pump clips of previously featured beers are displayed on beams in the public bar, which has a pool table and Sky TV. Guest beers change regularly and showcase local micro-breweries; a summer beer festival is held. The outdoor terrace houses long alley skittles. Parking is difficult; the town centre is nearby. Catch the No. 91 or 92 Derby-Mansfield bus or Red Arrow.

Ashford in the Water

Bull's Head

Church Street, DE45 1QB

11-3, 6-11; 12-3, 7-10.30 Sun

(01629) 812931

Robinson's Unicorn, Old Stockport, seasonal beers Ⓗ

This 460 year old stone-built coaching inn was once on the Manchester Road. The traditional two-roomed layout is served by a central bar. The pub has been run by the same family for more than 50 years and the wall in the lounge bears photographic evidence of this. Look in the lounge for the collection of tankards and bank notes, also the coins in cracks in the beams. No evening meals are served Thursday in winter.

P

Ashover

Old Poets' Corner

1 Butts Road, S45 0EW

✪ 12-2.30, 5-11; 12-11 (Fri & Sat); 12-10.30 Sun

☎ (01246) 590888 website: www.oldpoets.co.uk

Greene King Abbot Ⓗ/Ⓖ**; guest beers** Ⓗ

Beautiful, mock-Tudor building with old village photographs adorning the walls, open fires, wooden beams and hops above the bar. As well as two house beers – Ashover Gold from Leatherbritches and Old Poets' Ale from Tower – there is an ever-changing range of beers from regional and microbreweries (usually including one strong dark ale), real ciders, Belgian beers and fruit wines. This enterprising establishment also hosts regular live music, poetry readings, folk evenings, three seasonal beer festivals a year and monthly quiz nights. Dogs are welcome. ⛫Q❀◗♿⛺🍎P

Barlborough

Pebley Inn

Rotherham Road, S43 4TH OS481792

✪ 12-11; 12-10.30 Sun

☎ (01246) 810327

Stones Bitter; Taylor Landlord; guest beers Ⓗ

This former coaching inn, which dates from 1770, stands on the ancient Sheffield-Newark-London turnpike just a few hundred yards from the county boundary. A friendly two-roomed free house, it features a guest beer, often from a micro-brewery, and occasional real cider. Fresh home-cooked food is available in the bar and the smoke-free dining room (except Mon-Tue lunchtime), and there is a Sunday lunchtime carvery. A fun quiz is held on Thursday and an age-old ring the bull game can be played. Children (and dogs) are welcome.
⛫❀◗⊟♣🍎P⊁⊡

Belper

Cross Keys ✔

Market Place, DE56 1FZ

✪ 12-11; 12-10.30 Sun

☎ (01773) 599191

Draught Bass; Bateman Mild, XB, XXXB, seasonal beers; guest beer Ⓗ

This early 19th-century pub was formerly used as accommodation for visiting theatre troupes, and as a meeting place for Druids and Oddfellows. It has also witnessed at least one murder! Two-roomed, with a central bar, the pub has enjoyed a renaissance since being bought by Bateman, all of whose beers have proved popular locally; a summer beer festival is held. A real fire warms the lounge. Bar billiards and shove-ha'penny are played. Catch the R61-64/71 bus from Derby. ⛫Q❀⊟♿⥂♣

Queen's Head

29 Chesterfield Road, DE56 1FF

✪ 4 (12 Fri & Sat)-11; 12-10.30 Sun

☎ (01773) 825525

Caledonian Deuchars IPA; Tetley Bitter, Burton Ale; guest beers Ⓗ

Built during the Victorian era, this popular roadside inn comprises three rooms with a central bar, an upstairs function room and a pleasant patio area, providing panoramic views over the town and countryside. The public bar has a real fire and old photographs of Belper. Reputedly haunted, the pub hosts regular themed beer festivals, quizzes and entertainment, usually blues or folk, at the weekends. It is a short walk uphill from the market place. Catch the R61-64/71 bus from Derby. ⛫Q❀⊟♣🍎

Bolsover

Blue Bell

57 High Street, S44 6HF

✪ 12-3.30, 6.30-11; 12-3, 7-10.30 Sun

☎ (01246) 823508

website: www.bolsover.uk.com/index.html

Camerons Strongarm; Marston's Burton Bitter; guest beers Ⓗ

This thriving, two-roomed pub can be found between the parish church and historic Bolsover Castle. The garden is perched precariously on a clifftop, affording uninterrupted views to the Peak District and Crich Stand lighthouse. This former coaching house, built in 1747, retains some original features including low, beamed ceilings. Beer festivals are held twice yearly. Drinkers should be prepared to rub shoulders with knights in armour participating in events at the castle. Q❀⊟♣P

Bonsall

Barley Mow

The Dale, DE4 2AY

✪ 6-11; closed Mon; 12-midnight Sat; 12-10.30 Sun

☎ (01629) 825685

website: www.barleymowbonsall.co.uk

Greene King Abbot; Whim Hartington Bitter; guest beers (occasional) Ⓗ

The Barley Mow is featured in Wendy Holden's best-selling novel Pastures Nouveaux. A small pub, very big on character, there is always something different going on here: UFO spotting, live music, the landlord's guided walks, hen races or just relaxing in the sun on the south-facing patio. The extraordinary use of such a small space makes the pub quite tardis-like. The pool room has just enough space for the table and two people; on match nights the rest of the team watch from the bar on CCTV.
⛫Q❀◗⛺♣P

INDEPENDENT BREWERIES

Brunswick Derby
Danelaw Chellaston
Derby Derby
Edale Edale
Falstaff Derby
Funfair Ilkeston
Haywood Ashbourne
Howard Town Glossop
Leadmill Denby
Leatherbritches Fenny Bentley
John Thompson Ingleby
Peak Ales Chatsworth
Thornbridge Ashford in the Water
Toll End Tipton
Townes Staveley
Whim Hartington

King's Head
62 Yeoman Street, DE4 2AA
12-2.30 (not Mon), 6.30-11; 12-2.30, 7-10.30 Sun
☎ (01629) 822703
Bateman XB, seasonal beers; guest beers ℍ
One of Bateman's furthest flung pubs, this 17th-century stone local sits right at the heart of the village. The first innkeeper, John Abell, engraved his name on a wooden beam just inside the entrance to the pub when his first son was born. Sunday quizzes are warmed by log fires in the winter. Food is recommended and based around fish and grill dishes in hearty portions, with special children's choices.
♨Q❀◐◑Å♣P⊁

Brassington

Olde Gate Inne ☆
Well Street, DE4 4HJ (off A5023)
12-2.30, 6-11; 12-3, 7-10.30 Sun
☎ (01629) 540448
Marston's Pedigree, seasonal beers; guest beer ℍ
Family-run, ivy-clad gem, built in 1616, now Grade II listed and reputedly haunted. Oak beams feature throughout, with gleaming copper utensils hanging around three open fireplaces. The main bar boasts pewter jugs and a black-leaded range, while a pipe rack in the snug dates from the 17th century. An extensive menu includes home-cooked dishes and game in season (no food Mon eve). Boules is played here. The tourist attraction of Carsington Water is nearby. No children under 10 are admitted.
♨Q❀◐◑♿Å♣P⊁

Buxton

Baker's Arms
26 West Road, SK17 6HN
12-2, 6-11 (4 Fri; 7 Sat); 12-3, 7-10.30 Sun
☎ (01298) 24404
Burtonwood Bitter, Top Hat; guest beers ℍ
Small and friendly two-room town-centre pub entered via a welcoming porch. The simple bench seating and small tables surround a central L-shaped bar. If you are confident in playing in confined spaces, you can try a game of darts, just one of many sports supported by the pub. The success of the pub teams is evident from the impressive contents of the trophy cabinet. Constantly changing guest beers are complemented by a selection of foreign bottled beers. ❀Å⇛♣P

Buckingham Hotel (Ramsey's Bar)
1 Burlington Road, SK17 9AS
12-2, 6-11; 12-3, 6-10.30 Sun
☎ (01298) 70481
website: www.buckinghamhotel.co.uk
Wells Bombardier; guest beers ℍ
An extensive, family-run hotel with an outstanding public bar that feels like a well-appointed gentlemen's club. A range of interesting beers, usually from independent and micro-breweries, makes the bar popular with real ale drinkers. The name stems from the fact that number one Burlington Road used to be the studio and home of noted local artist George Ramsey. The food here is well above average pub quality, with an a la carte selection or a hearty carvery.
❀⇔◐◑⊟Å⇛⊖●P

George Hotel
The Square, SK17 6AZ
11-11; 12-10.30 Sun
☎ (01298) 24711
Kelham Island Pale Rider; Taylor Landlord; guest beers ℍ
Centrally located and spacious inside, the George continues to make friends and expand its trade. Always bustling, especially in the evenings when live music is a regular feature, the afternoon or early evening is often the best time to sample the constantly changing range of interesting guest beers. Outdoor drinking is possible in summer on the pleasant patio. Good, home-cooked food is served all day and is highly recommended.
❀⇔◐◑⊟Å⇛♣

Caldwell

Royal Oak
Main Street, DE12 6RR
12-11; 12-10.30 Sun
☎ (01283) 761486
Marston's Pedigree; guest beers ℍ
Friendly, 18th-century free house with a real community feel. There is a small, narrow bar with low-beamed ceiling at the front, and stairs leading to a smart split-level lounge with log fire and beamed ceiling at the rear. Cyclists and ramblers are welcome, as are families in the lower part of lounge. No meals are served but occasional themed food evenings for charity are held, and free snacks are often available. Locally-made preserves can be bought. Limited parking at the pub is supplemented in dry weather by a field beyond.
♨❀⊟Å♣P

Calver

Bridge Inn ✔
Calver Bridge, S32 3XA (on A623)
11.30-3 (3.30 Sat), 5.30-11; 12-3.30, 7-10.30 Sun
☎ (01433) 630415
Hardys & Hansons Bitter, Olde Trip, seasonal beers ℍ
This pub stands on the bank of the River Derwent, close to the huge Calver Mill, built by Arkwright in 1803-4 and recently converted into luxury apartments. The landlord has been here since the Bridge was a Stones pub in the 1980s and has built up a strong local trade as well as attracting visitors. The two cosy rooms house a display of fire-fighting equipment and more recently the landlord has started to build up a collection of hats. No evening meals are served on Monday or winter Sunday.
♨Q❀◐◑♿ÅP⊁⊓

Chelmorton

Church Inn
Main Street, SK17 9SL
12-3.30, 7-11 (11-11 summer Sat); 12-3, 7-10.30 (12-10.30 summer) Sun
☎ (01298) 85319

Adnams Bitter; Marston's Burton Bitter, Pedigree; guest beer (summer)
Set in beautiful surroundings opposite the church, this village pub caters for both walkers and locals alike. Even though the main room is laid out with dining tables, and good, home-cooked, food is on offer, a cosy pub atmosphere is maintained. The low ceiling and welcoming fire make this an excellent pub serving great beer, more so in summer when a guest beer is also available. A well-attended quiz is held on Monday evening.
⌂Q❀◑♣

Chesterfield

Derby Tup

387 Sheffield Road, Whittington Moor, S41 8LS
(on B6057)
✪ 11.30-3, 5-11; 11.30-11 Fri & Sat; 12-10.30 Sun
☎ (01246) 454316
Archers Golden; Bateman XXXB; Burton Bridge Top Dog Stout; Oakham JHB; Taylor Landlord; guest beers 🄷
What more can be said about a pub that has featured every year in the Guide for more than 20 years? A well-established, no frills drinkers' pub with an ever-changing menu of guest ales, a wide variety of bottled continental beers, and a selection of ciders, even the most discerning drinker is spoilt for choice here. Simple bar snacks are available, including pizzas. Quiz night is Sunday. Two smoke-free areas are provided in the snug and back room.
Q◖⊟♣●⍻

Market Hotel

New Square, S40 1AH
✪ 11-11; 7.30-10.30 Sun
☎ (01246) 273641
Marston's Pedigree; Taylor Landlord; Tetley Bitter; guest beers 🄷
Busy town-centre local with views of New Square market place and the historic Market Hall. Inside you will find a large L-shaped room with dark wood fittings, flagstone floors and a central bar with nine handpumps. The pub can be busy on market days and Friday and Saturday nights. Reasonably-priced food is served at lunchtimes. ⌂◖

Peacock

412 Chatsworth Road, Brampton, S40 3BQ
(on A619)
✪ 12-4, 5.30-11; 12-10.30 Sun
☎ (01246) 275115
Adnams Broadside; Black Sheep Best Bitter; Caledonian Deuchars IPA; Tetley Bitter; guest beer 🄷
Popular, friendly two-room pub with an open fire in the lounge. The central bar offers a good selection of real ales, including a guest beer. To the rear is a large garden ideal for families in summer, with an additional seating area at the front. Entertainment includes darts, dominoes and a Monday night quiz. Locally-made pickles and chutneys are sold here. Well worth a visit for a pleasant night out, it was winner of Derbyshire CAMRA Pub of the Year 2005.
⌂Q❀♣

Portland Hotel ✔

West Bars, S40 1AY
✪ 10-11; 12-10.30 Sun (opens 7am for breakfast; 8am at weekend)
☎ (01246) 245410
Greene King Abbot; Marston's Burton Bitter, Pedigree; guest beers 🄷
This architecturally impressive former railway hotel is now a bustling town-centre Wetherspoon, just off the smaller market square. It has a spacious and modern open-plan interior with reserved dining areas, where children are allowedto have a meal. The hotel offers a good range of cask ales, food and accommodation. It is the only place in the town centre that regularly stocks beers from the local Townes Brewery.
Q❀⊭◖◑♿

Red Lion

570 Sheffield Road, Whittington Moor, S41 8LX
✪ 12-11; 12-10.30 Sun
☎ (01246) 450770
Old Mill Mild, Bitter, Bullion, seasonal beers 🄷
An interesting, mid-Victorian sandstone edifice, built as an ale house. It has a large public bar with a wide-screen TV and a snug often used for live music. The interior is decorated with old photographs of Chesterfield's trams which used to terminate just outside. The monthly guest beers are from Old Mill, for which this is the southernmost outlet. A popular pub, it can be noisy.
⊟♣P

Royal Oak

1 The Shambles, S40 1PX
✪ 11-11 (7 Mon & Tue); 12-10.30 Sun
☎ (01246) 237700
Caledonian Deuchars IPA; Greene King Abbot; Stones Bitter; guest beers 🄷
Located in the Shambles area of the town, this is reputed to be Chesterfield's most historic pub. Made up of two distinct buildings, the older dates back to the 16th century. Each building is accessible by a separate entrance but both are served by a central bar. The top bar room is completely no-smoking and has an impressive, high, timbered ceiling. A range of up to eight cask ales is available. ◖⊟⍻

Cromford

Boat Inn

Scarthin, DE4 3QF
✪ 12-3, 6-11; 12-11 Sat; 12-10.30 Sun
☎ (01629) 823282
website: www.theboatatcromford.co.uk
Whim Hartington Bitter; guest beers 🄷
Popular free house tucked away behind the market place close to Cromford Dam. The bare stone walls, low beamed ceiling, beer barrel tables and open fires create a cosy, cave-like atmosphere. Regular live music including a folk night on Tuesday, summer barbecues and three beer festivals a year add to its appeal. Guest ales are usually sourced from local breweries such as Leatherbritches. The food is recommended, making this gem well worth seeking out.
⌂❀◑♿⛺⇌♣

Darley Abbey

Abbey Inn

Darley Street, DE22 1DX

11.30-2.30, 6-11; 12-11 Sat; 12-10.30 Sun

(01332) 558297

Samuel Smith OBB H

This erstwhile, 15th-century guesthouse is all that remains of the Augustinian Abbey of St Mary De Pratis, the most powerful abbey in Middle England before the Dissolution. Rescued from long neglect in 1978, it won a national award for the conversion to its present use. The upper level bar is reached by an impressive stone spiral staircase and boasts original church pews for seats. This complements a lower-level bar, with stone-flagged floor and roaring fire. Darley Park is nearby.

Q P

Denby

Leadmill Old Stables Bar

Park Hall, Park Hall Road, DE5 8PX (off B6179)

5 (12 Sat)-11 (closed Mon-Thu); 12-10.30 Sun

(01332) 883577

website: www.leadmillbrewery.co.uk

Leadmill range; guest beers H

Set in the grounds of the imposing Park Hall, this converted stable building now acts as the tap for the Leadmill Brewery, directly opposite. With an original stable door, sawdust-covered floor, wooden furniture, low lighting and much brewery memorabilia, the place has real atmosphere. Awarded Derbyshire CAMRA Pub of the Year in 2004, the bar boasts an impressive range of 11 handpumps. Catch the No. 91/92 Derby-Mansfield bus. Denby Pottery is nearby.

Q P

Derby

Alexandra Hotel

203 Siddals Road, DE1 2QE

11-11; 12-3, 7-10.30 Sun

(01332) 293993

Draught Bass; Castle Rock Harvest Pale; York Yorkshire Terrier; guest beers H

Named after the Danish princess who married the Prince of Wales (later Edward VII) in 1863, the Alex was originally the Midland Coffee House. The end wall once advertised Zacharia Smith's Shardlow Ales, but both sign and brewer have slipped into history. Long a Shipstone's house, it subsequently went to Bateman's and latterly to Tynemill, since when it has been a strong champion of small breweries. Two roomed, with a central bar; the pub was the birthplace of Derby CAMRA in 1974.

Q P

Babington Arms

11-13 Babington Lane, DE1 1TA (off St Peter's St)

11-11; 12-10.30 Sun

(01332) 383647

Beer range varies H

One of the best Wetherspoon's houses in the country, showcasing Wyre Piddle beers, plus an amazing range of guests from its 14 handpumps, with regular themed brewery weekends. Originally a furniture store, now fronted with a verandah for fair-weather drinking, the pub stands in the former grounds of Babington House. The first performance of Bram Stoker's Dracula was given in the neighbouring Grand Theatre in 1924. It was local CAMRA City Pub of the Year 2005.

Q

Bishop Blaise

114 Friargate, DE1 1EX

11 (12 Sun)-midnight

(01332) 297065

Draught Bass; Burton Bridge Bitter; Oakham JHB, Bishops Farewell; Whim Hartington IPA; guest beers H

Near the town centre on one of Derby's older streets, now a modernised cafe bar quarter, the former Friargate pub offers a good range of real ales. The stylish venue includes comfortable sofas, piped music and an outdoor patio drinking area. This Victorian tavern replaced the Sun, a much older timber-framed inn, and lies almost opposite the now-defunct church where Dr Samuel Johnson married Tetty Porter in 1735.

P

Brunswick Inn

1 Railway Terrace, DE1 2RU

11-11; 12-10.30 Sun

(01332) 290677

Second Brew, Railway Porter, Triple Gold, Father Mike's, Rambo; H guest beers G/H

Originally built as the centrepiece of a railway village, the building was closed in 1974 and fell into disrepair. Eventually rescued and restored, it opened as Derby's first multiple real ale house some 14 years later. A purpose-built brewery was added and it rapidly became one of the best-known free houses in the country before being sold to Everards in 2002. Things remain unchanged however and the pub was crowned Local CAMRA City Pub of the Year 2004.

Q

Crompton Tavern

45 Crompton Street, DE1 1NX

11-11; 12-10.30 Sun

(01332) 733629

Marston's Pedigree; Taylor Landlord; guest beers H

Tucked away in a cul-de-sac off Green Lane and picked out at night by a fringe of fairy lights, the former Queen's Hotel was originally a guest house for visiting thespians at the nearby Grand Theatre. Two doors open on to different sides of the same U-shaped room, with lower level wings on each side of a central bar. The walls frequently double as a gallery for local artists. A pleasant rear garden provides a welcome fair-weather haven.

Falstaff

74 Silverhill Road, Normanton, DE23 6UJ

12-11; 12-10.30 Sun

(01332) 342902

Falstaff 3 Faze, Phoenix, Smiling Assassin, seasonal beers; guest beers H

Known locally as 'the Folly' and reputedly haunted, this former Allied pub was originally a latter-day coaching inn before the surrounding area was built up, closing it in. Now free, the re-opening of its on-site brewery has made it the

best real ale house in Normanton. The curved bar is flanked on one side by a small lounge, with a real fire in winter, and on the other by a games room with occasional entertainment. Not posh, but a real local.
⛬Q❀⊟♣⚟

Flowerpot

23-25 King Street, DE1 3DZ

⏲ 11-11; 12-10.30 Sun

☎ (01332) 204955

Draught Bass; Ⓖ Marston's Pedigree; Whim Arbor Light, Hartington Bitter, IPA; Ⓗ guest beers Ⓖ/Ⓗ

Just up from the cathedral and round Clockhouse Corner, this is one of the pubs that spearheaded Derby's free trade expansion in the 1990s to become a virtual showcase for small breweries. Much extended from its original premises, it reaches far back from the small, roadside frontage and divides into several interlinking rooms. The furthest provides the stage for a lively, ongoing gig scene and another houses a glass cellar wall, revealing row upon row of stillaged firkins. Q❀◑⊟♿●

Furnace Inn ✔

9 Duke Street, DE1 3BX

⏲ 11-11; 12-3, 6.30-10.30 Sun

Hardys & Hansons Mild, Bitter, Olde Trip, seasonal beers Ⓗ

Just off St Mary's Bridge with its 15th-century chapel, the pub stands on the west bank of the Derwent at the edge of Darley Park. The name preserves its close connection with Handyside's Britannia foundry of which it was once part. Although opened out, it retains distinct drinking areas around a central bar. Scenes of bygone Derby adorn the walls and bar top. A bustling community local, it provides a handy watering-hole for riverside cyclists and walkers. ❀♿♣P

Olde Dolphin Inne ☆ ✔

5A Queen Street, DE1 3DL

⏲ 10.30-11; 12-10.30 Sun

☎ (01332) 267711

Adnams Bitter; Draught Bass; Black Sheep Best Bitter; Caledonian Deuchars IPA; Greene King Abbot; guest beers Ⓗ

Standing below the great gothic tower of the cathedral, the timber-framed Dolphin is Derby's most picturesque and oldest surviving pub, although much restored latterly. The beamed interior divides into bar, upper and lower lounges, snug and an upstairs steak bar, each with its own character. Reputedly haunted, regular themed evenings are supplemented by an annual beer festival in July, which spreads out on to a splendid, raised rear patio. It is a real gem and not to be missed.
⛬Q❀◑⊟♿P⚟

Rowditch Inn

246 Uttoxeter New Road, DE22 3LL

⏲ 12-2 (not Mon-Thu), 7-11; 12-2, 7-10.30 Sun

☎ (01332) 343123

Hardys & Hansons Bitter, Olde Trip, seasonal beers; Marston's Pedigree; guest beers Ⓗ

The pub stands on the borough's ancient boundary, once marked by a defensive dyke or rough ditch (hence Rowditch). A plain-fronted, warmly welcoming roadside pub, its unexpectedly deep interior divides into two drinking areas and a small snug. A downstairs cellar bar opens occasionally, and the long rear garden is a positive haven in warmer weather. An ever-changing range of guest ales is borne out by a large collection of pump clips which adorns the walls of the bar area.
⛬❀♣⚟

Smithfield

Meadow Road, DE1 2BH

⏲ 11-11; 12-10.30 Sun

(01332) 370429 website: www.thesmithfield.co.uk

Burton Bridge Top Dog Stout; Oakham JHB, Bishops Farewell; Phoenix Arizona; Whim Hartington IPA; guest beers Ⓗ

Bow-fronted riverside pub built to serve the cattle market, which has since moved to a new site, leaving the Smithy in a bit of a backwater. A long, basic bar is flanked on one side by a games/TV room that admits children until 9pm, and on the other by a cosy lounge with stone fireplace and old settles, overlooking a pleasant riverside patio. Exceptional beer helped earn the pub local CAMRA's Pub of the Year award in 2003. ⛬⛴❀◑⊟♣P

Station Inn ✔

12 Midland Road, DE1 2SN

⏲ 11.30-2.30, 5 (7 Sat)-11; 11.30-11 Fri; 12-3, 7-10.30 Sun

☎ (01332) 608014

Draught Bass; Ⓖ Black Sheep Best Bitter; Caledonian Deuchars IPA; guest beers Ⓗ

Elaborate frontage and stained glass apart, this is a modest pub, named after the Midland Railway's classical station nearby, which was needlessly swept away in 1983 to be replaced by the present uninspiring edifice. A traditional bar, with panelled counter, cast iron footrail and quarry-tiled floor, it is flanked by a games area to the right and a large lounge to the rear which acts as a dining area and function room. Many cellar awards attest to the skills of the licensee.
◑⊟♿⚌♣▯

Earl Sterndale

Quiet Woman

SK17 9SL (off B5053)

⏲ 12-3.30, 7-11; 12-3.30, 7-10.30 Sun

☎ (01298) 83211

Banks's Mansfield Dark; Marston's Burton Bitter, Pedigree; guest beers Ⓗ

The epitome of the rural village inn, this totally unspoilt and charming pub appears to have been caught in a time warp. Hard to find in the idyllic setting of the Peak District National Park, efforts to track it down will be amply rewarded with a great pint and settles around the fire. It is popular with walkers, who stock up on the local eggs and cheese on sale. A folk club is hosted on Sunday. Why the Quiet Woman? The answer is on the pub sign outside.
⛬Q⛴❀◑⛺♣P

Fenny Bentley

Bentley Brook Inn

DE6 1LF (on A515)

⏲ 11-11; 12-10.30 Sun

☎ (01335) 350278 website: www.bentleybrookinn.co.uk

Leatherbritches Goldings, Ashbourne Ale, Hairy Helmet, Bespoke; Marston's Pedigree; guest beers
Just inside the National Park and set back off the main road, this attractive inn is home to Leatherbritches Brewery, an award-winning restaurant, a smokehouse, a Victorian kitchen garden, a bakery and a shop selling local produce, plants and bottled real ales. The annual spring bank holiday Peak Booze and Blues festival, featuring over 150 beers, is held in a large marquee in its extensive grounds, with camping facilities. With fine views and superb facilities the pub is the ideal base for Derbyshire's major tourist attractions.

Glossop

Crown Inn
142 Victoria Street, SK13 8HY
5-11; 11.30-11 Fri & Sat; 12-10.30 Sun
(01457) 862824
Samuel Smith OBB
A fine example of a pub serving the community, this friendly, corner, terraced local is on the Hayfield Road out of the town. Built in 1846, it has been a Sam Smith's house since 1977 – the only one in the entire High Peak area. An attractive central bar serves two side snugs (one no-smoking), and a sizeable pool/games room. Old pictures of Glossop and prints of local country scenes add to a traditional pub atmosphere. Its beer prices are by far the cheapest in the area.

Friendship
3 Arundel Street, SK13 7AB
4 (3 Fri)-11; 12-11 Sat; 12-3, 7-10.30 Sun
(01457) 855277
website: www.thefriendship.co.uk
Robinson's Unicorn, Hatters, seasonal beers
Street-corner local with an open-plan lounge and a rear tap room, which retains its 1950s look through ongoing sympathetic refurbishment. It is popular with spectators of Glossop's cricket and football clubs, which are both nearby. A secluded and well-stocked garden is open to children until 8pm. A choice of 30-plus malt whiskies complements the well-kept ales. Over the front door is one of the diminishing number of the brewery's impressive lamps dating from around 1900.

Old Gloveworks
Unit 1 Riverside Mill, George Street, SK13 8AY
12-11 (not Mon-Wed); 12-10.30 Sun
(01457) 858432
website: www.thegloveworksglossop.com
Beer range varies
This converted mill building, which formerly manufactured gloves, is completely free of tie, with six ever-changing guest ales from micro-breweries and regionals far and wide. A roof terrace and front patio give views of Glossop Brook and Harehills Park. There is a late licence on Friday and Saturday, with no admittance after 10.45pm, and a lower age limit of 25, although children are allowed in the daytime at the landlord's discretion. Entertainment includes discos (Fri & Sat) and a cabaret on Sunday. Bar snacks are available 12-2pm. An upstairs function room is available to hire.

Star Inn Ale House
2 Howard Street, SK13 7DD
12 (11 Fri & Sat)-11; 12-10.30 Sun
(01457) 853072
Beer range varies
Highly regarded by locals and the first and last stop off for visitors by public transport – bus and train termini are within yards of the door. Now run by long-standing CAMRA members, the pub offers a choice of two or more real ciders alongside the six handpumps that dispense beers from local breweries such as Shaws, Pictish and Phoenix. Pictures of bygone Glossop, wood floors and a tap room served by a hatch add to the atmosphere.

Great Hucklow

Queen Anne Inn
Main Road, SK17 8RF
12-2.30 (not Tue), 6.30 (6 Fri)-11; 12-3, 6-11 Sat; 12-3, 7-10.30 Sun
(01298) 871246
website: www.thequeenanne.net
Marston's Burton Bitter; guest beers
The only pub in the village, this was an ale house as early as 1577, but was granted a licence in 1704 and has recently celebrated its tercentenary. The village thrived on lead mining in the 18th century and was also on a salt route from Cheshire to Yorkshire. The pub has low ceilings, beams and brasses, and a high backed settle. Pets and walkers are welcome. The guest beers often come from the Storm Brewery. The pub is closed all day Monday between New Year and Easter.

Hathersage

Little John Hotel
Station Road, S32 1DD
12-11; 12-10.30 Sun
(01433) 650225
Beer range varies
Popular, family-run free house serving four regularly changing beers from micro-breweries. Food is home cooked and portions are generous; meals are served all day Saturday and Sunday. There are four seating areas: a lounge, a bar with bar billiards, a family area and a function room, all smartly furnished. Visitors are accommodated in hotel rooms and holiday cottages. Folk singers travel by train from Manchester on the second Saturday of each month to perform in the pub.

Hayfield

Kinder Lodge
10 New Mills Road, SK22 2JE
12-11; 12-10.30 Sun
(01663) 743613
website: www.kinderlodge.hi-peak.net
Taylor Best Bitter; guest beers
Stone pub close to the village centre, which blends in naturally with its Peak District

environment. Formerly known as the Railway, its open plan interior allows for a separate games area. Busy and comfortable, it is a popular and well-used pub by locals and visitors. Situated at the end of the Sett Valley trail (the route of the former New Mills-Hayfield railway), it is well placed for walkers and cyclists. ❀⇌◑♣

Royal Hotel

Market Street, SK22 2EP

✪ 11-11; 12-10.30 Sun

☎ (01663) 742721

Boddingtons Bitter; Hydes Bitter; guest beers Ⓗ

A former vicarage, this imposing stone pub stands near the church and cricket ground in an attractive Peak District village. In front of the pub, the River Sett flows down from Kinder Scout. The traditional interior boasts original oak panels and pews that create a relaxing atmosphere, further enhanced by real fires in winter. A restaurant and function room complete the facilities. There is an annual beer festival in early October. ♔Q❀⇌◑◐♿▲P⁄

Holbrook

Dead Poets Inn

38 Chapel Street, DE56 0TQ

✪ 12-2.30, 5-11; 12-11 Fri & Sat; 12-10.30 Sun

☎ (01332) 780301

Greene King Abbot; Marston's Pedigree; guest beers Ⓖ/Ⓗ

Built in 1800 and formerly known as the Cross Keys, the pub has undergone a remarkable transformation in recent times to create an inn with a real medieval feel. Its two rooms contain high-backed pews, stone-flagged floors, low lighting, a real fire and inglenook. Now an Everards house, it was re-named because its former owner believed that many of our famous poets gained inspiration for their work from atmospheric taverns such as this; poetry readings are held on the first Tuesday of the month. Catch the R71 Derby-Belper bus.
♔Q❀◑♣●P

Holymoorside

Lamb Inn

16 Loads Road, S42 7EU

✪ 12-3 (not Mon-Fri), 7-11; 12-3, 7-10.30 Sun

☎ (01246) 566167

Adnams Bitter; Fuller's London Pride; John Smith's Bitter; guest beers Ⓗ

Cosy and immaculate local in a village on the edge of the Peak District National Park, close to Chesterfield. This proud holder of numerous local CAMRA awards boasts up to seven ales on the bar, three ever changing – quite an achievement for a small pub. A roaring fire welcomes in winter, while the pleasant outdoor drinking area is perfect for summer evenings. Note that lunchtime opening is restricted to weekends and bank holidays.
♔Q❀♣P

Hope

Cheshire Cheese

Edale Road, S33 6ZF

✪ 12-3, 6-11; 12-11 Sat; 12-4, 6-10.30 Sun

☎ (01433) 620381 website: www.cheshire-cheese.net

Black Sheep Best Bitter; Blackpool Bitter; Jennings Ward's Best Bitter; guest beers Ⓗ

Within this 16th-century free house are three seating areas furnished with upholstered chairs and benches; the lower section becomes a restaurant at mealtimes. Food is served all day on Sunday. Guest beers are supplied by Archers, Cottage and Wentworth, among others. Children are welcome, except in the immediate vicinity of the bar. The accommodation has been extended – three bedrooms are available. Take care outside: the car park is small and the road narrow. ♔Q❀⇌◑◐▲P⁄

Horsley Woodhouse

Old Oak Inn

176 Main Street, DE7 6AW (on A609)

✪ 5 (4 Fri)-11; 12-11 Sat; 12-10.30 Sun

☎ (01332) 881299

Leadmill range; guest beers Ⓗ

Once a farmhouse, the Old Oak was under threat of demolition when it was acquired and renovated by the Denby-based Leadmill Brewery in 2003. Four interconnected rooms and a courtyard provide a variety of drinking spaces with real fires and hanging hops giving the pub a genuine homely atmosphere. The house beer, Old Oak, is brewed by Leadmill. Eight handpumps, occasional beer festivals and live music help to make it another example of a recent, successful village pub revival. The Derby-Heanor No. 125 bus stops right outside (daytime). ♔Q❀♣●P⁄◻

Hulland Ward

Black Horse Inn

DE6 3EE (on A517)

✪ 12-2.30, 6-11; 12-3, 7-10.30 Sun

☎ (01335) 370206

Beer range varies Ⓗ

This traditional, 300-year-old country inn stands in an elevated village, in some of the most picturesque country outside the Peak, close to Carsington Water. Its split-level, multi-roomed drinking area, with low beamed ceilings and quarry-tiled floors, is served by a central bar, offering rotating guest ales. An extensive bar menu is complemented by a popular Sunday carvery in the restaurant. Some guest rooms boast four-poster beds. Catch the No. 109 Derby-Ashbourne bus. ❀⇌◑◐♣P⁄

Nag's Head

Main Road, DE6 3EF (on A517)

✪ 12-3, 5-11; 12-11 Fri & Sat; 12-10.30 Sun

☎ (01335) 372865

Draught Bass; Caledonian Deuchars IPA; Marston's Pedigree; guest beers Ⓗ

Smart, bay-fronted roadhouse at the heart of a long, straggling village. Open-plan inside, it has distinct drinking areas either side of a central U-shaped bar. A bustling and lively community local that caters for all age groups, there is a side room towards the rear housing pool and Sky Sports TV. The licensees have transformed the pub with the introduction of guest beers and, together with its near neighbour the Black Horse, have made the village an exceptional place to drink.
☋❀◑◐♿♣P

Ilkeston

Dewdrop

24 Station Street, DE7 5TE

12-2.30 (4 Sat), 7-11; 12-4, 7-10.30 Sun

(0115) 932 9684

Draught Bass; Taylor Best Bitter; guest beers H

This unspoilt local retains the original lobby from its Middleton Hotel days, where inventor of the 'bouncing bomb' Barnes Wallis stayed during WWII. The bar has a pool table and a free juke box, while the no-smoking snug and the lounge both feature real fires. Guest beers are usually from local micro-breweries including Mallard, Oakham and Glentworth. Various cobs, including a hot black pudding filling, are available at all times. The No. 27 bus passes nearby. This was local CAMRA Pub of the Year for 2004 and 2005.

Ilford Club

93 Station Road, DE7 5LJ (on A6096)

2-5.30 (not Mon-Fri), 7.30 (7 Sat)-11; 12-10.30 Sun

(0115) 930 5789

Beer range varies H

Situated by the Erewash Canal with boat moorings nearby, this is a private club but access can be gained by showing a CAMRA membership card or a copy of the Good Beer Guide. Whim beers are usually prominent but beers from other micros are also stocked. Filled cobs are sold at weekends. Children are allowed on Saturday and Sunday lunchtimes but must be supervised by parents at all times. Should you wish to play snooker or any of the gaming machines, membership is £1.

Needlemakers' Arms

Kensington Street, DE7 5NY (off A6007)

6.30-11; 12-11 Fri & Sat; 12-10.30 Sun

(0115) 932 2561

Caledonian Deuchars IPA; guest beers H/G

Created by knocking two former workers' cottages into one, this traditional pub, with a quarry-tiled floor, is just a 10-minute walk from the town centre. The beer range usually consists of frequently-changing guest beers on handpump, plus beers jugged from the cellar. There is a quiet lounge area to one side, with a family area and a pool room to the rear. Traditional pub games are also popular. Local bus services stop right outside. The pub gets its name from the former needlemaking factory nearby.

Q P

Spanish Bar

76 South Street, DE7 5QJ

11-11; 12-10.30 Sun

(0115) 930 8666

Whim Hartington IPA; guest beer H

A warm welcome awaits at this small, bustling café-style bar, which features a changing guest beer, a brew from Mallard and a small selection of bottled Belgian beers. Tuesday is quiz night and a regulars' card school is held on Sunday lunchtimes, with cheese sandwiches and pickles on the bar for customers to enjoy. Comfortable armchairs surround a log-burning fire in winter. The bar is easily accessible to disabled customers but a key to the WC must be requested from the bar staff. Outside there is a small garden next to the skittle alley.

Ingleby

John Thompson Inn

Ingleby Lane, DE73 1HW (off A514)

10.30-2.30, 5-11; 12-2, 7-10.30 Sun

(01332) 862469

John Thompson JTS Bitter, Porter, Summer Gold; Tetley Burton Ale H

John Thompson is the former fruit grower who revived Derbyshire's brewing industry in 1977, having made his family home into a highly individual pub eight years earlier. Comprising a large, comfortable lounge with smaller rooms opening off, the pub is rich in local interest, displaying many prints and watercolours. Close to the banks of the River Trent, in open country just outside the village, it also has a spacious patio and large garden with the brewery housed in outbuildings.

P

Kirk Ireton

Barley Mow ☆

Main Street, DE6 3JP (off B5023)

12-2, 7-11; 12-2, 7-10.30 Sun

(01335) 370306

Hook Norton Old Hooky; Marston's Pedigree; Whim Hartington IPA; guest beers G

Set in an olde-worlde village overlooking the Ecclesbourne Valley, this traditional gabled Jacobean building was originally a farmhouse. Several interconnecting rooms of different sizes and character have low, beamed ceilings, mullioned windows, slate-topped tables, well-worn woodwork and open fires set in stone fireplaces. A small serving hatch reveals a stillage with beer dispensed straight from the cask. There are few pubs remaining like this rural gem. Q P

Litton

Red Lion

Main Street, SK17 8QU

12-3, 6-11; 12-11 Fri & Sat; 12-10.30 Sun

(01298) 871458

Black Sheep Best Bitter; Oakwell Barnsley Bitter; Shepherd Neame Spitfire; guest beer H

This is the only pub in the village and a hive of local activity. It dates from the 17th century and faces the village green, complete with stocks. There are three small rooms, two of which are separated by an enormous fireplace. You can take a look at the collection of guide books of local interest over your pint. On Monday evenings, monthly in winter and more frequently at other times, there is a quiz. Walkers and dogs are welcome. There are three guest bedrooms. No meals are served on Sunday evening. Q P

Long Eaton

Hole in the Wall

6 Regent Street, NG10 1JX

10.30-11; 12-10.30 Sun

(0115) 973 4920

Draught Bass; guest beers Ⓗ
The only free house in Long Eaton offers an excellent range of beers, mostly from micro-breweries around the country. Situated in a side street away from the main centre of town, this 100-year old local has two rooms: a raised, quiet lounge and the main bar with a pool table. Breweriana adorns both rooms along with local CAMRA awards. Outside there is an enclosed skittle alley and barbecue area. Use the pay and display car park opposite. ❀⊟♣

Longshaw

Grouse Inn

S11 7TZ (on A625)
✪ 12-3, 6-11; 12-11 Sat; 12-10.30 Sun
☎ (01433) 630423
Banks's Bitter; Caledonian Deuchars IPA; Marston's Pedigree; guest beers Ⓗ
A free house in the same family since 1965, with a gradually improving beer range. Although it stands in isolation on a bleak moorland, it is on a main road crossing from Sheffield into the Derwent Valley and easily accessible for motorists. It is also popular with walkers enjoying the local countryside. There is a large lounge at the front and a smaller bar and conservatory at the rear. The walls are decorated with fine colour photographs of local gritstone features, taken with the weather at its best. No evening meals are served on Monday. ♔Q⛭❀◐◑♣P▯

Lullington

Colvile Arms

Main Street, DE12 8EG
✪ 12-2 (not Mon-Fri), 6-11; 12-3, 7-10.30 Sun
☎ (01827) 373212
Draught Bass; Marston's Pedigree; guest beer Ⓗ
Popular 18th-century free house, leased from the Lullington Estate, at the heart of an attractive hamlet at the southern tip of the county. The public bar comprises an adjoining hallway and snug, each featuring high-backed settles with wood panelling. The bar and a comfortable lounge are situated on opposite sides of a central serving area. A second lounge/function room overlooks the garden and bowling green. Two quiz teams and the local cricket and football teams meet here, provoking lively conversation. ❀⊟♣P

Makeney

Holly Bush Inn

Holly Bush Lane, DE56 0RX OS352447
✪ 12-3, 5-11; 12-11 Fri & Sat; 12-10.30 Sun
☎ (01332) 841729
Greene King Ruddles County; Ⓗ **Marston's Pedigree;** Ⓖ **guest beers** Ⓗ/Ⓖ
Grade II listed, and once a farmhouse with a brewery on the Strutt Estate, this late 17th-century, former Offilers' house positively oozes character. It stood on the Derby turnpike before the Strutts opened the valley route in 1818; Dick Turpin is known to have drunk here. The enclosed wooden snug is sandwiched between two bars. Up to five guest beers are offered, supplemented by regular beer festivals. It is a short 10 minute walk from the R61-64 Derby-Belper bus route. ♔Q⛭❀⊟P

Melbourne

Blue Bell

53 Church Street, DE73 1EJ
✪ 11-11; 12-10.30 Sun
☎ (01332) 865764
Shardlow Special Bitter, Golden Hop, Reverend Eaton's Ale, seasonal beers; guest beers (occasional) Ⓗ
In the prime spot close to the hall and Norman church, in a well-pubbed locality, the Blue Bell stands out as the Shardlow Brewery tap, although it is several miles from the brewery itself. The bar of this old country pub bears a sporting emphasis, while the lounge opens on to a patio with barbecue. Run on traditional lines with seasonal beers and a house mild, occasional guests are available too. The regular Derby-Swadlincote bus No. 69/69A stops nearby. ❀⛟◐◑⊟▲♣

Monsal Head

Monsal Head Hotel

DE45 1NL (on B6465)
✪ 11.30-11; 12-10.30 Sun
☎ (01629) 640250 website: www.monsalhead.com
Abbeydale Moonshine, Absolution; Taylor Landlord; Theakston Best Bitter, Old Peculier; Whim Hartington Bitter; guest beer Ⓗ
Real ale is served mainly in the Stables Bar, which lies behind the main hotel. This building survives from an earlier inn on the same spot, which did not live into the railway age when the Derby to Manchester line was driven through the limestone gorge below. The Stables Bar retains its original floor and vestiges of individual stalls; it has a warm stove and can get crowded, especially when the weather does not allow the many visitors to spill outside. The house beer, Monsal Bitter, is from Lloyds. Meals are served all day. ♔Q❀⛟◐◑▲♣P

Morley Smithy

Three Horseshoes

Main Road, DE7 6DF (on A608)
✪ 11.30-11; 12-10.30 Sun
☎ (01332) 834395
Marston's Pedigree, seasonal beers; guest beers Ⓗ
An attractive, white painted, rural pub on the main Derby-Heanor road and H1 bus route. Modestly modernised inside, its long, narrow, single room is divided by an archway separating a food-oriented lounge from the plainer, quarry-tiled bar with open fire and fake beams. An old photo shows the original thatched inn that also served as a smithy, which was pulled down around 1910. Real farm eggs can be bought at the bar. No meals are served on Sunday evening. ♔Q❀◐◑♿♣P

New Mills

Pack Horse Inn

Mellor Road, SK22 4QQ
✪ 12-3, 5-11; 12-11 Sat; 12-10.30 Sun
☎ (01663) 742365

website: www.packhorseinn.co.uk
Tetley Bitter; guest beers Ⓗ
Whether reaching the pub by car or a stiff uphill walk from New Mills, all visitors will agree that it is well worth the effort. The enterprising owners choose their own guest beers and do so with the touch of connoisseurs. A sympathetically designed stone extension has recently added more guest bedrooms and a new dining room – both are recommended.
♛Q❀⇄◑♿P

New Whittington

Wellington

162 High Street, S43 2AN
✪ 11-11; 12-4, 7-10.30 Sun
☎ (01246) 450879
Camerons Strongarm; Marston's Pedigree; guest beers Ⓗ
Within easy reach of Chesterfield (buses 25 and 50 regularly stop outside), this friendly two-roomed community local now offers a choice of up to six real ales and occasional mini beer festivals. Good value bar meals (including daily specials and vegetarian options) are served at lunchtime and early evening Monday-Saturday, and Sunday lunch. Quizzes on Wednesday and Sunday, a free pool table at weekends and twice monthly live entertainment complete the line-up at this local CAMRA award-winner.
❀◑⊟♿♣P⊡

Oakerthorpe

Anchor Inn

DE55 7LP (on B6013)
✪ 12-3, 6.30-11; 12-11 Sat; 12-10.30 Sun
(01773) 833575
Cropton Two Pints, Honey Gold, Monkmans Slaughter, seasonal beers Ⓗ
This mid 18th-century bay fronted building is marked at the roadside by a huge 18ft dredger's anchor. Long and rambling inside, it has four distinct areas separated by stonework archways. A stone wall surrounding the fireplace and beams believed to originate from ship's timbers remain from the pub's original features. Beers are dispensed by an unusual reverse swan-neck handpull system. The Castle Hill Roman camp fortlet is just a short walk away. No evening meals are served on Sunday or Monday.
Q☕❀◑⊟♿P⊬

Ockbrook

Royal Oak

55 Green Lane, DE72 3SE (off A52)
✪ 11.30-2.30 (3 Sat), 6-11; 12-3, 7-10.30 Sun
☎ (01332) 662378
Draught Bass; guest beers Ⓗ
Set back from the road across a cobbled courtyard, this fine pub, local CAMRA Country Pub of the Year 2003, was the regional award winner in 2000. In the same family since coronation year and little changed since then, each of the five rooms has its own distinctive character and clientele. Three ever-changing guest beers are supplemented by an annual beer festival in October. Excellent home-cooked food is served. Separate gardens cater for adults and families.
Catch the No.9 bus from Derby, daytime only.
Q❀◑♿♣P⊬

Old Brampton

George & Dragon

Main Road, S42 7JG OS336718
✪ 12-4, 7-11.30 Mon; 12-11 Tue-Sat; 12-10.30 Sun
☎ (01246) 567826
Adnams Bitter; Marston's Pedigree; guest beers Ⓗ
Situated opposite the medieval church with its 63-minute clock face, this 200-year-old pub has intriguing ghost stories to tell. A haven for walkers, it is within easy reach of the Peak Moors, woodland and local reservoir. Dogs are welcome. The landlady's enthusiasm for real ale results in frequent weekend festivals. Weston's Old Rosie cider and half a dozen malt whiskies complement the changing guest beers. There is regular live music, a Tuesday quiz and entertainment on Saturday evening.
♛❀▲●P⊡

Over Haddon

Lathkil Hotel

School Lane, DE45 1JE (off B5055) OS216665
✪ 11.30-3, 6.30-11; 11.30-11 Sat; 12-10.30 Sun
☎ (01629) 812501
website: www.lathkil.co.uk
Marston's Pedigree; Wells Bombardier; Whim Hartington Bitter; guest beers Ⓗ
Free house in an idyllic setting affording superb views over Lathkill Dale nature reserve. A welcoming atmosphere awaits with real fires, an oak-panelled bar and wooden settles. Bar meals are available at lunchtime, the restaurant is open in the evening (booking recommended). A family room is available at lunchtime. A good choice of real ales is on offer, including two guests. Popular with walkers, visitors and locals alike, this is a pub not to be missed by lovers of real ale. ♛Q☕❀⇄◑♣P⊡

Ripley

George Inn

20 Lowes Hill, DE5 3DW
✪ 4 (12 Fri & Sat)-11; 12-10.30 Sun
☎ (01773) 748719
Banks's Mansfield Dark, Cask; Sarah Hughes Dark Ruby; Whim Hartington IPA; guest beers Ⓗ
Back-street local, half a mile from the busy town centre. Owned by several breweries over the years, the pub is now free of tie and the licensees serve a large range of real ales and ciders. The last alterations rendered it almost open-plan but with distinct drinking spaces and a clear division between games and lounge areas. A skittle alley is outside. Sir Barnes Wallis, famous for the bouncing bomb, was born nearby and the Midland Railway Centre lies just down the road at Butterley.
Q⊟♣●P

Pear Tree Inn

4 Derby Road, DE5 3HR
✪ 11-11; 12-10.30 Sun
☎ (01773) 742468
Hardys & Hansons Mild, Bitter, Olde Trip, seasonal beers Ⓗ

Busy, traditional, two-roomed tied house in a well-pubbed town. It is one of the few to stock the full range of the brewery's draught beers, with a long-standing reputation for beer quality. The rear lounge is usually quiet. No sign of the eponymous tree these days though, as the pub is just a few steps away from the market place and buses to most other East Midland towns. From Derby catch the Red Arrow or 91/92 or R62/63 bus.
⛼❀⊟♣P

Sawley

Harrington Arms ✔

392 Tamworth Road, NG10 3AU (on B6540)
11-11; 12-10.30 Sun
☎ (0115) 973 2614
Hardys & Hansons Best Bitter, Olde Trip, seasonal beers Ⓗ
Standing near the River Trent and Trent & Mersey Canal, this former coaching inn is a regular entry in this Guide. Panelled walls, low, beamed ceilings and a wood-burning stove add to the charm of this large roadside pub. The restaurant serves an excellent choice of freshly-cooked international cuisine all day, and there is also a wide range of bar meals. The patio and large garden host a successful and popular August bank holiday beer festival.
⛼❀◐◑⇌(Long Eaton) P

Nag's Head

1 Wilne Road, NG10 3AL (on B6540)
11-11; 1-10.30 Sun
☎ (0115) 973 2983
Banks's Mansfield Cask; Marston's Burton Bitter; Pedigree; guest beers Ⓗ
Early 19th-century, traditional, two-roomed local with a central bar close to the River Trent and Sawley Marina. The present landlord has been resident here for 14 years and is only the fourth incumbent since WWII. The bar is heated by a wood-burning stove during the colder months and the lounge has a homely, comfortable feel. Traditional pub games are played, including long alley skittles. Guest beers are selected from Wolverhampton and Dudley's list and change monthly.
⛼Q❀⊟⇌(Long Eaton) ♣P

Scarcliffe

Horse & Groom

Rotherham Road, S44 6SU (on B6417)
12-11; 12-3, 7-10.30 Sun
☎ (01246) 823152
Draught Bass; Greene King Abbot; Stones Bitter; Tetley Bitter; guest beers Ⓗ
Excellent country pub where the art of conversation is preferred to loud music and slot machines (neither are found here). This past Derbyshire CAMRA Pub of the Year consists of a tap room where pub games are played, and a lounge with a copper-topped bar. Up to six real ales are available as well as an impressive range of malt whiskies. Children are welcome in the covered verandah behind the pub. Accommodation is in three self-catering cottages.
Q❀⇋⊟♿Å♣P

Shirland

Hay Inn ✔

135 Main Road, DE55 6BA
4.30 (6 Mon)-11; 12-3, 6-11 Sat; 12-10.30 Sun
☎ (01773) 835383
Hardys & Hansons Mild, Bitter; guest beers Ⓗ
Traditional local with one room and a central bar, offering a refreshing selection of real ales. Situated on the A61, this previously keg-only pub is now run by long-standing award-winning CAMRA members. Three ever-changing guests include many ales not normally seen in the area. There is also a good choice of Belgian bottled beers and English country wines to enjoy. Well worth seeking out. Å♣●P

Smalley

Bell Inn

35 Main Road, DE7 6EF (on A608)
11.30-3, 5-11; 11-11 Sat; 12-10.30 Sun
☎ (01332) 880635
Adnams Broadside; Mallard Duckling; Oakham JHB; Whim Hartington Bitter, IPA; guest beers Ⓗ
This mid 19th-century inn has three rooms and a large, attractive child-friendly garden. Brewing and other memorabilia adorn the walls. Top quality beer and food helped make the Bell a past local CAMRA Pub of the Year. Situated near Shipley Country Park, it can be reached via the Derby-Heanor H1 bus service, which stops right outside. Accommodation is offered in three flats in a converted stable adjoining the pub.
⛼Q❀⇋◐◑⊟♿P

Smisby

Smisby Arms

Main Street, LE65 2UA
12-3, 6 (5.30 Fri)-11; 12-11 Sat; 12-4, 7-10.30 Sun
☎ (01530) 412677
Marston's Pedigree; guest beers Ⓗ
While parts of this popular village free house are thought to be 350 years old, the pub originates in the 19th century and was formerly called the Nelson Inn. Despite extension and renovation in recent decades, it still retains much of its original character. There is an upper lounge with brick pillars and beamed ceiling, then steps down to the former snug, which is now linked to a new dining room. The pub has a good reputation for food; no meals are served on Sunday evening.
Q⛼❀◐◑P⚟

South Normanton

Clock Inn ✔

107 Market Street, DE55 2AA
11-11; 12-10.30 Sun
☎ (01773) 811396
website: www.theclockinn.co.uk
Everards Tiger; Marston's Bitter; guest beer Ⓗ
A free house with a no-smoking lounge, traditional bar and a beer garden to the rear. CAMRA awards adorn the walls. Customers are attracted by popular lunches (currently served on Sunday only), guest beers (available at the weekend) and the selection of malt whiskies. Also worth looking out for are beer festivals featuring 20 real ales and ciders that are held each May and October. Q☎❀◐⊟♿P⚟

Royal Oak
78 Water Lane, DE55 2EE
11-11; 12-10.30 Sun
☎ (01773) 861337
Greene King Abbot; guest beers Ⓗ
A worthy new entry to this Guide that should not be missed for a number of reasons. These include three well-kept real ales, the selection of bottled beers, occasional real cider and quality whiskies. Quiz nights are held every Thursday and traditional pub games are available. Look out for the collection of ornamental brass around the bar and the famous quotes that adorn the wooden beams. A minibus service is available for parties of six or more. ♨❀◑⊟♣P

South Wingfield

Old Yew Tree
51 Manor Road, DE55 7NH (on B5035)
5-11; 12-3, 6.30-11 Sat; 12-4, 7-10.30 Sun
☎ (01773) 833763
Cottage seasonal beers; Marston's Pedigree; guest beers Ⓗ
A regular Guide entry, this busy, family-run free house is situated near the magnificent remains of the 15th-century Wingfield Manor, destroyed by Cromwell during the Civil War. Guest beers regularly showcase local micro-breweries. Good home-cooked food, including excellent Sunday lunches (no food Sun eve), has drawn people from near and far. The pub has won the Amber Valley Clean Air award in the past. There is limited parking space. ♨❀◑♿▲P⅟

Stanley Common

White Post Inn
237 Belper Road, DE7 6FT (on A609)
11-11; 12-10.30 Sun
☎ (0115) 930 0194
Black Sheep Special; Taylor Landlord; guest beers Ⓗ
This large, white-painted, roadside inn on the main thoroughfare is surrounded by some fine countryside, away from the built-up sprawl. Three interlinking rooms are served by a central bar. One is used as a dining area where good home-cooked food is served. An interesting range of ever-changing guest beers is supplemented by occasional beer festivals, which in summertime spill out on to the pleasant rear garden. Catch the No. 59 Derby-Ilkeston bus, daytime only.
♨Q⊗❀◑⊟♿♣P⅟

Staveley

Speedwell Inn
Lowgates, S43 3TT
6-11; 6-10.30 Sun
☎ (01246) 474665
Townes Speedwell Bitter, Lowgate Light, Staveley Cross, IPA, Staveleyan; guest beer (occasional) Ⓗ
Home of the Townes Brewery since 1998, this unassuming pub is a two-time winner of the local CAMRA Pub of the Year award. Simple and comfortable surroundings provide real ale lovers with a desirable venue. Townes' regular special brews and bottle-conditioned beers feature at the bar. Occasional guest beers are also offered. Bus services 70, 74 (eve only) and 77 from Chesterfield stop near the pub. Q♣⅟

Sutton Cum Duckmanton

Arkwright Arms
Chesterfield Road, S44 5JG
(on A632 between Chesterfield and Bolsover)
11-11; 12-10.30 Sun
☎ (01246) 232053
website: http://thearkers.mysite.wanadoo-members.co.uk
Marston's Pedigree; guest beers Ⓗ
A warm welcome awaits visitors to this mock-Tudor fronted free house. A central horseshoe bar separates the bar and lounge with the dining area towards the rear. The five guest beers are normally from local micro-breweries and change regularly. Beer festivals are held on the Easter and August bank holidays and generate a great atmosphere with an excellent range of ales. Three open fires add to the cosy feel at this great watering-hole, which was local CAMRA Pub of the Year 2004. ♨❀◑⊟♣●P

Swanwick

Steam Packet Inn ✔
Derby Road, DE55 1AB (on B6179)
2 (12 Thu & Fri; 10 Sat)-11; 12-10.30 Sun
☎ (01773) 602172
Adnams Bitter; Jennings Cumberland Ale; guest beers Ⓗ
Land-locked Swanwick does not see many steam packets come or go. And a rumour that the name arose from the use of the pub as a pay office by the steam railway sounds improbable. Situated at the heart of the village, next to the church, this traditional 19th-century inn has not been drastically altered inside. A selection of rotating guest beers is complemented by beer festivals in April and October. Lunches are served Thursday-Sunday, evening meals Wednesday-Saturday. Catch the No 91/92 Derby-Mansfield bus or the Red Arrow.
❀◑⊟♿♣●P

Tideswell

Star
High Street, SK17 8LD
12-11; 12-10.30 Sun
☎ (01298) 872397
Tetley Bitter; guest beers Ⓗ
Traditional village local consisting of three small rooms (one recently made no-smoking) around a central bar. The pub has low ceilings and is smartly furnished and decorated. The opening hours have been extended over recent years. The pub has its own pizza oven, which is in action on Thursday, Friday and Saturday evenings until 10pm. Despite the address, the pub is not on the main road through the village, but up a side street. ⇌◑♿▲♣⅟

Troway

Gate Inn
Main Road, S21 5RU
(from B6056 Snowdon Lane, turn off at Black-a-Moor pub)
12-3, 7-11; 12-3, 7-10.30 Sun
☎ (01246) 413280

Burtonwood Bitter, Top Hat; guest beer Ⓗ
A hidden gem to be found up a narrow country lane in North Derbyshire. Relax and soak up the charm of this small, friendly pub in good walking country on the south side of the Moss Valley. Now in its 11th year under the current tenants, it has featured in this Guide for the past 10. The real ales may be enjoyed beside a real fire in winter or in the award-winning garden in the summer. ♨Q❀⊟♣P⊟

Wardlow Mires

Three Stags Heads ☆
SK17 8RW
✪ 7-11 Fri; 12-11 Sat; 12-10.30 Sun
☎ (01298) 872268
Abbeydale Matins, Absolution Ⓗ
A listed building that is remarkable for its simplicity, the pub features in CAMRA's National Inventory. The small bar is furnished with well-scrubbed tables and settles, gathered round a coal-fired range. A second, larger room is similarly furnished. Black Lurcher, from Abbeydale, is brewed exclusively for this pub (however, the landlord now has three whippets). Real cider is sold occasionally. Fines are levied for using mobile phones. Note limited opening hours and that no meals are served on Friday. ♨Q◑▲♣●P

Whaley Bridge

Dog & Partridge
Buxton Road, Bridgemont, SK23 7NL
✪ 11-3, 5-11; 11-11 Fri & Sat; 12-10.30 Sun
☎ (01663) 732284
Cains Mild; Caledonian Deuchars IPA; Greene King Abbot, Old Speckled Hen; Tetley Bitter Ⓗ
Welcoming pub standing on what was once part of the A6 road prior to construction of the nearby bypass. The location is handy for boaters and walkers as the pub stands adjacent to the Peak Forest Canal. Although open plan it has distinct areas, each with its own coal fire. There is an excellent restaurant and an annual beer festival which is well worth looking out for. ♨Q❀◑⇌♣P

Wirksworth

Royal Oak
North End, DE4 4FG (off B5035)
✪ 8-11; 12-3, 7.30-10.30 Sun
☎ (01629) 823000
Draught Bass; Taylor Landlord; Whim Hartington IPA; guest beer Ⓗ
Excellent, small, ultra-traditional local in a stone terrace near the market place. The bar features some interesting breweriana and old local pictures. Genuinely free, the Oak combines a long-standing reputation for Bass with a choice of guests. Wirksworth (or Wuzzer, as it is affectionately known) is well pubbed and the rest are worthy of a visit too, if staying nearby. The Ecclesbourne Valley railway line should be open during 2006. Catch the No. R61 Derby-Bakewell bus. Q♣

Woodville

Nelson Inn
26 High Street, DE11 7EH (on A511)
✪ 1-4.30, 7-11 (not Mon); 1 (12 Sat)-11 Fri; 12-10.30 Sun
☎ (01283) 216696
Marston's Pedigree; guest beer Ⓗ
This lively locals' pub was once a coaching inn and dates back to the mid-19th century. The public bar features some old photographs of the area, but is now dominated by a large Sky Sports TV screen. There is a smaller, quieter lounge, a games room to the rear, and a recently refurbished function room upstairs. Very much a community pub, it runs several games teams, regular bingo and karaoke evenings, plus the occasional disco.
❀⊟♣P

Youlgreave

George Hotel
Church Street, DE45 1VW
✪ 11-11; 12-10.30 Sun
☎ (01629) 636292
Greene King Old Speckled Hen; John Smith's Bitter; Theakston Mild; guest beer Ⓗ
Situated opposite the church, this traditional and welcoming village pub has three rooms around a central wood-panelled bar. A wide selection of award-winning, home-cooked food is available seven days a week, ranging from bar snacks to main meals (game dishes are a speciality). Accommodation (three en-suite rooms) is available at a reasonable price, making the pub an ideal base for exploring the Derbyshire Dales.
Q❀⇔◑⊟▲♣P

Olde Gate Inn, Brassington

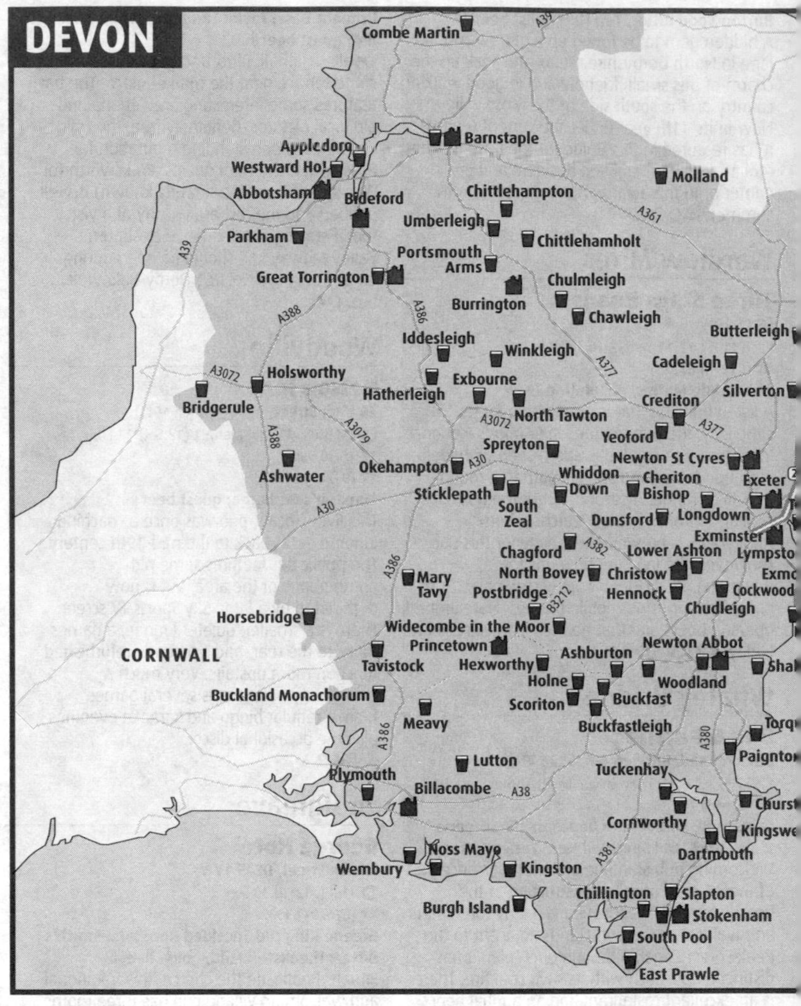

Appledore

Coach & Horses

5 Market Street, EX39 1PW

11-11; 12-10.30 Sun

(01237) 474470

Country Life Old Appledore; Courage Directors; Fuller's London Pride; guest beers H

Attractive and established local in the heart of a pretty maritime village. The pub is quite handy for the local Maritime Museum and passenger ferry to Instow (summer only). Samples of the five beers usually available can be requested. The bar is small but incorporates several seating areas. Winkleigh cider is stocked.

Ashburton

Exeter Inn

26 West Street, TQ13 7DU

11-3, 6-11; 12-3, 7-10.30 Sun

(01364) 652013

Badger Best; Greene King IPA H

Friendly local, and the oldest public house in Ashburton, built in 1131 (with additions in the 17th century) to house the workers that built the nearby church. The inn was used by Sir Francis Drake on his journeys to London. The main room has a rustic, wood-panelled, L-shaped bar with a canopy and two drinking areas. A lounge bar at the rear is served by a small hatch. The drink dispensing area is a disused fireplace edged by two old millstones.

Q

Ashwater

Village Inn

EX21 5EY (off A388, midway between Launceston and Holsworthy)

12-2.30 (3 Sat), 6-11; 12-3, 6-10.30 Sun

(01409) 211200 website: www.villageinnpub.co.uk

Exmoor Ale; Sharp's Doom Bar; guest beers H

Busy pub set on the village green where a well-maintained, Mediterranean-style patio and a conservatory add to its appeal. There is a large car park to the rear. A games room is just one of several drinking areas. On the green is a children's play area. Facilities for disabled patrons are good. Although off the main road, it is easy to find and well worth the effort.

P

Axmouth

Harbour Inn

EX12 4AF

⚙ 11-3, 6-11; 12-3, 7-10.30 Sun

☎ (01297) 20371

Draught Bass; Flowers IPA, Original; Otter Bitter Ⓗ

The tidal part of the River Axe, just around the corner from this old pub, is a well known spot for birdwatchers, and the pub is also near the end of the famous Undercliffe walk from Lyme Regis. The current landlord has been here for 30 years, and the menu usually offers lamb from his farm. The main area features an enormous fireplace, always alight in winter, and there is more dining space beyond the bar.
ᗑQ♉❀◑▲P

Barnstable

Marshals

95 Boutport Street, EX31 1SX

⚙ 11-11; 12-10.30 Sun

☎ (01271) 376633

Draught Bass; Ⓗ **guest beers** Ⓗ/Ⓖ

Typical town pub, situated on one of Barnstaple's main shopping streets, near the Queen's Theatre. A true local, stocking changing guest beers, the pub is popular for lunchtime food – all the meals are home cooked using local ingredients. It is well known for its support of charities, so beware of the fines for using a mobile phone. The pub is on the Tarka Rail Ale Trail. ◑⇌♣●

Reform Inn

Reform Street, Pilton, EX31 1PD

⚙ 11.30-11; 12-10.30 Sun

☎ (01271) 323164

Beer range varies Ⓗ

Well established local at the heart of the Pilton community. Pool and music are played in the larger bar, while the smaller, wood-panelled bar on the right is quieter. The pub frequently hosts live music and runs annual events such as a conker championship and a chutney making competition. It also holds occasional beer festivals, the main one being during Pilton's Green Man festival in July. The beers are from Barum Brewery, located behind the pub.
❀⇌♣●

Bridgerule

Bridge Inn

EX22 7EJ OS274029

⚙ 12-2.30 (not Mon-Fri), 6.30-11; 12-3.30, 6.30-10.30 Sun

☎ (01288) 381316

Flower's Original; Sharp's Own; guest beers Ⓗ

True community pub in a village on the Devon/Cornwall border. The pub is just to the west of the bridge over the Tamar and a few miles from the Cornish coast, making it an ideal escape, and the most westerly pub in North Devon. In winter visitors are greeted by an open fire in the middle of the main bar. The pub boasts its own skittle alley. No evening meals are served Sunday. ᗑ♉❀◑▲♣

Buckfast

Abbey Inn ✔

TQ11 0EA (off A38)

⚙ 11-2.30, 6-11; 11-11 Sat & summer; 12-10.30 Sun

☎ (01364) 642343

INDEPENDENT BREWERIES

Barum Barnstaple
Beer Engine Newton St Cyres
Blackdown Dunkeswell
Branscombe Vale Branscombe
Burrington Burrington
Clearwater Great Torrington
Country Life Abbotsham
Exe Valley Silverton
Jollyboat Bideford
O'Hanlon's Whimple
Otter Luppitt
Princetown Princetown
Scattor Rock Christow
South Hams Stokenham
Summerskills Billacombe
Teignworthy Newton Abbot
Topsham & Exminster Exminster
Warrior Exeter

St Austell Dartmoor Best, Tribute, HSD Ⓗ
Large inn within Dartmoor National Park, close to the famous Buckfast Abbey. The traditionally-furnished oak-panelled bar is spacious, warm and welcoming. The inn benefits from a beautiful setting next to the River Dart; the terrace overlooks the river, and provides a glimpse of the abbey. The large dining room offers an excellent range of food. There are many visitor attractions in the vicinity.
Q P

Buckfastleigh

White Hart Inn

2 Plymouth Road, TQ11 0DA (near top of main st)
12-11; 12-10.30 Sun
(01364) 642337
Princetown Jail Ale; guest beers Ⓗ
Friendly, town-centre pub: a single, open-plan bar, plus a dining area to the left of the entrance. Down the alleyway to the rear of the pub is a courtyard that provides extra seating and a barbecue area in summer. A room at the rear is used for special functions. The pub serves a house beer, White Hart Best Bitter, brewed by Teignworthy.

Buckland Monachorum

Drake Manor Inn

The Village, PL20 7NA
11-2.30, 6.30-11; 12-3, 7-10.30 Sun
(01822) 853892 website: www.drakemanorinn.co.uk
Courage Best Bitter; Greene King Abbot; Sharp's Doom Bar Ⓗ
Cosy, 16th-century, two-bar pub in a small Dartmoor village. The public bar is where the locals can be found enjoying the good beer, while the second bar is used for food, which is based on local produce as far as possible. A small cellar room behind the bar admits children. A stream runs through the peaceful garden and the pub stands next to the church in the village centre. Parking is limited.
Q P

Burgh Island (Bigbury)

Pilchard Inn

TQ7 4BG (walk from Bigbury car park, or take half-hourly sea tractor at high tide)
11.30-11; 12.30-10.30 Sun
(01548) 810514
Beer range varies Ⓗ
This ancient, atmospheric and supposedly haunted pub is located on a tidal island. There are always three ales on tap, with the emphasis on West Country beers. Heron Valley cider is always stocked. Evening meals are served Thursday-Saturday. Listen out for the pre-1960s background music and Oscar the African Grey parrot in the bar where children are admitted. Please note this is a no-smoking pub.
Q

Butterleigh

Butterleigh Inn

EX15 1PN
12-2.30, 6-11; 12-3, 7-10.30 Sun
(01884) 855407 website: www.butterleighinn.co.uk
Butcombe Bitter; Cotleigh Tawny; guest beers Ⓗ
Great pub in a charming rural location. This splendid 400-year-old Devon cob building is full of character. There is a main bar and lounge with a modern but sympathetically-styled dining room. The open fire in the bar and the woodburner in the lounge make this a warm, welcoming place in winter. In summer, you can sit in the attractive, secluded garden and enjoy the views of the surrounding rolling hills. The food (not served Sun eve) is recommended.
Q P

Cadeleigh

Cadeleigh Arms

EX16 8HP
11-11; 12-10.30 Sun
(01884) 855238
Otter Bitter; guest beers Ⓗ
Real country pub in a pleasant setting, close to National Trust ancient woodland and watermeadows, popular with walkers. Log fires and stone-flagged floors entice you in on a dark, wet winter evening. Skittles, pool and darts are played here. On summer days, enjoy the wonderful views from the garden. The house beer is from Sharp's Brewery.
Q P

Chagford

Ring O' Bells

44 The Square, TQ13 3AH
11-3, 5-11; 12-3, 5-10.30 Sun
(01647) 432466 website: www.ringobellschagford.co.uk
Butcombe Bitter; Exmoor Ale; guest beer Ⓗ
This 400-year-old country inn, a former courthouse, is full of character: a huge fireplace, exposed beams and comfortable furnishings. An extensive and reasonably-priced wine list accompanies a daily changing menu of local produce. A good selection of bottled beers is stocked; the cider varies. The main bar and lounge are supplemented by a dining area and lawned courtyard at the rear. Accommodation is available – breakfasts are served when the pub opens at 8.30am. Q

Sandy Park Inn

Sandy Park, TQ13 8JW (on A382, Moretonhampstead-Whiddon Down road)
12 (5.30 Mon)-11; 12-10.30 Sun
(01647) 433267
Otter Ale; St Austell Tribute; guest beer Ⓗ
Thatched free house, circa 17th century, near Castle Drogo (NT). A stone-flagged bar, log fire, exposed beams and pews around the tables indicate its character. A spacious, no-smoking snug off the bar boasts a huge table while the no-smoking restaurant offers an intimate atmosphere and a menu of mainly local produce, with the accent on game and fish; the specials board changes daily. It keeps an extensive wine list, but a limited bottled beer range. Parking is limited.
Q P

Chardstock

George Inn

Chard Street, EX13 7BX (1 mile NW of A358, between

Axminster and Chard) OS308045
⚙ 12-3, 6-11; 12-3, 7-10.30 Sun
☎ (01460) 220241 website: www.george-inn.co.uk
Otter Bitter; guest beers Ⓗ
Grade II listed, attractive, 15th-century thatched church house at the heart of a rural village. The drinking area is divided by panels into three distinct areas, supplemented by a pool room and large dining room. Interesting features include superb linen-fold panelling and graffiti from 1640. An excellent range of good food is mostly sourced locally, as are the two guest beers. The accommodation is highly recommended.
Q❀⇌◑♣P

Chawleigh

Earl of Portsmouth

The Square, EX18 7HJ (on B3042)
⚙ 11-3, 5.30-11; 11-11 Sat; 12-10.30 Sun
☎ (01769) 580204
website: www.earlofportsmouth-pub.co.uk
Beer Engine Rail Ale; Country Life Old Appledore; guest beers Ⓗ
Delightful village local, refurbished by the current occupants. Originally called the London Inn, which burned down in 1869, the pub was rebuilt by the Earl of Portsmouth (hence the name). It boasts two skittle alleys. The cosy single bar supplies three real ales from local brewers and cider from Winkleigh. Local home-cooked produce is available from the restaurant; the fish on Friday's menu comes from Clovelly. It is frequented by walkers on the nearby Ridge and Valley walk.
♨❀◑⇌(Eggesford)♣●P

Cheriton Bishop

Old Thatch Inn

EX6 6JH (½ mile off A30)
⚙ 11.30-3, 6-11; 12-3, 6-10.30 Sun
☎ (01647) 24204 website: www.theoldthatchinn.com
Otter Ale; Sharp's Doom Bar; guest beers Ⓗ
Friendly, 16th-century free house situated on the north-eastern edge of Dartmoor. The bar and no-smoking dining area have beamed ceilings and are separated by a lovely open stone fireplace. The four ales are all from south-western independent breweries. The extensive menu is based on locally-sourced produce which is freshly cooked to order; the pub is deservedly popular with diners.
♨❀⇌◑▲P⊁

Chillington

Open Arms

TQ7 2LD (on A379, E of Kingsbridge)
⚙ 11-2.30, 6-11; 12-3, 7-10.30 Sun
☎ (01548) 581171
Draught Bass; Exmoor Ale; Princetown Jail Ale; guest beer Ⓗ
Unpretentious free house, a village local on the narrow Kingsbridge to Slapton main road. An excellent range of ales includes well-chosen guests, or try a glass of real Devon cider. Home-cooked food is served all day. Daily specials are chalked up – depending on the fish catch. Family friendly, the pub hosts occasional live music.
♨Q♉❀◑▲♣●⊁

Chittlehamholt

Exeter Inn

EX37 9NS (off B3226, SW of S Molton)
⚙ 11.30-2.30, 7-11 (11.30-11 summer); 12-3, 7-10.30 Sun
☎ (01769) 540281
Greene King Abbot; St Austell Dartmoor Best Ⓗ
The quintessential Devon pub: thatched roof, beams and a warm welcome. Fine ales are accompanied by good food and good conversation. This village pub, dating from the 16th century, is well worth a visit; when in the area why not also try the Old George Inn at High Bickington, the Portsmouth Arms and the Rising Sun in Umberleigh (the latter two are listed in this Guide). Accommodation is in self-catering cottages. Q⇌◑

Chittlehampton

Bell Inn

The Square, EX37 9QL (off B3227, opp. church)
⚙ 11-3, 6-11; 11-11 Sat; 12-10.30 Sun
☎ (01769) 540368
Beer range varies Ⓗ/Ⓖ
True free house and a focus for the village community. The central bar serves all areas, including the no-smoking conservatory. Up to 10 real ales are sold – three on handpump, the rest on gravity, so always ask what is available. Cider is Sam's Dry from Winkleigh and there are some 150 whiskies to choose from. Excellent food is served throughout, ordered from the blackboard menu. Families with children are welcome and there is free Internet access for customers. A wheelchair WC is provided. ❀◑♿▲⇌♣●P

Chudleigh

Bishop Lacy

52-53 Fore Street, TQ13 0HY
⚙ 11-11; 12-10.30 Sun
☎ (01626) 854585 website: www.thebishoplacy.com
O'Hanlons Firefly; Ⓗ **Princetown Jail Ale;** Ⓖ
Skinner's Cornish Knocker; guest beers Ⓗ/Ⓖ
Grade II listed, this 14th-century church house is now a bustling local. It has built up a reputation for serving a good selection of real ales, including some on gravity. The pub has two bars, both warmed by real fires. Home-cooked food is served in a no-smoking restaurant area. Beer festivals are a regular event at this local CAMRA Pub of the Year 2000 (and regional winner in 1998). Children and dogs are welcome. ♨Q◑⊡▲♣⊁

Chulmleigh

Old Court House

South Molton Street, EX18 7BW
(200 yards from town centre)
⚙ 11.30-11; 12-10.30 Sun
☎ (01769) 580045 website: www.oldcourthouseinn.co.uk
Draught Bass; Cotleigh Tawny; guest beer Ⓗ
Thatched country inn with an Internet cafe. The upper level once formed the great hall and court house where Charles I stayed in 1643 – his coat of arms now dominates one of the rooms. Three real ales are served in the cosy bar, one chosen by locals, along with Thatchers traditional cider. Regular quizzes support various charities and BBC Radio Devon has broadcast charity events

from here. Children are welcome in the skittle alley. The dining room may be used by non-smokers outside mealtimes.
(Eggesford/Kings Nymton)

Churston

Weary Ploughman

Brixham Road, TQ5 0LL (on A3022, between Paignton and Brixham)
11-11; 12-10.30 Sun
(01803) 844702
John Smith's Bitter; Sharp's Doom Bar; guest beers

Next to the preserved steam railway, this pub has rapidly gained a reputation for its variety of high quality ales, sourced mainly from local breweries, and its top of the range pub grub served at reasonable prices. There are usually three guest beers. It has a large, open-plan bar with a no-smoking section and a child-friendly area. Voted South Devon CAMRA's Pub of the Year 2004, it hosts a small beer festival in August. (Steam Rlwy) P

Cockwood

Anchor

EX6 8RA (on A379 between Starcross and Dawlish)
11-11; 12-10.30 Sun
(01626) 890203
Draught Bass; Fuller's London Pride; Greene King Abbot, Old Speckled Hen; Otter Ale; Wadworth 6X

Highly photogenic pub, both outside and in, overlooking an ancient harbour. In summer drinkers sit on the harbour wall. Inside, admire the lovely old high-backed settles and dark panelling, but beware of low beams. The seafood is nationally renowned and is a regular winner of prestigious awards. Six ales, including one local brew and one on gravity, make this a really good pub to visit, and the staff are well experienced in coping with busy times.
Q (Starcross) P

Colyton

Gerrard Arms

Rosemary Lane, EX24 6LN
11-3, 5.30 (6 Sat)-11; 12-3, 7-10.30 Sun
(01297) 552588
Draught Bass; Branscombe Vale Branoc; guest beer

Busy, one-bar pub next to the church in this delightful little town with lots of lovely old cottages and tangled narrow streets and alleyways. Popular with locals, it has a well-used skittle alley at the rear and a courtyard garden. The home-made food is good value, with a roast available on Sundays; in winter evening meals are served Friday and Saturday. Colyton Station on the Seaton tramway is a level walk.

Combe Martin

Castle Inn

High Street, EX34 0HS
12-11; 12-10.30 Sun
(01271) 883706 website: www.castleinn.info
Draught Bass; Fuller's London Pride; guest beers

Situated about halfway along the High Street, the Castle has a long-standing reputation for its ales. It attracts local sports fans, due to a large projector screen in the main bar. There is a restaurant and a 150 seat function room at the rear, housing two skittle alleys. A beerfest is held during carnival week. P

Cornworthy

Hunter's Lodge Inn

TQ9 7ES (off A381, between Totnes and Kingsbridge)
12-2.30, 6.30-11; 12-2.30, 7-10.30 Sun
(01803) 732204
Teignworthy Reel Ale; guest beers

This South Devon CAMRA Pub of the Year for 2003 has maintained its variety and quality of beers. Mentioned in the Domesday Book, it boasts a resident ghost, low, beamed ceilings, a log fire and a comfortable and welcoming atmosphere. Three real ales are normally available and it enjoys an excellent reputation for home-cooked food using local ingredients.
Q P

Crediton

Crediton Inn

28a Mill Street, EX17 1EZ (opp. Somerfield)
11-11; 12-2, 7-10.30 Sun
(01363) 772882 website: www.crediton-inn.co.uk
Fuller's London Pride; Sharp's Doom Bar; guest beers

Just off the town centre, this well-established, friendly, free house is a regular entry in this Guide. Four ales are always available, with guests normally coming from regional independent brewers. The skittle alley doubles as a function room and the pub runs its own angling club and pool team. It hosts occasional quiz and theme nights. The menu is modest, but the food is good at local CAMRA's Pub of the Year 2005. P

Culmstock

Culm Valley Inn

EX15 3JJ
12-4, 6-11; 11-11 Sat; 12-10.30 Sun
(01884) 840354
Beer range varies

You will find this 300-year-old village inn by the River Culm, where it emerges from the Blackdown Hills. The car park was formerly the railway sidings of the Tiverton light railway and the pub was previously called the Railway Inn. For the excellent food, local produce is used – often free range and organic. Children are welcome for meals. Up to eight beers are stillaged on automatic tilters and dispensed by gravity from the temperature controlled cellar behind the bar. Q

Dartmouth

Cherub Inn

13 Higher Street, TQ6 9RB
11-11; 12-10.30 Sun
(01803) 832571 website: www.the-cherub.co.uk
Sharp's Doom Bar; guest beers

This Grade II listed pub is the oldest building in Dartmouth, and dates from 1380. It has a small, cosy, beamed bar that offers meals every lunchtime and evening. The restaurant is open every night and has earned a good reputation for local fish and seafood as well as steak, poultry and game. Three beers (two in winter) supplement the house beer from Summerskills. A wonderful atmosphere prevails in this fine old building.
Q◐◑▲♠

Dawlish

Smugglers' Inn

27 Teignmouth Road, EX7 0LA (on A379 coast road)
⏲ 11-11; 12-10.30 Sun
☎ (01626) 862301
Draught Bass; Scattor Rock Devonian; Teignworthy Reel Ale; guest beers Ⓗ
This large roadhouse, half a mile from Dawlish, benefits from a massive car park and lovely coastal views. Nautical artefacts, plenty of comfortable seating and carpets throughout give a warm welcome for visitors. It also draws a good local trade to its regular games evenings, occasional live music and its excellent no-smoking restaurant. Regular beer festivals are held. The pub is fully accessible to disabled customers.
♨Q♉❀◐◑♿▲⇌♣P

Dunsford

Royal Oak

EX6 7DA (follow B3212 from Exeter)
⏲ 12-2.30 (not Mon), 6.30 (6 Fri)-11 (7-10.30 Mon); 12-2.30, 7-10.30 Sun
☎ (01647) 252256 website: www.troid.co.uk
Greene King Abbot; Princetown Jail Ale; Sharp's Cornish Coaster; guest beers Ⓗ
Well supported popular village local on the edge of Dartmoor National Park, comprising three main areas: a dining room, bar with adjoining bar room, and family section. Accommodation is in converted barns. It hosts quiz nights on most Thursdays and is active in regional competitions. Tuesday is fish and chips night (booking is advised), Friday is mystery ale night at £1.50 a pint. Children are welcome. Bottled Grays cider is stocked.
♨Q♉❀🛏◐◑♣P

East Budleigh

Sir Walter Raleigh

22 High Street, EX9 7ED (off A376)
⏲ 11.45-3, 6-11; 12-3, 7-10.30 Sun
☎ (01395) 442510
Adnams Broadside; Otter Bitter; Wells Bombardier Ⓗ
Pleasant community-minded pub situated in the village, close to Sir Walter Raleigh's birthplace of Hayes Barton. Opened in the 16th century, it displays many original features, such as exposed beams. It offers a wide selection of good food and real ales. A no-smoking area is provided for diners; dogs are welcome in the bar area, but children are not encouraged.
Q◐◑♣

East Prawle

Pig's Nose Inn

TQ7 2BY
⏲ 12-2.30, 7-11 (closed winter Mon); 12-2.30, 7-11 (not winter eve) Sun
☎ (01548) 511209 website: www.pigsnoseinn.co.uk
Fuller's London Pride; South Hams Devon Pride, Ⓖ **Eddystone** Ⓗ
Old, three-roomed smugglers' inn, set on the village green. Children and dogs are welcome in its cluttered interior with a maritime ambience. Occasional live music, performed at weekends in a hall adjoining the pub, draws a crowd. The beer, largely on gravity, is stored in a specially-made rack behind the bar in an old alcove. It is a haven for birdwatchers and coastal walkers alike. Home-made, wholesome food is provided using local ingredients. Local CAMRA Pub of the Year 2005. ♨♉❀◐◑▲♣♠

Exbourne

Red Lion Inn

High Street, EX20 3RY (next to church)
⏲ 12-3 (not winter), 6 (7 Oct-March)-11; 12-3, 6-11 (10.30 winter) Sun
☎ (01837) 851640
Skinner's Betty Stogs, Figgy's Brew; guest beer Ⓗ
This 16th-century free house is a friendly village local. Skinner's supplies all three real ales, but food is limited to bar snacks. Low ceilings and exposed beams are evident throughout with a wood-burning stove in the bar area. The interior may seem familiar to some as it features in the BBC series Down To Earth. A warm welcome awaits, providing you do not mind the friendly ghost. ♨Q♣P

Exeter

Brook Green Tavern

31 Well Street, EX4 6QL
(near St James Park Station and football ground)
⏲ 4 (12 Sat & summer Fri)-11; 12-10.30 Sun
☎ (01392) 495699
Butcombe Bitter; Fuller's London Pride; Taylor Landlord; guest beers Ⓗ
Traditional pub serving the local community where the friendly landlady always offers six beers. Close to St James Park football ground, it is also student-friendly. It fields two league darts teams and hosts meetings of the Victorian cricket team. Recently upgraded kitchens now allow for good value meals, including Sunday lunches. A small garden has also been added. Parking is difficult, but it is close to St James Station and a five-minute walk from the city centre. Q❀◐◑⇌(St James)♣

City Gate

City Gate Hotel, Iron Bridge, North Street, EX4 3RB
⏲ 11-11; 12-10.30 Sun
☎ (01392) 495811 website: www.citygatehotel.co.uk
Young's Bitter, Special, Waggle Dance; guest beers Ⓗ
A short walk from the High Street, the City Gate is popular with locals. The bar area is open plan, with an impressive conservatory/dining area serving good food. Upstairs there are 15 guest rooms. The large patio garden is enclosed by

part of Exeter's old city wall. It is worth remembering that as well as a good selection of Young's draught ales it also stocks many bottled ales that you can buy to take away.
⌂Q❀🛏◐♿⇌(Central)🍏⊘

Double Locks Hotel ✔

Canal Bank, EX2 6LT (road access from Marsh Barton trading estate) OS932900
⏲ 11-11; 12-10.30 Sun
☎ (01392) 256947
Branscombe Vale Branoc; O'Hanlons Royal Oak; Otter Bright; Ⓖ Young's Bitter, Special; Ⓗ guest beers Ⓖ
Historic, characterful pub on the banks of the famous Exeter Ship Canal. The building dates back to the 18th century, when it was a lock-keeper's cottage. All day food and a pleasant location make it popular during the summer. Note the ceiling drawings in the main bar executed by Chris Noton around 1994. Camping is available (phone ahead). A children's play area is provided. A good selection of guest ales is supplemented by a cider in summer. Children (and dogs) are welcome. ⌂Q❀◐♿▲♣🍏P

Globe Inn

39 Clifton Road, Newtown, EX1 2BL
⏲ 11-11; 12-10.30 Sun
☎ (01392) 256491
Greene King IPA, Abbot; Topsham Ferryman Ⓗ
Good value, community pub near the city centre where the emphasis is on live music five nights a week as the landlord is a keen musician who previously ran a CAMRA award-winning pub in Leeds. Quiz night is Sunday. It is currently the only regular Exeter outlet for the new Topsham and Exminster Brewery's Ferryman. ◐🚌♣

Great Western Hotel

St David's Station Approach, EX4 4NU
⏲ 11-11; 12-10.30 Sun
☎ (01392) 274039 website: www.greatwesternhotel.co.uk
Adnams Broadside; Branscombe Vale Branoc; O'Hanlon's Yellowhammer, Royal Oak; Taylor Landlord; guest beers Ⓗ
The Great Western is a traditional railway hotel with lots of character, and is certainly the place to meet other real ale enthusiasts. It has won the local CAMRA's Pub of the Year award twice for its fantastic choice of real ales. It stages live music and entertainment throughout the year and has a wide-screen TV for sporting events. There are a few benches outside by the road.
❀🛏◐⇌(St David's)🍏P

Well House Tavern

Cathedral Yard, EX1 1HO
⏲ 11-11; 12-10.30 Sun
☎ (01392) 223611
Otter Ale; guest beers Ⓗ
The Royal Clarence Hotel, Michael Caine's Restaurant and its ale house, the Well House Tavern, occupy a stunning location overlooking the cathedral green. While major refurbishments took place at the hotel during 2005, the tavern has just had minor redecoration and its character remains intact. Six handpumps serve mainly local beers and there is a choice of ciders on gravity. This is a drinkers' haven set at the historic heart of the city.
Q◐⇌(Central/St David's)🍏

Exmouth

Bicton Inn

5 Bicton Street, EX8 2RU
⏲ 11-11; 12-10.30 Sun
☎ (01395) 272589
Draught Bass; Branscombe Vale Branoc; guest beers Ⓗ
Characterful local with wooden floors and stained glass; the games room offers darts and pool. It started life as the New Inn in 1836, originally a coach stop; the name was changed in 1856. Live music is usually staged on the first Thursday of each month – folk with some jazz. A friendly atmosphere prevails in this free house, where generally the real ale is priced at £1.20-£2 a pint. ⇌♣

Grove

The Esplanade, EX8 1AS
⏲ 11 (12 winter)-11; 12-10.30 Sun
☎ (01395) 272101
Young's Bitter, Special, seasonal beers Ⓗ
Large Young's house, at the western end of the Esplanade, just beyond the town centre. This fine, late Victorian building is designed on the lines of a Bavarian house. Upstairs, a no-smoking restaurant affords panoramic views across the sea and Exe estuary. Good food is served 12-9pm every day, including in the bar, which also has a no-smoking area. Large gardens with tables and chairs encourage families and it can get busy in the tourist season. It has a disabled WC.
⌂❀◐♿⇌⊘

Powder Monkey ✔

2-2a The Parade, EX8 1RJ
⏲ 11-11; 12-10.30 Sun
☎ (01395) 280090
Blackawton Headstrong; Exmoor Ale; Greene King Abbot; Marston's Burton Bitter; Shepherd Neame Spitfire; guest beers Ⓗ
JD Wetherspoon's house opened in 1999. A linear pub, warmed by open fires in winter, a patio at the front has heaters or sunshades as required. Popular with all ages, beer is usually sold quite cold here, but in good variety. Often busy for theme nights (curry night and during the summer), it has no TV or music. It has good wheelchair access; no dogs are admitted. Food and beer are competitively priced. ⌂Q👶❀◐♿⇌⊘

Great Torrington

Torrington Arms

170 New Street, EX38 8BX (on A386)
⏲ 11-11; 12-10.30 Sun
☎ (01805) 622280
Clearwater Cavalier; guest beer Ⓗ
Originally the Railway Inn, it was renamed the Torrington Arms after the railway's demise. Now very much a local community pub, the bar wall is covered in photos of bonfire events organised by the Cavaliers – English Civil War themed charity fundraisers – over the last 35 years. At the rear is a patio and a newly converted barn function room for skittles and pool. 'Proper' food, served at lunchtime, is good value.
⌂Q❀🛏◐♣

Hatherleigh

Tally Ho!

14 Market Street, EX20 3JN (opp. church)

11-3, 6-11; 12-3, 6-10.30 Sun

☎ (01837) 810306 website: www.hatherleigh.org.uk/tallyho

Clearwater Cavalier, Torridge Best; guest beers Ⓗ

Wonderful, 15th-century inn serving the local community in this small market town, featuring low beams and woodblock flooring. One central bar containing a wood-burning fire serves all the drinking and dining areas. Three real ales are always on tap and the cider is from nearby Winkleigh, but not stocked in winter. New for this year is the refurbished garden and additional seating behind the pub. Efforts are ongoing to resurrect the redundant brewery. ⚠Q❀⇔◐◑●⊁

Hennock

Palk Arms

Church Road, TQ13 9QB

12-2, 7-11; 12-10.30 Sun

☎ (01626) 836584

Princetown Jail Ale; guest beers Ⓗ

Set high above the Teign Valley, this is the quintessential rustic pub, reputedly dating from the 16th century. After a long period of hibernation, it has taken on a new lease of life thanks to the quality of its ever-changing real ales. It incorporates a small shop and post office. You are assured of a warm welcome from locals – and the cavernous log fire. Bar billiards, bar skittles and shove-ha'penny are played here. The menu is limited.
⚠Q⛒❀◐◑♣

Hexworthy

Forest Inn

PL20 6SD (off B3357, Two Bridges-Dartmeet Road)

11.30-2.30, 6-11; 11-2.30, 6-10.30 Sun

☎ (01364) 631211 website: www.theforestinn.com

Teignworthy Reel Ale, Springtide; guest beers Ⓗ

Country inn situated in the Dartmoor forest; although off the beaten track it is worth seeking out. Walkers, riders, anglers, canoeists, children and dogs are all welcome. Devon beers and cider are offered as well as a wide range of food and accommodation, including en-suite guest rooms and a bunkhouse. The bars are furnished with comfortable chesterfields. Horses can be stabled by prior arrangement.
⚠Q⛒❀⇔◐◑●P⊁

Hockworthy

Staple Cross Inn

TA21 0HN

11-11; 12-10.30 Sun

☎ (01398) 361374

Cotleigh Tawny; Exmoor Ale; guest beers Ⓗ

Unspoilt, 400-year-old local. This lively country pub on the Somerset border comprises two bar areas, one with quarry-tiled floor and the other a carpeted lounge. It offers a friendly welcome and is popular for food, served in the dining area. A recent extension has provided a bigger cellar and inside toilets.
⚠Q❀◐◑⛺♣P

Holcombe Rogus

Prince of Wales

TA21 0PN

12-3 (not Mon), 6-11; 11-11 Sat; 12-10.30 Sun

☎ (01823) 672070

Beer range varies Ⓗ

Not far from the Grand Western Canal, which is popular with cyclists and walkers, this 17th-century country pub boasts unusual restored cash register handpumps. The recently extended restaurant area includes smart new toilets. Home-cooked food caters for vegetarians. A large log-burning stove warms the bar area. Pool and darts facilities are well used by local teams. The attractive walled garden is a bonus. Up to four real ales change often; cider is sold in summer. ⚠Q❀◐◑♣●P

Holne

Church House Inn

TQ13 7SJ

12-2.30 (3 Sat), 7 (6.30 Sat)-11; 12-3, 7-10.30 Sun

☎ (01364) 631208 website: www.churchhouse-holne.co.uk

Butcombe Bitter; Teignworthy Reel Ale; guest beers Ⓗ

Grade II listed building in Dartmoor National Park. The 14th-century building has a small leat running down one side. It enjoys an excellent reputation for food and accommodation, and is a regular entry in this Guide. Guest beers come from local breweries. Seating is provided outside and the pub is a must during any visit to Dartmoor. Two bars: one leads to the dining area, the other is basically for drinkers. Families with children, dogs and walkers are all welcome. ⚠Q❀⇔◐◑⛺●⊁

Holsworthy

Rydon Inn

Rydon Road, EX22 7HU (½ mile W of Holsworthy on A3072, Bude road)

11.30-3, 5.30-11 (closed winter Mon); 12-3, 6-10.30 (not winter eve) Sun

☎ (01409) 259444 website: www.rydon-inn.com

Sharp's Doom Bar Ⓗ

Extensively refurbished by the current owners, this free house and restaurant encompass an original Devon longhouse. The central bar serves all sections, which include a conservatory and a large no-smoking area offering award-winning food. The Triple H Bitter is based on Dreckly and Bodmin Boar ales from Ring o' Bells Brewery. The cider is Thatchers Dry. Vaulted pine beams support the ceilings, while the bar, unusually, is thatched. Families with well-behaved children are welcome. ⚠Q❀◐◑♿●P⊁

Horsebridge

Royal Inn

PL19 8PJ (off A388, Tavistock-Launceston road)

11.30-3, 6.30-11; 12.30-3, 6.30-10.30 Sun

☎ (01822) 870214 website: www.royalinn.co.uk

Draught Bass; Sharp's Doom Bar; Ⓗ **guest beers** Ⓖ

Originally built by monks as a nunnery, the pub overlooks an old bridge over the River Tamar, connecting Devon and Cornwall. The main bar is half panelled, while the lounge is decorated with hops and horse brasses. A further, larger room is no-smoking. The terraced garden is suitable for children, who are welcome until 9pm. The food is recommended. You can try your hand at bar billiards here. ⛼Q❀◐▶♣P⊬

Iddesleigh

Duke of York

EX19 8BG (off B3217, next to church) OS570083

⏲ 11-11; 12-10.30 Sun

☎ (01837) 810253

Adnams Broadside; Cotleigh Tawny; guest beer Ⓖ

Free house situated in a quiet village, converted from four cottages that housed the craftsmen building the church next door. A welcoming atmosphere is enhanced by the large log fire and rocking chair in the bar. Cider is from nearby Winkleigh. Some food is supplied from the landlord's farm and served in the bar or restaurant. Although remote, this 15th-century pub can get busy with locals and walkers on the Tarka Trail. ⛼❀⛟◐▶♣●

Kilmington

New Inn

The Hill, EX13 7SF (100 yds S of A35)

⏲ 11-2.30, 6-11;12-3, 7-10.30 Sun

☎ (01297) 33376

Palmer Copper Ale, IPA, Dorset Gold Ⓗ

Neat, 14th-century thatched Devon long house that has been in every edition of this Guide. It was burnt out in 2004, but has been sympathetically rebuilt by the owners, Palmer of Bridport, with new indoor toilets and twice the seating area. There is a safe garden that houses some aviaries and offers views across the Axe Valley. Well supported by local teams most nights in winter, it has a good skittle alley. Q❀◐▶♿⛺P

Old Inn

EX13 7RB

⏲ 12-2.30 (3 Sat), 6-11;12-3, 7-10.30 Sun

☎ (01297) 32096

Branscombe Vale Branoc; St Austell Tinners, Tribute; guest beer Ⓗ

Thatched village pub on the main road. It changed hands in 2004, and has gone upmarket in the food department. The landlord is determined about his beer and goes to great lengths to serve it well. Outside at the back there is a patio and a raised lawn with tables; inside is a restaurant, a no-smoking lounge and a bar displaying cricketing memorabilia. The beers and food are from the south-west, except for the Czech Budvar lager. No evening meals are served on Sunday in winter. ⛼Q❀◐▶P⊬

Kingston

Dolphin Inn

TQ7 4QE

⏲ 11-3.30 (2.30 winter), 6-11; 12-3.30, 7-10.30 Sun

☎ (01548) 810314

Courage Best Bitter; Sharp's Doom Bar; Wadworth 6X; guest beer Ⓗ

This 16th-century quintessential country pub is frequented by locals and walkers as well as visitors from further afield. It is stone built, and the two open fires blend well with the pleasant low lighting. Note the foreign currency bills attached to some of the exposed beams. The beer quality is consistently high and the food is good. The gents' toilets and the family room are across the road, as is the garden. ⛼Q☋❀⛟◐▶P

Kingswear

Ship Inn

Higher Street, TQ6 0AG (near steam railway station)

⏲ 12-3, 6-11; 12-3, 7-10.30 Sun

☎ (01803) 752348

Adnams Bitter; Greene King IPA; Otter Ale Ⓗ

Look uphill from the steam railway station and next to the church you will see this cosy, 15th-century pub. On the left is the basic public bar, with darts and other games; on the right is a small, comfortable, lounge bar. Some walls are panelled in wood, the rest are hung with local pictures. Up some stairs is a larger dining room, affording excellent views of the River Dart (no food Sun or Mon in winter). Inches cider is sold in summer. ⛼Q❀◐▶⛺⇌(Steam Rlwy)●

Longdown

Lamb Inn

EX6 7RS (on B3212)

⏲ 12-3, 6-11; 12-3, 7-10.30 Sun

☎ (01392) 811711

Teignworthy Reel Ale; guest beers Ⓗ

Large, open-plan village pub, part of which is a no-smoking restaurant serving reasonably priced, home-cooked food. The main area, with a central bar housing four handpumps, is carpeted and furnished with comfortable settees, chesterfields and plenty of bar stools. There is always a wide range of both draught and bottled Belgian beers on offer. ⛼❀◐▶♿♣●P

Manor Inn

EX6 7QL (off B3193, between Dunsford and Chudleigh) OS844843

⏲ 12-2, 6.30-11; closed Mon; 12-2.30, 7-10.30 Sun

☎ (01647) 252304 website: www.themanorinn.co.uk

Princetown Jail Ale; RCH Pitchfork; Teignworthy Reel Ale; guest beers Ⓗ

Small, traditional pub, well supported by the local community. Two bars are warmed by open fires. A good choice of ales comes from a variety of breweries and draught Grays cider is always available. Ale is sold in four-pint jugs. The garden to the front offers beautiful views over the Teign Valley and Dartmoor National Park. The inn serves an extensive menu of freshly-prepared local produce. The pub is dog friendly, but no children under 14 are admitted. ⛼Q❀◐▶⊟⛺♣●P

Lutton

Mountain Inn ✔

Old Chapel Road, PL21 9SA (off Plympton-Cornwood road)

⏲ 12-3, 6.30 (6 Fri & Sat)-11.30; 12-3, 7-11.30 Sun

☎ (01725) 837247

Draught Bass; Princetown Jail Ale; guest beers Ⓗ

Two-roomed village pub on the edge of Dartmoor; visitors are welcome including horse

riders, walkers and their dogs. The bar area is simple with cob walls and a real fire creating a homely atmosphere. The second room is comfortable, set with dining room furniture. There is also a family room off the bar. The pub name is a corruption of a local landowner's family name, Montain. Thatchers cider is sold. No food is served Tuesday.
♨Q☺❀◐◑♣●P⊬

Lympstone

Redwing

Church Road, EX8 5JT (off A376 before Exmouth)
⏲ 11.30-3, 6-11; 11.30-11 Sat; 12-10.30 Sun
☎ (01395) 222156
Greene King Abbot; Otter Bitter; Palmer IPA; guest beer Ⓗ
Village free house, that successfully combines good food custom in the restaurant area with a lively pub trade in the public bar. Locals, dogs, trad jazz musicians on Tuesday and visitors together make a lively atmosphere. Thatchers cider is sold. Regular quiz nights are staged.
❀◐◑⇌●P

Mary Tavy

Elephant's Nest

Horndon, PL19 9NQ
⏲ 12-3, 6.30-11; 12-3, 6.30-10.30 Sun
☎ (01822) 810273
Palmer Copper Ale, IPA; guest beers Ⓗ
Intriguingly renamed, from the New Inn, by a previous landlord. The bar, despite many references to elephants in a mural, figures and curios, is traditional and comfortable. Two further rooms off the bar are suitable for children. It supports local cricket, rugby and pony clubs. The large garden affords magnificent views over Dartmoor. ♨Q☺❀◐◑♣●P⊬

Royal Standard

PL19 9QB
⏲ 11-11; 12-10.30 Sun
☎ (01822) 810289
Beer range varies Ⓗ
Compact family pub welcoming locals and visitors (and their dogs). The main bar is supplemented by an adjoining dining area. The changing choice of four ales is sourced from the south-west penisular, and beer festivals are becoming part of the calendar. Camping can be arranged in a field next to the pub, which is also used as an overflow car park. Disabled access is by a dedicated door. A special pensioners' menu is available. ♨Q❀◐◑♿▲♣P

Meavy

Royal Oak Inn

PL20 6PJ (off A386 to Yelverton)
⏲ 12-3, 6.30-11; 12-3, 6.30-10.30 Sun
☎ (01822) 852944
Otter Bitter; Princetown Dartmoor IPA, Jail Ale Ⓗ
Cosy inn, at the heart of the village. A cobbled area with bench seating in front of the pub overlooks the green where the eponymous oak tree stands. The lounge bar is comfortable, with exposed beams, settles, a table and chairs. The public bar has a flagstone floor and roaring log fire in winter. Varied lunch and evening menus are supplemented by a specials board, and a large choice of traditional puddings. Worth seeking out, the inn stocks Westons Scrumpy.
♨Q❀◐◑⊟●

Molland

London Inn

EX36 3NG
⏲ 12-2.30, 6-11; 12-2.30, 7-10.30 Sun
☎ (01769) 550269
Cotleigh Tawny; Exmoor Ale Ⓖ
Delightful old pub next to the church in a village on the edge of Exmoor, attracting locals and visitors alike. The pub comprises several small rooms and a restaurant; it can be busy during the shooting season – the inn is full of displays connected with shooting, hunting and fishing. The pub has a skittle alley situated across the road.
♨Q☺❀◐

Newton Abbot

Locomotive Inn ✔

35-37 East Street, TQ12 2JP (100 yds from hospital)
⏲ 12-11; 12-10.30 Sun
☎ (01626) 365249
Adnams Broadside; Draught Bass; guest beers Ⓗ
Cosy, three-roomed, 17th-century inn at the town centre. There is a main bar with a large open fire, a pool room at the rear, and a fine example of an old sherry bar. Four real ales are always on offer, as well as Westons Old Rosie cider. Children (and dogs) are welcome.
♨⊟♿⇌♣●

Wolborough Inn

55 Wolborough Street, TQ12 1JQ (on Totnes road)
⏲ 5.30 (12 Thu; 11 Sat)-11; 12-4, 7-10.30 Sun
☎ (01626) 361667
Beer range varies Ⓗ
This cosy, terraced pub, the smallest in Newton Abbot, is well worth the few minutes' walk from the main shopping area. The faithful local clientele, who are often encouraged to help choose guest beers, gather around the bar for conversation; there are also a few tables and seats. Two ales are generally available, while draught Budvar and a small but tempting bottled selection adds to the drinkers' choice. ♣

Newton St Cyres

Beer Engine

EX5 5AX (off A377, near station)
⏲ 11-11; 12-10.30 Sun
☎ (01392) 851282
Beer Engine Rail Ale; Piston Bitter; Sleeper Heavy; seasonal beers Ⓗ
Built as a railway hotel at the time the Barnstaple–Exeter (Tarka Line) branch line was under construction, the pub is now home to Devon's oldest brewery (opened in 1983). The single room has a bar and dining area (children welcome), decorated with hops and photographs of village life. Voted local CAMRA Pub of the Year 2003, the landlord is justly proud of the beer produced on the premises and the convivial atmosphere that the pub generates; good food is served.
♨Q❀◐◑♿▲⇌♣P☐

North Bovey

Ring of Bells

TQ13 8RB

11-11; 12-10.30 Sun

(01647) 440375

Draught Bass; St Austell Dartmoor Best; guest beer H

Large restaurant/pub but with many attributes of a smaller establishment. In the centre of the village, it stocks a good local selection of beers, a regular guest ale and a local cider. Worth the short drive from Moretonhampstead to the village centre, parking is available around the village green.

North Tawton

Railway Inn

Whiddon Down Road, EX20 2BE (1 mile S of village)

OS666001

12-2 (not Mon-Thu), 6-11; 12-3, 7-10.30 Sun

(01837) 82789

Teignworthy Reel Ale; guest beers H

Local CAMRA Pub of the Year 2004; set in a rural location, the Railway is a friendly, single-bar pub – part of a working farm. It stands next to the former North Tawton Station (closed 1971), which it predates; the bar decor includes railway memorabilia and old photos. The beer range is generally West Country based, as is the cider stocked in summer. The dining room is popular in the evening (no food Thu); light meals are served at lunchtime. Q P

Noss Mayo

Ship Inn

PL8 1EW

11.30-11; 12-10.30 Sun

(01752) 872387 website: www.nossmayo.com

Butcombe Blonde; Princetown Jail Ale; Shepherd Neame Spitfire; Summerskills Tamar; guest beers H

This former Plymouth CAMRA Pub of the Year is situated on the River Yealm, with its own tidal moorings (check with pub regarding tides). Comfortable seating inside and out allows guests to enjoy the atmosphere, and gaze at the river. The pub's ethos is to support local producers and brewers wherever possible. Now totally no-smoking inside, children are welcome until 7pm. Q P

Okehampton

Plymouth Inn

26 West Street, EX20 1HH

12-11; 12-10.30 Sun

(01837) 53633

Beer range varies G

Former coaching inn dating back to the 16th century, it stands near the bridge over the West Okement River. The Plymouth is a friendly pub that brings the welcome and atmosphere of a village pub to an old market town. Two beer festivals are held each year (normally May and November). The changing beer range places the accent on West Country breweries. Occasional live music is performed in the bar, usually acoustic, sometimes impromptu.

Paignton

Isaac Merritt

54-58 Torquay Road, TQ3 3AA (near post office)

10-11; 12-10.30 Sun

(01803) 556066

Courage Directors; Greene King Abbot; Marston's Burton Bitter, Pedigree; guest beers H

This busy, town-centre pub was local CAMRA Pub of the Year in 2001 and a Wetherspoon's award-winner in 2004. It is easily accessible to wheelchair users, and has a designated ground-floor toilet. The changing range of up five guest beers is augmented by mini-beer festivals every Sunday and Monday, when a chosen brewery's beers are offered at reduced prices. A house beer, Isaac's Tipple, is brewed by Blackawton. Good value meals are served all day.

Q

Parkham

Bell Inn

EX39 5PL (off A39, between Bideford and Bude)

12-3, 6-11; 12-3, 7-10.30 Sun

(01237) 451201

Fuller's London Pride; Greene King IPA; guest beer H

Thatched, 13th-century cottage where the modernised bar area is split into two sections. A pub that is really at the centre of village life, the village store is in a converted part of the pub. A small extension houses a restaurant; bar food is also available. Visitors to the locality might also like to try the Coach and Horses at Buckland Brewer or the Hoops Inn at Horns Cross, which both sell real ale. Q

Plymouth

Artillery Arms

6 Pounds Street, Stonehouse, PL1 3RH

(behind Stonehouse Barracks and Millbay Docks)

11-11; 12-10.30 Sun

(01752) 262515

Draught Bass; guest beers H

Opening at 9am for breakfast (no alcohol), this corner pub at the rear of the Brittany Ferries Terminal has a single bar, plus a no-smoking dining area where good value home-made food is served. This is very much a community pub, sponsoring charity fundraising events, including monkey races. Although not the easiest pub to locate in the back streets of Stonehouse, it is well worth the effort.

Blue Peter

68 Pomphlett Road, Plymstock, PL9 7BN

11-11; 12.30-10.30 Sun

(01752) 402255

Beer range varies H/G

Two-bar pub in a part of Plymouth where real ale is scarce. The design of the pub is comfortable; the lounge area has alcove seating, while the public bar contains a large sports screen and games area, and can be used for live entertainment. Beer festivals are held – check with the pub for details. Locally brewed beer is usually available, as well as two or more others, at this Plymouth CAMRA Pub of the Year winner, on bus route No. 7A/7 from the city centre.

Q P

Boringdon Arms

Boringdon Terrace, Turnchapel, PL9 7TQ

11-11; 12-10.30 Sun

(01752) 402053 website: www.bori.co.uk

Draught Bass; Butcombe Bitter; Princetown Jail Ale; RCH Pitchfork; Summerskills Best Bitter; guest beers H

Recent renovations have made this former regional CAMRA Pub of the Year even more popular. Situated in a waterside village on the coastal footpath, Turnchapel is well served by road and water taxis. Beer festivals are held on the last weekend of odd numbered months. The enclosed garden is part of the redundant quarry for which the 'Bori' was the manager's house many years ago. Nearby are memorials to Civil War battles and AC Shaw (Lawrence of Arabia) who was stationed here. ⩩Q❀⇌◑Ʌ♣

Britannia ✔

1 Wolseley Road, Milehouse, PL2 3AE (near football ground)

11-11; 11-10.30 Sun

(01752) 607596

Greene King Abbot; Marston's Burton Bitter, Pedigree; Shepherd Neame Spitfire; guest beers H

Friendly Wetherspoon's house near the football ground, offering a good selection of ales and the usual diverse Wetherspoon's menu. It has a no-smoking area and superior disabled access. It is quite a big pub, with a large bar area and good seating. It gets busy at weekends, but not oppressively so. Car parking is fairly limited, but it is easy to get to by bus. ⩩Q❀◑♿⇌P⊬

Cider Press

7 Quay Road, Barbican, PL1 2JZ

12 (10 summer)-11; 12-10.30 Sun

(01752) 205151

Beer range varies G

The landlord of this friendly, basic pub is enthusiastic about real ale, which is reflected in the interesting range. On two levels, it gets lively when live music is staged and at weekends, although the upstairs can be more quiet. The cider will be either Westons Old Rosie or Old Cobble Kisser. Food is served in summer; also in that season, check out Smokey Joe's next door for gravity ales and cider. ⩩◑●

Dolphin Hotel

14 The Barbican, PL1 2LS

10-11; 12-10.30 Sun

(01752) 660876

Draught Bass; G

The most famous pub on the Barbican, not only is it the only unspoilt and unmodernised pub, but it has featured in the Dawn French/Beryl Cook cartoon series. The Tolpuddle Martyrs stayed here on their return to England and Plymouth's brewing heritage is remembered in the original Octagon Brewery windows. It stands near the Mayflower Steps from where the Pilgrim Fathers left for a new life in the New World. ⩩Q

Fawn Private Members Club

39 Prospect Street, PL4 8NY

12-11; 12-10.30 Sun

(01752) 660546

Courage Best Bitter; guest beers H

Named after the now-scrapped HMS Fawn, this private members club always welcomes CAMRA members carrying a current membership card. Cheap prices make the club popular with the locals and it also has a good following of rugby players and supporters. The house beer is supplied by Sharp's and two guest ales are also available as well as Inches cider. ❀⇌♣●

Fortescue ✔

37 Mutley Plain, Mutley, PL4 6JQ

11-11; 12-10.30 Sun

(01752) 660673

Draught Bass; Greene King Abbot; guest beers H

This lively local is situated in a student area, but is frequented by a cross-section of the community. It has a bohemian feel, and conversation flourishes in this TV-free zone. Musically themed evenings take place in the cellar bar several times a month. The patio garden at the rear is popular in summer. There are normally two or three changing guest beers, showcasing some unusual brews. Home-cooked roast lunches are served on Sunday. ❀⇌

Lounge

7 Stopford Place, PL1 4QT

11-2.30, 6-11; 12-2.30, 6-10.30 Sun

(01752) 561330

Draught Bass; guest beers H

Located on the edge of Devonport Park, this is a comfortable, old-fashioned pub with a relaxed, welcoming atmosphere. The floor is carpeted, and paintings by local artists cover the walls – many of these can be purchased in the pub. The guest beers are changed regularly, and lunchtime food is available Tuesday-Saturday. The Plymouth Albion rugby ground is located nearby at the Brickfields. Q❀◑⇌(Devonport)

Minerva

31 Looe Street, Bretonside, PL4 0EA (near bus station)

11 (12 Sat)-11; 12-10.30 Sun

(01752) 223047

Draught Bass; Greene King Abbot; Sharp's Doom Bar; Wychwood Hobgoblin H

Built before the Spanish Armada in 1588, it is not known exactly when the Minerva became an inn, however it is recognised as the oldest pub in Plymouth. It boasts a fine leaded window, picturesque lantern and a curious wooden spiral staircase made from the mast of a captured Spanish galleon. Live music is staged on weekend evenings, also impromptu jam sessions on Wednesday evening. ⩩

New Inn

1 Boringdon Road, Turnchapel, PL9 9TB (on A379, follow signs to Mountbatten and Turnchapel)

12-3, 6-11; 12-11 Sat; 12-10.30 Sun

(01752) 402675

Draught Bass; Sharp's Doom Bar; Taylor Landlord; guest beers H

This quaint, welcoming village pub stands at the waterside looking out across the Cattewater to Plymouth Hoe. It is decorated on a nautical theme and is popular with yachtsmen. It enjoys an excellent reputation for both beer and food. Some of the inn's five quiet, en-suite guest rooms benefit from sea views. ⩩Q❀⇌◑♿P

Prince Maurice

3 Church Hill, Eggbuckland, PL4 6RJ

11-3, 7-11; 11-11 Fri & Sat; 12-4, 7-10.30 Sun

☎ (01752) 771515

Adnams Broadside; Badger Tanglefoot; Draught Bass; RCH East Street Cream; Summerskills Best Bitter; guest beers Ⓗ

Cosy, friendly pub redolent of its village status, before Plymouth's expansion incorporated Eggbuckland. Close to the church and village green, a warm welcome is extended to both visitors and locals. Four times local CAMRA Pub of the Year, it sells eight beers, including two guests, plus Thatchers Cheddar Valley cider. The pub is named after the Royalist general who beseiged Parliamentary Plymouth and whose HQ was nearby.

Pym Arms

16 Pym Street, Devonport, PL1 4RG (between Devonport Park and Albert Rd)

11-11.30 (4-11 Mon-Wed); 12-10.30 Sun

☎ (01752) 561823

Princetown Jail Ale; guest beers Ⓖ

A long, single-roomed pub at the end of a terrace, with bare beams and floorboards. Hidden away below the main road, it is worth finding to sample the guest beers from local breweries. The clientele tends to be locals and workers from the nearby Devonport Dockyard. All beer is gravity dispensed. Real cider is normally available from a variety of producers.

Rising Sun

138 Eggbuckland Road, Higher Compton, PL3 5JT

11-3, 6-11; 12-11 Sat; 12-10.30 Sun

☎ (01752) 774359

Courage Best Bitter; Greene King Abbot; guest beers Ⓗ

Situated to the north of the city centre, this welcoming two-bar pub has a quirky olde-worlde charm and can rightly be described as a country pub in the city. Originally three 18th-century cottages, it became Harpers Alehouse in 1814. Interestingly, part of it was used as a chapel of rest for the adjacent church during WWI. It is popular for its home-made pub grub including Sunday roast lunches. Dogs are welcome.

Thistle Park Brewhouse

32 Commercial Road, Coxside, PL4 0LE (next to National Aquarium and Vue Cinema)

11-2am; 12-12.30am Sun

☎ (01752) 204890

South Hams Devon Pride, XSB, Sutton Comfort, Eddystone, seasonal beers Ⓗ

Friendly, basic pub that can be reached via the swingbridge from the Barbican. It has retained bare floorboards and a village pub feel. All beers, including the house beer, are from the South Hams Brewery at its new base in Stokenham, after the old Sutton Brewery moved there. Try the biltong if you have a strong jaw – a delicacy from South Africa, the licensee's original home. Live music is staged – ring for details; note the late licence.

Plymtree

Blacksmith's Arms

EX15 2JU

12-2.30 (not Mon or Tue; 12-3 Sat), 6-11; 12-4, 7-10.30 Sun

☎ (01884) 277474

Donks's Hanson's Mild; O'Hanlon's Firefly; guest beers Ⓗ/Ⓖ

Village free house that has gained a reputation for good reasonably-priced food sourced locally. It hosts occasional live music, quiz nights and summer barbecues; skittles, boules, pool and darts are played. Open fires and oak beams are as expected in an 18th-century pub; while blacksmiths' tools add a decorative touch. Children are welcome in the main bar and have their own menu.

Portsmouth Arms

Portsmouth Arms

EX37 9ND (on A377 between Umberleigh and Eggesford)

12-3, 6-11; closed Mon; 12-3, 7-10.30 Sun

☎ (01769) 651117

Jollyboat Grenville's Renown, Main Brace Ⓗ

Early 16th-century post inn situated alongside the Tarka Line – the station is nearby. There are two bars: the first, with bare boards, beams and a log fire is to the left of the entrance and is no-smoking; the lower bar, with a pool table, leads to the garden. The inn is named after the Earl of Portsmouth who owned a large amount of land locally. The Taw River nearby has good fishing. The pub is dog-friendly. The cider is Thatchers.

Postbridge

Warren House Inn

PL20 6TA (on B3212, Two Bridges-Moretonhampstead road)

11-3, 6-11; 11-11 Fri, Sat & summer; 12-10.30 Sun

☎ (01822) 880208

Butcombe Gold; Ringwood Old Thumper; Sharp's Doom Bar; guest beers Ⓗ

The third highest inn in England, isolated in the middle of Dartmoor, a granite hostelry where no other civilisation exists. Allegedly the open fire in the bar has not gone out since 1845. The dining area, which opens for groups in summer, is no-smoking. Traditional home-made food, including a range of vegetarian dishes, is provided, made mostly from locally-sourced ingredients. It stocks a range of malt whiskies and rums. Outside drinking is on the moor.

Scoriton

Tradesman's Arms

TQ11 0JB (on Holne road)

12-3 (not winter Mon or Tue), 6-11; 12-4, 7-10.30 (closed winter) Sun

☎ (01364) 631206

Princetown Dartmoor IPA, Jail Ale; Teignworthy Reel Ale Ⓗ

Village pub, originally an ale house built for the tin miners in the 17th century. It comprises a single, open-plan L-shaped bar, with a small additional seating area for diners, plus a room for families or meetings. A quiz night is held on Thursday. Good food is served and special dietary needs are catered for, especially diabetic and gluten-free. ♨Q☎❀◗⛺♣●P⚡

Shaldon

Clifford Arms

34 Fore Street, TQ14 0DE

⚙ 11-11; 12-10.30 Sun

☎ (01626) 872311

Teignworthy Reel Ale; guest beers Ⓗ

Lovely, traditional, U-shaped village pub with a single, extended semi-circular bar. There is a seating area for diners on the left, while drinkers gather around the bar. Sofas provide additional comfort. An excellent range of food is served and the pub is popular with the locals. Up to three guest ales are on tap, frequently from Teignworthy and other Devon breweries. Shaldon gets busy in summer; Green Man cider is available then. ❀◐◗⛺♣●⚡

Sidmouth

Dukes

The Esplanade, EX10 8AR

⚙ 11-11; 12-10.30 Sun

☎ (01395) 513320

Branscombe Vale Branoc; guest beers Ⓗ

This recently refurbished hotel has comfortable lounge and dining areas with a large south-facing patio. The accommodation is in 14 upstairs rooms. Food is served from 12-9 daily. There are normally three real ales on offer. In winter, the warmth and comfort of the bar and conservatory offer the perfect place to escape the elements. ☎❀🛏◐◗♿⚡

Silverton

Lamb Inn

Fore Street, EX5 4HZ

⚙ 11.30-2.30, 6-11; 11-11 Sat; 12-10.30 Sun

☎ (01392) 860272 website: www.lamb-inn.com

Draught Bass; Ⓗ **Exe Valley Dob's Best Bitter; guest beers** Ⓖ

Family-run village pub characterised by stone floors, stripped timber and old pine tables and chairs. Most ales served are by gravity from a temperature controlled stillage behind the bar. A multi-purpose function room/skittle alley and bar is well used by local teams. Good value, home-cooked food includes a specials board with vegetarian options; monthly steak nights are held, with low prices. ♨◗♣

Slapton

Queen's Arms

TQ7 2PN (800 yds from beach, off A379)

⚙ 11-3, 5-11; 12-3, 6-10.30 Sun

☎ (01548) 580800

Princetown Dartmoor IPA; South Hams Devon Pride; Teignworthy Reel Ale Ⓗ

South Devon free house with a single bar where the traditional mood is enhanced by a large open fire. Two or three real ales are stocked, depending on the time of year, plus a good range of bottled beers. A full menu includes a take-away service. Many old photos depict wartime evacuation. The walled garden allows for alfresco drinking. Children (and dogs) are welcome. ♨❀◐◗⛺♣●P

South Pool

Millbrook Inn

TQ7 2RW (off A379 at Chillington, E of Kingsbridge) OS776402

⚙ 12-3, 6-11; 12-3, 6-10.30 Sun

☎ (01548) 531581

Draught Bass; Ⓖ **Palmer IPA; guest beers** Ⓗ

This pub is situated at the head of the Salcombe estuary, accessible by boat. The main section dates back to the 17th century, with the top bar, where children are welcome, added later. It is busy in summer with most of its trade coming from boaters and walkers. It is famed for its crab sandwiches. Dogs are also welcome. At the back you can watch ducks swimming in the stream. Heron Valley cider is stocked in summer. ♨Q❀◐◗⊟♣●⚡

South Zeal

Oxenham Arms

EX20 2JT

⚙ 11-3, 5-11; 12-2.30, 7-10.30 Sun

☎ (01837) 840791 website: www.theoxenhamarms.co.uk

Beer range varies Ⓗ/Ⓖ

First licensed in 1477, the Oxenham Arms was once described as the stateliest and most ancient abode in the hamlet. That is still a fair description, although the hamlet has grown into a village. The building has the unspoilt atmosphere of an old country inn – low beams, flagged floors, open fires and mullion windows – yet a visit to the small lounge behind the bar will reveal even more ancient roots as the monastic builders incorporated a prehistoric standing stone into the wall. ♨Q☎❀🛏◐◗⛺♣P

Spreyton

Tom Cobley Tavern

EX17 5AL (leave A30 at Whiddon Down, follow A3124 and Devon lanes)

⚙ 12-2.30 (not Mon), 6 (6.30 Mon)-11; 12-2.30, 7-10.30 Sun

☎ (01647) 231314

Cotleigh Tawny; Ⓗ **Greene King Old Speckled Hen; Keltek Magik; Otter Ale;** Ⓖ **St Austell Tribute; guest beers** Ⓗ/Ⓖ

This long-standing Guide entry returns after three years' absence. The free house is now in the hands of an enthusiastic family, offering eight ales on handpump and gravity. The warm feel of a true Devon village pub is apparent as soon as you push the door and the chimes welcome you in. The food is excellent quality and good value. Study the history of Tom Cobley who travelled to Widecombe Fair, and was laid to rest in the churchyard here. ♨Q❀🛏◐◗⛺♣P

Sticklepath

Devonshire Inn

EX20 2NW (on old A30)

⚙ 11-3, 5.30-11; 11-11 Fri & Sat; 12-3, 7-10.30 Sun

☎ (01837) 840626

Draught Bass; St Austell Tinners, HSD Ⓖ

At the end of what was originally a terrace of Elizabethan cottages in a North Dartmoor village, the Devonshire is an unspoilt thatched local with low beams and a large open fire. A leat running past the back wall helps cool the stillage for the gravity dispensed beer, as well as powering the waterwheels of the NT's Finch Foundry Museum nearby. The Exeter-Okehampton bus stops outside and a number of footpaths access the Dartmoor countryside nearby. Dogs are welcome. Q P

Taw River Inn
EX20 2NW

12-3, 5-11; 11-11 Wed-Sat; 12-10.30 Sun

(01837) 840377 website: www.tawriver.co.uk

Draught Bass; Greene King Abbot; Sharp's Doom Bar [H]

The Taw River is an active village local on the old A30 where it skirts the north of Dartmoor. The large single bar is usually lively as numerous sports and pub games are pursued by the locals. The area is popular for walking in summer, while the Finch Foundry Museum (NT) is just across the road. The pub does not offer accommodation, but there is an associated holiday cottage next door. The Exeter-Okehampton (X9) bus stops nearby. Local CAMRA Pub of the Year 2005. P

Stockland

King's Arms Inn
EX14 9BS

12-3, 6.30-11; 12-3, 6.30-10.30 Sun

(01404) 881361 website: www.kingsarms.net

Exmoor Ale; Otter Bitter Ale; guest beers [H]

Busy, 16th-century, thatched former coaching inn, near the centre of a pretty village on the eastern edge of the Blackdown Hills. The large public bar stages live music on Saturday and Sunday evenings. A lounge leads off the bar and there is a skittle alley. Good, locally-sourced food is served; see the extensive blackboard menus. Two guest beers are supplied by O'Hanlon's, and Jack Rat cider is served in summer. P

Stokenham

Tradesman's Arms
TQ7 2SZ (250 yds from A379)

11.30-3, 6-11; 12-3, 7-10.30 Sun

(01548) 580313

Brakspear Bitter, Special; Draught Bass; South Hams Devon Pride [H]

Pleasant free house in the South Hams, frequented by local drinkers. Reputed to be 500 years old, with beamed ceilings and a real fire, interconnecting rooms off the bar provide ample seating and tables. The quiet pub permits an excellent atmosphere in which to savour the Brakspear ales on offer or local breweries' products, and the extensive menu. The landlord hails from Oxfordshire, hence the Brakspear connection. Q

Talaton

Talaton Inn
EX5 2RQ

12-3, 7-11; 12-3, 7-10.30 Sun

(01404) 822214

Fuller's London Pride; O'Hanlon's Yellowhammer; Otter Bitter; guest beer [H]

Charming, 16th-century pub in a small village where the large bar draws in the locals. The restaurant, with a no-smoking bar area, serves a good value menu, including a specials board and weekday lunchtime offers; evening meals are served Tuesday-Saturday. The large skittle alley is well used. It always has four real ales on tap, two from local brewers; the guest is normally Badger Tanglefoot. Q P

Tavistock

Trout & Tipple
Parkwood Road, PL19 0JS (on A386 to Okehampton, past Kelly College)

12-2.30 (not Tue), 6-11; 12-2.30, 6 (7 winter)-10.30 Sun

(01822) 618886 website: troutandtipple.co.uk

Princetown Jail Ale; guest beers [H]

Just a mile north of Tavistock, this hostelry features a traditional bar with a large no-smoking conservatory and dining area. A small games room and patio complete the picture. Nearby is a trout fishery from which the pub takes its name. Children are welcome until 9pm. This friendly pub, with a warm atmosphere, stocks a changing cider and seasonal beers from Teignworthy. It stages an established bi-annual beer festival. Q P

Topsham

Bridge Inn ☆
EX3 0QQ (by River Clyst on Exmouth road)

12-2, 6-10.30 (11 Fri & Sat); 12-2, 7-10.30 Sun

(01392) 873862 website: www.cheffers.co.uk

Beer range varies [G]

This Grade II listed building overlooking the River Clyst is the only public house the Queen has officially visited (in March 1998). The inn has been owned and run by the same family since 1897. All bars are no-smoking at lunchtime and most in the evening, too. Very little changes in this timeless gem apart from the beers, with around eight to choose from. Soup and ploughmans lunches are available; picnic tables are provided by the river. Q P

Globe Hotel
Fore Street, EX3 0HR (5 minutes' walk from station)

11-11; 12-10.30 Sun

(01392) 873471 website: www.globehotel.com

Draught Bass; Butcombe Bitter; Sharp's Doom Bar; guest beers [H]

Former coaching inn dating from the 17th century, where some of the walls are wood panelled and there is a real fire in winter. A folk club meets on Sunday evening and skittles can be played in the Malt House, a separate building. Food is served in the restaurant or the bar. Situated at the heart of Devon, it is easy to locate, although parking is limited, especially in the tourist season. Q P

Torquay

Buccaneer
43 Babbacombe Downs Road, TQ1 3LN (off B3199)

11-11; 12-10.30 Sun

(01803) 314661 website: www.staustellbrewery.co.uk

St Austell Tribute, HSD [H]

Recently refurbished and improved, family-run St Austell house overlooking the clifftop gardens, with superb views across Lyme Bay. The single, spacious, comfortable bar offers a friendly welcome and admits children until 7pm. There is a wide choice of food, with fish a speciality. A function room upstairs and a front forecourt provide extra space for drinkers. It is a short walk from the model village and cliff railway, and the steep descent to Babbacombe Beach is nearby. ❀◑♿♣⊬

Crown & Sceptre
2 Petitor Road, St Marychurch, TQ1 4QA

⊙ 11-3 (12-4 winter), 5.30-11; 11-11 Fri; 12-4, 6.30-11 Sat; 12-4, 7-10.30 Sun

☎ (01803) 328290

Courage Best Bitter; Fuller's London Pride; Greene King Old Speckled Hen; Theakston Old Peculier; Young's Special; guest beers Ⓗ

The landlord has chalked up 30 years in charge here (29 in this Guide). This 200-year-old coaching house is a well supported and much loved community local; families (and dogs) are welcome. Candlelit tables and ceilings adorned with pennants and chamber pots add character. Two enclosed gardens are a bonus. Snacks are available on request (no meals Sun). It hosts several live music evenings: jazz (Tue and Sun), varied live music (Sat) and a folk session most Fridays; Torquay folk club meets here, too. ♨Q❀◑⊟♣P

Hole in the Wall
6 Park Lane, TQ1 2AU (off end of Torwood St)

⊙ 11-11; 12-10.30 Sun

☎ (01803) 200755

Courage Best Bitter; Greene King IPA, Abbot; Sharp's Doom Bar; Shepherd Neame Spitfire; Wells Bombardier; guest beers Ⓗ

Tucked away behind the harbour, Torquay's oldest inn (circa 1540), with its beamed ceilings and listed cobbled floors, is a real ale oasis in the town centre. For hundreds of years its hospitality has been enjoyed by all, from generations of seafarers to modern-day business types, locals, and the many people who visit the town on holiday. During the day, the restaurant doubles as a no-smoking area for drinkers. ❀◑⊬

Tuckenhay

Maltster's Arms
Bow Creek , TQ9 7EQ

(signed from A381, Totnes-Kingsbridge road)

⊙ 11-11; 12-10.30 Sun

☎ (01803) 732350 website: www.tuckenhay.com

Princetown Dartmoor IPA; guest beers Ⓗ

Superb old pub, overlooking the peaceful Bow Creek, with boat moorings available on the tidal River Dart and ample waterside seating. It hosts excellent barbecues and occasional live music outdoors. The two cosy rooms are linked by a long, narrow bar. Live music is sometimes staged on Friday evenings. The pub fields a cricket team. The restaurant serves good food and boasts fine views of the wooded valley. A discount applies to accommodation for card-carrying CAMRA members. Heron Valley cider is sold in summer. ♨Q♉❀⛟◑♿♣●P

Umberleigh

Rising Sun Inn
EX37 9BU

⊙ 12-3, 6-11 (11-11 summer); 12-3, 6-10.30 Sun

☎ (01769) 560447 website: www.risingsuninn.com

Cotleigh Tawny, Barn Owl Ⓗ

Famous old sporting inn, dating back to the 13th century, this attractive hotel overlooks the River Taw. The bar and lounge boast exposed beams, an inglenook, a log-burning stove, an impressive mural and abundance of fishing memorabilia. Facilities for golf, fishing, shooting, cycling and walking are all available within an easy distance. ♨♉❀⛟◑▲⇌♣P

Wembury

Odd Wheel
Knighton Road, PL9 0JD

⊙ 12-3, 6.30-11; 12-11 Sat; 12-4, 7-10 Sun

☎ (01752) 862287

Courage Best Bitter; Princetown Jail Ale; Shepherd Neame Spitfire; Skinner's Spriggan Ale; South Hams XSB Ⓖ

Friendly village pub where the comfortable lounge bar offers an extensive menu, with game a speciality. The dog-friendly public bar is simply furnished, housing a pool table and dartboard. Live jazz sessions take place on Thursday evenings. The bus stop outside is on a regular route to Plymouth. Ducks and chicken roam freely on the small patio, while the orchard is home to ponies, goats and pot-bellied pigs – a favourite with children. Q❀◑⊟▲P

Wembury Club ✔
Southland Park Road, PL9 0HH (off Church Rd)

⊙ 7.30 (8 Fri; 4 Sat)-11; 12-11 Sun

☎ (01752) 862159

Moorhouses Premier; guest beers Ⓖ

Although this is a private club, CAMRA members and their families are made most welcome in this excellent drinking establishment. It offers changing guest beers that are generally rarely available elsewhere, sold at sensible and uniform prices, regardless of strength. The landlord relishes the opportunity to obtain more uncommon beers on request. The club is near a picturesque marine conservation area, which is popular with walkers. ♨Q♉❀◑⊟♿▲♣●P

Westcott

Merry Harriers
EX15 1SA (S of Cullompton on B3181)

⊙ 11.30-3, 6-11; 12-3, 6-10.30 Sun

☎ (01392) 881254

Cotleigh Tawny; O'Hanlon's Firefly, Yellowhammer; guest beers Ⓗ

The Merry Harriers is a food-oriented road pub with a warm, friendly welcome. There is a log fire in the lounge and a large skittle alley, that doubles as a function room, at the rear. Fish and steaks are specialities on the pub's menu. Motel-style accommodation is available in a bungalow behind the pub. Addlestones cider is sold. ♨Q❀⛟◑♣●P

Westward Ho!

Pig on the Hill
Pusehill, EX39 5AH OS426282

⊙ 12-3, 6.30-11; 12-3, 7-10.30 Sun

☎ (01237) 425889

Country Life Old Appledore, Wallop, Golden Pig, Country Bumpkin Ⓗ
Converted farmhouse with a porcine theme. The pub is family- and dog-friendly with a bar area and two dining areas. Outside is a sheltered patio and a large garden; the pub hosts a petanque club in the grounds. Formerly the home of the Country Life Brewery, the bar still stocks its beers. The coastal footpath is within easy reach. The pub has holiday cottages to rent. The cider sold here is Addlestones.
❀◑♿▲♣●P

Whiddon Down

Post Inn

EX20 2QT (close to A30, Whiddon Down roundabout)
⏲ 11-11; closed Tue; 12-10.30 Sun
☎ (01647) 231242
Beer range varies Ⓗ
Built in the 16th century as a post office on the old coaching road to the west, the Post is a pleasantly refurbished country pub. Handy for the A30, it is keen to cater for modern travellers (meals are served 11-11); food is home cooked, using local produce and game in season. The central bar serves three rooms; the two side rooms, although generally laid out for diners, are available for no-smoking drinkers. The ales follow a West Country theme and the cider (Grays) is local. ♨Q❀◑▲●P

Whimple

New Fountain Inn

Church Road, EX5 2TA (leave A30 E of Exeter at Daisymount, follow signs)
⏲ 12-3, 6.30-11; 12-3, 7-10.30 Sun
☎ (01404) 822350
O'Hanlon's Firefly; Teignworthy Reel Ale; guest beers Ⓖ
A good, if small, Devon village pub, with two bars and an open fire. One bar has recently been refurbished in old elm panelling to maintain the warm, welcoming atmosphere. A varied menu with reasonable prices is based on local produce. Community activities are centred on the pub and a village heritage centre is housed in the pub's car park. ♨Q❀◑♣P

Widecombe-in-the-Moor

Rugglestone Inn

TQ13 7TF (¼ mile from village centre) OS721766
⏲ 11.30-3, 6.30-11; 12-3, 6.30-10.30 Sun
☎ (01364) 621327
Butcombe Bitter; St Austell Dartmoor Best; guest beers Ⓖ
Unspoilt, cosy pub in a splendid Dartmoor setting. The small bar area has seating and a stone floor; beer is also served through a hatch in the passageway. The lounge, with an open fire, welcomes children. The pub is named after a local 'logan' stone. Across the stream, a large grassed seating area has a shelter for use in bad weather. A wide selection of home-cooked food is served. The large car park is just down the road. ♨Q☋❀◑⊟♿▲●P⚟

Winkleigh

King's Arms

Fore Street, EX19 8HX
⏲ 11-11; 12-10.30 Sun
☎ (01837) 83384
website: www.hatherleigh.org.uk/kingsarms
Butcombe Bitter; Flowers IPA; Skinner's Cornish Knocker Ale Ⓗ
At the heart of Winkleigh village, this old thatched inn is well worth visiting, with low ceilings and a log fire warming the single bar. Three real ales are served plus Winkleigh's Sam's Dry cider. Freshly-prepared meals made from local produce are ordered from the blackboard above the fire, or the restaurant menu. Look for the well in the dining area.
♨Q❀◑♣●

Woodland

Rising Sun

TQ13 7JT (signed from Plymouth-bound A38) OS790697
⏲ 11.45-3, 6-11; closed Mon; 12-3, 7-10.30 Sun
☎ (01364) 652544 website: www.risingsunwoodland.co.uk
Princetown Jail Ale; guest beer Ⓗ
Food-oriented, rural pub that has been awarded many accolades for its cuisine and is renowned for its pies. It comprises a spacious, open-plan area used mainly by diners, with a long, single bar where small screens offer some privacy. The children's area is off the main bar. The extensive grounds are pleasant, with a children's play area. Accommodation is recommended but you may be woken by the peacocks.
♨Q☋❀⇌◑♿▲P

Yeoford

Mare & Foal

The Village, EX17 5JD
⏲ 12-2 (not Mon or Tue), 6-11; 12-3, 7-10.30 Sun
☎ (01363) 84348 website: www.mareandfoal.co.uk
Beer range varies Ⓗ
Although built in the 1830s to serve the expanding railway, this is a pub not a railway hotel. An open fire, interconnecting rooms, a skittle alley and a no-smoking dining room give it character. The food is sourced locally and is cooked to order, featuring traditional country fare, plus a curry night on Thursday (no food Tue eve). The two or three ales are usually from local breweries, including Sharp's and Cotleigh, while the cider is Thatchers.
♨☋❀◑⇶●P⚟

By George!

It was my Uncle George who discovered that alcohol was a food well in advance of modern medical thought.

P G Wodehouse, The Inimitable Jeeves

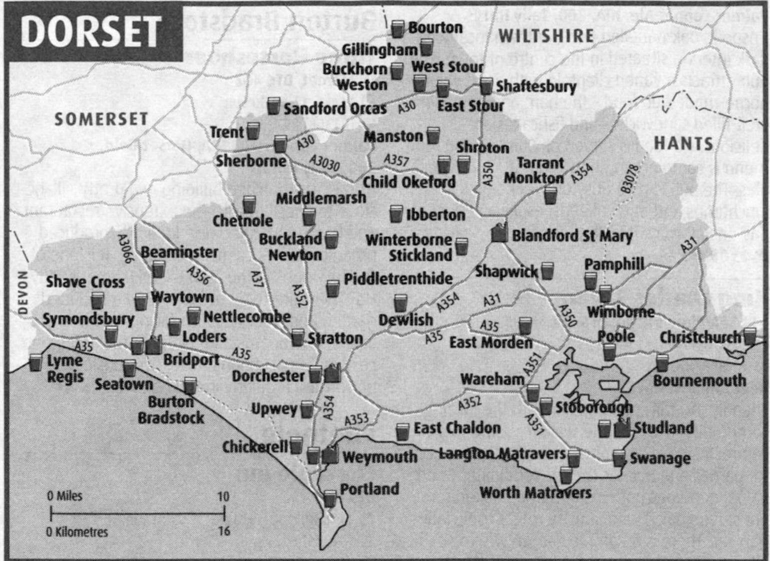

Beaminster

Greyhound Inn

The Square, DT8 3AW

11.30-3, 6.30-11; 12-3, 7-10.30 Sun

☎ (01308) 862496

Palmer Copper Ale, IPA, Dorset Gold (summer), **200, Tally Ho!** (winter)

Picturesque, rendered pub with a lichen-spotted roof and slatted window shutters. The attractive, 18th-century interior features a spacious flagstoned bar room, with a stone fireplace, leading to a comfortable dining area. A corridor, hung with local photos and Guinness adverts, leads to the family/function room. The pub caters for regulars and visiting trade with a varied menu including local fish, steaks, pasta and vegetarian dishes. Dogs are welcome.

Q

Bournemouth

Goat & Tricycle

27-29 West Hill Road, BH2 5PP

12-3, 6-11; 12-3, 7-10.30 Sun

☎ (01202) 314220

Wadworth IPA, 6X, JCB; guest beers

Sensibly joined together 12 years ago by Wadworth's, the Goat used to be two neighbouring pubs. The bar boasts a row of 11 handpumps and on the wall is a huge blackboard with tasting notes carefully chalked up. The full Wadworth range is supplemented by seven guest ales, with two or three firkins of each at a time. The delightful flower-filled courtyard is heated and can be used all year round at East Dorset CAMRA Pub of the Year 2004. Q

Porterhouse

113 Poole Road, Westbourne, BH4 8BY

11-11; 12-10.30 Sun

☎ (01202) 768586

Ringwood Best Bitter, Fortyniner, Old Thumper, seasonal beers; guest beer

Cosy, Ringwood-owned pub with a bustling atmosphere, featuring a wood floor, oak panelling and hops adorning the bar. It sells the full range of Ringwood beers and an excellent choice of changing guests plus Cheddar Valley cider. The pub was voted East Dorset CAMRA Pub of the Year six times in the last eleven years, as well as spring Pub of the Season 2004.

Q (Branksome)

Bourton

White Lion

High Street, SP8 5AT

(1 mile off A303 between Zeals and Wincanton)

12-3, 6-11; 12-3, 7-10 (closed eve Jan/Feb) Sun

☎ (01747) 840866

Fuller's London Pride; Greene King IPA; guest beers

Traditional inn dating from 1763 with three flagstoned bar areas separated by wood panel and glass partitions. This popular village local serves regular and guest ales, often including Hop Back seasonal brews. Bar meals are available and top quality meals are served in the Bush restaurant. The large garden and children's play area are popular in summer. Accommodation in double and four-poster en-suite rooms is available. Q P

Bridport

George Hotel

4 South Street, DT6 3NQ

11-11; 12-3, 7-11 Sun

☎ (01308) 423187

INDEPENDENT BREWERIES

Badger Blandford St Mary
Dorset Weymouth
Goldfinch Dorchester (brewing suspended)
Isle of Purbeck Studland
Palmer Bridport

Palmer Copper Ale, IPA, 200, Tally Ho! [H]
Unspoilt, oak-panelled two-bar town local with a dark interior, situated in the centre of town. The pub attracts a varied clientele with good value home-made pub food – the ham and pork joints, well-filled sandwiches and fishcakes are delicious. No food is served on Sunday. The food menu is complemented by a range of excellent ales. The pub can be busy on weekday lunchtimes and at weekends, especially market day on Saturday. It is dog friendly.
♕♞◐♣P⁄

King Charles Tavern
114 St Andrews Road, DT6 3BL (on B3066)
☼ 11-3, 6-11; 11-11 Sat; 12-3.30, 7-10.30 Sun
☎ (01308) 422911
Beer range varies [H]
Friendly, no-frills pub popular with the local community, a 15-minute walk from the town centre. Inside is one room with plenty of space for games and quieter corners for dining. Good value, generous portions of home-cooked food are served daily, with Sunday roasts especially popular. There is an ample garden with a skittle alley next to it. One real ale is served which changes frequently and is often from regional or local breweries. Westons Traditional Scrumpy is stocked.
♕❀⇌◐♣●

Buckhorn Weston

Stapleton Arms
Church Hill, SP8 5HS
(Wincanton exit off A303 or A30) OS757247
☼ 11-3. 6-11; 12-3, 6-10.30 Sun
☎ (01963) 370396 website: www.thestapletonarms.co.uk
Butcombe Bitter; Ringwood Best Bitter; [H] **guest beers** [H] /[G]
Popular, welcoming village pub at the hub of the community. Usually three guest ales are available, mostly from micros. One is dispensed by gravity, increasing to 12 for the annual beer festival in July. Excellent home-prepared food, from bar snacks to full meals, is served in the large single bar or the two no-smoking dining areas. There is a large garden with a children's play area. Westons Old Rosie cider is supplemented by guests and the occasional perry.
Q❀⇌◐♣●P

Buckland Newton

Gaggle of Geese
DT2 7BS (600 yds from B3143)
☼ 12-2.30, 6.30-11; 12-3, 7-10.30 Sun
☎ (01300) 345249
website: www.gaggleofgeese.co.uk
Badger Best (occasional); **Butcombe Bitter; Ringwood Best Bitter, Fortyniner; guest beers** [H]
Large, traditional village pub at the top of the Piddle Valley. The bar has wooden floors and exposed beams, with several drinking areas and a restaurant where an extensive menu of home-cooked food is offered. A genuine free house, it offers occasional guest beers. Internet access is available here. The large garden is popular in summer and the adjacent caravan club site is also run by the pub.
♕Q♞❀◐♿▲♣P⁄

Burton Bradstock

Three Horseshoes
Mill Street, DT6 4QZ
☼ 11-11; 12-10.30 Sun
☎ (01308) 897259
Palmer Copper Ale, IPA, Dorset Gold, 200, Tally Ho! [H]
Attractive, thatched building in a pretty village close to Chesil Beach. The extensive restaurant and bar menus specialise in locally produced organic meat, local fish and game. It is one of the few pubs in the area to sell Palmer's Tally Ho! There are two outdoor areas: a secluded garden and a set of south-facing benches. Inside, low beams and a log fire make the pub cosy in winter. Good quality live music is performed regularly in the bar. ♕❀◐▲P

Chetnole

Chetnole Inn
DT9 6NU
☼ 11-2.30, 6.30-11; 12-3, 7-10.30 Sun
☎ (01935) 872337
Branscombe Branoc; Butcombe Bitter; Palmer IPA; guest beer [H]
This classic country pub, opposite the church, is a 20-minute stroll along country lanes from Chetnole Halt on the Weymouth to Bristol line, and makes an excellent day out. The public bar is warmed by a blazing fire, and there is a skittle alley behind. Excellent food includes a Sunday curry night and fish and chips on Wednesday evening (no food Wed lunchtime). Guest beers come from west country brewers, and there is a beer festival at Easter. ♕Q❀⇌◐⊟♿≋♣P

Chickerell

Lugger Inn
West Street, DT3 4DY
☼ 11-11; 12-10.30 Sun
☎ (01305) 766611 website: www.luggerinn.co.uk
Palmer Dorset Gold; guest beers [H]
Closed for 10 years, the pub has recently been extensively rebuilt as part of a housing project. Bearing little resemblance to the original, it now resumes its place as the only true pub in the village. It has a flagged bar area, restaurant and function room. Local beers feature prominently: the house beer (rebadged Weymouth Best) comes from the Dorset Brewing Company. Accommodation includes five holiday cottages. Wheelchair access is to the side.
♞❀⇌◐♿●P

Child Okeford

Saxon Inn
Gold Hill, DT11 8HD
☼ 12-3, 7-11; 12-3, 7-10.30 Sun
☎ (01258) 860310
Butcombe Bitter; Ringwood Best Bitter; guest beers [H]
Tucked peacefully away at the north end of the village, the pub was originally three farm cottages until the early 1950s. Nestling under Hambleden Hill iron age fort, it is in good walking country. A corner bar serves both the main room, with its open fire, and the low-beamed, panelled lounge. Old prints and early

photographs decorate both rooms. Excellent meals are cooked to order (no food Sun eve). A large garden overlooks the scenic Dorset countryside. ♨Q❀◑P

Christchurch

Olde George Inn ✔

2A Castle Street, BH23 1DT

11-11; 12-10.30 Sun

☎ (01202) 479383

Brains Dark; Ringwood Fortyniner; guest beers H

Former coaching inn boasting a 600-year history, located at the bottom of Christchurch high street, near the Priory. It has two rooms with low ceilings, each served by its own bar. The smaller front room is no-smoking. A mild beer is usually available. A partly-covered courtyard has patio heaters and extra seating. Curries on Thursday and roasts on Sunday are served in the barn bar at the bottom of the courtyard. Q❀◑⚟

Ship in Distress

66 Stanpit, BH23 3NA

(400 yds from Purewell Cross towards Mudeford)

11-11; 12-10.30 Sun

☎ (01202) 485123 website: www.theshipindistress.com

Adnams Broadside; Ringwood Best Bitter; Wells Bombardier; H **guest beers** H/G

Delightful, 300-year-old pub which was formerly home to John Streeter, a notorious smuggler. Original wooden beams remain in the bars, with comfortable seating and a cosy atmosphere. A fascinating mix of old photographs, sea-faring memorabilia and fishing tools decorates the interior. As well as the regular beers there is a vigorous guest beer policy. The adjoining restaurant specialises in seafood. This is a fine pub in which to drink real ale, chat with friends and laugh at the pace of life. Q❀◑⊟♿♣P

Thomas Tripp

10 Wick Lane, BH23 1HX

11-11; 12-10.30 Sun

☎ (01202) 490498

Ringwood Fortyniner H

Named after a legendary local smuggler, the pub is situated just round the corner from the busy high street, the tranquil Priory and the old trolleybus turntable. Good food is available at lunchtimes. Frequent live bands play in the evening and the pub can be quite boisterous, but always friendly. Usually just one cask ale is offered – from the local Ringwood Brewery – always in pristine condition. ❀◐

Dewlish

Oak at Dewlish

DT2 7ND (signed 2 miles NW of A354) OS776983

11.30-2.30, 6-11; 12-3, 7-10.30 Sun

☎ (01258) 837352

Ringwood Best Bitter, seasonal beers; guest beer H

Attractive, small village pub with an L-shaped bar, traditional tiling, stripped pine furnishings and settle seating. Outside is a large, pleasant garden. Good food is served in the bar area and small dining room, featuring local produce and including vegetarian options. Two real ales from Ringwood are usually available, as well as a guest from a smaller brewery. Real cider comes straight from the cask. Dogs are welcome. ♨Q❀◑♣●

Dorchester

Blue Raddle

9 Church Street, DT1 1JN

11.30-3 (not Mon), 6.30-11; 12-3 (closed eve) Sun

☎ (01305) 267762

Otter Bitter; Sharp's Doom Bar; guest beers H

Friendly, town-centre free-house with dark wood wainscots, and two realistic flame-effect gas fires. Popular with drinkers and diners, young and old, there are always vegetarian options on the excellent menu. The guest ales are usually sourced from west country breweries. There is no parking at the pub but the town car park is adjacent. ◑♿⇌

East Chaldon

Sailor's Return

DT2 8DN (1 mile S of A352) OS791834

11-11; 12-10.30 Sun

☎ (01305) 853847 website: www.sailorsreturn.com

Hampshire Strong's Best Bitter; Ringwood Best Bitter; guest beers H

This large, thatched inn on the fringe of a small hamlet provides a welcome break for ramblers on the nearby Dorset Coastal Path. It can be busy on summer weekends. Inside is a large beamed bar at one end and a stone-walled dining room at the other with flagstone floors throughout. The food menu is extensive and renowned for its high quality and generous portions. Up to seven beers are offered in high season, as well as a cask cider. A tented beer festival is held in late spring. ❀◑♣●P

East Morden

Cock & Bottle ✔

BH20 7DL (on B3075, off A35 near Wareham)

11-3, 6-11; 12-3, 7-10.30 Sun

☎ (01929) 459238

Badger K&B Sussex, Best, Tanglefoot H

Lovely, unspoilt village pub. An open fire is the main feature in the public bar. Well-used by locals, the pub attracts a lot of custom for its award-winning food, served in the cosy dining area. (Booking is recommended for weekend meals.) Reasonably-priced bar snacks are also served. The garden is well situated to enjoy a summer pint. Disabled facilities are good with easy wheelchair access. ♨Q◑⊟♿♣P

East Stour

King's Arms

The Common, SP8 5NB (on A30, W of Shaftesbury)

12-3, 5.30-11; 12-3, 7.30-10.30 Sun

☎ (01747) 838325

Butcombe Bitter; Palmer Copper Ale; guest beer H

Large, single-bar country pub alongside the A30. Good value, home-cooked food is served in the quiet, comfortable lounge/dining area, decorated with chickens and cockerels (no food Sun eve). There is also a games room. Live, acoustic music is played on the first Sunday of the month, and folk music on the third Sunday –

bring your own instrument. Comfortable accommodation is available in four recently-refurbished en-suite rooms. Basic camping facilities are offered and well-behaved dogs are welcome. Q❀⇌◑▲♣P⊬

Gillingham

Buffalo ✔
Lydfords Lane, Wyke, SP8 4NS
(100 yds from B3081, Wincanton road)
✪ 12-2.30, 5.30 (7 Sat)-11; 12-10.30 Sun
☎ (01747) 823759
Badger K&B Sussex, Best, seasonal beers Ⓗ
The Buffalo is at the heart of the community, hosting meetings of several local societies, and has the feel of a rural village pub. Good food is served in the pleasant dining area (not Sun eve). A buffalo was the logo of the nearby former Matthews Brewery, hence its name, and beer bottles from that firm are displayed in the main bar. The former Matthews buildings, now flats, can still be seen. ⛰Q❀◑♣P

Phoenix Inn ✔
The Square, SP8 4AY
✪ 10-2.30 (3 Sat), 7-11; 12-3, 7-10.30 Sun
☎ (01747) 823277
Badger K&B Sussex, Best, seasonal beers Ⓗ
Busy town-centre pub in the high street, adorned with award-winning floral displays. Built in the 15th century and added to in the 17th century, it was originally a coaching inn complete with its own brewery. A cosy, friendly, one-bar pub, it has a separate dining area as well as an outside drinking area in the square. ⛰Q❀◑▲≹♣

Ibberton

Crown Inn
Church Lane, DT11 0EN (4 miles off A357)
✪ 12-2 (not Mon), 7-11; 12-2, 7-10.30 Sun
☎ (01258) 817448
Butcombe Bitter; guest beer Ⓗ
Delightful, unspoilt pub in a peaceful lane near the village church. Entrance to the two bars is via a terrific old oak door. The main bar, with its original flagstone floor, is dominated by a large inglenook and the walls are decorated with old photographs. The rear bar is mostly used for dining. A small brook runs alongside the idyllic lawned garden. Nearby are Woolland Heath and Bulbarrow Hill viewpoint, with plenty of walks to earn your pint. ⛰Q♉❀◑♣P

Langton Matravers

King's Arms Hotel ✔
27 High Street, BH19 3HA
✪ 12-3, 6-11; 12-3, 7-10.30 Sun
☎ (01929) 422979
Ringwood Best Bitter; Fortyniner; guest beer Ⓗ
Dating back to 1743, this lovely four-room pub features the original flagstone floors. Adorning the walls are paintings and photographs of the local area. In the early days the front room was formally the village morgue and the rest of the building was the inn! Outside is a large garden with a shed housing a pool table. The pub is ideally situated for exploring the Purbecks. ⛰Q♉❀◑⊟≹♣

Loders

Loders Arms
DT6 3SA
(approx 2 miles NE of Bridport, via A35 or A3066) OS493942
✪ 11.30-3, 6-11 (11.30-11 summer Sat); 12-3, 6-10.30 (12-10.30 summer) Sun
☎ (01308) 422431 website: www.lodersarms.co.uk
Palmer Copper Ale, IPA, 200 Ⓗ
Charming inn standing in a pretty village in the River Asker Valley, a short drive from Bridport and the coast. The garden affords pleasing views of the surrounding hills which are etched with ancient field terraces. The pub comprises a long, beamed bar and a dining room at one end, with an enviable reputation for home-cooked food. Well supported by the locals, the pub has seven skittles teams. The caravan/camp site lies beyond the car park. Children (and dogs) are welcome. ⛰❀⇌◑▲♣●P

Lyme Regis

Harbour Inn
Marine Parade, DT7 3JF
✪ 11-11 (11-3, 6-11 winter Mon-Fri); 11-11 Sun
☎ (01297) 442299
Otter Bitter, Ale; St Austell Tribute Ⓗ
Next to the world-famous Cobb, this spacious beachside pub is laid out in modern café style. The emphasis is on food here – although three west country ales are always available. The front verandah overlooks the beach and harbour, and there is a reserved seating area on the beach (plastic glasses only here). The enviable location means higher prices, but it is worth it to feel the sand between your toes. Q❀◑▲⊬

Nag's Head
32 Silver Street, DT7 3HS (400 yds up hill from Broad St)
✪ 11-2, 5-11; 11-11 Fri & Sat; 12-10.30 Sun
☎ (01297) 442312
Butcombe Bitter; Otter Ale; guest beers Ⓗ
Old coaching inn a short walk from the town centre. It has two linked bar areas and a games room. Two regular local ales are available plus a range of guests. Occasional mini-beer fests are held. The pub is renowned for Saturday night gigs with visiting bands. Food is served at Sunday lunchtime only. The restaurant and garden enjoy magnificent views along the Jurassic Coast. Booking is recommended for the B&B accommodation. ⛰❀⇌▲♣

Volunteer
31 Broad Street, DT7 3QE
✪ 11-11; 12-10.30 Sun
☎ (01297) 442214
Draught Bass; Fuller's London Pride; guest beers Ⓗ
Historic, centuries-old pub named after the regiment founded in 1794. Double fronted with a low ceiling, there is an atmospheric bar and a no-smoking family/dining room. Two regular beers are served plus the house beer Donegal, which is Branscombe Vale BVB, available on stillage behind the bar. A varying guest beer is also on offer. Bar meals are recommended (not served Sun eve or Mon). The sound system plays mainly 1960s and 70s music, low enough not to detract from the merry banter between the locals. ♉◑▲⊬

Manston

Plough

Shaftesbury Road, DT10 1HB
(on B3091, 2½ miles NE of Sturminster Newton)
⏲ 11.30-2.30, 6.30-11; 12-10.30 Sun
☎ (01258) 472484
Palmer Copper Ale, IPA; 🄷 guest beers 🄷 /🄶
The pub is situated in a prominent position on a sharp bend between Shaftesbury and Sturminster Newton. Inside is a single large bar with a no-smoking conservatory extension. Note the ornate plasterwork ceiling and unusual relief panels on the bar front and walls, said to be fertility symbols. Two guest ales are usually on gravity dispense. There is a petanque rink in the large garden where the July beer festival is held.
♨Q❀◑◗♿⛺♣P⚞

Middlemarsh

Hunter's Moon

DT9 5QN (on A352)
⏲ 11-2.30, 6-11; 12-3, 7-10.30 Sun
☎ (01963) 210939 website: www.thehuntersmoon.co.uk
Beer range varies 🄷
The charming owner has transformed the derelict former White Horse into a quality pub with a homely and welcoming atmosphere. Brewery memorabilia lines the walls, with jugs, cups and tankards hanging from the ceiling. Many small alcoves and cosy corners fill the interesting L-shaped room. The menu is not extensive, but the food is good and local game is a speciality. The beers come from Palmer, St Austell and Sharp's. ♨Q❀⛟◑◗♿P

Nettlecombe

Marquis of Lorne

DT6 3SY (approach from A3066 to Powerstock) OS517956
⏲ 11.30-2.30, 6.30-11; 12-2.30, 6.30-10.30 Sun
☎ (01308) 485236
website: www.marquisoflorne.com
Palmer Copper Ale, IPA, 200 🄷
Lovely stone pub tucked away in the heart of west Dorset. The wood-panelled main bar is cosy and attractive with a real fire. The pub enjoys a good reputation for food, served in the bar and the dining area. The pretty garden has a children's play area. B&B accommodation is available and the location is ideal for exploring the surrounding countryside and coastal area. This unspoilt pub is well worth seeking out.
♨Q♘❀⛟◑◗⛺P

Pamphill

Vine Inn ☆

Vine Hill, BH21 4EE (off B3082)
⏲ 11-2.30, 7-11 (10.30 winter Mon-Wed); 12-3, 7-10.30 Sun
☎ (01202) 882259
Fuller's London Pride; 🄷 guest beer 🄶
Delightful pub, built as a bakehouse over 200 years ago, close to the National Trust's Kingston Lacey House and Badbury Rings. Run by the same family for three generations, it has two small bars (one no-smoking) and a games room. The garden has ample seating and is popular with walkers and cyclists. Sandwiches and ploughman's are served at lunchtime. Bulmers cider is served on gravity at local CAMRA Rural Pub of the Year 2004.
Q❀◑⌸♣●P⚞⊓

Piddletrenthide

Poachers Inn

DT2 7QX
⏲ 12-11; 12-10.30 Sun
☎ (01300) 348358
website: www.thepoachersinn.co.uk
Butcombe Bitter; Fuller's London Pride; Palmer 200; Ringwood Fortyniner 🄷
Set in the heart of the beautiful Piddle Valley, with sloping lawns leading down to the River Piddle at the bottom of the garden, the pub has gone from strength to strength since the new owners took over in 2004. Three real ales are always available, and the beer range varies at the request of customers. Farmers in boots mingle happily with diners who have come for the fine cuisine and residents staying in the attractive en-suite accommodation.
♨Q❀⛟◑◗♿P

Poole

Bermuda Triangle

10 Parr Street, Lower Parkstone, BH14 0JY
⏲ 12-2.30, 5-11; 12-11 Sat; 12-10.30 Sun
☎ (01202) 748087
Beer range varies 🄷
This lively pub sells four guest ales, the frequency with which they are changed bearing testimony to their popularity. Taped music in the evening adds to the atmosphere and the wood-panelled walls are covered with artefacts and stories relating to the pub's name. A former CAMRA East Dorset Pub of the Year – do not miss this mecca for real ale drinkers if you are in the area. ❀◑⇌ (Parkstone)

Blue Boar

29 Market Close, BH15 1NE
⏲ 11-3, 5-11; 12-11 Sat; 12-10.30 Sun
☎ (01202) 682247 website: www.blueboarpub.co.uk
Cottage Southern Bitter; Courage Best Bitter, Directors; guest beers 🄷
Built in 1750 as a merchant's house, this popular free house is a minute's walk from the high street. The lounge bar offers comfortable seating. The atmospheric cellar bar features live music on Wednesday, which is folk night, and Friday. On Saturday Claire and Jim's disco plays an eclectic selection of music. Both bars, and passageways, are covered in nautical artefacts and photographs. There are tables out on the pavement in summer. Q❀◑⇌♣

Branksome Railway Hotel

492 Poole Road, BH12 1DQ
⏲ 11-11; 11-10.30 Sun
☎ (01202) 769555
Hampshire Strong's Best Bitter; Fuller's London Pride; Hop Back Summer Lightning 🄷
This Victorian building was built to service the rail network as it extended from Bournemouth to Poole and still enjoys excellent public transport links. Some of the original architectural features survive, although significant alterations have been made. Internally, the layout is open-plan but divided into a vibrant saloon with pool

table, quieter seating area and a high-ceilinged, long-windowed lounge overlooking the railway line. Good en-suite accommodation is available. 🛏◐⊟♿≋♣P

Brewhouse

68 High Street, BH15 1DA
⌚ 11-11; 12-10.30 Sun
☎ (01202) 685288
Milk Street Mermaid, Beer, seasonal beers 🄷
Popular town-centre pub owned by Frome's Milk Street Brewery. Formerly the home of the now-defunct Poole Brewery, this split-level room is served by a single bar. The front area overlooks the High Street; at the rear are two pool tables and a classic rock juke box. CAMRA Pub of the Season for the past two years, it sells excellent beers at the best price in town. ≋♣

Oakdale

Kingsmill Road, BH17 8RQ
⌚ 11-11; 12-10.30 Sun
☎ (01202) 672055
Ringwood Best Bitter, Old Thumper, seasonal beers 🄷
Welcoming pub visible from the A350 but tricky to get to, although worth the effort to track down. This spacious, modern pub has two entrances: one to the public bar with its pool table and dartboard, the other a ramp to the lounge where there is a large open fire to welcome you on a cold day. Sunday lunches are popular. ♨❀◐◑⊟♿♣P

Poole Arms

The Quay, BH15 1HJ
⌚ 11-11; 12-10.30 Sun
☎ (01202) 672309
Ringwood Best Bitter, Fortyniner 🄷
This traditional, old-fashioned pub, overlooking the harbour, stands out from the others on Poole Quay with its distinctive green tiled frontage. You can enjoy your pint sitting outside and watching the world go by. Inside are wood-panelled walls featuring pictures of different ships at Poole Quay, old and new. Q❀◐◑

Royal Oak & Gas Tavern

25 Skinner Street, BH15 1RQ
⌚ 11-11; 12-10.30 Sun
☎ (01202) 672022
Hampshire Strong's Best Bitter; Hook Norton Old Hooky; Ringwood Best Bitter 🄷
Local back-street inn, dating from 1798. Many original features remain – note the windows and wood-panelled walls. An enclosed garden can be used in summer as an extra function room. Close to Poole quay, the pub is off the beaten track in the old town and a haven of peace during the busy summer holiday season. ❀≋♣

Portland

George Inn

133 Reforne, Easton, DT5 2AP
⌚ 11-11; 12-10.30 Sun
☎ (01305) 820011
Adnams Bitter; Greene King Abbot; guest beer 🄷
This 17th-century pub lies just across the road from the cricket ground – a location much appreciated by visitors and locals alike, particularly on warm summer evenings. The original bar is built from timbers of long-gone sailing ships and is a place for conversation. In contrast, the more recently built extension hosts occasional live music, quizzes and darts matches. Food is excellent with the popular weekly gourmet evenings offering good value. A beer festival is held on the weekend nearest to St George's Day. Q❀◐◑⊟♣

Sandford Orcas

Mitre Inn

DT9 4RU (village signed from B3148) OS626205
⌚ 11.30-2.30 (not Mon), 7-11; 12-2.30, 7-10.30 Sun
☎ (01963) 220271
Greene King Abbot; guest beers 🄷
Mind your head when you enter the Mitre! The welcome is warm, home-cooked food is excellent, there is plenty of comfortable seating including armchairs in the bar, and there is fine real ale to enjoy. Flagged floors extend from the bar area to the dining room and outside is an elevated garden. Children are welcome. No food is served on Monday. ♨Q❀◐◑♿♣P

Seatown

Anchor Inn

DT6 6SU (at Seatown beach) OS420919
⌚ 11-3, 6-11 (11-11 summer); 12-10.30 Sun
☎ (01297) 489215
Palmer Copper Ale, IPA, 200 🄷
Dramatically situated on the edge of the beach, nestling under the 600ft Golden Cap on the coastal path, this comfortable pub is predictably busy in summer. Out of season it is quieter and this is a good time to take a look at the photographs on the walls and fossils on display. Opening hours vary according to the season and the weather conditions. ♨Q❀◐◑⊟⛺♣P

Shaftesbury

Crown ✔

40 High Street, SP7 8JG
⌚ 10-11; 12-10.30 Sun
☎ (01747) 852902
Badger K&B Sussex, Best Bitter, seasonal beers 🄷
Friendly single-room, single-bar town pub in the heart of historic Shaftesbury. Originally a far larger, 19th-century coaching inn, an interesting feature is the brick and wood fireplace, reputedly from the old abbey. Seating is mainly a long fixed settle down one wall. Major changes are planned for 2006. ♨❀♣

Shapwick

Anchor

West Street, DT11 9LB (off B3082)
⌚ 11-3, 6-11; 12-3, 7-10.30 Sun
☎ (01258) 857269
Ringwood Best Bitter; guest beers 🄷
In the heart of the delightful Stour Valley lies the village of Shapwick and opposite the village cross is this 19th-century, family-run pub. The main bar is light and open-plan with a central serving area and a small games room. Home-cooked meals are prepared to order, with vegetarians catered for and local Dorset dishes a speciality. An annual beer festival is held in a

marquee in the garden. This is a popular halt for walkers and cyclists on the Stour Valley way in summer. ❀◐◑♣♠P

Shave Cross

Shave Cross Inn ✔

DT6 6HW

(2½ miles W of B3162 Bridport-Broadwindsor road) OS415980

11-3, 6-11 (11-11 summer); 12-3, 7-10.30 (12-10.30 summer) Sun

☎ (01308) 868358

Branscombe Vale Branoc; guest beer Ⓗ

A quintessential rural pub – stone built, stone-flagged, thatched and steeped in history. It was the resting place for pilgrims who had their heads shaved here to visit St White's shrine two miles away. The lovely garden has a new children's play area and the thatched skittle alley doubles as a family/function room. The house beer, Marshwood Vale, is from the Dorset Brewing Company. Local English and Caribbean food is served in the bar and dining room (not Mon, or winter Sun eve) at this CAMRA regional Pub of the Year 2004. ♨Q☺❀◐◑♿⛺♣♠P

Sherborne

Digby Tap

Cooks Lane, DT9 3NS

11-2.30, 5.30-11; 12-3, 7-10.30 Sun

☎ (01935) 813148

Beer range varies Ⓗ

The town's only remaining true free house is situated close to the abbey, railway station and town centre. It has four drinking areas, all with flagged floors and cosy corners. A popular locals' pub but visitors are made welcome, however, mobile phones are discouraged and an inadvertent ring will incur a 'fine'. Three or four ever-changing beers are served, mostly from independent brewers in the south west. Basic but wholesome food is served on weekday lunchtimes. Q☺❀◐♿⇌♣♠

Shroton (Iwerne Courtney)

Cricketers ✔

Main Street, DT11 8QD (off A350)

11.30-3, 6.30-11; 12-3, 7-10.30 Sun

☎ (01258) 860421

Butcombe Bitter; Wadworth 6X; guest beers Ⓗ

This traditional village pub is well worth visiting. As the name suggests, it has a cricket theme, with pictures, artefacts and cricket bat style handpumps. Ideally located for those who like to walk up a thirst, the village nestles below Hambledon Hill. The pub has established a good reputation for its meals and customers come from near and far to dine here. Daily specials are on a blackboard.
Q❀⛟◐◑♿♣P⚟

Stoborough

King's Arms

3 Corfe Road, BH20 5AB (adjacent to B3075)

11-3, 5-11; 11-11 Sat; 12-10.30 Sun

☎ (01929) 552705

Ringwood Best Bitter; guest beers Ⓗ

A 400-year-old listed building, the King's Arms ironically played host to Cromwell's troops in1642 at the time of the siege of Corfe Castle. A long, slim pub renowned for its food, it has a large no-smoking restaurant and a split-level bar. The riverside dining area is popular with families in summer. An annual beer festival is hosted. ♨Q☺❀◐◑⊞P⚟

Stratton

Saxon Arms

The Square, DT2 9WG

11-2.30, 5.30 (6 Sat)-11; 12-3, 6.30-10.30 Sun

☎ (01305) 260020

Caledonian Deuchars IPA; Fuller's London Pride; Ringwood Best Bitter; Young's Special Ⓗ

Attractive and spacious stone pub built in 2001 with a thatched roof and large suntrap patio at the front with benches. The extensive menu plus specials board feature a wide range of fresh and well-prepared dishes including vegetarian choices, all served with a smile by efficient staff. It is no surprise that the pub is popular, so it is advisable to book if you wish to dine here.
♨❀◐◑♿P

Studland

Bankes Arms Hotel

Watery Lane, BH19 3AU

11-11; 12-10.30 Sun

☎ (01929) 450225

Isle of Purbeck Fossil Fuel, Solar Power, Studland Bay Wrecked; guest beers Ⓗ

Built of Purbeck stone and covered in virginia creeper, this famous pub overlooks the bay towards Bournemouth. A huge garden is across the lane from the pub. A range of nine ales is on offer including three from the Isle of Purbeck Brewery, opened in 2003 next to the pub. Owned by the National Trust and run by the same family for many years, the pub hosts an annual beer festival in August. Superb food is served all day in summer. ♨Q❀⛟◐◑⛺♠

Swanage

Red Lion

63 High Street, BH19 2LY

11-11; 12-10.30 Sun

☎ (01929) 423533

Caledonian Deuchars IPA; Taylor Landlord; Ringwood Best Bitter; guest beer Ⓗ

Thriving, two-room real ale pub in the town centre, dating back to the 17th century and retaining many traditional features. A range of good value meals is served all week, with curry night on Wednesday. The pub hosts quiz nights, games nights and occasional live music. The outside drinking area is busy in summer; well worth a visit. ♨❀◐◑⊟♣♠P

Symondsbury

Ilchester Arms

DT6 6HD

11.30-3 (not Mon), 6-11; 12-3, 6-10.30 Sun

☎ (01308) 422600

Palmer Copper Ale, IPA, Dorset Gold (summer), **200 or Tally Ho!** Ⓗ

Popular, stone-flagged pub situated at the heart of good walking country. In winter the low-beamed bar has a welcoming roaring fire burning in the inglenook. Home-cooked meals are served in the bar or dining room (booking recommended). Children are welcome in the skittle alley and the pretty stream-side garden. Two beers from Palmer are always available plus a real cider.

Tarrant Monkton

Langton Arms

DT11 8RX

11.30-11; 12-11 Sun

(01258) 830225

website: www.thelangtonarms.co.uk

Ringwood Fortyniner; guest beers [H]

Sadly, the old, thatched part of the pub was burned down in a major fire in March 2004, but following a major rebuild and with a new phoenix logo, the Langton Arms is again a highly successful enterprise and a gem of a pub. Set in a peaceful village in the north Dorset countryside, the pub offers excellent food, real ales, including a house beer, and accommodation. It now has a no-smoking restaurant, tap room and large dining room/function room with skittle alley. Wedding catering is a speciality.

Trent

Rose & Crown

DT9 4SL OS590184

12-3, 7-11; closed Mon; 12-3 (closed eve) Sun

(01935) 850776

Butcombe Bitter; Exmoor Ale; Otter Ale [H]

Originally two 15th-century cottages, this attractive rural pub has a true rustic feel. To the right is a cosy family room with a huge fireplace and shelves of books and there is a dining area in the conservatory. Beers are from brewers in the south-west. There is a selection of good food available – though not much for vegetarians. Bar snacks are not available on Friday and Saturday evenings, or Sunday lunchtime, but full meals are served at these times. Period bedrooms feature four-posters.

Upwey

Royal Standard

700 Dorchester Road, DT3 5LA

11-3, 6-11; 12-10.30 Sun

(01305) 812558

Butcombe Gold; Fuller's London Pride; Hop Back Summer Lightning [H]

Compact pub on the outskirts of town serving beer in top condition. It has a public bar and separate lounge, with a small amount of outdoor seating in summer. A magnificent eagle owl is housed in an aviary at the rear. The interior features much railway memorabilia (the landlord is a GWR railway modeller) and vintage motorcycles too – another of the licensee's passions. Although customers are welcome to use the Internet facilities here, acceptance of technology does not extend to mobile phones – you risk a fine if yours rings.

Wareham

Duke of Wellington

7 East Street, BH20 4NN

11-11; 12-10.30 Sun

(01929) 553015

Camerons Castle Eden Ale; Isle of Purbeck Fossil Fuel; Ringwood Best Bitter; guest beers [H]

Delightful, cosy pub, about 400 years old, in the middle of the town. Inside, the dark, wood-panelled walls feature photographs of old Wareham. Copper and brass ornaments surround the large, open fireplace. An extensive menu is available in the no-smoking restaurant. Outside is an attractive courtyard leading to the public car park.

Waytown

Hare & Hounds

DT6 5LQ

11.30-2.30 (not Mon), 7 (6.30 summer)-11; 12-2.30, 7-10.30 Sun

(01308) 488203

Palmer Copper Ale, IPA, 200 (summer) [G]

Attractive village local set in beautiful countryside, popular with walkers. On either side of the cosy bar is a children's room with a TV and a small restaurant. The garden, with lovely views, has a children's play area. The interesting menu uses mostly local ingredients including fresh fish. Taunton traditional cider is stocked. Evening meals are served Tuesday-Saturday.

West Stour

Ship Inn

SP8 5RP (on A30)

12-3, 6-11; 12-3, 7-10.30 Sun

(01747) 838640 website: www.shipinn-dorset.co.uk

Palmer Dorset Gold; Ringwood Best Bitter; guest beer [H]

Cask Marque

Cask Marque, whose symbol appears alongside many pubs in the Good Beer Guide, is an organisation financed by the brewing industry to improve the quality of cask beer in pubs. When a pub displays a Cask Marque plaque it means inspectors have been satisfied by the cleanliness and temperature of pub cellars and the quality of the beer at the bar. The plaque is removed if quality falls. The plaque is given to licensees and accreditation lapses when a publican leaves a pub.

Popular roadside inn affording superb views over Blackmore Vale. The imposing stone premises were built in 1750 as a coaching inn providing accommodation and a last chance to change horses before the steep climb to nearby Shaftesbury. The dog-friendly public bar has changed little over the years and the pub is believed to be haunted by a ghost who has a liking for banging doors. The pleasant gardens include a tranquil water feature.
⚔Q❀⇌◑⊟♣P

Weymouth

Boot Inn

High West Street, DT4 8QT
✪ 11-11; 12-10.30 Sun
☎ (01305) 770327
Ringwood Best Bitter, Fortyniner, Old Thumper, seasonal beers; guest beers Ⓗ
Weymouth's oldest pub is hidden behind the fire station. The bare-boarded bar area leads to small rooms at each end with comfortable seating and warming fires. The full Ringwood beer range is supplemented with guest beers and Cheddar Valley cider. The pub's popularity can lead to a spillage of customers on to the pavement where seating is provided in fine weather. An old-fashioned pub where conversation dominates. It was voted local CAMRA Pub of the Year 2005.
⚔Q❀⇌♣●⚟

Queen's Hotel

7 King Street, DT4 7BJ
✪ 11-11; 12-10.30 Sun
☎ (01305) 786326
Dorset Weymouth Harbour Master, Steam Beer Ⓗ
For years a keg beer only establishment, a change of licensee has rejuvenated this multi-room pub opposite the station. It is now considered the main outlet for local Dorset Brewing Company beers, with two offered in winter and three in summer. The main bar area is simply furnished and leads to a spacious games and family room. The lounge is more comfortable and has its own bar. Good value, wholesome food is served.
❀⇌◑⊟♿⇌♣●⚟

Wellington Arms

15 St Alban Street, DT4 8PY
✪ 12-11; 12-10.30 Sun
☎ (01305) 786963
Tetley Bitter, Burton Ale; Wadworth 6X Ⓗ
Homely and comfortable family-run oasis in the centre of the busy town, with a wood-panelled interior largely unchanged for the last 40 years. Grade II listed, with a green and gold faience-tiled frontage, the pub is a real gem dating from around 1850; an old-fashioned place to escape from the noisy, crowded pubs all around. Good value meals include the excellent Wellington brunch grill. Beer choice may vary.
⚔Q◑♿⇌⚟

In July 2005, Hall & Woodhouse (Badger) launched a new beer First Gold that may replace Badger Best in some pubs.

Wimborne

Crown & Anchor ✔

Walford Bridge, BH21 1NN
✪ 11-2.30, 6-11; 12-3, 7-10.30 Sun
☎ (01202) 841405
Badger Best, seasonal beers Ⓗ
This riverside pub overlooks Walford Craft Mill. A comfortable and friendly local, it serves some of the finest Badger beer in east Dorset. Built in 1823, it is somewhat plain from the outside but attractively decorated inside with an L-shaped bar. Popular for its home-cooked food, this is a quiet pub where conversation can be enjoyed. There is a small garden by the river which you can walk alongside to the town centre.
⚔Q❀◑P

Oddfellows Arms ✔

2 Church Street, BH21 1JH
✪ 10.30-11; 11.30-10.30 Sun
☎ (01202) 885067
Badger K&B Sussex; Best Ⓗ
Situated in a narrow street between the Minster and the town centre, this is the smallest pub in Wimborne. Frequented mainly by locals, conversation flourishes in the cosy bar. China jugs and brass ornaments hang around the bar and old photographs adorn the walls. Bar snacks are available at lunchtime. Note the colourful hanging baskets outside this lovely pub. ♣

Winterborne Stickland

Crown

North Street, DT11 0NJ
(2½ miles N of A354)
✪ 12-2.30, 6.30 (7 Mon)-11; 12-3, 7-10.30 Sun
☎ (01258) 880838
Ringwood Best Bitter, Fortyniner, seasonal beers; guest beer Ⓗ
This 18th-century Grade II listed inn sits in the middle of a peaceful Dorset village. It reverted to its original name when purchased by Ringwood Brewery. A two-room pub, the inglenook dominates the front bar, with a low, beamed dining room at the back. The original well remains beside the back door, and there is an unusual thatched games room in the courtyard. Good, home-cooked food is available.
⚔Q❀◑♿⛺♣P⚟

Worth Matravers

Square & Compass ☆

BH19 3LF (off B3069) OS974777
✪ 12-3, 6-11; 12-11 Sat;
12-3, 7-10.30 (closed winter eve) Sun
☎ (01929) 439229
Ringwood Best Bitter; guest beer Ⓖ
Perched atop the Jurassic coastline, this old Purbeck stone inn truly is a gem. Character flows from every nook and cranny, with a wealth of history stretching back 100 years. The tiny pub hosts beer and cider festivals, live music and eccentric events, all with spectacular views. Well worth seeking out – ring the landlord if you would like to camp. It is one of only a few pubs in the country to be in every edition of this Guide. ⚔Q❀⛺♣●

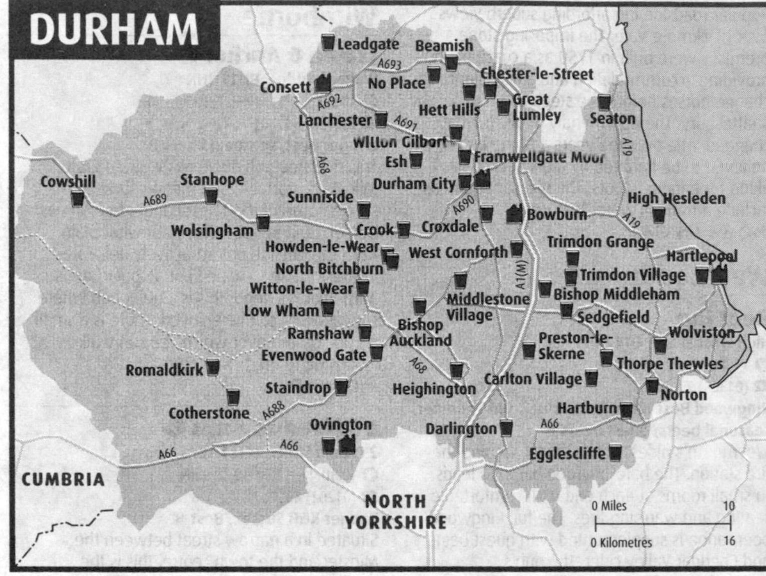

Co Durham incorporates part of the former county of Cleveland

Beamish

Sun

Beamish Open Air Museum, DH9 0RG
(follow signs for Beamish, then catch tram)
✪ 11-3.30 (4.30 summer); 12-3.30 (4.30 summer) Sun
☎ (0191) 370 2908
Theakston Old Peculier; guest beers ⊞
Traditional pub, formerly situated in Bishop Auckland. Step back in time in an authentic replica of a 1913 pub with sawdust on the floor and an antique till on the bar. Mounted animals on display represent the taxidermist's art. Sample Temperance drinks here, including sarsparilla. Serial killer, Mary Ann Cotton, stayed here during her incarceration at Durham. Note the original vessels. ♣P⊬

Bishop Auckland

Derby

1 Tenters Street, DL14 7AB
(immediately S of bus station)
✪ 11-11; 12-10.30 Sun
☎ (01388) 603981
John Smith's Bitter; guest beers ⊞
Busy, town-centre pub next to the bus station. The landlord is enthusiastic about his cask ale and now has three active hand pumps, although the range at present is restricted to Enterprise Inns guest list. Popular with shoppers at lunchtime for good value meals, it can be busy at weekends and for live sports on TV. ⇌

Grand Hotel

Holdforth Crest, DL14 6DU (near Asda car park)
✪ 6 (12 Fri & Sat)-11; 12-10.30 Sun
☎ (01388) 601956 website: www.the-grand-hotel.co.uk
Camerons Strongarm; Jennings Cumberland Ale; guest beers ⊞
Since its first mention in this Guide last year, this large free house has gone from strength to strength. Up to seven handpumps provide a varying beer range, mostly from independent brewers, plus a cider (usually from Westons). Beer festivals are held throughout the year. Live music is performed every Saturday and occasionally on Friday (details on the website). Budget accommodation is available. It is a five minute walk from Asda's rear car park and the station. ⇌♣P

Station Hotel

201 Newgate Street, DL14 7EJ
✪ 11-11; 12-10.30 Sun
☎ (01388) 605780
John Smith's Magnet ⊞
Popular, town-centre pub near Asda and Morrison's where shoppers can rest for a bite and a pint or relax while waiting for the train to Darlington. The provision of large-screen and plasma TVs ensures that this pub can be popular when sporting events are shown. Located at the opposite end of Newgate Street to the bus station, any bus to Asda will drop you nearby. ⇌♣

Tut 'n' Shive

68 Newgate Street, DL14 7EQ
✪ 11-11; 12-10.30 Sun
☎ (01388) 603252
Beer range varies ⊞
Former Guide regular, now under new management and returning to its old glories. Up to three ales are on offer from a wide range from independent brewers. Good value meals are popular with Newgate Street shoppers and live music evenings are a regular feature that attract the predominantly young clientele who make this place busy at weekends and holiday

INDEPENDENT BREWERIES

Camerons Hartlepool
Derwent Rose Consett
Durham Bowburn
Four Alls Ovington
Hill Island Durham City

periods. Take any bus to Bishop Auckland bus station (100 yards), or buses to Darlington stop at the door. Evening meals finish early. ◑≹

Bishop Middleham

Cross Keys

9 High Street, DL17 9AR (1 mile from A177)

✪ 12 (5 Mon)-11; 12-10.30 Sun

☎ (01740) 651231

Marston's Pedigree; Theakston's Black Bull Bitter; Wells Bombardier Ⓗ

Busy village pub with a warm, friendly atmosphere; this is a family-run business. A spacious open-plan lounge/bar with exposed beams is complemented by a large (80 covers) restaurant/function room serving an extensive menu of freshly-prepared meals. A three-mile circular village walk starts opposite (leaflets available in the pub). It supports a quiz night Tuesday, Teeside Tornados Bike Club on Wednesday and its own football team. ⩕❀◐◑⊟

Carlton Village

Smith's Arms

TS21 1EA

✪ 12-11; 12-10.30 Sun

☎ (01740) 630471

Caledonian Deuchars IPA; guest beer Ⓗ

Fine Victorian, red-brick end-of-terrace pub at the village centre. The Smith's Arms is the focus for village life. The staff provide a cheery welcome to one and all. The plain public bar, bustling on big-match days, contrasts with the cosy, comfortable lounge. The newly refurbished restaurant in the old stables, offering an upmarket menu, is recommended. Q❀◐◑⊟♣P

Chester-le-Street

Butcher's Arms

Middle Chare, DH3 3QD (off Front St)

✪ 11-3, 6.30-11; 7-10.30 Sun

☎ (0191) 388 3605

Camerons Strongarm; Marston's Pedigree; guest beers Ⓗ

Ideal for the discerning drinker and diner, this pub enjoys a good reputation for beer and home-cooked food. Pies and freshly delivered fish are specialities. Bedrooms are available for weary travellers. Tea and coffee are served here. Small meetings can be accommodated. Note the fine array of porcelain. ❀⇌◐≹

Cotherstone

Fox & Hounds ✔

DL12 9PF

✪ 12-3, 6.45-11; 12-3, 6.45-10.30 Sun

☎ (01833) 650241 website: www.cotherstonefox.co.uk

Black Sheep Best Bitter; guest beer Ⓗ

On the B6277, a quiet route to Scotland, overlooking the village green, this 200-year-old coaching inn is convenient for walkers and frequented by shooters. The beamed bar displaying local photographs has a log fire and cushioned wall seats. Say hello to the two unusual feathered lavatory attendants Reva, a parrot, and Charlie, a conure. Two no-smoking dining rooms serve meals produced from local ingredients. Accommodation in good quality, en-suite rooms, or a cottage, is recommended. ⩕Q❀⇌◐◑ÅP

Cowshill

Cowshill Hotel

DL13 1JQ

✪ 12-2.30 (may vary), 7-11; 12-2.30, 7-10.30 Sun

☎ (01388) 537236

Tetley Bitter Ⓗ

High in the North Pennines area of outstanding natural beauty, this establishment has been in the same family since the early 1960s. Food is served Sunday lunchtime and Friday and Saturday evenings; booking is strongly recommended. The area provides excellent terrain for hillwalkers and cyclists but the weather can be extreme at this altitude. This free house is served by the Weardale 101 bus from Stanhope, but check return times before travelling. ⩕Q◐◑Å♣P

Crook

Colliery

High Jobs Hill, DL15 0UL

✪ 12-11 (may vary Mon); 12-10.30 Sun

☎ (01388) 762511

Camerons Strongarm; Courage Directors; Wells Bombardier Ⓗ

High above Crook on the Durham road and far enough out of town to be off the 'circuit', this large, but quiet hostelry offers three ales to wash down meals prepared with local Weardale meat and home-grown organic vegetables. Still without a juke box, this is a place to relax and converse. The Arriva 46 bus from Durham stops near the door. Q◐◑P

Croxdale

Daleside Arms

Front Street, DH6 5HY

(on B6288, 3 miles S of Durham, off A167)

✪ 3 (6 Tue; 12 Sat)-11; 12-8 Sun

☎ (01388) 814165

Beer range varies Ⓗ

Gut-busting meals are freshly cooked to order to accompany some unusual beers, but there is more to this rural roadside hostelry. The pub takes its name from one of the first cask ales sold here after conversion from a guest house. Special one-off brews from Darwin and other northern micros feature. Try the chilli if you dare. Sporting ephemera decorate the bar and many awards are on display. Frequent beer festivals are now held at this gem. Lunches are only served Sunday. Q❀⇌◐◑⊟♿P

Darlington

Binns Department Store

1-7 High Row, DL3 7HH

✪ 9-5.30 (7 Thu; 6 Sat); 11-5 Sun

☎ (01325) 462606

House of Fraser department store with a fabulously-stocked bottled beer section in the basement, highly commended in the British Guild of Beer Writers Take Home Beer awards. Over 400 quality beers are available, including scores of Belgian and British bottle-conditioned ales: micros are a speciality. It stocks a good choice of badged glasses too. If the store does not have what you want, the manager, John, will try to get it for you. Occasional Saturday tasting sessions are hosted by different brewers. ♿≠

Britannia

Archer Street, DL3 6LR
(next to ring road, W side of town centre)
11.30-3, 5.30-11; 11.30-11 Fri & Sat; 12-10.30 Sun
☎ (01325) 463787
Camerons Strongarm; John Smith's Bitter; guest beers H
Warm, friendly, much-loved local, well removed from the frenetic 'circuit'. A bastion of cask beer for 140 years, it is a frequent Guide entry. The pub retains much of the appearance and layout of the private house it originally was: a modestly enlarged bar and domestic-proportioned parlour (used for meetings) sit either side of a central corridor. Listed for historic associations, it was the birthplace of teetotal, 19th century publisher, JM Dent. Up to four guest beers are available. ≠♣P

Darlington Snooker Club

1 Corporation Road, DL1 6AE (¼ mile N of centre)
11-11; 12-10.30 Sun
☎ (01325) 241388
Beer range varies H
This first-floor, family-run, private club offers a friendly welcome to family groups as well as individuals. Up to three guest beers are available in the single bar, while a small, comfortable TV lounge is provided for those not playing on one of the 10 top quality snooker tables. Twice yearly, the club plays host to a professional celebrity. CAMRA's north-east Club of the Year 2004 always welcomes CAMRA members on production of a current membership card or this Guide. ≠(North Rd) ♣

Number Twenty-2

22 Coniscliffe Road, DL3 7RG
11.30-11; closed Sun
☎ (01325) 354590 website: www.villagebrewer.co.uk
Village White Boar, Bull, Old Raby; guest beers H
Town-centre ale house, showing a rare passion for cask ale; it has won numerous CAMRA awards since opening in 1995. Huge curved windows and a high ceiling give it an airy spaciousness even when packed, which is often. Thirteen handpumps serve ten beers: five regulars and five guests, mainly from small independents. This is the home pub of Village Brewer beers, commissioned from Hambleton by the licensee. Hambleton Nightmare is sold here as Yorkshire Stout and Burton Bridge Festival as Classic Burton Ale. ♿≠

Old Yard Tapas Bar

98 Bondgate, DL3 7JY
11-11; 12-10.30 Sun
☎ (01325) 467385 website: www.tapasbar.co.uk
John Smith's Magnet; Theakston Cool Cask, Old Peculier; guest beers H
Interesting mixture of small town-centre bar and Mediterranean-style taverna, where a range of six real ales is sold alongside the sangria, ouzo, tapas and mezes. Three guest beers are stocked and it is perfectly acceptable to simply pop in for a pint. It is licensed for pavement drinking in summer, when tables are set out. The TV is used for football only. Public car parks are within 50 yards. ≠

Quakerhouse

1-3 Mechanics Yard, DL3 7QF
(off High Row, through alley next to Binns)
11-11; 12-10.30 Sun
☎ (07818) 848213 website: www.quakerhouse.net
Darwin Ghost Ale; guest beers H
Hidden jewel, based in one of Darlington's oldest buildings. A regular local CAMRA award winner, where Ghost Ale (the house beer named after Ethel the pub ghost) brewed by Darwin, is found alongside up to nine guests from micro-breweries countrywide, plus a cider. It hosts live music Wednesday and Friday evenings (door charge after 8pm), however the music-free upstairs bar is open on Friday nights, with an excellent range of up to four guests. Lunchtime food (not served Sun or Tue) is reasonably priced. ♿≠

Durham City

Colpitts

Colpitts Terrace, DH1 4EG
(on A690, near St Margaret's Hospital)
12-11; 12-10.30 Sun
☎ (0191) 386 9913
Samuel Smith OBB H
This gem of a pub remains little changed and sits in a time warp in the heart of the city. Situated on a corner, this local still boasts an off-sales hatch. In line with Sam Smith's policy it has no music or live bands, and entertainment is provided by conversation, however the jury is still out on this one as the folk nights have been discontinued. If you love unpretentious and interesting pubs then this is a must.
Q≠♣

Dun Cow

37 Old Elvet, DH1 3HN
11-11; 12-10.30 Sun
☎ (0191) 386 9219
Boddingtons Bitter; Camerons Castle Eden Ale; guest beer H
Dating from the 17th century, a friendly welcome is assured in this atmospheric two-roomed pub. The front snug is cosy and intimate, while the larger lounge is accessed further down an alleyway. Note the plaque bearing the tale of the Dun Cow on the alley wall. This pub boasts the highest sales of Castle Eden in the country. A small no-smoking area is provided in the lounge bar. Q♣

Elm Tree

12 Crossgate, DH1 4PS
12-2, 6-11; 12-11 Sat; 12-10.30 Sun
☎ (0191) 386 4621
Adnams Bitter; Camerons Strongarm; Greene King IPA; guest beers H
This former Vaux pub has an extensive range of guest ales from the Punch Taverns portfolio and has been run by the same tenant for over 10 years. A couple of minutes' walk from the city centre, up a cobbled road, the Elm Tree has

been on this site since the 16th century. Wheelchair access is via the back door. ❀⇌⊟♿⇌♣P⊬

Half Moon

New Elvet, DH1 3AQ (end of Elvet Bridge)
⌚ 11-11; 12-10.30 Sun
☎ (0191) 383 6981
Draught Bass; Taylor Landlord; guest beer Ⓗ
This deservedly popular city-centre pub continues to thrive under its long-established licensee. Its listed interior is split in two halves: the upper half is favoured by locals and the lower half, accessed by steps, is the place for big-screen sporting occasions and discerning real ale drinkers. The pub hosts regular mini-beer festivals; the rest of the time a beer from the Durham Brewery features as a guest. A recent refurbishment has provided good wheelchair access. ❀⊟♿⊬

Market Tavern

27 Market Place, DH1 3NL
⌚ 11-11; 12-10.30 Sun
☎ (0191) 386 2069
McEwan's 80/; Theakston Old Peculier; guest beers Ⓗ
Award-winning bare-boarded ale house, run by an enthusiastic manager. As well as guests from the Scottish Courage list, a wide range of ales is featured, with Houston beers a frequent sight on the bar. The L-shaped bar hugs Durham's indoor market. A newcomer to this Guide, it has become popular with young and old alike and can be busy at weekends. More handpumps are planned to be in place by the time this Guide appears, offering up to eight beers. ◐♿⇌

Queen's Head Hotel

2 Sherburn Road, Gilesgate, DH1 2JR
(1 mile E of city centre)
⌚ 12-11; 12-4, 7-10.30 Sun
☎ (0191) 386 5649
Black Sheep Special; Greene King Old Speckled Hen; Marston's Pedigree Ⓗ
Friendly pub, with a spacious no-smoking dining area where a varied menu, supplemented by specials, offers good value food. The broth starter is a meal in itself. Pool is played in the bar where there is also a TV. A pleasant back garden, housing an aviary, provides further space in which families can relax. The pub is served by Arriva and Go Northern buses from the city centre; ask the driver for Sherburn Road end. ☋❀⇌◐⊟♣P

Victoria Inn ☆

86 Hallgarth Street, DH1 3AS
⌚ 11.45-3, 6-11; 12-3, 7-10.30 Sun
☎ (0191) 386 5269
Beer range varies Ⓗ
This authentic Victorian pub has listed status. Its quaint decor, tiny snug and coal fires enhance the warm olde-worlde atmosphere. Superb real ales, often from local micro-breweries, are sold alongside a varied range of malt and Irish whiskies. Excellent toasties are also on offer. This friendliest of establishments has earned glowing and deserved praise from the north-eastern press and is simply a must for visitors to the city. Awarded Durham CAMRA Pub of the Year 2005. ♨Q⇌⊟♣⊬

Water House

65 North Road, DH1 4TM (opp. bus station)
⌚ 10-11; 12-10.30 Sun
☎ (0191) 370 6540
Courage Directors; Marston's Burton Bitter, Pedigree; Mordue Workie Ticket; Shepherd Neame Spitfire; guest beers Ⓗ
Situated in the former local waterboard offices, the Water House is a long, narrow building with a bar to the rear. The interior is on three levels, the lower level serving as the family area during the day. It took several attempts for Wetherspoon's to arrive in Durham City, but it was well worth the wait. The pub gets crowded at weekends, but is deservedly popular all day for meals. Twice yearly beer festivals are held, usually in May and October. Q☋◐♿⇌⊬

Woodman Inn

23 Gilesgate, DH1 1QW
⌚ 12-11; 12-10.30 Sun
☎ (0191) 386 7500
Beer range varies Ⓗ
Ten minutes' walk from Durham centre, it is well worth the stroll. Now mainly no-smoking, the Woodman showcases micro-brewery beers from far and wide, and serves as the tap for Durham Brewery. Regular beer festivals have returned, but be prepared for the unusual. The rear garden is now in use as an outdoor drinking area. The licensee's love of border terriers is evident by the pictures on the wall – staff and dogs are all friendly at local CAMRA's Pub of the Year 2002. ❀⊬

Egglescliffe

Pot & Glass

Church Road, TS16 9DQ
⌚ 12-2 (not Mon), 6 (5.30 Fri)-11; 12-10.30 Sun
☎ (01642) 651009
Draught Bass; Caledonian Deuchars IPA; Jennings Cumberland Ale; guest beers Ⓗ
Fine village pub in a quiet cul-de-sac opposite the church. The graveyard is the last resting place of former licensee Charlie Abbey who, using his skills as a cabinet maker, crafted the ornate bar fronts from old country house furniture. The Pot & Glass has two bars and a small function room that can be used by families. Darts and cricket teams are supported. The two rotating guest beers are from micro-breweries or independents. Evening meals are served Tuesday-Saturday. ♨☋❀◐⊟♿♣P⊓

Esh

Cross Keys

Front Street, DH7 9QR (3 miles off A691, between Durham and Consett)
⌚ 12-3, 7 (6.30 Sat)-11; 7-10.30 Sun
☎ (0191) 373 1279
Boddingtons Bitter; Tetley Bitter Ⓗ
Pleasant, 18th-century pub in a picturesque village where a varied menu offers vegetarian and children's choices. A comfortable locals' bar is complemented by a lounge that affords views across the Browney Valley. Delft racks display porcelain artefacts, some of which portray the old village. The No. 725 bus from Chester-le-

Street and the No. 52 from Durham pass the door; if walking, telephone for directions.
◐◑⊟♿P⊬

New Board Inn

Hill Top, DH7 9RL OSN77144

✪ 11-11; 12-10.30 Sun

☎ (0191) 373 6924

Beer range varies Ⓗ

Traditional country house, commanding a prominent position overlooking the Brownley Valley. It offers all the charm and atmosphere you would expect from a bygone era: the inn reputedly dates back to the 1500s. In late 2003 a major refurbishment took place making it the prestigous place you will find today. The bar stocks six beers from local breweries.
ᘎ❀◐◑⊟♿⛺♣P⊬

Evenwood Gate

Brown Jug Inn

DL14 9NW

✪ 11-11 (may vary); 12-10.30 Sun

☎ (01388) 833180

Black Sheep Best Bitter; guest beers Ⓗ

Rural free house where the landlord is keen to expand cask sales. Located on the Bishop Auckland to Barnard Castle road, this is a popular destination for diners wanting to get out of town for a quiet night's refreshment. Go Northern bus No. 82 and buses from Bishop Auckland to Barnard Castle serve the pub. Note that the opening hours may vary on weekdays.
Q❀◐◑P⊬

Framwellgate Moor

Tap & Spile

Front Street, DH1 5EE

✪ 12-3 (not Mon), 6 (5 Fri)-11; 12-3, 7-10.30 Sun

☎ (0191) 386 5451

Beer range varies Ⓗ

With its wooden floors and interior, this is a typical ale house offering up to eight beers. Multi-roomed, it has a no-smoking back room and bar billiards in the family room. The Enterprise Inns' guest list is put to good use here. Why not have a go at the quiz on Wednesday evening? A friendly welcome awaits in this real ale paradise.
Qᘎ⊟♿♣●⊬

Great Lumley

Old England

Front Street, DH3 4JB (near Co-op)

✪ 11-11 (lounge: 6.15-11, plus 11-3 Fri & Sat); 12-10.30 (lounge: 12-3, 6.30-10.30) Sun

☎ (0191) 388 5257

Beer range varies Ⓗ

This friendly, family-run pub usuallly has three guest beers on tap, including ales from Northumberland and Durham. The spacious, comfortable, split-level lounge is divided into distinct areas by stylish panels. The atmosphere is peaceful, attracting a regular clientele, including diners (no-smoking tables available). The public bar is more lively, with a pool table, dartboard, satellite and projection TV. Other entertainment includes a quiz held twice a week. ◐◑⊟♿♣P

Smiths Arms

Brecon Hill, Castle Dene, DH3 4HE (over Lumley new bridge, past golf course, left after roundabout)

✪ 4 (12 Sat)-11; 12-10.30 Sun

☎ (0191) 385 6915

Black Sheep Best Bitter; Courage Directors; Taylor Landlord; guest beer Ⓗ

Popular, country pub. Despite being tucked away and having a small car park, it gets busy at weekends, especially in the high quality restaurant upstairs. Regulars gather in the cosy public bar where a real fire is alight through the winter. There is a comfortable lounge, where the floor slopes disconcertingly – so it may not be the drink. The games room houses a pool table. A guest beer appears at the weekend.
♨Q◑⊟♣P

Hartburn

Masham Hotel

87 Hartburn Village, TS18 5DR

✪ 11-11; 12-6, 7-10.30 Sun

☎ (01642) 580414 website: www.themasham.co.uk

Draught Bass; Black Sheep Special; Taylor Landlord Ⓗ

Fine village terraced local clearly displaying its public house origins. Recently refurbished, without loss of character, a bustling public bar is flanked by two side rooms, one of which is no-smoking. Good garden facilities provide a warm weather alternative. The first Monday of each month is acoustic night, the third Sunday evening hosts jazz. A small, but impressive, menu of home-cooked food is served lunchtime (except Sun) and evening. Q❀◐◑⊟♣P⊬

Parkwood Hotel

64-66 Darlington Road, TS18 5ER

✪ 12-3, 5-11; 11-11 Sat; 12-10.30 Sun

☎ (01642) 587933

Cameron's Strongarm; Greene King Abbot; guest beer Ⓗ

One of three pubs in Hartburn featured in this Guide, the Parkwood was once the home of the local shipowning Ropner family. The large, open-plan pub is set in extensive grounds and offers quality accommodation. The conservatory has been extended and the dining room is a no-smoking area. Evidence of the licensee's enthusiasm for real ale is reflected in ever-growing demand. Arriva Stockton-Darlington buses Nos. 98 and 99 stop nearby. ❀⇄◐◑P

Stockton Arms

24 Darlington Road, TS18 5BH

✪ 11-11; 12-10.30 Sun

☎ (01642) 571901

Draught Bass; guest beer Ⓗ

Imposing red-brick roadhouse at the junction of the main road into the village. The 1930s-style exterior opens into a warm and friendly atmosphere. The layout is open plan with a TV area and a dining alcove, also used by non-smokers. A large garden hosts regular barbecues in summer. The menu is imaginative, offering vegetarian and children's options (no food Sun eve). For long a Bass stronghold, it now stocks a guest beer. Stockton-Darlington buses 98 and 99 stop nearby.
♨❀◐◑♿P⊬

Hartlepool

Causeway

Vicarage Gardens, Stranton, TS24 7QT (beside Stranton Church)

⊙ 11-11; 12-10.30 Sun

☎ (01429) 273954

Banks's Original, Bitter; Camerons Strongarm; Marston's Old Empire Ⓗ

This fine Victorian watering-hole, with red brick façade and Camerons etched windows (despite W&DB ownership) has long been regarded as a Camerons Brewery tap. Featuring wood panelling, globe lighting and cast iron figurine tables in the spacious bar, the pub also boasts two smaller rooms (one no-smoking), served by a passageway hatch. Vibrant and lively, staging live music several times a week, the pub accounts for a massive real ale turnover of more than 500 barrels a year. No food is served Sunday. Q❀◑⊟⇌♣⅍⊓

Jackson's Arms

Tower Street, TS24 7HH (S of Church Sq)

⊙ 12-11; 12-10.30 Sun

☎ (01429) 862413

Beer range varies Ⓗ

Excellent, street-corner pub, marked by a hanging sign depicting Ralph Ward Jackson, founder of West Hartlepool. Two bustling bars have leather wall seating; one caters for pool and darts players. Four handpulls dispense an ever-changing choice of guest ales, often from small or micro-breweries. The pub has a strong sense of local identity, but provides a warm and friendly welcome to regulars and strangers alike. Q⊟⇌♣

White House

Wooler Road, TS26 0DR (at Grange Rd roundabout)

⊙ 11-11; 12-10.30 Sun

☎ (01429) 224392

Draught Bass; Camerons Strongarm; guest beers Ⓗ

Once an RC boys' grammar school, its former pupils would surely approve of the Ember Inns conversion of their alma mater. Relax and read the newspapers in comfortable leather armchairs in one of the eight or so areas, warmed by gas or open fires and decorated with abundant old photographs and descriptions. Good food is served until 8pm. Occasional beer festivals are held.
⩕Q❀◑P⅍

Heighington

Bay Horse

28 West Green, DL5 6PE

⊙ 11-11; 12-10.30 Sun

☎ (01325) 312312 website: www.bay-horse-restaurant.co.uk

John Smith's Magnet; Theakston Cool Cask; guest beers Ⓗ

Picturesque, historic, 300-year-old pub overlooking the village's largest green. Its exposed beams and stone walls offer traditional surroundings, partitioned into distinct drinking and dining areas. Food plays a prominent role, with excellent home-cooked meals available as well as bar food; a large restaurant extends from the lounge. The bar area gives drinkers the chance to enjoy the pub's beer range in the evening, which includes up to three guest ales; the cider is Westons Old Rosie.
❀◑⊟♿♣●P⊓

George & Dragon

4 East Green, DL5 6PP (behind church)

⊙ 12-3 (not Mon), 5-11; 11-11 Fri & Sat; 12-10.30 Sun

☎ (01325) 313152

Black Sheep Best Bitter; Caledonian Deuchars IPA; Wells Bombardier; guest beers Ⓗ

Friendly village pub where locals warmly welcome visitors. An old coaching inn, complete with stables, it has been refurbished in a modern style, with a bar and spacious lounge. Meals are served in the lounge, while a conservatory-style restaurant area offers excellent home-cooked food. It hosts regular live music and quiz nights on alternate Sundays. Two guest ales help ensure this is a pub for lovers of good beer.
❀◑⊟♣P⊓

Locomotion No. One

Heighington Station, DL5 6QG

⊙ 11-11; 12-10.30 Sun

☎ (01325) 320132 website: www.locomotionone.co.uk

Marston's Pedigree; John Smith's Magnet; guest beers Ⓗ

This family-run pub occupies the former stationmaster's house at Heighington Station, next to the level crossing where the first-ever locomotive to haul a passenger train was hoisted on to the lines in 1825. An excellent range of real ales is enjoyed by locals and visitors alike. A terrace occupies the original platform with an additional courtyard for outdoor drinking. An extensive menu is served in the pub or upstairs restaurant (no food Sun eve). Beware, the last train leaves early.
⩕❀◑♿⇌♣P

Hett Hills

Moorings

DH2 3JU (from Chester-le-Street, follow B6313 under viaduct) OSNZ2451

⊙ 11.45-11; 11.45-10.30 Sun

☎ (0191) 370 1597 website: www.themooringsdurham.com

Theakston Cool Cask; guest beers Ⓗ

Impressive pub on two levels bearing a nautical theme. The bar and bistro serve food all day, with a wide choice of traditional home-cooked English fare. The upstairs restaurant, with a conservatory overlooking the west Durham hills, offers classical French cuisine, including such exotic items as lobster and other seafood. The guest beers are sourced from local micro-breweries. ⛟❀◑♿P⅍

High Hesleden

Ship Inn

TS27 4QD (½ mile off B1281)

⊙ 12-3, 6-11; 12-3, 7-10.30 Sun

☎ (01429) 836453

Beer range varies Ⓗ

After years of neglect this amazing pub is becoming quite a regular in this Guide. The combination of quality ales and good food is a simple, winning formula. Refurbished accommodation and rebuilt facilities show what can be done to revive the fortunes of a village

local. An extensive lounge/dining area and cosy bar display nautical memorabilia. Micro-breweries are well supported here.
♔Q♨❀⇌◐◑⊟♿⛺●P⊬Ū

Howden-le-Wear

Plantation

40 High Street, DL15 8EZ

(road leading E at Crook end of village)

⏲ 6 (7 Tue & Thu)-11; 12-3, 7-10.30 Sun

☎ (01388) 810904

Beer range varies ⊞

Popular village local, offering five ales from a variety of breweries and winner of local CAMRA's Pub of the Season award on several occasions. Evening meals are served (not Tue or Thu), plus Sunday lunch. The Thursday night quiz is well attended. Although a little hard to find, a good evening's refreshment is guaranteed in this true free house. Weardale 101 and Arriva/Go Northern 1B buses to Howden-le-Wear stop just a four-minute walk away.
❀◐◑♣P

Lanchester

Queen's Head

17 Front Street, DH7 0LA

(on A691, Consett road, 7 miles from Durham)

⏲ 11-11; 12-10.30 Sun

☎ (01207) 520200

Beer range varies ⊞

Comfortable, stone Grade II listed country pub, apparently haunted by a ghost named Charlotte. Consett and Durham buses pass the door. An outdoor area is available for balmy summer days. The Coast-to-Coast cycle route passes nearby. An ATM facility is provided in the bar. Sunday quizzes are popular. Home-cooked food is served in the homely no-smoking restaurant. The three beers may come from anywhere in the country. ♔❀◐◑♣P⊬

Leadgate

Jolly Drovers

DH8 6RR (at A692/Ebchester Rd jct)

⏲ 11-11; 12-10.30 Sun

☎ (01207) 503994

Beer range varies ⊞

Two cask ales are sold at this pleasantly situated country pub; Black Sheep Best Bitter often features. Home-made food adds to the good reputation the pub has gained. Full of rural charm, the Jolly Drovers is further proof of how pubs can be successful outside major towns by doing the simple things well. Q❀◐◑⊟P⊬

Low Wham

Malt Shovel

DL13 5JE (off B6282, E of Butterknowle)

⏲ 12-3, 5-11 (may vary); 12-11 Fri & Sat; 12-10.30 Sun

☎ (01388) 710033

Beer range varies ⊞

Free house, now owned by a cask ale fan and returned to the past splendour of the time when the pub was the unofficial tap house for the much missed Butterknowle Brewery. Three handpumps now operate, and it is worth enquiring about meals before setting off. This true rural gem is set amid tranquil countryside and entails a half mile walk from the 'egg factory' or a mile from the nearest bus stop.
❀◐◑P

Middlestone Village

Ship Inn

Low Road, DL14 8AB

⏲ 4 (12 Fri & Sat)-11; 12-10.30 Sun

☎ (01388) 810904

Beer range varies ⊞

This thriving village free house was saved by a concerted local campaign after Vaux closed it for being unviable – the brewery has disappeared but the Ship continues to win local and regional CAMRA awards. Six ales from a changing range of breweries are on offer, supplemented by twice-yearly beer festivals. A true community hostelry, its regular clientele comes from far and wide. On clear days enjoy magnificent views from the rooftop patio. Take bus No. 7/7A from Spennymoor or Shildon. ♔❀◑♣PŪ

No Place

Beamish Mary Inn ✔

DH9 0QH (off A693, Chester-le-Street-Stanley road)

⏲ 12-11; 12-10.30 Sun

☎ (0191) 370 0237

Beer range varies ⊞

Family-run pub in a former mining village, boasting open fires and a collection of memorabilia from the 1920 and '30s. Live music is performed at least thrice weekly and a folk club meets on Wednesday in the stables. Up to 10 ales are stocked, including a Big Lamp house beer. A beer festival is staged in January. The pub whose theme is 'all dressed up and no place to go', has received many CAMRA awards.
♔❀⇌◐◑⊟♿♣●P

North Bitchburn

Red Lion

North Bitchburn Terrace, DL15 8AL

⏲ 12-3, 7-11; 12-3, 7-10.30 Sun

☎ (01388) 763561

Beer range varies ⊞

Popular village pub with three ales on offer, usually from lesser known breweries. The house ale – Jenny Ale – comes from Camerons; a contribution to the local hospice is made for every pint sold. The pub retains its reputation for excellent food and the dining room affords superb views over rural Weardale. The 1B bus route (Darlington-Bishop Auckland-Tow Law) serves the pub. ♔❀◐◑♣P

Norton

Unicorn

High Street, TS20 1AA

⏲ 12-3.30, 5.30-11; 11-11 Fri & Sat; 12-10.30 Sun

☎ (01642) 643364

John Smith's Magnet ⊞

Known to locals as Nellie's after a previous long-serving licensee, the Unicorn stands as an oasis of stability in a world in which pub fashions alter all the time. Unnecessary change is unwelcome here; plans to cover a girder bearing the name of famous steelmakers Dorman Long were

successfully resisted. In this Guide, where many pubs boast a huge range of real ales, the Unicorn serves one – superbly. Magnet is also sold as keg, so remember to ask for cask.
Q🍼❀◑⊟♿♣

Ovington

Four Alls

The Green, DL11 7BP (2 miles S of Winston and A67)
⌚ 7 (6 Fri)-11; 12-11 Sat; 12-10.30 Sun
☎ (01833) 627302
Tetley Bitter; guest beer Ⓗ
Friendly 18th-century inn opposite the green in what is known as the 'Maypole village'. Note the unusual Victorian sign, denoting The Four Alls: 'I govern all (Queen), I fight for all (Soldier), I pray for all (Parson), I pay for all (Farmer). The pub consists of a bar, games room and restaurant serving excellent value food. The pub is the home of the Four Alls Brewery, whose beers alternate with guests from micros countrywide; phone first if wanting to try the popular Four Alls beers as they tend not to last.
🔥🍼❀🛏◑♣P

Preston-le-Skerne

Blacksmiths Arms

Preston Lane, DL5 6JH
(½ mile from A167 at Gretna Green)
⌚ 11.30-2, 6-11; closed Mon; 12-10.30 Sun
☎ (01325) 314873
Beer range varies Ⓗ
Welcoming, recently extended free house, known locally as the Hammers, situated in a rural location. A long corridor separates the bar, lounge and restaurant. The beamed lounge is designed in a farmhouse style complete with Welsh dresser. It has an excellent reputation for home-cooked food, while up to three guest beers come from micro-breweries countrywide. It has been a previous local CAMRA Rural Pub of the Year winner. 🍼❀◑⊟♿♣P

Ramshaw

Bridge Inn

1 Gordon Lane, DL14 0NS
⌚ 11-11; 12-10.30 Sun
☎ (01388) 832509
Beer range varies Ⓗ
True village community business that includes a fish and chip shop, tuck shop and bingo. This free house is in a pleasant riverside location and the accommodation provides an ideal base for those exploring rural Teesdale and Weardale, including the spectacular High Force waterfalls. The two beers tend to come from small independents, with a north-eastern brew usually on tap. Go Northern bus No. 82 from Bishop Auckland will drop you at the door.
🔥❀🛏◑♿⛺P

Romaldkirk

Kirk Inn

The Green, DL12 9ED
⌚ 12-3 (not Tue), 6-11; 12-3, 7-10.30 Sun
☎ (01833) 650260
Black Sheep Best Bitter; Hambleton Bitter; Taylor Landlord Ⓗ
Overlooking the large green, surrounded by many fine houses, this one-roomed, friendly inn is in an Upper Teesdale village, voted the second most desirable in the country. The inn serves as the village post office until midday, but it is impossible to detect this at other times. The range of real ales and meals makes it a popular stop for walkers and cyclists. A motorclub meets here monthly (first Sun). Evening meals must be booked.
🔥Q❀🛏◑♿♣P

Seaton

Seaton Lane Inn

Seaton Lane, SR7 0LP (on B1404, just off A19)
⌚ 11.30-11; 12-10.30 Sun
☎ (0191) 581 2038
Black Sheep Best Bitter; Taylor Landlord; Young's Special; guest beer Ⓗ
An oasis in a beer desert, originally a 17th-century blacksmith's cottage. Major refurbishment has taken place since last in this Guide 12 years ago. A new kitchen has been built and the restaurant extended. A contemporary bar and refurbished lounge lead to a split-level restaurant and garden. Note the pictorial history of the village on the bar wall. Live bands perform in the garden in summer. Meals are served 12-9pm; families are well catered for here.
🔥Q❀◑⊟P

Sedgefield

Ceddesfeld Hall

Sedgefield Community Association, Rectory Row, TS21 2AE (behind church in centre)
⌚ 7-10.30; 8-11 Sat; 8-11 Sun
☎ (01740) 620341
Beer range varies Ⓗ
Private club where CAMRA members and guests are most welcome. Originally built as the parsonage in 1791, it is now home to the ghostly Pickled Parson. Set in its own grounds, it is ideal for a summer evening. There is a policy of rotating ales regularly and reasonable prices. The club has a small bar, a comfortable, spacious lounge and a large function room. Awarded local CAMRA Club of the Year 2005, it is a credit to the volunteers of Sedgefield Community Association who stage an annual beer festival in July.
Q❀♿P🗑

Nag's Head

8 West End, TS21 2BS
⌚ 12-2.30 (not Mon or Tue), 5-11; 12-11 Sat; 12-10.30 Sun
☎ (01740) 620234
Taylor Landlord; Theakston Cool Cask; guest beers Ⓗ
Situated in an attractive village, close to Sedgefield racecourse, this free house is run as a traditional local to attract all age groups; families with well-behaved children are most welcome. There is a comfortable bar and a smaller lounge, while the restaurant serves local and international dishes prepared with fresh local produce, and seafood meals are also served in the bar (eve meals Tue-Sat). The landlord and landlady both come from the village.
❀◑♣P⚟

Staindrop

Wheatsheaf Inn ✔

42 South Green, DL2 3LD

⏲ 12-11; 12-10.30 Sun

☎ (01833) 660129

Camerons Strongarm; Black Sheep Best Bitter; guest beer (occasional) Ⓗ

Welcoming, tudor-style former coaching inn overlooking the green in a picturesque Teesdale village. Consisting of a linked bar/lounge and a games room, this popular pub is home to many clubs and the village carnival committee. It has a fabulous garden with water features. A quiz is held every Tuesday. Handy for exploring Teesdale, bus Nos. 8 and 75 stop right outside the door. Q ❀ ♿ ⛺ ♣

Stanhope

Grey Bull

17 West Terrace, DL13 2PB

⏲ 2 (12 Sat)-11; 12-10.30 Sun

☎ (01388) 528177

Jennings Cumberland Ale; guest beer Ⓗ

Popular Jennings local at the west end of town, near the ford and open air swimming pool. From the pub, the road north to Consett starts on its route across spectacular high moorlands through an area well used by walkers and cyclists. This hostelry can become busy, especially on darts nights. The Weardale No. 101 bus to Horn Hall serves the pub.

♨ ❀ ⛺ ♣

Sunniside

Moss Inn

78 Front Street, DL13 4LX

⏲ 11-11; 12-10.30 Sun

☎ (01388) 730447

Black Sheep Best Bitter; guest beer Ⓗ

Village free house where the landlord has built up a reputation for excellent service in a cask ale desert. A spacious restaurant and function room are available; diners are advised to ring in advance. This local offers that rare experience of quality and value for money and is well worth seeking out. The Arriva/Go Northern bus 1B stops 50 yards away.

♨ Q ◑ ◐ ♣

Thorpe Thewles

Hamilton Russell Arms

Bank Terrace, TS21 3JW

⏲ 11-11; 12-10.30 Sun

☎ (01740) 630757 website: www.hamiltonrussell.co.uk

John Smith's Magnet; guest beer Ⓗ

Named in honour of the marriage of Gustavson Hamilton and Emma Maria Russell in 1928, and formerly part of the Marchioness of Londonderry's estate, this impressive pub overlooks the green in an attractive village now mercifully bypassed by the busy A177. There are several distinct drinking areas, a snug and a games room, and a spacious no-smoking area, as well as a large, sunny garden. An extensive menu includes many fish and vegetarian options for diners who travel far to eat here.

♨ ❀ ◑ ◐ ⊟ ♿ P ⊬

Trimdon Grange

Dovecote Inn

Salters Lane, TS29 6EP (on B1278)

⏲ 7 (12 Fri & Sat)-11; 12-11 Sun

☎ (01429) 880391

Marston's Old Empire; guest beer Ⓗ

The landlord of this free house hails from Charles Wells country; his twin passions are Rugby Union and real ale. Situated on the outskirts of a former mining village, the pub dates back to at least 1820, growing an extra storey in 1927, resulting in a distinctive tall but narrow appearance. There used to be a dovecote on one corner – hence the name. Its single large room houses a popular pool table and dartboard; quiz night is Tuesday. ♨

Trimdon Village

Bird in Hand

Salters Lane, TS29 6JQ (on B1278 Fishburn)

⏲ 11-11; 12-3, 7-11 Mon; 12-10.30 Sun

☎ (01429) 880391

Black Sheep Best Bitter; guest beers Ⓗ

Large, friendly, 1950s local on the village outskirts. It has a central serving area, a bar with a pool table at one side and a spacious lounge/restaurant at the other. The landlord is a real ale enthusiast, offering some 280 beers to date. He stages six themed beer weekends a year as well as putting on old-fashioned games nights, while live bands and singers provide additional entertainment. August bank holiday sees the Battle of the Bands played out (rock and blues). ⛯ ❀ ◑ ◐ ♣ P

West Cornforth

Hare & Hounds Inn

Garmondsway, DL17 9DT (1 mile S of Coxhoe on A177)

⏲ 12-3, 6-11; closed Mon; 12-11 Sat; 12-10.30 Sun

☎ (01740) 654661

Beer range varies Ⓗ

The pub's origins go back to 1771, when it was called the Fox Inn, forming part of a farm and coaching inn. Now owned by Enterprise Inns and run by tenants who appreciate real ale, it comprises a large L-shaped bar, and a restaurant that doubles as a lounge; exposed beams feature throughout. It specialises in meals based on locally sourced produce, particularly beef.

♨ ❀ ◑ ◐ ⊟ P ⊬

Square & Compass

7 The Green, DL17 9JQ (off Coxhoe-W Cornforth road)

⏲ 11.30-2.30, 6.30-11.30; 12-11.30 Fri & Sat; 12-11 Sun

☎ (01740) 653050

Beer range varies Ⓗ

Thriving local situated at the top of the green, in the oldest part of the village and quite different from the rest of 'Doggy' (the locals' name for the place). The pub comprises a large, L-shaped, open-plan bar/lounge and a smaller games room. This is a free house, hosting a popular quiz on Thursday and entertainment on Saturday.

❀ ♿ ♣ P

Witton Gilbert

Glendenning Arms

Front Street, DH7 6SY (off A691, 3 miles from Durham)

❂ 4 (3 Fri; 12 Sat)-11; 12-10.30 Sun
☎ (0191) 371 0316
Draught Bass; Tetley Bitter; guest beer Ⓗ
Two rooms in contemporary style, this pub is an old Guide favourite. Recently refurbished inside and out, it is popular with local clubs and football teams. The cosy, quiet lounge contrasts with the bar, which is the hub of pub activity. Note some interesting paintings on the walls and original 1970s Vaux handpulls on the bar. Toasties are available at lunchtime.
♔Q❀◐⊟♣P

Travellers Rest

Front Street, DH7 6TQ (off A691, 3 miles from Durham)
❂ 11-11; 12-10.30 Sun
☎ (0191) 371 0458
Theakston Best Bitter; guest beers Ⓗ
Country-style, multi-room pub, popular for the food on its eclectic menu, served throughout the pub. Most of the pub is no-smoking including the conservatory which is ideal for meals with children. The outdoor seating area makes it even more appealing for families in summer. The bar area is partitioned into three sections, adjoining the restaurant. The decor is contemporary with plenty of ornaments. Q❀◐P⚟

White Tun

Sacriston Lane, DH7 6QU (on road to Sacriston)
❂ 12-3, 5-11; 12-11 Fri & Sat; 12-10.30 Sun
☎ (0191) 371 0734
Camerons Nimmos XXXX; guest beers Ⓗ
Estate-style, two-room pub with a spacious, comfortable bar and a smaller, quieter lounge. It persists with cask beer in an area not noted for discerning drinkers, and attracts customers from the village and nearby estate. Popular for functions, it gets busy at weekends for food, which is available during most opening hours (except Sun eve). The bar houses a large-screen TV and a pool table. Tables in the car park allow for some outdoor drinking. Q❀◐◑P

Witton-le-Wear

Dun Cow

19 High Street, DL14 0AY (off A68)
❂ 6 (12.30 Fri & Sat)-11; 12-10.30 Sun
☎ (01388) 488294
John Smith's Bitter; Wells Bombardier Ⓗ
Dating from 1799, this village free house is a pleasant community-focused pub, where pool, juke box and bandits are banned, although it can get noisy when Sunderland's football team are on TV. Just a few hundred yards from the main A68, the inn is situated on the 'top road' and offers a pleasant stop for those travelling north or visiting the nearby Low Barns nature reserve. Go Northern bus Nos. 85 and 88 run a limited daytime service to the door. ♔Q❀▲P

Wolsingham

Black Bull

27 Market Place, DL13 3AB
❂ 12-11; 12-10.30 Sun
☎ (01388) 527332
Young's Bitter; Caledonian Deuchars IPA Ⓗ
Former coaching house in the market place, providing first-rate food and lodging, both of which are often fully booked well in advance (no eve meals winter Sun). The beer range has changed and is proving even more popular, while Westons Old Rosie cider from containers is now regularly in stock. At the centre of historic Wolsingham, the hotel is under a mile's walk from the steam operated Weardale Railway. Weardale bus No. 101 stops at the market place (No. X21 runs from Newcastle on Saturday).
♔Q❀⇔◐◑⊟▲♣●

Wolviston

Ship

50 High Street, TS22 5JX
❂ 12-3, 5-11; 12-3, 7-10.30 Sun
☎ (01740) 644420
Black Sheep Best Bitter; guest beer Ⓗ
On the main Stockton-Sunderland road, the Ship, once a coach stop, now serves a more local clientele, although the home-cooked meals, with no hint of portion control or bleeping microwave, draw diners from a wide area. The present buildings date from the early 1900s, but the old stables can still be seen to the rear. The licensee keenly supports real ale, changing the guest beer every couple of days.
❀◐◑♣P⚟

Wellington

31-33 High Street, TS22 5JY
❂ 11-11; 12-10.30 Sun
☎ (01740) 646901
Draught Bass; Taylor Landlord; guest beer Ⓗ
Whitewashed and pantiled in typical northern style, this pub guards the old main road to the north. Bass Burton Ales are advertised on the façade. The pub is open plan, with a busy public bar leading into a comfortable lounge. The large upstairs function room is often used for live music. The licensee has a long, unswerving commitment to real ale, welcoming visitors and regulars alike. ❀◐◑♣P

Your shout

We would like to hear from you. If you think a pub not listed in the Guide is worthy of consideration, please let us know. Send us the name, full address and phone number (if known). If a pub in the Guide has given you poor service, we would also like to know. Write to Good Beer Guide, CAMRA, 230 Hatfield Road, St Albans, Herts, AL 14 LW or email **camra@camra.org.uk**

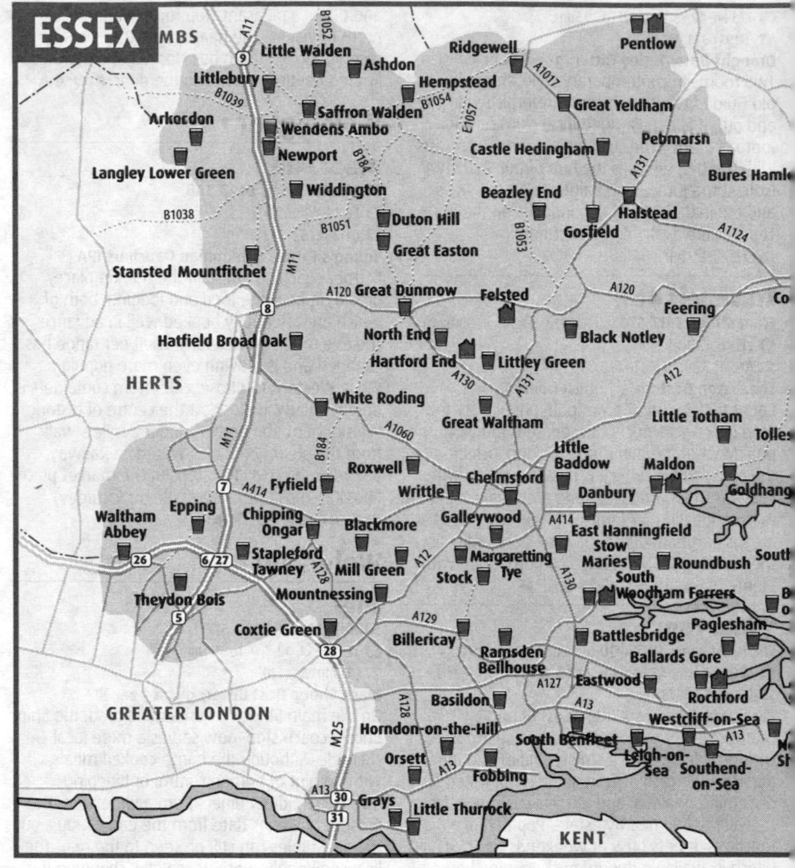

Arkesden

Axe & Compasses ✔

Wicken Road, CB11 4EX (2 miles N of B1038) OS483344

11.30-2.30 (12-3 Sat), 6-11; 12-3, 7-10.30 Sun

☎ (01799) 550272 website: www.axeandcompasses.co.uk

Greene King IPA, Abbot, Old Speckled Hen Ⓗ

Partly thatched, 17th-century village inn, with a public bar and an award-winning restaurant. A community pub with a friendly atmosphere, it is the centre for much of village life and locals actually talk to strangers here. It is frequented by walkers on the extensive footpath network in this beautiful locality, which includes a long distance path, the Harcamlow Way. Q ❀ P

Ashdon

Rose & Crown

Crown Hill, CB10 2HB

(5 miles NE of Saffron Walden) OS587422

12-2, 6-11; 12-4, 7-10.30 Sun

☎ (01799) 584337

Adnams Bitter; Greene King IPA, Abbot Ⓗ

This 16th-century, three-roomed pub reveals much character of historical interest. Reputedly haunted, the Cromwell Room still has its original decoration. Access at the front is via steps. Evening meals are served Tuesday-Saturday; the weekly fish and chips night is a speciality. The main bar is no-smoking. Q ❀ P

Ballards Gore

Shepherd & Dog

Gore Road, SS4 2DA (between Rochford and Paglesham)

12-3, 6-11; 12-4, 6.30-10.30 Sun

☎ (01702) 258279 website: www.shepndog.com

Beer range varies Ⓗ

Fine, family-run, rural pub in comfortable cottage style. Local CAMRA's Pub of the Year 2004, it was also voted Rural Pub of the Year. Four real ales generally come from micro-breweries and are often unusual for the area. The no-smoking restaurant serves excellent meals, and snacks are available in the bar. Cider is stocked in summer. Children over 12 are allowed in the restaurant. Q ❀ P

Basildon

Moon on the Square ✔

1-15 Market Pavement, SS14 1DF

(near station and bus station)

10-11; 12-10.30 Sun

☎ (01268) 520360

Marston's Burton Bitter, Pedigree; Courage Directors; De Koninck Ambrée; Greene King Abbot; guest beers Ⓗ

Excellent Wetherspoon's outlet serving a superb choice of guest beers, many of which do not appear on the regular Wetherspoon's guest list. Easily accessible, it is close to the railway and bus stations. Curry nights and beer festivals are

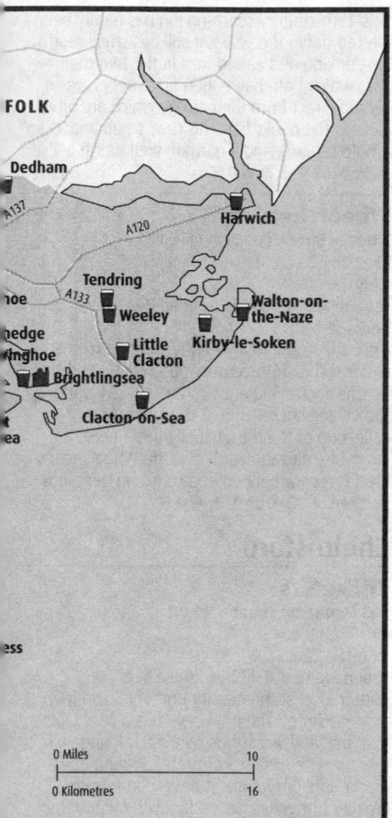

especially popular at this oasis in the keg desert. Meals are served all day. Q◐ ♿ ⇌ ⚟

Battlesbridge

Barge Inn

Hawk Hill, SS11 7RE
(off A130, follow signs to antiques centre)
✪ 11-11; 12-10.30 Sun
☎ (01268) 732622
Adnams Bitter, Broadside; Greene King Abbot; Marston's Pedigree; guest beer 🄷
Opposite an antiques and craft centre in an historic village on the River Crouch, this 400-year-old weatherboarded pub is a Grade II listed building. A regular beer festival is held on St George's Day and another around Guy Fawkes Night. A cosy atmosphere encourages both the local trade and visitors alike. Food is served all day and children are welcome.
♨ ❀◐ ♿ ⇌ ♣ ● ⚟

Beazley End

Cock Inn

CM7 5JH (on B1053, 4 miles N of Braintree) OS743289
✪ 12-11; closed Mon; 12-10.30 Sun
☎ (01371) 850566
Greene King IPA; Woodforde's Wherry; guest beers 🄷
This country pub, set back from the road, featured in TV's Lovejoy series. Good local trade

In July 2005 Greene King bought Ridley's Brewery and planned to close it within three months. Some of the Ridley's brands may be retained, but the beers available in pubs in Essex are liable to change

and a friendly, knowledgeable landlord make the pub a welcoming hostelry. This cosy free house has three bars, including a small snug, and a restaurant. Three or four real ales are stocked, plus Biddenden cider. Excellent food, sourced locally, includes game and fish dishes as bar meals or in the restaurant. ♨Q❀◐ ⊟ ● P

Billericay

Coach & Horses

36 Chapel Street, CM12 9LU (near B1007)
✪ 11-11; 12-10.30 Sun
☎ (01277) 622873
Adnams Bitter; Greene King IPA, Abbot; 🄷 **guest beers** 🄷/🄶
Welcoming beer drinkers' pub close to the High Street. This regular Guide entry caters for all ages. It stands on the site of the tap room of the Crown, a one-time coaching inn. The bright, comfortable bar is adorned with prints and photographs, plus impressive collections of jugs and elephants. Good quality food is served, specialising in home-made pies. ♨❀◐ ⇌P

Black Notley

Vine Inn

105 The Street, CM77 8LL
✪ 12-2, 6.30-11; 12-4, 7-10.30 Sun
☎ (01376) 324269
Adnams Bitter, Broadside; guest beers (summer) 🄷
The Vine is a 16th-century establishment, comprising an open-plan bar/restaurant with log-burning stoves at each end. An unusual feature is the compact mezzanine galleried area with seating for six people, accessible via a steep, straight, wooden staircase. The restaurant side is a designated no-smoking area. Parking is limited. ♨◐P

Blackmore

Leather Bottle

Horsefayre Green, CM4 0RL OS603009
✪ 11-11; 12-10.30 Sun
☎ (01277) 821891
Adnams Bitter; Ridleys IPA; 🄷 **guest beers** 🄷/🄶

INDEPENDENT BREWERIES

Blanchfields Rochford
Crouch Vale South Woodham Ferrers
Felstar Felsted
George & Dragon Foulness Island
Maldon Maldon
Mersea Island East Mersea
Mighty Oak Maldon
Nethergate Pentlow
Railway Tavern Brightlingsea
Ridleys Hartford End: will close Autumn 2005

Large village pub with a small, flagstone-floored bar and a larger restaurant offering good deals on high quality, freshly-prepared food. Two guest beers are on tap at all times, with a third served by gravity at weekends – the choice always includes a stronger option. The cider is Westons Old Rosie. An annexe to the bar houses a pool table, dartboard and silent fruit machine. Sunday meals are served 12-4pm.
♨❀◑◐⊟♣●P

Brightlingsea

Railway Tavern

58 Station Road, CO7 0DT (on B1029)
⊙ 5 (3 Fri; 12 Sat)-11; 12-10.30 Sun
☎ (01206) 302581 website:
www.geocities.com/famousrailway
Crouch Vale Crouch Best; Railway Tavern Crab & Winkle Mild, seasonal beers; guest beers Ⓗ
Traditional local unspoilt by modern pressures with a real fire in winter, but no TV or music. It is worth seeking out for its laid-back style, but especially for the beers produced in the back room micro-brewery – all vegan-friendly and seldom seen elsewhere. The mild is usually available, plus seasonal stout and porter and guests. ♨Q♉❀⊟♿⛺♣●

Bures Hamlet

Eight Bells

Colchester Road, CO8 5AE (on B1508)
⊙ 11.30-3, 5-11; 12-5, 7-10.30 Sun
☎ (01787) 227354
Greene King XX Mild, IPA, Abbot; Tetley Bitter; guest beers Ⓗ
Large, friendly pub situated by the River Stour on the Essex/Suffolk border. Three drinking areas include a spacious games room, that supports regular darts and pool teams. It is popular with diners for its good value food. Horse riding regalia adorns the lounge walls. One of the few pubs in the area to offer a regular mild, the guest beers also come from the Greene King stable. ♨◑◐♿⇌♣P

Burnham on Crouch

Ship Inn

52 High Street, CM0 8AA (on B1021 opp. clock tower)
⊙ 11-11; 12-10.30 Sun
☎ (01621) 785057
Adnams Bitter, Broadside, seasonal beers Ⓗ
Traditional Adnams tied pub in a small riverside town, a friendly local where visitors and regulars enjoy food and ales in tip-top condition. The Ship is a smart, comfortable pub with a nautical theme running throughout. The outside drinking area at the front of the pub allows drinkers to sit and watch the world go by. Upstairs are three guest bedrooms. No food is served Sunday evening. ❀⛍◑◐♿P

Castle Hedingham

Bell Inn

10 St James Street, CO9 3EJ (1 mile from A1017)
⊙ 11.30-3, 6-11; 11.30-11 Fri & Sat; 12-10.30 Sun
☎ (01787) 460350
Adnams Bitter; Greene King IPA; Mighty Oak Oscar Wilde; guest beer Ⓖ
This 15th-century coaching inn has hardly been altered down the years. It still has small rooms for drinking and eating beside the two main bars which both have open fires. Beers are served direct from the barrels, which are all on view in the public bar. This Gray's pub boasts an ample car park and a garden; well worth a visit.
♨♉❀◑◐⊟♿♣●P⚡

Wheatsheaf ✔

2 Queen Street, CO9 3EX (1 mile from A1017)
⊙ 12-2.30, 5-11; 12-11 Sat; 12-10.30 Sun
☎ (01787) 460555
Greene King IPA, Old Speckled Hen; guest beers Ⓗ
Once the home of a wealthy wool merchant this characterful, 16th-century pub boasts carved beams and an inglenook. As the headquarters of the village cricket club, it displays a fine collection of trophies. Usually three beers are available, plus Budvar lager. The Wheatsheaf's food is recommended and comes in generous portions. ♨Q❀◑◐⊟♿♣●P

Chelmsford

Cricketers

143 Moulsham Street, CM2 0JT
⊙ 11-11; 12-10.30 Sun
☎ (01245) 261157
Greene King IPA, Abbot; guest beers Ⓗ
Corner local at the quieter end of this heavily-pubbed street. The public bar has a pool table, juke box and Sky sports, while the lounge bar is quieter with more comfortable seating and a piano. One or two guest beers come from smaller breweries generally, with Mighty Oak products a frequent choice. Note the pub's two different signs and the corner mural outside.
❀◑⊟♣

Endeavour

351 Springfield Road, CM2 6AW
⊙ 11-11; 12-10.30 Sun
☎ (01245) 257717
Greene King IPA, Abbot; Mighty Oak Maldon Gold; guest beers Ⓗ
Three-roomed local about a mile from the town centre. There are usually two guest beers on tap and in the colder months one of these is normally a mild. Real cider is a new addition to the drinks range. Fresh Lowestoft fish and chips are available on Friday and Saturday evenings and local, hung, steaks are served on Saturday evening; there are no evening meals on other days. A meat raffle is held on Sunday.
♨◑◐♣●⚡

Original Plough

28 Duke Street, CM1 1HY
⊙ 12-11; 12-10.30 Sun
☎ (01245) 250145
Greene King IPA; Taylor Landlord; guest beers Ⓗ
Friendly staff in this spacious open-plan pub attract a varied clientele and it is popular with office staff and commuters. Friday and Saturday evenings can be noisy. Major sports events are shown on TV (the landlord is a rugby fan). It stages live rock and soul music. Mild and other dark beers are often available. Meals are served 12-7pm (12-3 Fri-Sun); the no-smoking area only applies at lunchtime. ◑⇌♣P⚡

Queen's Head

30 Lower Anchor Street, CM2 0AS (300 yds from New London Rd, B1007)
12 (11 Sat)-11; 12-10.30 Sun
(01245) 265181 website: www.queensheadchelmsford.co.uk
Crouch Vale Crouch Best, Brewers Gold; guest beers Ⓗ
Six guest beers, including a mild and a stronger dark beer, tended by an enthusiastic landlord is the recipe for success at this street-corner town pub. Four times CAMRA's local Pub of the Year, it welcomes customers from far and wide. Good value lunches (not served Sun), monthly live jazz, weekly quizzes and an annual beer festival add to its appeal. It is popular with cricket followers and Essex players from the nearby ground. Spot the difference between the two sides of the pub sign.

Chipping Ongar

Cock Tavern

218 High Street, CM5 9AB (on A128)
11-11; 12-10.30 Sun
(01277) 362615 website: www.thecocktavernongar.co.uk
Greene King IPA; guest beers Ⓗ
Typical Gray's house over 400 years old, frequently by all age groups and a loyal bunch of locals. A public car park is next to the pub; bus services after 8pm are limited. A function room with handpumps is available for hire and live music is staged most Saturdays. The landlord has been experimenting with real cider, which should become a regular feature.

Clacton-on-Sea

Old Lifeboat House

39 Marine Parade East, CO15 6AD (near A133, almost on seafront)
11-11 (closed winter Mon); 12-10.30 Sun
(01255) 688004
Shepherd Neame Best Bitter, Spitfire, seasonal beers Ⓗ
It is not every day that you are offered a pub on the way to work. The new landlord of the Old Lifeboat House was and has since brought back to life a pub that had been closed for several years. He is a professional magician and a member of the Magic Circle. The formerly run-down pub is now fully refurbished. It really was the old lifeboat house but do not expect the horses to arrive when the maroon goes up.
P

Colchester

Bricklayers

27 Bergholt Road, CO4 5AA (on A134/B1508, near station)
11-3, 5.30-11; 11-11 Fri & Sat; 12-3, 7-10.30 Sun
(01206) 852008
Adnams Bitter, Broadside, seasonal beers; guest beers Ⓗ
Friendly Adnams house, attracting a loyal local clientele. The nearest port of call from North Station, it comprises a comfortable, split-level saloon, a sun lounge and a public bar with pool and darts. The full range of Adnams seasonal beers is offered, plus guests and a real cider. Excellent, good value, home-cooked food is served, but arrive early for the popular Sunday roast. (North) P

British Grenadier

67 Military Road, CO1 2AP (opp. military church)
11-2.30, 6-11, 11-11 Sat; 12-3, 7-10.30 Sun
(01206) 500933
Adnams Bitter, Broadside, seasonal beers; guest beers Ⓗ
Warm, traditional local with an open fire in the front bar and a pool table in the small back bar. The landlord is committed to real ale and was awarded local CAMRA's Town Pub of the Year in 2004. Darts is played regularly in the front bar and frequent charity quiz nights are held for fun, on a Sunday evening. (Town)

Dragoon

82 Butt Road, CO3 3DA (on B1026, near police station,)
11-11; 12-10.30 Sun
(01206) 573464
Adnams Bitter, Broadside, seasonal beers; guest beers Ⓗ
Edge-of-town local with a spacious lounge and a public bar area, housing a pool table. A large-screen TV shows sports; the pub is popular with football fans on match days and welcomes supporters from visiting teams. Try the famous chilli served on match days; a great value Sunday roast lunch is served. The pub dates back to the 1800s and boasts a lovely garden.
(Town)

Fox & Fiddler

1 St Johns Street, CO2 7AA
11-11; 12-10.30 Sun
(01206) 560520
Greene King IPA; guest beers Ⓗ
Friendly, town-centre pub dating back to 1420. Allegedly haunted, it is a stop-off point on the town's Thursday evening ghost trail. A small front bar leads to two larger drinking areas, also used for dining at lunchtime when good value food is served (no meals Mon). This free house offers a changing range of beers from local micros. The entertaining landlord stages live music some Saturday evenings. An enclosed patio allows for outdoor drinking. (Town)

Hospital Arms

123-125 Crouch Street, CO3 3HA (opp. Essex County Hospital, near A1134)
11-11; 12-10.30 Sun
(01206) 573572
Adnams Bitter, Broadside, seasonal beers; Fuller's London Pride; guest beers Ⓗ
Strongly committed to real ale, 'Ward 9' eschews loud music, darts and pool, but still attracts a lively, eclectic clientele. Four drinking areas are supplemented by the patio, a real suntrap in fine weather. It offers excellent home-cooked food and occasional summer barbecues. All Adnams seasonal beers are offered, plus guests, making it well worth the 10-minute walk from the High Street. Q

Odd One Out

28 Mersea Road, CO2 7ET (on B1025)
4.30 (12 Fri; 11 Sat)-11; 12-10.30 Sun
(01206) 578140
Beer range varies Ⓗ

If you are serious about real ale, you really cannot visit Colchester without experiencing the 'Oddy'. At least five beers, including a dark ale, are always on tap, but check which ones are running low, or you might miss your favourite due to the high turnover. With usually three ciders, and numerous malt whiskies, this is one of the cheapest pubs in town. A front room atmosphere prevails throughout this multi-award-winning pub. ♨Q❀⇌(Town)♣●⚟

Prettygate

102 The Commons, CO3 4NW (near B1022)
✪ 11-11; 12-10.30 Sun
☎ (01206) 563501
Courage Best Bitter; guest beers 🄷
Late 1950s estate pub, refurbished in 2002, benefiting from a frequent bus service (No. 1) from the town centre. The four guest ales change often and are mainly from smaller breweries. It hosts regular karaoke evenings and occasional live music. Good value food is available and booking is advisable for the steak and music quiz evening on Tuesday. ❀◐♿P

Stockwell Arms

18 West Stockwell Street, CO1 1HN
(off High St, behind town hall)
✪ 11-11; 11-5, 6.30-11 Sat; 12-4, 7-10.30 Sun
☎ (01206) 575560
Caledonian Deuchars IPA; Nethergate Suffolk County, Augustinian Ale; Shepherd Neame Spitfire; guest beers 🄷
Situated in the historic Dutch Quarter, this 14th-century local provides a welcome change from the theme pubs in the High Street. Untouched by modern refurbishment, oak beams are visible inside and out. The long-serving landlord provides his customers with four regular and one or two guest ales. Ask to see the album of old Colchester photos – the pub has not changed much from its image in the Victorian pictures. Monthly country walks are organised (last Sat), and booking is recommended for Sunday lunch. ❀◐♣

Coxtie Green

White Horse

173 Coxtie Green Road, CM14 5PX
(1 mile W of A128) OS564959
✪ 11.30-11; 12-10.30 Sun
☎ (01277) 372410
Adnams Bitter; Fuller's London Pride; Ridleys Rumpus; guest beers 🄷
Excellent, two-bar country local keeping up the high standards of the last few years; the atmosphere is always relaxed and friendly. The three guest beers come from anywhere in the United Kingdom; darts and cribbage are played and regular golf and angling competitions are organised, as well as occasional quizzes and cycle rides. Good value lunches are served Monday-Saturday. A large lawned garden has a children's play area and seating. Cider is sometimes on sale. ❀◐♿♣●P

Danbury

Griffin

64 Main Road, CM3 4DH (on A414)
✪ 12-11; 12-10.30 Sun
☎ (01245) 222905
Adnams Broadside; guest beers 🄷
Food-oriented Chef and Brewer benefiting from a beer-loving landlord who makes the most of his ability to source guests from far and wide through Beer Seller. The building dates back to the 1500s and has been an inn since 1744. Sir Walter Scott stayed here (it is mentioned in the introduction to Waverley). Fish features prominently on the all-day menu and regular food themed evenings are held. The Griffin is no-smoking throughout.
♨❀◐P⚟

Dedham

Sun Inn

High Street, CO7 6DF (on B1029, opp. church)
✪ 12-11; 12-10.30 (6 winter eve) Sun
☎ (01206) 323351 website: www.thesuninndedham.com
Adnams Broadside; guest beers 🄷
This extended 15th-century inn has a large, no-smoking bar, a wood-panelled smoking room, a spacious, recommended restaurant and a garden to the rear. Guest ales are mainly sourced from local micros. The menu is seasonal and sourced from local produce. The pub is handily placed for walks in Constable country. The pub keeps a plentiful supply of board games. One of the four en-suite, no-smoking guest rooms has a four-poster bed.
♨Q❀⇆◐♣P⚟

Duton Hill

Three Horseshoes

CM6 2DX (½ mile W of B184, Dunmow-Saffron Walden Road OS606268
✪ 12-2.30 (not Mon-Wed; 12-3 Sat), 6-11; 12-3, 7-10.30 Sun
☎ (01371) 870681
Archers Village; guest beers 🄷
Cosy village local, where the large garden overlooks the Chelmer Valley and open farmland. It hosts an open-air theatre in July (the landlord is a former pantomime dame). The wildlife pond is home to frogs and newts. A millennium beacon, breweriana and a remarkable collection of Butlins' memorabilia are features of this unpretentious pub. A beer festival is held over the late spring bank holiday at local CAMRA's Pub of the Year 2003 and 2004. Guest beers include Mauldons and Mighty Oak.
♨❀♣P

East Hanningfield

Windmill Tavern

The Tye, Main Road, CM3 8AA OS771012
✪ 11-11; 12-10.30 Sun
☎ (01245) 400315
website: www.thewindmilleasthanningfield.co.uk
Crouch Vale Brewers Gold; Greene King IPA; guest beer 🄷
Pub on the village green selling good, home-made food seven days a week (not Mon eve). The restaurant area is open Friday evening, all day Saturday and Sunday lunchtime. Special prices apply to meals on Wednesday and Thursday lunchtimes for the over 55s. Wednesday is quiz night. The guest beer is usually from a small brewery.
♨❀◐♣P

Eastwood

Oakwood

564 Rayleigh Road, SS9 5HX (on A1015)
⏲ 11-11; 12-10.30 Sun
☎ (01702) 429000 website: www.theoakwood.co.uk
Fuller's London Pride; Greene King IPA Ⓗ
Spacious pub, comprising two bar areas. The larger bar houses several pool tables, a dartboard and two big screens showing sport. The smaller bar is quieter, with comfortable seating and a piano. It hosts various entertainment on Friday and Saturday evenings, plus a quiz on Monday. This local CAMRA Town Pub of the Year 2002 is served by bus routes Arriva 9 and First 20 from Southend and Rayleigh. Meals are served 12-8pm daily. ❀◑ ♣P

Epping

Forest Gate

Bell Common, CM16 4DZ (off B1393, Ivy Chimneys road) OS451011
⏲ 10-2.30, 5.30-11; 12-3 (3.30 summer), 7-10.30 Sun
☎ (01992) 572312
Adnams Bitter, Broadside, seasonal beers; Ⓗ **Ridleys IPA,** Ⓗ **Woodforde's Wherry** Ⓖ
Timeless, 17th-century, genuine country free house, owned and run by the same family for many years. Situated on the edge of Epping Forest, it is popular with walkers. It specialises in real ale; the juke box, music and fruit machines are remarkable for their absence. Snacks are usually available and a renowned turkey broth is served all year round. A large, lawned area at the front of the pub is used for summer drinking. Dogs are welcome. Q❀P

Feering

Sun Inn

3 Feering Hill, CO5 9NH (on B1024, off A12)
⏲ 11-3, 6-11; 12-3, 6-10.30 Sun
☎ (01376) 570442
Beer range varies Ⓗ
Beautifully maintained pub, a short walk from Kelvedon Station. Full height exposed beams separate the three cosy drinking areas, with log fires in winter. A changing range of beers, usually includes at least one dark ale, plus real cider. Micro-breweries are always well represented. The extensive menu ranges from snacks and wholesome favourites to more exotic fare, but do leave room for the fantastic puddings. The garden offers seating and a barbecue area. Q❀◑ ≠(Kelvedon) ♣P

Fingringhoe

Whalebone

Chapel Road, CO5 7BG
(take B1025 to Mersea, turn left at Abberton)
⏲ 11-3, 5.30-11; 11-11 Sat; 11-10.30 Sun
☎ (01206) 729307
Greene King IPA; Mauldons White Adder; Mighty Oak Maldon Gold; Young's Special; guest beers Ⓗ
Grade II listed, early 1700s pub at the village centre, comprising a large, open, single bar/eating area and a no-smoking dining room. The varied menu offers quality food, prepared and cooked on the premises. An extensive garden affords fine views over the Roman river valley. Nearby stands the 12th-century church that suffered damage in the 1884 earthquake. A popular area with walkers and nature reserve visitors. Dogs are welcome at the pub, which stages a summer beer festival. ❀◑ P⊬

Fobbing

White Lion

Lion Hill, SS17 9JR (near B1420) OS716839
⏲ 12-3, 5.30-11; 12-11 Fri & Sat; 12-10.30 Sun
☎ (01375) 673281
Archers Village; Greene King Old Speckled Hen; guest beer Ⓗ
Circa 17th-century, friendly village pub with 18th-century extensions, incorporating beams from Thames sailing barges. Barge owners stored their sails in the pub's loft. The building was also used to house masons building a nearby monastery; part of an old underground tunnel connecting the two buildings still exists. The village is associated with the Peasants Revolt against the poll tax in 1381. Home-cooked lunches are served (not Sun), a designated no-smoking area applies at lunchtime only. Children are welcome until 9pm.
❀◑ P⊬

Foulness Island

George & Dragon

Church End, SS3 9XQ
⏲ 11-2.30 (not Mon or Tue), 6-11; 12-10.30 Sun
☎ (01702) 219460
website: www.georgeanddragonpub.co.uk
Greene King IPA Ⓗ
The George and Dragon stands on MoD property as does the whole of Foulness – visitors need to phone to make arrangements; this can be done at short notice by calling the pub. Greene King is always on tap, but now the pub brews its own beers, including a mild and two excellent bitters. The 17th-century pub is well worth a visit; it houses a small but interesting heritage centre. The walled garden once served as an arena for bare fist fighting. Sunday meals are served all day.
Q❀◑ ♣P

Fyfield

Queen's Head

Queen Street, CM5 0RY (by B184) OS570068
⏲ 11-3.30 (4 Sat), 6-11; 12-4, 7-10.30 Sun
☎ (01277) 899231
Adnams Bitter, Broadside; guest beers Ⓗ
Busy, 15th-century country pub in the middle of the village. It retains a cosy feel, with a long bar, some partitions, a beamed ceiling and two real fires. Popular for food, which is a cut above standard pub fare, it can get crowded at lunchtime; evening meals are served Monday-Saturday. The garden backs on to the River Roding (you can feed the ducks). The guest beers – normally four – are usually from micro-breweries. The cider is Westons Old Rosie.
❀◑ P

Galleywood

Horse & Groom

Horse & Groom Lane, CM2 8PL (off B1007 from Chelmsford at Goat Hall Lane, then left) OS701030

11.30-3, 6-11; 12-10.30 Sun

☎ (01245) 261653

Greene King IPA, Abbot; Mighty Oak Oscar Wilde; guest beer H

Two-bar local, tucked away on Galleywood Common overlooking the old racecourse. This pub was awarded local CAMRA's Most Improved Pub award for 2004. The public bar can be noisy with a juke box, pool table and big-screen TV sports, but the lounge bar is quieter. The guest beer comes from the Gray's list. Note the collection of old champagne bottles. Evening meals are served Wednesday-Sunday.

Goldhanger

Chequers

The Square, CM9 8AS (400 yds from B1026)

11-11; 12-10.30 Sun

☎ (01621) 788203 website: www.thechequersgoldhanger.co.uk

Caledonian Deuchars IPA; Flowers IPA; York Stonewall; guest beers H

Busy, but welcoming 15th-century village pub with exposed beams. The central bar is surrounded by a diversity of characterful rooms including a dining area, tap, no-smoking snug, a games room and a public bar, bearing an abundance of village and rural memorabilia. It offers an extensive, reasonably-priced menu; no food is served Sunday evenings, except monthly curry evenings (third Sun). Quiz night is Thursday. Annual events include a beer festival (March), vintage car rally (Oct) and a sloe gin competition (Feb).

Cricketers

33 Church Street, CM9 8AR (on B1026)

11-11; 12-10.30 Sun

☎ (01621) 788468

Adnams Bitter; Greene King IPA; guest beers H

Virtually inaccessible by public transport, this unspoilt, tiny village now has two pubs in this Guide. The Cricketers is full of nooks and crannies. One bar doubles as a restaurant, the other is more lively, with a juke box and dartboard. A good range of food and beer is served, with regular guests often including a dark ale. Young, but knowledgeable staff offer a warm welcome.

Gosfield

King's Head

The Street, CO9 1TP (on A1017)

12-3, 6-11 (12-11 summer Sat); 12-10.30 Sun

☎ (01787) 474016

Greene King IPA; guest beers H

At the centre of a truly communal village, this charming, 16th-century pub has been faithfully restored. The public bar has a wood floor; bar snacks are listed on a blackboard. The lounge, adjoining restaurant and conservatory feature oak panelling with bookshelves, polished wood tables and sofas. Imaginative meals are all freshly prepared; food is available all day (12-8) Sunday and summer Saturdays. Guest beers are usually well known names, such as Marston's Pedigree. Do not miss the August scarecrow festival.

Grays

Grays Athletic Football Club

Bridge Road, RM17 6BZ (S end of ground, Bridge Rd entrance)

5 (12 Fri & Sat)-11; 12-10.30 Sun

☎ (01375) 377753 website: www.graysathletic.co.uk

Greene King IPA; guest beers H

The social club of Grays Athletic FC admits card-carrying CAMRA members and bearers of this Guide. Local CAMRA's Club of the Year 2003, 2004 and 2005 has recently introduced Bridge Road Bitter, brewed exclusively for the club by Cox and Holbrook. It also offers two guest beers and Belgian beers (30 bottled and two on draught). Live blues bands are featured fortnightly on Thursday (see website for details). An annual beer festival is held at the end of January. Use the public car park opposite.

Theobald Arms

141 Argent Street, RM17 6HR

(5 mins' walk from Grays Station, down King's Walk)

11-3, 5-11; 11-11 Fri & Sat; 12-4, 7-10.30 Sun

☎ (01375) 372253

Courage Best Bitter; guest beers H

A real traditional pub with a public bar and an unusual hexagonal pool table. The changing selection of three guest beers showcases local independent breweries. In addition to real ales it stocks a range of unusual bottled beers. It is popular with office workers at lunchtime for weekday meals.

Great Dunmow

Saracen's Head Hotel

High Street, CM6 1AG

12-11; 12-10.30 Sun

☎ (01371) 873901 website: www.thesaracenshead.biz

Adnams Bitter; Greene King IPA; guest beers H

Handy for Stansted Airport, this coaching inn, recommended for food and accommodation, is now privately owned. Built in 1560, it incorporates an 18th-century façade with Georgian and Tudor architecture; the bar area has been modernised. An ancient flitch of bacon ceremony is held every leap year opposite the hotel. Landlords here have been recorded since 1620; one of the earliest was a Roundhead. Mighty Oak guest beers are supplemented by beers from other micros supplied by Mighty Oak. The car park is approached via Chequers Lane.

Great Easton

Swan

The Endway, CM6 2HG

(3 miles N of Dunmow near B184) OS606255

12-3, 6-11; 12-3, 7-10.30 Sun

☎ (01371) 870359 website: www.swangreateason.co.uk

Adnams Bitter; guest beer H

A warm welcome is assured in this 15th-century free house in an attractive village. A log-burning stove, exposed beams and comfortable sofas feature in the lounge; pool and darts are played in the public bar. Occasional French classes are held here. All meals are prepared to order, the majority home made (including the chips) from fresh local produce; no frozen ingredients are used. The chef looks after the beer that complements the food. The restaurant is no-smoking (no meals Sun eve). ⌂Q❀◑◗⊟♣P

Great Waltham

Rose & Crown

Minnows End, Chelmsford Road, CM3 1AG (400 yds W of B1008)

✪ 11.30-3, 5.30-11; 11.30-11 Sat; 12-10.30 Sun

☎ (01245) 360359 website: www.roseandcrowngreatwaltham.co.uk

Draught Bass; Fuller's London Pride; guest beers Ⓗ

Country pub where a log fire burns in the inglenook. Old flintlock and percussion guns on the walls reflect the rural heritage of this part of Essex. It offers good ales and home-cooked food. It organises monthly racing trips, with breakfast in the pub, a coach to the racecourse and dinner at the pub on return. A front patio provides outdoor seating for summer drinking. Previously known as the Great Waltham, the pub has a congenial family room. ⌂Q❀◑◗P

Great Yeldham

Waggon & Horses

High Street, CO9 4EX (on A1017)

✪ 11-11; 12-10.30 Sun

☎ (01787) 237936 website: www.waggonandhorses.net

Greene King IPA, Abbot; guest beers Ⓗ

Guest beers are only sourced from local brewers, such as Mauldons or Wolf, and Storm cider, also produced locally, is always available. This 16th-century inn is a busy village hostelry, but everyone is made welcome. Food, served every day, is especially popular at weekends. Sixteen rooms in an annexe overlooking the garden provide overnight accommodation. The friendly landlord is a long-term supporter of real ale. ⛟◑◗♣●P

Halstead

Dog Inn

37 Hedingham Road, CO9 2DB (on A1124)

✪ 4 (11 Sat)-11; 12-10.30 Sun

☎ (01787) 477774

Adnams Bitter, Broadside; guest beers Ⓗ

The Dog Inn is ideal for a quiet pint after walking in the country or hunting antiques in the villages along the Essex/Suffolk border. Adnams staples are offered alongside at least two guest ales, usually including a mild. Good accommodation is provided in en-suite rooms. Bar snacks and more substantial meals are served, as well as barbecues in summer, alongside the petanque court. Regular buses run from Sudbury, Colchester and Braintree. A beer festival is held in spring. ⌂Q❀⛟◑♣P▯

Harwich

New Bell Inn

Outpart Eastward, CO12 3EN

(200 yds from eastern end of A120)

✪ 11-2.30, 7-11; 12-4, 7-10.30 (12-10.30 summer) Sun

☎ (01255) 503545

Greene King IPA; Nethergate Priory Mild; guest beers Ⓗ

Friendly local, a good stopping-off point on a walk round historic old Harwich. The front bar is the hub and buzzes with conversation, while the quieter back bar and seating area provide somewhere to enjoy a quiet pint or a meal. Food is basic but wholesome and hearty. The beer list features guests from East Anglian micro-brewers. A strong supporter of community events, it was voted local CAMRA's Most Improved Pub in 2005.

❀◑⊟⇌(Town) P

Hatfield Broad Oak

Cock

High Street, CM22 7HF (on B183)

✪ 12-2.30, 6-11; 12-4, 7-10.30 Sun

☎ (01279) 718306

Adnams Bitter; Fuller's London Pride; guest beer Ⓗ

Interesting pub in a charming village. The main bar is smart but bare, displaying film posters on the walls. Frequented by ramblers and cyclists as well as regulars, this large pub comprises many sprawling rooms. Food does tend to dominate at times, but the beer range is good and rings the changes with extra guests.

Q◑◗♿P

Hempstead

Bluebell Inn

High Street, CB10 2PD

(on B1054, between Saffron Walden and Haverhill)

✪ 11.30-3.30, 6-11 (closed winter Mon); 11-11 Sat; 12-10.30 Sun

☎ (01799) 599199

Adnams Bitter, Broadside; Woodforde's Wherry; guest beers Ⓗ

Late 17th-century village pub with 18th-century additions, reputed to be the birthplace of Dick Turpin; the bar displays posters about his life. The restaurant serves meals of excellent quality from an extensive menu. The large bar has a log fire in winter. Ample seating is provided outside for summer, with a children's play area at the rear. Five real ales often include a guest from a Fenland brewery; the Aspall cider comes from Suffolk. Local CAMRA's Pub of the Year 2005 hosts a folk evening on Tuesday.

⌂Q❀◑◗♣●P⚟

Horndon-on-the-Hill

Bell Inn

High Road, SS17 8LD (near B1007) OS671833

✪ 11-2.30 (3 Sat), 5.30 (6 Sat)-11; 12-4, 7-10.30 Sun

☎ (01375) 642463 website: www.bell-inn.co.uk

Draught Bass; Ⓖ **Greene King IPA; guest beers** Ⓗ

Busy, 15th-century coaching inn, where the beamed bars feature wood panelling and carvings. The unusual hot cross bun collection hanging in the saloon bar was started about 100 years ago; a hot cross bun is still added every Good Friday. The hilltop village, now relieved by a bypass, has a restored woolmarket. The award-winning restaurant is no-smoking. The pub boasts five honeymoon

suites. Up to five guest ales are stocked, including beers from Essex breweries.
⛰Q❀⇌◐◗⊟P⚟

Kirby-le-Soken

Red Lion

32 The Street, CO13 0EF (on B1034)
✪ 11-11; 12-10.30 Sun
☎ (01255) 674832
Greene King IPA; guest beers 🄷
This ancient pub is set in a picturesque village opposite the church. The new landlord has brought a change of emphasis to the pub's beer range; a wide choice of beers from micro-breweries has made it a magnet for real ale lovers. A weekly quiz is held in the split-level bar and it hosts two beer festivals a year. Even the poltergeist approves of the change, as did local CAMRA, voting it Pub of the Year 2005. Note the wide range of oversized festival glasses.
⛰❀◐◗⇌♣●P⊓

Langley Lower Green

Bull

CB11 4SB (turn N off B1038 at Clavering) OS436345
✪ 12-2 (3 Sat), 6-11; 12-3, 7-10.30 Sun
☎ (01279) 777307
Greene King IPA, Abbot, Old Speckled Hen 🄷
Classic, Victorian village local, with its original cast iron lattice windows and fireplaces. It sits in a tiny isolated hamlet, less than a mile from the Hertfordshire border, and just a bit further from Cambridgeshire. The pub is supported by a devoted band of regulars, including local football and cricket teams. This friendly pub lies in beautiful rolling countryside. Meals can be arranged with advance notice. ⛰Q❀⊟♣P

Leigh-on-Sea

Broker

213-217 Leigh Road, SS9 1JA
✪ 11-3, 6-11; 11-11 Wed-Sat; 12-10.30 Sun
☎ (01702) 471932
Everards Tiger; Fuller's London Pride; Ridleys IPA; Shepherd Neame Spitfire; Young's Bitter; guest beers 🄷
Family-run free house that has featured in every edition of this Guide since 1996. It has a garden at the rear and a small pavement seating area. This sporty, community pub organises local charity fundraising events, including quizzes or live music on Sunday evening. Bar and restaurant meals are served lunchtime and Tuesday-Saturday evenings. Children are welcome until 7.30pm in a sectioned-off, no-smoking area of the bar. Two guest beers are stocked. ❀◐◗⇌(Chalkwell)♣

Elms ✔

1060 London Road, SS9 3ND (on A13)
✪ 10-11; 12-10.30 Sun
☎ (01702) 474687
Courage Best Bitter; Hop Back Summer Lightning; Marston's Burton Bitter, Pedigree; Shepherds Neame Spitfire; guest beers 🄷
Busy roadhouse on the A13. The name originates from the farmhouse that previously occupied the site. Wetherspoon's refurbishment has created a spacious, comfortable pub with many alcoves providing seating. The large front garden has a deep hedge to reduce the noise from the main road. Many photographs and pictures recall past inhabitants, the history of Leigh-on-Sea and the old town. Food is available 10-11 (9.30 Sun). Q❀◐◗♿P⚟

Little Baddow

Rodney

North Hill, CM3 4TQ OS778080
✪ 12-3, 6-11; 12-10.30 Sun
☎ (01245) 222385
Greene King IPA, Old Speckled Hen; guest beer 🄷
A pub since the early 1800s, when it sold beer from the old Chelmsford Brewery, the Rodney was built as a farmhouse around 1650 and has served as a grocer's and bakery. This comfortable, two-roomed, beamed building comprises a public bar with a pool table, a small snug and a compact drinking/dining area, displaying brasses, posters, pump clips and seafaring prints. The food is all home made and includes good value daily specials. Q❀◐◗⊟♣P

Little Clacton

Apple Tree

The Street, CO16 9LF (on B1441)
✪ 12-11; 12-7 Sun
☎ (01255) 861026
Fuller's London Pride; Greene King Abbot; Mighty Oak Oscar Wilde 🄶
Little Clacton's renowned pub continues to win plaudits for the quality of its beer, many years after it was first described as an oasis in a real ale desert, and its real ale club continues to thrive. The big difference now is that the beer is served by gravity dispense and there is usually a mild available. The introduction of Sky sports and a pool table has encouraged a younger clientele to try real ale. Three bus routes regularly pass the door. ❀♣P⚟⊓

Little Thurrock

Traitor's Gate

40-42 Broadway, RM17 6EW
(on A126, 1 mile E of Grays town centre)
✪ 12-11; 12-10.30 Sun
☎ (01375) 372628
Beer range varies 🄷
Friendly, one-bar local that has been sympathetically refurbished to retain its original features. Two changing ales are sourced from small and micro-breweries. With comfy sofas and a pool table at the rear, it fields football and darts teams and shows major sporting events on a large-screen TV. Bar snacks are available and the patio hosts barbecues in summer. Lively at weekends, it is quieter during the week. The No. 320 Lakeside to Tilbury Asda bus stops outside. ❀♣

Little Totham

Swan

School Road, CM9 8JL (2 miles SE of B1022, between Tiptree and Gt Totham) OS889117
✪ 11-11; 12-10.30 Sun
☎ (01621) 892689 website: www.theswanpublichouse.co.uk

Adnams Bitter; Caledonian Deuchars IPA; Crouch Vale Brewers Gold; Mighty Oak Oscar Wilde, Maldon Gold; guest beers [G]
Archetypal, 17th-century, heavily beamed village pub: the unspoilt public bar has billiards and darts, while the comfortable saloon has open fires and an air filtration system. National CAMRA Pub of the Year 2002 and Essex winner 2005, it has a large, enclosed garden; muddy boots and dogs are welcome. The food here is recommended, but walkers may eat their own food by arrangement. It stocks country fruit wines and some Belgian beers; the house beer Totham Parva is brewed by Mighty Oak. A beer festival is held in June. No evening meals are served on Sunday. ⛫Q❀◐◑⊟♿⛺♣●P⊬⊡

Little Walden

Crown

High Street, CB10 1XA (on B1052, 2 miles NE of Saffron Walden)
⏲ 11.30-2.30 (3 Sat), 6-11; 12-10.30 Sun
☎ (01799) 522475
Adnams Broadside; City of Cambridge Boathouse Bitter; Greene King IPA; guest beers [G]
Charming, beamed country pub, boasting a large walk-through fireplace. The pub offers an extensive menu, with evening meals available Tuesday–Saturday. Racked cask stillage is used for dispensing an excellent range of beers. This recently extended, 18th-century pub, in a quiet country hamlet, attracts locals and business customers from Saffron Walden. It is used for club meetings and hosts trad jazz on Wednesday evening.
⛫Q⛹❀◐◑♿♣P⊬

Littlebury

Queen's Head

High Street, CB11 4TD (on B1383, approx 1 mile N of Audley End House)
⏲ 12-3, 5.30-11; 12-3, 7-10.30 Sun
☎ (01799) 522251
website: www.queensheadinnlittlebury.co.uk
Greene King IPA, Morland Original; guest beer [H]
Once a strategic roadhouse on the old A11, it is now a homely, 15th-century village-centre pub supporting local football and cricket teams, as well as its own golf society. The spacious single bar has many period features – an inglenook, exposed beams and a large, fixed settle, dominated by an imposing circular bar counter. The landlord is keen to promote the guest beers supplied by Greene King. The dining room offers home-cooked meals (Tue-Sun), based on local produce. ⛫Q❀◐◑♿♣P⊬

Littley Green

Compasses

CM3 1BU (turn off B1417 at Ridleys Brewery, Hartford End)
OS699172
⏲ 12-3, 6 (7 Sat)-11; 12-3, 7-10.30 Sun
☎ (01245) 362308
Ridleys IPA, Rumpus, Old Bob [G]
Ridley's brewery tap is an isolated and unspoilt country pub with tiled floors and simple wood furniture. The beers are drawn direct from the cask and carried up from a half-cellar. Huffers (giant baps) and jacket potatoes, both with a wide variety of fillings, and soup, are available at all sessions. There are seats and tables outside the bar and picnic tables in the large garden. A folk evening is held monthly on a Monday. ⛫Q⛹❀♣P⊬

Maldon

Blue Boar Hotel

Silver Street, CM9 4QE (off High St opp. All Saints Church)
⏲ 11-11; 12-11 Sun
☎ (01621) 855888 website: www.blueboarmaldon.co.uk
Adnams Bitter; Maldon Blue Boar Bitter, Pucks Folly, seasonal beers [G]
Privately-owned, 15th-century, two-bar coaching inn in the centre of historic Maldon. It boasts original period furniture with other antiques. Beer is served by gravity in the back bar, which is also no-smoking. Three beers from the Maldon Brewing Company, operating from stables at the rear, are always available. Good quality bar food is served. Regular jazz sessions take place in the upstairs function room (Thu eve and Sun lunchtime). ⛫Q❀⛟◐◑P⊬⊡

Queen's Head

The Hythe, CM9 5HN
⏲ 10.30-11; 12-10.30 Sun
☎ (01621) 854112
Greene King IPA, Abbot; Mighty Oak Maldon Gold, Burntwood; guest beer (occasional) [H]
Pleasant pub, some 600 years old, on the quay where the sailing barges are moored. The rear bar overlooks the River Blackwater, and a spacious outdoor seating area with sun umbrellas, an outside bar and barbecue. The front bar, warmed by a log fire, is a local meeting place. Food can be consumed in the restaurant or elsewhere; seafood is a speciality on the extensive menu that offers daily specials. Children are allowed in the restaurant. Good disabled access and WC facilities are provided.
⛫Q❀◐◑⊟♿●P⊡

Warwick Arms

185 High Street, CM9 5BU
⏲ 12-11; 12-10.30 Sun
☎ (01621) 850122
Greene King IPA; Mighty Oak Maldon Gold; guest beers [H]
Dating from the late 1830s, it became the Warwick Arms in 1899. Settle down by the log fire or on the comfortable sofa in the bay window. A choice of hot food and snacks is offered at lunchtime. With a welcoming landlord and friendly bar staff, it was awarded Most Improved Pub of the Year by local CAMRA in 2004. Darts and pool teams meet here regularly, and a function room draws various groups for meetings. Stowford Press cider is sold.
⛫◐♿●P⊡

White Horse

26 High Street, CM9 5PJ
⏲ 11-11; 12-10.30 Sun
☎ (01621) 851708
Shepherd Neame Master Brew Bitter, Spitfire, Bishops Finger, seasonal beers [H]
This Shepherd Neame tied house has one long bar with a small screened restaurant area at one end. One of the town's oldest inns, it remains

unspoilt by modernisation. Well-behaved children are admitted, if accompanied by an adult. Pool is available. Live music is performed at weekends, and it hosts a Friday disco. Home-cooked food is served daily, with special deals for pensioners. Parking is limited – use the public car park at the rear. 🛏◑◐♿♣

Margaretting Tye

White Hart Inn

Swan Lane, CM4 9JX (off Galleywood Rd) OS684011
⏲ 11.30-3, 6-11; 12-10.30 Sun
☎ (01277) 840478 website: www.thewhitehart.uk.com
Adnams Bitter, Broadside; Mighty Oak IPA; 🄷
guest beers 🄶
Large pub comprising an L-shaped bar and a conservatory, hidden away in farmland between Chelmsford and Ingatestone. Six guest beers are always available on gravity, all served from the temperature-controlled cellar. Home-made daily specials supplement the regular menu; food is served all day Sunday. The expansive grounds include a children's play area and a pets' corner. Beer festivals are held in June and at the end of October. ⛰Q🚶❀◑◐♿▲♣P⚟

Mill Green

Viper ☆

Mill Green Road, CM4 0PT OS641018
⏲ 12-3, 6-11; 11-11 Sat; 12-10.30 Sun
☎ (01277) 352010
Mighty Oak Oscar Wilde; Ridleys IPA; 🄷
guest beers 🄷/🄶
A long-standing Guide entry, the Viper now has a new owner, but he has not altered the unspoilt nature of this isolated pub. The only significant changes are longer weekend opening hours, an expanded lunchtime food range and the removal of the door between the snug and the lounge bar. Alas, no more chilli pickled eggs! House beers (Viper Ales) are commissioned from the local Mighty Oak Brewery, and a beer festival is held in September. Wilkins cider is stocked. ⛰Q❀◑🀫♣●P

Mountnessing

Prince of Wales

199 Roman Road, CM15 0UG (on B1002)
⏲ 12-3, 5-11; 12-3, 7-10.30 Sun
☎ (01277) 353445
Ridleys IPA, Tolly Original, Old Bob 🄷
This former Ridleys' tied house stands opposite a windmill and a large cricket field. The timbered interior divides into two distinct drinking areas, one of which has a no-smoking section, with individual partitioned tables. Evening meals are served Monday–Saturday. ◑◐🀫♣P⚟

Newport

Coach & Horses

Cambridge Road, CB11 3TR (on B1383, old A11)
⏲ 11-3, 6-11 (11-11 summer); 12-3 (10.30 summer) Sun
☎ (01799) 540292
Adnams Bitter, Broadside; Ridleys IPA; Young's Bitter; guest beers 🄷
An attractive and friendly pub dating from 1520. It has a large open fire in the main bar to warm customers on cold winter days. Separate family and dining areas, together with a fine and varied range of food have made this a popular place to dine. The landlord's two Great Danes are large but also friendly. ⛰🚶❀◑◐♿P⚟

North End

Butcher's Arms ✔

Dunmow Road, CM6 3PJ (on A130, SE of Gt Dunmow)
⏲ 11-11; 12-10.30 Sun
☎ (01245) 237481
Ridleys IPA, Old Bob, seasonal beers 🄷
The 500-year-old Butcher's Arms is a friendly, family pub, divided into three well-defined areas: a public bar housing a pool table, a central bar with tables for eating and drinking, and a no-smoking dining area. Children are welcome inside and in the award-winning garden. Snacks and an extensive menu of home-cooked food are usually available, but phone to check for any variations. The field to the rear is available for tents and caravans (booking essential). ⛰❀◑◐🀫♿▲♣P

North Shoebury

Angel

Parsons Corner, SS3 8UD (at A13/B1017 roundabout)
⏲ 11-3, 5.30-11; 12-3, 7-10.30 Sun
☎ (01702) 589600
Greene King IPA, Abbot 🄷
Excellent pub with flagstone floor, free from machines. Much of the original, thatched 16th-century building survives. It was for years a post office. The bar staff are friendly. The carved angel in the restaurant is of particular note. It can be busy at weekends, showing what a popular venue this is. An hourly bus, operated by Arriva sometimes stops near the pub (limited evening service). It holds occasional beer festivals. Q❀◑◐♿P🗑

Orsett

Foxhound

18 High Road, RM16 3ER (on B188)
⏲ 11-3.30, 6-11; 11-11 Sat; 12-3.30, 7-10.30 Sun
☎ (01375) 891295
Courage Best Bitter; Greene King IPA; guest beer 🄷
Two-bar village local that is at the centre of social life in Orsett. It has a comfortable saloon and a basic, but characterful public bar. The guest beers are usually from the Crouch Vale portfolio. The Fox's Den restaurant provides excellent meals at lunchtime and Wednesday-Saturday evenings (booking necessary); it is also available for functions. Quiz nights are held regularly. ⛰❀◑◐🀫♿♣P

Paglesham

Punch Bowl

Church End, SS4 2DP
(from A127, head for Rochford then follow signs)
⏲ 11.30-3, 6.30-11; 12-3, 6.30-10.30 Sun
☎ (01702) 258376
Adnams Bitter; Ridleys Old Bob; guest beers 🄷
Dating from the 16th century, this former sailmaker's house in white Essex board is situated in a quiet, one-street village. The single, low, beamed bar displays a large collection of

mugs, old pictures and other artefacts and serves two guest beers. The small, no-smoking restaurant offers a reasonably priced, changing menu. Tables at the front of the pub face south; a large children's garden at the rear is also set out with dining tables. Q❀◖◗P

Pebmarsh

King's Head

The Street, CO9 2NH (4 miles NE of Halstead) OS851335
☉ 12-3, 6-11 (closed Mon); 12-10.30 Sun
☎ (01787) 269306
Greene King IPA; Woodforde's Wherry; guest beers Ⓗ
Based in the tiny village of Pebmarsh, this pub is popular with locals, walkers and cyclists. The building is over 500 years old, with bowed ceilings and oak beams. Locals sit at the bar or play pool, while many visitors head for the restaurant to sample the home-cooked fare. Benches at the front and rear provide an alternative in summer. A good range of guest beers mainly come from micro-breweries.
♨❀◖◗♣P

Pentlow

Pinkuah Arms

Pinkuah Lane, CO10 7JW
(off B1064, down narrow lane) OS816448
☉ 5-11; 12-3, 7-11 Sat; 12-4.30, 7-10.30 Sun
☎ (01787) 280857
Greene King IPA; guest beer Ⓗ
Hard to find, this quiet country pub is 350 years old. It was named after two spinster sisters who lived here in the late 1800s; see their photo in the bar. The well-kept and established, secluded garden is an added attraction. Monthly quiz nights are held in the heavily-beamed, open-plan bar on Sunday evening. Children, walkers and dogs are welcome; warm up by the big open fire in winter. ♨❀♣P

Ramsden Bellhouse

Fox & Hounds

Church Road, CM11 1PW
(50 yds from the railway bridge)
☉ 11.30-11, 12-10.30 Sun
☎ (01268) 710286 website:
www.foxandhoundsramsdenheath.co.uk
Greene King IPA, Old Speckled Hen; guest beers Ⓗ
Recently refurbished, this classy mock-Tudor pub is both a friendly local and ideal for people passing through the village. It usually offers a good choice of ales; guests include Archers'. The pub is situated in a rural location with plenty to keep children amused. The restaurant offers a good menu all day, specialising in pies of the day, plus vegetarian options. Every summer the pub hosts a well-attended beer festival in the spacious garden. ❀◖◗P

Ridgewell

White Horse

Mill Road, CO9 4SG (on A1017) OS737410
☉ 11-11; 12-10.30 Sun
☎ (01440) 785532
Beer range varies Ⓖ
A recently-installed stillage behind the bar serves a wide range of beers from local and nationwide breweries, all on gravity with cooling jackets; real cider is always available. It offers good value compared to many pubs in the vicinity. As well as bar snacks a charming restaurant offers a wide choice, with occasional seafood specialities. The comfy sofa in front of the log fire is especially welcoming. A newly-built motel has spacious, well-furnished rooms overlooking the garden. ♨❀⇌◖◗♿♣●P

Rochford

Golden Lion ✔

35 North Street, SS4 1AB
☉ 11.30-11; 12-10.30 Sun
☎ (01702) 545487
Adnams Bitter; Crouch Vale Brewers Gold; Greene King Abbot; guest beers Ⓗ
Unspoilt, 16th-century pub, featuring Essex weatherboard and stained-glass windows. South-East Essex CAMRA Pub of the Year 2005, this is an award it has won many times, due to its excellent beer and lively atmosphere. It generally keeps two or three guest beers, one of which is usually dark, plus a real cider. It can get busy on Friday evening. Dogs are welcome, but not children. Meals are served Tuesday-Friday.
❀◖⇌♣●Ū

Roundbush (Purleigh)

Roundbush

Fambridge Road, CM9 6NN (on B1010)
☉ 11-3, 6 (5 Fri & Sat)-11; 12-10.30 Sun
☎ (01621) 828354
Greene King IPA; guest beers Ⓖ
Traditional, friendly Gray's house with all beers on gravity dispense. The main bar has a relaxed, cottagey style where conversation is the entertainment, while the second bar is more basic and houses a TV. An extensive menu is on offer, and a third room is used by diners. The pub also owns the adjoining café.
♨Q❀◖◗⊟♣P

Rowhedge

Albion

High Street, CO5 7ES (approx. 3 miles S of Colchester)
☉ 12-3 (not Mon), 5-11; 12-11 Thu-Sat; 12-10.30 Sun
☎ (01206) 728972
Adnams Bitter; Ⓗ **guest beers** Ⓗ/Ⓖ
Village free house; look for the noose – the Customs and Excise man was hanged here. Benefiting from river views and decorated with seafaring artefacts, the interior is on a split level. It always stocks two guest beers and offers real, home-made food on a weekly changing menu. Traditional pub games are played, as well as boules. ◖◗♣

Roxwell

Chequers Inn

The Street, CM1 4PD (next to church)
☉ 5-11; 12-2.30, 6-11 Sat; 12-3.30, 7-10.30 Sun
☎ (01245) 248240
Greene King IPA, Abbot; Mighty Oak seasonal beers Ⓗ
Friendly, 17th-century village inn, retaining

several original beams in the single bar. The background music is subdued, the TV frequently extinguished, and the pool table is in a separate room; the most noticeable sound is the hum of conversation. The landlord will open weekday lunchtimes by prior arrangement for parties.
⌂❀▲♣P⊁⊡

Saffron Walden

Old English Gentleman

11 Gold Street, CB10 1EJ (50 yds E of B184/B1052 jct)
✪ 11-11; 12-10.30 Sun
☎ (01799) 523595
Adnams Bitter; Greene King IPA; guest beers Ⓗ
This 18th-century, town-centre pub, has log fires and a welcoming atmosphere. It serves a selection of guest beers and an extensive tapas-style lunchtime menu that changes regularly. Filled baguettes and sandwiches are also available in the bar or the no-smoking dining area where a variety of works of art are on display. Saffron Walden is busy on Tuesday and Saturday – market days. The pub has a pleasant patio at the rear. ⌂❀◑

Temeraire ✔

55 High Steet, CB10 1AA (on B184)
✪ 10-11; 12-10.30 Sun
☎ (01799) 516975
De Koninck Ambrée; Greene King IPA, Abbot; Marston's Burton Bitter, Pedigree; guest beers Ⓗ
Spacious Wetherspoon's house in a former workingmen's club on the main thoroughfare of this attractive market town. Named after a battleship, featured in a famous painting by Turner, its tenuous local connection is explained in displays around the pub. Beer festivals are staged three times a year. The well-trained staff assiduously apply a 'try before you buy' policy. A pleasant, secluded outside drinking area at the rear is a bonus. It draws a young crowd evenings and weekends. Q❀◑◐♿P⊁

South Benfleet

Hoy & Helmet ✔

24-32 High Street, SS7 1NA (on B1014)
✪ 11-11; 12-10.30 Sun
☎ (01268) 792307
Adnams Broadside; Courage Directors; Greene King IPA, Old Speckled Hen; guest beers Ⓗ
Situated in a conservation area, close to Benfleet Station, this Grade II listed pub has many rooms on different levels, including a pool room and a designated no-smoking area. Televised sport and fruit machines contrast with an open fireplace and low beams. It benefits from a large garden and car park and attracts both commuters and locals. It stocks various guest beers. An extensive menu is served until 9.30pm; a seafood stall sells its wares nearby at times. ⌂❀◑◐⇌(Benfleet)♣P⊁

South Woodham Ferrers

Railway

50 Hullbridge Road, CM3 5NG (near B1012)
✪ 11-11; 12-10.30 Sun
☎ (01245) 320262
Crouch Vale Brewers Gold Ⓗ
Substantial, brick-built 1850s hotel next to the station, it was probably the first building in South Woodham Ferrers. Quiet during the day, this pub becomes lively in the early evening and at weekends. Live music is performed on Friday, karaoke Saturday. There is an emphasis on darts in the open-plan bar area. The Railway acts as the brewery tap for the ever-reliable Crouch Vale flagship beer.
❀♿⇌♣P

Southend-on-Sea

Cork & Cheese

10 Talza Way, Victoria Plaza, SS2 5BG (near A13/A127)
✪ 11-11; closed Sun
☎ (01702) 616914 website: www.corkandcheese.co.uk
Draught Bass; Nethergate IPA; guest beers Ⓗ
Large, friendly pub located on the lowest level of the Victoria Plaza shopping centre within easy reach of two local railway stations. The walls and ceiling are adorned with breweriana collected by the current owner. Local CAMRA Pub of the Year on five occasions, it offers a changing range of guest beers – over 2,700 to date; the cider is Cheddar Valley. Good quality, home-cooked lunches are served weekdays in the upstairs restaurant.
❀◑⇌(Victoria/Central)●

Southminster

Station Arms

39 Station Road, CM0 7EW (near B1020/B1021 jct)
✪ 12-2.30, 6 (5.30 Thu-Fri)-11; 12-11 Sat; 12-4, 7-10.30 Sun
☎ (01621) 772225 website: www.thestationarms.co.uk
Adnams Bitter; Crouch Vale Brewers Gold; Mighty Oak Oscar Wilde; guest beers Ⓗ
Unpretentious, weatherboarded pub, recognised for the quality of its changing beer range. The three beers listed are more often on tap than not, while one or two guest ales frequently showcase local breweries. The single bar is decorated with memorabilia to reflect its railway connections. Beer festivals are held in January, late May and August bank holidays in the pub's restored barn. It stages a monthly blues evening. The cider is Westons. The enclosed patio garden is a plus.
⌂Q❀⇌♣●

Stansted Mountfitchet

Rose & Crown

31 Bentfield Green, CM24 8HX
(½ mile W of B1383, old A11) OS507255
✪ 11.30-3.30, 6-11; 12-3.30, 7-10.30 Sun
☎ (01279) 812107
Adnams Bitter; Fuller's London Pride Ⓗ
Typical Victorian pub near a duckpond on the edge of a small hamlet, now part of Stansted Mountfichet village. This free house has been modernised to provide one large bar, but maintains the caring atmosphere of a village local. Attractive floral displays brighten the front of the pub. The landlady, who seems to know every customer's name, makes everyone welcome and the pub is well used by locals. Food is simple but reliably excellent and good value (no eve meals Sun).
❀◑◐♣P

Stapleford Tawney

Moletrap

Tawney Common, CM16 7PU (3 miles E of Epping, 1½ miles from Toot Hill. Left turn on Epping road after Toot Hill to Tawney Common) OS501014

11-2.30 (3 summer), 6.30 (6 summer)-11; 12-4, 7-10.30 Sun

☎ (01992) 522394

Fuller's London Pride; guest beers Ⓗ

Great country pub, enjoying good views and a fine reputation for real ale and food. Three guest beers mostly come from small micro-breweries. A lovely selection of home-made dishes represents good value; no food is served Sunday evening. Warm and inviting in winter, in summer everyone sits outside while goats, geese and chickens wander around.

Q P

Stock

Hoop

21 High Street, CM4 9BD (by B1007)

11-11; 12-10.30 Sun

☎ (01277) 841137 website: www.thehoop.co.uk

Adnams Bitter; Ⓗ **guest beers** Ⓗ/Ⓖ

Starting life as weavers' cottages circa 1460 and converted into an ale house 450 years ago, this small pub is a long-standing Guide entry and frequent local CAMRA Pub of the Year winner. Four or five guest beers change regularly and a real cider or perry is always stocked. Home-cooked food is served all day. The large garden hosts the famous annual beer festival in late May; regular events include Monday night food specials. The Hoop is served by the No. 100 Lakeside-Chelmsford bus. Q ♣

Stow Maries

Prince of Wales

Woodham Road, CM3 6SA (near B1012) OS830993

11-11; 12-10.30 Sun

☎ (01621) 828971 website: www.powstowmaries.co.uk

Beer range varies Ⓗ

Attractive, 17th-century, weatherboarded pub in a tiny village. Three separate but open-plan drinking areas are warmed by open fires in winter; in summer meals may be served in the converted barn outbuildings. The beer range is eclectic and includes several Belgian ales; Westons Old Rosie cider is sold. Themed menu evenings add variety to the good value food range. The annual firework display is awesome. Occasional live music is performed on Sunday afternoon. Q P

Tendring

Cherry Tree Inn

Crow Lane, CO16 9AP (on B1035)

11-3, 6-11; closed Mon; 12-7 (variable) Sun

☎ (01255) 830340

Adnams Bitter; Greene King IPA; guest beers Ⓗ

Rural roadside free house located at a quiet junction, served by the local village-link bus service. Inside you will find a beamed and timber-clad bar, with a brick fireplace in the dining area. An extensive menu complements the four real ales on tap. In fine weather there is roadside and garden seating areas outside. P

Theydon Bois

Sixteen String Jack

Coppice Row, CM16 7DS (on B172)

12-3, 5-11; 12-11 Sat; 12-10.30 Sun

☎ (01992) 813182

McMullen AK, Country Ⓗ

This elegant, two-bar Georgian pub takes its name from Jack Mann, a highwayman who managed to be acquitted six times for highway robbery but was found guilty and hanged after his seventh trial. The pub is on the western edge of the village as it peters out into Epping Forest, and is just three-quarters of a mile from Theydon Bois underground station. The lounge is a no-smoking area between midday and 4pm.

P

Tollesbury

King's Head

1 High Street, CM9 8RG (on B1023, 5 mile SE of Tiptree)

12-11; 12-10.30 Sun

☎ (01621) 869203

Greene King IPA; Ridleys IPA; guest beers Ⓗ

Tucked away in rural Essex on the Blackwater Estuary, the King's Head forms the heart of village life, with regular visits by motor-cyclists, and hosting monthly folk and 'open mike' nights. A large screen at the end of a long bar shows Sky Sports, but the way the three bars are separated prevents this intruding on the rest of the pub. A pool table and dartboard are located in the public bar, but it is the strong beer range (usually five beers) that makes it special. ♣P

Waltham Abbey

White Lion

11 Sun Street, EN9 1ER (near B194)

11-11; 12-10.30 Sun

☎ (01922) 718673

McMullen AK Ⓗ

Small, one-bar pub in the pedestrianised shopping area of the town centre, a short walk from the abbey and the Abbey Gardens. The pub fields a number of darts teams (both male and female) in the local leagues. This is a rare McMullen pub that does not use cask breathers. Live music is performed some Saturday evenings. ♣

Walton-on-the-Naze

Queen's Head

76 High Street, CO14 8AD (near B1034)

11-11; 12-10.30 Sun

☎ (01255) 676700

Ridleys IPA, Old Bob; Tolly Original Ⓗ

Recent refurbishment has created a friendly, comfortable environment in this family-run pub. Its front backs on to the main street and its back is adjacent to the market and the town car park. The interior consists of a pool room, a bar area and a small, discrete restaurant area. Weather watchers will note the barometers and all should see the memorial to Dr Barnardo, dated 1905. The pub is a great supporter of local charities.

♣

Walton Tavern

30-31 The Parade, CO14 8AP (near B1034)

⌚ 11-11; 12-10.30 Sun

☎ (01255) 676000

Adnams Bitter, Broadside; Nethergate IPA, Old Growler Ⓗ

Once a small, intimate drinking house overlooking the sea, now it is a busy community pub that has been rebuilt to satisfy the needs of the locals throughout the year and holidaymakers in summer. The large main bar, on any night, plays host to various darts and pool teams. This seaside pub still caters for those who sit and sup while watching the ships go by on the North Sea. Parking can be difficult in summer. ❀◐◑≠♣

Weeley

White Hart ✓

Clacton Road, CO16 9ED (on B1441)

⌚ 12-2.30, 4.30-11 (10 Mon); 12-11 Fri; 11-11 Sat; 12-10.30 Sun

☎ (01255) 830384

Beer range varies Ⓗ

The White Hart has had a topsy-turvy year. The necessary space for a growing family finally meant that an extension had to be built. Fortunately the bar was not a hard hat area and the landlord continued to supply a range of micro-brewed beers to satisfy the most ardent of real ale lovers. At last he has four handpumps in action. Regular bus services pass the pub and Weeley Station is walkable distance.

❀Å♣P⊽

Wendens Ambo

Bell

Royston Road, CB11 4JY (on B1039)

⌚ 11.30-2.30, 6-11; 11.30-11 Sat; 12-10.30 Sun

☎ (01799) 540383

Adnams Bitter; guest beers Ⓗ

Classic, country pub at the centre of a picturesque village near Saffron Walden. A past winner of local CAMRA's Pub of the Year award, it boasts an enormous garden, with crazy golf to occupy the children. Audley End Station on the Liverpool Street to Cambridge line is five minutes' walk. A mild ale usually features among the guest beers, rare in the area.

♨Q❀◐◑≠(Audley End)P

Westcliff-on-Sea

Cricketers

225 London Road, SS0 7JG (on A13 at Milton Rd jct)

⌚ 11-11; 12-10.30 Sun

☎ (01702) 343168

Fuller's London Pride; Greene King IPA, Abbot; guest beers Ⓗ

Occupying a corner site on the main London road, a comfortably furnished, spacious interior makes this pub look bigger than it appears outside. There are usually two guest beers on tap plus a real cider – Westons at time of survey. The pub has a no-smoking area and caters for diners. In adjoining premises – Club Riga – there is an emphasis on music with live rock and blues most Friday and Saturday evenings. Parking is limited. Q◐◑♿≠P⅄

White Roding

Black Horse

Chelmsford Road, CM6 1RF

(on A1060, opp. Abbess Roding jct)

⌚ 11.30-3 (not Mon), 5.30 (6 Sat)-11; 12-3, 7-10.30 Sun

☎ (01279) 876322

Ridleys IPA, Ⓗ **Old Bob** Ⓖ

Run by an experienced couple, this local caters well for the various preferences of its community. The 400-year-old public bar fields two pool teams and offers other pub games. The more modern saloon, partly a no-smoking area, is mainly used for dining, including traditional Sunday lunches and fish nights (Thu-Sat); no food is served Sunday evening. Legend has it that George, the ghost, can be heard playing a piano on occasion. Q❀◐◑⊟♣P⅄

Widdington

Fleur de Lys

High Street, CB11 3SG (off B1383)

⌚ 12-2.30, 6-11; 11-11 Sat; 12-10.30 Sun

☎ (01799) 543280

Adnams Bitter; Greene King IPA; guest beers Ⓗ

This beamed pub, 450 years old, has a large inglenook where a fire is lit in winter. A small menu is supplemented each Friday and at the weekend fresh fish served in large portions in the restaurant area. There is a games room with darts, pool and table football.

♨Q❀◐◑Å♣P⅄

Wivenhoe

Horse & Groom ✓

55 The Cross, CO7 9QL

(on Colchester-Wivenhoe road, B1028)

⌚ 10.30-3, 5.30 (6 Sat)-11; 12-4.30, 7-10.30 Sun

☎ (01206) 824928

Adnams Bitter, Broadside, seasonal beers; guest beer Ⓗ

Friendly local at the edge of a pleasant fishing village. The pub, dating from the 1700s, comprises a cosy saloon bar and a large public bar. Adnams beers are always served in top form, accompanied by a guest beer. Good value, home-cooked food is served lunchtimes, except Sunday. It is easy to get to by bus from Colchester, but the train station is quite a distance. ❀◐⊟♣P

Writtle

Wheatsheaf

70 The Green, CM1 3DU (off A1060)

⌚ 11-2.30, 5-11; 11-11 Fri & Sat; 12-10.30 Sun

☎ (01245) 420695

website: www.wheatsheafph-writtle.co.uk

Greene King IPA, Abbot; Mighty Oak Oscar Wilde, Maldon Gold, Burntwood Ⓗ

Small, traditional pub near the village green, converted from a pair of pre-Victorian cottages. There is no piped music, and the TV is used only for occasional sporting events. A varied but friendly clientele gathers here, creating a vibrant and convivial atmosphere. The Gray and Sons sign in the public bar was rescued from the brewery when it closed in 1974. A roadside patio allows for some outdoor drinking.

Q❀⊟♣P

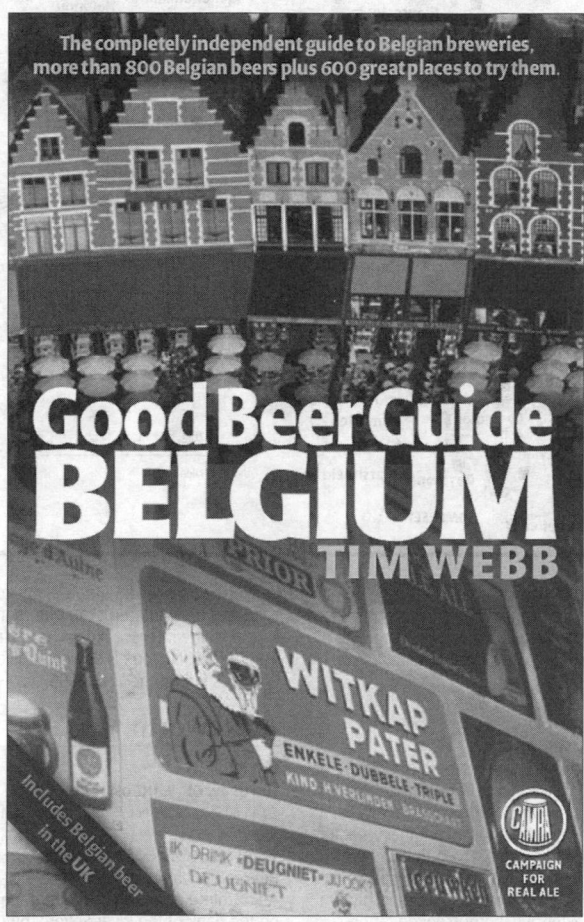

GLOUCESTERSHIRE & BRISTOL

Alderton

Gardeners Arms ✔

Beckford Road, GL20 8NL (follow brown signs from B4077)

⏲ 12-2.30, 6-11; 12-2.30, 6.30-10.30 Sun

☎ (01242) 620257

Beer range varies Ⓗ

Listed, 16th-century, oak beamed free house at the heart of a quiet village. Four handpumps serve a changing range of beers from a weekly menu. The lounge features an original well, local photographs and a piano. The pub hosts Whitsun and Christmas mini-beer festivals (focusing on local brewers), charity events and monthly fun quizzes. An extensive, home-cooked range includes bar meals, fresh fish specials, theme nights and takeaways. Live music is performed on Friday evening. ⛫❀◐◑♿♣P⊁

Ampney St Peter

Red Lion ☆

GL7 5SL (on A417)

⏲ 12-2 (not Mon-Fri), 6-10; 12-2, 7-10.30 Sun

☎ (01285) 851596

Hook Norton Best Bitter; Taylor Golden Best, Landlord Ⓗ

Still bearing a (now defunct) Stroud Brewery sign, this superb, 400-year old pub is caught in a time warp. The two tiny flagstoned rooms with open fires are superbly preserved and little appears to have changed since the veteran landlord was a child. Without a bar counter, service is from the corner of one room. One beer is available winter weekdays, an extra beer at other times. No food is served at all at local CAMRA's Pub of the Year 2005. ⛫Q❀⊞P

Ashleworth

Boat Inn

The Quay, GL19 4HZ OS819251

⏲ 11.30-2.30 (3 Sat; not Wed), 7-11; closed Mon; 12-3, 7-10.30 Sun

☎ (01452) 700272 website: www.boat-inn.co.uk

Beer range varies Ⓖ

An absolute gem – an unspoilt, tranquil haven on the bank of the River Severn, owned by the same family for 400 years. It serves beer direct from the cask, the range coming from smaller local breweries. Several rooms are furnished with antiques. The courtyard has some tables under cover. A rare no-smoking pub, it is a frequent local CAMRA award-winner. Rolls and ploughman's are available at lunchtime. ⛫Q❀◐●P⊁

Avening

Bell

29 High Street, GL8 8NP (on B4014)

⏲ 12-3, 5.30-11; 12-5.30 (3 Jan-Feb), 7-10.30 Sun

☎ (01453) 836422

Wickwar BOB; Young's Bitter; guest beer Ⓗ

Pleasantly refurbished, old stone inn located at

the centre of the village. Efficiently run and comfortable, the exposed stone walls, adorned with horse brasses and tankards, lend a traditional, rustic appearance to the two rooms, one a pleasantly open bar with a wood-burning stove, the other a candlelit dining area. The competitively priced menu is recommended.
⩩ᑕ◗ ♣

Awre

Red Hart

GL14 1EW (off A48 S of Newnham on Severn) OS709080
⏲ 12-3.30, 6 (6.30 winter)-11 (closed winter Mon); 12-3.30, 6.30-10.30 (closed winter eve) Sun
☎ (01594) 510220
Fuller's London Pride; guest beers Ⓗ
This cosy, atmospheric pub is a little off the beaten track, but well worth finding. It boasts a well in the middle bar. Sample the good food from an interesting, varied menu. Up to four guest beers come from the Wye Valley Brewery. Three river walks of different lengths start from the pub, which stands next to a lovely old church in the quaint hamlet of Awre. Two en-suite guest bedrooms should be available by the time of publication. ❀⛟ᑕ◗ P

Blaisdon

Red Hart Inn

GL17 0AH (signed from A4136, E of Longhope) OS703169
⏲ 11.30-3, 6-11; 12-3.30, 7-10.30 Sun
☎ (01452) 830477
Hook Norton Best Bitter; Tetley Bitter; guest beers Ⓗ
Busy village pub on the outskirts of the Forest of Dean. The inviting bar has flagstoned floors and window seating with a real log fire. Great food ranges from sandwiches to main meals. A popular venue for a special occasion, the pub is full of character and charm. The large garden and patio have a barbecue and an extensive wooden play area for children. Two guest beers are usually on tap. ⩩ᘔᑕ◗ ♣P

Bledington

King's Head

The Green, OX7 6XQ
⏲ 11-3, 6-11; 12-3, 6.30-10.30 Sun
☎ (01608) 658365 website: www.kingsheadinn.net
Hook Norton Best Bitter; guest beers Ⓗ
This delightful, 16th-century inn on the village green with its brook and ducks, boasts Prince Rupert of the Rhine as one of its first guests, prior to the Battle of Stow in 1646. The pub is adorned with old beams, an inglenook with kettle and military brasses, flagstone floors and high-backed settles and pews. Archers and North Cotswold breweries provide regular guest beers. Both accommodation and food are top quality.
⩩Qᘔ❀⛟ᑕ◗ 🀫⇚(Kingham) ♣P

Bridgeyate

White Harte

111 London Road, BS30 5NA (on A420, between Warmley and Wick)
⏲ 11-2.30, 5 (6 Sat)-11; 12-3, 7-10.30 Sun
☎ (0117) 967 3830
Draught Bass; Butcombe Bitter; Courage Best Bitter; Marston's Pedigree Ⓗ
Consistently good roadside inn, extended in 1987, sometimes known as the Inn on the Green. This is a friendly meeting place where conversation is the rule. The decor incorporates a variety of woods, including an unusual bar with old spice drawers. Some stone walls mix in well, as do the comfy red sofas. Lunches are served Monday-Saturday in an area that becomes no-smoking. Children are allowed until 9pm. It stages a quiz on Monday. Q❀ᑕP

Bristol

Adam & Eve

7 Hope Chapel Hill, Hotwells, BS8 4ND
⏲ 12-11; 12-10.30 Sun
☎ (0117) 929 1508 website: http://home.btconnect.com/Adam---Eve/adameve.htm
Sharp's Doom Bar, Eden Ale; guest beers Ⓗ
This pub, with its wood floors and panelling on some walls, its nooks and crannies and candlelit tables, attracts a mixed clientele. It stocks up to four changing guest beers. It offers a selection of board games and, more unusually, a book exchange. The interesting menu caters for carnivores, fish-lovers and vegetarians alike, even with the Sunday roasts. The food is made on the premises using fresh organic ingredients where possible. Meals are served 12-9 (12-5 Sun). ᑕ◗

Bag o' Nails

141 St Georges Road, Hotwells, BS1 5UW
⏲ 12-2, 5.30-11; 12-11 Fri & Sat; 12-10.30 Sun
☎ (0117) 940 6776 website: www.bagonails.org.uk
Beer range varies Ⓗ
Tiny gaslit pub with wood panelling and bare floorboards, with unusual viewing portholes to the cellar. It is close to College Green and the cathedral. A changing range of eight beers from far and wide is the main attraction, complemented by a good choice of bottled beers. Now fully back to its best after several changes of licensee, it hosts 'Port & Stilton' nights fortnightly and occasional beer festivals. Sandwiches are served at lunchtime. Q

Bell ✔

Hillgrove Street, Stokes Croft, BS2 8JT (off Jamaica St)
⏲ 12-2 (not Sat); 5 (4.30 Sat)-11 (midnight Thu-Sat); 12-11 Sun
☎ (0117) 909 6612
Bath Gem; Butcombe Bitter, Blonde, Gold Ⓗ
Classic, central Bristol two-roomed pub, 15 minutes' walk from the Broadmead shopping

INDEPENDENT BREWERIES

Bath Ales Bristol
Bristol Beer Factory Bristol
Cotswold Spring Dodington Ash
Donnington Stow-on-the-Wold
Freeminer Cinderford
Goff's Winchcombe
Home County Wickwar (brewing suspended)
Stanway Stanway
Uley Uley
Whittington's Newent
Wickwar Wickwar
Zerodegrees Bristol

centre. The pub was purchased and carefully refurbished by Butcombe Brewery in 1995. Both rooms have wood flooring and panels; to the rear is an attractive patio drinking area. Background music often features and a DJ appears most evenings from 9pm. The meals are good value. ❀◐◑

Black Swan

92 Stoke Lane, Westbury on Trym, BS9 3SP
⌚ 12-3, 5-11; 12-11 Sat; 12-10.30 Sun
☎ (0117) 962 5111
Draught Bass; Brakspear Bitter; Courage Best Bitter; Wychwood Hobgoblin; 🄷 guest beer 🄶
A new entry in this Guide, the pub has three drinking areas at the front, as well as a large back bar, where families are welcome. The garden has a play area, an ornamental pond, and parking spaces nearby. Sunday lunches, which must be booked, are served in two sittings – 12.30 and 3pm. ⌂Q❀◐⊞P⊬

Bridge Inn

16 Passage Street, BS2 0JF
(over river bridge from fire station)
⌚ 11.30 (12 Sat)-11; 7-10.30 Sun
☎ (0117) 949 9967
Bath SPA, Gem; guest beers 🄷
Small and friendly, this one room pub enjoys good business on weekday lunchtimes, as it is surrounded by offices; the jacket potatoes and chilli dishes go down well then. The walls are adorned with film stills and posters. Continuous but not deafening background pop music is played. The pub has close ties with Bath Ales, who often supply the guest beer. GWR radio station stands opposite. ◐⇌ (Temple Meads)

Cornubia

142 Temple Street, BS1 6EW
(opp. fire station by former Courage Brewery)
⌚ 12 (6.30 Sat)-11; closed Sun
☎ (0117) 925 4415
Beer range varies 🄷
The Cornubia has survived a few changes of leaseholder and the closure of Smiles Brewery and remains as popular as ever, now with up to seven handpumps plus a changing cider. Twice local CAMRA Pub of the Year, it was once the Courage tasting rooms. Cornubia is the Latin name for Cornwall. Built in 1773, the front is Grade II listed. The pub is small and gets crowded, especially early evenings. A limited, but changing menu is served weekdays. ❀◐⇌ (Temple Meads) ●P

Coronation

18 Dean Lane, Southville, BS3 1DD (off Coronation Rd)
⌚ 3 (12 Sat)-11; 12-10.30 Sun
☎ (0117) 940 9044
Hop Back GFB, Best Bitter, Crop Circle, Summer Lightning; guest beer 🄷
A hotel until the 1930s, this local, comprising a bar and elevated snug, is now owned by Hop Back Brewery, stocking a good range of its beers on tap, plus four Hop Back bottle-conditioned ales. Minipins and polypins are available to take away, a cheeseboard is offered on Sunday and pizzas are available every day after 6pm. A quiz is held on Monday evening. It gets busy on Friday and Saturday evenings. ⇌(Temple Mead/Bedminster) ♣●

Cotham Porter Stores

15 Cotham Road South, Cotham, BS6 5TZ
⌚ 12-11; 12-10.30 Sun
website: www.cothamporterstores.co.uk
Sharps Doom Bar; Shepherd Neame Spitfire 🄷
Sometimes smoky, but oozing character, this famous cider house, located atop a steep hill, is increasingly popular for real ale. A narrow main room is complemented by a snug at the far end. Note the rustic cider frieze painted around 30 years ago; see, too the framed plan of the pub from 1935. Games are popular, teams include a cricket eleven. Sport is shown on the TV, and the juke box is often in use. Ciders are Thatchers Dry and Cheddar Valley. ♣●

Hare on the Hill

41 Thomas Street, North Kingsdown, BS2 8LX
⌚ 12-2.30, 5-11; 12-11 Fri ; 11-11 Sat; 12-10.30 Sun
☎ (0117) 908 1982
Bath SPA, Gem, Barnstormer, seasonal beers; guest beers 🄷
The pub is situated in Kingsdown, Bristol's foremost Georgian suburb, overlooking Stokes Croft and the city. It stocks a good range of British and continental bottled beers. The L-shaped bar houses a dartboard and plasma TV (for Sky sports). It displays paintings and photographs by local artists for sale. It normally keeps a guest ale from an independent brewery, occasionally replaced by a seasonal brew. Good food is served. ◐◑♣

Highbury Vaults

164 St Michael's Hill, Kingsdown, BS2 8DE
⌚ 12-11; 12-10.30 Sun
☎ (0117) 973 3203
Brains SA; Young's Bitter, Special, seasonal beers; guest beers 🄷
This busy Young's pub is popular with both locals and students. There is a small front bar and a larger, wood-panelled back room, split into smaller areas. Heating and covering allows the rear walled garden to be used all year round. Good value, home-cooked food is served at lunchtime and weekday evenings. Guest beers have replaced the long-standing Smiles' offerings. Bar billiards can be played here. Q❀◐◑♣

Hillgrove Porter Stores

53 Hillgrove Street North, Kingsdown, BS2 8LT
(off Dove St)
⌚ 5 (7 Sat)-11; 7-10.30 Sun
☎ (0117) 944 4780
Butcombe Bitter; Wadworth 6X; guest beers 🄷
Friendly, Victorian, brick-built community street-corner pub that has recently undergone a refurbishment to create three distinct drinking areas. Old keg brewery memorabilia adorn the bar, which is candlelit at night to create a cosy, relaxed atmosphere. Note that there is no lunchtime opening. The rock juke box has an excellent selection. A no-smoking area is available until 9pm. ❀⊬

Hope & Anchor

38 Jacobs Well Road, Hotwells, BS8 1DR
⌚ 12-11; 12-10.30 Sun
☎ (0117) 929 2987
Beer range varies 🄷

Popular free house where six changing beers often include Goff's, Moles, Bath Ales and other West Country brews. An extensive food menu is served all day until 10pm. It is a good refreshment stop after scaling nearby Brandon Hill and tower, affording panoramic views of Bristol. The raised garden at the back is steep and not accessible to all. The pub was the home of the short-lived Lucifer Brewery. ❀◑◗

Horts

49 Broad Street, BS1 2EP

11-11; 12-10.30 Sun

☎ (0117) 925 2520

Young's Bitter, Special, seasonal beers Ⓗ

Large, town-centre pub comprising a single bar and several distinct drinking areas. A raised area at the rear has a projection screen TV used for major sporting events, and doubles as the restaurant. Entertainment includes live jazz on Sunday afternoon and regular quizzes. Two ciders are stocked – Thatchers Dry and Cheddar Valley. No meals are served Sunday evening. The pub has a wheelchair WC. ❀◑◗♿●

Inn on the Green

2 Filton Road, Horfield, BS7 0PA

(on A38, opp. sports centre, near Memorial Stadium)

11-3, 6-11; 11-11 Sat; 12-10.30 Sun

☎ (0117) 952 1391

Draught Bass; Fuller's London Pride; Sharp's Doom Bar; guest beers Ⓗ

Open-plan pub, offering seven guest beers, where three distinct sections have successfully been created, to cater for the community it serves. At the centre is the bar, with a mix of seating and tables; to the left is a quiet, comfy lounge. To the right is the old skittle alley, with seating, tables, pool, fruit machines, juke box and big TV screens. Independent chefs supply a wide variety of meals, oriented towards the beer drinker. Children are welcome at lunchtime. Q❀◑◗P

Kings Head ☆

60 Victoria Street, BS1 6DE

11 (7.30 Sat)-11; 12-3, 7-10.30 Sun

☎ (0117) 927 7860

Draught Bass; Courage Best Bitter; Sharp's Cornish Coaster, Doom Bar Ⓗ

Possibly on a medieval site, the pub dates back to the 1600s but boasts an outstanding late Victorian interior. The single narrow bar leads to a cosy 'tramcar' snug. Photographs and drawings of old Bristol adorn the walls. Frequented by office workers at lunchtime and locals in the evening, four pavement tables are available in summer. Good food is served weekdays. This little gem is listed in CAMRA's National Inventory.

❀◑⇌ (Temple Meads)

Merchants Arms

5 Merchants Road, Hotwells, BS8 4PZ

12-2.30, 5-11; 12-11 Fri & Sat; 12-10.30 Sun

☎ (0117) 904 0037

Bath SPA, Gem, Barnstormer; guest beers Ⓗ

Small but perfectly restored example of a Victorian street-corner local, saved from almost certain closure in 2000 by Bath Ales. The pub retains much of its 19th-century character. There is a single, wood-panelled bar with glazed screens, and two cosy drinking areas. The full range of Bath Ales' regular beers is always available, plus a guest from another micro-brewery. Impromptu folk music sessions take place on Tuesday evening in the back bar.

Orchard Inn

12 Hanover Place, BS1 6XT (off Cumberland Rd)

12-3, 5-11; 12-4, 7-10.30 Sun

☎ (0117) 926 2678

Bath Gem; Butcombe Gold; Courage Best Bitter Ⓗ

Street-corner free house, pleasantly located near the SS Great Britain, frequented by locals (many of whom are seafarers) and passing trade. It is known for the quality of its ciders, Thatchers Dry and Cheddar Valley – see the two-handled cider mugs behind the bar. Excellent lunches are served weekdays. Note the Georges Brewery pictures. Quiz night is Tuesday. Aardman Animations, creator of Wallace and Gromit, is based nearby. ❀◑♣●

Port of Call

3 York Street, Clifton, BS8 2YF

(near top of Blackboy Hill)

12-2.30, 5.30-11; 12-11 Sat; 12-5 Sun

☎ (0117) 973 3600

Draught Bass; Butcombe Blonde; Caledonian Deuchars IPA; Hop Back Summer Lightning; Sharp's Cornish Coaster; guest beers Ⓗ

This delightful L-shaped bar is a real beer drinker's haven. Visitors are rewarded with a choice of six regular and six changing guest beers. The quality of the beer is equalled by the traditional home-made fare, especially the Sunday lunches. This smart, friendly pub, joint local CAMRA Pub of the Year 2005, dates from around 1776 and bears a maritime mood. The fine patio garden is a bonus in summer. No children are admitted.

Q❀◑◗⇌(Clifton Down)♣⚟

Portwall Tavern

Portwall Lane, Redcliffe, BS1 6NB

11.30 (12 Sat)-11; closed Sun

☎ (0117) 922 0442

Adnams Broadside; Draught Bass; Courage Best Bitter; guest beer Ⓗ

This pub, popular with shoppers, office workers and drinkers alike, is located opposite the imposing St Mary Redcliffe Church. Real ale is a feature here, with over 200 guest beers from around the country served in the last 12 months. The pub is tidy and smartly furnished. Soft background music adds to the atmosphere, and an unobtrusive TV usually shows the news or major sporting events with subtitles. No food is served Saturday. A public car park is adjacent.

◑⇌(Temple Meads)♣

Red Lion ✔

26 Worrall Road, Clifton, BS8 2UE (off Blackboy Hill)

12-11; 12-10.30 Sun

☎ (0117) 903 0989

Draught Bass; Bath SPA; Courage Best Bitter Ⓗ

Built in 1846, this traditional, two-bar pub has been a part of the local community since early Victorian times. With its lively, hop-adorned bar and impressive flagstoned floor, it is popular for watching major sporting events on TV. In addition, a quiz is held every other Thursday

evening. For a more peaceful drink, try the comfortable, well-presented, wood-panelled lounge bar. Thatcher's cider is sold.
Q◑⊟⇌(Clifton Down) ♣●

Shakespeare

1 Henry Street, Totterdown, BS3 4UD
⏲ 4.30 (12 Sat)-11; 12-10.30 Sun
☎ (0117) 907 8818 website: www.theshakey.co.uk
Greene King Old Speckled Hen; guest beers Ⓗ
This well-established, street-corner pub features up to four guest beers, mainly from local and regional breweries. Over 100 years old, it houses a pool table at the far end of the U-shaped bar, with plenty of seating throughout the rest of the pub. The outside drinking area at the rear is heated and a small front patio provides extra seating. Food is limited to rolls and snacks during the week, but a full Sunday lunch is served (booking advised).
❀♣⇌(Temple Meads)

Victoria ✔

20 Chock Lane, Westbury on Trym, BS9 3EX
(150 yds off Eastfield Rd)
⏲ 12-2.30, 5.30-11; 12-3, 7-10.30 Sun
☎ (0117) 950 0441
Draught Bass; Butcombe Bitter; Wadworth IPA, 6X; guest beers Ⓗ
Hidden away behind the parish church, the Victoria is a welcoming local. Its elevated garden catches the evening sun. The bar has a no-smoking area. The pub is known for its excellent food. See the pictures of Westbury when it was a village and quite separate from Bristol. It hosts regular social and food events, with occasional live music.
Q❀◑◗♣⅍

Wellington

Gloucester Road, Horfield, BS7 8UR
(on A34 by Horfield Common, near Memorial Stadium)
⏲ 12-2.30, 5-11; 12-11 Fri & Sat; 12-10.30 Sun
☎ (0117) 951 3022
Bath SPA, Gem, Barnstormer, seasonal beers; guest beers Ⓗ
Traditional pub that attracts a wide range of customers of all ages. Local CAMRA's Pub of the Year 2004 (and joint 2005 winner) is divided into several drinking areas, with a large no-smoking area (smoking is not permitted at the bar). The garden is the venue for a beer festival in May. It stocks a fine range of bottled beer, organic cider and continental beers on draught. Free live music is performed: jazz on Monday, blues Sunday. Try the superb food at this popular haunt of rugby and football supporters. The accommodation is recommended.
❀⊭◑◗P⅍

White Horse

24 High Street, Westbury on Trym, BS9 3DZ
⏲ 11-11; 12-10.30 Sun
☎ (0117) 950 7622
Draught Bass; Sharp's Cornish Coaster; Ⓖ **guest beers** Ⓗ
The pub is known locally as the Hole in the Wall, as one bar is served via a window of the original building into the Georgian extension. The main bar has a flagstone floor. The beers, served direct from the barrel, are kept cool in a 14th-century vault. The seating mixes modern styles with ancient carved wooden settles. Children are allowed in the rooms without a bar until 7pm. It can be smoky and busy at weekends. Q❀◑♣●

Zerodegrees

53 Colston Street, BS1 5BA (opp. Bristol Royal Infirmary)
⏲ 12-midnight; 12-11.30 Sun
☎ (0117) 925 2706 website: www.zerodegrees.co.uk
Zerodegrees Wheat Ale, Pale Ale, Pilsner, Black Lager, seasonal beers Ⓟ
And now for something completely different! Opened in 2004, the company built its second pub around an old tramshed at the top of the famous Christmas Steps. The high-tech brewery is on full view. A 200-seat restaurant is spread over two floors with an open kitchen on the lower one. The drinking area around the bar has limited seating, except in summer when the balconies and patio are opened. TVs are set on silent sports channels. Music can be loud; live jazz is performed (Wed and Sun). All beers are served at cool temperatures. ❀◑◗⊓

Broad Campden

Bakers Arms

GL55 6UR (signed from B4081)
⏲ 11.30-2.30, 4.45-11; 11.30-11 Fri, Sat & summer; 12-10.30 Sun
☎ (01386) 840515
Donnington BB; Stanway Stanney Bitter; Taylor Landlord; Wells Bombardier; guest beer Ⓗ
Dating from 1724, this fine old country pub was voted local CAMRA Pub of the Year in 2003 and county winner in 2005. A former bakery and grainstore, it is characterised by Cotswold stone walls, exposed beams, an inglenook and an oak bar counter where beers from local breweries can be tried. Reasonably-priced, home-cooked food can be taken in the no-smoking dining room, but debit or credit cards are not accepted.
♨Q❀◑◗⛺♣●P⊓

Broadwell

Fox Inn

The Green, GL56 0UF (off A429)
⏲ 11-2.30, 6-11; 12-2.30, 7-10.30 Sun
☎ (01451) 870909
Donnington BB, SBA Ⓗ
Pleasant, one-bar, stone pub overlooking the large green of this charming village. Original flagstone flooring remains in the main bar area, where jugs hang from the beams. Good, home-cooked food is served (not Sun eve) in the no-smoking dining area of this friendly, family-run pub. In the rear garden Aunt Sally is often played, while behind that is a field with a caravan site. ♨Q❀◑◗⛺

Chedworth

Seven Tuns

Queen Street, GL54 4AE (near church)
⏲ 12-3.30, 6-11; 11-11 Sat & summer; 12-10.30 Sun
☎ (01285) 720242
Young's Bitter, Special, seasonal beers Ⓗ
Unspoilt, spacious pub attractively located in one of England's longest villages. A rare outlet for Young's in Gloucestershire, bottled beers such as Ramrod and Double Chocolate Stout are also stocked. Various rooms and dining areas are well

furnished, displaying local artefacts and photographs. The pub has an attractive garden and a skittle alley available for hire.
⩋Q❀◐▶♣P⊬

Cheltenham

Adam & Eve

8 Townsend Street, GL51 9HD (near Tesco superstore)
✪ 10-2, 4-11; 10-11 Sat; 12-2, 4-10.30 Sun
☎ (01242) 690030
Arkells 2B, Moonlight, seasonal beers ⊞
This friendly, unpretentious terraced local was Cheltenham CAMRA's Pub of the Year in 2003/4. Close to Tesco superstore, it is 15 minutes' walk from the centre, and is readily accessible by bus (Stagecoach C, H and 41). The public bar, with an adjoining skittle alley and separate lounge form a strong community focus. The pub is home to skittle and quiz teams. Run by the same landlady for 26 years, it always provides a relaxing atmosphere. ⊟♣

Cheltenham Motor Club

Upper Park Street, GL52 6SA
(access from London Rd, A40 is via Crown Passage)
✪ 12-3 (not Mon-Fri), 7-midnight; 12-2, 7-midnight Sun
☎ (01242) 522590
Draught Bass or Fuller's London Pride; guest beers ⊞
Just outside the town centre in the former Crown Inn, pedestrian access from the A40 London Road is via Crown Passage. This friendly club is open to all; regular visitors will be asked to join. The steward normally keeps three ales, including two guests, one is usually a local beer. Thatchers cider is sold. The club has a bar with a games room leading off. The decoration consists of motoring paraphernalia and an extensive collection of pump clips. Parking is limited.
Q●P

Jolly Brewmaster

39 Painswick Road, GL50 2EZ
✪ 12-11; 12-10.30 Sun
☎ (01242) 772261
Caledonian Deuchars IPA; Donnington SBA; Greene King IPA; guest beers ⊞
Hidden oasis, waiting to be discovered. Built as a coaching inn in 1854, it has kept the distinctive etched windows. This busy pub has been sympathetically modernised, yet retains the feel of an old-fashioned local, with two original real fires and an unusual horseshoe-shaped bar, boasting six handpumps. The atmosphere is bright, airy and convivial and the pub welcomes both smokers and dog-owners. A brick paved courtyard at the rear provides a perfect retreat for summer evenings. Sunday lunch is served.
⩋❀♣●

Kemble Brewery Inn

27 Fairview Street, GL52 2JF
✪ 11.30-2.30 (3 Fri), 5.30-11; 11.30-11 Sat; 12-4, 7-10.30 Sun
☎ (01242) 243446
Taylor Landlord; Whittington's Cats Whiskers; Wye Valley Hereford Pale Ale; guest beers ⊞
This former Cheltenham CAMRA Pub of the Year is a small but deservedly popular back-street local, hard to find but well worth the effort. It offers six real ales, including a local beer, and good value, home-made lunches. The first owner came from Kemble and made cider pressed from apples grown in the back garden, now an attractive walled drinking area. Tuesday is quiz night. The pub can become smoky on race days or if near neighbours, Cheltenham Town are at home. Q❀◐

Restoration Inn

55-57 High Street, GL50 1DX
(end of pedestrianised zone)
✪ 11-11; 12-10.30 Sun
☎ (01242) 522792
Beer range varies ⊞
This Barracuda-owned, city-centre pub has up to six handpumps serving rotating beers from St Austell, Wychwood, Wye Valley and a local micro-brewery. The 16th-century black and white facade hides a large open-plan interior with two snugs (one no-smoking) at the front. One area has a large screen for sports, while a raised section for diners is at the back, although meals can be eaten throughout (12-9 daily); Sunday roasts are good. No children are admitted. ◐▶⊬

Royal Oak

43 The Burgage, Prestbury, GL52 3DL
✪ 11.30-2.30, 5.30-11 (11.30-11 summer Sat); 12-3.30, 7.10.30 (12-10.30 summer) Sun
☎ (01242) 522344 website: www.royal-oak-prestbury.co.uk
Archers Best Bitter; Taylor Landlord; guest beers ⊞
Small, popular local in Prestbury, which is reputed to be Britain's most haunted village. The public bar features exposed beams, while the lounge serves as a dining room until 9pm; all food is home made and regularly features fresh fish and Cotswold game. The large rear garden leads to a skittle alley-cum-function room. It holds at least two beer festivals and a cider festival annually. Stagecoach service A stops nearby; it is handy for the race course.
⩋Q❀◐▶●P

Sudeley Arms

25 Prestbury Road, GL52 2PN (near Pittville Gates)
✪ 11-11; 12-10.30 Sun
☎ (01242) 510697
Camerons Castle Eden Ale; Goff's Jouster; Taylor Landlord; guest beers ⊞
Built in 1826, this friendly, welcoming pub is close to Cheltenham Town football ground and away fans are well looked after here. The pub is loosely divided into three rooms: public bar, lounge and snug. Westons draught cider and perry are always available. The friendly pub dog is named Misty. Five handpumps are in regular use, including one for the local Goff's Jouster. Stagecoach service A passes the pub, which is a five-minute walk from the town centre.
Q❀⊟●

Swan

37 High Street, GL50 1DX
✪ 12-11; 12-10.30 Sun
☎ (01242) 584929
website: www.theswan-cheltenham.co.uk
Beer range varies ⊞
Cheltenham CAMRA's Pub of the Year 2005, this local close to the town centre has a bright, contemporary ambience that attracts a cosmopolitan crowd. The wood-floored interior

has been sympathetically refurbished and divided into three distinct areas; the large courtyard is a bonus. See the changing displays of work by local artists in the no-smoking conservatory. It hosts a Monday quiz, live music twice monthly (Thu) and regular theme nights. A superior choice of wines and spirits is stocked; the varied menu offers local produce (weekend meals served 12.30-4pm). ❀◐♿♣⍻

Chipping Campden

Volunteer Inn

Lower High Street, GL55 6DY

✪ 11.30-3, 5 (6 Sat)-11; 12-3, 7-10.30 Sun

☎ (01386) 840688 website: www.thevolunteerinn.com

Hook Norton Best Bitter; North Cotswold Genesis; Stanway Stanney Bitter; guest beers Ⓗ

In 2005 the family owners celebrated their 20th anniversary of running this fine 300-year-old stone inn. Named the Volunteer in the mid-1800s when men used to sign on here for the volunteer armies, the front bar has a huge stone fireplace and cushioned seats in the bay windows. The owners are big supporters of local breweries; the cider is Cheddar Valley. This former county CAMRA Pub of the Year boasts a pretty garden by a stream. ♨Q❀⛟◐⊟♣●

Cirencester

Twelve Bells

Lewis Lane, GL7 1EA (off A435 roundabout)

✪ 11-3, 5-11; 12-3.30, 6.30-10.30 Sun

☎ (01285) 644549

Beer range varies Ⓗ

Beer drinkers' haven, an old, panelled pub warmed by open fires in all three rooms. The landlord, who has a wry sense of humour, holds court in the lively front bar, but the rear rooms are quieter. Choose from five changing guest beers and an excellent, wide-ranging menu of freshly prepared meals using ingredients from local suppliers. Portions are substantial – abandon all diets ye who enter here!
♨♉❀◐♿⛺

Coaley

Fox & Hounds

The Street, GL11 5EG

✪ 12-3 (not Mon or Tue), 7-11; 12-3, 7-10.30 Sun

☎ (01453) 890366

Uley Bitter; guest beers Ⓗ

Situated in an attractive country village, this 300-year-old Cotswold stone free house has one cosy bar with a low, beamed ceiling and a wood-burning stove. The function room houses a skittle alley and dining area, which serves an extensive home-cooked menu at reasonable prices. At the front is an outdoor, roadside seating area. The pub is famous for its jazz, Irish and Cajun music performed on Saturday and occasionally on Friday. ♨Q❀◐♣●P

Cranham

Black Horse Inn

GL4 8HP (off A46 or B4070)

✪ 12-3 (possibly not Mon), 6.30-11 (not Mon); 12-3, 7 (8.30 winter)-10.30 Sun

☎ (01452) 812217

Archers Special; Hancock's HB; Sharp's Doom Bar; Wickwar BOB; guest beers Ⓗ

Unspoilt, stone-built, 17th-century free house almost hidden up a side road in the lower part of Cranham village. An open log fire and the landlord's endless fund of puns contribute to lively conversation in a music-free environment. A blackboard offers country-style dishes aimed at satisfying hearty appetites. Local CAMRA's country Pub of the Year 2005, it serves no food on Sunday evening, and seldom opens on Monday lunchtime.
♨Q❀◐⊟♣P

Didmarton

King's Arms

The Street, GL9 1DT (on A433)

✪ 11-3, 6-11; 11-11 Fri & Sat; 11-11 Sun

☎ (01454) 238245

Uley Bitter; Wickwar Cotswold Way; guest beer Ⓗ

The plain frontage belies the warm, welcoming interior of this sympathetically refurbished 17th-century coaching inn. The style and comfort of the interior gradually increase as you progress around the central counter from the hop-strewn games/public bar to the excellent restaurant. The food is imaginative but pricey; half portions are available for children. The recommended accommodation includes three self-catering cottages. The well-maintained walled garden is an added attraction. ♨❀⛟◐⊟♣P⍻

Doynton

Cross House Inn

High Street, BS30 5TF

(1 mile N of A420, on outskirts of Wick)

✪ 11.30-3, 6-11; 12-4, 7-10.30 Sun

☎ (0117) 937 2261

Draught Bass; Courage Best Bitter; Fuller's London Pride; Greene King Old Speckled Hen; guest beer (summer) Ⓗ

Built 300 years ago and serving as an inn for 200 years, this pub plays a pivotal role in the local rural community, with cricketers and darts players meeting here. An open log fire in the bar creates a welcoming ambience. An excellent selection of food is available both here and in the restaurant, which is on a lower level. In its early history the building is thought to have been associated with the nearby Dyrham Park estate. ♨❀◐♣P

Duntisbourne Abbots

Five Mile House ☆

Old Gloucester Road, GL7 7JR

(on old A417; follow services sign from new road)

✪ 12-3, 6-11; 12-3, 7-10.30 Sun

☎ (01285) 821432

Beer range varies Ⓗ

Refurbishments of pubs with Grade II listed interiors are rarely as successful as this. The tiny bar, virtually unchanged and offering three ales, leads to a smart no-smoking dining room where the meals are deservedly popular. Left of the entrance is a small tap room created by two venerable curving settles around a wood-burning stove; steps lead down to a snug and

the old converted cellar. Moving the main road a few yards has left the old Ermin Street empty, if not exactly quiet.
₼Q❀◑♣P

Dursley

Old Spot Inn

Hill Road, GL11 5JQ (next to bus station)
⏲ 11-11; 12-10.30 Sun
☎ (01453) 542870
Uley Old Ric; guest beers Ⓗ
CAMRA award-winning free house named after the Gloucester Old Spot pig. Sympathetically restored by the owner, Ric, this 100-year-old pub's intimate atmosphere is enhanced by log fires and brewery memorabilia. Two of the four drinking areas are no-smoking. Four guest beers and a good lunchtime menu are offered here. A convivial local on the Cotswold Way, the secluded garden has a boules piste. This gem stands next to a free car park.
₼Q❀◐⚟

Filton

Rate Payers Arms

Filton Sports & Leisure Centre, Elm Park, BS34 7PS
(signed from mini-roundabout on A38 by police station)
⏲ 12-2.30, 6.30-11; 12-11 Sat; 12-3, 7-10.30 Sun
☎ (01454) 866697
Butcombe Bitter; guest beers Ⓗ
This pub is unusual in being part of the sports centre, and an excellent place to drink, whether you have come to use the wide range of sports facilities provided or watch sport on the big-screen TV. It keeps up to four guest beers and food is available at all times. It hosts events most Sundays, including a monthly charity quiz (third Sun) and live jazz (fourth Sun). Look out for occasional real ale promotions.
◑♿⇌(Abbey Wood) P

Ford

Plough Inn

GL54 5RU (on B4077, 5 miles W of Stow-on-the-Wold)
⏲ 11-11, 12-10.30 Sun
☎ (01386) 584215 website: www.ploughinnatford.co.uk
Donnington BB, SBA Ⓗ
This Cotswold stone inn dates back to the 16th century when it was used as a courthouse, with cellar dungeons for prisoners. Today it overlooks the racing gallops of trainer Jonjo O'Neill, and the racing connection is evident around the pub. Excellent home-cooked food is served (all day Sat and Sun). The olde-worlde atmosphere within the three bars, with low beamed ceilings, flagstone floors and inglenooks, can be enjoyed while sampling the superb Donnington ales in local CAMRA's Pub of the Year 2004. ₼❀⟺◑♿♣●P

Forthampton

Lower Lode Inn

GL19 4RE OS878317
⏲ 12-3 (not winter Mon or Tue), 6-11; 12-11 Sat; 12-10.30 Sun
☎ (01684) 293224
Donnington BB; Black Sheep Best Bitter; Goff's Tournament; Hook Norton Old Hooky; guest beers Ⓗ
Standing in three acres of lawned river frontage, looking across the River Severn to Tewkesbury Abbey, this brick-built pub has been licensed since 1590. A popular stop-over for boaters using the public mooring facilities, it has a private slipway on to the river. There is a Camping and Caravan Club hideaway site and day fishing is available. A ferry operates across from Tewkesbury to Lower Lode's picnic area (April-Oct); the approach roads are liable to winter flooding.
₼Q☋❀⟺◑♿▲♣P⚟

Frampton Cotterell

Globe

366 Church Road, BS36 2AB
⏲ 12-3, 6-11; 12-10.30 Sun
☎ (01454) 778286
Draught Bass; Butcombe Bitter; Courage Best Bitter; St Austell Tribute; guest beers Ⓗ
Spacious Georgian pub, set back from the main street, with a friendly atmosphere, where six real ales and Black Rat cider feature. The L-shaped bar is wood panelled with a beamed ceiling. The rear part is no-smoking. The pub is food oriented so there are two dining areas, including a marquee at the rear. The large garden has a play space; children are welcome until 9pm. Good walks can be taken along the adjacent Frome Valley walkway.
₼❀◑●P⚟

Rising Sun

43 Ryecroft Road, BS36 2HN
⏲ 11.30-3, 5.30-11; 11.30-11 Fri & Sat; 12-10.30 Sun
☎ (01454) 772330
Draught Bass; Bath Gem; Butcombe Bitter; Sharp's Doom Bar; Wadworth 6X; guest beers Ⓗ
Family-run, award-winning free house, a former local CAMRA Pub of the Year. It usually has six beers on tap, many from local breweries. The three rooms include an upper dining area for smokers, while the conservatory is a no-smoking restaurant. The main bar has a flagstone floor and walls adorned with prints and brewery memorabilia. The adjacent skittle alley doubles as a function room. Children are welcome until 8.30pm. ❀◑♣P⚟

France Lynch

King's Head

GL6 8LT
⏲ 12-2.30, 6-11; 12-4, 7-10.30 Sun
☎ (01453) 882225
Hook Norton Best Bitter; St Austell Tribute; Sharp's Doom Bar; Young's Bitter Ⓗ
Friendly, single-bar pub, hidden away at the heart of a village of winding streets, but well worth finding. The village name implies Huguenot connections; French and Flemish weavers came to this wool-rich area in search of work. The superb reclaimed garden has a safe play area for children and a crèche is provided on Friday evening (7-9pm). Live music is performed on Monday evening – jazz, blues and folk. No food is served Sunday evening.
₼Q☋❀◑♣P

Gloucester

Dick Whittington

100 Westgate Street, GL1 2PE
⏲ 11-11 (1am Fri & Sat); 12-10.30 Sun
☎ (01452) 502039
St Austell Tribute; guest beers Ⓗ
Grade I listed building where the frontage is an early Georgian enhancement to the 14th-century structure. From 1311 to 1546 it was the town-house of the Whittington family and the four-times Mayor of London would certainly have visited. A recent refurbishment has given the interior a contemporary feel with attractive lighting. A free house of growing popularity, it was voted local CAMRA City Pub of the Year 2005. Three guest beers mainly come from small local brewers; the food is good.
Q❀◐◑

Fountain Inn ✔

53 Westgate Street, GL1 2NW
⏲ 10.30-11; 12-10.30 Sun
☎ (01452) 522562
website: www.fountainglos.co.uk
Caledonian Deuchars IPA; Fuller's London Pride; Greene King Abbot; Wickwar BOB; guest beer Ⓗ
Approached through a passage from Westgate Street, this popular, 17th-century inn occupies a site whose pub pedigree has been traced back to 1216. Its flower-bedecked courtyard is packed in summer. A comprehensive selection of food is home cooked to order and is available throughout the day (except winter Sun eve). The Orange Room restaurant opens Thursday-Saturday evenings and Sunday lunchtime. The long room is available for private functions. The cider is Addlestones. Q❀◐◑♿♣●⚟

Linden Tree ✔

73-75 Bristol Road, GL1 5SN (on A430, S of docks)
⏲ 11.30-2.30, 6-11; 11.30-11 Sat; 12-10.30 Sun
☎ (01452) 527869
Wadworth IPA, 6X, JCB, seasonal beers; Ⓗ **guest beers** Ⓖ
The end property of this Grade II listed Georgian terrace is a popular community hostelry. Its modest entrance masks an interior not untypical of a Cotswold pub. The open fire, warm colour scheme and slightly eccentric decorative features contribute to a homely atmosphere. The popular skittle alley opens up to create extra space when required. Guest ales are mainly from southern family brewers. It offers substantial home-made meals (not Sat or Sun eves) and bargain accommodation.
♨Q❀⇄◐◑♣

New Inn

16 Northgate Street, GL1 1SF
⏲ 11-11 (1am Thu; 1.45am Fri & Sat); 12-10.30 Sun
☎ (01452) 522177 website: www.newinnglos.com
Palmer IPA; Wychwood Hobgoblin; guest beers Ⓗ
The finest medieval galleried inn in Britain, this Grade I listed building is a major social venue in the city as reflected in its late weekend opening hours. The ale bar offers up to seven guest beers from small brewers. The cider is Black Rat from Moles. The inn has a coffee shop, restaurant and function room. Its accommodation has recently been upgraded to a high standard; weekend concessionary rates are available for CAMRA members at this local Pub of the Year 2002-4.
❀⇄◐◑⇌♣●

Gretton

Royal Oak

GL54 5EP (1½ miles from Winchcombe)
⏲ 12-3, 6-11; 12-4, 7-10.30 Sun
☎ (01242) 604999
Goff's Jouster; Hook Norton Best Bitter; Taylor Landlord; guest beer Ⓗ
Very much a country pub once more, now run by a family of brothers, where a friendly, laid-back welcome is assured. Bar areas have a mix of wood and flagstone floors, while the no-smoking conservatory, benefiting from outstanding views across the vale, acts as the dining area (good food). Beers from nearby Goff's Brewery feature. In the garden, where a beer festival is held in June, you may play tennis or even spot a steam train on the nearby Gloucestershire-Warwickshire line.
♨Q❀◐◑♣P

Hawkesbury Upton

Beaufort Arms

High Street , GL9 1AU
⏲ 12-11; 12-10.30 Sun
☎ (01454) 238217
Wickwar BOB; guest beers Ⓗ
Cotswold stone, two-bar pub, frequented by locals and passing customers. Note the period dentist's chairs and collection of brewery and local memorabilia. The no-smoking dining area offers good value food. Added attractions include a skittle alley/function room and an attractive garden, boasting a six-foot wood carving of a silver yale (mythical beast). The pub has been local CAMRA's Pub of the Year four years running and won the Gloucestershire award in 2004. ♨Q☕❀◐◑⊟♿♣●P

Littleton-on-Severn

White Hart

High Street, BS35 1NR (signed from B4461)
⏲ 12-2.30, 6-11; 12-11 Sat; 12-10.30 Sun
☎ (01454) 412275
Young's Bitter, Special, seasonal beers Ⓗ
Flagstoned gem, surrounded by countryside and enjoying views over the Severn Estuary, but easily accessible from the M48 motorway (junction 1). Dating back to the 1680s, the pub was originally a farmhouse; many features survive including two inglenooks. The interior has six distinct areas including a games room and a family room. A sunny patio and large front garden add to its appeal. Well worth a visit, the food and accommodation here are recommended. ♨Q☕❀⇄◐◑⊟♣P

Longford

Queen's Head

84 Tewkesbury Road, GL2 9EJ (on A38 N of A40 jct)
⏲ 11-3 (2.30 Mon & Tue), 5.30 (6 Sat)-11; 12-3, 7-10.30 Sun
☎ (01452) 301882
Ringwood Best Bitter; guest beers Ⓗ
Partly timber-framed building, dating from the 1730s, that was a blacksmith's before becoming

a pub a century ago. With atmospheric lighting and an efficient ventilation system, it is popular with local drinkers and diners. For the former, up to five guest ales are sourced from small and family brewers; for the latter, award-winning food includes outstanding Longford lamb. The lounge area is smoke-free. Children are not admitted. Flower baskets brighten the exterior in summer.
Q◐◑⊟P⍁

Marshfield

Catherine Wheel

High Street, SN14 8LR
⏲ 12-3, 6-11; 12-11 Sat; 12-3, 7-10.30 Sun
☎ (01225) 892220
Archers Village; Draught Bass; Courage Best Bitter; guest beer Ⓗ
Beautifully restored Georgian pub on the village High Street. When entering, peek into the pretty dining room on the left of the front door. The extensive main bar leads down from the original wood-panelled area, via stone-walled rooms to the cosy patio garden at the rear. In winter there is usually a superb open fire to warm your feet at. Food, served in the bar or garden, is imaginative and well presented (no lunches Mon or eve meals Sun).
⛫Q❀⊭◐◑P

May Hill

Glasshouse

GL17 0NN (off A40 W of Huntley) OS710213
⏲ 11.30-3, 6.30-11; 12-3, 7-10.30 Sun
☎ (01452) 830529
Draught Bass; Butcombe Bitter; Whittington's Cats Whiskers Ⓗ
Charming old pub where an extension, incorporating reclaimed timbers and stonework added two years ago, blends in well. Divided into three bar areas, one houses an old, black-leaded range, and another a roaring open fire. The new, improved kitchen provides excellent fare. Of the three real ales on tap, one is usually a guest. An historic yew hedge with a seat makes a lovely focal point in the garden. Local CAMRA members voted it Pub of the Year in 2004.
⛫Q❀◐◑♣P

Mayshill

New Inn

Badminton Road, BS36 2NT
(on A432, between Coalpit Heath and Nibley)
⏲ 11.45-3, 5.30-11; 12-10.30 Sun
☎ (01454) 773161
Draught Bass; guest beers Ⓗ
Warm and cosy, 17th-century roadside inn, where the original parts date back to 1550. Carpeted throughout, the front bar is warmed by a real fire in winter. The main bar area features settles and window seats; note the collection of model cars above the bar. The Chestnut Lounge serves as a restaurant (5.30-9pm Mon-Sat, 12-8pm Sun). Children are welcome until 8.45pm. Guest beers come from far and wide.
⛫Q❀◐◑P

Minchinhampton

Old Lodge

Minchinhampton Common, GL6 9AQ
(in middle of common, signed from main road)
⏲ 12-3, 6-11; 12-4 Sun
☎ (01453) 832047
Sharp's Cornish Coaster, Doom Bar, Special; Theakston XB Ⓗ
Old stone house in the middle of the common, next to Minchinhampton Golf Club (old course). It affords fantastic views of the Stroud valleys and River Severn in the distance. Good food can be eaten in the restaurant or the bar area. The pub, formerly the golf clubhouse, is a large building, frequented by walkers; it is a joy to visit on a summer's evening. Q❀◐◑P

Moreton-in-Marsh

Inn on the Marsh

Stow Road, GL56 0DW (on A429)
⏲ 12-2.30, 7-11; 11-3, 6-11 Fri, Sat & summer; 12-3, 7-10.30 Sun
☎ (01608) 650709
Banks's Original; Marston's Burton Bitter, Pedigree; guest beer Ⓗ
This charming pub is a rare outlet in the area for the Wolverhampton & Dudley Brewery. It has comfortable armchairs, old photographs, duck prints and hanging hops, while baskets on the rafters are a reminder of Moreton's former trade of basket weaving. Food, served in the conservatory, bears the Dutch East Indies influence of the landlady. Try your hand at the Dutch game of schoolen. The duckpond in the garden is a former coach wash.
Q❀◐◑♿⛺⇌♣P⍁

Moseley Green

Rising Sun

GL15 4HN (off B4431, Blakeney-Parkend road) OS632087
⏲ 11-3, 6.30-11 (11-11 summer Sat); 12-3, 7-10.30 (12-10.30 summer) Sun
☎ (01594) 562008
Freeminer Speculation; Greene King Abbot; guest beers Ⓗ
Built in the early 1800s to serve the coal mining community, it was renovated and extended in 1982, adding a skittle alley-cum-function room and a balcony. A patio, seating 50, was created in 1989 to commemorate 50 years service at the inn by the same family. A children's play area and barbecue have since been added. The latter is used when local brass bands play on summer evenings. Family meals are always available. Enjoy the panoramic views of the Forest of Dean. ❀◐◑♣●P⍁⊓

Nailsworth

George Inn

Newmarket, GL6 0RF
⏲ 11-3, 6-11; 12-3, 7-10.30 Sun
☎ (01453) 833228
Moles Tap Bitter; Taylor Landlord; Uley Bitter, Old Spot Ⓗ
Village local, looking south over the valley above Nailsworth. The George is a 15-minute walk from the Forest Green Rovers ground. Three chimneys confirm that the inn was originally

three cottages, becoming a pub in 1820 and renamed in 1910 to honour the incoming King (George V). The food is renowned and can be eaten in the small restaurant or in the bar (booking is advisable). Q❀◑P

Naunton

Black Horse

GL54 3AD (off B4068) OS119234
⏲ 11-3, 6-11; 11-11 Sat; 12-10.30 Sun
☎ (01451) 850565
Donnington BB, SBA Ⓗ
Traditional Cotswold stone village inn offering a friendly welcome to locals and visitors alike. Interior features include black beams, stripped stonework, flagstone flooring, wooden settles and cast iron framed tables. The old snug dining area is no-smoking (no eve meals Sun or Mon in winter). Unspoilt Naunton boasts a magnificent dovecote and an old mill. The Black Horse walk is a day's ramble – a leaflet is available at the pub. ❀⇌◑♿▲♣P

Nettleton Bottom

Golden Heart

GL4 8LA (on A417)
⏲ 11-3, 5.30-11; 11-11 Fri & Sat; 12-10.30 Sun
☎ (01242) 870261
Marston's Pedigree; Taylor Golden Best; guest beers Ⓗ
This 300-year-old Cotswold free house stands beside the only single-carriageway section of the Swindon to Gloucester road. Little changed in appearance in a century, it has, however, absorbed two adjoining cottages to create a series of rooms with a log fire, bare stone walls, mixed furniture and assorted mementos. Reasonably-priced national award-winning food attracts locals and passing motorists alike. A large stone-paved patio abuts cow pastures. An August bank holiday beer festival is staged. ⌂Q❀⇌◑P⊬

Newent

George

Church Street, GL18 1PU (off B4215 and B4216)
⏲ 11-11; 12-10.30 Sun
☎ (01531) 820203 website: www.georgehotel.uk.com
Hancock's HB; Whittington's Cats Whiskers; guest beers Ⓗ
Lively, town-centre hotel bar with a central serving area and seating. It is quiet at the front while a dartboard, fruit machines and TV screens are provided at the rear. The restaurant is reached by a corridor behind the bar (no food Sun eve). A games room above the restaurant has snooker and table football. There is a large patio in the courtyard of this former coaching inn. A beer festival takes place during Newent Onion Fair in September. ⌂❀⇌◑♣P

Old Down

Fox

The Inner Down, BS32 4PR (1½ miles from A38)
⏲ 12-3 (2.30 Sat), 6-11; 12-10.30 Sun
☎ (01454) 412507
Draught Bass; Flowers IPA; Moles Best Bitter; Sharp's Cornish Coaster, Doom Bar; guest beer Ⓗ
Welcoming, single-bar, 18th-century small village pub. The bar is pleasantly decorated with low ceilings, exposed beams and a real fire; one part is sectioned off for non-smokers. A covered verandah at the rear has seating overlooking the well-kept garden. A children's climbing frame with bark floor is provided and there is a small children's room to the back of the pub. The food is recommended. Moles Black Rat cider is served from the barrel. ⌂ᐅ❀◑♣●P⊬

Oldbury on Severn

Anchor Inn

Church Road, BS35 1QA
⏲ 11.30-3, 6.30-11; 11.30-11 Sat; 12-10.30 Sun
☎ (01454) 413331
Draught Bass; Ⓖ **Butcombe Bitter; Theakston Old Peculier; Wickwar BOB; guest beer** Ⓗ
Converted riverside mill, built in the 16th century. The main bar is L-shaped and comfortable, but the public bar is where the locals gather for village gossip. Children are allowed in the dining room; excellent food is served in the pub and restaurant. The large rear garden is safely fenced and has a boules piste at the end. ⌂Q❀◑⊟♣P

Pucklechurch

Star Inn ✔

37 Castle Street, BS16 9RF (opp. village playing fields)
⏲ 11-11; 12-10.30 Sun
☎ (0117) 937 2391
Draught Bass; Ⓖ **Wadworth 6X** Ⓗ
Excellent village pub, and a real focus for the local community. A Guide regular, an annual beer festival is held in June to coincide with the 'Revels', a local charity event. Bass is brought from the cellar to the bar in jugs, and the pub is renowned for its three ciders – Thatchers Dry, Cheddar Valley and Taunton Traditional. Good food is served (not Sun eve). A recently-built conservatory provides additional dining space. The No. 689 Bristol-Yate bus stops outside daytime (not Sun). ⌂❀◑♣●P

Sheepscombe

Butchers Arms ✔

GL6 7RH (signed from A46/B4070) OS892104
⏲ 11.30-3, 6.30 (6 Fri & Sat)-11; 12-3.30, 7-10.30 Sun
☎ (01452) 812113 website: www.cotswoldinns.co.uk
Moles Best Bitter; Otter Ale; Wye Valley Bitter Ⓗ
Cosy, 17th-century village pub and restaurant cooking fresh produce. It is part of Blenheim Inns, a privately-owned company that breathes life into tired pubs. Quoits is played here. The pub sign of a butcher supping ale with a pig tied to his leg is probably the most photographed in the country. It is thought that butchering went on here when Henry VIII hunted deer in Sheepscombe Valley. Enjoy the staggering views from the outside tables above and behind the pub. ⌂Q❀◑♣P⊬◻

Slad

Woolpack

GL6 7QA (on B4070)
⏲ 12-3, 6-11; 11.30-11 Sat; 12-10.30 Sun
☎ (01452) 813429

Uley Bitter, Laurie Lee's Bitter, Old Spot, Pig's Ear ⊞
Local CAMRA Pub of the Year 2004 and '05, this popular, 16th-century inn affords superb views of the Slad Valley. It achieved fame through the late Laurie Lee, author of Cider with Rosie, who was a regular customer. The building has been thoughtfully restored, with wood settles in the end bar where children are welcome. The beers are served in three rooms. No evening meals are served Monday.
⛬Q♈❀◐◑⊟♣●P

Slimbridge

Tudor Arms

Shepherd's Patch, GL2 7BP
(from A38 1 mile beyond Slimbridge village)
⌚ 11-11; 12-10.30 Sun
☎ (01453) 890306
Uley Pig's Ear; Wadworth 6X; Wickwar BOB; guest beers ⊞
Family-owned and -operated free house, close to the Wildfowl and Wetlands Trust site and the Gloucester-Sharpness Canal. Licensed in the early 1800s to cater for navvies digging the canal, it remained a beer and cider house until the 1950s. Now much enlarged, it offers accommodation in the modern brick-built lodge alongside, and a caravan and camping park behind. Children are welcome. Disabled facilities have recently been added. The two guest beers come from small brewers. The food is recommended.
❀⊭◐◑♿⛺♣P⊁

Stow-on-the-Wold

Queen's Head

The Square, GL54 1AB
⌚ 11-11; 12-10.30 Sun
☎ (01451) 830563
Donnington BB, SBA ⊞
This 17th-century Cotswold pub in the town square attracts locals and visitors alike. The excellent Donnington ales can be tried in either bar area, the back one being no-smoking. There are fascinating pictures, clocks and other artefacts throughout, while flowers on the dining tables are a nice touch. There is plenty of room for parking in the town square.
Q❀◐◑♣⊁

Stratton

Drillman's Arms

34 Gloucester Road, GL7 2JY (on old A417)
⌚ 11-2.30, 5.30-11; 11-11 Sat; 12-4, 7-10.30 Sun
☎ (01285) 653892
Archers Best Bitter; Sharp's Doom Bar; Wickwar Cotswold Way; guest beer ⊞
Do not be put off by the looming fruit machines in the lounge. The low, beamed ceilings, open fire, horse brasses, brewery pictures and excellent beer more than compensate. A pool table is in the rear bar, while the function room houses a skittle alley. The menu is limited, but reasonably priced (no food Sun eve). A small beer festival is staged in summer. Outside seating is in the small car park at the front.
⛬❀◐◑♣P

Stroud

Golden Fleece

Nelson Street, GL5 2HN
⌚ 12-3, 5-11; 11.30-11 Sat; 12-10.30 Sun
☎ (01453) 764850
Adnams Broadside; Badger Tanglefoot; Caledonian Deuchars IPA; Fuller's London Pride ⊞
The single main bar has two alcoves decorated with musical instruments and jazz memorabilia; live music is performed on Thursday. An open fire and a south-facing walled garden add to this homely pub. The nearest public car park is only 50 yards away and charges do not apply after 6pm. ⛬Q❀◐⇌♣

Lord John ✔

Russell Street, GL5 3AA
⌚ 11-11; 12-10.30 Sun
☎ (01453) 767610
Beer range varies ⊞
Wetherspoon's sympathetic conversion of the old postal sorting office has produced an L-shaped bar with a south-facing patio. A comfortable bar, with a no-smoking area, free from piped music, produces a relaxing atmosphere in which to enjoy the real ales (there is a rotating range). The food is good value. Q❀◐◑⇌⊁

Queen Victoria

5 Gloucester Street, GL5 1DG
⌚ 10-11; 12-10.30 Sun
☎ (01453) 762396
Beer range varies ⊞
This imposing building formerly housed the Gloucester Street forge and records show that it was owned by the Nailsworth Brewery in 1891. The large, single bar houses a pool table and wide-screen TV. This community pub fields quiz, darts and pool teams in local leagues. The spacious function room hosts beer festivals at least once a year and regular live music on three evenings a week. Four handpumps serve a changing range of ales, mainly drawn from micro-breweries. ⛬❀⇌♣

Swineford

Swan

Bath Road, BS30 6LN (1 mile from Bitton on A431)
⌚ 11-3, 5-11; 11-11 Fri; 12-3.30, 7-10.30 Sun
☎ (0117) 932 3101
Draught Bass; ⓖ **Butcombe Bitter; Courage Best Bitter; Sharp's Doom Bar** ⊞
Free house in a tiny hamlet between Bath and Bristol, the Swan is frequented by locals, walkers and residents of nearby villages. A no-smoking room, between the main bar and the restaurant, is used by drinkers and those enjoying bar meals (no food Sun eve). Children are welcome. The open log fire provides a pleasant focal point, while in summer flowers brighten the frontage.
⛬Q❀◐◑P⊁

Tewkesbury

Berkeley Arms

8 Church Street, GL20 5PA
⌚ 11.30-3, 5-11; 11-11 Fri & Sat; 12-4, 7-10.30 Sun
☎ (01684) 293034

Wadworth IPA, 6X, JCB; guest beers Ⓗ
Superb, 15th-century, half-timbered Grade II listed building. The public bar entrance is on the street, while the lounge is accessed via one of Tewkesbury's many alleyways at the rear. A barn, believed to be the oldest non-ecclesiastical building in this historic town, is used for dining in summer. Good value food includes specials (no meals Mon). Live music is performed on Saturday evening at Tewkesbury CAMRA's Pub of the Year 2005. Q◐◑⊟♣

White Bear

Bredon Road, GL20 5BU (N of High St)
11-11; 12-10.30 Sun
☎ (01684) 296614
Beer range varies Ⓗ
On the edge of the town centre, this good value, family-run lively pub attracts a varied clientele and can be noisy on busy evenings. The single L-shaped bar houses a dartboard and pool table. The three guest beers change often and include many from smaller breweries. Near Tewkesbury Marina, the pub is popular with river users. Crib, darts, skittles and pool teams compete in local leagues. The cider is Thatchers. ❀▲♣●P

Todenham

Farriers Arms

GL56 9PF
12-3, 6.30-11; 12-3, 7-10.30 Sun
☎ (01608) 650901 website: www.farriersarms.com
Hook Norton Best Bitter; guest beers Ⓗ
Cosy, friendly red-brick pub next to the old village smithy. A huge inglenook is set off by hops on beams, polished flagstones and a Cotswold stone bar counter. One annexe is full of books, photos and board games, while another is a dining area where regular theme nights are held. Guest ales include seasonal beers from nearby North Cotswold Brewery. The pub has a small front terrace and back garden; Aunt Sally is played in the car park.
⌂Q❀◐◑♣P

Tormarton

Portcullis

High Street, GL9 1HZ (close to M4 jct 18)
12-3, 6-11; 12-3, 7-10.30 Sun
☎ (01454) 218263
Draught Bass; Otter Bitter; guest beers Ⓗ
The focal point of the village, built in the 1700s, the modest virginia creeper-covered stone frontage belies its spacious, unassuming main bar, frequented by locals. The friendly landlord extends a warm welcome to strangers, and takes great pride in his fine selection of beers, including three guests. The oak-panelled, no-smoking restaurant provides freshly cooked meals at reasonable prices; evening meals are served Monday-Friday. Q❀⇌◐◑♣P

Uley

Old Crown

The Green, GL11 5SN
11.30-3, 7-11; 12-3, 7-10.30 Sun
☎ (01453) 860502
Uley Bitter, Pig's Ear; guest beers Ⓗ
Attractive, whitewashed, 17th-century free house set in the picturesque Uley Valley in a pleasant walled garden. The main bar has low, timbered ceilings and a bar billiards table. Close to the Cotswold Way, it is popular with walkers. Run by a landlady who prides herself on obtaining beer from unusual micro-breweries, the regular ales are from neighbouring Uley Brewery. Good value food and en-suite accommodation complete the picture here.
⌂Q❀⇌◐◑♣P

Waterley Bottom

New Inn

GL11 6EF (signed from North Nibley; OS map recommended) OS758964
12-2.30 (not Mon), 6 (7 Mon)-11; 12-11 Sat; 12-10.30 Sun
☎ (01453) 543659
Bath SPA, Gem; Cotleigh Tawny; Greene King Abbot; guest beers Ⓗ
Welcoming free house, nestling in a tiny hamlet in a scenic valley surrounded by steep hills. During the 19th century it was a cider house frequented by mill workers taking the footpath to Dursley. It has a cosy lounge/dining area with a pair of ancient beer engines on display. Darts and cards are played in the small public bar. The attractive, child-friendly garden has a boules piste. It offers an imaginative menu (not Mon) and en-suite accommodation. Thatchers cider is sold. ⌂Q❀⇌◐◑⊟♣●P

Whitecroft

Miners Arms

New Road, GL15 4PE
(on B4234, between Lydney and Parkend) OS619062
12-11; 12-10.30 Sun
☎ (01594) 562483
website: www.minersarmswhitecroft.co.uk
Freeminer Speculation; Holden's Bitter; guest beers Ⓗ
This traditional free house derives its name from the proximity of two coal mines. It has been restored as the hub of the community. The skittle alley doubles as a function room; quoits is played in the bar and boules in one of the gardens. The back garden is safe for children, while the front one runs down to the River Lyd. Enjoy the blues club on alternate Mondays. The Dean Forest Railway passes behind the pub. Three draught ciders are stocked.
⌂Q❀◐⊟♿♣●P

Wick

Rose & Crown

44 High Street, BS30 5QH
12-11; 12-10.30 Sun
☎ (0117) 937 9198
Courage Best Bitter; Greene King Old Speckled Hen; guest beers Ⓗ
Dating from around 1640, this large, rambling pub, trading under the Chef and Brewer group, is renowned for its high quality food (served 12-9.30pm, 9pm Sun). The real fire, low beams and candles on the tables make this a cosy pub, the many rooms adding to the effect. One of the two guest beers changes often. Children are permitted up to 6pm. The famous prize fighter John Gully was born here in 1783.
⌂Q❀◐◑P

Winchcombe

Corner Cupboard Inn

83 Gloucester Street, GL54 5LX (near parish church)

11-11; 12-10.30 Sun

☎ (01242) 602303 website: www.cornercupboard.co.uk

Greene King IPA; Hook Norton Old Hooky; Stanway Stanney Bitter; guest beer (occasional)

This former farmhouse dates from at least 1550 and has been a pub since the 1860s. It was built with Cotswold stone from the ruins of Winchcombe Abbey. The local Stanney Bitter is the most popular of the three regular ales. Corner cupboards were a feature of the old farmhouse; two remain in the main bar which boasts a big wood-burning stove. The games room is home to local crib and darts teams. The no-smoking restaurant's extensive menu features fresh fish. Q P

Winterbourne Down

Cross Hands Inn

85 Down Road, BS36 1BZ

12 (11 Sat)-11; 12-10.30 Sun

☎ (01454) 850077

Draught Bass; Courage Best Bitter; Greene King Old Speckled Hen; guest beers

Friendly, street-corner free house set in 17th-century converted cottages. The main bar is spacious and airy, with a snug and an alcove where traditional games are played. Children are admitted until 9.30pm. It hosts live music on Friday evening. There is a large garden at the rear and a small patio with seating at the front of the pub.

Withington

King's Head

King's Head Lane, GL54 4BD (off Yanworth road, SE of village) OS036153

11-2.30, 6-11; 12-3, 7-10.30 Sun

☎ (01242) 890216

Hook Norton Best Bitter; Wickwar Cotswold Way, seasonal beers

Unspoilt village local that can be hard to find but is worth the effort. The pub has been run by the same family for over 90 years and is a true free house full of interesting pictures. Food is not normally available but sandwiches can be ordered in advance. This stone-built pub is popular with walkers, cyclists and visitors to nearby Chedworth Roman Villa. Children are allowed in the lounge anteroom. Nine men's morris and quoits are played here.

Q P

Woolaston Common

Rising Sun

GL15 6NU (1 mile off A48 at Woolaston) OS590009

12-2.30 (not Wed), 6.30-11; 12-3, 7-10.30 Sun

☎ (01594) 529282

Fuller's London Pride; Robinson's Unicorn

The Rising Sun is a 350-year-old country pub that benefits from some fine views, as it lies on the circular pub walk of the Forest of Dean. Popular with both ramblers and cyclists, the pub has undergone many sympathetic changes over the years, and now features a large bar and a small snug. Good value, home-cooked meals are an added bonus (no food is served Wed).

Q P

Wotton Under Edge

Falcon

Church Street, GL12 7HB

11-11; 12-10.30 Sun

☎ (01453) 521005 website: www.easywell.co.uk/falcon/

Bath SPA; Sharp's Cornish Coaster; guest beers

This 17th-century listed inn on the Cotswold Way was sympathetically restored in 2002 and has gained a reputation for its real ales, cider and wines. The public and lounge bars have wood-burning stoves for a cosy atmosphere. Food of a high standard is served in no-smoking areas at lunchtime and in the evenings. The pub also features live music regularly. A minimum of four real ales includes guests that change frequently.

Q

Red Lion, Ampney St Peter

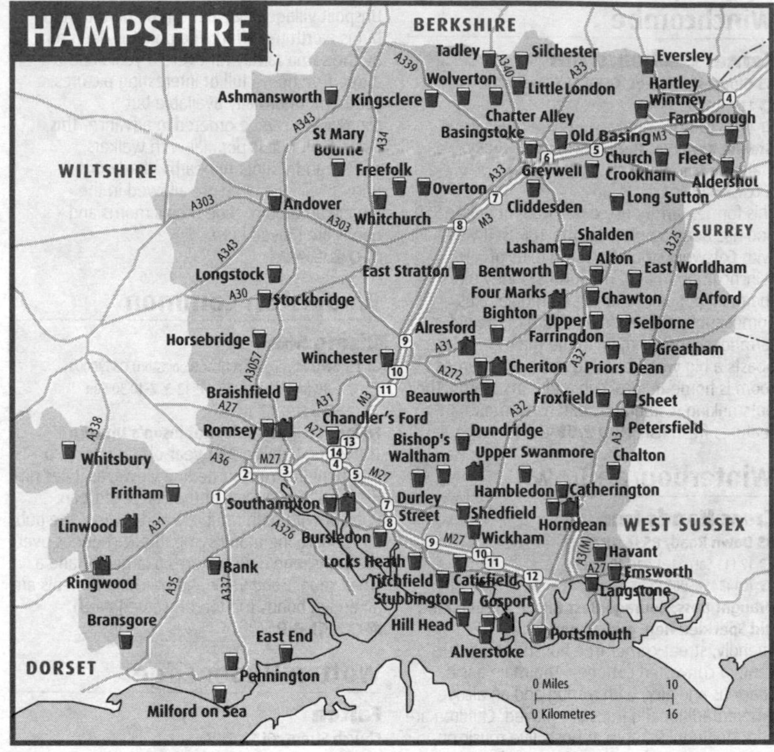

Aldershot

Royal Staff ✓

37A Mount Pleasant Road, GU12 4NN

12-3, 5-11; 11-11 Sat; 12-10.30 Sun

☎ (01252) 408012

Fuller's London Pride, seasonal beers Ⓗ

This impressive-looking pub has a relaxed cosy atmosphere. Close to the top end of Aldershot Town football ground, it can get busy with both local discerning drinkers and visiting supporters. A Fuller's seasonal ale is often on tap. The interior boasts half-wainscotting with other traditional features, notably etched windows throughout. The patio leads into a garden suitable for children. The pub has regular golfing activities and darts teams. ❀

Alton

Eight Bells

33 Church Street, GU34 2DA

11-11; 12-10.30 Sun

☎ (01420) 82417

Ballard's Best Bitter; Hogs Back TEA; guest beers Ⓗ

Excellent free house, just outside the town centre on the old Alton to Oldham turnpike. The building dates from 1640 and is steeped in history. Opposite stands the ancient St Lawrence Church, around which the Civil War battle of Alton was fought. The pub has one small, oak-beamed bar with a further drinking area and a bijou garden, housing a well. The house ale, Leaping Trout is brewed by Archers and may be accompanied by hearty filled rolls.

⛫Q❀⇌♣

French Horn

The Butts, GU34 1RT (near A31 western jct)

11-11; 12-10.30 Sun

☎ (01420) 83269

Courage Best Bitter; Wells Bombardier; Wadworth 6X; Young's Bitter; guest beers Ⓗ

Delightful, historic pub overlooking the medieval archery butts and within sight and sound of steam trains on the nearby Watercress Line. The beamed bar has a roaring fire in winter. The excellent food may be enjoyed in the restaurant. There is a garden and skittle alley. Once part of Chawton, the pub has gained an excellent reputation for its beer and hands-on approach of the management. Children (over eight) are welcome. Two chalets round off the facilities here. ⛫Q❀⇔◑♣P⚡

Market Hotel

3 Market Square, GU34 1HD

11-11 (midnight Thu-Sat); 12-10.30 Sun

☎ (01420) 82350

INDEPENDENT BREWERIES

Cheriton Cheriton
Gale's Horndean
Hampshire Romsey
Itchen Valley Alresford
Oakleaf Gosport
Red Shoot Linwood
Ringwood Ringwood
Stumpy's Upper Swanmore
Triple fff Four Marks
White Star Southampton
Winchester Southampton

Courage Best Bitter; Hogs Back TEA; Ringwood Best Bitter; guest beers 🄷
As a former coaching inn, the Market Hotel forms an impressive sight in the market square. There are two bars: a lounge with comfortable seating and no-smoking section; and a refurbished public bar with fireplace and a striking mural commemorating Alton's extinct livestock market. Good food, served daily is sensibly priced. The pleasant patio boasts a recently-discovered well.

Railway Arms

26 Anstey Road, GU34 2RB (400 yds from station)
11-11; 12-10.30 Sun
☎ (01420) 82218
Triple fff Alton's Pride, Pressed Rat, Moondance, seasonal beers; guest beers 🄷
Close to the Watercress Line and main line station, the U-shaped bar has one side divided into cosy areas. Owned by the proprietor of Triple fff Brewery, his beers are supplemented by ales from a host of micros. A recent function room extension at the rear, leads to a small, pleasant garden. There are also tables outside the front of the pub under a striking sculpture of a steam locomotive.

Alverstoke

Alverbank

Stokes Bay Road, PO12 2QT
11-11; 12-10.30 Sun
☎ (023) 9251 0005 website: www.alverbankhotel.co.uk
Caledonian Deuchars IPA; guest beers 🄷
Victorian country house hotel bar in an attractive setting overlooking Stokes Bay, once frequented by Lillie Langtry. As well as two restaurants, the property has recently been extended to include a function suite for weddings and other events. Uusually one guest beer from the Courage range is always available with more at busy times. Special themed food evenings are held throughout the winter.

Andover

Wyke Down Country Pub & Restaurant

Picket Piece, SP11 6LK (follow signs for Wyke from A303)
11-2.30, 6-11; 12-3, 6-10.30 Sun
☎ (01264) 352048 website: www.wykedown.co.uk
Exmoor Ale; guest beers 🄷
The main part of the pub is housed in a converted 19th-century barn in which many old rural items are displayed. A modern, well-appointed restaurant is a more recent addition, along with a large, comfortable conservatory and adjacent games rooms. Outside the pub's attractions include a campsite, children's play area, golf driving range and a swimming pool. Some hard-standing pitches are provided for caravans. Excellent food is served in the bars and restaurant.

Arford

Crown

Arford Road, GU35 8BT (200 yds N of B3002) OS826365
11-3, 6-11; 12-3, 7-10.30 Sun
☎ (01428) 712150
Adnams Bitter; Fuller's London Pride; Greene King Abbot; guest beer 🄷
Excellent example of a typical, small, country village inn, serving the local community for over two centuries. Named the Crown since 1876, this former Friary Meux pub has three distinct drinking areas; one is slightly raised and functions as a no-smoking restaurant. Good food is available at all sessions. The guest beer is often from a local micro-brewery. Do not miss the sunken riverside garden opposite the pub for a glorious summer drink. Q P

Ashmansworth

Plough Inn

RG20 9PU (1 mile off A343) OS415575
12-2.30, 6-11; closed Mon & Tue; 7.30-10.30 Sun
☎ (01635) 253047
Archers Village, Best Bitter, Golden; guest beer 🄶
Superb, unspoilt, country local in a small village near Highclere Castle. The nearby Ridgeway gives good views from the Downs and makes the pub popular with walkers. Beers are all gravity drawn from the L-shaped bar. Food is limited to snacks and rolls. The pub is Hampshire's highest and is a former local CAMRA Pub of the Year. There is a risk of closure which would mean the loss of a fine hostelry, and the village's last community facility, so a visit is highly recommended. Q

Bank (near Lyndhurst)

Oak Inn

Pinkney Lane, SO43 7FE (1¼ miles W of Lyndhurst) OS287072
11-2.30, 6-11; 11-11 Sat & summer; 12-10.30 Sun
☎ (023) 8028 2350
Ringwood Best Bitter; guest beers 🄿
This 18th-century pub is situated just off the main A35 route through the New Forest, but is a world apart from the busy road. Four guest beers are normally available, many from small brewers, plus local cider. Two beer festivals are held each year, one in early July, the other the weekend before Christmas. Excellent food is served with seafood a speciality. The X35 Southampton to Bournemouth bus stops at the bank turn nearby.

Basingstoke

Basingstoke & North Hants Cricket Club

May's Bounty, Fairfields Road, RG21 3QU (5 mins walk from the old town)
12-3, 5-11; 12-11 Fri & Sat; 12-10.30 Sun
☎ (01256) 473646
website: www.basingstoke-sports-club.co.uk
Fuller's London Pride, ESB; Greene King IPA; Ringwood Best Bitter; guest beers 🄷
The club was founded by Colonel John May, owner of May's Brewery, which ceased brewing in the late 1940s. Although a members' only club visitors are welcome (show a valid CAMRA membership card). The club fields cricket, squash, football, snooker and darts teams. The bar area is strictly no-smoking. The atmosphere is more pub that club at this regular CAMRA

award winner. A serious fire nearly put an end to it last year; it was luckily saved by staff and the fire brigade. ❀◐♣P⊬▯

Bounty Inn

81 Bounty Road, RG21 3BZ (follow signs for Fairfields Art Centre)

✪ 12-11; 11-1am Sat; 12-10.30 Sun

☎ (01256) 320071 website: www.thebountyinn.co.uk

Courage Best Bitter; Greene King Abbot; guest beers Ⓗ

Although at the top of town this pub has the ambience of a traditional country inn, helped by a beautiful garden. Originally called the Cattle Market, the name now reflects its proximity to Mays Bounty cricket ground – a gift to the people of Basingstoke by Col. John May the town's great benefactor. Good ales, good food and live music co-exist here in a friendly atmosphere. Guest ales often include Young's Bitter and Wells Bombardier.

♨Q❀◐▶⊟≠♣P⊬

Soldier's Return

80 Upper Sherborne Road, RG21 5RP (near the hospital jct of the ring road)

✪ 11-2.30, 5.30-11; 11-11 Fri & Sat; 12-10.30 Sun

☎ (01256) 322449

Courage Best Bitter; guest beers Ⓗ

Beer house built in the 1860s on the main road, it was extended in the 1920s and again in the '60s. The road has now been cut off by the Basingstoke ring road to provide a quiet environment overlooking a large playing field with a children's play area. The popular public bar boasts pool and a Wurlitzer; the contrasting lounge has a long, sociable bar counter. The three guest beers come from micros and local regional breweries. Weekday lunches are served. ❀◐⊟P

Beauworth

Milbury's

SO24 0PB (S of A272, 1 mile beyond Beauworth hamlet) OS570246

✪ 11-3, 5.30-11; 11-11 Sat & summer; 12-10.30 Sun

☎ (01962) 771248 website: www.themilburys.co.uk

Caledonian Deuchars IPA; Theakston Old Peculier; guest beer Ⓗ

Hilltop inn, well worth finding: a wealth of beams, flagstones, antique brick walling, ancient settles and gnarled tables give it charm. One room features an amazing 300ft hand-dug well, with a manpowered wheel to raise the bucket; the restaurant boasts a minstrels' gallery. A skittle alley is available for games and functions. An extensive menu is served in the restaurant or bar. The Triple fff house beer is a 3.8% ABV bitter. Accommodation is in one double room.

♨Q❀⇌◐♣P⊬

Bentworth

Star

Church Street, GU34 5RB (off A339)

✪ 12-3, 5 (6 Sat)-11; 12-4, 7-11 Sun

☎ (01420) 561224 website: www.star-inn.com

Fuller's London Pride; Ringwood Best Bitter; guest beers Ⓗ

This is a typical country pub and village local, warmed by open fires. It has a central bar, a games area and a no-smoking dining room offering an extensive range of freshly-prepared meals, including award-winning fish dishes, and a good choice of bar snacks. It is in an ideal location for ramblers and cyclists who would like to start or finish an excursion with a drink or a meal. It hosts live music on Friday evenings.

♨❀◐▶⊟♿♣P

Bighton

Three Horseshoes

Alresford Road, SO24 9RE (2 miles NE of Alfresford, off B3046) OS614344

✪ 12-2.30 (not Mon), 6 (6.30 Sat)-11; 12-2.30, 7-10.30 Sun

☎ (01962) 732859

Gale's Best, HSB; Fuller's London Pride; guest beer (summer) Ⓗ

Friendly, multi-roomed village free house with wide appeal. The small, cosy no-smoking lounge bar is suitable for families. The larger public bar houses the dartboard; the pub fields two teams. Children are also allowed in the games room, with pool table and other games. The menu is varied but uncomplicated; meals are freshly prepared (no eve meals Mon). Monthly live music is staged (Fri or Sat). Disabled access is through the side entrance. Ropley Watercress Line station is two miles away.

♨◐▶⊟♿♣P⊬

Bishop's Waltham

Bunch of Grapes

St Peter's Street, SO32 1AD

✪ 11-2, 6-11; 12-2, 7-10.30 Sun

☎ (01489) 892935

Courage Best Bitter; Greene King IPA; guest beer (occasional) Ⓖ

This ancient pub stands in a narrow street, leading to the churchyard. The pub was purchased two years ago by the licensee, whose family has run it for over 90 years. The small bar is a place for good ale and conversation. The pub's golfing society, which has been in existence for over 15 years, has 120 members (and a waiting list). It is intended that the pub will become smoke-free in February 2006.

Q❀♣

Braishfield

Newport Inn

Newport Lane, SO51 0PL (lane opp. phone box)

✪ 11-3, 6-11; 12-2.30, 7-10.30 Sun

☎ (01794) 368225

Gale's Butser, HSB, Festival Mild or seasonal beers Ⓗ

The world changes, but the Newport stays the same: an attractive late Victorian house, set in a rambling unrestrained garden and car park. The beer is probably the best Gale's in south-west Hampshire. The sandwiches and ploughmans (ham/cheese/tomato) are better than home made. Singalongs around the old festooned piano take place on Saturday evenings, and often folk jam sessions on Thursday. The pub has a loyal following, come and see for yourselves.

♨Q❀⊟♣P

Bransgore

Three Tuns ✓

Ringwood Road, BH23 8JH (take Hinton turn off A35 between Lyndhurst and Christchurch)

11.30-3, 6-11; 12-10.30 Sun

☎ (01425) 672232

Caledonian Deuchars IPA; Hop Back Summer Lightning; Ringwood Best Bitter, Fortyniner; Taylor Landlord H

Well worth the five-minute detour from the main road, this 17th-century inn looks delightful outside, and the interior does not disappoint. The spacious main bar accommodates drinkers and diners, while the restaurant area has tables laid and welcomes well-behaved children. The menu has a modern touch, featuring fresh soups and local ingredients. Smoking is permitted in the snug, warmed by a roaring wood-burning stove. Its annual real ale festival is in late summer. Braille signage is used here.

⚔Q❀◐◑♿P

Bursledon

Jolly Sailor ✓

Land's End Road, Old Burlesdon, SO31 8DN (park at Bursledon Station, follow signed footpath)

11-11; 12-10.30 sun

☎ (023) 8040 5557

Badger K&B Sussex, Best, Tanglefoot, seasonal beers H

Friendly, sympathetically refurbished, multi-room waterside pub. All are welcome – from both land and water. Enjoy the splendid views across the River Hamble to a busy marina, from the pub, patio and covered jetty. The open log fires give a warm welcome in winter. Superb food, from a comprehensive menu, including fresh seafood, suits all tastes. ⚔Q❀◐◑⇌⚟

Catherington

Farmer Inn

300 Catherington Lane, PO8 0TD

12 (5 Mon)-11; 12-10.30 sun

☎ (023) 9259 2402

Gale's Butser, HSB H

Small, traditional, village pub, constructed in typical Gale's pre-war style. Close to the ancient Catherington Down and church, it is popular with walkers. This family-friendly pub welcomes well-behaved children in the bar and the large garden that has a play area, next to a donkey paddock. The comfortable public bar has an unusual raised, fenced darts stage. The lounge doubles as a Thai restaurant, Thursday-Saturday evenings, however daily lunches, including Sunday roasts are English cuisine.

⚔Q❀◐◑⊟♣P⚟

Catisfield

Limes

34 Catisfield Lane, PO15 5NN

12-2.30 (not Tue or Wed), 5-11; 12-3, 7-11 Sat; 12-3, 7-10.30 Sun

☎ (01329) 842926

Fuller's London Pride; Gale's HSB; Hop Back Summer Lightning; Ringwood Fortyniner, Old Thumper H

This pub is located on the road which is said to have the oldest road bridge in the country; this does not seem to stop vehicles clouting the parapets on a regular basis. Once in the pub the impression is of entering someone's home. The public bar is on the right, whereas the small lounge is along a corridor and has a conservatory attached.

Q❀◐◑⊟♣P

Chalton

Red Lion ✓

PO8 0BG OS231160

11-3, 6-11; 12-3, 7-10.30 Sun

☎ (023) 9259 2246

Gale's Butser, Best, HSB, seasonal beers; guest beers H

Reputedly the oldest pub in the county, it was built in the 12th century in conjunction with the church across the road. After 300 years it became a popular stop on the coaching route from Portsmouth to London. One of the most attractive pubs in the area, nestling cosily in the Downs, it retains two bars; the public boasts a large inglenook. It remains popular with all despite its remoteness and lack of public transport. No food is served Sunday evening.

⚔❀◐◑⊟♿P⚟

Chandler's Ford

Cleveland Bay ✓

Pilgrim Close, Valley Park, SO53 4TQ (between Kingsmead leisure centre and Valley Park shops) OS421200

11.30-11; 12-10.30 Sun

☎ (023) 8026 9814

Wadworth IPA, 6X, JCB, seasonal beers or guest beers H

A rarity: a successful estate house in a real ale desert. This spacious, modern pub is named after Britain's oldest breed of carriage horse. The roomy L-shaped bar has various large alcoves off it, two are no-smoking: a family room with TV, and a dining area. An extensive menu is served daily except Sunday, when there is a lunchtime carvery and a popular quiz in the evening. Guest beers are from Wadworth's list.

❀◐◑♿P⚟

Charter Alley

White Hart

White Hart Lane, RG26 5QA (1 mile W of A340, 1 mile E of A339) OS593577

12-2.30 (3 Sat), 7-11; 12-3, 7-10.30 Sun

☎ (01256) 850048

website: www.whitehartcharteralley.com

Butts Jester; Otter Ale; Taylor Landlord; West Berkshire Maggs Mild; guest beers H

The oldest building in the village, put up next to the forge in 1819, it was the meeting point for folk to stop and natter, hence 'chatter alley' which later became Charter Alley. A delightful rural ambience is enhanced by exposed oak beams and log fires in winter. In summer still cider is stocked. The menu offers a variety of steaks, the speciality – home-made pies (made with real ale) – plus vegetarian meals and children's portions (eve meals Tue-Sat).

⚔Q❀⇔◐◑⊟♣●P⚟⊓

Chawton

Greyfriar ✓

Winchester Road, GU34 1SB (opp. Jane Austen's cottage)

12-11, 12 10.30 Sun

☎ (01420) 83841 website: www.thegreyfriar.co.uk

Fuller's London Pride, ESB, seasonal beers Ⓗ

This award-winning Fuller's house is a welcoming hostelry, attracting locals and visitors alike for the full range of Fuller's beers. Originally three cottages, the pub includes a no-smoking restaurant and dedicated no-smoking areas in the bar. The menu changes daily and has gained an excellent reputation. Look out for the special themed evenings throughout the year. A pleasant garden and function room round off the facilities at this attractive pub.

Cheriton

Flower Pots

SO24 0QQ (½ mile N of A272 between Winchester and Petersfield)

12-2.30, 6-11; 12-3, 7-10.30 Sun

☎ (01962) 771318

Cheriton Pots Ale, Best Bitter, Diggers Gold Ⓖ

Two-bar, red-brick Victorian pub, adjoining but commerically separate from the Cheriton Brewhouse. On the southern edge of the village, the pub is close to the source of the Itchen and only a mile from the Civil War battlefield (1644); it is popular with walkers. Good food is served daily (not Sun eve); Wednesday is curry night and quality ice-creams are another speciality. A converted barn provides four, high-class accommodation units. Seasonal and occasional Cheriton brews are also available.

Church Crookham

Foresters

Aldershot Road, GU52 9EP (on road linking B3013 and A323)

12-11; 12-10.30 Sun

☎ (01252) 616503

Fuller's London Pride; Taylor Landlord Ⓗ

This individual pub stands at the edge of the village, tucked into the woodland ranges. The sylvan theme continues in the traditional, yet at the same time modern-style interior. The public bar flows into the dining area, with wood and flagstone floors, to an impressive open fire. Subdued lighting throughout promotes an adult ambience. Local produce and suppliers are used as far as possible for the varied menu; a fish special is regularly offered (booking is recommended for weekend meals).

Cliddesden

Jolly Farmer

Farleigh Road, RG25 2JL (on B3046, near Basingstoke)

12-3, 5.30-11; 12-11 Fri & Sat; 12-10.30 Sun

☎ (01256) 473073

Brains Rev James; guest beers Ⓗ

Traditional country pub, full of character with black beams and a good selection of interesting beers plus a local cider. This award-winning village local has a second room that can be used for children if there is no function on. A large garden at the rear provides a quiet, secluded area with a covered, heated deck for cooler evenings. The pub is well separated from Basingstoke by the motorway, but is still accessible by a footbridge.

Dundridge

Hampshire Bowman

Dundridge Lane, Bishop's Waltham, SO32 1GD (1½ miles E of B3035) OS578184

12-3, 6-11; 12-11 Fri & Sat; 12-10.30 Sun

☎ (01489) 892940

Beer range varies Ⓖ

This fine Victorian rural pub is an absolute gem, the like of which are few and far between these days. Two real fires and a brick floor combine to give a warm, friendly atmosphere. It stocks up to seven cask ales, all of which are gravity dispensed from a beautiful oak stillage. An interesting selection of reasonably-priced food is served (not Sun eve) and camping is possible in the neighbouring field. A beer festival is held in the summer.

Durley Street

Robin Hood

Durley Street, SO32 1AA (at crossroads between Durley and Bishop's Waltham) OS527177

10-3, 5-11; 10-11 Fri & Sat; 12-10.30 Sun

☎ (01489) 860229 website: www.robinhooddurley.co.uk

Greene King IPA, Ruddles County, Old Speckled Hen; guest beer Ⓗ

From the outside this is a simply modernised 19th-century inn; inside an L-shaped bar serves three immaculate rooms: a public bar and a small lounge, both with open fires, and an elegant dining room overlooking a spacious patio and garden to fields and trees beyond. The whole pub is furnished in a restrained, modern style with much light wood. The bar and dining room menus offer high quality food (not Sun eve). The loos are well hidden – behind a false bookcase.

East End

East End Arms

Main Road, SO41 5SY (2¼ miles E of IOW ferry terminal) OS361968

11.30-2.30, 6-11; 12-9 Sun

☎ (01590) 626223

Ringwood Best Bitter, Ⓗ **Fortyniner; guest beer** (occasional) Ⓖ

New Forest pub where two bars are warmed by log fires: the cosy, rustic public bar (dogs welcome, not children) is frequented by customers of a sociable bent; the comfortable, uncluttered lounge (children welcome, not dogs) is the haunt of diners (booking recommended; no food Sun eve or Mon) and patrons wanting a quiet drink. Children's portions are available at lunchtime. Infrequent weekday daytime bus 112 (Hythe-Lymington) serves East End Pond (three-quarters of a mile).

East Stratton

Northbrook Arms

SO21 3DU (off A33, 8 miles N of Winchester)

11-11; 12-10.30 Sun

(01962) 774150 website: www.northbrookarms.co.uk

Gale's HSB; Otter Bitter; guest beers H

Set in an attractive village among thatched cottages, the pub overlooks the green where there are plenty of tables, and petanque and vollyball are played. Inside is a bar with tiled floor, plus two further rooms, one no-smoking, used mainly for dining. Food is served daily, 12-8.45pm and there are two interesting guest beers. A skittle alley at the rear with bar billiards, darts and bar, is used for functions. Children are welcome. Planned extensions include disabled facilities.

East Worldham

Three Horseshoes

Cakers Lane, GU34 3AE (on B3004)

12-3, 6-11; 12-3, 7-10.30 Sun

(01420) 83211

Gale's Butser, Best Bitter, HSB, seasonal beers or guest beers H

This Victorian pub, reputedly haunted, has a single bar, comfortably broken up into informal areas. A no-smoking section for drinkers leads to a small, attractive restaurant serving daily home-made specials (no eve meals Sun). A useful pit-stop if walking the ancient Hanger's Way from Aton to Selbourne, and beyond, the pub once provided refreshment for workers in the long-gone, hop-growing district.

P

Emsworth

Coal Exchange

21 South Street, PO10 7EG

10.30-3, 5.30-11; 10.30-11 Fri & Sat; 12-10.30 Sun

(01243) 375866

Gale's Butser, Best, HSB, seasonal beers; guest beers H

Unusual (for Gale's), green tiled building built in the 17th century as a pork butchers and ale house. As the name suggests, it was also used as a place for locals to trade goods with coal delivered to the nearby harbour. Now that the commercial traffic has ended, the harbour is popular with yachtsmen and those enjoying walks along the shoreline. Local CAMRA's 2005 Pub of the Year has recently been recognised for its food: the curry (Tue) and international evenings (Thu) are especially recommended.

Lord Raglan

35 Queen Street, PO10 7BJ

11-3, 6-11; 12-10.30 Sun

(01243) 372587 website: www.thelordraglan.com

Gale's Butser, HSB, seasonal beers; guest beers H

Located at the eastern edge of the town by the estuary of the River Ems, this flint-built pub has a single bar (the other has been converted into a cosy restaurant) and a pleasant garden offering views of the river and harbour. In addition to traditional beer and cider, good value home-cooked meals are available. Every Sunday, the pub hosts live music from some of the best local bands.

Eversley

White Hart

Reading Road, RG27 0PJ (from A30 take A327 towards Reading, two miles)

11-11; 12-10.30 Sun

(0118) 973 2817

Courage Best Bitter; Fuller's London Pride; Hogs Back TEA or seasonal beer; guest beer H

Oak-beamed, 17th-century rural pub comprising three small bar areas, and a significant amount of padded bench seating. The cosy front bar has log fires at each end in winter, and displays of the pub's internationally-renowned sevens rugby team, Marauders. The snug middle bar (with even lower beams) leads to the Village Bar used for darts and cards and housing a large, drop-down TV screen for major sports events.

Q P

Farnborough

Thatched Cottage

122 Prospect Road, Cove, GU14 8NU (¼ mile W of Farnborough main station)

11.30-11; 12-10.30 Sun

(01252) 543118

Adnams Broadside; Courage Best Bitter; Hogs Back TEA, Hop Garden Gold; guest beer H

This Grade II listed building (still thatched) was originally a 16th-century cottage and only converted into a pub in the 1960s. Exposed oak beams throughout give an appealing warmth, but beware the low ceiling in parts. Two main bars are supplemented by a smaller no-smoking lounge area. A real community pub, it fields a darts league team, and hosts quizzes on Thursday and Sunday evenings. P

Prince of Wales

184 Rectory Road, GU14 8AL (near North Station)

11.30-2.30, 5.30-11; 12-10.30 Sun

(01252) 545578

Badger Tanglefoot; Fuller's London Pride; Hogs Back TEA; Ringwood Fortyniner; Young's Bitter; guest beers H

Local CAMRA Pub of the Year 2005; a single U-shaped room, made up of several discrete drinking areas including a snug, where up to five guest beers are found. South of England micros are well represented and the range includes a lower priced session beer that changes monthly. Milds are featured in May and strong ales in December. The annual beer festival (Oct) is one of many events held throughout the year. Lunches are served Monday-Saturday.

(North) P

Fleet

Prince Arthur

238 Fleet Road, GU51 4BX

10-11; 12-10.30 Sun

(01252) 622660

Courage Best Bitter; Hogs Back TEA; Ringwood Fortyniner, Old Thumper; Marston's Burton Bitter, Pedigree H

Situated towards the southern end of Fleet's

high street, the Prince Arthur is a Wethespoon's on a human scale. It stocks a wide range of real ales, including Greene King Abbot and De Koninck Ambrée in addition to those listed, plus two or three guests which often include Itchen Valley Fagin's. The usual Wetherspoon's menu is served until an hour before closing, and the pub opens at 10am on Sunday for unlicensed sales including breakfast.
Q◑♿⚟

Freefolk

Watership Down

RG28 7NJ (off B3400)
11.30-3, 6-11; 12-3, 7-10.30 Sun
☎ (01256) 892254
Young's Bitter; guest beers Ⓗ
Welcoming free house with one bar but several drinking areas, including a large, no-smoking conservatory. Named after the famous Richard Adams book – if you have read the book, seen the film, now visit the pub. Five pumps serve a changing range of ales, always including a real mild. See the impressive collection of penny arcade machines or try a game of table football. The pub is popular with walkers and cyclists, and buses stop close to local CAMRA's Pub of the Year 2005 winner.
❀◑♣P

Fritham

Royal Oak ✔

SO43 7HJ (1 mile S of B3078) OS232141
11.30-2.30 (11-3 summer), 6-11; 11-11 Sat ; 12-10.30 Sun
☎ (023) 8081 2606
Hop Back Summer Lightning; Ringwood Best Bitter, Fortyniner; guest beers Ⓖ
Small, thatched gem at the end of a New Forest track. The main bar leads into several interconnecting rooms (one no-smoking), served through a hatchway. Beers from the cask are from small brewers; five usually available. Black beams, low doorways, boarded floors and colour-washed walls blend perfectly. Lunchtime food is simple but real. A vast, tabled garden hosts barbecues, hog roasts and a mid-September beer festival. The log fires are delightful. Perfect for walkers, cyclists and equestrians (facilities provided); dogs abound.
⚫Q❀◑

Froxfield

Trooper

Alton Road, GU32 1BD OS727273
12-3, 6-11; 12-3, 7-10.30 Sun
☎ (01730) 827293 website: www.trooperinn.com
Beer range varies Ⓗ
Dating from the 17th-century, this old inn is set high in Hampshire's rolling countryside. Although opened up inside, the single bar serves several distinct areas. Walls are adorned with photographs of film stars while classical music is quietly played in the background. The atmosphere is enhanced by the candlelit bar and tables. There are generally three beers on offer, sometimes four, mainly from local breweries. The extensive food menu makes it popular with country folk.
⚫⛟◑P

Gosport

Clarence Tavern

1 Clarence Road, PO12 1BB
11-11 (may close 2-4 Mon-Thu winter afternoons); 12-10.30 Sun
☎ (023) 9252 9726
Oakleaf Bitter, Hole Hearted, Blake's Gosport Bitter, seasonal beers Ⓗ
The Clarence is the tap for the Oakleaf Brewery, just across the road. The main bar area is supplemented by a room whose roof comes from an old chapel on the Isle of Wight, plus an upstairs restaurant. Beer festivals take place over the Easter and August bank holiday weekends. A folk group meets on Thursday evening for a jam session. Accommodation is planned for summer 2005. An area outdoors allows for some alfresco drinking. ⚫❀◑P

Queen's Hotel

143 Queen's Road, PO12 1LG
11.30-2.30 (not Mon-Thu), 5-11; 11.30-11 Sat; 12-3, 7-10.30 Sun
☎ (023) 9258 2645
Ringwood Fortyniner; Rooster's Yankee; Young's Bitter; guest beers Ⓗ
Back-street local, a winner of many CAMRA awards, that draws regular visitors from all over the country. Up to three guest beers are provided by Beer Seller. The focal point of the bar is an old open fireplace with a carved wood surround. Bar snacks are served on Friday lunchtime. The beer festival is an established event in October. An upstairs function room is available. Real cider is served in summer, while dark beers often appear in winter.
⚫♣●

Greatham

Greatham Inn

Petersfield Road, GU33 6AD
12-3, 6-11; 12-11 Sat; 12-10.30 Sun
☎ (01420) 538016
Courage Directors; guest beers Ⓗ
Previously the Queen, this pub was closed for two years and its future looked doubtful, but renamed and refurbished it re-opened in May 2004 and is busy once more, serving three cask ales, with guests from local breweries such as Hogs Back, Triple fff or Itchen Valley. A wide range of food is served (all day at weekends). The original pub is a no-smoking/dining area; the larger area at the back was once a barn.
⚫Q❀◑♿P

Greywell

Fox & Goose

The Street, RG29 1BY (1 mile S of M3 jct 5)
11-11; 12-10.30 Sun
☎ (01256) 702062
Courage Best Bitter; Wychwood Hobgoblin; Young's Bitter; guest beers Ⓗ
Popular, 16th-century pub set in a charming village, with a large field behind used for camping and village events. The area is good for walking and Basingstoke Canal is nearby. Child-friendly, customers with well-behaved dogs are also welcome in the pub and garden. Games are provided along with local newspapers. Good

home-cooked food often features local game in season. Meals are served all day Sunday. ⛫❀◑⛺♣P

Hambledon

Bat & Ball

Hyden Farm Lane, PO8 0UB (2½ miles from village on Clanfield road)) OS677167
✪ 11.30-3 (12-3.30 Sat), 6-11; 12-4, 7-10.30 Sun
☎ (023) 9263 2692
Gale's Butser, Best, HSB 🄷
Despite its remote setting, high on Broadhalfpenny Down, this is one of the most famous pubs in the country: as every cricket fan will know, this is the cradle of the great game. The bar also serves as a museum, displaying photographs and artefacts, including lyrics written by Richard Stilgoe to commemorate the visit of the late Brian Johnston. Another notable feature is the parish boundary marked on the floor, most important in the days when licensing hours were not uniform. ⛫❀◑♿♣P

Vine

West Street, PO7 4RW
✪ 11.30-3.30, 6-11; 12-4, 7-10.30 Sun
☎ (023) 9263 2419
Ballard's Trotton; Ringwood Best Bitter; guest beers 🄷
Comfortable, 16th-century pub that has been opened up inside to give a single bar serving several distinct drinking areas. It boasts exposed beams, old fireplaces and a glass-covered well. The walls are heavy with bric-à-brac, mainly relating to rural life. Its relaxed atmosphere attracts mainly local customers. A shove-ha'penny board is fixed to one wall. No meals are served Sunday evening. Addlestones cloudy cider is stocked. ⛫Q❀◑●⚟

Hartley Wintney

Waggon & Horses

High Street, RG27 8NY
✪ 11-11; 12-10.30 Sun
☎ (01252) 842119
Courage Best Bitter; Gale's HSB; guest beers 🄷
True village pub where the lively public bar contrasts with a quieter lounge. Although packed on weekend evenings, it is still a great place to drink after browsing the many antique shops in the village. A winner of many local CAMRA awards, it is as welcoming to first-timers as it is to all the regulars. At the rear of the pub is a pleasant courtyard garden. No food is served Sunday. ⛫❀◐⊟♣

Havant

Old House at Home ✔

2 South Street, PO9 1DA
✪ 11-11; 12-10.30 Sun
☎ (023) 9248 3464
Gale's Butser, Best, HSB, seasonal beers; guest beers 🄷
This is one of the oldest buildings in town, although the 1339 date on the outside is early by some 200 years. It was built using beams recovered from the Spanish Armada and was one of the few buildings to survive the 1760 fire. It is reputed to have shown the last dancing bear in England. Originally cottages, the building was converted into a bakery, then a comfortable pub that luckily retains two bars and a splendid hidden garden. ⛫❀◐⊟⇛♣

Robin Hood

6 Homewell, PO9 1GE
✪ 11-11; 12-10.30 Sun
☎ (023) 9298 2779
Gale's Butser, HSB, seasonal beers; 🄶 **guest beers** 🄷
Originally this could have been described as a 'pub in your lounge' as it was so small. It has now been considerably enlarged, but has not lost its character. All the regular beers are served direct from the cask, with a lone handpump supplying the guest beer. Havant was once a centre for parchment making; water drawn from a nearby underground stream was used in making the parchment for both the Magna Carta and the Treaty of Versailles. ⛫❀◐⇛

Hill Head

Crofton

48 Crofton Lane, PO14 3QF
✪ 11-11; 12-10.30 Sun
☎ (01329) 314222
Caledonian Deuchars IPA; Greene King Old Speckled Hen; 🄷 **guest beers** 🄶/🄷
Modern estate pub in a housing area that once used to be strawberry fields. The guest beers are from Punch Taverns (Innspired) and Oakleaf Hole Hearted has appeared regularly. Normally two guest beers are on handpump and one or two more on gravity at weekends. It comprises a public bar, a large, no-smoking lounge area, a function room and a skittle alley that gets booked up well in advance. Food is served all day at weekends. ❀◑⊟♣P⚟

Horndean

Brewers Arms

1 Five Heads Road, PO8 9NW
✪ 12-2 (not Mon; 12-4 Sat); 5 (6 Sat)-11; 12-3, 7-10.30 Sun
☎ (023) 9259 1325
Courage Directors; Fuller's London Pride; Ringwood Best Bitter; guest beers 🄷
Pre-war, half-brick tiled pub, set back off the main Portsmouth road. it is referred to by regulars as 'a proper pub' – a genuine local where people come to drink and talk. See plans in the lounge of the previous 1929 layout, prior to internal alterations carried out by previous owners, Gale's, in the early 1970s. Three regular beers are stocked and two guests are added each Friday evening, generally from small breweries. This is a dog-friendly pub. Q❀⊟♣P

Horsebridge

John O' Gaunt

SO20 6PU (½ mile W of A3057) OS346304
✪ 11-3, 6-11; 11-11 Sat; 12-10.30 Sun
☎ (01794) 388394
Palmer IPA; Ringwood Best Bitter, Fortyniner; guest beer (summer) 🄷
Victorian building, that stood by the scenic LSWR branch line to Andover (now the Test Way footpath). Definitely a pub, not a restaurant, but it offers an extensive, frequently changed menu

of home-cooked meals, often using local produce including game (no food Sun eve or Mon). Set near the idyllic (and expensive) Test trout stream and some game-rearing estates, the pub is often busy with devotees of country pursuits, mingling with the loyal regulars. The bar can supply trout flies. ♨Q❀◑▶P

Kingsclere

Swan Hotel

Swan Street, RG20 5PP

⏲ 11-3, 5.30-11; 12-3, 7-10.30 Sun

☎ (01635) 298314 website: www.swankingsclere.co.uk

Hampshire King Alfred's; Young's Bitter; guest beers Ⓗ

Traditional bar, frequented by an eclectic mix of customers, serving four handpumped beers. One of the country's oldest coaching inns dating from 1449, retaining many original oak beams and fireplaces, it is a Grade II listed building. Owned by Winchester College for 300 years, it has been a pub since 1600. As befits a true inn, food is served in the bar or dining room, and there are nine en-suite bedrooms. ♨Q❀🛏◑▶♿♣P

Langstone

Ship Inn ✔

Langstone Road, PO9 1RD

⏲ 11-11; 12-10.30 Sun

☎ (023) 9247 1719

Gale's Butser, Best, HSB, seasonal beers; guest beers Ⓗ

Situated at the crossings to Hayling Island, this pub offers views of the harbour and is an ideal starting (or finishing) point for walks along the shore, or into Havant via the track of the much-missed railway to the island. The remains of the railway bridge can still be seen and more intrepid explorers may find traces of the Roman Wade Way to Hayling and the berth of the train ferry to the Isle of Wight (last in service in 1888). ♨❀◑▶♿⛺P⚟

Lasham

Royal Oak ✔

GU34 5SJ

⏲ 12-11; 12-10.30 Sun

☎ (01256) 381213 website: www.royaloak.uk.com

Hogs Back TEA; Triple fff Alton's Pride, Moondance; guest beers Ⓗ

The Royal Oak is a 200-year-old free house with two bars. It is situated in the centre of a quiet village next to Lasham Airfield, well known for its gliding club. Quality fresh food is served daily lunchtime and evening, and all day on Sunday. A large car park, beautiful garden and picturesque surroundings make this pub popular with ramblers and cyclists. Triple fff's Moondance alternates with a Hogs Back TEA. ♨Q❀◑▶⊟♣P

Little London

Plough Inn

Silchester Road, RG26 5EP (1 mile off A340, S of Tadley)

⏲ 12-2.30, 5.30-11; 6-11 Sat; 12-3, 7-10.30 Sun

☎ (01256) 850628

Ringwood Best Bitter, seasonal beers; Ⓗ **guest beers** Ⓖ

Wonderful, popular village pub, with an informal atmosphere. This is a sympathetically restored cottage where in winter you can enjoy a glass of porter in front of a cheery log fire. A good range of baguettes is usually available (not Sun eve). Musicians perform popular songs monthly (second Tue). A lovely secluded garden at the side of the pub is an added attraction. The location is ideal for ramblers visiting the Roman ruins at nearby Silchester or Pamber Wood. ♨Q❀♣P

Locks Heath

Sir Joseph Paxton

272 Hunts Pond Road, PO14 4PF

⏲ 12-11; 12-10.30 Sun

☎ (01489) 572125

Caledonian Deuchars IPA; Fuller's London Pride; guest beer Ⓗ

The area in which this pub is located is famous for its strawberries. The pub is in fact named after Sir Joseph Paxton who developed a variety of strawberry. A small display detailing Paxton's life can be seen near the entrance. The pub was sympathetically extended a couple of years ago in keeping with its character. No food is served Sunday evening or Monday lunchtime. ♨❀◑▶P

Longstock

Peat Shade

SO20 6DR (1 mile N of Stockbridge)

⏲ 11.30-3, 6.30-11; closed Mon; 12-3 (closed eve) Sun

☎ (01264) 810612

Beer range varies Ⓗ

The emphasis here is on dining, featuring organic vegetables and local meat, but there is a welcome for beer drinkers. The regularly changing beer selection comes from Hampshire, Hop Back, Ringwood and Archers; the cider is Thatchers. The pub is handy for walkers on the Test Way and visitors to Danebury Ring. There is a no-smoking room. Note the pub is closed Sunday evening and Monday. ♨Q❀◑▶♿●⚟

Long Sutton

Four Horseshoes ✔

The Street, RG29 1TA (1 mile E of village) OS748471

⏲ 12-2.30, 6.30-11; 12-3, 7-10.30 Sun

☎ (01256) 862488

Beer range varies Ⓗ

CAMRA's local Pub of the Year 2004, this exemplary single bar pub offers good food (not Sun eve) and friendly conversation. Cyclists and car clubs regularly meet here. The changing beer range often features Fuller's London Pride, Gale's and a mild. The conservatory welcomes children, who also appreciate the extensive garden with climbing frame and petanque terrain. The landlord's claim to fame was completing the 1987 London marathon in 2 hours 35 minutes. Ramps assist wheelchair users. ♨Q⚇❀🛏◑▶⛺P

Milford on Sea

Red Lion ✔

32 High Street, SO41 0QD

⏲ 11.30-2.30, 6-11; 12-3, 7-10.30 (not winter eve) Sun

☎ (01590) 642236

website: www.redlionmilford.co.uk
Fuller's London Pride; Ringwood Best Bitter, seasonal beers Ⓗ
Friendly, comfortable, 18th-century village pub with a relaxed atmosphere, notable for its feature fireplace and photographs of submarines on the walls. The no-smoking dining area can be used by drinkers after the diners finish. A central ramp enables wheelchair access. Pool and darts are played and occasional bands perform. The large, lawned garden is away from traffic. Real cider is sold in summer. Accommodation is in two double and one twin room.
❀⇌◐◑♿⛺♣●P⊁

Old Basing

Crown
The Street, RG24 7BW
11-3, 5.30-11; 11-11 Sat; 12-10.30 Sun
☎ (01256) 321424
Fuller's London Pride; guest beers Ⓗ
In an attractive village, the pub sits alongside the remains of Old Basing House. Cromwell's troops are said to have attacked the house over the wall at the rear of the pub. Many of the picturesque dwellings around the pub were built using bricks from the ruins. The pub has two main bars, one no-smoking, and a cosy snug. Two changing guest beers are normally chosen from independent breweries. On Sunday food is served until 6pm.
♨❀◐◑P⊁

Overton

Greyhound
46 Winchester Street, RG25 3HS
11-1.30, 4.30-11; 11-2, 6-11 Sat; 12-2, 7-10.30 Sun
☎ (01256) 770241
Caledonian Deuchars IPA; Greene King IPA, Abbot; Wadworth 6X Ⓗ
A few hundred yards from the village centre and shops, this popular single-bar pub offers a genuine welcome to locals and visiors alike. With a pool table and dartboards, the pub supports enthusiastic teams in district darts, pool, cribbage and quiz leagues. In winter months a blazing log fire compensates for the somewhat chilly walk across the rear courtyard to the outside loos.
♨❀♣

Pennington (Lymington)

Musketeer
26 North Street, SO41 8FZ (off A337, at White Hart roundabout)
11.30-3, 5.30-11; 11-11 Fri & Sat; 12-10.30 Sun
☎ (01590) 676527
Courage Best Bitter; Ringwood Best Bitter, Fortyniner; guest beers Ⓗ
This pub underwent extensive internal building work in 2005, resulting in a spacious rectangular bar with plenty of tables for drinkers and diners. The menu (served Mon-Sat) offers freshly-prepared meals; evening meals are promised. Wheelchair users can now enjoy full access including a designated WC. Despite the changes, the Musketeer remains a community local, hosting a quiz (Tue), fortnightly meat draws (Sun) and supporting a darts team. Pennington is on bus routes 117, 119 and 121 from Lymington. ♨◐♣P

Petersfield

Folly Wine & Ale House
10-12 College Street, GU31 4AD
10-11; 12-10.30 Sun
☎ (01730) 264816
Young's Bitter; guest beer Ⓗ
French-style, bistro bar in part of the Folly Market, just off the high street. It opens at 9am for coffee and bacon sandwiches. The guest beer is from the Cheriton Brewhouse and changes regularly. Apart from the upstairs restaurant, cakes and muffins are available in the bar and are freshly cooked all day. It offers an extensive wine list, including off-sales. Fortnightly on Monday, the comedy club presents national and international acts.
❀♿⇌⊁

Good Intent ✔
40-46 College Street, GU31 4AF (near Old London Rd/Station Rd jct)
11-3, 5.30-11; 12-3, 7-10.30 Sun
☎ (01730) 263838 website: www.stuartinns.com
Gale's Butser, Best, HSB, seasonal beers Ⓗ
Just off the town centre, this 16th-century, beamed pub is known as the 'country pub in the town'. The single bar serves a split-level room with candlelit tables. Hop vines hang from the beams and two log fires set the scene. Further rooms leading off the main room include the restaurant. The pub has won awards for its food, including fresh fish (weekends), and is well known for its sausages. Live music is performed Sunday evening. ♨Q❀◐◑⇌⊁

Portsmouth

Fifth Hampshire Volunteer Arms ✔
74 Albert Road, Southsea, PO5 2SL
12-11; 12-10.30 Sun
☎ (023) 9282 7161
Gale's Best, HSB, Festival Mild, seasonal beers; guest beers Ⓗ
As the pub where the local CAMRA branch was founded, it is good to report that the Fifth Hants has managed to retain its separate lounge bar in what is essentially a local. The relaxing lounge complements the more lively public bar, with its sports TV and juke box. The public bar continues to expand its decorative display of tin hats.
Q⊟♣

Florence Arms
18-20 Florence Road, Southsea, PO5 2NE (near Pyramid Centre)
12-11; 12-10.30 Sun
☎ (023) 9287 5700
Adnams Broadside; Young's Bitter, Special; guest beers Ⓗ
Although basically a street-corner pub, near shops, the seafront and Southsea Gardens, this pub is more than merely traditional. Maroon glazed tiled and etched windows characterise the exterior; inside are three quite distinct bars. One houses a pool table and a TV; another serves as a comfortable, quiet lounge, while the third (and largest) doubles as a restaurant and

function room. Beers unusual to the area are featured. No meals are served Saturday or Sunday evening. Q◖⊞♿●⚟

Hole in the Wall

36 Great Southsea Street, PO5 3BY

12-2 (not Mon-Thu), 4-11; 12-11 Sat; 12-10.30 Sun

(023) 9229 8085

Oakleaf Nuptu'ale, Hole Hearted; guest beers ⊞

Small pub but well laid out on two levels; the lounge bar is basically a large table with seats around it. This is a quiet local for those who appreciate good beer; for a change a small selection of bottled Belgian beers is available. The cider varies. The Thursday night quiz can be busy. The dog has moved on with the previous tenants. Evening meals are served 5-8pm, except Sunday when lunch continues until 5pm. Q◖◗⊞⇌♣●⚟

Old House at Home ✔

104 Locksway Road, Milton, PO4 8JR

11-11; 12-10.30 Sun

(023) 9273 2606

Adnams Broadside; Fuller's London Pride; Gale's HSB; Taylor Landlord; guest beer (occasional) ⊞

Thriving, two-bar community local. The lounge bar is a real step back in time; at weekends it doubles as a restaurant. The pub stocks four regular beers and the occasional guest. This is the pub's first inclusion in this Guide, and it is well merited. ♨❀◖◗⊞♣P

Sallyport Hotel

57-58 High Street, Old Portsmouth, PO1 2LU

12-11; 12-10.30 Sun

(023) 9282 1860

Draught Bass; Fuller's London Pride; Gale's HSB; Young's Special; guest beer ⊞

Situated at the south-western end of Old Portsmouth's historic High Street, this hotel is overlooked by the cathedral church of St. Thomas. A collection of chamber pots decorates the bar, along with paintings and lithographic engravings of local scenes. It makes an ideal base for exploring the nearby Gunwharf Quays and historic dockyard of Portsmouth's maritime England. Parking is difficult, except for residents. ⇆◖◗⚟

Sir Loin of Beef

152 Highland Road, Southsea, PO4 9NH

11-11; 12-10.30 Sun

(023) 9282 0115

Hop Back GFB, Summer Lightning; guest beers ⊞

True free house with a café-style feel. The walls are adorned with naval paraphernalia while a klaxon behind the bar is used to call time. The beer selection is mainly taken from southern independent breweries, with some unusual guest beers, including seasonal brews when available. The pub is not far from Eastney which has a caravan park, pumping station and the Royal Marines Museum on the seafront. ⛺♣●

Still & West ✔

2 Bath Square, Old Portsmouth, PO1 2JL

10-11; 12-10.30 Sun

(023) 9282 1567

Gale's Butser, Best, HSB, seasonal beer or guest beer ⊞

One of the oldest pubs in the old part of the city, this house benefits from stunning views across the harbour and its environs. The spacious downstairs bar bears interesting ceilings and an eclectic display of maritime memorabilia, as would be expected in the heart of maritime England. ⛴❀◖◗♿♣⚟

Priors Dean

White Horse (Pub with no name) ✔

GU32 1DA (signed from Petersfield-Alton road, 2nd lane from main road, 400 yds) OS714290

12-3, 6-11; 12-11 Sat; 12-10.30 Sun

(01420) 588387 website: www.stuartinns.com

Gale's Butser, HSB; Ringwood Fortyniner; guest beers ⊞

Well known old pub in the middle of a field. A bit easier to find compared to yesteryear, although there is still no pub sign; it is well worth seeking out. The two small bars have exposed beams and tiled floors, the restaurant is through the left-hand room. Eight beers come from Gale's (who supply the two house ales) and Ringwood. ♨Q❀◖⊞P

Romsey

Abbey Hotel ✔

11 Church Street, SO51 8BT

11-3, 6-11; 12-3, 7-10.30 Sun

(01794) 513360 website: www.abbeyhotelromsey.co.uk

Courage Best Bitter, Directors; Young's Bitter ⊞

Handsome pub, opposite Romsey Abbey, built in the late 19th century to replace an earlier establishment that fell victim to road widening. It passed from Fuller's to Strong's before acquisition by Courage (note the lintel above the entrance) in 1905. The interior is divided into two: one part is no-smoking during food service (no meals Sun eve), but both are peaceful havens for conversation. The splendid floral displays are a joy to behold and have deservedly won awards. ♨Q❀⇆◖◗⇌P⚟

Old House at Home

62 Love Lane, SO51 8DE (next to Waitrose car park)

11-3, 5 (6 Sat)-11; 12-4, 7-10.30 Sun

(01794) 513175

Gale's Butser, Best, HSB, seasonal beers ⊞

Romsey's only thatched pub is a welcoming, well-managed establishment. The three discrete areas, two of which are reserved for non-smokers, offer comfortable settings in which to enjoy good quality English food that makes much use of locally-sourced ingredients. Those who prefer to take their pleasures alfresco may do so on the large, secluded and heated patio. Sunday is quiz night. ❀◖◗⇌♣P⚟

Star Inn

13 Horsefair, SO51 8EZ

12-2.30, 5-11; 12-11 Sat; 12-3, 7-10.30 Sun

(01794) 516353

Wadworth IPA, 6X, JCB, seasonal beers ⊞

Located just north of the town centre, outside the old Strongs Brewery gates, the pub was once the brewery tap, although it started life in the 17th century as a weaver's house. A broad single bar has a dartboard at one end and an inglenook with easy chairs at the other. Evening entertainment includes varied live music (Sat), folk sessions (Wed) and a Sunday quiz. Reasonably-priced food is available Wednesday-Sunday lunchtimes, and Wednesday-Friday early evening. ⌂❀⇌◑⇌♣

St Mary Bourne

Coronation Arms ✔

SP11 6AR (on B3048, NW side of village)

11-30-2.30 (not Mon), 6.30-11; 12-3, 7-10.30 Sun

☎ (01264) 738432

Fuller's London Pride; guest beers Ⓗ

Comfortable free house on the edge of a small Hampshire village close to some of the county's famous watercress beds. Look out, too for the picturesque dovecot located near the narrow bridge at the village centre. The roomy bar features a log fire. Two further rooms serve mainly as dining areas, where families with children are welcome. Good quality home-cooked food is served at all sessions (except Sun eve and Mon). ⌂❀◑♣P⊭

Selborne

Selborne Arms ✔

High Street, GU34 3JR

11-3, 6 (5.30 Fri)-11 (11-11 summer Sat); 12-10.30 Sun

☎ (01420) 511247

Cheriton Pots Ale; Courage Best Bitter; Ringwood Fortyniner; guest beers Ⓗ

Traditional village pub retaining log fires and other original features in a building that dates back to the 1600s. It is located at the bottom of Selborne Hanger and the famous zigzag path carved by naturalist Gilbert White. The guest beers in this free house showcase local micro-breweries' products, while the award-winning menus also feature local produce. The extensive, grassed garden is popular in summer; it boasts a children's play area and a fantastic barbecue.

⌂Q❀◑⊞P

Shalden

Golden Pot ✔

Odiham Road, GU34 4DJ (on B3349, 1 mile N of village)

12-11; 12-10.30 Sun

☎ (01420) 80655

Greene King IPA, Ruddles County, Abbot, Old Speckled Hen; guest beer Ⓗ

This pub continues to demonstrate how Greene King beer should taste. The pub name is derived from the local area, its origin the subject of whimsical theories. Several ghosts reputedly haunt the premises, including two Polish airmen who crashed in the garden during WWII. The food, enjoyed in the light, airy, L-shaped dining area, has acquired an excellent reputation; the menu changes daily – try the fish. It hosts monthly folk evenings (second Tue). ⌂❀◑♣P

Shedfield

Wheatsheaf Inn

Botley Road, SO32 2JG

12-11; 12-10.30 Sun

☎ (01329) 833024

Cheriton Pots Ale, Diggers Gold; Oakleaf Farmhouse Ale; Ringwood Best Bitter, seasonal beers; guest beers Ⓖ

Lively, friendly pub with a comfortable public and small lounge bar. Beer is served straight from casks mounted on an impressive stillage behind the bar. Beers are sourced from Hampshire breweries and from Hobson's in Worcestershire. A beer festival is held annually over the late spring bank holiday. Dogs on leads are admitted. Children are welcome at lunchtime. The car park is across a busy main road. Blues/jazz is staged Saturday evening. All food is home made. Q❀◑♣P

Sheet

Queen's Head

Sheet Green, GU32 2AH

11-2.30, 5.30 (6 Sat)-11; 12-3, 7-10.30 Sun

☎ (01730) 264204

Brakspear Bitter; Fuller's London Pride; Hampshire Strong's Best Bitter; guest beer Ⓗ

Typical local, in a pleasant setting, next to the village green. The public bar is 400 years old, with a stone floor, exposed beams and a log fire. The lounge was added later (the front part was once the village butcher's). The restaurant, open Tuesday–Saturday evenings, has an Italian chef who serves up traditional dishes from his country. Bar snacks are available at lunchtime. The pub has been in the same family since 1959.

⌂Q❀◑⊞P

Silchester

Calleva Arms

Little London Road, RG7 2PH

(2 miles E of A340 at Tadley)

11-3, 5.30-11; 11-11 Sat; 12-10.30 Sun

☎ (0118) 970 0305

Gale's Butser, Best, HSB, seasonal beers; guest beers Ⓗ

Adjacent to the village green, the pub is popular with cyclists and walkers. It also attracts visitors to the Iron Age and Roman settlement of Calleva Atrebatum, which has some of the finest examples of Roman walls; do not miss the amphitheatre. Parts of the pub date back to the 18th century. A pleasant conservatory caters for non-smokers wanting a quiet drink (no music here). A large garden and good food are added attractions.

⌂Q❀◑♣P

Southampton

Bevois Castle

63 Onslow Road, SO14 0JL

11-11; 12-10.30 Sun

☎ (023) 8033 0350

Beer range varies Ⓗ

Cosy pub that manages to create a variety of moods in a relatively small space. There is a comfortable lounge, a games area and a bar with room – and stools – for drinkers. The immaculate courtyard garden allows for secluded outdoor drinking. Food, particularly the traditional breakfast and new brunch option, is competitively priced and popular. On the bar, local (Hampshire and Itchen Valley) beers compete with more travelled brews. For a change, check the range of brandies.

⌂❀◑♣P⊡

Bitter Virtue (off licence)

70 Cambridge Road, SO14 6US (take Alma Rd from The Avenue, by church, 250 yds)

⏲ 10.30-8.30 (not Mon); 10.30-2 Sun

☎ (023) 8055 4881 website: www.bittervirtue.co.uk

Beer range varies Ⓖ

The 2005 drinks retailing awards ceremony featured Bitter Virtue as one of the top three independent beer retailers in the country, recognising its ever-expanding bottled beer range. It stocks beers from the UK, Belgium, Germany, USA, Australia and now France. Draught beer is also available from local (and not so local) breweries such as Cheriton, Taylor and Robinson's. Many of the beers can be served in the appropriate vessel, all sold at reasonable prices.

Crown

9 Highcrown Street, SO17 1QE (off Highfield Lane)

⏲ 11-11; 12-10.30 Sun

☎ (023) 8031 5033

Draught Bass; Flowers Original; Fuller's London Pride; Hampshire Strong's Best Bitter; Ringwood Best Bitter Ⓗ

Imposing, brick-built pub, long converted from its original multi-bars to a single, welcoming space, with an impressive (possibly original) bar. Close to the university, food is popular and reservations are sensible at weekends. Children are welcome in the heated and covered patio area; dogs on leads are allowed in the pub.
❀◐◑P

Dolphin ✔

30 Osborne Road South, St Denys, SO17 2EZ (by footbridge from St. Denys Station)

⏲ 12-11; 12-10.30 Sun

☎ (023) 8039 9369

Adnams Broadside; Cheriton Pots Ale; Fuller's London Pride; Gale's HSB; Ringwood Best Bitter; guest beers Ⓗ

Large, single-bar pub by the station, formerly owned by the old Coopers Brewery. The interior features comfortable corners and nautical prints; the cellar door in the middle of the floor shows the original bar position. A varied clientele enjoys the changing guest beer selection, which usually includes Wychwood and Taylor Landlord. Live music is performed at least twice weekly. The landlady's imaginative menu is served daily. Pleasant summer drinking can be enjoyed in the undulating garden. ⛫❀◐◑⇌(St Denys) P⊬

Duke of Wellington ✔

36 Bugle Street, SO14 2AH (off A33, Town Quay Road)

⏲ 11-11; 12-10.30 Sun

☎ (023) 8033 9222

Ringwood Best Bitter; Wadworth IPA, 6X, seasonal beers; guest beers Ⓗ

Probably Southampton's oldest pub, with parts dating back to the 13th century, located a short walk from the docks, Town Quay and Bargate. An extensive menu of home-cooked food is served lunchtime and evening (except Sun eve). Six handpumps serve four regular and two guest ales. A room is available for private functions. A terrace by the pavement allows for some outdoor drinking. Wheelchair access is via the back door.
⛫☕❀◐◑⊟♿⊬

Guide Dog ✔

38 Earl's Road, Bevois Valley, SO14 6SF (100 yds W of Bevois Valley road)

⏲ 3 (12 Sat)-11; 12-10.30 Sun

☎ (023) 8022 5642

Beer range varies Ⓗ

Like many small, back-street Victorian pubs, the 'Valley' closed in 1981, but happily reopened as a genuine free house in 1983. The new name is in honour of a previous landlady who raised £14,000 for the charity. The single bar has five handpumps offering a changing choice of beers plus a good selection of bottled beers. A superb place for a drink before or after a Saints match at St. Mary's Stadium, food is served on match days. ♣

Park Inn ✔

37 Carlisle Road, Shirley, SO16 4FN (off Romsey Rd)

⏲ 11.30-3, 5-11; 11.30-11 Thu-Sat; 12-10.30 Sun

☎ (023) 8078 7835

Wadworth IPA, 6X, JCB, seasonal beers; guest beers Ⓗ

Compact, neat, unpretentious pub that attracts a cosmopolitan clientele and supports two darts teams and a football side. The single bar is split into distinct lounge and public areas. Dating from the 1860s, it has been owned by Barlow's Victoria, Brickwoods and Whitbread breweries before being purchased by Wadworth in the 1980s. On Sunday try your luck at the lunchtime meat draw or evening quiz. Sandwiches are available at lunchtimes. The forecourt has tables for summer drinking.
Q❀♣

Platform Tavern

Town Quay, SO14 2NY

⏲ 12-11; 12-10.30 Sun

☎ (023) 8033 7232 website: www.platformtavern.com

Fuller's London Pride; Itchen Valley Godfathers; guest beers Ⓗ

This pub, built in 1872 incorporates parts of the 14th-century city walls and is close to the Isle of Wight ferry terminal. The single, stone-flagged bar has a carpeted section with a leather sofa and chairs. Pub ornaments bear an African theme and candlelight adds to the ambience. Sunday roast lunches are served (12-5pm) accompanied by live jazz during the afternoon. Live blues features on Tuesday and Thursday evenings. ◐◑

Richmond Inn ✔

108 Portswood Road, Portswood, SO17 2FW

⏲ 11-11; 12-10.30 Sun

☎ (023) 8055 4523

Greene King IPA, Abbot; guest beer Ⓗ

Dating from the 1870s, it was once owned by the Winchester Brewery, later Marston's and now Greene King. It comprises two quite distinct bars: a public with darts, TV and a juke box, and a quiet, comfortable lounge. Many pictures of the great liners associated with Southampton are displayed. A pleasant, well-maintained garden houses a function room that is used by local groups, including CAMRA. The helpful staff happpily remove sparklers on request.
❀⊟⇌(St Denys) ♣

South Western Arms

38-40 Adelaide Road, St Denys, SO17 2HW (next to St Denys Station)

3.30 (1.30 Fri; 12 Sat)-11; 12-10.30 Sun

(023) 8032 4542 website: www.southwesternarms.com

Caledonian Deuchars IPA; Fuller's London Pride; Hop Back Summer Lightning; Ringwood Best Bitter; guest beers H

Not to be missed – a thriving ale house on two floors, mainly wood-panelled with interesting features. Local CAMRA Pub of the Year three years running and a national finalist in 2003, it stocks a consistently impressive selection of at least six guest ales from all over the UK. Occasional beer festivals enhance the choice; the cider varies. Food is limited to snacks, with summer barbecues in the garden. The upstairs area houses pool, table football and a TV. (St Denys) P

Stile

163 University Road, Highfield, SO17 1TS (at Burgess Rd, A35 jct)

11 (12 Sat)-11; 12-10.30 Sun

(023) 8058 1124 website: www.thestile.com

Young's Bitter; Theakston Old Peculier; guest beers H

Great pub with a lovely atmosphere and friendly staff. Located at the edge of the university campus, it is popular with both students and locals. The pub normally serves six real ales, but the range is sometimes reduced to maintain quality during university holidays. The landlord takes pride in his ales and holds a beer festival annually on the early May bank holiday weekend. Guest beers may be seasonal brews. Games such as chess and backgammon may be played.

Waterloo Arms

101 Waterloo Road, Freemantle, SO15 3BS

12-11; 12-10.30 Sun

(023) 8022 0022

Hop Back GFB, Best Bitter, Crop Circle, Entire Stout, Summer Lightning, seasonal beers; guest beers H

True real ale pub, attracting locals and, thanks to its proximity to Southampton and Millbrook stations, travellers from afar. The L-shaped main bar can get busy. The spacious conservatory-styled back room is no-smoking and allows children until 9pm, although it is also used for private meetings and parties. Biannual real ale festivals in the secluded garden may be threatened by new licensing regulations. The pub is on a residential road and bus route; parking is restricted. (Millbrook)

Wellington Arms

56 Park Road, Freemantle, SO15 3DE (Mansion Rd jct)

12-11; 12-10.30 Sun

(023) 8022 7356

Adnams Bitter; Fuller's London Pride; Greene King Abbot, Old Speckled Hen; Ringwood Best Bitter; guest beers H

Dating from the 1860s, it was called the Swan Inn until 1975. Owned by Barlow's Victoria Brewery in the early 20th century, later by Brickwoods and Whitbread, it is now a Punch Group house. The pub is a treasure trove of Iron Duke memorabilia; also note the many old coins set into the bar counter. There are two bars, with a designated no-smoking area and a garden/patio area.

(Central/Millbrook)

Stockbridge

Three Cups

High Street, SO20 6HB

12-11; 12-10.30 Sun

(01264) 810414 website: www.the3cups.co.uk

Fuller's London Pride; Ringwood Best Bitter; guest beer H

This 15th-century coaching inn, boasting low black beams and pillars, is in an attractive village with the River Test flowing through it. The pub has a dining room and a no-smoking area. The guest beer is normally from a small brewery and around 4.5-5% ABV. The Three Cups is noted for its interesting food, served daily. The large garden is an added attraction. Q P

Stubbington

Golden Bowler

122 Stubbington Lane, PO14 2NQ

11-11; 12-10.30 Sun

(01329) 662845

Draught Bass; guest beers H

1960s free house, originally a Victorian country property attached to a nursery, and under the same ownership for 25 years. Three guest beers mostly come from small, independent breweries, with occasional dark beers in the winter. The main bar is divided in two, with a separate restaurant and TV/function room. Families are welcome in some areas before 8pm. Live music is performed occasionally on Saturday evening. No food is served on Monday evening. P

Tadley

Bishopswood Golf Club

Bishopswood Lane, RG26 4AT (6 miles N of Basingstoke, off A340) OS591617

11-11 (9.30 Mon; winter hours vary); 12-7 Sun

(0118) 981 2200

Beer range varies H

A golf club is not generally a place to find any, not to mention good quality, real ale, but this is an exception and also offers a warm, friendly atmosphere. There is a public bar and a comfortable lounge (dress code applies), with an unusual central fireplace. Snooker is played. Outside, a pleasant raised terrace overlooks the course. Visitors are welcome to local CAMRA's Club of the Year 2004 and 2005. Guest beers are often from Brains, Gale's and West Berkshire. P

Titchfield

Wheatsheaf

East Street, PO14 4AD

12-3, 5 (6 Sat)-11; 12-11 Fri; 12-3, 7-10.30 Sun

(01329) 842965

Fuller's London Pride; guest beers H

Near the centre of the picturesque village, this three-roomed, 17th-century, cosy pub is usually full of village folk enjoying the roaring fire and the ales (three of which are guests). The pub is

blessed with a public bar, a tiny snug and a dining area that was added a few years ago. Meals are served Wednesday-Saturday. There is a large seating space outside; the car park is down the narrow street next to the pub.
⌂❀◑◐⊟P

Upper Farringdon

Rose & Crown Inn

Crows Lane, GU34 3ED (off A32)
⌚ 12-3, 6-11; 12-11 Sat; 12-10.30 Sun
☎ (01420) 588231
Adnams Bitter; Courage Best Bitter; Greene King IPA; Triple fff Moondance, Stairway Ⓗ
In a village just off the beaten track, this friendly pub, with an L-shaped bar, progresses from a seating area near a log fire through formal tables to a modern restaurant (no food Mon eve). Families are welcome, there is a large garden and boxed games in the bar. Imaginative food is supplemented by lunchtime bar snacks. Dogs and walkers are always welcome. It stages regular Monday jazz evenings. ⌂Q❀◑◐⊟♣P

Whitchurch

Prince Regent

104 London Road, RG28 7LT (on Basingstoke road)
⌚ 11-11; 12-10.30 Sun
☎ (01256) 892179
Hop Back Summer Lightning; Otter Bitter; Stonehenge Pigswill Ⓗ
Unspoilt town pub catering for a local clientele. The single bar overlooks one of England's smallest towns and is well worth the walk up from the Square. Be prepared for some lively and good-humoured banter. The pub fields crib, quiz and pool teams, and the Ferret Club meets here in the private cellar bar. Buses stop outside for the nearby towns of Winchester, Andover and Basingstoke. ⌂♣P

Red House Inn

21 London Street, RG28 7LH
⌚ 11.30-3, 6-11; 12-3, 7-10.30 Sun
☎ (01256) 895558
Cheriton Pots Ale; guest beers Ⓗ
This 16th-century pub has become renowned for its hospitality and for catering for a wide range of custom. From the award-winning restaurant to the stone-flagged public bar, all are welcome. Local beers are given pride of place in the unpretentious atmosphere. The large garden has an area set aside for young children. If visiting Whitchurch, with its silk mill, trout streams and fine river walks, the Red House makes an excellent stop – before the other seven pubs.
⌂❀◑◐⊟♣P

Whitsbury

Cartwheel

SP6 3PZ (2½ miles W of A338 at Breamore) OS129188
⌚ 11.30-2.30 (3 Sat), 5.30-11; 12-10.30 Sun
☎ (01725) 518362 website: www.cartwheelinn.co.uk
Ringwood Best Bitter; Fortyniner, Old Thumper, seasonal beers Ⓗ
Part 18th-century building in a village known for its racing stables, the Cartwheel was acquired by Ringwood and reopened after refurbishment in 2004. The bar is divided into several sections and there is a no-smoking dining room (children welcome). The Salisbury to Bournemouth/Poole bus serves Breamore every day; take a map and enjoy a walk which may take in Breamore's church, house and mizmaze, and arrive at this cheerful pub. Rockbourne's Roman Villa remains can be seen nearby ⌂🐕❀◑◐♿♣P⚟

Wickham

Greens

The Square, PO17 5JQ
⌚ 11-3, 6-11; closed Mon; 12-3, 6-10.30 Sun
☎ (01329) 833197 website: www.btinternet.com/~a.kingshott/greens/greens.htm
Fuller's London Pride; Young's Special; guest beer Ⓗ
Advertised as a restaurant with a gourmet menu, and pub, the building is about 100 years old. The modern interior is divided into several areas including a function room. The emphasis on food has resulted in real ale being served in oversized glasses (rare in the area), keeping spillage to a minimum. The garden overlooks Wickham water meadows and hosts special events in summer. The guest beer is usually from Beer Seller. A no-smoking policy applies throughout the premises. Q❀◑◐♿⚟🍷

Wickham Wine Bar

The Square, PO17 5JN
⌚ 12-2.30, 6-11; closed Sun
☎ (01329) 832732
website: www.wickham-bar-rest.demon.co.uk
Cheriton Diggers Gold Ⓗ
Grade II listed, 15th-century timber-framed building, a wine bar and restaurant that also sells real ale (no keg). The ground-floor bar boasts original vaulted oak beams and an open log fire. The two-storey upstairs restaurant extends over the shop next door and features an original 16th-century wall painting and an open gallery overlooking the bar. The menu generally offers fresh fish and local game. Live jazz is performed on Wednesday evening. ⌂Q❀◑◐

Winchester

Bell ✔

83 St Cross Road, St Cross, SO23 9RE (on B3335 at edge of the city)
⌚ 11-3, 5-11; 11-11 Fri, Sat & summer; 12-4, 7-10.30 Sun
☎ (01962) 865284
Greene King IPA, Old Speckled Hen; guest beer Ⓗ
Different bars allow a choice of drinking atmosphere in this comfortable pub. A quiet, carpeted, conversational lounge (no-smoking at lunchtime) contrasts with a busy, flag-stoned public bar. The large, safe garden with play equipment is reached via the public bar. The Bell adjoins the Hospital of St Cross, England's oldest (1132) almshouse; it is a tranquil riverside stroll from the city through meadows that inspired Keats' Ode to Autumn. Good food served daily (except Wed eve), includes Sunday roasts.
⌂Q❀◑◐⊟♿♣P⚟

Black Boy ✔

1 Wharf Hill, SO23 9NQ (off B3330, Chesil St)
⌚ 11-3, 5-11; 12-3, 7-10.30 Sun
☎ (01962) 861754

Cheriton Pots Ale; Hop Back Summer Lightning; Ringwood Best Bitter; guest beers 🄷
Centuries old, rambling building where many interconnecting rooms of different styles surround a central bar. A converted barn becomes a restaurant Tuesday–Saturday, another room is a complete farmhouse kitchen with functioning Aga. Decor throws up constant surprises – a lathe on a mantelpiece, a wall of buckets, ceilings of keys, pipes and watches – many visits would be needed to notice everything. Guest beers are from local breweries. No food is served Sunday evening or Monday and Tuesday lunchtimes. ⛰Q❀◐◑♣

Fulflood Arms ✔

28 Cheriton Road, SO22 5EF (W of station, N of prison)
⏲ 12-2 (not Tue), 5-11; 12-11 Fri; 11-11 Sat; 12-10.30 Sun
☎ (01962) 622006
Greene King IPA, Abbot, seasonal beers; guest beer 🄷
Splendid, back-street corner community local, in a quiet residential area. The exterior is enhanced by much glazed brickwork, beautiful etched windows, and signs of its earlier association with the long-defunct Winchester Brewery. It hosts a monthly music quiz or live music, on most Sunday evenings, and a general knowledge quiz on Wednesday. Various darts teams and discussion groups meet here; a bar billiards table is a recent addition. ❀⥴♣⚟

Hyde Tavern ✔

57 Hyde Street, SO23 7DY (on B3047)
⏲ 12-2 (3 Sat), 5 (6 Sat)-11; 12-10.30 Sun
☎ (01962) 862592
Greene King IPA, guest beer 🄷
Classic, small, medieval, timber-framed building, dominated by dormer windows. In a street where ale has been sold for over 700 years, this unspoilt pub is below street level – beware low beams and ceilings, undulating floors and walls. A place for conversation, it is frequented by a mature clientele. The public bar has another cosy bar leading off, which bears a sports theme. A ghost's footsteps are reputedly sometimes heard in the bar. Snacks are normally available. Q❀⊡⥴♣

St James Tavern ✔

3 Romsey Road , SO22 5BE (on B3040, near county hospital)
⏲ 11.30-2.30, 5.30-11; 11.30-11 Sat; 12-3, 6.30-10.30 Sun
☎ (01962) 861288
Butcombe Bitter; Wadworth IPA, 6X, seasonal beers 🄷
Close to the historic Westgate and Castle, this pub lies just outside the city centre. Bare floorboards, light wood panelling and lofty ceilings help create a relaxed atmosphere, with a raised no-smoking extension and plenty of seating at tables. At one end of the L-shaped bar is a TV for sport, together with board games and newspapers. Fun quiz nights are held every Monday. Popular with students and hospital staff, it serves good value food.
❀◐◑⥴♣⚟

Wykeham Arms ✔

75 Kingsgate Street, SO23 9PE (by the Cathedral Close and college gates)
⏲ 11-11; 12-10.30 Sun
☎ (01962) 854411
Gale's Butser, Best, HSB, Festival Mild (summer); **guest beer** 🄷
Rambling, many-roomed Georgian pub by the old city Kingsgate. Deluged in bric-a-brac – it claims to have over 2,000 pewter mugs – old school desks make convenient tabling, Nelsonia abounds and every square inch of wall and ceiling displays some interesting artefact. It can be busy but service is quick and the clientele always civilised. Food (not Sun eve) has earned awards (evening booking is advised) as has the high quality accommodation. Even your crisps will be served in a bowl.
⛰Q❀⛟◐◑♿

Wolverton

George & Dragon

Wolverton Townsend, RG26 5ST (1 mile E of A339, 3½ miles SW of Tadley)
⏲ 12-3, 5.30-11; 12-3, 7-10.30 Sun
☎ (01635) 298292
Brakspear Special; Fuller's London Pride; Wadworth IPA; West Berkshire Mr Chubb's; guest beers 🄷
Oak beams festooned with dried hops, and a huge open fireplace burning logs in winter characterise this 300-year-old inn; altogether a superb setting in which to relish the good selection of beers. Diners sit at candlelit tables to enjoy good home-cooked cuisine in a romantic atmosphere. Outside, the large garden is set in an orchard where children can play. The function room, with bar and skittle alley, caters for parties. ⛰Q❀⛟◐◑♣P

Harrow, Steep

Beer Festival Calendar 2006

The Campaign for Real Ale's beer festivals are magnificent shop windows for cask ale and they give drinkers the opportunity to sample beers from independent brewers rare to particular localities. Beer festivals are enormous fun: many offer good food and live entertainment, and – where possible – facilities for families. Some seasonal festivals specialise in spring, autumn and winter ales. Festivals range in size from small local events to large regional ones. The Campaign holds two national festivals, for winter beers in January, and the Great British in August; the latter features around 500 beers. The festivals listed are those planned for 2006. For up-to-date information, contact the CAMRA website: www.camra.org.uk and click on 'CAMRA Near You'. By joining CAMRA – there's a form at the back of the Guide – you will receive 12 editions of the Campaign's newspaper What's Brewing, which lists every festival on a month-by-month basis. Dates listed are liable to change: check with the website or What's Brewing

JANUARY
Great British Winter Beer Festival, Manchester, 19-21
Atherton Bent Bongs Beer Bash
Burton winter festival
Cambridge winter festival
Chelmsford winter festival
Exeter winter festival
Hitchin winter festival
St Neots winter festival

FEBRUARY
Ashfield winter festival
Battersea
Bishops Auckland
Bradford
Chesterfield
Derby winter festival
Dorchester
Dover winter festival (no beers under 5%)
Fleetwood
Gosport
Hucknall
Liverpool
Richmond & Hounslow
Rotherham
Salisbury
Sussex/Brighton
Tewkesbury
Wear Valley

MARCH
Banbury
Bristol
Darlington spring festival
Ely
Hitchin
Leeds
Leicester
Loughborough
London Drinker
Oldham
South Devon
Wigan
York

APRIL
Bury St Edmunds
Chippenham
Coventry
Dunstable
Farnham
Fife (Glenrothes)
Maldon
Mansfield
Newcastle upon Tyne
Paisley
Walsall

MAY
Alloa
Cambridge
Chester
Colchester
Doncaster
Ealing, West London
Hitchin
Macclesfield
Newark
Reading (May Day Bank Holiday weekend)
Rugby
St Ives, Cornwall
Stockport
Stourbridge
Wolverhampton
Yapton

JUNE
Catford
Colchester
Doncaster
Hereford
Kingston (Surrey)
Northampton
North Devon
Plymouth (also July)
Salisbury
Scottish Traditional Beer Festival, Edinburgh
Stalybridge
Southampton
South Downs (Sussex)
Thurrock
Woodchurch, near Ashford, Kent: Rare Breeds

JULY
Ardingly
Boston
Boxmoor (Hemel Hempstead)
Bromsgrove
Canterbury: all Kent branches
Chelmsford
Cotswold
Derby
Devizes
Eden Valley (Kent)
Fenland
Louth
Much Wenlock
Plymouth
Woodcote Steam Rally

The Great British Beer Festival is CAMRA's flagship event

AUGUST
Great British Beer Festival, London, Earls Court, 1-5
Barnsley
Clacton
Heart of Warwickshire
Harbury
Moorgreen
Peterborough
Moorgreen
Mumbles, Swansea
Worcester

SEPTEMBER
Abergavenny at Food Festival
Ayrshire
Birmingham
Bridgenorth/SVR (also October)
Burton-on-Trent
Chappel (Essex)
Darlington
Hull
Ipswich
Keighley
Letchworth
Maidstone
Melton Mowbray
Norths Notts
Northwich
Portsmouth
St Albans
St Ives, Cambs
Scunthorpe
Sheffield
Shrewsbury
Somerset
Southport
South Devon
Tamworth
Troon
Ulverston
Quorn

OCTOBER
Alloa
Bath
Bedford
Birkenhead/Wirral
Bridgenorth/SVR
Carmarthen
Cardiff Great Welsh & Cider Festival
Croydon
Dunfermline
Eastbourne
Falmouth
Gravesend
Harlow
Huddersfield
Jersey
Middlesbrough
Norwich
Nottingham
Overton
Oxford
Poole
Quorn (Leicestershire)
Redhill
Solihull
Stoke-on-Trent
Swindon
Twickenham
Wakefield
Westmorland/Kendall
Worthing

NOVEMBER
Aberdeen
Accrington
Barnsley winter festival
Belfast
Dudley winter festival
Eastleigh (Hants)
Erewash
Great Welsh Beer & Cider Festival (Cardiff: also December)
Hull
Loughborough
Luton
Medway
Rochford
Watford
Wirral
Woking
Wolverton, near Milton Keynes

DECEMBER
Cockermouth
Great Welsh Beer & Cider Festival (Cardiff)
Harwich
Ipswich winter festival

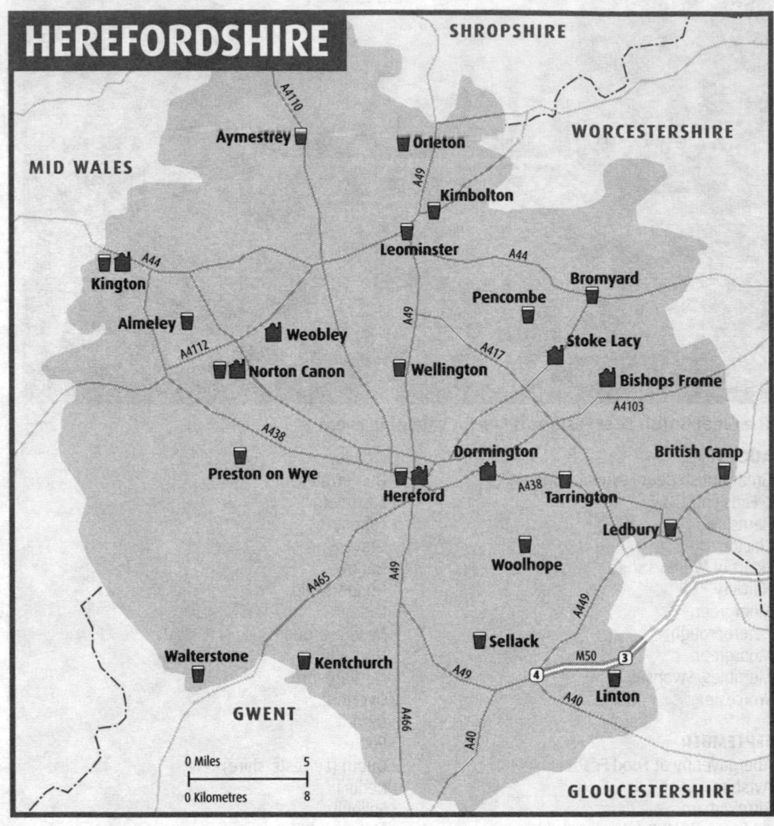

Almeley

Bells Inn

HR3 6LF

12-3 (not winter Tue or Thu), 7-11; 12-3, 7-10.30 Sun

(01544) 327216

Wye Valley Bitter; guest beer Ⓗ

From the car park, where horses may sometimes be seen at the hitching rail, this unpretentious stone-built village pub is entered through the former 'jug and bottle'. It has a large, low-ceilinged bar, always popular with locals, and a second, no-smoking room that doubles as a family room and dining area. Outside is a double petanque piste. Traditional bar snacks and meals are served at lunchtime (Sun only in winter) and evenings (Thu–Sat). The guest beer is generally from local brewers. There is live music on some Saturday evenings.

Aymestrey

Riverside Inn

HR6 9ST (on A4110)

11-3, 6-11; closed winter Mon; 12-3, 6-10.30 (not winter eve) Sun

(01568) 708440

website www.theriversideinn.org

Beer range varies Ⓗ

The restaurant is always a popular venue for evening and weekend diners, but the Riverside does not neglect drinkers, with its stylish bar areas. Using local meat and home-grown produce, an interesting menu of well-presented dishes is available, with the accent on traditional English cuisine. Regular beers are one each from the Wood and Wye Valley breweries, sometimes replaced by a seasonal brew. Delightfully situated on the River Lugg, with its own mile of fishing rights, it is close to the Mortimer Trail footpath and a number of circular walks.

British Camp

Malvern Hills Hotel

Jubilee Drive, WR13 6DW

11-11; 12-10.30 Sun

(01684) 540690

website www.malvernhillshotel.co.uk

Malvern Hills Black Pear; Wye Valley Bitter, Hereford Pale Ale; guest beers Ⓗ

Large landmark hotel located high on the Malvern Hills, near the British Camp Hill Fort. It is popular with locals and particularly with walkers

INDEPENDENT BREWERIES

Bridge Street Kington
Dunn Plowman Kington
Marches Dormington
Mayfields Bishops Frome
Shoes Norton Canon
Spinning Dog Hereford
Wild's Weobley
Wye Valley Stoke Lacy

(dogs and children welcome – the latter until 5.30pm). There is a genuine commitment to quality cask beers: five pumps adorn a single main bar, with guest beers from local breweries. A modernised airy restaurant offers affordable dining, and meals can be taken in the main bar. A rooftop patio and outside seating make this an ideal venue for a fine day.
⛰❀⇄◑♿♣P⅟

Bromyard

Rose & Lion ✔
5 New Road, HR7 4DE
☉ 11-3, 5-11; 11-11 Fri & Sat; 12-10.30 Sun
☎ (01885) 482381
Wye Valley Bitter, Hereford Pale Ale, Butty Bach; guest beer Ⓗ
Situated just off the High Street, this multi-roomed pub was Herefordshire CAMRA Pub of the Year 2001 and has all the necessary ingredients: a friendly public bar, a cosy lounge and a garden providing a pleasant environment in which to drink good ale. It enjoys a loyal following among locals while always welcoming visitors. A folk jam session is held on Sunday evening. Rent for the garden is paid annually to owners Wye Valley in home-grown parsnips.
Q❀⊟♣P

Hereford

Barrels ✔
69 St Owen Street, HR1 2JQ
☉ 11-11; 12-10.30 Sun
☎ (01432) 274968
Wye Valley Bitter, Hereford Pale Ale, Butty Bach, Dorothy Goodbody's Wholesome Stout, seasonal beers Ⓗ
The Barrels was once home to Wye Valley Brewery, and is still the company's flagship outlet, stocking most of the beer range, plus Thatchers Traditional cider. Voted Herefordshire CAMRA Pub of the Year 2003, its four rooms cater for all age groups. A pool table occupies one bar, and another has a large-screen TV for major sporting events – otherwise conversation rules. Freed from brewery activities, the rear courtyard now provides a great outdoor drinking area, and is the venue for the August bank holiday charity music and beer festival.
❀⊟⇌♣●

Kings Fee ✔
49-53 Commercial Road, HR1 2BJ
☉ 10-11; 12-10.30 Sun
☎ (01432) 373240
Greene King Abbot; Marston's Burton Bitter, Pedigree; guest beers Ⓗ
This one-time garage and former supermarket has undergone a remarkable transformation by Wetherspoon; a conversion highly commended in the 2004 CAMRA National Pub Design Awards. The large, open-plan main bar leads to an elevated family area (children welcome until 5pm) and a courtyard. Decor is contemporary in style, and features local history panels and woodcut prints by a local artist. It has brought to Hereford a welcome choice of guest ales at reasonable prices. Good value food is served all day. Q☋❀◑♿⅟

Victory ✔
88 St Owen Street, HR1 2QD
☉ 11-11; 12-10.30 Sun
☎ (01432) 274998
Spinning Dog Chase Your Tail, Mutleys Dark, Herefordshire Light Ale, Top Dog; guest beers Ⓗ
Home of Hereford's Spinning Dog Brewery and serving most of its beers, the pub also offers the city's best range of real ciders including Thatchers and Broome Farm. The main bar is made of timber with bare wooden floors, and the bar servery is in the shape of a galleon. The nautical theme continues through to a large narrow bar and skittle alley to the rear. A key venue for local bands on Saturday and Sunday evenings, it holds mini-beer festivals twice a year. ⛰☋❀◑⊟⇌♣●P

Kentchurch

Bridge Inn
Kentchurch, HR2 0BY (on B4347)
☉ 12-3 (not Mon or Tue), 5-11; 12-3, 7-10.30 Sun
☎ (01981) 240408
Beer range varies Ⓗ
Beautifully situated close to the Welsh border on the banks of the River Monnow, the building probably dates from the 14th century. Recently refurbished, it comprises a welcoming single front bar plus a restaurant affording excellent views. It boasts riverside gardens and a petanque piste for summer days. The freshly prepared food ranges from bar snacks to a full menu (not served Sun eve). The three beers are from regional and local breweries, with always one from Wye Valley.
⛰Q❀⇄◑♿Å♣P

Kimbolton

Stockton Cross
HR6 0HD (on A4112, W of village)
☉ 12-3, 7-11 (not Mon eve); 12-3 Sun
☎ (01568) 612509
Teme Valley This; Wye Valley Hereford Pale Ale, Butty Bach Ⓗ
This black and white pub with just one bar dates from the 16th century and retains some interesting features. Long and narrow, it has a drinking area at one end of the bar while the eating area at the other end features two cosy alcoves set either side of the large fireplace. The food, including a good vegetarian choice, is mainly sourced locally and freshly prepared – not to be rushed, but worth the wait.
⛰❀◑P⅟

Kington

Olde Tavern
22 Victoria Road, HR5 3BX
☉ 6.30-11; 12-3, 6-11 Sat; 12-3, 7-10.30 Sun
☎ (01544) 230122
Dunn Plowman Brewhouse Bitter, Sting, Shirehorse Ale Ⓗ
Pub for the connoisseur, voted Herefordshire CAMRA Pub of the Year in 2004. The Olde Tavern has gone from strength to strength following a successful refurbishment in 2002 that was greeted with universal local approval. The side room has been opened up, with a serving hatch

through to the central bar. The totally untouched main room retains much character, displaying old drawings and photographs of the pub, and many interesting curios. It is now the tap for the nearby Dunn Plowman Brewery. Q❀⊟♣

Ledbury

Prince of Wales

Church Lane, HR8 1DL

⏲ 11-11; 12-10.30 Sun

☎ (01531) 632250

Banks's Original, Bitter; Greene King Abbot; St Austell Tribute; guest beer Ⓗ

Tucked away in a beautiful, narrow, cobbled street, this superb 16th-century timbered pub comprises front and back bars and a dining area. Always bustling with locals and visitors alike, it hosts a well-attended folk jam session (Wed eve) and is popular for pub games. Good value home-cooked bar meals and Sunday roasts are served. Weston's First Quality cider is stocked, plus Weston's Perry (summer only). ⚘❀◖⊟⇌♣●

Talbot Hotel

14 New Street, HR8 2DT

⏲ 11.30-3, 5-11; 11.30-11 Sat; 12-4, 7-10.30 Sun

☎ (01531) 632963

website www.talbotledbury.co.uk

Wadworth IPA, 6X; Wye Valley Hereford Pale Ale, Butty Bach Ⓗ

This excellent black-and-white half-timbered hotel dates back to 1596. The heavily beamed bar surrounds an island servery, offering a range of relaxing and comfortable drinking areas. The beautiful oak-panelled dining room, with its fine carved overmantle, was once the scene of fighting between Cavaliers and Roundheads. Traditional English bar snacks and meals are served to a high standard using local ingredients. The hotel is an ideal place to spend a relaxing short break. Occasional live music is played on Thursday. On-street parking is available nearby. ♨⛟◖◗⇌♣P

Leominster

Bell Inn

39 Etnam Street, HR6 8AE

⏲ 12-11; 12-10.30 Sun

☎ (01568) 612818

Taylor Landlord; Wye Valley Bitter; guest beers Ⓗ

Friendly pub with a single U-shaped bar recently refurbished in a modern style to give a light and airy feel, plus a pleasant yard to the rear. Live music features every Tuesday evening (folk) and Thursday evening (band). On-street parking outside is free and there is a large car park nearby. Reasonably-priced, home-made pub food is served at lunchtimes. The regular beers are complemented by guests drawn mainly from local micro-breweries. ♨❀◖⇌♣

Black Horse

74 South Street, HR6 8JF

⏲ 11-2.30, 6-11; 11-11 Sat; 12-3, 7-10.30 Sun

☎ (01568) 611946

Dunn Plowman Brewhouse Bitter; Hobsons Town Crier; guest beers Ⓗ

Former coach house to the south of the town centre. Once home to the Dunn Plowman Brewery, and still noted for the range and quality of its beers, it has a public bar, a narrow lounge area resplendent with 1980s decor, and a dining area to the rear. Bar snacks and meals are served (not Sun eve), with Sunday lunches a speciality. Games include petanque, table skittles and quoits. Car park access is via the narrow courtyard entrance. Addlestones cider is served. ⚘❀◖◗⊟⛺⇌♣●P

Grape Vaults ✔

Broad Street, HR6 8BS

⏲ 11-11; 12-10.30 Sun

☎ (01568) 611404

Banks's Original, Bitter; Marston's Pedigree; guest beers Ⓗ

Herefordshire CAMRA Pub of the Year runner-up for 2004, this is a wonderfully unspoilt pub that was once a 'hard-core' cider house. Behind an unassuming exterior is a delightfully intimate wood-panelled pub, resplendent with snug, roaring fire and original bench seating. Conversation rules in this tiny pub – TV is only allowed to intrude for home international rugby matches. Conventional English pub food is served (not Sun) at affordable prices, with local ingredients where possible. One of the beers is always from Wood Brewery. ⚘❀◖⊟⇌●

Linton

Alma Inn

HR9 7RY (off B4221, W of M50 jct 3) OS659255

⏲ 12-3 (not Mon-Fri), 6.30 (6 Fri & Sat)-11; 12-3, 7-10.30 Sun

☎ (01989) 720355 website www.almainnlinton.co.uk

Butcombe Bitter; RCH Pitchfork; guest beers Ⓗ

Herefordshire CAMRA Pub of the Year 2002, and Best Country Pub in 2001 and 2004, the Alma demonstrates that rural pubs have a future without being converted into restaurants. A large lounge with comfortable furniture contrasts with a pool room and a less-used no-smoking bar. Run with a real passion, the Alma champions small and local breweries. The extensive hillside gardens are the venue for an ambitious and successful Music and Ale festival every June, which attracts people from near and far. ♨Q❀⛺♣P⊬

Norton Canon

Three Horseshoes

HR4 7BH (on A480)

⏲ 12-3 (Wed & Sat only), 6-11; 12-3, 7-10.30 Sun

☎ (01544) 318375

Shoes Norton Ale, Canon Bitter Ⓗ**, Farriers Beer** Ⓖ

Home of the Shoes Brewery, this traditional roadside pub is also run by the brewer. A public bar leads through to a larger pool room, in contrast to the small, cosy lounge which is furnished with an ad hoc collection of comfortable old sofas, chairs and a piano. Farriers Beer at 15.4% ABV is now available on draught as well as in bottles, served by gravity despite the handpump. The bus stop (services 461/462 from Hereford) is half a mile from the pub; alight at the 'Weobley Turn'. ♨Q⚘❀⊟⛺♣P

Orleton

Boot Inn

SY8 4HN (off B4361) OS494672
⏲ 12-3, 6-11; 12-3, 7-10.30 Sun
☎ (01568) 780228
Hobsons Best Bitter, Town Crier or guest beer Ⓗ
Popular 17th-century black and white village pub with a distinctive and comfortable public bar, lounge and restaurant. The large, attractive garden houses a children's play area and a barbecue. The home-cooked food ranges from bar snacks to a full menu with interesting daily specials. A charity quiz is held monthly on a Tuesday. Town Crier alternates with a second guest beer, usually from local breweries. Local bottled cider is stocked. The Hereford-Ludlow bus No. 492 stops outside.
⛼Q❀◐◑⊟♣P

Pencombe

Wheelwrights

HR7 4RN OS598528
⏲ 12-2.30 (not Mon), 6-11; 12-4, 7-10.30 Sun
☎ (01885) 400358
Adnams Broadside; Black Sheep Best Bitter; Greene King Abbot; Taylor Landlord; guest beer Ⓗ
This excellent and sensitively modernised 17th-century single-bar establishment is everything a thriving village pub should be. Local CAMRA Country Pub of the Year 2003, it serves a good selection of ales, and features straightforward, good value pub food (Wed-Sun). It is at the nexus of village life with activities including a regular Friday teatime farmers' market (not in winter), and folk and poetry jam sessions on the first Tuesday of the month. No lunches are served on Wednesday. ⛼❀⛟◐◑♣P

Preston On Wye

Yew Tree

HR2 9JT OS385414
⏲ 7-11; 12-3, 7-10.30 Sun
☎ (01981) 500359
Beer range varies Ⓖ
A pleasantly eccentric and unspoilt single-bar, drinkers' establishment located in a quiet hamlet near the River Wye. Comfortable and welcoming, it fields boules, pool and quiz teams, while in the summer, it is popular with anglers and canoeists. The single beer, which tends to alternate from local or regional breweries, is served direct from a cask behind the small bar. Draught Thatchers Heritage cider is also available. Often open on Saturday lunchtime in summer; it also hosts monthly live music on Saturday. ⛼Q❀⛺♣●P

Sellack

Loughpool Inn

HR9 6LX (1 mile NW of A49 at Peterstow) OS558268
⏲ 11.30-2.30, 6.30-11 (not winter Mon eve); 12-2.30, 6.30-10.30 (not winter eve) Sun
☎ (01989) 730236
Courage Best Bitter; Wye Valley Bitter, Butty Bach; guest beer Ⓗ
This superb 16th-century black and white half-timbered inn, set behind attractive lawns, affords exceptional views over the delightful countryside. The single long opened-out bar has the original flagstone floor, wooden tables and kitchen chairs. There is also a restaurant. The accent is unashamedly on food to a high standard, using local produce where possible – but not to the exclusion of drinkers. Booking is advisable for meals. The guest beer is usually sourced locally. ⛼Q❀◐◑♿P

Tarrington

Tarrington Arms

HR1 4HX (on A438)
⏲ 12-3, 7-11; 12-3, 7-10.30 Sun
☎ (01432) 890796
Wood Shropshire Lad; guest beer Ⓗ
The reinvention of this late Georgian red brick ex-hotel continues apace. An imposing roadside building with interesting colonnade entrance, it has two bars and a restaurant with a distinctly modern refectory atmosphere. The smaller lounge bar features fascinating photographs of the local hop picking industry over the years. The guest beer is from small regional or micro-breweries. The good value food is of a high standard, with the emphasis on steaks and seafood (not served Sun eve). The Hereford-Ledbury bus No. 476 stops outside.
⛼❀⛟◐◑⊟♣P⚡

Walterstone

Carpenters Arms

HR2 0DX OS340251
⏲ 12-11; 12-10.30 Sun
☎ (01873) 890353
Breconshire Golden Valley; Wadworth 6X Ⓖ
Known locally as the Gluepot, this lovely old pub, situated by the church in a scattered

Cask Marque

Cask Marque, whose symbol appears alongside many pubs m the Good Beer Guide, is an organisation financed by the brewing industry to improve the quality of cask beer in pubs. When a pub displays a Cask Marque plaque it means inspectors have been satisfied by the cleanliness and temperature of pub cellars and the quality of the beer at the bar. The plaque is removed if quality falls. The plaque is given to licensees and accreditation lapses when a publican leaves a pub.

hamlet, is a favourite of ramblers. The front garden looks out to the Skirrid Mountain over the border in Wales. The ales are served direct from the cask, which is not on view from the tiny bar. Two small drinking areas, warmed by a welcoming fire, contrast with the restaurant to the rear. Good value home-cooked food is served, including Sunday evening. If the pub appears to be closed, try knocking on the door!
⚠Q❀◐▶P

Wellington

Wellington Inn

HR4 8AT (½ mile W of A49)
✪ 12-3 (not Mon), 6-11; 12-3, 7-10.30 Sun
☎ (01432) 830367
Hobsons Best Bitter; Wye Valley Butty Bach; guest beers Ⓗ
Thriving, traditional village hostelry with a welcoming public bar, where wooden benches contrast with opulent leather sofas. A separate barn-style restaurant is popular with diners. Commended in the Tastes of Herefordshire awards 2004, food is a real speciality, with bar snacks, an elaborate lunchtime and evening menu, and carvery on Sunday. The bar has interesting local photographs, board games and newspapers. Guest beers are mainly from micro-breweries, and Westons First Quality cider is served. The Hereford-Ludlow bus No. 492 stops outside. ⚠❀◐▶♣●P

Woolhope

Butchers Arms

HR1 4RF (E of village) OS618358
✪ 12-3, 6.30 (6 Sat)-11; 12-3, 6.30-10.30 Sun (shorter hours in winter)
☎ (01432) 860281
Hook Norton Best Bitter; Shepherd Neame Spitfire; Wye Valley Butty Bach; guest beers Ⓗ
Formed in Victorian times by combining a butcher's shop and a beer house, there are original beams much in evidence, including some at head height in the public bar (beware!). Popular with customers not just for drinking but for dining too; home-prepared food is served in both bars, as well as the dining room. Guest beers are from local breweries. A stream runs past the pub, garden and newly constructed car park. Bus service 453 from Hereford stops outside.
⚠❀⇔◐▶ᗡP⚟

Crown Inn

HR1 4QP OS611357
✪ 12-2.30, 6.30 (7 winter)-11; 12-3, 6.30 (7 winter)-10.30 Sun
☎ (01432) 860468
Whittington's Cats Whiskers; Wye Valley Bitter Ⓗ
Situated next to the church, the Crown is deservedly popular with out of town diners, but also welcomes drinkers. The large bar, adorned with brewery memorabilia, where children are welcomed, is complemented by a restaurant and a drinking area in the conservatory by the front door. The food is home prepared and the extensive, appetising menu includes a large choice of imaginative vegetarian dishes. Booking for weekend meals is strongly advised. Bus No. 453 from Hereford stops outside.
❀◐▶♣P⚟

Sun, Leintwardine

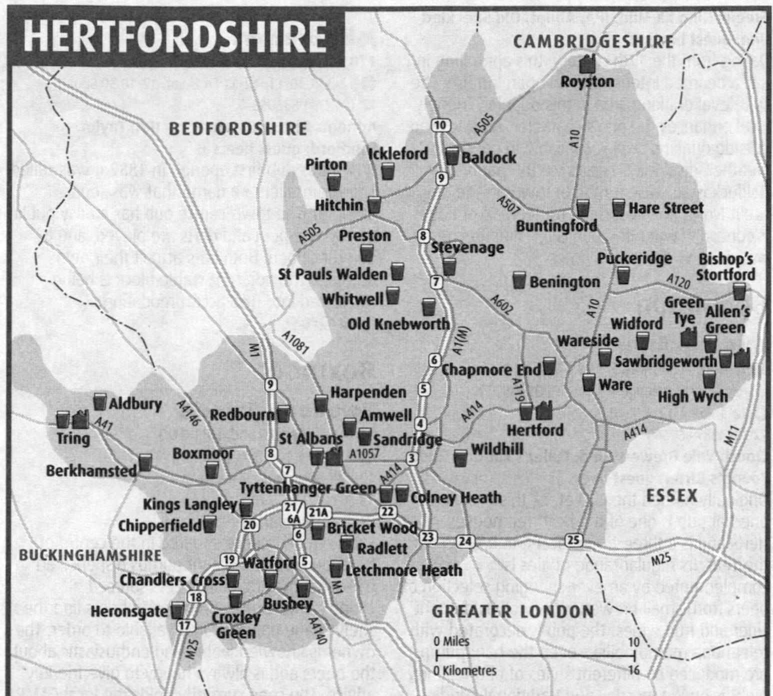

Aldbury

Valiant Trooper

Trooper Road, HP23 5ER OS964121
11.30-11; 12-10.30 Sun
☎ (01442) 851203
Fuller's London Pride; Taylor Landlord; guest beers H

Dating back to 1753, then known as the Royal Oak, it became the Valiant Trooper in 1852. The central bar has original low beams and is decorated with military prints. Two regular beers are supplemented by three guests, one usually from Tring Brewery. A converted stable adjoining the pub has seating for 40 diners. Good ale and food makes this a popular destination for cyclists and walkers. No evening meals are served on Sunday or Monday. Dogs are welcome. Q P

Allen's Green

Queen's Head

CM21 0LS (take W road from double roundabout in Sawbridgeworth) OS455168
12-2.30 not Mon or Tue), 5-11; 12-11 Sat; 12-10.30 Sun
☎ (01279) 723393
website: www.shirevillageinns.co.uk
Fuller's London Pride; H **Mighty Oak Oscar Wilde;** G **guest beers** H /G

Friendly, traditional, village local with a bar opening into a cosy parlour where conversation reigns supreme in a peaceful environment. The London Pride is usually accompanied by three guests which are regularly rotated including a dark mild or porter plus two real ciders and a perry. Bar meals are served at all times. There is a family-friendly patio and garden where the May and August bank holiday beer festivals are held. Q P

Amwell

Elephant & Castle

Amwell Lane, AL4 8EA OS167132
12-2.30, 5.30-11; 12-10.30 Sun
☎ (01582) 832175
Greene King IPA, Morland Original, Abbot; guest beer H

Welcoming and deservedly popular 18th-century inn beautifully situated in a peaceful setting. See the 200ft well in the back bar and the two real fires that warm the pub in colder weather. With the added asset of two large gardens (the back garden is for adults only), this is an excellent example of a successful country pub. Lunches are served daily and evening meals Tuesday to Saturday. P

Baldock

Cock

43 High Street, SG7 6BG
12-1.30 Wed; 12-3 Sat; 5-11 Mon-Sat; 12-3.30, 7-10.30 Sun
☎ (01462) 892366

INDEPENDENT BREWERIES

Buntingford Royston
Green Tye Green Tye
McMullen Hertford
Red Squirrel Hertford
Sawbridgeworth Sawbridgeworth
Tring Tring
Verulam St Albans

Greene King XX Mild, IPA, Abbot, Old Speckled Hen; guest beers Ⓗ
Dating from the 17th century, this appealing inn has a beamed interior and an open log fire. The split-level drinking area in this popular, friendly local enhances the pub's character. An enclosed outside drinking area is available in good weather; disabled access is via the patio. Baldock is an ancient market town on the old Great North Road coaching route. Market day is Wednesday when the pub is open at lunchtime. ♕Q❀♿≡♣

Benington

Lordship Arms

42 Whempstead Road, SG2 7BX
(3 miles E of Stevenage via B1037) OS308227
✪ 12-3, 6-11; 12-3, 7-10.30 Sun
☎ (01438) 869665
Crouch Vale Brewers Gold; Fuller's London Pride; Young's Bitter; guest beers Ⓗ
Originally named the Cricketers, this excellent one-bar pub is one of the best free houses in Herts and is a three-times local CAMRA Pub of the Year. Its regular range of ales is complemented by an ever-changing selection of beers from small breweries, as well as draught cider and fruit wines. The pub is decorated with telephone memorabilia – even the handpumps are modelled on different styles of phone. Curry night is on Wednesday and traditional Sunday roasts are popular. ♕❀◖●P▯

Berkhamsted

Lamb

277 High Street, HP4 1AJ
✪ 11-11, 12-10.30 Sun
☎ (01442) 862615
Adnams Bitter; Fuller's London Pride; Greene King IPA; Tring Ridgeway Ⓗ
The two front doors of this traditional old-school pub lead to a public bar and a lounge, joined inside by an open doorway. A welcoming and friendly local, the emphasis here is on drinking, with meals only served at weekday lunchtimes. However, the superb home-made food comes in generous portions and should not be missed. The public bar area is dominated by the dartboard. It is a regular outlet for the local Tring Brewery. Q❀◖≡♣

Bishop's Stortford

Half Moon

31 North Street, CM23 2LD
✪ 11-11; 12-10.30 Sun
☎ (01279) 834500
Caledonian Deuchars IPA; Fuller's London Pride; Wychwood Hobgoblin; guest beers Ⓗ
A warm welcome from the landlady awaits you at this 16th-century former coaching inn. The large lower bar is no-smoking and hosts folk music every other Sunday, while a separate function room is used as a live music venue with a blues night and an acoustic club. There is an extensive cheese menu to complement the superb range of beers, with different guest ales mainly from micro-breweries. Westons Old Rosie cider is also available.
Q❀◖⊟≡♣●P⚟

Jolly Brewers

170 South Street, CM23 3BQ
✪ 12-3, 5.30-11; 12-11 Fri & Sat; 12-10.30 Sun
☎ (01279) 836055
Adnams Bitter; Greene King IPA; Taylor Landlord; guest beers Ⓗ
When this pub first opened in 1882 it was called The Teetotallers – a name that was soon dropped! The town-centre pub has a busy public bar, where pool and darts are played, and a quieter saloon. Both bars attract their own regulars. The adjacent stable block is being converted into B&B accommodation.
❀◖◗⊟≡P

Boxmoor

Boxmoor Vintners

25-27 St Johns Road, HP1 1QQ
✪ 9.30-1, 4.30-9.30 (9 winter);
12-2 (1.30 winter), 7-9 Sun
☎ (01442) 252171
Beer range varies Ⓗ
Excellent off-licence situated in the centre of Boxmoor. The three handpumps dispense an ever-changing range of beers sourced countrywide. Bottle-conditioned beers line the shelves and polypins are available to order. The owner is knowledgeable and enthusiastic about the beers and is always happy to give friendly advice. The shop currently holds the local CAMRA award for 'services to real ale'. There is a public car park nearby. ≡ (Hemel Hempstead)

Bricket Wood

Black Boy

79 Old Watford Road, AL2 3RU (off A405)
✪ 10.30-11; 12-10.30 Sun
☎ (01923) 672444
Fuller's London Pride; Young's Special; guest beers Ⓗ
Dating from 1751, this Grade II listed building has had extensions added in the 1930s. The bar area has original oak beams and a flagstoned floor with two seating areas at either end. A genuine local, it is a serious games pub with two darts teams, four football teams and a flourishing golf society. Outdoor drinking can be enjoyed in the sloping garden which is set on three levels. Meals are served Friday lunchtime; rolls available the rest of the week. ❀♣

Buntingford

Crown

17 High Street, SG9 9AB
✪ 12-3, 6-11; 12-3, 7-10.30 Sun
☎ (01763) 271422
Archers Best Bitter; Ridleys IPA; guest beers Ⓗ
A Guide entry for the last 16 years, this town-centre pub has a large front bar, cosy back bar and a function room. Outside are a covered patio and a secluded garden. Although the emphasis at this pub is on drinking, rather than dining, there are regular themed speciality food nights as well as traditional fish and chips on Thursday and Friday. Crossword fans find the large collection of dictionaries and reference books useful! ♕❀◖◗

Bushey

Swan

25 Park Road, WD23 3EE (off A411)
11-11; 12-10.30 Sun
(020) 8950 2256
Greene King Old Speckled Hen; Jennings Cumberland Ale; Young's Bitter, Special H
Small, one-bar, back-street local. The walls are covered with old photographs, CAMRA awards and other items of interest. The ladies' loo is outside, accessed via the garden. The real fires are welcoming and the dartboard and pub games popular. This is the Swan's 31st appearance in the Guide.

Chandlers Cross

Clarendon Arms

Redhall Lane, WD3 4LU (off Sarratt Road, N of Croxley Green)
11-11; 12-10.30 Sun
(01923) 262924
Courage Best Bitter; Greene King Old Speckled Hen; Wells Bombardier; guest beers H
Country pub with an L-shaped bar which appeals to drinkers and diners. A pleasant hour's stroll from Watford through woods and parkland, it is popular with walkers. There is a quiz night and live music evening, both monthly. Two small beer festivals are held each year, and the pub runs a lawn mower racing team. The pub is difficult to access by public transport but during the day the No. 352 bus passes the end of Redhall Lane. P

Chapmore End

Woodman

30 Chapmore End, SG12 0HF
(off B158, ¼ mile SW of A602) OS328164
12-2.30 (not Mon), 5.30-11; 12-11 Sat; 12-10.30 Sun
(01920) 463143 website: www.woodmanpub.com
Greene King IPA, Abbot, seasonal beers; guest beers G
In a quiet hamlet off the B158, this totally unspoilt gem has been sensitively updated. The two-bar pub has gravity dispensed real ale from cooled casks in the cellar behind the public bar. A local favourite is 'Mix': half IPA, half Abbot. Speciality themed meal evenings are held on alternate Thursdays. The large gardens to the rear have a safe children's play area. The pub holds numerous special events including music, carol singing and fireworks in season.
Q P

Chipperfield

Royal Oak

1 The Street, WD4 9BH
12-3, 6-11; 12-3, 7-10.30 Sun
(01923) 266537
Adnams Broadside; Draught Bass; Fuller's London Pride; Young's Bitter H
Long-standing Guide entry situated on the lower edge of the village. The public bar has many upholstered beer casks as seating, and walls adorned with old car photographs, local drawings and a large matchbook collection. The saloon is more open, furnished with horse brasses and brewery mirrors; children are admitted for meals. There is a patio area outside. No lunches are served on Sunday.
Q P

Colney Heath

Crooked Billet

88 High Street, AL4 0NP (signed from A414)
11-2.30, 5.30-11; 11-11 Sat; 12-10.30 Sun
(01727) 822128
Beer range varies H
Popular and friendly cottage-style village pub dating back over 200 years. A genuine free house stocking a selection of three to five guest beers from national, regional and micro breweries, it offers a wide selection of good value food. An ideal place to stop off for walkers on the many local footpaths, families are welcome in the large garden with children's play equipment. P

Croxley Green

Sportsman

2 Scots Hill, WD3 3AD (on A412)
12-11; 12-10.30 Sun
(01923) 443360
website: www.croxleygreen.com/sportsman
Draught Bass; Tring Side Pocket for a Toad; guest beers H
Situated on a mini-roundabout between Rickmansworth and Watford, and handy for the green, this is a popular destination for locals 'taking the dog for a walk'. Although there is a strong sporting theme to the pub, darts and pool often play second fiddle to live music – usually blues, jazz or folk. A separate 'shed' is used for occasional beer festivals and private functions. A regular Guide entry for many years, this was local CAMRA Pub of the Year in 2005. P

Hare Street

Beehive

Near Buntingford, SG9 0DX (jct of B1368/B1038)
12-3 (not Tue), 5-11 (8 Tue); 12-11 Sat; 12-6 Sun
(01763) 289355
Greene King IPA; McMullen AK; guest beers (summer) H
This traditional 200-year-old roadside free house was an ale house until 1956. It is an appealing, cosy pub with a single bar, no fruit machines or juke box. A small TV will be turned on for sporting events by request. Pub games, including darts and cribbage, are popular. The Beehive achieved fame as the last pub in the world in The Hitchhiker's Guide to the Galaxy movie. P

Harpenden

Carpenters Arms

14 Cravells Road, AL5 1BD
(off A1081, Southdown Rd at mini roundabout) OS143133
11-3, 5.30-11; 12-3, 7-10.30 Sun
(01582) 460311
Adnams Bitter; Courage Best Bitter; Greene King Abbot; guest beers H
Harpenden's smallest pub was South Herts CAMRA Pub of the Year 2005. As well as awards for its beer, the pub has been recognised by the council for its services to the community and

wonderful floral displays in summer. Inside, the atmosphere is cosy and comfortable. The pub is adorned with motoring memorabilia from all over the world. The landlord, who has been in residence for 20 years, is a staunch supporter of mild and local micro-breweries. No food is served on Sunday. ⌂Q❀◐♣P

Heronsgate

Land of Liberty, Peace & Plenty

52 Long Lane, WD3 5BS (N from M25, jct 17) OS023949
✪ 11-11; 12-10.30 Sun
☎ (01923) 282226
website: www.landoflibertypub.com
Fuller's London Pride; Young's Bitter; guest beers H
Traditional country free house, divided into distinct drinking areas. Guest beers come from a variety of local micros, often rare to the area. Breweriana on display shows the landlord's commitment to real ale. Regular events include quiz nights and live music plus occasional beer festivals. The pub has a large garden where families are welcome. ⌂❀◐P

Hertford

Black Horse

29-31 West Street, SG13 8EZ
✪ 12-2 (2.30 Fri; not Mon), 5-11; 12-11 Sat; 12-10.30 Sun
☎ (01992) 583630 website: www.blackhorseherts.co.uk
Greene King IPA, Abbot, seasonal beers; guest beers H
You will receive a warm welcome at this early 19th-century timbered pub situated in one of Hertford's most attractive streets. Handy for Hertford Town football club supporters, the pub also supports rugby union and fields its own team. Seasonal and guest beers are always available. Good value home-made food is served – times vary so check on the website. ⌂❀◐◑≠ (North/East) ♣

Old Cross Tavern

8 St Andrew Street, SG14 1JA
✪ 11.30-11; 12-10.30 Sun
☎ (01992) 583133
Crouch Vale Brewers Gold; Fuller's London Pride; Mighty Oak IPA; Taylor Landlord; guest beers H
Superb town pub offering a friendly welcome to all. Eight real ales – four regulars and four guests – usually including a dark beer of some distinction, come from brewers large and small. A choice of good house wines and country wines is offered. Lunches are served from Monday to Saturday including the famous fish pie and a full board of daily specials. ⌂Q◐≠ (North/East) ●

White Horse

33 Castle Street, SG14 1HH
✪ 12-2.30, 5.30-11; 12-11 Fri & Sat; 12-10.30 Sun
☎ (01992) 501950
Adnams Bitter; Fuller's Chiswick, London Pride, ESB, seasonal beers; guest beers H
Charming old timber-framed building with two downstairs bars and no-smoking rooms upstairs (where well-supervised children are welcome until 9pm). Alongside the Fuller's beers are guests of character from leading brewers. Country wines are also stocked. Twice yearly beer festivals are held offering 50 or more ales. Reasonably-priced lunches are served every day. Monday night features a set menu of dishes from around the world.
⌂Q◐◑⊟≠ (North/East) ♣⁄

High Wych

Rising Sun

High Wych, CM21 0HZ OS465141
✪ 12-2.30, 5.30-11; 12-3, 5-11 Fri & Sat; 12-2.30, 7-10.30 Sun
☎ (01279) 724099
Courage Best Bitter, guest beers G
A mecca for real ale lovers in the area. Owned by the same family for many years, it is known locally as 'Sid's' by regulars. Divided into a bar room, lounge with a serving hatch and a games room, it is considered by some to be stuck in a time warp: unchanged decor, no piped music, no mobile phones (fine payable if used). However the service from smiling staff is sublime – with sarcasm the unofficial pub game. All beers are on gravity with guests from micros. The garden is newly landscaped and a pleasant place for a pint. ⌂Q⊃❀♣P

Hitchin

Half Moon

57 Queen Street, SG4 9TZ
✪ 12-2.30, 5-11; 12-11 Fri & Sat; 12-10.30 Sun
☎ (01462) 452448
Adnams Bitter; Young's Special; guest beers H
This friendly, split-level, one-bar pub dates back to 1748 and survived a fire which burnt down the stables next door. Once owned by Hitchin brewer W&S Lucas, its current mock-Tudor façade was added in the 1930s. Two regular beers and one guest are always available, plus a real cider and a good choice of wines. The landlady provides an interesting selection of home-prepared food.
⌂❀◐◑♣●P⁄

King's Arms

16 Bucklersbury, SG5 1BB
✪ 11-2.30, 5.30-11; (1am Fri & Sat); closed Mon; 11-2, 7-11 Sun
☎ (01462) 459544
Adnams Bitter, Broadside; Caledonian Deuchars IPA; guest beer H
Run by the same landlord for the past 30 years, it was first opened in 1806 in a much older Grade II listed building and still retains the feel of a multi-roomed old-style pub despite being butchered in the 1960s. To the rear is a conservatory and patio heated in winter. The pub gets popular with younger drinkers at the weekends due to its late opening hours. Substantial meals are served. ⌂◐◑P

Sunrunner

24 Bancroft, SG5 1JW
✪ 12-3, 5-11; 12-11 Fri & Sat; 12-10.30 Sun
☎ (01462) 440717
Fuller's London Pride; Potton Shannon IPA; guest beers H
The Sunrunner is a mini-beer festival in its own right. With two regular and six ever-changing guest beers, mainly from small or

new micros, including stouts and milds, there is always something different to try. Pauliner and Leffe are dispensed from fonts. Cider drinkers have Westons Old Rosie and one other guest. Fruit wines are also sold. Live music is hosted on Wednesday night. The pub has built up a loyal clientele and visitors are always made to feel welcome. ◑ ●

Ickleford

Plume of Feathers

Upper Green, SG5 3YD
(400 yds from A600 down Turnpike Lane)
✪ 11.30-3, 6-11; 11-11 Fri & Sat; 12-10.30 Sun
☎ (01462) 432729
Adnams Bitter; Flower's IPA; Fuller's London Pride; Shepherd Neame Spitfire; Wadworth 6X; guest beers H

Welcoming pub that has been run by two sisters for 10 years. It has changed little over the years and retains its public bar. A lively place, it is popular with enthusiastic rugby union fans. The excellent food is prepared to order (not Sun eve) and served in the no-smoking restaurant. There is a pleasant, secluded garden in which to enjoy a pint on a summer's day. Q❀◑♣P⚟

Kings Langley

Saracen's Head

47 High Street, WD4 9HU
✪ 11-2.30 (3 Sat), 5 (6 Sat)-11; 12-3, 7-10.30 Sun
☎ (01923) 400144
Fuller's London Pride, ESB; Tring Ridgeway; guest beer H

Enter through the low doorway of this building, which dates from 1619, and step down into the cosy atmosphere of the single-bar pub. It features low ceilings, beams, a wood-burning open fire and collections of beer bottles, water jugs and antique telephones. Outside are award-winning hanging basket displays. There is an active golf society. Lunches are served Monday to Saturday. No children are admitted. ⛰◖P

Letchmore Heath

Three Horseshoes

The Green, WD25 8ER
✪ 11-11; 12-10.30 Sun
☎ (01923) 856084
Adnams Bitter, Broadside; Shepherd Neame Spitfire; guest beers H

A beer house since the 18th century, the earliest part of the building is the 16th-century timber hall, with its 17th-century frontage. Substantial reconstruction took place in 1803. The pub has featured in films since the 1920s, and numerous TV programmes. Facing the common, it has two bars: a flagstoned public and an oak beamed lounge. Q◑●⊞P

Old Knebworth

Lytton Arms

Park Lane, SG3 6QB OS229202
✪ 11-11; 12-10.30 Sun
☎ (01438) 812312
Adnams Bitter, Broadside; Fuller's London Pride; guest beers H

Situated on the edge of the Knebworth House estate, this 19th-century Lutyens house has been recently refurbished. Appealing to all, the pub is frequented by village locals, visitors and those who have come to enjoy the good food. An interesting range of continental beers supplements the real ale and cider. The two bars are complemented by a no-smoking conservatory and attractive garden seating areas. Regular beer festivals are held at least twice a year.
❀◑●P⚟

Pirton

Fox

37 High Street, SG5 3PS
✪ 3 (12 Thu-Sat)-11; 12-10.30 Sun
☎ (01462) 711101
Adnams Broadside; Fuller's London Pride; Greene King IPA, Abbot; Taylor Landlord; Wells Bombardier H

True village pub at the heart of the local community. The emphasis is on quality real ale rather than serving food. Two new handpumps have been added. It has a bright, open feel and part of the pub can be curtained off for functions. Pictures of old Pirton folk adorn the walls. Traditional music sessions are held monthly (second Wednesday), run by local morris men. ❀P

Preston

Red Lion

The Green, SG4 7UD (signed from B651)
✪ 12-3, 5.30-11; 12-3, 7-10.30 Sun
☎ (01462) 459585
Greene King IPA; guest beers H

Attractive Georgian-style free house on the village green. It was the first community-owned pub in Great Britain. The guest beers, many from micro-breweries, are constantly changing. The landlord and landlady, Tim and Jane, continue to prepare the fresh home-cooked food (no meals Tue eve), with many of the ingredients supplied locally. The pub runs several cricket teams and is involved in fundraising events.
⛰Q❀◑♿♣●P

Puckeridge

Crown & Falcon

33 High Street, SG11 1RN
✪ 11.30-2.30, 5.30-11; 12-3, 6.30-11 Sat; 12-4.30, 7-10.30 Sun
☎ (01920) 821561
Adnams Bitter; Greene King Abbot; McMullen AK; guest beers H

A public house since around 1530, with the 'Crown' half of the name taken much later from a defunct pub in the village. Changes to the interior layout of the pub can be traced on plans displayed in the bar. It is now one large, open-plan room with a separate no-smoking restaurant. A collection of Allied Breweries memorabilia is on display. The guest beer changes weekly. Darts and bar billiards are popular. The Falcon is mentioned in Samuel Pepys' diary of 1662 – he bought the landlord's boots for four pence.
⛰❀◑♣P

Radlett

Red Lion

78-80 Watling Street, WD7 7NP
11-11; 12-10.30 Sun
☎ (01923) 855341
Young's Bitter, Special, seasonal beers H
This Victorian hotel opposite the station was originally a temperance house. Things have changed and it now has a large, split-level bar plus a 60-seater restaurant. There are 14 guest rooms and a function room. Meals are served in both bar and restaurant. A flower-bedecked patio is at the front of the building overlooking the street. ❀⇌◖◗♿⇌P

Redbourn

Hollybush

Church End, AL3 7DU (in cul-de-sac by St Mary's Church)
12-11; 12-10.30 Sun
☎ (01582) 792423
Adnams Bitter; Brakspear Bitter; Gale's HSB; Greene King Abbot; guest beer H
Charming traditional pub, dating from 1595, set within a Grade II listed conservation area in picturesque Church End, just off Chequer Lane with former alms houses opposite. A free house, the pub is now owned by Brakspear which supplies the guest beer. It offers a wide selection of food, and has a no-smoking dining area. ♔Q❀◖◗P

St Albans

Boot

4 Market Place, AL3 5DG
12-11; 11-11 Wed & Sat; 12-10.30 Sun
☎ (01727) 857533
Draught Bass; Young's Special; guest beers H
Charming 16th-century, low-ceilinged pub at the heart of the city's market place opposite the Clock Tower. It has recently been refurbished and the fruit machines removed, making it a pleasant refuge from the youth circuit pubs. Food is traditional and freshly made with roasts on Sunday (eve meals Tue-Thu). Champagne is available by the glass. Live acoustic music can be heard on Tuesday night. It stages occasional beer festivals. ♔❀◖◗

Farmer's Boy

134 London Road, AL1 1PQ
11-11; 12-10.30 Sun
☎ (01727) 766702
Verulam Best, Clipper IPA, Farmers Joy, seasonal beers H
Cosy, cottage-style pub, now the home of the Verulam Brewery, which moved here from Harpenden in 1996. All the beers are brewed on site, now using floor-malted barley. An assortment of German and Belgian bottled beers is also available. The food is home made, with roasts on Sundays and barbecues on the patio in summer. There is a no-smoking area at the rear. Note the unusual ashtrays on the bar.
♔❀◖◗⇌ (City) ♣⊁

Farriers Arms

35 Lower Dagnall Street, AL2 4MJ (off A5183)
12-2.30 (not Mon), 5.30-11; 12-10.30 Sun
☎ (01727) 851025
McMullen AK, Country, seasonal beer; guest beer H
Originally a grocer's and butcher's shop in the 19th century, this building became a pub in 1920 and is now a classic back-street local. It is the only pub in St Albans never to have forsaken real ale. A plaque on the wall marks the first meeting of the Hertfordshire branch of CAMRA. The split-level interior has a small area fronting the bar for stand-up drinking, darts and card players. The back room has more comfortable seating. Both bars are free of gaming machines and muzak. ◖♣

Garibaldi ✓

61 Albert Street, AL1 1RT
12-11; 12-10.30 Sun
☎ (01727) 855046
Fuller's Chiswick, London Pride, ESB, seasonal beers; guest beers H
Traditional, welcoming, back-street local acquired by Fuller's in the 1980s. The pub is named after the Italian patriot who unified Italy in the 19th century. Mauritian food – a mix of oriental, Asian and creole dishes – is available at lunchtimes and evenings (not Sun eve). Sunday roasts are also served, plus barbecues in summer. The pub is within walking distance of the cathedral. Q❀◖◗⇌ (Abbey) ♣⊁

Lower Red Lion

34-36 Fishpool Street, AL3 4RX
12-2.30, 5.30-11; 12-11 Sat; 12-10.30 Sun
☎ (01727) 855669 website: www.lowerredlion.com
Fuller's London Pride; Oakham JHB; guest beers H
Two-bar, 17th-century coaching inn near the cathedral and Roman Verulamium. This genuine free house serves seven varying guest beers from micro breweries, Dutch, Czech and Belgian beers on draught, Belgian bottled beers and malt whiskies. Regular beer festivals are held on May and August bank holidays, plus other small festivals at weekends. The pub runs beer and cheese clubs; quiz night is on Wednesday and chess night on Monday.
♔Q❀⇌◖♣P

Mermaid

98 Hatfield Road, AL1 3RL
12-11 (midnight Fri & Sat); 12-7 (closed evening) Sun
☎ (01727) 837758
Adnams Bitter, Everards Tiger; guest beers H
Former Everards pub, now owned by a small independent pub chain, Old English Inns. Guest beers come from smaller breweries including Nethergate and Tring. No food is served. The pub is open until midnight on Friday and Saturday at the landlord's discretion if it is busy. There is a satellite TV and live bands play every fortnight on Saturday. ❀⇌ (City) ♣P

Portland Arms

63 Portland Street, AL3 4RA
12-3, 5.30-11; 12-11 Sat; 12-10.30 Sun
☎ (01727) 844574
Fuller's Chiswick, London Pride, ESB, seasonal beers H
Warm and welcoming traditional back-street community pub tucked away in a residential area. It was acquired by Fullers from Whitbread in 1990 and has since been refurbished. The

tenants are members of the Campaign for Real Food and the pub serves a wide range of food with meat supplied by a local farm, including Sunday roasts. Takeaway fish and chips is also available. There are no meals on Sunday evening which is music night. ⌂Q❀◐◑♣P

White Hart Tap

4 Keyfield Terrace, AL1 1QJ

12-11; 12-10.30 Sun

☎ (01727) 860974 website: www.whiteharttap.co.uk

Caledonian Deuchars IPA; Fuller's London Pride; guest beers H

Much-improved one-bar, back-street local which features two guest beers a week. Meals are served every lunchtime including roasts on Sunday. Barbecues are held in the spacious garden in summer. There are foreign food nights on Wednesday. Live music, featuring local bands, can be heard on Saturday nights. Computers with Internet access are available. The pub is twinned with the 'Bar No Limit' in Belgrade. A public car park is opposite the pub. ⌂❀◐⇌ (Abbey) ♣

St Pauls Walden

Strathmore Arms

London Road, SG4 8BT (on B656)

12-2.30 (not Mon); 5 (6 Mon)-11; 12-11 Sat; 12-10.30 Sun

☎ (01438) 871654

Fuller's London Pride, Chiswick; guest beers H

Refurbished pub on the Bowes-Lyon estate divided into drinking, dining and games areas. The landlord keeps not just a fine selection of beers but cider on handpump, available in summer. The pub is close to the church and is popular with the bellringers. It holds a beer festival at least once a year. The pub does a lot for the area, raising money for good causes and was local CAMRA Pub of the Year for 2004. Q❀◐◑▲♣●P

Sandridge

Green Man

High Street, AL4 9DD

11-3, 5.30-11; 11-11 Fri & Sat; 12-10.30 Sun

☎ (01727) 854845

website: www.thegreenman-sandridge.co.uk

Adnams Bitter, H **Broadside; Bateman XXXB;** G **Greene King IPA,** H **Abbot** G

One-bar Victorian 1880s red-brick pub in the centre of the village. Run by the same landlord for the last 18 years, this locals' pub extends a warm welcome to all discerning ale drinkers. There are five beers, three of them served straight from the cask from a cellar area located nearby at floor level. The pub is a meeting point for cyclists and mountain biker groups. ⌂Q❀◐◑♣P

Sawbridgeworth

Gate

81 London Road, CM21 9JJ

11.30-2.30, 5.30-11; 11-11 Fri & Sat; 12-10.30 Sun

☎ (01279) 722313 website: www.the-gate-pub.co.uk

Adnams Bitter; Caledonian Deuchars IPA; Gale's HSB; Taylor Landlord; Young's Bitter; guest beers H

First a beer house in 1838, it remained one until it was bought by Flowers Brewery in 1953. Run by the same family since 1988, it is a real community pub and runs sports and pub game teams. Several beer festivals are held every year, the biggest in a marquee in the car park on August bank holiday. A popular destination for its changing guest ales, the pub will soon sell its 3,000th real ale. Real cider from Saxon Mill is stocked. The Sawbridgeworth Brewery is at the rear of the pub. ❀◐⊟♿⇌♣●P⚟

Stevenage

Our Mutual Friend

Broadwater Crescent, SG2 8EH

(off A602 at Esso garage)

12-11; 12-3, 7-10.30 Sun

☎ (01438) 312282

Caledonian Deuchars IPA; Tetley Dark Mild; guest beers H

Friendly pub whose name is derived from the Dickens novel. The thriving two-bar pub hosts pool and darts matches and quiz nights. Stevenage Borough FC ground is nearby. Three permanent beers, including one mild, are available as well as three guests and real perry. A beer festival is held in January at this former CAMRA Pub of the Season and most improved pub award winner.
Q❀◐⊟♣●P▯

Tring

King's Arms

King Street, HP23 6BE

12-2.30 (3 Fri), 7-11; 11.30-3, 7-11 Sat; 12-4, 7-10.30 Sun

☎ (01442) 823318

Wadworth 6X; guest beers H

The striking fuchsia pink façade and impressive pillared entrance of the 'KA' welcome you into this back-street beer haven, a winner of many CAMRA awards. It serves an ever-changing array of five ales and occasional cider. The half-panelled interior displays a large collection of brewery plaques and mirrors. There are two real fires in winter and a secluded, heated patio with canopies for outdoor drinking. The home-cooked food is based on an imaginative international menu. A takeaway beer service is offered. Children are welcome at lunchtime.
⌂Q❀◐◑♣●⚟

Robin Hood ✔

1 Brook Street, HP23 5ED (at B4635/B486 jct)

11-2.30 (3 Sat), 5.30 (6.30 Sat)-11; 12-3, 7-10.30 Sun

☎ (01442) 824912

Fuller's Chiswick, London Pride, ESB, seasonal beers H

Pristine, town-centre Fuller's pub with a country feel dating from the 1800s. The single bar gleams with an array of handpumps featuring the brewery's beers, including seasonal and special brews. A raised no-smoking area to the rear has exposed rafters displaying a variety of brasses and breweriana. Two solid fuel burners add to the rural feel. The menu specialises in seafood. There is a courtyard with seating.
⌂Q❀◐◑♿⚟

Tyttenhanger Green

Plough

AL4 0RW (off A414 via Highfield Lane)

11.30-2.30 (11-3 Sat), 6-11; 12-3.30, 7-10.30 Sun

(01727) 857777

Fuller's London Pride, ESB; guest beers H

Deservedly busy country free house with an ever-changing range of up to six guest beers as well as the Fuller's staples. Excellent value food makes it a popular lunchtime destination. The large garden has children's play equipment and there is a conservatory for families. Look out for the impressive collection of bottled beers and the landlord's self-deprecating beermats.

Q P

Ware

Crooked Billet

140 Musley Hill, SG12 7NL (via New Rd from High St)

12-2.30 (not Mon, Wed or Thu), 5.30-11; 12-11 Sat; 12-10.30 Sun

(01920) 462516

Greene King XX Mild, IPA; guest beer H

This justifiably popular local is well worth tracking down. There are two main bar areas, one relaxed and cosy, the other more lively with a pool table and Sky Sports on TV. Carlisle United fans will be given the red carpet treatment! The beers usually include the hard-to-find Greene King Mild, although it may not be available on tap in the summer.

Wareside

Chequers Inn

SG12 7QY (between Ware and Widford on B1004) OS395155

12-3, 6-11; 12-10.30 Sun

(01920) 467010

Beer range varies G

Situated in a pretty part of east Hertfordshire, this low-beamed pub dates from the 16th century and offers excellent beers, mostly from smaller breweries, straight from the barrel. Guests often include a mild, stout or porter. The restaurant menu offers a good choice of food including a vegetarian option. The pub is welcoming and friendly to all; children are allowed until 9pm. Q P

Watford

Nascot Arms

11 Stamford Road, WD17 4QS

11-11; 12-10.30 Sun

(01923) 231336

Greene King IPA, Abbot; guest beers H

Comfortable and popular, street-corner local in a residential part of town. The emphasis is on sports and games and there is a big screen for watching live matches, especially rugby and football. Food is served at lunchtime and evenings. Guest beers come from independent breweries such as Bateman and Brains, or from Greene King. Look out for the 'Top Corner Club' library by the bar. (Junction)

Southern Cross

41 Langley Road, WD17 4PP

11-11; 12-10.30 Sun

(01923) 256033

Caledonian Deuchars IPA; Courage Best Bitter; Wells Bombardier; guest beers H

Large, comfortable pub five minutes walk from Watford Junction railway station and 20 from the town centre. Three guest beers from the Beer Seller list are usually available. Food is served until 9pm, including blackboard specials. This remains a popular locals' pub and is also busy with students from the nearby college. A quiz is held on Tuesday, Thursday and Sunday evenings. Accommodation is available.

(Junction) P

Whitwell

Maiden's Head

67 High Street, SG4 8AH

12-3, 5-11; 12-3, 7-10.30 Sun

(01438) 871392

McMullen AK, Country; guest beers H

One of the flagship McMullen pubs, the Maiden's Head has been a regular Guide entry for the last 21 years. The public bar in this two-bar pub has recently been carpeted, and there are photographs, paintings and awards adorning the walls. There is also a fine collection of Dinky toys. The pub has won the 'Ted and Josie' award for best community pub and also the CAMRA East Anglian Pub of the Year. P

Widford

Green Man

High Street, SG12 8SR (on B1004)

12-3, 5.30-11; 12-11 Fri & Sat; 12-10.30 Sun

(01279) 842846

Adnams Bitter; McMullen AK; guest beers H

Now the only pub remaining in this small village, popular with locals, cyclists and ramblers, the emphasis here is on drinking. However, simple, high quality and reasonably priced food is served at lunchtime, along with a good range of guest ales; guests are normally from small, independent breweries. The B&B accommodation here is popular and must be booked. The local bus service No. 351 Bishop's Stortford-Hertford stops outside the pub.

Q P

Wildhill

Woodman

Wildhill Road, AL9 6EA

(between A1000 and B158) OS265068

11.30-2.30, 5.30-11; 12-2.30, 7-10 Sun

(01707) 642618

Greene King IPA, Abbot; McMullen AK; guest beers H

This small, friendly village pub specialises in beers from micro-breweries near and far and offers up to three guests at a time. Popular with office workers for lunch, it is also busy on Sunday lunchtime, although no food is served at that time. The large garden is lovely in summer. It is a favourite watering hole for Saracens rugby fans – the landlord is a keen supporter. The pub has won many awards including CAMRA local Pub of the Year a record five times. Well worth a visit – look out for God's Waiting Room!

Q P

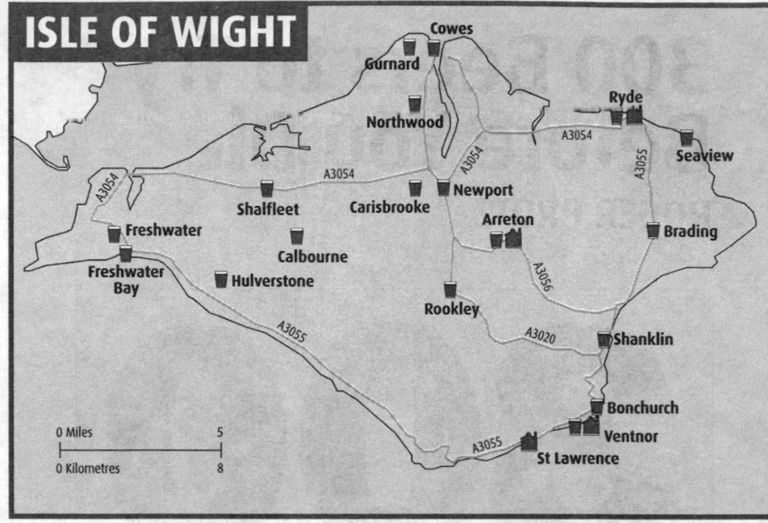

Arreton

White Lion

Main Road, PO30 3AA

✪ 11-11; 12-10.30 Sun

☎ (01983) 528479 website: www.white-lion-arreton.com

Badger Best; Fuller's London Pride; Taylor Landlord; guest beer Ⓗ

Lovely old staging inn within a short distance of the 13th-century church of St George. Beamed ceilings and brassware complement the assortment of old signs and bric-a-brac. There is a stable room available for private parties up to 35 people. The pub has achieved a high reputation for good quality food, which is served every day from 12-9pm. Well-behaved children are always welcome. ♨❀◑P⍻

Bonchurch

Bonchurch Inn

The Chute, PO38 1NU (off Shanklin to Ventnor road)

✪ 11-3, 6.30-11; 12-3, 7-10.30 Sun

☎ (01983) 852611 website: www.bonchurch-inn.co.uk

Courage Best Bitter, Directors; Greene King Ruddles Best Ⓗ

Superbly preserved stone pub, tucked away in a Dickensian courtyard, formerly the stables of the adjacent Manor House. Little has changed since first gaining its licence in the 1840s, making this one of the most unspoilt pubs on the island. As well as featuring in an episode of TV's The Detectives, there are mementos and keepsakes from many of the stars who have visited. There is an Italian restaurant across the courtyard. Q❀⇌◑♣P⍻

Brading

Yarbridge Inn

Yarbridge, PO36 0AA

(left at traffic lights between Brading and Sandown)

✪ 11-11 (11-3, 5-11 winter); 12-10.30 Sun

☎ (01983) 404212 website: www.yarbridge.co.uk

Moorhouses Pendle Witches Brew; Oakleaf Hole Hearted; RCH East Street Cream; Taylor Landlord; Ventnor Golden; guest beer Ⓗ

Previously known as the Anglers, this is a very pleasant single-bar pub that keeps an interesting selection of changing ales. It provides a dining area, where the menu includes a specials board and a choice of roast on Sunday. There is plenty of railway memorabilia, its own model train and the Brading to Sandown line at the bottom of the garden. ❀◑▲≠♣●P⍻▯

Calbourne

Sun Inn

Sun Hill, PO30 4JA

✪ 11-3, 5-11 (11-11 summer); 12-3, 6-10.30 (12-10.30 summer) Sun

☎ (01983) 531231 website: www.suninn-calbourne.co.uk

Adnams Broadside; Butcombe Bitter; Greene King Old Speckled Hen; Taylor Landlord; guest beer Ⓗ

Friendly village pub, overlooking Westover cricket ground, with a traditional public bar. Splendid views can be had of Westover, Brighstone Forest and of Freshwater Cliffs in the distance. A garden, patio and a very large car park are added attractions. Good home-made food includes a daily roast. Four ales are always available as well as an ever-changing range of guest beers. Winkle Street is but a short stagger away. Well-behaved children are welcome. ❀◑⊟▲♣P

Carisbrooke

Waverly

2 Clatterford Road, PO30 1PA

✪ 11-11; 12-10.30 Sun

☎ (01983) 522338 website: www.thesportsmansrest.com

Archers Best Bitter; Hampshire Ironside, seasonal beers; Ventnor Golden; Yates' Undercliff Experience; guest beer Ⓗ

Large local at the village crossroads that has retained its individual rooms. The present incumbent, with a record of successful pubs in the area, has quickly built a reputation for good quality food and interesting beer. Real cider is available during the summer months. Local memorabilia is displayed around the walls and a large-screen TV is switched on for big occasions. There is plenty of room for well-behaved children. ♔Q❀⇌◐◑⊟♣●P⊬

Cowes

Union Inn

Watchhouse Lane, PO31 7QH (off the Parade)

⊛ 11-11 (11-3, 6-11 winter); 12-10.30 Sun

☎ (01983) 293163

Gale's Butser (summer), **HSB, seasonal beers; guest beer** (summer) ⊞

One three-sided bar services the lounge, a snug, a dining area and an airy conservatory that had originally been the yard. The guest ale in summer comes from the Gale's portfolio. Note the interesting collection of photographs associated with the sea. The specials board has some tasty offerings; meals are served all day in the summer. A roaring fire in the winter adds to the overall cosy atmosphere. ♔❀⇌◐◑♿

Freshwater

Prince of Wales

Princes Road, PO40 9ED

⊛ 11-11; 12-10.30 Sun

☎ (01983) 753535

Archers Dark Mild, Best Bitter; Greene King Abbot; Ringwood Fortyniner; Wadworth 6X; guest beer ⊞

This fine, unspoilt town pub is run by possibly the longest-serving landlord on the island. A strong games section adds to the lively atmosphere. Just off the main Freshwater shopping centre, it has a large garden for hot summer days and a pleasant snug bar to sample the ales in winter. It now has a barrel of cider out the back. No need to phone for a taxi – the landlord has one. Q❀⊟⅄♣●P⊬⊓

Freshwater Bay

Fat Cat

Sandpipers, Coastguard Lane, PO40 9QX

⊛ 11-11; 10.30-10.30 Sun

☎ (01983) 758500 website: www.sandpipershotel.com

Black Sheep Best Bitter; Mordue Workie Ticket; Ringwood Best Bitter, Old Thumper; guest beer ⊞

A real gem, tucked away within the Sandpipers Hotel and situated between Freshwater Bay and the Afton Nature Reserve. It stocks an ever-changing range of ales. This is well worth a visit, especially at the end of March for the biggest real ale festival on the island with 60 ales on offer. For the children, there is an adventure playground and a cosy playroom with games and amusements.

♔Q♉❀⇌◐⊟♿⅄♣●P⊬⊓

Gurnard

Woodvale Hotel

1 Princess Esplanade, PO31 8LE (on the seafront)

⊛ 11-11; 12-10.30 Sun

☎ (01983) 292037 website: www.the-woodvale.co.uk

Badger Tanglefoot; Fuller's London Pride; Greene King Abbot, Old Speckled Hen; Taylor Landlord; guest beers ⊞

Just a short walk along the esplanade from Cowes stands the splendid former Mew Langton Hotel. Within yards of the water's edge it offers a grandstand view of the racing yachts and shipping movements, not to mention the odd power boat race. Recently renovated to a high standard, it now has a function room upstairs and five spectacular letting rooms. Enjoy summer days or balmy evenings in the large garden. An excellent selection of food is available all day. ♔♉❀⇌◐◑♣P

Hulverstone

Sun Inn

Main Road, PO30 4EH

⊛ 11-11; 12-10.30 Sun

☎ (01983) 741124 website: www.sun-hulverstone.com

Badger Best; Goddards Special Bitter; Taylor Landlord; Ventnor Golden; guest beer ⊞

This 600-year-old building at the heart of the rural west Wight boasts a charming garden and uninterrupted views to sea. It has now been restored to its former glory after a few years of uncertainty and also plans to provide a restaurant. It has built up a strong following for food, which is served all day, with a weekly curry night and music evening. Well-behaved children are welcome.

♔❀◐◑♿⅄♣P

Newport

Prince of Wales

36 South Street, PO30 1JE (opp. bus staton)

⊛ 10.30-11; 12-10.30 Sun

☎ (01983) 525026

Ushers Best Bitter; guest beers ⊞

Formerly the tap to the now demolished Green Dragon, this excellent mock-Tudor, single-bar, street-corner local has established a fine reputation for its ales. Although in the centre of town, this is very much a local, which has resisted the temptation to be 'tarted up', and still retains the atmosphere of a public bar.

♔◐♣●

Northwood

Travellers Joy

85 Pallance Road, PO31 8LS

(on A3020, Yarmouth road out of Cowes)

⊛ 11-2.30, 5-11; 11-11 Fri & Sat; 12-3, 7-10.30 Sun

☎ (01983) 298024

Adnams Broadside; Caledonian Deuchars IPA; Goddards Special Bitter; Greene King Abbot; Oakleaf Nuptu'ale ⊞

Offering one of the best choices of cask ales on the island, this well renovated and extended old country inn was the island's first beer exhibition house. Local drinkers owe much to the Travellers Joy, and CAMRA members have voted it local Pub of the Year on no fewer than five occasions. It always has at least eight beers on offer from national, local and micro-breweries. A good range of home-cooked food is also served.

♔♉❀◐◑⅄♣P⊬⊓

INDEPENDENT BREWERIES

Goddards Ryde
Scarecrow Arreton
Ventnor Ventnor
Yates' St Lawrence

Rookley

Chequers Inn

Niton Road, PO38 3NZ (on A3020, Rookley road)
✪ 11-11; 12-10.30 Sun
☎ (01983) 840314
website: www.chequersinn-iow.co.uk
Draught Bass; Courage Best Bitter; Gale's HSB; Goddards Fuggle-Dee-Dum; Ventnor Golden; guest beers Ⓗ
This country pub at the heart of the island benefits from beautiful views. Considering its present popularity after an extensive rebuild, it is astonishing that Whitbread closed the pub and sold it. Dating back to the mid-1880s, it was once a customs and excise house. These days it is heavily food- and family-oriented but still retains a flagstone-floored public bar and a fine pint of beer. Good children's facilities include a large outdoor play area and a baby changing room. ♨Q☺❀◐◑⊟♿▲♣●P

Ryde

S. Fowler's ✔

41-43 Union Street, PO33 2LF
✪ 10-11; 10-10.30 Sun
☎ (01983) 812112
Courage Directors; Greene King Abbot; Marston's Pedigree; Shepherd Neame Spitfire; guest beer Ⓗ
Although not the most charismatic pub in the Wetherspoon chain, this converted drapery store offers one of the most varied ranges of beers you will find anywhere. Fowler was the surname of one of CAMRA's most ardent campaigners in the early days and at the invitation of Wetherspoon's this connection has been marked with a testimonial to his life. After the addition of an upstairs restaurant, there is now a children's menu and this area is family friendly. Q☺◐◑♿⇌(Esplanade) ⊬

Simeon Arms

21 Simeon Street, PO33 1JG
(opp. swimming pool and canoe lake)
✪ 11-11; 12-10.30 Sun
☎ (01983) 614954
Courage Directors; Goddards Special Bitter; Ventnor Golden; guest beer Ⓗ
Thriving, yet unlikely, gem tucked away in Ryde's back streets, with a Tardis-like interior and a separate function hall. The pub is immensely popular with the local community, participating in all the various indoor leagues such as darts, crib and pool, plus petanque on the enormous floodlit pitch during the summer. Evening meals are served Friday-Saturday. ☺❀◐▲⇌(Esplanade) ⊬⊟

Solent Inn

7 Monkton Street, PO33 1JW (by parade of shops)
✪ 11-11; 12-10.30 Sun
☎ (01983) 563546
Banks's Bitter; Oakleaf Hole Hearted; Blake's Gosport Bitter; Ventnor Wight Spirit; guest beers Ⓗ
Excellent, street-corner local, with a warm, welcoming atmosphere. The pub has an impressive record for excellence and was the 2004 Isle of Wight CAMRA Pub of the Year, offering an ever-changing range of six ales. Live music is performed at least three times a week and a friendly quiz is staged on one night. Q❀◑⊟♿▲⇌(Esplanade) ♣

Seaview

Seaview Hotel

High Street, PO34 5EX
✪ 11.30-2.30, 6-11; 12-3, 7-10.30 Sun
☎ (01983) 612711 website: www.seaviewhotel.co.uk
Goddards Special Bitter; guest beer Ⓗ
It may not seem right to rave about a hotel when it is the beer that we are tasting, but in this hostelry, the two are intertwined. From the moment you walk in through the front or back entrances, you will be taken in by the history of the sea that is all around you. The public bar is quite small, but during the summer months it really buzzes. Recent alterations have added a no-smoking bar.
♨Q❀⇌◐◑⊟♿⊬

Shalfleet

New Inn

Mill Road, PO30 4NS
✪ 12-3, 6-11; 12-3, 6-10.30 Sun
☎ (01983) 531314
Badger Tanglefoot; Goddards Special Bitter; Marston's Pedigree; Ventnor Golden Ⓗ
The New Inn has stood at the entrance to Mill Road for 300 years. It is an ancient and largely unspoilt country local with a flagstone floor and huge log fire, where the seafood, for which the pub is noted, continues to entice locals from inland and yachtsmen from Shalfleet Creek. The roaring log fire is a delight in the winter and, for the summer, there is a sheltered garden to the rear. Well-behaved children are welcome.
♨❀◐◑P

Shanklin

Chine Inn

Chine Hill, PO37 6BW
✪ 11.30-midnight (12-4, 7-11; 11.30-11 Sat winter); 12-10.30 Sun
☎ (01983) 865880
Archers Village; Draught Bass; Greene King Abbot; Oakleaf Hole Hearted; Taylor Landlord; guest beer Ⓗ
This pub is a gem. The building, which has stood since 1621, must have some claim to being one

Join CAMRA

The Campaign for Real Ale has been fighting for more than 30 years to save Britain's proud heritage of cask-conditioned ales, independent breweries, and pubs that offer a good choice of beer. You can help that fight by joining the Campaign: use the form at the back of the Guide or see: **www.camra.org.uk.**

of the oldest buildings with a licence on the island. Completely refurbished with a new kitchen, it has retained plenty of the original charm for which it was well known. On a summer's day when the sky is blue and the sun's rays are dancing on Sandown Bay, there is no finer view in England than from here.

King Harry's Bar

6 Church Road, Old Village, PO37 6NU

11-11; 12-10.30 Sun

(01983) 863119

Fuller's London Pride; guest beers H

Charming, 19th-century, thatched property with two established Tudor bars and Henry VIII Kitchen that specialises in steaks and grills. The large garden, floodlit at night, boasts a stream, natural wild flowers and ferns, and offers an opportunity to see the rare red squirrel. Adjacent, Shanklin Chine leading to the beach was once the route of PLUTO (the wartime Allied pipeline). A totally refurbished bar area has seen an increase in the number of handpumps. Well-behaved children are welcome.

P

Ventnor

Spyglass Inn

Esplanade, PO38 1JX

10.30-11; 10.30-10.30 Sun

(01983) 855338

website: www.thespyglass.com

Badger Best, Tanglefoot; Ventnor Golden; guest beers H

This inn has considerable character and displays a grand collection of seafaring memorabilia. Wisely, the temptation was avoided to knock all the rooms into one, instead they have been skilfully incorporated into the overall layout. Local seafood is a speciality. It hosts a small beer festival every year and regular entertainment every evening and sometimes Sunday lunchtime, either piano or classical guitar. It has an extensive outdoor drinking area; food is served all day and families are welcome.

P

Volunteer

30 Victoria Street, PO38 1ES (near bus terminus)

11-11; 12-10.30 Sun

(01983) 852537

website: www.volunteer-inn.co.uk

Courage Best Bitter, Directors; Greene King Abbot; Ventnor Golden; guest beers H

Built in 1866, the Volunteer is probably the smallest pub on the Isle of Wight. It operated as a beer house between 1869 and 1871 and retains many original features of the traditional drinkers' pub. Always highly rated in the annual local CAMRA Pub of the Year awards, it achieved first place in 2003. No chips, no children, no fruit machines, no video games, just a pure adult drinking house; this is one of the few places where you can still play rings.

Q♣

The language of beer

Nose: the aroma. Gently swirl the beer to release the nose. You will detect malt: grainy, biscuity, sappy. When darker malts are employed the nose will have powerful hints of chocolate, coffee, nuts, vanilla, liquorice, molasses and such dried fruits as raisins and sultanas. Hops add superb aromas of resins, herbs, spices, fresh-mown grass and tart citrus fruit – lemon and orange are typical with intense grapefruit hints from American varieties. Sulphur may also be present when waters are 'Burtonised': ie gypsum and magnesium have been added to replicate the famous spring waters of Burton-on-Trent.

Palate: the appeal in the mouth. The tongue can detect sweetness, bitterness and saltiness as the beer passes over it. The rich flavours of malt will come to the fore but hop bitterness will also make a substantial impact. The tongue will also pick out the natural saltiness from the brewing water and fruit from darker malts, yeast and hops. Citrus notes often have a major impact on the palate.

Finish: the aftertaste, as the beer goes over the tongue and down the throat. The finish is often radically different to the nose. The aroma may be dominated by malt whereas hop flavours and bitterness can govern the finish. Darker malts will make their presence felt with roasty, chocolate or coffee notes; fruit character will linger. Strong beers may end on a sweet or biscuity note but in mainstream bitters, bitterness and dryness come to the fore.

KENT

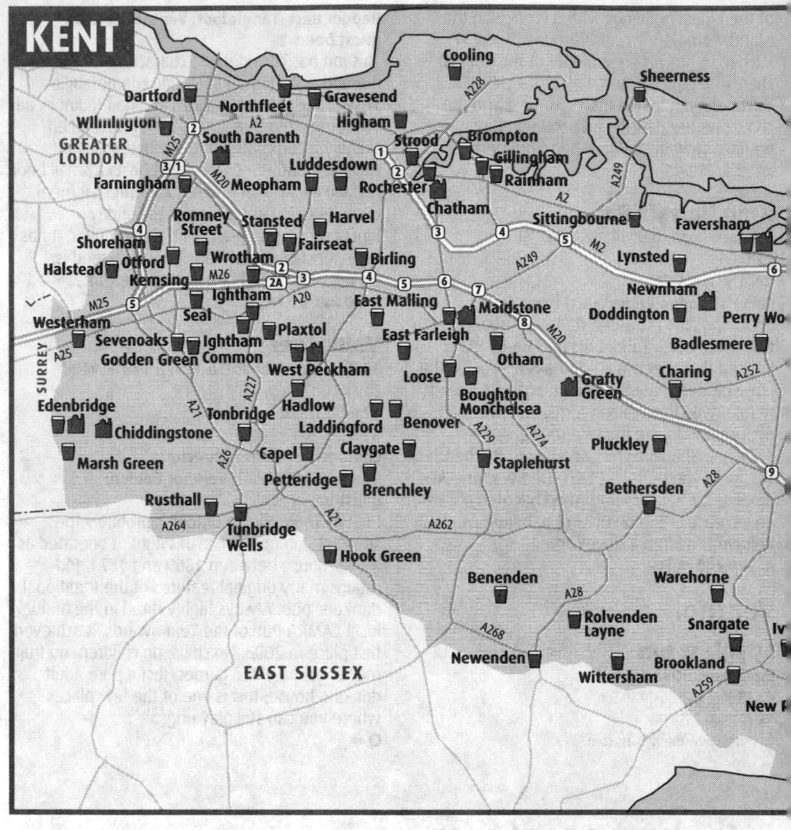

Badlesmere

Red Lion

Ashford Road, ME13 0NX

(on A251, 5 miles S of Faversham)

✪ 12-3 (not Mon), 5-11; 12-11 Fri & Sat; 12-3, 5-10.30 Sun

☎ (01233) 740320

Fuller's London Pride; Greene King Abbot; Shepherd Neame Master Brew Bitter; guest beers Ⓗ

Welcoming roadside local of exposed beams and low ceilings. It dates from 1546 and boasts a naturally cool cellar that once doubled as a morgue. There are normally up to three guest beers. Beer festivals are held over the Easter and August bank holiday weekends. Food is usually sourced from local producers. Johnson's cider from the Isle of Sheppey goes under the name of Marsh Monkey. Bands perform most Friday evenings. The large garden is an added attraction. ♨✿◑▲♣●P

Benenden

Bull

The Street, TN17 4DE

✪ 12 (11.30 Sat)-11; 12-10.30 Sun

☎ (01580) 240054

Harveys BB; Larkins Traditional; Rother Valley Level Best; guest beers Ⓗ

Sizeable, 17th-century pub in the village centre, at the corner of a large triangular green where the village team plays cricket. The Bull's comfortable interior features wood floors, oak beams and a large inglenook. Meals can be taken in the bar or restaurant, which serves a popular Sunday lunchtime carvery. Later on Sunday afternoon performances of live music are staged in the public bar. Guest accommodation is of a high standard.

♨✿⇌◑▲♣●P

Benover

Woolpack Inn

Benover Road, ME18 6AS (1 mile S of Yalding, on B2162)

✪ 12-3, 6-11; 12-3, 7-10.30 Sun

☎ (01892) 730356

Shepherd Neame Master Brew Bitter, Spitfire, seasonal beers Ⓗ

A welcome return to the Guide for this 15th-century wayside inn. A locals' haunt, this rural Shepherd Neame tenancy is run by friendly staff. The single bar has seating for diners, and a brick floor; a second open room boasts an inglenook. Set well back from the road, the Woolpack has a large garden at the back and parking in front. Apart from some unobtrusive music, the inn is blissfully free of electronic distractions. No evening meals are served Sunday.

♨Q✿◑♣P

Bethersden

George Inn

The Street, TN26 3AG (off A28)

✪ 12-3, 4.30-11; 12-11 Fri & Sat; 12-10.30 Sun

☎ (01233) 820235

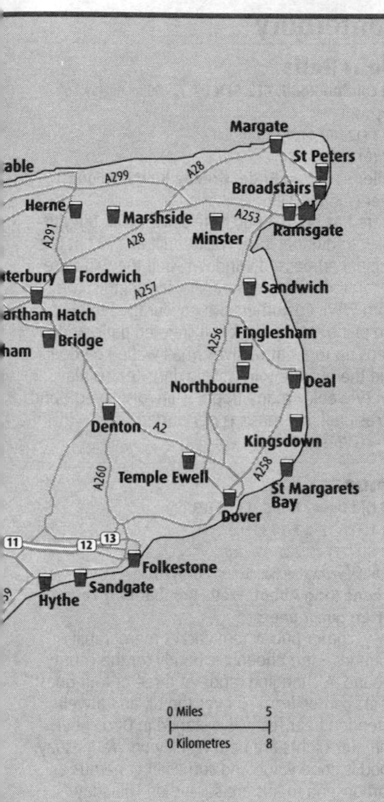

Greene King Old Speckled Hen;
Ⓖ Harveys BB; Ⓗ Rother Valley Level Best;
Ⓖ guest beers Ⓗ/Ⓖ
Two-bar village local serving up to six real ales and good, home-cooked food. Dating from the early 18th century, 1960s cladding has recently been removed from the interior to expose the original brick walls and open fires. Beer festivals are held to celebrate St George's day and over the last weekend in July. The No. 400 bus between Ashford and Tenterden stops outside. No food is served on Sunday evenings or Monday. Biddenden cider is sometimes available in summer.
⛫Q✿◑♣●P

Birling

Nevill Bull

1 Birling Road, ME19 5JW
⏲ 11-3 (not Mon), 6.30-11; 12-3, 7-10.30 Sun
☎ (01732) 843193
Adnams Bitter; Ringwood Best Bitter;
guest beers Ⓗ
Spacious, well-appointed pub at the centre of a dormitory village. The name change to Nevill Bull dates from 1953, in memory of a local noble, Michael Nevill, killed in WWII. The main, mock-beamed bar area has comfortable, red upholstered bench seating; the restaurant is no-smoking. The same varied menu is available in both sections. Absence of TV and low volume on the hidden fruit machines help make for a relaxed visit. ⛫Q✿◑P

Boughton Monchelsea

Cock Inn

Heath Road, ME17 4JD
⏲ 11-11; 12-10.30 Sun
☎ (01622) 743166
Young's Bitter, Special, seasonal beers Ⓗ
Former coaching inn, brought back to life by Young's after many years as a dull Beefeater. It was built in 1604 by Canterbury Diocese to provide lodgings for travellers on their way to the cathedral. Oak beams in the drinking areas are adorned with hops. An excellent menu, served in the bar or the good-sized restaurant, specialises in seafood; children are welcome in restaurant. No food is served Sunday evening.
⛫✿◑P

Brenchley

Halfway House ✔

Horsmonden Road, TN12 7AX
⏲ 12-3 (4 Sat), 5.30-11 (12-11 summer); 12-10.30 Sun
☎ (01892) 722526
Adnams Broadside; Elgood's Black Dog; Harveys BB; Westerham Black Eagle; guest beers Ⓖ
Presenting all the ambience of an old Kentish pub, complete with open fires, beams and hops, this pub is a pleasure to visit. The landlord took over recently and has refurbished the pub to allow beers to be served direct from the cask, and opened up more rooms for drinking. Draught Chiddingstone cider is also available. Beer festivals take place on May and August bank holiday weekends; quiz nights are held every fortnight. The large garden is a bonus.
⛫Q☕✿⛟◑♣●P⚟

Bridge

Plough & Harrow

86 High Street, CT4 5LA
⏲ 11-3, 5-11; 11-11 Sat; 12-3, 7-10.30 Sun
☎ (01227) 830455
Shepherd Neame Master Brew Bitter Ⓗ
This 300-year-old former maltings has no garden, food or music, but is home to over 30 clubs and teams, including art, cribbage, literature and chess groups. It also has a bar billiards table. The vicar works behind the bar here once a month. The emphasis in the pub is on conversation; visitors are always made welcome. The pub is a wireless broadband hotspot with Internet access available to customers.
⛫Q⚃♣P

INDEPENDENT BREWERIES

Goacher's Maidstone
Hopdaemon Newnham
Larkins Chiddingstone
Millis South Darenth
Nelson Chatham
Ramsgate Ramsgate
Shepherd Neame Faversham
Swan West Peckham
Westerham Edenbridge
Whitstable Grafty Green

Broadstairs

Brown Jug

204 Ramsgate Road, CT10 2EW
⌚ 12-3, 6-11; 12-11 Sat; 12-10.30 Sun
☎ (01843) 862788
Greene King IPA; guest beers Ⓗ
Delightful olde-worlde pub in the Dumpton district between Margate and Ramsgate. Shuttered, leaded windows, a flint façade, outside toilets and separate saloon and public bars combine to create an absolute time warp. A selection of board games is always available and it fields strong quiz and petanque teams. Lunchtime opening hours may vary. The Thanet loop bus service stops outside.
♨Q☕❀⊟≢(Dumpton Pk) ♣P

Neptune's Hall ☆

1-3 Harbour Street, CT10 1ET
⌚ 11-11; 12-10.30 Sun
☎ (01843) 861400
Shepherd Neame Master Brew Bitter, Spitfire, seasonal beers Ⓗ
Lively old fishermen's pub, not far from the town's picturesque harbour. Built in 1815 the building is listed and the interior is on CAMRA's National Inventory. Note the fine panelling behind the bar and the large collection of bottled beers on display. Regular music nights and jam sessions are held, and the pub plays a large part in Broadstairs folk week, held every August. ❀◐⊟♣

Brompton

King George V ✔

1 Prospect Row, ME7 5AL (left end of Gillingham High St, first right)
⌚ 11.45-11; 12-10.30 Sun
☎ (01634) 842418
Adnams Bitter; guest beers Ⓗ
This Grade II listed, single bar is a classic, back-street, unspoilt local. The wood-panelled walls display around 100 military plaques denoting its association with the local army barracks and nearby Chatham Dockyard. The pub serves three or four changing ales of varying strengths, plus a monthly mild. It also offers a small selection of Belgian beers in a relaxed and cosy atmosphere. No food is served Monday evening or Sunday.
◐⊭

Brookland

Woolpack

Beacon Lane, TN29 9TJ (off A259, 1 mile SW of Brookland) OS978245
⌚ 11-3, 6-11; 11-11 Sat; 12-10.30 Sun
☎ (01797) 344321
Shepherd Neame Master Brew Bitter, Spitfire, seasonal beers Ⓗ
Ancient timber-framed, hall house in the beautiful rural area of Walland Marsh. Old furniture is arranged in front of a large open fire. Shove-penny and -ha'penny are etched into an old, long table. Good value food is served daily; all day (12-9) at weekends. Note the spinning wheel on the ceiling once used to allocate contraband and wool. It is well worth finding for the warm welcome.
♨Q☕❀◐⊟♣P

Canterbury

Eight Bells

34 London Road, CT2 8LN (off A2050 roundabout on ring road)
⌚ 3 (12 Sat)-11; 12-10.30 Sun
☎ (01227) 454794
Fuller's London Pride; Greene King IPA; guest beer (summer) Ⓗ
There has been a pub here since 1708, but this cosy, traditional local was rebuilt in 1902. It has original embossed windows, and the walls are decorated with memorabilia, including some from WWI. Customers are encouraged to play the piano. At the back is a covered patio and steps up to an attractive, small walled garden and the outside toilets. Five darts teams play every week – many trophies are displayed – and occasional live music is performed.
❀≢(West) ♣

Phoenix

67 Old Dover Road, CT1 3DB
⌚ 11-11; 12-4, 7-10.30 Sun
☎ (01227) 464220
website: www.thephoenix-canterbury.co.uk
Greene King Abbot, Wells Bombardier; Young's Bitter; guest beers Ⓗ
Cosy, corner pub where cricket memorabilia abounds – the Phoenix is handy for the county ground. A changing range of three or four guest beers comes from all over the UK and a well-attended beer festival is staged in December. Fun quiz nights are held weekly on Wednesday. Food is good value and comes in generous portions; no meals are served on Thursday evening. ♨Q❀⇌◐♿≢(East) ♣P⊭

Unicorn Inn

61 St Dunstans' Street, CT2 8BS (by level crossing)
⌚ 11 (12 Mon)-11; 12-10.30 Sun
☎ (01227) 463187
Caledonian Deuchars IPA; Shepherd Neame Master Brew Bitter; Taylor Landlord; guest beers Ⓗ
This 1604 pub stands near the ancient Westgate. A comfortable pub, it boasts an attractive suntrap garden. Bar billiards is played, and a quiz is held weekly on Sunday evening. An excellent range of beers usually includes one from a local brewery, while Hopdaemon produces a house beer, Unicorn Ale. There is a wide range of reasonably-priced home-cooked food that includes daily specials such as sea bass (no meals Sun eve or Mon).
♨❀◐≢(West) ♣⊭

Westgate Inn ✔

1-3 North Lane, CT2 7EB (off A290, opp. Westgate Towers)
⌚ 10-11; 12-10.30 Sun
☎ (01227) 464329
Courage Directors; Marston's Pedigree; guest beers Ⓗ
This popular Wetherspoon outlet was created from old commercial premises and features separate drinking areas with exposed brickwork, oak floors, beams and a partitioned dining space. Standing opposite the historic 14th-century Westgate Towers, it is close to the main shopping centre and the cathedral. The River Stour and Westgate Gardens are close by; punt

trips can be taken in summer. It offers a varied range of seasonal beers and food specials. The pub is now no-smoking throughout.
(West/East)

Capel

Dovecote Inn

Alders Road , TN12 6FU (½ mile W of A228, between Colts Hill and Tudeley) OS643441
12-3, 5.30-11; 12-4, 7-10.30 Sun
(01892) 835966
Adnams Broadside; Badger K&B Sussex; Harveys BB; Larkins Chiddingstone; guest beer G
In an idyllic rural location between rows of cottages, enjoy the welcoming atmosphere of the inn's traditional, bare brick-walled interior. Four or more ales are served from the cask, plus Chiddingstone cider. Good value food (not Sun eve) is popular; the dining area and one end of the bar are no-smoking. Themed nights include steak or curry nights and quizzes. The attractive garden houses a dovecote, children's climbing frame, patio dining area and a barbecue for summer weekends. Q P

Charing

Bowl Inn

Egg Hill Road, TN27 0HG (at Five Lanes jct) OS950514
5 (12 Fri & Sat)-11; 12-10.30 Sun
(01233) 712256 website: www.bowl-inn.co.uk
Fuller's London Pride; guest beers H
Historic pub in a remote location at the top of the North Downs. Its large garden has facilities for camping (please book). The Bowl is a regular CAMRA award-winner. It stages a beer festival in mid-July. Three guest beers are always on tap. A small but varied snack menu is available until 9.45pm. Pub games include an unusual hexagonal pool table. The pub is signposted from both the A20 and the A251.
Q P

Chartham

Artichoke Inn

Rattington Street, CT4 7QP (just past paper mill)
11-2.30 (5 Sat), 7-11; 12-5, 7-10.30 Sun
(01227) 738316
Shepherd Neame Master Brew Bitter, Spitfire, seasonal beers H
This 14th-century hall house has been beautifully restored, with a notable half-timbered exterior. In the dining room, a well has been converted into a table. The pub is very much a community local, hosting quiz and race nights, darts, bat & trap and rounders, and occasional live music. It is on the Stour Valley Walk; hikers and well-behaved dogs are welcome. Traditional English cooking includes pub favourites; in winter evening meals are served Friday and Saturday. P

Chartham Hatch

Chapter Arms

The Street, CT4 7LT
11-3, 6.30-11; 12-10.30 Sun
(01227) 738340
Shepherd Neame Master Brew Bitter, Spitfire (summer); **guest beers** H
Overlooking orchards and oasts, this attractive pub is popular with walkers, and has earned an excellent reputation for food. The large gardens boast a colourful display of tubs and hanging baskets. It hosts live jazz on Monday evenings, and two candlelit dinners with live music every month. Cream teas are served on Sunday afternoon and a barbecue Sunday 7-9pm. The pub which dates from the 19th century, is named after the former summer retreat of Canterbury's Dean and Chapter.
P

Chilham

White Horse

The Square, CT4 8BY (15 min walk from station)
11-11 (opens 8.30am Tue-Sun for food); 12-10.30 Sun
(01227) 730355
Beer range varies H
Facing the castle, this 15th-century pub is just one of the beautiful houses in the charming surroundings of Chilham's square. It is adjacent to the 15th-century St Mary's Church, and was the home of a 17th-century vicar whose ghost is said to haunt the superb inglenook; his story is explained fully by the window next to the gents' toilet. The pub opens for breakfast at 8.30am (except Mon) but shuts from 10.30-12 on Sunday morning (no food is served Sun eve or Mon).

Claygate

White Hart

TN12 9PL (on B2162, between Yalding and Horsmonden)
11-11; 12-10.30 Sun
(01892) 730313 website: www.thewhitehart.biz
Shepherd Neame Master Brew Bitter; Goacher's Light; guest beers H
Quaint old Victorian inn, set in open orchards and hop gardens. It comprises two simply furnished bars, one large, one small. The rest of the pub is given over to diners, seating up to 60. Excellent home-cooked food caters for diabetic and gluten-free requirements. A large garden provides a pleasant retreat, with frequent barbecues and pig roasts. Darts may be played here; children are welcome.
Q P

Cooling

Horseshoe & Castle

The Street, ME3 8DJ (follow B2000 to Cliffe, turn right to Cooling)
11.30-3, 7-11; 12-4, 7-10.30 Sun
(01634) 221691 website: www.horseshoeandcastle.co.uk
Adnams Bitter; Larkins Chiddingstone; guest beers H
This quiet pub nestles in the peaceful village of Cooling, close to an RSPB bird and nature reserve. Seafood is a speciality on an interesting menu; evening meals are not served Monday. The graveyard of St James' Church boasts the tombstones that were described by Dickens in Great Expectations. The nearby ruined castle was once owned by Sir John Oldcastle, on whom Shakespeare's Falstaff was modelled.
Q P

Dartford

Stage Door

37 Hythe Street, DA1 1BE
✪ 11-11; 12-3 Sun
☎ (01322) 311200
Shepherd Neame Master Brew Bitter, Spitfire, seasonal beer 🄷
Formerly the Smith's Arms, this town-centre pub was renamed several years ago after the opening of the nearby Orchard Theatre. Carefully refurbished by Shepherd Neame, it displays pictures and artefacts autographed by various stars, including a brick signed by Fred Dibnah and a cap by Sir Norman Wisdom. Darts is played in a raised area (stage left). The garden is within sight of the theatre. The landlord is the licensee of the annual Dartford Beer Festival in Central Park.
❀◐≠♣

Deal

Bohemian

47 Beach Street, CT14 6HY (on seafront, by pier)
✪ 11-3, 6-11; 11-11 Fri, Sat & summer (closed winter Mon); 12-10.30 Sun
☎ (01304) 374843
Beer range varies 🄷
No low beams or horse brasses here – the modern pub is alive and well, exemplified by wood floors and comfy furniture. The landlord's cheerful disposition is all-pervasive, all the more remarkable for a Norwich City fan! Bottled beers from around the world accompany Belgian beers on tap, a good selection of wines and an occasional draught cider. The upstairs restaurant overlooks the 'downs' as the sea in this area is confusingly known.
❀◐◑≠●

Deal Hoy

16 Duke Street, CT14 6DU (north end of town)
✪ 12-11; 12-7.30 Sun
☎ (01304) 363972 website: www.dealhoy.co.uk
Shepherd Neame Master Brew Bitter, Spitfire, Bishops Finger, seasonal beers 🄷
Open-plan, Shepherd Neame pub with a central bar, tucked away in Deal's conservation area. It is a rare outlet for the Kent brewery's porter, and stocks an excellent range of wines, many available by the glass. Especially popular at weekends, comfy sofas and a small garden add to the welcoming atmosphere of this pub, five minutes from the station.
❀≠

Prince Albert

187-189 Middle Street, CT14 6LW
✪ 5-11; 12-10.30 Sun
☎ (01304) 375425
Beer range varies 🄷
Well worth the walk out from the town centre, this 18th-century inn is situated in Deal's conservation area on the corner of Alfred Square, between the main shopping street and the seafront. The small, congenial, wood-panelled local is definitely a pub with a restaurant, rather than a restaurant with a bar. The ales tend to come from smaller breweries, and usually include one from Kent; its deep cellar is naturally cooled. ◑

Ship

141 Middle Street, CT14 6JZ (off seafront, north end of town)
✪ 11-11; 12-10.30 Sun
☎ (01304) 372222
Fuller's ESB; Hop Back Summer Lightning; Shepherd Neame Master Brew Bitter; guest beers 🄷
Cosy, two-bar pub in the conservation area, with a piano in the front bar and nautical prints on the walls; bare wood floors feature throughout. To the rear of the pub, down some steps is a small garden housing children's play equipment. Smoking is allowed throughout, but each bar has a ceiling-mounted air cleaner. The Ship is free from gaming machines or juke box.
❀≠

Denton

Jackdaw

The Street, CT4 6QZ
✪ 11-11; 12-10.30 Sun
☎ (01303) 844663
Ringwood Best Bitter; Shepherd Neame Spitfire; guest beers 🄷
At the centre of the small village of Denton the pub lies on the busy Canterbury to Folkestone road. Although catering for a substantial food trade, it maintains an inviting and relaxing front bar, with five real ales from small breweries all over the country. Formerly the Red Lion, it featured in the early 1970s film, Battle of Britain. Buses for Folkestone and Canterbury stop outside. ❀◐◑P

Doddington

Chequers Inn

The Street, ME9 0BG
✪ 11-3, 7 (6 Fri)-11; 11-11 Sat; 12-3, 7-10.30 Sun
Shepherd Neame Master Brew Bitter, seasonal beers 🄷
Classic, timeless pub nestling in a fold of the North Downs. It has two bars: the public has a pool table and the saloon is entered via an old stable-type door. In winter a cosy fire burns in the large fireplace. Popular with cyclists and walkers, it is also home to the Norton motorcycle owners' club. Locally-made cheese and sausages are on the menu, among other delights. Folk music is performed now and again. Outside seating is provided.
♨❀◐◑⊟♣P

Dover

Blakes

52 Castle Street, CT16 1PS (from market square, head towards castle)
✪ 10.30-11; 12-10.30 Sun
☎ (01304) 202194 website: www.blakesofdover.com
Beer range varies 🄷
When the Mogul closed last year the stillage moved down the hill and the locals followed! Six self-tilting casks and handpumps feature in the cellar bar, plus 52 malt whiskies. A restaurant (not open Sun) and accommodation are also available here. Convenient for Dover Castle, the port, seafront and town centre, it has a pleasant

rear drinking area. Merry banter make this a pub not to miss; especially as it often serves Gadds beers from Ramsgate Brewery.
❀⇌◗ ⥱ (Priory) ♣

Golden Lion

11 Priory Street, CT17 9AA (on roundabout at A256/B2011 jct)
⌚ 10-11; 12-10.30 Sun
☎ (01304) 202919
Draught Bass; Marston's Pedigree; guest beer Ⓗ
Known locally as the Golden Roarer, this pub provides a refuge from the town centre. It enjoys a good, regular trade, but visitors are made welcome. Maritime and Royal Marine prints are joined by details of the local Winkle Club, which has raised thousands of pounds for local children in need; the new Lord Warden of the Cinque Ports is its president. Inexpensive filled rolls are available. Occasional karaoke and live music sessions are staged. ⥱ (Priory) ♣

Red Lion

Charlton Green, CT16 2PS
⌚ 11-11; 12-10.30 Sun
☎ (01304) 202899
Fuller's London Pride; Wells Bombardier Ⓗ
Cosy, two-bar pub, tucked away in a cul-de-sac off the main Dover one-way system. Popular with locals and staff from the postal sorting office nearby, it has a good-sized secluded rear garden with a skittle alley. An open fire, big-screen TV and darts draw drinkers into the public bar. It hosts regular darts and skittles matches, plus a Friday night meat raffle.
⛼❀◖◘♣⚟

White Horse

St James Street, CT16 1QF (50 yds SE from foot of Castle Hill)
⌚ 1-11; 1-10.30 Sun
☎ (01304) 242974
Taylor Landlord; guest beers Ⓗ
With origins dating back to the 14th century, the pub stands at the top end of what remains of St James Street, next to the ruins of the old church. A convenient stop for visitors to Dover Castle and cross-channel travellers, it also retains a strong local following. Refurbished a few years ago, it comprises a front bar and bar servery, with a raised bar area at the back. To the rear, a garden at first-floor level is popular. ⛼❀⚟

East Farleigh

Bull Inn ✔

Station Road, ME15 0HD (200 yds uphill from station)
⌚ 11-11; 12-10.30 Sun
☎ (01622) 726282
Adnams Bitter, Broadside; Fuller's London Pride; Goacher's Gold Star, seasonal ales Ⓗ
Family-friendly pub in a lovely rural setting that is home to farm animals and an aviary. Goacher's Maidstone ales can often be found here. The pub is the focus for the local community, hosting live music on Sunday, special charity nights and occasional beer festivals. A function room is available for local groups. The traditional home-cooked carvery is a speciality for Sunday lunch. A cider is sometimes sold.
⛼❀◖◗♿⥱♣P⚟

East Malling

King & Queen

1 New Road, ME19 6DD OS702571
⌚ 11-2.30, 6-11; 11-11 Fri & Sat; 12-3.30 Sun
☎ (01732) 842752
Shepherd Neame Master Brew Bitter; Marston's Pedigree; Hook Norton Old Hooky; guest beers Ⓗ
Popular, 16th-century pub in a semi-rural setting, next to the well-known horticultural research centre. A changing selection of ales complements a wide choice of menus served in a spacious lounge, no-smoking dining room, function room or large garden – weather permitting. Special occasion menus are available for romantic and family dates, as well as grill nights on Monday and Tuesday.
❀◖◗⥱P⚟

Rising Sun

125 Mill Street, ME19 6BX (½ mile from station)
⌚ 12-11; 12-10.30 Sun
☎ (01732) 843284
Goacher's Light; Shepherd Neame Master Brew Bitter; guest beer Ⓗ
Close to a Victorian mill, this large bar with mock-Tudor interior has been in the same family for the last 15 years and is a genuine free house. A popular venue for local football teams, the Sky sports screen always shows the big matches. A rotating guest beer policy, regular Goacher's ales and, above all, competitive bar prices ensure its popularity. No children under 14 are admitted. Weekday bar lunches are basic but good value.
❀◖⥱♣

Edenbridge

White Horse Inn

High Street, TN8 5AJ
⌚ 11-2.30, 5.30-11; 12-2.30, 7.30-10.30 Sun
☎ (01732) 862208
Shepherd Neame Master Brew Bitter, Spitfire Ⓗ
Recently refurbished, the pub dates back to 1574 when it was a coaching inn, under Royal Charter from Elizabeth I. A courtyard garden and rooms to let add to its appeal. Regular functions include darts nights, charity and family events. It has no set menu, however food is available on request. The landlord coaches at the local rugby club, and is involved with the local bonfire society, so expect a good community appeal.
⛼Q❀⇌◖◗♿⥱♣

Fairseat

Vigo

Gravesend Road, TN15 7JL (on A227, 1 mile N of A20)
⌚ 12-4 (not Mon-Fri), 6-11; 7-10.30 Sun
☎ (01732) 822547
Harveys BB; Westerham Black Eagle; Young's Bitter; guest beers Ⓗ
Traditional ale drinkers' haven that has recently undergone refurbishment to provide a new wood floor and bar fittings. Now no-smoking throughout, the Vigo has retained its quiet atmosphere. There is a large open fireplace at one end. Daddlums, a rare form of Kentish table skittles, is still played in the smaller bar, which boasts a brick fireplace, Harveys' mirror and

large prints of country scenes. Other beers from Westerham Brewery are usually available.
⩩Q⊞⅄♣P⚟⊓

Farningham

Chequers

87 High Street, DA4 0DT (250 yds from A20, off M25 jct 3)

✪ 11 (12 Sat)-11; 12-10.30 Sun

☎ (01322) 865222

Fuller's London Pride, ESB; Oakham JHB; Taylor Landlord; guest beers ⊞

Thriving, one-bar, small corner local in a charming riverside village, complete with family butcher, grocer, post office and curry house. It is close to the Darent Valley footpath and accessible by major roads, although parking is difficult. Up to eight beers include a rotating range of guests, especially from smaller regional and micro-breweries. Nearby cottages display notable flower arrangements in spring and summer. No food is served on Sunday. ◖♣

Faversham

Anchor

52 Abbey Street, ME13 7BP

✪ 12-11 (12-3, 6-11 Mon); 12-10.30 Sun

☎ (01795) 536471

Shepherd Neame Master Brew Bitter, Best Bitter, Spitfire, seasonal beers ⊞

Old pub at the end of historic Abbey Street, well worth the five-minute walk from the town centre. Around the corner is Standard Quay, with its ancient wooden warehouses and sailing barges. The pub is noted for its range of beers and fine menu, which has some unusual offerings as well as more standard fare; fish dishes are a speciality. The Anchor takes on a different personality on Friday evening when bands play. It benefits from a large, sheltered garden. ⩩❀◖◗⊞⥶♣

Bear Inn

3 Market Place, ME13 7AG

✪ 10.30-3, 5.30-11; 10.30-11 Sat; 12-3.30, 7-10.30 Sun

☎ (01795) 532668

Shepherd Neame Master Brew Bitter, Spitfire, seasonal beers ⊞

Stunningly evocative, late Victorian interior: three rooms are accessed from a side corridor. It is patiently awaiting inclusion in CAMRA's National Inventory of pubs of outstanding historic interest. Fine English food is served. The front bar is small but light and airy; the snug in the middle is a classic. The cosy, comfortable lounge bar was once a small bar with the landlord's dining room. A wonderful piece of vernacular architecture opposite the historic Guildhall, some tables are provided for outdoor drinking. ❀◖◗⊞⥶

Crown & Anchor

41 The Mall, ME13 8JN

✪ 10.30-3, 5.30-11; 10.30-4, 6-11 Sat; 12-3.30, 7-10.30 Sun

☎ (01795) 532812

Shepherd Neame Master Brew Bitter ⊞

Step back in time and rediscover the joy of conversation in this true community pub, with no TV or background music. Run by one of the longest-serving landlords in the area, it has been a regular entry in this Guide for over 10 years. It is located just five minutes from the station. Everybody is guaranteed a warm welcome. There is a large single bar area with side section for darts and pool. Q◖⥶♣

Elephant

31 The Mall, ME13 8JN

✪ 3 (12 Sat)-11; 12-10.30 Sun

☎ (01795) 590157

Nelson seasonal beers; guest beers ⊞

One of the few free houses in Faversham, the Elephant is under the same ownership as the Nelson Brewery in Chatham Dockyard. The result of this connection is that Nelson beers are always on offer, although other brewers are represented. Another exclusive offering in the town is the bottled Honeyhole Farm Cider. ⩩❀◖⥶♣●

Mechanics Arms

44 West Street, ME13 7JG

✪ 11-11; 12-10.30 Sun

☎ (01795) 532693

Shepherd Neame Master Brew Bitter ⊞

Small, traditional local. The licensee is the holder of Shepherd Neame's Master of Beer award. In the summer months the almost-secret garden is a haven of solitude. Sporting events are often screened on the TV. No food is served Sunday. ❀◖⥶♣

Phoenix

98-99 Abbey Street, ME13 7BH

✪ 11-3, 6-11; 12-4 Sun

☎ (01795) 532757

Beer range varies ⊟

Friendly old pub at the town end of historic Abbey Street with its many fine, ancient buildings. Wood panelling and beams abound. Two or three guest beers are offered, often including something from Rother Valley Brewery. An inglenook provides a warming glow in winter, and the sheltered rear garden, with its aviary, is a haven in summer. The landlord's wife is from Thailand and this shows in the quality of the Thai cuisine (supper licence until midnight; no food Sun eve). ⩩Q❀⇌◖◗⥶P⚟

Shipwright's Arms

Hollowshore, ME13 7TU (off Ham Road) OS017636

✪ 11-3, 6-11 (closed winter Mon); 12-3, 6-10.30 Sun

☎ (01795) 590088

Goacher's Mild; guest beers ⊟

This romantic wooden pub sits at the confluence of Faversham and Oare creeks and is surrounded by marshes. There are normally five beers, sourced only from Kentish breweries; Shipwrecked is a house beer from Goacher's who sometimes supply the pub with beer in wooden barrels. A previous CAMRA south-east region Pub of the Year, it has received the local accolade many times. No food is served Sunday evening or Monday. ⩩Q❀◖◗♣P⚟

Sun Inn

10 West Street, ME13 7JE

✪ 11-11; 12-10.30 Sun

☎ (01795) 535098

Shepherd Neame Master Brew Bitter, Spitfire, seasonal beers ⊞

The focal point of market town life during the day, by evening the average age of the drinkers drops and it assumes the role of a vibrant meeting point. The well-preserved wood panelling is notable, as is the beautiful and ancient fireplace, especially in winter when it serves its purpose. For summer there is the garden, or tables at the front in historic West Street which is pedestrianised. In 2003 the pub was extended into the adjacent premises to provide a new restaurant. ⛫❀⇌◐◑♿⚟

Windmill Inn

Canterbury Road, Preston, ME13 8LT

12-3, 6-11; 12-11 Fri & Sat; 12-4, 7-10.30 Sun

☎ (01795) 536505

Shepherd Neame Master Brew Bitter, seasonal beers Ⓗ

This friendly, two-bar pub, retaining many original features, is well worth the 10-minute walk from the centre of town. Situated on Watling Street, the old Roman road from London to Dover, it still fulfills its original purpose as a residential inn. The pub's name is derived from the mill that stood opposite until demolished in the early 1940s. There is a separate no-smoking area.

⛫⇌◐◑⊟⇌♣P⚟

Fingelsham

Crown

The Street, CT14 0NA (signed from the Deal-Sandwich road)

11-3, 6-11; 11-11 Sat; 12-10.30 Sun

☎ (01304) 612555

website: www.thecrownatfinglesham.co.uk

Greene King Old Speckled Hen; Shepherd Neame Master Brew Bitter; guest beers Ⓗ

Welcoming village pub and 16th-century restaurant that is the hub of the community. The regularly-changing specials board puts an emphasis on home-made food. Dogs are welcome outside mealtimes. Local Kentish micros provide regular guests, and a good selection of wines by the glass is available. The recently-installed smoke filtration system helps keep the environment pleasant for smokers and no-smokers alike. Bat and trap is played in summer; crib and quizzes throughout winter. The Crown is Caravan Club certified.

❀◐◑⛺♣P

Folkestone

British Lion

10 The Bayle, CT20 1SQ

11-4, 7-11; 12-5, 7-10.30 Sun

☎ (01303) 251478

Greene King IPA, Abbot, Old Speckled Hen; guest beers Ⓗ

An ale house was first recorded on this site in 1460. It is situated close to the town centre but manages to retain a comfortable and relaxed atmosphere. The pub fields a quiz team, and crib and chess are played regularly. The pub is decorated with some fine old prints from former Whitbread days, including a scene from the Chiswell Street brewery. The food is notable for generous portions; no meals are served on Tuesday evening.

⛫❀◐◑♣

Chambers

Radnor Chambers, Cheriton Place, CT20 2BB

12-11; 12-10.30 Sun

☎ (01303) 223333

Beer range varies Ⓗ

Surprisingly spacious cellar bar with a café upstairs. Lots of activities make this a lively venue. Four beers including local brews are supplemented by a cider from Biddenden. It stands just a few yards back from Folkestone's delightful promenade, the Leas, where the concert hall has recently been refurbished, and on a good day, the French coast can be glimpsed across the Channel. ◐◑⇌(Central) ●

East Cliff Tavern

13-15 East Cliff, CT19 6BU

12-3, 6-11; 11-11 Sat; 12-10.30 Sun

☎ (01303) 251132

Beer range varies Ⓗ

Two-bar, split-level pub hidden along a terraced street. It is a recent convert to real ale, which has proved very popular. Well worth searching for above Folkestone's harbour, which is due for redevelopment. ♣

Guildhall ✔

42 The Bayle, CT20 1SQ (off pedestrian precinct, top of the old High St)

12-11; 12-10.30 Sun

☎ (01303) 251393

Draught Bass; Greene King IPA; guest beers Ⓗ

Traditional pub, close to the town centre, with a single bar that splits neatly into two halves. Usually two guest beers are on tap at all times. Large windows give the pub a light, airy feel. The Bayle is an attractive old area of town, where Charles Dickens once lived and started working on Little Dorritt. It is handy for the shops and cinema. ❀◐♣

Happy Frenchman

Christchurch Road, CT20 2SX (by clock tower at west end of town)

11-11; 12-10.30 Sun

☎ (01303) 259815

Adnams Broadside; guest beers Ⓗ

Spacious, one-bar pub with a large area for pool and darts. The pub's interior was refreshed in 2005 and the exterior is now enhanced by colourful hanging baskets. Varied live music draws a young audience on Friday and Saturday evenings. It is just a few minutes' walk to the Leas and the town centre. ⇌(Central) ♣

Fordwich

Fordwich Arms

King Street, CT2 0DB (500 yds from A28 at Sturry)

11-11; 12-3, 7.30-10.30 sun

☎ (01227) 710444

Flowers Original; Shepherd Neame Master Brew Bitter; Wadworth 6X; guest beers Ⓗ

Classic 1930s pub that replaced an older building, destroyed by fire. The main features are its superb fireplace, a long bar and a woodblock floor. The garden and terrace overlook the River Stour. This friendly, popular local is opposite the tiny town hall of what is proudly claimed to be England's smallest town. The pub is on the Stour Valley walk. It hosts regular live folk, blues and country music. Excellent food is served in the bar or dining room (not Sun eve). ⩩Q❀◑▶⇌♣P

Gillingham

Barge

63 Layfield Road, ME7 2QY

7 (12 Fri & Sat)-11; 12-10.30 Sun

☎ (01634) 850485

website: www.myofficesecretary.com/thebarge

Draught Bass; guest beers Ⓗ

Three of the five handpumps in this traditional, single-bar town house regularly dispense beer from micro-breweries. The house ale, Joshua, is a beer brewed by the local Nelson Brewery. Well-known as a folk venue (Mon eve), a friendly welcome is assured. Decking and a compact garden afford excellent views of the River Medway. Charity barbecues are held in the summer months. The pub is candlelit in the evenings. ❀⇌♣

Frog & Toad ✔

Burnt Oak Terrace, ME7 1DR

11-11; 12-10.30 Sun

☎ (01634) 852231 website: www.thefrogandtoad.com

Fuller's London Pride; guest beers Ⓗ

This thriving town house was Medway CAMRA Pub of the Year 2001-03. It offers up to four real ales, Biddenden cider and a range of 30 bottled Belgian beers. The pub holds four beer festivals a year, including one celebrating draught Belgian beers, in the recently extended garden. Meals are served early evening, Monday-Thursday, and sandwiches are available at other times. No juke box or fruit machines disturb the peace here. Q❀▶⇌●

Upper Gillingham Conservative Club

541 Canterbury Street, ME7 5LF

11-2.30 (3 Sat), 7-11; 12-2.30, 7-10.30 Sun

☎ (01634) 851403

Shepherd Neame Master Brew Bitter; guest beers Ⓗ

The small lounge (formerly the ladies' lounge) was refurbished in 2005, and a wheelchair ramp added to the entrance. A previous runner-up in CAMRA's Club of the Year competition, the beers are kept below mid-4% ABV, as this suits the membership. A copy of this Guide or your CAMRA membership card will allow you to be signed in as a guest. A single U-shaped bar is supplemented by rooms for TV and snooker. ♿⇌♣

Will Adams

73 Saxton Street, ME7 5EG (off lower end of Canterbury St)

12-3 (not Mon-Fri), 7-11; 12-4, 8-10.30 Sun

☎ (01634) 575902

Hop Back Summer Lightning; guest beers Ⓗ

This friendly, one-bar local is a long-standing entry in the Guide, named after a local navigator/adventurer. Up to three real ales (two of which are changed frequently), a real cider, Bitburger lager and 27 malt whiskies are stocked. The pub can get busy when Gillingham FC play at home; the hours can be extended. Good value basic pub food is served. ❀◑⇌♣●

Godden Green

Buck's Head

Park Lane, TN15 0JJ (off A25 at Seal, S along Park Lane for 1 mile) OS553551

11-4, 6-11; 12-4, 6.30-10.30 Sun

☎ (01732) 761330

Shepherd Neame Master Brew Bitter, Best Bitter, Spitfire Ⓗ

Located in a hamlet near Knole Park, due east of Sevenoaks, this is a good place to seek refreshment when exploring the many footpaths in this area. The main bar has whitewashed walls, exposed beams and wood panelling, decorated with framed pictures, horse brasses and large copper kettles hanging from the ceiling. The food ranges from sandwiches to full meals that may be eaten in the restaurant area beside the main bar (eve meals Tue-Sat). ⩩❀◑▶♣P⍁

Gravesend

Crown & Thistle

44 The Terrace, DA12 2BJ (off inner ring road, near River Thames)

11-11; 12-10.30 Sun

☎ (01474) 326049 website: www.crownandthistle.org.uk

Daleside Shrimpers; guest beers Ⓗ

Small Georgian terraced pub near the River Thames and the town centre. A convivial atmosphere prevails, with newspapers and magazines provided, but no TV, fruit machines or children admitted. Chinese, Indian and Thai meals can be ordered at the bar to eat on or off the premises. Three rotating guest beers, from a vast range of small breweries, are supplied by AVS Beer Agency of Gravesend. Westons cider is served at CAMRA's National Pub of the Year 2003. ❀◑▶⇌●⍁

Hadlow

Rose Revived

Ashes Lane, TN11 0AN

12-3 (may vary), 5.30-11; 12-11 Fri, Sat & summer; 12-10.30 Sun

☎ (01732) 850382

Adnams Bitter; Fuller's London Pride; Harveys BB Ⓗ

Built in 1509, this free house was converted from two cottages and called the Rose & Crown; a more detailed history may be found inside. The oak beamed single bar is divided into a number of self-contained areas: note the collection of old keys. A large log fire burns in winter. Food is served daily (not Sun eve). There is a large garden for summer use. A regular bus service from Tonbridge Station stops outside, and runs until late evening. ⩩Q❀◑▶P

Halstead

Rose & Crown

Otford Lane, TN14 1 7EA OS489611

12-11; 12-10.30 Sun

☎ (01959) 533120

Courage Best Bitter; Larkins Traditional; Westerham British Bulldog; guest beers Ⓗ

Two-bar, flint-faced free house, dating from 1860 then named the Crown. It was part of Fox and Sons' estate and later owned by Style and

Winch. The bars show pictures of the pub and village in earlier times. In this Guide for 11 consecutive years, it has a policy of offering three regularly-changing guest ales. A mainly home-made menu is served daily; Sunday lunch is recommended and well-behaved children are welcome. ₼Q≋❀◐◑⊟♿♣P

Harvel

Amazon & Tiger

Harvel Street, DA13 0DE

12-3, 6-11; 12-11 Fri & Sat; 12-10.30 Sun

☎ (01474) 814705

Beer range varies Ⓗ

Lively village local at the heart of its community. This rather austere, 1914 brick building was reputedly deliberately styled as a private house to avoid offending the sensibilities of those attending services in the village hall. It hosts a quiz evening (Mon) and curry night (Thu 7-9pm). Three guest beers come from independent brewers. The two bars are comfortably furnished; one admits children. It enjoys a close association with Harvel cricket club whose ground is behind the pub. No evening meals are served Sunday-Wednesday. ₼❀◐⛺♣P

Herne

First & Last

Herne Common, CT6 7JU (on A291)

11-11; 12-10.30 Sun

☎ (01227) 364465

Fuller's London Pride; Harveys BB; guest beer Ⓗ

This comfortable roadhouse dates back to the 1700s. It is popular for food, but regulars and visitors are made welcome in the bar area. Food is served all day (12-9pm) on Saturday, and 12-6pm Sunday, when booking is advised. The function room holds up to a hundred. The pub is situated on the Herne Bay-Canterbury bus route, with buses about every 15 minutes at peak times. A good place to stop on your way for a paddle in the sea.
₼❀◐◑⛺♣P

Smuggler's Inn

1 School Lane, CT6 7AN

11-11; 12-10.30 Sun

☎ (01227) 741395

Shepherd Neame Master Brew Bitter, seasonal beers Ⓗ

True local, offering a friendly welcome in an attractive village with a smuggling history, situated just inland from Herne Bay. Parts of the pub are 400 years old; the saloon bar is characterised by hanging hops, wood panelling and a ship's binnacle. The public bar is more modern and has pool and darts. Bat & trap is played in the garden in summer. Regular buses from Canterbury, Whistable and Herne Bay pass the door. Q≋❀⊟♿♣

Hernhill

Three Horseshoes

46 Staple Street, ME13 9UA (follow Bull Lane from Boughton, then right) OS080601

12-3, 6-11; 12-11 Fri & Sat; 12-3, 7-10.30 Sun

☎ (01227) 750842

Shepherd Neame Master Brew Bitter, Spitfire, seasonal beers Ⓖ

Cosy pub dating from 1690 in a small hamlet among the fruit orchards and hop gardens, close to Mount Ephraim House and gardens and also Farming World. The beers are served direct from casks behind the bar. A warm welcome is extended to all who visit this friendly village local. Home-cooked food is served; no meals are available Sunday evening or Monday. Live music (jazz/blues) is performed monthly (last Sat); regular quiz nights and other events are staged.
₼Q❀◐◑⛺♣P

Higham

Stonehorse

Dillywood Lane, ME3 8EN (150 yds off B2000)

11-3, 6-11; 11-11 Fri & Sat; 12-3, 7-10.30 Sun

☎ (01634) 722046

Courage Best Bitter; guest beers Ⓗ

Classic pub on the edge of the Medway Towns, surrounded by fields and handy for country walks. The unspoilt, wood-panelled public bar boasts a wood-burning range, darts and a rare bar billiards table. A quiz is held on Sunday evening in the quiet saloon. Good value food is served Monday-Saturday. The large garden to the rear is a bonus in fine weather.
₼Q❀◐◑♣P

Hook Green

Elephant's Head

Furnace Lane, TN3 8LJ (on B2169, near Bayham Abbey) OS807313

12-3, 5-11; 12-11 Sat; 12-10.30 Sun

☎ ((01892) 890279

Harveys Pale Ale, BB, Armada, seasonal beers Ⓗ

Making a welcome return to the Guide last year, this Harvey's pub is situated on the road from Tunbridge Wells to Lamberhurst, near Bayham Abbey. It offers good food to accompany the full range of Harveys' ales. Evening meals are served Tuesday-Saturday (booking advised for Sunday lunch). As well as the conservatory and garden there is a children's play area.
₼Q❀◐◑P

Hythe

King's Head

117 High Street, CT21 5JJ

11-3, 6-11; 11-11 Thu-Sat; 12-10.30 Sun

☎ (01303) 266283 website: www.kingsheadhythe.co.uk

Shepherd Neame Master Brew Bitter, Spitfire, seasonal beers Ⓗ

Pleasant High Street pub offering a warm welcome to all. It serves good value food and hosts regular theme nights and special events. Enjoy a traditional pub atmosphere in this hospitable meeting place, convenient for Hythe's shops and within walking distance of the Military Canal. ₼◐◑

Ightham

Chequers

The Street, TN15 9HH

11-3, 6-11; 12-3, 7-10.30 Sun

☎ (01732) 882396

Greene King IPA, Abbot, seasonal beer; guest beer 🄷
Charming 17th-century village-centre pub, with an excellent local reputation for good food (booking essential). Diners are accommodated throughout, with a no-smoking section at one side; the other is dominated by a large stone fireplace. The Greene King range is supplemented by a guest beer from a regional brewery. The Chequers supports various charities including Kent Air Ambulance. ⌂Q❀◖◗♿P

Ightham Common

Old House ☆
Redwell Lane, TN15 9EE (½ mile SW of Ightham Village, between A25 and A227) OS590559
⏲ 12-3 (not Mon-Fri), 7-11 (9 Tue); 12-3, 7-10.30 Sun
☎ (01732) 882383
Daleside Shrimpers; 🄶 **Flowers IPA;** 🄷 **Oakham JHB; guest beers** 🄶
Hidden away in a steep, narrow, country lane, this red brick cottage is a gem. It has no pub sign and entering through a small lobby gives the feeling of a private house. The main bar, part 16th century, features a large inglenook and exposed beams, while the other bar resembles a quiet parlour. At least four beers are served from gravity stillage in a room behind the bar; guests come from independent breweries. This is an unchanging, timeless survivor from a bygone era. ⌂Q⊟♣P

Ivychurch

Bell Inn
Ashford Road, TN29 0AL
⏲ 12-2 (not Mon; 3 summer), 6-11; 12-4, 7-10.30 Sun
☎ (01797) 344355
Fuller's London Pride; Greene King IPA; guest beers (occasional) 🄷
Church house pub situated on former glebe land. Frequented by walkers and cyclists, a warm welcome is assured at this rural inn that has retained its traditional atmosphere. Both the pub and the church next door were once used by owlers as contraband warehouses. Lunches are served Friday-Sunday. ❀◖▲♣P

Kemsing

Bell
High Street, TN15 6NB
⏲ 11-11; 12-10.30 Sun
☎ (01732) 761550
Greene King XX Mild, IPA, Abbot; guest beers 🄷
Traditional village local, near the parish church. The main bar has a no-smoking area for diners, wood panelling and a glass showcase displaying ceramic bells. The public bar, housing the dartboard, is separated by a sliding door and step down. Mild is a regular favourite, while guest beers come from Greene King's range and regional family brewers. Good food includes special meal deals (eve meals Tue-Sat). The small garden is home to the local league bat & trap team. ❀◖◗⊟▲♣P

Rising Sun
Cotmans Ash Lane, TN15 6XD (phone for directions) OS563599
⏲ 11-3, 6-11; 12-3, 7-10.30 Sun
☎ (01959) 522683
Beer range varies 🄷
Isolated hilltop hostelry in scenic downland near several local footpaths. The main bar area is a converted hunting lodge displaying old agricultural implements. An ancient African Grey parrot lives by the large open fireplace. Five ales from independent small breweries complement the excellent home-cooked English food; generous portions are served every lunchtime and evening. Children are welcome in the restaurant. Ring for directions, the current beer range and to book a meal. ⌂Q♉❀◖◗▲♣P🗑

Kingsdown

King's Head
Upper Street, CT14 8BJ (approx 1 mile E of A258)
⏲ 12-2.30 (not Mon-Thu), 5-11; 12-3, 6-11 Sat; 12-10.30 Sun
☎ (01304) 373915
Fuller's London Pride; Greene King IPA; guest beer 🄷
Split-level pub, partly dating back to the turn of the 18th/19th century, next to the village shops. The lower bar has a display of old firearms, the upper bar barrel taps and pictures of local scenes. Note the frosted glass door bearing the name of a defunct local brewery, Thompson of Walmer. An excellent home-cooked menu includes local sausages; Sunday lunch is served 12-6. Walmer castle is less than a mile away; families are welcome here. ⌂♉❀◖◗♣⚟

Laddingford

Chequers Inn ✔
Lees Road, ME18 6BP
⏲ 12-3, 5-11; 12-11 Sat; 12-10.30 Sun
☎ (01622) 871266
Adnams Bitter; Fuller's London Pride; guest beers 🄷
Typical 15th-century village pub that is truly at the heart of its community. The frontage is a picture in summer, festooned with hanging baskets. A warm welcome is assured inside, in the bar or dining areas. A beer festival is held in late April, showcasing some 30 beers, in a marquee in the garden. The food is excellent, with a variety of sausages, daily specials and theme nights. Off the beaten track, it is a pub well worth finding. ⌂Q❀⇌◖◗P

Loose

Walnut Tree
657 Loose Road, ME15 9UX (on A229, S of Maidstone) OS762524
⏲ 11-3 (4 Fri), 6-11; 12-3, 7-10.30 Sun
☎ (01622) 743493
Shepherd Neame Master Brew Bitter, Spitfire, seasonal beers 🄷
Popular local, consisting of two bars in an L-shape, separated by a realistic log-effect fire. The main area is decorated with horse brasses, WWII prints, caricatures and an unusual collection of chamber pots and shaving mugs. The other bar has a selection of water jugs and a dartboard. The landlord has been here for 20 years. Reasonably priced bar snacks, and hot meals including vegetarian dishes, are available every day except Sunday. Petanque can be played in the garden. Q❀◖◗♣P

Luddesdown

Cock Inn ✔

Henley Street, DA13 0XB (1 mile S of Sole Street Station)
OS664672
⌚ 12-11; 12-10.30 Sun
☎ (01474) 814208
Adnams Bitter, Broadside; Goacher's Mild; Harveys BB; Shepherd Neame Master Brew Bitter; guest beers Ⓗ

Enterprising, independently-owned free house offering at least six real ales, including one from Westerham Brewery, and three draught ciders. The landlord devises and hosts a quiz on Tuesday evenings. The saloon bar features WWII memorabilia, the public bar has a classic car theme and four types of dartboard, and the conservatory doubles as a function room. Petanque is played in the garden. Deservedly popular and well worth finding; no food is served Sunday evening.
♨Q❀◐◑⊟▲♣●P

Lynsted

Black Lion

ME9 0RJ
⌚ 11-3, 7-11; 11-11 Sat; 12-3, 7-10.30 Sun
☎ (01795) 521229
Adnams Bitter; Goacher's Mild, Light, Crown Imperial Stout Ⓗ

Friendly pub sought out by drinkers. There are two real fires at either end of the main room; a second room houses a pool table and dartboard. For the summer there is a large garden at the side of the pub. Wooden floors throughout the pub add to its character.
♨Q❀◐◑P

Maidstone

Druid's Arms

24 Earl Street, ME14 1PP (almost opp. Hazlitt Theatre)
⌚ 11-11; 12-10.30 Sun
☎ (01622) 758516
Fuller's London Pride; Greene King Abbot; guest beers Ⓗ

Conveniently situated, town-centre pub near the established shops and the new Fremlin Walk shopping centre, as well as all three rail stations. Standing almost opposite the Hazlitt Theatre, it is handy for a drink before or after a performance. Good value food is served daily until 7pm. The courtyard is popular and hosts occasional barbecues. Guest beers are usually from Gale's, Timothy Taylor or Charles Wells.
♨❀◐♿⇌

Fox

85 Hartnup Street, ME16 8LT (SW of Maidstone off A26 to Tonbridge)
⌚ 12-11; 12-10.30 Sun
☎ (01622) 729530
Flowers IPA; Fuller's London Pride; Goacher's Dark; Young's Bitter Ⓗ

Typical, back-street community pub serving the locals, both young and old. The pool table is moved out of the way for live music on most Saturday evenings. You cannot escape the many TV screens showing sport unless you go outside to relax or play petanque in the garden. Occasionally extra ales from Goacher's are available via polypins including a mild (ask at the bar). No meals are served Sunday; small portions can be provided for children. ♨❀◐♣P

Rifle Volunteers

28 Wyatt Street, ME14 1EU
⌚ 11-3, 6 (7 Sat)-11; 12-3, 7-10.30 Sun (opening hours may vary)
☎ (01622) 758891
Goacher's Mild, Light, Crown Imperial Stout Ⓗ

This quiet, street-corner, single-bar pub is one of two owned by the local Goacher's Brewery. Its three beers include the rarely seen stout, which is available here all year round. Good value, no-nonsense lunches are provided mainly for the regular customers from the nearby retirement flats; evening meals can be arranged. The pub runs two quiz teams. Toy soldiers are used as beer tokens for customers not yet ready for their refill. Q❀◐⇌(East)♣

Swan Inn

2 County Road, ME14 1UY
(200 yds from East Station, past County Hall)
⌚ 11-11; 12-10.30 Sun
☎ (01622) 751264
Shepherd Neame Master Brew Bitter, seasonal beers Ⓗ

The Swan has become a Guide fixture now, thanks to the landlord's passion for serving his beer in superb condition. Situated opposite the prison, this quiet, street-corner pub offers lunchtime snacks and hosts occasional barbecues in the summer. For distraction, there is a bar billiards table at one end of the bar and a few shelves of paperbacks at the other. A range of country wines and local honey is sold.
Q❀⇌(East)♣⊓

Margate

Mechanical Elephant ✔

28-30 Marine Terrace, CT9 4DE
⌚ 11-11; 12-10.30 Sun
☎ (01843) 234100
Marston's Burton Bitter, Pedigree; Shepherd Neame Spitfire; guest beers Ⓗ

Former amusement arcade on Margate's Golden Mile, given the Wetherspoon's makeover. The name stems from a mechanically-powered elephant that gave rides along the seafront in the 1920s. The pub becomes a waiting room for night-clubbers on Friday and Saturday evenings, but some quiet corners and comfy sofas provide a welcome retreat for those seeking a beer and a chat. ◐◑♿⇌

Spread Eagle

25 Victoria Road, CT9 1LW
⌚ 11-3, 5-11; 11-11 Sat; 12-10.30 Sun
☎ (01843) 293396
Greene King IPA; Fuller's London Pride; guest beers Ⓗ

Popular, street-corner local, offering a changing range of guest beers. Making a welcome and deserved return to this Guide following a change of ownership, the pub has served the locality since becoming a beer house in 1838. A Victorian frontage was added to the Georgian façade, and two adjoining cottages have been incorporated over the years. No food is served on Sunday. ♨❀◐⇌♣

Marsh Green

Wheatsheaf Inn

TN8 5QL

⚙ 11-11; 12-10.30 Sun

☎ (01732) 864091 website www.thewheatsheaf.net

Harveys BB; guest beers Ⓗ

The focal point for its village community, the pub stocks up to eight real ales, including a mild, that change regularly. Biddenden cider is stocked. An annual beer festival is held in early summer, to coincide with the village fête, offering over 30 ales on gravity and a hog roast. The pub has several rooms, including a conservatory. Home-cooked food includes vegetarian options. Darts, cribbage and shove-ha'penny are played. ♨Q✿❀◑◐⊞♿♣●P

Marshside

Gate Inn

Boyden Gate, CT3 4EB (take Chislet turning off A28 at Upstreet)

⚙ 11-2.30, 6-11; 12-4, 7-10.30 Sun

☎ (01227) 860498

Shepherd Neame Master Brew Bitter, Spitfire, seasonal beers Ⓖ

Village pub that has been in this Guide for 30 years under the same landlord. His commitment to the local community includes organising fundraising events and hosting traditional entertainment such as mummers' plays, hoodeners and morris dancing. The bars have tiled floors, log fires and hanging hops. The excellent, good value food (not winter Mon or Tue) is based on fresh local ingredients. It is handy for Kent's new international airport at Manston. The pretty garden features a stream with ducks. ♨Q✿❀◑◐▲♣P⚟

Meopham

George

Wrotham Road, DA13 0AH (200 yds from parish church on A227)

⚙ 11-11; 12-10.30 Sun

☎ (01474) 814198

Shepherd Neame Master Brew Bitter, Spitfire, seasonal beers Ⓗ

Attractive former coaching inn located in the centre of a long village. Believed to date from the 15th century, it reopened in the late 1990s following a rescue by Shepherd Neame from semi-dereliction. Inside the Kentish weatherboarded exterior are two bars with differing styles, and a restaurant serving excellent quality food until 9pm. There is a paved, heated courtyard, a large garden and a floodlit petanque pitch. ♨❀◑◐♣P

Minster (Thanet)

New Inn

2 Tothill Street, CT12 4AG

⚙ 11.30-3, 6 (5 Tue)-11; 11.30-11 Wed-Sat; 12-10.30 Sun

☎ (01843) 821294

Greene King IPA, Abbot; guest beer Ⓗ

Welcoming village local built in 1837 as a replacement for the original hostelry in William Buddell's pleasure gardens. The pub retains its Cobb's Brewery windows, while an extensive garden houses an aviary, rabbit warren and climbing frame. A sympathetic extension provides a dining area and space for live music. No food is served on Sunday evening or Monday. ❀◑◐⇌♣P

New Romney

Prince of Wales

Fairfield Road, TN25 8HW (off A259, near Sainsbury's)

⚙ 12-3, 6 (5 Thu)-11; 12-11 Fri & Sat; 12-10.30 Sun

☎ (01797) 362012

Shepherd Neame Master Brew Bitter; guest beers Ⓗ

Traditional, two-bar local: the public bar houses a pool table and juke box, the lounge has a piano and dartboard. At least one guest beer is usually available. The pub is home to quiz and crib teams and hosts the occasional impromptu piano singalong. ♨⊞♣

Newenden

White Hart

Rye Road, TN18 5PN (on A28)

⚙ 11-11; 12-10.30 Sun

☎ (01797) 252166

Fuller's London Pride; Harveys BB; Rother Valley Level Best; Young's Bitter Ⓗ

You may be joined by a ghostly diner in this 500-year-old inn. A short stroll from Northiam Station on the Kent and East Sussex Light Railway, there are connections to Tenterden and Bodiam for the NT castle. The pub runs summer boat trips to the castle and back. A magnificent inglenook with seats greets you on entry. The restaurant area is no-smoking and serves excellent food. Six bedrooms and a boules pitch complete the facilities.

♨Q❀⊨◑◐▲⇌(Northiam K&ES Rlwy) ♣P

Northbourne

Hare & Hounds

The Street, CT14 0LG (signed from A258 and A256)

⚙ 11-3, 6-11; 12-3, 7-10.30 Sun

☎ (01304) 365429

Fuller's ESB; Harveys BB; Shepherd Neame Master Brew Bitter, Spitfire; guest beers Ⓗ

In a pretty village location near an ancient church and cricket ground, the pub's pleasant garden has children's play equipment. Guest ales include Gadds from Ramsgate Brewery and others. Monthly quiz nights are held in winter in aid of the cricket club and other worthy causes. The completely no-smoking hostelry has an open layout, with hops around the bar, and open fires in cold weather. It is served by local buses during the day. ♨Q❀◑◐♣P⚟

Northfleet

Campbell Arms

1 Campbell Road, DA11 0JZ

⚙ 12-11; 12-10.30 Sun

☎ (01474) 320488

Courage Best Bitter; Daleside Shrimpers; guest beers Ⓗ

Friendly, back-street corner local in an old residential area on the boundary between Gravesend and Northfleet. A community pub, it gets busy early on weekday evenings; it fields darts and football teams, and has a pool table.

Note the Mann Crossman and Paulin Brewery mirror behind the bar. Two guest beers always include a draught mild; the beer prices are exceptionally good value. A basic pub, it is worth seeking out away from the town-centre hustle. ❀⇌(Gravesend) ♣

Otford

Bull

High Street, TN14 5PG
⌚ 11-11; 12-10.30 Sun
☎ (01959) 523198
Wells Bombardier; guest beers Ⓗ
A Victorian exterior fronts a timber-framed Tudor building. Of note are the chiming of the old grandfather clock, the 17th-century wood panelling and two large stone fireplaces. Principally functioning as a large restaurant with several dining areas (some no-smoking), it serves a varied menu all day until one hour before closing time (booking preferred). Fresh fish dishes are the house speciality. Three changing guest beers come from small independent breweries. ♨Q❀◐⇌P

Otham

White Horse

White Horse Lane, ME15 8RG (¾ mile N of A274)
OS796528
⌚ 12-11; 12-10.30 Sun
☎ (01622) 861304
Courage Best Bitter; Fuller's London Pride; Harveys BB; Wells Bombardier Ⓗ
Spacious, one-bar pub with the air of a country local. Built in 1848, it replaced a pub of the same name less than a mile away. One end of the pub is set aside as a restaurant area, although the reasonably-priced food is also served in the main bar; a carvery is offered Sunday lunchtime. The landlord stocks a good choice of malt whiskies and hosts occasional live music evenings. The garden is to the rear of the pub. ❀◐♣P

Perry Wood

Rose & Crown

ME13 9RY (1 mile S of Selling) OS042552
⌚ 11-3, 6.30-11; 12-3, 7-10.30 Sun
☎ (01227) 752214
Adnams Bitter; Goacher's Mild; Harveys BB; guest beer Ⓗ
Remote pub, once a woodcutter's cottage, in the midst of ancient Perry Wood, next to the highest point in East Kent. Nowadays it is noted for its good beer and food (not served Sun eve or Mon). On summer days the award-winning garden fills right up; in winter, warm up by the wood fire, also an award-winner. Unsurprisingly, it has been voted local CAMRA Pub of the Year several times. Outside is a children's play area and a pitch for the traditional Kentish game of bat and trap. ♨Q❀◐♣P

Petteridge

Hopbine

Petteridge Lane, TN12 7HE OS668413
⌚ 12 (11 Sat)-2.30, 6-11; 12-3, 7-10.30 Sun
☎ (01892) 722561
Badger K&B Sussex, Best; guest beer Ⓗ
Splendid Badger Brewery house, offering a fine range of home-cooked food and snacks along with a daily specials board. Well-behaved children are welcome to dine and there is a safe garden for their use. No food is served on Wednesday. Westons Old Rosie cider is also served. The Hopbine has been in this Guide for 16 years so a visit is certainly recommended. ♨Q❀◐♣●P

Plaxtol

Golding Hop

Sheet Hill, TN15 0PT
(E off A227, into Bewley Lane, 1st right)
⌚ 11-3, 6 (5.30 Fri)-11; 11-11 Sat; 12-3.30 (4 summer), 7-10.30 Sun
☎ (01732) 882150
Adnams Bitter; Young's Special, seasonal beers; guest beers Ⓖ
Particularly attractive, ancient country pub surrounded by orchards, notable for its range of ciders, one of which is made on the premises. The homely interior, on three levels, features whitewashed walls, oak beams and log-burning stoves. Good bar food is available (not Mon or Tue eves). Petanque and bar billiards are played. Outside is a flower-filled terraced garden and a tranquil seating area by a stream. Eggs are often for sale from the resident ducks, geese and chickens. ♨❀◐♣●P

Pluckley

Dering Arms

Station Road, TN27 0RR (outside station)
⌚ 11.30-3, 6-11; 12-3, 6-10.30 Sun
☎ (01233) 840371
Goacher's Gold Star Ⓗ
Once a hunting lodge for the Dering estate, with stone-flagged floors, the pub is very attractive and easy to find, opposite Pluckley Station. The regular house beer, Dering Ale, is brewed by Goacher's. The pub is renowned for its good food, especially fish, and hosts regular gourmet evenings. ♨Q☺⇆◐⊟⇌

Rainham

Angel

Station Road, ME8 7UH (from station head N to river)
⌚ 12.30 (12 Sat)-11; 12-10.30 Sun
☎ (01634) 360219
Adnams Bitter; guest beers Ⓗ
Semi-rural pub on the outskirts of Rainham, this popular local has a large L-shaped bar area. Of the three handpumps one offers Adnams, the other two constantly change and sometimes showcase rare beers. Medway CAMRA's Pub of the Year 2004 and 2005 is dog-friendly and welcoming to humans. ♨❀♣P

Mackland Arms

213 Station Road, ME8 7PS (400 yds N of station)
⌚ 10-11; 12-10.30 Sun
☎ (01634) 232178
Shepherd Neame Master Brew Bitter; guest beers Ⓗ
Small, true local, set in a terrace. The L-shaped bar area offers a quiet corner if this suits your mood. The long-standing landlord and his wife

cater for a mixed group of customers, including fans of TV sport. The seasonal ales from Shepherd Neame are rotated along with the brewery's other regular beers. ❀⇌♣

Ramsgate

Artillery Arms
36 Westcliff Road, CT11 9JS
11-11; 12-10.30 Sun
☎ (01843) 853282
Beer range varies H
Unpretentious, street-corner pub dating from 1812, formerly used as an officer's billet and a brothel (although not simultaneously). Note the superb leaded bow windows depicting soldiers, artillery and memorabilia from the Napoleonic Wars. The doorstep sandwiches are a must. An impressive, ever-changing roster of six real ales is always available. ▲●

Churchill Tavern
19-22 The Paragon, CT11 9JX
11.30-11 (midnight Fri & Sat); 12-10.30 Sun
☎ (01843) 587862 website: www.churchilltavern.co.uk
Fuller's London Pride; Ringwood Old Thumper; Wells Bombardier; guest beers H
The Churchill combines a modern, brasserie-style restaurant with a traditional English pub. Affording superb views across the English Channel and busy harbour, it is popular with locals, visitors and students from the nearby language school. The current owners rebuilt the interior in 1986 as an English country pub, using authentic reclaimed materials, including stained glass; the bar was built from 19th-century oak church pews. ⩩◑◗♣

Foy Boat
8 Sion Hill, CT11 9HZ
11-11; 12-10.30 Sun
☎ (01843) 591198
Greene King IPA, Abbot; Ramsgate Gadds No. 5; Young's Bitter H
This former Thomson & Wotton house boasts a unique name and a prime site overlooking the picturesque harbour. The building is a sympathetic late 1940s replacement for the old Foy Boat Tavern that was bombed in 1941. It is reputed to be the model for the Channel Packet referred to in Ian Fleming's Goldfinger. Good value food includes deservedly popular Sunday roasts served until 6pm. ⇄◑◗♣

Montefiore Arms
1 Trinity Place, CT11 7HJ
12-2.30 (not Wed), 7-11; 12-3, 7-10.30 Sun
☎ (01843) 593265
Beer range varies H
Busy, friendly local named after a local Jewish philanthropist, Sir Moses Montefiore, who is buried in a mausoleum nearby. Regular theme nights are held throughout the year and it fields flourishing quiz and darts teams. The pub also gives outstanding support to CAMRA's mild month. It is easily reached by the Thanet loop bus service. ⇌ (Dumpton Pk) ♣

St Lawrence Tavern
High Street, St Lawrence, CT11 0QN
11-11; 12-10.30 Sun
☎ (01843) 592337
Beer range varies H
Now owned by the local Thorley Taverns chain, this lively pub and restaurant was once known as the White Horse and was part of the Cobb's estate. The original pub was sited some 300 yards nearer the church but settled in its present position in 1969. CAMRA's mild month and pubs week are both keenly supported.
❀◑◗▲⇌♣P⁄

Rochester

Britannia Bar Café
376 High Street, ME1 1DJ
11-11; 12-10.30 Sun
☎ (01634) 815204 website: www.britannia-bar-cafe.co.uk
Beer range varies H
Busy at lunchtimes, attracting a mainly business clientele, the pub serves an extensive and popular daily menu, plus traditional Sunday lunches. Breakfasts are also served (10-12pm). A friendly, cosy atmosphere extends into the evening. A stylish bar leads out into a small walled garden that is a suntrap in summer. Live music is performed every Monday evening and occasionally on other nights; a monthly quiz is held. Q❀◑⇌(Rochester/Chatham)

Cooper's Arms
10 St Margaret's Street, ME1 1TL (behind cathedral)
11-2.30, 5.30-11; 11-11 Fri & Sat; 12-10.30 Sun
☎ (01634) 404298
Courage Best Bitter, Directors; guest beers H
Within stumbling distance of the cathedral and castle, this ancient inn features in the Domesday Book and is a contender for the oldest pub in Kent. It has an overhanging upper storey and weatherboarded sides. Two bars hold items of historical interest, including the original fireplace uncovered a few years ago during renovation work. Good quality food includes barbecues on Friday evenings in summer. ⩩Q❀◑⇌P

Good Intent
John Street, ME1 1YL
11-11; 12-10.30 Sun
☎ (01634) 843118
Beer range varies H
The only original building left in a completely redeveloped area, this two-bar local in Rochester's Troy Town area sources its three changing beers mainly from small brewers. It is a short walk from the castle and cathedral. Traditional pub games are played in the public bar, including bar billiards. The entrance to the quieter saloon bar is via the garden gate.
Q❀⊡⇌♣P

Man of Kent
6-8 John Street, ME1 1YN (behind police station)
12-11; 12-10.30 Sun
☎ (01634) 818771
Goacher's Light, Gold Star; guest beers H
Small, back-street pub with a single L-shaped bar. The exterior offers a splendid example of tiling advertising the long-gone Style & Winch Brewery of Maidstone. Five handpumps showcase beers from Kent micro-breweries. Two Kentish ciders are also stocked – one on handpump, one top pressure. Three Belgian and two German draught beers, plus an expanding

range of bottled Belgian beers, add yet more variety. Occasional summer barbecues are held in the garden.

What the Dickinns

1 Ross Street, ME1 2DF

11.30-11; 12-10.30 Sun

(01634) 409912

Beer range varies H

Friendly little back-street local, completely renovated and reopened in 2001. A horseshoe-shaped bar dominates the room with a no-smoking area at one end of the horseshoe and a pool area at the other. Four of the six handpumps are in constant use. Top quality food, using only organic ingredients with vegetarian options, is served daily. A comedy night is staged every Wednesday.

Rolvenden Layne

Ewe & Lamb

26 Maytham Road, TN17 4LN

11-11; 12-5 Sun

(01580) 241837

Adnams Bitter; Greene King Old Speckled Hen; Harveys BB H

Traditional, beamed, country pub with log fire and polished floorboards. The single bar is complemented by a formal no-smoking restaurant, offering traditional French and English cooking. A former Hooden Horse pub, it has undergone a sympathetic refurbishment, revealing many original features, and reverted to its previous name. P

Romney Street

Fox & Hounds

TN15 6XR (2 miles up hill from A225 Eynsford war memorial) OS550614

12-3, 6-11; 11-11 Fri & Sat; 12-10.30 Sun

(01959) 525428

Beer range varies H

Remote country pub in a hamlet in the hills east of Otford village; a welcoming watering-hole for ramblers and loyal regulars. A pool table and dartboard are supplemented by shove-ha'penny and shut-the-box. The pub welcomes children and has a large, peaceful garden. Food is good and plentiful. Four handpumps dispense beers from regional family brewers and smaller independents. It is wise to ring for directions and beer range; a wheelchair ramp is available.

Q P

Rusthall

Beacon

Tea Garden Lane, TN3 9JH (400 yds off A264, opp. cricket pitch)

11-11; 12-10.30 Sun

(01892) 524252 website: www.the-beacon.co.uk

Harveys BB; Larkins Traditional; Taylor Landlord H

Set in 17 acres of grounds on a sandstone outcrop, the view from the Beacon's decked seating area is magnificent. The main bar is arranged like a comfy front room, with two large sofas in front of a fireplace surrounded by a collection of old wirelesses. Specialising in seafood, the varied menu of largely locally-sourced produce can be enjoyed in one of four dining rooms. The downstairs bar caters for functions and is licensed for weddings. Fishing and camping are possible in the grounds.

P

St Margaret's Bay

Coastguard

The Bay, CT15 6DY

(follow winding road down from clifftop)

11-11; 12-10.30 Sun

(01304) 853176

Beer range varies H

Pubs in renowned scenic locations can often be a let-down, but thankfully here is one exception. In a prime site in St Margaret's Bay overlooking the Straits of Dover at England's nearest point to France, it is well worth a visit for the beer, too. The selection features smaller breweries, usually from Kent, but sometimes from Scotland, plus a good range of continental bottled beers. Formerly known as the Green Man, the pub was rebuilt in the 1950s after wartime shelling.

P

St Peters

White Swan

17 Reading Street, CT10 3AZ

11-2.30, 7-11; 12-3, 7-10.30 Sun

(01843) 863051

Beer range varies H

Old smuggling inn situated in a quiet backwater of the Isle of Thanet. A former Thomson and Wotton house, its 1970s-style interior belies its 17th-century origins. The changing beer roster underlines the pub's commitment to quality real ale for its loyal local clientele, however strangers are always warmly welcomed. Q

Sandgate

Clarendon

Brewers Hill, CT20 3DH (up steep footpath from Sandgate Esplanade, A259)

11.45-3 (may close early), 6-11; 12-5 Sun

(01303) 248684

Shepherd Neame Master Brew Bitter, seasonal beers H

Well worth the climb to this rare gem, not only for the stunning views to France on a fine day, but mostly for the Shepherd Neame beers with always two on tap, plus possibly a seasonal offering. A good choice of foreign bottled beers is also stocked. Lovely home-cooked food uses the best local ingredients; fish is a speciality, plus lobster in season. Be warned – do not ask what 'YCUCYFPFTPU' stands for at this local CAMRA Pub of the Year 2005. Q

Sandwich

Fleur de Lis

6-8 Delf Street, CT13 9BZ

(between Guildhall and Market St)

10-11; 11-10.30 Sun

(01304) 611131

Fuller's London Pride; Greene King IPA; guest beers H

Town-centre hotel offering a fine selection of beers, including regular guests from micros such

ENGLAND

as Ramsgate and Hopdaemon both in East Kent. Live music is performed at weekends. An extensive menu is served all day. The pub dates from at least as far back as 1642 and retains many interesting features (take a look at the ornate cupola in the restaurant), with wood panelling much in evidence. Friendly staff and touches such as armchairs and newspapers add to the ambience of this popular local. ⇄◑◗⇌

Market Inn
7 Cattle Market, CT13 9AE (opp. Guildhall)
⌚ 10-11; 12-10.30 Sun
☎ (01304) 615173
Shepherd Neame Master Brew Bitter, Spitfire, seasonal beers [H]
Historic, town-centre pub opposite the Guildhall. A good representation of Shepherd Neame beers includes seasonals such as porter. The pub is divided into two halves – the left-hand side is popular with regulars who enjoy the wide-screen TV and bar billiards, while the other offers a restaurant and no-smoking area for drinkers. Beams, inglenooks, armchairs and newspapers complete the picture at this welcoming pub, which is within easy walking distance of the station. ♨◑◗♿⇌⊬

Seal

Five Bells
25 Church Street, TN15 0AU (100 yds N of High St, A25)
⌚ 11.30-11; 12-10.30 Sun
☎ (01732) 761503
Greene King IPA; Harveys BB [H]
Friendly free house frequented by locals and many groups. Formerly three 18th-century cottages, the wood-panelled interior displays old photos of village life. There is a piano for impromptu entertainment. Barbecues are hosted on most summer bank holidays. A quiz is held on a number of occasions during the year. Three changing guest ales are stocked and a lunchtime snack menu is offered weekdays. Roadside tables allow for outdoor drinking. ❀♣

Sevenoaks

Anchor
32 London Road, TN13 1AS
⌚ 11-3 (10.30-4 Fri; 10.30-4.30 Sat), 6 (7 Sat)-11; 12-5, 7-10.30 Sun
☎ (01732) 454898
Harveys BB; guest beer [H]
The guest beers at this traditional pub are often uncommon for the area, frequently sourced from the smaller breweries. Good value food is served – the Christmas lunches are recommended. The pub has recently been sympathetically refurbished, retaining the unusual curved entrance doors – the inner and outer doors form an almost completely circular lobby. Live blues music is performed monthly (first Wed). The licensee is the longest serving in Sevenoaks and local chairman of the Licensed Victuallers Association. ◑◗♣

Sheerness

Red Lion
61 High Street, Blue Town, ME12 1RW
⌚ 11-11; 12-10.30 Sun
☎ (01795) 664354
Beer range varies [H]
Set in the historic Blue Town area of Sheerness, the pub faces the dockyard wall. The interior features various items of maritime memorabilia, including old photographs of naval ships associated with the local area. Three changing beers are usually available, mostly from independent and micro-breweries – it is also an outlet for Johnson's cider made locally on the Isle of Sheppey. Pavement tables are set out in summer.
♨❀◑◗⇌●

Shoreham

Olde George Inne
Church Street, TN14 7RY
⌚ 11 (5 Mon)-11; 12-10.30 Sun
☎ (01959) 522017
Brains Bitter; Shepherd Neame Master Brew Bitter; guest beers [H]
Shoreham is approximately halfway along the Darent Valley path that runs from Westerham to Dartford through some picturesque scenery. This old pub is located on the edge of the village opposite the church. A painting reputed to be by Samuel Palmer is hidden on a wall in the side bar. When in this area, a visit to the interesting aircraft museum at the other end of the village is highly recommended. No food is served Sunday evening; lunch continues until 4pm.
♨❀◑◗⇌♣P

Sittingbourne

Long Hop
80 Key Street, ME10 1YU
⌚ 11-11; 12-10.30 Sun
☎ (01795) 425957
Shepherd Neame Master Brew Bitter; Fuller's London Pride [H]
This rustic looking local is situated on the busy A2 about a mile and a half from the town centre. Once inside, however you would hardly know there was a main road outside. Originally known as the British Queen, the new name was chosen in a competition organised by Courage. Parts of the pub date back 200 years, although it was totally refurbished around 20 years ago. Gore Court cricket ground stands directly opposite.
♨❀◑◗♣P

Snargate

Red Lion ☆
TN29 9UK (on B2080, 1 mile W of Brenzett) OS990285
⌚ 12-3, 7-11; 12-3, 7-10.30 Sun
☎ (01797) 344648
Goacher's Mild, Light; guest beers [G]
Beautiful, unspoilt, award-winning pub on the remote Walland Marsh. It hosts several beer festivals annually – the main one in June. The walls are decorated with WWII and Women's Land Army posters. This pub is run with love and devotion, preserving the character of an inn from a largely bygone age for the enjoyment of current and future generations. Not to be missed, try your hand at a game of toad in the hole. Dogs are welcome.
♨Q❀♿♣●P

Stansted

Black Horse

Tumblefield Road, TN15 7PR (1 mile N of A20)
OS606621
11-11; 12-10.30 Sun
☎ (01732) 822355
Larkins Traditional; guest beers H
Imposing Victorian building in a secluded downland village near Brands Hatch, the focus of local community life and welcoming to walkers and visitors. A large natural garden includes a safe children's play area. The pub hosts an annual Kent week in early July, when all real ales, ciders and wines are from Kent producers. Biddenden cider is available and local small breweries are supported. Authentic Thai food (Tue-Sat eves) and excellent Sunday lunches are recommended, as is the accommodation.

Staplehurst

Lord Raglan

Chart Hill Road, TN12 0DE (1 mile N of A229 at Cross at Hand garage) OS786472
12-3, 6-11; closed Sun
☎ (01622) 843747
Goacher's Light; Harveys BB; guest beer H
A real gem of a country pub, popular with locals and visitors alike. The main area, occupying the full width of the building, contains the hop-strewn bar and is warmed by log fires at each end. Excellent snacks and full meals are available at all times and may be eaten in comfort in the bar or dining area. Well-behaved children (and dogs) are welcome. The large garden catches the evening sun. Double Vision cider is sold.

Strood

Cecil Arms

14 Cliffe Road, ME2 3DS
12-11; 12-10.30 Sun
☎ (01634) 730812
Harveys BB; Greene King Old Speckled Hen; guest beers H
A recent convert to real ale, this spacious, enterprising pub is just off the town centre. The large games section has two pool tables; a quieter area for drinkers is to the left of the bar. This pub can get busy when there is live music. No food is served on Sunday.

Temple Ewell

Fox

14 High Street, CT16 3DU (downhill from old Dover-Canterbury road)
11-3.30, 6-11; 12-4, 7-10.30 Sun
☎ (01304) 823598
Caledonian Deuchars IPA; guest beers H
This pub, normally stocking four draught ales, is heavily involved in village activities. Outside is a skittle alley and children's play area; inside cribbage, dominoes and darts are played regularly. Quiz night is Tuesday. Food is available but the layout allows drinkers and diners to remain separate. Popular with locals, walkers and cyclists, Kearsney Abbey and Russell Gardens are nearby. Booking is recommended for the popular Sunday lunch carvery at local CAMRA's Pub of the Year 2005.
(Kearsney)

Tonbridge

Cask & Glass (off-licence)

64 Priory Street, TN9 2AW
12-3, 5-9.30; 11-10 Sat; 12-9.30 Sun
☎ (01732) 359784
Harveys BB; Larkins Best; guest beers H
Off-licence specialising in real ales, five minutes' walk from the station. At least one, and normally two draught beers are kept, often including a dark ale in winter; guest ales are from independent and micro-breweries. Draught Biddenden cider is stocked, plus an extensive range of bottled cider and beer, including organic and bottle-conditioned ales, foreign beers and wine. Polypins and mini-pins can be ordered. The licensee offers well-informed and friendly advice.

New Drum

54 Lavender Hill, TN9 2AU (off A26, Pembury Road)
11-11; 12-10.30 Sun
☎ (01732) 365044
Courage Best Bitter; Greene King IPA; Harveys BB; guest beers H
Thriving community local, tucked away down a quiet side-street. The New Drum consists of two Victorian terraced cottages, knocked through into one. Although opened up and enlarged in recent years, the pub retains a homely feel. It attracts a cross-section of regulars, united by a common interest in sport, which is shown on several TV screens. The pub has seen several changes of name and ownership over the past two decades, but cask ale has always been a priority.

Tunbridge Wells

Crystal Palace

69 Camden Road, TN1 2QL
11-11; 12-10.30 Sun
☎ (01892) 548412
Harveys Pale Ale, BB, seasonal beers H
Traditional pub, convenient for the shops. It is popular with regulars who compete with other local teams for cribbage, darts and bar billiards trophies. This sports-minded pub shows national events on TV. A friendly atmosphere helps you relax over a fine pint. The garden, winner of Harvey's Best Town Garden award, boasts a water feature and a childrens' play area. Lunchtime snacks are available.

Grove Tavern

19 Berkley Road, TN1 1YR
12-11; 12-10.30 Sun
☎ (01892) 526549
Harveys BB; guest beers H
This pub is one of the oldest buildings in the village area near Mount Sion. It fields busy pool, darts and crib teams, but always has room for those wanting a quiet drink. The landlord keeps a good cellar and the beer range is likely to include Timothy Taylor's Landlord.

Kelsey Arms

St John's Road, TN4 9TH

✪ 12-11; 12-10.30 Sun

☎ (01892) 614709

Adnams Bitter; Fuller's London Pride; Shepherd Neame Master Brew Bitter; Young's Bitter Ⓗ

Comfortable, one-bar, family-run local, originally a roadhouse, named after the defunct Kelsey Brewery, which brewed locally. Team games – crib, darts and bar billiards – are played while quiz night is Thursday. Live music is staged every Saturday. Sky sports fans are catered for here. Sunday lunch and evening meals are home cooked. The top floor now offers overnight accommodation once more. ♨❀🛏◑♣P

Rose & Crown

47 Grosvenor Road, TN1 2AY

✪ 10.30-11; 12-3.30, 6-10.30 Sun

☎ (01892) 522427

Greene King IPA; Wadworth 6X; guest beers Ⓗ

This Victorian, town-centre pub offers a good choice of real ales, making it popular with the locals. Brains Mild is nearly always on tap. Food is home-made and served in generous portions, so it gets busy at lunchtime. Major sporting events are shown on TV, and bar billiards is played. ◐≠♣

Sankey's

39 Mount Ephraim, TN4 8AA

✪ 10-11; 12-10.30 Sun

☎ (01892) 511422

Harveys BB; Larkins Traditional Ⓗ

Quirky pub selling continental draught beers – 16 on tap at time of survey. It is one of just 10 outlets in the UK selling Belgian Trappist Chimay on draught. The street-level bar is informal and relaxed, displaying lots of pub memorabilia. The menu specialises in fish dishes; evening meals are served in the restaurant. ❀◐◑≠

Warehorne

Woolpack Inn ✔

TN26 2LL (off B2067, between Hamstreet and Woodchurch)

✪ 11.30-3 (not Mon), 6-11; 12-4, 7-10.30 Sun

☎ (01233) 733888

Harveys BB; guest beer Ⓗ

Rural, 16th-century free house, opposite the village church. Two welcoming log fires warm the hop-strewn bar and side room, while subdued lighting and candles help create a relaxed, intimate mood in this vibrant and popular pub. It is ideally situated for a variety of walks on Walland Marsh; dogs are welcome. The restaurant is at the rear. The inn offers a changing guest ale and a house bitter brewed by Goacher's. ♨🚼❀◐◑P

Westerham

Grasshopper on the Green

4 The Green, TN16 1AS

✪ 11.30-11.30; 12.30-10.30 Sun (hours may vary)

☎ (01959) 562926

Courage Best Bitter; Westerham seasonal beers Ⓗ

Overlooking the green and Sir Winston Churchill's statue, the pub welcomes locals, tourists and walkers. Over 600 years old, the low ceilings decorated with antique jugs, the log fire in winter and peaceful garden in summer, give a homely feel. Fresh fish, succulent steaks, home-made pies and casseroles can be enjoyed in one of three bars or the no-smoking restaurant. The house beer is brewed by local Westerham Brewery. The pub is handy for nearby Chartwell (National Trust) and Hever Castle. ♨❀◐◑⊟P

West Peckham

Swan on the Green

The Green, ME18 5JW

(1 mile W of B2016, Seven Mile Lane) OS644525

✪ 11-3, 6-11; 12-5 Sun

☎ (01622) 812271 website: www.swan-on-the-green.co.uk

Swan Whooper Pale, Trumpeter, Bewick, seasonal beers Ⓗ

Parts of the building date from 1526 and it has been licensed since 1685. It stands close to the church, opposite the village green where cricket is played. The beams and brickwork have been exposed and it has a bare wood floor; log fires provide winter warmth. Six handpumps supply beers from the Swan micro-brewery, situated at the rear. Lager and wheat beer are on tap from tanks. Excellent bistro-style meals are available at this popular lunch stop for walkers. ♨Q❀◐◑P

Whitstable

Four Horseshoes

62 Borstal Hill, CT5 4NA (on Canterbury road)

✪ 12 (11 Sat)-11; 12-10.30 Sun

☎ (01227) 273876

Shepherd Neame Master Brew Bitter, Best Bitter Ⓗ

Charming, quiet pub halfway up a steep hill about 10 minutes' walk from the town centre. It attracts a loyal crowd of regulars who also join in with the quiz, darts and bat & trap teams that compete in local leagues. The typically Kentish building, with its long, low weatherboarded front, dates from 1638 and was originally a blacksmith's forge. Inside are several small interconnecting rooms, warmed in winter by real fires, while to the rear is a pleasant garden. ♨❀♣P

New Inn

30 Woodlawn Street, CT5 1HQ

(side street opp. harbour entrance)

✪ 11-11; 12-4, 7.30-10.30 Sun

☎ (01227) 264746

Shepherd Neame Master Brew Bitter Ⓗ

Rare, traditional, back-street local, part of Whitstable's heritage. The long narrow bar was originally divided into tiny drinking areas; etched glass windows provide clues to the old layout. A small snug room can be used by families. Note the original matchboarded walls and ceiling, dotted with coins. Darts and pool are played. A good Chinese takeaway will deliver to the pub when you are ready to leave. Use the large public car park in Cromwell Road. Q🚼≠

Prince Albert

Sea Street, CT5 1AN (opp. Horsebridge Gallery)

✪ 11.30-11; 12-10.30 Sun

☎ (01227) 273400

Fuller's London Pride; Greene King IPA; guest beer Ⓗ

Just a few yards from the beach and popular restaurants, this small, friendly, one-bar pub stands opposite the new Horsebridge development. Note the original Thomson and Wotton windows and the line showing the level reached by the 1953 flood. The small, secluded garden is a real suntrap and a pleasant summer lunch venue. The excellent home-cooked food includes fisherman's pie, steak and oyster pie and specials. The guest beer changes regularly. A public car park is in Terry's Lane opposite.
❀◐◑ ⇌

Ship Centurion ✓

111 High Street, CT5 1AY (opp. Whitstable Playhouse)
11-11; 12-7 Sun
☎ (01227) 264740
Adnams Bitter; Elgood's Black Dog; guest beers Ⓗ

The only pub in town always to serve mild, this busy, central free house is festooned with colourful hanging baskets in summer. Fascinating photographs of old Whitstable hang in the bar. Entertainment includes Sky TV and live music on Thursday evening. Home-cooked bar snacks often feature authentic German produce (the only food on Saturday is schnitzel). A public car park is in Middle Wall nearby.
◐ ⇌

Wilmington

Cressy Arms

1 Hawley Road, DA1 1NP (on A225, Dartford boundary)
11-11; 12-10.30 Sun
☎ (01322) 287772
Courage Best Bitter; guest beers Ⓗ

Small, friendly, corner pub at traffic lights on the A225 on the Wilmington border. New landlords took over in 2003 and have transformed and pleasantly redecorated this pub, which previously had a poor reputation. The bar is a truncated V-shape and dispenses two interesting guest beers on a rotation basiss. One side of the pub is covered with pictures of Ford cars and three glass cabinets contain model Ford cars.
❀♣

Wittersham

Swan Inn

1 Swan Street, TN30 7PH
11-11; 12-10.30 Sun
☎ (01797) 270913
website: www.swan-wittersham.co.uk
Goacher's Mild, Light; Harveys BB; guest beers Ⓗ/Ⓖ

This 17th-century drovers' pub has been CAMRA's local Pub of the Year and continues to delight with its range of ales. Two bars serve seven beers, including a mild, several on gravity dispense. Special events staged here include summer and winter beer festivals and regular live music. Good value food is served, and a warm welcome is assured at all times. Q❀◐◑♣P

Wrotham

Rose & Crown

High Street, TN15 7AE
12-3, 5.30 (6 Sat)-11; 12-4, 7-10.30 Sun
☎ (01732) 882409 website: www.rose-crown.co.uk
Shepherd Neame Master Brew Bitter, Spitfire, seasonal beers Ⓗ

Popular, traditional local in a pleasant village that still maintains four pubs. Near the M20 junction at the foot of the North Downs, it originally had three rooms. The 18th-century pub has been sympathetically altered to give a spacious area around the central bar with a dining section to the rear. Good quality food is served lunchtime and Friday and Saturday evenings. Home to many social and sporting activities including a quiz on Thursday evening, local morris dancers are based here. ❀◐◑♣P

Neptune's Hall, Broadstairs

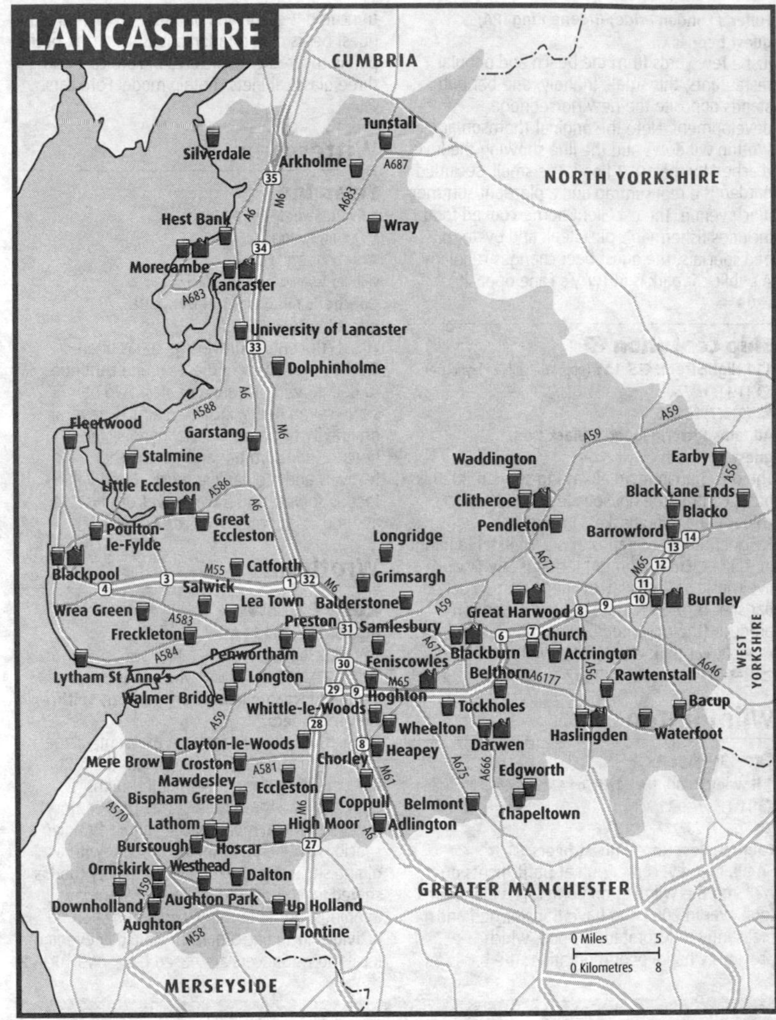

Accrington

Great Eastern

Arnold Street, BB5 1AN

7 (12 Fri & Sat)-11; 12-10.30 Sun

(01254) 234483

Thwaites Original

The Great Eastern is an unspoilt local, having retained most of the original layout, complete with the public bar at the front. It is popular with various games teams based here, and is also well used for meetings of various organisations. In addition to the downstairs rooms, there is a larger room upstairs which is available for meetings.

Peel Park Hotel

Turkey Street, BB5 6EW

12-11; 12-10.30 Sun

(01254) 235830

Lees Bitter; Tetley Bitter; guest beers

Neither Thwaites nor Mitchells could make this pub work. After being closed for 18 months it was bought as a free house in 2003 by the present family owners. It has since gone from strength to strength. A function room/restaurant has been added and the beer range has been steadily increasing, now offering four guests. Regular quiz nights are held and teams are supported in the local dart and dominoes leagues. Food is served every day except Monday; Sunday meals are 12-7.30pm.

P

Sydney Street Working Men's Club

Sydney Street, BB5 6EG

4.30 (7 Wed; 11.30 Fri & Sat)-11; 12-10.30 Sun

(01254) 233194

John Smith's Bitter; Hydes seasonal beers; guest beers

The Sydney Street Club has a spacious, open-plan layout, typical of working men's clubs in the area. It is divided by a screen to form a lounge with a small stage, and a games area with a full-sized snooker table. The club is on the site of the long-gone Sidney Street Brewery. The two guest beers change regularly and the Hydes pump changes with the seasons to offer the best real ale choice in Accrington. ⇌♣

Victoria
161 Manchester Road, BB5 2NY (on A680)
✪ 3-11 (1am Fri & Sat); 1-10.30 Sun
☎ (01254) 237727
Thwaites Mild, Original Ⓗ
Large, open-plan pub on the main road to Manchester, a short distance out of the town centre. The single, U-shaped room has a central bar, while a small games area with pool table is to the left. This pub is popular with both the local community and passers-by and is primarily frequented by drinkers. Easily reached from Accrington town centre, buses to Rawtensall and Bacup pass the Victoria every 10 minutes during the day. ⊖♣

Adlington

Spinners Arms
23 Church Street, PR7 4EX (on A6)
✪ 12-2 (not Mon), 5-11; 12-11 Wed-Sat; 12-10.30 Sun
☎ (01257) 481170
Coniston Bluebird; Taylor Landlord; guest beers Ⓗ
Situated on the main road that runs through Lower Adlington, the Spinners is a cosy local dating from 1838. It has a sizeable bar area with alcoves, plus a no-smoking dining area. At the front of the pub is an attractive outdoor drinking space. The bar's six handpumps offer a dark mild and Saxon cider. The guest beers are mostly sourced from northern and Scottish micros. There is another Spinners in the upper part of the village so be sure to get the right one!
⋒❀◑⇌●P⊁

Arkholme

Bay Horse
LA6 1AS (on B6254)
✪ 11.30-3 (not Mon), 6-11; 12-3, 6-10.30 Sun
☎ (01524) 221425
Boddingtons Bitter; guest beer Ⓗ
This old village inn retains a homely, rustic feel. The three-roomed pub boasts a bowling green and seats in front for outdoor drinking. Most of the pub's customers now arrive in cars for meals, but you can get here by bus Nos. 286, 443, 445 or L2.
Q❀◑▶P⊁

Aughton

Derby Arms ✔
Prescot Road, L39 6TA
(midway between Kirkby and Maghull)
✪ 11.30-11; 12-10.30 Sun
☎ (01695) 422237
Tetley Mild, Bitter; guest beers Ⓗ
Rural pub that is hard to find, being away from the village centre, but worth the effort; you will receive a warm welcome here. Now a free house, the landlord seeks out ales from smaller, more obscure brewers. A no-smoking room, housing a real fire, gives a cosy atmosphere in winter. This unspoilt pub serves good home-cooked food at reasonable prices.
⋒❀◑▶⊟♣P⊁

Stanley Arms
24 St Michael Road, L39 6SA (off A59 opp. church)
✪ 11-3, 5-11; 12-10.30 Sun
☎ (01695) 423241
Taylor Landlord; Tetley Dark Mild, Bitter Ⓗ
One bar serves this popular local in the centre of the village opposite the imposing church. Just off the A59, it is popular for food especially in the evening. A children's play area and garden are busy in summer. Music nights feature often and are well attended. On two levels, the upper level offers the best wheelchair access. The free juke box is a bonus.
❀◑▶⇌(Town Green) P⊁

Aughton Park

Dog & Gun
233 Long Lane, L39 5BU
(near Aughton Park Merseyrail Station)
✪ 5 (11 June-Sept)-11; 12-10.30 Sun
☎ (01695) 423303
Burtonwood Bitter, Top Hat Ⓗ
A mecca for the real ale drinker in Ormskirk. Regulars travel from miles around for the excellent beers, always changing and many from micro-breweries. Originally a farmhouse and then a restaurant, the Hayfield became derelict for four years, reopening in 1994. Since then it has won many CAMRA awards including the Pub of the Year. Meals are excellent value, and games include chess, shove-ha'penny and bowls. Many young customers make it a busy place at weekends.
⋒Q❀♿⇌♣P

Bacup

Crown
19 Greave Road, OL13 9HQ
(½ mile up Todmorden Rd turn right)
✪ 7 (5 Fri; 12 Sat)-11; 12-10.30 Sun
☎ (01706) 873982
Pictish Bare Arts, IBA; guest beers Ⓗ
Fascinating, traditional, stone pub built in the vernacular style of the mid-Pennines. A welcoming, cosy atmosphere prevails, with the emphasis on a quiet, social evening for adults; no children are allowed or dogs. A unique range of beer is featured, specially brewed for the pub by Pictish Brewery. The patio fronts on to a quiet road and there is also a garden. Bar skittles is played here. Sandwiches are usually available.
⋒Q❀♣P

INDEPENDENT BREWERIES

Blackpool Blackpool
Bowland Clitheroe
Bryson's Morecambe
Hart Little Eccleston
Hopstar Darwen
Lancaster Lancaster
Moonstone Burnley
Moorhouses Burnley
Porter Haslingden
Red Rose Great Harwood
Three B's Feniscowles
Thwaites Blackburn

Balderstone

Myerscough

Whalley Road, BB2 7LE (on A59, opp. BA Samlesbury)
12-2.30, 5-11; 12-10.30 Sun
(01254) 812222
Robinson's Hatters, Unicorn, seasonal beers H
Homely country inn, close to the entrance of Samlesbury Aerodrome. It comprises a wood-panelled lounge with bay windows and authentic beams, and a small no-smoking room with a real fire; pictures of aeroplanes abound. It is the base for many clubs including car enthusiasts, anglers and motorcyclists. There is a large garden to the rear. Accommodation is provided in three en-suite rooms. Home-cooked food includes Lancashire dishes (served all day Sunday until 7pm).

Belmont

White Bear

Gisburn Road, BB9 6EP (on A682)
11.30 (11 Sat)-11; 12-10.30 Sun
(01282) 440931
Draught Bass; Taylor Landlord; Thwaites Original; Young's Special; guest beers H
This stone-built inn, dating from 1607, is approached from a steeply cobbled patio overlooking the park. A pub aimed at the over 30s, it places a strong emphasis on food, which is served daily between 12 and 8pm. Quiz night is Tuesday. It stages an annual, month-long beer festival in October/November.

Belmont

Black Dog Hotel

Church Street, BL7 8AB (on A675)
12-11; 12-10.30 Sun
(01204) 811218
Holt Mild, Bitter, seasonal beers H
Popular village local, part of the Holt estate, which is unusual for East Lancashire. The brewery's mild and bitter are always available, along with the occasional seasonal beer. Bar meals are reasonably priced, a dining area is available at busy times. Part of the main bar has been used as a court in the past, dating back to the 1750s. A small cobbled area allows for some outside drinking. Buses from Bolton and Blackburn stop here.

Belthorn

Grey Mare

Elton Road, BB3 2PG (on A6177, 1½ miles S of M65 jct 5)
12-2.30, 6-11; 11-11 Fri & Sat; 12-10.30 Sun
(01254) 53308
Thwaites Mild, Original, Lancaster Bomber H
Traditional roadside inn standing 1163 feet above sea level on the Grane road between Blackburn and Haslingden. Visitors are attracted by the spectacular views towards the coast and the successful combination of reasonably-priced, award-winning food and the ales on offer, including Thwaites' excellent Dark Mild, a rarity in its home area. Food is served daily until 9pm. There is a small outdoor drinking area. A number of buses pass during the day, and the pub has a large car park.

Bispham Green

Eagle & Child

Malt Kiln Lane, L40 3SG
(off B5246, between Parbold and Mawdesley)
12-3, 5.30-11; 12-10.30 Sun
(01257) 462297
Thwaites Original; guest beers H
Outstanding, 16th-century local, boasting antique furniture and stone-flagged floors. Renowned for its food, a popular feature is the monthly themed menu evening (first Mon) when booking is advisable. An annual beer festival is held over the first May bank holiday in a marquee behind the pub. Tables around the bowling green offer wonderful views of the surrounding countryside, while the front of the pub overlooks the village green.

Blackburn

Navigation Inn

2 Canal Street, Mill Hill, BB2 4DL
(off A6062 , by bridge No. 96A on Leeds/Liverpool Canal)
10.30-11; 12-10.30 Sun
(01254) 53230
Thwaites Mild, Original H
Unpretentious, good value local run by the same landlady for more than 20 years. The pub has retained all its character as a result of sympathetic refurbishment. There is a sloped cobbled parking area adjacent, plus a number of boat moorings. A couple of benches at the front enable drinkers to watch passing canal craft. Mill Hill's main shopping area is close by as is Ewood Park, home of Blackburn Rovers. Bus Nos. 21 and 22 run from the town centre.
(Mill Hill)

Postal Order

15-19 Darwen Street, BB2 2BY (next to cathedral)
10-11; 10-10.30 Sun
(01254) 676400
Boddingtons Bitter; Courage Directors; De Koninck Ambrée; Marston's Burton Bitter, Pedigree; guest beers H
This impressive building sits next to the cathedral. A former post office, offering the largest selection of cask beer in Blackburn, beers from Three B's and Moorhouses feature alongside the usual Wetherspoon's range. The spacious, open room has alcove seating, while raised areas at both ends cater for non-smokers and family dining. A drop-screen TV is used for major sporting events. Many local people meet here after work to relax.

St Mark's Conservative Club

Preston Old Road, Witton, BB2 2SS (on A674, 1 mile W of town centre)
11.30-2.30 (not Mon-Fri), 6.30-11; 12-3, 7-10.30 Sun
(01254) 52962
Thwaites Mild, Original; guest beer H
Built in 1923, this welcoming club has two lounges, a games room housing two full-sized snooker tables and a concert room extension. Entertainment takes place on Saturday evening – usually a vocalist – while on Sunday evening dancing or karaoke is the norm. The guest beer is generally a session bitter from an independent brewer. Show this Guide or CAMRA

membership card to gain admission. Buses 123 and 124 to Chorley and No. 152 to Preston pass the door. Q ⇌ (Mill Hill) ♣ P

Black Lane Ends

Hare & Hounds

Skipton Old Road, BB8 7EP
(on old road between Colne and Skipton) OS929432
12-11; 12-10.30 Sun
☎ (01282) 863070
Black Sheep Best Bitter; Taylor Golden Best, Landlord; Tetley Bitter; guest beers Ⓗ
Remote country pub on the edge of Kelbrook Moor, just half a mile from the Yorkshire boundary. There is a strong emphasis on home-made food, which is available all day and uses locally-produced ingredients. Popular with walkers, boot washing facilities are provided. Six ales are always on tap.
♣ P ⊁

Blacko

Rising Sun

330 Gisburn Road, BB9 6LS (on A682)
4.30 (7 Mon; 2 Fri; 12 Sat)-11; 12-10.30 Sun
☎ (01282) 612173
Copper Dragon Black Gold, Best Bitter; John Smith's Bitter; guest beers Ⓗ
This friendly pub displays old photos of surrounding towns and villages in the main bar. The no-smoking parlour has Internet access. The almost impossible to find local delicacy of 'stew an' hard' is usually on the pub's popular menu. Watch the sun setting over Pendle Hill from the elevated front patio.
Q ♣ P ⊁

Blackpool

Churchills ✔

83-85 Topping Street, FY1 3AY
10.30-11 (midnight Fri & Sat); 12-midnight Sun
☎ (01253) 622036
Greene King Ruddles County, Old Speckled Hen; Marston's Pedigree; Wells Bombardier Ⓗ
Lots of nostalgic posters and Guinness memorabilia adorn this split-level, traditional pub at the centre of Blackpool. Both the bar and the floor are varnished wood while the front windows hold the original curved glass; comfortable seating is plentiful. It stages entertainment at the weekend and sometimes evenings during the week which means the pub can get busy, with an extremely lively atmosphere. Food is served during the day until 6pm. ⇌ (North) ♣

Blackpool

Dunes

561 Lytham Road, FY4 1RD (500 yds from airport)
11-11; 12-10.30 Sun
☎ (01253) 403854
Boddingtons Bitter; guest beers Ⓗ
True local community pub with a separate public bar. The Dunes offers up to four guest beers, usually sourced from micro-breweries and it nearly always has a beer on tap from the local Hart Brewery. The pub holds a quiz on Thursday and Sunday evenings. Meals finish at 7.30pm. A front patio allows for outside drinking. It stands on the No. 11 bus route from the town centre.
♣ P

New Road Inn

244 Talbot Road, FY1 3HL
(near North Station at Elizabeth St jct)
11-11;12-10.30 Sun
☎ (01253) 628872
Jennings Dark Mild, Cumberland Ale, Sneck Lifter; guest beers Ⓗ
In the early 1840s Talbot Road was the new road in to Blackpool and the first railway followed nearby in 1846. This friendly 1930s local has not only consistently good real ale but also an impressive Art Deco interior, retaining many original features. The single, central bar serves the main lounge, a games room and a comfortable no-smoking room. A local CAMRA Pub of the Year, it was a silver award-winner in 2005. ⇌ (North) ⊁

Pump & Truncheon

Bonny Street, FY1 5AR (opp. police station)
10.30-11 (midnight Fri & Sat); 12-midnight Sun
☎ (01253) 751176 website: pumpandtruncheon.co.uk
Boddingtons Bitter; guest beers Ⓗ
Busy, town-centre local, a magnet for discerning tourists. Furnished in the Hogshead style, with brick walls and bare floorboards, photos of old Blackpool and the police through the years abound. It stages live entertainment every week during the season and often has beer promotions. This local CAMRA award-winner offers beer discounts to CAMRA members. The home-cooked lunches are good value. Look out for the horse racing on Sunday evening. ♣

Saddle Inn ✔

286 Whitegate Drive, FY3 9PH
(on A583/Preston Old Rd jct)
12-11;12-10.30 Sun
☎ (01253) 607921
Draught Bass; guest beers Ⓗ
Blackpool's oldest pub, established 1770, has a main bar and two side rooms: the first is a cosy, wood-panelled room, displaying pictures of sporting heroes, the second is used as a no-smoking dining area and features pictures of the brewing art. The menu includes daily specials; no evening meals are served at the weekend but Sunday lunch is available 12–5pm. A large patio with tables is pleasant for summer drinking. Q P ⊁

Shovels ✔

260 Commonedge Road, FY4 5DH
(on B5261, ½ mile from A5230 jct)
11.30-11; 12-10.30 Sun
☎ (01253) 762702
Beer range varies Ⓗ
This large, award-winning pub, twice local CAMRA Pub of the Year, offers six ever-changing beers, often from small micros and brew-pubs. The Shovels is home to many sports teams and has a large-screen TV; Thursday is quiz night. It holds a week-long beer festival at the end of October. An extensive menu (served 12-9.30) offers daily specials, all freshly cooked. The pub is on the No. 14 bus route from the town centre.
▲ ♣ P ⊁

Burnley

Bridge Bier Huis

2 Bank Parade, BB11 1UH (behind shopping centre)
12 (11 Sat)-11; closed Mon & Tue; 12-10.30 Sun
☎ (01202) 411304 website: www.thebridgebierhuis.co.uk
Hydes Bitter; guest beers Ⓗ

Mainly micro-breweries' beers can be tried from five handpumps; the Hydes Bitter is on the sixth. This smart pub caters for beer connoisseurs, offering five draught foreign beers, along with over 40 bottled beers from around the world. No juke box or slot machines disturb the conversation, although occasional live music is performed (frequently acoustic). Occasional beer festivals are held. It opens exceptionally on Tuesday evening when Burnley FC play at home. Q◖⇌(Central) ♣

Coal Clough

41 Coal Clough Lane, BB11 4PG
(200 yds E of M65 jct 10)
12-11; 12-10.30 Sun
☎ (01282) 423226 website: www.coalcloughpub.co.uk
Cains Bitter; Worthington's Bitter; guest beers Ⓗ

This end-of-terrace community local is always busy. In the games room the most popular card game is Don. The pub is a well-attended venue for entertainment on Tuesday and Thursday evenings and Sunday teatime. The Massey's Bitter on tap is brewed to an old recipe from a defunct Burnley brewery. Two guest beers, usually from micro-breweries, are stocked at this CAMRA award-winner.
⇌(Barracks) ♣

Ministry of Ale

9 Trafalgar Street, BB11 1TQ
(off A682, Manchester Rd, near station)
5 (12 Fri & Sat)-11 (closed Wed); 12-10.30 Sun
☎ (01282) 830909 website: www.ministryofale.co.uk
Moonstone Black Star; guest beers Ⓗ

A friendly welcome is guaranteed at this small local where the emphasis is on good beer and conversation. The home of Moonstone beers, the micro-brewery can be viewed in the front room of the pub. The beers are available on a rotating basis, with the popular mild (Black Star) the best-seller. Two guests from other micros are sold. The pub hosts regular alternative art exhibitions. It stands 100 yards from Manchester Road Station.
⇌(Manchester Rd)

Burscough

Slipway

48 Crabtree Lane, L40 0RN (off A59) OS432123
12-11; 12-10.30 Sun
☎ (01704) 897767
Thwaites Original, Lancaster Bomber, seasonal beers Ⓗ

Canalside tavern, with a slipway for trailer boats. The large single room adorned with boating memorabilia, is also used for dining; try the Sunday carvery. There is an extensive garden with seating and children's play equipment from where you can watch boats negotiate the adjacent swing bridge. Next door is Burscough Motor Boat Club, with moorings nearby.
Q❀⇔◖◗♿⇌♣P

Catforth

Running Pump

Catforth Road, PR4 0HH (S off B5269 at Woodsfold, then 1 mile on left) OS477362
11-11; 12-10.30 Sun
☎ (01772) 690265
Robinson's Unicorn; guest beers Ⓗ

Traditional country pub refurbished in a sympathetic manner, with an exceptional dining room showcasing a good selection of home-prepared food. Background music is unobtrusive and there are no games machines or TV to disturb the calm atmosphere. The eponymous pump is built into the front wall of the building, and constantly flows. The pub is set in open countryside, boasting clear views to the Bowland Hills, on bus route 182 Fleetwood-Preston. ⛰❀◖◗P

Chapeltown

Chetham Arms

83 High Street, BL7 0EW (on B6391)
12-11; 12-10.30 Sun
☎ (01204) 852274
Greene King Old Speckled Hen; Taylor Landlord; guest beer Ⓗ

Large, comfortable, multi-roomed village pub, convenient for walkers. Built in the 18th century, the Chetham Arms has been considerably extended. Lighting is kept at a low level, as are the ceilings. The food menu is varied and caters for most tastes. The pool room is hidden to the left of the bar. The rear lounge displays an interesting collection of teapots alongside photographs of local sights. Quiz night is Thursday. ❀◖◗P⚟

Chorley

Malt & Hops

50-52 Friday Street, PR6 0AH (behind station)
11.30-11; 12-10.30 Sun
☎ (01257) 260967
Beartown Kodiak Gold, Bearskinful; guest beers Ⓗ

Although it resembles a long-standing, street-corner local, this has only been a pub for about 15 years, having been converted from a corner shop. The Victorian-style decor gives a period ale house atmosphere emphasising its purpose as a place for people who like to drink in convivial surroundings. A quiz takes place on Wednesday evening. Now owned by Beartown Brewery, the eight handpumps usually offer four guests. At Chorley Station, take the platform two exit. ♿⇌

Plough

136 Pall Mall, PR7 3NE (on B5251, just S of town centre)
11-11; 12-10.30 Sun
☎ (01257) 232944
Banks's Original; Mansfield Dark, Bitter; Camerons Bitter Ⓗ

A Banks's house and previous Guide entry, the Plough is a traditional, two-roomed pub situated just to the south of Chorley town centre. The spacious lounge and games room are in fact the result of a refurbishment some 10 years ago, which reconverted the inside from a large, single room – vastly improving the appearance and ambience of the place (a lesson there for other breweries and pubcos). Cask beers on the bar include Camerons dark and Banks's light mild. ❀◐⊟♣P⚟

Potter's Arms

42 Brooke Street, PR7 3BY (next to Morrisons)
✪ 12 (7 Wed)-11; 12-5, 7-11 Sat; 12-5, 7-10.30 Sun
☎ (01257) 267954
Moorhouse's Premier; Tetley Bitter; guest beers Ⓗ
Small, friendly free house named after its owners, situated at the bottom of Brooke Street, alongside the railway line. The central bar serves two games areas, while the two comfortable lounges are popular with locals and visitors alike. The Potter's displays a fine collection of photographs from the world of music and local history. Guest beers are sourced from a mix of family and micro-breweries. ♿≹♣P

Prince of Wales ✔

9-11 Cowling Brow, PR6 0QE (off B6228)
✪ 11-11; 12-10.30 Sun
☎ (01257) 413239
Jennings Dark Mild, Bitter, Cumberland Ale, seasonal beers; guest beers Ⓗ
This stone terraced pub stands in the south-eastern part of town, not far from the Leeds–Liverpool Canal. Its unspoilt interior incorporates a traditional tap room, a games area, a large lounge and a comfortable snug, complete with real fire. There is photographic evidence of the licensee's love of jazz plus collections of brewery artefacts and saucy seaside postcards. A fine selection of malt whiskies is stocked. Sandwiches are on sale at lunchtime. ♨❀⊟♣⚟▯

Church

Stag Inn

1 Bank Street, BB5 4HH (off A679)
✪ 12-11; 12-10.30 Sun
☎ (01254) 399906
Holt Mild, Bitter; guest beers Ⓗ
Typical, street-corner local, comprising a comfortable lounge and a busy tap room. The regulars enjoy games such as dominoes and darts, which are played competitively against other local pub teams. The area has a number of homes for the elderly and the pub organises many events to cater for them. This is a perfect example of a successful community pub. ⊟≹♣

Clayton Le Woods

Halfway House

470 Preston Road, PR6 7JB (on A6, N of Chorley)
✪ 11-11; 12-10.30 Sun
☎ (01772) 334477
Lees GB Mild, Bitter, Moonraker, seasonal beers Ⓗ
Taking its name from its location, the Halfway House is situated on the A6 road just north of Chorley, reputedly halfway between London and Glasgow. A former Banks's pub, now owned by JW Lees, this large roadside inn has been refurbished in traditional style to give a tap room with games area, a large lounge, dining room and a no-smoking area. Most of Lees' beers can be sampled here.
♨♉❀◐◑⊟♿♣P⚟

Clitheroe

King's Arms

144 Bawdlands, BB7 2LA (on B6243, towards Edisford Bridge)
✪ 1-11 (midnight Fri, Sat and summer); 1-10.30 Sun
☎ (01200) 425751
Beer range varies Ⓗ
The two beers change often in this lively, deceptively large pub. Semi-open plan it has four distinct areas for sitting, watching the TV, playing pool or table football, or listening (and dancing) to live bands (every Fri and two Sats each month). Children can play on the slide and swings on sunny days, or they can play table football, if the weather is inclement. Meals are served in the summer. ♨❀◐⅄♣P

Coppull

Red Herring

Mill Lane, PR7 5AN (off B5251)
✪ 12-11; 12-10.30 Sun
☎ (01257) 470130
Theakston Best Bitter; guest beers Ⓗ
Cask oasis in a village dominated by keg outlets; the building was the offices of the imposing mill next door. Converted to a pub some years ago, the bar serves a large single room and extension. TV sports addicts are catered for, along with the fishing fraternity who use the millpond at the pub. Regular music nights and free barbecues are a feature of the pub that attracts train spotters, being alongside the West Coast main line. Weekday lunches are served 1-2pm. ❀◐♿♣P

Croston

Crown Hotel

Station Road, PR26 9RN
✪ 11.30-11; 12-10.30 Sun
☎ (01772) 600380
Thwaites Mild, Original, Lancaster Bomber, seasonal beers Ⓗ
Welcoming pub in the picturesque prize-winning village of Croston. Ivy clad, its paved frontage is adorned with flowers, while at the rear is a large garden, car park and boules pitch. There is a comfortable lounge with a real fire and a split-level vault. Excellent, home-cooked food is good value, offering daily specials and roasts; steak night is Thursday, curry on Friday. No food is served Monday (Sun meals 12-7). Thwaites' seasonal beers go down a treat here.
♨❀◐◑⊟♿⅄≹♣P

Grapes ✔

67 Town Road, PR26 9RA
✪ 12-11; 12-10.30 Sun
☎ (01772) 600225
Boddingtons Bitter; guest beers Ⓗ
Old whitewashed pub, situated close to the cross from which the village takes its name. The Grapes has been an inn since at least 1799; the building also having been used as a custom house and a magistrate's court in the past. A small bar serves a compact lounge, but there are also two rooms at the front, plus a restaurant at the back. Four interesting guest beers are usually on tap.
❀◐◑⅄≹♣P

Dalton

Prince William

Beacon Lane, WN6 7RU (from A577 at Upholland, take road to Beacon Country Park) OS623989
⌚ 12-11; 12-10.30 Sun
☎ (01695) 623989
Burtonwood Bitter; guest beers Ⓗ
Sandstone pub built in 1803. It is popular with walkers and drivers who take a run out here to visit nearby Ashurst Beacon with its great views over the Lancashire plain, North Wales and the Lake District. Recently refurbished, it offers excellent, freshly-prepared meals. Adults only may use the garden, but there is a separate children's play area. Dalton Cricket Club is next door and the pub has two pool tables.
♨☋❀◐◑♿P⊬

Darwen

Black Horse

72 Redearth Road, BB3 3DE (near Sainsbury's)
⌚ 12-11; 12-10.30 Sun
☎ (01254) 873040
Bank Top Flat Cap; Hopstar Lush; Three B's Stoker's Slake; guest beers Ⓗ
Lively community local that stocks quality ales and cider. Its annual rare beer festivals, showcasing over 30 ales, held in January, late May bank holiday and November, draw visitors from far and wide. Monthly mini-festivals also take place. Darwen's own brewery, Hopstar's products take pride of place on the bar. Meal deals on Sunday afternoons and at beer festivals are a speciality. Picnic tables cover the large, enclosed flagged yard. ❀◐♿⇌♣●

Dolphinholme

Fleece ✔

Bay Horse, LA2 9AQ (on Galgate-Oakenclough road) OS509532
⌚ 12-11; 12-10.30 Sun
☎ (01524) 791233 website: www.fleeceinn.co.uk
Boddingtons Bitter; guest beers Ⓗ
At first sight, this former farmhouse appears in the middle of nowhere, but as the nearby village and the country beyond have no pubs, it is the local for quite a large community. The old-fashioned hall features an antique settle; on the right is the oak-beamed main bar; on the left the restaurant. There are two rooms off the bar, one for families. Up to five guest beers are offered, with Moorhouse's and Dent favoured breweries. ♨☋❀⊭◐◑♣P

Downholland

Scarisbrick Arms ✔

2 Black-a-Moor Lane, L39 7HX (at A5147 jct)
⌚ 12-3, 5-11; 12-11 Sat; 12-10.30 Sun
☎ (0151) 526 1120
Beer range varies Ⓗ
Family pub, made up of three good-sized rooms, with moorings on the Leeds-Liverpool Canal. A natural oasis for travellers, it has a huge garden and children's play area. Eat in the pub or in the garden while watching canal craft float sedately by. The kitchen enjoys a reputation for producing good reasonably-priced food daily, with meals served all day Saturday and Sunday. A smallish bar serves up to four cask ales with interesting selections from both near and far. It hosts folk music on Wednesday evening.
♨Q☋❀◐◑⊟P⊬

Earby

Red Lion

70 Red Lion Street, BB18 6RD (follow signs to youth hostel from A56)
⌚ 12-3, 5-11; 12-11 Sat; 12-10.30 Sun
☎ (01282) 843395
Copper Dragon Black Gold, Best Bitter; Tetley Bitter; Theakston Best Bitter; guest beers Ⓗ
Friendly, two-roomed village local next to the youth hostel and popular with walkers. It offers an extensive menu, and food is served in the lounge bar every day (12-2, and 6-9). The home-made pies are a speciality. It was voted Pub of the Year by local CAMRA in 2004.
Q❀◐◑⊟♣P

Eccleston

Original Farmers Arms

Towngate, PR7 5QS (on B5250)
⌚ 11-11; 12-10.30 Sun
☎ (01257) 451594
Boddingtons Bitter; Taylor Landlord; Tetley Bitter; guest beers Ⓗ
This white-painted village pub has expanded over the years into some cottages next door, allowing for a substantial dining area. However, the original part of the pub is still used mainly for drinking. The three guest ales change often. Meals are served throughout the day, seven days a week and there are four guest rooms. Buses 113 Preston to Wigan, 347 Chorley to Southport and C7 from Chorley serve the pub.
⊭◐◑P

Edgworth

Black Bull

167 Bolton Road, BL7 0AF
⌚ 11.30-11; 12-10.30 Sun
☎ (01204) 852811
Lees Bitter; Tetley Bitter; guest beers Ⓗ
Traditional, country pub – two cottages joined together. Until 1995 only the front rooms were licensed, but not for spirits, and no women were admitted; they had to use the back 'Nanny Pen' kitchen (now the lounge). In these more enlightened times the bar unites both areas, with handpumps each end. Tap room pump clips often face inwards as the guest beers change regularly. The award-winning bistro restaurant provides excellent food. Ornate floral decorations at the front complete the picture.
❀◐◑⊟♣P

Fleetwood

Steamer

1-2 Queens Terrace, FY7 6BT (next to market)
⌚ 11-11 (midnight Fri & Sat); 12-10.30 Sun
☎ (01253) 771756 website: www.sugarvine.com
Wells Bombardier; guest beers Ⓗ
This former Matthew Brown outlet is situated next to Fleetwood's market; it opens at 10am on market days. Snooker, darts, pool and dominoes can be played here. Good value meals are

available and children are welcome until 7pm. Evening meals are served Thursday-Saturday (until 7pm). The yard at the rear was used as a stable area until the police station opposite was demolished. Winner of local CAMRA's Pub of the Season, the Steamer is handy for buses and trams. ◐◑♿⊖(Ferry Terminal) ♣⊬

Thomas Drummond

London Street, FY7 6JY (between Lord St and Dock St)
⏲ 10-11; 12-10.30 Sun
☎ (01253) 775020
Theakston Mild, Best Bitter; Marston's Burton Bitter, Pedigree; Shepherd Neame Spitfire; guest beers 🄷
Fleetwood's newest pub was formerly a church hall and a warehouse before being converted by Wetherspoon. Inside, see the display celebrating the founding fathers of Fleetwood. Famous for good value meals and its curry nights, there is always a mild on offer. This past winner of local CAMRA's Pub of the Season award welcomes children until 6pm.
Q ఠ❀◐◑♿⊖(Preston St) ⊬

Wyre Lounge Bar ✔

Marine Hall, The Esplanade, FY7 6HF
⏲ 12-3.30 (4 Fri, Sat & summer), 7-11; 12-4, 7-10.30 Sun
☎ (01253) 771141
Courage Directors; Moorhouses Pendle Witches Brew; Phoenix Navvy; guest beers 🄷
Located within the Marine Hall on Fleetwood's seafront, it has won local CAMRA's Pub of the Year award twice and Pub of the Season in 2004. It affords great views of Morecambe Bay and the distant Lakeland fells. The outside drinking area is popular in summer due to its location near the beach; crazy golf, pitch and putt and crown green bowls can be played in the nearby gardens. Beers are sourced from breweries that are local and further afield.
❀♿⊖(Ferry Terminal) P

Freckleton

Coach & Horses ✔

6 Preston Old Road, PR4 1PD (behind war memorial, off A584)
⏲ 11-11; 12-10.30 Sun
☎ (01772) 632284
Boddingtons Bitter; guest beers 🄷
In the centre of a large village, the pub has undergone recent refurbishment. The main lounge has a welcoming fire in winter and a corner glass cabinet to show off sporting and local brass band trophies. Another side room has a TV but no juke box or pool table. It is reached by bus Nos. 68-69 (and No. 7 on Sun and bank holidays) from Blackpool, Kirkham and Preston. No meals are served on Sunday. ♨Q❀◐P

Garstang

Royal Oak

Market Place, PR3 1ZA
⏲ 11-3 (4 Thu), 6-11; 11-11 Fri & Sat; 12-10.30 Sun
☎ (01995) 603318
Robinson's Hatters, Hartleys XB, Unicorn 🄷
This 17th-century inn, sympathetically renovated, retains four small rooms around the main bar and restaurant. It has been run by the same family since 1959. Seats are set outside on the former market square. Bus Nos. 40, 41 and 42 stop nearby on Bridge Street (southbound) and Park Hill Road (northbound).
♨Qఠ❀🛏◐◑⛺♣P

Wheatsheaf

Park Hill Road, PR3 1EL
⏲ 11-11; 12-10.30 Sun
☎ (01995) 603398
Courage Directors; Jennings Cumberland Ale; Theakston Best Bitter; guest beers 🄷
The Wheatsheaf was extended and altered in 2002 to give a modern but cosy style with pine furnishings. The low ceiling bears oak beams – some older ones mark the original bar. The floors are a mix of flagstones and carpet. The large, central bar serves distinct areas, one no-smoking. It hosts a disco on Sunday and monthly live music (Mon). It stocks three guest beers – expect one from Moorhouses. For buses, see the Royal Oak above. Sunday meals are served 12-7.30pm. ❀◐◑♿♣P⊬

Great Eccleston

White Bull

The Square, PR3 0ZB
⏲ 11 (6 Tue)-11; 12-10.30 Sun
☎ (01995) 670203
Black Sheep Best Bitter; Tetley Bitter; guest beers 🄷
Comfortable, village-centre pub where the landlord takes great pride in the quality and choice of his beers the range is carefully selected to give the drinker a full range of beer styles. This former coaching inn favours wood and stone over plastic and concrete. Winner of a local CAMRA Pub of the Season award, it serves lunches in summer (Wed, Fri and Sat), and Sunday lunch all year. ♨Q❀◐♿⛺

Great Harwood

Royal Hotel

Station Road, BB6 7BE (opp. gasometers)
⏲ 12-11; 12-10.30 Sun
☎ (01254) 883541 website: www.royalblues.co.uk
Beer range varies 🄷
Brewery tap for the Red Rose Brewery, its range of seven ales includes up to five guests from near and far, supplemented by a choice of bottled beers and malt whiskies. It hosts the annual Great Harwood beer festival over May Day bank holiday. Lovers of good music enjoy weekly live entertainment in the concert room (see website). Well served by public transport, it is a handy stop when visiting the Ribble Valley or Pendle Witches trail. ❀🛏⛺♣🍶

Victoria ☆

St John's Street, BB6 7EP (behind St John's Church)
⏲ 4.30 (3 Fri, 12 Sat)-11; 12-10.30 Sun
☎ (01254) 885210
Beer range varies 🄷
Built in 1905 by Alfred Nuttall, the Vic or 'Butcher Brig' is the archetypal multi-roomed pub. Four rooms, including a no-smoking snug, are accessed from a central drinking area served by a horseshoe-shaped bar. Admire the floor-to-ceiling glazed tiling and original woodwork throughout. Up to eight ales are offered; local beers are well represented. Enjoy fine views

from the rear lounge and garden; the pub sits next to a disused railway line, now a delightful cycleway. Q ♣ ⅟

Grimsargh

Plough

187 Preston Road, PR2 5JR (on B6243)
11-11; 12-10.30 Sun
(01772) 652235 website: www.theplough-grimsargh.co.uk
Beer range varies H
Dating from 1785, this award-winning hostelry is just a few miles from Preston and the M6. It retains many original features, including oak beams, open fires and antique furniture. The lounge is no-smoking throughout. Good, home-cooked food is served, using local ingredients whenever possible (children's portions available). Up to four cask ales, often from regional and micro-breweries, are stocked. A bowling green, outdoor drinking area, regular theme nights and social events are added attractions. ♣P

Haslingden

Griffin

86 Hudrake, BB4 5AF (off A680)
12-11; 12-10.30 Sun
(01706) 214021
Porter Dark Mild, Bitter, Rossendale Ale, Porter, Sunshine, seasonal beers H
This fine community pub is the home of the Porter Brewing Company. The pub is open plan with a separate games section. In the large lounge area, a picture window overlooks the countryside to the north and the valley below; the window in the bar area has views of the hills across the valley to the west. The most outstanding aspect here is the beer, with the brewery in the cellar. A changing cider is stocked. ♣

Foresters

12 Pleasant Street, BB4 5LG
12-11; 12-10.30 Sun
(01706) 219066
Beer range varies H
The Foresters has three rooms, plus the bar area. There are two sitting rooms, one with a bar, and a pool room. One of the few cask beer outlets in the town centre, it is popular with the locals. It remains a homely place, despite the real fires in all rooms having been replaced with realistic gas fires. ♣

Heapey

Top Lock

Copthurst Lane, PR6 8LS
(alongside canal at Johnson's Hillock)
12-11; 12-10.30 Sun
(01275) 263376
Black Sheep Best Bitter; Coniston Bluebird; Taylor Best Bitter; guest beers H
An annual beer festival is held each October at the picturesque Top Lock which sits beside the Leeds–Liverpool Canal at the series of locks called Johnson's Hillock. This fine country pub comprises a single bar downstairs and an upstairs dining area. Frequented by walkers and narrow boat-owners, the eight handpumps serve at least five guest beers, including a dark mild and a stout. An authentic Indian menu is served alongside more traditional pub fare. P

Hest Bank

Hest Bank

2 Hest Bank Lane, LA2 6DN (near canal bridge 116)
11.30-11; 12-10.30 Sun
(01524) 824339
Boddingtons Bitter; Greene King IPA; Taylor Landlord; guest beer H
Once the last stop for travellers beginning the perilous crossing of the sands, transport developments and suburban sprawl have cut it off from the sea, but left it with a pleasant canalside garden. The locals' bar is in the older part of the pub, with the oldest room behind; to the right various linked spaces on different levels are used mainly by diners. Buses No. 5 (on the main road A5109) and 55A can be used to get here. Meals are served 12-9pm daily. Q ♣P

High Moor

Rigbye Arms

2 Whittle Lane, WN6 9QB (off B5209 along Robin Hood Lane, left along High Moor Lane)
12-3, 5.30-11; 12-10.30 Sun
(01257) 462354
Greene King Old Speckled Hen; Marston's Pedigree; Taylor Landlord; Tetley Bitter H
Although only three miles from the M6 (junction 27) this pub nestles in the heart of rural Lancashire. Always a hostelry, it was built in the 17th century and retains the character and distinct flavour of those bygone days. A Lancashire Life award winner for its food, the Foxhole snug is popular with ramblers. A well-kept bowling green sits behind the car park. Q P

Hoghton

Royal Oak

Blackburn Old Road, Riley Green, PR5 0SL
(at A675/A674 jct)
11.30-3, 5.30-11; 11.30-11 Sat; 12-10.30 Sun
(01254) 201445
Thwaites Mild, Original, Lancaster Bomber, seasonal beers H
Stone pub on the old road between Preston and Blackburn, near the Riley Green basin on the Leeds–Liverpool Canal. The Royal Oak is popular with diners and drinkers alike: rooms and alcoves radiate from the central bar, and it has a separate dining room. The pub features low, beamed ceilings and horse brasses. This Thwaites' tied house is a regular outlet for their seasonal beers. Visitors may want to visit nearby Hoghton Tower, which is steeped in history. Q P

Sirloin

Station Road, PR5 0DD (off A675, near level crossing)
12 (4 Mon)-11; 12-10.30 Sun
(01254) 852293
Beer range varies H
250 years old, this pub, and its award-winning restaurant (closed Mon), cater for both the

community and passing trade. King James I knighted a loin of beef in nearby Hoghton Tower, hence the name. Sirloin steak is a feature, as is the King's coat of arms above one of the three fireplaces. Exposed beams and wood panelling abound. Three handpumps dispense beers, often from Lancashire micro-breweries; a dark beer, either mild or porter, is usually available. ⋒❀◐◑♣P

Hoscar

Railway Tavern

Hoscar Moss Road, L40 4BQ
(next to station, 1 mile from A5209)
✪ 12-11; 12-10.30 Sun
☎ (01704) 892369
Jennings Bitter; Tetley Mild, Bitter; guest beers Ⓗ
The pub dates back to around the opening of the railway between Southport and Wigan in the 19th century. It is a perfect stop for cyclists and walkers, and is far from the Leeds-Liverpool Canal. The pub was refurbished in 2004 and is an ideal rural local, with three rooms served by a central bar, decorated with railway pictures and old local views. The pleasant garden at the back gets busy in summer. Parties are welcome, but no trains stop on Sunday. ⋒❀◐◑⊟♿⥵P

Lancaster

Golden Lion

31 Moor Lane, LA1 1QD (uphill from Duke's Playhouse)
✪ 2-11; 3-10.30 Sun
☎ (01524) 824195
Caledonian Deuchars IPA; Greene King Old Speckled Hen; Theakston Best Bitter; Webster's Green Label Ⓗ
Close to Duke's Theatre, this 300-year-old pub is sometimes referred to as the Whittle, after the old Whittle Springs Brewery. A pool room at the back attracts younger customers and there is room for non-smokers. Live music includes acoustic blues (Sun), folk (Tue), 'open mike' on Thursday and a band or singer Saturday. The clientele is a mix of regulars, Goths, and those seeking that rare thing – a pub free of recorded music. Q♣⚟

Sun

63 Church Street, LA1 1ET (off A6)
✪ 11-11; 12-10.30 Sun
☎ (01524) 66006
Beer range varies Ⓗ
A pub of two rather similar halves. The old Sun Inn was transformed in 2004, taken back to bare walls and floorboards and given a new bar and minimalist furnishings. Less than a year later, the shop next door was added to the drinking space. A number of interesting features have been left exposed by the renovations. Eight handpumps always have at least one Thwaites' beer; otherwise, north-western micros are favoured. ⛟◐♿⥵

Three Mariners

Bridge Lane, LA1 1EE (between bus station and St George's Quay)
✪ 11-11; 12-10.30 Sun
☎ (01524) 388597
Jennings Cumberland Ale; guest beers Ⓗ
Commonly claimed to be the oldest pub in Lancaster. It certainly looks old, and many of the beams and stones are original, but it has undoubtedly undergone some rebuilding and the restaurant area was refurbished recently. It is built into the side of a hill and the cellar is excavated at first-floor level. The strip of cobbles at the front, now occupied by tables, is Bridge Lane, once a main route. The pub, formerly hemmed in by buildings, now stands alone. Evening meals finish at 7.30pm.
❀◐◑⥵♣

Water Witch

Tow Path, Aldcliffe Road, LA1 1SU
(off A6 at Penny St canal bridge; follow canal south)
✪ 11-11; 12-10.30 Sun
☎ (01524) 63828
Beer range varies Ⓗ
This former canal company stable block assumed its present function in 1978 – the first true canalside pub on this waterway. Wedged between the towpath and a retaining wall, it is long and narrow. The decor is spartan: bare stonework predominates. A mezzanine floor and the space beneath is used mainly for dining – the pub's food has some reputation – this area is no-smoking. Eight handpumps always offer a Thwaites' beer; others mainly come from north-western micro-breweries. ❀◐◑

Yorkshire House

2 Parliament Street, LA1 1PB
(facing S end of Greyhound Bridge)
✪ 7 (2 Sat)-11; 2-10.30 Sun
☎ (01524) 64679 website: www.yorkshirehouse.enta.net
Everards Beacon, Tiger; guest beers Ⓗ
On the fringe of the city centre, it draws a mainly regular clientele. Bare floorboards contrast with pictures of old rock stars and film posters. It boasts the best juke box in town and a large room upstairs is used for live music, approximately three days a week. Two guest beers are mainly sourced from Yorkshire and Lancashire breweries. Westons organic vintage cider alternates with perry. Table football is played at this dog-friendly pub. A public car park is nearby; the bus station is a little further on.
⋒❀●

Lathom

Ship

4 Wheat Lane, L40 4BX
(off A5209, by Leeds-Liverpool Canal)
✪ 11.30-11; 12-10.30 Sun
☎ (01704) 893117
Moorhouse's Black Cat, Pendle Witches Brew; John Smith's Bitter; Theakston Best Bitter, Old Peculier; guest beers Ⓗ
The 200-year-old pub stands next to canal locks close to where the Leeds-Liverpool Canal branches off. The Ship has made itself a popular port of call for walkers in summer because of its range of beers. Although partly opened up, it retains an attractive small room feel to its bars. It is reputedly haunted, presumably by a customer who could not bear to leave. The pub is known locally as the 'Blood Tub' because of its past dealings, involving makers of black puddings.
Q☗❀◐◑♿♣●P⚟

Lea Town

Smith's Arms

Lea Lane, PR4 0RP (opp. BNFL East Gate) OS476312
12-2, 5-11; 11-11 Sat; closed Mon; 12-10.30 Sun
☎ (01772) 726906
Thwaites Mild, Original, seasonal beers Ⓗ
Friendly Thwaites' house, close to a large nuclear fuel factory. A refurbishment in 2005 is the first major work here since 1952. Its nickname the Slip Inn, dates from the time when Fylde farmers walked their cattle past, en-route to Preston market and would slip in for a drink. It has two outdoor drinking areas – one is covered; camping is possible in an adjacent field. The Christmas 'humbug corner' is now a year-round feature.
P

Little Eccleston

Cartford Hotel

Cartford Lane, PR3 0YP (½ mile off A586 by toll bridge)
12-3, 6.30-11; 12-10.30 Sun
☎ (01995) 670166 website: www.cartfordinn.co.uk
Boddingtons Bitter; Fuller's London Pride; guest beers Ⓗ
Local CAMRA and Lancashire 2004 Pub of the Year and a frequent West Pennines regional winner, this 17th-century, riverside, former farmhouse is now a free house. One or two Hart beers, and up to six guest beers are usually on offer. The Hart Brewery is at the rear of the hotel. Cyclists and caravanners enjoy the river views from the bankside tables in summer, while guests staying overnight can make use of the pub's fishing rights. Cider is stocked in summer.
P

Longridge

Forrest Arms

1 Derby Road, PR3 3JR
4 (12 Fri & Sat)-11; 12-10.30 Sun
☎ (01772) 782610
Beer range varies Ⓗ
The stone exterior of this pub gives way to a bright, modern interior without losing character. In keeping with its contemporary look, it is painted in light colours and examples of modern art hang alongside football memorabilia. From the central island bar, an unusual feature for Lancashire, three handpumps dispense cask ale. The house beer Thyme is Bank Top GSM, rebadged by the brewery. Good value food is served, often locally sourced.

Old Oak

111 Preston Road, PR3 3BA
12-11; 12-10.30 Sun
☎ (01772) 783648
Theakston Mild, Best Bitter; guest beers Ⓗ
Community local, recently extended to open up the underused rear part of the bar. The comfortable lounge has a real fire, while the large games room houses a big screen for sport. It offers at least three guest beers, usually from family or micro-breweries. The pub runs its own Beer Appreciation Society and holds competitions for giant onions and other eccentricities. The small patio is a suntrap. The landlord organises a 20-pub annual charity walk. Meals are served daily, 12-4, except Monday.
P

Longton

Dolphin

Marsh Lane, PR4 5JY
(1 mile down Marsh Lane, take right fork)
12-11; 12-10.30 Sun
☎ (01772) 612032
Beer range varies Ⓗ
Two-bar pub with real fires in both. A large no-smoking conservatory caters for families and diners. The bar areas are also used for dining where smoking is permitted. Food is served 12-8pm every day. An outside area for children has play equipment; a paved area has seating, tables and windbreaks. An annual beer festival is held at the end of August. One of the four guest beers is usually a mild. The pub is two miles from Longton with no bus service.
P

Lytham St Anne's

Hastings

26 Hastings Place, FY8 2LZ
12-11; 12-10.30 Sun
☎ (01253) 732839
Black Sheep Best Bitter; Moorhouses Pride of Pendle, Pendle Witches Brew; Wadworth 6X; guest beers Ⓗ
CAMRA National Club of the Year 2005, this former conservative club is now privately owned. It features wood flooring and large, comfortable chairs. The club usually offers four guest beers, normally from micro-breweries, plus a range of bottled foreign beers. Show your CAMRA card for entry (or just join – membership is free).

Taps

Henry Street, FY8 5LE
11-11; 12-10.30 Sun
☎ (01253) 736226 website: www.thetaps.com
Boddingtons Bitter; Greene King IPA; guest beers Ⓗ
Snug, multiple award-winning ale house off the main square, decorated in Hogshead style, with bare floorboards and brick. It is regularly turfed wall-to-wall for major golf tournaments. Look out for the portraits of regulars and locals. It serves home-cooked food and a good selection of ales; the house mild and bitter are brewed by Titanic. Service is always fast and friendly, even when busy. It was runner-up CAMRA national Pub of the Year in 2004. Q

Mawdesley

Black Bull

Hall Lane, L40 2QY (off B5246)
12-11; 12-10.30 Sun
☎ (01704) 822202
Cains Mild; Boddingtons Bitter; Jennings Cumberland Ale; guest beers Ⓗ
A pub since 1610, the low-ceilinged, stone building boasts some magnificent oak beams. Older village residents know the pub as 'Ell 'Ob – a reference to a coal-fired cooking range. There is a games room upstairs and a boules pitch

outside. Certificates in the bar record the pub's success in the Lancashire Best-Kept Village competition. The two guest beers are from regional breweries. Bus No. 347, Chorley-Southport passes four times a day (not Sun). Evening meals are served Tuesday-Sunday.
⌂❀◐◑♿♣P

Robin Hood

Bluestone Lane, L40 2QY (off B5250) OS506163
⌚ 11.30-11; 12-10.30 Sun
☎ (01704) 822275 website: www.robinhoodinn.co.uk
Boddingtons Bitter; Caledonian Deuchars IPA; Taylor Landlord; guest beers Ⓗ
Charming, white-painted inn at the crossroads between the three old villages of Mawdesley, Croston and Eccleston. The 15th-century building was substantially altered in the 19th century. In the same family for over 30 years, the pub enjoys a reputation for good food, but still finds room for drinkers, with three guest ales on tap. Bar food is served all day at the weekend; Wilsons Restaurant, upstairs, is open Tuesday–Sunday evenings. For buses, see Black Bull above. ◐◑P⚟

Mere Brow

Legh Arms ✔

82 The Gravel, PR4 6JX (near A565/B5246 jct)
⌚ 12-11; 12-10.30 Sun
☎ (01772) 812359
Boddingtons Bitter; Taylor Landlord; Tetley Bitter; Wells Bombardier Ⓗ
Quiet, friendly local country inn near the leisure lakes complex just off the main road between Southport and Preston. A former Higson's pub, it retains a popular public bar where games are played, plus a small snug with a TV at the rear. The house beer, Fetlers, is brewed by Tetley. The three coal fires help to create a cosy atmosphere in winter. Children are not admitted.
⌂Q❀◐◑⊟♿♣P⚟

Morecambe

New Inn

2 Poulton Square, LA4 5PZ (off B5274, near police station)
⌚ 11-11; 12-10.30 Sun
☎ (01524) 418179
Boddingtons Bitter; guest beers Ⓗ
Back when Boddingtons was a family brewery, this was one of its classic pubs. The beer range has changed, the place has been smartened up a bit, but the essence remains in this pub for locals to sink pints. There are two small rooms, one nominally the public bar, with a TV, the other has piped music. A third room, where children are welcome, has another TV and a dartboard. It has long been the base for local pigeon-fanciers. ❀⊟♣

Ormskirk

Hayfield

22 County Road, L39 1NN (on A59)
⌚ 12-11, 12-10.30 Sun
☎ (01695) 571157
John Smith's Bitter; guest beers Ⓗ
About 200 years old, the pub saw off its last competitor, the Aughton Arms in 1907. Now under new management after 34 years, the new landlady provides an extremely warm welcome. A classic, proper pub with a superb bowling green and two real coal fires, this is the perfect winter and summer pub rolled into one. Sunday meals are served 12-7.30pm.
Q❀◐◑♿⇌●P⚟

Yew Tree ✔

Grimshaw Lane, L39 1PD (off A59)
⌚ 11.30-3; 6-11; 12-11 Sat; 12-4, 7-10.30 Sun
☎ (01695) 572261
Cains Mild, Bitter; Robinson's Unicorn; guest beers Ⓗ
Superb 1950s survival in a pleasant housing estate, a haven for those seeking unusual beers in a suburban area. There is a perfectly preserved post-war lounge and an excellent tile floored traditional tap room. The lounge opens onto a walled garden with overhanging plants. Despite being some distance from the town centre, it is worth seeking out. No food is served Sunday. Q❀◐◑⊟♿♣P

Pendleton

Swan with Two Necks

Main Street, BB7 1PT (off A59)
⌚ 12-2 (not Mon), 7-11; 12-2.30, 6-11 Fri & Sat; closed Tue; 12-10.30 Sun
☎ (01200) 423112
Phoenix Arizona; guest beers Ⓗ
Lying on the northern slopes of Pendle Hill, this is the only pub in the picturesque village. Formerly a Whitbread house, it was bought by the incumbent licensee and is now a true free house. Partially opened out, it is small, and a little old-fashioned, but feels very welcoming. The food is superb, freshly home cooked (no meals Mon). One of the guest beers is nearly always from Copper Dragon. Due to its rural location, the pub attracts walkers.
⌂Q❀◐◑♿♣P

Penwortham

Black Bull

83 Pope Lane, PR1 9BA
⌚ 11-11; 12-10.30 Sun
☎ (01772) 752953
Greenalls Bitter; John Smith's Bitter; Theakston Mild Ⓗ
Attractive, cottage-style pub that has managed to retain a village atmosphere, despite being situated in a well-populated area. On entering, a narrow passageway leads through to a central bar serving a number of drinking areas. The pub is making a welcome return to this Guide after a 20-year gap, it has continued to serve a real mild, and is a rare outlet for the fast disappearing Greenalls Bitter. ◐♣P

Poulton-le-Fylde

Grapevine

19-21 Market Place, FY6 7AS
⌚ 5-11; closed Mon; 6-10.30 Sun
☎ (01253) 896700
Thwaites Original, Lancaster Bomber; guest beer (occasional) Ⓗ
Not so much a pub, more a soul music bar named after the Marvin Gaye song. The

Grapevine features northern soul memorabilia and music. It occupies three floors of a building dating back to 1754 that was formerly the longest trading ironmongery shop in Wyre. The ground floor is a wine and cocktail bar, the first floor has the main bar and the second floor is a comfortable gallery seating area. Cask ales are sold at a lower price before 8pm. ⅄≢

Thatched House

12 Ball Street, FY6 7BG (200 yds from station)

✪ 11-11; 12-10.30 Sun

Boddingtons Bitter; Theakston Best Bitter; Wells Bombardier; guest beers Ⓗ

This popular, half-timbered pub stands in the grounds of a Norman church. The half-wood-panelled walls display photos of Blackpool FC's glory days, plus cricketing heroes of the past. There is no music, food, or children allowed in; as such it is a relaxing place for conversation at lunchtime, but it can get busy at weekends. ⩩Q⊟≢

Preston

Ashton Institute

10-12 Wellington Road, PR2 1BU

(nr Slingers Motorcycles)

✪ 7 (4 Fri & Sat)-11; 2-10.30 Sun

☎ (01772) 726582

Thwaites Original; guest beers Ⓗ

Formerly two terraced houses, this club is the oldest in Preston still in its original premises, founded 4-4-44. Comprising two rooms: the main room features pool and snooker, while the second room is used for functions (choose your own beers). An annual beer festival on the last weekend of October celebrates its tenth anniversary in 2005. Show a CAMRA membership card or this Guide to be signed into this CAMRA multi-award winner. ♣

Black Horse ☆

166 Friargate, PR1 2EJ

✪ 10.30-11; 12-4 (closed eve) Sun

☎ (01772) 204855

Robinson's Hatter's, Unicorn, Double Hop, seasonal beers Ⓗ

Classic, Grade II listed pub in the main shopping area, close to the historic open market. With its exquisite tiled bar and walls, and superb mosaic floor, it is an English Heritage/CAMRA award winner. The two front rooms bear photos of old Preston; the famous 'hall of mirrors' seating area is to the rear. See the memorabilia of a previous landlord set in a glass partition. The modern upstairs bar (no real ale) is usually open at weekends. ≢

Finney's Sports Bar

1 East View, Deepdale Road, PR1 5AS

✪ 12-11; 12-10.30 Sun

☎ (01772) 250490

Tetley Bitter; guest beers Ⓗ

Multi-screen, multi-channel sports venue at the town end of Deepdale Road, it has a large bar area and raised games sections to the right and left, plus a small dance floor. Handy for Preston North End, a collection of football shirts adorns the walls. The bar commemorates the Preston legend, Tom Finney. It hosts karaoke on Friday and Saturday evenings when tracksuit-wearers are not admitted. Usually two guest beers come from small breweries and micros. ❀♣

Fox & Grapes

15 Fox Street, PR1 2AB (off Fishergate)

✪ 11-11; 12-10.30 Sun

☎ (01772) 561149

Beer range varies Ⓗ

Small, friendly, back-street oasis close to the bustling shopping centre. Six handpumps dispense a changing range of real ales, listed on a blackboard, and the occasional cider. A large collection of beermats, motorcycle memorabilia, table football, and the 60-year-old framed press articles on old Preston pubs (many now long-gone) all add interest. Customers are welcome to bring in their own food, or use the delivery service of a nearby sandwich bar. ≢♣

Limekiln

288 Aqueduct Street, PR1 7JP (off Fylde Road, A583)

✪ 11-11; 12-10.30 Sun

☎ (01772) 793247

Banks's Hanson's Mild, Bitter; guest beers Ⓗ

This tile-fronted local welcomes visitors as well as regulars. The aqueduct which carried the Lancaster Canal into Preston centre was demolished in the 1960s and the canal terminus is now only 200 yards from the pub. A central bar serves four drinking areas, including a pool room. Entertainment ranges from karaoke (Fri eve) to an organ singalong (Sun). In summer, tables are set up outside the pub. ❀♣P

Market Tavern

33-35 Market Street, PR1 2ES

✪ 10.30-11 (9 Mon-Wed); 12-9 Sun

☎ (01772) 254425

Beer range varies Ⓗ

Small, but friendly, town-centre local overlooking the Victorian outdoor covered market. Over 300 different guest beers from far and wide were served through four handpumps during 2004. It stocks a good selection of German and Belgian bottled beers and a German wheat beer on draught. No juke box or TV interferes with conversation at this former local CAMRA Pub of the Year. ≢

New Britannia

6 Heatley Street, PR1 2XB (off Friargate)

✪ 11-3, 6-11; 11-11 Sat; 7-10.30 Sun

☎ (01772) 253424

Boddingtons Bitter; Camerons Castle Eden Ale; Goose Eye Brontë Bitter; Marston's Pedigree; guest beers Ⓗ

This CAMRA multi-award winning single bar, town-centre pub attracts real ale enthusiasts from a fair distance. It enjoys an excellent reputation for the high quality and range of its beers. Note the splendid Britannia windows. The tasty home-made food represents good value; weekday lunches are served. Saxon cider is sold. A small patio to the rear allows for some outdoor drinking. ❀◑≢●

Old Black Bull ✔

35 Friargate, PR1 2AT

✪ 10.30-11; 12-10.30 Sun

☎ (01772) 823397

Boddingtons Bitter; Cains Bitter; guest beers Ⓗ

Mock-Tudor-fronted, city-centre pub. A small front vault, a main bar with distinctive black and white floor tiles, two comfortable lounge areas and a pool table, combine to make it a popular venue, with its patio a bonus in summer. Live music is performed Saturday evening and Sky Sports is viewed. Up to seven guest beers are usually from micros or small independents. Twice winner of local CAMRA's Pub of the Year, it serves a good range of food at competitive prices. ❀◖⊟♿≷♣

Olde Dog & Partridge

44 Friargate, PR1 2AT

11-2, 6-11; 11-11 Sat; 12-4, 7-10.30 Sun

☎ (01772) 252217

Fuller's London Pride; Highgate Dark Mild; guest beers Ⓗ

Internationally renowned bikers pub, near the university, but attracting a varied clientele. The decor mainly features military memorabilia. A rare outlet for both real mild and cider; this shows how a Punch Taverns pub can be run with a bit of effort. Handy for fast food takeaways and late buses, the DJ has been at the pub over 20 years, nearly as long as the landlord. Guest ales are often from the White Shield Brewery (formerly Bass Museum). No food is served Sunday. ◖≷♣●

Stanley Arms

24 Lancaster Road, PR1 1DD (next to Guild Hall)

12-11; 12-10.30 Sun

☎ (01772) 254004

Courage Directors; Theakston Mild, Best Bitter; guest beers Ⓗ

This pub is close to but not part of the 'circuit'. A rare outlet for mild in the city centre, three guest beers are available; the 'landlord's choice' may come from anywhere in the country. The single lounge bar tends to be busy; meals are served 12–6 (5 Sun). An impressive, ornate listed building, the pub's name refers to the Earls of Derby, once landowners in the area. Pavement tables allow for summer drinking. ❀◖◗≷

Rawtenstall

Craven Heifer

264 Burnley Road, BB4 8HY (on A682)

6 (4 Fri)-11; 12-10.30 Sun

☎ (01706) 214757

Moorhouses Black Cat, Premier, Pride of Pendle, Pendle Witches Brew Ⓗ

One of Moorhouses latest acquisitions: a modern, comfortable, two-roomed pub. Typical of a Moorhouses renovation it has been vastly improved since the take-over. The handpumps overshadow all other bar fittings as they should, and offer a good range of Moorhouses' beers. The pub is popular with the locals who like to watch TV sport.

Salwick

Hand & Dagger

Treales Road, PR4 0SA

(on crossroads, 1 mile N of station) OS463330

12-11; 12-10.30 Sun

☎ (01772) 690306

Black Sheep Best Bitter; Jennings Cumberland Ale; guest beer Ⓗ

Comfortable country pub, with a well-deserved reputation for good home-cooked food, catering for locals and occasional visitors alike. The games room is served by a hatch from the main bar, while the dining room can be used for functions. Situated alongside the Lancaster Canal, the pub offers a tranquil outdoor drinking area for summer evenings; in winter, a real fire lends a rosy glow. ♨☺❀◖◗⊟♣P⊬

Samlesbury

New Hall Tavern

Cuerdale Lane, PR5 0XA (on B5230)

11.30-11; 12-10.30 Sun

☎ (01772) 877217

Boddingtons Bitter; guest beers Ⓗ

Welcoming pub at a rural crossroads close to Interbrew's 'megakegery'. The attractive white pub has a large rear car park where outdoor drinking is possible. Inside, the bar serves a single room with areas separated for dining. The excellent range of guest beers (usually four) complements the good, home-cooked food prepared with local produce. Meals are available all day. The infrequent No. 217 Preston-Mellor bus passes the pub. ♨❀◖◗♿⛺P

Silverdale

Woodlands

Woodlands Drive, LA5 0RU (up driveway, opp. end of Emesgate Lane)

7 (12 Sat)-11; 12-10.30 Sun

☎ (01524) 701655

Beer range varies Ⓗ

Country house, backing on to Eaves Wood, easily overlooked by the casual visitor, so most of the trade is local. Even when you find it, it still does not look much like a pub – the impressive entrance hall shows no sign of a bar, but go through the door on your left, through a lounge and voila! The beer list displays four ales from near and far. The bar has a big fireplace, great views and usually a dog or two. ♨⛺♣P

Stalmine

Seven Stars Hotel

Hallgate Lane, FY6 0LA

12-11; 12-10.30 Sun

☎ (01253) 700207

Boddingtons Bitter; Worthington's Bitter; guest beers Ⓗ

Originally a row of four cottages, the pub was later a coaching house and post office. This quiet village-centre inn retains four distinct public rooms. Locals and summer visitors enjoy a changing range of up to six cask ales (less in winter). Full meals and bar snacks are served daily. Accommodation is available in six en-suite double rooms, refurbished in 2005. It has been awarded Pub of the Season by local CAMRA. Q⇌◖◗⛺P⊬

Tockholes

Royal Arms

Tockholes Road, BB3 0PA

12-11; closed Mon; 12-10.30 Sun

☎ (01254) 705373

Three B's Bobbin's Bitter; guest beers Ⓗ

This village pub is the closest to Darwen Tower and Roddlesworth walks. Two houses knocked into one, with back-to-back fireplaces, this is a four-roomed, cosy little retreat. Hops hang from beams; walls reveal original stonework; wood or stone floors welcome walkers and dogs. The beers come from local micros. A local newspaper competition winner for service and cuisine (booking advisable), meals are served until 9pm (not Tue). Regular special theme nights are a feature. ⌂❀◐▶P

Victoria Hotel

Golden Soney Top O'th Low, BB3 0NL

✪ 12-2.30 (not Tue), 7.30 (6.30 Fri & Sat)-11; closed Mon; 12-10.30 Sun

☎ (01254) 701622

Theakston Best Bitter, Old Peculier; guest beer Ⓗ

Charming, 18th-century, family-owned pub, where the original stone fireplace and beams have been carefully renovated over the years. It offers a superb range of traditional, home-cooked food with such rarities as fresh vegetables and home-made chips. Just right for that special occasion or party, the function room has a bar and space for dancing. It is ideal for walkers' refreshments after exploring Roddlesworth's nature trail or Darwen Tower. ❀◐▶P

Tontine

Delph Tavern

WN5 8UJ (off B5206, then right at lights) OS525045

✪ 11.30-11; 12-10.30 Sun

☎ (01695) 622239

Caledonian Deuchars IPA; Hydes Bitter; Moorhouses Pride of Pendle; Phoenix Arizona; guest beers Ⓗ

Large multi-roomed pub that has been opened out but retains a separate vault. It has bags of local atmosphere, capped off with a warm friendly welcome. It caters for all ages. The dining area serves good value meals (all day Sat and Sun). The beers are also reasonably priced. Children are welcome, except in the vault. Dominoes and darts are played here. ❀◐▶ ♿ ⇌(Orrell) ♣P⊁

Tunstall

Lunesdale

LA6 2QN (on A683)

✪ 11-3, 6-11; closed Mon; 12-3, 6-10.30 Sun

☎ (01524) 274203

Black Sheep Best Bitter; guest beer Ⓗ

Clean, modern decor characterises this pub: white walls, scrubbed tables and varnished floorboards. There is a small servery surrounded by several rooms: one has pool and table football; one at the other end is furnished as a restaurant, but food dominates everywhere. Bus Nos. 81 and 276 call infrequently. ◐▶P

University of Lancaster

Furness College Bar ✔

Bailrigg, LA1 4YG (first college on south spine)

✪ 12 (6 Sat)-11; 7-10.30 Sun

☎ (01524) 592564

Beer range varies Ⓗ

Student bar of early 1970s vintage: matchboarding and teal paint, chiaroscuro and lots of standing room. Eight handpumps, not always all in use, dispense mainly micro-brewed beers from all over the country. The university is served by buses 2, 2A, X2, 3, 4 and 4A. Furness is near the middle of the campus, well signposted. The bar is directly off the main concourse. Tables are put out on the quad in the summer. ❀

Graduate College Bar

LA2 0PF (Alexandra Park, off A6)

✪ 7 (6 Thu & Fri)-11; 8-10.30 Sun

☎ (01524) 65201 website: www.gradbar.co.uk

Beer range varies Ⓗ

Modern student bar, more like a pub than most and (as the name suggests), the age range is slightly higher than other campus bars. Only university members, staff, guests and people carrying a copy of this Guide are served. The Graduate College lies in a confusing cluster of buildings south-west of the main campus, served by buses X2, 3, 4 and 4A. Look for the Gradbar sign. Phoenix, Jennings, Goose Eye and Bazens feature regularly; the cider varies. ●

Up Holland

Old Dog

6 Alma Hill, WN8 0NW (off A577)

✪ 5 (4 Sat)-11; 4-10.30 Sun

☎ (01695) 623487

Boddingtons Bitter; guest beers Ⓗ

Halfway up the steep Alma Hill, this small stone pub is worth the climb from the village conservation area. It retains an original Greenall Whitley etched window and one showing the pub name. Its three small, heavily beamed rooms are all on different levels; the small bar area shows pump clips from the many guest ales. In the lower lounge, pictures are displayed, while the rear rooms benefit from wonderful views across Wigan to the West Pennines. Q❀♣

Waddington

Lower Buck

Edisford Road, BB7 3HU

✪ 12-11; 12-10.30 Sun

☎ (01200) 423342

Black Sheep Best Bitter; Moorhouses Black Cat, Premier; Taylor Landlord; guest beers Ⓗ

Situated just outside the village centre, the Lower Buck is a free house, featuring six handpumps. Two of these are for guest ales, often from local micro-breweries, such as Bowland or Three B's. There are three drinking rooms, each with a real fire in winter, plus a pool room. Food is served either in the bar or in the restaurant upstairs; note the extensive specials board. ⌂Q◐▶⊁

Walmer Bridge

Walmer Bridge Inn ✔

65 Liverpool Old Road, PR4 5QE

✪ 4 (12 Sat)-11; 12-10.30 Sun

☎ (01772) 612296

Robinson's Unicorn; guest beers Ⓗ

Brick-built village local in a central location,

comprising a comfortable lounge and a lower level vault. Pictures of bygone Walmer Bridge and Longton include some of the old Wilkins Brewery. The large garden has children's play equipment. The two guest beers on sale are sourced from regional or micro-breweries. Buses stop outside. ❀⊟♣P

Waterfoot

Boot & Shoe

Millar Barn Lane, BB4 7AU

7(12 Sat)-11; 12-10.30 Sun

☎ (01706) 213828

Beer range varies Ⓗ

This pub started life as a club some 20 years or more ago. The same landlady has run it since it became a pub; the barman has also worked here all this time. The pub consists of four areas: a lounge, bar and a games area, with a dining section to the rear.

Jolly Sailor

Booth Place, BB4 9BD

5-11 (midnight Fri & Sat); 12-10.30 Sun

☎ (01706) 226340

Caledonian Deuchars IPA; Jennings Cumberland Ale; Taylor Landlord; Tetley Dark Mild; guest beers Ⓗ

The name may commemorate the first landlord's seafaring life; the pub was originally built in 1825, but has been rebuilt once and extended since. The Jolly Sailor now features a semi-open-plan layout, with a separate games room served from the bar via a hatch. There is a raised stage in the main bar room, used for live music. Freshly-prepared food includes snacks and a roast lunch on Sunday. ❀◐♣

Westhead

Prince Albert

109 Wigan Road, L40 6HY (2 miles E of Ormskirk, on A577)

12-11; 12-10.30 Sun

☎ (01695) 573656

Tetley Dark Mild, Bitter; guest beer Ⓗ

Multi-roomed, small village pub situated on the main Ormskirk to Skelmersdale road. The bus stop outside has a regular service every 10 minutes daytime (less frequent eves and Sun) to Ormskirk and Wigan. Home-cooked food is available at lunchtime, also bed and breakfast should you want to stay longer. Real coal fires in winter give everyone a warm welcome. The guest beer changes weekly. It hosts two weekly quizzes; darts and dominoes are played. Q❀◐⊟♿♣P

Wheelton

Dressers Arms

Briers Brow, PR6 8HD (off A674)

11-11; 12-10.30 Sun

☎ (01254) 830041

Boddingtons Bitter; Taylor Landlord; Tetley Bitter; Worthington's Bitter; guest beers Ⓗ

The pub has been converted over the years from a row of terraced cottages into a spacious multi-roomed establishement. The bar is supplemented by a lounge, games room and snug, plus a no-smoking room behind the bar. Eight handpumps serve three guest beers and a house beer, Big Franks, brewed by Pictish. Good food is served downstairs, while an authentic Chinese restaurant upstairs is an added attraction. ❀◐♿P⊬

Whittle-le-Woods

Royal Oak

216 Chorley Old Road, PR6 7NA (off A6)

2.30-11; 12-10.30 Sun

☎ (01257) 276485

Black Sheep Best Bitter; Jennings Cumberland Ale; Taylor Landlord Ⓗ

This small, single-bar, terraced village local was built in 1820 to serve the adjacent branch of the Leeds–Liverpool Canal (now filled in). A local CAMRA award-winner, it has been in this Guide for 30 years consecutively. Long and narrow, with a small bar and a games room, it is very much a community pub and the haunt of mature motorcycle enthusiasts. ❀♣

Wray

George & Dragon

Main Street, LA2 8Q4

12-2.30, 5-11; 12-11 Sat; 12-10.30 Sun

☎ (01524) 221403

Everards Beacon; Jennings Bitter; guest beers Ⓗ

Genuine village local that is gaining a reputation for food; meals are served all day Sunday. It comprises two bar rooms of very different sizes and a restaurant. This dog-friendly establishment hosts a weekly quiz on Wednesday; other pub games include shove ha'penny. ❀◐♣⊬

Wrea Green

Villa

Moss Side Lane, PR4 2PE (on B5259, S of village)

11-11; 12-10.30 Sun

☎ (01772) 684347

Jennings Cumberland Ale; Copper Dragon Scotts 1816; guest beer Ⓗ

Attractive, 19th-century country house hotel set in its own grounds. Smart and elegant, the Villa has leather sofas in front of the fire. It hosts Murder Mystery weekends twice a year, and offers quality accommodation, conference facilities and a restaurant. All this is matched by real enthusiasm for cask ales shown by the staff. Look out for the impressive monolithic chairs in the entrance lobby. ❀◐♿P⊬

LEICESTERSHIRE & RUTLAND

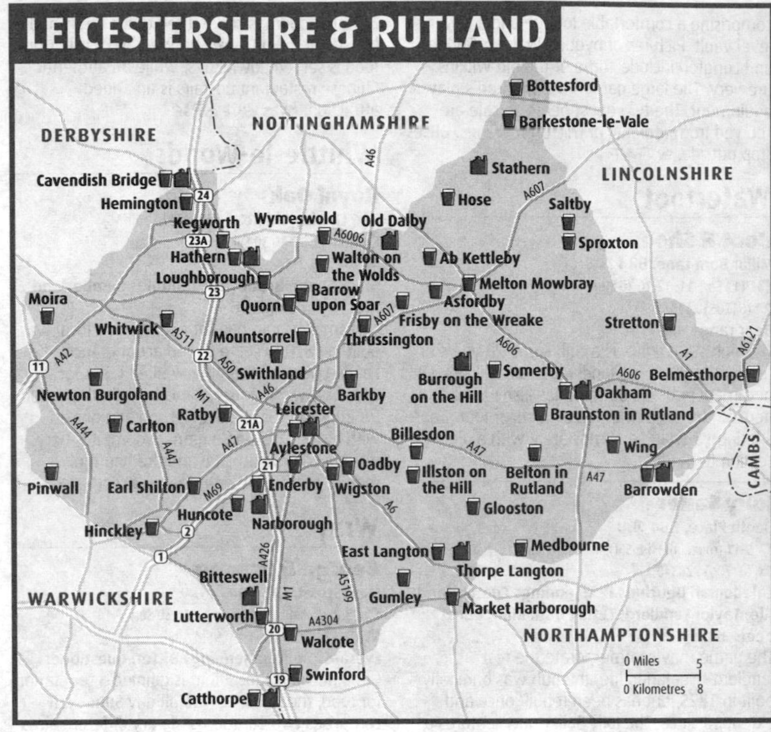

Ab Kettleby

Sugar Loaf

Nottingham Road, LE14 3JB

⊛ 11-11; 12-10.30 Sun

☎ (01664) 822473

Draught Bass; Belvoir Beaver; guest beers Ⓗ

This 17th-century coaching inn with a Georgian facade has recently been refurbished but retains its character and atmosphere. Inside is a bar, lounge/dining area and conservatory. It is the tap for Belvoir Brewery, and two guest beers are also always available. Home-cooked food of excellent quality and value is served all day. Daytime buses from Melton and Nottingham serve the pub. ⚞Q❀◑♣P

Asfordby

Blue Bell

178 Main Street, LE14 3TT

⊛ 12-3, 6-11; 12-11 Fri & Sat; 12-10.30 Sun

☎ (01664) 812232

website: www.bluebell.fsbusiness.co.uk

Greene King IPA; Tetley Bitter; Wells Bombardier; guest beer Ⓗ

Village local with a difference, combining excellent ale with an extensive Thai menu (not Tue), courtesy of the landlord's wife. The pub has two rooms plus a restaurant, and features low-beamed ceilings, comfortable seating and an open fire. The guest beer is usually from a micro-brewery, often local. Buses from Leicester and Melton Mowbray serve the pub.
⚞Q❀◑⊟P⚟

Crown

106 Main Street, LE14 3SA

⊛ 6.30 (4 Fri; 12 Sat)-11; 12-10.30 Sun

☎ (01664) 812175

Beer range varies Ⓗ

An 18th-century, friendly local with low, beamed ceilings and nooks to sit in. Saved by locals from becoming a private residence a few years ago, it has been sympathetically renovated and refurbished. A free house with an ever-changing beer range, more than 500 different beers have been enjoyed here. Evening meals are served on Friday and Saturday, lunches Sunday only. It stands on the bus route from Leicester and Melton Mowbray.
⚞Q⛾❀◑♿♣P

Aylestone

Black Horse

65 Narrow Lane, LE2 8NA

⊛ 5 (12 Fri & Sat)-11; 12-10.30 Sun

☎ (0116) 283 2811

INDEPENDENT BREWERIES

Bells Bitteswell
Belvoir Old Dalby
Blencowe Barrowden
Brewster's Stathern
Dow Bridge Catthorpe
Everards Narborough
Grainstore Oakham
Hoskins Leicester
Langton Thorpe Langton
Parish Burrough on the Hill
Shardlow Cavendish Bridge
Wicked Hathern Hathern

Everards Beacon, Tiger, seasonal beers; guest beers Ⓗ
Cracking three-bar community local dating from late Victorian times. It offers a comfortable lounge and smoke-free snug. All bars have open log fires in winter. There is a function room upstairs and a large garden with a children's play area. A long alley skittles room is available for hire. A short distance from the Grand Union Canal and Great Central Way, the pub is popular with boaters and walkers. ♨Q❀⊟♣⚟

Barkby

Brookside

35 Brookside, LE7 3QO (off Barkby Holt Lane)
⏲ 12-2.30 (not Tue), 6-11; 12-4, 7-10.30 Sun
☎ (0116) 260 0092
Burtonwood Bitter, Top Hat; Marston's Pedigree; guest beer Ⓗ
Cheery and welcoming pub with the air of a country local. Two-roomed, with a traditional bar and a comfy lounge, log fires blaze on cold winter nights. There is a no-smoking restaurant leading from the lounge. Meals are not served on Saturday lunchtime, Sunday evening or Tuesday. The pub has a picturesque setting with a brook at the front and plenty of ducks. Dogs and horses are welcome. ♨❀◑⊟♣P

Malt Shovel

27 Main Street, LE7 3QG
⏲ 11-3, 5.30 (5 Fri)-11; 10.30-11 Sat; 12-10.30 Sun
☎ (0116) 269 2558
Banks's Original, Bitter; Marston's Pedigree; guest beer Ⓗ
This pub offers seven real ales, including a mild, and a cider, all on handpump. Shelves around the main room are filled with unopened bottles of British and European beers. There is also a restaurant. Access to the bar is via the car park under cover of a stable block roof. Petanque is popular in summer. ♨❀◑♿♣●P

Barkestone-le-Vale

Chequers

2 Rutland Square, NG13 0HN
⏲ 12-3, 6-11; 12-11 Sat; 12-10.30 Sun
☎ (01949) 842947
Banks's Bitter; Marston's Pedigree; guest beers Ⓗ
Tucked away in a small village in the heart of the Vale of Belvoir, this pub can be difficult to find. However, it is well worth seeking out this friendly, family-run hostelry. A traditional interior features plain terracotta paintwork and natural wood floors. The layout is open plan, with a central bar and a raised area with a pool table at the back. ❀♿♣

Barrow upon Soar

Hunting Lodge

38 South Street, LE12 8LZ
⏲ 11.30-11; 12-10.30 Sun
☎ (01509) 412337
website: www.thehuntinglodgebarrowonsoar.co.uk
Greene King Old Speckled Hen; Marston's Pedigree; Taylor Landord; guest beer Ⓗ
Three-storey granite hotel, restaurant and bar. The spacious bar has a contemporary style with large, comfortable leather chairs, wooden floors and open log fires. Drinkers and diners are equally welcome. There is a large garden at the rear. Each of the six bedrooms has a unique design, ranging from an ethnic theme to the more traditional four-poster bed. Regular buses and trains to Loughborough and Leicester serve the hotel. ♨❀🛏◑♿⚠≷P

Billesdon

New Greyhound

2 Market Place, LE7 9AJ
⏲ 12-3 (not Thu), 5-11; 12-11 Fri & Sat; 12-10.30 Sun
☎ (0116) 259 6226
Banks's Original; Marston's Bitter, Pedigree Ⓗ
Sarah Jordan become the pub's first landlady in the 1840s, following 10 years assisting her late husband who was landlord of the 'old' Greyhound. The pub is situated across the market place, just inside Long Lane. While both pubs were trading, the prefixes 'old' and 'new' were added to distinguish them. The single storey part of the building was formerly the village blacksmith's workshop. A recent refurbishment has given the pub a more modern feel. Q♉❀

Bottesford

Bull

5 Market Place, NG13 0BW
⏲ 12-2, 5.30 (5 Fri)-11; 12-11 Sat; 12-10.30 Sun
☎ (01949) 842288
Greene King IPA; Theakston Best Bitter; Taylor Landlord; guest beers Ⓗ
One of three excellent pubs in a delightful village, well served by public transport. This popular pub in the village centre has a spacious bar with open fire and a comfortable seated area with TV and pool table. The lounge features many photographs of Laurel and Hardy – Stan Laurel's sister was a previous landlady and the duo stayed here, apparently causing much mayhem. There is a function room which hosts occasional beer festivals. ♨❀⊟♿≷♣P⚟

Carlton

Gate Hangs Well

Barton Road, CV13 0DB
⏲ 12-3, 6-11; 12-4, 7-10.30 Sun
☎ (01455) 291845
Draught Bass; Marston's Pedigree Ⓗ
Cosy, welcoming roadside inn in a village near Market Bosworth. Comfortable seating is arranged around a central bar. Singers provide entertainment on Wednesday and Saturday evenings. There is a pleasant garden for summer evenings and a conservatory where families with children are welcome until mid evening. Q❀♣P

Catthorpe

Cherry Tree

Main Street, LE17 6DB
⏲ 12-3 (Fri only), 5-11; 6-11 Sat; 12-10.30 Sun
☎ (01788) 860430
Ansells Best Bitter; Draught Bass; Hook Norton Best Bitter; guest beers Ⓗ
Situated between the old Roman road (Watling

Street A5) and a major motorway interchange (M1/M6), this small, rural free house is easy to find and well worth a detour. The bar and lounge/games room with table skittles are popular with locals. Guest beers include those from Catthorpe's Dow Bridge viewing of the brewery can be arranged by appointment. Filled rolls are available at lunchtime. ⩩Q❀♣P

Cavendish Bridge

Old Crown

DE72 2HL

☼ 11-11; 12-10.30 Sun

☎ (01332) 792392

Burtonwood Bitter, Top Hat; Draught Bass; Marston's Pedigree; guest beers Ⓗ

Coaching inn on the banks of the River Trent, dating from the 17th century. The original oak-beamed ceiling displays an extensive collection of old jugs. The walls are covered with pub mirrors, brewery signs and railway memorabilia, which even extend into the toilets. The cosy, open-plan interior is divided into two areas and there is a large inglenook. Daytime buses from Derby and Loughborough pass by. ⩩❀⇐◖P

Earl Shilton

Dog & Gun

72 Keats Lane, LE9 7DR (100 yds from A47)

☼ 12-2.30 (not Mon-Thu), 5.30-11; 11.30-3.30, 5.30-11 Sat; 12-3, 7-10.30 Sun

☎ (01455) 842338

Banks's Original; Marston's Burton Bitter, Pedigree Ⓗ

Built behind the original pub, which was demolished in 1932, the pub is set back from the rest of the buildings on the street. It has three rooms including a bar with a tiled floor and a large log fire, and a snug. Meals are served at lunchtimes and evening. With a number of walking routes in the area, the pub runs its own rambling club, as well as participating in many charity events. The attractive garden is a regular award winner. ⩩❀◖◗⊟♣P

East Langton

Bell Inn

Main Street, LE16 7TW

☼ 12-2.30, 7 (6 Fri; 6.30 Sat)-11 (closed Mon in winter); 12-4, 7-10.30 (not winter) Sun

☎ (01858) 545278

Greene King IPA, Abbot; Langton Caudle Bitter, Bowler Strong Ale Ⓗ

This 17th-century listed building is in the heart of Leicestershire's hunting country. Low beams and an open log fire add to the pub's appeal. Food is freshly prepared from local ingredients (no food Sun eve). The Langton Brewery commenced brewing behind the pub in November 1999. ⩩Q❀⇐◖◗♿♣P

Enderby

New Inn

51 High Street, LE19 4AG

☼ 12-2.30 (not Mon; 12-3 Sat), 7 (5.30 Fri)-11; 12-2.30, 5.30-11 Fri; 12-3, 7-10.30 Sun

☎ (0116) 286 3126

Everards Beacon, Tiger; guest beers Ⓗ

Friendly, low-beamed village local, dating from 1549. This pub has two main rooms with a central bar, plus a lounge. Acquired by founder William Everard in 1887, it was the first for the family brewery, although it had already gained its current name owing to a transfer of licence from a previous location nearby. Long alley skittles, darts and a full-size snooker table are part of the games culture here. Guest beers are from Everards Old English Ale Club. ⩩Q❀◖⊟♣P

Frisby on the Wreake

Bell Inn

2 Main Street, LE14 2NJ

☼ 12-2.30, 6-11; 12-2.30, 7-11 Sat; 12-3, 7-10.30 Sun

☎ (01664) 434237

Greene King IPA, Abbot; guest beers Ⓗ

This welcoming village local, dating back to 1759, is situated in a small village on the south side of the River Wreake. The comfortable lounge/bar features oak beams, flagstone floors and an open fire. There is a family room/restaurant (no food Wed lunch or Sun eve). Above the bar is a collection of Vaux Brewery pottery tankards. Two regular beers are complemented by three guests. A daytime bus service runs from Melton and Leicester. ⩩Q♉❀◖◗P

Glooston

Old Barn Inn

Andrews Lane, LE16 7ST

☼ 12-2.30 (not Mon), 6.30-11; 12-2.30, 7-10.30 Sun

☎ (01858) 545215

Fuller's London Pride; Greene King IPA; guest beers Ⓗ

This 16th-century rural inn is set in the heart of Leicestershire's hunting country. Low ceilings, oak beams and an open fire add to the welcoming ambience. Three guest beers are usually available. No food is served on Sunday evening. ⩩Q❀◖◗

Gumley

Bell Inn

2 Main Street, LE16 7RU

☼ 11-3, 6-11; 12-3 (closed eve) Sun

☎ (0116) 279 2476

Draught Bass; Bateman XB; Greene King IPA; guest beers Ⓗ

This early 19th-century free house is popular with locals as well as a commuting urban clientele. Cricketing memorabilia adorns the entrance hall and fox hunting scenes hang on the walls of the bar and dining room. The beamed interior has an L-shaped bar and a no-smoking dining room serving an extensive menu. The pub has a large patio garden but children and dogs are not permitted here. ⩩Q❀◖◗♣P

Hathern

Dew Drop Inn ✔

49 Loughborough Road, LE12 5HY

☼ 12-2.30, 6-11; 12-3, 7-11 Sat; 12-3, 7-10.30 Sun

☎ (01509) 842438

Hardys & Hansons Mild, Bitter, seasonal beers Ⓗ
Traditional two-room local run by a friendly, long-established landlord who makes all visitors feel like regulars. The large bar has a beamed ceiling, comfortable seating and a real fire. There is also a small, cosy lounge. A visit to the toilets is a must to see the tiled walls and original features. A good range of malt whiskies is available, and cobs are served at lunchtime. Regular buses from Loughborough, Nottingham and Derby serve the pub. ⛼Q❀⊟♣P

Hemington

Jolly Sailor

21 Main Street, DE74 2RB
11.30-2.30, 4.30-11; 11-11 Sat; 12-10.30 Sun
☎ (01332) 810448
Draught Bass; Greene King Abbot; M&B Mild; Marston's Pedigree; guest beers Ⓗ
This 17th-century building is thought to have once been a weaver's cottage. A pub since the 19th century, it retains many original features including old timbers, open fires and a beamed ceiling – a convenient place to hang the collection of blow lamps and beer mugs. The restaurant is also available for functions and meetings. Cider is dispensed on gravity. Evening meals are served on Friday and Saturday; there is no food on Sunday. Daytime buses run from Castle Donington and Long Eaton.
⛼Q❀◐◑♿♣●P

Hinckley

Railway Hotel

Station Road, LE10 1AP
12-11; 12-3.30, 7-11 Sat; 12-3.30, 7-10.30 Sun
☎ (01455) 615285
Banks's Original; Marston's Burton Bitter, Pedigree Ⓗ
Basic, spacious two-room local opposite Hinckley railway station – the bar is adorned with railway pictures. A comfortable lounge features regular live music and the conservatory/family room houses a pool table. There is a function room, and B&B accommodation is available.
Q❀⇌♣P

Hose

Black Horse

21 Bolton Lane, LE14 4JE
12-2 (not Mon & Tue), 6-11; 12-4, 7-10.30 Sun
☎ (01949) 860336
Adnams Bitter; Castle Rock Harvest Pale; Fuller's London Pride; guest beers Ⓗ
Traditional pub with a lounge featuring wooden beams and a brass-ornamented brick fireplace. Pictures and blackboard menus for food and drink surround a wooden corner bar. The unspoilt public bar, decorated with pictures and mirrors, has a tiled floor, wooden furniture and a brick fireplace. The rustic, wood-panelled restaurant serves good food using local produce.
⛼Q❀◐◑⊟♿♣P⚟

Huncote

Red Lion

Main Street, LE9 3AU
12-2, 5-11; closed Mon; 12-11 Sat; 12-10.30 Sun
☎ (0116) 286 2233 website: www.red-lion.biz
Everards Beacon, Tiger; guest beers Ⓗ
Built in 1892, the Red Lion is a friendly local with beamed ceilings throughout. It has a cosy lounge with a wooden fireplace and log fire. The bar has an adjoining dining area and a separate pool room. The sizeable garden has picnic tables and a children's play area. The pub serves good value home-cooked lunches. Long alley skittles can be played by prior arrangement.
⛼❀◐♣P⚟

Illston on the Hill

Fox & Goose

Main Street, LE7 9EG (off B6047 near Billesdon)
12-2.30 (not Mon or Tue), 5.30 (7 Mon)-11; 12-2.30, 7-10.30 Sun
☎ (0116) 259 6340
Everards Beacon, Tiger, Original; guest beer Ⓗ
Cosy, unspoilt pub with a timeless feel, tucked away in the village and well worth seeking out. A fascinating collection of local mementos and hunting memorabilia is on display. In 1997, when structural work was needed, every item on the walls was photographed and later returned to exactly the same place. That's how unchanged it is! Popular annual events include a conker championship, onion-growing competition and a fundraising auction for local charities. ⛼Q❀⊟♣

Kegworth

Red Lion

24 High Street, DE74 2DA
11-11; 12-10.30 Sun
☎ (01509) 672466
Adnams Bitter; Archers Golden; Banks's Original; Courage Directors; Greene King Abbot; guest beers Ⓗ
Georgian building with three small bars retaining many original features. There is also a no-smoking family/function room. Various flavoured Polish and Ukrainian vodkas, a good selection of malt whiskies, and up to four guest beers are stocked. There is a skittle alley and petanque courts. Outside is a large garden with children's play area. Part of the award-winning Tyne Mill pub company, the Red Lion was local CAMRA Pub of the Year 2005.
⛼Q❀⇌◐◑⊟♣●P⚟

Leicester

Ale Wagon

27 Rutland Street, LE1 1RE (on Charles St)
11-11; 12-10.30 Sun
☎ (0116) 262 3330
website: www.alewagon.co.uk
Hoskins Hob Best Mild, Bitter, Ⓗ **White Dolphin, Tom Kelly's Stout,** Ⓟ **EXS; guest beers** Ⓗ
A friendly local atmosphere pervades the 1930s interior of this pub, run by the Hoskins family. It boasts an original oak staircase and has two rooms with tiled and parquet floors and a central bar. There is always a varied selection of Hoskins Brothers ales and guests available. A function room is available. The pub is popular with rugby fans and real ale drinkers visiting the town. It was voted Leicester CAMRA Pub of the Year 2004. ⛼⊟⇌♣⚟

Black Horse

1 Foxon Street, LE3 5LT (on Braunstone Gate)
3 (12 Sat)-11; 7-10.30 Sun
(0116) 254 0030
Elgood's Black Dog; Everards Beacon, Tiger; guest beers
Small street-corner pub, the only traditional one left on Braunstone Gate, now surrounded by wine bars. With all the character of a lively local, it has two rooms and a central bar. There is a general knowledge quiz on Wednesday and Sunday – the longest running in Leicester – and live music on Tuesday, Thursday and Saturday evening. Up to four guest beers are from Everards Old English Ale Club, and Westons Old Rosie cider is sold.

Criterion

44 Millstone Lane, LE1 5JN
12-11; 12-10.30 Sun
(0116) 262 5418
Hardys & Hansons Bitter; Oakham JHB, Bishops Farewell; guest beers
Thriving, modern city-centre pub offering a good range of real ales and foreign bottled beers. The front bar is basic and the comfortable lounge dominated by a long, dark wood bar. Between six and 12 real ales are available. Home-baked Italian-style pizzas are the house speciality (no food Sun). Beer festivals are a regular event, some held jointly with the nearby Swan & Rushes. Free live music plays from 3-5pm on Saturday. P

Globe

43 Silver Street, LE1 5EU (300 yds from clock tower)
11-11; 12-10.30 Sun
(0116) 262 9819
Everards Beacon, Tiger, Original; guest beers
Almost 30 years ago, this city-centre pub was hailed as Everards' first pub to return to a full real ale range after seven years as keg only. Major renovations in 2000 moved the bar to the centre of the pub and created four drinking areas. The yard became part of the pub interior. There is a snug, and gas lighting throughout (electric too!). An upstairs room is regularly used for Leicester CAMRA meetings; its first meeting was held here in 1974, as well as its 25-year bash.

Leicester Gateway

52 Gateway Street, LE2 7DP
11-11; 12-10.30 Sun
(0116) 255 7319
Castle Rock Harvest Pale; guest beers
Friendly, air-conditioned local in a converted hosiery factory, frequented by nearby infirmary and university staff, visitors and students. Close to both Leicester City football and Tigers rugby grounds, the pub supports local teams. Up to five real ales, including bottled beers, are always available, and up to eight beers are on tap for special events. A popular carvery is offered on Sunday at lunchtime.

Out of the Vaults

24 King Street, LE1 6RL
12-11; 12-10.30 Sun
website: www.outofthevaults.com
Beer range varies
Opened in March 2004 by the management of the original Vaults, which closed six months earlier, this pub is just a stone's throw away from the old premises. It is popular with visitors to the city as well as locals. The interior has one long bar with a wooden floor and basic seating, offering 12 beers all from micro-breweries. Regular beer festivals are held at Leicester CAMRA City Pub of the Year 2005.

Shakespeare's Head

Southgates, LE1 5SH
12-11; 12-10.30 Sun
(0116) 262 4378
Oakwell Old Tom Mild; Barnsley Bitter
This two-room local was built alongside the underpass in the 1960s and has changed little since then – it retains all the charm of a typical town pub of its era. It has two large glass doors leading to an off-sales area with a bar to the left and lounge to the right. Formerly a Shipstones pub, it now sells Oakwell beers at reasonable prices. Sunday lunch and Saturday night curries are popular.

Swan & Rushes

19 Infirmary Square, LE1 5WR
12-11; 12-10.30 Sun
(0116) 233 9167
Hardys & Hansons Bitter; Oakham JHB; guest beers
Triangular in shape, this comfortable two-bar 1930s pub is now a shrine to great beer from Britain and beyond. Between seven and 10 real ales are usually on tap, including a mild, four imported draughts and a large selection of imported bottled beers. Regular beer festivals are held. Close to Leicester football and rugby grounds, the pub can be busy on match days.

Talbot

4 Thurcaston Road, LE4 5PF
11.30-3 (4 Fri & Sat), 6-11; 12-4, 7-10.30 Sun
(0116) 266 2280
Ansells Mild; Banks's Bitter; Marston's Pedigree; guest beers
There has been a pub on this site since the 15th century and the cellars date back to the 12th century, owned by the church until the 19th century. This friendly local in the heart of old Belgrave consists of two lounge areas. Handy for the historic Belgrave Hall (reputed to be haunted), Abbey pumping station and the National Space Centre, it is a 10-minute walk from the Great Central Railway (steam) Leicester North station which connects with Rothley, Quorn and Loughborough.
P

Tudor

100 Tudor Road, LE3 5HT
12-3, 5-11; 11-11 Thu-Sat; 12-10.30 Sun
(0116) 262 0087
Everards Beacon, Tiger
Corner pub in a terraced area with a Victorian exterior. Inside are two rooms – a bar and a lounge. There is a function room upstairs with table skittles. Darts and pool are also played.

Loughborough

Albion

Canal Bank, LE11 1QA

⌚ 11-3 (4 Sat), 6-11; 12-3, 7-10.30 Sun

☎ (01509) 213952

Archers Best Bitter; Brains Dark; guest beers 🄷

This canalside pub was built in the late 18th century at the same time as the Loughborough Canal. It has a bar, darts room and quiet lounge (no-smoking until 8pm). Outside is a patio with an aviary. The house beer, Albion Special, is brewed for the pub by the local Wicked Hathern Brewery. Take care if driving to the pub along the narrow towpath.

♨Q❀◖◗≠♣P⊬

Boat Inn

47 Meadow Lane, LE11 1JU

⌚ 11-11; 12-10.30 Sun

☎ (01509) 214578

Banks's Original; Marston's Pedigree, Old Empire; guest beers 🄷

Built in the 18th century, this canalside pub has been much extended and modernised. One large room, it has been made more cosy by the use of partitions to create smaller seating areas. Guest beers have been introduced and there are regular beer festival weeks, when over 30 real ales are available. The pub is popular in the summer when boaters (moorings available) and students mix to enjoy the sun in the outside seating area.

❀◖◗♿≠P⊬

Swan in the Rushes

21 The Rushes, LE11 5BE

⌚ 11-11; 12-10.30 Sun

☎ (01509) 217014

Adnams Bitter; Archers Golden; Castle Rock Rushes Gold, Harvest Pale; guest beers 🄷

Popular, three-room Tynemill pub. Upstairs is a skittle alley/function room which hosts live music and twice-yearly beer festivals. A range of up to six guest beers is on offer, always including a mild, plus a real cider and perry. There is also a limited range of continental bottled and draught beers, as well a selection of malt whiskies and country wines. The dining/family room is no-smoking and the Garendon Room is no-smoking until the evening.

♨Q♉❀⛟◖◗◫♿≠♣●P⊬

Tap & Mallet

36 Nottingham Road, LE11 1EU

⌚ 12-2.30, 5-11; 11.30-11 Sat; 12-10.30 Sun

☎ (01509) 210028

Church End Gravediggers; Courage Best Bitter; guest beers 🄷

Genuine free house situated on a direct route from the railway station to the town centre. The five guest beers are from micro-breweries, often local, and usually brews that are rarely seen in this area. The pub has a single room split into two, and there is a pool table. The lounge can be partitioned off for private functions. Outside, the secluded walled garden has children's play equipment and a pets' corner. Cobs are available all day.

♨❀≠♣●

Lutterworth

Fox Inn

34 Rugby Road, LE17 4BN (off M1 jct 20 on A426)

⌚ 12-3, 5-11; 12-11 Fri & Sat; 12-3, 7-10.30 Sun

☎ (01455) 552677

Adnams Best Bitter; Greene King Old Speckled Hen; Taylor Landlord 🄷

A welcome return to the Guide for an old favourite. The new landlord has rejuvenated this pub, which is now adorned with many items of motor racing and rallying memorabilia, plus rugby football collections and displays of RAF and other aircraft photographs. Lunchtime food is served daily. ♨❀◖P

Unicorn Inn

29 Church Street, LE17 4AE

(on one-way system near church)

⌚ 10.30-11; 12-10.30 Sun

☎ (01455) 552486

Draught Bass; Greene King IPA; M&B Brew XI; Robinson's Best Bitter 🄷

Traditional, town-centre corner pub, run by the same landlord for 25 years. The small entrance lobby still has the old off-sales hatch. The large public bar area has skittles tables and a dartboard; the pub fields several teams. The lounge area features a central fireplace.

♨❀⛟◖◫♣P⊬

Market Harborough

Cherry Tree

Church Walk, Kettering Road, Little Bowden, LE16 8AE

⌚ 12-3, 5-11; 11-11 Fri & Sat; 12-10.30 Sun

☎ (01858) 463525

Everards Beacon, Tiger, Original, seasonal beers; guest beers 🄷

This spacious pub has low beams and a thatched roof. Drinkers and diners can choose from many small alcoves and seating areas. Although the pub is situated in Little Bowden it is very much part of the Market Harborough community. A beer festival is held over the August bank holiday. Guest beers are from Everards Old English Ale Club. ❀◖◗≠♣⊬

Medbourne

Nevill Arms

12 Waterfall Way, LE16 8EE

⌚ 12-2.30, 6-11; 12-3, 7-11 Sun

☎ (01858) 565 288

Adnams Bitter; Fuller's London Pride; Greene King Abbot; guest beers 🄷

The initials MGN over the door are those of Captain Nevill, who was heir to the nearby Holt estate when this former coaching inn was rebuilt in 1863, after the original building was destroyed by fire in 1856. Folklore suggests that a spark caused the fire after the village blacksmith wagered that he could support an anvil on his chest while a horseshoe was forged on it. A warm welcome awaits inside the heavily-beamed bar with its large inglenook.

♨❀⛟◖◗♣P

Melton Mowbray

Crown Inn

10 Burton Street, LE13 1AE

11-3, 7-11; 11-11 Sat; 12-4, 7-10.30 Sun
☎ (01664) 564682
Everards Beacon, Tiger, Original; guest beer Ⓗ
Sociable, two-room town pub, run by a long-serving landlord. The pub is popular with office workers and shoppers at lunchtime, and a varied clientele during the evening. Smoking is not permitted in the lounge when lunches are being served. Photographs of old Melton Mowbray adorn the walls. Daytime buses from Loughborough, Grantham and Nottingham serve the pub. No food is served on Sunday and Monday, or Friday and Saturday evenings.
⌂◐◑ ⇌

Harboro Hotel
49 Burton Street, LE13 1AF
11-11; 12-10.30 Sun
☎ (01664) 560121 website: www.harborohotel.com
Beer range varies Ⓗ
An 18th-century coaching inn close to the station and town centre. The comfortable bar serves four guest beers and a range of draught and bottled German and Belgian beers. There are two lounges, one with sofas and the other more traditional, with tables and chairs. Meals and bar snacks are served except on Sunday evening. There is a no-smoking area at lunchtimes. Petanque is played here. There are good bus links to Leicester, Loughborough, Grantham and Nottingham. Q ◐◑ ♿ ⇌ ♣ P ⊁

Moira

Woodman
1 Shortheath Road, DE12 6AL
12-11; 12-10.30 Sun
☎ (01283) 218316
Greene King Abbot; Marston's Pedigree; Wells Bombardier; guest beer Ⓗ
Formerly called the Rawdon Arms after the local mine which closed in the 1980s, this popular pub was local CAMRA Pub of Autumn 2004. It has a large L-shaped single room with comfortable seating. The walls are covered with commemorative plates depicting local coal mines, the last of which closed in 1990. Food is served at lunchtime and there is a separate pool room that can be converted to a dining area or meeting room. Daytime buses from Ashby-de-la-Zouch pass nearby. ❀◐ ♣ P

Mountsorrel

Swan Inn
10 Loughborough Road, LE12 7AT
12-2.30, 5.30-11; 12-11 Sat; 12-3, 7-10.30 Sun
☎ (0116) 230 2340 website: www.jvf.co.uk/swan
Greene King Ruddles County; Theakston Best Bitter, XB, Old Peculier; guest beer Ⓗ
Traditional 17th-century coaching inn, formerly called the Nag's Head. It has been under the present ownership since 1990. The split-level bar has stone floors, bench seating and low ceilings. There is a small dining area with a polished wood floor which leads off a further room that can be used for eating or drinking. Westons bottled cider is stocked. Good quality, interesting food is cooked to order and the menu changes fortnightly. Outside is a secluded riverside garden with moorings available locally.
⌂❀◐◑ P

Newton Burgoland

Belper Arms
Main Street, LE67 2SE
12-3, 6-11; 12-11 Fri & Sat; 12-10.30 Sun
☎ (01530) 270530
Hook Norton Best Bitter; Marston's Pedigree; guest beers Ⓗ
Traditional village free house, dating from 1290, with a warm, friendly atmosphere. Reputed to be the oldest pub in Leicestershire, it has many historical artefacts, even a ghost, '5 to 4 Fred'. The pub has one large, low-beamed bar with several alcoves. Three guest beers are always available. Food, from snacks to an a la carte menu, is served every lunchtime and evening, either in the bar or separate, spacious restaurant. The location is ideal for exploring the surrounding countryside. ⌂Q ❀◐◑ ▲P

Oadby

Cow & Plough
Stoughton Farm Park, Gartree Road, LE2 2FB
12-3, 5-11; 12-10.30 Sun
☎ (0116) 272 0852
Fuller's London Pride; Steamin' Billy Bitter, Skydiver; guest beers Ⓗ
Situated in a converted farm building with a no-smoking conservatory, the pub is decked out with breweriana, pub and brewery mirrors, signs and fittings from old pubs. It is home to Steamin' Billy beers, named after the owner's Jack Russell featured on its logo, and brewed under licence by Grainstore of Oakham. A guest mild and Westons cider are always available. Occasional beer festivals are held. Twice CAMRA's East Midlands Pub of the Year, it was Leicester Pub of the Year 2005.
Q ❀◐◑ ♿ ♣ P ⊁

Pinwall

Red Lion
Main Road, CV9 3NB
(at B4116/B5000 jct, 1 mile from A5)
12-11; 12-10.30 Sun
☎ (01827) 712223
Draught Bass; Marston's Pedigree; Taylor Landlord; guest beers Ⓗ
This rural, cosy, unspoilt locals' pub is one of only five or six buildings that make up Pinwall – a village so tiny that it does not even appear on most maps. The Red Lion includes a restaurant and six-room accommodation; room prices may be negotiated at weekends. Usually there are three guest beers on tap. Evening meals are not served on Sunday. ⌂Q ❀◐◑ ♣ P

Quorn

White Hart ✔
32 High Street, LE12 8DT
12-2, 5-11; 12-11 Fri & Sat; 12-10.30 Sun
☎ (01509) 412704
Caledonian Deuchars IPA; Greene King IPA; Taylor Landlord; Wadworth 6X; guest beer Ⓗ
The oldest pub in Quorn, the White Hart dates from 1690 and once had its own brewhouse. However, over the years it has been modernised and little evidence remains to show its true age. The L-shaped bar and central chimney split the

pub into three drinking areas, each with a real fire. Outside there is an illuminated, sheltered seating area and a petanque court. Regular buses run from Loughborough and Leicester. ♔❀◐⛺♣P

Ratby

Bull's Head

23 Main Street, LE6 0LN

⊙ 11-3, 5-11; 11-11 Fri & Sat; 12-5, 7-10.30 Sun

☎ (0116) 239 3256

Everards Beacon, Tiger, Original; guest beers Ⓗ

This white-painted village pub is much larger than it appears from the outside. It has a cosy, quiet lounge, a large front bar and a smaller rear bar with a piano – the use of which is actively encouraged. The pub has a darts team and there is also a skittles alley. Excellent home-made food is served in the large restaurant. The spacious garden has a children's play area plus a patio to one side, where petanque can be played. ♔Q❀◐⊟♣P

Railway Inn

191 Station Road, LE6 0JR

⊙ 4 (12 Thu-Sat)-11; 12-10.30 Sun

☎ (0116) 239 2493

Everards Beacon, Tiger Ⓗ

Traditional, family-run drinkers' pub built to serve the long-gone Leicester and Swannington railway – now a bridle path. Originally called the Wharf and doubling as a ticket office, it was renamed the Railway in 1862. It has a large, L-shaped bar and a cosy snug named Leander lounge after the steam locomotive whose memorabilia adorns the walls. The pub has darts and cribbage teams, and dominoes is regularly played. ❀◐◑⊟♣P

Saltby

Nag's Head

1 Back Street, LE14 4RN

⊙ 12-3, 6.30 (6 Fri & Sat)-11; closed Mon; 12-3, 7-10.30 Sun

☎ (01476) 860491

Fuller's London Pride; guest beers Ⓗ

This attractive, stone-built pub set on the edge of the Vale of Belvoir has three rooms, an open fire and a restaurant. It is popular with locals and visitors alike. The owners' commitments to both CAMRA and the Campaign for Real Food shine through. Three real ales are usually available, at least one from a local brewer. Food is prepared to high standards, using local produce where possible. Occasional beer festivals are always popular. ♔❀◐◑⊟♣P⊬

Somerby

Stilton Cheese

High Street, LE14 2QB

⊙ 12-3, 6-11; 12-3, 7-10.30 Sun

☎ (01664) 454394

Grainstore Ten Fifty; Marston's Pedigree; Tetley Bitter; guest beers Ⓗ

Late 16th-century pub built in the local ironstone, as are most of the buildings in the village. Tall customers in particular, as they bang their heads, will notice the wide range of handpump labels fixed to the low beams. There are two rooms, one no-smoking, both with low doorways. Real cider is always available. A popular pub for dining, booking is advisable. There is a function room upstairs. ♔Q❀◐◑♣●P⊬

Three Crowns Inn

39 High Street, LE14 2PZ

⊙ 12-2.30, 6.30 (5.30 Fri)-11; 12-10.30 Sun

Draught Bass; Greene King IPA; Parish Special; guest beer Ⓗ

Formerly called the Old Brewery Inn, the pub has reverted to its original name now that the Parish Brewery has moved back to Borough on the Hill. This 15th-century pub was given by Sir Richard Sutton to Brasenose College, Oxford, in 1508. The interior has changed very much since then, but it remains a cosy place with lots of character. Although the Parish Brewery has moved, its beers are still available on draught. There is live music on the first Saturday of the month. ♔Q❀◐◑♿⛺♣P

Sproxton

Crown Inn

Coston Road, LE14 4QB

⊙ 5 (12 Sat)-11; 12-10.30 Sun

☎ (01476) 860035

Greene King XX Mild, IPA, Ruddles County, Abbot Ⓗ

Unspoilt, creeper-covered, stone building on the edge of the Vale of Belvoir, the pub is popular with locals and visitors. The bar has several comfy chairs, an open fire and a small TV in the corner. Five handpumps serve beers from the Greene King stable, including the cask mild. A full food menu is offered and there is a room set aside for dining. ♔❀◐◑⊟♿♣P

Swinford

Chequers

High Street, LE17 6BL

⊙ 12-2.30 (not Mon), 6 (7 Mon)-11; 12-3, 6-11 Sat; 12-3, 7-10.30 Sun

☎ (01788) 860318

Adnams Bitter; guest beers Ⓗ

This popular, comfortable village pub is welcoming and family friendly. The inside has been opened out with a dining area and wood-floored bar, chairs and tables. Three cask beers are usually available, including a regularly changing guest. Bar food is served, including vegetarian options and children's meals. Pub games include table skittles. The large garden and extensive children's play area are popular in summer. Stanford Hall is nearby. ❀◐◑⛺♣P

Swithland

Griffin Inn

174 Main Street, LE12 8TJ

⊙ 11-2.30, 5.30-11; 11-11 Sat; 12-10.30 Sun

☎ (01509) 890535

Everards Beacon, Tiger, Original; guest beers Ⓗ

Friendly local with three comfortable rooms, a restaurant and long alley skittles. Set in the heart of Charnwood Forest, there are many cycling and walking routes nearby. Swithland Reservoir and the preserved Great Central Railway are also close. Guest beers are from the

Everards Old English Ale Club. Meals are served all day on Saturday and Sunday. ♨Q❀◐◑♿♣P

Thrussington

Blue Lion

5 Rearsby Road, LE7 4UD

⌚ 12 (6 Mon)-11; 12-3, 7-10.30 Sun

☎ (01664) 424266

Marston's Burton Bitter, Pedigree, seasonal beers; guest beer Ⓗ

Late 18th-century rural pub which was once two cottages. It has a comfortable lounge where you can enjoy good value pub food including meat provided by the local butcher. The bar is the heart of the pub, where locals meet to challenge each other to darts and dominoes matches. The pub also fields strong petanque teams who play on the pitch outside. Note the extensive collection of teapots –160 at the last count. Daytime buses run from Leicester and Melton Mowbray. Q❀◐◑⊟▲♣P

Walcote

Black Horse

25 Lutterworth Road, LE17 4JU

(on A4304 1 mile from M1 jct 20)

⌚ 12-2, 5-11; 12-11 Fri & Sat; 12-10.30 Sun

☎ (01455) 552684

Greene King Abbot; Oakham JHB; Taylor Landlord; guest beers Ⓗ

It is well worth taking a detour off the M1 to visit this friendly, welcoming village free house. Refurbished in 2004, it has a single bar and is comfortably furnished. A speciality of the house is home-cooked Thai food. Guest beers are sourced from independent breweries. ♨❀◐◑P

Walton on the Wolds

Anchor Inn

2 Loughborough Road, LE12 8HT

⌚ 12-3 (not Mon), 7-11; 12-3, 7-10.30 Sun

☎ (01509) 880018

Adnams Bitter; Marston's Pedigree; Taylor Landlord; guest beer Ⓗ

The pub is situated in an elevated position in the centre of the village. It has an open-plan, comfortable L-shaped lounge with a real fire. Prints and photographs of classic cars and village scenes adorn the walls. One corner is dedicated to sporting memorabilia and trophies. Good quality food is served Tuesday to Saturday, and a roast on Sunday lunchtime. Daytime buses serve the pub from Loughborough. ♨Q❀◐◑P

Whitwick

Man within Compass

Loughborough Road, LE67 5AS

⌚ 12 (6 Mon)-11; 12-10.30 Sun

☎ (01530) 811813

Greene King IPA; Marston's Pedigree; Taylor Landlord Ⓗ

Built from local granite, this comfortable pub was originally two rooms, but these were opened up to form a large U-shaped room, retaining the open fires. It is known locally as the Rag and Mop after a previous landlady who constantly cleaned the pub using a mop made from old rags. Food is served from lunchtime to early evening Tuesday-Saturday, and lunchtime on Sunday. The pub is served by regular buses from Coalville, Loughborough and Leicester. ♨❀◐◑♣P

Three Horseshoes ☆

11 Leicester Road, LE67 5GN

⌚ 11-3, 6.30-11; 12-2, 7-10.30 Sun

☎ (01530) 837311

Draught Bass; M&B Mild; Marston's Pedigree Ⓗ

Recently granted Grade II listed status, this building features in CAMRA's National Inventory of pubs with interiors of outstanding historic interest. Its nickname, 'Polly's', is thought to come from a former landlady, Polly Burton. Originally two separate buildings, they were joined possibly in 1882. The long bar has a quarry tiled floor and open fires, plus wooden bench seating and pre-war fittings. There is no till: the change is kept on a back shelf. The small snug is equally full of character. The original outside toilets are still in use. There are regular buses from Coalville, Loughborough and Nottingham. ♨Q⊟♣

Wigston

Star & Garter

114 Leicester Road, LE18 1DS

⌚ 11-3, 5-11; 11-11 Fri & Sat; 12-10.30 Sun

☎ (0116) 288 2450

Everards Beacon, Tiger, Original, seasonal beers; guest beers Ⓗ

Fully refurbished in March 2004, this award-winning pub retains two rooms with a central bar. Very much a community local with a regular following, it also offers a warm welcome to visitors. It has both long alley and table skittles, and darts and dominoes are played. Guest beers come from Everards Old English Ale Club. Thursday is curry night. ❀◐⊟♣P

Wymeswold

Three Crowns

45 Far Street, LE12 6TZ

⌚ 12-3, 5.30-11; 12-3, 7-10.30 Sun

☎ (01509) 880153

Adnams Bitter; Highgate Dark; Marston's Pedigree; guest beers Ⓗ

Cosy, traditional 18th-century village pub with an exposed, beamed ceiling and open fires. This multi-room pub has two cosy snugs, a bar with traditional games and a lounge which is split level with a raised no-smoking area. Up to four guest beers are available each week, often from the Belvoir Brewery. Food is served at lunchtimes and some evenings. A large beer garden is popular in summer and has a petanque pitch. Dogs are welcome. ♨Q❀◐⊟♣P⊁

RUTLAND

Barrowden

Exeter Arms

28 Main Street, LE15 8EQ

⌚ 12-2, 6-11; 12- 3, 7-10:30 Sun

☎ (01572) 747247

Blencowe Beach Boys, seasonal beers; guest beers Ⓗ

The pub is built of stone with a Collyweston tiled roof. It overlooks the village green and duckpond, with southerly views across the Welland Valley to Wakerley Woods. Inside, there is one long room with a dining area at one end and the bar at the other. Smoking and the use of mobile phones are not allowed inside the pub. A barn at the end of the garden is home to the Blencowe Brewery. ♕Q❀⇌◑♣P⊬

Belmesthorpe

Blue Bell

Shepherds Walk, PE9 4JG

⏲ 12- 2.30, 6 (5 Fri)-11; 12-10.30 Sun

☎ (01780) 763859

Draught Bass; Greene King Abbot; Hop Back Summer Lightning; guest beer Ⓗ

This limestone pub has original oak beams and an award-winning inglenook. The main entrance is from the car park, which brings you into the bar area, with a dining area behind and a games room situated beyond the fireplace. The pub reputedly has a resident ghost in the form of a monk. Visitors can play an unusual game which involves trying to drive nails into large tree trunk in one hit using the small end of the hammer provided. ♕Q❀◑⊟♣P

Belton in Rutland

Sun Inn

24 Main Street, LE15 9LB (½ mile from A47)

⏲ 12-2, 6-11; 12-10.30 Sun

☎ (01572) 717227

Banks's Original; guest beer Ⓗ

This cosy pub is tucked away in a small, quiet village and is well worth a detour from the nearby A47. It was originally a Phipps pub until it was swallowed up by Watneys in the early 1970s. On three floor levels, including a games room, little has changed since the 1960s. It has an unusual washer on nail system for recording when drinks are left in by the locals. This typical country local is unspoilt by the passage of time. ♕Q❀♣

Braunston in Rutland

Old Plough Inn

2 Church Street, LE15 8QY

⏲ 11-3, 6-11; 11-11 Fri & Sat; 12-10.30 Sun

☎ (01572) 722714

Grainstore Cooking; guest beers Ⓗ

Now one of the few pubs owned by the Grainstore Brewery, it has a bar and cosy, low-beamed lounge, conservatory, restaurant and patio garden. Not all the pub's spirits come in bottles: footsteps and slamming doors have been heard long after closing time. ♕Q❀◑⊟♣P

Oakham

Grainstore

Station Approach, LE15 6RE

⏲ 11-11; 12-10.30 Sun

☎ (01572) 770065

Grainstore Rutland Panther; Cooking, Triple B, Ten Fifty, seasonal beers; guest beers Ⓗ

Situated next to Oakham Station, this pub and brewery derive their name from the former Victorian railway grainstore they are located in. The large bar is on the ground floor and the brewery on the first. Two sets of handpumps are in use, one set with swan necks and one without. There is also a good selection of Belgian bottled beers on offer. The hardstanding area in front of the pub is used for outdoor drinking in summer. ❀◑♿⇌♣P

Stretton

Jackson Stops Inn

Rookery Lane, LE15 7RA

⏲ 12-2:30, 6:30-11; closed Mon; 12-3 Sun

☎ 01780 410237

Oakham JHB; guest beer Ⓗ

This 17th-century inn is located in the heart of the small village of Stretton, conveniently situated just off the A1. There are four dining rooms and a traditional public bar area which contains a small but interesting bottled beer collection. Traditional games include nurdling, which is played in only one other pub in the country. Ask about the story of how the pub got its name. ♕Q❀◑⊟♿♣P⊡

Wing

King's Arms

Top Street, LE15 8SE

⏲ 12-3, 6-11; 12-10:30 Sun

☎ 01572 737634 website: www.thekingsarms-wing.co.uk

Grainstore Cooking; Taylor Landlord; Marston's Pedigree; guest beer Ⓗ

This 17th-century coaching inn is situated on the highest road in the village of Wing. Not far from Rutland Water Reservoir, it is popular with visitors and locals who want a quiet drink or meal. The inn comprises two dining rooms, a bar area and snug which is separated from the bar by an impressive inglenook. ♕Q❀⇌◑⊟⛺P⊡

Open all hours?

The new Licensing Act for England and Wales was due to come into effect in the autumn of 2005. In spite of media frenzy over '24-hour opening', only a handful of pubs and hotels had applied for such extensions as the Guide went to press. It is likely that most pubs will opt for existing hours or for late-night extensions at weekends. The hours listed for pubs were correct when the Guide went to press but are liable to change.

CAMRA's Beers of the Year

The beers listed below are CAMRA's Beers of the Year. They were short-listed for the Champion Beer of Britain competition in August 2005, and the Champion Winter Beer of Britain competition in January 2005. The August competition judged Dark and Light Milds; Bitters; Best Bitters; Strong Bitters; Golden Ales; Speciality Beers; and Real Ale in a Bottle, while the winter competition judged Old Ales and Strong Milds; Porters and Stouts; and Barley Wines. Each beer was found by panels of trained CAMRA judges to be consistently outstanding in its category, and they all receive a 'full tankard' [■] symbol in the Breweries section.

DARK AND LIGHT MILDS
Bateman's Dark Mild
Brains Dark
E&S Elland First Light
Elgood's Black Dog
Grainstore Rutland Panther
Moorhouse Black Cat
Triple fff Pressed Rat & Warthog

BITTERS
Belvoir Star
Castle Rock Harvest Pale
Dark Star Hop Head
E&S Elland Bargee
Harviestoun Bitter & Twisted
Holden's Black Country Bitter
Marble Manchester Bitter
RCH PG Steam
Sharp's Doom Bar
Thwaites Bitter
Triple fff Alton's Pride
Woodforde's Wherry
Wolf Golden Jackal
York Bitter

BEST BITTERS
Bath Barnstormer
Cotleigh Barn Owl
Fuller's London Pride
Grainstore Triple B
Harvey's Sussex Best Bitter
Hogs Back TEA
Mighty Oak Burntwood Bitter
Olde Swan Entire
Phoenix Arizona
Reepham Rapier
Robinson's Unicorn
Skinner's Betty Stoggs
Timothy Taylor Landlord
Wickwar Cotswold Way

STRONG BITTERS
Berrow Topsy Turvey
Bullmastiff Son of a Bitch
Fuller's ESB
Hanby Nutcracker
O'Hanlon's Royal Oak
Porter Sunshine
Tring Colley's Dog

GOLDEN ALES
Breconshire Golden Valley
Crouch Vale Brewers Gold
Hop Back Summer Lightning
Jarrow Rivet Catcher
Kelburn Goldihops
Oakham JHB
Storm Bosley Cloud

OLD ALES AND STRONG MILDS
Abbeydale Absolution
Bath Festivity
Chalk Hill Flintknappers Mild
Sarah Hughes Dark Ruby
King Old Ale
Ramsgate Gadds Dark Ale
Young's Winter Warmer

PORTERS AND STOUTS
Bateman's Salem Porter
Big Lamp Summerhill Stout
Crown Stannington Stout
Goacher's Crown Imperial Stout
Salamander Stout
Spectrum Old Stoatwobbler
Tomas Watkin Merlin Stout

BARLEY WINES
Bass No 1
Big Lamp Blackout
Milton Mammon
Moor Old Freddy Walker
Orkney Skullsplitter
Woodforde's Headcracker

SPECIALITY BEERS
Cairngorm Trade Winds
Daleside Morocco
Nethergate Umbel Ale
Ridley's Rumpus
Titanic Iceberg
Williams Fraoch
Young's Waggledance

REAL ALE IN A BOTTLE
Beartown Pandamonium
Black Isle Organic Porter
Bridge of Allan Brig O'Allan
Durham Evensong
E&S 1872
Fuller's 1845
O'Hanlon's Port Stout
RCH Pitchfork
Ringwood Fortyniner
Titanic Stout
Wye Valley Dorothy Goodbody's Wholesome Stout
Young's Special London Ale

CHAMPION WINTER BEER OF BRITAIN
Robinson's Old Tom

CHAMPION BEER OF BRITAIN 2005
Crouch Vale Brewers Gold

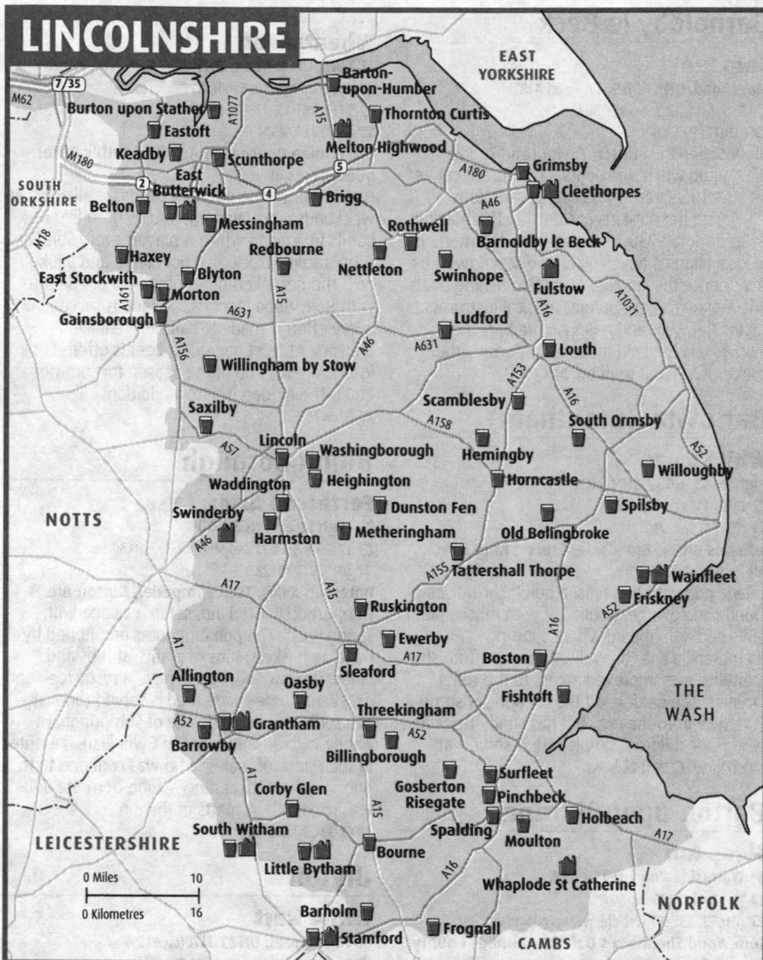

Allington

Welby Arms ✪

The Green, NG32 2EA

(1 mile from A1 Gonerby Moor roundabout)

12-2.30, 6-11; 12-4, 6-10.30 Sun

☎ (01400) 281361

Draught Bass; John Smith's Bitter; Taylor Landlord; guest beers Ⓗ

The Welby Arms makes a good base for visiting the Vale of Belvoir, Belton House and the former home of Sir Isaac Newton, Woolsthorpe Manor. Stamford is only a 30-minute drive down the A1. It usually has six beers on tap and a good wine list. The monthly quiz (third Mon) is reckoned to be the best in the county. Excellent meals are available daily plus special menus for events such as Mother's Day and Christmas. The rear door is wheelchair accessible.

Q P

Barholm

Five Horseshoes

Main Street, PE9 4RA (off sharp bend in main street)

5 (12.30 Sat)-11; 12-10.30 Sun

☎ (01778) 560238

Adnams Bitter; Oakham JHB; guest beers Ⓗ

This 18th-century, three-roomed pub, situated in a quiet hamlet, is constructed from locally-quarried barnack stone, with a creeper-covered patio and large attractive gardens. Open fires greet visitors on chilly evenings. The pub concentrates on selling real ales, with four guest beers always on offer, frequently including strong brews. The pub supports micro-breweries and stocks an occasional house beer, brewed by Rooster. P

INDEPENDENT BREWERIES

Bateman Wainfleet
Blue Bell Whaplode St Catherine
Blue Cow South Witham
DarkTribe East Butterwick
Fugelestou Fulstow
Melbourn Stamford
Newby Wyke Little Bytham
Oldershaw Grantham
Poachers Swinderby
Riverside Wainfleet
Willy's Cleethorpes
Tom Wood Melton Highwood

Barnoldby le Beck

Ship Inn

Main Road, DN37 0BG (1 mile off A18)
❂ 12-3, 6-11; 12-3, 6-10.30 Sun
☎ (01472) 822300
Black Sheep Best Bitter; Taylor Landlord Ⓗ
Dining pub where the popular restaurant caters for customers from well beyond Barnoldby village, on the outskirts of Grimsby. The building dates back to 1730, and was named in memory of local pilgrims travelling on the Mayflower; by coincidence the landlord owns two fishing boats. Bric-a-brac (rackets, pumps, musical instruments) covers the walls and ceiling in the bar. The owners take pride in the food, especially the choice of fish and seafood. ♨Q❀P

Barrowby (Grantham)

White Swan

High Road, NG32 1HN (off A1 and A52)
❂ 11.30-11; 12-10.30 Sun
☎ (01476) 562375
Adnams Bitter, Broadside; Greene King IPA; Wells Bombardier Ⓗ
Village pub with two bars: a quiet, comfortable lounge and a larger public bar with music, pool table and a dartboard where sporting memorabilia line the walls. A recent refurbishment includes improved access to the toilet facilities. The garden, off the car park, is some little way from the pub, but has shady trees and swings for children. Simple fare is served at lunchtime. Q❀◑⊟♿P

Barton-upon-Humber

Sloop Inn

81 Waterside Road, DN18 5BA
❂ 11-11; 12-10.30 Sun
☎ (01652) 637287 website: www.sloopinn.net
Tom Wood Shepherd's Delight, Bomber County, seasonal beers Ⓗ
Multi-roomed pub, away from the town centre, where a nautical theme is enhanced by stained glass windows showing sailing scenes. Boating equipment is displayed and each area is named as part of a ship. Three Tom Wood ales are usually available, including a seasonal beer. The bar area houses pool and darts, others are designated for dining, including one no-smoking room. The Sloop is near Far Ings nature reserve and Water's Edge visitors centre. A wheelchair ramp is available. Q❀◑◗⊟♿⇌♣P⊁

Belton

Crown

Church Lane, Churchtown, DN9 1PA (off A161)
❂ 4 (12 Sat)-11; 12-10.30 Sun
☎ (01427) 872834
Marston's Pedigree; John Smith's Bitter; Theakston Best Bitter Ⓗ
Difficult to find – situated behind All Saints' Church – but well worth the effort, this friendly local is a haven for the discerning beer drinker. No smooth beers are kept and no food is served. Beers from the nearby Glentworth Brewery have proved popular and are served on a rotating basis. A games room is located at the back of the pub. ♨❀♣P

Wheatsheaf

152 Westgate Road, DN9 1QB (from A161 follow Westgate Rd towards Sandtoft)
❂ 5 (12 Sat)-11; 12-10.30 Sun
☎ (01427) 872504
Caledonian Deuchars IPA; John Smith's Bitter; guest beers Ⓗ
Family-run village pub that caters for all ages. At weekends entertainment ranges from live rock bands to a piano which is played every Sunday. Other facilities include a pool table and a juke box. The decor combines photos of old Belton with Hollywood legends. No food is served but every effort is made to cater for real ale drinkers. At least one guest beer is offered at local CAMRA's Pub of the Season for summer 2003. The garden is a new addition.
♨❀♣P

Billingborough

Fortescue Arms

27 High Street, NG34 0QB
❂ 12-2.30, 6-11; closed Mon; 12-3, 7-10.30 Sun
☎ (01529) 240228
Bateman XXXB; Tetley Imperial, Burton Ale Ⓗ
Fine, Grade II listed inn, set in a village with spring wells. The pub exterior is brightened by hanging baskets, tubs of plants, shrubs and vines. The bar and lounge have a rustic feel, and excellent home-made food is served (booking advised). Nearby is the site of Sempringham Abbey with a monument to Gwenllian, daughter of the Prince of Wales, who was confined to the priory in the 12th century. Stone from the abbey was used to build parts of the inn.
♨Q❀◑◗⊟♿▲P

Blyton

White Hart

66 High Street, DN21 3LA (on A159)
❂ 5 (3 Fri; 1 Sat)-11; 12-10.30 Sun
☎ (01427) 628683
Tom Wood Best Bitter; John Smith's Bitter Ⓗ
Friendly village pub where the large comfortable front bar has a small serving area in the corner. The long rear bar is bright and adjoins the patio. This room is used for dining; large steaks are the house speciality (no food Mon eve). The pub hosts busy theme nights and many activities are planned for the future. ♨❀◗P

Boston

Ball House ✔

Wainfleet Road, PE21 9RL (on A52, 2 miles from centre)
❂ 11.30-3, 6.30-11; 12-3, 7-10.30 Sun
☎ (01205) 364478 website: www.the ballhouse.co.uk
Draught Bass; Bateman XB, XXXB; guest beers Ⓗ
Mock-Tudor, 13th-century pub that stands on the site of an old cannonball store. Stunning award-winning floral displays greet you during the summer; there is outdoor seating and an enclosed play area for children. An excellent, varied menu is based on fresh and home-grown produce; small portions are always available. Monthly theme nights are hosted from January-July and the landlord is a big supporter of the Boston beer festival.
♨Q❀◑◗♿P

Coach & Horses ✔

86 Main Ridge East, PE21 6SY

5 (6 Fri)-11; 11-3, 7-11 Sat; 12-3, 7-10.30 Sun

☎ (01205) 362301

Bateman XB, XXXB

Friendly, one-roomed pub just off the town ring road (John Adams Way), near Boston United foootball ground – arrive early on match days. It is well used by the local community; trophy cabinets record the pub's successful participation in various games. It serves no food but is near the famous 'Eagles' fish and chip café and several takeaways. The pub is run by a long-serving landlord and his family and is famed for its XXXB. Q ♣

Cowbridge

Horncastle Road, PE22 7AX (on B1183, N of town)

11-3, 6-11; 12-4, 7-10.30 Sun

☎ (01205) 362597

Greene King Old Speckled Hen; Theakston Mild, Best Bitter; guest beers

Just out of town, this pub is popular with drinkers and diners. It splits into three main areas: the public bar is a no-nonsense drinking and darts environment, displaying a large collection of football scarves; the smaller lounge is warm and cosy with a welcoming open fire – here the display is baseball caps; beyond the lounge is the restaurant serving excellent, home-cooked food. The pub is handy for Boston Golf Club. Q ♣P

Duke of York Inn ✔

Lincoln Lane, PE21 8RU

12-3 (not Mon), 5-11; 2-11 Wed; 12-11 Fri & Sat; 12-10.30 Sun

☎ (01205) 363120

Draught Bass; Bateman XB; guest beers

A warm welcome awaits customers old and new to this small friendly pub, 2005 winner of the Bateman Cellar Management competition. It fields 11 pub teams: darts, pool, dominoes, quiz and football. Recently refurbished, and with a log fire, it has a cosy atmosphere. Home-cooked food is served. Occasional music is performed by local bands. It has a large-screen TV. Popular on match days, it is on the route from the nearby station to the football ground. ♣P

Eagle

West Street, PE21 8RE (250 yds from station)

11-11; 12-10.30 Sun

☎ (01205) 361116

Banks's Bitter; Castle Rock Harvest Pale; Taylor Landlord; guest beers

Part of the Tynemill chain, the Eagle is known as Boston's real ale pub. The L-shaped bar has a pool table and large screen for live sports events. Next door is a cosy lounge with an open fire. The pub stocks a changing range of guest ales, with at least one Castle Rock beer. Cider comes from Biddenden and Stowford Press. The function room is home to Boston Folk Club.
Q ♣

Moon Under Water ✔

6 High Street, PE21 8SH

10-11; 10 (12 for alcohol)-10.30 Sun

☎ (01205) 311911

Greene King Abbot; Marston's Burton Bitter, Pedigree; Shepherd Neame Spitfire; guest beers

This busy town-centre pub, close to the tidal section of the River Witham, has the usual mix of drinking/dining areas, customers, atmosphere and helpful staff associated with a Wetherspoon conversion. Formerly a government building, an imposing circular staircase leads from the central lounge area to the toilets. There are two dining areas: one is no-smoking and child-friendly. With four guest ales and plenty of promotional material, cask beer is properly highlighted here.

Ship Tavern

Custom House Lane , PE21 6HH (off South Sq)

11-11; 12-10.30 Sun

☎ (01205) 358156

Bateman Mild, XB; Greene King IPA; guest beer

Town-centre pub near the quayside in the historic and cultural quarter, near the Guild Hall and theatre. This is a traditional pub, comprising one large L-shaped room where plenty of brewery memorabilia is on display. It is popular with students and gets busy with football supporters on match days. A small patio to the rear gives extra space for summer drinking.
♣

Bourne

Smith's

25 North Street, PE10 9AE

11-11; 12-10.30 Sun

☎ (01778) 426819 website: www.smithsofbourne.co.uk

Fuller's London Pride; Oakham JHB; guest beers

Winner of the national CAMRA/English Heritage conversion to pub use award, this former grocers, in a three-storey listed Georgian building, is now a superb pub. Bars are situated downstairs (front and rear), while several attractive drinking areas take up the rest of the ground and first floors. There is a large, well-equipped patio and garden. The pub regularly has promotions and guests to showcase micro-breweries. If you miss lunch, a cheeseboard is available until 7pm.

Brigg

Black Bull

3 Wrawby Street, DN20 8JH (in main shopping street)

11-3 (4 Thu), 7-11; 11-11 Sat; 12-3, 7-10.30 Sun

☎ (01652) 652153

John Smith's Bitter; Tom Wood Harvest Bitter; guest beers

Popular, recently refurbished town-centre pub, that gets busy on market days (Thu & Sat). It has a no-smoking dining room where children are welcome. It stocks a regular beer from the local Tom Wood (formerly Highwood) Brewery, plus a changing guest beer. The patio adjoins the car park at the rear. Brigg can be reached from Scunthorpe and Barton by bus; also by train, but only on Saturday. ♣P

Yarborough Hunt

49 Bridge Street, DN20 8NF

(across bridge from tourist information)

⏲ 10-11; 10.30-10.30 Sun
☎ (01652) 658333
Greene King IPA; Tom Wood Best Bitter; guest beers Ⓗ
Formerly Sargeant's Brewery tap, built in the early 1700s, the pub has been carefully restored to retain original features. Four rooms (two no-smoking) are furnished in simple style, with brewery memorabilia around the walls. Three rotating guest ales are supplemented by draught Belgian beers and 50 malt whiskies. Wood-burning stoves and a heated patio in the garden keep you warm all year. No food is served but you are welcome to bring sandwiches. The train only runs on Saturday. ♔Q❀♿⇶♣●⊬

Burton upon Stather

Ferry House
Stather Road, DN15 9DJ (follow campsite signs)
⏲ 7 (11 Sat)-11; 12-10.30 Sun
☎ (01724) 721783
Beer range varies Ⓗ
Friendly village local situated low down in the village alongside the River Trent. The pub has been run by the same family for 46 years. The large L-shaped bar houses a pool table and local memorabilia is displayed. A no-smoking lounge/family room overlooks the river bank. Regular seasonal beer festivals are held. A large grassed seating area next to the pub allows for outdoor drinking in summer. ❀♿⛺♣P⊬

Cleethorpes

No. 2 Refreshment Room
Station Approach, DN35 8AX (on station)
⏲ 10-11; 12-10.30 Sun
☎ (07905) 375587
Fuller's London Pride; M&B Mild; Worthington's Bitter; guest beers Ⓗ
Known as Under the Clock because of its position under the station clock tower, this should be your first port of call when arriving by train. The single-roomed free house boasts up to five real ales, and was voted local CAMRA Pub of the Year 2004. It probably has the best-kept pub toilet facilities in the area. A quiz night on Thursday and a free buffet on Sunday evening add to its appeal. ❀⇶

Nottingham House
5-7 Seaview Street, DN35 8EU
⏲ 12-11; 12-10.30 Sun
☎ (01472) 505150
Fuller's London Pride; Tetley Mild, Bitter Ⓗ
Prominently located at the town's highest point, it stands at the end of a narrow, timeless street overlooking the promenade. The new luxury apartments adjacent provide a startling contrast to the frontage of the 'Notts', which positively invites you to enter. Once inside, you will find two distinctive rooms either side of the entrance lobby, while at the rear is a room suitable for informal meetings, served by means of a hatch. One to savour. Q⊟⇶♣

Willy's
17 Highcliff Road, DN35 8RQ
⏲ 11-11; 12-10.30 Sun
☎ (01472) 602145
Bateman XB; Willy's Original; guest beers Ⓗ
An ever-present regular in this Guide, Willy's is run by beer enthusiasts for beer enthusiasts. The seafront location makes it a must for locals and visitors alike. The attached brewhouse can be viewed from the bar. The front patio is handy for sunny days. Great value home-cooked food is served daily at lunchtime, plus Monday, Tuesday and Thursday evenings. ❀◑◗⇶

Corby Glen

Coachman
2 Bourne Road, NG33 4NS (on A151)
⏲ 12-3, 5-11; 12-11 Sat; 12-10.30 Sun
☎ (01476) 550316
Caledonian Deuchars IPA; Fuller's London Pride; Greene King Abbot; guest beers Ⓗ
Two real fires, stripped stone and brick walls and beamed ceilings characterise the Coachman. Two restaurant areas – the Post Horn and the Farrier Room – cater for diners, the larger being available for functions (no food Sun eve). Disabled access is from the car park, and there is a designated WC. Recently refurbished to a high standard, soft chairs and sofas are set by the fires. Caledonian Deuchars IPA alternates with Gale's HSB. The pub benefits from an enclosed garden. ♔Q❀⇄◑◗♿P

Dunston Fen

White Horse Inn
LN4 3AP (6 miles E of B1188) OS138663
⏲ 12-3, 7-11; 12-11 Sat; 12-10.30 Sun
☎ (01526) 398341 website: www.dunstonfen.co.uk
Beer range varies Ⓗ
Remote, family-run, free house on the banks of the River Witham. There is always at least one beer from Poachers Brewery available, with one or two from other micros, depending on the time of year. A popular tented beer festival is held over the August bank holiday weekend. The menu changes often as it incorporates fresh local produce whenever possible. The large garden includes a children's play area. Free overnight moorings are available to customers. ♔❀⇄◑◗⛺P

East Butterwick

Dog & Gun
High Street, DN17 3AJ (off A18, at Keadby Bridge, follow river bank road))
⏲ 6 (5 Thu-Sat)-11; 12-10.30 Sun
☎ (01724) 782324
John Smith's Bitter; guest beers Ⓗ
Old-fashioned village local by the River Trent, recently acquired by DarkTribe Brewery, which has relocated to the rear of the premises. In summer drinkers sit on the bank, or in the courtyard, where seating is provided. Basic, but welcoming, the central bar serves three distinct areas, one with a pool table. Renowned for its real fire in winter, it regularly serves up a real from Dark Tribe, plus a changing guest beer. A busy hub of village life, visitors are always made welcome. ♔Q❀⊟♣P

East Stockwith

Ferry House
27 Front Street, DN21 3DJ

⏲ 11.30-3, 6.30-11; closed Mon; 12-10.30 Sun
☎ (01427) 615276
John Smith's Bitter; Webster's Bitter; guest beers Ⓗ
Village free house on the River Trent which caters for locals and has a thriving food trade (booking is sometimes necessary). Prices are reasonable for the good quality food that is cooked on the premises. The large bar has facilities for pool, darts and dominoes. There is a separate dining room and a function room. Three guest bedrooms with Trent views provide keenly-priced B&B. Two guest beers from independent brewers are offered. A quiz night is held on alternate Wednesday evenings.
♨❀⇌◑♣P

Eastoft

River Don Tavern

Sampson Street, DN17 4PQ (On A161)
⏲ 5 (7.30 Mon & Tue; 12 Sat)-11; 12-10.30 Sun
☎ (01724) 798040
John Smith's Bitter; guest beers Ⓗ
Rural pub located in the Isle of Axholme. The open-plan design has retained discrete areas for eating and drinking. A country inn ambience is enhanced by dark beams and agricultural implements. It generally offers two guest ales in winter, three in summer and autumn. It is popular for good value meals, including a hot skillet menu and Sunday carvery. Food is served Wednesday-Friday 5-9pm (12-9 Sat and Sun). An annual beer festival is staged in the summer.
♨❀◑♿♣P

Ewerby

Finch Hatton Arms

43 Main Street, NG34 9PH
⏲ 12-3, 6-11; 12-3, 6-10.30 Sun
☎ (01529) 460363
Everards Tiger; Riverside Dixon's Major Bitter; guest beers Ⓗ
Substantial country inn built in the early 1870s. It was bought by Lord Winchelsea in 1875 and given his family name until the mid-1960s. The pub sign includes the Finch Hatton family motto, 'with a clear conscience'. Previously a traditional brewery-owned pub, it is now a free house and fully-equipped, small hotel, but it retains its charm and displays local artefacts both inside and out. The extensive menu is varied in both taste and price. ♨Q❀⇌◑⊟♣P

Fishtoft

Red Cow Inn

Gaysfield Road, PE21 0SF
⏲ 5.30 (11 Sat)-11; 12-10.30 Sun
☎ (01205) 367552
Bateman Mild, XB Ⓗ
Well-established village pub extending a warm welcome to customers old and new. Various teams, including pool, darts and dominoes, represent this small but charismatic pub. Occasional entertainment evenings might include music or local bands. Close to the Pilgrim Fathers memorial, it offers an opportunity to call in after a spot of birdwatching, angling or walking.
♨Q❀⛺♣P⊓

Friskney

Barley Mow

Sea Lane, PE22 8SD
(on A52, between Boston and Skegness)
⏲ 12-3, 6.30-11; 12-11 Sat; 12-10.30 Sun
☎ (01754) 820883
Bateman XB; guest beers Ⓗ
This 300-year-old hostelry, known locally as the Barley Mow (rhymes with cow) is situated on the busy Boston-Skegness road. Frequented by visitors and locals alike, it is especially popular during the summer months. An imaginative selection of home-cooked meals is offered at reasonable prices. A lovely conservatory leads to the garden, making this pub even more enjoyable in fine weather.
♨Q❀◑⊟♿♣P

Frognall

Goat

155 Spalding Road, PE6 8SA
(on B1525, E of Deeping St James)
⏲ 11.30-2.30, 6-11; 6-10.30 Sun
☎ (01778) 347629
Beer range varies Ⓗ
Friendly pub, which consists of one bar and two dining areas (one is a separate room). The low-ceilinged bar serves four cask beers including a low gravity brew and, usually, a strong, dark ale. A large (and growing) range of single malt whiskies is also stocked. The pub is popular for its good quality food, cooked to order. The large garden has a children's play area and another just for toddlers. A beer festival is held in late July. ♨Q☺❀◑♿P⊓

Gainsborough

Eight Jolly Brewers

Ship Court Silver Street, DN21 2DW (off market place)
⏲ 11-11; 12-10.30 Sun
Glentworth Lightyear; Maypole May Fly Bitter; guest beers Ⓗ
This town-centre pub was converted from a carpenter's workshop. The bar is on the ground floor; a quiet upstairs room is split by the staircase – one half is no-smoking. A former CAMRA national Pub of the Year runner-up, it is a real ale haven, featuring eight draught beers, Biddenden cider, and Belgian Leffe on draught, plus a wide selection of foreign bottled beers and fruit wines. Two beers are always heavily discounted. Look out for other Maypole Brewery beers. Thursday is music night.
Q❀⊟♣●P⚟⊓

Sweyn Forkbeard ✔

Silver Street, DN21 2AJ
⏲ 11-11; 12-10.30 Sun
☎ (01427) 675000
Beer range varies Ⓗ
Spacious Wetherspoon's house with open-plan seating and glass walls to the street on two sides. Frequented by all age groups, a varied menu is served all day, with curry nights and other promotions on Thursday. The patio overlooks the river boulevard in the town centre. The beer range is always changing, with at least four guests on tap at any time. ❀◑♿⚟

Gosberton Risegate

Duke of York

105 Risegate Road, PE11 4EY

12-2.30 (not Mon), 6-11; 12-11 Fri & Sat; 12-2.30, 7-10.30 Sun

(01775) 840193

Bateman XB; Black Sheep Best Bitter; guest beers Ⓗ

This lively pub plays an active role in the local community, supporting charities, sports teams and social activities. It has a well-established reputation for its interesting and varying range of competitively-priced cask ales and quality food. There is a no-smoking dining room and a games room. A Bateman's house many years ago, note the arch above the bar, a feature from that period. The garden, with play area, goats and other animals is an added attraction.

Grantham

Beehive

10-11 Castlegate, NG31 6SE (between Guildhall and St Wulfram's Church on one-way street)

11.30-11; 12-10.30 Sun

(01476) 404554

Everards Tiger; Newby Wyke Bear Island; guest beer Ⓗ

A famous feature of this busy, 16th-century pub is its living sign in the tree on the street, so beware of the bees. Also of note, indoors, are the original pub sign displayed behind the bar and the one-line sayings that are painted on the walls of the low-ceilinged rooms. Plain fare is served at lunchtime.

Blue Pig

9 Vine Street, NG31 6RQ (near St Wulfram's Church and the Beehive pub)

11 (10.30 Sat)-11; 12-10.30 Sun

(01476) 563704 website: www.bluepiginn.com

Caledonian Deuchars IPA; Flowers Original; Ⓗ **Oldershaw Old Boy; Wadworth 6X;** Ⓖ **York Yorkshire Terrier** Ⓗ

Old, Tudor-style pub that boasts lashings of history and a fine collection of pigs. There has been a hostelry on this site for hundreds of years, reflected in the timber framing of the building. A log fire creates a warm welcome in the winter months, while in summer the enclosed garden with an outdoor bar comes into its own. The pub offers a good range of bar food, served all day at the weekend; high chairs are provided.

Q

Nobody Inn

9 North Street, NG31 6NU (on corner near Asda car park)

12-11; 12-10.30 Sun

(01476) 5665288 website: www.nobodyinn.com

Beer range varies Ⓗ

Small, friendly pub where the six handpumps support local breweries. Grantham Gold is brewed by Newby Wyke especially for the pub. On a split-level with bare wood floors, an unusual feature is the access to the toilets gained through the bookcase. Outside, café-style tables are set out on the pavement for fair weather drinking.

Grimsby

Hope & Anchor

148 Victoria Street, DN31 1NX

12-11; 12-10.30 Sun

(01472) 500706

Flowers Original; Tetley Bitter; Tom Wood Best Bitter; guest beers Ⓗ

One-roomed pub where a central bar manages to create the feeling of a multi-roomed house. Situated just away from the town centre, it is quiet in the week, but more lively at the weekend, featuring regular entertainment. A welcome return to this this Guide for an old favourite, which serves restaurant-quality food on an interesting menu at pub prices.

(Town)

Millfields

53 Bargate, DN34 5AD

11-11; 12-10.30 Sun

(01472) 356068 website: www.millfieldshotel.co.uk

Fuller's London Pride; John Smith's Bitter Ⓗ

Hotel and bar situated on one of the main routes into Grimsby. For those wanting more than a bar meal, there is a quality restaurant attached, with a range of prices, including some special offers in the early evening and at lunchtime. The overnight accommodation is also recommended here. (Town) P

Royal Oak

190 Victoria Street, DN31 1NX

12-11; 12-10.30 Sun

(01472) 354562

Theakston Mild; guest beer Ⓗ

The attractive Tudor-style front and leaded lights suggest a traditional interior, and despite some changes over the years, it still retains two distinct rooms. A pleasant lounge complements the bar, with its working man's feel – demonstrated by the clatter of dominoes and the thud of darts. Here you may view the tropical fish and have a chat without having to shout. The Oak is 300 yards from the town-centre bus station and seven minutes' walk from the rail station. (Town)

Tap & Spile

Haven Mill, Garth Lane, DN31 3AF (rear of Freshney Place shopping precinct)

11-11; 12-10.30 Sun

(01472) 357493

Bateman XB, XXXB; Caledonian Deuchars IPA; Wychwood Hobgoblin; guest beers Ⓗ

Spacious, one-roomed, open-plan pub, a former flour mill where old stone, brick and woodwork have been retained. Good quality, wholesome food is served Monday-Saturday. It stages quiz nights on Monday and Thursday and regular music most weekends, including acoustic blues. A welcome retreat away from the brash town centre disco bars. The pub's balcony overlooks the river. (Town)

Wheatsheaf

47 Bargate, DN34 5AD

11.30-11; 12-10.30 Sun

(01472) 246821

Bateman XXXB; Taylor Landlord; Tetley Bitter; guest beer Ⓗ

Formerly a girls' school, the Wheatsheaf has

been a pub for many years. Recently refurbished by Mitchells and Butlers as an Ember Inn, it is considered a flagship for these establishments. The emphasis is on comfort, good food at reasonable prices (served all day) and a fine selection of real ales and other beverages. The split-level interior encompasses many seating areas – some are no-smoking. Beer festivals are held twice a year and include beers from small breweries. ❀◐◑♿⇌(Town) P⊬

Harmston

Thorold Arms

High Street, LN5 9SN (off A607)

⏲ 12-3 (not Mon), 6-11; 12-3, 7-10.30 Sun

☎ (01522) 720358 website: www.thoroldarms.co.uk

Beer range varies Ⓗ

Stone-built, village pub where the bar combines a traditional counter area with comfortable sofas and an open fire. Four handpumps regularly offer Archers' beers, Poachers and other Lincolnshire micros also often feature. Around 110 different beers were served in 2004. Food is available until 8.45pm (not Sun eve or Mon), including a roast, 'potluck' Tuesday, and fish and chips (Wed). The Lincoln-Grantham bus stops 400 yards away; the Viking Way footpath runs through village. ♔Q❀◐◑⊟♿P⊬

Haxey

Loco

31-33 Church Street, DN9 2HY (from A161, follow B1396 into village)

⏲ 2 (12 Sat)-11; 12-10.30 Sun

☎ (01427) 752879

John Smith's Bitter; guest beers Ⓗ

Unusual pub, converted from the village Co-op and chip shop during the 1980s. Decorated with railway memorabilia, including an engine smokebox, it is a must for railway buffs. Further interest is added by Kashmir Sidings, the pub's Indian restaurant and takeaway, which is open Tuesday-Sunday evenings. At least one guest beer is always available, with local breweries often represented. The pub participates in the annual local Haxey Hood game on January 6th. ◑♣

Heighington

Butcher & Beast ✔

High Street, LN4 1JS

⏲ 11-11; 12-10.30 Sun

☎ (01522) 790386

Bateman XB, XXXB, seasonal beers; guest beers Ⓗ

Stone-built Bateman's house in an attractive village setting. Open plan, but with distinct areas, the bar has old photographs of the village on display, and an open fire. There is a no-smoking dining room where meals and snacks from a wide-ranging menu are served 12-2 daily and 5-9 Tuesday-Saturday. The pub has won awards for its floral displays. The village has a bus service from and to Lincoln. ♔Q♘❀◐◑⊬

Hemingby

Coach & Horses

Church Lane, LN9 5QF (1 mile from A158, turn in Baumber)

⏲ 12-2 (not Mon or Tue), 7 (6 Wed-Fri)-11; 12-3, 7-10.30 Sun

☎ (01507) 578280

website: www.coachandhorses.mysite.freeserve.com

Bateman Mild; Riverside Dixon's Major Bitter; guest beers Ⓗ

Situated in the foothills of the Wolds and sitting comfortably at the side of the church, this low, white building looks (and is) charming. On entry the central fire separates the pool area from the bar proper, which is cosy and welcoming; beams and comfortable settles abound. Mind your head if you are tall. No food is served on Sunday evening. ♔Q❀◐◑▲♣P

Holbeach

Red Lion

6 Spalding Road, PE12 7HG

⏲ 11.30-2.30, 5.30-11; 12-2.30, 6-10.30 Sun

☎ (01406) 425534

Greene King Old Speckled Hen; Marston's Pedigree; Tetley Bitter Ⓗ

This attractive, old building apparently started life as a farmhouse; the large open fire in winter betrays something of its origins. However it is now a friendly, unpretentious pub with one bar and three distinct seating areas. The adjoining dining room is popular for the Sunday carvery. An upstairs room with a bar is ideal for functions. Wheelchair access is via the back door. ♔❀◐◑♿♣P

Holbeach St Johns

Plough

1 Jekils Bank, PE12 8RF (4 miles S of Holbeach on B1168)

⏲ 12-11; 12-10.30 Sun

☎ (01406) 540654

Adnams Bitter; Marston's Burton Bitter; Oakham Bishops Farewell; guest beers Ⓗ

The landlord's determination and enthusiasm for real ale and good food have revitalised this village local. Popular with all ages, it is at the centre of village life, with pub games playing an important part without being too dominant. A skittle alley is available, but only by prior arrangement, as some furniture reorganisation is necessary. Guest beers are generally from Oakham Brewery – the landlord is a big fan. No food is served Tuesday, Sunday meals are 12-5pm. ❀◐◑♿▲♣P

Horncastle

Fighting Cocks

West Street, LN9 5JF

⏲ 11-3, 7-11; 12-3, 7-10.30 Sun

☎ (01507) 527307

Draught Bass; Black Sheep Best Bitter; Greene King IPA, Old Speckled Hen Ⓗ

This comfortable, friendly pub has a bright and cheery atmosphere. See the impressive collection of chickens displayed throughout. Good value food is served every day except Sunday. Four real ales are usually available, making this a pub worth seeking out. Q❀⇋◐◑♿♣P

Keadby

Auld South Yorkshire

Trentside, DN17 3EF

(turn right at foot of Keadby Bridge, W side)

✪ 12 (4 Sat)-11 (closed winter Mon); 12-10.30 Sun

☎ (01724) 783518

Beer range varies Ⓗ

Village pub by the junction of the South Yorkshire Canal and River Trent. The pleasant interior has been refurbished in traditional style with a comfortable bar, and separate dining and pool areas. Good food is served, with locally renowned Sunday lunch. A handpulled real ale is usually stocked from a rotating selection ranging from large national to local micro-breweries. Popular with locals, it also attracts visitors, especially at weekends when live music is performed. Note: reduced hours operate in winter.

♨❀◐◑⊟♿♣P

Lincoln

Dog & Bone ✔

10 John Street, LN2 5BH (off Monks Rd)

✪ 12-2, 7-11; 12-3, 7-10.30 Sun

☎ (01522) 522403

Bateman Mild, XB, XXXB, seasonal beers; guest beers Ⓗ

The short walk from the city centre to this friendly local is not wasted – some travel miles to visit. A wide range of Bateman's draught and bottled beers is sold, plus guests. Beer festivals are held to celebrate independent family brewers and national pub weeks. Occasional feature nights often include pub games. Lunchtime visitors are welcome to bring their own food. Bateman's memorabilia adorns both parts of the bar and a coal fire cheers in winter. Summer barbecues are popular. ♨❀⇌♣P

Golden Eagle

21 High Street, LN5 8BD (S of town centre)

✪ 11-11; 12-10.30 Sun

☎ (01522) 521058

Draught Bass; Castle Rock Harvest Pale; Everards Beacon; guest beers Ⓗ

This Tynemill pub, offering up to six guest beers, was once a coaching inn dating back to around 1780. Located south of the city, it is convenient for the football ground. The lounge is the quieter room at the front, while the livelier bar is at the rear. A meeting room is provided upstairs. Friday is quiz night, while throughout the year occasional beer festivals and events are staged. The large garden contains a petanque pitch.

Q❀⊟♣●P

Jolly Brewer

27 Broadgate, LN2 5AQ

✪ 12-11; 12-10.30 Sun

☎ (01522) 528583

Greene King Abbot; Taylor Landlord; Young's Bitter; guest beers Ⓗ

Popular, city-centre local returned to its former glory under new management. There is one long bar, decorated in Art Deco style, together with a corridor and covered outdoor drinking area. An adventurous menu, combining British and foreign cuisines, is available at lunchtime and early evening. Live music is performed on Saturday evening and Wednesday is 'open mike' night. Cider is sold occasionally.

♨❀◐◑⇌♣●P⊡

Lord Tennyson ✔

72 Rasen Lane, LN1 3HD

✪ 11-2.30, 5.30-11; 12-2.30, 7-10.30 Sun

☎ (01522) 889262

Draught Bass; Black Sheep Best Bitter; Greene King IPA; guest beer Ⓗ

Victorian, purpose-built pub, named after the Lincolnshire poet. It benefits from a garden and a small area with benches at the front – most pleasant in full summer bloom. Originally two rooms, it is now open plan, with the bar in the middle. The trend is towards quiet conversation with a pint, or a good value, home-cooked meal. A recent extension to the rear gets slightly livelier with quiet music and games. Near the tourist area, visitors who stumble upon it often pledge to return. ❀◐◑♣P

Morning Star

11 Greetwell Gate, LN2 4AW

✪ 11-11; 12-10.30 Sun

☎ (01522) 527079

Draught Bass; Greene King Ruddles Best, Abbot; Tetley Bitter; Wells Bombardier; guest beer Ⓗ

Busy, friendly, back-street pub, drawing a mixed clientele, close to the cathedral and hospital. In the bar, which has an open fire, pub games are provided, a quiz is held on Tuesday and the piano is played on Saturday. Framed sheet music of old popular songs decorates the walls. A small, comfortable lounge, where children are allowed, is a no-smoking area. Occasionally, live music is performed in the garden in summer. Sandwiches are sold at lunchtime.

♨Q☋❀⊟♣P⚟

Portland

50 Portland Street, LN5 7JX

✪ 11-11; 12-10.30 Sun

☎ (01522) 560564

Greene King IPA; John Smith's Bitter; guest beers Ⓗ

Welcoming, city-centre pub where the lively bar/games area contrasts with the quieter lounge. Six guest beers (including a mild) are usually available, the majority from micro-breweries. Two beer festivals are held annually, in summer (last week of July) and winter (early December). Situated midway between the station and the Imps football ground, the Portland refreshes both home and away supporters on match days. Westons Old Rosie is joined by a guest cider in summer.

❀⊟⇌♣●P

Sippers

26 Melville Street, LN5 7HW (opp. bus station)

✪ 11-11; 12-3, 7-10.30 Sun

☎ (01522) 527612

Hop Back GFB, Summer Lightning; John Smith's Bitter; guest beers Ⓗ

Close to bus and rail stations, a warm welcome is assured as visitors take in the nautical decorations, including a cased model sailing ship in the lounge. The guest beers vary in strength from 4% ABV upwards, and a selection of Hop Back bottle-conditioned beers is stocked. Efficient smoke extraction ensures that meals can be consumed in comfort; evening meals must be booked. The pub's darts and dominoes teams are well supported. Q◑◐⊟⇌♣

Strugglers Inn ✔

83 Westgate, LN1 3BG

✪ 11-11; 12-10.30 Sun

☎ (01522) 535023

Draught Bass; Bateman Mild; Black Sheep Best Bitter; Fuller's London Pride; Taylor Landlord; guest beers Ⓗ

This multi-award-winning pub stands in the shadow of Lincoln Castle's wall, where in the past the scaffold stood, hence the pub's name – look at the sign. The suntrap patio garden is popular in summer; in winter it is covered and heated. Freshly home-cooked food, served Tuesday-Saturday, often has seafood on the menu. A fortnight-long beer festival is held in October, and themed evenings are staged throughout the year. ♨Q❀◑⊟

Treaty of Commerce ✔

173 High Street, LN5 7AF

✪ 11-11; 12-10.30 Sun

☎ (01522) 541943

Bateman XB, XXXB; guest beers Ⓗ

Conveniently located for the station and main shopping area, the pub's attractive frontage stands out among the surrounding shops. The interior has extensive wood panelling throughout. The single room has two seating sections separated by the bar area, the one at the back having a vaulted wooden ceiling. Two changing guest ales are offered plus either the dark mild or porter from Bateman. Home-cooked lunches are served Tuesday-Sunday. Dogs are welcome after 3pm. ❀◑⇌ (Central)

Victoria

6 Union Road, LN1 3BJ

✪ 11-11; 12-10.30 Sun

☎ (01522) 536048

Bateman XB; Castle Rock Harvest Pale; Taylor Landlord; guest beers Ⓗ

A long-time entry in this Guide, this small pub is a favourite with locals. Part of the Tynemill chain, a long, thin public bar is augmented by the small lounge, which is no-smoking at lunchtime (11-4pm). Five changing guest beers, including a mild, come from regional and micro-brewers. Beer festivals are held in summer and at the city's Christmas market. The outside seating area is by the castle's west gate. Home-cooked food is available (booking advisable for the upstairs restaurant). Q❀◑⊟⍻

Little Bytham

Willoughby Arms

Station Road, NG33 4RA (off A1)

✪ 12-2.30, 5-11; 12-11 Sat; 12-10.30 Sun

☎ (01780) 410276 website: www.willoughbyarms.co.uk

Newby Wyke White Squall, Sidewinder; guest beers Ⓗ

Village pub to the south of Grantham, surrounded by open countryside, which was voted Lincolnshire CAMRA Pub of the Year 2004. It stages regular mini-beer festivals throughout the year, and stands next to Newby Wyke Brewery, whose beers regularly feature on the bar. Westons Old Rosie cider is normally stocked. The large garden to the rear affords rural views. The blackboard menu offers a wide choice; meals are served all day at the weekend. The overnight accommodation is also recommended. ♨❀⇔◑◐♠P⊓

Louth

Boar's Head

12 Newmarket, LN11 9HH

✪ 12-2 (9.30-3 Wed; 11-3 Thu), 5-11; 12-11 Sat; 12-4, 7-10.30 (12-10.30 summer) Sun

☎ (01507) 603561

Bateman Mild, XB, seasonal beers; guest beers Ⓗ

Situated next to the cattle market a short distance from the town centre, the Boar's Head features real fires in winter and a warm welcome. Pub games include darts, pool, shove-ha'penny and dominoes. There are two main rooms (one no-smoking), plus the old snug which now houses the pool table. It opens early on Wednesday to cater for the cattle market traders. Once again under the auspices of the Bateman Brewery, a council car park is next to the pub. ♨❀⇔◑◐♣

Lord Tennyson Inn ✔

Northolme Road, LN11 0JF (100 yds from N end of Louth bypass, signed A16 Grimsby)

✪ 11-11; 12-10.30 Sun

☎ (01507) 603555

Draught Bass; Boddington Bitter; John Smith's Bitter; guest beer Ⓗ

Large, suburban public house and restaurant where the Tennyson theme is abundant in pictures and verse written on beams. The bright, airy, no-smoking restaurant seats 40 and serves an à la carte menu all day. This family-friendly pub has a free bouncy castle in the garden and barbecues in the summer.

Q♉❀◑◐⊟♿♣P⍻

Mason's Arms Hotel

Cornmarket, LN11 9PY

✪ 11-11; 12-10.30 Sun

☎ (01507) 609525 website: www.themasons.co.uk

Bateman XB, XXXB; Marston's Pedigree; Taylor Landlord; guest beers Ⓗ

Grade II listed, early 18th-century posting inn. Formerly a meeting place for the local masonic lodge, note the various artefacts and signs on display around the building. Good quality home-cooked food is served lunchtime (except Sun) and Wednesday-Saturday evenings. Well-behaved children are welcome while food is being served. It makes an ideal place to stay for race meetings at Cadwell or Market Rasen.

⇔◑◐

Newmarket Inn

LN11 9EG (corner of Queen St)

✪ 7 (6 Wed & Fri)-11; 12-3 Sun

☎ (01507) 605146

Adnams Bitter; Robinson's XB Ⓗ

The laid-back atmosphere is appreciated by a loyal set of locals. The two real ales change occasionally. Note the pub only opens in the evenings, plus Sunday lunchtime. Cosy, warm and friendly, it now has a new restaurant, Hurdles, serving good evening meals, leaving the bar for its true purpose – drinking quality real ale. ♨Q◐♿

Old Whyte Swanne

45 Eastgate, LN11 9NP (near market place)

✪ 9.30-11; 10-10.30 Sun

☎ (01507) 601312

website: www.louth.org/swan/swan.html

Black Sheep Best Bitter; Greene King Old Speckled Hen; Theakston Old Peculier Ⓗ

This 16th-century coaching inn offers a friendly welcome at the heart of a busy market town. Both the bar and dining room are warmed by real fires. It serves food throughout the day, all based on local produce and listed on several blackboards in the cosy bar. It has recently changed hands and some alterations are being planned, such as adding another guest pump. The pub is a short walk from St James Church. The overnight accommodation is recommended. ♨Q⇌◐◑♿P

Wheatsheaf Inn

62 Westgate, LN11 9YD (close to St James Church)

✪ 11-3, 5-11; 11-11 Sat; 12-4, 7-10.30 Sun

☎ (01507) 606262

Caledonian Deuchars IPA; Flowers Original; Taylor Landlord; guest beers Ⓗ

Attractive, traditional inn dating back to 1625. It is located in a Georgian terrace on the west side of town, close to St James Church which boasts the tallest spire of any parish church in England. The three rooms are all warmed by coal fires during the winter months. Well-behaved dogs are welcome in the outside drinking area. A 'beer and banger' festival is held every year at the end of May. Daily specials are offered on the home-cooked menu. ♨❀◐P

Woolpack Inn

Riverhead Road, LN11 0DA (1 mile E of town centre, at head of canal)

✪ 11-3 (not Mon), 5-11; 11-11 Sat; 11-10.30 Sun

☎ (01507) 606568

Bateman Mild, XB, XXXB, seasonal beers; Greene King IPA, Abbot; guest beers Ⓗ

Friendly pub, a Grade II listed building, away from the town centre. Dating from the early 1770s, it was built to serve the trade from the newly-constructed canal, storing wool as well as quenching thirsts. It is a recommended starting point for the 'Round Louth Walk'. The Woolpack is a regular Guide entry, comprising two L-shaped bars, with open fires, and a dining area serving home-cooked food (no food Mon). A good-sized garden to the rear is a bonus. ♨Q❀◐◑⊟♿♣P⊬

Ludford

White Hart Inn

Magna Mile, LN8 6AD (on A631, between Louth and Market Rasen)

✪ 12-2 (not Tue), 5-11; 12-3, 6-11 Sat; 12-4, 7-10.30 Sun

☎ (01507) 313489

Hardys & Hansons Bitter; guest beers Ⓗ

Allegedly used as a public house since 1742, this two-roomed village pub lies close to the Viking Way, and is popular with hikers and ramblers. There are five handpumps, offering four changing guest beers. In this age of multi-national brands, the licensees pride themselves on supporting micro-brewers both local and further afield. All the food sold is home made from local suppliers. The guest rooms are all en-suite and separate from the pub. Well-behaved dogs are welcome. ♨Q⇌◐◑⊟P

Messingham

Bird in the Barley

Northfield Road, DN17 3SQ (on A159 to Gainsborough)

✪ 11-3 (not Mon), 5.30-11; 12-3, 6-10.30 Sun

☎ (01724) 764744

Marston's Pedigree; guest beers Ⓗ

Spacious, open-plan, roadside inn, served from a central bar, traditionally styled with oak beams and panels, and rural artefacts. Although the emphasis is on good quality meals (not served Sun eve or Mon), the beer is also given prominence, with guest ale tasting notes and a sampling policy. Two guest beers are normally available plus Hoegaarden on draught. Frequented by diners and drinkers of all ages, it offers a friendly and relaxed atmosphere. Quizzes are hosted on Sunday and Monday evenings. ♨❀◐◑♿P

Horn Inn

61 High Street, DN17 3NU

✪ 11-11; 12-10.30 Sun

☎ (01724) 762426

John Smith's Bitter; guest beers Ⓗ

The Horn may well have been continuously serving beer since 1798. Obviously much changed, it is a friendly, family-run local, extending a warm welcome to passing trade. The open-plan layout is TV and music-free. It enjoys a reputation for good value lunches. Guest beers are drawn from the SIBA list, with two on tap at all times – the more unusual choices do not last long. It hosts a quiz (Mon) and popular live music (Wed). Buses 351 and 353 pass the pub. ♨Q❀◐♿♣P

Metheringham

Londesborough Arms

Middle Street, LN4 3EY

✪ 2 (12 Fri; 11 Sat)-11; 12-10.30 Sun

☎ (01526) 320637

Bateman XB, XXXB Ⓗ

Village local designed as a Swiss chalet; beware of the step on entry and other steps in the pub. One long bar serves a mixed bunch of locals and visitors. Pub games are played regularly. Popular food is served every evening. Make sure you read the landlord's tale. The village is on the No. 631 Lincoln-Sleaford bus route. ♨❀◑≠♣P

Morton

Crooked Billet

1 Crooked Billet Street, DN21 3AG

✪ 12-11; 12-10.30 Sun

☎ (01427) 612584

Beer range varies Ⓗ

This three-roomed village pub, with a central bar and a large games room, is home to several sports teams – darts, dominoes, pool and angling. Open fires burn in two rooms of this former local CAMRA Pub of the Season. A real ale success story – casks now outsell keg beers here. Occasional live music is performed, and one room is kept for quiet conversation. ♨Q⊟♣⊡

Moulton

Swan

13 High Street, PE12 6QB
11-11; 12-10.30 Sun
☎ (01406) 370349

Tetley Bitter; Wells Bombardier; guest beers Ⓗ

An open fire in each bar ensures a warm welcome in this family-run pub. Perfectly situated, it stands opposite the tallest windmill in the country, the church, and the butcher who supplies the meat for the cook, who serves up some of the best food for miles. The pleasant garden has a bouncy castle in summer to keep everyone happy in this family-friendly establishment. The windmill, currently undergoing extensive restoration, is set to become a major attraction. ⛬❀◑ ⊟♿♣P

Nettleton

Salutation Inn

Church Street, LN7 6NP (on A46)
12-3, 6-11; 12-3, 7-10.30 Sun
☎ (01472) 851228

Flowers IPA; Taylor Landlord; Wadworth 6X; guest beers Ⓗ

Friendly, relaxing pub on the A46 Grimsby-Lincoln road, not only popular with locals but also with walkers – the Viking Way and Lincolnshire's highest point (near Normanby-le-Wold radar station) are close by. There is a dining area adjacent to the bar and a family room. The pub hosts a monthly themed food night. A large garden houses a variety of farm animals, rabbits and guinea pigs.
⛬⛽❀◑♿▲P⚟

Oasby

Houblon Arms Inn

Village Street, NG32 3NB (between A15 and B6403)
12-2, 7-11; 12-2.30, 6-11 Sat; 12-3, 7-10.30 Sun
☎ (01529) 455215

Black Sheep Special; Everards Tiger; guest beers Ⓗ

Village pub that has recently undergone extensive refurbishment, providing a new stone-flagged floor. Real fires, a large inglenook with seating and a stuffed, sleeping fox all add character. Beware the low beam in front of the bar. Families are welcome, and traditional board games are provided to keep the children amused. The spacious restaurant offers a superb menu.
⛬Q◗P

Old Bolingbroke

Black Horse Inn

Moat Lane, PE23 4HH
12.30 (3.30 winter Mon-Fri)-11; 12.30-10.30 Sun
☎ (01790) 763388

Bateman Mild; Young's Bitter; guest beers Ⓗ

This old country inn has history literally on its doorstep. The castle remains and the roses of Henry IV and the Duke of Lancaster from 1366 are features of this lovely village. The inn gives a warm welcome and the new owners have already held several successful beer festivals. Good food is based on local produce and organic vegetables; Friday is Grimsby fish night. It is advisable to check opening hours and food serving times, which may vary. ⛬Q❀◑♿P

Pinchbeck

Bull Inn

1 Knight Street, PE11 3RA (on B1356)
12-2.30, 5.30 (5 Fri)-11; 12-11 Sat; 12-10.30 Sun
☎ (01775) 723022

Greene King Old Speckled Hen; John Smith's Bitter; guest beers Ⓗ

The Bull is a cosy, friendly pub retaining two drinking areas. The lounge is comfortable, with tables set mainly for dining, while the traditionally-furnished bar has a real fire and a notable bullhorn bar rail. Outside is a seating area and patio for summer use. Situated on the main road through Pinchbeck, this pub is easy to find. ⛬❀◑ ⊟♿P

Redbourne

Red Lion Hotel

The Green, DN21 4QR (4 miles S of M180 jct 4, off A15)
12-11; 12-10.30 Sun
☎ (01652) 648302 website: www.redlion.org

Greene King IPA, Abbot; Tom Wood Shepherd's Delight Ⓗ

Traditional, 17th-century coaching inn situated in the picturesque village of Redbourne, overlooking the green. The large drinking area is divided into a snug, bar and a no-smoking area. The house beer is Duckpond Bitter (source undisclosed!). The sympathetically refurbished hotel serves home-cooked food and fine wines in the restaurant; sandwiches are available at lunchtime in the bar. Should you wish to extend your visit, there are 11 guest rooms.
⛬Q❀⛿◑ ⊟♿P⚟

Rothwell

Blacksmith's Arms

Hill Rise, LN7 6AZ
11.30-3, 5-11; 12-10.30 Sun
☎ (01472) 371300

Bateman XB; Greene King Abbot; Tom Wood Shepherd's Delight; guest beer Ⓗ

Warm, welcoming pub on the edge of the Lincolnshire Wolds, popular with walkers, as it stands close to the Viking Way. White walls, low beams and an open fire set in the centre of the pub, give a cosy feel to the 'Blackies'. It offers a good range of beer and the food is excellent; the function room at the rear doubles as a restaurant during busy periods (ring to check meal times). ⛬Q❀◑♿♣P

Ruskington

Potter's

3 Chestnut Street, NG34 9DL
12 (11 Fri & Sat)-3 (not Mon), 5-11; 12-3, 7-10.30 Sun
☎ (01526) 832777

Black Sheep Best Bitter; Tetley Bitter; guest beers Ⓗ

In its former life, the building formed part of a garage and car showroom. It was converted into a snooker club, hence the name, and has a couple of tables in a room adjoining the bar. The bar and restaurant are open to non-members and provide a convivial atmosphere for drinkers and diners. There is a Sunday lunchtime carvery. ◑◐≋P

Saxilby

Anglers

65 High Street, LN1 2HA

✪ 11.30-2.30 (3 Sat), 6 (5 Fri; 7 Sat)-11; 12-3, 7-10.30 Sun

☎ (01522) 702200

Greene King IPA; Theakston Best Bitter; guest beers Ⓗ

This comfortable, bustling village pub, for drinkers – no food – fields darts, dominoes, cribbage, pool and golf teams. In quieter times ask for the shove ha'penny or skittles boards. The advertised hours may be extended if important football matches are played. In 1900 the pub attracted hordes of anglers, travelling by rail to fish in the nearby Fossdyke Canal, and its name was changed from the original Railway. Ask about the gnome! ❀⊟≋♣P

Scamblesby

Green Man

Old Main Road, LN11 9XG (off A153, Horncastle-Louth road)

✪ 12-11; 12-10.30 Sun

☎ (01507) 343282

Black Sheep Best Bitter; Young's Bitter; guest beer Ⓗ

The pub sits almost end-on to the main street. It is a traditional house with a flat roof extension that houses the games area. You step up into the bar in the original building, which is cosy and warm from a real fire. The lounge is just as pleasant. It is frequented by walkers and visitors to Cadwell Park Racing Circuit.
♨Q♉❀⛟◑◐⊟⛺♣P

Scunthorpe

Berkeley

Doncaster Road, DN15 7DS (on A18, ½ mile from end of M181 W)

✪ 11.30-3, 5-11; 11.30-11 Fri & Sat; 12-10.30 Sun

☎ (01724) 842333 website: www.the-berkeleyhotel.co.uk

Samuel Smith OBB Ⓗ

Conveniently situated on the western side of town, this prominent hotel is five minutes' walk from the centre. Recently refurbished to retain its 1930s features and style, it comprises three rooms: a bar with games, a lounge with a dining area and a no-smoking dining room where drinkers are also welcome. This room can be booked for private functions. It serves exceptionally good home-cooked meals and bar snacks (no food Sat). Friendly staff provide good service. A patio is behind the pub.
Q♉❀⛟◑◐⊟♿♣P⊁

Blue Bell ✔

1-7 Oswald Road, DN15 7PU

✪ 10-11; 10-10.30 Sun

☎ (01724) 863921

De Koninck Ambrée; Greene King Abbot; Marston's Burton Bitter, Pedigree; guest beers Ⓗ

Town-centre Wetherspoon's house of open-plan design. The large bar serves a general drinking area, plus a raised area for non-smokers and families dining (until early evening). It opens at 10am each day but alcohol is not served before midday on Sunday. Four regular real ales are supplemented by up to three guests and an annual beer festival. The patio is popular in summer and the pub can get busy with clubbers on weekend evenings. Q❀◑◐♿≋⊁

Honest Lawyer

70 Oswald Road, DN15 7PG

✪ 11-11; 12-10.30 Sun

☎ (01724) 849906

Daleside Bitter; guest beers Ⓗ

The pub interior has a legal theme and is decorated in an old-fashioned style, with much wood. The bar area is long and narrow with a snug area at the end, housing a large TV (popular with football fans); daily newspapers are provided. Six real ales are offered – five are rotating guest beers. Addlestones cider is also sold. Upstairs has recently been converted into the Gallows Restaurant. The pub can get busy on Friday and Saturday evenings. It is handy for the station. ❀◑♿≋●

Malt Shovel

219 Ashby High Street, DN16 2JP

✪ 11-11; 12-10.30 Sun

☎ (01724) 843318

Bateman XXXB; Courage Directors; John Smith's Bitter; Theakston Old Peculier; guest beers Ⓗ

Spacious, pleasantly furnished lounge with a private snooker club under the same roof. The lounge bears a country feel, with beams and a brick fireplace. Four permanent beers are supplemented by three rotating guests from small breweries – often Rooster's, Abbeydale or Glentworth. It is close to a shopping centre, but is usually quiet except at lunch and evening mealtimes when the good value, home-cooked food is rightly popular. Q❀◑◐

Queen Bess

Derwent Road, Ashby, DN16 2PE (near A18/Grange Lane Sth jct)

✪ 11.30-3.30 (4 Sat), 6-11; 12-3.30, 7-10.30 Sun

☎ (01724) 840827

Samuel Smith OBB Ⓗ

Estate pub making its 24th (not consecutive) Guide appearance. Its loyal local following is a testament to consistent beer quality and the brewery's renowned good value. It comprises a bar and lounge, plus a large function room used for private events and live Country and Western (Thu eves). The long-standing licensee is one of the few to retain a music licence and TV in the face of increasingly eccentric brewery restrictions. The bay window in the entrance was part of the original off-sales. ♨❀⊟♣P

Sleaford

Barge & Bottle ✔

Carre Street, NG34 7TR

✪ 11-11 (11.30 Thu-Sat); 12-10.30 Sun

☎ (01529) 303303 website: www.thebargeandbottle.co.uk

Bateman XB; Greene King IPA, Abbot, Old Speckled Hen; Marston's Pedigree; Tetley Bitter; guest beers Ⓗ

Modern, open-plan pub where the separate dining area provides a wide range of meals at reasonable prices. This independently-owned hostelry is modelled on a pub group design, and stocks a range of nine real ales. The spacious conservatory may be used for private functions; the patio overlooks the river. A footbridge leads to the new Hub regional arts centre, making the pub popular with tourists as well as locals. ❀◑♿≢⚟

Marquis of Granby

Westgate, NG34 7PU

☼ 11-11; 12-10.30 Sun

☎ (01529) 303223

Greene King IPA, Abbot; guest beer [H]

No-frills, small, back-street local, a short distance from the market place. Although recently refurbished, its single bar retains a cosy atmosphere. A former private house, the pub has an interesting history, which is described on a display above the fireplace. There is a strong sports connection, with teams entering all the traditional pub games leagues. ♨≢♣

South Ormsby

Massingberd Arms

Brinkhill Road, LN11 8QS (1½ miles from A16 turn at Swaby)

☼ 12-3 (not Mon), 6-11; 12-5, 7-10.30 Sun

☎ (01507) 480492

Beer range varies [H]

Named after the lord of the manor, the pub has now been voted local CAMRA Pub of the Year for three consecutive years. It is well worth seeking out, whether walking, cycling or passing by car, as it stands in a beautiful area of the country. The beers change frequently and the food is home-cooked; no meals are served Sunday evening. No dogs except guide dogs are admitted. ♨Q❀◑♣P⚟

Spalding

Birds

108 Halmergate, PE11 2EL (½ mile from town bridge, take Church St)

☼ 11-11; 12-10.30 Sun

☎ (01775) 723329 website: www.hungryhorse.co.uk

Greene King IPA, Abbot, Old Speckled Hen [H]

Spacious, modern, one-bar, community-style pub/restaurant, on the outskirts of town, near the bypass. Popular with families, the emphasis is on food, served all day, although beer drinkers and sports fans are well catered for with a big-screen TV and themed evenings, as well as pool and darts. A no-smoking dining section is available. Customers can enjoy a relaxing summer pint in the extensive outdoor area. ❀◑♣P

Lincoln Arms

4 Bridge Street, PE11 1XA (off market place)

☼ 11-3, 7-11; 11-3.30, 7-11 Sat; 12-4, 7.30-10.30 Sun

☎ (01775) 722691

Banks's Mansfield Dark, Riding Bitter, Mansfield Cask; guest beers [H]

Popular with locals of all ages, this traditional, 18th-century pub is located by the town bridge, overlooking the River Welland, and offers a welcoming atmosphere. The open-plan layout features an L-shaped bar and a serving hatch to the pool area. Other games played are darts (Mon eve league) and cribbage. The function room upstairs hosts Spalding Folk Club (first Wed in month). Consistent beer quality has kept the pub in this Guide for 12 consecutive years. ⊭≢♣

Olde White Horse

Churchgate, PE11 2RA (opp. town-centre bridge)

☼ 11.30-11; 12-10.30 Sun

☎ (01775) 766740

Samuel Smith OBB [H]

Originally built as a residence, using bricks from the former Spalding Priory, this 450-year-old thatched coaching inn overlooks the River Welland. Historic Ayscoughfee Hall and gardens are nearby. A meeting place for customers of all ages, it has a cosy lounge and adjoining no-smoking dining room. The flagstoned public bar attracts a young clientele. This Samuel Smith's house offers good value beer and a wide range of snacks, meals and all-day Sunday roasts. Q❀◑⊟≢P

Red Lion Hotel

Market Place, PE11 1SU

☼ 10.30-11; 12-10.30 Sun

☎ (01775) 722869

website: www.redlionhotel-spalding.co.uk

Draught Bass; Fuller's London Pride; Greene King Abbot; Marston's Pedigree; guest beer (occasional) [H]

Bustling oasis in the corner of the market, two minutes from a pleasant riverside stroll. The cosy interior welcomes both its many regulars and visitors alike. There is a sense of history and community about the hotel. It is home to the Spalding Blues Club, which presents fortnightly bands in the Blues Café. It gets a little smoky when busy, but traditional food is served in a no-smoking dining room (no meals Sun eve). ♨Q❀⊭◑≢

Spilsby

Nelson Butt

10 Market Street, PE23 5JT

☼ 11-3 (not Tue), 7-11; 12-3, 7-10.30 Sun

☎ (01790) 752258

Bateman XB, XXXB; guest beers [H]

The Nelson Butt offers a friendly welcome to locals and visitors to the small market town of Spilsby. A real fire, traditional pub games and the absence of a juke box number among the attractions of this genuine free house that stocks two guest beers. A growing reputation for great value food makes this a pub not to be missed. ♨Q☕❀◑⊟♿♣P

Stamford

Crown Hotel ✔

6 All Saints Place, PE9 2AG

☼ 11-11; 12-10.30 Sun

☎ (01780) 763136

website: www.thecrownhotelstamford.co.uk

Adnams Bitter; Draught Bass; Black Sheep Best Bitter; Taylor Landlord [H]

The owner of the Crown also runs the Ufford Brewery, so look out for his beers appearing in the bar. Due for refurbishment, the solid, three-storey building in the town centre has a mosaic tiled lobby leading to the bar and dining rooms. Smoking is only permitted in the bar, which is decorated to celebrate local rural pursuits. The hotel stocks a good range of wines and whiskies. ⛫Q🛏◖◗≹⊬

Green Man

29 Scotgate, PE9 2YQ
⊙ 11-11; 12-10.30 Sun
☎ (01780) 753598
Caledonian Deuchars IPA; Newby Wyke Stamford Gold; Theakston Best Bitter; guest beers Ⓗ
Stone-built, former coaching inn dating from 1796 and now a real ale house not to be missed, with guest ales from Newby Wyke, often Rooster's and always micro-breweries. Two beer festivals are held each year (Easter and Sept) on the secluded patio that is reached from the split-level, L-shaped bar. A good range of European bottled beers and two ciders are sold and perry is stocked in summer. No food is served Sunday; children's portions are available. ⛫❀🛏◖≹♣●⊡

Otter's Pocket

20 All Saints Street, PE9 2PA
⊙ 11-midnight; 12-11 Sun
☎ (01780) 755228 website: www.theotterspocket.co.uk
Fuller's London Pride; Hop Back Summer Lightning; Oakham Bishops Farewell; Taylor Landlord; Wells Bombardier Ⓗ
Formerly the Albion, the bar is one long room leading to a raised drinking area. Over-21s only are admitted to this sports-oriented pub. Three draught Belgian beers are always stocked, as well as Belgian bottled beers. The pub hosts live jazz on summer Sundays. ⛫◖≹⊡

Periwig

7 All Saints Place, PE9 2AG
⊙ 11-11 (midnight Wed & Thu; 1am Fri & Sat); 12-10.30 Sun
☎ (01780) 762169
Adnams Bitter; Fuller's London Pride; Oakham JHB; guest beers Ⓗ
The old Marsh Harrier sold no real ale, but this renamed pub has been completely updated to allow the first floor also to be used by drinkers. Popular with youngsters, it now boasts four plasma screens for live sports coverage, an array of disco lighting and a late licence at the weekends. In the daytime it is less frantic. Excellent guest beers are usually sourced from micro-breweries. A no-smoking area is available at lunchtime when the menu includes a good cheeseboard. ◖♿≹⊬

Surfleet

Ship Inn

Reservoir Road, PE11 4DH (1 mile off A16; turn W at brown sign, near A152 roundabout)
⊙ 11-3, 6-11; 11-11 Sat; 12-10.30 Sun
☎ (01775) 680547
Adnams Bitter; guest beers Ⓗ
This two-storey building replaced the old single-storey Ship a few years ago. On the bank of the tidal part of the River Glen, it features flagstones, oak beams and stonework from the original pub. The spacious single bar serves food, all made on the premises, from local produce wherever possible. There is also a no-smoking restaurant on the upper floor overlooking the river. It stages live music some evenings. ⛫Q❀🛏◖◗♿P

Swinhope

Click'em Inn

LN8 6BS (on B1203, 2 miles N of Binbrook)
⊙ 12-3 (not Mon), 7-11; 11.30-11 Sat; 12-3, 7-10.30 Sun
☎ (01472) 398253
Theakston XB; guest beers Ⓗ
Country pub set in the picturesque Lincolnshire Wolds. It is popular with diners, who come for the good home-cooked food served in the conservatory, and with locals enjoying a drink at the bar. The pub serves a house beer called Click'em Bitter, as well as changing guest beers and a real cider (varies). Well worth seeking out, it was local CAMRA's Country Pub of the Year for the last three years. Q❀◖◗♣●P

Tattershall Thorpe

Bluebell Inn

Thorpe Road, Woodhall Spa, LN4 4PE
⊙ 12-2.30, 7-11; 12-2.30, 7-10.30 Sun
☎ (01526) 342206
Poachers Pathfinders Ale; Tom Wood Bomber County; guest beers Ⓗ
This delightful 13th-century inn, one of the oldest in Lincolnshire, comes complete with beamed ceilings and a wealth of olde-worlde charm. The large open fire adds cosiness to the low ceilings, which are inscribed with many RAF personnel signatures, as this was the watering-hole for the famous Dambusters 617 Squadron during WWII. The walls are covered in wonderful photos depicting another era. ⛫Q❀◖◗⊟♿♣P

Thornton Curtis

Thornton Hunt Inn

Main Street, DN39 6XW (on A1077, between Wooton and Barton)
⊙ 12-3, 6-11; 12-10.30 Sun
☎ (01469) 531252 website: www.thornton-inn.co.uk
Taylor Landlord; Tetley Bitter; guest beer Ⓗ
Well-appointed village local set opposite a picturesque church. The interior has a country-style decor of dark wood, brasses, toby jugs and rural pictures; the bar is L-shaped. Bar meals are served and the pub has its own bistro (open on Sat eve). Three real ales are stocked, one of which is a guest from Tom Wood. An attractive garden offers children a fun trail play area. The pub lies close to the ruins of Thornton Abbey. The accommodation is recommended. ❀🛏◖◗♿P

Threekingham

Three Kings Inn

Salters Way, NG34 0AU
⊙ 12-3 (not Mon or Tue), 6-11 (not Mon); 12-3, 6-10.30 Sun
☎ (01529) 240249
Draught Bass; Taylor Landlord; guest beer Ⓗ
A pub at the centre of village life that caters for visitors, too. An inn has stood on the site since 871 but this building is around 400 years old. With its wood-panelled rooms, it imparts a cosy atmosphere. A family-run business, it provides home-cooked food from local produce. The name derives from three Danish chieftains, or kings, killed at the nearby Battle of Stow in the 8th century. Look for the stone effigies above the entrance. ⛫Q❀◖◗⊟♣P⊡

Waddington

Three Horseshoes

High Street, LN5 9RF

12-4, 7-11; 12-11 Fri & Sat; 12-10.30 Sun

☎ (01522) 720448

Fuller's London Pride; John Smith's Bitter; guest beers Ⓗ

Popular village local that serves a wide range of guest beers as well as hosting brewery feature nights. The single large bar area is supplemented by a smaller back room. Many pub games are played here. Note the Grimsby Town FC mirror, which is proudly displayed. No food is served at any time. ♣P

Wainfleet

Bateman's Visitor Centre ✔

Salem Bridge Brewery, PE24 4JE

11.30-3.30 (not winter Mon or Tue); eves by appointment

☎ (01754) 880317 website: www.bateman.co.uk

Bateman Mild, XB, Salem Porter, XXXB, seasonal beers Ⓗ

An excellent way to sample those 'good honest ales' at source – the brewery's core brands are always available, plus one or two from the seasonal special range. The Mill Bar is situated inside the famous mill; its circular layout and proximity to the 'Brewery Experience' with its many artefacts, makes this an interesting place to drink. Indoor and outdoor games attract families, and a good selection of local food is served. Q♣P

Washingborough

Royal Oak

Main Road, LN4 1AU

2 (1 Sat)-11; 12-10.30 Sun

☎ (01522) 794412

Adnams Bitter; Banks's Mansfield Cask; Greene King Abbot Ⓗ

This village local has a large L-shaped bar, where the pub's sporting connections are immediately apparent from the many trophies and pictures on display. The pub fields two football teams and two cricket teams, offers pool and crib, and hosts a golf society. The smaller lounge area has a homely feel, with comfortable sofas and a real fire in winter. ♣P

Willingham by Stow

Half Moon

23 High Street, DN21 5JZ (off B1241)

6 (11 Fri & Sat)-11; 12-10.30 Sun

☎ (01427) 788340

Black Sheep Best Bitter; Brains Bitter; Wells Bombardier; guest beers Ⓗ

Converted farm labourer's cottage, where a central bar serves the lounge and bar. Local CAMRA Pub of the Year 2004, it serves three regular beers, plus an alternating guest beer. A typical village pub, used for local functions, it offers home-cooked fish and chips on Friday and Saturday evenings and bar snacks at weekend lunchtimes. Quiz night is Thursday. It supports darts, dominoes and football teams. A summer beer festival showcases up to 15 beers. Occasional entertainment by local musicians is staged on Friday evening. Q♣P

Willoughby

Willoughby Arms

Church Lane, LN13 9SU

12-2 (not Mon; 12-3 Sat), 7-11; 12-3, 7-10.30 Sun

☎ (01507) 462387

Bateman XB; guest beers Ⓗ

Village pub with an L-shaped drinking area. Two guest beers are stocked and often reflect seasonal or calendar events. Themed nights are held throughout the year. The recently opened restaurant, separate from the bar, has a varying weekly menu (served Tue-Sat eves); booking is essential due to its popularity. The pub is proud of the village's links to Captain John Smith of Pocahontas fame; the bell from his ship, Godspeed, hangs above the fire. Well-behaved dogs are welcome in the games room. ♣P

Smith's, Bourne

GREATER LONDON

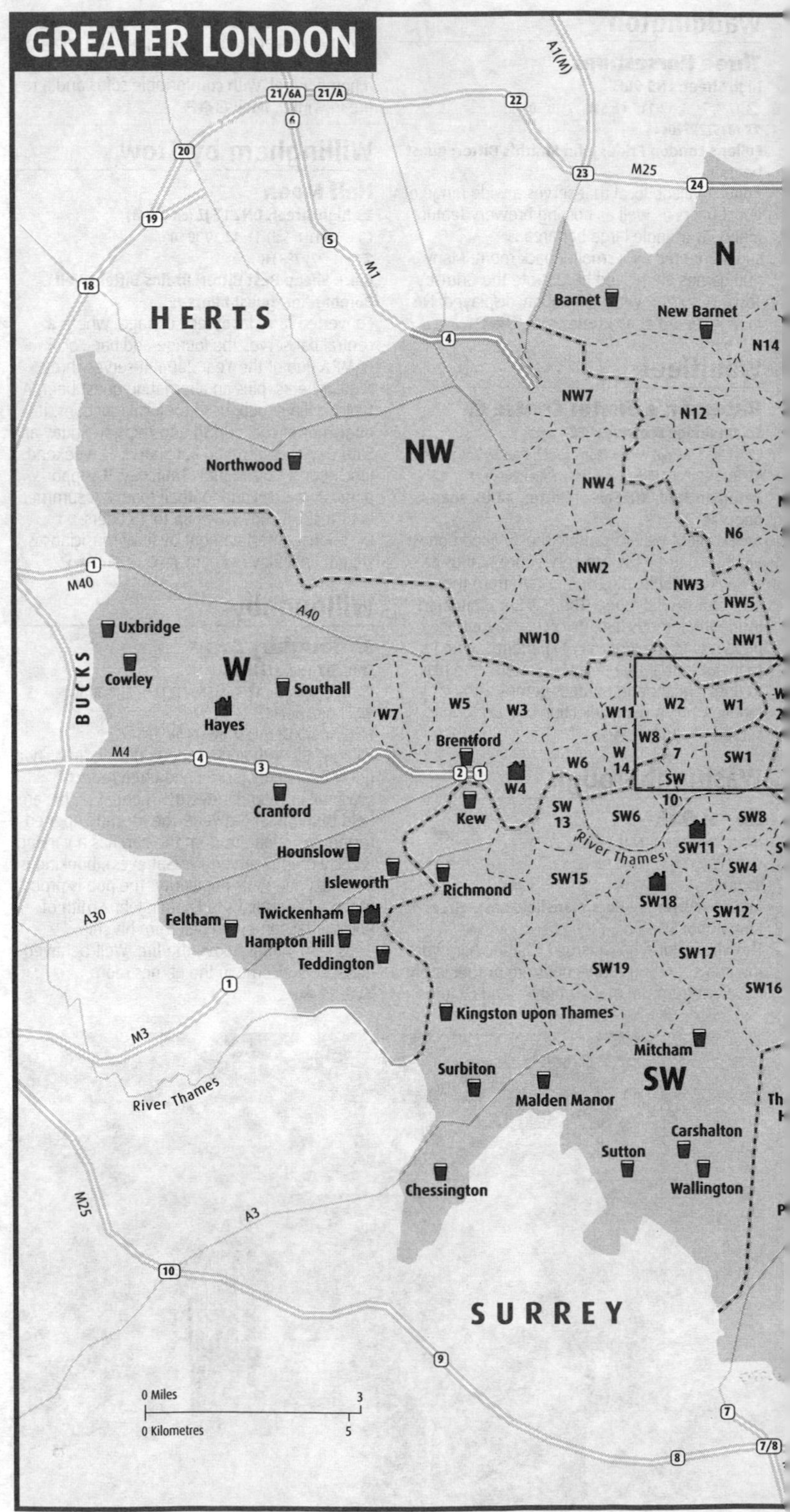

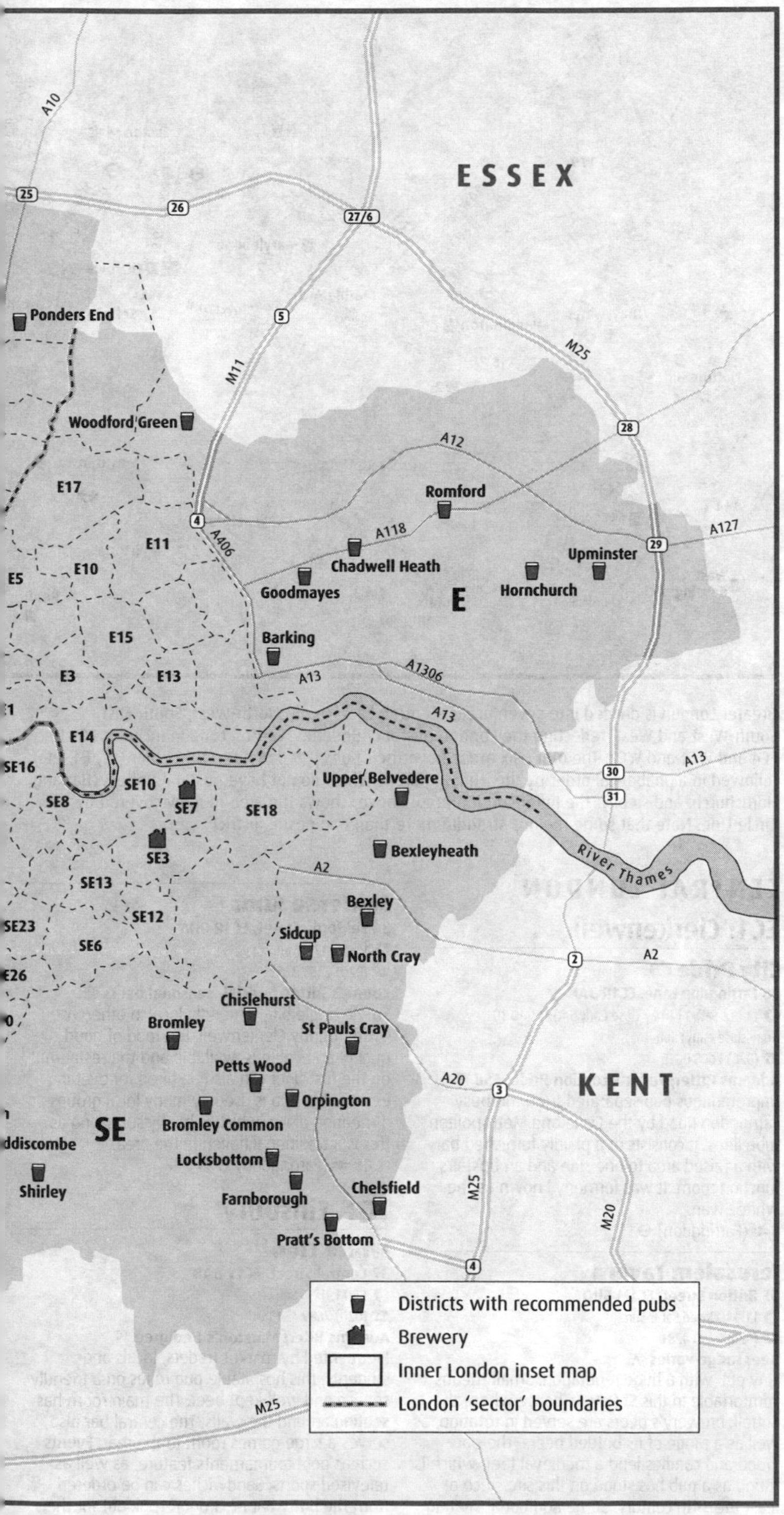
ESSEX
E
KENT
SE
Ponders End
Woodford Green
Romford
Chadwell Heath
Goodmayes
Hornchurch
Upminster
Barking
Upper Belvedere
Bexleyheath
Bexley
Sidcup
North Cray
Chislehurst
Bromley
St Pauls Cray
Petts Wood
Orpington
Bromley Common
Locksbottom
Farnborough
Chelsfield
Pratt's Bottom
Shirley
ddiscombe
E17
E11
E10
E5
E15
E3
E13
E14
SE16
SE10
SE7
SE8
SE18
SE3
SE13
SE12
SE23
SE6
E26
River Thames
A10
M11
M25
A12
A118
A127
A406
A13
A1306
A2
A20
M20
25
26
27/6
5
28
4
29
30
31
2
3
Districts with recommended pubs
Brewery
Inner London inset map
London 'sector' boundaries

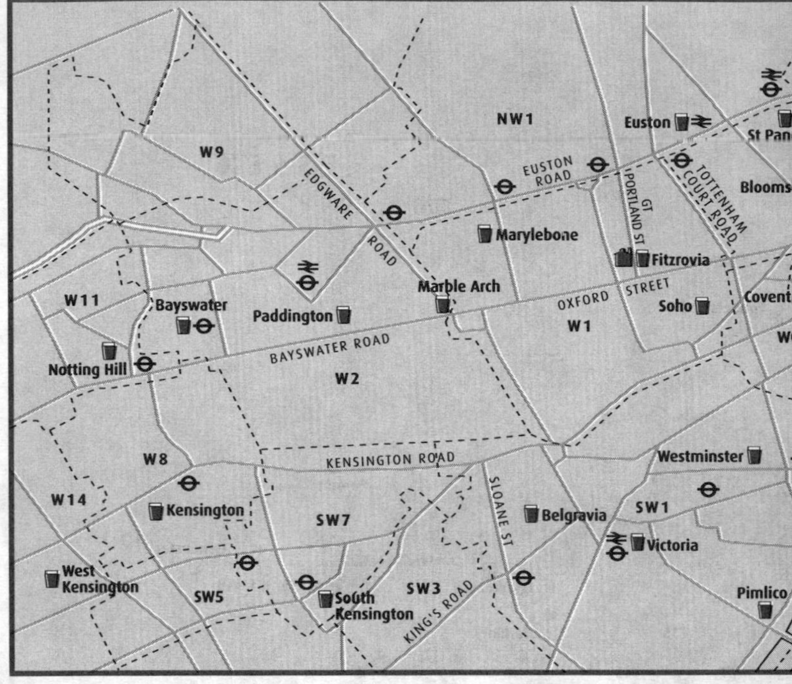

Greater London is divided into seven areas: Central, East, North, North-West, South-East, South-West and West, reflecting the London postal boundaries. Central London includes EC1 to EC4 and WC1 and WC2. The other six areas have their pubs listed in numerical order (E1, E4, etc) followed in alphabetical order by the outlying areas which do not have postal numbers (Barking, Hornchurch, and so on). The Inner London map, above, shows the area roughly covered by the Circle Line. Note that some regions straddle more than one postal district.

CENTRAL LONDON

EC1: Clerkenwell

City Pride ✓

28 Farringdon Lane, EC1R 3AN

11 (12 Sat)-11 (may close early Sat); 12-10.30 (may close early) Sun

☎ (020) 7608 0615

Adnams Bitter; Fuller's London Pride, ESB H

Unpretentious pub separated from the busy Farringdon Road by the Circle and Metropolitan tube lines. It consists of a plainly furnished bar with a raised area to one side and an upstairs function room. It was formerly known as the White Swan.

◐ ⇌ (Farringdon) ⊖

Jerusalem Tavern

55 Britton Street, EC1M 5UQ

11-11; closed Sat & Sun

☎ (020) 7490 4281

Beer range varies A

Tiny pub with a huge reputation. Small means comfortable in this St Peter's house where the Suffolk brewery's beers are served in rotation, as well as a range of its bottled beers. The bare wood and candles lend a medieval feel, which is fitting as a pub has stood on this site since at least the 14th century. Some additional seating is provided on the pavement.

Q ◐ ⇌ (Farringdon) ⊖

Sekforde Arms

34 Sekforde Street, EC1R 0HA

11-11; 12-4 Sun

☎ (020) 7253 3251

Young's Bitter, Special, seasonal beers H

Small, single bar, a friendly local in otherwise overly trendy Clerkenwell. Bar food of good quality and value is available and the restaurant on the first floor can also be hired for evening events. The pub is used by many local groups as a meeting place, which is hardly surprising as this is a traditional haven in the area.

❀ ◐ ◑ ⇌ (Farringdon) ⊖ ♣

EC1: Finsbury

White Lion

37 Central Street, EC1V 8AB

11-11; 12-6 Sun

☎ (020) 7689 4313

Adnams Biter; Marston's Pedigree H

Frequented by market traders, locals and students, this hospitable pub relies on a friendly service and well-kept beer. The main room has seating around the walls. The central bar also serves a large games room to the rear. Events such as pool tournaments feature, as well as televised sports. Sandwiches can be ordered from the butty bar next door. Look out for the lonely fish behind the bar.

❀ ♿ ⇌ ⊖ (Barbican)

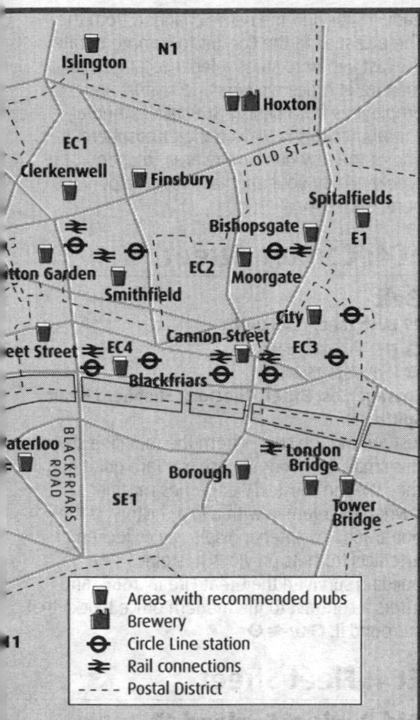

EC1: Hatton Garden

Old Mitre ☆

1 Ely Court, Ely Place, EC1N 6SJ

11-11; closed Sat & Sun

☎ (020) 7405 4751

Adnams Bitter, Broadside; Tetley Bitter; guest beer (occasional) Ⓗ

Hidden away down the alleyway at the side of Ely Place, this was originally the servants' quarters of the Bishop of Ely's Palace and so part of Cambridgeshire. Built in 1546 and refurbished in the 18th century, it has a rich history: a piece of cherry tree round which Elizabeth I danced the maypole is on display, along with other antiquities, and is there any London pub not frequented by Dr Johnson? Tasty snacks include toasties, sausages and scotch eggs.

Q ≠(Farringdon/City Thameslink) ⊖(Chancery Lane)

EC1: Smithfield

Butchers Hook & Cleaver

61 West Smithfield, EC1A 9DY

11-11; 12-6 Sat; 12-6 Sun

☎ (020) 7600 9181

Fuller's Chiswick, London Pride, ESB, seasonal beers Ⓗ

Just behind Smithfield Market stands this Fuller's 'Pie and Ale' house. Expect the large downstairs area to be filled with city workers winding down with a drink. It is particularly busy on Thursday and Friday. Food is available all day Monday-Friday and a winding staircase leads to a function area often used for office parties. The decor reflects the local market, displaying pictures of the meat industry. Bar billiards may be played here.

≠(Farringdon) ⊖

EC2: Bishopsgate

Dirty Dicks

202 Bishopsgate, EC2M 4NR

11-10.30; closed Sat & Sun

☎ (020) 7283 5888

Young's Bitter, Special, seasonal beers Ⓗ

This pub appears small at first, but is actually spread over three floors. The main bar is dedicated to perpendicular drinking with plenty of leaning posts and butts to rest your beer, while the basement (with its own street entrance) is more relaxed, providing seating and tables. Upstairs is a busy restaurant and bar.

≠(Liverpool St) ⊖

EC2: Moorgate

Red Lion

1 Eldon Street, EC2M 1LS

11-11; closed Sat & Sun

☎ (020) 7247 5381

Courage Directors; Fuller's London Pride; Greene King IPA, Abbot; Young's Bitter; guest beers Ⓗ

Small, two-bar corner pub that hosts occasional beer festivals. Regular guest beers come from the larger micros. Food is served until 9pm, with speciality pies and sausages changing daily. The upstairs bar is no-smoking with (sadly) unused handpumps, however the friendly staff are happy to have beer sent upstairs. The downstairs bar features snob screens (not original) and Victorian brass water fountains. This is one of the cheaper pubs in the city.

Q ≠(Liverpool St/Moorgate) ⊖

EC3: City

Counting House ✔

50 Cornhill, EC3V 3PD

11-11; closed Sat & Sun

☎ (020) 7283 7123

Fuller's Chiswick, London Pride, ESB, seasonal beers; guest beers Ⓗ

One-bar pub with an upstairs seating area in converted bank premises. The former manager's offices are used as function rooms. A war memorial dedicated to the bank staff who fell in the Great War of 1914-1918 is reported to be the only memorial in a public house in England. The building dates back to 1893 and part of it is built on to a Roman basilica that was incorporated into the walls of the strong room in the basement (now the toilets).

Q ≠(Liverpool St) ⊖(Monument/Bank)

INDEPENDENT BREWERIES

Battersea SW11
Bunker WC2
Fuller's W4
Grand Union Hayes
Mash W1
Meantime SE7
Pitfield N1
Twickenham Twickenham
Young's SW18
Zerodegrees SE3

Elephant
119 Fenchurch Street, EC3M 5BA
11-9; closed Sat & Sun
☎ (020) 7623 8970
Young's Bitter, Special, seasonal beers Ⓗ
The bare-boarded, small room on the ground floor is ideal for a quick drink, while the spacious, comfortable basement bar provides ample seating for a longer stay. The televisions downstairs are not obtrusive, and the menu is excellent. An old pub in a modern office building – look out for the unusual pub sign.
◖⇌(Fenchurch St) ⊖(Tower Hill)

Lamb Tavern
10-12 Leadenhall Market, EC3V 1LR
11-9; closed Sat & Sun
☎ (020) 7626 2454
Young's Bitter, Special; seasonal beers Ⓗ
Magnificent Grade II listed pub in an unusual setting: Leadenhall Market is full of small retailers of quality produce and the Lamb fits in perfectly. The main bar and mezzanine floor are frequently packed, and drinkers spill out into the market, which is covered. The splendidly tiled basement bar is open only during the day; there is another bar on the first floor.
Q❀◖⇌(Liverpool St) ⊖(Monument/Bank)

Swan ✔
Ship Tavern Passage, 78 Gracechurch Street, EC3V 1LY
11-11; closed Sat & Sun
☎ (020) 7283 7712
Fuller's Chiswick, London Pride, ESB, seasonal beers; guest beers Ⓗ
This must be one of the smallest two-bar pubs. It was awarded the 2004 City Pub of the Year in Fuller's annual competition. The ornate ground-floor bar is barely wide enough for two people to pass, and is often supplemented with a small covered area in the passage outside. The second, slightly larger, bar is upstairs.
Q❀◖⇌(Fenchurch St) ⊖(Monument/Bank)

Wine Lodge
Sackville House, 145 Fenchurch Street, EC3M 6BL
11-10; closed Sat & Sun
☎ (020) 7626 0918
Young's Bitter, Special Ⓗ
Do not be misled by the name – this is no modern wine bar, having served Young's beers since 1933. Formerly Chapman's Wine Lodge, it does maintain its links to the grape, but the beer is excellent. The narrow entrance leads past the stairs to the lower bar into the hall-like main bar, which is dominated by a single, central table. A skylight offers the only natural light. A shelf around the room has stools, but this is basically a standing bar.
◖⇌(Fenchurch St) ⊖(Monument/Bank)

EC4: Blackfriars

Cockpit
7 St Andrews Hill, EC4V 5BY
11-11 (9 Sat); 12-4, 7-10.30 Sun
☎ (020) 7248 7315
Adnams Bitter; Courage Best Bitter, Directors; Marston's Pedigree Ⓗ
The present building was constructed in the early 1840s and the name changed from the Three Castles to the Cockpit to commemorate the last venue to stage a legal cockfight. A mixture of office workers and visitors and employees from nearby St Paul's Cathedral, contributes to the welcoming atmosphere. It is one of the few pubs in the area to open at the weekend. Try your hand at shove-ha'penny here. ◖⇌⊖♣

EC4: Cannon Street

Bell
29 Bush Lane, EC4R 0AN
11-9; closed Sat & Sun
☎ (020) 7626 7560
Courage Best Bitter, Directors; Shepherd Neame Spitfire Ⓗ
Just around the corner from the mainline station, this small, two-room house is a rare quiet pub in the city – no music, TV or games machines. Owned by a family with a long history in the pub trade, the interior displays a collection of artefacts from its previous hostelries. The building survived the Great Fire in 1666, and offers a contrast to the modern office blocks that surround it. Q❀⇌⊖

EC4: Fleet Street

Old Bank of England ✔
194 Fleet Street, EC4 2LT
11-11; closed Sat & Sun
☎ (020) 7430 2255
Fuller's Chiswick, London Pride, ESB, seasonal beers Ⓗ
The name says it all: this magnificently ornate bar was the law courts' branch of the Bank of England until 1975. The balcony (which may be hired for private functions) and the ground-floor side rooms provide additional space. A great place to celebrate if you have just been acquitted in the nearby courts, meals are served all day until 9pm (8pm Fri).
◖◗⊖(Temple/Chancery Lane)

WC1: Bloomsbury

Calthorpe Arms
252 Grays Inn Road, WC1X 8JR
11-11; 12-10.30 Sun
☎ (020) 7278 4732
Young's Bitter, Special, seasonal beers Ⓗ
Located on the corner of Wren Street, this is a comfortable, friendly, single bar, popular with locals and office workers alike. It was once used as a temporary magistrates' court after the first recorded murder of an on-duty policeman in 1830. The upstairs dining room is open at lunchtime and evening meals are served weekdays. Although now a tenancy, the landlord has been in charge for the past 16 years at local CAMRA's Pub of the Year 2004.
❀◖◗⇌(King's Cross) ⊖(Russell Sq)

Lamb ☆
94 Lamb's Conduit Street, WC1N 3LZ
11-11; 12-4, 7-10.30 Sun
☎ (020) 7405 0713
Young's Bitter, Special, seasonal beers Ⓗ
Attractive Grade II listed Georgian building. It has a basically Victorian front with green tiling and

entrance mosaics either side showing the name of the pub. It boasts notable intact snob screens that allowed posh drinkers not to be seen by hoi polloi, green leather banquettes, photos of past celebrities, and an island bar. The pub's name commemorates William Lambe who built a conduit to take water from a tributary of the River Fleet to what is now Snow Hill. The polyphon works and can be played in aid of charity. Food is served 12-2.30 all week and 6-9pm Monday-Thursday and Saturday.
Q ❀◑◗ ⇌(Kings Cross) ⊖(Russell Sq) ⊬

Rugby Tavern

19 Great James Street, WC1N 3ES
✪ 11-11; closed Sat & Sun
☎ (020) 7405 1384
Shepherd Neame Master Brew Bitter, Best Bitter, Spitfire, seasonal beers Ⓗ
This welcoming street-corner pub was acquired by Shepherd Neame several years ago. It serves the local residential and office community, and gets busy in the late afternoon and early evening. The semi-pedestrianised location makes it an ideal place to enjoy an outdoor drink in summer. Inside, photographs celebrate the game of rugby. The food is highly recommended and reasonably priced. The pub also fields an active dart team.
❀⊖(Russell Sq) ♣

WC1: Holborn

Cittie of Yorke ☆

22 High Holborn, WC1V 6BS
✪ 11.30 (12 Sat)-11; closed Sun
☎ (020) 7242 7670
Samuel Smith OBB Ⓗ
Situated next to the gatehouse to Gray's Inn, a pub has stood on this site since 1430. Grade II listed, the last rebuilding was in 1923-34 and the result has led to the pub's listing in CAMRA's National Inventory of Historic Pub Interiors. The cellar bar (closed 3-5pm) is the old cellar of the original coffee house. The front bar (on the left as you enter) is wood-panelled with plenty of seating. However, the real splendour lies in the rear bar, with its unusual vaulted ceiling, long bar, handsome screenwork, compartments (similar to carrels in a library) for private drinking and massive, mounted vats. A full menu is served weekdays, snacks on Saturday.
⾕Q◑◗⊖(Chancery Lane)

Penderel's Oak ✔

283-288 High Holborn, WC1V 7HJ
✪ 10-11; 12-10 Sun
☎ (020) 7242 5669
Fuller's London Pride; Greene King Abbot; Marston's Burton Bitter, Pedigree; guest beers Ⓗ
Named after Richard Penderel who helped Charles II escape from Worcester in 1651; a painting of the monarch hiding in an oak tree in Boscobel Wood can be seen in the National Gallery. This large Wetherspoon's serves four changing guest beers. Although the upstairs bar, the former premises of the Meteorological Office, is quiet, the downstairs bar features several large TV screens, mainly for sport. Food is available 10am-10.30pm.
⾕Q◑◗♿⊖⊬

Princess Louise ☆

208 High Holborn, WC1V 7EP
✪ 11 (12 Sat)-11; 12-10.30 Sun
☎ (020) 7405 8816
Samuel Smith OBB Ⓗ
Grade II listed Victorian masterpiece. Built in 1854, with an interior by WB Simpson dating back to the end of the 19th century, this pub is an essential part of any visit to central London. The visitor will find an interior of stained and gold embossed glass, polychrome tile work, a patterned ceiling, and the original mahogany bar. Features of particular note are the four-faced clock at the centre of the bar, cast iron Corinthian columns, and downstairs the contemporary gents' WC. Selling a very affordable Samuel Smith's OBB on draught, this pub is always popular. Q◑◗⊖

WC1: St Pancras

Mabel's Tavern

9 Mabledon Place, WC1H 9AZ
✪ 11-11; 12-10.30 Sun
☎ (020) 7387 7739
Shepherd Neame Master Brew Bitter, Best Bitter, Spitfire, Bishops Finger, seasonal beers Ⓗ
Comfortable pub within easy walking distance of both Euston and King's Cross stations. The raised bar occupies most of the length of the pub, with a no-smoking alcove at one end. A raised seating area at the other end has a coal-effect gas fire. The pub attracts mainly office staff at lunchtime, while in the evening and at weekends its character changes when tourists take over. If offers a good selection of affordable food. A few seats are available outside for summer use. ❀◑◗⇌(Kings Cross/Euston) ⊖⊬

Skinners Arms

114 Judd Street, WC1H 9NT
✪ 11-11; closed Sat & Sun
☎ (020) 7837 6521
Greene King IPA, Abbot; guest beer (occasional) Ⓗ
Despite the ubiquitous Greene King's livery, the Skinners is now independently run. It is a comfortable pub where low lighting enhances the lavish mock-Victorian interior of drapes, bar back, entrance, mirrored pillar, stained glass, flock wallpaper and framed Dickensian characters. Popular with office workers, the no-smoking section is at the rear.
⾕Q◑◗⇌(Kings Cross/Euston) ⊖⊬

WC2: Covent Garden

Harp

47 Chandos Place, WC2N 4HS
✪ 11-11; 12-10.30 Sun
☎ (020) 7836 0291
Black Sheep Best Bitter; Harveys BB; Taylor Landlord; guest beers Ⓗ
One of the best pubs in Covent Garden for its changing selection of cask ales. It also offers a good choice of traditional sausages from O'Hagans. This bustling, mirror-lined pub is popular with musicians from theatreland. The committed landlady has brought in many interesting beers from independents and micro-breweries in the last few years. Children are

welcome in the function room. All sorts of board games may be played here.
Q ◑ ⇌ (Charing Cross) ⊖ (Embankment) ♣

EAST LONDON

E1: Spitalfields

Pride of Spitalfields

3 Heneage Street, E1 5LJ
11-11; 12-10.30 Sun
☎ (020) 7247 8933
Fuller's London Pride, ESB; guest beers H
Located just off curry house-filled Brick Lane, the Pride of Spitalfields is a cosy, friendly, neat East End pub. The interior is chock-full of old pictures of the area, stone jugs and mugs. There is a coal-burning fireplace, a TV and big screen for catching the weekend or evening sporting events. The small bar offers excellent guest beers, making this the perfect place for a pre- or post-curry pint.
⌂ ◐ ⇌ (Liverpool St) ⊖ (Aldgate East/Shoreditch)

Shooting Star ✔

125-129 Middlesex Street, E1 7JF
11-11; closed Sat & Sun
☎ (020) 7929 6818
Fuller's Chiswick, London Pride, ESB, seasonal beers H
Although this pub is outside the Central London postal area, it is literally only just around the corner, and so is well used by city office workers. The spacious, open, ground-floor bar reflects the clientele, being packed with sofas and low coffee tables. A smaller bar downstairs is often booked for private parties. Evening meals finish at 8pm.
◑ ⇌ (Liverpool St) ⊖

E1: Whitechapel

Black Bull

199 Whitechapel Road, E1 1DE
11-11; 12-10.30 Sun
☎ (020) 7247 6707
Adnams Broadside; Nethergate Suffolk County, seasonal beers H
One of the last true free houses in the East End, where a large, open-plan bar serves excellent beers from Nethergate Brewery – a must for real ale zealots. Easily spotted by its dominant mock-Tudor exterior, it is a retreat for market traders and staff from the Royal London Hospital. Major sports events are shown on a big screen. Ask the bar staff which games are available. It was awarded local CAMRA Pub of the Year 2005.
⊖ (Whitechapel) ♣

E3: Bow

Coborn Arms

8 Coborn Road, E3 2DA
11-11; 12-10.30 Sun
☎ (020) 8980 3793
Young's Bitter, Special, seasonal beers H
The pub in Bow with all the charms – an oasis in a changing world. So say the signs outside and who are we to argue? The bar area is bigger than you might expect from the outside and is step-free (apart from the side room on the right). This friendly local serves good food (all day Sat and Sun). The names of the street and the pub come from Priscilla Coborn – a 17th-century benefactor.
❀ ◑ ♿ ⊖ (Mile End/Bow Rd) ♣

E5: Clapton

Princess of Wales

146 Lea Bridge Road, E5 9BQ
11-11; 12-10.30 Sun
☎ (020) 8533 3463
Young's Bitter, Special; seasonal beers H
This Young's pub has been a regular Guide entry since 1993. It is popular with locals as well as walkers, canal boaters and skaters from the nearby ice rink. The public bar has a pool table, while the comfortable main bar overlooks the canal. It makes an ideal base for exploring the Lea Valley Park. ❀ ◑ ⊟ ⇌ ♣ P

E8: Hackney

Baxters Court ✔

282 Mare Street, E8 1HE
10-11; 12-10.30 Sun
☎ (020) 8525 9010
Courage Directors; Greene King Abbot; Marston's Burton Bitter, Pedigree; guest beers H
This spacious Wetherspoon's pub opened only three years ago, but is already one of the most popular in the area. The entrance, opposite the Hackney Empire, opens into a small, open-air atrium, ideal for a quiet drink in dry weather. The ground floor is open plan, but booths on the side walls allow privacy, while carefully arranged furniture helps create a buzzing atmosphere. The upstairs bar is more trendy.
Q ❀ ◑ ♿ ⇌ (Hackney Central) ⚟

E10: Leyton (Bakers Arms)

Drum ✔

557-559 Lea Bridge Road, E10 7EQ
10-11; 12-10.30 Sun
☎ (020) 8539 1985
Courage Directors; Greene King Abbot; Marston's Burton Bitter; guest beers H
Modest, street-corner pub, quite unlike the usual Wetherspoon style, but with its famously keen prices. A recent East London CAMRA Pub of the Year, the Drum is a deservedly popular, pleasant local. It is well served by bus routes Nos. 48, 55, 56 and 69. Meals are served all day until 10pm.
Q ❀ ◑ ⇌ (Leyton Midland Rd) ⚟

E11: Leytonstone

Birkbeck Tavern

45 Langthorne Road, E11 4HL
11-11; 12-10.30 Sun
☎ (020) 8539 2584
Beer range varies H
This ever-popular, back-street local specialises in serving beers from micro-breweries. The pub has a distinct sporting culture: several darts teams call it home, and supporters of Leyton Orient are frequently to be found celebrating (or drowning their sorrows) on match days. In summer the large garden provides a pleasant spot to sink a pint. In the colder months take your pick from the smaller public bar or the high ceilinged lounge. ❀ ⊟ ⊖ (Leyton) ♣

North Star

24 Browning Road, E11 3AR
✪ 12-11; 12-10.30 Sun
☎ (020) 8989 5777
Adnams Broadside; Fuller's London Pride; guest beer Ⓗ
Originally a pair of cottages, this 19th-century, two-bar pub stands in Leytonstone's old village. Railway and steamship memorabilia commemorate the famous North Star name. TV sport is shown unobtrusively in both bars. The games room is served through the old off-sales hatch, and the garden is popular in summer.
❀◑⊟⊖♣

E11: Wanstead

Duke of Edinburgh

79 Nightingale Lane, E11 2EY
✪ 11-11; 12-10.30 Sun
☎ (020) 8989 0014
Adnams Broadside; Draught Bass; Young's Bitter Ⓗ
A proper, back-street pub that has recently been refurbished. A small screen has been added to separate off one end of the sizeable bar as a no-smoking area. The other end is dedicated to pool and televised sports. An unusual feature is the shove-ha'penny board against the wall. Tables are set outside for summer drinking. Food is served 11-9pm (11-5pm Sat).
❀◑ ⊖(Snaresbrook) ♣P⊬

George ✔

159 High Street, E11 2RL
✪ 10-11; 12-10.30 Sun
☎ (020) 8989 2921
Beer range varies Ⓗ
Just when you think you have seen all that this large Wetherspoon house has to offer, it throws up another surprise. Entering through the marble porch you find several distinct drinking areas. Upstairs is an airy balcony space, which gets busy on Friday and Saturday evenings when the upstairs bar is open. As you might expect, the 'George' theme is reflected in the decor with many famous Georges depicted. Wondering where you will find the dragon – just look up.
⚔Q❀◑♿⊖⊬

Nightingale ✔

51 Nightingale Lane, E11 2EY
✪ 11-11; 12-10.30 Sun
☎ (020) 8530 4540
Courage Best Bitter; Fuller's London Pride; Greene King Old Speckled Hen; Wells Bombardier; guest beers Ⓗ
On entering this pub the eye is drawn to the central bar with its six handpumps and large array of whiskies. The pub has a palatial sitting room with plush curtains and upholstered seats around polished tables. Behind the bar, service is through hatches. The no-smoking lounge is often used for meetings by local community groups. An excellent menu of international cuisines is offered. Q❀◑ ⊖(Snaresbrook) ⊬

E13: Plaistow

Black Lion

59-61 High Street, E13 0AD
✪ 11-3, 5.30-11; 11-11 Wed-Sat; 12-10.30 Sun
☎ (020) 8472 2351
Courage Best Bitter, Directors; guest beers Ⓗ
Although rebuilt in the early 18th century, a coaching inn has stood on this site for over 600 years. The long public bar shows TV sport. The quieter lounge bar is accessed by the door to the side of the pub. At the rear, the old stables have been converted to a function room with its own bar. A cobbled yard leads to the garden of this historic pub. ⚔❀◑ ⊟⊖♣P

E14: Limehouse

Grapes

76 Narrow Street, E14 8BP
✪ 12-3, 5.30-11; 12-11 Sat; 12-10.30 Sun
☎ (020) 7987 4396
Adnams Bitter; Draught Bass; Marston's Pedigree Ⓗ
A former haunt of Charles Dickens, it was named the Six Jolly Fellowship Porters in his novel Our Mutual Friend. The Grapes is the quintessential riverside pub: warm, cosy (and dog-friendly), with a fine interior and great views of the Thames from the wee deck at the back. It serves excellent traditional pub food and the best chips in town; an award-winning seafood restaurant upstairs is a bonus. A pub not to be missed.
⚔Q❀◑ ⇌(Limehouse/West Ferry DLR) ⊖♣▯

E15: Stratford

King Edward VII

47 Broadway, E15 4BQ
✪ 12-11; 12-10.30 Sun
☎ (020) 8534 2313 website: www.kingeddy.co.uk
Wells Bombardier; guest beers Ⓗ
The low-ceilinged front bar boasts a flagstone floor, pew seating on one side and comfortable leather sofas around the fire on the other. To the right, a wood and etched glass screen bears the new name of the pub (it was once called the Prussia). Beyond this a magnificent, Victorian tiled passage leads to the saloon bar. The upstairs seating area is now a restaurant. Bombardier is always available and up to five other ales are rotated. ⚔◑ ⊟⇌⊖

E17: Walthamstow

Village

31 Orford Road, E17 9NL
✪ 12-11; 12-10.30 sun
☎ (020) 8521 4398
Adnams Broadside; Courage Best Bitter, Directors; Greene King IPA; guest beers Ⓗ
It is hard to believe that this comfortable local in a quiet side street has only been a pub for about 15 years. Set in the heart of a conservation area it has a spacious main bar and a cosy snug. The paved yard behind the pub will appeal on sunny days. ❀◑⇌(Central) ⊖

Barking

Britannia

1 Church Road, IG11 8PR (near A123)
✪ 12-3, 5-11; 11-11 Sat; 12-10.30 Sun
☎ (020) 8594 1305
Young's Bitter, Special, Winter Warmer Ⓗ
The architecture of the Britannia is a tribute to

Barking's nautical past, once boasting England's largest fishing fleet. The saloon bar is a comfortable home-from-home for most locals, and is normally quiet, in contrast to the noisier public bar with its bare boards, juke box, darts and pool. Basic bar meals representing excellent value, are available weekdays and a set Sunday lunch is served. Entertainment is also occasionally staged in this friendly local.
Q❀ᗡ⊟≠⊖♣P

Chadwell Heath

Eva Hart ✔

1128 High Road, Romford, RM6 4AH (at A118/Station Rd jct)
✪ 10-11; 12-10.30 Sun
☎ (020) 8597 1069
Greene King IPA, Abbot; Marston's Burton Bitter, Pedigree; Shepherd Neame Bishops Finger; guest beers Ⓗ
Large, friendly, comfortable Wetherspoon's house converted from a former police station, on the site of the old village stocks. A great range of at least five guest beers is usually on tap, plus Westons Old Rosie cider. It has extensive no-smoking areas on both the ground floor and balcony, where children are welcome until 7pm. The pub is named after a local musical lady who was the oldest Titantic survivor. Food is served 12-10pm daily. ❀ᗡ◗♿≠P⊬

Goodmayes

Standard Bearer ✔

7-13 Goodmayes Road, IG3 9UH
✪ 10-11; 12-10.30 Sun
☎ (020) 8597 7624
Greene King Abbot; Marston's Burton Bitter, Pedigree; guest beers Ⓗ
Multi-levelled Wetherspoon house that hides its origin as a shop. Now, more like a café-bar in appearance, it attracts all sections of the community and shows that the pub has a future, rather than being stuck in the past. Wireless internet facilities are provided. Breakfast is served from 10am incuding Sunday.
Q❀ᗡ◗♿≠⊬

Hornchurch

Chequers

North Street, RM11 1ST (near A124 at Billet Lane jct)
✪ 11-11; 12-10.30 Sun
☎ (01708) 442094
Ansells Best Bitter; Draught Bass; Tetley Bitter; Young's Bitter Ⓗ
Genuine local that has managed to retain much of its character. Situated on a large traffic island, it sells excellent value beers and is definitely a drinkers' pub. This busy local enjoys a keen darts following, fielding several teams. A TV in an area at the end of the bar shows sporting events. It is a regular local CAMRA Pub of the Year winner. Note: the nearby railway station closes just before 8pm and is not open on Sunday.
ᗡ≠(Emerson Pk)♣P

JJ Moon's ✔

46-62 High Street, RM12 4UN (on A124)
✪ 10-11; 12-10.30 Sun
☎ (01708) 478410
Greene King Abbot; Marston's Burton Bitter, Pedigree; guest beers Ⓗ
Late 1993 Wetherspoon's bar, stocking up to eight guest beers, mostly from small independent breweries. An extended no-smoking area permits children to eat until 6pm. Framed prints show old Hornchurch scenes and local history. Sunday breakfasts are served from 10am with soft drinks; curry night is Thursday. Two beer festivals are staged annually in May and October. Three real ciders are served straight from the cask. Emerson Park Station is closed Sunday and from 8pm other days.
Qᗡ◗♿≠(Emerson Park)●⊬

Romford

Golden Lion ✔

2 High Street, RM1 1HR
✪ 11-11; 12-10.30 Sun
☎ (01708) 740081
Adnams Broadside; Courage Best Bitter; Greene King IPA, Old Speckled Hen; Shepherd Neame Spitfire; Theakston Old Peculier Ⓗ
This town-centre pub is a Grade II listed building, which was refurbished about 20 years ago, but retains many ancient timbers in its structure. There has been a pub on this site since the 15th century and Sir Francis Bacon was a notable former owner. Although prices are on the high side, it can get quite busy on market days. 'Southern' beers are sometimes dispensed using a tight sparkler; ask for it to be removed when ordering. Evening meals finish at 8pm.
❀ᗡ◗≠

Upminster

Crumpled Horn ✔

33-37 Corbets Tey Road, RM14 2AJ (on B1421)
✪ 11-11; 12-10.30 Sun
☎ (01708) 226698
Adnams Broadside; Marston's Pedigree; Ridleys IPA; guest beer Ⓗ
Opened in September 2000, this Pathfinder Inn (formerly Wizard) is an attractive conversion of three former shop units, near the centre of Upminster. The guest ale changes monthly and provides a welcome boost to the limited local real ale scene. A prize quiz is held on Tuesday evening. The pub's name was chosen in a competition, and was taken from a nearby dairy – which was long-defunct and sadly demolished at the end of 2003. ᗡ◗♿≠⊖⊬

Woodford Green

Cricketers ✔

299-301 High Road, IG8 9HG (on A1099)
✪ 11-11; 12-10.30 Sun
☎ (020) 8504 2734
McMullen AK, Country; guest beer Ⓗ
Pleasant, comfortable pub whose basic public bar houses a dartboard. The roomy, cosy saloon bar has a relaxed atmosphere and displays insignia plaques for most of the county cricket clubs. Also featured are several photos of Sir Winston Churchill who was for many years the local MP – his statue stands on the green almost opposite. A guest beer is usually available and hearty lunchtime food is served on weekdays.
❀ᗡ⊟♿♣P

Traveller's Friend

496-498 High Road, IG8 0PN (on A104)

11-11; 12-4, 7-10.30 Sun

(020) 8504 2435

Adnams Broadside; Courage Best Bitter; Greene King Abbot; Ridleys IPA; guest beers H

Excellent, characterful one-bar pub on a slip road off the busy main road. The friendly Welsh couple in charge have welcomed allcomers for many years. The main features of the interior are its oak-panelled walls and the original snob screen at one end of the bar. A great little local with one guest beer always available, it hosts an annual beer festival in April. Limited parking, but several routes stop at the nearby bus stop. No food is served Sunday.

Q ❀ ☾ ♣ P

NORTH LONDON

N1: Hoxton

Beershop

14 Pitfield Street, N1 6EY

11-7; closed Mon; 10-4 Sat; closed Sun

(020) 7739 3701 website: www.pitfieldbeershop.co.uk

Beer range varies

Specialist off-licence, one of the few remaining outlets for home-brewing and wine-making supplies in London. Organic wine, bottled cider, glasses and breweriana are also stocked, though most visit to choose from the vast range of bottled beers on display. The organic and historic bottled-conditioned ales from the adjoining Pitfield Brewery take pride of place, but a changing range of bottled micro-brewed beer is sourced from around the country. The range of Belgian specialities is especially noteworthy.

≈ (Old St) ⊖

Prince Arthur

49 Brunswick Place, N1 6EB

11-11; 12-6.30 Sun

(020) 7253 3187

Shepherd Neame Master Brew Bitter, Best Bitter, Spitfire H

Cosy, single-bar, back-street local near Pitfield Street, consisting of two distinct areas: glass-panelled windows and table seating to the front; a dartboard in the sunken area to the rear. The pub fields its own darts teams. Pictures of racehorses feature throughout, and photographs of the landlord's days as a boxer add interest to the fireplace at the rear. Background music plays, and a TV shows occasional sporting events, but neither intrudes on the convivial atmosphere.

❀ ≈ (Old St) ⊖ ♣

Wenlock Arms ✔

26 Wenlock Road, N1 7TA

12-11; 12-10.30 Sun

(020) 7608 3406 website: www.wenlock-arms.co.uk

Adnams Bitter; Crouch Vale Brewers Gold; Pitfield East Kent Goldings; guest beers H

This 1830s back-street pub has been North London CAMRA Pub of the Year four times. It stocks six or eight real ales, always including a mild, plus a real cider and a good range of draught and bottled continental beer. It hosts live jazz over three evenings at the weekend. Food in this cosy pub consists of substantial sandwiches, including the famous salt beef.

♛ ≈ (Old St) ⊖ ♣ ●

N1: Islington

Barnsbury

209-211 Liverpool Road, N1 1LX

12-11; 12-10.30 Sun

(020) 7607 5519 website: www.thebarnsbury.co.uk

Fuller's London Pride; Taylor Landlord; guest beer H

Originally the Windsor Castle, later Houricans, this gastro-pub features a horseshoe bar, wine glass chandeliers, bare boards and a changing collection of artwork (for sale). Usually three ales are on tap, plus a draught German wheat beer. The outdoor decked area is a bonus in good weather. Light lunchtime snacks are available, with a wider menu (including vegetarian options) served in the evening.

❀ ◗ ≈ (Highbury & Islington) ⊖ (Angel) ⁄

Compton Arms

4 Compton Avenue, N1 2XD

11-11; 12-10.30 Sun

(020) 7359 2645

Greene King IPA, Abbot, Morland Original; guest beer H

Small, attractive, cottage-style building in a quiet, narrow side street that belies its proximity to the hectic bustle of Islington. Compact dimensions and beams heighten the country pub atmosphere. The main area is bare-boarded, with bottle-glass windows. To the rear of the bar is a small dining area; a lower lounge area leads to the patio courtyard. The guest beer changes regularly and the home-cooked traditional meals are recommended. It can get crowded before kick-off when Arsenal play at home.

❀ ☾ ◗ ≈ (Highbury & Islington) ⊖

Island Queen ☆ ✔

87 Noel Road, N1 8HD

12-11; 12-10.30 Sun

(020) 7704 7631

Fuller's London Pride; Taylor Landlord; Young's Bitter H

Built in 1851, despite being in trendy Islington, this little gem has avoided most refit fashions. Formerly five sections, now one, plus a rear no-smoking area; note the three-sided bar, exuberant multi-bay windows and elaborate gilt mirrors. It offers premium Belgian bottled beers and an extensive wine list. The upstairs TV lounge is the only modern area. Dogs are welcome. Outside seating is provided in summer. The food is recommended.

Q ☾ ◗ ⊖ (Angel)

N4: Harringay

Oakdale Arms

283 Hermitage Road, N4 1NP

12-11; 12-10.30 Sun

(020) 8800 2013

website: www.individualpubs.co.uk/oakdale

Milton Minotaur, Jupiter, Pegasus; guest beers H

Large two-bar inter-war pub in the back streets between Harringay and South Tottenham. The lounge bar hosts a rank of handpumps, with up to eight real ales; guests often come from East

Anglian micros. Real cider (typically organic Cassels from Cambridgeshire) is served from the cellar. There is a selection of mainly Belgian bottled beer and a nice line in single malts. The bare-boarded public bar houses a pool table and dartboard. Toasties and jacket potatoes are sold and the landlord's excellent curry is served Friday lunchtime. Football matches and the like are shown on a big screen. Two beer festivals are held each year at this true community local, voted North London CAMRA Pub of the Year 2005. ❀⊟♣●⊡P

Salisbury ☆

1 Grand Parade, Green Lanes, N4 1JX

12-1am (2am Thu-Sat); 12-midnight Sun

☎ (020) 8800 9617

Fuller's Chiswick, London Pride, ESB, seasonal beers H

Almost worth visiting just for an architectural feast alone, this Grade II listed pub has a glorious interior, used as a location for the 1992 film Chaplin. The tiled walls, mosaic floors, stained glass windows, wonderful skylight in the no-smoking restaurant area (an old billiards room) and two snugs add interest. It stocks Czech lager, continental bottled beer and a good range of malts. A fine selection of food comes at reasonable prices, not quite 'gastro' but more than just usual pub food, prepared by talented chefs. With quiz night (Mon) and comedy club (Thu), the Salisbury has a lot to offer, not forgetting the late licence.

◑▶♿≈(Green Lanes) ⊖(Turnpike Lane) ⊬

N6: Highgate

Flask ☆ ✔

77 Highgate West Hill, N6 6BU

12-11; 12-10.30 Sun

☎ (020) 8348 7346

Adnams Broadside; Taylor Landlord; guest beers H

Built 1663 and later modified, it was originally used as a stop-off point for drinkers taking flasks of water from the nearby Hampstead spring. Now a well established part of the Highgate community, its single bar offers lots of interesting side alcoves and quiet drinking rooms. The large garden has heaters, an outside bar and a barbecue. Choose traditional, home-cooked food from a varied menu, or select one of the wide range of bottled European beers, or draught German beer.

♨Q❀◑▶⊖♣⊬

N8: Crouch End

Harringay Arms

153 Crouch Hill, N8 9QH

12-11; 12-10.30 Sun

☎ (020) 8340 4243

Adnams Broadside; Courage Best Bitter; guest beers H

Small, narrow, friendly, if at times rather smoky local at the centre of Crouch End. Old photographs and maps show the area's development since the 18th century. In summer, use can be made of a bijou garden at the rear. Quiz night is on Tuesday. Filled rolls are available from lunchtime until early evening.

❀≈(Crouch Hill) ♣

King's Head

2 Crouch End Hill, N8 8AA

12-11; 12-10.30 Sun

☎ (020) 8340 1028

Caledonian Deuchars IPA; guest beers H

Bustling pub in the centre of Crouch End, decorated in modern style, consisting of the bar and a second room separated by a curtain. The back room has more comfortable seating. This is very much a pub for drinking, although good food is served. Background music plays, but is never loud. There is an excellent range of bottled foreign beers. Downstairs is a large room that is a well known comedy and music venue, and which always has one cask ale.

◑▶≈

N8: Hornsey

Three Compasses

62 High Street, N8 7NX

11-11; 12-10.30 Sun

☎ (020) 8340 2729

Draught Bass; Fuller's London Pride; Taylor Landlord; guest beers H

Friendly, welcoming pub that has been recently refurbished. The main bar is light and airy, especially when the double doors are opened out in warm weather. The back bar has a different feel, with a pool table and skylight. Major sporting events are shown in the back bar, which hosts occasional live music. Food is served daily until one hour before closing. Quiz night is Monday.

◑▶♿≈♣⊬⊡

Tollgate ✔

26 Turnpike Lane, N8 0PS

10 (11 Sat)-11; 12-10.30 Sun

☎ (020) 8889 9085

Courage Directors; Greene King Abbot; Marston's Burton Bitter, Pedigree; Shepherd Neame Spitfire; guest beers H

The interior of this large Wetherspoon shop conversion will induce nostalgia in those who remember 'Spoon's early book-lined heyday. During succeeding refurbishments the pub has been maintained as a community ale house – cask Belgian De Koninck often features – and the management aims to stock up to five guest ales. Even by this competitive company's standards beer here is good value. Food is served from opening until an hour prior to closing.

Q❀◑▶≈⊖(Turnpike Lane) ⊬

N12: North Finchley

Tally Ho

749 High Road, N12 0BP

9-11; 12-10.30 Sun

☎ (020) 8445 4390

Greene King Abbot; Marston's Burton Bitter, Pedigree; Shepherd Neame Spitfire; guest beers H

In noisy, bustling North Finchley where every other pub is fake Irish, this is a welcome and quiet retreat. The mixed clientele divide themselves among the five different areas, including two bars and two no-smoking areas (one doubles as a family room-cum-restaurant). This Wetherspoon's had seen better times but has risen again under new management. The pub opens early for breakfast (no alcohol) and serves food until 10.30pm. Q ❀ ◑ ♿ ⚟

N14: Southgate

New Crown ✔

80-84 Chase Side, N14 5PH

⌚ 10-11; 12-10.30 Sun

☎ (020) 8882 8758

Greene King Abbot; Marston's Burton Bitter; Shepherd Neame Spitfire; guest beers Ⓗ

Large, Wetherspoon's conversion of a former supermarket with no-smoking and children's areas to the rear. The open-plan room has snugs around the edge. Up to five guest beers and the Belgian ale De Koninck are usually on tap. It generally attracts a mixed clientele but a younger crowd dominates on Friday and Saturday evenings. It opens for breakfast from 10am. Q ◑ ⊖ ⚟

Woolpack

52 High Street, N14 6EB

⌚ 11-11; 12-10.30 Sun

☎ (020) 8886 5051

Courage Best Bitter; Greene King Old Speckled Hen; guest beer Ⓗ

Split-level Victorian pub close to the shopping centre and historic village green. It has designated areas for darts and pool. Good home-cooked food is served, except on Sunday evening. Quiz night is Thursday and live music is staged most weekends. An atttractive garden lies to the rear. Tables offer a view on to the busy High Street. The TV is switched on for sport. ❀ ◑ ⊖ ♣

N16: Stoke Newington

Rochester Castle ✔

145 Stoke Newington High Street, N16 0NY

⌚ 10-11; 12-10.30 Sun

☎ (020) 7249 6016

De Koninck Ambrée; Fuller's London Pride; Greene King Abbot; Marston's Burton Bitter; Ridleys Old Bob; guest beers Ⓗ

Cavernous yet cosy Wetherspoon house that draws a broad and lively cross-section of drinkers from the local area. The substantial choice of up to seven guest beers can be enjoyed in three distinct areas; the no-smoking conservatory is popular with chess players. Meals start at 10am with breakfast and continue until 10pm; Thursday is curry night.

Q ❀ ◑ ⇌ ♣ ⚟

Rose & Crown

199 Stoke Newington Church Street, N16 9ES

⌚ 11.30-11; 12-10.30 Sun

☎ (020) 7254 7497

Adnams Bitter; Marston's Pedigree; guest beer Ⓗ

After an invigorating walk in nearby Clissold Park you will find the Rose & Crown at the western end of Stoke Newington's eating and drinking centre. This distinctive former Truman's house retains a largely unspoilt, wood-panelled interior, featuring many details from this lost London brewer's past. A 'hockeystick' bar serves a good mix of customers from sports fans to crossword puzzlers. Seating around the large 'bottle-glass' corner section is popular with people watchers. The food and en-suite accommodation are recommended.

⊭ ◑ ♿ ⇌ ♣

N21: Winchmore Hill

Dog & Duck

74 Hoppers Road, N21 3LH

⌚ 12 (11 Fri & Sat)-11; 12-10.30 Sun

☎ (020) 8886 1987

Greene King IPA, Abbot; Taylor Landlord; Wadworth 6X Ⓗ

Built in the late 19th century on the site of an earlier pub, this country-style local originally had three small rooms, now converted to one. The pub was refurbished a few years ago creating a new ambience. Although there is a big screen for golf and football, this pub has great character, including a magical secluded garden.

❀ ⇌

Orange Tree

18 Highfield Road, N21 3HA

(off Green Lanes, opp. Sainsbury's)

⌚ 11-11; 12-10.30 Sun

☎ (020) 8360 4853

Greene King IPA; guest beer Ⓗ

Easy to miss, although just yards from a main bus route, this lively community pub is a regular winner of local CAMRA awards. A former Taylor Walker house, now operated by Punch, it benefits from a long-standing management and bar team. A long bar serves the main lounge and side areas, one of which is well used by pool and darts players. Several TV screens attract sports fans for all the main events. The large, family-friendly garden hosts barbecues. Parking is limited. ❀ ◑ ⇌ ♣ P

Winchmore Hill Cricket Club

The Paulin Ground, Fords Grove, N21 3ER

⌚ 7 (12 Sat)-11; 12 (may vary)-10.30 (6 winter) Sun

☎ (020) 8360 1271 website: www.winchmorehill.org

Greene King IPA; guest beers Ⓗ

The land was part of the Paulin family estate and became a sports ground in 1880; permission was granted in that year for cricket to be played. Football and other sports can also be enjoyed. Five cask ales are on tap. A function room can be booked. Local CAMRA's Club of the Year 2003 and 2004, it hosts a cricket week in August with a mini-beer festival. Lunches are served at the weekend in summer. Sport is shown on TV; darts and pool are played. CAMRA membership card or current Guide advised for for entry. ❀ ◑ ♣ P

Barnet

Lord Nelson

14 West End Lane, EN5 2SA

⌚ 11-3, 5-11; 11-11 Thu-Sat; 12-10.30 Sun

☎ (020) 8449 7249

Young's Bitter, Special, seasonal beers Ⓗ

Back-street local, hidden away off Wood Street, a recent addition to the Young's estate. A cosy, traditional hostelry popular with locals, the pub is decorated with model sailing ships above the bar and other Nelson memorabilia, plus collections of plates and whisky miniatures. The TV at the rear of the pub is mainly for sport (special requests are considered). A seasonal

Young's beer is usually stocked. A steak meal is available on Wednesday evening; no lunches are served on Sunday. ❀◐♣

Mitre Inn

58 High Street, EN5 5SJ

✪ 12-11; 12-10.30 Sun

☎ (020) 8449 6582

Adnams Bitter; Tetley Bitter; guest beers Ⓗ

One of the oldest pubs in Barnet, it was once two pubs back-to-back. There are now three bars: two small ones at the front (one no-smoking), and a spacious room at the back with a large TV for football. Food is served 12-8pm (12-6pm at the weekend). The pub is wood-panelled throughout; note the thought-provoking inscriptions on the walls. The guest beers change often. Parking is limited.

❀◐◑ ≇ ⊖ (High Barnet) P⚟

Sebright Arms

9 Alston Road, EN5 4ET (off St Albans Rd)

✪ 12 (5 Mon)-11; 12-10.30 Sun

☎ (020) 8449 6869

McMullen AK, Country, seasonal beer or guest beer Ⓗ

Although only five minutes' walk from Barnet High Street, you could be in another world here. A traditional two-bar local, this McMullen's tenancy does not use the cask breather. The public bar is popular for darts and crib as well as TV which is mainly for sport. The saloon is available for functions. A guest or seasonal beer is usually stocked. Fish and chips is served on Friday, and meals are laid on for Christmas and other special occasions. ⛫❀⊟♣P

Enfield

Wonder ✔

1 Batley Road, EN2 0JG

✪ 11-11; 12-10.30 Sun

☎ (020) 8363 0202

McMullen AK, Country Ⓗ

Although the present building dates back to circa 1929, there has been a licensed premises on this site since 1838. The two-bar pub, converted from two Victorian cottages, is at the end of an alley. Acquired in 1867, it was McMullen's first pub in Enfield. With a piano in the public bar, it hosts a pianist or sing-along/boogie-woogie on Friday and Sunday afternoons and Saturday evening. It stages jazz on Sunday evening while soloists or duos play on Friday evening at this football-free pub. The menu is limited to pie'n'mash or chilli.

⛫Q❀◐◑⊟♿≇ (Gordon Hill) ♣P

New Barnet

Railway Bell ✔

13 East Barnet Road, EN4 8RR

✪ 10-11; 12-10.30 Sun

☎ (020) 8449 1369

Courage Best Bitter; Greene King Abbot; Marston's Burton Bitter, Pedigree; Shepherd Neame Spitfire; guest beers Ⓗ

Long-established Wetherspoon's benefiting from strong local support. Divided into different areas – the front is a smoking area and the rear the no-smoking, dining and family area – the pub is decorated with railway pictures and memorabilia. It regularly offers four guest beers besides the usual Wetherspoon range, including Belgian De Koninck. Be prepared to wait for food during busy periods; in summer you can watch the trains go by from the garden.

Q❀◐◑≇P⚟

Ponders End

Picture Palace ✔

Howards Hall, Lincoln Road, EN3 4AQ (Hertford Rd jct)

✪ 10-11; 12-10.30 Sun

☎ (020) 8344 9690

Courage Directors; Fuller's London Pride; Greene King Abbot; Marston's Burton Bitter, Pedigree; guest beers Ⓗ

1920s listed building, formerly a cinema, that has been sympatheticly restored by Wetherspoon. A large mural above the bar depicts Laurel and Hardy, while other silent movies stars are remembered in various items. This is the only pub in the vicinity with any real ale, let alone 10 handpumps. Not only that, loud music is eschewed and no-smoking areas are provided.

Q❀◐◑♿≇ (Southbury Rd/Ponders End) P⚟

NORTH-WEST LONDON

NW1: Euston

Head of Steam

1 Eversholt Street, NW1 1DN

✪ 11-11; 12-10.30 Sun

☎ (020) 7383 3359 website: www.theheadofsteam.com

Banks's Original; Holt Bitter; Hop Back Summer Lightning, seasonal beers; guest beers Ⓗ

Located at the east side of the bus station right in front of the railway station, with a single bar on the first floor reached by two entranceways. This pub boasts an impressive collection of railway artefacts, and some impressive old enamel advertising signs. Bus passengers are catered for as the raised no-smoking bar area presents a bird's eye view of the bus station. Regular beer festivals are held. The range can extend to 10 draught beers plus real cider always on sale (Westons) and seasonal perries. Evening meals are served 5-8 weekdays.

◑≇⊖●⚟

NW1: Primrose Hill

Princess of Wales

22 Chalcot Road, NW1 8LL

✪ 11-11; 12-10.30 Sun

☎ (020) 7722 0354

Adnams Bitter; Fuller's London Pride; guest beer Ⓗ

Delightful corner pub (in a pleasant area of London), reminiscent of a bistro, with large windows that open out on to the pavement in the summer. The cosy, friendly pub has a central bar with a seating area at the rear and a brick-walled basement bar leading to a 'sunken' garden. The pub prides itself on good, honest food at reasonable prices (unlike many premises in this affluent area) that is freshly cooked. Sunday meals are served 12-5.30pm. Live jazz is performed Thursday evening and Sunday afternoon.

❀◐◑⊖ (Chalk Farm)

NW2: Cricklewood

Beaten Docket ✔

50-56 Cricklewood Broadway, NW2 3DT

⏲ 11-11; 12-10.30 Sun

☎ (020) 8450 2972

De Koninck Ambrée; Greene King Abbot; Marston's Burton Bitter, Pedigree; guest beer Ⓗ

Due, in Wetherspoon's terms, to an uncommonly long period under the same management, this typical conversion of a retail premises has become a beacon for real ale. A series of well-defined drinking areas disguises the vastness of the place. The pub's name refers to a losing betting slip: plenty of prints and paraphernalia reinforce the theme. Benches are outside all year long for the hardy. A local CAMRA Pub of the Season winner, it offers a children's family food area and menu – last orders 5pm.
Q❀◐◑♿⇌⊁

NW3: Hampstead

Duke of Hamilton

23 New End, NW3 1JD

⏲ 12-11; 12-10.30 Sun

☎ (020) 7794 0258

Fuller's London Pride, ESB; guest beer Ⓗ

Twice local CAMRA Pub of the Year (2002 and 2003), this is a rarity for London – a wonderful community pub. Tucked away in a side-street, it is patronised by everyone from builders to judges. The pub's decor has a strong sporting theme – it also fields its own rugby and cricket teams. The Duke of Hamilton was a Civil War Royalist. This 200-year-old building has a single bar and a lovely terrace often busy during warmer weather. There is a cobbled yard and downstairs cellar bar for functions. It stocks Czech lager and a wide range of malts; remarkably good value for the area.
❀◑⊖♣●

Flask ☆

14 Flask Walk, NW3 1HE

⏲ 11-11; 12-10.30 Sun

☎ (020) 7435 4580

Young's Bitter, Special, seasonal beers Ⓗ

A fine example of a Young's pub in an attractive side street in Hampstead Village. With two separate drinking areas, sports are shown on TV in the smaller public bar; a comfortable place to warm up and relax after a bracing walk over the Heath. Seasonal beers Winter Warmer and Waggledance are sometimes replaced by guest beers. Q☕◐◑⊞♿⊖

Holly Bush ☆ ✔

22 Holly Mount, NW3 6SG

⏲ 12-11; 12-10.30 Sun

☎ (020) 7435 2892 website: www.thehollybushpub.com

Adnams Bitter, Broadside; Harveys BB; guest beer Ⓗ

This local is a true gem, situated in a quiet residential area just off the High Street. Frequented by celebrities, the pub itself is a Grade II listed building, which has endured various threats to its existence over the years. Now a multi-roomed building, real fires and original features combine with a varied and extensive history to draw the visitor to Hampstead. Reputedly haunted, many stories abound. The menu is based on organically produced ingredients. ♨Q◐◑⊖♣

NW4: Hendon

Greyhound

52 Church End, NW4 4JT

⏲ 11-11; 12-10.30 Sun

☎ (020) 8457 9730

Young's Bitter, Special, Waggledance, Winter Warmer Ⓗ

The Greyhound is set in an area of Hendon that has a village atmosphere, next to the Church Farmhouse Museum. Three main drinking areas cater for all members of the community – old and young alike. A large-screen TV shows sporting events. Great blues is played at closing time. Food ranges from bar snacks to more substantial fare. Friday's curry night offers three starters and three main courses – original recipes from the pub's Indian chef and superb value.
♨❀◐◑♣

NW5: Dartmouth Park

Dartmouth Arms

35 York Rise, NW5 1SP

⏲ 11 (10 Sat)-11; 10-10.30 Sun

☎ (020) 7485 3267 website: www.dartmoutharms.co.uk

Adnams Bitter; guest beers Ⓗ

This popular local is split into a front bar and rear seating area, featuring attractive wood and copper. It provides a warm and friendly atmosphere in which to enjoy an excellent pint from various micros. Chess, chequers, dominoes and backgammon are played to the rear of the pub where a regular quiz takes place. Meals include a weekly steak night (Wed), 'Fishy Fursday' and tapas on Sunday and Monday evenings.
♨◐◑⇌(Gospel Oak)⊖(Tufnell Pk)♣●

NW5: Kentish Town

Junction Tavern

101 Fortess Road, NW5 1AG

⏲ 12-11; 12-10.30 Sun

☎ (020) 7485 9400

Caledonian Deuchars IPA; guest beers Ⓗ

Attractive, spacious Victorian corner pub of three rooms. At the front is a restaurant with galley kitchen where table reservation is recommended (although food is served throughout the pub). To the rear is a bright, spacious conservatory overlooking a large garden, crowded with picnic tables. In between is a traditional wood-panelled bar room, complete with big mirrors, a fireplace and an ornate ceiling. Beer festivals are held over the May and August bank holiday weekends.
❀◐◑⇌⊖(Kentish Town/Tufnell Pk)

NW7: Mill Hill

Rising Sun ☆

137 Marsh Lane, Highwood Hill, NW7 4EY

(¾ mile from A41/A1 jct)

⏲ 12-11; 12-10.30 Sun

☎ (020) 8959 1357

Adnams Bitter; Greene King Abbot; Young's Bitter Ⓗ

Country pub situated at the top of a steep hill in the old village of Mill Hill. Work had to be done after a bus crashed through a wall into the bar. Supposedly haunted, it was once owned by Sir Stamford Raffles, founder of Singapore and London Zoos. The pub comprises three areas: a charming small front bar, a cosy snug and a barn conversion restaurant. The outside toilets can be chilly in winter. ❀◑ ♣P

NW10: Harlesden

Grand Junction Arms

Acton Lane, NW10 7AD

11-11 (midnight Fri & Sat); 12-10.30 Sun

☎ (020) 8965 5670

Young's Bitter, Special Ⓗ

Imposing pub alongside the Grand Union Canal (moorings available), offering three contrasting bars together with extensive gardens, a patio and children's amusments. The front bar, most likely the old public bar, has pool tables and a TV for sport. The middle bar is more intimate and regularly features sport on a smaller TV. The beamed back bar, which stays open late, opens on to the canal and welcomes children until 7pm at weekends. Music is played on alternate Friday evenings. Sunday meals are served 12-4pm. ❀◑ ♿⇌⊖P

Northwood

Olde Northwood

142 Pinner Road, HA6 1BP

11-10; 12-10 Sun

☎ (01923) 804862

Beer range varies Ⓗ

Grade II listed corner local with newly-painted signage adorning its somewhat jaded frontage. This pub started life in 1901 as the Clifton, then changed to the Ironbridge before adopting its current title. A warm welcome awaits within this local, but beware the 'exotic dancers' 2-10pm Mon-Sat. The guest beer is always from the Nethergate Brewery – most unusual for the area. A couple of outside benches are provided for summer drinking. Q❀⊟⊖P

SOUTH-EAST LONDON

SE1: Borough

Duke of York

47-48 Borough Road, SE1 1DR

12-11 Mon-Fri; closed Sat & Sun

☎ (020) 7403 3590

Shepherd Neame Master Brew Bitter, Spitfire, Bishops Finger Ⓗ

This pub used to be the Goose & Firkin, which was the first in the original Firkin chain. Since being taken over and refurbished by Shepherd Neame it has quickly established a reputation for quality ale and a wide range of imported beers including Leffe on tap. Friendly staff cater for all age groups. ◑⇌(Elephant & Castle) ⊖

Lord Clyde ☆ ✔

27 Clennam Street, SE1 1ER

11 (12 Sat)-11; 12-7 Sun

☎ (020) 7407 3397

Adnams Bitter; Fuller's London Pride; Greene King IPA; Shepherd Neame Spitfire; Young's Bitter Ⓗ

Charming, friendly, back-street traditional London local. Unchanged, a single bar serves the public and saloon. Classic decor features large mirrors and London history. A TV is in the saloon bar. ◑ ⊟♿⇌(London Bridge) ⊖(Borough) ♣

Market Porter ✔

9 Stoney Street, SE1 9AA

6-8.30am Mon-Fri; 11-11; 12-10.30 Sun

☎ (020) 7407 2495

Beer range varies Ⓗ

Traditional pub that has served Borough Market for many years. The old licence permits it to open at 6am weekdays for the convenience of market and postal workers (and handy for clubs closing); breakast is served. The cosy bar is divided by decorative glass partitions offering discrete seating areas; the ceiling is lined with oak beams. It draws a good cross-section of customers from locals and tourists to city and market workers. ◑⇌(London Bridge) ⊖♣

Royal Oak ✔

44 Tabard Street, SE1 4JU

11 (6 Sat)-11; 12-6 Sun

☎ (020) 7357 7173

Harveys XX Mild, Pale Ale, BB, seasonal beers Ⓗ

The only London pub owned by Harveys of Sussex, and a regular in this Guide since being rescued from dereliction by the brewery in 1997. Superbly restored, this pub was a deserving winner of CAMRA's 2003 London Pub of the Year award. Good quality home-cooked food is served including Sunday lunch until 5pm. Although tucked away in a back street, anyone seeking it out will not be disappointed. Q◑ ⊟⇌(London Bridge) ⊖

SE1: London Bridge

Shipwrights Arms ☆ ✔

88 Tooley Street, SE1 2TF

11-11; 12-10.30 Sun

☎ (020) 7378 1486

Beer range varies Ⓗ

Single-room pub close to the riverside that has seen much recent development, including the Mayor of London's office. It is convenient for tourist attractions around London Bridge and Tower Bridge. There are usually three ales on tap. Look out for the large tiled picture of local maritime activity in one corner.
◑⇌⊖

SE1: Tower Bridge

Bridge House ✔

218 Tower Bridge Road, SE1 2UP

11-11; 12-10.30 Sun

☎ (020) 7407 5818

Adnams Bitter, Broadside, seasonal beers; guest beer Ⓗ

Modern Adnams pub and restaurant on Tower Bridge approach where the decor is stylish and neat. The upstairs bar is open as a restaurant on weekdays and for private functions, affording a great view of the Pool of London. Note the interesting effect of the exposed metal roof structure in the upper bar.
◑ ⇌(London Bridge) ⊖(Tower Hill)

Pommelers Rest ✓
196-198 Tower Bridge Road, SE1 2UN
10-11; 12-10.30 Sun
☎ (020) 7378 1399
Beer range varies Ⓗ
Street-corner Wetherspoon's close to Tower Bridge, enjoying an excellent view over the Pool of London, convenient for the Tower of London and the Thames path. An enterprising beer range is usually on offer, together with the usual all-day food. There is a spacious family/no-smoking area.
Q ≈(London Bridge) ⊖(Tower Hill)

SE1: Waterloo

Hole in the Wall
5 Mepham Street, SE1 8SQ
11-11; 12-10.30 Sun
☎ (020) 7928 6196
Fuller's London Pride; guest beers Ⓗ
Possibly the nearest pub in this Guide to public transport, this great little pub occupies one of the railway arches in between Waterloo East and Waterloo Stations. It has two bars, a small room to the side and a large main bar with six handpumps; both are decorated with old brewery mirrors. ≈⊖

King's Arms
25 Roupell Street, SE1 8TB
11-11; 12-10.30 Sun
☎ (020) 7207 0784
Adnams Bitter; Fuller's London Pride; Young's Special Ⓗ
Traditional local set in a surprisingly undisturbed residential area near Waterloo; very cosy and friendly. The bar serves two rooms that are wood-panelled and plainly decorated. By contrast, a third room to the rear – The Court Yard – is a bit like a museum, with old pictures and signs; its jolly atmosphere makes it popular with visitors.
Q ≈⊖(Waterloo/Southwark)

SE6: Catford

Catford Ram
9 Winslade Way, SE6 4JU
11-11; 12-10.30 Sun
☎ (020) 8690 6206
Young's Bitter, Special, Winter Warmer Ⓗ
At the Broadway entrance to the Catford shopping centre, near the street market, this pub is popular with shoppers. There is a large, raised seating area and plenty of standing space. Despite having no windows it has a light, airy feel created by the comfortable spaciousness, light decor and air-conditioning. Sporting events are shown on the big-screen TV. It is handy for the Broadway Theatre where the Catford beer festival is held every June. No evening meals are served Sunday (roast lunches 12-4). ≈

London & Rye
109 Rushey Green, SE6 4AF
10-11; 12-10.30 Sun
☎ (020) 8697 5028
Courage Best Bitter, Directors; Greene King Abbot; Marston's Pedigree; Shepherd Neame Spitfire; guest beers Ⓗ
With a more modern touch to the design than is usual, this Wetherpoon's pub is tucked away in a busy parade of shops. It caters for a wide variety of customers. All the usual Wetherspoon features are here: curry club, affordable prices, engaging bar staff. It opens for breakfast at 10am. Q ≈

SE8: Deptford

Dog & Bell ✓
116 Prince Street, SE8 3JD
12-11; 12.30-3.30, 7-10.30 Sun
☎ (020) 8692 5664
Fuller's London Pride, ESB; guest beers Ⓗ
Excellent community local, voted 2004 CAMRA London Regional Pub of the Year after winning the South-East London award three times. It was also Pub of the Year from the Society for Preservation of Beers from the Wood twice, so this is definitely a pub to seek out. It boasts an extensive range of malt whiskies and Belgian bottled beers. Quiz night is Sunday and bar billiards is played here. Q ≈

SE10: Greenwich

Ashburnham Arms
25 Ashburnham Grove, SE10 8UH
11-11; 12-10.30 Sun
☎ (020) 8692 2007
Shepherd Neame Master Brew Bitter, Best Bitter, Spitfire, Bishops Finger, seasonal beers Ⓗ
Just behind the bustle of central Greenwich in the area locally known as the Ashburnham Triangle stands this delightful, back-street Shepherd Neame public house. The beers, which include a selection of the range plus a seasonal brew, accompany the varied choice of food served Tuesday-Sunday. It benefits from a rear garden and a front patio drinking area. The local Blackheath morris group meets here regularly.
≈⊖♣

Plume of Feathers
19 Park Vista, SE10 9LZ
11-11; 12-10.30 Sun
☎ (020) 8858 1661
Adnams Bitter; Fuller's London Pride; guest beers Ⓗ
Welcome refuge from the hubbub of central Greenwich, yet close to the park and the National Maritime Museum. Green exterior tiling, awnings and hanging baskets provide a colourful façade, while the interior is comfortably upholstered and warmly lit. A rear room for dining and a walled garden with the children's summer playroom add to its appeal. It offers an extensive choice of good quality meals (not Sun or Mon eves) and guest beers rare for the area. Quiz night is Wednesday and sports events are shown on TV.
Q ≈(Maze Hill) ⊖(DLR Cutty Sark)

Richard I (Tolly's)
52-54 Royal Hill, SE10 8RT
11-11; 12-10.30 Sun
☎ (020) 8692 2996
Young's Bitter, Special, Winter Warmer, seasonal beers Ⓗ
Traditional two-bar pub, formerly a cottage dating back to the 18th century. It gets its

alternative name from once being owned by the Tolly Cobbold Brewery and is now owned by Young's. A small patio in front of the pub and a large rear garden are ideal for summer drinking.
❀◐♿⇌⊖

Trafalgar Tavern
Park Row, SE10 9NW
⏲ 12-11; 12-10.30 sun
☎ (020) 8858 2909 website: www.trafalgartavern.co.uk
Draught Bass; Fuller's London Pride; Nelson Trafalgar; guest beers Ⓗ
Historic pub by the Thames, next to the Old Royal Naval College, full of real character, appreciated by locals and tourists alike. The bar links the main room to the restaurant area behind, both furnished in classic style; the pub has changed little over time. Large windows offer a great river view; in summer they allow a gentle breeze into the pub, while outside benches offer a pleasant alternative. Beer prices reflect the area and tourist trade.
♛❀◐◑⇌(Maze Hill) ⊖(DLR Cutty Sark)

SE12: Lee

Crown
117 Burnt Ash Hill, SE12 0AJ (off A205)
⏲ 11-11; 12-10.30 Sun
☎ (020) 8857 6607
Young's Bitter, Special, seasonal beers Ⓗ
In a residential area, this spacious but friendly Young's house lies within walking distance of the South Circular. Both the garden and veranda provide space for outdoor drinking when the weather is fine. A wide range of food, from bar snacks to main course meals, is served at lunchtime and during the evening.
❀◐◑⇌♣P

SE13: Lewisham

Dacre Arms
11 Kingswood Place, SE13 5BU
⏲ 12-11; 12-10.30 Sun
☎ (020) 8852 6779
Courage Best Bitter; Greene King IPA; guest beers Ⓗ
Hidden away gem within walking distance of local buses. This superb local, although small, has bags of atmosphere and room for everybody. The two regular real ales are supplemented by two guests from independent breweries. The pub is friendly and welcoming – whether you are a first-time visitor or one of the lucky locals.
Q❀⇌(Blackheath) ♣

Jordan
354 Lewisham High Street, SE13 6LE
⏲ 11-11; 12-10.30 Sun
☎ (020) 8690 2054
Beer range varies Ⓗ/Ⓖ
In such a densely populated area, few local pubs take the trouble to keep a real pint for the thinking drinker. The Jordan has changed little since its days as a Hogshead, with the same bare floorboards and pub fittings. There are at least three real ales on sale (more at busier times), two of which can be on gravity. Bar food is served 12-6 weekdays.
❀◐⇌(Ladywell)

Watch House ✔
198-204 Lewisham High Street, SE13 6JP
⏲ 10-11; 12-10.30 Sun
☎ (020) 8318 3136
Courage Directors; Greene King Abbot; Shepherd Neame Spitfire; guest beers Ⓗ
Large Wetherspoon's outlet in its original style located in the shopping area and popular with a wide-ranging clientele; it is often busy, particularly on Saturday afternoon. Wooden partitions and seating on different levels help to break up the large floor area and avoid the warehouse effect. The pub is named after Watch House Green, the original village green. The usual good value food is available, together with a range of guest beers.
◐◑♿⇌⊖⚟

SE15: Peckham

Gowlett
62 Gowlett Road, SE15 4HY
⏲ 11 (12 Fri & Sat)-11; 12-10.30 Sun
☎ (020) 7635 7048
Adnams Bitter; guest beers Ⓗ
Stylishly renovated pub; a welcome addition to the area. The wood-panelled interior, large windows and sofas give it a contemporary feel. 'Chilled' background music and occasional DJs playing laid-back music make it a popular place for the younger set. Ale fans have three regularly-changing guest beers. Home-made stone-baked pizzas are served on Saturday and Sunday and the wine is of the organic, vegetarian variety. Children are welcome until 9pm. It was South-East London CAMRA's Pub of the Year 2005.
❀◐◑♿⇌(Peckham Rye) ♣

SE16: Rotherhithe

Blacksmith's Arms ✔
257 Rotherhithe Street, SE16 5EJ
⏲ 12-11; 12-10.30 Sun
☎ (020) 7237 1349
Adnams Broadside; Fuller's London Pride, ESB Ⓗ
The Blacksmith's Arms is often described as the Village Pub. Regulars include people who have lived in the area forever and new residents moving into the upmarket apartments and houses, who quickly feel at home in this friendly pub. It has traditional wood panelling, low ceilings and a mock-Tudor black and white frontage. A plaque on the side of the bar shows the level of the floodwater in 1928. It stands next to the Holiday Inn and close to the Isle of Dogs ferry crossing, convenient for the 225 bus route. Sunday lunch is served. ❀◑ ⊖♣

SE18: Woolwich

Prince Albert (Rose's Free House)
49 Hare Street, SE18 6NE (near Woolwich Ferry)
⏲ 11-11; 12-3 (closed eve) Sun
☎ (020) 8854 1538
Beer range varies Ⓗ
This fantastic free house used to be owned by EJ Rose and Co. many moons ago – hence the nickname. A superb place to try changing beers in a friendly atmosphere. Filled rolls, available at most times, are excellent value and the

customers are often heard to complain about the lack of bread around the generous fillings. Good value B&B is also offered if you have one too many or just don't fancy catching that last bus home. Q ⇌ (Woolwich Arsenal)

SE19: Crystal Palace

Railway Bell

14 Cawnpore Street, SE19 1PF

12-11; 12-10.30 Sun

☎ (020) 8670 2844

Young's Bitter, Special, seasonal beers Ⓗ

Built in 1865 and a Young's house since 1885, this comfortable, friendly local lies not far from Crystal Palace Park. It is decorated with railway pictures and posters, numerous miniature bottles and ornamental teapots. A homely atmosphere prevails here and children are welcome until 7pm. It boasts an award-winning patio garden. Food is served 12-3 and 6-8pm; 1-5pm on Sunday. ⇌ (Gipsy Hill) ♣

SE20: Penge

Moon & Stars

164-166 High Street, SE20 7QS

10-11; 12-10.30 Sun

☎ (020) 8776 5680

Courage Directors; De Koninck Ambrée; Greene King Abbot; Hop Back Summer Lightning; Marston's Burton Bitter, Pedigree; guest beers Ⓗ

Purpose-built Wetherspoon's of some character, attracting a diverse range of customers and offering the best value and choice of beers for miles (usually five or six guests from independents). The spacious interior comprises an L-shaped front bar dominated by an imperious lion statue and a raised rear section with much wood panelling, with numerous tables and more private alcoves throughout. Meals range from breakfasts to all-day Sunday roasts. A patio garden and tables are at the rear. Q ⇌ (Penge E/Clock House) ⊖ (Beckenham Rd Tramlink) P ⅍

SE22: East Dulwich

Herne Tavern ☆

2 Forest Hill Road, SE22 0RR

11-11; 12-10.30 Sun

☎ (020) 8299 9521

Courage Best Bitter, Directors Ⓗ

Handy for Peckham Rye, this attractive two-bar, wood-panelled pub with notable architectural features is listed in CAMRA's London Regional Inventory. It draws a good local following, with customers of all ages. TV sport is shown in the smaller bar. A quiz is held on Thursday evening. The pub has a popular, large garden, and is dog-friendly. Children are welcome until 9pm; meals are served 12-8pm. Regular No. 63 and 363 buses stop close by.

♣

SE23: Forest Hill

Blythe Hill Tavern ☆

319 Stanstead Road, SE23 1JB

11-11; 12-10.30 Sun

☎ (020) 8690 5176

Courage Best Bitter; Fuller's London Pride; guest beer Ⓗ

Lovely, proper Irish pub on the South Circular, but don't let that location put you off, as once inside you could be many miles away. There are three separate rooms, some with TV showing sport and, at the back, a decent-sized garden. It hosts a quiz on Monday and a good Irish traditional music session on Thursday evening. Toasted sandwiches are available at lunchtime. ⇌ (Catford/Catford Bridge)

Capitol

11-21 London Road, SE23 3TW

10-11; 12-10.30 Sun

☎ (020) 8291 8921

Marston's Pedigree; guest beers Ⓗ

Large Wetherspoon converted from a cinema, combining modern decor with many of the original features. The large bar at the back provides a sense of being on stage, as you look back up at the old cinema circle. Below this, the room offers a selection of seating; from open areas to cosy, semi-circular booths. It opens at 10am for breakfast. ⇌ ⅍

SE25: South Norwood

Alliance

91 High Street, SE25 6EA

11-11; 12-10.30 Sun

☎ (020) 8653 3604

Courage Best Bitter; Greene King Abbot; guest beers Ⓗ

Corner pub dating from 1864, bearing an unspoilt exterior. Standing opposite the clock tower, it is close to the shops and station. The L-shaped bar is comfortable and features much brass and copperware and pictures of old Norwood. Very much a locals' pub for beer and conversation, it can become busy with football supporters travelling to and from Crystal Palace. No food is served. Two guest ales from micro-breweries are always available.

⇌ (Norwood Jct) ♣

SE26: Sydenham

Dulwich Wood House

39 Sydenham Hill, SE26 6RS

12-11; 12-10.30 Sun

☎ (020) 8693 5666

Young's Bitter, Special, seasonal beers Ⓗ

Popular, large and comfortable pub that serves excellent food (no meals Sun eve). It was designed as a private residence in 1857 by Sir Joseph Paxton, the architect of the nearby Crystal Palace, home of the Great Exhibition in 1851. In summer there are barbecues in the garden and an outside bar. Located in a leafy part of south-east London, it was awarded a certificate for 25 years in the Good Beer Guide in 2004. Wheelchair access is via the garden. Q ⇌ (Sydenham Hill) ♣ P ⅍

Addiscombe

Claret Free House

5a Bingham Corner, Lower Addiscombe Road, CR0 7AA (on A222, W of tram crossing)

11.30 (11 Sat)-11; 12-10.30 Sun

☎ (020) 8656 7452 website: www.claretfreehouse.co.uk

Beer range varies Ⓗ
Small, privately-owned free house in an attractive shopping parade. The changing ales are mainly sourced from small breweries. Good public transport helps to attract drinkers from far and wide, joining a dedicated band of locals. The house beer is Palmer IPA; cider is brought up from the cellar. Two TVs mean it gets busy during televised sporting events, but Croydon CAMRA's Pub of the Year 2004 is rarely empty. Buses 289, 312 and 494 and trams stop close by. ⊖(Tramlink) ♣●

Bexley

Black Horse
63 Albert Road, DA5 1NT
11.30-11; 12-4, 7-10.30 Sun
☎ (01322) 523371
Courage Best Bitter; Daleside Shrimpers; guest beer Ⓗ
Friendly, back-street local, worth finding. Good value lunches are served in comfortable, uncrowded surroundings. The front and left part of the open-plan bar houses the dartboard; the right side offers a smaller, more intimate, area with bar, which leads to the garden. The pub supports a golf society. The publican aims to put on a different beer every time a barrel runs out: a noble ambition. ❀◑⇌

Old Wick
9 Vicarage Road, DA5 2AL
12-11; 12-10.30 Sun
☎ (01322) 524185
Shepherd Neame Master Brew Best Bitter, Spitfire, seasonal beers Ⓗ
Excellent pub on the road from Bexley Village to Dartford. It changed its name from the Rising Sun in 1996. The welcoming, cosy interior is enhanced by subdued lighting and friendly, knowledgeable staff. It benefits from a regular, local clientele, but has a no dogs rule, presumably to avoid upsetting the resident dog and cat. A rare outlet for Shepherd Neame Porter in season, it always has special meal deals. ♨❀◑◗⇌♣P

Bexleyheath

Robin Hood & Little John
78 Lion Road, DA6 8PF
11-3, 5.30 (7 Sat)-11; 12-4, 7-10.30 Sun
☎ (020) 8303 1128
Adnams Bitter; Brains Rev James; Brakspear Bitter; Fuller's London Pride; Harveys BB; guest beers Ⓗ
A warm welcome awaits at this excellent little back-street pub, dating from the 1830s when it sat amid fields and farms. Eight real ales are stocked. It enjoys a well-earned reputation for home-cooked lunches (not served Sun), with themed specials and regular Italian pasta dishes. Eat at tables converted from old Singer sewing machines at this regular CAMRA award-winner. Over 21s only are admitted. ❀◑

Rose
179 Broadway, DA6 7ES (opp. Christ Church)
11-11; 12-10.30 Sun
☎ (020) 8303 3846
Adnams Broadside; Greene King IPA; Harveys BB; Tetley Bitter Ⓗ
Double bay-windowed building, conveniently located on the main shopping street. A small U-shaped bar is surrounded by comfortable stools and bench seating. A small drinking area outside at the front and patio at the rear add to its appeal. Good lunches include daily specials (not served Sun). Over 21s only are admitted. Watch Sky sports here. ❀◑

Royal Oak (Polly Clean Stairs)
Mount Road, DA6 8JS
11-3, 6-11; 11-11 Sat; 12-3, 7-10.30 Sun
☎ (020) 8303 4454
Courage Best Bitter; Fuller's London Pride; guest beers Ⓗ
Highly attractive brick and weatherboarded pub, once the village store, which has managed to keep its rural character, despite being overtaken by 1930s housing. The country charm continues inside with cosy seating areas and plates and tankards adorning the walls and ceiling. The nickname derives from a house-proud landlady who used to wash the front steps every day. Lunchtime snacks (not served Sun) are prepared to order. Children are allowed in the garden. The pub is on the B13 bus route. Q❀P

Yacht
167 Long Lane, DA7 5AE
11-11; 12-10.30 Sun
☎ (020) 8303 4889
Courage Best Bitter, Directors; Shepherd Neame Spitfire; guest beer (occasional) Ⓗ
Popular, spacious roadhouse that opened in 1938, and is now a Steak and Ale pub. Converted to one bar, it has dedicated areas for sports fans (TVs and pool tables), families, smokers and non-smokers. A big garden contains a children's play area. Quality food is available all day, with steaks a speciality, plus pub favourites, a children's menu, Sunday lunches and specials. The No. 401 bus stops nearby. ❀◑◗♿P

Bromley

Bitter End (off-licence)
139 Masons Hill, BR2 9HW
12-3 (not Mon), 5-10 (9 Mon); 11-10 Sat; 12-2, 7-9 Sun
☎ (020) 8466 6083 website: www.thebitterend.biz
Beer range varies Ⓖ
Just the job, whether you simply fancy a couple of pints at home or are planning a party or larger function. This off-licence keeps a good selection of beers and ciders and, given a little notice, polypins and firkins can be obtained from a range of over 500 beers. It stocks an interesting choice of British and imported bottled beers (some bottle-conditioned). Glasses and equipment can be hired or loaned. ⇌(South)

Bricklayers Arms
143 Masons Hill, BR2 9HY
11-3, 5.30 (7 Sat)-11; 12-3, 7-10.30 Sun
☎ (020) 8460 4552
Shepherd Neame Master Brew Bitter, Spitfire, Bishops Finger, seasonal beers Ⓗ
This traditional, pleasant, comfortable local is situated right on the main A21 road. It has recently been extended and refurbished and

offers tasty bar meals weekdays, and a good Sunday roast. A past Shepherd Neame Pub of the Year, it benefits from a patio garden. ❀◑⇌(South)

Bromley Labour Club

HG Wells Centre, St Marks Road, BR2 9HG

11-11, 12-10.30 Sun

☎ (020) 8460 7409

Shepherd Neame Master Brew Bitter; guest beer Ⓗ

This former CAMRA South-East London Club of the Year is a friendly community club with one main bar and a function room (with its own bar). A few minutes' walk from the bustling town centre, it has a good seating area, plus pool table and darts; a perfect place to escape the shopping crowds. ❀♿⇌(South) P

Partridge ✓

194 Bromley High Street, BR1 1HE

11-11, 12-10.30 Sun

☎ (020) 8464 7656

Fuller's London Pride, ESB, seasonal beers Ⓗ

High quality bank conversion that still retains its grand feel. It is popular with a wide range of customers. The main bar shows live sports on a number of TV screens, while club and dining rooms allow for peace and quiet. A good range of Fuller's bottled beers is stocked. ◑◐⇌(North/South)

Red Lion

10 North Road, BR1 3LG

11-11, 12-10.30 Sun

☎ (020) 8460 2691

Greene King IPA, Abbot; Harveys BB; guest beers Ⓗ

Popular, welcoming pub in the back streets near Bromley North Station. It was taken over by Greene King when they bought the Beard's pub company, but continues to serve two guest ales, with a huge collection of pump clips around the bar testifying to the number of beers that have featured. The interior is in traditional style with some original tiling and a large collection of books. The TV is used for major sporting events but does not dominate. Evening meals are served until 7pm. Q❀◑◐⇌(North)♣

Bromley Common

Bird in Hand

62 Gravel Road, BR2 8PF (short walk from Bromley bus garage on A21)

11-11; 12-10.30 Sun

☎ (020) 8462 1083

Courage Best Bitter; Fuller's London Pride; Greene King IPA; guest beers Ⓗ

A favourite local where horse racing and football are followed avidly on TV. Originally a Stile and Wynch tied house, with a traditional wood-panelled bar, this friendly, busy, back-street pub serves home-cooked lunches in the dining area. Q❀

Two Doves

37 Oakley Road, BR2 8HD

12-3, 5.30 (5 Mon & Fri; 6 Sat)-11; 12-3, 7-10.30 Sun

☎ (020) 8462 1627

Young's Bitter, Special, Winter Warmer Ⓗ

Now part of Young's estate, this community local has retained the features that have made it so popular. A cheerful façade boasts notable floral-design leaded-light windows. A friendly welcome in the company of a mostly mature clientele provides for a civilised atmosphere. The tranquil rear conservatory leads into a garden haven, festooned with flowers. Opening hours may be extended in summer. Occasional sports events are shown on TV and quiz nights held. A limited lunchtime menu is served. Q❀◑♣⚟

Chelsfield

Bo Peep

Hewitts Road, BR6 7QL

11-2.30, 6-11; 12-11 Sat; 12-10.30 Sun

☎ (01959) 534457

Courage Best Bitter, Directors; Greene King IPA Ⓗ

Dating back to the 16th century, this mainly brick, flint and clay tiled pub used to be called the White Hart, as can be seen from two surviving etched window panes. Customers are attracted from miles around by the extensive, imaginative menu, served in the bar and cosy restaurant. Bus R3 stops outside. ❀◑◐P

Chislehurst

Bull's Head

Royal Parade, BR7 6NR

11-11; 12-10.30 Sun

☎ (020) 8467 1727

Young's Bitter, Special, Winter Wamer Ⓗ

Impressive, creeper-clad hotel, comfortably furnished throughout, particularly the smart lounge bar. Much wood-panelling and subtle lighting results in a cosy atmosphere. Meals include a Sunday carvery in the ballroom (no food Sun eve) and summer barbecues. Children are welcome in the no-smoking lounge until 6.30pm. Terrestrial TV sports are shown in the public bar. Wedding guests, salsa dancers and blood donors can leave the function room and head for the bars for a well-deserved drink. Q❀◑◐P⚟

Croydon

Beer Circus

282 High Street, CR0 1NG

12-11; 6-10.30 (closed lunchtime) Sun

☎ (07910) 095945 website: www.thebeercircus.co.uk

Dark Star Hophead; guest beers Ⓗ

Genuine free house that is a welcome addition to Croydon. This specialist beer bar serves up to three real ales from local micro-breweries, four regular foreign beers, two guests on draught and two real ciders. The friendly staff and regulars can help you choose from the extensive menu of over 250 foreign bottled beers. Good value, beer-related food is served weekdays. Dutch shuffleboard can be played in the downstairs bar. Occasional beer and cider festivals are held at Croydon CAMRA's Pub of the Year 2005. Q◑♣●

Dog & Bull

24 Surrey Street, CR0 1RG

(off High St, behind Grants multiplex)

11-11; 12-10.30 Sun
(020) 8667 9718
Young's Bitter, Special, Winter Warmer, seasonal beers H
Splendid local at the heart of Croydon's famous Surrey Street market, which has Royal Charter status; Prince Charles visited the pub in the 1990s. It probably has the best pub garden in central Croydon (no dogs allowed). Parts of the pub date from the 18th century. Lively and full of character especially at weekends, it serves good quality food at lunchtime when the front area becomes no-smoking. The famous Beanos secondhand record store is nearby in Middle Street. ❀ⅎ⇌(East/West) ⊖(George St/Church St Tramlink) ⅟

Porter & Sorter ✔

Billington Hill, CR0 6BT (left out of station and left down hill)
11-11; 12-10.30 Sun
(020) 8688 4296
Fuller's London Pride; Hogs Back TEA; Marston's Burton Bitter, Pedigree; Young's Special; guest beer H
Tucked between the station and the sorting office, this externally interesting building was originally built in 1880 as the Station Hotel. Renamed in 1971 and later extended, it is hugely popular with commuters and local workers. Noisy, with large TVs and piped music, but the management shows a strong commitment to traditional quality products. The beer range may increase with guest beers. Food is served all day. A small patio allows for outside drinking.
❀ⅎ◗♿⇌(East) ⊖(Tramlink) ⅟

Princess Royal

22 Longley Road, CR0 3LH (off A213/A235)
12-3.30, 5.30-11; 12-11 Fri; 12-3.30 Sun
(020) 8689 7862
Adnams Broadside; Banks's Original; Fuller's London Pride; Greene King IPA, Abbot H
Brought back to life by new management, this genuine local is also known as the Glue Pot. Secluded from the bustle of Croydon, it has a welcoming, friendly atmosphere enhanced by the coal-effect fire. A good range of home cooking includes popular Sunday lunches. The garden is ideal for relaxing in good weather. It is well-stocked, featuring a pergola, climbing honeysuckle and a Koi carp pond. The pub fields a darts team.
❀ⅎ◗⇌(West)

Royal Standard ✔

1 Sheldon Street, CR0 1SS (behind Wandle Road car park by flyover)
11-11; 12-10.30 Sun
(020) 8688 9749
Fuller's Chiswick, London Pride, ESB, seasonal beers H
Excellent back-street local, virtually under the flyover and behind the ugly multi-storey car park. It can get crowded early evenings, with the 'suited' brigade, but attracts a more cosmopolitan clientele later in the evening and at weekends. The garden by the flyover allows you to watch the traffic whistle by. Regulars are keen on rugby union, with most games shown. A cricket bat signed by the 2002 Surrey team (after playing at nearby Whitgift School) takes pride of place in the bar. ❀ⅎ⇌(East/West) ⊖(George St/Church St Tramlink) ♣

Ship ✔

47 High Street, CR0 1QD
11-11; 12-10.30 Sun
(020) 8688 2810 website: www.theship.org.uk
Banks's Bitter; Marston's Pedigree; Shepherd Neame Spitfire; Young's Bitter; guest beers H
Grade II listed building at the centre of Croydon, one of Wolverhampton and Dudley's Wizard Inns. The interior is designed to resemble an old sailing ship. This friendly pub is quiet during the day, serving excellent home-cooked food until 7pm (3pm Sun). It gets lively in the evenings when DJs play a variety of rock and alternative music, six nights a week; Monday is quiz night. Occasional fancy dress theme nights are staged for charity.
ⅎ⇌(East/West) ⊖(George St Tramlink)

Ship of Fools ✔

9-11 London Road, CR0 2RE (on A235, opp. W Croydon station)
11-11; 12-10.30 Sun
(020) 8681 2835
Hop Back Summer Lightning; Marston's Burton Bitter, Pedigree; guest beers H
Large, bustling town-centre Wetherspoon's, with an imposing Victorian façade. The entrance, with bare boards, leads to a carpeted smoke-free area at the rear. The all-day Sunday roasts, Tuesday steak club and Thursday's curry club are popular with diners; children eat for free, two per adult. Belgian and Czech bottled beers are stocked, plus Westons cider. This friendly pub hosts seasonal beer festivals, and has five rotating guest ales; a must for thirsty shoppers and commuters.
Qⅎ◗♿⇌(West) ⊖(Tramlink) ⅟

Skylark ✔

34-36 South End, CR0 1DP
11-11; 12-10.30 Sun
(020) 8649 9909
Courage Directors; Greene King Abbot; Hop Back Summer Lightning; Marston's Pedigree; Shepherd Neame Spitfire; guest beers H
The 1990s conversion of a former gym and health club has created a spacious pub on two floors. The usual Wetherspoon's decor commemorates the former Croydon Airport and other aspects of local interest. Meals are served until 10pm; children are allowed in with diners until 6pm in the two no-smoking areas downstairs. Upstairs is a second bar, more seating and three large screens for showing sport. A jazz ensemble plays on Sunday lunchtime in the lower bar.
Q❀ⅎ◗♿⇌(South) ⅟

Farnborough

Woodman

High Street, BR6 7BA
11-11; 12-10.30 Sun
(01689) 852563
Shepherd Neame Master Brew Bitter, Spitfire, Bishops Finger, seasonal beers H
A real community local, this friendly village hostelry caters for all ages. Food is excellent

value and goes down easily with a pint of Shepherd Neame. A welcoming pub, the garden provides a nice place to relax in the summer.
Q❀◑P

Locksbottom

Olde Whyte Lion

Farnborough Common, BR6 8NE (on A21 next to hospital)
⏲ 11-11; 12-10.30 Sun
☎ (01689) 852631
Shepherd Neame Master Brew Bitter, Spitfire, seasonal beers Ⓗ
Bright, comfortable, friendly local on the main road. This large pub, divided into different areas, includes a spacious dining room. The garden at the back is pleasant in the summer. This cosy establishment offers a good range of beers brewed in Kent. ⅏❀◑♿P

North Cray

White Cross

146 North Cray Road, DA14 5EL (access is off northbound carriageway)
⏲ 11-11; 12-10.30 Sun
☎ (020) 8300 2590
Courage Best Bitter, Directors; guest beers Ⓗ
A survivor of the dual carriageway development of the 1960s, the pub was known as the Red Cross from 1730 until 1935. The front bar bears an impressive array of copper and brass utensils; this is where the locals gather. The pub is popular for food, particularly at lunchtime, and meals are served all day at the weekend. The guest beer is always something interesting. The pub is on the No. 492 bus route. Q❀◑P

Orpington

Cricketers

93 Chislehurst Road, BR6 0DQ
⏲ 12-3, 5-11; 12-11 Sat; 12-10.30 Sun
☎ (01689) 812648
Adnams Bitter, Broadside; Wadworth 6X; guest beer Ⓗ
Family-run local that has demonstrated a commitment to good quality real ale for many years, offering a homely atmosphere to those who venture the few minutes' walk from the High Street. It provides a pleasant diversion after a hard day's work or a dog walk on Broomhill Common. An attractive wisteria-covered patio and garden lie to the rear beyond a sizeable family/games rooom. A retractable screen for terrestrial TV sports events and a juke box are added attractions in the front bar. ♉❀♣P⚟

Petts Wood

Sovereign of the Seas

Queensway, BR5 1DG
⏲ 10-11; 10-10.30 Sun
☎ (01689) 891606
Greene King Abbot; Marston's Burton Bitter, Pedigree; Shepherd Neame Spitfire; guest beers Ⓗ
Smaller than the usual Wetherspoons but maintaining high standards, the pub features wood-panelled walls and local history. Various seating arrangements including alcoves, allow an intimate atmosphere. There is a garden at the back of the pub for outdoor drinking.
Q❀◑♿⇄⚟

Pratt's Bottom

Bull's Head

Rushmore Hill, BR6 7NQ
⏲ 11-11; 12-10.30 Sun
☎ (01689) 852553
Beer range varies Ⓗ
This 16th-century, former coaching inn faces the village green. After many years of uninspired management, a thriving local has emerged under an enterprising new landlord. Ramblers, children and dogs are all welcome. It comprises three distinct bar areas, plus a small no-smoking restaurant. Good value, home-cooked food is available until 8pm every day. Three guest beers are sourced from independent breweries. The large enclosed garden has bat and trap in summer and indoor board games are available. It stands on No. R5 bus route. ❀◑P

Purley

Foxley Hatch ✔

8-9 Russell Hill Parade, Russell Hill Road, CR8 2LE (on one-way system near Purley Cross)
⏲ 11-11; 10-10.30 sun
☎ (020) 8763 9307
Greene King Abbot; Marston's Burton Bitter, Pedigree; guest beers Ⓗ
Small Wetherspoon's where a strong commitment to real beers is demonstrated by the growing display of pump clips around the bar. Five or six changing guest beers come from a variety of independents, and a real cider is usually stocked at this friendly local. Helpful staff help attract a broad range of drinkers of all ages – something to be applauded. Display boards highlight local history and characters, and the usual Wetherspoon's menu is served.
Q◑♿⇄●⚟

St Pauls Cray

Bull Inn

Main Road, BR5 3HS
⏲ 11-11; 12-10.30 Sun
☎ (01689) 821642
Flowers Original; Greene King Old Speckled Hen; Shepherd Neame Master Brew Bitter Ⓗ
Partly-weatherboarded 18th-century, two-bar pub near the Cray River, popular with locals as well as customers from the neighbouring offices and golf courses. The cosy saloon bar has a no-smoking area for drinkers and diners; disabled access is via Sandy Lane into this bar. Food is served until 2.45pm. The main road has no restrictions on parking. ⅏❀◐⊟♿⚟

Shirley

Orchard

116 Orchard Way, CR0 7NN (between A232 and A214 on corner of Radnor Walk)
⏲ 12-11; 12-10.30 Sun
☎ (020) 8777 9011
Harveys BB; Fuller's London Pride; guest beer (occasional) Ⓗ
Modern, open-plan local with private alcoves in

the Monk's Orchard district of Shirley. Sky sports compete with more traditional pub games such as darts and cribbage – the pub is in the local league. A keen pricing policy is in force at one of Croydon's few genuine free houses. The nearest tramstop is Arena (three-quarters of a mile); the No. 367 bus stops in the Glade, a 10-minute walk away. Look out for the cedar tree that conceals the pub. ◐♣P

Sidcup

Alma

10 Alma Road, DA14 4EA
11-2.30, 5.30 (6 Sat)-11; 11-11 Fri; 12-3, 7-10.30 Sun
☎ (020) 8300 3208
Courage Best Bitter; Fuller's London Pride; Shepherd Neame Spitfire H
Back-street local, near Sidcup Station, popular with commuters recovering from their journey home. The pub dates from 1868 when it was called the Railway Tavern. In 1897 a large billiards room was added, now used for functions. It has a fair-sized garden that is popular in summer. The interior retains some of its Victorian character; a designated bar area is used for games. Lunches are served on weekdays. Parking is limited. Q ❀◐⇌♣P

Portrait

7 Elm Parade, Main Road, DA14 6NF
11-11; 12-10.30 Sun
☎ (020) 8302 8757
Fuller's London Pride; Greene King Old Speckled Hen; guest beers H
Barracuda Group pub, converted from retail premises. Drinking areas on two levels provide a choice of booths and open-plan seating. Becoming popular with diners, special meal and drink deals are offered. The evening customers are mainy young, but the atmosphere is friendly. Guest beers at the time of survey were supplied by Fuller's and Archers. ◐◑

Thornton Heath

Lord Napier

111 Beulah Road, CR7 8JG (off B273)
12-11; 12-10.30 Sun
☎ (020) 8653 2286
Young's Bitter, Special H
Excellent revival of this famous jazz pub by the friendly landlord and his staff has resulted in a good local following. The large bar and music room bear distinctive jazz-related murals. Jazz is played on Sunday lunchtime and Thursday evening, with a 16-piece big band on the first and third Thursday of the month. The music room is used for pool during non-music sessions. Good value Sunday lunch is the only food provided. ⚞❀⇌♣

Upper Belvedere

Fox

79 Nuxley Road, DA17 5JU
11-11; 12-10.30 Sun
☎ (01322) 435557
Courage Best Bitter; Sharp's Special H
This building, which dates from 1853, was given a facelift in 1921 creating an attractive, bold appearance. The interior is one large, L-shaped bar with plentiful seating. Meals are served daily between 11 and 5pm. A children's playground is to the rear of the pub. Occasional live music is staged on Saturday. ❀◐

Victoria ✓

2 Victoria Street, DA17 5LN
11-11; 12-10.30 Sun
☎ (01322) 433773
Adnams Bitter; Shepherd Neame Spitfire; guest beer H
Cheery, back-street local run in a traditional manner. A cosy horseshoe-shaped bar displays sporting memorabilia on one side and old local photographs on the other. The leaded windows warrant a close look. A pleasant outside drinking area is ideal for summer evenings. ❀◐♣

SOUTH-WEST LONDON

SW1: Belgravia

Duke of Wellington

63 Eaton Terrace, SW1W 8TR
11-11; 12-10.30 Sun
☎ (020) 7730 1782
Shepherd Neame Master Brew Bitter, Spitfire, Bishops Finger H
Built in 1862 and named after the title of Arthur Wellesley to celebrate the Battle of Waterloo, the pub, a former Whitbread house, is now owned by Shepherd Neame of Faversham and is popular with customers from all walks of life. The pub is carpeted, with a central bar and Sky TV, which is always at a low volume, allowing for conversation and to catch up with the headlines in the newspapers. This is a dog-friendly pub. ◐◑⊖(Sloane Square)

Horse & Groom

7 Groom Place, SW1X 7BA
11-11; closed Sat & Sun
☎ (020) 7235 6980
Shepherd Neame Master Brew Bitter, Spitfire H
Licensed in 1846 as a beer house, this pub, until recently owned by Greene King, is now part of Shepherd Neame, which owns several outlets in the area. Small and compact, and hidden down a mews, it is frequented by a loyal band of regulars and embassy staff all enjoying an atmosphere redolent of a rural pub. The pub can be booked for functions at the weekend.
◐◑⊖(Hyde Pk Corner)

Nag's Head

53 Kinnerton Street, SW1X 8ED
11-11; 12-10.30 Sun
☎ (020) 7235 1135
Adnams Bitter, Broadside, seasonal beers H
Dating from circa 1833, this pub boasts the lowest bar counter in London and is full of collectibles, including a 'what the butler saw' slot machine. The pub attracts locals, tourists and celebrities to its cosy atmosphere. There is a downstairs back bar where more seating can be found. Food is served all day until 9.30pm. The use of mobile phones is discouraged.
⚞Q◐◑⊖(Hyde Pk Corner/Knightsbridge)

Star Tavern ✓

6 Belgrave Mews West, SW1X 8HT
11-11; 12-10.30 Sun

☎ (020) 7235 3019
Fuller's Chiswick, London Pride, ESB, seasonal beers Ⓗ
Small, one-bar, back-street pub, just off busy Knightsbridge. This carpeted pub, dating back to 1826, has a central dividing bookcase and two small snugs. The lower back room can be booked for functions. The pub has received many floral awards; photographs on the back bar show hanging basket displays as well as a rare London heavy snow scene.
⊖ (Knightsbridge/Hyde Pk Corner)

SW1: Pimlico

Morpeth Arms
58 Millbank, SW1P 4RW
11-11; 12-10.30 Sun
☎ (020) 7834 6442
Young's Bitter, Special, seasonal beers Ⓗ
Small, rather smoky Victorian bar, plus a back bar and upstairs dining room/private room for hire. Look out for some good glass, 19th-century prints and photos, and an interesting history of the pub that stood near the old Millbank prison. It is now convenient for the Tate Gallery and MI6. A simple one-choice supper is served in the evening. A few seats are provided outside on the pavement if you can stand the roar of traffic along Millbank. Q ⇌ (Vauxhall) ⊖

SW1: Victoria

Cask & Glass
39 Palace Street, SW1E 5HN
11-11; 12-8 Sat; closed Sun
☎ (020) 7834 7630
Shepherd Neame Master Brew Bitter, Best Bitter, Spitfire Ⓗ
First licensed in 1862 as a beer house, the pub used to serve beer only in half-pints. Now owned by Shepherd Neame, this is the smallest pub in Westminster, noted for its attractive floral display at the front. Inside, the small pub appears roomy, with upholstered bench seating. Caricatures of political figures and model aeroplanes decorate the bar. The TV in one corner is mainy turned low, and is used by the locals for racing fixtures. ⇌ ⊖ ♣

Jugged Hare
172 Vauxhall Bridge Road, SW1V 1DX
12-11; 12-10.30 Sun
☎ (020) 7828 1543
Fuller's Chiswick, London Pride, ESB, seasonal beers Ⓗ
Formerly a NatWest bank and now a Fuller's Ale and Pie house, this pub is more of a local's bar than a venue for business types. It is situated in a partly residential and shopping area with Tachbrook Street market nearby. The decor is in the usual Ale and Pie house style with chandeliers and an upstairs balcony seating area that can be booked for functions. The no-smoking area at the back of the pub used to be the bank manager's office.
⇌ ⊖ (Pimlico/Victoria)

SW1: Westminster

Buckingham Arms
62 Petty France, SW1H 9EU
11-11 (5.30 Sat); 12-5.30 Sun
☎ (020) 7222 3386
Young's Bitter, Special, seasonal beers Ⓗ
Well-deserved regular Guide entry: a large main bar with tables and benches at the back and a drinking corridor (with TV) where the servants could drink out of sight of their masters. The usual pub prints are enlivened by an amusing note as to how the bar staff like to be treated. At 10pm you can listen to the Last Post or a lament from Wellington Barracks opposite.
⊖ (St James's Pk)

Royal Oak
2 Regency Street, SW1P 4BZ
11-11; closed Sat; 12-4 Sun
☎ (020) 7834 7046
Young's Bitter, Special, seasonal beers Ⓗ
Former Watney's house, this local was nearly demolished when the building adjoining the pub was redeveloped. The pub has been radically rebuilt by Young's with an open-plan interior, satellite tables and stools, clear windows and a smaller bar. One side of the pub has more comfortable bench seating where customers can have an intimate chat. Outside by the taxi rank, spot the Grade II listed gents' lavatory.
⇌ (Victoria) ⊖ (St James's Pk)

Sanctuary House Hotel ✔
33 Tothill Street, SW1H 9LA
11-11; 12-10.30 Sun
☎ (020) 7799 4044 website: www.sanctuaryhousehotel.com
Fuller's Chiswick, London Pride, ESB, seasonal beers Ⓗ
Situated on the site of a monastery and formerly the MI5 offices during WWII, this is now a 34-bedroom hotel and pub offering sanctuary for tourists and business people relaxing after experiencing the hectic pace of London life. The pub offers good beer and food from the large bar where a raised seating area has a frieze depicting monks working the land before building development destroyed the marshland where the pub stands. ♿ ⊖ (St James's Pk)

Speaker ✔
46 Great Peter Street, SW1P 2HA
12-11; closed Sat; 12-4 Sun
☎ (020) 7222 1749
Gale's HSB; Shepherd Neame Spitfire; Young's Bitter; guest beer Ⓗ
Formerly the Elephant and Castle and first licensed in the 19th century, this popular, small, street-corner pub attracts a mix of locals and office workers. In close proximity to the seat of government, there are caricatures of past and present politicians on the walls and a photograph of Betty Boothroyd, recent Speaker of the House of Commons. As with most local pubs it has a division bell to call the MPs back to the house. Q ⊖ (St James's Pk)

SW4: Clapham

Windmill on the Common
Clapham Common South Side, SW4 9DE
11-11; 12-10.30 Sun
☎ (020) 8673 4578
Young's Bitter, Special, seasonal beer Ⓗ
A Clapham institution, a pub has stood on this site since 1665, although the current buildings

are Victorian. The pub is spacious in a cool 1920s style, with a conservatory that doubles as a function room. A popular quiz is held on Sunday evening. The pub gets busy at weekends and in the summer. This pub features as the Pontefract Castle in Graham Greene's novel The End of The Affair. The full range of Young's bottled beers is stocked.
♛Q♨❀⇌◑◐⊟♿⊖(Common/South) P⊬

SW6: Parsons Green

White Horse ✔

1-3 Parsons Green, SW6 4UL

⏲ 11-11; 12-10.30 Sun

☎ (020) 7736 2115 website: www.whitehorsesw6.com

Adnams Broadside; Fuller's ESB; Harveys BB; Oakham JHB; Rooster's Yankee; guest beers Ⓗ

This is a special pub for beer enthusiasts and is well worth going out of your way to visit. It hosts regular beer festivals and stocks many specialist foreign beers. Good food is served in the bars and in the small (no-smoking) restaurant at the back. Nicknamed by regulars as the Sloany Pony, it is always busy and can be crowded at weekends. ♛❀◑◐⊖

SW7: South Kensington

Anglesea Arms ✔

15 Selwood Terrace, SW7 3QG

⏲ 11-11; 12-10.30 Sun

☎ (020) 7373 7960

Adnams Bitter, Broadside; Brakspear Bitter; Fuller's London Pride; Young's Bitter; guest beers Ⓗ

One of the few free houses in London to sell real ale in CAMRA's early days, it was built in 1827 and licensed in 1829. Later tied to Meux for more than 100 years, it became free and was subsequently bought by Maxwell Joseph's Taverns. The traditional, wood-panelled pub is adorned with pictures in oils and various photos. Meals are served all day in the no-smoking dining room, and the bar menu changes regularly. Q❀◑◐⊖⊬

SW8: South Lambeth

Mawbey Arms

7 Mawbey Street, SW8 2TT

⏲ 11-11; 12-10.30 Sun

☎ (020) 7622 1936

Shepherd Neame Master Brew Bitter; Young's Bitter; guest beer Ⓗ

Listed, friendly, family-run pub, a South London local where customers are known for impromptu singalongs. A few years ago it was given a major refurbishment. Regulars play cribbage and darts, and four darts teams meet at the pub. It gets busy at weekends, especially for televised sports.
❀◑⇌(Vauxhall) ⊖(Stockwell/Vauxhall) ♣P

Priory Arms ✔

83 Lansdowne Way, SW8 2PB

⏲ 11-11; 12-10.30 Sun

☎ (020) 7622 1884 website: www.priory-arms.com

Adnams Bitter; Harveys BB; Hop Back Summer Lightning; guest beers Ⓗ

This remains a genuine free house despite a change of ownership. Regulars and visitors will still find two constantly-changing guest beers from micro-breweries, plus a large choice of foreign bottled beers and real cider. Things are always developing here, with the introduction of evening meals a case in point.
◑◐⊖(Stockwell) ♣

SW9: Brixton

Beehive ✔

407-409 Brixton Road, SW9 7DG

⏲ 10-11; 10-10.30 Sun

☎ (020) 7738 3643

Courage Best Bitter; Hop Back Summer Lightning; Marston's Pedigree; Shepherd Neame Spitfire; guest beers Ⓗ

Thriving, single-bar pub that attracts a wide ranging clientele. This typical Wetherspoon's outlet boasts a high turnover of cask beers with always at least four guests on tap. The rear is a quiet no-smoking area. Panelled walls display pictures of the locality around the 1930s. Tables in booths allow people to meet and linger. Food is served all day, including breakfast from 10am. Westons Old Rosie draught cider is stocked.
◑◐⇌⊖♣⊬

Trinity Arms

45 Trinity Gardens, SW9 8DR

⏲ 11-11; 12-10.30 Sun

☎ (020) 7274 4544

Young's Bitter, Special, seasonal beers Ⓗ

Traditional pub, built in 1850, in a quiet, residential square a few hundred yards from the bustling centre of Brixton. The name derives from the Trinity Asylum, founded in 1824 for poor women who professed belief in the Holy Trinity. Today, a good mix of customers includes loyal locals, town hall staff and rock fans enjoying a drink before a concert at the Brixton Academy. The Trinity Arms was voted SW London CAMRA Pub of the Year for 2004. Weekday lunches are served. ❀◑⇌⊖

SW9: Clapham

Landor

70 Landor Road, SW9 9PH

⏲ 12-11; 12-10.30 Sun

☎ (020) 7274 4386 website: www.landortheatre.co.uk

Fuller's London Pride; Greene King IPA; guest beers Ⓗ

Spacious and airy, yet charming Victorian pub with ample seating and busy pool tables around an ornate central bar. Crimson pillars, old pictures and curios add atmosphere. A large, enclosed patio opens in summer for families; the bar is strictly for over-18s. An intimate theatre upstairs (Tue-Sat) offers a new act or show every fortnight. The enterprising licensee serves at least two guest beers in winter, often from Rebellion and Battersea breweries. Sunday meals are served 1-5pm.
❀◑◐⇌(High St) ⊖(North)

SW10: West Brompton

Chelsea Ram

32 Burnaby Street, SW10 0PL

⏲ 11-11; 12-10.30 Sun

☎ (020) 7351 4008

Young's Bitter, Special, seasonal beers Ⓗ

Large, open-plan establishment with bare floorboards and extending tables and chairs. Some of the windows are frosted glass etched with the ram motif. An extensive food menu changes bi-monthly. The pub can get busy towards the weekend. There is a room upstairs that is used for dining, but can also be booked for meetings. Newspapers are provided. Children are welcome. The pub is close to Chelsea Harbour. Q ❀ ◐ ◑ ♿ ⚟

SW11: Battersea

Beehive ✔

197 St John's Hill, SW11 1TH

11-11; 12-10.30 Sun

☎ (020) 7564 1897

Fuller's London Pride, ESB Ⓗ

Located on St John's Hill among trendy drinking and dancing venues, this Fuller's pub remains an excellent local. A recent refurbishment has replaced the wall benches and worn carpet with wooden furniture and bare boards. A large-screen TV shows major sporting events. Home-cooked food is served lunchtime (except Tue). The amiable landlord and his staff have substantially increased sales of real ale in the past year. ◐ ♣

Castle

115 Battersea High Street, SW11 3HS

12-11; 12-10.30 Sun

☎ (020) 7228 8181

Young's Bitter, Special, seasonal beers Ⓗ

In an area where, in many pubs, style now triumphs over substance, this 1960s house continues to provide good beer, unpretentious cuisine and friendly service. A relaxed atmosphere prevails throughout the three distinct areas including a conservatory popular with diners and one bar furnished with sofas and decorated with vintage posters. The pub's patio, yard and pavement seating come into their own in the warmer months.
❀ ◐ ◑ ≋ (Clapham Jct) P

Eagle Ale House

104 Chatham Street, SW11 6HG

11-11; 12-10.30 Sun

☎ (020) 7228 2328

Fuller's London Pride; Taylor Landlord; guest beers Ⓗ

This local seems to change its personality when major sporting events are shown on the large-screen TV. Normally though, it is a haven for real ale drinkers from the weekend hustle and bustle of trendy Northcote Road. Its relatively unspoilt, chaotic interior features old carpets, big leather sofas and dusty book and bottle collections. Changing guest ales help tempt the discerning drinker. The garden is covered by a heated marquee for winter use.
⛫ ❀ ≋ (Clapham Jct/Wandsworth Common) ♣

Prince Albert

85 Albert Bridge Road, SW11 4PF

12-11; 12-10.30 Sun

☎ (020) 7228 0613

Battersea Bitter; Greene King IPA, Old Speckled Hen; guest beer (occasional) Ⓗ

Comfortable, spacious, open-plan, Victorian pub, overlooking Battersea Park, just south of Albert Bridge. A pleasant 15-minute walk across the park takes you to Battersea Park and Queenstown Road railway stations. It is a rare outlet for locally brewed Battersea Bitter. The pub was sympathetically refurbished in 2003. Outside seating is provided in summer. An adventurous menu is served all day until 9.30pm. The No. 19 bus terminates nearby. ❀ ◐ ◑ ♿

SW12: Balham

Nightingale

97 Nightingale Lane, SW12 8NX

11-11; 12-10.30 Sun

☎ (020) 8673 1637

Young's Bitter, Special, seasonal beer Ⓗ

Still far away the best bet in Balham for atmosphere and good beer, the 'Bird' is an unchanging haven of peace and quiet that attracts regulars in large numbers. A small conservatory is no-smoking and acts as a children's room until the warmer weather when the garden, which is a real suntrap, comes into its own. Lunches are served daily and evening meals at the weekend.
Q ⛀ ❀ ◐ ◑ ♿ ≋ (Wandsworth Common)
⊖ (Clapham Sth) ♣ ⚟

SW13: Barnes

Coach & Horses

27 Barnes High Street, SW13 9LW

11-11; 12-10.30 Sun

☎ (020) 8876 2695

Young's Bitter, Special, seasonal beers Ⓗ

One of only 28 Young's pubs known to have sold beers from the Ram Brewery since before 1831 when the Young family took control. A regular in this Guide, it remains a cosy, welcoming local. The small single bar retains fine etched windows and dark wood panelling. The large garden, which hosts barbecues in summer, has a well-equipped children's area. Excellent lunches and early evening meals are offered. The large function room is an asset to the community.
❀ ◐ ◑ ≋ (Barnes Bridge)

Red Lion ✔

2 Castelnau, SW13 9RU

11-11; 12-10.30 Sun

☎ (020) 8748 2984

Fuller's London Pride, ESB, seasonal beers Ⓗ

Large roadside pub by the entrance to the Wetlands Centre. Extended over the years and recently sympathetically refurbished, it has been opened out to provide one spacious drinking and eating area with comfortable seating. Close to Barnes Common and pond, it has a village atmosphere and is dog- and family-friendly. Excellent food is available from a wide, upmarket menu; arrive early for Sunday lunch (no bookings). Barbecues are held in summer.
⛫ ❀ ◐ ◑ ♿ ≋ P

SW15: Roehampton

Angel

11 Roehampton High Street, SW15 4HL

11-11; 12-10.30 Sun

☎ (020) 8788 1997

Young's Bitter, Special Ⓗ

Easily the best pub for miles around, it is

situated in the old-fashioned High Street, which is well worth exploring. The pub draws regulars from the area but is welcoming to visitors. The small public bar with TV and loud games contrasts with a more sedate saloon bar that is often crowded in the evenings and weekends. The beer quality is exceptional. ◐◗⊟♣

SW16: Streatham

Pied Bull

498 Streatham High Road, SW16 3BQ
⊛ 11-11; 12-10.30 Sun
☎ (020) 8764 4003
Young's Bitter, Special, seasonal beers Ⓗ
Despite a change of management since last year, this Guide regular is still the best bet for beer drinkers. Situated just past the common, its coaching origins remain evident. The locals support the pub in large numbers drawn by the beer, food, entertainment and large-screen TV for sporting events. In such a large pub it is possible to find quiet areas away from it all, and the garden is popular in summer. ❀◐◗⇌

SW17: Tooting

Hope ✔

1 Bellevue Road, SW17 7EG
⊛ 12-11; 12-10.30 Sun
☎ (020) 8672 8717
Beer range varies Ⓗ
Revitalised under new management in 2004, this wedge-shaped pub on Wandsworth Common had a spell as the Faith & Firkin, but has reverted to its original name. The pub runs a beer club staging events such as 'meet the brewer' evenings and brewery trips. Four cask ales are available – sparklers are removed on request. Undecided customers may try before they buy. The menu has been developed with an eye on the local gastro-pub market. Food is served 12-10pm daily.
❀◐◗⇌(Wandsworth Common)

SW17: Wimbledon (Summerstown)

Prince of Wales ☆

646 Garratt Lane, SW17 0NT
⊛ 11-11; 12-10.30 Sun
☎ (020) 8447 3190
Young's Bitter, Special Ⓗ
Spacious, comfortable, two-bar corner pub, traditionally decorated with old photographs around the walls and a pleasant wood and frosted glass vestibule. Mostly serving locals, the pub's proximity to Wimbledon Stadium and its main road location mean it benefits from the passing trade as well. The lounge bar boasts an upright piano. ⛫◐⊟

SW18: Southfields

Gardeners Arms

266-268 Merton Road, SW18 5JL
⊛ 11-11; 12-10.30 Sun
☎ (020) 8874 7624
Young's Bitter, Special, seasonal beer Ⓗ
Popular corner house, built in 1931 and distinguished by green tiling, 10 minutes' walk from Southfields tube or central Wandsworth (156 bus route). Drinking areas either side of the U-shaped bar are supplemented by a large seating area from a 1989 refurbishment, taking in what had been a shop next door. A thriving community pub, it hosts a quiz on Tuesday evenings. No food is served on Sunday. ◐◗⊖♣

SW18: Wandsworth

Alma ☆

499 Old York Road, SW18 1NN
⊛ 11-11; 12-10.30 Sun
☎ (020) 8870 2537 website: www.thealma.co.uk
Young's Bitter, Special, seasonal beers Ⓗ
A mixed crowd frequents this lively, open-plan pub just opposite the railway station. Despite its modern layout, many original and exquisite features remain, including painted mirrors, external tiling and internal mosaics. The pub can get busy at the weekend. International rugby is shown on a big screen, but no other sport or musical/game machine noise intrudes. The restaurant serves excellent meals, with a new innovation – breakfast, served 8-11am.
⛫◐◗♿⇌(Wandsworth Town)

Freemasons

2 North Side, SW18 2SS
⊛ 12-11; 12-10.30 Sun
☎ (020) 7326 8580 website: www.freemasonspub.com
Everards Tiger; Taylor Landlord Ⓗ
This pub has had many guises over the past decade, recently as a fish restaurant, but now enters the Guide for the first time due to the quality of the real ales, served through unusual canister-style handpumps. Restored to its original name, the Freemasons retains some original features. It has become a lively gastro-pub, drawing a mainly young crowd on busy weekend evenings. A slightly calmer atmosphere prevails during the week. Worth the short trek up the hill from Clapham Junction, buses 77 and 219 stop outside.
❀◐◗♿⇌(Clapham Jct)⊭

Grapes

39 Fairfield Street, SW18 1DX
⊛ 11-11; 12-10.30 Sun
☎ (020) 8874 3414
Young's Bitter, Special Ⓗ
Unspoilt corner pub from the early-19th century, runner-up SW London CAMRA Pub of the Year 2004. The single, U-shaped bar has a piano at one end – occasional impromptu recitals can be heard on a Saturday. At other times unobtrusive background music is played. The superb garden and observatory open in the summer. This is a great local not to be missed. ❀◐⇌

SW19: South Wimbledon

Sultan

78 Norman Road, SW19 1BT
⊛ 12-11; 12-10.30 Sun
☎ (020) 8542 4532
Hop Back GFB, Entire Stout, Summer Lightning, seasonal beer or guest beer Ⓗ
Hop Back's only tied house in London is an attractive, 1950s two-bar pub that has won numerous CAMRA awards and Time Out's Eating and Drinking Best Pub award in 2004. As might be expected it attracts committed real ale

drinkers and runs a beer club on Wednesday (6-9pm), when all cask beers are sold at discounted prices. A beer festival is held in September. Quiz night is Tuesday.
❀⊟♿⊖(Colliers Wood)♣

SW19: Wimbledon

Brewery Tap ✔
68-69 High Street, SW19 5EE
⏲ 11-11; 12-10.30 Sun
☎ (020) 8947 9331
Adnams Bitter; Fuller's London Pride; guest beers Ⓗ
Open-plan, café-style enterprise that is still very much a pub where good quality beer is prized. The three changing guests often include a mild or dark beer and northern micro-breweries are strongly represented. Evening food is limited to a tapas night on Wednesday, but there is a good choice of snacks – try the marinated anchovies. The pub is a gathering point for watching rugby internationals, or for playing games. ◑♣

Crooked Billet
15 Crooked Billet, SW19 4RQ
⏲ 11-11; 12-10.30 Sun
☎ (020) 8946 4942
Young's Bitter, Special; seasonal beers Ⓗ
Popular pub on the edge of Wimbledon Common that has been selling Young's beers for over a century although the brewery did not acquire the freehold until 1928. A side corridor leads to a barn-like dining area at the rear, offering a varied menu that changes regularly. In summer many customers can be found drinking outside on the green opposite the pub. ❀◐◑⛔

Hand in Hand
6 Crooked Billet, SW19 4RQ
⏲ 11-11; 12-10.30 Sun
☎ (020) 8946 5720
Young's Bitter, Special, seasonal beers Ⓗ
Much altered and enlarged since Young's bought it in 1974, after 100 years as a beer house, this pub retains distinct drinking areas around and away from the large bar/servery, including a no-smoking family and games room. Outside tables are popular with diners in summer. Plastic glasses are a sensible requirement for parties spilling out on to the green opposite at busy times. This former SW London CAMRA Pub of the Year is a delightful country pub at the corner of Wimbledon Common. ♛Q♉❀◐◑♣⛔

Carshalton

Greyhound Hotel
2 High Street, SM5 3PE
⏲ 11-11; 12-10.30 Sun
☎ (020) 8647 1511
Young's Bitter, Special, Winter Warmer, seasonal beers Ⓗ
Handsome Young's hotel enjoying an enviable location by Carshalton pond. Once two buildings, the older, timbered part now houses the comfortable Swan Bar, warmed by an open fire. Elsewhere, rooms have been opened out during a 2000 refit (when a sympathetic hotel extension was added), but this pub is large enough to cater for its varied clientele. Notable features are the old cellar, now a dining area, the wonderful greyhound mosaic in the entrance and an old horse mounting block. It was local CAMRA Pub of the Year in 2005.
♛Q⇄◐◑⇛P⛔

Railway Tavern ✔
47 North Street, SM5 2HG
⏲ 12-2.30, 5-11; 11-11 Sat; 12-10.30 Sun
☎ (020) 8669 8016
Fuller's London Pride, ESB Ⓗ
This Fuller's pub – acquired from Bass Charrington in a long-ago pub swap – lies just north of the railway; the opposite side from the station entrance. A small street-corner building housing a single U-shaped bar, it is decorated with various items of railway memorabilia, Sutton-on-Bloom award certificates and an ever-increasing collection of Fuller's Master Cellarman certificates. There is a small outdoor drinking area. Bridge, crib and dominoes are played.
❀⇛

Windsor Castle
378 Carshalton Road, SM5 3PT (at A272/B271 jct)
⏲ 11-11; 12-10.30 Sun
☎ (020) 8669 1191 website: www.windsorcastlepub.com
Fuller's London Pride; Hancock's HB; Taylor Landlord; guest beers Ⓗ
Large, open-plan pub where the beams and walls are adorned with pump clips from the many micro-brewery beers that have been sold. One end is a wood-panelled restaurant area. Beers are available in four-pint jugs at 10% discount and a beer of the week is sold at a reduced price. A beer festival is held in May. Live music is staged every Saturday evening. Children are welcome in the garden until 9pm.
❀◐◑♿⇛(Carshalton Beeches)♣P

Chessington

North Star ✔
271 Hook Road, Hook, KT9 1EQ (on A243)
⏲ 12-11; 12-10.30 Sun
☎ (020) 8391 9811
Adnams Bitter; Draught Bass; guest beers Ⓗ
Busy community pub, whose real ale enthusiast barman has served for over 30 years. The layout is open plan, but there are several discrete areas, including one for non-smokers. The background music is not intrusive; quizzes are held on Sunday and Tuesday. Food is served all day until 8pm. A spring beer festival is an annual event. ❀◐◑♿P⛔

Kew

Coach & Horses Hotel ✔
8 Kew Green, TW9 3BH
⏲ 11-11; 12-10.30 Sun
☎ (020) 8940 1208 website: www.coachhotelkew.co.uk
Young's Bitter, Special, seasonal beers Ⓗ
This is a wonderful 17th-century coaching inn, opposite the Royal Botanic Gardens and close to the Public Records Office. Its function room, capable of accommodating up to 80 people, adjoins an atrium licensed to hold civil weddings. Good quality home-cooked food includes an extensive fresh fish menu that changes daily, served in the bar or the wood-panelled no-smoking dining area.
♛❀⇄◐◑♿⇛(Bridge/Gardens)⊖(Gardens)P

Kingston upon Thames

Albert Arms

57 Kingston Hill, KT2 7PX (on A308)
⌚ 11-11; 12-10.30 Sun
☎ (020) 8546 7669
Young's Bitter, Special, seasonal beers ⊞
Imposing pub opposite Kingston Hospital whose workers and visitors make it busy at times. Split into three partly wood-panelled areas, once separate bars, the no-smoking space is adjacent to the food servery. A quiz is held once a month and occasional live music is staged. Evening meals are served Monday-Friday; Sunday lunch continues until 5pm. Q ✿ ◐◑ ⇌ (Norbiton) ♣ P ⊬

Park Tavern

19 New Road, KT2 6AP (off B351)
⌚ 11-11; 12-10.30 Sun
Fuller's London Pride; Taylor Landlord; Young's Bitter; guest beers ⊞
Friendly, cosy, free house near Richmond Park's Kingston Gate. This homely establishment was originally three cottages. The long narrow bar has seating at either end; live TV sport is shown on occasion at one end. An attractive open fire for winter months, and a floral patio in summer add to its appeal. Take time to look at the pub memorabilia, including a classic 'God save the King' poster. ⛬ Q ✿

Willoughby Arms ✔

47 Willoughby Road, KT2 6LN
⌚ 10.30-11; 12-10.30 Sun
☎ (020) 8546 4236 website: www.thewilloughbyarms.com
Caledonian Deuchars IPA; Fuller's London Pride; Marston's Pedigree; guest beers ⊞
Cheery Victorian pub that deserves its reputation for quality ale, as the real ale cause is something the landlord supports strongly. Beer festivals are held for St George's Day and Halloween, while the Society for the Preservation of Beer from the Wood meets here regularly. Two almost separate bars comprise one for live TV sport, pool and darts, the other is a cosier saloon. The function room upstairs hosts live bands. The garden is used for summer barbecues. ✿ ♿ ♣

Wych Elm ✔

93 Elm Road, KT2 6HT
⌚ 11-3, 5-11; 11-11 Sat; 12-10.30 Sun
☎ (020) 8546 3271
Fuller's Chiswick, London Pride, ESB, seasonal beers ⊞
Homely, traditional pub in a residential area, renowned for its excellent beer quality. Under the stewardship of its long-standing Spanish landlord, the Wych Elm exudes a friendly air. There is a public bar and a characterful garden for warmer months; pretty floral displays add colour. It hosts occasional jazz evenings (with barbecues in summer). Good quality, home-made lunches are served Monday-Saturday at this outstanding advert for the Fuller's organisation. ✿ ◐ ⊟ ⇌ ♣

Malden Manor

Manor

Manor Drive North, KT3 5PW (off B284)
⌚ 12-11; 12-10.30 Sun
☎ (020) 8335 3199
Courage Best Bitter; Shepherd Neame Spitfire; guest beer ⊞
This pub stands next to Malden Manor Station in the shadow of the national grid. Built in the 1930s it comprises three largely unspoilt bars. Set within a large suburban housing area, the pub thrives on local trade. The guest beer regularly changes and is sometimes from a micro-brewery. The Hodgsons' Brewery coat of arms appears above all three entrances. Bus K1 passes the pub. Cribbage, darts and dominoes are played here. ⛬ Q ✿ ⊟ ⇌ ♣ P

Mitcham

Queen's Head

70 Cricket Green, CR4 4LA (on A239)
⌚ 11-11; 12-10.30 Sun
☎ (020) 8648 3382
Shepherd Neame Master Brew Bitter, Spitfire, seasonal beers ⊞
Two-roomed pub, reputedly patronised by Nelson, overlooking part of the historic cricket green area. Sports TV and games machines are in the smaller room with volume kept at reasonable levels. It hosts an occasional disco or acoustic act in the main room. A quiz is held on Sunday evening and regular charity events are organised. Home-cooked lunches including chef's specials, are served daily except Saturday. In warm weather a barbecue is held on Saturday afternoons. ✿ ◐ ⊖ (Tramlink)

Richmond

Red Cow

59 Sheen Road, TW9 1YJ
⌚ 11-11; 12-10.30 Sun
☎ (020) 8940 2511
website: www.redcowpub.activehotels.com
Young's Bitter, Special, seasonal beers ⊞
Sympathetically restored, this popular local is a few minutes' walk from Richmond's shops and station. There are three distinct drinking areas where rugs on bare floorboards and period furniture create a traditional atmosphere. The first floor has four en-suite bedrooms. Good lunches are served daily, and evening meals Monday-Thursday until 8.30pm. Tuesday is quiz night and live music is performed on Thursday evening. ⛬ ✿ ⛟ ◐◑ ⇌ ⊖

Roebuck

130 Richmond Hill, TW10 6RN
⌚ 11-11; 12-10.30 Sun
☎ (020) 8948 2329
Beer range varies ⊞
Overlooking the World Heritage view of Petersham Meadows and the Thames, this 200-year-old, reputedly haunted pub is close to Richmond Park Gate. Patrons are welcome on the terrace opposite to enjoy the view cherished by their forbears and highwaymen for 500 years. Three beers change regularly, and award-winning pies and sausages form the basis of an extensive menu (served all day Sat and Sun). Bar billiards is played. ✿ ◐◑ ⊟ ♣

Triple Crown

15 Kew Foot Road, TW9 2SS
⌚ 11-11; 12-10.30 Sun
☎ (020) 8940 3805

Beer range varies Ⓗ
True free house serving four regularly changing ales. It stands by Richmond Athletic Ground, close to Old Deer Park and Kew Gardens and is convenient for the station. A fairly small, narrow pub, it is popular for the Tuesday evening quiz and Sunday afternoon jazz. There are a couple of tables on the front pavement and an upstairs function room has its own bar (with handpumps) and a small balcony. Lunches are served Monday-Saturday. ❀◖≠⊖

Watermans Arms

12 Water Lane, TW9 1TJ
✪ 11-11; 12-10.30 Sun
☎ (020) 8940 2893
Young's Bitter, Special, seasonal beers Ⓗ
Historic pub, one of the oldest in Richmond (rebuilt 1895), retaining its Victorian two-bar layout. In a lane leading to the White Cross and the river, generations of watermen have drunk here and some, along with others in riparian occupations, still do. In the 1950s it was a lunchtime stop for the Swan Uppers en-route from Blackfriars to Henley. Full of character, it has a truly local feel – good Thai food is served all day until 10pm. The upstairs room hosts a Monday folk club. ⩕Q◖◗≠⊖

White Cross

Riverside, Water Lane, TW9 1TJ
✪ 11-11; 12-10.30 Sun
☎ (020) 8940 6844
Young's Bitter, Special, seasonal beers Ⓗ
A prominent feature on Richmond's waterfront, the pub dates from 1835, but a stained glass panel is a reminder that it stands on the site of a former convent of the Observant Friars, whose insignia was a white cross. It is reached by steps for good reason – the river often floods here. An island bar serves two side rooms (one a mezzanine); an unusual feature is a working fireplace beneath a window. A ground-level patio bar opens at busy times. ⩕Q❀◖≠⊖

Surbiton

Cap in Hand ✔

174 Hook Rise North, KT6 5DE (at A3/A243 jct)
✪ 10-11; 10-10.30 Sun
☎ (020) 8397 3790
Fuller's London Pride; Greene King Abbot; Hop Back Summer Lightning; Marston's Burton Bitter; Shepherd Neame Spitfire; guest beers Ⓗ
Imposing pub at the Ace of Spades roundabout, built in 1934. Acquired by Wetherspoon in 1998, the large, airy conservatory at the front overlooks the A3 heading into the green belt. Beer festivals are held in May and October; there is generally a guest beer from Itchen Valley. Alongside the mainly 1930s memorabilia, Chessington-born singer Petula Clark is celebrated. Alcohol is not served until midday on Sunday. Q♉❀◖◗♿P⍁

New Prince ✔

117 Ewell Road, KT6 6AL (on A240)
✪ 11-11; 12-10.30 Sun
☎ (020) 8296 0265
Gale's Butser, Best Bitter, HSB, seasonal beers Ⓗ
Typical, old-fashioned local with a friendly atmosphere. The enclosed garden has a patio and small children's play area; barbecues are held in summer. Major sporting events are covered on the TV. The comfortable pub features exposed beams, with dark wooden furniture. The area to the rear can be used for functions. ❀◖≠

Waggon & Horses

1 Surbiton Hill Road, KT6 4TW (on A240)
✪ 11-11; 12-10.30 Sun
☎ (020) 8390 0211
Young's Bitter, Special, Waggledance or Winter Warmer Ⓗ
Large old-style pub divided into several distinct bar areas, including a basic public bar, a room for diners and a split-level bar with ample seating. The function area admits children until early evening. Apart from the small car park, parking may be difficult but the frequent, nearby Surbiton-Kingston bus route is convenient. Meals are served 12-9pm (12-4pm Sat and Sun). Q❀◖◗≠P⍁

Sutton

Little Windsor ✔

13 Greyhound Road, SM1 4BY (E of centre)
✪ 11.30-11; 12-10.30 Sun
☎ (020) 8643 2574
Fuller's London Pride, ESB; guest beer Ⓗ
Popular local in Sutton's well-pubbed New Town district. This small corner house can get busy, especially when sport is on TV, but the consistently good beer has resulted in several local CAMRA awards. The present building has been licensed since the 1890s and became a Fuller's house some 25 years ago. A patio garden to the rear and small drinking area to the front provide an overspill in summer. Shove-ha'penny can be played here. ❀◖≠♣

Lord Nelson

32 Lower Road, SM1 4QP (E of town centre)
✪ 12-11; 12-4, 7-10.30 Sun
☎ (020) 8642 4120
Young's Bitter, Special Ⓗ
Traditional local situated in the New Town area of Sutton. A Young's hostelry since 1888, it has changed remarkably little over the years. Green and brown exterior tiling and etched windows recall a bygone Victorian era. It retains two of the three original bars. Darts and crib are played in the public bar and it hosts regular quizzes. The saloon bar is cosy and there is a pleasant garden. It stands on bus route 154. Lunches are served Monday-Saturday. ❀◖⊟♣

Robin Hood

52 West Street, SM1 1SH (one block W of cinema/shopping complex)
✪ 11-11; 12-10.30 Sun
☎ (020) 8643 7584
Young's Bitter, Special, Winter Warmer, seasonal beers Ⓗ
Pleasant, open-plan local just off the main shopping areas of Sutton, run by a friendly landlord who welcomes all. The national home-brewing championships are held here every November (contact the pub for details). Games include shove-ha'penny and dominoes. It is lovely and cosy in the winter so settle in, buy a four-pint jug and you will get a pound off. ⩕Q❀◖◗≠♣

Wallington

Whispering Moon ✔
25 Ross Parade, Woodcote Road, SM6 9QT
11-11; 12-10.30 Sun
☎ (020) 8647 7020
Greene King Abbot, Old Speckled Hen; Marston's Burton Bitter, Pedigree; guest beers ⊞
The Wetherspoon formula has been applied to a former small cinema premises and offers all the company's usual price promotions and beer festivals. The layout inside comprises an L-shaped drinking area and a smaller raised section. It is handy for the station across the road and Wallington Hall – home of Croydon & Sutton CAMRA's annual October beer festival.
Q◐◑♿⇌⚡

WEST LONDON

W1: Fitzrovia

Hope
15 Tottenham Street, W1T 2AJ
11-11; 12-6 Sun
☎ (020) 7637 0896
Adnams Bitter; Fuller's London Pride; Gale's HSB; Taylor Landlord ⊞
Once ornate pub dating back to 1892, which was refurbished during Whitbread ownership in an open-plan layout. The Real London pub company now owns this former Hogshead house. Just off Tottenham Court Road, it can get busy at any time and the upstairs lounge bar may be booked for functions. Old prints dominate the walls. Note the portrait located over a doorway of gentlemen from the society of Goffers of Blackheath. Lunchtime food consists of speciality sausages. ◐⊖(Goodge St)

One Tun
58 Goodge Street, W1T 4ND
11-11; 12-10.30 Sun
☎ (020) 7209 4105
Young's Bitter, Special, seasonal beers ⊞
The One Tun used to be a Finch's pub until Young's took it over; the Bass mirrors remain to remind us of those days. An island bar has seating along the walls; a dartboard is at the rear and Sky TV satisfies the sports fans. Bench seating is available outside when it gets crowded with local office workers. Quiz night is Tuesday. ❀◐⊖(Goodge St)

W1: Marylebone

Carpenters Arms
12 Seymour Place, W1H 7NE
11-11; 12-10.30 Sun
☎ (020) 7723 1050
Fuller's London Pride; Gale's Best; Harveys BB; guest beers ⊞
Free house just five minutes' walk from Marble Arch, providing a welcome respite from West End shopping. A popular venue for viewing all major sporting events; darts matches are played on Thursday evening. The beer range changes with guests from independents and micros. The interior is split level towards the back and the room upstairs also has a bar. Lunchtime meals are served Monday-Friday.
Q❀◐⊖(Marble Arch) ♣

Duke of Wellington ✔
94A Crawford Street, W1H 2HQ
11-11; 12-10.30 Sun
☎ (020) 7724 9435
Adnams Bitter; Wells Bombardier ⊞
You could be forgiven for walking past this pub thinking it was an antique shop. Most of the memorabilia and curios displayed in the window commemorate the Duke of Wellington. Inside, a pillar acts as a signpost directing the eyes to the sites of Wellington's many victories. A display case contains a collection of Belgian and British beers. Some are from breweries that no longer exist. Scrabble and playing cards are available.
Q◐◑⊖(Edgware Rd)

Wargrave Arms
40-42 Brendon Street, W1H 5HE
11-11; 12.30-10.30 Sun
☎ (020) 7723 0559
Young's Bitter, Special, seasonal beers ⊞
Back-street local just a few minutes' walk from cosmopolitan Edgware Road. An L-shaped bar displays bottles and trophies on its shelves. A framed sweatshirt, presented to the landlord by the Wallabies rugby team, is mounted on the far wall. If you visit on a Tuesday evening you may find yourself invited to play a game of chess, as that is when the chess club meets.
◐◑⇌(Paddington) ⊖(Edgware Rd) ♣

W1: Soho

Coach & Horses ☆
29 Greek Street, W10 5DH
11-11; 12-10.30 Sun
☎ (020) 7437 5920
Fuller's London Pride; Marston's Pedigree; Tetley Burton Ale ⊞
Famous Soho institution run by Norman Balon since the 1960s and a regular in Private Eye magazine – spot the many cartoons depicting the landlord, the pub and Jeffrey Bernard being carted off in an ambulance. The pub attracts a mix of young folk and local workers enjoying the entertaining atmosphere, and it gets busy with theatregoers. Norman announced his retirement in July 2005. ⊖(Leicester Sq)

Dog & Duck ☆ ✔
18 Bateman Street, W1D 3AF
11-11; 12-10.30 Sun
☎ (020) 7437 4447
Fuller's London Pride; Greene King IPA; Taylor Landlord ⊞
A pub has existed on this site since 1732 when the land was bought by Lord Bateman (hence Bateman Street). The area was mainly meadows where fox hunting used to take place, giving rise to the name of Soho after the huntsman's cry. This small, street-corner local boasts ceramic tiles along the main walls, two early 1900s advertising mirrors and in the rear snug, a large fireplace displaying two ornamental Cleopatra's needles. The upstairs bar is now a restaurant.
Q◐⊖(Tottenham Ct Rd)

Ship ✔
116 Wardour Street, W1F 0TT
11-11; closed Sun
☎ (020) 7437 8446

Fuller's London Pride, ESB; guest beers Ⓗ
The Ship is the only Fuller's pub in Soho. It is close to where the old Marquee Club used to stand and Lennon, Hendrix and the Who are reputed to have supped here. Would-be pop singers should note that 'you haven't made it 'til you've fallen over in the Ship'. The long, narrow bar has undergone some excellent renovations since a gas explosion destroyed most of the original interior. The music can be very loud in the evening. ◐⊖(Tottenham Ct Rd)

W2: Bayswater

King's Head

33 Moscow Road, W2 4AH
⏲ 11-11; 12-10.30 Sun
☎ (020) 7229 4233
Fuller's London Pride; Young's Bitter; guest beers Ⓗ
A single, large room incorporating a small, no-smoking area, popular with young people and tourists from the busy Queensway shopping precinct. It can get noisy and smoky later in the evening. An attractive bar holds five handpumps offering a changing range of beers that are listed together with forthcoming ales. It also stocks a good range of foreign beers. Photographs of the Bernard brewery are displayed. Sporting events are shown on TV. ◐◑ ⊖(Bayswater/Queensway)

Prince Edward

73 Princes Square, W2 4NY
⏲ 11-11; 12-10.30 Sun
☎ (020) 7727 2221
Fuller's London Pride; Greene King Abbot; Marston's Pedigree; guest beers Ⓗ
Situated on a Regency square, with some outdoor tables and chairs, the Prince Edward was refurbished some years ago to give an island bar. Note the fine black and white photographs, etched glass mirrors and coloured, leaded glass panels. The no-smoking restaurant area, offering daily specials, is open Wednesday-Friday and all day Saturday and Sunday; children are welcome for meals. Once Whitbread-owned, then acquired by Hall & Woodhouse, it became a free house in 2004. ❀◐◑ ⊖⚟

W2: Marble Arch

Tyburn ✔

18-20 Edgware Road, W2 2EN
⏲ 10-11; 12-10.30 Sun
☎ (020) 7723 4731
Fuller's London Pride; Marston's Burton Bitter, Pedigree; guest beers Ⓗ
The Tyburn is a large, open-plan pub with generous seating and table arrangements. It opens for breakfast and serves meals throughout the day to within an hour of closing, with various themed food menus during the week. The large windows look directly on to Edgware Road; the cinema down the road provides the theme for some of the photographic decor. ◐◑♿⊖⚟

W2: Paddington

Mad Bishop & Bear ✔

First Floor, The Lawn, Paddington Station, W2 1HB
(accessible via escalator from main station concourse)
⏲ 10 (7.30 breakfast)-11; 12 (8.30 breakfast)-10.30 Sun
☎ (020) 7402 2441
Fuller's Chiswick, London Pride, ESB, seasonal beers; guest beers Ⓗ
This Fuller's pub is situated above Paddington Station with access via an escalator. Furnished and fitted to a high standard, attractive mirrors and lighting, including a prominent chandelier, create a sophisticated impression; many prints depict clerical and aristocratic subjects. It is a relaxing refuge from the hustle and bustle of the station below, despite the piped music. Breakfast is served from 7.30am (8.30 Sun).
❀◐◑♿⇌⊖⚟

Victoria ☆ ✔

10A Strathearn Place, W2 2NH
⏲ 11-11; 12-10.30 Sun
☎ (020) 7724 1191
Fuller's Chiswick, London Pride, ESB, seasonal beers Ⓗ
This mid-Victorian pub is a classic of its period. Richly fitted out, notable features include decorated mirrors and an elaborate bar back. The main bar has two comfortable areas and an impressive fireplace. The library and theatre bar upstairs may be hired for functions. It is said that Queen Victoria once visited the pub; a print of Victoria and Albert hangs over the fireplace. A varied food menu is served. Outdoor tables are shielded from the road by plants.
❀◐◑ ⇌⊖(Paddington/Lancaster Gate)

W3: Acton

Castle ✔

140 Victoria Road, W3 5NY
⏲ 11-11; 12-10.30 Sun
☎ (020) 8992 2027
Fuller's London Pride, ESB, seasonal beers Ⓗ
Spacious, comfortable pub on the edge of North Acton industrial estate. Pictures celebrate the heyday of BBC radio. The no-smoking area is by the window in the lounge. Two TVs show live sporting events. Live jazz is performed on Sunday afternoon and a quiz is held on Monday evening. It can be busy and lively in the evenings. ❀◐◑ ⊖(North Acton) ♣⚟

W4: Chiswick

Bell & Crown

11-13 Thames Road, Strand-on-the-Green, W4 3PL
⏲ 11-11; 12-10.30 Sun
☎ (020) 8994 4164
Fuller's Chiswick, London Pride, ESB, seasonal beers Ⓗ
Located near Kew Bridge on the bank of the River Thames, the Bell & Crown can be found alongside the Riverside Walk – a seating area is provided for drinkers who pop in for a pint then carry on with their walk. The pub has two glass-fronted extensions that provide a great view of the river in any weather, one of these is for non-smokers. Meals are freshly prepared on the premises. ♨❀◐◑ ⇌(Kew Bridge) ⚟

George & Devonshire ✔

8 Burlington Lane, W4 2QE
⏲ 11-11; 12-10.30 Sun
☎ (020) 8994 1859

Fuller's Chiswick, London Pride, ESB, seasonal beers [H]
Right next to Fuller, Smith & Turner's Griffin Brewery in Chiswick, the George & Devonshire is a rare type of pub in this area. Where most pubs have had their partitions between bars removed, it has retained separate saloon and public bars with individual entrances. The function room (accessed through the saloon bar) doubles as a no-smoking area, when not booked. Some outdoor seating is provided in front of and behind the pub. ❀◖⊟♣P⚟

Old Pack Horse
434 Chiswick High Road, W4 5TF
✪ 11-11; 12-10.30 Sun
☎ (020) 8994 2872
Fuller's Chiswick, London Pride, ESB, seasonal beers [H]
Set on a busy corner near Chiswick Park tube station, the Old Pack Horse has a sizeable passing trade. The pub is U-shaped, with what used to be three separate bars (the partitions were removed a few years ago) making up the 'L' part and the Thai restaurant towards the rear making up the remainder of the U shape.
❀◖◗⊖(Chiswick Pk)

W5: Ealing

Castle
36 St Mary's Road, W5 5EU
✪ 11-11; 12-10.30 Sun
☎ (020) 8567 3285
Fuller's Chiswick, London Pride, ESB, seasonal beers [H]
A traditional local, opposite Thames Valley University. The snug bar at the front is tiny. The main bar area has a stone-flagged floor. Mainly open-plan, it does have a few quiet corners and a partly divided-off area at the rear. A large-screen TV is used for sports broadcasts. The menu features Thai food. ❀◖◗♿⊖(South)

Fox & Goose ✔
Hanger Lane, W5 1DP
✪ 11-11; 12-10.30 Sun
☎ (020) 8998 5864
Fuller's Chiswick, London Pride, ESB, seasonal beers [H]
Large, roadside pub just off the A40 – the Fox & Goose has been a local landmark since the 17th century. Although converted to an English Inns house in the 1990s it retains much of its original structure throughout, with the addition of a restaurant and a separate hotel block. It caters for nearby office staff during the day, but has a vibrant local atmosphere in the evening. All major televised sporting events are shown in the public bar.
⛺❀⇆◖◗♿⊖(Hanger Lane) P

Questors Grapevine Club ✔
12 Mattock Lane, W5 5BQ
✪ 7-11; 12-2.30, 7-10.30 Sun
☎ (020) 8567 0011
website: www.questors.org.uk/grapevine
Fuller's London Pride, seasonal beers, guest beers [H]
Friendly theatre bar, located just south of the town centre. The staff are all volunteers and real ale fans, which shows in the quality of the beer. A session bitter is always available alongside the London Pride, with other guests often appearing. Beer festivals and whisky nights are a regular feature in the calendar. Although primarily for members of the Questors Theatre, guests are welcome – just sign the visitors' book on arrival. Bar skittles can be played here.
Q♿⇌⊖(Broadway) ♣P⚟

Red Lion ✔
13 St Mary's Road, W5 5RA
✪ 11-11; 12-10.30 Sun
☎ (020) 8567 2541
Fuller's Chiswick, London Pride, ESB, seasonal beers; guest beers [H]
A serial winner of local CAMRA's Pub of the Year contest, this single-bar institution was much enlarged in a 2002 refurbishment. While this has allowed a greater emphasis to be placed on food, the essential character of the original front section remains virtually unchanged. The alternative name, Stage 6, derives from the nearby Ealing Studios – a link reinforced by old photographs lining the walls. The door has been known to be relocated without warning. No evening meals are served Sunday.
❀◖◗⇌(Broadway) ⊖(South)

Wheatsheaf ✔
41 Haven Lane, W5 2HZ
✪ 11-11; 12-10.30 Sun
☎ (020) 8997 5240
Fuller's Chiswick, London Pride, ESB, seasonal beers [H]
Friendly local, tucked away up a side street, just north of Ealing town centre. Inside, it is deceptively large and appears to be constructed almost entirely of wood. A small semi-partitioned area at the front leads to a comfortable saloon that itself leads on to an open space at the rear. Several TVs show sport, but it is possible to escape them.
◖◗⇌(Broadway) ⊖

W5: South Ealing

Ealing Park Tavern
222 South Ealing Road, W5 4RL
✪ 11-11; 12-10.30 Sun
☎ (020) 8758 1879
Beer range varies [H]
Large 18th-century pub, rescued from mediocrity by its recent conversion into a gastro-pub, which also saw a reversion to its original name. Five handpumps in the spacious front bar serve an ever-changing variety of beers, often from unusual breweries. The restaurant serves excellent contemporary English/European dishes and unusual bar snacks are available in the other areas; no food is served Monday lunchtime.
⛺❀◖◗♿⊖

W6: Hammersmith

Andover Arms ✔
57 Aldensley Road, W6 0DL
✪ 12-11; 12-10.30 Sun
☎ (020) 8741 9794
Fuller's Chiswick, London Pride, ESB, seasonal beers [H]
Tucked away in the side streets of Hammersmith you will find the Andover Arms.

Although quite small by modern standards, the pub is well run. During the day the kitchen serves traditional pub fare, but in the evening it turns into a Thai restaurant serving good food at reasonable prices, however this does not affect the pub as it has its own dining area.
Q ◑ ⊖ (Ravenscourt Pk)

Brook Green Hotel

170 Shepherd's Bush Road, W6 7PB

11 (breakfast 7am Mon-Fri; 8am Sat)-11; 12 (breakfast 8am)-10.30 Sun

☎ (020) 7603 2516

Young's Bitter, Special, seasonal beers ⊞

Dating from 1886, this Victorian pub conveys an impression of grandeur with large windows, high ceilings and chandeliers. Sympathetically refurbished, many imposing features remain, including much woodwork, ornate mirrors and an impressive fireplace. Comfortable lounge-style seating and a real fire are provided in the main bar. The basement bar is a function room and entertainment venue, staging comedy, jazz and blues. The overnight accommodation is competitively priced. ♨❀⇌◑♿
⊖ (Hammersmith/Goldhawk Rd) ⚡

Cross Keys ✔

57 Black Lion Lane, W6 9BG

11-midnight; 12-10.30 Sun

☎ (020) 8748 3541

Fuller's London Pride; guest beer ⊞

The Cross Keys is located in a side street off King Street, with very little through traffic. The pub has a traditional looking bar at the front with some fine wood-panelling. Walk through the bar to the rear room, which is quite different from the rest of the pub with its high ceiling. Behind the pub is an outside seating area which is partially covered.
❀◑⊖ (Stamford Brook)

Dove ✔

19 Upper Mall, W6 9TA

11-11; 12-10.30 Sun

☎ (020) 8748 9474

Fuller's London Pride, ESB, seasonal beers ⊞

Probably dating from the 18th-century, this well-known pub boasts an enviable riverside position. Choose from several diverse drinking areas: the two front bars are the most historic, while the tiny snug is said to be the smallest public bar in Britain. The saloon bar is the place to be on a winter's evening with its fireplace (gas fire) and wood panelling.
Q ❀◑ ⊟⊖ (Ravenscourt Pk)

Salutation ✔

154 King Street, W6 0QU

11-11; 12-10.30 Sun

☎ (020) 8748 3668

Fuller's Chiswick, London Pride, ESB, seasonal beers ⊞

Built on the site of an old coaching inn, the Salutation is a welcoming pub. Although the interior has seen a few alterations in the past years, it retains a traditional feel with a wooden floor, hard seating and old-fashioned lamps, however there are two soft seating areas. Towards the rear, you can enjoy your pint during the summer in a large open space with outdoor seating. ❀◑⊖

W7: Hanwell

Fox

Green Lane, W7 2PJ

11-11; 12-10.30 Sun

☎ (020) 8567 3912

Caledonian Deuchars IPA; Fuller's London Pride; Taylor Landlord; guest beer ⊞

Family-owned and -run free house serving the local community, but visitors are always made to feel welcome. It stands 50 yards from the junction of the River Brent and Grand Union Canal. An annual beer festival is held at Easter and regular barbecues take place in the garden in summer. Well-behaved children (and dogs) are welcome. Although now all one bar, it has distinct saloon (carpeted) and public bar areas. The Fox was once owned by Brentford's Royal Brewery. ♨Q❀◑⇌♣P

W8: Kensington

Britannia

1 Allen Street, W8 6UX

11-11; 12-10.30 Sun

☎ (020) 7937 6905

Young's Bitter, Special, seasonal beers ⊞

A short walk from Kensington High Street, this pub was situated next door to the Britannia Brewery that was closed by Young's Brewery in the 1920s. Formerly Britannia's tap, after the brewery closed it exchanged names with what is now the Britannia Tap in nearby Warwick Road. The pub has recently undergone a refurbishment, losing the public bar and regaining the rear conservatory (bookable for functions), which was the former brewery stable block. Quiz nights are held on alternate Thursdays. ◑ ⊖ (High St)

Churchill Arms ☆ ✔

119 Kensington Church Street, W8 7LN

11-11; 12-10.30 Sun

☎ (020) 7727 4242

Fuller's Chiswick, London Pride, ESB, seasonal beers ⊞

This renowned Fuller's pub has genuine character in abundance. A huge range of memorabilia and bric-a-brac cover the walls and ceiling, including chamber-pots, Irish sporting items from Gaelic football and hurling, and a collection of framed butterflies. Reminders of Sir Winston Churchill are also much in evidence. Food is a strong theme in the pub which has a franchised Thai restaurant; dine in the conservatory, among the numerous plants.
Q◑ ⊖ (Notting Hill Gate)

Uxbridge Arms

13 Uxbridge Street, W8 7TQ

12-11; 12-10.30 Sun

☎ (020) 7727 7326

Fuller's London Pride; Greene King IPA; Young's Bitter ⊞

Popular, back-street local a stone's throw from busy Notting Hill Gate, offering three small drinking areas. The pub displays an interesting collection of bric-a-brac above the bar and many prints along the wood-panelled walls. Until a few years ago the pub was under threat before a petition was organised by the locals to save it.
Q❀⊖ (Notting Hill Gate)

W11: Notting Hill

Cock & Bottle ☆
17 Needham Road, W11 2RP
⌚ 12-11; 12-10.30 Sun
☎ (020) 7229 1550
Fuller's London Pride; Hogs Back TEA ⊞
Relaxing haven, close to the busy thoroughfare of Westbourne Grove. The pub has preserved its local character and heritage: upon entering, the visitor's gaze is immediately drawn to the ornate bar back with its rich decoration. One of the three rooms has snob screens at the bar. Previously called the Swan, the stained glass panels in the front bar depict swans. Bar food is available 12-2.30pm weekdays.
❀◖⊖(Notting Hill Gate/Westbourne Pk)

W14: West Kensington

Crown & Sceptre
34 Holland Road, W14 8BA
⌚ 11-11; 12-10.30 Sun
☎ (020) 7602 1866
Beer range varies ⊞
The closest pub in this Guide to the Olympia Exhibition Centre, the Crown & Sceptre offers an ever-changing guest beer line up. Apart from the beer, the interior is also of interest. Although the pub was refurbished a few years ago, the existing traditional bar was retained, as was an inscription of the pub name carved into wood with a glass frontage above the bar. Picnic tables allow for some outdoor drinking. Meals represent good value.
❀◖◗♿⇌(Olympia)⊖♣⚡

Radnor Arms
247 Warwick Road, W14 8PX
⌚ 12-11; 12-10.30 Sun
☎ (020) 7602 7708
Everards Tiger; guest beer ⊞
Located on the busy Earl's Court one-way system, the building stands out because of redevelopment all around it. This single-bar pub is unusual in an area of trendy bars and gastro-pubs, as it has a very traditional feel, with wooden floors and a collection of beer bottles, glasses and jugs. This is the only regular stockist of Everards Tiger in West London.
⇌(Olympia)⊖♣

Brentford

Brewery Tap
47 Catherine Wheel Road, TW8 8BD
⌚ 11-11; 12-10.30 Sun
☎ (020) 8560 5200
Fuller's Chiswick, London Pride, ESB, seasonal beers; guest beers ⊞
Originally the tap of the William Gomm Brewery (acquired by Fuller's in 1908, but subsequently closed). The pub is of Victorian origin, and it is reached by steps from road level as the river used to flood here. Well-known for its jazz (Tue and Thu eves), it now stages a Monday quiz and other music at the weekend. Lunches are popular (book Sun); on weekdays, last food orders are taken at 7.45pm Mon-Fri. There are patios to the front and rear.
❀◖◗⇌♣

Express Tavern
56 Kew Bridge Road, TW8 0EW
⌚ 11.30-3, 5.30 (6.30 Sat)-11; 12-10.30 Sun
☎ (020) 8560 8484
Draught Bass; Young's Bitter; guest beers ⊞
Over 200 years old, the Express is associated with the origins of Brentford FC, the former Brentford market, the 'Buffalos' and CAMRA. Locally renowned for its Bass, supplemented by the Young's and two changing guest beers, it provides a haven from the busy road, with its two bar areas, quiet rear lounge and garden – but please keep off the grass.
Q❀◖⊟⇌(Kew Bridge)

Magpie & Crown
128 High Street, TW8 8EW
⌚ 11-11; 12-10.30 Sun
☎ (020) 8560 5658
Beer range varies ⊞
Mock-Tudor pub, set back from the High Street, which allows for an outside drinking area. Four regularly-changing ales (over 1,300 in nine years) have made it a magnet for real ale lovers. A varying cider (occasionally perry) is offered, plus draught Budvar, Hoegaarden and Paulaner, and continental bottled beers. CAMRA's local Pub of the Year 1999 and 2000 offers bar billiards, shove-ha'penny and shut the box. ❀⇌♣●

Cowley

Paddington Packet Boat
High Road, UB8 2HT
⌚ 12-11; 12-10.30 Sun
☎ (01895) 442392
Fuller's London Pride, ESB, seasonal beers ⊞
Spacious 200-year-old pub which, despite having been completely modernised, retains some old fittings and mirrors, and displays memorabilia relating to the old packet boat service to Paddington. It draws a good passing trade, although most of its customers are local, and include workers from the almost adjacent Grand Union Canal. It hosts live music on Friday and Saturday and a quiz on Tuesday. Meals are served Sunday from 12–4pm. ❀⇆◖◗♿♣P⚡

Cranford

Jolly Gardeners
144 High Street, TW5 9PD
⌚ 11-11; 12-10.30 Sun
☎ (020) 8897 6996
Beer range varies ⊞
Small, predominantly locals' pub with a warm welcome for all. It offers hearty lunches Sunday-Friday. Its single beer often comes from the Cottage Brewery stable. Most activities, including occasional live music on Saturday evening, take place in the larger public bar but, through a doorless arch, is a cosier lounge complete with a verdant (private) conservatory. ♨❀⇆◖♣P

Queen's Head
123 High Street, TW5 9PB
⌚ 11-11; 12-10.30 Sun
☎ (020) 8897 0722
Fuller's Chiswick, London Pride; ESB, seasonal beers ⊞

This large roadhouse was the first pub in the country to be granted a full licence from inception in 1604. Rebuilt in the 1930s it was the venue for the formation of the local CAMRA branch in 1974. Try to spot the certificate presented after a commemorative dinner held in 2004. Rolls are usually available; evening meals are served weekdays. ♨Q❀◐◑♣P

Feltham

Moon on the Square ✔

30 The Centre, High Street, TW13 4AU
⏲ 11 (10 breakfast)-11; 12-10.30 Sun
☎ (020) 8893 1293
Greene King Abbot; Marston's Pedigree; Shepherd Neame Spitfire; guest beers Ⓗ
Flourishing real ale oasis, where up to eight different beers are stocked at a time. Pictures and history panels depict the changing Feltham landscape over 90 years, perhaps foretelling the latest development plans that may require the pub to be re-sited in the near future. Families with children are welcome in the no-smoking area. Q◐◑♿⇌🚭

Hampton Hill

Roebuck

72 Hampton Road, TW12 1JN
⏲ 11-11; 12-10.30 Sun
☎ (020) 8255 8133
Badger K&B Sussex, Best, Tanglefoot; guest beers Ⓗ
Work continues on improving this pub, now with a function room and small but award-winning garden. A friendly, welcoming place, it is festooned with bric-a-brac and transport-related memorabilia – ships, trains, buses and working traffic lights that change for last orders and closing time. Two guest beers change monthly; lunches are served weekdays. Bus Nos. 285 and R68 pass by. ♨❀🛏◐⇌(Fulwell)

Hounslow

Cross Lances ✔

236 Hanworth Road, TW3 3TU (on A314)
⏲ 11-11; 12-10.30 Sun
☎ (020) 8570 4174
Fuller's London Pride, ESB, seasonal beers Ⓗ
Dark-red tiled Victorian local, with an extended saloon giving wheelchair access from the award-winning garden. Excellent beers are complemented by the huge lunches (including Sunday roasts – best to book). Fielding football, pool and darts teams, it also hosts crib, quiz and music evenings, plus occasional Sunday barbecues. ❀◐◑⊟♿⇌♣P

Moon under Water ✔

84-88 Staines Road, TW3 3LF
⏲ 11 (10 breakfast)-11; 12-10.30 Sun
☎ (020) 8572 7506
Greene King Abbot; Hop Back Summer Lightning; Marston's Burton Bitter, Pedigree; guest beers Ⓗ
Local history panels feature in this early Wetherspoon's outlet, since enlarged. It enjoys a good regular following, and some customers travel a fair distance. Its beer range is more extensive than most, with up to three guests usually on tap. At festival times all 12 handpumps may have different beers. The large, no-smoking area accommodates families. Q❀◐◑♿⇌⊖(Central)🚭

Isleworth

Coach & Horses

183 London Road, TW7 5BQ (on A315)
⏲ 11-midnight (11 Wed); 12-10.30 Sun
☎ (020) 8560 1447
Young's Bitter, Special, seasonal beers Ⓗ
First leased by Young's in 1831, this is one of the few remaining coaching houses that were once abundant on this road. There have been a few changes since it was mentioned by Dickens in Oliver Twist, but it is still a pub of great character. Music evenings are regular – usually jazz Monday, folk or blues Tuesday, and various bands Thursday–Saturday; Wednesday is quiz night. Meals are served (not Sun eve) either in the bar or the Thai-influenced restaurant. ♨❀◐◑⇌(Syon Lane)♣P

Red Lion

92-94 Linkfield Road, TW7 6QJ
⏲ 11-11; 12-10.30 Sun
☎ (020) 8560 1457 website: www.red-lion.info
Young's Bitter; guest beers Ⓗ
Spacious, two-bar free house with a strong community focus. There is often something going on: a production on stage or in the garden by their own theatre group; live music (weekend eves); a quiz (Thu), or darts and pool competitions. It has summer barbecues and twice-yearly beer festivals featuring champion beers. You will often see as many as eight beers here, usually with tasting notes provided. Lunches are served weekdays at local CAMRA's Pub of the Year 2003 and 2004. ❀◐⊟⇌♣

Royal Oak

128 Worton Road, TW7 6EP
⏲ 12-11; 12-10.30 Sun
☎ (020) 8560 2906
Fuller's Chiswick, London Pride, ESB; seasonal beers or guest beer Ⓗ
The Royal Oak (circa 1843) is a gem in an entirely residential area by the Duke of Northumberland's River. It is very traditional with dark wood partitions, etched glass and bric-à-brac, including a miniature bottle collection. Old photos of local interest adorn the walls and ceiling alongside the long-serving landlord's many awards. It has a riverside patio, TV at the back for sports, and food is served all day. It is on bus route H20. ❀◐◑

Southall

Conservative & Unionist Club

Fairlawn, High Street, UB1 3HB
⏲ 11.30-2.30 (3 Fri & Sat), 7-11; 12-3, 7-10.30 Sun
☎ (020) 8574 0261
Rebellion IPA, seasonal beers; guest beers Ⓗ
Between Southall's old and new fire stations, this hidden gem welcomes all, regardless of political persuasion. Card-holding CAMRA members or those with a copy of this Guide can gain entry to take advantage of reasonably-priced weekday lunches, and evening activities most nights. A recent innovation has been

monthly live music (last Sat). Rebellion beers predominate but other breweries are featured. The club has four snooker tables. ❀◖≢♣P

Red Lion

94-100 High Street, UB1 3DN

⌚ 11-11; 12-10.30 Sun

☎ (020) 8813 8948

Draught Bass; Brakspear Bitter; Grand Union Bitter; guest beers Ⓗ

Georgian coaching inn on the edge of Southall Park, this former keg-only establishment has been rescued from a period of closure by a licensee from the same family which ran the Beaconsfield Arms in the town. Seasonal Grand Union beers are often substituted for the regional and international brewery offerings as there are only three handpumps. Regular events pepper the weekly schedule including big-screen sports coverage. ≢♣

Teddington

Lion ✔

27 Wick Road, TW11 9DN

⌚ 12-11; 12-10.30 Sun

☎ (020) 8977 6631 website: www.thelionpub.co.uk

Caledonian Deuchars IPA; Fuller's London Pride; Greene King Abbot; Young's Bitter; guest beer Ⓗ

Victorian single-bar pub, sympathetically modernised and recently extended to give additional (no-smoking) space for dining and other activities, as well as disabled facilities. Food (not served Sun eve) is from a modern menu, but traditional favourites are also available. Live music on Saturday evening is blues based. Twice-yearly beer festivals are held; barbecues are hosted in the large garden. It is a short walk from Hampton Wick Station. ♛❀◖◗♿≢(Hampton Wick)⊁

Teddington Arms ✔

38-40 High Street, TW11 8EW

⌚ 12-11; 12-10.30 Sun

☎ (020) 8973 1510 website: www.capitalpubcompany.com

Fuller's London Pride; Greene King IPA; guest beers Ⓗ

New pub, opened in 2003, in a former Italian restaurant – previously a tyre depot. The bar area is high-ceilinged and tends to be noisy, but to the right is a quieter lounge area furnished with rugs and sofas, and the restaurant. The lounge and restaurant areas have dark panelling displaying old drinks posters and photos. One of the guest beers is usually from Adnams and at least one comes from a micro-brewery. ◖◗♿≢

Twickenham

Fox ✔

39 Church Street, TW1 3NR

⌚ 11-11; 12-10.30 Sun

☎ (020) 8892 1535

Caledonian Deuchars IPA; Fuller's London Pride; Grand Union Special; Hogs Back TEA; guest beers Ⓗ

Twickenham's oldest pub (known originally as the Bell) dates from around 1670 and changed its name to the Fox in the early 1700s. Its function room was built as the Assembly Rooms around 1900. Step down from the street into the small bar where a good selection of real ales is always available, and try the home cooking. The Fox is favoured by the locals in this attractive area. ♛Q❀◖≢

Prince of Wales

136 Hampton Road, TW2 5QR (on A311)

⌚ 11-11; 12-10.30 Sun

☎ (020) 8894 5054

Greene King IPA; Twickenham Original; guest beer Ⓗ

An inn has existed on this site for over 150 years, and served as the final staging post on the Windsor-London stagecoach route. The original stables still survive and are listed. Now a single-bar pub it offers three ales including one or two from the new local brewery. Soon to be refurbished, the pub is home to a golf society and a rugby team. Children are welcome until 7.45pm. ♛❀◖≢(Strawberry Hill) ♣

St Margaret's Tavern ✔

107 St Margaret's Road, TW1 2LJ

⌚ 11-11; 12-10.30 Sun

☎ (020) 8892 2369 website: www.st-margarets-pub.com

Adnams Bitter; Caledonian Deuchars IPA; Fuller's London Pride; Greene King IPA; Marston's Pedigree; Wells Bombardier Ⓗ

It started life 150 years ago as a temperance hotel, the Lord Lyon, changing to its present name in 1881. After a rather dismal period as a station pub, it has recently been extended, restyled and regenerated, causing local residents to return in droves. They can choose from three distinct areas in which to relax with a quiet drink or sample the comprehensive menu, served all day. Live music is staged Sunday evening. ♛❀◖◗♿≢(St Margaret's) P

Turk's Head ✔

28 Winchester Road, TW1 1LF

⌚ 12-11; 12-10.30 Sun

☎ (020) 8892 1972

Fuller's London Pride, ESB, seasonal beers Ⓗ

Beatles fans (some even from Japan) come here to see the pub location for a scene from A Hard Day's Night. The Bearcat Comedy Club has been bringing top comedians every Saturday night to the function room for over 20 years. Rugby fans form human pyramids on match days and try to stick stamps on the high ceiling! Recently much renovated, this is still a genuine local corner pub offering fine food and beers, hosting live R&B on Friday. ♛❀◖◗♿≢(St. Margaret's)

Uxbridge

Load of Hay

33 Villier Street, UB8 2DU

⌚ 11-11; 12-10.30 Sun

☎ (01895) 234676

Fuller's London Pride; guest beers Ⓗ

Genuine free house that sells a changing range of beers. There are usually three guest ales, mostly sourced from small, independent breweries. The building was originally the officers' mess of the Elthorne Light Militia, becoming a pub in the 1870s. The main part of the pub was originally the stable block. The small, quiet front bar is the venue for frequent darts matches. A quiz is held each Tuesday and there is live music on Saturday. ❀◖◗♣P⊁

CAMRA's National Inventory

of Pub Interiors of Outstanding Historic Interest

The pubs listed here have interiors or internal features of national historic significance. They are a diverse group ranging from basic street-corner locals to some of the most ornate pubs in the land. Most, but by no means all, of them sell real ale.

National Inventory Part 1

Part 1 emphasises intactness. It lists pubs whose interiors have remained largely unaltered since World War Two and also certain exceptional examples from the post-War era (up to 1975)

ENGLAND

BEDFORDSHIRE
Luton: Painters Arms

BUCKINGHAMSHIRE
West Wycombe: Swan

CAMBRIDGESHIRE
Peterborough: Hand & Heart

CHESHIRE
Alpraham: Travellers Rest
Barthomley: White Lion
Bollington: Holly Bush
Gawsworth: Harrington Arms
Macclesfield: Castle
Wheelock: Commercial

CORNWALL
Falmouth: Seven Stars

CUMBRIA
Broughton Mills: Blacksmiths Arms
Carlisle: Cumberland Inn

DERBYSHIRE
Brassington: Gate Inn
Derby: Old Dolphin
Elton: Duke of York
Kirk Ireton: Barley Mow
Wardlow Mires: Three Stags' Heads

DEVON
Drewsteignton: Drewe Arms
Luppitt: Luppitt Inn
Topsham: Bridge Inn

DORSET
Pamphill: Vine
Worth Matravers: Square & Compass

COUNTY DURHAM
Durham City: Shakespeare; Victoria

ESSEX
Mill Green (Ingatestone): Viper

GLOUCESTERSHIRE & BRISTOL
Ampney St Peter: Red Lion Inn
Bristol: (centre) King's Head
Purton: Berkeley Arms
Willsbridge: Queen's Head

HAMPSHIRE
Steep: Harrow

HEREFORDSHIRE
Leintwardine: Sun Inn
Leysters: Duke of York

KENT
Broadstairs: Neptune's Hall
Ightham Common: Old House
Snargate: Red Lion

LANCASHIRE
Great Harwood: Victoria
Preston: Black Horse
Stacksteads: Commercial

LEICESTERSHIRE
Hinckley: Holly Bush
Whitwick: Three Horseshoes

GREATER LONDON
Central London: (Hatton Garden, EC1) Old Mitre; (Smithfield, EC1) Hand & Shears; (Bloomsbury, WC1) Duke of York; (Holborn, WC1) Cittie of York
East London: (Ilford) Doctor Johnson
North London: (Harringay, N4) Salisbury; (Crouch End, N8) Queen's Hotel
North West London: (Harrow) Castle; (South Kenton) Windermere
South East London: (Kennington, SE11) Old Red Lion
South West London: (West Brompton, SW10) Fox & Pheasant; (Mortlake, SW14) Charlie Butler
West London: (Soho, W1) Argyll Arms; (Hammersmith, W8) Hope & Anchor; (Kensington, W8) Windsor Castle; (West Ealing, W13) Forester

GREATER MANCHESTER
Altrincham: Railway
Ashton-under-Lyne: March Hare
Chorlton on Medlock: Mawson
Eccles: Grapes; Lamb; Royal Oak; Stanley Arms
Farnworth: Shakespeare
Gorton: Plough
Heaton Norris: Nursery Inn
Manchester: (centre) Briton's Protection, Circus Tavern, Hare & Hounds, Peveril of the Peak
Rochdale: Cemetery Hotel
Salford: Coach & Horses
Stockport: Alexandra; Arden Arms; Swan with Two Necks
Westhoughton: White Lion

MERSEYSIDE
Birkenhead: Stork Hotel
Liverpool: (centre) Nook, Peter Kavanagh's, Philharmonic, Vines; (Walton) Prince Arthur
Lydiate: Scotch Piper
Waterloo: Volunteer Canteen

NORTHUMBERLAND
Berwick upon Tweed: Free Trade
Netherton: Star Inn

NOTTINGHAMSHIRE
Nottingham: (centre) Olde Trip to Jerusalem; (Sherwood) Five Ways

OXFORDSHIRE
Steventon: North Star
Stoke Lyne: Peyton Arms

SHROPSHIRE
Edgerley: Royal Hill
Halfway House: Seven Stars Inn
Selattyn: Cross Keys
Shrewsbury: Loggerheads

SOMERSET
Bath: Old Green Tree; Star
Faulkland: Tucker's Grave Inn
Midsomer Norton: White Hart
Witham Friary: Seymour Arms

STAFFORDSHIRE
Rugeley: Red Lion
Tunstall: Vine

SUFFOLK
Brent Eleigh: Cock
Bury St Edmunds: Nutshell
Ipswich: Margaret Catchpole
Laxfield: King's Head ('Low House')

SUSSEX (EAST)
Hadlow Down: New Inn

SUSSEX (WEST)
The Haven: Blue Ship

TYNE & WEAR
Newcastle upon Tyne: (centre) Crown Posada

WARWICKSHIRE
Five Ways: Case is Altered

WEST MIDLANDS
Birmingham: (Aston) Britannia; (Digbeth) Anchor, Market Tavern, White Swan; (Handsworth) Red Lion; (Nechells) Villa Tavern; (Small Heath) Samson & Lion; (Sparkbrook) Marlborough; (Stirchley) British Oak
Bloxwich: Romping Cat; Turf Tavern
Dudley: Shakespeare
Oldbury: Waggon & Horses
Rushall: Manor Arms
Sedgley: Beacon Hotel
Wednesfield: Vine

WILTSHIRE
Easton Royal: Bruce Arms
Salisbury: Haunch of Venison

WORCESTERSHIRE
Clent: Bell & Cross
Defford: Cider House ('Monkey House')
Worcester: Paul Pry Inn

YORKSHIRE (EAST)
Hull: (centre) Olde Black Boy; Olde White Harte

YORKSHIRE (NORTH)
Beck Hole: Birch Hall Inn
Harrogate: Gardeners Arms
York: Blue Bell; Golden Ball; Royal Oak; Swan

YORKSHIRE (SOUTH)
Barnburgh: Coach & Horses
Doncaster: Plough
Sheffield: (centre) Bath Hotel

YORKSHIRE (WEST)
Bradford: (centre) New Beehive
Leeds: (centre) Adelphi, Whitelock's; (Burley) Cardigan Arms, Rising Sun; (Hunslet) Garden Gate; (Lower Wortley) Beech

WALES

MID WALES
Llanfihangel-yng-Ngwynfa: Goat
Llanidloes: Crown & Anchor
Welshpool: Grapes

NORTH EAST WALES
Ysceifiog: Fox

NORTH WEST WALES
Bethesda: Douglas Arms
Conwy: Albion Hotel

WEST WALES
Llandovery: Red Lion Inn
Pontfaen: Dyffryn Arms

SCOTLAND

BORDERS
Selkirk: Town Arms

DUMFRIES & GALLOWAY
Stranraer: Grapes

FIFE
Kincardine: Railway Tavern
Leslie: Auld Hoose

GRAMPIAN
Aberdeen: (centre) Grill

THE LOTHIANS
Edinburgh: (centre) Abbotsford, Bennet's Bar, H P Mather's Bar, Oxford Bar; (Newington) Leslie's Bar

STRATHCLYDE
Auldhouse: Auldhouse Arms
Glasgow: (centre) Horseshoe Bar, Old Toll Bar, Steps Bar; (Shettleston) Portland Arms
Larkhall: Village Tavern
Lochgilphead: Commercial ('The Comm')
Paisley: Bull

TAYSIDE
Dundee: Clep; Speedwell Bar; Tay Bridge Bar

NORTHERN IRELAND

COUNTY ANTRIM
Ballycastle: House of McDonnell
Ballyeaston: Carmichael's
Bushmills: Bush House
Camlough: Carragher's

COUNTY ARMAGH
Portadown: Mandeville Arms (McConville's)

BELFAST
Belfast: (centre) Crown; (west) Fort Bar (Gilmartin's)

COUNTY FERMANAGH
Irvinestown: Central Bar

COUNTY LONDONDERRY
Limavady: Owen's Bar

National Inventory Part 2

Part 2 lists pub interiors that although altered have exceptional rooms or features of national historic importance. We also include (in italics)a number of outstanding pub-type rooms in other kinds of establishment, such as hotel bars.

ENGLAND

BEDFORDSHIRE
Broom: Cock

BERKSHIRE
Aldworth: Bell

DEVON
South Zeal: *Oxenham Arms*

ESSEX
Bishop's Stortford: Nag's Head

GLOUCESTERSHIRE & BRISTOL
Bristol: (centre) Palace Hotel
Duntisbourne Abbots: Five Mile House

KENT
Cowden Pound: Queen's Arms

GREATER LONDON
Central London: (Blackfriars, EC4) Black Friar; (Holborn, EC4) Olde Cheshire Cheese; (Holborn, WC1) Princess Louise; (Covent Garden, WC2) Salisbury
South East London: (Southwark, SE1) George Inn; (Herne Hill, SE24) Half Moon
South West London: (St James's, SW1) Red Lion; (Battersea, SW11) Falcon; (Tooting, SW17) King's Head
West London: (Fitzrovia, W1) Tottenham; (Marylebone, W1) Barley Mow; (Soho, W1) Dog & Duck; (Maida Vale, W9) Prince Alfred, Warrington Hotel; (Notting Hill, W11) Elgin Arms

GREATER MANCHESTER
Manchester: (centre) Marble Arch, Mr Thomas's
Stalybridge: *Railway Station Buffet*
Stockport: Queen's Head

MERSEYSIDE
Liverpool: (centre) Crown, Lion

NORFOLK
Warham: Three Horseshoes

NORTHUMBERLAND
Blyth: King's Arms

NOTTINGHAMSHIRE
Arnold: Vale Hotel
West Bridgford: Test Match Hotel

SOMERSET
Huish Episcopi: Rose & Crown ('Eli's')

SUSSEX (EAST)
Brighton: King & Queen
Hastings: Havelock

TYNE & WEAR
Gateshead: Central Hotel
Sunderland: Dun Cow; Mountain Daisy

WEST MIDLANDS
Birmingham: (Aston) Bartons Arms; (Hockley) Rose Villa Tavern; (Northfield) Black Horse
Coventry: Biggin Hall Hotel
Netherton: Old Swan ('Ma Pardoe's')
Smethwick: Waterloo Hotel

WORCESTERSHIRE
Hanley Castle: Three Kings

YORKSHIRE (EAST)
Beverley: White Horse Inn ('Nellie's')
Hull: (centre) White Hart

YORKSHIRE (NORTH)
Middlesbrough: (centre) Zetland Hotel

YORKSHIRE (EAST)
Bridlington: *Railway Station Buffet*

YORKSHIRE (SOUTH)
Sheffield: (Carbrook) Stumble Inn

YORKSHIRE (WEST)
Heath: King's Arms

WALES

GLAMORGAN
Cardiff: (centre) Golden Cross

MID-WALES
Rhayader: *Lion Royal Hotel*

SCOTLAND

BORDERS
Oxton: *Tower Hotel*
Tweedsmuir: Crook Inn

FIFE
Kirkcaldy: Feuars Arms

THE LOTHIANS
Edinburgh: (centre) Cafe Royal, Kenilworth
Leith: Central Bar
Prestonpans: Prestoungrange Gothenburg

NORTHERN IRELAND

COUNTY FERMANAGH
Enniskillen: Blake's Bar

■Pub Heritage Group maintains a further list of pubs that are closed or undergoing refurbishment and will require reappraisal. Details are published from time to time in CAMRA's newspaper What's Brewing.

The National Inventory is compiled by CAMRA's Pub Heritage Group

GREATER MANCHESTER

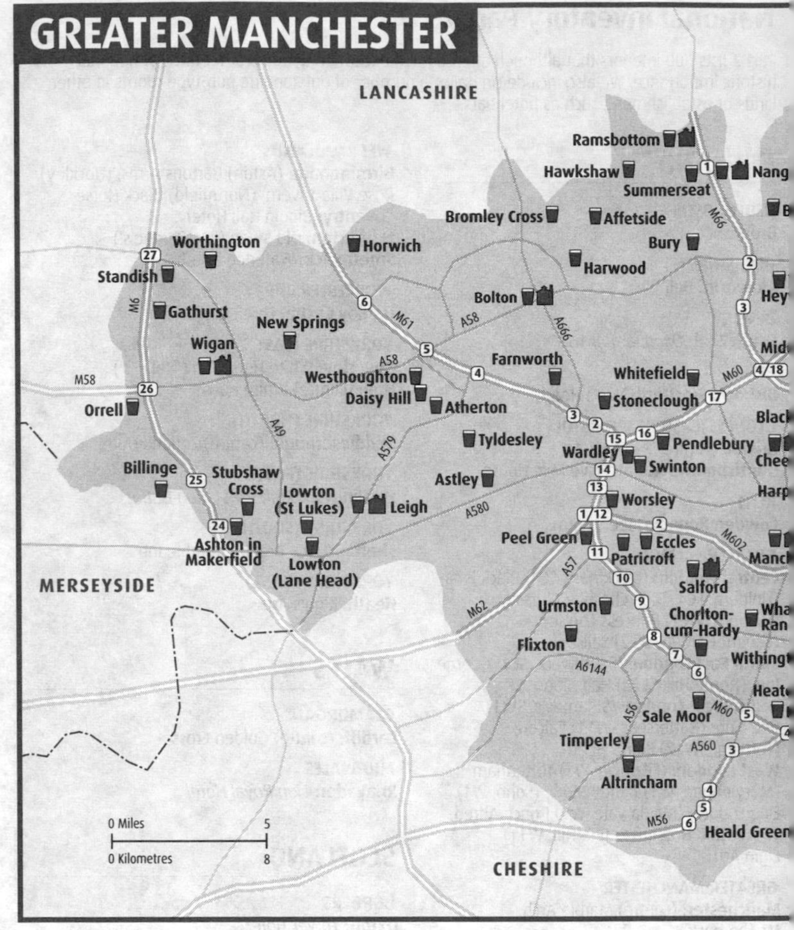

Affetside

Pack Horse

52 Watling Street, BL8 3QW

(approx 2 miles NW of Walshaw) OS755136

✪ 12-3, 5-11; 12-11 Sat; 12-10.30 Sun

☎ (01204) 883802

Hydes Light, Bitter, Jekyll's Gold, seasonal beers Ⓗ

This country pub benefits from panoramic views, thanks to its situation, high up on a Roman road. The bar area and cosy lounge (with real fire), are the original parts of the pub, dating from the 15th century. It has a function and pool room, while the Hightop Bar is used as a family room. Many stories are told relating to the ghost of the local man whose skull is on view behind the bar. Excellent food is served (all day Sat and Sun).

⚔Q❀◐▲P

Altrincham

Old Market Tavern

Old Market Place, WA14 4DN (uphill from metro station)

✪ 12-3, 5-11; 12-11 Fri & Sat; 12-10.30 Sun

☎ (0161) 927 7062

Beer range varies Ⓗ

Large black and white coaching inn on the main A56 road, only five minutes' walk from the bus, rail and tram stations. Opened out in the early 1990s to give a bare-boarded beer house style, a recent refurbishment has made it brighter. It stocks the largest selection of cask ales in the area. There are usually up to three real draught ciders. In winter Robinson's Old Tom is on sale by gravity dispense. Heavy rock music is performed on Sunday evening.

⚔≠⊖●⚡

Orange Tree

15 Old Market Place, WA14 4DE

(outskirts of town centre)

✪ 12-11; 12-10.30 Sun

☎ (0161) 928 2935

Boddingtons Bitter; Tetley Bitter; guest beers Ⓗ

A favourite with older drinkers and diners, the Orange Tree was the result of joining three old buildings together; it is said to be haunted. The upstairs function room, which holds about 30 people, was the venue for Altrincham's first (and, so far, only) beer festival in 2003. Do not miss the 'Wilson's shrine', a collection of breweriana in a glazed alcove. Usually two guest beers are on tap here. Chess and backgammon can be played.

⚔Q❀◐≠⊖♣⚡

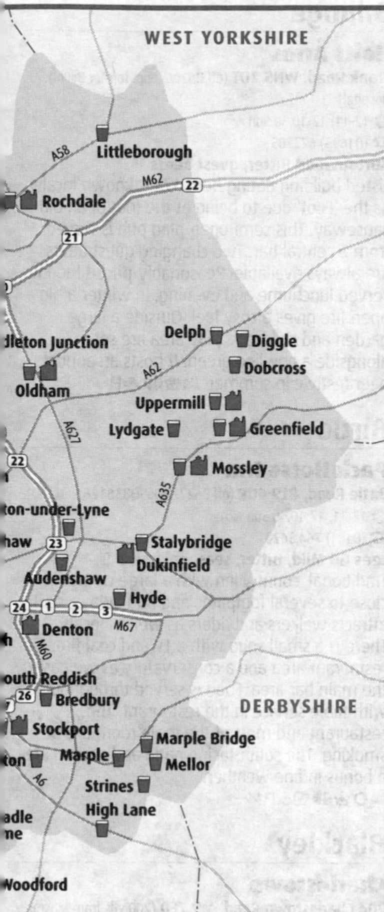

Ashton-in-Makerfield

Jubilee Club

167 Wigan Road, WN4 9ST

(on A49, ½ mile from town centre)

8 (7.30 Fri & Sat)-midnight; 7.30-midnight Sun

☎ (01942) 202703

Beer range varies Ⓗ

Warm, welcoming private members' club with a friendly atmosphere. The single changing cask ale is consistently good quality and competitively priced. It offers the usual social club entertainment (quiz, karaoke, bingo, themed nights) and live entertainment, most Saturdays, in the main function room. There is a games room and a small lobby bar area. Smoking is allowed throughout. Contact the club for further information and details of events, CAMRA members are welcome.

♿ ≹(Bryn) ♣P

Ashton-under-Lyne

Dog & Pheasant

528 Oldham Road, Waterloo, OL7 6PQ

12-11; 12-10.30 Sun

☎ (0161) 330 4894

Banks's Original; Marston's Burton Bitter, Pedigree; guest beers Ⓗ

Nicknamed the Top Dog, this popular, friendly, local stands near the Medlock Valley Country Park. A large bar serves three areas, plus another room at the front. Good value food is available (not Sun eve), the extensive menu includes vegetarian options. On Tuesday and Thursday evenings it stages a quiz. The pub is home to a local hiking group known as the Bog Trotters. The No. 409 bus, from Ashton centre, Oldham and Rochdale, stops outside. ⛰❀◑P

Junction Inn

Mossley Road, Hazlehurst, OL6 9BX

12-11; 12-10.30 Sun

☎ (0161) 343 1611

Robinson's Hatters, Unicorn, seasonal beers Ⓗ

Small pub of great character that remains little changed, close to open countryside and Ashton golf course. Built of local stone in the 19th century, it is the first building out of town that is not of brick construction. The small, cosy rooms make it welcoming and the unpretentious tap room is traditional in every respect. The home-made rag puddings are well worth a try.

Q◑♣P

Oddfellows Arms

1-7 Alderley Street, Hurst, OL6 9LJ

11-11; 12-10.30 Sun

☎ (0161) 330 6356

Robinson's Hatters, Unicorn, seasonal beers Ⓗ

The 'Oddies', on a corner terrace, has been run by the same family since 1914. A small hatch and screen leads to the fine polished bar with its stained glass and nooks and crannies; a small tap room and vestry are to the left. Adjoining the lounge is the no-smoking Tom's Room, named after the late landlord. There is a walled patio to the side, used for free barbecues in summer, which houses a Koi carp pool. Q❀≹⚟

Witchwood

51 Old Street, OL6 7SF

12-11; 12-10.30 Sun

☎ (0161) 344 0321 website: www.thewitchwood.co.uk

INDEPENDENT BREWERIES

Bank Top Bolton
Bazens' Salford
Boggart Hole Clough Moston
Facer's Salford
Greenfield Greenfield
Holt Cheetham
Hydes Manchester
Lees Middleton Junction
Leyden Nangreaves
Lowes Arms Denton
McGuinness Rochdale
Marble Manchester
Mayflower Wigan
Merlin Leigh
Millstone Mossley
Owl Oldham
Phoenix Heywood
Pictish Rochdale
Ramsbottom Ramsbottom
Robinson's Stockport
Saddleworth Uppermill
Shaws Dukinfield
Three Rivers South Reddish

Holt Bitter; John Smith's Bitter; Marston's Pedigree; guest beers Ⓗ
Thriving and deservedly popular urban pub on the edge of the town centre. The area is due to be redeveloped, but the pub has been saved from demolition by a grass roots campaign of impressive scale. A great choice of beers, usually sourced from independent breweries is offered. The major attraction is the award-winning concert room at the rear with an extended licence, which hosts local, national and international artists. Regular beer festivals are also held. ❀⇌

Astley

Cart & Horses

221 Manchester Road, M29 7SD
❂ 12-11; 12-10.30 Sun
☎ (01942) 870751
Holt Mild, Bitter Ⓗ
Popular roadside local with a busy vault, large lounge and a raised no-smoking area away from the bar. It fields an active quiz team and stages regular quiz nights. The large garden is used by families in the summer and hosts frequent barbecues. Regular Tapas nights are a more unusual feature. The pub is home to Astley golf society. ♨ᘓ❀ℂ◗⊟♿♣P⊬

Atherton

Atherton Arms

6 Tyldesey Road, M46 9DD
❂ 11.30-11; 12-10.30 Sun
☎ (01942) 875996
Holt Mild, Bitter, seasonal beers Ⓗ
This spacious, former labour club has various rooms for entertainment: regular karaoke nights are held in the lounge, snooker and pool are played in the tap room, while regular turns (acts) are staged in the concert room. For a quiet pint there are a few seats in the corridor.
ᘓ❀⊟⇌P

Pendle Witch

2-4 Warburton Place, M46 0EQ (alley off Market St)
❂ 4 (12 Sat)-11; 12-10.30 Sun
☎ (01942) 884537
Moorhouses Black Cat, Premier, Pendle Witches Brew, seasonal beers; guest beers Ⓗ
Small, town-centre local, one split-level room with a pool table, which is moved to allow room for rock discos. The small garden is popular in summer. The pub holds regular beer festivals. ♣

Audenshaw (Guide Bridge)

Boundary

2 Audenshaw Road, M34 5HD
❂ 11-11; 12-10.30 Sun
☎ (0161) 330 1677
Beer range varies Ⓗ
Bustling, friendly pub on a busy road junction next to Guide Bridge Station and the Ashton Canal. Good value meals are a feature at the pub, which hosts an annual beer festival in June. All-in-all this is an enterprising pub doing a good job. A changing range of beers is sourced from micro-breweries to nationals. Tables are set outside in summer.
❀ℂ◗⊟⇌(Guide Bridge) ♣P

Billinge

Holts Arms

Crank Road, WN5 7DT (off B5206, opp. former Billinge Hospital)
❂ 12-11; 12-10.30 Sun
☎ (01695) 622705
Burtonwood Bitter; guest beers Ⓗ
Listed building dating from 1721, known locally as the 'Foot' due to being at the foot of an old causeway. This semi-open-plan pub is served from a central bar. Two changing guest beers are always available. Reasonably-priced food is served lunchtime and evening. In winter a big open fire gives a cosy feel. Outside a large garden and children's play area are set alongside a bowling green. It hosts an annual beer festival in summer. ♨❀ℂ◗♣P

Birtle

Pack Horse Inn

Birtle Road, BL9 6UR (off B6222) OSSD836126
❂ 12-11; 12-10.30 Sun
☎ (0161) 764 3620
Lees GB Mild, Bitter, seasonal beers Ⓗ
Traditional, country inn with a large car park, close to several footpaths and bridleways, so it attracts walkers and riders as well as locals. There is a small snug with a TV and coal fire, a restaurant area and a conservatory as well as the main bar area. Food is served throughout, with table service in the restaurant. The restaurant and most of the main room are no-smoking. The south-facing patio and garden are a bonus in fine weather.
♨Q❀ℂ◗⊟♿P⊬

Blackley

Charlestown

204 Charlestown Road, M9 7ED (200 yds from Moston Lane jct)
❂ 12-11; 12-10.30 Sun
☎ (0161) 740 7966
Lees GB Mild, Bitter Ⓗ
Former Tetley house, transformed by Lees Brewery to a friendly community local. Situated on the large White Moss housing estate, it is the only pub on a long, straight stretch of road. A massive 1930s pub (spot the flagpole), it has a large vault (with TV and pool) and an even bigger lounge with a stage, hosting live entertainment on Friday and Saturday evenings. Bar snacks are available during the week and Sunday roasts are served. The disabled WC is by the lounge. Q❀⊟♿♣P

Golden Lion

47 Old Market Street, M9 8DX
(200 yds off Rochdale Rd)
❂ 11-11; 12-10.30 Sun
☎ (0161) 740 1944
Holt Mild, Bitter, seasonal beers Ⓗ
Large, corner Edwardian pub facing the parish church. Recently refurbished both inside and out, it is one of the few pubs to retain its bowling green (the last surviving pub green in north Manchester/Salford). A central bar serves the L-shaped lounge (with large TV screen) and the vault, where the mild handpump can be found. Entertainment is staged on Friday and Saturday

evenings. The sunny patio, overlooking the bowling green, is popular in the warmer weather. ❀⊟♣

Bolton

Ainsworth Arms ✔

606 Halliwell Road, BL1 8BY (at A58/A6099 jct)

11.30-2 (not Tue-Thu), 5-11; 11.30-11 Sat; 12-10.30 Sun

☎ (01204) 840671

Taylor Landlord; Tetley Mild, Bitter; guest beers H

Near Smithills Hall, a Grade I listed building, this is a dog-friendly local. The bar serves three areas: one is raised with alcoves, another is a basic tap room complete with bell pushes in use until 1981. It has a long association with football, and is the meeting place for many local sports teams; the juke box is only switched on by request. Lunches are served Friday–Sunday and breakfasts are strongly recommended. Guest beers come from small, independent breweries. Q❀◐♣

Bob's Smithy Inn

1448 Chorley Old Road, BL1 7GX (on B6226, ½ mile uphill from A58 ring road)

4.30 (12 Sat)-11; 12-10.30 Sun

☎ (01204) 842622

Boddingtons Bitter; Taylor Best Bitter; Tetley Bitter; guest beers H

Cosy, dog-friendly, stone hostelry on the edge of the moors affording a panoramic view over Bolton. It is handy for walkers and visitors to the Reebok Stadium (2½ miles away). A genuine free house, run by friendly, enterprising owners, the pub has been in existence for around 200 years. It is named after a regular, Bob the blacksmith, who used to work across the road. The guest beers are usually from small independent breweries; a Bank Top beer is always available. ♨❀P

Dog & Partridge

22 Manor Street, BL1 1TV

6 (12 Sat)-11; 6-10.30 Sun

☎ (01204) 388596 website: www.dogandpartridgepub.com

Thwaites Original, Lancaster Bomber H

This unspoilt, three-roomed local is situated on the edge of the town centre. The pub dates from the 18th century and features a traditional vault with a curved bar. The small back room has an acid-etched Cornbrook Ales window. The larger side room houses a pool table and hosts weekend discos and popular live acoustic music sessions on Sunday evening. Public car parks are nearby. ⊟≈♣

Hen & Chickens ✔

143 Deansgate, BL1 1EX (near Moor Lane bus station)

11.30-11; 7.30-10.30 Sun

☎ (01204) 389836

Cains Mild; Tetley Bitter; guest beers H

Traditional, friendly, town-centre local where a central bar serves two areas. See the pump clips displayed to show the many guest beers served; there are always three available. A reasonably-priced, tasty home-cooked menu is popular; children dining at lunchtime are welcome, when a no-smoking area is set aside. ◐≈♣

King's Head

52-54 Junction Road, Deane, BL3 4NA (off A676)

12-11; 12-10.30 Sun

☎ (01204) 62609

Taylor Landlord; Tetley Mild, Bitter; guest beers H

This 300-year-old Grade II listed pub stands by the Deane Clough nature trail. Three distinct drinking areas (the largest of which has a stone floor and authentic-looking range) are served from a long bar. A well-used crown bowling green adjoins a children's play space and outdoor seating. This dog-friendly pub welcomes children until 7.30pm. Piped music and TV underlie the buzz of conservation. It hosts a weekly quiz (Wed) and monthly acoustic sessions (last Mon). ❀◐♣P⊬

Lodge Bank Tavern

260 Bridgeman Street, BL3 6SA

12-11; 12-10.30 Sun

☎ (01204) 531946

Lees Bitter H

Welcoming local, near Bobby Heywood's Park (with free use of floodlit pitches). The main room is conveniently divided into three small areas, and there is a pool room at the back of the bar. Karaoke, on Friday and Saturday evenings, and the quiz on Wednesday are always well-attended. The only Lees pub in Bolton, it was the last to change its ale house status to a full licence. Well-behaved dogs are welcome. ❀≈♣P

Sweet Green Tavern

127 Crook Street, BL3 6DD (opp. Sainsbury's, off A579)

11-11; 12-10.30 Sun

☎ (01204) 392258

Tetley Bitter; guest beers H

This friendly local is situated on the edge of the town centre close to the bus/rail interchange. It comprises four small rooms served by a long bar, including an unspoilt vault. Its name reflects the original character of the area, 'a place of fragrant gardens', prior to 19th-century industrial development, which has in turn been replaced by a supermarket. Five guest beers are regularly served, usually featuring a mild. Meals are served 12-7pm daily.
♨❀◐◑⊟≈♣●

Bredbury

Traveller's Call

402 Stockport Road West, SK6 2DT

12-11; 12-10.30 Sun

☎ (0161) 430 2511

Lees Bitter, seasonal beers H

The only Lees outlet in Stockport has become a regular entry in this Guide. It is one of a handful of Lees pubs to stock the brewery's seasonal beers throughout the year. Despite extensive renovation, the pub has maintained a traditional look and now has broadened its appeal to include a wide age range, firmly establishing itself as a community local. Regular bus services from Stockport make the pub easily accessible. Evening meals, served weekdays, finish at 7pm. ❀◐◑♿≈P⊬

Bromley Cross

Flag Inn ✔

50 Hardmans Lane, BL7 9HX (off B6472)

⏲ 12-11; 12-10.30 Sun

☎ (01204) 598267

Boddingtons Bitter, guest beers Ⓗ

Enterprising management and changing guest beers, sourced from small independent breweries, make this beer drinker's mecca well worth seeking out. Although not immediately apparent, the building's history has been traced back over 300 years; the old brick-arched cellars were originally stables. In a spacious open-plan interior, TV screens attract sports enthusiasts, but do not dominate or impede conversation. It gets busy at weekends. ⛰❀≠

Bury

Dusty Miller

87 Crostons Road, BL8 1AL (at B6213/B6214 jct)

⏲ 12-11; 12-10.30 Sun

☎ (0161) 764 1124

Moorhouses Black Cat, Premier, Pendle Witches Brew; guest beer Ⓗ

Typical local drawing a mixed clientele. A central bar serves the two rooms: a basic public bar and a comfortable lounge. Outside a covered courtyard leads to an open rear yard with seating. A guest beer is usually available from a local brewery. No food is served Monday-Wednesday; at the weekend meals are available 12-6pm. ❀◐◑⊟

Rose & Crown

36 Manchester Old Road, BL9 0TR

⏲ 5 (12 Sat)-11; 12-10.30 Sun

☎ (0161) 764 6234

Caledonian Deuchars IPA; Jennings Cumberland Ale; guest beers Ⓗ

Attractive end-of-terrace pub, just five minutes' walk from the bus and metro stations. Six cask ales are kept and the pub is deservedly popular with locals and visitors alike. One cosy room is split into various distinct drinking areas. It is frequented by Bury FC fans as it is the nearest good pub to the stadium and has a relaxed atmosphere. Q⊖♣

Trackside

East Lancs Railway, Bolton Street Station, BL9 0EY

⏲ 12 (11 Sat)-11; 12-10.30 Sun

☎ (0161) 764 6461

Beer range varies Ⓗ

Free house with nine handpumps and draught cider (varies) from the cellar. Simple wooden tables and chairs impart a traditional railway buffet bar mood. The vast array of pump clips on poles attached to the ceiling bear testimony to the beers that have been sold here. It stocks a good choice of foreign bottled beers. It can be busy at weekends when the ELR holds special events. Food is served all day on Saturday and Sunday, from 9.30am until 5pm.
Q❀◐♿≠(Bolton St) ⊖●

Wyldes

4 Market Street, BL9 0LH

⏲ 12-11 (midnight Fri & Sat); 12-10.30 Sun

☎ (0161) 797 2000

Holt Mild, Bitter, seasonal beers Ⓗ

Large, modern two-storey pub, right at the centre of town. Once a bank, it has been impressively converted by Manchester brewer, Joseph Holt. A long bar on the ground floor is supplemented by a smaller one upstairs; seating is a mix of chairs and comfortable sofas. A no-smoking mezzanine area is the perfect place to dine; food is served until 7pm Monday-Saturday and until 6pm Sunday. Several TVs show music videos. It can get busy at times. ◐◑♿⊖⚟

Cheadle Hulme

Cheadle Hulme

47 Station Road, SK8 7AA (next to station, on A5149)

⏲ 11-11; 12-10.30 Sun

☎ (0161) 485 4706

Holt Mild, Bitter, seasonal beers Ⓗ

Situated next to the railway station, the pub was refurbished in early 2004 to give it an ultra-modern interior, with contemporary furnishings and plasma TV screens. The L-shaped bar serves the open-plan sectioned lounge bar and vault. A large, no-smoking area is provided in the dining area of the lounge bar, where an interesting choice of food is served. It attracts a good, mixed clientele but retains a local pub atmosphere. ❀◐◑⊟♿≠♣P⚟

Church Inn

90 Ravenoak Road, SK8 5HP (on A5149)

⏲ 11-11; 12-10.30 Sun

☎ (0161) 482 5221

Robinson's Hatters, Old Stockport, Unicorn, seasonal beers Ⓗ

This inviting Robinson's house has been run by the same family for over 30 years. It comprises three rooms: the panelled front lounge, decorated with brass and ceramics, with a welcoming fire; the rear lounge which doubles as Edwardo's Restaurant, and a small vault behind the bar. Despite increasing competition in the area, this pub remains as popular as ever, providing excellent service. Seasonal beers are sold in place of Old Stockport as available.
⛰Q❀◐◑⊟♣P⚟

Ryecroft Arms ✔

Turves Road, SK8 6AJ (near Highfield Rd jct)

⏲ 12-11; 12-10.30 Sun

☎ (0161) 485 2655

Hydes Bitter, Jekyll's Gold, seasonal beers Ⓗ

Known as the Conway until early 2004; the renaming acknowledges the local tennis club. The interior was also remodelled along clean lines that better reflect the age and style of the building. Pastel paint and pine abound, with Art Nouveau vases in display units that partition the lounge into cosy booths. The vault is the domain of the livelier younger generation, while the lounge has a more laid-back atmosphere for drinkers and diners to relax in. ❀◐◑⊟♿♣P⚟

Cheetham

Queen's Arms

6 Honey Street, M8 8RG (300 yds from A665 at top of Red Bank)

⏲ 12-11; 12-10.30 Sun

☎ (0161) 834 4239

Phoenix Bantam; Taylor Landlord; guest beers Ⓗ

Just outside Manchester's northern quarter, this well-established, two-roomed free house, bearing an impressive tiled Old Empress Brewery façade, justly rewards the uphill walk from the city centre. A large garden to the rear has a children's play area overlooking the industrialised Irk Valley. Up to six guest beers are usually available from micro-breweries, together with a wide selection of bottled and draught continental beers. A quiz is held on Tuesday.
⚙❀ᗡ⇌(Manchester Victoria) ⊖♣●

Chorlton-cum-Hardy

Bar

533 Wilbraham Road, M21 0UE
✪ 12-11; 12-10.30 Sun
☎ (0161) 861 7576
Marble Manchester Bitter, Ginger Marble; guest beers ⊞
As the name implies, this is a modern bar, not a traditional pub. Unlike many of its competitors in this fashionable suburb, it offers a range of cask ales from Marble and other independent breweries. It is increasingly sought out by lovers of good ale and food, based on local ingredients and served 12-8pm daily. The no-smoking area has grown as the bar moves towards a smoke-free future. It attracts a predominantly, but not overwhelmingly young clientele. ᗡ◗♣⚟

Beech Inn

72 Beech Road, M21 9EZ
✪ 11-11; 12-10.30 Sun
☎ (0161) 881 1180
Caledonian Deuchars IPA; Marston's Pedigree; Taylor Best Bitter, Landlord; ⊞
Thriving, three-roomed pub, popular with drinkers of all ages, close to the village green. There is a garden at the rear and a pavement seating area at the front. A TV is installed in each room, including a large pull-down screen in the back room; all are used mainly for sporting events. Irish musicians get together on Monday evenings and a quiz is held every Thursday at local CAMRA's Pub of the Season for spring 2005. ❀⊟♣

Marble Beer House

57 Manchester Road, M21 9PW
✪ 12-11; 12-10.30 Sun
☎ (0161) 881 9206
Marble Bitter, Manchester Bitter, Ginger Marble, Lagonda IPA, seasonal beers; guest beers ⊞
The full range of Marble's organic beers is supplemented by changing seasonals and guests in this distinctive café-bar style beer house. In front of the bar, successfully converted from a beer shop, is an outdoor seating area, which is busy during the day and into the evening. No meals are served but snacks from the award-winning Unicorn Wholefood Co-operative are available, while the celebrated Barbakan Deli, a few doors away, is one of many eating places nearby. Q❀

Daisy Hill

Rose Hill Tavern

321 Leigh Road, BL5 2JQ (on B5235)
✪ 12-11; 12-10.30 Sun
☎ (01942) 815776
Holt Mild, Bitter ⊞
Large, welcoming pub, now opened out, but retaining the original room plan, with two rooms taken up by games of all sorts. It is often referred to by locals as the 'Bug' since an orphanage (the Bug House) was demolished to make way for the pub in 1899, a year after the railway came to the village. Originally an Oldfield Brewery (of Poolstock, Wigan) tavern, its crest can still be seen over the front door.
❀⇌P

Delph

Royal Oak (Th'heights)

Broad Lane, OL3 5TX
(1 mile above Denshaw Rd) OS982090
✪ 7-11; 12-5, 7-10.30 Sun
☎ (01457) 874460
Black Sheep Best Bitter; guest beers ⊞
Isolated, 250-year-old stone pub on a packhorse route overlooking the Thame Valley. In a popular walking area, it benefits from outstanding views. It comprises a cosy bar and three rooms, each with an open fire. The refurbished side room boasts a hand-carved stone fireplace, while the comfortable snug bears exposed beams. Good home-cooked food (eve meals Fri-Sun) often features game and home-bred pork. The house beer is brewed by Moorhouses. Guests include brews from Phoenix and Millstone.
⚙Q❀◗P⚟

Didsbury

Fletcher Moss ✔

1 William Street, M20 6RQ (off Wilmslow Rd, A5145)
✪ 12-11; 12-10.30 Sun
☎ (0161) 438 0073
Hydes Mild, Bitter, Jekyll's Gold, seasonal beers ⊞
Formerly the Albert, the pub was renamed in 1998 after Alderman Fletcher Moss, who was responsible for building Didsbury Library and whose name was also given to the nearby park. One of the last pubs in Didsbury to retain a strong local identity, it does not pander to the young people who pack many of the pubs on the Wilmslow Road. A comfortable interior offers a variety of different areas; a large conservatory features mock adverts for local firms.
Q♿P⚟

Royal Oak

729 Wilmslow Road, M20 6WF (on A5145)
✪ 11-11; 12-10.30 Sun
☎ (0161) 434 4788
Banks's Mansfield Dark; Marston's Burton Bitter, Pedigree; guest beers ⊞
Built around 1850 this multi-roomed pub is now the community centre for the village. The large, central horseshoe-shaped bar displays an impressive collection of old spirit vats and posters promoting long-gone boxing legends. Despite a serious arson attack a few years ago, the pub has now bounced back stronger and better than ever. On a weekday, try the extensive range of cheese and pâté at lunchtime, which many have tried to copy but none have surpassed for choice or value.
ᗡ⇌(East)

Diggle

Diggle Hotel

Station Houses, OL3 5JZ (½ mile off A670) OS011081
⊛ 12-3, 5-11; 12-11 Sat; 12-10.30 Sun
☎ (01457) 872741
Black Sheep Best Bitter; Boddingtons Bitter; Taylor Landlord; Theakston Mild; guest beer Ⓗ
Stone pub in a pleasant hamlet near the Standedge canal tunnel under the Pennines. Built as a merchant's house in 1789, it became an ale house and general store on the construction of the railway tunnel in 1834. Affording fine views of the Saddleworth countryside, this makes a convenient base in a popular walking area. With a bar area and two rooms, the accent is on home-cooked food (served all day Sat and Sun). Brass bands play on alternate summer Sundays. Q❀⇆◑♣P

Dobcross

Navigation Inn

21-23 Wool Road, OL3 5NS (on A670)
⊛ 12-2.30, 5-11; 12-11 Sat; 12-10.30 Sun
☎ (01457) 872418
Black Sheep Best Bitter; Phoenix Arizona; Taylor Landlord; Theakston Best Bitter; Wells Bombardier; guest beer Ⓗ
Next to the Huddersfield Narrow Canal, this stone pub was built in 1806 to slake the thirsts of the navvies cutting the Standedge tunnel. The open-plan bar and L-shaped interior feature a fine collection of old brass band photos; live concerts are staged on alternate Sunday afternoons in summer. It is the venue for annual events such as the beer walk (May-June) and the Saddleworth Rushcart Festival (Aug). Home-cooked meals with weekday special offer lunches are popular (no food Sun eve).
Q❀◑P⊬

Swan Inn (Top House)

The Square, OL3 5AA
⊛ 12-3, 5.30-11; 12-4, 7.30-10.30 Sun
☎ (01457) 873451
Jennings Dark Mild, Bitter, Cumberland Ale, Cocker Hoop, Sneck Lifter; guest beers Ⓗ
Built circa 1765, for the Wrigley family of chewing gum fame, part of the building was later used as a police court and cells. Overlooking the attractive village square, the pub has been well renovated, with flagged floors and three distinct drinking areas, plus a fine function room that caters for 80 people. It gets busy during the Whit Friday brass band contest and the August Rushcart Festival. Good quality, home-cooked food includes Indian dishes (no food Sun eve); booking advisable.
♨Q❀◑⊬

Eccles

Albert Edward

142 Church Street, M30 0LS (opp. library)
⊛ 12-11; 12-10.30 Sun
☎ (0161) 707 1045
Samuel Smith OBB Ⓗ
The pub closed for several months in 2003/4 when it was extensively rebuilt, following the original plans. There are now four rooms: a front bar, a snug to the right, a no-smoking room behind this, and at the rear a lounge, displaying Lowry prints. The garden occupies an enclosed yard behind the no-smoking room. A company-wide 'diktat' early in 2005 saw the removal of all TV sets, juke boxes and piped music. Beer prices are among the lowest in town.
♨Q❀⊟♿⇌⊖(Terminus) ♣⊬

Lamb Hotel ☆

33 Regent Street, M30 0BP (opp. tram terminus)
⊛ 11.30-11; 12-10.30 Sun
☎ (0161) 787 7297
Holt Mild, Bitter Ⓗ
Arguably the jewel in the crown among Holt's collection of Edwardian drinking palaces, the Lamb glories in finely etched glass and rich mahogany, professionally finished by Holt's own french-polisher. There are four rooms, including a vault and a billiards room with a full-size table. The pub is handy for the tram terminus, bus station and nearby retail park.
Q⊟⇌⊖(Terminus) ♣P

Royal Oak ☆

34 Barton Lane, M30 0EN (behind library)
⊛ 11-11; 12-10.30 Sun
☎ (0161) 707 0732
Holt Mild, Bitter, seasonal beers (occasional) Ⓗ
Another of Holt's Edwardian monuments, the Royal Oak attracts a following of regular, enthusiastic drinkers. The large vault and spacious bar lobby are particularly popular, but there is also a front snug, a pool room and a former billiards room that now serves as a family room until 5.30pm.
Q♘❀⊟⇌⊖(Terminus) ♣

Farnworth

Britannia

34 King Street, BL4 7AF (opp. bus station, off A6053)
⊛ 11-11; 12-10.30 Sun
☎ (01204) 571629
Moorhouses Premier Ⓗ
Busy local near the market, with a basic, but spacious vault and a small lounge, both served by a small central bar. The pub offers well-priced Moorhouses Premier and inexpensive, home-cooked lunches every day. Mini-outdoor beer festivals on May and August bank holidays are well attended. Behind the pub is a free car park. Children are welcome until 4.30pm.
❀◑⊟⇌♣

Flixton

Church Inn

34 Church Road, M41 6HS
⊛ 11-11; 12-10.30 Sun
☎ (0161) 748 2158
Coach House Coachman's Best Bitter; guest beers Ⓗ
Comfortable, village-style pub, next to the church, within five minutes' walk of the station on the Manchester-Warrington line. The bar serves three seating areas; the raised part at the rear is for non-smokers while the section on the left by the main entrance is used for traditional games such as darts and cribbage. A good selection of cooked meals is available, 12-8pm daily; the Sunday lunches are popular.
♨❀◑⇌♣P⊬

Gathurst

Navigation
162 Gathurst Lane, WN6 8HZ
(on B5206 by Leeds-Liverpool canal)
⏲ 12-11; 12-10.30 Sun
☎ (01257) 252856
Greene King Abbot; Taylor Landlord; Tetley Bitter; guest beers Ⓗ
Extended canalside pub, next to Bridge 46 on the Leeds–Liverpool Canal, popular with boaters, walkers and cyclists. Named after the Douglas Navigation Company who kept the adjacent River Douglas navigable during the 19th century, the point of transfer for barges from river to canal is still visible alongside the nearby locks. Food is available daily in the pub and restaurant (lunches in summer only). Westons Old Rosie cider is sold. ⩩❀◐◗≠♣●P⊬

Greenfield

King William IV ✔
134 Chew Valley Road, OL3 7DD (on A669)
⏲ 11-11; 12-10.30 Sun
☎ (01457) 873933
Lees Bitter; Tetley Mild, Bitter; guest beers Ⓗ
Detached stone pub at the village centre, comprising a central bar area and two rooms. A cobbled forecourt with benches allows for outdoor drinking. It offers two changing guest beers and food is served until 7pm each day. Handy for walks over the Moors, the Nos. 180 and 183 buses from Manchester and Oldham pass by. The pub is the centre of village life, participating in the annual beer walk and Ruschart Festival (Aug) and hosting the Whit Friday brass band contest. ❀◐◗≠♣P

Railway
11 Shaw Hall Bank Road, OL3 7JZ (opp. station)
⏲ 12-11; 12-10.30 Sun
☎ (01457) 872307
Caledonian Deuchars IPA; John Smith's Bitter; Taylor Landlord; Wells Bombardier; guest beer Ⓗ
Unspoilt pub where the central bar and games area draw a good mix of old and young. The tap room boasts a log fire and old Saddleworth photos. In a picturesque area, it provides a good base for various outdoor pursuits and affords beautiful views across Chew Valley. The venue for live Cajun, R&B, jazz and pop music on Thursday, Friday (unplugged night) and Sunday, it also hosts top class entertainment every month. Lunches are served at weekends.
⩩❀⇄◐⊟⚠≠♣●P

Harpurhey

Junction Inn
1-5 Hendlam Vale, Queen's Road, M9 5SF (on A6010, near A664 jct)
⏲ 11-11; 12-10.30 Sun
☎ (07910) 472403
Beartown Bearskinful, Black Bear Ⓗ
Pathos and pints are the order of the day in this lively local, taken over by the Beartown Brewery in 2002. The hosts here have made this pub well known for its inexpensive quality beers; on weekdays 5-8pm, they are sold at £1 a pint. The building is crescent-shaped, with the vault and two rooms, retaining many original features. Discos are held on Saturday evening.
⩩⊟⊖(Woodlands Rd) ♣

Harwood

House without a Name
75-77 Lea Gate, BL2 3ET (on B6196, near A676 jct)
⏲ 2 (11 Sat)-11; 12-10.30 Sun
☎ (01204) 300063
Holt Bitter; guest beers Ⓗ
Traditional, cosy, two-roomed village local. Several guest beers are always available and changed regularly, making it well worth visiting. Known as the 'No Name', it was historically an un-named drinking den. When a licence was applied for, no-one knew what to call it, so the magistrate declared it a house without a name. Take No. 506 or 507 bus from Moor Lane bus station in Bolton town centre. Well-behaved children (and dogs) are welcome. ❀⊟♣

Hawkshaw

Red Lion
81 Ramsbottom Road, BL8 4JS (on A676)
⏲ 12-3, 6-11; 12-11 Sat; 12-10.30 Sun
☎ (01204) 856600 website: www.redlion-hawkshaw.co.uk
Jennings Bitter, Cumberland Ale; guest beers Ⓗ
Attractive stone pub, nestling in a picturesque village. Inside you will find a single, large room, friendly locals and an excellent menu. Popular with diners, you can choose to eat either in the pub or the adjacent restaurant, which offers an extensive range of freshly prepared delights (meals all day Sat and Sun). The pub is on the outskirts of Bury but is frequented by locals and those from further afield. ⇄◐◗

Heald Green

Griffin
124 Wilmslow Road, SK8 3BE (Finney Lane jct)
⏲ 11-11; 12-10.30 Sun
☎ (0161) 437 1596
Holt Mild, Bitter, seasonal beers Ⓗ
Although there has been a pub on this site for over 100 years, the Griffin is a 1960s building, whose exterior belies the warmth inside. There is a thriving vault, a large lounge for TV football and regular entertainment, and a comfortable snug where customers are asked not to smoke, especially when lunch is served. By the time this Guide is published a conservatory should be finished as part of a general refurbishment, and evening meals should be available. ❀◐⊟♣P⊬

Heaton Norris

Navigation
11 Manchester Road, SK4 1TY
(on A626 roundabout by flour mill)
⏲ 12-11; 12-10.30 Sun
☎ (0161) 480 6626
Beartown Kodiak Gold, Bearskinful, Polar Eclipse, Bruins Ruin, Wheat Bear, Black Beer Ⓗ
Situated between a busy roundabout and a flour mill, this is the only Beartown Brewery outlet in Stockport, and is well worth seeking out. A former local CAMRA Pub of the Year, the full selection of Beartown beers is sold, along with occasional guest beers and various ciders. A

small, comfortable, two-roomed local with a central bar serving both the vault and best room, there is a courtyard for fair weather drinking. The pub hosts monthly folk nights and occasional quizzes. ❀

Nursery ☆

258 Green Lane, SK4 2NA (off A6 by Dunham Jaguar garage)

✪ 11.30-3, 5.30-11; 11.30-11 Fri & Sat; 12-10.30 Sun

☎ (0161) 432 2044

Hydes Mild, Bitter, Jekyll's Gold, seasonal beers 🄷

CAMRA's national Pub of the Year 2001, and a Guide regular, the Nursery is a classic, unspoilt 1930s pub, hidden away in a pleasant suburb. The multi-roomed interior includes a traditional vault with its own entrance, and a spacious wood-panelled room, used by diners at lunchtime. The home-made food draws customers from miles around, particularly on Sunday; children are welcome if dining. The pub's immaculate bowling green – an increasingly rare feature – is well used by local league teams. ❀◖⊟♣P

Heywood

Wishing Well

89 York Street, OL10 4NS (on A58 towards Rochdale)

✪ 12-11; 12-10.30 Sun

☎ (01706) 620923

Black Sheep Best Bitter; Phoenix Pale Moonlight, White Monk; Moorhouses Pride of Pendle; Taylor Landlord; guest beers 🄷

Popular free house, on the Rochdale side of the town centre, where the wide range of beers and clientele make the pub well worth visiting. Each of several comfortable drinking areas is equipped with a smoke filter unit. The efforts of the long-standing landlord are reflected in the quality of the beer and various awards received over the years. The beers can be served in the adjoining award-winning restaurant. The frequent No. 471 Bury-Rochdale bus stops outside.

High Lane

Royal Oak

Buxton Road, SK6 8AY (2 miles from Hazel Grove)

✪ 12-3, 5.30-11; 12-3, 6-10.30 Sun

☎ (01663) 762380

Burtonwood Bitter; guest beer 🄷

Well-appointed pub, with a pleasing exterior, on a busy main road. Although open-plan, there are three distinct drinking areas – one is used for games. Live entertainment is staged most Fridays. An interesting menu is served at all sessions. Burtonwood beers make a welcome addition to the choice in the locality. The garden and play area are added attractions.

Q❀◖◗♿P

Horwich

Crown

1 Chorley New Road, BL6 7QJ (at A673/B6226 jct)

✪ 11-11; 12-10.30 Sun

☎ (01204) 690926

Holt Mild, Bitter, seasonal beers 🄷

Large pub on the edge of town, handy for the Reebok Stadium, Rivington Pike and the West Pennine moors. Mainly open plan, it comprises a well-furnished drinking area, a vault and a games room at the rear. This friendly pub serves good value food. Sunday evening is busy, when locals take part in free and easy singalongs; Wednesday is quiz night. The pub is a well known and imposing local landmark.

❀◖⊟♿⇌(Blackrod) ♣P

Hyde

Queen's

23 Clarendon Place, SK14 2ND

✪ 11-11; 12-10.30 Sun

☎ (0161) 368 2230

Holt Mild, Bitter, seasonal beers 🄷

A new addition to the gently expanding estate of the highly respected Manchester brewers Joseph Holt. The Queen's has been rescued from a run-down, tawdry hovel to a well laid-out and welcoming community pub. Good use of an understated theme makes the pub warm and welcoming. The well-priced beers add to its appeal. Look out for the attractive brewery showcard in the lobby.

⊟♿⇌(Central/Newton for Hyde) ♣

Sportsman

57 Mottram Road, SK14 2NN

✪ 11-11; 12-10.30 Sun

☎ (0161) 368 5000

Moorhouses Black Cat; Phoenix Bantam; Pictish Brewers Gold; Plassey Bitter; Taylor Landlord; Whim Hartington Bitter 🄷

True free house, offering an excellent and varied beer range that includes a guest from an independent or micro-brewery, but the pub is so much more. A loyal regular crowd keeps it firmly at the heart of the community, but passing visitors slip in seamlessly, and are soon involved in the bar chat if they wish. Sports teams feature highly, and there is a full-sized snooker table. This frequent local CAMRA Pub of the Year should not be missed.

⛼❀⊟⇌(Newton for Hyde/Central) ♣P

Leigh

Waggon & Horses

68 Wigan Road, WN7 5AY (1 mile from town centre)

✪ 7 (5 Fri; 12 Sat)-11; 12-10.30 Sun

☎ (01942) 673069

Hydes Light, Dark, Bitter 🄷

Warm, friendly local on the outskirts of Leigh town centre. The lounge, with an open fire, has a large-screen TV that shows main sporting events. There is standing space around the bar and a cosy snug. The large games room is where the pub's darts and dominoes teams regularly play and there is also a pool table. The garden patio offers the possibility of alfresco drinking.

⛼❀♣

Musketeer ✔

15 Lord Street, WN7 1AB (5 mins' walk from bus station)

✪ 11-11; 12-10.30 Sun

☎ (01942) 701143

Boddingtons Bitter; Jennings Cumberland Ale; guest beers 🄷

Comfortable lounge with three distinct parts including a snug. The large tap room is popular

with local rugby fans. Children are welcome until 9pm in the main lounge area. Four guest beers change weekly at this busy local where food is served every lunchtime. Note the display of Lancashire pit plates and photographs of local rugby teams. Parking is limited, but it is close to town-centre car parks and the bus station.
☋◐⊟♿♣⚟

Littleborough

Moorcock Inn

Halifax Road, OL15 0LD (on A58)
11.30-11; 11.30-10.30 Sun
☎ (01706) 378156
Taylor Landlord; guest beers Ⓗ
Built as a farmhouse in 1641 and first licensed in 1840, this gem, nestling in the Pennine foothills, is worth a visit for the view alone. Although boasting a fine 80-seat restaurant, the pub section is kept apart by clever use of floor space. Three guest beers, usually from local brewers, are served in agreeable surroundings. The pub is close to the Pennine Way so ramblers and equestrians stop by; tethers are provided for horses. Six guest rooms are a recent addition.
⩩❀⊏◐◑♿▲P

White House

Blackstone Edge, Halifax Road, OL15 0L6 (on A58, top of hill)
12-3, 6.30-11; 12-10.30 Sun
☎ (01706) 378456
Theakston Best Bitter; guest beers Ⓗ
The Pennine Way passes by this old coaching house, situated 1,300 feet above sea level. A landmark that dates from 1671, it benefits from panoramic views of the surrounding moors and Hollingworth Lake far below. This family-run hostelry gives a warm friendly welcome in its two bars, with a real fire in each. Guest beers and Belgian bottled beers complement the excellent menu and daily specials board; food is served all day Sunday. It has a comfortable family room. ⩩Q☋❀◐◑▲P⚟

Lowton (Lane Head)

Red Lion

324 Newton Road, WA3 1HE
12-11; 12-10.30 Sun
☎ (01942) 671429
Boddingtons Bitter; Marston's Pedigree; Tetley Mild; Thwaites Original; Wells Bombardier; guest beers (occasional) Ⓗ
Large, ivy-clad local frequented by all ages. Several drinking areas are supplemented by a lounge used by diners. It hosts regular quiz nights, and crown green bowls is played; the green can be hired for private parties. The Lion is a good base for Haydock Park Racecourse and Pennington Country Park. ❀⊏◐◑♣P

Travellers' Rest

443 Newton Road, WA3 1NX (on A572 between Lowton and Newton)
12-11; 12-10.30 Sun
☎ (01925) 224391
Marston's Pedigree; guest beers Ⓗ
Pub and restaurant split into discrete areas, with different menus for each, specialising in game and Greek cuisine. The guest beer adds variety to the regular ales. The chatty locals enhance the atmosphere of this friendly pub. For a roadside pub at the centre of a small hamlet, it gets quite busy. The kitchen's game supplier can often be found at the bar, for anybody wanting to swap notes on dogs and hunting. ❀◐◑♣P

Lowton (St Luke's)

Hare & Hounds

1 Golborne Road, WA3 2DP
11-11; 12-10.30 Sun
☎ (01942) 728387
Tetley Bitter; guest beers Ⓗ
Attracting a good mix of local customers, the central bar provides a barrier between the various drinking and dining areas. The original part of the pub houses the tap room and comfortable lounge; families are catered for in the no-smoking section next to the children's play room. In summer the two patios are well used, the largest houses a children's playground.
☋❀◑⊟♣P⚟

Lydgate

White Hart

51 Stockport Road, OL4 4JJ (at A669/A6050 jct)
12-11; 12-10.30 Sun
☎ (01457) 872566 website: www.thewhitehart.co.uk
Lees Bitter; Taylor Landlord; Tetley Bitter; guest beers Ⓗ
Detached, stone, free house dating from 1788, commanding impressive views over the hills above Oldham. Adjoining the village church and school, the pub has four rooms, two used for dining. The small snug has its own servery and the main bar boasts eight handpumps. A new extension, with bar, is used for gourmet meals and weddings. It makes an excellent base for visiting Saddleworth's moors and villages, with 18 en-suite rooms and food from an award-winning chef. Buses from Manchester and Oldham to Greenfield pass nearby.
⩩Q❀⊏◐◑♿P

Manchester City Centre

Bar Fringe

8 Swan Street, M4 5JN (50 yds from A665/A62 jct)
12-11; 12-10.30 Sun
☎ (0161) 835 3815
Beer range varies Ⓗ
Excellent example of a Belgian 'brown bar'. Expect a friendly, yet robust and occasionally boisterous experience in this characterful pub, with its ever-changing wall posters, framed cartoons and bare floorboards. Stocking an extensive selection of continental draught and bottled beers alongside its four handpumps with their local micro-brewery offerings, the pub is an alternative to the other nearby free houses in the northern quarter. A secluded patio can be found to the rear. Meals finish at 6pm (4pm Sat and Sun). ❀◐⇌(Victoria) ⊖(Shudehill) ●

Beer House

6 Angel Street, M4 4BR (off Rochdale Road, A664)
12-11; 12-7 Sun
☎ (07868) 897075
Black Sheep Best Bitter; Brains SA; Moorhouses Black Cat, Pendle Witches Brew; guest beers Ⓗ

Famous free house being returned to its former glory by new licensees from the now-closed Pot of Beer nearby. The bar dominates a single, bare-boarded room, dispensing up to six guest beers, putting the pub firmly back on the northern quarter 'drinking circuit'. Real cider and perry, plus an interesting range of bottled beers complete the picture. A function room is available upstairs. ≷ (Victoria) ⊖ (Shudehill) ●

Britons Protection ☆
50 Great Bridgewater Street, M1 5LE (by Bridgewater Hall)
✪ 11-11; 12-10.30 Sun
☎ (0161) 236 5895
Jennings Bitter; Robinson's Unicorn; Tetley Bitter; guest beers Ⓗ
Friendly, city-centre pub with a long, narrow bar leading to two more cosy rooms at the rear. Deserving of its listing on CAMRA's National Inventory, it boasts beautiful preserved tiling inside and out. The food consists mainly of speciality pies, including venison and game, plus specials. Situated next to the Bridgewater Hall, it is also handy for the G-Mex exhibition centre.
♔Q ❀ ◑ ⊟ ≷ (Deansgate) ⊖ (G-Mex)

City Arms
46-48 Kennedy Street, M2 4BQ (near town hall)
✪ 11.30-11; 12-9 Sun
☎ (0161) 236 4610
Tetley Dark Mild, Bitter; guest beers Ⓗ
Local CAMRA Pub of the Season for winter 2005, this listed, two-roomed city pub is sandwiched between the Vine Inn and the Waterhouse. Hectic at lunchtime with office workers, it combines good value food with fast service. The early evening is again busy, slowly giving way to a quieter period when the 'local' mood is regained. The six changing guest beers include a 'guess the mystery ale' on Friday.
◑ ≷ (Oxford Rd) ⊖ (St Peters Sq)

Dutton Hotel
37 Park Street, M3 1EU (200 yds from A665/A6042 jct)
✪ 11.30-11; 12-10.30 sun
☎ (0161) 834 4508
Hydes Bitter, seasonal beers Ⓗ
Next to the site of the former Boddingtons Strangeways Brewery, this triangular, street-corner pub appears deceptively small from the outside. A central bar serves three rooms, each of differing character, with their collections of various bric-a-brac including an anvil (Hydes' trademark), brass blowtorches and weather barometers. Handy for visitors to events at the nearby MEN Arena, this is basically a locals' pub where a friendly welcome is guaranteed.
Q ❀ ≷ ⊖ (Victoria) ♣

Font Bar
7-9 New Wakefield Street, M1 5ND
✪ 12-1am; 5-12.30am Sun
☎ (0161) 236 0944 website: www.fontbar.com
Black Sheep Best Bitter; guest beers Ⓗ
This is a rare, real ale bar to be open late every night. The Font is a distinctively modern drinking place built into a railway arch alongside Oxford Road Station, handy for the BBC's new Broadcasting House. Food is available at all hours. It stages regular live music and the downstairs bar can be hired for parties. Guest beers are often from York Brewery. A lift connects the different levels.
◑◐ ♿ ≷ (Oxford Rd) ⊖ (St Peters Sq)

Hare & Hounds ☆
46 Shudehill, M4 4AA (opp. transport interchange)
✪ 11 11, 12 10.30 Sun
☎ (0161) 832 4737
Holt Bitter; Tetley Bitter Ⓗ
Maxine Doyle, in her tenth year as licensee, knows exactly which real ales please her customers. Affectionately known as the 'H&H', it is Mancunian through and through, having kept a market-style Edwardian atmosphere. Listed in CAMRA's National Inventory, it has a vault, lobby and lounge with 1930s mahogany, tiles and leaded glass. Piano singalongs take place (Wed and Sun at 6.30pm); Full Circle folk club meets on Friday evening. Butties and home-made pickled eggs are always available. Wheelchair access is at the rear.
Q ♿ ≷ (Victoria) ⊖ (Shudehill) ♣

Jolly Angler
47 Ducie Street, M1 2JW (behind Piccadilly Station)
✪ 12-3, 5.30-11; 12-11 Sat; 12-6, 8-10.30 Sun
☎ (0161) 236 5307
Hydes Bitter, seasonal beers Ⓗ
Genuine Irish pub, in the same family for nearly 20 years, the Angler is small, basic and welcoming. A cosy snug in front of the bar features a real fire which sometimes burns peat. Live folk and Irish music are regularly performed. The bar opens on to a larger room with seating at the front and a pool table to the rear. It is handy for a last drink before catching the train home. You can try your hand at table football here. ♔ ≷ ⊖ (Piccadilly) ♣

Knott
374 Deansgate, M3 4LY (opp. station)
✪ 12-11 (midnight Thu; 1am Fri & Sat); 12-11 Sun
☎ (0161) 839 9229
Marble Manchester Bitter, Ginger Marble, seasonal beers; guest beers Ⓗ
Built into a railway arch in historic Castlefield, the Knott has established itself as a pub for good beer lovers from all walks of life. Its unusual layout, furniture and outside balcony (best tried in summer) all add to the atmosphere. As well as guests from local micros, draught and bottled beers from Belgium and Germany and a couple of ciders are stocked. The unusual open kitchen serves up a menu as varied as the selection on the juke box, 12-8pm daily.
❀ ◑◐ ≷ (Deansgate) ⊖ (G-Mex) ●

Marble Arch ☆
73 Rochdale Road, M4 4HY
(on A664, ½ mile from town centre)
✪ 11.30 (12 Sat)-11; 12-10.30 Sun
☎ (0161) 832 5914 website: www.marblebeers.co.uk
Marble Bitter, Manchester Bitter, Ginger Marble, Lagonda IPA, seasonal beers; guest beers Ⓗ
A street-corner entrance takes you into a narrow sloping lounge, featuring tiled walls, a McKenna Brewery mirror, old stone bottles, barrel-vaulted ceiling and a mosaic floor. The doorway in the bottom corner leads through to a no-smoking room and the Marble Brewery. In addition to Marble's own organic vegan beers, guests from far and wide are always on tap, plus a changing

guest cider or perry. Excellent quality meals are available throughout the day until 8pm (6pm Sun). ◐◑ ≠ (Victoria) ⊖ (Shudehill) ♠ ⊁

Peveril of the Peak ☆

127 Great Bridgewater Street, M1 5JQ
✪ 12-3, 5-11; 12-11 Fri; 4-11 Sat; 7-10.30 (hours may vary) Sun
☎ (0161) 236 6364
Taylor Landlord; Wells Bombardier; guest beer Ⓗ
Built in 1834 and run by the same family for 34 years, the pub was named after an old coaching run. Quite rightly, it is listed in CAMRA's National Inventory – any visitor will have no problem guessing why. Look for the many unusual original features, especially the tiles. Having fought off developers, the pub is now surrounded by trendy bars and apartments, but its many regulars and visitors still regard it as a haven. It opens early on Saturday when United play at home.
Q ❀◐ ≠ (Oxford Rd) ⊖ (G-Mex/St Peters Sq) ♣

Sinclairs Oyster Bar

2 Cathedral Gates, M3 1SW (by cathedral)
✪ 11-11; 12-10.30 Sun
☎ (0161) 834 0430
Samuel Smith OBB Ⓗ
Painstaking recreation five years ago of a pub of the same name that stood on a site approximately 100 yards away. The mock-Tudor exterior houses two floors linked by a central staircase, each with its own bar; the downstairs one boasts a marble top. Low beams and wood panelling abound in this totally no-smoking environment. The restaurant offers an extensive menu that naturally includes oysters and is served until 8pm (6pm Sun).
Q ❀◐◑ ♿ ≠ (Victoria) ⊖ (Shudehill) ⊁

Smithfield Hotel & Bar

37 Swan Street, M4 5JZ (100 yds SE of A664/A665 jct)
✪ 12-11; 12-10.30 Sun
☎ (0161) 839 4424
Robinson's Hatters; guest beers Ⓗ
Busy hotel bar at the heart of Manchester's northern quarter. Six of the eight handpumps dispense a changing array of unusual beers from far and wide. At regular beer festivals the handpumps are supplemented by even rarer beers served in jugs from the cellar. The house beer is Phoenix Smithfield Bitter. A pool table is sited towards the front of the narrow single room, while a TV dominates the rear. Good value accommodation makes this an ideal base if visiting the city.
⇄ ≠ (Victoria) ⊖ (Shudehill) ♣

Marple

Hare & Hounds ✔

Dooley Lane, SK6 7EJ (on the Marple-Romiley road at Chadkirk)
✪ 11.30-11; 12-10.30 Sun
☎ (0161) 427 0293
Hydes Bitter, seasonal beers Ⓗ
Riverside pub with its own parking. Many years ago it stood at the end of the terrace. The open-plan interior is on split levels and comfortable seating adds to a welcoming atmosphere. The pub is now one of Hydes' flagship dining houses.
❀◐◑ P ⊁

Hatters Arms

81 Church Lane, SK6 7AW
✪ 12-11; 12-10.30 Sun
☎ (0161) 427 1529
Robinson's Hatters, Unicorn, Old Tom, seasonal beers Ⓗ
At the end of a row of hatters' cottages, this small stone pub is everyone's idea of a local, replete with small rooms and wooden panelling. Service bells are still nominally in use and it pursues an active social life. This is one of only 20 pubs that qualify to serve Robinson's Old Tom on draught. A patio allows for some outdoor drinking. ❀◐◑ ♿ ♣ ⊁

Railway

223 Stockport Road, SK6 3EN
✪ 11.45-11; 12-10.30 Sun
☎ (0161) 427 2146
Robinson's Hatters, Unicorn Ⓗ
This impressive pub opened in 1878, alongside Rose Hill Station, whose Manchester commuters still number among its customers. The pub is little changed externally and is handy for walkers and cyclists on the nearby MIddlewood Way. There are two airy, open-plan, relaxing rooms and an outside drinking area. It is deservedly popular. ❀◐ ♿ ≠ (Rose Hill) P

Marple Bridge

Lane Ends

Glossop Road, SK6 5DD
✪ 12-3, 5.30-11; closed Mon; 12-10.30 Sun
☎ (0161) 427 5226
Caledonian Deuchars IPA; guest beer Ⓗ
It is a long uphill pull here from Marple Bridge, but the Glossop–Hazel Grove bus passes the door. This stone pub borders on some lovely countryside and benefits from delightful views from the front. It became open plan four years ago, but its window spaces, a hint of two levels with some secluded seating, give it a fairly intimate feel. Children are welcome. Take time to look at the old local photos. Home-cooked food comes in enormous portions. Q◑ ⊞ ♿ P

Mellor

Oddfellows Arms ✔

73 Moor End Lane, SK6 5PT (2 miles out of Marple Bridge on New Mills road)
✪ 12-3, 5.30-11; closed Mon; 12-3, 7-10.30 Sun
☎ (0161) 449 7826
Adnams Bitter; Boddingtons Bitter; Phoenix Arizona; guest beer Ⓗ
Elegant, ivy-clad, three-storey building of considerable character. Inside you will find flagged floors, exposed beams and blazing fires in cold weather. Meals, of extremely good quality, are served in the pub and upstairs restaurant (no-smoking). Tables and benches are set out in the front patio for outdoor drinking. This is a good pub for all the family.
⛫ Q ❀◐◑ ♿ P

Royal Oak

134 Longhurst Lane, SK6 5PJ (1 mile from Marple Bridge)
✪ 5.30 (12 Sat)-11; 12-10.30 Sun
☎ (0161) 427 1655

Robinson's Hatters, Unicorn, Double Hop, ⒽOld Tom, Ⓖ seasonal beer Ⓗ
Convivial village pub serving a choice of Robinson's beers. The excellent rear garden boasts impressive views. An integral Thai restaurant serves authentic cuisine in the evening (bar snacks are available during lunchtime sessions). It is one of a sadly diminishing band of Robinson's pubs that serves the authentic, and apparently unchanging winter warmer, Old Tom direct from the cask.
⌂Q❀◗⚡

Middleton

Old Boar's Head

111 Long Street, M24 6UE
✪ 12-11; 12-10.30 Sun
☎ (0161) 643 3520
Lees GB Mild, Bitter Ⓗ
Charming and atmospheric, half-timbered, multi-roomed pub with flagstoned floors. It dates back to at least 1632 and a varied past includes stints as a magistrates' court and a resting place for stage coaches on the way to Manchester. Assorted rooms, including the large sessions room, break the pub into distinct drinking areas, providing something for everyone. Excellent hot lunches are an added attraction.
❀◖P

Tandle Hill Tavern

14 Thornham Lane, Slattocks, M24 2HB
(1 mile along unmetalled road off A664 or A627) OS898091
✪ 8 (7 summer; 12 Sat)-11; closed Mon & Tue; 12-10.30 Sun
☎ (01706) 345297
Lees Bitter Ⓗ
This hidden gem is reached by way of an unmade pot-holed lane from either the Middleton or Royton end of the lane. Small and welcoming, with two simply furnished but comfortable rooms, it is a haunt of farmers and walkers who come for beer and banter. Dogs are welcome and simple home-made soup and sandwich lunches are available at weekends. Lees GB Mild is on a cask breather. Check opening times before travelling, especially in winter. ⌂❀

Mossley

Britannia Inn

217 Manchester Road, OL5 9AJ
✪ 11-11; 12.30-10.30 Sun
☎ (01457) 832799
Marston's Burton Bitter, Pedigree or Old Empire; guest beers Ⓗ
This impressive grit-stone building dates from 1857. It was owned by Shaw & Bentley's, Rothwell's, then Marston's before passing to the Pyramid Pub Company. The interior is semi-open plan. The pub faces the Manchester to Huddersfield railway line and is only a few yards from Mossley Station. There is a small patio drinking area at the front of the building. Food is served until 7pm (5pm Sun). ❀◖◗⇌♣

Rising Sun

235 Stockport Road, OL5 0RQ
✪ 5 (4 Fri)-11; 2-10.30 Sun
☎ (01457) 834436
Black Sheep Best Bitter; Taylor Landlord; guest beers Ⓗ
This is Mossley's only surviving truly free house. From its lofty position to the north of the town it affords fine views over the Tame Valley to Saddleworth Moor. The interior is open plan, with a games room (used by the local Blue Grass Boys on Tue). The pub is popular with all ages. Local micro-breweries' beers are often served. An extensive range of genuine East European, flavoured vodkas is available and many malt whiskies are stocked. A pavement patio allows for outdoor drinking. ⌂❀♣P

Nangreaves

Lord Raglan

Mount Pleasant, BL9 6SP OS810154
✪ 12-2.30, 7 (5 Fri)-11; 12-11 Sat; 12-10.30 Sun
☎ (0161) 764 6680
Leyden Nanny Flyer, Crowning Glory; guest beers Ⓗ
This inn is the home of the Leyden Brewery and several of its beers feature on the bar. The Leyden family has run this charming country local for half a century. It is decorated throughout with many items of interest, including antique glassware and pottery, old photographs and pictures. The pub is renowned for its good food; the chef is also the head brewer. Meals are served all day at weekends (until 9.30pm Sat and 8.30pm Sun). ❀◖◗P

New Springs

Colliers Arms

192 Wigan Road, WN2 1DU
(on B5238, betweeen Wigan and Aspull)
✪ 1.30-5.30 (not Wed or Thu), 7.30-11; 1.30-11 Sat; 1-5, 7.30-10.30 Sun
☎ (01942) 831171
Burtonwood Bitter Ⓗ
Known locally as the Stone, this popular, two-roomed inn is making its 22nd consecutive appearance in this Guide – a feat unrivalled by any other pub in this area. A striking mock-Tudor building dating from 1700, much memorabilia from former local collieries is on show, including a pit helmet used to illuminate the lounge fireplace. Oak beams are apparent throughout. It is handy for the nearby Haigh Country Park and the Leeds–Liverpool Canal. There is limited parking space. ⌂QP

Offerton

Victoria

125 Hall Street, SK1 4HE (on A626)
✪ 12-11; 12-10.30 Sun
☎ (0161) 480 3983
Banks's Original, Bitter; Greene King Old Speckled Hen; guest beers Ⓗ
Situated mid-terrace, the Victoria draws a local following from neighbouring residential areas. Up to five cask beers may be on tap at any time. The two-roomed vault throngs with games and sports' fans. Decorated with local artists' work (for sale) and painted plates on aviation and equestrian themes, the smaller lounge is just as busy. Three rare stone pub signs are located in the front wall and beer garden. The children's playground is enclosed for safety. ❀◖⊟♣P

Oldham

Ashton Arms

28-30 Clegg Street, OL1 1PL (below town square shopping centre)

✪ 12-11; 12-10.30 Sun

☎ (0161) 630 9709

Beer range varies Ⓗ

A friendly welcome awaits in this mid-terrace, split-level, traditional pub. Situated in the town-centre conservation area, opposite the old town hall, this free house provides up to six real ales plus a permanent cider and various continental beers. A seat by the 200-year-old stone fireplace makes a change from the trendy outlets nearby. An array of guest beers, many from independent breweries, make this pub well worth a visit. Good value meals finish at 6pm.

⛫Q◑⇌(Mumps)♣●

Bank Top Tavern

King's Square, King Street, OL8 1ES (next to Mecca Bingo)

✪ 11-11; 12-10.30 Sun

☎ (0161) 624 8603

Lees GB Mild, Bitter, seasonal beers Ⓗ

Town-centre pub with a restaurant and function room. It caters for students from the nearby college at lunchtime and more mature customers in the evening and at the weekend. The interior is open plan with a raised area for dining. A flagged floor by the bar, together with wrought iron and spindles, enhance the mill theme apparently inspired by the former Bank Top mill. Sunday meals are served 12-5pm. A huge car park adjoins the pub.

❀◑◐P

Gardener's Arms

Dunham Street (Millbottom), Lees, OL4 3NH (near Huddersfield Rd)

✪ 12-11; 12-10.30 Sun

☎ (0161) 624 0242

Robinson's Hatters, Unicorn Ⓗ

About two miles out of Oldham centre, near the Waterhead bus terminus, the pub stands in a dip on the original route to Yorkshire, right next to the River Medlock and overshadowed by one of the many old mills in this area. Most of the pub's original room layout and features remain from rebuilding in the 1930s – plenty of wood and tilework, fireplaces and some leaded windows, typical of pubs of the day. A collection of brassware adds to the atmosphere.

❀♣P

Royal Oak

172 Manchester Road, Werneth, OL9 7BN (on A62 opp. Werneth Park)

✪ 2-11; 12-5.30, 8-11 Sat; 12-10.30 Sun

☎ (0161) 624 5795

Robinson's Hatters, Unicorn Ⓗ

Traditional pub, retaining separate rooms around a central bar. This popular, community local boasts wood panelling, old-fashioned cast iron radiators and an old Gledhill cash register, which is still in use. Regular bus services stop nearby, and Werneth Station is about 15 minutes' walk. Although the pub is in a restricted parking zone, a small car park is nearby.

Q♿♣

Openshaw

Legh Arms

741 Ashton Old Road, M11 2HD (on A635)

✪ 11-11; 12-10.30 Sun

☎ (0161) 223 4317

Moorhouses Black Cat, Pride of Pendle; guest beer Ⓗ

Welcoming, friendly atmosphere in a pub with several distinct drinking areas, ranging from a comfy snug at the front to a games/pool room to the rear. It appeals to all – from the young to the young at heart. The hardworking, enterprising landlord is introducing an interesting selection of beers to an area devoid of real ale; Black Cat Mild outsells the bitter. Within walking distance of the City of Manchester Stadium, the Legh Arms was local CAMRA Pub of the Year 2005. ❀⇌(Ashburys)♣

Railway

2 Manshaw Road, Higher Openshaw, M11 1HS (off Ashton Old Road, A635)

✪ 12-11; 12-10.30 Sun

☎ (0161) 371 5184

Holt Mild, Bitter Ⓗ

Typical Holt's multi-roomed pub, modernised sensitively, so that many original Victorian features are still evident. An archetypal community pub, it attracts a cross-section of regulars, who come in to enjoy the friendly banter, Manchester log-end darts, karaoke and quizzes, but especially the beer. The licensee's welcome makes you feel you are joining friends in the best parlour. It is hidden away down a side road, but worth searching out.

❀⇌(Fairfield)♣P⍁

Orrell

Robin Hood

117 Sandy Lane, WN5 7AZ

✪ 2 (12 Thu-Sat)-11; 12-10.30 Sun

☎ (01695) 627479

Beer range varies Ⓗ

Small, unspoilt, two-roomed family-oriented pub, built of sandstone. Themed on the well-known freedom fighter from Sherwood Forest, the ladies' cloakroom is romantically designated 'Damsels'. Home-cooked food (Thu-Sun) is popular, so you may need to book; meals are served all day Sunday, 12-8pm. Three rotating guest beers ensure the pub attracts drinkers as well as diners. Q◑◐⊟♿⇌♣P⍁

Patricroft

Stanley Arms

295 Liverpool Road, M30 0QN (on A57, near fire station)

✪ 12-11; 12-10.30 Sun

☎ (0161) 788 8801

Holt Mild, Bitter Ⓗ

Ignore the corner door and use the side one on Liza Ann Street. Here is a tiny lobby with a single table. Across the bar is the vault and just on the left, the best room. At the end of the corridor is another room with a reproduction cast iron kitchen range. The Stanley is one of Holt's smallest pubs and one of its rare tenancies. It is an essential stop on the nine-pub Peel Green to Eccles, Holt's Pub Crawl (Grapes to the Lamb).

⊟⇌♣

Peel Green

Grapes Hotel

439 Liverpool Road, M30 7HD (on A57, near M60 jct 11)

11-11; 12-10.30 Sun

(0161) 789 6971

Holt Mild, Bitter H

The Grapes shares many features with Holt's Lamb and Royal Oak in Eccles: etched glass, polished mahogany, wall tiling and mosaic floors, as well as a billiards room (although nowadays this contains just a pool table). It has a large vault and three lounges, the back one converted from private quarters a few decades ago. One of the earlier Edwardian palaces, it dates from 1903. The family room is open until 7pm. Q ⇌(Patricroft) ♣P

Pendlebury

Newmarket

621 Bolton Road, M27 4EJ (on A666 Bolton-Manchester road)

11-11; 12-10.30 Sun

(0161) 794 3650

Holt Mild, Bitter H

Traditional local: on entering, there is a large lounge on the left with a small vault area to the right of the bar where the theme of sporting photos includes an image of Swinton RLFC Championship winners 1962-63. It hosts a quiz (Wed eve) and a live artist on Saturday. A small, basic games room is to the left of the bar. Q⇌(Swinton) ♣P

Ramsbottom

Hare & Hounds

400 Bolton Road West, Holcombe Brook, BL0 9RY (at B6214/A676 jct)

12-11; 12-10.30 Sun

(01706) 822107

Beer range varies H

Large, open-plan coaching house, with separate pool and dining areas, plus a no-smoking room at the rear. Twelve handpumps fed by water cooled lines mostly offer beers from local breweries. A lively mix of customers means it can be loud and bustling. Large-screen TVs are provided for sports coverage. This is a traditional gathering place at Easter, when crowds spill out into the pub's courtyard and car park. P

Reddish

Thatched Tavern

54 Stanhope Street, SK5 7AQ (behind Houldsworth Sq off B6167)

11-11; 12-10.30 Sun

(0161) 285 0900

Boddingtons Bitter; Tetley Dark Mild, Bitter H

Could it be the Thatched Tavern's location, hidden away from the main roads in Reddish that has helped to preserve it as a gem of a street-corner local? Once you have found the pub you will find it warm and welcoming, with a comfortable lounge and a traditional vault. On the wall is a photo of the workmen who built the pub in 1882, standing outside the original Thatched Tavern when it really was thatched and in a far more rural setting. ♣

Rochdale

Albion

600 Whitworth Road, OL12 0SW

12-2.30, 5-11; 12-11 Sat; 12-10.30 Sun

(01706) 648540

Lees Bitter; Taylor Golden Best, Best Bitter, Landlord; guest beers H

A true free house with a bistro attached. The pub's growing reputation for good food makes it popular with locals and visitors alike. There is always a good range of real ales with three guest beers on tap. The pub offers good value bar food as well as bistro meals, many having an African flavour; a good selection of wine is also stocked. The walls are hung with paintings by a local artist, which are for sale.

Cask & Feather

1 Oldham Road, OL16 1UA

11-11; 12-10.30 Sun

(01706) 711476 website: www.mcguinnessbrewery.com

McGuinness Feather Pluckers Mild, Best Bitter, Junction Bitter, seasonal beers H

This busy, town-centre pub is situated near the station on many bus routes. Stone built, it has an open-plan layout with a long bar and pool table annexe. The McGuinness Brewery, at the rear of the pub, is visible from the bar. This pub is the brewery's sole tied outlet, serving up to five handpumped beers of a range of strengths and types, all at reasonable prices. It is popular for bar meals at lunchtime. ⇌

Healey Hotel

172 Shawclough Road, OL12 6LW (on B6377)

3-11 (midnight Fri & Sat); 12-10.30 Sun

(01706) 645453

Robinson's Unicorn, seasonal beers H

This terraced stone pub is perfectly situated, near Healey Dell nature reserve. A popular local, it retains many architectural features including the original bar, tiled walls and oak doors in a traditional layout. The quiet, no-smoking room displays paintings of the area by local artists. The rear gentleman's room features sporting photographs, while the bar/lounge is decorated with film star portraits. The extensive garden boasts a well-used petanque piste. Q♣

Merry Monk

234 College Road, OL12 6AF (at A6060/B6222 jct)

12-11; 12-5, 7.30-10.30 Sun

(01706) 646919

Hydes Mild, Bitter, Jekyll's Gold; guest beers H

A gem in an inner-city area; this small traditional local attracts all those for whom good ale is important. Two rooms in an open-plan setting draw a good sports following. There is often a guest from a small (usually local) brewery. The atmosphere is welcoming to young and old, to singles and groups, and to regulars and visitors. CCTV watches the small car park, yet the ethos is friendly. Petanque and ring the bull can be played here. ♣P

Regal Moon

The Butts, OL16 1HB (next to central bus station)

10-11; 12-10.30 Sun

(01706) 657434

Boddingtons Bitter; Greene King Abbot; Shepherd Neame Spitfire; guest beers H

This Wetherspoon's outlet was sympathetically converted from the Art Deco Regal Cinema. It retains original features, such as ornamental pillars with uplights. A tail-coated mannequin sits at an organ over the bar, while many pictures of Rochdale notables and old film stars feature. A raised family area doubles as the no-smoking dining section. The pub faces the Town Hall Square and is next to the central bus station. Up to 10 cask ales are regularly on tap. Breakfast is served 10am-midday. Q ❀ ◐ ◑ ♿ ⚟

Sale Moor

Legh Arms

178 Northenden Road, M33 2SR (at A6144/B5166 jct)

⏲ 11.30-11; 12-10.30 Sun

☎ (0161) 973 7491

Holt Mild, Bitter Ⓗ

Spacious, multi-roomed local where an island bar serves lounges on the right and left as you enter, a large room at the rear, a vault and a lobby area. The rear lounge acts as a concert room at weekends and overlooks the bowling green. It is roughly 15 minutes' walk to both Sale and Brooklands metrolink stations. Lunches are served Wednesday-Sunday, evening meals Wednesday-Friday. Q ❀ ◐ ◑ ⊟ ♣ P

Salford

Albert Vaults

169 Chapel Street, M3 6AD (near central station and A6/A34 jct)

⏲ 11-11; 12-10.30 Sun

☎ (0161) 819 1368

Beer range varies Ⓗ

Bazens' of Salford and Phoenix of Heywood feature prominently, with keen prices at this pub. Now under the Wolverhampton and Dudley Brewery wing, the pub while it was a Burtonwood house did not sell their beers. After refurbishment in the main room and kitchen area, a more extensive food range is planned. A local, frequented by the more mature drinker, it is a Salford pub to the core.

♨ ◐ ⊟ ⇌ (Central) ♣

Crescent

18-21 Crescent, M5 4PF (on A6, near university)

⏲ 11.30-11; 12-10.30 Sun

☎ (0161) 736 5600

Bazens' Black Pig Mild; Hydes Bitter; Phoenix Thirsty Moon; guest beers Ⓗ

Thriving terraced free house near Salford University, attracting an eclectic mix of locals, students and real ale fans. A long-standing Guide entry, one central bar serves three drinking areas, plus a side vault. Guest ales from micro-breweries are complemented by Thatchers cider and a range of draught and bottled foreign beers. Additional beers are served from the cellar at the regular festivals. Wednesday's curry night is the highlight of the excellent value food (serving times vary).

♨ ❀ ◐ ◑ ⇌ (Crescent) ● P ⊡

King's Arms

11 Bloom Street, M3 2AN (off A6, near Central Station & A34 jct)

⏲ 12-11; 12-6 Sun

☎ (0161) 832 3605 website: www.studiosalford.com

Bazens Black Pig Mild, Pacific Bitter; Caledonian Deuchars IPA; guest beers Ⓗ

The pub has a reputation for showcasing new micro-breweries, such as Merlin from Leigh, as well as Bazens' and Facers. This traditional pub houses a modern bar and hosts live bands, plays, cinema and poetry nights in a domed function room upstairs. Jazz is also performed on Wednesday evening. Good value lunches are served (not Sat). Phone to check if open if travelling far as it occasionally hosts private parties. Q ❀ ◐ ⇌ (Central) P

Star Inn

2 Back Hope Street, Higher Broughton, M7 2FR (near A56/B6187 jct)

⏲ 1.30-11; 1.30-10.30 Sun

☎ (0161) 792 4184

Robinson's Hatters, Unicorn, seasonal beers Ⓗ

Resembling a row of cottages, this characterful pub is located in a conservation area known as 'the Cliff'. Hidden away along a narrow, cobbled alleyway, the front entrance with its half-hinged door opens into a small vault with a tiny bar and a central lounge. To the left is the pool/games room and beyond that the gents (unusually ladies have to go outside and cross the courtyard). Nearby is the Bazens'/Facers Salford brewery syndicate. Sunday is quiz night. ❀ ⊟ ♣

Stalybridge

British Protection

Hough Hill Road, SK15 2HB

⏲ 4.30 (3 Fri, 12 Sat)-11; 12-10.30 Sun

☎ (0161) 338 5432

Burtonwod Bitter; guest beers Ⓗ

True community local in the urban heart of Stalybridge, a town much improved since Engels passed through! Several welcoming rooms include a traditional tap room. Frequented by all ages, this former free house is now tied to Burtonwood, which provides the guest beers that are surprisingly varied. Its proximity to the Huddersfield Narrow Canal makes it popular with passing boaters. ♨ Q ⊟ ⇌ ♣

Stalybridge Station Buffet Bar ✔

Platform 1, Stalybridge Station, Rassbottom Street, SK15 1RF

⏲ 11-11; 12-10.30 Sun

☎ (0161) 303 0007

Boddingtons Bitter; Flowers IPA; guest beers Ⓗ

A national institution among discerning drinkers, the Buffet Bar continues to bring new beers to the good people of Stalybridge. Far enough away from the brash concentration of youth-oriented venues in the town, which have earned it the sobriquet of 'Staly-Vegas', the Buffet Bar remains popular, due to its late Victorian charm. Four rooms each have their attractions, and the wholesome food well complements the beer. It hosts a folk club on Saturday evening.

♨ Q ◐ ◑ ⊟ ⇌ ● P

Standish

Dog & Partridge

33 School Lane, WN6 0TG (off A49, towards M6 jct 27)

⏲ 1-11; 12-10.30 Sun

☎ (01257) 401218

Tetley Mild, Bitter; guest beers Ⓗ

Popular drinkers' pub offering several guest beers, mostly from micro-breweries, and a real cider. One central bar serves both sides of the pub which is popular for football and rugby matches shown on several TVs. There is a quieter corner on one side of the bar. A heated, covered patio to the rear can be used in fine weather. Definitely the best pub in Standish for its selection of ales, it hosts an annual charity beer festival.
❀♿P

Horseshoe

1 Wigan Road, WN6 0BG (on A49)
✪ 12-11; 12-10.30 Sun
☎ (01257) 400716
Burtonwood Bitter; Marston's Pedigree Ⓗ
Renovated to give a modern, open-plan look, there is a pool table at one end of the pub, while darts can be played at the opposite end. The central bar area has TVs and snob screens much in evidence. Popular with diners, it can get busy at weekends. The home-cooked food (served until 8pm) represents excellent value. The guest beers are from the Pub Company's list. Children are welcome until 8pm. A small car park lies behind the pub.
◖◗♿♣P

Stockport

Arden Arms ☆

23 Millgate, SK1 2LX (behind Asda)
✪ 12-11; 12-10.30 Sun
☎ (0161) 480 2185
Robinson's Hatters, Unicorn, Double Hop, Ⓗ
Old Tom (winter), Ⓖ **seasonal beers** Ⓗ
Lying below the market place, this National Inventory listed Grade II building, was CAMRA's runner-up for national Pub of the Year 2004. A full range of Robinson's ales, the convivial atmosphere and lunchtime food of restaurant quality make this a pub not to miss. Note the superb glassed-in bar, chequerboard floor tiling and grandfather clocks. The tiny snug at the rear of the bar and real fires make it cosy in winter.
♨Q❀◖P⊬

Bakers Vaults

Castle Yard, Market Place, SK1 2LY
✪ 11 (6 Wed)-11; 5-10.30 Sun
☎ (0161) 477 7312
Robinson's Hatters, Unicorn, Ⓗ/Ⓟ **seasonal beers** Ⓗ
New licensees have put this pub back on track after several fallow years. Architecturally imposing, both inside and out, a central bar divides the comfortable interior in two. Local artists regularly exhibit on the walls and the pub is also regaining its reputation for an eclectic range of live music. Lunchtime food is available on market days (Tue, Fri and Sat). ◖≋

Blossoms

2 Buxton Road, Heaviley, SK2 6NU (at A6/A5102 jct)
✪ 12-3, 5-11; 11.30-11 Sat; 12-10.30 Sun
☎ (0161) 477 2397
Robinson's Hatters, Unicorn, Ⓗ
Old Tom (winter) Ⓖ
Situated at a busy road junction, this multi-roomed Victorian gem, built as a coaching house, has a lobby bar and four rooms. The rear room is of special interest, boasting a carved fireplace and etched window panes. It is one of the few Stockport pubs to offer a pinball game. The food includes some excellent pies made on the premises. Q◖⊟♿≋(Davenport) ♣P

Crown

154 Heaton Lane, SK4 1AR (on A560, 200 yds from A6 under viaduct)
✪ 6-11; 12-3, 6-11 Thu; 12-11 Fri & Sat; 3-10.30 Sun
☎ (0161) 429 0549
Black Sheep Best Bitter; guest beers Ⓗ
This thriving pub has two entrances: the first door opens into the pool room directly off the bar; the other opens into the bar where 14 handpumps dispense a changing range of beers. Five rooms altogether reside behind an impressive façade, including a no-smoking room. To the rear the large cobbled yard hosts live music in summer. During the week, the pub hosts regular musical events (four evenings). A good mix of customers mingle at this Three Rivers Brewery tap. Lunches are served Thursday-Saturday. ❀◖≋●⊬

Olde Vic

1 Chatham Street, Edgeley, SK3 9ED (behind station)
✪ 5 (7 Sat)-11; 7-10.30 Sun
☎ (0161) 480 2410
Beer range varies Ⓗ
Jolly, welcoming one-roomed free house run in irrepressible style. Particularly busy when Sale Sharks play at home, no-one is a stranger for long in this well-run pub (strictly no swearing). Five handpumps dispense a changing range of guest beers, usually from micros; see all the pump clips on the ceilings. Pub dog Molly can hear a crisp packet rustle from half a mile away. Note that the pub is closed at lunchtime.
♨❀≋●

Olde Woolpack

70 Brinksway, SK3 0BY (off M60 jct 1, by blue pyramid)
✪ 11.30-3, 5-11; 11.30-11 Fri; 11.30-4, 7.30-11 Sat; 12-10.30 Sun
☎ (0161) 476 0688
Theakston Best Bitter; guest beers Ⓗ
Rescued from dereliction in the late 1980s, its fortunes started to turn under the present licensee. Standing 200 yards from the M60 motorway junction, pavement tables in summer overlook the River Mersey. Children are welcome if dining. It attracts lunchtime custom from workers at the landmark blue pyramid that dwarfs the pub. Past winner of local and regional CAMRA Pub of the Year awards, it offers three guest beers. Tuesday is quiz night.
❀◖⊟♣P

Pineapple

159 Heaton Lane, SK4 1AQ (on A560)
✪ 11.30-11; 12-10.30 Sun
☎ (0161) 480 3221
Robinson's Hatters, Cumbria Way, Unicorn, seasonal beers Ⓗ
Coaching house, dating back to the 1820s – the building itself is considerably older. Later, in the 19th century it became the HQ of the Stockport Botanical Society, until Bells Brewery turned it into a public house in the early 1900s. The undulating floor, beamed ceiling and walls, decorated with ornamental plates, give this

warm, friendly, multi-roomed pub a really traditional feel. Handy for the Stockport Hat Museum, it is known locally as the Chunky. Lunches are served Monday–Saturday.
❀◐⊟⇌♣

Railway

1 Avenue Street, Portwood, SK1 2BZ (on A560, opp. Peel Centre shops)
⏲ 12-11; 12-10.30 Sun
☎ (0161) 429 6062
Porter Dark Mild, Floral Dance, Bitter, Railway Sleeper, Rossendale Ale, Porter Ⓗ
The way this CAMRA award-winning, street-corner pub is so well run, masks the fact that the encroaching shopping development brings the bulldozers ever closer to the door of the jewel in Porter's crown. The Railway must have the largest selection of cask ales, real ciders, bottled foreign beers, whiskies, mead and fruit wines under one roof for many a mile. Watch out for the three guest ales at the weekend, and summer barbecues. The comfortable, single room surrounds a central bar. ❀◐♣●

Red Bull

14 Middle Hillgate, SK1 3AY
⏲ 11.30-11, 12-10.30 Sun
☎ (0161) 480 2087
Robinson's Hatters, Unicorn Ⓗ
The entrance to this whitewashed building is up some well worn steps. The interior, featuring dark wood panels, is served by a large three-sided bar. The pub has a country atmosphere in its various areas include a snug at the front, with a stone-flagged floor, open fire and pew seating. The plush lounge has its own bar for busy times; mirrors, brass and old drawings of Stockport abound. The pub is popular with Robinson's directors especially at lunchtime for the weekday meals. ⩩Q❀◐⇌P

Tiviot

8 Tiviot Dale, SK1 1TA (Princes St jct)
⏲ 11-11; 12-3.30 (closed eve) Sun
☎ (0161) 480 4109
Robinson's Hatters, Unicorn, Ⓟ **Old Tom** (winter) Ⓖ
A rarity: a four-roomed (including vault and dining room), old fashioned, no-nonsense pub that caters predominantly for a lunchtime trade of shoppers from nearby Merseyway, and a loyal band of regular topers. Prints of steam locos recall the days of long-closed Tiviot Dale Station, while pen and ink drawings and monochrome photos of local scenes lend a reassuring and homely warmth. ◐⊟⊟

Stoneclough

Market Street Tavern

131 Market Street, M26 1HF (on A667)
⏲ 12-11; 12-10.30 Sun
☎ (01204) 572985
Bank Top Flat Cap; Tetley Bitter Ⓗ
Busy, main road pub with a long lounge and a smaller vault, where the beers are keenly priced. Benches and tables provide a pleasant outside drinking area to the front. A car park is available to the rear. A free juke box and Monday evening quiz add to the appeal of this well-run, friendly local. ❀⊟⇌(Kearsley) P

Strines

Sportsman's Arms

105 Strines Road, SK6 7GE
⏲ 12-3, 5-11; 12-11 Sat; 12-10.30 Sun
☎ (0161) 427 2888
Boddingtons Bitter; Cains Bitter; guest beers Ⓗ
So attractive are the views down the Goyt Valley, that this pub has had a massive picture-window installed. The patio at the side also overlooks the valley. For the winter, a monumental fireplace houses log fires. In an area where beer variety is at a premium, this pub stocks an enterprising choice. The food here is also recommended; Sunday meals are served all day (until 8pm).
⩩Q❀◐◑⊟♿♣P

Stubshaw Cross

Cross Keys

76 Golborne Road, WN4 8XA (on B5207, off A58)
⏲ 4 (6 Mon; 12 Fri & Sat)-11; 12-10.30 Sun
☎ (01942) 727965
Burtonwood Bitter; guest beers Ⓗ
Built in 1893, this is the only pub in Stubshaw Cross. An old-fashioned local, it offers a warm, friendly welcome. It has rooms for pool and darts, with the main room opened up around the bar. In 2003 it won Wigan CAMRA's New Cask Outlet award. Sports fans can watch rugby league football on TV; most Saturdays it hosts karaoke. Families with children are welcome until 8pm. Snacks are available on request. Beware, this is a heavy smokers' pub.
❀♿♣

Summerseat

Footballers Inn ✔

28 Higher Summerseat, BL0 9UG OS788145
⏲ 2 (12 Sat)-11; 12-10.30 Sun
☎ (0120) 488 3363 website: www.footballersinn.co.uk
Black Sheep Best Bitter; Boddingtons Bitter; Taylor Landlord; guest beers Ⓗ
In the quiet village of Summerseat, this friendly, family-run pub caters for all. One large room is divided into several drinking areas. The bar boasts six cask ales, including a guest beer from a micro-brewery. The pub runs numerous social events, including a popular quiz evening. Enjoy the excellent views from the rear garden or you can play petanque, or even practise your golf swing on the covered driving range. Dog-friendly, this pub has it all, including bar snacks.
❀⇌(E Lancs Steam Rlwy) ♣P

Swinton

White Lion

242 Manchester Road, M27 4TS (at A6/A572 jct)
⏲ 3 (12 Sat)-11; 12-10.30 Sun
☎ (0161) 288 0434
Robinson's Hatters, Unicorn, seasonal beers Ⓗ
Built in the late 1700s in what was then the centre of Swinton, it has seen many internal changes. The main front lounge has comfortable upholstered seating, and a small basic room leads through to a conventional vault. A large back room is dedicated to the history of Swinton RLFC which originated in this pub, hence their nickname, Lions. Usually three or four beers are

available, with seasonal brews alternating with Cumbria Way. There is folk singing on Monday evenings.
Q🍺❀⊟P

White Swan
186 Worsley Road, M27 5SN (on A572, N of A580)
12-11; 12-10.30 Sun
☎ (0161) 794 1504
Holt Mild, Bitter Ⓗ
Circa 1926, the pub was built on the site of the original inn and refurbished in the 1990s when two side rooms were opened up. The comfortable main lounge has wood-panelled walls and stained glass windows. The small bar area dates back to the days of waiter service. The traditional vault at the front has its own gents' toilet. The large back room, where children are allowed, is available for functions and shows live football on a large-screen TV.
🍺⊟♣P

Timperley

Moss Trooper
Moss Lane, WA15 6JU
11-11 (midnight Fri & Sat); 12-10.30 Sun
☎ (0161) 980 4610
Boddingtons Bitter; Webster's Bitter; Wells Bombardier; guest beers Ⓗ
Large, former Wilson's pub dating back to 1957; despite its size, it can get crowded in the evening. Three guest beers are normally sourced from independent breweries. The Tuesday quiz is well attended. Meals are served all day (until 9pm); the pub stocks a selection of 18 wines. Scrabble and other board games are played. Warmed in winter by living flame gas fires, the outdoor area has gas heaters, too.
❀◑♿⇌(Navigation Rd) ⊖P⊁

Tyldesley

Half Moon
115-117 Elliot Street, M29 8FL
11-4, 7-11 including Sun
☎ (01942) 873206
Holt Bitter Ⓗ
Long-established, town-centre local, in the middle of the 'monkey run', the town 'crawl' that starts at the Mort Arms and takes in the pubs along Elliot Street. The main lounge has various seating areas and there is a second lounge. In summer the patio is a pleasant spot for a drink, to take in the panoramic views of Winter Hill.
❀♣

Mort Arms
235-237 Elliot Street, M29 8FL
12-11; 12-10.30 Sun
☎ (01942) 883481
Holt Mild, Bitter Ⓗ
Splendid 1930s Holt's emporium, not as large as some of its contemporaries, but well worth a visit. The beers are served in the lounge via a bowed mahogany bar, complete with etched glass. The lounge is in two halves; the original ex-living quarters are comfortably laid out. Dominoes and darts are played in the bright tap room.
⊟♣

Uppermill

Cross Keys
OL3 6LW (off Running Hill Gate)
11-11; 12-10.30 Sun
☎ (01457) 874626
Lees GB Mild, Bitter, Moonraker, seasonal beers Ⓗ
Overlooking Saddleworth Church, this attractive, 18th-century stone building has exposed beams throughout. The bar boasts a stone-flagged floor and a Yorkshire range. The centre for many activities, including mountain rescue, a clay pigeon club and the Saddleworth Runners, it is busy during annual events, such as the folk festival (July), the road and fell race, and Rushcart Festival (Aug). It hosts folk nights (Wed and Sun) in the barn. Good value home-cooked food is served until 6.45pm. Children are welcome. ⌂Q🍺❀◑◑⊟♣P

Waggon Inn
34 High Street, OL3 6HR
11.30-11; 12-10.30 Sun
☎ (01457) 872376
Robinson's Old Stockport, Unicorn, seasonal beers Ⓗ
This mid-19th-century stone pub in a picturesque village, stands opposite Saddleworth Museum and the Huddersfield Narrow Canal. With a central bar, three rooms and a restaurant, it now offers high quality, en-suite B&B. The venue for many annual events, including the Whit Friday brass band contest, and in August, the 'Yanks' weekend and Rushcart Festival; live music is regularly performed every Friday evening. Good quality home-cooked food includes seniors and early bird specials (no eve meals Thu). Q❀⇆◑◑⊟▲⇌(Greenfield) ♣P

Urmston

Urmston
292 Stretford Road, M41 9WE
12-11; 12-10.30 Sun
☎ (0161) 865 2568
Lees GB Mild, Bitter, Moonraker, seasonal beers Ⓗ
Community pub bought by Lees in 2001 and refurbished, it now has a new landlady, who is keen on keeping top class cask ale. The vault has a big-screen TV for sports. The larger main room is broken into more secluded sections by partitions. The Urmston welcomes a mixed clientele, not skewed to any age range, and is particularly popular with owners of vintage traction engines – watch out for them over May bank holiday when the town holds a steam rally. Weekend meals are served 12-5pm.
❀◑◑⊟♿⇌(Humphrey Pk) ♣P

Wardley

Morning Star
520 Manchester Road, M27 9QW (on A6 near motorway flyover)
12-11; 12-10.30 Sun
☎ (0161) 794 4927
Holt Mild, Bitter Ⓗ
Situated between Swinton and Walkden on the A6, this Holt's pub serves the local community, but a warm welcome is assured to visitors

calling in from the busy main road. Dating from the Edwardian era, the main lounge was extended in the late 20th century. On the left of the main central bar is a traditional vault for the darts and dominoes teams. Excellent food is served weekday lunchtimes from the award-winning kitchen. ❀ᑫ⊟⇌ (Moorside) ♣P

Westhoughton

Brinsop Country Inn

584-592 Chorley Road, BL5 3NJ (on A6, 500 yds from A6027 roundabout)

12-3, 5.30-11; 12-11 Fri & Sat; 12-10.30 Sun

☎ (01942) 811113

Thwaites Bitter; guest beers Ⓗ

Spacious free house standing on the A6 out of Westhoughton. On entering the pub, the bar to the left serves the main central drinking area, which has wooden floors and is comfortably furnished. To the right of the bar, the restaurant serves home-cooked food; to the left is the no-smoking area. Just 20 minutes' walk from the Reebok Stadium, it can be busy on match days. Q❀ᑫ◗⊟⇌(Horwich Park Way) P⚟

Whalley Range

Hillary Step ✔

199 Upper Chorlton Road, M16 0BH

4 (12 Sat)-11; 12-10.30 Sun

☎ (0161) 881 1978

Thwaites Thoroughbred, Lancaster Bomber; guest beers Ⓗ

Café-bar style pub, one of only two in a beer starved district. Ten minutes' walk from Chorlton, it is popular with students and young people. Its small size means it can get crowded at peak times. The no-smoking premises offers two guest beers and bottled Belgian beers. No meals are served but bar snacks include nuts, olives and salamis – no children are admitted. It hosts occasional folk music on Sunday and a monthly quiz night. The name comes from a plateau on Mount Everest. ❀⚟

Whitefield

Eagle & Child

Higher Lane, M45 7EY

12-11; 12-10.30 Sun

☎ (0161) 766 3024

Holt Mild, Bitter, seasonal beers Ⓗ

Large, black and white pub set back from the road. It has an L-shaped main bar and a cosy back room. The well-kept bowling green at the rear is popular in summer. The building dates from 1936, replacing the original hostelry built in 1802, which was the first hostelry on Higher Lane. The other five pubs have long gone. Once a Whitefield Brewery pub, it has been a Holt's house since 1907. ❀ᑫ⊟⊖(Besses o' th' Barn) P

Wigan

Anvil ✔

Dorning Street, WN1 1ND (by bus station)

11-11; 12-10.30 Sun

☎ (01942) 239444

Hydes Mild, Bitter; Phoenix Arizona; Roosters Yankee; guest beers Ⓗ

Plain, modern bar that still manages to generate a great atmosphere and attracts a good, mixed clientele. A large room on the right shows TV sport, but the rest of the pub is dedicated to conversation. The guests are from micros and should include the nearby Allgates Brewery beers when production starts. The real ale is augmented by seven draught Belgian beers, plus bottles. The pub has already won Wigan CAMRA's Alan Ball Pub of the Year award twice this century. ❀ᑫ⇌(North Western/Wallgate)

Bowling Green

106 Wigan Lane, WN1 2LF

11-11; 12-10.30 Sun

☎ (01942) 251167

Caledonian Deuchars IPA, 80/-; Greene King Old Speckled Hen; Tetley Dark Mild, Bitter; guest beers Ⓗ

The guest ales change frequently at this popular pub, comprising a lively vault and two large lounges. The attractive garden at the rear of the pub gets busy in summer, especially for barbecues. Daily newspapers are provided. Food is served at lunchtime and late into the evening. The quiz on Tuesday evening is well attended. ⅏Q❀ᑫ◗⊟

Brocket Arms ✔

Mesnes Road, Swinley, WN1 2DD

11-11; 12-10.30 Sun

☎ (01942) 403500

Courage Directors; Marston's Burton Bitter, Pedigree; guest beers Ⓗ

This former small hotel has been restored to its original use as a Wetherlodge. The spacious, light, airy, open-plan room provides a choice of intimate booths and flexible seating to accommodate groups of all sizes. A large, no-smoking area and a patio for use in good weather are added attractions. ❀⛟ᑫ◗♿P⚟

Moon under Water ✔

5-7A Market Place, WN1 1PE

11-11; 12-10.30 Sun

☎ (01942) 323437

Courage Directors; Marston's Burton Bitter, Pedigree; Theakston Best Bitter; guest beers Ⓗ

The former Halifax Building Society office was converted into Wigan's first Wetherspoon's pub. The no-smoking area on the first floor is also accessible from the Wiend (Wigan's historic shopping street). Situated in the centre of town, it gets extremely busy at weekends. Selected sports programmes are shown on a large screen. Qᑫ◗♿⇌ (North Western/Wallgate) ⚟

Old Pear Tree

44 Frog Lane, WN1 1HG (400 yds from town centre and bus station)

12-11; 12-10.30 Sun

☎ (01942) 243677

Burtonwood Bitter; Marston's Pedigree; guest beers Ⓗ

Welcoming and traditional hostelry, reputed to be the oldest purpose-built pub in Wigan. A five-minute walk from the town centre, its low ceiling and imposing beams create an impression of a local country inn. An authentic vault offers a dartboard and dominoes tables, along with interesting old football and rugby photographs. The Pear Tree also has some quiet, comfortable alcoves and open coal fires. A

strong cask policy ensures interesting guest beers. Sunday meals finish at 5pm.
♨Q❀◐◑⊟♿⇌(Wallgate/North Western) ♣

Royal Oak

Standishgate, WN1 1XL (on A49, N of centre)
⏲ 12 (4 Mon & Tue)-11; 12-10.30 Sun
☎ (01942) 323137 website: www.royaloakwigan.co.uk
Everards Tiger; Mayflower Dark Oak, Myles Best Bitter; Merlin Astley Gold; Tetley Bitter ⊞
Multi-roomed pub, served by a long bar stocking foreign draught and bottled beers and draught cider. The Royal Oak is the Mayflower Brewery tap, and hosts live music, beer and food festivals. The attractive, well-kept garden is available for summer barbecues.
❀◐◑♿⇌♣🍎⚟🗑

Swan & Railway

80 Wallgate, WN1 1BA (opp. North Western Station)
⏲ 11-11 12-10.30 Sun
☎ (01942) 495032
Banks's Original, Bitter; guest beers ⊞
A magnificent mosaic floor and tiled passageway lead you into this superbly traditional urban pub, facing the station. The bar features much wood and an impressive stained glass window (not original). The walls of the atmospheric narrow vault are adorned with railway memorabilia from the golden age of steam, while the passageway to the toilets show old seaside posters and photos of obscure cricketers. There is a pool room, plus a large lounge. Keenly-priced food is served 12-10pm.
♉❀⇆◐◑⊟⇌(North Western/Wallgate) ♣

Withingon

Victoria ✔

438 Wilmslow Road, M20 3BW (on B5093)
⏲ 11.30-11; 12-10.30 Sun
☎ (0161) 434 2600
Hydes Mild, Bitter, Jekyll's Gold, seasonal beers ⊞
This popular pub has been owned by Hydes for over 100 years. Scattered around the walls, numerous photographs show its heritage. Its regulars range from students to pensioners. It has a games room and the licensee hosts a Thursday quiz, when up to 14 teams take part. The outdoor drinking area is a real suntrap in summer. The pub is well served by buses from the centre of Manchester. Lunches are served Saturday and Sunday. ❀◐♣

Woodford

Davenport Arms (Thief's Neck)

550 Chester Road, SK7 1PS (on A5102)
⏲ 11-3.30, 5.15-11; 11-11 Sat; 12-3, 7-10.30 Sun
☎ (0161) 439 2435
Robinson's Hatters, Unicorn, Old Tom (winter), **seasonal beers** ⊞
A real pub in an area dominated by 'identikit' dining venues, run by the same family for over 70 years. Resembling an old red-brick Cheshire farmhouse, it features impressive floral displays in spring and summer. Inside, the cosy rooms are warmed by real fires in winter; the interior is entirely no-smoking, apart from the tap room. The excellent food is mostly home made, with some adventurous specials. The large, attractive garden to the rear is set well away from the road. ♨Q♉❀◐⊟♣P⚟

Worsley

Bridgewater

23 Barton Road, M28 2PD (on B5211, 200 yds from Worsley Court House)
⏲ 11-11; 12-10.30 Sun
☎ (0161) 794 0589
Boddingtons Bitter; Phoenix Arizona; guest beer ⊞
Spacious, roadside inn near the Bridgewater Canal. The tiled floor main room has space round the bar for drinkers who prefer to stand. Seating is in several rooms branching off from this area, most of which are at a raised level. The large outdoor drinking area can get crowded on summer weekends. The guest beer is usually from Poenix or Bank Top. Wheelchair access is via a ramp at the rear. Meals are served until 8pm daily. ❀◐◑♿P⚟

Worthington

Crown Hotel

Platt Lane, WN1 2XF
⏲ 12-11; 12-10.30 Sun
☎ (01257) 421354
website: www.thecrownatworthington.co.uk
Moorhouses Black Cat; Mayflower Myles Best Bitter; guest beers ⊞
Enjoying a new lease of life, the Crown Hotel now offers five cask beers. The landlord sources guest ales from micro-breweries around the country. It is also a rare outlet for Mayflower beers – food is served in the bar and no-smoking conservatory/restaurant. A large, decked sun terrace has patio heaters. The upstairs function room and 10 en-suite bedrooms have recently been refurbished. The large car park is a bonus.
♉❀⇆◐◑♿P

White Crow

Chorley Road, WN1 2XL
⏲ 12-3, 5.30-11; 12-11 Fri & Sat; 12-10.30 Sun
☎ (01257) 474344
Boddingtons Bitter; Theakston Best Bitter; guest beers ⊞
Commodious country pub, refurbished in olde-worlde style. One end is a large, no-smoking, family dining area, while the central bar area offers room for further diners, and a no-smoking dining area. At the other end there is a games area with a large TV. It serves an extensive menu and has earned a deserved reputation for its food. Close to Worthington Lakes, the pub has a large car park and children's play area. Two guest beers are regularly sourced from micro-breweries. ♨♉❀◐◑♿♣P⚟

Priorities

No tea, Mrs Morgan. In training he is. A glass of beer if you please.

Barry Fitzgerald in John Ford's film How Green Was My Valley.

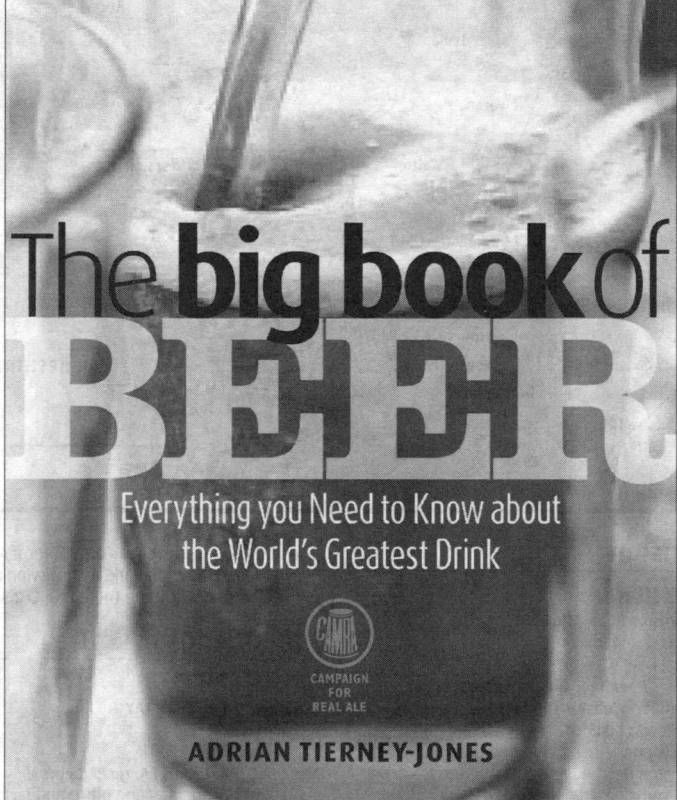

MERSEYSIDE

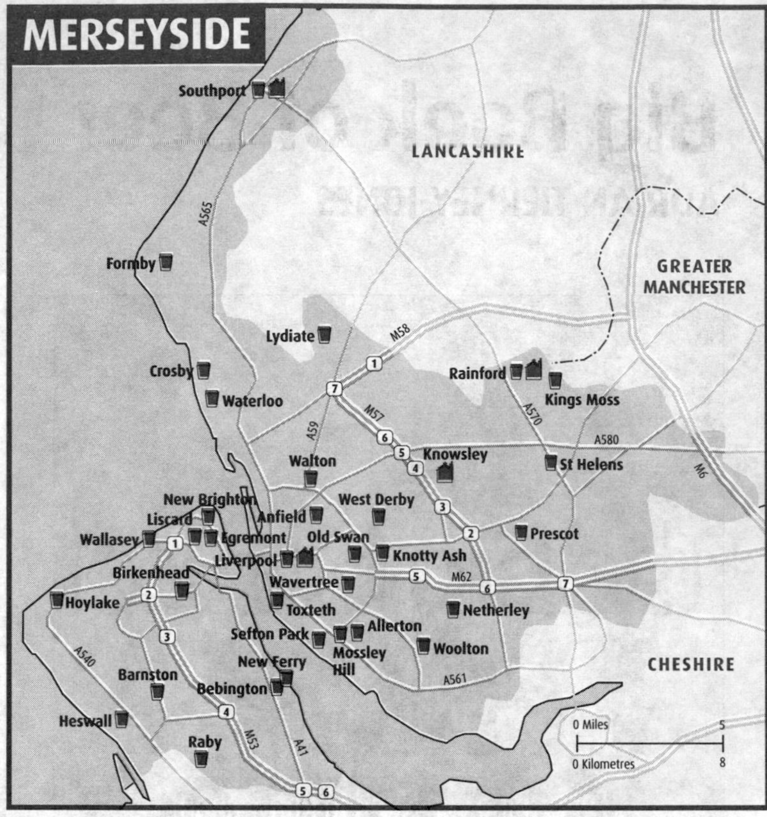

Barnston

Fox & Hounds

107 Barnston Road, CH61 1BW
11-11; 12-10.30 Sun
☎ (0151) 645 7685
Marston's Pedigree; Theakston Best Bitter, Old Peculier; Webster's Bitter; guest beer H
This pub was built in 1911 by Birkenhead Brewery, on the site of a former pub at the top of Barnston Dale. A lounge, converted from tea rooms, complements the original snug and traditional tiled bar. Plenty of local photographs add interest and each room has a warming real fire during winter months. The flowery courtyard is a welcoming stop-off on the local CAMRA summer pubs walk. Q ♣P

Bebington

Traveller's Rest

169 Mount Road, CH63 8PJ
12-11; 12-10.30 Sun
☎ (0151) 608 2988
Boddingtons Bitter; Caledonian Deuchars IPA; Flowers IPA; Greene King Abbot; Taylor Landlord; guest beers H
Former coaching inn, reputed to be over 300 years old; this popular hostelry has a country pub feel, decorated throughout with brasses and bric-a-brac. Beers are obtained from a central bar serving two other rooms (one no-smoking), and regularly include brews from local micros. A regular winner of local CAMRA awards, it is frequented by fans visiting nearby Tranmere Rovers' ground, Prenton Park. Award-winning food is served at lunchtime (not Sun). Q

Birkenhead

Old Colonial ✔

167 Bridge Street, CH41 1AY
11-11; 12-10.30 Sun
☎ (0151) 647 1560
Cains Mild, IPA, Bitter, FA; guest beers H
Friendly town pub attracting office and factory workers at lunchtime, loyal regulars at night. Tastefully restored in typical Cains style, entertainment is provided most evenings including a jazz band on Thursday. Beware Heritage trams crossing the car park entrance; the first street tramway in Europe was introduced in Birkenhead in 1860. The pub is a 10-minute walk from both the Merseyrail network and bus station. ♣P

Crosby

Crosby Conservative Club

1 Glenn Buildings, Moor Lane, L23 2UN

INDEPENDENT BREWERIES

Cains Liverpool
Cambrinus Knowsley
Southport Southport
Wapping Liverpool
George Wright Rainford

3 (1 Thu-Sat)-11; 1-10.30 Sun
(0151) 924 1486
Beer range varies H
Friendly club that welcomes CAMRA members on production of a membership card. It has two weekly-changing guest beers; the Phoenix Brewery features most regularly on the handpumps. The lounge is geared for drinking and conversation. The small pool room displays a stern-looking portrait of Sir Winston Churchill who casts a critical eye over the players. The snooker room boasts two full-sized tables and its own bar access.
Q (Blundellsands/Crosby)

Crow's Nest
63 Victoria Road, L23 7XY
11.30-11; 12-10.30 Sun
(0151) 924 6953
Cains Bitter; guest beers H
This popular local, housed in a Grade II listed building, is one of the best pubs on Merseyside. It offers a cosy bar with a tiny snug and comfortable lounge. The interior has several interesting features, including a tiled floor and original etched windows. Friendly staff ensure a warm welcome for locals and visitors alike. Outside tables are available for summer drinking. A blackboard of forthcoming ales is displayed; you are bound to want to return to this suburban gem.
Q (Blundellsands/Crosby) P

Stamps Wine Bar
4 Crown Buildings, L23 5SR
10.30-11; 12-10.30 Sun
(0151) 286 2662
Beer range varies H
Bistro-type bar that was once the local post office, hence its name. The upper floor is a pleasant, peaceful place to spend time chatting and reading. The lower floor with bare bricks and floorboards provides a comfortable and inviting ambience. The four handpumps dispense a diverse range of ales. Food is served until 9pm, freshly cooked to order. The pub is well known for its support of live music sessions and attracts a varied mix of customers.
(Blundellsands/Crosby)

Egremont

Magazine Hotel
Magazine Row, CH45 1HP
11-11; 12-10.30 Sun
(0151) 639 3381
Draught Bass; guest beers H
Multi-roomed pub of great character, dating from 1759, the Mags makes a welcome return to this Guide after 20 years. Situated above the Seaforth Promenade, in the Magazine Row conservation area, it affords extensive views over the River Mersey. A main central bar serves two no-smoking rooms and a snug. Renowned over many years for its Draught Bass, there are now three additional guest beers. Good value bar meals are served every lunchtime and early evening meals on Thursday and Friday.
Q P

Formby

Freshfield Hotel
1A Massams Lane, Freshfield, L37 7BD
12-11; 12-10.30 Sun
(01704) 874871
Boddingtons Bitter; Caledonian Deuchars IPA; Camerons Castle Eden Ale; Taylor Landlord; guest beers H
The National Red Squirrel Reserve and a beach are situated near this unpretentious open-plan pub with wooden floors and a hearty real fire in winter. Up to 12 real ales are regularly available. A local gem – the large function room is used for frequent events including the comedy club, guitar club and local charity fundraisers. The pub is a 10-minute walk from the Merseyrail Station.
(Freshfield) P

Heswall

Dee View
Dee View Road, CH60 0DH
11-11; 12-10.30 Sun
(0151) 342 2320
Boddingtons Bitter; Caledonian Deuchars IPA; Taylor Landlord; guest beer H
Homely local with a single bar, offering a warm welcome and six handpulled beers, many from micro-brewers. It sits on a hairpin bend opposite the war memorial and famous mirror. Monday is curry night, while Tuesday offers a popular and entertaining pub quiz. Excellent Sunday lunches are served until 3pm (booking recommended); evening meals are available Monday-Thursday.
P

Johnny Pye
Pye Road, CH60 0DB (next to bus station)
11-11; 12-10.30 Sun
(0151) 342 8215
Banks's Original, Bitter; Marston's Burton Bitter H
Situated on the site of the old bus depot, this lively, modern pub is named after a local entrepreneur. Johnny Pye is also associated with other buildings nearby, and he was responsible for starting the local bus service. An autographed cartoon of footballer Gordon Banks adorns the bar; the pub has a wide-screen TV, a strong football following and a darts team. Well-priced food is on offer with authentic curries on Thursday night (no meals Sun eve).
P

Hoylake

Plasterer's Arms
35 Back Seaview, CH47 2DJ (opp. Grove Park)
11-11; 12-10.30 Sun
(0151) 632 3023
Cains Bitter; Caledonian Deuchars IPA; Greene King Abbot; Jennings Bitter H
Traditional, unspoilt back-street pub that is well worth finding. One bar serves the main room and cosy snug. Note the etched glass mirrors on the ceiling depicting local landmarks. It hosts a busy quiz night on Thursday, and Irish music night every fourth Friday of the month. The pub regularly fundraises for local charities and in particular supports the Hoylake lifeboat. There is patio seating close by. (Manor Rd) P

Ship Inn
Market Street, CH47 3BB
🕘 11.30-11; 12-10.30 Sun
☎ (0151) 632 4319
Caledonian Deuchars IPA; Fuller's London Pride; Jennings Bitter; Wells Bombardier; guest beers 🄷
Popular, town-centre pub, first licensed in 1754 (recent testing has dated the building to 1730). Although modernised in recent years into one L-shaped bar area, old beams have been retained in the back lounge. Twelve real ales are on offer, with good value bar meals served 12-2.30pm (4pm Sun) and 5.30-8pm (Mon-Sat). The large, secluded garden at the rear boasts a pond. On Monday night a jazz band plays.
❀◖◗⇌(Manor Rd) P

Kings Moss

Collier's Arms ✔
57 Pimbo Road, WA11 8RD
(off B5205 to Rainford, follow Houghwood Golf Club signs)
🕘 12-11; 12-10.30 Sun
☎ (01744) 892894
Beer range varies 🄷
Nestling in a tiny hamlet between Billinge and Rainford, this cosy pub is part of a row of traditional miners' cottages. The interior has stone floors and mining memorabilia. There are three guest beers available. This food-oriented pub has an extensive menu and can get busy with diners. Families are welcome and high chairs are available (no eve meals Sun). The garden has a children's play area.
♨Q❀◖◗♣P⊘

Liscard

Clairville ✔
48 Wallasey Road, CH45 8PB
🕘 10-11; 12-10.30 Sun
☎ (0151) 346 8960
Marston's Burton Bitter; Greene King Abbot; guest beers 🄷
Recently converted supermarket in the Wetherspoon pub chain, with an interesting guest beer policy. This large, airy, modern establishment has a no smoking/family area. Meals are served all day, including a children's menu until 8.30pm. Popular with daytime shoppers and workers, it is a short walk from the main shopping area and town-centre bus stops. Wi-fi Internet access is available.
◖◗♿⊘

Liverpool: Allerton

Allerton Hall (Pub in the Park)
Clarke's Gardens, Springwood Avenue, L25 7UN
🕘 11.30-11; 12-10.30 Sun
☎ (0151) 494 2664
Cains Bitter; guest beers 🄷
Allerton Hall stands in the grounds of the pleasant Clarke's Gardens. Up to five guest beers come from the Cellarman's Reserve list, usually including Marston's Pedigree. The hostelry is a Miller's Kitchen. It boasts two outdoor drinking areas, one of which features a children's playground. Bus 86B passes the pub during the day (except Sun). Note: the new South Liverpool Parkway interchange will replace the old Allerton and Garston stations from December 2005. Q☺❀◖◗♿⇌⊖(Garston) P⊘

Liverpool: Anfield

Strawberry Tavern
Breckfield Road South, L6 5DR
🕘 11.30-11; 12-10.30 Sun
☎ (0151) 260 6158
Oakwell Old Tom Mild, Barnsley Bitter 🄷
Now in its fourth year as an Oakwell house, the Strawberry continues to serve two of its beers. The interior is divided to give a separate games area with a pool table and dartboard. Lying between Breck Road and West Derby Road, the pub is a welcome oasis for thirsty fans visiting Liverpool Football Club. ❀⊟♿♣P

Liverpool: City Centre

Augustus John
Peach Street, L3 5TX (on University campus)
🕘 11-11; closed Sat & Sun
☎ (0151) 794 5507
Cains Bitter; guest beers 🄷
Located on the University of Liverpool campus, the pub is open plan with a large juke box and pool table. A changing range of guest beers, along with low prices, makes this pub popular with both staff and students. Cains Brewery occasionally supplies a house beer, AJ Bitter. Beer festivals have recently been added to the pub's schedule of events. The entrance has a wheelchair ramp and there is a designated WC.
❀♿⇌(Lime St) ⊖(Central)

Baltic Fleet
33 Wapping, L1 8DQ
🕘 12-11; 12-10.30 Sun
☎ (0151) 709 3116
Wapping Bitter, Summer Ale, Stout; guest beers 🄷
Located near the Albert Dock, the building is Grade II listed and designed on the 'flat iron' principle. The interior bears a nautical theme and mysterious tunnels in the cellar have led to much speculation among the customers of a dark period in history involving smuggling and press gangs. The beer range comes from the pub's own Wapping brewery, supplemented by two guest ales. Food is served downstairs most lunchtimes, while an upstairs restaurant caters for evening meals and Sunday roasts.
♨Q◖⊖(James St) 🍎⊘

Cracke
13 Rice Street, L1 9BB (near Philharmonic Hall)
🕘 12-11; 12-10.30 Sun
☎ (0151) 709 4171
Cains Bitter; Phoenix Old Oak Ale, Wobbly Bob; guest beers 🄷
This back-street pub is almost impossible to find unless you know where it is. Dating from around 1850, it gets its name because it was originally so small, consisting of what is now the tiny public bar. It features a back room called The War Office where people who wanted to bore about the Boer War were despatched. Food is served until 6pm and the garden is licensed until 9pm. Biddendens cider is sold straight from the cask.
❀◖⊟⇌(Lime St) ⊖(Central) 🍎

Crown Hotel

43 Lime Street, L1 1JQ
11-11; 12-10.30 Sun
(0151) 707 6027
Fuller's London Pride; guest beers H
This architectural gem is just a few seconds' walk from Lime Street Station. The Grade II listed building boasts an Art Nouveau-style interior; the two downstairs rooms retain the original decoration. A function room is available upstairs. A small range of beers is served from a large bar. Reasonably-priced food is available until the early evening. The friendly staff welcome a wide variety of patrons.
(Lime St) (Central)

Dispensary

87 Renshaw Street, L1 2SP
12-11; 12.30-10.30 Sun
(0151) 709 2160
Cains Mild, IPA, Bitter, FA; guest beers H
Originally called the Grapes (the old name is displayed above the bar), when bought by Cains it was converted into a replica of a one-room Victorian street-corner local. The brewery was rewarded with the CAMRA/English Heritage Refurbishment award. Although a tied house, it sells two constantly-changing guest beers; the cider is Addlestones. The pub is frequented by both regulars and shoppers.
(Lime St) (Central)

Doctor Duncan's

St John's House, St John's Lane, L1 1HF
(on Queen's Square)
11.30-11; 12-10.30 Sun
(0151) 709 5100
Cains Mild, IPA, Bitter, FA, seasonal beers; guest beers H
Cains' flagship managed house, usually serving the full range of its beers plus four guests on handpump. A small bar leads to back lounges and the Grade II-listed tiled room, which was the original entrance to the Pearl Assurance building, designed by Alfred Waterhouse in 1896-8. Dr Duncan implemented a public health policy to combat cholera epidemics in Liverpool around 1850. This friendly pub can get busy, and is often crowded on Friday and Saturday evenings with people enjoying a night out.
(Lime St)

Everyman Bistro

5-9 Hope Street, L1 9BH
(beneath the Everyman Theatre)
12 (11 Sat)-midnight (2am Thu-Sat); closed Sun
(0151) 708 9545 website: www.everyman.co.uk
Cains Bitter; guest beers H
This cellar pub has a theatre attached. Some years ago the theatre went bust and the Bistro bought the freehold to the entire building. It comprises three rooms: the first has a bar, the second serves award-winning food, and the third is used as an overflow for the first two as well as a function room for the folk club, poetry readings and other events. No attempt is made to separate diners from drinkers. The middle room is now no-smoking except after 9pm on Friday and Saturday.
Q (Lime St) (Central)

Flute

35 Hardman Street, L1 9AS
12-11 (midnight Wed & Thu; 2am Fri & Sat); 12-10.30 Sun
(0151) 707 6485
Beer range varies H
Located among the numerous restaurants and bars of the Hardman Street area, the Flute is a spacious, open-plan pub frequented by younger drinkers taking advantage of its longer opening hours at weekends. Formerly a part of the Firkin chain of pubs, the decor is a mixture of old and new and is dominated by several large screens showing satellite TV. A DJ plays popular music on Friday and Saturday evenings. Food is served all day.
(Lime St) (Central)

Fly in the Loaf

13 Hardman Street, L1 9AS
12-11 (midnight Fri & Sat); 12-10.30 Sun
(0151) 708 0817
Okells Bitter, Maclir, Dr Okells IPA, seasonal beers; guest beers H
The second Manx Cat inn was opened on the mainland in 2004 by the IOM brewer Okells. The previous Kirklands bakery, whose slogan was 'no flies in the loaf', has been tastefully refurbished to a Steve Holt design with ecclesiastical fittings. There are usually four guest beers from micro-breweries and a good selection of foreign bottled beers. The Fly attracts a wide cross section of customers from students to theatregoers. The home-cooked meals (served until 6.45pm) are excellent, especially the Sunday roasts.
(Lime St) (Central)

Globe

17 Cases Street, L1 1HW (opp. Central Station)
11-11; 12-10.30 Sun
(0151) 707 0067
Cains Mild, Bitter; guest beers H
Small, two-roomed Victorian pub in the city centre, close to Central Station and Clayton Square shopping area. Offering a good selection of real ales, this friendly little pub is popular with regulars and thirsty shoppers, and can get busy. However, it is well worth a visit; watch out for the sloped floor between the two rooms. A plaque commemorating the inaugural meeting of the Merseyside branch of CAMRA hangs in the small, quiet back room.
(Lime St) (Central)

Head of Steam

7 Lime Street, L1 1RJ (inside Lime St Station)
11-11; 12-10.30 Sun
(0151) 707 9559
Beer range varies H
Located inside Lime Street Station, in part of the former Great North-Western Hotel development, the pub comprises four bars, one of which is no-smoking and displays railway memorabilia. The largest bar contains several handpumps and a large-screen TV for football matches or pop videos. Studio 58 is a modern café-type bar while the Display Bar is designed as a traditional railway bar.
Q (Lime St)

Lion Tavern ☆

67 Moorfields, L2 2BP

11-11; 12-10.30 Sun

☎ (0151) 236 1734

Caledonian Deuchars IPA; Highgate Dark; Lees Bitter; guest beers H

The Lion Tavern is an original Robert Cain house named after the locomotive that first worked the Liverpool to Manchester railway. An architecturally splendid Grade II listed building (featured on the front cover of CAMRA's National Inventory), the Lion stands proud on a street corner in an area of rapid redevelopment. It attracts a mixed clientele throughout the day including local office staff and journalists. Bar food is available; the speciality cheeses and hand-made pork pies particularly recommended. ≠(Lime St) ⊖(Moorfields)

Peter Kavanagh's ☆

2-6 Egerton Street, L8 7FY (off Catherine St)

12-11; 12-10.30 Sun

☎ (0151) 709 3443

Cains Bitter; Greene King Abbot; guest beers H

The original terraced structure of this wonderful back-street pub, with stained glass windows and wooden shutters, is more than 150 years old. Over the years the pub has expanded into two adjoining houses, resulting in lots of small, interestingly shaped rooms. Two snugs boast period wall paintings by Eric Robertson, and wooden benches with carved arms, said to be caricatures of Peter Kavanagh. The staff are happy to tell visitors about the pub's history, and point out its many features.

Q

Philharmonic ☆

36 Hope Street, L1 9BX

12-11; 12-10.30 Sun

☎ (0151) 707 2837

Beer range varies H

The Philharmonic is a Grade II listed, ornate pub located across the road from the Philharmonic Hall. Up to 10 guest beers are stocked. The pub is split into five areas: the main bar, Vaults bar, Grand Lounge, Brahms and Liszt (no-smoking room). The pub has been refurbished and a disabled WC added. The first floor now boasts a restaurant. A visit to the spectacular gents is a must for anyone, but women should check with the bar staff first.

Q ≠(Lime St) ⊖(Central)

Poste House

23 Cumberland Street, L1 6BU

11-11; 12-10.30 Sun

☎ (0151) 236 4130

Cains Mild, Bitter; guest beer H

Compact, busy pub dating back to 1820, tucked away just off Dale Street. It has two cosy rooms and a warm, welcoming environment. It was saved from demolition by a campaign led by regular customers, local newspapers and CAMRA members. This hospitable little pub will now be integrated into the development scheme that was meant to replace it. Charles Dickens is one of a number of famous people who are said to have visited this characterful pub over the years. ≠(Lime St) ⊖(Moorfields)

Roscoe Head

24 Roscoe Street, L1 2SX

11.30 (12 Sat)-11; 12-10.30 Sun

☎ (0151) 709 4365

Jennings Bitter; guest beers H

Run by the same family for more than 20 years, this quiet, back-street local has appeared in every edition of the Guide. The unspoilt interior includes four separate rooms, all quite small. The front snug features Art Deco prints and the back room has a Walkers mirror. There are usually two guest beers on at any time. Lunches are served Monday-Friday. Q ≠(Lime St) ⊖(Central)

Ship & Mitre

133 Dale Street, L2 2HJ (by Birkenhead tunnel entrance)

12-11; 12-10.30 Sun

☎ (0151) 236 0859 website: www.shipandmitre.com

Beer range varies H

Just down the hill from Lime Street, this pub features an impressive Art Deco exterior. Unfortunately someone decided the interior could be improved by converting it into a representation of upturned boats. Twelve beers plus two ciders or perries are normally served, alongside around 100 different imported bottles. To provide yet more variety, the pub holds quarterly beer festivals when around 70 beers are available. As well as lunchtime food, tea-time snacks are served Wednesday-Friday. ≠(Lime St) ⊖(Moorfields)

Swan Inn

86 Wood Street, L1 4DQ

12-11; 12-10.30 Sun

☎ (0151) 709 5281

Hydes Bitter; Phoenix Best Bitter; Wobbly Bob; guest beers H

Once tucked away in a back street, this is now in a more prominent position since the FACT Arts Centre was built next door. Ranging over three floors, only the ground floor has real ale. Four guest beers are normally stocked. The pub is well known for its rock juke box. A quiet room or smoke-free environment are unthinkable here. Traditionally thought of as a bikers' pub, it now seems to be attracting a wider range of customers. ≠(Lime St) ⊖(Central)

Thomas Frost

177-187 Walton Road, Kirkdale, L4 4AJ

(opp. Aldi on A59)

10-11; 12-10.30 Sun

☎ (0151) 207 8210

Beer range varies H

This branch of Wetherspoon's occupies the ground floor of a former drapery store. Thomas Frost had a single shop on the site in 1885 and later expanded to occupy the whole block. The layout is open plan, broken only by a few supporting pillars, providing a light and airy feel to this pleasant venue. It usually has a larger selection of real ales on dispense than most Wetherspoon outlets. The pub has a family area but children are not admitted on Liverpool or Everton home match days.

Thomas Rigby's

23-25 Dale Street, L2 2EZ

11.30-11; 11.30-10.30 Sun

☎ (0151) 236 3269

Okells Mild, Bitter, Maclir, seasonal beers; guest beers Ⓗ
Sensitively restored, friendly pub, formerly part of warehouses and other buildings owned by Thomas Rigby since 1852. The façade of the building was changed in the early 1800s although the interior walls date from the 18th century. Legend has it that Horatio Nelson drank here when it was a coffee house. An extensive world beer range is stocked, both in bottles and on draught. Hot and cold food is served all day until 7pm, including daily specials. Daily newspapers are provided.
❀◐◑⊟≉(Lime St) ⊖(Moorfields) ⚟

Welkin ✔
7 Whitechapel, L1 6DS
⊛ 10-11; 12-10 Sun
☎ (0151) 243 1080
Beer range varies Ⓗ
A Wetherspoon house, the Welkin is situated in the busy city-centre shopping area, close to the Cavern Quarter. No-smoking throughout, it offers a changing choice of beers, including seasonal options, and holds a series of beer festivals throughout the year. Good value food is available all day; look out for the ever-popular curry nights, steak nights and Sunday roasts. The pub opens at 10am each day for breakfast, with tea or coffee.
◐◑♿≉(Lime St) ⊖(Central) ⚟

Wetherspoon's ✔
1-2 Charlotte Row, L1 1HU
⊛ 11-11; 12-10.30 Sun
☎ (0151) 709 4802
Marston's Burton Bitter; Greene King Abbot; guest beers Ⓗ
Spacious and modern, this is a typical Wetherspoon's outlet. A long bar services a single room with an area dedicated to serving good value food. It is busier in the evenings now that it shows televised sports. Two guest beers are usually on tap and the pub regularly takes part in the chain's beer festivals. Meals are served all day.
☕◐◑♿≉(Lime St) ⊖(Central) ⚟

White Star ✔
2-4 Rainford Gardens, L2 6PT
⊛ 11.30-11; 12-10.30 Sun
☎ (0151) 231 6861 website: www.thewhitestar.co.uk
Beer range varies Ⓗ
Rare, traditional pub, located among the more trendy establishments of the Mathew Street area, the White Star abounds with local memorabilia and pictures of White Star liners. Twinned with bars in the Czech Republic and Norway, it has a strong sporting theme, and regularly broadcasts football matches on a big screen. House beers are from Lancashire's Bowland Brewery range.
◑⊟≉(Lime St) ⊖(Central/Moorfields)

Liverpool: Knotty Ash

Wheatsheaf
186 East Prescot Road, L14 5NG
⊛ 12-11; 12-10.30 Sun
☎ (0151) 228 5080
Cains Bitter Ⓗ
Multi-roomed pub that has retained the etched windows of the nearby Joseph Jones Brewery some 80 years after its demise. It is probably the only pub in Liverpool still offering a table service in the lounge and snug. The bar shows televised sports. Bus routes 8, 9 and 10 pass the pub from the city centre to Huyton & St Helens; service 61 from Bootle to Aigburth also stops nearby.
Q⊟P

Liverpool: Mossley Hill

Storrsdale
43-47 Storrsdale Road, L18 7JY
⊛ 12-11; 12-10.30 Sun
☎ (0151) 724 3464
Taylor Landlord Ⓗ
Sizeable two-roomed local with a comfortable wood-panelled lounge and a bar housing a dartboard and juke box. No piped music is played in the lounge. Leaded windows and attractive exterior tiling reflect the 1930s construction. Popular with a mix of locals, students and thirsty sporty types from the nearby playing fields, all are drawn by the friendly, relaxed atmosphere. Sky football is shown. A small yard to the side has tables and benches for outdoor drinking in summer.
Q❀⊟≉♣

Liverpool: Netherley

Falcon
Caldway Drive, L27 0YB
⊛ 12-11; 12-10.30 Sun
☎ (0151) 498 9994
Oakwell Barnsley Bitter Ⓗ
Spacious pub on the edge of the Netherley estate. This Oakwell tied house is the only outlet for some distance serving real ale. It hosts karaoke on Saturday evening and bingo on Tuesday and Friday afternoons. Bus Nos. 165, 169 and 883 pass the pub, along with the 166/188/266/288 Garston circular services. A patio allows for outdoor drinking. ❀⊟♿♣P

Liverpool: Old Swan

Wetherspoon's ✔
694 Queens Drive, L13 5UH (corner of Prescot Rd)
⊛ 11-11; 12-10.30 Sun
☎ (0151) 220 2713
Greene King Abbot; Marston's Burton Bitter, Pedigree; guest beers Ⓗ
The pub consists of a large single room, with a dining area at the back. There are usually at least four guest ales available, which makes this outlet very welcome in the suburbs. Televised sports are now shown. The standard Wetherspoon's menu is available all day. ◐◑♿⚟

Liverpool: Sefton Park

Albert
66-68 Lark Lane, L17 8UU
⊛ 12-11; 12-10.30 Sun
☎ (0151) 726 9119
Black Sheep Best Bitter; Fuller's London Pride; Greene King Old Speckled Hen; Taylor Landlord; guest beers Ⓗ
Impressive corner pub in a conservation area, popular with locals and students. Built in 1873 by Robert Cain, it retains some original fittings,

glass woodwork and mosaic floor tiling in its side entrance. It was sympathetically refurbished in 2004 to provide disabled facilities, a no-smoking room and a rear courtyard garden. The large central bar with 11 handpumps serves three rooms. A varied menu is available lunchtimes and evenings, and all day at the weekend. Sky Sports is shown in the front bar. ❀◐◑♿⇌(St Michaels)⚟

Liverpool: Toxteth

Brewery Tap ✔

35 Grafton Street, L8 5XJ (adjoins Cains Brewery)

11-11; 12-10.30 Sun

☎ (0151) 709 2129

Cains Mild, IPA, Bitter, FA, seasonal beers Ⓗ

Cains' tap, set within the walls of the brewery, usually has the full range of its beers on handpump. Addlestones cider is also sold. Formerly the Grapes (the name remains in the terracotta façade), it hosts brewery tours. An interesting collection of breweriana, especially beer labels from former Merseyside breweries, is on display. Meals are served until 6pm. The Tap is just up Stanhope Street from the Smartbus 4 stop after it exits the Albert dock. ❀◐●P

Liverpool: Walton

Raven ✔

72-74 Walton Vale, L9 2BU (on A59)

10-11; 12-10.30 Sun

☎ (0151) 524 1255

Greene King Abbot; Marston's Burton Bitter, Pedigree; guest beers Ⓗ

This suburban Wetherspoon pub, close to Aintree racecourse, was previously a Kwik Save supermarket. Situated in something of a beer desert, it provides welcome relief for those with a thirst in the area. Although, like many Wetherspoon's, the interior is one large room, it has something of the feel of a traditional local. Meals are served all day and an area is designated for family use.
Q◐◑♿⇌(Orrell Pk)⚟

Liverpool: Wavertree

Willowbank

329 Smithdown Road, L15 3JA

12-11; 12-10.30 Sun

☎ (0151) 733 5782

Greene King IPA; Shepherd Neame Spitfire; guest beers Ⓗ

Now part of the Spirit Group, this Victorian pub is a classic ale house. New management has maintained the quality of the beer, with several guests available, and a real cider. The pub is popular with residents as well as numerous students who live locally. All football matches and other sports are shown on the TVs situated around the pub. Weekend meals are served 12-6pm. Beer festivals are held in March, June, October and December. ❀◐◑⊟♿●P

Liverpool: West Derby

Crown Inn

2 Leyfield Road, L12 9HA

12-11; 12-10.30 Sun

☎ (0151) 228 9943

Caledonian Deuchars IPA Ⓗ

Welcoming, unspoilt, suburban pub, retaining much of its original decor. The pub has two rooms: a comfortable lounge with a large-screen TV, and a spacious bar, which lists the honours of the Crown Inn Bowling Club. The well-kept bowling green and garden are found to the rear of the pub. The Crown Inn is easily reached by the No. 61 bus. ❀⊟♣P

Halton Castle

96 Mill Lane, L12 7JD

12-11; 12-10.30 Sun

☎ (0151) 270 2013

Cains Bitter; Marston's Pedigree Ⓗ

Traditional Victorian pub divided into several rooms, including a public bar. An outside area provides a pleasant place for drinking in good weather. A rare outlet for real ale in the suburbs, the pub is supplied with bitter from the local Cains Brewery. It is serviced by the Nos. 12 and 13 bus routes from the city centre. ❀⊟P

Liverpool: Woolton

Gardeners Arms

101 Vale Road, L26 7RW

4 (2 Thu; 1 Fri & Sat)-11; 12-10.30 Sun

☎ (0151) 428 1443

Cains Bitter; Caledonian Deuchars IPA; Theakston Mild Ⓗ

Small, back-street local hidden behind flats but easily accessible from the city centre on the 176 or 177 bus routes (alight at Allerton Golf course, walk through flats). A warm and friendly community pub, the atmosphere is relaxed and visitors are made welcome. It caters for local sports and is home to a number of teams including golf and women's netball. Sky TV is available and a quiz is held on Tuesday evening. Almost half the pub is no-smoking. Q⚟

White Horse

2 Acrefield Road, L25 5JL

12-11; 12-10.30 Sun

☎ (0151) 428 1862

Cains Bitter; guest beers Ⓗ

This cosy local dates from the time when Woolton was a proper village, and has been run for many years by the same landlord. Three drinking areas, one of which is no smoking, and a central bar with wood panelling create a warm, relaxed atmosphere. Good value food is available 12-8pm (12-5pm Sun) and includes a daily special. Customers can watch Sky TV. Two guest beers are available, often from Black Sheep and Charles Wells. ❀◐◑⚟

Lydiate

Scotch Piper ☆

Southport Road, L31 4HD

12-3, 5.30-11; 12-11 Sat; 12-10.30 Sun

☎ (0151) 526 0503

website: www.fortunecity.com/millenium/ellerburn/53/

Banks's Bitter; guest beer Ⓗ

This picturesque Grade II listed pub is on the Southport road (A5147) just outside Lydiate. The No. 300 bus from Liverpool or Southport stops outside the door. Each of the three rooms has its own real fire, but most regulars try to squeeze into the tiny front bar! With a warm welcome for

all, the Piper is popular with locals and visitors alike; bikers congregate on Wednesday.
♨Q❀♣P

New Brighton

Clarence Hotel ✔

89 Albion Street, CH45 9JQ (behind Hotel Victoria)
⌚ 11.30-11; 12-10.30 Sun
☎ (0151) 639 3860
Cains Bitter; Caledonian Deuchars IPA; guest beers Ⓗ
Friendly, suburban pub with a bar, lounge and dining/function room. Handpumps situated in the lounge, not the bar, dispense a varied range of up to three guest beers, and showcase micro-breweries. No meals are served on Monday or Tuesday, or Sunday evening. Winner of many local CAMRA awards, the pub holds an excellent annual beer festival every July. It is a five minute walk from the Merseyrail station. ᘐ❀◑⊟⇌

New Ferry

Freddie's Club

36 Stanley Road, CH62 5AS (off New Chester Rd)
⌚ 5 (12 Sat)-11; 12-10.30 Sun
☎ (0151) 645 3023
Beer range varies Ⓗ
Small, cosy club in the back streets of New Ferry, Freddie's is a welcome addition to this Guide in an area considered to be a beer desert. Entry is either by showing a CAMRA membership card or Good Beer Guide. A comfortable lounge bar serves two changing guest beers. It was voted Wirral CAMRA Club of the Year 2004 for its consistently good beer quality. An attached snooker room houses two full-sized tables.
Q♿P

Prescot

Clock Face

54 Derby Street, L34 3LL (off jct 2 M57)
⌚ 11-11; 12-10.30 Sun
☎ (0151) 292 4121
Thwaites Original, Lancaster Bomber Ⓗ
Located on the hillside approach to Prescot from the M57, this elegant former mansion house on the Lord Derby estate was converted in the 1980s, yet retains much of its former splendour, with sympathetic decor and furnishings. The central bar serves several areas. Lancaster Bomber is now a permanent feature, with Thwaites seasonal beers appearing occasionally. In the evenings a cold platter is available until 8.30pm. Quiz night is Monday. The Clock Face is reputedly home to three ghosts. ❀◑P

Raby

Wheatsheaf Inn

Raby Mere Road, CH63 4JH (from M53 jct 4 take B5151)
⌚ 11-11; 12-10.30 Sun
☎ (0151) 336 3416
Greene King Old Speckled Hen; Theakston Mild, Best Bitter, Old Peculier; Thwaites Original; Wells Bombardier; guest beer Ⓗ
Locally known as the Thatch, it is probably the oldest pub on the Wirral. Catering for all tastes, customers can enjoy a pint of one of the nine cask ales by an inglenook fire, in the loose box or in the garden suntrap. No evening meals are served on Sunday or Monday. Children are admitted at lunchtime. It was voted Wirral CAMRA Pub of the Year runner-up 2004. Morris dancing takes place during the local Scarecrow Festival. The Wheatsheaf is home to an award-winning restaurant, the Cowshed.
♨Qᘐ❀◑⊟♿♣P

Rainford

Junction

News Lane, WA11 7JU
(from A570 follow Rainford Jct Station signs)
⌚ 12-11; 12-10.30 Sun
☎ (01744) 882876
website: www.thejunctionrainford.co.uk
Weetwood Old Dog Bitter; guest beers Ⓗ
Located opposite Rainford Junction Station, this friendly community local offers rotating beers from the Weetwood Brewery and occasional guest beers. A central bar serves the lounge and games room, with darts, dominoes and pool. A popular live music venue, it hosts bluegrass on Wednesday and folk nights Thursday and Sunday. Several clubs gather at the Junction. Quiz night is Monday. Sunday meals are served 12-8pm. Outside is a large car park with a children's play area. ❀◑⊟⇌♣P

St Helens

Abbey Hotel

1 Hard Lane, Denton's Green, WA10 6TL
(off A570, 1 mile N of St Helens town centre)
⌚ 12-11; 12-10.30 Sun
☎ (01744) 25649
Holt Mild, Bitter, seasonal beers Ⓗ
Late 19th-century former coaching inn on the north side of town, this Holt's pub has been recently refurbished but retains many of the original features. One central bar area serves five rooms (one no-smoking). Traditional pub games are played (including dominoes and pool) and a large-screen projector caters for most popular sporting broadcasts. A quiz night is held on Thursday. Evening meals are available Thursday-Sunday. Rooms are available to hire for private parties. Q❀◑♣P⊬

Beecham's Bar ✔

Water Street, WA10 1PZ (under Beecham's clock tower)
⌚ 12-11; closed Sun
☎ (01744) 623420
Beer range varies Ⓗ
Although no longer a brew-pub, the bar, based in a listed building next to St Helen's College, remains a haven for real ale lovers. It features at least four guest beers and offers CAMRA members 10% discount on production of a membership card; students also receive 10% discount. Televised sports events are screened. Sandwiches are available at lunchtime. Beecham's Crystal Wheat, originally brewed here, is now brewed under licence by Three Rivers Brewery. ♿⇌(Central)⊬⊟

Griffin Inn

Church Lane, Eccleston, WA10 5AD
(from A570 St Helens take B5201 to Prescot)
⌚ 12-11; 12-10.30 Sun
☎ (01744) 27907 website: www.griffininn.co.uk

Cains Bitter; Marston's Pedigree; guest beers Ⓗ
Situated on the outskirts of St Helens at Eccleston, the current building dates back to 1812, with an impressive sandstone frontage. A rotating guest beer complements the regular ales. Bar meals are available, and the restaurant serves a full menu. A decked patio area to the rear, and additional benches, overlook the recently-built children's play area. A central bar serves all areas, including a no-smoking lounge with a large-screen TV. Quiz night is Wednesday.
❀⇆◑◗P⍁

Sutton Oak ✔

73 Bold Road, WA9 4JG (on B5204)
✪ 4 (12 Fri & Sat)-11; 12-10.30 Sun
☎ (01744) 813442
website: www.suttonoak.co.uk
Black Sheep Best Bitter; guest beers Ⓗ
Cosy, family-friendly pub close to the station serving at least three guest beers, usually from independent breweries, including one dark beer plus a cider. A large-screen TV shows sports events in the lounge. An extensive garden with children's play area hosts barbecues in summer and a marquee is erected for a beer festival over the August bank holiday. Other seasonal beer festivals are held inside. The pub hosts quiz nights and runs an angling club. Smoking is not permitted at the bar.
❀⊟♿⇌(Junction) ♣●P⊽

Southport

Barons Bar (Scarisbrick Hotel) ✔

239 Lord Street, PR8 1NZ
✪ 11-11; 12-10.30 Sun
☎ (01704) 543000
website: www.baronsbarbeerfestival.co.uk
Moorhouses Pride of Pendle; Tetley Bitter; guest beers Ⓗ
Barons Bar is a friendly, relaxed and comfortable lounge bar set within Southport's premier hotel. The decor resembles a medieval baronial hall with knights and shields on the wall. Eight handpumps occupy the centre of the bar. Flag & Turret is the house beer. The bar is renowned for its annual beer festival, usually beginning on May Day at 6am. Children are welcome in the Victoria Room until 6pm. Parking is for hotel residents.
Q⛱❀⇆◑♿⇌●P

Berkeley Arms

19 Queens Road, PR9 9HN
✪ 4 (12 Fri & Sat)-11; 12-10.30 Sun
☎ (01704) 500811
website: www.berkeley-arms.com
Adnams Bitter; Banks's Bitter; Hawkshead Bitter; Marston's Pedigree; Moorhouses Black Cat; guest beers Ⓗ
Small residential hotel, the Berkeley specialises in excellent beer and home-made fresh pizzas baked on the premises. The bar even has a pizza hot line to phone in your order. Well worth a detour from town, it is handy for visitors to the YMCA, police station, magistrates' courts and fire station. One of the cheapest pubs in town, beer in the Berkeley is excellent value. Regular No. 42/44 buses from Southport to Crossens stop outside the pub.
Q⛱❀⇆◗⇌♣P⍁

Bold Arms

59-61 Botanic Road, Churchtown, PR9 7NE
(2 miles N of town, near Botanic Gardens)
✪ 11.30-11; 12-10.30 Sun
☎ (01704) 228192
Tetley Dark Mild, Bitter; guest beers Ⓗ
Situated at the heart of the historic village of Churchtown, this 17th-century former coaching house offers a warm welcome in winter, with its many coal fires, and a garden for summer days. The oldest pub in Southport, it retains many original features, including a stable block to the rear. Just a short walk from the Botanic Gardens and the manorial Meols Hall, it can be easily reached from Southport town centre by the regular No. 49/49A bus to Crossens.
♨⛱❀◑◗⊟♿♣P⍁

Cheshire Lines

81 King Street, PR8 1LQ
✪ 11-11; 12-10.30 Sun
☎ (01704) 532178
Tetley Dark Mild, Bitter Ⓗ
This small, half-timbered property with unchanged frontage is reputed to be Southport's third oldest pub and has attractive hanging baskets in season. A genuine local, it was named the Cross Keys until 1884 when the Cheshire Lines railway station terminus opened opposite. The first livery stables in Southport opened behind the pub in 1817. The interior has been opened up but there is a pleasant snug with newspapers and the pub serves excellent value food (eve meals finish at 7.30pm; Sun meals are served 12-5pm). ♨❀◑◗⇌♣

Falstaff

68 King Street, PR8 1LG
✪ 11.30-11; 12-10.30 Sun
☎ (01704) 530123
Greene King Old Speckled Hen; Theakston Best Bitter; Wells Bombardier; guest beers Ⓗ
The Falstaff is an essential stop for real ale aficionados in Southport. The pub has an adventurous beer purchasing policy, offering a widely varying range. It has comfortable open-plan seating and is popular with locals and mature visitors because of the excellent food bargains on offer (Sun lunch is served 12-4pm; no food Sun eve). Outdoor tables are provided at the front for summer use. Q❀◑◗♿⇌♣

Guest House

16 Union Street, PR9 0QE (side street off Lord St)
✪ 11-11; 12-10.30 Sun
☎ (01704) 537660
Boddingtons Bitter; Cains Bitter; Theakston Old Peculier; guest beers Ⓗ
Charming Edwardian pub with a tiled entrance hall, decorated glass tiling above the bar and wooden panelling throughout. The Guest House is one of the most popular spots in Southport for those who appreciate a good range and quality of real beers, serving three rotating beers in addition to those listed. CAMRA's Winter Pub of the Season 2004, it has three comfortable drinking areas with newspapers provided. Festooned with flower baskets in summer, a hidden courtyard drinking area is at the rear. Light snacks and soup are available at lunchtime (not Sun). Q❀⇌

London

14 Windsor Road, PR9 0SR (near Asda)

⚲ 12-11; 12-10.30 Sun

☎ (01704) 542885

Oakwell Old Tom Mild, Barnsley Bitter Ⓗ

Southport's only outlet for Oakwell Brewery's famous Barnsley Bitter and Old Tom Mild, it sells probably the cheapest beer in Southport and the best kept. A traditional community pub with a large, comfortable, open-plan lounge, a family room and a tap room, it also has a bowling green. Darts, dominoes and pool are played and a full trophy cabinet is evidence of the success of the pub teams. ♘❀≉♣P

Masons Arms

44 Anchor Street, PR9 0UT (off London St)

⚲ 11-11; 12-10.30 Sun

☎ (01704) 534123

Robinson's Unicorn; seasonal beers Ⓗ

Small back-street pub just two minutes' walk from the railway station and central bus stops. The Masons is the only remaining old-fashioned beer house in Southport and the town's only outlet for local brewer Robinson's beers. The pleasant snug to the left of the entrance features a real fire; this is a comfortable and relaxing place to reflect on the quality of the beer. ⩨❀≉

Sands Hotel

Shore Road, Ainsdale, PR8 2QB

(follow directions to beach from station)

⚲ 11-11; 12-10.30 Sun

☎ (01704) 578084

Moorhouses Premier, Pride of Pendle; Theakston Best Bitter; guest beer (occasional) Ⓗ

Still officially known as a hotel, its name harks back to the days when it provided residential holiday accommodation at the now defunct Edwardian resort of Ainsdale-on-Sea. Nowadays, the Sands is a pleasant pub with a large conservatory area overlooking a freshwater lake where water birds abound amid the sand dunes. Popular with holidaymakers at nearby Pontins, with day trippers as well as locals, the Sands is family-friendly and spacious. It offers good food at reasonable prices (eve meals in summer). ♘❀◖◗⊟♿≉ (Ainsdale) ♣P⚟

Wallasey

Cheshire Cheese

2 Wallasey Village, CH44 2DH

⚲ 12-11; 12-10.30 Sun

☎ (0151) 630 3641

Tetley Bitter; Theakston Mild; guest beers Ⓗ

Much improved pub where the landlord is committed to real ale and allows regulars to vote for guest beers. The multi-room layout includes a snug; the handpumps are in the lounge, not the bar. It supports darts, golf and other sports teams, and stages regular quizzes. This true community local is a charity fundraiser. Meals are served 12-7.30pm (6pm Sun). A well-preserved Victorian ale house, it has a courtyard for outdoor drinking.

❀◖◗⊟≉ (Wallasey Village) ♣

Farmers Arms

225 Wallasey Village, CH45 3LG

⚲ 11.30-11; 12-10.30 Sun

☎ (0151) 638 2110

Cains Mild, Bitter; Tetley Bitter; Theakston Best Bitter; guest beer (occasional) Ⓗ

With a string of local and regional CAMRA awards, including local Pub of the Year 2004, the pub's licensee of 20 years has achieved consecutive entries in this Guide for more than 10 years. A front bar, side snug and back lounge cater for all ages and tastes. Quiz night is on Tuesday and the pub runs its own golf society. Good food is served on weekday lunchtimes.

Q❀◖⊟≉(Grove Rd)

Nelson Hotel ✔

60 Grove Road, CH45 3MN

⚲ 11.30-11; 12-10.30 Sun

☎ (0151) 639 7102

Cains Bitter; guest beers Ⓗ

Extensive refurbishment of this large pub has meant the loss of the bar, but there are still plenty of drinking areas, including a no-smoking section. Great emphasis is placed on food and a fine wine selection but not at the expense of the beers – the pub is a local CAMRA Pub of the Month winner. Piped music, a Monday quiz and summer barbecues on the rear patio add to the attraction. It has a large function room upstairs.

❀◖◗♿≉(Grove Rd) P⚟

Waterloo

Volunteer Canteen ✔

45 East Street, L22 8QR

⚲ 12-11; 12-10.30 Sun

☎ (0151) 928 4676

Cains Bitter; guest beer Ⓗ

A real gem in the back streets of old Waterloo. This cosy, traditional local has a central bar serving both the public bar and the lounge, where photographs of old Liverpool, Crosby and Waterloo decorate the walls. The 'Volly' provides table service, a rarity these days. The pub runs its own golf society and darts team. A relaxed atmosphere exists without the intrusion of a juke box; just good banter and the rustle of newspapers. Q⊟≉

Sailors Arms

Up the street, in the Sailors Arms, Sinbad Sailors, grandson of Mary Ann Sailors, draws a pint in the sunlit bar. The ship's clock in the bar says half past eleven. Half past eleven is opening time. The hands of the clock have stayed still at half past eleven for fifty years. It is always opening time in the Sailors Arms.

Dylan Thomas, Under Milk Wood,

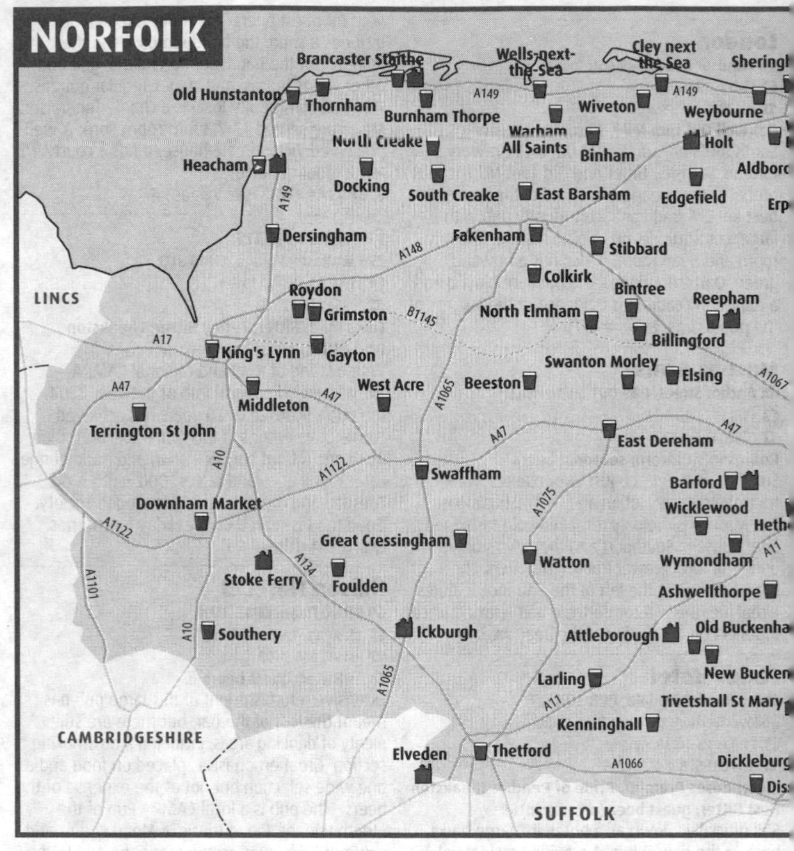

Aldborough

Old Red Lion

The Green, NR11 7AA

☼ 11-11; 12-10.30 Sun

☎ (01263) 761451

Winter's Golden; guest beers Ⓖ

This pub is a marvellous old building, overlooking the impressive and very large Aldborough village green. There has been a beer house here since the mid-19th century. The present pub was closed in the late 1960s but reopened again for business in 1985 as a free house. The regular beers sold here come from Winter's Brewery, plus between one and three guests from other breweries. The main bar has an adjoining restaurant where meals can be booked. Cider is sold in summer.

♛❀⇌◑◐♣●P⚟

Ashwellthorpe

White Horse

51-55 The Street, NR16 1AA

☼ 12-3.30 (not Mon-Fri), 5.30-11; 12-3.30, 7-10.30 (not winter eve) Sun

☎ (01508) 489721

Fuller's London Pride; guest beers Ⓗ

Free house and village local with an active and mixed clientele. The drinking areas have a low-beamed wooden ceiling. There is a flame-effect fire in a small inglenook with an armorial fireback. The dining area has a woodburner. It has a large garden at the rear and tables at the front. The woman trying to get into the pub through a bricked-up door is the resident ghost. Guest beers come from both regional and micro-breweries. Q❀◑◐♣P⚟

Barford

Cock Inn

Watton Road , NR9 4AS

☼ 12-3, 6-11; 12-4, 7-10.30 Sun

☎ (01603) 757646

Blue Moon Easy Life, Sea of Tranquillity, Hingham High, seasonal beers; guest beers Ⓗ

Formerly a coaching inn, this two-bar pub and restaurant is home to the Blue Moon Brewery whose premises are shared by the Spectrum Brewery. Good food is served throughout, with the kitchen specialising in fresh fish. Use of mobile phones results in a fine, which is donated to the Lifeboat appeal. In addition to shove-ha'penny and skittles, there is a bowls green-cum-croquet lawn and garden.

♛❀◑◐⛺♣P

Beeston

Ploughshare

The Street, PE32 2NF

☼ 12-2.30 (3 Sat), 6-11; 12-3, 6-10.30 Sun

☎ (01328) 701845 website: www.theploughshare.co.uk

Greene King IPA; Spectrum Wizzard; Tindall Norfolk'n'Good; guest beers Ⓗ

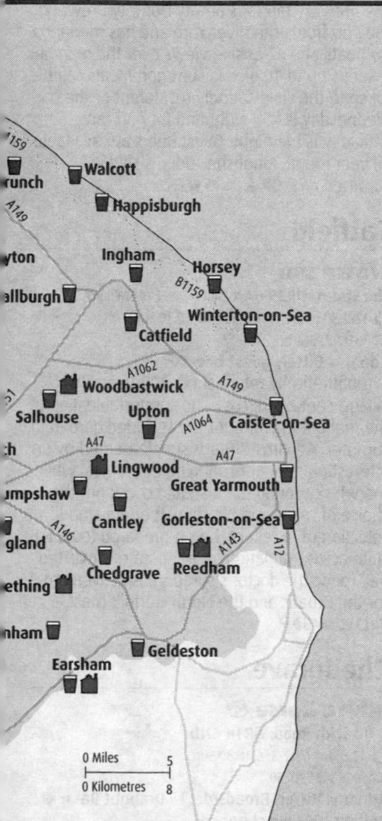

Parts of this pub date back to as early as the 17th century, although much of the building was built more recently. Records show that an ale house has existed on this site from as far back as 1575. The interior of the brick and whitewashed building consists of a small front bar, used mainly as a games room, a main lounge and a spacious restaurant at the rear. There is a large garden where barbecues are held on Wednesday evening during the summer months.
⛼Q❀⇌◑◐⊟♣P⊬

Billingford

Forge

Bintree Road, NR20 4AJ

⌚ 11-2.30, 7-11; 12-3, 7-10.30 Sun

☎ (01362) 668720

Adnams Bitter, Broadside; guest beers Ⓗ

As the name suggests, the building was a forge before becoming a pub in 1980. The bar is long and narrow, on several levels with characterful exposed beams. The pub car park is on the opposite side of the road, while the large garden stands next to the village cricket field where you can watch a match every summer Sunday. Local attractions include Gressing Hall Rural Life Museum and Pensthorpe Waterfowl Park. Home-cooked food can be enjoyed in the no-smoking dining room.
Q❀◑◐⊟Ⓐ̂P

Binham

Chequers Inn

45 Front Street, NR21 0AL OS007438

⌚ 11.30-2.30, 6-11; (closed winter Tue); 12-2.30, 7-10.30 Sun

☎ (01328) 830297 website: www.chequersinnbinham.co.uk

Beer range varies Ⓗ

A gem of a pub. The village charity, the enthusiasm and skills of the former brewer and his wife who run the pub and the creative and customer-focused chef all combine to create an excellent experience here. Real ales mostly come from local micros, supplemented by an extensive selection of bottled beers from around the world; as you would expect, Belgian brews feature heavily. It has no regular menu. All meals, mostly using local produce, are cooked to order. ⛼❀◑◐♿P⊬

Bintree

Royal Oak

The Street, NR20 5AH (off A1067, Norwich-Fakenham Road)

⌚ 11-3, 5.30-11; 12-4, 7-10.30 Sun

☎ (01362) 683326

Adnams Bitter; Greene King IPA; guest beer Ⓗ

Village local built in the mid-19th century, just off the Norwich-Fakenham road and not far from Bintree Mill. The interior is horseshoe-shaped and houses a large real fire and a pool table; one end is sectioned off mainly for eating, and is a no-smoking area. Food provided here is home cooked. It has its own ghost who resides in the cellar. There is a car park at the front and a large garden at the rear. ⛼❀◑◐ÅP

Brancaster Staithe

Jolly Sailors

Main Road, PE31 8BJ

⌚ 11-11; 12-10.30 Sun

☎ (01485) 210314 website: www.jollysailors.co.uk

Brancaster IPA, Old Les; guest beers Ⓗ

Popular with sailors, walkers and birdwatchers, the pub's own brewery produces the house beers on site. Retreat from the bitter east wind to the open fire in the bar in winter or enjoy the

INDEPENDENT BREWERIES

Blue Moon Barford
Brancaster Brancaster Staithe
Buffy's Tivetshall St Mary
Chalk Hill Norwich
Elveden Elveden
Fox Heacham
Humpty Dumpty Reedham
Iceni Ickburgh
Norfolk Cottage Norwich
Reepham Reepham
Spectrum Barford
Tindall Seething
Tipples Norwich
Uncle Stuarts Lingwood
Waveney Earsham
Winter's Norwich
Wissey Valley Stoke Ferry
Wolf Attleborough
Woodforde's Woodbastwick
Yetman's Holt

garden in summer. At all seasons excellent food is available, 12-9pm; the seafood is particularly recommended. Three smallish bar areas, a restaurant and a conservatory suit customers' different needs.

White Horse
Main Road, PE31 8BY
11-11; 12-10.30 Sun
☎ (01485) 210262
website: www.whitehorsebrancaster.co.uk
Adnams Bitter; Fuller's London Pride; Woodforde's Wherry; guest beers 🄷
The bar of this award-winning hotel and restaurant maintains a genuine pub feel. Bare floors and scrubbed pine furniture set off the walls covered in local photographs and artists' exhibits. The feel is bright but cosy. From the outside terrace, enjoy glorious views across the saltmarsh to Scolt Head Island. Bar billiards is played here. The accommodation is in 15 comfortable, en-suite rooms.

Burnham Thorpe

Lord Nelson
Walsingham Road, PE31 8HL
11-3 (12-2.30 winter Mon-Fri), 6-11; 12-3, 6.30-10.30 Sun
☎ (01328) 738241 website: www.nelsonslocal.co.uk
Greene King IPA, Abbot; Woodforde's Wherry, Nelson's Revenge; guest beer (summer) 🄶
The new owners of this historic pub are continuing the good work done by previous tenants. Modern additions have not spoilt the character of the pub, which is close to Nelson's birthplace and full of his memorabilia. The homely bar dates back over 300 years and boasts old settles and a flagstone floor. Beer is brought to your table direct from the casks. The restaurant was voted Restaurant of the Year 2004 by the Eastern Daily Press; the fish, meat and game are sourced locally.

Caister-on-Sea

Ship Inn
2 Victoria Street, NR30 5HA (off High St, down Tan Lane)
10.30-11; 12-10.30 Sun
☎ (01493) 728008
Greene King IPA, Old Speckled Hen; guest beers 🄷
This cosy pub has a good local trade with a single L-shaped bar divided into several drinking areas, and a real fire. Food is served in the dining section. The pub has won awards for its hanging baskets; over 100 adorn the pub walls and patio area. The beach is 300 yards east, past the only independent all-weather offshore lifeboat in the UK. The pub and the lifeboat station are both well worth a visit.

Cantley

Reedcutter
Station Road, NR13 3SH (near level crossing)
12-3 (not winter Mon or Tue), 7-11 (12-11 summer); 12-10.30 Sun
☎ (01493) 701099
Humpty Dumpty Reed Cutter, Cheltenham Flyer; 🄷 **guest beers** 🄷/🄶
The brewery tap for Humpty Dumpty Brewery, the pub fronts the River Yare and has moorings for boats and extensive views over the marshes. It keeps up to 10 ales in summer. Meals can be taken in the child-friendly restaurant or the bar. Wednesday is folk night and for quiz fans Thursday is the night. Guest beers are available all year round; Kingfisher cider is sold in summer.

Catfield

Crown Inn
The Street, NR29 5AA (S of A149, E of Stalham)
12-2.30 (3 Sat), 7-11; 12-3, 7-10.30 Sun
☎ (01692) 580128
Adnams Bitter; guest beers 🄷
Sympathetically refurbished, 300-year-old village-centre inn, cosy and comfortable. Enjoy the real fire in winter or the secluded garden in summer. Adnams Bitter is supplemented by an interesting range of changing guest ales, while the whisky connoisseur should check out the choice of malts and bourbon. It offers a good selection of excellent, home-prepared food. En-suite accommodation, in a separate converted hall (once the doctor's surgery), is convenient for the Broads and the North Norfolk coast.

Chedgrave

White Horse ✔
5 Norwich Road, NR14 6ND
11-3, 6-11; 12-3, 6-10.30 Sun
☎ (01508) 520250
Adnams Bitter, Broadside; 🄷 **Draught Bass;** 🄶 **Ridleys IPA; guest beer** 🄷
Turn of the century, typical country pub now with connecting bars and restaurants, no-smoking dining room, a family room that can be used for private parties and functions, plus an area for pool and darts. Outside a charming decking area overlooks the bowls green. A good selection of whiskies is an added attraction.

Cley next the Sea

Three Swallows
Newgate Green, NR25 7TT (½ mile S of A149, coast road)
11-3, 5.30-11; 11-11 Sat; 12-10.30 Sun
☎ (01263) 740526
Adnams Bitter; Greene King IPA, Abbot 🄷
Alongside the village green and parish church, a short walk away from the internationally important Cley marshes, this three-roomed pub will delight ramblers, birdwatchers and beer lovers alike. Children are welcome and the extensive menu only adds to the pub's allure. There is en-suite accommodation for those wanting a longer stay. Benches for an outdoor pint on a sunny summer afternoon complete the perfect location.

Colkirk

Crown
Crown Road, NR21 7AA (follow signs from B1146)
11-2.30, 6-11; 12-3, 7-10.30 Sun
☎ (01328) 862172

Greene King IPA, Abbot; guest beer ⊞
Attractive, two-roomed pub with some wood-panelled walls and areas of tiled floor. There is a large garden at the rear. All beers sold here are supplied by Greene King and it offers an extensive menu. Dominoes is played. Local photographic prints are offered for sale. Close to the historic market town of Fakenham, it has ample parking space. ♛Q❀◑♣P⊬

Dersingham

Feathers Hotel

Manor Road, PE31 6LN
⏲ 11-11; 12-10.30 Sun
☎ (01485) 540207 website: www.thefeathershotel.co.uk
Adnams Bitter; Draught Bass; guest beers ⊞
This large carrstone hotel is close to the royal residence of Sandringham and offers something for everyone. The main building has two wood-panelled bars, the Saddle bar being no-smoking. There are two large gardens, which include a children's play area and seating. Separate from the main building is the Stable bar where the younger folk can go and listen to loud music, sometimes live bands. Food is available in all the bars, or the quiet restaurant, with views over the gardens. ♛❀⇌◑♣P

Dickleburgh

Crown

The Street, IP21 4NQ
⏲ 12-3, 7-11; 12-11 Fri & Sat; 12-10.30 Sun
☎ (01379) 741475
Greene King IPA; guest beers ⊞
This village pub, built in the 1500s, bears many original features, including exposed oak beams. A large, log-burning brick fireplace separates the main bar from the comfortable lounge area. The cosy, no-smoking dining room on the other side of the bar is a spacious room with pool table, TV and seating. At the rear is a garden where drinks can be enjoyed in summer. A varied menu is served, Tuesday-Sunday. ♛Q❀◑⊟P

Diss

Cock Inn

63 Lower Denmark Street, IP22 4BE
⏲ 12 (1.30 winter Mon-Thu)-11; 12-10.30 Sun
☎ (01379) 643633
Adnams Bitter; Greene King Abbot; guest beer ⊞
The 16th-century beamed pub faces a large green, which acts as an outdoor drinking area, on the south side of this market town. It has one bar, serving three real ales to three comfortable drinking areas, with wood furniture and leather sofas. A good drinkers' pub (no food), it gets busy at weekends when music is provided. The locals are keen on a game of spin the wheel (on the ceiling). ♛Q❀♿♣

Docking

Railway Inn

Station Road, PE31 8LY (on B1153 Brancaster road)
OS766374
⏲ 12-3, 6-11.30; 12-11.30 Sat; 12-10.30 Sun
☎ (01485) 518620
Buffys Bitter, Norwegian Blue; guest beers ⊞
Genuine local in the same ownership for more than 20 years. The warmth and friendliness of the staff and regulars make visitors feel at home. A log fire in winter and always a full pint make this pub a must. A high-level LGB model railway in the restaurant is operated when children are present. A bowling green and remains of a former railway line add interest. An excellent menu includes additional curries on a Tuesday evening. ♛ᗢ❀⇌◑⊟P

Downham Market

Crown Hotel

12 Bridge Street, PE38 9DH
⏲ 10-11; 12-10.30 Sun
☎ (01366) 382322
Adnams Bitter; Greene King IPA, Abbot; guest beers ⊞
This 17th-century coaching inn is a favourite with local ale drinkers. It is situated at the centre of this small market town. In the single bar, with its beamed ceiling, there are always two guest ales from independent breweries. In 1816 the Crown Hotel was the scene of one of the 'bread riots' when hungry agricultural workers kept the justices of the peace 'prisoners' there until the militia arrived. ♛Q❀⇌◑⇌P

Earsham

Queen's Head

Station Road, NR35 2TS
⏲ 12-3, 5-11; 12-3, 7-10.30 Sun
☎ (01986) 892623
Waveney East Coast Mild, Lightweight; guest beers ⊞
Village-centre 17th-century inn, close to the Suffolk border. The main bar has red tiled floors, exposed beams and a ceiling covered with beer mats. There is a welcoming real fire at one end, which leads into a games room. The dining room also has a real fire. In 2004 it opened up its own brewery in an outhouse. There is normally a choice of four real ales available, two from the pub's Waveney Brewery and two guests. ♛❀◐⛺♣P⊡

East Barsham

White Horse Inn

Fakenham Road, NR21 0LH
⏲ 11.30-3, 6.30-11; 12-3, 6.30-10.30 Sun
☎ (01328) 820645 website: www.norfolkinns.co.uk
Adnams Bitter, Broadside; Wells Eagle ⊞
This Grade II listed pub stands next to the historic East Barsham Hall where Henry VIII stayed while on a pilgrimage to Walsingham. It has an open-plan bar with traditional furnishings and an inglenook, leading to a restaurant featuring original beams. Note the hay feeders on the wall and old agricultural tools. Birdwatching tours are run from the pub, and a diary of daily bird sightings is kept inside the entrance porch. The food and accommodation here are recommended. ♛Q❀⇌◑P⊬

East Dereham

George Hotel

Swaffham Road, NR19 2AZ (near cenotaph)
⏲ 11-11; 12-10.30 Sun
☎ (01362) 696801 website: www.lottiesrestaurant.co.uk

Adnams Bitter, Broadside; Fuller's London Pride; Greene King Old Speckled Hen; Woodforde's Wherry; guest beers 🄷
Comfortable hotel bar open to non-residents offering a good selection of regular beers and interesting guests. It enjoys an excellent reputation for food, with pub meals served in the bar and an a la carte restaurant on the premises. Friendly staff and comfortable surroundings make the George well worth a visit. The town has a station served by vintage diesel trains on the mid-Norfolk Railway; still being restored, the line connects to the main line at Wymondham. ♨❀⇄◑◐♿P⚟

King's Head Hotel
42 Norwich Street, NR19 1AD
⏲ 10-11; 12-10.30 Sun
☎ (01362) 693842
Adnams Broadside; Greene King IPA, Abbot; guest beer 🄷
Situated in the town centre, the hotel has a cosy, carpeted, non-residents lounge bar plus a small function room. The three regular beers are supplemented by a guest. Meals are served in the adjoining no-smoking dining area. At the rear of the building there is a large garden, which is set out with tables and chairs during summer months. ❀⇄◑◐♣P⚟

Edgefield

Three Pigs ✔
Norwich Road, NR24 2RL
⏲ 11-3, 6.30-11; 12-3, 6.30-10.30 Sun
☎ (01263) 587634
Adnams Bitter, Broadside; Greene King IPA; Woodforde's Wherry; guest beers 🄷
Traditional village free house, just three miles from the beautiful Georgian town of Holt. This two-roomed pub has a no-smoking room next to the bar and an excellent dining room where renowned home-cooked meals are served. Jazz sessions are held once a month. The pub offers up to five guest beers. It owns a touring caravan park next to its own large car park.
♨Q❀◑◐⊟⛺♣P⚟

Elsing

Mermaid
Church Street, NR20 3EA
⏲ 12-3, 7 (6 Fri & Sat)-11; 6-10.30 Sun
☎ (01362) 637640
Adnams Broadside; Woodforde's Wherry; guest beers 🄶
Lovely, 17th-century free house set in the Wensum Valley, standing opposite a large 14th-century church, which boasts the widest nave in a parish church in England. The pub has one long bar with a log fire and dartboard at one end and pool table at the other. The restaurant serves meals lunchtime and evening; try the 16oz steak special served on Tuesday evenings. All beers are from local breweries. ♨❀◑◐♣P

Erpingham

Spread Eagle
Eagle Lane, NR11 7QA
⏲ 11-11; 12-10.30 Sun
☎ (01263) 761591
Adnams Bitter, Broadside; Woodforde's Wherry; guest beers 🄷
The original building dates back to the early decades of the 18th century and it became a licensed premises at the end of that century. The building stands opposite the old Woodforde's brewery; it was the brewery tap until it moved to Woodbastwick in 1989. The interior consists of one long, open-plan room with a no-smoking dining area at one end, where home-cooked meals are served. The main bar is in the middle of the pub and a games area at the other end.
♨♉◑◐⛺P

Fakenham

Bull
41 Bridge Street, NR21 9AG
⏲ 10-11; 12-10.30 Sun
☎ (01328) 853410
Elgood's Black Dog; Woodforde's Wherry; guest beers 🄷
Pleasant pub, popular with all ages. Completely refurbished in 2004 by the present owners, the modern decor is of a high quality with an impressive solid ash bar, oak plank flooring, leather sofas and attractive artworks. The open-plan interior is divided into three sections: the bar, a no-smoking zone and an area where children are made welcome. Accommodation in four guest rooms should be ready by the time of publication. No food is served Monday. Excellent WCs include a separate wheelchair facility.
♨♉❀⇄◑♿⛺⚟⊡

Star
44 Oak Street, NR21 9DY
⏲ 12-2.30 (11-3 Thu-Sat), 7-11; 12-2.30, 7-10.30 Sun
☎ (01328) 862895
Greene King Ruddles County; Tetley Imperial 🄷
Traditional, comfortable, friendly local. This 16th-century listed building has one bar plus a pool room. Unusual wood features, which could be several hundred years old, enhance the interior. There is a large rear garden with an extensive range of children's play apparatus. In summer, a cooked lunch is served on Thursday, and barbecue facilities are provided for the use of customers, who bring their own food. ❀⛺♣P

Foulden

White Hart
White Hart Street, IP26 5AW
⏲ 11-11; 12-10.30 Sun
☎ (01366) 328638
Greene King IPA, Abbot; guest beers 🄷
Ever-changing guest beers and a warm welcome await you at this family-run village pub. Excellent home-cooked food is available (roast only on Sun). Children are welcome in the conservatory at local CAMRA's Pub of the Year in 2003. Four handpumps serve some of the best-kept ales in the area. Petanque is played in the grounds. ♨Q♉❀⇄◑◐♣P⚟

Gayton

Crown ✔
Lynn Road, PE32 1PA
⏲ 12-3, 6 (5.30 Fri)-11; 11-11 Sat; 12-10.30 Sun
☎ (01553) 636252

Greene King XX Mild, IPA, Abbot; Old Speckled Hen; guest beer Ⓗ
This pub was voted local Pub of the Year in 2004, and with good reason. The food is excellent, however, the pub layout, and the size of the dining room means there is plenty of space left for drinkers. It is well supported by locals and special events, such as music nights, ensure that it is at the centre of village life. In summer sit in the garden; in winter see how close you dare get to the massive log fire. ♨❀◐♣P

Geldeston

Locks ✔

Locks Lane, NR34 0HW (take Station Rd out of village, then left at signpost to pub)
✪ 6-11 (not Mon-Wed); 11-11 Sat & summer Mon-Fri; 12-10.30 Sun
☎ (01508) 518414
Green Jack Canary, Orange Wheat, Grasshopper, Gone Fishing, Ⓗ **seasonal beer** Ⓖ
Early-17th century smugglers' haunt, beautifully situated by the River Waveney and accessible by boat, foot or cart track – the most remote pub in Norfolk. Soak up the genuine olde-worlde atmosphere, enhanced by stone flagged floors, gas lighting and candles – no mains electricity. The large riverside garden has free moorings, regular live music includes a folk session (Thu) in the extended family/music room. The spacious no-smoking restaurant area serves home-cooked pub grub. ♨❀◐⊞P

Wherry

7 The Street, NR34 0LB (opp. boatyard)
✪ 12-3, 7-11; 12-11 Sat; 12-10.30 Sun
☎ (01508) 518371
Adnams Bitter, Broadside, seasonal beers Ⓗ
Traditional, 18th-century inn, with two bars and a no-smoking restaurant. The attractive garden and suntrap courtyard in the centre of the pub add to its appeal. The games area has a dartboard and on Monday evenings phat is played. Home-cooked meals are served daily. ♨❀◐⊞♿♣P

Gorleston-on-Sea

Dock Tavern

Dock Tavern Lane, NR31 6PY
✪ 12-11; 12-10.30 Sun
☎ (01493) 442255
Adnams Broadside; Elgood's Black Dog; Fuller's London Pride; Greene King IPA; Woodforde's Wherry; guest beers Ⓗ
Close to the River Yare and the docks, the road was named after the pub. The decor is traditional apart from the upturned rowing boat above the bar. It hosts occasional weekend entertainment. The pub is close to the High Street and is served by regular buses from Great Yarmouth. A large-screen TV, used mainly for sporting events, does not seem to detract from the convivial atmosphere. ❀

Lord Nelson

Trafalgar Road West, NR31 8BS
✪ 11-11; 12-10.30 Sun
☎ (01493) 301084 website: www.lordnelsonph.co.uk
Adnams Bitter, Broadside; Ⓗ **seasonal beers; guest beers** Ⓖ
Surprisingly spacious, back-street, corner pub, comprising two large bars and a quiet room used for card games. A Nelson theme with interesting memorabilia, plus an amazing lighter collection are special features. A gravity beer bar has 12 beers from the cask, plus eight on handpump. The wide range of guest beers changes regularly, offering a national range, but always some products from East Anglian micro-breweries. Cider is sold in summer. This independent free house is highly recommended. ♨Q❀⊞●

New Entertainer

80 Pier Plain, NR31 6PG
✪ 12-11; 12-10.30 Sun
☎ (01493) 441643
Greene King IPA, Old Speckled Hen; guest beers Ⓗ
Close to the river and harbour mouth, this pub was built in the 1800s, and retains a Victorian ambience. The long, single bar is divided into lounge bar areas, housing a pool table. The unusual, rounded end features an original Lacon's window. Old pictures of Gorleston line the walls. In addition to seven real ales, a range of Belgian beers is stocked. ♣

Great Cressingham

Windmill Inn

Water End, IP25 6NN
✪ 11-3, 6-11; 12-3, 6.30-10.30 Sun
☎ (01760) 756232
Adnams Bitter; Greene King IPA; guest beers Ⓗ
If you are looking for a place to suit all tastes, the Windmill Inn has to be it. Each room has a different emphasis: one bar caters for music (Tue and Thu most weeks); another has plenty of windows, useful for keeping an eye on children playing in the safe garden area, complete with sandpit. The rest of the drinking and dining areas are full of character. In the same family ownership for more than 45 years, you are bound to want to return.
♨Q❀◐♿⛺♣P⊬

Great Yarmouth

Gallon Pot ✔

1 Market Place, NR30 1NB
✪ 10-11; 12-10.30 Sun
☎ (01493) 842230
Adnams Bitter; Fuller's London Pride; Greene King Old Speckled Hen; Woodforde's Wherry Ⓗ
There has been a pub on this site since the 18th century, the last one having been destroyed by the Luftwaffe. Rebuilt in 1960, this is a large, smart town-centre pub with two spacious bars. Although there is an emphasis on food, drinkers should not be deterred from trying the four ales on offer, as there is plenty of room – and a welcome – for all. Children are welcome in the no-smoking Burroughs bar.
◐⇌(Vauxhall)⊬

St John's Head

58 North Quay, NR30 1JB
✪ 11-11; 12-10.30 Sun
☎ (01493) 843443
Elgood's Cambridge; guest beers Ⓗ

Quayside pub with a single bar, convenient for the station. A 'sale price' quality ale is a regular feature among the three guests and Addlestones cider is always stocked. The pub dates back to the 18th century and is said to be built on land confiscated from the Carmelite Order. Outside seating is provided in summer. ❀≋(Vauxhall) ♣●P

Grimston

Bell

1 Gayton Road, PE32 1BG

12-2 (not Mon-Thu), 5-11; 11-11 Sat; 12-10.30 Sun

☎ (01485) 601156 website: www.bellinngrimston.com

Greene King IPA, Abbot; guest beer H

This village pub has had to adapt to survive. The original pub has been converted to guest accommodation, and a conservatory at the back is now the Walnut Tree Farm Tearooms, ideal for a family visit. Sandwiched between the two is a small bar, which serves two or three beers (generally at least one from Greene King, and one from a small brewery). The landlord is keen on motorbikes; you may see his monster truck in the car park, converted into the ultimate mobile home. ⇄◐P

Happisburgh

Hill House

NR12 0PN

12-3, 7-11; 12-11 Thu-Sat & summer; 12-10.30 Sun

☎ (01692) 650004

Beer range varies H

A 16th-century inn with a 21st-century purpose: real ale and lots of it. Six changing guest beers come from all over Britain. In June it hosts a four-day beer festival, selling over 40 ales, ciders and perry. Good, reasonably-priced food and loads of atmosphere complete the picture. Sir Arthur Conan Doyle wrote a Sherlock Holmes novel here, and fans still meet at the pub from time to time. One of the pub's guest bedrooms is a converted signal box. ♛♉❀⇄◐▲♣P⊬

Heacham

Fox & Hounds

22 Station Road, PE31 7EX

12-11; 12-10.30 Sun

☎ (01485) 570345

website: www.foxbreweryandphheacham.fsnet.co.uk

Adnams Broadside; guest beers H

Thriving local and home of Fox Brewery; three of the five beers come from the brewery itself and one guest is generally from another micro-brewery. It stages live music on Tuesday evening and a pub quiz on Thursday. Two beer festivals are held here each year, in March and mid-July. ❀◐♣P

Hedenham

Mermaid

Norwich Road, NR35 2LB

12-2, 7-11; 12-10.30 Sun

☎ (01508) 482480

Adnams Bitter; Greene King IPA; Tindall Best Bitter; guest beers (summer) H

Terracotta-coloured, 17th-century coaching inn on the main Bungay to Norwich road. Access into the pub for customers is via a side entrance from the car park. There is a large terrace at the rear. The pub is open plan, with brick floors, exposed beams and a large log fire; it retains distinct areas of bars and lounges with a pool table in one section. A number of guest beers are added to the beer list in the summer season. ♛♉❀◐P⊬

Hethersett

King's Head ✔

36 Old Norwich Road, NR9 3DD

11-3, 5.30-11; 11-11 Fri & Sat; 12-4, 6.30-10.30 Sun

☎ (01603) 810206

Adnams Bitter; Fuller's London Pride; Greene King IPA, Abbot; Theakston Old Peculier (winter); **guest beer** (summer) H

Attractive former coaching inn. The no-smoking public bar is relaxed and characterful, with exposed beams, pamment floor and an unusual brick inglenook. Note the collection of old bottles and details of the arrest inside the pub of a local murderer in 1817. By contrast, the lounge bar is larger, more comfortable and has a real fire. The dining room is no-smoking and all the food is home cooked. There is a play area in the garden. ♛Q❀◐⊟♣P⊬

Horsey

Nelson's Head

Beach Road, NR27 3LT (300 yds off B1159)

11-3, 6-11 (10 winter); 12-3, 7-10.30 Sun

☎ (01493) 393378

Woodforde's Wherry, Nelson's Revenge H

Near Horsey Mere and the landmark windmill (NT), the pub attracts a mix of holidaymakers and locals in the summer. In winter the surroundings evoke memories of the local 'Black Shuck' a fearsome giant hound that roams the marshes in Norfolk mythology. Inside, though, all is mellow and welcoming, with good food and a log fire to complement the local brews. ♛❀◐♣P

Ingham

Swan

Sea Palling Road, NR12 9AB (1 mile NE of Stalham on B1151) OS390260

12-3, 6-11 (closed Mon winter); 12-10.30 (12-3 winter) Sun

☎ (01692) 581099

Woodforde's Wherry, Great Eastern, Nelson's Revenge, Admiral's Reserve H

Delightful, thatched, flint-built pub, part of a 14th-century terrace, in a pleasant rural setting near the village church and close to the north Norfolk coast and the Broads. The split-level interior features a wealth of warm brick, flint and beams. A wide choice of excellent home-prepared meals is served in the dining room, and in summer a special alfresco menu is available in the secluded courtyard. High quality en-suite accommodation is available all year. Q❀⇄◐▲♣P

Kenninghall

Red Lion ✔

East Church Street, NR16 2EP

(take West Church St from village centre)

✪ 12-3, 6.30-11; 12-11 Fri & Sat; 12-10.30 Sun
☎ (01953) 887849
Greene King IPA; Woodforde's Wherry; Ⓗ guest beers Ⓗ/Ⓖ
This lovely pub, believed to be 400 years old and licensed since 1722, has a main bar, a wood-panelled snug and a large dining room, all retaining their original fireplaces. It has wood and tiled floors throughout. Note the burn marks above the fire in the dining room where hot pokers were used to mull the ale. Bed and breakfast is available in the former stable block at the rear next to the bowling green. The pub offers three guest ales. ⌂Q❀⇌⦷◗⊟P

King's Lynn

Live & Let Live ✔
18 Windsor Road, PE30 5PL
✪ 12-11; 12-10.30 Sun
☎ (01553) 764990
Beer range varies Ⓗ
Traditional community pub that can be found just off London Road. There are two bars: a small cosy lounge and a larger public bar with TV and a pool table. Four real ales are available here, generally including a beer from Wolf Brewery and a mild; it is one of a few outlets in the area to offer these products on a regular basis. Westons cider is also sold, ask at the bar. ⊟♣●⊔

Lord Napier
1 Guanock Terrace, PE30 5QT
✪ 11-11; 12-10.30 Sun
☎ (01553) 760049
Shepherd Neame Spitfire; guest beer Ⓗ
Back-street corner local, off London Road in the south end of Lynn, near the South Gates. Two of the three beers stocked by this popular free-house are changing guests. Regulars often gather to watch football, and live music is staged once a month. Tables at the front of the pub allow customers to sit outside and enjoy a drink. ❀⇌♣P

Stuart House Hotel
35 Goodwins Road, PE30 5QX
✪ 7-11; 12-3, 7-10.30 Sun
☎ (01553) 772169 website: www.stuart-house-hotel.co.uk
Beer range varies Ⓗ
Follow the sign down a gravel drive off Goodwins Road, close to the Walks football ground and park. The comfortable hotel bar offers three beers, from Greene King, Adnams or Woodforde's, together with something from further afield. Regular live music – blues (Fri), and jazz on Sunday luchtime – draws in the crowds, as does the annual beer festival in the garden in July. Check the website for details of events. The bar is closed most lunchtimes, but may open by arrangement for groups. ⌂❀⇌◗P

Tudor Rose Hotel
St Nicholas Street, PE30 1LR
✪ 11-11; 12-10.30 Sun
☎ (01553) 762824
Fuller's London Pride; Greene King IPA; guest beers Ⓗ
There are two bars in this attractive hotel, just off the Tuesday Market Place, which dates back to the 15th century. A cosy lounge at the front is in the older part of the building, while a livelier public bar at the rear houses a juke box. Four beers are on sale here, two being guest beers, generally from Archers, Bateman or Hook Norton. Q☎❀⇌⦷◗⊟⇌P

White Horse
9 Wootton Road, PE30 4EZ
✪ 11-3, 5.30-11; 11-11 Fri & Sat; 12-10.30 Sun
☎ (01553) 763258
Greene King IPA; Wychwood Hobgoblin; guest beers Ⓗ
Typical two-bar drinkers' pub, located near the Gaywood Clock. The public bar has a TV and a large screen, where regulars often gather to watch the football. Of the four beers available here, two are changing guest ales, one of which is generally from a micro-brewery. ⊟♣P

Larling

Angel Inn
NR16 2QU
(just off A11, 1 mile S of Snetterton market/track)
✪ 10-11; 12-10.30 Sun
☎ (01953) 717963
Adnams Bitter; guest beers Ⓗ
Snetterton circuit nearby has its pits; the superb Angel Inn should be your pit-stop off the A11. Five ales await, including a mild, to be drunk either in the lively public bar or the comfortable lounge bar. You can dine in the restaurant where booking is advisable for the excellent home-cooked food. The Angel is a watering-hole for the local farming community; football fans are also welcome, the landlord is an avid Norwich City supporter. A beer festival is held in summer. ⌂❀⇌⦷◗▲⇌(E Harling) ♣P⊔

Middleton

Gate
Fair Green, PE32 1RW
✪ 12-2.30, 7-11; 12-3, 7-10.30 Sun
☎ (01553) 840518
Greene King IPA; guest beer Ⓗ
Situated in Fair Green, near Middleton, a couple of miles to the east of Kings Lynn, the Gate's beer range is limited, but well kept, and this thriving village local has something for everyone. There is a games room with a pool table, a cosy bar with a roaring fire in winter, and a small dining area. In summer, the award-winning hanging baskets add to the attraction of the garden. No evening meals are served Sunday. ⌂❀⦷◗P

New Buckenham

King's Head
Market Place, NR16 2AN
(5 miles from Attleborough on B1077)
✪ 12-3, 7-11; 12-3, 7-10.30 Sun
☎ (01953) 860487
Adnams Bitter; guest beers Ⓗ
Centrally located free house facing the village green. This friendly, conversational pub dates from 1502, serving as a coaching inn between London and Norwich. Consisting of two bars, the larger rear bar has a stone floor and is warmed by a real fire in the large inglenook. Traditional

home-cooked food includes Sunday lunch (12-2). Parking is available around the village green. Close by is a 12th-century Norman castle. ⌂Q❀◖◗⛺♣⚟

North Creake

Jolly Farmers

1 Burnham Road, NR21 9JW (on B1355)

⏲ 12-2.30 (not Tue), 7-11; closed Mon; 12-3, 7-10.30 Sun

☎ (01328) 738185 website: www.jolly-farmers.com

Adnams Bitter, Broadside; Woodforde's Wherry Ⓖ

This welcoming old coaching inn maintains a cosy feel throughout. There are two bar areas, plus the Red Room for families and no-smokers. The public bar houses a pool table, while the rest of the pub has homely farmhouse-style tables and chairs. All the real ales are drawn directly from the cask in the cellar. An interesting range of home-cooked meals makes use of fresh local produce. ⌂☕◖◗⊟P⚟

North Elmham

Railway

40 Station Road, NR20 5HH

(on B1145, 200 yds E of old rail crossing)

⏲ 11-11; 12-10.30 Sun

☎ (01362) 668300

Beer range varies Ⓗ

Set back from the road, this brick and flint building, formerly the Railway Hotel, is now a comfortable village local, showing excellent community spirit. It offers five beers, including ales from micro-breweries, mainly East Anglia. The open fire is surrounded by comfortable armchairs. This area and at the bar are no-smoking. Just off the bar is the small restaurant where home-cooked food is served. Real cider is occasionally available in summer. A beer festival is held August bank holiday. ⌂❀◖◗♿⛺P⚟

Norwich

Alexandra Tavern

16 Stafford Street, NR2 3HH (off Dereham Rd)

⏲ 10.30-11; 12-10.30 Sun

☎ (01603) 627722

Chalk Hill Tap, CHB, Flintknapper's Mild; guest beers Ⓗ

Small, corner local divided into two drinking areas. Chalk Hill beers are sold here along with a selection of guest ales. Situated just off the Dereham Road, the landlord is well known in the pub trade for fighting, and winning, the battle against the Courage leasing terms in the early 1990s. Food is served daily, and in the summer the outside patio area can be used. An interesting mix of memorabilia adorns the walls. ⌂❀◖◗●

Beehive

30 Leopold Road, NR4 7PJ (between Newmarket and Unthank Roads, outside ring road)

⏲ 12-2.30, 5.30-11; 12-11 Sat; 12-3, 7-10.30 Sun

☎ (01603) 451628 website: www.beehivenorwich.com

Fuller's London Pride; Greene King IPA; Wolf Golden Jackal, Bitter; guest beers Ⓗ

Traditional city local: a public bar and pleasant lounge with lots of comfortable sofas. It hosts regular quiz nights and barbecues in summer. Monthly speciality wine tasting evenings (last Wed) are accompanied by food from the appropriate region. As well as the regular beers it offers over 40 guest beers a year, from a wide range of breweries, which change every week. No food is served Sunday. ❀◖⊟♣P

Champion ✔

101 Chapelfield Road, NR2 1SE (opp. shopping mall)

⏲ 11-11; 12-10.30 Sun

☎ (01603) 765611

Beer range varies Ⓗ

Typical Victorian town local, conveniently situated immediately to the south of Norwich's shopping centre, frequented by locals, shoppers and city-centre office workers. The interior consists of two main bars plus a small snug at the rear. The six real ales vary, most are supplied by local breweries. Hot and cold lunchtime meals are now sold Monday to Saturday. The pub was recently voted Eastern Counties Newspapers Norwich Pub of the Year. ◖♣

Coach & Horses

82 Thorpe Road, NR1 1BA (400 yds from station)

⏲ 11-11; 12-10.30 Sun

☎ (01603) 477077

Chalk Hill Tap, CHB, Dreadnought, Flinknapper's Mild, Old Tackle; guest beers Ⓗ

Home of the Chalk Hill Brewery which is situated next door, the brewery is visible from within the pub. The L-shaped bar serves the entire range of Chalk Hill beers and up to two guests. Food is practical – served all day in generous portions. Just a short walk from the station up the Thorpe Road, look out for the balcony and windows above the main entrance, it is popular with all sorts, especially on match days as it is only a few minutes from the football ground. Banham cider is sold. ⌂❀◖◗⇌●P

Coachmakers Arms

9 St Stephen's Road, NR1 3SP

⏲ 11-11; 12-10.30 Sun

☎ (01603) 662080

Greene King IPA, Abbot; Wolf Golden Jackal; Woodforde's Wherry Ⓖ

Former coaching inn, where the stables now form a roofed courtyard, dating from the 17th century. The pub stands on the site of an old asylum, five minutes' walk from the main shopping area. Popular with local office workers and students, the main drinking area has Sky TV and darts. In the airy courtyard further tables are available, while the flower-filled patio is pleasant in summer. All beers are served by gravity from a wall-mounted stillage behind the main bar. Sunday meals are served 12-6pm. ⌂❀◖◗♣

Duke of Connaught

60 Livingstone Street, NR2 4HC

⏲ 12-4 (not Mon-Fri), 7.30-11; 12-4, 7-10.30 Sun

☎ (01603) 629805

Winter's Mild, Bitter, Golden, Revenge, Storm Force Ⓗ/Ⓖ

This pub was a Victorian local corner pub situated in the Norwich suburbs. The original building however, was destroyed in a bombing raid in 1942. It traded from a shed until 1954 when the present pub was rebuilt, consisting of two rooms, a bar and a lounge. Real ale comes from Winter's Brewery, opened in Norwich in 2001 by Dave Winter, a former brewer at Woodforde's and Chalk Hill. The pub effectively acts as Winter's tap, usually selling most of its beer range. ♣P

Duke of Wellington

91-93 Waterloo Road, NR3 1EG

12-11; 12-10.30 Sun

☎ (01603) 441182

Elgood's Black Dog; Fuller's London Pride; Wolf Golden Jackal; [H] guest beers [H]/[G]

About 10 minutes' walk north of the city centre, this pub supplies a huge range of real ales served either by handpump at the bar or by gravity from the adjoining tap room. There are usually about 20 beers available at any one time. Although the interior is spacious, it is split into a number of small drinking areas, including a snug, giving the pub a friendly, convivial atmosphere. It was voted Norfolk CAMRA Pub of the Year in 2003. ❀♣P

Fat Cat ✔

49 West End Street, NR2 4NA (off Dereham Rd)

12-11; 12-10.30 Sun

☎ (01603) 624364 website: www.fatcatpub.co.uk

Adnams Broadside; Caledonian Deuchars IPA; Fuller's ESB; Taylor Landlord; Woodforde's Wherry; guest beers [H]

CAMRA National Pub of the Year 1998 and 2004, it is the only pub ever to win this trophy twice. A treasure trove of a pub and a real ale drinker's paradise, it sells regular beers and a range of over 15 changing guests, served by gravity or handpump from breweries all over the country. Belgian beers, draught and bottled, and local cider are also stocked. The Fat Cat is a 10-minute walk from the city centre. ❀●

Glass House ✔

11-13 Wensum Street, NR3 1LA

10-11; 10-10.30 Sun

☎ (01603) 877650

Greene King Abbot; Marston's Burton Bitter, Pedigree; guest beers [H]

Busy city-centre Wetherspoon's house, built on the site of the old Norwich Glass Company. Several distinct areas include two family rooms and no-smoking zones; parts of the upstairs family room date back to the 15th century. Outside is a large, attractive patio with gas heaters. Lunchtimes are quiet, catering to mixed age groups, whereas evenings tend to be more lively and popular with younger customers. Q❀◐◑♿⇌⊬

King's Arms

22 Hall Road, NR1 3HQ

11-11; 12-10.30 Sun

☎ (01603) 766361

Adnams Bitter; Bateman Mild, XB, XXXB; Wolf Coyote; guest beers [H]

Formerly an award-winning free house, now a Bateman's tenanted pub, but still carrying the wide range of ales from East Anglia and further afield. The pub always has a dark beer on tap, including milds, stouts and porters. Food is available at lunchtime and if nothing on the menu appeals you can bring in your own from local takeaways (plates provided). Mini-themed beer festivals are run alternate months. The pub can be busy, especially on match days, as it is only a short walk from the football ground. ❀◐

Nelson

122 Nelson Street, NR2 4DR (off Dereham Rd)

12-11; 12-10.30 Sun

☎ (01603) 626362 website: www.nelsonpub.co.uk

Caledonian Deuchars IPA; Woodforde's Wherry; Wychwood Hobgoblin; guest beers [H]

Spacious two-roomed pub with a TV in one bar, pool and darts, and a quieter area to the front. Folk music is performed (Tue, Thu and Sun) and regular bands play on Monday. Spring and autumn beer festivals feature beers from Norfolk and surrounding areas. It sells a wide range of rums and gins plus bottled Kingfisher cider. Very much involved with the Nelson bicentennial celebrations in 2005, this community-oriented plub fields football, darts and pool teams. The large garden hosts summer barbecues. Traditional Sunday roast lunches are served. ❀♿♣P

Rosary Tavern

95 Rosary Road, Thorpe Hamlet, NR1 4BX

(5 mins' walk from station)

11.30-11; 12-10.30 Sun

☎ (01603) 666287 website: www.rosarytavern.cwc.net

Black Sheep Best Bitter; Caledonian Deuchars IPA; Fuller's London Pride; guest beers [H]

Local football and darts teams support this friendly pub that serves the community and nearby office workers as well. A pleasant atmosphere extends to the back garden and conservatory/function room, which is available for meetings. A variety of beers from around the country are available, from a changing range. Convenient for City home games at Carrow Road, it welcomes visiting supporters. No food is served Sunday. Bar billiards, crib and shut the box are all played here. ❀◐⇌♣●

Trafford Arms ✔

61 Grove Road, NR1 3RL

11-11; 12-10.30 Sun

☎ (01603) 628466 website: www.traffordarms.co.uk

Adnams Bitter; Tetley Bitter; Woodforde's Wherry [H]

Situated close to the city centre behind Sainsbury's, this welcoming pub has great community spirit. Its diverse customers enjoy the friendly atmosphere and relish the choice of three regular ales, two ciders and up to seven guests. The pub is divided into two: a quiet, no-smoking area and another for TV and pool. The Valentines beer festival is a highlight not to be missed. The Terry Storer cycle rack outside reminds us of his devotion to CAMRA. Awarded Norwich and Norfolk CAMRA Pub of the Year 2005. ❀◐◑●P⊬

Wig & Pen

6 St Martins at Palace Plain, NR3 1RN

(near Law Courts)

11.30-11; 12-5 Sun

☎ (01603) 625891 website: www.thewigandpen.com

Adnams Bitter; guest beers [H]

A 'village' pub in the heart of the city, close to the cathedral and law courts. It stocks a wide variety of ales from around the country. Good food is available at lunchtime and early evening, including Sunday, offering daily home-made specials. Popular with tourists and local office workers, the pub has an evident community feel to it. It hosts occasional themed beer festivals, and is well situated to watch the annual Lord Mayor's street procession. A Buffy's beer is always available. ⛼❀◑♣⅟

Old Buckenham

Gamekeeper ✔

The Green, NR17 1RE

✪ 11.45 (11 Sat)-11; 12-10.30 Sun

☎ (01953) 860397

Adnams Bitter, Broadside; Ⓗ guest beers Ⓖ

Free house, dating from 1639, in a typical village setting on the green next to the duck pond. The traditional charm continues inside with open fires, stone floors and dried hops. House beers are provided by Adnams and Wolf and it stocks a variety of Belgian bottled beers. When available, guest beers are served from gravity behind the bar. The restaurant offers a comprehensive menu, including traditional Sunday lunch. It stages a beer festival in August. ⛼Q❀◑P

Old Hunstanton

Ancient Mariner

Golf Course Road, PE36 6JJ

✪ 11-11 (11-3, 6-11 winter Mon-Thu); 12-10.30 Sun

☎ (01485) 534411 website: www.lestrangearms.co.uk

Adnams Bitter, Broadside; guest beers Ⓗ

This cosy pub was converted from an old barn attached to the Lestrange Arms Hotel and has a timbered interior on a nautical theme. Busy, and child-friendly, with two family rooms, extensive gardens lead to a sandy beach. As Old Hunstanton faces west you can watch the sun set over the sea with a pint in your hand. A good menu includes locally-caught fish.
⛼❀◑♿♣P⅟

Poringland

Royal Oak

44 The Street, NR14 7JT

✪ 12-3, 5-11; 12-11 Fri & Sat; 12-10.30 Sun

☎ (01508) 493734

Adnams Bitter; Mauldons Moletrap; Woodforde's Wherry; Ⓗ guest beers Ⓖ

Victorian pub with a large car park in the village centre about five miles south of Norwich. Essentially one large open-plan bar with distinct drinking areas, it serves four regular ales, and anything up to ten guests. There is a tendency to specialise in local brews although some beers come from further afield. Prominent blackboards display the beers on sale. The pub does not serve cooked food but there is a fish and chip shop next door. ❀♣P

Reedham

Reedham Ferry Inn

Ferry Road, NR13 3HA (off B1140)

✪ 11-3, 6.30-11 (11-11 summer); 12-10.30 Sun

☎ (01493) 700429 website: www.archerstouringpark.co.uk

Adnams Bitter, Broadside; Woodforde's Wherry; guest beers (summer) Ⓗ

Equidistant between Norwich and Great Yarmouth, in the heart of the Broads countryside sits this delightful award-winning 17th-century inn replete with beamed ceilings and a collection of rural craftsmen's tools. Right beside the River Yare, you can relax and watch rivercraft and wildlife as well as the historic car chain ferry that crosses the river all year round. The inn specialises in locally-caught fish, game and seafood. Themed evenings provide dishes and wine from around the world. Cider is sold in summer. ⛼Q❀◑♿⛺≉♣●P⅟

Reepham

King's Arms

Market Place, NR10 4JT

✪ 11-3, 5.30-11; 12-3, 7-10.30 Sun

☎ (01603) 870345

Adnams Bitter; Courage Directors; Greene King Abbot; Woodforde's Wherry Ⓗ

Built in 1667, this pub is centrally situated in a corner of Reepham's old market place. The interior has been converted into a large open-plan design with lots of drinking areas on split levels. However, it has retained plenty of charm in its many original beams and fireplaces. At the rear is a conservatory with an old glass-topped well and a small garden. The pub stocks a range of about six real ales including its own house beer. Parking space is available on the market place. ⛼Q❀◑♣

Roydon

Blacksmith's Arms

30 Station Road, PE32 1AW

✪ 4 (12 Mon, Fri & Sat)-11; 12-10.30 Sun

☎ (01485) 601347

Greene King IPA; guest beers Ⓗ

A rare sight these days – a drinkers' pub, in a rural location serving no food. Three beers are sold here, two being varying guest beers at around 4% ABV, which are selected after consultation with the regulars. Beer festivals are held here twice a year, one in May and the other in late August/September.
⛼❀♣P

Salhouse

Bell

3 Lower Street, NR13 6RW (set back from B1140)

✪ 12-3, 5.30-11; 12-11 Fri, Sat & summer; 12-10.30 Sun

☎ (01603) 721141

Adnams Bitter; Wolf Golden Jackal; guest beers Ⓗ

Low, beamed 17th-century country pub in a Broadland village with two well-defined bars and a small restaurant area. The Bell served as the local for American servicemen stationed at nearby Rackheath airfield; see the photos and mementoes that still line part of the public bar. Regular beer festivals are held and two guest ales from local breweries are stocked. Unusually the patio is designed as a chess/draughts board.
❀◑≉♣P

Sheringham

Lobster

13 High Street, NR26 8JB

✪ 11.30-11; 12-10.30 Sun

☎ (01263) 822716 website: www.the-lobster.com

Adnams Bitter, Broadside; Greene King Abbot; Marston's Pedigree; guest beers 🄷
Old, three-bar pub with a 50-cover restaurant offering modern English cuisine in converted stables to the rear, the Lobster is at the seaward end of the High Street. A lively public bar with pool table, comfortable wood-panelled lounge with open fire and plenty of outdoor seating, it stocks a wide range of malts, and a rotating beer range (on average 15 per week). Local sports teams are supported and there is a Lobster Potties Morris group. It hosts five beer festivals a year. ⛫Q❀◐◑⊟♿⇌♣●P⊬

Windham Arms
Wyndham Street, NR26 8BA (off High St)
⊙ 11-11; 12-10.30 Sun
☎ (01263) 822609
Adnams Bitter, Broadside; Woodforde's Wherry; guest beers 🄷
Confusingly located on Wyndham Street and tucked away off the High Street, this friendly, early 19th-century pub retains a two-bar layout with two outdoor seating areas, popular in summer. Food is traditional English, offering local seafood in season. The Windham's first recorded landlord, Robert Sunman, besides being a carpenter, wheelwright and fishmonger, also built the town's first lifeboat, Augusta in 1838. The family room is open in summer. Pool is played in the public bar. ⛀❀◐◑⊟⇌P⊬

Skeyton

Goat Inn
Long Road, NR10 5DH OS250244
⊙ 11-3, 6-11; 12-3, 6.30-11 Sun
☎ (01692) 53860 website: www.goatinnskeyton.co.uk
Adnams Bitter; Woodforde's Wherry; guest beers 🄷
Greatly extended 16th-century thatched country pub set in over seven acres of grounds, serving a wide rural community. Many events are held in the grounds, including a classic car show in May. Farm implements and old photographs of local interest are displayed. Excellent snacks and meals are served in the bar and restaurant from an adventurous menu with daily specials. A house beer is produced by Woodforde's for summer. ⛀❀◐◑▲P⊬

Smallburgh

Crown
NR12 9AD (on A149 between North Walsham and Stalham)
⊙ 12-3 (not Mon), 5.30 (7 Sat)-11; 12-3 (closed eve) Sun
☎ (01692) 536314
Adnams Bitter; Greene King IPA, Abbot; guest beers 🄷
Friendly and characterful, this comfortable thatched, village local started life as a 15th-century coaching inn and retains some original timbers. The log fire in winter enhances the already cosy atmosphere. A good selection of home-prepared meals, using local produce when available, is served in the bar or dining room. A tranquil, tree-fringed garden at the rear is a bonus at this locally renowned pub, close to the North Norfolk coast and the Broads; a gem. ⛫Q❀⛾◐◑♣P

South Creake

Ostrich ✔
NR21 9PB (on B1355, Burnham Market-Fakenham road) OS864355
⊙ 12-3, 6-11 (12-11 summer); 12-3, 5-10.30 Sun
☎ (01328) 823320 website: www.ostrichinn.co.uk
Greene King IPA, Abbot; Woodforde's Wherry; guest beer 🄷
Family-run, homely, country inn dating from 1680s, attracting a cross-section of drinkers and food-lovers due to the care and attention given to every aspect. A local farm owned within the family supplies fresh seasonal ingredients that the chef uses to full advantage. This pub has everything – superb ales, excellent food, a delightful snug with leather sofas, newspapers and a woodburner. A lovely patio area and a restored, heated barn, lit by candelabra for atmosphere complete the picture. ⛫❀◐◑♿P⊬

Southery

Old White Bell
20 Upgate Street, PE38 0NA
⊙ 11 (3 Wed)-11; 12-10.30 Sun
☎ (01366) 377057 website: www.oldwhitebell.co.uk
Adnams Broadside; City of Cambridge Rutherford IPA; guest beer 🄷
True local free house serving a village community on an 'island' in the fens, close to the City of Ely and just off the busy A10. The pub is open plan and has a small dining room. It is home to the village football team, White Bell Wanderers, for which the landlord is part of the management team. ❀◐◑♣P

Stibbard

Ordnance Arms
Guist Bottom, NR20 5PF (on A1067)
⊙ 12-3 (not Mon-Fri), 5.30-11; 12-3, 7-10.30 Sun
☎ (01328) 829471
Adnams Bitter; Greene King Abbot 🄷
This country free house welcomes you into a cosy front room warmed by a log fire. The adjoining pool room leads through to a rear bar, with quarry tiled floor and old pews. Photographs, maps and sketches of the pub are displayed. The name is said to refer to the fact that the original ordnance surveys of the area were carried out from the barn. The pub is well known for its Thai restaurant, offering an extensive authentic menu, Tuesday-Saturday evenings.
⛫Q❀◑⊟♣P

Strumpshaw

Shoulder of Mutton
Norwich Road, NR13 4NT
⊙ 11-11; 12-10.30 Sun
☎ (01603) 712274
Adnams Bitter, Broadside; Greene King IPA; guest beer 🄷
Village pub and restaurant, set back from the road, boasting a large garden and petanque courts. Booking is advisable for the restaurant. Note no food is served Sunday evening, however the pub does sell kippers to take home. ❀♣P

Swaffham

Lydney House Hotel

Norwich Road, PE37 7QS

⏲ 10.30-2.30, 7-11; 7-10.30 Sun

☎ (01760) 723355

website: www.lydney-house.demon.co.uk

Woodforde's Wherry; guest beers Ⓖ

This small, family-run hotel continues its tradition of keeping excellent ales straight from the barrel. The guest beer is usually from Iceni. The comfy bar has many traditional pub games including bagatelle. A full menu is served as well as bar meals (no food Sun). The hotel is situated on the eastern side of Swaffham's grand medieval church. Look out for the town's two giant wind turbines and visit Ecotech for an environmental treat. Q❀⇌◖◗♣P⚡

Swanton Morley

Darby's

142 Elsing Road, NR20 4NY

⏲ 11.30-3, 6-11; 11.30-11 Sat; 12-10.30 Sun

☎ (01362) 637647

Adnams Bitter, Broadside; Badger Tanglefoot; Theakston Mild; Woodforde's Wherry; guest beers Ⓗ

Darby's features a lovely wood floor and tables, bar stools made from old tractor seats with cushions, walls of exposed brick or stone with some wood panelling, an inglenook and beams aplenty. Pump clips are displayed on the ceiling; the selection of real ales is one of the best to be found in a Norfolk country pub. There is a good choice of non-alcoholic drinks. Bar staff are friendly and helpful. A garden play area is provided for children. ⌂❀◖◗♿▲♣

Terrington St John

Woolpack

Main Road, PE14 7RR

⏲ 11.30-2.30, 6.30-11; 12-3, 7-10.30 Sun

☎ (01945) 881097

Wells Eagle; guest beers Ⓗ

Take a short detour off the Wisbech to Kings Lynn road to check out this amazing village pub. Famous in the area for food, it may well be worth booking if you want to eat, as it can get busy. Lucille, the Australian landlady, ensures that there is never a dull moment, especially if there is any kind of celebration. She is passionately interested in art, and you can admire her own paintings, as well as others here. The jewel is the dining room built recently in Art Deco style, with specially commissioned glass and tapestry. Q❀◖◗P

Thetford

Albion ✔

93-95 Castle Street, IP24 2DN (opp. Castle Hill)

⏲ 11-2.30 (3 Fri & Sat), 6 (5 Fri)-11; 12-3, 7-10.30 Sun

☎ (01842) 752796

Greene King IPA, Abbot; guest beers (occasional) Ⓗ

Situated in a quiet area in a row of cottages, this well-established local looks out over Castle Park, towards the ramparts of Castle Hill. A small comfortable pub, consisting of two rooms, you will always find a friendly welcome here. The main bar offers conversation, in the lower bar pool and darts are on offer and there is an intimate patio for relaxed summer drinking. The IPA and Abbot are the best pints you will find for many a mile. ⌂Q❀P

Thornham

Lifeboat

Ship Lane, PE36 6LT

⏲ 11-11; 12-10.30 Sun

☎ (01485) 512236 website: www.lifeboatinn.co.uk

Adnams Bitter; Greene King IPA, Abbot; guest beer Ⓗ

Popular pub, beautifully situated on the edge of the salt marsh in the quiet village of Thornham. The well-preserved bar is dark and cosy and lit by hanging oil lanterns. Walkers, children and dogs are all made very welcome. The historic bar is complemented by an extensive restaurant and hotel facilities. The hearty restaurant menu is based on local ingredients, including Brancaster mussels in season. The cider is Westons Old Rosie. ⌂Q❀⇌◖◗♿♣●P⚡

Trunch

Crown ✔

Front Street, NR28 0AH

⏲ 12-3 (3.30 Sat), 5.30-11; 12-3.30, 7-10.30 Sun

☎ (01263) 722341 website: www.trunchcrown.co.uk

Bateman Dark Mild, Ⓗ/Ⓖ **XB, XXXB; Greene King IPA; guest beers** Ⓗ

Welcoming, traditional pub providing beers not normally seen in the area, Dark Mild is always available (on gravity at quiet times). Check the website for details of the beer festival and other events. 'Old gits corner' still attracts regulars and visitors for a chat about this, that and, well who knows. Meals are served Wednesday-Sunday (but ring for Sunday evening food). ⌂❀◖◗▲P

Upton

White Horse

17 Chapel Road, NR13 6BT

⏲ 11-11; 12-10.30 Sun

☎ (01493) 750696

Adnams Bitter, Broadside; Ⓗ **guest beers** Ⓗ/Ⓖ

Popular village local, close to the Norfolk Broads, where the friendly atmosphere is enhanced by a large fireplace. Delicious, home-made food is served in the restaurant at reasonable prices. Friday evening's take-away fish and chips is unmissable. A conservatory provides another drinking area. Camping facilities are provided at the rear of the pub. ⌂❀◖◗▲♣P

Walcott

Lighthouse ✔

Coast Road , NR12 0PE (on B1159, ½ mile S of seafront)

⏲ 11-11; 12-10.30 Sun

☎ (01692) 650371 website: www.lighthouseinn.co.uk

Adnams Bitter; Greene King IPA; guest beers Ⓗ

Coastal pub, benefiting from a garden and newly-extended function and family rooms. Two real ales are sold all year round, with at least two guests at busier times. Home-cooked food is available all day until 10.30pm every day. Bonfire night sees probably the best display in East Anglia. ⌂❀◖◗▲●P⚡

Warham All Saints

Three Horseshoes ☆

Bridge Street, NR23 1NL

✪ 11.30-2.30, 6-11; 12-2.30, 6-10.30 Sun

☎ (01328) 710547

Greene King IPA; Ⓗ Woodforde's Wherry; guest beer Ⓖ

Step back in time, in the three rooms of this 1725 flint-built Norfolk gem. The gaslit bar, with its log fire, stone floors and old wooden furniture, is as traditional as you will find in Norfolk, while the rooms are adorned with many old local photographs, documents and artefacts. The hearty, generous meals feature local produce and game. The 1991 edition of this Guide said it was unspoilt and it still is, thanks to the landlord who has been here ever since. ♛Q♉❀⇔◖◗♿♣P⚟

Watton

Breckland Wines

80 High Street, IP25 6AK

✪ 9-9; 9-9 Sun

☎ (01953) 881592

Beer range varies Ⓖ

Friendly off-licence that caters for the beer lover. Draught ales are available to take away, local Iceni beers are to be found among others from East Anglian micro-brewers. From the same micros comes a superb range of bottled beers (mostly bottle-conditioned), and products from further afield are also on the shelves. A small number of Belgian and foreign beers are also stocked, and a good choice of sweets to keep the children happy.

Wells-next-the-Sea

Edinburgh

Station Road, NR23 1AE

✪ 11-2.30, 7-11; 11-11 Sat; 12-3, 7-10.30 Sun

☎ (01328) 710120

Draught Bass; Hancock's HB; guest beer Ⓗ

In the heart of this lovely seaside town, this long-established pub has two bars, and an open fire with an unusual pebblestone surround. At one end, the restaurant serves a wide range of food in smoking and no-smoking areas. Wells boasts one of the finest beaches in the UK and is extremely popular with birdwatchers and walkers. The quaint streets with small shops are delightful and should not be missed. The Wells-Walsingham Light Railway station is nearby. ♛Q❀⇔◖◗◘⛺⇌(Wells-Walsingham Light Rlwy) ♣⚟♁

West Acre

Stag

Low Road, PE32 1TR 05782154

✪ 12-2.30, 7-11; closed Mon; 12-3, 7-10.30 Sun

☎ (01760) 755395

Beer range varies Ⓗ

The village of West Acre is famous for the summer theatre in the ruins of the Priory, and now in the old chapel too. However, close behind comes the village local, transformed over the last few years with the addition of a dining room. There always seems to be something going on – maybe a hog roast, quiz night or a beer festival. Even on an ordinary day there will be three interesting beers to choose from, with increasingly adventurous selections. The food is good, too, at West Norfolk CAMRA's Pub of the Year 2005. ♛❀◖◗♣P

West Beckham

Wheatsheaf Inn

Church Road, NR25 6NX (1 mile S of A148, Cromer-Holt road)

✪ 12-3, 6.30-11; 12-3, 7-10.30 Sun

☎ (01263) 822110 website: www.wheatsheaf.org.uk

Greene King IPA; Woodforde's Wherry, Nelson's Revenge; guest beers Ⓗ

Old farmhouse, converted into a public house in the 1980s. Inside are many exposed beams and old brickwork. Beers are mainly from local brewers, with Woodforde's being one of the most prominent suppliers. There is a games room down the corridor from the main bar. The pub is conveniently situated, near the picturesque Sheringham Park (NT). Three self-catering cottages are available within the grounds of the pub. ♛Q❀⇔◖◗⛺♣●P

Weybourne

Ship

The Street, NR25 7SZ (A149 coast road)

✪ 12-3, 6 (7 winter)-11; 11-11 Sat; 12-3, 7-10.30 Sun

☎ (01263) 588721 website: www.shipinnweybourne.co.uk

Beer range varies Ⓗ

Opposite the church (and priory remains) on the coast road, the Ship was originally a Georgian creation. It was modernised in Edwardian Norfolk's heyday and exhibits Stewart & Patterson Brewery windows and an impressive veranda. Divided into a small restaurant, no-smoking lounge, bar and sports room, this pub offers a changing beer range (often from local micros) and an annual beer festival. The food, locally sourced where possible, has devotees from way outside the local area. The Coastliner bus service stops outside. ♛❀◖◗◘⛺♣P⚟

Wicklewood

Cherry Tree

116 High Street, NR18 9QA

✪ 12-3, 6-11; 12-11 Sat; 12-10.30 Sun

☎ (01953) 606962 website: www.buffys.co.uk

Buffy's Bitter, Hopleaf, Norwegian Blue; guest beer Ⓗ

This comfortable pub is essentially the Buffy's Brewery tap, frequented by locals and real ale enthusiasts alike. The L-shaped layout comprises a drinking space with sofas and a dining area at the end. A choice of up to nine ales (four on gravity) is laid on for some special functions. A deep cellar helps to keep the beer at a consistent temperature throughout the year. Regular events include live music, quiz nights and food themes. Home-made pies are the house speciality. ❀◖◗⛺●P⚟

Winterton-on-Sea

Fisherman's Return

The Lane, NR29 4BN (off B1159)

✪ 11-2.30, 6-11; 11-11 Sat; 12-10.30 Sun

☎ (01493) 393305 website: www.fishermans-return.com

Adnams Bitter, Broadside; Greene King IPA; Woodforde's Wherry, Ⓗ **Norfolk Nog;** Ⓖ **guest beers** Ⓗ

An absolute gem, five minutes' walk from the beach, benefiting from an extensive front terrace for outdoor drinking. The 17th-century, flint-faced pub serves a good range of ales, and snacks or full restaurant meals. Popular with holidaymakers, ramblers and birdwatchers, the pub is handy for the Broads and just eight miles from Great Yarmouth. ♨☕❀⛺◐♣♣P

Wiveton

Bell

Blakeney Road, NR25 7TL

(4 miles from Holt on B1156, signed Glanford)

⏲ 12-2.30, 6-11 (closed winter Mon); 12-2.30 (closed eve) Sun

☎ (01263) 740101 website: www.wivetonbell.co.uk

Woodforde's Wherry, Nelson's Revenge; guest beer (summer) Ⓗ

The Wiveton Bell, formerly known as the Bluebell, is set in a quiet village in the picturesque Glaven Valley, close to the North Norfolk coast. The pub is a few hundred years old with a whitewashed exterior and a beautiful open, beamed interior fitted out with pews and settles. There is a no-smoking conservatory/restaurant offering highly recommended cuisine, presented by the Danish chef/patron; meals can also be enjoyed alfresco in the secluded garden (no food Sun eve or Mon).
♨Q❀◐♿♣P⊁

Wymondham

Feathers

13 Town Green, NR18 0PN

⏲ 11-2.30, 7 (6 Fri)-11; 12-2.30, 7-10.30 Sun

☎ (01953) 605675

Adnams Bitter; Greene King Abbot; Marston's Pedigree; guest beers Ⓗ

A short walk from the historic town centre, this is the place to find a good selection of consistently well-kept real ale in Wymondham. The general theme is rustic, the walls being adorned with a curious mixture of farm implements, old metal signs and photos. An ARP warden's bike hangs beside the door leading to the quiet courtyard. Monthly folk nights are held in the upstairs clubroom (last Sun). Elgood's supplies the house beer. ❀◐♣

Three Horseshoes, Warham All Saints

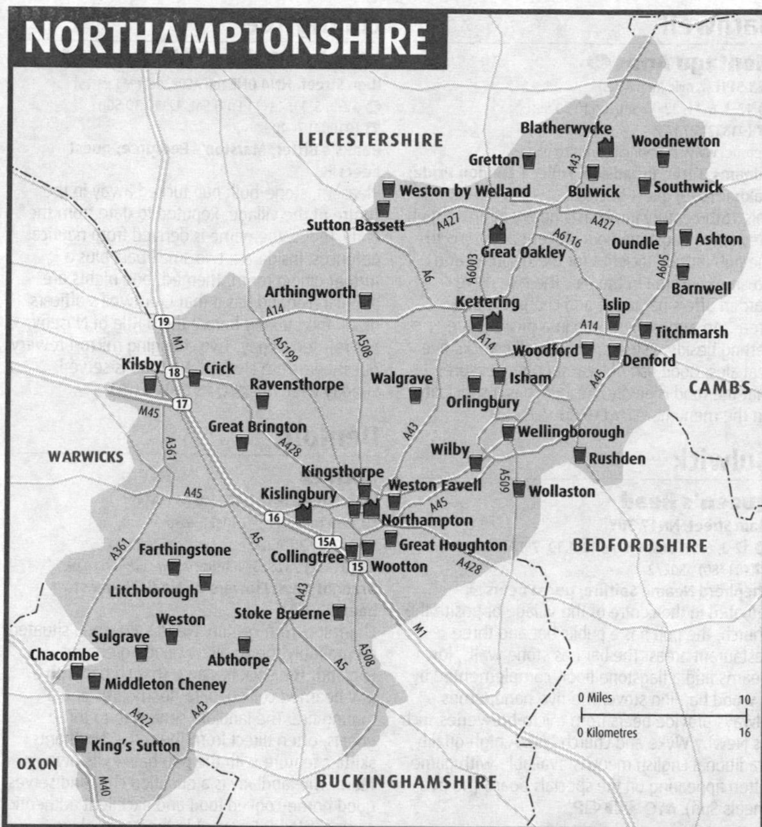

Abthorpe

New Inn

Silver Street, NN12 8QR (off A43/B4525)
12-3, 6-11; 12-10.30 Sun
☎ (01327) 857306
Hook Norton Best Bitter, Old Hooky, seasonal beers; guest beer Ⓗ
Quiet, country pub, hidden in a cul-de-sac off a corner of the village green, providing the villagers with a popular amenity. Built from mellow sandstone, the New Inn was once a thatched farmhouse, although it is now tiled. The comfortable interior has an inglenook in the bar area and a restaurant on a lower level in the Elton John snug. A beer festival is held over bank holiday in August. Aunt Sally can be played here.
Q P

Arthingworth

Bull's Head

Kelmarsh Road, LE16 8JZ (off A508)
12-3, 6-11; 12-10.30 Sun
☎ (01858) 525637
Everards Tiger; Wells Eagle; guest beers Ⓗ
Large, thriving 19th-century brick village pub, converted from a former farmhouse. The spacious L-shaped bar has log fires and a beamed ceiling. Fresh, home-cooked meals are served in the restaurant or on the patio. An August bank holiday beer festival runs Friday-Monday. The pub hosts speciality evenings, such as an Australian night when crocodile is on the menu. Up to four guest beers supplement the regular range. There are eight en-suite rooms for overnight stops. Q P

Ashton

Chequered Skipper

The Green, PE8 5LD
11.30-3, 6-11; 11.30-11 Sat; 11.30-10.30 Sun
☎ (01832) 273494
Oakham JHB; guest beers Ⓗ
Attractive, thatched pub in the heart of the Rothschild's model village of Ashton. A fire nine years ago meant that the whole of the interior had to be refurbished, and the pub now has a modern, clean appearance. Usually four real ales and Aspalls Suffolk cider are available all year round. The outside drinking area is the village green, scene of the annual World Conker Championship held in October. The food is highly recommended; booking is advised at weekends.
Q P

INDEPENDENT BREWERIES

Frog Island Northampton
Great Oakley Great Oakley
Hoggleys Kislingbury
Nobby's Kettering
Potbelly Kettering
Rockingham Blatherwycke

Barnwell

Montagu Arms ✔

PE8 5PH (¼ mile from A605)
⏲ 12-3, 6-11; 12-11 Sat; 12-10.30 Sun
☎ (01832) 273726
website: www.themontaguarms.co.uk
Adnams Bitter, Broadside; Fuller's London Pride; Oakham JHB; guest beers Ⓗ

This 16th-century inn boasts heavy beams, open fires and a flagstone floor. Recent additions to the pub include facilities for the disabled and a no-smoking area in the bar. The extensive garden offers petanque and children's play areas. An atmospheric pub in a picturesque setting beside a stream, it normally stocks five real ales. Good use of local suppliers ensures that the food is always fresh; fish is a speciality on the menu here. ♨Q❀◑⊟♿▲P

Bulwick

Queen's Head

Main Street, NN17 3DY
⏲ 12-3, 6-11; closed Mon; 12-4.30, 7-10.30 Sun
☎ (01780) 450272
Shepherd Neame Spitfire; guest beers Ⓗ

Situated in the centre of the village opposite the church, the pub has a public bar and three restaurant areas. The bar has stone walls, low beams and a flagstone floor, complemented by a wood burning stove. The five handpumps always provide beers from micro-breweries such as Newby Wyke and Church End. A high quality, traditional English menu is available with game often appearing on the specials board (no eve meals Sun). ♨Q❀◑⊟P

Chacombe

George & Dragon

Silver Street, OX17 2JR
⏲ 11-11; 12-10.30 Sun
☎ (01295) 711500
Everards Beacon, Tiger; guest beers Ⓗ

Excellent pub, recently purchased by Everards, overlooking the village green, with parts of the building dating from the 17th century. Inside there is a public bar, popular with the locals, and a lounge which features an old well, covered with glass and illuminated. There are two dining areas, the larger is no-smoking and can be used for functions. ♨Q❀◑⊟P

Crick

Royal Oak

22 Church Street, NN6 7TP (off M1 jct 18)
⏲ 3.30 (12 Sat)-11; 12-10.30 Sun
☎ (01788) 822340
Banks's Mansfield Cask; guest beers Ⓗ

Friendly, welcoming, beamed cottage-style free house, hidden from the main A428 near the village church. The ever-changing beer range includes eight to ten guests weekly. Open fires in the three main drinking areas give the pub a cosy feel. Traditional skittles and darts are played in the games room. Quiz nights and occasional entertainment are hosted, together with regular beer festivals. A separate function room seating 50 can be booked with catering provided on request. ♨Q❀♣●

Collingtree

Wooden Walls of Old England

High Street, NN4 0NE (off A508, near M1 jct 15)
⏲ 12-3, 5-11; 11-11 Fri & Sat; 12-10.30 Sun
☎ (01604) 764082
Banks's Bitter; Marston's Pedigree; guest beers Ⓗ

Pleasant, stone-built pub tucked away in the centre of the village. Reputed to date from the early 1600s, the name is derived from nautical defences. Inside are two small bars plus a further dining room. Themed food nights are popular. Legend has it that Cromwell's officers drank the pub dry before the battle of Naseby, but refused to pay. Two changing micro-brewery guest beers are stocked. No food is served Sunday evening. ♨Q☕❀◑⊟♣P

Denford

Cock ✔

High Street, NN14 4EC (off A45/A14)
⏲ 12-3 (not Mon), 5.30-11; 6.30-11 Sat; 12-3, 7-10.30 Sun
☎ (01832) 732565 website: www.cock-inn.co.uk
Draught Bass; Flowers Original; Ⓗ **guest beers** Ⓖ/Ⓗ

Charming 16th-century Nene Valley pub situated on probably the smallest village green in England. The Cock has an L-shaped bar with a low beamed ceiling, bare floorboards and a roaring fire. The landlord serves up to three guests, often direct from the cellar. Northants skittles feature with the pub having its own team. The landlady is a qualified chef and serves good home-cooked food and excellent authentic curries (Wed & Fri eves) in the no-smoking restaurant. Friendly staff and good beer make this local CAMRA Pub of the Season and Year 2004 well worth visiting.
♨Q❀◑⊟♣●

Farthingstone

King's Arms

Main Street, NN12 8EZ
⏲ 12-3 (not Mon-Fri), 7-11 (not Mon & Wed); 12-3, 9-10.30 Sun
☎ (01327) 361604
Beer range varies Ⓗ

Picturesque 18th-century building located in time-honoured tradition opposite the church, with a warm and welcoming atmosphere. The L-shaped bar has a country cottage feel, with chintzy armchairs and a piano as you come in, a fireplace, and walls and beams covered in china plates and ornaments. Popular, weekend lunches feature quality farm produce. Northants skittles is played in an adjoining room. The long terraced garden is a riot of herbs and shrubs. The loos are worth a visit. ♨Q❀◐▲♣

Great Brington

Althorp Coaching Inn (Fox & Hounds)

Main Street, NN7 4EW (2 miles W of A428)
⏲ 11-11; 12-10.30 Sun
☎ (01604) 770651
Fuller's London Pride; Greene King IPA, Abbot, Old Speckled Hen; guest beers Ⓗ

This is exactly the sort of olde-worlde pub where you would take a visitor from overseas. It is a listed, stone-built and thatch-roofed village inn with oak beams, flagstoned floors and a huge inglenook. Outside is a courtyard surrounded by stabling, a cellar restaurant and an enclosed floral garden which is a delight in summer. Meals are served every lunchtime and evening. The menu is quite adventurous and attracts a lot of diners, but the pub maintains the feel of a village local. Up to five guest beers are available.
⛼❀◐◑P

Great Houghton

White Hart

39 High Street, NN4 7AF (off A428)
⌚ 12-3, 5-11; 12-3, 6-11 Sat; 12-4, 7-10.30 Sun
☎ (01604) 762940
Greene King IPA; Hook Norton Best Bitter; guest beers Ⓗ
Just outside the borders of Northampton, this stone-built, thatched village pub provides a warm and cosy atmosphere with its exposed walls, beams and low ceilings. Once five rooms, they were knocked through to provide one rambling and divided room on several levels. Good, reasonably priced food (not served Mon eve) and three changing guest beers ensure that the White Hart is a popular pub throughout the week. Home to the cricket club, to the rear is an attractive garden. Q❀◐◑⊟P⚟

Gretton

Blue Bell Inn

90 High Street, NN17 3DF (off A6003)
⌚ 5 (3 Fri; 12 Sat)-11; 12-10.30 Sun
☎ (01536) 770404
Greene King IPA, Abbot; guest beers Ⓗ
Formerly a bakehouse, this three-roomed, comfortable pub is set in a row of 15th-century houses, and has a real fire in the winter. Up to three guest beers are available. It stages occasional live music and has an outdoor drinking area that is put to good use during the Welland Valley Beer Festival in June. Nearby is Welland Viaduct. ⛼❀◐◑⊟♣⚟

Isham

Lilacs

39 Church Street, NN14 1HD (off A509)
⌚ 12-3, 5.30-11; 12-11 Fri & Sat; 12-4, 7-10.30 Sun
☎ (01536) 723948
Greene King IPA, Ruddles Best Bitter, Abbot; guest beers Ⓗ
A three-room 17th-century ironstone village pub, right at the heart of the community. It hosts various car clubs and a monthly singles club. The Lilacs refers to a breed of rabbit, pictured on the pub sign. It has a cosy snug, a bay-fronted lounge and a large games room with pool and Northants skittles.
⛼♨❀◐⊟♣P

Islip

Rose & Crown

1 High Street, NN14 3JS (off A14/A6116)
⌚ 12-2.30, 4.30-11; 12-11 Sat; 12-5, 7-10.30 Sun
☎ (01832) 733118
Draught Bass; Courage Directors; Newby Wyke Bear Island; Young's Bitter Ⓗ
Situated in the centre of the village, this warm, cosy pub dates from 1691 and is built of local ironstone with a Collyweston tiled roof. The two rooms have low, beamed ceilings with a welcoming fire for winter nights. Outside is a small patio with a long garden sloping down to the River Nene. The Nene Valley Way passes through the garden, which contains children's play equipment. Four beers are always available, with a regular guest ale.
⛼Q♨❀◐P

Kettering

Alexandra Arms

39 Victoria Street, NN16 0BU (near bus station)
⌚ 2 (12 Sat)-11; 12-10.30 Sun
☎ (01536) 522730
Beer range varies Ⓗ
Back-street pub reborn as a real ale mecca. This genuine free house has a constantly-changing range of beers, with usually 10 on handpump, adding up to 1,000 different beers in just two years. There is a busy lounge at the front and a larger back bar which doubles as a games room with darts and Northants skittles. The bar has an antipodean rugby theme whereas the lounge is full of brewery memorabilia. The small rear courtyard is used for summer drinking and has an aviary. A beer festival is held in October at this runner up local CAMRA Pub of the Year 2004.
Q❀⛟⊟⚌♣⚟

Piper ✔

Windmill Avenue, NN15 6PS
(off A6003, by Wicksteed Park)
⌚ 11-3 (4 Sat), 5 (6 Sat)-11; 12-10.30 Sun
☎ (01536) 513870
Hook Norton Best Bitter; guest beers Ⓗ
Excellent 1950s, two-room pub, a previous local CAMRA Pub of the Year. The landlord supplies a changing guest beer range, six in all with a scrumpy cider and a good choice of fruit wines. The bar/games room is lively and popular with the young, while the lounge is quieter with a no-smoking policy. A beer festival is held in August. On Sunday evening there is a quiz. Good value pub meals are served every night. Wicksteed Park is close by.
❀◐◑⊟♣●P⚟

Sawyers

44 Montague Street, NN16 8RU (near bus station)
⌚ 12-11; 12-10.30 Sun
☎ (01536) 484800
Marston's Pedigree; guest beers Ⓗ
Formerly known as the Swan, this lively pub dates back to the 1600s. After a recent refurbishment it has reopened as Sawyers, which was the name of the owners in olden times. This busy, town-centre pub has a large single bar room on three levels. Presently four ales are available, always including a Newby Wyke brew, but the new management is looking to increase the range of beers. No food is served. Live music is played on Friday and Saturday evenings and jam nights are on Tuesday. ⚌♣P

Kilsby

George ✔

Watling Street, CV23 8YE (at A361/A5 jct)

⏲ 11.30-3, 5.30-11; 11.30-3, 6-11 Sat; 12-10.30 Sun

☎ (01788) 822229

Greene King IPA, Abbot; Fuller's London Pride; guest beers 🄷

This Guide regular is one of the finest pubs in the west of the county. It offers an excellent range of real ales and home-cooked food. A wood-panelled lounge and no-smoking dining room are joined by a public bar at the rear. It makes an ideal venue to watch rugby and football, while the dining room can be used for private functions. The George is an ideal stop-off for journeys on the A5 or M1. No food is served Sunday evening. Q❀⇌◐◑⊟♣P

King's Sutton

Butchers Arms

Whittall Street, OX17 3RD

⏲ 11-3 (4 Sat), 6-11; 12-4, 7-10.30 Sun

☎ (01295) 810898

Hook Norton Best Bitter, Old Hooky, seasonal beers; guest beer 🄷

Small, attractive stone pub, dating from the 17th century. Once two cottages, it was converted into a combined pub and butcher's shop. Both bars boast inglenooks, the main bar area has stone walls and a ceiling covered with spirit jugs and mugs. The garden is an orchard and ideal for children, it contains an Aunt Sally game. Meals are served Tuesday to Saturday.

⌂Q❀◐◑⊟♿≉♣P

Kingsthorpe

Queen Adelaide

50 Manor Road, NN2 6QJ

⏲ 11.30-3, 5.30-11; 11.30-11 Fri & Sat; 12-3, 7-10.30 Sun

☎ (01604) 714524

website: www.queenadelaide.com

Adnams Bitter, Broadside; Hook Norton Best Bitter; Webster's Bitter 🄷

Pub in the heart of the village, which has been swallowed up by Northampton. Popular with the locals, this pretty, white-painted pub has an ironstone frontage and brick rear. Inside, a split-level front bar has Northants skittles in the lower room, while the upper area retains a welcoming snug, and there is a lounge/dining area. Outside is a pleasant back garden as well as seating to the front.

❀◐◑⊟♿♣P

Litchborough

Old Red Lion

4 Banbury Road, NN12 8JF

⏲ 11-3, 6.30-11; 12-3, 6.30-10.30 Sun

☎ (01327) 830250

Banks's Bitter; Marston's Pedigree; guest beer 🄷

Traditional stone village pub providing a warm welcome to locals and tourists alike. Flagstone floors, wooden beams and a real fire in a large inglenook feature in the main bar. There are further rooms for pool, darts and Northants skittles. The pub is the only village amenity and attracts walkers and cyclists from the rolling countryside around this attractive part of the county. Visit this time warp – one of a dying breed. ⌂Q❀♣P⊓

Middleton Cheney

New Inn ✔

45 Main Road, OX17 2ND

⏲ 12-3, 5-11; 12-11 Sat; 12-10.30 Sun

☎ (01295) 710399

Fuller's London Pride; Hook Norton Best Bitter; Marston's Pedigree; Wadworth 6X; guest beers 🄷

Built in the 17th century, this traditional stone pub is on the main road through the village. Inside there is a long open bar, a no-smoking restaurant to the rear and a smaller eating area. In the summer, relax in the extensive garden, favoured by families, where Aunt Sally may be played. ⌂Q❀◐◑♣P⊬

Northampton

Fish Inn ✔

11 Fish Street, NN1 2AA

⏲ 11-11; 12-10.30 Sun

☎ (01604) 234040

Courage Directors; Frog Island Best Bitter; Marston's Pedigree; Theakston Old Peculier; Wells Bombardier; guest beers 🄷

This large pub in the pedestrianised town centre is spacious and comfortable with wood floors. The single-room pub has a central bar where up to 200 Bernards of Edinburgh beer bottles fill shelves throughout. Five regular and four guest beers are served, including the local Frog Island brew. ⇌◐≉

Malt Shovel Tavern

121 Bridge Street, NN1 1QF (opp. Carlsberg Brewery)

⏲ 11.30-3, 5-11; 12-3, 7-10.30 Sun

☎ (01604) 234212

website: www.maltshoveltavern.com

Banks's Bitter; Frog Island Natterjack; Fuller's London Pride; Tetley Bitter; guest beers 🄷

This award-winning free house is full of brewery memorabilia from Phipps and NBC who brewed oppposite (now Carlsberg). Apart from the nine beers regularly available, including a mild, there are bottled and draught Belgian beers, English country wines and up to 50 single malts, making this a discerning drinkers' paradise. Home-cooked food is sold and top live blues bands perform on Wednesday evening. There are regular beer festivals, based on counties, at CAMRA's Regional Pub of the Year 2004.

Q❀◐♿≉●

Racehorse

15 Abington Square, NN1 4AE (N of shopping precinct)

⏲ 12-11; 12-10.30 Sun

☎ (01604) 631997

Beer range varies 🄷

Lively, town-centre pub with a mixed clientele and excellent beer range. The pub is divided into two and has a large back room for live bands and other functions. The large rear garden is a fun place to be in the summer, especially when barbecues are held. Children are not allowed in the pub but are welcome in the garden – a great place to escape from the shops. ❀●P

Romany

Trinity Avenue, NN2 6JN
(½ mile E of Kingsthorpe Village)
⏲ 11.30-11; 12-10.30 Sun
☎ (01604) 714647
Caledonian Deuchars IPA; Fuller's London Pride; Harvieston Bitter & Twisted; Newby Wyke Bear Island; guest beers ⊞
This former Northants Pub of the Year is a 1930s two-room community pub situated one and a half miles from the town centre (bus No. 8 or 25). An excellent choice of ales is available, sourced from all over the country. The landlord organises many events and stages live bands in the lounge. The public bar has Northants skittles, pool and darts and is always lively. Card-carrying CAMRA members receive a 10% discount on ales on Tuesday and Wednesday evenings.
❀◐⊟♣●P

Victoria Inn

2 Poole Street, NN1 3EX
⏲ 4 (12 Sat)-11; 12-10.30 Sun
☎ (01604) 633660
Vale Best Bitter, Edgar's Golden Ale; guest beers ⊞
Popular, corner terraced, back-street pub with wood panelling throughout. This one-bar pub offers Northants skittles and bar billiards. Tuesday and Wednesday evening are quiz nights and folk and blues are performed on Friday. Having featured in the Guide over a decade ago, the Victoria Inn now returns to its former glory and makes an ideal stop for visitors to the Balloon Festival in August. ♣

Orlingbury

Queen's Arms

11 Isham Road, NN14 1JD (off A43, S of Kettering)
⏲ 11-2.30, 5.30-11; 11-3, 5-11 Sat; 12-3, 6-10.30 Sun
☎ (01933) 678258
Adnams Bitter; Caledonian Deuchars IPA; Fuller's London Pride; Taylor Landlord; Tetley Bitter; guest beers ⊞
Drive around the village green looking for signs to Isham to find this fine village pub. Recently refurbished, the central lounge has three distinct areas plus a no-smoking snug and dining room. The sizeable garden has trestle tables and children's play equipment. Look out for Brian on the bar. The pub dates back to about 1750, and was originally called the King's Arms but changed its name in 1840 for the coronation of Queen Victoria. Up to three guest beers are available. No food is served Sunday evening.
❀◐◑P⊁

Oundle

Ship Inn

18 West Street, PE8 4EF
⏲ 11-11; 12-10.30 Sun
☎ (01832) 273918
website: www.theshipinn-oundle.co.uk
Draught Bass; Oakham JHB; guest beers ⊞
Grade II listed building in the main street, 100 yards from the town centre. The pub is reputedly haunted by a previous landlord who threw himself from an upstairs window. The Ship is divided into several drinking areas, and has a homely and cosy atmosphere. It is often busy with live jazz on the last Sunday of each month, quiz nights on Tuesday and jam sessions on most Wednesdays. Good food is served 12-9 daily. ♨☕❀⇌◐◑⊟♿P⊁

Ravensthorpe

Chequers

Chequers Lane, NN6 8ER (off A428)
⏲ 12-3, 6-11; 12-11 Sat; 12-3, 7-10.30 Sun
☎ (01604) 770379
Acorn Barnsley Bitter; Fuller's London Pride; Greene King IPA; guest beers ⊞
The Chequers is in a rural village in rolling Northants countryside near three reservoirs. In the shadow of the Church of Dionysius tower, this Grade II listed building started life as a farmhouse. It features an L-shaped bar and a dining room at the rear. The bar's stone fireplace adds to the welcoming warmth in winter, pictures and knick-knacks make it homely. Across the yard is a games room housing Northants skittles and a pool table. Excellent food is served. ☕❀◐◑♣P

Rushden

Rushden Historical Transport Society

Station Approach, NN10 0AW (off inner ring road)
⏲ 12-3 (not Mon-Fri), 7.30-11; 12-3, 7-10.30 Sun
☎ (01933) 318988 website: www.rhts.co.uk
Fuller's London Pride; guest beers ⊞
Wonderfully preserved old LMS station on the former Wellingborough to Higham Ferrers branch. Purchased by the local transport society some 20 years ago, the gas-lit bar and museum have many railway artefacts on display. The society has the honour of being CAMRA's joint National Club of the Year 2000 and regional winner in 2002 to 2004. It holds five steam-ups a year with barbecue, hog roast and a jazz band. These weekends are open house, otherwise day membership is 50p. Six changing guests from micro-breweries are available, with one normally from Oakham Ales.
♨Q❀⊟P▯

Southwick

Shuckburgh Arms

Main Street, PE8 5BL
⏲ 12-2 (not Mon or Tue), 6-11; 12-10.30 Sun
☎ (01832) 274007
Fuller's London Pride; Oakham JHB; guest beer (summer) ⊞
Located at the centre of the village next to the village hall, this cosy pub has two rooms, one housing the bar and a real fire. The large, enclosed garden at the rear, with wooden benches, is adjacent to the village cricket pitch. The traditional home-cooked food is popular and well priced. Up to three beers are available in the summer. ♨Q❀◐◑♿P⊁

Stoke Bruerne

Boat Inn

Shutlanger Road, NN12 7SB (opp. canal museum)
⏲ 11-3, 6-11; 11-11 Fri, Sat & summer; 12-10.30 Sun
☎ (01604) 862428 website: www.boatinn.co.uk

Adnams Bitter; Banks's Bitter; Frog Island Best Bitter; Marston's Burton Bitter, Pedigree; guest beers (summer) Ⓗ
This popular thatched canalside pub is opposite the Waterways Museum. It contains many drinking areas, the most delightful being the original two front bars with low ceilings, stone flagged floors, chequered tiles and Northants skittles. To the rear is a lounge and bistro on several levels which provides a no-smoking environment. Upstairs is a further restaurant that overlooks the canal. The pub is home to the Rose & Castle morris dancers who regularly perform on the lock side. Children are welcome in the bistro and lounge.
⌂Q⊟♣P

Sulgrave

Star Inn

Manor Road, OX17 2SA (off A43)
✪ 11-3, 6-11; 12-5 Sun
☎ (01295) 760389
website: www.starinnsulgrave.com
Hook Norton Best Bitter, Old Hooky, seasonal beers; guest beer Ⓗ
Beautiful, ivy-clad stone-built pub set in an idyllic village. In summer the 300-year-old Star Inn is festooned with hanging baskets. The front bar is relatively unchanged with its flagged floor, beamed ceilings, settles, glass partitions and an inglenook. The restaurant serves excellent well-priced meals. The pub is almost opposite Sulgrave Manor, the ancestral home of George Washington's family. A skittle alley is available on request.
⌂Q✿⇌◐◑♣P

Sutton Bassett

Queen's Head

Main Street, LE16 8HP (on B664)
✪ 12-3, 5-11; 12-11 Sat & summer; 6-10.30 Sun
☎ (01858) 463530
Adnams Bitter; Greene King IPA; Taylor Landlord Ⓗ
Quiet, rural pub overlooking the Welland Valley which specialises in high quality food. It has a central bar between two small, low, beamed rooms. The pub opens all day in summer. The outdoor drinking area benefits from fabulous views over the valley.
Q✿◐◑♣P⚡

Titchmarsh

Dog & Partridge

6 High Street, NN14 3DF
✪ 12-3, 6-11; 12-11 Sat; 12-10.30 Sun
☎ (01832) 732546
Adnams Broadside; Marston's Pedigree; Wells Eagle, Bombardier; guest beer Ⓗ
Centrally situated in the village, the pub interior consists of one long room, with a raised games area where table football and Northants hood skittles are played. A major refurbishment has resulted in new pipework and interior decoration, and pub food is a welcome recent introduction. Outside is a pleasant patio. This regular Guide entry is well worth a visit.
⌂Q✿◐◑♣P

Walgrave

Royal Oak

Zion Hill, NN6 9PN (2 miles off A43)
✪ 12-3, 5.30-11; 12-10.30 Sun
☎ (01604) 781248
Adnams Bitter; Greene King Abbot; guest beers Ⓗ
This old ironstone building has been on the main street for many years, but it has only been a pub since 1840. The smart lounge has a dining section, and the front bar now has three distinct areas. There are usually three guest ales, plus an extensive menu with reasonable prices. Outside in the yard is a games room containing Northants table skittles; the garden has a children's play area.
⌂Q✿◐◑♣P

Wellingborough

Locomotive

111 Finedon Road, NN8 4AL (on A510 next to industrial estate)
✪ 11-11; 12-3, 7-10.30 Sun
☎ (01933) 276600
Bateman XB; Wychwood Hobgoblin; guest beers Ⓗ
Originally three cottages, this three-room pub is a warm, cosy and homely local, dating back to circa 1830. Friendly and welcoming, this free house has a policy of three rotating guest beers. The ambitious and innovative management is gradually developing the range of meals available. Featuring much interesting railway memorabilia including a constantly running train set above the bar, it is also a fascinating place to visit. ⌂Q✿◐⊟♣P

Old Grammarians Association

46 Oxford Street, NN8 4JH (off one-way system)
✪ 12-2.30, 7-11; 12-11 Fri-Sat; 12-10.30 Sun
☎ (01933) 226188
Greene King IPA; Hook Norton Best Bitter, Old Hooky; guest beers Ⓗ
Close to the town centre, this sports and social club is friendly and welcoming. The main bar is quite spacious and there is a compact TV lounge plus a function/games room. As well as the regular beers, three or four guest beers are available. Access is from the large rear car park with a stairlift for wheelchair users. Although the club is open to everyone, regular visitors will be asked to join.
☕◐♿P

Weston

Crown

2 Helmdon Road, NN12 8PX
✪ 12-3 (not Mon-Thu), 6-11; 12-3, 7-10.30 Sun
☎ (01295) 760310
Greene King IPA; Hook Norton Best Bitter; guest beers Ⓗ
Well run local pub at the heart of the village, with a good community atmosphere. It has a no-smoking family restaurant serving good food (Fri-Sun) and a beamed function room which can be booked for special occasions. There is a games room where table football and Northants skittles can be played.
⌂Q✿⇌◑⊟♣

Weston by Welland

Wheel & Compass

Valley Road, LE16 8HZ (off B664)
12-3, 6-11; 12-10.30 Sun
☎ (01858) 565864
Banks's Bitter; Greene King Abbot; Marston's Bitter, Pedigree; guest beer Ⓗ
A multi-roomed pub in a rural location which specialises in good value food from an extensive menu. Popular with visitors and locals, it participates in the Welland Valley beer festival held in June. The large rear garden has benches and seats plus swings and slides for children. Q P

Weston Favell

Bold Dragoon

48 High Street, NN3 3JW (off A4500)
11-11; 12-10.30 Sun
☎ (01604) 401221
Fuller's London Pride; Greene King IPA, Abbot; guest beers Ⓗ
Thirties pub hidden away down the High Street of a village that has been swallowed up by Northampton. This popular pub features a main bar to the front complete with pool table, plus a comfortable lounge to the rear adjoining the conservatory which is used by diners. The pub has a full time chef with food served all day. The 'Bold' is a sporty pub with both a cricket team and golf society, plus Northampton Saints supporters corner. Three guest beers are available. Q ♣P

Wilby

George Inn

Northampton Road (on A4500)
12-11; 12-10.30 Sun
☎ (01933) 222902
Bateman XB; Courage Best Bitter; guest beers Ⓗ
Stone-built pub situated on the former A45. The cosy lounge is warmed by an open fire. Above the fireplace is a list of upcoming events including the well-supported live music played on Thursday, Friday and Sunday evenings. To the rear of the pub is an adjoining dining area, as well as a garden and children's area with views of open countryside. The landlord serves up to three guest beers, mainly from micros. Evening meals are served Tuesday, Wednesday and Saturday. ♣P

Wollaston

Crispin Arms

14 Hinwick Road, NN29 7QT (off A509)
12-11; 12-10.30 Sun
☎ (01933) 664303
Black Sheep Best Bitter; Fuller's London Pride; Shepherd Neame Spitfire; guest beers Ⓗ
Small, compact, cosy and welcoming, this two-room pub is popular with locals, particularly at tea time and early evening. Six real ales are available, with the guest beers regularly changed. A variety of prints and posters plus relics of the boot and shoe industry make this an interesting place to visit. Crib, darts and quiz nights feature in this lively pub. Outside there is a small patio area for summer. Q P

Woodford

White Horse

Club Lane, NN14 4EY (off A14/A510 jct)
12-2 (not Mon), 6 (6.30 Mon)-11; 12-4, 7-10.30 Sun
☎ (01832) 732646
Draught Bass; Black Sheep Best Bitter; Greene King Abbot; guest beers Ⓗ
On the far corner of the village green, enter the pub through the archway. The slightly raised bar area, adorned with pictures of local and national celebrities, stocks up to five ales. English and Thai food are served in the conservatory restaurant. The 'white room' is a function room with Northants skittles. It also serves as a music venue, and the bar extends into this room. A friendly landlord and staff make this pub well worth visiting. Look out for the playful dog. Q ♣P

Woodnewton

White Swan

22 Main Street, PE8 5EB
12-2.30, 5.30-11; 12-11 Sat; 12-10.30 Sun
☎ (01780) 470381
Adnams Bitter; Draught Bass; Fuller's London Pride; guest beer Ⓗ
Located at the centre of the village, this pub consists of one long room with a wooden partition separating the bar and drinking area by the entrance, and the popular restaurant at the far end. The food is good quality and cooked to order (eve meals served Wed-Sat). Coco the Clown used to frequent this pub and is buried in the local churchyard. Of the five beers available, one is a guest and one a real ale brewed exclusively for the pub. Q P

Wootton

Wootton Working Men's Club

High Street, NN4 6LW (near M1 jct 15, off A508 towards Northampton)
12-2 (not Thu, 12-3 Sat), 7-11; 12-3.30, 7-10.30 Sun
☎ (01604) 761863
Greene King IPA; guest beers Ⓗ
Formerly the Red Lion, this club is a mecca for real ale drinkers. Five guest beers are regularly rotated to give a varied choice. The club has a bar, a quiet lounge, concert room and a games room featuring Northants skittles. It is a long-standing entrant in this Guide, and justifiably so. Show this Guide or CAMRA membership card for admittance. Q ♣P

The waiting inn

Prince, it is dark to left and right.
Waits there an inn for you
and me?
Fine hoppy ale and red firelight?
These things are at the
Fleur-de-Lys.

Rupert Brooke

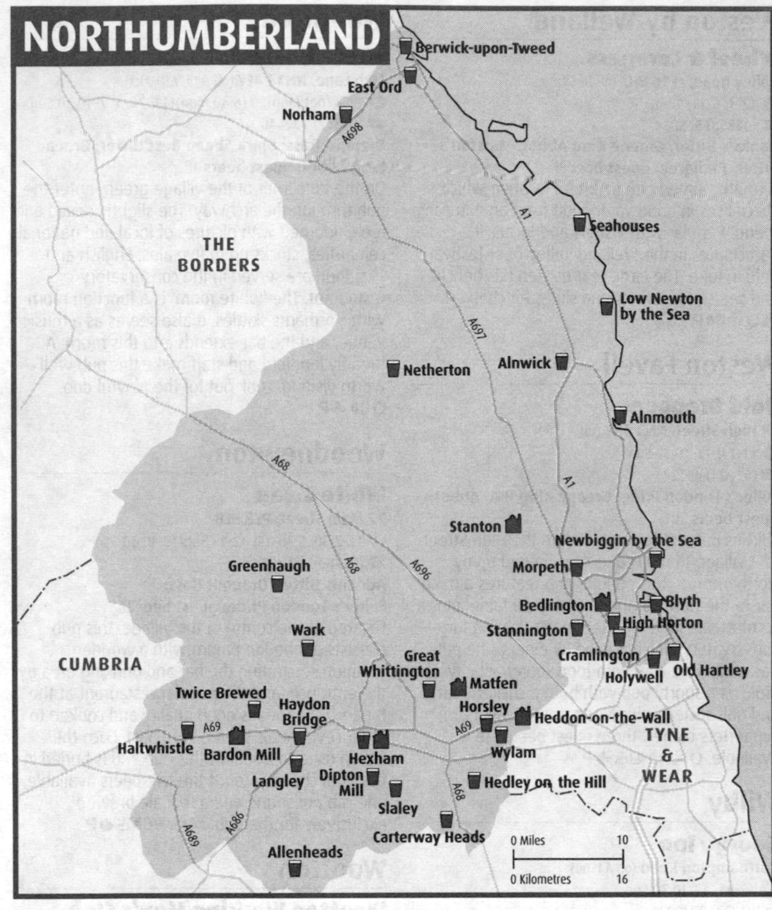

Allenheads

Allenheads Inn

NE47 9HJ

⏲ 12-4, 7-11; 12-11 Fri & Sat; 12-10.30 Sun

☎ (01434) 685200

website: www.theallenheadsinn.co.uk

Black Sheep Best Bitter; Greene King Abbot; guest beers Ⓗ

Built in the 18th century as the family home of Sir Thomas Wentworth, the inn is now the social heart of a village claiming to be the highest in England. It features an extensive, eclectic assembly of memorabilia, antiques and equipment throughout its many rooms – public bar, games, lounge and dining. A good selection of guest beers attracts hikers, walkers and cyclists on the Coast-to-Coast cycle route that runs nearby. Bus No. 688 to Hexham passes regularly. ♨❀🛏◑◗♣P

Alnmouth

Red Lion Inn

22 Northumberland Street, NE66 2RT

⏲ 12-3, 6-11 (closed winter Mon); 12-11 Sat; 12-10.30 Sun

☎ (01665) 830584

Black Sheep Best Bitter; guest beers Ⓗ

Former coaching inn with a cosy, wood-panelled lounge bar. The wood is reputed to have come from the Carpethia – the first ship to reach the ill-fated Titanic. The dining room features two red lions in the windows. Check out the murals depicting Northumbrian scenes in the gents. Great views over the River Aln estuary can be enjoyed from the raised decking in the garden. The pub is on the No. 518 bus route, close to the town golf course and some of the best sandy beaches in the country. ♨❀🛏◑◗♣P

Alnwick

John Bull Inn

12 Howick Street, NE66 1UY

⏲ 7-11; 12-3, 7-11 Sat; 12-3, 7-10.30 Sun

☎ (01665) 602055 website: www.john-bull-inn.co.uk

Beer range varies Ⓗ

Self-styled as a 'back street boozer', the inn was purpose-built in 1832, possibly as the Alnwick Brewery tap. As well as offering a wide range of

INDEPENDENT BREWERIES

Font Valley Stanton
Hexhamshire Hexham
High House Matfen
Northumberland Bedlington
Redburn Bardon Mill
Wylam Heddon on the Wall

quality real ales, often from local micro-breweries, it also stocks over 100 malt whiskies and a large selection of Belgian bottled beers. There are no gaming machines, electronic music or juke box, but it does have a board games corner for 'big kids' including Triominoes (three-sided dominoes). The pub holds a leek show and annual beer festival to coincide with the Alnwick Fair. Q❀♣

Tanner's Arms

Hotspur Place, NE66 1QF

12-3 (summer), 5-11; 12-11 Sat; 12-10.30 Sun

☎ (01665) 602553

Wells Bombardier; guest beers H

Situated on a street corner in a residential area just away from the shops on Bondgate Without. A single-room, it has bare, rough, stone-block walls, beams, a flagstone floor and seating around the walls, plus a well-used juke box. Note the tree in the centre serving as a shelf. The Tanner's hosts the famous annual Alnwick Strongman competition and occasional beer festivals. It is handy for visiting Hotspur Tower and not far from the entrance to Alnwick Gardens.

Berwick-upon-Tweed

Barrels

Bridge Street, TD15 1ES

11.30 (4 Tue-Thu Jan-Mar)-11; 12-10.30 Sun

☎ (01289) 308013

website: www.thebarrelsalehouse.com

Boddingtons Bitter; Taylor Landlord; guest beers H

Aimed at 'the more discerning bar fly', the Barrels is situated by Berwick's oldest, lowest bridge over the River Tweed. The ground floor is full of eclectic furniture including an old-fashioned dentist's chair, intricately carved wooden throne and a space invaders machine. The basement bar is mainly used for live music, particularly funk, jazz and soul. Singer-songwriters are always popular. Meals are served in summer. ◐≉

Foxtons

26 Hide Hill, TD15 1AB

10-11; closed Sun

☎ (01289) 303939

Caledonian Deuchars IPA, 80/-; guest beer H

Despite looking more like a coffee shop than a pub, this busy, enterprising establishment is indeed a venue for real ale as well as cakes. The emphasis is on food and wine, but non-diners are most welcome too. The location is handy for a pre- or post- Maltings Art Centre performance drink, as well as taking a stroll to see the Elizabethan town walls or the River Tweed and its famous swans. ❀◐◑≉

Pilot

31 Low Greens, TD15 1LZ

12-3, 6-11; 11-11 Fri, Sat & summer; 12-10.30 Sun

☎ (01289) 304214

Beer range varies H

The early 20th-century wood-panelled public bar features nautical artefacts plus traditional beams and a real fire. Two lounges are accessed by a central drinking corridor. The pub hosts a wide variety of regular music ranging from easy listening to folk – there is even a guitar club. Fiddles, mouth organs and penny whistles can often be heard. The pub fields two quoits teams. ⌂⇌◐◑⊟≉

Blyth

Oliver's Bar

60 Bridge Street, NE24 2AP

11 (1 Sat)-11; 12.30-10.30 Sun

☎ (01670) 540356

Greene King Ruddles Best; guest beers H

A welcome oasis in a town that is a real ale desert; the landlord created a one-room pub in a former newsagent's shop. Three real ales are available, one usually sourced locally. The pub has a welcoming, friendly atmosphere free from juke box or gaming machines. No main meals are served but freshly-prepared sandwiches are available at lunchtimes. The location is handy for visiting the recently revitalised Blyth Quayside. Q

Carterway Heads

Manor House Inn

DH8 9LX (on A68 S of Corbridge)

12-3, 6-11; 12-3, 6-10.30 Sun

☎ (01207) 255268

Courage Directors; Greene King Old Speckled Hen; Theakston Best Bitter; Wells Bombardier; guest beer H

Welcoming country inn near Derwent Reservoir which enjoys splendid views over the Derwent Valley. Guest ales usually come from local micro-breweries, and Westons Old Rosie cider is stocked. Excellent home-cooked food is served in the restaurant. The accommodation is also recommended here. ⌂❀⇌◐◑●P

Cramlington

Plough

Middle Farm Buildings, NE23 9DN

11-3, 6-11; 11-11 Thu-Sat; 12-10.30 Sun

☎ (01670) 737633

Theakston XB; guest beers H

In the centre of a former mining village, this fine pub stands opposite the parish church. Once a farm, the old buildings were sympathetically converted to the present establishment some years ago. The bar is small and busy with a door to the outside seating area. The lounge, containing the handpumps, is large and comfortable with a round 'gin gan' acting as an extra sitting room. Guest beers are often from local micro-brewers. The village is well served by buses from Newcastle. ❀◐◑⊟♿≉P

Dipton Mill

Dipton Mill Inn

Dipton Mill Road, NE46 1YA

(2 miles from Hexham on Whitley Chapel road)

12-2.30, 6-11; 12-4, 7-10.30 Sun

☎ (01434) 606577

Hexhamshire Devil's Elbow, Shire Bitter, Devil's Water, Whapweasel, Old Humbug; guest beers (occasional) H

The tap for Hexhamshire Brewery, this is a small low-ceilinged pub with a cosy atmosphere and a warm welcome. The landlord brews excellent

beers which must be sampled. Occasional guest beers are also available. Great home-cooked meals complement the ales. The large garden has a stream running through it and there is plenty of countryside to explore.
⛫Q❀◑🍎

East Ord

Salmon Inn

TD15 2NS

🕒 11-3, 5-11; 11-11 Fri & Sat; 12-10.30 Sun

☎ (01289) 305277

Caledonian Deuchars IPA, 80/-; guest beers 🄷

Although many customers are attracted here by the home-cooked food made with locally sourced ingredients – game is a speciality – the pub and particularly the area around the fire is still very much a focal point for drinkers. A large marquee in the garden caters for the frequent overspill. Handy for the Tweed Cycle Way and fishing on the River Tweed; dogs are welcome. The No. 23 Berwick-Kelso bus passes the door.
⛫❀◑⛺P

Great Whittington

Queen's Head Inn

NE19 2HP

🕒 12-2.30, 6-11; closed Mon; 12-3, 7-10.30 Sun

☎ (01434) 672267

Hambleton Bitter; guest beers 🄷

Dating from the 15th century, the Queen's Head is reputedly the oldest inn in the county. It is the only regular outlet in Northumberland for Hambleton Brewery who provide the house beer, Queen's Head Bitter. Set in the heart of Hadrian's Wall country, the pub is popular with tourists. The extensive food menu is recommended – all made with local produce where possible. The small, friendly bar is warmed by a roaring fire.
⛫Q◑P

Greenhaugh

Hollybush Inn

NE48 1PW

🕒 5.30-11 (closed Mon winter); 12-11 Sat; 12-3, 7-10.30 Sun

☎ (01434) 240391

High House Nel's Best; guest beer 🄷

Formerly a drovers' inn, the pub is in a row of cottages and dates back to the 17th century. It is the only public house in England's largest and least populated parish. Cosy and welcoming, do not be surprised if you are invited to share a table with friendly locals. The emphasis is on conversation here: there is no television, piped music or gaming machines. Note the Victorian range: its oven is still in regular use. The garden offers marvellous views of the local scenery.
⛫Q❀🛏◑

Haltwhistle

Black Bull

Market Square, NE49 0RL

🕒 12 (7 Mon)-11 (12-3, 5-11 winter Tue-Fri); 12-10.30 Sun

☎ (01434) 320463

Big Lamp Prince Bishop Ale; guest beers 🄷

Noted for its fine ale and food, this compact pub is situated just off the market place in the town that claims to be at the geographic centre of Britain. A disused room has now become a dining room to cater for the growing popularity of the freshly prepared meals. Beer drinkers are well catered for too with ever-changing guest ales, mainly from northern England micros and usually at least one from the local Redburn Brewery. ⛫Q❀◑🚌≠♣🍎

Haydon Bridge

General Havelock

9 Ratcliff Road, NE47 7HU

🕒 12-2.30, 7-11; closed Mon; 12-2.30, 7-10.30 Sun

☎ (01434) 684376

Beer range varies 🄷

A pub with a well-deserved reputation for fine food, with the emphasis on local produce. There are usually one or two of northern England's finest micro-brewed ales on offer here. The rear garden extends down to the River Tyne. Hadrian's Wall is just a few miles to the north. Haydon Bridge lies halfway between Hexham and Haltwhistle and is served by the No. 685 Newcastle-Carlisle bus. ⛫Q👶❀◑≠♣

Hedley on the Hill

Feathers

NE43 7SW

🕒 6-11; 12-3, 6-11 Sat; 12-3, 7-10.30 Sun

☎ (01661) 843607

Beer range varies 🄷

Outstanding pub set in a hamlet high above the Tyne Valley with views of the surrounding three counties. There are two bars, both with exposed stone walls and wood beams. High quality home-made food complements the four real ales on offer. The pub holds a mini beer festival at Easter culminating on Monday with the famous uphill barrel race – the winners are rewarded with a prize of real ale. ⛫Q❀◑♣P

Hexham

Forum ✔

Market Place, NE46 3BP

🕒 10-11; 12-10.30 Sun

☎ (01434) 609190

Courage Directors; Shepherd Neame Spitfire; Theakston Best Bitter; guest beers 🄷

Standard Wetherspoon's conversion of part of the town's cinema – films are still shown upstairs. What is unusual is the wide selection of real ales offered alongside the regulars, including guests from the Darwin, Mordue and Wylam Breweries. This is possibly the best Wetherspoon's pub in the north-east of England. Situated directly opposite the town's market place (market day is Tuesday), a friendly welcome awaits you. Q👶◑♿≠⚟

Tap & Spile ✔

1 Eastgate, NE46 1BH

🕒 11-11; 12-3, 7-10.30 Sun

☎ (01434) 602039

Black Sheep Best Bitter; Caledonian Deuchars IPA; guest beers 🄷

Classic town-centre, street-corner pub split into two drinking areas, both served from a central bar. Guest beers reflect the owning pub company's limited choice, but there should always be something to take your fancy. No food is served on Sunday. Regular live music nights are held. Situated in the centre of Hexham, the abbey is nearby. Q◑⊟⇌♣

High Horton

Three Horseshoes

Hatherley Lane, NE24 4HF
(off A189 N of Cramlington, follow A192) OS276794
⏲ 11-11; 12-10.30 Sun
☎ (01670) 822410
Tetley Bitter, Burton Ale; Greene King Abbot; guest beers Ⓗ
Much extended former coaching inn at the highest point in the Blyth Valley, affording excellent views of the Northumberland coast. The pub is open plan with bar and dining areas plus a conservatory. Known locally as the 'Shoes', it is dedicated to real ale with seven handpumps serving three regular beers and a constantly changing list of guests. It offers an extensive range of meals and snacks. Occasional beer festivals are held. Arriva bus Nos. X25 and 26 pass the end of the lane. Q♉❀◑◐P⊁

Holywell

Fat Ox

NE25 0LJ
⏲ 12-11; 12-10.30 Sun
☎ (0191) 237 0964
Mordue Workie Ticket; guest beers Ⓗ
Traditional pub in the heart of the village, serving quality cask ales. Guests include beers from the Scotco list and local micro Mordue. The cosy half-timbered bar offers a warm welcome to all. The pub's owners are winners of the local Village in Bloom competition. ❀

Horsley

Lion & Lamb ✔

NE15 0NS
⏲ 12-3, 6-11; 12-11 Fri & Sat; 12-10.30 Sun
☎ (01661) 852952
Caledonian Deuchars IPA; High House Nel's Best; Marston's Pedigree; guest beers Ⓗ
Well-appointed multi-roomed roadside pub in the centre of the village. Parts of the building date from 1718 with resulting low beamed ceilings – the inscription to 'Mind ya heed' is not there for decorative purposes. Despite an emphasis on food (no meals Sun eve), drinkers are well catered for by the six handpumps in the bar. A garden to the rear offers stunning views along the Tyne Valley. Bus No. 685 Newcastle-Carlisle stops outside. ♨Q♉❀◑◐⊟♿P⊁

Langley

Carts Bog Inn

NE47 5NW (3 miles off A69 on A686 to Alston)
⏲ 12-3, 5-11; 12-11 Sat; 12-3, 7-10.30 Sun
☎ (01434) 684338
Jennings Cumberland Ale; Yates Bitter; guest beers Ⓗ
Traditional, unspoilt country pub which serves a discerning local community as well as visitors to the area. Dating from 1730, it is built on the site of an ancient brewery (circa 1521). A large, unusual open fire divides the two rooms. The name is derived from a steeply-banked corner on the old road where, on wet days, the horse-drawn carts were invariably bogged down. Popular for Sunday lunch, you are assured a warm welcome at any time. ♨Q❀◑◐P

Low Newton by the Sea

Ship Inn

Newton Square, NE66 3EL (off B1340)
⏲ 11-3, 8 (6 Fri)-11; 11-11 Sat & summer; 12-10.30 (5 winter) Sun
☎ (01665) 576262
Black Sheep Best Bitter; guest beers Ⓗ
Despite its location in a quiet village with a tiny population, the Ship can be busy most of the time, even in winter. Set among a row of old whitewashed stone fishermen's cottages around the village green, it is almost on the beach. It is easier to access on foot by walking along the Northumberland coastline rather than road, as car drivers must use the village car park at the entrance to Low Newton and walk down the hill to the hamlet itself. An excellent choice of guest ales is available, from local micro-breweries. Evening meals must be booked.
♨Q♉❀⊏◑◐▲♣⊁

Morpeth

Joiners Arms

3 Wansbeck Street, NE61 1XZ
⏲ 12-11; 11-11 Fri & Sat; 12-10.30 Sun
☎ (01670) 513540
Draught Bass; Caledonian Deuchars IPA; Fuller's London Pride; Tetley Bitter; guest beers Ⓗ
This Fitzgerald's owned pub, just a short stroll from the town centre, is a friendly place to enjoy a good pint of real ale. Its guest list often features beers from local micro-breweries. The lounge has a pleasant view of the River Wansbeck. It is popular with locals and visitors. Quiz addict? Tuesday is the night for you. Q⊟

Tap & Spile

23 Manchester Street, NE61 1BH
⏲ 12-2.30, 4.30-11; 12-11 Fri & Sat; 12-10.30 Sun
☎ (01670) 513894
Beer range varies Ⓗ
If you like Tap & Spile pubs then this one will certainly appeal. Popular with locals and visitors alike, the pub boasts eight handpumps serving a variety of real ales and Westons Old Rosie cider. There is a bar and comfortable, quiet lounge where children are welcome. Northumbrian pipers play on Sunday lunchtime. Snacks are served Thursday to Sunday lunchtime, at other times you are welcome to bring your own food.
Q⊟●

Netherton

Star Inn ☆

NE65 7HD (off B634 from Rothbury)
⏲ 8-10 Wed; 8-10.45 Fri; 8-10 Sun
☎ (01669) 630238
Camerons Castle Eden Ale Ⓖ
Entering this inn feels like going into the living room of a private house rather than a pub. Unchanged for the last 80 years, the beer is

served on gravity straight from the cellar at a hatch in the panelled entrance hall. The bar area is basic with benches around the wall. It is the only pub in Northumberland to appear in every edition of this Guide. Children are not allowed in the bar. Opening hours may be extended in summer; please ring to check first. QP

Newbiggin by the Sea

Queen's Head

7 High Street, NE64 6AT

10-11; 12-10.30 Sun

(01670) 817293

John Smith's Bitter; guest beers H

Multi-roomed, traditional pub with lots of character and some unusual oval tables. The landlord introduced guest ales, often from local micro-breweries, when he took over the pub two years ago and has now sold over 500 different brews. The large collection of pump clips behind the bar makes an interesting topic of conversation – how many of the ales have you tried?

Norham

Mason's Arms

16 West Street, TD15 2LB

12-3, 7-11; 12-3, 7-10.30 Sun

(01289) 382326

Belhaven 80/-; Caledonian Deuchars IPA; guest beer H

Cosy, wood-panelled bar with a welcoming real fire at its heart and an eclectic assembly of tools, water jugs and fishing equipment hanging from the ceiling. The pub hosts regular ceilidh music evenings reflecting both northern Northumbrian and southern Scottish musical traditions. It also runs a leek club. The pub, on the No. 23 bus route, is well situated for attractions including the 12th-century castle at the end of the village, the Tweed Cycle Way, and local golf courses.

Old Hartley

Delaval Arms

NE26 4RL (at jct of A193/B1325)

12-3, 6-11; 12-11 Sat; 12-10.30 Sun

(0191) 237 0489

Beer range varies H

Multi-roomed Grade II listed building dating from 1748 with a listed water storage tower in the garden and great views up and down the Northumberland coast. To the left as you enter the pub there is a room served through a hatch from the bar and to the right a room where children are welcome. In the public bar the landlord has introduced guest ales, often from local micros. Good quality, affordable meals (not served Sun eve) complement the beer.

Q P

Seahouses

Olde Ship Hotel

7-9 Main Street, NE68 7RD

11-11; 12-10.30 Sun

(01665) 721383

website: www.seahouses.co.uk

Draught Bass; Black Sheep Best Bitter; Courage Directors; Greene King Ruddles County, Old Speckled Hen; guest beers (H)

Built around 1745 as a farmhouse, this hotel was bought by the current owner's family in 1910. Its saloon and cabin bars are maritime themed with ships' decking floors, brass instruments, diving helmets, figureheads and other nautical artefacts. Most notable is a nameplate from the wrecked SS Forfarshire of Victorian heroine Grace Darling fame. Evening meals are served in summer. Adjacent to the harbour, the hotel is well situated for boat trips to the Farne Islands. Infrequent buses run to Newcastle, Berwick and Alnwick.

Q P

Slaley

Travellers' Rest

NE46 1TT (on B6306, 1 mile N of village)

12-11; 12-10.30 Sun

(01434) 673231

Black Sheep Best Bitter; Marston's Pedigree; guest beers H

Licensed for over 100 years, this welcoming inn started life in the 16th century as a farmhouse. Living up to its name, it offers visitors an excellent choice of guest beers, wonderful food and accommodation. The bar has several cosy areas and a large open fire, stone walls, flag floors and comfortable furniture. Food is served in the bar as well as the restaurant – the menu is extensive and meals are made using local produce (no food Sun eve). Children are welcome and there is a safe play area beside the pub. Q P

Stannington

Ridley Arms

NE61 6EL

11.30-11; 12-10.30 Sun

(01670) 789216

Black Sheep Best Bitter; Taylor Landlord; guest beers H

Another excellent Fitzgerald house with several rooms, some of which are no-smoking. Ramps and wide doors ensure easy access for disabled visitors. Eight handpumps and good food cater for all tastes. Efficient air conditioning ensures a pleasant atmosphere for drinkers and diners who do not wish to be disturbed by smoking or food smells. A quiz night is held on Tuesday.

Q P

Twice Brewed

Twice Brewed Inn

Military Road, NE47 7AN (on B6318)

11-11; 12-10.30 Sun

(01434) 344534

website: www.twicebrewedinn.co.uk

Yates Bitter; guest beers H

This pub in the middle of nowhere has a surprisingly long list of facilities available to customers. The inn is a rural transport interchange with several bus routes stopping here, and offers an IT suite with Internet connection for use by locals and visitors alike. There is full disabled access and staff are trained in sign language. The guest ales regularly include a brew from the Redburn Brewery in nearby Bardon Mill. Due to its proximity to Hadrian's Wall, it can be busy, particularly in summer. It is open all year except Christmas Day. Q P

Wark

Battlesteads Hotel

NE48 3LS

11-11; 12-10.30 Sun

(01434) 230730

website: www.battlesteads-hotel.co.uk

Wylam Gold Tankard; guest beers H

Traditional 17th-century farmhouse inn close to Hadrian's Wall and the national park. The cosy bar room has an interesting bar front converted from a 200-year-old dresser, and a big inglenook. Live folk music is played on most evenings and there is a large garden. The excellent accommodation includes ground-floor rooms designed to provide disabled access. Q P

Wylam

Black Bull

Main Street, NE41 8AB

4-11; 12-10.30 Sun

(01661) 853112

Camerons Castle Eden Ale; Taylor Landlord; guest beers H

Recently refurbished, lively local in the middle of the village. The landlord has introduced cask ale including beers from the local Wylam Brewery which has proved very popular. The pub has its own restaurant with regular theme nights. It offers something for everyone including music evenings, pool, darts and sport on TV. Cherryburn, the birthplace of George Stephenson, is within walking distance.

Boathouse

Station Road, NE41 8HR

11-11; 12-10.30 Sun

(01661) 853431

Taylor Landlord; Wylam Gold Tankard; guest beers H

Outstanding two-room pub located next to the level crossing at Wylam railway station. The bar groans under the constant use of its nine handpumps. The Boathouse is the tap for Wylam Brewery and offers all of its beers as available. The chances are that you will be rubbing shoulders with the brewers themselves as you order your pint. George Stephenson of Rocket fame was born nearby; his cottage can be visited just across the River Tyne. Meals are served at the weekend at CAMRA Northumberland Pub of the Year 2005.

Q P

News from beer's front line

CAMRA members receive a free monthly newspaper, with its special Beer supplement. It's packed with information about beer, brewing and pubs, and will keep you informed about all the latest developments in the world of beer. The paper also lists CAMRA beer festivals and branch activities.

What's Brewing is worth the price of CAMRA membership alone. Sign up for membership, using the forms at the back of the Guide.

BEER

August 2005

Heritage Pub: O

What's Brewing

NEWSPAPER OF THE CAMPAIGN FOR REAL ALE

August 2005

CAMRA CAMPAIGN FOR REAL ALE

Christmas pub threat

Greene King under pressure to keep Ridleys brewery open

CAMPAIGN FIGHTS TO STOP CLOSURE

by TIM HAMPSON

Book now for awards

I'll be back...

NOTTINGHAMSHIRE

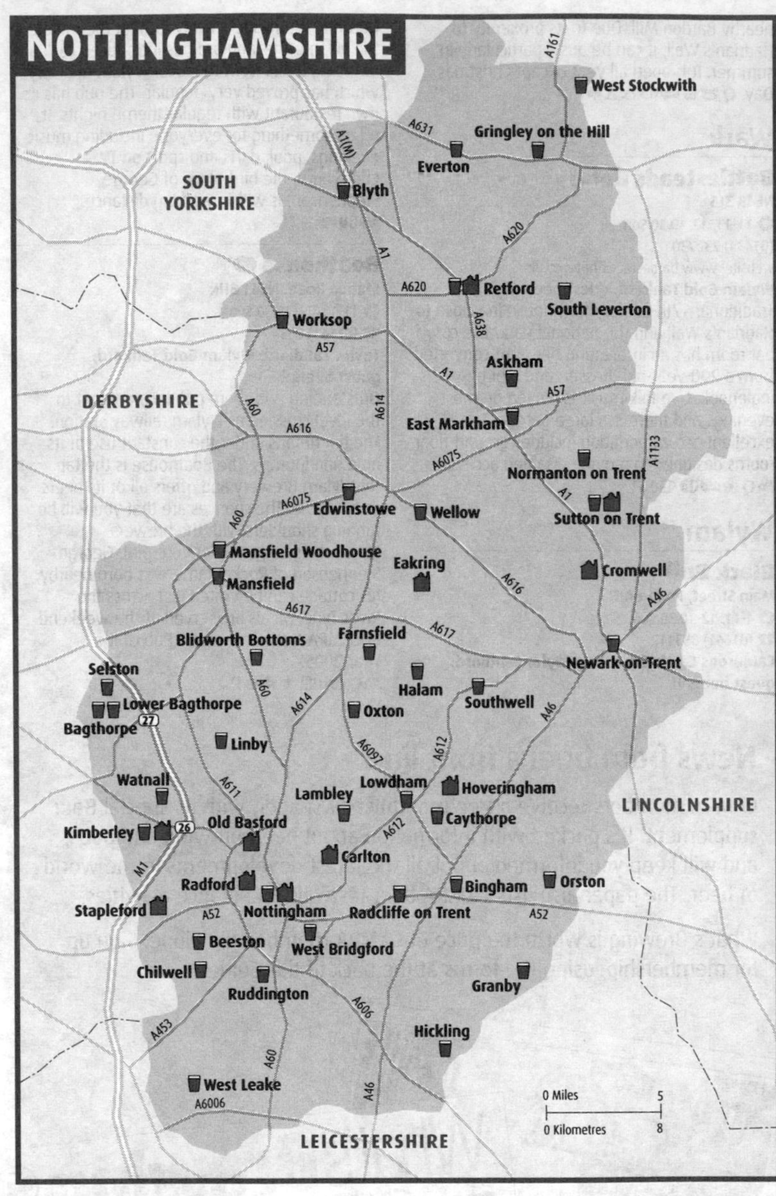

Askham

Duke William

Town Street, NG22 0RS

(4 miles from Retford)

12-11; 12-10.30 Sun

(01777) 838564

Taylor Landlord; guest beers H

The small quarry tiled front bar displays farming implements on the walls and ceiling. Fresh food is served lunchtimes and evenings and there is a small dining area to the rear of the lounge. Guest ales are always available and normally include beers from Acorn Brewery at Barnsley. It won local CAMRA Winter Pub of the Season 2004/2005.

Q P

Bagthorpe

Red Lion

134 Church Lane, NG16 5HD (off B600)

12-3, 5.30-11; 12-11 Fri & Sat; 12-10.30 Sun

(01773) 810482

Caledonian Deuchars IPA; Marston's Pedigree; guest beers H

A popular pub at any time of the year. The open-plan bar area is attractive with beams and a raised area for diners, although meals are served throughout the pub. Locals tend to gather around the bar where a frequently-changing range of guest beers is always on offer. The patio and tables outside are busy on summer evenings and there is a children's play area.

Q P

Beeston

Crown Inn ✔

Church Street, NG9 1FY

11-11; 12-10.30 Sun

☎ (0115) 925 4738

Hardys & Hansons Bitter, Olde Trip, seasonal beers Ⓗ

Multi-roomed town pub, the 'Shambles' has a darts room with exposed beams and wood panelling, a snug with high-backed seating and a service hatch, and a third room with wood panelling, etched windows and a sloping bar top. A further screened area features old photographs of Beeston. A comfortable lounge completes the layout. Quiz nights are on Tuesday and Thursday. ❀◖⊟⇌♣P

Victoria Hotel

85 Dovecote Lane, NG9 1JG (off A6005 by station)

11-11; 12-10.30 Sun

☎ (0115) 925 4049

website: www.victoriabeeston.co.uk

Castle Rock Harvest Pale, Hemlock; guest beers Ⓗ

Popular with drinkers and diners alike, this multi-roomed pub serves up to 12 beers, mainly from regionals and micros. A mild and a stout, and two real ciders, are always available, and there are more than 100 whiskies and a wide selection of wines to choose from. The food menu offers freshly-cooked food with plenty of vegetarian choice, served all day. Beer and music festivals are hosted during the year at Nottingham CAMRA Pub of the Year 2005. ♨Q❀◖◗♿⇌♣●P

Bingham

Horse & Plough ✔

25 Long Acre, NG13 8AF

11-11; 12-10.30 Sun

☎ (01949) 839313

Caledonian Deuchars IPA; Wells Bombardier; guest beers Ⓗ

Warm, friendly one-room free house with an olde-worlde cottage-style interior and flagstone floor. Six cask ales are always available including four frequently changing guests. The pub, which has a 'try before you buy' policy, is housed in a former Methodist chapel and was once a bookies and a butchers. The first floor restaurant serves a varied menu and is popular with diners from near and far. Bar food is served weekday lunchtimes (no eve meals Mon). ◖◗♿⇌

Blidworth Bottoms

Fox & Hounds ✔

Calverton Road, NG21 0NS

(off B6020 S of Blidworth Old Village) OS589548

11-3, 5.30-11; 11-11 Fri & Sat; 12-11 Sun

☎ (01623) 792383

Hardys & Hansons Bitter, Olde Trip, seasonal beers Ⓗ

Isolated, late-Victorian building set in grounds overlooking fields in a hamlet in Sherwood Forest. Recently refurbished and opened up, it has retained its original character and atmosphere. The unspoiled public bar seats two dozen drinkers. An extensive open lounge attracts a wide clientele of drinkers and diners. Reasonably priced home-cooked food is served in a no-smoking section. Folk musicians play on Thursday evening. A 'Plough Play' is enacted annually in early January. ♨Q❀◖◗⊟♿P

Blyth

White Swan

High Street, S81 8EQ

12-3, 6-11; 12-3, 7-10.30 Sun

☎ (01909) 591222

Black Sheep Best Bitter; guest beer Ⓗ

Attractive one-room village pub with low beams and flagstone flooring, situated in the heart of the village overlooking the village green. Two handpulls dispense Black Sheep Bitter and a changing guest ale. Good, reasonably-priced, home-cooked food is served in the dining room at lunchtimes and evenings every day except Sunday. ♨Q❀◖◗P

Caythorpe

Black Horse Inn

29 Main Street, NG14 7ED

12-2.30, 5 (6 Sat)-11; closed Mon; 12-4, 7 (8 winter)-10.30 Sun

☎ (0115) 966 3520

Caythorpe Dover Beck Bitter; guest beers Ⓗ

This 18th-century free house has been in the same family for 35 years. It features a comfortable lounge, a gem of a snug bar with hatch servery, inglenook, bench seats, beams and wood panelling. A private dining room is available for dinner parties. Bar food, mostly cooked to order using fresh ingredients, is popular and booking is essential. Guest beers often come from local micro-breweries. ♨Q❀◖◗⊟♣P

Chilwell

Cadland Inn

342 High Road, NG9 3EG

11.30-11, 12-10.30 Sun

☎ (0115) 951 8911

Draught Bass; guest beers Ⓗ

Friendly Ember Inns house with an open-plan layout but retaining a real pub ambience. Quiz nights and other events, as well as the annual beer fest, are hosted. A varied menu offers full meals, snacks and vegetarian choices. The 'drinks menu' has a well-chosen guest beer list and 20 house wines. Muzak and a large screen are unobtrusive. ♨❀◖◗♿P⊬

INDEPENDENT BREWERIES

Alcazar Old Basford
Broadstone Retford
Castle Rock Nottingham
Caythorpe Hoveringham (brewing suspended)
Full Mash Stapleford
Hardys & Hansons Kimberley
Holland Kimberley
Mallard Carlton
Maypole Eakring
Milestone Cromwell
Nottingham Radford
Springhead Sutton on Trent

East Markham

Queen's Hotel

High Street, NG22 0RE (½ mile from A1)
12-11; 12-10.30 Sun
(01777) 870288
Adnams Bitter; Black Sheep Best Bitter; Everards Tiger H
One of two pubs in East Markham selling real ales, this cosy house has a friendly atmosphere enhanced by an open fire in the winter. A single bar serves the lounge, pool room and dining area. Food, ranging from hot and cold snacks to full home-cooked meals, is available Tuesday-Sunday. There is a large garden area at the rear of the premises where you can enjoy a drink on a warm summer day. ⌂Q❀◐▲♣P

Edwinstowe

Forest Lodge Hotel

2-4 Church Street, NG21 9QA (at A6075/B6034 jct)
11-11; 12-10.30 Sun
(01623) 824443 website: www.forestlodge.co.uk
Wells Bombardier; guest beers H
Charming rural pub in Robin Hood country, near the heart of Sherwood Forest and its visitors' centre. This 17th-century coaching house retains the character and atmosphere that have been enjoyed by travellers throughout its long history. A log fire welcomes in winter. Good food is available in the cosy bar and restaurant. Families are welcome. ⌂❀◐♿♣P

Everton

Blacksmith's Arms

Church Street, DN10 5BQ
12-2, 5-11; 12-10.30 Sun
(01777) 817281
website www.blacksmiths-everton.co.uk
John Smith's Bitter; Theakston Old Peculier; guest beers H
Regular winner of local CAMRA Pub of the Season awards, this 18th-century free house stands at the heart of the village. Drinking areas include the locals' bar with its original tiled floor and the games room (formerly the old smithy). The comfortable lounge area leads to a large restaurant where the emphasis is on fresh, home-cooked food (booking is advisable). Outside is a Mediterranean-style garden; en-suite accommodation is available in the converted stables.
⌂Q❀◐♿P

Farnsfield

Red Lion

Main Street, NG22 8EY
11-3, 6-11; 11-3, 6-10.30 Sun
(01623) 882304
Banks's Riding Bitter, Mansfield Cask; Marston's Pedigree; guest beers H
Friendly, family-run local on the main street of a rural village close to Sherwood Forest. Popular with locals and visitors, it serves good home-cooked food in its no-smoking restaurant area. An open fire is welcoming in winter. Dominoes is played on Sunday and Monday evenings. A rare outlet for Riding Bitter, the regular beers are supplemented by a changing guest. ⌂Q❀◐♿♣P

Granby

Marquis of Granby

Dragon Street, NG13 9PN
12-2.30 (not Mon-Wed), 5.30-11; 12-11 Sat; 12-4.30, 7.30-10.30 Sun
(01949) 850461
Brewster's Marquis, guest beers H
Believed to be the original Marquis of Granby, dating back to 1760 or earlier, this inn has risen from near extinction to the award-winning pub it is today. York stone floors throughout the two wood-beamed rooms complement the naturally-shaped yew bar tops. A frequently changing range of beers is served by the friendly landlord and landlady – in the last year more than 300 different ales have been sold. A past East Midlands CAMRA Pub of the Year, it was national runner-up in 2003. ⌂❀◐♿♣P

Gringley on the Hill

Blue Bell

High Street, DN10 4RF
6 (12 Sat)-11; 12-10.30 Sun
(01777) 817406
Adnams Bitter; Courage Directors; John Smith's Bitter; guest beers H
At the heart of the village, an open fire welcomes you in winter. One small bar serves all rooms. The pub is busy and prides itself on its food, which is served daily except Monday. Tuesday is quiz night and several times during the season the Retford-based Rattlejack morris dancers entertain the customers. ⌂Q❀◐

Halam

Waggon & Horses

The Turnpike, NG22 8AE
11.30-3, 5.30-11; 11.30-11; 12-10.30 Sun
(01636) 813109
Thwaites Original, Thoroughbred, Lancaster Bomber; guest beers H
Situated in an unspoilt village, the pub has a rustic charm with its low-beamed ceiling and exposed brickwork. It is close to Southwell with its historic minster and restored workhouse, and near Sherwood Forest. The full range of Thwaites beers is on offer. Good quality, home-cooked food is served at reasonable prices.
Q❀◐♣P

Hickling

Plough Inn

Main Street, LE14 3AH
12-3, 5.30-11; 12-11 Fri & Sat; 12-10.30 Sun
(01664) 822225
website: www.plough-hickling.co.uk
Adnams Broadside; Caledonian Deuchars IPA; Greene King Ruddles Best; Taylor Landlord H
Situated opposite the Hickling Basin, part of the Grantham canal, this attractive pub is popular with walkers and cyclists using the towpath. The main bar is upstairs while downstairs is a second bar, a small function room and a pool room. Four cask beers are usually on offer and an annual beer festival is held over the August bank holiday. Food is served every lunchtime and evening except on Sunday night.
⌂❀◐♿♣P

Kimberley

Nelson & Railway ✔

12 Station Road, NG16 2NR

✪ 11-11; 12-10.30 Sun

☎ (0115) 938 2177

Hardys & Hansons Bitter, Olde Trip, seasonal beers Ⓗ

Traditional local, less than 150 yards from Hardys & Hansons Brewery, run by the same family for more than 30 years. The friendly bar offers a warm welcome to all and there is a cosy beamed lounge with an adjoining dining area. A no-smoking area is available until 9pm. The front garden is popular in summer and a rear garden is a recent addition. The pub is renowned for its good value food and accommodation. Q❀⇌◐▶⊟♿♣P⊬

Stag Inn ✔

67 Nottingham Road, NG16 2NB (on A610)

✪ 5 (4.30 Fri; 1.30 Sat)-11; 12-10.30 Sun

☎ (0115) 938 3151

Adnams Bitter; Boddingtons Bitter; Marston's Pedigree; Taylor Landlord; Tetley Dark Mild; guest beer Ⓗ

Full of character, this two-room village pub dates from 1537. The interior features low beams and settles, old-fashioned slot machines in full working order and old photographs of Shipstones – the former brewery that once owned the pub. A superb rear garden and children's play area are popular in summer and during the end-of-May annual bank holiday weekend beer festival. Quiz night is on Wednesday. The R1 bus from Nottingham stops outside. Q❀⊟♣P

Lambley

Robin Hood & Little John

82 Main Street, NG4 4PP

✪ 12-3, 5-11; 12-11 Fri & Sat; 12-4, 7-10.30 Sun

☎ (0115) 931 2531

Banks's Mansfield Dark, Bitter, Mansfield Cask; Marston's Pedigree Ⓗ

Centrally located and probably the older of the two pubs in the village, this white-painted building has a traditional multi-room interior. The small lounge offers a quiet retreat while the main bar, decorated in mock-Tudor style, bustles with village life. A function room to the rear accommodates the darts team and there is a skittle alley outside. The landlord is justly proud that cask beers account for over 90 per cent of his sales. Lunches are served on Friday only or by arrangement. ⛫Q⊟♣P

Linby

Horse & Groom

Main Street, NG15 8AE

✪ 12-11; 12-10.30 Sun

☎ (0115) 963 2219

Beer range varies Ⓗ

Grade II listed and set in a tranquil, picturesque village, this is a lovingly nurtured olde-worlde pub that dates back to the 1800s. The public bar boasts an inglenook while the snug and red room also have open fires. The green room is no-smoking. There is a conservatory and outdoor patio. The garden has picnic and play areas where families are welcome. Good quality food from an extensive and varied menu is served Monday-Saturday. A Sunday lunch menu is also popular. ⛫Q☋❀◐▶⊟P⊬

Lowdham

World's End

Plough Lane, NG14 7AT (just off A6097)

✪ 12-3, 5.30-11; 12-11 Fri & Sat; 12-10.30 Sun

☎ (0115) 966 3857

Mansfield Cask; Marston's Burton Bitter, Pedigree Ⓗ

Pleasing, white-painted village inn dating from around 1744 with a fine display of flowers in summer. The single room interior has a cosy feel with exposed beams and memorabilia on display. Look for the boxed World's End golf society plate. Excellent home-cooked food ranges from imaginative baguettes and snacks to a full menu with daily specials (not served Sun eve). The last Thursday of the month is fish night. The garden is dominated by a flagpole purchased from Nottingham Forest FC. ⛫Q❀◐▶⇛P

Lower Bagthorpe

Dixies Arms

School Road, NG16 5HF (1½ miles from M1 jct 27)

✪ 12-11; 12-10.30 Sun

☎ (01773) 810505

Greene King Abbot; Theakston Best Bitter; guest beer Ⓗ

Built in the late 1700s, Dixies offers a friendly welcome to all. Locals and visitors alike can be found warming themselves around the real fires in the public rooms, playing darts or dominoes, or gossiping in the snug. The pub's unspoilt character and amiable atmosphere attract a big following, with full houses at weekends for the live music on Saturday and quiz on Sunday. On weekdays it is quieter and a haven for real ale drinkers who can enjoy lively debate or just a quiet chat. ⛫❀Ʌ♣P

Shepherds Rest

Wansley Lane, NG16 5HF (2 miles from M1 jct 27)

✪ 12-11; 12-10.30 Sun

☎ (01773) 811337

Greene King Abbot; Wells Bombardier; guest beer Ⓗ

Family-run pub, dating back to the 1700s and reputedly haunted. An extensive garden includes a children's play area and benches in an idyllic countryside setting. The freshly prepared and home-cooked food can be enjoyed in the garden, weather permitting. Exposed beams, flagstone floors and open fires in the bar and restaurant add to the ambience. Evening meals are served Tuesday-Saturday. ⛫❀◐▶⊟♣P⊬

Mansfield

Bold Forester ✔

Botany Avenue, NG18 5NF (on A38 ½ mile from station)

✪ 11-11; 12-10.30 Sun

☎ (01623) 623970

Greene King IPA, Ruddles County, Abbot, Old Speckled Hen; guest beers Ⓗ

Large, popular, modern pub, run by a genial host, that appeals to a varied clientele. Divided

into smaller areas, the pub has an intimate feel despite its size. Frequent quizzes are held and there is live music on Sunday – weekday lunchtimes are the best time for a quiet pint. In summer the patio area is busy, too. Beer festivals are held in April and October. A range of six guest beers from regional and micro breweries is always on offer.
❀◐◗♿⇌♣●P⅟

Court House ✔

Market Place, NG18 1HX.
☺ 10-11; 12-10.30 Sun
☎ (01623) 412720
De Koninck Ambrée; Greene King Abbot; Marston's Burton Bitter, Pedigree; guest beers Ⓗ
This Weatherspoon's is a converted stone-built multi-room former courthouse, with a central bar. The family area is spacious and children are welcome. Good value specials augment the standard Wetherspoon's menu. Guest beers are sold at the best price in the area. The pub attracts a varied clientele from dedicated drinkers to shoppers taking a break.
Q◐◗♿⇌⅟

Nell Gwyn

117 Sutton Road, NG18 5EX (on A38)
☺ 12-4 (3 Mon; not Tue-Thu), 7-11; 12-3, 7-10.30 Sun
☎ (01623) 659850
Beer range varies Ⓗ
A free house with a homely atmosphere offering a warm welcome to all, whether you want to join in with the traditional pub games or enjoy a peaceful drink with friends. Two rooms – a comfortable lounge and games room – are served from a central bar. Home-cooked lunches are available on Saturday only at reasonable prices. Q♿♣

Railway Inn

9 Station Street, NG18 1EF
☺ 11-11 (5 Tue); 12-5 Sun
☎ (01623) 623086
Bateman XB, seasonal beers; guest beers Ⓗ
It is no surprise that this community pub continues to flourish with its new landlady – she has worked behind the scenes here for the last eight years. Excellent, reasonably priced pub food is served at lunchtime. The beer is mainly from Bateman with a varying guest ale and there is a range of bottled and canned beers. Worryingly, the pub is under threat of closure at the time of writing, but CAMRA and locals are fighting for its survival. Q❀◐⇌♣⅟

Widow Frost ✔

Leeming Street, NG18 1NB
☺ 10-11; 10-10.30 Sun
☎ (01623) 666790
Bateman XXXB; Marston's Burton Bitter; Pedigree; guest beers Ⓗ
Excellent Wetherspoon's pub with a spacious layout, including a larger than usual drinking area and no-smoking section for families. A good range of beers from near and far is on handpull at reasonable prices. The usual potted pub history is displayed on the wall. Good food includes daily specials and a Sunday roast lunch. The pub opens at 10am on Sunday for breakfast but no alcohol is served until noon.
Q◐◗♿⇌⅟

Mansfield Woodhouse

Greyhound Inn

82 High Street, NG19 8BD
☺ 12-11; 12-10.30 Sun
☎ (01623) 464403
Greene King Abbot; Mansfield Cask; Theakston Mild; Webster's Bitter; guest beers Ⓗ
This popular, friendly stone-built pub, reputedly dating from the 17th century, has been a regular Guide entry for more than 13 years. Situated near the old market square, it has two rooms – a quiet, comfortable lounge and a lively tap room with pool table, dartboard and other games. Up to six real ales are on offer. Quizzes are held twice a week. Do not miss this pub if you are in the area. Q❀⊞♿⇌♣P⊡

Newark-on-Trent

Castle & Falcon

10 London Road, NG24 1TW
(50 yds from Beamond Cross)
☺ 12 (11 Fri)-3 (not Tue-Thu), 7-11; 12-3, 7-10.30 Sun
☎ (01636) 703513
John Smith's Bitter; guest beers Ⓗ
On the outskirts of the town centre, this friendly local has the old James Hole Brewery in the background. Dating from the 19th century, it was once a coaching inn on the London-York run. Inside is a bar, lounge and conservatory, and outside a patio and skittles area. The pub runs darts, dominoes and pool teams, and is always lively. It offers a wide selection of guest beers, with testers to help you decide. ❀⊞⇌(Castle)♣

Fox & Crown

4-6 Appletongate, NG24 1JY
☺ 11-11 (midnight Fri & Sat); 12-10.30 Sun
☎ (01636) 605820
Draught Bass; Castle Rock Harvest Pale, Hemlock; Everards Tiger; guest beer Ⓗ
This open-plan pub divides into five areas: bar, lounge, snug, restaurant and seating for drinkers. Serving what is possibly the best quality and most consistent beer in Newark, the pub hosts regular brewery nights and live entertainment. As well as draught beer, real perry and cider are available during the summer months. Q◐◗♿⇌(Northgate/Castle)●

Mail Coach

13 London Road, NG24 1TN
(25 yds from Beamond Cross)
☺ 11.30-3, 5.30-11; 11.30-11 Fri & Sat; 12-3, 7-10.30 Sun
☎ (01636) 605164
Caledonian Deuchars IPA; Flowers IPA, Original; guest beers Ⓗ
Dating from 1778, this free house is not far from the town centre. The roomy interior has three main drinking areas with two real fires and an entrance hall, all served from a central bar. Three regular beers are supplemented by two guests. Hot food and baguettes are served at lunchtime. There is a small patio for outdoor drinking. Live music is played occasionally.
⌂❀⊟◐⇌(Castle)P

Old Malt Shovel ✔

25 Northgate, NG24 1HD (400 yds from Newark castle)
☺ 11.30-3, 5.30-11; 12-11 Wed-Sat; 12-10.30 Sun
☎ (01636) 702036

website: www.theoldmaltshovel.co.uk
Wells Bombardier; guest beers 🄷
A genuine local where visitors return again and again to enjoy the beer and ambience. The pub also has a well deserved reputation for good food. Standing close to the River Trent, on the site of a 16th-century bakery, it is the only survivor of the five pubs originally situated here. It has its own RATS club (real ale tasting society) and holds an annual snail racing competition. It was local CAMRA Pub of the Year in 2002.
⚐❀◑◐ ⇌(Castle/Northgate)♣

Normanton on Trent

Square & Compass

Eastgate, NG23 6RN (10 miles N of Newark via A1)
✪ 12-11; 12-10.30 Sun
☎ (01636) 821439
website: www.squareandcompass.co.uk
Adnams Bitter; Black Sheep Best Bitter; guest beers 🄷
Friendly village free house, parts of which date back 500 years, with a low-beamed ceiling and open log fires. Good value food from a varied menu is highly recommended. There is a no-smoking dining area and a garden with an imaginative children's play area. Table skittles night is Tuesday and dominoes is played on Thursday. Occasional live music is hosted. Wheelchair access is good throughout.
⚐❀⇔◑◐♿⅄♣P

Nottingham: Central

Bell Inn ✔

18 Angel Row, Old Market Square, NG1 6HL
✪ 10.30-11; 12-10.30 Sun
☎ (0115) 947 5241
website: www.thebell-inn.com
Hardys & Hansons Mild, Bitter, Olde Trip, seasonal beers; guest beers 🄷
Three-room, traditional pub in the market square, owned by local brewer Hardys & Hansons. A wide selection of guest ales is available, many from micros. Under the pub is a labyrinth of Norman caves – a tour of the cellar can be arranged. Food is served in the bars as well as the Belfry restaurant. During the summer there is a café-style drinking area on the pavement outside. The back bar hosts live music and frequent beer festivals.
Q❀◑◐ ⊟⊖(Old Market Sq)

Cock & Hoop

25-27 High Pavement, Lace Market, NG1 1HF
✪ 12-11 (midnight Thu; 1am Fri & Sat); 12-10.30 Sun
☎ (0115) 852 3231
Fuller's London Pride; guest beers 🄷
This no-smoking, air-conditioned, split-level pub is situated opposite the Galleries of Justice in the Lace Market area and attracts a varied clientele. Downstairs is a comfortable lounge created out of a former cellar room. The unusual solid pewter bar top has five handpumps dispensing regular and guest beers, some from local breweries. Cock & Hoop house bitter is brewed by Nottingham Brewery. A good choice of wines is also available. Freshly-cooked food is served daily. Quiz nights and gourmet evenings are regular events.
Q◑◐ ⊖(Lace Market)⅍

Fellows, Morton & Clayton

54 Canal Street, NG1 7EH
✪ 11-11 (midnight Fri & Sat); 12-10.30 Sun
☎ (0115) 950 6795
website: www.fellowsmortonandclayton.co.uk
Camerons Castle Eden Ale; Fellows Bitter, Post Haste; Fuller's London Pride; guest beers 🄷
One-room, split level pub, converted from a warehouse, situated next to Nottingham canal, 10 minutes from the city centre. Home of the city's first brew-pub (note: malt extract is used), it has won awards for its floral displays. Good food from a wide and varied menu is available in the pub and restaurant. Sports are shown on TV. ❀◑◐ ⇌⊖(Station St)

Langtrys

4 South Sherwood Street, NG1 4BY
✪ 11-11; 12-10.30 Sun
☎ (0115) 947 2124
Boddingtons Bitter; Caledonian Deuchars IPA; guest beers 🄷
This old, split level, single room pub is a friendly locals' pub, despite being in the middle of the town centre. Named after Lillie Langtry, the pub is opposite the Theatre Royal. It serves up to 40 different beers a month, all voted on by customers in the 'beer of the month' competition. A full and varied all-day menu is offered. ⚐❀◑◐ ⊖(Royal Centre) ●

Lincolnshire Poacher

161 Mansfield Road, NG1 3FR
(on A60 500 yds N of city centre)
✪ 11-11; 12-10.30 Sun
☎ (0115) 941 1584
Bateman XB, XXXB; Castle Rock Poacher's Gold, Harvest Pale; guest beers 🄷
Two-room, traditional pub, with a no-smoking room and conservatory to the rear, plus an enclosed patio. The pub is popular with diners and the real ale fraternity doing the Mansfield Road crawl. Probably the first pub in Nottingham to sell an ever-changing range of up to 10 real ales from micro-breweries on a regular basis, it also stages regional brewery themed nights. An extensive food menu is available. ❀◑◐ ♣●⅍

Olde Trip to Jerusalem ☆ ✔

1 Brewhouse Yard, NG1 6AD (below castle)
✪ 11-11; 12-10.30 Sun
☎ (0115) 947 3171
website: www.triptojerusalem.com
Hardys & Hansons Mild, Bitter, Olde Trip, seasonal beers; guest beers 🄷
The world famous Olde Trip to Jerusalem is reputed to date from 1189. It has a number of rooms downstairs, some cut out of the castle rock. Upstairs, the rock lounge is home to a cursed galleon and a modern tapestry depicting Nottingham's history. Meals are served until 6pm. The top bar can be reserved for private functions. This must-visit pub was winner of the English Heritage/CAMRA award 2004.
Q❀◑◐ ⇌⊖(Station St) ♣⅍

Old Moot Hall Inn

27 Carlton Road, NG3 2DG (near ice stadium)
✪ 10.30-11; 12-10.30 Sun
☎ (0115) 954 0170

Oakham JHB; guest beers 🄷
Formerly a chapel, and retaining some of its original features, this two-storey building has been beautifully converted to a warm and friendly local. Eight guest handpumps offer up to 30 ales from many different micro-breweries each week. A family-run business, this real ale mecca is worth seeking out. ⌂◐●

Rose of England ✔

36-38 Mansfield Road, NG1 3GY
⏲ 11-11; 11.30-midnight Wed-Sat; 12-10.30 Sun
☎ (0115) 947 2739
Adnams Broadside; Greene King Abbot; Tetley Dark Mild; Wells Bombardier; guest beer 🄷
This interesting building was built by local architect Fothergill Watson in 1898. The exterior is a fine example of his work. A friendly welcome awaits you in this popular pub. A weekly quiz is held, along with many other events, and live music is often played in the function room upstairs. Food is served at lunchtime, Monday-Saturday. ◐⊖(Royal Centre)

Vat & Fiddle

12-14 Queen's Bridge Road, NG2 1NB
⏲ 11-11; 12-10.30 Sun
☎ (0115) 985 0611
Castle Rock Meadows Gold, Harvest Pale, Hemlock; guest beers 🄷
Popular, friendly single-room pub, handy for the station. Ten handpumps offer an ever-changing selection of beers including up to four from the Castle Rock Brewery next door. Traditional cider and around 70 whiskies are also stocked plus a range of German and Belgian beers. There are plans to install two new rooms with viewing panels into the brewery.
Q✿♿⇌⊖(Station St) ●

Nottingham: East

Lord Nelson ✔

13 Thurgaton Street, Sneinton, NG2 4GU
⏲ 11-3, 5-11; 11-11 Sat; 12-10.30 Sun
☎ (0115) 911 0069
Hardys & Hansons Bitter, Olde Trip, seasonal beers 🄷
A 10-minute walk from the National Ice Arena, situated in the heart of Sneinton, the pub is set within a lovely garden. Some of its four beamed rooms are warmed by coal fires. Popular with a diverse range of customers, a friendly welcome is guaranteed from staff and regulars alike. A varied menu includes a Sunday roast. Quizzes and other entertainment are staged. ⌂Q✿◐⊟

Nottingham: North

Fox & Crown

33 Church Street, Old Basford, NG6 0GA
⏲ 12-11; 12-10.30 Sun
☎ (0115) 942 2002
Alcazar Ale, Nottingham Nog, New Dawn, Vixen's Vice, Windjammer, seasonal beers; guest beer 🄷
This pub, the Alcazar Brewery tap, attracts beer lovers from afar, but remains a true local. Around six brewery beers are supplemented by seasonal ales. A large selection of bottled continental and fruit beers are stocked along with Alcazar bottled beers. Two regular beer festivals are held. The food choice is either Thai or pizzas (unusual for this area). An enclosed rear patio is a pleasant spot for a summer drink.
⌂✿◐◑⊖(David Lane/Basford) P

Gladstone

45 Loscoe Road, Carrington, NG5 2AW
(off A60 Mansfield road)
⏲ 5 (12 Sat)-11; 12-10.30 Sun
☎ (0115) 912 9994
Fuller's London Pride; Greene King IPA; Nottingham EPA; Taylor Landlord; guest beer 🄷
Small, friendly, two-room back-street hostelry dating from around 1880, serving the local community. The public bar displays sporting memorabilia and screens sports events on TV, while the lounge holds many books for customers to read. A quiz is held on Thursday and the Carrington Folk Club meets on Wednesday. The pub is a regular outlet for Nottingham Brewery beers.
✿⊟♣

Horse & Groom ✔

462 Radford Road, New Basford, NG7 7EA
⏲ 11-11; 12-10.30 Sun
☎ (0115) 970 3777
website: www.horseandgroombasford.co.uk
Caledonian Deuchars IPA; Courage Directors; Wells Bombardier; guest beers 🄷
In the shadow of the former Shipstone's Brewery, and at one time the firm's social club, this pub enjoys a reputation for quality and choice that has spread far and wide. Four or five guest beers from micro-breweries are always available. The pub is divided into several areas, including a snug and a function room at the rear, where occasional live music is staged.
⌂◐⊖(Shipstone St)

Lion Inn ✔

44 Mosley Street, New Basford, NG7 7FQ
(off Radford Rd)
⏲ 12-11; 12-10.30 Sun
☎ (0115) 970 3506
Draught Bass; Bateman XB, XXXB; guest beers 🄷
Busy pub that is both a genuine local and a very popular music venue. Blues, rock and jazz bands play live on Friday and Saturday, with a Sunday lunchtime jazz session too. The interior is one large room, but the central bar gives a feel of distinct areas. Nationwide breweries and local micros are well represented. Meals are served throughout the day Friday-Sunday.
⌂✿◐◑♿⊖(Shipstone St) ♣●P

Nottingham: South

Globe

152 London Road, NG2 3BQ
⏲ 11-11; 12-10.30 Sun
☎ (0115) 986 6881
Beer range varies 🄷
Light, airy, popular pub near to Nottingham's cricket and football grounds. The function room caters for up to 100 people and occasionally shows matches on a big screen. The varied menu is competitively priced; Sunday meals are served 12-5pm. Recently refurbished, up to six handpumps provide ales from mainly local breweries. Seating ranges from bar stools to

sofas in a cosy alcove, with a fire in winter. Ask about the CAMRA discount. Frequent buses run from the city centre. ◑ ≹ P

Nottingham: West

Falcon Inn ✔

Canning Circus, NG7 3NE

12-11; 12-10.30 Sun

☎ (0115) 978 2770 website: www.thefalconinn.co.uk

Adnams Bitter, Broadside; Wells Bombardier; guest beer Ⓗ

Small, traditional public house with a regular local clientele. It is situated at the top of Derby Road/Alfreton Road, where the traffic system has created an oasis of calm, allowing an outdoor pavement drinking area to flourish in summer. Limited on-street parking is available after 6pm. The main bar has a discreet TV in the corner dedicated to rugby and cricket, and there is a 30-seater restaurant upstairs serving top quality food (booking recommended). Q ❀ ◑

Johnson Arms ✔

59 Abbey Street, Lenton, NG7 2NZ

12-11; 12-10.30 Sun

☎ (0115) 978 6355 website: www.johnsonarms.co.uk

Wadworth 6X; guest beers Ⓗ

Large, single-bar pub with three seating areas, situated near the QMC Hospital. Popular with locals and appealing to all ages, it fosters a good community spirit. The pub is run by four partners who work as a co-operative. There are up to five changing guest ales. A special food menu is available on live music nights and on Sunday meals are served 12-4pm. The pub benefits from a large, tranquil garden. Frequent beer festivals are held. ♔ ❀ ◑ ♣

Moulders Arms

Bovill Street, Radford, NG7 3PG

11-11; 12-10.30 Sun

☎ (0115) 924 9736

Oakwell Brewery Old Tom Mild; Barnsley Bitter Ⓗ

Back-street pub which has earned a Lord Mayor's Charter award for its services to the local community. Food is served in the lounge from 11-4pm and no smoking is allowed during that time. Children are permitted in the lounge. The public bar has plenty of seating and a pool table; a fine example of a locals' pub. ◑ ⊟ ♿ P

Plough

17 St Peters Street, Radford, NG7 3EN (off Ilkeston Rd)

12-2.30, 5-11; 12-11 Thu-Sat; 12-10.30 Sun

☎ (0115) 942 2649

website: www.nottinghambrewery.com

Nottingham Rock Ale Mild, Rock Ale Bitter, Legend, Extra Pale Ale, Bullion; guest beers Ⓗ

This splendid 1840s local is the tap for Nottingham Brewery which is situated at the rear. Tuesday is curry night and free chilli is served on Thursday evening. Live music is hosted occasionally, and barbecues are popular in summer. The outdoor skittles alley is an added attraction. As well as the range of Nottingham ales, draught Dutch and Belgian beers are served (not cask conditioned). Local CAMRA Pub of the Year 2004, it was the Mild Trail winner in 2003 and 2004.

♔ ❀ ⊟ ♣ P

Orston

Durham Ox

Church Street, NG13 9NS

12-3, 6-11; 11.30-11 Sat; 12-3, 6-10.30 Sun

☎ (01949) 850059

Fuller's London Pride; Greene King IPA; Marston's Burton Bitter, Pedigree; guest beers Ⓗ

Delightful village pub, popular with locals and visitors alike. It has a garden and pavement café tables in summer and a roaring fire in winter. There is ample parking and hitching rails for horses (and ferrets!). The bar room has an interesting whisky collection in one half and aviation pictures and memorabilia in the other. There is no hot food but filled rolls can be made to order. Pub games are often played here.

♔ Q ❀ ⊟ ≹ ♣ P ⁄

Oxton

Olde Bridge Inn ✔

Nottingham Road, NG25 0SE (off A6097 roundabout)

12-2.30, 6-11; closed Mon; 12-11 Sat; 12-5 (10.30 summer) Sun

☎ (0115) 965 2013

Adnams Broadside; Caledonian Deuchars IPA; Taylor Landlord; Wells Bombardier; guest beers Ⓗ

Elegant example of Arts and Crafts architecture in a rural setting. The interior comprises a bar, lounge, snug, garden room and a restaurant. A minimum of four beers are available, plus a varied wine and spirits range. The creative menu features excellent local produce including vegetarian options prepared by the resident chef. The pub is popular with cyclists and ramblers exploring the area. The large garden has three patio areas. ❀ ◑ ♿ P ⁄

Radcliffe on Trent

Black Lion

Main Road, NG12 2FD

12 (11 Sat)-11; 12-10.30 Sun

☎ (0115) 933 2138

Courage Directors; Greene King IPA; Taylor Landlord; guest beers Ⓗ

Popular, spacious pub in the village centre, serving three guest ales. Food is served in the comfortable lounge with home-cooked dishes and an extensive specials board. The lively public bar has a large-screen TV for sport and regular live music is featured in the Den upstairs. The large, enclosed garden has a children's play area and is also the setting for the annual spring bank holiday beer festival and spectacular bonfire night display. Traditional cider is sold in summer at local CAMRA Pub of Excellence award winner 2003. ♔ ❀ ◑ ⊟ ♿ ≹ ♣ ● P ⁄

Retford

Rum Runner

Wharf Road, DN22 6EN (50 yds from fire station)

11.30-11, 12-10.30 Sun

☎ (01777) 860788

Bateman XB, XXXB; guest beers Ⓗ

This town-centre pub, now owned by Bateman Brewery, was local CAMRA Pub of the Year 2002 and is a regular Pub of the Season winner. The local Broadstone Brewery is situated in outbuildings at the rear and the brewer can be seen at work from the lounge area or garden. Three guest ales are always available and will often include a Broadstone product; in addition there is a good selection of foreign bottled beers. The lounge area has a couple of soft sofas, but can get busy at the weekends. In winter you will be welcomed by a roaring fire. ♛❀◐ ⇌♣

Turks Head

Grove Street, DN22 6LA (200 yds from market square)

✪ 11-3, 7-11; 11-11 Sat; 12-3, 7-10.30 Sun

☎ (01777) 702742

Adnams Bitter; Courage Directors; Tetley Bitter 🄷

Attractive, oak-panelled pub off the town centre. A warm welcome is assured at this supporter of real ales. Food is served daily and the pub is noted for the quality of its Sunday roasts. While there is a pool table, there are also plenty of quiet corners where you can sit and enjoy conversation. Wednesday is quiz night. ♛Q◐♣

Ruddington

Three Crowns

23 Easthorpe Street, NG11 6LB

✪ 12-3, 5-11; 12-11 Sat; 12-10.30 Sun

☎ (0115) 921 3226

Adnams Bitter; Nottingham Rock Ale Mild, EPA; Taylor Landlord; guest beers 🄷

Friendly village pub – known locally as Top House. Newly refurbished, with a large, single bar, the pub boasts six handpumps including two guest beers. The restaurant specialises in Thai cuisine and Thai bottled beers are also available. Look out for the tuk-tuk. The country park is nearby and the pub is popular with walkers. ◐

Selston

Horse & Jockey

Church Lane, NG16 6FB OS464539

✪ 12-3, 5-11; 12-3, 7-10.30 Sun

☎ (01773) 781012

Draught Bass; 🄷 **Greene King Abbot; Taylor Landlord;** 🄶 **guest beers** 🄷

This friendly village local, dating back to 1664, is reputedly haunted. The interior has a main bar, snug and lounge with cast iron range. Low-beamed ceilings, flagstone floors and open fires give a warm and cosy feel. You are welcome to play pool or a selection of pub games in the games room. Winner of several local CAMRA awards and Nottinghamshire CAMRA Pub of the Year 2004, two beers are always served from the cellar in jugs. ♛Q❀♿♣P

South Leverton

Plough Inn

Town Street, DN22 0BT

✪ 4 (12 Sat)-11; 12-10.30 Sun

☎ (01427) 880323

Greene King Ruddles County; guest beers 🄷

Small, friendly village inn that also houses the post office. You could drive through the village and not see the pub, opposite the village hall, but then you would miss out on a little gem. Some of the seating appears to be old church pews. The locals will make you feel welcome and there certainly cannot be many pubs where you can drink a pint and buy your stamps at the same time. It was a recent local CAMRA Pub of the Season award winner.

Q❀⛺♣P

Southwell

Bramley Apple

51 Church Street, NG25 0HQ

✪ 12-2.30, 6 (5 Fri & Sat)-11; 12-10.30 Sun

☎ (01636) 813675 website: www.thebramleyapple.co.uk

Springhead Bitter; guest beers 🄷

Somewhere between a pub and a restaurant, the Bramley offers good home-cooked food and an excellent choice of beers: seven pumps serve two Springhead ales and five guests. Wholesome, freshly-prepared lunchtime and evening meals are available from a varied menu and live entertainment is staged every Sunday. The pub is well situated for discovering Southwell's rich history. ❀⛟◐♿⛺♣●

Old Coach House

69 Easthorpe, NG25 0HY (on A612 heading to Upton)

✪ 5 (4 Fri; 12 Sat)-11; 12-10.30 Sun

☎ (01636) 813289

Draught Bass; guest beers 🄷

This traditional pub has a long-established commitment to beer, with five guest ales, including a mild, largely from micros, always on offer. The central bar serves several drinking areas and there is a cast iron range fire in winter. An imaginatively-designed patio provides a pleasant outdoor drinking area. This genuine local offers a friendly welcome to all and was voted Newark CAMRA Pub of the Year 2005. ♛Q❀⊟♣●

Sutton on Trent

Memory Lane

35 Main Street, NG23 6PF

✪ 12-2 (not Wed); 5-11; 12-11 Sat; 12-10.30 Sun

☎ (01636) 821071

Everards Tiger; guest beers 🄷

Opaque windows hide a friendly village local with a public and lounge bar/family room. The public bar has five areas each themed with a different sport. The walls are covered with photographs and memorabilia. Guest beers come from micro-breweries and local brews are well represented. There is a small restaurant area at the rear of the lounge. Outside is a patio and garden with a children's play area. ❀⛟◐⊟♣P

Watnall

Royal Oak ✔

25 Main Road, NG16 1HU (on B600)

✪ 12-11; 12-10.30 Sun

☎ (0115) 938 3110

Hardys & Hansons Bitter, Olde Trip, seasonal beers 🄷

Friendly roadside local with an interesting collection of dog ornaments and photographs. A cosy, relaxing upstairs lounge is open at weekends. The log cabin at the back now holds regular beer festivals and occasional live 1960s nights. Pool is played in the back room and sport is shown on TV. Freshly-made rolls are readily available. The No. 331 bus passes the door.

❀⊟P

Wellow

Olde Red Lion

Eakring Road, NG22 0EG

⏲ 11.30-3.30, 6-11; 11-11 Sat; 12-10.30 Sun

☎ (01623) 861000

Black Sheep Best Bitter; Shepherd Neame Spitfire; Wells Bombardier Ⓗ

Regular winner of local CAMRA Pub of the Season awards, this 400-year-old pub, with exposed beams, stands opposite the village green and maypole. The walls of the bar are covered in old photographs and maps which depict the history of both the pub and the village. There is a small lounge bar and restaurant where good home-cooked food is served daily. It is situated close to Clumber and Rufford country parks and Center Parcs Holiday Village. May Day is busy when children from the village dance round the maypole.

Q❀◑▲♣P⚟

West Bridgford

Southbank Bar

1 Bridgford House, Trent Bridge, NG2 5GJ

⏲ 11-11; 10-midnight Thu-Sun

☎ (0115) 945 5541

website: www.southbankbar.co.uk

Caledonian Deuchars IPA; Mallard Duck 'n' Dive; guest beers Ⓗ

Large, lively bar on Trent Bridge, handy for the cricket and both football grounds. It has comfortable seating and a patio overlooking the Trent. An independently owned free house, it always offers a beer from Mallard. The Globe, its sister pub, is just over the bridge. A varied selection of food is available all day, including breakfast at the weekend from 10am. Live music is played on Thursday-Sunday evenings. Several TVs show sport and there is a large screen for major games. ❀◑♿

Stratford Haven

2 Stratford Road, NG2 6BA

⏲ 10.30-11; 10.30-midnight Fri & Sat; 12-10.30 Sun

☎ (0115) 982 5981

Adnams Broadside; Bateman XB; Caledonian Deuchars IPA; Castle Rock Harvest Pale, Hemlock, Nottingham Gold; guest beers Ⓗ

Busy, gimmick-free Tynemill pub, tucked away next to the Co-op, between the town centre and Trent Bridge cricket ground. Named as the result of a competition in the local press, the winning entry is on display. The beer range includes at least one mild and Castle Rock house beers. Monthly brewery nights feature all the selected brewery's beers, and are usually accompanied by live music. A good menu is served 12-8pm (6pm Sun), including vegetarian options.

Q❀◑♿P⚟

West Leake

Star

Melton Lane, LE12 5RQ

⏲ 11-11; 12-10.30 Sun

☎ (01509) 852233

Caledonian Deuchars IPA; Draught Bass; guest beers Ⓗ

Also known locally as the Pit House after nearby disused gypsum excavations, this pretty, white-painted pub has a quintessentially English country bar complete with beams, high-backed settles, open fire and quarry-tiled floor. There is an adjoining no-smoking family room. The lounge features a central stone hearth, wood-panelled walls supporting a fine array of tankards and old bottles, and plenty of polished brassware. No food is served on Sunday evening. ⌂Q☺❀⇌◑⊟♿P⚟

West Stockwith

White Hart

Main Street, DN10 4ET

⏲ 11.30-11; 12-10.30 Sun

☎ (01427) 890176

Taylor Landlord; guest beers Ⓗ

Small country pub with a little garden overlooking the River Trent, Chesterfield Canal and West Stockwith Marina. One bar serves the through bar, lounge and dining area. Daleside beers are often available to accompany the freshly cooked food. The area is especially busy during the summer, due to the volume of river traffic. West Stockwith is where the Chesterfield Canal joins the River Trent. Q❀◑♿▲♣P

Worksop

Mallard

Station Approach, S81 7AG

⏲ 5 (2 Fri; 12 Sat)-11; 12-4 Sun

☎ (01909) 530757

Beer range varies Ⓗ

Local CAMRA Pub of the Year 2004 and regular winner of Pub of the Season awards. Formerly Worksop Station Buffet, this pub offers a warm welcome. Two real ales are always available together with a large selection of foreign bottled beers and country fruit wines. A further room is available downstairs for special occasions such as the three beer festivals the pub holds each year. Q▲⇌P

Regency Hotel

Carlton Road, S81 7AG (opp. station)

⏲ 11-2, 7-11; 12-2, 7-10.30 Sun

☎ (01909) 474108

John Smith's Magnet; guest beers Ⓗ

Situated opposite the station, on the edge of the town centre, this large hotel has one bar and a dining area. Following its inclusion in CAMRA's 2005 Good Beer Guide, the Regency has now added a third handpull, allowing it to dispense two guest ales as well as the regular John Smith's Magnet. It is popular at lunchtimes due to the good selection of reasonably priced food.

Q❀◑▲⇌P

Shireoaks Inn

Westgate, S80 1LT (200 yds from market)

⏲ 11.30-4, 6-11; 11.30-11 Sat; 12-4.30, 7-10.30 Sun

☎ (01909) 472118

Beer range varies Ⓗ

Warm, friendly pub, converted from cottages. The public bar houses a pool table and large screen TV. There is a comfortable lounge bar and dining area where tasty home-cooked food represents good value. The two handpulls dispense varying guest ales. A small outside area with tables is available in the summer.

Q❀◑⊟▲⇌♣⚟

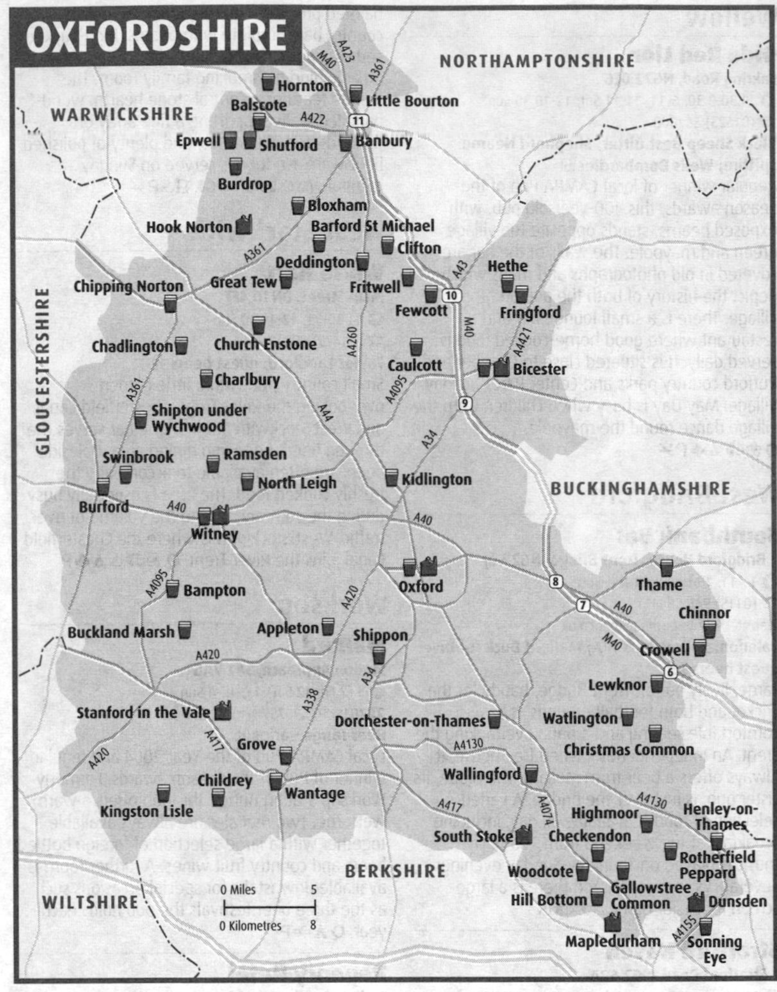

Appleton

Plough Inn

Eaton Road, OX13 5JR

12-3, 6-11; 12-3, 6-10.30 Sun

☎ (01865) 862441

Greene King XX Mild, IPA, Morland Original H

Convivial, 17th-century stone-built pub in the centre of the village. Visitors are assured of a warm welcome as soon as they set foot inside the door. There are three interconnected rooms served from a single bar. The small public bar – almost a snug – has a coal fire in winter. The landlord sees no need for either a juke box or gaming machine; earnest debate and lively conversation are the main sources of entertainment here – with the landlord playing a prominent part in both. Q P

Balscote

Butcher's Arms

Shutford Road, OX15 6JQ

(½ mile S of A422 Banbury-Stratford road)

12-2 (3.30 Sat; not Mon-Tue), 6.30-11; 12-3.30, 7-10.30 Sun

☎ (01295) 730750

Hook Norton Best Bitter, seasonal beers; H **guest beers** G

Situated in picturesque countryside, this welcoming pub is built of local Hornton stone. Comfortably furnished, the bar is enhanced with a small library, TV, pool table and friendly dog. In the summer the garden provides a relaxing, quiet area and is a good finishing point for a country walk. Aunt Sally is played in season. Folk music sessions are held every second Wednesday. Meals are served on Friday, Saturday, and Sunday lunchtime. P

INDEPENDENT BREWERIES

Brakspear Witney
Butler's Mapledurham
Hook Norton Hook Norton
Loddon Dunsden
Meesons Oxford
Ridgeway South Stoke
White Horse Stanford in the Vale
Wychwood Witney

Bampton

Morris Clown

High Street, OX18 2JW

5 (11 Sat)-11; 12-10.30 Sun

☎ (01993) 850217

Brakspear Bitter; Courage Best Bitter; guest beer H

Formerly run by the landlord's father, this has been a great pub with good beer for many years. The single bar is decorated with Toulouse-Lautrec style murals, and there is a juke box with music supplied by the landlord and locals. The pub's name reflects its morris dancing connections – the village has upheld the tradition for 600 years and a major morris dancing festival is held every Whit Monday. ♔❀♣●P

Banbury

Bell Inn ✔

Middleton Road, Grimsbury, OX16 4QJ

(from town and rail station over Bridge Street)

1-3.30, 7-11; 12-11 Sat; 12-5, 8-10.30 Sun

☎ (01295) 253169

Adnams Bitter; Bateman XB; Hancock's HB; Highgate Dark; Jennings Cumberland Ale; guest beers H

Dave and Shirley have been running the Bell for 20 years. A regular entry in this Guide, this traditional two-room pub is the only one in the area to sell Highgate Mild. It was voted North Oxon CAMRA Mild Pub of the Year in 2004. In winter the real fire adds to the appeal. Ideally situated close to the canal, rail and coach stations, the pub is well worth a visit. ♔❀⊟⇌P

Olde Reindeer

47 Parsons Street, OX16 5NA

11-11; 12-3 (closed eve) Sun

☎ 01295 264031

Hook Norton Hooky Dark, Best Bitter, Old Hooky, seasonal beer; guest beers H

Oliver Cromwell is said to have held councils of war in this 15th-century Hook Norton-owned pub. The Globe Room is famous for its old panelling which was retrieved from an Islington factory and brought back to Banbury in the mid-1960s. This warm, welcoming pub has high, beamed ceilings, a wooden floor and an open fire in winter. Home-cooked food is served at lunchtimes. A range of Hook Norton beers is on offer, as well as a selection of fruit wines plus mulled wine in winter. ♔Q♘❀◐⊟♿⇌♣P⚡

Barford St Michael

George Inn

Lower Street, OX15 0RH

(1½ miles off B4031 6 miles SW of Banbury)

7-11; 12-4 & 7-10 summer) Sun

☎ (01869) 838226

Greene King IPA; guest beers H

Charming, thatched village inn dating from 1672. There is a pool table in the back bar and regular quiz evenings are held. Live folk or pop bands play occasionally. Themed food evenings are also popular. Weddings and celebrations can be catered for in a marquee in the large rear garden with scenic countryside views. Aunt Sally is played in the garden. Look out for Dillon, the pub dog – he loves to investigate handbags! ♔❀♿⛺♣P

Bicester

Swan Inn

13 Church Street, OX26 6AY

11-11; 12-3, 7-10.30 Sun

☎ (01869) 369035

Brakspear Bitter, seasonal beers H

Refurbished by Brakspear in 2003, this comfortable, stylish bar has given a much-needed boost to the local pub scene. The split-level bar has now been opened out into one room, with a contemporary feel enjoyed by drinkers and diners alike. The imaginative and reasonably priced pub food is popular, as is the excellent choice of local Brakspear's ales. The Swan is the only pub in Bicester to stock real cider. ♔⇄◐◑⇌●

Bloxham

Elephant & Castle

Humber Street, OX15 4LZ

(off A361 4 miles W of Banbury)

11-3, 5-11; 11-11 Sat; 12-10.30 Sun

☎ (01295) 720383

Hook Norton Best Bitter, seasonal beers; guest beers H

Welcoming 16th-century coaching inn with a wide carriage entrance to the garden, car park and front doors. Open fires blaze in winter. Home-cooked meals and snacks are available at lunchtime Monday-Saturday. The original bread oven remains in the restaurant area. There is a pleasant terrace overlooking the Aunt Sally pitch. Chas, the friendly landlord, has run this pub for more than 30 years. ♔❀⇄◐⊟♿P

Buckland Marsh

Trout at Tadpole Bridge

SN7 8RF (off A420 towards Bampton) OS335004

11.30-3, 6-11; 12-3 (12-10.30 July & Aug) Sun

☎ (01367) 870382 website: www.troutinn.co.uk

Young's Bitter; White Horse Oxfordshire Bitter; guest beers H

Splendid pub in an idyllic setting next to the upper reaches of the River Thames. Visitors travel from afar to enjoy the excellent cuisine, mostly made using locally-sourced ingredients. Fresh fish, landed in the West Country and delivered the next day, is a speciality. The Trout provides an ideal refreshment stop for walkers along the Thames footpath, and there are moorings for those travelling by boat. En-suite accommodation is available, with disabled facilities. ♔❀⇄◐◑♿♣P

Burdrop, Sibford Gower

Bishop Blaize Inn

OX15 5RQ (½ mile W of B4035 between Sibford Gower and Sibford Ferris) OS359379

12-2.30, 6-11; 12-3, 7-10.30 Sun

☎ (01295) 780323

website: www.bishopblaize.co.uk

Vale Best Bitter; Theakston Best Bitter; guest beer H

Warm and friendly, family-run, 17th-century village inn set on the edge of the hamlet of Burdrop. The landscaped gardens have extensive views along the deep Sib Valley and over to Sibford School. The main bar is oak beamed with an inglenook and wood-burning stove; to one side of the fireplace is Sam's library – with plenty of good reading. The sympathetically extended restaurant has an excellent pub food menu, and meals can also served in the garden. ♔Q❀◐◑⊟♣P

Burford

Royal Oak

26 Witney Street, OX18 4SN (off A361)
✪ 11-2.30 (not Tue), 6.30-11; 11-11 Sat; 11-3, 7-10.30 Sun
☎ (01993) 823278
Wadworth IPA, 6X; guest beer Ⓗ
Tucked away in a side street, this is a genuine local with a traditional pub atmosphere. The flagstoned front bar leads to a long, carpeted side bar with a bar billiards table. The walls are decorated with photographs and memorabilia. An ancient clock chimes melodiously. Around 1,000 tankards hang from the ceilings. Excellent home-made food using local produce is served. Walkers are welcome and can make use of the special boot scraper.
♔Q❀⇄◐◑▲♣●P

Caulcott

Horse & Groom

Lower Heyford Road, OX25 4ND
(on B4030 between Middleton Stony and Lower Heyford)
✪ 11-3, 6-11; 12-3, 7-10.30 Sun
☎ (01869) 343257
Hook Norton Best Bitter; guest beer Ⓗ
A small country pub with a big welcome and cosy atmosphere. Three frequently changing guest beers are available with the trend now towards brews from local small and micro-breweries, giving an excellent choice. Good a la carte meals and speciality sausages are served in the bar or restaurant at this twice local CAMRA Pub of the Year winner.
♔Q❀◐◑♿

Chadlington

Tite Inn

Mill End, OX7 3NY (off A361 2 miles S of Chipping Norton)
✪ 12-2.30, 6.30-11; closed Mon; 12-3, 7-10.30 Sun
☎ (01608) 676475
website: www.titeinn.com
Butcombe Bitter; Young's Bitter; guest beers Ⓗ
Cotswold stone free house run by the same family for 18 years. The attractive garden offers fine views, and colourful shrubs line the path from the car park. Two comfortably-furnished connecting bars and a restaurant are supplemented by the garden room in summer. Excellent, freshly prepared food and five real ales are served. Guinness has been replaced by a micro-brewery draught stout. The pub is a focus for village activities including an annual pantomime, cricket team and Easter egg rolling. Check out the immaculate toilets.
♔Q❀◐◑♿▲♣●P

Charlbury

Rose & Crown ✔

Market Street, OX7 3PL
✪ 12 (11 Sat)-11; 12-10.30 Sun
☎ (01608) 810103
Young's Bitter; guest beers Ⓗ
Popular, traditional, town-centre free house, 19 years in this Guide. Simply furnished, it has a split-level bar with separate no-smoking lounge, plus a patio courtyard. On the Oxfordshire Way long-distance path, walkers are welcome to bring their own food. A pub for the discerning drinker, six real ales are offered – the best selection in the area. A strong supporter of micro-breweries, the Rose & Crown has twice been North Oxon CAMRA Pub of the Year.
❀▲⇌●⚡

Checkendon

Black Horse

Burncote Lane, RG8 0TE (off A4074, through village, second left after red phone box) OS667481
✪ 12-2, 7-11; 12-2, 7-10.30 Sun
☎ (01491) 680418
Butler's Oxfordshire Bitter; West Berkshire Old Father Thames, Good Old Boy Ⓖ
Old equestrian inn deep in the South Chiltern woodlands, run by the same family for over a century. Hard to find – the unnamed lane it is on is very narrow and easy to miss. The pub has three rooms, each with its own character. Ale is served by gravity from casks in the dairy adjacent to the bar. Ramblers and horse riders are welcome. Baguettes are usually available at lunchtime. ♔Q❀▲P

Childrey

Hatchet

Main Street, OX12 9UF (on B4001)
✪ 12-2.30 (3.30 Sat), 7-11; 12-3.30, 7-10.30 Sun
☎ (01235) 751213
Greene King Morland Original; guest beers Ⓗ
Situated not far from the duckpond in this picture postcard village, the Hatchet offers a warm welcome and a fine array of ales to suit all tastes. The interior of the pub is open plan with a quieter drinking and dining area off to one side. As well as the usual pub games, there is shove-ha'penny and an Aunt Sally pitch. A well-deserved winner of local CAMRA Pub of the Year in 2004, it lies on the Wantage-Farringdon bus route. ❀◐◑▲♣P

Chinnor

Red Lion ✔

3 High Street, OX39 4DL (on B4009)
✪ 12-3, 5-11; 12-11 Fri & Sat; 12-10.30 Sun
☎ (01844) 353468
Adnams Bitter; Draught Bass; Greene King IPA; guest beers Ⓗ
This 300-year-old friendly village local was originally three cottages. It is situated near the village centre but within easy access of the fine Chiltern countryside and a local steam railway. The outside drinking area has recently been refurbished and wooden decking added. The pub supports an Aunt Sally team. Guest ales change three times a week. ♔Q❀◐◑⊟♣P

Chipping Norton

Chequers ✔

Goddards Lane, OX7 5NP
⌚ 11-11; 12-10.30 Sun
☎ (01608) 644717
website: www.chequers-pub.co.uk
Fuller's Chiswick, London Pride, ESB, seasonal beers 🄷
Town-centre pub with a warm, welcoming atmosphere and friendly service from an efficient team. Divided into four seating areas, it has a separate meeting room and covered courtyard restaurant. A mix of traditional and Thai food is served. A convenient meeting point for the adjacent theatre, it is a popular venue for all ages and a frequent award winner. ⌂Q◑◐

Christmas Common

Fox & Hounds

OX49 5HL (off B480/B481 and B4009) OS715932
⌚ 11-3.30, 6-11; 11.30-11 Sat; 12-10.30 Sun
☎ (01491) 612599
Brakspear Bitter, Special, seasonal beers 🄷/🄶
Although the emphasis here is on good food, drinkers are always welcome. Organic food is a speciality and bar snacks are available. The barn conversion restaurant is popular and booking is advised. Meals are served lunchtime and evening (except Sun eve). Beer can be dispensed by gravity or handpump on request. In front of the pub is an outdoor drinking area, and there is a small front garden, making it a popular destination for walkers and cyclists.
⌂Q✿◑◐⊟▲P

Church Enstone

Crown

OX7 4NN (off A44)
⌚ 12-3 (not Mon), 6-11; 12-3 (closed eve) Sun
☎ (01608) 677262
website: www.crowninnenstone.co.uk
Hook Norton Best Bitter; guest beers 🄷
Picturesque Cotswold stone pub in a quiet village dating from the 17th century. An inglenook and local photographs add to the character. The separate no-smoking restaurant features fresh fish, seafood and game (in season), and uses local produce (no food Mon). Popular with locals and visitors who can enjoy pleasant conversation without intrusive music or games machines, it is an ideal place to enjoy a well-earned drink after a walk in the delightful surrounding countryside. ⌂Q✿◑◐P

Clifton

Duke of Cumberland's Head

Main Street, OX15 0PE (on B4031)
⌚ 12-2.30 (not winter Mon), 6.30-11; 12-2.30, 6.30-10.30 (not winter eve) Sun
☎ (01869) 338534
Caledonian Deuchars IPA; Hook Norton Best Bitter; guest beers 🄷
Built in 1645, this attractive, peaceful pub, situated close to the canal, is popular, especially at weekends. Named after Prince Rupert, who led the King's troops in the Battle of Edgehill in 1642, the low-beamed lounge has a large fireplace with a cosy log fire. The no-smoking dining room has exposed stone walls – none of which is straight, nor is the ceiling! Three excellent real ales, together with over 30 whiskies, await you at this warm, welcoming pub.
⌂Q✿⇌◑◐♿P

Crowell

Shepherd's Crook

The Green, OX39 4RR
(off B4009 between Chinnor and M40 jct 6) OS744997
⌚ 11.30-3, 5-11; 11-11 Sat; 12-10.30 Sun
☎ (01844) 351431
Batham Best Bitter; Taylor Landlord; Young's Bitter; guest beers 🄷
In the foothills of the Chilterns, this comfortable inn was known as the Catherine Wheel until 1991. The current landlord, who took over in 1996, is a real ale fanatic and this is one of the few pubs in the area to sell Batham Bitter, as well as stocking Loddon ales. A former fish merchant, his fresh fish comes direct from the West Country, while excellent steak and kidney pies and steaks come from the local butcher. It was voted local CAMRA Pub of the Year 2004.
⌂Q✿◑◐♣P

Deddington

Deddington Arms Hotel

Horsefair, OX15 0SH
(50 yds off A4260 towards Market Square)
⌚ 10-11; 12-10.30 Sun
☎ (01869) 338364
website: www.oxfordshire-hotels.co.uk
Caledonian Deuchars IPA; Greene King IPA; Tetley Bitter; guest beers 🄷
This 16th to 17th-century gabled and stuccoed hotel has been refurbished and enlarged in keeping with its age and character. In the flagstone-floored bar are window seats overlooking the picturesque market square, plus an open fire in winter. Two of the bedrooms have four-poster beds. There is a no-smoking restaurant and two functions rooms to hire. Tables on the pavement in front of this south-facing hotel are popular in summer for outdoor drinking.
⌂✿⇌◑◐♿P⊬

Dorchester-on-Thames

White Hart Hotel

26 High Street, OX10 7HN (off A4074)
⌚ 11-11; 12-10.30 Sun
☎ (01491) 340074
website: www.white-hart-hotel-dorchester.co.uk
Fuller's London Pride; Greene King IPA; Tetley Bitter 🄷
Situated in the middle of the village, this 17th-century hotel is close to the 12th-century abbey. The inn was sensitively refurbished, maintaining its old beams and olde-worlde atmosphere. The hotel has a good reputation for food: the restaurant is open every day, lunchtime and evening, and bar snacks are also available. Dorchester-on-Thames is an attractive village with many fine old buildings, and is near the rivers Thames and Thame.
⌂Q⇌◑◐♿P⊽

Epwell

Chandler's Arms

Sibford Road, OX15 6LH

(off B4039 Banbury to Shipston Road) OS353403

⏲ 11.30-11; 12-10.30 Sun

☎ (01295) 780394

Hook Norton Best Bitter, Old Hooky, seasonal beers; guest beer Ⓗ

On the Warwickshire border, in a popular walking area, this traditional two-room village pub has a cosy, lived-in feel. The pub has evolved over the years but has retained its original character and remains a rural idyll. Small but comfortable, there is a lounge area where rugby internationals are screened. Pub games are available, including the locally popular Aunt Sally. Food is served all day every day.

Q❀◐◑⊟♣P

Fringford

Butchers Arms

Main Street, OX27 8EB

⏲ 12-3.30, 6-11; 12-11 Sat; 12-4.30, 7-11 Sun

☎ (01869) 277363

Draught Bass; Caledonian Deuchars IPA; Marston's Pedigreee Ⓗ

Small, village-centred, stone-built pub overlooking the cricket green. Open-plan bars are separated into three areas: a 'public' area with a large TV, juke box and dartboard, a quieter, beamed, fireside 'lounge' and a small area by the restaurant. Meals include simple bar snacks, home-made pies, steaks and daily specials, in addition to an extensive, regular menu. Meals are served in the bar and the adjoining no-smoking restaurant.

⛰❀◐◑♿⛺P⚡

Fewcott

White Lion

Fritwell Road, OX27 7NZ

(near jct 10, M40, 300 yds off B4130) OS539279

⏲ 7 (5.30 Fri; 12 Sat)-11; 12-6.30 Sun

☎ (01869) 346639

Beer range varies Ⓗ

Village pub with a cosy and spacious bar, popular for sports, with a games room for darts and pool. A true free house, the White Lion has constantly changing guest ales, often including a porter, stout or mild. Families are welcome, and there is a large, quiet garden at the rear.

⛰❀♿♣P

Fritwell

King's Head

92 East Street, OX27 7QF

(2 miles W of jct 10, M40)

⏲ 12-midnight; 12-10.30 Sun

☎ (01869) 346738

website: www.thekingsheadfritwell.co.uk

Fuller's London Pride; Hook Norton Best Bitter; guest beers Ⓗ

Typical Oxfordshire village pub with a welcoming cosy fire. The well-kept real ales are often available on gravity, if you ask. A popular bottled beer festival is held in the spring, and the landlord holds many other pub events – check the website for details. Food is served daily, except Monday – the casseroles are highly recommended.

⛰❀◑P

Gallowstree Common

Reformation

Horsepond Road, RG4 9BP

(1 mile E of A4074 at Cane End)

⏲ 11-3, 6-11; 12-5 (closed eve) Sun

☎ (0118) 972 3126

Brakspear Bitter, Special, seasonal beers Ⓗ

Excellent local pub serving good value food, lunchtimes and evenings. Fish and steaks are specialities. Families are welcome – there is a children's play area in the garden. Twice monthly folk evenings are held as well as singing and jam sessions when locals bring in their own instruments. The pub hosts an annual log splitting competition where teams of four try for the quickest time – raising money for charity.

Q❀◐◑⊟♣P

Great Tew

Falkland Arms ✔

19-21 The Green, OX7 4DB (off A361 and B4022)

⏲ 11.30-2.30 (3 Sat), 6-11 (11.30-11 summer Sat); 12-3, 7-10.30 (12-10.30 summer) Sun

☎ (01608) 683653

website: www.falklandarms.org.uk

Wadworth IPA, 6X; guest beers Ⓗ

Set in a quiet thatched village, this pub is a haven for drinkers, with an unspoilt, relaxed atmosphere where mobile phones are banned. Oak-panelled walls, flagstone and board floors, and an inglenook fire to warm you in winter, add to the olde-worlde character. Old farm tools and drinking vessels hang from the oak beams. A regular CAMRA award winner, it offers up to four guest ales. A range of whiskies, country wines and snuffs are available, and high quality food is served (not Sun eve). ⛰Q❀🛏◐●

Grove

Volunteer

Station Road, OX12 0DH (on A338, 2 miles N of Wantage)

⏲ 11-11; 12-10.30 Sun

☎ (01235) 769557

Hook Norton Hooky Dark, Best Bitter, Generation, Old Hooky, seasonal beers; guest beer Ⓗ

Popular, open-plan pub, one of Hook Norton's more remote outposts. The Volunteer was originally built to serve the former Wantage Road station and the terminus of the old Wantage tramway. In the courtyard, there is a pitch for Aunt Sally, the traditional pub game peculiar to this part of Oxfordshire. Buses pass by regularly on their way to Oxford and Wantage. Westons Old Rosie cider is served in summer. No food is served on Monday.

❀◐♣●P▯

Henley-on-Thames

Bird in Hand

61 Greys Road, RG9 1SB (200 yds SW of A4155)

⏲ 11.30-2.30, 5-11; 11.30-11 Sat; 12-10.30 Sun

☎ (01491) 575775

Brakspear Bitter; Fuller's London Pride; Hook Norton Hooky Dark; guest beers Ⓗ
Henley's only genuine free house, this friendly, one-bar, town-centre local is popular with regulars and visitors. Pub quizzes are held fortnightly. The large, secure garden has an aviary, pond and pets, and is reached through the family room. Two guest beers often come from micro-breweries. The pub has teams in both men's and ladies' local darts leagues. Reasonably priced lunches are served weekdays. Henley is famed for the Royal Regatta and its Festival (both July) and its River and Rowing Museum.
Q❀◐Ă⇌♣🗑

Hethe

Whitmore Arms

Main Street, OX27 8ES
7 (6 Fri)-11; 12-3, 7-11 Sat; 12-3, 7-10.30 Sun
☎ (01869) 277654
Brakspear Bitter; Ⓗ **Fuller's London Pride;** Ⓖ **Hook Norton Best Bitter,** Ⓗ **seasonal beers** Ⓖ
Quiet and unassuming, this 18th-century, stone-built village local has a welcoming and relaxed atmosphere. Old farm implements and memorabilia hang on the walls of the single bar room, which has a large inglenook at one end and a comfortable lounge area at the other. There is a games room for darts, pool and table football. Excellent value home-cooked meals are served.
❀◐Ă♣P🗑

Highmoor

Dog & Duck

RG9 5DL (on B481)
11.30-3, 6-11; 12-3, 7-10.30 (closed Oct-Mar eve) Sun
☎ (01491) 641261
Brakspear Bitter, Special Ⓗ
Unspoilt, country-cottage style pub dating from the 17th century. It has three rooms – a traditional snug, a bar and dining room with quarry-tiled floor, benches and wood panelling, and a further dining room. The pub is popular with locals and visitors alike; families, walkers and dogs are all welcome. The food menu is varied and reasonably priced, with good home-made dishes. The notable selection of fresh fish comes direct from Cornwall.
Q❀◐♣P

Hill Bottom

Sun

RG8 7PU (½ mile E of B471) OS644793
12-11; 12-10.30 Sun
☎ (0118) 984 2260
Brakspear Bitter, Special; Hook Norton Hooky Dark Ⓗ
Despite the hamlet's name, this pub is not at the foot of a hill. Hill Bottom adjoins Whitchurch Hill to the east. The pub is ideally situated on the edge of the Chilterns in an area of outstanding natural beauty, and is popular with walkers. Excellent meat dishes are recommended – the landlord was previously a butcher. No food is served on Sunday-Monday evening. Children are welcome in the large garden.
❀◐♿P

Hornton

Dun Cow

OX15 6DA
7-11; 12-3, 7-11 Sat; 12-3, 7-10.30 Sun
☎ (01295) 670524
Hook Norton Best Bitter; Wells Bombardier; guest beers Ⓗ
Classic, hidden-away, thatched, low beamed and flagstone-floored pub in a remote village close to the Warwickshire border. It was a butcher's slaughterhouse until 1840 and retains much of its character. Part of the Drunken Monk company, it specialises in occasional reproductions of historic ales. There are beer festivals in February and July. Food is cooked to order at evening and weekend lunchtime sessions. The pub will open at weekday lunchtime by prior arrangement.
Q❀◐♣P⚡

Kidlington

King's Arms

4 the Moors, OX5 2AJ
11-2.30, 6-11; 11-11 Sat; 12-10.30 Sun
☎ (01865) 373004
Greene King IPA; Wells Bombardier; guest beer Ⓗ
Cosy, two-room local situated in the old part of Kidlington. With good value lunchtime food, various pub sports teams and excellent beer, it is popular, particularly at the weekend and when football matches are on. A previous local CAMRA Country Pub of the Year, the landlord serves an interesting range of guest beers. Q❀◐♣P

Kingston Lisle

Blowing Stone Inn

OX12 9QL (follow B4507 W out of Wantage)
12-3, 6-11; 12-11 Fri & Sat; 12-10.30 Sun
☎ (01367) 820288
website: www.theblowingstoneinn.com
Beer range varies Ⓗ
Welcoming local pub, with a pleasant atmosphere, affordable bar food and comfortable accommodation. Close to the Ridgeway and the White Horse at Uffington, it is a favourite with walkers and riders. The conservatory restaurant offers an a la carte menu, which complements the well-kept range of frequently changing beers from local breweries. Horse racing photographs decorate the walls. A large ornamental pond is a feature of the rear garden.
Q❀◐♣P

Lewknor

Olde Leatherne Bottel

1 High Street, OX49 5TW
(W of B4009, near M40 jct 6)
11-2.30, 6-11; 12-3, 7-10.30 Sun
☎ (01844) 351482
Brakspear Bitter, Special, seasonal beers Ⓗ
Archetypal English country inn, over 400 years old, with three fireplaces including an attractive inglenook. The two bars are separated by a central servery and there is a no-smoking lounge and family area. The well-tended garden, with children's play area, is busy in

summer. An extensive food menu, with daily home-made specials, is displayed on blackboards, with many vegetarian options. The 'Oxford Tube' (express coach service Oxford-London) stops on the B4009 two minutes' walk away. This pub has only missed one edition of the Guide. ⚠❀◑P⊬

Little Bourton

Plough

OX17 1RH (on A423 Southam Road 1½ miles from Banbury)
✪ 12-2.30, 6.30-11; 12-2.30, 7-10.30 Sun
☎ (01295) 750222
Adnams Broadside; Hook Norton Best Bitter; Wadworth 6X; guest beer 🄷
A warm welcome awaits visitors to this free house where locals and visitors are equally at home. The one-room pub is partially divided between the bar and dining areas, however drinkers may sit anywhere. Reasonably priced food includes many specials – look on the blackboard. Note the collection of pigs mixed in with other artefacts decorating the pub. ❀◑P

North Leigh

Woodman Inn

New Yatt Road, OX29 6TT
✪ 12-3, 5.30-11; 12-11 Sat; 12-10.30 Sun
☎ (01993) 881790
Brakspear Bitter; Wadworth 6X; guest beer 🄷
Popular, comfortable, community pub with a spacious bar with simple wooden furniture and plenty of space for drinkers and diners. Food is served lunchtime and evening – authentic Indian cuisine is a speciality. The well-kept garden is a pleasure in summer. The pub is home to a number of local societies and clubs. In the bar is an impressive 30ft-deep illuminated well. Beer festivals are held during the Easter and August bank holiday weekends. ⚠❀⇄◑♣P

Oxford

Angel & Greyhound

30 St Clements Street, OX4 1AB
✪ 11-11; 12-10.30 Sun
☎ (01865) 242660
Young's Bitter, Special, seasonal beers 🄷
Once known as the Oranges and Lemons, famous for its live rock music, then a wine bar, the pub is now one of the city's finest. Named after the local Angel meadow, this spacious open-plan pub attracts a varied clientele. Good pub food is served lunchtime and evening. Patios front and rear are popular, particularly when this busy pub becomes crowded. ⚠Q◑♣

Butcher's Arms ✔

5 Wilberforce Street, OX3 7AN
✪ 12-2.30, 5-11; 12-11 Fri & Sat; 12-10.30 Sun
☎ (01865) 761252
Fuller's Chiswick, London Pride, seasonal beers 🄷
Not the easiest pub to find, but worth the effort to seek out this friendly, back-street local. A recent overhaul means the pub is more spacious than it once was. Though the pub serves a good range of food and sandwiches at lunchtime, the main attraction is the well-kept range of Fuller's ales. Regular barbecues and the Sunday night quiz, set by the previous week's winners, are also popular. ⚠❀◑♣

Far from the Madding Crowd

10 Friars Entry, OX1 2BY
✪ 11-11; 11-10.30 Sun
☎ (01865) 240900
Black Sheep Best Bitter; Taylor Landlord; Wells Bombardier; guest beers 🄷
Tucked away down an alleyway in the city centre, the pub was converted from a shop in 2002. A free house, it has become popular with real ale drinkers and hosts regular small beer festivals. There are usually three guest ales, often from local small breweries. There is an interesting menu (not Sun) and food is served with plenty of salad on the side. Contemporary art for sale is exhibited on the walls. Live jazz is occasionally held on Thursday evening. Q◑♿⊬

Harcourt Arms

Cranham Terrace, Jericho, OX2 6DG
✪ 12-2.30, 5.30-11; 12-2.30, 7-10.30 Sun
☎ (01865) 310630
Fuller's Chiswick, London Pride, ESB, seasonal beers 🄷
Relaxed, welcoming corner pub in the middle of Jericho, with subdued lighting and two roaring log fires. This is a pub for conversation, reading (help yourself to Private Eye and New Scientist) and playing board games (Scrabble is popular), with a little background jazz to mellow the atmosphere further. The three established beers, including ESB, are now supplemented by a Fuller's seasonal. It is handy for Walton Street restaurants and the Phoenix cinema. ⚠Q❀♿♣

Hobgoblin

172 Cowley Road, OX4 1UE
✪ 12-11; 12-10.30 Sun
☎ (01865) 439496
Beer range varies 🄷
Vibrant pub with a single open-plan bar and a large garden with covered patio. There are six handpumps offering a constantly changing range of guest beers, usually one or two from local breweries. The clientele tends to be a mix of locals and students. Indie music plays most of the time except when sporting events are shown on the large screen. The pub appeals to younger drinkers but all ages are welcome. ❀

King's Arms

40 Holywell Street, OX1 3SP
✪ 10.30-11; 12-10.30 Sun
☎ (01865) 242369
Young's Bitter, Special, seasonal beers; Wadworth 6X; guest beers 🄷
Historic Oxford institution dating from 1607, with a lively front bar, lounge that serves morning coffee, and some atmospheric, quieter rooms and snugs to the rear. Located at the heart of the city, opposite the Sheldonian Theatre, the 'KA' is owned by Young's and serves its full range of draught and bottled beers, plus a good choice of guest ales and wines. Meals are served all day at the weekend. Outdoor seating is limited to a few pavement benches. Q❀◑⇌⊬

Lamb & Flag

12 St Giles, OX1 3JS

11-11; 11-10.30 Sun

(01865) 515787

Fuller's London Pride; Palmer IPA; Shepherd Neame Spitfire; Skinner's Betty Stoggs; Theakston Old Peculier; guest beers H

Originally a 15th-century coaching inn, now owned by St John's College next door, this pub can be quite lively during term time. A rambling pub with low ceilings, it has two bars, one more formal overlooking St Giles, the other a lounge bar with three drinking areas. Up to eight real ales are available, always including Skinner's and Palmer's beers. The Lamb & Flag house beer is brewed by Palmer.

Masons Arms

2 Quarry School Place, Headington Quarry, OX3 8LH

5 (11 Sat)-11; 12-4, 7-10.30 Sun

(01865) 764579

Black Sheep Best Bitter; Caledonian Deuchars IPA; guest beers H

Friendly, welcoming free house just off the ring road but tucked away in an old quarry. A community pub that puts great emphasis on its real ales; it opened its own brewery in January 2005. The weekly quiz and meat raffle, plus darts and Aunt Sally teams, mean the pub is always busy. Real cider is sold all year round. Home of the Headington Beer Festival, it was Oxford CAMRA city Pub of the Year in 2004.

Q P

Rose & Crown

14 North Parade Avenue, OX2 6LX

11-3, 5 (6 Sat)-11; 12-4, 7-10.30 Sun

(01865) 510551

website: www.rose-n-crown.co.uk

Adnams Bitter, Broadside; Hook Norton Old Hooky H

Unspoilt, three-room, single bar pub located to the north of the city in a smart Victorian suburb – beer prices reflect the affluent nature of the area. The current licensees have run the pub for 22 years and have a loyal following of students, locals and academics. The ambience is relaxed and conversation and lively debate remain uninterrupted by background music, gaming machines and mobile phones (banned). A covered and heated garden is popular all year round.

Q

St Aldates Tavern

108 St Aldates, OX1 1BU (opp. town hall)

11-11; 12-10.30 Sun

(01865) 250201

White Horse Oxfordshire Bitter; guest beers H

This year sees another name change for the pub originally known as the Bulldog, and more recently the Hobgoblin. There are usually five real ales on handpump, often from small independent and micro-breweries. Beers from White Horse, West Berkshire and Titanic are popular choices. Card-carrying CAMRA members and students get a discount on draught beer. Home-cooked food is served throughout the day. Thursday is live acoustic music night.

Turf Tavern

7 Bath Place, OX1 3SU

(between Holywell St and New College Lane)

11-11; 12-10.30 Sun

(01865) 243235

website: www.theturftavern.co.uk

Beer range varies H

Tucked away between the old city wall and surrounding colleges, this famous pub is sought out by students, tourists and real ale lovers. Two bars with low ceilings supply up to 11 varying ales plus Westons Old Rosie cider. Three flagstone patios, heated by coal braziers in winter, ease the pressure during busy term times. Traditional English food is served 12-7.30pm. Check the website for popular 'meet the brewer' evenings. Q

Wharf House

14 Butterwyke Place, St Ebbes, OX1 1TT

(jct of Thames St and Speedwell St)

11.30-3, 6-11; 11.30-11 Sat; 12-4, 7-10.30 Sun

(01865) 728318

RCH Pitchfork; guest beers H

A warm welcome is guaranteed at this community local, a short walk from the town centre, and one of the last remaining buildings from the old St Ebbes district. A basic, single-bar pub, it is one of Oxford's few, true free houses. Guest beers always include a brew from a local brewery. A large range of foreign beer is always available, along with ciders and perries from small producers.

P

Ramsden

Royal Oak

High Street, OX7 3AU

11-3, 6.30-11; 12-3, 7-10.30 Sun

(01993) 868213

Hook Norton Best Bitter; Young's Special; guest beer H

Popular 17th-century free house run by the same owners for 18 years with an excellent reputation for good food and well-kept ales. Comfortably furnished in traditional style, the main bar has an inglenook. A small snug is at the rear, and a spacious restaurant opens onto a courtyard for summer drinking. No music, fruit machines, TV or games, this is a pub for relaxation and conversation. Children, dogs and walkers are welcome.

Q P

Rotherfield Peppard

Unicorn

Colemore Lane, Kingwood, RG9 5LX

(off B481, towards Stoke Row)

12-3, 6-11; 12-3, 6-10.30 Sun

(01491) 628452

Brakspear Bitter, seasonal beers; Hook Norton Hooky Dark H

Originally the village blacksmith's around 1850, this convivial village pub was closed in 2002, to be put to housing use. However a successful campaign led by the locals, with support from their councillors, MP and the Prince of Wales, resulted in its re-opening in August 2003. Facilities include comfortable leather seating

around the log fire and a dining area (no food Sun eve), with wooden floorboards throughout.
⌂❀◑♣P⊬

Shippon

Prince of Wales ✔

60 Barrow Road, OX13 6JQ
⏲ 11.30-2.30, 6.30-11; 11-11 Fri & Sat; 12-10.30 Sun
☎ (01235) 520845
Black Sheep Best Bitter; Caledonian Deuchars IPA; guest beers ⊞
An oasis on the western side of Abingdon in a town where good pubs and quality beer are hard to find. There are usually two or three frequently changing and interesting beers to choose from, often brews that are rare for the area and a good complement to the regular beers. The pub, with its traditional public bar and quiet, comfortable lounge, is run by a friendly and well-informed landlord. Lunches are served Monday-Saturday.
Q❀◑⊟♣P

Shipton under Wychwood

Shaven Crown

High Street, OX7 6BA
(on A361 between Burford and Chipping Norton)
⏲ 12-2.30, 5-11; 12-11 Sat; 12-10.30 Sun
☎ (01993) 830330
website: www.theshavencrown.co.uk
Hook Norton Best Bitter; guest beers ⊞
Situated in the heart of the village, this 700-year-old free house with a warm and friendly atmosphere welcomes drinkers and diners. Many original features remain including the 14th-century gateway. The Monks Bar is traditionally furnished with booth seating and a heavily beamed ceiling. It has a large open fire and many interesting pictures on the walls. Leaded windows look out onto the delightful courtyard garden. Well-behaved children are welcome. Three real ales are always available.
⌂Q❀⇔◑⊟⇌P

Shutford

George & Dragon

Church Lane, OX15 6PG
(3 miles off A422 Banbury-Stratford road)
⏲ 12-2.30, 6-11; closed Mon; 12-10.30 Sun
☎ (01295) 780320
Hook Norton Best Bitter; guest beers ⊞
This ancient village inn, part of which dates back to the 1300s, sits in the shadow of the nearby church. It was once threatened with closure but is now a thriving pub and has recently had a sympathetic refurbishment. The bar is furnished in a traditional style with an inglenook and quarry tiled floor, and there is a separate restaurant. Wholesome food from an ever changing menu draws local diners.
⌂Q❀◑⊟♣

Sonning Eye

Flowing Spring

Henley Road, RG4 9RB
(on A4155, 2 miles E of Caversham)
⏲ 11.30-11; 12-10.30 Sun
☎ (0118) 969 3207
Fuller's Chiswick, London Pride, ESB, seasonal beers ⊞
Traditional country local which has had a sympathetic extension with a balcony overlooking the large garden. The bar is effectively an island surrounded by drinking areas. Traditional pub food, including vegetarian options, is served every lunchtime and Wednesday-Saturday evenings. Occasional barbecues are popular too. Walkers come from footpaths in the surrounding countryside and the Thames long distance footpath a mile away. The garden has swings for children. Quiz night is Sunday from late September to March.
⌂Q◑▲♣P⊬

Swinbrook

Swan Inn

OX18 4DY (off A40)
⏲ 11.30-3, 6.30-11; 12-3, 7-10.30 Sun
☎ (01993) 822165
Archers Village; Greene King IPA; Wadworth 6X; Wychwood Hobgoblin ⊞
Unspoilt, 16th-century country pub with wisteria over the door in an idyllic setting by the River Windrush. The comfortable tap room has a flagstone floor, old settles, a corner cupboard and a log-burning stove in the inglenook. The main bar features hops, an attractive mirror and beams supported by ancient oak pillars. An open fire burns in the cosy dining room with its unusual alcove seats. The pub has an excellent reputation for its food as well as its ale. Westons vintage organic draught cider is sold. Outdoor drinking can be enjoyed in the large garden or seating at the front. ⌂Q❀◑♣●P

Thame

Swan Hotel

9 Upper Street, OX9 3ER
⏲ 11-11; 12-10.30 Sun
☎ (01844) 261211
website: www.swanhotelthame.com
Hook Norton Best Bitter; Taylor Landlord; guest beers ⊞
The Swan is a genuine market town pub with excellent beers including frequently changing guests, good food and the kind of ambience that makes you stay longer than you intended. The large open fire and deep settees help make you feel at home. Upstairs is the restaurant with a painted Tudor ceiling. Outside seating is in a small shopping street. Note the boar's head and paintings of past customers.
⌂❀⇔◑

Wallingford

Cross Keys

48 High Street, OX10 0DB
⏲ 12-3, 5-11; 12-11 Fri & Sat; 12-10.30 Sun
☎ (01491) 826377
Brakspear Bitter, Special, seasonal beers ⊞
Award-winning, unspoilt, 17th-century, four-room pub near Wallingford Museum and town parks. Predominantly a beer drinkers' local, it fields teams in crib, darts and dominoes. Low beams and polished wood floors feature. The public bar has steps up to a games room; a small lounge bar leads through to another room

that is used as either a games area or function room. Live music is staged twice a month. The large, fenced garden, with children's play area, stands on what are believed to be Saxon town ramparts. ♛❀◐⊟⛺♣●P

Wantage

Royal Oak Inn

Newbury Street, OX12 8DF

(300 yds from Market Place along Hungerford Rd A338)

✪ 5.30-11; 12-2.30, 7-11 Sat; 12-2, 7-10.30 Sun

☎ (01235) 763129 website: royaloakwantage.tripod.com

Wadworth 6X; Ⓗ/Ⓖ **West Berkshire Maggs Mild,** Ⓖ **Dr Hexter's Wedding Ale, Dr Hexter's Healer; guest beers** Ⓗ/Ⓖ

Thriving corner pub with a beer-loving landlord of many years' standing, whose name features on two West Berkshire ales served here. Photographs of ships bearing the Royal Oak name adorn the walls, as do many CAMRA awards. The smaller public bar with table football is frequented by a younger crowd. The larger lounge has a bar front of oak leaves and acorns formed from wrought iron, although it is hidden by more than 200 real ale pump clips. ⛟⊟♣●

Shoulder of Mutton

38 Wallingford Street, OX12 8AX

(200 yds E of Market Square on A417)

✪ 3.30 (12 Sat)-11; 12-10.30 Sun

Butcombe Bitter; Taylor Landlord; guest beer Ⓗ

Popular, town pub, split into three bars: there is a cosy snug, a slightly bigger public bar and a larger lounge housing a computer with Internet access in one corner – making it the first and, at the moment, only cyber pub in the area. The furnishings and decor are traditional, with an interesting selection of prints and photographs adorning the walls. Do not miss the small paved drinking area at the back, festooned with hanging baskets. A friendly welcome is assured. ♛Q❀⊟♣

Watlington

Carriers Arms

Hill Road, OX49 5AD (off B4009, from town hall follow signs for public car park, continue 50 yds)

✪ 11-11; 12-10.30 Sun

☎ (01491) 613470

Beer range varies Ⓗ

Good, basic free house with the cheapest beer in the area, and a range of up to three ales to choose from. Good meals in generous portions are served every lunchtime and evening, and filled rolls are available most of the time. The pub is popular with old and young alike. A meat raffle is held on Sunday lunchtime. Situated close to the Ridgeway long distance footpath, from the garden there is a good view of the White Mark, a chalk triangle of dubious origin on Watlington Hill. Q❀◐◑⛺♣P

Witney

House of Windsor

11 West End, OX28 1NQ

✪ 12-3 (not Mon-Thu), 6-11; 12-10.30 Sun

☎ (01993) 704277

Caledonian Deuchars IPA; Taylor Landlord; guest beers Ⓗ

This free house, situated in the old, historic part of Witney, was originally called the King of Prussia but changed its name during the first World War. The warm welcome and excellent range of beers makes it popular with all ages. Rumours of closure still persist but it would be a sad loss for the community if this this lively, vibrant pub were to close. ♛❀◑

New Inn ✔

111 Corn Street, OX28 6SU

✪ 5 (4 Fri; 12 Sat)-11; 12-10.30 Sun

☎ (01993) 703807

Adnams Broadside; Brakspear Bitter; Black Sheep Best Bitter; Taylor Landlord; guest beer Ⓗ

Voted Oxford City CAMRA Country Pub of 2004, the New Inn has fast become a favourite haunt of local real ale drinkers since new licensees took over in late 2003. The barn attached to this former 19th-century farmhouse is the venue for the pub's beer festival – in 2004 it showcased 40 Cornish brews. More festivals are promised for the future. The pub supports darts, cribbage, Aunt Sally teams and other local events. It hosts live music on alternate Saturday nights. ♛❀♿♣P

Woodcote

Black Lion

Greenmore, RG8 0RB (1 mile SW of A4074)

✪ 5-11; 11.30-11 Sat; 12-10.30 Sun

☎ (01491) 680625

Butler's Oxfordshire Bitter; Courage Best Bitter Ⓗ

At the edge of the village, this free house is the tap for the local Butler's Brewery. The regulars are proud of their new micro-brewery and the pub is popular, particularly when sports are shown on TV in the one-room bar. Sandwiches and baguettes are available on Saturday lunchtime. Ideally situated for walks in the surrounding woods, there are extensive scenic views from Greenmoor Hill at the rear of the pub. ♛❀P

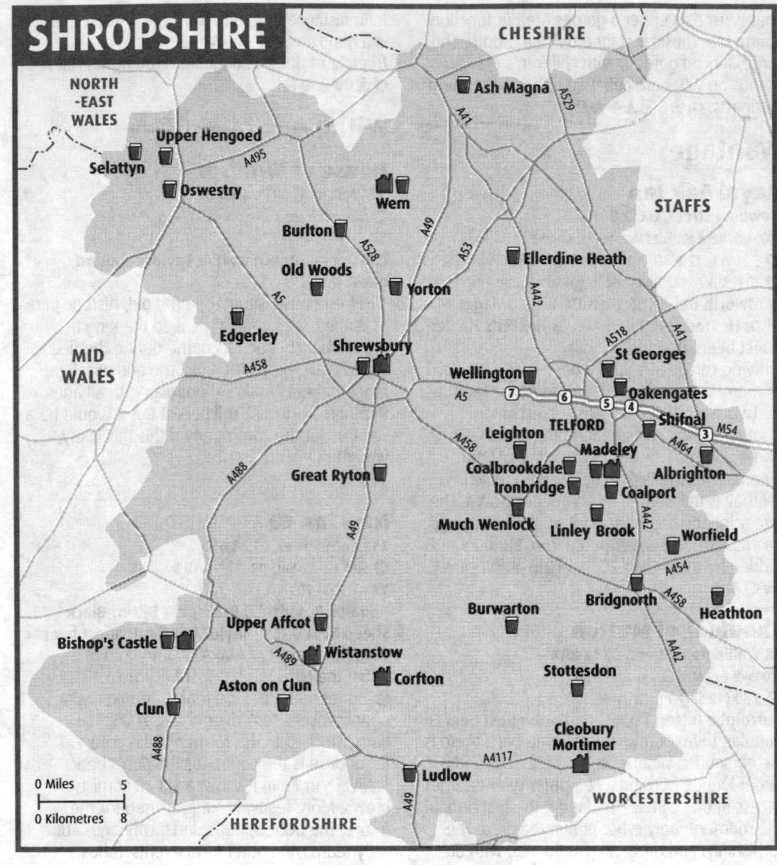

Albrighton

Harp

40 High Street, WV7 3JF
✪ 12-11; 12-10.30 Sun
☎ (01902) 374381
Holden's Bitter; guest beers Ⓗ
Terry and his dog Max will make you feel welcome at this basic two-room pub. As well as Holden's offerings there are three guest beers available, plus traditional cider from the bar dispenser. The pub is a must for jazz lovers on Sunday lunchtime and Tuesday evening, and country and western fans on Thursday evening. Photographs of international artists who have played here in the past are displayed on the walls. Two mini-beer festivals are held annually. When the weather is fine why not sit outside by the village green? ❀⊟♿⇌♣●P

Ash Magna

White Lion

SY13 4DR
✪ 12-3 (not Mon-Fri), 6-11; 12-5, 7-10.30 Sun
☎ (01948) 663153
Draught Bass; Worthington's Bitter; guest beers Ⓗ
A welcome return to the Guide for this lively two-bar pub just a few miles from Whitchurch. The White Lion has a busy bar and comfortable lounge full of real ale and golf memorabilia. The menu (served Tue-Sat eves) specialises in German food, home cooked by the landlady at this former local CAMRA Pub of the Year.
♨Q❀◗⊟♣P⊡

Aston on Clun

Kangaroo

Clun Road, SY7 8EW (on B4368 between Craven Arms and Clun)
✪ 12-3 (not Mon or Tue), 6-11; 2-11 Fri; 12-11 Sat; 12-10.30 Sun
☎ (01588) 660263 website: www.kangarooinn.co.uk
Holden's Mild; Six Bells Roo Brew; Wells Bombardier; guest beers Ⓗ
The unusual name dates from the 19th century. This cosy village local has a public bar, games room and a large garden and patio. Home-cooked food is served (not Sun-Tue eves); try

INDEPENDENT BREWERIES

All Nations Madeley
Corvedale Corfton
Dolphin Shrewsbury
Hanby Wem
Hobsons Cleobury Mortimer
John Roberts Bishop's Castle
Salopian Shrewsbury
Six Bells Bishop's Castle
Wood Wistanstow
Worfield Madeley

the themed evenings. Roo Brew is brewed exclusively to the publican's recipe. The pub and locals support the nearby annual Arbor tree redressing ceremony at the end of May, summer barbecues, the pub's own beer festival on August bank holiday and Clun Valley beer festival at the beginning of August. The Bike-roos meet here on Sunday afternoon.
⊕Q⊛◑Ⓓ Å⇌ (Broome)♣P⊬

Bishop's Castle

Castle Hotel

Market Square, SY9 5BH
⊙ 12-2.30, 6-11; 12-2.30, 7-10.30 Sun
☎ (01588) 638403
website: www.thecastlebishopscastle.com
Hobsons Mild, Best Bitter; Six Bells Big Nev's ⊞
Welcoming 18th-century hotel at the top of the town. It is popular with locals and visitors who enjoy the beers and excellent home-cooked food, especially Sunday lunch, while soaking up the timeless ambience of the public bar, lounge, small snug and dining room, with much original woodwork and open fires. There are six bedrooms and the hotel is ideal for a short break. The Castle fully supports the local beerfest and offers a good range of beers. Enjoy the fine views from the garden across the town to the South Shropshire Hills. ⊕Q⊛⇄◑Ⓓ ⊟♣P

Six Bells

Church Street, SY9 5AA
⊙ 12-2.30 (not Mon), 5-11; 12-11 Sat; 12-10.30 Sun
☎ (01588) 630144
Six Bells Big Nev's, Marathon Ale, Cloud Nine, Duck & Dive, seasonal beers ⊞
Very much a community local and popular with visitors, too, this 17th-century coaching inn has the added attraction of the Six Bells Brewery with its fine range of hoppy beers. Freshly cooked meals are served in the dining room (eve meals Tue-Sat). The public bar has exposed stonework, beams and an inglenook. It has a warm, welcoming feel, as befits a CAMRA award-winning pub. It supports the town's beer festival in July with a much extended selection of beers. ⊕Q⊛◑Ⓓ ⊟♣P

Three Tuns

Salop Street, SY9 6BW
⊙ 12-11; 12-10.30 Sun
☎ (01588) 638797
John Roberts Three 8, XXX, Castle Steamer, Cleric's Cure ⊞
One of the truly historic pubs in the country; it was one of the famous four brew-pubs who were still brewing in the early 1970s. Together with the adjoining John Roberts Brewery, from where it gets all its beers, it has been on this site since 1640. It has three rooms: on one side is the dining lounge, there is a small middle bar and on the other side a public bar. As well as good food it offers music, including jazz, in the top room on a regular basis. ⊕Q◑Ⓓ ⊟●⊬

Bridgnorth

Bell & Talbot

2 Salop Street, High Town, WV16 4QU
⊙ 12-2.30 (not Mon-Fri), 5-11; 12-2.30, 5-10.30 Sun
☎ (01746) 763233
Batham Best Bitter; Hobsons Town Crier; Holden's Bitter; guest beers ⊞
Old coaching inn with bags of character. A modern conservatory at the rear, separate from the main bars, complements rather than contrasts. The pub is renowned for its friendliness and it really comes alive during the Bridgnorth Folk Festival on August bank holiday when it is an official venue. There is an emphasis on local Shropshire and Black Country beers alongside a changing guest list from further afield Meals are served Thursday-Sunday.
⊕⊛⇄Ⓓ ⇌(SVR)♣

Black Boy

58 Cartway, WV16 4BG
⊙ 5 (12 Sat)-11; 12-10.30 Sun
☎ (01746) 764691
Banks's Bitter, Wells Bombardier; guest beers ⊞
Compact and cosy with a friendly atmosphere and warm welcome from the lively landlord who is the 'youngest in town'. This 17th-century inn is in a prime location between Hightown and Lowtown. It has two distinct drinking areas both served by a central bar. The unusual 18th-century fireplace was found in a skip in Shrewsbury 25 years ago. The patio affords outstanding views over the River Severn and Bridgnorth landscape.
⊕⊛♣

Friars Inn

St Mary's Street, WV16 4DW
(in passageway between St Mary's St and High St)
⊙ 12-2.30, 6-11; 12-11 Sat; 12-7.30 Sun
☎ (01746) 762396
Enville Ale; Holden's Golden Glow; guest beers ⊞
This tranquil oasis in the heart of the busy market town can be found in an ancient pedestrian-only area. Inside is a large bar room and a smaller no-smoking dining room with a comfortable atmosphere. Steaks are a speciality (no meals Sun eve). There is a pleasant seating area outside brightened by hanging baskets for warmer days. The guest beers come from local independents. The Cliff Railway and the Severn Valley Railway are nearby.
⊕Q⊛⇄◑Ⓓ Å⇌(SVR)

Railwayman's Arms

Severn Valley Railway Station, Hollybush Road, WV16 5DT (signed SVR)
⊙ 11.30-4, 6-11; 11-11 Sat; 12-10.30 Sun
☎ (01746) 764361 website: www.svr.co.uk
Batham Best Bitter; Hobsons Best Bitter; guest beers ⊞
A licensed refreshment room since before 1900, owned by SVR and attracting steam railway enthusiasts from around the country. The three guest beers are from local breweries. Note the original Cheshire Brewery (Smethwick) mirror in the bar. Baguettes and snacks are served. This exceptionally busy free house hosts a CAMRA beer festival every September in the car park. Not to be missed are the 1940s themed weekends held on the trains where everyone dresses up in '40s style – a real step back in time.
⊕Q⊛⇌(SVR) ●P⊡

Burlton

Burlton Inn

SY4 5TB (on A528 between Shrewsbury and Ellesmere)
11-3, 6-11; 12-3.30, 7-10.30 Sun
(01939) 270284
website: www.burltoninn.co.uk
Beer range varies Ⓗ
Attractive rural free house situated near the North Shropshire lakes between Shrewsbury and Ellesmere. Recently refurbished, it offers three changing guest beers along with award-winning home-cooked food featuring local produce. Although the emphasis is on food here, drinkers are welcome in the quiet drinking area and comfy lounge. Tucked away behind the inn is cottage accommodation with six en-suite bedrooms.
Q P

Burwarton

Boyne Arms

WV16 6QH (on B4364 Bridgnorth-Ludlow road)
10-3, 6-11; 10-11 Sat; 12-10.30 Sun
(01746) 787214
Hobsons Town Crier; Taylor Landlord; Wood Shropshire Lad; guest beers Ⓗ
There is a five foot frog on a bike at the front of this popular 18th-century coaching inn. Inside, the two bars offer seven handpulls. Restaurant and bar snack menus cater for all tastes and pockets. Food is available daily from 10am. In the garden is a fully-enclosed ROSPA-certified children's play area with unusual animal sculptures. There is a stables bar for functions and skittles. The pub is popular with walkers and the en-suite accommodation is recommended.
Q P

Clun

White Horse Inn

The Square, SY7 8JA
12-11; 12-10.30 Sun
(01588) 640305
website: www.whi-clun.co.uk
Hobsons Best Bitter; John Roberts XXX; Salopian Shropshire Gold; Wye Valley Butty Bach; guest beers Ⓗ
Comfortable, 18th-century coaching inn and post house that stands in the old market square at the centre of a wonderful, timeless town – described by A E Housman as 'one of the quietest places under the sun'. This friendly local, two minutes from the castle, has an L-shaped bar with low beams. A range of board games can be borrowed and the excellent, reasonably-priced food is home made. Westons First Quality cider is stocked. Relax over a quiet pint in the secluded garden at the rear. The attractive guest rooms are recommended.
Q

Edgerley

Royal Hill ☆

SY10 8ES (midway between Pentre and Melverley) OSSJ3517
12-2, 6-11; 12-11 Sat; 12-10.30 Sun
(01743) 741242
Salopian Shropshire Gold; guest beers Ⓗ
Set on a quiet road, with its garden bordering the River Severn, this delightful pub dating from the 18th century looks out towards the Breidden Hills and is well worth seeking out. The recently extended but well-preserved building comprises a number of cosy rooms and a tiny bar. Visitors are warmly welcomed. Camping is possible at the back of the pub's grounds, caravans are admitted too.
Q

Ellerdine Heath

Royal Oak

TF6 6RL (midway between A53 and A442) OS603226
12 (11 Sat)-11; 12-10.30 Sun
(01952) 250300
Hobsons Best Bitter; Salopian Shropshire Gold; Wye Valley Hereford Pale Ale; guest beers Ⓗ
The Tiddly, as it is known locally, is not so tiddly now. A new extension with disabled access has made the pub more spacious, but without losing any of its traditional feel or friendly atmosphere. Lively conversation is the order of the day and visitors are made to feel welcome by the regulars. The pub has built its reputation by offering good quality beer and no-nonsense food (not served Tue) at reasonable prices. Long may it continue to do so!
Q P

Great Ryton

Fox Inn

SY5 7LS
(5½ miles S of Shrewbury, 1 mile E of A49) OSSJ4903
12-2.30 (not Mon), 7-11; 12-3.30, 7-11 Sat; 12-3.30, 7-10.30 Sun
(01743) 718499
Hobsons Mild, Town Crier; Salopian Shropshire Gold; Worfield Dabley Ale; guest beers Ⓗ
Country pub overlooking the Stretton Hills. At the heart of the local community, the Fox is popular with locals and visitors from neighbouring villages. It hosts music nights, quizzes and special cuisine evenings. Shropshire beers are always stocked. A bar menu offers tasty meals at lunchtime and there is an extensive food menu for the evening.
Q P

Heathton

Old Gate

WV5 7EB (between B4176 and A458 near Halfpenny Green) OS814923
12-2.30 (not Mon), 6.30-11; 12-3, 7-10.30 Sun
(01746) 710431
website: www.oldgateinn.co.uk
Enville White; Taylor Landlord Ⓗ
Busy pub in a rural area, serving good quality food. The extensive menu is well priced and caters for all, including children; no meals are served on Sunday evening. A typical 16th-century inn, the two bars are decorated in traditional style with welcoming log fires and a cosy atmosphere. Music is played but quietly, so conversation can prevail. Addlestones cider is sold. Children are welcome and there is a safe play area in the well-maintained garden.
P

Leighton

Kynnersley Arms
SY5 6RN (on B4380) OS610055
⊕ 12-2 (Tue-Thu summer only), 5-11; 12-11 Fri & Sat; 12-10.30 Sun
☎ (01952) 510258
Banks's Original; Draught Bass; Tetley Bitter; guest beer Ⓗ
An out of the way Grade II listed inn well worth seeking out. This former mill and forge is close to Ironbridge and the old Roman town of Wroxeter. Three regular beers are joined by a weekly guest ale, all on handpull. The French chef chooses local organic produce for the restaurant where vegetarian dishes and crepes are a speciality; no food is served on Sunday evening or Monday.
♔Q❀◐◑♣P⊬

Linley Brook

Pheasant
Britons Lane, WV16 4TA (400 yds off B4373) OS680979
⊕ 12-2, 7 (6.30 summer)-11; 12-3, 7 (6.30 summer)-10.30 Sun
☎ (01746) 762260 website: www.the-pheasant-inn.co.uk
Beer range varies Ⓗ
Traditional inn, idyllically situated in beautiful walking countryside. The pub provides a choice of ales, mostly sourced from local independents, and excellent, good value food. Inside is a lively main bar with real fire and a quieter lounge area, and a second room where traditional games including bar billiards are played. Featuring in this Guide for 22 consecutive years, this is exactly what an unspoilt country pub should be. Not to be missed. ♔Q❀◐◑⊡P

Ludlow

Church Inn
The Buttercross, SY8 1AW
⊕ 12-11; 12-10.30 Sun
☎ (01584) 872174 website: www.thechurchinn.com
Hobson Mild, Town Crier; Hook Norton Best Bitter, Old Hooky; Weetwood Eastgate Ale; Wye Valley Bitter; guest beers Ⓗ
Situated in the centre of Ludlow, close to the castle and market square, the Church is the only free house within the town walls. The landlord is a former mayor of Ludlow and also owns the reopened Charlton Arms at Ludford Bridge. He is a great advocate of real ale; guests always supplement the inn's regular beers. The upstairs bar affords a wonderful view of the South Shropshire Hills and the church. Four of the pub's guest rooms feature spa baths.
♔Q⇌◐◑▲≢⊬▯

Nelson Inn
Rocks Green, SY8 2DS (on A4117 Kidderminster road)
⊕ 12-2.30, 5 (7 Tue)-11; 12-11 Fri & Sat; 12-10.30 Sun
☎ (01584) 872908
Banks's Original; St Austell Tribute; Nottingham Extra Pale Ale; guest beers Ⓗ
On the outskirts of Ludlow, the Nelson dates back some 300 years and is a fine example of a traditional beer house. The bar has a pool table, darts, quoits and a juke box featuring 1970s and '80s music. The lounge is decked out with musical instruments on the walls. Occasionally, spontaneous musical events occur. The tasty real chips on the menu are highly recommended. Real cider and, from time to time, perry are sold.
♔Q❀◐◑⊡▲♣●

Much Wenlock

George & Dragon
2 High Street, TF13 6AA
⊕ 12-11; 12-10.30 Sun
☎ (01952) 727312
Hobsons Town Crier; Greene King IPA, Abbot; Taylor Landlord; guest beer Ⓗ
An intimate bar and snug restaurant are hidden behind an attractive but unassuming frontage. Dating from 1714, this friendly market town local welcomes regulars and visitors alike, and is a focal point for the area. The pub is involved in many of the town's festivals and holds regular quiz nights. Four regular ales and one guest are all on handpull. The cosy, alcoved restaurant bases its excellent menu on local produce (no eve meals Sun or Wed). Every effort is made to accommodate wheelchairs within the limits of the aged building. Q◐◑

Old Woods

Romping Cat
SY4 3AX (4 miles NW of Shrewsbury, off A528)
⊕ 12-2.30 (not Mon, Wed or Fri), 6-11; 12-3.30, 7-11 Sat; 12-2.30, 7-10.30 Sun
☎ (01939) 290273
Draught Bass; Black Sheep Best Bitter; Boddingtons Bitter; guest beers Ⓗ
Originally the Railway Inn but, for reasons lost in time, it became known locally as the Cat and adopted its present name during the late 80s. This cosy, comfortable free house is supported by the local community and has raised many thousands of pounds for charities. The three staple beers are on an ever-changing cycle supplemented by three guests. During the winter an open fire blazes. A paved area is popular in the summer, enhanced by attractive floral displays. ♔Q❀P▯

Oswestry

Fox Inn
Church Street, SY11 2SU
⊕ 12-3, 7-11 Mon; 11.30-11 Tue-Sat; 12-10.30 Sun
☎ (01691) 679669
Banks's Bitter; Marston's Old Empire; guest beers Ⓗ
Town-centre pub with timber-beamed rooms. A small front bar leads to a larger room with a big table by the log fire. Behind this room is a small no-smoking room. At the rear of the pub is a courtyard where barbecues are held in the summer. A mini-art gallery of local artwork is displayed here which is for sale. The cider is Westons Old Rosie. No food is served Sunday evening or Monday. ♔Q❀◐◑ ♣●⊬

Selattyn

Cross Keys ☆
Glyn Road, SY10 7DN
(on B4579, between Oswestry and Glyn Ceiriog)
⊕ 7 (6 Fri)-11; 12-4, 7-10.30 Sun
☎ (01691) 650247

Salopian Shropshire Gold; guest beers 🄷
This 17th-century CAMRA National Inventory listed pub is close to Offa's Dyke and is a classic village local. The garden affords a splendid view over the Shropshire Plain. The small bar has a quarry-tiled floor and real fire. There is a cottage attached to the pub which was once a shop – it can now be rented for self-catering accommodation for the night or longer.
⛫Q♨❀⇔⊞⛺ ♣P

Shifnal

White Hart

4 High Street, TF11 8BH
✪ 12-3, 5.30-11; 12-11 Fri & Sat; 12-10.30 Sun
☎ (01952) 461161
Cotleigh Barn Owl; Enville Ale; Holden's Mild, Bitter; guest beers 🄷
Superb, half-timbered, 16th-century local with a relaxed and welcoming atmosphere. Seven ales are on offer – and seven wines – much appreciated by the inn's friendly customers. Some of the more mature regulars have formed a Thursday club; the minutes are available to peruse and well worth a look. Four times local CAMRA Pub of the Year and deservedly so.
Q❀◑⇌ ♣P

Shrewsbury

Admiral Benbow

24 Swan Hill, SY1 1NF
✪ 12-2.30 (not Mon-Wed), 5-11; 12-11 Sat; 7-10.30 Sun
☎ (01743) 244423
Greene King IPA; guest beers 🄷
Early records from 1835 show that this pub was once called the Talbot Tap but it was renamed in 1861 as a tribute to the gallant local sailor. The free house currently specialises in a choice of Shropshire-brewed ales, five of which are normally on tap. A draught cider is occasionally available too. There is a room off the main bar, served via a hatch, which is available for private functions. Note that an age policy exists: under-30s are served at the discretion of the management. ⛫Q❀⊞⇌♣●

Armoury

Victoria Quay, Victoria Avenue, SY1 1HH (near Welsh Bridge)
✪ 12-11; 12-10.30 Sun
☎ (01743) 340525
website: www.armoury-shrewsbury.co.uk
Boddingtons Bitter; Caledonian Deuchars IPA; Salopian Icon; Wood Shropshire Lad; guest beers 🄷
Four regular and four changing guests aim to please a wide range of palates. Tasting notes are provided on chalkboards. Some 70 malt whiskies are also available. Excellent food is served and children are welcome until 9pm. Once an armoury, the building was renovated in 1995 and renamed. A quiet pub during the day, it becomes much livelier in the evening. Board games are available on request. ⛫◑◐♿

Coach & Horses ✔

Swan Hill, SY1 1NP (near Music Hall)
✪ 11-11; 12-10.30 Sun
☎ (01743) 365661
website: www.vixentrading.com/odley/
Salopian Shropshire Gold; Phoenix Arizona; guest beers 🄷
Set in a quiet street just off the main shopping area, the Coach & Horses provides a quiet haven. In summer it has magnificent award-winning floral displays. Victorian in style, the pub has a wood-panelled bar, a small side snug area and a large lounge where meals are served at lunchtime and in the evening. Light dishes are available until 2.30pm. Addlestones cider is also sold. ⛫◑◐⊞♿⇌●

Loggerheads ☆

1 Church Street, SY1 1UG
✪ 11-11; 12-3, 8-10.30 Sun
☎ (01743) 355457
Banks's Original, Bitter; Draught Bass; guest beers 🄷
This friendly, family-managed, town-centre local was CAMRA Pub of the Year winner in 2004. Food and guest beer menus are shown on chalkboards. The Grade II listed building has a small bar as a servery to three rooms, one with 'scrubbed top' tables and settles as well as a shove-ha'penny board. The larger lounge is a venue for darts and dominoes matches, spontaneous folk music and CAMRA meetings. Evening meals are served in summer (no food Sun). Q◑◐⊞⇌♣

Prince of Wales

30 Bynner Street, SY3 7NZ
✪ 12-2 (not Mon), 5-11; 12-11 Fri & Sat; 12-10.30 Sun
☎ (01743) 343301
website: www.princeofwaleshotel.co.uk
Ansells Mild; Greene King IPA; Salopian Golden Thread; guest beers 🄷
A well-deserved return to the Guide. Locals and visitors are attracted by the friendly and relaxed atmosphere at this pub which is just a short walk from the town centre. Inside is a main room with a warming fire and a smaller room with pool table. Lunchtime meals are reasonably priced and home prepared with fresh local produce where possible. Evenings are reserved for social drinking.
⛫♨❀◑⊞♿♣P⚡

Three Fishes ✔

Fish Street, SY1 1UR
✪ 11.30-3, 5-11; 11.30-11 Fri & Sat; 12-4, 7-10.30 Sun
☎ (01743) 344793
Caledonian Deuchars IPA; Fuller's London Pride; Taylor Landlord; guest beers 🄷
A warm welcome awaits you at this CAMRA award-winning pub. The 15th century building stands in the shadow of two churches, St Alkmond's and St Julian's, within the maze of streets and passageways in the medieval quarter of the town. Freshly-prepared food is available at lunchtime and early evening (except Sun eve). The pub offers a range of up to six local and national beers, one of which is usually a mild or dark beer. It proudly defends its no-smoking policy throughout. Q◑◐⇌⚡

Wheatsheaf

50 High Street, SY1 1ST
✪ 11-11; 12-10.30 Sun
☎ (01743) 272702
Banks's Bitter; Marston's Old Empire, seasonal beers; guest beers 🄷

This town-centre, street-corner local has recently been refurbished and the landlord has now increased the range of real beer on offer. The L-shaped bar divides the pub into three distinct seating areas for youngsters, shoppers and regulars. Meals are served at lunchtime (except Sun), making this the perfect place to eat, drink, chat and watch the world go by through the attractive leaded windows. If the juke box is too loud for you, ask the landlord to turn it down.
◖⇌ ♣

Woodman Inn

32 Coton Hill, SY1 2DZ
(½ mile from train station on Ellesmere road, A528)
2 (4 winter Mon-Fri)-11; 12-11 Sat; 12-10.30 Sun
☎ (01743) 351007
Theakston Mild, Best Bitter; Greene King Old Speckled Hen; guest beers Ⓗ
Half brick, half timbered black and white corner pub originally built in the 1800s but destroyed by fire in 1923 and rebuilt in 1925. It has a wonderful oak-panelled lounge with two log fires and traditional settles. The bar has original stone-tiled flooring, wooden seating and listed leaded windows. The courtyard seating area is decorated with award-winning floral displays. The pub is reputedly haunted by the landlady who died when the pub burnt down.
♔Q❀◖⊟♿⇌♣

Stottesdon

Fighting Cocks

1 High Street, DY14 8TZ
6 (5 Fri, 12 Sat)-11; 12-11 Sun
☎ (01746) 718270
Hobsons Best Bitter, Town Crier; guest beers Ⓗ
Fine example of a popular community pub which also attracts visitors from far and wide. Set deep in the Shropshire countryside, it is well worth seeking out for its ale and food (eve meals Tue-Sat). Ingredients for the home-cooked food are sourced locally and are on sale in the shop in a converted building by the side of the pub. There is live music every other Saturday night.
♔Q❀◖◗Ⴤ♣P

Telford: Coalbrookdale

Coalbrookdale Inn ✔

12 Wellington Road, TF8 7DX
12-11; 12-10.30 Sun
☎ (01952) 433953
Adnams Broadside; Highgate Mild; Hobsons Town Crier; Wye Valley Hereford Pale Ale; guest beers Ⓗ
This former CAMRA National Pub of the Year is back in the Guide with new licensees at the helm. The welcome is friendly and you can soak up the atmosphere just by listening to the banter between the locals. There are seven handpulls, all 'free of tie', that showcase local brews alongside regional and micro beers. Freshly prepared, home-cooked food is available, served in the bar or no-smoking lounge/dining room. The Museum of Iron is close by.
♔Q❀⇆◖◗P⚟⊡

Telford: Coalport

Shakespeare Inn

High Street, TF8 7HT (next to Tar Tunnel)
5 (12 Sat)-11 (not Mon); 12-10.30 Sun
☎ (01952) 580675 website: www.shakespeare-inn.co.uk
Enville Ale; Everards Tiger; guest beers Ⓗ
A new conservatory was added to this delightful World Heritage Site pub in the summer of 2005. Inside the original inn an open brick interior is complemented by old artefacts and pictures of Coalport, Ironbridge and the surrounding area. The four real ales, fine wines and excellent value food ensure that this friendly family inn appeals to all. The sizzlers are to die for. No food is served on Sunday evening or Monday.
Q❀⇆◖◗P⚟

Telford: Ironbridge

Golden Ball

Newbridge Road, TF8 7BA
(near jct Madeley Rd/Wesley Rd)
12-11; 12-10.30 Sun
☎ (01952) 432179 website: www.goldenballinn.com
Everards Tiger; Hook Norton Old Hooky; guest beers Ⓗ
Set in spectacular countryside, this inn serves fine ale and food, and is handy for the museums. With its wooden floors and real fires it exudes comfort. An inn since 1728, part of an old brewery is on display in one of the many rooms. Shropshire ales are given preference as guest beers, though there is a fine selection of Belgian bottled beers. Fresh, home-made food is served all day using local produce where possible. ♔Q❀⇆◖◗⊟P⚟⊡

Robin Hood Inn

33 Waterloo Street, TF8 7HQ
11-11; 12-10.30 Sun
☎ (01952) 433100
Holden's Bitter, Golden Glow, Special; guest beers Ⓗ
A welcome return to the Guide for the Robin Hood, now a Holden's tied pub but also offering guest beers. This historic hostelry combines a strong local trade mixed with many tourists. There are two main bars plus three no-smoking smaller rooms. The pub offers a fine view of the modern Jackfield Bridge and River Severn, especially from the elevated outdoor drinking areas. Meals are served 12-7pm daily.
❀⇆◖●P⚟

White Horse ✔

Lincoln Hill, TF8 7NX
12-2.30 (not Mon-Thu), 6-11; 12-5, 6.30-11 Sat; 12-5, 7-10.30 Sun
☎ (01952) 432369
website: www.thewhitehorse-ironbridge.co.uk
Banks's Mild, Bitter; guest beers Ⓗ
Off the beaten track and hard to find, but well worth the effort to seek out, this friendly, welcoming hostelry has recently been refurbished. The real ale is strongly promoted and the guest beers change frequently. Cider is also sold in summer. Reasonably-priced food, served in the bar or dining area, is made from ingredients sourced locally as much as possible. No evening meals are served on Sunday. Traditional games are played. ♔❀◖◗P

Telford: Madeley

All Nations Inn

20 Coalport Road, TF7 5DP

12-3, 5-11; 12-11 Fri & Sat; 12-10.30 Sun

☎ (01952) 585747

Highgate Dark; Worfield Dabley Ale; guest beers [H]

A pub since 1831, this one-roomed, 1789-built gem with exposed ceiling beams and a real fire is famous as one of the last home-brew pubs in Britain. An early landlord's sign is on display inside. Worfield Brewery sits behind the pub and provides the Dabley house beers. You will also find the traditional toilets outside. The pub is popular with locals as well as tourists visiting Blists Hill Museum and other sites of Ironbridge Gorge. The outside drinking areas are tranquil with views of the wooded valley but inside can be busy and crowded, especially on quiz night on Monday. The tasty rolls are recommended. ᗑQ❀⛺♣●P⍽

Telford: Oakengates

Compasses

72 Beverley Road, Ketley, TF2 6SD

(just off Holyhead Rd at Ketley)

12-11; 12-10.30 Sun

☎ (01952) 617997

Hobsons Bitter; Archers Golden; guest beers [H]

Originally a coaching inn dating back around 350 years, the Compasses lies on the Watling Street Roman road. This free house offers quality beer and excellent food. The restaurant serves a variety of traditional foods all home prepared (not Sun eve). The landlord was once a member of the British freestyle skiing team. A warming fire welcomes you in winter. ᗑ❀◑◐♣●P

Crown Inn ✔

Market Street, TF2 6EA

12.30-3, 5-11; 12-11 Thu-Sat; 12.30-10.30 Sun

☎ (01952) 610888

website: www.crown.oakengates.com

Hobsons Best Bitter, Town Crier; guest beers [H]

Popular pub featuring 14 handpulls serving a good range of British and continental draught and bottled beers including mild and a stout or porter. There is also an excellent selection of malt whiskies and country wines available. The Crown hosts many regular events including live music on Thursday and quiz night on the last Sunday of the month. Beer festivals, with up to 34 ales, are held on the first weekends of May and October. ᗑ❀◑⊟≠♣●P⚟

Station Hotel

42 Market Street, TF2 6DU

11-11; 12-3.30, 7-10.30 Sun

☎ (01952) 612949

website: www.station-hotel.net

Enville Ale; Fuller's London Pride; Salopian Shropshire Gold; guest beers [H]

Town-centre pub with a public bar, pool room and lounge. No smoking is allowed in the lounge during the week until 8pm and at any time at the bar. Bar snacks are available. There is an excellent range of beers including two Belgian brews on tap and 15 bottled beers. A beer festival is held on May bank holiday with a cider and perry festival during the first week of July and a Belgian beer festival in August. ❀⊟♿≠♣●⚟

Telford: St Georges

St Georges Sports & Social Club

Church Road, TF2 9LU

7 (12 Sat)-11; 12-10.30 Sun

☎ (01952) 612911

Banks's Original, Bitter; guest beers [H]

A cosmopolitan club where CAMRA guests are made welcome. It overlooks one of the county cricket grounds and is a delightful setting for a pint during the summer while watching the matches. At least one guest beer comes from within the county. There is great support at the club for various local sports teams and social functions are often held here. ☎❀♣P

Telford: Wellington

Cock Hotel

148 Holyhead Road, TF1 2DL

4 (12 Thu-Sat)-11; 12-4, 7-10.30 Sun

☎ (01952) 244954

website: www.cockhotel.net

Hobsons Best Bitter; guest beers [H]

Originally an 18th-century coaching inn, the old stable courtyard is now an outdoor drinking area. A lively, popular pub attracting a good mix of customers, it has won local CAMRA Pub of the Year a number of times in the last few years, as well as county and regional awards. Six guest beers are stocked, always including a mild and a stout. One handpump is reserved for cider, often from Westons. Two out of the three rooms are no-smoking.

ᗑQ❀⛟⊟≠●P⚟⍽

Upper Affcot

Travellers Rest Inn

SY6 6RL (on A49 between Church Stretton and Craven Arms)

11-11; 12-10.30 Sun

☎ (01694) 781275

website: www.travellersrestinn.co.uk

Draught Bass; Hobsons Mild, Best Bitter; Wood Shropshire Lad; guest beers [H]

A warm welcome for travellers and locals alike is offered at this large roadside inn on the busy A49. You will find a good selection of real ales, including a house beer from Wood, and a varied food menu served all day. There is a spacious new no-smoking conservatory for diners and a games area with a pool table and darts. Children are welcome. Overnight accommodation includes two rooms adapted for wheelchair users. Q❀⛟◑◐♿⛺♣●P⚟

Upper Hengoed

Last Inn

Upper Hengoed, SY10 7EU

(off B4579, 3 miles N of Oswestry) OS680979

7-11; 12-3, 7-10.30 Sun

☎ (01691) 659747

Beer range varies [H]

A large pub standing on its own by the crossroads at Upper Hengoed. This former cobbler's workshop now sells beer from micro and regional breweries. The Last has a large games room with pool tables and darts as well as a function room hosting folk evenings. The pub is also home to an amateur athletics club. Various items of brewery memorabilia, including some from French micros, are on display. No meals are served on Tuesday. ₾Q≿◗♣P

Wem

Albion

2 Aston Street, SY4 5AY (opp. station)
✪ 11-11; 12-10.30 Sun
☎ (01939) 233933
Draught Bass; Tetley Bitter; guest beers Ⓗ
Large, red-brick, mid-19th-century former coaching inn. It is a busy local, offering four real ales and serving good quality, locally produced food. A 200-year-old barn at the side of the pub has been converted into a restaurant. Outside, the large garden is a pleasant place to enjoy a drink in summer. The pub is situated at the start of the Shropshire Way, making it popular with walkers. ₾❀◖◗⊟♿⅄≷♣P⅟

Worfield

Dog Inn (Davenport Arms)

Main Street, WV15 5LF (off A454 3 miles E of Bridgnorth)
✪ 12-2.30, 7-11; 12-3, 7-10.30 Sun
☎ (01746) 716020
Courage Best Bitter; Theakston Mild; Wells Bombardier; guest beers (summer) Ⓗ
Charming, typically English village pub in a quiet, secluded lane. There are two bars; the lounge has been extended into an attractive dining area. Home-made food is served with fresh fish a speciality. Families are welcome. If you are in the area, it is well worth making a diversion off the main road to the Dog.
₾Q❀◖◗⊟♿♣P⅟

Yorton

Railway Inn

SY4 3EP (200 yds from station)
✪ 12-3.30, 6.30-11; 12-3.30, 7-10.30 Sun
☎ (01939) 220240
Archers Golden; Holden's Golden Glow; Salopian Heaven Sent; Wadworth 6X; Wood Special Bitter, Shropshire Lad Ⓗ
Near the picturesque village of Clive, this small, friendly country pub has been run by the same family for 68 years. The simple bar, with settles, quarry-tiled floor, dartboard and dominoes, is favoured by locals. The well-appointed lounge displays a collection of trophies including 'Pinkie', a large carp caught at a local pool long ago. Due to its proximity to the station the pub is popular with railway travellers awaiting the next train. A previous regional CAMRA Pub of the Year winner. ₾Q≿◗⊟≷●P⊡

Star Inn, Netherton (Northumberland)

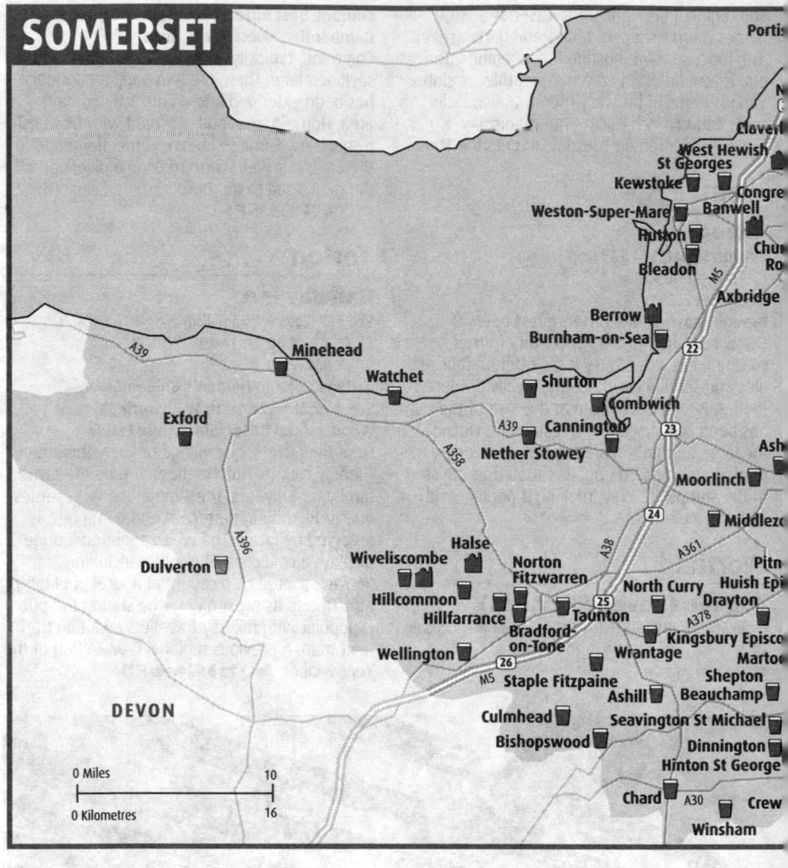

Ash

Bell

3 Main Street, TA12 6NS

12-2.30, 6-11 (closed winter Mon & Tue); 12-3, 7-10.30 Sun

☎ (01935) 822727 website: www.thebellatash.co.uk

Sharp's Doom Bar; Butcombe Bitter; Greene King IPA; guest beers Ⓗ

An attractive, buttressed frontage is made a little unusual by its sign, showing a different picture on each side. The main bar is split into two by the judicial use of furniture, soft chairs and a sofa clustered around a piano which sees considerable use. This is hardly surprising in a pub that frequently hosts main line British and American blues bands in the skittle alley-cum-function room. ⌂❀◑◐♿♣P

Ashcott

Ring O'Bells

High Street, TA7 9PZ (off A39)

12-2.30, 7-11; 12-2.30, 7-10.30 Sun

☎ (01458) 210232 website: www.ringobells.com

Beer range varies Ⓗ

Central village pub near the church and village hall, with a large garden to the rear. The pub has been run by the same family for 17 years. There is a busy function room and a no-smoking dining room. The pub serves award-winning food and ales, usually including a local brew from Moor or Glastonbury, and local cider from Wilkins. It was voted Somerset CAMRA Pub of the Year in 1998. ❀◑◐♿♣●P⊁

Ashill

Square & Compass

Windmill Hill, TA19 9NX (off A358, near Ilminster) OS310166

12-2.30 (not Tue-Thu), 6.30-11; 12-3, 7-10.30 Sun

☎ (01823) 480467

Exmoor Ale; St Austell HSD; guest beer (occasional) Ⓗ

Inviting country pub situated off the A358 near Ashill, towards Windmill Hill. The menu offers a wide range of home-cooked food. Superb views over the Blackdown Hills are a bonus. The pub has a function room with its own bar for up to 250 people. The house beer is WHB (Windmill Hill Bitter, from Interbrew) and guest beers are sometimes available. ⌂Q❀◑◐♣●P

Axbridge

Crown Inn

St Mary's Street, BS26 2BN

12-3, 5-11; 12-11 Sat; (hours vary summer); 12-10.30 Sun

☎ (01934) 732518 website: www.axbridgecrown.co.uk

Sharp's Doom Bar; guest beers Ⓗ

Free house just off the main square of this historic Somerset village. Table skittles is the central feature of the front bar where local

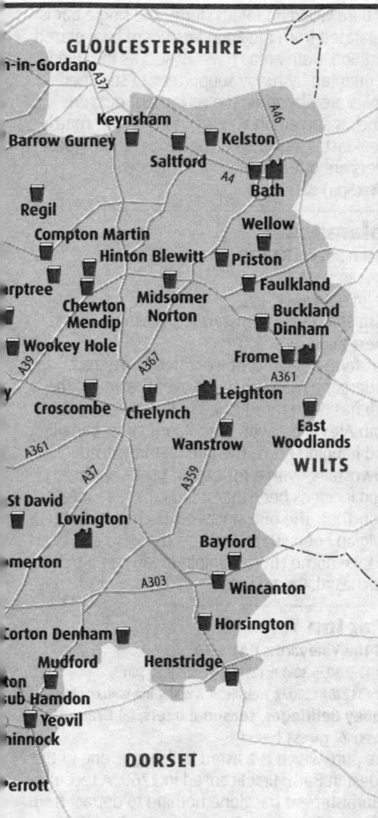

teams gather regularly for competitive games. Reasonably-priced bar food is served all day. The skittle alley doubles as a family room. Takeaway beer is available in four-pint containers. The house beer Crown Glory is brewed by Sharp's; up to four beers are on tap at any time. The cider is Thatchers. ⌂ ♨ ❀ ⊟ ♣ ●

Barrow Gurney

Princes Motto

Barrow Street, BS48 3RY (½ mile NW of A38/B3130 jct)

✪ 11-11; 12-10.30 Sun

☎ (01275) 472282

Draught Bass; Butcombe Bitter; Wadworth IPA, 6X, seasonal beers Ⓟ

Converted from three stone cottages, the Princes Motto has all the attractions of a country pub. Games are played in two of the three rooms while the third, long room is ideal for a quiet chat or a meal; food is available weekday lunchtimes. In winter the real fire in the main bar provides a focal point for all customers. At the rear of the pub is a small garden with a patio. Westons cider is sold. ⌂ Q ❀ ◑ ♣ ● P

Barton St David

Barton Inn

TA11 6BZ

✪ 12.30-2, 4-11; 12-11 Sat; 12-10.30 Sun

☎ (01458) 850451

Beer range varies Ⓗ

A 1930s red-brick pub, retaining most of its original features. A good range of bottled beers and soft drinks, many of them organic, support the handpumped ales (mainly West Country, but not usually the common ones) and, in summer, cider. The menu is limited but imaginative and relies on mainly local produce – organic where possible. A little off the beaten track but well worth the effort, dogs are requested to leave room at the bar for paying customers.
⌂ ◑ ♿ ♣ ● P ⊁ ⊓

Bath

Bell

103 Walcot Street, BA1 5BW

✪ 11.30-11; 12-10.30 Sun

☎ (01225) 460426 website: www.walcotstreet.com

Abbey Bellringer; Bath Gem; Otter Bitter; RCH Pitchfork; Stonehenge Danish Dynamite; guest beers Ⓗ

City-centre pub drawing a mixed clientele, the Bell has live bands on Monday and Wednesday evenings and Sunday lunchtime. There is a long main bar and a collection of smaller rooms at the rear. At the back is a large, terraced garden with plenty of seating. Posters for local gigs and forthcoming events in the Walcot area are displayed. Walcot Street is well known for its bohemian atmosphere. Vegetarian sandwiches are available. ❀ ⥱ (Spa) ♣

Hobgoblin

47 St James Parade, BA1 1UQ

✪ 11-11; 12-10.30 Sun

☎ (01225) 460785

Wychwood Hobgoblin; guest beers Ⓗ

This is a large, noisy, friendly place, popular with students, and selling an excellent range of four guest ales, plus Westons cider. The dark, woody atmosphere of the two main drinking areas – on the ground floor and in the cellar – gives this pub a slight 'retro' feel. Upstairs are two pool tables, well away from those wanting a quiet pint. The young landlord has recently introduced mini-beer festivals. ◑ ⥱ (Spa) ●

Hop Pole

Albion Buildings, Upper Bristol Road, BA1 3AR (opp. Victoria Park)

✪ 12-2.30, 5-11; 12-11 Fri & Sat; 12-10.30 Sun

☎ (01225) 446327

Bath SPA, Gem, Barnstormer, seasonal beers; Butcombe Gold; guest beers Ⓗ

INDEPENDENT BREWERIES

Abbey Ales Bath
Berrow Berrow
Blindmans Leighton
Butcombe Wrington
Cotleigh Wiveliscombe
Cottage Lovington
Exmoor Wiveliscombe
Glastonbury Somerton
Milk Street Frome
Moor Ashcott
Newmans Banwell
RCH West Hewish
Somerset Electric Halse

Bath Ales' first pub in Bath, the Hop Pole is a friendly place, situated between Victoria Park and the River Avon. Normally six real ales are available – four from Bath; a range of bottled foreign beers and cider is also stocked. High quality food is available lunchtimes (not Mon), and Tuesday Saturday evenings until 9pm. A restaurant has been added by converting the skittle alley. An alleyway connects to the river towpath, part of the Bath-Bristol cycle path. Games include backgammon and boules. Children are not admitted. ❀◐◑♣⊬

King William IV

54 Combe Road, Combe Down, BA2 5HY

11-11; 12-6 Sun

☎ (01225) 833137

Butcombe Bitter; guest beers Ⓗ

Built in 1825, it was named in honour of William IV for commissioning the local Bath stone for Buckingham Palace. The recently refurbished L-shaped bar is decorated with real ale themed posters and beermats. In additon to the skittle alley, there is an enclosed courtyard which is used in summer with more seating in the yard opposite. The range of beers is constantly changing, with forthcoming brews listed beside the bar alongside a record of all the past offerings. Booking is advised for Sunday lunch (served 12-3pm). ❀◐♣P

Old Green Tree ☆

12 Green Street , BA1 2JZ

11-11; 12-10.30 Sun

☎ (01225) 448259

RCH Pitchfork; Wickwar BOB; guest beers Ⓗ

This is a classic, traditional, unspoilt pub. Situated in a 300-year-old building in a narrow street near the centre of Bath, its atmosphere of dim cosiness pervades all three of the small, oak-panelled rooms. The panelling dates from the 1920s. The comfortable lounge bar at the front is decorated with pictures of WWII aircraft. During Bath's annual Fringe Festival, these are replaced by the works of selected local artists. The back bar is no-smoking. ♨Q◐⇌♣⊬

Pig & Fiddle

2 Saracen Street, BA1 5PL

11-11; 12-10.30 Sun

☎ (01225) 460868

Abbey Bellringer; guest beers Ⓗ

Large, busy but friendly town-centre pub. One end is an old shop front, the other an outside courtyard with drinking benches. Inside is a long room on two levels, plus an annexe. The decor is an esoteric mix of rugby memorabilia, such as signed shirts, a pair of signed Olympic skis and an oar from the coxed eight Olympic gold medalists. Useful for the rugby ground, meals are served 12-7pm (6pm Sat and Sun). Four beers are mostly from local breweries. ❀◐◑⇌(Spa)♣●

Ram

20 Widcombe Parade, Claverton Buildings, BA2 4LD

11-2.30, 5-11; 11-11 Fri & Sat; 12-7 Sun

☎ (01225) 421938

Draught Bass; Courage Best Bitter; guest beers Ⓗ

Popular local accessed by footbridge from the main station. The spacious interior is dominated by bare wood and Bath stone. The single bar is separated from the Founders Room by a glazed partition. Both areas have TV sets as the pub is frequented by rugby supporters. In summer tables are placed on the pavement outside. Lunch is served on weekdays and a pre-match breakfast is available on Saturday. Three guest beers are offered; the cider is Thatchers. ◐⇌(Spa)●

Salamander

3 John Street, BA1 2JL

11.30-11; 12-10.30 Sun

☎ (01225) 428889

Bath SPA, Gem, Barnstormer, seasonal beers; guest beers Ⓗ

This former 18th-century coffee house has undergone many changes over the years. The pub has been refurbished in the now familiar Bath Ales style, with bare floorboards, panelling and hanging hops. The pub is subtly divided downstairs, with a restaurant upstairs where food includes beer-themed meals (eve meals Mon-Thu). The pub stocks a selection of bottled Belgian beers; Bath Ales merchandise and beers to take home (from minipin to kil) can also be purchased. ◐◑⇌(Spa)⊬

Star Inn ☆

23 The Vineyards, BA1 5NA

12-2.30, 5.30-11; 12-11 Sat; 12-10.30 Sun

☎ (01225) 425072 website: www.star-inn-bath.co.uk

Abbey Bellringer, seasonal beers; Ⓗ **Draught Bass;** Ⓖ **guest beers** Ⓗ

The pub, which is a listed building, is one of the oldest in Bath, first licensed in 1760. A recent refurbishment has done nothing to detract from the superb interior. The many small rooms feature oak panelling and 19th-century bar fittings. Now owned by Abbey Ales it serves seasonal offerings alongside its regular ales and at least three guests. Bass is served, as it has been for many years, from jugs. ♨Q⇌(Spa)♣

Bayford

Unicorn Inn

BA9 9NL (on old A303, 1 mile E of Wincanton)

12-2 (not Mon), 7-11; 12-2.30, 7-10.30 Sun

☎ (01963) 32324 website: www.theunicorninnbayford.com

Draught Bass; Butcombe Bitter; guest beers Ⓗ

Former coaching inn that sits beside the old A303, and has become the hub of this friendly village. It usually offers two guest beers at keen prices. The inn serves exceptionally good food – fish is a speciality (no meals Sun eve). The single bar, with identifiably separate areas in one room, is entered via the old courtyard. The en-suite accommodation comprises four rooms, one with a four-poster. The inn gets busy on Wincanton race days. Ask about the hidden well. ♨Q❀⊏⊐◐◑P⊬

Bishopswood

Candlelight Inn

TA20 3RS (½ mile N of A303)

12-2.30, 7 (6.30 Fri & Sat)-11; 12-2.30, 7-10.30 Sun

☎ (01460) 234476

Butcombe Bitter, Gold; guest beer Ⓖ

A free house, dating back to the 17th century, that serves mainly West Country cask ales by gravity dispense. It is a friendly village pub, combining a social centre and meeting place with good quality food and drink. There is a garden by the River Yarty and a skittle alley that doubles as a function room. Meals are cooked to order and the pub also offers a take-away menu. ♨❀◑▲♣P

Bleadon

Queen's Arms

Celtic Way, BS24 0NF (¼ mile from A370)
✪ 11.30-3, 5.30-11; 11-11 Fri & Sat; 12-10-30 Sun
☎ (01934) 812080
Butcombe Bitter, Blonde, Gold; Fuller's London Pride; guest beer Ⓖ
Originally three cottages, built in the 17th century, this delightful stone pub is the centre of village life. Its four connecting rooms give a certain traditional ambience, and have a friendly feel. The village is situated just off the A370 Weston-Super-Mare to Burnham-on-Sea road. All beers are gravity-fed. Although the pub is owned by Butcombe Brewery, its guest beer policy observes customers' requests. The cider is from Thatchers. ♨Q❀◑⊟♣●P⊬

Bradford-on-Tone

White Horse Inn

Regent Street, TA4 1HF (off A38, Taunton-Wellington road)
✪ 11.30-3, 5.30-11; 12-3, 7-10-30 Sun
☎ (01823) 461239
Cotleigh Tawny; guest beers Ⓗ
Very much a community pub at the village centre, the post office and shop are in outbuildings. One or two guest beers are sourced from micros and national breweries. Real fires warm both bars; bar billiards can be played in the main one. The bar/restaurant serves excellent home-cooked food using local produce (booking advised). The skittle alley (with its own bar) doubles as a function room. The beautiful large garden hosts barbecues in summer; children and dogs are welcome.
♨❀◑♣P⊬

Buckland Dinham

Bell ✔

High Street, BA11 2QT
(on A362 between Frome and Radstock)
✪ 12-3, 6-11; 12-2.30, 7-10.30 Sun
☎ (01373) 462956 website: www.bellatbuckland.co.uk
Butcombe Bitter; Fuller's London Pride; guest beers Ⓗ
This 16th-century inn is the base for most village activities. It has won an award from the trade paper, Morning Advertiser for the best pub website for the whole of the South-West. The bar boasts four real ales along with Addlestones cider. An ancient barn has been converted to acccommodate live music and beer festivals.
♨❀◑♿▲♣●P

Burnham-on-Sea

Dunstan House

8 Love Lane, TA8 1EU (next to hospital)
✪ 11-11; 12-10.30 Sun
☎ (01278) 784343
Young's Bitter, Special, Waggledance, seasonal beers Ⓗ
Spacious roadside pub owned by Young's, which has been recently refurbished. It has a long bar with split-level eating areas. A garden room has been added to the side. There is outside seating and a play area for children. The pub caters for all ages and attracts a good mix of customers. The food and accommodation are both recommended. ♨♉❀⇌◑♿▲P⊬

Cannington

Rose & Crown

30 High Street, TA5 2HF (off A39)
✪ 12-11; 12-10.30 Sun
☎ (01278) 653190
Caledonian Deuchars IPA; Greene King IPA, Abbot, Old Speckled Hen; guest beers Ⓗ
Atmospheric pub, with a tiled floor, dating back to the 17th century. The single bar has a loyal following of locals and lively conservation is the norm. Talking points are the large collection of clocks set to the landlord's year of birth, and beams covered in trinkets and trivia. A wood-burning stove adds to the friendly ambience. The garden has won the Pubs in Bloom competition for three years running. Table skittles can be played here. ♨❀⇌♣P

Chard

Bell & Crown

Coombe Street, Crimchard, TA20 1JP
✪ 12-2.30 (not Mon), 7-11; 12-3, 7-10.30 Sun
☎ (01460) 62470
Otter Bitter; Branscombe Vale Draymans; guest beers Ⓗ
Originally converted from cottages, offering six ales, mostly West Country brews, this pub fits nicely into this Guide and its inclusion is abetted by the mini-beer festivals, held on the first weekend of every month throughout the winter. Food is served at lunchtimes only, which gives the landlord more time to promote his beer and his dedication to running a village pub in a town.
Q❀◑♣●P

Cheddar

White Hart

The Bays, Cheddar Gorge, BS27 3QW
(behind Fortes Ice Cream Parlour)
✪ 12-2.30 (not winter Mon-Wed), 6-11;
12 (11 summer)-11 Sat; 12-10.30 (hours may vary) Sun
☎ (01934) 741261
Butcombe Bitter; Greene King Old Speckled Hen; Wadworth 6X Ⓗ
Friendly, welcoming, back-street local near Cheddar Gorge. The single, large but cosy bar with a stone fireplace displays memorabilia of White Hart charabanc trips of the 1930s. The small snug doubles as a no-smoking family room. Regular music and quiz nights are staged. The cider is Thatchers. ♉❀◑♣●P⊬

Chelynch

Poachers Pocket

BA4 4PY
✪ 12-3, 6-11; 12-3, 7-10.30 Sun
☎ (01749) 880220 website: www.poachers-pocket.co.uk

Butcombe Bitter; Cotleigh Tawny; Wadworth 6X; guest beers 🄷
A part 14th-century village pub with an emphasis on food. Bare flagstone floors, plain wood furniture and a real fire create a welcoming atmosphere. The bar area and adjacent function room/skittle alley are popular with locals. The pub offers a good choice of three regular real ales, plus a guest beer and Wilkins cider. In recent years it has hosted annual beer and cider festivals and also supports local arts and folk music events.
⛼❀◐◑♣●P

Chewton Mendip

Waldegrave Arms

High Street, BA3 4LL (on A39)
11.30-2.30, 6-11; 12-10.30 Sun
☎ (01761) 241384 website: www.waldegravearms.co.uk
Butcombe Bitter; Courage Best Bitter; guest beers 🄷
Two-bar, stone free house with an award-winning garden in a village on the edge of the Mendip Hills. Like most of the surrounding area, the pub used to be part of the Waldegrave estate. The lounge is no-smoking, but diners are given priority. Home-cooked food includes fish on Friday and Sunday roasts. Two local guest beers are usually available. The accommodation represents good value – check the informative website.
Q❀⛼◐◑⊟♣P⚟

Churchill

Crown Inn

The Batch, Skinners Lane , BS25 5PP
(off A38, ¼ mile S of A368 crossroads)
11.30-11; 12-10.30 Sun
☎ (01934) 852995
Draught Bass; Bath SPA; Newmans Wolvers Ale; Palmer IPA; RCH Hewish IPA, PG Steam; guest beers 🄶
Long-standing CAMRA favourite, popular with all age groups. An increasingly rare example of an unspoilt, pre-war country pub, the decor may be somewhat tired and those in search of the creature comforts of central heating, fitted carpets and inside toilets could be disappointed. Howevers, lovers of bare stone floors and walls, hard wooden seats and log fires will be delighted. It always stocks at least seven real ales including two guests, plus Thatchers cider. Good value, home-prepared food is served.
⛼Q❀◐●P

Clapton-in-Gordano

Black Horse

Clevedon Lane, BS20 7RH OS472739
11-2.30, 5-11; 11-11 Fri & Sat; 12-10.30 Sun
☎ (01275) 842105
Draught Bass; 🄷 **Butcombe Bitter; Courage Best Bitter; Shepherd Neame Spitfire; Webster's Green Label;** 🄶
Fine, traditional village local – a real community pub. This 14th-century building was once the village lock-up. It features flagstone floors, exposed beams and settles. A single bar serves an L-shaped drinking area; there is also a snug, which is no-smoking at lunchtime. The attractive garden has a play area for children. Food is not served on Sunday. Dogs are welcome. Thatchers cider is sold. ⛼Q❀◐●P⚟

Claverham

Claverham Village Hall

Bishop's Road, BS49 4NP (½ mile off A370 at Cleeve)
12-2 (not Mon-Thu), 7-11; 12-10.30 Sun
☎ (01934) 830020 website: www.claverhamvillagehall.co.uk
Butcombe Bitter; guest beer 🄷
The bar and its adjoining skittle alley form part of the village hall, which was completed in October 1999. Run by volunteers, it is a focus for the community. Comfortable seating aids the pleasant, relaxed atmosphere. Pump clips of previous beers hang above the bar; some have been sourced from far and wide. Skittles, crib and bar skittles are all played here. ❀♿⛺♣P

Combwich

Anchor Inn

39 Riverside, TA5 2RA
6.30 (12 Fri & Sat)-11; closed Mon; 12-11 Sun
☎ (01278) 653612
Cotleigh Golden Eagle; guest beers 🄷
Situated on the riverside of a former port serving Greenland whalers, its Art Deco exterior belies the genuinely ancient interior. Enjoy the panoramic views from South Wales to the Mendip Hills or a walk on the River Parrett trail. The nearest pub to Steart nature reserve, it serves good food and usually at least two cask beers. The skittle alley is combined with the function room at this warm, comfortable pub.
⛼Q☕❀◐◑⊟♿⛺♣P

Compton Martin

Ring O' Bells ✔

Main Street, BS40 6JE (on A368)
11-3, 6.30-11; 12-3, 7-10.30 Sun
☎ (01761) 221284
Butcombe Bitter, Gold; guest beers 🄷
Under the ownership of Butcombe Brewery, this is an attractive village pub comprising several bars – the largest has a log fire and a no-smoking rule. The varied, reasonably-priced menu is extended with special dishes; a good selection of competitively priced wines is stocked. A large, well-equipped family room has toys and baby changing facilities. The garden boasts a fine floral display in summer.
⛼Q☕❀◐◑⊟♣P⚟

Congresbury

Plough Inn

High Street , BS49 5JA
(off A370 at Ship & Castle turning on bend)
11-2.30, 4.30-11; 11-11 Sat; 12-10.30 Sun
☎ (01934) 832475 website: www.plough-inn.co.uk
Draught Bass; Butcombe Gold; RCH PG Steam; guest beers 🄶
Friendly, characterful village pub, complete with several themed drinking areas and many original features, including flagstone flooring. No food is served except lunchtime rolls and sandwiches. Popular with local clubs, it is HQ of the Mendip morris men. Sunday is quiz night. An annual summer dog show is held at this dog-

friendly pub. Guest beers are always available, alongside Thatchers cider. A regular bus service from Weston and Bristol provides access (services XI and 354). P

Corton Denham

Queen's Arms

DT9 4LR (3 miles from A303) OS636225

11-3, 6-11; 11-11 Sat; 12-10.30 Sun

(01963) 220317

Adnams Bitter, Fisherman; Butcombe Bitter; guest beers H

Village pub, well decorated throughout with fires at both ends, wood and flagstone flooring and a trendy ambience. It stocks an excellent selection of bottled beers, non-alcoholic drinks and whiskies and boasts an extensive wine list. Cheddar Valley cider is sold; mulled wine appears on the bar in winter. There is a no-smoking dining room, but food is served throughout and families are welcome. Q P

Crewkerne

Old Stagecoach Inn

Station Road, TA18 8AL

11-2 (not Sat), 6-11; 12-3, 7-10.30 Sun

(01460) 72972 website: www.stagecoach-inn.co.uk

Glastonbury Mystery Tor; guest beers H

Comfortable, relaxed free house, run by a friendly Belgian landlord, who stocks nearly 30 bottled beers from home, plus five on draught. He is also a supporter of West Country breweries, as indicated by the real ales on offer. Good food is served whenever the pub is open, including some interesting beer-based dishes; the restaurant is no-smoking. Due to the landlord's lifelong interest in motorcycles, visiting bikers are always welcome. This is a pleasant place to wait for a train. P

Croscombe

Bull Terrier

Long Street, BA5 3QJ

12-2.30, 7-11; (closed winter Mon); 12-2.30, 7-10.30 Sun

(01749) 343658 website: www.bullterrierpub.co.uk

Butcombe Bitter; guest beers H

Originally a 15th-century priory, what was then the Rose and Crown was first granted a licence to sell ale in 1612. It was renamed the Bull Terrier in 1976. The fine beams and inglenook in the main bar date back to the 16th century. Two main rooms at the front of the pub are mainly used by diners (no food Sun eve in winter). Locals congregate in the common bar at the back. The landlord offers a good choice of four real ales plus Thatchers cider. Q P

George Inn

Long Street, BA5 3QH

12-2.30, 7-10.30 (6-11 Wed-Fri); 11.45-3, 7-11 Sat; 12-3, 7-10.30 Sun

(01749) 342306

Butcombe Bitter; guest beers H

An early landlord, Mr James George, introduced his own coinage in 1666, depicting George and the Dragon. This 17th-century former coaching inn has been sympathetically refurbished since 2000 by the present landlord whose use of personal photographs and mementos gives the feel of being welcomed into a family home. It comprises a large main bar with smaller, adjacent no-smoking area and a dining room. A skittle alley is in an outbuilding in the back garden. Limited parking is available in front of the pub. P

Culmhead

Holman Clavel

TA3 7EA (¼ mile off B3170, about 5 miles S of Taunton)

12-11; 12-3, 7-10.30 Sun

(01823) 421432

Butcombe Bitter, Gold; guest beer H

The only pub in England to bear this unusual name, the eponymous Clavel is a lintel above the fireplace made of Holm Oak. The menu features local fish and game in season and has dishes to suit all tastes and budgets. Guest ales come from both micro and regional independent brewers. The pub is allegedly haunted by the ghost of a defrocked monk, but a warm, friendly welcome is assured. Q P

Dinnington

Rose & Crown (Dinnington Docks)

Lower Street, TA17 8SX

(1 mile off Ilminster-Crewkerne road)

11.30-3.30, 6-11; 12-3, 7-10.30 Sun

(01460) 52397

Butcombe Bitter; Wadworth 6X; guest beers H

Traditional country pub, which is well supported by locals. An extensive range of food includes lunch-time specials at unbelievable prices. You can get your hair cut in the pub on the fourth Tuesday of each month. Happy hours, 6-7pm Saturday and 7-8pm Sunday, offer reduced prices. The bar area is full of transport memorabilia and the pub has a skittle alley. The cider is Burrow Hill. Q P

Drayton

Drayton Arms

Church Street, TA10 0JY

12-2.30, 5.30 (6.30 Sat)-11; 12-3, 7-10.30 Sun

(01458) 250233

Exmoor Ale; Fuller's London Pride; guest beers G

A warm welcome is assured at this recently refurbished, Georgian pub in the heart of the village. Although open plan, it is divided into four distinct areas. There is a varied menu to suit all tastes at reasonable prices (no meals Tue lunchtime). All beers are served on gravity; two or three guest beers come from a wide range of both small and large breweries around the country. Skittles and board games can be played here. P

Dulverton

Rock House Inn

1 Jury Road, TA22 9DU

11-11; 12-11 Sun

(01398) 323131

Cotleigh Tawny; guest beers H

Lively free house at the top of this bustling

Exmoor town. Built on the side of a rock face, it was first licensed in 1837, although part of the property is said to be much older. The single bar is where locals congregate and it can get smoky, but there is an adjoining lounge area and a no-smoking family room. Food is simple, homely stuff such as baguettes, pork and beans or a Sunday roast; evening meals are served Thursday-Saturday. ⛼◑◗⛺●

East Harptree

Castle of Comfort

BA40 6DD (on B3134, between Wells and Burrington)

✪ 12-3, 6-11; 12-10.30 Sun

☎ (01761) 221321

Butcombe Bitter; Cotleigh Barn Owl; guest beers Ⓗ

High in the Mendip Hills, this 17th-century inn is close to Wells, the Wookey Hole caves and Cheddar Gorge. It was reputedly a stopping-place for convicts on their way to the gallows. The lower bar with log fire, and upper bar (mainly for diners) serve a rolling programme of West Country ales, Thatchers cider and food from a comprehensive menu. Outside, a deck and children's play area are available in summer. ⛼❀◑◗♣●P

East Woodlands

Horse & Groom

BA11 5LY (1 mile S of A361/B3092 jct) OS792446

✪ 11.30-2.30 (not Mon), 6.30-11; 12-3, 7-10.30 Sun

☎ (01373) 462802

Branscombe Vale Branoc; Butcombe Bitter; guest beers Ⓖ

A warm welcome awaits at this pub on the edge of Longleat estate and safari park; listen carefully and you may hear a lion roar. The pub boasts an open fire and flagstone floors, an intimate public bar and no piped music. The conservatory has been turned into a restaurant and snacks are available; no food is served Sunday evening. The large garden provides good views of the country. ⛼Q❀◑◗⊟♿⛺♣P

Exford

Exmoor White Horse Inn

TA24 7PY (by bridge over River Exe)

✪ 11-11; 12-11 Sun

☎ (01643) 831229

Exmoor Ale, Fox, Gold; Greene King Old Speckled Hen; guest beers (summer) Ⓗ

Ivy-covered hotel at the heart of Exmoor, popular with locals and visitors. The Dalesman Bar is cosy and compact, while the tap bar is larger and has rustic settles, benches, tables, old beams, log fires in winter, antlers and foxes' heads. See the many photos of Exmoor, taken by the landlord. In summer enjoy a pint overlooking the River Exe. Children and dogs are welcome. ⛼❀⛟◑◗⛺●P⚞

Faulkland

Tucker's Grave ☆

BA3 5XF (on A366, 1 mile E of village) OS752552

✪ 11-3, 6-11; 12-3, 7-10.30 Sun

☎ (01373) 834230

Draught Bass; Butcombe Bitter Ⓖ

This is a real treasure of a local that has not changed much since it was built in the mid-17th century. All beers and ciders are served direct from the cask in an alcove rather than a bar. A good clientele is drawn from all walks of life and many visitors come from miles around. Tucker hanged himself in 1747 and is buried at the crossroads, as recorded in song the Tucker's Grave by the Stranglers. ⛼Q❀♣●P

Frome

Griffin Inn

Milk Street, BA11 3DB

✪ 5 (11 Sat)-11; 12-10.30 Sun

☎ (01373) 467766

website: www.milkstreetbrewery.co.uk

Milk Street Nick's, Beer, seasonal beers; guest beers Ⓗ

Situated in the older part of Frome, the inn is owned by the Milk Street Brewery. A small brewhouse was constructed out the back, in a former adult cinema, producing a wide range of ales, which are on sale alongside guest beers. The single bar has retained many original features – open fires, etched glass windows and wood floors – in this basic but popular pub. Live music is performed regularly. The small garden is open in the evenings. ⛼❀⥂♣P⊡

Henstridge

Bird in Hand

2 Ash Walk, BA8 0RA (100 yds S of A30/A357)

✪ 11-2.30, 5.30-11; 11-11 Sat; 12-3, 7.30-10.30 Sun

☎ (01963) 362255

Wadworth 6X; guest beers Ⓗ

This cosy village pub, of thick stone walls, low ceilings and exposed beams is a gem. It caters for all, with its skittle alley/function room and games room which is separate from the main bar. Two or three real ales are always on tap, including a changing guest ale, plus Taunton cider. Do try the excellent bar snacks as well as the beer. ⛼Q❀◑◗♣●P

Hillcommon

Royal Oak

TA4 1DS (on B3227)

✪ 11.30-3, 6 (6.30 winter)-11; 12-3, 6 (6.30 winter)-11 Sun

☎ (01823) 400295

Cotleigh Tawny; RCH Pitchfork; guest beer Ⓗ

Village pub on the main road, frequented by local drinkers as well as diners. The single large, open-plan bar is set for diners, but there is always seating for drinkers, plus designated smoking and no-smoking areas. A selection of bottled beers supplements the three handpumps. There is a beautiful, large garden, a bus stop outside is for routes 25 and 307 (925 Sunday). Food is locally sourced; Tuesday and Thursday are senior citizen discount days. ❀◑◗♣P⚞

Hillfarrance

Anchor

TA4 1AW (1 mile off A38 or A358 near Oake) OS166246

✪ 11-11; 12-10.30 Sun

☎ (01823) 461334

Branscombe Vale Branoc; O'Hanlon's seasonal

beers; guest beers 🄷
Four handpumps serve two regular and two guest beers at this village hostelry. Food is locally sourced and home made; try the Sunday carvery. Several rooms include a cosy bar, a dining room and a function room. Accommodation consists of four double rooms. Outside is a car park, garden and camping facilities (caravan licence applied for). A beer festival is held on August bank holiday. Children (and dogs) are welcome. ⌂☺❀⇄◑♿▲P⚟

Hinton Blewitt

Ring o' Bells

Upper Road, BS18 5AN (about 2 miles from A37 at Temple Cloud)
⏲ 11.30-3.30, 5 (6 Sat)-11; 12-3.30, 7-10.30 Sun
☎ (01761) 452239
website: www.ringobells.net
Butcombe Bitter; guest beers 🄷
Small pub situated on the village green benefiting from views over the Chew Valley. A yard with seating and toilets at the front leads to a small bar with a log fire and dining area. Several guest beers are normally available. The popular, reasonably priced menu offers a vegetarian option. It can be busy, especially in summer with walkers and cyclists enjoying the surrounding countryside.
⌂Q❀◑▲♣●

Hinton St George

Lord Poulett Arms

High Street, TA17 8SE OS417127
⏲ 12-3, 6.30-11; 12-3, 6.30-11 Sun
☎ (01460) 73149
website: www.lordpoulettarms.co.uk
Butcombe Bitter; 🄷 **guest beers** 🄶
Stone-flagged floors and a bar-mounted gravity stillage are immediately noticeable on entering. Further inspection shows an unusually furnished dining room, featuring much antique furniture, where an imaginative menu can be enjoyed. The bar has a well-stocked magazine rack and library. Outside, a charming Mediterranean garden, complete with petanque court, leads to a secluded garden with a pelota wall that dates from Napoleonic times.
⌂Q❀⇄◑⊟♣●P

Horsington

Half Moon

BA8 0EF (200 yds off A357, between Wincanton and Templecombe)
⏲ 12-2.30 (3 Sat), 6-11; 12-3, 7-10.30 Sun
☎ (01963) 370140
Beer range varies 🄷
Unspoilt free house in the Blackmore Vale dating back to the 1700s. Originally a barn used for making cider, it became a pub in the 19th century. The large, bare-boarded bar, heated in winter by two log fires, boasts up to six real ales at any one time. Local micro-breweries are always well represented here, alongside more widely known brands. Facilities now include new en-suite accommodation, with three rooms adapted for disabled visitors. No food is served Sunday evening.
⌂☺❀⇄◑♿♣●P

Huish Episcopi

Rose & Crown (Eli's)

TA10 9QT (on A372, 1 mile E of Langport)
⏲ 11.30-2.30, 5.30-11; 11.30-11 Fri & Sat; 12-10.30 Sun
☎ (01458) 250494
Teignworthy Reel Ale; guest beers 🄷
Traditional cider and ale house of a type rarely found nowadays. The 17th-century thatched pub has been in the same family for several generations. The central flagstoned tap room does not have a bar; several rooms lead off this area, including a cosy space for non-smokers. Home-cooked food is available, but check first if you hope to eat after 7.30pm (no food Sun eve). Camping is possible if you do not mind 'roughing it'. Local cider and ales are always available.
⌂Q❀◑♿▲♣●P⚟

Hutton

Old Inn

Main Road, BS24 9QQ
⏲ 11.30-11; 12-10.30 Sun
☎ (01934) 812336
Draught Bass; Greene King IPA, Old Speckled Hen; Taylor Landlord; guest beers 🄷
Popular local situated in the heart of the village, carefully refurbished in the recent past. Now owned by Greene King, the landlord is keen to rotate weekly guest beers; it stages occasional beer festivals. An extensive menu aims to suit most tastes and budgets. Live music is performed at weekends. Locally the village is well known as a regular winner in the regional Britain in Bloom contest held each year. The front patio has bench seats for you to admire the flowers. ⌂❀◑P

Kelston

Old Crown

Bath Road, BA1 9AQ (3 miles from Bath, on A431)
⏲ 11.30-2.30, 5-11; 11-11 Sat; 12-10.30 Sun
☎ (01225) 423032
Draught Bass; Bath Gem; Butcombe Bitter, Gold; Wadworth 6X 🄷
Low ceilinged, hop-strewn, multi-roomed, 18th-century former coaching inn owned by Butcombe Brewery. Flagstone floors, open fires and settles provide cosy drinking areas. The main bar contains an original beer engine. This busy pub serves good food (eve meals Tue-Sat). There is a large attractive garden, plus a roadside drinking area. No children under 14 years are admitted. Bath to Bristol buses stop right outside (Nos. 319 and 332). ⌂Q❀⇄◑P

Kewstoke

Castle Inn ✔

2 Kewstoke Road, BS22 9YD
(end of Weston-Kewstoke toll road)
⏲ 12-2.30, 7-11 (closed winter Mon); 12-11 Sat; 12-11 (3.30 winter) Sun
☎ (01934) 414850 website: www.the-castle.co.uk
Newmans Red Stag Bitter, Wolvers Ale, Bite 🄷
Friendly, early 20th-century crenallated bar/bistro of two rooms, acting as the brewery tap for Newmans' ales, with up to four of their beers on handpump. An interesting wine list is an added attraction. Excellent quality food is

served, accompanied by piped jazz and live performances on Friday evening. No food is served Sunday evening or Monday. An outside terrace for alfresco dining/drinking in summer affords beautiful views of the Severn coast. ❀◑⛺

Keynsham

Ship

93 Temple Street, BS31 1ER

☼ 12-3, 6.30-11; 12-11 Sat; 12-10.30 Sun

☎ (0117) 986 9841

Abbey Bellringer; Draught Bass; Courage Best Bitter; Theakston Best Bitter; guest beers [H]

Lovely pub – a community local that is popular with all ages. The large public bar is supplemented by a small lounge and a small, split-level dining area; evening meals are served Tuesday-Saturday. Darts and shove-ha'penny are played in the bar. For warm days there is a garden set with tables, giving views down through the park to the river at the bottom. Children are allowed in the dining area and garden. ♨❀◑⊟⥬♣P

Kingsbury Episcopi

Wyndham Arms

TA12 6AT

☼ 12-3, 6.30-11; 12-3, 7-10.30 Sun

☎ (01935) 823239 website: www.wyndhamarms.com

Fuller's London Pride; Worthington's Bitter; guest beers [H]

Hamstone inn circa 17th century, with open fires, flagstone floors, traditional decor and a thriving village pub ambience. Frequented by walkers and cyclists visiting the Somerset Levels, a good range of food is available at all sessions (no table reservations). There is a garden and courtyard seating. Two guest beers typically come from Glastonbury, Otter or Teignworthy; local Burrow Hill cider is sold. The Wyndham Blues & Roots Club based here regularly features international artists. Resident skittles and darts teams play here. ♨❀◑♣●P

Martock

White Hart Hotel

East Street, TA12 6JQ (at B3165 jct)

☼ 12-2 (not Mon; 12-3 Sat), 5.30-11; 12-3 (closed eve) Sun

☎ (01935) 822005

website: www.whiteharthotelmartock.co.uk

Beer range varies [H]

Grade II listed coaching inn dating from 1735 near the A303 trunk road. This family-run free house keeps three guest beers – Dorset, Otter and Sharp's are regulars. Bar and wide-ranging restaurant menus offer quality meals, including special dishes (no food Mon eve). The hotel has several bedrooms, some en-suite. The comfortable bar has high ceilings and chesterfield sofas around the fireplace. Some outside tables are set out in the courtyard in summer. The pub has a skittle alley. ⛟◑⛺♣P

Middlezoy

George Inn

42 Main Road , TA7 0NN (1 mile from A372/A361 jct in Othery)

☼ 12-2.30 (not Mon; 12-3 Sat), 7-11; 12-3, 7-10.30 Sun

☎ (01823) 698215

Butcombe Bitter; guest beers [H]

This 17th-century pub has retained many of its original features, such as exposed beams, fireplaces, and the stone-flagged floor. Home-cooked food is served in the no-smoking dining room (eve meals Tue-Sat). An excellent selection of changing real ales includes frequent appearances by Otter, Hop Back and Church End beers. Beer festivals are a regular features at Somerset CAMRA's Pub of the Year 2000. ♨Q❀⛟◑⛺●P⚟

Midsomer Norton

White Hart ☆

The Island, BA3 2HQ

☼ 11-11; 12-10.30 Sun

☎ (01761) 418270

Draught Bass; Butcombe Bitter [G]

This pub is a gem of Victorian design. Its multi-room layout has not changed in years and it is worth a visit for this alone. In addition to the Victoriana, memorabilia from the past mining heritage of the area are displayed alongside old pub pictures. The beers are served direct from the cask and there is usually a choice of two ciders. This popular local in the centre of town provides good bar snacks. ♨❀⛟◑⊟♿♣●

Minehead

Queen's Head

Holloway Street, TA24 5NR (off The Parade)

☼ 12-3, 6.30 (5 Fri & Sat)-11; 12-3, 6.30-11 Sun

☎ (01643) 706000

Draught Bass; Exmoor Gold, Hart; Greene King IPA; guest beers [H]

Situated in a side street, just off The Parade, this popular town pub often sells up to eight ales. The spacious single bar has a raised seating area for dining and families. There is a games room at the rear. The decor features pine furniture and old photographs of Minehead. Twice yearly beer festivals are held. The varied menu represents good value. ♨◑⛺⥬(W Somerset Rlwy) ♣

Moorlinch

Ring O'Bells

TA7 9BT (signed from A39)

☼ 12-2 (not Mon), 5 (4.30 Fri)-11; 12-11 Sat; 12-10.30 Sun

☎ (01458) 210358

Beer range varies [H]

Set in the heart of the village, this pub has a large, carpeted public bar housing a pool table, dartboard and juke box. The lower lounge bar acts as the restaurant, where good value home-cooked meals are served (opening hours are flexible and often extended at busy lunchtimes). Three real ales are available most days. The no-smoking area is in the lower lounge. The pub has a skittle alley. Moorlinch Vineyard is not far away. ♨Q⛵❀◑⊟♿♣●P⚟

Mudford

Half Moon

Main Street, BA21 5TF (on A359)

☼ 12-11; 12-10.30 Sun

☎ (01935) 850289

website: www.visitwestcountry.com/thehalfmoon
RCH Hewish IPA, Pitchfork, East Street Cream Ⓖ
This 17th-century inn has recently undergone a five-year restoration, which has retained and enhanced its character, and added an eclectic collection of artefacts. Under skilled management, it has become a local for residents of neighbouring villages as well as Mudford itself. It is a rare outlet in south Somerset for RCH Ales on gravity dispense. Excellent food is served all day, with snacks offered until 6pm. There is a large courtyard for summer drinking. En-suite accommodation is available. ♨❀⇌◐◗♿P⚡

Nailsea

Blue Flame

West End, BS48 4DE (access from Backwell, A370 via Chelvey – 2 miles)
✪ 12-3, 6-11 (12-11 summer Sat); 12-5, 7-10 (12-10.30 summer) Sun
☎ (01275) 856910
Draught Bass; Fuller's London Pride; RCH East Street Cream; guest beer Ⓗ
Lovely, rustic, 19th-century pub, unaltered for many years, comprising two rooms, one with a bar, and a snug. Coal fires help create a cosy atmosphere in winter. The large rear garden is ideal for families in summer. Food is limited to filled rolls. Thatchers cider is available. This free house is well worth seeking out. ♨Q❀▲♣●P

Nether Stowey

Rose & Crown

St Mary's Street, TA5 1LJ (off A39, Bridgwater-Minehead road)
✪ 12-11; 12-10.30 Sun
☎ (01278) 732265
Beer range varies Ⓗ
Large, friendly 16th-century pub set in a quiet historic village beneath the Quantock Hills. It has a large garden. The pub sells a wide range of real ales with seasonal guests, and real cider. The restaurant serves fruit and vegetables from the pub's garden (no food Sun eve). Full of local history, many old photographs are displayed. There are no-smoking areas for drinking and dining. Dogs are welcome – even in the guest bedrooms. Coleridge Cottage is nearby.
♨Q☕❀⇌◐◗⊟♣●⚡

North Curry

Bird in Hand

Queen's Square, TA3 6LT (off main road)
✪ 12-3, 6 (5.30 Fri)-11; 12-4, 7-11 Sat; 12-3, 7-10.30 Sun
☎ (01823) 490248
Otter Bitter; guest beers Ⓗ
Renovated village local with low, beamed ceilings and a central fireplace in the front bar. A restaurant area is situated to the rear of the pub. The varied menu includes meals using local produce and offers good quality at reasonable prices. Outside drinking areas are provided at the front and rear of the pub. The two guest beers change often. ♨Q◐◗▲♣●P

North Perrott

Manor Arms

Middle Street, TA18 7SG
✪ 11-11; 12-10.30 Sun
☎ (01460) 72901 website: www.manorarmshotel.co.uk
Butcombe Bitter; guest beers Ⓗ
Six or eight real ales are usually on handpump at this 16th-century village inn; they mainly come from West Country breweries. Do not let the a la carte restaurant and bar food signs put you off, you will be made welcome if just calling in for a beer. With eight en-suite bedrooms, and long hours – open all day, every day – this is a must when visiting the West Country.♨Q❀⇌◐◗♿P

Norton Fitzwarren

Cross Keys ✔

TA2 6NR (at A358/B3227 jct W of Taunton)
✪ 11-11; 12-10.30 Sun
☎ (01823) 333062
Courage Best Bitter; guest beers Ⓗ
Large Chef and Brewer house that extends a warm welcome to all. A wide-ranging menu is supplemented by chef's specials, often featuring fresh fish. There is an extensive wine list and guest beers change regularly. Bottled Belgian and German beers are also stocked. A beer festival is held annually. The large garden offers a pleasant drinking area. Regular buses from Taunton stop outside. ♨❀◐◗P

Pitney

Halfway House

Pitney Hill, TA10 9AB
(on B3153, between Langport and Somerton) OS451278
✪ 11.30-3, 5.30-11; 12-3.30, 7-10.30 Sun
☎ (01458) 252513
Branscombe Vale Own Label; Butcombe Bitter; Hop Back Crop Circle, Summer Lightning; Teignworthy Reel Ale; guest beers Ⓖ
Traditional village pub serving a wide variety of local ales, alongside a range of international bottled beers. There is no juke box or fruit machine at CAMRA's national Pub of the Year 1996 (and frequent Somerset winner). A real gem of a pub. The No. 54 bus stops outside (Taunton to Yeovil service) including Sunday (No. 954). ♨Q❀◐◗▲♣●P

Portishead

Windmill Inn

58 Nore Road, BS20 6JZ (off M5, jct 19)
✪ 11-11; 12-10.30 Sun
☎ (01275) 843677
Butcombe Gold; Draught Bass; Courage Best Bitter; RCH Pitchfork; guest beers Ⓗ
Spacious free house on the coast road, next to a golf course and coastal footpath. The earliest part of the building dates from 1832. A major refurbishment in 2000 divided the pub into three levels. The large patio overlooks the Severn estuary and second Severn crossing. A good, varied menu, including a specials board is served all day, every day. It supports local breweries by showcasing regular guest ales; Thatchers cider is sold. ☕❀◐◗♿●P

Priddy

Hunter's Lodge

BA5 3AR (at crossroads of Old Bristol/Hillgrove Road) OS549500

❂ 11.30-2.30, 6.30-11; 12-2, 7-10.30 Sun
☎ (01749) 672275
Butcombe Bitter, Gold; Exmoor Ale Ⓖ
Atop the Mendip Hills, the pub stands at an unmarked crossroads close to Priddy. It appears unloved from the outside, but inside is like stepping back in time. It is a real gem, warmed by coal fires, where simple, inexpensive food is accompanied by beer served under gravity from the barrel. The landlord has been in residence for over 30 years, so there appears to be no danger of modernisation. Locals, walkers and cavers all make their way here.
♔Q❀◐◑⛺♣●P

Queen Victoria Inn

Pelting Drove, BA5 3BA
(3 miles off A39 at Green Ore)
❂ 7-11; 12-11 Sat & school holidays; 12-10.30 Sun
☎ (01749) 676385
Butcombe Bitter, Blonde, Gold Ⓖ
Creeper-clad, stone pub by the village green. The single bar is broken up by three stone fireplaces where log fires give a wonderful, warming olde-worlde feel. Stone floors throughout blend well with low wood ceilings, church pews and walls covered in agricultural implements. A children's playground is in the car park opposite the pub. New owners took over after 35 years in the same hands, and have kept everything much the same. No food is served Sunday.
♔Q❀◑♣P

Priston

Ring of Bells

BA2 9EE
❂ 7-11; 12-3, 6.30-11 Sat; 12-3, 7-10.30 Sun
☎ (01761) 471467
Draught Bass; Greene King IPA, Ruddles Best, Morland Original, Abbot Ⓗ
Traditional old English pub, providing a real fire, real ale and real atmosphere. A cheerful landlord and friendly customers combine to make this a welcome stop. Substantial bar meals are served in convivial surroundings. A pub set in the heart of a pretty village, it is well worth visiting for several good rural walks, or to try your hand at skittles or shove ha'penny.
♔❀◐◑⛺♣P

Regil

Crown Inn

Crown Hill, Regil Lane, BS40 8AY
(off Winford-Chew Magna road; take first turn for Ridgehill)
❂ 11-3, 6-11; 12-10.30 Sun
☎ (01275) 472388
Butcombe Bitter; Wadworth IPA, 6X Ⓗ
This hostelry, built in the 1750s, started life as a cottage and bakery, continued in various guises, to finish as it is now – a delightful stone, olde-worlde pub, in rural Somerset, yet only five minutes from Bristol Airport via the A38. It has an authentic laid-back feel and serves good, reasonably-priced meals. Unusually, the skittle alley is upstairs and can be booked for functions. Note the photos and paintings of previous customers in the bar.
♔Q♉❀◐◑♿♣P⚡

Rowberrow

Swan Inn ✔

Rowberrow Lane, BS25 1QL (E of A38, ¾ mile S of A368 jct)
❂ 12-3, 6-11; 12-3, 7-10.30 Sun
☎ (01934) 852371
Draught Bass; Butcombe Bitter, Blonde, Gold Ⓗ
Welcoming country pub in a peaceful setting. There are two spacious bar areas with seating arranged around assorted large pine dining tables. The emphasis is on good value, home-cooked food which is available seven days a week. A log fire crackles in winter. The large garden opposite the pub affords fine views of Dolebury iron age hillfort to the north. The pub is well situated for some excellent walking on the Mendip Hills. Thatchers cider is sold.
♔Q❀◐◑●P

St George's

Woolpack Inn

Shepherds Way, BS22 7XE (off M5 jct 21, signed from the old A370 on to B3440)
❂ 12-2.30, 6-11; 12-3, 7-10.30 Sun
☎ (01934) 521670
Beer range varies Ⓗ
This 17th-century stone-built pub started life as a woolpacking station (hence the name) on what was the old main road. It later became four railway cottages, as it stood so close to the south-west main line. The Stables function room has been added in the same style. Four changing beers are mostly sourced from local micro-breweries and regionals. Situated only five minutes from the M5, it is worth a detour.
♔Q❀◐◑⇌(Worle Parkway)♣P

Saltford

Bird in Hand

58 High Street, BS31 3EJ (follow signs for Saltford Hall, continue to river)
❂ 11-3 (3.30 Sat), 6-11; 12-3.30, 6-10.30 Sun
☎ (01225) 873335
Abbey Bellringer; Butcombe Bitter; Courage Best Bitter; guest beer Ⓗ
Built in 1869 as three cottages, coinciding with the advent of the Midland Railway to Bath, this fine country pub lies in a pleasant setting among the older cottages of Saltford, close to the River Avon. The Bristol-Bath cycle track runs alongside the car park and is good for walks. Home-cooked food is served at reasonable prices in the no-smoking conservatory extension. Children are welcome in the small family area. The garden has a pond and petanque pitch. Local Thatchers cider is stocked. ❀◐◑♿♣●P

Seavington St Michael

Volunteer

TA19 0QE (2 miles from A303, E of Ilminster)
❂ 12-2.30, 6.30-11; 7-10.30 Sun
☎ (01460) 240126
St Austell Tinners, Tribute, HSD Ⓗ
Roadside pub in the village of Seavington St Michael near Ilminster. The main bar is kept nicely warm by a large log-burner in the original inglenook. There is a no-smoking dining room off the bar where a good range of food is

served, including curry night on Tuesday; booking is recommended for Sunday lunch. The smaller public bar, which houses the TV and dartboard, is open Thursday-Sunday. 🔥Q❀🛏◑⊟♿♣P

Shepton Beachamp

Duke of York

North Street, TA19 0LW

⏲ 12-3, 6-11; 12-11 Sat; 12-10.30 Sun

☎ (01460) 240314

Teignworthy Reel Ale; Wells Bombardier; guest beers Ⓗ

Tables on a raised pavement outside the split-level bar make the ideal place to watch leisurely village life unfold, when weather permits. Inside dark wood abounds, with a discreet monitor tucked away showing forthcoming village events and the current standings of the active darts and skittles teams, along with the high and low points of the latest matches. Dogs (if quiet) are welcome. At the rear is the restaurant and a pool room with the garden beyond. 🔥☕❀◑♣●P

Shurton

Shurton Inn

TA5 1QE

⏲ 12-3 (3.30 Sat), 6-11; 12-3.30, 7-10.30 Sun

☎ (01278) 732695

Butcombe Bitter; Exmoor Ale; guest beers Ⓗ

Old, slate-roofed pub set in its own garden, handy for Bridgwater Bay nature reserve and the Quantock Hills. It has a no-smoking garden room and restaurant. The varied food menu draws much local trade, but it still leaves plenty of room for discerning drinkers, sampling the beers provided by four handpumps. Skittles is played here. 🔥Q❀◑♣P⊘

Somerton

Half Moon

West Street, TA11 6QQ

⏲ 11-3, 6.30-11; 12-3, 6.30-10.30 Sun

☎ (01458) 272401

Otter Ale; guest beers Ⓗ

Large public house, built in 1903, set in a small shopping district of Somerton. The public bar is sports oriented, with two dartboards and a pool table, which are well supported by local teams. The skittle alley can be accessed from both bars. Usually four real ales are on tap, plus a cider from Burrow Hill. The extensive menu offers Tuesday night steak specials; Sunday lunches are popular, and booking is advisable for the no-smoking dining room. ❀🛏◑⊟♿♣●⊘

South Petherton

Brewer's Arms ✔

18 St James Street, TA13 5BW (½ mile off A303)

⏲ 11.30-2.30, 6-11; 12-10.30 Sun

☎ (01460) 241887

Otter Bitter; guest beers Ⓗ

This 17th-century coaching inn encourages dogs and locals. One thousand ales have been sold here in 10 years. It organises trips to the races, Somerset cricket and two beer festivals a year (one national and one Somerset beers and ciders). The adjoining restaurant is recommended – attentive staff ensure that your glass will not be empty for long. A couple of minutes from the A303, this is not a pub to be missed. Bus Nos. 630/2/3 pass (but not Sun or eves). 🔥Q❀◑♣●

Staple Fitzpaine

Greyhound Inn ✔

TA3 5SP (4 miles S of Taunton)

⏲ 12-3, 6-11.30; 12-10.30 Sun

☎ (01823) 480227

website: www.thegreyhoundinn.fsbusiness.co.uk

Adnams Broadside; Camerons Castle Eden Ale; Otter Ale; guest beer Ⓗ

Grade II listed 16th-century, former hunting lodge in a lovely rural setting between Taunton and the Blackdown Hills. There is a flagstoned bar area and several connected rooms, revealing old timbers and natural stone walls. It offers an extensive menu and the food is freshly prepared to order. Thatchers cider is also served. 🔥❀◑⊟●P

Stoke sub Hamdon

Prince of Wales

Ham Hill, TA14 6RW OS479169

⏲ 11-2.30, 7-11; 11-11 Fri, Sat & summer (closed winter Mon); 11-5 Sun

☎ (01935) 822848

Beer range varies Ⓗ

Situated in Ham Hill Country Park, high above the surrounding countryside, magnificent views are the order of the day; ample outside benches encourage their enjoyment. As the pub is right on the Leland Trail it is as well that the flagstones fashioned from locally quarried hamstone cope with both muddy boots and dogs. A conservatory dining area leads to the restaurant in an old chapel. Beers come mainly from West Country micros. 🔥☕❀◑♿●P

Taunton

Harpoon Louies

75 Station Road, TA1 1PB (200 yds from station)

⏲ 6 (5 Fri)-11 (11.30 diners); 7-10.30 Sun

☎ (01823) 324404

Otter Ale; guest beers Ⓗ

Friendly bar/restaurant, where three or four real ales are sourced from micro-breweries, both locally and further afield – Cotleigh and Otter are particularly well represented. The subtly-lit restaurant (specialising in fish) is on split levels, with wooden floors and stone walls. Bar meals are also available. Close to the cricket ground, it is a favourite haunt of fans. Sunday is quiz night, when no food is served. Cider is stocked in summer. ❀◗≋●

Wyvern Club

Mountfields Road, TA1 3BJ (off B3170)

⏲ 7-11; 12-2.30, 7-10.30 Sun

☎ (01823) 284591 website: www.wyvernclub.co.uk

Exmoor Ale; guest beers Ⓗ

This large, busy sports and social club offers a variety of West Country beers, which change frequently. Normally three different breweries' ales are on offer at club prices. Meals are available until 10pm, plus Sunday lunchtime and during home rugby, football and cricket matches. The club premises are also available for daytime meetings. Show this Guide or your CAMRA membership card to be signed in as a guest. A real ale festival is held in October.

Wanstrow

Pub

Station Road, BA4 4SZ

12-2.30 (not Mon; 12-3 Sat), 6-11; 12-3, 7-10.30 Sun

(01749) 850455

Draught Bass; Blindmans Mine Beer, seasonal beers; Greene King IPA; H guest beers H/G

This is a gem, a friendly village local where the lounge bar with open fire and flagstone floors leads to a small restaurant. The pub is a regular outlet for the nearby Blindmans' Brewery and in addition can serve up to six guest beers on handpump or gravity. Blindmans' seasonal beers are also offered, plus two ciders from Thatchers. Games include skittles, bar billiards and ring the bull. A limited but imaginative menu is served; all food is home made. Q P

Watchet

Star Inn

Mill Lane, TA23 0BZ

12-3, 6.30-11; 12-3, 7-11 Sun

(01984) 631367

Beer range varies H

Tucked away, 250 yards from the marina, this pub is well worth searching out. Three cottages dating from the 15th century make up this welcoming, cosy inn. The beer range is constantly changed, putting an emphasis on local and West Country brews. Home-cooked food, served in generous portions, is a feature of this pub that is well supported by locals and visitors alike.
(W Somerset Rlwy) P

Wellington

Cottage Inn

31 Champford Lane, TA21 8BH (200 yds from Wellesley Cinema, up a side street)

11-3 (3.30 Sat), 6-11; 12-4, 7-10.30 Sun

(01823) 664650

Cotleigh Tawny; Fuller's London Pride; St Austell Tribute; guest beers H

Friendly, back-street local behind the Wellesley Theatre and Cinema. Five beers are normally on tap, including two rotating guests with often one from Cotleigh. With black beams and brass knick-knacks, the main bar area is divided in two by a large chimney breast to provide a lounge and public-style area where conversation flourishes. The Cottage is home of darts and skittles teams, as well as a local carnival club. Good value basic bar lunches are served (not Sun). Q P

Wellow

Fox & Badger

Railway Lane, BA2 8QG

11.30-3.30, 6-11; 11.30-11 Fri & Sat; 12-10.30 Sun

(01225) 832293 website: www.foxandbadger.co.uk

Badger Best; Draught Bass; Butcombe Bitter H

Cosy pub in the village centre. The lounge and public bar both have flagstones. There is a skittle alley at the rear. It sells King & Barnes Sussex rebadged as Fox Ale and Thatchers cider. An extensive and good value menu offers traditional and more unusual dishes. Meals can be taken in a no-smoking dining room. A quiz night is held once a month. It can be difficult to park.

West Chinnock

Muddled Man

Lower Street, TA18 7PT

11-2 (not winter Mon), 7-11 ; 11-11 Fri & Sat; 12-10.30 Sun

(01935) 881235

Beer range varies H

Recently upgraded with the addition of a new skittle alley-cum-function room – the extra space has improved the cellar facilities so that the more unusual of the local brews (which are a speciality) are given the conditions they need to satisfy serious real ale drinkers. The food is locally sourced where possible, and the meat can normally be traced to an individual animal. This is a charming pub in an attractive village.

Weston-super-Mare

Off the Rails

Station Approach, BS23 1XY (on railway station)

10-11; 11-10.30 Sun

(01934) 415109

RCH Hewish IPA; guest beers H

Part of the buffet facilities at Weston-Super-Mare railway station. RCH Hewish IPA is the permanent ale, while two guests are usually sourced from West Country breweries. Local Thatchers traditional cider is stocked. Sandwiches, snacks and magazines are available for the weary traveller, and a free juke box for music lovers. The landlord is applying for a late licence, so opening hours may extend.

Raglan Arms

42-44 Upper Church Road, BS23 2DX (from seafront turn up Greenfield Place)

11-11; 12-10.30 Sun

(01934) 418470

Draught Bass; Butcombe Blonde; Newmans Red Stag; RCH Pitchfork; guest beers H

Corner Victorian pub in a quiet part of town, 150 yards from the seafront. It has a pool table, darts and a big-screen TV. The lounge bar has a real fire, comfortable seating and all the handpumps; acoustic live music is performed on Friday evenings and occasionally, Sunday. The landlord supports real ales, especially new brews from local micros, and welcomes recommendations from CAMRA members to expand the range at this genuine free house. Q

Wincanton

Nog Inn

South Street, BA9 9DL

10.30-2.30, 5-11; 10.30-11 Sat; 12-10.30 Sun

(01963) 32159

Draught Bass; Greene King IPA; guest beer (occasional) **H**

Known for 150 years as the New Inn, this 18th-century pub had a name change in 1949. The patio garden and pool room are reached by a cobbled path, which may predate the pub. Home-cooked food enjoys a good reputation here; vegetarian options are available and the Sunday roast is served all day. Q❀◐◑♣P

Winsham

Bell Inn

11 Church Street, TA20 4HU

12-2.30 (not Mon; 12-3 Sat), 7-11; 12-3, 7-10.30 Sun

☎ (01460) 30677

Branscombe Vale Branoc; Young's Special; guest beers Ⓗ

Popular pub at the village centre, comprising a large, open-plan bar and a function room where darts and skittles are played. The patio hosts many village activities in summer. This pub offers good value food and drink; the home-made pies are a speciality. Children are welcome at this pleasant village local. Q❀◐◑♣

Wiveliscombe

Bear Inn

10 North Street , TA4 2JY

11-11; 12-11 Sun

☎ (01984) 623537

Cotleigh Tawny, Golden Eagle; Otter Bitter; guest beers Ⓗ

Former coaching inn and lively community pub just away from the town centre. It has a comfortable bar with a pool area. Children are welcome; there is a large garden and play space at the back. The old brewing centre of Wiveliscombe is ideal as a base for exploring Exmoor and the Bredon Hills. Guest beers include seasonals from nearby Cotleigh Brewery. ❀◐◑♿P

Wookey

Burcott Inn

Wookey Road, BA5 1NJ (on B3139, 2 miles W of Wells)

11.30-2.30 (12-3 Sat), 6-11; 12-3, 7-10.30 Sun

☎ (01749) 673874

Beer range varies Ⓗ

On the outskirts of the village, within easy reach of Wells and Wookey, this popular pub serves bar snacks as well as an extensive menu. No evening meals are available Sunday or winter Monday. The games room is no-smoking. A good range of beers is always on offer, including West Country ales. The garden houses the remains of an old cider press and benefits from good views of the Mendip Hills.
Q❀◐◑♣P

Wookey Hole

Wookey Hole Inn

BA5 1BP (near entrance to caves)

12-3, 6-11; 12-4 Sun

☎ (01749) 676677 website: www.wookeyholeinn.com

Beer range varies Ⓗ

Unusual conversion of an old village pub, where the single bar has been divided into a split-level dining room and two drinking areas, one with sofas and low tables. The impression is more of a café-bar than a country pub. It stocks four guest beers from micro-breweries, plus several draught Belgian beers. High quality food includes a good vegetarian choice. It hosts live jazz Sunday lunchtime and middle of the road music Friday evening. The large garden is a bonus. ❀◐◑P

Wrantage

Canal Inn

TA3 6DF (on A378, 4 miles SE of Taunton)

12-2 (not Mon), 5-11; 12-3, 7-10.30 Sun

☎ (01823) 480210 website: www.canalinn.com

Beer range varies Ⓗ

Roadside country pub, reopened in 2003 after a long campaign. The house beer is Canal Ditchwater brewed by Blackdown, with guest beers from West Country breweries. Belgian beers are also sold, plus a good selection of wines to go with the award-winning home-cooked food. It won Somerset CAMRA's Pub of the Year 2005 and Taste of the West award in 2004. A beer festival is held here in the summer. A skittle alley and a large garden complete the picture. Q❀◐◑♣P

Yeovil

Great Western

47 Camborne Grove, BA21 5DG (next to Pen Mill Station)

12-2, 5-11; 12-11 Fri & Sat; 12-10.30 Sun

☎ (01935) 431051 website: www.greatwestern-pub.co.uk

Butcombe Bitter; Wadworth 6X; guest beers Ⓗ

This previous Guide entry is now back on form, under friendly licensees who are new to the trade, but doing a great job. The comfortable, bare-boarded bar has recently been redecorated, but the railway memorabilia, mostly relating to the Great Western Railway, have been retained. The pub is very much a local, and hosts league matches in its skittle alley. Good, home-cooked food includes Sunday lunch, served from 12-6pm.
❀◐◑ ⇌ (Pen Mill) ♣

Pall Tavern

15 Silver Street, BA20 1HW

(down hill from St John's Church)

11-11; 12-10.30 Sun

☎ (01935) 476521

Greene King Ruddles Best, Old Speckled Hen; guest beer Ⓗ

Closed for more than two years, until being reopened and revitalised by experienced licensees, this town-centre local is now a shining light in the main shopping area. Named after a funeral pall, its name is pronounced 'pal', which well describes the pub's character. The music, mostly 1950s and '60s, is kept fairly quiet, and the TV is usually mute, to encourage conversation. The guest beer is generally from a West Country micro-brewery. Good value home-cooked food comes in generous portions.
❀◐◑♣

Sky's the limit

'Beer is the proof God loves us'
– **Benjamin Franklin**

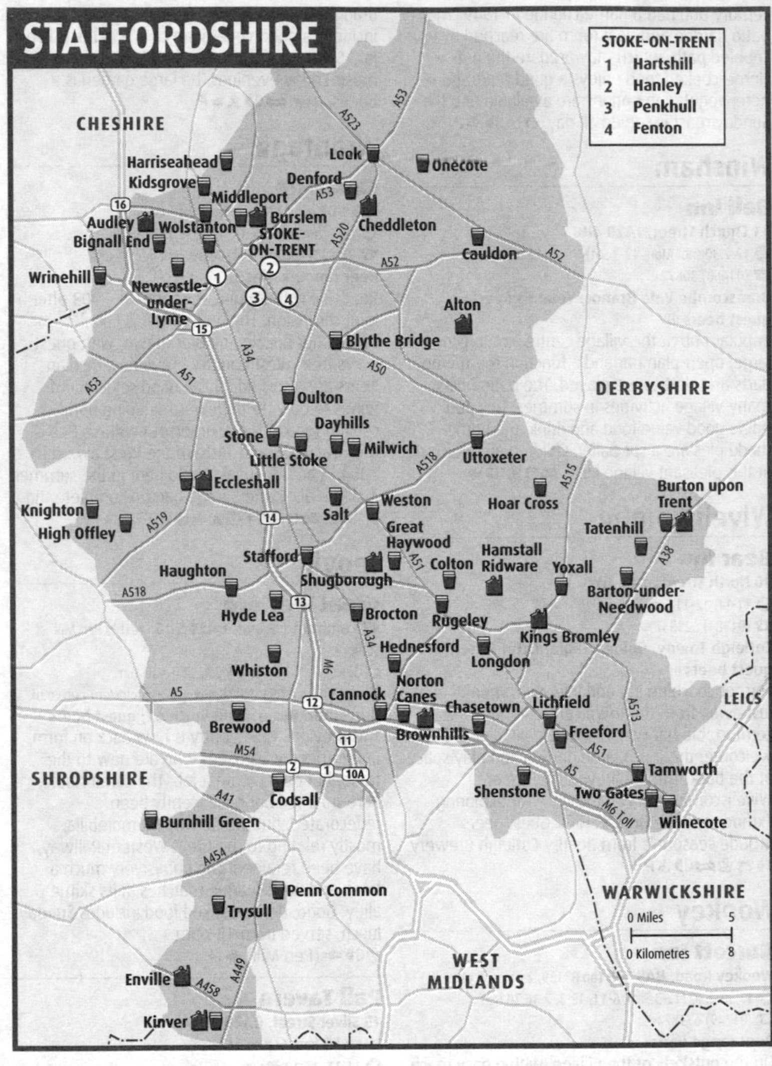

Barton-under-Needwood

Royal Oak ✔

74 The Green, DE13 8JD

(½ mile from B5016 via Wales Lane)

11.45-11; 12-3, 7-10.30 Sun

☎ (01283) 713852

Marston's Pedigree; guest beers H /G

Bustling, community local situated on the southern edge of the village, home to many traditional pub games and an over-40s football team. While parts of the building date back to the 16th century, the pub has only existed since the late 1800s. Public bar and lounge customers are served from a central sunken bar, the floor being below the level of the rest of the ground floor. Beers are available on handpump or on gravity direct from the cask on request. The pub is noted for its annual summer beer festival and bonfire night celebrations. A conservatory serves as a family room.

P

Bignall End

Bignall End Cricket Club

Boon Hill, ST7 8LA (off B5500)

7-11 (all day Sat in cricket season); 12-3, 7-10.30 Sun

☎ (01782) 720514

Fuller's London Pride; Wells Bombardier; guest beers H

Traditional village cricket club, in a semi-rural location, established over 100 years. The large club house comprises a comfortable lounge bar and a billiard room with full-sized snooker table downstairs, plus a spacious function room upstairs. Enjoy panoramic views across Cheshire from the cricket field. The club hosts a popular annual beer festival and 'biker' rallies. CAMRA members are admitted as guests. P

Plough

2 Ravens Lane, ST7 8PS (on B5500, ½ mile E of Audley)

12-3, 7-11; 12-11 Fri & Sat; 12-10.30 Sun

☎ (01782) 720469

Beer range varies H

Ever-popular, family-owned village pub, twice CAMRA Potteries Pub of the Year (1995 and 2002). The local Town House Brewery beers are regularly on sale along with Banks's Bitter and a changing range of guest ales, mainly from micros. It also stocks a selection of bottled beers. The busy bar supports darts and dominoes teams and in the split-level lounge good value meals are served; no food Sunday evening. ❀◐◑⊟♣P

Blythe Bridge

Black Cock ✔
393 Uttoxeter Road, ST11 9NT

✪ 12-3, 5-11; 12-2.30, 7-11 Sun

☎ (01782) 392388

Beer range varies Ⓗ

Unspoilt village pub renowned for its good beer and traditional lunches. The bar has seven handpulls offering a frequently-changing choice of ales, making this the hardest decision of your visit. Stand-up drinkers congregate by the bar of this two-room, totally smoke-free pub while comfortable seating is provided for the rest. The pub boasts a busy social schedule: two quizzes each week and an acoustic night, which draws local talent to entertain all evening. Q❀◐⇌P⊬

Brewood

Bridge Inn
22 High Green, ST19 9BD

✪ 11 (12 winter)-11; 12-10.30 Sun

☎ (01902) 851999

Burtonwood Bitter; guest beers Ⓗ

Popular with boaters and walkers, the inn stands on the Shropshire Union Canal and the Staffordshire Way. Dogs are welcome in the bar, which gets busy when national sporting events are shown on Sky. Home-cooked food from a daily changing blackboard menu is available in the comfortable lounge and the no-smoking restaurant; the kitchen closes at 4pm on Sunday. Regular live music and theme nights are held in the lounge or restaurant. ♨Q❀◐◑⊟♿P

Swan Hotel
15 Market Place, ST19 9BS

✪ 11.45-2.30 (4 Sat), 7-11; 12-10.30 Sun

☎ (01902) 850330

Courage Directors; Theakston XB; guest beers Ⓗ

This village-centre, former coaching inn has a low, beamed bar area warmed by a log fire, supplemented by two cosy snugs and a skittle alley in the room above the car park entrance. Two, usually interesting, guest beers are available alongside Swan Bitter (Courage Best rebadged). A regular award-winner at local level, the Swan is a former Regional CAMRA Pub of the Year. Hourly buses from Wolverhampton stop outside; in the evening some buses run from Stafford. ♨Q♣P

Brocton

Chetwynd Arms
Cannock Road, ST17 0ST (on A34)

✪ 12-11; 12-10.30 Sun

☎ (01785) 661089

Banks's Original, Bitter; Marston's Pedigree; guest beer Ⓗ

The bustling public bar, offering pub games, is a haven for drinkers, while the comfortable lounge accommodates both drinkers and diners; meals are served all day until 9.30pm. The garden includes a children's play area. Brocton is an ideal base for exploring Cannock Chase, an area of natural beauty. The pub supports local charities, the highlight event being the annual harvest festival. It was voted local CAMRA Pub of the Year 2004. ❀◐◑⊟♿⛺♣P

Burnhill Green

Dartmouth Arms
Snowdon Road, WV6 7HU

✪ 6-11 Mon; 12-3, 6-11 Tue-Sat; 12-3, 6-10.30 Sun

☎ (01746) 783268

Hobsons Best Bitter, Town Crier Ⓗ

Originally the estate pub for the Earl of Dartmouth's Patshull Park, the pub retains its rural atmosphere with two low rooms filled with hops, horse brasses and memorabilia. Excellent home-cooked food is served in a no-smoking area, including Sunday evening (not Mon lunchtime). There is access from a courtyard to a children's playground. A recently restored barn with a gallery is available for functions. Weston's perry is stocked in summer. ♨❀◐◑♿●P⊬

Burton upon Trent

Burton Bridge Inn
24 Bridge Street, DE14 1SY

(on A511 at town end of Trent Bridge)

✪ 11.30-2.15, 5-11; 12-2.15, 7-10.30 Sun

☎ (01283) 536596

Burton Bridge Golden Delicious, Bridge Bitter, Porter, Festival, seasonal beers; guest beer Ⓗ

This 17th-century pub fronting the brewery is the flagship of the Burton Bridge Brewery estate. Sensitively renovated and extended in 2000 to provide two rooms, both served from a central bar, the smaller front room has wooden pews, and walls covered with awards and brewery memorabilia. The oak beamed and panelled back room is no-smoking, and furnished with oak tables and chairs. It stocks a fine selection of malt whiskies and fruit wines. A function room and skittle alley are upstairs. No meals are served Sunday. ♨Q❀◐♣⊬

Coopers Tavern
43 Cross Street, DE14 1EG (off Station St)

INDEPENDENT BREWERIES

Beowulf Brownhills
Blythe Hamstall Ridware
Burton Bridge Burton upon Trent
Eccleshall Eccleshall
Enville Enville
Kinver Kinver
Leek Cheddleton
Marston's Burton upon Trent
Old Cottage Burton upon Trent
Peakstones Rock Alton
Quartz Kings Bromley
Shugborough Shugborough
Titanic Burslem
Tower Burton upon Trent
Town House Audley

12-3, 5-11; 6.30-10.30 Sun
☎ (01283) 523551
Draught Bass; G Castle Rock Harvest Pale H Marston's Pedigree; G guest beers H/G
Originally the Bass Brewery bottle store, this classic, unspoilt 19th-century ale house, later regarded as the Bass Brewery tap, is now operated by Tynemill. The intimate inner tap room has barrel tables and bench seats; the beer is served from a small counter, next to the cask stillage, using a mixture of gravity and handpumps. The more comfortable lounge often hosts impromptu folk music (usually Tue eve), other musical events and quizzes. A small no-smoking/meeting room is found off the lounge. No food is served Sunday. Q

Coors Visitor Centre (Burton Bar) ✔
PO Box 220, Horninglow Street, DE14 1YQ
(on A511, at Guild St jct)
10-7 (5 Sat); 12-5 Sun
☎ (01283) 513513 website: www.coorsvisitorcentre.com
White Shield St Modwen, Worthington E, seasonal beers; guest beers H
Large, comfortable, L-shaped, single-roomed bar within the Visitor Centre and Museum of Brewing, accessed via the reception. The bar, adorned with brewery memorabilia, is adjacent to the Wheelwrights Restaurant, while an L-shaped conservatory (The Cloisters) overlooks the garden and children's play area; families are welcome. There are normally six real ales on offer, and food is served from 8am for breakfast until 4.30pm every day. Entry to the museum, which includes the Coors White Shield Brewery, is free to card-carrying CAMRA members.
P

Devonshire Arms
86 Station Street, DE14 1BT
11.30-2.30, 5.30-11; 11-11 Fri & Sat; 12-3, 7-10.30 Sun
☎ (01283) 562392
Burton Bridge Golden Delicious, Bitter, Porter, Stairway to Heaven; guest beer H
Popular old pub, dating from the 19th century and Grade II listed: one of four Burton Bridge Brewery hostelries in the town. It comprises a small public bar and a larger, comfortable lounge with a no-smoking area off to one side. Note the 1853 map of Burton, old photographs, and unusual arched wooden ceilings. The rear patio features a fountain. A number of continental bottled beers and English fruit wines are stocked. Food is served all day Friday and Saturday; no meals Sunday. Derby and Uttoxeter bus services stop outside. P

Lord Burton ✔
154 High Street, DE14 1JE (near Station St jct)
10-11; 12-10.30 Sun
☎ (01283) 517587
De Koninck Ambrée; Greene King Abbot; Marston's Burton Bitter, Pedigree; guest beers H
Spacious, busy, single-roomed, typical Wetherspoon's pub, formerly a Woolworths store, close to the town's main shopping area. Old photographs of Burton adorn the walls. The wide selection of real ales now includes De Koninck from Belgium as well as guest offerings from UK micro-breweries. Food, from the standard Wetherspoon's menu, is available all day (last orders an hour before closing). The attractive, enclosed mixed grass and paved area to the rear allows access to the Memorial Gardens overlooking the River Trent.
Q

Oak & Ivy
119-122 Wellington Street, DE14 2DP
(100 yds from town hall)
10.30-11; 12-10.30 Sun
☎ (01283) 532508
Marston's Pedigree; guest beers H
Busy but welcoming mid-terrace local on the western side of town, a short walk from the station. A central bar serves a comfortable lounge and lively public bar. Burton's brewing history is illustrated by photographs and brewery memorabilia. The regular exchange of gossip and rumour once gave rise to the pub being known locally as The Jungle (from 'jungle telegraph'). Guest beers come from the Wolverhampton & Dudley list. Simple bar snacks are supplemented on Sunday lunchtime by a speciality cheeseboard.

Plough
7 Ford Street, Stapenhill, DE15 9LE (off Rosliston Rd)
12-3.30 (4.30 Sat), 7-11; 12-3.30, 7-10.30 Sun
☎ (01283) 548160
Marston's Pedigree; H guest beers H/G
Free house in the suburb of Stapenhill, on the other side of the River Trent from the town centre. Dating back to the 19th century, the pub is thought to be a converted farm building. The single, large room is partitioned into distinct areas, served from a central counter where the guest beers (up to 10, including a mild) are listed on a board. It hosts live music on Saturday evening. Beer festivals are held late May and early December at CAMRA Staffordshire Pub of the Year 2004. P

Cannock

Stumble Inn
264 Walsall Road, Bridgtown, WS11 3JL
(200 yds from A34/A5/M6 toll jct)
11-3, 6 (5 Fri)-11 (7-12 Sat); 12-10.30 Sun
☎ (01543) 502077
Banks's Original; guest beers H
Comfortable, one-room pub where the split-level interior includes a pool/darts area and a small function room. Popular with the local community, the pub stages regular charity events, a lively disco every Friday and live music on Saturday. It also hosts showcase nights (last Tue of month) for new local bands; worth checking out. Lunches (served weekdays) represent excellent value. P

Cauldon

Yew Tree
ST10 3EJ (1 mile S of A523 at Waterhouses)
11-2.30, 6-11; 12-3, 7-10.30 Sun
☎ (01538) 308348
Draught Bass; Burton Bridge Bridge Bitter; Grays Dark Mild H
You will never visit a pub quite like this one. The 300-year-old inn gets its name from the large yew tree right outside the front door. Go in and you enter a pub full of bygones and

memorabilia: a collection of pianolas, music boxes, ancient guns and a penny farthing. A monthly folk music evening is held (first Tue). Bar snacks are sandwiches and pies. The pub is handy for the Manifold Valley and Alton Towers. ⌂Q☕◐◑♿⛺♣P

Chasetown

Uxbridge Arms

2 Church Street, WS7 8QL (opp. Spot Garage)

⌚ 12-3, 6-11; 12-11 Fri & Sat; 12-10.30 Sun

☎ (01543) 674853

Draught Bass; guest beers [H]

Busy, corner local, close to Chasewater Country Park. The large public bar features an unusual round pool table. An extended lounge caters for diners, as the does the Haycroft restaurant upstairs; no food is served Sunday evening. Four guest beers, mostly from micro-breweries, are always available and the pub offers a full range of fruit and country wines, plus 50 malt whiskies. The cider varies. The forecourt is used for summer drinking. ❀◐◑⊟♣●P

Codsall

Codsall Station

Chapel Lane, WV8 2EJ

⌚ 11.30-2.30, 5-11; 11.30-11 Fri & Sat; 12-10.30 Sun

☎ (01902) 847061

Holden's Mild, Bitter, Golden Glow, Special, seasonal beers; guest beer [H]

Local CAMRA Pub of the Year 2005, this sensitively restored Grade II listed building is a working station on the Wolverhampton-Shrewsbury line. A comfortable interior, displaying worldwide railway memorabilia, comprises bar, lounge, snug and conservatory. It hosts a beer festival the weekend after August bank holiday and the landlord seeks out imaginative guest ales. Outside is a floodlit boules pitch and raised patio, where you can sit in peace and watch the trains. Evening meals are served Tuesday-Saturday.

⌂Q❀◐◑♿⇌♣P

Colton

Greyhound

Bellamour Way, WS15 3LN

⌚ 5.30 (12 Sat)-11; 12-10.30 Sun

☎ (01889) 586769

Banks's Original; Fuller's London Pride; Greene King Abbot; guest beer [H]

Classic unspoilt village pub, dating back to the early 1800s, and refurbished in the mid-1980s. The attractive bar features a brick-lined fireplace, red tiled floor and authentic beams. The lounge, with some settles, has a similar homely feel and doubles as a dining room; meals are served Thursday-Saturday evenings and Sunday lunchtime. Dogs are welcome in the public bar, and children allowed in the lounge until 8pm. A mile north of Rugeley Trent Valley Station, it is near the Staffordshire Way. ⌂❀◐◑⊟♣P

Dayhills

Red Lion

Uttoxeter Road, ST15 8RU

(3½ miles E of Stone on B5027)

⌚ 6-11; 12-4, 6.30-10.30 Sun

☎ (01889) 505474

Draught Bass; [H] **/**[G] **Worthington's Bitter; guest beer** [H]

This welcoming country pub is known locally as the Romping Cat. Unspoilt and full of character, along with the adjoining farm it has been in the same family since 1920. The main room has a timeless feel, with its quarry tiled floor, meat hooks in the ceiling and inglenook. The atmosphere is undisturbed by music, gaming machines or TV. A back room is opened at busy times. Draught Bass may be served straight from the cask during winter months.

⌂Q♣P

Denford

Holly Bush

Canal Side, ST13 7JT

(south of A53 between Stoke on Trent and Leek)

⌚ 11-11; 12-10.30 Sun

☎ (01538) 371819

Courage Directors; Tetley Burton Ale; guest beers [H]

Popular canalside free house at the end of a terrace of buildings situated beside the restored Caldon Canal. A traditional bar area leads to a comfortable lounge and dining extension at the rear. It has a large car park and children's play area. The pub attracts boaters, walkers and cyclists – it even sells puncture outfits. The two regular beers are complemented by changing guests, with up to six cask ales on tap at a time.

☕❀◐◑⊟♿P

Eccleshall

George

Castle Street, ST21 6DF

⌚ 11-11; 12-10.30 Sun

☎ (01785) 850300

website: www.thegeorgeinn.freeserve.co.uk

Eccleshall Slaters Bitter, Original, Top Totty, Premium, Supreme, seasonal beers [H]

As the home of the Eccleshall Brewery, the George is best known for stocking nearly the full range of Slater's award-winning hoppy ales. Bought by the Slater family 15 years ago, the neglected 17th-century coaching inn has been thoughtfully renovated. It now has attractive bar and lounge areas, excellent meals all day which can be taken in the pub's own café bar, and 10 luxurious guest rooms. Deservedly popular, the George is situated at Eccleshall's main crossroads.

⌂⛟◐◑P

Freeford

Horse & Jockey

Tamworth Road, WS14 9JE (on A51)

⌚ 11-2.30, 5-11; 11-11 Fri & Sat; 12-10.30 Sun

☎ (01543) 262924

Marston's Pedigree; Taylor Landlord; guest beer [H]

The pub name is one of the remaining clues that Lichfield racecourse used to exist nearby. The interior consists of a no-smoking dining room and a bar for drinkers. The latter is carpeted at one end, with bare floorboards and a dartboard at the other. The reasonably-priced food is of an excellent standard (booking advised). The bar is often packed on alternate Monday evenings when Irish folk music is performed. ❀◐◑⊟♣P

Great Haywood

Clifford Arms

Main Road, ST18 0SR (off A51)

⏲ 12-3, 5-11; 12-11 Sat; 12-10.30 Sun

☎ (01889) 881321

Draught Bass; Worthington's Bitter; Greene King Old Speckled Hen; guest beers Ⓗ

This village-centre pub has a large bar with plenty of seating and a no-smoking restaurant adorned with past photos of the pub. Darts, dominoes and quiz teams are based at the pub. It is popular with walkers, cyclists and visitors to the nearby Shugborough Estate (National Trust). The Staffordshire Way and Bridge 73 of the Trent and Mersey Canal are 200 metres along Trent Lane. The pub is dog friendly and has a garden. ♔❀◐◑♿♣P⊬

Harriseahead

Royal Oak

42 High Street, ST7 4JT

⏲ 12-3 (not Mon-Fri), 7-11; 12-3, 7-10.30 Sun

☎ (01782) 513362

Copper Dragon Black Gold; Courage Directors; Fuller's London Pride; John Smith's Bitter; guest beers Ⓗ

Two-roomed, 19th-century free house, deservedly popular with locals. Two changing guest beers come from small micro-breweries. An upstairs function room provides extra space during beer festivals. A selection of 15 Belgian bottled beers is supplemented by a Belgian draught. Monthly quizzes are held in aid of local charities. Air-conditioning filters the smoke. Access to the car park is through the door marked Ladies. ♔⊟♣●P

Haughton

Bell

Newport Road, ST18 9EX (on A518)

⏲ 12-3, 6-11; 12-10.30 Sun

☎ (01785) 780301

Banks's Original; Marston's Burton Bitter, Pedigree; guest beers Ⓗ

This friendly local free house has one large L-shaped room; the lounge area is no-smoking and serves excellent food (no meals Sun eve). The bar has Sky TV for football and horse racing fans. The building is over 200 years old and was originally a farm; photos and memorabilia are on display. Two guest beers change regularly. ❀◐◑P⊬

Hednesford

Queen's Arms

37 Hill Street, WS12 1DJ (250 yds off A460, on B154)

⏲ 12-3, 6.30 (7 Sat)-11; 12-3, 7-10.30 Sun

☎ (01543) 878437

Draught Bass; Highgate Dark, Old Ale (Christmas); **Worthington's Bitter** Ⓟ

Small, friendly, two-roomed local, a regular Guide entry. The current landlord has been here for more than 20 years. The bar of this traditional pub is decorated with many brasses. Darts and dominoes are the popular sports. Excellent home-made lunches are provided Monday-Saturday at reasonable prices. Weekly quizzes are held. Q❀◐⊟♿⇌♣P

High Offley

Anchor

Peggs Lane, Old Lea, ST20 0NG (by bridge 42 of Shropshire Union Canal) OS775256

⏲ 12-3 (not winter Mon-Fri), 7-11 (not winter Mon-Thu); 12-3, 7-10.30 (not winter eve) Sun

☎ (01785) 284569

Wadworth 6X Ⓖ

On the Shropshire Union Canal, this Victorian inn is a rare example of an unspoilt, country pub. It has two small bars where the cask ale and cider are served from jugs. This free house has been run by the same family since 1870, when it was called the Sebastopol. It boasts a large, award-winning garden with a canalware gift shop at the rear. Not easily found by road, it is well worth seeking out. ♔Q❀⊟⛺♣●P

Hoar Cross

Meynell Ingram Arms

Abbots Bromley Road, DE13 8RB

⏲ 12-11; 12-10.30 Sun

☎ (01283) 575202

Marston's Pedigree; Taylor Landlord; guest beer Ⓗ

Unspoilt village pub, with original beams and quarry-tiled floors, in a pleasant rural setting. Once a farmhouse, it dates from the early 16th century when it formed part of the Earl of Shrewsbury's estate. The pub was named after the Meynell family who owned nearby Hoar Cross Hall (now a health spa). There are smoking and no-smoking bar areas, a tiny snug served through a hatch, an intimate restaurant and an attractive paved courtyard. It enjoys a good reputation for food based on local produce. No meals are available on Sunday evening, when live music is staged. Q❀◐◑⊟P⊬

Hyde Lea

Crown ✔

ST18 9BG (1 mile off A449, 2½ miles SW of Stafford town centre)

⏲ 12-11; 12-10.30 Sun

☎ (01785) 253332

Banks's Original, Bitter; Black Sheep Special; Caledonian Deuchars IPA; guest beers Ⓗ

Welcoming village pub with traditional bar, which is equally popular with the local community and visitors from surrounding areas. The refurbished smoke-free lounge can be used for private functions. Good value bar meals rely on produce that is sourced locally (no food Sun eve or Tue lunch). The pub also sells general convenience items as the village has no shop. ♔❀◐◑⊟♿♣P⊬

Kidsgrove

Blue Bell

25 Hardingswood, ST7 1EG (off A50, near Tesco)

⏲ 7.30-11 (not Mon); 1-4.30, 7-11 Sat; 12-4.30, 7-10.30 (12-10.30 summer) Sun

☎ (01782) 774052

Beer range varies Ⓗ
This canalside pub was Staffordshire CAMRA Pub of the Year 2000–02 and a frequent Potteries winner. Six ever-changing cask beers are on tap from a wide variety of breweries. This genuine free house has stocked over 1,900 different beers in seven years. Real cider and/or perry plus German and Czech draught beers provide real choice. No juke box, TV or games machines disturb the peace. On Sunday evening folk musicians perform at this dog-friendly pub.
Q❀⇌●P⊭

Kinver

Constitutional Social Club

119 High Street, DY7 6HL
5 (11.30 Sat)-11; 12-10.30 Sun
☎ (01384) 872044
Banks's Original, Bitter; Wye Valley Hereford Pale Ale; guest beers Ⓗ
Rambling building on the High Street, comprising three main areas. A smart restaurant serves inventive home-made food at excellent prices, while the main bar dispenses up to four reasonably-priced guest beers from myriad breweries. The club enjoys an excellent sporting reputation, as testified by the trophies on display. A snooker hall is attached. Quiz and music nights are a regular feature. Current card-carrying CAMRA members are welcome but must be signed in. ◐&♣P

Plough & Harrow

82 High Street, DY7 6HD
4 (2 Fri)-11; 12-10.30 Sun
☎ (01384) 872659
Batham Mild, Best Bitter, XXX Ⓗ
Full of character, this local, situated on the main village thoroughfare, is affectionately named the Steps. The central bar dominates; the front bar sees locals and casual visitors, including cyclists and walkers, engaging in lively conversation. This contrasts with the smarter lounge, bedecked in Batham's breweriana and old advertising posters. Basic hearty fare is served 12-9pm at weekends at keen prices. Cider is stocked in summer. ❀◐⊟♣●P

Royal Exchange

High Street, DY7 6ER
11-11; 12-10.30 Sun
☎ (01384) 872683
Banks's Bitter; guest beers Ⓗ
Basic, no-nonsense pub at the top end of the High Street, offering a choice of guest ales from Marston's seasonal range and larger regional breweries. Two fires dominate either end of the small bar, which markedly contrasts with the plusher lounge adorned with pictures of old Kinver. This homely pub has real character but limited capacity. Live music is performed most Thursdays. Accessible on the No. 227/228 bus route from Stourbridge, it is well worth a visit in conjunction with the other Guide entries in the village. ♨❀♣P⊟

Knighton

Haberdasher's Arms

ST20 0QH (between Adbaston and Knighton) OS753275
12.30 (5 Wed)-11; 12-10.30 Sun
☎ (01785) 280650
Banks's Original, Bitter; guest beer Ⓗ
Traditional community pub, built about 1840, offering a warm, friendly welcome. This former local CAMRA PUb of the Year has four compact rooms all served from a small bar. The large garden is used for events such as the annual potato club show. It is well worth the drive through leafy country lanes to get here.
♨Q❀⊟▲♣P

Leek

Bull's Head

35 St Edward Street, ST13 5DN
5 (12 Wed, Fri & Sat)-11; 12-10.30 Sun
☎ (01538) 370269
Leek Staffordshire Gold, Bitter, St Edwards; guest beers Ⓗ
Snuggled in a row of terraced properties, the Bull's Head is the main purveyor of Leek Brewery ales. This elongated pub has three slightly different levels, creating areas for various activities. The pool table is on the third level, the bar and seating are on the second level, with more seating on the ground level. Look out for Jack the Hallowe'en puppet on the bar. Westons Old Rosie cider is sold. ♣●

Den Engel

11-13 Stanley Street, ST13 5HG
11 (5 Mon & Tue)-11; 12-10.30 Sun
☎ (01538) 373751
Beer range varies Ⓗ
This building has been refurbished in contemporary Belgian bar style. The centrally-situated bar stocks 11 draught Belgian beers, with four handpumps for guest beers and 150 different bottled Belgian beers (plus matching glasses) so there is no shortage of choice. The bar has two rooms: the front room overlooks the street and is no-smoking; the room at the rear overlooks the courtyard. ❀⊭

Quiet Woman

73 St Edward Street, ST13 5DN
11-11; 12-10.30 Sun
☎ (01538) 398190
Phoenix Arizona, Pale Moonlight Ⓗ
At the foot of this wonderful pub crawl street sits the Quiet Woman. Dating from the 17th century, what was then the White Hart Inn gained its present name from a barmaid who was beheaded on this site. The spacious lounge has a no-smoking section. Towards the rear is a courtyard section that doubles as a dining area; children's portions can be provided. Look out for the original hotel glass behind the bar. The house beer is supplied by Phoenix. ◐⊭

Wilkes' Head

16 St Edward Street, ST13 5DS
12 (3 Tue)-11; 12-11 Sun
☎ (01538) 383616
Whim Arbor Light, Hartington Bitter, IPA, seasonal beers; guest beers Ⓗ
The town's second oldest pub, a former coaching inn dating back to 1704. On entry you have a choice of three rooms. The room on the right houses the bar and seating, with access to the rear snug, WC and outside stage area that hosts summer music festivals. The room on the

left is a sitting room that doubles as a music venue – Mondays is acoustic night, although music can be staged on any night. Real cider is stocked occasionally. ☺❀♣P

Lichfield

Earl of Lichfield Arms

10 Conduit Street, WS13 6JR

⊙ 11-11; 12-10.30 Sun

☎ (01543) 251020

Marston's Burton Bitter, Pedigree; guest beer Ⓗ

Known locally as the Drum, this split-level, bare-boarded bar is popular with visitors and locals alike. Conveniently situated at the corner of the market place, the frontage is partly hidden behind a row of brick arches. Good value cooked lunches are served Monday-Saturday. An enclosed rear patio provides a welcome retreat in the summer.

❀◑≹(City)

George & Dragon

28 Beacon Street, WS13 7AJ

⊙ 11-11; 12-10.30 Sun

☎ (01543) 253667

Banks's Original, Bitter; Ⓟ Marston's Pedigree; guest beer Ⓗ

Welcoming, two-roomed pub where a public bar to the right is complemented by a cosy lounge to the left. The lounge tells the story of the second siege of Lichfield in 1643 when Royalists led by Prince Rupert bombarded the cathedral from a mound in the pub gardens. Close to Beacon Park, it is just five minutes' walk from the city centre.

❀⊟≹(City)♣P

Queen's Head

4 Queen Street, WS13 6QD

⊙ 12-11; 12-3, 7-10.30 Sun

☎ (01543) 410932

Adnams Bitter; Marston's Pedigree; Taylor Landlord; guest beers Ⓗ

A mecca for real ale lovers from near and far, this bustling, elongated, single-roomed pub is well worth the short walk from the market place. Two guests, often from micros, supplement the three regular beers. Good value, home-cooked lunches are served Monday-Saturday, while bread, cheese and paté are available during all sessions from a specialist counter beside the bar.

Q◑≹(City)♣

Little Stoke

Little Stoke Cricket Club

The Sid Jenkins Cricket Ground, Uttoxeter Road, ST15 8RA (on B5027, 1 mile SE of Stone)

⊙ 5 (12 Sat; 3 winter Sat)-11; 12-10.30 Sun

☎ (01785) 812558

Thwaites Original, Mild, Lancaster Bomber, seasonal beers Ⓗ

The bar is in the main room of the club house. A spacious room with plenty of seating, it looks out on to the cricket pitch and houses a large TV with Sky channels. As well as cricket the club is home to crib, darts and dominoes teams. Non-members are welcome. Sandwiches and snacks are available at the bar.

❀♿♣P

Longdon

Swan with Two Necks

40 Brook End, WS15 4PN (off A51)

⊙ 12-2.30 (3 Sat), 7-11; 12-3, 7-10.30 Sun

☎ (01543) 490251

Adnams Bitter, Broadside; Marston's Pedigree; guest beer Ⓗ

Run by a French landlord and his English wife, the pub has been in this Guide for over 25 years. An excellent example of a village local, it plays a central role in this rural community. High standards are maintained for both the beers, which include a guest from a micro, and the food. The restaurant is open 7-9pm on Friday and Saturday evenings. Real fires are lit during the winter months. ⩩Q❀◑◐P

Milwich

Green Man

ST18 0EG (on B5027)

⊙ 12-2.30 (not Mon), 5-11; 12-11 Sat; 12-10.30 Sun

☎ (01889) 505310 website: www.greenmanmilwich.com

Adnams Bitter; Marston's Pedigree; guest beers Ⓗ

A pub since 1775, this free house offers guest beers from regional and micro-breweries nationwide, with two on tap at weekends. See the website for information on Milwich and forthcoming guest beers. Westons or Thatchers cider is also stocked. The current licensee is in his 15th year at the pub and a list of his predecessors, dating back to 1792, hangs in the bar. The pub is popular with walkers and cyclists. Lunches are served from Tuesday to Sunday.

⩩❀◑♣●P⊁

Newcastle-under-Lyme

Museum ✔

29 George Street, ST5 1JU (on A52)

⊙ 12-11; 12-10.30 Sun

☎ (01782) 623866

Draught Bass; Worthington's Bitter; guest beers Ⓗ

Excellent, traditional, two-roomed pub with a basic bar and quiet, cosy lounge. It takes its name from a Museum of Curiosities once located here. In the bar you may play pub games, watch televised sport or just join in the friendly banter. A rapidly-growing collection of clocks and pictures of Newcastle are assembling in the lounge. Pies and the local delicacy, oatcakes, are available at lunchtime. Try the new patio area in summer. Q❀♣●

Old Brown Jug ✔

41 Bridge Street, ST5 2RY

⊙ 6-11 (1am Wed); 12-1am Fri & Sat; 12-11.30 Sun

☎ (01782) 711393 website: www.theoldbrownjug.co.uk

Marston's Pedigree; guest beers Ⓗ

This popular drinking venue, although central, is slightly off the beaten track. The interior has been opened up over the years. Regular jazz nights are hosted on Wednesday and varied music is performed on Sunday. A late licence has been granted for entertainment. This is a rare local outlet for real cider, with two normally on sale (usually from Westons). The Jug holds occasional food events and mini-beer festivals.

❀●

Norton Canes

Railway Tavern

63 Norton Green Lane, WS11 9PR (off Walsall Rd)
🕘 12-2, 5-11; 12-11 Fri & Sat; 12-10.30 Sun
☎ (01543) 279579
Banks's Original, Bitter; Greene King IPA; Highgate Dark; guest beers Ⓗ
One-roomed pub divided into two distinct drinking areas. The fully enclosed garden contains a well-fitted children's play area. Plans have been approved for interior alterations, to include an additional no-smoking area at the rear. A warm welcome is guaranteed by the friendly staff and customers at local CAMRA's Pub of the Year 2003 and 2004. ❀◑ ♣ ●P⊬

Onecote

Jervis Arms

ST13 7RU (on B5053, N of Leek-Ashbourne road)
🕘 12-3, 7-11; 12-10.30 Sun
☎ (01538) 304206
Draught Bass; Titanic Iceberg; Worthington's Bitter; guest beers Ⓗ
First class, family-friendly country pub set within the Peak District national park and not far from Alton Towers. The beer choice varies. Regular beer festivals, when camping is possible, focus on micro-breweries. Food ranges from bar snacks to a full menu to satisfy the most hungry walker. A small river runs between the good-sized car park and the garden, which on a hot summer's day is popular with locals and tourists. Just how a country pub should be.
❀◑ ⊟♣P⊬

Oulton

Brushmaker's Arms

8 Kibblestone Road, ST15 8UW (500 yds W of A520, 1 mile NE of Stone)
🕘 12-3, 6-11; 12-3, 7-10.30 Sun
☎ (01785) 812062
Marston's Pedigree; Worthington's Bitter; guest beer Ⓗ
Built in 1865 and thought to be named after a local cottage industry, this pub is an example of a local that has retained its traditional public bar and lounge. The unspoilt bar has photos of the area going back in time and a TV; the lounge is intimate and comfortable. There are no gaming machines or juke box. Guest ales include favourites from Archers and Black Sheep. A small patio garden at the rear is popular in summer, especially at lunchtime. ⩩Q❀⊟♣P

Penn Common

Barley Mow

Pennwood Lane, WV4 5JN (follow signs for Penn Golf Club from A449) OS949902
🕘 12-2.30, 6-11; 12-11 Sat; 12-10.30 Sun
☎ (01902) 333510
Banks's Original; Flowers Original; Greene King Abbot; guest beers Ⓗ
Small pub situated on the West Midlands county border, which dates back to the 1600s with a small extension added in the early 1990s. The range of real ales is complemented by an extensive food menu including meat supplied from the landlord's own butcher's shop. If you are over 5'5" tall you need to duck when entering the pub. Next to the local golf course, the pub is a short walk over seven cornfields from Wolverhampton. ❀◑P

Rugeley

Talbot Inn ✔

187 Main Road, Brereton, WS15 1EE
(on A51, Lichfield road)
🕘 4 (12 Sat)-11; 12-10.30 Sun
☎ (01889) 575512
Draught Bass; Marston's Pedigree; guest beer Ⓗ
Cosy, roadside pub in the village of Brereton, just over a mile from Rugeley Station. A real fire makes the split room a welcoming retreat on a cold day. In the couple of years the landlord has been here, he has certainly moved the pub forward. It is popular with locals and visitors alike. A regular bus service, Arriva 825, stops right outside. Brereton Town Football Club stands behind the Talbot. ⩩♣P

Salt

Holly Bush

ST18 0BX
🕘 12-2.30, 6-11; 12-11 Sat; 12-10.30 Sun
☎ (01889) 508234 website: www.hollybushinn.co.uk
Adnams Bitter; Marston's Pedigree; guest beer Ⓗ
Dating back to 1190, the Holly Bush is said to be not only the second oldest inn in England but also, having been granted a licence in 1610, the first fully licensed inn in the country. The oldest part is still thatched but there have been many alterations and extensions over the years resulting in three distinct areas: a bar towards the middle of the pub, a no-smoking dining room and a snug which is mainly occupied by diners; try the award-winning food. Q❀◑P

Shenstone

Fox & Hounds

42 Main Street, WS14 0SB
🕘 12-2.30, 5-11; 12-11 Sat; 12-10.30 Sun
☎ (01543) 480257
Adnams Bitter; Highgate Dark; Marston's Pedigree; Taylor Landlord Ⓗ
Friendly village local, consisting of a lounge at the rear and a welcoming split-level snug to the front. A large area of the lounge is reserved for diners only during food serving times, but the snug is always for drinkers only. During the summer a patio area provides a welcome retreat for fresh air fans. Meals are served Monday-Saturday evenings, and Sunday lunchtime until 4.30pm. Q❀◑ ⊟⇌P⊬

Stafford

Greyhound

12 County Road, ST16 2PU (opp. jail)
🕘 12-2.30 (not Mon-Fri), 5-11; 12-2.30, 7-10.30 Sun
☎ (01785) 222432
M&B Brew XI; guest beers Ⓗ
A few minutes' walk north of the town centre, the Greyhound has experienced a remarkable transformation. Formerly run down, then closed, it was rescued by the new owners who, with a thorough yet sympathetic refurbishment, have

revived it as one of very few genuine free houses in the area. Darts, dominoes and crib are again played in the bar, but the gaming machines, TV and juke box have been banished. Three guest beers tend to include one from Holden's and usually one from a local micro such as Blythe. Local CAMRA Pub of the Year 2005.
⅏❀⊟♣P

King's Arms

11-12 Peel Terrace, ST16 3HB (off B5066, Sandon road)
11-3, 5-11; 11-11 Fri & Sat; 12-10.30 Sun
☎ (01785) 249872
Beer range varies Ⓗ
One of several pubs now making the north end of Stafford an excellent drinking area, the King's Arms has increased its range to six ever-changing ales while maintaining quality. Converted long ago from two terraced houses, the pub has been further opened up in recent years, but retains separate bar and snug areas. Parking can be difficult. Although just a mile north of the town centre, the pub has a surprisingly large, well-maintained garden. ❀♣

Lamb ✔

Broad Eye, ST16 2QB
11-11; 12-10.30 Sun
☎ (07946) 403433
Banks's Original; Everards Tiger; Marston's Pedigree; guest beer Ⓗ
Although next to the busy Chell Road and surrounded by car parks and supermarkets, the Lamb retains something of the atmosphere of a street-corner local. Bought by Punch several years ago, the pub has since been carefully refurbished. Regular customers are joined during the evening by drivers stationed at the nearby lorry park and during the day by shoppers taking advantage of the good value meals served until 9pm (3pm Sat and Sun). ◐⇌♣

Luck Penny

62 Crab Lane, ST16 1SQ (2 miles NNW of centre on Trinity Fields estate)
11-11; 12-10.30 Sun
☎ (01785) 603503
John Smith's Bitter; Marston's Pedigree; guest beer Ⓗ
Deservedly popular estate pub that has been run by the same licensee for nearly a quarter of a century, making him currently the longest-serving pub landlord in the Stafford area. Built in the late 1960s at the same time as the surrounding houses, this community-based pub supports several sports and games teams. There is a particularly welcoming and comfortable lounge, plus a public bar. Great value food is served (no meals Sun eve). ❀◐⊟♿♣P

Railway

23 Castle Street, ST16 2EB
5 (12 Sat)-11; 12-10.30 Sun
☎ (01785) 605085
Draught Bass; Greene King Abbot; guest beer Ⓗ
Like the surrounding terraced housing of Castletown, the inn was built shortly after the Grand Junction railway reached Stafford, soon after Queen Victoria's coronation in 1837. The main bar now gives easier access to two other rooms, but the Railway remains Stafford's best example of a Victorian back-street local. Parking can be difficult, but it is just a five minute walk from the station and not much further from the town centre. ⅏❀⊟⇌♣

Spittal Brook ✔

106 Lichfield Road, ST17 4LP (1 mile SE of centre, in cul-de-sac off A34)
12-3, 5-11; 12-11 Sat; 12-4, 7-10.30 Sun
☎ (01785) 245268
Jennings Cumberland Ale; Marston's Pedigree; Tetley Bitter; guest beer Ⓗ
Formerly the Crown, this pub reverted to the original name of the locality in 1998. This thriving, traditional, two-roomed ale house, adjacent to the West Coast mainline, fields darts, cribbage, water polo and netball teams and a golfing society. The premises are licensed for civil weddings and the accommodation comprises three twin-bedded rooms. Entertainment includes a folk night (Tue) and a quiz (Wed). Addlestones Cloudy cask cider is sold. No food is served Sunday evening.
⅏❀⊭◐⊟♣●P

Tap & Spile

59 Peel Terrace, ST16 3HE (off B5066, ¾ mile N of centre)
4.30 (2 Fri; 12 Sat)-11; 12-10.30 Sun
☎ (01785) 223563
Beer range varies Ⓗ
Thriving beer house, selling an incredible volume and variety of cask ales from a wide range of regional and micro-breweries. Eight beers are usually on tap. Built early last century, the name change from the Cottage by the Brook, just over a decade ago, coincided with a sensitive refurbishment, four distinct drinking areas being retained. The first pub locally with a proper no-smoking area, the Tap & Spile also has a free bar billiards table and several sports teams. ⅏❀♣⚟

Stoke on Trent: Burslem

Bull's Head

14 St John's Square, ST6 3AJ
3 (12 Fri & Sat)-11; 12-10.30 Sun
☎ (01782) 834153
Titanic Best Bitter, Iceberg, Premium, White Star, seasonal beers; guest beers Ⓗ
The jewel in Burslem's crown, this two-roomed, town-centre pub is only 10 minutes' walk from Vale Park. The bar houses a juke box and bar billiards table, while the quieter wood-panelled lounge is warmed by a real fire. Serving by far the best selection of real ale in the town, this pub is busy at weekends and on match days. Although owned by Titanic Brewery, two guest ales are usually available; it also hosts occasional mini-beer festivals. ⅏Q❀⊟♣●

Stoke on Trent: Fenton

Malt 'n' Hops

259 King Street, ST4 3EJ
12-4, 7-11; 12-4, 7-10.30 Sun
☎ (01782) 313406
Beer range varies Ⓗ
One of the few free houses in the city, this long-established hostelry has been in the same ownership for almost two decades. Comprising a single room greatly extended over the years,

the split levels give the impression of a separate traditional bar and comfortable lounge. Ever-changing beers from small breweries and micros make this very much a beer oriented pub. The house beers are brewed by Tower. Belgian beers are also stocked.
⇌(Longton)

Potter
432 King Street, ST4 3DB (on old A50)
12 (11 Sat)-11; 12-10.30 Sun
☎ (01782) 311968
Coach House Dick Turpin; Fuller's London Pride; Greene King Abbot; guest beers Ⓗ
Established, genuine, traditional free house that appeals to customers of all ages. Three excellent guest beers are backed up by the regular ales. This three-roomed pub comprises a main bar, another room set aside for games, and a back snug that doubles as a meeting room. A minor refurbishment has not changed the original feel of this 100-year-old house. It gets busy for televised sport, but a warm welcome awaits all visitors. Longton bus garage is a half-mile walk.
Q ⇌(Longton) ♣

Stoke on Trent: Hanley

Coachmaker's Arms
65 Lichfield Street, ST1 3EA (off A5008, Potteries Way)
12-11; 7-10.30 Sun
☎ (01782) 262158
Draught Bass; guest beers Ⓗ
An excellent addition to this Guide, the Coachmaker's is one of a few Hanley pubs to have maintained its separate room layout. Coming off a tight drinking corridor are no less that four rooms, all with their own character. The pub retains many original features: the wall and floor tiling, fireplaces and seating. A rendition of acoustic music may be heard occasionally. Currently four different beers are available, with a further two planned. Q ♣

Unicorn
40 Piccadilly, ST1 1EG (opp. Regent Theatre)
12-11; 12-3, 7-10.30 Sun
☎ (01782) 281809
Fuller's London Pride; Marston's Pedigree; guest beer Ⓗ
Little gem at the heart of Hanley's cultural quarter, this pub is a traditional local with horse brasses and copperware hanging from the ceiling. It offers theatregoers an alternative interval drinks venue (drinks may be ordered in advance). It has a bar area and an alcoved seating area to the rear. The convivial surroundings offer a welcoming refuge from the busy city centre.

Stoke on Trent: Hartshill

Jolly Potters ✔
296 Hartshill Road, ST4 7NH (on A52, Newcastle road)
12-11; 12-10.30 Sun
☎ (01782) 845254
Greene King IPA; Taylor Landlord; guest beers Ⓗ
Situated within Hartshill's conservation area, near the hospital complex, this is a rare example of a typical Potteries pub, once owned by Joules. First licensed as a beer house in 1834, you can still enjoy a pint in traditional surroundings. The small public bar acts as a servery to three other small rooms, accessible from a central corridor, often full of standing drinkers during busy periods. The absence of juke box, pool table or gaming machines allows for friendly conversation. Q ♣

Stoke on Trent: Middleport

White Swan
107 Newport Lane, ST6 3PJ (300 yds from post office)
11-11; 11-5, 7-11 Sat; 12-4, 7-10.30 Sun
☎ (01782) 813639
Draught Bass; Boddingtons Bitter; Flowers IPA; guest beer Ⓗ
This warm, welcoming pub is just 15 minutes' walk from Burslem town centre and even closer to the Trent and Mersey Canal at Middleport. With five cask ales usually available this pub is well worth finding. It is dog-friendly and often hosts fundraising charity events; it even has its own golf society. Snacks are available during the day. ♣

Stoke on Trent: Penkhull

Beehive Inn
103 Honeywall, ST4 7HU (off A52, Hartshill road)
4 (12.30 Fri, 2 Sat)-11; 12-4, 7-10.30 Sun
☎ (01782) 846947 website: www.beehiveinn.com
Marston's Pedigree; guest beers Ⓗ
A welcome return for this pub halfway up Honeywall. This popular inn is festooned in Stoke City memorabilia, clocks and old pictures. A real community local, it hosts many charity events and runs trips. Tuesday evening can be busy due to the quiz. Lunchtime opening varies, especially for Stoke City home games (ring beforehand). The garden and beer tent are popular in summer. ⇌♣P

Greyhound Inn
5-6 Manor Court Street, ST4 5DW
11-3, 5-11; 11-11 Fri & Sat; 12-10.30 Sun
☎ (01782) 848978 website: www.thegreyhoundinn.co.uk
Greene King Old Speckled Hen; Marston's Pedigree; Taylor Landlord; guest beer Ⓗ
One of the oldest buildings in Penkhull, this former 15th-century manor courthouse has been a pub since the early 1800s. Read about the pub's history above the large fireplace. The bar plays host to darts and pool. The comfortable lounge allows for relaxed conversation and enjoying the freshly-cooked food. The award-winning community local hosts many events and supports a greyhound charity. A quiz is normally held on Monday and Tuesday is Balti night. Q ♣P

Stone

Red Lion
25 High Street, ST15 8AJ
10-11; 12-10.30 Sun
☎ (01785) 814500
Adnams Bitter; Everards Tiger; guest beers Ⓗ
With the earliest recorded licence in 1793, this is one of the oldest pubs in Stone. Joules Brewery memorabilia is displayed in the small, quiet lounge that overlooks the pedestrianised High Street. At the back of the pub is a spacious public bar that supports dominoes, darts, pool and quiz

teams. Stone Jazz Club meets here on Monday. The lunches, served Tuesday-Saturday 11.30-2.30pm, are good value. Q◖⊟≋♣

Swan Inn

18 Stafford Street, ST15 8QW (on A520, by Trent & Mersey Canal)
✪ 10-11; 12-10.30 Sun
☎ (01785) 815570
Coach House Gunpowder Mild; John Joule Old Knotty, Old Priory, Victory; guest beers ⊞
This fine, Grade II listed building was carefully renovated in 1999. It has one large L-shaped room with real fires at each end. To date over 300 guest beers have been served up by the landlord. Tuesday is quiz night and live music is performed up to three nights a week. A free buffet is served every Sunday at 12.30pm and lunchtime snacks are offered Tuesday-Saturday. Be sure not to miss the beer festival held annually in the second week of July.
♨❀◖≋●

Tamworth

Albert

32 Albert Road, B79 7JS (near station)
✪ 12-11; 12-10.30 Sun
☎ (01827) 64694
Banks's Bitter; Marston's Pedigree; guest beer ⊞
A warm welcome is guaranteed at this popular local that is handy for the railway station. This former local CAMRA Pub of the Year has roadside seating and a garden for outdoor drinking in summer. The guest beer is usually from the Wolverhampton & Dudley portfolio. Regular mini-beer festivals are held. Sunday meals are served until 5pm. Bus route 776 to Atherstone and Nuneaton stops directly outside the front door.
❀⇄◖◗⊟♿≋♣P

Sir Robert Peel

13-15 Lower Gungate, B79 7BA (in pedestrian area opp. Gungate shopping centre)
✪ 11-11; 12-10.30 Sun
☎ (01827) 300910
Beer range varies ⊞
Although the building has been a pub for less than 20 years, it is one of the older properties in a town that has not been very kind to preservation. The pub is named after the former Prime Minister and founder of the modern police force who was born in Tamworth. A warm welcome is assured by the friendly landlord. The changing guest beers are usually from local micros, making this a popular haunt for CAMRA members. ≋♣

White Lion

1 Aldergate, B79 7JJ (next to borough council offices)
✪ 11-11; 12-10.30 Sun
☎ (01827) 64630
Banks's Original; Greene King Old Speckled Hen; Marston's Pedigree; guest beers ⊞
Three-roomed pub on the edge of the town centre. The split-roomed main bar is popular with sports fans, due to its large-screen Sky TV at one end of the bar. A pool room with two tables always seem to be busy. Note the interesting old plan of the White Lion and its sister pub that was demolished in the early 1960s. A small car park is next to the pub. The Tamworth beer festival takes place a mere stroll away. ≋♣P

Tatenhill

Horseshoe Inn

Main Street, DE13 9SD
✪ 11-11; 12-10.30 Sun
☎ (01283) 564913
Marston's Pedigree ⊞
This old village coaching inn, dating back to the late 17th-century, has retained much of its charm despite extensive renovation over the years. The public bar has a homely, comfy feel (note the list of tenants going back to 1860), and the linked rooms feature low, beamed ceilings, breweriana and agricultural artefacts. It is locally renowned for its meals, which are available all day; ramblers and cyclists are welcome. The garden includes a children's play area and pets' corner. ❀◖◗⊟♿P

Trysull

Bell

Bell Lane, WV5 7JB
✪ 11.30-3, 5-11; 11.30-11 Sat; 12-10.30 Sun
☎ (01902) 892871
Batham Best Bitter; Holden's Bitter, Golden Glow, Special; guest beer ⊞
This 18th-century building stands on the site of a much older pub alongside the medieval church of All Saints at the village centre. It comprises three cosy rooms: the lounge with an inglenook and two distinct seating areas, the more basic bar, popular with locals and ramblers, and a restaurant serving good value meals, mostly home made (Sun available 12-6). The Staffs & Worcs Canal is about 20 minutes' walk away. The guest beer usually comes from a micro-brewery. ❀◖◗⊟♿P⊡

Two Gates

Bull's Head

446 Watling Street, B77 1HW (at A51/B5404 jct)
✪ 12-2.30, 6-11; 12-3, 7-11 Sat; 12-2.30, 7-10.30 Sun
☎ (01827) 287820
Banks's Original; Marston's Pedigree ⊞
Friendly local, convenient for public transport, being close to Wilnecote Station. Although situated in a built-up area, it has the appearance of a country pub. Excellent value meals are served every lunchtime, except Sunday. The two-roomed pub has a split-level cosy lounge, a small, friendly public bar and a patio bar overspill. The pub hosts weekly sports quizzes. Situated on the old Watling Street, it attracts both locals and passing trade.
Q❀◖⊟≋(Wilnecote) P

Railway Inn

409 Watling Street, B77 5AD
✪ 12-11; 12-10.30 Sun
☎ (01827) 262937
Draught Bass ⊞
Excellent drinking establishment next to Wilnecote Station, and a mere stone's throw from the Bull's Head. The popular public bar is full of railway photographs and memorabilia. Those wanting their pint of Bass in a peaceful

setting head for the lounge, which is called the Club Room. A pool room completes the trio of rooms in this welcoming local.
⛫Q ⊟ ⇌ (Wilnecote) ♣P

Uttoxeter

Bank House Hotel

Church Street, ST14 8AG (opp. St Mary's Church)
⌚ 11-11; 12-10.30 Sun
☎ (01889) 566922 website: www.bankhousehotel.info
Hardys & Hansons Bitter, Olde Trip; Marston's Pedigree; guest beer Ⓗ
Built in 1776 and situated just a short distance from the town centre, this fine looking building was once the first bank in Uttoxeter. The original bank vault can still be seen in what is now the restaurant, but instead of holding cash it now contains condiments. The Bank House has also served as a dental practice and a private house and boasts an impressive unsupported staircase. The 14 en-suite bedrooms make it a handy base for Uttoxeter racecourse. ⛫❀⇌◑◗♿▲⇌P

Weston

Woolpack

The Green, ST18 0JH
⌚ 11-11; 12-10.30 Sun
☎ (01889) 270238
Banks's Original, Bitter; Marston's Pedigree; guest beer Ⓗ
Known locally as the Inn on the Green, the Woolpack is a welcoming village local with an extensive dining area. Four bays inside reflect the pub's origins as a row of cottages, and it is recorded as having been owned by the Bagot family in the 1830s. Over the years the pub has been thoughtfully extended, retaining the original bar area. The outdoor drinking space is popular during good weather; meals are served all day in summer. ⛫❀◑◗⊟♣P

Whiston

Swan

ST19 5QH (2 miles W of Penkridge) OS895144
⌚ 12-3 (not Mon), 6-11; 12-10.30 Sun
☎ (01785) 716200
Holden's Mild, Bitter; guest beer Ⓗ
With an emphasis on excellent beer and superb food, the Swan, although remotely situated, is now a thriving pub and was extended a couple of years ago. As much local produce as possible is used for the wide range of meals. Midlands micro-brewers supply most of the guest beers. Built in 1593, the oldest part of the pub is the small bar that caters well for the local farming community. The six acres of grounds include a children's obstacle course. ⛫❀⇌◑◗⊟▲♣P

Wilnecote

Globe Inn

91 Watling Street, B77 5BA (on B5404)
⌚ 1-3.30, 7-11; 12-10.30 Sun
☎ (01827) 280885
Marston's Pedigree Ⓗ
One-roomed, L-shaped pub, cosy and friendly, situated on the ancient Roman road. A real community pub with time for everyone, it fields darts, dominoes and football teams. The pub stands opposite the Red Lion, within 15 minutes' walk of the Railway and Bull's Head at Two Gates making an ideal pub crawl, accessible from Wilnecote Station. ❀♣

Red Lion Inn

Quarry Hill, B77 5BS
⌚ 12-3, 5 (7 Sat)-11; 12-11 Thu & Fri; 12-3, 7-10.30 Sun
☎ (01827) 280818
Draught Bass; guest beers (occasional) Ⓗ
Typical community pub with a quiet lounge and livelier public bar where games are played. It is situated on the ancient Roman road close to the Globe Inn. You will be welcomed by friendly staff and customers alike, plus the landlord's dogs. ❀⊟♣P

Wolstanton

New Smithy

21 Church Lane, ST5 0EH
⌚ 12 (11 Sat)-11; 12-10.30 Sun
☎ (01782) 740467
Everards Beacon, Tiger; Marston's Pedigree; guest beers Ⓗ
This one-roomed, open-plan pub has a split level that is a useful divider for those times when rugby is shown on the TV. A continuing feature is a monthly brewery night showcasing three or four beers from independent breweries; this occurs on the third Thursday of the month. The patio offers an escape on summer evenings. Westons Old Rosie cider is sold. ❀♣🍎P⊡

Wrinehill

Crown Inn ✔

Den Lane, CW3 9BT (off A531, between Newcastle and Crewe)
⌚ 12-3 (not Mon), 6-11; 12-4, 6-10.30 Sun
☎ (01270) 820472
Adnams Bitter; Banks's Original; Marston's Bitter, Pedigree; guest beer Ⓗ
Busy, family-owned village free house with a commitment to real ale. It won the 'Britain in Bloom' regional gold award for licensed premises in 2003 and 2004. No pool, TV or games machines spoil the peace. The excellent varied menu includes steaks, fresh fish, vegetarian and vegan options. There are two no-smoking areas in the comfortable lounge bar, complete with open fires. ⛫❀◑◗♿P⊁

Yoxall

Golden Cup

Main Street, DE13 8NQ (on A515)
⌚ 12-3, 5-11; 12-11 Sat; 12-10.30 Sun
☎ (01543) 472295 website: www.thegoldencup.com
Marston's Pedigree; guest beer Ⓗ
Impressive, 300-year-old inn at the village centre, opposite St Peter's Church, bedecked with attractive floral displays for much of the year. The smart, L-shaped lounge primarily caters for diners where an extensive home-cooked menu is on offer. The separate public bar features 'witticisms' on the walls, in keeping with the locals' friendly banter. The award-winning pub gardens stretch down to the River Swarbourn and include a camping area (caravans and motor-homes only). Regular beer festivals are held. ⛫❀⇌◑◗⊟♿▲♣P

SUFFOLK

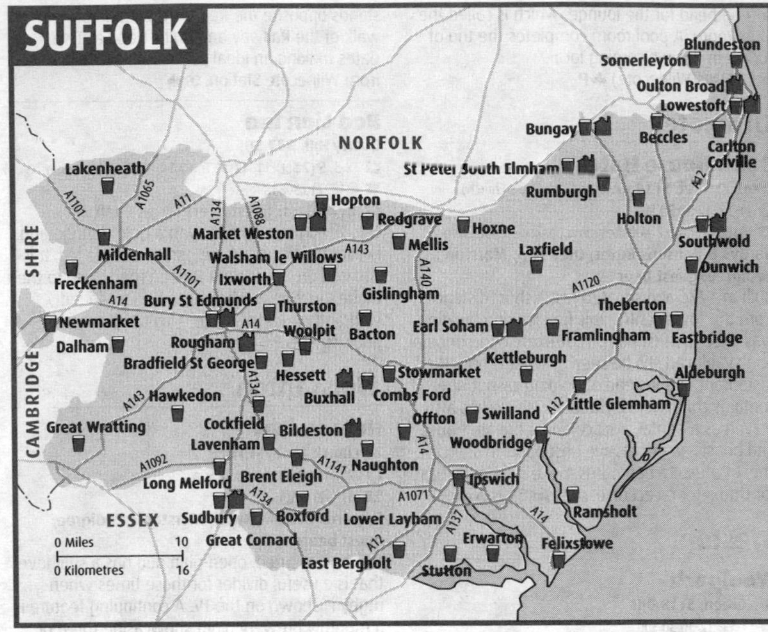

Aldeburgh

Mill Inn

Market Cross Place, IP15 5BJ (opp. Moot Hall)

11-2.30, 6-11; 11-11 Fri-Sat; 12-10.30 Sun

(01728) 452563 website: www.themillinn.com

Adnams Bitter, Broadside; seasonal beers [H]

Delightful two-bar inn with a small restaurant close to the sea. Simply decorated and furnished, it offers a friendly welcome at any time of the year. Popular not just with visitors but also many locals including some of the lifeboat crew. There is regular folk music on Thursday. A welcome haven for good beer after a walk over the shingle beach to see the scallops on a blustery day, no food is served Sunday evening or Monday. Q ❀ ⇌ ◐◑ ♣ ⁄

White Hart

222 High Street, IP15 5AJ

11-11; 12-10.30 Sun

(01728) 453205

Adnams Bitter, Broadside; seasonal beers [H]

A former public reading room which is now used as a small, cosy public bar. It is always a favourite with both locals and tourists, especially at weekends and during the summer. An interesting selection of nautical memorabilia adorns the wood-panelled walls. At one end of the room an open fire is a delight on cold nights. There is regular live music on Saturday and Thursday. The pub is also 'dog friendly' so is popular with many walkers. Alterations are expected soon to provide full disabled access. ⚔ ❀ ♿

Bacton

Bull Inn

Church Road, IP14 4LJ

11-3, 6-11; closed Tue; 11.30-11 Sat; 12.30-10 Sun

(01449) 781159

Greene King IPA, Abbot, Old Speckled Hen; [H] **guest beer** [G]

This busy village local boasts a popular public bar area, a spacious dining section and a lounge bar. The pub serves three beers from handpump and a changing guest beer which is served by gravity dispense from the cellar. The main part of the building is timber framed with many exposed oak beams. Despite relatively recent refurbishment, the pub has retained its olde-worlde charm. The well-kept beer is complemented by an outstanding menu (not served Sun eve). Bar snacks are also available. ❀ ◐◑ ⊟ ♿ ♣ P

Beccles

Bear & Bells

Old Market, NR34 9AP (adjacent to bus station)

11.30-3, 5.30-11; 12-3, 7-10.30 Sun

(01502) 712291

Adnams Bitter; Greene King IPA; guest beers [H]

This fine Victorian pub is located in the old town square, convenient for users of the River Waveney. There is a spacious drinking area and

INDEPENDENT BREWERIES

Adnams Southwold
Bartrams Rougham
Cox & Holbrook Buxhall (brewing suspended)
Earl Soham Earl Soham
Green Dragon Bungay
Green Jack Lowestoft
Greene King Bury St Edmunds
Kings Head Bildeston
Mauldons Sudbury
Old Cannon Bury St Edmunds
Old Chimneys Market Weston
Oulton Oulton Broad
St Peter's St Peter South Elmham

dining room attached with a central bar. The pub is renowned for wholesome food (not served Mon). A refurbished function room with skittle alley and stage is available for hire. Guest beers are sourced from local micros, generally including a dark beer in winter months. Mobile phones must be switched off.
Q❀◑⇌P

Blundeston

Plough

Market Lane, NR32 5AN
⌚ 12-2 (3 Sat), 6-11; 12-3, 6-10.30 Sun
☎ (01502) 730261
Adnams Bitter; Greene King IPA; guest beers Ⓗ
Spacious inn close to the village hall with an attractive garden. This mock-Tudor style inn with exposed beams consists of a restaurant, a main bar and a pool room. The parish features in Dickens' works as 'Blunderstone', the birthplace of David Copperfield – hence the Dickensian memorabilia. Every August bank holiday there is a beer festival and music weekend with barbecue. Quiz nights are held on Wednesday and live music most Friday evenings.
♨❀◑⊟♣P

Boxford

White Hart

Broad Street, CO10 5DX
⌚ 12-3, 6-11; 12-3, 7-10.30 Sun
☎ (01787) 211071
website: www.white-hart.co.uk
Adnams Bitter; Greene King IPA; Woodforde's Great Eastern; guest beers Ⓗ
Not many pubs can claim to have a lion buried in the front garden! Briton the Lion was part of 'Tornado' Smith's wall of death act in the 1930s when Tornado's mother ran the White Hart. The current landlord brought history to life with a modern wall of death in the back yard a few years ago and owns a restored 1930s bike. The pub is situated beside the River Box in the centre of the pretty village of Boxford.
♨❀⇔◑P

Bradfield St George

Fox & Hounds

Felsham Road, IP30 0AB
⌚ 12-2.30, 6-11; 12-2.30, 7-10.30 Sun
☎ (01284) 386379
Bartrams Premier Bitter; Ridleys IPA; guest beers Ⓗ
On the village outskirts, close to the historic coppiced woodland of the Suffolk Wildlife Trust stands this beautifully restored Victorian free house and country restaurant. The comfortable, attractive interior is fronted by a glazed dining area. The public bar has a woodblock floor, wood-burning stove and pine seating. Service throughout is excellent. ♨Q❀◑⊟P

Brent Eleigh

Cock ☆

Lavenham Road, CO10 9PB
⌚ 12-3, 6-11; 12-3, 7-10.30 Sun
☎ (01787) 247371
Adnams Bitter; Greene King IPA, Abbot Ⓗ
An absolute gem! This pub manages to transport you back to a time most of us have long forgotten. In winter both the tiny bars are snug and warm; in summer, with the doors open, the bar is at one with its surroundings. Good conversation is guaranteed – sit and listen and you will soon become involved. Close to Lavenham and the beautiful Brett Valley, the comfortable accommodation is recommended. The pub is 'CAMROT' (Campaign for Real Outside Toilets) approved. Do not miss it.
Q❀⇔⊟♣●P

Bungay

Green Dragon

29 Broad Street, NR35 1EE
⌚ 11-3, 4.30-11; 11-11 Fri-Sat; 12-3, 7-10.30 Sun
☎ (01986) 892681
Green Dragon Chaucer Ale, Bridge Street Bitter Ⓗ, seasonal beers Ⓖ / Ⓗ
Home of the Green Dragon Brewery which is situated in outbuildings adjacent to the car park. It is a lively town pub with public bar and lounge plus a dining room which doubles as a family room leading to a side garden surrounded by hops. Meals are served from Monday to Friday with some speciality evenings. During the summer the pub stays open all day at weekends. Occasional bottle-conditioned beers are brewed to supplement the quality draught ales. ♨☋❀◑⊟▲♣P

Bury St Edmunds

Bushel ✔

28 St John's Street, IP33 1SW
⌚ 11-2.30, 5-11; 11-11 Sat; 12-4, 7-10.30 Sun
☎ (01284) 754333
Greene King IPA, Abbot, Old Speckled Hen Ⓗ
Situated on a busy main street, this 15th-century coaching inn is just a short walk from the Abbey Gardens. Three drinking areas are offered and a separate restaurant. Sky Sports is available and pool and darts are played. Accommodation is provided in 12 en-suite rooms. No evening meals are served Sunday. ❀⇔◑⇌♣P

Kings Arms ✔

23 Brentgovel Street, IP33 1EB
⌚ 11-11; closed Sun
☎ (01284) 761874
Greene King IPA, Abbot, Old Speckled Hen; guest beers Ⓗ
Large one-room pub popular with a mixture of young and older customers. The friendly, helpful staff offer a warm welcome. The outdoor patio is heated on cooler evenings. Meals are served 12-5pm. A 'happy hour' operates early weekday evenings. ❀◐

Old Cannon Brewery

86 Cannon Street, IP33 1JR
⌚ 12-3 (not Mon), 5-11; 12-3, 7-10 Sun
☎ (01284) 768769
website: www.oldcannonbrewery.co.uk
Adnams Bitter; Old Cannon Best Bitter, Gunner's Daughter, seasonal beers; guest beers Ⓗ
Formerly the St Edmund's Head, this brew-pub is on the same site as the original Cannon Brewery. It reopened several years ago and now offers an excellent range of its own beers,

brewed on site, as well as guest beers and foreign beers which change frequently. The Cannon serves good quality food (not Sun eve) and accommodation is available but booking is essential.
⛫Q❀⛟◑♿≠P☐

Rose & Crown ✔
48 Whiting Street, IP33 1NP
⌚ 11.30-11; 11.30-3, 7-11 Sat; 12-2.30, 7-10.30 Sun
☎ (01284) 755934
Greene King XX Mild, IPA, Abbot; guest beer Ⓗ
Listed, red-brick, street-corner pub, run by the same family for 29 years. It has two bars and a rare off-sales counter. The pub is in sight of Greene King Brewery in Westgate Street. It is said to have the best kept mild in town. Good value lunches are available from Monday to Saturday at this popular pub offering a friendly welcome. ◐⊟♣

Carlton Colville

Bell
The Street, NR33 8JR
⌚ 11-3, 7-11; 11-11 Fri-Sat; 12-10.30 Sun
☎ (01502) 582873
Oulton Bitter, Nautilus, Gone Fishing; guest beer Ⓖ
Friendly, traditional village pub with a relaxed atmosphere. This Oulton Ales inn has a central fireplace separating the drinking area from the restaurant. The original flagstone floor has been well maintained. The no-smoking area doubles as a family room. Ample parking is available at the front with a large garden at the rear that can be viewed from the conservatory. Just a mile away, the East Anglian Transport Museum is well worth a visit. ⛫Q♉❀◑P⍻

Cockfield

Three Horseshoes
Stow's Hill, Lavenham Road, IP30 0JB (on A1141)
⌚ 11-3, 6-11; 12-3, 7-10.30 Sun
☎ (01284) 828177
website: www.threehorseshoespub.co.uk
Theakston Best Bitter; guest beers Ⓗ
Part-thatched, 14th-century inn with a large conservatory. One of the bars has an unusual crown post roof. The restaurant serves good home-cooked food with a wide choice of meals; no food is served Tuesday. Pub games such as ring the bull are played. Camping and caravanning facilities are available on site.
⛫❀◑⊟♿⛺♣P

Combs Ford

Gladstone Arms
2 Combs Ford, IP14 2AP (on Stowmarket-Ipswich road)
⌚ 11-3, 5 (7 Sat)-11; 12-4, 7-10.30 Sun
☎ (01449) 612339
Adnams Bitter, Broadside; guest beer Ⓗ
This regular Guide entry is situated in the hamlet of Combs Ford once separate from, now attached to, Stowmarket. It boasts a mounting stone at its north-west corner which was used to assist people climbing on their horses. The beers include a guest from another independent brewer or a seasonal offering. The pub is noted for generous portions of real home-made traditional food, including vegetarian dishes. No food is served on Sunday or Monday evenings. ⛫❀◑♿P

Dalham

Affleck Arms
Brookside, CB8 8TG
⌚ 5-11, 12-3; 6.30-11 Sat; 12-10.30 Sun
☎ (01638) 500306
Adnams Bitter; Greene King IPA; guest beers Ⓗ
Two continually changing guest ales complement the two regulars at this attractive thatched free house in rural Suffolk. How many pubs have a small river at their front door? This one does and with tables and chairs along the bank for spring and summer drinking, the setting is idyllic. Random happy hours and offers reduce the keenly-priced drinks even further. Excellent food and self-contained accommodation are available at this friendly pub (eve meals Tue-Fri). ⛫❀⛟◑♿P

Dunwich

Ship
St James Street, IP17 3DT
⌚ 11-11; 12-10.30 Sun
☎ (01728) 648219
Adnams Bitter, Broadside; Mauldons seasonal beers Ⓗ
Situated in what is now a small village, but was once a sizable medieval town until it was lost to the sea, this pub is a mixture of ages going back as far as Tudor times. The spacious bar is well served by the wood-burning stove in winter and very welcome after a windy walk along the beach. There is a dining room and a conservatory where children are welcome. The large garden at the rear has a fine and ancient fig tree. Dogs are welcome in the bar and the guest bedrooms. ⛫Q❀⛟◑⛺P

Earl Soham

Victoria
The Street, IP13 7RL (on A1120)
⌚ 11.30-3, 6-11; 12-3, 7-10.30 Sun
☎ (01728) 685758
Earl Soham Victoria Bitter, Sir Roger's Porter, Albert Ale; Empress of India; guest beers Ⓗ
Traditional, down-to-earth pub with simple wooden furnishings which appeals to all. Good value home-cooked meals are served at lunchtime and evenings alongside the superb beers brewed just down the road in the village. Outside drinking takes place on the green in front of the pub. The neighbouring Victoria Terrace was formerly a barley maltings.
⛫Q❀◑♣P

East Bergholt

Hare & Hounds
Heath Road, CO7 6RL
⌚ 12-11; 12-10.30 Sun
☎ (01206) 298438
Adnams Bitter; guest beers Ⓗ
Friendly pub in the village where John Constable, possibly the greatest English landscape painter, was born in 1776. Built in the 15th century it retains a pargetted (deep plaster relief) ceiling,

circa 1590, in the lounge. A fine pub that caters for all and offers a family room, pleasant garden and a separate public bar. Guest beers change frequently. Food is served at lunchtime, 12-4pm. Sadly, Constable's house no longer stands but nearby Flatford Mill, immortalised in The Haywain, is well worth a visit. ♛Q❀◑⊟▲♣P

Eastbridge

Eel's Foot

Leiston Road, IP16 4SN

⏲ 12-3, 6-11; 11-11 Sat & summer; 12-10.30 Sun

☎ (01728) 830154

website: www.theeelsfootinn.co.uk

Adnams Bitter, Broadside; seasonal beers [H]

Traditional brick inn which was originally three small workman's cottages. The pub is enjoyed by locals and visitors to the Minsmere Bird Reserve. Good food complements the fine beer. The large garden has plenty of seating for warm summer evenings and children are welcome. Acoustic music is played every Thursday and everyone is welcome to join in. There is new accommodation for 2006 and plenty of camping space at the rear. Dogs are permitted.

♛Q❀⇌◑▲♣P

Erwarton

Queen's Head

IP9 1LN OS215346

⏲ 11-3, 6-11; 12-3, 7-10.30 Sun

☎ (01473) 787550

Adnams Bitter; Greene King IPA; [H]

guest beers [H] / [G]

This heavily timbered pub has a spacious bar with a split-level floor to the family room. An extensive food menu (with good vegetarian options) is served daily. Bar billiards and shove ha'penny are played. The walls are adorned with seafaring and local photographs and nautical maps. The pub is a great base for walkers on the Shotley Peninsula. Tradition has it that the heart of Anne Boleyn is buried in the local church. ♛♉❀◑⊟♿♣P

Felixstowe (Walton)

Half Moon

303 Walton High Street, IP11 9QL

⏲ 12-2.30 (not winter Mon), 5-11; 12-11 Sat; 12-3, 7-10.30 Sun

☎ (01394) 216009

Adnams Bitter, Broadside; guest beers [H]

This friendly two-bar community local retains the feel of a pub of yesteryear, where traditional pub games can be played and good conversation enjoyed. Part of one bar is a no-smoking area and there are no games machines or muzak. Books are available for customers to read and quiz nights are held. Buses from Felixstowe and Ipswich stop right outside the door. Spot the humorous messages on the pavement blackboard. ♛Q❀⊟▲♣P⚟

Framlingham

Station

Station Road, IP13 9EE (on B1116)

⏲ 12-2.30, 5-11; 12-2.30, 7-10.30 Sun

☎ (01728) 723455

Earl Soham Gannet Mild, Victoria Bitter, Albert Ale, seasonal beers [H]

Railway-themed memorabilia reflect the link with the old station, which was adjacent to the pub and closed to passenger traffic in 1952. Prominent in the main bar is a fine five-handpull font. The pub is a short walk from the town's market square and castle, where Mary Tudor was proclaimed Queen. An excellent, varied menu is available every day except Sunday evening. ♛Q❀◑♣P

Freckenham

Golden Boar Inn

The Street, IP28 8HZ

(2½ miles from A11, on B1102 from Mildenhall)

⏲ 12-11; 12-4.30 Sun

☎ (01638) 723000

Adnams Bitter, Broadside; Fuller's London Pride; guest beer [H]

Former coaching inn with 16th-century origins. Many old features have been exposed during refurbishment; most impressive is the fireplace to the left when entering. Newer additions to the building are the guest rooms to supplement the two self-contained chalets. The dining room extension is now able to cope with the growing demand from the much acclaimed kitchens. Meals are prepared using the freshest ingredients with a range of blackboard specials clearly on display, including fish dishes in season. ❀⇌◑♿P

Gislingham

Six Bells

High Street, IP23 8JD

⏲ 12-3, 7-11; closed Mon; 12-3, 7-10.30 Sun

☎ (01379) 783349

Adnams Bitter; guest beers [H]

Although off the beaten track, this free house is very much the centre of the community and, unlike many village pubs, is well supported by locals who recognise that it provides a much needed facility. The affable landlord will welcome you into the one-roomed bar area where you can marvel at the large collection of pump clips from guest ales while enjoying your pint of well-kept cask beer, or indulging in some simple home-cooked food.

❀◑♿♣P

Great Cornard

King's Head

115 Bures Road, CO10 0JE (on B1508)

⏲ 4 (12 Fri & Sat)-11; 12-10.30 Sun

☎ (01787) 319253

Greene King IPA, Abbot, Old Speckled Hen; guest beers [H]

This traditional community pub serves what, with a population of nearly 10,000, must be one of the largest villages in the country. The building dates from the early 1500s. It has been a coaching inn and in the late 1800s had its own brewery. Greene King bought the pub in the 1930s. Guest beers are from the Greene King list. The pub fields many teams in darts, crib and pool. Evening meals are served Tuesday-Sunday.

♛❀◑▲♣P

Great Wratting

Red Lion

School Road, CB9 7HA (just off the A143 N of Haverhill)
11-2.30, 5-11; 11-11 Sat; 12-3, 7-10.30 Sun
☎ (01440) 783237
Adnams Bitter, Broadside, seasonal beers Ⓗ
You may feel like Jonah as you enter this pub through the jaw bones of a whale arched over the door, but once inside, the friendly atmosphere will prevail. Check out the amazing collection of brass and copper in the bar. A full range of Adnams beers, including all the seasonals, is available, together with good food served in either the bar or restaurant. A huge back garden, with various attractions, provides great views over the surrounding countryside.
P

Hawkedon

Queen's Head

Rede Road, IP29 4NN
5 (12 Sat)-11; 12-10.30 Sun
☎ (01284) 789218
Adnams Bitter; Greene King IPA; guest beers Ⓗ
It is worth the effort to find this 15th-century gem in the charming rural village of Hawkedon. Low beams, uneven flagged and board floors and a huge fire in winter complement the wonderful range of up to five guest beers, real cider and perry. Meals (served Fri and Sat eves; Sat and Sun lunch) are excellent and imaginative. They are made using locally sourced ingredients, as is the produce on sale in the shop recently opened in an outbuilding. Occasional events such as live music, theatre, suppers and games evenings are held.
Q P

Hessett

Five Bells

The Street, IP30 9AX
12-3, 5-11; 12-4, 7-10.30 Sun
☎ (01359) 270350
Greene King IPA, Abbot; Wadworth 6X Ⓗ
To say that the most impressive feature of the Five Bells is the massive Tudor brick post holding the sign above the entrance is not to detract from the pub itself. The sign's post is said to be all that remains of the entry to a long-demolished stately home. Two bars are both heavily beamed and have welcoming log fires. A record of the Bell's landlords back to 1753 is framed in the bar. No food is served Sunday evening or Monday. Q P

Holton

Lord Nelson

Mill Road, IP9 8PP
11.30-3, 6.30-11; 12-3, 7-10.30 Sun
☎ (01986) 873275
Adnams Bitter; guest beer Ⓗ
Traditional village local with a large garden and warm welcome for all. The interior is divided into two bars, one with a pool table and the main bar decorated with seafaring and Nelson artefacts. Sunday lunches, prepared with local produce, are good value for money – it is no surprise that they are popular and booking is recommended. The pub offers a takeaway service for food and off-sales.
P

Hopton

Vine

High Street, IP22 2QX (near Diss)
12-11; 12-10.30 Sun
☎ (01953) 681466
Adnams Bitter; Greene King IPA; guest beer Ⓗ
A magnet for all-day drinkers, this is a no-nonsense village pub, mostly with standing room only, bare floorboards, simple decor and a roaring log fire. The pool table and dartboard are both well used, but the emphasis is on good quality beer and simple, inexpensive food. There is a small, intimate restaurant at the rear and basket meals are available at all other times. A wide range of food is available to take away. Live entertainment features occasionally.
P

Hoxne

Swan

Low Street, IP21 5AS
11-3, 6-11; 12-10.30 Sun
☎ (01379) 668275
Adnams Bitter, Broadside Ⓖ**; guest beers** Ⓗ
Situated in an ancient village with a considerable history, this 15th-century pub has impressive fluted beams and a high ceiling in the main bar. Excellent home-cooked food features dishes in keeping with the character of the building, such as venison, wild boar and rabbit stew, on a frequently changing menu. Legend has it that the East Anglian King Edmund was killed nearby by the invading Danes in 870. The large garden is a pleasant place for a drink in summer. Q P

Ipswich

Brewers Arms

18-20 Orford Street, IP1 3NS
11-11; 12-10.30 Sun
☎ (01473) 406048
Greene King IPA, Ruddles Best Ⓗ
An old-style, side-street pub run by a long-serving landlord. It is deceptively large inside. A popular meeting place on Ipswich Town match days, it can be busy at these times. Sky TV and pool are available and accommodation is offered. The pub is a rare outlet for Ruddles Best in this area and is certainly worth the effort to seek out. P

Dove Street Inn

76 St Helens Street, IP4 2LA
12-11; 12-10.30 Sun
☎ (01473) 211270
website: www.dovestreetinn.co.uk
Beer range varies Ⓗ / Ⓖ
A welcome addition to the local free house scene. This Grade II listed traditional pub has three rooms, including one that is no-smoking. A superb array of up to 20 beers is available from handpumps in the bar and gravity dispense from the tap room. At least two real ciders are also always available. Hot, home-made traditional

snacks are served. Three beer festivals are held each year – in May, August and November.
❀♿♣●P⊁⊟

Emperor

293/295 Norwich Road, IP1 4BP

⏲ 11-11; 12-10.30 Sun

☎ (01473) 743600

Young's Bitter; Ansells Mild; guest beers [H]

Alterations and extensions over the years have made this pub unrecognisable as the three cottages it once was. Nevertheless, it continues to serve its purpose as a welcoming establishment for locals and visitors alike. In addition to the excellent beer, always including a mild, there is something for everyone's taste – pool, darts, TV sports, conversation and occasional music. Steel quoits is played at the rear of the building beyond the patio drinking area. The local CAMRA quoits team is based here. ♨❀◐♿♣P⊁

Fat Cat

288 Spring Road, IP4 5NL

⏲ 12 (11 Sat)-11; 12-10.30 Sun

☎ (01473) 726524

website www: fatcatipswich.co.uk

Adnams Bitter; [H] **Crouch Vale Brewers Gold; Fuller's London Pride; Woodforde's Wherry; guest beers** [G]

Superb reconstruction of a basic bareboards pub, decorated with tin advertising signs and posters. A wide range of guest ales is always on offer and is reasonably priced. Although only reopened in its present format in the mid-1990s, the Cat is regarded as an institution by real ale drinkers in the Ipswich area; definitely worth a visit. Q❀⇌ (Derby Rd) ●

Greyhound

9 Henley Road, IP1 3SE

⏲ 11-2.30, 5-11; 11-11 Sat; 12-10.30 Sun

☎ (01473) 252862

Adnams Bitter, Broadside, seasonal beers; guest beers [H]

Busy pub, a short walk from the town centre and close to Christchurch Park, with its splendid mansion. A traditional-style public bar is complemented by a larger lounge and outdoor patio drinking area. Well used by locals, it is also a popular meeting place for town-centre workers. Food is of a high quality with an interesting menu that changes regularly.
❀◐⊟♣P

Lord Nelson

81 Fore Street, IP4 1JZ

⏲ 11-2.30 (not Sat unless Ipswich Town are at home), 5-11; 12-4, 7-10.30 Sun

☎ (01473) 254072 website: www.ipswichlordnelson.com

Adnams Bitter, Broadside, seasonal beers [G]

Originally two timber-framed cottages, this Grade II listed pub was completely refurbished in the mid-1990s in a style appropriate to its age and location – there has been a pub on the site since at least 1672. An unusual gravity dispense system is used that incorporates a row of wooden casks to good effect. As you might expect there is an array of naval memorabilia on display. Its location, close to the rejuvenated historic wet dock, attracts varied clientele.
☋❀◐♿⇌♣⊁

Mannings ✔

8 Cornhill, IP1 1DD

⏲ 11-11; 12-5 Sun

☎ (01473) 254170

Adnams Bitter, Broadside; Fuller's London Pride; guest beer [H]

A gem of a pub on the Cornhill by the town hall in the town centre. It is a welcome haven from the shops and bustling thrice-weekly market. The frontage is quite small but the building stretches back a long way. Take a seat in the large front window and watch the world pass by while enjoying your pint. Good, hot meals are served at lunchtime until 5.30pm (4pm Sun). A superb pub. ❀◐♿⇌

Milestone Beer House

5 Woodbridge Road, IP4 2EA

⏲ 12-2.30, 5-11; 12-11 Fri-Sat; 12-10.30 Sun

☎ (01473) 252425

website: www.milestonebeerhouse.co.uk

Adnams Bitter, Broadside; Greene King IPA, Abbot, Old Speckled Hen; [H] **guest beers** [G] / [H]

There is a heated patio at the front of this award-winning, mock-Tudor, open-plan pub situated near the Odeon and Regent Theatre. A wide variety of up to 15 beers is available on handpump and gravity dispense from the tap room, plus a couple of ciders. Excellent, good value food is served, as well as traditional Sunday lunches (12-7pm on Sun). Live music from local bands is played at weekends.
❀◐♿♣●P⊟

Ixworth

Greyhound

High Street, IP31 2HJ

⏲ 11-2.30, 6-11; 12-3, 7-10.30 Sun

☎ (01359) 230887

Greene King XX Mild, IPA, Abbot [H]

Situated in Ixworth's pretty High Street, which is now free from traffic since the bypass, this traditional pub has three bars including a lovely central snug. The whole community is made welcome here. The heart of the building dates back to Tudor times. At the rear of the car park the stable block bears witness to its historic past. It is one of the few remaining outlets for XX Mild in west Suffolk. Good value lunches and early evening meals are served in the no-smoking restaurant. Q❀◐⊟♣P⊁

Kettleburgh

Chequers

The Street, IP13 7JT

⏲ 12-2.30 (3.30 Sat), 6-11; 12-3.30, 7-10.30 Sun

☎ (01728) 723760 website: www.thechequers.net

Adnams Bitter; Elgood's Black Dog; Greene King IPA; guest beers [H]

Situated in a delightful location with a large garden leading down to the River Deben. The atmosphere is relaxed with old photos of the pub and village adorning the partially wood-panelled walls. This is the third pub on the site, built in 1912 after the previous building burnt to the ground. The long-gone Deben Brewery used to be adjacent to the pub. Self-catering accommodation is now available.
♨❀⛟◐⛺♣P

Lakenheath

Brewer's Tap

54 High Street, IP27 0AU

12-11; 12-4.30, 7-10.30 Sun

☎ (01842) 862328

Beer range varies H

Village-centre pub of character; a good find for real ale fans being truly 'free' in an area dominated by one brewer (Greene King). Local beers are usually available and some from 'abroad' (Suffolk dialect for anything not local) are allowed. Do not be put off by the small frontage – an extension and patio at the rear make the pub more spacious than it appears. A public car park is nearby.

Lavenham

Angel

Market Place, CO10 9QZ

11-11; 12-10.30 Sun

☎ (01787) 247388

website: www.lavenham.co.uk/angel

Adnams Bitter, Broadside; Greene King IPA; Nethergate Suffolk County H

A 15th-century, family-run inn at the heart of England's finest medieval village. It sits opposite the Guildhall and overlooks the market cross. Now fully no-smoking throughout, it is a busy place for food and the menu changes daily. All meals are prepared from fresh ingredients on the premises. There are eight comfortable, well-equipped guest rooms with good value mid-week breaks available. Q P

Laxfield

King's Head (Low House) ☆

Gorams Mill Lane, IP13 8DW

11-3, 5.30-11; 12-3, 7-10.30 Sun

☎ (01986) 798395

Adnams Bitter, Broadside, seasonal beers; Fuller's London Pride G

Superb, unspoilt country pub with its origins in the 16th century. It is timber framed and plastered, with the plaster lined to imitate stonework. There is no bar and the ales are dispensed by gravity from the tap room at the back. A choice of rooms (including a dining area) and outdoor drinking provide convivial space for all. There is a notable absence of machines, electronic music or TV, just plenty of real atmosphere. Featuring in CAMRA's National Inventory, this pub should not be missed. Q P

Little Glemham

Lion Inn

Main Road, IP13 0BA (on A12)

12-2.30, 6-11; closed Mon; 12-3, 7-10.30 (not winter eve) Sun

☎ (01728) 746505

Adnams Bitter, Broadside; guest beers H

Welcome, deceptively large stopping-off point on the A12 for customers from afar as well as for locals. The owners previously ran a CAMRA award-winning pub in Shropshire and are continuing the same high standards here. An entirely smoke-free establishment, it serves good food. The monthly Tuesday night quiz is popular; likewise the monthly Friday themed food evening. Apparently the kitchen is occasionally frequented by a friendly ghost dressed in a long black skirt. Perhaps she likes g(h)oulash! P

Long Melford

Swan

Hall Street, CO10 9JQ

11.30-2.30, 5-11; 12-3, 7-10.30 Sun

☎ (01787) 378740

Greene King IPA, Abbot; guest beer H

Opened in 1767 as a brew-pub, part of the two-storey brewhouse remains as a garage. Very much a village pub, many teams are supported and it is home to the Swan Knights who raise money for local charities. A display of local history in the lounge has been collected by the landlord. Part of the rear bar, designated Tudor Corner, is used by participants in Kentwell Hall's Tudor recreations – just one of Melford's attractions.

Lower Layham

Queen's Head

The Street, IP7 5LZ

12-3 (Fri-Sat), 7-11; 12-3, 7-10.30 Sun

☎ (01473) 827789

Beer range varies H

This pub dates back over 700 years. Full of character, with lots of beams, the collection of wall-mounted ephemera includes a photo of every villager who took part in WWII, a picture of a former customer whose ghost now reputedly haunts the premises and a pair of fascinating antique darts scorers. Usually four beers are on offer, often rare. Superb food is served including vegetarian dishes (eve meals Wed-Sun). Do not miss this friendly rural free house. Q P

Lowestoft

Oak Tavern

Crown Street West, NR32 1SQ

10.30-11; 12-10.30 Sun

☎ (01502) 537246

Adnams Bitter; Greene King Abbot; guest beers H

Back street local on the northern side of town with a car park at the rear. It is popular with all ages and dog friendly. This jovial, open-plan pub has pool, darts, a large-screen TV at one end and a display of Belgian memorabilia at the other. A range of Belgian bottled beers is stocked and four handpumps all sell draught beers at the same price. Dark beers are often served during winter months. P

Triangle Tavern

29 St Peter's Street, NR32 1QA

11-11; 12-10.30 Sun

☎ (01502) 582711

Green Jack Canary, Orange Wheat, Grasshopper, Gone Fishing, seasonal beers; H **guest beers** H / G

Popular twin-bar pub with Green Jack Brewery attached, situated on Triangle Market Place. The cosy front bar has a wooden floor and open fire with a corridor leading to a back bar. The walls are adorned with brewery memorabilia. Beer festivals are held quarterly. New seasonal beers have been brewed using real fruits and elderflowers. Live music is staged twice weekly. Customers are welcome to bring their own food from nearby takeaways. It was local CAMRA's Pub of the Year 2005. ♨⊟⇌●

Market Weston

Mill Inn

Bury Road, IP22 2PD

✪ 12-3 (not Mon), 5-11; 12-3, 7-11 Sun

☎ (01359) 221018

Adnams Bitter; Greene King IPA, Morland Original; Old Chimneys Military Mild, Great Raft Bitter [H]

It is difficult to miss this striking brick pub standing at the crossroads of the B1111. There is always a warm welcome here, and the pub is the closest outlet for Old Chimneys Brewery on the other side of the village. The pub is free of tie and boasts an interesting range of beers. The excellent beer choice is complemented by a menu of home-cooked food. ♨Q◐◑♣P

Mellis

Railway Tavern

The Common, IP23 8DU

✪ 12-3.30 (2.30 Sat), 5-11; 3.30-11 Mon & Tue; 12-3, 5.30-10.30 Sun

☎ (01379) 783416

Adnams Bitter, Broadside; Greene King IPA; guest beers [H]

Adjacent to the main London to Norwich railway line and a stone's throw from what is reputed to be the largest common in England, this village watering-hole offers newly refurbished, comfortable surroundings. The landlord is proud to serve well-known regional ales, plus a changing selection from breweries further afield. Local micro-breweries are also well supported. Have a game of pool, treat yourself to some home-cooked food, or simply sit back, relax and enjoy the beer. ♨Q⇋◐◑⊟♿▲♣P

Mildenhall

Queen's Arms ✔

42 Queensway, IP28 7JW

✪ 12-2.30, 5-11; 12-11 Fri-Sat; 12-10.30 Sun

☎ (01683) 713657

Greene King XX Mild, IPA, Abbot; guest beer [H]

Comfortable local, popular with many regulars. Visitors are welcome and it is favoured by the annual cycle rally. A community centre in every respect, it fields darts teams and many pub games are played; monthly quiz nights are well supported. Excellent home-cooked food is available at lunchtime and most evenings (phone first); Sunday lunches are recommended. A good-sized garden is a bonus. Guest beers are from the Greene King list. ❀⇋◐◑▲♣P

Naughton

Wheelhouse

Whatfield Road, IP7 7BS (400 metres from B1078)

✪ 5 (12 Fri-Sat)-11; 12-10.30 Sun

☎ (01449) 740496

Beer range varies [H]

People come here from miles around, attracted by the quality and variety of interesting beers – usually three or four are available. A range of sandwiches and baguettes complements the ale. Low beams and a lovely inglenook give character to this rural gem. The main bar is no-smoking. A pool table, darts and pub games are popular. ♨Q❀♿♣P⚟

Newmarket

Five Bells

15 St Mary's Square, CB8 0HZ

(behind the Rookery shopping centre)

✪ 11-11; 12-10.30 Sun

☎ (01638) 602868

Greene King IPA, Abbot; guest beer [H]

Two streets away from the hustle and bustle of Newmarket High Street, you will find the Five Bells with its open fire and warm atmosphere. Local artists' work adorns the walls, much of which is for sale. The regulars are active in all pub games including petanque. Through the French windows there is a large garden with two petanque pitches and a barbecue that is pressed into service most summer Sunday afternoons. ♨❀♿▲⇌♣

Offton

Limeburners

Willisham Road, IP8 4SF

✪ 4.30 (12 Mon, Fri & Sat)-11; 12-10.30 Sun

☎ (01473) 658318

Adnams Bitter, Broadside; Greene King IPA; guest beer [H]

This roadside pub takes its name from a disused lime kiln in the old quarry opposite. Built on split levels, it has a ramp to provide wheelchair access. A room off the main bar has a pool table. New to the pub is a fish and chip restaurant serving meals and takeaways (not Wed). Busy in the early evening with workers stopping off on the way home, the pub is also lively on Sunday night when it hosts a folk jam evening. ❀◐◑♿P

Ramsholt

Ramsholt Arms

Dock Road, IP12 3AB (signed off B1083) OS307415

✪ 11.30-11; 12-10.30 Sun

☎ (01394) 411229

Adnams Bitter, Broadside, seasonal beers; guest beers [H]

Once known as Dock Farm, this fine inn is in a splendid location, enjoying superb views of the River Deben. Although it is in an isolated spot, it is popular with walkers, birdwatchers and sailors; families and dogs are welcome too. Meals are served all day. Photographs on the wall show past scenes of village life from this idyllic hamlet. ♨Q❀⇋◐◑P

Redgrave

Cross Keys ✔

The Street, IP22 1RW

✪ 12-2.30 (not Mon), 6-11; 12-3, 7-10.30 Sun

☎ (01379) 898510

Ridleys IPA, Tolly Original [H]

Delightful village pub ideally situated on the village green and benefiting from its

proximity to the Redgrave and Lopham Fen which is popular with ramblers and naturalists. The pub was recently bought by Essex brewers Ridleys and showcases a range of its real ales. A number of Ridleys' bottled beers are also on sale. The landlord and landlady concentrate on beer sales but also offer a menu of pub food which, although simple, is unpretentious and tasty.
⛫❀◖◗⊟♣P

Rumburgh

Rumburgh Buck

Mill Road, IP19 0NT
✪ 11.45-3, 6.30-11; 12-3, 7-10.30 Sun
☎ (01986) 785257
Adnams Bitter, seasonal beers; guest beers Ⓗ
Full of character, this pub was originally the guest house for a medieval priory. Refurbishments and extensions have added a number of interlinked areas around the original historic core. Two dining areas and one bar are no-smoking; the rest of the pub permits smoking. One of the guest beers is always from Woodforde's; dark beers are served in the winter months. At the heart of village life, the pub's folk music evenings, quiz nights and darts matches are well attended.
Q❀◖◗⊟▲♣P⚟

St Peter South Elmham

St Peter's Hall

NR35 1NQ
✪ 11-11; 12-10.30 Sun
☎ (01986) 782322
website: www.stpetersbrewery.co.uk
St Peter's beer range Ⓗ
15th-century moated farmhouse conversion using architectural salvage materials. The pub has a churchlike entrance with a traditional-style bar and a small area for drinking. There is a dining room (booking recommended) plus a second eating area. When busy, a spacious, comfortable room upstairs is opened solely for drinkers. Three varying St Peter's ales are always available, all priced the same. The Brewery is across the courtyard with a shop attached; brewery visits by appointment.
⛫Q❀◖◗P⚟

Somerleyton

Duke's Head

Slugs Lane, NR32 5QR
✪ 11-3, 6.30-11; 11-11 Sat; 12-10.30 Sun
☎ (01502) 730281
Adnams Bitter; Greene King IPA; Oulton Bitter, seasonal beers; guest beer Ⓗ
This pub has taken on a new lease of life since coming under the ownership of Herringfleet Inns. The public bar has been retained with a refurbished lounge and restaurant which has a good reputation (booking advisable). All produce is sourced locally. A large garden overlooks the marshes and River Waveney, making the pub convenient for Broads users (it is open all day in summer). A visit to Somerleyton Hall in this picturesque village with its famous maze is also recommended.
⛫❀◖◗⊟▲≠P

Southwold

Lord Nelson

42 East Street, IP18 6EJ
✪ 10.30-11; 12-10.30 Sun
☎ (01502) 722079
Adnams Bitter, Broadside, seasonal beers Ⓗ
Always a busy and lively pub, it is popular with locals and visitors enjoying the coastal views from the nearby cliff top. Children and well-behaved dogs are welcome in the small side room and the partly-covered patio at the rear. The main bar, with flagstone flooring and a roaring log fire in winter, is always welcoming. As the name suggests, there is a lot of memorabilia relating to England's greatest naval hero. Reasonably priced food is served.
⛫❀◖◗▲

Sole Bay

7 East Green, IP18 6JN
✪ 11-11; 12-10.30 Sun
☎ (01502) 723736
Adnams Bitter, Broadside, seasonal beers Ⓗ
Excellent L-shaped single room pub situated close to the lighthouse. Recently refurbished, it retains the original wooden flooring in the bar but now has disabled access and baby changing facilities. As befits the nearest pub to the Adnams Brewery, the ales are dispensed in fine form from a bank of handpumps. Evening meals are served on Thursday, Friday and Saturday.
◖◗♿▲

Stowmarket

Royal William

53 Union Street East, IP14 1HP
✪ 11-3, 6 (5 Fri; 7 Sat)-11; 12-3, 7-10.30 Sun
☎ (01499) 674553
Greene King IPA; St Austell Tribute Ⓖ
Good, basic, back-street local with a single bar. It is situated behind late medieval buildings on Stowupland Street and is part of an area of 19th-century development in a town that grew after the arrival of the railway. One of just a handful of pubs in Suffolk still serving beers by gravity, the casks are kept on a stillage in a small room behind the bar. Stowmarket was an important malting centre and the old maltings can be seen nearby; the modern maltings is out of town. ≠♣

Stutton

Gardeners Arms

Manningtree Road, IP9 2TG
✪ 12-3, 6-11; 12-11 Sat; 12-5 Sun
☎ (01473) 328868
Adnams Bitter; Greene King IPA; guest beers Ⓗ
This friendly local offers a warm welcome to all. The main bar extends back to the garden and there is a separate restaurant. You will be blown away by the size of the bellows! Excellent food is served at lunchtime and early evening. An ideal destination for walkers and travellers to the locality, dogs are welcome in the bar. The outside seating area is a perfect place for a pint.
⛫Q❀◖◗♣P

Sudbury

Waggon & Horses

Acton Square, CO10 1HJ

11-3.30, 7 (5 Wed-Fri)-11; 11-4, 7-11 Sat; 12-4, 7-10.30 Sun

☎ (01787) 312147

Greene King IPA; guest beers Ⓗ

Local in the town's back streets, behind Market Hill. As well as several drinking areas, there is a games section with pool and darts and a small dining area. Food is home cooked with frequent special menus (booking is advisable). The new Phoenix Court flats nearby are built on the site of the defunct Phoenix Brewery, so named because it rose from the ashes of a fire in 1890. Guest beers are from the Greene King list.

Q ❀ ♣

Swilland

Moon & Mushroom

High Road, IP6 9LR

11.30-2.30 (not Mon), 6-11; 12-2.30, 7-10.30 Sun

☎ (01473) 785320

Buffy's Norwich Terrier, Hopleaf; Crouch Vale Brewers Gold; Nethergate Umbel Ale, Wolf Bitter; Woodforde's Wherry, Norfolk Nog Ⓖ

Oak beams, low ceilings and an open fire make this a cosy pub in winter and the pleasant patio is perfect for enjoying a pint in warmer weather. An excellent range of beers from some of East Anglia's smaller breweries is served by gravity dispense from cooled casks. The food is of the good, wholesome variety, with vegetarian options. This award-winning pub is certainly worth a visit. Q ❀ ♣

Theberton

Lion

The Street, IP16 4RU

12-2.30, 6-11; 12-3, 7-10.30 Sun

☎ (01728) 830185

website: www.thelioninn.co.uk

Adnams Bitter; Woodforde's Wherry; guest beers Ⓗ

A regular entry to the Guide, you will find this pub opposite the fine, thatched, round-towered church. With camping facilities at the rear, it is well situated for exploring the Suffolk coast and surrounding countryside. The single bar serves the main area and the no-smoking dining room, with guest beers usually from local East Anglian breweries. It is always worth checking the website to see when your favourite ale is on. Monthly popular jazz nights are held (first Sun).

❀ ♣P

Thurston

Fox & Hounds ✔

Barton Road, IP31 3QT (opp. station)

12-2.30, 5-11; 11-11 Fri-Sat; 12-10.30 Sun

☎ (01359) 232228

Adnams Bitter; Greene King IPA, Old Speckled Hen; guest beers Ⓗ

Busy village pub, a listed building from the 1800s. Regular real ales are supplemented by two guests at the weekends. Good home-cooked food is served (Tue-Sun; not Sun eve). Sky Sports is on in the public bar. ❀ P

Walsham le Willows

Blue Boar

The Street, IP31 3AA

11.30-2.30, 5-11; 11.30-11 Sat; 12-10.30 Sun

☎ (01359) 258533

Adnams Bitter, Broadside; Woodforde's Wherry; Ⓖ **guest beers** Ⓗ

An ale house most of the time since 1420, the rare wooden crown post roof can still be seen in the attic. Good home-cooked food (eve meals Thu-Sat) and a fine selection of ales are available. The house beer is brewed by Bartrams. The large, enclosed garden is safe for children and families are welcome. Quiz night is Wednesday; live entertainment is hosted fortnightly. A beer festival is held on May bank holiday in a large marquee. ❀ ♣P

Woodbridge

Cherry Tree ✔

73 Cumberland Street, IP12 4AG

11-3, 5-11; 11-11 Sat; 12-10.30 Sun

☎ (01394) 384627 website: www.thecherrytreepub.co.uk

Adnams Bitter, Broadside, seasonal beers; guest beer Ⓗ

Opposite a large garden centre and just a short walk from the town centre and station, this single-bar pub is popular with a varied mix of customers. Despite having many internal walls removed, it retains a cosy atmosphere in which to enjoy the splendid beers and varied food menu. Regular live music is hosted on Friday and the Thursday evening quiz is well attended. A Grade II listed barn to the rear has been converted into accommodation.

♣P

Olde Bell & Steelyard ✔

103 New Street, IP12 1DZ

12-3, 6-11; 12-11 Sat; 12-10.30 Sun

☎ (01394) 382933

Greene King IPA, Abbot, Ruddles County, Old Speckled Hen Ⓗ

Impressive, timber-framed building with the historic 'steelyard' on the front wall overhanging the street. It has two bars with bare wood floors and high ceilings, an airy conservatory and a garden at the back. Among its many attractions, appealing to a wide range of customers, are the good food, traditional games, children's area and live music. A quiz is held every other Sunday. This friendly, cosy pub is always worth a visit. ❀ ♿ ♣

Woolpit

Bull

The Street, IP30 9SA

11 (11.30 Sat)-3, 6-11; 12-2.30, 7-10.30 Sun

☎ (01359) 240393 website: www.bullinnwoolpit.co.uk

Adnams Bitter; guest beers Ⓗ

Large inn, on the main Ipswich to Cambridge road through the centre of this historic village. A garden with a children's play area leads off the car park beside the pub. Inside, choose between the community-minded front bar, hosting varied charity events throughout the year, a games room, a comfortable conservatory and spacious restaurant at the rear. Wholesome home-cooked food is served (not Sun eve). ❀ ♣P

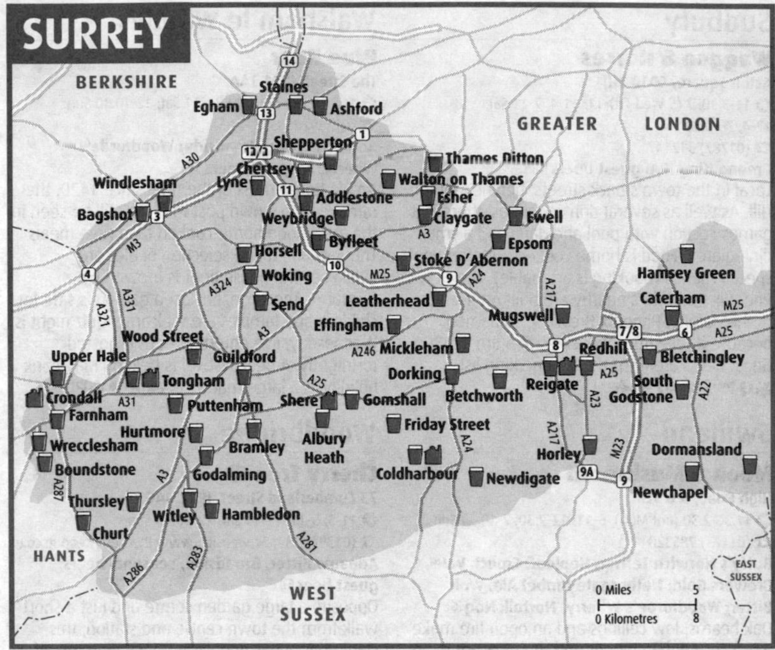

Addlestone

Waggon & Horses

43 Simplemarsh Road, KT15 1QH (off A318)
⏲ 11-11; 12-10.30 Sun
☎ (01932) 828488
Ushers Best Bitter; guest beers Ⓗ
Comfortable and welcoming local dating from 1912. In winter the cosy atmosphere is enhanced by the open fire. A long defunct outside gents' toilet with a corrugated iron roof is commemorated by the pub's 'tin house golf society'. Quiz night is on Tuesday and there is occasional live music at the weekend. Guest beers are from the Punch portfolio. No evening meals are served on Sunday or Monday. Visit in the summer to enjoy the pub's award-winning floral displays. ᗰ❀◐◑♣P⊬

Albury Heath

William IV

Little London, GU5 9DG
⏲ 11-3, 5.30-11; 12-3, 7-10.30 Sun
☎ (01483) 202685
Archers Best Bitter; Flowers IPA; Greene King Abbot; Hogs Back TEA, Hop Garden Gold Ⓗ
Originally dating from the 16th century, the building boasts beams, flagstones and a large fireplace where a welcoming wood fire burns in winter. Situated in a quiet lane adjoining extensive woodland, the area is popular with walkers. There are two traditional bars with a dining room up a few steps and a function room upstairs. Excellent home-made meals are served (not Sun eve or Mon eve in winter).
ᗰQ❀◐◑♣P

INDEPENDENT BREWERIES

Crondall Crondall
Hogs Back Tongham
Leith Hill Coldharbour
Pilgrim Reigate
Surrey Hills Shere

Ashford

Ash Tree ✔

Convent Road, TW15 2HW (on B378)
⏲ 11-11; 12-10.30 Sun
☎ (01784) 424610
Fuller's Chiswick, London Pride, ESB, seasonal beers Ⓗ
Large, boisterous 1960s-built local with a sprawling bar area filled with comfortable nooks and crannies to sit in. It serves a range of Fuller's cask beers including occasional seasonal ales. Good value food, both traditional English and Thai, is available except on Sunday evening and Monday. Pool is popular – with pub teams playing in the local league – and quiz night is on Thursday. Well served by local bus routes, the stop is right outside. ❀◐◑♣P⊬

King's Fairway ✔

91 Fordbridge Road, TW15 2SS (on B377)
⏲ 12-11; 12-10.30 Sun
☎ (01784) 424801
Fuller's London Pride; Young's Bitter; guest beers Ⓗ
There is a friendly feel to this comfortable Ember Inns establishment with a constant buzz of conversation from locals and visitors in the warren of interlinked drinking areas. The six handpumps sport up to four guest beers, often from smaller regionals or micros. An all-day menu serves food until 8pm. A notice behind the bar tells customers that pints will gladly be topped up. Quiz nights are on Sunday and Wednesday. ᗰQ❀◐◑P⊬

Bagshot

Foresters Arms

173 London Road, GU19 5DH (on A30)
12-2.30, 5.30-11; 12-3, 7-10.30 Sun
☎ (01276) 472038
Courage Best Bitter; Fuller's London Pride; Hogs Back TEA; Taylor Dark Mild; guest beers Ⓗ
Cosy, uncomplicated little pub serving an excellent choice of beers including three guests. Good pub food ranges from sandwiches to curries and roasts. The pub competes in a local darts league and has a golf society. The skittle alley with its own bar can be used for parties and private events. Every summer the landlord's proverbial green fingers transform the pub frontage into a glorious floral display.
❀◐♣P

Betchworth

Dolphin Inn

The Street, RH3 7DW (off A25, opp. church)
11-3, 5.30-11; 11-11 Sat; 12-10.30 Sun
(01737) 842288
Young's Bitter, Special, Waggledance (summer), **Winter Warmer** (winter) Ⓗ
The Dolphin is said to be over 400 years old, although the earliest written record of the pub dates from 1785. The present building, with a flagstone floor and two wood-burning inglenooks, dates from the 18th century. A busy local, the pub also attracts many visitors, especially at weekends. Outside is a pleasant seating area and a garden. The meals are good value, with specials always available.
⩋Q❀◐◑♣P

Bletchingley

William IV

Little Common Lane, RH1 4QF
(off A25, N of village) OS322509
12-3, 6-11; 12-11 Sat; 12-10.30 (3 winter) Sun
☎ (01883) 743278
Adnams Bitter; Fuller's London Pride; Greene King Ruddles County; Harveys BB Ⓗ
Cosy, quiet low-beamed Victorian pub that was originally built as two cottages in the 1850s. It is entered via steps from a narrow country lane although there is a ramp for easier access at the side of the pub. Plenty of seating can be found in the two unpretentious bars which are separated by a connecting door. A restaurant, open all day Saturday and Sunday (not winter afternoons), lies to the rear and even provides a takeaway service. Q❀◐◑P

Boundstone

Bat & Ball

Bat & Ball Lane, GU10 4SA
(via Upper Bourne Lane off Sandrock Hill Rd)
11-3, 5.30-11; 11-11 Fri & Sat; 12-10.30 Sun
☎ (01252) 792108
website: www.thebatandballfarnham.co.uk
Hogs Back TEA; Young's Bitter; guest beers Ⓗ
Excellent free house with wood-panelled walls, a tiled floor and real fire. The large garden includes a children's play area. The delicious home-cooked food is served in generous portions (available all day in summer). Road access is via a bumpy private road or on foot via the signposted footpath and steep steps off Shortheath Road, which can be reached by bus. The house beer, Bat & Ball Bitter, is Hampshire Ironside rebadged. ⩋Q♉❀◐◑♿P⚟

Bramley

Jolly Farmer

High Street, GU5 0HB (on A281)
11-11; 12-10.30 Sun
☎ (01483) 893355 website: www.jollyfarmer.co.uk
Badger Best; Hogs Back TEA; guest beers Ⓗ
Genuine free house consisting of a single room that seems to go on forever, eventually ending in a raised dining area. It is decorated with a bewildering array of artefacts including ceramic tiles, business cards, bank notes, puppets, stuffed birds and animals and a fish tank. An extensive range of regular beers is supplemented by up to five guests, with Surrey, Hampshire and Sussex breweries well represented. Regular buses run nearby seven days a week, including evenings. Q⇌◐◑P

Byfleet

Plough ✔

104 High Road, KT14 7QT (off A245)
11 (12 Sat)-3, 5-11; 12-3, 7-10.30 Sun
☎ (01932) 353257
Courage Best Bitter; Fuller's London Pride; guest beers Ⓗ
Enduringly popular free house with up to seven guest beers. A real haven, this comfortable establishment offers a choice of three drinking areas, two with blazing fires. The conservatory is no-smoking and welcomes children (access via the car park). In summer, try the tranquil garden. Interestingly, the pub sign is indoors over the bar. ⩋Q♉❀◐♣P⚟

Caterham

Clifton Arms

110 Chaldon Road, CR3 5PH (on B2031)
11.30-2.30, 4-11; 12-11 Sat; 12-10.30 Sun
☎ (01883) 343525
Fuller's London Pride; Young's Bitter; guest beers Ⓗ
Former Charrington house, host to a fantastic collection of artefacts relating to local history and militaria which has to be seen to be believed – it even rivals Caterham's East Surrey Museum! The wooden bar back is also most impressive. A comfortable and cosy place to while away your time and enjoy a drink, whether it is beer or one of the fine selection of ciders and sometimes perry. The back room doubles as a restaurant (eve meals served Tue-Sat) and, on Saturday, a rock 'n' roll disco.
❀◐◑♣●P

King & Queen ✔

34 High Street, CR3 5UA (on B2030)
11-11; 12-10.30 Sun
☎ (01883) 345438
Fuller's Chiswick, London Pride, ESB Ⓗ
Wonderful 400-year-old red brick and flint pub that has evolved since the 1840s from three former cottages, one of which was a bakery. The pub was one of Caterham's early ale houses and

still retains three distinct areas – a front bar facing the main road, a high-ceilinged wooden beamed middle room with inglenook, and a small lower level rear area leading to a patio. Its name refers to Britain's only joint monarchy, William and Mary. No meals are served on Sunday. ⚑Q❀◖◗♣P

Chertsey

Coach & Horses ✔

14 St Anns Road, KT16 9DG (on B375)
⏲ 12-11; 12-5, 7-10.30 Sun
☎ (01932) 563085
Fuller's Chiswick, London Pride, ESB 🄷
Situated off the main high street, this building dates from the 1800s. Consistently appearing in the Guide, this well-run pub with friendly staff serves the full range of Fuller's beers. The drinking area is divided by a raised bar into one quieter side and the other with TV and darts area. Food is not served at the weekend or Monday evening. There is limited accommodation available. ⚑Q❀⛾◖◗♣P

Churt

Crossways

Churt Road, GU10 2JE (on A287)
⏲ 11-3.30, 5-11; 11-11 Fri & Sat, 12-4, 7-10.30 Sun
☎ (01428) 714323
Cheriton Best Bitter; Courage Best Bitter; Ringwood Fortyniner; 🄷 **guest beers** 🄶
Home from home for locals and welcoming for visitors, this is everything a good pub should be. A good line up of guest beers (up to 500 a year) is always served, drawn straight from the cask in the cellar, and four real ciders are on stillage. Good home-cooked food is available at lunchtime, Monday-Saturday. The interior is comfortable with a quarry tile floor in the public bar. A popular beer festival is held every year. It was local CAMRA Pub of the Year for 2005. Q❀◖⊟⛺♣●P

Claygate

Foley Arms

Hare Lane, KT10 0LZ OS153636
⏲ 11-11; 12-10.30 Sun
☎ (01372) 462021
Young's Bitter, Special, seasonal beers 🄷
Comfortable, traditional two-bar Victorian village pub, named after local landowners. Alongside the quieter lounge is a hall that hosts a Friday night folk club. A quiz is held every three months. The large garden has a children's play area. No food is served on Sunday evening. The old stables is the gymnasium and boxing ring for the Foley Amateur Boxing Club. It lies on the K3 bus route. ⚑❀◖◗⊟⇌♣P

Coldharbour

Plough Inn

Coldharbour Lane, RH5 6HD
(on Dorking-Leith Hill road) OS152441
⏲ 11.30-11; 12-10.30 Sun
☎ (01306) 711793 website: www.ploughinn.com
Leith Hill Crooked Furrow, Tallywhacker; Ringwood Old Thumper; Shepherd Neame Master Brew Bitter, Spitfire 🄷
Home of the Leith Hill Brewery, which is situated in an outbuilding at the rear of the building, this is a gem of a rural brew-pub. Despite being tucked away in a small, sleepy village, the restaurant serves first rate meals. In summer the large garden is popular, as is the converted barn that has become a family room. An ideal stop on a country walk, six en-suite guest rooms are available. ⚑☋❀⛾◖◗●P

Dorking

Cricketers ✔

81 South Street, RH4 2HU
(on A25 one-way system, westbound)
⏲ 11-11; 12-10.30 Sun
☎ (01306) 889938
Fuller's Chiswick, London Pride, ESB, seasonal beers 🄷
Comfortable, town-centre one-bar pub with bare brick walls decorated with old pictures and photographs. Real ale is very much the favourite tipple here. A television is switched on for sporting occasions, particularly rugby. Outside is an attractive walled garden – a real suntrap in the summer. Just down the road is another Fuller's pub, the Queen's Head, which is well worth a visit. Weekday lunches are served. ❀◖♣

King's Arms

45 West Street, RH4 1BU
(on A25 one-way system eastbound)
⏲ 11-11; 12-3, 7-10.30 Sun
☎ (01306) 883361
Fuller's London Pride; Greene King IPA; guest beers 🄷
Attractive, old-fashioned pub with low beams situated in a street of antique shops. Inside, a choice of drinking areas leads to an excellent restaurant at the rear (eve meals Tue-Sat). Up to four guest beers are available, mostly sourced from micro-breweries. Live music is played on Sunday and Wednesday evenings; the first Wednesday of the month is jam night. ❀◖◗⇌(West)P

Old House at Home

24 West Street, RH4 1BY (on A25 one-way system eastbound)
⏲ 11-11; 12-10.30 Sun
☎ (01306) 889664
Young's Bitter, Special, seasonal beers 🄷
One-bar 15th-century inn which has been well refurbished with bare wooden floors and exposed beams. Plasma-screen TVs show sports matches (the landlord is a staunch Chelsea supporter). Outside is a surprisingly large garden – a popular place to while away a sunny summer afternoon. Meals are served 12-6pm (3pm Mon; 5pm Sat). ⚑❀◖♣⚟

Dormansland

Old House At Home

63 West Street, RH7 6QP (off Dormans Road) OS402422
⏲ 11-3, 6-11; 12-4.30, 7-10.30 Sun
☎ (01342) 832117
Shepherd Neame Master Brew Bitter, 🄷 **Best Bitter,** 🄶 **Spitfire, seasonal beers** 🄷
Friendly, traditional 16th-century inn, somewhat

hidden but worth seeking out. The log fire is a focal point for the lounge with its beamed walls and ceiling. A cosy side room houses a dartboard. The pub attracts locals from far and wide for its fine home-made food as well as the beer. Convenient for Lingfield Park races; no food is served on Sunday evening.
⩕Q❀◐◑⊟♣P⊁

Effingham

Plough

Orestan Lane, KT24 5SW OS118538
⚙ 11-3, 5.30-11; 12-5, 7-10.30 Sun
☎ (01372) 458121
Young's Bitter, Special, seasonal beers 🄷
Welcoming country pub, 200 years old. A central bar divides the pub into two distinct areas: one frequented by drinkers enjoying the Young's, the other is a no-smoking dining area where high quality home-cooked food is served. Bar meals are also available at lunchtime. The extensive garden is an added attraction in summer. Mid-week evenings are a good time for a quiet pint.
Q❀◐◑♿P⊁

Egham

Crown

38 High Street, TW20 9DP
⚙ 11.30-11; 12-10.30 Sun
☎ (01784) 432608
Adnams Bitter, Broadside; Fuller's London Pride; Greene King Abbot; guest beers 🄷
Large one-bar pub at the west end of the High Street near to Strodes College. This friendly pub is popular with all ages. A no-smoking conservatory at the rear leads to a delightful garden. The two guest beers come from regional brewers including Adnams, Archers and Fuller's. Beer festivals are held two or three times a year. The car park is small. Meals are served 12-9pm daily. ❀◐◑⇌P⊁

Epsom

Barley Mow

12 Pikes Hill, KT17 4EA (off A2022, Upper High St)
⚙ 11-11; 12-10.30 Sun
☎ (01372) 721044
Fuller's Chiswick, London Pride, ESB, seasonal beers 🄷
Converted from three cottages, this pub is situated in the back streets of Epsom close to the town centre. The interior is divided into three distinct drinking areas, and there is a conservatory which leads to the pleasant garden. The pub is highly regarded for its good food, most of which is prepared on the premises. This is complemented by barbecues in the summer. Use Upper High Street public car park; a short walk along an alley to the pub.
⩕Q❀◐◑⇌

Railway Guard

48 Church Road, KT17 4DZ (off A2022)
⚙ 11.30-11; 12-10.30 Sun
☎ (01372) 721143
Fuller's London Pride; guest beers 🄷
Small locals' pub close to the town centre. A large-screen TV shows sporting events, at other times the juke box is popular. The bar serves a good range of single malt whiskies to complement the real ales. Outside there is a small triangular patio with seating. The pub hosts a golf society. ❀⇌

Rifleman ✔

5 East Street, KT17 1BB (on A24)
⚙ 11-11; 12-10.30 Sun
☎ (01372) 726079
Greene King IPA, Ruddles County, Abbot 🄷
Situated in the shadow of a railway bridge, this small one-bar town-centre pub is popular with locals. Photographs of bygone Epsom decorate the walls. A TV occupies part of the bar area. Barbecues are held in the summer months. No food is served at weekends. ❀◐

Esher

Bear

71 High Street, KT10 9RQ (at A307/A244 jct)
⚙ 11-11; 12-10.30 Sun
☎ (01372) 469786
Young's Bitter, Special, seasonal beers 🄷
Dating back to the 18th century, this former coaching inn is centrally located. It gets its name because the pub was built on the site of the Earl of Warwick's hunting lodge, whose crest featured bears, which look down from the roof. The pub can be busy on race days at nearby Sandown Park. The single bar serves several different areas, including one for diners. Sport is shown on the large-screen TV in the front bar area. Seven en-suite rooms are available for overnight stays. ⚇❀⊯◐◑♣P⊁

Ewell

Wheatsheaf

34 Kingston Road, KT17 2AA (off A240/B2200)
⚙ 11-11; 12-10.30 Sun
☎ (020) 8393 2879
Young's Bitter; Webster's Green Label Best; guest beer 🄷
Rebuilt in 1858, there has been an ale house on this site since 1456. A popular pub with locals, it has two comfortable, carpeted rooms with open fires served by one bar and retains a traditional atmosphere. Around the walls are pictures of old Ewell and behind the bar are windows commemorating the long-gone Isleworth Brewery. Occasional sport, particularly rugby, is shown on TV and there is live music on Saturday. Good home-made food is served at lunchtime.
❀◐⇌(West) ♣

Farnham

Hop Blossom ✔

Long Garden Walk, GU9 7HX (off A287)
⚙ 12-3, 5-11; 11-11 Fri & Sat; 12-10.30 Sun
☎ (01252) 710770
Fuller's Chiswick, London Pride, ESB, seasonal beers; guest beer 🄷
A gem of a pub in a side street in the centre of town. Four Fuller's beers are served as well as one guest. On Friday one Fuller's beer is usually available from a barrel on the bar. Food is themed from Monday to Thursday, a la carte on Friday and Saturday, and a roast is served on Sunday. The pub promotes live music with

acoustic sessions on Tuesday and jazz on Thursday. There is a large no-smoking room at the rear for diners and drinkers.
⛫☎◖◗ ⇌⊬

Lamb
43 Abbey Street, GU9 7RJ (off A287)
✪ 11-2.30, 5-11; 11-11 Sat; 12-10.30 Sun
☎ (01252) 714133
Shepherd Neame Master Brew Best Bitter, Spitfire, Ⓖ **seasonal beers** Ⓗ
Situated down a side street between the town centre and the station, this one-room pub displays its wares via both handpump and gravity. It is well known and popular in the area for good value hearty food and live bands every alternate Friday night. The courtyard garden, with a wrought iron staircase leading to an upstairs haven with tables and chairs, is a delightful place to sit in summer. No food is served on Sunday or evening meals Tuesday.
⛫❀◖◗ ⇌♣

Friday Street

Stephan Langton
RH5 6JR
(1 mile S of A25 at Wotton) OS128456
✪ 11-3 (not Mon), 5-11; 11-11 Sat; 12-8 Sun
☎ (01306) 730775
Adnams Bitter; Fuller's London Pride; Hogs Back TEA Ⓗ
Named after an archbishop of Canterbury involved in the Magna Carta who was reputedly born in Friday Street. Situated in good walking country and the only pub with Michelin Bib Gourmand recognition in Surrey, it gets especially busy at weekends. The freshly-cooked food changes daily and booking is essential for Sunday lunch, and advisable at all times. There is a nearby car park if the pub's limited spaces are full. ⛫❀◖●P

Godalming

Red Lion
1 Mill Lane, GU7 1HF
✪ 11-11; 12-10.30 Sun
☎ (01483) 415207
Harveys BB; guest beers Ⓗ
Wonderful free house at the top end of the high street offering up to five guest beers. Dating from 1696, the building served time as the Oddfellows Hall and a grammar school. It is divided into a historic public bar and a saloon with wood-panelled bar and pump clips on the ceiling which testify to the enormous range of beers served over time. Always worth a visit just to experience a different real ale, themed beer festivals are held at Easter and Hallowe'en. Evening meals are served Tuesday-Saturday.
Q❀◖◗⊟♿⇌♣

Gomshall

Compasses
50 Station Road, GU5 9LA (on A25)
✪ 11-11; 12-10.30 Sun
☎ (01483) 202506
Marston's Pedigree; guest beers Ⓗ
Situated on the bank of the Tillingbourne River, this pub is an ideal place to break your journey. Divided into a bar and restaurant, it serves three guest beers which change monthly, usually from micro-breweries, and home-made food is cooked to order (no food Sun eve). Live music – blues, rock or folk – is played on Friday evening. The garden is reached via a bridge over a stream. ☎❀⛟◖◗⇌P

Guildford

Keystone
3 Portsmouth Road, GU2 4BL (on A3100)
✪ 12-11; 12-10.30 Sun
☎ (01483) 575089 website: www.thekeystone.co.uk
Black Sheep Best Bitter; Wadworth 6X; guest beer Ⓗ
Friendly, town-centre pub with a stylish, minimalist interior. Popular with local office workers, it enforces a strict over 21s policy. The welcoming staff and relaxed atmosphere provide a welcome respite from the bustle of the surrounding area. All the food, including the Sunday roast, is prepared on the premises (meals served 12-5pm Sat and Sun). There is live jazz on the first Wednesday of the month and an acoustic set every alternate Saturday. The small rear terraced garden has a heated patio. ❀◖◗⇌

Plough
16 Park Street, GU1 4XB (on central one-way system)
✪ 11-11; 12-10.30 Sun
☎ (01483) 570167
Fuller's London Pride; Harveys BB; guest beer Ⓗ
Small, friendly, down-to-earth pub popular with locals on the busy Guildford one-way system, five minutes' walk from the High Street. With just one bar – or two if you count the 'dry' brick island built by one of the regulars – the pub is simplicity itself. There is always a welcoming atmosphere, whether you want to chat or watch one of the two TVs at either end of the bar showing sporting events. Food is only served at lunchtime during the week. ⛟◖⇌♣

Varsity Bar
University of Surrey, Egerton Road, GU2 7XU
(off A3 at university exit, near hospital)
✪ 12-11; 12-8.30 Sat; 12-10.30 Sun
☎ (01483) 689974
website: www.unisport.co.uk/varsity_bar.htm
Beer range varies Ⓗ
University sports bar open to all; the entrance is through the shop. Three varying beers are always available, including one strong ale. Future offerings are displayed on a board. Sports matches are shown on a large-screen TV and the bar can get busy on match days (Wed and Sat) but can be quiet at other times. Quiz night is the first Monday of the month. A British cask and international bottled beer festival is held annually in November. ◖◗P

White House
8 High Street, GU2 4AJ (off A3100)
✪ 12-11 (midnight Fri & Sat); 12-10.30 Sun
☎ (01483) 302006
Fuller's Chiswick, London Pride, ESB, seasonal beers Ⓗ
Spacious pub situated just off the bottom end of the High Street. Smartly decorated in shades of soft cream, it has wooden floorboards, rugs and

comfortable settees to relax in. An impressive staircase leads to an upper drinking balcony. At the bar you will find a full range of Fuller's ales. At the back of the pub a door leads to a heated patio overlooking the River Wey – an especially popular place to drink on summer evenings.
❀◑◗♿⇌

Hambledon

Merry Harriers

Rock Hill, Hambledon Road, GU8 4DR
(1 mile off A283)
⊛ 11-3 (4 Sat), 6-11; 12-4, 7-10.30 Sun
☎ (01428) 682883
Greene King IPA; Hogs Back TEA; Hop Back Crop Circle; guest beer Ⓗ
Compact 16th-century pub which has been in the hands of the Beasley family for 38 years. Ignore the sign outside declaring 'warm beer and lousy food' – both beer and food are excellent in this unpretentious country pub (no eve meals Sun, Mon or Thu). Notable features include the use of traditional wooden Surrey slats on the walls and the collection of old chamber pots and stamped pint-measure ceramic mugs on the ceiling. Camping and caravan facilities are opposite. Addlestones cider is served. ᗑQ❀◑◗▲♣●P

Hamsey Green

Good Companions

Limpsfield Road, CR6 9RH (on B269)
⊛ 11-11; 12-10.30 Sun
☎ (020) 8657 6655
website: www.thegoodcompanions.com
Beer range varies Ⓗ
Large pub split into a main bar, a restaurant and a no-smoking lounge area with comfortable sofas for drinkers. The three beers change frequently but are all from the Westerham brewery and of varying strengths. The main bar has a pool table and a large-screen TV showing the major sporting events. Tuesday is 'open mic' night and there is a disco on the last Saturday of the month. Food is available all day in the bar (not Sun eve). ᗑ❀⇆◑◗♿♣P⅍

Horley

Coppingham Arms

263 Balcombe Road, RH6 9EF (on B2036, S of town)
⊛ 11.30-11; 12-10.30 Sun
☎ (01293) 782283
Greene King Old Speckled Hen; Harveys BB Ⓗ
Originally two cottages, this pub is more than 300 years old. The bright, airy, open-plan bar is popular with locals for the good food it serves. To one side of the entrance is a public bar area with a pool table. There are four double rooms available for accommodation, one en-suite.
ᗑ⇆◑◗♿♣P

Horsell

Crown

104 High Street, GU21 4ST
⊛ 11-11, 12-10.30 Sun
☎ (01483) 771719
Adnams Bitter; Fuller's London Pride; Wells Bombardier; guest beers Ⓗ
Unpretentious village pub on the edge of Woking. A constant flow of interesting guest beers sits alongside the regular offerings – Sharp's Brewery often features. Popular with locals, the bustling main bar occasionally stages live music. The lounge is quieter and more relaxing. Outside, in the garden dominated by a wonderful willow tree, there is a petanque terrain. Beer festivals are held twice a year in a marquee. The No 28 Woking-Guildford bus stops outside. ❀⊟P

Hurtmore

Squirrel Inn ✔

Hurtmore Road, GU7 2RN (off A3)
⊛ 11-11; 12-10.30 Sun
☎ (01483) 860223
Fuller's London Pride; guest beers Ⓗ
Cosy bar with comfortable seating spread between two lounge areas. There is a good choice of food ranging from sandwiches to main meals, including vegetarian options. A TV shows sporting events, but is not intrusive. In summer the garden is popular and the heated patio allows outside drinking on cooler evenings. Quiz night is Tuesday and there are live bands every alternate Saturday. ᗑ❀⇆◑◗♣P⅍

Leatherhead

Running Horse

38 Bridge Street, KT22 8BZ (off B2122)
⊛ 11.30-11; 12-10.30 Sun
☎ (01372) 372081
Fuller's London Pride; Greene King IPA, Old Speckled Hen; Taylor Landlord; Young's Bitter, Special Ⓗ
Full of character, this Grade II listed pub can trace its roots back to Tudor times. It sits just above the River Mole, close to the town centre. The historic lounge bar has been extended at the rear to provide various seating areas and there is a courtyard for outdoor drinking in summer. The smaller public bar has live sport on TV. No meals are served on Sunday evening. Regular bus No. 465 passes the door.
Q❀◑◗⊟⇌♣P⅍

Lyne

Royal Marine

Lyne Lane, KT16 0AN OS012663
⊛ 12-2.30, 5.30-11; 12-3 (closed eve) Sun
☎ (01932) 873900
Courage Best Bitter; Hogs Back TEA, seasonal beers; guest beers Ⓗ
A cosy, rural gem that is only three miles from the M25 but could be a world away. Converted from two cottages over 150 years ago, it is filled with marine bric-a-brac as well as 100 ale tankards. Very much the centre of village social life, it doubles as the headquarters of the Lyne Mountain Rescue Team! Guest beers change frequently and often include a mild. ᗑ❀◑◗P

Mickleham

King William IV

Byttom Hill, RH5 6EL (off A24, southbound) OS174538
⊛ 11-3, 6-11; 12-10.30 Sun
☎ (01372) 372590

Adnams Bitter; Badger First Gold; Hogs Back TEA; guest beer (summer) [H]
Nestling on the edge of the scenic North Downs, this 18th-century rural pub provides great views over Norbury Park and the Mole Valley. Full of character, it has just two small bars but the secluded garden provides more room for drinkers in summer. As well as the range of beers, food is a major attraction (no eve meals are served on Sun). Worth seeking out, the pub is served by the regular 465 bus route.
♛Q✿◖◗

Mugswell

Well House Inn ✔
Chipstead Lane, CR5 3SQ
(off A217, approx 1 mile from M25 jct 8) OS258553
⊙ 12-11; 12-10.30 Sun
☎ (01737) 830640 website: www.wellhouseinn.com
Archers Best Bitter; Fuller's London Pride; Hogs Back Hair of the Hog; Wadworth 6X; guest beers [H]
Named after the well in its garden, the pub is a listed building said to date possibly from the 14th century. Mag's Well, mentioned in the Domesday Book, also gave the area its name. Inside, the pub is divided into four areas: two bars, a small no-smoking conservatory and a restaurant (no eve meals on Sun). The guest beers change weekly and usually come from small independents or micros. In summer Addlestones cider replaces one of the beers. The popular quiz night is on Tuesday and occasional live music is staged.
♛✿◖◗♣●P⊬

Newchapel

Blacksmith's Head ✔
Newchapel Road, RH7 6LE (on B2028, off A22)
⊙ 11-3, 5.30 (6 Sat)-11; 12-3 (closed eve) Sun
☎ (01342) 833697
website: www.theblacksmithshead.co.uk
Fuller's London Pride; Harveys BB; guest beers [H]
Single bar with two wood-burning stoves and a restaurant area. The two guest beers are usually from small independents or micros and change frequently. The garden is well worth admiring; its attractive design a testament to the owners' previous occupation as landscape gardeners. Food is freshly prepared with a la carte, bar and tapas menus to choose from. Accommodation is in five en-suite rooms.
♛✿⛟◖◗⛺♣P

Newdigate

Surrey Oaks
Parkgate Road, RH5 5DZ
(between Newdigate and Leigh) OS205436
⊙ 11.30-2.30, 5.30-11; 11.30-3, 6-11 Sat; 12-3, 7-10.30 Sun
☎ (01306) 631200
website: www.surreyoaks.co.uk
Caledonian Deuchars IPA; Harveys Sussex BB; Taylor Landlord; guest beers [H]
The 'Soaks' continues to lead the way locally in its support of micro-breweries, with a different beer arriving on average every day. Stouts and old ales are favoured in winter and light beers are popular in summer. Dating from the 16th century, the pub has retained many period features including an inglenook. There are various drinking areas, each attracting its own set of regulars. Good food is available in the restaurant (no eve meals Sun or Mon). Outside is a large garden with swings and a boules pitch. A beer festival is held over the August bank holiday at local CAMRA Pub of the Year 2005.
♛Q✿◖◗♣●P⊬

Puttenham

Good Intent ✔
62 The Street, GU3 1AR (off B3000)
⊙ 11-3, 6-11; 11-11 Sat; 12-10.30 Sun
☎ (01483) 810387
Theakston Old Peculier; Young's Bitter; guest beers [H]
Relaxing retreat in an unspoilt village yet easily accessible from the busy A31 (Hogs Back) that passes nearby. Dominated by a magnificent fireplace and a hop-adorned bar, the three drinking areas include a lower level dining section where children are permitted (no food Mon eve). The pub offers a warm welcome to walkers from the North Down Way and their dogs too. There are five regular guest beers, including one from the Ringwood Brewery, and a choice of ciders including Mr Whitehead's Boxing Dog.
♛Q✿◖◗●P

Redhill

Garland ✔
5 Brighton Road, RH1 6PP (on A23, S of town centre)
⊙ 11-11; 12-3, 7-10.30 Sun
☎ (01737) 760377
Harveys Sussex XX Mild, Pale Ale, BB, Armada, seasonal beers [H]
A short distance from the town centre, this friendly local serves the full range of Harveys' beer from its eight handpumps (if they are offering a ninth beer it is sold from the cellar). Good, inexpensive food is sold at weekday lunchtimes. Darts is popular with the regulars. Note the large collection of clowns around the bar – they are not immediately obvious. The pub community raises a lot of money for charity.
✿◖⇌♣P

Reigate

Prince of Wales
2 Holmesdale Road, RH2 0BQ
⊙ 12-11; 12-10.30 Sun
☎ (01737) 243112
Shepherd Neame Master Brew Bitter, Best Bitter, Spitfire [H]
Unassuming pub conveniently located beside Reigate train station. The interior is divided into three drinking areas, each served from the same U-shaped bar. Food is served on weekday lunchtimes. A large TV screen is used for major sporting events. If you are looking for a place to escape the bustle, go all the way to the back room where you will find large, comfortable sofas and high backed chairs to relax in. The garden backs on to the railway line.
♛✿◖⇌♣P

Send

New Inn

Send Road, GU23 7EN (on A247)
11-11; 12-10.30 Sun
(01483) 762736
Adnams Bitter; Fuller's London Pride; Greene King Abbot; Young's Special; guest beer Ⓗ
The present New Inn, which was originally a mortuary, has replaced what used to be the New Inn on the opposite side of the road. It is situated on the Wey Navigation, one of Britain's oldest man-made waterways dating from the 1660s. Once used to move flour to London markets, this stretch of water is now dominated by recreational boaters. It is no surprise that in summer the garden, with its outdoor weekend bar and barbecues, is a popular attraction. The guest beer changes weekly and is usually from a local brewery. Q❀◐◑P

Shepperton

Barley Mow

67 Watersplash Road, TW17 0EE (off B376)
12-11; 12-10.30 Sun
(01932) 225326
Courage Best Bitter; Hogs Back TEA; guest beers Ⓗ
Friendly, welcoming side-street local with an extensive, fast moving beer range. Favourite breweries include Archers, Grand Union and Twickenham. One real cider is normally available too. Beer festivals are held in summer and winter. Quiz night is on Thursday, jazz is performed Wednesday as well as other occasional live music. Meals are served at lunchtimes only; with the exception of Friday night fish and chips. It was local CAMRA Pub of the Year in 2004. ⋒Q❀◐♿♣P

South Godstone

Fox & Hounds

Tilburstow Hill Road, RH9 8LY (½ mile W of A22)
OS354494
12-3, 6-11; 12-3, 7-10.30 Sun
(01342) 893474
Greene King IPA, Abbot; guest beer Ⓗ
Attractive, beamed 14th-century building which was originally a brew-pub at the beginning of the 17th century. With a long history of involvement in smuggling, on the wall you will find a smuggler's gaiter belonging to John Trenchman (his ghost is reputedly still a regular today!). The pub serves an excellent selection of home-made food in the old-fashioned bar and no-smoking restaurant. Both rooms feature a real fire. The guest beer is supplied by Greene King.
⋒Q❀◐◑♣P⚟

Staines

Bells

124 Church Street, TW18 4YA (off B376)
11-3, 5-11; 11-11 Fri & Sat; 12-10.30 Sun
(01784) 454240
Young's Bitter, Special, seasonal beers Ⓗ
Comfortable 18th-century pub at the quieter end of town opposite St Mary's Church. Friendly staff serve the full range of Young's ale, including seasonals and a good selection of bottled beers. The pub has been a local CAMRA Pub of the Year for three consecutive years. Good food using fresh produce is served daily except Sunday evening. The pleasant rear garden is popular in summer. It is within easy walking distance of the town centre and River Thames.
Q❀◐◑♿

George ✔

2-8 High Street, TW18 4EE (on A308)
10-11; 10-10.30 Sun
(01784) 462181
Courage Best Bitter; Greene King Abbot; Marston's Burton Bitter, Pedigree; Shepherd Neame Spitfire; guest beers Ⓗ
Popular town-centre pub opposite the old town hall. The large, comfortable ground-floor main bar includes a dining area and is decorated with photographs illustrating the local history of Staines. Upstairs is a smaller, quieter bar. The pub gets busy on weekend evenings. An array of handpumps serves a good range of real ales including one from the Loddon Brewery, as well as another guest beer.
Q◐◑♿⥤⚟

Hobgoblin

14 Church Street, TW18 4EP (off B376)
12-11; 12-10.30 Sun
(01784) 452012
Beer range varies Ⓗ
Impressive town-centre pub serving four real ales that change so frequently the same beer is rarely served twice. Outside the pub is a small, secluded patio garden. The pub can be busy and noisy, particularly when sporting events are shown on the large-screen TV. There is a juke box and regular live music. Thai food is served throughout the day. ❀◐◑♿⥤

Wheatsheaf & Pigeon

Penton Road, TW18 2LL (off B376)
11-11; 12-10.30 Sun
(01784) 452922
Courage Best Bitter; Fuller's London Pride; Hogs Back TEA; guest beers Ⓗ
Comfortable out of town pub situated close to the Thames towpath to Laleham. An important part of the local community, the pub offers a warm welcome to visitors. Guest beers are now making a regular appearance on the bar. Activities include a well-supported quiz night on Tuesday evening and annual street parties complete with tug-of-war and barbecue. ❀◐◑

Stoke D'Abernon

Old Plough ✔

2 Station Road, KT11 3BN (on A245)
11-11; 12-10.30 Sun
(01932) 862244
website: www.dabernons-restaurant.co.uk
Courage Best Bitter; guest beers Ⓗ
Reputed to date possibly from the late 16th century, this traditional building has been opened out but retains its character with distinct areas. The guest beers usually come from micros all over the UK. Food is served in the bar area and a more extensive menu is available in the restaurant, however food does not dominate (no eve meals Sun). The garden is popular with

families in summer and children are welcome inside until 7.30pm. It was voted local CAMRA Pub of the Year in 2004.
(Cobham/Stoke D'Abernon) P

Thames Ditton

George & Dragon

High street, KT7 0RY (on B364)
11-11; 12-10.30 Sun
(020) 8398 2206
Shepherd Neame Master Brew Bitter, Best Bitter, Spitfire, seasonal beers H
Retaining its appeal as a village local, the pub is divided into several areas with cosy wood panelling. Set back from the road, it has its own garden and car park. A ramp has been fitted to the front steps to allow wheelchair access, although the toilets have not yet been upgraded. The pub is popular with local clubs for meetings and functions. Evening meals are served Wednesday to Saturday.
Q P

Thursley

Three Horseshoes

Dye House Road, GU8 6QD (off A3)
12-3, 5.30-11; 12-11 Sat; 12-10.30 Sun
(01252) 703268
Fuller's London Pride; Hogs Back TEA; guest beer H
The locals fought long and hard to save the only pub in the village when it was under threat of closure in 1999 for conversion to housing. Purchased by 24 supporters, it was reopened in 2004 after sensitive refurbishment, including the addition of an unobtrusive restaurant at the back of the building. A short drive from the A3, the pub is situated in popular walking country. No food is served on Sunday evening or Monday.
Q P

Tongham

Hogs Back Brewery Shop

Manor Farm, The Street, GU10 1DE (off A31)
10-6 (8.30 Wed-Fri); 9-6 Sat; 10-4.30 Sun
(01252) 784495 website: www.hogsback.co.uk
Beer range varies G
Off-licence attached to the award-winning brewery. The shop sells Hogs Back beers on draught to take away as well as more than 300 bottled beers from all over the world. Three ciders are also available, as well as a range of Gales and Lurgashall wines. The brewery can be viewed from a gallery in the shop. A discount on draught beers is available to card-carrying CAMRA members. P

Upper Hale

Ball & Wicket

104 Upper Hale Road, GU9 0PB
4 (12 Sat)-11; 12-10.30 Sun
(01252) 735278
B&T Dragonslayer; Hogs Back TEA; Itchen Valley Fagin's; Young's Bitter H
Roadside pub opposite the village green where cricket is played in the summer. The bar has exposed beams and comfortable seating. A strong following among locals ensures the pub is always buzzing with conversation. There is a TV for viewing major sporting events. A quiz is held every alternate Sunday night and a meat raffle on Friday. The pub enters a float in the local carnival every year. P

Walton on Thames

Regent

19 Church Street, KT12 2QP (on A3050)
10-11; 12-10.30 Sun
(01932) 243980
Greene King Abbot; Marston's Burton Bitter, Pedigree; Shepherd Neame Spitfire; guest beers H
A typical Wetherspoon's conversion of what was the Regent Cinema in the 1920s and more recently a furniture shop. Walton was an early centre for the film industry in the 1920s and 30s, and some photographs and memorabilia are displayed in the pub, which has a relaxing and convivial atmosphere. Up to four guest beers are served, usually one from the Itchen Valley Brewery.
Q

Weybridge

Jolly Farmer

41 Princes Road, KT13 9BN (off A317)
11-3, 5.30-11; 12-3, 7-10.30 Sun
(01932) 856873
Hop Back Best Bitter, Summer Lightning; guest beers H
Comfortable, friendly, back-street, mid-Victorian pub with a low, beamed ceiling. The L-shaped bar is surrounded by upholstered bench seats. There are large mirrors and photographs of old Weybridge decorating the walls. The large garden is popular in summer.
Q

Old Crown

83 Thames Street, KT13 8LP (off A317)
10-11; 12-10.30 Sun
(01932) 842844
Courage Best Bitter, Directors; Young's Bitter, seasonal beers H
Attractive, weatherboarded pub sited at the confluence of the rivers Thames and Wey. The interior is divided into three wood-panelled areas. The garden overlooks the river. An interesting range of food is served at this welcoming family-run pub (no eve meals Sun-Tue). The pub can be reached via the River Thames ferry from Shepperton when the service is operating.
Q P

Windlesham

Bee

School Road, GU20 6PD (on B386)
11-midnight; 12-10.30 Sun
(01276) 479244
Brakspear Bitter; Courage Best Bitter; Hop Back Summer Lightning; Young's Bitter; guest beer H
A village inn since the mid-1800s, this unspoilt rural pub continues to be popular with the local community. It offers four regular ales and one guest. Food is available from Tuesday to Saturday. It hosts live music, mainly

jazz or blues, on selected Saturday evenings. There is a children's play area in the garden and occasional barbecues are held in summer, weather permitting. ❀◑P⊟

Witley

White Hart

Petworth Road, GU8 5PH (on A283)
11-3.30, 5.30-11; 12-3.30, 7-10.30 Sun
(01428) 683695
Shepherd Neame Master Brew Bitter, Spitfire, seasonal beers Ⓗ
Family-run pub dating from Elizabethan times. The attractive building has a large garden with views of the surrounding coutryside. Inside there is the buzz of a congenial village pub. Dogs are welcome in the comfortable lounge with its large fireplace. There is also a cosy side bar with TV and another open fire. The dining room serves tasty home-made food (no eve meals on Sun). ❀◑P

Woking

Wetherspoon's

51-57 Chertsey Road, GU21 5AJ
10-11; 12-10.30 Sun
(01483) 722818
Courage Directors; Hogs Back TEA; Marston's Burton Bitter, Pedigree; Shepherd Neame Spitfire; guest beers Ⓗ
Wonderful, open-plan, town-centre pub unofficially referred to by locals as the 'waiting room' for the nearby train station. The guest beers change frequently, with up to four available at any one time. Westons Vintage cider is also served. The pub can be busy on Friday and Saturday evenings. Time literally flies here with a time machine clock on the ceiling and an invisible man peering down on drinkers.
Q◑

Wood Street

Royal Oak

89 Oak Hill, GU3 3DA
11-3 (3.30 Sat), 5-11; 12-3.30, 7-10.30 Sun
(01483) 235137
Courage Best Bitter; Hogs Back TEA; guest beers Ⓗ
Superb free house, local CAMRA Pub of the Year for two years running. The landlord, carefully supervised by his cat Oliver, runs a friendly, welcoming pub serving a range of six ales, always including a mild. The pump clips displayed behind the bar include beers brewed especially for the pub. A board displays forthcoming ale attractions. Thatchers cider is also sold. Hearty lunches are available from Monday to Saturday in three seating areas. A large back garden has swings and a windmill for children. Q❀◑♣P

Wrecclesham

Sandrock

Sandrock Hill, Upper Bourne, GU10 4NS
(off B3384) OS830444
12-11; 12-10.30 Sun
(01252) 715865
website: www.thesandrock.com
Batham Best Bitter; Cheriton Pots Ale; guest beers Ⓗ
The commitment to variety and quality of the beers served in this unpretentious local is a tribute to the cellarman and his passion for real ale. Vying for bar space among the regular eight ales are a selection of frequently-changing guests. The excellent food is an easy match for the best that British beer has to offer, both from the regular menu and occasional specials (for example a game evening with guest chef). Live music is sometimes hosted.
Q❀◑♣

The wonder of yeast

Yeast is a fungus, a single cell plant that can convert a sugary liquid into equal proportions of alcohol and carbon dioxide There are two basic types of yeast used in brewing, one for ale and one for lager. (The yeasts used to make the Belgian beers known as gueuze and lambic are wild yeasts in the atmosphere). It is often said that ale is produced by 'top fermentation' and lager by 'bottom fermentation'. While it is true that during ale fermentation a thick blanket of yeast head and protein is created on top of the liquid while only a thin slick appears on top of fermenting lager beer, the descriptions are seriously misleading. Yeast works at all levels of the sugar-rich liquid in order to turn malt sugars into alcohol. If yeast worked only at the top or bottom of the liquid, a substantial proportion of sugar would not be fermented. Ale is fermented at a high temperature, lager at a much lower one. The furious speed of ale fermentation creates the yeast head and with it the rich fruity aromas and flavours that are typical of the style.
It is more accurate to describe the ale method as 'warm fermentation' and the lager one as 'cold fermentation'.

Alfriston

Smugglers Inn

Waterloo Square, BN26 5UE

11-2.30 (3 Sat), 6.30-11; 12-3, 7-10.30 Sun

☎ (01323) 870241

Courage Directors; Harveys BB, seasonal beers Ⓗ

Dating from 1358, this village local was originally a dwelling. Sympathetically extended, its past connection with smuggling in the Cuckmere Valley is reflected in the name it has carried for over 70 years. The cosy bar area is decorated with hops and various country items. Tasty, fresh bar food is available at all sessions and is much appreciated by walkers on the South Downs Way. Q❀◐◑⚟

Battle

Chequers Inn

Lower Lake, TN33 0AT (at A2100/Marley Lane jct)

11-11; 12-10.30 Sun

☎ (01424) 772088

Fuller's London Pride; Harveys BB; guest beer Ⓗ

This busy, 15th-century inn is once more a haven for real ale drinkers and lovers of fine food. South of the High Street, it has a long, rectangular bar, exposed beams, open fires and a no-smoking dining room, which features a large inglenook. The garden at the rear overlooks the site of the Battle of Hastings. Very much part of the community, summer concerts are often performed by local musicians on the terrace. Professionally prepared food includes an extensive bar menu. ⌂❀◐◑⇌♣P

Beckley

Rose & Crown

Northiam Road, TN31 6SE (at B2188/B2165 jct)

11-3, 5.30-11; 11-11 Fri & Sat; 12-10.30 Sun

☎ (01797) 252161

Fuller's ESB; Harveys BB; Taylor Landlord; guest beers Ⓗ

First-class free house serving a great range of beers, many are sourced from distant breweries. This spacious family pub maintains separate areas for drinkers and diners. The long bar is noted for its wood floor and decorative hops. Locals and visitors alike are made most welcome in this country pub that offers an excellent menu. The fine views from the garden are an added bonus. ⌂Q❀◐◑♣P

Bells Yew Green

Brecknock Arms ✔

TN3 9BJ

12-3, 5.30-11; 12-3, 7-10.30 (not winter eve) Sun

☎ (01892) 750237

Harveys Pale Ale, BB Ⓗ

Popular village ale house with a cosy, rural feel, dating from the 1850s, whose landlord specialises in lower strength ales. Most drinkers frequent the snug, wood-panelled public bar. The saloon bar is no-smoking, where diners are able to enjoy excellent home-cooked food, including traditional English dishes as well as more exotic choices. The pub takes its name from the Earl of Camden and Brecknock who owned a large local estate. ⌂❀◐◑⇌P⚟

Berwick

Cricketers ✔

BN26 6SP (S of A27, W of Drusilla's roundabout)

11-11; 12-10 Sun

☎ (01323) 870469 website: www.cricketersberwick.co.uk

Harveys BB, Armada, seasonal beers Ⓖ

Cricket bats and prints decorate the walls of this friendly pub, close to the South Downs Way. Formerly two cottages, it became an ale house in the 18th century. Real ales are served from barrels stored in the scullery behind the small bar. In a peaceful location, with cottage gardens front and rear, it provides a popular lunch stop for locals and tourists. Two open fires create a warm welcome in winter. ⌂Q❀◐◑♿♣P⚟

Blackham

Sussex Oak

TN3 9UA (on A264 between East Grinstead and Tunbridge Wells)

✪ 11-3, 6-11; 12-3, 6.30-10.30 Sun
☎ (01892) 740273
Shepherd Neame Master Brew Bitter, Best Bitter, Spitfire Ⓗ
Excellent country pub, the Sussex Oak was a deserving winner of the local CAMRA Pub of the Year award in 2003. It is run by a friendly couple who offer a good range of meals, often with an Asian or Irish accent to reflect their origins. Occasional food themed nights are held – however, the pub is worth seeking out at any time for a quiet pint in convivial surroundings.
Q (Ashurst) P

Bodiam

Castle

TN32 5UB (opp. castle entrance)
✪ 11-3, 6-11; (11-11 summer Sat); 12-10.30 Sun
☎ (01580) 830330
Shepherd Neame Master Brew Bitter, Spitfire, seasonal beers Ⓗ
Rural Shepherd Neame pub in the scenic Rother Valley on the Kent border. Bodiam Castle, the impressive NT property, is opposite; it is well worth visiting both castles. An extensive menu, featuring local produce, is displayed in the main bar above the imposing fireplace. This pleasant, quiet pub is ideal for a peaceful pint.
Q (Kent & E Sussex Rlwy) P

Boreham Street

Bull's Head ✔

BN27 4SG (on A271)
✪ 12-3, 6-11 (11-11 summer); 12-10.30 Sun
☎ (01323) 831981
Harveys BB, seasonal beers Ⓗ
After an internal renovation completed in early 2002, this village local has a bar divided into two parts, both with open fireplaces. The decor is predominantly wood, with hops around the bar and windows. Food is served during all sessions except Sunday evening, with an augmented Saturday menu and the regular menu replaced by fish and chips on Thursday evenings. Darts and shove-ha'penny can be played; quiz night is Monday. Q P

Brighton

Basketmakers Arms ✔

12 Gloucester Road, BN1 4AD
✪ 11-11; 12-10.30 Sun
☎ (01273) 689006
Gale's Butser, Best Bitter, HSB, Festival Mild, seasonal beers; guest beers Ⓗ
A rare local in the North Laines area of Brighton, worth a visit when in the area. A Gale's tied house, it stocks a great range of whiskies. Read all the signs as some contain secret messages. The pub is convenient for the Theatre Royal and is popular for its food. Q

Evening Star

55-56 Surrey Street, BN1 3PB (400 yds S of station)
✪ 12 (11.30 Sat)-11; 12-10.30 Sun
☎ (01273) 328931 website: www.eveningstarbrighton.co.uk
Dark Star Hophead, seasonal beers; guest beers Ⓗ
Former home of the Dark Star Brewery, the Evening Star boasts a changing selection of Dark Star beers, plus guests from micro-breweries. A good array of Belgian and German beers, in bottles and on draught, add to the attraction of this friendly pub, as do the two real ciders and annual beer festivals (spring and December). Live music is performed most Sundays. This former local CAMRA Pub of the Year is a magnet for real ale drinkers of all ages.

Lord Nelson Inn ✔

36 Trafalgar Street, BN1 4ED
(under bridge outside station)
✪ 11.30 (11 Sat)-11; 12-10.30 Sun
☎ (01273) 695872 website: www.thelordnelsoninn.co.uk
Harveys XX Mild, Pale Ale, BB, Armada, seasonal beers Ⓗ
Set in the bohemian North Laines area, this welcoming tied house serves the full range of Harvey's regular and seasonal beers. The Nelson has two small bars: one with a pull-down screen for sporting events; the other leads on to a back room, then to a conservatory drinking area that doubles as an art gallery/function room, displaying works by local artists. Well worth a visit for the ambience alone, it is a regular on local CAMRA's ale trail.
Q

Prestonville Arms ✔

64 Hamilton Road, BN1 5DN
✪ 5 (12 Fri & Sat)-11; 12-10.30 Sun
☎ (01273) 701007
Gale's Butser, Best Bitter, HSB, seasonal beers Ⓗ
Street-corner local on a triangular site in a residential area – its bar is on two levels, reflecting its hilly location. A sister pub to the Basketmakers, it features old adverts on the walls and has plenty of seating, which extends into the garden. It hosts a music quiz on Tuesday and one for general knowledge on Sunday. At least four Gale's beers are usually on offer, together with a good choice of well-presented, home-cooked food (no meals Sun).

Sir Charles Napier ✔

50 Southover Street, BN2 9UE
✪ 4 (12 Fri & Sat)-11; 12-10.30 Sun
☎ (01273) 601413
Gale's Butser, Best Bitter, HSB, seasonal beers; guest beers Ⓗ
Superb street-corner local in the Hanover area of the city, replete with old photos of the local area, maps, bottles and golfing memorabilia. A well-attended quiz is held on Sundays, and various theme nights are staged, such as St George's, St Patrick's, Chinese New Year and Beaujolais Nouveau night. Bar snacks are served all day at weekends and good value Sunday lunches are popular. In summer there may be a barbecue in the small garden.

INDEPENDENT BREWERIES

1648 East Hoathly
Filo Hastings
Harveys Lewes
Kemptown Brighton
Rectory Streat
Rother Valley Northiam
White Bexhill

Waggon & Horses

109 Church Street, BN1 2PS (near library)

⏲ 11-11; 12-10.30 Sun

☎ (01273) 602752

Adnams Broadside; Fuller's London Pride; Harveys BB Ⓗ

Single bar, town-centre pub close to the Theatre Royal. Built around 1846 as a gymnasium, it became a pub in 1848. It features wooden floors, wood-panelled walls and a variety of seating, including pavement tables in summer. It can get busy and smoky on weekend evenings; there is a fruit machine and usually music playing. Do not believe the three clocks on the wall as none of them seems to show the right time. ❀◐⇌

Coleman's Hatch

Hatch Inn

TN7 4EJ (400 yds S of B2110) OS452335

⏲ 11.30-2.30, 5.30-11 (11-11 summer Sat); 12-10.30 Sun

☎ (01342) 822363 website: www.hatchinn.co.uk

Harveys BB; Larkins Traditional; guest beers Ⓗ

Originally three cottages dating from the 15th century, it has been a pub for the past 200 years. Inside the attractive, weatherboarded exterior is a cosy bar with scrubbed tables and low beams. A real fire keeps customers warm in winter, but outdoor drinkers and diners are also well catered for. Handy for the Ashdown Forest and Winnie the Pooh country, the Hatch is much appreciated by walkers, but is popular at all times. Local breweries are well supported. No food Sunday evening.

♨Q❀◐◑P⊁

Cowbeech

Merrie Harriers Inn

BN27 4JQ (off A271, NE of Hailsham) OS147619

⏲ 11.30-3 (4 Sat), 6-11; 12-4, 6-10.30 Sun

☎ (01323) 833108 website: www.merrieharriers.co.uk

Harveys BB; guest beers Ⓗ

Delightful white clapboarded village inn at the heart of the Sussex Weald. This Grade II listed building, circa 1624, offers a quintessential English experience. The comfortable beamed and panelled public bar has wooden floors and a large inglenook. The lounge bar is set for dining and has an open fire; there is also a no-smoking restaurant. Excellent food is freshly prepared on the premises and is sourced locally where possible. Well-kept gardens offer country views.

♨❀◐◑♿P

Crowborough

Cooper's Arms

Coopers Lane, TN6 1SN (follow St. John's Rd from Crowborough Cross for ½ mile)

⏲ 12-2.30 (not Mon or Tue; 3 Sat), 6-11; 12-3, 6-10.30 Sun

☎ (01892) 654796

Greene King IPA; guest beers Ⓗ

This excellent, friendly drinking establishment offers a varied selection of guest ales, including milds throughout May. Occasional themed beer festivals, often with live music, are held. A good bottled beer menu (mainly continental) is available as is Budweiser Budvar on tap. There is one long, L-shaped bar and a games room with pool, shuffleboard and darts. Views across Ashdown Forest and the Weald can be enjoyed from the garden. Q❀♿▲♣P

Wheatsheaf ✔

Mount Pleasant, Jarvis Brook, TN6 2NF

⏲ 12-3, 5-11; 12-1 Fri & Sat; 12-10.30 Sun

☎ (01892) 663756

Harveys XX Mild, Pale Ale, BB, seasonal beers Ⓗ

Charming, unspoilt, early Victorian beer house that probably dates from the 18th century, although the building may have moved up the hill when the railway arrived in 1868. Three distinct drinking areas are served by one delightful square bar. The front room is no-smoking at lunchtime and features an unusual copper fireplace, originally designed for an upmarket yacht. Seasonal celebrations are held with live music, including a beer festival in late May. ♨❀◐⇌♣P

Crowhurst

Plough Inn

TN33 9AW (near recreation ground)

⏲ 11.30-3, 6-11; 11-11 Sat; 12-10.30 Sun

☎ (01424) 830310

Harveys XX Mild, BB, Armada, seasonal beers Ⓗ

Well-deserved new entry to this Guide. When the Plough came on the market in 2004 it was bought by a local who has always lived in the village. Although a free house, the owner has opted to sell four Harveys' ales. A warm welcome awaits all here, including pets. There is a small restaurant and a no-smoking area. The pub supports local sports teams; toad in the hole and boules are played. Live music is staged occasionally. ♨❀◐◑♣P⊁

Danehill

Coach & Horses

School Lane, RH17 7JF

(1 mile E of village crossroads from A275)

⏲ 12-3, 6-11; 12-4, 7-10.30 Sun

☎ (01825) 740369

Harveys BB; guest beers Ⓗ

This rural, two-bar free house boasts a large, award-winning restaurant and is popular with diners as well as drinkers. An extensive front garden houses a children's play area, while the new rear patio is strictly for adults only. The bar offers a changing range of guest beers. Well-behaved dogs are welcome. The No. 270 bus stops outside. No meals are served Sunday evening. ♨Q❀◐◑⊟▲P

Ditchling

White Horse ✔

16 West Street, BN6 8TS

⏲ 11-11; 12-10.30 Sun

☎ (01273) 842006

Harvey's BB; guest beers Ⓗ

Dating from the 16th century, this fine village pub is situated opposite the church, with Anne of Cleves' house, the village pond and museum all close by. A Guide regular, the White Horse consists of a spacious bar leading to an open games area and patio garden. The pub is dog friendly, and children are allowed in the games room. The changing guest beers are complemented by bottled Leffe Blond. Home-made food is served in the bar or restaurant. ❀◐≠♣

Eastbourne

Buccaneer

10 Compton Street, BN21 4BW (between Devonshire Park Theatre and Winter Gardens)

⏲ 11-11; 12-10.30 Sun

☎ (01323) 732829

Draught Bass; Greene King Abbot; Tetley Bitter; guest beers Ⓗ

Situated in the town's theatreland, the single bar of this pub has a spacious feel. It attracts a mix of ages and offers a bar billiards table and inexpensive food (no meals Sun eve). There is a no-smoking raised seating area at the rear of the bar, which overlooks the Devonshire Park tennis courts. Up to three guest ales are served, which helped it win local CAMRA's Pub of the Year award in 2002. ◐◑≠⊬

Hurst Arms ✔

76 Willingdon Road, BN21 1TW (on A2270, 1½ miles N of centre)

⏲ 11-11; 12-10.30 Sun

☎ (01323) 721762

Harveys BB, Armada, seasonal beers Ⓗ

This small, friendly, Victorian corner pub possesses the atmosphere of a neighbourhood local. The wide-screen TV in the public bar fills the place up on weekends and match days; pool, darts and bar billiards can be played and there is a juke box. The quieter, homely saloon bar offers ample seating. A small rear garden and front patio by the road provide extra drinking areas in summer. ❀⊟♿♣

Terminus ✔

153 Terminus Road, BN21 3NU (½ mile from station towards seafront)

⏲ 10-11; 12-10.30 Sun

☎ (01323) 733964

Harveys XX Mild, Pale Ale, BB, Armada, seasonal beers Ⓗ

Located in the town centre with the railway station and seafront a few minutes' walk away, this friendly, traditional pub attracts a varied clientele. The landlord prides himself on offering the complete range of Harveys' beers. Good value food is available all day until early evening. A large bar, with ample seating, forms the main drinking area, while a veranda with tables and chairs in the pedestrian precinct is a pleasant spot on a sunny day.
❀◐◑♿≠

East Hoathly

Foresters Arms ✔

6 South Street, BN8 6DS (off A22)

⏲ 11.30-3 (not Mon), 5-11; 11.30-11 Sat; 12-10.30 Sun

☎ (01825) 840208

Harves Pale Ale, BB, seasonal beers Ⓗ

Dating from 1780, this village local is sympathetically furnished throughout. A central bar sits between a quiet drinking area and a public bar decorated with a musical theme, where live music is performed on Thursday evening. A range of freshly prepared food, including some seafood specialities, is available at all sessions; try the fish from Hastings fishmarket, coated in beer batter.
♨Q❀◐◑⊟⛺♣P

King's Head

1-3 High Street, BN8 6DR (½ mile off A22)

⏲ 11-11; 12-4, 7-10.30 Sun

☎ (01825) 840238 website: www.1648brewing.co.uk

1648 Original; seasonal beers; guest beers Ⓗ

Situated in the village centre and once the stables that served the London stagecoach, the King's Head is now home to the 1648 Brewery. At least one guest beer is stocked, often Harveys Best. The comfortably furnished bar is decorated with Sussex hops. A wide-ranging menu of fresh food, cooked to order, is available lunchtime and evening. It was voted local Pub of the Year for 2003 by local CAMRA members.
♨Q❀◐◑P⊬

Glynde

Trevor Arms ✔

The Street, BN8 6SS (½ mile N of A27, near station)

⏲ 11-11; 12-10.30 Sun

☎ (01273) 858208

Harveys Pale Ale, BB, seasonal beers Ⓗ

Conveniently located close to Glynde railway station, this multi-roomed village pub lies in a great walking area. The Trevor has an excellent menu for both adults and children. The world-famous Glyndebourne Opera House is within comfortable walking distance, and it is not unknown for members of the orchestra to play on a summer Sunday in the pub's extensive garden. Q♝❀◐◑⊟≠♣P⊬

Hailsham

Grenadier ✔

67 High Street, BN27 1AS

⏲ 11-11; 12-10.30 Sun

☎ (01323) 842152 website: www.thegrenny.com

Harveys XX Mild, BB, Armada, seasonal beers Ⓗ

Ex-Grenadier Guards' drinking house, built in 1803, which it has retained to this day much of its Georgian splendour. The pub is welcoming to all, including children. The public bar can be lively at times with drinkers playing toad in the hole, shove-ha'penny, skittles and darts, but the saloon is much quieter. The Mild and Ale Club raises funds for Guide Dogs for the Blind by holding many unusual events throughout the year. ❀◐⊟♣P

Hastings

First In Last Out

14 High Street, Old Town, TN34 3ET (near Stables Theatre)

⏲ 11-11; 12-10.30 Sun

☎ (01424) 425079

website: www.thefilo.co.uk

Filo Crofters, Cardinal (winter)**, Ginger Tom, Gold** (summer)**; guest beers** Ⓗ

This brew-pub has been dispensing beer since at least 1896 and parts of the building date back to the 1500s. It is situated in the scenic Old Town where TV's Foyle's War was filmed. Customers have the choice of sitting at the bar or occupying one of the unusual booths. An amazing fireplace roars into life in the winter making the pub cosy.

A covered courtyard garden at the back is enjoyed all year round and hosts bank holiday beer festivals.
♨Q❀◖⛺♣

Hove

Hangleton Manor Hotel

Hangleton Valley Drive, BN3 8AN

🕘 11-3, 6-11; 12-3, 7-10.30 Sun

☎ (01273) 413266

Harveys BB; Tetley Burton Ale; guest beers Ⓗ

Beautiful, listed stone building, which was the original manor house, circa 1540, and is set in spacious grounds, featuring a restored 17th-century dovecote. The entrance is via a Tudor stone archway into the original flagstoned hallway, with the magnificently panelled Tudor Bar (also used as a function room) and Garden Bar on the left and the main bar on the right. This genuine free house has been in the same ownership for over 20 years. 🛏❀◖⊟♿P

Sussex Cricketer

Eaton Road, BN3 3AF (next to Sussex cricket ground)

🕘 12-11; 12-10.30 Sun

☎ (01273) 771645

Draught Bass; Harveys BB; Young's Bitter; guest beers Ⓗ

Single bar, refurbished four years ago to a good standard, with comfortable sofas and modern art prints. At least three real ales are normally stocked and food is served from noon until 8pm. The garden is actually inside the Sussex County Cricket Club ground. As part of the Ember Inns group, the pub usually holds a six-week beer festival in the autumn. ♨❀◖◗♿⇌⊬

Icklesham

Queen's Head

Parsonage Lane, TN36 4BL (off A259, opp. village hall)

🕘 11-11; 12-10.30 Sun

☎ (01424) 814552 website: www.queenshead.com

Beer range varies Ⓗ

Splendid example of a traditional country pub, complete with beams, horse brasses, farm implements, a collection of unusual beer bottles and antique bikes hanging over the bar. Three log fires blaze in winter. With five ales on tap, 124 different brews were sold in 2004; the cider is from Biddenden. The garden has a children's play area. Home-cooked food is served all day on Saturday and Sunday (small portions available). Live music is performed every Tuesday at local CAMRA's Pub of the Year 2005.
♨❀◖◗♣🍎P⊬⍗

Isfield

Laughing Fish

Station Road, TN22 5XB (W of A26, 2 miles S of Uckfield)

🕘 11.30-3, 4.30-11; 11.30-11 Fri; 12-11 Sat & summer; 12-10.30 Sun

☎ (01825) 750349 website: www.laughingfishonline.co.uk

Greene King IPA, Morland Original, Old Speckled Hen, seasonal beers; guest beers Ⓗ

Victorian pub in a small village between Lewes and Uckfield, situated next to the Lavender Line heritage railway. The garden has a patio and pergola. One bar is no-smoking for the comfort of diners, where good home-made food is served. Guest beers tend to feature from Thursday onwards. Toad in the hole is played here. ♨Q❀◖◗⛺♣P⊬

Jevington

Eight Bells

High Street, BN26 5QB (on Polegate-Friston road)

OS563017

🕘 11-11; 12-10.30 Sun

☎ (01323) 484442

Adnams Broadside; Flowers Original; Harveys BB, Old Ⓗ

Frequented by ramblers, this deservedly popular village free house lies at the heart of the South Downs. The traditional and inviting interior boasts an impressive fireplace; note the antique cash register (sadly not in use) on the bar. The pleasant restaurant/children's room displays interesting photographs. Good, home-cooked food is served (all day Sun). The large garden, with secluded areas, plays host to the local cricket and stoolball teams. 🛏❀◖◗P

Lewes

Brewers Arms

91 High Street, BN7 1XN

🕘 10-11; 12-10.30 Sun

☎ (01273) 479475

Harveys BB; guest beers Ⓗ

This celebrated pub situated in the historic High Street has two contrasting bars. The larger public bar has a pool table and a large-screen TV, while the more sedate and plush front bar features old photographs and an architect's drawing of the pub from days gone by. Outside the pub, spot the Page and Overton ceramic plaques, revealing one of its former owners. Biddenden cider is served on handpump; the guest beers come from small independent breweries.
Q◖◗⊟⇌🍎

Elephant & Castle

White Hill, BN7 2DJ (behind the castle)

🕘 11.30-11; 12-10.30 Sun

☎ (01273) 473797

Brakspear Bitter; Fuller's London Pride; Greene King Old Speckled Hen; Harveys BB Ⓗ

Built in 1838 for the former Southdowns and East Grinstead Brewery as a hotel on the new approach road into Lewes, the Elephant & Castle is now a spacious pub with plain wood floors, long tables and benches. It has been the HQ of the Commercial Square Bonfire Society since the early 1850s. The home-made organic beef 'Eliburgers' are a house speciality in this child- and dog-friendly establishment. ♨Q◖♣

Gardener's Arms

46 Cliffe High Street, BN7 2AN

🕘 11-11; 12-10.30 Sun

☎ (01273) 474808

Harveys BB; guest beers Ⓗ

A deservedly popular free house stocking up to four beers and a cider on handpump. It is situated almost opposite Harveys Brewery, near the River Ouse, which has caused flooding problems in the past – see the photographs on the panelled walls. Visitors are made welcome and soon find themselves feeling at home and involved in conversation. ♣🍎

Lewes Arms ✓
1 Mount Place, BN7 1YH
11-11; 12-10.30 Sun
☎ (01273) 473152
Greene King IPA, Abbot; Harveys BB, seasonal beers Ⓗ
This historic, curved-fronted pub is built into the castle ramparts. Features include a tiny front bar and a rear patio accessible via the stairs. The function room houses a miniscule stage and is home to a folk club and drama groups. The pub holds many charity fundraising events, including the world pea throwing championships. Well-behaved children are welcome until 8pm in the games room where toad in the hole and darts are played. Be advised: do not use your mobile phone here.
⌂Q❀◑⊟≠♣

Milton Street

Sussex Ox
BN26 5RL (signed off A27) OS534041
11-3, 6-11; 12-3, 6-10.30 (12-5 winter) Sun
☎ (01323) 870840
Dark Star Hophead; Harveys BB; Hop Back Summer Lightning; guest beers Ⓗ
Superb free house in the small hamlet of Milton Street. It affords great views of the Cuckmere Valley and South Downs and is handy for the South Downs Way. Its traditional wooden interior boasts a fine array of sepia-tinted photographs in the bar. The Sussex Ox is well worth seeking out.
Q❀◑▶P⊬

Newhaven

Jolly Boatman
133-135 Lewes Road, BN9 9SJ
11-11; 12-10.30 Sun
☎ (01273) 510030
Harveys BB; King Horsham Best Bitter, seasonal beers; guest beer Ⓗ
This street-corner pub is popular among the locals and draws a good, regular clientele. An ex-Harveys pub, now a free house, it fields football and darts teams; pool and cribbage are also played here. The current real ales are displayed on a blackboard, showing ABV and price. A good basic pub, albeit slightly scruffy in appearance.
≠(Town) ♣

Plumpton

Half Moon
Ditchling Road, BN7 3AF
(on B2116, between Ditchling and Cooksbridge)
12-3, 6-11 (12-11 summer Sat); 12-3, 6-10.30 (12-10.30 summer) Sun
☎ (01273) 890253
Harveys BB, seasonal beers; Welton Old Cocky Ⓗ
Just off the South Downs Way, the pub is ideal for ramblers, with a large garden for families and a play area. Children are also allowed in the bar, under parental supervision. A typical country pub, it welcomes well-behaved dogs. The Half Moon is convenient for Plumpton College and the station (half a mile).
⌂❀◑▶♿▲♣P⊬

Plumpton Green

Plough ✓
BN7 3DF (1½ miles from station and racecourse)
11.30-11; 12-10.30 Sun
☎ (01273) 890311
Harveys BB, seasonal beers Ⓗ
Family-oriented village pub near the former airfield, where a monument is dedicated to Polish airmen and an airshow is staged in August. The Plough has a large garden where children are welcome under adult supervision, dogs too. Camping is permitted in the field next

What is Real Ale?

Real ale – or cask-conditioned beer – is a natural product that is neither filtered nor pasteurised in the brewery. At the end of the brewing process, when malt sugars have been turned into alcohol by fermentation, the beer is run or 'racked' into casks. Additional hops may be added for aroma and, either in the brewery or the pub, finings are added to clear the beer In the pub cellar.
Cask beer enjoys a secondary fermentation, with yeast turning remaining malt sugars into alcohol and natural carbon dioxide. The casks are vented with wooden pegs or spiles to allow excess gas to escape. Venting is carefully controlled to ensure that sufficient gas remains in the beer to give it sparkle or 'condition'. When fermentation is complete and the beer is clear or 'dropped bright', plastic tubes known as lines are attached to taps in each cask and the beer is then drawn by the action of beer engines to the bar and in to the drinkers' glasses.

to the pub. Bar billiards is played here. No meals are served Sunday evenings.
♨Q❀◑▣⛺♣P⊬

Portslade

Stanley Arms

47 Wolseley Road, BN41 1SS
⊙ 2 (12 Sat)-11; 12-10.30 Sun
☎ (01273) 430234 website: www.thestanley.com
Beer range varies Ⓗ
Intimate, friendly back-street local, showcasing real ales from three small and micro-breweries, as well as a choice of 10 bottled Belgian beers and Biddenden cider. It hosts popular beer festivals in February and September. A large-screen plasma TV shows major sporting events, and live music is performed in the main bar twice a month. At the rear is a small garden, where barbecues are offered in summer. It is a frequent winner of the local CAMRA Pub of the Year award. ♨Q❀▣⇌(Fishersgate)♣●▯

Rottingdean

Black Horse ✔

65 High Street, BN2 7HE (off A259)
⊙ 10.30-11; 12-10.30 Sun
☎ (01273) 302581 website: www.theblackhorse.co.uk
Greene King IPA, Morland Original, Abbot, seasonal beers Ⓗ
Rottingdean is an attractive coastal village, three miles east of Brighton, and the Black Horse is the oldest pub of five. There are three bars: a compact snug joins the public to the saloon which has been extended at the rear. This is the place for the popular Tuesday night quiz when tables may be reserved. Food of good quality and value is served weekdays.
◑▣♣

St Leonards

Bull

530 Bexhill Road, TN38 8AY (on A259, E of Glynde Gap shops)
⊙ 12-11; 12-10.30 Sun
☎ (01424) 424984 website: www.the-bull-inn.com
Shepherd Neame Master Brew Bitter, Best Bitter, Spitfire, seasonal beers Ⓗ
Welcoming roadside pub, noted for its range of Shepherd Neame beers. This local also offers an excellent menu (book at weekends; no food Sun evening). There is a dining room and a large car park at the rear, which offers much more space than appears at first. At the western end of St Leonards, it is convenient for the Glynde Gap shops. ♨Q◑♿♣P

Dripping Spring

34 Tower Road, TN37 6JE (off A2100)
⊙ 11-11; 12-10.30 Sun
☎ (01424) 434055
Goacher's Light; Wells Bombardier; Young's Bitter; guest beers Ⓗ
In autumn 2004, this CAMRA award-winning local changed ownership and landlord. The good news is, however, that the beer range and quality remain excellent, with seven beers catering for all tastes and strengths. Beer festivals are planned for May and September, and a dark beer festival each autumn. Locals and visitors can be reassured that this treasured pub, tucked away in the bohemian part of St Leonards, remains a must for real ale fans.
❀⇌(Warrior Sq)♣●▯

Horse & Groom

4 Mercatoria, TN38 0EB
⊙ 11-11; 12-10.30 Sun
☎ (01424) 420612 website: www.sussex200.com
Adnams Broadside; Greene King IPA; Harveys BB; guest beers Ⓗ
The town of St Leonards was created in the 1820s and this, its first pub, was built in 1829 mainly for the benefit of the builders. A first-class free house, it is welcoming and comfortable with olde-worlde charm and manners. The horseshoe-shaped bar serves two separate bars and there is a futher, quieter room to the rear. Outdoor seating is provided on a small patio. Good lunchtime food is served Monday-Saturday.
♨❀◐⇌(Warrior Sq)

Seaford

Wellington ✔

33 Steyne Road, BN25 1HT
⊙ 11-11; 12-10.30 Sun
☎ (01323) 890032
Greene King IPA, Abbot, Old Speckled Hen; Harveys BB; guest beers Ⓗ
This is a large, Victorian Greene King house, situated on the southern edge of the town centre and about 200 yards from the seafront. It tends to be busy at weekends. There is a spacious main bar, a small bar with TV for sport with its own street entrance, a games room with pool table, and a further no-smoking room with dining tables and sofas. It offers a good selection of real ales. ◑⇌

Southwick

Romans

Manor Hall Road, BN42 4NG (400 yds from A27)
⊙ 12 (11 Sat)-11; 12-10.30 Sun
☎ (01273) 592147
Beer range varies Ⓗ
Red-brick, 1930s public house, comprising two large bars: one has traditional pub games, while the other is a quieter, more spacious area with plenty of comfortable seating. A small, no-smoking restaurant is to one side. The large garden houses an aviary with a variety of small birds. An annual beer festival is held in the spring.
♨❀◑▣♿⇌(Fishersgate)♣P▯

Udimore

King's Head

Rye Road, TN31 6BG (on B2089, W of village)
⊙ 11-4 (not winter Mon), 5.30-11; 12-4, 7-10.30 (not winter eve) Sun
☎ (01424) 882349
Harveys BB; guest beers Ⓗ
Built in 1535, and extended in the 17th century, this traditional village ale house boasts exposed beams, two open fires and a very long bar, which was installed in the 1930s and has to be seen (and leant on) to be believed. The pub serves excellent, home-cooked food and has a

no-smoking dining room. Lunches are served Tuesday-Sunday, evening meals Monday-Saturday. Situated in an area of outstanding natural beauty, there are many scenic walks nearby. ⌂Q⚲❀◑◗♿♣P

Westfield

Old Courthouse

Main Road, TN35 4QE

✪ 12-11; 12-10.30 Sun

☎ (01424) 751603

Harveys BB; guest beers Ⓗ

The Courthouse, formerly known as the New Inn, is a welcome addition to this year's Guide. With two bars, this large pub is central to the village and very community focused. Mind your head on the low ceiling. Note the unusual ten pin billiards played in the public bar.

⌂Q❀◑⊟♣P

Whatlington

Royal Oak

TN33 0NJ (on A21, between Robertsbridge and Sedlescombe)

✪ 11-11; 12-10.30 Sun

☎ (01424) 870492 website: www.whatlington.com

Harveys BB; guest beers Ⓗ

Pleasant, weatherboarded inn, five miles from Hastings. The split-level interior has beams aplenty and low ceilings. The restaurant area is no-smoking. A deep indoor well is an unusual feature and a splendid large inglenook holds a roaring fire in winter. It stages occasional music sessions, including a wassail in January that involves toasting the good health of the apple tree, when much fun is had by all. An extensive menu is served.

⌂Q❀◑◗P⊬

Wilmington

Giant's Rest

BN26 5SQ (off A27)

✪ 11.30-3, 6-11; 11.30-11 Sat; 12-10.30 Sun

☎ (01323) 870207 website: www.giantsrest.co.uk

Harveys BB, seasonal beers; Hop Back Summer Lightning (summer); **Taylor Landlord** Ⓗ

Taking its name from the ancient downland chalk figure that overlooks the village, this pub specialises in fresh food, with a varied three course menu, but is also recommended for its real ale. Beryl Cook prints adorn the walls, otherwise wood predominates in the decor. The wood floors, bar, tables and chairs are complemented by wooden table puzzles and games.

⌂❀◑◗ÅP⊬

Withyham

Dorset Arms ✔

TN7 4BD (on B2110, between Hartfield and Groombridge)

✪ 11-3, 6-11; 12-3, 7-10.30 Sun

☎ (01892) 770278 website: www.dorset-arms.co.uk

Harveys Pale Ale, BB, seasonal beers Ⓗ

Popular with walkers and visitors to nearby Ashdown Forest, this attractive village pub is set back from the road behind a small green with picnic tables. The pub dates back to the 15th century: a cosy bar with oak floors and a large fireplace is complemented by a small, no-smoking saloon bar that leads to the restaurant. Roast lunches only are available on Sunday; evening meals are served Tuesday-Saturday (booking is advised at weekends, especially in summer).

⌂Q❀◑◗⊟♣P⊬

New Inn, Hadlow Down

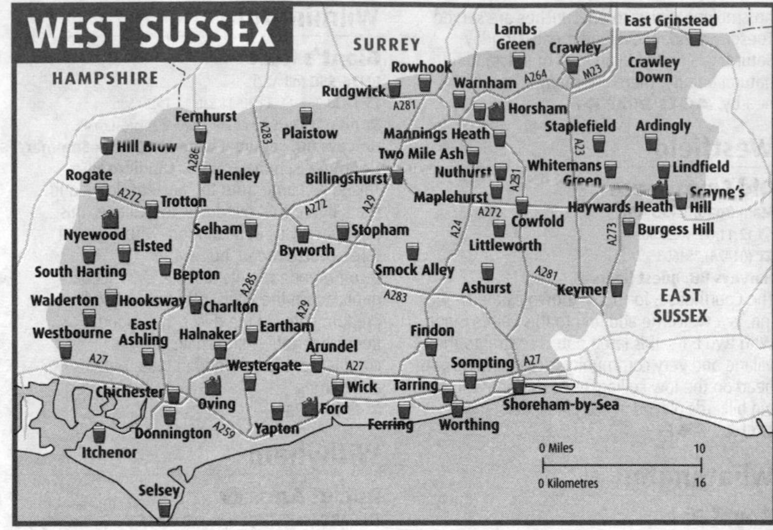

Ardingly

Oak Inn

Street Lane, RH17 6UA

12-3, 5-11 winter; 11-11 Fri, Sat & summer; 12-10.30 Sun

☎ (01444) 892244 website: www.theoakardingly.co.uk

Harveys BB; King Red River; guest beer Ⓗ

Formed out of three labourers' cottages dating from the 16th century, the pub's characterful interior features an inglenook and many low beams. It is said that the ghost of a grey lady sometimes joins customers at the bar. The restaurant serves a wide range of food (not Sun eve). Walkers are welcome here. It is handy for Ardingly Showground and there are bus links to Crawley and Haywards Heath.

Q❀◐◑⊟P

Arundel

King's Arms

36 Tarrant Street, BN18 9DN

11-3, 5.30-11; 11-11 Sat; 12-10.30 Sun

☎ (01903) 882312

Fuller's London Pride; Hop Back Summer Lightning; Young's Special; guest beer Ⓗ

Warm, welcoming pub, popular with locals and visitors alike. A true free house, it has been a pub for about 500 years. Although bar food is available at lunchtime, this pub's priority is the beer. Built on a split level, the top bar is the lounge, where the handpumps can be found; the public bar has a juke box for 1970s rock fans. Fines are imposed for mobile phone use. The pub is dog-friendly; look out for Sultan.

❀◐⊟⛺≠♣

Swan Hotel

27 High Street, BN18 9AG (opp. riverside bus stop)

11-11; 12-10.30 Sun

☎ (01903) 882314

Gale's Best Bitter, HSB Ⓗ

A dominant old white building which is difficult to miss, thus making it an ideal meeting place. The single bar is smart, with bare floorboards. Currently leased to Gale's Brewery, the selection of ales is limited; HSB is regular, and arguably the best in the area. Food is served all day, with a choice of good quality bar snacks or the separate restaurant; vegetarians are catered for.

⊭◐◑≠

White Hart ✔

3 Queen Street, BN18 9JG

12-3, 5-11; 12-11 Sat; 12-10.30 Sun

☎ (01903) 882374

Harveys Pale Ale, BB, seasonal beers Ⓗ

Built around 1790, this quiet Harveys' pub has a homely bar, separated by an open fireplace from the restaurant area. The relaxing ambience is enhanced by oak beams, horse brasses and assorted bric-a-brac, which lend a 'village' feel to this pub that lies east of the River Arun. Children are not permitted in the bar area after 9pm. ♨❀≠

Ashurst

Fountain

Horsham Road, BN44 3AP (on B2135, between Steyning and Partridge Green)

11.30-2.30, 6-11; 12-3.30, 7-10.30 Sun

☎ (01403) 710219

Black Sheep Best Bitter; Brakspear Bitter; Fuller's London Pride; Harveys BB; guest beer Ⓗ

Fine example of a 16th-century pub and restaurant, complete with oak beams, flagstone floors and selected ales on stillage behind the bar. Multiple rooms help to preserve the cosy front bar as a drinking area, with its homely inglenook fire. The back bar accommodates both drinkers and diners, while the recommended restaurant is a discrete entity in the pub. This helps to ensure a restaurant ambience for diners, and the atmosphere of a village local for imbibers. ♨Q⛟❀◐◑♿P

Bepton

Country Inn

Severals Road, GU29 0LR

(1 mile SW of Midhurst) OS870206

11.30-3, 5-11; 11.30-11 Fri & Sat; 12-10.30 Sun

☎ (01730) 813466

Ballard's Midhurst Mild; Taylor Landlord; Young's Bitter; guest beers ⊞
Popular local, serving ever-changing guest beers from independent brewers, an easy one-mile walk down the lane from Midhurst (via A286, or No. 60 bus from Chichester). With a single bar and a dining area with log fire, it enjoys a busy weekend food trade, but no meals are served Sunday evening (reservations are required for Sun lunch); the specials board changes monthly. There are outside tables at the front and an extensive rear garden for long summer afternoons. ⛫Q❀◐◑♣P

Billingshurst

King's Arms

80 High Street, RH14 9QS
⏲ 11-11; 12-10.30 Sun
☎ (01403) 782072
Fuller's London Pride; Welton Kid & Bard ⊞
Friendly, two-bar, town-centre pub with oak beams throughout. It fields teams in several local sports leagues. When guest beers are available it tries to support local brewers, particularly independents and micros, and maintains good value on prices. The pub is a fair walk from the railway station, but hourly buses from Horsham stop nearby. ⊟♣P

Burgess Hill

Watermill Inn

1 Leylands Road, World's End, RH15 0QF
(100 yds E of Wivelsfield Station)
⏲ 11-11; 12-10.30 Sun
☎ (01444) 241088
Fuller's London Pride; Greene King Old Speckled Hen; Young's Bitter; guest beers ⊞
Community pub with a single bar, situated in the World's End area of Burgess Hill. It is a regular on the local CAMRA ale trail. The guest beer, which comes from a southern independent brewery, varies each month. An enclosed garden provides a safe area for families. Sky TV is turned on for major sporting events. A pub quiz is held on Thursday evening and occasional live music is staged. ❀◐⇌(Wivelsfield) ♣P

Byworth

Black Horse

RH15 0QF (off A283, 1 mile from Petworth)
⏲ 11.30-3, 5-11; 12-10.30 Sun
☎ (01798) 342424
Arundel ASB; Cheriton Pots Ale; King Horsham Best Bitter ⊞
Unspoilt, popular, rural pub (circa 1564) in the hamlet of Byworth. The traditional bar room features old floorboards, exposed ceiling beams, a large log fire and darts. Several other rooms are for diners, as well as an Elizabethan dining room (booking essential). The extensive menu is based on fresh local produce. ⛫Q☕❀◐◑⊟P

INDEPENDENT BREWERIES

Arundel Ford
Ballard's Nyewood
Custom Haywards Heath
Dark Star Haywards Heath
Gribble Inn Oving
Hepworth Horsham
King Horsham
Welton Horsham

Charlton

Fox Goes Free

PO18 0HU (¾ mile E of A286 at Singleton) OS889130
⏲ 11-11; 12-10.30 Sun
☎ (01243) 811461 website: www.thefoxgoesfree.com
Arundel Stronghold; Ballard's Best Bitter; guest beers ⊞
Fine Sussex flint pub in a downland valley below Goodwood racecourse. With red brick floors, inglenooks and many original features retained during its 400-year history, it oozes character. A former village bakery and a stable block now form part of the popular restaurant. Benefiting from five en-suite bedrooms and fine views from the large garden, this is an excellent base for tourists. Meals are served all day at the weekend. Live music is performed Wednesday. The house ale is supplied by Arundel Brewery. ⛫Q❀⇄◐◑⛺♣●P

Chichester

Bell Inn

3 Broyle Road, PO19 6AT (on A286, just N of city)
⏲ 11.30-3, 5-11; 12-3, 7-10.30 Sun
☎ (01243) 783388
Beer range varies ⊞
Attractive city local near the Festival Theatre. Timber panelling, exposed brickwork and beams all contribute to the homely atmosphere. Popular with theatregoers and locals alike, a good selection of typical pub fare is available at all sessions, except Sunday evening. To the rear, the small sheltered patio garden with tables is a real suntrap in summer. Handpumps deliver two guest beers from the Enterprise range and one from a local independent or micro-brewery. Q❀◐◑⇌♣P

Four Chesnuts

243 Oving Road, , PO19 4EQ (900 yds E of market cross)
⏲ 12-11; 12-10.30 Sun
☎ (01243) 779974
Caledonian Deuchars IPA; Oakleaf Hole Hearted; Tetley Dark Mild; guest beer ⊞
Slightly away from the city centre, this corner pub is easy to find and well worth the visit. Converted to a single bar some time ago, it still retains its distinctive drinking areas. At busy times the skittle alley is also used for dining and drinking, and hosts an annual beer festival early in the year. In addition to the darts, pool and quizzes, local musicians perform on Monday and Saturday evenings. ⛫❀◐♣P

Cowfold

Hare & Hounds

Henfield Road, RH13 8DR
⏲ 11.30-2.30 (3 Sat), 6-11; 12.30-3, 7-10.30 Sun
☎ (01403) 865354
Harveys BB; King Horsham Best Bitter; guest beers ⊞
Large, Victorian village pub, which was sensitively refurbished ten years ago. The bar top was made from local timber after the 1987

storm. The large flagstoned main bar leads to a cosy saloon at one end. Real fires add a homely touch during winter months. Guest beers are rotated regularly. Tasty meals are served at all sessions. A bus service runs from Horsham.

Crawley

Swan

1 Horsham Road, West Green, RH11 7LY

12 (11 Sat)-11; 12-10.30 Sun

(01293) 527447

Flowers Original; Wells Bombardier; guest beers

This enterprising Enterprise Inns' pub stocks a changing range of strong guest ales, as evidenced by the impressive array of pump clips above both bars. Westons Old Rosie cider is also on tap. Live rock music at the weekend is complemented by a juke box by the pool table, which holds a further two million tunes. There is also a quieter bar to retreat to.

Crawley Down

Royal Oak

Grange Road, RH10 4JT

11-11; 12-10.30 Sun

(01342) 713170

Greene King Old Speckled Hen; Harveys BB; guest beer

This Victorian railway hotel has undergone a complete refurbishment and has been vastly improved. After the railway line closed in 1967 the pub suffered mixed fortunes, but now the local customers are returning, attracted by the bright and clean interior. All meals are freshly prepared and there is a dining area. A mixed clientele of all ages creates a friendly atmosphere.

Donnington

Blacksmith's Arms

Selsey Road, PO20 7PR (on B2201, 2 miles S of Chichester)

11-3, 5.30-11; 11-11 Sat; 12-10.30 Sun

(01243) 783999

Fuller's London Pride; Greene King IPA, Abbot; Oakleaf Bitter

Cosy, cottage-style, 17th-century, part Grade II listed pub. It attracts an equal split of diners and drinkers, and is worth seeking out for the Oakleaf beer, which is rare for the area. Dine in the bar or the excellent restaurant where fresh fish is a speciality. Everything is home-made daily, using locally-sourced produce (no eve meals Sun or Mon in Jan or Feb). The large, safe garden offers activities for children (including swingboats) – ideal for visiting after a day at the beach. Q P

Eartham

George

PO18 0LT

11-11; 12-10.30 Sun

(01243) 814340

Greene King IPA, Ruddles County; guest beers

Attractive old country pub at the village centre, benefiting from a large, pleasant garden. The spacious interior provides plenty of seating for both drinkers and diners. A range of guest beers showcases Butcombe and local breweries. Food is available in the restaurant or dining area, where the menu always includes fish, game and vegetarian main courses, alongside more adventurous fare. A beer festival is held in spring. P

East Ashling

Horse & Groom

PO18 9AX (on B2178, 2½ miles NW of Chichester)

12-3, 6-11; 12-6 (closed eve) Sun

(01243) 575339

website: www.horseandgroom.sageweb.co.uk

Dark Star Hophead; Harveys Pale Ale; Hop Back Summer Lightning; Young's Bitter

Local CAMRA's Pub of the Year 2005, this 17th-century inn has been skilfully extended, using knapped Sussex flints. The large fireplace (once a forge) houses a fine old range, while the flagstone floor, old settles and half-panelled walls in the bar underpin its character. Diners enjoy a diverse, high quality menu of home-made dishes in the comfortable restaurant (no food Sun eve). Accommodation is offered in oak-beamed, en-suite rooms converted from a 17th-century flint barn. Q P

East Grinstead

Ship Inn

RH19 4EG (London Rd/High St jct)

11-11; 12-10.30 Sun

(01342) 312089

Young's Bitter, Special

Just out of the town centre, the Ship has two large bars: one is used for food, the other houses the TV. A fairly quiet pub with no loud music, the decor features sea scenes and pictures of boats. There is a pleasant garden to the rear of the pub, but the car park is a little small. The Ship is a good option for a drink when visiting East Grinstead. P

Elsted

Three Horseshoes

GU29 0JY

11-2.30, 6-11; 12-3, 7-10.30 Sun

(01730) 825746

Ballard's Best Bitter; Cheriton Pots Ale; Fuller's London Pride; Taylor Landlord

Former drovers' inn – perfect for cosy winter evenings with its small low-beamed rooms and open fires, or equally so in summer for the view of the Downs or the garden. It serves as the village local but one room is set aside for dining, where a good range of home-cooked traditional country fare is always on offer; game is a speciality. Q P

Fernhurst

King's Arms

Midhurst Road, GU27 3HA (on A286, ¾ mile S of village)

11.30-3, 5.30 (6.30 Sat)-11; 12-3.30 (closed eve) Sun

(01428) 652005

website: www.kingsarmsfernhurst.com

King Horsham Best Bitter; Ringwood Fortyniner; guest beers

Sussex sandstone free house, set below Henley Hill. A pub since the 17th century, the wood-panelled interior is divided into a bar and restaurant, plus a separate private dining room. Guest beers are always sourced from micro-breweries. The regularly changing menu usually features local fish and game (no meals Sun eve). Outside is an enclosed garden and a camping field (24 hours notice required) and a Sussex barn for functions. The pub is served by No. 70 Midhurst–Haslemere bus. Q❀◑ ⛺♣P

Red Lion ✔

8 The Green, GU27 3HY (¼ mile E of A286 crossroads)

✪ 11.30-3, 5-11; 11.30-11 Thu-Sat; 12-10.30 Sun

☎ (01428) 643112

Fuller's Chiswick, London Pride, ESB, seasonal beers; guest beers (occasional) 🄷

Idyllically set beside the village green, the Red Lion has been a pub since 1592. Inside is a single bar with a low, timbered ceiling and two side rooms. Outside, customers can drink at the front overlooking the green or in the large rear garden. The pub is popular with both locals and diners, but no food is served on Sunday or Monday evenings. It is a short walk from the A286 and the No. 70 Midhurst-Haslemere bus. ♨☕❀◑♣P⚟

Ferring

Henty Arms

2 Ferring Lane, BN12 6QY (N of level crossing)

✪ 11-11; 12-10.30 Sun

☎ (01903) 241254

Caledonian Deuchars IPA; Greene King Ruddles County; Wells Bombardier; Young's Bitter; guest beers 🄷

Friendly, two-bar pub where the public bar houses the juke box, darts, pool and TV, while the lounge bar is quiet, with a no-smoking restaurant area. It hosts a Sunday night quiz. The large rear garden is the venue for an annual beer festival which coincides with the vintage bus running day from Worthing. The nearest station, Goring, is 10 minutes' walk along the path on the north side of the railway. ♨Q☕❀◑⛽P

Findon

Findon Manor Hotel

High Street, BN14 0TA

✪ 12-2.30, 6-11; 12-10.30 Sun

☎ (01903) 872733 website: www.findonmanor.com

Black Sheep Best Bitter; Fuller's London Pride; Greene King Abbot; Harveys BB 🄷

The Findon Manor was built in the 16th century, originally as the village rectory. Real ale can be found in the the Snooty Fox bar adjacent to the main building. Enjoy log fires in winter, extensive gardens in summer; children are always welcome (but not dogs). This cosy, quiet establishment attracts a cross section of villagers and urbanites. A quiz is held annually on Boxing Day. A regular bus service (No. 1) runs from Worthing. ♨Q❀🛏◑P⚟

Halnaker

Anglesey Arms

Stane Street, PO18 0NQ

(3 miles NE of Chichester, on A285)

✪ 11-3, 5.30-11; 12-4, 7-10.30 Sun

☎ (01243) 773474 website: www.angleseyarms.co.uk

Adnams Bitter; Caledonian Deuchars IPA; Young's Bitter; guest beer 🄷

Family-run Georgian pub consisting of a flagstone-floored public bar with log fire and a comfortable restaurant. A large, enclosed garden at the rear is ideal in summer (petanque is played). The restaurant is renowned for good food using local produce; steaks and fresh fish are specialities. It is served by bus routes No. 99 and 55 from Chichester.

♨Q❀◑♣P

Henley

Duke of Cumberland Arms

GU27 3HQ (off A286)

✪ 11-11; 12-10.30 Sun

☎ (01428) 652280

Adnams Broadside; Brakspear Bitter; Hook Norton Best Bitter; Shepherd Neame Spitfire; guest beers 🄶

Dating from the 15th century, the Duke used to be on the main road from London to Chichester but was bypassed in the 1800s. Now it sits in four acres of garden with trout ponds coming from a spring-fed pool. The small bar is little altered and still partly lit by gas lamps and warmed by a roaring fire in winter. Fine traditional food is served in the bar or in the function room to the rear (eve meals Tue-Sat).

♨Q❀◑♣🍎P

Hill Brow

Jolly Drover

GU33 7QL (at B2070/B3006 jct)

✪ 11-2.30, 6-11; 12-3 (closed eve) Sun

☎ (01730) 893137

Draught Bass; Ringwood Best Bitter, Fortyniner; Taylor Landlord; guest beer 🄷

Built in 1820 by a drover, this watering-hole lies midway between Petersfield and Liphook on the old A3, just outside Liss. A family-run, country local, the atmosphere is enhanced by original beams, huge log fire and two chesterfield sofas; note the bar price list from the 1950s. The well-proportioned bar and dining area offer over 20 home-made daily specials. Swamp Donkey cider is pressed on the premises.

♨Q❀◑🍎P

Hooksway

Royal Oak

PO18 9JZ (¼ mile NE of B2141, near North Marden)

OS815162

✪ 11.30-2.30, 6 (7 winter)-11; closed Mon; 12-3, 7-10.30 (not winter eve) Sun

☎ (01243) 535257

Beer range varies 🄷

Tucked away in a valley close to the South Downs Way, this 15th-century rural gem became a lunch stop for the 'guns' on West Dean Estate shoots. King Edward VII was a frequent patron, but now walkers and cyclists enjoy its peaceful setting. Reasonably-priced, home-cooked food complements the four ales which include Hooksway Bitter from Hampshire Brewery, and usually a strong dark beer.

♨Q☕❀◑⛺♣P⚟

Horsham

Black Jug

31 North Street, RH12 1RJ (opp. arts centre)
⏲ 12-11; 12-10.30 Sun
☎ (01403) 253526
Caledonian Deuchars IPA; Greene King Old Speckled Hen; Marston's Pedigree; guest beers Ⓗ
Lively, bustling, town-centre pub, with a friendly atmosphere; over half the pub is no-smoking. A large conservatory leads to an outside sitting area, and there is plenty of seating in both bars. An ideal meeting place and easy to get to, it offers good quality meals at affordable prices; try the Sunday roasts. The house beer, Black Jug, comes from Horsham brewery, Welton.
♨Q❀◑◐ ≈⊬

Itchenor

Ship

The Street, PO20 7AH (100 yds from harbour)
⏲ 11.30-11; 12-10.30 Sun
☎ (01243) 512284
Ballard's Best Bitter; Gale's HSB; Itchen Valley Godfathers; guest beer Ⓗ
New to this Guide, the old building was replaced in 1933 by the present brick and tiled pub that has mellowed nicely. The oak panelled interior is decorated with yachting memorabilia and is divided into three rooms. In summer the garden fills with visitors and yachtsmen. A three-roomed suite will be ready for bed & breakfast accommodation by 2006. The guest beer is always from a local micro. The home-cooked food is recommended. ♨Q❀⇌◑◐ ⊟♣P

Keymer

Greyhound Inn

Keymer Road, BN6 8QT (opp. church)
⏲ 11-3, 6-11; 11-11 Fri & Sat; 12-10.30 Sun
☎ (01273) 842645
Gale's Best Bitter; Harveys BB; guest beers Ⓗ
Traditional village pub of two bars: the lounge bar leads to the dining area and garden. The main features of this bar are the panelled walls, inglenook and beamed ceiling, festooned with ceramic beer and beverage mugs. The smaller public bar is also panelled, displaying action photographs of greyhound meetings. Well-behaved children are allowed to stay until 9pm. Evening meals are served Tuesday-Saturday.
♨Q❀◑◐ ⊟♿♣P

Lambs Green

Lamb Inn

RH12 4RG (2 miles N of A264)
⏲ 11.30-3, 5.30-11; 12-3, 7-10.30 Sun
☎ (01293) 871336 website: www.thelambinn.info
King Horsham Best Bitter, Red River, seasonal beers Ⓗ
This delightful country pub is WJ King's only tied house. The dining area extends into a large no-smoking conservatory while drinkers are surrounded by dark oak beams and cosy nooks in the bar. Traditional home-cooked food is available daily. Biddenden's cider and mulled wine are offered, along with a range of King's bottled beers. Regular quiz nights are held. ♨❀◑◐ ♣P

Lindfield

Linden Tree

47 High Street, RH16 2HN
⏲ 11-3, 6-11; 12-2.30, 7-10.30 Sun
☎ (01444) 482995
Arundel Gauntlet; Gale's HSB; Harveys BB; Young's Winter Warmer, seasonal beers Ⓗ
In a pretty village near the pond, the pub could be missed as it looks like a shop front. A no-smoking policy applies at the bar but smoking is allowed elsewhere. There are always Sussex ales on tap, including seasonal brews from Arundel and Dark Star, but no food is served. A great pub for locals and visitors alike. The Linden Tree has a small garden. ♨Q❀♿⊬

Littleworth

Windmill ✔

Littleworth Lane, RH13 8EJ (from A24 or A272 head for Partridge Green) OS193205
⏲ 11.30-3, 5.30 (6 Sat)-11; 12-3, 7-10.30 Sun
☎ (01403) 710308
Badger K&B Sussex, Tanglefoot; guest beers Ⓗ
Still proudly displaying the old King & Barnes livery, this unspoilt rural gem offers two contrasting bars. A comfortable saloon caters for diners, while an uncompromising public bar has bar billiards and darts. Its walls and ceiling are festooned with an extensive collection of esoteric agricultural implements. The pleasant garden is blessed with an idyllic setting. The menu is based mostly on home-cooked dishes; fish and chips are on offer Friday and a traditional roast on Sunday. ♨❀◑◐ ⊟♿♣P

Mannings Heath

Dun Horse Inn

Brighton Road, RH13 6HZ
⏲ 11-3, 5.30-11; 11-11 Sat; 12-10.30 Sun
☎ (01403) 265783
Fuller's London Pride; Taylor Landlord Ⓗ
Roadside, two-bar pub on the A281 at Mannings Heath, now offering overnight accommodation. The exterior is notable for its stained glass windows promoting Rock Ales, while the interior has a beamed ceiling. A varied menu of excellent food is available during all sessions. The house is on the Horsham-Brighton bus route No. 107. ♨Q❀⇌◑◐ ⊟♿♣P

Maplehurst

White Horse Inn

Park Lane, RH13 6LL
⏲ 12 (11.30 Sat)-2.30, 6-11; 12-3, 7-10.30 Sun
☎ (01403) 891208
Harveys BB; Welton Pride'n'Joy; guest beers Ⓗ
Wonderful country pub where the large bar area has several areas rambling off it, with numerous artefacts on display. The conservatory doubles as a family room, while the spacious garden provides activities for children. Although the pub offers a wide range of food (Tue-Sun), the emphasis is on conversation and good beer, with many guest ales coming from small independent brewers. Local cider (JB's) is always

available at local CAMRA's Pub of the Year 2004, now in its 21st year in this Guide.
♨Q❀◖◗⊟♣●P⊬

Nuthurst

Black Horse Inn ✔

Nuthurst Street, RH13 6LH

⏲ 12-3, 6-11; 12-11 Sat; 12-10.30 Sun

☎ (01403) 891272

Fuller's London Pride; Harveys BB; guest beers Ⓗ

Split-level, 17th-century village pub with a flagstone floor and inglenook in the main bar; step down to a further bar area, and step up to a small room with access to the no-smoking dining room. A glass panel on one wall of the dining room shows a section of the wattle and daub construction. Beer festivals are often held on bank holidays with all-day opening. Regular quiz evenings are staged on Thursday. Guest beers often come from local breweries – King, Hepworth or Welton. ♨Q❀◖◗P⊬

Plaistow (nr Billingshurst)

Sun Inn

The Street, RH14 0PX

⏲ 12-3 (not Mon), 7-11; 12-3, (closed eve) Sun

☎ (01403) 871313

Gale's Best Bitter Ⓗ

Quiet, friendly, village local, comprising two small bars: a sunken, corner bar to the left and a bar to the right that is dominated by an inglenook. A small room off this bar is mainly used for dining. Brick floors and exposed beams feature throughout. Evening meals are served Thursday-Saturday and Sunday lunches are available by prior arrangement. ♨Q❀◗⊟♣P

Rogate

White Horse Inn ✔

East Street, GU31 5EA (on A272)

⏲ 11.30-3, 6-11; 11.30-11 Sat; 12-10.30 Sun

☎ (01730) 821333

Harveys Pale Ale, BB, Armada (summer), **seasonal beers** Ⓗ

A coaching inn since 1598, now a popular village pub boasting oak beams, a flagstone floor and a huge log fire in its large bar. It recently became a Harveys' tied house, stocking all its regular and seasonal beers; the Armada is replaced in winter by Old. The car park backs on to the village sports field. The pub supports its own cricket, soccer and darts teams. An excellent restaurant serves home-made snacks and meals (no food Sun evening). ♨Q❀◖◗♣P

Rowhook

Chequers

RH12 3PY

⏲ 11.30-3, 6-11; 12-3, 7-10.30 Sun

☎ (01403) 790480

Fuller's London Pride; Harveys BB; Young's Bitter; guest beer Ⓗ

Pubs are just not made like this any more! The Chequers is an archetypal traditional, rural British pub, complete with low beams and the statutory inglenook. The bar food and restaurant are recommended; the chef is a member of the 'Master Chefs of Great Britain'. The Chequers can be challenging to find but is rewarding when you do get there.
♨Q❀◖◗⊟P

Rudgwick

King's Head

Church Street, RH12 3EB

⏲ 11-11; 12-10.30 Sun

☎ (01403) 822200

Fuller's London Pride; Gale's HSB; Shepherd Neame Spitfire; guest beers Ⓗ

This 18th-century, low-beamed pub can be found at the northern end of the village, close to the church. Friendly owners ensure a warm welcome for all customers. All food is freshly prepared (no lunches Mon), and a Thai restaurant is open early evening except Sunday. Enjoy pleasant views across the Sussex countryside – the pub is close to the Downslink footpath. ❀◖◗♣P

Scayne's Hill

Sloop

Sloop Lane, RH17 7NP

(1½ miles along road to Danehill) OS385244

⏲ 12-3, 6-11; 12-10.30 Sun

☎ (01444) 831219 website: www.sloopcountry.com

Greene King XX Mild, IPA, Abbot; seasonal beers Ⓗ

Off the beaten track, the Sloop lies near the river and now-defunct canal that brought bricks for the Balcombe railway viaduct. The Bluebell Railway is nearby. Low-ceilinged cottages were converted into a pub in 1815. The Sloop is food-oriented but is proud of its Greene King beers; a seasonal brew is usually available – sometimes a guest as well. The stylish English menu is a cut above normal pub fare. In July a 10-day music and drinking festival is staged.
♨Q❀◖◗♿♣P⊬

Selham

Three Moles

GU28 0PN (1 mile S of A272, midway between Midhurst and Petworth) OS935206

⏲ 12-2, 5-11; 11.30-11 Sat; 12-10.30 Sun

☎ (01798) 861303 website: www.thethreemoles.co.uk

Skinner's Betty Stogs; guest beers Ⓗ

Moles abound at this characterful bijou country pub hidden in the Rother Valley, serving Selham Station since 1872. The railway may be defunct, but the pub has grown in stature since becoming a free house, sporting a mild, plus three guest beers from southern and south-western micro-breweries. The name relates to the coat of arms of owners, the Mitford family. A frequent CAMRA Pub of the Year winner, it holds a garden beer festival in June. ♨Q❀⛺♣P

Selsey

Lifeboat

Albion Road, PO20 0DJ (near lifeboat station on seafront)

⏲ 11-3, 6-11; 12-4, 7-10.30 Sun

☎ (01243) 603501

Arundel ASB; Fuller's London Pride; guest beer Ⓗ

Situated close to the beach and lifeboat slipway, this pleasant, friendly pub comprises two bars

and an adjoining restaurant that serves home-cooked meals, including locally-caught fish and Selsey crab salads. The garden and patio area are popular in summer with both locals and holidaymakers. Nautical photographs abound at this favourite watering-hole of lifeboat crew and local fishermen. Car parking is limited.
Q❀◖◗⊟♿♣P

Shoreham-by-Sea

Buckingham Arms

35-39 Brunswick Road, BN43 5WA
⏲ 11-11; 12-10.30 Sun
☎ (01273) 453660
Badger Best; Greene King XX Mild, Abbot; Harveys BB; Hop Back Summer Lightning; Taylor Landlord; guest beers Ⓗ
Superb town pub next to the station. The Buckingham boasts an array of 11 handpumps with up to six changing guest beers, mainly from micros and smaller breweries, plus an occasional cider on the back bar. The pub hosts monthly live music and popular beer and cider festivals in February and August each year. The L-shaped bar leads on to a pleasant patio garden, which is a suntrap in summer. Good food is served. ❀◖⇌P

Red Lion

Old Shoreham Road, BN43 5TE (opp. old toll bridge)
⏲ 11.30-11; 12-10.30 Sun
☎ (01273) 453171
Beer range varies Ⓗ
Situated at the western end of Old Shoreham Road, this 16th-century free house serves six different real ales and a good choice of food. There is a garden at the back, while the front patio overlooks the River Adur. Two beer festivals are held annually, at Easter and for the Shoreham Air Show. The pub is reputedly haunted by a ghost called George, an unfortunate soul who was hanged, drawn and quartered, his coffin laid on tables in the bar.
♛❀◖◗⊟P⚟

Royal Sovereign

6 Middle Street, BN43 5DP
⏲ 11-11; 12-10.30 Sun
☎ (01273) 451518
Badger K&B Sussex; Camerons Castle Eden Ale; Fuller's London Pride; Hook Norton Old Hooky; Taylor Landlord; guest beer Ⓗ
Classic town pub, an oasis of calm set in a quiet side street off the bustling town centre. Notable for its original green tiles, flint frontage and leaded Portsmouth United Brewery windows, the Royal Sovereign attracts a mature clientele. Conversation and displays of wit rule the roost here. Close to the Norman church and town museum, a pay and display council car park is next door on the one-way system. ♛Q◖⇌

Smock Alley

Five Bells

RH20 2QX (signed from Storrington-W. Chiltington road)
OS091172
⏲ 12-3, 6-11; 12-4.30, 7-10.30 Sun
☎ (01798) 812143
website: www.thefivebellsinsmockalley.co.uk
Harveys XX Mild; Palmer Copper Ale; guest beers Ⓗ
The genial landlord of this Guide regular offers an imaginative range of three guest ales, as well as Biddenden cider straight from the barrel. Food (not served Sun or Mon eves) is served in both the bar and adjacent conservatory restaurant overlooking the garden. En-suite accommodation is available for those wishing to spend more than the odd hour or two savouring the delights of this rural gem and the surrounding area. Enquire at the bar if you wish to try a game of devil among the tailors.
♛Q❀⊏◖◗♣●

Sompting Village

Marquis of Granby

1 West Street, BN15 0AP
⏲ 11-11; 12-10.30 Sun
☎ (01903) 231102
Fuller's London Pride; Harveys BB; Shepherd Neame Spitfire; guest beer Ⓗ
The Marquis is a friendly 1930s family-run village pub. At the front it retains the original attractive United Brewery bay windows, to the rear is an extensive, safe garden with a marquee for hire. The lounge bar has a flagstone floor, eating area and numerous comfy sofas. Food is available all day – try the Sunday roasts – to eat in or take away. The public bar is popular with sports fans. Sompting morris men cavort about on Boxing Day. Dogs on leads are welcome.
❀◖◗⊟♿♣P⚟

South Harting

Ship

North Lane, GU31 5PZ
⏲ 11.30-3, 6-11; 11-11 Sat; 12-10.30 Sun
☎ (01730) 825302
Ballard's Wassail; Cheriton Pots Ale; Palmer IPA; guest beer Ⓗ
Cosy, old village-centre local built in 1684 from ships' timbers. It features a small regulars' bar and a larger lounge/restaurant. Good value meals are served (not Sun eve); booking is advised at weekends. Outside, an enclosed garden flanks the main road. The guest beer is always from a small independent brewer.
♛Q❀◖◗⊟♣P

Staplefield

Jolly Tanners

Handcross Road, RH17 6EF
⏲ 11-3, 6-11; 11-11 Sat; 12-10.30 Sun
☎ (01444) 400335
Elgood's Black Dog; Fuller's Chiswick, London Pride; Harveys BB; guest beer Ⓗ
This friendly free house stocks an ever-changing range of guest beers and serves a good selection of home-cooked meals. It is a traditional village pub, popular with both locals and visitors alike. The main bar is on two levels and another room is used by diners. Admire the horse brasses that surround the roaring fire. The cider is Addlestones.
♛❀◖◗●P

Stopham

White Hart

(by A283, 1 mile W of Pulborough), RH20 1DS

(signed at Stopham bridge)

11-3, 6-11; 10-11 Sat; 12-11 Sun

☎ (01798) 873321

Fuller's London Pride; Greene King Old Speckled Hen; Welton Sussex Pride, seasonal beers Ⓗ

Situated next to the River Arun at the ancient Stopham bridge, this superb old establishment is a popular restaurant as well as a pub. The single bar serves four real ales. There is a choice of comfortable rooms with a log fire in the west lower lounge; ceiling beams abound. A varied menu offers good pub food. Morris dancers perform in July and August. ⛰❀◐◗⊟⅄P⁄

Tarring

George & Dragon

1 High Street, BN14 7NN (opp. post office)

11-11; 12-10.30 Sun

☎ (01903) 202497

Courage Directors; Harveys BB; Hop Back Summer Lightning; Wells Bombardier; guest beers Ⓗ

There has been a tavern on this site since at least 1610, when the landlord was Moses Brian and the pub was called the White Horse. This venerable, timber-framed building consists of one rambling bar, including a games area and a secluded snug for diners. Popular, with friendly staff, it attracts an eclectic mix of punters; vertical drinking is sometimes obligatory.

❀◐⇌(Worthing) ♣P

Vine

27 High Street, BN14 7NN

11-11; 12-10.30 Sun

☎ (01903) 202891

Badger Best, Tanglefoot; guest beers Ⓗ

Situated at the centre of the well-preserved Tarring village High Street since 1882, the Vine serves a selection of up to nine real ales. A wide range of home-made food is available lunchtime and evenings. It hosts live music on Monday evening and a quiz on Thursday evening; morris dancers perform the annual wassail along the High Street in January. Children are welcome in the courtyard and large secluded rear garden, but not in the pub.

❀◐◗♿P

Trotton

Keeper's Arms

GU31 5ER (on A272, between Rogate and Midhurst)

12-3; 6.30-11; closed Mon; 12-3 (closed eve) Sun

☎ (01730) 813724 website: www.keepersarms.co.uk

Ballard's Best Bitter, Nyewood Gold; Cheriton Pots Ale; guest beer Ⓗ

Delightful country pub, close to the River Rother. An oak floor, wood-panelled walls, beams and homely soft furnishings around a log fire allow for total relaxation. Note the private collection of intriguing ornaments and artefacts from the landlady's travels. Reservations are recommended for the excellent restaurant. The patio is popular in summer. The beer range includes seasonal brews.

⛰Q❀◐◗♿♣P

Two Mile Ash

Bax Castle

Two Mile Ash Road, RH13 0LA

(off A24, take B2237 then first left)

11.30-3, 6-11; 11-11 Sat; 12-3, 6.30-10.30 Sun

☎ (01403) 730369

Brakspear Bitter; Harveys BB; Hepworth Pullman; King Horsham Best Bitter Ⓗ

Large house, turned into a pub; it is frequented by walkers and cyclists using the nearby Downslink (former rail line), as well as staff from nearby Christ's Hospital School. The friendly, large bar has several adjoining rooms including a restaurant. Two open fires keep the bar cosy during the winter months. Local breweries are well supported. ⛰Q❀◐◗♿P

Walderton

Barley Mow

PO18 9ED (300 yds E of B2147) OS790106

11-3, 6-11; 12-3, 7-10.30 Sun

☎ (023) 92631321

Ringwood Fortyniner, Old Thumper; guest beers Ⓗ

This unspoilt, 18th-century country pub nestles in a downland valley. Choose from four ales to enjoy by one of the real fires or book a skittles evening (minimum 20 people; a buffet or hot food can be ordered). On sunny days, relax by the stream in the secluded garden. Sandwiches, bar snacks and daily specials, plus a weekday £4.99 menu, provide a good food choice. Children are welcome in the skittle alley when not in use. ⛰Q❀◐◗P⁄

Warnham

Sussex Oak ✔

Church Street, RH12 3QW

11-11; 12-10.30 Sun

☎ (01403) 265028 website: www.thesussexoak.co.uk

Adnams Bitter; Fuller's London Pride; Taylor Landlord; Young's Bitter; guest beers Ⓗ

Spacious, 16th-century pub opposite the village church. The attractive, beamed interior boasts an inglenook that is appreciated on winter days. For summer outdoor drinking, you can opt for the large garden. Diners enjoy good quality meals in the no-smoking restaurant (eve meals Tue-Sat). The pub has a strong community feel and supports many local charities. This pub is the best bet for a good pint in the area and bar billiards can be played. ⛰❀◐◗♿⅄⇌♣P⁄

Westbourne

Cricketers

Commonside, PO10 8TA (northern edge of village)

5 (11 Fri & Sat)-11; 12-10.30 Sun

☎ (01243) 372647

Beer range varies Ⓗ

At the edge of a large village, this 300-year-old pub is well worth seeking out. Now a thriving free house, it offers at least three guest beers from micro-breweries; the regular Angry Trout is brewed by Hampshire. The large, L-shaped bar has partly-panelled walls and hops hanging from the ceiling. Darts and bar billiards are played. The south-facing garden gives extra drinking space in summer. ⛰❀♣P

Westergate

Labour in Vain

Nyton Road, PO20 3UG (A29/B2233 jct)

⏲ 11-3, 6-11; 11-11 Fri; 12-4, 7-10.30 (summer varies) Sun

☎ (01243) 543173

Badger K&B Sussex, Dollard's Best Bitter; Harveys BB; King Horsham Best Bitter; guest beers Ⓖ

Step back in time at this pub formed 200 years ago from two 16th-century tied cottages, with its flagstone floor, exposed beams and a large open fire. The two-bar local has a no-smoking eating area where pub food is served in generous portions at reasonable prices (no food Mon). Drinkers and diners mix in a cosy atmosphere, where locals and seasonal visitors enjoy beer from Sussex and monthly changing guest ales. ⌂Q☋❀◖◗♿♣P

Whitemans Green

Ship Inn

RH17 5BY (N of Cuckfield at B215/B2114 jct)

⏲ 12-2.30, 5.30-11; 12-11 Sat; 12-3, 7-10.30 Sun

☎ (01444) 413219

Caledonian Deuchars IPA; Courage Directors; King Horsham Best Bitter; guest beers Ⓖ

Single-bar, village local close to Haywards Heath rugby club. The numerous handpumps are not used as all the real ales are gravity dispensed from the cool room behind the bar. This family-run free house has a cosy interior furnished with sofas. Good food is served and there is a no-smoking dining area. A games room can be found at the rear.

⌂Q❀⇌◖◗▲♣P

Wick

Dewdrop Inn

96 Wick Street, BN17 7JS

⏲ 10.30-3, 5.30-11; 10.30-11 Sat; 10.30-10.30 Sun

☎ (01903) 716459

Gale's Butser; Ringwood XXXX Porter Ⓗ

This is a rare find: an uncompromisingly basic free house with no pretensions whatsoever. Dating from 1860 as part of a Victorian terrace, it features a large public bar and a tiny saloon. Very much a locals' pub, with the accent on traditional games, a warm welcome is nevertheless guaranteed. Q◖⊟♣

Worthing

Coach & Horses

Arundel Road, BN13 3UA (on A27, W of Worthing)

⏲ 11-3, 5.15-11; 11-11 Sat; 12-10.30 Sun

☎ (01903) 264665

Fuller's London Pride; Greene King Abbot; Harveys BB Ⓗ

Former coaching inn on the Arundel road, dating from 1741. The interior is divided into three areas: bar, restaurant and family room. The middle part of the pub is a long bar, with the family room off to the right. In the restaurant area food is served daily at lunchtime and 6.30-9 evenings, except Sunday and Tuesday. A good selection of full meals and bar snacks is available, including children's and vegetarian options.

Q☋❀◖◗P

Old House at Home

77 Broadwater Street East, BN14 9AX (left after Broadwater pub on A24)

⏲ 11.30-11; 12-10.30 Sun

☎ (01903) 232661

Draught Bass; Harveys BB; Wells Bombardier Ⓗ

Reputedly haunted, but nonetheless popular, two-bar, wood-panelled village pub in traditional Sussex style with flint-faced exterior walls. A quiet saloon and conservatory contrast with the lively public bar where the dartboard is in use most of the time. Open fires warm both bars. Families are welcome and good pub meals cater for children. A car park is provided in a difficult area for parking.

⌂Q☋❀◖⊟♣P

Selden Arms ✔

41 Lyndhurst Road, BN11 2DB (near Worthing Hospital)

⏲ 11 (12 Sat)-11; 12-10.30 Sun

Beer range varies Ⓗ

The Selden has been at the vanguard of Worthing's real ale scene for several years. A genuine free house, selling six ever-changing ales, plus Belgian bottled beers, it hosts an annual beer festival in January. A community pub in every sense, it has been local CAMRA's Pub of the Year since 2000. Live music occasionally rattles the walls, which are adorned with photos of old Worthing hostelries. Children are admitted during the day. Dogs are welcome – but not at mealtimes.

⌂◖≠(Central) ♣

Swan

79 High Street, BN11 1DN (opp. Waitrose)

⏲ 11-2.30, 6-11; 11-11 Sat; 12-10.30 Sun

☎ (01903) 232923

Greene King Abbot; Harveys BB; Shepherd Neame Spitfire; guest beer Ⓗ

Five minutes from the town centre, this 19th-century one-bar pub offers a warm welcome and caters for a diverse clientele. The decor is country-inn style, with lots of beams, brasses, agricultural implements and two open fires. There is plenty going on with darts, bar billiards and regular music nights. The food is good, too.

⌂❀◖≠♣

Yapton

Maypole Inn

Maypole Lane, BN18 0DP (off B2132, N of village. Pedestrian access from Lake Lane) OS978041

⏲ 11.30-11; 12-10.30 Sun

☎ (01243) 551417

Arundel Sussex Mild; Ringwood Best Bitter; Skinner's Betty Stoggs; guest beers Ⓗ

Regional CAMRA Pub of the Year 2004, this small, flint-built pub is tucked away from the village centre. Maypole Lane was cut off by the railway in 1846 and the pub has enjoyed quiet isolation ever since. The cosy lounge boasts a log fire and an imposing row of seven handpumps, dispensing beers from local and West Country independents. The public bar houses a juke box, darts and pool, and a skittle alley can be booked.

⌂Q☋❀◖⊟♿▲♣●P

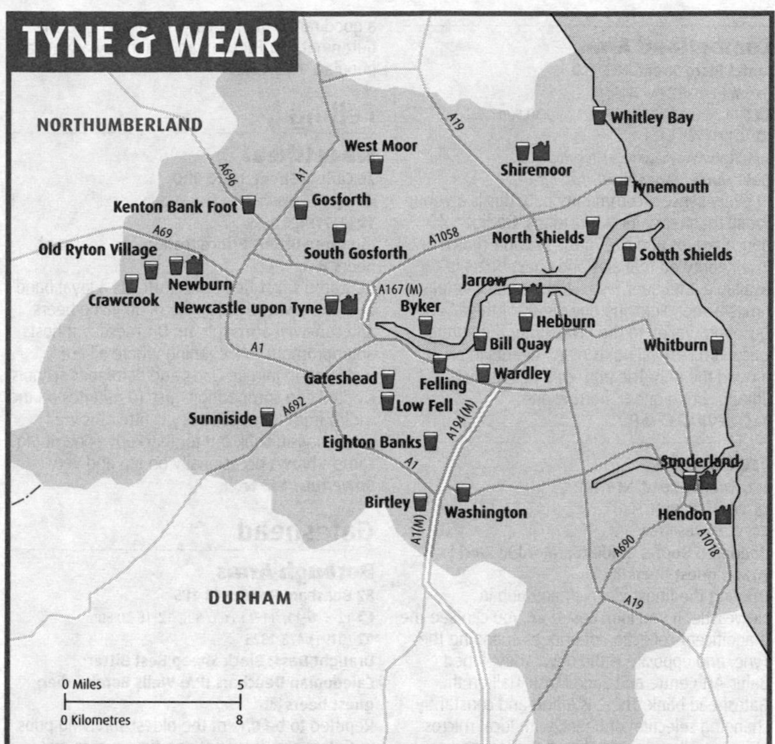

Bill Quay

Albion

Reay Street, NE10 0TY

4 (12 Sat)-11; 12-10.30 Sun

(0191) 469 2418

Jarrow Bitter, Swinging Gibbet, Old Cornelius, seasonal beers; guest beers H

One of only three pubs owned by the local Jarrow Brewery, it stocks not just its own multiple CAMRA award-winning real ales but those from other micros from the north east too. Overlooking the widest part of the River Tyne, the comfortable lounge bar, with large-screen TV, has fascinating views across heavily-industrialised Tyneside. There is a pool table in the conservatory. Regular live music and weekly quizzes are hosted. The Coast-to-Coast cycle route and Keelman's Way Walk run nearby. ⊖ (Pelaw) ♣P

Birtley

Moulders Arms

Peareth Terrace, Birtley Lane, DH3 2LW

11-3, 5.30-11; 12-3, 7-10.30 Sun

(0191) 410 2949

Boddingtons Bitter; Flowers Original; guest beer H

Just off the main road, this community pub is at the centre of the local social scene. Managed by a tenant with many years' experience of running Good Beer Guide favourites, it has a large, comfortable split-level lounge and a smaller, livelier public bar with wooden beams. A strong supporter of local charities, it runs its own long-standing golf society and darts teams and hosts a weekly quiz. The pub is reputed to be home to a ghost whose main activity seems to be moving things about! P

Byker

Cluny

36 Lime Street, NE1 2PQ

12-11 (1am Fri & Sat); 12-10.30 Sun

(0191) 230 4474

Black Sheep Best Bitter; Taylor Landlord; Young's Bitter; guest beers H

Owned by the locally-based pub chain Head of Steam, although the first not to be on or near a railway station, the pub is in fact a restored 19th-century industrial building and retains many of its original features. It has developed a reputation as one the busiest and best live music venues in the area. The ales change constantly and there are also imported beers and ciders sold. Good, home-made food is also served. Occasional themed beer festivals are hosted and the upper, no-smoking area holds regular art displays. In the summer visitors can enjoy their pint on the village green.

INDEPENDENT BREWERIES

Big Lamp Newburn
Bull Lane Hendon
Darwin Sunderland
Hadrian & Border Newcastle upon Tyne
Jarrow Jarrow
Mordue Shiremoor

Cumberland Arms
James Place Street, NE6 1LD
(below E end of Byker Bridge)
✪ 5 (4.30 Fri; 12.30 Sat)-11; 12-10.30 Sun
☎ (0191) 265 6151
website: www.thecumberlandarms.co.uk
Beer range varies Ⓗ/Ⓖ
In every sense a community pub, this is a venue for all manner of local musicians, traditional dance groups and live music. A wide choice of locally-brewed real ales and guest beers is available, and beer festivals are held several times a year. Enjoying fine views of the Ouseburn Valley to the River Tyne, the annual Ouseburn Festival holds many events in or around the pub. The pub even has its own library – bring one to borrow one.
♨Q✿◐◑⊟⊖●P

Free Trade
St Lawrence Road, NE6 1AP
✪ 11-11; 12-10.30 Sun
☎ (0191) 265 5764
Hadrian & Border Gladiator; Mordue Workie Ticket; guest beers Ⓗ
Offering the finest views of any pub in Newcastle, if you look upstream you can see the magnificent collection of bridges spanning the Tyne, and opposite is the newly developed Baltic Art Centre and Sage Music Hall on the Gateshead bank. There is a fine and constantly changing selection of beers, with local micros always well represented, and Archers and Cropton providing frequent guests. There are no fruit machines but a free juke box plays classic rock. ♨✿

Crawcrook

Rising Sun
Bank Top, NE40 4EE
✪ 11-11; 12-10.30 Sun
☎ (0191) 413 3316
Black Sheep Best Bitter; guest beers Ⓗ
Lively, well-run community local with a warm, friendly atmosphere. It offers the best choice of beers for miles around including an interesting range of guests. An extensive food menu is available and the conservatory provides a comfortable place for dining. Drinkers can choose between the lounge and pool table area or a quieter room upstairs. The pub, served by Go Northeast bus No. 10, is situated half a mile south of the main village crossroads.
✿◐◑P

Eighton Banks

Lambton Arms ✔
Rockliffe Way, NE9 7XR
✪ 11-11; 12-10.30 Sun
☎ (0191) 487 8137
website: www.lambtonarms.co.uk
Greene King IPA, Abbot, Old Speckled Hen; guest beers Ⓗ
Following a refurbishment this pub is now an established pub/restaurant as well as being north-east England's first no-smoking pub. Although largely a food establishment – meals are served all day – it proudly claims to be a cask ale specialist too, with four handpumps offering a good range of ales varying in strength. The quiz nights on Tuesday and Thursday are always popular. ✿◐◑⊟●P

Felling

Wheatsheaf
26 Carlisle Street, NE10 0HQ
✪ 5 (12 Fri & Sat)-11; 12-10.30 Sun
☎ (0191) 420 0659
Big Lamp Bitter, Prince Bishop Ale, seasonal beers Ⓗ
Big Lamp's first tied house attracts a loyal band of followers who enjoy the good value beers and convivial atmosphere. On Tuesday it hosts an impromptu folk evening where all are welcome to join in. Darts and dominoes schools create keen competition. Just 10 minutes on the metro from Newcastle city centre, it is well worth a visit. Look out for Blackout – one of Big Lamp's brews occasionally on tap and very powerful. ♨⊖●

Gateshead

Borough Arms
82 Bensham Road, NE8 1PS
✪ 12-3, 6-11; 11-11 Fri & Sat; 12-10.30 Sun
☎ (0191) 478 1323
Draught Bass; Black Sheep Best Bitter; Caledonian Deuchars IPA; Wells Bombardier; guest beers Ⓗ
Reputed to be one of the oldest surviving pubs in Gateshead, it was at one time a corn mill. Situated in a residential area, this single room, no-frills local offers the only real ale in the area, including the nearby town centre. A popular live music venue, it plays mostly blues, jazz and soul. It also hosts regular buskers' nights and weekly pop music and general knowledge quizzes. Close to the main public transport interchange, it is on the town trail and near the historic Windmill Hills Park. ♨✿⊖♣P

Gosforth

County ✔
70 High Street, NE3 1HB
✪ 12 (11 Fri & Sat)-11; 12-10.30 Sun
☎ (0191) 285 6919
Courage Directors; Greene King Old Speckled Hen; McEwan's 80/-; Theakston Best Bitter; Wells Bombardier; guest beers Ⓗ
An impressive listed building at the southern end of Gosforth High Street. Once a 'dwelling house' to the gangland Boulmer family in the 19th century, the pub is now a firm favourite of drinkers throughout the area. Relatively unspoilt, its L-shaped bar serves up to five regular and three guest beers. One of the guests is usually from the Houston Brewery in Scotland. A small room provides a no-smoking area. Food is available from noon to 8pm daily.
♨Q◐◑⇌(Regent Centre)P⊘

Gosforth Hotel
Salters Road, NE3 1HQ
✪ 12-11; 12-10.30 Sun
☎ (0191) 285 6617
Black Sheep Best Bitter; Fuller's London Pride; Marston's Pedigree; Taylor Landlord; Wells Bombardier; guest beers Ⓗ

On the corner of a busy road junction, this lively pub is building a reputation for its variety and quality of cask ales. Recently refurbished to a high standard, it has a cafe/bar approach that allows drinkers to relax in comfy sofas while trying out the six regular and up to two guest beers on offer. A more traditional bar at the back opens in the evenings only. Meals are served 12-7 (5 Fri & Sat). (Regent Centre)

Hebburn

Lakeside

East Fellgate Farm, NE10 8YD (on A194)
12-11; 12-10.30 Sun
(0191) 428 3030
Beer range varies
The Lakeside is a stone-built pub adjacent to a well-stocked fishing lake. It offers a warm welcome to all and is particularly popular with families, with a children's play area in the garden. The restaurant opens daily and features a wide range of good value meals (no food Sun eve). The choice of beers usually includes one from the nearby Jarrow Brewery. A quiz is held on Monday evening. (Fellgate) P

Jarrow

Robin Hood

Primrose Hill, NE32 5UB (off A194)
(0191) 428 5454
Jarrow Bitter, Rivet Catcher, Swinging Gibbet, McConnell's Stout, seasonal beers; guest beers
Two years after opening, the local CAMRA branch chose this tap of Jarrow Brewery as Pub of the Year in 2004. It contains a public bar, lounge and restaurant serving Italian food plus a conservatory. The bar is reached through an impressive set of oak doors and the brewery can be seen at the rear. Five beers in the range are usually available, as well as Westons Old Rosie cider, and beer festivals are held in March and October. No meals are served on Sunday evening or Monday. (Fellgate) P

Kenton Bank Foot

Twin Farms

22 Main Road, NE13 8AB
11-11; 12-10.30 Sun
(0191) 286 1263
Mordue Workie Ticket; Taylor Landord; guest beers
Newly built on the site of an old farm in traditional style, this is a large, open-plan room. However, the use of alcoves gives the feel of several small rooms. Two real fires, plus a huge kitchen range, add character. The air conditioning helps to provide a pleasant environment for all. Guest beers change weekly and are often from local micros; occasional beer festivals are held. Food is served all day.
Q (Bank Foot) P

Low Fell

Aletaster

706 Durham Road, NE9 6JA
12 (11 Sat)-11; 12-10.30 Sun
(0191) 487 0770
Draught Bass; Bateman XXXB; Jennings Cumberland Ale; Marston's Pedigree; Theakston Best Bitter; guest beers
Styled as an ale house, this suburban pub has bare boards in the public bar but carpet in the cosy snug. It is still recognisable as a member of the Scottish & Newcastle T&J Bernard chain that it once was. With 10 cask conditioned beers available at all times it offers the widest selection of real ales in the area. A real cider (Westons Old Rosie) is served too – a rarity in Tyneside. Occasional beer festivals are held as well as a weekly quiz and, from time to time, live music.
P

Newburn

Keelman

Grange Road, NE15 8NL
11-11; 12-10.30 Sun
(0191) 267 1689
Big Lamp Bitter, Summerhill Stout, Prince Bishop Ale, seasonal beers
Big Lamp's brewery tap was opened in 1997 in a converted water pumping station. A Grade II listed building, a conservatory was recently added providing a relaxed dining area and the bar area extended to accommodate a growing band of Big Lamp converts. Quality and value are key here and this is reflected in the excellent beer range and good food. Situated on the Coast-to-Coast cycle way and the newly opened Hadrian's Wall Path, the Keelman is well worth stopping off for.
P

Newcastle upon Tyne

Bacchus

High Bridge, NE1 6BX
11.30-11; 7-10.30 Sun
(0191) 261 1008
Harviestoun Bitter & Twisted; Taylor Landlord; guest beers
Recently refurbished to a high standard, the interior features lots of wood, model ships, photographs of the shipbuilding industry and comfortable seating areas. A good range of regular beers is available, generally with four guests, as well as an ever-growing number of interesting bottled beers. High quality food is served at lunchtime Monday to Saturday. The pub only opens on Sunday lunchtime if Newcastle United are playing at home.
(Monument)

Bodega

125 Westgate Road, NE1 4AG
11-11; 12-10.30 Sun
(0191) 221 1552
Big Lamp Prince Bishop Ale; Durham Magus; Mordue Workie Ticket; guest beers
A multiple winner of local CAMRA Pub of the Year awards, this large single-roomed pub with two fine original stained glass ceiling domes is slightly to the west of the city centre. One of two pubs in the theatre village, it is handy for events at the Journal Tyne Theatre. It is also popular with football fans going to and from the match or watching live on TV. A recent convert to real cider, it is one of the few pubs in

Newcastle where this is available. Lunches are served Monday to Saturday.
◖⇌(Central) ⊖

Bridge Hotel

Castle Garth, NE1 1RQ

✪ 11.30-11; 12-10.30 Sun

☎ (0191) 232 6400

Black Sheep Best Bitter; Caledonian Deuchars IPA; Mordue Workie Ticket; guest beers Ⓗ

Sitting hard up against the high level bridge and facing the keep of the 'new' castle which gave the city its name, the pub, and in summer the garden, offer fine views of the River Tyne. Inside, the main room is divided into a number of seating areas, while still allowing plenty of standing room around the bar. There is always a good selection of real ale here to enjoy. The upstairs lounge hosts many live music events including what is possibly the longest established folk session in the country.
✿◖⇌(Central) ⊖

Crown Posada ☆

33 the Side, NE1 3JE

✪ 11 (12 Sat)-11; 7-10.30 Sun

☎ (0191) 232 1269

Draught Bass; Jennings Bitter; Taylor Landlord; guest beers Ⓗ

Architecturally the finest pub in Newcastle with beautiful stained glass windows, an unusual high ceiling and wood-clad walls. The front snug was formerly the preserve of captains and chief engineers in the days when the quayside was bustling with shipping and trade; now it is a pleasant resting place for all. Visitors who struggle beyond the narrow, often packed, front bar will discover a larger lounge area. Here there are no distractions other than a gramophone to interrupt the beer drinking.
Q⇌(Central) ⊖(Monument)

Duke

High Bridge, NE1 1EN

✪ 11-11; 12-10.30 Sun

☎ (0191) 261 8852

Caledonian Deuchars IPA; Tetley Bitter; guest beers Ⓗ

Bustling city-centre pub supporting up to 10 cask ales at any one time. Formerly the Duke of Wellington, pictures of the man and his soldiers line the walls. Although the pub is situated close to the infamous Bigg Market, the atmosphere here is relaxed and friendly. The lane on which it stands appears to be gradually turning into the retail music centre of the city, so if you are in the area, do not miss this pub.
◖⇌⊖(Monument)

Hotspur

103 Percy Street, NE1 7RY

✪ 11-11; 12-10.30 Sun

☎ (0191) 232 4352

Courage Directors; McEwan's 80/-; Theakston Old Peculier; guest beers Ⓗ

Beers from Scottish independent brewers are well represented here alongside an interesting mix of well-known and unusual English ales. The pub's central location close to Newcastle's university, hospital and major bus station provides a varied mix of clientele including students, staff, shoppers, travellers waiting for a bus and discerning drinkers. The atmosphere is lively and friendly and the pub can be crowded, particularly when live football and rugby are shown on TV. ✿◖◗⇌⊖(Haymarket)

North Shields

Magnesia Bank

Camden Street, NE30 1NH

✪ 11-11 (midnight Thu-Sat); 12-10.30 Sun

☎ (0191) 257 4831 website: www.magnesiabank.co.uk

Durham Magus; Mordue Workie Ticket; guest beers Ⓗ

Opened in 1989 in a converted Georgian bank, this excellent town-centre pub is a past winner of local CAMRA Pub of the Year. It is the brewery tap for Mordue and stocks up to six guest ales at any one time. Excellent meals are served in the Garden restaurant and themed international food nights are a speciality. It is also a venue for comedy nights, country music and performances by local bands. ♨Q◖◗⊖⊬

Oddfellows

7 Albion Street, NE30 2RJ

✪ 11-11; 12-10.30 Sun

☎ (0191) 257 4288

Hadrian & Border Gladiator; Jarrow Bitter Ⓗ

The walls of this friendly, small, single-room lounge bar are covered with historic maps, photographs of pre-war North and South Shields and newspaper cuttings of former local boxing heroes. The pub has strong sporting connections and football matches are shown on the large-screen TV. The landlord fundraises for charities and the darts team has most of the top 16 professional players signed up to play when in the area. ♿⊖♣

Porthole

11 New Quay, NE29 6LQ

✪ 11-11; 12-10.30 Sun

☎ (0191) 257 6645

Courage Directors; guest beers Ⓗ

Dating from 1834 and rebuilt around 1900, the Porthole is situated close to the North and South Shields ferry landing. It has two bars, separated by a food serving area. Local breweries are chosen to provide the guest ales. A lunchtime jazz club is held on Wednesday and there is also live entertainment on Friday and Sunday evenings. ✿◖⊖♣⊬

Prince of Wales

2 Liddell Street, NE30 1HE (follow Fish Quay signs)

✪ 12-11 (closed Tue lunchtime); 12-10.30 Sun

☎ (0191) 296 2816

Samuel Smith OBB Ⓗ

There are records of this pub dating back to 1627, but the current building, faced with green glazed brick, dates from 1927. The premises lay empty for some years before being restored in traditional style by Sam Smith's and reopened in 1992. A rare outlet for Sam Smith's this far north, it is well worth a visit. Crab sandwiches and fish and chips are served at lunchtime and are highly recommended. ♨QႦ✿◖⌸⊖♣⊬

Tap & Spile ✔

184 Tynemouth Road, NE30 1EG

✪ 12-11; 12-10.30 Sun

☎ (0191) 257 2523

Caledonian Deuchars IPA; Greene King Ruddles County; guest beers H
A past winner of CAMRA Tyneside & Northumberland Pub of the Year, this inn continues to delight the beer enthusiast, offering two regular ales and an ever-changing guest list from all over the country. Two traditional ciders are also available. The pub's two rooms are served from one bar; the bar area offers live TV coverage of major sporting events. The lounge is part no-smoking and remains the quiet zone. No meals are served on Sunday.
◐⊟⊖♣●

Old Ryton Village

Old Cross

Barmoor Lane, NE40 3QP (off B6317)
✪ 4 (12 Sat)-11; 12-10.30 Sun
☎ (0191) 413 4689
Black Sheep Best Bitter; Caledonian Deuchars IPA; Camerons Strongarm; Wells Bombardier; guest beer H
Originally a coaching house that served the Gateshead-Hexham route, this lively local gets its name from its location overlooking the village green and cross. It has a large one-room bar with a raised area to the rear and doors opening onto the patio. There is a function room on the upper floor. The clientele are mainly locals and very friendly. Guest beers come from micro-breweries in the region. Thursday is quiz night.
ざ✿◐●P⊁

Shiremoor

Shiremoor Farm

Middle Engine Lane, NE29 8DZ
✪ 11-11; 12-10.30 Sun
☎ (0191) 257 6302
Mordue Workie Ticket; guest beers H
An award-winning conversion of derelict stone farm buildings, this Fitzgerald pub retains many original features including a conical, raftered 'gin gan' which is now the highly recommended restaurant. No-smoking areas and superb air conditioning ensure comfort for drinkers and diners alike. Food is served all day. Children are welcome in the Granary. An excellent pub, it is well worth seeking out.
Qざ✿◐◑P⊁

South Gosforth

Victory

Killingworth Road, NE3 1SY
✪ 12-11; 12-10.30 Sun
☎ (0191) 285 1254
Courage Directors; John Smith's Bitter; Taylor Landlord; Wells Bombardier; guest beers H
A lively roadside local, this pub is almost 150 years old. Patronised in past years by generations of coal miners, the many pictures and mining memorabilia reflect the industrial heritage of the Victory and surrounding area. Two guest beers are on constant rotation. A quiz night is held every Tuesday. During summer, the benches on the paved area outside are popular.
♨Q✿◐⊖P

South Shields

Alum Ale House

River Drive, NE33 1JR (by ferry landing)
✪ 11-11; 12-10.30 Sun
☎ (0191) 427 7245
Banks's Bitter, Mansfield Cask; Marston's Pedigree; guest beers H
Old-fashioned, small pub at the heart of the market docks area. The Alum has always been a firm favourite with local real ale drinkers. The present management have featured over 100 guest ales throughout the last year, including hosting various beer festivals. The pub prides itself on being a quiet haven for good beer and conversation.
✿⊖

Bamburgh

Bamburgh Avenue, NE34 6SS (on main coast road)
✪ 11-11; 12-10.30 Sun
☎ (0191) 454 1899
Flowers Original; Greene King Abbot, Old Speckled Hen; guest beer H
Spacious, modern pub with splendid views out over the North Sea. The open-plan bar has a raised seating area for dining, a space for two pool tables, and a separate family room. Two overhead projectors supply live football action on match days. In summer there is further seating outside at the front of the pub.
ざ✿◐◑⅄P

Beacon

Greens Place, NE33 2AQ
✪ 11-11; 12-10.30 Sun
☎ (0191) 456 2876
Adnams Broadside; Caledonian Deuchars IPA; Marston's Pedigree H
Traditional pub with a nautical feel providing wonderful views over the River Tyne. The interior is roughly split into three areas and the decor also reflects connections with the local Roman occupation of South Shields. Away from the main hubbub of the city centre, the pub is the perfect place for a peaceful pint.
✿◐◑⅄⊖♣

Dolly Peel

137 Commercial Road, NE33 1SH
✪ 11-11; 12-10.30 Sun
☎ (0191) 427 1441
Black Sheep Best Bitter; Caledonian Deuchars IPA; Courage Directors; Taylor Landlord; guest beers H
Named after a local fishwife whose husband and sons were pressganged into the navy, here you will receive a friendly welcome from the landlord and staff at this local riverside pub. It is quiet during the week but, as a popular part of the circuit with the Mill Dam pubs, it can get busy at weekends. A former CAMRA local Pub of the Year.
✿◐♿⊖(Chichester)P⊔

Lord Ashley

267 Stanhope Road, NE33 4SS
✪ 11-11; 12-10.30 Sun
☎ (0191) 427 1682
Courage Directors; Jarrow Swinging Gibbet, McConnell's Stout; guest beers H
Former working men's club that was part of the

small pub estate of the Federation Brewery. This locals' pub is located on a street corner close to West Park. It has a ground-floor bar area dominated by TV sport and a lounge/function room upstairs. Three cask beers are usually available with at least one from the local Jarrow Brewery. Quiz night is on Sunday.
⊖(Tyne Dock)

Riverside ✔
3 Mill Dam, NE33 1EQ
✪ 12-11; 12-10.30 Sun
☎ (0191) 455 2328
Courage Directors; John Smith's Bitter; Taylor Landlord; guest beers Ⓗ
A splendid place, popular with older drinkers, situated just outside the market square, next to two other pubs where real ale is sold. Particularly lively at weekends, this well-maintained bar keeps an appealing selection of beers including three guests and one real cider. There is a quiz night once a week with free nibbles. Sandwiches are available at lunchtime. Local CAMRA Pub of the Year in 2003.
≠⊖●

Stag's Head
45 Fowler Street, NE33 1NS
✪ 11-11; 12-10.30 Sun
☎ (0191) 427 2911
Draught Bass; Stones Bitter; guest beers (occasional) Ⓗ
Contrary to popular belief, the Stag's Head has been selling real ale for longer than any other pub in the town. Even in the fallow days of the 1970s, the Stag continued to sell real beer. A small yet busy pub, popular with young and old alike, it has had several refurbishments over the years but retains its original character. There is always a warm welcome at this 'holy grail' for those in search of a good pint of Bass. On 'disco' nights there is not enough room to swing a cat.
⩩⊖

Steamboat
51 Coronation Street, Mill Dam, NE33 1EQ
✪ 11-11; 12-10.30 Sun
☎ (0191) 454 0134
Black Sheep Best Bitter; Greene King Abbot, Old Speckled Hen; guest beers Ⓗ
One of the oldest pubs in town, this traditional riverside tavern features nautical memorabilia throughout. On the Mill Dam circuit, it is busy at weekends. The location is handy for a pre- or post-performance drink for visitors to Custom House Theatre. The landlord and staff offer a friendly welcome. ⩩◑⊖♣

Trimmers Arms
34 Commercial Road, NE33 1RW
✪ 11.30-11; 12-10.30 Sun
☎ (0191) 454 5550
website www.trimmers-arms.co.uk
Bateman XXXB; Boddingtons Bitter; Courage Directors; Jarrow Bitter; John Smith's Bitter; Taylor Landlord; guest beers Ⓗ
A trimmer is the person who had to level and tidy up coal after it had been dropped into the holds of a ship – thirsty work. This pub, recently opened, is a conversion from a shop and another pub, and is under the same ownership as the Riverside. The high-ceilinged bar area is decorated with an eclectic collection of bric-a-brac. Swing doors separate the bar from the Lobster Pot restaurant. The small Nelson's Boardroom is available for private functions. Two guest beers from micro-breweries are usually available. Quiz night is Tuesday.
◑♿⊖(Chichester) ●P

Sunderland

Cliff
Mere Knolls Road, SR6 9LG
✪ 11-11; 12-10.30 Sun
☎ (0191) 548 6200
Courage Directors; guest beers Ⓗ
Tucked away in a quiet residential area, the Cliff is conveniently placed near the coastal and park areas of Roker and Seaburn. It has a games area and TV, but the volume is kept at a low level. Monitors on the beer fonts allow TV fans to continue viewing while ordering their beer. Wednesday is quiz night. Courage Directors is supplemented by two guest ales – micro-breweries are usually well represented.
⊖(Stadium of Light)

Fitzgerald's
10-12 Green Terrace, SR1 3PZ
✪ 11-11; 12-10.30 Sun
☎ (0191) 567 0852
Beer range varies Ⓗ
Always bustling, Fitzgerald's appeals to a wide variety of customers. Two bars with a total of 10 handpumps make the pub a year-round mini-beer festival. A supporter of north-east micro-breweries, the pub is probably the best place to find specials from the local Darwin Brewery. One real cider is usually available too. A past CAMRA local Pub of the Year, it was regional winner in 2003. ❀◑≠⊖(University) ●

Ivy House
Worcester Street, SR2 7AW
✪ 11-11; 12-10.30 Sun
☎ (0191) 567 3399
Black Sheep Best Bitter; Darwin Evolution Ale; Taylor Landlord; guest beers Ⓗ
This popular pub is a short walk from Park Lane interchange and worth discovering. Quiet during the day, it can become crowded in the evening with students from the nearby university. Football match days are also busy and the pub can be very smoky. Wednesday is quiz night and live music is performed on Wednesday and Thursday evenings. No food is served Sunday. Regular beers are supplemented by three guests with micro-breweries occasionally represented.
◑≠⊖(Park Lane)

King's Arms ✔
Beach Street, Deptford, SR4 6BU
(near B&Q warehouse)
✪ 11.30-11; 12-10.30 Sun
☎ (0191) 567 9804
Taylor Landlord; guest beers Ⓗ
Unspoilt, traditional pub with a 150-year-old history that is written on the wall next to the fireplace. A free house with an ever-changing range of beers from a variety of suppliers, independent and micro-brewers feature prominently. There are six real ales on at any one time. The pub has two rooms and a garden

with a marquee where live music is played on occasion. With two fires in winter and friendly staff and regulars, the welcome here is always warm. ♔❀⊖(University/Millfield) ♣

Lambton Worm ✔
Victoria Buildings, SR1 3QA
⏲ 10-11; 12-10.30 Sun
☎ (0191) 568 9910
Marston's Burton Bitter; guest beers Ⓗ
Modern Wetherspoon pub opened in 2003, with a friendly, relaxed atmosphere. The large, one-room interior features a sculpture of the Lambton Worm, a mythical dragon. Attractively decorated with low lighting, there is a long bar, raised no-smoking area and a small side room for quieter drinking. A large-screen TV shows sporting events but the volume is not excessive. Up to six cask ales are available, often from local micro-breweries. ◑♿⇌⊖ (University)

Rosedene ✔
Queen Alexandra Road, SR2 9BT
⏲ 11-11; 12-10.30 Sun
☎ (0191) 528 4313
Beer range varies Ⓗ
Large, converted Georgian house with an Edwardian-style drawing room and conservatory overlooking spacious grounds. The restaurant offers a high quality menu and food is also available in the bar. A function room can be hired for private parties. Q❀◑♿P⊬

Saltgrass ✔
Hanover Place, Deptford, SR4 6BY
⏲ 11-11; 12-10.30 Sun
☎ (0191) 565 7229
Black Sheep Best Bitter; Caledonian Deuchars IPA; Draught Bass; guest beers Ⓗ
A haven for the discerning drinker looking for a quiet pint, this is an old fashioned two-room pub with a real fire. The bar is furnished in traditional style and the small, pleasant, no-smoking dining room is decorated with numerous old photos of Deptford. Meals are popular, particularly at the weekend so it is advisable to book. In the summer outside seating is available.
♔❀◑⊟⊖(Millfield) ♠P

Sunniside

Potter's Wheel
Sun Street, NE16 5EE
⏲ 11.30-11; 12-10.30 Sun
☎ (0191) 488 3628
Caledonian Deuchars IPA; guest beers Ⓗ
Part of the Fitzgerald's chain, this spacious village pub has several seating areas served by one main bar. It offers continually rotating guest ales from all parts of the country, with local breweries featuring regularly. Food is available all day. In previous times the building was a nightclub with a star attraction – Mandy Rice-Davies! ◑♿P

Tynemouth

Cumberland Arms ✔
17 Front Street, NE30 4DX
⏲ 12-11; 12-10.30 Sun
☎ (0191) 257 1820
website: www.cumberlandarms.co.uk
Courage Directors; McEwan's 80/-; Theakston Best Bitter; guest beers Ⓗ
Split-level pub with two bars each dispensing six real ales. The dining area is at the rear of the building, serving good value meals (12-8; 12-5 Fri-Sun). One of the guest ales is often a mild. The pub can become busy at weekends when live football matches are shown on the large-screen TV – the manager is a big football fan himself. ◑♿⊖

Tynemouth Lodge Hotel
Tynemouth Road, NE30 4AA
⏲ 11-11; 12-10.30 Sun
☎ (0191) 257 7565
website: www.tynemouthlodgehotel.co.uk
Draught Bass; Belhaven 80/-; Caledonian Deuchars IPA; guest beer Ⓗ
This attractive, externally-tiled free house, built in 1799, has been in every issue of this Guide since 1984 when it was taken over by the present owner, now celebrating 21 years at the pub. The comfortable, single-room lounge bar is noted in the area for always having Scottish real ales on tap, and for selling reputedly the highest volume of Draught Bass on Tyneside. It is next to Northumberland Park and near the Coast-to-Coast cycle route. Q❀⊖P

Wardley

Green
White Mare Pool, NE10 8YB (at A184/B1288 jct)
⏲ 11.30-11; 12-10.30 Sun
☎ (0191) 495 0171
Caledonian Deuchars IPA; Courage Directors; Taylor Landlord; guest beers Ⓗ
Resembling a large bungalow, adjacent to a golf course and near a motorway junction, this Guide regular is an oasis for beer drinkers in an area not noted for the availability of real ale. Well-furnished throughout, it has a plush, Victorian-style public bar (closed during the day) with a large-screen TV, a spacious lounge and a highly-regarded restaurant. The pub holds occasional mini-beer festivals, and weekly sport and general knowledge quizzes. ❀◑⊟♿♣P

Washington

Courtyard ✔
Arts Centre, Biddick Lane, Fatfield, NE38 8AB
⏲ 11-11.30; 12-10.30 Sun
☎ (0191) 417 0445
Taylor Landlord; guest beers Ⓗ
Located within the council-run Arts Centre, this open-plan café-bar has a light, airy feel and a friendly welcome from the bar staff. Four handpumped beers are on offer from various independent and micro-breweries. Food is served during the day and curry night is Friday. In the summer, drinks can be enjoyed outside in the courtyard. Take a look at the local arts and crafts on sale within the centre.
Q❀◐♿♣P⊬

Sir William de Wessyngton ✔
2-3 Victoria Road, Concorde, NE37 2SY
⏲ 10-11; 12-10.30 Sun
☎ (0191) 418 0100
Courage Directors; Greene King Abbot; Shepherd Neame Spitfire; guest beers Ⓗ

A typical Wetherspoon pub with an open-plan layout but divided into several areas, including a dining section. Although it follows the Wetherspoon's philosophy of no loud music or noisy gaming machines, on match days the large-screen TV follows all the live football action. The pub can be busy and crowded at weekends. ☎◐◑♿⚟

Steps

Spout Lane, NE38 7HP

⏲ 11-11; 12-10.30 Sun

☎ (0191) 416 7396

Beer range varies Ⓗ

Part of the John Fitzgerald chain, this is the only pub in Washington village selling real ale. The warm, homely pub has a main bar with a large TV and smaller seated area decorated with old Washington memorabilia. A real ale club meets on Tuesday and quiz night is on Wednesday. Close to Washington Old Hall, the pub serves plenty of American tourists. ◐♣

West Moor

George Stephenson ✔

Great Lime Road, NE12 0NJ

⏲ 12-11; 12-10.30 Sun

☎ (0191) 268 1073

Caledonian Deuchars IPA; McEwan's 80/-; guest beers Ⓗ

Much altered over its 100 years, this extended pub retains two largely separate areas which, when required, can become a single room by opening the dividing doors. Two frequently changing guest beers are served, usually from smaller local breweries. An established music venue, live bands play on Wednesday, Thursday and Saturday evening, plus the occasional Sunday afternoon. Buskers' night is on Tuesday. ❀P⊡

Whitburn

Jolly Sailor

East Street, SR6 7BZ (on A183)

⏲ 11-11; 12-10.30 Sun

☎ (0191) 529 3221

Black Sheep Best Bitter; Courage Directors Ⓗ

Once one of three coaching houses in the village, the Jolly Sailor is the only one that remains. A typical, traditional village pub dating from Victorian times, it is situated on the main road between the two seaside resorts of South Shields and Seaburn. It has a maze of small rooms on the ground floor, where food is available at lunchtime, and an upper function room where meals are served on Thursday-Saturday evenings.

♨❀◐◑⊟

Whitley Bay

Briar Dene

71 The Links, NE26 1UE

⏲ 11-11; 12-10.30

☎ (0191) 252 0926

Beer range varies Ⓗ

Every day is a beer festival at this Fitzgerald's pub, with eight handpumps dispensing constantly-changing beers from all over the country, including many that are not usually available in this area. Once a toll house, it enjoys a well-earned reputation for good quality beer and food (not served Sun eve). The pub is a former Tyneside and Northumberland CAMRA Pub of the Year. The attractively-lit lounge has coloured, leaded glass above the bar and overlooks the links, St Mary's lighthouse and the sea. The smaller rear bar has a TV, pool and darts.

❀◐◑⊟♿▲⊖P⚟

Rockliffe Arms

Algernon Place, NE26 2DT

⏲ 11-11; 12-10.30 Sun

☎ (0191) 253 1299

Beer range varies Ⓗ

A compact Sir John Fitzgerald one-roomed community pub offering old-style drinking in pleasant surroundings. Enter by the snug or the lounge doors attractively decorated with stained glass. The single bar is divided to serve two distinct drinking areas. Regular darts and dominoes nights are popular; Tuesday is quiz night.

❀⊖♣

Crown Posada, Newcastle

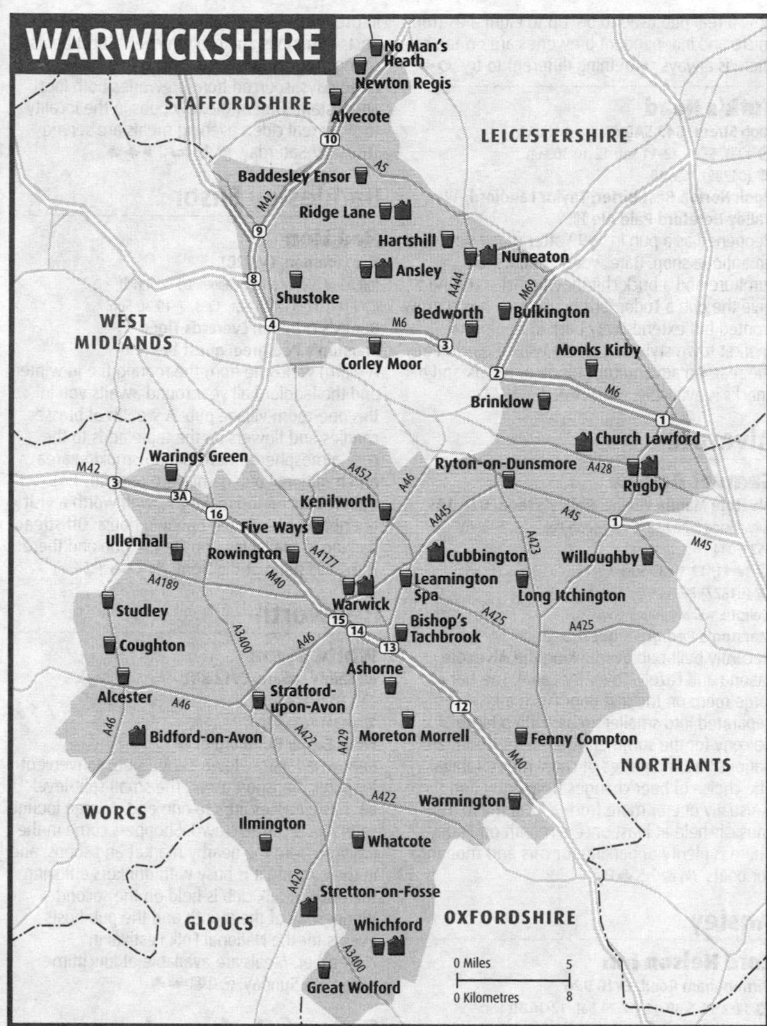

Alcester

Holly Bush

Henley Street, B49 5QX (behind church and town hall)
✪ 12-11; 12-10.30 Sun
☎ (01789) 762482
Black Sheep Best Bitter; Cannon Royall Fruiterer's Mild; Greene King Abbot; Uley Bitter; guest beers Ⓗ
Former hotel hidden behind the town hall and the church in this delightful market town. It boasts five rooms (one no-smoking) plus a function room and walled garden with a barbecue. Eight real ales are always available and beer festivals are held in October and June – the latter as part of the Alcester and Arden Folk Festival. Enjoy the regular music sessions, singarounds and frequent informal music making.

Three Tuns

34 High Street, B49 5AB (next to post office)
✪ 12-11; 12-10.30 Sun
☎ (01789) 762626
Goff's Jouster; Hobsons Best Bitter; guest beers Ⓗ
Do not be fooled by the double-fronted bull's eye windows that make the Tuns look like an antique shop. Inside there are original low beams, flagstone floors and a glass panel in one wall where the wattle and daub construction is revealed. There is no music, no pool and no food at this local CAMRA award-winning pub – just

INDEPENDENT BREWERIES

Church End Ridge Lane
Fantasy Nuneaton
Frankton Bagby Church Lawford
North Cotswold Stretton-on-Fosse
Rugby Rugby
Shakespeares Bidford-on-Avon
Slaughterhouse Warwick
Tunnel Ansley
Walsh's Bakehouse Warwick
Warwickshire Cubbington
Wizard Whichford

how a real pub used to be. Up to eight ales from micro and independent breweries are on tap so there is always something different to try. **Q♣**

Turk's Head

High Street, B49 5AD (near the church)
🕔 12-3, 5-11; 12-11 Sat; 12-10.30 Sun
☎ (01789) 765948
Hook Norton Best Bitter; Taylor Landlord; Wye Valley Hereford Pale Ale Ⓗ
Reopened as a pub in 1999 after many years as an antique shop. Bare wooden floors, old furniture and a brick chimney breast combine to give the pub a Tudor farmhouse feel. It is narrow fronted but extends way back in traditional market town style to a lovely walled garden at the rear. An adventurous range of meals and bar snacks is available. ⛫❀◖◗♿♣

Alvecote

Samuel Barlow

Alvecote Marina Village, Robey's Lane, B78 1AS
(signposted from B5000 Tamworth-Polesworth road)
OS245044
🕔 12-11; 12-10.30 Sun
☎ (01827) 898175
website: www.samuelbarlow.co.uk
Marston's Pedigree; guest beers Ⓗ
Recently built pub overlooking the Alvecote Marina and Fazely-Coventry Canal. The bar is a large room on the first floor (with a lift) separated into smaller areas, with a large balcony for the summer. Around the room are various bits and pieces of canal memorabilia. The choice of beer changes frequently and there is usually one or more from a local micro. Live music is held at least once a month on Friday. There is plenty of parking for cars and moorings for boats. ⛫❀◖♿♣**P**

Ansley

Lord Nelson Inn

Birmingham Road, CV10 9PG
🕔 12-2.30, 5.30-11; 12-11 Sat; 12-10.30 Sun
☎ (024) 7639 2305
Draught Bass; M&B Brew XI; Taylor Landlord; guest beers Ⓗ
Family-run free house with over 30 years' experience. It is the home of the Tunnel Brewery (named after the nearby Ansley Railway Tunnel), a separate, new brewing venture. Decorated throughout with a naval theme, the sloping floors give an authentic feel. Four draught beers are available in the public bar. The pub is also renowned for the food served in its two restaurants. Regular bus services stop outside. ❀◖◗🚌**P**

Ashorne

Cottage Tavern

CV35 9DR (1½ miles from B4100 at Fosse Way island)
OS303577
🕔 12-3 (not Mon or Tue), 5-11; 12-11 Sat; 12-4.30 Sun
☎ (01926) 651410
John Smith's Bitter; guest beers Ⓗ
Friendly, popular village pub with a welcoming atmosphere. A cosy log fire warms the traditional drinking area at one end of the bar; at the other is a no-smoking dining area. When not in use for the great value food, the dining area hosts dominoes and crib matches. Guest beers change regularly, mostly selling out in two or three days, sourced from breweries both local and distant. One of the few pubs in the locality to stock real cider; evening meals are served Thursday-Saturday. ⛫❀🛏◖◗♣●

Baddesley Ensor

Red Lion

The Common, CV9 2BT
(off A5 at Grendon roundabout, up Boot Hill)
🕔 7-11; 12-3, 7-11 Sat; 12-3, 7-10.30 Sun
Banks's Original; Everards Tiger; Marston's Pedigree; guest beers Ⓗ
A warm welcome from the roaring fire in winter and the landlord all year round awaits you in this one-room village pub. A wealth of brasses, candles and flowers on the table adds to the cosy atmosphere. There is a no-smoking area and traditional pub games are popular. Two guest beers on tap make this well worth a visit but note the restricted opening hours. Off street parking is available opposite the pub and there is a small patio at the front. ⛫ **Q♣ P**⊁

Bedworth

White Swan

All Saints Square, CV12 8NL
🕔 11-11; 12-10.30 Sun
☎ (024) 7631 2164
Wells Eagle; Bombardier Ⓗ
Renowned, large, town-centre pub, convenient for public transport users. The small split-level bar has a games area to one end. A large lounge caters for a mixed crowd. Shoppers come in the daytime from the nearby market and shops, and in the evening it is busy with drinkers enjoying the disco. A folk club is held on the second Wednesday of the month and the pub hosts events for the National Folk Festival in November. Meals are available at lunchtime except on Sunday. ❀◖🚌⇌♣

Bishop's Tachbrook

Leopard

Oakley Wood Road, CV33 9RN
(On B4087, near jcts 13 and 14 of M40)
🕔 12-3, 6-11; 12-11 Sat; 12-10.30 Sun
☎ (01926) 426466
Draught Bass; Caledonian Deuchars IPA; Greene King IPA, Abbot; Hook Norton Best Bitter or Old Hooky Ⓗ
Grade II listed building with exposed beams. The bar area, popular with locals, allows smoking but the rest of the pub, which is food oriented, is no-smoking. There is a dining/function room serving high quality food on an extensive menu (no meals Sat lunchtime or Sun eve). The cosy lounge features a large open fireplace hiding the skeleton of the pub's celebrated 'Doris'.
⛫❀◖◗🚌**P**⊁

Brinklow

White Lion Inn

Broad Street, CV23 0LN (main road through village B4027)
🕔 11-3, 5.30-11; 11-11 Fri & Sat; 12-10.30 Sun
☎ (01788) 832579 website: www.thewhitelioninn.co.uk

Banks's Mild; Everards Tiger; Greene King IPA, Abbot, Old Speckled Hen 🄷
Black and white timbered, 17th-century coaching inn with a cosy, traditional interior retaining many original features. The pub is in a quaint village on Fosse Way with a large garden. Skittles, darts and dominoes are popular with locals in the bar and there is a quiet, comfortable lounge and a no-smoking conservatory. Bed and breakfast accommodation is available as well as two self-catering cottages. A beer festival is held on August bank holiday and a folk weekend in July.
⛰❀⇌◐⊟♣P⊁

Bulkington

Olde Chequers Inn

Chequers St, CV12 9NH
12-3.30, 7-11; 12-11 Thu-Sat; 12-10.30 Sun (opening times may vary)
☎ (024) 7631 2182
website: www.oldechequersinn.com
Draught Bass; M&B Brew XI, guest beers 🄷
There is always a friendly welcome in this picturesque village free house with a small, cosy bar which offers two guest beers from local micro-breweries. A well-appointed restaurant serves excellent food from Thursday to Sunday. The popular, community pub runs two football teams and two darts teams. Bus Nos. 56 and 775 stop in the village. ⛰❀◐◑♿♣P

Weavers Arms

12 Long Street, CV12 9JZ (100 yards from Wolvey Rd)
⏲ 12-4, 5-11; 12-11 Fri & Sat; 12-5, 7-10.30 Sun
☎ (024) 7631 4415
Draught Bass; M&B Brew XI, guest beers 🄷
Popular family-run traditional free house, particularly picturesque in the summer with its hanging baskets. The split-level slate floored bar has an open fire giving it a comfortable feel. Leading off the bar is a small wood-panelled games room with a bar billiards table. Darts, crib and dominoes are also played. Lunches are served Wednesday to Saturday. ⛰❀◐⊟♣

Corley Moor

Bull & Butcher ✔

Common Lane, CV7 8AQ (1½ miles from B4098)
⏲ 11-12-30; 12.30-10.30 Sun
☎ (01676) 540241
Draught Bass; Greene King Abbot; M&B Brew XI; guest beer 🄷
Friendly country pub serving traditional English food – try the home-made pies – and ale. Meals, including breakfast, are served every day (all day at the weekend). There is a superb range of dishes available in the snug, which is still occasionally used for cooking. Opposite the range is a fine settle – the ideal place to be on a cold winter's night. ⛰ Q❀◐◑⊟♿P⊁

Coughton

Throckmorton Arms

B49 5HX (on A435, between Studley and Alcester)
⏲ 12-11; 12-10.30 Sun
☎ (01789) 766366
Hook Norton Best Bitter; St Austell Tribute; Wye Valley Butty Bach; guest beers 🄷
Large, roadside hotel with a warm, welcoming atmosphere due to the friendly staff and the real fire. It is situated close to Coughton Court of 'gunpowder plot' fame. The lounge and snug are served from a single bar. The hotel is popular with business people for overnight stops and visitors on weekend breaks. A pleasant no-smoking restaurant is next to a large patio overlooking fields to the west, serving meals (all day Sun) from snacks to full home-cooked meals. ⛰❀⇌◐◑♿P⊁

Fenny Compton

Wharf Inn

Wharf Road, CV47 2FE (on A423 Banbury-Southam road)
⏲ 11-11; 12-10.30 Sun
☎ (01295) 770332
Adnams Broadside; Brakspear Bitter; Wells Bombardier; guest beers 🄷
Recently refurbished canalside pub, popular with drinkers and diners, offering friendly and comfortable surroundings in a modern, trendy interior. The pub is noted for good value meals and regular guest ales. One long room, it has a restaurant at one end and bar at the other. There are also two snugs with comfortable sofas. A campsite is next door and there is plenty of parking space. The large west-facing garden is perfect for watching summer sunsets. ⛰Q❀◐◑⊟♿⛺P

Five Ways

Case is Altered ☆

Case Lane, CV35 7JD
(off Five Ways Road near A4141/A4177 jct) OS225701
⏲ 12-2.30, 6-11; 12-2, 7-10.30 Sun
☎ (01926) 484206
Greene King IPA; Hook Norton Dark, Old Hooky; 🄶 guest beers 🄷
Rural 350-year-old gem with two separate drinking areas. The lounge, with old-style comfy sofas, is only occasionally open at weekends. The regular beers, stillaged behind the bar, are served by unusual antique cask pumps. One guest beer is usually from a Warwickshire brewery. In the bar, look out for relics from long-gone Leamington breweries, the Sopwith Pup aeroplane propeller and a bar billards table which takes old 6d pieces. A quiet pub: mobile phones, computers, dogs and children are barred. There are two courtyards for outdoor drinking. ⛰Q❀♿P

Great Wolford

Fox & Hounds

CV36 5NQ (on road to Moreton-in-Marsh)
⏲ 12-2.30, 6-11; closed Mon; 12-2.30, 7.30-10.30 Sun
☎ (01608) 674220
website: www.thefoxandhoundsinn.com
Hook Norton Best Bitter; Taylor Landlord; guest beers
Ancient, unspoilt stone-built village inn which has been trading since 1540. It is set back from the road around a central courtyard. Inside, the main bar is stone-flagged with an inglenook open fire and high backed settles. The ceiling is decorated with garlands of hops. As well as interesting guest beers there is a selection of 200 malt whiskies available. Diners can enjoy

modern British cuisine with local produce. There is something for everyone from a bar menu to traditional Sunday lunch as well as blackboard specials. ⩩❀🛏◖◗♿▲♣P

Hartshill

Stag & Pheasant

The Green, CV10 0SW

⏲ 12 (3 Mon-Wed)-11; 12-10.30 Sun

☎ (024) 7639 3173

Draught Bass; Flowers Original; Marston's Pedigree; guest beer Ⓗ

Two-roomed pub overlooking the village green, ideally situated for walkers using the nearby Hartshill Hayes Park and canal users. The guest beer is always from Church End Brewery. Traditional Sunday lunch is served, and bar meals on Friday and Saturday afternoons. Monday is curry night and Chinese food is featured the rest of the week. A summer beer festival is held every June. Bus Nos. 48 and 776 stop outside.

❀◖◗⊟♣ P

Ilmington

Howard Arms ✔

Lower Green, CV36 4LT

⏲ 11-2.30 (3 Fri & Sat), 6-11; 12-3.30, 6-10.30 Sun

☎ (01608) 682226 website: www.howardarms.com

Everards Tiger; North Cotswold Genesis; guest beers Ⓗ

Rambling, mellow, stone inn built over 400 years ago in an idyllic setting on the green of this lovely Cotswold village. It is now no-smoking throughout. It has won several awards for its cuisine and, with three very individual guest bedrooms, it is an ideal base for walking or touring the Cotswolds and Shakespeare country. Both regular beers are quite unusual for the area. ⩩Q❀🛏◖◗▲♣ P⊬

Kenilworth

Old Bakery Hotel

12 High Street, CV8 1LZ (near A429/A452 jct)

⏲ 5-11; 12-2, 5-11 Sat; 12-2, 7-10.30 Sun

☎ (01926) 864111

website: www.theoldbakeryhotel.co.uk

Black Sheep Best Bitter; Hook Norton Best Bitter; Taylor Landlord Ⓗ

Situated in the heart of old Kenilworth, this is the perfect place for a pint after a walk round Abbey Fields or the castle ruins. The hotel was restored from an old bakery and the bar divided into two areas, welcoming residents and visitors alike. The open-plan main area is free from fruit machines, music and TV so friendly conversation dominates. There is a small rear patio with seating around a well. Disabled access is from the rear car park. Q❀🛏♿P

Virgins & Castle

7 High Street, CV8 1LY (at A429/A452 jct)

⏲ 11-11; 11-10.30 Sun

☎ (01926) 853737

Adnams Bitter; Wadworth 6X; Wells Bombardier; Young's Bitter Ⓗ

Medieval pub reputed to be known in the 1500s as the Two Virgins Inn until its merger with the Castle Tavern. The pub has low, exposed beams and a bar that serves the lounge and three snugs. A converted courtyard houses an adjacent bar popular with diners. The menu offers traditional dishes but the more adventurous may be tempted by Filipino or Japanese cuisine including sushi. There is limited parking in the High Street. ⩩Q❀◖◗⊬

Leamington Spa

Bowling Green ✔

18-20 New Street, CV31 1HP

⏲ 12-11; 12-10.30 Sun

☎ (07816) 907398

Black Sheep Best Bitter; Caledonian Deuchars IPA; M&B Brew XI; guest beers Ⓗ

Traditional, small, welcoming local pub, well worth the effort to find down a back street south of the River Leam and north of Radford Road. Comfortable and friendly, it is popular, especially with students. A varied clientele supports the crib and darts teams and a regular Sunday evening quiz. The prize-winning garden is a suntrap in the summer. Scottish breweries feature regularly on the guest beer list.

❀⊟⇌♣

Somerville Arms

4 Campion Terrace, CV32 4SX (off Leicester St)

⏲ 5.30 (12 Sat)-11pm; 12-10.30 Sun

☎ (01926) 426746

Adnams Broadside; Fuller's London Pride; Greene King IPA, Abbot, Old Speckled Hen; M&B Mild Ⓗ

Friendly Victorian local with a busy bar at the front and small cosy lounge at the rear. 'Real ale for your health' and 'Abound in hops all ye who enter here' are prominently displayed drinking mottos. First opened in 1868, the pub is named after a local magistrate. At one time there was a glass canopy at the front, which explains why the pub is set back from the other buildings in the street. Impromptu music sessions are held every other Wednesday evening. Q❀⊟♿♣

Long Itchington

Harvester Inn

6 Church Road, CV47 9PG

(off A423 at village pond, then first left)

⏲ 11-3, 6-11; 12-3, 7-10.30 Sun

☎ (01926) 812698 website: www.theharvesterinn.co.uk

Hook Norton Best Bitter, Old Hooky; guest beers Ⓗ

Traditional village pub making its 21st consecutive entry in this Guide. Originally two 19th-century cottages, it became a free house in 1976. The present owners took over in 1984 and have built a reputation for good quality and value home-cooked food. There is a main L-shaped bar with a small games room and a restaurant. Booking is advised for Sunday lunches.

❀◖◗⊟♿▲♣P

Monks Kirby

Denbigh Arms

Main Street, CV23 0QX (opp church)

⏲ 12-3 (not Mon), 6.30-11; 12-3, 6.30-10.30 Sun (opens all day summer Sat & Sun)

☎ (01788) 832303

ENGLAND

Caledonian Deuchars IPA; Greene King Abbot; Taylor Landlord; Theakston XB; guest beer Ⓗ
Beautiful, unspoilt, traditional village inn dating back to the 17th century, standing opposite the second largest church in Warwickshire. The central bar serves all the linked rooms, and there is a no-smoking snug. An extensive range of meals is served. Outside there is seating on the front and rear lawns and a children's play area. ⌂Q❀ⒹⒹ♣P⊬

Moreton Morrell

Black Horse

CV35 9AR (near Fosse Way and M40 jct 12)
✪ 11.30-3, 7-11; 12-3, 7-10.30 Sun
☎ (01926) 651231
Hook Norton Best Bitter; guest beer Ⓗ
Village pub set in a time warp from the 1960s. Wooden settles are arranged around the walls of the cosy bar. Artefacts in the room belonged to the landlord's mother and have never been moved. Music on the juke box is mostly from the Beatles era. There is a popular pool table. The guest beer is usually from a small independent brewery. In summer the peaceful rear garden overlooking the countryside is a lovely spot to enjoy a pint. Q❀⊟▲

Newton Regis

Queen's Head

Main Road, B79 0NF
✪ 11-2.30, 6-11; 12-3, 6.30-10.30 Sun
☎ (01827) 830271
Draught Bass; guest beers Ⓗ
Dating from the 16th century, this two-roomed village local with oak beams and open fires has attractive gardens to the front and rear. Guest beers are changed every 10 days or so. Traditional pub games are popular and there is a quiz night every other Monday. The pub has a well-deserved reputation for value-for-money, good food, but bookings are not taken so go early as it can be busy at times. ⌂❀ⒹⒹ♣P

No Man's Heath

Four Counties

Ashby Road, B79 0PB (on B5493, near M42 jct 11)
✪ 11.30-3, 6.30-11; 12-3, 7-10.30 Sun
☎ (01827) 830243
Banks's Original; Everards Original; Marston's Pedigree; guest beers Ⓗ
Rumoured to once have been a highwayman's retreat, this free house is situated where four counties meet. Nowadays it is in Warwickshire, just. The charming landlady and her husband provide a warm welcome to all. Notices on the doors advise disabled customers to call the bar where staff will be most happy to help. The guest beer is almost always from a micro-brewery. A no-smoking room adjoins the bar. ⌂Q☺❀ⒹⒹ♿♣P⊬

Nuneaton

Lloyds

10 Bond Street, CV11 4BX
✪ 11-11; 12-3, 7-10.30 Sun
☎ (024) 7637 3343
Beer range varies Ⓗ
Well placed for both town centre and railway station, Lloyds is the home of the Fantasy Brewery. On entering the split-level bar you are greeted by the welcoming sight of 10 handpulls including Fantasy brews. The walls make good reading, decorated with many pump clips from beers that have been served in the past. Regular beer festivals are held throughout the year. ⒹⒹ⇌

Ridge Lane

Church End Brewery Tap

109 Ridge Lane, CV10 0RD
(2 miles SW of Atherstone) OS295947
✪ 6 (12 Fri & Sat)-11; 12-10.30 Sun
☎ (01827) 713080
Beer range varies Ⓗ/Ⓖ
Converted from a working men's club, the brewery is visible from the bar of this popular tap. Four handpulled beers are served, some straight from the cask, plus traditional cider. The no-smoking pub has been awarded a silver certificate in the National Clean Air Award scheme. A large meadow-style garden offers alfresco drinking at all times. Hidden behind houses, look for the sandwich board opposite the unmarked drive. Lunches are served on Friday and Saturday at CAMRA Warwickshire Pub of the Year 2004. Q❀Ⓓ♣●P⊬

Rowington

Cock Horse

Old Warwick Road, CV35 7AA
(on B4439 S of Rowington)
✪ 12-11; 12-10.30 Sun
☎ (01926) 842183
Adnams Broadside; Fuller's London Pride; Hook Norton Best Bitter; guest beer Ⓗ
Situated just south of Rowington, this 300-year-old traditional inn offers a good choice of ales and food. The pub has a single oak-beamed bar and an intimate restaurant. There is a regular beer festival on August bank holiday weekend, live music on Friday evening, and a monthly folk club. Voted local CAMRA Most Improved Pub of the Year 2003, this is a popular local with a warm welcome for visitors.
⌂❀ⒹⒹ●P

Rugby

Alexander Arms

James Street, CV21 2SL (next to multi-storey car park)
✪ 11.30-3, 5-11; 11-11 Fri & Sat; 12-10.30 Sun
☎ (01788) 578660
website: www.alexandraarms.co.uk
Fuller's London Pride; Greene King IPA, Abbot; guest beers Ⓗ
Awarded Rugby CAMRA Pub of the Year in 2004 for the sixth time. The L-shaped lounge is a comfortable place where lively debate flourishes among the locals. The games room is a favourite with rock fans attracted by the well-stocked juke box. Skittles and bar billiards are also played. The garden serves as a venue for summer beer festivals with both open and covered seating. Guest beers include milds, stouts and porters from a wide range of breweries. Addlestones cider is available too. No food is served Sunday evening. Q❀ⒹⒹ♿⇌♣●

Merchant's Inn
5-7 Little Church Street, CV21 3AW
⏲ 12-11 (midnight Tue; 1am Fri & Sat); 12-10.30 Sun
☎ (01788) 571119
website: www.merchantsinn.co.uk
B&T Shefford Bitter; Everards Tiger; quest beers 🄷
Warwickshire CAMRA 2003 Pub of the Year, this well-established ale house has a warm, cosy atmosphere, wooden seating and comfortable sofas, flagstone floors and an abundance of brewery memorabilia. The pub stocks two regular beers, six guest ales and a superb selection of Belgian beers, cider, wines and malt whiskies. Home-cooked food is served every lunchtime. On Tuesday evening the pub becomes a popular live music venue. Actively involved with the Brewery History Society, the pub hosts regular beer festivals.
◖♿≋♣ ●P⊬

Raglan Arms
50 Dunchurch Road, CV22 6AD
⏲ 5-11; 11.30-3.30, 7-11 Sat; 12-3.30, 7-10.30 Sun
☎ (01788) 544441
Ansells Mild, Best Bitter; Fuller's London Pride; Greene King Abbot; Marston's Pedigree; guest beers 🄷
Small, friendly local near Rugby School run by an ex-England rugby player. This regular Guide entry serves one of the best beer ranges in town and is one of the very few still to stock mild. The pub runs darts, dominoes, crib, football and hockey teams. Folk evenings are staged monthly, and impromptu quiz nights every now and again. At the back of the pub are a few bench tables for outdoor drinking.
❀⊟♣P

Victoria
1 Lower Hillmorton Road, CV21 3ST
⏲ 12-2.30, 6 (5.30 Fri)-11; 1-11 Sat; 12-4, 7-10.30 Sun
☎ (01788) 544374
Greene King IPA; guest beers 🄷
Traditional street-corner local on the edge of town. The basic public bar area has a pool table, dartboard and TV. Excellent lunches are served in the Victorian-style comfy lounge. Good value guest beers are sourced from anywhere and everywhere. A jazz night is held on Monday in the lounge and a quiz on Wednesday.
◖⊟≋♣

Ryton-on-Dunsmore

Old Bull & Butcher
Oxford Road, CV8 3EP
(on A423, 1½ miles SE of Peugeot factory)
⏲ 12-2.30 (not winter Mon or Tue), 5-11 (11-11 summer Sat); 12-10.30 Sun
☎ (024) 7630 1400
Highgate Dark; guest beers 🄷
Large, country free house, a former farmhouse, with two rooms. The wood and tile-floored front bar has an open fire and the lounge leads to an adjoining conservatory which is no-smoking. The spacious garden has children's play equipment; baby changing facilities and high chairs are provided. Nearby are Ryton Pools Country Park and Ryton Organic Gardens.
♨❀◖◗⊟♿ P⊬

Shustoke

Griffin Inn
Church Road, B46 2LB (on B4114)
⏲ 12-2.30, 7-11; 12-3, 7-10.30 Sun
☎ (01675) 481205
Banks's Original; Marston's Pedigree; RCH Pitchfork; Theakston Old Peculier; guest beers 🄷
Local CAMRA Pub of the Year for several years, the Griffin is one of the few unspoilt rural pubs remaining unchanged. Set in the Warwickshire countryside, it has fine views from the garden, a spacious conservatory where families are welcome and three open fires. Lunches are served from Monday to Saturday. Alongside the four regular beers are six guests. Real cider is available in summer. Attracting locals and visitors from near and far, this is one pub not to be missed. ♨Q♉❀◖▲ ● P

Stratford-upon-Avon

Garrick ✔
25 High Street, CV37 6AU
⏲ 11-11; 12-10.30 Sun
☎ (01789) 292186
Flowers Original; Greene King Abbot; guest beer 🄷
One of the oldest buildings in town, this traditional black and white pub dates back to the early 1400s. An inn since 1718, original timber beams and old wood are found throughout. The small, cosy, oak-panelled front bar has bottle glass windows. Food is served throughout the day. The pub is completely no-smoking. ♉◖◗⊟≋⊬

Studley

Little Lark
108 Alcester Road, B80 7NP
(on A435/Tom's Town Lane jct)
⏲ 12-3, 6-11; 12-11 Sat; 12-3, 6.30-10.30 Sun
☎ (01527) 853105
Ansells Mild; Ushers Best Bitter; Wadworth 6X; guest beers 🄷
Popular village local with three drinking areas served by a central bar. The pub's interior has a newspaper theme, with framed front pages adorning the walls. Good quality, reasonably-priced meals, cooked by the landlord, are served – try the cow pie. Traditional country wines and a selection of single malt whiskies are available. The pub hosts two beer festivals and cheese festivals every year. Q❀◖◗♣

Ullenhall

Winged Spur
Main Street, B95 5PA
⏲ 12-11; 12-10.30 Sun
☎ (01564) 792005
Flowers IPA; guest beers 🄷
Unassuming, traditional pub in a quiet village. The name comes from the spur on the crest of the Knight family, who were associated with Ullenhall from 1554. The single open-plan room is split into different areas. The outdoor seating area overlooks the car park and is not very inviting. Up to three guest beers are stocked at local CAMRA's Most Improved Pub 2004. Dogs are allowed in the pub if on a lead. No food is served on Sunday evening. ♨❀ ◖◗●P

Warings Green

Blue Bell Cider House

Warings Green Road, B94 6BP

(S of Cheswick Green – off Ilshaw Heath Rd) OS129742

⏲ 11-11; 12-10.30 Sun

☎ (01564) 702328

Caledonian Deuchars IPA; guest beers [H]

Friendly canalside free house offering two or three real ales and five draught ciders, including a house special from Westons. Eight temporary moorings make it popular with boaters, and walking, cycling and fishing parties are catered for. Both the large lounge and cosy bar have real fires during winter. Reasonably-priced food includes a children's menu and vegetarian options. Regular quiz nights and occasional live music are hosted. Some locals remember when a former landlady used to brew her own beer.

♨Q ☈❀◑◗ ⊟♿♣● P⚡

Warmington

Plough Inn

Church Hill, OX17 1BX

(off B4100 between Gaydon and Banbury)

⏲ 12-3, 6-11; 12-10.30 (9 winter) Sun

☎ (01295) 690666

Beer range varies [H]

A genuine free house, this red ironstone pub, in a village on the Edgehill Escarpment, dates from the Civil War. It is a real gem with a warm and welcoming atmosphere, low ceilings, and heated in winter by an open copper-hooded fire. The beer range includes five guest beers and the food is good value and tasty (no evening meals served Sun or Mon). The pub is popular with locals, ramblers and cyclists. The village boasts a fine 'sloping' duckpond. The pub motto is 'Goode Olde Menu, Goode Olde Real Ales and Goode Olde-fashioned pub.'

♨Q❀◑◗P

Warwick

Cape of Good Hope

66 Lower Cape, CV34 5DP

⏲ 12-11; 12-10.30 Sun

☎ (01926) 498138

website: www.capeofgoodhope.co.uk

Greene King IPA, Abbot; Tetley Bitter; Walsh's Bakehouse Two LLocks; [H] **Weatheroak Keystone Hops;** [G] **guest beers** [H]

Friendly canalside pub, adjacent to Cape top lock on the Grand Union Canal. There are two bars: a traditional public bar and a lounge. Good value food is served and live music is regularly hosted. It is the nearest pub to Walsh's Bakehouse Brewery and Two LLocks, named after the two locks between the pub and brewery, was voted Beer of the Festival at Harbury in 2004. The pub also won local CAMRA Pub of the Year award in 2004.

❀◑◗⊟♣P

Old Fourpenny Shop

27-29 Crompton Street, CV34 6HJ

(near racecourse, between A429 and A4189)

⏲ 12-2.30 (3 Sat), 5.30-11; 12-11 Fri; 12-3, 6-10.30 Sun

☎ (01926) 491360

website: www.fourpennyshophotel.co.uk

RCH Pitchfork; guest beers [H]

One-time racing inn and stables, this fine Georgian pub was a favourite for the navvies building the Warwick canals. A coffee and tot of rum was sold for four old pennies – hence the name. Today the pub is famous for its ever-changing range of guest beers, prominently displayed on the blackboard behind the bar. Diners can enjoy good quality food served in the restaurant (eve meals Tue-Sat). Some of the accommodation is converted from the old stables at the back. Q⇌◑◗P⚡

Whatcote

Royal Oak

CV36 5EF

⏲ 12-2 (not Mon), 5.30-11; 12-10.30 Sun

☎ (01295) 680319

Hook Norton Hooky Dark, Best Bitter, Old Hooky; guest beer [H]

Dating back to 1168, this is one of the oldest pubs in the country and was originally built to serve workers constructing the local church. Inside the chimney are large rungs leading to a hideaway. In 1642 Cromwell and his officers had temporary lodgings and reputedly sojourned to the Royal Oak after the battle of Edgehill to slake their thirsts and fill their bellies. A cosy bar and a warm welcome still await visitors today. Special food evenings are a regular feature. Although off the beaten track, this is definitely a pub worth finding. ♨❀◑◗ ⊟♿P⚡

Whichford

Norman Knight

CV36 5PE

⏲ 12-2.30 (not Mon), 7-11; 12-2.30, 7-10.30 Sun

☎ (01608) 684621

website: www.thenormanknight.co.uk

Wizard Apprentice, One for the Toad; seasonal beers [H]

Overlooking the extensive village green, this traditional pub boasts exposed beams and flagged floors. It is named after Sir John de Mohun, a medieval garter knight who is buried in the nearby church. Wizard Brewery set up here in 2003 and at least two of its beers are always available. The pub has two holiday cottages and a touring caravan site. Lunches are available from Wednesday to Sunday and evening meals on Friday and Saturday. Unusual pub games, including Aunt Sally, are played here. ♨❀◑◗ ⛺♣P

Willoughby

Rose Inn

Main Street, CV23 8BH (600 yds from A45)

⏲ 12-2.30, 6.30-11; closed Mon; 12-3, 7.30-10.30 Sun

☎ (01788) 891464

Greene King Abbot; Flower's Original; Black Sheep Best Bitter; guest beers [H]

Reopened in 2004 after refurbishment, this picturesque 16th-century part-thatched country local has an attractive interior with a tiled floor, wood surroundings and two wood-burning stoves. There are three big rooms including a restaurant for drinking and dining. Meals range from bar snacks to a Sunday carvery. Cheese skittles is played.

♨❀◑◗♿♣P⚡

WEST MIDLANDS

Amblecote

Swan

10 Brettel Lane, DY8 4BN (on A461, ⅓ mile from A491 jct)

12-2.30 (not Tue-Thu), 7-11; 12-11 Sat; 12-3, 7-10.30 Sun

☎ (01384) 76932

Beer range varies Ⓗ

This friendly, two-roomed pub has a comfortable lounge and a basic public bar where traditional pub games are played. Regular raffles are held for local charities and the air ambulance service. The garden is a delightful sun-trap and provides an ideal fair weather setting for sampling the ever-changing three real ales on offer. ❀⊟♣

Balsall Common

Railway

547 Station Road, Berkswell, CV7 7EF

12-11; 7-10.30 Sun

☎ (01676) 533284

Adnams Broadside; Draught Bass; Taylor Landlord Ⓗ

One-roomed pub, formerly railway workers' cottages owned by the London and Birmingham Railway, dating from 1846. Divided into two sections, one part is the comfortable Lords, the other, called Commons, houses a pool table and dartboard that attract a young crowd. The pub hosts regular karaoke nights and occasional live music. Lunches are served Monday-Saturday. ⋒❀ᑕ⇌♣P

Barston

Bull's Head ✔

Barston Lane, B92 0JU

11-2.30, 5-11; 11-11 Sat; 12-10.30 Sun

☎ (01675) 442830

Adnams Bitter; M&B Brew XI; guest beer Ⓗ

Genuine village local, in part dating back to 1490. Split into three rooms, all beamed, the two bars feature real fires and horse racing memorabilia; the restaurant is in the oldest part of the building. The pub has featured in this Guide for 13 consecutive years, also winning the local CAMRA Pub of the Year award three times. It offers a choice of high quality food with a regularly-changing menu; no food is served on Sunday evening. ⋒Q❀ᑕᑐ♣P

Bilston

Olde White Rose

20 Lichfield Street, WV14 0AG

12-11; 12-10.30 Sun

☎ (01902) 498339

Beer range varies Ⓗ

Wolverhampton CAMRA's City Pub of the Year 2005 is handy for bus and metro stations. It offers up to 12 real ales, a wide variety of foreign beers, plus Westons cider and perry. Many improvements have been made, including a conservatory, conference room, bierkeller (hosting live folk music Thu eve) and a play area where children are welcome until 9pm. In

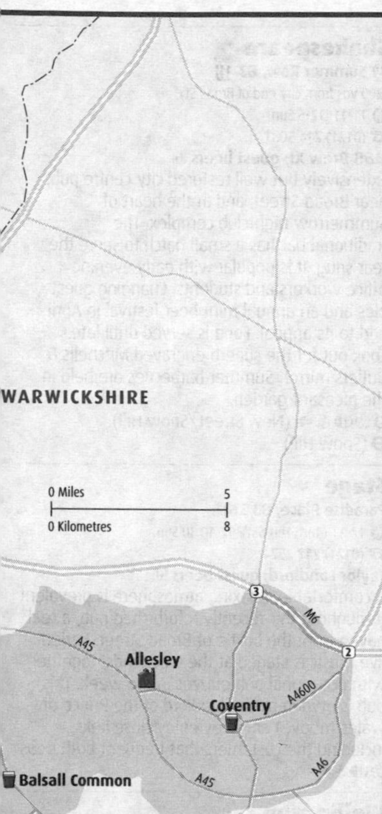

addition to the menu served 12-9pm, a carvery is offered lunchtime and evening (12-5pm Sun). ❀◑♿⊖(Bilston Central) 🍎

Trumpet
58 High Street, WV14 0EP
⏲ 11-3, 7.30-11; 12-3, 7.30-10.30 Sun
☎ (01902) 493723 website: www.trumpetjazz.org
Holden's Mild, Bitter, Golden Glow, Special; guest beer Ⓗ
This well-known pub started life as the Royal Exchange. Its name was changed to the Trumpet to reflect its popularity as a jazz venue. A different style of jazz is showcased here every evening and Sunday lunchtime. Entry is free, but a collection plate is passed around. The walls and ceiling are covered in jazz memorabilia. Both the bus and metro station are only minutes away. ⊖(Bilston Central)

Birmingham: Balsall Heath

Old Moseley Arms ✔
Tindal Street, B12 9QU
⏲ 12-11; 12-10.30 Sun
☎ (0121) 440 1954
Enville Ale; Greene King Abbot; guest beer Ⓗ
Back-street pub, set on the end of a terrace surrounded by the local play area. Live music is staged every Sunday upstairs in the pool room. Most Tuesdays and Thursdays are curry nights. The pub fields one cricket team and is regularly visited by a second. A community pub with a loyal following, it is 10 minutes' from Edgbaston cricket ground. ❀⊟

Birmingham: Billesley

Covered Wagon
298 Yardley Wood Road, B13 9UW
(¼ mile S of B4217)
⏲ 12 (11 Sat)-11; 12-10.30 Sun
☎ (0121) 442 0911
Caledonian Deuchars IPA; M&B Mild, Brew XI; Marston's Pedigree; guest beers Ⓗ
Typical Ember Inns house in its decor and furniture: the spacious open-plan pub is served from a single bar. It has a patio area at the front, with plenty of parking at the front and rear. A quiz is held on Monday and Wednesday evenings. Music is played throughout the pub, but is not intrusive. Guest beers are taken from the pub's guest of honour list. Beer festivals are held in line with the chain's policy.
◑♿P⚡

Birmingham: City Centre

Bull
1 Price Street, B4 6JU (off St Chads Queensway)
⏲ 12-1am; closed Sun
☎ (0121) 333 6757
Adnams Broadside; Ansells Mild; Marston's Pedigree; guest beer Ⓗ
Friendly, unspoilt, back-street local near Aston University and the hospital. Two main rooms share a bar in the middle. A smaller, quieter room is at the rear. One cannot miss the extensive collections of plates, cups and water jugs alongside old photographs of Birmingham. The guest beer changes frequently at one of the oldest pubs in Birmingham; note the etched Ansells Ales windows. A wheelchair WC is provided.
Q❀⇄◑♿⇌(Snow Hill) ⊖♣▯

Corner House ✔
29a Newhall Street, B3 3PU
⏲ 12-11; 12-10.30 Sun
☎ (0121) 200 2423
Beer range varies Ⓗ
Formerly known as the Hogshead and renamed the Corner House, this pub continues to serve beer from a wide range of regional brewers including Caledonian, Enville and Greene King. The pub is frequented by office workers at lunchtime/early evening and by students during term-time. All enjoy the relaxed, comfortable atmosphere with unobtrusive music played most weekdays. The pool table sees a lot of action.
◑♿⇌(Snow Hill/New St) ⊖(Snow Hill) ⚡

INDEPENDENT BREWERIES
Banks's Wolverhampton
Batham Brierley Hill
Black Country Lower Gornal
Highgate Walsall
Holden's Woodsetton
Sarah Hughes Sedgley
Olde Swan Netherton
Rainbow Allesley
Toll End Tipton
Windsor Castle Lye

Old Fox

54 Hurst Street, B5 4TD
11.30-1am (2am Thu-Sat); 12-midnight Sun
(0121) 622 5080
Everards Tiger; Greene King Old Speckled Hen; Marston's Pedigree; Tetley Bitter; guest beers Ⓗ
Situated opposite the Hippodrome Theatre, the Old Fox is popular with theatregoers in the evening. The central bar serves the bar and lounge, which are connected by an open doorway. The walls are decorated with photographs of the stars, including Charlie Chaplin, who reputedly drank here. On the edge of the Chinese quarter, it is also close to the recently restored Victorian back-to-back houses in Inge Street. Meals are served 12-8pm.
(New St)

Old Joint Stock

4 Temple Row West, B2 5NY (opp. St. Philip's Cathedral)
11 (12 Mon)-11; closed Sun
(0121) 200 1892
Fuller's Chiswick, London Pride, ESB, seasonal beers Ⓗ
Grade II listed building, formerly the Joint Stock Bank, bearing an impressive illuminated façade. The interior mixes Victorian gothic and classical styles with Roman statuettes, colonnades and a cupola, set around an island bar. Its three rooms and upper level have been recently refurbished. Food is served 12-8pm. It stocks an ever-changing range of Beowulf beers and hosts quarterly beer festivals and themed celebrations.
(New St/Snow Hill) (Snow Hill)

Old Royal

53 Church Street, B3 2DP (off Colmore Row)
12-11; 12-10.30 Sun
(0121) 200 3841
Fuller's London Pride; guest beer Ⓗ
Sympathetically refurbished, 150-year-old pub, retaining old stained glass windows and other features. The busy single bar is popular with city-centre workers at lunchtime and early evening. On-street car parking is possible. An excellent, large upstairs function room (available for hire) doubles as a restaurant at lunchtime; food is served 12-8 weekdays and 12-6 on Saturday. A large-screen TV is provided.
(New St/Snow Hill) (Snow Hill)

Prince of Wales

84 Cambridge Street, B1 2NP (behind international convention centre)
11-11; 12-10.30 Sun
(0121) 643 9460
Adnams Broadside; Banks's Bitter; Greene King Abbot; Taylor Landlord; Wells Bombardier; guest beers Ⓗ
The Prince of Wales makes a welcome return to this Guide after an absence in 2005 due to a change of landlord. The new host is as committed to real ale as his predecessor. This intimate, wooden-floored, one-bar pub stands just behind Broad Street, surrounded by modern buildings. Up to eight real ales can be found on sale, making it popular with cask beer enthusiasts throughout Brum. Live music is performed most Sundays, when it can become crowded.
Q (New St/Snow Hill) (Snow Hill)

Shakespeare

31 Summer Row, B3 1JJ
(200 yds from city end of Broad St)
11-11; 12-6 Sun
(0121) 214 5081
M&B Brew XI; guest beers Ⓗ
Extensively but well restored city-centre pub, near Broad Street, and at the heart of Summerrow nightclub complex. The traditional bar has a small hatch to serve the rear snug. It is popular with early evening office workers and students. Changing guest ales and an annual mini-beer festival in April add to its appeal. Food is served until late. Look out for the superb engraved Mitchells & Butlers mirror. Summer barbecues are held in the pleasant garden.
Q (New Street/Snow Hill)
(Snow Hill)

Stage

Paradise Place, B3 3HJ
12-11 (1am Thu-Sat); 12-10.30 Sun
(0121) 212 2524
Taylor Landlord; guest beers Ⓗ
A comfortable, relaxing atmosphere is prevalent throughout this recently refurbished pub, a real haven from the bustle of Broad Street. Varied live music is staged at the weekends, together with occasional pub quizzes in the week. This pub is owned by the landlord of the Prince of Wales (above) and they enjoy close links, including the customers that frequent both pubs.

Wellington

37 Bennetts Hill, B2 5SN
10-11; 12-10.30 Sun
(0121) 200 3115
Black Country Bradley's Finest Golden, Pig on the Wall, Fireside; guest beers Ⓗ
Birmingham's newest real ale pub has proved phenomenally popular with beer drinkers. It consistently sells 50 different guest ales a week, supplementing the three regulars from the new West Midlands brewery, Black Country Ales. No meals are served, however you can bring your own food. Cider is stocked from Saxon. It is five minutes' walk from both New Street and Snow Hill railway stations.
(New St/Snow Hill)

Birmingham: Digbeth

Anchor ☆

308 Bradford Street, B5 6ET
11-11; 12-10.30 Sun
(0121) 622 4516 website: www.the-anchor-inn.fsnet.co.uk
Ansells Mild; Tetley Bitter; guest beers Ⓗ
Grade II listed, four-roomed Victorian pub, built by James and Lister Lea (famous for several Birmingham pubs), next to Digbeth coach station. The latest room to have been opened is a no-smoking room free from music or fruit machines. The pub's range of cask ales has helped it win local CAMRA's Pub of the Year award three times. It stocks a selection of foreign bottled and draught beers, plus Cheddar Valley cider. Evening meals finish at 8pm.
Q (New St/Moor St)

Horans Tavern

92 Floodgate Street, B5 5SR
11-11; 12-3 (closed eve) Sun
(0121) 643 3851
Ansells Mild; Taylor Landlord; guest beer Ⓗ
This traditional street-corner pub is situated on the edge of Birmingham's Irish quarter, and is frequented by the Irish community and workers from the many local light industries in this area. There are two rooms: a basic bar and a comfortable lounge with a small alcove for diners – hot meals are served at lunchtime, bar snacks in the evening.
Q (New St/Moor St) ♣

White Swan ☆

276 Bradford Street, B12 0QY
11-2, 4-11; 11-11 Fri & Sat; 12-10.30 Sun
(0121) 622 2586
Banks's Original, Bitter; Marston's Burton Bitter, Pedigree Ⓗ
The CAMRA National Inventory listed White Swan was built by famous architects James and Lister Lea who were also responsible for the Anchor, Woodman and the Bartons. The Irish Centre is located just minutes away and the pub is lively when Ireland are on TV or Birmingham City are at home. The large-screen TV sits in the bar, but there is a small lounge at the rear if you are not a fan.
(Moor St)

Birmingham: Edgbaston

MAC (Midlands Arts Centre)

Cannon Hill Park, B12 9QH (opp. Edgbaston cricket ground)
12-11; 12-10.30 Sun
(0121) 440 4221 website: www.macarts.org.uk
Beer range varies Ⓗ
Bar area inside a mixed-use arts centre, with theatre, cinema and displays; the bar walls are employed as gallery space. Next to Cannon Hill Park's boating lakes and acres of managed parkland, it is particularly suitable for families. The courtyard stages live music and barbecues in summer. Pizzas are served, and a café in the centre opens during the day. It has good disabled access. Two beers are picked from a list of around five.
Q P

Birmingham: Five Ways

City Tavern

38 Bishopsgate Street, B15 1EJ (next to cinema)
11-11; 12-10.30 Sun
(0121) 643 8467
Highgate Dark, Special Bitter, Davenports Bitter, Saddlers; guest beer Ⓗ
Rare Highgate outlet in Birmingham, this welcoming pub off busy Broad Street is a fine example of a friendly community pub. Missed out by the circuit drinkers, it is frequented by local residents and city-centre workers and can get busy at lunchtime and early evening. The pub was rescued by Highgate Brewery after a lengthy period of closure, when some of the bar fittings were stolen. It is handy for the cinema on the corner.
(Snow Hill/Five Ways) (Snow Hill)

Birmingham: Harborne

Bell Inn

11 Old Church Road, B17 0BB (100 yds from A4040)
12-11; 12-10.30 Sun
(0121) 427 0934
Beer range varies Ⓗ
Dating from the 17th century, this old farmhouse has a village-like feel. It stands next to St Peter's Church, boasting a bowling green and a heated parasol area at the rear. Oak beams in the front lounge and a small rear snug help create a cosy, intimate atmosphere. It is popular in summer, when children are welcome outside. Food is served until 8pm weekdays; occasional summer barbecues are held. P

White Horse

2 York Street, B17 0HG (off High St)
11-11; 12-10.30 Sun
(0121) 427 2063
website: www.whitehorseharborne.homestead.com
Adnams Bitter; Greene King IPA, Abbot; Marston's Pedigree; Wells Bombardier; guest beers Ⓗ
Built in 1861, the traditional but plainly decorated interior displays old brewery trade pictures, sports posters and banners. A narrow front bar area leads to some seating at the rear used for big-screen sports fixtures; most major terrestrial TV events are shown to a lively audience, as well as the resident cat. A good range of substantial pub grub is served, steaks in particular are good value. This regular Guide entry is a rare outlet in the city for real cider.

Birmingham: Highgate

Lamp

257 Barford Street, B5 6AH (off Pershore St)
12-11; 12-10.30 Sun
(0121) 622 2599
Church End Gravediggers; Everards Tiger; Stanway Stanney Bitter; guest beers Ⓗ
Back-street pub that continues to cater for all, and can be busy some evenings. Two guest beers, often from micros, complement the ale choice. The single bar room can get smoky. A large function room at the rear doubles occasionally as a live music venue. The city's only outlet for Stanway beers has twice been Birmingham CAMRA's Pub of the Year. Photos of old Birmingham adorn the walls alongside a brief history of the pub. Nos. 35, 45 and 47 buses stop nearby. Q (New St)

Birmingham: Hockley

Black Eagle

16 Factory Road, B18 5JU (near Soho House Museum)
11.30-3, 5.30-11; 11.30-11 Fri; 12-3, 7-11 Sat; 12-3 (closed eve) Sun
(0121) 523 4008
Ansells Mild, Best Bitter; Marston's Pedigree; Taylor Landlord; guest beers Ⓗ
Highly sociable pub, rebuilt in 1895, retaining most of the original features, including Minton tiles. It has been a loyal supporter of Beowulf, the brewery that originated in Birmingham. It is Birmingham's only entry in CAMRA's Good Pub Food guide, and is convenient for the Soho

House Museum and the famous Jewellery Quarter and museum. An annual beer festival is held in July. ❀◑◗⊟⊖(Soho Benson Rd)

Church Inn

22 Great Hampton Street, B18 6AQ (take A41 from city centre)

⏲ 11.45-11; 12-3, 6-11 Sat; closed Sun

☎ (0121) 515 1851

Batham Best Bitter; Greene King Old Speckled Hen; Jennings Cumberland Ale ⊞

This 160-year-old pub is a former Birmingham CAMRA Pub of the Year. The front bar has a cosy atmosphere and the rear section is served through a hatch. The lounge displays many old photographs. The menu offers a wide selection of steaks, grills and roasts and portions are huge. The Batham's is legendary, but the pub also stocks an extensive range of whiskies, mostly single malts.
◑◗⊟⇌(Jewellery Qtr/Snow Hill) ⊖(St Pauls)

White House

99 New John Street West, B19 3TZ

⏲ 10-11; 12-10.30 Sun

☎ (0121) 523 0782

Holden's Mild, Bitter, Special ⊞

Imposing, white, two-roomed, corner pub that is hard to miss. It has a basic bar and a roomy lounge, with an alcove for diners. The walls feature a number of photos of old Birmingham. The pub serves the local community and business people. The food is not fancy, but reasonably priced and available 10-2pm weekdays. The only regular outlet for Holden's beers in Birmingham, its prices are low compared to city-centre outlets.
❀◑⊟♿⊖(Jewellery Qtr)

Birmingham: Moseley

Highbury

Dads Lane, B13 8PG (Dogpool Rd jct)

⏲ 11-11; 12-10.30 Sun

☎ (0121) 414 1525

Banks's Original; Draught Bass; M&B Brew XI ⊞

Traditional, spacious M&B triangular-shaped pub that has kept many of its original 1920s features. Popular with both locals and the passing trade, there is always one quiet room, depending on events taking place (normally in the lounge). Note the impressive original bar back with M&B logo. The pub is handy for the No. 69 bus route and five minutes' walk from the 45 and 47 stop on Pershore Road. It sells Westons Old Rosie cider. Q♨❀◑⊟♿●P

Birmingham: Nechells

Villa Tavern ☆

307 Nechells Park Road, B7 5PD

⏲ 11.30-2.30, 5-11; 11.30-11 Fri & Sat; 12.30-10.30 Sun

☎ (0121) 326 7466

Ansells Mild, Best Bitter; Marston's Pedigree ⊞

Situated a short walk from Aston Station and the busy Lichfield Road, this splendid Victorian-style pub is easily accessible from the city centre. The interior, consisting of bar, lounge and function room, remains unchanged – note the bowed, stained glass window in the lounge. The pub is community-oriented, supporting pool and dominoes teams. Lunches are served Monday-Friday. Q◑⊟⇌(Aston) ♣P

Birmingham: Selly Oak

Country Girl

1 Raddlebarn Road, B29 6JH (off A38)

⏲ 11-11; 12-10.30 Sun

☎ (0121) 414 9921

M&B Brew XI; Marston's Pedigree; guest beers ⊞

Ember Inns pub, refurbished into an open-plan area with alcoves and mixed seating spaces. Comfortable and modern, the bright, cheerful environment attracts locals and students plus staff and visitors from the nearby hospital. Busy most evenings, it is also a good Sunday lunch venue. A quiz is held on Monday and Wednesday evenings. A decent menu is served until 8pm. The guest beer range includes seasonal brews. Patio seating is a bonus.
❀◑◗♿⇌(Selly Oak) P⊁

Blackheath

Bell & Bear

71 Gorsty Hill Road, Rowley Regis, B65 0HA (on A4099, Halesowen Road)

⏲ 11.30-11; 12-4, 7-10.30 Sun

☎ (0121) 561 2196

Taylor Landlord; guest beers ⊞

Country-style pub between Blackheath and Halesowen. The building is over 400 years old making it just about the oldest pub in the area. Inside, the opened-up bar/lounge area retains an olde-worlde feel. The seven real ales are mostly national brands, such as Adnams Broadside or Flowers Original. Food is good here (no meals Sun eve), although there is room for drinkers, too. Do not miss the panoramic view from the patio in summer. ❀◑◗⇌(Old Hill) P⊁

Bloxwich

Lamp Tavern

34 High Street, WS3 2DA (by leisure centre)

⏲ 12-11; 12-10.30 Sun

☎ (01922) 479681

Holden's Mild, Bitter, Special; guest beers ⊞

Lively local with pleasantly decorated drinking areas, created out of former farm buildings and stables. The pub still has much charm and is a focus for the community, staging regular quizzes and theme nights. Sunday lunch is the only food available, served in the adjoining restaurant.
♨❀⇌♣⊡

Turf Tavern ☆

13 Wolverhampton Road, WS3 2EZ (opp. Bloxwich Park)

⏲ 12-3, 7-11; 12-3, 7-10.30 Sun

☎ (01922) 407745

RCH Pitchfork; Titanic Mild, Iceberg; guest beers ⊞

Grade II listed building, an unspoilt gem known locally as Tinky's that has been in the same family ownership for over 130 years. A tiled floor is a feature of the bar, while the other two rooms are steeped in nostalgia and offer a haven for those who enjoy a quiet drink and the art of conversation. Q❀⊟♿⇌⊁

Brierley Hill

Vine (Bull & Bladder)

10 Delph Road, DY5 2TN

12-11; 12-10.30 Sun
(01384) 78293
Batham Mild, Best Bitter, XXX H
'Blessings of your heart, you brew good ale' from Shakespeare's Two Gentlemen of Verona, is proclaimed across the frontage of this famous Black Country pub, welcoming visitors from near and far. On entering the Batham's Brewery tap, choose from the unspoilt front bar on the right, a comfortable lounge to the left, or down the corridor, the small family room or larger lounge-bar. Excellent good value hot and cold food is served weekday lunchtimes. Q ❀ ⊟ ♣ P

Brownhills

Prince of Wales

98 Watling Street, WS8 7NP
7 (5 Mon; 4 Fri)-11; 12-11 Sat; 12-10.30 Sun
(01543) 372551
Beowulf Heroes Bitter H
Cheerful, friendly corner local on the A5, near Chasewater Park and the light railway. The single U-shaped room bears Laurel & Hardy memorabilia, and a large TV screen shows sporting events. It can be busy on Wednesday, when a free buffet is served, Friday and Saturday evenings. Filled rolls are generally available. Parking can be difficult. ♨ ❀ ♣

Royal Oak

68 Chester Road, WS8 6DU (on A452)
12-3 (3.30 Sat), 6-11; 12-3.30, 7-10.30 Sun
(01543) 452089 website: www.theroyaloakpub.co.uk
Ansells Mild; Caledonian Deuchars IPA; Greene King Abbot; Tetley Bitter; Taylor Landlord; guest beers H
The Middle Oak, as it is known locally, is a large, well-decorated Art Deco-style pub. Traditional games are played in the welcoming bar, while the comfortable lounge has a more relaxed atmosphere, with a no-smoking dining room to the rear. The guest beer changes frequently. Q ❀ ◑ ⊟ ♿ ♣ P ⍻

Coseley

New Inn

35 Ward Street, WV14 9LQ (off A4123)
4 (12 Sat)-11; 12-10.30 Sun
(01902) 676777
Holden's Mild, Bitter, seasonal beers H
Although the front entrance of the pub is tucked away on peaceful Ward Street, its rear and car park are accessed from the busy Birmingham New Road. Inside is one large room, cosily bedecked in standard issue mock-Victoriana, and dominated by an imposing, well-lit modern bar counter. Around it, the regulars engage in jovial banter. Evening meals are served including home-made Black Country specialities. Thatchers cider is sold in summer. ♨ ❀ ◗ ♿ ⚌ ♣ ● P ⍻

Painters' Arms

33 Avenue Road, WV14 9DJ (off A4123)
11-11; 12-10.30 Sun
(01902) 883095
Holden's Mild, Bitter, P **Special, seasonal beers** H
Lively, Black Country local on the edge of 'the village' of Roseville. Its main room is a long L-shaped bar running the length of the pub. Tile-floored, with a bar room atmosphere at the front, it resembles a plush lounge at the back. There is also a tiny snug. The double-bay frontage has been remodelled since its last appearance in these pages. It is handy for Coseley Station and Birmingham Canal. ♨ ❀ ⊟ ⚌ ♣ P ⊓

White House

1 Daisy Street, WV14 8QQ
12-3, 6-11; 12-3, 7-10.30 Sun
(01902) 402703
Everards Mild, Beacon, Tiger, Old Original; guest beer H
Welcoming, family-run free house dominating a suburban crossroads halfway between Dudley & Bilston. Both its tiny bar and comfy lounge are the epitome of cosiness, in contrast to the imposing exterior. Good value meals are served at lunchtime and bar snacks until 7.30pm (not Sun). The pub is served by the Nos. 525 (daytime only) and 544 buses from Dudley or Bilston and it is about a mile from Loxdale Midland metro stop. ♨ ❀ ◖ ⚌ ♣

Coventry

Albany

24 Albany Road, Earlsdon, CV5 6JU
11-11 (2am Thu-Sat); 11-2am Thu-Sat; 12-midnight Sun
(024) 7671 5227
Marston's Burton Bitter, Pedigree, Old Empire, seasonal beers; guest beers H
Large Edwardian pub comprising a recently-refurbished, split-level lounge with a juke box, a public bar housing darts and a pool table, and an upstairs function room. The wide choice of up to six beers is mainly sourced from the Marston's portfolio with varied guests. The outside drinking area is due to be enlarged and improved, but the stables will remain as the venue for occasional mini-beer festivals. Food is served daily 12-9.30pm. A quiz is held weekly. ❀ ◑ ⊟ ♣

Beer Engine

35 Far Gosford Street, CV1 5DW (off ring road jct 3)
12-11; 12-10.30 Sun
(024) 7626 7239
Black Sheep Best Bitter; guest beers H
This formerly failing pub has been transformed by the landlord who has kicked out the Carling and introduced six handpumps dispensing a variety of real ales. The pub walls have become a constantly-changing art gallery. The piano in the corner gives a clue to the Saturday night music and Sunday afternoon jam sessions. All the food is home made, including hand-cut chips. The Nos. 17 and 27 bendibus from the city centre and railway station stop outside. ❀ ◖

City Arms ✔

1 Earlsdon Street, Earlsdon, CV5 6EP
10-11; 12-10.30 Sun
(024) 7671 8170
Greene King Abbot; Marston's Burton Bitter, Pedigree; guest beers H
Popular Wetherspoon's house at the centre of Earlsdon, particularly busy at weekends. It is a large open-plan pub with no-smoking throughout; children are welcome until 8pm. The patio, with awning, provides an outdoor

smoking area. An imaginative range of beers is served from 10 handpumps and regularly includes micro-brewery products. The house beer, Ma Cooper's Ale, named after a previous landlady, is brewed by Church End. ❀◑◗♿P⚟

Craven Arms

58 Craven Street, Chapelfields, CV5 8DW (1 mile W of city centre, off Allesley Old Road)

11 (4 Tue)-11; 12-4, 7-10.30 Sun

☎ (024) 7671 5308

Flowers Original; Taylor Landlord; guest beers Ⓗ

Traditional pub on a street corner in a conservation area, which is the home of the now defunct watchmaking industry. It forms an integral part of the renowned 'Craven Street crawl'. The pub comprises a lounge and an area for pool and darts. Popular barbecues are held on the patio in summer. Live entertainment is provided on Sunday evening. ♨❀◑♣

Farmhouse ✔

215 Beechwood Avenue, CV5 6HB (300 yds from Canley station)

11-11; 12-10.30 Sun

☎ (024) 7671 4332

Hardys & Hansons Bitter, Olde Trip, seasonal beers Ⓗ

Large house converted to an open-plan pub, Coventry's only Hardys & Hansons' house. It provides a restaurant area on one side and a comfortable drinking area with pool table and TV on the other. A monthly changing beer from the brewery at Kimberley is usually available. The pub gets busy when there is a fair on Hearsall Common opposite and on warm summer days when the large garden, with its play area for children, attracts families.

❀◑◗♿⇌(Canley) P

Gatehouse Tavern

46 Hill Street, CV1 4AN (near jct 9 of inner ring road)

11-3, 5-11; 11-11 Thu-Sat; 12-10.30 Sun

☎ (024) 7663 0140 website: www.gatehousetavern.com

Draught Bass; guest beers Ⓗ

Single bar conversion by the landlord from the disused gate house of long-gone Leigh Mill, a huge Victorian weaving mill (a framed picture shows its former impressive scale). Rugby dominates on international match days when it is strictly standing room only. The garden with its lovely summer flower displays is a city-centre oasis. The pub is a rare consistent outlet for Church End brews and attracts fans from a wide area. Good food in generous portions is served Monday-Friday. ❀◑◗

Graduate Bar

Union South Central Campus, University of Warwick, CV4 7AL (opp. campus arts centre)

12 (8 Sat)-11 (7-11 Mon-Fri vacations); 7-10.30 Sun term-time

☎ (024) 7657 2777

Everards Tiger; Ⓗ **guest beers** Ⓖ

Situated on the third floor of the Student Union south building, this thriving single-bar real ale oasis disproves the theory that students are not interested in cask beer. As well as regular beers from Everards and Church End who brew Graduate Ale for the bar, it keeps a changing selection of micro-brewery beers on cooled gravity stillage. Card-carrying CAMRA members and guests are always welcome. Telephone for term dates and rare student-only nights before visiting. ❀♿●

Greyhound Inn

Sutton Stop, Hawkesbury Junction, Longford, CV6 6DF (1 mile along Blackhorse Rd from B4113 jct)

11-11; 12-10.30 Sun

☎ (024) 7636 3046 website: www.thegreyhoundinn.com

Highgate Dark; Marston's Pedigree; guest beers Ⓗ

Lovely old inn, dating back to around 1837, situated at the junction of the Oxford and Coventry canals. Winter days and evenings can be cheered by a roaring fire, a key feature of the old bar area, which retains its olde-worlde charm. The cosy restaurant is no-smoking in this traditional canalside inn that offers real ale, real food and real character. Half portions of meals are available for children.

♨Q❀◑◗⊟♣P

Nursery Tavern

38-39 Lord Street, Chapelfields, CV5 8DA (1 mile W of city centre, off Allesley Old Rd)

11-11; 12-10.30 Sun

☎ (024) 7667 4530

Courage Best Bitter; Highgate Dark; John Smith's Bitter; guest beers Ⓗ

Popular community pub set in the old watchmaking district, which has been run by the same family team for over 10 years. A central bar serves three rooms; the rear room welcomes families and hosts traditional pub games and other social events. The pub holds two well-attended beer festivals under cover on the rear patio in June and December. Excellent value Sunday roasts are served – booking is recommended. Thatchers dry cider is stocked.

Q⛭❀◑♣●

Rose & Woodbine

40 North Street, Stoke Heath, CV2 3FN

12-4, 7-11; 12-11 Fri & Sat; 12-5, 7-10.30 Sun

☎ (024) 7645 1480

Banks's Original; Draught Bass; M&B Brew XI; Tetley Bitter Ⓗ

Unpretentious, Victorian, back-street pub on a residential street corner about one and half miles north-east of the city centre. This friendly pub assures visitors of a warm welcome to its cosy, comfortable lounge. Loved by the locals for its national beers, the large bar features pool and darts. Meals on Friday and Saturday continue until 8pm; no food Sunday. ❀◑⊟♣

Town Wall Tavern

Bond Street, CV1 4AH (behind Belgrade Theatre)

11-11; 12-10.30 Sun

☎ (024) 7622 0963

Adnams Bitter, Broadside; Draught Bass; M&B Brew XI; guest beer Ⓗ

Pub with a traditional layout, including the almost famous donkey box, which although small, will house a donkey (just). The area is now being redeveloped so the pub may take some finding at times. The rolls baked by the landlord are popular with actors, journalists and shoppers alike. No food is served Sunday. Smoking restrictions apply weekday lunchtimes. Westons Old Rosie cider is served.

♨◑⊟⇌●⚟

Whitefriars Olde Ale House

114-115 Gosford Street, CV1 5GN

11-11; 12-10.30 Sun

(024) 7625 1655

Beer range varies H

Built circa 1335 and sympathetically renovated, this popular, city-centre pub is Coventry's only true free house, serving beers mostly from micro-breweries. The beer menu indicates what awaits in the cellar. With two (and a bit) rooms downstairs and a labyrinth of rooms upstairs, each floor boasts a roaring log fire in winter. Exposed brickwork, beams and subtle lighting create atmosphere. A quiz is held on Tuesday evening, acoustic night is Wednesday and occasional live music is performed on Saturday.

Q

Darlaston

Boat

20 Bentley Road South, WS10 8LW

12-2.30, 6-11; 12-11 Fri; 12-3, 7-10.30 Sun

(0121) 526 5104

Greene King IPA; guest beers H

Traditional, two-roomed pub, displaying a super mirrored boat above the bar. Next to Bentley Bridge and the Walsall Canal, the Boat sells seven real ales including a terrific range of guests. The bar has a TV just for sport and is the base for several clubs. It holds occasional barbecues and an annual beer festival in the garden. Local CAMRA members voted it Pub of the Year 2004. The cider is Westons.

QP

Prince of Wales

74 Walsall Road, WS10 9JT

2 (12 Fri & Sat)-11; 12-10.30 Sun

(0121) 526 6244

Holden's Bitter, Golden Glow, seasonal beers H

The long narrow bar is decorated with advertising mirrors; darts is played at one end. The small, comfortable lounge displays a number of photos of the local swimming club and football teams; this room is popular with families. At the rear is a garden with a play area and bench seating. The conservatory may be hired by small parties. Good value food is served.

Dorridge

Railway

Grange Road, B93 8QA

11-3, 4.30-11; 11-11 Sat; 12-10.30 Sun

(01564) 773531

Draught Bass; M&B Brew XI; guest beers H

Popular pub that has been run by the same family for almost a century. Up to three guest beers are available, as well as a real cider. Good value food is served (all day Sunday and bank holidays); game is a speciality when in season. The garden, with children's play area, is busy on summer evenings, while the real fire in the public bar provides a warm welcome in winter.

QP

Dudley

Lamp Tavern

116 High Street, DY1 1QT

12-2.30, 5-11; 12-11 Fri & Sat; 12-10.30 Sun

(01384) 254129

Batham Mild, Best Bitter, XXX H

Lively Batham's local: a large, welcoming, dog-friendly front bar, a comfortable lounge and a dining area where good value traditional pub lunches are served weekdays. At the rear of the pub, the old Queen's Cross Brewery has been converted into a venue, the Brewhouse, staging regular music and comedy nights. Bed and breakfast accommodation is in the adjacent Lamp Cottage (discount for CAMRA members).

P

Halesowen

Coombs Wood Sports & Social Club

Lodgefield Road, B62 8AA (off A4099 to Blackheath)

7.30 (7 Fri)-11; 12.30-11 Sat; 12-10.30 Sun

(0121) 561 1932

Beer range varies H

Originally created as a facility for employees of the local steel works, the steel plant is long gone but the social club continues to prosper. It runs various sports teams, and overlooks a cricket pitch; a pool table and big-screen TV provide entertainment for the less energetic. Five real ales, including a mild, are normally on tap. Bar snacks are available Friday-Sunday evenings. Visitors should show a CAMRA membership card or copy of this Guide to gain admission.

Hawne Tavern

76 Attwood Street, B63 3UG (off A458 ½ mile W of town centre)

4.30 (12 Sat)-11; 12-10.30 Sun

(0121) 602 2601

Banks's Original, Bitter; Batham Best Bitter; guest beers H

In contrast to many struggling local pubs, this free house has thrived, largely due to the availability of six ever-changing guest beers, plus three regulars. It attracts some out-of-town real ale fans. On one side is a popular but quiet lounge. The other room is large including a pool table separated by a partition, plus TV and a darts corner. Stourbridge CAMRA members voted it Pub of the Year 2005. Sandwiches only are served on Sunday. Q

Somers Sports & Social Club

The Grange, Grange Hill, B62 0JH (at A456/B4551 jct)

12-2.30, 6-11; 12-2, 7-10.30 Sun

(0121) 550 1645

Banks's Original; Batham Mild, Best Bitter; Enville Ale; Olde Swan Original; guest beers H

Thriving club set in its own extensive grounds on the outskirts of town. Somers is a three-times winner of CAMRA's National Club of the Year award, with six regular and six guest ales normally available. In summer, enjoy the extensive patio area overlooking the bowling green. Show a CAMRA membership card or this Guide to gain admission. Groups of five or more should phone in advance to confirm they can be admitted. QP

Waggon & Horses

21 Stourbridge Road, B63 3TU (on A458, ¼ mile from bus station)

⌚ 12-11; 12-10.30 Sun

☎ (0121) 550 4989

Batham Best Bitter; Nottingham Extra Pale Ale; Oakham White Dwarf; guest beers Ⓗ

Its 14 cask beers, many from micros and small local brewers, make this regular Guide entry a must for real ale lovers. The bustling traditional bar with its long row of handpumps is complemented by quieter seating areas at each side. Along with the real ale and cider, Belgian beer and a good choice of fruit wines are sold, and if you are peckish, tasty home-made sandwiches are available 12-6.30pm. Q●

Kingswinford

Park Tavern

182 Cot Lane, DY6 9QG (off A4101 and A491)

⌚ 12-11; 12-3, 7-10.30 Sun

☎ (01384) 287178

Batham Best Bitter; Tetley Bitter; guest beer Ⓗ

Two-roomed local 10 minutes' walk from the village centre. The bar clientele tends to be sports fans. Sky TV and darts feature here and the pub has a golf society. The lounge is popular for a quiet drink and conversation. The guest beer is usually from an independent brewery. Broadfield House Glass Museum is nearby. The 264/5 and 274/5 Stourbridge-Kingswinford route buses stop outside.

❀⊟♣P

Knowle

Vaults

St John's Close, B93 0JU

⌚ 12-2.30, 5-11; 12-11 Fri & Sat; 12-10.30 Sun

☎ (01564) 773656

Ansells Mild; Greene King IPA; Tetley Bitter, Burton Ale; guest beers Ⓗ

Just off the High Street, this pub was voted Solihull CAMRA Pub of the Year 2003 and 2004. It offers a warm welcome in traditional surroundings. Guest beers showcase micro-breweries rarely seen in the area, and a real cider (from Westons) is also available. Occasional beer festivals are held, as well as an annual pickled onion competition. Lunches are served Monday-Saturday. There is a public car park nearby. ◐●

Langley

Crosswells

Whyley Walk, B69 4SB

⌚ 12-11.30 (midnight Fri & Sat); 12-10.30 Sun

☎ (0121) 552 2626

M&B Mild; Marston's Pedigree; Olde Swan Entire; guest beer Ⓗ

Recently refurbished and enlarged pub close to Langley Green Station. The pub retains its bar and lounge, but the addition of a carvery restaurant has enhanced the facilities, without detracting from its cosiness. The beers are served from a centrally-positioned bar. A large function room occupies the rear of the pub and regularly features local bands.

◐◑⊟♿⇌(Langley Green)⚡

Lower Gornal

Black Bear

86 Deepdale Lane, DY3 2AE (off A459)

⌚ 5 (4 Fri)-11; 12-11 Sat; 12-10.30 Sun

☎ (01384) 253333

Beer range varies Ⓗ

Originally an 18th-century farmhouse, this hillside local now overlooks the surrounding new housing estate, affording wide-ranging views beyond. The split-level interior has an eclectic charm, stemming from gradual evolution. Four or more changing guest beers make this free house an essential port of call on the Lower Gornal real ale circuit. It is 10 minutes' walk from Gornal Wood bus station for buses to Dudley, Wolverhampton and Stourbridge (daytime); the No. 257 bus stops outside.

♛❀♣

Five Ways

Himley Road, DY3 2PZ (at B4175/4176 jct)

⌚ 12-11; 12-10.30 Sun

☎ (01384) 252968

Batham Best Bitter; guest beer Ⓗ

Vibrant roadside hostelry named after one of two local intersections known as Five Ways. Batham's amber nectar is the only regular ale, usually joined by a guest. The pub's one J-shaped room sweeps round from the large-screen TV to a quieter lounge-end at the front of the pub. Good value no-nonsense food is served weekday lunchtimes. The No. 257 bus goes past, and Gornal Wood bus station is a short walk away.

❀◐♣P

Fountain

8 Temple Street, DY3 2PE (on B4157, near Gornal Wood bus station)

⌚ 12-11; 12-10.30 Sun

☎ (01384) 242777

Enville Ale; Greene King Abbot; RCH Pitchfork; guest beers Ⓗ

Excellent free house serving up to six guests from micros and regional breweries. Popular with locals and visitors, the vibrant bar is complemented by an elevated dining area serving a good choice of imaginative food 12-9pm, except Sunday evening. Twice winner of Dudley CAMRA's Pub of the Year award, it hosts beer festivals at Easter and in October. It offers draught and bottled Belgian beers plus real cider to complete the taste experience.

❀◐◑♿♣●P⚡

Old Bull's Head

1 Redhall Road, DY3 2NU

⌚ 4 (12 Sat)-11; 12-10.30 Sun

☎ (01384) 231616 website: www.oldbullshead.co.uk

Black Country Bradley's Finest Golden, Pig on the Wall, Fireside Ⓗ

Impressive, late Victorian pub dominating its corner site. It has one large bar with a raised area to the left of the serving area that doubles as a stage several evenings a week for live entertainment, and a no-smoking area at other times. There is also a games room. Since late 2004 it has been the home of Black Country Ales Brewery. Filled cobs are often available. The No. 541 Dudley-Wolverhampton bus stops nearby.

♛❀⊟♣P⚡

Minworth

Kingsley

Kingsbury Road, B76 9DP (on A4097, between Minworth and Curdworth)
✪ 11-11; 12-10.30 Sun
☎ (01675) 470808
Marston's Pedigree; guest beers Ⓗ
Situated between the A4097 and the Birmingham and Fazeley Canal, the outdoor seating benefits from views of the canal and countryside. Meals are served in the no-smoking restaurant or the bar; food is available all day in summer (call for times in winter). Children are allowed in the bar area until 9pm. The new management is committed to real ales, with two guest beers constantly changing, and plans to increase the number of guests. ❀◑P⊬

Netherton

Olde Swan ☆

89 Halesowen Road, DY2 9PY (on A459)
✪ 11-11; 12-4, 7-10.30 Sun
☎ (01384) 253075
Olde Swan Original, Dark Swan, Entire, Bumble Hole Bitter, seasonal beers Ⓗ
Characterful brewery tap on the main Dudley–Old Hill road. The front bar is an unspoilt gem, while the cosy rear snug is the perfect place for conversation. The restaurant caters for all tastes with its varied menu including Black Country favourites. Diners are advised to book; a lower age limit of 14 applies (no evening meals Sun). It was national CAMRA Pub of the Year runner-up in 2004. ♛Q❀◑⊟♿P⊬

Oldbury

Waggon & Horses ☆ ✔

17a Church Street, B69 3AD (off A4034, 1 mile from M5 jct 2)
✪ 12-11; 12-10.30 Sun
☎ (0121) 552 5467
Enville White; Olde Swan Entire; guest beers Ⓗ
Popular local, pleasantly refurbished in 2003. Notable for its splendid tiled walls, panelled ceiling and Holt Brewery etched windows, these architectural features account for the pub's place on CAMRA's National Inventory. The cavernous interior offers several pleasant drinking areas for its clientele of office workers and locals. Good food is served at reasonable prices (no meals Sun). It is accessible by bus from Dudley, Birmingham and West Bromwich. Sky TV and a monthly quiz provide entertainment.
♛♘◑⇌(Sandwell/Dudley) P

Sedgley

Beacon Hotel ☆

129 Bilston Street, DY3 1JE (on A463)
✪ 12-2.30 (3 Sat), 5.30 (6 Sat)-10.45 (11 Fri & Sat); 12-3, 7-10.30 Sun
☎ (01902) 883380
Sarah Hughes Pale Amber, Surprise Bitter, Dark Ruby, Snow Flake; guest beers Ⓗ
Fantastic Victorian pub – a national institution in the pub world. Faithfully restored, the tiny central bar dispenses the full range of home-brewed ales, plus two guests via a hatchway from larger micros. Four distinctive rooms lend a comfortable if labyrinthine quality. Families are well catered for with a children's play area outside. The No. 545 bus stops outside and the more frequent 558 Dudley-Wolverhampton service passes nearby. A true gem, not to be missed. Q♘❀♣P

Bull's Head

27 Bilston Street, DY3 1JA (on A463)
✪ 12 (11 Thu & Fri)-11; 12-10.30 Sun
☎ (01902) 578905
Holden's Bitter, Golden Glow, Special, seasonal beers Ⓗ
Open-plan, L-shaped house, recently refurbished. This basic, no-nonsense community pub is popular with the locals and gets crowded at weekends, but a warm welcome is guaranteed. Despite its open-plan layout, the comfortable, boisterous bar contrasts with the more sedate, smarter extension. New licensees have maintained the relaxed atmosphere. Traditional Thatchers cider is served. Quiz night is Sunday. Filled rolls are available. ❀⊟♿♣●⊓

Shelfield

Four Crosses

11 Green Lane, WS4 1RN (off A461)
✪ 12-11; 12-3, 7-10.30 Sun
☎ (01922) 682518
Banks's Original, Bitter; Ⓟ **guest beers** Ⓗ
Imposing detached pub over 200 years old; part of the building was once a blacksmith's. On entering note the mosaic flooring and stained glass, remnants of a bygone age. The traditional saloon bar is warmed by a coal fire. The guest beers are dispensed in the quieter, comfortable lounge. This pub is the nearest thing to a good old basic local in the area. Children, accompanied by adults, may use the passageway. ♛Q❀⊟♣P

Shirley

Bernie's Real Ale Off-Licence

266 Cranmore Boulevard, B90 4PX
✪ 12-2 (not Mon), 6-10 (5.30-9 Fri); 11.30-1.30 (closed eve) Wed; 11-3, 5-9 Sat; 12-2, 7-9 Sun
☎ (0121) 744 2827
Beer range varies Ⓗ
The business of Bernie's is to sell real ale of quality and diversity. It has the most interesting range of beers from micro-breweries that you will find anywhere in the Solihull area. Its owners have built a reputation for always serving a perfect pint. If you are unsure which beer to buy, a sampling service is offered together with advice and a warm welcome. Do not pass it by.

Red Lion

171 Stratford Road, B90 3AX
✪ 11-2.30, 5.30-11; 11-11 Fri & Sat; 12-10.30 Sun
☎ (0121) 744 1030
Highgate Dark; Marston's Pedigree; Tetley Bitter; guest beers Ⓗ
On the main road linking Shirley and Birmingham, this is a haven for shoppers. Do not be put off by the exterior, for the interior is traditional, comfortable, and has three drinking areas. Part of the lounge is no-smoking. There is a games area with a large-screen TV, the other

two TVs also cater for the sporting fraternity. The guest beer is usually low gravity with a good range of breweries featured. A few tables and chairs are set out on the pavement in summer. Parking is available in front of the shops. ❀◐♣

Short Heath

Duke of Cambridge

82 Coltham Road, WV12 5QD

12-3.30 (not Mon or Tue), 7-11; 12-3.30, 7-10.30 Sun

☎ (01922) 408895

Greene King Old Speckled Hen; Highgate Dark; Taylor Landlord; Worthington's Bitter; guest beers Ⓗ

Convivial, family-run free house converted from 17th-century farm cottages but licensed for nearly 200 years. The main rooms benefit from electronic air cleaners. The public bar has a solid fuel stove. The lounge is split into two halves by a wall containing an aquarium; the front half showing the original exposed beams. Both rooms feature display cases of model commercial vehicles. The large family room houses pool and bar football tables.
⚗Q♘⊟♣P

Solihull

White Swan ✔

32-34 Station Road, B91 3SB

11-11; 12-10.30 Sun

☎ (0121) 711 5180

Greene King Abbot; Marston's Burton Bitter, Pedigree; Shepherd Neame Spitfire; guest beers Ⓗ

Interestingly converted shop, mixing some Art Deco design with open seating and cosy alcoves. It is ideally located between Solihull Station and the Touchwood shopping and entertainment complex. A welcome addition to Solihull's growth as a cosmopolitan town, it offers a changing choice of real ales. The front dining area includes relaxing leather sofas by the large French windows to watch the world whizzing by. Q❀◐◗⇌⊬

Stourbridge

Garibaldi

19 Cross Street, DY8 3XE (take Greenfield Ave exit from New Road, third left)

2 (1 Sat)-11; 12-4.30, 7-10.30 Sun

☎ (01384) 373390 website: www.thegaribaldi.info

Banks's Original, Bitter; Marston's Pedigree Ⓗ

This pub is hard to find but worth the effort. Three rooms provide a choice for different tastes. The traditional bar offers the opportunity to play cards or darts, or you can play pool in the family room. Live music can be enjoyed on most evenings in the comfortable lounge; local and overseas performers are featured. Full details can be found on the website. ♘⊟♣P

New Inn

2 Cherry Street, Norton, DY8 3YQ (off B4186 via Glebe Lane)

2 (12 Sat)-11; 12-11 Sun

☎ (01384) 393323

Adnams Bitter; Draught Bass; Enville Ale; Greene King IPA, Abbot Ⓗ

Community-focused local, the lounge is decorated with diverse themes including golf and clowns. The pub has a classic bar where everyone is made welcome and you can enjoy a game of darts, or watch sport on TV. In addition to the real ales, there are more than 130 whiskies. Various outings are organised, such as golf trips and Ascot Ladies Day. ❀⊟♣P

Plough & Harrow

107 Worcester Street, DY8 1AX (at Heath Lane jct, B4186)

12-2.30, 6-11; 12-11 Sat; 12-3.30, 7-10.30 Sun

☎ (01384) 397218 website: www.ploughandharrow.net

Enville White; Greene King IPA; Marston's Pedigree; guest beer Ⓗ

Originally opened in 1840 to supply beer to the local glass industry, the former brewhouse at the rear of the pub has sadly not been used for many years. This popular one-room pub, near Mary Stevens Park, serves four real ales. The guest pump clips are displayed above the bar, forming quite a collection now, with over 250 different beers in the last three years. Meals are served Wednesday-Sunday (no evening meals Sun); snacks available at other times. ⚗Q❀◐◗

Royal Exchange

75 Enville Street, DY8 1XW (on A458)

1 (12 Sat & summer)-11; 12-10.30 Sun

☎ (01384) 396726

Batham Mild, Best Bitter, seasonal beers Ⓗ

Popular pub in the Batham's estate with a lively bar and small, quiet lounge, plus a large paved patio area, all accessed from a narrow passageway. The upstairs room is not normally open, but is available for private hire. There is a public car park opposite. Snacks are usually available. Q❀⊟♣

Shrubbery Cottage

28 Heath Lane, DY8 1RQ (near Oldswinford lights)

11.30-11; 12-10.30 Sun

☎ (01384) 377598

Holden's Mild, Bitter, Golden Glow, Special, seasonal beers Ⓗ

Cosy, welcoming pub, recently refurbished to create a spacious, more open bar area. The pub has a barbecue in the garden and its own putting green. The boss is a golf fanatic and the front TV area with Sky sports will likely be showing a golf tournament or a football match. The pub now has full disabled access and is all on one level. ❀♿⇌(Junction) P

Sutton Coldfield

Bishop Vesey ✔

63 Boldmere Road, B73 5UY (in Boldmere central shopping area)

10-11; 12-10.30 Sun

☎ (0121) 355 5077

Courage Directors; De Koninck Ambrée; Greene King Abbot; Marston's Burton Bitter; Shepherd Neame Spitfire; guest beers Ⓗ

Typical Wetherspoon's interior; previously a camping and outdoor shop, the restructured building is named after the Sutton Coldfield benefactor (hence the pulpit feature in the bar area). Service is efficient and friendly. The usual open-plan layout has upstairs seating, and a book-lined conservatory at the end of the bar opens on to a patio with seating. Children are

allowed to eat in the family area until 7pm. A main bus route is within 200 yards.
Q✿◑◐♿≋(Wylde Green)⚡

Crown ✔

Walsall Road, Four Oaks, B74 4RA (at Crown Lane jct)
✪ 12-11; 12-10.30 Sun
☎ (0121) 323 2715
M&B Brew XI; guest beers [H]
Large, warm and comfortable Ember Inn, decorated in contemporary style. It attracts a good mix of age groups who fit easily into the spacious accommodation. There is a large car park and convenient heated patio area to the front. Changing guest beers are from the company's broad list. The food, which is always good quality, is available 12-8pm daily.
♨✿◑◐♿≋(Butler's Lane)P⚡

Laurel Wines

63 Westwood Road, Banners Gate, B73 6UP
(200 yds off A452, near Sutton Park)
✪ 5 (3 Fri)-10; 12-10.30 Sat; 12-6 Sun
☎ (0121) 353 0399
Batham Best Bitter; Enville Ale; Taylor Landlord; guest beers [G]
This real ale off-licence is a well-frequented outlet for its constantly-changing range of beers sourced from Cornwall to Scotland. Requested ales can be obtained and sample tasting before purchase is encouraged. With an extensive range of British bottled beer, wine, spirits and cider, plus other off-licence commodities, it offers something for everyone. It now caters for parties and provides a glass hire service.

Station Hotel

Station Street, B73 6AT
✪ 12-11; 12-10.30 Sun
☎ (0121) 362 4961
Taylor Landlord; guest beer [H]
Convenient for Sutton station, its location draws commuters after work to eat and drink from the interesting selection of food and beer. Regulars enjoy the outside patio areas for the impromptu music sessions. On Thursday evening you need to book early for the comedy club. Weekends are busy and lively. ♨✿◑◐♿≋

Tipton

Rising Sun

116 Horseley Road, DY4 7NH (off B4517)
✪ 12-2.30, 5-11; 11-11 Fri & Sat; 12-3, 7-10.30 Sun
☎ (0121) 530 2308 website: www.therisingsunpub.com
Banks's Original; Oakham JHB; guest beers [H]
Victorian hostelry, retaining two distinct rooms. The bright bar, adorned with pictures of local sporting heroes, is warmed by a log-burning stove. Two open fires provide a similar function in the comfortable lounge. In summer, the back yard opens for drinking and occasional functions. There are usually four guest beers and two guest ciders on tap. The pub is 10 minutes' walk from Great Bridge bus station, with frequent services to Dudley, West Bromwich and Birmingham. Weekday lunches are served. ♨✿◑⊟♣●

Waggon & Horses

131 Toll End Road, Ocker Hill, DY4 0ET (on A461)
✪ 5 (12 Fri & Sat)-11; 12-3.30, 7-10.30 Sun
☎ (0121) 502 6453
Banks's Original; Burton Bridge Stairway to Heaven; Olde Swan Entire; guest beers [H]
Mock-Tudor brew-pub of contrasting character. The busy public bar, with darts and a real fire, has an open-plan feel. The spacious, comfortable lounge displays a collection of Burton Bridge monthly beer cards. Toll End Brewery at the rear is set in a landscaped garden with a conservatory providing a peaceful drinking area. Guests from micros are often available. Food is limited to summer barbecues and rolls. Bus Nos. 311 and 312 pass outside.
♨✿⊟♿⊖(Wednesbury Parkway)♣●

Upper Gornal

Britannia

109 Kent Street, DY3 1UX (on A459)
✪ 4 (12 Fri & Sat)-11; 12-4, 7-10.30 Sun
☎ (01902) 883253
Batham Mild, Best Bitter [H]
Batham's house, with a decidedly local feel, where you are transported back in time. The front bar has a cosy fire and old pictures of Upper Gornal. The original tap room resembles a homely lounge where pictures relate the pub's history and handpumps dispense beer at busy times. A converted TV room to the right doubles as a live music venue at weekends. The wonderful back garden is a relaxing drinking area in summer. Cobs are served.
♨Q✿⊟♿♣⚡

Jolly Crispin

25 Clarence Street, DY3 1UL (on A459)
✪ 4 (12 Fri & Sat)-11; 12-3, 7-10.30 Sun
☎ (01902) 672220 website: www.jollycrispin.co.uk
Beer range varies [H]
In the beer heaven of Lower and Upper Gornal and Sedgley, this is the brightest star. It serves nine changing ales, chosen to suit all tastes. The friendly staff are helpful and knowledgeable at local CAMRA'S Pub of the Year 2005. Three steps lead down to the cosy front bar, containing a tiny 'snug' created by leaded glass panels. At the rear is a large, comfortable lounge. Dogs are welcome throughout. The cider comes from Thatchers; perry is also sold. Q⊟●P

Walsall

Rose & Crown

55 Old Birchills, WS2 8QH (off A34 ½ mile N of town)
✪ 12-11; 12-10.30 Sun
☎ (01922) 720533
Black Country Pig on the Wall; guest beers [H]
Dasting from 1901, this three-roomed corner pub has recently achieved Grade II listing because of its ornate tilework and original bar features. Note the unusual clock above the corner bar entrance. Two guest beers from independent breweries are usually on tap, together with a real cider from the Thatchers range. A function room is available for use on the first floor. ♨⊟≋♣●

Walsall Arms

17 Bank Street, WS1 2EP (behind Royal Hotel)
✪ 12-2 (3 Fri & Sat), 6-11; 12-5, 7-10.30 Sun
☎ (01922) 725848
Banks's Mansfield Dark Mild, Mansfield Cask; Marston's Burton Bitter, Pedigree; guest beer [H]

Cheerful, traditional, back-street local, comprising a basic saloon bar with quarry tiled floor, a small, intimate snug and a corridor drinking area at the rear. It also boasts a permanent skittle alley. Images of old Walsall adorn the walls throughout.
Q⊞♣

Walsall Cricket Club

Gorway Road, WS1 3BE (off A34, by university campus)
⌚ 7.30 (12.30 Sat)-11; 12-10.30 Sun
☎ (01922) 622094 website: www.walsallcricketclub.com
Banks's Mansfield Dark; Marston's Burton Bitter, Pedigree; guest beers Ⓗ
Well-appointed, comfortable, single-roomed clubhouse bar displaying photographs of past teams and club achievements. On match days the cricket can be viewed via panoramic windows. There are plans to hold a regular beer festival, following the success of its 2004 event. Entry to the club for non-members is by showing this Guide or a CAMRA card.
❀P▯

White Lion ✔

150 Sandwell Street, WS1 3EQ
⌚ 12-11; 12-10.30 Sun
☎ (01922) 628542
Adnams Bitter; Fuller's London Pride; Greene King IPA, Old Speckled Hen; Highgate Dark; guest beer Ⓗ
Imposing, Victorian, back-street local. The classic and lively L-shaped bar is probably the best in town. A plush, comfortable lounge caters for the drinker who wants to languish, while the pool room has two tables. This pub is a great community melting-pot, caught at the right moment an instant party. The cider is Westons Old Rosie. ❀⊞♣●

Warley

Plough

George Road, Oldbury, B68 9LN
⌚ 12-3, 5.30-11; 12-11 Fri & Sat; 12-10.30 Sun
☎ (0121) 552 3822
Adnams Bitter; Banks's Original; Marston's Pedigree; guest beer Ⓗ
Pub with a distinctly local accent. It began life as a farmhouse and maintains a distinctive rustic feel. Different drinking areas on various levels lend a cosy, intimate and relaxed atmosphere around the central bar. Note the large bottle collection. The busy bar offers games and hosts occasional live music. ❀⊞♣P

Wednesbury

Old Blue Ball

19 Hall End, WS10 9ED
⌚ 12-3, 5-11; 12-11 Fri; 12-4.30, 7-11 Sat; 12-3.30, 7-10.30 Sun
☎ (0121) 556 0197
Everards Original; Highgate Dark; Taylor Landlord; guest beers Ⓗ
Traditional three-roomed pub. The bar is decorated with brewery mirrors, toby jugs and chamber pots. A family room and small snug complete the accommodation internally, but the garden offers plenty of seating and has a play area for children. Simple snacks are boosted by barbecues in summer. Q☎❀⊞⇌⊖♣

Wednesfield

Pyle Cock ✔

Rookery Street, WV11 1UN (on old Wolverhampton road)
⌚ 10.30-11; 12-10.30 Sun
☎ (01902) 732125
Banks's Original, Bitter; guest beers Ⓗ
Fine, small pub, a rare surviving Victorian local. It attracts a wide mix of customers to its three rooms. The public bar with its wooden settles is popular, and you can expect to be drawn into conversation. The small smoke room and rear lounge have their own regulars. It lies on showcase bus route No. 559 from the city, with frequent service day and evening. ❀⊞P

Royal Tiger ✔

41 High Street, WV11 1ST
⌚ 11-11; 12-10.30 Sun
☎ (01902) 307816
Banks's Original; Greene King Abbot; Marston's Burton Bitter; guest beers Ⓗ
In the centre of Wednesfield, this Wetherspoon's pub was built on the site of a former bakery in 2000. Its one room extends back to the patio. The dining area is available for families until early evening. The building next door was the original Royal Tiger that closed in 1994. The pub has no car park, but it is well served by showcase route No. 559 with its regular service.
Q❀◑♿⚟

West Bromwich

Old Crown

56 Sandwell Road, B70 8TJ (200 yds off High St)
⌚ 12-4, 5-11; 12-11 Sat; 12-3.30, 7-10.30 Sun
☎ (0121) 525 4600
Beer range varies Ⓗ
Local ale drinkers received an early Christmas present in December 2004 when a fourth handpull sprouted up on the bar of this popular back-street free house. The home-made curries and baltis continue to be an additional draw for the pub's varied clientele; no food at the weekend or Monday evening. Various bus services pass nearby. ◑⊖(Dartmouth St)♣

Vine

152 Roebuck Street, B70 6RD
⌚ 11.30-2.30, 5-11; 11.30-11 Fri; 12-11 Sat; 12-10.30 Sun
☎ (0121) 553 2866
Beer range varies Ⓗ
This pub has a Tardis-like interior: a tiny snug, smoke room and back bar opens out into a large glass-roofed extension, with further dining room beyond, complete with a huge indoor barbecue. It is popular for good quality food: spicy curries, barbecues and traditional pub fare (served all day Sat and Sun). Handy for the metro pub-crawl (details from www.travelwm.co.uk), from the metro stop head for the motorway bridge then follow the footpath alongside it.
◑⇌(Smethwick Galton Bridge)⊖(Kenrick Pk)▯

Wheatsheaf

379 High Street, B70 9QW
⌚ 11-11; 12-10.30 Sun
☎ (0121) 553 4221
Holden's Mild, Ⓟ **Bitter;** Ⓟ/Ⓗ **Golden Glow, Special; seasonal beers** Ⓗ

Behind the handsome frontage is a long front bar, comfortable lounge and rear patio. Classic pub food is served in generous portions, including 'doorstep' roast pork sandwiches. It can be busy on WBA match days, when traditional Black Country dishes, such as faggots and peas and 'gray paes' and bacon are served. Another 'metro crawl' pub: alight at Guns Village, then a short walk past the clock tower into Carter's Green. The cider is Thatchers Cheddar Valley.
❀◐⊟⊖ (Guns Village/Dartmouth St) ♣●⊡

Willenhall

Falcon

Gomer Street West, WV13 2NR
⊙ 12-11; 12-10.30 Sun
☎ (01902) 633378
Greene King Abbot; Oakham JHB; RCH Pitchfork; guest beers Ⓗ
Genuine free house, a short walk from the town centre, providing up to eight cask beers. Originally built in 1936, this two-roomed pub is welcoming to all and popular with the local community. The lively bar is countered by a quieter rear lounge. The Falcon fields darts, crib and cricket teams. ⊟♣⊡

Robin Hood

54 The Crescent, WV13 2QR (200 yds from A462/B4464 jct near railway line)
⊙ 12-3; 5 (7 Sat)-11; 12-3, 7-10.30 Sun
☎ (01902) 608006
Courage Directors; Taylor Landlord; Tetley Bitter, Burton Ale; guest beer Ⓗ
Although this cosy, friendly little pub has a single U-shaped room, the internal layout still offers tables with a little privacy. Appropriately, the local archery club practises on the adjacent common ground. A popular quiz takes place every second Monday and it hosts regular charity events. The guest beer is often Fuller's London Pride or Spitfire from Kentish brewer Shepherd Neame. Q❀♿♣P

Wollaston

Unicorn

145 Bridgnorth Road, DY8 3NX (on A458 towards Bridgnorth)
⊙ 12 -11; 12-4, 7-10.30 Sun
☎ (01384) 394823
Batham Mild, Best Bitter, seasonal beers Ⓗ
This former brewhouse was purchased by Batham some 12 years ago and has earned a reputation for serving one of the best pints in the estate. The old brewhouse remains intact but, sadly, it will never brew again as costs are prohibitive. The pub itself is a basic two-roomed drinkers' house. A sandwich may be ordered at most times. The small front annexe is now smoke-free, but this is a pub that is genuinely unspoilt by progress. Q❀⊟♿♣P⁄⁄

Wolverhampton

Chindit ✔

113 Merridale Road, WV3 9SE
⊙ 12 (2 winter weekdays)-11; 12-10.30 Sun
☎ (01902) 425582
Caledonian Deuchars IPA; guest beers Ⓗ
The Chindit opened after WWII as a tribute to local men who served with the South Staffordshire Regiment, taking part in the 1944 Chindit campaign in Burma. The pub comprises two rooms: a comfortable lounge and a bar with pool table. Three cask beers are usually available, rising to four at weekends. Live music is staged on Friday evening and an outdoor beer festival held over Mayday weekend. ❀⊟P

Combermere Arms

90 Chapel Ash, WV3 0TY (at A41/A454 jct)
⊙ 11-3, 5.30-11; 12-11 Fri & Sat; 12-10.30 Sun
☎ (01902) 421880
Banks's Original, Bitter; guest beers Ⓗ
Renowned for the tree growing in the gents, this small, terraced pub is invariably busy. The bar, family room and snug are served by a single bar. The passageway and enclosed courtyard act as additional drinking areas. To the rear, a small garden hosts live music during the warmer months. Quizzes are put on every Tuesday evening. Two guest ales change at least twice a month. ≿❀◐⊟P⁄⁄

Great Western

Sun Street, WV10 0DJ
⊙ 11-11; 12-3, 7-10.30 Sun
☎ (01902) 351090
Batham Best Bitter; Holden's Mild, Bitter, Golden Glow, Special; guest beers Ⓗ
Local CAMRA 2004, and former national Pub of the Year, this listed historic railway pub stands opposite the gates of the now disused GWR station. This is Wolverhampton's only outlet for Batham and Holden's beers. The good value meals (not served Sun) usually arrive quickly. The railway and Wolverhampton Wanderers memorabilia is well worth a look. ❀◐♿⇌♣P

Homestead

Lodge Road, Oxley, WV10 6TQ (off A449 at Goodyear island)
⊙ 2 (12 Sat)-11; 12-10.30 Sun
☎ (01902) 787357
Adnams Broadside; Tetley Bitter; guest beer Ⓗ
Originally an old farmhouse, this large estate pub has been a consistent Guide entry for over two decades. The sizeable bar is popular for pub games, while the spacious lounge serves substantial portions of home-cooked food (no meals Sun eve). Bus Nos. 503, 504 and 506 stop on the main Stafford Road (stop after the Goodyear island). Note the restricted lunchtime opening and limited guest beers due to closure of the nearby Goodyear factory. ❀⇆◐◑⊟♣P

Moon under Water ✔

53-55 Lichfield Street, WV1 1EQ (opp. Grand Theatre)
⊙ 10-11; 10-10.30 Sun
☎ (01902) 422447
Banks's Original; Greene King Abbot; Marston's Burton Bitter, Pedigree; guest beers Ⓗ
Typical, open-plan Wetherspoon's pub conversion, from the former Co-op store, in 1995. It attracts a wide mix of customers and is popular with theatre patrons before and after shows at the Grand Theatre opposite. On Friday and Saturday evenings it can be crowded with the younger set starting their night out. It is close to both the railway and bus stations.
◐◑⇌ (Wolverhampton) ⁄⁄

Muldoons

Wheelers Fold, WV1 1HN (off Princess St behind Posada)
10-11 (may vary); 12-6 Sun
(01902) 221745
Beer range varies Ⓗ
When this quirky Irish pub opened in September 2003 it became the first licensed premises in this ancient Fold for over 120 years. This one-roomed bar is not a typical fake Irish bar with fake plastic fittings. Its furniture consists of old church pews and covered empty casks used as stools and tables. Popular with the Irish community, it is also an occasional music venue. It usually offers a rare beer for the area.
Q ⚘ ♿ ⇌ (Wolverhampton) ⊖ (St. George's) ●

Newhampton

19 Riches Street, WV6 0DW
11-11; 12-10.30 Sun
(01902) 745773
Caledonian Deuchars IPA; Courage Best Bitter, Directors; Greene King Abbot; Theakston Old Peculier; guest beer Ⓗ
This newly refurbished, multi-roomed local boasts an unexpectedly large garden where games facilities include a bowling green and boules piste. The Newhampton serves its local community and customers from further afield, as its function room is a thriving venue for folk and other music. Its bar, smoke room, pool room and bowls pavilion bar allow for different environments. The home-made food is recommended. ⚘ Q ⚘ ◐ ◑ ⊟ ● ♣

Posada

48 Lichfield Street, WV1 1DG (opp. art gallery)
12-11; closed Sun
(07967) 185830
Jennings Cumberland Ale; guest beers Ⓗ
Grade II listed, city-centre hostelry behind an imposing tiled frontage. The interior of this small, narrow pub features more original tiling, a magnificent bar back and a tiny, intimate alcove. The pub has been revitalised by new management and regularly stocks five guest beers, of which one is usually a mild. Meals are available. ⚘ ◐ ◑ ⇌ (Wolverhampton)

Royal Oak

7 School Road, Tettenhall Wood, WV6 8EJ
12-11; 12-10.30 Sun
(01902) 754396
Banks's Original, Bitter Ⓟ
Attractive, 200-year-old Grade II listed pub benefiting from a large garden and function room. Situated in the Tettenhall Wood area, its handsome exterior befits a winner of the national hanging baskets competition. The cosy lounge is no-smoking at lunchtime. The bar has cable TV for sport and fields a local league dominoes team. Meals are available 12-2pm (all day in summer) and beers are still served in oversized glasses despite brewery policy. Bus No. 510 from the city stops outside. ⚘ ◐ ◑ ⊟ ♣ ⊓

Stile

3 Harrow Street, Whitmore Reans, WV1 4PB
(off Newhampton Road East)
12-11; 12-10.30 Sun
(01902) 425336
Banks's Original, Bitter Ⓟ
Late Victorian pub that has been given local listing status. With its small smoke room, club room and public bar, it is a real community-focused place. An old stable block dating back to the 1860s (which is the only reminder of the previous pub on the site) overlooks the unusual L-shaped bowling green. It gets crowded on Wolves match days as it is only a short walk from the football ground. ⚘ ⊟ ♣

Swan (at Compton)

Bridgnorth Road, Compton, WV6 8AE
11-11; 12-10.30 Sun
(01902) 754736
Banks's Original, Bitter; Marston's Pedigree Ⓗ
Grade II listed inn in the Compton area of the city. A basic unspoilt gem with a convivial atmosphere, the traditional bar features wooden settles, exposed beams and a faded painting of a swan dating from 1777. The bar and L-shaped snug are both supplied from a central servery. The lounge has Sky TV for sports, and doubles as a games room, with bar billiards and a dartboard. Bus No. 510 from the city centre stops right outside. Q ⚘ ⊟ ♣ P

Tap & Spile

35 Princess Street, WV1 1HD
11-11; 12-10.30 Sun
(01902) 713319
Banks's Original, Bitter; guest beers Ⓗ
Busy, city-centre pub consisting of a small narrow bar and two snugs. There is also a small paved area at the back where you can sit outside. Due to its central location, it is popular with both weekend clubbers and Wolves fans on match days. A large-screen TV and three others dominate the pub, showing sporting events or music videos all day.
⚘ ♿ ⇌ (Wolverhampton) ⊖ (St. George's) ♣ ●

Wheatsheaf Hotel

Market Street, WV1 3AE (next to Bilston St police station)
11 (10.30 Sat)-11; 12-5 Sun
(01902) 424446
Banks's Original, Bitter Ⓗ
The Wheatsheaf Hotel is a traditional, city-centre Banks's house which, as its name suggests, also offers accommodation. The pub is particularly busy during the day, but less so in the evening. Although not large, it has three rooms and a conservatory all served by a single bar. A small corridor acts as a further standing area for drinkers. The pub is within five minutes' walking distance of rail, bus and metro stations.
⇌ (Wolverhampton) ⊖ (St. George's)

Woodsetton

Park Inn

George Street, DY1 4LW (on A457, 200 yds from A4123)
12-11; 12-10.30 Sun
(01902) 661279
Holden's Mild, Bitter, Golden Glow, Special, seasonal beers Ⓗ
Holden's Brewery tap revolves around its light and airy main bar, with its huge TV screen and raised dining area. From here you can access the conservatory (available for functions) and a small games room. Competitively priced food is available daily. The useful but infrequent No. 545 bus passes the pub. ⚘ ◐ ◑ ♣ P

The Book of Beer Knowledge

JEFF EVANS

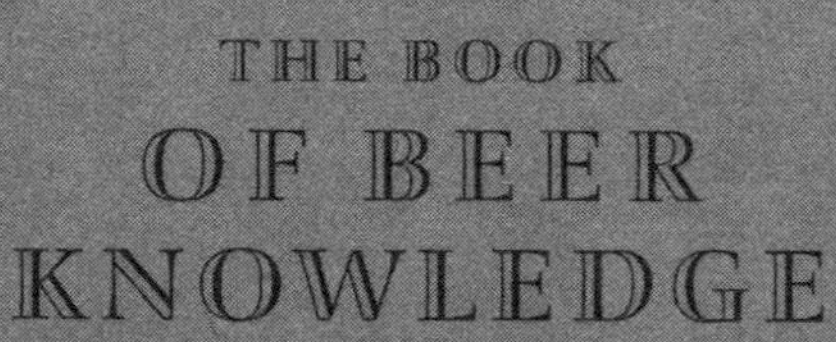

ESSENTIAL WISDOM FOR
THE DISCERNING
DRINKER

JEFF EVANS

A unique collection of entertaining trivia and essential wisdom, this is the perfect gift for beer lovers everywhere. More than 200 entries cover everything from the fictional 'celebrity landlords' of soap pubs to the harsh facts detailing the world's biggest brewers; from bizarre beer names to the serious subject of fermentation.

£9.99 ISBN 1 85249 198 1

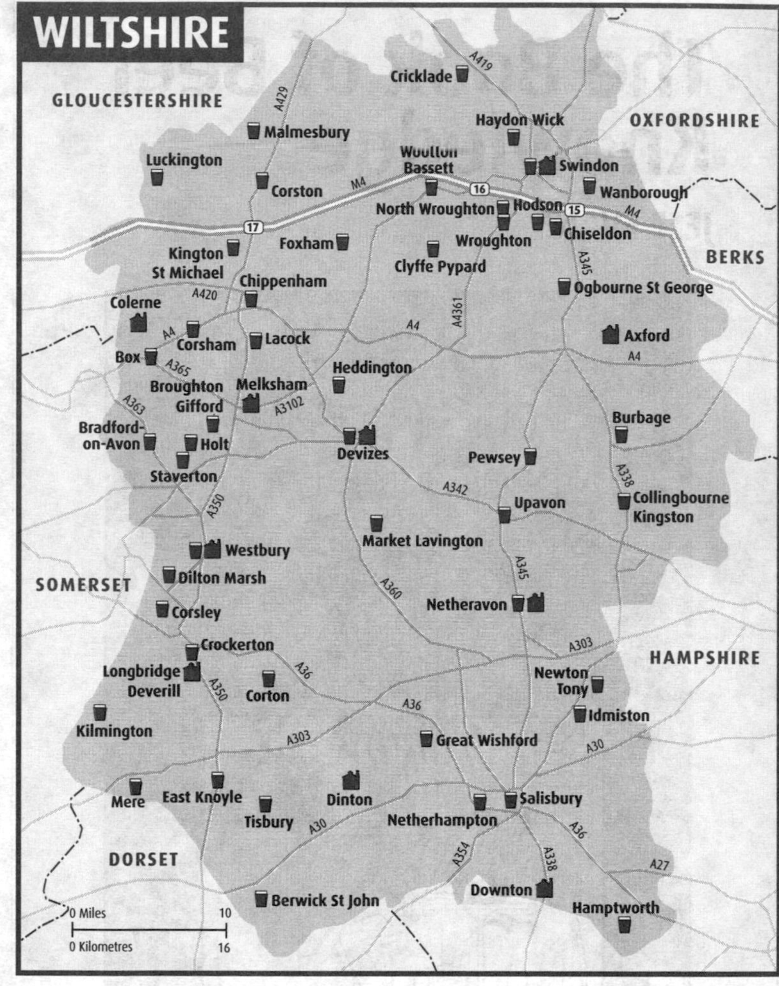

Berwick St John

Talbot

The Cross, SP7 0HA (5 miles E of Shaftesbury)
12-2.30, 6.30-11; closed Mon; 12-5 Sun
(01747) 828222
Draught Bass; Ringwood Best Bitter; Wadworth 6X; guest beers Ⓗ
Stone-built free house dating from the 16th century with low ceilings, wooden beams and a huge inglenook. The dining area is tucked away at one end of the long, comfortable bar. The pub, nestling in the centre of the village, is situated in spectacular countryside on the northern edge of Cranborne Chase. Not far away at Fovant are the famous regimental badges carved into the chalk hillsides. ⌂Q❀◐♣P

Box

Bear

High Street, SN13 8NJ (on A4)
11-3, 5-11; 11-11 Fri & Sat; 12-10.30 Sun
(01225) 743622
Box Steam Rev Awdry, Tunnel Vision, Blind House; Wadworth 6X; guest beers Ⓗ
Having spent 12 years as 'Baileys', then regaining its proper name a few years ago, this village pub with an upmarket air has now acquired its own brewery, Box Steam, although not actually on the premises. The landlord's brews feature in the pub, as well as further guests on tap. The food enjoys a good reputation. Paintings by local artists are displayed on the walls.
⌂❀◐P

INDEPENDENT BREWERIES

Archers Swindon
Arkells Swindon
Box Steam Colerne
Downton Downton
Hidden Dinton
Hop Back Downton
Moles Melksham
Ramsbury Axford
Stonehenge Netheravon
Wadworth Devizes
Wessex Longbridge Deverill
Westbury Westbury

Bradford-on-Avon

Bunch of Grapes
14 Silver Street, BA15 1JY
12-11; 12-10.30 Sun
☎ (01225) 863877
Young's Bitter, Special, seasonal beers 🄷
Town-centre pub, easily recognisable by the grapevine growing over the side. This welcoming pub has been a well-deserved regular in the Guide for years. It has three drinking areas plus a restaurant upstairs (booking advisable) serving good value food. There is a carvery every Sunday and theme nights once a month. The small pub can get busy at times, making it feel crowded. It is a rare Young's pub in the area. ❀◐◑⇌

Rising Sun
231 Winsley Road, BA15 1QS
12-11; 12-10.30 Sun
☎ (01225) 862354
Draught Bass; guest beers 🄷
Popular local on the outskirts of Bradford at the top of a hill. Inside are two bars: the lounge, which is small and quiet with pictures of various cricket pavilions adorning the walls, and the larger and livelier saloon, with a big TV screen. Live music is played at weekends. ♨❀♣●▽

Broughton Gifford

Bell on the Common
SN12 8LX (2 miles W of Melksham, off B3107)
11-11; 12-10.30 Sun
☎ (01225) 782309
Wadworth IPA, 6X, seasonal beers 🄷
Handsome old pub standing on the edge of the extensive village green. Choose between two contrasting bars: the smart bar, with a copper top, attached to the restaurant, or the public bar which is very much a locals' hangout, complete with wooden settles and old tables. A games room is next to the public bar. The garden is large and safe for families, and in summer there are barbecues here. The food in the restaurant is highly rated. ♨ぢ❀◐◑⊟♣P

Burbage

Three Horseshoes ✔
1 Stibb Green, SN8 3AE (off A346 bypass, through village)
12-2 (not Mon), 6-11; 12-2, 7-10.30 Sun
☎ (01672) 810324
Wadworth IPA, 6X; guest beer 🄷
Traditional thatched pub by the village green, near to the Savernake Forest and the Kennet & Avon canal. The food is highly recommended; a variety of pies and other traditional dishes are served (no meals Mon). Guest beers come from Wadworth's list.The pub is adorned with railway pictures and other artefacts. ♨Q❀◐◑⊟P⚟

Chippenham

Four Seasons
6 Market Place, SN15 3HD
11-11 (1am Thu; 2am Fri & Sat); 11-midnight Sun
☎ (01249) 444668
Fuller's London Pride, ESB; guest beer 🄷
Lively, town-centre pub in the market place next to the Buttercross, serving fine Fuller's real ales. Reasonably-priced lunchtime meals are excellent. Live local bands feature as part of a regular programme of evening entertainment – mid-week karaoke is always popular. A big screen shows sports fixtures. This is an ideal spot to take time out from the busy town centre. ◐♿⇌

Chiseldon

Patriots Arms ✔
6 New Road, SN4 0LU
12-2, 5.30-11; 12-11 Sat; closed Mon; 12-10.30 Sun
☎ (01793) 740331 website: www.patriotsarms.co.uk
Courage Best Bitter; Wadworth 6X; West Berkshire Mr Chubb's; guest beers 🄷
There is something for everyone at this multi-room pub which welcomes families and diners alongside casual drinkers. A large no-smoking family room opens on to the secure garden where a huge wooden playship, HMS Patriot, is berthed. The lounge bar leads to a no-smoking restaurant and a public bar. On the menu is a mixture of traditional and modern dishes; fresh meat is supplied by the local butcher. The beer is no after-thought, either. No food is served on Sunday evening. Qぢ❀⇔◐◑⊟⛺♣P⚟

Clyffe Pypard

Goddard Arms
Wood Street, SN4 7PY OS074769
12-2.30, 7-11; 11-11 Sat; 12-10.30 Sun
☎ (01793) 731386
Wadworth 6X; guest beers 🄷
A real community local in this small village, the pub is the focus for many local activities. Guest beers are mainly from smaller breweries. New for this year is the YHA hostel in what was once the skittle alley. The White Horse trail passes nearby. This pub is well worth seeking out. ♨Q⇔◐◑⊟♣P

Collingbourne Kingston

Barleycorn
SN8 3SD
12-3, 7-11; 12-3, 7-10.30 Sun
☎ (01264) 850368
Wadworth IPA; guest beers 🄷
Large roadside pub in an elevated position on the main road from Swindon to Salisbury. The pub is popular with locals as well as travellers passing through. Inside is a cosy, comfortable lounge with a restaurant and games area. Up to four guest beers are available, with local breweries often represented. Quiz night is on Sunday. ♨Q❀◐◑♿♣P

Corsham

Hare & Hounds
48 Pickwick, SN13 0HY
12-3, 6-11; 12-11 Fri & Sat; 12-10.30 Sun
☎ (01249) 701106
Caledonian Deuchars IPA; Fuller's London Pride; Wychwood Hobgoblin; guest beers 🄷
This busy community pub on the old London to Bath coaching road is on a bus route and in easy reach of many tourist attractions including Bath itself, the medieval village of Lacock and Castle Combe. Divided into three drinking areas, there

is a large lounge and two public bars. Constantly changing guest beers are on offer at weekends and occasional beer festivals are hosted. A varied selection of good food is always on the menu. ⚑Q❀◐◑⊞♿P⚟

Two Pigs
38 Pickwick, SN13 9BU
⏲ 7-11; 12-2.30, 7-10.30 Sun
☎ (01249) 712515
website: www.twopigs.freeserve.co.uk
Hop Back Summer Lightning; Stonehenge Pigswill, Danish Dynamite; guest beers Ⓗ
A real gem, this lively free house has a rustic bar, flagstone floor and wood panelled walls. The outside covered seating area is called 'the Sty'. With a strong commitment to real ale and an ever-changing range of guest beers, the pub has featured in the Guide for the last 17 years, and has been local CAMRA Pub of the Year several times. Live blues is staged on Monday evening. Over-21s only are admitted. ⚑❀

Corsley

Cross Keys
Lyes Green, BA12 7PB (off A362 Corsley Heath roundabout, Frome-Warminster road) OS821462
⏲ 12-3, 6.30-11; 12-4, 7-10.30 Sun
☎ (01373) 832406
website: www.crosskeyscorsley.co.uk
Wadworth IPA, 6X, JCB; guest beer Ⓗ
A warm welcome is guaranteed at this 18th-century pub with friendly, helpful staff and a beautiful, large open fire in the bar. An improving portfolio of guest beers makes the pub popular with locals as well as visitors to the nearby Longleat House and safari park. Good bar snack and restaurant meals are served. Traditional pub games are played including crib, dominoes and skittles – housed in a new function room/skittles alley.
⚑Q❀◐◑♿▲♣P⚟

Corston

Radnor Arms
SN16 0HD (on A429 between Malmesbury and Chippenham)
⏲ 11-11; 12-10.30 Sun
☎ (01666) 823389
Hook Norton Best Bitter; Young's Bitter; guest beers Ⓗ
Welcoming, 19th-century pub on the main road through the village with a friendly landlord and bar staff. Good value food is served including 12 different sausage dishes. The pub runs two darts teams and is planning to build a skittles alley. The garden is popular in summer.
⚑Q❀◐◑♿♣P

Corton

Dove
BA12 0SZ (on Wylye Valley road, S of Sutton Veny) OS934405
⏲ 12-3 (3.30 Sat), 6.30-11; 12-4, 7-10.30 Sun
☎ (01985) 850109
website: www.thedove.co.uk
Butcombe Bitter; Hop Back GFB; Taylor Landlord; guest beer Ⓗ
Village pub in the Wylye Valley. Recent improvements have given drinkers a larger bar area with a polished wood floor and central fireplace. Four ales are usually on handpump. Food is excellent with a varied range of lunchtime meals and a more sophisticated evening menu using local ingredients including game and fish. There is a large garden and children are also welcome in the candlelit conservatory and restaurant. Corton is situated on the Wiltshire cycleway.
⚑Q❀⛼◐◑♿▲♣●P⚟

Cricklade

Red Lion
74 High Street, SN6 6DD
⏲ 12-11; 12-10.30 Sun
☎ (01793) 750776
Moles Best Bitter; Ramsbury Gold; Wadworth 6X; guest beers Ⓗ
Friendly, 16th-century ale house serving a variety of up to nine real ales from small local breweries. Up until last year the pub survived on real ale sales alone, but now food is served in what used to be the back bar (no food on Mon). It was voted CAMRA South West regional Pub of the Year in 2003.
⚑❀⛼◐◑♿

Crockerton

Bath Arms
Clay Street, BA12 8AJ
(off A350 N of Longbridge Deverill) OS863422
⏲ 11-4, 6-11; 12-4, 6-10.30 Sun
☎ (01985) 212262
Courage Best Bitter; Wessex Crockerton Classic; guest beers Ⓗ
Fairly large yet cosy and inviting, the pub is on the edge of Crockerton. Popular with locals as well as visitors from further afield, it has a single, long bar with a restaurant at one end, known for its good quality food. The pub boasts a picturesque garden where barbecues and village events are often held. A fine outlet for beers from the nearby Wessex brewery, it also offers one or two guests, and is handy for the Longleat estate. ⚑Q❀◐◑▲P

Devizes

British Lion
9 Estcourt Street, SN10 1LQ
⏲ 11-11; 12-10.30 Sun
☎ (01380) 720665
Beer range varies Ⓗ
The archetypal working man's pub, this basic free house has a friendly atmosphere, good bar staff and a dedicated landlord. The pub is a winner of many awards and a Guide regular. The selection of current beers is displayed on a blackboard by the door. Four handpumps dispense eight to 12 beers a week, mostly from small, local breweries, often including stouts or milds. ❀♣●P

Hare & Hounds ✔
Hare & Hounds Street, SN10 1LZ
⏲ 11-3, 7-11; 12-3, 7-10.30 Sun
☎ (01380) 723231
Wadworth IPA, 6X, seasonal beers Ⓗ
A traditional back-street local that has been knocked about a few times over the years while

losing none of its original charm. Its community atmosphere, friendly landlady and band of loyal locals give it the feel of a village pub and it provides a benchmark for what Wadworth beers should taste like. ♨❀◖♣P

Southgate
SN10 5BY (on A360 Potterne road)
⊛ 12-11; 12-10.30 Sun
☎ (01380) 722872
Beer range varies Ⓗ/Ⓖ
Small, refurbished, warm, comfortable and welcoming pub with three drinking areas around a central bar. One Hop Back and three constantly changing guest beers are on handpump or gravity. The ciders, perry and range of foreign beers attract visitors from afar. Outside is a small patio with tables and a function room where live music is staged occasionally at the weekend. The pub can be crowded on weekend evenings. A beer festival is held at Easter. Meals are served Thursday-Saturday and Sunday lunchtime. ♨Q❀♿♣●P

Dilton Marsh

Prince of Wales
94 High Street, BA13 4DZ
⊛ 12-2.30 (not Mon & Tue; 12-3 Sat), 7 (5.30 Fri)-11; 12-3, 7-10.30 Sun
☎ (01373) 865487
Wadworth 6X; Young's Bitter; guest beers Ⓗ
Friendly village local with a single bar serving two drinking areas plus a small pool table annexe and a skittle alley. It offers a wide variety of guests, mostly session beers. The pub participates in local skittles, crib and pool leagues. There is a weekly Sunday evening quiz. The original pub sign is factually incorrect and has featured in a Japanese pub sign guide. ❀◖◗≉♣P

East Knoyle

Seymour Arms
The Street, SP3 6AJ
⊛ 12-3, 7-11; closed Mon; 12-3, 7-10.30 Sun
☎ (01747) 830374
Wadworth IPA, 6X, JCB Ⓗ
This 16th-century stone pub is in the heart of the village, and was formerly a farmhouse. East Knoyle was the birthplace of Sir Christopher Wren, whose father was rector of the parish church. The pub is named after the family of Jane Seymour, third wife of Henry VIII. It is very much a community pub at the heart of village life. No food is served on Sunday evening. ♨Q❀⇌◖◗♿P⚟

Foxham

Foxham Inn
SN15 4NQ (follow signs to Foxham off B4069 Chippenham to Lyneham road)
⊛ 12-2.30 (3 Sat), 7-11; closed Mon; 12-3, 7-10.30 Sun
☎ (01249) 740665 website: www.thefoxhaminn.co.uk
Bath Gem; Wadworth 6X; guest beer Ⓗ
Renovated two years ago, this pub in the centre of a small village is a free house with a friendly atmosphere, concentrating mainly on local beers. An extensive menu of home-cooked food features produce from local high quality suppliers – fish is a speciality in summer. The pub has a single bar with a separate dining area. Slightly off the beaten track, it is well worth a detour for an excellent pint and good food. ♨Q❀◖◗♿P

Great Wishford

Royal Oak
Langford Road, SP2 0PD
(½ mile off A36 at Stoford) OS078355
⊛ 11.30-2.30, 6-11; 12-3, 7-10.30 Sun
☎ (01722) 790079
Beer range varies Ⓗ
A traditional local that is the focus for village life, including celebrating Oak Apple Day on May 29th. There are up to four real ales available, usually including two local brews. The bar is panelled and has an open fire and separate restaurant. Good food ranges from bar meals to an a la carte menu. ♨❀⇌◖◗⛺♣P

Hamptworth

Cuckoo Inn
Hamptworth Road, SP5 2DU
⊛ 11.30 2.30, 5.30-11; 11.30-11 Sat; 12-10.30 Sun
☎ (01794) 390302
Cheriton Pots Ale; Hop Back GFB, Summer Lightning; Ringwood Best Bitter; guest beers Ⓖ
Beautiful, thatched pub on the edge of the New Forest. Inside are four small rooms, three of which are served from the same bar. Ales are dispensed direct from the cask, racked in the ground floor cellar. Frams Scrumpy cider is stocked, as well as at least three guest ales – more in summer. The large garden has an area for children with swings and a quiet, adults-only space. Look out for the annual beer festival in late summer. ♨Q☕❀◖◗♣●P

Haydon Wick

Fox & Hounds
10 High Street, SN25 1HX OS135878
⊛ 11-11; 12-10.30 Sun
☎ (01793) 724749
Courage Best Bitter; Fuller's London Pride; guest beers Ⓗ
Traditional two-bar pub that has been serving ales for well over a century. The village of Haydon Wick has now been swallowed up by Swindon's northern expansion. The older part of the building is now the lounge, which features a low ceiling with exposed beams. Hunting pictures hang on the walls. The public bar is in the modern, flat roofed extension, where regular quiz nights and other entertainment take place. Q❀◖◗⊟♣P

Heddington

Ivy
Stockley Road, SN11 0PL (2 miles off A4 from Calne)
⊛ 12-3, 6.30-11; 12-4, 7-10.30 Sun
☎ (01380) 850276
Wadworth IPA, 6X Ⓖ
This outstanding thatched village local was originally three 15th-century cottages and it remains a focal point for the surrounding area. To complement the beer, it has a well-deserved reputation for ample portions of high quality

food (booking for the restaurant is advisable; eve meals Thu-Sat). The village is situated at the foot of the North Wessex Downs, and there are a number of footpaths crossing this area of outstanding natural beauty. ⛫Q❀◑◐♣P

Hodson

Calley Arms

SN4 0QG (off B4005)
✪ 12 (11.30 Sat)-2.30, 6.30 (5.30 Thu & Fri)-11; 12-4, 7-10.30 Sun
☎ (01793) 740350
Wadworth IPA, 6X, seasonal beer; guest beers Ⓗ
This cosy pub has a large board outside with directions for a 2½ mile walk to Coate Water Country Park. Those on two wheels will find a cycle path to the same destination starts half a mile down the road to Chiseldon. Inside is a bar with a real fire and a raised dining area. A varied menu, including plenty of specials, is available every day except Sunday evening. ⛫Q❀◑◐P

Holt

Tollgate Inn

Ham Green, BA14 6PX
(on B3105 between Bradford on Avon and Melksham)
✪ 11.30-2.30, 5.30-11; closed Mon; 12-2.30 (closed eve) Sun
☎ (01225) 782326 website: www.tollgateholt.co.uk
Beer range varies Ⓗ
A gem of an old village pub with an upmarket atmosphere with sofas in the bar. The range of four to five ales, which changes every week, is imaginative with a good selection of local beers and many from smaller brewers from further away. The food in both the upstairs restaurant and bar is excellent. The garden at the rear overlooks a pretty valley. ⛫❀🛏◑◐⛺P⍉

Idmiston

Earl of Normanton

Tidworth Road, SP4 0AG (on A338)
✪ 11-3, 6-11; 12-3, 7-10.30 Sun
☎ (01980) 610251
Cheriton Pots Ale, Best Bitter; Hop Back Summer Lightning; guest beers Ⓗ
This popular roadside pub boasts an enviable selection of real ales. The five handpumps feature local breweries with Triple fff and Hop Back popular guests. Appetising and good value food is served and there is a small but pleasant garden, albeit a little steep. Accommodation is available separately from the pub. This was Salisbury CAMRA Pub of the Year in 2002. ⛫Q❀🛏◑◐P

Kilmington

Red Lion Inn ✔

BA12 6RP (on B3092 to Frome 3 miles N of A303 at Mere)
✪ 11.30-2.30, 6.30-11; 12-3, 7-10.30 Sun
☎ (01985) 844263
Butcombe Bitter; Butts Jester; guest beers Ⓗ
National Trust owned, the pub was originally a farmworker's cottage and is over 400 years old. Nestling in the lee of the Wiltshire Downs, and close to Stourhead Gardens, it is popular with walkers, and dogs are welcome. The single bar is mainly stone-flagged with a real fire at each end. A smaller no-smoking room is for diners. Excellent, value for money food is served at lunchtime. Accommodation is good value too. ⛫Q❀🛏◑♣●P

Kington St Michael

Jolly Huntsman

Kington St Michael, SN14 6JB (¾ mile from A350)
✪ 11.30-2.30, 6-11; 12-3, 7-11 Sun
☎ (01249) 750305
Greene King IPA; Wadworth 6X; Wychwood Hobgoblin; guest beers Ⓗ
This friendly village pub has stone walls and wonderful flowers outside. At night the pub is partly lit by candles and an open fire adds warmth in winter. At the centre of the local community, the pub holds a quiz night on Monday, live music on Wednesday and whist on Sunday, as well as occasional theme nights. Two or three guest ales are usually available. A wide selection of fresh, home-cooked meals is served. ⛫🛏◑◐⛺♣P⍉

Lacock

Bell Inn

The Wharf, Bowden Hill, SN15 2PJ
✪ 11-2.30 (closed eve Mon-Fri); 11.30-11 Sat; 12-10.30 Sun
☎ (01249) 730308
Wadworth 6X; Wells Eagle; guest beers Ⓗ
A warm welcome is guaranteed at this free house. There is a large garden with a play area for children, a boules piste and plenty of seating. A summer beer festival is held on the nearest weekend to mid-summer. Situated close to the Chippenham to Melksham cycle path, the pub is popular with walkers, passers by and locals. The Bell was local CAMRA Pub of the Year 2003 and 2004. ❀◑◐♿⛺♣●

Rising Sun

32 Bowden Hill, SN15 2PP (1 mile E of Lacock)
✪ 12-3 (not Mon), 6-11; 12-11 Sat; 12-10.30 Sun
☎ (01249) 730363
Moles Tap Bitter, Best Bitter, Molecatcher, seasonal beers Ⓗ
Lovely stone-built pub, with flagstone floors, now with a spacious, no-smoking conservatory and a large garden, both affording spectacular views over the Avon Valley. The tap for Moles, the Melksham-based brewery, the full range of their beers is usually on offer. There is live music on Wednesday and alternate Sundays. A good range of pub food is available and customers with special dietary requirements can be catered for – telephone in advance for requests or booking. ⛫Q❀◑◐♣P

Luckington

Old Royal Ship

SN14 6PA
✪ 11.30-2.30, 6-11; 11-11 Sat; 11-4, 7-10.30 Sun
☎ (01666) 840222
Archers Village; Draught Bass; Wadworth 6X; guest beer Ⓗ
Popular, friendly and welcoming pub set on the edge of the green in this south Cotswold village. The pub offers three real ales as well as a frequently changing guest beer. An extensive

menu is available throughout the week. Badminton is just up the road and Gatcombe Park close by. Q❀◐◗♿♣P

Malmesbury

Whole Hog

8 Market Cross, SN16 9AS

11-11; 12-10.30 Sun

☎ (01666) 825845

Archers Best Bitter; Wadworth 6X; Young's Bitter; guest beers H

Located between the historic 15th-century market cross and Abbey church, the 'Hog', a former cottage hospital and café/restaurant, popular with a broad mix of Malmesbury locals, has a warm, friendly atmosphere. After completing the tourist trail, this is the ideal place to relax with a newspaper and enjoy the latest guest beer or a tasty meal from the interesting menu (no meals Sun eve). There is a separate dining area but meals can also be eaten in the bar. Be discreet with the mobile phone. Cider is sold in summer. Q◐◗●

Market Lavington

Green Dragon ✔

26-28 High Street, SN10 4AG

(on B3098, 1½ miles E of A360)

12-3, 6.30 (5.30 Thu-Sat)-11; 12-3.30, 7-10.30 Sun

☎ (01380) 813235

Wadworth IPA, 6X, seasonal beers; guest beer (occasional) H

An impressive portico leads to this thriving village local which is equally welcoming to regulars and visitors. The pub has a well-deserved reputation for good food. Bar snacks are available as well as main meals in the restaurant area. For the children there is a play area in the garden and a pets' corner. ⛼❀⇌◐◗♿♣●P⚟

Mere

Old Ship Hotel

Salisbury Road, BA12 6JE

11-3, 6-11; 11-11 Fri & Sat; 12-3, 7.30-10.30 Sun

☎ (01747) 860258

Draught Bass; Wessex Naughty Ferret; guest beer H

A coaching inn since 1785, situated in the centre of Mere. The hotel lounge boasts an interesting old fireplace. The public bar is closed at lunchtime during the week. There is a large restaurant upstairs which opens in the evening. A rare outlet for the local Wessex Brewery, in the summer the pub often opens all day. ⛼Q❀⇌◐◗⊟♿P

Netheravon

Dog & Gun

Salisbury Road, SP4 9RQ (on A345)

11-3, 6-11; 11-11 Sat; 12-10.30 Sun

☎ (01980) 671287

Courage Best Bitter; Greene King Old Speckled Hen; guest beers H

Typical village inn with a friendly atmosphere. A community pub, it plays a part in local events such as Top Hat Day in early summer. Guest beers usually include one or two brews from Stonehenge Ales, the local village brewery. The house beer, Dog and Gun Ale, is Morrells Oxford Blue rebadged. Good food is served at reasonable prices. The pub is ideally located for exploring Salisbury Plain, Stonehenge and Avebury. ⛼❀◐◗♣P

Netherhampton

Victoria & Albert

SP2 8PU

11-3, 5.30 (5 Fri & Sat)-11; 12-3, 7-10.30 Sun

☎ (01722) 743174

Beer range varies H

This small country pub, built in 1540, has a thatched roof and a large garden. Log fires and low beams add to the cosy atmosphere. The four constantly changing real ales are mostly from small, independent brewers – over 700 different beers have been drunk in the last two years. All food is prepared in the pub and the menu ranges from snacks to restaurant meals. Dogs are welcome at Salisbury CAMRA Pub of the Year 2005. ⛼Q☕❀◐◗⛺♣●P

Newton Tony

Malet Arms

SP4 0HF (1 mile off A338)

11-3, 6-11; 12-3, 7-10.30 Sun

☎ (01980) 629279

Stonehenge Spire Ale; Wadworth 6X; guest beers H

Classic country pub named after a local family who are well represented in the village churchyard. There are two comfortable bars and a restaurant – the larger bar features a huge fireplace and a window reputed to come from an old galleon. Wadworth 6X is always served from the wood; Butts Barbus Barbus is often one of the two guests. A blackboard menu based on fresh, local ingredients changes daily. ⛼Q❀◐◗P

North Wroughton

Check Inn

79 Woodland View, SN4 9AA

11.30-3, 6-11; 11.30-11 Fri & Sat; 12-10.30 Sun

☎ (01793) 845584

website: www.checkinn.co.uk

Beer range varies H

Genuine free house serving eight real ales plus imported lager and bottled beers. Guest beers change frequently and are usually from local and independent breweries. The roadside pub has been cut off by the M4 and isolated in a cul-de-sac. It has a terraced drinking area at the front and boules can be played in the back garden. Good home-cooked food is available at a reasonable price. Local CAMRA Pub of the Year 2005, it was South West regional runner up in 2004. ⛼Q❀⇌◐◗♿♣●P⚟⊓

Ogbourne St George

Inn with the Well

Marlborough Road, SN8 1SQ (off A346)

12-2.30 (not Mon), 6-11; 12-2.30 (closed eve) Sun

☎ (01672) 841445

website: www.theinnwiththewell.co.uk

Wadworth 6X; guest beer G

Formerly known as the Old Crown, the pub takes its name from the 90ft well in the dining room. A comfortable pub with a relaxed feel, it is well placed for walking the Ridgeway or the Og Valley. Good food and a comprehensive menu complement the changing guest beer (no food Sun eve or Mon). All real ales are drawn straight from the barrel in the cellar rather than the handpumps on the bar. The St George's Day weekend beer festival has now become a regular event.

Pewsey

Coopers Arms

37-39 Ball Road, SN9 5BL (off B3087) OS168600

6 (12 Sat)-11; 5-midnight Fri; 12-10.30 Sun

(01672) 562495

Fuller's London Pride; Wadworth 6X; guest beers H

This thatched pub takes some finding, but is well worth the effort to seek out. In the main bar there is an open fire in winter, and there are rooms for pool and TV. Cider is served in summer. Live music is performed regularly. It is ideally situated for walkers on the White Horse Trail.

Salisbury

Deacons

118 Fisherton Street, SP2 7QT

5 (4 Fri; 12 Sat)-11.30; 12-10.30 Sun

(01722) 504723

Hop Back GFB, Summer Lightning; guest beers H

This traditional, friendly drinkers' pub, popular with a mixture of locals and visitors, is convenient for the city centre and railway station. The front bar has an open gas fire in a traditional hearth and woodblock flooring. The back bar has table football and a TV showing sport. Guest beers change frequently. Traditional pub games are played occasionally.

King's Arms

99 Fisherton Street, SP2 7SP

12-11; 12-4 Sun

(01722) 337811

Hop Back GFB; Ringwood Best Bitter; guest beer H

Family-run pub with two long rooms – one with comfortable seating ideal for a quiet pint; the other more lively with pool and darts. The large garden is a real suntrap and barbecues are held in summer. Pub teams play in local crib, darts and pool leagues, and live music is occasionally hosted. The guest beers are often from Moles, Gale's, or Ringwood Fortyniner.

Rai d'Or

69 Brown Street, SP1 2AS

12.30-2 (not Mon-Thu), 5-11; closed Sun

(01722) 327137

Beer range varies H

Historic free house dating from 1292 with open fires, wooden floors and panelled benches. The bar retains its original atmosphere despite changes such as serving Thai food at all times. Previously known as the Star, it has reverted to the name it had for 500 years when it was a brothel and tavern in the old red light district. Now all you will find here is beer from small local breweries, usually including Stonehenge, a welcoming landlord and 700 years of history.

Village Freehouse

33 Wilton Road, SP2 7EF

(on A36 near St Paul's roundabout)

12 (3 Mon & Tue)-11; 12-10.30 Sun

(01722) 329707

Abbey Bellringer; Taylor Landlord; guest beers H/G

This friendly city local serves four ever-changing guest beers chosen by its customers. It specialises in beers unusual in the area and normally includes a mild or a stout, making it the only regular outlet for such ales in the city. Close to the station, it is popular with visitors by rail, and railway memorabilia adorns the walls. Cricket, rugby and football are shown on a small TV at CAMRA local Pub of the Year 2001 and 2004.

Winchester Gate

113-117 Rampart Road, SP1 1JA

12-11; 12-10.30 Sun

(01722) 322834

The soul of beer

Brewers call barley malt the 'soul of beer'. While a great deal of attention has been paid to hops in recent years, the role of malt in brewing must not be ignored. Malt contains starch that is converted to a special form of sugar known as maltose during the brewing process. It is maltose that is attacked by yeast during fermentation and is converted into alcohol and natural carbon dioxide. Other grains can be used in brewing, notably wheat. But barley malt is the preferred grain as it gives a delightful biscuity note to beer. Unlike wheat, barley has a busk that works as a natural filter during the first stage of brewing, known as mashing. Cereals such as rice and corn are widely used by some brewers of mass lagers, but craft brewers avoid them.

Hop Back Crop Circle; Taylor Landlord; guest beers 🄷
Welcoming and popular two-room former 17th-century coaching inn on the site of the city's east tollgate. It is now separated from the city centre by the ring road. A large garden, complete with petanque terrain, is unusual in Salisbury and very attractive in summer. Hop Back and other local breweries feature at this free house, and it stocks a large range of bottled beer. Live music is played on Friday and Saturday evenings.
P

Wyndham Arms
27 Estcourt Road, SP1 3AS
4.30 (3 Fri)-11; 11-11 Sat; 12-10.30 Sun
☎ (01722) 331026
Downton seasonal beers; Hop Back GFB, Crop Circle, Summer Lightning, seasonal beers; guest beer 🄷
The original home of the Hop Back brewery, although brewing has long since moved to nearby Downton. A genuine local, it caters for all. Inside is a small bar and two further rooms; one is no-smoking and admits children. This pub is all about beer, with six real ales available and a fine selection of bottled beers on offer.

Staverton

Old Bear
BA14 6PB (opp. Nestle factory) OS934405
11.30-3, 5.30 (5 Fri)-11; 11.30-11 Sat; 12-10.30 Sun
☎ (01225) 782487 website www.theoldbear.co.uk
Draught Bass; Wadworth 6X; guest beers 🄷
Originally four weavers' cottages, this pub is now one large building with four separate drinking areas. The pub prides itself on traditional food in a peaceful environment with no music or games machines. The interior is light and clean. A welcome port of call for those using the Kennet & Avon canal. Dogs are permitted. QP

Swindon

Gluepot
5 Emlyn Square, SN1 5BP
11-11; 12-10.30 Sun
☎ (01793) 523935
Hop Back GFB, Best Bitter, Summer Lightning; guest beers 🄷
Small, no-frills, friendly one-bar pub. Built in the mid-19th century, it was part of Brunel's railway village. Located close to the steam museum, it is a short walk from Swindon station. Four Hop Back beers are served as well as four guest beers and five traditional ciders. On Sunday there is a regular meat raffle and buffet. Food is served Tuesday-Saturday. Dogs are welcome.
Q

Steam Railway ✔
14 Newport Street, SN1 3DX
12-11; 12-10.30 Sun
☎ (01793) 538048
Fuller's London Pride; Wadworth 6X; Wells Bombardier; guest beers 🄷
Large pub that was expanded years ago and can be quite noisy at weekends. The traditional real ale bar has a low ceiling and wood panelling; it has nine handpumps offering a regularly changing selection of guest beers. The bar gets busy when major sporting events are shown on TV but at other times you can enjoy a quiet drink here. Meals are served daily including a roast on Sunday. The pub is home to RATS (real ale tasting society) and the RATS beer festival is held in May. P

Tisbury

Boot Inn
High Street, SP3 6PS
11-2.30, 7-11; 12-4 Sun
☎ (01747) 870363
Beer range varies 🄶
This fine village pub, built of Chilmark stone, has been licensed since 1768. The landlord has been here since 1976 and maintains a relaxed, friendly atmosphere appealing to locals and visitors alike. Three beers are served direct from the casks stillaged behind the bar. Good food is available and there is a spacious garden.
P

South Western Hotel
Station Road, SP3 7JT
12-3, 6-11; 11-11 Fri & Sat; 12-10.30 Sun
☎ (01747) 870160
Fuller's London Pride; Ringwood Best Bitter; Young's Bitter 🄷/🄶
Opposite the station, this Victorian railway inn offers a warm and vibrant welcome to regulars and visitors alike. There are several drinking areas so a quiet corner can always be found, or just join in the conversation at the bar. Handpumps are in place but the beer is often served from the cask in the ground floor cellar. The garden has picnic tables. Wardour Castle ruins is two miles away. Food is served daily except Thursday.
P

Upavon

Antelope
3 High Street, SN9 6EA
11-3, 5.30-11; 11-11 Sat; 12-10.30 Sun
☎ (01980) 630206 website: www.antelope-inn.co.uk
Wadworth IPA, 6X, JCB; guest beers 🄷
Once a coaching inn, the pub is popular with locals as well as visitors, and has a real community feel to it. It has a large, cosy lounge with an open fireplace. The restaurant features an interesting, changing menu: Monday is curry night, Tuesday is Italian night and Wednesday and Thursday are steak nights. Two guest beers are available. B&B is provided. QP

Wanborough

Harrow Inn ✔
High Street, SN4 0AE
12-2.30 (3 Sat), 6-11; 12-3, 7-10.30 Sun
☎ (01793) 790622
website: www.theharrowinnwanborough.com
Adnams Bitter; Wadworth 6X; guest beers 🄷
The oldest pub in Wanborough, this charming thatched village inn dates back to the 16th century. A brew-pub in the 19th century, it now

has two inglenooks which burn enormous logs. It still retains many of the original features from its days as a coaching inn, with a split-level village bar and a separate dining room. A wide range of home-made food is served (not Sun eve). ₼Q❀◐◑P⊬

Plough

High Street, SN4 0AE

✪ 12-3, 5-11; 12-11 Fri; 12-3, 7-10.30 Sun

☎ (01793) 790523

Draught Bass; Fuller's London Pride; Greene King Old Speckled Hen; Moles Tap Bitter; Wadworth 6X 🄷

This thatched Grade II listed building is the only pub in Wanborough that has always served real ale. It has a cosy interior with beams and open fireplaces. A full menu offers plenty of variety (no food Sat lunchtime or all day Sun). The pub hosts a boules competition each May on its own piste. ₼Q❀◐◑♿♣P

Westbury

Horse & Groom

Alfred Street, BA13 3DY

✪ 12-2.30, 7-11; 12-11 Sat; 12-10.30 Sun

☎ (01373) 822854

Westbury Amber Daize, Pale Storm, Midnight Mash; guest beers 🄷

This pub now boasts its own brewery and usually features three of its ales along with a couple of guests. There is a public and a lounge bar, the latter with a no-smoking area. This is a locals' pub offering crib and quiz nights as well as skittles. The food is good, honest pub grub and the welcome is genuine. It is a fine place to take a rest after a hike up to the Westbury White Horse. ₼Q❀◐◑⇌♣P⊬

Wootton Bassett

Five Bells

Wood Street, SN4 7BD

✪ 12-2.30, 5-11; 12-11 Sat; 12-10.30 Sun

☎ (01793) 849422

Fuller's London Pride; Young's Bitter; guest beers 🄷

Cosy, thatched local with a low, beamed ceiling. The Five Bells opened before 1841 and absorbed the adjoining cottage in 1921. The bar sports five handpumps and a large blackboard with a good selection of lunchtime meals. Themed food evenings are held on Wednesday. The pub features a fine display of flowers and in 2004 won the Bassett in Bloom competition. A beer festival, offering more than 20 beers, is held in August.

₼❀◐♣🍎

Wroughton

Carters Rest

High Street, SN4 9JU

✪ 12-3, 5-11; 12-11 Sat; 12-10.30 Sun

☎ (01793) 812288

Adnams Bitter; Fuller's London Pride; Hop Back Crop Circle; Taylor Landlord; guest beers 🄷

Built some time after 1866, this large, two-room pub with a friendly atmosphere was extensively refurbished in the early 1990s when it was owned by Archers. Decorated with plenty of beer-related memorabilia, it keeps up to eight real ales. It hosts a quiz night every Thursday – get there early to find a seat.

₼Q❀⊟♣P

Haunch of Venison, Salisbury

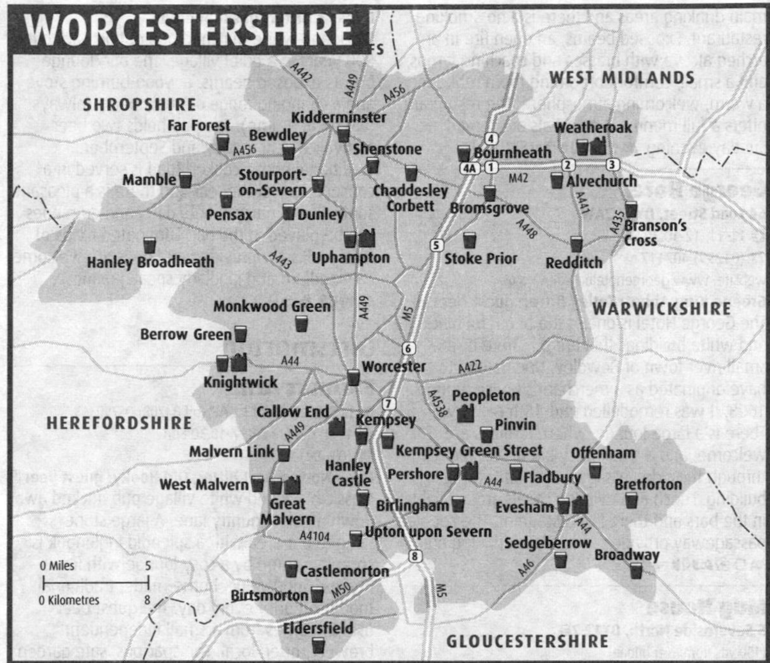

Alvechurch

Weighbridge

Scarfield House, Scarfield Hill, B48 7SQ

(follow signs to marina, from village)

12-3 (4.30 summer), 7-11; 12-3, 7-10.30 Sun

☎ (0121) 445 5111

website: www.the-weighbridge.co.uk

Beer range varies Ⓗ

Converted from a house four years ago, the Weighbridge won the 2004 British Waterways gold award for the Best Waterside pub. With its small but comfortable no-smoking rooms and a public bar, it is rapidly establishing itself as a popular canalside hostelry for rail travellers, boaters and motorists. Good value food is available from a daily changing menu (no hot food Tue or Wed lunchtime). Tillerman's Tipple is brewed especially for the pub by the Weatheroak Brewery. A beer festival is held in the autumn. ♨Q❀◐◑⊟≠P⊬

Berrow Green

Admiral Rodney

WR6 6PL (near Martley)

12-3 (not Mon), 5-11; 11-11 Sat; 12-10.30 Sun

☎ (01886) 821375 website: www.admiral-rodney.co.uk

Wye Valley Bitter; guest beers Ⓗ

This light, airy country pub welcomes all the family. Usually there are three guest ales to choose from, often from local micro-breweries, as well as real cider. There are three main bar areas all serving excellent meals, from home-made bread to fresh Cornish fish. The pub also has a three-tier restaurant (booking recommended), a skittle alley and a floodlit garden. Good accommodation makes the pub a popular night stop with walkers. A disabled WC and baby changing facilities are provided. ♨Q❀◐◑♿♣●P⊬

Bewdley

Black Boy ✔

50 Wyre Hill, DY12 2UE

(follow Sandy Bank from B4194 at Welch Gate)

12-3, 7-11; 12-11 Sat; 12-10.30 Sun

☎ (01299) 403523

Banks's Original, Bitter, seasonal beers; Marston's Pedigree Ⓗ

Traditional and comfortable local in an old part of Bewdley. It is a steep climb from the town centre but the rewards for taking on the hill are there to be seen, from the building itself, which dates back several hundred years, to the many awards for cellarmanship which are proudly on display. There are several rooms including a small games area that may be used by families at the landlord's discretion. ♨Q❀⊟♣

Black Boy Hotel

Kidderminster Road, DY12 1AG

(on B4190 close to river)

11-11; 12-10.30 Sun

☎ (01299) 402119 website: www.blackboyhotel.co.uk

Enville Ale; Greene King Abbot; guest beer Ⓗ

Near the River Severn, this 15th-century former coaching inn is named after its Royalist connection in the Civil War. A single bar serves two

INDEPENDENT BREWERIES

Brandy Cask Pershore
Cannon Royall Uphampton
Evesham Evesham
Malvern Hills Great Malvern
Mayfields Bishop Frome
St George's Callow End
Teme Valley Knightwick
Weatheroak Weatheroak
Wyre Piddle Peopleton

main drinking areas and there is a no-smoking restaurant. Exposed beams, an open fire in an arched alcove with brasses and coaching lamps, and a small, comfortable sitting room make for a warm, welcoming atmosphere. The restaurant offers a full menu but no meals are served Sunday evening. ⊯❀⇔◑ ⇌(SVR)♣P

George Hotel

64 Load Street, DY12 2AW

✪ 11-11; 12-10.30 Sun

☎ (01299) 402117

website: www.georgehotelbewdley.co.uk

Greene King Abbot; Tetley Bitter; guest beer Ⓗ

The George Hotel is one of the beautiful black and white buildings that are a feature of the small river town of Bewdley. Understood to have originated as a merchant's house around 1608, it was remodelled mid-18th century. There is a large lounge, where families are welcome, and a small, cosy bar accessible through the side passage to the left of the building. Lunch and evening meals are available in the bars and there is a restaurant. The cobbled passageway provides an outdoor drinking area. ⊯Q❀⇔◑ ⇌(SVR) P

Mug House

5 Severnside North, DY12 2EE

(150 yds from river bridge)

✪ 12-11; 12-10.30 Sun

☎ (01299) 402543

website: www.mughousebewdley.co.uk

Taylor Landlord; Wye Valley Pale Ale; guest beers Ⓗ

The new Severn Flood Barrier has thankfully made it worthwhile for a sympathetic refurbishment of this 18th-century pub with its riverside frontage. Comfortable, with a welcoming fire, it was originally the venue for deals between trow haulers and trow owners – negotiated over a mug of ale. The restaurant (closed Sun eve) offers live lobsters. Guest beers are normally from local independents; the house beer, Mug's Gayme is brewed by Wye Valley. Local English wine is also stocked. In May a beer festival is held in the garden. ⊯❀⇔◑ ⇌(SVR) ♣

Waggon & Horses

91 Kidderminster Road, DY12 1DG

(on Bewdley-Kidderminster road, Wribbenhall side of river)

✪ 12-3, 6-11; 12-11 Fri & Sat; 12-10.30 Sun

☎ (01299) 403170

Banks's Original, Bitter; guest beer Ⓗ

Friendly town pub retaining its Victorian charm where a single bar serves two rooms. The snug has exposed beams and an open fire with settles and tables. The larger main room has comfy seating and adjoins a third room with a quarry-tiled floor and kitchen range. This is a real community pub – when it was under threat of closure the locals campaigned to save it. The guest beers are from independents. Bar snacks are available at lunchtime and early evening – no food Sun. ⊯Q❀◑ ⇌(SVR) ♣⬤P

Birlingham

Swan ✔

Church Street, Pershore WR10 3AQ

✪ 12-3, 6.30-11; 12-3, 6.30-10.30 Sun

☎ (01386) 750485 website: www.theswaninn.co.uk

Banks's Bitter; guest beers Ⓗ

Black and white thatched pub dating back over 500 years in a quiet village. The bar/lounge boasts exposed beams, a wood-burning stove and a changing range of guest beers (always two on at a time). The pub holds two beer festivals a year in May and September. Traditional home-cooked food is served in a conservatory at the rear and there is a pleasant south-facing garden. Crib, darts and dominoes can be played in the bar. Laminated maps of local walks are provided and dogs are welcome. The landlord and landlady speak Japanese. ⊯❀◑ ♣⬤P⍁

Birtsmorton

Farmers Arms

Birts Street, WR13 6AP (off B4208) OS790363

✪ 11-4, 6-11; 12-4, 7-10.30 Sun

☎ (01684) 833308

Hook Norton Best Bitter, Old Hooky; guest beer Ⓗ

Classic black and white village pub, tucked away down a quiet country lane. A large stone-flagged bar area with a splendid inglenook is complemented by a cosy lounge with low beams. Good value, home-made, traditional food is on offer every day. The guest beer usually comes from a small independent brewery, often local. The spacious, safe garden with swings provides fine views of the Malvern Hills in the distance. ⊯Q❀◑ ⊟P

Bournheath

Nailers Arms

62 Doctors Hill, B61 9JE

✪ 12-11; 12-10.30 Sun

☎ (01527) 873045 website: www.thenailersarms.com

Enville White; Greene King Old Speckled Hen; guest beers Ⓗ

Dating from the 1780s, this whitewashed three gabled building was once a nail makers' workshop-cum-brewery. It has a traditional quarry tiled bar with a real fire. The lounge/restaurant is accessible via a corridor or a separate entrance (no eve meals Sun). The decor, with comfortable seating and sofas, creates a distinctive, modern Mediterranean feel. Two guest ales and real cider are usually available. ⊯ざ❀◑ ⊟♿♣⬤P⍁

Branson's Cross

Cross & Bowling Green

Alcester Road, B98 9DR (A435/B4101 jct)

✪ 12-11; 12-10.30 Sun

☎ (01564) 742472

Ansells Mild; Young's Bitter; guest beer Ⓗ

Although on a busy main road, the Cross and Bowling Green is well worth stopping off for. It is quiet during the day but in the evenings you will find a busy local atmosphere, with pub games to the fore. The long public bar is dominated at one end by the well-used dartboard. There is a comfortable snug as well as a restaurant serving meals from Wednesday to Saturday. An unusual feature is that all three rooms have their own bars. The garden is well away from the road. ⊯❀◑ ⊟♿♣P

Bretforton

Fleece ☆

The Cross, WR11 7JE (near church)
12-3, 6-11; 11-11 Sat; 12-10.30 Sun
☎ (01386) 831173 website: www.thefleeceinn.co.uk
Hook Norton Best Bitter; Uley Pig's Ear; guest beers Ⓗ
Famous old National Trust pub untouched by the passage of time until a fire in February 2004 gutted the upstairs living area. Fortunately the public area escaped almost unscathed – inglenooks, three open fires, antique furniture and its world-famous collection of 17th-century pewter all survived. The pub is one of the stars of CAMRA's National Inventory of Historic Pub Interiors. Families can enjoy the large garden with play area and orchard. There is a famous asparagus auction in its season. An informal folk music gathering is held on Thursday in the Pewter Room. Fruit wines are available.
⛼Q❀◐◑⊟♣●

Broadway

Crown & Trumpet

Church Street, WR12 7AE
11-3, 5-11; 11-11 Fri & Sat; 12-10.30 Sun
☎ (01386) 853202
website: www.cotswoldholidays.co.uk
Hook Norton Old Hooky; Stanway seasonal beers; Taylor Landlord; guest beers Ⓗ
Fine 17th-century Cotswold stone inn on the road to Snowshill, complete with oak beams and log fires along with plenty of Flowers Brewery memorabilia. The menu includes specials using locally grown fruit and vegetables, making the pub popular with locals, tourists and walkers alike. It offers an unusual range of pub games, and live music mainly on Saturday evening. The Stanway seasonal beers rotate throughout the year; some are brewed exclusively for the pub.
⛼Q❀⇌◐◑▲♣P

Bromsgrove

Hop Pole

78 Birmingham Road, B61 0DF
12-11; 12-10.30 Sun
☎ (01527) 870100 website: www.hop-pole.com
Worfield OBJ; guest beers Ⓗ
This revitalised one-room pub was local CAMRA Pub of the Autumn in 2004. The daytime atmosphere is light and bright with a tasty lunchtime menu offering freshly prepared soup, salads, sandwiches and hot snacks including burgers. The inviting enclosed garden is a sunny spot to relax in the afternoons. In the evenings from Wednesday to Sunday the pub hosts local live bands performing many musical styles. ❀◐

Ladybird Inn

2 Finstall Road, Aston Fields, B60 2DZ (on A448)
11-11; 12-10.30 Sun
☎ 01527 (878014)
Batham Best Bitter; Hobsons Bitter Best; guest beer Ⓗ
After a thorough refurbishment this thriving local now boasts a front bar and extensive lounge area with a light, airy feel. There is a restaurant and a function room as well as a garden. A hotel extension has just been added. Situated on the outskirts of town, next to the station, it is an ideal base from which to explore the region.
❀⇌◐◑⊟♿⇌P⊬

Red Lion ✔

73 High Street, B61 8AQ
10.30-11; 12-10.30 Sun
☎ (01527) 835387
Banks's Hanson's Mild, Original, Bitter; guest beers Ⓗ
Busy (it can get smoky) one-room pub in the main shopping street, well known locally for its slogan, 'Smooth pour is never sold'. Seven real ales are available, including four guests, as well as two Belgian beers on draught. Bar food is available at lunchtime, with hot food on Thursday, Friday and Saturday; Monday is curry night. The patio area to the rear is covered when necessary. The pub was local CAMRA Pub of the Year for 2003 and 2004. Beer festivals are held regularly. ❀◐♣P

Castlemorton

Plume of Feathers

Gloucester Road, WR13 6JB (on B4208) OS788388
12-11; 12-10.30 Sun
☎ (01684) 833554
website: www.plumeoffeathers.co.uk
Batham Best Bitter; Greene King Old Speckled Hen; Hobsons Best Bitter; guest beer Ⓗ
Situated on the edge of Castlemorton Common, with fine views of the Malvern Hills from the garden, this classic country pub provides an ideal base for walks across the common or up on the hills. A friendly welcome is assured in the main bar, with its wealth of beams and decorative hops, while the no-smoking dining area provides a good value menu of home-cooked food. A beer festival is held in the early summer and the pub also occasionally plays host to local musicians. Local bus services pass the door on Saturday. ⛼Q♉❀◐◑P

Chaddesley Corbett

Fox Inn

Bromsgrove Road, DY10 4QN (on A448 past village)
11.30-2.30, 5-11; 11-11 Sat; 12-10.30 Sun
☎ (01562) 777247
Enville Ale; Theakston Best Bitter; guest beer Ⓗ
Roadside pub to the south of this attractive village with a tidy L-shaped lounge and a pool room to the side. An air-conditioned no-smoking restaurant area serves a popular, good value carvery (Tue- Sun lunchtimes; Wed and Fri eves). A comprehensive range of main meals and snacks is available every day. Bottle-conditioned beers are normally available. The guest beer is usually from an independent micro-brewery.
⛼♉❀◐◑♣P

Swan ✔

High Street, DY10 4SD
11-3, 6-11; 11-11 Sat; 12-3, 7-10.30 Sun
☎ (01562) 777302
Batham Mild, Best Bitter, XXX Ⓗ
Built in 1606, this comfortable village pub is set in a picturesque black and white timbered village. The large, traditional bar enjoys a good atmosphere and there is a snug to the rear and a restaurant to the side. No food is served on

Monday lunchtime; evening meals are available Thursday-Saturday. A jazz band plays every Thursday evening. Dogs are welcome in the pub and in the extensive garden. Good walks can be enjoyed in the vicinity. Westons Old Rosie cider is stocked. ₼Q❀⊂D⊟♣⬤P⅍

Dunley

Dog Inn

Stourport Road, DY13 0UE (on A451 Stourport-Great Witley road)

⌚ 11-3, 5-11, 12-11 Fri & Sat ; 12-10.30 Sun

☎ (01299) 822833

Banks's Original; Hobsons Best Bitter; guest beers Ⓗ

Friendly village pub with a small snug, bar and lounge. The L-shaped lounge has exposed beams, a real fire and a no-smoking dining area. The pub has a reputation for fine, home-cooked food from a varied menu. The garden has a playground for children and a bowling green for hire. A function room is available as well as accommodation with three en-suite rooms.

₼Q❀⊯⊂D⊟♣P

Eldersfield

Greyhound

Lime Street, GL19 4NX (N of B4211/B4213 jct) OS814305

⌚ 11.30-2.30 (3 Sat), 7 (6 Fri & Sat)-11; 12-3, 7-10.30 Sun

☎ (01452) 840381 website: www.greyhoundinn.co.uk

Butcombe Bitter; Ⓖ **guest beers** Ⓗ

Worth the considerable effort needed to find it, the Greyhound offers a traditional country pub experience with wood-burning stoves and pub games including quoits. The beer is dispensed straight from the barrel and up to three guests join the permanent Butcombe. There is a public bar and lounge with both bars no-smoking, although smoking is permitted in the skittle alley and garden. A wide range of food is available (eve meals Tue-Sat). The accommodation is a holiday cottage in the grounds. A beer festival is held in June.

₼Q❀⊯⊂D⅄♣P⅍

Evesham

Old Swanne Inn

66 High Street, WR11 4HG (near bus station)

⌚ 11-11; 12-10.30 Sun

☎ (01386) 442650

Greene King Abbot; Marston's Burton Bitter, Pedigree; Shepherd Neame Spitfire; guest beers Ⓗ

The Swanne opened as a Wetherspoon's in late 1998, the latest in a series of changes since it first appeared as an inn in 1586. Evesham Civic Society commended the refurbishment which 'transformed a scruffy and derelict building into one which is an asset to the town'. It offers two or three guest beers, and holds several mini-beer festivals through the year. It is an ideal spot to pop into after the shopping.

Q❀⊂D♿⅄⥱⅍

Far Forest

Plough ✔

Cleobury Road, DY14 9TE

(½ mile from A456/ B4117 jct) OS730744

⌚ 12-3, 6-11.30; 11-11 Sat; 12-10.30 Sun

☎ (01299) 266237)

website: www.englandsnumber1.com

Wye Valley Hereford Pale Ale; Enville Ale; guest beers Ⓗ

This busy, country pub/restaurant has a number of drinking and eating areas served from the main bar. The front room is for drinkers only and there is a dining room that extends into a conservatory. The guest beer range varies – up to six different ales are on tap in summer. For diners, there is a renowned carvery and extensive menu. Children are allowed in the dining areas. Food is served all day Sunday.

₼❀⊂D♿⅄♣P

Fladbury

Chequers Inn

Chequers Lane, WR10 2PZ

⌚ 11.30-3, 5.30-11; 12-3 (closed eve) Sun

☎ (01386) 860276

Black Sheep Best Bitter; Hook Norton Best Bitter, Old Hooky; guest beer Ⓗ

Large, welcoming inn dating from 1372, set back from the village green. The spacious open bar, once three rooms, boasts exposed beams and a range fire at one end. The restaurant, at the rear of the pub, serves a wide range of food, making best use of locally produced ingredients. Seven bedrooms are available for overnight guests.

₼Q❀⊯⊂D⬤P

Great Malvern

Great Malvern Hotel

Graham Road, WR14 2HN (by crossroads with Church St)

⌚ 10-11; 11-10.30 Sun

☎ (01684) 563411

website: www.great-malvern-hotel.co.uk

Draught Bass; Flowers IPA; guest beer Ⓗ

Town-centre, Victorian hotel bar situated near the Malvern Theatre complex, making it ideal for pre- or post- performance refreshment. The guest beer often comes from a local brewery, including the nearby Malvern Hills Brewery. The beer pricing policy reflects the bar's location. Beers and meals can be enjoyed in the bar, or in the no-smoking brasserie (food not served Sun). The 1950s themed Great Shakes bar downstairs is keg-only. There is limited parking but public car parks are nearby.

Q❀⊯⊂D⥱P⅍

Hanley Broadheath

Fox Inn

WR15 8QS (on B4204)

⌚ 5 (12 Fri & Sat)-11; 12-10.30 Sun

☎ (01886) 853189

Batham Best Bitter; Hobsons Best Bitter; guest beers Ⓗ

This busy, 400-year-old, timbered rural village pub is a gem well worth seeking out. It has become a community focal point to the extent that a local resident delivers the Batham's! Many different social events are held here including the Foxstock beer and music festival (first weekend Aug) and lawnmower Grand Prix in the adjacent field. The Thai landlady serves

authentic Thai food from Thursday to Saturday evenings. Camping is by prior arrangement. There are two guest beers and cider is served in summer.
♔Q♉❀◐◑⊟⛺♣●P

Hanley Castle

Three Kings Inn ☆

Church End, WR8 0BL (signposted off B4211)
⏲ 12-3, 7-11; 12-3, 7-10.30 Sun
☎ (01684) 592686
Butcombe Bitter; Hobsons Best Bitter; guest beers Ⓗ
A gem of an unspoilt country pub run by the same family for 95 years. A former CAMRA National Pub of the Year, it also features in the National Inventory of Historic Interiors. Free from any tie, the three guest ales are always interesting, often from local breweries and, from time to time, can be first brews or other rarities. Both the small snug and the larger Nell's Lounge feature open inglenook fires. Regular music sessions are held on Sunday evening, sometimes on a Saturday and informally at any other time. A popular beer festival is held every November.
♔Q♉❀◐◑●P

Kempsey

Walter de Cantelupe

34 Main Road, WR5 3NA
⏲ 12-2 (2.30 Sat), 6-11; closed Mon; 12-2.30, 7-10.30 Sun
☎ (01905) 820572
website: www.walterdecantelupeinn.com
Cannon Royall King's Shilling; Hobsons Best Bitter; Taylor Landlord; guest beer Ⓗ
Interesting free house with an attractive walled garden where dogs are welcome. The bar features a large inglenook and there is a busy dining area. The high quality food complements the wide selection of beers and wines; ploughmans and sandwiches made with local bread and cheeses are a speciality. Evening meals are not served on Sunday. Regular events hosted throughout the year include an outdoor paella party in June. There are three en-suite rooms available for overnight stays.
♔Q❀⇔◐◑P⊔

Kempsey Green Street

Huntsman Inn

Green Street, WR5 3QB (take Post Office Lane off A38 at Kempsey)
⏲ 12-2 (3 Sat; not Mon), 5.30-11; 12-3.30, 6.30-10.30 Sun
☎ (01905) 820336
Batham Best Bitter; Everards Beacon, Tiger Ⓗ
Comfortable and welcoming free house. Exposed beams and open fires throughout the bar and restaurant area make it a deservedly popular venue for locals and visitors alike. The bar area consists of several rooms around a central bar. The restaurant serves a wide range of reasonably-priced, home-cooked food. An extensive open garden to the rear is an added attraction. The impressive skittle alley has its own bar. ♔Q♉❀◐◑⊟P

Kidderminster

Boar's Head

39 Worcester Street, DY10 1EW
⏲ 11.30-11 (12.30am Thu-Sat); 7-11.30 Sun
☎ (01562) 68776
Banks's Original, Bitter; Mansfield Cask; guest beers Ⓗ
Town-centre Victorian pub with a number of drinking areas. As well as the main bar there is a cosy wood-panelled lounge with a wood-burning stove. Outside are a large covered and heated courtyard where regular live music is staged and a tented garden area for the summer. The guest beers change frequently and a free mineral water dispenser is provided for drivers. Note the Pop Art style paintings dotted around the pub. ♔Q❀◑♿⇌●

King & Castle

SVR Station, Comberton Hill, DY10 1QX
⏲ 11-3, 5-11; 11-11 Sat; 12-10.30 Sun
☎ (01562) 747505
Batham Best Bitter; Enville Nailmaker Mild; guest beers Ⓗ
Deservedly a Guide regular, this recreation of a GWR refreshment room of the 1930s is popular with locals and visitors to the Severn Valley Railway. There are plenty of seating areas with railway photographs and memorabilia. The carpet is a reproduction of an original with the GWR logo. The beer is good value with Royal Piddle brewed especially for the pub by the local Wyre Piddle Brewery. Evening meals are served Friday-Sunday when trains are running. A wheelchair WC is available on the platform.
♔Q❀◐◑⇌

Knightwick

Talbot

WR6 5PH (on B4197, 400 yds from A44 jct) OS572560
⏲ 11-11; 12-10.30 Sun
☎ (01886) 821235 website: www.temevalley.co.uk
Hobsons Best Bitter; Teme Valley This, That, seasonal beer Ⓗ
Nestling beside the River Teme, this pub is all that a classic 14th-century coaching inn should be. Behind the pub is the Teme Valley Brewery; both are owned by the same family. The ingredients on the food menu are locally sourced – sometimes even home-grown. The local hop fields provide the brewery with some of the raw material for the Green Hop Festival held early in October. A farmers' market is held on the second Sunday of the month outside the pub where the brewery sells its bottled beers.
♔Q❀⇔◐◑⊟●P

Malvern Link

Nag's Head

Bank Street, WR14 2JG
(uphill from Malvern Link station, left at traffic lights)
⏲ 11-11; 12-10.30 Sun
☎ (01684) 574373
website: www.nagsheadmalvern.co.uk
Banks's Bitter; Batham Best Bitter; Greene King IPA; Marston's Pedigree; Wood Shropshire Lad; guest beers Ⓗ
Local CAMRA Pub of the Year for 2004, this popular pub usually has at least eight ales on

tap, often 10 or 11. Excellent food is served in the Nag's Tail, 6.30-8.30, after which the room reverts to a bar. The landlord invests heavily in making the pub comfortable and attractive for all seasons. Real fires, patio heaters and marquees stave off the winter cold before giving way to abundant spring and summer colour in the hanging baskets and garden.
♨❀◑◐≠♣●P

Mamble

Sun & Slipper

DY14 9JL (signed from A456, approx ¼ mile)
⊛ 12-3, 6.30-11; closed Mon; 12-4, 7-10.30 Sun
☎ (01299) 832018
Banks's Original, Bitter; Hobsons Best Bitter; guest beer Ⓗ
In the centre of the village, close to Mamble Craft Centre, this solid country pub has a cosy bar with pool table and a dining room with log burning stove. With a blazing fire in the grate the atmosphere is warm and welcoming. Recently refurbished, old photos of village life enliven the hallway, while the bar benefits from new seating, a bar of light oak and floral displays. The food is good; menus change monthly (no food Sun eve). ♨❀◑◐♣P▯

Monkwood Green

Fox

WR2 6NX (follow signs to Wichenford, off A443 at Hallow) OS803601
⊛ 12-2.30 (not Mon-Thu), 5-11; 12-5, 7-11 Sat; 12-5, 7-10.30 Sun
☎ (01886) 889123
Cannon Royall Arrowhead, Muzzle Loader; guest beer Ⓗ
Friendly, single-bar village local dating from Georgian times, affording good views of the Malvern Hills to the south. The pub is a rare outlet for Barker's farmhouse cider and award-winning perry. The guest beer usually comes from a local micro. A venue for many local events, including indoor air rifle shooting, and a skittle alley is available. Music nights are held every last Friday of the month. Opening hours and food availability are flexible – phone ahead. Camping requires prior arrangement.
♨Q❀◑▲♣●P

Offenham

Bridge Inn ✔

Boat Lane, WR11 8QZ (signed Riverside Pub)
⊛ 11-11; 12-10.30 Sun
☎ (01386) 446565 website: www.bridge-inn.co.uk
Caledonian Deuchars IPA; Donnington BB; guest beers Ⓗ
Ancient riverside inn with its own moorings and a garden leading down to the Avon, known locally as the 'Boat' since the bridge was washed away in the 17th century and replaced by a ferry. With extensive improvements in recent years, the Bridge features a vibrant public bar and enjoys an excellent reputation for meals produced with locally grown fruit and vegetables. Regular mini beer festivals are held over the year. Westons cider is sold and the house Boat Bitter is from Theakston.
♨Q❀◑◐⊟▲♣●P

Pensax

Bell

WR6 6AE (on B4202, Clows Top-Great Witley road)
⊛ 12-2.30 (not Mon), 5-11; 12-10.30 Sun
☎ (01299) 896677
Hobsons Best Bitter; guest beers Ⓗ
Winner of numerous awards including CAMRA's Regional Pub of the Year 2003, the bar serves at least four guest beers, usually from local independents, as well as Herefordshire perry and Westons cider. Children are welcome in the snug and no-smoking dining room. The food is prepared using local produce where possible. A beer festival is held on the last weekend of June and a monthly farmers' market is on the fourth Saturday. ♨Q☎❀◑◐▲●P

Pershore

Brandy Cask

25 Bridge Street, WR10 1AJ
⊛ 11.30-2.30 (3 Sat), 7-11; 12-3, 7-10.30 Sun
☎ (01386) 552602
Brandy Cask Whistling Joe, Brandy Snapper, John Baker's Original; guest beers Ⓗ
Busy, town-centre free house, home of the Brandy Cask Brewery. The large, landscaped garden running down to the River Avon is popular in summer. Ale Mary occasionally joins the regular Brandy Cask brews but there are usually four further guests. Real cider direct from the barrel is sometimes stocked. Bar food and a good restaurant complete the package (no food winter Tue).
♨Q❀◑◐

Pinvin

Coach & Horses

Main Street, WR10 2ES
⊛ 12-11; 12-10.30 Sun
☎ (01386) 552858
Cannon Royall Arrowhead; M&B Brew XI; Wyre Piddle Piddle in the Hole Ⓗ
Classic village pub truly at the hub of its community. The games room and skittle alley bear witness to the fact that the spirit of friendly competition lives on. Two of the regular beers are from nearby micro-breweries, which adds to the 'local' feeling. Families are welcome. Sandwiches are served at lunchtime.
❀⊟▲≠(Pershore) ♣P⊬

Redditch

Bramley Cottage ✔

Callow Hill Lane, Hunt End, B97 5QB
⊛ 12-11; 12-10.30 Sun
☎ (01527) 541464
Beer range varies Ⓗ
Rambling, modern estate pub with many areas, including no-smoking zones. A large central bar serves three or four real ales; one is always a major national brew and the others a varying range of guests, although these also tend to be well-known national and regional brews. Pub food is served daily until 8pm, including vegetarian options. Children over 14 are welcome if dining with adults, but younger children are restricted to the garden.
❀◑◐P⊬

Steps ✔
163 Evesham Road, Headless Cross, B97 5EN
⏲ 12-2.30, 5.30-11; 12-11 Fri; 11-11 Sat; 12-10.30 Sun
☎ (01527) 550448
website: www.stepsbarandbistro.co.uk
Hobsons Town Crier; guest beers Ⓗ
Bright, smart and modern cafe bar with a long single bar divided into sections, and sofas dominating in the no-smoking area. The place can become busy some evenings with live bands on Saturday, soul disco on Friday and a quiz Thursday, but this friendly local is more peaceful at other times. The well planted conservatory leads to a pleasantly decked patio and garden. Guest beers are mainly from local independents. Breakfasts are available on Saturday and Sunday from 9.30am-noon.
❀◐♠⅟

Sedgeberrow

Queen's Head
1 Main Street, WR11 7UE (on B4078)
⏲ 12-3, 5.30-11; 12-4, 6.30-10.30 Sun
☎ (01386) 881447
Wickwar Cotswold Way; guest beers Ⓗ
Recently renovated to a high standard, this village pub on the southern edge of the Vale of Evesham offers a warm welcome from the friendly landlord. The regular Wickwar beer is unusual for the area, and is complemented by up to two guest beers that often come from local micros, as well as a traditional cider from Thatchers. A good menu is available (no food Mon) and children are allowed in the no-smoking lounge area.
◐▯♣♠⅟

Shenstone

Plough
DY10 4DL (off A450/A448)
⏲ 12-3, 6-11; 12-3, 7-10.30 Sun
☎ (01562) 777340
Batham Mild Ale, Best Bitter, XXX Ⓗ
Tucked away just off the main road, this Batham's beer house (snacks are the only food available) is a traditional pub with a real fire. A single bar serves the cheery public bar and walk-through lounge, which is divided into two sections and displays pictures relating to the Falkland War. Children are not allowed inside, but are permitted in the spacious, enclosed, covered courtyard. The pub, with its Led Zeppelin connections, is well worth seeking out, not least for its excellently priced ales.
♔Q❀▲≠P⅟

Stoke Prior

Navigation Inn
Hanbury Road, Stoke Wharf, B60 4LB (on B4091)
⏲ 11-11; 12-10.30 Sun
☎ (01527) 870194
Fuller's London Pride; John Smith's Bitter; guest beers Ⓗ
Traditional pub by the Worcester & Birmingham canal offering a spacious bar with pool table, a comfortable lounge and a dining area. Good value food is served, except on Sunday evening. Thursday is paella night, courtesy of the Spanish chef. Two guest beers at premium prices are normally served. A portable ramp is available on request for wheelchair users. Q❀◐▯♣P

Stourport-on-Severn

Angel ✔
14 Severnside, DY13 9EW (off Lion Hill, into Hart Lane, left at river)
⏲ 11-11; 12-10.30 Sun
☎ (01299) 822661
Banks's Original, Bitter; guest beer Ⓗ
Two-roomed, 18th-century riverside pub in the old part of town built as a watering-hole for the navvies working on the canals. Its ancient nickname of The Virgins is ironic – alcohol was not the only service provided here! The cosy locals' bar has an open fire and the quieter second room, used for dining, its own feature fireplace. Meals are served 12-3 daily and 6-9 every evening except Sunday. Arrive by boat and you can tie up at the pub's moorings.
♔Q❀◐▲♣♠P

Bird in Hand
Holly Road, DY13 9BA (off B4193 by canal)
⏲ 11-11; 12-10.30 Sun
☎ (01299) 822385
Enville Ale; Flowers IPA; Tetley Dark Mild; Wadworth 6X Ⓗ
This canalside pub is a 10-minute walk along the towpath from the town. Enjoy the warm, comfortable atmosphere in its small snug and main room divided into three with plenty of seating. The pub serves good value food with special themed food nights. In summer, you can take a pleasant walk or cycle ride here, and drink a well-deserved pint sitting outside by the canal. Saturday is quiz night. ♔❀◐▯P⅟

Old Crown ✔
8 Bridge Street, DY13 8XB
⏲ 10-11; 12-10.30 Sun
☎ (01299) 825693
Banks's Original; Greene King Abbot; Marston's Burton Bitter; guest beers Ⓗ
The outside drinking area at this Wetherspoon pub overlooks Brindley's historic river basins and the river bridge. Inside is one large room with a long single bar down one side. On the walls are some old photos of canal basins of note. The family area is at the back; children are welcome until 9pm and there is plenty of seating. The pub is popular with weekend visitors.
Q❀◐♿▲P⅟

Uphampton

Fruiterer's Arms
Uphampton Lane, WR9 0JW
(off A449 at Reindeer pub) OS839649
⏲ 12.30 (12 Sat)-3, 7-11; 12-3, 7-10.30 Sun
☎ (01905) 620305
Cannon Royall Fruiterer's Mild, Arrowhead, Muzzle Loader, seasonal beers; John Smith's Best Bitter Ⓗ
This unspoilt country pub and brewery tap, down a short country lane, is a little gem worth seeking out. It has a central dispense serving a cosy, homely lounge and a public bar. The Cannon Royall Brewery is situated alongside the pub. Local CAMRA awards, old local pictures,

antique sporting guns and horse brasses adorn the walls. Basic home-cooked food, including excellent sandwiches and baguettes, is served at lunchtimes. ⌂Q❀◖⊟♣P

Upton upon Severn

White Lion Hotel

High Street, WR8 0HJ

⏲ 11-11; 12-10.30 Sun

☎ (01684) 592551 website: www.whitelionhotel.biz

Greene King Abbot; guest beers Ⓗ

Traditional hostelry, dating from the 16th century that featured in Henry Fielding's novel Tom Jones. The resident owners go out of their way to make you feel welcome. Three guest ales are available, usually including one from a local micro. Bar meals are not available on Saturday evening or Sunday lunchtime but the high quality restaurant is open daily. Regular beer events are held to complement Upton's many riverside music festivals.
Q❀⇌◖◗♿▲P

Weatheroak

Coach & Horses

Weatheroak Hill, Alvechurch, B48 7EA

⏲ 11.30-2.30, 5.30-11; 11.30-11 Sat; 12-10.30 Sun

☎ (01564) 823386

Black Sheep Best Bitter; Everards Original; Weatheroak Light Oak, Ale, Redwood; Wood Shropshire Lad; guest beers Ⓗ

Attractive rural pub with its own brewery. A quarry-tiled bar with a real fire and functional seating is complemented by a two-level lounge and modern restaurant (with wheelchair access) to the side. The surrounding gardens make it ideal for a summer outing. The pub received an outstanding achievement award from the local CAMRA branch in 2003. ⌂Q❀◖◗⊟▲♣P

West Malvern

Lamb Inn

87 West Malvern Road, WR14 4NG (on B4232)

⏲ 4.30 (12 Sat)-11; 12-10.30 Sun

☎ (01684) 577847

Adnams Broadside; Greene King Abbot; Hook Norton Old Hooky; Taylor Landlord; guest beers Ⓗ

Thriving village local that is regularly packed for music nights on Saturday and sometimes Friday, with 'open mike' sessions on Thursday. The main bar room is festooned with flags and inflatable toys. A quieter second room has a skittle alley and is often used for practice sessions by local musicians. The only food served is on Sunday lunchtime – a popular menu featuring 10 vegetables. The road to the car park is very steep and not recommended for large vehicles. ❀♣●P

Worcester

Bell

35 St Johns, WR2 5AG (W side of the Severn off A44)

⏲ 10.30-2, 5-11; 10.30-4, 7-11 Sat; 12-3, 7-10.30 Sun

☎ (01905) 424570

M&B Brew XI; guest beers Ⓗ

Busy community local comprising a main bar and two small side rooms, one of which doubles as a family room. At the rear is a function room and a well-used skittle alley. Worcester St John's cycling club, founded in 1888, is once again using the pub to meet, after a break of 66 years. The guest beers are either Fuller's London Pride or Wells Bombardier, with others frequently from local micro-breweries.
❀♣

Berkeley Arms

School Road, St Johns, WR2 4HF

⏲ 11.30-3, 5-11; 11.30-11 Fri & Sat; 12-3, 7-10.30 Sun

☎ (01905) 421427

Banks's Hanson's Mild, Original, Bitter; Ⓟ **guest beer** Ⓗ

Friendly pub where two rooms are served from a single bar. The public bar has a small TV for sports fixtures and pub games are played, while the lounge is more comfortably furnished and suitable for a quiet drink. A third room at the back is used for darts, games and meetings, but can also accommodate families. The guest beer is usually from one of the larger independent breweries.
❀⊟♣P

Bush

4 Bull Ring, St Johns, WR2 5AD

⏲ 10.30-3, 5.30-11; 10.30-11 Sat; 12-3, 7-10.30 Sun

☎ (01905) 421086

Banks's Bitter; guest beers Ⓗ

The outstanding feature of this pub is its public bar with ornate carvings on the front of the Victorian bar, and etched and stained glass windows. The lounge is served from a hatch at the back of the bar, and there is a further small room which doubles as an overflow for the upstairs restaurant. Mulbury's restaurant, open every evening except Sunday, is no-smoking and caters for vegetarians. Up to four guest ales range from the mundane to the obscure. ◖◗⊟

Cap 'n' Gown

45 Upper Tything, WR1 1JZ

⏲ 11-11; 12-10.30 Sun

☎ (01905) 24208

Hook Norton Hooky Dark, Best Bitter, Old Hooky, seasonal beers Ⓗ

This is Hook Norton's first pub in Worcester. Inside is a single room bar, where you may meet the landlady's dog. Be warned, he's a big one! A big screen shows the main sporting events, but at other times it is conversation that fills the air rather than cheers or cries of despair from the sports fans.
⇌(Foregate St) ♣

Dragon Inn

51 The Tything, WR1 1JT (on A449)

⏲ 12-3, 4.30-11; 12-11 Sat; 12-3, 7-10.30 Sun

☎ (01905) 25845

website: www.thedragoninn.com

Beer range varies Ⓗ

This Grade II listed Georgian inn is a real ale paradise and has won many awards for the quality of its beer. The six changing guests always include a stout or porter, as well as a cider or perry. The website is updated daily with the current range and cellar stock. Most of the ales are from micros, many of which are collected personally from the breweries by the landlord.
Q❀◖⇌(Foregate St)♣●

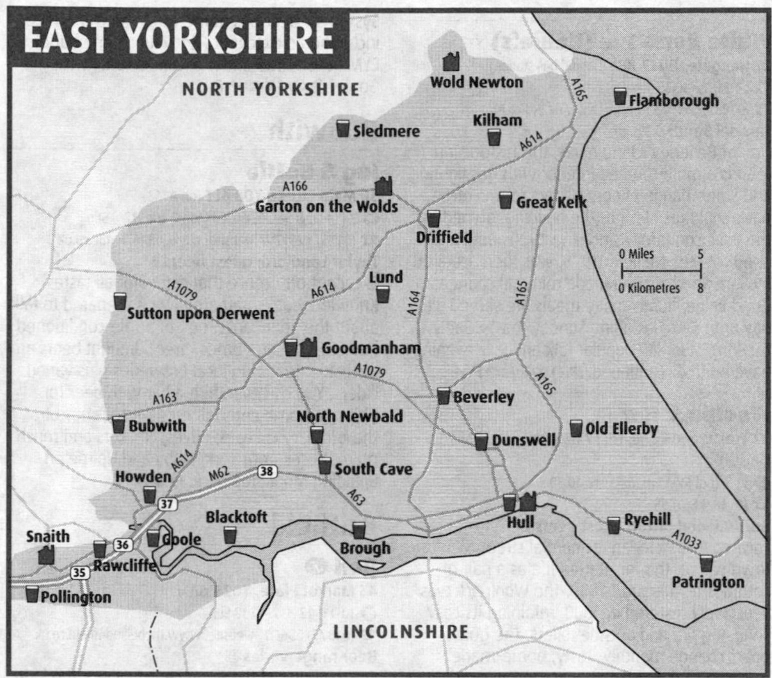

YORKSHIRE (EAST)

Beverley

Cornerhouse

2 Norwood, HU17 9ET (near bus station)
12-2.30, 5-11; 12-11 Fri; 11-11 Sat; 12-10.30 Sun
(01482) 882652
Black Sheep Best Bitter; Greene King Abbot; Rooster's Yankee; Taylor Landlord; Tetley Bitter; guest beers H

Former Tetley pub, known as the Valiant Soldier, this historic listed building was gutted by the previous owners before its rebirth as the Cornerhouse in 1999. This well-respected pub/café bar serves quality food in colourful surroundings. Guest beers, Westons Old Rosie cider, plus malt whiskies and cocktails add variety. Food is a speciality, mostly home made and served until 8pm. Tuesday is curry night and the pub opens early on weekends for English breakfast. ❀◖◗ ♠P

Dog & Duck Inn

33 Ladygate, HU17 8BH
11-4, 7-11; 11-11 Sat; 12-3, 7-10.30 Sun
(01482) 862419
Caledonian Deuchars IPA; Greene King Abbot; John Smith's Bitter; guest beer H

Just off the main Saturday market, next to the historic picture playhouse, the Dog & Duck, built in the 1930s, has been in the same family for over 30 years. It comprises a former tap room, with a period brick fireplace and bentwood seating, a lounge and a rear snug area, but dividing walls have been removed. The good value, home-made lunches are popular and include pensioners' specials. Guest accommodation is in six purpose-built, self-contained rooms to the rear. ♨⇌◖♣

Durham Ox

48 Norwood, HU17 9HJ (300 yds E of bus station)
10.30-11; 12-10.30 Sun
(01482) 679444
John Smith's Bitter; Tetley Bitter; guest beers H

Two-roomed Victorian local near the new Tesco store that was built on the site of the former cattle market. The pub was refurbished about five years ago after consultation with CAMRA's local pub preservation officer. The lounge was extended to include a games area, but thankfully it retains its original etched windows, public bar with wooden floor and off-sales hatch in the entrance lobby. The pub fields four darts and two dominoes teams. Off-street parking is possible directly opposite. Q◖⊟♣

Royal Standard Inn ✔

30 North Bar Within, HU17 8DL
12-11; 12-10.30 Sun
(01482) 882434
Jennings Cumberland Ale; Tetley Bitter; guest beer H

Classic town local by the historic North Bar and close to the racecourse. The small front bar features bentwood seating from the 1920s, but the Darley's window is a recent reproduction. The comfortable lounge to the rear hosts occasional live music. Award-winning hanging baskets and a bench on the pavement are a summer attraction. No food is served, but you can bring your own sandwiches. Q❀⊟

INDEPENDENT BREWERIES

Garton Garton on the Wolds
Goodmanham Goodmanham
Old Mill Snaith
Whalebone Hull
Wold Top Wold Newton

White Horse Inn (Nellie's) ☆

22 Hengate, HU17 8BL (behind bus station)

11-11; 12-10.30 Sun

(01482) 861973 website: www.nellies.co.uk

Samuel Smith OBB H

One of Beverley's landmarks, this historic inn retains a multi-roomed interior with gas lighting and stone-flagged floors; all five rooms often have coal fires blazing. The building, owned by the Collinson family since the 1920s until the death of Miss Nellie in 1975, was then acquired by Sam Smith's, who made minimal changes. Good value, home-made meals are served all day until 5pm, including Sunday roasts. Sadly, the long-standing popular folk and jazz evenings have been discontinued. Q P

Woolpack Inn

37 Westwood Road, HU17 8EN (near Westwood, S of hospital)

12-2 (not Mon-Fri), 6-11; 12-10.30 Sun

(01482) 867095

Burtonwood Bitter; guest beers H

Located in a Victorian residential street, W of the town centre, this inn started life as a pair of cottages built around 1830. The Woolpack was sensitively restored in 2000, retaining its cosy snug, log fire and outside toilets. The guest beers change monthly. Tasty, home-made meals, based on fresh produce, are served Wed-Sat, 6-8pm plus Sunday roasts (12-2pm). It hosts a folk night (Tue), quiz night (Thu) and live music on Sunday evening. Children are welcome, dogs too. Q

Blacktoft

Hope & Anchor

Main Street, DN14 7YW (3½ miles S of Gilberdyke station)

4-11; 12-10.30 Sun

(01430) 440441

John Smith's Bitter; Theakston Mild; guest beer H

Village local with a recently added conservatory that, like the outdoor tables, looks out across the River Ouse to Blacktoft Sands bird sanctuary. To the side is a children's play area. On the Trans-Pennine trail link, the pub is popular with walkers and cyclists, and with seamen who tie up at the nearby jetty. Note the collection of Laurel and Hardy figures. Old Mill Mild sometimes replaces the Theakston's. The village is served by South Cave-Goole, EYMS No. 160 bus (Wed and Sat only). P

Brough

Buccaneer

47 Station Road, HU15 1DZ

12-2.30, 5-11; 12-11 Fri & Sat; 12-10.30 Sun

(01482) 667435

Black Sheep Best Bitter; Tetley Dark Mild, Bitter; guest beer H

Friendly pub at the heart of the old village, it dates back to 1870 when it was the Railway Tavern. The pub was renovated in 2000 to provide a bar-lounge (displaying old local photos) and a comfortable 45-seater dining room. The present name was introduced in 1968 in honour of the aircraft company (now BAE Systems). Delicious home-made food is served, including an excellent Friday lunchtime buffet. EYMS buses 155 and X62 connect Hull with Goole. P

Bubwith

Jug & Bottle

50 Main Street, YO8 6LT (on A163)

5 (11 Fri & Sat)-9; closed Mon & Tue; 12-8 Sun

(01757) 289707 website: www.jugandbottle.co.uk

Taylor Landlord; guest beers H

Excellent off-licence that caters for all tastes. Knowledgeable staff are always prepared to talk about the abundant range of bottle-conditioned beers. Two (sometimes three) draught beers are available, featuring local breweries plus various ciders. You can even hire a bar with beer for ultimate home entertainment. It sells out-of-the-ordinary cheeses, olives, crackers and much more. Buses from York, Selby and Holme on Spalding Moor stop here. Q

Driffield

Bell ✓

46 Market Place, YO25 6AN

10-11; 12-3, 7-10.30 Sun

(01377) 256661 website: www.thebellindriffield.co.uk

Beer range varies H

Coaching inn at the town centre where the long, wood-panelled bar's red leather seating, substantial fireplaces, antiques and paintings lend a quality feel. Two or three beers are kept, usually from Wold Top, Hambleton or Highwood breweries, but other micros are also represented. Over 300 malt whiskies are stocked. A covered courtyard has bistro seating. A splendid lunchtime carvery buffet is served Mon-Sat; the restaurant opens 7-9.30pm; Sunday lunch must be booked. Children are welcome until 7.30pm; the no-smoking area is available 10-6pm. Q P

Foundry

7 Market Walk, YO25 6BW (down passageway off market place)

10-3 (not Wed; 10-4 Fri), 7-11; 10-11 Tue & Sat; 12-3 (closed eve) Sun

(01377) 253874

Beer range varies H

Café and bar housed in the only building that remains of the old Victoria Foundry complex. The ground floor is divided in two: a front area with a tiled floor, comfortable bench seating, tables and chairs; the raised rear area is known as 'the comfort zone' because of the sofas and low tables. The walls throughout are bare brick with original heavy beams. Daily papers are provided for customers. Up to five beers are available at weekends in this completely no-smoking hostelry. P

Mariner's Arms

47 Eastgate South, YO25 6LR (near cattle market)

3 (12 Sat)-11; 12-4.30, 7-10.30 Sun

(01377) 253708

Burtonwood Bitter; guest beer H

This street-corner local is well worth seeking out as an alternative to the John Smith's outlets that dominate the 'capital of the Wolds'. Formerly part of the Hull Brewery estate, its four small rooms have now become two: a basic bar and more comfortable lounge. The long-standing licensees create a friendly atmosphere. Note at time of survey the pub had just been purchased by W&D. Driffield is well served by buses – the EYMS No. 121, Hull-Scarborough being the most frequent. ❀⊟⇌♣P

Rose & Crown ✔

North Street, YO25 6AS (400 yds N of centre)

⌚ 11 (12 autumn & winter)-11; 12-10.30 Sun

☎ (01377) 253041

John Smith's Bitter; guest beers ⊞

Family-run pub, opposite the town's Green Flag awarded park. It comprises a main bar/lounge and a pool room. Televised live sport is shown and Thursday is quiz night. Numerous sports teams represent the pub throughout the week. The two guest beers change every few days and include one from an independent brewery. Table service is available Thursday-Saturday nights. Bar lunches are served weekdays. Benches are provided outside for summer drinking. The EYMS No. 121 Hull-Scarborough bus and other services run regularly. ❀◐♣P

Dunswell

Ship Inn

Beverley Road, HU6 0AJ

⌚ 11-11; 12-10.30 Sun

☎ (01482) 859160

John Smith's Bitter; Taylor Landlord; guest beer ⊞

Attractive, homely, white-painted roadside pub fronting the old Hull-Beverley road. It once served traffic on the nearby River Hull – hence the name. Log fires warm the convivial interior that is divided to form a dining area with church pew seating. Events include occasional beer festivals, held in the adjoining paddock. Meals are served from 11-7pm. Accommodation will be available from autumn 2005. The pub lies on the main bus route serving Hull, Beverley and Scarborough. ⋒❀◐◑♣P

Flamborough

Seabirds

Tower Street, YO15 1PD

⌚ 12-3, 7 (6 summer)-11; 12-3, 7 (6.30 summer)-10.30 Sun

☎ (01262) 850242

John Smith's Bitter; guest beer ⊞

Once two rooms, this pub changed ownership in 2003 and has been refurbished, resulting in a clean, contemporary look. The guest beer often comes from a local brewery. A range of home-cooked food, with vegetarian options, is based on local produce whenever possible. Varied camping options are available nearby; the pub is popular with walkers and bird enthusiasts – spectacular cliffs and Bempton RSPB Sanctuary are close by. EYMS buses 510 and 502 from Bridlington provide an occasional service.
⋒❀◐◑⛺P⊬

Goodmanham

Goodmanham Arms ✔

Main Street, YO43 3JA

⌚ 4 (12 Fri, Sat & summer)-11; 12-10.30 Sun

☎ (01430) 873849 website: www.goodmanhamarms.co.uk

Goodmanham Randy Monk, seasonal beers; Theakston Best Bitter; guest beer (occasional) ⊞

On the Wolds Way opposite the Norman church, a mile from Market Weighton, this classic village pub serves beers from its own micro-brewery. The welcoming open fire, basic furnishings, tiled floor, outside gents' toilet and absence of recorded music all contribute to the sense of stepping back in time. No food is served, but the summer Sunday barbecues are a good feature. It hosts monthly traditional folk sessions (first Thu). Ring to check opening times if travelling far. Dogs are welcome.
⋒Q❀⊟♣P

Goole

Macintosh Arms

13 Aire Street, DN14 5QE

⌚ 11-11; 12-10.30 Sun

☎ (01405) 763850

John Smith's Bitter; Tetley Bitter, Imperial; guest beer ⊞

Opposite Goole docks and once part of a courthouse, this long-standing Guide entry attracts a varied clientele. It can be busy weekend evenings, but the host and locals are always welcoming. Home to the Wobbly Goolies motorcycle club, see the evidence of their exploits and themed charity events on the notice board. Pavement benches are provided for warm weather. The guest beer is changed often at one of the few authentic real ale pubs left in the town.
❀⊟⇌♣P

Great Kelk

Chestnut Horse

Main Street, YO25 8HN (follow signs for Kelk)

⌚ 6 (5.30 Fri & Sat; 5 summer)-11; 12-10.30 Sun

☎ (01262) 488263

John Smith's Bitter; guest beers ⊞

Built in 1793, this delightful Grade II listed, rural community pub is situated between the Wolds and Holderness. Darts, dominoes and chess are played here. It comprises a cosy bar with real fire, a comfortable games room that doubles as a daytime family room and a restaurant serving lunches Friday-Sunday and evening meals. Food is also available in the bar Sunday lunchtime and every evening. Up to three guest beers are sold alongside draught Hoegaarden; Belgian bottled beers are served in authentic glasses.
⋒❀◐◑⊟♣P

Howden

Barnes Wallis

Station Road, North Howden, DN14 7LF (on B1228, next to station)

⌚ 12-2 (3 Sat), 5-11; closed Mon; 12-10.30 Sun

☎ (01430) 430639 website: www.barneswallis.co.uk

John Smith's Bitter; guest beers ⊞

Recently refurbished, one-roomed pub, adjacent to Howden Station, but over a mile from the town centre. Yorkshire micro-breweries feature in the guest ales. Aviation memorabilia decorate the bar, including the inn sign that commemorates the Wellington Bomber designed by Barnes Wallis. Quizzes are held on Sunday afternoon and Wednesday evening. People travel from all over to visit this thriving semi-rural pub. ♨❀◑♿⇌♣P

Hull

Bay Horse

113 Wincolmlee, HU2 8AH (400 yds N of North Bridge on W bank of river)

✪ 11-11; 12-10.30 Sun

☎ (01482) 329227

Bateman Mild, XB, XXXB, seasonal beers Ⓗ

Well worth a stroll from the centre, this former Bass street-corner local is the most northern, and Hull's only, Bateman's house. The mostly original L-shaped bar displays photos of the city's two rugby league teams. To the right is a lofty stable lounge – an extension that was added when Bateman's purchased the pub in 1990. This room, decorated with brewery memorabilia, is also used as a restaurant and for functions. The large stove is a real attraction; especially in winter. ♨Q☋⊟♣P

Editorial

48 Spring Bank, HU3 1AB

✪ 12-11; 12-10.30 Sun

☎ (01482) 327738

Tetley Bitter; guest beers Ⓗ

The pub takes its name from the nearby Hull Daily Mail newspaper offices. This conversion is one of just a few free houses in the city. A narrow, middle bar has a seating area where live entertainment is staged at weekends. The rear part is mainly used for Sunday lunches. Tuesday is quiz and curry night. A recent refurbishment has regrettably seen many of the historical newspaper extracts removed in favour of a minimalist theme. A Hydes beer is often available. ❀♿⇌♣●

Gardeners Arms

35 Cottingham Road, HU5 2PP

✪ 11-11; 12-10.30 Sun

☎ (01482) 342396

Tetley Bitter; guest beers Ⓗ

Hull CAMRA Pub of the Year 2004 and a finalist since 1999, it is situated on a main bus route. The original front bar has seen many alterations, but retains the matchwood ceiling that blends with the current ale house style. The large rear extension is comfortably furnished, housing several pool tables. Good value food is served 12-2.30pm and 5-7pm (12-6pm at weekends). The six guest beers in the front bar usually include one each from Bateman and Cropton. It hosts three weekly quizzes. ❀◑⊟♿♣●P⊬

Green Bricks

9 Humber Dock Street, HU1 1TB

✪ 1-11; 12-10.30 Sun

☎ (01482) 591961

Tetley Bitter; guest beers Ⓗ

Benefiting from panoramic views over the marina, this pub attracts those interested in boats. The former Humber Dock Tavern was extended in the 1990s into a large one roomer with comfy sofas for chilling out, and plenty of dining space. Good value traditional food is served daily until 9pm. There are designated no-smoking areas. Guest beers (usually two) are mainly obtained from Yorkshire micro-breweries; real perry is stocked. A space can be sectioned off for private functions. ❀◑♿●⊬

Hole in the Wall

115 Spring Bank, HU3 1BH

✪ 1 (12 Fri & Sat) 11; 12 10.30 Sun

☎ (01482) 580354

Old Mill Mild; Rooster's Yankee; guest beers Ⓗ

Former amusement arcade, converted in 2001, it offers up to four guest beers, mainly sourced from independents, including local breweries. All real ales are reduced in price Monday-Thursday. Featuring wood floors throughout, the spacious front bar has plenty of standing room and comfortable leather upholstered bench seating. Sports enthusiasts prefer the rear bar for its large-screen TV and pool table. It is handy for the KC Stadium and railway station – both 15 minutes' walk away. ❀⇄♿⇌♣

Oberon

44-45 Queen Street, HU1 1UU

✪ 5 (12 Fri & Sat)-11; closed Tue; 12-10.30 Sun

☎ (01482) 217557

Black Sheep Best Bitter; Tetley Bitter; Wentworth WPA Ⓗ

This traditional two-roomed pub has thankfully reverted to its original name. It is situated a short distance from the Corporation Pier, affording excellent views of 'the Deep' across the mouth of the River Hull. Two rotating guest beers are available. Fish and chips are a speciality for Friday and Sunday lunch. This atmospheric pub, which is also handy for Hull Marina, has been rejuvenated by its jovial landlord. ◑⊟♣

Olde Black Boy ☆

150 High Street, HU1 1PS

✪ 12-11; 12-10.30 Sun

☎ (01482) 326516 website: www.yeoldeblackboy.co.uk

Caledonian Deuchars IPA; guest beers Ⓗ

Licensed in 1729, this town pub on the medieval cobbled High Street is a five-minute walk from 'the Deep'. Note the leaded display front window and the carved head above the fireplace in the front snug; the upstairs bar and dining room both feature stained glass windows and Victorian fireplaces. Six guest ales, Gale's fruit wines and foreign beers are available. It hosts live piano and folk music. The pub is a Grade II listed building following a successful local CAMRA campaign. ♨Q⊟♣●

Old English Gentleman

Mason Street, HU2 8BH (beind New Theatre)

✪ 11-11; 12-10.30 Sun

☎ (01482) 324659

website: www.theoldenglishgentleman.com

Banks's Riding Bitter; guest beers Ⓗ

This former shop was 200 years old in 2005. It became a pub in 1831 and now consists of one single U-shaped room divided by a double-sided fireplace. Its attractive, dark wood panelled walls feature dozens of pictures of artistes who have appeared at the New Theatre. Its proximity to the stage door ensures regular visits from actors and musicians. Two guest beers are available in this revitalised, family-run, atmospheric pub. Evening meals finish at 7pm. ❀◑⇌♣

Olde White Harte ☆

25 Silver Street, HU1 1JG

⏲ 11-11; 12-10.30 Sun

☎ (01482) 326363

Caledonian Deuchars IPA; McEwan's 80/-; Theakston Best Bitter, Old Peculier Ⓗ

Historic, 16th-century courtyard pub, reputedly the residence of the Governor of Hull when he resolved to deny Charles I entry to the city. An impressive staircase leads to the 'plotting room'. The ground floor comprises two distinct areas, with both bars open at busy times. Award-winning floral displays, superb dark woodwork, stained glass windows and sit-in fireplaces feature. At the heart of the old town's commercial centre, it has a covered, heated outdoor drinking area. An extensive range of single malts is stocked. Q❀◑⇌

Pave

16-20 Princes Avenue, HU5 3QA

⏲ 11 (12 Mon)-11; 12-10.30 Sun

☎ (01482) 333181 website: www.pavebar.co.uk

Theakston Best Bitter, XB; guest beer Ⓗ

Cosmopolitan café bar; the result of a conversion in 2002. Single roomed, it incorporates a raised stage area with real fire. Comfy sofas and leather seating attract diverse drinkers; it is especially popular at weekends. Live jazz is played on Sunday afternoons. A secluded garden and front patio are pleasurable in warmer months. A varied range of European draught and bottled beers is stocked. The menu, including vegetarian options, is served from opening until 7pm daily. ♨❀◑♿

Three John Scotts ✔

Lowgate, HU1 1XW

⏲ 10-11; 12-10.30 Sun

☎ (01482) 381910

Greene King Abbot; Hop Back Summer Lightning; Marston's Pedigree; Tetley Bitter; Theakston Old Peculier; guest beers Ⓗ

Converted from the Edwardian post office opposite St Mary's church in the old town area, this open-plan Wetherspoon's features modern decor. It was named after three past incumbents of the church. It draws a mixed clientele at lunchtime and circuit drinkers at weekends. A large rear courtyard has plentiful seating. Up to five guest beers are on tap, plus Westons Old Rosie cider. Food offers include a steak club (Tue) and curry club (Thu).
❀◑♿●⚟

Wellington Inn

55 Russell Street, HU2 9AB (on N edge of city centre)

⏲ 12-11; 12-10.30 Sun

☎ (01482) 329486

Tetley Bitter; guest beers Ⓗ

Back-street free house established in 2004 in a former Hull Brewery house dating from 1861. Refurbished to a high standard, it boasts a walk-in cooler with a stock of more than 80 European bottled beers and up to eight traditional ciders and perries; see the glass-fronted display in the back bar. Up to six guest beers mainly come from Yorkshire and Lincolnshire independents. No food is available but you are welcome to bring your own sandwiches. Outdoor drinking is next to the car park. ❀●P⚟

Whalebone

165 Wincolmlee, HU2 0PA (500 yds N of North Bridge on W bank of river)

⏲ 12-11; 12-10.30 Sun

☎ (01482) 327980

Tom Wood Best Bitter; Taylor Landlord; Whalebone Diana Mild, Neckoil, seasonal beers; guest beer (occasional) Ⓗ

Built in 1796 on the site of the old Lockwood's Brewery, the pub is situated on the former harbour in an old industrial area – look for the illuminated M&R Ales sign. The comfortable saloon bar is adorned with photos of bygone Hull pubs and the city's sporting heritage; several CAMRA awards are also displayed. The Whalebone Brewery, housed in the adjacent building, started brewing in 2003. Two real ciders and Gale's country wines are available, plus hot bar snacks. ♨♣●

Kilham

Old Star

Church Street, YO25 4RG

⏲ 12-2 (not Sat), 5.30 (5 summer)-11 (12-11 summer Sat); 12-10.30 Sun

☎ (01262) 420619

John Smith's Bitter; guest beers Ⓗ

Village pub at the heart of the Wolds. Dark oak panelling has been retained throughout the central bar and four rooms. Three real fires keep everyone cosy in winter. One of the guest beers is likely to come from Archers; Westons Old Rosie cider is sold in summer. Food is always freshly prepared – a varied menu, including vegetarian options, is available throughout the week. EYMS bus No. 126 (to Driffield) offers an occasional service. ♨❀◑◐⊟●P

Lund

Wellington Inn

19 The Green, YO25 9TE

⏲ 12-3 (not Mon), 6.30-11; 12-3, 6.30-10.30 Sun

☎ (01377) 217294

Black Sheep Best Bitter; John Smith's Bitter; Taylor Landlord; guest beer Ⓗ

The Wellington boasts a prime site on the green in this award-winning Wolds village. Most of its trade comes from the local farming community. It was totally renovated by the present licensee, and features stone-flagged floors, beamed ceilings and three real fires. This multi-roomed pub includes a no-smoking room, a games room and a candlelit restaurant serving evening meals, Tuesday-Saturday. Good quality food can be enjoyed at lunchtime from the bar menu and specials board. ♨◑⊟♿♣P⚟

North Newbald

Tiger

The Green, YO43 4SA

⏲ 12-11; 12-10.30 Sun

☎ (01430) 827759

Black Sheep Best Bitter; John Smith's Bitter; Taylor Landlord Ⓗ

Overlooking the village green, in a picturesque setting in the Yorkshire Wolds, the Tiger is a Grade II listed building. The layout comprises a public bar, a recently introduced no-smoking lounge and a family/games room with a pool table. It is especially popular with walkers; the Wolds Way footpath passes nearby. Sunday lunches must be booked, sandwiches are available at other times. The EYMS bus No. 143 provides an occasional service from Beverley and Drough. ♨Q☕❀P

Old Ellerby

Blue Bell Inn

Crabtree Lane, HU11 5AJ

✪ 12-4.30 (not Mon-Fri), 7-11; 12-5, 7-10.30 Sun

☎ (01964) 562364

Black Sheep Best Bitter; Tetley Bitter; guest beers Ⓗ

The single room in this 16th-century inn has a rear games area and a snug to the right of the L-shaped bar. Tiled floors, beamed ceilings and horse brasses are features of this community-based pub that holds many fundraising events. Morris dancers visit in summer and before Christmas. The large garden houses a bowling green and a children's play area. EYMS Hull-Hornsea bus 230/240 runs twice daily (not Sun). It was CAMRA's East Yorkshire Pub of the Year in 1998, 2000 and 2003. ♨Q❀▲♣●P

Patrington

Hildyard Arms

1 Market Place, HU12 0RA

✪ 12-11; 12-10.30 Sun

☎ (01964) 630234

Draught Bass; Tetley Bitter; guest beer Ⓗ

Former coaching inn at the village centre. A central bar serves a no-smoking restaurant, a pool and games room, and a public bar; each room has a real fire and cottage decor. All food is freshly prepared, including daily specials and both lunch and evening carveries on Sunday. The pub is convenient for Patrington Haven holiday park and Spurn Point nature reserve. A regular bus service operates between Hull and Withernsea, EYMS Nos. 71, 75, 76 and 77.
♨Q❀◐◑⊟♣P

Pollington

King's Head

Main Street, DN14 0DN (signed from A19)

✪ 5.30-11; 12-5, 7-10.30 Sun

☎ (01405) 861507

Daleside Bitter; Tetley Bitter; guest beer Ⓗ

Old village pub, at the Snaith end of Main Street, that surprises the visitor on entry as modernisation has resulted in one large airy room, with a games area occupying one quarter, and which is served by the original V-shaped bar. Very much a community pub, its friendly hosts create a relaxed atmosphere. Well worth the detour from the nearby A645 Knottingley-Snaith road; the guest beer is normally from Daleside. The garden has a play area.
❀⛟♣P

Rawcliffe

Jemmy Hirst at the Rose & Crown

26 Riverside, DN14 8RN

✪ 6 (5 Fri; 12 Sat)-11; 12-10.30 Sun

☎ (01405) 831038

website: www.goolelink.co.uk/Pubs_and_Clubs

Taylor Landlord; guest beers Ⓗ

A shining example of how commitment to real ale pays off. This pub was taken over and transformed by CAMRA members four years ago. This includes educating locals about the delights of proper beer. The number of handpumps has increased to four, serving a changing range of beers, promoting regional micros and interesting ales from further afield. Their dedication has been rewarded by already winning local CAMRA Pub of the Year twice in a row. Sunday lunch must be booked. ♨❀◑♣P

Ryehill

Crooked Billet

Pitt Lane, HU12 9NN (400 yds off A1033, E of Thorngumbald)

✪ 11-11; 12-10.30 Sun

☎ (01964) 622303

Burtonwood Bitter, guest beer Ⓗ

Unspoilt, 17th-century coaching inn featuring a stone-flagged floor, comfortable upholstered seating areas, horse brasses and old pictures of the pub. This two-roomed inn is a peaceful retreat. Guest beers are from Burtonwood's monthly list. Good quality, home-cooked food is served from Tuesday evening through to Sunday. At the heart of the local community, it supports cricket and darts teams and a Scrabble club. Regular buses run on the Hull-Withernsea route, EYMS Nos. 71, 75, 76 and 77.
♨Q◐◑♣P

Sledmere

Triton Inn

Main Street, YO25 3XQ

✪ 12-3, 5-11; 12-11 Sat; 12-10.30 Sun

☎ (01377) 236644 website: www.thetritoninnsledmere.co.uk

Camerons Bitter; Taylor Landlord; Wold Top Bitter, Falling Stone, seasonal beers; guest beers Ⓗ

This 18th-century coaching inn formed part of the Sykes family estate; see their motto and coat of arms on the pub sign. The main bar features a real fire, oak panelling and settles; the beams display horseshoes from classic winners bred at the nearby Sledmere stud. A meeting place for the village football team, it fields darts, pool and dominoes teams and the local art club meets here. Lunches are served Friday-Monday (evening meals Mon, Fri and Sat); sandwiches are usually available.
♨Q❀⛟◐◑⊟♣●P⚟▯

South Cave

Fox & Coney ✔

52 Market Place, HU15 2AT

✪ 11.30-2.30, 4.30-11; 11.30-11 Sat; 12-10.30 Sun

☎ (01430) 424336 website: www.foxandconey.com

Caledonian Deuchars IPA; Taylor Landlord; Theakston Cool Cask; guest beer Ⓗ

Dating from 1739, this coaching inn is the second oldest building in the village. The second landlord, a furrier, added the eponymous coney, and it is thought to be the only pub in England with this name. This friendly pub is warmed by three real fires in winter. Good food is served in generous portions – try the mixed grill or

gammon steak (booking is advisable at weekends when it can get busy). The village is served by EYMS bus service 155 (Hull-Goole).
⌂❀⊭◑P

Sutton upon Derwent

St Vincent Arms

Main Street, YO41 4BN (follow B1228 beyond Elvington)
⏲ 11.30-3, 6-11; 12-3, 7-10.30 Sun
☎ (01904) 608349
Fuller's Chiswick, Old Mill Bitter; Taylor Landlord; Wells Bombardier; York Yorkshire Terrier; guest beers Ⓗ
Quintessential country inn, renowned for its range of Fuller's beers, including ESB direct from the barrel. Owned and run by the same family for many years, it combines a village local with an excellent restaurant. The striking, whitewashed building contains several rooms: a cosy bar, little-changed over the years and often busy with groups of regulars; a smaller bar/dining room and two further dining areas. Note the large Fuller, Smith & Turner mirror.
Q❀◑ ⛺P

YORKSHIRE (NORTH)

Appletreewick

New Inn

Appletreewick, BD23 6DA
⏲ 12-3 (not Mon; 12-3.45 Sat), 7-11; 12-3, 7-10.30 Sun
☎ (01756) 720252
Daleside Bitter; John Smith's Bitter; Theakston Old Peculier Ⓗ
Small, friendly, unspoilt village local, affording fine views of the surrounding fells, in this Guide since 1988. It stocks a large range of bottled beer from around the world with three foreign beers on tap. The Dales Way long distance footpath and the Yorkshire Dales cycle way close by make it an excellent stop for walkers and cyclists who can make use of the pub's cycle livery for any maintenance. The No. 74 Ilkley-Grassington bus passes (not Sun).
⌂♘❀⊭◑ ⛺P

Beck Hole (near Goathland)

Birch Hall Inn ☆

YO22 5LE (1 mile N of Goathland) OSN28202
⏲ 11-3, 7.30-11 (not Mon eve); 11-11 May-Aug; 12-10.30 Sun
☎ (01947) 896245
Black Sheep Best Bitter; Theakston Black Bull; guest beer Ⓗ
Hidden gem, worth seeking out. The pub dates from the 1860s and has had just three licensees in the past 80 years. It has been deliberately left unchanged: two bars are separated by a small shop. The snug is served by hatch from the shop. The outside sign is a painting by Algernon Newton RA. The terrace is reached by steep stone steps to the side, but seats are also provided outside the pub. See the little train in the bar. ⌂Q❀⊟⛺⇌(Goathland NYMR)

Beckwithshaw

Smith's Arms

Church Row, HG3 1QW (on B6161)
⏲ 11-11; 12-10.30 Sun
☎ (01423) 504871
Courage Directors; Theakston Best Bitter; guest beer Ⓗ
In a pretty village just outside Harrogate, this large food-oriented pub has earned an excellent reputation for its menu. The three real ales include a guest beer that often changes. Both the interior and car park are spacious and there is a garden to the rear. Children are welcome.
⌂Q❀◑♿P

Bedale

Three Coopers

2 Emgate, DL8 1AH (between High St and station)
⏲ 12-11; 12-10.30 Sun
☎ (01677) 422153
Black Sheep Best Bitter; Jennings Bitter, Cumberland Ale Ⓗ
Fascinating town pub in a side street, near the market cross and just off the main street of Bedale – the 'Gateway to the Dales'. Decorated in a rustic style with bare stone and brick walls and floorboards, it has been opened out into three main drinking areas on different levels. The nearby Wensleydale Railway station reopened in 2004 after 50 years with no trains.
⌂❀⇌(Wensleydale Rlwy) ♣

Bishop Monkton

Lamb & Flag

Boroughbridge Road, HG4 3QN (off A61)
⏲ 12-3 (not Mon), 5.30-11; 12-3, 7-10.30 Sun
☎ (01765) 677322
Daleside Bitter; Tetley Bitter; guest beer Ⓗ
This cosy country pub is the centre of activity for the village. It supports many local clubs and societies, and is an active fundraiser for the cricket team. Its two rooms are filled with knick-knacks and brasses. The nearby stream hosts the August bank holiday plastic duck race.
⌂Q♘❀◑⛺♣P

Bishopthorpe

Ebor Inn

Main Street, YO23 2RB
⏲ 11-11; 12-10.30 Sun
☎ (01904) 706190
Samuel Smith OBB Ⓗ
Good-sized local in a picturesque village, close to the palace of the Archbishop of York. Two large rooms lie either side of the entrance and bar area, bearing decor typical of this local independent brewery. Good wholesome food is freshly cooked; a speciality being fresh fish from Whitby on the Yorkshire coast. This family-friendly pub benefits from a large, well-equipped garden where village fetes and bonfire parties are held. ⌂Q❀◑⊟♿♣P

Blakey Ridge

Lion Inn

YO62 7LQ (6 miles N of Hutton le Hole on Castleton road)
⏲ 11-11; 12-10.30 Sun
☎ (01751) 417320 website: www.lionblakey.co.uk
Greene King Old Speckled Hen; John Smith's Bitter; Theakston Best Bitter, Black Bull Bitter, XB, Old Peculier Ⓗ

NORTH YORKSHIRE

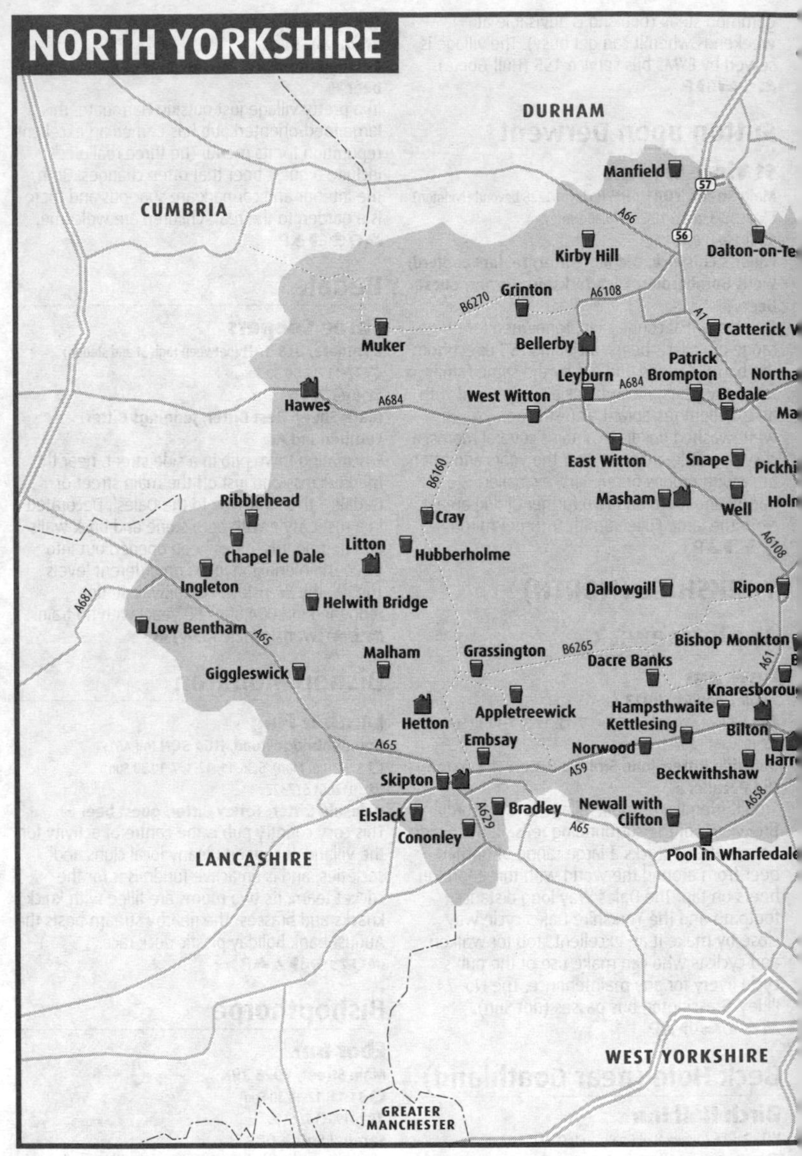

Remote moorland inn on a ridge between Rosedale and Farndale. The fourth highest pub in England, it was founded by priors in the 16th century, near a Neolithic burial mound. Business boomed in the 19th century due to the local iron mining industry. Recently extended, with a separate dining room, the beamed ceilings, open fires and various drinking areas make the inn popular with walkers and visitors who come especially for the food, served in generous portions. ⚑❀⇄◐◑ ⛺P

Boroughbridge

Black Bull Inn

6 St James Square, YO51 9AR
✪ 11-11; 12-10.30 Sun ☎ (01423) 322413
John Smith's Bitter; Theakston Best Bitter; guest beer Ⓗ

The inn is situated in the town square, opposite where St James Church used to stand until it was moved 500 yards to its present site many years ago. The oak-framed building, with many parts dating back to 1262, is steeped in history. It has three rooms (one no-smoking) and is said to be haunted by a monk-like figure who disappears through walls. A restaurant has been added at the rear where the stables used to be. The car park holds four vehicles.
⚑Q⇄◐◑ ⛺♣P⚟

Borrowby

Wheatsheaf

YO7 4QP (1 mile off A19, trunk route)
✪ 5.30 (12 Sat)-11; 12-4, 7-10.30 Sun
☎ (01845) 537274 website: www.borrowbypub.co.uk
Daleside Bitter; Tetley Bitter; guest beers Ⓗ

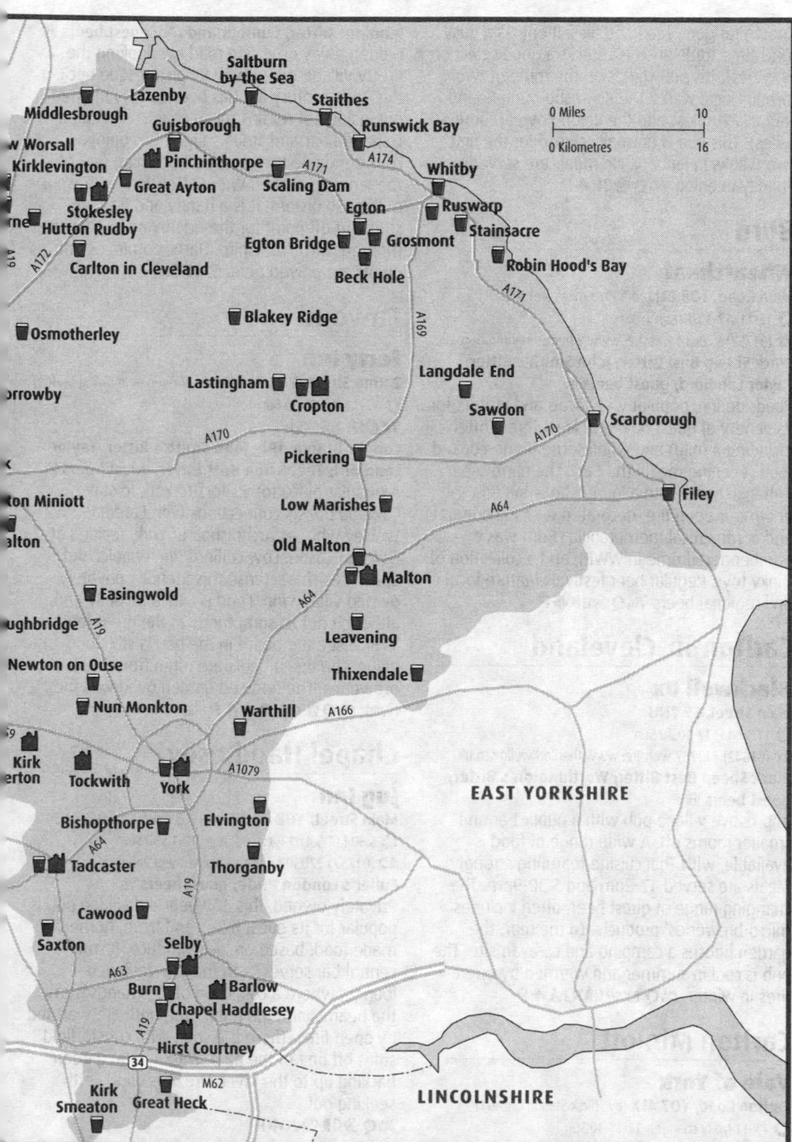

In a pretty village, the jewel of this Grade II listed inn is its splendid public bar, which has changed little since Victorian times and remains the hub of activity. Dominated by an unusual and attractive fireplace, the room is decorated with antique brass and copperware. There is a dining room and a no-smoking room behind the bar. The landlord successfully weaned locals from the ubiquitous John Smith's onto his Daleside and guest beers. Evening meals are served Tuesday-Saturday.

Bradley

Slaters Arms

Crag Lane, BD20 9ER OS003481

12-3, 5-11; 12-10.30 Sun

☎ (01535) 632179

Black Sheep Best Bitter; John Smith's Bitter; Tetley Bitter; Wells Bombardier Ⓗ

Two-roomed local at the eastern end of a quiet country village, half a mile from the Leeds-Liverpool canal. The traditional style lounge has an open fireplace with real fire. A smaller back room is near the exit to the car park and garden, which give extensive views of the Aire Valley. The high quality meals, served in the lounge, attract visitors from afar. P

Brearton

Malt Shovel Inn

Main Street, HG3 3BX (off B6165, Ripley road)

12-2.30, 6.45-11; closed Mon; 12-2.30, 6.45-10.30 Sun

☎ (01423) 862929

Black Sheep Best Bitter; Daleside Bitter; Theakston Best Bitter; guest beers Ⓗ

Little inn on the outskirts of Harrogate, well

known for good food and ales. It enjoys a busy lunchtime trade and also stocks a good selection of wines. This pub stands on the route of two famous local walks: the Knaresborough Round (about 22 miles) and the Ripon Rowel (about 50 miles). This pub is normally closed for the first two weeks in January. No meals are served Sunday evening. ♨Q✿◐◑♣P

Burn

Wheatsheaf

Main Road, YO8 8LJ (on A19, 3 miles S of Selby)
⏲ 12-11; 12-10.30 Sun
☎ (01757) 270614 website: www.wheatsheafburn.f9.co.uk
Black Sheep Best Bitter; John Smith's Bitter; Taylor Landlord; guest beers Ⓗ
Roadside inn, popular with locals and visitors for its variety of guest beers (at least three, often including a mild) and wholesome home-cooked food (evening meals Thu-Sat). The narrow bar entrance opens into a lounge boasting an enormous open fire, decorated with agricultural and aeronautical memorabilia (Burn was a bomber aerodrome in WWII), and a collection of Dinky toys. Regular beer festivals feature local and regional beers. ♨Q✿◐◑♣P

Carlton-in-Cleveland

Blackwell Ox

Main Street, S9 7NU
⏲ 11.30-11; 12-10.30 Sun
☎ (01642) 712287 website: www.theblackwellox.co.uk
Black Sheep Best Bitter; Worthington's Bitter; guest beers Ⓗ
Impressive village pub with a public bar and smaller rooms off. A wide range of food is available, with Thai cuisine featuring strongly. Meals are served 12-2pm and 5.30-9pm. The changing range of guest beer, often includes micro-breweries' products. To the rear, the garden houses a camping and caravan site. The pub is cool in summer and warmed by open fires in winter. ♨Q☺✿◐◑⊟▲♣P

Carlton Miniott

Vale of York

Carlton Road, YO7 4LX (by Thirsk Station on A61)
⏲ 11-11 (may change); 12-10.30 Sun
☎ (01845) 528161
Black Sheep Best Bitter; John Smith's Bitter; Samuel Smith OBB; Taylor Landlord Ⓗ
Warm, comfortable and friendly pub on the outskirts of Thirsk with a quiet, relaxed atmosphere, popular with locals. Four Yorkshire-brewed ales are always on tap, including Sam Smith's – rare in this area. The 15 en-suite rooms plus bar meals and restaurant service combine to give good value for money; the restaurant provides a Sunday lunchtime carvery. The pub is adjacent to Thirsk's mainline station and a mile from the town's racecourse.
♨Q✿⛟◐◑⊟♿▲≢♣P⊘▯

Catterick Village

Bay Horse

38 Low Green, DL10 7LP (off A6136, facing village green)
⏲ 12-11; 12-10.30 Sun
☎ (01748) 811383
Jennings Bitter, Cumberland Ale; guest beers Ⓗ
Hidden away on a side road overlooking the pretty village green with its picturesque beck, this 19th-century inn has been largely opened out inside but retains much character with an L-shaped bar and small snug. It has enjoyed a commendable revival since becoming part of the Jennings estate. With Catterick racecourse a mile or so distant, it is a handy and tranquil stopping-off point for the nearby main A1 route through North Yorkshire. Darts, dominoes and quoits are played here. ✿◐◑♿♣

Cawood

Ferry Inn

2 King Street, YO8 3TL (S side of river, near swing bridge)
⏲ 12-11; 12-10.30 Sun
☎ (01757) 268515
Copper Dragon IPA; John Smith's Bitter; Taylor Landlord; Theakston Best Bitter; guest beers Ⓗ
A popular place for visitors to York to stay, Cawood boasts connections with Cardinal Wolsey who, as Archbishop of York, resided at Cawood Castle. Low ceilings, inglenooks and open fires characterise this friendly, privately-owned village inn. Food is available daily and, although not as sumptuous as the great feast of 1464 – see the board in the bar, is still good value. The guest beers are often from local breweries. The terraced garden overlooks the river. ♨Q✿⛟◐◑▲♣P

Chapel Haddlesey

Jug Inn

Main Street, YO8 8QQ (on A19, 5 miles N of M62 jct 34)
⏲ 5.30 (12 Sat)-11; closed Mon; 12-10.30 Sun
☎ (01757) 270307 website: www:thejuginn.co.uk
Fuller's London Pride; guest beers Ⓗ
Privately owned, this 300-year-old village pub is popular for its guest beers and fresh, home-made food, based on local produce. A small central bar serves both the low-ceilinged lounge, where a collection of jugs hangs from the beams, and the public bar; both are warmed by open fires. There is a snug with chesterfield sofas off one of the bars. With a large garden backing up to the River Aire, it is well worth seeking out.
♨Q✿◐◑⊟♿♣P

Chapel-le-Dale

Hill Inn

LA6 3AR (on B6255)
⏲ 12-2.30, 6-11; 12-11 Sat & summer; closed Mon; 12-10.30 Sun (phone for winter opening: Tue & Wed may be closed)
☎ (015242) 41256
Black Sheep Best Bitter, Special; Dent Bitter, Aviator; Theakston Best Bitter Ⓗ
Beloved of generations of hikers and potholers: well-worn paths run from here to both Whernside (Yorkshire's highest peak) and Ingleborough (its best known). It is also a destination for diners (booking advisable); puddings are a speciality here. Lots of exposed wood features in the bar, and some stonework. It hosts a monthly folk evening (last Fri). The nearest public transport is at Ribblehead Station (two miles).
♨✿◐◑▲P

Cononley

New Inn
Main Street, BD20 8NR
⌚ 12-3, 5.30-11; 12-11 Sat; 12-10.30 Sun
☎ (01535) 636302
Taylor Golden Best, Best Bitter, Landlord, seasonal beers ⊞
Historic inn, situated in a Dales village between Keighley and Skipton, with mullioned windows and low, beamed ceilings. Always busy, as a real local community pub it has earned a reputation for serving excellent good value meals. The New Inn is just a short walk from Cononley Station – if catching a train south, allow time to cross the level crossing. Bus route (78A/67/67A) runs between Keighley and Skipton. ⩕Q❀◑≠♣

Crathorne

Crathorne Arms
TS15 0BA
⌚ 11.30-2.30, 5-11; 11.30-11 Sat; 12-2.30, 7-10.30 Sun
☎ (01642) 701931
Black Sheep Best Bitter; Hambleton Bitter ⊞
Known locally as Free House Farm, the pub forms part of Lord Crathorne's estate and displays photographs of village life and of famous people from his own collection. The pub, all Yorkshire farmhouse outside and warmly welcoming inside, lies a short drive from the busy A19. Diners come from near and far to sample the locally-sourced, freshly-prepared food that includes meat from the neighbouring farm, which has been run hand-in-hand with the pub for over a century. ⩕Q♨❀◑♿♣P⊁▯

Cray

White Lion Inn
BD23 5JB (on B6160 N of Buckden)
⌚ 11-11; 12-10.30 Sun
☎ (01756) 760262 website: www.whitelioncray.com
Taylor Landlord; guest beers ⊞
This traditional Dales inn boasts stone-flagged floors, an open fire and welcoming atmosphere. Popular with walkers, cyclists and anyone exploring the countryside, the accommodation provides an excellent base for those who enjoy the outdoors. The bar is situated in the main drinking area with raised seating at the back; there is a no-smoking room to the left. Copper Dragon beers feature regularly here.
⩕Q❀⇔◑♣P⊁

Cropton

New Inn
Woolcroft, YO18 8HH (5 miles off A170, Pickering-Kirkby Moorside road)
⌚ 11-11; 12-10.30 Sun
☎ (01751) 417330 website: www.croptonbrewery.co.uk
Cropton Two Pints, Honey Gold, Yorkshire Moors, Monkmans Slaughter, seasonal beers; guest beers ⊞
Charming old country inn on the edge of the North Yorkshire Moors national park. It enjoys strong local support and is welcoming to visitors, old and new. A good base for walkers, cyclists and horse riders, with good value accommodation, it is convenient for access to the North Yorkshire Moors Railway and the many attractions of Whitby, York and an abundance of other locations. Cropton Brewery, in the grounds, supplies most of the pub's ales; guided tours are available.
Q♨❀⇔◑♿▲♣●P⊁▯

Dacre Banks

Royal Oak Inn
Oak Lane, HG3 4EN
⌚ 11.30-3, 5-11; 12-3, 7-10.30 Sun
☎ (01423) 780200 website: www.the-royaloak-dacre.co.uk
John Smith's Bitter; guest beer (summer) ⊞
Affording fine views over the River Nidd, this family-run Grade II listed pub was built in 1752. Close to Fountains Abbey, Brimham Rocks and the Dales, it is popular with locals, holidaymakers and ramblers, who enjoy the open fires and cosy bars. Note the food and drink quotations painted on the beams. The garden has a cobbled seating area and a boules piste. Rudgate beers are sold here and the extensive menu features local produce and fish. One bar and the restaurant are no-smoking.
⩕❀⇔◑♿♣P⊁

Dallowgill

Drovers' Inn
HG4 3RH (2 miles W of Laverton on road to Pateley Bridge)
OS210720
⌚ 12-3 (summer only), 7-11; closed Mon; 12-3, 6.30-11 Sat; 12-3, 6.30-10.30 Sun
☎ (01765) 658510
Black Sheep Best Bitter; Hambleton Bitter; Old Mill Bitter ⊞
High on the hills above Laverton, this traditional stone-built inn is used by walkers, shooting parties and the local farming community. All are made welcome at this small one-roomed pub. In winter there is a blazing coal fire adjacent to the tiny bar. Good pub food is available. On Friday evening after 9pm a darts and dominoes tournament is played. Tables are provided for outdoor drinking. ⩕Q❀◑▲♣P

INDEPENDENT BREWERIES

Abbey Bells Hirst Courtney
Black Sheep Masham
Brown Cow Barlow
Captain Cook Stokesley
Copper Dragon Skipton
Cropton Cropton
Daleside Harrogate
Franklin's Bilton
Hambleton Holme-on-Swale
Litton Litton
Malton Malton (brewing suspended)
Marston Moor (brewed by Rudgate)
Moorcock Hawes
North Yorkshire Pinchinthorpe
Rooster's Knaresborough
Rudgate Tockwith
Selby Selby
Samuel Smith Tadcaster
Theakston Masham
Wensleydale Bellerby
Wharfedale Hetton
York York

Dalton

Jolly Farmer

Main Street, YO7 3HY (off A19)
⏲ 12-3 (not Mon or winter Tue-Wed), 7-11; 12-3, 7-10.30 Sun
☎ (01845) 577359
John Smith's Bitter; guest beer Ⓗ
Family-run pub at the heart of a picturesque village. Constantly enthusiastic about converting regulars to real ale, it usually has three cask beers on tap. The menu represents good value for money and a no-smoking dining room is open Thursday-Saturday evenings and for Sunday lunch.
Q❀⇌◑◐⛺P⊬

Moor & Pheasant

YO7 3JD
⏲ 12-11; 12-10.30 Sun
☎ (01845) 577268
John Smith's Bitter; guest beer Ⓗ
This pub lies on the southern outskirts of the village, five miles south of Thirsk. A front bar with a pool table shares a servery with the lounge, which doubles as a dining area. Both rooms have an open fire. Good value meals are available (not Sun eve). Outside is a large play area for children and a private static caravan site.
♨❀◑◐⊟♣P⊡

Dalton-on-Tees

Chequers Inn

DL2 2NT
⏲ 12-3, 5.30-11; 12-10.30 Sun
☎ (01325) 721213 website: www.chequers.org.uk
Jennings Bitter; guest beers Ⓗ
Traditional inn dating back to the 1840s, consisting of a bar, lounge and restaurant, where a warm welcome is always guaranteed. Formerly known as the Crown and Anchor, this was once part of the now-defunct Fryer's Brewery estate. The landlord is passionate about real ale and at least two guest beers are sourced from micros countrywide. Regular gourmet evenings take place and a quiz is held every Wednesday.
♨Q❀⇌◑◐⊟♿♣P⊬

Easingwold

George at Easingwold ✔

Market Place, YO61 3AD
⏲ 11-2.30, 5-11; 12-2.30, 5-10.30 Sun
☎ (01347) 823448 website: www.the-george-hotel.co.uk
Black Sheep Best Bitter; Taylor Landlord; Tetley Bitter; guest beers Ⓗ
Characterful, 18th-century coaching inn on Easingwold's market square, featuring oak beams and horse brasses. Connected areas formed from small rooms now provide a friendly meeting place, popular with residents and visitors alike. This family-run inn offers a wide range of food from bar snacks to special meals in the restaurant. A central bar serves both the dining area (formerly an open courtyard) and a cosy lounge, with open fires in the winter.
♨Q❀⇌◑◐♿P⊬

East Witton

Cover Bridge Inn

DL8 4SQ (½ mile N of village on A6108)
⏲ 11-11; 12-10.30 Sun
☎ (01969) 623250 website: www.thecoverbridgeinn.co.uk
Black Sheep Best Bitter; Copper Dragon Golden Pippin; John Smith's Bitter; Taylor Landlord; Theakston Old Peculier; guest beers Ⓗ
This classic Dales inn can trace its origins at least as far back as 1670 and has character by the bucketful in an unspoilt interior – if you can negotiate the novel door latch! Situated by a bridge over the River Cover, which runs by the delightful garden, it lies close to its confluence with the larger River Ure. A CAMRA multi-award winner, its eight cask beers include interesting guests. The home-cooked food is also recommended. Camping is possible in the garden by arrangement.
♨Q☊❀⇌◑◐⊟⛺♣P⊡

Egton

Wheatsheaf Inn

YO21 2TZ
⏲ 11-3 (not Mon), 5.30-11; 11.30-11 Sat; 12-10.30 Sun
☎ (01947) 895271
Black Sheep Best Bitter; Theakston Black Bull; guest beer Ⓗ
Grade I listed pub at the centre of a two-pub village. The no-smoking dining room has been sympathetically refurbished and now has windows. The original church pew-style seats occupy the bar area, which is warmed by a coal fire. There is a large grassed area to the front for warmer seasons. Becoming popular with visitors to the agricultural show, walkers and anglers, it is well worth including on a tour, or for a special meal. ♨Q☊❀⇌◑◐⊟⛺♣P⊬

Egton Bridge

Horseshoe Hotel

YO21 1XE (down hill from Egton Station, over bridge) OS801052
⏲ 11.30-3, 6.30-11; 12-3, 7-10.30 Sun
☎ (01947) 895245
John Smith's Bitter; Theakston Black Bull Bitter; guest beers Ⓗ
This hidden gem is popular with locals and visitors alike. The cosy bar, with coal fire, is furnished with old-fashioned settles. A small room away from the bar is no-smoking. Large grassy areas make outdoor dining a pleasure in summer, although the restaurant is also comfortably furnished. Many walks can be started or finished from here. Easily reached from the station via the road or stepping stones across the Esk, there are campsites nearby on the moors. ♨Q☊❀⇌◑◐⛺≠♣P⊬

Elslack

Tempest Arms ✔

BD23 3AY (off A56, Skipton-Colne road)
⏲ 11-11; 12-10.30 Sun
☎ (01282) 842450
Black Sheep Best Bitter; Copper Dragon Scotts 1816; Taylor Best Bitter, Landlord; Theakston Best Bitter; guest beer Ⓗ
Large, popular, upmarket country pub, just off

the A56, serving excellent food from an extensive menu. The decor is a mix of traditional and contemporary, and the rear no-smoking room bears pictures and historical items relating to the Tempest family and the Broughton estate. There is a dining area/restaurant; conference facilities and a function room are available for hire. The guest beer is usually from Wharfedale Brewery. Pennine bus 215, Burnley-Skipton, passes on the main road.
⛫❀⇄◑◗P⊬

Elvington

Grey Horse

Main Street, YO41 4AG (on B1228 6 miles SE of York)
✪ 12-2.30 (not Mon, Tue or Thu); 5.30-11; 12-11 Sat; 12-10.30 Sun
☎ (01904) 608335
Black Sheep Best Bitter; John Smith's Bitter; Taylor Landlord; guest beers Ⓗ
Small pub, where two rooms are served from a central bar. In summer outdoor seating is provided at the front and in the yard; in winter wood-burning stoves add to the comfortable atmosphere. The lounge displays photographs of the WWII bombers that used to fly from Elvington Aerodrome, adjacent to the village, now the Yorkshire Air Museum. Recent renovations have provided accommodation and a restaurant. The guest beers change regularly. No evening meals are served Monday.
⛫❀⇄◑◗⊟▲♣P

Embsay

Elm Tree Inn

5 Elm Tree Square, BD23 6RB
✪ 11.30-3, 5.30-11; 12-3, 7-10.30 Sun
☎ (01756) 790717
Black Sheep Best Bitter; Goose Eye No-Eye Deer; Wells Bombardier; guest beers Ⓗ
Former coaching inn situated in the village square. Inside it has an open feel with oak beams and horse brasses. The large main bar is supplemented by a smaller no-smoking side room mainly used by diners (no eve meals Mon). Look for the worn mounting steps outside. Well situated for walking on the edge of the Yorkshire Dales National Park; Embsay and Bolton Abbey steam railway line are nearby. Hourly daytime buses run from Skipton Monday-Saturday. ❀⇄◑◗♿⇌P⊬

Filey

Bonhommes Bar

Royal Crescent Court, The Crescent, YO14 9JH (500 yds past the bandstand)
✪ 11-11; 12-10.30 Sun
☎ (01723) 512034
Caledonian Deuchars IPA; John Smith's Bitter; guest beers Ⓗ
The bar is to the side of the fine Victorian Royal Crescent Hotel complex, now private flats. From the 1950s it was known as the American Bar. The present name celebrates John Paul Jones, father of the American navy. His ship, the Bonhomme Richard, was involved in a battle off nearby Flamborough Head during the War of Independence. Live music is provided most Friday evenings, quizzes on Tuesday and Sunday evenings and an afternoon fun quiz on Saturday.
⇌♣

Giggleswick

Hart's Head Hotel ✔

Belle Hill, BD24 0BA (from Settle take B6480 for ½ mile N towards Kirby Lonsdale)
✪ 12-2.30 (not Thu), 5.30-11; 11-11 Sat; 12-10.30 Sun
☎ (01729) 822086 website: www.hartsheadhotel.co.uk
Copper Dragon Scotts 1816; Tetley Bitter; guest beers Ⓗ
Welcoming 18th-century coaching inn, transformed by the owners since 1997. The open-plan bar retains a multi-room feel and a no-smoking area. Changing guest beers often come from Yorkshire micro-breweries. Freshly prepared meals use local ingredients, while 10 en-suite rooms make it an ideal base to explore the Dales. There is a full-sized snooker table in the refurbished cellar. Serving the community well, it is also popular with visitors.
⛫Q❀⇄◑◗⊟♣P⊬

Grassington

Foresters Arms ✔

20 Main Street, BD23 5AA
✪ 11-11; 12-10.30 Sun
☎ (01756) 752349
Black Sheep Best Bitter; Taylor Best Bitter, Landlord; Tetley Mild; guest beers Ⓗ
Just off the main village square, this friendly local now has an opened-out feel from its coaching inn origins. The bar and pool/TV area are to the left and further seating to the right leads to the dining room. Quizzes are held Monday and traditional pub games include shove-ha'penny and devil among the tailors. Up to four guest beers, usually from local micros, supplement the regular ales which include a brew from Wharfedale. ⛫ᘔ❀⇄◑◗♣P

Great Ayton

Whinstone View Country Club

Langbaurgh, TS9 6AG
(along B1292 between Great Ayton and A172) OS555123
✪ 11-11; closed Mon; 11-11 Sun
☎ (01642) 723285 website: www.whinstoneview.co.uk
Beer range varies Ⓗ
Converted old cow byre traditionally decorated in cream to show off the exposed wood beams. In a secluded location on the B1292 around half a mile from Great Ayton, this large, open-plan pub has several fires and a function room upstairs. It enjoys a reputation for good home-cooked food, so booking is often necessary; the small bar is complemented by a spacious dining area. New guest beers appear every week.
⛫Q❀◑◗♿▲P⊡

Great Heck

Bay Horse

Main Street, DN14 0BQ (follow signs from A19)
✪ 12-2, 5-11; 12-10.30 Sun
☎ (01977) 661125 website: www.bay-horse.co.uk
Old Mill Bitter, Bullion Ⓗ
Another outlet for the local Old Mill Brewery, the pub was converted from cottages and is

prominently sited. It is surprisingly light and bright but retains some old features, such as exposed beams, pottery and brassware. Although open-plan, it still keeps three distinct areas; the raised restaurant offers an extensive menu. The patio is ideal for warm weather and makes a convenient stop for boaters on the nearby Aire and Calder Canal. Bullion may be replaced by a seasonal beer. ❀◖P⚟

Grinton

Bridge Inn

DL11 6HH (on B6270 1 mile E of Reeth)
✪ 12-11; 12-10.30 Sun
☎ (01748) 884224 website: www.bridgeinngrinton.co.uk
Jennings Dark Mild, Cumberland Ale, Cocker Hoop; guest beer Ⓗ
Family-run pub in beautiful Swaledale, prime walking country in the Yorkshire Dales National Park. The pub focuses on fine beer and quality food sourced from local produce; its changing guest is usually drawn from the Jennings micro-brewery scheme. The pub has its own accommodation but there is also nearby camping and a youth hostel. For entertainment, investigate the unusual wall-mounted games in the pool room, an 'open mike' evening is held on Thursday.
♨Q♉❀🛏◖◗⊟▲♣P

Grosmont

Crossing Club

Front Street, YO22 5QE (next to Co-op)
✪ 7-11; 7-11 Sun
☎ (01947) 895040
Black Sheep Best Bitter; Tayor Landlord; guest beers (summer) Ⓗ
Interesting conversion of the old Co-op delivery bay to a room full of old Grosmont and railway memorabilia, transformed and run by volunteers. Situated on the main street near the station, access is gained through glass doors (ring the bell), up a few stairs into the one-roomed bar, which feels like part of a bygone era. Well-behaved children and pets are welcome. It opens in summer for special events outside the posted opening times. Two guest beers are stocked in summer. ▲⇌

Guisborough

Cross Keys Inn

Middlesbrough Road, TS14 6RW (on A171 Nunthorpe road)
✪ 11-11; 12-10.30 Sun
☎ (01287) 610035
North Yorkshire Prior's Ale, Ruby Ale Ⓗ
Originally a farmhouse selling refreshments to passing coachmen, it was converted to an inn during the 1820s, with the construction of the Middlesbrough and Guisborough railway. It became a Chef & Brewer establishment in 2002. The inn is divided into family and adult areas, using wood panelling and lintels, creating semi-secluded spaces for dining and drinking; salvaged pine furniture enhances the effect. Up to eight ales are stocked in summer – try a free tasting. Game and fish are specialities.
♨❀🛏◖◗♿P⚟

Globe

81 Northgate, TS14 6JP (opp. general hospital)
✪ 4 (2 Thu & Fri; 12 Sat)-11; 12-10.30 Sun
☎ (01287) 280799
Camerons Strongarm; guest beers Ⓗ
Old-fashioned community local, originally the first hotel in Guisborough, with railway connections. The bar features brasses and red leather upholstered furniture. A lounge/function room hosts entertainment throughout the week: bankhouse country & western (Mon), jazz night (Wed) and folk club (Fri). The large, rear yard doubles as a car park or garden. It supports local darts and dominoes teams; games played include shove-ha'penny, bar skittles and bagatelle. Snacks, tea and coffee are available all day. Q❀⊟♿♣P

Tap & Spile

11-13 Westgate, TS14 6BG (near market cross)
✪ 11.30-11; 12-10.30 Sun
☎ (01287) 632983
John Smith's Bitter; Jennings Cumberland Ale; guest beers Ⓗ
One of the oldest pubs in Guisborough, this traditional dinking house was previously known as the Mermaid. Sailors from Teeside used this and other Guisborough pubs as a refeshment stop en-route to Whitby to board ship. The snug and bar area, with pool table, is decked out with wooden flooring, seating and exposed beams. The back room is no-smoking and used for families or functions. Live music is staged: blues/soul (Wed) and jazz or young bands (alternate Sun). Lunchtime snacks are available weekdays. Q♉❀◖♣●⚟

Hampsthwaite

Joiners Arms

High Street, HG3 2EU (off A59)
✪ 11.30-2.30, 5.30-11; 11.30-11 Sat; 11.45-10.30 Sun
☎ (01423) 771673
John Smith's Bitter; Tetley Bitter; guest beer Ⓗ
Close to the A59 and Nidderdale Way, this 200-year-old pub has a central bar serving the lounge and tap room. These rooms are connected by an unusual snug that was once the cellar and retains its original stone floor and arched ceiling. The lounge features an inglenook discovered during refurbishment. The no-smoking dining room displays a rare collection of gravy boats. Evening meals are served Wednesday-Saturday. ◖◗⊟P

Harrogate

Coach & Horses ✔

16 West Park, HG1 1BJ
✪ 11-11; 12-10.30 Sun
Daleside Bitter, Blonde; Taylor Landlord; Tetley Bitter; guest beers Ⓗ
A central bar serves two guest beers, one of which is often another Daleside brew. The pub is popular and maintains a friendly atmosphere with seating arranged into snugs and alcoves. The food is good: a curry night is held every Wednesday, while Tuesday is 'championship pie and peas' night, with the profits going to local charities. Look out for the cartoon drawings of local characters. ◖⇌⚟

Old Bell Tavern

6 Royal Parade, HG1 2SZ

✪ 12-11; 12-10.30 Sun

☎ (01423) 507930

Black Sheep Best Bitter; Caledonian Deuchars IPA; Taylor Landlord; guest beers [H]

Five changing guest beers supplement the three regulars and three continental draught beers on tap. A Rooster's beer and a mild are always available, plus an extensive range of foreign bottled beers. The inn dates back to 1846, gaining extra space with an extension into an old Farrah's toffee shop – see the memorabilia. Top quality food is available daily in the bar area, and a dining room upstairs opens evenings (ring for times). The pub is no-smoking throughout. Q◖◗≉⁄

Tap & Spile ✔

Tower Street , HG1 1HS (off West Park, opp. multi-storey car park)

✪ 11.30-11; 12-10.30 Sun

☎ (01423) 526785

Fuller's London Pride; Rooster's Yankee; Theakston Old Peculier; guest beers [H]

Well-established, quality ale house. A central bar links the three drinking areas, one of which is no-smoking. A mix of wood panelling and bare brick walls are used to display many old photographs of Harrogate. Popular with all ages, the pub stages folk music on Tuesday and rock on Thursday. Basic lunches are served Monday-Saturday. The cider is Westons Old Rosie. Some outdoor seating is provided.
❀◖≉♣●⁄

Winter Gardens ✔

4 Royal Baths, HG1 2WH

✪ 10-11; 12-10.30 Sun

☎ (01423) 877010

Courage Directors; Greene King Abbot; Marston's Bitter, Pedigree; Theakston Best Bitter; guest beers [H]

Set in the Royal Baths complex on the main route through town, this impressive conversion from the old lounge hall retains all the grandeur of the magnificent Victorian building, while adding some modern touches in a way that complements the style. A particularly fine feature is the sweeping double stone staircase leading from the main entrance to the bar area. As with all Wetherspoon's pubs value for money in beer and food is the byword here.
Q⛟❀◖◗♿≉⁄

Helwith Bridge

Helwith Bridge

BD24 0EH

✪ 11-11; 12-10.30 Sun

☎ (01729) 860220 website: www.helwithbridge.com

Greene King Old Speckled Hen; McEwan's 80/-; Theakston XB; Webster's Bitter; Wells Bombardier; guest beers [H]

Friendly, stone-flagged pub, full of character. It has been divided into a number of rooms to suit different clientele. Backing onto the River Ribble, it affords good views of the Settle-Carlisle Railway and Pen-y-Ghent. Railway paintings and photographs abound and a roaring fire is guaranteed in winter. A full food menu is served Tuesday-Sunday, 12-3 and 6-9. Guest beers are mainly from the Scottish Courage guest list.
♨Q❀◖◗▲♣●P

Hubberholme

George Inn

Kirk Gill, BD23 5JE (opp. church)

✪ 12-2.30, 6.30-10.30 (11 Fri & Sat; closed Mon eve); 11.30-11 summer Mon-Sat; 12-3 (10.30 summer) Sun

☎ (01756) 760223 website: www.thegeorge-inn.co.uk

Black Sheep Best Bitter, Special; Copper Dragon seasonal beers [H]

Sitting snugly alongside a river, this hamlet was named after a Viking chieftain called Hubba. This remote and unspoilt 18th-century inn was reputedly the author J. B. Priestley's favourite watering-hole. It boasts two rooms of genuine character with heavy oak beams and walls stripped back to the bare stone and hung with antique plates and photos. An open stove in a big fireplace welcomes visitors to the stone-flagged bar. Wholesome bar food is available at reasonable prices. ♨Q❀⇆◖◗▲P

Hutton Rudby

King's Head

36 North Side, TS15 0DA

✪ 12-11; 12-10.30 Sun

☎ (01642) 700342

Mansfield Cask; Camerons Strongarm; guest beer [H]

Come and walk the River Leven through this historic village, and try the ale at its traditional local. It comprises a small, U-shaped bar on the left, and a small no-smoking snug on the right, where children are welcome. The bar has a beamed ceiling and brasses on the wainscotting, and is partially divided. Quizzes are held on Tuesday. ♨Q⛟❀⇆♣⁄▯

Ingleton

Wheatsheaf ✔

22 High Street, LA6 3AD

✪ 12-11; 12-10.30 Sun

☎ (01524) 241275 website: www.wheatsheaf-ingleton.co.uk

Black Sheep Best Bitter, Special; Taylor Golden Best; Tetley Bitter [H]

One long, narrow bar is divided into different areas. There is also a restaurant, similar in size, and an attractive garden, home to birds of prey. The pub is popular with tourists, who come especially for the accommodation and food. It is handy for the finish of the Waterfalls Walk.
♨❀⇆◖◗▲♣P

Kettlesing

Queen's Head

HG3 2LB (off A59 west of Harrogate)

✪ 11-3, 6.30-11; 11-3, 6.30-10.30 Sun

☎ (01423) 770263

Black Sheep Best Bitter; Theakston Old Peculier; guest beer [H]

Located in a quiet village, the Queen's Head is noted for its food. An entrance lobby dominated by images of Queen Elizabeth leads to two bars, one decorated with cricketing memorabilia, presumably to baffle the regulars from the nearby American base. Outdoor facilities include benches at the front of the pub and a large patio at the rear. ⩩Q☕❀⇌◑P

Kirkby Hill (Richmond)

Shoulder of Mutton

DL11 7JH (2½ miles from A66, 4 miles NW of Richmond)
✪ 12-3 (not Mon-Fri), 6-11; 12-3, 6-10.30 Sun
☎ (01748) 822772 website: www.shoulderofmutton.net
Black Sheep Best Bitter; Daleside Bitter; Jennings Cumberland Ale; guest beer Ⓗ

Ivy-fronted country inn in a beautiful hillside setting, overlooking Lower Teesdale and the ruins of Ravensworth Castle. Situated opposite the church, the pub consists of an opened-out front bar linking through to the lounge and no-smoking restaurant to the rear. The guest beer is chosen by the regulars. It hosts live music every Monday. Popular with walkers, there are also five en-suite guest bedrooms. Evening meals are served Wednesday-Sunday.
⩩Q❀⇌◑♿♣P⅍⊓

Kirklevington

Crown

Thirsk Road, TS15 9LT (on A67, near Crathorne A19 interchange)
✪ 5 (12 Sat)-11; 12-10.30 Sun
☎ (01642) 780044
Draught Bass; John Smith's Magnet Ⓗ

Welcoming village pub with two drinking areas: the lounge is no-smoking during food service and has a massive log fire blazing in winter. The local environmental health officer caused much mirth when the gas tap for this fire could not be located. Only fresh ingredients are used in the small but impressive menu; meals are served Tuesday-Saturday evenings and Sunday lunch, which must be booked. The pub may seem remote, but is well worth seeking out.
⩩❀◑⊟♿♣P

Kirk Smeaton

Shoulder of Mutton

Main Street, WF8 3JY
✪ 12-2, 6-11; 12-11 Fri & Sat; 11.30-10.30 Sun
☎ (01977) 620348
Black Sheep Best Bitter; guest beer Ⓗ

Attractive village pub, frequented by locals and walkers from the nearby Went Valley and Brockadale nature reserve. The traditional layout comprises a large lounge with two open fires and a cosy, dark-panelled snug. Good drinking facilities can be enjoyed outside, too. Probably the best pint of Black Sheep you will ever taste is served here, sourced direct from the brewery. The changing guest beer is obtained from mainly local independent breweries. A quiz is held on Tuesday evening.
⩩❀P

Knaresborough

Blind Jack's

18A Market Place, HG5 8AL
✪ 4 (5.30 Mon; 3 Fri)-11; 12-11 Sat; 12-10.30 Sun
☎ (01423) 869148
website: www.blindjacks.villagebrewer.co.uk
Black Sheep Best Bitter; Copper Dragon IPA; Taylor Landlord; Village White Boar; guest beers Ⓗ

When you enter, it is difficult to appreciate that this pub has only existed since the 1990s. The award-winning ale house is based around an existing Georgian building with dark wood panelling and bare floorboards. This gem of a pub has a serving area downstairs with an adjacent comfortable room. Upstairs are two smaller rooms, including a no-smoking area. A Rooster's beer is a regular feature.
Q⇌⅍⊓

So Bar & Eats

1 Silver Street, HG5 8AJ (opp. bus station)
✪ 11-11; 11-10.30 Sun
☎ (01423) 863202
Black Sheep Best Bitter; guest beers Ⓗ

Spacious, open, bistro-style bar that caters for all. Imaginative, innovative food, served 12.30-9.30pm, and relaxed fine dining take equal priority with the ale. The bar stocks a good selection of New World wines. Seating ranges from giant bean bags to comfortable sofas and a conventional dining area. Staff are friendly and helpful. The pub sits on a busy corner. This is a regular outlet for Black Sheep and Rooster's beers. It hosts live music on Thursday.
◑♿⇌♣⅍

Langdale End

Moorcock Inn

YO13 0BN OS938913
✪ 11-2, 6.30-11 (phone for winter hours); 12-3, 6.30-10.30 Sun
☎ (01723) 882268
Beer range varies Ⓗ/Ⓖ

Sympathetically restored, classic village pub, well off the beaten track but only four miles from Scarborough near the end of the Dalby Forest Drive. Beers are usually sourced from local breweries, such as Hambleton, Daleside and Wold Top. Beer is served through a hatch to both bars that can be busy when the local cricket team plays in summer. In idyllic surroundings, the pub is now completely no-smoking, and is well worth a detour.
⩩Q❀◑⛺♣P⅍

Lastingham

Blacksmith's Arms

Front Street, YO62 6TL (4 miles N of A170 between Helmsley and Pickering)
✪ 12-2.30 (not Tue), 6-11; 12-11 Fri, Sat & summer; 12-10.30 Sun
☎ (01751) 417247
Theakston Best Bitter; guest beers Ⓗ

Pretty pub in a conservation village opposite St Mary's Church, famous for its 11th-century Saxon crypt. It was once run by the vicar's wife, who had 13 children; they are gone, but you may encounter the ghost called Ella. The single bar has an old range, lit in winter; the adjoining room is served by a hatch. A snug and two dining rooms complete the interior but do not miss the secluded rear garden. Food is of the highest quality.
⩩Q❀⇌◑♣🍎

ENGLAND

Lazenby

Half Moon

High Street, TS6 8DX (off A174 by Wilton works)
⏲ 11-11; 12-10.30 Sun
☎ (01642) 452752
Black Sheep Best Bitter; Greene King Old Speckled Hen; Taylor Landlord; guest beers 🄷
The pub is located beneath the Eston Hills and the view from the rear patio is spectacular. An Enterprise Inns house, this is a traditional village pub, enjoying an excellent reputation for home-cooked food, served daily from 12 noon until 9pm. Visit the Half Moon to enjoy a meal or drink in a completely smoke-free environment; it offers five cask ales, of which two vary regularly. Children are welcome in the restaurant. ☋❀◐◑♿P⊘

Leavening

Jolly Farmers

Main Street, YO17 9SA
⏲ 7 (6 Fri; 12 Sat)-11; 12-10.30 Sun
☎ (01653) 658276
John Smith's Bitter; Taylor Landlord; Tetley Bitter; guest beers 🄷
Former York CAMRA Pub of the Year, dating from the 17th century, lying between York and Malton on the edge of the Yorkshire Wolds. The cosiness of its original multi-room layout has been retained despite extensions, with two small bars, plus family and dining rooms. Guest ales often include stronger beers from independent breweries, while the restaurant offers a wide range of dishes and specialises in locally-caught game.
♨☋❀◐◑♣P▯

Leyburn

Black Swan Hotel

Market Place, DL8 5AS
⏲ 11.30-11; 12-10.30 Sun
☎ (01969) 623131
Black Sheep Best Bitter; John Smith's Bitter; Taylor Landlord; guest beer 🄷
Market town inn at the centre of a popular Dales tourist destination, now served by the revived Wensleydale Railway. The opened-out interior is divided into several distinct areas, with a cosy bar tucked away towards the rear. The pub is noted for its Sunday lunchtime carvery and it hosts occasional traditional music and jamming sessions – call for details. Children (and dogs) are welcome. ♨☋❀🛏◐◑⇌(Wensleydale Rlwy)

Low Bentham

Punch Bowl

LA2 7DD (on B6480, near county boundary)
⏲ 12-3 (not Mon), 6.30-11; 12-4, 7-10.30 Sun
☎ (01524) 261344
Black Sheep Best Bitter; Everards Beacon; guest beers 🄷
Small country pub, 400 years old, run by and for locals, but strangers are welcome. Various nooks and crannies are warmed by two open fires, including a cosy bar and a room down some steps with games and extra seating. The no-smoking restaurant opens at the weekend: no food is served on Monday. Two guest beers are normally on tap, from a large number of possible sources but Okells and Copper Dragon have featured recently. ♨❀◐◑P

Low Marishes

School House Inn

YO17 6RJ (800 yds from A169, Malton-Pickering road)
⏲ 11.30-3, 6-11; 12-10.30 Sun
☎ (01653) 668247
Hambleton Nightmare; Tetley Bitter; guest beers 🄷
Quiet, unspoilt, multi-roomed pub just off the A169, offering up to four guest beers in summer (less in winter). Superb, home-cooked food can be enjoyed in the dining room or conservatory. Pool and darts are available in the games room along with three on-line computers. Children (and dogs) are welcome; expect an enthusiastic welcome from the landlord's two Great Danes. Electricity for caravans is available on site, or camp on the lawn; there is a spacious patio and garden. ♨Q❀◐◑⊟⛺♣P

Low Worsall

Ship

Low Worsall, TS15 9PH
⏲ 11-11; 12-10.30 Sun
☎ (01642) 780314
Taylor Landlord; guest beer 🄷
Busy roadside inn on the B1264 between Yarm and Richmond. It places a strong emphasis on food, but has an equally dedicated commitment to real ale. Food is available all day, every day. The garden is home to rabbits and guinea pigs. A pub called the Ship this far inland – how come? Well, in distant times, Low Worsall was the limit of navigation on the River Tees. Occasional beer festivals are held. ❀◐◑♿♣P

Malham

Lister Arms

Gordale Scar Road, BD23 4DB
⏲ 12-3, 7-11; 12-11 Fri & Sat; 12-10.30 Sun
☎ (01729) 830330 www.listerarms.co.uk
Black Sheep Best Bitter; Boddingtons Bitter; Caledonian Deuchars IPA; Taylor Landlord; guest beers 🄷
Set opposite the village green, this 17th-century coaching inn takes its name from Thomas Lister, the first Lord of Ribblesdale. The tiled entrance opens to a main bar with a large inglenook and many other original features. There is a bottled foreign beer list and a cider in summer. The food and recently extended accommodation are of the best quality. Internet access is available in the bar. Look out for the magnificent resident tabby cats. ♨❀🛏◐◑⛺♣🍎P

Malton

Crown Hotel (Suddaby's)

12 Wheelgate, YO15 0JJ
⏲ 11-11; 12-10.30 Sun
☎ (01653) 692038 website: www.suddabys.co.uk
Malton Double Chance, Golden Chance, Auld Bob, seasonal beers; John Smith's Bitter; guest beers 🄷
Grade II listed market town-centre pub that has been in the Suddaby family for five generations.

At present no brewing takes place on the premises – beers are contract brewed at Hambleton and Brown Cow. It stages beer festivals in July and December, plus a mini version at Easter. Malt'on Hops off-licence, now on the premises, stocks over 350 bottled beers from around the world, plus wines. All may be drunk in the bar for a small corkage charge. Sandwiches are available. ♨Q☋❀⇌⇛P⊬

Manfield

Crown Inn

Vicars Lane, DL2 2RF (500 yds from B6275)
✪ 6 (12 Sat)-11; 12-10.30 Sun
☎ (01325) 374243
Village White Boar, Bull; guest beers Ⓗ
Attractive, 18th-century inn consisting of two bar areas, a games room and a no-smoking lounge; the bar design allows all areas to be served. The mix of locals and visitors give the pub a friendly atmosphere. Up to six guest beers come from micro-breweries countrywide; a rotating guest wheat beer on draft and bottled Belgian beers are stocked. Local CAMRA Pub of the Year 2005, it stages two annual beer festivals. Dogs are welcome in this rural gem. ♨Q❀◐◑♣P⊬Ū

Masham

Black Sheep Brewery Visitors Centre ✔

Wellgarth, HG4 4EN (follow brown tourist signs on A6108)
✪ 11-11; closed Mon & Tue in Jan/Feb; 12-5.30 Sun
☎ (01765) 680100 website: www.blacksheep.co.uk
Black Sheep Best Bitter, Special, Riggwelter, seasonal beers Ⓗ
This popular visitor attraction is housed in the spacious and historic setting of the former North of England maltings. There is a 'sheepy' shop and a bistro, serving coffees to full meals. Tours around the recently expanded brewery can be arranged. Various entertainments are staged throughout the year from Victorian fairs to plays. A small garden overlooks scenic rolling countryside. Q❀◐◑♿P

White Bear

12 Crosshills, HG4 4EN
✪ 11-11; 12-10.30 Sun
☎ (01765) 689319
Caledonian Deuchars IPA; Theakston Best Bitter, Black Bull Bitter, Old Peculier; guest beer Ⓗ
This is a solid stone, typical Dales country inn. The lively, traditional public bar benefits from a roaring fire in winter. The spacious, rustic lounge is the venue for high quality meals, and occasional live music. This friendly pub has a strong local community feel, but is always welcoming to the many visitors to this beautiful area of Lower Wensleydale. ♨Q❀◐◑⊟♣P

Maunby

Buck Inn

YO7 4HD (signed from A167 at South Otterington and Kirby Wiske)
✪ 5 (12 Fri & Sat)-11; 12-10.30 Sun
☎ (01845) 587777 website: www.buckinnmaunby.co.uk
John Smith's Bitter; Theakston Best Bitter; guest beer Ⓗ
Former 18th-century dower house, now a genuine free house with oak beams and log fire. Warm, comfortable and inviting, it offers a good range of beers and wines. There is an additional no-smoking bar and a restaurant, serving a full menu seven evenings a week (booking recommended). Situated a little off the beaten track, it is popular with the fishing fraternity and well used by locals. Children are welcome. Quoits and darts are played here. ♨Q❀◐◑⊟♣P⊬

Middlesbrough

Star & Garter

14 Southfield Road, TS1 3BZ
✪ 11-11; 12-10.30 Sun
☎ (01642) 245307
Beer range varies Ⓗ
Spacious, two-roomed pub, once a dockers' club. The pub offers four, constantly-changing guest beers, often sourced from micro-breweries and including seasonal beers. A large-screen TV in the lounge shows Sky football, but there are areas where customers can escape. It can get busy at the weekend. Tables outside are next to the car park. ❀◐◑⊟♣P

Muker

Farmers Arms ✔

DL11 6QG
✪ 11-11; 12-10.30 Sun (may close late afternoon in winter)
☎ (01748) 886297
Black Sheep Best Bitter; John Smith's Bitter; Theakston Best Bitter, Old Peculier; guest beer Ⓗ
Situated in the remote but beautiful surroundings of Upper Swaledale, this village local possesses plenty of character and charm, with its stone-flagged floor and welcoming open fire. Its traditional surroundings are enjoyed by locals, seasoned walkers and daytrippers alike, allowing for a refreshing break on the long-distance Coast-to-Coast walk and a short detour from the Pennine Way. ♨Q❀◐◑⛺♣PŪ

Newall with Clifton

Spite

Roebuck Terrace, LS21 2EY (on B6451)
✪ 12-3, 6-11; 12-11 Thu-Sat; 12-10.30 Sun
☎ (01943) 463063
Copper Dragon Black Gold, Best Bitter, Golden Pippin; Tetley Bitter Ⓗ
Solid stone country inn just north of Otley, set in pleasant rural surroundings. Although the pub has been opened out, it preserves the feeling of separate areas with the use of various levels; exposed beams and an open fireplace have been retained. Despite the pub's unusual name, it is well worth visiting this friendly inn. Meals are served in the restaurant area daily, except Monday. ♨Q❀◐◑⛺♣P

Newton on Ouse

Blacksmith's Arms

Cherry Tree Avenue, YO30 2BN
✪ 12-3 (not Mon-Thu), 5.30-11; 12-11 Sat; 12-10.30 Sun
☎ (01347) 848249
Camerons Bitter, Strongarm; guest beers Ⓗ
The pub was originally the blacksmith's

workshop for the Beningbrough estate – see the hall by the village, now owned by the NT. This comfortable local stands in the centre of a quiet village next to the church. A single bar serves the central lounge and dining area, plus the adjacent raised games room. Football and other sporting items reflect the family connections with professional sport. A wide choice of food is available evenings and all day at weekends.
⛰❀⇌◐◑♣P

Northallerton

Tithe Bar

2 Friarage Street, DL6 1DP (off High St)
⏲ 12-11; 12-10.30 Sun
☎ (01609) 778482
Taylor Landlord; guest beers Ⓗ
Part of the small but expanding Market Town Taverns chain, this traditional bar serves a changing range of five guest beers, often from Yorkshire micro-breweries. A wide choice of bottled and draught Belgian and German beers is also stocked; you will not find any boring lagers here. Much of the CAMRA award-winning bar is no-smoking and there is a restaurant upstairs. The selection of board games will help you while away the time; play in exchange for a charity donation.
Q◐◑⊟≈♣⍁

Norwood

Sun Inn

Brame Lane, Norwood, HG3 1SZ (on B6451 about ½ mile S of A59)
⏲ 11-11; 12-10.30 Sun
☎ (01943) 880220
Greene King Old Speckled Hen; Theakston Best Bitter, Old Peculier; guest beer Ⓗ
Large, popular country inn affording fine views over the surrounding countryside. The original part of this stone building dates back to the 18th century. The extension, which includes the main dining area, blends in well, although it was added in the last century. The three regular real ales are supplemented by a changing guest beer. The garden provides customers with an ideal opportunity to enjoy a summer evening's beer in a rural setting. Saturday meals are available all day; 12-5pm on Sunday.
❀◐◑♣P

Nun Monkton

Alice Hawthorn

The Green, YO26 8EW (off A59, York-Harrogate road)
⏲ 12-2, 6-11; 12-10.30 Sun
☎ (01423) 330303 website: www.alicehawthorn.co.uk
John Smith's Bitter; Taylor Landlord; guest beers Ⓗ
The village is tucked away at the end of a country lane, complete with a maypole and a duckpond on the green. The cosy pub enjoys views of this idyllic scene and offers a varied range of home-cooked food. A firm favourite with the fishing and boating fraternity from the nearby rivers Ouse and Nidd, walkers are also most welcome – local routes can be supplied on request. Outside are patio tables and a children's playground.
⛰❀◐◑⊟⛺♣P

Old Malton

Wentworth Arms

Town Street, YO17 7HD (200 yds off A64, Malton bypass)
⏲ 11.30-2.30, 5-11; 11.30-11 Sat & summer; 12-10.30 Sun
☎ (01653) 692618
Theakston Best Bitter; guest beers Ⓗ
Former coaching inn dating from the 18th century, situated just off the busy A64, making it an excellent stop between York and Scarborough. The main drinking area is a low, beamed, L-shaped space. A no-smoking restaurant has been converted from an adjoining barn, where good value, home-cooked meals are based on locally-sourced produce and feature daily specials. Guest beers come mainly from northern micro-breweries.
⛰Q❀⇌◐◑⛺♣P

Osmotherley

Golden Lion

6 West End, DL6 3AA (1 mile off A19, at A684 jct)
⏲ 12-3.30, 6-12; 12-10 Sun
☎ (01609) 883526
John Smith's Bitter; Taylor Landlord; guest beer Ⓗ
Old stone pub overlooking the village cross in this popular tourist centre at the edge of the National Park's walking country. It has earned a far-reaching reputation for fine food; the single bar room serves largely as a dining area, but drinkers are made very welcome and it enjoys a strong local trade. Many mirrors adorn the walls and candlelit tables enhance the mood. There is also an upstairs restaurant – booking for meals is recommended. Outdoor tables are at the front of the pub.
⛰❀◐◑⛺

Patrick Brompton

Green Tree ✔

DL8 1JW
⏲ 12-3 (not Mon or Tue), 6.30 (7 Sat)-11; 12-3, 7-10.30 Sun
☎ (01677) 450262
Black Sheep Best Bitter; Taylor Landlord; guest beer Ⓗ
Set in gently rolling countryside at the entrance to Wensleydale, this pleasant Grade II listed free house makes a perfect partner to the picturesque church next door. A small garden overlooks the main A684; motorists entering the car park should beware the narrow entrance. Inside is a simple but cosy bar with brick-built counter and fireplace plus an adjoining dining room. ⛰Q❀◐◑⊟♣P

Pickering

Royal Oak

Eastgate, YO18 7DW
⏲ 11-11; 12-10.30 Sun
☎ (01751) 472718
John Smith's Bitter; guest beers Ⓗ
Popular, bustling pub near a roundabout and bus stops, and five minutes' walk from the North York Moors Railway station. Guest beers are sourced from SIBA breweries/Unique Inns initiative. An extensive car park and lawned garden lie to the rear, with a children's play area. Food is available until 7pm. The pub now

has a no-smoking room. Occasional live music is staged.
Q ❀ ◐ ⛺ ⇌ (North York Moors Rlwy) ♣ P ⁄

Pickhill

Nag's Head

YO7 4JG (off A1, between Thirsk and Masham) OS346835
✪ 11-11; 12-10.30 Sun
☎ (01845) 567391 website: www.nagsheadpickhill.co.uk
Black Sheep Best Bitter, Special; Theakston Black Bull Bitter; guest beer 🄷
Comfortable country inn that strikes a perfect balance between food service and locals' bar. In the same hands for more than 30 years and a long-standing Guide entry, its restaurant has an outstanding reputation for food. The public bar remains a distinct entity, well supported by local customers. A CAMRA award-winner, it was Hambleton Ales' first outlet and a Hambleton beer is always on tap. Good accommodation is available and the landlord can arrange various activities for guests. ♨ Q ❀ ⛟ ◐ ⊟ ♿ ⛺ ♣ P ⁄

Pool in Wharfedale

Hunter's Inn

Harrogate Road, LS21 2PS (on A658, Harrogate-Bradford road)
✪ 11-11; 12-10.30 Sun
☎ (0113) 284 1090
Tetley Bitter; Theakston Best Bitter; guest beers 🄷
Real ale haven with ample parking facilities: a single-room pub with a raised dining area at one end and a pool table at the other. Two permanent real ales are complemented by seven guests sourced from local and national breweries. A good wine selection is stocked. Cooked meals are available at lunchtime when a no-smoking area is provided; sandwiches in the evenings. Children are welcome until 9pm.
♨ ❀ ◐ ♣ P ⁄

Ribblehead

Station

LA6 3AS (where Settle-Carlisle line crosses B6255)
✪ 11-11; 12-10.30 Sun
☎ (01524) 241274 website: www.thestationinn.net
Black Sheep Best Bitter; Copper Dragon IPA; Theakston Old Peculier; guest beer 🄷
Homely bar and restaurant, whose walls carry plenty of references to the Settle-Carlisle Railway, including a timetable for the nearby station. In a bleak and lonely location, it caters mainly for tourists and trippers, and is a convenient starting point for the ascent of Whernside – the famous path passes close to the famous viaduct. Bunkhouse accommodation is available. No buses serve this dog-friendly hostelry. ♨ ❀ ⛟ ◐ ⛺ ⇌ ♣ P

Ripon

One-Eyed Rat

51 Allhallowgate, HG4 1LQ (near bus station)
✪ 12-3.30 (not Mon-Wed), 6 (5.30 Fri)-11; 12-11 Sat; 12-3, 7-10.30 Sun
☎ (01765) 607704 website: www.oneeyedrat.co.uk
Black Sheep Best Bitter; Taylor Landlord; guest beers 🄷
This cosy pub, situated in one of the oldest parts of the town, has been a Guide regular for many years. It is well known for its four changing guest ales from independent breweries and large selection of bottled beers from many countries. Rugby memorabilia adorn the walls and a roaring coal fire gives a warm welcome in winter. Biddenden cider is sold. Bar billiards can be played here. ♨ Q ❀ ⛺ ♣ ●

Robin Hood's Bay

Dolphin

King Street, YO22 4SH
✪ 11 (12 winter)-11; 12-10.30 Sun
☎ (01947) 880337
Caledonian Deuchars IPA; Tetley Bitter; Wychwood Hobgoblin; guest beers 🄷
Friendly, old-fashioned village pub boasting an open coal fire and beamed bar. It has just the one room downstairs, but an upstairs room accommodates children. Home-cooked food is available lunchtime and evening. The Friday folk club is open to all; quiz night is Sunday. Benches at the front allow drinkers to sit and enjoy the village atmosphere. The Coast-to-Coast walk ends here. Local CAMRA's Pub of the Season 2003 puts on a second guest beer in summer.
♨ Q ☋ ❀ ◐ ⛺ ♣

Runswick Bay

Royal Hotel

TS13 5HT (off A174 at Hinderwell, down steep bank, left past lifeboat station)
✪ 12-3, 6-11; 12-11 Fri & Sat; 12-10.30 Sun
☎ (01947) 840215
website: www.theroyal-runswickbay.co.uk
Black Sheep Best Bitter; Tetley Bitter; guest beer (summer) 🄷
Tables on the small front patio overlook the beach at Runswick Bay. Quite old-fashioned, the bar, a rather long, narrow room, has a fireplace, while the back room has recently been refurbished with settles in traditional tap room style. The dining room is upstairs. The licensee plans to restrict smoking. On the Cleveland Way, the tiny village of Runswick is a renowned beauty spot, popular with walkers; take some ale to fortify yourself for the climb up the bank.
♨ Q ☋ ❀ ◐ ♣ ⁄

Ruswarp

Bridge Inn

High Street, YO21 1NJ (by bridge over River Esk). OS889091
✪ 7 (6 Fri)-11; 12-3, 6-11 Sat; 12-10.30 Sun
☎ (01947) 602780
Greene King IPA; guest beer (summer) 🄷
A friendly welcome is assured at this traditional local, in the middle of a pleasant village; you can walk here from Whitby along a mostly flagged path in 30 minutes. Take a trip on the Esk Valley Railway or the miniature steam trains, or row to Sleights. Step down from pavement level into the bar, decorated with old railway photos. There is a pool room and a snug on the right, and a back garden overlooking the river.
♨ ❀ ⊟ ⇌ ♣

Saltburn by the Sea

New Marine

Marine Parade, TS12 1DZ (on the top promenade)
⚙ 12-11; 12-10.30 Sun
☎ (01287) 622695
Beer range varies H
Converted from a small hotel, the bar caters for young or livelier folk with juke box, TV and pool tables, while the lounge is quiet. Both rooms are comfortably furnished and have a warm and relaxed atmosphere. An upstairs restaurant doubles as a bar and function room. The patio affords a vista from the Durham coastline across the Tees estuary to the cliffs of North Yorkshire. Nearby is the most northerly pier in England and a water-powered funicular rail lift.
Q❀◑⊟♿⛺≠⊡

Saltburn Cricket, Bowls & Tennis Club

Marske Mill Lane, TS12 1HJ (by Saltburn leisure centre)
⚙ 8 (2 summer Sat)-11; 12-3, 8-10.30 Sun
☎ (01287) 622761
Adnams Bitter; guest beer H
Private sports club, fielding cricket, tennis and bowls teams in local leagues. It has a spacious, well-furnished lounge and games room; both areas afford a magnificent view of the cricket field. The club is open all day on match days. Lounge/games rooms are available for special occasions. Casual visitors are welcome without joining. It stocks a large range of guest beers and runs occasional beer festivals. Snacks are available at Cleveland CAMRA's frequent Pub of the Season winner. ❀⛺≠♣P

Sawdon

Anvil

Main Street, YO13 3DY (off A170, Scarborough-Pickering road)
⚙ 12-11; 12-10.30 Sun
☎ (01723) 859896 website: www.theanvil.co.uk
Black Sheep Best Bitter; guest beers H
Sympathetically restored in 1986, this former blacksmith's forge features the original anvil and local village memorabilia. Voted Scarborough CAMRA Rural Pub of the Year in 2004, it stocks up to seven guest ales, plus Westons Old Rosie cider. Beer festivals are held in January and August bank holiday. The dining area provides excellent value, home-cooked meals; the Sunday carvery includes wild boar. Try the hog roasts in summer. Accommodation, all en-suite, is convenient for the moors.
♔Q☕❀⛟◑⛺♣●P

Saxton

Greyhound

Main Street, LS24 9PY (W of A162, 5 miles S of Tadcaster)
⚙ 11-3, 5.30-11; 11-11 Sat; 12-10.30 Sun
☎ (01937) 557202
Samuel Smith OBB H
This picturesque Grade II listed, 13th-century, whitewashed village inn is favoured by locals and walkers. Originally a teasle barn, it nestles by the village church (it is said that some occupants of the graveyard still drop in for a quick one!). Entry is through a low-ceilinged, stone-flagged corridor to the tiny bar. Real fires blaze in two of the three rooms in winter; admire the extensive collection of colourful wall plates in one bar. ♔Q❀⊟♣

Scaling Dam

Grapes

TS13 4TP (on A171, opp. reservoir)
⚙ 11.30-3 (not winter Mon), 6.30-11; 12-3, 6-10.30 Sun
☎ (01287) 640461
Black Sheep Best Bitter; guest beer H
Old sandstone pub, opposite the reservoir at Scaling Dam. The bar, on the left of the entrance, boasts a beamed ceiling, decorated with brasses, an old range, and pictures of butterflies. In the restaurant smoking restrictions apply on Sunday. Scaling is a tiny village in the middle of the moors, where people go to sail or watch birds on the reservoir. Good views can be had from Ridge Lane towards Staithes (five miles away – unsuitable for large vehicles).
♔❀⛟◑P

Scarborough

Angel Inn

46 North Street, YO11 1DF
⚙ 11-11; 12-10.30 Sun
☎ (01723) 365504
John Smith's Bitter; Tetley Bitter; Wells Bombardier H
Friendly, town-centre local where the single horseshoe bar room displays an excellent collection of saucy seaside postcards. An interest in sport and games is reflected in the impressive array of trophies won by various pub teams and the large-screen TV used for major events on one side of the bar. Note the 'clocking-in' machine for use by the regulars who get a free pint for time served at the bar! ≠♣

Cellars

35-37 Valley Road, YO11 2LX
⚙ 12 (4 Mon)-11; 12-10.30 Sun
☎ (01723) 367158
Tetley Bitter; guest beers H
Family-run pub, converted from the cellars of an elegant Victorian house (now holiday flats). The busy bar area keeps at least three guest beers. It hosts live music Saturday evening and an 'open mike' night Wednesday, when the whole pub is no-smoking. Bar meals are available and there is a restaurant upstairs; all food is made on the premises from locally-sourced supplies. Beer festivals are staged in spring and autumn. The patio and gardens give a pleasant alfresco drinking experience. ❀◑⛺≠♣P⊬

Cricketers ✔

119 North Marine Road, YO12 7HU
⚙ 12 (3 winter Mon-Fri)-11; 12-10.30 Sun
☎ (01723) 365864
Caledonian Deuchars IPA; Taylor Landlord; Tetley Bitter; guest beers H
Local CAMRA Pub of the Year for the past three years, it stands opposite the cricket ground, overlooking the North Bay. Cricketing memorabilia (naturally) adorn the walls. It offers up to three guest beers (more in season), Weston's Old Rosie cider, draught Hoegaarden and bottled fruit beers. It hosts an annual beer festival in July. The function room doubles as a

family room in summer. Try the landlord's chilli (made with home-grown chillies in season) and the Riggwelter casserole. ☎❀◑◗⛺⇌♣♠P

Indigo Alley

4 North Marine Road, YO12 7PD

✪ 4-11; 4-10.30 Sun

☎ (01723) 381900

Beer range varies Ⓗ

Lively, popular, one-roomed pub, offering six constantly-changing real ales, including a regular Rooster's brew. Belgian Leffe blonde and brown beers as well as Hoegaarden are all sold on draught. Live music is performed several times a week. It was voted local CAMRA Pub of the Year for three consecutive years. A real gem – not to be missed; note opening time, 4pm daily. ⇌

Old Scalby Mills

Scalby Mills Road, YO12 6RP

✪ 11-11; 12-10.30 Sun

☎ (01723) 500449

Brains Rev James; Wychwood Hobgoblin; guest beers Ⓗ

Favoured by walkers and tourists, in a seafront location, the building was originally a watermill but has seen many uses over the years; old photographs and prints chart its history. Admire the superb views of the North Bay and castle from the sheltered patio or lounge. The Cleveland Way reaches the seafront at this point and there is a Sea Life Centre nearby. Children are welcome in the lounge until 6pm, when smoking restrictions are lifted. Q☎❀◑⊟⛺♣⚟

Scholars

Somerset Terrace, YO11 2PW

✪ 12-11; 12-10.30 Sun

☎ (01723) 360084 website: www.bedfordhotel.info

Daleside Blonde; York Yorkshire Terrier; guest beers Ⓗ

Part of the Bedford Hotel, situated in an elegant Regency crescent, this large, one-roomed pub was recently refurbished and has a warm, friendly atmosphere. The three guest ales include regular offerings from Durham, York and Daleside breweries; Hoegaarden wheat beer is also on tap. The Scarborough Jazz Club presents live performances on Tuesday evening and acoustic sets on Wednesday. Home-cooked food is available all day until early evening.

Q☎❀⛟◑◗♿⇌♣

Tap & Spile ✔

94 Falsgrave Road, YO12 5AZ

✪ 11-11; 12-10.30 Sun

☎ (01723) 363837

Adnams Broadside; Big Lamp Bitter; Caledonian Deuchars IPA; Everards Tiger; Taylor Landlord; Wychwood Hobgoblin Ⓗ

Sympathetically restored coaching inn, not far from the town centre, serving 13 cask ales. Three rooms, including a no-smoking snug, display local memorabilia. Excellent value meals are served lunchtime and early evening (not Wed). Barbecues are held on the patio during summer Sunday afternoons. Live music, every Tuesday evening and Sunday, is often blues-oriented. This thriving local has a friendly atmosphere; TV sports is shown in one bar.

Q❀◑◗⇌♣♠P⚟

Valley

51 Valley Road, YO11 2LX

✪ 12-11; 12-10.30 Sun

☎ (01723) 372593

Beer range varies Ⓗ

Multi-roomed pub, its cellar bar offers a welcoming atmosphere to regulars and visitors alike. The beers are often sourced from local micros: Wold Top, Abbey Bells, Daleside, Rudgate and Acorn. Entertainment includes quizzes and live music (Tue). Evening meals are served 5.30-7.30. The food is home-cooked from locally-sourced produce. Local fish dishes are a speciality; Friday is curry night. Barbecues are held in summer on the spacious patio.

❀⛟◑◗⛺⇌♣⚟

Selby

Albion Vaults

New Street, YO8 0PT (on A19, town side of the swing bridge)

✪ 12-11; 12-10.30 Sun

☎ (01757) 213817

Old Mill Bitter Ⓗ

Two-roomed pub just off the town centre, close to the River Ouse swing bridge. The pleasing Edwardian decor is characteristic of the style of this local independent brewery. The public bar has a pool table and TV for sporting events. Food is not served, but an upstairs room is available for functions and meetings. Although the house bitter is the only regular beer, occasionally the brewery's seasonal specials are available.

♨Q❀⊟⇌♣

Skipton

Cock & Bottle ✔

30 Swadford Street, BD23 1RD

✪ 11.30 (11 Sat)-11; 12-10.30 Sun

☎ (01756) 794734 website: www.cockandbottle.co.uk

Camerons Castle Eden Ale; Tetley Bitter; guest beers Ⓗ

Former 18th-century coaching inn with a single, long, split-level bar, original exposed beams and fireplace. Note the unusual ground-floor beer 'cellar' visible through windows both from the bar and the street outside. Beware of the low beam above the step halfway along the bar. The guest beers are from the Enterprise specialist cask range and often include ales rarely found in Yorkshire from as far afield as Orkney and Sussex.

♨❀◑⇌♣

Narrow Boat

38 Victoria Street, BD23 1JE (alley off Coach St near canal bridge)

✪ 12-11; 12-10.30 Sun

☎ (01756) 797922 website: www.markettowntaverns.co.uk

Beer range varies Ⓗ

Popular free house near the canal basin. The no-smoking pub is furnished with old church pews and decorated with canal-themed murals, old brewery posters and mirrors; no piped music, juke-box or gaming machines. Of the eight ales, one is usually from the local Copper Dragon Brewery; it stocks a good selection of continental bottled beers. It hosts monthly jazz (first Tue) and folk (alternate Sun eves); Wednesday is quiz night. Evening meals are served Sunday-Thursday. Q❀◑≠♣⊬

Snape

Castle Arms ✔

DL8 2TB (off B6268, Bedale-Masham road) OS267844

✪ 12-3, 6 (7 winter)-11; 12-3, 7-10.30 Sun

☎ (01677) 470270

Black Sheep Best Bitter Ⓗ

Named after Snape Castle, once home of Catherine Parr, this 14th-century inn with exposed beams, a magnificent fireplace in the bar and stone-flagged floor provides good food from local produce and offers accommodation in a converted barn. It sits in the middle of this quiet picturesque village on the bus route from Bedale to Masham. Quoits is played in summer. Camping and caravan facilities are available to CC members. ⩩Q❀⇆◑▲♣P

Stainsacre

Windmill Inn

Mill Lane, YO22 4LT (off A171 from Whitby) OS912086

✪ 12 (7 Tue)-11; 12-10.30 Sun

☎ (01947) 602671

Camerons Strongarm; Theakston Best Bitter Ⓗ

Traditional village pub, with one large bar, a quiet, no-smoking dining room off to the right and a garden. It hosts bingo on Monday, pool is played on Tuesday, and Thursday is games night, with darts, pool and dominoes. It is popular with visitors staying the weekend at nearby Stainsacre Hall. Just off the old railway line, it is convenient for people walking and cycling from Whitby to Scarborough; cycles can be hired about three-quarters of a mile away. ⩩Q❀⇆◑♿▲♣P⊬⊡

Staithes

Captain Cook Inn

60 Staithes Lane, TS13 5AD (about ¼ mile from A174)

✪ 11-11; 12-10.30 Sun

☎ (01947) 840200 website: www.capitaincookinn.co.uk

Marston's Burton Bitter, Pedigree; Rudgate Viking Bitter; guest beers Ⓗ

Originally known as the Station Hotel, this 19th-century building stands at the top of the steep bank above the village. The garden affords great views of Boulby and the harbour. The village is popular with holidaymakers and walkers. The pub has a main bar area decorated with local memorabilia and pump clips, a snug and a games room, where children are welcome. The beer choice includes products not often seen in this area. Occasional beer festivals are staged at this regular Cleveland CAMRA award winner. ⩩Q☋❀⇆⊟▲♣●P

Stokesley

Spread Eagle

39 High Street, TS9 5AD (near town hall)

✪ 11-11; 12-10.30 Sun

☎ (01642) 710278 website: www.thespreadeagle.net

Banks's Original; Camerons Strongarm; Marston's Pedigree; guest beer Ⓗ

Small, unspoilt, town-centre pub with friendly regulars and a relaxed atmosphere. Excellent, home-cooked food is available all day from an interesting menu with meat, game and poultry from the family butcher, real vegetables and imaginative salads (booking is advisable). An enclosed rear garden leads down to the River Leven. In the front room, only the fire is permitted to smoke. Live music is performed Tuesday evening in this otherwise quiet pub. ⩩Q❀◑♿⊬

White Swan ✔

1 West End, TS9 5BL (on road from centre towards Hutton Rudby)

✪ 11.30-3 (not Tue), 5.30 (5 Fri)-11; 12-3, 7-10.30 Sun

☎ (01642) 710263

website: www.thecaptaincookbrewery.co.uk/swan/htm

Captain Cook, Sunset, Slipway, Black Porter; guest beer Ⓗ

Old-fashioned town pub with a J-shaped bar (no-smoking area at the back). An outlet for the adjacent prize-winning Captain Cook's Brewery, it also has a great cheeseboard – and an award to prove it. Just off West Green, it stands in maybe the prettiest part of this fine little market town. No juke box or fruit machines disturb the peace. Served by buses from Hutton Rudby, Great Ayton, Redcar, Guisborough and Middlesbrough, it was local CAMRA's Pub of the Year 2003. ⩩Q◐♣⊬

Tadcaster

Royal Oak

8 Wighill Lane, LS24 8EX

✪ 10.30-4, 6-11; 10.30-11 Fri; 12-4, 7-10.30 Sun

☎ (01937) 832283

Samuel Smith OBB Ⓗ

Very much a local, just outside the town centre, the unusual layout of this 17th-century building features an L-shaped tap room and lounge, giving four drinking areas, each with access to the central bar. Real fires in winter, low beams and collections of old flat irons and cobblers' lasts lend a homely feel, typical of pubs owned by this independent Yorkshire brewery. A warm welcome is assured by the landlord; only the third in 50 years. ⩩Q❀♣

Thirsk

Golden Fleece Hotel

Market Place, YO7 1LL

✪ 11-3, 6-11; 12-2, 7-10 Sun

☎ (01845) 523108 website: www.goldenfleecehotel.com

Hambleton Bitter, Stud; guest beer Ⓗ

This comfortable hotel, now part of the Best Western group, has been a coaching inn for nearly 400 years. Facing onto the main Market Place of this bustling centre, the Paddock Bar is on a split level and follows a distinct horse racing theme as befits a racecourse town. The former surgery of Alf Wight – better known as fictional vet, James Herriot – is now an award-winning museum in nearby Westgate. The guest beer is another from the Hambleton stable. ⩩Q☋⇆◐◑P

Thixendale

Cross Keys

YO17 9TG OS842612

✪ 12-3, 6-11; 12-3, 7-10.30 Sun

☎ (01377) 288272
Jennings Bitter; Tetley Bitter; guest beers 🄷
Remote, but worth seeking out, Thixendale is a picturesque village in the heart of the Yorkshire Wolds at the junction of several typical Wolds dry valleys. Inhabited since the Stone Age, many tracks established in Roman times are still used today by walkers in the dramatic surrounding countryside. The hostelry is an unspoilt, unpretentious village local with a single bar, serving guest beers from independent breweries and good value, home-cooked food. Children are welcome in the garden. ♛❀🛏◐◑♣

Thorganby

Ferryboat Inn

YO19 6DD (1 mile NE of village, SE of York) OS697426
⊛ 7 (12 Sat)-11; closed Mon; 12-3, 7-10.30 Sun
☎ (01904) 448224
Old Mill Bitter; guest beers 🄷
Set beside the River Derwent, this family-run inn is a haven of tranquillity. One bar and an excellent family room lead out to the large lawn that slopes down to the tree-lined river. Families, walkers, cyclists, boaters and anglers enjoy the varied Durham Brewery beers and local brewery selection. Signposted from the main road down a narrow lane, it is home to the local dominoes and quiz teams, and hosts folk music nights. ♛Q♞❀♿▲♣P⊽

Warthill

Agar Arms

YO19 5XW (off A166, 5 miles NE of York)
⊛ 11.30-2.30, 6.30-11; 12-3, 7-10.30 Sun
☎ (01904) 488142
Samuel Smith OBB 🄷
This could almost be the subject of a Constable painting: the pub stands on a bank overlooking the village pond where, on lazy summer days, you can sit, enjoy a beer from this Yorkshire brewery and watch the ducks. Alternatively, choose a sumptuous meal from the wide range of food available within, where there are open fires in winter. A well in the floor of the bar reveals the building's origins as a blacksmith's shop.
♛Q♞❀◐◑P⊁

Well

Milbank Arms

Church Street, DL8 2PX (off B6267, Masham-Thirsk road) OS267819
⊛ 12-3, 6.30-11; closed Mon; 12-3, 6-10.30 Sun
☎ (01677) 470411
Black Sheep Best Bitter; Rudgate Viking Bitter; guest beer (summer) 🄷
Warm, comfortable and friendly country inn between the market towns of Bedale and Masham. Over 300 years old, the name derives from the original owners, the Milbank family. A recent major refurbishment has resulted in a relaxing atmosphere. Two Yorkshire-brewed traditional ales are joined by a guest in summer. A full menu is served in the restaurant or bar, booking is recommended. Thorpe Perrow Arboretum is a mile away. The local quoits team plays here in summer.
♛Q❀◐◑♿♣P

West Witton

Fox & Hounds

Main Street, DL8 4LP (on A684)
⊛ 12-4, 6.30-11; 12-4, 6.30-10.30 Sun (may open all day in summer)
☎ (01969) 623650 website: www.foxwitton.com
Black Sheep Best Bitter; John Smith's Bitter; guest beers 🄷
On the main A684 Wensleydale route, this welcoming yet down-to-earth inn is frequented by walkers and other Dales visitors as well as its loyal regulars. The CAMRA award-winning landlord serves two guest beers, often from Salamander or Eastwood & Sanders, and the pub is popular for its home cooking. The bar is split into two small areas, divided by a chimney breast; the dining room boasts an attractive inglenook. Cider is sold in summer.
♛❀◐◑▲♣🍎P⊽

Whitby

Shambles

Shambles Market Place, YO22 4DD
⊛ 11-11 (midnight summer); 12-10.30 Sun
☎ (01947) 600306
Camerons Strongarm; Theakston XB; guest beer 🄷
Originally this building was a meat factory, hence the pub name, although it later became a Burberry factory. Climb the steps from the market place to enter this refurbished pub: a central bar with an adjoining smoke-free family room and dining area. The main bar area retains the exposed, 200-year-old, original beams and is furnished with large, comfortable chairs and sofas. Relax with a beer and watch the traffic pass by or admire the magnificent view of Whitby Harbour. ♞◐◑⇌⊁

White House Hotel

Upgang Lane, YO21 1JJ
⊛ 11-11; 12-10.30 Sun
☎ (01947) 600469
Courage Directors; Greene King Old Speckled Hen; Theakston Best Bitter 🄷
Small, friendly hotel, with overnight accommodation, overlooking the sea and golf course. It was extensively refurbished in 2004. The two spacious bars have a modern appearance and a comfortable atmosphere. Food is available in the adjacent restaurant; the no-smoking area is the lower bar. The propellor in the upper bar comes from a Sopwith Camel, but there is no truth in the rumour that the remainder of the plane is just behind the wall.
❀🛏◐◑♿P⊁

York

Ackhorne

9 St Martins Lane, YO1 6LN (up cobbled lane by church at bottom of Micklegate)
⊛ 12-11; 12-10.30 Sun
☎ (01904) 671421 website: www.ackhorne.com
Caledonian Deuchars IPA; Rooster's Yankee; guest beers 🄷
A refuge from the city centre. The current layout resulted from a major refurbishment in 1993, which sensibly retained the stained glass windows. At the same time it reverted to its

original name (from the Acorn). The bare-boarded bar, with comfortable bench seating, leads to a carpeted snug that houses a collection of Civil War memorabilia based around local hero, Sir Thomas Fairfax. The garden is tiny, but a real suntrap. No meals are served Sunday. Q❀◐≠♣●

Blue Bell ☆

53 Fossgate, YO1 9TF

🕐 11-11; 12-10.30 Sun

☎ (01904) 654904 website: www.bluebellyork.co.uk

Adnams Bitter; Caledonian Deuchars IPA; Greene King Abbot; Taylor Landlord; Tetley Mild; guest beers Ⓗ

Tiny, glazed brick-clad pub (dating back to 1798) with York's only perfect surviving Edwardian interior – courtesy of a 1903 refurbishment by then owners CJ Melrose. Fully panelled throughout, the drinking corridor, bar and snug have a cosy, timeless atmosphere, providing a welcome haven from the nearby tourist spots. Twice local CAMRA Pub of the Year, its generosity has resulted in a Morning Advertiser fundraising Pub of the Year award too. Good value sandwiches are sold 11-6pm. Q⊟≠♣

Golden Ball ☆

2 Cromwell Road, YO1 6DU

🕐 4 (12 Fri & Sat)-11; 12-10.30 Sun

☎ (01904) 652211 website: www.goldenball-york.co.uk

Caledonian Deuchars IPA; Marston's Pedigree; John Smith's Bitter, Magnet; Wells Bombardier; guest beers Ⓗ

This recent York CAMRA Pub of the Year is a fine, Victorian, street-corner local in the Bishophill residential area. The impressive, glazed brick facade leads to a multi-roomed interior where the layout owes much to a 1929 refurbishment by John Smith's. The public bar, unusual bar-side alcove and rear lounge all have their devotees, as does the bar billiards/TV room created recently from former living accommodation. The well-kept garden is a delightful refuge. Live music is staged Thursday. Q❀⊟⅄≠♣

Golden Slipper

20 Goodramgate, YO1 7LG

🕐 11-11; 12-10.30 Sun

☎ (01904) 651235 website: www.goldenslipper.co.uk

Caledonian Deuchars IPA; Greene King Old Speckled Hen; John Smith's Bitter; Wells Bombardier; guest beer Ⓗ

Deceptively small from the outside, this pub is made up of two buildings, curiously overlapping its neighbouring pub. There are small rooms beyond the entrance passage and bar leading to a patio at the rear, where you can sit peacefully and enjoy the varied range of beers or maybe choose a book from the library. An interesting place, with plenty of exposed timberwork, it was recently sympathetically refurbished. The food is recommended. ❀⇔◐♣⚟

Last Drop Inn

27 Colliergate, YO1 8BN

🕐 11-11; 12-10.30 Sun

☎ (01904) 621951

York Guzzler, Stonewall, Yorkshire Terrier, Centurion's Ghost Ale, seasonal beers; guest beers Ⓗ

Only five years old, but now a well-established attraction for visitors and locals, this York Brewery/Tynemill conversion of a former solicitors' office stands opposite King's Square, where live entertainers may be observed through the pub's large, plain glass windows. The split-level interior was crafted using mainly good quality local materials creating a more permanent feel than expected in a new pub. There are no electronic amusements and children are not admitted. Q❀◐≠

Maltings

Tanners Moat, YO1 6HU (below Lendal Bridge)

🕐 11-11; 12-10.30 Sun

☎ (01904) 655387 website: www.maltings.co.uk

Black Sheep Best Bitter; guest beers Ⓗ

First or last (or both) port of call for many visitors to York, due to its proximity to the station, the Maltings is highly regarded locally too. The idiosyncratic interior – now over 10 years old – is wearing well, as is the ebullient management in whose capable hands the pub has been since its conversion from the Lendal Bridge. The huge portions of food served from the Dragon's Pantry enjoy a devoted following, as do the annual beer festivals. ◐≠●

Minster Inn ✔

24 Marygate, YO30 7BH (off Bootham, A19, next to Museum Gardens)

🕐 12 (11 Fri & Sat)-11; 12-10.30 Sun

☎ (01904) 624499 website: www.minsterinn.co.uk

Marston's Burton Bitter; guest beers Ⓗ

Traditional, multi-roomed local, tucked away behind the old abbey walls. A central corridor with a bar leads to three other rooms (one no-smoking). It offers an adventurous choice of guest ales and frequent beer festivals. Families are especially welcome here. Table games, such as nine men's morris, are dotted around the pub. It is a place to while away time with good beer and friendly locals, and to enjoy what most pubs used to offer. ♨Q⛐❀⊟≠♣⚟

Rook & Gaskill

12 Lawrence Street, YO10 3WP (near Walmgate Bar)

🕐 12-11; 12-10.30 Sun

☎ (01904) 674067

Caledonian Deuchars IPA; York Guzzler, Yorkshire Terrier, Centurion's Ghost Ale, seasonal beers; guest beers Ⓗ

York CAMRA's 2005 Pub of the Year boasts 12 beers, a mix from York Brewery and interesting guests; a welcome outlet for local, independent brewers. The single bar has terrazzo flooring (note the brewery insignia), comfortable bench seating and sporting pictures. There is a conservatory at the rear. Youthful management, together with a policy of no children, piped music or gaming machines, make this a haven for the discerning drinker. Evening meals are served Monday-Thursday. Q❀◐◗≠♣

Saddle Inn

Main Street, Fulford, YO10 4PJ (on A19, 2 miles S of York centre)

🕐 11.45-4, 5.45-11; 12-4, 5.45-10.30 Sun

☎ (01904) 633317

Banks's Bitter; Camerons Bitter; guest beers Ⓗ

Although it has been on this site for more than 150 years, the original Saddle stood on the opposite side of the street. The comfortable

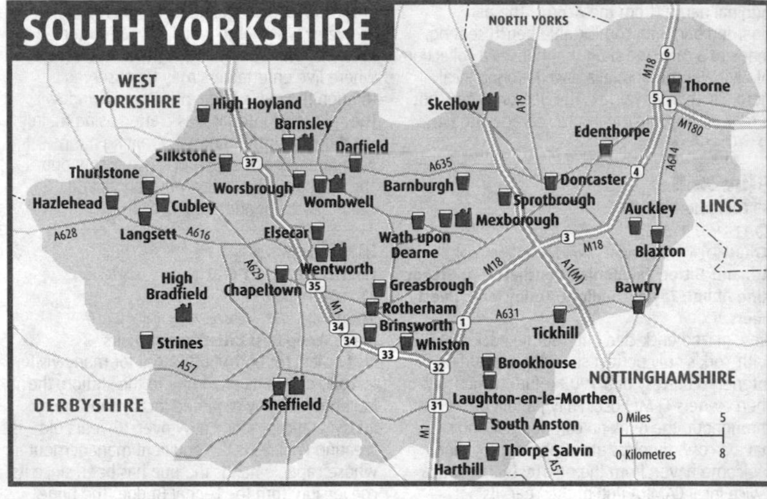

L-shaped lounge has an adjacent dining area, where children are welcome. In the bar there are darts and pool; beyond the car park the attractive garden boasts a petanque terrain. No lunches are served on Monday.

Sun Inn

The Green, Acomb, YO26 5LL (on B1224, York to Wetherby road))

11-11; 12-10.30 Sun

(01904) 798500

John Smith's Bitter; guest beers

Overlooking Acomb village green in York's western suburb, the Sun has all the traditional hallmarks of a real pub. Sensitive refurbishments have enhanced the three drinking areas while patio tables are provided outside to the front and rear. Displays of local street scenes add interest. Quality home-made food (lunchtime and early eve) is described as 'classic dishes with a modern twist'.

Swan Inn ☆

16 Bishopgate Street, YO23 1JH

4 (12 Sat)-11; 12-10.30 Sun

(01904) 634968

Caledonian Deuchars IPA; Taylor Landlord; Tetley Bitter; guest beers

The entrance leads into a drinking lobby with servery and two rooms, supplied from the main bar. This classic, street-corner local has a 'West Riding' layout, unusual for York. One of the three pubs in York included in CAMRA's National Inventory as having outstanding historic interest, this Tetley Heritage Inn is popular in the evening with the younger generation, but usually quieter in the early evening and at weekends. The sunny, walled garden is large by York's standards.

Tap & Spile

29 Monkgate, YO31 7PB

11.30-11; 12-10.30 Sun

(01904) 656158

Rooster's Yankee; guest beers

Imposing, Flemish-style pub dating from 1897, built by then local brewers JJ Hunt of nearby Aldwark. Formerly the Black Horse, it was renamed in 1988 when it became one of the first Tap & Spiles of the chain. The spacious, split-level interior, with a carpeted lounge area featuring bookshelves and an elegant fireplace, has recently been pleasantly refurbished. The annual pork pie festival in September is typical of the pub's occasional off-beat events.

Three-Legged Mare

15 High Petergate, YO1 7EN

11-11; 12-10.30 Sun

(01904) 638246 website: www.thethreeleggedmare.co.uk

York Guzzler, Stonewall, Yorkshire Terrier, Centurion's Ghost Ale, seasonal beers; guest beers

The eponymous mare is actually a triangular device which once stood on the York Knavesmire for the purpose of hanging three criminals simultaneously; take a look at the replica in the garden. Converted from a shop in 2001, this York Brewery pub bears the most modern look of its four tied houses. The single bar – free from electronic gimickry – leads to a pleasant conservatory. Toilets are down a twisting spiral staircase.

York Beer & Wine Shop

28 Sandringham Street, YO10 4BA (off A19/Fishergate)

11 (6 Mon; 10 Sat)-10; 6-10 Sun

(01904) 647136

Taylor Landlord; guest beers

One of the original breed of pioneering off-licences, it is now more than 20 years old and was a recent award-winner in Off-Licence News' Independent Beer Retailer of the Year competition. The draught beer and cider (to be taken away in any quantity), classic bottled beers (from home and abroad) and artisanal cheeses, complemented by friendly and knowledgeable staff, provide an unbeatable combination.

YORKSHIRE (SOUTH)

Auckley

Eagle & Child

24 Main Street, DN9 3HS (on B1396)

⏲ 11.30-3, 5-11; 11.30-11 Sat; 12-4, 7-10.30 Sun
☎ (01302) 770406
Black Sheep Best Bitter; John Smith's Bitter; Theakston Cool Cask; guest beers Ⓗ
Attractive, traditional village inn, well supported by the local community and well placed for Doncaster's Robin Hood Airport. Guest beers are usually from local independent breweries – visits to them are organised regularly. The excellent, varied and reasonably priced meals can be taken in smoking or no-smoking areas. The Eagle received a special CAMRA award for services to Real Ale in 2000 and local Pub of the Season for autumn 2003. There is a regular bus service from Doncaster.
Q❀◖◗⊟♣P⊁

Barnburgh

Coach & Horses ☆
High Street, DN5 7EP (follow signs from A635)
⏲ 12-5.30, 7-11; 12-11 Sun
☎ (01709) 892306
John Smith's Bitter; guest beers Ⓗ
When Whitworth, Son & Nephew, brewers of Wath Upon Dearne, decided to build a pub in Barnburgh they specified a magnificent example. This four-roomed house opened in 1937 and remains unaltered. Whitworth's wheatsheaf motif can be seen in the leaded glass screens above the bar, while drawers on the bar back have polished brass handles. Guest beers often come from Springhead Brewery.
♛♉❀⊟♣P

Barnsley

George & Dragon
41-43 Summer Lane, S70 2NW (follow signs from Town End to hospital)
⏲ 12-11; 12-10.30 Sun
☎ (01226) 205609
John Smith's Bitter; guest beers Ⓗ
This brilliant, white, popular, edge-of-town pub is set on a busy road, a few minutes' walk from the town centre. The open-plan area is split into two: a darts and pool room and a drinking area with plenty of comfortable seating. TV sport is shown. Old photos of Barnsley cover the walls. Popular lunches are served Tuesday-Friday 12-2pm. The two changing guest beers are also well received at local CAMRA's Pub of the Year 2005. ❀◖⇌(Interchange) ♣P⊡

Keel Inn
18 Canal Street, S71 1LJ (next to Asda, 5 mins from town centre)
⏲ 12-3, 5-11; 12-10.30 Sun
☎ (01226) 284512
Beer range varies Ⓗ
Somewhat hidden pub, but just a few yards from the busy A61 and on the old Barnsley branch section of the Aire and Calder Navigation Canal. The pub is nautically themed to suit its location even though the canal closed in the 1950s. As one of the last pubs to serve the famous Barnsley Bitter from the original Oakwell Brewery, much Oakwell Brewery memorabilia are displayed. Barnsley CAMRA stages a beer festival here in October. Meals are served 12-2pm Tuesday-Friday.
♛❀⊨◖⇌(Interchange) ♣P

Moulders Arms
Summer Street, S70 2NU (off Summer Lane, heading to hospital)
⏲ 4.30 (2.30 Fri; 12 Sat)-11; 12-10.30 Sun
☎ (01226) 215767
John Smith's Bitter; guest beer Ⓗ
Detached pub on the edge of town. The small bar serves three open-plan areas offering a relaxed, friendly atmosphere. TV screens show sport, but the pub is often buzzing with friendly conversation. The garden provides a secure area for family drinking. The guest beer changes around twice a week; during May you can usually find a mild in support of CAMRA's mild campaign. It hosts a quiz and nostalgic disco Wed; buskers' night is Friday.
❀⇌(Interchange) ♣

Shaw Lane Sports Club (Barnsley RUFC)
Shaw Lane, S70 6HZ (next to Holgate School)
⏲ 5 (12 Sat)-11; 12-10.30 Sun
☎ (01226) 203509 website: www.barnsleyrufc.co.uk
Phoenix Wobbly Bob; guest beers Ⓗ
Local CAMRA's inaugural Club of the Year in 2004 has only existed in its present modern clubhouse since 2000. This successful real ale outlet now attracts a varied clientele from sports players to birthday parties and family gatherings. One room houses a cosy bar with large windows overlooking the cricket pitch, while the bigger lounge room has three handpulls that usually dispense micro-brewery beers. Sunday lunch is served.
❀♿P

Bawtry

Turnpike
28-30 High Street, DN10 6JE (on A638)
⏲ 11-11; 12-10.30 Sun
☎ (01302) 711960
Caledonian Deuchars IPA; Greene King Ruddles Best Bitter; John Smith's Bitter; guest beers Ⓗ
This L-shaped pub incorporates glass and wood-panelling, flagstones and carpeted floors, a cricket tie collection and photographs of the nearby former RAF Finningley base (now Robin Hood Airport). Originally one of Doncaster's Stocks' Brewery tied houses, the Turnpike has appeared in this Guide for 18 consecutive years and has received four local CAMRA Pub of the Season awards. A good choice of food is served lunchtime, plus Wednesday and Thursday evenings. Bus routes connect with surrounding towns. ❀◖◗

INDEPENDENT BREWERIES

Abbeydale Sheffield
Acorn Wombwell
Bradfield High Bradfield
Concertina Mexborough
Crown Sheffield
Glentworth Skellow
Kelham Island Sheffield
Oakwell Barnsley
Port Mahon Sheffield
Wellington Sheffield
Wentworth Wentworth

Blaxton

Blue Bell Inn

Old Thorne Road, DN9 3AL

⏲ 12-11; 12-10.30 Sun

☎ (01302) 770424

John Smith's Bitter; Taylor Landlord; Theakston Old Peculier Ⓗ

The Blue Bell is a cosy, yet deceptively large L-shaped pub, with the bar area directly ahead as you walk in. The lounge, to the left, leads to the restaurant. The pub is well decorated throughout, with a stone floor in the bar and old prints of the area's mining heritage. Although smoking is permitted throughout (except in the restaurant) the smoke level is not a problem. This friendly community pub is well worth a visit and is ideally situated for Robin Hood Airport. ❀♣P

Brinsworth

Phoenix Sports & Social Club

Pavilion Lane, S60 5PA (off Bawtry Rd)

⏲ 11-11; 12-10.30 Sun

☎ (01709) 363864

Wentworth Best Bitter; Worthington's Bitter; guest beer (summer) Ⓗ

Members of the public are welcome to be signed in at Rotherham's only club in this Guide. Set amid the club's 18-hole golf course, football and cricket pitches, the large, comfortable main bar features beers from Wentworth. A family room, TV room, snooker room with two full-sized tables and three function rooms complete the interior. The patio is especially popular in summer during the cricket season. No food is served on Monday. Q❀◐♣P⊬

Brookhouse

Travellers' Rest

Main Street, S25 1YA (½ mile from Laughton, near railway viaduct)

⏲ 12-3 (not Mon), 5-11; 12-11 Sat; 12-10.30 Sun

☎ (01909) 562661

Hardys & Hansons Bitter, Olde Trip, seasonal beers Ⓗ

Bungalow-style pub in a picturesque village, originally built as a house, using stone from an old watermill which stood on the site until the late 1960s. It is handy for walks to Roche Abbey and the impressive parish church at Laughton-en-le-Morthen, which dominates the hill above the village and is reached via the footpath beside the pub. The extensive garden alongside the brook is popular with families; catch the bank holiday duck races. It is a rare outlet for Hardys' beers in the area. ❀◐◑⊟♿♣P

Chapeltown

Commercial

107 Station Road, S35 2XF

⏲ 12-3, 5.30-11; 12-11 Fri & Sat; 12-10.30 Sun

☎ (0114) 246 9066

Wentworth Needles Eye, WPA, Oatmeal Stout; Ward's Best Bitter; guest beers Ⓗ

Former Strouts Brewery pub, built in 1890, it now stocks regular Wentworth beers including specials, plus four changing guests and a rotating cider. It is undergoing some refurbishment, but the snug retains its extensive pump clip collection. All three rooms are served by a central bar; the public bar has games. Successful beer festivals are held in May and November. No meals are served Sunday evening. ⛫❀◐◑⊟♿≠♣●P⊬⊡

Cubley

Cubley Hall Hotel ✔

Mortimer Road, S36 9DF (⅔ of a mile S of Penistone)

⏲ 11-11; 12-10.30 Sun

☎ (01226) 766086

Tetley Bitter, Imperial, Burton Ale; guest beers Ⓗ

Gentleman's residence, long since converted into a flourishing country hotel and restaurant known for its excellent food. The Carlsberg-dominated range of real ales is supplemented by a changing guest beer, often from a family or regional brewery. This popular venue for weddings and receptions caters for a mix of customers as diverse as its modern conservatory, high, moulded ceilings of the main room or old-fashioned mosaic tiles in the entrance hallway. ❀⇌◐◑♿P⊬

Darfield

Darfield Cricket Club

School Street, S73 9EZ

⏲ 7-11; 12-3, 6-11 Sat (12-11 Sat in cricket season); 12-10.30 Sun

☎ (01226) 752194

Beer range varies Ⓗ

Enjoying a pint of locally-brewed ale while listening to the thwack of leather on willow and watching fielders chase to the boundary is for many an ideal day. Here at this club, separated from Doncaster Road by its protective ring of trees, that ideal can be realised. Evenings in the clubhouse, with great food, make this club appealing all year. Food is served on Saturday and Sunday. Card-carrying CAMRA members and visitors with this Guide are welcome at local CAMRA's Club of the Year 2005. Q❀◐◑♣P

Doncaster

Leopard

1 West Street, DN1 3AA (near station)

⏲ 11-11; 12-10.30 Sun

☎ (01302) 363054 website: www.thegigguide.co.uk

Glentworth seasonal beers; John Smith's Bitter; guest beer Ⓗ

Traditional, large, street-corner pub, less than five minutes' walk from the station. An impressive tiled exterior recalls previous owners Warwick and Richardson's Brewery. It is now a long-standing regular outlet for the local Glentworth Brewery (one of its beers is always on tap). An eclectic mix of music is played on the juke box in both the comfortable lounge and the lively bar/games room. The upstairs music room hosts regular gigs. Tables by the car park cater for outdoor drinkers. ❀⊟≠♣●P⊬

Masons' Arms

22 Market Place, DN1 1ND

⏲ 11-11; 12-10.30 Sun

☎ (01302) 364391

Taylor Landlord; Tetley Bitter; guest beer Ⓗ

Market place pub, a Guide regular for many years. Once a Tetley Heritage pub, the additional beers have proved popular. Over 200 years old, it has maintained its multi-roomed layout. An outstanding public bar, where background music is sometimes played, is complemented by two quieter, comfortable rooms, one of which is the HQ of the local morris team. On busy market days it provides a haven from the bustle outside. Q❀⊟≹

Plough ☆

8 West Laith Gate, DN1 1SF (next to Frenchgate shopping centre)

⊛ 11-11; 12-3, 7-10.30 Sun

☎ (01302) 738310

Draught Bass; Blackpool Bitter Ⓗ

A recent addition to CAMRA's National Inventory of historic pub interiors, the Plough was altered in 1934 and remains much the same today. A drinkers' pub near the Frenchgate centre, it attracts mature, discerning clients. Long-standing hosts promote a comfortable, friendly atmosphere, making it an ideal break from shopping. Choose between the light, informal bar or the relaxing, comfy lounge. On warmer days, sit in the tiny, covered courtyard and admire the stained glass windows. ❀⊟≹♣

Salutation Hotel

14 South Parade, DN1 2DR

⊛ 12-11 (1am Fri & Sat); 12-10.30 Sun

☎ (01302) 340705

Tetley Bitter; guest beers Ⓗ

Coaching inn, built around 1780, that has retained its character, comprising a large bar plus a no-smoking area where you can enjoy a changing choice of guest beers, big-screen football or the popular Tuesday quiz. Meals are served daily. A function room upstairs has its own bar; the patio is ideal for summer days. ❀♿⊬

Tut 'n' Shive ✔

6 West Laith Gate, DN1 1SF (side of Frenchgate centre)

⊛ 11-11 (midnight Fri & Sat); 11-midnight Sun

☎ (01302) 360300

Black Sheep Best Bitter; Boddingtons Bitter; Greene King IPA, Abbot; Shepherd Neame Bishops Finger; guest beers Ⓗ

Traditional pub with stone floors and boarded ceilings where the walls are decorated with beer mats. The entertainment at the Tut 'n' Shive is rock music from the juke box, indie music played by a DJ on Tuesdays, football on the big screen, and pub quizzes on Sunday and Wednesday. This is a pub where everyone is welcome; up to six handpulled beers are available. ◐♿≹

Edenthorpe

Beverley Inn

Thorne Road, DN3 2JE (on A18)

⊛ 12-3, 5 (6 Sat)-11; 12-3, 7-10.30 Sun

☎ (01302) 882724

website: www.thebeverleyinn&hotel.co.uk

John Smith's Bitter, Magnet; guest beer Ⓗ

Popular, family-owned local, with a 200-year history. T'Bev was voted Pub of the Year 2004 in a local newspaper competition. Guest beers are often supplied by local breweries. The no-smoking restaurant offers mainly home-cooked food; the Sunday carvery is particularly popular. Accommodation is in 14 no-smoking three diamond-rated rooms. Buses on routes 87 and 88 from Doncaster stop outside. ❀🛏◐◑♿P

Eden Arms ✔

Edenfield Road, DN3 2QR (off A18, next to Tesco)

⊛ 12-11; 12-10.30 Sun

☎ (01302) 888682

Stones Bitter; Taylor Landlord; guest beers Ⓗ

An Ember Inn branded pub, the Eden offers a relaxed atmosphere, enhanced by friendly staff, homely furnishings and roaring fires throughout. An extensive menu is served all day, with no-smoking areas provided for both diners and drinkers. Weekly quizzes are held on Monday and Wednesday evenings. Two beer festivals are staged during the year, usually in May and October; three cask-conditioned ales are always on tap. A WC in the RADAR scheme is available. ⛰❀◐◑♿P⊬

Elsecar

Fitzwilliam Arms

42 Hill Street, S74 8EL (100 yds downhill from station)

⊛ 12-3.30 (not Mon), 7-11; 12-4, 7-10.30 Sun

☎ (01226) 742461

Tetley Bitter; guest beers Ⓗ

Two minutes' downhill walk from Elsecar Station, this traditional pub is decorated and furnished to an excellent standard, with the central bar separating the lounge/dining area from the games room. Two different guest ales are available from a constantly varying range. The games room plays host to darts and pool teams, and has TV for sporting events. The lounge area remains undisturbed and makes for a relaxing venue. Bus Nos. 227 and 325 call close to the pub. ❀◐◑♿≹♣P

Market Hotel

2-4 Wentworth Road, S74 8EP (¼ mile downhill from station)

⊛ 12 (11 Sat)-11; 12-10.30 Sun

☎ (01226) 742240

Copper Dragon Black Gold; Wentworth WPA; guest beer Ⓗ

Spacious, multi-roomed pub with a large garden. The well-presented and comfortable interior was originally stables – see the surviving stonework outside offering a horse and gig for hire. It is ideal for walkers and cyclists exploring the Trans-Pennine trail, or visitors to the Elsecar Heritage Centre next door. Many local clubs and societies meet here, including football and pool. Quizzes are held Wednesday and Sunday. The No. 227 bus stops outside. Q❀⊟≹♣

Greasbrough

Prince of Wales

9 Potter Hill, S61 4NU

⊛ 11-4, 7-11; 12-3, 7-10.30 Sun

☎ (01709) 551358

John Smith's Bitter; Ⓟ **guest beer** Ⓗ

Street-corner pub, with a spacious, well-decorated lounge and tap room. The friendly landlord is in his 26th year of tenancy and provides real ale from various breweries across the country; the guest beer can change up to

three times a day. Traditional pub games are available and in the summer tables and chairs allow customers to sit outside and watch the world go by. Close by are various take-away outlets.
Q⊟♣▯

Harthill

Beehive

16 Union Street, S26 7YH (opp. church on road from Kiveton crossroads)
✪ 12-3 (not Mon), 6 (6.30 Sat)-11; 12-3, 7-10.30 Sun
☎ (01909) 770205
Fuller's London Pride; Taylor Landlord; Tetley Bitter ⊞
Welcoming village pub with rooms for drinkers and diners (children welcome, if eating, until 9pm); last food orders 8.30pm. A full-sized snooker table is in the back room. Home to Harthill morris dancers and the local folk club, the function room upstairs can be reached by a chairlift. The pub is close to Rother Valley Country Park and is on the Five Churches walk.
Q◐◗♿♣P

Hazlehead

Dog & Partridge

Bord Hill, Flouch, S36 4HH (2 miles from the Flouch roundabout, westbound A628)
✪ 12-3, 6-11; Sat 12-11; 12-10.30 Sun
☎ (01226) 763173 website: www.dogandpartridgeinn.co.uk
Acorn Barnsley Bitter; Black Sheep Best Bitter; Tetley Bitter; guest beers ⊞
Large, roadside pub/hotel set in the northern section of the Peak District National Park (the Darke Peake) on an old medieval saltway route. The pub can be traced back to Elizabethan times; its first licence was in 1740. This isolated pub still offers shelter and refreshment to travellers crossing the hostile moors of the Pennines. Several buses call at the Flouch roundabout then it is a 15-minute walk. Accommodation in a converted barn includes a double room adapted for disabled visitors.
♔Q❀⇌◐◗♿P⍻

High Hoyland

Cherry Tree

Bank End Lane, S75 4BB (on main Huddersfield-Barnsley road)
✪ 12-3, 5.30-11; 12-11 Sat; 12-10.30 Sun
☎ (01226) 382541
Black Sheep Best Bitter; E&S Elland Best Bitter, Beyond the Pale; John Smith's Bitter; Tetley Bitter ⊞
Impressive rural pub that is popular with locals and visitors alike. A well-deserved reputation for both beer and food ensures a good turnout. The central bar and drinking area separate the two dining areas, with at least one area smoke-free. Spectacular views of the surrounding countryside can be enjoyed from the drinking area outside the front. The No. 235 Barnsley-Huddersfield bus stops right outside and there are public footpaths nearby. Meals are served all day Sunday until 9pm.
❀◐◗♿♣P⍻

Langsett

Waggon & Horses

Manchester Road, S36 4GY (on A616)
✪ 11-3, 7-11; closed Mon; 12-3 Sun
☎ (01226) 763147 website: www.langsettinn.com
Taylor Landlord; guest beer ⊞
Built in 1809, this Grade I listed pub has a warm, welcoming family atmosphere. Beside Langsett Reservoir, and benefiting from wonderful views of the Peak District, it makes an ideal meeting place for drinkers, walkers or holidaymakers. Accommodation is available in three individually-designed rooms. The legendary home-made meat and potato, and bilberry pies have been on the menu for over 30 years.
♔Q❀⇌◐◗⩓P

Laughton-en-le-Morthen

St Leger Arms

4 High Street, S25 1YF (1 mile from B6463 at Dinnington)
✪ 12-11; 12-10.30 Sun
☎ (01909) 562940
Blackpool Bitter; Boddingtons Bitter ⊞
The pub was named after the famous Doncaster horse race classic, said to have been first run in the fields between Laughton and nearby Firbeck as a wager between the Leger and Hatfield families. The other pub in the village is named after the Hatfields, and also sells real ale. Popular with locals, tourists and ramblers, walks from the car park lead to Roche Abbey and Brookhouse. Children are welcome in the restaurant until 9pm; a large play area is at the rear. ❀◐◗♣P⍻

Mexborough

Concertina Band Club

9A Dolcliffe Road, S64 9AZ
✪ 12-4, 7-11; 12-2, 7-10.30 Sun
☎ (01709) 580841
Concertina Club Bitter, Bengal Tiger; John Smith's Bitter ⊞
With the transfer of the Federation Brewery, the Tina, as it is known, is the sole remaining club brewery left. Photographs on the wall are a reminder of the days of the former band after which the club is named. Very much a traditional, old-fashioned place offering a warm, friendly welcome; show a CAMRA card or this Guide for entry. Occasional guest beers may be brewery specials or regular beers from independent brewers. ⇌♣▯

Rotherham

Blue Coat

The Crofts, S80 2DJ
✪ 10-11; 12-10.30 Sun
☎ (01709) 539500
De Koninck Ambrée; Marston's Burton Bitter; guest beers ⊞
This converted old school – hence the name – is a Wetherspoon's gem, hidden behind the town hall. The range on offer always includes Westons Old Rosie cider; the other seven pumps are given over to a huge variety of locally-sourced micro-breweries, including Acorn, Abbeydale and Wentworth, plus draught Leffe and Hoegaarden. It stocks a wide range of specialist

bottled beers. The pub is no-smoking; it has a disabled toilet and a large patio garden.
Q ❀ ◐ ♿ ≠ ● P ⊬

Hare & Hounds

52 Wellgate, S60 2LR
✪ 11.30-11; 12-10.30 Sun
☎ (01709) 821554
Greene King Abbot; guest beer Ⓗ
Situated on one of Rotherham's main shopping streets, the pub serves a local clientele. The single room is divided into three areas, with two housing large TV screens. Greene King Abbot is always served, with another changing guest ale; both beers enjoy a quick turnover. There is a small garden, a function room and the pub is flanked by municipal car parks. Traditional pub food is served at lunchtime. ❀ ◐ ♿ ≠ ♣ ● P

Sheffield: Central

Bath Hotel ☆

60 Victoria Street, S3 7QL
✪ 12-11; 7-10.30 Sun
☎ (0114) 249 5151
Abbeydale Moonshine; Acorn Barnsley Bitter; Tetley Bitter; guest beers Ⓗ
Does illicit beer taste better? The original 1867 lease on the land here states that it is not to be used for 'the business of an inn keeper, publican or beerhouse keeper' and there is a polite notice asking people not to direct the original landlord in the direction of the pub. The award-winning restoration of this pub has not involved any walls coming down, but left the two rooms commanded by the cubbyhole central bar. Lunches are served weekdays.
◐ ⊖ (University of Sheffield) ⊬

Devonshire Cat

49 Wellington Street, S1 4HG
✪ 11-11; 11-10.30 Sun
☎ (0114) 279 6700 website: www.devonshirecat.co.uk
Abbeydale Moonshine; Caledonian Deuchars IPA; Theakston Old Peculier; guest beers Ⓗ
Set in a large corner unit of a new building tucked back from the fashionable Devonshire Quarter, this is a fusion pub – a place for worshippers of real ale (and cider) to meet their unconverted friends and colleagues to baptise them. The sheer range of handpulled beer, draught and bottled continental lager means that there is always a chance they will find something to appeal to their taste. The house beer is brewed by Kelham Island.
♿ ⊖ (West St) ● ⊬

Fat Cat

23 Alma Street, S3 8SA
✪ 12-3, 5.30-11; 12-11 Fri & Sat; 12-3, 7-10.30 Sun
☎ (0114) 249 4801 website: www.thefatcat.co.uk
Kelham Island Bitter, Pale Rider, seasonal beers; Taylor Landlord; guest beers Ⓗ
What further is there to say in plaudit that has not been put in print before? It is in danger of running out of wall space to fit in all the awards for the pub, its food and the beer from Kelham Island, for which it is effectively the brewery tap. The old-fashioned pub provides clean air in the no-smoking room, a cosy public bar, a family-friendly upstairs room and a pleasant garden.
♛ Q ❀ ◐ ⊖ (Shalesmoor) ● P ⊬

Frog & Parrot ✔

Division Street, S1 4GF
✪ 11-11; 11-10.30 Sun
☎ (0114) 272 1280
Greene King IPA, Abbot, Old Speckled Hen; Ward's Best Bitter; guest beers Ⓗ
The most imposing external features of this corner pub are the seaside tea room windows for watching over the passing shoppers or night owls. The interior is dominated by a particularly baroque example of bar furniture behind the dark wood bar. Home of the darkly infamous Roger and Out, former holder of the Guinness record for world's strongest beer, it is now joined on the bar by a regular rotation of hand-pulled beers.
◐ ⊖ (West St)

Kelham Island Tavern ✔

62 Russell Street, S3 8RW
✪ 12-11; 12-3, 7-10.30 Sun
☎ (0114) 272 2482 website: www.kelhamislandtavern.co.uk
Acorn Barnsley Bitter; Pictish Brewers Gold; guest beers Ⓗ
Pub awards, including the CAMRA 2004 Yorkshire Pub of the Year, jostle for space with local and regional 'in bloom' certificates and reproductions of Hieronymous Bosch triptychs on the walls of this cosy, stylish pub. Recently extended, its no-smoking garden room is surrounded by the beautiful back yard. The beer range offers variety of style as well as brewery and generally includes at least one dark beer and/or mild. The real cider is kept cool in the cellar. Q ◐ ♿ ⊖ (Shalesmoor) ● ⊡

Museum

25 Orchard Street, S1 2GX
✪ 10-11; 12-10.30 Sun
☎ (0114) 275 5016
Greene King IPA, Abbot, Old Speckled Hen; Ward's Best Bitter Ⓗ
Recently refurbished pub, arranged on multiple levels served from one bar on the streetside ground floor. Set into the gateway of a quiet shopping precinct, the daytime crowd is predictably shoppers and lunchtime office workers; the latter crop up again for drinking in the evening along with theatregoers bound for the nearby City Hall and others preparing for a night out. It stocks a selection of Belgian beers.
◐ ♿ ≠ (Midland) ⊖ (Cathedral) ⊬

Red Deer ✔

18 Pitt Street, S1 4DD
✪ 11.30-11; 7.30-10.30 Sun
☎ (0114) 272 2890 website: www.red-deer-sheffield.co.uk
Adnams Broadside; Black Sheep Best Bitter; Caledonian Deuchars IPA Ⓗ
The front half of this pub is an L-shape tucked round the bar. To the rear, a raised seating area leads to a small but pleasant terrace. This cosy and enormously popular pub, while on the periphery of Sheffield University, maintains an atmosphere that is academic rather than studenty. The plethora of handpulls means there is always a good range of different beers available. No food is served Saturday evening or Sunday.
◐ ⊖ (West St) ⊬

Red Lion

109 Charles Street, S1 2ND

11.30-11; 11-3.30, 7-11 Sat; 12.30-2.30, 7-10.30 Sun

(0114) 272 4997

Caledonian Deuchars IPA; Black Sheep Best Bitter; Taylor Landlord; Ward's Best Bitter H

The Red Lion is in a side street between the railway station and the city centre near the new Winter Gardens. The pub's conservatory (no-smoking for lunchtime), although slightly small, is pleasant for summer supping. The two most notable features of the pub are the fact that it retains a separate snug in these days of knocking rooms together, and its abundance of theatrical posters and memorabilia.

Q (Midland) (Sheffield Station)

Riverside

1 Mowbray Street, Neepsend, S1 2BS

10-11; 10-10.30 Sun

(0114) 281 3621

Abbeydale Moonshine; guest beers H

Situated on the bank of the River Don, the Riverside truly shines when the sun does. The imposing french windows are flung open, giving access to the extensive terrace and allowing the breeze to flow into the spacious, high-ceilinged bar area decorated in a 'stripped and dipped salvage' style. Nonetheless it can seem just as inviting on a freezing winter evening with the fire bringing warmth to the stone flags. Evening meals are served weekdays. (Shalesmoor)

Rutland Arms

86 Brown Street, S1 2BS

11.30 (12 Sat)-11; 12-3, 7-10.30 Sun

(0114) 272 9003

website: www.rutlandarms-sheffield.co.uk

Adnams Bitter; Black Sheep Best Bitter; Cains Bitter; Caledonian Deuchars IPA; Greene King Abbot; guest beers H

Occupying a corner plot in the Cultural Industries Quarter near Sheffield's main railway station, this is a patch of greenery hidden behind city walls. To complement the multi-award winning garden, it has a comfortable interior, fitted into a corner shape, and including ample seating. There really is no descriptive term for the eclectic collection of paraphernalia that decorates the bar area. Evening meals are served weekdays; last orders 8pm.

(Midland) (Sheffield Station)

Ship Inn

312 Shalesmoor, S3 8UL

12-3, 7 (5 Fri; 7.30 Sat)-11; 12-3, 7.30-10.30 Sun

(0114) 281 2204

Hardys & Hansons Bitter, seasonal beers H

A grand, high-ceilinged lounge bar in two parts melds seamlessly into a low, cosy snug and games room, with the height changes replacing real walls. The theme of the name and the Anchor beers livery is continued inside by nautical memorabilia. The central box bar retains a traditional line of tankards and jug glasses while the general public are given lined, oversized glasses. (Shalesmoor) P

Three Cranes

74 Queen Street, S1 2DW

11-11; closed Sat & Sun

(0114) 273 1415

Stones Bitter; Taylor Landlord; guest beers H

A large, central horseshoe bar dominates two rooms. The larger lounge is fitted with booths suitable for the discussions of the local legal profession over lunch or between hearings. Dark wood panelling is inlaid with stained glass that lends an air of gravitas to an establishment that often has a young clientele mixing with more mature drinkers.

(Cathedral)

Sheffield: East

Carlton

563 Attercliffe Road, S9 3RA

11-11; 7-10.30 Sun

(0114) 244 3287

Acorn Barnsley Bitter; Kelham Island Pale Rider; Marston's Pedigree; guest beers H

Former Gilmours' pub dating from 1862 with a deceptively small frontage. A programme of careful renovation in traditional style has transformed the pub from a typical east end workmen's pub to a thriving community local catering for all. A comfortable lounge around the newly installed bar (salvaged from a recently closed country pub) leads to a pool room at the rear. The friendly atmosphere is enhanced by a strict no-swearing policy.

(Attercliffe/Woodbourn Rd)

Cocked Hat

75 Worksop Road, S9 3TG

11-11; 11-3, 7-11 Sat; 12-2, 7-10.30 Sun

(0114) 244 8332

Marston's Burton Bitter, Pedigree; guest beer H

Corner pub built in the 1840s, then at the heart of the steel industry, but now in the shadow of the Don Valley Stadium. The stalled seating area at the end of the bar is reserved for diners at lunchtime (served weekdays), decorated with pictures of bygone Attercliffe. One of Sheffield's few bar billiards tables occupies a raised area. It is frequented by players and fans from the sports stadium and walkers following the Five Weirs walk. (Attercliffe)

Sheffield: North

Cask & Cutler

1 Henry Street, Shalesmoor, S3 7EQ

12-2 (not Mon), 5.30-11; 12-11 Fri & Sat; 12-3, 7-10.30 Sun

(0114) 249 2295

Beer range varies H

Quiet, two-roomed pub at the centre of North Sheffield's acclaimed real ale circuit. Little changes at the Cask except the nine real ales from micros and small independents (always including a mild and stout or porter): nearly 6,000 have featured so far. Original leaded windows and many features remain from a 1940s refurbishment. The no-smoking room has a real fire where you will find Holly the dog and Magus the cat. A beer festival is staged in November. Q (Shalesmoor)

Gardener's Rest

105 Neepsend Lane, S3 8AT

3 (12 Fri & Sat)-11; 12-10.30 Sun

(0114) 272 4978 website: www.gardenersrest.co.uk

Taylor Golden Best, Best Bitter, Landlord;

Wentworth Needles Eye, WPA; Ⓗ
guest beers Ⓗ/Ⓖ
Combining the traditional with the modern, this pub appeals to all, with three rooms to choose from – a smoke-free lounge, a larger main room and a recently-built conservatory, plus a garden at the back overlooking the River Don. Throughout the pub are exhibitions and information on art, brewery memorabilia, local history, regeneration and the environment, plus a library and games, including bar billiards. It hosts live music most weekends, and a beer festival in early October.
Q❀♿⊖(Infirmary Road)♣●⊬☐

Hillsborough Hotel

54-58 Langsett Road, S6 2UB
✪ 6 (4.30 Thu-Sat)-11; closed Mon; 6-10.30 Sun
☎ (0114) 232 2100 website: www.crownbrewery.com
Crown HPA, Loxley Gold, Stannington Stout; Edale seasonal beers; Wellington seasonal beers; guest beers Ⓗ
Owned by the Edale Brewery, the Hillsborough is home to both Crown and Wellington whose beers are brewed in the cellar (tours available on request). Opening times have been extended and more than 20 guest ales now feature each week (bottled house beers are also on sale). Largely no-smoking (apart from the conservatory and raised sun terrace), Tuesday quiz night features a pie & peas supper; a wider range of dishes is offered on Wednesday (sandwiches at other times).
Q❀⇄◑⊖(Langsett/Primrose View)♣P⊬

New Barrack Tavern

601 Penistone Road, Hillsborough, S6 2GA
✪ 11-11; 12-10.30 Sun
☎ (0114) 234 9148 website: www.tynemill.co.uk
Abbeydale Moonshine; Acorn Barnsley Bitter; Castle Rock Harvest Pale; seasonal beers; guest beers Ⓗ
Just 15 minutes' walk from Hillsborough – a must for discerning visiting supporters and locals. Refurbishment has improved facilities and given an airier feel while maintaining character. New Castle Rock etched windows complement the original Gilmours panes. The garden has been paved for summer barbecues. Now family-run, children are welcome in the no-smoking room (bookable for functions). The nine real ales, continental beers and single malts are set off by home-cooked food (eve meals Mon-Fri). Live music is performed on Saturday.
♔Q❀◐◑⊖(Bamforth St)♣●⊬

Sheffield: South

Archer Road Beer Stop

57 Archer Road, S8 0JT
✪ 11 (10.30 Sat)-10; 5-10 Sun
☎ (0114) 255 1356
Taylor Landlord; guest beers Ⓗ
Small, corner shop-style real ale off-licence serving up to four beers on handpumps, generally sourced from independent and micro-brewers. It also stocks up to 200 bottled beers (many bottle-conditioned), including a considerable range of continental ales. The shop is the first winner of a new local CAMRA award for services to real ale and will soon celebrate 10 consecutive years in this Guide. Broadoak cider is sometimes available. ●

Old Mother Redcap

Prospect Road, Bradway, S17 4JA
✪ 12-3, 5.30-11; 12-11 Sat; 12-10.30 Sun
☎ (0114) 236 0179
Samuel Smith OBB Ⓗ
Large, modern, stone pub, built in the style of an old Yorkshire farmhouse. It features an L-shaped lounge, split into smaller drinking areas. One of just a handful of Samuel Smith's houses in Sheffield, it supplies the cheapest beer in the area. Although well patronised by all ages, it tends to attract more mature drinkers than most, especially midweek. On the outskirts of the city, it is worth seeking out. Evening meals are served Thursday and Friday. ❀◐◑♣

Prince of Wales

150 Derbyshire Lane, S8 8SE
✪ 11-11; 12-10.30 Sun
☎ (0114) 255 0960
Fuller's Original; Greene King Abbot; Ward's Best Bitter Ⓗ
Welcoming community local of open-plan design, but divided into small sections with a games area at the far end. Popular with all age groups, the regulars are keen on football; the pub fields its own Sunday team. There is a garden/play area and a comfortable upstairs function room. Entertainment includes two quizzes a week and fortnightly rock music on Saturday evening. ❀♿♣P

Sheaf View

25 Gleadless Road, Heeley, S2 3AA
✪ 12-11; 12-10.30 Sun
☎ (0114) 249 6455
Abbeydale Moonshine; Blackpool Bitter; Wentworth WPA; guest beers Ⓗ
Reopened in 2000, following expensive renovation, as a genuine free house, this has become one of Sheffield's premier real ale pubs. It always offers up to five changing ales, usually sourced from independent and micro-breweries, plus a large range of bottled and draught continental beers. This spacious, open-plan pub is adorned with breweriana. A no-smoking conservatory was added recently; the pub has excellent disabled access. It is close to Heeley City Farm. Q❀♿♣●P⊬

White Lion ✔

615 London Road, S2 4HT
✪ 12-11; 12-10.30 Sun
☎ (0114) 255 1500
Marston's Pedigree; Taylor Landlord; Tetley Mild, Bitter; guest beers Ⓗ
Superb, multi-roomed former Tetley heritage pub. Now owned by the Punch Group and leased to the Just Williams group, it is largely unspoilt, with parts of the interior Grade II listed. A tiled corridor opens onto several small rooms, including two snugs and a no-smoking lounge, displaying pictures of bygone Sheffield. Note the original windows and spelling of Windsor Ales. A large games and concert room at the rear caters for younger drinkers and hosts live music on Thursday.
❀♣●⊬

Sheffield: West

Cobden View

40 Cobden View Road, S10 1HQ

❂ 4 (12 Sat)-11; 12-10.30 Sun

☎ (0114) 266 1273

Abbeydale Moonshine; Black Sheep Best Bitter; Caledonian Deuchars IPA, 80/-; guest beers Ⓗ

Named after Sir Richard Cobden, a 19th-century Sheffield industrialist, this busy community pub has been revived from near closure three years ago, and now caters for a varied clientele, from students to retired folk. Although largely opened out, the original room layout is still discernible, with two bars and three distinct seating areas, one housing a pool table. It stages well-attended quizzes on Sunday and Tuesday, and live music on Thursday. Guest beers are usually from local micro-breweries. ❀♿♣

Freedom House

371 South Road, Walkley, S6 3TD

❂ 1 (11 Sat)-11; 12-10.30 Sun

☎ (0114) 234 3653

Caledonian Deuchars IPA; Kelham Island Easy Rider; Taylor Landlord; guest beer Ⓗ

Popular community pub at the heart of Walkley's commercial centre. The large tap room on the right of the entrance has pool and darts, while to the left is a cosy lounge. The garden at the rear has a children's play area where an attractive mural of cartoon characters was painted by a local artist. It hosts weekly pool matches, a quiz on Tuesday evening and a games night. ❀⊟♣

Porter Brook ✔

565 Ecclesall Road, S11 8PR

❂ 11-11; 12-10.30 Sun

☎ (0114) 266 5765

Caledonian Deuchars IPA; Greene King Abbot; Taylor Landlord; guest beers Ⓗ

Opened about 10 years ago in a converted house on the bank of the River Porter, originally as a Hogshead pub, it quickly became established as the leading real ale outlet on the Ecclesall Road. Up to 10 cask beers are sold, with guests mainly from regional brewers but sometimes local micros. Furnished in typical ale house style, with bare floorboards and exposed brickwork, it is popular, particularly with students. Quiz night is Monday, with live music some Sundays and regular beer festivals. ◐♿⚡

Robin Hood

Greaves Lane, Little Matlock, S6 6BG (from Hillsborough take Greaves Lane, via Myers Grove Lane)

❂ 12-2 (not Mon or Tue), 5-11; 12-10.30 Sun

☎ (0114) 234 4565

Beer range varies Ⓗ

Family-run pub, 200 years old, near the Peak District. With a two-roomed, split-level format, it was saved from developers in 2003 by the present owners. The pub offers two rotating guest beers. The tap room, with its original stone-flagged floor, displays old prints of the local area and the Robin Hood legend, plus work from the local college. Outside is a children's play area; occasional medieval pageants take place in summer. Muddy boots and dogs are always accepted.

Q☎❀◐⊟♣P

Walkley Cottage

46 Bole Hill Road, S6 5DD

❂ 11-11; 12-10.30 Sun

☎ (0114) 234 4968

Black Sheep Best Bitter; Greene King Abbot; Taylor Landlord; Tetley Bitter; guest beers Ⓗ

Spacious, roadhouse-style suburban local retaining two rooms. The tap room houses a snooker table and big-screen TV, while the comfortable lounge has a food servery and a no-smoking area for mealtimes (no food Sun eve). Built for Gilmours between the wars on a large site, the extensive garden affords panoramic views over the Rivelin Valley. A lively pub, with a quiz on Thursday evening, it usually offers three or four guest beers from regional and local brewers. ❀◐⊟♣P

Silkstone

Ring O' Bells

High Street, S75 4LN (½ mile W of church)

❂ 11-11; 12-10.30 Sun

☎ (01226) 790298

Hardys & Hansons Bitter, Olde Trip, seasonal beers Ⓗ

Lovely, traditional pub set in a picturesque village on the outskirts of Barnsley. The low entrance opens directly into the bar, with lounge and dining area to the right, and a cosy tap room on the left; note the comfy armchair nestling by the real fire. Under the present licensee the frontage has been vastly improved making a veritable suntrap for drinkers among the numerous flower baskets and wooden seating. Bus Nos. 21 and 22 from Barnsley stop outside (half-hourly).

♨❀⇌(Silkstone Common) ♣

South Anston

Loyal Trooper Inn

34 Sheffield Road, S25 5DT (off A57, 3 miles from M1 jct 31)

❂ 12-3, 6-11; 12-11 Sat; 12-3, 7-10.30 Sun

☎ (01909) 562203

Adnams Bitter; Taylor Landlord; Tetley Bitter; guest beers Ⓗ

Popular village local with a public bar, snug and lounge. It dates back to 1690 and gets its name from reputedly being used to house soldiers. The function room upstairs is home to many local groups, including a folk club and birdwatchers. The pub offers good value food (eve meals Mon-Thu). Children are welcome, if eating, until 8pm. This regular local CAMRA award winner stands on the Five Churches walk. Q❀◐⊟♣P

Sprotbrough

Boat Inn

Nursery Road, Lower Sprotbrough, DN5 7NB

❂ 11-11; 12-10.30 Sun

☎ (01302) 858500

Black Sheep Best Bitter; John Smith's Bitter; Tetley Bitter Ⓗ

Situated in a riverside location, this attractive pub is popular with drinkers and diners, and is convenient for walkers on the nearby Trans-Pennine Trail. Recently refurbished to a high standard, the pub is divided into various distinct drinking areas, some of which are smoke-free. The Boat has gained a good reputation for the quality of its food which is available throughout the day. Outside is a large courtyard drinking area. ⛫❀◐◑♿P⚟

Ivanhoe Hotel

Melton Road, DN5 7NS

⏲ 11-11; 12-10.30 Sun

☎ (01302) 853130

Samuel Smith OBB Ⓗ

Standing by the village crossroads, this community pub offers beer and food at reasonable prices. The spacious lounge leads to the conservatory, part of which is smoke-free, where children are welcome. The public bar houses snooker and pool tables. The garden includes a safe play area and adjoins the local cricket pitch. Evening meals are served Monday-Saturday; Sunday lunches are popular. Q☋❀◐◑⊟♿♣P⚟

Strines

Strines Inn

Bradfield Dale, Bradfield, S6 6JE (2 miles from A57) OS222906

⏲ 10.30-11 (10.30-3, 6-11 winter Mon-Fri); 12-10.30 Sun

☎ (0114) 285 1247

Banks's Riding Bitter; Marston's Pedigree; guest beers Ⓗ

Isolated stone building on the moors above Sheffield, served by a summer bus route. Some parts date from 1275 and it has been an inn since 1771, never being owned by a brewery. Two of the three drinking areas are no-smoking. Food is served all day in summer and at weekends at this pub for all: drinkers, families, diners, walkers and dogs. An unusual menagerie of animals includes 30 peacocks. It usually stocks two guest ales and has three double en-suite bedrooms. ⛫❀⛿◐◑⊟P⚟

Thorne

Punch Bowl Inn

Fieldside, DN8 4BE (on A614, near Thorne North Station and M18)

⏲ 11-11; 12-10.30 Sun

☎ (01405) 813580

Old Mill Bitter, Bullion, seasonal beers Ⓗ

Popular hotel situated five minutes' walk from Thorne North Station. Pleasant, well-appointed drinking areas (some smoke-free) include a conservatory, library room, function room and outside terrace. It has gained a good reputation for the quality of its food, available all day. There are excellent facilities for the disabled. Three Old Mill beers are always available. At the weekend, special lower rates are offered for accommodation.
❀⛿◐◑♿⇌(Thorne North) P⚟

Victoria Inn

South End, DN8 5QN (next to Thorne South Station)

⏲ 1-11; 12-10.30 Sun

☎ (01405) 813163

Beer range varies Ⓗ

Two minutes' walk from Thorne South Station, this multi-roomed pub offers guest beers from mainly local independent breweries. John Smith's Magnet is often also available. Meals, excellent value and quality, are served Thursday-Saturday evening, with a three course meal offered at £4.95 for early diners. Excellent outside drinking facilities, reasonably-priced accommodation and entertainment on Saturday in the public bar are added attractions.
⛫❀⛿◑⊟⇌(Thorne South) ♣P⚟

Thorpe Salvin

Parish Oven

Worksop Road, S80 3JU

⏲ 12-2, 5.30-11; 12-11 Sat; 12-10.30 Sun

☎ (01909) 770685

Black Sheep Best Bitter; guest beers Ⓗ

Rotherham CAMRA Pub of the Season, winter 2004, the pub has also won awards from Avebury Taverns. A popular venue for Sunday lunch and evening meals, it offers a good choice of home-cooked food. There is a large play area for children. The pub's wide range of changing guest beers makes it well worth a visit. It stands at the village centre, close to Chesterfield Canal and Rotherham Ring Walk. Q❀◐◑♣P

Thurlstone

Huntsman

136 Manchester Road, S36 9QW (on A628)

⏲ 6-11; 12-10.30 Sun

☎ (01226) 764892

Clark's Classic Blonde; guest beers Ⓗ

Pub at the heart of its community, hosting quizzes and acoustic nights. Set at the side of the main Barnsley to Manchester road (A628), it offers a friendly welcome to all visitors. Designed in cottage style, with exposed beams, it is comfortably furnished. With up to six real ales available, this multiple award-winning pub is well worth a call. ⛫Q❀⚟

Tickhill

Carpenter's Arms

Westgate, DN11 9NE

⏲ 12-3, 6-11; 12-11 Sat; 12-10.30 Sun

☎ (01302) 742839

Black Sheep Best Bitter; Jennings Cumberland Ale; John Smith's Bitter Ⓗ

Appealing pub, with a cosy front lounge and adjoining bar. A large no-smoking conservatory doubles as a family room and looks out over an award-winning garden. This is a pleasant setting for a summer afternoon or evening pint; there should also be a crazy golf course installed by the time this Guide is published. Other attractions include a regular music quiz and food freshly cooked on the premises. Regular buses serve Doncaster, Sheffield and Worksop.
☋❀⊟P⚟

Scarbrough Arms

Sunderland Street, DN11 9QJ (near Buttercross landmark)

⏲ 11-3, 6-11; 12-3, 7-10.30 Sun

☎ (01302) 742977

Courage Directors; Greene King Abbot; John Smith's Bitter; Theakston Old Peculier; guest beers Ⓗ

A deserving Guide entry since 1990, this three-roomed stone pub has won several awards from CAMRA, including Doncaster Pub of the Year

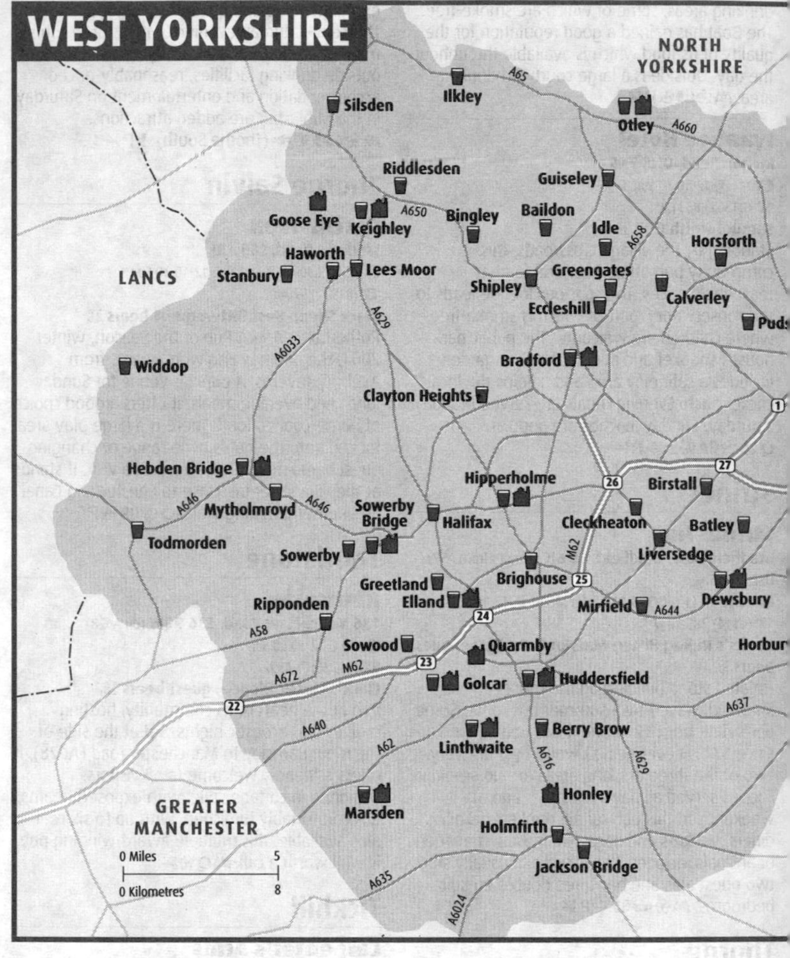

1997 and 2003. Originally a farmhouse, the building dates back to the 16th century, although structural changes have inevitably taken place over the years. The pub's no-smoking snug is a delight, with its barrel-shaped tables and real fire. This is one of the few pubs in the Doncaster district using oversized lined glasses. Food is served Tuesday-Saturday.
⌂❀◐⊟♣P⊬⊡

Wath upon Dearne

Church House ✔

Montgomery Square, S63 7RZ
✪ 10-11; 10-10.30 Sun
☎ (01709) 879518
Greene King Abbot; Marston's Burton Bitter, Pedigree; guest beers Ⓗ
This impressive Wetherspoon pub is set in a pedestrian square in the town centre. Serving a wide range of good value ales from around the country, the Church House also offers a variety of meals, including curry nights. Children are welcome until 6pm (last food orders for children is 5pm). This quiet pub is fully air conditioned over two floors. It is handy for the RSPB Wetlands Centre at Wombwell.
Q❀◐◗♿⊬

Wentworth

George & Dragon

85 Main Street, S62 7TN
✪ 10-11; 10-10.30 Sun
☎ (01226) 742440
Taylor Landlord; Wentworth WPA; guest beers Ⓗ
Part of the picturesque Wentworth estate, set back from the road to allow for generous gardens, this partly 16th-century pub serves a range of ales from Yorkshire breweries, featuring two changing ales from the nearby Wentworth Brewery, plus cask cider. Delicious home-cooked food includes children's meals and a curry night (Mon) as well as breakfast and traditional Sunday lunch. Pub snacks are available. ⌂Q❀◐◗⊟▲♣●P⊬

Rockingham Arms

8 Main Street, S62 7TL
✪ 11-11; 12-10.30 Sun
☎ (01226) 742075
Theakston Best Bitter, Old Peculier; Wentworth Needles Eye, WPA; guest beers Ⓗ
Country pub in the grounds of the Wentworth Estate, near Wentworth Brewery. Ideal for walkers, this pub offers accommodation, local entertainment, a range of home-cooked meals,

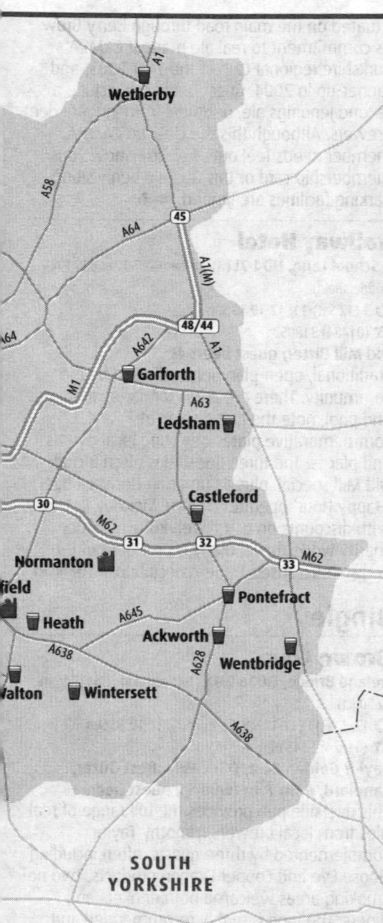

and 'dogs' dinners' for canine companions at only £1. A crown green bowling green is attached. This pub is welcoming with real fires in winter and a patio and garden for the summer. A wide range of local ales is kept at Rotherham CAMRA's Pub of the Year 2005.
⚐Q☐❀⇆(I)⊟♿P⊬

Whiston

Chequers Inn

Pleasley Road, S60 4HB (on A618 near Whiston crossroads)
⏲ 12-11; 12-10.30 Sun
☎ (01709) 829168
Taylor Landlord; Tetley Bitter; guest beers Ⓗ
Friendly local that has been rejuvenated by the current tenant. One side has a tap room with a dartboard and dominoes. It hosts regular entertainment. Children are welcome for meals (except Sun) until 7pm. The large garden includes a barbecue area. It stands in a picturesque village next to a 13th-century thatched barn and is handy for Ulley Country Park. ⚐❀(I)♣P⊬

Golden Ball

7 Turner Lane, S60 4HY (off A618, 1½ miles from M1 jct 33)
⏲ 12-11; 12-10.30 Sun
☎ (01709) 726911
Stones Bitter; Taylor Landlord; Tetley Bitter; guest beers Ⓗ
The second year in this Guide after refurbishment, this small cottage-style pub with a quiet snug dates back in part over 500 years. It boasts large gardens to the rear and sides. An extensive menu is served until 8pm. Children are not admitted. Real fires create a warm atmosphere in winter. You may find seasonal beers on tap here. ⚐❀(I)♿P⊬

Sitwell Arms

Pleasley Road, S60 4HQ (on A618, 1½ miles from M1 jct 33)
⏲ 12-11; 11.45-10.30 Sun
☎ (01709) 377003
Acorn Barnsley Gold; Greene King Abbot; Tetley Bitter; guest beer Ⓗ
Village pub of low ceilings and oak beams. It has a dartboard and hosts live entertainment. The garden houses a children's play area. Restaurant and bar meals are served; children are welcome. The new landlord is keen to promote CAMRA's aims. Situated at the heart of a picturesque village, the pub offers a lively but friendly atmosphere. ❀(I)♿P

Wombwell

Horseshoe

30 High Street, S73 0AA (next to main post office)
⏲ 10-11; 12-10.30 Sun
☎ (01226) 273820
Beer range varies Ⓗ
Barnsley area's only Wetherspoon outlet, providing up to five rotating guest beers and at least twice-yearly beer festivals. A large, raised no-smoking and family area is at the rear corner, while small alcoves dotted around afford more intimate seating in this busy pub. Easily reached by public transport, buses from Barnsley, Doncaster and Rotherham pass every 15-20 minutes; it is one mile uphill to Wombwell Station though! Q☐(I)♿⊬

Worsbrough

Edmunds Arms

25 Worsbrough Village Road, S70 5LW (opp. church)
⏲ 11.45-3, 6-11; 12-4, 7-10.30 Sun
☎ (01226) 206865
Samuel Smith OBB Ⓗ
Stone pub set in the centre of a picturesque village. It comprises a tap room and snug, plus a comfortable lounge that leads to the restaurant, which offers lunches and evening meals, Tuesday-Saturday. The outside area is wonderful during the summer months. A quiz is held on Tuesday evening. Buses to the pub include Nos. 227 and 265. ⚐Q❀(I)⊟♿♣P

YORKSHIRE (WEST)

Ackworth

Boot & Shoe

Wakefield Road, WF7 7DF (on A638, ¼ mile N of Moor Top roundabout)

⊛ 12-11; 12-10.30 Sun
☎ (01977) 610218
Marston's Pedigree; Samuel Smith OBB; John Smith's Bitter Ⓗ
Busy non-food pub, thought to date back to the late 16th century, with some original features exposed. It offers a choice of cask ales and is a rare outlet for Samuel Smith in the free trade. It has a reputation for live music but no juke box. Behind the pub is the village cricket field. This makes a good start/finish for country walks. ⚑❀⊟♿♣P

Rustic Arms
7 Long Lane, WF7 7EZ (off A639)
⊛ 12-3, 5-11; 12-10.30 Sun
☎ (01977) 794136
John Smith's Bitter; guest beers Ⓗ
Spacious, open-plan pub in idyllic surroundings next to a trout-fishing lake. The pub is divided into distinct spaces, including a games area with pool table. There is a dining room or meals can be taken in the bar areas (no food Mon). Well-behaved children are allowed in the pub, which has a well-equipped garden, with a climbing frame and go-karts. A function room is the latest addition to facilities here. ⚇❀◑♿♣P⊬

Baildon

Junction
1 Baildon Road, BD17 6AB
⊛ 12-11; 12-10.30 Sun
☎ (01274) 582009
Bob's White Lion; Oakham JHB; Taylor Landlord; Tetley's Bitter; guest beers Ⓗ
Traditional pub with a friendly atmosphere in its three rooms. Good quality beers are sold at low prices. The beers are changed regularly as Bill and Chris listen to their customers' requests. Features include a TV tuned to sport, pool room, free juke box (all the time), curry night every Tuesday and folk/Irish band most Sundays. The cider is from Saxon. ⚇❀≠(Shipley)●P⊬

Batley

Cellar Bar
51 Station Road, WF17 5SU (opp. station)
⊛ 12-11; 12-10.30 Sun
☎ (01924) 473705
Hambleton Bitter, Goldfield; Tetley Bitter; guest beer Ⓗ
Easily found, opposite Batley Station, this homely, one-room bar occupies the basement of a former Victorian mill trading office. A Hambleton's house for the past two years, it features bare brick, plaster and wood panelling, creating an atmosphere of bygone days, with well worn, comfy chesterfield sofas for lounging in while enjoying a pint, and long saddles for the traditional drinker. TV sports are shown at the weekend; Tuesday is quiz night. ≠♣

Berry Brow

Berry Brow Liberal Club ✔
6 Parkgate, HD4 7NF (on A616)
⊛ 8 (12 Sat)-11; 12-3.30, 8-10.30 Sun
☎ (01484) 662549
Jennings Cumberland Ale; guest beer Ⓗ
Compact, CIU-affiliated club, conveniently situated on the main road through Berry Brow. Its commitment to real ale made it CAMRA's Yorkshire regional Club of the Year 2003, and runner-up in 2004. Guest beers can include a second Jennings ale, or others from independent brewers. Although this is a club, no CAMRA member needs feel out of place – show your membership card or this Guide when visiting. Parking facilities are limited. ≠♣

Railway Hotel
2 School Lane, HD4 7LT (take bus No. 306 or 319 from Huddersfield)
⊛ 3 (12 Sat)-11; 12-10.30 Sun
☎ (01484) 318052
Old Mill Bitter; guest beers Ⓗ
Traditional, open-plan pub well-used by the community. There are areas for darts, dominoes and pool; note the fine display of commemorative plates depicting local events and places. The three guest ales often include an Old Mill special, plus a Cumbrian Derwent beer. 'Happy Hour' operates 4-7pm, Monday to Friday, with discounts on pints. Well-known for her charity work, the landlady is president of the Yorkshire Licensed Trade Association. ⚑❀≠♣

Bingley

Brown Cow
Ireland Bridge, BD16 2QX (100 yds along B6429 from A650 jct)
⊛ 12-3, 5-11 (12-11 Sat & summer); 12-10.30 Sun
☎ (01274) 564345
Taylor Golden Best, Dark Mild, Best Bitter, Landlord, Ram Tam (winter)**; guest beers** Ⓗ
This riverside pub provides the full range of real ales from local brewers, Timothy Taylor, complemented by three guests, often including Goose Eye and Copper Dragon products. Two no-smoking areas welcome both drinkers and diners. The food is highly recommended and booking is advisable. A few minutes' walk from the town centre, the Leeds & Liverpool Canal's three and five rise locks are nearby. ⚑❀◑♿≠(Bingley/Crossflatts)P⊬

Ferrands Arms
Queen Street, BD16 2JS
⊛ 11-11 (midnight Thu; 12.30am Fri & Sat); 12-10.30 Sun
☎ (01274) 563949
Taylor Golden Best, Best Bitter, Landlord Ⓗ
Town-centre pub that can get busy during extended hours at the end of the week. Part of the Timothy Taylor estate, this pub has been refurbished several times, but now provides a comfortable open-plan arrangement. Live TV sport is shown and live bands play once a month, on Thursday evening. Food is served 12-7pm (4pm Fri and Sat). Daily newspapers are provided and coffee is served. ◑≠

Myrtle Grove ✔
Main Street, BD16 1AJ
⊛ 10-11; 12-10.30 Sun
☎ (01274) 568637
Greene King Abbot; Marston's Burton Bitter, Pedigree; guest beers Ⓗ
Smaller than usual Wetherspoon outlet, this popular, one-roomed pub stands on the main road through the town. There are often 10 different real ales on tap, many from micro-

breweries, including regular beers from E&S Elland. The interior features a raised no-smoking family area and several seating booths. The folding glass doors along the front are sometimes opened in summer. Bradford CAMRA Pub of the Season, winter 2005 opens early every day for food. Q◖◗♿⇌⊬

Birstall

Black Bull

5 Kirkgate, WF17 9PB (off A652, near A643)
🕒 12-11; 12-3.30, 7-10.30 Sun
☎ (01274) 873039
Boddingtons Bitter; Worthington's Bitter; guest beer Ⓗ
Partly dating from the 17th century, with St Peter's Church opposite, this was the natural place for functions, which until 1839 included the magistrate's court. The courtroom upstairs retains the magistrate's box and prisoner's dock and is still used for social events. Downstairs, the snug is popular for small meetings, while the remainder is divided into cosy areas. Good food is served (eve meals Wed-Sat). The guest beer changes almost daily, any strength and style, usually from renowned small breweries.
❀◖◗♣P

Bradford

Castle Hotel

20 Grattan Road, BD1 2LU (off Westgate)
🕒 11.30-11; 2-10.30 Sun
☎ (01274) 393166
website: www.thecastlehotel.britain-uk.com
Blackpool Bitter; Fuller's ESB; Greene King Ruddles Best; guest beers Ⓗ
This imposing stone pub, complete with castellated battlements, was built in 1898. Formerly a Webster's house, it now sells a variety of beers in a relaxing atmosphere. This CAMRA award-winner has an open-plan interior. It is a rare outlet for ESB. The Castle is close to a busy shopping area and Bradford Colour Museum. ⇄⇌(Interchange/Forster Sq)

Corn Dolly

110 Bolton Road, BD1 4DE
🕒 11.30-11; 12-10.30 Sun
☎ (01274) 720219
Black Sheep Best Bitter; Everards Tiger; Taylor Landlord; guest beers Ⓗ
Popular, real ale oasis, a few minutes' walk from the city centre. Family run for many years, the four regular real ales are complemented by guests from the length and breadth of the country, and a house beer brewed by Moorhouses. The pub is split into two areas: a comfortable lounge one side, and a games area at the other. It is Bradford's most successful CAMRA award-winner – four times Pub of the Year to date. The food here is good value.
⌂❀◖⇌(Interchange/Forster Sq) ♣P

Fighting Cock

21-23 Preston Street, BD7 1JE (1 mile from city centre, off Thornton Road)
🕒 11.30-11; 12-10.30 Sun
☎ (01274) 726907
Copper Dragon Golden Pippin; Old Mill Bitter; Phoenix White Monk; Taylor Landlord; Theakston Old Peculier; guest beers Ⓗ
Surrounded by industry, this down-to-earth ale house is a haven for drinkers, only 15 minutes' walk from the city centre. Bare floorboards add character to the three drinking areas, where 12 real ales, ciders and fruit wines are appreciated by a loyal clientele. Busy at lunchtime with diners, televised football and rugby league also attract an enthusiastic following at Bradford CAMRA Pub of the Year 2004. ⌂◖♣

Haigy's

31 Lumb Lane, Manningham, BD8 7QU
🕒 5-10.30 (1am Fri & Sat); 12-10.30 Sun
☎ (01274) 731644
Greene King Abbot; Tetley Bitter; guest beers Ⓗ
Friendly local offering regular guest beers from Ossett, Phoenix and Newby Wyke breweries. A cosy lounge, pool and music areas offer customers a choice. A late licence operates on Friday and Saturday. Try the unusual hexagonal revolving pool table. A Bradford CAMRA Pub of the Season on more than one occasion, it was Pub of the Year for 2005.
❀⇌(Forster Sq/Interchange) ♣P

Melborn Hotel

104 White Abbey Road, BD8 8DP (on B6144, ½ mile from city centre)
🕒 4 (2 Mon)-midnight; 12-1am Sat; 2-10.30 Sun
☎ (01274) 726867 website: www.melborn.co.uk
Tetley Bitter; guest beers Ⓗ
An imposing, Art Deco exterior fronts this splendid, multi-roomed free house. The friendly, long-standing landlord has skilfully built a fine reputation around live music and cask ale. Look carefully in the glass cabinets for many reminders of its Melbourn Brewery past. The

INDEPENDENT BREWERIES

Anglo Dutch Dewsbury
Bob's Horbury
Briscoe's Otley
Clarke's Organic Dewsbury
Clark's Wakefield
E&S Elland Elland
Egyptian Dewsbury
Empire Quarmby
Fernandes Wakefield
Golcar Golcar
Goose Eye Keighley
Greenwood Bradford
Halifax Hipperholme
Linfit Linthwaite
Little Valley Hebden Bridge
Naylor's Keighley
Old Bear Keighley
Ossett Ossett
Riverhead Marsden
Rodham's Otley
Ryburn Sowerby Bridge
Salamander Bradford
Taylor Keighley
Tigertops Wakefield
Turkey Goose Eye
Upper Agbrigg Honley
WF6 Normanton
Whitley Bridge Wakefield

oldest folk club in the world, the Topic, meets here on Thursday evening. Guest beers frequently come from Coach House, Goose Eye and Slaters (Ecclesall) breweries.
🛏⊟⇌(Forster Sq) ♣P

New Beehive Inn ☆
171 Westgate , BD1 3AA
⏲ 11-11 (2am Fri & Sat); 6-10.30 Sun
☎ (01274) 721784
Kelham Island Best Bitter; Taylor Landlord; guest beers Ⓗ
Take a step back in time at this gaslit pub that fully merits its CAMRA National Inventory listing for its historic interior. The accommodation includes two main bars, a drinking area in the entrance hall, a games room and a no-smoking room. The cellar bar, where live music is played, is open at weekends. The range of guest beers often includes one from local brewer, Salamander.
♨Q❀🛏⇌(Forster Sq) ♣♣P⊭

Prospect of Bradford
527 Bolton Road, BD3 0NW
⏲ 2.30-5.30, 7-11; 2.30-11 Fri & Sat; 12-10.30 Sun
☎ (01274) 727018
Taylor Golden Best; Tetley Bitter Ⓗ
You can be assured of a friendly welcome from Richard and Albina, who have been running this Victorian pub for almost 20 years. There is a games room on the ground floor and a spacious bar area, where live music is a weekend speciality. The large, first-floor function room has its own real ale bar and quality catering can be provided. ♨⇌(Forster Sq) ♣P

Sir Titus Salt ✔
Unit B, Windsor Baths, Morley Street, BD7 1AQ (behind Alhambra Theatre)
⏲ 10-11; 12-10.30 Sun
☎ (01274) 732853
Greene King Abbot; Marston's Burton Bitter, Pedigree; guest beers Ⓗ
Splendid Wetherspoon's conversion of the original Windsor swimming baths, now named after the local industrialist and philanthropist. An upstairs seating area overlooks the main pub. Framed pictures portray the educational heritage, literature and art of the city. It draws a cosmopolitan clientele, including students from the nearby university and college and is ideally situated for theatregoers, clubbers, Indian restaurants and the National Museum of Photography, Film and Television.
Q☕◐◑♿⇌(Interchange/Forster Sq) ⊭

Steve Biko Bar
D floor, Richmond Building, University of Bradford, Richmond Road, BD7 1DP (off Gt Horton Rd)
⏲ 10 (6.30 Sat)-11; closed Sun
☎ (01274) 233257
Everards Tiger; Fuller's London Pride; Greene King Old Speckled Hen; Stones Bitter; guest beers Ⓗ
Situated in the university, this spacious bar is open to the general public. During student vacations the opening hours are restricted to 10-5pm Mon-Fri and closed at weekends. Up to four guest beers from local micros such as Salamander and Goose Eye are often available. A cask ale promotion runs on Monday evening. Understandably popular with students, its juke box and pool tables often create a lot of noise.
⇌ (Interchange)

Brighouse

Red Rooster
123 Elland Road, Brookfoot, HD6 2QR (on A6025)
⏲ 3 (12 Fri & Sat)-11; 12-10.30 Sun
☎ (01484) 713737
Caledonian Deuchars IPA; Rooster's Yankee; Taylor Landlord; guest beers Ⓗ
Small, stone pub on the inside of a sharp bend. Stone-flagged throughout, the former four-roomed layout is still apparent. The six guest beers always include one each from Ossett and Moorhouses, plus a dark beer. There is a small patio garden. Live music (blues) is featured on the afternoon of the last Sunday of each month. It was voted local CAMRA Pub of the Year in 2005. Parking is limited. ❀♣P

Roundhill Inn ✔
75 Clough Lane, Rastrick, HD6 3QL (on A6107, 400 yds from A643 jct)
⏲ 5 (7 Sat)-11; 12-3, 7-10.30 Sun
☎ (01484) 713418
Black Sheep Best Bitter; Taylor Golden Best, Landlord; guest beer Ⓗ
The 380/381 Brighouse-Huddersfield bus passes this genuine free house on the very edge of Rastrick, close to the M62 and the Calderdale/Kirklees boundary. This local overlooks Rastrick cricket ground, and the unusual hill from which it takes its name. There are spectacular views over Brighouse, about 1½ miles distant and beyond. The smaller, quiet lounge is no-smoking. The guest beer is normally from an independent brewery. Parking can be difficult. ♨Q❀P⊭

Calverley

Thornhill Arms
18 Towngate, LS28 5NF (on A657, near parish church)
⏲ 11.30-11; 12-10.30 Sun
☎ (0113) 256 5492
John Smith's Bitter; Theakston Best Bitter; guest beers Ⓗ
This Grade II listed, former coaching inn was called the Leopard until the 1830s when it changed ownership after a card game. It retains many old features including the stables, original beams and the stone fireplaces that lend a homely feel to this spacious, open-plan pub. It is thought that a secret passage links the pub to the church. Hearty meals are available at lunchtime (not Sun) and the no-smoking bistro is open weekday evenings, 5-8pm (booking advisable). ❀◑♿♣P

Castleford

Glass Blower ✔
15 Bank Street, WF10 1JD (400 yds N of station)
⏲ 10-11; 12-10.30 Sun
☎ (01977) 520390
Greene King Abbot; Marston's Burton Bitter, Pedigree; Theakston Old Peculier; guest beers Ⓗ
Former post office, converted into a popular Wetherspoon's establishment, stocking five regular beers alongside six guest ales. Children

are welcome until 7pm (5pm Fri-Sun). The pub opens at 10am on Sunday for food only. The toilets are on the first floor.
Q ❀ ◐ ◑ ⇌ (Castleford) ⚟

Griffin
Lock Lane, WF10 2LB
✪ 2 (12 Fri & Sat)-11; 12-10.30 Sun
☎ (01977) 557551
John Smith's Bitter; guest beer Ⓗ
Small, two-roomed, traditional local on the northern outskirts of the town, 100 yards from the renowned Lock Lane ARLFC and new sports centre. The landlord regularly rotates a guest beer from the Enterprise list. The pub hosts quiz nights (Wed and Sun) and bingo on Wednesday. A friendly greeting is provided by the pub dog.
Q ❀ ◐ ⊟ ♣ P

Shoulder of Mutton
18 Methley Road, WF10 1LX (off A6032)
✪ 11-4, 7-11; 12-4, 7-10.30 Sun
☎ (01977) 736039
Old Mill Old Curiosity; Tetley Dark Mild, Bitter Ⓗ
A great welcome awaits you here from the landlord and his loyal regulars who fought successfully to save the pub from closure. Now a genuine free house, dating from 1632, the building began life as a farmhouse and is probably the oldest licensed house in Castleford. The George Formby Society meets here regularly. It has no juke box, but acoustic music sessions are a frequent occurrence on Sunday, when the pub stays open all day.
⛫ ❀ ⊟ ♿ ⇌ ♣ P

Clayton Heights

Old Dolphin Inn
192 Highgate Road, BD13 1DR (on A647, Bradford side of Queensbury)
✪ 11-3, 5.30-11; 11-11 Fri & Sat; 11-10.30 Sun
☎ (01274) 882202
Beer range varies Ⓗ
This ancient coaching inn offers two guest beers from micro-breweries especially E&S Elland, Durham and Goose Eye. A good selection of home-cooked meals includes vegetarian options, large grills and enormous steaks; a barbecue facility is in the garden play area. Built as a hospital during the War of the Roses, it housed Cromwell's men in 1650. Note the Black Dyke Mills Band memorabilia. Mill owner, John Foster, performed here and cats eye inventor, Percy Shaw, was a regular visitor. ⛫ Q ❀ ◐ ◑ P

Cleckheaton

Commercial ✔
33 Bradford Road, BD19 3JN (on A638, almost opp. town hall)
✪ 12-11; 12-10.30 Sun
☎ (01274) 878745 website: www.thecommercialinn.com
Tetley Bitter; guest beers Ⓗ
Busy, but welcoming, town-centre pub, mainly knocked through but retaining several distinct drinking areas, including a no-smoking snug. The lounge has plenty of breweriana on display along with items commemorating the Panther motorcycle factory that once stood behind the pub. The home-cooked lunches are popular; on Sunday the upstairs function room is used to provide extra seating. A wide range of regional guest beers is served. ⛄ ◐ ♣ ⚟

Marsh
28 Bradford Road, BD19 5BJ (200 yds S of bus station on A638)
✪ 1 (12 Sat)-11; 12-10.30 Sun
☎ (01274) 872104
Old Mill Mild, Bitter, Bullion, seasonal beers Ⓗ
Friendly, wedge shaped pub catering for all ages, the Marsh is the only Old Mill tied house in the area. The drinking areas are open plan, but a homely feel prevails. Pub games are regularly played. Outside drinking is at benches adjacent to the car park; a side door from here allows wheelchair access to most of the pub. At quiet times the Bullion and seasonal beer are alternated, so only one may be available.
❀ ♣ P

Dewsbury

Huntsman ✔
Chidswell Lane, Shaw Cross, WF12 7SW (400 yds from A635/B6128 jct)
✪ 12-3 (not Mon), 5 (7 Sat)-11; 12-3, 7-10.30 Sun
☎ (01924) 275700
Taylor Landlord; guest beers Ⓗ
This gem of a traditional pub nestles in Chidswell, overlooking open countryside. Despite the rural outlook, it is easily reached by bus and a short walk. The interior reflects its rustic setting, with horse brasses and a Yorkshire range. The location makes it a popular stop for walkers and cyclists. Lunches are served Tuesday-Saturday; evening meals Tuesday-Friday. The house beer, Chidswell Bitter, is brewed by Highwood. ⛫ ❀ ◐ ◑ P

Leggers Inn
Robinsons Boatyard, Mill Street East, Saviletown, WF12 9BD (off B6409, S of town centre)
✪ 11-11; 12-10.30 Sun
☎ (01924) 502846
Everards Tiger; guest beers Ⓗ
First-floor bar, converted from a hayloft, in a busy canal basin overlooking residential narrowboats, it makes an ideal watering-hole for walkers along the towpath. Real cider and a good range of bottled beers are now available. This interesting pub has low, exposed beams and displays of pub memorabilia knick-knacks. Pie and peas and sandwiches are served all day. The pebbled courtyard, with picnic tables, is great for a summer pint.
⛫ ❀ ♣ ● P

Park at Earlsheaton
26 Park Road, Earlsheaton, WF12 8BE (400 yds off A638)
✪ 11-11; 12-10.30 Sun
☎ (01924) 465477
Tetley Bitter; guest beers Ⓗ
Situated next to the local park from which it takes its name, this pub is easily found, just off the A638 Wakefield road out of Dewsbury. One or two guest beers come from both national and regional breweries and change weekly. There is a quiz on Friday evening and Wednesday is curry night. It is advisable to book for Sunday lunch as space is limited.
❀ ♣ P

West Riding Licensed Refreshment Rooms ✔

Railway Station, Wellington Road, WF13 1HF (on platform 2 of Dewsbury Station)

✪ 11-11; 12-10.30 Sun

☎ (01924) 459193 website: www.wrlrr.co.uk

Black Sheep Best Bitter, Riggwelter; Taylor Landlord; guest beers 🄷

Take four steps from the train at platform two and pass through the Arabic arched doorway to find eight real ales on draught at this gem of a pub in the Grade II listed station building. There is always an Anglo-Dutch beer and usually a local mild on offer. Exceptionally good lunches are served Monday-Friday, pie & peas Tuesday evening and curry night on Wednesday. It hosts occasional live music and an annual beer festival in summer. ♨❀◑◐♿⇌P⍻

Eccleshill

Royal Oak

39 Stony Lane, BD2 2HN (¼ mile from A6176)

✪ 11-11; 12-10.30 Sun

☎ (01274) 639182

Taylor Landlord; Tetley Mild, Bitter; guest beer 🄷

Popular local in the main street of one of Bradford's urban villages. The comfortable, low-ceilinged lounge retains divided areas, while the rear tap room has darts and dominoes. The guest beer is from the Punch Taverns' list. Cellarmanship awards on the walls reflect the landlord's skill and enthusiasm for cask ales. Regulars enjoy quizzes and social events throughout the year. Outdoor summer drinking is enhanced by patio heating. ❀⊟♣P

Elland

Barge & Barrel ✔

10-20 Park Road, HX5 9AP (on A6025)

✪ 12-11; 12-10.30 Sun

☎ (01422) 373623

E&S Elland Bargee; John Eastwood Best Bitter; Phoenix Wobbly Bob; Rooster's Yankee; guest beers 🄷

Large canal/roadside pub with a central horseshoe-shaped bar. Many interior walls have been removed, and some replaced by glazed screens. The decor features Victoriana and breweriana. Up to five guest beers come from micro-breweries. Live music is performed occasionally on Sunday evening. Beer festivals are held over the spring bank holiday and a weekend in late autumn. No food is served Monday. ♨❀◑♣●P

Golden Fleece ✔

Lindley Road, Blackley, HX5 0TE (½ mile from M62 jct 24, off Blackley New Road)

✪ 12-2.30 (not Tue), 5-11; 12-11 Sat; 12-10.30 Sun

☎ (01422) 372704

Greene King IPA, Abbot; Jennings Cumberland Ale; guest beer 🄷

Rural pub with panoramic views over stunning countryside, backing onto Blackley Cricket Club. On the Calderdale/Kirklees boundary, this 16th-century building, the oldest in Blackley, has been a pub since 1861. With a two-roomed interior and a corridor drinking area, the smaller, quiet, no-smoking room can be used for functions. Food is mainly home cooked – the speciality is steak and ale pie. Quiz night is Monday. The 343/344 Halifax-Elland bus passes by. Q❀◑◐P⍻

Garforth

Gaping Goose

41 Selby Road, LS25 1LR

✪ 11-11; 12-10.30 Sun

☎ (0113) 286 2127

Tetley Mild, Bitter 🄷

Bustling, lively pub where the 1930s interior comprises three rooms: a main bar, a lounge – the Tudor Room – and a basic tap. Note the floor mosaic in the entrance and the doors featuring octagonal windows with the room names. A big screen shows live sport most evenings in the Tudor Room and a quiz is held on Tuesday. This is a fine example of a pub with an intact interior. ❀⊟♣P

Golcar

Rose & Crown

132 Knowle Road, HD7 4AN (off A62, into Milnsbridge, up Scar Lane and into Knowle Rd)

✪ 11.30-2.30, 5-11; 11.30-11 Fri & Sat; 11.30-10.30 Sun

☎ (01484) 460160

Golcar Mild, Bitter, Weavers Delight; guest beers 🄷

Picturesque, spacious, roadside pub: the Golcar Brewery tap. Its two main rooms are served by an L-shaped bar, and there is a function room. The lounge is warmed by a real fire in winter; a working model of a steam engine and a chaise longue are added attractions. A pool table and Sky sports TV are to be found in the tap room. This pub fields its own football team. Sunday lunch is served. The guest beers are Golcar brews. ♨❀♿♣P

Greengates

Albion Inn

25 New Line, BD10 9AS (on A657)

✪ 12-11; 12-10.30 Sun

☎ (01274) 613211

Oakwell Barnsley Bitter; Tetley Mild, Bitter; Wells Bombardier 🄷

This traditional inn on the main road from Leeds to Keighley lies near two business centres; bus No. 760 passes the front door. A warm, friendly atmosphere is created by staff and customers alike at this compact local. An L-shaped lounge leads to an old-fashioned games room, which can be cramped on darts evenings. It hosts a prize quiz with jackpot money questions on Sunday evenings. ⊟♣P

Greetland

Greetland Community & Sporting Association

Rochdale Road, HX4 8JG (on B6113)

✪ 5 (4 Fri; 12 Sat)-11; 12-10.30 Sun

☎ (01422) 370140

Beer range varies 🄷

Everyone is welcome in this modern, but cosy, sports and social club bar. Set back from the road at the top of Greetland village, an outside drinking area gives views over the extensive playing fields and distant hills. The bar lounge displays pictures and pump clips. A wide range of guest beers is sold at Yorkshire CAMRA's Club of the Year 2004. Duckworth's Delight (4.3% ABV) is a house beer from Coach House, always available at a low price. ❀♣P

Spring Rock ✔

Rochdale Road, Upper Greetland, HX4 8PT (on B6113 at Norland Rd jct)

✪ 12-11; 12-10.30 Sun

☎ (01422) 377722

Holt Bitter; Tetley Bitter; guest beers Ⓗ

Country pub, close to Norland Moor and open access land. The bar and lounge area have hard and soft seating, next door is a small, no-smoking room. The bar has a solid fuel stove. Three guest beers usually come from micros. A good choice of wines is sold by the bottle or glass, and a good range of bottled imported beers is stocked. A local football team and a fishing club meet here. An extensive menu is served (no meals Sun eve) and lunchtime snacks are available. ♨❀◐◑P⚟

Guiseley

Guiseley Factory Workers Club

6 Town Street, LS20 9DT

✪ 1-4, 7-11; 1-11 Fri; 11.30-11 Sat; 12-10.30 Sun

☎ (01943) 874793

Tetley Bitter; guest beers Ⓗ

Popular club with low prices and a changing guest beer on sale in the main lounge. The concert room has an interconnecting bar. Two snooker tables are available (play free on Tuesday). Entertainment is varied throughout the week with a quiz (Sun), bingo (Fri) and live acts (Sat). The TV is usually showing a sporting event. Show this Guide or CAMRA membership card to be signed in. ⇌♣P

Ings

45A Ings Lane, LS20 9HR (off A65 at Guiseley Town FC)

✪ 11-11; 12-10.30 Sun

☎ (01943) 873315

Black Sheep Best Bitter; Taylor Landlord; Tetley Bitter Ⓗ

Scenic views from the rear window of this pub, which overlooks the wet marshland area from which it derives its name. The three tiled fireplaces and suspended tabletop canopy lighting highlight a memorable collection of artefacts and pictures. Bus No. 97A drops passengers right outside the door. A music quiz (Tue) and general knowledge quiz plus 'open the box' (Thu) provide entertainment. ♨❀⇌P

Halifax

Big Six

10 Horsfall Street, Savile Park, HX1 3HG (off Skircoat Moor road, A646, at King Cross)

✪ 5 (1 Fri; 12 Sat)-11; 12-10.30 Sun

☎ (01422) 350169

Greene King IPA; guest beers Ⓗ

Busy local welcoming all, dogs included. Named after a mineral company once using the premises, it is set in a row of terraced houses. Many original features remain. The bar fills much of the main room, while two cosy lounges lie across the corridor, which displays whisky bottles. A tap room is beyond the bar. Four guest beers include products from smaller breweries. Close to the recreation ground, the pub has a good garden. ♨Q❀♣

Pump Room

35 New Road, HX1 2LH (250 yds from station)

✪ 12-11; 12-10.30 Sun

☎ (01422) 381465

Black Sheep Best Bitter; Caledonian Deuchars IPA; Taylor Golden Best, Landlord; guest beers Ⓗ

Traditional, two-bar ale house, close to the football/rugby ground, decorated with a collection of taps and other breweriana. It offers possibly the widest range of real ales in the area, with up to 13 available. The landlord hosts regular beer festivals and occasional live bands. A popular carvery is served at weekends (Fri, Sat and Sun) in the right-hand bar. Quiz night is Thursday. ❀◐◑⇌

Shears Inn

Paris Gates, Boys Lane, HX3 9EZ (behind flats opp. football ground)

✪ 11.30-11; 12-10.30 Sun

☎ (01422) 362936

Taylor Golden Best, Best Bitter, Landlord; guest beers Ⓗ

The Shears can take a little finding, but is worth it. By the side of the Hebble Brook, with a working mill towering over, this is a long-established inn. The central chimney breast effectively splits the main single room into what feels like more secluded niches. One of the guests is a dark beer from Timothy Taylor. Evening meals are served Monday-Friday. ♨❀◐◑⇌♣P

Haworth

Haworth Old Hall Inn ✔

8 Sun Street, BD22 8BP

✪ 12-11; 12-10.30 Sun

☎ (01535) 642709 website: www.hawortholdhall.co.uk

Jennings Bitter, Cumberland Ale, Cocker Hoop, Sneck Lifter, seasonal beers; Tetley Bitter Ⓗ

Lovely Tudor manor house, full of charm and character, located close to the famous main street. On entering through the substantial main door you will find stone floors, arches, mullioned windows, a huge fireplace and a splendid wood-panelled bar. Not forgetting the important stuff, the pub is a Jennings tied house and a good showcase for its beers. Good quality home-cooked food is available. It can get very busy at weekends. ♨☋❀⛟◐◑⛺⇌P⚟

Keighley & Worth Valley Light Railway Buffet Car

Haworth Station, BD22 8NJ

(join at any station on Worth Valley line)

✪ 11.25-5.20 Mon-Fri, July-Aug, & school hols; 11.15-5 Sat & Sun all year

☎ (01535) 645214 website: www.kwvr.co.uk

Beer range varies Ⓗ

Two to three beers are usually available (often from independent breweries) for the steam-hauled scenic journey. Beer is dispensed into tea urn-style containers from the cellar at Oxenhope Station, then served through handpumps on the train service departing every 90 minutes. An annual beer and folk festival happens at Oxenhope shed in October. Santa trains must be booked. A ticket to travel is required. Checking times before travelling is recommended. Q⛺≢P⊬

Heath

King's Arms

Heath Common, WF1 5SL (off A655, Wakefield-Normanton road)
⏲ 11.30-3, 5.30-11; 11.30-11 Sat; 12-10.30 Sun
☎ (01924) 377527
Clark's Classic Blonde; Taylor Landlord; Tetley Bitter; guest beers ⊞
Built in the early 1700s and converted into a pub in 1841, the King's Arms became one of the small number of pubs owned by Clark's Brewery. The pub consists of three oak-panelled rooms lit by gas lighting. It enjoys a good reputation for food, which is served all day Sunday. Children are welcome in the conservatory. There is a wheelchair WC. ♔Q♨❀◑◗♿♣P

Hebden Bridge

Fox & Goose

9 Heptonstall Road, HX7 6AZ (on A646, W of centre)
⏲ 11.30-3, 7 (6 Fri)-11; 12-10.30 Sun
☎ (01422) 842649 website: www.foxale.co.uk
Beer range varies ⊞
Local CAMRA's Pub of the Year 2004 is a family-owned, genuine free house, a haven for its discerning regulars. Popular beer festivals are held thrice yearly (ring for details), but the guest beers (over 800 from 300 breweries in the last two years) make this friendly, comfortable local something of a year-round festival. Good conversation is enjoyed throughout the three rooms (one no-smoking), and traditional games are played. The house beer, Slightly Foxed, is brewed by E&S Elland. Q❀≢♣●⊬▯

White Lion

Bridge Gate, HX7 8EX (on A6033)
⏲ 11-11; 12-10.30 Sun
☎ (01422) 842197 website: www.whitelionhotel.net
Boddingtons Bitter; Camerons Castle Eden Ale; Flowers Original; Taylor Landlord; guest beers ⊞
This 1657 coaching inn offers a relaxed atmosphere in historic surroundings. The Grade II listed building has been extensively refurbished, uncovering many original features. One of the two guest ales is from a small independent brewery. There are two good-sized, no-smoking areas and the patio garden overlooks Hebden Water. Meals are served 12-9 daily. Accommodation is in 10 en-suite rooms. ♔♨❀⛾◑◗♿≢P⊬

Hipperholme

Brown Horse

Denholme Gate Road, Coley, HX3 7SD (on A644, 1 mile N of A58)
⏲ 11-11; 12-3, 7-10.30 Sun
☎ (01422) 202112
Black Sheep Best Bitter; Greene King Ruddles Best; Taylor Landlord; Tetley Bitter ⊞
The same couple have run this pub for over 20 years, and it is well established as a popular dining venue, enjoying a strong local following; evening meals are served 5-7.30 weekdays. In addition to the bar area, there are three equally comfortable rooms for drinking or dining. With Coley Church to the rear, the Brown Horse stands at the head of Jum Hole Beck, in its wooded valley. ❀◑◗P⊬

Holmfirth

Farmers Arms

2-4 Liphill Bank Road, Burnlee, HD9 2LR (off A635, below Compo's Café)
⏲ 5 (12 Sat)-11; 12-10.30 Sun
☎ (01484) 683713
Adnams Bitter; Black Sheep Best Bitter; Fuller's London Pride; Taylor Landlord; Tetley Dark Mild; guest beer ⊞
Well worth seeking out, the pub stands in a quiet corner of Holmfirth between the Woodhead and Greenfield roads. The relaxed atmosphere is enhanced by discretely-sectioned seating areas. A central bar dominates the pub, which has a small function room. A tenanted house of the Punch Taverns chain, it caters well to its local trade, while its wide beer range appeals to serious and discerning drinkers. ♔❀♣P

Rose & Crown (Nook)

7 Victoria Square, HD9 2DN (down alley off Hollowgate)
⏲ 11-11; 12-10.30 Sun
☎ (01484) 683960 website: www.thenookpublichouse.co.uk
Moorhouses Black Cat; Taylor Best Bitter, Landlord; guest beers ⊞
Celebrating 30 years in this Guide, the 'Nook' becomes Yorkshire's longest-running entry. It is family-owned, now by the second generation, who have commendably retained the pub's status and identity as a basic, traditional free house, with minimal changes since 1976. Despite appearing small, it has some deceptively spacious rooms, plus an outdoor drinking area. Other attractions include monthly live music, continental beers and, now, an annual summer beer festival. ♔❀⊖♣

Horbury

Boon's

6 Queen Street, WF4 6LP (off High St)
⏲ 11-3, 5-11; 11-11 Fri & Sat; 12-10.30 Sun
☎ (01924) 280442
John Smith's Bitter; Taylor Landlord; Tetley Bitter; guest beers ⊞
One of the small number of tied houses owned by Clark's Brewery, this town-centre pub caters for all age groups and is a real community pub. Needless to say, there is always one beer from the Clark's range among the guest beers. The pub has a sizeable outdoor drinking area that is well used in summer. ♔❀♣

Horsforth

Town Street Tavern

16-18 Town Street, LS18 4RJ
⏲ 12-11; 12-10.30 Sun
☎ (0113) 281 9996
Black Sheep Best Bitter; Caledonian Deuchars IPA; Taylor Landlord; guest beers ⊞
Converted from a former off-licence at the heart

of Horsforth, this spacious bar offers eight real ales, and foreign draught beers. Located on a regular bus route (50/50A), the pub is no smoking throughout and has a small patio for alfresco drinking and dining. A connoisseurs' beer menu lists the many bottled beers available. This dog-friendly establishment offers an innovative dog menu all year round! No evening meals (for humans) on Sundays. Q❀◖◗♣●P⊬

Huddersfield

Albert Hotel

Victoria Lane, HD1 2QF (opp. library)

✪ 11-11; 12-5 Sun

☎ (01484) 536230 website: www.itsthealbert.com

Banks's Bitter; Black Sheep Best Bitter; Caledonian Deuchars IPA, 80/-; Taylor Landlord; guest beers 🄷

Designed in 1879 by Edward Hughest, the Albert boasts one of the finest remaining pub interiors in Huddersfield. The ornate rosewood bar features etched glass, mirrors and marble tops; Oscar Wilde's 'Work is the curse of the drinking classes' is inscribed overhead. Red leather seats are topped by stained glass panels. A large dining/function room is supplemented by three more functions rooms upstairs. Beers usually include a mild and handpulled cider is served; food options are extensive. ⛟◖◗⇌⊖♣●

Fieldhead

219 Quarmby Road, HD3 4FB (off A640, 3 miles out of town centre)

✪ 4 (12 Sat)-11; 12-10.30 Sun

☎ (01484) 654581

Tetley Bitter; guest beers 🄷

Large, inter-war pub, set back from the road. A wood-panelled and stained glass porch leads to a spacious, open-plan lounge, with a horseshoe-shaped bar, featuring two fireplaces, one in Arts and Crafts style. There are two further rooms, one for pool and the other for games. Enjoy the views of the Colne Valley from the rear of the pub and garden. Live music is staged on Tuesday evening. ❀♣P

Rat & Ratchet

40 Chapel Hill, HD1 3EB (on A616, below ring road)

✪ 12 (3.30 Mon & Tue)-11; 12-10.30 Sun

☎ (01484) 516734

Greene King Abbot; Ossett Pale Gold, Silver King, Excelsior; Taylor Best Bitter; guest beers 🄷

Former brew-pub that has become Ossett Brewery's second house. It has been sympathetically refurbished with new upholstered seating, but retains a traditional multi-roomed feel; the decor is enhanced by brewery adverts and music posters. The back room is now no-smoking, with a stove for warmth. Usually 12 beers include four permanent and one rotated Ossett beer, plus a mild. Lunches are served Wednesday-Saturday; Wednesday is curry night. The pub has clocked up 15 years in this Guide. ❀◖⇌♣●P⊬

Slubber's Arms

1 Halifax Old Road, Hillhouse, HD1 6HW (off A641)

✪ 12-3, 5.30-11; 12-3, 7-10.30 Sun

☎ (01484) 429032

Taylor Golden Best, Best Bitter; Landlord; guest beer 🄷

Huddersfield's only Timothy Taylor tied house, this solid, no-nonsense pub dates back 150 years and is located on the edge of town, the last of a terrace of dwellings overlooking Bradford Road. Inside, around a central bar, is a veritable glimpse into Huddersfield's past – relics of 'slubbing' and other skills adorn the rooms and seating areas.
♨Q❀◖⇌♣⊬

Star Inn ✔

7 Albert Street, Lockwood, HD1 3PJ (off A616)

✪ 5-11 (not Mon); 12-2, 5-11 Fri; 12-11 Sat; 12-10.30 Sun

☎ (01484) 545443 website: www.thestarinn.info

E&S Elland Best Bitter; Taylor Best Bitter, Landlord; guest beers 🄷

Back-street local enjoying deserved success since opening a few years ago. Emphasis is on quality ale, conversation and a friendly atmosphere, without juke boxes or games machines. Three drinking areas surround the bar and cosy, real fire. A phenomenal range of beers has been served here, resulting in numerous awards – it was CAMRA's Yorkshire Pub of the Year 2003, and runner-up in 2004. Regular beer festivals (two or more yearly) are staged in the garden marquee. ♨Q❀♿⇌(Lockwood)

Station Tavern

St George's Square, HD1 1JB (in train station buildings)

✪ 11.30-10 (11 Thu-Sat); 12-10.30 Sun

☎ (01484) 511058

Taylor Landlord or Best Bitter; guest beers 🄷

Formerly a station refreshment room in Grade I listed buildings, it has been a pub for well over 20 years, and is a noted free house, supporting local and regional micro-breweries. Up to eight beers are normally on sale. Open-plan, it boast a mosaic tiled floor, a snug with military pictures, and a side room with TV and piano. Live entertainment is staged from time to time. ♿⇌

White Cross Inn ✔

2 Bradley Road, Bradley, HD2 1XD (on A62)

✪ 11.45-11; 12-10.30 Sun

☎ (01484) 425728

Tetley Bitter; guest beers 🄷

Spacious, popular pub at the crossroads of Leeds Road and Bradley Road, near the Huddersfield Narrow Canal and the Calder and Hebble Navigation. As well as enjoying a strong local following, the pub's stock of up to four guest ales acts as a magnet for discerning drinkers. It has an extensive lounge and an upstairs function room, where an annual beer festival is held in February. Local CAMRA Pub of the Year 2004, the pub is well served by buses from Leeds.
❀◖♿♣P

Idle

Idle Working Men's Club

23 High Street, BD10 8NB

✪ 12-3 (not Tue-Thu), 7-11; 12-4, 7-10.30 Sun

☎ (01274) 613602 website: www.idleworkingmensclub.com

Tetley Mild, Bitter; guest beers 🄷

Club that attracts members because of its name – souvenir merchandise is sold. The concert room hosts live entertainment weekend evenings, while the lounge offers a quieter alternative. The downstairs games room houses two full-sized snooker tables, plus a large-screen

TV. It sometimes offers a different guest beer from upstairs. Show this Guide or CAMRA membership to be signed in. Parking is difficult. Bus Nos. 610 and 612 pass close by. Q♣

Symposium Ale & Wine Bar ✔

7 Albion Road, BD10 9PY

12-2.30, 5.30-11; 12-11 Fri & Sat; 12-10.30 Sun

☎ (01274) 616587

Taylor Landlord; guest beers H

At the heart of Idle village is this delightful ale and wine bar, one of the increasing chain of Market Town Taverns. The pub has kept its continuously-changing range of northern beers format, but also stocks an excellent range of foreign beers in bottle and on tap. In January 2005 the pub became no-smoking throughout. From the snug room you can access the verandah in warmer weather.

Q❀◑⊬

Ilkley

Bar T'at ✔

7 Cunliffe Road, LS29 9DZ

12-11; 12-10.30 Sun

☎ (01943) 608888

Black Sheep Best Bitter; Caledonian Deuchars IPA; Taylor Landlord; guest beers H

Popular, side-street pub renowned for its beer and food quality. Guest ales always include a Rooster's product and the pub regularly supports Yorkshire micro-breweries, such as Salamander. A good choice of foreign beers is available in bottle and on draught. Home-cooked food is available every day. This three-storey building has a music-free bar area as well as a no-smoking seating and dining area. Dogs are welcome.

Q❀◑≠⊬

Riverside Hotel

Riverside Gardens, Bridge Lane, LS29 9EU

11-11; 12-10.30 Sun

☎ (01943) 607338

Copper Dragon Best Bitter; Samuel Smith OBB; Tetley Bitter H

Family-run hotel, a mere 10 minutes' walk from the rail and bus interchange. A large lounge, refurbished in early 2005, has an open fire and forms the main drinking area where 'happy hour' is 4-8pm, Monday-Friday. Selected live football and rugby games are shown on TV. Meals are served until early evening and the attached fish and chip shop opens daily from 11.30am until evening. The hotel patio overlooks the river. Set in parkland, the hotel has 10 bedrooms. ⛼❀⇌◑≠P

Jackson Bridge

Red Lion ✔

Sheffield Road, HD9 7HB (on A616 from Huddersfield)

12-11; 12-10.30 Sun

☎ (01484) 683499 website: www.theredlioninn.com

Adnams Bitter; Caledonian Deuchars IPA; Greene King IPA; Tetley Bitter; guest beer H

In a quiet village in the Holme Valley, this former Victorian coaching house is well worth seeking out. A low, beamed lounge adorned with brassware is served by the central bar; it has its own dining room and a real fire during winter. With views across the valley to the row of cottages made famous in Last of the Summer Wine, this is an ideal place to relax, unwind and enjoy a fine drink. ⛼❀⇌◑♣

Keighley

Brewery Arms ✔

18 Longcroft, BD21 5AL (opp. Morrisons)

4 (11.30 Thu-Sat)-11; 12-10.30 Sun

☎ (01535) 603102

Clark's Classic Blonde; Goose Eye Barm Pot; Taylor Best Bitter; guest beers H

This free house is effectively a permanent beer festival, striving to have 10 real ales available, of which one is usually a mild. The bar area has a dartboard and a partially segregated no-smoking area. Upstairs is a fine restaurant (no-smoking) where draught ale can be served with your meal. Wheelchair access is now possible from the car park. ❀◑♿≠♣P⊬

Brown Cow

5 Cross Leeds Street, BD21 2LQ

4 (12 Fri & Sat)-11; 12-10.30 Sun

☎ (01535) 602577

Taylor Dark Mild, Golden Best, Best Bitter, Landlord; guest beer H

Family-run Taylor's tied house, run by a former Taylor's drayman and his wife. Three drinking areas around a central bar include a pool room and no-smoking area. Brewery memorabilia and old photos adorn the walls. Guest beers from local micros are a regular feature. It won local CAMRA's 'Pub of the Season' and 'Best Mild' on the Mild Trail in 2004. The pub's no-swearing policy draws favour from customers. ⛼♣P⊬

Cricketers Arms

Coney Lane, BD21 5JE

11.30-11; 12-10.30 Sun

☎ (01535) 669912

Moorhouses Premier; guest beers H

Single room, divided into two distinctly different areas: note the unusual tram seating, complete with luggage racks. Always worth a visit as the handpumps dispense a range of up to six regional and micro-brewed ales. The regular Moorhouses Premier may be swapped for a different beer from this Lancashire brewery from time to time. Bottled foreign beers are often available at reasonable prices. ♿≠

Ledsham

Chequers Inn

Claypit Lane, LS25 5LP

11-3, 5-11; closed Sun

☎ (01977) 683135 website: www.thechequersinn.f9.co.uk

Brown Cow Bitter, seasonal beers; John Smith's Bitter; Taylor Landlord; Theakston Best Bitter H

Historic multi-roomed inn dating from the 14th century. The cosy, candlelit interior of two main rooms with two smaller rooms, is served by a central bar. Low oak beams throughout are decorated with a variety of brasses, jugs, bottles and pictures of bygone Ledsham. The pub has a deserved reputation for its food. It is the only pub in Leeds to close on Sunday after Lady Elizabeth Hastings decreed so, 400 years ago.

⛼Q❀◑P

Leeds: City

Baroque

159 The Headrow, LS1 5RG

11-11; 12-10.30 Sun

(0113) 242 9674

Okells Bitter, Maclir, Dr Okells IPA; guest beer H

A welcome addition to the city centre drinking scene. The name says it all in terms of the decor – both internally and externally. A large no-smoking room at the back, plus two seating areas and a stand-and-sup counter near the bar make up the accommodation. It stocks a good 'world beer selection' – consult the beer list on the tables – both in bottles and on draught. It hosts live jazz on Friday evening. Meals are served 12-7pm daily.

Duck & Drake

43 Kirkgate, LS2 7DR

11-11; 12-10.30 Sun

(0113) 246 5806

Caledonian Deuchars IPA; John Smith's Bitter; Taylor Landlord; Theakston Best Bitter, Old Peculier; guest beers H

A regular Guide entry for many years, this basic ale house serves a good range of real ales to an eclectic mix of punters. There are two rooms, with the bar in between, both with wooden flooring and real fires. The back room has a dartboard and TV, while regular live music is staged in the larger front room. A small outdoor drinking area is open in the summer months.

George

67-69 Great George Street, LS1 3BB (opp. Leeds Infirmary)

12-11 (1am Fri & Sat); 7-10.30 Sun

(0113) 245 3232

Greene King Abbot; Tetley Bitter; guest beers H

Situated opposite the hospital, this pub is popular with staff there as well as from the nearby courts. Dark wood panelling and screens with stained glass inserts add interest. The central bar serves a public bar on two sides; a smaller snug-style room has its own servery. A cellar bar is available for functions. A range of lunchtime snacks is available weekdays; sandwiches made from meat carved from a joint are served Friday until 7pm.

North Bar

24 New Briggate, LS1 6NU

12-1am (2am Wed-Sat); 12-10.30 Sun

(0113) 242 4540 website: www.northbar.com

Beer range varies H

It is easy to pass by this narrow café bar near the North Bar – one of the city's old boundary stones. This would be a shame since, in addition to a regularly changed British cask ale, it keeps a cornucopia of foreign beer – either on draught or in one of the many well-stocked fridges. Modern, unassuming decor is complemented by young, enthusiastic staff. Guest DJs perform on Friday and Saturday evenings.

Palace

Kirkgate, LS2 7DJ

11-11; 12-10.30 Sun

(0113) 244 5882

Tetley Bitter; guest beers H

The Palace is in Leeds now, but at the parish Church of St Peter nearby you will find the East Bar Stone set into the churchyard wall, denoting the medieval eastern boundary of Leeds. It was first recorded as an inn in 1841, then passed on to the Castelow family who brewed their own beers. It was bought by the Melbourne Brewery in 1926, hence the original Melbourne tiling. In the forefront of the local ale scene, it serves meals 11.30 (12 Sun)-7pm.

Scarbrough Hotel

Bishopgate Street, LS1 5DY

11-11; 12-10.30 Sun

(0113) 243 4590

Tetley Bitter; guest beers H

Leeds CAMRA Pub of the Year 2003/4 and Pub of the Season, summer 2004, keeps usually five, but up to seven guest ales. It is also the only place in the city centre regularly selling real perry as well as cider. Yorkshire beers are normally well represented on the chalkboard, but not to the exclusion of all else. The range of ales can be doubled by the addition of a temporary bar when the pub holds its occasional beer festivals.

Town Hall Tavern

17 Westgate, LS1 2RA

11.30-11; closed Sun

(0113) 245 3966

Taylor Golden Best, Landlord; Tetley Bitter H

Opposite the courthouse and town hall, this establishment caters for the adjacent busy financial and legal sector of the city. A pleasant, open-plan venue, it is comfortably furnished and decorated with a changing display of memorabilia of the courts, old Leeds circa 1900 and other related subjects. Collections of pump clips, cigarette cards and old photos (including Leeds United from a happier era) complete the decor. Weekday lunches are served.

Victoria Family & Commercial

28 Great George Street, LS1 3DL

11-11; closed Sun

(0113) 245 1386

Black Sheep Best Bitter; Taylor Landlord; Tetley Mild, Bitter; guest beers H

Fine example of a Victorian pub, built in 1865 and situated behind the town hall. The main bar is a palace of finely detailed wood and glass, complete with snob screens and an Italian brass coffeemaker behind the bar. There is a comfortable, no-smoking room to the left of the entrance, and another room at the back of the bar. The permanent Yorkshire ales are supplemented by three changing guests. Live jazz is a regular Thursday evening event. Meals are served 12-6pm.

Whitelock's First City Luncheon Bar ☆

Turks Head Yard, LS1 6HB (hidden up an alley off Briggate)

11-11; 12-10.30 Sun

(0113) 245 3950

John Smith's Bitter; Theakston Best Bitter, Old Peculier; guest beers H

Largely untouched since its Victorian heyday, this, one of the oldest pubs in Leeds, is a

16th-century building that is listed on CAMRA's National Inventory of historic pub interiors. Whitelocks is quite simply about as traditional as it gets. Past generations of pubgoers would still be able to recognise the compact interior with its dark wood, brass fittings and engraved glass. It is an oasis in a bustling city where the atmosphere is second to none. ⛫Q❀◑◐⇌

Leeds: North

Arcadia Ale & Wine Bar

Arndale Centre, Otley Road, LS6 2UE

11-11; 12-10.30 Sun

☎ (0113) 274 5599

Black Sheep Best Bitter; Caledonian Deuchars IPA; Taylor Landlord; guest beers Ⓗ

Part of the excellent Market Town Taverns group, Arcadia attracts a combination of locals, discerning students and beer enthusiasts to sample the fine range of eight real ales and varied foreign beers. Situated in a row of shops and originally a bank, a careful conversion has made good use of limited space. There are no TVs or games machines, just the hum of conversation. Arcadia is no-smoking throughout. Q◑◐⚟

Bricklayers Arms

8 Low Close Street, LS2 9EG (off St Mark's Rd)

11-11.30; 12-10.30 Sun

☎ (0113) 245 8277

Caledonian Deuchars IPA; John Smith's Bitter; guest beers Ⓗ

Known locally as the Brickies, its policy of creating a true community pub results in attracting a mix of locals and students. It sponsors student archery and hockey, and fields football, darts and dominoes teams. Guest ales – normally three – come from a selected micro or independent brewery. Many a reunion is held here with students and locals who have left the area, travelling many miles for the event. Difficult to find, but do make the effort to visit. ❀◑◐♣P

Eldon ✔

190 Woodhouse Lane, LS2 9DX

11.30-11; 12-10.30 Sun

☎ (0113) 245 3591

Adnams Bitter; Greene King IPA, Abbot; Tetley Dark Mild; Wells Bombardier; guest beers Ⓗ

Traditional, welcoming pub that is popular with locals and students alike. It is busy most nights of the week, making for a great atmosphere. There is always a wide variety of up to nine ales on offer. The Eldon has recently undergone some light refurbishment and now boasts three wide-screen TVs, on which you can catch major sporting action almost every evening, in comfortable surroundings. ◑◐⇌⚟

New Roscoe

Bristol Street, Sheepscar, LS7 1DH

11-11; 1-10.30 Sun

☎ (0113) 246 0778 website: www.newroscoe.co.uk

Greene King Abbot, Old Speckled Hen; Tetley Bitter; guest beers Ⓗ

One of the few genuine free houses in central Leeds: a spacious establishment, renowned for its music. Local, national and foreign bands play in the concert room when a door charge is levied (ring for details). The public bar has three pool tables, while the Roscoe Room is a quieter lounge/TV room. Tetley memorabilia are displayed, the highlight being the two Tetley monocled huntsman lanterns in the public bar. Weekday lunches are served. Moorhouses brews the house ale. ❀◑⊟♣P

Leeds: South

Garden Gate ☆

Whitfield Place, Hunslet, LS10 2QB

11.30-11; 12-10.30 Sun

☎ (0113) 270 0379

Tetley Bitter Ⓗ

Victorian gem, hidden away in a modern housing estate, the Garden Gate is justifiably included in CAMRA's National Inventory. The pub has retained intact its multi-roomed layout, with a tiled drinking corridor, off which comes the tap room and two further rooms. The unspoilt features include a mosaic in the entranceway, fine mirrors and stained glass panels. It also boasts a splendid tiled exterior. ◑⊟♣

Grove Inn

Back Row, Holbeck, LS11 5PL

12-11; 12-10.30 Sun

☎ (0113) 243 9254

Adnams Broadside; Caledonian Deuchars IPA; Theakston Mild; Wells Bombardier; guest beers Ⓗ

Dwarfed by multi-storey developments rising all around this pub, the Grove continues to provide an oasis of real ale despite serious attempts by the developers to demolish it. The regular beers are supplemented by two rapidly-changing guests, plus a limited range of foreign bottled beers. An excellent example of an unspoilt West Riding corridor pub, with four rooms, it hosts regular live music, including the Friday folk club. Cider is sold in summer, no food Saturday. ⛫❀◑⇌●P⚟

Leeds: West

Jug & Barrel

56-58 Town Street, Stanningley, LS28 6EZ

12-11; 12-10.30 Sun

☎ (0113) 257 6877 website: www.jugandbarrel.com

John Smith's Bitter, Magnet; Taylor Landlord; Theakston Old Peculier; Wells Bombardier Ⓗ

This former nightclub has gone from strength to strength, becoming a favourite with locals and visitors alike. The large bar has stools and other seating, with the open fire being the focal point. Regular live music is performed in the concert room featuring acoustic, 'open mike' sessions (ring for details). ⛫❀◑◐♣P

Old Vic

17 Whitecote Hill, Bramley, LS13 3LB (set back from road)

4 (2 Fri; 11 Sat)-11; 7-10.30 Sun

☎ (0113) 256 1207

Black Sheep Best Bitter; Taylor Landlord; Tetley Bitter; guest beers Ⓗ

This genuine free house (rare in the Leeds area) was once a vicarage, hence the name, and serves real ale in an atmosphere packed with community spirit. The central bar serves a

comfortable lounge and two further rooms, one with a pool table. Dominoes is popular and it hosts regular quiz nights. A function room is available. Normally at least two guest ales are on tap here.
⌂❀♣P

West End House ✔
26 Abbey Road, Kirkstall, LS5 3HS (next to Kirkstall sports centre)
☉ 11.30-11; 12-10.30 Sun
☎ (0113) 278 6332
Beer range varies Ⓗ
An oasis of real ale in Kirkstall, this pub consists of a large bar surrounded by comfortable seating where you can enjoy a relaxing drink, either on its own or with a meal. This establishment is renowned for good food at reasonable prices. Quiz nights on Tuesday and Thursday are well attended. The TV in one corner regularly shows sporting events. ❀◐◑⇌(Headingley)

Lees Moor

Quarry House Inn
Bingley Road, BD21 5QE (off A629/A6033 jct)
☉ 12-3, 7-11; 12-10.30 Sun
☎ (01535) 642239
Taylor Golden Best, Best Bitter, Landlord; Tetley Bitter Ⓗ
Converted farmhouse affording extensive views across the surrounding area. Run by the same family since 1982, it has appeared in this Guide every year since 1986. It is slightly off the beaten track, but well worth seeking out to enjoy excellent real ale and food in comfortable, friendly surroundings. The bar is an old pulpit set in a cosy drinking area. The attached barn hosts functions. Q❀◐◑⊟P

Linthwaite

Sair Inn ✔
139 Lane Top, HD7 5SG (top of Hoyle Ing, off A62) OS100143
☉ 7 (5 Fri, 12 Sat)-11; 12-10.30 Sun
☎ (01484) 842370
Linfit Dark Mild, Bitter, Gold Medal, English Guineas Stout, seasonal beers Ⓗ
Renowned ale house, dating back to the 1800s; more recently, winner of numerous awards, most notably CAMRA's national Pub of the Year in 1997. The on-site brewery has been established for over 20 years, and up to 10 of its beers are normally available in the pub, making it an icon for locals, visitors, and beer-samplers alike. The inn enjoys a hilltop location overlooking the Colne Valley; although not large, it has four rooms, one quiet for non-smokers.
⌂Q♉❀♣●⚟

Liversedge

Black Bull
37 Halifax Road, WF15 6JR (on A649, 400 yds from A62 jct)
☉ 12-3, 5-11; 12-11 Wed-Sat; 12-10.30 Sun
☎ (01924) 403779
Osset Pale Gold, Excelsior; Taylor Landlord; guest beers Ⓗ
Owned by Ossett Brewery for three years, the success of this pub is such that a comfortable new no-smoking room has been added to accommodate the extra trade. The entrance to this 300-year-old building is narrow and a little difficult in busy periods, but it opens out to four homely rooms and the new room. Nine handpumps serve the regular beers, a house beer from Ossett, three guests including a mild, a German pils and a white beer. Sandwiches are available. ⌂❀♣P⚟

Marsden

Tunnel End Inn
Waters Road, HD7 6NF (near Standedge Visitor Centre)
☉ 12-3 (not Mon-Wed), 5 (8 Mon)-11; 12-11 Sat; 12-10.30 Sun
☎ (01484) 844636
Black Sheep Best Bitter; Taylor Landlord; Tetley Bitter; guest beer Ⓗ
Welcoming country pub, close to the Standedge tunnel – the longest, highest and deepest tunnel in this country. Situated amid fine Pennine countryside, near the Pennine Way and Kirklees Way, the pub enjoys patronage from hikers, cyclists, equestrians and canal enthusiasts who are drawn to the nearby Huddersfield Canal. The pub takes pride in its beers, as well as its home-cooked food. Accommodation is available – ring for details. ⌂❀⇔◐◑♿♣⚟

Mirfield

Navigation Tavern
6 Station Road, WF17 8NL (down narrow lane by railway embankment)
☉ 11.30-11; 12-10.30 Sun
☎ (01924) 492476
John Smith's Bitter; Theakston Mild, Best Bitter, XB, Old Peculier; guest beer (occasional) Ⓗ
This traditional canalside pub has been sympathetically renovated and extended to provide a large, modern function room while retaining the cosy features of the original building in its two open-plan rooms and games room. It fields a games team and a soccer team. Quiz night is Wednesday. Mooring for canal boats is available close by. ❀♿⇌♣P

Mytholmroyd

Robin Hood Inn
Cragg Road, Cragg Vale, HX7 5SQ (from Mytholmroyd follow B6138 towards Rochdale)
☉ 12-11; 12-10.30 Sun
☎ (01422) 885899
Holt Bitter; Taylor Golden Best, Landlord Ⓗ
The inn was only recently reopened by popular demand after a campaign by a group calling themselves the Merrymen. It is set in the picturesque Cragg Vale, opposite Bell House, the one-time home of David Hartley, the king of the infamous Cragg Vale coiners. An ideal starting point for scenic walks, local CAMRA's Pub of the Season, summer 2004 sells bottled Belgian beers and serves meals with a difference.
⌂Q❀◐◑▲

Shoulder of Mutton
36 New Road, HX7 5DZ (near station)
☉ 11.30-3, 7-11; 11-11 Sat; 12-10.30 Sun
☎ (01422) 883165

Black Sheep Best Bitter; Boddingtons Bitter; Caledonian Deuchars IPA; Castle Eden Ale; Greene King IPA; Taylor Landlord Ⓗ
Roadside village inn at the start of the longest continuous incline in England. Popular with locals and visitors alike, it provides a focal point for community sports teams. The spacious main bar relates the history of local 17th-century coin-clipping activities. The smaller cottage-style rooms are welcoming to families who come to enjoy the simple, but delicious, home-cooked meals that offer real value for money (not served Tue eve). A small outside drinking area lies next to the beck behind the pub.
❀◐◑⇌P

Ossett

Brewer's Pride

Low Mill Road, Healey, WF5 8ND (1½ miles from centre)
⏲ 12-3, 5.30-11; 12-11 Fri & Sat; 12-10.30 Sun
☎ (01924) 273865
Ossett Pale Gold, Excelsior; guest beers Ⓗ
Popular free house, adjacent to the Ossett Brewery, offering nine cask ales on handpull. The pub is five minutes' walk from the Calder and Hebble Canal; bus no. 121 stops nearby (daytime only). Home-cooked lunches are served and on Wednesday evening, curry, pies and steak feature on subsequent weeks. The local folk club meets on Thursday evening and monthly live music is performed (first Sun). The pub has received many awards from local CAMRA. A beer festival is held annually.
⛫Q❀◐●

Otley

Black Bull

Market Place, LS21 3AQ
⏲ 11-11; 12-10.30 Sun
☎ (01943) 462288
Taylor Best Bitter, Landlord; Tetley Bitter Ⓗ
Busy, market place pub, parts of which date from the 16th century. The low beams and stone-flagged floor give the place an olde-worlde feel. A single bar serves an L-shaped drinking area divided into three distinct alcoves. Good value lunches are served; Sunday lunches are particularly well received. Smoking is permitted throughout. Paintings depicting the English Civil War recall the pub's links with Cromwell who is reputed to have stayed here. Westons Old Rosie cider is sold.
⛫❀◐●

Bowling Green

18 Bondgate, LS21 3AB (near bus station)
⏲ 12-4 (not Mon & Tue), 7-11; 6-10.30 Sun
☎ (01943) 461494
Beer range varies Ⓗ
Genuine free house, serving beers mainly from micro-breweries, the pub consists of an L-shaped bar with a pool table at one end. An eclectic collection of items from around the world is displayed. The large outdoor area to the front is popular in summer and plays host to morris dancers during the annual September folk weekend. The building dates from 1757, but it was 1825 before it became a pub. Children are not admitted.
⛫❀♣

Junction

44 Bondgate, LS21 1AD
⏲ 11-11; 12-10.30 Sun
☎ (01943) 463233
Taylor Dark Mild, Best Bitter, Landlord; Tetley Bitter; guest beers Ⓗ
Friendly, vibrant pub occupying a prominent corner site on the approach from Leeds. The single room features a central fireplace and pictures of bygone Otley alongside beer and brewery posters. The odd stuffed animal, antlers and a high shelf of beer bottles complete the decoration. It hosts live music on Tuesday. A former local CAMRA Pub of the Year, this is a welcoming, traditional local. Roadside tables allow for some outdoor drinking. ⛫❀

Pontefract

Robin Hood

4 Wakefield Road, WF8 4HN (off A645, opp. major traffic lights)
⏲ 11.30-3.30 (4.30 Fri & Sat), 7-11; 12-3.30, 7-10.30 Sun
☎ (01977) 702231
John Smith's Bitter; Tetley Bitter; guest beers Ⓗ
Busy local near the town end traffic lights, comprising a public bar and three other drinking areas. It holds quizzes twice weekly and fields darts and dominoes teams in the local charities league. Winner of several local CAMRA awards, including 1998 Pub of the Year, the Robin Hood stages a beer festival over August bank holiday weekend.
⛫🀫⇌(Tanshelf-Baghill) ♣

Pudsey

Fleece

100 Fartown, LS28 8LU
⏲ 12-11; 12-10.30 Sun
☎ (0113) 236 2748
Taylor Landlord; Tetley Bitter; guest beer Ⓗ
Spacious, stone pub, set back from the main road. The Fleece, despite its name, greets you with a fibreglass pig over the front door. The porcine theme carries throughout, but does not detract from the homely feel. The lounge is comfy, with seats at a premium on busy evenings. The tap room is where sports fans can watch TV. Just outside Pudsey centre, the Fleece is a friendly local. The guest beer is usually from the Brown Cow stable.
❀🀫P

Riddlesden

Willow Tree Inn

Ilkley Road, BD20 5PN
⏲ 4 (12 Sat)-11; 12-10.30 Sun
☎ (01535) 210487
Tetley Bitter; guest beers Ⓗ
Two-roomed village pub, affording elevated views across the Aire Valley. The comfortable lounge is quiet while the public bar has both music and TV; both rooms are served from a central bar. There are usually two guest beers from the Enterprise range, one in each room. As you enter through the porch, note the old Heys Brewery stained glass windows and guest beer tasting notes on a blackboard. Q🀫P

ENGLAND

Ripponden

Old Bridge

Priest Lane, HX6 4DF (between A58 and B6113)
⏲ 12-3, 5.30-11; 12-11 Sat; 12-10.30 Sun
☎ (01422) 822595 website: www.porkpieclub.com
Black Sheep Best Bitter; Taylor Golden Best, Best Bitter, Landlord; guest beers Ⓗ
Picturesque, whitewashed, mostly single-storey building; one of Yorkshire's oldest pubs with a record dating from 1307. On three levels, the lowest room is no-smoking and boasts an exposed cruck beam. On the opposite bank of the River Ryburn to the parish church, the adjacent stone humpback bridge dates from the 16th century. It stands on the route of the 50-mile Calderdale Way (no dogs admitted). Evening meals are served Monday-Friday. Two guest beers are usually available. ♨Q❀◖◗P🚭

Shipley

Fanny's Ale & Cider House

63 Saltaire Road, BD18 3JN (on A657, opp. fire station)
⏲ 12 (5 Mon)-11; 12-10.30 Sun
☎ (01274) 591419
Taylor Golden Best, Landlord; guest beers Ⓗ
Formerly a shop, it was opened by the present owner firstly as a beer shop, then as a fully licensed free house, and has been a regular Guide entry since. The drinking area has a real fire and gas lighting; a comfortable upstairs room provides more seating. Up to nine real ales are on tap, some from local breweries. A selection of foreign beers is kept, both on draught and bottled, along with Biddenden cider. ♨Q⇶(Saltaire)♣

Shipley Club

162 Bradford Road, BD18 3PD (opp. A650/A6038 jct by Northcliffe Park)
⏲ 12-3 (not Mon, Tue or Thur), 7-11; 12-11 Sat; 12-3 Sun
☎ (01274) 201842
Beer range varies Ⓗ
Formed in 1900 as Shipley Bowling Green Club; now a thriving sports and social club, staging occasional live entertainment. Pub games and bowling are available, subject to members' commitments. The steward (a real ale enthusiast) has introduced three changing beers. Food is served Sunday lunchtime and midweek lunch and evening April-October (ring for times). Children are welcome until 9.30pm. Show this Guide or CAMRA membership card to be signed in. The outdoor drinking area is beside the bowling green. ❀◗♿⇶♣P

Shipley Pride

1 Saltaire Road, BD18 3HH (on A657)
⏲ 11.30 (11 Sat)-11; 12-10.30 Sun
☎ (01274) 585341
Taylor Landlord; Tetley Bitter; guest beer Ⓗ
Formerly the Bee Hive Hotel, built in 1870 as a Hammond Brewery house, this is a friendly local with two rooms around the central bar. Both rooms boast lovely stained glass windows. The lounge is comfortably appointed, while the games room is more functional for pool and darts. Quizzes are held on Thursday evening. Guest beers are from regional brewers. Home-made food is served weekday lunchtimes. ❀◖⇶(Shipley/Saltaire)♣P

Silsden

Bridge Inn

Keighley Road, BD20 0EA (on A6034)
⏲ 4 (12 Fri & Sat)-11; 12-10.30 Sun
☎ (01535) 653144
John Smith's Bitter; guest beers Ⓗ
Opened in 1799 as the Spoon and Slipper, it lies alongside the Leeds-Liverpool navigation. Most of the time it is a traditional, back-street local; on weekend evenings karaoke and disco prevail and major sporting events are shown on a large screen TV. The small, smoke-free snug acts as a dining room in summer for lunches. A pleasant canalside garden is reached through the cellar. ❀⇌◖⊟🚭

Sowerby

Rushcart

Sowerby Green, HX6 1JJ (1¼ miles off A58 at Triangle)
⏲ 12 (2 Mon & Tue)-11; 12-10.30 Sun
☎ (01422) 831956
Jennings Cumberland Ale, Cocker Hoop; guest beers Ⓗ
Busy village local, once a resting place for rushbearers and their cart on their annual tour of local churches. The main lounge features a large old fireplace, the bar area lots of hops and timber boarding. Note the rushcart design in the leaded window. Popular with hikers, it is a meeting place for various local organisations. An enclosed patio is to the front of the pub, which was voted Pub of the Season, winter 2005 by local CAMRA members.
♨❀◖◗♣P

Sowerby Bridge

Navigation

Chapel Lane, HX6 3LF (off A58/A6026 jct)
⏲ 12-3, 5-11; 12-11 Fri & Sat; 12-10.30 Sun
☎ (01422) 831636
Black Sheep Best Bitter; Taylor Landlord; Tetley Bitter Ⓗ
Set down a narrow lane in a valley bottom overlooking the Calder and Hebble Canal, the long lounge displays canal-related memorabilia and artefacts. There is an adjoining pool room to the left. The extensive menu, with food freshly prepared, makes the 'Navvi' popular with diners, although there is plenty of room for those who just want a drink. A fourth handpump always serves beer from E&S Elland.
❀◖◗⇶♣P

Puzzle Hall Inn

21 Hollins Mill Lane, HX6 2RF (400 yds from A58)
⏲ 12 (4 Mon)-11; 12-10.30 Sun
☎ (01422) 835547
Greene King IPA; Taylor Landlord; guest beers Ⓗ
Lively, friendly pub nestling between the canal and the river. Opened in the 1700s, this former brew-pub is dominated by the tower of the former Puzzle Hall Brewery. Although the pub is tiny, with just two rooms, it creates a wonderful atmosphere for live jazz every Tuesday, folk music on Wednesday and R'n'B on Saturday. Three music festivals are held every year with over 50 bands taking part. Curry is served on Wednesday.
♨Q❀◖⇶♣P

Ram's Head

26 Wakefield Road, HX6 2AZ (on A6026, 400 yds from A58)

12-2.30, 5-11; 12-11 Sat; 12-10.30 Sun

(01422) 835876 website: www.ryburnbrewery.co.uk

Ryburn Best Bitter, Numpty Bitter, Ryedale Bitter, Luddite, Stabbers Bitter; guest beer (occasional) H

Ryburn Brewery's only tied house has the brewery situated underneath it. The main space off the small bar is divided into several drinking areas, where brassware and plates adorn the stone walls; a door leads to an attractive garden. The larger L-shaped lounge doubles as the dining area, where fresh food is cooked to order (served all day Sat and Sun). As well as Ryburn's well-priced beers, the pub now offers an occasional guest from a micro-brewery. ❀ȸ▶P

White Horse

Burnley Road, Friendly, HX6 2UG (on A646, ¾ mile from centre)

12-11; 12-10.30 Sun

(01422) 831173

E&S Elland Beyond the Pale; Tetley Mild, Bitter H

This white-painted pub stands just back from the busy A646; in summer the prize-winning window boxes can be stunning. It is a welcoming, comfortable local with a tap room to the side of the bar, and a larger bar/lounge – once two rooms and still partially divided. A strong local following includes members of Friendly football club, Friendly brass band, and the pub's own dominoes club. ❀♣P

Sowood

Dog & Partridge

Forest Hill Road, HX4 9LB (¼ mile W of B6112)

7-11; 12-4.30, 7-10.30 Sun

(01422) 374249

Black Sheep Best Bitter; Taylor Landlord; guest beer H

This Pennine pub is a genuine rural local, and there are few like it remaining. It comprises just two simply furnished rooms: the bar and a smaller room, where the piano is sometimes played by the landlord. Run by the same family for many years (the mother of the present landlord was behind the bar into her nineties), the only noise is the hum of conversation. A no-smoking policy was introduced recently.

Q❀♣P⚟

Stanbury

Friendly

54 Main Street, BD22 0HB (on Colne road between Haworth and Colne)

12-11; 12-10.30 Sun

(01535) 645528

Goose Eye Brontë Bitter; Tetley Bitter; guest beer H

Friendly by name and nature, this village local offers a warm welcome. Two lounges with a central bar and a games room are comfortably decorated. Children are welcome throughout; the pub is directly opposite the village play area. Close to Top Withens and the Pennine Way, it is popular with hikers and walkers. Tea and coffee are available all day. Dogs are welcome at local CAMRA's Pub of the Season, winter 2003/4. No lunches are served winter Thursday.

❀ȸ♿⛺♣P

Todmorden

Top Brink Inn

Brink Top, Lumbutts, UL14 6JB (near Lumbutts Mill activity centre) OS956236

12-3 (not Mon-Fri), 6-11; 12-10.30 Sun

(01706) 812696

Boddingtons Bitter; Camerons Castle Eden Ale; Flowers Original; Taylor Landlord; guest beer H

Large country inn, popular with family diners, offering excellent, friendly service. The guest beer always comes from an independent brewery. Enjoy spectacular Pennine views from the conservatory or outdoor seating. Next to the Pennine Bridleway and handy for the Pennine Way and Stoodley Pike, it attracts passing walkers, cyclists and riders. Fell races and the annual New Year Lee Dam swim are hosted at the pub, which is festooned with flowers in summer. Children are welcome in the games room.

❀ȸ▶⛺P⚟

Wakefield

Alverthorpe WMC

111 Flanshaw Lane, Alverthorpe, WF2 9JG

11.30-3.30, 6.30-11; 12-10.30 Sun

(01924) 374179

Tetley Mild, Bitter H

This working men's club is a member of the official CIU. It has the usual indoor games along with a snooker table. Outdoor pursuits include football, cricket and bowls on a floodlit green. All the rooms are of adequate size. The lounge displays models of shire horses, while pictures and mirrors feature throughout the club. This club has a function room available for hire. Cottage beers are sometimes on tap.

❀♿♣P

Fernandes Brewery Tap

5 Avison Yard, Kirkgate, WF1 1VA (near George St/Kirkgate jct)

5-11; 11-11 Fri & Sat; 12-10.30 Sun

(01924) 369547

website: www.fernandes-brewery.gowyld.com

Fernandes Malt Shovel Mild, Butlers; guest beers H

This pub won the 2004 Wakefield CAMRA Pub of the Year to add to its endless list of awards from previous years. A real ale drinkers' paradise, it has most things to satisfy the serious drinker. It boasts a Belgian Genever Bar and stocks draught and bottled Belgian beers. The cider varies.

Q⇌(Kirkgate/Westgate) ●

Flanshaw Hotel

Flanshaw Lane, WF2 9JD (400 yds from Dewsbury Rd)

12-11; 12-10.30 Sun

(01924) 290830

John Smith's Bitter; Tetley Bitter; guest beers H

Spacious community pub that benefits from a strong local trade. A welcoming pub, with a fine selection of guest beers, it offers good disabled access and ample parking for coaches. Active in sports and charitable work, it hosts occasional family evenings in school holidays. It employs a

resident DJ and can cater for most requirements in its function room. CCTV monitors custom here.
♨ꝏ❀⌸♿♣P⊁⊓

Harewood Arms

101 Kirkgate, WF1 1JG
⊛ 12-11; 12-10.30 Sun
☎ (01924) 201321
Taylor Landlord; Tetley Bitter Ⓗ
Popular pub on the edge of the city centre. Recently opened out to give a central bar, it has retained two separate drinking areas with plain glass front windows and bright blue exterior paintwork. Despite the makeover, many of the 1830 fittings have been retained at this pub that appeals to women.
❀◐♿⇶

Harry's Bar

107B Westgate, WF1 1EL (near Westgate Station)
⊛ 5-11; 5-10.30 Sun
☎ (01924) 373773
Ossett Silver King, Excelsior; Taylor Landlord; guest beers Ⓗ
Small, one-roomed pub in an alleyway near the station. It draws many friendly regulars aged from 18 to 80. A real fire, bare brick and cosy wood interior are enhanced by vintage sporting pictures. Take in the fantastic view of Wakefield's famous 99-arch viaduct. The pub hosts live music every Wednesday. A selection of Belgian bottles adds to the temptation.
♨Q❀♿⇶(Westgate)

Labour Club (Red Shed)

18 Vicarage Street, WF1 1QX (opp. outdoor market car park)
⊛ 12-5 (not Mon-Thu; 11-4 Sat), 7-11; 12-5 Sun
☎ (01924) 215626 website: www.theredshed.org.uk
Ossett Pale Gold; guest beers Ⓗ
This truly is a red shed – a friendly, welcoming landmark in the city centre. A regular haunt of Wakefield CAMRA members, it boasts many awards. A changing selection of guest ales and bottled Belgian beers draws beer lovers from far and wide. Although the venue for Labour and union meetings, a wide cross-section of the community uses the Shed. The popular Wednesday night quiz and twice-yearly beer festivals are among the many events staged here.
❀⇶(Westgate/Kirkgate)♣P

Redoubt

28 Horbury Road , WF2 8TS (corner of Westgate)
⊛ 12 (11 Sat)-11; 12-10.30 Sun
☎ (01924) 377085 website: www.theredoubt.co.uk
Taylor Landlord; Tetley Mild, Bitter Ⓗ
One of the oldest pubs in Wakefield, this Tetley Heritage pub has four small but cosy rooms that display the historical and sporting heritage of the city. The Redoubt fields its own football and cricket teams. The pub has its own small outdoor drinking area. Children are welcome in the family room until 8pm.
♨Qꝏ❀⇶(Westgate)♣P

Six Chimneys ✔

41-43 Kirkgate, WF1 1HY (next to Woolworths, opp. cathedral precinct)
⊛ 10-11; 10-10.30 Sun
☎ (01924) 239449
Boddingtons Bitter; Greene King Abbot; Marston's Burton Bitter, Pedigree; Tetley Bitter; guest beers Ⓗ
A Wetherspoon's conversion of a former shop, it was a welcome addition to the real ale scene on Kirkgate when it opened five years ago. The ladies facilities won a Best Toilets competition a few years ago. It opens at 10am for tea, coffee and breakfast, then good value meals are served all day until 10pm. There is usually a choice of five guest beers.
◗♿⇶(Westgate/Kirkgate)⊁

Talbot & Falcon ✔

Northgate, WF1 3AP (100 yds from Bull Ring)
⊛ 11-11; 12-10.30 Sun
☎ (01924) 201693
Tetley Bitter; guest beers Ⓗ
A listed building at the heart of the city, the Talbot is popular with shoppers who can choose from a good selection of lunches at fair prices. It was completely refurbished in 2003 and can accommodate up to 11 people in six en-suite rooms, all with tea and coffee-making facilities and colour TV. The pub boasts a changing range of guest ales from an extensive cask list, and has recently added a cask cider. It also stocks a selection of fine wines.
⌸◐⇶(Kirkgate/Westgate)●

Walton

New Inn

144 Shay Lane, WF2 6LA
⊛ 12 (11 Sat)-11; 12-10.30 Sun
☎ (01924) 255447
Boddingtons Bitter; Caledonian Deuchars IPA; Jennings Cumberland Ale; John Smith's Bitter; Taylor Landlord Ⓗ
Well-appointed, community-spirited pub, where the manager, a real ale enthusiast, hopes to be able to feature guest ales from micro-breweries in the future. All sorts of events are staged, including quizzes on Sunday and Monday evenings. It opens for coffee and soft drinks at 10am. It is popular with ramblers as it stands in good walking country.
❀◐◗P⊁

Wentbridge

Blue Bell

Great North Road, WF8 3JP (1 mile off A1)
⊛ 11.30-11; 12-10.30 Sun
☎ (01977) 620697
Black Sheep Best Bitter; Taylor Landlord; Tetley Bitter Ⓗ
In the picturesque village of Wentbridge, on the old Great North Road, this former coaching inn was rebuilt in 1633; an original sign hangs in the entrance. It stands at the head of Brockdale, the smallest of the Yorkshire Dales. It is noted for excellent food, which includes vegetarian options (booking advisable at weekends). It is comfortably furnished with Mousey Thompson tables and chairs. The manager was Punch Tavern's national Cellarman of the Year in 1998.
Q❀⌸◐◗♿P⊁

Wetherby

Muse

16 Bank Street, LS22 6NQ

12 (11 Sat)-11; 12-10.30 Sun

(01937) 580201

Beer range varies Ⓗ

Four rotating guest beers, mainly from local breweries and usually including one from either Black Sheep or Timothy Taylor, are augmented by a changing range of foreign draft beers and an extensive bottled beer selection. The bar is to the left and a brasserie to the right; the excellent food is available in both. Muse is a wholly no-smoking venue and is also free of music and game machines.

Q◐◑P⚟

Royal Oak

60 North Street, LS22 6NR

12 (4 Mon)-11; 12-3, 7-10.30 Sun

(01937) 580508

John Smith's Bitter; Tetley Bitter; guest beer Ⓗ

Cheery, traditional local where old photos of Wetherby, internal stained glass and various statuettes draw the eye. The L-shaped room splits into two areas, both served from the same bar. There is a real fire and a small TV in the cosy left-hand bar. Unobtrusive background music means that everyone can enjoy a natter. No lunches are served Saturday. ⌂◐

Widdop

Pack Horse Inn (The Ridge) ✔

HX7 7AT

(midway between Hebden Bridge and Colne) OS952317

12-3 (not winter Tue-Fri), 7-11; closed Mon; 12-10.30 Sun

(01422) 842803

Black Sheep Best Bitter, Special; Greene King Old Speckled Hen; Thwaites Original; guest beer (summer) Ⓗ

Converted stone farmhouse next to the old packhorse route, and close to the Pennine Way. Isolated, but affording spectacular moorland views, it is popular with diners and walkers. Excellent food (no chips) comes in portions aimed at hearty eaters. The accommodation is useful if you plan to sample the 100-plus malt whiskies. Booking is recommended for the separate restaurant (open Sat). Stone fireplaces, exposed stone walls and old, well-fed, labradors add character here.

⌂Q❀⇌◐◑P

Wintersett

Anglers Retreat

Ferry Top Lane, WF4 2EB

(between Crofton and Ryhill) OS382157

12-3, 7-11; 12-11 Sat; 12-10.30 Sun

(01924) 862370

Acorn Barnsley Bitter; John Smith's Bitter; Samuel Smith OBB; Theakston XB; guest beer Ⓗ

Locally known as the Sett, this two-roomed pub has a tap room full of locals telling stories of their hunting days. This free house is popular with anglers and 'twitchers', as it is close to the Anglers Country Park. It is accessible by bus nos. 195 and 197 from Wakefield. The car park is opposite the pub.

⌂Q❀⊟♣P

Blue Bell, York

Wales

GLAMORGAN

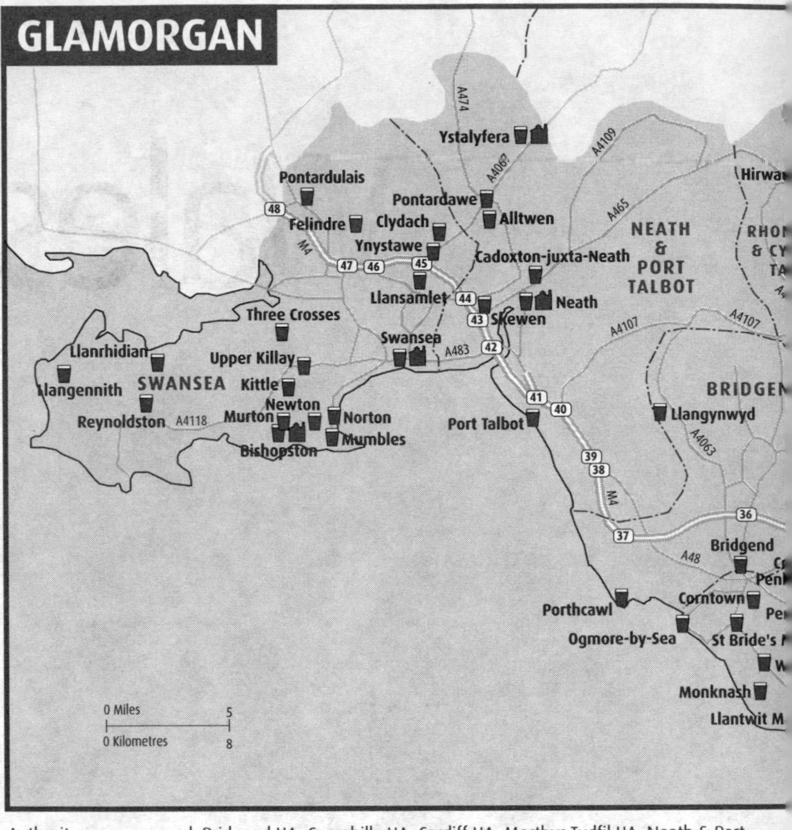

Authority areas covered: Bridgend UA, Caerphilly UA, Cardiff UA, Merthyr Tydfil UA, Neath & Port Talbot UA, Rhondda, Cynon, Taff UA, Swansea UA, Vale of Glamorgan UA

Abercarn

Old Swan

55 Commercial Road, NP11 5AJ

12-11; 12-10.30 Sun

(01495) 243161

Courage Best Bitter; H/G **guest beer** H

Welcoming, Valleys roadside local with a cosy bar and comfortable lounge. The atmosphere is enhanced by the bar's real fire. The pub has a strong community spirit and a deserved reputation for charity fundraising. Unusually for the area, the regular ale is offered via handpump and gravity – the latter known as 'cold tea'. ⌂◐♣

Aberdare

Cambrian Inn

60 Seymour Street, CF44 7DL

11-5, 7-11; 11-11 Fri & Sat; 12-10.30 Sun

(01685) 879120

Beer range varies H

Pleasant town pub just a short walk from the main shopping area. The comfy interior draws a mixed clientele. Only one ale is served, but this is invariably well sourced and changes frequently. The pub sign portrays a famous conductor from Aberdare, 'Caradog' or Griffith Rhys-Jones. Aberdare is situated at the railway terminus in the Cynon Valley. ◐≹♣

Aberthin

Farmers Arms

Cowbridge Road, CF71 7HB

12-3, 6-11; 12-2, 7-10.30 Sun

(01446) 773429

Wadworth 6X; guest beer H

Popular pub one mile from Cowbridge on the main road towards Ystradowen. It keeps one regular real ale plus one guest. Food, of excellent quality and value, is served all day. There is ample parking and extensive outdoor facilities for summer. The pub changed hands in 2003; the current owner was formerly licensee of the Barley Mow in Craig Penllyn. ❀◐◑⊟♿♣P⊬

Alltwen

Butchers Arms

Alltwen Hill, SA8 3BP

12-midnight; 12-10.30 Sun

(01792) 863100

Fuller's London Pride, ESB; John Smith's Bitter; Wadworth 6X; guest beers H

Set high above the Swansea Valley, the friendly atmosphere in this pub is enhanced by a real fire. The piano may be used by all customers. Pub food is available and a la carte meals are served in the recommended restaurant with waitress service. Live music is performed occasionally. ⌂❀◐◑P

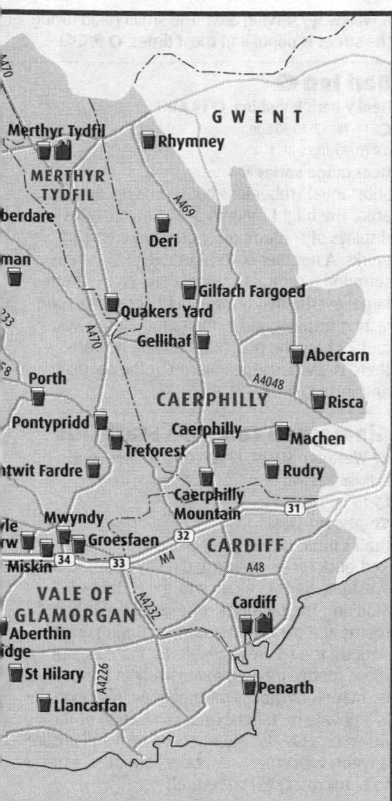

Bishopston

Joiner's Arms

50 Bishopston Road, SA3 3EJ

11.30-11; 12-10.30 Sun

☎ (01792) 232658

Courage Best Bitter; Marston's Pedigree; Swansea Bishopswood, Three Cliffs Gold, Original Wood; guest beers Ⓗ

Attractive, stone village pub, dating from the 1860s; the Swansea Brewing Company is based here. Popular with locals and always busy, the food enjoys a good reputation. Beer festivals are held occasionally, further extending the range at local CAMRA's Pub of the Year 2002 and 2003, and regional winner in 1999. The bus from Swansea to Bishopston stops outside; the car park is small – if full try 100 yards down the hill. ♨Q❀◐◑⊟♣P

Bridgend

Wyndham Arms ✔

Dunraven Place, CF31 1JE

10-11; 12-10.30 Sun

☎ (01656) 663608

Brains SA; Marston's Burton Bitter, Pedigree; guest beers Ⓗ

Originally an 18th-century coaching inn, although it may be older and have medieval foundations. It now caters for travellers of the 21st century as a Wetherlodge. Different areas add to the atmosphere of this old inn and the history of Bridgend is displayed around the walls. Regular guest beers make this an interesting place to visit. Q⇄◐◑♿⇌⊁

Cadoxton-juxta-Neath

Crown & Sceptre Inn

Main Road, SA10 8AP

12-3 (not Mon), 5-11; 11-11 Fri & Sat; 12-10.30 Sun

☎ (01639) 642145 website: www.crownandsceptreinn.co.uk

Draught Bass; Tomos Watkin OSB; guest beer Ⓗ

Built in 1835, as a tap for the nearby Vale of Neath Brewery, this former coach house has a public bar and lounge. The stable has been converted into a fine restaurant. It has an excellent reputation for its ale and freshly-cooked food (no food Sun eve or Mon). It is well run, trouble-free and has a pleasant atmosphere. Near Neath town centre, it is close to tourist attractions such as Aberdulais Falls and Neath Abbey. ⇄◐◑⊟♿P⊁

Caerphilly

Masons Arms

Mill Road, CF83 3FE

12-11; 12-10.30 Sun

☎ (029) 208 83353

Adnams Bitter; Brains Bitter; guest beer Ⓗ

Traditional suburban local, a short walk from the town centre and castle. A proper bar has pool, darts and a juke box, while the rear lounge is where food is served (not Sun eve). The lounge is divided into two, with smoking permitted in one part. The Masons offers a welcome refuge from the excesses of the town centre at weekends. The small garden opens up to a large public park at the rear. Q❀◐◑⊟♣P

Caerphilly Mountain

Black Cock Inn

CF83 1NF (off A469) OS145848

12-11; 12-10.30 Sun

☎ (029) 208 80534 website: www.blackcock-inn.com

Hancock's HB; Felinfoel Double Dragon; guest beer Ⓗ

Traditional pub in a rural setting, the bar has a wood floor, and is friendly to dogs and walkers. The combined lounge/restaurant is no-smoking throughout. All meals are freshly home cooked based on produce from local suppliers, daily specials include fresh fish. The large garden has children's activity frames for summer use. ♨Q❀◐◑⊟⋏♣P⊁

Cardiff

Albany

105 Donald Street, Roath, CF24 4TL (off Albany Rd at Woolworths)

12 (11 Sat)-11; 12-10.30 Sun

☎ (029) 203 11075

INDEPENDENT BREWERIES

Brains Cardiff
Bryncelyn Ystalyfera
Bullmastiff Cardiff
Eagles Bush Neath
Rhymney Merthyr Tydfil
Swansea Bishopston
Tomos Watkin Swansea

Brains Dark, Bitter, SA, seasonal beers Ⓗ
Local CAMRA's Pub of the Year 2005 stands on a street corner in a residential area. With something to suit all, its two distinct rooms are separated by the bar area. The public bar offers a lively environment, with a large-screen TV while the lounge has a much more relaxed atmosphere. A skittle alley is available via a doorway from the public bar. In summer a beer in the large garden is a must – see the rabbits, budgerigars, quails and zebra finches.
Q ❀ ◐ ⊟ ♣

Black Lion ✔

Cardiff Road, Llandaff, CF5 2DP (at A4119/High St jct)
11-11; 12-10.30 Sun
☎ (029) 205 67312
Brains Dark, Bitter, SA, Rev James Ⓗ
Well established, traditional pub on a busy street corner, identified by its Victorian half-timbered exterior. A fairly basic public bar and comfortable lounge each has its own entrance, but they are connected internally via a passageway. Frequent bus services run from the city centre and parking is available in a public car park off the High Street. Q ◐ ⊟ ⇌ (Fairwater)

Cayo Arms

36 Cathedral Road, CF11 9LL
12-11; 12-10.30 Sun
☎ (029) 203 91910
Tomos Watkin Brewery Bitter, Merlin Stout, OSB, seasonal beers; guest beers Ⓗ
Named after Julian 'Cayo' Evans, the infamous founder of the Free Wales Army, this popular pub was Cardiff CAMRA's Pub of the Year in 2001 and 2002. The single bar appeals to all. It is the only regular Cardiff outlet for Tomos Watkin beers; guest ales usually come from larger established brewers. Both front and rear outside drinking areas prove popular at busy periods and in summer. A 10-minute walk takes you to the city centre, across the river bridge.
Q ❀ ⇄ ◐ ◑ P

Chapter Arts Centre

Market Road, Canton, CF5 1QE (off Cowbridge road)
6 (5 Thu)-11; 1-12.30am Fri; 1-11 Sat; 1-10.30 Sun
☎ (029) 203 11050 website: www.chapter.org
Brains Rev James; guest beers Ⓗ
Thriving arts centre housing a single bar and a dining area that doubles as seating for drinkers during the inevitable busy evening. See a film, watch a play, join one of the many clubs or go there just to enjoy a drink in the contemporary surroundings. The three guest beers, often from local micro-breweries, are supplemented by an extensive range of continental beers and cider in summer. German beerfests are held in May and October. It is served by frequent buses.
Q ◐ ♿ ● P

Conway ✔

58 Conway Road, Pontcanna, CF11 9NW
12-11; 12-10.30 Sun
☎ (029) 202 32797
Beer range varies Ⓗ
Mainly frequented by locals in a residential area of bedsits and flats, the pub occupies a street-corner position. Up to six changing guest beers are on offer, mainly from long-established breweries. The bar and lounge are connected by a walkway/serving area. The small patio facing the street is popular at most times. Q ❀ ◐ ⊟

Deri Inn ✔

Heol y Deri, Rhiwbina, CF14 6UH
11-11; 12-10.30 Sun
☎ (029) 206 95051
Beer range varies Ⓗ
Substantial Ember Inns house in a residential area. The bright modern decor incorporates displays of contemporary glassware and art works. A number of comfortable public areas surround a central bar. Beers are usually from large, established brewers, but occasional long-lasting festivals add to the range. Buses Nos. 21 and 23 pass the pub, but if driving beware – there is a vicious speed ramp at the car park entrance. Q ❀ ◐ ◑ ⊟ P

Glamorgan Council's Staff Club

17 Westgate Street, CF10 1DD (opp. entrance to National Stadium)
10-11; 12-10.30 Sun
☎ (029) 202 33216
Brains Dark, Bitter; guest beers Ⓗ
Red-brick corner building, directly opposite the Westgate Street entrance to the National Stadium. The premises consists of a number of rooms and bars on two storeys. During quieter periods, rooms are available for families, but these rooms are used extensively in the evening by numerous groups for meetings. Although this is a private members' club, production of this Guide or a CAMRA membership card will ensure a warm welcome. Guest beers are often from local micros. Q ♘ ⇌ (Central)

Goat Major ✔

33 High Street, CF10 1PU (on corner of High St and Castle St, opp. castle)
11-11; 12-10.30 Sun
☎ (029) 203 37161
Brains Dark, Bitter, SA, seasonal beers Ⓗ
Occupying a prime position at a busy road junction, opposite Cardiff Castle, this traditional Brains pub comprises a single bar. Although it has undergone refurbishment in recent years, it retains its Victorian style and character. Strong connections link it with the Royal Regiment of Wales – as the name implies. Q ◐ ⇌ (Central)

Mochyn Du

Sophia Close, CF11 9HW (near Welsh Institute of Sport)
12-11; 12-10.30 Sun
☎ (029) 203 71599
Brains BItter, Rev James; guest beers Ⓗ
Single-storey building, the one-time lodge for a long-since demolished home for the gentry. Translated from the Welsh language its name is Black Pig, although there is no certainty as to how the name came about. The single bar is supplemented by an extensive dining area, displaying bi-lingual Welsh and English signage. A haunt of Welsh-speaking students, it is situated at the entrance to the National Cricket Centre and Welsh Institute of Sport. ❀ ◐ ◑

Old Cottage ✔

Cherry Orchard Road, Lisvane, CF14 0UE (100 yds W of Lisvane & Thornhill station)
11-11; 12-10.30 Sun
☎ (029) 207 64875

Beer range varies ⊞
Ember Inns house in the vicinity of Cefn Onn Park; a smart lounge bar with a plush, split-level seating area. While food forms a major part of the trade, a designated dining area ensures that this does not impinge upon the enjoyment of the pub atmosphere. Beers are mainly from established larger brewers.
Q❀◖◗⇌(Lisvane & Thornhill) P

Owain Glyndŵr
10 St John's Street, CF10 1GL (opp. St John's Church)
⏲ 12-11 (midnight Thu; 1am Fri & Sat); 12-6 Sun
☎ (029) 202 21980
Beer range varies ⊞
Situated in the city centre pedestrianised area, in the shadow of St John's Church, this split-level bar is within a larger keg-only premises, but makes a complete contrast. The three handpumps mainly feature beers from regional brewers. Popular with daytime shoppers and office workers, beware that in the early part of the week it may close early. Westons Old Rosie Cider is sometimes available.
❀◖♿⇌(Central) 🍏

Pendragon ✔
Excalibur Drive, Thornhill, CF14 9BB
⏲ 11-11; 12-10.30 Sun
☎ (029) 206 10550
Brains Dark, Bitter, SA, seasonal beers ⊞
Modern estate pub reached by a long driveway. The central bar serves three drinking areas: a lounge, pool room and a function room with TV. Its elevated position provides views over Cardiff, particularly from the garden and children's play area. The licensee and his wife preserve the best traditions – he is a supporter of cask ales and she is dedicated to good quality food at reasonable prices. Keen supporters of local charities, customers have raised many thousands for worthwhile causes.
Q❀◖◗⊟♿P⍻

Vulcan
10 Adam Street, CF24 2FH (opp. prison)
⏲ 12-11; 12-10.30 Sun
☎ (029) 204 61580
Brains Bitter, SA ⊞
In an area earmarked for redevelopment, the future of this pub hangs very much in the balance. Opened in the 1850s, it represents an excellent example of a traditional drinking house. The frontage is tiled, and the wood floor in the bar still receives a regular sprinkling of sawdust. At the rear is a lounge, served by a hatch from the bar. Good value, home-cooked lunches are available.
Q◖⊟⇌(Central/Queen St) ♣

Westgate
49 Cowbridge Road East, CF11 9AD
⏲ 12-11; 12-10.30 Sun
☎ (029) 203 03926
Brains Dark, Bitter, SA, Rev James ⊞
On the corner of a major road junction, just over the river bridge this is a 1930s design by the famous architect Percy Thomas. The pub was refurbished three years ago to attract a wider clientele, and now features a bar, lounge and skittle alley. Its proximity to the National Stadium makes it a popular gathering place on match days when entry may be restricted.
Q◖◗⊟⇌(Central) ♣

Yard
42-43 St Mary's Street, CF10 1AD
⏲ 10-1am; 11-12.30 Sun
☎ (029) 202 27577
Brains Dark, Bitter, SA, Rev James ⊞
Situated in the old brewery yard, the former Albert is now unrecognisable as such. A lively two-storey establishment, its somewhat unusual decor includes considerable use of steel for the staircase and other fittings. Its location and extended hours make it an ideal venue for those who wish to continue enjoying a drink after the usual closing time of other premises in the vicinity. Outside drinking is possible in a covered walkway.
❀◖◗♿⇌(Central)

Clydach (Swansea)

Carpenters Arms
High Street, SA6 5LN (on B4603 through Clydach)
⏲ 11-11; 12-10.30 Sun
☎ (01792) 843333
Adnams Broadside; Fuller's London Pride; Young's Special; guest beers ⊞
Award-winning, stone-fronted pub with a busy public bar and a split-level lounge/restaurant. Live music is played most Saturdays, and real ale festivals held on bank holidays. A wide range of meals is served in the restaurant. There is a pleasant patio garden and ample parking. The pub is used by the local cycle group for meetings and events.
❀◖◗⊟♣P

Corntown

Golden Mile
Corntown Road, CF35 5BA (off A48, between Cowbridge and Bridgend) OS928774
⏲ 11-3, 5.30-11; 12-4, 7-10.30 Sun
☎ (01656) 654884
Evan Evans BB; guest beer ⊞
Set down below road level, this pub has a lounge and restaurant which is complemented by a small cosy bar. A real fire in the lounge adds to the atmosphere. Brassware adorns the fireplace, and Dave the dog adds his friendly welcome to visitors in the bar. The outside drinking area affords fine views over adjacent fields. The award-winning chef completes this pub's appeal.
⩕Q❀◖◗⊟P

Cowbridge

Vale of Glamorgan
53 High Street, CF71 7AE
⏲ 11.30-11; 12-10.30 Sun
☎ (01446) 772252
Draught Bass; Hancock's HB; Greene King Old Speckled Hen; Wye Valley Hereford Pale Ale; guest beer ⊞
Busy, old, market town pub, ideally situated on the High Street. The friendly clientele can enjoy excellent food here throughout the day, washed down by a fine choice of real ales. The regular beer festivals are well attended. There is no music, and no gambling

or cigarette machines, but it is popular with the younger generation, particularly at the weekend. Q≿❀⇔◑◐♣P

Craig Penllyn

Barley Mow

CF71 7RT (1½ miles N of A48) OS978773
✪ 12-11 (12-12.30am Fri & Sat); 12-10.30 Sun
☎ (01446) 772555
Hancock's HB; guest beers Ⓗ
This old established inn retains a special atmosphere; the real ale is always in good condition and the pub continues to supply some of the finest guest beers. The bar meals are reasonably priced and of excellent quality. Families are welcome and there is plenty of space in the large car park opposite. The pub is heated in winter by roaring log fires while a small garden at the rear is a bonus in summer. Keep your mobile phones switched off.
≿❀◑◐⊟♣P

Cwmaman

Falcon Inn

1 Incline Row, CF44 6LU OS008998
✪ 11-11; 12-10.30 Sun
☎ (01685) 873758 website: www.thefalcon.co.uk
Beer range varies Ⓗ
Although close to the village, this rural pub feels quite isolated at the end of a lane. It is popular in summer due to its riverside setting. Three beers are usually on offer. Well-appointed accommodation is available. A pub to visit and remember; note its large bar, built with wood from a local chapel. ❀⇔♿P

Deri

Old Club ✔

93 Bailey Street, CF81 9HX
✪ 4 (12 Sat)-11; 12-10.30 Sun
☎ (01443) 830278
Beer range varies Ⓗ
Visitors are always welcome at this friendly, independent social club. Two guest beers are on offer, with a range and diversity which is unusual for the area. The cellar is managed by enthusiasts who take pride in quality and presentation. Cwm Darran Country Park is nearby and a direct bus service from Bargoed stops close to the club. A selection of bottled continental beers is always available and cider is sold in summer. ❀⊟♿⚠●P

Felindre (Swansea)

Shepherds Country Inn

18 Heol-myddfai, SA5 7ND (2½ miles N of M4 jct 46)
✪ 11.30-3, 6-11 (11.30-11 summer Sat); 12-3, 6-10.30 (12-10.30 summer) Sun
☎ (01792) 794715
Wadworth 6X; guest beers Ⓗ
Village community pub: a single bar and a restaurant – note the old photographs of the locality on display. A free house, serving two guest beers, it also offers good quality, reasonably-priced food with an interesting selection on the specials blackboard. A pleasant, large, decked patio overlooks a children's grassy play area. En-suite accommodation is useful for visitors to the Lliw Reservoirs Country Park nearby. No evening meals are served Sunday or Monday in winter. ❀⇔◑◐P

Gellihaf

Coal Hole

Bryn Road, NP12 2QE (on A4049, S of Heur de Lys)
✪ 12-3, 6.30-11; 11-11 Fri & Sat; 12-10.30 Sun
☎ (01443) 830280
Hancock's HB; Shepherd Neame Spitfire; guest beers Ⓗ
Set back from the road, this friendly, comfortable one-bar pub was converted from a farm during the 19th century. The bar now occupies the stable. It offers regularly-changing guest ales. Extensive views can be enjoyed over the Rhymney Valley. There is a no-smoking restaurant, and the pub can appear quite food-oriented, however the landlord takes pride in offering an excellent pint of real ale; well worth a visit. ♔◑◐P

Gilfach Fargoed

Capel Hotel ✔

Park Place, CF81 8LW
✪ 12-3, 7-11; 12-11 Fri & Sat; 12-4, 8-10.30 Sun
☎ (01443) 830272
Brains SA; John Smith's Bitter; guest beers Ⓗ
This award-winning pub is among the finest for miles around. Many original features give a homely touch, and it would be easy to imagine the bar full of tired colliers as it once was. Today's customers enjoy up to three guest beers, plus a guest cider. Mid-Glamorgan CAMRA's Pub of the Year 2004 displays an enthusiastic approach to real ale, with an annual beer festival held in early May. Note: the local station is a request stop. Q❀⇔⇛♣●⚟

Groesfaen

Dynevor Arms ✔

Llantrisant Road, CF72 8NS (off A4119) OS061810
✪ 11-11; 12-3, 7-10.30 Sun
☎ (029) 208 90530
Adnams Broadside; Draught Bass; Hancock's HB; guest beers Ⓗ
Popular, comfortable village pub, that caters for disabled customers and families. Well decorated on the inside, on the outside it is colourfully signposted and painted in traditional pub colours. Changing guest beers come from various brewers. An area is set aside for darts, dominoes and cards, and either live music or a quiz is staged on Sunday evening. A dining area enhances the open-plan bar facilities and the varied menu represents good value (no food Sun eve). ❀◑◐♿♣●P

Hirwaun

Glancynon Inn

Swansea Road, CF44 9PH
✪ 11-11; 12-10.30 Sun
☎ (01658) 811043
Beer range varies Ⓗ
Large country pub, with oak beams and a congenial atmosphere. Popular with drinkers and diners, it is the main real ale pub for a sizeable neighbourhood. Bookings are essential

for Sunday lunch (no meals Sun eve). The pub offers a well-appointed and pleasantly decorated lounge and a split-level bar. A little way off the main roads, it is nonetheless easy to find. ❀⊂◗ ⊟♣P

Kittle

Beaufort Arms ✔

18 Pennard Road, SA3 3JS

11-11; 12-10.30 Sun

☎ (01792) 234521

Brains Bitter, Buckley's Best Bitter, Rev James, seasonal beers H

Reputedly the oldest pub in Gower, the original part, now the lounge, boasts a beamed ceiling and some early stonework. A Brains' tenanted house with three bars and a function room, it also offers outdoor seating, a covered decked area and a children's playground. The pub has won various community and Gower in Bloom awards. A quiz is held on Monday and the pub hosts the local ladies darts team. An extensive menu is served; meals are available all day Friday-Sunday. ❀⊂◗ ⊟♣P

Llancarfan

Fox & Hounds

CF62 3AD

12-2.30, 6.30-11; 12-3, 7-10.30 Sun

☎ (01446) 781287

Brains Bitter, Rev James; guest beer H

Cosy traditional pub with a no-smoking dining area. Situated in an attractive part of the vale, it plays an important role in the village community. A recent addition is the B&B accommodation. Traditional wooden settles and a fine outside drinking area add to its appeal, while the fire is a welcome sight on a cold winter's night. No food is served Monday evening. ⌂Q❀⊂◗ ⊟P⊬

Llangennith

King's Head

SA3 1HX

11-11; 12-10.30 Sun

☎ (01792) 386212

Flowers IPA, Original; guest beers (summer) H

Historic pub on the village green, extended over the centuries as adjoining farm buildings have been incorporated. There are splendid views of nearby beaches that are within walking distance for the energetic. The pub is popular with visitors to nearby caravan and camping sites, especially in the holiday periods, and a games room is available. Food is served all day. Note the old pictures in the bar, including those of Phil Tanner, the legendary Gower folk singer. ⌂Q❀⊂◗ ⊟Δ♣P

Llangynwyd

Old House/Yr Hen Dŷ ✔

CF34 9SB (opp. church) OS858889

12-11; 12-10.30 Sun

☎ (01656) 733310

Flowers Original; Worthington's Bitter; guest beer H

Thatched pub that dates back to 1147, featuring a large fireplace with high-backed settles around it; do not get dazzled by the gleaming copper-topped tables and brasswork. The restaurant affords views of the Bryncynan Valley. A Welsh folk custom, the Mari Llwyd, is kept alive in the village and is represented on the pub sign. The extensive garden incorporates an adventure playground. A good range of whiskies is available, including Penderyn Welsh Whisky. Read about Wil Hopcyn (1701–41) and Ann Thomas, the Maid of Cefn Ydfa, here. ⌂❀⊂◗ ΔP

Llanrhidian

Greyhound Inn

Oldwalls, SA3 1HA

11-11; 12-10.30 Sun

☎ (01792) 391027

Draught Bass; Flowers IPA; Wadworth 6X; guest beer (occasional) H

Free house with an excellent atmosphere situated on the main north Gower road. The food is popular – especially local fish and the Sunday carvery. Families are welcome in the games room and food is served all day in the bars and the restaurant. There is a function room, a garden, and a welcoming fire in winter. Sometimes a guest beer replaces one of the regulars. ⌂Q❀⊂◗ ⊟Δ♣P

Llansamlet (Swansea)

Plough & Harrow

57 Church Road, SA7 9RL (off A48, 200 yds N of traffic lights)

12-11; 12-10.30 Sun

☎ (01792) 772263

Tomos Watkin, OSB, seasonal beers; guest beers H

Semi-rural, Celtic Inns pub where the large bar has seating arranged in comfortable groups, and an open fire at one end. It serves reasonably-priced bar meals downstairs and has a no-smoking dining room upstairs. Bench seating is provided in front of the pub for fine weather drinkers. Good disabled access and facilities are provided, family groups are especially welcome. A charity quiz is run by the vicar from the church next door on Wednesday evening. ⌂❀⊂◗ ♿P

Llantwit Fardre

Bush Inn

Main Road, CF38 2EP

11-11; 12-10.30 Sun

☎ (01443) 203958

Beer range varies H

Busy village local, recently extended, but still retaining its cosy atmosphere. Regular quiz, darts and sixties record nights are held. Guest beers usually change every few days, and come from far and wide. There is usually a locally brewed bitter available. The Pontypridd-Bridgend bus passes the pub. ❀♣P

Llantwit Major

King's Head

East Street, CF61 1XY

11.30-11; 12-10.30 Sun

☎ (01446) 792697

Brains Dark, Bitter, SA; guest beer H

WALES

Friendly, town-centre pub with a loyal local following. Sporting events are shown on a large screen in the public bar, which is lively with pool players, dominoes and chat. The lounge is quieter, except when a Wales rugby match is on, and is bright and airy. Both food and beer are of excellent quality and represent good value. ♛Q♉❀◐⊟⛺≠♣P

Old Swan Inn

Church Street, CF61 1SB

⏲ 12-11; 12-10.30 Sun

☎ (01446) 792230

Beer range varies Ⓗ

Local CAMRA's Pub of the Year 2005, its awards now include an accolade for pub food; eat here and you will find out why. A changing selection of beers from all over the country adds to the enjoyment of visiting this pub. With warming fires, large gardens and a varied clientele, the pub is suitable for all the family. A huge range of food, wine and ale gives everyone a superb choice. It is well worth a visit; cider is sold in summer. ♛❀◐◑⊟⛺≠♣●

Machen

White Hart

Nant-y-Ceisiad, CF83 8QQ (100 yds N of A468 at W end of village) OS203892

⏲ 12-3, 6.30-11 (12-11 summer Sat); 12-10.30 Sun

☎ (01633) 441005

Beer range varies Ⓗ

Independent free house offering four guest beers. This rambling old pub has been much extended over the years, incorporating panels and fittings from the classic liner Empress of France. A good range of food is served, but Sunday lunches can be busy so booking is advisable. Occasional beer festivals are held. Opening hours may vary in winter, so phone ahead. ❀⇄◐◑♣P⊬

Merthyr Tydfil

Rose & Crown ✔

Morgan Street, CF47 8TP (off Brecon Rd, S of Cyfarthfa Park)

⏲ 12-11; 12-10.30 Sun

☎ (01685) 723743

Brains Bitter; Rhymney Brewery Centenary Ale, Bevans Bitter; guest beers Ⓗ

Busy local, that also attracts many visitors – check for famous names in the visitors' book. Originally cottages, this many-roomed pub hosted prayer meetings in the 19th century. The beer range changes regularly and features nationally popular ales alongside less common ones. The former Giles & Harrap Brewery buildings are still standing further up Brecon Road. ◐♿≠

Miskin

Miskin Arms

Hensol Road, CF72 8JQ (off B4264)

⏲ 11.30-11; 12-10.30 Sun

☎ (01443) 224326

Brains Bitter; Everards Tiger; guest beers Ⓗ

The first mention in local records of the Miskin Arms was in 1741. Food is listed on a two-tier menu, with one operating 12-2pm and the other main menu taking over 2-9pm. Everards Tiger is considered to be the house beer; the guests are usually seasonal brews. The bar/lounge overlooks the large car park and garden; a small decked platform area has further seating. ❀◐◑♿≠(Pontyclun) P

Monknash

Plough & Harrow

CF71 7QQ (off B4265, between Wick and Marcross)

⏲ 12-11; 12-10.30 Sun

☎ (01656) 890209

Archers Golden; Draught Bass; Wye Valley Hereford Pale Ale; Worthington's Bitter; guest beer Ⓗ

A welcome return to the Guide for this well-known watering hole under its new licensee. The range and quality of ales remains excellent. The two-roomed pub is located in what was a medieval grange; the public bar having once been a mortuary. Visitors to the lounge are advised that the real ale is in the bar, including up to five guests in winter (seven in summer), plus Westons Old Rosie Cider. The food here also makes it well worth a visit. ♛❀◐◑⊟♿⛺♣●P

Mumbles

Mumbles Rugby Club

588 Mumbles Road, SA3 4DL

⏲ 6.30 (4 Sat)-11; closed Wed; 12-5 Sun

☎ (01792) 368989

Tomos Watkin OSB, seasonal beers; Worthington's Bitter Ⓗ

This fine old club, established in 1887, welcomes non-members. The licensees are committed to real ale here and Tomos Watkin's OSB and seasonal ales are available at all times. The large function room upstairs gets quite lively on international match days. Their 'cracker sevens' rugby tournament, held every year on August bank holiday weekend, coincides with the Mumbles beer festival. ⊟♣

Park Inn

23 Park Street, SA3 4DA

⏲ 4 (12 Fri & Sat)-11; 12-10.30 Sun

☎ (01792) 366738

Swansea Three Cliffs Gold; guest beers Ⓗ

Traditional back-street pub that is a favourite with real ale drinkers in the area. It offers four changing guest beers, with the accent on Welsh and West Country independent breweries. Cider is sold in summer. There is a separate room for darts and a quiz is held on Thursday. A fine collection of pump clips and pictures of old Mumbles add to the warm, welcoming atmosphere. Twice the Park Inn has been voted Swansea CAMRA Pub of the Year. Q♣●

Victoria Inn

21 Westbourne Place, SA3 4DB

⏲ 11-11; 12-10.30 Sun

☎ (01792) 380111

Draught Bass; Greene King Old Speckled Hen; Worthington's Bitter Ⓗ

Lovely, old back-street corner local dating from the mid-19th century, as the name implies. The pub has been sympathetically renovated, retaining the stained glass windows and making a feature of the old well, which was probably the water source in the days when the pub brewed its own beer. The single room is divided into two distinct areas – the bar area has darts and TV while the other end is a little quieter. ❀

Murton

Plough & Harrow

88 Oldway, SA3 3DJ

⊙ 11-11; 12-10.30 Sun

☎ (01792) 234459

Courage Best Bitter, Directors; guest beers [H]

One of the oldest pubs in Gower, it has been enlarged and renovated in recent times but has retained its character. The pub combines a busy food trade with its tradition as a village local. The bar has TV and a pool table, which attracts younger customers, while the lounge is a comfortable place to enjoy a quiet chat or a meal. Quiz night is Tuesday. Heaters in the garden are useful on chillier evenings.

Q❀◐◑♣P

Mwyndy

Barn at Mwyndy

Cardiff Road, CF72 8PJ (down lane opp. Corner Park Garage on A4119) OS056816

⊙ 11-11; 12-10.30 Sun

☎ (01443) 222333

Beer range varies [H]

Converted, 16th-century long barn displaying an array of country memorabilia, including a coracle. The split-level bar has a log fire. Amenities include a good no-smoking restaurant (reservations advised), a garden with children's play area, and a meeting room. Regular beer festivals, occasional music and a serious interest in petanque are added attractions. Up to six guest beers are stocked, usually including one from Bullmastiff, Tomos Watkin or other Welsh breweries. It won local CAMRA's Pub of the Year award in 2001 and 2002. ⩩❀◐◑♿P

Neath

Borough Arms

New Henry Street, SA11 1PH

⊙ 4 (12 Sat)-11; 12-10.30 Sun

☎ (01639) 644902

Beer range varies [H]

Traditional, back-street pub that has been transformed by the new owner into a brew-pub and real ale oasis in a town where the emphasis is on nitro-keg. The L-shaped bar keeps a choice of up to four real ales, including many from micro-breweries and always one beer from the Eagles Bush Brewery, established in September 2004 at the rear. The four beers brewed, named after birds of prey, are exclusive to the pub.

Q♉❀⇌♣●

Highlander

2-4 Lewis Road, SA11 1EQ (near Stockhams roundabout on A474)

⊙ 11-11; 12-10.30 Sun

☎ (01639) 633586

Draught Bass; Hancock's HB; guest beers [H]

Quiet pub with a split-level interior. A good range of beers is sold, with at least three real ales on at any time. Good bar food and snacks are available downstairs, there is a dedicated dining area on the upper level and a restaurant upstairs (eve meals served Tue-Sat). A quiz night is held every Sunday. The pub is within easy walking distance of the town centre. Q◐◑⇌

Newton (Swansea)

Newton Inn

New Well Lane, SA3 4SR

⊙ 12-11; 12-10.30 Sun

☎ (01792) 363226

Draught Bass; [H]/[G] Fuller's London Pride; Greene King Abbot; Worthington's Bitter; guest beers [H]

Refurbished, village local retaining the bar and lounge areas in a semi open-plan layout. The pub offers competitively-priced meals and is popular with diners at lunchtime and early evening. The bar has a big-screen TV, which is used for sporting events. The draught beers, particularly the Bass, can be drawn straight from the cask on request; the landlord regularly changes the guests. Quizzes are held on Monday and Wednesday. Roadside tables are placed outside for alfresco drinking. ❀◐◑⊟

Norton (Swansea)

Beaufort Arms

1 Castle Road, SA3 5TF (turn by Norton House Hotel, off Mumbles Rd)

⊙ 11.30-11; 12-10.30 Sun

☎ (01792) 401319

Draught Bass; Brains SA; Greene King Abbot [H]

Village local, dating from the 18th century, with a traditional public bar and a smaller, comfortable lounge, recently refurbished. Both rooms have real fires. The bar has darts and a TV and a quiz is held every Tuesday. See the photographs of the annual Mumbles Raft Race on the walls, including one splendid picture of a raft built to replicate the pub itself. The Beaufort retains a friendly charm. ⩩Q❀⊟♣

Ogmore-by-Sea

Pelican in her Piety ✔

CF32 0QP

⊙ 12-11; 12-10.30 Sun

☎ (01656) 880049

Draught Bass; Fuller's London Pride; Greene King Old Speckled Hen; Worthington's Bitter; Wye Valley Hereford Pale Ale [H]

Situated near Ogmore Castle, this is a welcoming village local with a cosy log fire in winter. A recent investment in a cooling system for cask ales shows the commitment to high standards of cellarmanship. The same care is applied to the food, adding to this pub's appeal. The locals continue to support charity events. Cask ales are served without a sparkler. ⩩Q❀◐◑▲P⚡

Sealawns

Slon Lane, CF32 0PN

⊙ 12-3, 6-11; 12-3; 6-10.30 Sun

☎ (01656) 880311

Felinfoel Double Dragon; Worthington's Bitter; guest beer (summer) [H]

Extended from a 16th-century cottage, this hotel benefits from superb views over the Bristol Channel. The small, cosy bar complements the restaurant and function room; outside is a large

garden. This is a regular outlet for Felinfoel and a guest beer is added in summer.
♨Q❀⇌◖◗⊟⋀♣P

Penarth

Bear's Head ⊘

37-39 Windsor Road, CF64 1JD

✪ 10-11; 12-10.30 Sun

☎ (02920) 706424

Marston's Burton Bitter, Pedigree; Brains SA; Bullmastiff Welsh Gold, Son of a Bitch; guest beer Ⓗ

This Wetherspoon's pub is popular with many people, including the brewers from Bullmastiff Brewery. Hardly an architectural gem, but the pub is a welcome change from the usual local outlets. The family area is upstairs, where modern art paintings add decorative appeal. The pub is named after the English translation of the town's name – Pen-arth meaning Bear's Head – but you will not find any bears here today and the head is on the top of your pint.
Q☋◖◗♿⇶⊬

Penllyn

Red Fox

CF71 7RQ (off A48 at Pentre Meyrick)

✪ 12-3 (not Mon), 6-11; 12-10.30 Sun

☎ (01446) 772352

Hancock's HB; Tomos Watkin OSB; guest beer Ⓗ

This charming country inn continues to enjoy a fine reputation for the quality of its real ale and excellent cuisine. It is now in its sixth year of business since reopening (with the help and support of CAMRA) and is gaining in popularity. It is a friendly local with much character; in winter it boasts a roaring log fire where roasted chestnuts are enjoyed by all. ♨Q❀◖◗♿♣P

Pontardawe

Pontardawe Inn

123 Herbert Street, SA8 4ED

✪ 12-11; 12-10.30 Sun

☎ (01792) 830791

Brains Buckley's Best Bitter, Rev James; guest beers Ⓗ

Attractive, two-bar village inn, known locally as the Gwachel. It stands alongside the River Tawe cycle path. Notes and artefacts relating to local history are displayed in one bar; the other houses a large-screen TV for sporting events. Busy during the Pontardawe music festival held during the third weekend in August, Wednesday is when the acoustic music club meets weekly. Boules is played. The riverside restaurant is busy (no meals Sun eve). The pub was previously a local CAMRA Pub of the Year. ❀◖◗♿P

Pontardulais

Fountain Inn

Bolgoed Road, SA4 8JP (on A48)

✪ 12 (5 Mon)-11; 12-10.30 Sun

☎ (01792) 882501

Greene King Abbot; Wells Bombardier; Worthington's Bitter Ⓗ

A first-time entry for this comfortable roadside pub with its award-winning adjoining restaurant where booking is recommended for evening meals and Sunday lunch. The pub bears strong historical connections with the Rebecca Riots, and a stone obelisk on the road opposite commemorates the burning of the nearby Bolgeod tollgate in July 1843. Bus service X13 runs every 20 minutes (daytime) from Swansea city centre. The beer range may vary. Q⇌◖◗P

Pontypridd

Bunch of Grapes

Ynysangharad Road, CF37 4DA (behind retail park, off A4054)

✪ 11-11; 12-10.30 Sun

☎ (01443) 402934

website: www.bunchofgrapes.org.uk

Black Sheep Best Bitter; Wye Valley Hereford Pale Ale; guest beers Ⓗ

A short walk from the town centre, you are assured of a warm welcome in this comfortable free house. Two guest ales supplement the regulars – an occasional Cornish bias may be evident. Home-cooked fare is available both in the bar and the award-winning no-smoking restaurant; booking is advised, particularly for Sunday lunch – (no meals Sun eve).
♨❀◖◗⇶♣P⊬

Llanover Arms

Bridge Street, CF37 4PE (opp. entrance to Ynysyharad Park)

✪ 12-11; 12-3, 7-10.30 Sun

☎ (01443) 403215

Brains Dark, Bitter; guest beer Ⓗ

Kept by the same family for over a century, this town pub is well sited for visitors to the town's historic centre and the renowned Ynysynharad Park. The three rooms are festooned with a miscellany of bric-a-brac, including equine paintings, old mirrors, maps and (non-working) clocks. A popular feature is the constantly-changing guest ale, which attracts a loyal following. Note: if using the car park obtain a ticket from the bar or risk clamping. Q❀⇶♣P

Porth

Rheola

Rheola Road, CF39 0LF (on A4058, 200 yds S of bus depot)

✪ 2 (1 Fri; 12 Sat)-11; 12-10.30 Sun

☎ (01443) 682633

Draught Bass; Butcombe Gold; guest beer Ⓗ

Comfortable, friendly pub with a lively bar and a smart lounge. A guest ale is offered each weekend to supplement the two regular beers. Situated at the 'Gateway to the Rhondda' and only a short distance north of the Rhondda Heritage Park, this is a pub not to be missed. Both rail and bus stations are a short walk away.
❀⊟⇶♣P

Porthcawl

Lorelei Hotel

36-38 Esplanade Avenue, CF36 3YU

✪ 12-2, 5-11; 11-11 Fri; 12-10.30 Sun

☎ (01656) 788342

Draught Bass; Ⓖ **Tomos Watkin OSB; guest beers** Ⓗ

In a terraced street, this inconspicuous hotel is a real ale oasis. Two guest beers and a spring and

autumn beer festival add to its appeal. The number of pump clips show the commitment to a wide range of guest ales, and Budvar is available on draught along with other European beers. Real cider is available in summer. The hotel has two drinking areas and a dining room where children are admitted.
ᘔ❀⇌◗⅄♠

Port Talbot

Lord Caradoc ✔

69-73 Station Road, SA13 1NW
✪ 10-11.30; 12-10.30 Sun
☎ (01639) 896007
Greene King Abbot; Marston's Burton Bitter, Pedigree; guest beers H
This Wetherspoon's has all the usual features: good value food served all day; competitively priced beer and coffee; occasional beer festivals; no music. It is a spacious, open-plan pub where an L-shaped bar has an elevated drinking area. Situated in the centre of Port Talbot, about two minutes' walk from the mainline station, there is a small outside patio for summer drinking.
Q❀◖◗♿≹(Parkway)⊬

Quaker's Yard

Glantaff Inn

Cardiff Road, CF46 5AH (off A4054)
✪ 12-4, 7-11; 12-4, 7-10.30 Sun
☎ (01443) 410822
Courage Best Bitter; John Smith's Bitter; guest beers H
Comfortable inn, where you can peruse a large collection of water jugs, boxing memorabilia, old photographs and other items of interest. The three guest ales are popular, both with locals, and walkers and cyclists travelling along the Taff Trail which runs from Cardiff to Brecon through the post-industrial landscape of the valley of the River Taff. No evening meals are served Sunday.
❀◖◗▽

Reynoldston

King Arthur

Higher Green, SA3 1AD
✪ 12-11; 12-10.30 Sun
☎ (01792) 390775
Draught Bass; Felinfoel Double Dragon; Worthington's Bitter H
Imposing pub and hotel/restaurant, popular with both locals and tourists. The King Arthur is named after 'Arthur's Stone', a prehistoric monument situated on the nearby Cefn Bryn Hill. The hotel is in a most pleasant spot in the middle of the Gower Peninsula and has a large outdoor area. It is reputedly haunted by two ghosts. Meals are served in the bar as well as the restaurant, the family room and outside. The hotel has recently been extended.
♛❀⇌◖◗⊟♿♣P

Rhymney

Farmers Arms ✔

Brewery Row, NP22 5EZ (off A465 at Rhymney jct then A469 for 1 mile)
✪ 12-11; 12-3.30, 7-10.30 Sun
☎ (01685) 840257
Brains Bitter; Fuller's London Pride; guest beers H
Local community pub furnished with a traditional look to reflect the pub's history. It was sited near the former Rhymney Brewery; among the photographs and breweriana is a superb, framed display of medals won by the old brewery. The lounge and dining area offer affordable food. A function room is available for up to 40 guests. A quiz night is held on Thursday. This pub is frequented by rail travellers. Q❀◖◗≹♣P

Risca

Commercial ✔

Commercial Street, NP11 6BA (on B4591)
✪ 11-11; 12-10.30 Sun
☎ (01633) 612608
Beer range varies H
Large, bustling pub at the southern end of Risca, easily accessible by bus from Newport. The single bar has two distinct areas: one side is devoted to pool and darts, the other a more comfortable and quieter lounge. The ales on offer change often – to the satisfaction of the clientele, many of whom travel from as far away as Newport to sample them. ❀♣

Fox & Hounds

Park Road, NP11 6PW (next to park)
✪ 11-11; 12-10.30 Sun
☎ (01633) 612937
Beer range varies H
Lively local just across the park from Risca shops. The large-screen TV can be intrusive, but the opposite bar offers some peace. The beers are from regionals and micro-breweries. Good value meals include children's choices (eve meals Mon-Thu). A busy pub, it can be noisy at weekends. The Monmouthshire Canal (Newport-Crumlin branch) runs along the hillside to the rear of the pub. ❀◖◗♣P

Rudry

Maenllwyd Inn ✔

CF83 3EB (500 yds SW of village) OS201867
✪ 12-11; 12-10.30 Sun
☎ (024) 208 82372
Courage Best Bitter; Wells Bombardier; guest beers H
Bustling Chef & Brewer restaurant, based around a former farmhouse and later, a Victorian inn. A pleasant rural retreat close to Rudry common, it is within easy reach of Cardiff and Caerphilly. Two guest beers are usually sourced from regional and family brewers. The majority of the premises is no-smoking. A bar menu is offered at lunchtime; the restaurant serves meals all day. ♛Q❀◖P⊬

St Bride's Major

Farmers Arms

Wick Road, Pitcot, CF32 0SE
✪ 12-3, 6-11; 12-10.30 Sun
☎ (01656) 880224
Courage Best Bitter; Greene King Old Speckled Hen; Hancock's HB; Marston's Pedigree; Ushers Best Bitter H
Hugely popular pub and restaurant known as

'the pub on the pond' – it is obvious why when you get there. It attracts a good mix of locals and visitors. The food enjoys a reputation for both quality and value; booking for the restaurant is advised. China jugs hang from the beams and the windows in the bar offer views of the pond. A word of warning – do not try to touch the swans on the pond or you risk losing a finger. ⌂Q❀◑⊟♣P

St Hilary

Bush

CP71 7AD (off A48, E of Cowbridge)

11.30-11; 12-10.30 Sun

☎ (01446) 772745

Draught Bass; Greene King Old Speckled Hen; Hancock's HB; guest beer Ⓗ

This 400-year-old thatched pub stands near the church in an attractive village. The small bar has larger rooms opening off either side – the restaurant is to the right. A pleasant outside drinking area adds to the appeal, while a display of hops around the fireplace enhances the cosy atmosphere. Ask about the guest beer; the pub is also a rare outlet for real cider (Westons Old Rosie). No meals are served Sunday evening, but this is another pub with a fine reputation for food. ⌂Q❀◑⊟●P

Skewen

Crown

216 New Road, SA10 6EW

11-11; 12-10.30 Sun

☎ (01792) 411270

Brains Dark, Bitter, SA, seasonal beers Ⓗ

Pleasant, centrally-located community pub consisting of a public bar, a lounge and upstairs snooker room. Televised horse racing in the bar is popular with the regulars. This pub is a busy, cheery place where live music is enjoyed on Friday evening. The decor is traditional and comfortable, displaying some interesting music memorabilia in the lounge. It keeps the best range of Brains beers in the area, which can also be enjoyed in fine weather in an enclosed outside drinking area. ❀⊟♿⇌♣⚡

Swansea

Brunswick

3 Duke Street, SA1 4HS

12-11; 12-10.30 Sun

☎ (01792) 456676

Brains SA; Courage Best Bitter; Ⓗ **guest beers** Ⓖ

Long-established pub on the fringe of the city centre, where bare woodwork and rural pictures add to the cosy mood. A quiz is held on Monday and live music is staged twice a month. It is popular for food, especially the lunches, evening meals are served 6-8.30 (not Sun). Guest beers are dispensed on gravity. This pub is a regular outlet for the Swansea Brewing Company. ◑♣

Eli Jenkins Ale House

24 Oxford Street, SA1 4HS

11-11; 12-10.30 Sun

☎ (01792) 630961

Badger Tanglefoot; Worthington's Bitter; guest beer Ⓗ

Modern, city-centre pub, named after a character in the play Under Milk Wood by Dylan Thomas. Wooden alcoves and niches feature throughout, while the walls are adorned with paintings of the local Swansea and Gower area. The two guest beers change frequently. The pub attracts many lunchtime diners, but is usually quieter in the evening. ◑♿

Queen's Hotel

Gloucester Place, SA1 1TY

11-11; 12-10.30 Sun

☎ (01792) 521531

Brains Buckley's Best Bitter; Theakston Best Bitter, Old Peculier Ⓗ

Situated on the edge of the city centre and marina, this is a high-ceilinged, one-bar outlet with a smaller drinking area towards the rear. The walls display photographs depicting Swansea's maritime history. Entertainment includes a Sunday quiz and bingo on Wednesday evening. Lunches are served daily (12-2.30pm). It is a rare local outlet for Old Peculier, and Theakston Mild is also available (on cask breather). ❀◐

Westbourne Hotel ✔

1 Bryn-y-mor Road, SA1 4JQ

12-11; 12-10.30 Sun

☎ (01792) 476637

Greene King Abbot; guest beers Ⓗ

Comfortable Enterprise Inn 'free' house with an internal layout that manages to retain lounge and bar areas. Guest beers change frequently, with Marston's Pedigree and/or Wells Bombardier often on tap, along with regular Addlestones cider. Four seasonal mini-beerfests showcase up to six real ales. Ten minutes' walk from the city centre, the pub is popular with locals; there is a dartboard and two TVs for sport in the bar. Meals are served 12-8pm daily, during mealtimes the dining area is no-smoking. ❀◑♿♣●

Three Crosses

Poundffald Inn

Tirmynydd Road, SA4 3PB

12-11; 12-10.30 Sun

☎ (01792) 873428

Brains SA; Greene King Abbot, Old Speckled Hen Ⓗ

The Poundffald is a popular village local where the traditional public bar is warmed by a welcoming fire; note the interesting collection of horse bits, and other rural implements. The name refers to the old circular animal pound that was incorporated into the lounge. 'Ffald' is the Welsh word for pound and so the name is in both languages together. The lounge is mainly oriented towards food, which is served all day. ⌂♨❀◑⊟P

Treforest

Otley Arms

Forest Road, CF37 1SY (100 yds from station)

11-11; 12-10.30 Sun

☎ (01443) 402033

Bullmastiff Welsh Gold; guest beers Ⓗ

Tardis-like, end-of-terrace pub that finds locals rubbing shoulders with students from the nearby university. Both enjoy the ambience, the eclectic range of guest ales and the multiple screens that provide a wide choice for sports fans. There are disabled toilet facilities, but at present access to the pub is difficult for an unaccompanied wheelchair user. Lunches are served 11-4.30 (5 Sat and Sun). ◖⇌♣

Tyle Garw

Boar's Head

Coedcae Lane, Talbot Green, CF72 9EZ
(turn off A473 opp. L'Oréal factory entrance) OS029891
11-11; 12-10.30 Sun
☎ (01443) 225400
Brains Rev James; RCH Pitchfork; guest beers Ⓗ
CAMRA's regional Pub of the Year 2003 was built in 1845 to serve the heavy industries; it now sits among modern light industry and housing. It retains a country pub feel in its small bar, pool room and lounge. Serving up to seven real ales, the beer prices have not increased for three years. The no-smoking restaurant has a reputation for value (book for Sunday lunch). Special deals are available on steak (Mon) and curry (Wed) evenings (no meals Sun or Tue eve).
⌂❀◖◗⊟⩘⇌(Pontyclun) ●P

Upper Killay

Railway Inn

553 Gower Road, SA2 7DS
12-2, 4-11; 12-11 Sat; 12-10.30 Sun
☎ (01792) 203946
Swansea Deep Slade Dark, Bishopswood, Original Wood; guest beers Ⓗ
Built in 1864 this is a rare gem, full of character. The former railtrack is now a foot or cycle way to the seafront. Usually, there is a good selection of guest beers. Visitors find this a friendly house which can be difficult to leave. Occasional beer festivals are held and, from time to time, beers not normally seen in the area are served. It was voted CAMRA regional Pub of the Year in 2004.
⌂❀⊟♣P

Wick

Lamb & Flag

Church Street, CF71 7QE
11.30-11; 12-10.30 Sun
☎ (01656) 890278
Hancock's HB; guest beer Ⓗ
Welcoming village pub, just off the main road, comprising a large, airy public bar with a wide-screen TV and dartboard, and a small cosy lounge, where the serving area, with traditional settles and open fire, leads to a comfortable seating area. The guest beer is often from Cottage or Bullmastiff. The food includes home-made pies and curries among many other dishes.
⌂Q◖◗⊟♿⩘♣P

Ynystawe

Millers Arms

634 Clydach Road, SA6 5AX (on B4609, next to school)
11-3, 6-11; 11-11 Sat; 12-3, 7-10.30 Sun
☎ (01792) 842614
Caledonian Deuchars IPA; Greene King Abbot; Tomos Watkin OSB Ⓗ
Relaxing, roadside pub where good, wholesome food is served in the bar and adjoining restaurant (booking is recommended for eve meals and Sun lunch). The beer range may change from that given but will always include one of a premium gravity. Note the unusual teapot collection above the bar. The pub is easily accessed from Swansea city centre on regular daytime bus services X20, X21 and 122.
Q◖◗♿P

Ystalyfera

Wern Fawr Inn

47 Wern Road, SA9 2LY
7 (6.30 Sat)-11; 12-3.30, 7-11 Sun
☎ (01639) 843625
website: www.bryncelynbrewery.co.uk
Bryncelyn Holly Hop, Buddy Marvellous, Oh Boy, seasonal beers Ⓗ
Home of the Bryncelyn Brewery, the pub is extremely popular with real ale buffs who enjoy the multi-award-winning beers – all named after Buddy Holly songs (the landlord is an ardent fan). The bar, which contains a multitude of artefacts from years gone including and an old-fashioned stove, has to be seen to be believed. There is also a comfortable lounge at Swansea CAMRA's Pub of the Year 2005. Real ale is available to take away.
⌂❀⊟♣

WALES

Corker

'Open two bottles of stout, Jack,' said Mr O'Connor. 'How can I?' said the old man, 'when there's no corkscrew?' 'Wait now, wait now!' said Mr Henby getting up quickly. 'Did you ever see this little trick?' He took two bottles from the table and, carrying them to the fire, put them on the hob. Then he sat down again by the fire and took another drink from his bottle. In a few minutes an apologetic 'Pok!' was heard as the cork flew out of Mr Lyons' bottle. Mr Lyons jumped off the table, went to the fire, took his bottle and carried it to the table.

James Joyce, Ivy Day in the Committee Room, from Dubliners, 1914.

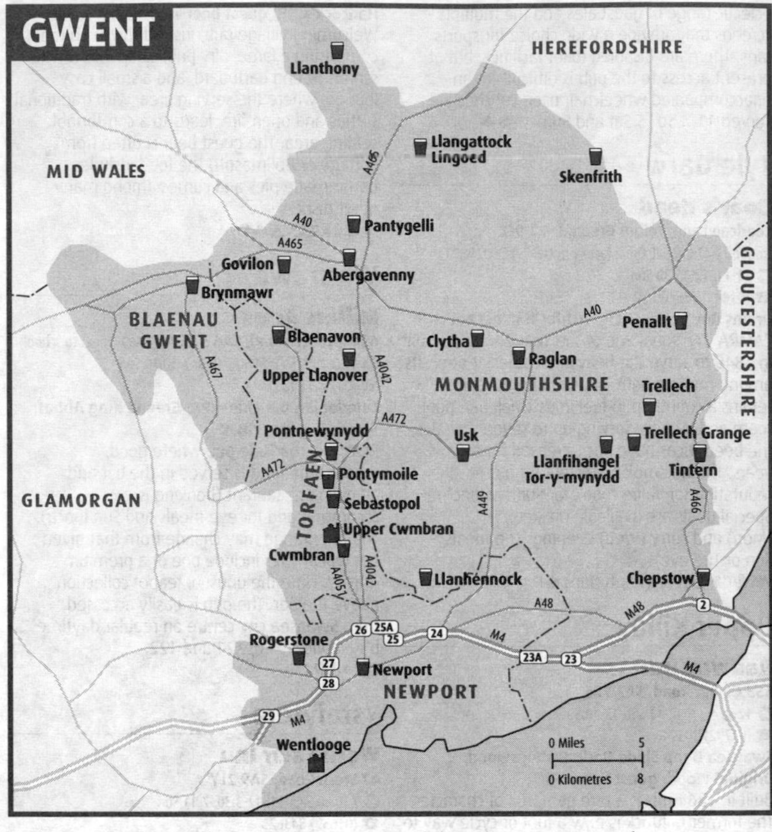

Authority areas covered Blaenau Gwent UA, Monmouthshire UA, Newport UA, Torfaen UA

Abergavenny

Angel Hotel

15 Cross Street, NP7 5EN

10-3, 6-11; 12-3, 7-10.30 Sun

(01873) 857121

website: www.angelhotelabergavenny.com

Draught Bass; Brains Rev James; guest beers H

The bar of the town's one-time coaching inn has been rejuvenated in line with the rest of the hotel to provide high-standard facilities for visitors. An excellent enclosed patio with heaters allows drinkers and diners to remain alfresco even on cooler summer evenings. A pianist plays in the bar at weekends and there is a beautifully-decorated lounge with armchairs that provides a relaxed atmosphere for those seeking a peaceful drink. ⌂Q❀⇌◖◗P

Cantreff Inn

61 Brecon Road, NP7 7RA

12-2.30, 6-11; 12-3, 7-10.30 Sun

(01873) 855827

Greene King Abbot; Wadworth 6X; guest beers H

A short walk from the town centre, situated on the road out to the hospital. The promotion of real ales by the landlord has seen a rise in their popularity and the changing guest beers are chosen by the regulars. There are separate drinking and dining areas either side of the entrance to the pub, while the enclosed garden provides a pleasant outdoor space for warm days. No children under five years are permitted. ❀◖◗P

Coliseum ✔

Lion Street, NP7 5DR

10-11; 12-10.30 Sun

(01873) 736960

Brains SA; Greene King Abbot; Marston's Burton Bitter, Pedigree; guest beers H

The biggest range of beers in town is the hallmark of this Wetherspoon pub. There is the usual formula of good value beers in a modern environment that appeals to drinkers of all ages. A former cinema, the cavernous bar with a high vaulted ceiling is often noisy, especially at weekends. Local beers from smaller breweries such as Cwmbran and Bullmastiff can often be found among the regular range. Q◖◗♿⍉

Hen & Chickens ✔

7 Flannel Street, NP7 5EG

10.30-11 (10 Tue & Fri); 12-10.30 Sun

(01873) 853613

Draught Bass; Brains Bitter; guest beer H

The Chicks is one of the best-known historic

INDEPENDENT BREWERIES

Cwmbran Upper Cwmbran

Warcop Wentlooge

pubs in South Wales, home to poetry and music groups and a venue for Abergavenny's food festival. Each room in the pub has its own character, from a small snug to a larger room with TV for match days. Outside tables create a continental café feel on warm days, while on Sunday afternoons a jazz band provides the entertainment. Guest beers are from the Brains brewery. ⛼☊❀◖♣

King's Head

60 Cross Street, NP7 5EU

⊛ 10.30 (10 Tue & Fri)-3, 7-11; 10.30-11 Sat; 12-3, 7-10.30 Sun

☎ (01873) 853575

Wells Bombardier; guest beer 🄷

Next door to the famous Victorian market hall – hence the early opening on two days a week – in the evening, when shoppers have gone, the pub reverts to serving local customers. On Friday nights it hosts live music sessions. The bar is one large, open-plan room with the dartboard in one corner and the fairly unobtrusive TV in another. Popular lunches are served Monday-Saturday. ⇌◖♣

Somerset Arms

Victoria Street, NP7 5DT (at Merthyr Rd jct)

⊛ 12-11, 12-10.30 Sun

☎ (01873) 852158

Brains Bitter; guest beers 🄷

Unashamedly a street-corner local, this cosy pub is one of a dying breed. It is a mecca for sports fans with TV screens showing Sky Sports offerings and a dartboard forever in use. Although popular with locals, visitors are always made to feel welcome. The quiet lounge is a comfortable place for conversation. Sunday night quizzes are well attended – giving the landlord a chance to show off his show-biz side! ❀⇌◖◗⊟♣

Blaenavon

Queen Victoria Inn

Prince Street, NP4 9BD

⊛ 11-11; 12-10.30 Sun

☎ (01495) 791652

Brains Rev James; guest beers 🄷

Built in 1837, the year Queen Victoria ascended the throne – hence its name. Inside you will find an intimate public bar and a separate lounge for families, diners and bookworms. Embracing the town's book culture, the shelves are stacked with titles covering all sorts of interests from military to cookery. One of the guest beers is usually from the Wychwood Brewery. With food and accommodation also available the pub is a convenient base from which to explore local heritage sites. ☊❀⇌◖◗⊟♣P⍻

Brynmawr

Hobby Horse Inn

30 Greenland Road, NP23 4DT (off Alma St)

⊛ 12-2.30, 7-11; 12-11 Sat; 12-10.30 Sun

☎ (01495) 310996

website: www.hobby-horse.co.uk

Beer range varies 🄷

Back-street local with a strong community feel named after the once-famous Rhymney Brewery symbol. The heart of the pub is the cosy, low, beamed bar where real ale is served in the 'inner sanctum'. This room displays drinking vessels and pump clips, and beer bottles line a shelf. The outer area, popular with diners, displays vessels of a different kind: unusual models of sailing ships. There is also a restaurant. Two small TVs show major sporting events. ❀⇌◖◗⊟♣P

Chepstow

Chepstow Athletic Club

Mathern Road, NP16 5JJ (off Bulwark Rd)

⊛ 7 (12 Sat)-11; 12-2.30, 7-10.30 Sun

☎ (01291) 622126

Boddingtons Bitter; Brains SA; Flowers IPA, Original; guest beers 🄷

Basic looking from the outside but inside is a spacious, smart lounge that opens on to a patio, popular with fair-weather cricket spectators as it overlooks the sports field. The bar team are long-term cask fans and ensure that six regular ales are always available from large and small Welsh breweries, plus an inspired selection from independents across Britain. Visiting CAMRA members are always warmly welcomed in this cheery haven (show your card for free entry). A large function room upstairs also serves cask ales. ❀♿♣P

Clytha

Clytha Arms

Old Raglan Road, NP7 8BW OS368089

⊛ 12-3 (not Mon), 6-11; 12-11 Sat; 12-4, 7-10.30 Sun

☎ (01873) 840206

website: www.clytha-arms.com

Draught Bass; Hook Norton Best Bitter; guest beers 🄷

Several times a local CAMRA Pub of the Year, the Clytha Arms is gaining a national reputation for the quality of its beer, cider and food. A former dower house, it is set in beautiful, extensive grounds. Six real ales are served including guests from a wide variety of independent breweries. These are complemented by draught ciders and perry. Highlights of the pub year are the festivals of Welsh beer and cheese and the Welsh cider festival, but every day is special here. ⛼Q❀⇌◖◗⊟♣●P

Cwmbran

Bush Inn

Graig Road, NP44 5AN

(off the top of Upper Cwmbran Rd)

⊛ 12-2 (not Mon & Tue), 7-11; 12-11 Sat; 12-10.30 Sun

☎ (01633) 483764

Cwmbran Crow Valley Bitter 🄷

Cosy hillside pub in one of Cwmbran's oldest communities. Cwmbran Brewery is a stone's throw away and Crow Valley Bitter sometimes gives way to other local beers. The split-level interior divides the lively public bar from a charming parlour-style room with a comfy settee and dresser displaying crockery. The inn is popular with all ages, including the Torfaen Folk Club who practise on Monday evenings. From the front patio there are superb views across to the Severn estuary. ⛼❀⊟♣P

Commodore Hotel

Mill Lane, NP44 8SH
(off Llanfrechfa Way behind Crow's Nest pub)
✪ 11-11; 12-10.30 Sun
☎ (01633) 484091
Cwmbran Crow Valley Bitter; guest beer 🄷
Family-run hotel known for its personal touch; a popular venue for tourists, business folk and locals alike. A staunch supporter of Cwmbran Brewery, it offers interesting local brews as well as, occasionally, beers from other small breweries. Comfortably furnished throughout, ales can be enjoyed in the relaxing Piliner's lounge or on the patio. Diners can choose from tasty bar meals or excellent seasonal dishes in Willows restaurant. ❀⇄◑◗P

Govilon

Bridgend Inn ✔

Church Lane, NP7 9RP
✪ 12-3.30; 7-11 (not Mon in winter); 12-3.30, 7-10.30 Sun
☎ (01873) 830177
Beer range varies 🄷
A pub at the heart of village life. The regulars are all members of the 'Yak and Penguin Appreciation Society', raising large amounts of money for charity. Real ales are served on a changing basis from a range of breweries. Friday nights from Easter to the autumn feature live music in the smoke-free lounge – the landlord often joining the musicians to demonstrate his considerable musical talent. ◑◗⊟♣P⁄

Llanfihangel Tor-y-mynydd

Star Inn

NP15 1DT (follow signs for Llansoy from Usk) OS459023
✪ 11-11 (11-5, 6-11 Mon-Thu winter); 12-10.30 Sun
☎ (01291) 650256
Draught Bass; Brains Rev James; Tomos Watkin OSB; guest beer 🄷
Situated in an area of outstanding natural beauty and with superb all-round views, this large inn at the centre of the hamlet hosts many local events. To the left of the entrance is a small lounge/dining area with an enormous log fire and on the right is the restaurant. Menus change regularly and food is cooked to order using seasonal local produce when possible. A public bar with a sporting theme and a large-screen TV runs off the lounge.
♨Q☎❀⇄◑◗⊟♿⛺♣P⁄

Llangattock Lingoed

Hunters Moon Inn

NP7 8RR (2 miles off B4521 Ross road at Llanvetherine)
✪ 12-3 (not Mon-Fri, Jan-Feb), 6.30-11; 12-3, 6.30-10.30 Sun
☎ (01873) 821499
website: www.hunters-moon-inn.co.uk
Brains Rev James; 🄷 **guest beers** 🄶
Dating from the 13th century, this pub offers visitors a warm and welcoming traditional atmosphere. Unusually for this area, the two guest beers come direct from casks set up behind the bar. Good food is served in the no-smoking, award-winning restaurant. Offa's Dyke Path passes through the next-door churchyard, so the pub is popular with walkers. There are two excellent places for outdoor drinking – a decking area looking up towards the church and a grassy garden with pool and waterfall. ♨❀⇄◑◗P

Llanhennock

Wheatsheaf Inn

NP18 1LT
(turn right 1 mile along Caerleon-Usk road) OS353927
✪ 11-11 (closed 3-5 Wed); 12-3, 7-10.30 Sun
☎ (01633) 420468
Draught Bass; Worthington's Bitter; guest beer 🄷
Unspoilt two-bar village pub, with fine views of the surrounding countryside. The public bar contains interesting local memorabilia and the lounge is cosy and welcoming. The pub has a hard core of loyal local regulars but is also popular with visitors who, having stopped off here once, make a point of returning. Food is served at lunchtime. Boules is played all year round in the car park. ♨❀◑⊟♣P

Llanthony

Half Moon

NP7 7NN (6 miles off A465 at Llanfihangel Crucorney) OS286279
✪ 12-3 (not Tue), 7 (6 Sat)-11; 12-3, 7-10.30 Sun (winter hours vary, ring to check)
☎ (01873) 890611
Bullmastiff Welsh Gold, Son of a Bitch; guest beers (summer) 🄷
In an area of outstanding natural beauty in the heart of the Black Mountains, the pub is just a few yards beyond the medieval ruins of Llanthony Priory. It opens only at the weekends in winter, but keeps more regular hours after Easter when walkers, trekkers and visitors boost the sparse population of this remote valley. This is a rare local outlet for Bulmastiff beers. The bar billiards table, bought secondhand 19 years ago, still operates on two shilling coins.
♨Q☎❀⇄◑◗⊟⛺♣●P⁄

Newport

Gladiator

Pillmawr Road, NP18 3QZ (eastbound, turn right before A4042 bridge)
✪ 11.30-11; 12-10.30 Sun
☎ (01633) 821353
Banks's Bitter; guest beers 🄷
Once a cottage but now well into its third decade as pub, the Gladiator has been firmly adopted by the local community. Set in spacious grounds with views out over the countryside, the pub has a vibrant public bar and a quieter lounge with prints of old military uniforms on wood-panelled walls. Meals are served Wednesday to Saturday and Sunday lunchtime only. A large function room is available.
❀◑◗⊟♣P

Godfrey Morgan

158 Chepstow Road, Maindee, NP19 8EG
✪ 10-11, 12-10.30 Sun
☎ (01633) 221928
Brains SA; Bullmastiff Welsh Gold; Greene King Abbot; Marston's Burton Bitter, Pedigree; guest beers 🄷

Spacious and welcoming conversion of a former cinema and bingo hall. Furnished in Art Deco style, there are photographs on the wall of erstwhile screen and stage stars with local connections. The pub is named after Godfrey Morgan who rode in the Charge of the Light Brigade and his picture also features. The light, airy front room opens up to the bar area; both have no-smoking sections. Situated in a lively area a mile and a half from the town centre, the pub is always busy. Q ☕ ◐ ◗ ♿ P ⚟

Old Murenger House

53 High Street, NP20 1GA

11-11; 7-10.30 Sun

☎ (01633) 263977

website www.murenger.com

Samuel Smith OBB Ⓗ

A perennial favourite that has stood the test of time; the pub's friendly atmosphere makes it popular with all ages. A building of Tudor origin, the interior has several linked areas but they are not as old as they look: testimony to Samuel Smith's excellence in authentic-looking, traditional-style pub refurbishments. Selling competitively priced beer, and in the midst of a medley of 'superpubs', the Murenger is well worth a visit. Q ❀ ◐ ⇌ ♣

Red Lion

47 Stow Hill, NP20 1JH

11-11; 12-10.30 Sun

☎ (01633) 264398

Beer range varies Ⓗ

Founding place of Gwent CAMRA in 1974 and still frequented by local members, this pub has retained its traditional character over the years. The open-plan interior offers plenty of space to drink and enjoy friendly banter. Note the barrels hanging above the bar and wall-mounted beer engine. A haunt of sports fans, particularly Rugby Union, as well as more leisurely activities: teams participate in the local shove-ha'penny league. Regular guest ales include Greene King Abbot and Wychwood Hobgoblin. A function room is available. ⩩ ❀ ⇌ ♣

St Julian Inn

Caerleon Road, NP18 1QA

11.30-11; 12-10.30 Sun

☎ (01633) 243548

Banks's Bitter; John Smith's Bitter; Wells Bombardier; guest beer Ⓗ

Well-run inn enjoying a scenic location on the rural outskirts of Newport, looking towards ancient Caerleon. With its commanding view of the river Usk and surrounding countryside, particularly from the riverside balcony, it is no surprise that this is a popular pub. Inside there is a choice of wood-panelled lounge with access to the balcony, public bar, games room and downstairs skittle alley that also serves as a function room. ❀ ◐ ◗ ⊟ ♣ P ⚟

Pantygelli

Crown Inn

Old Hereford Road, NP7 7HR

(off A465, 4 miles N of Abergavenny)

11-3 (not Mon), 6-11 (11-11 summer Sat); 12-3, 6-10.30 Sun

☎ (01873) 853314

Draught Bass; Brains Rev James; Hancock's HB; guest beers Ⓗ

A welcome return to the Guide for this old favourite – an excellent local enjoyed by the people in the hamlet as well as those from further afield. The secrets of its success lie in the warm welcome, the quality of the beer and food, and its location looking out towards the Skirrid Mountain. The patio, with comfortable chairs and tables, is a good place to relax with a drink and enjoy the view. Guest beers focus on local breweries. ⩩ ❀ ◐ ◗ ♣ P ⚟

Penallt

Boat Inn

Lone Lane, NP25 4AJ (across footbridge from Redbrook car park on A466) 0S535098

11-11; 12-10.30 Sun

☎ (01600) 712615

Greene King IPA; Wadworth 6X; guest beers Ⓗ

Unspoilt gem of a pub in a picturesque setting on the bank of the River Wye. The car park is across the river in the village of Redbrook, England, and the pub is approached along a footbridge next to the disused railway line. Inside, there is a bar with a flagstone floor and a small side room. A stream runs through the pub garden. Up to five ales are normally available, plus cider in summer. Live music is hosted here on Tuesday and Thursday. ❀ ◐ ◗ ♣ P

Pontnewynydd

Bridgend Inn

23 Hanbury Road, NP4 6QN (off Osborne Rd)

12-11; 12-10.30 Sun

☎ (01495) 757435

Beer range varies Ⓗ

Cosy community local formed out of two 17th-century cottages. Entry is down a wide set of steps leading to a low, beamed bar, games area and lounge leading off it. One or two beers are served from independent breweries, including Cwmbran. It is handy for walkers of the old railway track bed nearby. Meals can be served by prior arrangement only. ❀ ⊟ ♣

Pontymoile

Horse & Jockey

Old Usk Road, NP4 0JB (off A4042(T))

12-11; 12-10.30 Sun

☎ (01495) 762721

Adnams Broadside; Greene King Abbot or Old Speckled Hen; guest beers Ⓗ

Picture postcard pub, this classic rural inn with old thatched roof is situated beside an ancient church. Although it has been transformed in recent years from a boozer to a popular food venue, do not let that prevent you from stopping by for a beer. There is plenty of room in the bar area; you might even be unable to resist as the aroma of tasty food wafts past on its way to hungry diners. There is outside seating at the front and a pleasant rear garden where families are welcome.
❀ ◐ ◗ P

WALES

Raglan

Beaufort Arms ✔

High Street, NP15 2DY

⏲ 11-11; 12-10.30 Sun

☎ (01291) 690412

website: www.beaufortraglan.co.uk

Brains Rev James; Fuller's London Pride; guest beer Ⓗ

Imposing, upmarket but cosy, family-owned and run hotel at one end of the main street through Raglan. It has been at the heart of the village since the 15th century. Inside is a small flagstone floor bar at the front or a larger lounge at the rear where you can dine too. The Roundheads were stationed here during the siege of nearby Raglan Castle during the English Civil War. Local legend has it that a tunnel underneath the hotel connects to the castle.

❀⇌◑ ⊟♣P⊬

Rogerstone

Tredegar Arms

57 Cefn Road, NP10 9AQ

⏲ 12-3, 5.30-11; 12-11 Thu-Sat; 12-4, 7-10.30 Sun

☎ (01633) 664999

Draught Bass; Courage Best Bitter; guest beers Ⓗ

Roadside pub with strong local support augmented by passing trade. It is a handy watering hole for visitors of local attractions such as Cwmcarn Scenic Forest Drive. Inside is an intimate public bar with original flagstones and wood beams, plus a pleasant and spacious lounge with a dining room and family area. The lunchtime menu with tasty standard favourites gives way in the evening to a menu boasting a choice of exotic dishes.

Q♉❀◑ ⊟P

Sebastopol

Open Hearth

Wern Road, NP4 5DR (off Austin Rd)

⏲ 11.30-11; 12-10.30 Sun

☎ (01495) 763752

Caledonian Deuchars IPA; Greene King Abbot; guest beers Ⓗ

Winner of a clutch of CAMRA awards, this welcoming canalside favourite offers a range of up to nine beers from independent breweries as well as an extensive food menu. The pub has been greatly enlarged since its humble 17th-century days, but the intimate public bar was the original building which served first as a cowman's cottage, then a canal wash house known as the Clout. There is a spacious garden and play area for children.

❀◑ ⊟♣P

Sebastopol Social Club

Wern Road, NP4 5DU (on jct with Austin Rd)

⏲ 12-11; 12-10.30 Sun

☎ (01495) 763808

Hancock's HB; Wye Valley Butty Bach; guest beers Ⓗ

CAMRA's national Club of the Year in 2004, it continues to improve its facilities while maintaining an interesting and varied range of beers at highly competitive prices. A lively, sociable place, the main room displays award certificates and a colourful array of pump clips, while more breweriana decorates the comfortable and quieter rear bar. Downstairs there is a skittles alley and a pool table. Show your CAMRA membership card or a copy of this Guide to gain entry. ❀⊟♣P

Skenfrith

Bell

NP7 8UH

(on B4521, midway between Abergavenny and Ross-on-Wye)

⏲ 11-11 (not Mon); 12-10.30 Sun

☎ (01600) 730235

website: www.skenfrith.co.uk

Freeminer Bitter; Hook Norton Best Bitter; Taylor Landlord Ⓗ

Nestling on the bank of the River Monnow under the walls of the ancient Norman Skenfrith Castle, this former 17th-century village coaching inn has been transformed into a high quality hotel and restaurant while retaining a separate bar for locals and visitors. Beer comes from independent breweries and the draught cider is made at a farm just over the border in England.

♨Q❀⇌◑ ⊟●P⊬

Tintern

Cherry Tree Inn

Forge Road, NP16 6TH

(lane off A466 at Royal George Hotel)

⏲ 12-11 (supper licence until midnight); 12-10.30 Sun

☎ (01291) 689292 website: www.thecherry.co.uk

Hancock's HB; guest beers Ⓖ

A gravity-lover's delight, the fizz-free Cherry thrives in its enlarged 21st-century form after extensive redevelopment. The original bar remains for the serious business of drinking and conversation, both encouraged by an expansive stillage offering constantly changing choices from small breweries. Ciders include bottle-conditioned favourites plus Thatchers and Bulmers casks. With live music every Thursday and two beerfests a year, this ever-present entry in the Guide should not be missed.

♨Q❀⇌◑ ⊟⛺♣●P⊬

Moon & Sixpence

Monmouth Road, NP16 5SG

⏲ 11-11 (12-11 Oct-Easter); 12-10.30 Sun

(01291) 689284

website: www.themoonandsixpence.co.uk

Beer range varies Ⓗ

Perched above the river and a gentle 15-minute stroll from Tintern Abbey, this welcoming pub in the scenic Lower Wye Valley has gained high repute for its ale quality in recent years. Four cosy, interlinking rooms offer intimate places for drinkers and diners while an indoor spring makes an unusual feature. One or more Wye Valley or Archers ale is usually available alongside one or two interesting guests. A range of good value home-cooked meals is served.

❀◑ ⛺P⊬

Wye Valley Hotel

NP16 6SQ (on A466)

⏲ 11-3, 6-11; 12-3, 7-10.30 Sun

☎ (01291) 689441 website: www.wyevalleyhotel.co.uk

Wye Valley Bitter, Butty Bach; guest beers Ⓗ

Situated in an area of breathtaking natural

beauty in the heart of the Wye Valley, the hotel is a landmark at the north end of the village and invitingly close to the road for thirsty travellers. Inside is a hospitable bar area and large no-smoking dining room. Shelves around the bar display a huge and fascinating collection of bottled beers. Two local Wye Valley ales are always available. ⇄ⒹⒹ ΔP

Trellech

Lion Inn

NP25 4PA (on B4293, Chepstow-Monmouth road)

12-3, 6 (7 Mon; 6.30 Sat)-11 (hours vary in winter); 12-3 (closed eve) Sun

☎ (01600) 860322 website: www.lioninn.co.uk

Beer range varies Ⓗ

Gwent CAMRA Pub of the Year once and runner-up twice in the last three years, the Lion is a consistently excellent pub. With an open-plan interior, there is a small bar to the right and a slightly larger dining area to the left. An exhibition of foreign bottled beers was held in 2004, in addition to the regular summer beer festival. Up to four beers are always available, nearly always from micros. The food menu ranges from the simple to the exotic: Hungarian dishes are a speciality. ♔❀⇄ⒹⒹ♣P

Trellech Grange

Fountain Inn

NP16 6QW

(2½ miles down lane by George Hotel) OS503011

12-3, 7-11 (hours vary in summer); 12-3, 7-10.30 Sun

☎ (01291) 689303

website: www.fountaininn-tintern.com

Beer range varies Ⓗ

The owner of this 17th-century inn, determined to be sure of getting a decent pint, felt that the only way to do so would be to buy his own pub. This is the result, purchased in late summer 2004. Although the emphasis is on food, with a large restaurant off the main bar area, you are welcome to pop in for a pint and a game of darts. There is usually a choice of three beers, mainly from micros. ♔❀⇄ⒹΔ♣P

Upper Llanover

Goose & Cuckoo

NP7 9ER

(at end of a narrow lane off A4042 at Llanover) OS292073

11.30-3, 7-11; closed Mon; 11.30-11 Fri & Sat; 12-10.30 Sun

☎ (01873) 880277

Beer range varies Ⓗ

Proving that even the most isolated country pub can be a thriving, popular place, the Goose & Cuckoo is sought out by locals and visitors alike. Wind your way up a narrow, rising lane until you finally reach this venerable pub with its glorious views over the Vale of Usk. Many walkers and trekkers enjoy the pub's facilities. Twice yearly beer festivals, sometimes featuring live music, make the most of the large garden which is shared by the pub's goats and ducks. Gwent CAMRA Pub of the Year 2004 is a real gem. ♔Q❀⇄Ⓓ♣P⚟

Usk

Usk Conservative Club

The Grange, 16 Maryport Street, NP15 1AB

12-3, 7-11; 12-3, 7-10.30 Sun

☎ (01291) 672634

Hancock's HB; guest beers Ⓗ

Formerly a fine town house, the club has been enjoyed by members and their guests for some 50 years. Standard entry restrictions apply, but once signed in you too can savour the pleasant, relaxing surroundings and comfortable furnishings. The well-maintained bar is flanked by two seating areas, one with games, the other with a dining room. There is also a large function room. ❀Ⓓ♣P

King's Head Hotel

18 Old Market Street, NP15 1AL

11-11; 12-10.30 Sun

☎ (01291) 672963

Fuller's London Pride; Taylor Landlord Ⓗ

This 15th-century old English style inn features regularly in the Guide. Activity centres around the characterful bar, with its log-burning fire the focal point. Evidence of the landlord's fishing prowess is displayed on the walls among other interesting items dotted around the room. The tasty food and good beer make this a popular base for visitors exploring the locality. ♔⇄ⒹP

Nag's Head Inn ✔

Twyn Square, NP15 1BH

11-3, 5.30-11; 12-3, 6.30-10.30 Sun

☎ (01291) 672820

Brains Buckley's Best Bitter, SA, Rev James Ⓗ

Attractive old inn renowned for its good beer and fine, locally-sourced cuisine. Although the emphasis is on food, a warm welcome is always offered to those simply wishing to enjoy a drink. The front bar includes an intimate snug with etched glass windows and is pleasantly cluttered with all manner of artefacts and ornaments; the wood-panelled family room has a horse racing theme. A passageway leads to the pub's own coffee bar, Hoof's, built in the old entrance to the courtyard. Q❀Ⓓ⚟

Your shout

We would like to hear from you. If you think a pub not listed in the Guide is worthy of consideration, please let us know. Send us the name, full address and phone number (if known). If a pub in the Guide has given you poor service, we would also like to know. Write to Good Beer Guide, CAMRA, 230 Hatfield Road, St Albans, Herts, AL 14 LW or email **camra@camra.org.uk**

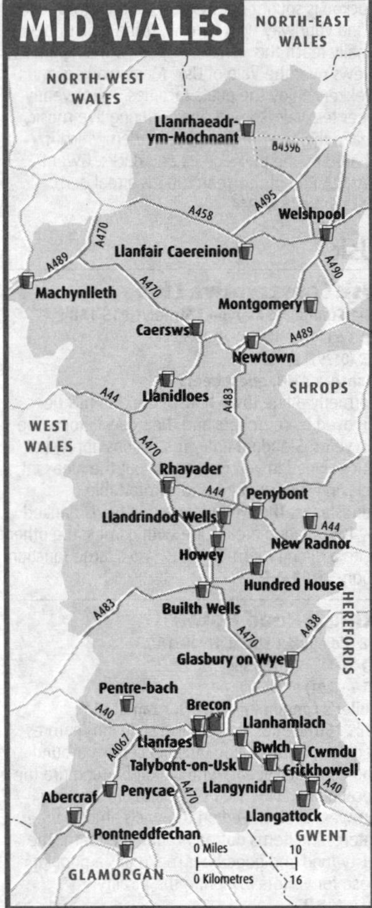

Abercraf

Copper Beech Inn

133 Heol Tawe, SA9 1XS
(off A4067 Swansea-Brecon road) OS824128
✪ 11.30-11; 12-10.30 Sun
☎ (01639) 730269
Draught Bass; guest beers Ⓗ
Recently refurbished, this large, friendly village-centre pub borders the Brecon Beacons National Park. The bar is dominated by a large fireplace and exposed beams. There is also a games room. Beers from micro-breweries feature regularly on the guest list. Excellent home-cooked food includes 12 curries of varying strengths.
⛫❀⇄◐◑♣P

Brecon

Boar's Head

Ship Street, LD3 9AL (by River Usk bridge)
✪ 12-11; 12-1am Fri & Sat; 12-10.30 Sun
☎ (01874) 622856
Breconshire Brecon County Ale, Golden Valley, Red Dragon, Ramblers Ruin, seasonal beers; Fuller's London Pride Ⓗ
The Breconshire Brewery tap is an extremely popular town-centre pub. The wood-panelled front bar displays a collection of old photographs of Brecon, and the larger, livelier back bar houses the busy pool table and a large screen for sporting events. Live music is hosted on Friday. The patio garden boasts views of the River Usk and over to the Beacons. Special events are held throughout the summer and during the jazz festival. Evening meals are served in summer. ⛫❀◐◑⊟♠P

Bull's Head

86 The Struet, LD3 7LS
✪ 12-3, 6.30-11; 12-3, 6.30-10.30 Sun
☎ (01874) 622044
Beer range varies Ⓗ
Now owned by Evan-Evans of Llandeilo, the beers are all sourced from them or Wolverhampton & Dudley breweries. A range of bottled beers is also stocked. This popular two-room pub has three drinking areas. An excellent menu featuring home-cooked food caters for all including vegetarians and vegans. Good value B&B accommodation is available.
⛫Q❀⇄◐◑⊟♠

Builth Wells

Greyhound Hotel

3 Garth Road, LD2 3AR
✪ 11-11 (11-3, 6-11 Mon-Fri winter); 12-10.30 Sun
☎ (01982) 553255
website: www.thegreyhoundhotel.co.uk
Fuller's London Pride; Greene King Abbot; guest beers Ⓗ
Early 20th-century hotel with open-plan bars, a large function room and a no-smoking restaurant. Guest beers are mainly from smaller breweries. The hotel has a reputation for the high quality of its food, and gets busy, particularly at weekends, when booking is essential. The Sunday lunchtime carvery is highly recommended. An engraved glass panel above the front door shows that a previous owner had a licence to brew, but sadly the brewery is no more. Quoits is played here.
Q❀⇄◐◑⊟♿♣P

Bwlch

New Inn

LD3 7LQ
(on A40 between Brecon and Crickhowell)
✪ 11-3, 6-11; 11-11 Sat & summer; 11-10.30 Sun
☎ (01874) 730215
Brains Rev James; guest beers Ⓗ
Vibrant village-centre pub with a large selection of pump clips and single malt whiskies reflecting the landlord's tastes. Beers are usually sourced from local breweries. A large fireplace dominates the room while a sadly under used piano lurks in a corner. The bar has a panel relating the story of the landlord's dog, the paint pot and the spirits in the cellar, which explains the pub's sign. Good food, fine ales and comfortable accommodation make this an ideal base for exploring the surrounding countryside.
⛫Q❀⇄◐◑▲P

INDEPENDENT BREWERIES

Breconshire Brecon

Caersws

Red Lion

SY17 5EL (off A470)
⌚ 3 (11 summer)-11; 12-11 Sun
☎ (01686) 688023
Banks's Original, Bitter; guest beer Ⓗ
Friendly village local with a small, cosy bar and a lounge/restaurant area. The wood-beamed pub has a comfortable, relaxed feel and attracts a varied clientele of all ages. Excellent home-cooked food is served and there is an attractive outdoor area for summer drinking.
♔❀◑▶⊟≠♣

Crickhowell

Bear Hotel

High Street, NP8 1BW
⌚ 11-3, 6-11; 11-3, 7-10.30 Sun
☎ (01873) 810408 website: www.bearhotel.co.uk
Draught Bass; Brains Rev James; Greene King Old Speckled Hen; Hancock's HB
Originally a 15th-century coaching inn, this is now a large, award-winning hotel. The multi-roomed bar is set in grand surroundings, with exposed beams, fine settles, several open fireplaces and architectural curiosities. The food menu boasts top-quality dishes made with local produce. The location is ideal for exploring the Brecon Beacons and Black Mountains, and the pub is on the Abergavenny-Brecon bus route.
♔Q❀◑▶⊟♿P

Cwmdu

Farmers Arms

NP8 1RU
(on A470 between Crickhowell and Builth Wells)
⌚ 12-3, 6-11; closed Mon; 12-3, 6-10.30 Sun
☎ (01874) 730464 website: www.thefarmersarms.com
Shepherd Neame Spitfire; guest beers Ⓗ
Exposed beams and an open fireplace containing an old iron stove dominate the bar area of this village-centre community pub. The hop-strewn bar separates the dining area at the front of the pub, where superb food is served. A wide-ranging menu features local produce and Welsh black steaks. Guest beers are sourced from local breweries as well as the occasional cask from well-known regional brewers. ♔Q❀◑▶P

Glasbury on Wye

Hollybush Inn

HR3 5PS (on B4350 between Glasbury and Hay) OS198403
⌚ 11-11; 11-10.30 Sun
☎ (01497) 847371
Breconshire Golden Valley; Greene King Abbot; Ⓗ **guest beer** (occasional) Ⓖ
Warm and friendly four-roomed pub. The two main rooms are part of the original building, with a slightly more modern annex at one end, and a newly-built dining room to the side. The exposed beams in the bar are bedecked with locally-grown hops. Superb home-cooked food includes dishes for vegans and vegetarians. Land beside the pub is taken up by a spacious camping and caravan park, next to the River Wye and complete with woodland walks and an adventure area. Views of the Black Mountains and the Begwn Hills mark the horizon.
♔Q❀◑▶⛺♣P⊭

Howey

Laughing Dog

LD1 5PT
⌚ 12-3, 6.30-11 (12-11 Fri & Sat summer); 12-3, 7-10.30 Sun
☎ (01597) 822406
website: www.thelaughingdog.ukpub.net
Dunn Plowman Early Riser; Wood Parish; Wye Valley Bitter; guest beers Ⓗ
Licensed since 1872, this is an 18th-century building housing a 19th-century pub. The no-nonsense public bar has sensible furniture and a collection of beer-related books and guides, plus comics for younger (and older) visitors. It has a games room. The area now occupied by the lounge/dining/function room was once the adjoining smithy; no meals are served Sunday evening or Monday lunchtime. The large stone outside the pub is said to have been used by customers dismounting from horses.
♔Q❀◑▶⊟♣P

Hundred House

Hundred House Inn

LD1 5RY
⌚ 11-11; 12-10.30 Sun
☎ (01982) 570231
Brains SA; Wood Parish; guest beers Ⓗ
First listed in 1823, this former drovers' inn is set in a prominent roadside position benefiting from fine views of the surrounding uplands. A detailed explanation of a hundred – an Anglo-Saxon administrative subdivision of a shire – is on display in the cosy bar, complete with its tiled floor and display of pump clips. All food on the menu can be served as a takeaway, but advance notice is required.
♔Q❀◑▶⊟♣P

Llandrindod Wells

Conservative Club

Lansdown South Crescent, LD1 5DH
(next to Glen Usk Hotel)
⌚ 11-2; 11-11.30 Fri & Sat; 11.30-10.30 Sun
☎ (01597) 822126
Banks's Mansfield Cask; Worthington's Bitter; guest beers Ⓗ
A quiet, comfortable haven overlooking the Temple Gardens. The 'Con' has a large lounge, TV room, games bar, snooker and pool tables and a small front patio. An excellent range of guest beers is available to complement the regular ales. Lunches are available Thursday-Saturday. Live entertainment is hosted occasionally in the evening. Non-members must be signed in. Q◑≠♣

Llanfaes

Drovers Arms

Newgate Street, LD3 8SN
⌚ 12-11; 12-10.30 Sun
☎ (01874) 623377
Tetley Bitter; Wadworth IPA; guest beer Ⓗ
Lively, community based local with a dedicated

WALES

following. The main bar is L-shaped with a side room with its own servery. Guest beers are sourced from the nearby Breconshire Brewery – either one of its own beers or the result of a beer swap or a foray further afield. A regular haunt of the walkers' club, the pub is also home to quoits and darts teams – it can be busy on match days. There is a secluded patio area for alfresco drinking. ❀◑◗♣

Llanfair Caereinion

Goat Hotel

High Street, SY21 0QS (on A458)

⚙ 11-11; 12-10.30 Sun

☎ (01938) 810428

Beer range varies Ⓗ

Excellent, beamed inn with a welcoming atmosphere. Popular with locals and tourists, the Goat has a plush lounge with comfortable leather armchairs and sofas. Three real ales are on offer including a house beer from the Wood Brewery. The lounge is dominated by a large inglenook with an open fire. There is a restaurant serving home-cooked food and a games room at the rear. ⛰❀⇌◑◗♣P

Llangattock

Vine Tree Inn

NP8 1HG (to the S of Crickhowell) OS215180

⚙ 12-3, 6-11 (extended in summer); 12-3, 6.30-10.30 Sun

☎ (01873) 810514

Fuller's London Pride; guest beer Ⓗ

Riverside pub where the emphasis is on food. However drinkers are welcome in the cosy, copper-covered bar, complemented by stone walls and quarry tiled floors. Cider is produced locally, exclusively for the pub. The impressive food menu boasts locally sourced meat and vegetables, and ever-changing specials which are always good. Booking is advisable as the pub can be busy. The riverside garden is an added attraction. ⛰Q❀◑◗♣P

Llangynidr

Red Lion

NP8 1NT (just off B4558)

⚙ 11.30-3.30, 6.30-11; 11.30-11 Fri & Sat; 12-10.30 Sun

☎ (01874) 730223

Draught Bass; Breconshire Golden Valley; guest beer (occasional) Ⓗ

Lively pub on the edge of the village. A real focus for the community, it hosts meetings and educational courses for local residents. The multi-roomed pub has a cosy main bar with a games room to one side and a dining room. Occasional guest beers come from the Breconshire Brewery. Food is home-made using local produce where possible, and curries are a speciality. The pub, with a patio and garden, can be busy in summer. ⛰Q❀◑◗⊞♣P

Llanhamlach

Old Ford Inn

LD3 7YB (on A40)

⚙ 12-11; 12-10.30 Sun

☎ (01874) 665220

Beer range varies Ⓗ

Built in the 12th century, the building has been much extended since then, but retains its original character. The public bar is in the centre and has some unusual copper-work features and a large collection of old half pint bottles from British brewers. A larger room is used mainly for dining and affords superb panoramic views of the Brecon Beacons. The beer range varies but often includes ales from local breweries. B&B accommodation is available. ❀⇌◑◗⊞P

Llanidloes

Crown & Anchor Inn

41 Long Bridge Street, SY18 6EF (on A470)

⚙ 11-11; 12-10.30 Sun

☎ (01686) 412398

Brains Rev James; Hancock's HB Ⓗ

Traditional no-frills town-centre local, with a relaxed and friendly atmosphere. This unspoilt pub with exposed beams retains its public bar, lounge, snug and two further rooms, one of which has a pool table and games machine. Old posters decorate the walls of the main bar. A central hallway separates the games room from the lounge and snug. ⛰⊞♣

Red Lion Hotel

Longbridge Street, SY18 6EE (on A470)

⚙ 12-11; 12-10.30 Sun

☎ (01686) 412270

Beer range varies Ⓗ

Wood-beamed, town-centre hotel with a relaxed, comfortable atmosphere. The plush lounge has red leather sofas and the bar area has table football and a pool table. Interesting fireplaces feature in both bars, as well as televisions – however, the volume is kept low or off in the lounge. No food is served on Sunday evening. ⛰❀◑◗⊞♣

Stag Inn

Great Oak Street, SY18 6BU (on B4518)

⚙ 11-3, 5.30-11; 11-11 Fri & Sat; 12-10.30 Sun

☎ (01686) 412392

Greene King Old Speckled Hen; Fuller's London Pride; guest beer Ⓗ

Pleasant, town-centre local with a varied clientele. The pub has a main bar and a separate back room, with two pool tables and gaming machines, accessed through an archway. Two regular ales and a guest are available, and the pub hosts occasional live music at the weekend. The town's museum, housed in the black and white former market hall, is worth a visit. ◑♣

Llanrhaeadr-ym-Mochnant

Tafarn Llaw

SY10 0JJ (off B4580)

⚙ 3 (12 Fri & Sat)-11; 12-10.30 Sun

☎ (01691) 780413

Beer range varies Ⓗ

Multi-roomed village pub with exposed beams and a tiled floor, frequented by friendly locals. The bar has a large inglenook with a real fire. The smaller, cosy lounge has a second inglenook. There is an additional no-smoking area and a large function room. Reasonably-priced accommodation is offered. ⛰❀⇌◑◗⊞▲♣P

Machynlleth

Skinners Arms

Main Street, SY20 8EB (on A487)
11-11; 12-10.30 Sun
(01654) 702354
Burtonwood Bitter; guest beer H
Town-centre pub where the plush lounge bar has exposed stone walls and a no-smoking dining area. The lounge is set around an impressive stone inglenook. The public bar is more basic and has a friendly, cosy feel with bare floorboards, subdued lighting and a pool table. A good selection of food is served in the lounge (not Sun eve) and snacks are available in the bar. There is a patio for summer drinking.

Montgomery

Dragon Hotel

Market Square, SY15 6PA
11-3, 6-11; 12-3, 7-10.30 Sun
(01686) 668359
website: www.dragonhotel.com
Beer range varies H
Small, cosy bar in a 17th-century coaching inn, situated in the centre of town. The beams and masonry are reputedly from the local castle, which was destroyed by Cromwell. The bar walls are covered with bric-a-brac. The beer range usually includes an ale from the Wood Brewery. The hotel itself has good facilities with an indoor heated pool and a function room for hire.
QP

New Radnor

Radnor Arms

LD8 2SP
12-3, 7 (5 Fri)-11; 11-11 Sat; 12-10.30 Sun
(01544) 350232
Beer range varies H
Set in the Welsh Marches and close to the English border, this cosy pub also offers accommodation, making it an ideal base for anyone looking for an away-from-it-all break. There is good walking, trekking and cycling, Offa's Dyke is nearby and Hereford 25 miles away. Food is served every day, with a popular Sunday carvery (booking advisable), and a children's menu. The restaurant is no-smoking and a take-away service is available, including excellent fish and chips.
QP

Newtown

Buck Inn

High Street, SY16 2NP (off A483)
11-11; 12-10.30 Sun
(01686) 622699
Banks's Bitter; guest beer H
Reputedly the oldest inn in Newtown, this town-centre local is crowded and noisy at weekends. The comfortable beamed pub has a large stone inglenook and is divided into distinct drinking areas. It attracts a varied clientele. Patios at the front and back are available for outside drinking.

Railway Tavern

Old Kerry Road, SY16 1BH (off A483)
12-2.30, 6-11; 11-11 Tue, Fri & Sat; 12-10.30 Sun
(01686) 626156
Draught Bass; Worthington's Bitter; guest beer H
Locals' bar with exposed beams and a rear stone wall, handy for the station. This unspoilt, compact one-bar hostelry has a good following, due to its friendly atmosphere and welcoming landlord and landlady, who have been at the Railway for over 20 years. The pub has a successful darts team and has recently had to clear out the trophy cabinet to make room for the next batch of silverware. Match nights can be crowded.

Pentre-bach

Shoemakers Arms

LD3 8UB (follow signs to 'country pub' from Sennybridge)
OS908328
12-2.30 (not Mon-Tue), 6-11; 12-2.30, 6-10.30 Sun (hours vary in summer)
(01874) 636508
Beer range varies H
Remote and welcoming country pub that lies close to the Eppynt firing ranges. However, as the signs on the approach road state, 'the road to Pentre-bach is always open'. A former Powys CAMRA Pub of the Year, it is owned by a co-operative of locals. It offers excellent food and an ever-changing selection of beers from local micros and regional breweries. Opening hours may vary depending on the time of year, but it is open every evening. QP

Penybont

Severn Arms

LD1 5UA
11-2.30, 6-11; 12-3, 7-10.30 Sun
(01597) 851224
Brains Rev James; Courage Directors; Theakston Best Bitter; guest beers H
This 18th-century coaching inn was named after John Cheesment Severn, a squire of Penybont Hall. It used to be the stop-off point on the route between Hereford and Aberystwyth. The spacious bar, with its large, open fireplace, opens on to rear gardens overlooking the River Ithon. Guests can fish for free on six miles of the river. There is a separate games room and a quiet, secluded restaurant – the Cheesments. Trotting races take place twice yearly on a nearby course. A good range of malt whiskies is an added attraction.
QP

Penycae

Ancient Briton

Brecon Road, SA9 1YY
11-11; 12-10.30 Sun
(01639) 730273
Beer range varies H
Busy roadside pub, providing a continuous unofficial beer festival, with up to six beers from far and wide at any one time, plus a traditional cider. The pub is open plan but divided by screens into a games area, a lounge and a restaurant. Quality, home-prepared food is

served (no meals Sun eve). There is a play area for children and camping facilities at the rear. The pub is popular with locals as well as visitors to the nearby Dan-Yr-Ogof caves and the Upper Swansea Valley.
⛫❀⇄◑◗♿⛺P

Pontneddfechan

Old White Horse Inn

12 High Street, SA11 5NP (off A465)
✪ 12-3, 6-11 (closed winter Mon); 12-11 Sat; 12-10.30 Sun
☎ (01639) 721219
Brains SA; guest beers Ⓗ
This building, built around 1600, has served as a coaching house, shop and B&B, before reverting to a pub in the early 1970s. It has a cosy public bar, lounge/restaurant and pool room. Good value food is served at lunchtime and evenings, except Sunday evening in winter. Three real ales are stocked in winter, five, plus a cider in summer, when the pub holds its annual beer festival. Budget hostel accommodation is available for up to 10 guests.
⛫Q❀⇄◑◗⊟♿♣●P

Rhayader

Cornhill

West Street, LD6 5AB
✪ 11 (12 winter)-11; 12-10.30 Sun
☎ (01597) 811015
website: www.cornhillinn.co.uk
Beer range varies Ⓗ
Despite alterations this early 16th-century pub retains not just its original character – with low ceilings and an inglenook – but reputedly a female ghost. Guest beers are mainly from smaller breweries and traditional cask and bottled cider is stocked. Vegan and vegetarian choices are included in the excellent menu of freshly-prepared meals. Self-catering accommodation is available in a detached former smithy. Children are welcome. No food is served January-March.
⛫Q❀⇄◑◗♣●

Crown

North Street, LD6 5BT
✪ 11-11; 12-10.30 Sun
☎ (01597) 811099
Brains Dark, Bitter, Rev James, seasonal beers; guest beers Ⓗ
This 16th-century building has always been a pub and, despite changes made in the 1970s, some of the original timber is still visible. The walls of the bar display a visual history of Rhayader, with some text look out for the item referring to Major Stanscombe, a former owner. The oak linen-fold bar front was saved from a demolished house in Caersws. The Crown is a rare outlet in the county for cask-conditioned mild.
Q❀⇄◑◗⊟⍻

Talybont-on-Usk

Star Inn

LD3 7YX (on B4558) OS114226
✪ 11-3, 6.30-11; 11-11 Sat & summer; 12-3, 6.30-10.30 Sun
☎ (01874) 676635
Beer range varies Ⓗ
Large and lively pub beside the Monmouthshire and Brecon Canal. A vast display of pump clips reflects the enormous number of ales served by this CAMRA award-winning pub over the years. Beers from the nearby Breconshire Brewery are often available, as well as a range of Westons ciders. Quiz nights and live music evenings are popular during the week. The large garden at the back, overlooking the canal, is busy in summer.
⛫❀⇄◑◗⊟⛺♣●

Welshpool

Talbot

High Street, SY21 7JP (on A458)
✪ 12-11; 12-10.30 Sun
☎ (01938) 553711
Banks's Original, Bitter; Greene King Abbot Ⓗ
Pleasant, town-centre local with a basic but comfortable tiled public bar and a small lounge with a relaxed, friendly atmosphere. The timbered brick walled public bar has tables displaying Welsh rugby tickets and unusual playing cards. Note the old Wolverhampton & Dudley Brewery notice from 1932. Food is served Friday-Sunday. An outside drinking area is available in summer.
❀◑◗⊟⇶♣P

Crown & Anchor, Llanidloes

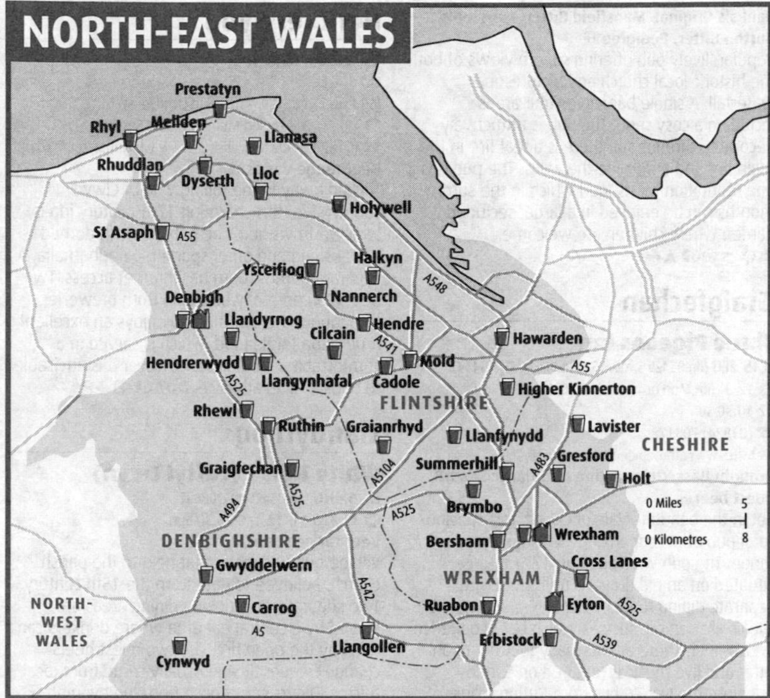

Authority areas covered Denbighshire UA, Flintshire UA, Wrexham UA

DENBIGHSHIRE

Carrog

Grouse Inn

LL21 9AT (close to river and jct of B5436/B5437) OS112436
⏲ 12-11; 12-10.30 Sun
☎ (01490) 430272
website: www.grouseinncarrog.co.uk
Lees Bitter; seasonal beers Ⓗ
Situated in a tranquil riverside location, the Grouse offers a friendly welcome to walkers, campers, passing motorists and passengers from the western terminus of the Llangollen Railway. Self-catering cottage accommodation is available nearby, for details telephone the pub. Carrog is twinned with Ploute, Brittany, and hosts visits during the international Eisteddfod. In recognition, Celtic flags hang from the beamed ceiling, supplementing the historic photographs, figurines and a number of framed brewery awards that adorn the walls. Why not ask for a take-away bottle of Draig Goch as brewed for Lees Welsh estate houses?
❀◑ ▲≋(Llangollen Rlwy) ♣P

Cynwyd

Blue Lion Hotel

Llandrillo Road, LL21 0LD (on B4401) OS057411
⏲ 12-3, 6-11; 12-11 Fri & Sat; 12-10.30 Sun
☎ (01490) 412106 website: www.bluelionhotel.co.uk
Plassey Bitter; guest beer Ⓗ
Comfortable, Grade II listed stone building, this popular and historic village-centre hostelry is close to Cynwyd Forest waterfall and Arche river bridge. The hotel no longer offers accommodation but is an established social centre for a range of rural pursuits and sports. Motorists are advised to park near the post office, a short stroll away. The interior includes a cosy dining room, complete with china shelf, pottery display and brass ornaments, and the main bar has two real fires. The original 19th-century leaded lights remain. ♨❀◑ ▲♣

Denbigh

Old Vaults

40 High Street, LL16 3RY
⏲ 11-11; 12-10.30 Sun
☎ (01745) 815142
Greene King Abbot, Old Speckled Hen Ⓗ
Town-centre pub with an L-shaped bar. The walls are adorned with pictures of a local nature; a Welsh dresser displays old jugs and bottles and a picture of HM Stanley the explorer, a son of the area. Denbigh Castle and town walls are of interest and worth a visit. A disco on Friday and Saturday is held in the upstairs function room. The No. 51 bus from Rhyl stops in the High Street next to the pub. ▲

Dyserth

New Inn

Waterfall Road, LL18 6ET
(on B5119 intersection from A5151) OS557995
⏲ 12-11; 12-10.30 Sun
☎ (01745) 570482

INDEPENDENT BREWERIES

Bryn Cyf Denbigh
Jolly Brewer Wrexham
Plassey Eyton

Banks's Original, Mansfield Bitter; Marston's Burton Bitter, Pedigree 🄷
Popular, lively pub offering superb views of both the historic local church and picturesque waterfall. A single bar serves four areas including a cosy snug. The pub is attractively decorated throughout; there is a real fire in the main bar and prints line the walls. The pub has a fine reputation for its food which in the summer months can be enjoyed in a large, secluded garden where children are welcome.
⩕Q⛵❀◐◑▲♣P

Graigfechan

Three Pigeons Inn

LL15 2EU (on B5429 3 miles S of Ruthin) OS14754547
⊛ 12-3 (not Mon or winter), 5.30-11; 12-11 Sat; 12-10.30 Sun
☎ (01824) 703178
website: www.threepigeonsruthin.co.uk
Draught Bass; Greene King IPA; Hancock's HB; guest beer 🄷
Set in the beautiful Vale of Clywd, this spacious rural pub offers superb views of the Clwydian range. The pub was rebuilt in 1777 and is situated on an old drovers' trail. There are separate dining rooms where excellent quality meals are served, such as Welsh beef cooked in Welsh beer. There are normally four beers on offer and live music is featured on Sunday evening. The No. 76 bus from Ruthin stops outside the pub. ⩕Q⛵❀◐◑▲♣P⊭

Graianrhyd

Rose & Crown

Llanarmon Road, CH7 4QW (on B5430, off A5104)
⊛ 4 (12 Fri & Sat)-11; 1210.30 Sun
☎ (01824) 780727
Flowers IPA; guest beers 🄷
200-year-old village pub, popular with the local community and walkers alike, where visitors are assured of a warm welcome from the cheery landlord. The bar area is split into two rooms served from one compact bar. The first room has an open fire and traditional copper-topped tables. The second, smaller room has a log-burning stove, a large table, benches and chairs. Freshly prepared food, using local produce is available lunchtime and evening.
⩕❀◐◑⊟♣P

Gwyddelwern

Ty Mawr

LL21 9DW (on A494 Corwen-Ruthin road) OS075469
⊛ 12-3, 5.30-11 (closed Mon-Tue); 12-11 Sat; 12-10.30 Sun
Beer range varies 🄷
This beautiful old roadside inn claims to be the oldest in Wales. Its main structure dates back to between 1386 and 1572. There are many original oak beams and in the bar area the ornate diamond patterned framing, which was once the end wall of the building, can still be seen. Upstairs is a cosy dining room with a medieval feel to it, where meals are served all day at weekends (no eve meals weekdays). Two real ales are available in summer, one in winter.
Q◐◑♣P⊭

Hendrerwydd

White Horse

LL16 4LL
(600 yds E of B5429, 1 mile S of Llandyrnog) OS121634
⊛ 12-3, 6-11; closed Mon; 12-10.30 Sun
☎ (01824) 790218 website: www.white-horse-inn.co.uk
Beer range varies 🄷
Tucked away in the rolling Vale of Clwyd countryside, this charming 17th-century inn is well worth visiting. The public bar is adorned with fishing and other sporting paraphernalia. A separate games room has Internet access. Two beers can normally be found from breweries throughout the UK. The pub enjoys an excellent reputation for its food, which is served in a comfortable dining area, however it is advisable to book well in advance. ⩕❀◐◑⊟♣P

Llandyrnog

White Horse (Ceffyl Cwyn)

LL16 4HG (on B5429) OS108652
⊛ 12-3, 6-11; 12-3, 6-10.30 Sun
Beer range varies 🄷
Village pub and restaurant next to the parish church, believed to date from the 15th century. Two separate no-smoking dining areas are served by a central bar area where drinkers can relax by the open fire. The two guest beers change frequently and usually come from local micros. Diners can choose from the evening specials board or the main menus. No evening meals are served on Monday. Local buses stop right outside. ⩕◐◑♿P

Llangollen

Corn Mill

Dee Lane, LL20 8PN
⊛ 12-11; 12-10.30 Sun
☎ (01978) 869555
website: www.cornmill.llangollen.co.uk
Boddingtons Bitter; Plassey Bitter; guest beers 🄷
Striking conversion of a former mill on the bank of the River Dee. The light and airy modern interior offers several distinct areas, including an upstairs restaurant. A spectacular terrace affords views of the river valley, while the steam railway station opposite runs the length of the building, past the functioning water-wheel. The three guest beers are usually from micro-breweries. Imaginative, home-cooked food is served all day. Q❀◐◑♿≹ (Llangollen Rlwy) ⊭

Sun Inn

49 Regent Street, LL20 8HN (head E on A5, near town centre)
⊛ 5 (3 Fri & Sat)-11; 3-10.30 Sun
☎ (01978) 860233
Beer range varies 🄷
The Grade II listed corner pub offers six real ales and a selection of continental beers. Coloured glass doors open into a large room with Welsh slate floor, three open fireplaces, school bench seating plus a stage area for live music (folk, jazz and rock). Behind the small bar, a small snug with a large plasma screen, leads to a covered courtyard for outside drinking. Friday and Saturday evenings may be busy when bands are playing. ⩕❀⊟▲≹(Llangollen Rlwy) ♣

Wynnstay Arms

20 Bridge Street, LL20 8PF

⏲ 12-3.30, 6-11; 12-11 Fri & Sat; 12-10.30 Sun

☎ (01978) 860710 website: www.wynnstay-arms.co.uk

Greene King IPA, Abbot; Tetley Burton Ale 🄷

Historic, popular, town-centre pub and former coaching inn. The interior remains largely unaltered, comprising many smal rooms. The main bar has large open fireplace. Opposite is a games room served through a hatch, while the rear rooms accommodate drinkers, diners or families as required. The steps at the front door originally provided a platform for mounting a horse or carriage; step-free access is through the courtyard via the rear door. For overnight guests there is a bunkhouse or en-suite accommodation.

♨Q♉❀⇌◐◑⇌(Llangollen Rlwy)

Llangynhafal

Golden Lion

LL16 4LN (off B5429 2 miles from Llandynog) OS129635

⏲ 6 (4 Fri; 12 Sat)-11; closed Mon; 12-10.30 Sun

☎ (01824) 790451

Holt Mild, Bitter 🄷

Pleasant, warm, welcoming pub and restaurant. An L-shaped bar serves two areas: the public bar with a pool table where smoking is allowed, and the no-smoking lounge with a restaurant with room for 22 diners. The pub is a welcome outlet for Holt's beers. The landlord collects the beer from the brewery himself and delivers it to a number of other outlets. A speciality of the restaurant is a choice of up to nine curries.

♨Q❀▲P⁄◻

Meliden

Miners Arms

23 Ffordd Talagogh, LL19 8LA

(on A547 Prestatyn to Ghuddlan road) OS063810

⏲ 12-11; 12-10.30 Sun

Marston's Burton Bitter, Old Empire; guest beer 🄷

Once the pay office for one of the last working lead mines on the north Wales coast. A single bar serves beer from the Marston's range. An inglenook-style fireplace housing a large wood-burning stove dominates the stone-floored lounge and snug to the right. The spacious dining area on the lower level has a reputation for fine food; booking is advisable for evening and Sunday meals.

♨Q♉❀◐◑P

Prestatyn

Royal Victoria

Sandy Lane, LL19 7SG (at A548 Coast Rd traffic lights)

⏲ 11.30-11; 12-10.30 Sun

☎ (01745) 854670

Marston's Burton Bitter; guest beer 🄷

Former hotel which is now a friendly local. A large L-shaped bar serves two drinking areas. To the rear of the pub is an area where children are allowed until 7pm. The pub runs keen darts and dominoes teams. It is situated close to Prestatyn railway and bus stations. Nearby is the northern end of Offa's Dyke.

♉▲⇌P

Rhewl (Llangollen)

Sun Inn

LL20 7YT (on B5103, follow signs from A542)

⏲ 12-2.30, 6-10; 12-10 Sun

☎ (01978) 861043

Beer range varies 🄷

This 14th-century former drover's cottage is a real gem. High above Dee Valley, four miles from Llangollen, it is popular with walkers and anglers. Three distinct rooms comprise a cosy bar, larger lounge with a range fire and a snug served from a hatch. The garden looks on to sheep-grazed Llantysilio Mountain. The beers are usually from regional or small breweries; the home-cooked food is recommended. A Rhewl OS map and enlarged postage stamp, plus a wall-mounted chess game add interest.

Q❀◐◑⊟♿▲♣P

Rhuddlan

King's Head

High Street, LL18 2TU (opp. Spar supermarket)

⏲ 9.30am-11pm; 9.30am-10.30pm Sun

☎ (01745) 590345

Banks's Mansfield Dark; Marston's Burton Bitter 🄷

Modern pub close to the historic castle and remains of the parliament building used by Charles I. The lively public bar has a large selection of photographs depicting local history as well as various social events held. A spacious lounge that can cater for various functions serves lunch (Wed-Sun) and breakfast is available daily between 9.30am and noon. Regular buses link Rhuddlan with Rhyl, Dyserth, St Asaph and Denbigh.

Q❀◐◑⊟♿▲♣P

Rhyl

Crown Bard

Rhuddlan Road, LL18 2RL

⏲ 11.30-11 (11.30-3, 5-11 winter); 12-10.30 Sun

Greene King IPA; guest beers 🄷

This popular pub is located on the southern outskirts of the town. It has a public bar and a large, comfortable lounge area. A quiet snug just off the lounge features a real coal fire and is the designated no-smoking area. The landlord is keen to ensure a mild is always available and guest beers are often from Welsh breweries. A well-attended quiz night takes place on Sunday evening.

♨❀◐⊟P⁄

Swan

13 Russell Road, LL18 3BS

⏲ 11-11; 12-10.30 Sun

☎ (01745) 336694

Thwaites Mild, Original, Lancaster Bomber 🄷

Busy, two-room pub close to the town centre, attractively decorated throughout with plenty of old photographs lining the walls. Lunches are served every day except Sunday in a dedicated area of the lounge. Reputedly the oldest pub in Rhyl, the name of the former, now defunct, brewery Wilderspool Ales is still displayed. The Swan was the first pub to hold a public TV licence in 1951.

◐⊟⇌♣

Ruthin

Castle Hotel

St Peters Square, LL15 1AA (off A525 at Ruthin)
☉ 12-11; 12-10.30 Sun
☎ (01824) 702479 www.castle-hotel-ruthin.co.uk
Greene King Old Speckled Hen; guest beers Ⓗ
Small public bar to the rear of the hotel, best approached from the car park. The hotel is in the main square of Ruthin, close to many historic attractions including the old gaol. Ruthin itself is situated in the spectacular Vale of Clwyd. The hotel boasts are two restaurants: Globetrotters serving dishes from around the world and the Castle Grill serving Welsh meats. ❀⇌◐◑▲P

St Asaph

Plough

The Roe, LL17 0LU (on A525 near A55 jct) OS033745
☉ 12-11 (11.30 Fri & Sat); 12-10.30 Sun
☎ (01745) 585080
Plassey Bitter; guest beers Ⓗ
Large central bar pub with a horse racing theme. It is popular for food but the emphasis here is on beer – the bar manager encourages young and old to drink real ale. The house beer, Graffiti, is brewed by Plassey. The tables on the ground floor are named after famous racehorses. The first floor has an Italian restaurant and a second restaurant called the Racecourse. A large patio at the front caters for outdoor drinking. St Asaph is an ancient city and has an interesting cathedral. ♨❀◐◑♿P⁄

FLINTSHIRE

Cadole

Colmendy Arms

Village Road, CH7 5LL (off A904, Mold-Ruthin road)
☉ 7 (6 Thu; 4 Fri; 12 Sat)-11; 12-10.30 Sun
☎ (01352) 810217
Beer range varies Ⓗ
Splendid red-brick local, convenient for the nearby Loggerheads Country Park. A small lounge exists for those who prefer a quiet drink, but the locals and those who like genial conversation use the main bar, which with its roaring fire and friendly atmosphere, is a fine place to cast away your cares. A welcome beer from Shepherd Neame and four interesting guests await you at local CAMRA Pub of the Year 2003 and 2004. Camping is by prior arrangement (no caravans). ♨Q❀▲P

Cilcain

White Horse

The Square, CH7 5NN (1 mile S of A541) OS177652
☉ 12-3, 6-11; 12-11 Sat; 12-10.30 Sun
☎ (01352) 740142
Banks's Bitter; guest beer Ⓗ
Mature village pub in the foothills of Moel Famau in the Clwydian range. Walkers and cyclists are welcome in the separate public bar but only children over 14 are allowed in the inn. Four log fires keep the pub warm in winter and food is served every lunchtime and evening. The guest beer often comes from the Marston's range. ♨Q❀◐◑⊟♣P

Halkyn

Blue Bell Inn

Rhosesmor Road, CH8 8DL (on B5123) OS209703
☉ 12-2.30 Wed-Fri summer; 5-11; 12-11 Sat; 12-10.30 Sun
☎ (01352) 780309
website: www.bluebell.uk.eu.org
Beer range varies Ⓗ
The real ale renaissance of the Blue Bell started in April 2003 and a blackboard displays the number of different cask beers sold since then. A house beer, Blue Bell Bitter, from Plassey is a regular, together with two changing guest beers usually from local micros, and a real cider, a rarity in north-east Wales. The pub is situated on top of Halkyn Mountain and is the focal point for guided walks organised by Walkabout Flintshire. Good value lunches are served at the weekend and evening meals are available Thursday-Saturday. Lunchtime weekday opening is restricted to Wednesday-Fridays only.
♨❀◐◑▲♣♠P

Hawarden

Fox & Grapes ✔

6 The Highway, CH5 3DH (on B5125 near A550 jct)
☉ 12-11; 12-10.30 Sun
☎ (0244) 532565 website: www.foxandgrapes.co.uk
Caledonian Deuchars IPA; Courage Directors; John Smith's Bitter; guest beer Ⓗ
Situated close to the home of former Prime Minister William Gladstone and Hawarden Castle, this pub offers a friendly, welcoming atmosphere and traditional features abound throughout. The garden is accessed through the large rear lounge. Four real ales include a rotating guest ale. If hunger strikes, an array of high quality meals is offered, all prepared with fresh ingredients. Q❀◐◑⊟▲♣≠P

Hendre

Royal Oak

Denbigh Road, CH7 5QE
(on A541 Mold-Denbigh road) OS191677
☉ 7-11; (also 12-3 Sat & Sun summer); 7-10.30 Sun
☎ (01352) 741466
website: www.royal-oak.wales.com
Tetley Bitter; guest beers Ⓗ
Roadside pub with two bars and a pool room. The lounge has the original air hooter from a nearby disused limestone mine. There is also a large display of coffee mugs from around the world, as well as old photographs of the area and bottles from long-gone breweries. The pub makes an ideal starting or finishing point for walkers on the nearby Clwydian hills; one route follows the old Mold to Denbigh railway line. The landlord likes to offer guest ales from local breweries. ♨Q❀⊟▲♣P

Higher Kinnerton

Royal Oak

Kinnerton Lane, CH4 9BE (8 miles SW of Chester off A55/A5104 jct)
☉ 12-11; 12-10.30 Sun
☎ (01244) 661395
Greene King IPA; Taylor Landlord; guest beer Ⓗ
One of the oldest coaching inns in North Wales,

it boasts a resident ghost and stands on the site of the famous tree where in 1644, King Charles I hid from Cromwell's troops. The tale is inscribed around the walls of the beamed snug. This is just one of many features here; note the ceiling covered with a large collection of pots and jugs. Three real ales are stocked and the restaurant sells a large selection of local dishes.
♨Q❀◑◗♿P

Holywell

Glan-yr-Afon

Milwr Road, Dolphin, CH8 8HE

(off A5026 signed Dolphin) OS195739

⏲ 12-3, 5.30-11; 12-10.30 Sun

☎ (01352) 710052

Tetley Bitter; guest beers Ⓗ

Extended Welsh long house with five separate areas including a games room popular with the younger set, extensive dining areas and a function room. The landlord promotes features of local geographical interest such as the red dragon and dolphin caves, and the pub fundraises for charities. The guest beers are usually from the Coach House range of one-offs and special beers. The accommodation is recommended. ♨👶❀🛏◑◗⊟♿⛺♣🍎P

Llanasa

Red Lion

CH8 9NE (off A5151 at Trelawnyd) OS105815

⏲ 12-11; 12-10.30 Sun

☎ (01745) 854291

Courage Directors; Webster's Bitter Ⓗ

Situated in the conservation village of Llanasa, this two bar inn has real fires and a homely feel. There is an extensive menu on offer in the no-smoking dining room. Meals are served all day every day. Disabled access is via the restaurant. There is outdoor seating in front of the pub overlooking the village church and surrounding hills. A guest ale is available at weekends.
♨❀🛏◑◗⊟♿♣P

Llanfynydd

Cross Keys

LL11 5HH (on B5101)

⏲ 7 (6 Fri & Sat)-11; closed Mon; 12-10.30 Sun

☎ (01978) 760333

Greene King IPA; guest beer Ⓗ

Attractive, traditional hostelry with a black and white exterior, which serves as a relaxing conclusion for a visit up Hope Mountain. A basic quarry-tiled bar leads to a restaurant, while a small, cosy lounge, once the village blacksmith's, features carved settles. An intimate snug is ideal for meetings. Apparently, the unprovoked clinking of the suspended pint mugs is a spooky premonition of an accident on the tricky bend outside. Sunday lunch and evening meals are served. ♨❀◗⊟♣P

Lloc

Rock Inn

St Asaph Road, CH8 8RD

(jct of A5026/A5151, 1 mile from A55) OS144766

⏲ 12-11; 12-10.30 Sun

☎ (01352) 710049

Burtonwood Bitter; guest beer Ⓗ

Village inn with two bars situated just outside Holywell and a mile from the A55. The lounge bar ceiling beams are hung with a large collection of teapots while the second bar has a racing theme. An unusual feature here is the traffic light on the bar. Both bars have real fires. There is a popular dining room off the lounge where meals are served Wednesday-Monday.
♨❀◑◗⊟♣P

Mold

Gold Cape ✔

8 Wrexham Road, CH7 1ES

(30 yds S of Market Square)

⏲ 9-11; 12-10.30 Sun

Brains Rev James; Courage Directors; Greene King Abbot; Marston's Burton Bitter, Pedigree; guest beers Ⓗ

A recent addition to the Wetherspoon's estate, the pub is named after the gold cape found nearby by workmen in 1831. A replica stands in the foyer. The manager is a keen real ale fan and keeps a good selection. Standard pub food is available until one hour before closing time. Stories of local interest are told on wall plaques, such as the Mold riots of 1869, and the life of novelist Daniel Owen, Mold's most famous son. The pub was awarded Welsh Loo of the Year 2004!
Q👶❀◑◗🍎

Nannerch

Cross Foxes

Village Road, CH7 5RD

(off A541 Mold-Denbigh road) OS167695

⏲ 6-11; 12-10.30 Sun

☎ (01352) 741293

Beer range varies Ⓗ

Traditional village pub with low, beamed ceilings and open fires in both bars. The smaller public bar has a tiled floor with a piano and brassware features in the lounge. A free house with two regularly changing beers, there is a full food menu at the weekend plus a range of filled baguettes. Curry and a pint is a popular Tuesday night attraction. The pub is a base for ramblers and fly fishermen.
♨Q◑◗⊟♣P

Ysceifiog

Fox Inn ☆

CH8 8NJ (signed from A541 and B5121) OS152715

⏲ 6 (9 Mon, 7.30 Tue in winter)-11; 12 (1 winter)-10.30 Sun

☎ (01352)720241

Beer range varies Ⓗ

In a peaceful setting opposite the village green, this Grade II listed pub is on CAMRA's National Inventory of pub interiors of outstanding historic interest. With four rooms and real fires in the lounge and bar, on winter nights the pub is warm and welcoming. It was a pilgrim stop on the trail from Shrewsbury to St Winifred's holy well at Holywell. Three real ales are usually available. Accommodation is planned for 2006. ♨❀◗⊟♣P

WALES

WREXHAM

Bersham

Black Lion ✔

Y Ddol, LL14 4HN
(off B5099 near Bersham Heritage Centre)
⏲ 12-11, 12-10.30 Sun
☎ (01978) 365588
website: www.blacklionpub.co.uk
Hydes Light, Mild, Bitter Ⓗ

This friendly pub, known by locals as the Hole in the Wall, is set on a wooded hillside above the picturesque River Clywedog on the eight-mile Clywedog industrial trail. A wood-panelled bar serves both the front room and the side lounge, and there is a separate games room. All rooms now have TV. A children's play area has been set up in the garden. Basic bar snacks are available all day. A quiz is hosted on Sunday evening. ♨❀⊟♣P

Brymbo

George & Dragon

Ael-Y-Bryn, LL11 5BA
⏲ 12-11; 12-10.30 Sun
☎ (01978) 758515
Lees Bitter Ⓗ

Bright, basic, no-frills local situated in a side road in a dormitory town for Wrexham. Sports TV dominates the cosy bar but the TV in the brightly-lit lounge shows alternatives. Live music is often hosted at weekends. This is a rare local outlet for John Willie's Bitter. ♨❀⊟♣P

Cross Lanes

Kagan's Brasserie

Bangor Road, Marchwiel, LL11 0TF
(on A525, 1 mile from Marchwiel)
⏲ 11-11; 12-10.30 Sun
☎ (01978) 780555
website: www.crosslanes.co.uk
Plassey Bitter Ⓗ

Located in a pleasant rural setting, this upmarket hotel lounge bar is a rare local outlet for Plassey. Served by a central bar, the drinking area comprises an airy, well-lit and comfortably furnished front room, with a more rustic back room featuring slate floors, solid oak tables and a superb log fire. Next to this is a dining area decorated with old prints and photographs. Visitors should note the magnificent 17th-century oak panelling in the front hall. ♨Q🛏◐◑P

Erbistock

Cross Foxes

Overton Bridge, LL13 0DR
(1 mile W of Overton on A528)
⏲ 12-11; 12-10.30 Sun
☎ (01978) 853525
website: www.crossfoxes-erbistock.co.uk
Banks's Original, Riding Bitter; Marston's Burton Bitter; guest beer Ⓗ

Splendidly located roadside pub overlooking one the most picturesque stretches of the River Dee. Dating back to 1748, the Cross Foxes has been extensively but sympathetically renovated to retain considerable character. Well-prepared, imaginative food is available and there is an extensive selection of wine and malt whiskies. For those who can resist the lure of nearby Bangor on Dee racecourse, the garden which leads down to the river is the perfect place to while away a sunny afternoon. Children are welcome until 7pm. Meals are served all day.
♨Q❀◐◑♿P🚭

Gresford

Griffin Inn

Church Green, LL12 8RG (on B5373)
⏲ 4 (3 Sat)-11; 3-10.30 Sun
☎ (01978) 582231
Tetley Bitter; guest beers Ⓗ

A step back 30 years, this is the kind of traditional local pub that is all too rare these days. Three irregular sized rooms run from the three-sided bar. Up to four real ales, normally from regional or small local breweries, are served by the friendly landlady who has presided over the pub for more than 32 years. Polished brass figurines, shell cases, a South African tortoise shell and domino clock are just some of the objects on display here. Across the road is All Saints Church, whose bells are one of the seven wonders of Wales. Q❀♣P

Pant-yr-Ochain

Old Wrexham Road, LL12 8TY
(follow sign to 'The Flash' from A534)
⏲ 12-11; 12-10.30 Sun
☎ (01978) 853525
website: www.pantyrochain-gresford.co.uk
Flowers Original; Plassey Bitter; Taylor Landlord; guest beers Ⓗ

This splendid, 16th-century manor house, overlooking a small lake, has been attractively refurbished and is now an elegant establishment offering cask ale and good food. The large, open-plan eating area features wooden floors, groups of tables, a wealth of fixtures and fittings and a newly rebuilt garden room. The policy of supporting local suppliers is reflected in the quality of food and the presence of Plassey beer. Smoking is allowed in the front bar. The pub is managed by the independent Brunning & Price group.
♨Q🐎❀◐◑♿P🚭🍷

Holt

Peal of Bells

12 Church Street, LL13 9JP
⏲ 12-11; 12-10.30 Sun
☎ (01829) 270411
Adnams Bitter; Marston's Pedigree; guest beers Ⓗ

This popular, family friendly pub is located next to St Chads Church on the English-Welsh border. The open-plan layout, which comprises three areas, is served from a central bar. Look out for the original Wurlitzer organ, often used as part of the regular evening entertainment. At the rear of the pub is a no-smoking restaurant area which looks out onto the sizeable garden leading down to the River Dee. Sunday lunch is popular and booking is recommended. ❀◐◑P

Lavister

Nag's Head

Old Chester Road, LL12 8SN
(on B5445, old Chester-Wrexham road)
✪ 5.30 (12 Sat)-11; 12-10.30 Sun
☎ (01244) 570486
Caledonian Deuchars IPA; Weetwood Best Bitter; Taylor Landlord; guest beers Ⓗ
Large, extended inn on the old Chester to Wrexham road. The pub has a plaque on its wall claiming it to be the birthplace of CAMRA. A small lounge area with an open fire welcomes you. The central bar serves a public bar with pool table, darts and Sky TV, and a larger no-smoking lounge popular with diners. The pub serves the busy local community as well as a good passing trade; meals are served all day. There is a large playground behind the pub, and adequate parking. ⩩❀◐▶P⚟

Ruabon

Wynnstay Arms

High Street, LL14 6BL (on B5605)
✪ 11.30-11; 12-10.30 Sun
☎ (01978) 822187
Robinson's Unicorn, seasonal beers Ⓗ
This late 18th-century coaching inn was enlarged and remodelled in 1841 into the grand public house and hotel that still exists to this day. The interior is split into many distinct rooms, each with its own character. The impressive library room is given over mainly to diners, while the drinker has a choice of the comfortable front lounge or back bar with its dartboard and TV. A function room is available to hire for special occasions.
⩩Q❀⛟◐▶⊟♿⇌♣P

Summerhill

Crown Inn

Top Road, LL11 4SR
(off Summerhill Rd, 1 mile from A483/A541 jct)
✪ 12-11; 12-10.30 Sun
☎ (01978) 755788
Hydes Dark, Bitter, seasonal beers Ⓗ
Real ale drinkers receive a hearty welcome from the landlord here who believes in his beers. The pub has a central bar with a lounge to one side, and a public bar with a pool table on the other. A Hydes metal anvil is displayed in the lounge, and a collection of pump clips behind the bar boasts the range of guest beers you have missed by not calling before. With stunning views of Alyn and Deeside, treat yourself – just ring the serving bell. Children are welcome until 7pm. ⩩Q☋◐▶⊟⇌(Gwersyllt)♣P

Wrexham

Albion Hotel

1 Pen-Y-Bryn, LL13 7HU
✪ 12-4, 7-11; 12-11 Thu-Sat; 12-10.30 Sun
☎ (01978) 364969
Lees Bitter Ⓗ
Impressive town-centre Edwardian pub with a traditional community atmosphere. It has a spacious lounge, and a more basic but friendly back bar with dominoes tables, dartboard and pool table. Both these rooms are served from a central bar. The pub is a popular venue on weekend evenings, featuring karaoke and live music. Good value accommodation makes the pub an ideal base from which to explore this area, rich in industrial heritage. ⛟⊟♿⇌♣▯

Horse & Jockey

Hope Street, LL11 1BD
✪ 10-11; 12-10.30 Sun
☎ (01978) 351081
Greene King Old Speckled Hen; Plassey Bitter; guest beers Ⓗ
Wonderful old thatched pub in the middle of Wrexham's shopping area. A central bar serves four areas, including a rear lounge where children are welcome during the day. The pub is always busy with escapees from the bustle of the shops during the day and aficionados of one of the few traditional pubs in Wrexham during the evening. ◐⊟♿⇌⚟▯

Your only man

We sat in Grogan's with our faded overcoats finely disarrayed on easy chairs in the mullioned snug. I gave a shilling and two pennies to a civil man who brought us in return two glasses of black porter, imperial pint measure. I adjusted the glasses to the front of each of us and reflected on the solemnity of the occasion. It was my first taste of porter. The porter was sour to the palate but viscid, potent. Kelly made a long noise as if releasing air from his interior. I looked at him from the corner of my eye and said: 'You can't beat a good pint!' He leaned over and put his face close to mine in an earnest manner. 'Do you know what I am going to tell you,' he said, with his wry mouth, 'a pint of Plain is your only man.'

Flann O'Brien, At Swim-Two-Birds, 1939. Plain is a Dublin term for porter.

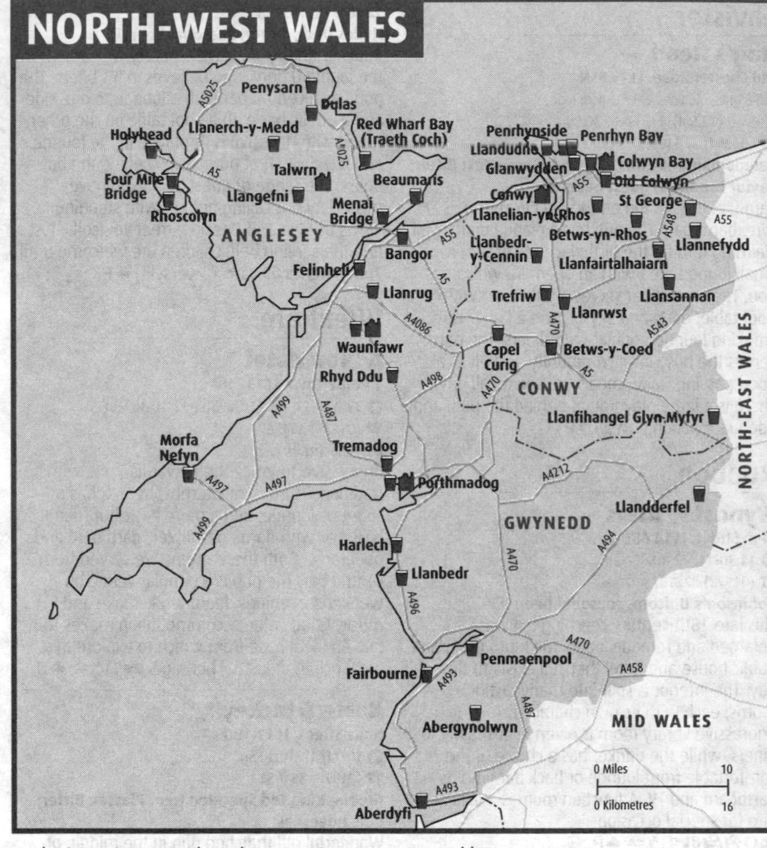

Authority areas covered: Anglesey UA, Conwy UA, Gwynedd UA

ANGLESEY/YNYS MÔN

Beaumaris

George & Dragon

Church Street, LL58 8AA

11-11; 12-10.30 Sun

☎ (01248) 810491

Robinson's Unicorn H

Welcoming local in the centre of town, a short walk from the Menai Straits, castle and other historic buildings. According to tradition, this timber-framed inn was built in 1410 but architectural details suggest a date in the more settled, prosperous days of Queen Elizabeth I. In the 1970s a remarkable series of wall paintings came to light during repair work. They have been restored and can be seen by appointment. ☾♣

Olde Bull's Head Inn

Castle Street, LL58 8AA

11-11; 12-10.30 Sun

☎ (01248) 810329

Draught Bass; Hancock's HB; Worthington's Bitter; guest beers H

Grade II listed building that was the original posting house of the borough. In 1645 General Mytton, a parliamentarian, commandeered the inn while his forces lay siege to the castle, which is a mere stone's throw away. The Royalists surrendered on 25th June 1646. Dr Samuel Johnson and Charles Dickens were famous guests and each individually-designed bedroom is named after a Dickens character. The beamed bar has a large open fire and many antiques. Not the cheapest pint but well worth the visit. Parking is limited. ⩕Q⇔P

Dulas

Pilot Boat Inn

LL70 9EX (on A5025)

11-11; 12-10.30 Sun

☎ (01248) 410205

Robinson's Unicorn H

Friendly, rural, family pub with a play area and converted double decker bus to keep the children amused. Originally a cottage-type building, now much extended, the lounge features an unusual bar created from half a boat. The pub is much used by walkers; the coastal path passes through the car park. It is worth visiting Mynydd Bodafon for its

INDEPENDENT BREWERIES

Conwy Conwy
Great Orme Colwyn Bay
Purple Moose Porthmadog
Snowdonia Waunfawr
Ynys Môn Talwrn

spectacular views and Traeth Lligwy for the sands. Meals are served all day. Q ❀◑◗ ⍋ ♣ P

Four Mile Bridge

Anchorage Hotel

LL65 3EZ (on B4545, just past bridge to Holy Island)
11-11; 11-10.30 Sun
Taylor Landlord; Theakston Cool Cask; guest beer Ⓗ
This family-run hotel is situated on Holy Island close to Trearddur Bay. There is a large, comfortable, lounge bar and a dining area serving a wide selection of meals all day. The hotel is close to some fine, sandy beaches and coastal walks. Its proximity to the A55 makes it a useful stopping off point for Holyhead Port. Bangor-Holyhead bus No. 4 stops nearby.
Q ⇌ ◑◗ ⍋ P

Holyhead

79

79 Market Street, LL65 1VW
11-11; 12-10.30 Sun
☎ (01407) 763939
Beer range varies Ⓗ
This is a comfortable, attractively furnished, town-centre pub enjoying a good year-round local trade, supplemented by visitors and rugby fans on their way through Holyhead to the Irish ferries. There are two bars, a pool room and a split-level dining area, affording views across to the ferry port. Beers are supplied by a local wholesaler, mostly from the large regional breweries, with occasional nationals. Good food, much of it prepared on the premises, is served all day.
◑◗ ≉ ♣

Llanerch-Y-Medd

Twr Cyhelun Arms

Twr Cyhelun Street, LL71 8DB
(on B5112)
7 (4 Fri; 12 Sat)-11; 12-10.30 Sun
Lees GB Mild, Bitter; guest beer Ⓗ
Situated in the heart of the island, Twr Cyhelun means Holly Tower. This friendly local is well worth a visit. The pub has a main bar, snug, games room and a dining area with real fires creating a cosy, welcoming environment. Guest beers are supplied by JW Lees. Food is served all day at weekends. Llanerch-y-Medd is on a cycle route and near Llyn Alaw. It is served by bus route 32 from Llanfefni and route 63 from Bangor.
⚠ Q ❀◗ ⊟ P

Llangefni

Railway Inn

48-50 High Street, LL77 7NA
(next to old railway station)
7 (12 Sat)-11; 12-10.30 Sun
Lees Bitter Ⓗ
Classic, small-town pub next to the old railway station displaying plenty of railway memorabilia and old photographs of Llangefni. The main bar is hewn out of the stone wall. The pub can get smoky. ♣

Menai Bridge

Liverpool Arms

St George's Pier, off Water Street, LL59 5DD
11.30-3, 5.30-11; 12-3, 7-10.30 Sun
☎ (01248) 713335
Flowers IPA, Original; guest beer Ⓗ
This 150-year-old pub has a good reputation for home-cooked food served all day. The conservatory is served by two central bars. Local photographs, antiques and maps adorn the walls. Well situated to explore the island of Anglesey and Snowdonia, the pub is popular with locals, the sailing fraternity and students. The narrow gauge Welsh Highland Railway is close by at Caernarfon. The guest bitter changes every few days. First class B&B (12 rooms) is provided. Q ❀ ⇌ ◑◗ ⍋

Victoria Hotel

Telford Road, LL59 5DR
(halfway between bridge and town centre)
11-11; 12-10.30 Sun
☎ (01248) 712309
Draught Bass; Ynys Môn Medra; guest beers Ⓗ
Situated 300 yards from the Menai suspension bridge, this 19-room hotel overlooks the strait and affords delightful views from the garden and patio. It is licensed for weddings and has a spacious function room with wide-screen TV for sports. The local independent brewery Ynys Môn supplies the hotel with excellent Welsh bitter. Regular live music is an added attraction. There is easy access to Snowdonia and the Welsh Highland Railway from Caernarfon, recently extended to the foot of Snowdon at Rhyd Ddu.
Q ❀ ⇌ ◑◗ ⊟ ♿ ⍋ P

Penysarn

Bedol

LL69 9YR (just off A5025)
12 (2 winter)-11; 12-10.30 Sun
☎ (01407) 832590
Robinson's Hatters, Hartleys XB, seasonal beers Ⓗ
The Bedol (Horseshoe) was designed by a local architect and built in 1985 to serve a small Welsh village, but the regulars now come from a much wider catchment area. The pub has changed breweries several times, but is now a Robinson's tied house, and unusually, serves most of the range on a rotating basis. Family run and friendly, it hosts regular live entertainment. Food is available all day except lunchtime in winter. Q ❀◑◗ ⊟ ⍋ ♣ P

Red Wharf Bay (Traeth Coch)

Ship Inn ✔

LL75 8RJ (1½ miles off A5025 near Benllech)
11-3, 6.30-11; 11-11 Sat & summer; 12-10.30 Sun
☎ (01248) 852568
Adnams Bitter; Brains SA; Greene King IPA; Tetley Dark Mild; guest beer Ⓗ
Previously known as the Quay, Red Wharf Bay was a busy port exporting coal and fertilizer in the 18th and 19th centuries. Enjoying an excellent reputation for restaurant and bar meals served all day, it gets busy with locals and holidaymakers in the summer. The garden affords panoramic views across the bay to

WALES

south-east Anglesey. The resort town of Benllech is two miles away and easy walks can be taken nearby. ♨Q♉❀◐◑⊟♿⅄P⊁

Rhoscolyn

White Eagle

LL65 2NJ

(off B4545 at head of lane marked Traeth Beach) OS270756

✪ 12-3.15, 6.30-11 (12-11 summer); 12-3, 6.30-10.30 (12-10.30 summer) Sun

☎ (01407) 860267

Marston's Pedigree; guest beer H

This pleasant, spacious pub gives a fine view over Caernarfon Bay and the Lleyn Peninsula to Bardsey Island. The nearby beach offers safe swimming; a warden is on duty in the summer months. The pub makes an ideal base for coastal walks. The bay provides moorings for small yachts and motor cruisers. Meals are served all day in summer. The infrequent No. 23 bus service runs from Holyhead. ♨♉❀◐◑♿⅄♣P⊁

CONWY

Betws-y-Coed

Glan Aber

Holyhead Road, LL24 0AB

✪ 11-11; 12-10.30 Sun

☎ (01690) 710325

Greene King Old Speckled Hen; Tetley Dark Mild, Bitter; guest beer H

Popular, family-run traditional Welsh stone-built hotel, in the middle of the picturesque village. The rear bar is open to visitors, as well as residents. There are a number of lounge areas, each with interesting features and located on varying levels, catering for all tastes. There is also a games room, with a display of plaques. Reasonably-priced bunkhouse accommodation is available. Q♉❀⇔◐◑⅄⇌♣P

Pont-y-Pair

Holyhead Road, LL24 0BN

(opp. Pont-y-Pair bridge over river Llugwy) OS791567

✪ 11-11; 11-10.30 Sun

☎ (01690) 710407

website: www.betws-y-coed.co.uk/acc/pontpair

Greene King Abbot; Marston's Pedigree; Tetley Bitter H

This family-run hotel is situated near the centre of Betws-y-Coed opposite the famous Ponty-y-Pair bridge. A warm welcome is offered to locals, visitors and guests and freshly-cooked meals are served in the no-smoking dining room, or the bar and lounge area. The games room with pool table looks out onto the patio; many interesting artefacts adorn the walls. At the side, a compact car park has space for three cars. The hotel has 10 guest rooms. ❀⇔◐◑⅄⇌♣P

Betws-yn-Rhos

Wheatsheaf Inn

LL22 8AH

✪ 12-3, 6.30-11; 12-3, 6.30-10.30 Sun

☎ (01492) 680218

Greene King IPA; Ruddles Best; Wadworth 6X H

Situated in an award-winning, picturesque village, famous for its twin-towered church, the Wheatsheaf was built in the 13th century, and licensed in 1640 as a coaching inn. This free house offers a quiet, welcoming atmosphere, good food and cosy, comfortable surroundings, with brass-strewn oak beams, stone pillars and its original hayloft ladder. A restaurant and function room, with full disabled facilities, is at the rear. Public bar beer prices are still cheaper than in the lounge. Q❀⇔◐◑⊟♿♣P

Capel Curig

Cobden's Hotel

Holyhead Road, LL24 0EE

✪ 11-11; 12-10.30 Sun

☎ (01690) 720243 website: www.cobdens.co.uk

Brains Rev James; Greene King Old Speckled Hen; guest beer H

An informal, 200-year-old hotel, set in its own grounds, centrally located in the village. Popular all year round, the well-appointed front lounge with multi-fuel stove, a rear terraced bar with feature natural rock face, and a restaurant cater for all visitors. The 16-bedroom hotel has built up a good reputation for its warm hospitality and comfortable informality, together with menus of freshly-prepared hearty and healthy food. ♨Q❀⇔◐◑⊟⅄♣P

Colwyn Bay

Pen-y-Bryn

Pen-y-Bryn Road, Upper Colwyn Bay, LL29 6DD

(top of King's Rd) OS842783

✪ 11.30-11; 12-10.30 Sun

☎ (01492) 533360

website: www.penybryn-colwynbay.co.uk

Thwaites Original; guest beers H

Built in old brick on the site of the former Colwyn Bay golf club, this large, modern, open-plan pub has oak floors, open fires and old furniture. Popular with locals and holidaymakers, outside a stunning garden terrace gives panoramic views over the bay and Great Orme. Imaginative bar food is served in a relaxed atmosphere; the menu is updated daily on the website. Five handpumps include guest beers from independent breweries. ♨Q❀◐◑♿♣P⊁▯

Wings Social Club

Station Square, LL29 8LF OS850791

✪ 12-3 (11-4 Fri), 7-11; 11-11 Sat; 12-4, 7-10.30 Sun

☎ (01492) 530682

Lees GB Mild, Bitter H

This former RAF social club is open to members and visitors, with CAMRA members particularly welcome. It is conveniently situated just off the main shopping area, opposite the station, the large, comfortably furnished lounge area has a stage for live entertainment; it is available for hire for special occasions. The club also has a games room for pool and darts and a snug with a TV. It has won numerous CAMRA awards including regional Club of the Year 2000. ⇌♣

Glanwydden

Queen's Head

LL31 9JP

(follow Penrhyn Bay sign from A470, 1 mile, second right)

⚙ 11-3, 6-11 (10.30 Mon); 12-10.30 Sun
☎ (01492) 546570
website: www.queensheadglanwydden.co.uk
Tetley Bitter; guest beers Ⓗ
Old pub, beautifully maintained with a cosy ambiance, well patronised by locals and holidaymakers. Formerly a wheelwright's cottage in the centre of this quiet village on the outskirts of Llandudno, the central bar serves a comfortable lounge/dining area on one side and welcoming locals' bar on the other. The restaurant serves award-winning food using local Welsh produce in an olde-worlde pub atmosphere. The same chef and landlord have been here for over 20 years. A luxury holiday cottage is available to let. ⛫Q❀◐⊟▲P

Llanbedr-y-Cennin

Olde Bull Inn

LL32 8JB (¾ mile from B5106 above Tal-y-Bont) OS761695
⚙ 12-2.30 (not Mon), 5-11; 12-11 Sat; 12-10.30 Sun
☎ (01492) 660508
Lees Bitter, seasonal beers Ⓗ
Small, 500-year-old drovers' inn on the steep incline above Tal-y-Bont (take lane off B5106 by side of Y Bedol) with splendid views over the Conwy Valley. It is popular with walkers and birdwatchers. Push hard on the original entrance door to reveal an interior with a low-beamed ceiling (some of the beams supposedly came from the Spanish Armada) and small copper-topped bar, where locals converse. The raised, 300-year-old extension, with flagstones and bare floorboards, serves as no-smoking dining room. ⛫❀◐▲♣P

Llandudno

King's Head

Old Road, LL30 2NB (next to Great Orme tramway)
⚙ 12-11; 12-10.30 Sun
☎ (01492) 877993
Greene King Abbot; Tetley Bitter Ⓗ
Over 300 years old, the King's Head is the oldest pub in Llandudno. It makes an ideal stop after walking on the Great Orme or riding on Britain's only cable-hauled tramway. The traditional, split-level bar is dominated by an open fire. The no-smoking dining area displays artefacts from the Great Orme mines. Char-grilled food is a speciality as well as traditional pub fare. The sun-trap patio is brightened by an award-winning flower display. A popular quiz is held on Wednesday evening. Phoenix brews the house beer, Tramdriver. ⛫❀◐▲⇌P

Queen Victoria

4 Church Walks, LL30 2HD
⚙ 11-11; 12-10.30 Sun
☎ (01492) 860952
Banks's Bitter; Marston's Pedigree, Old Empire; guest beers Ⓗ
Recently refurbished Victorian pub on the lower slopes of the Great Orme, close to the pier. An attractive green-tiled bay frontage, with patio seating, leads to a large, central bar with open-plan seating and dining areas, decorated with many portraits of Queen Victoria as well as historic Llandudno scenes. The pub's ambience attracts a more mature clientele. Upstairs is a no-smoking restaurant called Alberts. ❀◐♿▲⇌♣

Llanelian-yn-Rhos

White Lion Inn

LL29 8YA (off B583) OS863764
⚙ 11.30-3, 6-11; 12-4, 6-10.30 Sun
☎ (01492) 515807 website: www.whitelioninn.co.uk
Marston's Burton Bitter, Pedigree; guest beer Ⓗ
Traditional 16th-century inn located next to the church, in the hills above Old Colwyn. A slate-floored bar area with antique settles and real log fire ensures a warm welcome. Decorative stained glass is mounted above the bar of the tiny snug. The spacious, no-smoking dining area has a collection of jugs hanging from ceiling beams. White lion pottery lamps in the windows and two white stone lions guarding the door are a feature of this attractive, family-run inn. ⛫Q♉❀⇔◐⊟▲P

Llanfairtalhaiarn

Swan Inn

Swan Square, LL22 8RY
⚙ 12-3 (not Wed), 6-11; 12-11 Sat; 12-10.30 Sun
☎ 01745 720233
Banks's Original; Marston's Burton Bitter Ⓗ
In a peaceful village, this is an outstanding example of an unspoilt, traditional inn that is said to date from the 16th century. Exuding warmth and hospitality, at the front is a no-smoking dining room/bar, while the lounge, warmed by an open fire, has its own bar. The conservatory, housing a pool table, dartboard and juke box, doubles as a family room. Children are welcome in the garden and seating is provided out on the square. Occasional entertainment is hosted on Saturday evening. ⛫♉❀◐♣

Llanfihangel Glyn Myfyr

Crown Inn

LL21 9UL (On B5105, 3 miles from Cerrig-y-Drudion)
⚙ 7 (12 Sat)-11; closed Mon; 12-5, 7-10.30 Sun
☎ (01490) 420209
Beer range varies Ⓗ
Delightful rural gem, situated beside the Afon Alwen. The unspoilt interior of the front bar with its slate flooring area and open fire provides a warm welcome. Across the corridor is the pool room, with darts and portable TV. Monthly folk evenings are staged. Children are welcome in the pub and terraced gardens beside the river, where in summer bar meals are served. Permits are available for trout fishing – the licensees own the rights. Beers come from small independent breweries at this regular CAMRA award winner. ⛫Q❀▲♣P

Llannefydd

Hawk & Buckle Inn

LL16 5ED (signed from Henllan at B5382/B5429 jct) OS983706
⚙ 6-11; 12-3, 6-11 Wed; 12-3, 7-10.30 Sun
☎ (01745) 540249
Brains SA or guest beer Ⓗ
Welcoming, 17th-century coaching inn situated high in the hills on the old stagecoach route to Holyhead. This olde-worlde, multi-room pub has a black-beamed spacious bar, with comfy upholstered settles around the walls and by the

open fire. The locals' side bar has a pool table. A comfortable lounge and restaurant at the rear affords views over the hills to the coast. Excellent meals using local produce are also served in the front bar. ⛬Q◐◑⊟♿⛺♣P⊁

Llanrwst

New Inn

Denbigh Street, LL26 0LL

⏲ 11-11; 12-10.30 Sun

☎ 01492 640476

Banks's Original; Marston's Burton Bitter; guest beer [H]

Popular, recently refurbished, traditional terraced town pub, opposite the local balti house and just off the town square. The central bar serves the lounge and also a corner snug, with an open coal fire and TV. The rear games area has a pool table and juke box; in the evenings the volume can reach an amazing level! Outside is a small courtyard with a few picnic tables. This friendly pub appeals to all ages. ⛬❀⛺⇌♣

Pen-y-Bont

Bridge Street, LL26 0ET

⏲ 11-11; 12-10.30 Sun

☎ (01942) 640202

Beer range varies [H]

Full of character, this family-run, 14th-century free house with low beams and stone floors overlooks the elegant 17th-century stone bridge over the River Conwy. A small central bar serves both the public bar, with settle seating and collection of jugs, and the lounge with real fire and display of teapots. Further rooms are for family groups and traditional games. Two rotating guest beers are listed on the public bar blackboard. High river levels can result in flooding and temporary closure!

⛬Q☋◐◑⊟⛺⇌♣P

Llansannan

Red Lion (Llew Goch)

LL16 5HG

⏲ 5 (12 Sat)-11; 12-10.30 Sun

☎ (01745) 870256

Lees GB Mild, Bitter, seasonal beers [H]

Traditional village pub, popular with the locals. Its unusual layout features an original 14th-century secluded area around the stove, a raised lounge bar with large stone fireplace, and separate lower public bar, with pool table and TV. The dining room is normally no-smoking. A large garden lies beyond the courtyard. Good value food is available at most times.

⛬Q❀⛟◐◑⊟♣

Old Colwyn

Plough

282 Abergele Road, LL29 9LN

⏲ 12-3, 6-11; 12-11 Thu-Sat; 12-10.30 Sun

☎ 01492 515387

Courage Directors; Highgate Dark; Tetley Bitter; [H] **guest beers** [H]/[G]

Community pub in the town centre with a spacious lounge surrounding the bar, a dining area on the left and a games room on the right, where pool and darts are played. Guest beers are usually from independent breweries and include one on gravity dispense; Westons Old Rosie cider is also available. A popular quiz is held on Thursday evening. The landlord is a supporter of Colwyn Bay Football Club and holds regular fundraising events for the team.

Q❀◐◑⊟♣●

Red Lion

385 Abergele Road, LL29 9PL

⏲ 5 (4 Fri; 12 Sat)-11; 12-10.30 Sun

☎ (01492) 515042

Banks's Original; Marston's Burton Bitter; guest beers [H]

Serving up to seven, clearly listed ales from independent brewers, this ever-popular, recently sympathetically refurbished, genuine free house, boasts many CAMRA awards for its dedication to real ale. The cosy L-shaped lounge, warmed by a coal fire, features antique brewery mirrors and other breweriana. The traditional bar has a pool table, darts, TV and more breweriana. A rear stableyard is ideal for outdoor drinking, weather permitting. The pub lies on coastal bus route 12. ⛬Q❀⊟♣

Sun Inn

383 Abergele Road, LL29 9PL

⏲ 12-11; 12-10.30 Sun

☎ (01492) 517007

Banks's Mansfield Dark; Marston's Burton Bitter, Pedigree; guest beers [H]

The only original, unreconstructed pub building in Old Colwyn, dating from 1844, this is a genuine beer drinkers' local. A central bar serves a cosy lounge area with a welcoming real coal fire, paintings by a local artist on the walls and a piano for the prominent display of CAMRA literature. There is also a side bar with TV and juke box as well as a large rear games/meeting room where occasional live music can be heard. The pub is served by coastal bus route 12.

⛬Q❀♣

Penrhyn Bay

Penrhyn Old Hall

LL30 3EE OS816815

⏲ 12-3, 6-11; 12-3, 7-10.30 Sun

☎ (01492) 549888

Draught Bass; guest beer [H]

The Old Hall is a 16th-century building with a large wood-panelled Tudor bar serving a comfortable lounge area and a restaurant at the rear. Note the stone dated 1590 above the big, unused fireplace which hides a priest hole. The adjacent staircase is believed to be haunted by one of the two resident ghosts. The Hall has a nightclub that can be hired for functions and a Baronial Hall with a full-size skittle alley. ❀⛺♣P

Penrhynside

Penrhyn Arms

Pendre Road, LL30 3BY (off B5115)

⏲ 12-2 (not Mon-Thu), 5.30 (5 Wed-Fri)-11; 11-11 Sat; 12-10.30 Sun

☎ (01492) 541569

website: www.penrhynarms.com

Banks's Original, Bitter; Marston's Pedigree; guest beers [H]

A warm welcome is guaranteed at this

comfortable local. The spacious L-shaped bar has a pool table at one end, dartboard at the other and a wide-screen TV showing sport. The excellent website is updated regularly with a current list of beers, tasting notes, details of entertainment and fundraising events. An old Marston's mirror and framed pictures of noted drinkers such as Oliver Reed adorn the walls. Real Welsh cider is available as well as two guest beers, always from independents, and a winter ale on gravity at Christmas.

St George

Kinmel Arms

LL22 9BP (exit after Bodelwyddan, travelling W on A55)
12-3, 7-11; closed Mon; 12-5 Sun
(01745) 832207
website: www.thekinmelarms.co.uk
Moorhouses Black Cat; Tetley Bitter; guest beers H
Former coaching inn dating from the 17th century set on the hillside overlooking the sea. An L-shaped bar serves a combined dining and drinking area with a real log fire. Two independent guest ales change regularly, alongside a fine selection of Belgian beers, bottled and draught. A large, recently extended conservatory at the rear is mainly for diners. The pub has a reputation for good food, earning numerous awards including Best Dining Pub in Wales. Art by the owner Tim Watson adorns the walls. Q P

Trefriw

Old Ship/Yr Hen Llong

LL27 0JH (on B5106) OS 788638
12-3, 6-11; 12-11 Sat; 12-10.30 Sun
(01492) 640013
website: www.the-old-ship.co.uk
Banks's Bitter; Marston's Pedigree; guest beers H
Dating from the 16th century, this former customs house is now a busy village local. A small central bar serves the cosy L-shaped lounge with open fire, unusual period furniture, brass ornaments and pictures of historical and nautical interest. The no-smoking dining room boasts an inglenook. Note the saucy cartoons in the toilets. This genuine free house serves a fine range of guest beers and good home-cooked food. It lies on bus route 19 and 19a. A self-catering holiday cottage is available.
P

GWYNEDD

Aberdyfi

Penhelig Arms Hotel

Terrace Road, LL35 0LT
11-3.30, 6-11 (11-11 summer); 12-3.30, 6-10.30 Sun
(01654) 767215
Hancock's HB; guest beers H
Archetypal, small, friendly, seaside town hotel standing beside Penhelig harbour, affording superb views across the Dyfi estuary. The building is of some historic interest – today the 'Little Inn' has grown into a delightful hotel with its own well-earned reputation. Located in a self-contained part of the building is the rather stylish, nautically-themed Fisherman's public bar, with designated no-smoking area. Good food, including fish specialities and local meat dishes, is served in the excellent restaurant. The hotel has 14 comfortable bedrooms.
Q P

Abergynolwyn

Railway Inn

LL36 9YN (on B4405)
12-11; 12-10.30 Sun
Tetley Bitter; guest beers H
Friendly, two-roomed local in the village centre serving tourists and regulars alike. Ales come from the Enterprise Inns list, with one guest in winter and up to three in summer. An excellent range of food is served daily. Ideally situated for the Talyllyn Railway, children are welcome. The pub has a no-smoking dining section and outside drinking area.
Q (Talyllyn Rlwy)

Bangor

Belle Vue

Holyhead Road, LL57 2EU (in Upper Bangor)
11 (12 Sat)-11; 12.30-10.30 Sun
(01248) 364439
Draught Bass; Flowers IPA; Marston's Pedigree; guest beer H
Traditional town pub situated near the university, frequented by students, lecturers and locals. There is a wood-panelled lounge and the bar boasts an old Welsh range and a piano. Regular quiz nights and outdoor summer music events are held. Generous helpings of home-made food are served at lunchtime when a no-smoking area is available. Check on pub opening hours outside term time.

Black Bull/Tarw Du

107 High Street, LL57 1NS
10-11; 12-10.30 Sun
(01248) 387900
Courage Directors; De Koninck Ambrée; Greene King Abbot; Marston's Pedigree; guest beers H
Wetherspoon's pub in a converted church and presbytery at the top of the High Street. It offers spacious drinking areas including a large no-smoking section and a patio overlooking Upper Bangor and the university. It is busy during term time. A lift is available for disabled access. A number of pictures record the history of the university and the Menai Bridge.
Q

Harp Inn

80-82 High Street, LL57 1NS
11-11.30; 12-10.30 Sun
(01248) 361817
Greene King Abbot; Taylor Landlord; Tetley Bitter H
One of the oldest pubs in Bangor, the Harp has recently been refurbished. There is a large open-plan bar area, with steps leading to a games room, and a small snug to the side of the bar. Busy during term time, there tends to be loud music playing in the evening. Food is served 12-7pm, Friday-Sunday.

Tap & Spile

Garth Road, LL57 2SW (off old A5, follow pier signs)
⏲ 12-11; 12-10.30 Sun
☎ (01248) 370835
Draught Bass; guest beers [H]
Popular, split-level pub overlooking the renovated Victorian pier, offering superb views of the Menai Straits. The pub has a back-to-basics feel with old wooden tables and chairs and several church pews, but be prepared for the large-screen TV and fruit machines. It was voted local CAMRA Pub of the Year 2004. Food is served all day except Sunday evening. ◐◑♣

Fairbourne

Fairbourne Hotel

LL38 2HQ
⏲ 12-3, 6-11; 12-3, 6-10.30 Sun
☎ (01341) 250203
Greene King IPA; Marston's Pedigree; guest beer [H]
Situated on Mawddach estuary opposite Barmouth, this large 17th-century residential hotel with 20 comfortable bedrooms is renowned for its excellent food and friendly atmosphere. The long, narrow lounge bar is attractive, with subdued lighting and plenty of quiet corners. The terrace bar, which is no-smoking until 9pm, provides an ideal area for families. The restaurant has beautiful views over the hotel gardens and towards the sea. Live entertainment is often laid on on summer Saturday evenings. ♨Q⇄◐◑♿⇌P⚟

Felinheli

Gardd Fôn

Beach Road, LL56 4RQ (off main road by Menai Straits)
⏲ 11-11; 12-10.30 Sun
☎ (01284) 670359
Burtonwood Bitter; guest beer [H]
Nautically-themed ,18th-century, friendly pub that gets busy in summer and at weekends when locals are joined by numerous visitors. The bistro offers tasty food all day (booking is advisable at weekends). Splendid views of Anglesey and the Menai Straits can be enjoyed from the drinking area opposite the pub. The nearby marina is well worth a visit.
Q❀◐◑⊟♣⚟

Harlech

Lion Hotel

LL46 2SG
⏲ 12 (11 Sat)-11; 12-10.30 Sun
☎ (01766) 780731
Boddingtons Bitter; Flowers Original; Taylor Landlord [H]
Centrally located near the famous castle, this comfortable hotel offers a warm welcome. The lounge bar has an open fire and central heating with well-upholstered bench seating. A rear room has an electric stove in a large stone fireplace and the dartboard. The pool room houses a pool table, juke box and one-armed bandit. Popular bar meals are served from noon-8.30pm most days. Five bedrooms provide good value accommodation.
♨⇄◐◑⊟⇌♣

Llanbedr

Tŷ Mawr Hotel

LL45 2NH (take Cwm Bychan turn in village centre)
⏲ 11-11; 12-10.30 Sun
☎ (01341) 241440
Draught Bass; guest beers [H]
Small country hotel set in its own grounds. The modern lounge bar has a slate flagged floor and cosy wood-burning stove. Unusual flying memorabilia reflects connections with the local airfield. French windows lead on to a verandah and landscaped terrace with outdoor seating. The pub is popular with locals, walkers and real ale enthusiasts. Dogs and children are welcome. Meals are served all day.
♨❀⇄◐◑⛺⇌●

Llandderfel

Bryntirion Inn

LL23 7RA (on B4401 4 miles E of Bala)
⏲ 11-11; 12-10.30 Sun
☎ (01678) 530205
Jennings Cumberland Ale; guest beer [H]
Old coaching inn set in the countryside, with views to the River Dee. Off the pleasant public bar is a family room and there is a no-smoking lounge where meals are served in a quiet environment (booking advisable). Bar snacks are also served. A large function room is available. A few picnic tables stand near the small front car park; at the rear is a courtyard and a larger car park. Three bedrooms offer good value accommodation.
♨Q☋❀⇄◐◑♣P

Llanrug

Glyntwrog Inn

Caernarfon Road, LL55 4AN
(on A4086 towards Llanberis, approx ½ mile past Spar store)
⏲ 11-11; 12-10.30 Sun
☎ (01286) 671191
Greene King IPA; Young's Special [H]
This spacious local is situated just outside the village. It offers a games room, comfortable no-smoking area and a children's playground. Open all year round, it serves food served every lunchtime and evening. It is handy for Llanberis, Padarn Lake and Snowdonia National Park. The pub is served by regular buses from Caernarfon and Bangor. ◐◑⊟

Morfa Nefyn

Cliffs Inn

Beach Road, LL53 6BY OS283408
⏲ 12-3, 6-11; 11-11 Sat, July & Aug;
12-3 (10.30 July & Aug) Sun
☎ (01758) 720356
Beer range varies [H]
High on the cliffs overlooking the beautiful bay, the inn has views to Porth Dinllaen and far out to sea. Enjoy superb walks along the beach and out to the headland to watch the seals. Two beers are normally available: one may be Bass or Speckled Hen and the other often from Brains. The pub is closed on Sunday evening except in July and August. The conservatory is a no-smoking area.
Q☋❀⇄◐◑⊟♿P⚟

Penmaenpool

George III Hotel

LL40 1YD

⏲ 11-11; 12-10.30 Sun

☎ (01341) 422525

Black Sheep Best Bitter, Riggwelter; Theakston Best Bitter Ⓗ

This residential hotel built circa 1650 is situated beside the Mawddach estuary, at a toll bridge crossing, and adjacent to the old railway line which is now a cycleway and footpath. The Cellar Bar, open in the season, has a slate floor, oak-beamed ceiling and panelled benches. It is ideal for families, with a children's menu and no-smoking policy. Disabled access and WC are provided. Upstairs, the plush Dresser Bar lounge and restaurant benefit from fine views.

⛫Q❀⇆◑◐⊟♿P

Porthmadog

Spooner's Bar

Harbour Station, LL49 9NF

⏲ 11-11; 12-10.30 Sun

☎ (01766) 516032

website: www.festrail.co.uk

Banks's Bitter, Original; Marston's Pedigree; guest beers Ⓗ

Comfortable café bar forming part of the terminus of the world famous Ffestiniog Railway. Sit outside and watch the trains go by. Although Spooner's is renowned for its regular beer festivals (bank holidays and events to coincide with the railway), one or two beers from small independents are normally on tap all year round. Food is not always available in the evening out of season: telephone to check first. It was voted local CAMRA Pub of the Year 2003.

Q♉❀◑◐♿⇌P⍻

Rhyd Ddu

Cwellyn Arms

LL54 6TL

(on A4085 Caernarfon-Beddgelert road at foot of Snowdon)

⏲ 11-11; 11-10.30 Sun

☎ (01766) 890321

website: www.snowdoninn.co.uk

Beer range varies Ⓗ

This beamed, 200-year-old pub at the foot of Snowdon, with roaring log fire, is open all year round, serving an excellent all day menu including home-made curried pizza. A changing range of beers from smaller breweries makes this pub well worth a regular visit. B&B, bunkhouse and cottage accommodation is available. Railway enthusiasts will enjoy the Welsh Highland Railway which is only 250 yards away. A past winner of local CAMRA Pub of the Year, the beer is pricey but well worth sampling.

⛫♉❀⇆◑◐⇌P

Tremadog

Golden Fleece

Market Square, LL49 9RB

(on A487 1 mile N of Porthmadog)

⏲ 11.30-3, 6-11; 12.30-3, 6-10.30 Sun

☎ (01766) 512421

Draught Bass; guest beer Ⓗ

Situated in the old market square, this former coaching inn is now a friendly local on the main bus routes. Rock climbing and narrow gauge railways are nearby. The lounge bar has a no-smoking area at the rear and there is a snug which may occasionally be reserved for regulars. Outside, a covered area has decking and bench seats. An additional bistro is upstairs (booking advised). Guest beers are from smaller breweries. Children are welcome.

⛫Q♉❀⇆◑◐▲⍻

Waunfawr

Snowdonia Park

Beddgelert Road, L55 4AQ

(on A4085 Caenarfon-Beddgelert road S of village) OS527588

⏲ 11-11; 12-10.30 Sun

☎ (01286) 650409

website: www.snowdonia-park.co.uk

Banks's Mansfield Dark; Marston's Pedigree; Snowdonia Welsh Highland Bitter Ⓗ

Home of the Snowdonia Brewery, you will usually find one of its brews here, if not a guest beer is offered. Meals are served all day. There are children's play areas both inside (separate from the bars) and outside. The large campsite gives a discount to CAMRA members. The pub adjoins the station on the Welsh Highland Railway; stop off here before going on to Rhyd Ddu on one of the most scenic sections of narrow gauge railway in Britain. Meals are served all day.

Q♉❀◑◐⊟♿▲⇌(Welsh Highland Rlwy)♣P

WALES

Cask breather

When a pub entry states that some beers are served with the aid of cask breathers, this means that demand valves are connected to casks and cylinders of gas. As beer is drawn off, it is replaced by applied gas (either carbon dioxide or nitrogen, or both) to prevent oxidation. This method is not acceptable to CAMRA as it does not allow beer to condition and mature naturally. The Campaign believes brewers and publicans should use the size of casks best suited to the turnover of beer in order to avoid oxidation. If a pub in the Good Beer Guide uses cask breathers we list only those beers that are free of the device.

WEST WALES

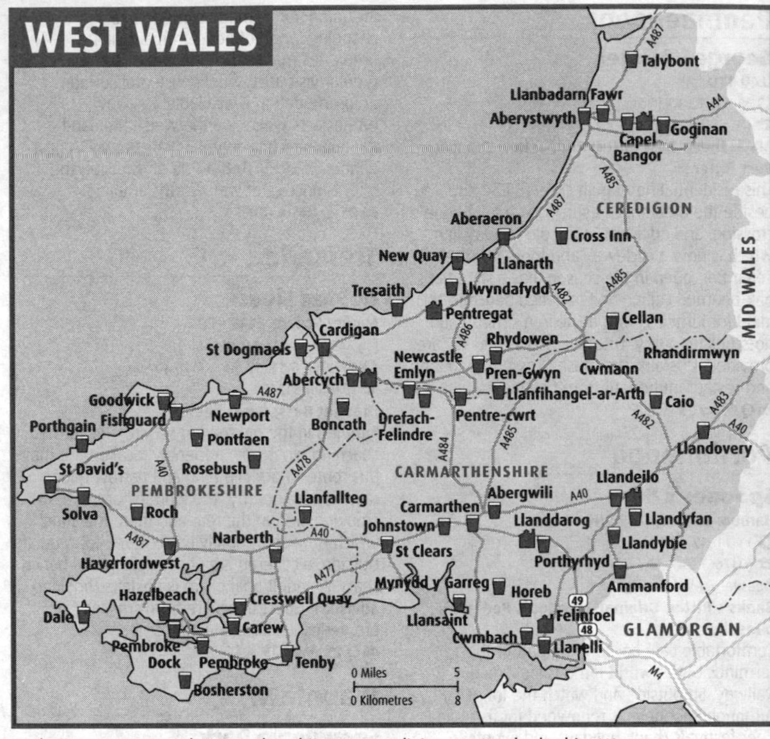

Authority areas covered: Carmarthenshire UA, Ceredigion UA, Pembrokeshire UA

CARMARTHENSHIRE

Abergwili

Black Ox

High Street, SA31 2JB

12 (5 Mon)-11; 12-10.30 Sun

(01267) 592598

Beer range varies H

Village local that has gained a reputation for its food. The bar is open plan but has three small, distinct drinking areas. The real ale is often provided by a Welsh brewer. There is a dining room, but meals may be taken in the bar (eve meals Tue-Sat). While no specific area is provided for children, families are welcome in the dining room. The former palace of the Bishop of St Davids – now a museum – can be visited nearby. ❀◐◑ ♿ ♣ P

Ammanford

Ammanford Hotel

Wernolau House, 31 Pontamman Road, SA18 2HX

5.30-11; 12-10.30 (7 winter) Sun

(01269) 592598

Brains Buckley's Best Bitter; guest beers H

On the outskirts of Ammanford, this was originally a colliery manager's house, and is set in five acres of landscaped grounds and woodlands. The hotel bar is open to non-residents. A varied guest list of up to five beers is often chosen by regulars. The Victorian theme is enhanced by open log fires in winter. A spacious function room caters for weddings. Families are welcome and food is available. Q ❀ ◐◑ P

Caio

Brunant Arms

SA19 8RD (approx 2 miles from Pumpsaint, off A482)

12 (6 Mon)-11; 12-10.30 Sun

(01558) 650483

Beer range varies H

Five rotating guest beers are kept at this pub in the centre of the village, near the Dolau Cothi goldmines. It hosts regular pool contests and quiz events. Good quality, home-cooked food is served. There is a pony-trekking centre nearby and a horse tethering rail is provided here. A legendary Welsh wizard is buried in the church opposite. ❀ ◐◑ P

Carmarthen

Queen's Hotel

Queen Street SA31 1JR

12-11; 12-10.30 Sun

(01267) 231800

Draught Bass; Worthington's Bitter; guest beers H

Town-centre pub noted for the quality of the Bass. There are discounted meal offers in the late afternoon. An upstairs meeting room is available. Numerous pump clips are displayed around the bar. A walled patio allows for alfresco drinking during summer months. The pub is situated beneath the remnants of the old castle. ❀◐ ≠ ♣

Stag & Pheasant

34 Spilman Street, SA31 1LQ

11-11; 12-10.30 Sun

(01267) 236278

Worthington's Bitter; guest beers ⊞
Popular town pub, especially favoured by office workers, serving good lunchtime and Sunday meals. The pub was once part of a stable block belonging to a nearby hotel. The bar is a single, open-plan room where the welcome is warm and fine beer is the norm. A TV in the corner is only used for sporting events. ◐⇌

Cwmann

Cwmanne Tavern

SA48 8DR (at A482/A485 jct)
✪ 5 (12 Sat)-11; 12-10.30 Sun
☎ (01570) 423861 website: www.cwmanntavern.co.uk
Beer range varies ⊞
Built in 1720 on a drovers' route, a quarter mile from Lampeter. All age groups are welcome here. The three drinking areas feature plenty of timber beams, posts and floors. New owners have improved the quality of the beer considerably since acquiring the premises in 2004. There are two guest beers, a draught cider, and a good selection of bottled British and European beers, including wheat beers (most bottle-conditioned). Live music on Saturday evening draws a crowd. No food is served Monday. ♨Q❀⇄◐◗♣●P

Cwmbach

Farriers

Trimsaran Road, SA15 4PN (on Llanelli road)
✪ 11-11; 12-10.30 Sun
☎ (01554) 774256
Draught Bass; Worthington's Bitter; guest beer ⊞
Small pub where the pretty garden is used as an additional drinking area in summer. The main entrance to the pub is by means of steps leading down to a suspended walkway. A good reputation for food is backed up by a varied and interesting menu. The owner is a keen golfer, as can be seen by memorabilia around the walls. Parking is possible in a side road opposite.
Q❀◐◗

Drefach-Felindre

John y Gwas

SA44 5XG (opp. St. Barnabus Church)
✪ 2 (3 Mon; 12 Sat)-11; 3-10.30 Sun
☎ (01559) 370469 website: www.johnygwas.co.uk
Beer range varies ⊞
Friendly village pub, previously the New Shop Inn. Extensive alterations have created a cosy, homely atmosphere, although it does get busy at times. Pool is particularly popular in the main bar where local farm implements and a collection of pewter mugs are on display. Note the pictures of local fallen heroes from the two world wars. Two restaurants (one no-smoking) serve good, locally-sourced meat dishes (Wed-Sat). The National Woollen Museum of Wales is a mile away. ♨Q◗⊟♣P

Horeb

Waunwyllt

Horeb Road, SA15 5AQ
(off B4309 at Five Roads, 3 miles from Llanelli)
✪ 12-3, 7 (6.30 Fri & Sat)-11; 12-3, 7-11 Sun
☎ (01269) 860209
Beer range varies ⊞
Superb country pub where a warm welcome is assured. A varied menu offers excellent food at a reasonable price, including daily specials. The pub is close to the cycle path that runs to Llanelli, and has developed a trade from passing cyclists. A recent local CAMRA Pub of the Year, it has overnight accommodation (booking is advisable). There are seats outside the pub and a garden to the rear.
Q❀⇄◐◗ ⛺P

Johnstown

Friends Arms

Old St Clears Road, SA31 3HH
✪ 4.30 (4 Fri; 11 Sat)-11; 12-2, 7-10.30 Sun
☎ (01267) 234073
Ansells Mild; Tetley Bitter, Burton Ale ⊞
Lively, welcoming, community local with a cosy, low, beamed bar. Adjoining a well-preserved toll house at the former western entry to Carmarthen, there has been a pub on this site for over 400 years. The extensive building once also housed a blacksmith's forge. Regular quiz nights provide entertainment. An interesting selection of bottled beers is stocked. ♨❀

Llandeilo

Angel Hotel

62 Rhosmaen Street, SA19 6EN (on A483)
✪ 11.30-3, 6.30-11; closed Sun
☎ (01558) 822765 website: www.angelbistro.co.uk
Evan-Evans BB, Cwrw; guest beers ⊞
Refurbished town-centre pub that has retained a rustic, olde-worlde charm. The central bar divides the large saloon into smaller, more segregated sections. Excellent food is served in the adjoining restaurant and in the bar. Diners and drinkers are normally treated to relaxing, easy listening jazz background music. The four cask ales include two local brews from Evan-Evans Brewery. Under-21s are discouraged after 6pm. Q❀◐◗⇌P

Salutation Inn

New Road, SA19 6DF
✪ 12-midnight; 12-11 Sun
☎ (01558) 823325
Tomos Watkin Brewery Bitter; guest beers ⊞
Vibrant pub in a market town. The central bar serves both the lounge and public bar. Although recently refurbished, it has retained its traditional character, with the large open fireplace being the focal point of the lounge area. The pub is popular, both with locals and visitors passing through this sleepy town. Live musical entertainment is arranged at least once a month.
♨Q❀⊟♿⇌♣⚟

INDEPENDENT BREWERIES

Ceredigion Pentregat
Coles Llanddarog
Evan-Evans Llandeilo
Felinfoel Felinfoel
Gwynant Capel Bangor
Nags Head Abercych
Penlon Cottage Llanarth

Llandovery

Castle Hotel

King's Road, SA20 0AP

⏲ 11-11; 12-3, 7-11 Sun

☎ (01550) 720343

Worthington's Bitter; guest beer ⊞

Built in the 18th century, the hotel has been extensively refurbished. As well as being close to the castle it is also handy for the town's livestock market. There is ample car parking for guests in the 23 rooms (two of which have four poster beds). An annual drovers' festival takes place in the town in September. ⇄◑◗⇌P

Llandybie

Ivy Bush

18 Church Street, SA18 3HZ

⏲ 12-11; 12-2.30, 7-10.30 Sun

☎ (01269) 850272

Greene King Old Speckled Hen; Tetley Burton Ale; guest beer ⊞

The oldest pub in the village, dating back nearly 300 years, now refurbished to an open-plan, it has lost none of its appeal. Darts is played Tuesday and Thursday, cards on Wednesday. Children (and dogs) are welcome. The pub is close to the Heart of Wales railway line. B&B accommodation in the adjacent holiday cottage includes an en-suite sauna. ⇄⇌

Llandyfan

Square & Compass

SA18 2UD OS652163

⏲ 5 (12 Sat)-11; closed Mon; 12-10.30 Sun

☎ (01269) 850402

Beer range varies ⊞

This 18th-century building was originally the village blacksmith's, converted into a pub during the 1960s. Nestling on the western edge of the Brecon Beacons national park, it offers magnificent panoramic views and plentiful walking opportunities. A traditional, family-oriented, country pub, it also extends a warm welcome to visiting discerning drinkers sampling the three real ales. The pub has a wonderful rustic charm and is packed with rural memorabilia. Good home-cooked food is served evenings (all day Sat and Sun).

Q⚲❀◑◗♿⛺P⚡

Llanelli

Lemon Tree

2 Prospect Place, SA15 3PT

⏲ 12-11; 12-10.30 Sun

☎ (01554) 775121

Brains Buckley's Best Bitter; guest beer ⊞

End-of-terrace establishment near the site of the former Buckley's Brewery. Popular with locals, it has a strong sports following. The interior has been refurbished and, although open plan, it feels as if the bar is still separate; there is a pool table at a lower level than the bar. The bowling green at the rear now hosts barbecues.

Llanfallteg

Plash Inn

SA34 0HN (off A40 at Llanddewi Velfrey)

⏲ 12-10.30 (6-11 winter Mon & Tue); 12-10.30 Sun

☎ (01437) 563472

Worthington's Bitter; guest beers ⊞

A truly local clientele gives this terrace-style cottage pub a homely feel. The regulars call it a 'talking pub'. A garden at the rear overlooks green fields and the River Taf. A small restaurant serves traditional home-made dishes. The attractive bar, rescued from an outfitters' shop, serves ales mainly from the Welsh border breweries, such as Wye Valley and Salopian. The new landlord has kept changes to a minimum, maintaining the pub's charm. ♨Q❀◑◗♣P

Llanfihangel-ar-Arth

Cross Inn

SA39 9HX

⏲ 5-11; closed Tue; 12-10.30 Sun

☎ (01559) 384838 website: www.crossinnwales.co.uk

Fuller's London Pride; guest beer ⊞

This 16th-century drovers' pub has now entered the 21st century as far as real ale is concerned. It comprises a single bar, with open fire, a pool room and a restaurant serving good quality food, all cooked on the premises. The specials menu offers a mouthwatering selection prepared from locally-sourced produce – the puddings will expand your waistline. The annual Easter beer fest, with over 14 beers, draws a crowd. The licensees organise regular events, ensuring this pub's role in village life.

♨Q❀◑◗⊟⛺♣●P

Llansaint

King's Arms

13 Maes yr Eglwys, SA17 5JE (behind church)

⏲ 12-2.30, 6.30-11 (closed winter Tue); 12-2.30, 6.30-10.30 Sun

☎ (01267) 267487

Worthington's Bitter; guest beers ⊞

A welcome as warm as the log fire that burns in winter is to be found at this 200-year-old pub, situated close to an 11th-century church. A collection of jugs adorns the low beams, while local photographs are displayed on the walls. The pub is reputedly built from stone recovered from the lost village of St Ishmaels. Children are welcome and good quality food is served. Carmarthen Bay holiday park is just a few miles away. ♨❀⇄◑◗⛺♣P

Mynydd y Garreg

Prince of Wales

SA17 4RP (1½ miles from Kidwelly bypass)

⏲ 7 (5 Sat)-11; 12-3 Sun

☎ (01554) 890522

Beer range varies ⊞

Small, isolated pub, well worth finding, where extensive movie memorabilia is featured throughout. The small, no-smoking restaurant offers good food. A changing choice of up to six beers comes from small and local breweries, and the pub does a good trade in takeaways (bring your own container). Children under 14 are not admitted. The town of Kidwelly, with its castle and industrial museum, is just a few miles away. It was voted Pub of the Year by the local CAMRA branch in 2003. ♨Q◑◗P

Newcastle Emlyn

Bunch of Grapes

Bridge Street, SA38 9DU (opp. provisions market, near castle entrance)
12-11 (closed winter Mon); 12-3, 7-10.30 (not winter eve) Sun
☎ (01239) 711185
Courage Directors; guest beers H

Excellent watering-hole at the town centre, with original exposed beams and flooring. This 17th-century pub was voted Pub of the Year by local CAMRA members in 2004. An unusual small indoor garden features a grapevine and advertising memorabilia. A restaurant serving excellent food is just off the bar area (lunches Thu-Sun, eve meals in summer). Live music is performed on Thursday evening. Pavement seating at the front gives a continental feel and a small, enclosed garden is at the rear.

Pentre-Cwrt

Plas Parke Inn

Plas Parke, SA44 5AX (on B4335, between Llandysul and Newcastle Emlyn)
4 (3 Fri; 1 Sat)-11; 12-10.30 Sun
☎ (01559) 362684
Draught Bass; guest beer H

Friendly local with two cosy bars and another area for a quiet drink. In summer sheltered seating is provided in the garden under gazebos. It is popular for evening meals (not Tue) and Sunday lunch: look for the specials. Generous portions are the norm in the restaurant. Nearby is the beauty spot, Alltcafan Bridge, which spans the 'Queen of Welsh rivers', fished for salmon and sewin. It is also handy for the canoeing centre in Llandysul, and the Teifi Valley narrow gauge railway at Henllan. P

Porthyrhyd

Mansel Arms

Banc y Mansel, SA32 8BS (off A48, Drefach-Llanddarog road)
6 (2 Sat)-11; 12-4 Sun
☎ (01267) 275305
Beer range varies H

Wood fires burn in each room of this friendly local and 18th-century former coaching inn beside the A48. The room where pool and darts are played to the rear was originally used for killing pigs. The limestone slabs have been broken up and used in the fireplace. Low beams have been put in to enhance the atmosphere, while a collection of jugs hanging in the bar adds a decorative touch to this welcoming pub.
Q P

Rhandirmwyn

Royal Oak

SA20 0NY
11.30-3, 6-11; 12-2, 7-10.30 Sun
☎ (01550) 760201
Beer range varies H

Remote, stone-flagged pub affording excellent views of the Towy Valley. CAMRA Pub of the Year for South Wales in 2002, it was built as a hunting lodge for the local landowner. The pub is frequented by ramblers and birdwatchers from the RSPB site nearby. Llyn Brianne Dam is just a couple of miles away. An excellent range of up to six beers is reduced to three to four in winter. A good choice of bottled beers and whiskies and wholesome food complete the picture. Q P

St Clears

Corvus

Station Road, SA33 4BG
11-11; 12-10.30 Sun
☎ (01994) 230965
Courage Best Bitter; Worthington's Bitter; guest beer H

Busy, two-bar local at the centre of the village. Caricatures of the pub's regulars cause amusement in the bar. Lots of brass and beer jugs decorate the lounge. The pub is the local haunt for sports people and it supports the village football team. An interesting food menu is available in the evening. Nearby, Weatherton adventure park offers a day out for all the family. Q

CEREDIGION

Aberaeron

Cadwgan

10 Market Street, SA46 0AU
12-11; 12-10.30 Sun
☎ (01545) 570149
Brains Buckley's Best Bitter; guest beer H

This cosy, one-roomed, carpeted pub near the harbour is seeing a revival in its fortunes following the arrival of an experienced licensee in autumn 2004. The customers are a harmonious mix of locals and (especially in summer) visitors to this charming Regency town. Fascinating local photographs decorate the walls. The single guest beer is sourced from a local wholesaler and may come from a wide range of (often micro-) breweries. Evening meals are served in the upstairs dining room.

Aberystwyth

Fountain Inn

Trefechan, SY23 1BE (S end of Trefechan Bridge)
12 (2 Mon-Fri Jan & Feb)-11; 12-10.30 Sun
☎ (01970) 612430
Boddingtons Bitter; Brains Dark, SA H

This cosy two-roomer is ideally situated for the harbour, marina and iron age hill fort at Pen Dinas (its ascent should prompt a healthy thirst). Reach it from the main shopping area by crossing the town's old stone bridge, or from the bus/rail station and public car parks via an elegant new footbridge. The pub was once the tap for the town's main brewery – a few remnants survive, and photographs evoke the past of this distinctive quarter of town.

Ship & Castle

1 High Street, SY23 1JG
2 (12 Sat)-11; 12-10.30 Sun
Brains SA; guest beers H

After a period of closure in 2004, this street-corner ale house has quickly re-established its position as the best place in town for a choice of quality draught beers. The L-shaped main drinking area is complemented by a back room area, featuring an attractive mural that illustrates the pub's name. The old 'perch' seating has been replaced by more comfortable benches. The pub attracts students, townsfolk and tourists. Irish session musicians congregate in the back room on Wednesday evening. ▲⇌

Capel Bangor

Tynllidiart Arms

SY23 3LR (on A44, 4 miles E of Aberystwyth)

11-midnight (11-3, 5-midnight winter); 12-11.30 Sun

☎ (01970) 880248

Gwynant Cwrw Gwynant; Hancock's HB; guest beer H

Home of probably the world's smallest commercial brewery, this village pub reopened in 2004 after some years' closure. Now largely food-led, it still enjoys a good following for the beers. The main room is open plan with bench seating, tables and chairs. The decking outside has gas heaters and pleasant views. There is a no-smoking restaurant upstairs. The house beer, Cwrw Gwynant, usually goes on at the weekend; if it sells out quickly, a second guest beer may be offered. ♣P

Cardigan

Black Lion/Llew Du

High Street, SA43 1JW

11-11; 12-10.30 Sun

☎ (01239) 612532

Tomos Watkin Cwrw Braf, OSB; Worthington's Bitter H

Historic coaching inn in a busy, characterful town. It dates back to the 12th century, but the present building is 18th century. There is a main drinking area, a small panelled snug and a rear dining section. It is a welcome outpost for Tomos Watkin beers. Good value food is available at this friendly meeting place. ♣

Red Lion/Llew Coch

Pwllhai, SA43 1DB (behind bus station)

11-11; 12-10.30 Sun

☎ (01239) 612482

Brains Buckley's Best Bitter, Rev James H

Homely local where Welsh is the first language. Visitors are made to feel most welcome. The main bar area is complemented by a smaller private lounge and a games room. Welsh music is sold here and weekly live entertainment is staged. Snacks are available at most times. Tucked away behind the bus station, this pub is worth seeking out. Q♣

Cellan

Fishers Arms

SA48 8HU (on B4343, S end of village, two miles from Lampeter)

4.30 (11 Sat)-11; 11-10.30 Sun

☎ (01570) 422895

Hancock's HB; guest beer H

Situated alongside the River Teifi, one of Wales' premier trout and salmon rivers, the Fishers dates from 1580 and was first granted a licence in 1891. The main bar has an open fire and flagstone floor; fly rods and antique guns hang from the beamed ceiling. The guest beer is usually from Tomos Watkin, but is occasionally Taylor Landlord or Marston's Pedigree. Buses from Lampeter and Tregaron, while hardly frequent, permit an afternoon or early evening visit. Q♣P

Cross Inn

Rhos-yr-Hafod

SY23 5NB (at B4337/B4577 crossroads)

12-2 (not winter), 6-11; 12 (6 winter)-11 Sat (closed Mon Jan & Feb); 12-3, 7-10.30 Sun

☎ (01974) 272644

Boddingtons Bitter; guest beers H

This sociable pub stands at a crossroads in the Ceredigion uplands. Small drinking areas cluster round the central bar. The back room, decorated with bird paintings and local photos, functions as a no-smoking family room; it also lacks loudspeakers, while the rest of the pub has quiet background music to set off the animated, bilingual conversation. There is a no-smoking restaurant (no eve meals Sun). Guest beers (usually two, one at quiet times) are from regional or larger micro-brewers.

♣P

Goginan

Druid

High Street, SY23 3NT (on A44, 6 miles E of Aberystwyth)

12 (11 summer)-11; 12-10.30 Sun

☎ (01970) 880650

Banks's Bitter, Brains SA; guest beer H

The focus for village life, but also a handy stop for travellers on the main east-west route across central Wales. Consisting of a series of linked rooms, the pub commands great views across the Melindwr Valley. Nearby attractions include Nant-yr-Arian Forest visitor centre and cycle trail and Llywernog Mining Museum. The guest beer (usually available) is generally from a micro-brewery in Wales or the borders. When quiet, ask to see the rock-hewn cellars. Buses run from Aberystwyth. The food and accommodation are recommended.

♣P

Llanbadarn Fawr

Black Lion

SY23 3RA (off A44, 1 mile E of Aberystwyth)

12-11; 12-10.30 Sun

☎ (01970) 623448

Banks's Original, Bitter; Marston's Pedigree; guest beer H

By the ancient church, the Black Lion, although greatly modernised over the years, retains a good atmosphere, with customers drawn from the village and nearby university campus. The long main bar has pool and darts at one end, bench seating at the other; the TV is switched on for major sporting events. The back bar accommodates families and non-smoking diners. The monthly guest beer is from the standard Wolverhampton & Dudley range. Lunches are served Thursday-Sunday (eve meals Thu-Sat). ♣P

Llwyndafydd

Crown Inn & Restaurant

SA44 6BU (off A487, 1 mile S of A486 jct)
✪ 12-3, 6-11; 12-3, 6-10.30 (not winter eve) Sun
☎ (01545) 560396
website: www.thecrowninnandrestaurant.co.uk
Enville Ale; Flowers IPA, Original; guest beers (summer) Ⓗ
Among the loveliest (if a little expensive) pubs in Wales, it offers good food, fine ales and a garden/play area in an idyllic village setting. Exposed beams and low ceilings make this Dylan Thomas Trail pub an intimate, friendly place in which to savour expertly prepared local produce. Other Enville beers sometimes replace the Ale; summer guests come from a wide range of micros. See the landlord's photographic gallery of mainly local scenes; reasonably-priced, limited edition prints are for sale.
Q ❀ ◑ ▲ ♣ P ⅄

New Quay

Cambrian Hotel

New Road, SA45 9SE (on B4342 at eastern approach to town)
✪ 11-11; 12-10.30 Sun
☎ (01545) 560295
Brains Buckley's Best Bitter or Hancock's HB; Felinfoel Double Dragon; guest beers Ⓗ
Behind the façade of an ordinary seaside-town hotel lurks a refuge for New Quay's discerning beer drinkers. Walk through the restaurant to the cosy rear bar, or use the entrance up the lane. A guest beer, often from a micro-brewery, is on all summer and at other busy times. The pub's beer festival (early July usually) has become a local institution. Entertainment on Friday and Saturday evenings, plus occasional jazz sessions, recalls the landlord's career as a session drummer. Q ❀ ◑ ▲ P

Pren-gwyn

Gwarcefel Arms

SA44 4LU (at A475/B4476 crossroads)
✪ 12 (6 Mon)-11; 12-10.30 Sun
☎ (01559) 362720
Brains Buckley's Best Bitter; Wadworth 6X; guest beer Ⓗ
Under new management, it is a pleasure to welcome this busy watering-hole back into the real ale fold. It is a popular eating place for locals throughout the year and the restaurant caters for parties and functions as well as normal trade. The bar's cosy, open fire enhances the relaxed, friendly atmosphere. It is a welcome stop for the many visitors to the area. ❀ ◑ ▲ ♣ P

Rhydowen

Alltyrodyn Arms

SA44 4QB (at B4459/A475 crossroads)
✪ 3 (12 Sat)-11; closed Mon; 12-10.30 Sun
☎ (01545) 590319
Fuller's London Pride; Oakham Bishops Farewell Ⓗ
This family-run village pub sells a changing range of real ales from micro-breweries and the better regionals; its early promise of 'class in a glass' has been maintained. With a warm welcome for all, well-behaved dogs can enjoy the open fire. Live music is now a feature. It offers some of the best meals locally, all freshly cooked, even the bread is home made. CAMRA beer tastings, Mild Day and mini-beer fests are now regular events. Q ❀ ◑ ▲ P

Talybont

White Lion/Llew Gwyn

SY24 5ER
✪ 11-11; 12-10.30 Sun
☎ (01970) 832245 website: www.whitelionhoteldyfed.co.uk
Banks's Original, Bitter Ⓗ
Refurbishment in 2004 only enhanced the appeal of this village green local. With flagstones and some bench seating, the main public bar is the heart of the pub, while a no-smoking extension has a local history display, with fascinating photos. Across the corridor, the extended and improved family/games room has oak flooring and two dartboards; a no-smoking dining room is at the rear. Occasional live music is staged. Local and Aberystwyth-Bangor buses stop outside (limited service Sun/eves/bank holidays).
❀ ◑ ♿ ▲ ♣ P ⅄

Tresaith

Ship Inn

SA43 2JL (bottom of lane leading to beach) OS279516
✪ 11-11 (11-3, 5-11 Jan-Feb if quiet); 12-10.30 Sun
☎ (01239) 810380
Brains Buckley's Best Bitter; guest beers Ⓗ
Considerably extended over the years, the Ship consists of a series of interlinked drinking and dining areas. While food is important (pizzas a speciality), it enjoys a healthy regular drinking trade too, particularly at weekends and early evening. The coastal views are glorious, especially from the extensive seating area at the front. Guest beers (generally two) may include one from the local Ceredigion Brewery. Buses from Cardigan call at the top of the lane (Mon-Sat daytime). ❀ ◑ ♿ ▲ ♣ P ⅄

PEMBROKESHIRE

Abercych

Nag's Head

SA37 0HT (on B4332, between Cenarth and Eglwyswrw)
✪ 11-3 (not Mon), 6-11; 12-10.30 Sun
☎ (01239) 841200
Nags Head Old Emrys; guest beers Ⓗ
Well restored old smithy, boasting a beamed bar, a riverside garden and a micro-brewery, where Old Emrys is brewed. The bar area is furnished with collections of old medical instruments, railway memorabilia and timepieces, giving the time in various parts of the world. Space is also found for an extensive display of beer bottles. Q ❀ ◑ P

Boncath

Boncath Inn

SA37 0JN (on B4332)
✪ 11-11; 12-10.30 Sun
☎ (01239) 841241
Hancock's HB; Salopian Shropshire Gold;

Worthington's Bitter; guest beer 🄷
Attractive pub, the centre of village life, dating back in part to the 18th century. Several distinct seating areas provide an intimate atmosphere. There is also a pleasant, no-smoking restaurant, serving home-cooked bar meals – try the steak and kidney pie. A wealth of local history is displayed in old pictures and photographs. The regular beers are supplemented by a changing, higher gravity guest ale. ⛫❀◑♿⛺♣P

Bosherston

St Govan's Inn

SA71 5AN (5 miles S of Pembroke, off B4319 to Castlemartin)
✪ 11-11; 11-10.30 Sun
☎ (01646) 661311
Fuller's London Pride; guest beers 🄷
Relatively modern, single-roomed pub that takes its name from the saint who built a chapel on the cliffs nearby. It is close to the Pembrokeshire coast path, the renowned lily ponds and Broadhaven's sandy beach. The inn is popular with walkers and climbers, who find the local cliffs irresistible. Look out for regular curry evenings. ⛫🛏◑⛺♣P

Carew

Carew Inn

SA70 8SL (take A477 to Carew, follow signs for Carew Cross)
✪ 11-11; 12-10.30 Sun
☎ (01646) 651267
Brains Rev James; Worthington's Bitter 🄷
This pub lies at the heart of the village, close to Carew's celtic cross, the castle and the tidal mill. The pub makes an ideal stop, with its central location in the national park, close to the Oakwood Adventure Park and many other attractions. Great food is accompanied on Thursday evening by live music.
⛫❀◑⊟♿♣P

Cresswell Quay

Cresselly Arms

SA68 0TE (follow signs for Lawrenny)
✪ 12-3, 5-11; 7-10.30 Sun
☎ (01646) 651210
Worthington's Bitter; guest beer 🄶
Situated on a tributary of the River Cleddau, the Cresselly, originally a one-roomed pub, has been sympathetically extended without losing any of its charm or character. Beer is still dispensed from barrels at the back of the bar via a jug. The guest beer arrives every Monday. The pub remains the hub of the community.
⛫Q❀P⚟

Dale

Griffin Inn

SA62 3RB (8 miles W of Milford Haven)
✪ 11-11; 12-10.30 Sun
☎ (01646) 636227
Felinfoel Double Dragon; Worthington's Bitter; guest beers 🄷
At the water's edge, close to the slipway, the Griffin is popular with visitors and locals alike. Some of the outside seats are right by the water. Inside have some fun with the table skittles. A rare local outlet for Felinfoel Brewery, the pub is ideally located for walkers on the Pembrokeshire coastal path. ⛫❀◑♣

Fishguard

Fishguard Arms

SA65 9QH
✪ 11-3, 7-11; closed Mon; 4-11 Tue; 4-midnight Sat; 12-10.30 Sun
☎ (01348) 872763
Worthington's Bitter; guest beer 🄶
Small local, behind a distinctive dark green painted exterior. There is no keg beer at all here, just a splendid rotation of guest ales. The main entertainment is conversation. A visit to this establishment is an experience not to be missed. The railway station for Fishguard is actually in nearby Goodwick. ⛫Q⊟⛺

Royal Oak

Market Square, SA65 9HA
✪ 11-11; 12-10.30 Sun
☎ (01348) 872514
Brains Dark, Bitter, SA, Rev James; guest beers 🄷
Charming, friendly pub with historic connections – French forces surrendered here, following the last invasion of mainland Britain in 1797. Note the fascinating memorabilia from this period on display. The Royal Oak is full of character and has a public bar, dining area and a garden. Home-cooked meals are served at affordable prices from a varied menu. Local folk singers meet here on Monday evenings. ⛫◑⊟⛺⚌♣

Goodwick

Rose & Crown

SA64 0BP
✪ 11-11; 12-10.30 Sun
☎ (01348) 874449
Brains Buckley's IPA; Worthington's Bitter; guest beer 🄷
Picturesque pub, close to the ferry port and benefiting from views of Goodwick Harbour and the beach. It has a no-smoking dining area and offers meals at each session. The landlord is an active member of the Royal British Legion. The local lifeboat volunteers use the pub as a meeting place. ⛫Q❀◑⛺⚌♣P

Haverfordwest

Bristol Trader

Quay Street, SA61 1BE
✪ 11-11; 12-10.30 Sun
☎ (01437) 762122
Worthington's Bitter; guest beers 🄷
As the name suggests, in the days of sail this was the highest point on the Cleddau River that coastal traders reached. Beware of the low ceiling in the bar area. Parking is on the quayside. Haverfordwest is an ideal base for exploring the Pembrokeshire area of West Wales.
Q❀◑⚌

Hotel Mariners

Mariners Square, SA61 2DU (near Castle Lake car park)
✪ 12-11; 12-10.30 Sun
☎ (01437) 763353

Hancock's HB; Worthington's Bitter; guest beer [H]
This establishment has been in existence since 1625 when coaches formed an important part of its trade. The hotel has been well modernised to provide a relaxing, informal atmosphere while retaining features such as exposed beams of an intriguing shape and massive stone walls. It now boasts conference facilities, no-smoking rooms and short mat bowls as well as the usual hotel amenities. ♨Q❀⇌◑⇌P

Pembroke Yeoman
Hill Street, St Thomas's Green, SA61 1QF
☉ 11-11; 12-3, 7-10.30 Sun
☎ (01437) 762500
Flowers IPA; [H] **guest beers** [H]/[G]
Well-supported, comfortable, town local that attracts a wide range of customers. It is popular with all age groups and is a meeting place for a variety of local organisations. The guest ale can be served by jug or gravity; the sparkler will be removed on request. Enjoy the peaceful atmosphere, fine ales and traditional pub games. An imaginative menu is offered. ♨◑♣

Hazelbeach

Ferry House Inn
SA73 1EG (take A477 to Neyland, then follow signs to Llanstadwell)
☉ 11-3, 6-11; 12-4, 7-10.30 Sun
☎ (01646) 600270
Hancock's HB; guest beer [H]
Situated on the Milford Haven Waterway, on the famous coastal path, the pub is convenient for Neyland Marina. The conservatory restaurant overlooks the river, and the menu features local fresh fish. Good accommodation makes this an ideal base for exploring the area. The pub lies across the river from the town of Pembroke Dock. Q⇌◑⊞P

Narberth

Angel Inn
High Street, SA67 7AS
☉ 11-3, 5-11; 7-10.30 Sun
☎ (01834) 860215
Brains Buckley's Bitter, Rev James; guest beer [H]
Cosy, modernised, town-centre pub that is popular for food. The lounge bar opens on to the split-level dining area. There is a public bar for customers who just want to drink. Narberth Station is some 20 minutes' walk from the town and is on the Carmarthen–Pembroke Dock line. Q◑⊞♿⇌

Newport

Castle Hotel
Bridge Street, SA42 0TB (on A487 through road)
☉ 11-11; 12-10.30 Sun
☎ (01239) 820742
Wadworth 6X; Worthington's Bitter; guest beer [H]
This friendly, popular local has an attractive bar with a real fire and a wealth of wood panelling. Food is served at all sessions in the extensive dining area. A large off-street car park is situated to the side and rear of the hotel. ♨☕❀⇌◑⊞P

Golden Lion
East Street, SA40 2SY (on A487)
☉ 11-11; 12-10.30 Sun
☎ (01239) 820321
Felinfoel Double Dragon; Tomos Watkin OSB; Worthington's Bitter [H]
Another of Newport's sociable locals – this one reputedly has a resident ghost. A number of internal walls have been removed to form a spacious bar area with distinct sections, thus retaining a cosy atmosphere. Car parking space is available on the opposite side of the road. Q◑♿P

Llwyngwair Arms
East Street, SA42 0SY (on A487)
☉ 5 (11 summer)-11 (closed winter Mon); 12-10.30 Sun
☎ (01239) 820267
Draught Bass; guest beers [H]
This popular local has not been altered for some considerable time. It has a dining area serving inexpensive food, with a focus on bar meals. Both food and ales have a distinctly Welsh emphasis. Parking is available through an archway on the opposite side of the road. ♨Q◑♿P

Pembroke

Old King's Arms Hotel
Main Street, SA71 4JS (next to town hall)
☉ 11-11; 12-10.30 Sun
☎ (01646) 683611 website: www.oldkingsarmshotel.co.uk
Worthington's Bitter; guest beer [H]
Olde-worlde hotel in the town centre close to Pembroke's Norman castle, birthplace of Henry VII. The hotel comprises a large public bar which can be busy at weekends and a small lounge. The recommended restaurant specialises in Welsh black steaks, fish and cockles with laver bread; a wide selection of bar snacks is also available. Q⇌◑⊞⇌P

Royal George Hotel
9 Northgate, SA71 4NR (on bridge over millpond)
☉ 11-3, 5-11; 11-11 Sat; 12-3, 7-10.30 Sun
☎ (01646) 682751
Worthington's Bitter; guest beers [H]
Pleasant, cheery local situated on the old south quay, just on the edge of the town centre. The building is part of the old town wall and is located directly below Pembroke Castle at what used to be the town's north gate. The interior consists of one large, split-level, L-shaped room with a single bar. Current and future guest ales are listed on a blackboard by the bar. ⇌⇌♣P

Pembroke Dock

Station Inn
Hawkestone Road, SA72 6DN (Pembroke Dock Station waiting room)
☉ 11-3.30, 5.30-11; 12-3, 7-10.30 Sun
☎ (01646) 621255 website: www.station-inn.com
Beer range varies [H]
Housed in a Victorian railway station with the trains still running on the adjoining tracks, this town-centre pub is close to both the Irish ferry terminal and the coast path. It serves excellent value lunches and evening meals (no food Sun eve). Every Tuesday a new beer is on tap and

two beer festivals are staged each year. Live music is performed on Saturday evening.
⛫Q❀◑◐⇌P

Pontfaen

Dyffryn Arms ☆

SA65 9SG (on B4313, Gwaun Valley road)
⊛ hours vary
☎ (01348) 881305
Draught Bass or Tetley Burton Ale Ⓖ
Fascinating bar that resembles a 1920s front room where time has stood still. The beer is still served by jug through a sliding hatch. Conversation is the main form of entertainment. The landlady is almost an octogenarian. A superb, relaxed atmosphere prevails in this pub, which lies at the heart of the scenic Gwaun Valley between the Preseli Hills and Fishguard (Abergwaun). ⛫Q⛺♣

Porthgain

Sloop Inn

SA62 5BN
⊛ 11.30-3, 6-11 (11-11 summer); 6-10.30 Sun
☎ (01348) 831449
Brains SA; Felinfoel Double Dragon; Worthington's Bitter Ⓗ
Sympathetically modernised old inn that has served both the locally-based fishing industry and the now-defunct quarrying and stone exporting industries. The pub displays quarrying and shipping artefacts as part of the decor. Holding hoppers for the stone can be seen on the opposite side of the harbour. Popular with both locals and visitors, it offers a good choice of beers and reasonably-priced food using local produce where possible. ⛫❀◑◐♣P

Roch

Victoria Inn

SA62 6AW
⊛ 11-11; 12-10.30 Sun
☎ (01437) 710426
Brains Rev James; Worthington's Bitter; guest beers Ⓗ
This is the last pub on the A487 before it descends to the coast at Newgale. It is within easy reach of the coastal footpath. The landlord is a great fan of real ale and his enthusiasm shows in the imaginative choice of ales. He also stages occasional mini-beer festivals.
⛫Q❀◑◐⛺P

Rosebush

Tafarn Sinc

SA66 7QU
⊛ 12-11 (not winter Mon); 12-10.30 Sun
☎ (01437) 532214
Worthington's Bitter; guest beer Ⓗ
Built of timber with a covering of corrugated iron on the outside, this was a popular establishment with American forces stationed locally during WWII. The bar area is modelled on the theme of a farmhouse kitchen, complete with sides of bacon hanging from the beams. Conversation is almost the only entertainment. The garden is based on the redundant station of the old Maenclochog Railway; memorabilia and sound effects help to reinforce this theme. The beer range includes a house ale brewed by Coles.
⛫Q❀◑◐⊟♿⛺P⍁

St David's

Farmers Arms

Goat Street, SA62 6RF
⊛ 11-11; 12-10.30 Sun
☎ (01437) 720328
Brains Rev James; Coles Dewi Sant; guest beer Ⓗ
Inviting, 19th-century stone hostelry that retains many old features. It is frequented by local farmers, anglers and young people, with many tourists calling in during the summer season. The pub serves an interesting range of good, wholesome, home-cooked food. Definitely worth a visit, there is often a singalong or folk sessions on a Sunday evening. ⛫Q❀◑◐⊟⛺

St Dogmaels

Ferry Inn

Poppit Road, SA43 3LF
⊛ 12-3, 7-11; 12-3, 7-10.30 Sun
☎ (01239) 615172
Greene King IPA, Old Speckled Hen; guest beer Ⓗ
An inn that sits on the very edge of the Teify estuary. Boat trips are run from a nearby quay in summer. It has been sympathetically developed so that both the open deck and the enclosed dining area enjoy panoramic views over the estuary. As the name implies, the inn has always been closely associated with the river, and boating ephemera features in the decor.
Q❀◑◐⊟⛺

Solva

Harbour Inn

SA62 6RF (on A487, adjoining harbour car park)
⊛ 11-11; 12-10.30 Sun
☎ (01437) 720013
Draught Bass; Greene King Old Speckled Hen; guest beer Ⓗ
This delightful harbourside hostelry retains a traditional atmosphere, having remained unaltered for a considerable time. It is used as a base for many community activities and is popular with the locals. Camping facilities close by cater for tents and caravans. Enjoy a quiet, relaxing pint in this welcoming local. Entertainment is organised on an ad hoc basis.
⛫Q❀⛟◑◐⛺

Tenby

Hope & Anchor

St Julian Street, SA70 7AS (on main approach to harbour)
⊛ 11-11; 12-10.30 Sun
☎ (01834) 842131
Brains Rev James; Worthington's Bitter; guest beers Ⓗ
Situated on the approach to the harbour and close to the sandy beaches, this friendly local caters for locals and tourists alike. An outside drinking area is provided in summer. A range of bar meals is offered, making it an ideal stop when walking to or from the beaches or harbour. The medieval town walls of Tenby can be seen nearby. ⛫Q❀◑◐⊟⛺⇌

Scotland

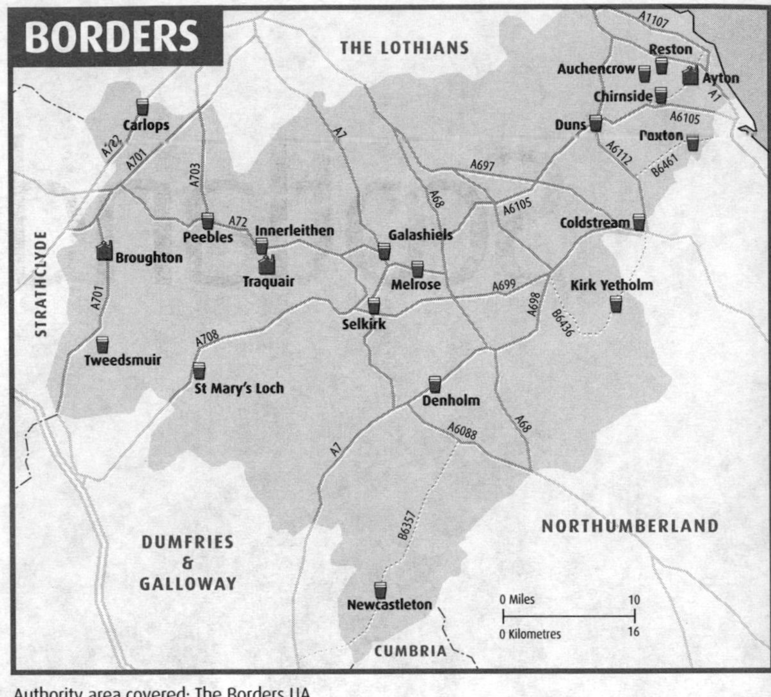

Authority area covered: The Borders UA

Auchencrow

Craw Inn

TD14 5LS (on B6438, follow signs from A1)
12-2.30, 6-11 (midnight Fri); 12-midnight Sat; 12.30-11 Sun
(01890) 761253
Beer range varies H

Friendly village inn, built circa 1680. The beamed bar has bench seating at one end and wooden tables and chairs by the log-burning stove at the other. The two beers are usually from smaller breweries, and change regularly. The no-smoking area at the back of the inn affords rural views and is divided into a lounge-cum-dining area and restaurant. Local produce is used in many dishes on the wide ranging menu. There are two areas for summer drinking: a patio and the garden opposite. Children are welcome. Q P

Carlops

Allan Ramsay Hotel

Main Street, EH26 9NF (on A702)
12-11 (1am Fri & Sat); 12.30-11 Sun
(01968) 660258
website: www.allanramsayhotel.co.uk
Caledonian Deuchars IPA; guest beer H

Hotel dating from 1792 set in a small village beside the Pentland hills. Several rooms have been knocked through into a single large area, retaining many original features including a fine stone fireplace. Tartan upholstery gives a Scottish feel. At one end is the restaurant, in the centre is the bar area and a pool table occupies the far end. The bar is inlaid with pre-decimal pennies. Children and dogs are welcome and food is served all day on Sunday and every day in summer. P

Chirnside

Waterloo Arms Hotel

Allanton Road, TD11 3XH (on B6437 S of village)
12-midnight (1am Fri & Sat); 12.30-midnight Sun
(01890) 818034 website: www.waterlooarms.com
Caledonian Deuchars IPA, Hadrian & Border Farne Island Pale Ale H

Comfortable village local, with bar and dining room, built circa 1820, but recently refurbished. The age is reflected in the ceiling beams but the wood panelling dates from the 1930s. The pub may be haunted by a farmer, who was shot after a feud with his brother, who himself died from a fall on his way to sea. If it is really chilly, the real fire in the bar burns like a furnace. Meals are served all day. Children are welcome until 9pm. P

Coldstream

Besom

75-77 High Street, TD12 4AE
11-midnight (1am Fri & Sat); 11-midnight Sun
(01890) 882391
Caledonian Deuchars IPA; guest beer H

This comfortable pub in the historic Borders town is the first in Scotland. The bar, with a real

INDEPENDENT BREWERIES

Broughton Broughton
Peelwalls Ayton
Traquair Traquair

fire, bookshelves, trophy cabinet and sofa-like seating, feels as much like a living room as a pub. The walls are decorated with a diverse range of memorabilia, some related to the Coldstream Guards. The rear lounge, where children are welcome, is divided into two areas, one no smoking. ♔Q◖◗⊟♣⊬

Denholm

Fox & Hounds Inn

Main Street, TD9 8NU (on A698)

✪ 11-3, 5-midnight (1am Fri); 11-1am Sat; 12.30-midnight Sun

☎ (01450) 870247

website: www.foxandhoundsinndenholm.co.uk

Wylam Gold Tankard; guest beers Ⓗ

Village local, circa 1750, overlooking the village green. The main bar is light and retains the original beams; a real fire gives it a cosy feel in winter. Pictures and memorabilia decorate the walls. The rear lounge has a coffee house feel. A dining room can be found upstairs. In summer the courtyard is used for sheltered outdoor drinking. Children are welcome until 8pm and dogs are also admitted. ♔❀⇔◖◗⊟♣

Duns

Black Bull Hotel

15 Black Bull Street, TD11 3AR

✪ 11-midnight (1am Fri & Sat); 12.30-midnight Sun

☎ (01361) 883379

Caledonian Deuchars IPA; guest beer Ⓗ

Recently improved 200-year-old hotel with bar, lounge area, restaurant and function room. The bar, popular with locals, has dark wood panelling. The lounge area, with bench seating, is more suited to families (children welcome) and is no-smoking. The restaurant has a good reputation and booking is recommended at weekends. Meals are served all day. Dogs are welcome in the bar. ❀⇔◖◗⊟▲♣P⊬

Galashiels

Salmon Inn

54 Bank Street, TD1 1EP (town centre, opp. the gardens)

✪ 11-11 (midnight Thu; 1am Fri & Sat); 12.30-11 Sun

☎ (01896) 752577

Draught Bass; Caledonian Deuchars IPA; guest beer Ⓗ

Welcoming pub with a mixture of old and modern decor including historic photos of the area. The single room is split into two areas, with more seating and a games machine towards the back of the bar. The guest beer, often from a smaller brewery, changes regularly. Lunchtime and evening meals are served except on Sunday. Children are welcome at lunchtime. Centrally situated by the fountain and gardens, National Cycle Route 1 passes the front door. Quizzes are held. ❀◖◗▲♣

Innerleithen

St Ronans Hotel

High Street, EH44 6HF

✪ 11-midnight (12.45am Fri & Sat); 12-midnight Sun

☎ (01896) 831487

Beer range varies Ⓗ

This village watering-hole takes its name from the local Saint who is also linked to a well in the village. The functional public bar is long and thin and has a brick and wooden fireplace. There are two alcoves, one with basic pub seating, the other with a dartboard. Leading off from here is a room with a pool table. Children are welcome. Food is served in summer. ♔❀⇔◖◗▲♣P

Kirk Yetholm

Border Hotel

The Green, TD5 8PQ

✪ 11-midnight; 11-1am Fri & Sat; 12-midnight Sun; (closes 1 hour earlier in winter)

☎ (01573) 420237 www.theborderhotel.com

Beer range varies Ⓗ

Built in 1750 as a coaching inn, its location at the end of the Pennine Way and on St Cuthbert's Way makes it popular with walkers. The wood-beamed bar has a practical feel, with stone flagged floor and red vinyl banquette seating, and the walls are decorated with photographs. A labyrinth of small rooms leads off, with two snugs, a pool room and a conservatory dining area. Meals are served all day in summer. Dogs and children are welcome. ♔Q❀⇔◖◗⊟▲P⊬

Melrose

Burt's Hotel

Market Square, TD6 9PL

✪ 11-2, 5-11; 12-2, 6-11 Sun

☎ (01896) 822285

Caledonian Deuchars IPA, 80/-; guest beer Ⓗ

Elegant, family-run hotel in the main square. The decor of this plush lounge bar reflects the country sports interests of many of the clientele. The restaurant is expensive but serves excellent food. The bar menu offers cheaper options. Children are welcome. About half the bar area is no-smoking. Melrose Abbey and the rugby ground are close by and National Cycle Route 1 passes the door. Real ale may not be available, and reservations are essential, during the Melrose 7's rugby week. ♔Q⇔◖◗▲P⊬

King's Arms Hotel

High Street, TD6 9PB

✪ 11-midnight; 12-11 Sun

☎ (01896) 822143

Caledonian Deuchars IPA; Tetley Bitter; guest beer Ⓗ

Coaching inn dating from 1793, close to Melrose Abbey and the rugby ground. The bar has a wooden floor and church pew seating, and is decorated with rugby memorabilia and old local photographs. There is a large-screen TV for sports events, and it can get smoky. The quieter lounge is comfortably furnished and has a lovely old carved door set into the ceiling. Children are welcome in the lounge until 8pm. ♔Q⇔◖◗⊟▲♣

Newcastleton

Liddesdale Hotel

Douglas Square, TD9 0QD

✪ 11-11 (1am Fri & Sat); 12-11 Sun

☎ (01387) 375255

Greene King Old Speckled Hen Ⓗ

Hotel in the main square of a remote 18th-century planned weavers' village, with a bright

SCOTLAND

and functional split-level bar. The upper level, with a real fire, serves as a dining area while the lower area near the bar is more basic with Art Deco style wooden panelling. Local pictures and railway prints, a few mirrors and an old map decorate the walls. Children are welcome until 10pm. The reception area and restaurant are no-smoking. ♨❀🛏◑♿▲♣⚟

Paxton

Cross Inn

TD15 1TE (off B6460)
⏲ 11-2.30, 6.30-midnight; closed Mon; 12.30-2.30, 6.30-midnight Sun (hours may extend in summer)
☎ (01289) 386267
Beer range varies 🄷
Pleasant, friendly village pub, dating from the 1870s. Recently renovated, it has now gone back to its original name following the restoration of the old cross outside. The narrow, wood-panelled bar has a sunny alcove and a mahogany-topped counter. There is also a comfortable dining room offering a good menu. Children are welcome and fishing permits are available. The real ale is often from the Wylam, Mordue or Atlas breweries. ❀◑♿♣P⚟

Peebles

Bridge Inn

Portbrae, EH45 8AW (W end of town centre)
⏲ 11 (12.30 Sun)-midnight
☎ (01721) 720589
Caledonian Deuchars IPA; guest beer (summer) 🄷
Cheerful, welcoming, single-room town-centre local, also known as the Trust. The mosaic floor in the entrance bears the pub's older name, the Tweedside Inn. The bright, comfortable bar is decorated with memorabilia of outdoor pursuits and photos of old Peebles. The gents is superb, with well-maintained original Twyford Adamant urinals. The house beer is Atlas Three Sisters, rebadged as Tweedside Ale. It was CAMRA Borders Pub of the Year in 2004 and 2005. ▲♣

Cross Keys Hotel

Northgate, EH45 8RS
⏲ 12-11 (midnight Fri & Sat); 12-11 Sun
☎ (01721) 724222
Beer range varies 🄷
Old coaching inn, just off the High Street, with a large L-shaped lounge bar. The ceiling is low but the light decor gives a spacious feel. The imposing bar and gantry were reclaimed from a demolished Edinburgh pub. Although generally relaxed, the pub can be lively during weekend evenings. One beer from the Atlas brewery is often available, the other is usually from another regional or micro-brewery. Children are welcome until 8pm. ♨❀🛏◑♿▲♣P⚟

Neidpath Inn

27-29 Old Town, EH45 8JF (on A72 W of town centre)
⏲ 11-midnight (10.30 Mon); 12.30-midnight Sun
☎ (01721) 721721
Caledonian Deuchars IPA; guest beer 🄷
Traditional town pub with an L-shaped bar; the area at the front is a cosy place to enjoy a relaxing drink while the section at the back has a pool table and juke box. Wood, musical instruments and glasswork add to the atmosphere. A comfortable lounge leads into a dining area which in summer spills onto an outdoor decked area. Meals are served all day at weekends. Children are welcome in the lounge and garden until 7pm. ♨❀🛏◑🚉▲♣

Reston

Red Lion

Main Street, TD14 5JP
⏲ 12-2.30 (not Mon), 5.30-11; 12-1am Sat; 12.30-11 Sun
☎ (01890) 761266
website: www.a1redlionreston.co.uk
Beer range varies 🄷
Comfortable pub well signposted from the A1. An area is set aside for eating and the menu is good and varied. The lounge bar features wooden bench seating, a real fire and an intriguing collection of vintage cameras. The beer is usually from a Scottish brewery such as Broughton or Harviestoun. Wheat beers are also available. Children are welcome. ♨❀◑P

Selkirk

Town Arms

1 Market Place, TD7 4BT
⏲ 11-11 (1am Fri & Sat); 12.30-midnight Sun
☎ (01750) 20185
Greene King Old Speckled Hen 🄷
Small, typical working men's pub, situated just off the market square within the historic centre of Selkirk. Its interior is unusual in that a large island bar dominates the main room. The decor is traditional with wood-panelled walls adorned with numerous brewery mirrors. The pub is often crowded and can be smoky.

St. Mary's Loch

Tibbie Shiels Inn

TD7 5LH (off A708 at southern end of loch) OS241205
⏲ 11-11 (midnight Fri & Sat); (closed winter Mon-Wed); 12.30-11 (6 winter) Sun
☎ (01750) 42231 website: www.tibbieshielsinn.com
Belhaven 80/-; Broughton Greenmantle IPA 🄷
Cosy, isolated, historic inn situated on the isthmus of two lochs in the Yarrow Valley, once the home of Tibbie Shiels (1782-1878). A haven for outdoor enthusiasts; the Southern Upland Way and a water sports centre are close by. Outside drinking is available in the grounds but be prepared to sit on the grass. Good food is served all day with daily specials. Children are welcome until 8.30pm.
♨Q❀🛏◑🚉♿▲♣P⚟

Tweedsmuir

Crook Inn ☆

ML12 6QN (on A701 between Moffat and Broughton)
⏲ 11-11; 12-11 Sun; (closed last two weeks Jan)
☎ (01899) 880272 website: www.crookinn.co.uk
Beer range varies 🄷
Originally dating back to 1604, the current building is mainly 1930s Art Deco. The large, well-appointed lounge areas are at the front. The bar is in the older part of the building at the back, which retains its splendid fireplace, although the fire is now gas powered. The beer is usually from the Broughton Brewery. Children are welcome. ♨Q❀🛏◑🚉♣P⚟

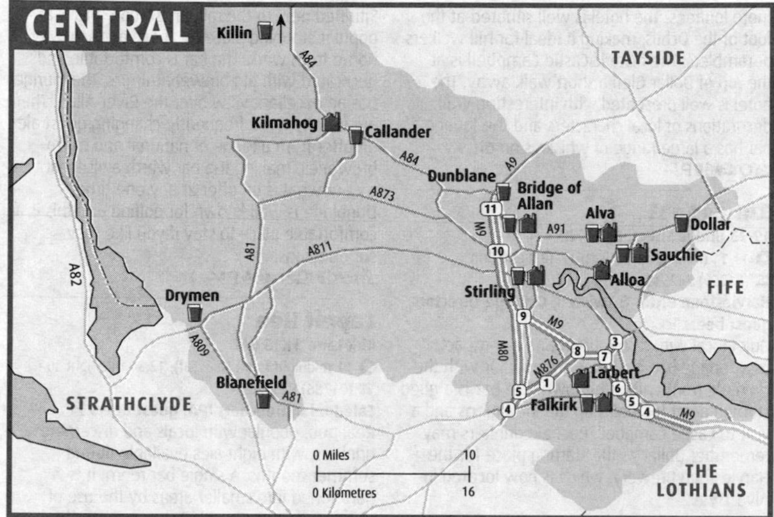

Authority areas covered Clackmannan UA, Falkirk UA, Stirling UA

Alva

Cross Keys

Stirling Street, FK12 5EH

11-11 (midnight Thu; 1am Fri & Sat); 11-11 Sun

(01259) 760409

Beer range varies H

Situated at the base of the Ochil Hills, this is a popular local, especially with young people at the weekends. It can be noisy on Friday and Saturday evenings when occasional live music and theme nights are held, which are advertised locally. The pub is well known in the area for the quality and value of its food. To avoid disappointment, it is best to book ahead for meals.

Blanefield

Carbeth Inn

Stockiemuir Road, G63 9AY

(on A809 N of Milngavie, near B821 jct) OSNS524791

11-11 (midnight Fri & Sat); 12.30-11 Sun

(01360) 770002

Belhaven 80/- H

Cheery pub drawing a local clientele from nearby fishing huts and farms. It is also popular with visitors from north-west Glasgow, particularly motorcyclists who fill up the outside seating in summer. Regular live music and a Sunday quiz are occasionally augmented by food-oriented events. The main bar, with an unobtrusive large-screen TV, is kept warm in winter by two wood-burning stoves. The cosy, spacious restaurant is available for private functions. P

Bridge of Allan

Crooked Arms

2 Allanvale Road, FK9 4NU

11-midnight (1am Fri & Sat); 11-midnight Sun

(01786) 833830

Caledonian 80/-; Courage Directors H

Small, cosy pub just off the main street, accessed via a few steps. This is a traditional, friendly local, where the atmosphere is jovial – but smoky too. It is mainly used by regulars but with the occasional student thrown in, or is it out! With the welcoming fire and a good pint of ale it is a pleasant place to spend a cold winter's day.

Callander

Waverley Hotel

88-94 Main Street, FK17 8BD

11-midnight (1am Fri & Sat); 11-midnight Sun

(01827) 330245

website: www.thewaverleycallander.com

Beer range varies H

Real ales are served in the Claymore bar. There is normally a good range to choose from, particularly in the summer when there can be up to eight beers stocked. The town, close to the Trossachs and the Central Belt, is well placed for tourists. A large dining area serves good food, and accommodation is also available. Cider is sold from May to October. Two, week-long, beer festivals normally take place in September and December. Q

Dollar

Castle Campbell Hotel

11 Bridge Street, FK14 7DE

11-11.30 (1am Fri & Sat); 12.30-11 Sun

(01259) 742519

Harviestoun Bitter & Twisted; guest beer H

Pleasant hotel with one lounge bar and two

INDEPENDENT BREWERIES

Bridge of Allan Bridge of Allan
City of Stirling Stirling
Devon Sauchie
Eglesbrech Falkirk
Harviestoun Alva
Trossachs Craft Kilmahog
Tryst Larbert
Williams Alloa

SCOTLAND

more lounges. The hotel is well situated at the foot of the Ochils, making it ideal for hill walkers or ramblers. The historic Castle Campbell is at the top of Dollar Glen a short walk away. The hotel is well presented with interesting wall decorations of local characters and the lounge bar has a large range of whiskies on offer.
♛Q⇌◑P⊬

King's Seat
19-23 Bridge Street, FK14 7DE
☼ 11-11 (midnight Fri & Sat); 12.30-11.00 Sun
☎ (01259) 742515
Harviestoun Bitter & Twisted; Courage Directors; guest beers Ⓗ
Quiet local with a restaurant and a compact, cosy lounge bar. Cask ales are popular with the clientele from within the town. The bar is a good starting point for walks up the local glens and a visit to Castle Campbell. Real ale drinkers may remember Dollar as the starting place for the Harviestoun Brewery, which is now located in Alva. ◑▲

Strathallan Hotel
6 Chapel Place, FK14 7DW
☼ 5-11.30 (12.30am Fri); 12-2.30, 5-12.30am Sat; 12-2, 5-11.30 Sun
☎ (01259) 742205
Fuller's London Pride; Harviestoun Bitter & Twisted; guest beers Ⓗ
Small, country hotel with a bistro-style restaurant and a cosy lounge run by cheerful staff. An outlet for Harviestoun Brewery's beers, special brews are also served when available. If you feel like earning your pint by taking a stroll first, there are pleasant walks in Dollar Glen. Or take a look at Castle Campbell, owned by the National Trust, which is just a short walk away – dating back to the 15th century, it was burned by Cromwell's troops in the mid-17th century, and is well worth a visit. ❀⇌P⊬

Drymen

Winnock Hotel
The Square, G63 0BL
☼ 11-midnight (1am Fri & Sat); 12-midnight Sun
☎ (01360) 660245
website: www.winnockhotel.com
Caledonian Deuchars IPA, 80/-; guest beer Ⓗ
Originally an 18th-century coaching inn, this Best Western hotel welcomes travellers to the east side of Loch Lomond and walkers on the West Highland Way. The bar and reception areas were recently refurbished to accommodate the frequent large family and corporate events hosted by the hotel. Friendly and professional staff ensure that locals and visitors are equally welcome. The restaurant serves Scottish specialities in the evenings and Sunday lunchtimes; standard bar food is also available.
♛⛫❀⇌◑♣P⊬

Dunblane

Dunblane Hotel ✔
10 Stirling Road, FK15 9EP
☼ 11-midnight (1am Fri & Sat); 11-midnight Sun
☎ (01786) 822178
Caledonian Deuchars IPA; Greene King Abbot; Taylor Landlord; guest beers Ⓗ
Situated next to the railway station, this is a popular stopping place for those on their way home from work. The bar is comfortable and decorated with old brewery mirrors. The lounge has an excellent view over the River Allan. There are usually three frequently-changing guest ales on offer from a range of national and micro-breweries, making the bar worth a visit just to try out what is on offer at any one time. Dunblane is well known for golfing and this is a comfortable place to stay if you like cosy surroundings.
❀⇌◑⊟♿⇌♣P⊬

Tappit Hen
Kirk Lane, FK15 0AL
☼ 11-midnight (1am Fri & Sat); 12.30-midnight Sun
☎ (01786) 825226
Caledonian Deuchars IPA; guest beers Ⓗ
Real pub, popular with locals and discerning drinkers, with eight ales available during summer months. A single bar room, it is partitioned into smaller areas by the use of screens. The town, with its imposing cathedral, is in an ideal position to visit Gleneagles and the Highlands and the pub is just a five-minute walk from the station. ♿⇌♣

Falkirk

Behind the Wall
14 Melville Street, FK1 1HZ
☼ 11-midnight (1am Fri & Sat); 12-midnight Sun
☎ (01324) 633338
website: www.behindthewall.co.uk
Beer range varies Ⓗ
Established in 1985, the pub is still managed by the original owners. It has a bar, restaurant and micro-brewery under one roof. The style is a mix of traditional and contemporary with a bistro/restaurant area. Its own beer is kept under blanket pressure, however it does excel in its guest beers, normally with four on offer. Products from Williams Brothers of Alloa appear regularly on the bar. ❀◑⇌

Wheatsheaf Inn
16 Baxters Wynd, FK1 1PF
☼ 11-11 (12.30am Fri & Sat); 12.30-11 Sun
☎ (01324) 623716
Caledonian Deuchars IPA; guest beers Ⓗ
This public house started off as a coaching inn in the 18th century and has retained much of its character over the years. The bar is long and narrow with stools and small tables. The walls are decorated with old brewery mirrors and caricatures of local worthies. A good selection of whiskies is stocked. Well used by locals, the pub retains its quiet atmosphere as there is no music and the TV is only turned on for football matches. ⇌ (Grahamston or Falkirk High)

Killin

Falls of Dochart Inn
Gray Street, FK21 8SL
☼ 11-1am (midnight Fri & Sat); 12-11 Sun
☎ (01567) 820270
Beer range varies Ⓗ
Under new management since 2002, this traditional Jacobite-style pub has undergone major refurbishment. Traditional food and good

beer make for a great night out in front of the blazing fire on cold nights. The stunning setting in rural Perthshire next to the Falls of Dochart lends plenty of atmosphere. An excellent range of single malts is served.
⛫🚂❀⇌◑▲P

Sauchie

Mansfield Arms ✔

7 Main Street, FK10 3JR

⏲ 11-11 (12.30 Fri & Sat); 12.30-11 Sun

☎ (01259) 722020

Devon Original, Thick Black, Pride Ⓗ

This pub has a typical public bar, well used by locals, providing a comfortable atmosphere. The lounge/restaurant is frequented mainly by families and those looking for good value, quality meals. Behind the pub is the compact brewery where three standard ales are made, sold only on its own premises. Brewery tours can be arranged. ◑⊟♿P

Stirling

Portcullis Hotel

Castle Wynd, FK8 1EG

⏲ 11.30 (12.30 Sun)-midnight

☎ (01786) 472290

website: www.portcullishotel.com

Orkney Dark Island; guest beer Ⓗ

Built in 1787 as a grammar school, the Portcullis is a quiet but busy bar, situated next to Stirling Castle. Reasonably-priced food is served, and it is well worth booking for the evenings and weekends during the tourist season as it can become busy. A peaceful pub that is popular with locals and tourists, the relaxed atmosphere is enhanced in the evening by candle-lit tables. A sheltered walled garden is available for food and drinks.
Q❀⇌◑P

Settle Inn

91 St Mary's Wynd, FK8 1BU

⏲ 12-midnight (1am Fri & Sat); 12.30-midnight Sun

☎ (01786) 474609

Beer range varies Ⓗ

Claimed to be the oldest pub in Stirling, dating from 1733, the Settle Inn is a peaceful but lively pub, popular with locals, students and visitors alike. The visitors' book bears witness to the friendliness of the welcome, the quality of the beer and the traditional cosy atmosphere. This is a pub with good community links, hosting a Hallowe'en bash and a Burns Supper for regulars, as well as a Christmas party for pensioners. Sunday is quiz night, 'open mike' sessions feature on Tuesday and folk on Thursday evening. Look out for the two ghosts that have made the Settle Inn their home. ⛫●

Hops: the essential flavouring

Hops are famous for adding bitterness to beer. But this remarkable perennial climbing plant – a member of the hemp family, Cannabinaceae – also contains acids, oils and resins that impart delightful aromas and flavours to beer. These can be detected in the form of pine, spice, sap and tart, citrus fruit. Fruit is often similar to lemon and orange, while some English hop varieties give powerful hints of apricots, blackcurrants and damsons. American hop varieties, the Cascade in particular, are famous for their grapefruit aroma and flavour. Many British brewers now use hops from mainland Europe – such as Styrian Goldings from Slovenia and Saaz from the Czech Republic – that have been developed primarily for lager brewing. They impart a more restrained aroma and flavour, with a gentle, resinous character. Lager hops used in ale brewing are usually added late in the copper boil to give a fine aroma to the finished beer. Kent is often thought of as the main hop-growing area of Britain but in 2004 it was overtaken by Herefordshire. The main hop varieties used in cask beer production are the Fuggle and the Golding, but First Gold, introduced in the 1990s, is now a major variety. First Gold was one of the first dwarf or hedgerow hops that grow to only half the height of conventional varieties. As a result they are easier to pick, are less susceptible to disease and aphid attack, and therefore use fewer agri-chemicals. In 2004, a new hop variety called Boadicea was introduced: it is the first aphid-resistant hop and therefore needs fewer pesticides. The hop industry is working on trials of new varieties that need no pesticides or fertilisers and should gain Soil Association approval as organic hops.

DUMFRIES & GALLOWAY

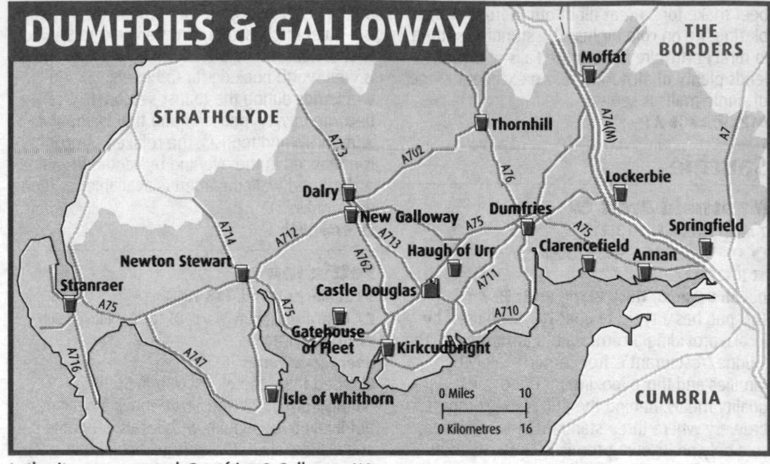

Authority area covered: Dumfries & Galloway UA

Annan

Bluebell Inn

10 High Street, DG12 6AG

11-11 (midnight Thu-Sat); 12.30-11 Sun

(01461) 202385

Caledonian Deuchars IPA; guest beers H

Fine old coaching inn retaining original panelling and features from its time as a Gretna & District State Management house. This friendly pub offers the best selection of beers between England and Dumfries, with three guest ales from both sides of the border. It also has pool, darts and large-screen TV. During the summer you can drink outside in the rear courtyard.

Clarencefield

Farmers Inn

Main Street, DG1 4NF (on B724)

11-2.30, 6-11.30 (12.30am Fri); 12-12.30am Sat; 12.30-11.30 Sun

(01387) 870675

website www.farmersinn.co.uk

Beer range varies H

Late 16th-century coaching inn with a varied history. The current building opened in 1983 with the original bar area still in use. It was the post office and also housed the village's first telephone exchange. Robert Burns was a customer when he came on a visit to the Brow Well for health reasons. Nearby tourist attractions include the world's first savings bank at Ruthwell and the 8th-century Ruthwell Cross. Clarencefield is served by a regular bus service between Dumfries and Annan.

P

Dalry

Clachan Inn

8-10 Main Street, DG7 3UW (on A713)

11 (12 Sun)-midnight

(01644) 430241

website www.clachaninn.com

Greene King Abbot; guest beers H

The Clachan Inn is set in the picturesque village of St. John's Town of Dalry, which straddles the A713. The area has a growing reputation for country pursuits and walkers are particularly welcome at this stopping off point along the Southern Upland Way. A year-round special walkers' rate is available for accommodation. The pub has a varied menu and prides itself on using local produce as much as possible. There are usually two real ales on tap.

P

Dumfries

Cavens Arms

20 Buccleuch Street, DG1 2AH

11-11 (12.30am Fri & Sat); 12.30-11 Sun

(01387) 252896

Caledonian Deuchars IPA; Greene King Abbot; guest beers H

The Cavens Arms is a welcome addition to the real ale scene in Dumfries. Two regular beers are supplemented by four or more guests from all parts of the country. Beer festivals, held several times a year, are well publicised in the local area. Good value meals are available all day on Saturday, but not served on Monday. The pub hosts regular quiz nights and if you are lucky you may chance upon one of the occasional live traditional music sessions.

New Bazaar

39 Whitesands, DG1 2RS

11-11 (midnight Thu-Sat); 11-11 Sun

(01387) 268776

McEwan's 80/-; Sulwath Knockendoch; guest beers H

Traditional pub, boasting a superb Victorian bar. The lounge is warmed by a welcoming fire during the winter months and benefits from great views across the River Nith to the Camera Obscura. A back room is available for meetings. There is plentiful free parking in the nearby public car parks. It is conveniently located for a

INDEPENDENT BREWERIES

Sulwarth Castle Douglas

number of tourist attractions and buses depart from across the road to all parts of the region.
♛Q⇌♣

Robert the Bruce ✔
81-83 Buccleuch Street, DG1 1DJ
⌚ 11 (12.30 Sun)-midnight
☎ (01387) 270320
Caledonian Deuchars IPA; guest beers Ⓗ
Former Episcopalian church originally consecrated in 1817 and sold 50 years later to local Methodists. It remained empty and roofless for many years before a sympathetic conversion by Wetherspoon. With its relaxed atmosphere the Bruce has quickly established itself as a favourite meeting place, handy for the town centre. Beers from Scottish brewers can be found among the guests.
◐⇌

Tam O'Shanter
113-117 Queensberry Street, DG1 1BH
⌚ 11-11 (midnight Fri& Sat); 12.30-11 Sun
☎ (01387) 254055
Caledonian Deuchars IPA; guest beers Ⓗ
The Tam is a 17th-century former coaching inn named after one of Rabbie Burns' famous poems. The bar is small and a corridor leads to further rooms and an outdoor drinking area. A no-smoking room containing the original hearth is housed in a former kitchen. Guest beers include Belhaven and Houston, with a fine selection of ales from both sides of the border.
Q❀⇌♣⚡

Gatehouse of Fleet

Masonic Arms
Ann Street, DG7 2HU
⌚ 11.30-2.30, 5.30-11.30 including Sun
☎ (01557) 814335
website www.themasonic-arms.co.uk
Beer range varies Ⓗ
The Masonic Arms bar, brasserie and restaurant is in the picturesque town of Gatehouse. The coast is nearby with cliffs and sandy beaches to explore. Exposed beams are a feature in the comfortable bar area. The house beer, Masonic Boom, is brewed by Sulwath. Renowned for its food, meals are served in the bar, as well as the no-smoking conservatory and restaurant.
Q❀◑◐♿▲♣

Haugh of Urr

Laurie Arms Hotel
11-13 Main Street, DG7 3YA (on B794, 1 mile S of A75)
⌚ 11.45-2.30, 5.30-11 (midnight Thu-Sat); 11.45-3.30, 6-midnight Sun
☎ (01556) 660246
Beer range varies Ⓗ
Award-winning pub where a warm welcome is extended to all customers. Situated on the main street of this quiet village in the Urr Valley, the pub is renowned for the quality of both the food and the beer. You may find up to four real ales on the bar here depending on the time of year; the local preference is for session beers from across Britain. A regular bus service connects the village with Castle Douglas and Dumfries.
♛❀◑◐♣P

Isle of Whithorn

Steampacket Inn ✔
Harbour Row, DG8 8LL
⌚ 11-11 (1am Fri; midnight Sat); (11-2.30, 6-11 Mon-Thu winter); 12-11 Sun
☎ (01988) 500334
Theakston XB; guest beers Ⓗ
Attractive harbourside inn with a small public bar featuring stone-clad walls, a large fireplace and flagstone floor. The larger lounge incorporates a pool room. Picture windows give good views of the harbour, which attracts sailing craft from near and far. Both the Isle of Man and the Lake District can be seen from this attractive and historic village. The menu is based mainly on local produce. The pub was awarded the local CAMRA Pub of the Year award in 2004.
♛Q♉❀⛿◑◐⊟♣

Kirkcudbright

Masonic Arms
19 Castle Street, DG6 4JA
⌚ 11 (12.30 Sun)-midnight
☎ (01557) 330517
Beer range varies Ⓗ
This small, sociable bar is welcoming to both locals and visitors. The tables and bar fronts are made from old malt whisky casks from Islay's Bowmore Distillery. One real ale is available throughout the year with up to two more during the summer months. The Masonic also offers draught Budvar, a selection of 30 bottled beers from all over the world, and 100 malt whiskies. The town is picturesque with a variety of tourist attractions. There are bus services to Dumfries and Gatehouse. ♛Q▲♣

Lockerbie

Somerton House Hotel
35 Carlisle Road, DG11 2DR
⌚ 11-11 including Sun
☎ (01576) 202583
Caledonian Deuchars IPA Ⓗ
Situated on the B723 on the southern outskirts of this ancient royal burgh, the hotel is about a mile from the A74(M) northbound junction 18. The real ale can be found in the comfortable lounge bar to the left of the entrance hall and is available all year round. The atmosphere is quiet and relaxed with a no-smoking area. Meals are served in the restaurant.
⛿◑◐▲⇌P⚡

Moffat

Balmoral Hotel
High Street, DG10 9DL
⌚ 11 (12.30 Sun)-11
☎ (01683) 220288
Caledonian 80/-; guest beers Ⓗ
Traditional hotel with a long lounge bar serving a choice of ales, usually including one from Broughton Brewery. Good value meals, served from noon until 9pm, include vegetarian options. Moffat is a good starting point for the scenic route to Edinburgh via the famous Devil's Beef Tub. There are good walking routes in the area and the Southern Upland Way passes nearby. ♛❀⛿◑◐♿▲P

Black Bull Hotel

Church Gate, DG10 9EG
⏲ 11-midnight (11 Sun)
☎ (01683) 220206
Theakston Best Bitter; McEwan's 80/-; guest beers Ⓗ
Historic inn dating from the 16th century, with two bars both serving two regular ales plus up to two guest beers. The lounge bar with adjoining Burns Room is in the main building. Across the courtyard is the public bar, known as the Railway Bar, which is furnished with railway memorabilia. The hotel has 12 modern en-suite guest rooms. Ample parking is provided by nearby public car parks.
❀♣

New Galloway

Cross Keys Hotel

High Street, DG7 3RN
⏲ 12-2, 6-11; 12-10.30 Sun
☎ (01644) 420494
Beer range varies Ⓗ
The Cross Keys, local CAMRA Pub of the Year 2004, has a warm, friendly and welcoming atmosphere. Situated close to the north end of Loch Ken and on the edge of the Galloway Forest Park, the secluded village and surrounding area offer many attractions including fishing, sailing and walking. Usually two real ales are stocked in winter and three in summer.
Q❀P

Newton Stewart

Creebridge House Hotel

Minigaff, DG8 6NP (on old main road)
⏲ 12-2.30, 6-11.30 (midnight Sat); 12.30-11 Sun
☎ (01671) 402121
website www.creebridge.co.uk
Beer range varies Ⓗ
Superb country house hotel set in three acres of idyllic gardens and woodland. Built in 1760 as the home of the Earl of Galloway, it has been sympathetically converted and is renowned for fine food and warm hospitality. Three real ales (four in summer), including some from the local Sulwath brewery, are available in the Bridge Bar. Meals are served in the brasserie as well as in the more formal garden restaurant.
❀♣P

Springfield

Queen's Head

Main Street, DG16 5EH
⏲ 5 (12 Sat)-11 (midnight Thu-Sat); 12.30-11 Sun
☎ (01461) 337173
Caledonian Deuchars IPA Ⓗ
This single-room village pub, although slightly off the beaten track, is actually little more than a stone's throw from Gretna, wedding capital of the country. It is close to the A74(M) and about a mile from Gretna Green railway station. There is always one real ale served in this friendly, unpretentious local. Please note there is no lunchtime opening on weekdays.
❀♣P

Stranraer

Ruddicot Hotel

London Road, DG9 8AJ
(on A751, 400 yds E of town centre)
⏲ 12-2.30, 5-11 (midnight Thu-Sat); 12.30-2.30, 6.30-11 Sun
☎ (01776) 702684
Beer range varies Ⓗ
A former girls' school, this is now a friendly, family hotel close to the Irish ferry terminal and Stranraer FC's football ground. It serves good value snacks and meals. The bar retains traditional wooden screens that divide the room into what were originally the dining and drinking areas. It is frequented by locals, ferry travellers and users of neighbouring sports facilities. Q❀P

Thornhill

Buccleuch & Queensberry Hotel

112 Drumlanrig Street, DG3 5LU
⏲ 11-midnight (1am Thu-Sat); 12-midnight Sun
☎ (01848) 330215
website www.buccleuchhotel.co.uk
Caledonian 80/-; guest beers Ⓗ
You may well find yourself swapping stories with friendly locals or visitors from all over Europe and beyond in this cheery hotel. The food is always hearty – watch the blackboard for special dishes. The nearby Drumlanrig Castle is worth a visit and regularly hosts special events. The area is an ideal location for country pursuits. There is a regular bus service between Thornhill and Dumfries. QP

Closing time

Keats once bought a small pub in London and one day he was visited by Dr Watson, confrere of the famous Baker Street sleuth. Watson came late in the evening accompanied by a friend and the pair of them took to hard drinking in the back snug. When closing time came, Keats shouted out the usual slogans of urgent valediction such as 'Time now, please!, 'Time gents!, 'The licence, gents!', 'Fresh air now gents! ' and 'Come on now, all together!' But Watson and his friend took no notice. Eventually Keats puts his head into the snug and roared, 'Come on now, gents, have yez no Holmes to go to!'. The two topers left in that lofty vehicle, high dudgeon.

Flann O'Brien, Irish Times

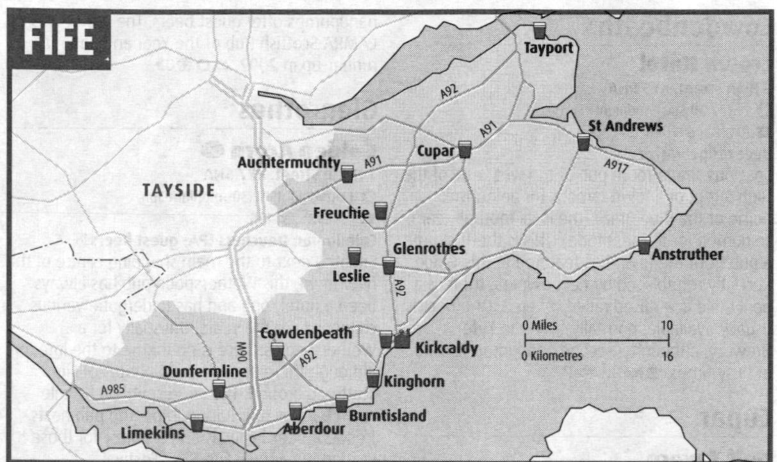

Authority area covered: Fife UA

Aberdour

Aberdour Hotel

38 High Street, KY3 0SW

4-11 Mon-Thu; 3-11.45 Fri; 11-11.45 Sat; 12-11 Sun

☎ (01383) 860325

website: www.aberdourhotel.com

Caledonian Deuchars IPA; guest beers Ⓗ

Family-run small hotel in a popular tourist and commuter area. The hotel started life as a coaching inn and many of the original features remain including stables to the rear. It has a separate public and lounge bar; the latter is used more as a restaurant and is open 6-9 each evening and lunchtime at weekends. There is one handpump in use during winter, increasing to two in spring and summer.

♨ ◑ ♿ ≠ P

Cedar Inn

20 Shore Road, KY3 0TR

11-2.30, 5-midnight; 11-midnight Fri & Sat; 12.30-midnight Sun

☎ (01383) 860310

Caledonian Deuchars IPA; guest beers Ⓗ

A short stroll from the scenic harbour, this small family-run hotel is situated in a quiet side street of Aberdour, on the north shore of the Forth. The public bar has a large-screen TV and pool table. The small side bar, lounge and no-smoking conservatory are quieter; there is a separate restaurant. One regular and three guest beers are available, changing on an almost daily basis.

Q ◑ ♿ ≠ P ⍻

Anstruther

Dreel Tavern

16 High Street, KY10 3DL

11 (12.30 Sun)-midnight

☎ (01333) 310727

Orkney Dark Island; guest beers Ⓗ

Old stone building in the East Neuk of Fife with crow step gables, a pan tile roof and beamed ceilings. It started life as a 16th-century coaching inn, reputedly visited by James V. The public and lounge bars are separated by an open fire and the conservatory provides a dining/family/no-smoking area. The pub gets busy at lunchtime and early evening. Good quality meals include locally caught fresh seafood. One regular and two guest beers are served from three handpumps. The Dreel is a previous winner of Kingdom of Fife CAMRA Pub of the Year. ♨ ◑ ♣ ⍻

Auchtermuchty

Cycle Tavern

75 Burnside, KY14 7AJ

11-11 Mon-Sat; 12.30-midnight Sun

☎ (01337) 828326

Beer range varies Ⓗ

Friendly two-room pub in the town probably best known as the home of Jimmy Shand and The Proclaimers. The bar has a pool table and a large TV screen. The sporting nature of the pub community is evident from the cabinets of trophies on show. The more comfortable lounge is busy at meal times, serving a good selection of keenly priced home-made food.

◑ ♿ ♣ P

Burntisland

Crown Tavern

17 Links Place, KY3 9DY

11 (12.30 Sun)-midnight

☎ (01592) 873697

Beer range varies Ⓗ

Traditional town pub with a lively, spacious public bar and even larger lounge. An attractive gantry, wood panelling and splendid etched glass windows create an old-fashioned and relaxed atmosphere in the bar. The sports-minded tend to gravitate to the pool table in the lounge. Three handpumps offer an exclusive blended beer, Bachanal, from Inveralmond Brewery and two guest beers.

♿ ≠ ♣

INDEPENDENT BREWERIES

Fyfe Kirkaldy

SCOTLAND

Cowdenbeath

Crown Hotel

6 High Street, KY5 9NA

11 (12.30 Sun)-midnight

(01383) 610540

Beer range varies H

Spacious single-room pub at the west end of the High Street of a town famous for being the home of the Blue Brazil (the local football team, so named for its ineptitude). This is the first time a pub from the town has featured in this Guide. Recently refurbished by new owners, there is a pool table in a raised railed-off area. One beer is usually available, normally from the Fyfe Brewery, although a second handpump is used at busy times.

Cupar

Golf Tavern

11 South Road, KY15 5JF

11-midnight (1am Fri & Sat); 12.20-11 Sun

(01334) 654233

Beer range varies H

Part of a low-set terrace on the main road south out of Cupar, this is a small, traditional bar. The modern interior has a seating area to the right of the main entrance with the bar counter to the left. This friendly local usually offers one beer during the week, two at the weekend. Good quality home-cooked bar meals are available at lunchtime including a dish of the day. Q

Dunfermline

Commercial Inn

13 Douglas Street, KY12 7EB

11-11 (midnight Fri & Sat); 12.30-11 Sun

(01383) 733876

website: www.commercialinn.co.uk

Caledonian Deuchars IPA; Courage Directors; McEwan's 80/-; Theakston Old Peculier; guest beers H

Cosy town-centre pub with a long history as an ale house and coaching inn dating back to the 1820s. Along with four regular Scottish Courage beers, four varying guest ales from all over Britain are served, augmented by a selection of continental bottled beers. The bare floorboards and mellow paintwork create a warm, relaxed atmosphere, and on weekdays the emphasis is on conversation not music. However, match day afternoons can get busy, as can Friday and Saturday evenings at Kingdom of Fife CAMRA Pub of the Year 2005.

Freuchie

Albert Tavern

2 High Street, KY15 7EX (W of A92)

11-2, 5-11; 12-1am Fri & Sat; 12.30-11 Sun

(01337) 857192

Beer range varies H

Family-friendly village local that probably started life as a two up, two down house. Reputedly a coaching inn when nearby Falkland Palace was a royal residence, an old photograph shows the property as a tavern some time in the 19th century. Both the bar and lounge have beamed ceilings, the bar has wainscot panelling; a small upstairs restaurant seats about 20. Three handpumps offer guest beers. The Albert was CAMRA Scottish Pub of the Year and national runner-up in 2002. Q

Glenrothes

Golden Acorn

1 North Street, KY7 5NA

11-midnight; 12.30-midnight Sun

(01592) 751175

Caledonian Deuchars IPA; guest beers H

Situated next to the main shopping centre of the new town, this Wetherspoon pub has always been a hotel/pub and has undergone various changes over the years. Unusually for a Wetherspoon's there is no theme to the interior although there are some old photos of Fife scattered around. The large split-level single room bar has four handpumps. The pub hosts frequent beer festivals and is handy for those visiting the annual Fife Beer Festival.

P

Kinghorn

Auld Hoose

6-8 Nethergate, KY3 9SY

(off main street, down a flight of stairs)

12 (11 Sat)-midnight; 12.30-midnight Sun

(01592) 891074 website: www.theauldhoose.co.uk

Broughton Greenmantle; Caledonian Deuchars IPA; H **guest beers** H/A

Lively village pub popular with locals and visitors situated on a steep side street leading off Kinghorn main street. The main bar has a TV and pool table to keep the sports fans happy and features dominoes competitions at the weekends; the lounge is quieter and more comfortable with a relaxed atmosphere. Two regular and two guest beers are sold from the three handpumps and one Scottish upright font on air pressure. The pub is handy for the station and Kinghorn beach.

Crown Tavern

55-57 High Street, KY3 9UW

11 (12.30 Sun)-midnight

(01592) 890340

Beer range varies H

Good, honest town local situated at the west end of the main street between Burntisland and Kirkcaldy. This two room bustling pub is always busy with regulars and visitors. Two frequently-changing ales are dispensed by the cheery bar staff.

Ship Tavern

2 Bruce Street, KY3 9JT

12 (12.30 Sun)-midnight

(01592) 890655

website: www.shiptavern.com

Caledonian Deuchars IPA; guest beers H

One of the older buildings in Kinghorn, originally built as a house for Bible John who printed the first bibles in Scotland. The rather unobtrusive entrance door, which faces the main road, opens into a fine timber-panelled interior with a long bar counter and ornate gantry. The small jug bar is probably one of the finest surviving traditional interiors in Fife; a brass pressure gauge at one end of the gantry is evidence of an old water engine for the beer. A separate back room is ideal for meetings and private parties. Meals may be available in summer; call first to check.

Kirkcaldy

Harbour Bar

471-475 High Street, KY1 1JL

11-3, 5-midnight; 11-midnight Thu-Sat; 12.30-midnight Sun

(01592) 264270

Beer range varies H

Situated on the ground floor of a tenement building, this unspoilt local has been described by regulars as a 'village local in the middle of town'. Murals in the public bar depict the town's whaling past while the comfortable, recently refurbished lounge features model sailing ships in glass cases. Six ales from micros all over Britain are on tap, along with those from the Fyfe Brewery, which is situated to the rear of the pub, and a fine selection of malt whiskies. Snacks include locally made pies and bridies. It was CAMRA Scottish Pub of the Year in 2000 and a national runner-up.

Leslie

Burns Tavern

184 High Street, KY6 7DD

12 (11 Fri & Sat)-midnight; 12.30 to midnight Sun

(01592) 741345

Taylor Landlord; guest beers H

Typical Scottish two-room main street local. The public bar is on two levels, the lower lively and friendly, the upper with a large-screen TV and pool table. The lounge bar is quieter and more spacious. There are pub quizzes on Wednesday and Thursday evenings and dominoes, darts and pool competitions on Sunday afternoon. There is one guest beer on tap, sometimes two, usually from a small independent brewery.

Limekilns

Ship Inn

Halketts Hall, KY11 3HJ (on promenade)

11-11 (midnight Fri & Sat); 12.30-11 Sun

(01383) 872247

Beer range varies H

Single room pub in a historic village on the north shore of the River Forth. This ever-improving inn serves a varied beer range, usually from Scottish micros, and a great lunch menu. In summer, real cider is sometimes available on one of the three handpumps. Wonderful views across the Forth can be enjoyed from the outdoor seating area.

St Andrews

Aikman's Cellar Bar

32 Bell Street, KY16 9UK

6-midnight; 1-1am Thu-Sat; 6-midnight Sun

(01334) 477425

website: www.cellarbar.co.uk

Beer range varies H

Basement lounge bar selling around 300 real ales each year, as well as a variety of continental bottled beers. The rolled copper bar top was salvaged from the White Star liner Oceanic (the same shipping line as the Titanic). Opening hours outside term time can vary; the bar is closed most lunchtimes but cask ales are available on request in the bistro upstairs. The bar is popular with students and can get busy. A week-long beer festival at Easter offers 20 ales. The bar has been a regular in this Guide since 1987.

Central Bar

77-79 Market Street, KY16 9NU

11-11.45 (1am Fri & Sat); 12.30-11.45 Sun

(01334) 478296

Caledonian Deuchars IPA; McEwan's 80/-; Greene King Old Speckled Hen; Theakston Best Bitter, Old Peculier; guest beers H

Town-centre pub popular with students and locals. The Victorian-style island bar, large windows and ornate mirrors give it a late 19th-century feel. It is the only pub in town that serves food after 9pm and can be busy. On a pleasant summer evening the pavement tables are ideal for watching the world go by while enjoying a good range of regular and guest ales.

Whey Pat Tavern

2 Argyle Street, KY16 9EX

11-11.30 (11.45 Fri & Sat); 12.30-11.30 Sun

(01334) 477740

Beer range varies H

Friendly, welcoming pub on a busy road junction just outside the old town walls. There has been a hostelry on this site for several centuries; it was taken over by Belhaven in 2002 but minimal changes have been made. This cheery pub is popular with students, academics and townspeople alike, and the superb sandwiches freshly made to order at lunchtimes are no doubt part of the attraction. Three handpumps offer an ever-changing range of beer.

Tayport

Bell Rock Tavern

4-6 Dalgleish Street, DD6 9BB

11-midnight (1am Thu-Sat); 12.30 to midnight Sun

(01382) 552388

Caledonian Deuchars IPA; guest beers H

Near the harbour, this friendly local has a bar on three levels, each with a mainly nautical theme of artefacts including old charts and photographs of ships and aircraft, old Dundee and the Tay ferries. One real ale is served throughout the year, with two in the summer and during the festive season. A welcoming pub that dispenses good cheer along with good ales and excellent value home-cooked meals, mince and tatties is a favourite at lunchtimes. It makes an ideal stop for walkers on the Fife coastal path. Q

Timely advice

'I think now would be a good time for a beer' – **Franklin Delano Roosevelt**, 15 December 1933, on the day Prohibition ended.

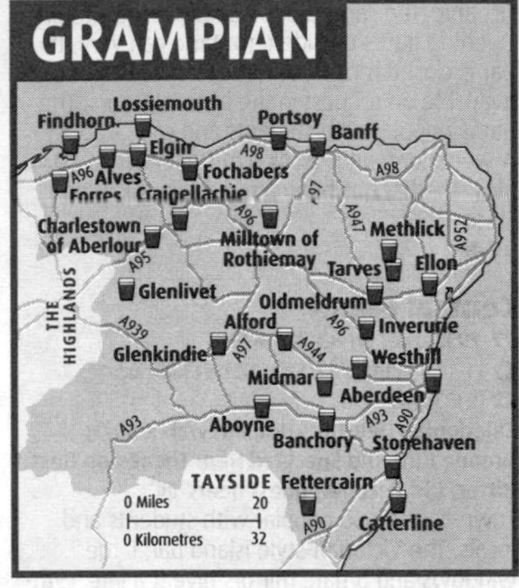

Authority areas covered: Aberdeenshire UA, City of Aberdeen UA, Moray UA

Aberdeen

Carriages

101 Crown Street, AB11 6HH

✪ 11-2.30, 4.30-midnight; 6-11 Sun

☎ (01224) 595440

website: www.brentwood-hotel.co.uk

Draught Bass; Boddingtons Bitter; Fuller's London Pride; guest beers Ⓗ

Basement bar set below the Brentwood Hotel offering the biggest selection of real ales in town in comfortable and relaxed surroundings. The adjoining restaurant serves excellent meals in the evenings (booking advised) and lunches are available in the lounge bar. As the hotel attracts mainly midweek oil firm residential business, the weekends are usually a quieter time to savour the choice of 10 ales. It was local CAMRA City Pub of the Year in 2005. ⇄◑≋ P

Grill ☆

213 Union Street, AB11 6BA

✪ 10-midnight (1am Fri & Sat); 12-30-midnight Sun

Caledonian 80/-; Courage Directors; Isle of Sky Red Cullin; guest beer Ⓗ

Superb, wood-panelled bar which is the only CAMRA National Inventory pub north of Dundee. A once men-only bar, it does now have a ladies' toilet! The lighting has become more subtle, concealed above the gantry, rather than the garish fluorescent tubes of previous years. Situated opposite the Music Hall, you may spy various musicians from rock to classical, passing the intervals of their respective gigs here. A large choice of malt whiskies will delight the connoisseurs and a variety of snacks (Stovies and pies) are also available. ≋

Old Blackfriars

52 Castle Street, AB11 5BB

✪ 11-midnight (1am Fri & Sat); 12:30-11 Sun

☎ (01224) 581922

Belhaven Sandy Hunter's Ale, St Andrew's Ale; Caledonian Deuchars IPA, 80/-; Inveralmond Ossian's Ale, guest beers Ⓗ

The pub creates the ambience of a high quality continental café with its well-balanced mixture of bar and restaurant. There are religious overtones to the eclectic furnishings and decor: note the back-lit stained glass. A multiple local CAMRA award winner, it supplies food throughout the pub until 9pm (8pm Fri & Sat). ◑♿≋

Prince of Wales

7 St Nicholas Lane, AB10 1HF (lane opp. M&S)

✪ 10-midnight; 12-midnight Sun (meals only from 12, alcohol from 12:30)

☎ (01224) 640597

Caledonian 80/-; Theakston Old Peculier; guest beers Ⓗ

Eight handpumps dominate the centrepiece of this long, original bar which has undergone various refurbishments in past years but kept its traditional feel. A carpeted, seated area near the entrance and a flagstoned section with private booths to the rear, makes it feel like two different pubs. The house beer, Prince of Wales Ale, is brewed by Inveralmond. Monday is quiz night and a folk session takes place on Sunday evening. It was local CAMRA City Pub of the Year 2002 and 2005. Q◑≋♣

Tilted Wig

55–56 Castle Street, AB11 5BA (opp. Court House)

✪ 12-midnight (1am Fri & Sat); 12:30-11 Sun

☎ (01224) 583248

Caledonian Deuchars IPA; Courage Directors; Marston's Pedigree; guest beers Ⓗ

Long, narrow bar (once called the Lang or Saloon Bar, and in the 1970s, the Welly Boot) with a small, elevated snug area at the front and a seated area at the rear where rock bands sometimes play. The menu is limited but food is served all day. ◑≋

Under The Hammer

11 North Silver Street, AB10 1RJ (off Golden Sq)

✪ 5 (4 Fri; 2 Sat)-midnight (1am Thu-Sat); 6.30-11 Sun

☎ (01224) 640253

Caledonian Deuchars IPA; Inveralmond Ossian's Ale; guest beers Ⓗ

Small, intimate basement bar, so named due to its proximity to the city auction rooms. It tends to get busy with patrons before and after shows at the nearby Music Hall (Union Street) or HM Theatre (Rosemount Viaduct) and only opens on Sunday if a major event is taking place at one of these venues. Art displays decorate the walls and are available to purchase while the large noticeboard has posters advertising forthcoming events in town. An acoustic 'open mike' session is held every second Monday. ≋

Aboyne

Boat Inn

Charleston Road, AB34 5EL

(N bank of River Dee next to Aboyne Bridge)

✪ 11-2.30, 5-11 (midnight Fri); 11-midnight Sat; 11-11 Sun

☎ (013398) 86137

Draught Bass; guest beers Ⓗ

Popular, riverside inn with a food oriented lounge featuring a log-burning stove and spiral staircase leading to the upper dining area. Junior diners (and adults!) may request to see the model train, complete with sound effects, traverse the entire pub at picture-rail height upon completion of their meal. The local Rotary Club regularly meets here. Two guest beers are supplied by Scottish micros. Accommodation is in a self-catering flat. ⛰Q⇌◑⊟♿⛺♣P

Alford

Forbes Arms Hotel

Bridge of Alford, AB33 8QJ
(1½ miles from Alford on A944)
☉ 11-11 (1am Fri & Sat); 11-midnight Sun
☎ (019755) 62108
Beer range varies Ⓗ
Family-run hotel in an attractive riverside setting with a small, comfortable lounge and sports-dominated public bar. There is one handpump in each bar, dispensing a different beer. Fishing parties are catered for and it is close to the Grampian Transport Museum, dry ski slope and Craigievar Castle. ⛰Q❀⇌◑⊟P

Alves

Crooked Inn

Burghead Road, IV30 8UU
☉ 12-2, 5.30-11 (11.30 Fri; midnight Sat); 12.30-11.30 Sun
☎ (01343) 850646
Beer range varies Ⓗ
This labyrinthine pub has low ceilings and obscure bric-a-brac filling every available space. It offers keenly-priced bar food contrasting well with the meals served in the restaurant. A friendly, efficiently run establishment, it tends to offer a rotating choice from Scottish micro-breweries. The wee snug is 'Nae Smokin'. ◑♣P⊬

Banchory

Douglas Arms Hotel

22 High Street, AB31 5SR
11-midnight (1am Sat); 11-midnight Sun
☎ (01330) 822547
Beer range varies Ⓗ
A small, budget hotel with public bar and lounge separated by a pool area. The former is a classic Scottish long bar with etched windows on to the High Street and vintage mirrors at either end. The latter contains a large fireplace and Chesterfield settees, and is in the east half of the hotel along with a function room and restaurant. There are usually two guest beers from Kelburn and Houston. Benches are provided on the street for summer drinking. ⛰ Q☕❀⇌◑⊟⛺♣P

Ravenswood Club (Royal British Legion)

25 Ramsay Road, AB31 5TS (up Mount St from A93, second right)
☉ 11-2.30, 5-midnight (11 winter); 11-midnight Sat & Sun
☎ (01330) 822347 website: www.banchorylegion.com
Beer range varies Ⓗ
Large British Legion Club which welcomes CAMRA members and bearers of this Guide as guests. A comfortable lounge adjoins the pool and TV room and there is a spacious function room well utilised by local clubs and societies as well as members. Darts and snooker are also played. The two handpumps offer excellent value as the beer is the cheapest in the area. A terrace is available for outdoor drinking. ❀⇌◑♿⛺♣P

Banff

Ship Inn

Deveronside, AB45 1HP (on seafront near harbour)
☉ 11-11 (12.30am Fri & Sat); 1-11 Sun
☎ (01261) 812620
Courage Directors Ⓗ
Traditional 200-year-old public house overlooking Banff bay towards Macduff. The public bar is decorated with nautical artefacts and its interior featured in the film Local Hero. A blocked carriage arch at the front hints at the pub's history. Both bar and lounge are wood-lined and have tremendous sea views although the windows are small. The inn is close to the baroque mansion of Duff House which is now home to one of Scotland's National Gallery collections. Golf and sailing are available close by. ⛰Q⊟

Catterline

Creel Inn

AB39 2UL
(on coast off A92, 5 miles S of Stonehaven) OS868781
☉ 12-11 (midnight Fri & Sat); 12-11 Sun
☎ (01569) 750254 website: www.thecreelinn.co.uk
Beer range varies Ⓗ
Compact village inn in a stunning cliff-top position, built in 1838 and now incorporating adjacent cottages which provide two en-suite guest rooms. An excellent menu is available in the restaurant (reservations recommended) and lounge, with local seafood a speciality (meals served all day Sun). A large selection of specialist bottled beers is stocked, mainly Belgian. Crawton Bird Sanctuary lies two miles to the north. Phone to check winter opening times before travelling.
⛰Q❀⇌◑⊟P⊬

Charleston of Aberlour

Mash Tun

8 Broomfield Square, AB38 9QP
☉ 11-11 (11.45 Thu; 12.30am Fri & Sat); 11-11.45 Sun
☎ (01340) 881771
website:www.speyside.moray.org/Aberlour/mashtun.htm
Belhaven 80/-; Cairngorm Highland IPA; guest beers Ⓗ
Built in 1896 as the Station Bar, this unusual, round-ended building has a light interior with extensive use of timber. The Speyside Way runs past the door and patrons may drink out on the former station platform in summer. Up to three beers are available during the tourist season and a wide variety of bottled beers is stocked at this former local CAMRA Country Pub of the Year.
❀⇌◑⛺

Craigellachie

Highlander Inn

10 Victoria Street, AB38 9SR
☉ 11-11 (midnight Fri); 11-11 Sun
☎ (01340) 881446
Cairngorm Trade Winds; Taylor Landlord Ⓗ
Cosy cellar bar on the Speyside Way and Whisky Trail with a fishing theme. The cuisine is a big attraction in the tourist season, as is the frequent live music. The inn runs an outdoor bar at the local 'Couthie Doo' and uses pins (35-pint

SCOTLAND

casks) in winter to maintain beer freshness. An extensive collection of malt whiskies is stocked. ⇌◑P

Elgin

Flanagan's

Shepherd's Close, 48a High Street, IV30 1BU
11-12.30am (1.30am Fri & Sat); 12-midnight Sun
☎ (01343) 549737
Beer range varies Ⓗ
Situated up an old close, this friendly pub has a long, narrow bar with a choice of two beers. At one end there are wooden benches, tables and a large screen TV while at the other are three large comfortable sofas. In the corner are a jukebox and two gaming machines. Occasional live music is staged at weekends. You can take your beer upstairs to the Tapas restaurant. The pub is within walking distance of Elgin cathedral, destroyed by the 'Wolf of Badenoch' (Alexander Stewart, Earl of Moray) in 1390. ◑≋

Muckle Cross ✔

34 High Street, IV30 1BU
11-12.30 (midnight Wed & Thu; 1am Fri & Sat); 12.30-11.45 Sun
☎ (01343) 559030
Caledonian 80/-; Courage Directors; Theakston Best Bitter; guest beers Ⓗ
Fairly typical small Wetherspoon pub converted from what used to be a bicycle repair shop and latterly a branch of Halfords. The long, wide bar offers a choice of up to five ales and can get busy, especially at weekends. It opens at 10am for coffee. ◑♿≋⚟

Sunninghill Hotel

Hay Street, IV30 1NH
11-11.15 (12.15am Fri & Sat); 11-11.15 Sun
☎ (01343) 547799
website: www.sunninghillhotel.com
Taylor Landlord; Tetley Burton Ale; guest beers Ⓗ
This small, family-run hotel is situated in a quiet residential area, a few minutes' walk from the railway station and the town centre. A comfortable lounge includes a dining area with additional tables in the attached conservatory and offers a varied menu making it a popular venue for families. Guest handpumps usually offer a choice of two or three beers. A large selection of whiskies can also entice the traveller slightly off the beaten track to this hostelry. Q❀ ⇌◑♿≋P⚟

Ellon

Station Hotel

Station Brae, AB41 9BD (½ mile W of village centre)
11-11 (1am Fri; 11.45 Sat); 11-10.45 Sun
☎ (01358) 720209
website: www.s-h-systems.co.uk/a14027.html
Beer range varies Ⓗ
Small Victorian hotel, family run since 1891, serving two regularly changing beers in the basic public bar. Excellent food is served which is also available in the no-smoking Arches Restaurant upstairs. The hotel has good function facilities and fishing and shooting can be arranged. A golf course is adjacent and Haddo Country Park is five miles distant. ⇌◑ ⊟♣P

Tolbooth

21-23 Station Road, AB41 9AE
11-2.30, 5-11 (midnight Thu & Fri); 11-11.45 Sat; 6.30-11 Sun
☎ (01358) 721308
Beer range varies Ⓗ
Comfortable lounge bar, split on two levels, with a spacious conservatory on the lower level leading to an enclosed patio. The generally older clientele and the pub's refusal to admit children ensures a fairly relaxed and quiet atmosphere. A smaller attic bar is available for meetings. The four beers are mainly from the larger English regionals with the occasional Scottish micro-brew. Q❀♿♣

Fettercairn

Ramsay Arms

Burnside Road, AB30 1XX
12-2.30, 5-11 (12-11.30 Fri & Sat); 12.30-11 Sun
☎ (01561) 340334
website: www.ramsayarmshotel.co.uk
Inveralmond Independence; Ossian's Ale Ⓗ
Situated in the shadow of the Victoria Commemorative Arch, erected in recognition of the Queen's first trip to the north-east of Scotland when she spent the night in the hotel. Traditional fare, using produce from the local area including Aberdeen Angus beef, game, fish and shellfish, is served in the open, modern lounge. Close to Fasque Estate, residence of Sir William Gladstone, it is also near the visitor centre at the Fettercairn distillery. ⇌◑

Findhorn

Crown & Anchor Inn

44 Findhorn, IV36 3YF
11-midnight (1.30am Fri & Sat); 11-12.30am Sun
☎ (01309) 690243
Draught Bass; Marston's Pedigree; Orkney Dark Island; Taylor Landlord; guest beers Ⓗ
Overlooking picturesque Findhorn Bay, this inn is situated in a listed building dating from 1739. Inside are two bars, and the outside seating area with benches is popular with families and water sports enthusiasts. A wide variety of food is served all day. Children are welcome until 9pm. ♛Q☕❀⇌◑⊟⛺♣P⚟

Kimberley Inn

94 Findhorn, IV36 3YG
11-midnight (1.30am Fri & Sat); 12-midnight Sun
☎ (01309) 690492
Taylor Landlord; guest beers Ⓗ
Specialising in local, fresh seafood, this popular, friendly bar stocks mainly English beers in winter and Scottish ones in summer. The patio offers glorious views of Findhorn Bay, famous for water sports. The nearby shop at the Findhorn Foundation is well worth a visit for its excellent selection of organic bottled beers. ♛Q❀◑♿⛺♣● ⚟

Fochabers

Gordon Arms Hotel

80 High Street, IV32 7DH (on A96)
11-11; 12-11 Sun
☎ (01343) 820508

website: www.gordonarmshotel.com
Caledonian Deuchars IPA; Marston's Pedigree; guest beers Ⓗ
This rambling coaching inn with low ceilings is on the main street of village. It offers an up-market restaurant and accommodation and is the home of many local societies. Real ale pumps are in the public bar but beer can be served in the lounge bar. Meals are available 12-2pm and 5-7pm. The hotel is adjacent to Speyside Way and Baxter's factory village.
❀⇌◐◑⊟P

Forres

Red Lion

2-6 Tollboth Street, IV36 1PH
✪ 11-12.30am (1.30am Fri & Sat); 12-12.30am Sun
☎ (01309) 672716
Beer varies Ⓗ
Dating from 1838 and known locally as the 'Beastie', this is one of the longest-established real ale outlets going back to the 1970s. Following CAMRA's lead it began to favour cask beer over keg and championed the now long-gone Younger's XXPS. Ale is now found in the more modern lounge but check out the original public bar. One changing guest ale is served. Food is available between noon and 2pm.
◐⊟⇌

Glenkindie

Glenkindie Arms Hotel

AB33 8SX (on A97, at E edge of village)
✪ 12-2, 5-midnight (1am Fri); 12-midnight Sat; 12-11 Sun
☎ (01975) 641288
website: www.glenkindiearms.co.uk
Beer range varies Ⓗ
Tiny 400-year-old former drovers' inn occupying a listed building. It is known locally as 'The Lodge' due to its former Masonic use, evidence of which is still visible on the outer wall. An extensive food menu specialises in local dishes as well as some with a far eastern flavour. The hotel stands on the Castle Trail with Kildrummy three miles away and is convenient for the Lecht Ski Centre. It is best to check winter opening hours before travelling.
ᗢ❀⇌◐◑P

Glenlivet

Croft Inn

AB37 9DP (on B9009 Dufftown-Glenlivet road)
✪ 12-11 (midnight Sat); 12.30-11 Sun (hours vary in winter)
☎ (01807) 590361 website: www.croft-inn.co.uk
Beer range varies Ⓗ
Small, single-room bar in a building dating from 1770 which was originally an alms house, then used for crofting, until it became an inn in 1973. Stocking over 50 malt whiskies, it is on the Whisky Trail with 50 distilleries within a 15-mile radius. It is close to the ski slopes at the Lecht. A light beer from the Cairngorm range is usually stocked and a dark brew from a Scottish micro. It is advisable to check winter hours in advance. Lunches are served in summer.
ᗢ⇌◐◑♿P

Inverurie

Edwards

2 West High Street, AB51 3SA
✪ 10 (12.30 Sun)-1am
☎ (01467) 629788
Beer range varies Ⓗ
Elegant cafe-bar, completely redesigned in 2001, with modern yet classic decor featuring gleaming wood, brass and subtle lighting, but comfortable too with cosy snugs. This venue is frequented by a range of customers, including business types, locals and young people. Good coffee, pastries, soup, pasta, sandwiches and snacks cater to all tastes. Inverurie is a thriving market town near hill-walking country and the Castle Trail. ◐♿⇌

Lossiemouth

Skerry Brae Hotel

Stotfield Road, IV31 6QS
✪ 11-11 (12.30am Fri & Sat); 12-11 Sun
☎ (01343) 812040
website: www.skerrybrae.co.uk
Beer range varies Ⓗ
Roomy lounge bar in an old granite hotel with a recently refurbished dining area and large bench-seated patio. Up to three beers are available to customers who, as suggested by the large collection of badges and stickers, come largely from the nearby RAF base. Children are allowed until 9.30pm in the conservatory, dining room and terrace. ⇌◐◑P

Methlick

Ythanview Hotel

Main Street, AB41 7DT
✪ 11-2.30, 5-11 (1am Fri); 11-12.30am Sat; 11-11 Sun
☎ (01651) 806235
website: www.ythanview.com
Beer range varies Ⓗ
Comfortable family-run hotel comprising a welcoming restaurant enlivened by a real fire and a smaller public bar. It has a real village local feel, with its own cricket team and new ground, organising community fundraising events. Inexpensive meals tempt visitors' appetites – the landlord's hot chicken curry is both a speciality and something of a challenge! The house beer, McLairds Ale, is from Atlas Brewery.
ᗢQ❀⇌◐◑⊟♿♣P⚟

Midmar

Midmar Inn

AB51 7LX (on B9119, 2 miles W of Echt)
✪ 11-2.30 (not Mon), 5-11; 11-midnight Thu-Sat; 12.30-11 Sun
☎ (01330) 860515
Beer range varies Ⓗ
Isolated country pub with plans for an extensive renovation and expansion to increase its dining capacity, which may be complete by the time you visit. It can be busy at weekends and especially on Thursday's ceilidh night. The reasonably-priced meals are popular and booking, especially at weekends, is advisable.
Q❀◐◑⊟P⚟

Milltown of Rothiemay

Forbes Arms Hotel

AB54 7LT

12-2.30, 5-11 including Sun

(01466) 711248

Beer range varies H

Dating from 1760, this charming two-bar hotel is in a picturesque setting on the bank of the River Deveron – noted for its salmon and trout fishing. Good, home-cooked food is a speciality and traditional music is featured once a month on a Thursday night. Guest beers are often from the Atlas Brewery range.

Q P

Oldmeldrum

Redgarth Hotel

Kirk Brae, AB51 0DJ (off A947 towards golf course)

11-2.30, 5-midnight; 12-2:30, 5-11 Sun

(01651) 872353

website: www.redgarth.com

Beer range varies H /G

Traditional, wood-panelled lounge bar sited in an imposing position at the top of the village, enjoying panoramic views of the eastern Grampian mountains. It offers an imaginative selection of seasonal guest ales and a varied menu of home-cooked food. Occasional 'Brewer-In-Residence' evenings are an added attraction. The main bar has designated smoking and no-smoking areas and the dining/meeting room is also no-smoking. Children are welcome at this local CAMRA Pub of the Year, awarded for the last three years.

Q P

Portsoy

Shore Inn

Church Street, AB45 2QR

10-11 (midnight Thu; 12.30am Fri & Sat); 10-11 Sun

(01261) 842831

Beer range varies H

Coastal inn dating from the 18th century situated at the oldest harbour on the Moray coast. It exudes an olde-worlde atmosphere with its low ceiling and dark wooden bar fittings. Up to three ales are stocked (only one in winter) and the selection is unpredictable. The village hosts an annual boat festival for which the pub runs an outdoor bar – the Shore Out!

Stonehaven

Marine Hotel

9-10 Shorehead, AB39 2JY

11-11 (midnight Thu; 1am Fri & Sat); 11-midnight Sun

(01569) 762155

Beer range varies H

This hotel's picturesque harbour-front location makes it a must, particularly in summer. Downstairs there is a simple, wood-panelled bar serving five frequently-changing ales selected from both micro-breweries and the more enterprising regionals. The adjacent lounge, with a huge fire in winter, makes a comfortable contrast to the bustle of the small bar. Upstairs is the main dining area specialising in fresh, local produce, particularly seafood dishes. The house beer is Dunottar Ale brewed by Inveralmond. Children are allowed upstairs or in the downstairs lounge at this former Scottish CAMRA Pub of the Year.

Tarves

Aberdeen Arms Hotel

The Square, AB41 7GX

12-2.30 (not Mon), 5-11 (1am Fri); 12-11.45 Sat; 12.30-11 Sun

(01651) 851214

website: www.geocities.com/aberdeenarmshotel

Beer range varies H

Small, family-run hotel in the village conservation area. Note the fine mirrors in the public bar. Regular folk music evenings featuring bagpipes and zither are well attended. Food ranges from the cuisine of the North East to the Far East. Children are welcome until 8pm. The location is handy for visiting Tolquhon Castle and Pitmedden Gardens, which were laid out in the 17th century by Sir Alexander Seddon with elaborate flower beds, fountains and pavilions.

Q P

Westhill

Shepherds Rest

10 Straik Road, Arnhall Business Park, AB32 6HF

11-11; 12.30-11 Sun

(01224) 740208

Courage Directors; guest beers H

An unusually well-designed kit-built pub with an enterprising guest ale policy as shown by the extensive pump clip display. Food dominates and is served all day, so the pub is particularly popular with families, especially at weekends. Accommodation is provided in the adjacent Premier Travel Inn. P

Open all hours?

The new Licensing Act for England and Wales was due to come into effect in the autumn of 2005. In spite of media frenzy over '24-hour opening', only a handful of pubs and hotels had applied for such extensions as the Guide went to press. It is likely that most pubs will opt for existing hours or for late-night extensions at weekends. The hours listed for pubs were correct when the Guide went to press but are liable to change.

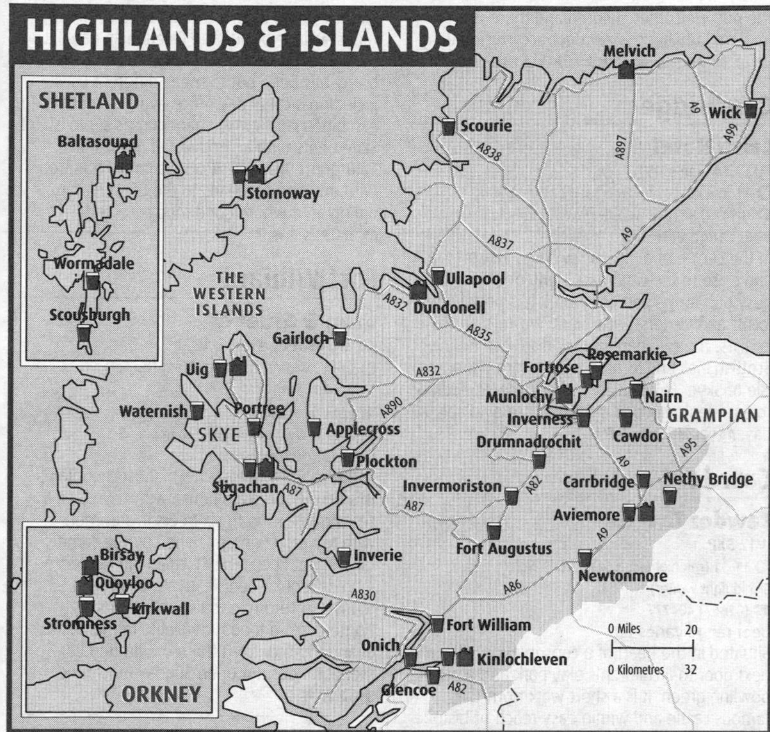

Authority areas covered: Highland UA, Orkney Islands UA, Shetland Islands UA, Western Islands UA

Applecross

Applecross Inn

Shore Street, IV54 8LR

(on unclassified road off A896) OS711445

11-11.30 (midnight Fri); 12.30-11.30 Sun

☎ (01520) 744262

Beer range varies H

Spectacularly situated on the shore of the Applecross Peninsula and enjoying views of the Isles of Skye and Raasay. Owned by the same family since 1989, it is reached by a single track road over the highest vehicular ascent in Britain, or by a longer scenic route. Two handpumps dispense beer from the Isle of Skye brewery and the food speciality is shellfish. It features regular ceilidhs and the area is ideal for climbing, walking and wildlife watching.

Aviemore

Cairngorm Hotel

Grampian Road, PH22 1PE (opp. station)

11-midnight (1am Fri & Sat); 11.30-midnight Sun

☎ (01479) 810233

website: www.cairngorm.com

Beer range varies H

The lounge of this 31-room privately owned hotel, though large, has a cosy feel. It is enhanced by the two bay windows, distressed wooden furniture and a large coal-effect fire. Although the trade is mainly holidaymakers, the bar is also popular with locals. The single handpump serves beer from the local brewery. There is a Scottish theme throughout the hotel with tartan wall coverings and Scottish entertainment many afternoons and evenings. A large-screen TV shows sport.

P

Old Bridge Inn

Dalfaber Road, PH22 1PU

(100 yds from jct with Cairngorm Ski Road, B970)

11-midnight (1am Fri); 11-midnight Sun

☎ (01479) 811137

website: www.oldbridgeinn.co.uk

Beer range varies H

Busy pub serving good quality food. Originally a cottage and now greatly enlarged, it lies to the south of the village on the road leading to the Strathspey Steam Railway and is popular with outdoor enthusiasts. It has three handpumps offering a range of ales from Scottish and English breweries and a good selection of malt whiskies.

INDEPENDENT BREWERIES

An Teallach Dundonell
Atlas Kinlochleven
Black Isle Munlochy
Cairngorm Aviemore
Cuillin Sligachan
Highland Birsay
Far North Melvich
Hebridean Stornoway
Isle of Skye Uig
Orkney Quoyloo
Valhalla Baltasound

SCOTLAND

The pub welcomes children and there is a modern bunkhouse next door accommodating up to 40 guests. ♨Q❀🛏◐♿⛺⇌P

Carrbridge

Cairn Hotel

PH23 3AS (on B9153)
⌚ 11-midnight (1am Fri & Sat); 12.30-11 Sun
☎ (01479) 841212 website: www.cairnhotel.co.uk
Beer range varies Ⓗ
In the centre of a pleasant village, just off the A9 and close to the Landmark Heritage Park, this busy pub forms part of a hotel. It is popular with locals and visitors, particularly walkers and cyclists. The two handpumps dispense mainly Scottish ales and include brews from Cairngorm, Isle of Skye, Caledonian and Kelburn. In addition to bar meals, soup and toasties are available all day. ♨❀🛏◐⇌♣P🚭

Cawdor

Cawdor Tavern

IV12 5XP
⌚ 11-11 (midnight Fri & Sat); 11-11 Sun (11-3, 5-midnight winter)
☎ (01667) 404777
Beer range varies Ⓗ
Situated in the heart of a conservation village next door to a children's play park and a public bowling green. It is a short walk from the famous castle and within easy reach of historic Fort George and Culloden battlefield. Family owned, the pub is full of character featuring a large lounge bar, cosy public bar and a 70-seater restaurant. The public bar has an antique mahogany bar and a ceiling covered in old maps. Both bars are wood panelled and have log fires. Two handpumps serve beers from the prize winning Cairngorm Brewery.
♨❀◐🍺♿♣P🚭

Drumnadrochit

Benleva Hotel

IV63 6UH (435 yards from A82)
⌚ 12-midnight (1am Fri; 11.45 Sat); 12.30-11 Sun
☎ (01456) 450080 website: www.benleva.co.uk
Beer range varies Ⓗ/Ⓖ
Popular, friendly village hotel catering for locals and visitors. A 400-year-old former manse, it is convenient for the Great Glen Way and searching for the Loch Ness Monster. The sweet chestnut tree was a former hanging tree. Three handpumps sell mainly Highland beers with one from the Isle of Skye and occasional beer from the wood. The hotel serves good evening meals and lunches (limited in winter). It hosts the Loch Ness Beer Festival in September and has occasional quiz nights and traditional music. It was voted local CAMRA pub of the year in 2003 and 2005. ♨Q❀🛏◐🍺⛺♣P🚭

Fort Augustus

Bothy

Canalside, PH32 4AU
⌚ 11-1am (12.30am Sat); 12.30-midnight Sun (hours vary in winter)
☎ (01329) 366710
Beer range varies Ⓗ
Situated in an ideal location in the centre of a tourist village beside the Caledonian Canal, Loch Ness and the Great Glen Way, this thick stoned bothy has been put to many different uses including a canal pay office, waiting rooms and exhibition centre. Two handpumps serve Isle of Skye beers with an occasional guest from Cairngorm Brewery. A cosy, friendly bar area with an open fire leads to the conservatory dining area where good food is served.
♨❀◐♿⛺♣P

Fort William

Grog & Gruel ✔

66 High Street, PH33 6AE
⌚ 11 (12 winter)-midnight (1am Thu-Sat); 5-midnight Sun
☎ (01397) 705078
website: www.grogandgruel.co.uk
Beer range varies Ⓗ
In the shadow of Britain's highest mountain, this bare-floored ale house with church pew seating keeps up to six beers in summer, with fewer in winter. Owned by the same family that keeps the Clachaig Inn in Glencoe, it holds regular beer festivals. Busy with tourists in summer, it also attracts locals. Home-cooked food is available in the upstairs dining room or from the more limited bar menu. It does not open Sunday lunchtime.
❀◐⛺⇌

Nevisport Bar

Tweedale, PH33 6EJ
(N end of High Street, under sports shop)
⌚ 11.30-11.30 (1am Fri & Sat); 11.30-11.30 Sun
☎ (01397) 704921
Beer range varies Ⓗ
At the end of the West Highland Way, convenient for Ben Nevis and Aonach Mor, this lively bar is a favourite meeting place for walkers, climbers and skiers. A large, warming open fire welcomes winter visitors. The walls of the informal lounge-style bar are adorned with a collection of classic mountaineering photographs and mountain sports equipment, giving an interesting insight into times gone by. Mainly Scottish beers are served, often from the Isle of Skye Brewery.
♨🍼◐♿⛺⇌

Fortrose

Anderson

Union Street, IV10 8TD
⌚ 11-11.30; 12.30-11 Sun
☎ (01381) 620236
website: www.theanderson.co.uk
Beer range varies Ⓗ
This cosy, homely bar, features a bare stone wall and has two settees in front of an open fire. It is part of a nine bedroom B-listed hotel. The owner is an international beer writer and self-confessed 'beer geek'. Serving only independent Scottish brewery beers, this beer drinkers' mecca also offers 60-plus Belgian bottled beers, backed by 170-plus malts. The food is reasonably priced, high quality, international cuisine available in the lounge bar and restaurant.
♨🍼❀🛏◐🍺⛺♣P

Gairloch

Old Inn

Flowerdale, IV21 2BD (opp. harbour) OSNG811751
11-1am (11.30 Sat); 12.30-11 Sun
☎ (01445) 712006
website: www.theoldinn.net
Beer range varies [H]
Traditional, family-run Highland coaching inn situated in a delightful setting on the magnificent Wester Ross coast at the foot of Flowerdale Glen. Close to Loch Maree and convenient for Inverewe Gardens and the Beinn Eighe Nature Reserve, this is an ideal base for outdoor activities. Two bars stock up to eight mainly Scottish beers (three in winter). The enticing menu of home-cooked seafood and game includes shellfish freshly landed at the busy harbour opposite. It was local CAMRA Pub of the Year 2004.

Glencoe

Clachaig Inn ✔

PH49 4HX (½ mile off A82) OSNN128567
11-11 (midnight Fri; 11.30 Sat); 11-11 Sun
☎ (01855) 811252 website: www.clachaig.com
Beer range varies [H]
A famous, almost legendary highland hostelry, popular with climbers, walkers and tourists who are lucky enough to find it. It has a large, stone-floored public bar with several sitting rooms off it, plus a lounge at the other side of the building. There are normally four beers from Scottish micros on sale, but this goes up to 15 during beer festivals in February, June and October. Live music is hosted most weekends. Britain's most rugged scenery is an added bonus.

Inverie

Old Forge

Knoydart, by Mallaig, PH41 4PL
(accessible by ferry from Mallaig or a very long walk!)
11-midnight (including Sun)
☎ (01678) 462267 website: www.theoldforge.co.uk
Beer range varies [H]
This is the most remote pub on mainland Britain and is reached by ferry or a 15-mile, hilly walk from Kinloch Hourn. In a spectacular setting on the shore of Loch Nevis, it provides an ideal base for walking the 'rough bounds' of Knoydart; moorings welcome waterborne visitors. An excellent hub of the local community, it has two pumps serving mainly Isle of Skye beers. Specialities on the all-day menu include locally caught seafood. An informal atmosphere prevails – dress code is wellies, waterproofs and midge cream. The landlord can arrange accommodation.

Invermoriston

Glenmoriston Arms Hotel

IV63 7YA (at A82/A887 jct)
11-11 (including Sun); closed Jan & Feb
☎ (01320) 351206
website: www.glenmoriston-arms-hotel.co.uk
Beer range varies [H]/[G]
Parts of this thick-walled hotel date from 1740 when it was a drovers' inn. Over the years it has been visited by Johnson and Boswell, Gavin Maxwell (author of Ring of Bright Water) and Charlie Chaplin. It is an ideal stopping off point on the Great Glen way, Loch Ness and the road to Skye. Isle of Skye beers are served by handpump in the Tavern Bar, where there is a pool table, TV and restaurant, and from the wood in the Moriston bar which is more comfortable and relaxed.

Inverness

Blackfriars

93–95 Academy Street, IV1 1LU
11-midnight (12.30am Fri; 11.45 Sat); 12.30-11 Sun
☎ (01463) 233881
website: www.blackfriars.50megs.com
Beer range varies [H]
Traditional, town-centre pub, comprising one spacious room with a large standing area by the bar and ample seating in comfortable alcoves. Guest ales usually come from local Scottish breweries. Good value meals are home cooked using local produce and a vegetarian dish is always available. This music-oriented pub stages evenings of ethnic music, dancing and poetry, often with bagpipes. Local bands perform regularly.

Clachnaharry Inn

17-19 High Street, IV3 6RB
(on A862 Beauly road, on outskirts of town)
11-11 (midnight Thu-Sat); 12.30-11.45 Sun
☎ (01463) 239806
website: www.clachnaharryinn.co.uk
Adnams Broadside; guest beers [H]/[G]
A friendly welcome is guaranteed in this popular, CAMRA award-winning 17th-century coaching inn. A selection of up to 10 real ales is served, including Isle of Skye beers on rotation, with at least one from the wood. Good value meals are available all day in the cosy bars which are warmed by real log fires in winter. The lounge and garden afford fine views over the Caledonian Canal sea lock and the Beauly Firth. Families are always welcome here.

Snowgoose

Stoneyfield, IV2 7PA (on A96, 1½ miles from city centre)
11-11; 12.30-10.30 Sun
☎ (01463) 701921
Draught Bass; Caledonian Deuchars IPA [H]
One of Mitchells & Butlers' Vintage Inns, this traditional eating house also supports a popular bar trade. Though set right next door to a Holiday Inn and Travel Lodge, most customers are from the local area. It has just one large L-shaped room but alcoves and log fires give it a cosy feel. The building is a converted and extended 1788 coach house retaining some of the old features and has carpeted and flagged flooring. The wide variety of food offered is reasonably priced and served all day.

Kinlochleven

Tailrace Inn

Riverside Road, PH40 4QH (on B863)
11-11.30 (12.30am Thu-Sat); 12-11.30 Sun
(01855) 831777
website: www.tailraceinn.co.uk
Beer range varies H
Surrounded by the Mamore mountains, it lies midway between Ben Nevis and Glencoe, on the West Highland Way. Two handpumps sell Atlas beers and the brewery is a short walk away. This modern inn serves food daily until 8pm in winter and 9pm in summer and stages entertainment in summer on Thursday and Friday. A bunkhouse just up the road is an ideal base for outdoor enthusiasts with the new Ice Factor indoor climbing centre across the road.
P

Kirkwall

Bothy Bar (Albert Hotel)

Mounthoolie Lane, KW15 1HW
(100 yds from harbour along Junction Rd)
11-11 (1am Thu-Sat); 12-1am Sun
(01856) 876000
website: www.alberthotel.co.uk
Highland Scapa Special; Orkney Red MacGregor, Dark Island; guest beers H
With its flagstone floor, fire and photos showing scenes of old Orkney crofting days, this is a good place to meet for a chat, a pint and a bite to eat. Situated in the middle of town, it is handy for shops, buses and ferries to the outer isles. Popular after work, it forms part of the night scene at weekends.

West End Hotel

14 Main Street, KW15 1BU
11-11 (midnight Sat); 12.30-midnight Sun
(01856) 872368
website: www.orkneyisles.co.uk/westendhotel
Orkney Red MacGregor H
The bar is on the first floor of what was originally a hospital from 1845 until 1927. During the winter the open fire creates a cosy atmosphere and in summer the garden is the place to be. There is an adjoining restaurant. All the amenities of Kirkwall are within easy walking distance along the narrow streets, with the cathedral and Earl's Palace being of note.
Q

Nairn

Invernairne Guest House

Thurlow Road, IV12 4EZ
11-11 (11.30 Fri & Sat); 11-11 Sun; (closed Oct-March)
(01667) 452039 website: www.invernairne.com
Beer range varies H
Family-owned business with reasonably-priced accommodation, tucked away in secluded gardens overlooking the Moray Firth. The baronial-style lounge bar has cosy nooks, oak panelling and a roaring log fire. The real ale is usually supplied by the Isle of Skye brewery. A garden path leads to the beach and a promenade. This is an ideal base for the 'whisky trail', and it is close to Nairn's two championship golf courses. Jazz and folk music evenings are staged occasionally. P

Nethy Bridge

Heatherbrae Hotel

Dell Road, PH25 3DG (off B970, on outskirts of village)
5-11 (1am Fri); 12-1am Sat; 12-11 Sun
(01479) 821345
website: www.strathmorehotels.com/neth_site/index.htm
Cairngorm Stag, Trade Winds H
Busy, welcoming pub forming part of a small hotel that supports many local activities. It is also popular with visiting birdwatchers, walkers, anglers, golfers and skiers. All meals are served in the dining room adjoining the bar. A bunkhouse and a variety of other accommodation is available nearby. Dogs are welcome. P

Newtonmore

Glen Hotel

Main Street, PH20 1DD (S end of village)
11 (12.30 Sun)-midnight
(01540) 673203 website: www.theglenhotel.co.uk
Beer range varies H
Set in 'Monarch of the Glen' country, the main bar of this small 10-room hotel has been fully refurbished by the new owners and features a games room alcove. The bar is developing a thriving local trade, and hill-walkers and other visitors are well catered for. Two handpumps serve 'Glenbogle', a house ale from Isle of Skye, while the other two serve a variety of guest beers. The extensive bar menu is enhanced by a table d'hote menu in the restaurant.
P

Onich

Four Seasons

PH33 6SE
6-11.45 (12.45am Thu-Sat); 6-11.45 Sun;
(closed Sun-Thu Nov-Jan)
(01885) 821287 website: www.inchreecentre.co.uk
Atlas Latitude; Isle of Skye Red Cuillin H
Set in the Inchree holiday centre, halfway between Ben Nevis and Glencoe, with plenty of chalets, camping and bunkhouse accommodation available. It offers superb views of Loch Linnhe and the Ardgour Hills. The business has been run by the same family for 30 years. It is not open at lunchtime. The small bar area opens out into a large tabled area where there is regular entertainment. Check in winter for availability of real ale. P

Nether Lochaber Hotel

Nether Lochaber, PH33 6SE
(by E terminal of Corran ferry, 200 yds from A82)
11-2.30, 5-11 (midnight Fri & Sat); 12.30-2.30, 6-11 Sun
(01855) 821235
Draught Bass; guest beers H
All are made to feel welcome in the delightful little bar, tucked away at the rear of the hotel and sitting at the side of the slipway for the Corran ferry, only a few yards from the busy A82. Once a temperance hotel, and not allowed to serve alcohol on the premises, the bar was built on to the rear of the building, only accessible from an outside door. It is convenient for Glencoe and the Ben Nevis mountain range.
Q P

Plockton

Plockton Hotel

Harbour Street, IV52 8TN

⏲ 11-midnight; 12.30-11 Sun

☎ (01599) 544274

website: www.plocktonhotel.co.uk

Caledonian Deuchars IPA; Isle of Skye Red Cuillin [H]

Situated among a row of traditional buildings on the picturesque Plockton waterfront, the hotel boasts spectacular views across Loch Carron to the mountains of Applecross beyond. An award-winning menu of locally landed seafood is on offer in the large but comfortable bar. Close to the Isle of Skye and the mountains of Torridon, the village has much to offer and is a regular haunt for outdoor enthusiasts. Palm trees take advantage of the Gulf Stream warmed coastline.

Q ❀ ◐ ♿ ♣ P

Plockton Inn

Innes Street, IV52 8TW (50 yds from seafront)

⏲ 11-1am (12.30am Sat); 11-11 Sun

☎ (01599) 544222

website: www.plocktoninn.co.uk

Beer range varies [H]

This busy, family-run inn in the centre of Plockton is popular with both locals and visitors. Meals and snacks are served all day in the lounge bar and award-winning restaurant, where locally-caught fish and shellfish take pride of place on the menu. Live traditional music is played in the public bar and all are welcome to join in. Enjoy real log fires in winter or take advantage of the garden in summer.

Q ❀ ◐ ♿ ♣ P

Portree

Bosville Hotel

9-11 Bosville Terrace, IV51 9DG

⏲ 11 (12.30 Sun)-11

☎ (01478) 612846

website: www.bosvillehotel.co.uk

Beer range varies [H]

Town-centre hotel and bar, close to the bus station and picturesque harbour. The tastefully decorated bar with open fire has one handpump serving Isle of Skye beers in rotation. Relax and unwind in the friendly atmosphere after your day's sightseeing, climbing or walking on the island. Enjoy the excellent bar food or try the delicious fresh food served in the restaurant which was awarded Scottish Restaurant of the Year in 2004. ◐ ♿ P

Rosemarkie

Plough Inn

48 High Street, IV10 8UF (E end of main street)

⏲ 11-11.30 (12.30am Fri); 12.30-11.30 Sun; (closed 2.30-6pm in winter)

☎ (01381) 620164

Beer range varies [H]

Beautiful old country pub in a pretty seaside village. Hard to miss with its distinctive leaning gable, it has a cosy wood-lined bar with an ancient marriage stone lintel (dated 1691) over the fireplace. Owned by an American, the pub now serves up to five beers, mainly Scottish and usually at least one from the Cairngorm Brewery. The food menu specialises in seafood. Gardens lead to a sandy beach and a path takes you to the Fairy Glen, a local beauty spot.

❀ ◐ ♣ P

Scourie

Scourie Hotel

IV27 4SX (on A894 Between Laxford Bridge and Kylesku)

⏲ 11-2.30, 5-11; 11-2.30, 6.30-10.30 Sun

☎ (01971) 502396 website: www.scourie-hotel.co.uk

Beer range varies [H]

Popular with fishermen and hill-walkers, this converted 1640 coaching inn overlooks Scourie Bay. It lies close to the bird reserve of Handa Island and the peaks of Arkle and Foinavon. The bar has a fishing theme with 1940s fishing nets as decoration. Meals in the hotel restaurant and bar are freshly cooked and feature seafood; the menu changes daily.

Q ❀ ◐ ♣ P

Scousburgh

Spiggie Hotel

ZE2 9JE (signed off A970)

⏲ 12-2, 5-11; 12-midnight Fri & Sat; 12-11 Sun

☎ (01950) 460409

website: www.thespiggiehotel.co.uk

Beer range varies [H]

The original terminus of the Northern Isles Ferries, this small, family-run hotel situated above the Spiggie Trout Loch is convenient for exploring the archaeological sites of Scatness and Jarlshof as well as bird and whale watching from Sumburgh head. The single bar is stone floored and there are usually four new beers each week. Requests may be catered for if enough notice is given. Summer beers usually include at least one beer from the local Valhalla brewery. Children are welcome. Opening hours may be extended in summer.

Q ❀ ◐ ♿ ♣ P

Sligachan

Sligachan Hotel

IV47 8SW (at A850/A863 jct)

⏲ 8am (11 Oct-Apr)-11; 11-11 Sun; (closed Jan)

☎ (01478) 650204

website: www.sligachan.co.uk

Beer range varies [H]

In a spectacular setting next to the Cuillin Hills, this famous family-run hotel is a haven for walkers, climbers and tourists. It has recently opened its own brewery, using water from the Cuillin. It also runs a campsite and bunkhouse. Food is available all day in the large lounge bar where numerous handpumps dispense a variety of beers alongside the hotel's own brews. It is an ideal spot for those touring the Isle of Skye.

❀ ◐ ♣ P

Stornoway

Whaler's Rest

19 Francis Street, HS1 2ND

⏲ 11-1am (11 Mon); 11-11 Sun

☎ (01851) 701265

Hebridean Clansman Ale, Islander Strong Premium Ale; guest beers (occasional) [H]

Traditional local situated one minute from the

town centre of the largest town in the Hebrides, providing an excellent base for touring the spectacular Outer Hebrides. The lounge bar has recently been redesigned and modernised with a raised seating area for diners while, thanks to popular demand from the locals, the public bar remains unchanged. Occasional guest beers are also available in addition to the two regulars.
❀⇄◐◑⊟▲P⚟

Stromness

Ferry Inn

John Street, KW16 3AA (100 yds from ferry terminal)
✪ 9am-midnight (1am Thu-Sat); 9.30am-midnight Sun
☎ (01856) 850280
website: www.ferryinn.com
Highland Scapa Special; Orkney Northern Light, Red MacGregor, seasonal beers; guest beers Ⓗ
A welcoming sight after a rough crossing, this is the first pub you see when alighting from the ferry and often a first port of call. The wrecks of Scapa Flow attract divers from far and wide, many of whom use the Ferry as a base, which creates a lively scene during the season. At all times the pub is popular with the locals.
⇄◐◑▲

Stromness Hotel

15 Victoria Street, KW16 3AA
(100 yds from ferry terminal)
✪ 11-11 (1am Fri & Sat); 12-11 Sun
☎ (01856) 850298 website: www.stromnesshotel.com
Highland Scapa Special; Orkney Red MacGregor, Dark Island, seasonal beers; guest beers Ⓗ
On the first floor of this imposing hotel is the large Hamnavoe Lounge with a small balcony overlooking the harbour. The hotel hosts jazz, blues and a beer festival annually and plays a full part in the local folk festival in May. There is a large Victorian garden at the rear which basks in summer sunshine. Popular historic sites within easy reach include the Ring of Brodger and Maise Howe. ♨❀⇄◐◑▲P

Uig

Uig Hotel

IV51 9YE
(halfway down hill on approach to village) OS397634
✪ 11 (12.30 Sun)-11
☎ (01470) 542205 website: www.uighotel.com
Beer range varies Ⓗ
This attractive and imposing old coaching inn has spectacular views across Uig Bay to the ferry terminal for the Western Isles. The cosy lounge bar dispenses Isle of Skye beers from two handpulls in summer and one in winter. The friendly staff provide excellent service and meals are available in both the bar and adjoining restaurant. The hotel keeps its own highland cattle in a field beside the car park. It is close to the Isle of Skye Brewery.
♨Q♉❀⇄◐◑⊟♿P

Ullapool

Ferry Boat Inn

Shore Street, IV26 2UJ (on the shore)
✪ 11 (12.30 Sun)-11
☎ (01854) 612366
website: www.ferryboat-inn.com
Beer range varies Ⓗ
This lively. family-run 18th-century waterfront inn is a short stroll from the Western Isles ferry terminal. A mix of locals and regularly returning visitors enjoy the friendly atmosphere in this busy bar, which has an old-fashioned feel and is warmed in winter by an open fire. The bar and restaurant afford glorious views across Loch Broom to the mountains of Wester Ross. Local fresh produce is served in the bar all year round and the restaurant is open from spring to late autumn.
♨Q♉⇄◐◑▲

Waternish

Stein Inn ✔

Stein, IV55 8GA
(N of Dunvegan on B886, 4½ miles from Fairy Bridge)
✪ 4 (12 summer)-11 (midnight Fri & summer); 12-12.30 Sun
☎ (01470) 592362
website: www.steininn.co.uk
Beer range varies Ⓗ
This family-run, traditional Highland hostelry, located in a picturesque setting on the shores of Loch Bay, is the oldest inn on the Isle of Skye. An open central fireplace warms the cosy, low, beamed bar, which has fine views over the loch to Rubha Maol. Locally-caught seafood is served from Easter to October in both the bar and restaurant. Facilities for seafarers include council moorings, showers, food supplies (by arrangement) and message relay services.
♨Q❀⇄◐◑▲♣P

Wick

Alexander Bain ✔

Market Place, KW1 4BS
✪ 10-midnight (1am Fri & Sat); 10-11.30 Sun
☎ (01955) 609920
Caledonian Deuchars IPA, 80/-; guest beers Ⓗ
This former telephone exchange is now a popular town-centre Wetherspoon pub with one large bar in the centre and several alcoves providing no-smoking and quiet areas. The large-screen TV is popular with sports fans. Two regular ales are supplemented by one frequently changing guest. Good value food is served and the Thursday evening curry club is a main attraction.
❀◐◑♿⇌⚟

Wormadale

Westings Inn

ZE2 9LJ (On A971, 2 miles past Tingwall airstrip) OS402464
✪ 12-3, 5-11; 12-midnight Fri & Sat; 12-3, 5-11 Sun
☎ (01595) 840242
website: www.originart.com/westings
Beer range varies Ⓗ
Friendly local pub, located centrally in the main island with stunning views over the islands to the west of Shetland. It is a convenient spot for visitors to stay and is close to Tingwall airstrip for those who wish to take a trip to the outer isles. Beers comprise a rotation of Valhalla products, plus guests. The local brewery's beers are also available in bottles and Shetland gin and vodka are stocked.
Q♉❀⇄◐◑⊟♿▲♣P⚟

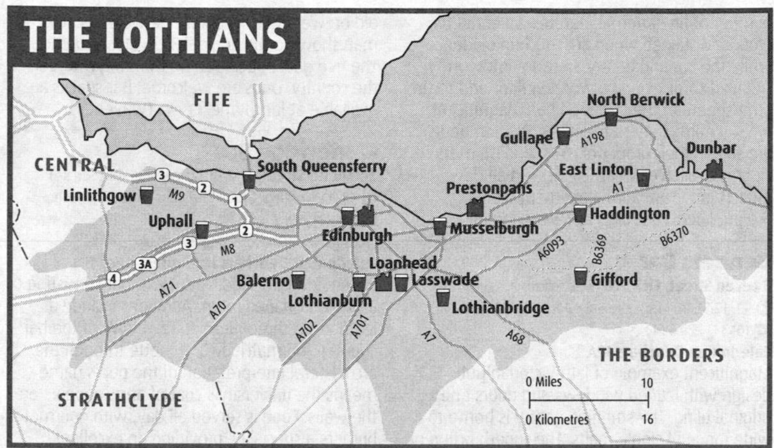

Authority areas covered: City of Edinburgh UA, East Lothian UA, Midlothian UA, West Lothian UA

Balerno

Johnsburn House

64 Johnsburn Road, EH14 7BB
(Off A70 on NW side of village)
12-3 (not Mon), 6-midnight (1am Fri); 12-1am Sat; 12.30-midnight Sun
☎ (0131) 449 3847
Caledonian Deuchars IPA; Marston's Pedigree; guest beers H
Grade B listed baronial mansion, circa 1760, once owned by Professor Adam Fergusson who reputedly brought together the two great men of Scottish literature, Robert Burns and Sir Walter Scott. The low ceilinged, cosy bar has a convivial atmosphere with varied memorabilia and exposed beams. A passageway leads to a dark wood-panelled dining room beyond which are further rooms for diners. It has a good reputation for award-winning meals. Children and dogs are welcome. ⌂Q❀◐◑♣P

East Linton

Bridgend Hotel

3 Bridge End, EH40 3AF
12-2, 7-11 (1am Thu); 12-1am Fri & Sat; 12-midnight Sun
☎ (01620) 860202
Beer range varies H
Village pub with public bar and comfortable lounge. Ownership connections to the Hadrian & Border Brewery mean its beers usually feature on the bar. The stained glass windows and roof top statue hint that the pub was once the Red Lion. The bar has a light wood counter, musical instruments hanging on the wall and a pool table. The lounge/dining room (eve meals Fri and Sat only) has a display of poaching pictures and plaid decor. Children are welcome. Dogs are admitted to the bar.
◐◑♿♣

Drovers Inn ✔

5 Bridge Street, EH40 3AG
11-11 (1am Thu-Sat); 12.30-midnight Sun
☎ (01620) 860298
Adnams Broadside; Caledonian Deuchars IPA; guest beers H
A village bar, bistro and restaurant full of rustic charm. The tiny bar boasts a wooden floor and marble-topped counter. The wood-panelled, claret-coloured walls are adorned with memorabilia, with a stuffed goat's head taking pride of place. There are always three or four serious ales to choose from and it is also a haven for foodies, with a bistro leading off the bar and a first class restaurant upstairs. At weekends meals are served all day. Children and dogs are welcome. ⌂❀◐◑♣

Edinburgh

Abbotsford Bar & Restaurant ☆

3 Rose Street, EH2 2PR
11-11; closed Sun
☎ (0131) 225 5276
Broughton Greenmantle IPA; guest beers H
Traditional Scottish bar with a magnificent island bar and gantry that was rescued from a nearby derelict pub back in 1902. The ornate plasterwork and corniced ceiling are highlighted by subdued lighting. The house beer, Abbotsford Ale, is Atlas Three Sisters rebadged and the guest beers are often from Scottish micros. If you are eating in the restaurant upstairs, the staff are happy to fetch you a pint from downstairs. Children are welcome until 3pm in the bar and at any time in the restaurant.
Q◐◑⇌(Waverley)

Barony Bar

81-83 Broughton Street, EH1 3RJ (E edge of New Town)
11-midnight (1am Fri & Sat); 12.30-11 Sun
☎ (0131) 557 0546
Caledonian Deuchars IPA, 80/-; Courage Directors Bitter, guest beers H
Full of character, this suburban pub has a

INDEPENDENT BREWERIES

Belhaven Dunbar
Caledonian Edinburgh
Fowler's Prestonpans
Innis & Gunn Edinburgh
McCowans Edinburgh
Stewart Loanhead

SCOTLAND

number of fine internal features. Splendid tile work and stained wood are much in evidence while the bar and gantry are also noteworthy. Detailed cornices and a wooden floor add to the atmosphere of the L-shaped bar. Magnificent whisky mirrors adorn the walls. Belgian beers are sold in their proper glasses, and Bulmers cider is available. Meals are served all day until 10pm (7pm Sun). Pavement tables are provided. ⚬⚬⚬⚬≠(Waverley) ⚬

Bennets Bar ☆

8 Leven Street, EH3 9LG (near Tollcross)

⚬ 11-12.30am (1am Thu-Sat); 11.30-11.30 Sun

☎ (0131) 229 5143

Caledonian Deuchars IPA H

Magnificent example of late Victorian pub design with leaded windows and doors and original tiling. The stunning gantry is home to a wide range of single malts. The superb brewery mirrors reflect Edinburgh's fast disappearing brewing heritage, including the once nearby Taylor & McLeods. Sadly, the tall founts adorning the bar are for decoration only. A visit is an absolute must for anyone interested in pub architecture. Children are admited to the green room for meals (no food Sun eve). ⚬⚬

Bert's Bar

29-31 William Street, EH3 7NG (West End)

⚬ 11-11 (midnight Thu-Sat); closed Sun

☎ (0131) 225 5748

Caledonian Deuchars IPA, 80/-; Taylor Landlord, guest beers H

Recreation of a traditional Scots' bar with quality wood and tile work. There is ample standing room and two sitting areas furnished with well-sprung banquettes finished in synthetic leather. A small, cosy snug at the front has a serving hatch. Brewery mirrors feature and complement an excellent gantry. Meals are served most lunchtimes and evenings, at other times try a pie.

⚬≠(Haymarket) ♣

Blue Blazer

2 Spittal Street, EH3 9DX (W of centre)

⚬ 11-1am; 12.30-1am Sun

☎ (0131) 229 5030

Caledonian Deuchars IPA A**, guest beers** A/H

Local CAMRA Edinburgh Pub of the Year in 2004, nestling in the shadow of Edinburgh Castle. The interior window opposite the bar reflects the pub's previous life as a Bernard's Brewery house. Attracting a wide range of customers, the atmosphere is cosmopolitan. The six guest beers are often sourced from Scottish micros. A wide range of exotic rums is available. Dogs with well-behaved owners are welcome.

Bow Bar

80 West Bow, EH1 2HH (Old Town, off Grassmarket)

⚬ 12-11.30; 12.30-11 Sun

☎ (0131) 226 7667

Belhaven 80/-; Caledonian Deuchars IPA; Taylor Landlord; guest beers A

Classic Scottish ale house for which the 2002 Champion Beer of Britain, Deuchars IPA, was originally brewed as the house ale. This one-roomed bar, in the centre of the historic Old Town, is dedicated to perpendicular drinking and traditional Scottish air pressure dispense. Rare old brewery mirrors adorn the walls, as does a map showing the original 33 Scottish counties. The five guest beers can be from anywhere in the country. Dogs are welcome. Bar snacks are available at lunchtime. Q ≠ (Waverley)

Cambridge Bar

20 Young Street, EH2 4JB (near Charlotte Square)

⚬ 11-11 (midnight Thu; 1am Fri & Sat); 12-11 Sun

☎ (0131) 226 2120

website: www.thecambridgebar.co.uk

Caledonian Deuchars IPA; guest beer H

Recently refurbished New Town bar consisting of a single L-shaped room. Additions include a leatherette three-piece suite in front of the bar counter and matching banquette through the arch. Literal interpretation of the pub's name means the university's coat of arms appears on the walls. Food is served all day, with gourmet burgers a speciality, providing an excellent alternative to the town's fast-food establishments. Expect a longer preparation time! ⚬⚬

Cask & Barrel

115 Broughton Street, EH1 3RZ (E edge of New Town)

⚬ 11-12.30am (1am Thu-Sat); 12.30-12.30am Sun

☎ (0131) 556 3132

Atlas Latitude; Caledonian Deuchars IPA, 80/-; Draught Bass; Hadrian & Border Cowie; guest beers H

Spacious and extremely busy ale house drawing a mainly local clientele of all ages, ranging from business people to football fans. The interior features an imposing horseshoe bar, bare floorboards, a splendid cornice and a collection of brewery mirrors. Old barrels act as tables for those who wish to stand up, or cannot find a seat. The guest beers, often from smaller Scottish breweries, come in a range of strengths. Sparklers can be removed on request. Pavement tables allow for alfresco drinking.

⚬⚬⚬≠ (Waverley)

Cloisters Bar

26 Brougham Street, EH3 9JH

(½ mile S of city centre, near Tollcross)

⚬ 12-midnight (12.30am Fri & Sat); 12.30-midnight Sun

☎ (0131) 221 9997

Caledonian Deuchars IPA; Greene King IPA; Taylor Landlord; guest beers H

Busy ale house converted from a former parsonage. A selection of old Scottish brewery mirrors adorns the walls and the large range of malt whiskies does justice to the impressive gantry, which was built with wood from a disused church. Good value lunches are served every day, augmented by traditional or vegetarian breakfasts and a roast on Sunday. The five guest beers are from all over the country. Dogs are welcome. Q ⚬

Cumberland Bar

1-3 Cumberland Street, EH3 6RT (New Town)

⚬ 11-1am; 12.30-1am Sun

☎ (0131) 558 3134

website: www.cumberlandbar.co.uk

Caledonian Deuchars IPA, 80/-; Taylor Landlord; guest beers H

Elegant but functional New Town pub with half wood panelling, exquisite, ornate brewery mirrors on the walls and framed, decorative and

illustrative posters. The wood finish is complemented by dark green leather seating. There are two drinking areas linked by a wide corridor where people stand when it is busy. Children are welcome in the rear room during the day. Dogs are also welcome. A meeting room is available for hire.
⛰Q❀◗♣⚟

Guildford Arms ✔

1 West Register Street, EH2 2AA
(off E end of Princes Street)
✪ 11-11 (midnight Fri & Sat); 12.30-11 Sun
☎ (0131) 556 4312
Caledonian Deuchars IPA, 80/- Ⓟ; Harviestoun Bitter & Twisted; Orkney Dark Island; guest beers Ⓗ
Busy, well-run city centre pub notable for its ornate plasterwork. The high ceiling, cornices and friezes are spectacular, as are the window arches and screens. An unusual gallery above the main bar, which serves as a restaurant, is also noteworthy. There are areas for standing and others with comfortable seating. The extensive range of regularly changing guest beers is usually dominated by beers from Scottish micro-breweries.
◗▶⇌(Waverley) ♣

Halfway House

24 Fleshmarket Close, EH1 1BX
(up steps opp. station's Market St entrance)
✪ 11-11.30 (1am Fri & Sat); 12.30-11.30 Sun
☎ (0131) 225 7101
Harviestoun Bitter & Twisted; guest beers Ⓗ
Cosy little bar full of character hidden away halfway down an old town close, with pavement tables. Old railway memorabilia and current timetables adorn the interior of the bar, which can get crowded. Usually there are three interesting guest beers from smaller Scottish breweries. Card-carrying CAMRA members get a discount on their first pint. Opening hours may extend to 1am at busy times of the year. Dogs and children are welcome at regional CAMRA Pub of the Year 2005. ❀◗▶⇌ (Waverley) ♣

Kay's Bar ✔

39 Jamaica Street, EH3 6HF
✪ 11-midnight (1am Fri & Sat); 12.30-11 Sun
☎ (0131) 225 1858
Belhaven 80/-; Caledonian Deuchars IPA; Theakston Best Bitter; guest beers Ⓗ
Small, cosy and convivial pub, the haunt of lawyers in the early evening. There is an impressive range of beers for the size of the bar. One wall is decorated with whisky barrels, and a good whisky selection is stocked behind the bar. An even smaller back room holds a well-stocked library. Traditional Scottish meals are available at lunchtime. The building was once used as a wine merchant's and the remains of the pipes can still be seen around the light rose. Dogs are welcome. ⛰Q◗♣

Leslie's Bar ☆ ✔

45 Ratcliffe Terrace, EH9 1SU
(Newington, 1½ miles S of city centre)
✪ 11-11 (11.30 Thu; 12.30am Fri & Sat); 12.30-11.30 Sun
☎ (0131) 667 7205
Caledonian Deuchars IPA, 80/-; Taylor Landlord; guest beers Ⓗ
Victorian pub, listed in CAMRA's National Inventory of pubs of outstanding historic interest. It retains its fine ceiling, cornice, leaded glass work and half wood panelling. The island bar has a spectacular snob screen which divides the pub. Small 'ticket window' hatches allow customers to order drinks. A plaque near the fire gives further details of this busy, vibrant but orderly pub. The three guest beers are usually from smaller breweries. Trad jazz is regularly played on Monday evening.
⛰Q⊞♣

Malt & Hops

45 The Shore, Leith, EH6 6QU
✪ 12-11 (midnight Wed & Thu; 1am Fri & Sat); 12.30-11 Sun
☎ (0131) 555 0083
Caledonian Deuchars IPA; Marston's Pedigree; Tetley Bitter; guest beers Ⓗ
One-room public bar dating from 1749 and in the heart of Leith's riverside restaurant district. Wood panelling gives an intimate feel with numerous mirrors, artefacts and a large oil painting adding interest. The superb collection of pump clips, many from now defunct breweries, indicates the ever-changing range of guest beers served. Addlestones Cloudy cider is stocked. The real fire is welcoming in winter. No meals are served on Saturday or Sunday. Children are welcome until 6pm.
⛰❀◗♣●

Old Dock Bar

3-5 Dock Place, Leith, EH6 6LV
✪ 12-11 (1am Fri & Sat); 12.30-11 Sun
☎ (0131) 555 4474
website: www.spidacom.co.uk/olddockbar/
Atlas Latitude; Taylor Landlord; Young's Bitter; guest beers Ⓗ
A true free house offering a mix of the old and new. The building has been a bar since 1813, and claims to be Leith's oldest. The traditional bar area has an excellent selection of ales and the comfy bistro area offers food and fine wines. The walls are decorated with maritime prints and photographs of old Leith. The bar is ideally situated for visitors to the Scottish Executive building and Ocean terminal shopping centre. Meals are served all day. Children and dogs are welcome.
❀◗▶♿⚟

Oxford Bar

8 Young Street, EH2 4JB
(New Town, off Charlotte Square)
✪ 11-1am; 12.30-midnight Sun
☎ (0131) 539 7119
website: www.oxfordbar.com
Belhaven 80/-; Caledonian Deuchars IPA; guest beer (summer) **Ⓗ**
Small and vibrant New Town drinking shop decorated with Burns memorabilia. It is where the 'Professor' holds court in Ian Rankin's Inspector Rebus novels. The bar has been the haunt of many famous and infamous characters over the years and you never know who you might bump into. Why not visit the website and contribute a story? A real taste of New Town past. Simple bar snacks are available. Dogs are welcome. ♣

Regent

2 Montrose Terrace, EH7 5OL (¾ mile E of centre)
11-1am; 12-1am Sun
☎ (0131) 661 8198
Caledonian Deuchars IPA, 80/-; guest beers Ⓗ
Large, comfortable tenement bar with two rooms, all on one level. One of the rooms is music free. Comfortable seating consists of banquettes, leather sofas and armchairs. A new slant on pub games is a gymnastic pommel horse between the ladies and gents toilets. CAMRA Lesbian & Gay group meet here on the first Monday of each month. Bar snacks are available and dogs are welcome.

Starbank Inn

64 Laverockbank Road, EH5 3BZ
(on foreshore near Newhaven)
11-11 (midnight Thu-Sat); 12.30-11 Sun
☎ (0131) 552 4141
Belhaven Sandy Hunter's Ale, 80/-; Caledonian Deuchars IPA; Taylor Landlord; guest beers Ⓗ
Bright, airy, bare-boarded ale house, with an extended U-shaped layout and superb views across the Firth of Forth to Fife. The walls sport several rare brewery mirrors. The pub is proud that it does not sell any keg ales but you can try a pint of prawns with your beer! Four interesting guest ales are usually available. The restaurant is no-smoking. Children are welcome until 8.30pm. Dogs are also permitted if on a leash. Occasional jazz is played on Sunday. Q◐◑♿♣

Thomson's

182-184 Morrison Street, EH3 8EB (W edge of centre)
12-11.30 (midnight Thu-Sat); 4-11 Sun
☎ (0131) 228 5700
Atlas Latitude; Caledonian Deuchars IPA, 80/-; guest beers Ⓐ
Award-winning refurbishment of a pub modelled on the style of Glasgow's forgotten architect, Alexander 'Greek' Thomson, and dedicated to traditional Scottish air pressure dispense. The walls are liberally decorated with old adverts and rare mirrors from long defunct Scottish breweries. Up to five guest beers are available. Food is limited to pies and is not served on Saturday or Sunday. Dogs are permitted here. Q⇌(Haymarket)

Gifford

Goblin Ha' Hotel

Main Street, EH41 4QH
11-2.30, 4.30-11; 11-midnight Fri & Sat; 11-11 Sun
☎ (01620) 810244 website: www.goblinha.com
Caledonian Deuchars IPA; Hop Back Summer Lightning; Taylor Landlord; guest beer Ⓗ
Long-established inn near the village green. With colourful decor and light stained wood, the smart, contemporary lounge bar and conservatories focus on dining, although there is an area for drinking. Drinkers will probably prefer the smaller and more rustic public bar, with its wood and stone walls. A games room leads off the bar. The garden is a favourite in summer. Children are welcome in the lounge until 8pm or in the conservatory all day.
⛼Q❀⇌◐◑⊞Å♣⁄

Tweeddale Arms Hotel

High Street, EH41 4QU
11-11 (midnight Fri & Sat); 11-11 Sun
☎ (01620) 810240
website: www.tweeddalearmshotel.co.uk
Beer range varies Ⓗ
Attractive hotel overlooking the village green and a 300-year-old avenue of lime trees. The public bar with its banquette seating and fire is favoured by drinkers, while the modern L-shaped lounge bar is popular for bar meals. High teas are served at weekends and there is an elegant restaurant for quality meals. Check the blackboard for the real ale selection as there are pumps in both the lounge and public bar. Children and dogs are welcome.
⛼Q⇌◐◑⊞♣

Gullane

Old Clubhouse

East Links Road, EH31 2AF
(W end of village, off main road)
11-11 (midnight Thu-Sat); 12-11 Sun
☎ (01620) 842008
website: www.oldclubhouse.com
Caledonian Deuchars IPA, Taylor Landlord, guest beer Ⓟ
Spacious, well appointed pub looking out over the golf links to the Lammermuir Hills. Decorated in natural woods, golfing memorabilia, stuffed birds and animals adorn the walls. Caricature-style statuettes including the Marx Brothers and Laurel and Hardy are among the many objects on display. Food features highly, and is served all day. An extensive menu and wine list are offered in both the bar and restaurant. Children are welcome until 8pm. Dogs are admitted.
⛼❀◐◑♿

Haddington

Tyneside Tavern

10 Poldrate, EH41 4DA
(on A6137, ½ mile S of town centre near river)
11-11 (midnight Thu; 12.45am Fri & Sat); 12.30-midnight Sun
☎ (01620) 822221
website: www.tynesidetavern.co.uk
Caledonian Deuchars IPA; Courage Directors; guest beer Ⓗ
Cosy, convivial community pub, close to the River Tyne, attracting a varied local clientele. The bar is long and narrow, with a stone fireplace beside the door. Rustic-style woodwork fronts the bar counter, which boasts a mahogany top and gantry. The quieter lounge bar focuses on food until around 9pm. Children are welcome until 8pm. ⛼❀◐◑⊞♣

Lasswade

Laird & Dog Hotel

5 High Street, EH18 1NA (on A768 near river bridge)
11-11.30 (11.45 Thu; 12.30am Fri & Sat); 12.30-11.30 Sun
☎ (0131) 663 9219
Beer range varies Ⓗ
Comfortable village local catering for all tastes, from music-loving pool players to those who enjoy a quiet drink or meal. The walls are

decorated with horse brasses and pictures reflecting local life. Food is served all day, with an extensive menu, daily specials and cheaper bar snacks to satisfy most tastes. An unusual bottle-shaped well, a real fire surrounded by armchairs, and two real ales, usually from smaller breweries, complete the picture. Children are welcome until 8pm. ⛰❀⇌◑♿♣P

Linlithgow

Four Marys ✔

65-67 High Street, EH49 7ED

☉ 12-11 (12-11.45 Thu-Sat); 12.30-11 Sun

☎ (01506) 842171

Belhaven 80/-, St Andrew's Ale; Caledonian Deuchars IPA; guest beers Ⓗ

Built around 1500 as a dwelling house and named after the four ladies-in-waiting of Mary, Queen of Scots, who was born in nearby Linlithgow Palace. The pub has seen several uses over the years; for a time it was a chemist's shop run by the Waldie family whose most famous member, David, established the anaesthetic properties of chloroform in 1847. It opened as a pub in 1975 and hosts beer festivals in May and October when the handpumps are increased from eight to 18. ◑⇶

Platform 3 ✔

1a High Street, EH49 7AB

☉ 11-midnight Mon-Thu (1am Fri & Sat); 12.30-12 Sun

☎ (01506) 847405

Caledonian Deuchars IPA; guest beer Ⓗ

Small, friendly pub on the railway station approach, originally the public bar of the hotel next door. It was purchased and renovated in 1998 as a pub in its own right and stages occasional live music. Note the interesting memorabilia displayed around the walls and look out for the train running above the bar. The guest ale rotates on one pump. ⇶

Lothianbridge

Sun Inn

EH22 4TR (on A7, near Newtongrange)

☉ 11 (12 Sun)-midnight

☎ (0131) 663 2456

website: www.thesuninndalkeith.com

Caledonian Deuchars IPA; guest beer Ⓗ

Originally built around 1870, and situated in the shadow of the impressive, but disused, 23-span Waverley line viaduct. A friendly welcome is offered to both locals and travellers alike. The comfortable bar caters for drinkers and diners and is tastefully decorated throughout. Local art on the walls and a suspended model railway system provide added interest. There is a no-smoking dining area. Food is served all day Friday to Sunday. Children are welcome.
⛰❀⇌◑▲P

Lothianburn

Steading

118-120 Biggar Road, EH10 7DU (on A702, S of bypass)

☉ 11-midnight; 12.30-11 Sun

☎ (0131) 445 1128

Atlas Three Sisters; Caledonian Deuchars IPA; Orkney Dark Island; Taylor Landlord Ⓗ

The pub was converted from farm cottages into an attractive bar and restaurant with a large conservatory extension and a no-smoking area. Good food is served in the restaurant and a more limited menu is available in the bar. The outside drinking area has excellent views of the Pentland Hills and the pub is ideally placed for a relaxing pint after walking in the hills or visiting the nearby dry ski-slope. Children and dogs are welcome. It may close early if quiet.
⛰❀◑♿P⊬

Musselburgh

Levenhall Arms

10 Ravensheugh Road, EH21 7PP

(on B1348, near racecourse roundabout)

☉ 12-11 (midnight Thu; 1am Fri & Sat); 12.30-midnight Sun

☎ (0131) 665 3220

Atlas Latitude; Caledonian Deuchars IPA Ⓟ

Busy pub, popular with locals and racegoers. This three-roomed hostelry dates from 1830 and was once a stopping point for the Edinburgh to London stagecoach. The lively public bar is half timber panelled and carpeted. A smaller area, with a dartboard, leads off. The quieter lounge area has vinyl banquettes and tables and is used for food, which is served all day until 8pm. Dogs are welcome. Children are also welcome until 8.30pm in the lounge.
Q◑⊟▲⇶ (Wallyford) ♣P

Volunteer Arms (Staggs)

81 North High Street, EH21 6JE (behind Brunton Hall)

☉ 12-11 (11.30 Thu); 11-midnight Fri & Sat; 2-11 Sun

☎ (0131) 665 9654

Caledonian Deuchars IPA, 80/-; guest beer Ⓗ

Three-roomed pub run by the same family since 1858. The main bar is traditional with a lino-tiled floor, dark wood panelling, wood and glass screens, and mirrors from defunct local breweries. A superb gantry is topped with old casks. The snug has a growing history collection on local breweries. A rear lounge opens at the weekend. The single guest beer changes regularly, up to four times on a Saturday. It was voted CAMRA Lothian Pub of the Year 2005.
❀⊟♣

North Berwick

Nether Abbey Hotel

20 Dirleton Avenue, EH39 4BQ

(on A198, ½ mile W of town centre)

☉ 11-11 (midnight Thu; 1am Fri & Sat); 12-11 Sun

☎ (01620) 892802

website: www.netherabbey.co.uk

Caledonian Deuchars IPA; guest beers Ⓟ

Comfortable family-run hotel in a stone built villa. The ground floor is now one room, split into a bar and eating area. It has a light and modern feel with pine and steel decor. The marble-topped bar counter has a row of chrome founts. The middle ones, with horizontally moving levers, dispense the real ales. The pleasant bar area expands outside under a retractable canvas roof on warmer days. Food is served all day in summer and at weekends. Children are welcome until 9pm.
❀⇌◑♿▲⇶♣P

SCOTLAND

Ship

7-9 Quality Street, EH39 4HJ

⏲ 11-11 (midnight Thu; 1am Fri & Sat); 12-11 Sun

☎ (01620) 890676

Caledonian Deuchars IPA; guest beers Ⓗ

Open-plan bar, split into three areas, with pine floorboards, a mahogany counter and a dark-stained wooden gantry. Real ale is dispensed from founts, which look similar to those dispensing the keg beers. Nautically-themed throughout; note the dado tile work and maritime tableaux dotted on shelves around the bar. Popular for food, which is served until at least 4pm at weekends, there is a designated no-smoking area in the daytime only. Children are welcome until 8pm. Dogs are also welcome.

❀ ◖▲≋♣⚡

South Queensferry

Ferry Tap ✔

36 High Street, EH30 9HN

⏲ 11.30-11.30 (midnight Thu; 12.30am Fri & Sat); 12.30-11.30 Sun

☎ (0131) 331 2000

Caledonian Deuchars IPA, 80/-; Orkney Dark Island; guest beer Ⓗ

Ground-floor bar in a 329-year-old building in the historic centre of a town overshadowed by mighty bridges. The comfortable, one-roomed L-shaped bar boasts an unusual barrel-vaulted ceiling. Dark wood gives an intimate feel and numerous artefacts, many from bygone breweries, add interest. A varied selection of meals is served at lunchtime. Evening meals are available on Monday (not winter), Wednesday and Friday. No children are admitted.

◖◗≋(Dalmeny)

Uphall

Oatridge Hotel

2-4 East Main Street, EH52 5DA (at A899/B8046 jct)

⏲ 11-midnight (1am Fri & Sat); 11-midnight Sun

☎ (01506) 856465

Caledonian Deuchars IPA; guest beers Ⓗ

Originally a 19th-century coaching inn, the hotel still provides a warm welcome for the thirsty traveller. A varied selection of real ales is served from a stylish bar with an Art Deco feel. Behind the bar is a large collection of ceramic drink vessels – and look out for the large mirror etched with a scene depicting life of yesteryear. Sport on TV is popular at the weekend and pool is also played.

⌘❀⇄◖⊟P

Bennets Bar, Edinburgh

Strathclyde comprises Argyll and Bute, Ayrshire and Arran, Dunbartonshire, Glasgow, Lanarkshire and Renfrewshire

ARGYLL AND BUTE

Arrochar

Village Inn

Shore Road, G83 7AX

(On A814, ¾ mile S of A83 jct)

11 (12 Sun)-midnight (1am Fri & Sat)

☎ (01301) 702279

Orkney Dark Island; guest beers H

Idyllic inn, built in 1827 as the local manse, offering breathtaking views over Loch Long, the Cobbler and Arrochar Alps. Inside, the bar and restaurant are decorated in traditional Scottish country style with wooden furniture, including many round tables. The clientele is a mixture of friendly locals and day tripping, hill walking or week-ending tourists. Food is served in the bar, garden and restaurant at lunchtime; in the evening only in the restaurant.

Q P

Bridge of Orchy

Bridge of Orchy Hotel ✔

PA36 4AD (on A82 at north end of Glen Orchy) OSNN 298396

11 (12 Sun)-11 (midnight Fri & Sat)

☎ (01838) 400208 website: www.scottish-selection.co.uk

Caledonian Deuchars IPA, 80/-; guest beers H

Large, whitewashed building on the road north to Rannoch Moor and well placed for walking the hills, or canoeing down white water. The bar areas are on the left, walkers congregate around a warming stove and admire pictures of local scenes. There is a more comfortable seating area by the bar itself, leading to a new, large dining room at the rear, surrounded by windows to give excellent views down Glen Orchy.

P

Cairnbaan

Cairnbaan Hotel

PA31 8SJ (on A816 from Lochgilphead, near junction with B841 & Crinan Canal) OSNR 839908

11-11 including Sun

☎ (01546) 603668 website: www.cairnbaan.com

Fyne Piper's Gold, Highlander H

This grey stone hotel was originally a coaching inn built in the latter part of the

INDEPENDENT BREWERIES

Arran Brodick
Clockwork Glasgow
Fyne Cairndow
Houston Houston
Islay Bridgend
Isle of Mull Tobermory
Kelburn Barrhead
Oyster Easdale

18th century during the construction of the Crinan Canal. The wood-panelled lounge is housed in a modern building on the side. There is also a comfortable conservatory that looks out onto Lock No.5 of the canal. Views of the canal locks may also be enjoyed from the restaurant and outside patio. A popular stop for tourists travelling by land or water, the menu includes local seafood.
Q ❀ ⇌ ◑ ◨ ♿ P

Campbeltown

Commercial Inn
Cross Street, PA28 6HU
✪ 11 (12.30 Sun)-1am (2am Fri & Sat)
☎ (01586) 553703
Caledonian Deuchars IPA; guest beers Ⓗ
Lively, family-run pub, in a quiet square in the centre of a town which once boasted no fewer than 36 distilleries. The handpump is located in the busy public bar, where sporting types can enjoy the pool table and dartboard, plus a TV that always shows sports channels but with the sound down. Aside, for the less energetic, there is a more relaxed and peaceful lounge bar, lit by ample natural light from ceiling skylights. ◨

Clachan Seil

Tigh-an-Truish
Isle of Seil, by Oban, PA34 4QZ (on B844 just across the Atlantic via Clachan Bridge) OSNM785197
✪ 11 (12 Sun)-11 summer; 11 (12 Sun)-2.30, 5-11 Winter
☎ (01852) 300242
Beer range varies Ⓗ
Located next to the world famous 'Bridge over the Atlantic'. The name means 'House of the Trousers' and islanders had to change out of the forbidden kilt here, before crossing to the mainland. There is an unusual bar counter and possibly the world's only modern George Younger pub sign. Beers from Fyne and Atlas are usually available in the summer, but in the quiet season, the locals seem to prefer Courage Directors and Flowers. Evening meals are served in summer.
⛬ ♉ ❀ ⇌ ◑ ◨ ⛺ P ⚡

Cove

Knockderry Hotel
204 Shore Road, G84 0NX
(on B833, 1 mile N of Cove) OSNS216834
✪ 11.30-midnight; 12.30-11 Sun
☎ (01436) 842283
website: www.knockderryhotel.co.uk
Atlas Latitude; Fyne Piper's Gold; Houston Peter's Well; guest beers Ⓗ
Built circa 1851, this former Glasgow merchant's house boasts one of the best examples of works by architect William Leiper and designer Daniel Cottier. It is a stunning building with a recurring theme of the four seasons, in both stained glass and wood. Situated on the rural Rosneath Peninsula, it offers superb views over Lock Long towards Blairmore and Strone. It has a safe anchorage with five moorings and a large garden. Local ales are regularly available. An hourly bus service runs from Helensburgh.
⛬ ❀ ⇌ ◑ ● P

Inveraray

George Hotel
Main Street East, PA32 8TT
✪ 11 (12 Sun)-midnight
☎ (01499) 302111
website: www.thegeorgehotel.co.uk
Beer range varies Ⓗ
Long-established hotel built in 1770 in the centre of an historic small town. The present family took over in 1860 and the seventh generation is currently serving its apprenticeship. The recently-added restaurant complements the two bars, the large stone-floored lounge and a smaller, lively public bar (with more restricted opening hours). There is always at least one beer from the local Fyne Brewery.
⛬ ♉ ❀ ⇌ ◑ ◨ ♿ ⛺ P ⚡

Kilceggan

Kilcreggan Hotel
Argyll Road, G84 0JP
✪ 11.30-midnight (1am Fri & Sat)
☎ (01436) 842 243
Fyne Piper's Gold, guest beers Ⓗ
Stone Victorian village mansion, at the southern end of the rural Rosneath Peninsula with stunning view over the Clyde estuary to Arran. Built by a Glasgow stockbroker, it contains fine wood panelling with stained glass windows, ornate bargeboards and balconies, and features a curious gabled and battlemented tower. It is close to the pier with regular passenger-only ferries to Gourock and an hourly bus service to Helensburgh. The paddle-steamer 'Waverley' calls on Fridays in summer.
♉ ❀ ⇌ ◑ ◨ ♿ ⛺ ♣ P ⚡

Kilmartin

Kilmartin Hotel
PA31 8RQ
✪ 5-11 (11-1am summer); 12-1am Fri & Sat; 12-midnight Sun
☎ (01546) 510250
website: www.kilmartin-hotel.com
Caledonian 80/-; guest beers Ⓗ
Attractive, whitewashed hotel built on a small rise overlooking an historic glen, filled with barrows, standing stones and other religious symbols. The hotel has a small, cosy public bar overflowing to a larger games room at the rear, with dining areas leading off. An excellent museum across the road traces the development of habitation in the glen from prehistoric days through to modern times.
❀ ⇌ ◑ P

Loch Eck

Coylet Inn
PA23 8SG (on A815 at S end of Loch Eck) OSNS143885
✪ 11 (12 Sun)-11 (midnight Fri & Sat)
☎ (01369) 840426
website: www.coylet-locheck.co.uk
Caledonian Deuchars IPA; Fyne Highlander; guest beers Ⓗ
Coaching inn dating from 1650, formerly called the Lock Eck Inn. The name coylet means a wooded inlet (or maybe a narrow inlet). It was

reopened in 2002 after refurbishment. There is a cosy little bar on the left as you go in and a much larger dining area to the right. The accommodation is highly recommended and the food is extremely sought after for somewhere miles from the nearest town. P

Oban

Oban Inn

1 Stafford Street, PA34 5NJ (near the pier)
11 (12.30 Sun)-12.45am
(01631) 562484
Atlas Three Sisters H
Late 18th-century coaching inn on the front of a harbour used by ferries to the many islands. The unspoilt public bar retains its old stone floors and dark wood panelling. Maritime artefacts are displayed on the walls and currency notes from many nations cover the wooden beams. The lounge upstairs (closed in Jan) boasts a collection of stained glass panels which reputedly came from an Irish monastery.

Port Bannatyne

Port Royal Hotel

37 Marine Road, PA20 0LW
(2 miles N of Rothesay and ferry terminal) OSNS072672
12-1am (2am Sat); 12.30-1am Sun
(01700) 505073 website: www.russiantavern.co.uk
Beer range varies G
Scottish CAMRA Pub of the Year 2005, this family-run recreation of a Russian tavern must not be missed if you are in the area. Local ales, served on gravity, are supported by a good range of foreign beers, Russian vodkas, real fruit drinks and real cider and perry. The Russian-style food, prepared from local ingredients, is available all day. The windows provide a fine view of the bay and mainland mountains. It is sometimes booked for functions, so phone before you set out on your train or ferry trip.
Q

Port Charlotte

Port Charlotte Hotel

Main Street, PA48 7TU
12-1am (11 Sun)
(01496) 850360 www.portcharlotte.co.uk
Black Sheep Best Bitter, guest beers H
Prominent white-painted seaside hotel in the middle of the village. Originally built as two houses and a shop in 1829, they were knocked together to become a hotel 60 years ago. The two guest beers are regular or seasonal beers from the new Islay Brewery and sit alongside a surprising regular from Yorkshire. Nearby is the Museum of Islay Life where descendants can trace their Islay heritage.
P

Rhu

Ardencaple Hotel

Shore Road G84 8LA (on A814)
11-11 (midnight Fri & Sat); 11-11 Sun
(01436) 820200
Caledonian Deuchars IPA, 80/- H
Attractive, white-painted 250-year-old former coaching inn with fine views over The Gare Loch and River Clyde. The Caple bar caters for traditional pub games and has a large TV projection screen, regularly used for sporting events. Real ale is only dispensed in this bar, but can be supplied to the comfortable lounge near the main entrance. P

Rhu Inn

49 Gareloch Road, G84 8LA (near village church)
11-midnight (1am Fri & Sat); 12.30-11 Sun
(01436) 821048 website: www.therhuinn.co.uk
Caledonian Deuchars IPA; Fyne Piper's Gold H
Coaching inn dating from 1648, formerly known as The Colquhoun Arms, taken from the ruling family. With possibly the smallest bar in Strathclyde, it features wonderful use of mahogany in the gantry, Tiffany-style windows and a flagstone floor. A snug is adjacent. Pictures of old village life and the local football team adorn the walls in this popular community local. Guitars are available for instant gigs. Excellent refurbishment in 1998 produced a modern lounge bar with Fyne ales handpump. Live music is staged at the weekend. A wee gem of a pub!
P

Strachur

Creggans Inn

PA27 8BX (on A815) OSNN087024
11 (12.30 Sun)-11 (midnight Fri & Sat)
(01369) 860279
Beer range varies H
Charming old hotel with a multi-room pub and separate restaurant. The public bar has a tiled floor, curious S-shaped counter and numerous photos of the local shinty team. There are fine views across Loch Fyne but the pub will probably always be associated with former owner Fitzroy Maclean, the famous WWII hero. Two guest beers are available, often from local micros.
Q P

Tayvallich

Tayvallich Inn

PA31 8PL (on B8025)
11-1 (midnight Sun) summer; 12.30-2.30, 5.30-11 (1am Fri & Sat) winter
(01546) 870282
Beer range varies H
This low, whitewashed building is one of the first you encounter on entering the small fishing village on Loch Sween down a quiet road from the Crinan Canal. It was converted from a bus garage in 1976 and after a gap is now back in the hands of the original family. The cosy, modern public bar squeezes in a pool table in winter, but there are tables throughout in summer serving high quality meals featuring seafood caught in the loch. Guest beers tend to come from Fyne Ales. Q P

AYRSHIRE AND ARRAN

Ayr

Cariston Hotel

11 Miller Road, KA7 2AX
11 (12 Sun)-midnight
(01292) 262474 website: www.caristonhotel.com
Beer range varies H

SCOTLAND

Upmarket hotel close to Ayr's main shopping area. The real ale is usually from Caledonian or one of the local micros. High quality meals are served in the comfortable lounge or the adjoining restaurant, for which booking is advisable at weekends. The hotel is an ideal base for the local golf courses (golfing breaks are offered) and for the Burns Heritage Park. ❀⇌◐◑♿⇌P

Chestnuts Hotel

52 Racecourse Road, KA7 2UZ (on A719, 1 mile S of centre)
⊛ 11 (12 Sun)-midnight
☎ (01292) 264393
Beer range varies [H]
The wood-panelled lounge of this family-run hotel features a large collection of water jugs and golfing memorabilia, reflecting its proximity to local courses. Three changing guest ales are offered with at least one from a local micro. High quality meals are available in the bar or adjoining restaurant. The garden includes an excellent children's play area.
♕❀⇌◐◑♿P

Geordie's Byre

103 Main Street, KA8 8BU
⊛ 11-11 (midnight Thu-Sat); 12.30-11 Sun
☎ (01292) 264925
Caledonian Deuchars IPA; guest beers [A]
Traditional, town-centre pub whose rather ordinary exterior hides a wealth of memorablia, particularly in the lounge (open Thu-Sat eves). Up to four guest ales come from a wide range of breweries, with both regionals and micros well represented. The pub also boasts a selection of over 100 malt whiskies and 28 rums – ask for the menu. Local CAMRA Pub of the Year on numerous occasions, it was Scottish Pub of the Year 2003. ⊟⇌ (Newton-on-Ayr)

Old Racecourse Hotel

2 Victoria Park, KA7 2TR (on A719 1 mile S of centre)
⊛ 11 (12 Sun)-midnight
☎ (01292) 262873
website: www.oldracecoursehotel.co.uk
Beer range varies [H]
This family-run hotel's name refers to the nearby former horse racing course, now playing fields. The comfortable lounge features an unusual pot still-shaped fire as a centrepiece. Up to four guest ales are offered with regional brewers and local micros usually well represented. The hotel provides an ideal base for visiting the Burns Heritage Park and the many local golf courses.
♕❀⇌◐◑♿P

Blackwaterfoot

Blackwaterfoot Lodge

KA27 8EU
⊛ 6.30-11; 12-2, 6.30-11 Sat & Sun (open Easter to end Oct only)
☎ (01770) 860202
website: www.blackwaterfoot-lodge.co.uk
Arran Ale; guest beers [H]
The Mariners pub is a small, cosy bar in what used to be a temperance hotel. Home-cooked food using local produce is available in the bar, the conservatory dining room or the garden. Local amenities include a golf course and the hotel swimming pool, open to the public. The village benefits from stunning views across to Campbeltown Loch, Kintyre and, on clear days, Northern Ireland. Closed during the winter, but it may open for special occasions. The guest ale is from Arran Brewery.
Q❀⇌◐◑⛺♣P

Brodick

Ormidale Hotel

Knowe Road, KA27 8BY (off A841 at W end of village)
⊛ 12-2.30 (summer only), 4.30-midnight; 12-midnight Sat & Sun
☎ (01770) 302293 website: www.ormidale-hotel.co.uk
Arran Ale, Blonde; guest beers [A]
This fine sandstone building, overlooking the sports field, has a small, friendly bar plus a large attached conservatory, which is a real suntrap. The original tall founts on the boat-shaped bar serve beers, including guests, from the nearby Arran brewery, although the prices do not reflect the proximity. There are discos and folk music in the conservatory at weekends, and quizzes Tuesday and Thursday evenings. Highly recommended home-cooked bar meals are served daily. Accommodation is available in summer. ♕❀⇌◐◑⊟♣P

Catacol

Catacol Bay Hotel

KA27 8HN
⊛ 11-midnight (1am Thu-Sat); 11-midnight Sun
☎ (01770) 830231 website: www.catacol.co.uk
Arran Blonde; guest beers [H]
This picturesque white building nestles among the hills opposite the shore, affording grand views across the Kilbrannan Sound towards Kintyre. It is adjacent to the Twelve Apostles, a listed terrace of former estate houses. It was a manse originally and has been run by the present owner for 27 years. Ideally situated for walking and climbing, there is a richness of wildlife to discover; glimpses of red deer and golden eagles are not unusual.
♕♉❀⇌◐◑⊟♣P

Craigie

Craigie Inn

KA1 5LY (off B730)
⊛ 12-2, 5-midnight; 11-midnight Sat & Sun
☎ (01563) 860286
website: www.craigieinn.com
Caledonian Deuchars IPA [H]
Located in a small village south of Kilmarnock, this attractive country pub has a single handpump. Meals featuring local fish and game are served in the bar and restaurant, and there is also an outside seating area which can be popular on a summer evening. Occasional Scottish nights are hosted. ♕❀◐◑P

Dundonald

Old Castle

29 Main Street, KA2 9HH
⊛ 11 (12.30 Sun)-midnight
☎ (01563) 851112
Beer range varies [H]

Popular, family-friendly local with great views of the historic medieval castle, once home to Scottish kings. Two guest beers are served in summer, one in winter, normally from Houston Brewery. The premises have been refurbished recently and there is a separate restaurant. The bar features an original stone well with natural spring water, and the building is reputed to be haunted by several ghosts. The pub used to be called the Castleview and the castle is well worth a visit too. ❀◐◗ ⊟♿P

Failford

Failford Inn ✔

KA5 5TF (on B743 Mauchline-Ayr road)

✪ 12-3, 5-midnight; 12-12.30am Fri & Sat; 12.30-midnight Sun

☎ (01292) 540117

website: www.failfordinn.co.uk

Beer range varies Ⓗ

Country pub set on the bank of the River Ayr, featuring a low-ceilinged bar with an old tiled range. Both restaurant and garden overlook the river. Meals are prepared by the chef/owner with an emphasis on freshly-cooked food. There is limited parking across the road, but the 43 Ayr-Cumnock bus stops outside the pub. This inn is a good starting point for River Ayr gorge walks in a nature reserve. ⚠Q❀◐◗⧋

Fairlie

Mudhook ✔

46 Bay Street, KA29 0AL (on A78, 3 miles S of Largs)

✪ 11-midnight (1am Fri & Sat); 12-midnight Sun

☎ (01475) 568432

Draught Bass, Greene King Abbot Ⓗ

This friendly village pub enjoys a lovely position overlooking the Isles of Cumbrae and Arran. It has two bars plus a restaurant with a conservatory. Bar meals are available and the restaurant offers an extensive menu. There is also a garden and a large car park.

❀◐◗⊟♿⇌♣P

Gateside

Gateside Inn

39 Main Road, KA15 2LE (on B777, 1 mile E of Beith)

✪ 11-11 (midnight Fri & Sat); 12.30-11 Sun

☎ (01505) 503362 website: www.thegatesideinn.co.uk

Caledonian Deuchars IPA, guest beers Ⓗ

Comfortable, village pub, with some regulars travelling from a distance to enjoy the friendly ambience. The guest beer is usually from a Scottish brewery, although some from further afield are now appearing. Beers sold are usually less than 4.5% ABV. The pub also stocks a wide range of bottled beers and malts and offers an interesting wine list. Food is served all day in the bar or a no-smoking dining area. There is a patio for summer drinking. The No. 337 bus passes every two hours. ❀◐◗P

Girvan

Royal Hotel

36 Montgomery Street, KA26 9HE

✪ 11-12.30am; 12.30-midnight Sun

☎ (01465) 714203 website: www.royalhotelgirvan.com

Beer range varies Ⓗ

Small hotel in Clyde coast town which still clings to the fishing and tourist trades. The traditional public bar attracts locals as well as fishing, cycling and walking groups. World-renowned Turnberry golf course is five miles away and the hotel is a good stopping off place for travellers to and from the Irish ferries. The regular beer is from Houston Brewery, with a second guest in summer only.

❀⇔◐◗⊟♿⧋⇌♣P

Kildonan

Breadalbane Hotel

KA27 8SE

✪ 11-midnight (1am Thu-Sat); 11-midnight Sun; (closed 2nd and 3rd weeks of Jan)

☎ (01770) 820284

website: www.breadalbanehotel.co.uk

Beer range varies Ⓗ

This white-painted hotel sits just behind the shore in a scattered village at the south end of the island. It enjoys extensive views, especially from the front sun lounge and new outside terrace, to Pladda and its lighthouse, Ailsa Craig, South Ayrshire and Loch Ryan. The main bar has a large stone fireplace, a corner bar and a pool table. The two guest ales are often from Scottish breweries; food is served all day. En-suite rooms and self-catering flats are available. The hotel is close to beaches renowned for seal spotting. Children are welcome until 8pm.

Q❀⇔◐◗⧋♣P⚟

Kilmarnock

Brass & Granite

53 Grange Street, KA1 2DD

✪ 11-midnight (1am Thu-Sat); 12.30-midnight Sun

☎ (01563) 523431

Caledonian Deuchars IPA; guest beers Ⓗ

Modern, open-plan, town-centre pub situated in a quiet street behind the post office. It is popular with a varied mix of customers. Belgian fruit beers are available on draught and Belgian bottled beers are a speciality. Take too long to order your beer and you may be asked to pay 20p at the parking meter (automatically refunded). The large-screen TV is used mostly for sporting events.

◐◗⧋♣⚟

Hunting Lodge

14-16 Glencairn Square, KA1 4AH

✪ 11 (12.30 Sun)-midnight(1am Thu-Sat)

☎ (01563) 522920

Beer range varies Ⓗ

This is a large bar with various rooms leading off it, one of which is no-smoking. There are up to five beers in the range from all over Britain. The bar is dominated by a large TV. One room has a pool table with competitions each Thursday. There are also two function rooms, hosting many different club events including Kilmarnock Folk Club. ◐◗⚟

Wheatsheaf ✔

Unit 5, Portland Gate, KA1 1JG

✪ 11 (12.30 Sun)-midnight

☎ (01563) 572483

Caledonian Deuchars IPA; guest beers Ⓗ

SCOTLAND

Large, modern open-plan pub with a no-smoking dining and drinking area. To the front there is a large, covered patio overlooking the impressive railway viaduct. Food is served all day, including early breakfast available before licensing hours. The door to the original Wheatsheaf at the rear of the pub allows it to claim to be the only licensed premises 'in the toun' to be visited by Rabbie Burns. The pub tends to be busy on Thursday to Saturday evenings due to its proximity to nightclubs.
Q ❀ ◖◗ ♿ ≢ ⚡

Largs

Charlie Smith's

14 Gallowgate Street, KA30 8LX (on seafront)
✪ 11-1am; 12.30-midnight Sun
☎ (01475) 672250
Beer range varies Ⓗ
Friendly, town-centre pub that prides itself on its excellent bar meals. It is situated at the corner of the seafront and Main Street, opposite the pier and ferry terminal – a good place for catching (or missing) the ferry to Cumbrae and, in summer, the Waverley paddle steamer. Live music is staged on Saturday and a quiz every Wednesday. Largs is home to two fine golf courses and the Vikingar Centre.
◖◗ ♿ ≢ ♣

Lochranza

Lochranza Hotel

KA27 8HL
✪ 11 (4 Nov-Feb)-midnight (1am Fri & Sat); 11-midnight Sun
☎ (01770) 830223
website: www.lochranza.co.uk
Arran Blonde; guest beers Ⓗ
This traditional hotel is located in a tranquil village affording spectacular views to Lochranza Castle and across the sea loch. The bar comprises two inter-connecting rooms and stocks over 100 malt whiskies. The front of the hotel has a large grassed area with tables, an ideal place for watching the local wildlife. There are good walks in the area, and the hotel is handy for the summer car ferry to Kintyre and onward to Islay, Gigha and other islands. Children are welcome.
♨ ♞ ❀ ⛟ ◖◗ ⛺ ♣ P ⚡

Saltcoats

Salt Cot ✔

7 Hamilton Street, KA21 5DS
✪ 11-midnight (1am Thu-Sat); 12.30-midnight Sun
☎ (01294) 465924
Beer range varies Ⓗ
A good conversion of a former cinema by Wetherspoon, decorated with photographs of the cinema in its heyday and of old Saltcoats. Children are allowed in one area and there is a family menu. Unusually for Wetherspoon, there are no regular beers, but Theakston Old Peculier and Greene King Old Speckled Hen are frequently on tap. The pub's name comes from the original cottages at the salt pans.
Q ◖◗ ♿ ≢ ⚡

Stair

Stair Inn

KA5 5HW (on B730, 7 miles E of Ayr, 4 miles W of Mauchline)
✪ 12 (12.30 Sun)-11 (1am Sat)
☎ (01292) 591650
website: www.stairinn.co.uk
Beer range varies Ⓗ
Family-run inn nestling at the foot of a glen on the bank of the River Ayr. The bar has an open log fire and a separate snug. Built around 1700, it serves a widespread area and is close to the historic Stair Bridge (single track on a tight corner – take care crossing). The area has many connections with Robert Burns and is well located for walks, golf and fishing. Houston beers are regulars, and the food is exceptionally good.
♨ Q ❀ ⛟ ◖◗ ♿ P

Troon

Ardneil Hotel

51 St Meddans Street, KA10 6NU (next to station)
✪ 11-midnight; 12-midnight (11 winter) Sun
(01292) 311611
Beer range varies Ⓗ
Well situated for Troon station and the local municipal golf courses; the bar is popular with locals and visitors alike, with regular golf parties staying at the hotel. The bar hosts up to four changing ales and Houston Brewery supplies a specially-blended house ale. There is a weekly quiz on Wednesday evening. The pool table and dartboard are situated in a lowered seating area within the bar.
❀ ⛟ ◖◗ ≢ ♣ P

Dan McKay's Ale House

69 Portland Street, KA10 6QU
✪ 11-12.30am; 12.30-midnight Sun
☎ (01292) 311079
Beer range varies Ⓗ
Comfortable one-roomed, town-centre bar with three real ales available in winter and four the rest of the year, supplemented by a range of Belgian and other foreign bottled beers. The pub hosts occasional live music on Sunday. There is a display of beer mats above and behind the bar demonstrating the numerous real ales sold over the years. It was highly commended in the local branch CAMRA Pub of the Year awards in 2004.
❀ ◖◗ ≢

Lonsdale Bar

15 Portland Street, KA10 6AA
✪ 11-midnight (12.30am Thu-Sat); 12.30-midnight Sun
☎ (01292) 311355
Beer range varies Ⓗ
Traditional town-centre pub with attractive wooden gantries and slabbed flooring in both the lounge and public bars. Two handpumps dispense beer in the public bar, which has TVs in two corners showing sport. There is usually one beer available midweek, with two on at weekends and over the summer. The real ales are from Scottish breweries, and the bar has a fine selection of malt whiskies. The lounge hosts regular karaoke and music nights.
⊟ ≢ ♣

DUNBARTONSHIRE

Balloch

Tullie Inn

Balloch Road, G83 8SW
11- midnight (1am Fri); 12.30-midnight Sun
(01389) 752052
website: www.tullieinnballoch.com
Caledonian Deuchars IPA; guest beers H
Staff offer local and tourist clientele a friendly welcome at this lively, modern pub in a busy village at the southern tip of Loch Lomond. There is entertainment most nights, including quizzes and live music by well-known local bands. It is also a venue for the Loch Lomond folk festival in July. Sited by Balloch rail station, with half-hourly trains from Glasgow, the Tullie is an ideal place to end a day out at Balloch Country Park and Loch Lomond. ❀⇄◐◑⊟⅄⇌P⚟

Bearsden

Burnbrae ✔

281 Milngavie Road, G61 3TA (on A81)
11-11.30 (12.30am Fri); 12.30-11 Sun
(0141) 942 5951
Courage Directors; Theakston Best Bitter; guest beers H
Situated on the edge of a former Roman frontier town on the road to the Trossachs, this modern faux traditional pub has a reputation for good food. An extensive specials menu of traditional and fusion dishes is displayed on blackboards throughout. Within a few minutes walk are two lodge-style hotels, three footpath networks, Milngavie town centre and a range of sporting facilities. ♨Q◐◑♿P⚟

Milton of Campsie

Kincaid House Hotel

Birston Road, G66 8BZ
(signed on B757, ½ mile S of village) OSNS650759
12-midnight (1am Fri); 12- midnight Sun
(0141) 776 2226
website: www.kincaidhouse.com
Caledonian Deuchars IPA; guest beers H
After the long, wooded driveway, this white, stone, castle-like hotel makes an impressive sight. However, the bar is in a low, modern building to the rear where the dark furniture, beams with horse brasses and fireplace provide a cosy, mock olde-worlde atmosphere. In summer the door is opened to the safe, hedge-enclosed garden. A varied menu makes the bar popular with families and a good stop for tourists and walkers of the nearby Campsie or Kilsyth Hills. ♨❀⇄◐◑♿♣P

Twechar

Barrhill Tavern

Main Street, G65 9QE (S of Forth & Clyde Canal)
11-11.30 (1am Fri); 12.30-11.30 Sun
(01236) 821496
Taylor Best Bitter; Thwaites Bitter; guest beers H
Originally The Quarry, after nearby workings, then Lock, Stock & Barrel and 'The Billy' to locals. The name may change, but this traditional pub has always been an oasis for those climbing Bar Hill to the Roman fort, or travelling the Antonine Way and Forth & Clyde Canal. The basic bar has a pool table, darts, Maclay Brewery mirror and a large-screen TV for sports. There is a separate lounge. Regular beer festivals are held with up to four ales stocked. ♨Q⊟♣P

GLASGOW

Glasgow

1901 Bar & Bistro

1534 Pollokshaws Road, G43 1RF (Haggs Road jct)
11.45-11 (midnight Fri & Sat); 12:30-11 Sun
(0141) 632 0161
Caledonian Deuchars IPA; guest beers H
Situated on the ground floor of a red sandstone tenement opened in 1901 as The Old Swan Inn, the bar is now French owned which is reflected in the food served in the attached bistro and also available in the bar. There is ample standing room and plenty of seating in the wood-panelled and floored bar, where a jazz band plays on Sunday afternoon. A good range of German Weiss beer is stocked and Addlestones cider. Pollok Country Park, which houses Glasgow's famous Burrell Collection, is nearby. ◐◑♿⇌ (Pollockshaws/W Shawlands) 🍎

Aragon ✔

151 Byres Road, G12 8TT
11-11 (midnight Fri & Sat); 12.30-11 Sun
(0141) 339 3252
Caledonian Deuchars IPA; McEwan's 80/-; guest beers H
Small, popular, L-shaped pub frequented by locals and others seeking a welcome relief from the trendy West End bustle. Once a T&J Bernards pub, the effects can still be seen in the use of mock rustic seating and multiple blackboards. There is a busy quiz on Tuesday evening and a flourishing fantasy football league. Up to four guest beers are on offer from small and medium sized brewers. ◐◑⊖ (Hillhead)

Babbity Bowster

16-18 Blackfriars Street, Merchant City, G1 1PE
(between High St and Walls St/Albion St)
11 (12.30 Sun)-midnight
(0141) 552 5055 website: www.babbity.com
Caledonian Deuchars IPA; guest beers P
Traditional meets classy in this airy, bright pub, located in the heart of Glasgow's Merchant City. With three permanent pumps and real cider, there is plenty for the enthusiast. The large, converted front room in this period house, with its high ceilings and fire at one end, has a spacious feel, with enormous windows to the front. Guest beers change regularly. A small garden at the side is well used in summer. Excellent food is served until 10pm daily. ♨Q❀⇄◐◑⇌ (High St/Argyle St/Queen St) ⊖ (Buchanan St) ♣🍎P

Blackfriars

36 Bell Street, Merchant City, G1 1LG
(corner of Albion St)
12 (12.30 Sun)-midnight
(0141) 552 5924 website: www.blackfriarsonline.co.uk
Courage Directors; Theakston Best Bitter; H
guest beers H/P

SCOTLAND

Cosmopolitan pub with a cosy, cafe bar atmosphere and flowers and candles on the tables. An open, raised area affords a good view of the local Merchant City streets. Large wall mirrors give the interior seating areas a more spacious feel. International draught and bottled beers are available and local micro-breweries feature among the three guest beers. Entertainment is provided by jazz on Saturday and Sunday, a Tango bar on Wednesday and a comedy club downstairs on Saturday evening.
(High St/Argyll St/Queen St)
(Buchanan St)

Bon Accord

153 North Street, G3 7DA
(between Mitchell Library and Argyle St)
11-midnight; 12.30-11 Sun
(0141) 248 4427
website: www.thebonaccord.freeserve.co.uk
Caledonian Deuchars IPA; Marston's Pedigree; guest beers H
Busy pub attracting locals and real ale fans from near and far. The long bar features 10 handpumps – over 600 different beers from independent brewers are served every year. There is also a large range of malt whiskies on offer as well as good choices of other spirits and wines. Live bands are featured on Saturday night with an open stage on Tuesday and a quiz on Wednesday evening.
(Charing Cross/Anderston)

Clockwork Beer Co.

1153-1155 Cathcart Road, Mount Florida, G42 9BH
(Kings Park Rd jct, by rail bridge)
11-11 (11.30 Tue; midnight Thu-Sat); 12.30-11 Sun
(0141) 649 0184
Caledonian Deuchars IPA, 80/-; guest beers P
Popular bar on Glasgow's South-side, only a goal kick from Hampden Park, Scotland's national football stadium. It has an open-plan interior with a spiral staircase leading to an upper seated area which is often used for live music. There is a five-barrel brewery opposite the bar. A wide range of drinks encompasses German and Belgian bottled beers, draught Belgian and Czech beers and Clockwork Beer Co's own beers, which include fruit beers. Westons cider is sold.
(Mount Florida) P

Crystal Palace

36 Jamaica Street, G1 4QD (100yds S of Argyle St jct)
11 (12.30 Sun)-midnight
(0141) 221 2624
Caledonian Deuchars IPA; Courage Directors; guest beers H
Ex-furniture store with huge shop windows, where friendly staff welcome you to the spacious bars on both floors. The ground floor has two raised areas and a quiet rear room. Upstairs, imaginative use of garden-style furniture and a stone slab floor give an 'outdoor' feel. The original cage lift allows access upstairs for the disabled. A varied clientele includes city workers, pre-clubbers and theatregoers. Unusually for a Wetherspoon's, a large-screen TV sometimes shows sports. The bar opens at 10am for ('dry') breakfast.
Q (Central) (St Enoch)

Horseshoe Bar ☆

17-21, Drury Street, G2 5AE (in street linking Renfield St/W Nile St)
11 (12.30 Sun)-midnight
(0141) 229 5711
Caledonian Deuchars IPA, 80/-; H **guest beers** H/P
Busy, city-centre establishment housing Britain's longest continuous bar, which stands horseshoe-shaped in the ground-floor drinking hall. The pub contains many decorative features of historical interest including clocks and mirrors, as well as new additions such as the photographs and gold discs of some of its more famous clientele. In addition to the wide and varying beer range, the Horseshoe is well known for its traditional food and keenly-priced menu.
(Central) (St Enoch/Buchanan St.)

Pot Still

154, Hope Street, G2 2TH
11-11 (midnight Thu-Sat); 6-11 Sun
(0141) 333 0980
website: www.thepotstill.co.uk
Caledonian Deuchars IPA, 80/-; guest beers H
Bustling and largely unspoilt city-centre pub which has retained original features including cornice work and stained glass panels at the entrance. A small, raised lounge at the rear provides an ideal spot to view the impressive gantry, stacked to the ceiling with malt whiskies, for which the pub has established a worldwide reputation. At the last count there were 540 whiskies in stock and occasional tastings are organised.
(Central/Queen St) (Buchanan St)

Samuel Dow's

69 Nithsdale Road, G41 2PZ
11-11 (midnight Fri & Sat); 12.30-11 Sun
(0141) 423 0107
Caledonian Deuchars IPA; guest beers H
Popular bar in Strathbungo, Scotland's first railway suburb. Built in the 1860s, Sammy's is renowned for its reasonable prices. Bench seating borders the bar and the gantry features two Ind Coope Brewery mirrors advertising Skol lager and Double Diamond. The guest beer usually rotates between Charles Wells Bombardier, Marston's Pedigree and Adnams Broadside. Meals are served at lunchtime and snacks are available until 10pm. The function room at the rear regularly features live bands including Scottish folk.

State Bar

148 Holland Street, G2 4NG (near King's Theatre)
11 (12.30 Sun)-midnight
(0141) 332 2159
Caledonian Deuchars IPA, 80/-; Houston Killellan; Marston's Pedigree; guest beers H
Although dating from 1902, few original features are still visible. The imposing island bar was installed in the 1990s. Note the display of old photographs and theatrical memorabilia. Situated close to the King's Theatre and Centre for Contemporary Arts, this welcoming city-centre pub attracts local office workers and students, who enjoy reasonably-priced lunches. Three guest ales are sourced from throughout

the UK. The basement bar hosts a comedy club on Saturday and blues bands on Tuesday. ◑ ⇌ (Charing Cross)

Station Bar

55 Port Dundas Road, G4 0HF (corner with McPhater St)
11-midnight; 12.30-11.45 Sun
☎ (0141) 332 3117
Caledonian Deuchars IPA; guest beers Ⓗ
Though just a few strides from the busy city centre, the Station provides a retreat for locals, real ale lovers and thirsty concertgoers from the nearby Theatre Royal. The name comes from the long-gone Buchanan Street station and the railways are remembered in photographs and pictures on the walls and in stained glass panels over the bar, along with panels depicting the present day trades nearby. The two guest beers are often supplied by small local brewers. ◑ ⇌ (Queen St) ⊖ (Cowcaddens/Buchanan St)

Tennents ✔

191 Byres Road, G12 8TN (corner with Highburgh Road)
11-11 (midnight Fri & Sat); 12.30-11 Sun
☎ (0141) 341 1024
Broughton Old Jock; Cairngorm Wildcat; Caledonian Deuchars IPA; Harviestoun Brooker's Bitter & Twisted; Taylor Landlord; guest beers Ⓗ
Large West End tenement corner pub, popular with workers, locals and Glasgow university staff and students. From the U-shaped bar you can admire the high ceiling, with its original cornice work around the beams and pillars. Seating is arranged mainly along one wall, which is adorned with old paintings. Eight regular beers and four guests are usually available. Good value meals are served until 9pm. The eight TV screens sometimes show two top sports events simultaneously. ◑ ♿ ⊖ (Hillhead)

Three Judges

141 Dumbarton Road, G11 6PR (jct with Byres Rd)
11-11 (midnight Fri; 11.45 Sat); 12.30-11 Sun
☎ (0141) 337 3055
Beer range varies Ⓗ
With nine handpumps dispensing an ever-changing list of new ales from Britain's micros alongside established favourites, this corner tenement pub is a magnet for real ale fans. It is also a popular local, where new faces are made welcome. The previous owners were keen boxing fans (hence the name). It has now been tastefully refurbished by current owners, Maclay, who allow the experienced licensee a free hand in the choice of ales, occasional real ciders and foreign beers available. The only food sold is locally-made pork pies, but hungry customers are welcome to bring food from nearby takeaways. ⇌ (Partick) ⊖ (Kelvinhall) 🍎

LANARKSHIRE

Castlecary

Castlecary House Hotel

Castlecary Road, G68 0HD
11-11 (11.30 Thu-Sat); 12.30-midnight Sun
☎ (01324) 840233
website: www.castlecaryhotel.com
Beer range varies Ⓗ
This hotel in the village of Castlecary stands on the site of one of the major forts on the Antonine Wall close to the restored Forth & Clyde Canal and the Castlecary Viaduct. There are three distinct drinking areas in the main building with a selection of real ales in the Castle Lounge. Food is excellent and high teas are highly recommended. A beer festival is held in November. ⌂ Q ☺ ❀ ⊟ ◑ ⊞ ♿ P ⊬

Coatbridge

St Andrews Bar

27 Sunnyside Road, ML5 3DG (near Central station)
11-midnight (1am Fri & Sat); 12.30-midnight Sun
☎ (01236) 423773
Beer range varies Ⓗ
Once a run-down, nondescript pub, this bar has recently been transformed, partly by reversing some uninspired 20th-century renovation and partly by introducing high quality beer and spirits. A wide range of malt whiskies is sold in addition to fine real ale. There is a small and lively public bar, where the low-level background music is often drowned by conversation, and an even smaller, quieter lounge. The pub is handy for the renowned Summerlee Industrial Museum.
⇌ (Central/Sunnyside)

Hamilton

George

18 Campbell Street, ML3 6AS
11-11.45 (1am Fri); 12.30-11.45 Sun
☎ (01698) 424225
Beer range varies Ⓗ
Family-run local, now well established as among the staunchest supporters of real ale in the region. The interior is decorated by a collection of awards from CAMRA. It can become busy and noisy on Friday nights, but is less hectic at other times. The small room to the rear is quieter and no-smoking on request. Two beer festivals are held annually. An outside drinking area has been added (local weather permitting!).
❀ ◑ ♿ ⇌ (Central) P ⊬

Lanark

Horse & Jockey

56 High Street, ML11 7ES
11-11 (1am Fri; 11.45 Sat); 12.30-midnight Sun
☎ (01555) 664 825
Beer range varies Ⓗ
A pub has been standing on the site of this small, town-centre local for the past 300 years. The public bar is at the front of the building and the lounge/dining area is through a low, narrow passageway to the rear. The racecourse, which gave the pub its name, has now joined William Wallace and Robert Owen in the mists of Lanark's rich history. Lunches are served Monday-Saturday, evening meals Saturday.
◑ ⚠ ⇌

Motherwell

Brandon Works ✔

45-60 Merry Street, ML1 1JJ
11-midnight (1am Fri & Sat); 12.30-midnight Sun
☎ (01698) 210280
Caledonian Deuchars IPA; guest beers Ⓗ

Possibly the most welcomed Wetherspoon pub in Britain. When it opened towards the end of 2001, it brought a serious commitment to real ale to the country's most notorious beer desert. Usually about four beers are on sale in this single long bar with separate seating areas on several levels. It is named after an iron works which once stood in the area now occupied by the car park behind the pub. Q ♿ ⇌ ⍻

Strathaven

Waterside Bar & Restaurant

31 Waterside Street, ML10 6AE

11-midnight (1.30am Thu-Sat); 11-midnight Sun

☎ (01357) 522588

Greene King Old Speckled Hen; guest beers H

Situated, predictably, by the burn running through the centre of town, this family-run operation comprises a comfortable lounge bar with an adjoining restaurant. The building dates from the 19th century but there are more recent extensions and the interior has been thoroughly modernised. It offers a varied menu including snacks, bar meals and three-course dinners, although customers only here for the beer are equally welcome. ❀ ⍻

Weavers

1 Green Street, ML10 6LT

12-11.45 Mon; 4-12.45am Tue-Thu; 12-12.45 Fri & Sat; 7-12.45 Sun

Beer range varies H

Family-run pub in the centre of a small, historic town with links to the 19th-century weaving industry. An old exterior houses a modern, single public room decorated with pictures of Hollywood stars. The pub has no television but the music can be loud on Friday and Saturday nights. Beers are mainly sourced from the Scottish micro-breweries, but Timothy Taylor, Marston's and Greene King are no strangers. There is also a selection of Belgian and other imported bottled beers.

Wishaw

Wishaw Malt ✔

62-66 Kirk Road, ML2 7BL

10-midnight; 10-1am Fri & Sat; 12-midnight Sun

☎ (01698) 358806

Beer range varies H

The pub takes its name from the distillery, founded in 1800, which produced Clydesdale single malt whisky (to critical acclaim, but without financial success – partly as a result of the disapproval of a strong, local temperance movement). The pub consists of one large hall, divided into many sections of different sizes. The decoration and menu is consistent with Wetherspoon's usual standards and there are usually three guest ales to support the two principal beers. Q ❀ ♿ ⇌ ⍻

RENFREWSHIRE

Barrhead

Cross Stobs Inn

4 Grahamston Road, G78 1NS (on B7712)

11-11 (midnight Thu; 1am Fri; 11.45 Sat); 12.30-11 Sun

☎ (0141) 881 1581

Kelburn Misty Law H

This inviting 18th-century coaching inn is on the edge of town on the road to Paisley. The public bar has a real coal fire and retains much of its original charm with antique furniture and service bells. The lounge has been recently attractively refurbished. There is an outside drinking area at the front of the pub and an enclosed garden with a table tennis table at the rear. A self-contained pool room and a function suite are also available. Children are allowed at lunchtime. A second beer from Kelburn is occasionally available.

❀ ⇌

Busby

Busby Hotel

Field Road, G76 8RX (off Busby Rd)

11-midnight (1am Thu-Sat); 12.30-midnight Sun

☎ (0141) 644 2661

website: www.busbyhotel.co.uk

Beer range varies H

Friendly and helpful staff provide a warm welcome at this hotel situated on a tree-lined avenue overlooking the River Cart. The public bar, with its genuinely aged wood panelling, low level lighting and leather couches, offers a relaxed eating and drinking experience. A long bar dominates one side of the room with chalkboards promoting the ale on offer. Roomy but still cosy pub with excellent service.

❀ ⇌ P

White Cart ✔

61 East Kilbride Road, G76 8HX (on A726 100yds SE of station)

11 (12.30 Sun)-11

☎ (0141) 644 2711

Beer range varies H

Rebuilt in 1996, this pub from the Chef & Brewer chain has a spacious interior divided mainly by large oak beams into several cosy nooks. The decor is from an earlier period incorporating a grandfather clock, dressing tables and a wealth of bric-a-brac. Part of the stone walls to the rear of the pub are thought to be from the stables which formerly stood on the site. One beer is from the local Kelburn Brewery and the other from the Scottish Courage range.

Q ❀ ♿ ⇌ P ⍻

Gourock

Spinnaker Hotel

121 Albert Road, PA19 1BU

11-11:30 (midnight Thu;1am Fri & Sat); 12.30-midnight Sun

☎ (01475) 633107 website: www.spinnakerhotel.co.uk

Beer range varies H

Warm and friendly hotel popular with both locals and day trippers. Situated on the sea front, it offers great views across the Firth of Clyde from its bay windows and patio tables. The menu includes vegetarian and children's choices, and one dining room is no-smoking. Handy for Gourock to Dunoon ferries, it is also a good spot to see the submarines heading up and down the Clyde. There are usually two real ales available, served from the cosy bar.

Q ❀

Greenock

James Watt ✔

80-92 Cathcart Road, PA15 1DD

⏲ 11-11 (midnight Thu; 1am Fri & Sat); 12.30-12.30am Sun

☎ (01475) 722640

Courage Directors; guest beers Ⓗ

Easy to find Wetherspoon near the railway station, providing a much-needed real ale outlet in the town. Named after the town's famous inventor, it offers the usual JDW trimmings. There is good access for wheelchair users and a small garden and heated patio area for outside drinking. Guest ales from local breweries and regular English beers are served by the attentive, friendly staff. Families are accommodated in a separate area of the bar and the all-day food is popular with locals.
Q ❀ ◐◑ ♿ ⇌ (Central) P ⚞

Houston

Fox & Hounds

South Street, PA6 7EN

⏲ 11-midnight (12.30am Fri & Sat); 12.30-midnight Sun

☎ (01505) 612448

website: www.houston-brewing.co.uk/fox_hound.htm

Houston Killellan, Barochan, Peter's Well, Warlock Stout, seasonal beers; guest beers Ⓗ

This 17th-century coaching inn is also the home of the Houston Brewing Co, which can be seen through a viewing window in the recently-decorated lounge. Both spacious, comfortable lounge and public bars are decorated with hunting memorabilia. The Huntsman bar and restaurant upstairs has full a la carte and bar menus served all day at weekends with Sunday traditional roast. The toilets are wheelchair accessible. ♨ Q ☕ ◐◑ ⊟ ♿ P ⚞

Houston Inn

North Street, PA6 7HF

⏲ 11-11.45 (12.45am Fri & Sat); 12.30-midnight Sun

☎ (01505) 614315

Beer range varies Ⓗ

An 18th-century inn in the centre of the village which appeals to a wide clientele, young and old. The L-shaped bar has original stonework exposed on the main wall and sells one ale from the local Houston brewery. The modern decor in the new restaurant contrasts well with the traditional feel of the remainder of the pub. The pub is co-owned by Walter Smith, Scotland's football manager. ❀ ◐◑ P

Inverkip

Inverkip Hotel

Main Street, PA16 0AS (off A78 Greenock-Largs road)

⏲ 11-11.30; 12.30-11 Sun

☎ (01475) 521478 website: www.inverkip.co.uk

Caledonian Deuchars IPA; guest beers (summer) Ⓗ

Originally an old coaching inn, this two-bar hotel sits by a marina in the small conservation village of Inverkip on the Clyde coast. It is cosy and welcoming, with excellent meals made using locally-sourced food served in both the lounge and restaurant (booking recommended). Some guest ales arrive by boat and are served during the summer months to meet seasonal demand, in addition to the regular ale. Q ⛟ ◐◑ ⊟ ⇌ P

Johnstone

Coanes ✔

26-28 High Street, PA5 8AH

⏲ 11-11:30 (1am Fri; midnight Sat); 12.30-11.30 Sun

☎ (01505) 322925

Boddingtons Bitter; Caledonian Deuchars IPA; guest beers Ⓗ

Friendly, town-centre pub with a welcoming atmosphere. The cosy bar has fake beams and bric-a-brac. The raised part of the lounge doubles as a restaurant (Wed-Sat eve). Lunchtime meals are available Monday to Thursday and meals are served all day on Friday and Saturday (no food Sun). Seven ales are normally on tap including one from the local Kelburn Brewery.
Q ◐◑ ♿ ⇌ ⚞

Kilbarchan

Glenleven Inn

25 New Street, PA10 2LN (off A737)

⏲ 11-11 (midnight Wed & Thu; 1am Fri Sat); 12.30-11 Sun

☎ (01505) 702481

Beer range varies Ⓗ

Traditional village pub with a warm and friendly atmosphere run by helpful staff. It retains its original dark wood beams and the walls are decorated with pictures of the area. A wide range of snacks is served. Houston and Kelburn breweries supply one beer each. Local bands provide the entertainment at weekends and there are regular quiz nights and a range of traditional pub games. Children are welcome during the daytime and for meals. Take Arriva bus No. 35.
♨ ❀ ◐◑ ♿ ♣ P

Trust Inn

8 Low Barholm, PA10 2ET

⏲ 11.45-11.30; 11-1am Fri & Sat; 11.45-11.30 Sun

☎ (01505) 702401

Caledonian Deuchars IPA; guest beers Ⓗ

This pleasant and lively village pub is decorated in traditional olde-worlde oak-beam style. It aims to please all its many and varied customers and has friendly, helpful staff. Both a standard and large-screen TV, folded away when not in use, provide entertainment. Added attractions are the local folk band sessions and quiz nights. Children are welcome.
◐◑ ♿ ⇌ (Milliken Park)

Lochwinnoch

Brown Bull

33 Main Street, PA12 4AH

⏲ 12-11 (midnight Fri; 11.45 Sat); 12.30-11 Sun

☎ (01505) 843250

website: www.lochwinnoch.info/Business/brownbull/

Beer range varies Ⓗ

Welcoming staff and a warm atmosphere await you at this friendly village pub situated in an old coach house. Retaining all of its traditional charm, the original stone walls and oak beams remain and the old stone cellar is still in use. It is popular with both visitors and locals due to its place in village history, and a good place to seek out local information. Four real ales are sourced from all over the UK.
♨ ◐◑ ♿ ⇌

Newton Mearns

Osprey

Stewarton Road, G77 6NP (off M77)
11-11; 12.30-11 Sun
(0141) 616 5071
Boddingtons Bitter; Caledonian Deuchars IPA; guest beers H
An olde-worlde feel prevails at this Mitchells & Butlers Vintage Inn owing to the judicious use of wood, brick and stone. The oak bar strewn with hops adds to the effect, along with an oak-beamed ceiling and stone flagged floor. Quiet areas within the bar allow privacy while the main pub is oriented to family dining. Three handpumps serve the two regular beers and one guest.

Paisley

Bull Inn ☆

7 New Street, PA1 1XU
11-midnight (1am Fri & Sat); 12.30-midnight Sun
(0141) 849 0472
Caledonian Deuchars IPA; Kelburn Red Smiddy; guest beers H
Dating back to 1901, this pub, designed by local architect WD McLennan, is rich in art detail. The pillared back fitment acts as a support for elongated whisky barrels, now disused. There are three sitting rooms at the rear and a fourth is now the ladies. The bar room would possibly benefit from less old curiosity shop clutter added by a previous owner, but do not let that put you off. Children are welcome until 4.30pm.
(Gilmour St)

Gabriels

33-35 Gauze Street, PA1 1EX
11-midnight (1am Fri & Sat); 12.30-midnight Sun
(0141) 887 8204
Beer range varies H
A variety of real ales from local micro-breweries Kelburn and Houston is regularly available in this pub now owned by Belhaven. It features an oval shaped bar with two handpumps. The TV and music are kept to reasonable noise levels and there is a quiz night held on Tuesday evening. It is situated near Paisley Abbey and Gilmour Street station. (Gilmour St)

Hogshead

45 High Street, PA1 2AH
11-midnight (1am Fri & Sat); 12.30-midnight Sun
(0141) 840 4150
Caledonian Deuchars IPA, 80/-; guest beers H
This lively, city-centre pub is open plan with a raised area for the pool table. Meals are served all day until 8pm and the efficient bar staff provide table service when the pub is quiet. Customers range from ale enthusiasts to students. Four TVs provide football coverage and music videos – it can often be loud at weekends.
(Gilmour St)

Wee Howff

53 High Street, PA1 2AN
11-11 (midnight Fri & Sat); closed Sun
(0141) 889 2095
Caledonian Deuchars IPA; guest beers H
Small town pub near the university, frequented by students and other discerning cask ale drinkers, showcasing guest beers from Houston and Kelburn breweries. The present publican has been in the last 18 editions of this Guide and was the first Burton Master Cellarman in Scotland.
(Gilmour St)

Uplawmoor

Uplawmoor Hotel

66 Neilston Road, G78 4AF
12-2:30, 5 – 11; 12-midnight Sun
(01505) 850565
website: www.uplawmoor.co.uk
Beer range varies H
Hotel bar and restaurant situated in the highest village in Renfrewshire. Originally opened in 1750 to serve travellers between Glasgow and the Clyde coast, it still performs that function admirably well but also serves as a meeting place for locals – a true village pub. Try the public bar for its homely atmosphere, the cocktail bar for something more upmarket and the restaurant for its excellent menu. Frequent diners can join the 'Smugglers Club' for a range of discounts. Beer choice is usually from local breweries.
P

Auldhouse Arms, Auldhouse

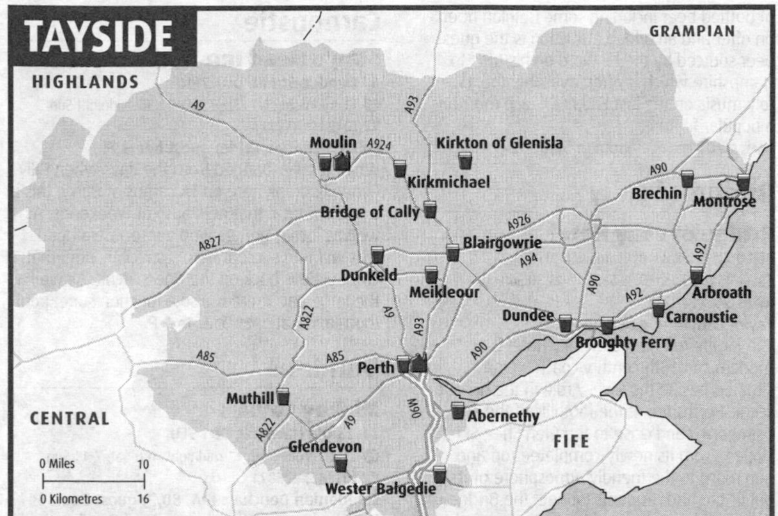

Authority areas covered: Angus UA, City of Dundee UA, Perth & Kinross UA

Abernethy

Crees Inn
Main Street, PH2 9LA
11-2.30, 5-11; 11-11 Sat; 12.30-11 Sun
☎ (01738) 850714
website: www.creesinn.co.uk
Beer range varies H
Formerly a farmhouse, this listed building has been sympathetically renovated to provide a homely pub with a long L-shaped lounge and small restaurant area. It lies in the shadow of a 12th-century round tower in the quiet village of Abernethy, once the Pictish capital of Scotland. Up to five ales are available with a good mix of different Scottish and English beers on offer. A varied menu is provided at lunchtime and evening in the busy restaurant using fresh local produce. Q ❀ ⇌ ◐ ◑ ♿ P ⁄

Arbroath

Lochlands Bar
14 Lochlands Street, DD11 3AB
11-midnight (1am Fri & Sat); 12.30-midnight Sun
☎ (01241) 873286
Beer range varies H
Classic, street-corner pub with strong sporting associations. The large public bar has a selection of sporting memorabilia adorning the walls plus two large TVs which dominate when football and rugby matches are shown. For those customers not interested in sport there is a smaller, quieter lounge area. Two ales are always on tap. ⊟ ⇌ ♣

Blairgowrie

Ericht Alehouse
13 Wellmeadow, PH10 6ND
11-11 (11.45 Fri & Sat); 12.30-11 Sun; best to phone as times may vary
☎ (01250) 872469
Beer range varies H
Established in 1802, this traditional, town-centre pub has a friendly atmosphere. The pub has two seating areas split by a well-stocked bar. The lounge area boasts a log-burning open fire. Up to six beers are on tap from Scottish and English Breweries – Inveralmond beers are a local favourite. Addlestones cider is available along with Liefmans Frambozen on tap and a good selection of bottled beers. Although no food is available customers are welcome to take their own. Weekends can be busy with occasional live music. ♨ Q ♿ ● ⊓

Rosemount Golf Hotel
Golf Course Road, PH10 6LJ
11-11 (11.45 Fri & Sat); 12-11 Sun
☎ (01250) 872604
website: www.rosemountgolf.co.uk
Beer range varies H
Situated in a quiet area to the south end of Blairgowrie, this traditional hotel has a comfortable lounge area with open fire and a restaurant. Popular with locals and visitors alike, it is an ideal base for walking and golf. Note the unusual array of golf tags over the bar. A large selection of malt whiskies is available and up to two ales. Inveralmond and Houston beers are regularly on tap.
♨ Q ❀ ⇌ ◐ ◑ ♿ P ⊓

Brechin

Caledonian Hotel
42 Esk Street, DD9 6D2 (opp. Caledonian Station)
11.30-2.30 (not Mon), 5-midnight (11.30 Mon; 1am Fri); 11.30-1am Sat; 12.30-midnight Sun
☎ (01365) 624345
Inveralmond Thrappledouser, guest beers H
Extensively refurbished hotel that takes its name from the privately run railway whose terminus is opposite. The Hotel has a large bar and a separate function room/restaurant (eve meals Wed-Sun). There is a large range

INDEPENDENT BREWERIES

Inveralmond Perth
Moulin Moulin

SCOTLAND

of bottled beer including some Belgian beer on offer and an added attraction is the guest beer sourced by the landlord on his trips to Hampshire which is often available too. Live folk music on the last Friday of each month is a popular feature.
(Caledonian Station)

Bridge of Cally

Bridge of Cally Hotel

PH10 7JJ (6 miles N of Blairgowrie on A93)
11-11 (12.30am Fri & Sat); 12-11.30 Sun
(01250) 886232
Taylor Landlord; guest beers H

The family-run Bridge of Cally Hotel is a modernised 18th-century coaching inn situated beside the River Ardle in the heart of scenic Perthshire at the foothills of the Cairngorms and close to the Glen Shee Ski slopes. From its newly-completed rod and gun room to the friendly atmosphere of its public bar and residents lounge, the Bridge of Cally Hotel provides an ideal base from which to enjoy local pastimes and attractions. Bar food is available for most of the day and evening, while the restaurant offers local produce including home-grown vegetables. Two ales are available with Houston beers a regular choice.
Q P

Broughty Ferry

Fisherman's Tavern

10-12 Fort Street, DD5 2AD
11-midnight (1am Fri & Sat); 12.30-midnight Sun
(01382) 775941
website: www.fishermans-tavern-hotel.co.uk
Beer range varies H

First opened in the early 19th century as the Buckie Tavern by a fisherman who harvested buckies (whelks), over the years the pub has expanded into a small hotel. The original interior and atmosphere are largely maintained in the public bar, and there are three further rooms, one no-smoking. The pub is a former Scottish and British CAMRA Pub of the Year and has been in this Guide every year since 1975. There is traditional music every Thursday and a quiz on the first Monday of the month. A beer festival is held every year in the secluded garden.
(limited service)

Royal Arch

258 Brook Street, DD5 2DS
11-midnight; 12.30-11 Sun
(01382) 779741
Caledonian Deuchars IPA; guest beers H

Busy, street-corner bar and adjoining lounge in the centre of the main shopping area of this historic suburb of Dundee. Its name comes from a former Masonic establishment that was once opposite. The bar's impressive gantry was recovered from the Craigour Bar, a former Dens Road Dundee pub; its walls are adorned by pen caricatures of a number of regulars as well as photographs of famous footballers. Meals (not served Sun) are popular and are usually served in the lounge.
(limited service)

Carnoustie

Stag's Head Inn

61 Dundee Street, DD7 7PN
11-midnight (1am Fri & Sat); 12.30-midnight Sun
(01241) 858777
Fuller's London Pride; guest beers H

While totally changed from the days when Billy Connolly drank here on TA camps at Barry, this is a popular local that gets busy at weekends. As well as locals, golfers who appreciate a good pint will find succour here, especially now that Carnoustie is back on the Open circuit. As well as the large bar, there is also a function suite, pool room and patio. P

Dundee

Mickey Coyle's

21-23 Old Hawkhill, DD1 5EU
11-3, 5-midnight; 11-midnight Fri & Sat; 7-11 Sun
(01382) 225871
Caledonian Deuchars IPA, 80/-; guest beers H

Popular bar near the University of Dundee, named after a previous owner. Closed for many years, it re-opened as a medical students' club, then became a pub called the Blue Mountain after a local area of tenements, and has now been altered to its present form with a split-level lower bar. Always noted for its cask ales, it now serves two guests in addition to the regular ones. Good food is served (not Sun or Fri-Sat eves) and there is traditional music after 9.15pm on Monday evening.

Phoenix

103 Nethergate, DD1 4DH (W of city centre)
11-midnight; 12.30-midnight Sun
(01382) 200014
Caledonian Deuchars IPA; Orkney Dark Island; Taylor Landlord; guest beers H

A popular howff for town and gown (a former name), only the ceiling and supporting pillars remain of the original building, but the mixture of stained glass, solid furniture, fruit machines, classic bar and gantry, Greek lettering, animal heads and bric-a-brac has created one of the few pubs of real character in the city centre. Look out for the rare mirror of Ballingall's, Dundee's long lost brewery. Good bar food is available including the legendary chilli.

Speedwell (Mennie's) ☆

165-167 Perth Road, DD1 1AS
11-midnight; 12.30-midnight Sun
(01382) 667783
Beer range varies H

The Speedwell is a fine example of an Edwardian pub, featuring in CAMRA's National Inventory of Pub Interiors of Outstanding Historic Interest. Named after William Speed, wine and spirits merchant, it is widely known as Mennie's after the family who ran the bar from the 1920s to the 1990s. The bar has an impressive moulded ceiling, etched glass dividing screens and mahogany gantry throughout. As well as two ales there are several foreign beers on draught and many more bottled beers.
Q

Dunkeld

Taybank

Tay Terrace, PH8 0HY

⏲ 11-11; 11-midnight Fri & Sat; 12-11 Sun

☎ (01350) 727340 website: www.thetaybank.com

Inveralmond Ossian's Ale Ⓗ

The Taybank, otherwise known as Scotland's Musical Meeting Place, is a haven for lovers of traditional Scottish and Irish music. The small public bar is comfortable and full of character with an open fire and equipped with a range of musical instruments (including piano) for those musicians who do not have their own. A small selection of bottled beer is available in addition to the beer on tap. The garden is on the bank of the River Tay looking across toward Birnam Hill. There is also a small music room where live events are held regularly. ⛫Q☎❀⇄◑⇌

Glendevon

Tormaukin Hotel

FK14 7JY

⏲ 11 (12 Sun)-11

☎ (01259) 781252

website www.tormaukin.co.uk

Beer range varies Ⓗ

Originally an 18th-century drover's inn, the Tormaukin (meaning 'hill of the mountain hare' in old Scots) is located in a peaceful rural setting surrounded by the Ochill Hills. With its warm, welcoming atmosphere, it makes an ideal base for a variety of outdoor activities such as walking, fishing and golf. It has two comfortable lounge bars in natural timber and stone along with log fires. An extensive menu includes traditional Scottish fare and international dishes. There is a restaurant with an a la carte menu. Up to three ales are available in the rear lounge; usually two are from Harviestoun.
⛫Q☎❀⇄◑P

Kirkmichael

Strathardle Inn

PH10 7NS (on A924 Bridge of Cally to Pitlochry road)

⏲ 12- 2, 6-11 (11.30 Fri & Sat); best to phone ahead as times may vary

☎ (01250) 881224 website: www.strathardleinn.co.uk

Beer range varies Ⓗ

This old coaching inn dating back to the late 1700s on the route from Balmoral to Pitlochry retains the original barn and stables. It was previously home to Aldchlappie, the smallest commercial brewery in Britain. The inn has an attractive woodland garden and a 700 yard beat of the River Ardle, which offers salmon and trout fishing. The Cataran Trail passes in front of the pub and the new Cairngorms National Park is a few miles north. Two ales are available, with a strong commitment to Scottish micros.
⛫Q☎❀⇄◑♿P⊡

Kirkton of Glenisla

Glenisla Hotel

PH11 8PH (on B591 10 miles N of Alyth)

⏲ 11 (12.30 Sun)-11 (closed afternoons and Mon in winter)

☎ (01575) 582223 website: www.glenisla-hotel.com

Beer range varies Ⓗ

Former coaching inn which has become a base for a variety of outdoor pursuits such as hill walking, skiing, shooting and pony trekking. The oak beamed bar to the back of the hotel is the focal point for locals and visitors alike, where bar lunches and suppers are served at oak and pine tables, and there is a no-smoking lounge and dining room serving traditional Scottish food. There is also an adjoining games room where children are welcome. ⛫Q❀⇄◑⛺♣P⍻

Meikleour

Meikleour Hotel

PH2 6EB

⏲ 11- 3, 6-11 (midnight Fri); 11-midnight Sat; 12-11 Sun

☎ (01250) 883206

website www.meikleourhotel.com

Beer range varies Ⓗ

Pleasantly refurbished country village inn with a stone-flagged bar and comfortable lounge serving two cask ales each. It is a popular venue for walkers and fishermen as well as those wanting a good meal or drink in a relaxing environment. The house beer Lure is brewed for the pub by Inveralmond Brewery. Nearby is the Meikleour Beech Hedge (100ft high and a third of a mile long) which was planted in 1745 and is recognised in the Guinness Book of Records as the tallest hedge in the world.
⛫Q❀⇄◑⊟♿P

Montrose

George Hotel

22 George Street, DD10 8EW

⏲ 11-2, 5-11; 11-11 Sat; 12-11 Sun

☎ (01674) 675050

Beer range varies Ⓗ

Small hotel in town centre with a two-level bistro style lounge/bar and an open gas fire and copper hood. At least one ale is available all year round and up to three in the summer. Meals may be eaten in the bar or in the restaurant. High tea is served Sunday to Thursday and dinner Friday and Saturday.
❀⇄◑⇌P

Moulin

Moulin Inn

11-13 Kirkmichael Road, PH16 5EH

(¾ mile NE of Pitlochry)

⏲ 12-11 (11.45 Fri-Sun)

☎ (01796) 472196

website: www.moulinhotel.co.uk

Moulin Light, Braveheart, Ale of Atholl, Old Remedial Ⓗ

First opened in 1695, 50 years before the '45 Jacobite Rebellion, the Inn is the oldest part of the Moulin Hotel. Furnished in a traditional style with two log fires, the pub has retained its character and charm since being extended into a hotel. The inn is situated within the village square of Moulin, an ancient Scottish crossroads near to Pitlochry – the 'gateway to the Highlands'. A varied menu of home-prepared local fare is available along with beer provided by the small brewery in the old coach house behind the hotel. An ideal base for a walking holiday; up to 16 routed walks pass nearby.
⛫Q☎❀⇄◑⊟♣P

SCOTLAND

Muthill

Muthill Village Hotel

6 Willoughby Street, PH5 2AB

✪ 11-11 (11.45 Fri & Sat); 12-2.30, 5.30-11 Jan-April; 12.30-11 Sun

☎ (01764) 681451

website: www.muthillvillagehotel.com

Orkney Dark Island; guest beers 🄷

Originally an 18th-century coaching inn, this traditional pub lies on the old drovers' road from the Highlands. It is located in the centre of the conservation village of Muthill which has more than 90 listed buildings. The Bothy Bar is full of character with a large open fire and walls adorned with farming implements. The restaurant area bears a hunting theme. Up to four ales are available with Scottish micros prominent, as well as the house beer Tapsman's Yill (Drover's Ale), brewed by Inveralmond. ⌂Q☕❀⇌◑P

Perth

Capital Asset ✔

26 Tay Street, PH1 5TS

✪ 11-11 (11.45 Fri & Sat); 12.30-11 Sun

☎ (01738) 580457

Caledonian Deuchars IPA, 80/-; guest beers 🄷

Large, open-plan pub with modern decoration and a small split-level seating area. Situated overlooking the River Tay, it takes its name from the fact that it was once a bank and Perth was the ancient capital of Scotland. The ceilings are high and much of the original plaster cornicing has been retained. A number of photographs of old Perth adorn the walls. Up to five ales are available on tap. The pub can be especially busy at weekends. Q◑♿⚟

Cherrybank Inn

210 Glasgow Road, PH2 0NA

✪ 11-11 (11.45 Fri & Sat); 12.30-11 Sun

☎ (01738) 444962 website: www.cherrybankinn.co.uk

Inveralmond Independence, Ossian's Ale; guest beers 🄷

Former drovers' inn on the western outskirts of Perth, this busy local has a small public bar and two adjacent rooms. It is thought to be one of the oldest public houses in Perth. For over 200 years it has been a popular venue for passing travellers. Lunches and evening meals are served in the well-appointed lounge. Up to four real ales are available from Inveralmond and other Scottish micros. Accommodation is available in seven en-suite bedrooms. Q⇌◑⊟♿P⚟

Greyfriars

15 South Street, PH2 8PG

✪ 11-11 (11.45 Fri & Sat); 12-11 Sun

☎ (01738) 633036

website: www.greyfriarsbarperth.co.uk.tt

Caledonian Deuchars IPA; Taylor Landlord; guest beers 🄷

One of the smallest lounge bars within Perth city centre, it has a vibrant and friendly atmosphere. As a plaque above the bar says, it is, 'More of a club without membership'. Good value lunches are served in the bar and a small upstairs seated area (no food Sun). Up to four ales are available, one of which is the house beer Friars Tipple, brewed by Inveralmond and a popular choice with regulars. Ideally located with various attractions nearby such as the Victorian theatre, art gallery and museum or for a short walk along the banks of the 'Silvery Tay'. ◑⇶

Wester Balgedie

Balgedie Toll Tavern

Nr Kinross, KY13 9HE

✪ 11-11; 12.30-11 Sun

☎ (01592) 840212

Harviestoun Bitter & Twisted 🄷

Comfortable country tavern with low ceilings, oak beams, horse brasses, wooden settles and works of art by a local painter. It has three seating areas plus a small bar. The building was once a toll house, situated where travellers had to break their journey to pay road tolls before travelling on. The oldest part of the building, dating from circa 1534, is at the southern end. A good selection of meals and bar snacks is available. ⌂Q❀◑⊟♿P

Speedwell (Mennie's). Dundee

Northern Ireland
Channel Islands
Isle of Man

NORTHERN IRELAND

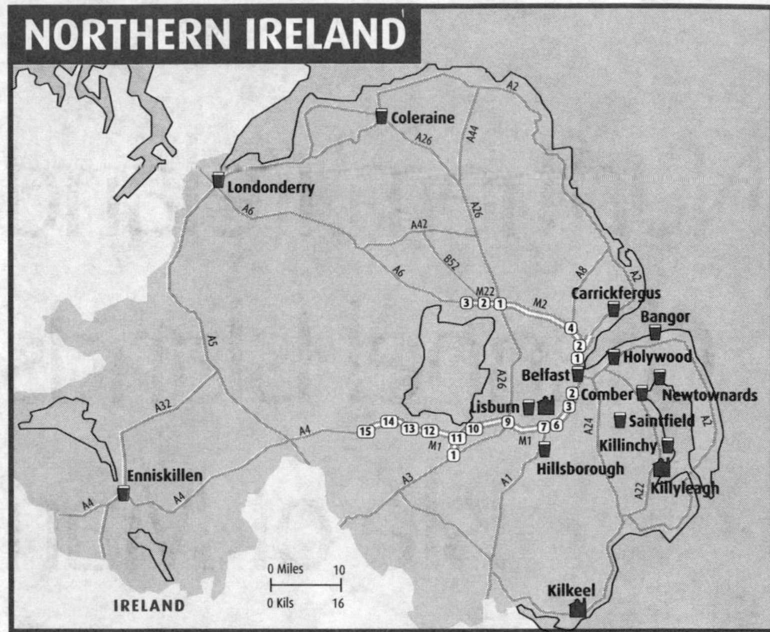

Bangor

Gillespie's Place

12 Ballyholme Esplanade, BT20 5LZ

11.30-11; 12.30-10 Sun

☎ (028) 9147 9584

website: www.gillespie-esplanade.com

Beer range varies H

Previously called The Esplanade (the name of the original hotel of which it remains a part), the bar has been completely refurbished with light wood fittings and an improved air-exchange system. There is always one ale from Whitewater Brewery available, alongside two guest ales. Food is served in the bar and staff will also serve ale in the hotel's restaurant and lounge.

Belfast

Bridgehouse

37-43 Bedford Street, BT2 4HF (opp. BBC)

10-1am; 12.30-midnight Sun

☎ (028) 9050 9740

Beer range varies H

Recently converted from a quiet Wetherspoon's into a far noisier Lloyd's No1. This popular bar can be very busy at weekends. There are TV screens upstairs and downstairs. The music is downstairs but you can hear it upstairs! Food is served from 10am and noon on Sunday.

(Gt Victoria St)

Botanic Inn

23-27 Malone Road, BT9 6RU

11.30-1am; 12-midnight Sun

☎ (028) 9050 9740

website: www.thebotanicinn.com

Whitewater Belfast Ale H

The 'Bot' is a large, busy pub about 500 yards from Queen's University. It is popular among students and sports fans. One real ale is available, kept in good order by the cellarman. The ale is usually served in dimpled pint pots unless you ask for a straight glass. Food is served from 12 to 8pm daily. Wednesday to Saturday are disco nights in the Record Club upstairs.

Crown Liquor Saloon ☆

46 Great Victoria Street, BT2 7BA

(opp. Gt Victoria St station)

11.30-12.30am; 12.30-11.30 Sun

☎ (028) 9027 9902

Whitewater Belfast Ale H

Dating from 1826, this is the UK's most ornate pub... possibly. Owned by the National Trust, the Crown is undergoing a sympathetic restoration to return it to its original glory. The house beer, Whitewater Crown Glory, is usually accompanied by a second local brew. Good pub food is available and there is a restaurant upstairs.

(Gt Victoria St)

King's Head

829 Lisburn Road, BT9 7GY (beside Balmoral station)

12-1am; 12-midnight Sun

☎ (028) 9050 9950 website: www.kingsheadbelfast.com

Whitewater Belfast Ale; guest beers H

Extensively refurbished and extended, this is a welcome return for a CAMRA favourite. Two handpumps have been reintroduced, serving mainly Whitewater beers. Food is a major feature of the pub and is served all day in the bar as well as the upstairs restaurant. The lounge is particularly comfortable, overlooking the King's Hall. Regular live music events are in an adjacent bar. Q (Balmoral) P

INDEPENDENT BREWERIES

Hilden Lisburn
Strangford Lough Killyleagh
Whitewater Kilkeel

Kitchen Bar

36-40 Victoria Square, BT1 4QB
11.30-11 (1am Fri & Sat); 11.30-11 Sun
(028) 9032 4901
Beer range varies Ⓗ
City centre pub in a converted shipping office. A contemporary replacement for the demolished Victorian original, the new bar has its own interesting features including impressive riveted pillars and ornate brickwork, as well as items salvaged from the old bar. Do not miss the Paddy pizza. (Central)

McHugh's

29-31 Queen's Square, BT1 3FG
11.30-1am; 12-midnight Sun & Mon
(028) 9024 7830
Whitewater Belfast Ale; guest beer Ⓗ
Busy, city-centre pub originally dating from 1711, which has recently been restored and extended. The basement bar hosts live music. Families are welcome and excellent food is available. It is convenient for Laganside bus station. (Central)

Carrickfergus

Central Bar

13-15 High Street, BT38 7AN
10-11 (1am Thu-Sat); 12.30-midnight Sun
(028) 9935 7840
Beer range varies Ⓗ
Basic, unpretentious pub overlooking the Norman castle. It is conveniently situated near the town centre and marina. The good value food is typical Wetherspoon's fare, and is served all day. There is a family area upstairs.

Coleraine

Old Courthouse

Castlerock Road, BT51 3HP (across the old bridge then 200 yds on)
10-11 (1am Thu-Sat); 12.30-midnight Sun
(028) 7032 5820
Beer range varies Ⓗ
Impressive, listed, former county courthouse dating from 1852. A standard Wetherspoon pub, it serves an ever-changing beer range. The large screens only come to life at 5pm. It has recently introduced music, although the sound level is not intrusive. There is a patio area surrounding the pub which is unusual for a town pub in this area. Good value food is served – try the Ulster fry.

Comber

North Down House

Belfast Road, BT23 5EW (Castle St roundabout)
12-midnight (1am Fri & Sat); 12.30-midnight Sun
(028) 9187 2242
Beer range varies Ⓗ
This pub is over 100 years old and its interior reflects the local history of the area. To one side of the main bar is the Comber Halt, with its railway-carriage style seats a reminder of the former railway station. The lounge bar is decorated with memorabilia from the Old Comber whiskey distillery. The bar staff offer a friendly welcome. Live music can be heard on Saturday night.

Enniskillen

Linen Hall

11-13 Townhall Street, BT74 7BD
10-11 (1am Fri & Sat); 12.30-midnight Sun
(028) 6634 0910
Beer range varies Ⓗ
Remote Wetherspoon's outlet in the far west of the province. Frequented by regulars and the many visitors drawn to this picturesque part of the country, it makes a good base for the superb fishing that can be enjoyed locally. A stairlift to the bar makes it accessible to all customers. Good value food is served all day.
Q

Hillsborough

Hillside

21 Main Street, BT26 6AE
12-11.30 (1am Fri & Sat); 12-11 Sun
(028) 9268 2765
Whitewater Belfast Ale; guest beers Ⓗ
Always a favourite with CAMRA members, this pub has sold real ale for years. There is a choice of local Whitewater Ale and beers from across the Irish Sea. Food is another attraction; meals are available all week in the bar and refectory, and on Friday and Saturday in the upstairs restaurant (served all day Sun). A beer festival is held in the summer. Quiz night is on Tuesday and jazz can be heard on Sunday.
Q

Holywood

Dirty Duck Ale House

3 Kinnegar Road, BT18 9JN
11.30-midnight (1am Fri & Sat); 12.30-midnight Sun
(028) 9059 6666
Beer range varies Ⓗ
This cheery pub on the County Down side of Belfast Lough is a previous N.I. CAMRA Pub of the Year. From the picture windows of the bar and upstairs restaurant you can enjoy superb views across the Lough, taking in shipping and the County Antrim coast. Four handpumps dispense a good range of beers. The pub hosts live music from Thursday to Sunday. Extra handpumps are in use for the late-August beer festival held in a temporary bar outside.

Killinchy

Daft Eddy's

Skettrick Island, BT23 6QH
(Whiterock Road, 2 miles N of Killinchy)
11.30-11.30 (1am Fri); 12-10.30 Sun
(028) 9754 1615
Whitewater Belfast Ale Ⓗ
Northern Ireland's most remote real ale pub shelters behind the ruins of Skettrick Castle and could be mistaken for a large bungalow from a distance. Both the public bar and restaurant have marvellous views of Whiterock Bay. The food is highly recommended, with seafood a speciality. Booking is advised as the restaurant can be busy. It is well worth the effort to find this genuine hidden gem. Q P

NORTHERN IRELAND

Lisburn

Tap Room
Hilden Brewery, Hilden, BT27 4TY
(from railway halt follow signs to brewery, 5 minutes' walk)
11.30-2.30, 5.30-9; closed Mon; 12.30-3 Sun
☎ (028) 9266 3863
Hilden Ale, Molly Malone's Porter H
The Tap Room is the bar/restaurant part of the adjacent Hilden Brewery. Tours can be arranged and there is an exhibition of brewing and Hilden's linen industry heritage. Good food is served in the restaurant. Special events including live music are staged here, and there is an annual beer festival in the brewery courtyard.
P

Tuesday Bell
Units 1-2 Lisburn Square, BT28 2TU
(adjacent to bus station)
10 (8 Tue & Sat)-11 (midnight Thu; 1am Fri & Sat); 12-11 Sun
☎ (028) 9262 7390
Beer range varies H
This large bar, spread over two floors, forms the centrepiece of the Lisburn Square shopping centre. It tends to be busy on Friday and Saturday nights when the upstairs is filled with young people. There are usually two real ales, mainly from Scottish breweries. The bar is named after the bell that used to open the local market. The bar opens early on Tuesday and Saturday to cater for the market trade but not alcohol is sold before 11.30am. Q

Londonderry

Diamond
23-24 The Diamond, BT48 6HP (centre of walled town)
10-11 (1am Thu-Sat); 12-midnight Sun
☎ (028) 7127 2880
Beer range varies H
Large Wetherspoon pub in the centre of Northern Ireland's historic city. The pub is split level and there is a children's room upstairs. It overlooks the city-centre war memorial and has views towards the River Foyle. The food is typical Wetherspoon's good value fare.

Ice Wharf
Strand Road, BT48 7AB
(approx. ¼ mile N of Guildhall Sq)
11-11 (1am Thu-Sat); 12-midnight Sun
☎ (028) 7127 6610
Beer range varies H
The first Lloyds No1 bar in Northern Ireland. This is a sizeable pub with a split-level main bar and a separate room for families. Standard Lloyds food is served.

Newtownards

Spirit Merchant
54-56 Regent Street, BT23 4LP
10-11 (1am Fri & Sat); 10-midnight Sun
☎ (028) 9182 4270
Beer range varies H
This Wetherspoon's pub, quiet in daytime, features plasma TV screens at night. These play restrained soul music in mid-week but at weekends can be noisy and attract a young crowd. The current manager is Scottish and serves ales from Scottish breweries. Meals are available from breakfast onwards.
P

Saintfield

White Horse
Main Street, BT24 7AB
11.30-11.30; 12-10 Sun
☎ (028) 9751 1143
Beer range varies H
Having undergone a complete renovation, the Horse, as it is known locally, is still a cosy, friendly pub, but is now more spacious with a wood-burning fire for the winter months. There is more seating, and a carvery as well as the Oast House restaurant downstairs. This Whitewater Brewery owned pub offers various beers, as well as its own, from five pumps. Northern Ireland CAMRA Pub of the Year, 2005, it hosts an annual beer festival showcasing 15-20 beers.

A pane in the neck

Pubs are dull enough places at any time though not so dull in Ireland as they are in England. I suppose I know most of them in Dublin and I'd rather have them than the pubs in London. I remember being in the Blue Lion in Parnell Street one day and the owner said to me, 'You owe me 10 shillings, you broke a glass the last time you were in here'. 'God bless and save us,' I said, 'it must have been a very dear glass if it cost 10 shillings. Tell us, was it a Waterford glass or something?' I discovered in double-quick time that it wasn't a glass you'd drink out of he meant – it was a pane of glass and I'd stuck somebody's head through it.

Brendan Behan

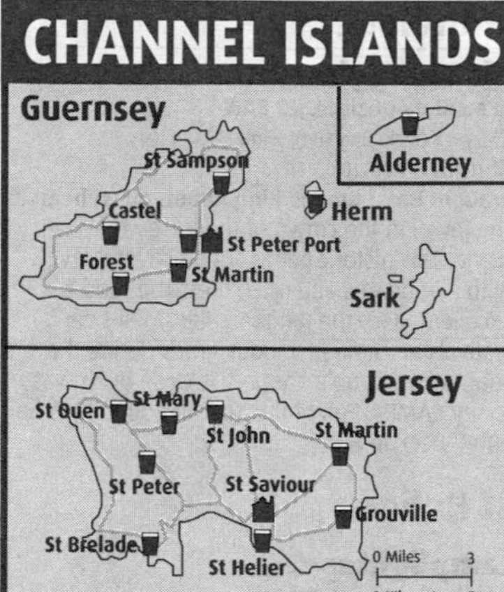

ALDERNEY

Alderney

Georgian House Hotel

Victoria Street, GY9 3UF

10-3, 6.30-midnight (10-12.30am summer); 10-4 Sun

☎ (01481) 822471

website: www.georgianhousealderney.com

Ringwood Best Bitter 🄷

Set on the main street, this imposing building extends a warm welcome to locals and visitors alike. It is a great place to enjoy a good pint or fine food from the extensive menu – from bar snacks to an a la carte meal. There is a good choice of seating in the bar area, in the orangery or in the gardens – the perfect place to while away a warm summer's afternoon.

GUERNSEY

Castel

Fleur du Jardin

Kings Mills, GY5 7JT

11.30-11.45 (including Sun); may close winter

☎ (01481) 257996

website: www.fleurdujardin.guernsey.net

Draught Bass; Tipsy Toad Guernsey Sunbeam 🄷

Country pub with a good-sized, sheltered garden in an attractive rural setting. There are two bars: one small and cosy, attached to the restaurant, the other a larger room where good quality food is served. The menus in both the bar and restaurant feature fresh, local produce. This popular pub can be very busy at weekends, particularly in the summer. Q P

Rockmount Hotel

Cobo, GY5 7HB

10-11.45 (12.45am Fri & Sat); 12-10.30 Sun

☎ (01481) 256757

Randalls Patois 🄷

This pub has a public bar situated to the rear of the building by the large car park and a lounge at the front by the road, with a warming fire during the winter. A good range of food is served in the lounge. The pub is just across the road from a popular beach – perfect for refreshments – and boasts one of the best views on the island of Guernsey's legendary sunsets. P

Forest

Venture Inn

New Road, GY8 0HG (near airport)

10.30-11.45; closed Sun

☎ (01481) 263211

Randalls Patois 🄷

Popular, traditional Guernsey hostelry. The busy public bar is to the side and there is a lounge where excellent food is served at lunchtime and every evening in summer; Friday and Saturday in winter. A new deck area has been created at the front, providing a pleasant spot for outdoor drinking when the weather is fine. P

St Martin

Ambassador Hotel

Route de Sausmarez, GY4 6SO

12-3, 6-11.45; 12-3.30 Sun

☎ (01481) 238356

website: www.ambassador.guernsey.net

Randalls Patois 🄷

The hotel is situated just down from Sausmarez Manor. A delicious range of meals is available, either in the bar, the newly-refurbished restaurant or in the Old Guernsey Conservatory when the weather is fine. There is also a patio area to the rear of the bar. The bar is open to hotel guests only on Sunday evening; the accommodation is good value. P

Captain's Hotel

La Fosse, GY4 6EF

10-11.45; 10-4 Sun

☎ (01481) 238990

Fuller's London Pride 🄷

In a secluded location down a country lane, this is a popular pub with locals who are a part of the lively, friendly atmosphere you will find here. There is a small outdoor area to sit in for the summer. Meals can be eaten in the bar or bistro. There is a car park but it fills up quickly.

St Peter Port

Cock & Bull

Lower Hauteville, GY1 1LL

11.30-2.30, 4-12.45am; 11.30-12.45am Fri & Sat; occasional Sun

☎ (01481) 722660

Beer range varies 🄷

Popular pub, just up the hill from the church. Five handpumps provide a choice of beers, including a brew created for the pub by Randalls called Sipping Bull. Beer festivals are hosted from time to time. Live music on Monday ranges from baroque to jazz, and Tuesday and Thursday nights are live microphone and Irish. Seating is on three levels and a large-screen TV shows sporting events.

Cornerstone Café

2 La Tour Beauregard, GY1 1LQ

10 (8am Thu & Fri)-12.45am; occasional Sun

☎ (01481) 713832

INDEPENDENT BREWERIES

Randalls St Peter Port Guernsey

Tipsy Toad St Saviour Jersey

Beer range varies Ⓗ
At this café there is a small bar area to the front with bar stools, and seating at tables to the rear. A Randalls beer is usually available. The menu offers a wide range of hot and cold meals, served all day. ◑

Ship & Crown
North Esplanade, GY1 2NB (opp. Crown Pier car park)
10-12.45am; 12-10 Sun
☎ (01481) 721368
Adams Broadside; Draught Bass; Fuller's London Pride Ⓗ
Situated just across the road from the Victoria Pier (known locally as the Crown Pier), the pub enjoys picturesque views of the harbour, the castle and the islands beyond. This busy pub attracts a varied clientele of all ages, including locals and tourists. Good quality bar meals are served in generous portions. ◑

St Sampson

La Fontaine Inn
Vale Road, GY2 4DS
10-11.45; 12-3.30 (6 summer) Sun
☎ (01481) 247644
Randalls Cynful Ⓗ
Popular with the local community, the inn has a small public bar where the handpumps are located. The bar adjoins an L-shaped lounge and both have access to a serving hatch, so you can obtain a drink wherever you are. Shove-ha-penny is played in the public bar. Cynful ale is named after Cindy, the landlady. ❀⊟♣P

HERM

Mermaid Tavern
Herm Island, GY1 3HR
10.30-10.45 (restricted hours during winter); 10.30-9 Sun
☎ (01481) 710170
Randalls Patois Ⓗ
Named after an old cargo ship used to carry supplies to Herm, the pub is popular with locals and tourists, whether staying on Herm or over from Guernsey. The bar is busy, with plenty of seating, and there is a large patio area outside, where food can be purchased. It is advisable to reserve ahead for the restaurant. During the holiday season it is also advisable to book for the ferry over to Herm. ❀

JERSEY

Grouville

Pembroke Inn
La Grande Route des Sablons, JE3 9FR
10-11; 11-11 Sun
☎ (01534) 855756
Draught Bass; Courage Directors; Wells Bombardier Ⓗ
The Pembroke is a large, friendly pub. Real ale is only available in the public bar so ask if you do not see it. Food is popular here, and booking is recommended. The public bar can get quite boisterous at times – it has a pool table and a range of games. The car park is small but there is plentiful parking nearby.
⚲Q❀◑⊟♿♣P

St Brelade

Old Smugglers Inn
La Mont du Ouaisne, JE3 8AW
11-11 (including Sun); winter hours vary
☎ (01534) 741510
Draught Bass; Greene King Abbot; guest beers Ⓗ
The jewel in the crown of the Jersey real ale scene. This historic pub is set on several levels with low beams and open fires. The food is excellent, as is the range of ales. Mini-beer festivals are held at various times during the year. A large public car park is close by. It was Jersey CAMRA Pub of the Year in 2002, 2003 and 2004. ⚲Q◑●

St Helier

Lamplighter ✓
9 Mulcaster Street, JE2 3NJ
10-11; 11-11 Sun
☎ (01534) 741510
Draught Bass; Ⓖ **Ringwood Best Bitter,** Ⓗ **Fortyniner, Old Thumper;** Ⓖ **Theakston XB; Wells Eagle IPA;** Ⓗ **guest beers** Ⓗ/Ⓖ
A haven for real ale lovers in the centre of bustling St Helier, with an excellent choice of four beers on handpump and four on gravity. There is always a lively atmosphere here, with music and sports shown on the recently-introduced televisions. A varied menu of meals and snacks is served at lunchtime. The famous gas lamps that gave the pub its name are still in situ and often used. ◐⊟

Original Wine Bar
82-84 Bath Street, JE2 4SU
11-11; 3-11 Sun
☎ (01534) 871119
Draught Bass; Courage Directors; Ringwood Best Bitter; Tipsy Toad Jimmy's Bitter; Wells Bombardier; guest beers Ⓗ
Unlike most wine bars, the Original boasts an excellent range of real ales. The bar is on two levels; the lower room is no-smoking while food is served. A varied lunchtime menu is offered and the bar can be busy on Friday and Saturday evenings, with seating at a premium. Regular themed dining/drinking evenings are popular. ◐

Post Horn
Hue Street, JE2 3RE
11-11 (including Sun)
☎ (01534) 872853
Draught Bass Ⓗ
The Post Horn is tucked away in a corner of town. An ex-Bass house, it is restricted to serving Draught Bass, but thankfully does this very well. A large pub, set on two levels, it offers an excellent range of food and at lunchtimes is frequented by workers from offices nearby. This pub is well worth a visit if you are in town.
❀◐⊟♣

Prince of Wales Tavern
8 Hilgrove Street, JE2 4SL (next to central market)
11-11; 11-2 Sun
☎ (01534) 737378
Draught Bass; Courage Directors; Ringwood Best Bitter; Wadworth 6X; Wells Bombardier Ⓗ
Shoehorned into a gap between the central

market and an office block, this lively one-bar pub is an oasis in the centre of town. The bar boasts a classic six-pump beer engine, although at the time of writing only three work. The back yard is popular in summer and the pub can be quite busy at lunchtime, although it tends to be less hectic in the evening. Q❀◖

St John

Les Fontaines Tavern

La Route du Nord, JE3 4AJ

⏲ 11-11 (including Sun)

☎ (01534) 862707

Draught Bass; Wells Bombardier Ⓗ

Set in 17th-century granite buildings on the picturesque north coast, the Fontaines offers unparalled views of France and the other Channel Islands. With its low roof and exposed beams, it is a popular choice with locals, and families are welcome; a play area is provided. Renowned for the quality of its food, booking in advance is advisable, particularly at weekends. A large courtyard allows for alfresco dining. Q🐎❀◖◗P

St Martin

Rozel Bay Hotel

La Vallee de Rozel, JE3 6AJ

⏲ 11-11 (including Sun)

☎ (01534) 863438

Draught Bass; Courage Directors; Wells Bombardier Ⓗ

Tucked away in a picturesque valley, the Rozel is a gem. The quiet no-smoking snug boasts an open fire and a small bar. The larger public bar has a television and pool table. An excellent range of gourmet bar meals is available, or you can treat yourself in the restaurant; no evening meals are served Sunday. There is also a delightful garden and an outdoor dining area. Car parking is at a premium, but the summer bus service is decent. ⛰Q❀◖◗⊟▲P⚡

St Mary

St Mary's Country Inn

La Rue des Buttes, JE3 3DS

⏲ 11-11 (including Sun)

☎ (01534) 482897

Draught Bass; Tipsy Toad Jimmy's Bitter Ⓗ

This large, historic country inn has two bars, a conservatory and a large garden to the front. Real ale is only available in the lounge bar, which has an open fire. An excellent range of lunch and evening meals is served. Families are welcome. There is a large car park and patio to the rear of the pub, which is served by a regular bus service from town. ⛰Q❀◖◗⊟P

St Ouen

Farmer's Inn

La Grande Route de St Ouen, JE3 2HY

⏲ 10-11; 11-11 Sun

☎ (01534) 485311

Draught Bass; Tipsy Toad Jimmy's Bitter; guest beers Ⓗ

The Farmer's has a real country feel to it. Set in the heart of the village, the large public bar has an open fire and up to four real ales on tap. The cosier lounge has a small bar and a hatch through to the main bar. Meals are served in the summer but check beforehand if you want to dine. There is a large car park, and a regular bus service from town. ⛰Q❀◖◗⊟P

St Peter

Star

La Route de Beaumont, JE2 7BQ

⏲ 11-11 (including Sun)

☎ (01534) 485556

Tipsy Toad Jimmy's Bitter, seasonal beers Ⓗ

Formerly the home of the Tipsy Toad Brewery, this large pub in the centre of St Peter's village has several rooms set round a central bar. Food is popular here, and the award-winning Jimmy's Bitter is served, along with occasional seasonal brews from Tipsy Toad. ⛰Q❀◖◗♿♣P

Beers suitable for vegetarians and vegans

A number of cask and bottle-fermented beers in the Good Beer Guide are listed as 'suitable for vegetarians and vegans'. The main ingredient used in cask beer brewing that causes concern for people who avoid animal-derived products is isinglass. This is a fining or clearing agent made from the swim bladders of certain fish, the sturgeon in particular. Isinglass is added to a cask when it leaves the brewery: the finings attract yeast and protein, which fall to the bottom of the container. Other clearing agents – notably Irish moss derived from seaweed – can be used in place of isinglass. As the sturgeon is being fished to extinction as a result of the world demand for caviar, it would be sensible for brewers to switch to Irish moss or other alternatives. Vegans avoid dairy products: lactose or 'milk sugar' is a bi-product of cheese making and is used in milk stout, of which Mackeson is the best known example.

ISLE OF MAN

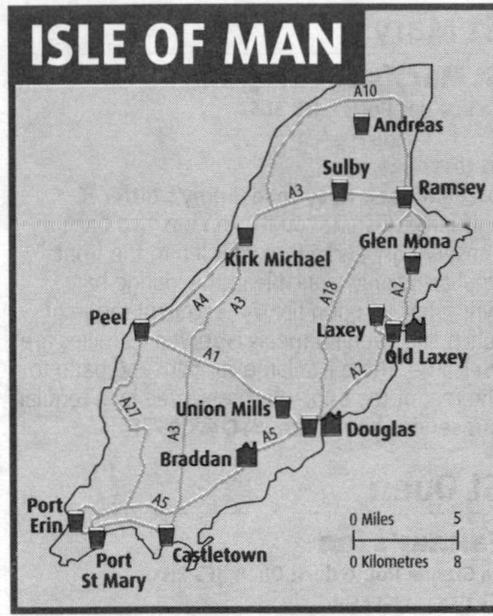

Andreas

Grosvernor Hotel

Kirk Andreas, IM7 4HE

12-3, 5-11 (midnight Fri & Sat); 12-4, 7.45-11 Sun

☎ (01624) 880576

Okells Bitter; guest beer Ⓗ

The most northerly pub on the island. The warm, friendly feel of the welcoming village pub makes the Grosvenor popular with real ale drinkers and diners alike. Reasonably-priced bar snacks and a full restaurant menu are available all year round. Unusual for the Isle of Man, disabled access is good. Public transport to this part of the island is limited to daytime.

Q ❀ ◑ ◐ ♣ P

Castletown

Castle Arms Hotel (Gluepot) ✔

Quayside, IM9 1LP (opp. castle entrance)

12-11 (including Sun)

☎ (01624) 874673

Okells Mild, Bitter Ⓗ

After a period of uncertainty, when this small quayside local was closed by the brewery, it underwent a transformation under new ownership. There is a maritime feel to the decor, with model ships and pictures of historic sea-going vessels. The building features on the back of the £5 note – on the bottom left-hand corner, which must be a unique accolade! Thai food is served on Friday and Saturday evenings. In summer, customers can drink on a paved area on the harbourside.

❀ ◑ ◐ ⇌ (IMR)

Sidings

Victoria Road, IM9 1EF (by station)

11.30-11 (midnight Fri & Sat); 11.30-10.30 Sun

☎ (01624) 823282

Bushy's Ruby Mild, Castletown Bitter; John Smith's Bitter; guest beers Ⓗ

Neglected under brewery ownership for many years as the Duck's Nest, this pub was refurbished and became a free house about 10 years ago. The bar, with an impressive and ornate woodern counter, serves up to 10 cask ales including mild, sourced from local breweries. During fine weather the garden is ideal for families. Excellent value food is served at lunchtimes except Sunday at local CAMRA's Pub of the Year 2003 and 2005. ⩩ ❀ ◑ ▲ ⇌ (IMR) ♣

Union Hotel

Arbory Street, IM9 1LJ (near castle)

11.30-11 (midnight Fri & Sat); 12-11 Sun

☎ (01624) 825286

Okells Mild, Bitter Ⓗ

Multi-roomed pub in the town centre – ideal for the serious drinker as no food is served so the emphasis here is on the ale. Well-supported by local residents, the Union is home to a branch of the Buffaloes as well as the Castletown Ale Drinkers' Society, a charitable organisation whose members take a dip in Castletown Harbour on New Year's Day.

⩩ ♣

Douglas

Albert Hotel ✔

3 Chapel Row, IM1 2BJ (near indoor market)

10-11 (midnight Fri & Sat); 12-10.30 Sun

☎ (01624) 673632

Okells Mild, Bitter Ⓗ

Close to the bus station and quayside, this busy, unspoilt local is home to a thriving social club. A central bar serves the spacious, wood-panelled lounge and smaller public bar. The atmosphere is lively and the bar is popular with bikers. The house brew Jough (Manx Gaelic for beer) is supplied by Okells. Q ⊟ ⇌ (IMR) ♣

Old Market Tavern

2 Chapel Row, IM1 2BJ

10-11; 12-4, 7-11 Sun

☎ (01624) 675202

Okells Bitter Ⓗ

Traditional back-street local, between the bus station and market hall, with two small wood-panelled rooms served by a central bar. It is a cheery, family-run pub with a strong community spirit. Dominoes, cribbage and darts are played. For many years (uniquely) it was owned by Castletown and Okells breweries. It is busy at weekends and visitors are always made to feel welcome. ⩩ Q ⊟ ⇌ (IMR) ♣

Prospect Hotel ✔

Prospect Hill, IM1 1ES

12-11; 12-midnight Fri; 6-midnight Sat; closed Sun

☎ (01624) 616773

Okells Bitter; guest beers Ⓗ

Busy pub located within the business sector of the Isle of Man and popular with office workers. A large, single room with plenty of seating; one area is no-smoking. A wide range of beers is available, from both on and off the island, and food is served throughout the day. Be warned: after 5pm on Friday the pub becomes crowded as the offices empty out! ◑ ◐ ⇌ (IMR) ⚟

INDEPENDENT BREWERIES

Bushy's Braddan
Okells Douglas
Old Laxey Old Laxey

Rovers Return

11 Church Street, IM1 2AG (behind town hall)
✪ 12-11 (midnight Fri & Sat); 12-11 Sun
☎ (01624) 676459
website: www.bushys.com
Bushy's Ruby Mild, Bitter, seasonal beers; guest beers 🄷
Extended again this year, more rooms have been added to this unusual multi-roomed establishment. There is now a downstairs bar stocking Bushy's, Archers and other real ales, and an area for bands with a video link to the bar. Real cider and perry are now available in the main bar. The Blackburn Rovers 'shrine' and snug have become no-smoking rooms. The unusual handpumps, fashioned from fire brigade brass branch pipes, remain unchanged. Live music staged most weekends draws the crowds in the evenings and substantial portions of food make the pub a popular lunchtime venue.
⛫❀◑⇌(IMR) ●⊬

Glen Mona

Glen Mona Hotel

IM7 1HF (near Glen Mona tram stop)
✪ 5 (12 Sun)-midnight
☎ (01624) 861263
Greene King IPA; guest beers 🄷
One-room free house in the north-east of the island with a spacious feel. Ample tables and seating are provided for dining as well as unusual bar stools for those just wishing to enjoy the choice of two real ales. Note the interesting window shutters decorated with a variety of floral designs and the delightful oil painting depicting the rural scenery outside. Glen Mona has its own electric railway tram stop and is well served by the No. 3 Douglas-Ramsey bus route.
❀◑◗▲⊖(MER) ♣P⊬

Kirk Michael

Mitre Hotel

Main Road, IM6 1AJ
✪ 12-2.30, 5-11 (midnight Fri); 12-midnight Sat; 12-11 Sun
☎ (01624) 878244
Okells Bitter 🄷
The only pub in the village and reputed to be the oldest pub on the island. It is located half way round the famous TT course. A popular local, it has a traditional public and lounge bar as well as a small snug. Old photographs of the TT and island are featured throughout. The large garden has children's play equipment. Events are held during the summer including live music weekends. A good selection of home-cooked meals will satisfy most tastes (not served Sun, or Mon eve). ❀◑◗⊟♿▲♣P

Laxey

Mines Tavern

Captains Hill, IM4 7AA (next to electric tram station)
✪ 12 (10.30 summer)-11 (midnight Fri & Sat); 12-11 Sun
☎ (01624) 861484
Bushy's Bitter; Okells Mild, Bitter; guest beer 🄷
Central village pub popular with locals and tourists. Enter the public bar from the garden and you will find a counter made from a Manx Electric Railway car. The Mines offers a wide range of good value lunches. The pleasant garden has seating, some under cover, and a children's play area. Situated close to several attractions, trips to the summit of Snaefell on the mountain railway, and the Lady Isabella waterwheel, recently renovated for her 150th birthday, are recommended.
❀◑⊟ ⊖(MER)

Queen's Hotel

New Road, IM4 7BP
✪ 12-11 (midnight Fri & Sat); 12-11 Sun
☎ (01624) 861195
Bushy's Ruby Mild, Castletown Bitter, Bitter; guest beers 🄷
Busy local sited on the edge of Laxey, popular with locals and bikers all year round. The interest in bikes is reflected in the numerous photos and pictures adorning the walls, including several of the late Joey Dunlop, famous TT rider. Live music is hosted every Saturday and barbecues are held on summer weekends on the patio. B&B accommodation is available. Note the large collection of beer mats and pump clips. The benches outside are handy if you are waiting for the No 3. bus to Douglas, which stops outside.
❀⇆⊖(MER) ♣ P

Old Laxey

Shore Hotel

IM4 7DA
✪ 12-midnight (including Sun)
☎ (01624) 861509
Old Laxey Bosun Bitter 🄷
Situated on the bank of the River Laxey, this popular local has an ideal location for summer drinking; picnic benches are provided next to the river. Beware of occasional harassment from the ducks. The large single room is decorated with faded fishing boat pictures and fishing equipment. There is a real fire in winter and comfortable seating adds to the cosy atmosphere. ◑◗

Peel

Peveril Hotel

Castle Street, IM5 1AS (off Promenade)
✪ 12-midnight (including Sun)
☎ (01624) 842381
Okells Mild, Bitter 🄷
Family-run pub on Peel Quay, on the west side of the island, a short distance from the new bridge built across the river to Peel Castle. Nearby are museums including a motor museum which is well worth visiting. The pub is popular with fishermen whose boats are moored across the road.
⛫Q⛀❀⊟♿▲♣●⊬

White House ✔

2 Tynwald Road, IM5 1LA (near bus station)
✪ 11-midnight (including Sun)
☎ (01624) 842252
Bushy's Bitter; Flowers Original; Okells Mild, Bitter; Taylor Landlord; guest beers 🄷
Multi-roomed, family-run town pub which has remained unaltered since the 1930s. The snug, public bar, pool room and music room are all around the central bar. Musicians meet most

Saturday evenings to play Gaelic music at this lively local. Serving one of the best pints on the island (awards adorn the walls), it also stocks over 120 malt whiskies. ⛫Q☕❀🍴⚠♣P

Port Erin

Bay Hotel

Shore Road, IM9 6HC (on road to lifeboat house)
12-11 (including Sun)
☎ (01624) 832084
Bushy's Ruby Mild, Bitter, Oyster Stout, Old Bushy Tail Ⓗ
The new Bay Hotel is the first-rate result of an 11th-hour restoration of a long-closed residential family-owned pub. Although you can no longer stay at the Bay, the ground-floor bars are very much worth a visit. Use of old and original materials gives the feel of a pub that has been around for years. Occasional live music and gigs are hosted at the weekend.
⛫☕◑🍴≠(IMR) ♣

Falcon's Nest Hotel

Station Road, IM9 6AF
10.30-11 (midnight Fri & Sat); 10.30-11 Sun
☎ (01624) 834077
website: www.falconsnesthotel.co.uk
Bushy's Bitter; Okells Bitter; guest beers Ⓗ
Family-run, seafront hotel on the south-west coast overlooking a sandy beach. It has two bars, a function room and a large restaurant. The attractive lounge, with polished wood and stained glass, and panoramic views of Port Erin bay, is where the cask ale is served. A wide range of highly recommended meals is served including the popular Sunday carvery.
⛫Q🛏◑🍴≠(IMR)♣P

Port St Mary

Albert Hotel

Athol Street, IM9 5DS (alongside bus terminal)
11-midnight (1am Fri & Sat); 12-midnight Sun
☎ (01624) 832118
Bushy's Old Bushy Tail; Okells Bitter; guest beers Ⓗ
Traditional free house overlooking the inner harbour. The bustling public bar has pool, darts and a juke box. The cosy lounge has a nautical theme; both bars have real fires. There is a small restaurant across the main hallway and bar meals are available. Both food and accommodation are recommended here.
⛫Q🛏◑♣P

Ramsey

Ellan Vannin

West Quay, IM8 1JU (200 yds from harbour swing bridge)
12-11 (midnight Fri & Sat); 12-11 Sun
☎ (01624) 812131
Bushy's Bitter, Castletown Bitter, seasonal beers; guest beers Ⓗ
Small, cosy Bushy's pub on the corner of the busy quay and market place; Ellan Vannin is the Manx name for the island. Recently refurbished, it offers a warm and friendly welcome to a varied mix of customers. Some foreign bottled beers are stocked, as well as Westons traditional scrumpy. Occasional live music is performed at the weekend.⛫♿⊖(MER) ♣

Trafalgar Hotel ✔

West Quay, IM8 1DW
(E of harbour swing bridge)
11-11 (midnight Fri & Sat); 12-3, 8-11 Sun
(01624) 814601
Okells Bitter; guest beers Ⓗ
Appealing freehold harbourside pub and a regular finalist for the island's CAMRA Pub of the Year award. The Trafalgar is one of the oldest pubs in Ramsey but has been refurbished in recent years without losing any of its cheery character and warm atmosphere. Guest ales are selected from a wide range of breweries.
⊖(MER) ♣

Sulby

Sulby Glen Hotel ✔

Main Road, IM7 2HR (Sulby crossroads, A3)
12-midnight (1am Fri & Sat); 12-11 Sun
☎ (01624) 897240
Bushy's Bitter; Okells Bitter; guest beers Ⓗ
Large, roadside hotel on the famous Sulby Straight section of the TT course. The bars display many photographs of riders through the ages and the pub is closely linked to a German motorcycle club in Waltrop. The hotel is a former local CAMRA Pub of the Year and usually has a choice of guest ales to sample. It is a popular place for food and offers a good, varied menu.
⛫☕❀🛏◑🍴♿⚠♣P

Union Mills

Railway Inn

Main Road, IM4 4NE
12-11 (including Sun)
☎ (01624) 853006
website: www.iomrailwayinn.com
Okells Mild, Bitter; guest beers Ⓗ
Roadside pub on the main Douglas to Peel road. Resolutely free of brewery control, and in the fifth generation of ownership by the same family, the Railway remains at the centre of village life. Inside are three rooms; the bar area is no-smoking. Two guest beers are usually served as well as local Manx ale. It is an excellent spot to watch the TT races while enjoying a good pint. P⚡

> **Look out**
>
> Mother's in the kitchen
> Washing out the jugs;
> Sister's in the pantry
> Bottling the suds;
> Father's in the cellar
> Mixing up the hops;
> Johnny's on the front porch
> Watching for the cops.
>
> **1920s American Prohibition song**

The Breweries

Wood clad brewing vessels at the Brunswick Inn, Derby

WaverleyTBS

Leading the way in Cask Beer provision

Given the certain pastiche associated with cask beer among its drinkers, and the extraordinarily wide range of beer and beer styles available, it is now more important than ever to make sure that the selection of cask beers on your bar is right for your outlet, and in turn, your customers.

WaverleyTBS has access to the widest range of cask beers in the marketplace, and our knowledgeable sales team are always on hand to advise you as to which beers will work best for your outlet, and how best to maximise sales.

Guest Beer Promotions

Our monthly **TotalCask** brochure gives you access to a wide range of seasonal, speciality, heritage and award winning beers from all over the country.

- Includes 45 different rotating beers per month
- Competitive pricing including 'price busters'
- Added value offers
- Directly delivered to your door each month
- Includes pump clip cards for instant use

The WaverleyTBS Cask Beer Directory
The WaverleyTBS Cask Beer Directory is a must for all stockists of real ale.
As well as an in-depth regional listing of hundreds of the top brands in the UK, you will find key information on which beers will work best for your outlet, how to maximise your cask sales, and current market and consumer trends.
Contact your local depot for your FREE copy or visit www.waverleytbs.co.uk
WaverleyTBS

How to use The Breweries section

Breweries are listed in alphabetical order. The Independents (regional, smaller craft brewers and brew-pubs) are listed first, followed by the Nationals, the Globals and finally the major non-brewing Pub Groups. Within each brewery entry, beers are listed in increasing order of strength. Beers that are available for less than three months of the year are described as 'occasional' or 'seasonal' brews. Bottle-conditioned beers are also listed: these are beers that have not been pasteurised and contain live yeast, allowing them to continue to ferment and mature in the bottle as a draught real ale does in its cask.

Symbols

🍺 A brew-pub: a pub that brews beer on the premises.

◆ CAMRA tasting notes, supplied by a trained CAMRA tasting panel. Beer descriptions that do not carry this symbol are based on more limited tastings or have been obtained from other sources.
Tasting notes are not provided for brew-pub beers that are available in fewer than five outlets, nor for other breweries' beers that are available for less than three months of the year.

🗌 A CAMRA Beer of the Year in the past three years.

■ One of the 2005 CAMRA Beers of the Year, a finalist in the Champion Beer of Britain competition held during the Great British Beer Festival at Olympia in August 2005, or the Champion Winter Beer of Britain competition held earlier in the year.

◎ The brewery's beers can be acceptably served through a 'tight sparkler' attached to the nozzle of the beer pump, designed to give a thick collar of foam on the beer.

⊗ The brewery's beer should NOT be served through a tight sparkler. CAMRA is opposed to the growing tendency to serve southern-brewed beers with the aid of sparklers, which aerate the beer and tend to drive hop aroma and flavour into the head, altering the balance of the beer achieved in the brewery.

Abbreviations

OG stands for original gravity, the measure taken before fermentation of the level of 'fermentable material' (malt sugars and added sugars) in the brew. It is a rough indication of strength and is no longer used for duty purposes.

ABV stands for Alcohol by Volume, which is a more reliable measure of the percentage of alcohol in the finished beer. Many breweries now only disclose ABVs but the Guide lists OGs where available. Often the OG and the ABV of a beer are identical, ie 1035 and 3.5 per cent. If the ABV is higher than the OG, ie OG 1035, ABV 3.8, this indicates that the beer has been 'well attenuated' with most of the malt sugars turned into alcohol. If the ABV is lower than the OG, this means residual sugars have been left in the beer for fullness of body and flavour: this is rare but can apply to some milds or strong old ales, barley wines, and winter beers.

*The Breweries Section was correct at the time of going to press and every effort has been made to ensure that all cask-conditioned and bottle-conditioned beers are included.

The Independents

✲Indicates new entry since the last edition; SIBA indicates member of the Society of Independent Brewers; IFBB indicates member of the Independent Family Brewers of Britain; EAB indicates member of the East Anglian Brewers Co-operative

1648 SIBA

1648 Brewing Co Ltd, Mill Lane, East Hoathly, near Lewes, East Sussex, BN8 6QB
Tel (01825) 840830
Email brewmaster@1648brewing.co.uk
Website www.1648brewing.co.uk

⊗ The 1648 brewery, set up in the old stable block of the King's Head pub in 2003, derives its title and some of the beer names from the time of the deposition of King Charles I. One pub is owned and between five and 10 outlets are supplied. Seasonal beers: Honey Beer (ABV 4%, summer), Armistice Ale (ABV 4.2%, Oct-Nov), Warrant (ABV 4.8%, summer), Winter Warrant (ABV 4.8%, winter).

1648 Original (OG 1040, ABV 3.9%)

Signature (OG 1044, ABV 4.4%)

Abbey Ales SIBA

Abbey Ales Ltd, Abbey Brewery, Camden Row, Bath, Somerset, BA1 5LB
Tel (01225) 444437
Fax (01225) 443569
Email enquiries@abbeyales.co.uk
Website www.abbeyales.co.uk
Shop via website
Tours by arrangement

⊗ Abbey Ales is the first and only brewery in Bath for nearly 50 years. It supplies more than 80 regular accounts within a 20-mile radius of Bath Abbey while selected wholesalers deliver beer nationally. One tied house, the Star Inn, Bath, is listed on CAMRA's National Inventory of heritage pubs. The one regular cask beer, Bellringer, has won several CAMRA Beer of Festival awards and was a finalist in the 2001 Champion Beer of Britain competition. Seasonal beers: Bath Star (ABV 4.5%, spring), Chorister (ABV 4.5%, autumn), White Friar (ABV 5%), Black Friar (ABV 5.3%, winter), Twelfth Night (ABV 5%, Christmas).

Bellringer (OG 1042, ABV 4.2%) 🗍 ◆
A notably hoppy ale, light to medium-bodied, clean-tasting, refreshingly dry, with a balancing sweetness. Citrus, pale malt aroma and dry, bitter finish.

Abbey Bells

Abbey Bells Brewery, 5 Main Road, Hirst Courtney, Selby, North Yorkshire, YO8 8QP
Tel (07940) 726658
Email enquiries@abbeybells.co.uk
Website www.abbeybells.co.uk
Tours for 12 persons or fewer only, by prior arrangement

⊗ The brewery was launched by Jules Dolan in 2002 and was financed by the sale of his motorbike. The 2.5-barrel plant has cellar tanks from the defunct Brigg Brewery and other parts from a dairy maker in Congleton. Some 30 outlets are supplied. Seasonal beers: Santa's Stocking Filler (ABV 4.5%), Black Satin (ABV 6.2%, winter).

Monday's Child (OG 1035, ABV 3.7%)
An easy-drinking session beer, made with Maris Otter malt and Goldings hops. Pale and refreshing.

Hoppy Daze (OG 1041, ABV 4.1%)
Similar in colour to Monday's Child, the beer is hopped with Target, giving a hoppy tang.

Cordelia's Gift (OG 1042, ABV 4.3%)
The combination of Pearl and chocolate malts and Fuggles hops imparts a flavour reminiscent of dandelion and burdock.

1911 Celebration Ale (OG 1048, ABV 4.8%)

Original Bitter (OG 1050, ABV 5.1%)
Made from Pearl malt with a dash of crystal and flavoured with Goldings hops.

Abbeydale SIBA

Abbeydale Brewery Ltd, Unit 8, Aizlewood Road, Sheffield, South Yorkshire, S8 0YX
Tel (0114) 281 2712
Fax (0114) 281 2713
Email admin@abbeydalebrewery.co.uk

⊗ Since its launch in 1996, Abbeydale has grown steadily and is now one of South Yorkshire's major breweries, supplying more than 200 outlets across the North and Midlands. Seasonal beers: Assumption (ABV 4.1%, August), Alchemy (ABV 4.2%), Black Bishop (ABV 4.2%), Devotion (ABV 4.4%), Wheat Beer (ABV 5.5%, summer), Belfry (ABV 4.5%), White Knight (ABV 4.5%), Stormbringer (ABV 4.7%), Reformation (ABV 4.8%), Epiphany (ABV 5.2%), Hells Bells (ABV 5.8%), Holy Water (ABV 6%, December).

Matins (OG 1034.9, ABV 3.6%)
Extremely pale and full flavoured, but light in alcohol; an excellent, hoppy session beer.

Best Bitter (OG 1039, ABV 4%)
A well-rounded beer, reddish in colour, not too bitter, with lots of aromatic hops.

Moonshine (OG 1041.2, ABV 4.3%)
Pale premium beer balancing hints of sweetness and bitterness with full hop aroma. Pleasant grapefruit traces may be detected.

Absolution (OG 1050, ABV 5.3%)
Strong, pale, sweetish beer.

Black Mass (OG 1065, ABV 6.6%)
Strong black stout, quite bitter and dry but full flavoured with a characteristic hop aroma.

Last Rites (OG 1097, ABV 11%)
A pale, strong barley wine bursting with flavour.

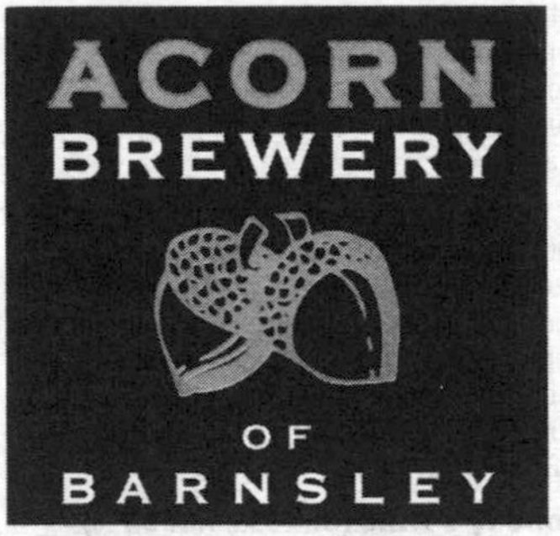

Acorn SIBA

Acorn Brewery of Barnsley Ltd, Unit 11, Mitchells Industrial Estate, Wombwell, Barnsley, South Yorkshire, S73 8HR
Tel (01226) 270734
Fax (01226) 270759
Email acornbrewery@tiscali.co.uk
Shop Mon-Fri 9-4pm
Tours by arrangement

Founded by Dave Hughes, former head brewer at the defunct Barnsley Brewery of Elsecar, Acorn started production in 2003, using a 10-barrel former Firkin plant. Beers are produced using the original Barnsley Bitter yeast strain, and the brewery currently has a 50-barrel a week capacity. Expansion will include a bottling plant and increasing brew length capacity to 70 barrels. 350 outlets are supplied. Seasonal beers: Forester (ABV 4.1%, autumn), Summer Pale (ABV 4.1%, summer), Winter Ale (ABV 4.5%, winter), 3rd Noel (ABV 5%, winter/Xmas).

Barnsley Bitter (OG 1038, ABV 3.8%)
Brewed using Maris Otter malt and English hops. Chestnut in colour, with a well-rounded, rich flavour and a lasting bitter finish.

Barnsley Gold (OG 1041.5, ABV 4.3%)
A well-balanced, golden malty bitter, with a mellow fruity nose and a dry hoppiness in the aftertaste.

Old Moor Porter (OG 1045, ABV 4.4%)

Special Pale Ale (OG 1046, ABV 4.7%)

Adnams IFBB

Adnams plc, Sole Bay Brewery, East Green, Southwold, Suffolk, IP18 6JW
Tel (01502) 727200
Fax (01502) 727201
Email info@adnams.co.uk
Website www.adnams.co.uk
Shop 9-5

⊗ The earliest recorded brewing on the site of Adnams was in 1345. The present brewery was taken over by George and Ernest Adnams in 1872 and turned into a public company in 1890. The Adnams family was joined by the Loftus family in 1902, and Adnams still has three members of the families working for the company. Real ale is available in 84 of its 85 pubs, and it also supplies some 750 other outlets. New fermenting vessels were installed in 2001, 2003 and 2005 to cope with demand. Seasonal beers: Regatta (ABV 4.3%, spring/summer), Mayday (ABV 5%, May), Fisherman (ABV 4.5%, autumn), Old (ABV 4.1%, Dec-Jan), Tally Ho (ABV 7%, Christmas G), Oyster Stout (ABV 4.3%, late winter).

Bitter (OG 1036, ABV 3.7%)
A well-balanced but complex beer with a distinctive sulphurous, hoppy nose. Copper coloured with an introductory bitterness that slowly gives way to a stronger hop presence. A low-key malty sweetness gives a good balance.

Broadside (OG 1049, ABV 4.7%)
Beguiling mix of flavours with a superb blend of malt and hops. The balance of bitter hoppiness is maintained by a mix of plum and malt. Long sustained finish.

Alcazar SIBA

Alcazar Brewery, Church Street, Old Basford, Nottingham, NG6 0GA
Tel (0115) 978 2282
Fax (0115) 975 4234
Email alcazarbrewery@tiscali.co.uk
Website www.alcazarbrewery.co.uk
Shop Tue-Sat, noon-7pm
Tours by arrangement

⊗ Alcazar was established in 1999 and is located behind its brewery tap, the Fox & Crown brew-pub. Alcazar means palace in Spanish, which relates to the crown in the pub name. The brewery is full mash with a 10-barrel brew length. Production is mainly for the Fox & Crown, with smaller quantities sold on demand to local free houses and beer festivals. Seasonal beers: Maple Magic (ABV 5.5%, winter), Black Fox (ABV 3.9%, spring), Desert Fox (ABV 4.3%, summer). Bottle-conditioned beer: Bombay Castle IPA (ABV 6.5%). It was planned to add to the bottle-conditioned range during 2005.

Ale (OG 1040, ABV 4%)
A session ale made with a blend of English and North American hops; pale, full-flavoured with a fruity aroma and finish.

Nottingham Nog **(OG 1042, ABV 4.2%)**
A dark session ale brewed with five kinds of malt and three varieties of hops; rich and smooth with fruit tones and a palate-pleasing finish.

New Dawn **(OG 1045, ABV 4.5%)**
Golden ale made with North American hops that give a unique fruit aroma and crisp, malty taste.

Foxtale Ale **(OG 1050, ABV 4.9%)**

Vixen's Vice **(OG 1052, ABV 5.2%)**
A pale, strong ale with a malt flavour balanced by a clean, crisp, hop taste.

Windjammer IPA **(OG 1060, ABV 6%)**

Ales of Scilly SIBA

Ales of Scilly Brewery, Higher Trenoweth, St Mary's, Isles of Scilly, TR21 0NS
Tel/Fax (01720) 422419
Email mark@alesofscilly.co.uk
Tours by arrangement

Opened in 2001 as a two-barrel plant and expanded in 2004 to five barrels, Ales of Scilly is the most south-westerly brewery in Britain. Nine local pubs are supplied, with regular exports to mainland pubs and beer festivals. Seasonal ales: Old Bustard (ABV 4.2%). Bottle-conditioned beer: Scuppered (ABV 4.6%).

Natural Beauty **(ABV 4.2%)**

Scuppered **(ABV 4.6%)**

All Nations

See Worfield

Alnwick Ales

See Hadrian

An Teallach

An Teallach Ale Co, Camusnagaul, Dundonnell, Little Loch Broom, by Garve, Ross-shire, IV23 2QT
Tel/Fax (01854) 633306
Email anteallachale@dundonell.freeserve.co.uk
Tours by arrangement

An Teallach was formed in the spring of 2001 by husband and wife team, David and Wilma Orr, on Wilma's family croft on the shores of Little Loch Broom, Wester Ross. With their growing range of ales, the business has grown steadily each year. An Teallach Ale (ABV 4.2%) and Beinn Dearg Ale (ABV 3.8%) were due be available bottle-conditioned in 2005. Sixty pubs are supplied.

Beinn Dearg Ale **(OG 1038, ABV 3.8%)** ◈
Sweetish, fruity beer but can vary while the brewery is still experimenting. Some malt and hop character.

Ale **(OG 1042, ABV 4.2%)** ◈
Somewhat variable as the brewery is still in the experimental stage. Generally a sweetish pint in the Scottish 80/- tradition.

Crofters Pale Ale **(OG 1042, ABV 4.2%)**

Brew House Special **(OG 1044, ABV 4.4%)**

Anglo Dutch SIBA

Anglo Dutch Brewery, Unit 12, Savile Bridge Mill, Savile Road, Dewsbury, West Yorkshire, WF12 9AF
Tel (01924) 457772
Fax (01924) 507444
Email mike@anglo-dutch-brewery.co.uk
Website www.anglo-dutch-brewery.co.uk
Tours by arrangement

Paul Klos (Dutch) set up the brewery with Mike Field (Anglo), who also runs the Refreshment Rooms at Dewsbury Station. The equipment came from the Rat & Ratchet in Huddersfield. Most beers contain wheat except for Spike and Tabatha, which contain lager malt. Seasonal beers: Devil's Knell (ABV 4.8%, January), Wild Flower (ABV 4.2%, September), No Doubt It's Stout (ABV 5.2, October).

Best Bitter **(ABV 3.8%)**

Kletswater **(OG 1039, ABV 4%)**
Pale-coloured beer with a hoppy nose and a good hop and citrus fruit flavour.

Mild Rabarber **(ABV 4%)** ◈
Light-coloured brown mild with a malty, fruity flavour and moderate hop character. Refreshing and light bodied.

Spike's on 't' Way **(OG 1040.5, ABV 4.2%)** ◈
Pale bitter with citrus/orange flavour and dry, fruity finish.

Spikus **(OG 1040.5, ABV 4.2%)**
Organic lager malt with New Zealand hops.

Jasperus **(OG 1042, ABV 4.4%)**

Jasper Ale **(OG 1043, ABV 4.4%)**

Ghost on the Rim **(OG 1043, ABV 4.5%)** ◈
Pale, dry and fruity.

At 't' Ghoul and Ghost **(OG 1048, ABV 5.2%)** ◈
Pale golden bitter with a strong citrus and hoppy aroma and flavour. The finish is long, dry, bitter and citrus.

Tabatha the Knackered **(OG 1054, ABV 6%)** ◈
Golden Belgian-style Tripel with a strong fruity, hoppy and bitter character. Powerful and warming, slightly thinnish, with a bitter, dry finish.

Ann Street

See Jersey

Archers

Archers Brewery, Penzance Drive, Swindon, Wiltshire, SN5 7JL
Tel (01793) 879929
Fax (01793) 879489
Email sales@archersbrewery.co.uk
Website www.archersbrewery.co.uk

⊗ Archers reached its 26th anniversary in 2005 and has continued to consolidate its position as

one of the leading regional breweries in the south, with major investment in the plant. Distribution to the free trade is via depots at Swindon, Warrington and Cambridge; regional brewers, micros and pub companies are also supplied. Some 2,500 free trade outlets are supplied direct; no wholesalers are used.

Dark Mild (OG 1036, ABV 3.4%)
A dark beer with a well-balanced hop character, malty roast flavour and rich aftertaste.

Village (OG 1036, ABV 3.6%)
A dry, well-balanced beer with a full body for its gravity. Malty and fruity in the nose, then a fresh, hoppy flavour with balancing malt and a hoppy, fruity finish.

Best Bitter (OG 1040, ABV 4%)
Slightly sweeter and rounder than Village Bitter, with a malty, fruity aroma and pronounced bitter finish.

Special Bitter (OG 1044, ABV 4.3%)
Tawny in colour, full-flavoured and well-balanced.

Golden (OG 1046, ABV 4.7%)
A full-bodied, hoppy, straw-coloured brew with an underlying fruity sweetness. A gentle aroma, but a strong, distinctive bitter finish.

Swindon Strong Bitter/SSB
(OG 1052, ABV 5%)
A copper-coloured ale, rich and full-flavoured. Brewed with Fuggles and East Kent Goldings hops.

Arkell's IFBB SIBA

Arkell's Brewery Ltd, Kingsdown Brewery, Swindon, Wiltshire, SN2 7RU
Tel (01793) 823026
Fax (01793) 828864
Email arkells@arkells.com
Website www.arkells.co.uk
Tours by arrangement

Arkells Brewery is 163 years old and still run by the family. The brewery continues to expand its estate and now owns 103 pubs in Berkshire, Gloucestershire, Oxfordshire and Wiltshire. Seasonal beers: Summer Ale (ABV 4.2%), JRA (ABV 3.6%), Noel Ale (ABV 5.5%). Bees Organic Beer (ABV 4.5%) is suitable for vegetarians and vegans.

2B (OG 1032, ABV 3.2%)
Light brown in colour, malty but with a smack of hops and an astringent aftertaste. It has good body for its strength.

3B (OG 1040, ABV 4%)
A medium brown beer with a strong, sweetish malt/caramel flavour. The hops come through strongly in the aftertaste, which is lingering and dry.

Moonlight (ABV 4.5%)

Kingsdown Ale (OG 1051, ABV 5%)
A rich, deep russet-coloured beer, a stronger version of 3B. The malty/fruity aroma continues in the taste, which has a hint of pears. The hops come through in the aftertaste where they are complemented by caramel tones.

Arran SIBA

Arran Brewery Co Ltd, Cladach, Brodick, Isle of Arran, Strathclyde, KA27 8DE
Tel (01770) 302353
Fax (01770) 302653
Email info@arranbrewery.com
Website www.arranbrewery.com
Shop 10am-5pm Mon-Sat, 12.30-5pm Sun in summer, reduced hours in winter
Tours by prior arrangement

The brewery opened in 2000 with a 20-barrel plant. Production has increased to 200 barrels a week with increased bottling capability. 50 outlets are supplied. Seasonal beers: Sunset (ABV 4.4%, Feb/March), Fireside (ABV 4.7%, Oct/Nov-Feb/March).

Ale (OG 1038, ABV 3.8%)
An amber ale where the predominance of the hop produces a bitter beer with a subtle balancing sweetness of malt and an occasional hint of roast.

Dark (OG 1042, ABV 4.3%)
A well-balanced malty beer with plenty of roast and hop in the taste and a dry, bitter finish.

Blonde (OG 1048, ABV 5%)
A hoppy beer with substantial fruit balance. The taste is balanced and the finish increasingly bitter. An aromatic strong bitter that drinks below its weight.

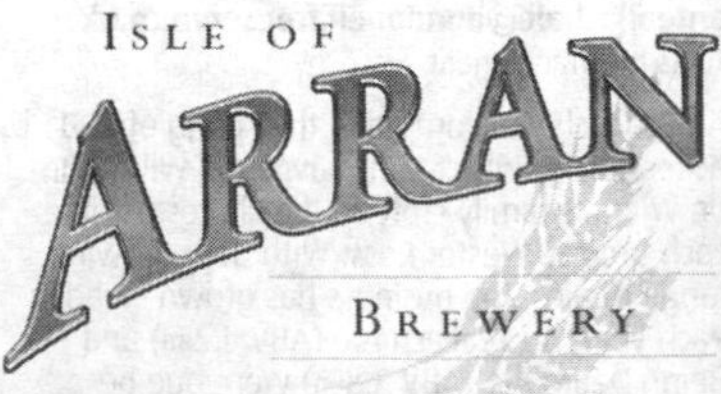

Arundel SIBA

Arundel Brewery Ltd, Unit C7, Ford Airfield Industrial Estate, Ford, Arundel, West Sussex, BN18 0HY
Tel (01903) 733111
Fax (01903) 733381
Email arundelbrewery@dsl.pipex.com
Shop No, but off-sales available

Mon-Fri 9-5pm at brewery
Tours Occasionally, by arrangement

⊗ Set up in 1992, the town's first brewery in 60 years, Arundel supplies around 70 outlets. Under new ownership since 2003, the brewery continues to improve its range of core brands and seasonal beers. A new steam boiler, copper and fermenter have been installed. Plans include doubling cold store space and obtaining a 20-barrel mash tun. Seasonal beers: Footslogger (ABV 4.4%, spring), Summer Daze (ABV 4.7%, summer), Black Beastie (ABV 4.9%, autumn), Old Knucker (ABV 5.5%, winter).

Gauntlet (OG 1035, ABV 3.5%)
A light, refreshing session beer. The blend of malt and hops produces an excellent initial flavour and a pleasant bitter finish.

Sussex Mild (OG 1037, ABV 3.7%)
A traditional dark and smooth mild.

Castle (OG 1038, ABV 3.8%) ◆
A pale tawny beer with fruit and malt noticeable in the aroma. The flavour has a good balance of malt, fruit and hops, with a dry, hoppy finish.

Gold (OG 1042, ABV 4.2%) ◆
A light golden ale with a malty, fruity flavour and a little hop in the finish.

ASB (OG 1045, ABV 4.5%)
A bitter beer with good hop and fruit aroma. A roast malt character gives way to a fruity, bitter-sweet finish.

Stronghold (OG 1047, ABV 4.7%)
A smooth, full-flavoured premium bitter. A good balance of malt, fruit and hops comes through in this rich brew.

Aston Manor

Aston Manor Brewery Co Ltd, 173 Thimble Mill Lane, Aston, Birmingham, West Midlands, B7 5HS
Tel (0121) 328 4336
Fax (0121) 328 0139
Email sales@astonmanor.co.uk
Website www.astonmanor.co.uk
Shop 10-6 Mon-Fri; 10-1 Sat

Aston Manor owns the Highgate Brewery in Walsall (qv). Its own plant concentrates on cider. Beer is bottled at Highgate but is not bottle-conditioned.

Atlantic*

Atlantic Brewery, Treisaac Farm, Treisaac, Newquay, Cornwall, TR8 4DX
Tel (01637) 880657/880326
Email stuart@atlanticbrewery.com
Website www.atlanticbrewery.com

Atlantic started brewing in 2005. Only bottle-conditioned beers are produced: Gold (4.6%), Red (ABV 5%), Blue (4.8%)

Atlas SIBA

Highlands and Islands Breweries, Lab Road, Kinlochleven, Argyll, PH50 4SG
Tel (01855) 831111
Fax (01855) 831122
Email info@atlasbrewery.com
Website www.atlasbrewery.com/www.hibreweries.com
Shop Open office hours
Tours by prior arrangement

⊗ Founded in 2002, Atlas is a 20-barrel brewery in a 100 year-old listed Victorian industrial building on the banks of the River Leven. It merged in 2004 with Orkney (qv) to form Highlands and Islands Breweries to improve distribution, but both sites remain in production. Atlas uses Scottish malts and local Highland water with whole hops from five different countries. Around 100 outlets are supplied. Seasonal beers: Equinox (ABV 4.5%, spring), Tempest (ABV 4.9%, autumn), Wayfarer (ABV 4.4%). Blizzard (ABV 4.7%, winter).

Latitude (OG 1036, ABV 3.6%) ◆
This golden ale has a light citrus taste with a hint of hops in the light, bitter finish.

Three Sisters (OG 1043, ABV 4.2%) ▯ ◆
A lightly malted beer with a short, hoppy, bitter finish.

Nimbus (ABV 5%) ◆
A well-balanced yellow/golden beer. Dry and fruity at the front, becoming slightly astringent with lasting fruit and a pleasant dry finish.

AVS

See Daleside

B&T SIBA EAB

B&T Brewery Ltd, The Brewery, Shefford, Bedfordshire, SG17 5DZ
Tel (01462) 815080
Fax (01462) 850841
Email brewery@banksandtaylor.com
Website www.banksandtaylor.com
Tours by arrangement

⊗ Banks & Taylor, founded in 1981, was restructured in 1994 under the name B&T Brewery. It produces an extensive range of beers, including monthly special brews together with contract brewing for wholesalers and individual public houses. Two pubs are owned. There is a wide range of seasonal beers (see website). Bottle-conditioned beers: Shefford Bitter, Goalden Hatter, Black Dragon Mild, Edwin Taylor Stout, Dragonslayer, SOS, SOD, Black Bat, Old Bat.

Two Brewers (OG 1036, ABV 3.6%)
Hoppy, amber-brown session beer.

Shefford Bitter (OG 1038, ABV 3.8%)
A pleasant, predominantly hoppy session beer with a bitter finish.

Shefford Dark Mild (OG 1038, ABV 3.8%) ◆
A dark beer with a well-balanced taste. Sweetish, roast malt aftertaste.

Goalden Hatter (OG 1040, ABV 4%)

Black Dragon Mild (OG 1043, ABV 4.3%)
Dark, rich in flavour, with a strong roast barley finish.

Dragonslayer (OG 1045, ABV 4.5%) ◆
A straw-coloured beer, dry, malty and lightly hopped.

Edwin Taylor's Extra Stout (OG 1045, ABV 4.5%)
A pleasant, bitter beer with a strong roast malt flavour.

Fruit Bat (OG 1045, ABV 4.5%)
Raspberry flavoured, hoppy fruit beer.

Shefford Pale Ale/SPA (OG 1045, ABV 4.5%)
A well-balanced beer with hop, fruit and malt flavours. Dry, bitter aftertaste.

SOS (OG 1050, ABV 5%)
A rich mixture of fruit, hops and malt is present in the taste and aftertaste of this beer. Predominantly hoppy aroma.

SOD (OG 1050, ABV 5%)
SOS with caramel added for colour, often sold under house names.

Black Bat (OG 1060, ABV 6%)
A powerful, sweet, fruity and malty beer for winter. Fruity, nutty aroma; strong roast malt aftertaste.

Old Bat (OG 1060, ABV 6%)
A powerful-tasting, sweet winter beer, with bitterness coming through in the aftertaste. Fruit is present in both aroma and taste.

Badger IFBB

Badger Brewery, Hall & Woodhouse Ltd, The Brewery, Blandford St Mary, Dorset, DT11 9LS
Tel (01258) 452141
Fax (01258) 459528
Email info@badgerbrewery.com
Website www.badgerales.com
Shop Mon-Sat For tours (ring 01258 452 231)
Tours by arrangement

⊗ The company was founded in 1777 as the Ansty Brewery by Charles Hall. Charles's son took George Woodhouse into partnership and formed Hall & Woodhouse. They moved to their present site at Blandford St Mary in 1899. Trading under the Badger name, it owns 260 pubs in the south of England. In 2000, Hall & Woodhouse bought King & Barnes of Horsham. The former Horsham company's 57 pubs now sell Badger beers, including Sussex Bitter, based on the K&B recipe. Hall & Woodhouse launched a visitor centre in 2002 and it is now a major attraction in Dorset. Seasonal beers: Festive Feasant (ABV 4.5%, winter), Fursty Ferret (ABV 4.4%, summer). The brewery is conducting trials of a new beer, First Gold (ABV 4.2%).

K&B Sussex (OG 1033, ABV 3.5%)
A thin, malty session beer, with little of its traditional hop bitterness. Mid-brown in colour with a moderate bitterness that lasts into a bitter, somewhat sharp finish. A beer that bears little resemblance to that brewed by the former King & Barnes Brewery.

Best (OG 1039, ABV 4%)
A fine best bitter whose taste is strong in hop and bitterness, with underlying malt and fruit. Hoppy finish with a bitter edge.

Tanglefoot (OG 1047, ABV 4.9%)
The beer was reformulated in 2004. The ABV has been dropped from 5.1% to 4.9%, crystal malt is now used, and the beer is dry hopped in cask with Goldings hops.

For Interbrew
Flowers IPA (OG 1035, ABV 3.6%)
Flowers Original Bitter (OG 1043, ABV 4.3%)

Ballard's SIBA

Ballard's Brewery Ltd, The Old Sawmill, Nyewood, Petersfield, Hants, GU31 5HA
Tel (01730) 821301/821362
Fax (01730) 821742
Email info@ballardsbrewery.org.uk
Website www.ballardsbrewery.org.uk
Shop 8-4 Mon-Fri
Tours by arrangement

⊗ Launched in 1980 by Carola Brown, one of the founders of SIBA, at Cumbers Farm, Trotton, Ballard's has been trading at Nyewood (in West Sussex, despite the postal address) since 1988 and now supplies around 60 free trade outlets. Seasonal beers: Golden Bine (ABV 4.2%, spring), Wheatsheaf (ABV 5%, summer), On the Hop (ABV 4.5%, autumn), Right Angler (ABV 9.5%, winter). Bottle-conditioned beers: Old Bounder series, plus Best Bitter, King's Table (ABV 4.2%), Nyewood Gold, Wassail and WMD (ABV 9.4%).

Midhurst Mild (OG 1035, ABV 3.5%)
Traditional dark mild, well-balanced, refreshing, with a biscuity flavour.

Trotton Bitter (OG 1036, ABV 3.6%)
Amber, clean-tasting bitter. A roast malt aroma leads to a fruity, slightly sweet taste and a dry finish.

Best Bitter (OG 1042, ABV 4.2%)
A copper-coloured beer with a malty aroma. A good balance of fruit and malt in the flavour gives way to a dry, hoppy aftertaste.

Wild (ABV 4.7%)
A blend of Mild and Wassail.

Nyewood Gold (OG 1050, ABV 5%)
Robust golden brown strong bitter, very hoppy and fruity throughout, with a tasty balanced finish.

Wassail (OG 1060, ABV 6%)
A strong, full-bodied, fruity beer with a predominance of malt throughout, but also an underlying hoppiness. Tawny/red in colour.

Bank Top SIBA

Bank Top Brewery Ltd, The Pavilion, Ashworth Lane, Bolton, Lancashire, BL1 8RA
Tel/Fax (01204) 595800
Email john@banktopbrewery.co.uk
Website www.banktopbrewery.co.uk
Shop Check website
Tours by arrangement

Bank Top was established in 1995 by John Feeney and has enjoyed gradual expansion. It relocated in 2002 and in 2004 John formed a partnership with David Sweeney. The beers are supplied to around 100 outlets locally and throughout the North-west and Yorkshire. Seasonal beer: Santa's Claws (ABV 5%, Christmas).

Bikes, Trikes and Beer (OG 1036, ABV 3.6%)

Brydge Bitter (OG 1038, ABV 3.8%)

Game, Set and Match (OG 1038, ABV 3.8%)

Dark Mild (OG 1040, ABV 4%)
Dark brown beer with a malt and roast aroma, rich mouthfeel and a complex taste, including roast malt and toffee. Roast, hops and bitterness in the finish.

Flat Cap (OG 1040, ABV 4%)
Amber ale with a modest fruit aroma leading to a beer with citrus fruit, malt and hops. Good finish of fruit, malt and bitterness.

Gold Digger (OG 1040, ABV 4%)
Golden coloured, with a citrus aroma, grapefruit and a touch of spiciness on the palate and a fresh, hoppy citrus finish.

Old Slapper (OG 1042, ABV 4.2%)

Samuel Crompton's Ale (OG 1042, ABV 4.2%)
Amber beer with a fresh citrus-peel aroma. Well-balanced with hops and a zesty grapefruit flavour, and a hoppy, citrus finish.

Volunteer Bitter (OG 1042, ABV 4.2%)
Brewed with American hops.

Orient Line (OG 1042, ABV 4.2%)

Pavilion Pale Ale (OG 1045, ABV 4.5%)

Port O Call (OG 1050, ABV 5%)

Smokestack Lightnin' (OG 1050, ABV 5%)

Banks's

See Wolverhampton & Dudley Breweries in New Nationals section

Barge & Barrel

See Eastwood

Barngates SIBA

Barngates Brewery Ltd, Barngates, Ambleside, Cumbria, LA22 0NG
Tel/Fax (015394) 36575
Email barngatesbrewery@drunkenduckinn.co.uk
Website www.drunkenduckinn.co.uk
Tours by prior arrangement

Barngates Brewery started brewing in 1997 as a one-barrel plant at the Drunken Duck inn. Expansion in 1999 saw a brand new five-barrel plant installed. Barngates supplies 60-70 outlets in Cumbria, 25 in Lancashire and 10 in North Yorkshire.

Cat Nap (OG 1037, ABV 3.6%)
A pale bitter with a strong hop aroma. Well-balanced bitterness leading to a long dry finish. A fruity, zesty character throughout.

Cracker Ale (OG 1038, ABV 3.9%)
Subtle hoppy aroma, clean, smooth and refreshing, developing into a long bitter finish.

Tag Lag (OG 1044, ABV 4.4%)
Light, golden bitter, citrus hints in the flavour with a slight dry finish.

Chester's Strong & Ugly (OG 1050, ABV 5.2%)
Slightly fruity, well-balanced roasted malt and hop flavours.

Barnsley

See Blackpool

Bartrams SIBA EAB

Bartrams Brewery, Rougham Estate, Rougham, Ipswich Road, Bury St Edmunds, Suffolk, IP30 9LZ
Tel (01449) 737655
Email netmarc@bartramsbrewery.co.uk
Shop Yes, with disabled access
Tours by arrangement

Marc Bartram moved his brewery to a new location on the same estate in 2004; it's signposted from the A14. There's a brewery shop where the full range of beer is available as well as beers from other members of the East Anglian Brewers Co-operative. Blackthorpe Bitter, Rougham Ready and Thurston Quencher are available for local distribution. As well as bottles, beer is available in carry-out containers, two pints to 18 gallons. Marld and Captain's Stout are suitable for vegetarians. Marc is seeking Soil Association accreditation for his organic beers. There was a Bartram's Brewery between 1894 and 1902 run by Captain Bill Bartram and a recreation of his image graces the pump clips. Beers are available in a selection of local pubs and there is a large amount of trade through local farmers' markets.

Marld (OG 1034, ABV 3.4%)
A traditional mild.

Rougham Ready (ABV 3.6%)

Blackthorpe Bitter (ABV 3.6%)

Premier Bitter (OG 1037, ABV 3.7%)

Little Green Man (ABV 3.8%)
Made with organic ingredients.

Red Queen (OG 1039, ABV 3.9%)

Pierrot (OG 1040, ABV 4%)

Green Man (ABV 4%)
An organic beer, using West Country floor-malted Maris Otter malt, New Zealand hops and coriander.

Cit'r'us, Lychee Limbo, Goosegog Grozet (ABV 4%)
Clear fruit beers using Green Man as a base beer.

Bees Knees (OG 1042, ABV 4.2%)

Jester Quick One (OG 1044, ABV 4.4%)
A darker than average best bitter that is more malty than hoppy, with hints of fruit in the aroma.

Stingo (ABV 4.5%)
A honey and coriander beer made using organic ingredients.

Coal Porter (ABV 4.5%)

Thurston Quencher (ABV 4.7%)

Captain's Stout (OG 1048, ABV 4.8%)
Overall champion at Cambridge Beer Festival 2002.

Captain Bill Bartrams Best Bitter (OG 1048, ABV 4.8%)

Damson/Cherry Stout (OG 1048, ABV 4.8%)

Beer Elsie Bub (ABV 4.8%)
A beer brewed for the local pagans.

Suffolk'n'Strong (ABV 5%)

Comrade Bill Bartrams Egalitarian Anti Imperialist Imperial Soviet Stout (ABV 6.4%)

Mother in Law's Tongue Tied (ABV 9%)
Originally brewed twice a year, the bulk goes in to bottle but is occasionally available at festivals and selected pubs.

Barum SIBA

Barum Brewery Ltd, c/o Reform Inn, Pilton, Barnstaple, Devon, EX31 1PD
Tel (01271) 329994
Fax (01271) 378338
Email info@barumbrewery.co.uk
Website www.barumbrewery.co.uk
Tours by arrangement

⊗ Barum started brewing in 1996 at the Reform Inn. Distribution is primarily within Devon. Seasonal beer: Gold (ABV 4%, summer), Barnstablaster (ABV 6.6%, winter). Bottle-conditioned beers: Original (ABV 4.4%), Breakfast (ABV 5.1%), Challenger (ABV 5.6%), Barnstablasta (ABV 6.6%).

XTC (OG 1039, ABV 3.9%)

Jester (OG 1042, ABV 4.2%)

Original (OG 1044, ABV 4.4%)

Breakfast (OG 1050, ABV 5%)

Firing Squad (ABV 5.3%)

Bateman IFBB SIBA

George Bateman & Son Ltd, Salem Bridge Brewery, Wainfleet All Saints, Lincolnshire, PE24 4JE
Tel (01754) 880317
Fax (01754) 880939
Email enquiries@bateman.co.uk
Website www.bateman.co.uk
Shop 11.30-3.30 daily
Tours by arrangement

⊗ Bateman's Brewery was established in 1874 and both the third and fourth generation of the original founder are involved with running the company. In 2000 Bateman's launched a visitor centre, which is open daily, and in 2002 a new brewhouse came on stream. The brewery owns 67 pubs, all huge cask beer establishments that sell other brewers' beers as well. Some 35 outlets are served. The seasonal beer range changes from year to year: see website. Special beers: Jesters IPA (ABV 3.5%), Hop Bine Bitter (ABV 3.6%), Summer Swallow (ABV 3.9%), Portugoal (ABV 4%), Spring Breeze (ABV 4.2%), Miss Luscious (ABV 4.3%), Combined Harvest (ABV 4.4%), Hooker (ABV 4.5%), Rosey Nosey (ABV 4.9%), Dark Lord Premium Beer (ABV 5%), Victory Ale (ABV 5.9%).

Dark Mild (OG 1032, ABV 3%)
Characteristic orchard fruit and roasted nut nose with hops evident. One of the classic mild ales, although the lasting bitter finish may not be entirely true to type; nevertheless, a ruby-black gem.

XB Bitter (OG 1037, ABV 3.7%)
A mid-brown balanced session bitter with malt most obvious in the finish. The taste is dominated by the house style apple hop, which also leads the aroma.

Salem Porter (OG 1048, ABV 4.7%)
Ruby black with a brown tint to the head. The aroma is liquorice with a subtle hint of dandelion and burdock; the initial taste is hoppy and bitter, with a mellowing of all the elements in the finish.

XXXB (OG 1048, ABV 4.8%)
A brilliant blend of malt, hops and fruit on the nose with a bitter bite over the top of a faintly banana maltiness that stays the course. A russet-tan brown classic.

Bath Ales SIBA

Bath Ales Ltd, Units 3-7, Caxton Industrial Estate, Tower Road North, Warmley,Bristol, BS30 8XN
Tel (0117) 947 4797
Fax (0117) 947 4790
Email hare@bathales.co.uk
Website www.bathales.com
Shop brewery hours 8-4
Tours by arrangement

⊗ Bath Ales started brewing in 1995, formed by two former Smiles brewers and a Hardington brewer. They began with rented equipment at the Henstridge Brewery near Wincanton, moved premises and upgraded to a full steam, 15-barrel plant in 1999. It now has a new, purpose-built site on the edge of east Bristol, with increased capacity of 50 barrels. Deliveries are direct to 260 outlets. Wholesalers are used in a limited way. Six pubs are owned, all serving cask ale. Seasonal beers: Festivity (ABV 5%), Spa Extra (ABV 5%). Bottle-conditioned beers: Gem Bitter (ABV 4.8%), Festivity.

SPA (OG 1037, ABV 3.7%)
Gold/yellow in colour, this is a light-bodied, dry, bitter beer with a citrus hop aroma. Long, pale, malty, bitter finish with some fruit and a slight sweetness.

Gem Bitter (OG 1041, ABV 4.1%)
Well-balanced and complex, this medium bodied bitter is malty (pale and crystal with a

tiny hint of chocolate), fruity and hoppy throughout. Amber-coloured, it is drier and more bitter at the end.

Barnstormer (OG 1047, ABV 4.5%)
Malt (roast and chocolate), hop and fruit aroma, with a similar taste. Mid-brown, well-balanced and smooth, with a complex malty and bitter, dry finish.

Batham IFBB

Daniel Batham & Son Ltd, Delph Brewery, Delph Road, Brierley Hill, West Midlands, DY5 2TN
Tel (01384) 77229
Fax (01384) 482292
Email info@bathams.com
Website www.bathams.com

A classic Black Country small brewery established in 1877. Tim and Matthew Batham represent the fifth generation to run the company. The Vine, one of the Black Country's most famous pubs, is also the site of the brewery. The company has 10 tied houses and supplies around 25 other outlets. Such is the demand for Batham's Bitter that the beer is delivered in 54-gallon hogsheads. Seasonal beer: XXX (ABV 6.3%, December).

Mild Ale (OG 1036.5, ABV 3.5%)
A fruity, dark brown mild with a malty sweetness and a roast malt finish.

Best Bitter (OG 1043.5, ABV 4.3%)
A pale yellow, fruity, sweetish bitter, with a dry, hoppy finish. A good, light, refreshing beer.

Bathtub*

Bathtub Brewery Co, Seven Stars Inn, Church Road, Stithians, Truro, Cornwall, TR3 7DH
Tel (01209) 860003

Bathtub is based in the backyard of the Seven Stars Inn and started brewing in 2004. It produces only one cask for the main bar each week from one of the beers listed below. The full range is supplied for the pub's two annual beer festivals in June and November, and CAMRA events at St Ives and Falmouth. There are plans to upgrade the plant to two barrels and supply other pubs.

Golden Ale (OG 1040, ABV 3.8%)

Tuckers Ale (OG 1044, ABV 4.2%)

Stithians Special (OG 1048, ABV 4.8%)

Pete's Porter (OG 1055, ABV 5.2%)

Battersea SIBA

Battersea Brewery Co Ltd, 43 Glycena Road, London, SW11 5TP
Tel/Fax (020) 7978 7978
Email enquiries@batterseabrewery.com
Website www.batterseabrewery.com
Tours by arrangement

The brewery was set up in Battersea in 2001 to produce hand-crafted specialist and historic beers using locally sourced English ingredients without additives. The beers are sold in London and SE England. Battersea Bitter, Powerstation Porter and Pagoda are available all year round and the brewery will produce limited availability and one-off beers for customers as requested. Powerstation Porter is available in bottle-conditioned form.

Pagoda (OG 1038, ABV 3.7%)

Bitter (OG 1040, ABV 4%)
A full-bodied, amber-coloured bitter with the hops balanced by a sweet malt character and soft fruit notes.

Power Station Porter (OG 1049, ABV 4.9%)
A traditional London porter.

Bazens' SIBA

Bazens' Brewery, The Rees Bazen Brewing Co Ltd, Unit 6, Knoll Street Industrial Park, Knoll Street, Salford, Greater Manchester, M7 2BL
Tel (0161) 708 0247
Fax (0161) 708 0248
Email bazensbrewery@mac.com
Website www.bazensbrewery.co.uk
Tours by arrangement for CAMRA groups

Bazens' Brewery is run by husband and wife team Richard and Jude Bazen. The brewery shares plant and premises with Facer's Brewery (qv), and together they form the Salford Brewery Syndicate. Flatbac gained the bronze medal in the 2004 SIBA awards. In 2004 the brewing plant increased in size and further expansion was scheduled for 2005. About 50 outlets are supplied. Seasonal beer: Knoll Street Porter (ABV 5.2%, winter). Bottle-conditioned beers: eXSB and Knoll Street Porter.

Black Pig Mild (OG 1037, ABV 3.6%)
A dark brown beer with malt and fruit aromas. Dark roast and chocolate flavours, with an underlying bitterness, lead to a dry, malty aftertaste.

Pacific Bitter (OG 1039, ABV 3.8%)
Gold-coloured bitter with a fruity nose. Hops and citrus fruit dominate the taste and there is a bitter, hoppy finish.

Flatbac (OG 1042, ABV 4.2%)

Zebra Best Bitter (OG 1043, ABV 4.3%)

Blue Bullet (OG 1045, ABV 4.5%)
Yellow in colour, this golden ale has a fruity aroma. Hops, fruit and bitterness are found in the taste and linger in the finish.

eXSB (OG 1055, ABV 5.5%)

Beartown SIBA

Beartown Brewery Ltd, Bromley House, Spindle Street, Congleton, CW12 1QN
Tel (01260) 299964
Fax (01260) 278895
Email sales@beartownbrewery.co.uk
Website www.beartownbrewery.co.uk
Tours by arrangement

Congleton's links with brewing can be traced back to 1272, when the town received charter status. Two of its most senior officers at the time were Ale Taster and Bear Warden, hence the name of the brewery. Both the brewery's Navigation in Stockport and the Beartown Tap have been named CAMRA regional pubs of the year. Plans are to extend the tied estate to 15 outlets over the next two years. Beartown supplies 50 outlets and owns nine pubs. Seasonal beers: Santa's Claws (ABV 4.5%, December), Blarney Bear (ABV 4.8%, March), St Georges Bear (ABV 4.2%, April). Most of the beer range is now available in bottle-conditioned form.

Ambeardextrous (OG 1038, ABV 3.8%)
Dark mild.

Bear Ass (OG 1040, ABV 4%)
Dark ruby-red, malty bitter with good hop nose and fruity flavour with dry, bitter, astringent aftertaste.

Ginger Bear (ABV 4%)
The flavours from the malt and hops blend with the added bite from the root ginger to produce a quenching finish.

Kodiak Gold (OG 1040, ABV 4%)
Well-balanced, straw-coloured beer with citrus fruit and hops aroma, and a sharp, bitter, clean, astringent aftertaste.

Bearskinful (OG 1043, ABV 4.2%)
A tawny, malty beer, with a clean hop finish.

Bearly Literate (OG 1045, ABV 4.5%)

Pandamonium (OG 1048, ABV 4.8%)

Polar Eclipse (OG 1048, ABV 4.8%)
A smooth and roasty dark stout, with light hoppy notes and dry, bitter finish.

Black Bear (OG 1050, ABV 5%)
Dark brown strong mild, some roast and malt flavours, with a mellow sweetish finish.

Bruins Ruin (OG 1050, ABV 5%)

Wheat Beer (OG 1050, ABV 5%)
A dry and bitter wheat beer. There is an initial fruitiness in aroma and taste with good wheat malt flavours. Long-lasting dry aftertaste.

Beckstones SIBA

Beckstones Brewery, Upper Beckstones Mill, The Green, Millom, Cumbria, LA18 5HL
Tel (01229) 775294
Email david.taylor@thelakes.org

Beckstones started brewing in 2003 on the site of an 18th-century mill with its own water supply. The beers are all malt brews.

Leat (OG 1038, ABV 3.6%)
A floral, fruity, thirst quencher.

Iron Town (OG 1040, ABV 3.8%)
A well-balanced, malt and hops session ale.

Border Steeans (OG 1042, ABV 4.1%)
Scottish Borders style, bitter-sweet with berry fruit undertones.

Hematite (OG 1058, ABV 5.5%)
Smooth with full malt throughout.

Beer Engine SIBA

Beer Engine Ltd, Newton St Cyres, Exeter, Devon, EX5 5AX
Tel (01392) 851282
Fax (01392) 851876
Email peterbrew@aol.com
Website www.thebeerengine.co.uk
Tours by arrangement

Beer Engine, run by Peter and Jill Hawksley, started brewing in 1983 next to the Barnstaple branch railway line. The brewery is visible behind glass downstairs. It uses the malts from Tuckers of Newton Abbot and English hops from Charles Faram of Newland. Some two-dozen other outlets are supplied regularly and the beers are also distributed via agencies. The Yuletide beer is Whistlemas (ABV varies) and occasional celebratory beers are produced.

Rail Ale (OG 1037, ABV 3.8%)
A straw-coloured beer with a fruity aroma and a sweet, fruity finish.

Piston Bitter (OG 1043, ABV 4.3%)
A mid-brown, sweet-tasting beer with a pleasant, bitter-sweet aftertaste.

Sleeper Heavy (OG 1052, ABV 5.4%)
A red-coloured beer with a fruity, sweet taste and a bitter finish.

For Agricultural Inn, Brampford Speke

Speke Easy (OG 1038, ABV 3.8%)

Belhaven

Belhaven Brewing Co Ltd, Spott Road, Dunbar, East Lothian, EH42 1RS
Tel (01368) 862734
Fax (01368) 869500
Email info@belhaven.co.uk
Website www.belhaven.co.uk
Shop open during tours
Tours by arrangement

Belhaven Brewery is located in Dunbar, some 30 miles east of Edinburgh on the East Lothian coast. The brewery claims to be the oldest independent brewery in Scotland and one of the oldest in Britain. Its history as a commercial brewery is well documented from 1719, although it's probable that a brewery existed there since at least the Middle Ages and is on the site of a former monastery where brewing took place. Belhaven owns 275 tied pubs and has about 2,500 direct accounts.

60/- Ale (OG 1030, ABV 2.9%)
A fine but virtually unavailable example of a Scottish light. This bitter-sweet, reddish-brown beer is dominated by fruit and malt with a hint of roast and caramel, and increasing bitterness in the aftertaste.

70/- Ale (OG 1038, ABV 3.5%) ◆
This pale brown beer has malt and fruit and some hop throughout, and is increasingly bitter-sweet in the aftertaste.

Sandy Hunter's Traditional Ale (OG 1038, ABV 3.6%) ◆
A distinctive, medium-bodied beer named after a past chairman and head brewer. An aroma of malt and hops greets the nose. A hint of roast combines with the malt and hops to give a bitter-sweet taste and finish.

80/- Ale (OG 1040, ABV 4.2%) ◆
One of the few remaining Scottish 80 Shillings, with malt the predominant flavour characteristic, though it is balanced by hop and fruit. Roast and caramel play a part in this complex beer. The soubriquet 'the claret of Scotland' hints at the depth and complexity of the flavours.

St Andrew's Ale (OG 1046, ABV 4.9%) ◆
A bitter-sweet beer with lots of body. The malt, fruit and roast mingle throughout with hints of hop and caramel.

For Maclay pub group (qv):

Signature (OG 1038, ABV 3.8%)
A pronounced malty note is followed by a digestive biscuit flavour. The beer has a late addition of Styrian and Goldings hops.

Kane's Amber Ale (ABV 4%)
A hoppy aroma gives way to a malty, yet slightly bitter flavour.

Wallace IPA (ABV 4.5%)
A classic IPA in both colour and style, with a long, dry finish.

Golden Scotch Ale (ABV 5%)
Brewed to an original Maclay's recipe, the emphasis is firmly on malt.

For Edinburgh Brewing Company (qv):

Edinburgh Pale Ale (ABV 3.4%)

Bells*

Bells Brewery & Merchants, Unit E3, Elms Farm Park, Ullesthorpe Road, Bitteswell, Leicestershire, LE17 4SD
Tel (01455) 558559
Email sales@bellsbrewery.co.uk
Website www.bellsbrewery.co.uk

Bells opened in 2004 and is run by former Man in the Moon Brewery owner Jon Hutchinson. Twenty outlets are supplied. Occasional seasonal beers are brewed.

Cosbys (OG 1037, ABV 3.7%)

Rainmaker (OG 1041, ABV 4.1%)

Dreamcatcher (OG 1046, ABV 4.7%)

Belvoir SIBA

Belvoir Brewery Ltd, 6B Woodhill Industries, Nottingham Lane, Old Dalby, Leicestershire, LE14 3LX
Tel/Fax (01664) 823455
Email sales@Belvoir-brewery.go-plus.net
Website www.belvoirbrewery.co.uk
Tours occasionally by arrangement

⊗ Belvoir (pronounced 'beaver') Brewery was set up in 1995 by Colin Brown, who previously brewed with Shipstone and Theakston. Long-term expansion has seen the introduction of a 20-barrel plant that can produce 50 barrels a week. Bottle-conditioned beers are now being produced using in-house bottling equipment. Up to 150 outlets are supplied. Seasonal beers: Whippling Golden Bitter (ABV 3.6%, spring/summer), Peacock's Glory (ABV 4.7%, spring/summer), Old Dalby (ABV 5.1%, winter). Bottle-conditioned beers: Star, Beaver Bitter, Peacock's Glory, Old Dalby.

Star Mild (OG 1034, ABV 3.4%) ◆
Reddish/black in colour, this full-bodied and well-balanced mild is at the same time both malty and hoppy with hints of fruitiness leading to a long, bitter-sweet finish.

Star Bitter (OG 1039, ABV 3.9%) ◆
Reminiscent of the long-extinct Shipstone's Bitter, this mid-brown bitter lives up to its name as it is indeed bitter in taste but not unpleasantly so.

Beaver Bitter (OG 1043, ABV 4.3%) ◆
A light brown bitter that starts malty in both aroma and taste, but soon develops a hoppy bitterness. Appreciably fruity.

Beowulf SIBA

Beowulf Brewing Co, Chasewater Country Park, Pool Road, Brownhills, Staffordshire, WS8 7NL
Tel/Fax (01543) 454067
Email beowulfbrewing@yahoo.co.uk
Tours Small tours by arrangement

After six successful years producing Birmingham's only cask beer in a converted shop, Beowulf moved to new premises in 2003. The beers appear as guest ales in the central region and across the country. Seasonal beers: autumn and winter – Hurricane (ABV 4%), Glutlusty (ABV 4.5%), Finn's Hall Porter (ABV 4.7%), Blizzard (ABV 5%), Grendal's Winter Ale (ABV 5.8%); spring and summer – Wergild (ABV 4.3%), Fifty Winters (ABV 4.4%), Wuffa (ABV 4.5%), Gold Work (ABV 5.1%). Bottling is imminent.

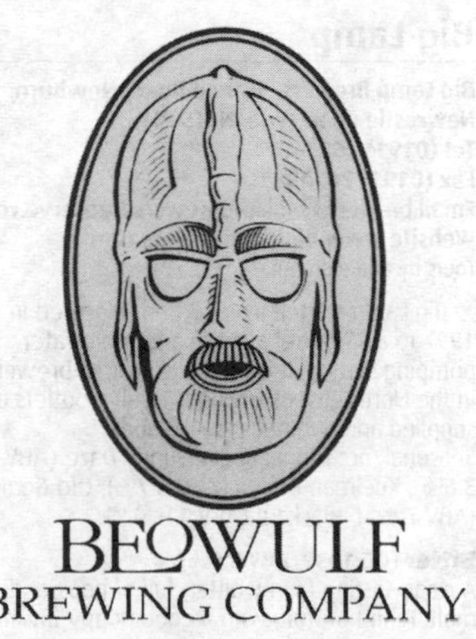

Beorma (OG 1038, ABV 3.9%)
A pale session ale with a malty hint of fruit giving way to a lingering bitterness.

Noble Bitter (OG 1039, ABV 4%)
Gold colour, fruity aroma, hoppy taste with a dry finish.

Wiglaf (OG 1043, ABV 4.3%)
A golden bitter, with a malty flavour married to a pleasing bitterness, with three hop varieties used.

Chasewater Bitter (OG 1043, ABV 4.4%)

Swordsman (OG 1045, ABV 4.5%)
Pale gold, light fruity aroma, tangy hoppy flavour. Faintly hoppy finish.

Dragon Smoke Stout (OG 1048, ABV 4.7%)

Heroes Bitter (OG 1046, ABV 4.7%)
Gold colour, malt aroma, hoppy taste but sweetish finish.

Mercian Shine (OG 1048, ABV 5%)
Pale gold colour, citrus flavour with a full body and hoppy, dry finish.

Berrow SIBA

Berrow Brewery, Coast Road, Berrow, Burnham-on-Sea, Somerset, TA8 2QU
Tel (01278) 751345
Off licence 9-9. Tours by arrangement, limited numbers

The brewery started brewing in 1982 and achieved success with the introduction of Topsy Turvy. Berrow Porter has also made its mark and is produced all year round. Berrow supplies 12 outlets. Seasonal beers: Christmas Ale (ABV 5%, winter), Carnivale (ABV 4.6%, Nov-Dec).

Best Bitter/4Bs (OG 1038, ABV 3.9%)
A pleasant, pale brown session beer, with a fruity aroma, a malty, fruity flavour and bitterness in the palate and finish.

Porter (OG 1047, ABV 4.7%)

Topsy Turvy (OG 1055, ABV 6%)
A gold-coloured beer with an aroma of malt and hops. Well-balanced malt and hops taste is followed by a hoppy, bitter finish with some fruit notes.

Big Lamp

Big Lamp Brewers, Grange Road, Newburn, Newcastle upon Tyne, NE15 8NL
Tel (0191) 2671689
Fax (0191) 2677387
Email brewers@biglampbrewers.freeserve.co.uk
Website www.biglampbrewers.com
Tours by arrangement

Big Lamp started in 1982 and relocated in 1997 to a 55-barrel plant in a former water pumping station. It is the oldest micro-brewery in the North-east of England. Twelve outlets are supplied and two pubs are owned.
Seasonal/occasional beers: Sunny Daze (ABV 3.6%), Keelman Brown (ABV 5.7%), Old Genie (ABV 7.4%), Blackout (ABV 11%).

Bitter (OG 1039, ABV 3.9%)
A clean-tasting tawny bitter, full of hops and malt. A hint of fruit, with a good hoppy finish.

Double M (OG 1043, ABV 4.3%)

Summerhill Stout (OG 1044, ABV 4.4%)
A rich, tasty stout, dark in colour with a lasting rich roast character. Malty mouthfeel with a lingering finish.

Prince Bishop Ale (OG 1048, ABV 4.8%)
A refreshing, easy-drinking bitter, golden in colour, full of fruit and hops. Strong bitterness with a spicy, dry finish.

Premium (OG 1052, ABV 5.2%)
A well-balanced, flavoursome bitter with a big nose full of hops. The sweetness lasts into a mellow, dry finish.

Embers (OG 1055, ABV 5.5%)

Blackout (OG 1100, ABV 11%)
A strong bitter, fortified with roast malt character and rich maltiness. Try it for its mouthfeel and lasting bitterness.

Bird in Hand

See Wheal Ale Brewery

Bitter End

Bitter End Pub & Brewery, 15 Kirkgate, Cockermouth, Cumbria, CA13 9PJ
Tel/Fax (01900) 828993
Email info@bitterend.co.uk
Website www.bitterend.co.uk
Tours by arrangement

The brewery opened in the back room of the Bitter End pub in 1995, using a one-barrel plant with former whisky casks as fermenters. The equipment was replaced in 2004 with a copper clad system imported from the US. There are plans to increase the range of cask beers to five. Beer is available only at the pub.

Cockermouth Pride (OG 1038, ABV 3.8%)

Farmers Ale (ABV 3.8%)
A pale brown, slightly thin, malty, bitter, fruity and sweet beer with a slight astringency in the finish.

Wheat Beer (ABV 4.1%)

Call Out (ABV 4.2%)
Brewed to raise funds for Cockermouth Rescue Team.

Czechumberland (ABV 4.5%)

Cuddy Lugs (ABV 4.7%)
A malty aroma and sweet start quickly lead to lingering bitter flavours.

Full English (ABV 5%)

Wordsworth 6X (ABV 5%)

Skinner's Old Strong (ABV 5.5%)

Black Bull

See Redburn

Black Country

Black Country Ales, Old Bulls Head, 1 Redhall Road, Lower Gornal, Dudley,

West Midlands, DY3 2NU
Tel (01384) 231616
Fax (01384) 237513
Email info@blackcountryales.co.uk
Tours by arrangement except Sundays

The brewery was set up in late 2004 by director Angus McMeeking and brewer Guy Perry. Guy was formally the brewer at nearby Sarah Hughes (qv). The brewery is situated in part of the pub's original tower brewery, dating from 1834, which produced its last brew in 1934. The plant is new, but it is hoped to refurbish the already existing oak vessels that were installed in 1900 and bring them into production to increase capacity. Production averages 10 barrels a week. One-off beers will be produced for distributors in the near future.

Bradley's Finest Golden (ABV 4.2%)

Pig on the Wall (ABV 4.3%)

Fireside (ABV 5%)

Black Isle SIBA

Black Isle Brewing Ltd, Old Allangrange, Munlochy, Ross-shire, IV8 8NZ
Tel (01463) 811871
Fax (01463) 811875
Email greatbeers@blackislebrewery.com
Website www.blackislebrewery.com
Shop 10-6 daily, closed Sundays in winter
Tours by prior arrangement

⊗ Black Isle Brewery was set up in 1998 in the heart of the Scottish Highlands. The five-barrel plant is based in converted farm buildings on the Black Isle. The company concentrates on organic production: the beers have Soil Association certification, while the bottle-conditioned beers are certified by both the SA and the Vegetarian Society. Bottled beers are available by mail order to anywhere in mainland Britain. 20 outlets are supplied. Bottle-conditioned beers (all suitable for vegetarians and vegans): Wheat Beer (ABV 4.5%), Scotch Ale (ABV 4.5%), Porter (ABV 4.5%) ◼, Blonde (ABV 4.5%).

Yellowhammer (OG 1042, ABV 4%) ◆
A delicious, fruity, hoppy summer ale bursting with citrus fruit and hops, and with caramel on the nose. A hoppy taste with some bitterness but sweetness predominates.

Red Kite (OG 1041, ABV 4.2%) ◆
Light malt and some hop on the nose and with summer fruits on the palate. Not as sweet as it once was, with a more lasting bitterness.

Hibernator (ABV 4.5%)

Wagtail Porter (ABV 4.5%)

Black Sheep SIBA

Black Sheep Brewery plc, Wellgarth, Masham, Ripon, North Yorkshire, HG4 4EN
Tel (01765) 689227 (brewery)
680100 (visitor centre)
Fax (01765) 689746
Email visitor.centre@blacksheep.co.uk
Website www.blacksheep.co.uk
Shop variable hours. Ring to check.
Tours by arrangement

⊛ Black Sheep was set up in 1992 by Paul Theakston, a member of Masham's famous brewing family, in the former Wellgarth Maltings. The company has enjoyed continued growth and now supplies a free trade of around 600 outlets in the Yorkshire Dales and in an 80-mile radius of Masham, but owns no pubs. A limited number of wholesalers are also supplied. All the output is fermented in two-storey Yorkshire square vessels; there are three slate ones and 10 stainless steel Yorkshire 'round' squares. The Black Sheep complex includes video shows of the brewing process, a brewery shop and a bistro. The second brewhouse was installed in 2004. Further developments were planned for 2005, which should increase capacity to around 75,000 barrels a year. The visitor centre offers brewery tours and incorporates a shop and bistro. Opening times vary according to season. Some 600 outlets are supplied direct.

Best Bitter (OG 1039, ABV 3.8%) ◻ ◆
A hoppy and fruity beer with strong bitter overtones, leading to a long, dry, bitter finish.

Special Ale (OG 1046, ABV 4.4%) ◆
A well-rounded and warming bitter beer with a good helping of hops and fruit in the taste and aroma, leading to a moderately dry, bitter aftertaste.

Emmerdale Ale (OG 1051, ABV 5%)
Brewed with pale malt, Goldings hops and Demerara sugar, it has a blood-orange fruitiness, juicy malt and a hint of rum in the finish.

Riggwelter (OG 1056, ABV 5.9%) ◆
A fruity bitter, with complex underlying tastes and hints of liquorice and pear drops leading to a long, dry, bitter finish.

Blackawton SIBA

Blackawton Brewery, Unit 7, Peninsula Park, Channon Road, Saltash, Cornwall, PL12 6LX
Tel (01752) 848777
Fax (01752) 848999
Email info@blackawtonbrewery.com
Website www.blackawtonbrewery.com
Tours by arrangement

⊗ Once Devon's oldest operating brewery, Blackawton relocated to Cornwall in 2000.

Ownership changed in 2004 but the brewery continues to operate from the same premises. New beers were planned for 2005 and Blackawton still produces a house beer for Wetherspoon's Isaac Merritt in Paignton. Some 50 outlets are supplied. Seasonal beers: Winter Fuel (ABV 5%). Bottle-conditioned beers: Headstrong, Winter Fuel.

Original Bitter (OG 1036, ABV 3.8%)

Westcountry Gold (OG 1038, ABV 4.1%)

44 Special (OG 1044, ABV 4.5%)

Exhibition Ale (OG 1046, ABV 4.7%)

Headstrong (OG 1048, ABV 5.2%)

For Wetherspoon

Frothblower (ABV 4.6%)

Blackdown

Blackdown Brewery Ltd, Unit C6, Dunkeswell Business Park, Dunkeswell, nr Honiton, Devon, EX14 4LE
Tel (01404) 891122
Fax (01404) 890097
Tours by arrangement for a maximum of 20

⊗ The brewery was established in 2002. It is a family-run business and covers Devon, Dorset and Somerset. Some 160 outlets are supplied and three regular beers are produced. Seasonal beer: Dark Side (ABV 5%, Christmas).

Devon's Pride (OG 1038, ABV 3.8%)

Gold Pale Ale (OG 1043, ABV 4.3%)

Premium (OG 1047, ABV 4.7%)

Blackpool

Blackpool Brewery Co Ltd, The Old Dairy, George Street, Blackpool, FY1 3SE
Tel (01253) 304999
Fax (01253) 304868

☺ The 20-barrel plant produces up to 80 barrels a week. The brewery supplies pubs as far away as London. It also produces beers for the now defunct Barnsley Brewery. Some 200 outlets are supplied. Seasonal beers: Golden Smile (ABV 3.7%), Bitter (ABV 4%), Crackle Porter (ABV 5%), Christmas Lights (ABV 4.3%).

Golden Smile
(OG 1036.5, ABV 3.7%) ◆
Pale-brown coloured beer with a hoppy aroma and a well-balanced flavour with the hop character staying right through to the finish, which is dry and slightly astringent.

Bitter (OG 1039, ABV 4%)
A golden beer with great depth of flavour.

BPA (OG 1041, ABV 4.2%) ◆
Amber-coloured best bitter with a flowery hop aroma. Clean and refreshing, hoppy taste with a dry, hoppy finish.

For Barnsley Brewery

IPA (OG 1041, ABV 4.2%)

Black Heart Stout (OG 1044, ABV 4.6%)

Ay Up It's Christmas (OG 1048, ABV 4.8%)

Blanchfields SIBA

Blanchfields Brewing Co, 3 Fleet Hall Road, Rochford, Essex SS4 1NF
Tel (01702) 530053
Fax (01702) 543999
Email richlunn@btinternet.com
Website www.blanchfields-brewery.com
Tours by arrangement

⊗ Blanchfields moved from north Norfolk to Essex in 2004. A new beer was added during the year and a total of 12 beers were due in 2005. 30 outlets are supplied. Seasonal beers: Killer Bull (ABV 6%, Jan-Feb), Spring Bull (ABV 4.2%, March), Jester Bull (ABV 4.4%, April), Black Bull Mild (ABV 3.6%, May-June), 9 Bull (ABV 4.9%, September), Black Witch (ABV 4.6%, October limited stock), Fire Bull Night (ABV 3.9%, November), Santa's Red Nose Bull (ABV 6%, December).

Black Bull Mild (OG 1040, ABV 3.6%) ◆
Light malty airs introduce this red-coloured, traditional mild. A dry fruity maltiness gives a hint of cocoa. The finish fades quickly although roasted malt remains.

Golden Bull (OG 1045, ABV 4.2%)

White Bull (OG 1044, ABV 4.4%)

Raging Bull Bitter (OG 1048, ABV 4.9%) ◆
Fruity strong ale with a perfumed aroma and a reasonably bitter finish.

Blencowe SIBA

♀ Blencowe Brewing Co, c/o Exeter Arms, Barrowden, Rutland, LE15 8EQ
Tel (01572) 747247
Email info@exeterarms.com
Website www.exeterarms.com
Tours by arrangement

⊗ The brewery was set up in 1998 in a barn behind the pub. The two-barrel plant was bought with the intention of supplying traditional beers for sale in the Exeter Arms bar and festivals only. An expansion programme in 2001 added one extra fermenting vessel but demand still outstrips production. The cask beers are also available in bottle-conditioned form.

Farmers Boy (OG 1036, ABV 3.6%)
A wheat beer.

Beach Boys (OG 1040, ABV 3.8%)
Fruit on the aroma; hoppy taste with a bitter finish.

Young Boy (OG 1042, ABV 4.1%)

Danny Boys (OG 1046, ABV 4.5%)
A rich, dark and creamy stout.

Golden Boy (ABV 5%)

Blindmans SIBA

Blindmans Brewery Ltd, Talbot Farm, Leighton, Frome, Somerset, BA11 4PN
Tel (01749) 880038
Fax (01749) 880379
Email info@blindmansbrewery.co.uk
Website www.blindmansbrewery.co.uk
Tours by arrangement

Blindmans brewery is a five-barrel plant based between Frome and Shepton Mallet in a converted milking parlour. The brewery has its own exclusive water spring and uses only locally-sourced ingredients. Following a change of ownership in 2004, Blindmans is undertaking a period of investment and expansion. Approximately 50 outlets are supplied. Seasonal beers: Conquest (ABV 3.8%, spring/summer/autumn), Eclipse (ABV 4.2%, autumn/winter), Siberia (ABV 4.7%, winter).

Golden Spring (OG 1040, ABV 4%)
A golden brew with a light, flowery aroma.

Mine Beer (OG 1042, ABV 4.2%)
A copper-coloured ale with full body, leading to a long finish. Fresh hoppy aroma.

Icarus (OG 1045, ABV 4.5%)

Blue Anchor SIBA

Blue Anchor Inn, 50 Coinagehall Street, Helston, Cornwall, TR13 8EL
Tel (01326) 562821
Fax (01326) 565765
Email theblueanchor@btconnect.com
Tours normally by arrangement

⊗ Dating back to the 15th century, this is the oldest brewery in Cornwall and was originally a monks' hospice. After the dissolution of the monasteries it became a tavern brewing its own uniquely flavoured beer called Spingo at the rear of the premises. Brewing has continued to this day and people travel from all over the world to sample the delights of this wonderful inn untouched by time. The brewery has undergone complete refurbishment and the pub is also due for improvement, with careful attention to preserving its special character. Five outlets are supplied. Seasonal beers: Spingo Bragget (ABV 6.1%, April-Oct), Spingo Easter Special (ABV 7.6%, two months), Spingo Christmas Special (ABV 7.6%, Dec-mid Jan). All draught beers are available in bottle-conditioned form. Bragget is a recreation of a medieval beer style.

Spingo Jubilee (IPA) (OG 1045, ABV 4.6%)

Spingo Middle (OG 1050, ABV 5.1%)
A deep copper-red beer with a big fruity aroma of raisins and sultanas, a hint of vanilla and an earthy, peppery note from the hops. The palate is nutty, with a fruit cake note. The long bitter-sweet finish has a raspberry-like fruitiness balanced by the dryness of the hops.

Spingo Special (OG 1066, ABV 6.7%)
Darker than Middle with a pronounced earthy character on the nose balanced by rich fruit. Fruit and peppery hops dominate the mouth, followed by a big finish in which malt, fruit and hops vie for attention.

Blue Bell

Blue Bell Brewery, Cranesgate South, Whaplode St Catherine, Lincolnshire, PE12 6SN
Tel/Fax (01406) 701000
Email enquiries@bluebellbrewery.co.uk
Website www.bluebellbrewery.co.uk
Tours by arrangement

⊗ Alan Bell, the owner of Blue Bell since 2004, has added two new beers, Mild and Olympic Gold. Olympic Gold was originally brewed for the Peterborough Beer Festival but has now become a permanent beer renamed Old Gold. Alan hopes to begin production of bottle-conditioned beers during 2006. Some 40 outlets are supplied. Seasonal beer: Mild (ABV 3.6%).

Moulton Mill Ale (OG 1037, ABV 3.7%)

Old Honesty (OG 1040, ABV 4.1%)

Old Gold (OG 1045, ABV 4.5%)

Old Fashioned (OG 1045, ABV 4.8%)

Old Comfort (OG 1050, ABV 5%)

Blue Cow

Blue Cow Inn and Brewery, 29 High street, South Witham, Grantham, Lincolnshire, NG33 5QB
Tel/Fax (01572) 768432
Email richard@thirlwell.fslife.co.uk
Website www.thebluecowinn.co.uk
Tours by arrangement

◎ Blue Cow started brewing in 1997 and only supplies the pub.

Thirlwell's Best (OG 1039, ABV 3.8%)

Thirlwell's Witham Wobbler (OG 1045, ABV 4.5%)

Blue Moon

Blue Moon Brewery, Cock Inn, Watton Road, Barford, Norfolk, NR9 4AS
Tel (01603) 757646

⊗ Pete Turner supplies the Cock and some 60 free trade outlets. A separate brewery, Spectrum (qv), run by Andy Mitchell, is now using the original Blue Moon kit.

Easy Life (OG 1040, ABV 3.8%)
A pale brown, easy-drinking session beer. A gentle toffee and malt aroma introduces a defined malty beginning. A soft fruity hoppiness supports the delicate balance of flavours to a swift but clean finish.

Sea of Tranquillity (OG 1042, ABV 4.2%)

A solid malty taste matches the nose of this mid-brown, complex bitter. A bitter-sweet hoppiness develops to soften the malt that lasts to the long, rounded finish.

Moon Dance (ABV 4.7%)
A rich elderberry aroma is matched by a solid fruity taste in which the nutty malt flavours are slightly topped by well-defined hoppy overtones.

Dark Side (OG 1048, ABV 4.8%)
Slightly scented, with fruit, hops and malt, this dark brown strong mild has plenty of body. A caramel sweetness gives balance to the dominant malty foundation. A long finish maintains the rich blend of flavours.

Hingham High (OG 1050, ABV 5.2%)
A malt-based beer with a good balance of hops and bitterness. Roast notes provide background flavour as the finish lingers to a dry richness befitting the red-brown colour.

Milk of Amnesia (OG 1055, ABV 5.2%)
A complex beer, mid-brown in colour but the light malty nose gives little away. The taste has a port-like note; cinnamon and ginger jostle with pepper and citrus as the flavours continue to hold up well.

Liquor Mortis (OG 1075, ABV 7.5%)
A heavy blackcurrant signature introduces this dark brown barley wine. A mature roast beginning counter-balances the fruity sweetness that carries through to a long, filling finish with more than a hint of hops.

Total Eclipse (ABV 9%)

Blythe

Blythe Brewery, Blythe House Farm, Lichfield Road, Hamstall Ridware, Rugeley, Staffordshire, WS15 3QQ
Tel (07773) 747724
Email info@blythebrewery.plus.com
Tours by arrangement

Robert Greenway started brewing in 2003 using a 2.5-barrel plant in a converted barn on a farm. As well as specials, seasonal beers are produced on a quarterly basis. Fifteen outlets are supplied. Seasonal beers: Old Horny (ABV 4.6%, Sept-Nov), Johnson's Ale (ABV 4.4%, June-Aug). Bottle-conditioned beers: as for cask beers listed below.

Bitter (OG 1040, ABV 4%)
Amber colour; caramel aroma with a touch of fruit and hops. Hoppy, fruity taste with a refreshing bitter finish.

Chase Bitter (OG 1044, ABV 4.4%)
Copper to tawny coloured, with a fruit and hop start with caramel sweetness developing; lingering bitterness with a sweet edge.

Palmer's Poison (OG 1045, ABV 4.5%)
Malt and caramel are the first characteristics of this mid-brown beer. Liquorice roast develops; hoppy throughout with a long, bitter finish.

Bob's*

Bob's Brewing Co Ltd, 25 Twitch Hill, Horbury, Wakefield, West Yorkshire, WF4 6NA
Tel (07789) 693597

Formerly Red Lion Ales, located at the rear of the Red Lion Inn in nearby Ossett. A new 15-barrel plant was installed in 2005. Ten outlets are supplied.

White Lion (OG 1043, ABV 4.3%)

Yakima Pale Ale (OG 1045, ABV 4.5%)

Chardonnayle (OG 1051, ABV 5.1%)

Boggart Hole Clough

Boggart Hole Clough Brewing Co, Unit 13, Brookside Works, Clough Road, Moston, Manchester, M9 4SP
Tel/Fax (0161) 277 9666
Email boggart@btconnect.com
Website www.boggart-brewery.co.uk
Tours by arrangement

The brewery was set up in 2001 by Mark Dade, former brewer at Marble (qv), next to Boggart Hole Clough Park in north Manchester. The park supplies timber from which the brewery's distinctive wooden pump clips are fashioned. Mark has increased the brew length to eight barrels. He has also set up the Workshop Brewery that enables visitors to design and produce beers to their own specifications on a dedicated 2.5-barrel plant. Boggart Distribution was launched in 2003 and this allows the beers to be sold to more than 250 free houses throughout the country. Monthly specials are produced. Bottle-conditioned beer: Steaming Boggart.

Bitter (OG 1038, ABV 3.8%)
An easy-drinking, light-coloured session beer with a unique hoppy, bitter aftertaste.

Light Mild (OG 1038, ABV 3.8%)
A classic light mild with a bitter edge.

Dark Mild (ABV 4%)

Standard Pioneer (ABV 4%)

Angel Hill (OG 1042, ABV 4.2%)
A premium, golden pale ale with an aromatic explosion of flavour.

Brew (OG 1043, ABV 4.3%)
A highly quaffable ruby red beer.

Dark Side (OG 1044, ABV 4.4%)
A classic porter with a smooth roast finish and subtle hop aftertaste.

Sun Dial (OG 1047, ABV 4.7%)
A pale beer with a refreshing, fruity hop taste and aroma.

Steaming Boggart (ABV 9%)

Borough Arms*

Borough Arms, 33 Earle Street, Crewe, Cheshire, CW1 2BG
Tel (01270) 254999

A new two-barrel brewery opened in March 2005 at the Borough Arms pub. The beer range was still being formulated as the Guide went to press.

Bowland SIBA

Bowland Beer Co Ltd, Bashall Barn, Twitter Lane, Bashall Town, nr Clitheroe, Lancashire, BB7 3LQ

Tel (07952) 639465
Fax (01200) 428825
Email richard@bowlandbeer.fsnet.co.uk
Website www.bowlandbrewery.com
Tours by arrangement

Bowland originally started brewing in 2003 and moved to Bashall Town in 2004 with a five-barrel plant that originally came from the Fuzz and Firkin in Southsea. Bottling and a visitor centre were planned for 2005. At least one new beer is brewed each month. 50 outlets are supplied.

Sawley Tempted **(OG 1038, ABV 3.7%)**
A copper-coloured beer with fruit and toffee flavours. American Mount Hood hops are used.

Hunters Moon **(OG 1039, ABV 3.7%)**
A dark mild with chocolate, coffee and biscuit flavours.

Golden Trough **(OG 1039, ABV 3.8%)**
A light session beer.

Gold **(OG 1039, ABV 3.8%)**
A pale session beer with intense citrus flavour and hoppy finish.

Centurion **(OG 1040, ABV 3.9%)**
Amber session bitter with a nutty finish.

Hen Harrier **(OG 1040, ABV 4%)**
Pale ale with citrus and peach tones.

Dragon **(OG 1043, ABV 4.2%)**
Slightly sweeter golden bitter that uses five hop varieties.

Box Steam*

Box Steam Brewery, Unit 2, Oaks Farm, Rode Hill, Colerne, Chippenham, Wiltshire, SN14 8AR
Tel (01225) 743622
Email marshallewart@ukonline.co.uk
Website www.boxsteambrewery.com
Tours by arrangement

The brewery was launched in 2004 on a farm between Bath and Box in Wiltshire. The copper is fired by a steam boiler. One pub is owned and 15 outlets are supplied. Seasonal beers: Rev Awdry (ABV 3.8%, spring and summer), Figgy Pudding (ABV 5%, winter only).

Tunnel Vision **(OG 1041, ABV 4.2%)**

Blind House **(OG 1048, ABV 4.6%)**

Bradfield*

Bradfield Brewery, Watt House Farm, High Bradfield, Sheffield, South Yorkshire, S6 6LG
Tel/Fax (0114) 2851 118
Email info@bradfieldbrewery.com
Website www.bradfieldbrewery.com

⊛ The brewery is based on a busy working farm in the Peak District in a picturesque village. Pure Peak District water from a bore hole on the farm is used in the brewing process.

Farmers Bitter **(OG 1039, ABV 3.9%)**

Farmers Stout **(OG 1045, ABV 4.5%)**

Farmers Pale Ale **(OG 1049, ABV 5%)**

Brains IFBB

S A Brain & Co Ltd, The Cardiff Brewery, PO Box 53, Crawshay Street, Cardiff, CF10 1SP
Tel (029) 2040 2060
Fax (029) 2040 3324
Email brains@sabrains.com
Website www.sabrain.com

⊛ S A Brain began trading at the Old Brewery in Cardiff in 1882 when Samuel Arthur Brain and his uncle Joseph Benjamin Brain purchased a site founded in 1713. The company has remained in family ownership ever since and in 1997 bought South Wales' other leading independent, Crown Buckley, formed from the merger of the Crown Brewery of Pontyclun with Buckleys of Llanelli. The full range of Brains Ales is now produced at the company's Cardiff Brewery (formerly Hancock's), bought from Bass in 1999. The company owns 230 pubs, has a sizeable free trade and a wholesale estate of more than 3,000 accounts since acquisitions of wholesalers James Williams of Narberth and Stedman's of Caerleon. Brains is the official sponsor of the Wales Rugby Union team. Bottle-conditioned beer: Brains Dark (ABV 3.9%)

Buckley's IPA **(OG 1033.5, ABV 3.4%)**

Dark **(OG 1035.5, ABV 3.5%)**
An award-winning, classic mild. Dark brown with a satisfying mix of malt, roast and caramel flavours. Initially sweet then becoming bitter-sweet, with a background of hops throughout and a lasting finish of malt and roast.

Bitter **(OG 1036, ABV 3.6%)**
Gentle hop and malt aroma. Amber coloured with a hop, malt and fruit flavour with increasing bitterness leading to a lasting bitter finish.

Buckley's Best Bitter **(OG 1036.5, ABV 3.7%)**

Bread of Heaven **(OG 1040, ABV 4%)**

SA **(OG 1042, ABV 4.2%)**
Amber-coloured beer with a malt and hop aroma. A mellow, full-bodied, mainly malty flavour with hops and fruit. The bitterness builds and complements the flavours.

Rev James **(OG 1045.5, ABV 4.5%)**
Pale brown with a faint malty and fruity aroma. Malt and fruit flavours dominate the taste with a balancing bitterness, making for an easy-drinking beer of deceptive strength.

Brakspear

Brakspear Brewing Co, Eagle Maltings, The Crofts, Witney, Oxon, OX28 4DP
Tel (01993) 890800
Fax (01993) 772553
Email info@brakspear-beers.co.uk
Website www.brakspear-beers.co.uk

Shop Merchandise available on-line
Tours by arrangement

Brakspear brewing came back to Oxfordshire in 2004 and has its own fermenting room within Wychwood Brewery (qv). The major development of the Wychwood site in 2004 saw the installation of the original Brakspear copper and fermenting vessels, including the famous 'double drop' fermenters. All the regular and seasonal beers are now brewed at Witney. Bottle-conditioned beers: Live Organic (ABV 4.5%), Triple (ABV 7.2%).

Bitter (OG 1035, ABV 3.4%)
A classic copper-coloured pale ale with a big hop resins, juicy malt and orange fruit aroma, intense hop bitterness in the mouth and finish, and a firm maltiness and tangy fruitiness throughout.

Special (OG 1045, ABV 4.3%)
Rich malt, hops and fruit aroma; biscuity malt and hop resins in the mouth; long bitter-sweet finish with orange fruit notes.

Brancaster EAB

Brancaster Brewery, Jolly Sailors, Main Road, Brancaster Staithe, Norfolk, PE31 8BJ
Tel (01485) 210314 Fax (01485) 210396
Email jayatjolly@aol.com
Shop open 11am-11pm

Brancaster opened in 2003 with a five-barrel plant in a converted ocean-going steel container adjacent to its own pub. It supplies beer to the pub in casks as well as to shops in bottle-conditioned form.

IPA (OG 1036, ABV 3.7%)

Old Les (OG 1049, ABV 5%)

Brandy Cask SIBA

Brandy Cask Pub & Brewery, 25 Bridge Street, Pershore, Worcestershire, WR10 1AJ
Tel/Fax (01386) 552602
Tours by arrangement

Brewing started in 1995 in a refurbished bottle store in the garden of the pub. It was run as a separate business until the retirement of the brewer in 1998. Brewery and pub now operate under one umbrella, with brewing carried out by the owner/landlord.

Whistling Joe (ABV 3.6%)
This tawny-coloured session bitter has powerful malt and fruity hops on the aroma and taste, which are still evident in the throat.

Brandy Snapper (ABV 4%)
Bitterness leads to a rich mix with the malt flavours on the tongue but with no lasting aftertaste.

John Baker's Original (ABV 4.8%)
An initial rich mix of malt, roast and fruitiness is joined by an underlying sweetness that remains through to the finish.

Ale Mary (ABV 4.8%)
A rich malt and fruit aroma leads on to an equally complex taste with no one flavour dominating. A dry finish.

Branscombe Vale SIBA

Branscombe Vale Brewery Ltd, Great Seaside Farm, Branscombe, Devon, EX12 3DP
Tel/Fax (01297) 680511
Email branscombe.brew@btconnect.com
Tours by arrangement

The brewery was set up in 1992 by former dairy workers Paul Dimond and Graham Luxton in cowsheds owned by the National Trust. Paul and Graham converted the sheds and dug their own well. The NT built an extension for the brewery to ensure future growth. Branscombe Vale currently supplies 60 regular outlets. Seasonal beers: Anniversary Ale (ABV 4.6%, Feb-March), Hells Belles (ABV 4.8%, winter), Summa That (ABV 5%, summer), Yo Ho Ho (ABV 6%, Christmas). Bottle-conditioned beer: Draymans.

Branoc (OG 1035, ABV 3.8%)
A classic session bitter, pale brown in colour with a fruity aroma and taste, and a dry, bitter finish.

Draymans (OG 1040, ABV 4.2%)
A mid-brown beer with hop and caramel notes, and a lingering finish.

BVB Own Label (OG 1046, ABV 4.6%)
Reddy/brown-coloured beer with a fruity aroma and taste, and bitter/astringent finish.

Breconshire SIBA

Breconshire Brewery Ltd, Ffrwdgrech Industrial Estate, Brecon, Powys, LD3 8LA
Tel (01874) 623731
Fax (01874) 611434
Email sales@breconshirebrewery.com
Website www.breconshirebrewery.com
Shop Mon-Fri 8.30-4.30
Tours by prior arrangement

Breconshire Brewery was founded by Howard Marlow in 2002 as part of C H Marlow, a wholesaler and distributor of ales in the South Wales area for more than 30 years. The 10-barrel plant uses Optic malts blended with a range of British whole hops. The beers are distributed throughout South, Mid and West Wales and the West of England. Seasonal beer: Winter Beacon (ABV 5.3%, Nov-Feb). Bottle-conditioned beers: Golden Valley, Red Dragon and Ramblers Ruin.

Brecon County Ale (OG 1037, ABV 3.7%)
An amber brown beer, well hopped with Fuggles, Goldings and First Gold.

Golden Valley (OG 1042, ABV 4.2%)
A welcoming aroma of hops, fruit and malt leads to a similar, balanced flavour with a good building bitterness. A lasting hoppy bitterness completes this well-crafted beer. CAMRA Champion Beer of Wales 2004/05.

Red Dragon (OG 1047, ABV 4.7%)
Large quantities of crystal malt are blended into a complex grist with a selection of unusual hops, including Pioneer and 93/50. Hop bitterness balances the biscuity malt characteristics of this easy drinking beer.

Ramblers Ruin (OG 1050, ABV 5%)
Dark amber, malty and well hopped. Large amounts of crystal and black malts create the

malt/biscuit undertones, with bitterness and aroma provided by Goldings and First Gold hops.

Brewster's SIBA

Brewster's Brewing Co Ltd, Penn Lane, Stathern, near Melton Mowbray, Leicestershire, LE14 4JA
Tel (01949) 861868
Fax (01949) 861901
Email sara@brewsters.co.uk
Website www.brewsters.co.uk
Tours by arrangement

⊗ Brewster is the old English term for a female brewer and Sara Barton is a modern example. A Master of Brewing trained at Heriot Watt Brewing School in Edinburgh, she worked with Courage before striking out alone. In 2000, she won the Small Business category of Country Living magazine's Enterprising Rural Women awards. Brewster's Brewery was set up in the heart of the Vale of Belvoir in 1998 with a five-barrel plant; this has since been upgraded to 10 barrels to cope with demand. Beer is supplied to some 250 outlets throughout central England and further afield via wholesalers. Seasonal beers: see website. Bottle-conditioned beer: Vale Pale Ale (ABV 4.5%).

Hophead (OG 1036, ABV 3.6%) ◈
A pale brew with a predominately floral, hoppy flavour. A refreshing session beer.

Marquis (OG 1038, ABV 3.8%) ◈
A well-balanced and refreshing session bitter with maltiness and a dry, hoppy finish. A SIBA award winner.

Daffys Elixir (OG 1042, ABV 4.2%)

Hop A Doodle Doo (OG 1043, ABV 4.3%)

Rutterkin (OG 1046, ABV 4.6%) ◈
A premium bitter with a golden appearance. A zesty hop flavour from American Mount Hood hops combines with a touch of malt sweetness to give a rich, full-bodied beer.

Wicked Woman Range (OG 1048, ABV 4.8%)
(Varies seasonally)

Belly Dancer (OG 1050, ABV 5.2%) ◈
Well-balanced, ruby-red ale having a full-bodied taste from crystal and roast malts, with a subtle hop finish from Bramling Cross and Fuggles. A beautifully smooth, warming beer.

Bridge of Allan SIBA

Bridge of Allan Brewery Ltd, The Brewhouse, Queens Lane, Bridge of Allan, Stirlingshire, FK9 4NY
Tel (01786) 834555
Fax (01786) 833426
Email brewery@bridgeofallan.co.uk
Website www.bridgeofallan.co.uk
Shop 11-6 daily
Tours by arrangement

☺ Bridge of Allan Brewery was founded in 1997 and is located in the leafy Victorian spa town in the Forth Valley, with Stirling Castle, the Wallace Monument and the Trossochs close by. The five-barrel plant has been expanded and the visitor centre is being refurbished to give better facilities and hopes to acquire a public house licence. The brewery sells to pubs in Scotland and also distributes to England and abroad via wholesalers. Seasonal beers: Wallace Monument Ale (ABV 4.8%, Nov & June), Stirling Summer Breeze (ABV 4%, July-Aug), Bramble Ale (ABV 4.2%, Oct-Nov), Stirling Dark Mild (ABV 3.2%, May). Bottle-conditioned beer: Brig O'Allan (ABV 4%) ▪, Champion Bottle-Conditioned Beer of Scotland 2004, is available only at the brewery but may soon be sold by mail order: check website. Lomond Gold, Glencoe Wild Oat Stout and Ben Nevis are suitable for vegetarians and vegans.

Stirling Bitter (OG 1039, ABV 3.7%)
A full-flavoured beer with a nutty and fruity taste and a dry aftertaste.

Ben Nevis Organic (OG 1042, ABV 4%) ◈
A traditional Scottish 80 Shilling, with a distinctive roast and caramel character. Bitter-sweet fruit throughout provides the sweetness typical of a Scottish Heavy.

Stirling Brig (OG 1042, ABV 4.1%)
Brewed to commemorate the 700th anniversary of the Battle of Stirling Bridge in 1297. Classic rich, dark, ruby red ale; a typical Scottish 80 Shilling.

Bannockburn Ale (OG 1044, ABV 4.2%)
Pale golden coloured beer with a complex hoppy and fruity aroma.

Glencoe Wild Oat Stout Organic (OG 1048, ABV 4.5%) ◈
A sweetish stout, surprisingly not dark in colour. Plenty of malt and roast balanced by fruit and finished with a hint of hop.

Lomond Gold Organic (OG 1054, ABV 5%) ◈
A malty, bitter-sweet golden ale with plenty of fruity hop character.

Bridge Street

Bridge Street Brewery, Bridge Street, Kington, Herefordshire, HR5 3DW
Tel (01544) 230685
Email deanewright@yahoo.co.uk

A brewery that uses equipment from Moss Brew, based on the site vacated by Dunn Plowman (qv).

Arrow Bitter (OG 1042, ABV 4%)

Quiver (OG 1050, ABV 5%)

Briscoe's

Briscoe's Brewery, 16 Ash Grove, Otley, West Yorkshire, LS21 3EL
Tel/Fax (01943) 466515
Email briscoe.brewery@virgin.net

The brewery was launched in 1998 by microbiologist/chemist Dr Paul Briscoe in the cellar of his house with a one-barrel brew length. The brew length increased to four barrels during 2002. The original one-barrel plant has been retained for special bottled beers. Following a serious injury, Dr Briscoe is currently brewing on his original plant but hopes to return to full production. Seasonal beers: Rombalds Reviver (ABV 3.8%), Runner's Ruin (ABV 4.3%), Shane's Shamrock Stout (ABV 4.6%), Chevinbrau Pilsner-style lager (ABV 5.2%), Puddled and Barmy Ale (ABV 5.8%).

Burnsall Classic Bitter (OG 1040, ABV 4%)
A full-flavoured, reddish-coloured bitter with a good hop flavour.

Chevin Chaser (OG 1043, ABV 4.3%)
A refreshing, pale-coloured, all-malt bitter with a distinct hop finish.

Dalebottom Dark (OG 1043, ABV 4.3%)
A smooth and malty strong dark mild with a good hop character.

Badger Stone Bitter (OG 1044, ABV 4.4%)
A classic English bitter, packed with the flavour of malt and hops.

Three Peaks Ale (OG 1045, ABV 4.5%)
A strong, pale premium bitter brewed with only pale malt and traditional hops.

Otley Gold (OG 1043, ABV 4.6%)
A pale, fairly full-flavoured but soft beer brewed in the style of a lager.

Victorian Velvet (OG 1049, ABV 4.9%)
A malty, fruity and smooth copper-coloured special bitter. Small amounts are available bottle-conditioned from the brewery at Christmas.

Bristol Beer Factory*

Bristol Brewing Co Ltd, The Beer Factory, Unit A, The Old Brewery, Durnford Street, Ashton, Bristol, B33 2AW
Tel (0117) 902 6317
Fax (0117) 902 6316
Email enquiries@bristolbeerfactory.co.uk
Website www.bristolbeerfactory.co.uk

The brewery was opened in the early 1800s by Thomas Baynton and was taken over in 1865 and registered as the Ashton Gate Brewing Co Ltd. There were a couple of name changes in the mid-to-late 1800s and in 1931 it was taken over by Georges & Co and was wound up in 1933. Bristol Brewing Co Ltd moved in and began brewing in 2004. The Beer Factory is a 10-barrel micro-brewery. The equipment has undergone major improvements. One outlet is supplied direct.

Red (ABV 3.8%)
Sultana fruit and malt loaf aroma with digestive biscuit maltiness in the mouth and dried fruit and light hops. Vinous fruit and rich malt finish with gentle hop bitterness.

No. 7 (ABV 4.2%) ◆
Mid brown, old-fashioned style, malty best bitter. Good body and mouthfeel, some apple-type fruit flavours, with a drying bitter and astringent finish.

Gold (ABV 5%) ◆
Full-bodied and strong-flavoured golden ale. Complex aroma of pineapple and unripe pale fruits with hints of butterscotch and pear drops. a dry and bitter beer with a long, astringent finish and little sweetness.

Broadstone SIBA

Broadstone Brewing Co Ltd, Waterside Brewery, Rum Runner, Wharf Road, Retford, Nottinghamshire, DN22 6EN
Tel (01777) 719797
Fax (01777) 719898
Email broadstone@btconnect.com
Website www.broadstonebrewery.com
Tours by arrangement

⊗ Alan Gill, who founded Springhead Brewery, set up Broadstone in an industrial unit in Tuxford in 1999. The brewery was relocated to the back of his former business partner's pub, the Rum Runner (now owned and run by Bateman's), in Retford, in 2002. From there, Alan supplies around 100 outlets. Broadstone began bottling in 2002 and supplies bottle-conditioned Black Abbot and Two Water Grog to two major supermarket chains, plus local off licences. Gardener's Tap (ABV 5.4%) is bottled for Chatsworth House and Gold is also available in bottle.

Best Bitter (OG 1039, ABV 3.8%) ◆
An orange-brown session beer with a good hop character, backed by a malty nose and a fairly bitter taste. The bitterness dries into a malty finish.

RPA (ABV 3.8%)

Stonebridge Mild (OG 1041, ABV 4%)

Priorswell Porter (OG 1041, ABV 4%)

Ladywell Ale (OG 1042, ABV 4%)

Two Water Grog (OG 1042, ABV 4%)

Black Abbot (OG 1052, ABV 5%)

Gold (OG 1052, ABV 5%)

Donjon (ABV 5.4%)

Warhorse (ABV 5.8%)

Donovan (ABV 6%)

Broughton SIBA

Broughton Ales Ltd, Broughton, Biggar, Peeblesshire, ML12 6HQ
Tel (01899) 830345
Fax (01899) 830474
Email beer@broughtonales.co.uk
Website www.broughtonales.co.uk
Shop 8-5 Mon– Fri
Tours by arrangement

⊛ Founded in 1979, the company went into receivership in 1995 and was taken over by Whim Brewery's owner Giles Litchfield along with managing director Alastair Mouat. They created the popular Clipper IPA and the new

Greenmantle Original as well as 16 other cask ales. Expansion into new markets in England is going well. 55 per cent of production is bottled (not bottle-conditioned), 10 per cent of it for export. A single tied house and 200 outlets in Scotland are supplied by the brewery. Seasonal beers: Scottish Oatmeal Stout (ABV 4.2%, winter), Ghillie (ABV 4.5%, summer), Black Douglas (ABV 5.2%, spring/autumn), Summer Ale (ABV 3.5%, summer), Winter Fire (ABV 4.2%, winter), Angel Lager (ABV 5%). All bottled beers are suitable for vegetarians and vegans.

Reiver (ABV 3.8%)

Border Gold Organic (OG 1042, ABV 4.2%)
Fruity hop aroma with citrus-lime hop flavour balanced by a malty sweetness. The finish is rich malt with grapefruit bitterness.

Clipper IPA (OG 1042, ABV 4.2%)
A light-coloured, crisp, hoppy beer with a strong hop character and a clean taste.

Merlin's Ale (OG 1042, ABV 4.2%) ◆
A well-hopped, fruity flavour is balanced by malt in the taste. The finish is bitter-sweet, light but dry.

Scottish Oatmeal Stout
(OG 1045, ABV 4.2%) ◆
A rare pleasure, this wonderfully dry stout has a bitter aftertaste dominated by roast malt. A distinctive malt aroma is followed by a prominent roast note. Fruit is evident throughout.

The Ghillie (OG 1043, ABV 4.5%) ◆
A full-bodied ale. Hops, malt and fruit dominate the palate. The finish is dry and dominated by hops.

The Black Douglas (OG 1053, ABV 5.2%)
Brewed using Maris Otter pale ale malt with the addition of roasted barley and maize, this ruby coloured beer has a full malty flavour with a warm, strong finish.

Old Jock (OG 1070, ABV 6.7%)
Strong, sweetish and fruity in the finish. A classic Scottish strong ale.

Brown Cow

Brown Cow Brewery, Brown Cow Road, Barlow, Selby, North Yorkshire, YO8 8EH
Tel (01757) 618947
Email susansimpson@browncowbrewery.co.uk
Website www.browncowbrewery.co.uk

Set up by Susan Simpson in 1997, the original 2.5-barrel plant was replaced by a five-barrel unit in 2002. Joined by husband Keith in 2004, they currently brew to a capacity of 12 barrels a week. In addition to the three well-established core beers, new one-off recipes are brewed regularly, selecting from the brewery hop stock of at least 20 varieties, especially the more unusual types. The beers are delivered throughout Yorkshire from the brewery and to a small number of outlets in the southern counties via a carefully selected agent. Bottled beers are now available and the range will be increased in 2006. Small-run specialist recipes, such as the After Dark Coffee Porter, are also brewed for Suddaby's of Malton. Seasonal beers: Nimbus Wheat Beer (suitable for vegetarians and vegans, ABV 4.8%, spring/summer), Wassail Warmer (ABV 5%, Christmas). Bottle-conditioned beer: How Now (ABV 5.1%), Nimbus Wheat Beer (ABV 4.8%), Wide Eyed and Legless (ABV 4.7%), Wassail Warmer (ABV 5%), Suddaby's After Dark Coffee Porter (ABV 5%). All bottle-conditioned beers are suitable for vegetarians.

Bitter (OG 1038, ABV 3.8%) ◆
A well-hopped traditional session bitter.

Old E'fer (OG 1042, ABV 4.4%)

Simpsons No. 4 (OG 1043, ABV 4.4%) ◆
Dark and bitter-sweet, full of roast barley character.

For Malton Brewery:

After Dark Coffee Porter

Brunswick SIBA

Brunswick Brewery Ltd, 1 Railway Terrace, Derby, DE1 2RU
Tel (01332) 290677
Fax (01332) 370226
Email grahamyates@work.gb.com
Tours by arrangement

⊠ The Brunswick is a purpose-built tower brewery that started brewing in 1991 and is now the city's oldest brewery. A viewing area allows pub users to watch production. Bought by Everards in 2002, it is now a tenancy supplying beers to local outlets and the Everards estate. Seasonal beer: Rambo (ABV 7.3%, winter).

Mild (OG 1038, ABV 3.6%) ◆
A light-bodied, well-balanced Midlands dark mild with liquorice and hints of coffee on the nose and balanced fruit, caramel and roast in the taste.

Second Brew (OG 1040, ABV 4%) ◆
This tawny best bitter, also known as 'The Usual', presents an aroma of sulphur and hops that continue throughout, accompanied by a striking bitterness and astringency.

Triple Hop (OG 1040, ABV 4%) ◆
A pale gold colour and citrus hop bouquet promise sweetness but the hops deliver a firm, dry, lasting bitterness.

Railway Porter (OG 1042, ABV 4.3%) ◆
A complex roast aroma can hint at coffee and vanilla, while roast malt dominates the taste, subsiding to a bitter aftertaste.

Triple Gold (OG 1044, ABV 4.5%) ◆
A smooth golden, full-bodied bitter with a pronounced hoppy aroma that develops into a complex fruity and hoppy taste with some sulphur. Long astringent finish.

Pilsner (ABV 5%)

Old Accidental (OG 1049, ABV 5%)
A well-balanced, malty beer leading to a bitter finish with warming aftertaste. A light, vinous floral hop has underlying malt notes.

Father Mike's Dark Rich Ruby (OG 1055, ABV 5.8%) ◆
A smooth, near black mild with a hint of red. Well-balanced and filled with sweet roast flavours that conceal its strength.

Black Sabbath (OG 1058, ABV 6%)

Bryncelyn

Bryncelyn Brewery, Wern Fawr Inn, 47 Wern Road, Ystalyfera, Swansea, SA9 2LX
Tel (01639) 843625
Email bryncelynbrewery@aol.com
Website www.bryncelynbrewery.co.uk
Tours by arrangement

A one-quarter barrel brewery was opened in 1999 by William Hopton (owner) and Robert Scott (brewer). Capacity was increased to its present three-quarter barrel capacity in the same year. As the beer names imply, the owner is fond of Buddy Holly: February 1959 commemorates the singer's death. One pub is owned; beer festivals and take away boxes are supplied. Seasonal beers: Feb 59 (ABV 3.7%), Peggy's Brew (ABV 4.2%, March), May B Baby (ABV 4.5%, May), That Will Be the Sleigh (ABV 6.6%, Dec-Jan).

Holly Hop (ABV 3.9%)

Buddy Marvellous (OG 1040, ABV 4%) ◆
Dark brown with an inviting aroma of malt, roast and fruit. Hop flavours add to this tasty blend with a gentle bitterness and lasting, complex finish.

Buddy's Delight (OG 1042, ABV 4.2%)

Cwrw Celyn (OG 1044, ABV 4.4%)

CHH (OG 1045, ABV 4.5%) ◆
A pale brown beer with hints of red malt and an inviting hop aroma, with fruit and bitterness adding to the flavour. The finish is clean and hoppy-bitter.

Oh Boy (OG 1045, ABV 4.5%) ◆
An enticing hop and fruit aroma, a golden colour and a taste full of hops and fruit. Good bitterness and underlying malt add to the flavour, with a long, hoppily-bitter finish.

Rave On (OG 1050, ABV 5%)

Buddy Confusing (OG 1050, ABV 5%)

Bryn Cyf*

Bragdy'r Bryn Cyf, Unit 2, Vale Park, Colomendy Industrial Estate, Denbigh, Clwyd, LL16 5TA
Tel (01745 812266)
Website www.bragdyrbryn.co.uk.

A brewery that was launched in May 2005 following five months of trial brews. Geraint Roberts was a home brewer who then worked for Sharp's in Cornwall (qv) before setting up his own business. He has a five-barrel plant and will add to the beer range.

Bitter (ABV 4%)

Bryson's

Bryson's Brewery Lancaster Ltd, Newgate Brewery, White Lund Industrial Estate, Morecambe, Lancashire, LA3 3PT
Tel (01524) 39481
Fax (01524) 382229
Email brysonbrews@supnet.com
Website www.brysonsbrews.co.uk

Bryson's closed in Heysham in 2004. The brewery moved to Morecambe and is now owned by Morecambe Bay Wines. The former brewer at Heysham, George Palmer, remains in charge of production. New beers will be added.

Shifting Sands (ABV 3.8%)

Barrows Bitter (ABV 4.2%)

Buffy's SIBA EAB

Buffy's Brewery Ltd, Rectory Road, Tivetshall St Mary, Norwich, Norfolk, NR15 2DD
Tel/Fax (01379) 676523
Email buffysbrewery@evemail.net
Website www.buffys.co.uk

Buffy's was established in 1993. The brewing capacity is 45 barrels, but a move to bigger premises is in hand. The brewery has one pub, the Cherry Tree at Wickerwood, and plans to buy a second pub closer to home: the brewery will eventually move to these premises. Julie Savory (one half of the business) won a national award from Publican newspaper in 2002 to mark her efforts to save and restore the Cherry Tree. Some 50 outlets are supplied. Seasonal beers: Sleigher (ABV 4.1%, Nov-Dec), Hollybeery (ABV 6% but changes each year), Festival 9X (ABV 9%, summer).

Norwich Terrier (OG 1036, ABV 3.6%) ◆
A fragrant peachy aroma introduces this refreshing, gold-coloured bitter. Strong bitter notes dominate throughout as hops mingle with grapefruit to produce a long, increasingly dry finish.

Bitter (OG 1039, ABV 3.9%) ◆
Copper coloured with a subtle hop and malt bouquet. Singularly bitter throughout, the mix of malt and hops adds a pleasant dry, biscuity background. A long, bitter ending.

Lite Relief (OG 1041.5, ABV 4.1%) ◆
Vanilla in both aroma and taste is the dominant feature of this amber brew. The basic maltiness is subdued by a dryish hop background. Flavour speedily diminishes to a sweet vanilla echo.

Mild (OG 1042, ABV 4.2%) ◆
A complex brew, deep red with a smooth but grainy feel. Caramel and blackcurrant bolster the heavy malt influence that is the main characteristic of this understated, deceptively strong mild.

Polly's Folly (OG 1043, ABV 4.3%) ◆
A jolly mixture of hoppiness, citrus fruit and malt gives this well-balanced offering a lively, satisfying feel. Grapefruit creeps into the flavour mix towards the end as the overall character becomes biscuity dry.

Mucky Duck (OG 1044, ABV 4.5%)

Hopleaf (OG 1044.5, ABV 4.5%) ◆
Clean tasting with a pronounced hoppy signature. The singular hop bouquet wanes slightly in the initial taste as malt combines with a sweet fruitiness to give greater depth. Consistent dry finish.

India Ale (OG 1046, ABV 4.6%) ◆
Amber coloured with the distinctive hoppy nose of a classic IPA. A subdued malt background does little to diminish the raw hoppiness. An increasingly bitter finale accentuates a grainy mouthfeel.

Norwegian Blue (OG 1049, ABV 4.9%) ◆
A gentle hoppy nose belies the rich warming character of this pale brown taste explosion. A complex, ever-changing mix of malt, hops, bitterness and fruit. A long, lingering, bitter-sweet ending.

Festival 9X (OG 1090, ABV 9.0%)
A fine, old-fashioned ale, dark amber in colour.

Bull Lane*

Bull Lane Brewing Company, Clarendon, 143 High Street East, Hendon, Sunderland, Tyne & Wear, SR1 2BL
Tel (0191) 510 3200

A new small brewery based in the cellar of the Clarendon pub and owned by the Beer Factory, which has a number of pubs in the area. The plant is 2.5 barrels in size and was bought from the Wylam Brewery (qv).

Bitter (ABV 3.9%)

Bullmastiff SIBA

Bullmastiff Brewery, 14 Bessemer Close, Leckwith, Cardiff, CF11 8DL
Tel/Fax (029) 2066 5292

⊗ An award-winning small craft brewery run by brothers Bob and Paul Jenkins since 1987. The name stems from their love of the bullmastiff breed. They have no ambitions for expansion or owning any pubs, preferring to concentrate on quality control. 30 outlets are supplied. Seasonal beers: Summer Moult (ABV 4.3%), Mogadog (ABV 10%, winter).

Welsh Gold (OG 1039, ABV 3.8%) ◆
A hoppy aroma invites you to taste the blend of hop and fruit flavours with balancing bitterness. A refreshing, juicy hop finish.

Jack the Lad (OG 1041, ABV 4.1%)

Thoroughbred (OG 1046, ABV 4.5%) ◆
A good hop aroma leads to a hoppy flavour with accompanying fruit, malt and balancing bitterness. There is a quenching hoppy bitterness in the finish of this amber brew.

Welsh Red (OG 1048, ABV 4.8%)

Welsh Black (OG 1050, ABV 4.8%)

Brindle (OG 1050, ABV 5.1%) ◆
A full-bodied, flavoursome pale beer. Good hop aroma with a mix of malt, hops, fruit and bitterness in the taste. A lasting and satisfying finish.

Son of a Bitch (OG 1062, ABV 6%) ◆
A warming amber ale, easy drinking for its strength. An aroma of hops, fruit and malt and a similar blend of flavours with a warming alcohol presence; the finish fades.

Bünker*

Bünker, 41 Earlham Street, Covent Garden, London, WC2H 9LD
Tel (0207) 240 0606
Fax (0207) 240 4422
Email info@bunkerbar.com
Website www.bunkerbar.com

Brew-restaurant that produces lager beers – Pils and Bock – but may add a wheat beer.

Buntingford SIBA

Buntingford Brewery Co Ltd, Greys Brewhouse, Therfield Road, Royston, Hertfordshire, SG8 9NW
Tel (01763) 250749
Email enquiries@buntingford-brewery.co.uk
Website www.buntingford-brewery.co.uk
Tours by arrangement

Buntingford relocated to a new site in 2005 and brewing was expected to be in progress by the summer utilising a new 15-barrel plant. The original five-barrel plant has been sold to a planned new brewery in Enfield. During the transitional period the beer was brewed by the Buntingford brewer at Belvoir Brewery (qv). Malt is used from barley that has been grown on an adjacent farm and natural spring water is used in the brewing process. All liquid waste is treated via a reed bed and the resultant clean water is fed into a wildlife habitat.

Challenger (ABV 3.8%)

No 1 Sweet Stout (OG 1040, ABV 4%)

Grey Partridge (OG 1040, ABV 4.1%)

Britannia (ABV 4.4%)

Buccaneer (ABV 4.6%)

Hayturner (ABV 5%)

Silence (OG 1050, ABV 5.2%)

Burrington SIBA

Burrington Brewery, Homelands Business Centre, Burrington, Devon, EX37 9JJ
Tel (01805) 622813 (m) 07986 009295
Email info@burringtonbrewery.co.uk
Website www.burringtonbrewery.co.uk
Tours by arrangement

Burrington Brewery was set up in the spring of 2003 by Craig Carter in a purpose-built unit in the heart of north Devon. The five-barrel brewery supplies some 80 outlets in Devon, Cornwall and pubs further afield through wholesalers. Bottle-conditioned beers: Newt Porter, Newt 'n' Wriggly, Parson Brown.

Mild (ABV 3.6%)

Tippled Newt (ABV 3.8%)

Azza Newt (ABV 4%)

Alchemy (ABV 4.2%)

Newt Porter (ABV 4.4%)

Newt 'n' Wriggly (ABV 4.6%)

Parson Brown (ABV 4.8%)

Liquid Newt-rition (ABV 5.2%)

Burton Bridge SIBA

Burton Bridge Brewery Ltd, 24 Bridge Street, Burton upon Trent, Staffordshire, DE14 1SY
Tel (01283) 510573
Fax (01283) 515594
Email bbb@burtonbridgebrewery.fsnet.co.uk
Shop Bridge Inn 11.30-2pm, 5-11pm
Tours by arrangement

☺ A brewery established in 1982 by Bruce Wilkinson and Geoff Mumford, two refugees from Allied Breweries who finished up at Ind Coope of Romford. Burton Bridge now has four tenanted pubs in the town, including an enlarged, CAMRA award-winning brewery tap. It also supplies 300 outlets. There are many seasonal beers. Bottle-conditioned beers: Burton Porter (ABV 4.5%), Empire Pale Ale (ABV 7.5%), Bramble Stout (ABV 5%), Tickle Brain (ABV 8%).

Golden Delicious (OG 1037, ABV 3.8%) ◆
Golden looks, exciting sulphurous aroma; hoppy and fruity with a bitter, mouth-watering finish.

XL Bitter (OG 1039, ABV 4%) ◆
A golden, malty bitter, with fruity and hoppy aromas. Hoppy and bitter finish with a characteristic astringent aftertaste.

Bridge Bitter (OG 1041, ABV 4.2%) ◆
Pale brown, good fruit and hop aroma. Hoppy start with a touch of caramel; good lingering bitter finish.

Burton Porter (OG 1044, ABV 4.5%) ◻ ◆
Amazingly red, with a faint roast aroma. The taste combines some liquorice flavour with hops and fruit; slightly sweet. A dry, astringent bite to finish.

Stairway to Heaven (OG 1049, ABV 5%) ◆
Golden bitter. A perfectly balanced beer. The malty and hoppy start leads to a hoppy body with some astringency.

Top Dog Stout (OG 1049, ABV 5%) ◆
Black and rich with a roast and malty start. Very fruity and abundant hops give a fruity, bitter finish with a mouth-watering edge.

Festival Ale (OG 1054, ABV 5.5%) ◆
Caramel aroma with hops and fruit. Sweet start, again with hops and fruit. Sweet finish that goes hoppy and fruity. Great mouthfeel and refreshing sparkle.

Thomas Sykes (OG 1095, ABV 10%) ◆
Very rich and warming, fruity, heady and hoppy. A true barley wine to be handled with caution.

Burtonwood

Thomas Hardy Burtonwood Ltd, Bold Lane, Burtonwood, Warrington, Cheshire, WA5 4PJ
Tel (01925) 220022
Fax (01925) 224562
Website www.thomashardybrewery.co.uk
Tours by arrangement (charge)

☺ Following the sale of 60% of its brewing operation to Thomas Hardy in 1998, Burtonwood sold the remaining 40% in 2004 to become solely a pub-owning group that was bought by Wolverhampton & Dudley (qv) in 2005. Burtonwood is now Thomas Hardy's only brewery, run by Peter Ward as a contract operation, principally for Scottish Courage.

For Wolverhampton & Dudley:

Burtonwood Bitter (OG 1036.8, ABV 3.7%) ◆
A well-balanced, refreshing, malty bitter, with good hoppiness. Fairly dry aftertaste.

Top Hat (OG 1046, ABV 4.8%) ◆
Soft, nutty, malty and a little sweet.

For Morrells of Oxford pub group (qv):

Oxford Blue (OG 1036, ABV 3.7%)

For Scottish Courage:

Webster's Green Label (OG 1032, ABV 3.2%)

Webster's Yorkshire Bitter (OG 1035, ABV 3.5%)

John Smith's Magnet (OG 1040, ABV 4%)

Bushy's SIBA

Mount Murray Brewing Co Ltd, Mount Murray, Braddan, Isle of Man, IM4 1JE
Tel/Fax (01624) 661244
Email bushys@manx.net
Website www.bushys.com
Shop Available from pubs
Tours by arrangement

☺ Set up in 1986 as a brew-pub, Bushy's moved to its present site in 1990 when demand outgrew capacity. It owns four tied houses and the beers are also supplied to 25 other outlets. Bushy's goes one step further than the Manx Pure Beer Law, that permits only malt, hops, sugar and yeast, preferring the German Reinheitsgebot (Pure Beer Law) that excludes sugar. Seasonal beers: Lovely Jubbly (ABV 5.2%, Dec-Jan), Piston Brew (ABV 4.5%, May-June).

Castletown Bitter (OG 1035, ABV 3.5%)

Ruby (1874) Mild (OG 1035, ABV 3.5%)

Bitter (OG 1038, ABV 3.8%) ◆
An aroma full of pale malt and hops introduces you to a beautifully hoppy, bitter beer. Despite the predominant hop character, malt is also evident. Fresh and clean-tasting.

Old Bushy Tail (OG 1045, ABV 4.5%)

Piston Brew (OG 1045, ABV 4.5%)

Butcombe SIBA

Butcombe Brewery, Cox's Green, Havyatt Road, Wrington, Somerset, BS40 5PA
Tel (01934) 863963
Fax (01934) 863903
Email info@butcombe.com
Website www.butcombe.com
Tours by arrangement

⊗ One of the most successful of the newer breweries, set up in 1978 by a former Courage Western director, Simon Whitmore, this West Country independent gained a considerable reputation for its quality beers. The brewery has doubled in size three times. Simon Whitmore sold the brewery to Guy Newell (the founder of the Beer Seller and now Butcombe's managing director) and friends in 2003. A new 10,000 sq ft brewery was built in 2004 on a new site. Butcombe has an estate of seven houses (although none is tied) and it also supplies 350 other outlets. Butcombe's beers contain no added sugars, colourings or preservatives, and are available from the brewery to outlets within a 50-mile radius and nationally via selected wholesalers and pub companies.

Bitter (OG 1039, ABV 4%) ◆
Amber-coloured, malty and notably bitter beer, with subtle citrus fruit qualities. Hoppy, malty, citrus and a very slightly sulphur aroma, and a long, dry, bitter finish with light fruit notes.

Blonde (ABV 4.3%) ◆
Crisp and refreshing pale, hoppy best bitter. Floral and fruity hops predominate, balanced by a slight sweetness, followed by a clean and quenching finish.

Gold (OG 1047, ABV 4.7%) ◻ ◆
Aroma of pale malt, citrus hops and fruit. Medium bodied, well-balanced, with good pale malt, hops and bitterness. Yellow-gold in colour, it is quite fruity, slightly sweet, with an abiding dryness.

Butler's SIBA

Butler's Brewery Co Ltd,
(Office) 23 Grimmer Way, Woodcote, Oxfordshire, RG8 0SN
(Brewery) Whittles Farm, Mapledurham, Oxfordshire, RG4 7UP
Tel/Fax (01491) 681974
Email butlerbrew@aol.com
Website www.Butlersbrewery.co.uk

The brewery was started by Mark and Sarah Butler in 2003. An old cart shed was converted into the brewery and a six-barrel plant was installed. Plans for the future include a new brew-house and the installation of a 15-barrel plant and bottling line. 40 outlets are supplied. Bottle-conditioned beer: Old Specific (ABV 5.8%).

Oxfordshire Bitter (OG 1036, ABV 3.6%)

Special Reserve (OG 1046, ABV 4.6%)

Butts SIBA

Butts Brewery Ltd, Northfield Farm, Wantage Road, Great Shefford, Hungerford, Berkshire, RG17 7BY
Tel (01488) 648133
Fax (01488) 648134
Email enquiries@buttsbrewery.com
Website www.buttsbrewery.com
Tours by arrangement

⊗ The brewery was set up in a converted Dutch barn in 1994. Apart from pubs, Butts also supplies a handful of local supermarkets with bottle-conditioned beers. In 2002, the brewery took the decision to become dedicated to organic production: all the beers brewed use organic malted barley and organic hops when suitable varieties are available. All beers are certified by the Soil Association. Some 60 outlets are supplied. Bottle-conditioned beers: Blackguard, Barbus Barbus, Golden Brown, Le Butts.

Jester Organic (OG 1035, ABV 3.5%) ◻ ◆
This amber-coloured beer is fruity and slightly buttery, with an excellent hop aroma supported by pale malt. Aroma and bittering hops balance in the mouth, leading to a dry, hoppy finish.

Traditional (OG 1040, ABV 4%)
A rich golden beer with a hint of fruitiness.

Blackguard (OG 1045, ABV 4.5%) ◆
A rich, fruity red-brown porter with hints of crystal and chocolate malt in the mouth. A blackcurrant aroma and taste are well-balanced with bitterness and malt characters, followed by a dry, bitter and roast finish.

Barbus Barbus (OG 1046, ABV 4.6%) ◻ ◆
The pale malt in this amber beer is tempered with a hint of crystal malt, well-balanced by hops and fruit, leading to a long, complex and bitter-sweet finish.

Golden Brown (OG 1050, ABV 5%)

Le Butts (OG 1050, ABV 5%)
Brewed with lager yeast and hops resulting in a crisp and refreshing European style beer.

Cains SIBA

Robert Cain & Co Ltd, Stanhope Street, Liverpool, Merseyside, L8 5XJ
Tel (0151) 709 8734
Fax (0151) 708 8395
Email info@cains.co.uk
Website www.cains.co.uk
Shop 9-5pm
Tours by arrangement

☺ The Dusanj brothers, Ajmail and Sudarghara, bought the brewery in 2002 and have invested heavily in the red-brick Victorian plant. They have won many awards for their beers. Cains launched 2008 Ale in support of Liverpool's successful bid for European Capital of Culture, while Fine Raisin Beer won the 2003 Tesco Beer Challenge. In 2004 the brothers launched Cains Lager, which is lagered (cold conditioned) for 90 days. A cask version was launched in 2005. Eleven pubs are owned, more are planned, and around 400 outlets are supplied by the brewery. Seasonal beers: Raisin Beer (ABV 5%, Dec-Jan), Victorian Winter Ale (ABV 6%, Feb-March), Triple Hop (ABV 4.5%, April-May), 2008 (June-July), Sundowner (ABV 4.5%, Aug-Sept), Dragonheart (ABV 5%, Oct-Nov).

Dark Mild (OG 1033.5, ABV 3.2%)
A smooth, dry and roasty dark mild, with some chocolate and coffee notes.

IPA (OG 1036, ABV 3.5%)

Traditional Bitter (OG 1038.5, ABV 4%)
A darkish, full-bodied and fruity bitter, with a good hoppy nose and a dry aftertaste.

Formidable Ale (OG 1048, ABV 5%)
A bitter and hoppy beer with a good dry aftertaste. Sharp, clean and dry.

2008 Ale (OG 1048, ABV 5%)

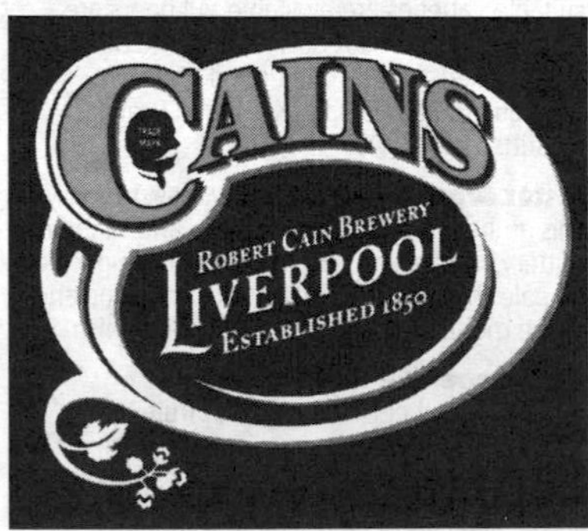

Cairngorm SIBA

Cairngorm Brewery Co Ltd, Unit 12, Dalfaber Industrial Estate, Dalfaber Drive, Aviemore, Highlands, PH22 1ST
Tel (01479) 812222
Fax (01479) 811465
Email info@cairngormbrewery.com
Website www.cairngormbrewery.com
Shop 9-430, Mon-Fri. On-line shop also available
Tours by arrangement

☺ Based in Aviemore in the shadow of the Cairngorms mountain range, the brewery has enjoyed much success since its formation, winning both Champion Beer of Scotland and a gold medal at GBBF in 2004. A regular range of seven cask beers is produced as well as a rolling programme of seasonal ales throughout the year: see website. Expansion was completed in spring 2005 and has taken the capacity to 90 barrels. The free trade is supplied as far as the central belt with national delivery via wholesalers. Seasonal beer: Highland IPA (ABV 3.6%, summer).

Stag (OG 1040, ABV 4.1%)
A drinkable best bitter with plenty of hop bitterness throughout. This tawny brew has some malt in the lingering bitter aftertaste.

Trade Winds (OG 1043, ABV 4.3%)
A truly intense, fruity, speciality beer with a strong hop character and grapefruit notes throughout. Bitter-sweetness does not come more intense than this Champion Beer of Scotland and winner of the Speciality class at GBBF 2004.

Black Gold (OG 1044, ABV 4.4%)

Nessies Monster Mash (OG 1044, ABV 4.4%)
A good, traditional, English-type bitter with plenty of bitterness and with light malt to balance. The sweetness diminishes in the aftertaste but the bitterness lingers.

Sheepshaggers Gold (OG 1044, ABV 4.5%)
A golden amber brew with some malt and hop character but balanced on the sweetish side.

Wildcat (OG 1049.5, ABV 5.1%)
This brew has varied but it is now generally strong on bitterness and at its best is a fine strong bitter. Some malt and fruit but with an accent on hops and bitterness throughout.

Caledonian

Caledonian Brewing Company Ltd, 42 Slateford Road, Edinburgh, EH11 1PH
Tel (0131) 337 1286
Fax (0131) 313 2370
Email info@caledonian-brewery.co.uk
Website www.caledonian-brewery.co.uk
Tours by arrangement

The brewery was formed in 1869 and operated as Lorimer & Clarke until a takeover by Vaux of Sunderland in 1919. In 1987, when Vaux planned to close the site, it was bought by its management and reformed as Caledonian Brewery. In 2004 the site was purchased by Scottish Courage but the brands are still owned and brewed by the existing management. Caledonian now brews McEwan's cask 80 Shilling with expansion in place for brewing further ScotCo beers. There is a rolling programme of monthly beers: see website. The brewery supplies more than 650 outlets but does not own any pubs.

Deuchars IPA (OG 1039, ABV 3.8%)
At its best, an extremely tasty and refreshing, amber-coloured session beer. Hops and fruit are

evident and are balanced by malt throughout. The lingering aftertaste is delightfully bitter and hoppy.

80/- (OG 1042, ABV 4.1%)
A predominantly malty, copper-coloured beer with underlying fruit. A Scottish heavy that now lacks the complex taste and hoppiness of old.

Golden Promise (OG 1044, ABV 4.4%)
The original organic beer, pale in colour, with pronounced hop character. Floral and fruity on the nose.

For Scottish Courage

McEwan's 80/- (OG 1042, ABV 4.2%)

Cambridge Moonshine*

Cambridge Moonshine Brewery, 28 Radegund Road, Cambridge, CB1 3RS
Tel (07906) 066794
Email mark.watch@ntlworld.com

A micro-brewery established in 2004. The first beers were launched at the 31st Cambridge Beer Festival where Mulberry Bitter was voted champion beer of the festival. Plans for the future are to increase brewing capacity and to move to larger premises. Two outlets are supplied direct. Bottle-conditioned beer: Porter (ABV 5.8%).

Harvest Moon Mild (OG 1040, ABV 3.8%)

Mulberry Bitter (OG 1040, ABV 4%)

Winter Moon Stout (OG 1044, ABV 4.5%)

Pigs Ear Porter (OG 1048, ABV 4.7%)

Moonrakers Golden Ale (OG 1050, ABV 5%)

Cambrinus SIBA

Cambrinus Craft Brewery, Home Farm, Knowsley Park, Knowsley, Merseyside, L34 4AQ
Tel (0151) 546 2226
Email cambrinus@ukonline.co.uk

Tours by prior arrangement

⊗ Established and run by John Aspinall since 1997, Cambrinus is housed in part of a former farm building on a private estate. It produces around 250 hectolitres a year on a five-barrel plant. Some 45 pubs are supplied on a regular basis in and around Lancashire, Cheshire and Cumbria. Seasonal beers: Bootstrap (ABV 4.5%, spring), St Georges Ale (ABV 4.5%, April), Clogdance (ABV 3.6%, May), Solstice (ABV 3.8%, June), Honeywheat (ABV 3.7%, July), Dark Harvest (ABV 4%, autumn), Hearts of Oak (ABV 5%, October), Lamp Oil (ABV 4.5%, winter), Celebrance (ABV 5.5%, Christmas).

Herald (OG 1036, ABV 3.7%)
Light summer drinking bitter, pale and refreshing.

Yardstick (OG 1040, ABV 4%)
Mild, malty and lightly hopped.

Deliverance (OG 1040, ABV 4.2%)
Pale premium bitter.

Endurance (OG 1045, ABV 4.3%)
IPA-style, smooth and hoppy, matured in oak.

Camerons

Camerons Brewery Ltd, Lion Brewery, Hartlepool, Co Durham, TS24 7QS
Tel (01429) 266666
Fax (01429) 868195
Website www.cameronsbrewery.com

Tours by arrangement 11-4 daily

Founded in 1865, Camerons has had a topsy-turvy existence from the 1970s, owned in turn by Ellerman Shipping Lines, the Barclay Brothers, Brent Walker, and Wolverhampton & Dudley. In 2002, the Castle Eden brewery bought Camerons and moved all production to Hartlepool. Nine pubs are owned, with four selling cask-conditioned beer. Some 40 outlets are supplied.

Bitter (OG 1036, ABV 3.6%)
A light bitter, but well-balanced, with hops and malt.

Strongarm (OG 1041, ABV 4%)
A well-rounded, ruby-red ale with a distinctive, tight creamy head; initially fruity, but with a good balance of malt, hops and moderate bitterness.

Castle Eden Ale (OG 1043, ABV 4.2%)
A light, creamy, malty sweet ale with fruit notes and a mellow dry bitterness in the finish.

Nimmos XXXX (OG 1045, ABV 4.4%)
Light golden beer with a well-balanced character derived from English malt and Goldings hops.

Cannon Royall SIBA

The Cannon Royall Brewery Ltd, Fruiterer's Arms, Uphampton Lane, Ombersley, Worcestershire, WR9 0JW
Tel (01905) 621161
Fax (01562) 743262
Email info@cannonroyall.co.uk
Website www.cannonroyall.co.uk

Tours CAMRA groups by arrangement

Cannon Royall's first brew was in 1993 in a converted cider house behind the Fruiterer's Arms. It has increased capacity from five barrels to more than 16 a week. The brewery supplies a number of outlets in Worcestershire and the West Midlands. There are occasional seasonal and special beers.

Fruiterer's Mild (OG 1037, ABV 3.7%)
A rich malt and roast aroma leads to sweet fruity undertones. The dry aftertaste stays with the drinker.

King's Shilling (OG 1038, ABV 3.8%) ◆
A golden bitter that packs a citrus hoppy punch throughout.

Arrowhead Bitter (OG 1039, ABV 3.9%) ◆
High alpha hops are the main characteristic of this pale golden bitter. From the aroma to the finish, this is for the lover of bitter bitters.

Muzzle Loader (OG 1042, ABV 4.2%) ◆
Also known as Tally Ho. Floral hops dominate the aroma, which then leads into a more subtle mix of tastes as the hops give way to the malts. Straw coloured.

Captain Cook SIBA

⚲ Captain Cook Brewery Ltd, The White Swan, 1 West End, Stokesey, North Yorkshire, TS9 5BL
Tel (01642) 710263
Fax (01642) 714245
Email joonanbri@aol.com
Website www.thecaptaincookbrewery.co.uk
Tours by arrangement

The 18th-century White Swan concentrated on promoting real ale for 10 years before taking on the challenge of becoming a brew-pub. The brewery, with a four-barrel plant, started operations in 1999 and was opened by White Swan regular James Cook on his 79th birthday. Seasonal beer: Black Porter (ABV 4.4%, autumn and winter).

Sunset (OG 1040, ABV 4%)
An extremely smooth light ale with a good balance of malt and hops.

Slipway (OG 1042, ABV 4%)
A light-coloured hoppy ale with bitterness coming through from Challenger hops. A full-flavoured ale with a smooth malt aftertaste.

Castle Rock SIBA

Castle Rock Brewery, Queens Bridge Road, Nottingham, NG2 1NB
Tel (0115) 985 1615
Fax (0115) 985 1611
Email castle.rock@btconnect.com
Website www.castlerockbrewery.co.uk
Shop in planning stage
Tours by arrangement

⊚ Castle Rock started brewing in 1996 as the Bramcote Brewery and moved to its present site next to the Vat & Fiddle pub in 1998, when its current name was chosen. In 2001 the Tynemill pub company (qv) took a 100% interest in the brewery. The brewery enjoyed considerable expansion in 2003, with production increasing from 30 barrels to 100 barrels a week. Some of the original equipment has been retained to enable one-off and special beers to be brewed. Future plans include a hospitality area, and windows between the brewery tap and the brewhouse to allow customers to see brewing in process. The beers are distributed throughout the Tynemill estate, local free trade and by reciprocal swaps with micro and regional brewers nationwide. A different beer in support of the Wildlife Trust is brewed every month, along with other occasional beers: see website. Seasonal beer: Nottingham Dark Stout (ABV 4.5%, winter).

Black Gold (ABV 3.5%)
A dark mild with a slight bitterness and without undue sweetness.

Nottingham Gold (ABV 3.5%)
A golden beer with a distinct hop character from Goldings. Launched in 2001, it's the house beer in many Tynemill pubs with a house name, such as Meadows Gold for the Vat & Fiddle.

Harvest Pale (ABV 3.8%) ■
SIBA champion bitter 2004. Gently kilned malt and an aromatic blend of American hops give this pale beer exceptional poise.

Hemlock (ABV 4%)
Mid-strength and full-bodied with fruity notes and a hop finish.

Elsie Mo (ABV 4.7%)
A blonde, single malt beer, light in colour and refreshing on the palate.

Caythorpe SIBA

⚲ Caythorpe Brewery, Walnut Cottage, Boat Lane, Hoveringham, Nottingham, NG14 7JP
Tel/Fax (0115) 966 4376

⊗ Caythorpe was set up in 1997 by ex-Home Brewery employee Geoff Slack and his wife Pam. The beers are brewed at the Black Horse, Caythorpe. Brewing was suspended in May 2005 when the Slacks decided to retire. The future of the brewery was uncertain when the guide went to press.

Ceredigion

Bragdy Ceredigion, Office: Bryn Hawk, New Quay, Ceredigion, SA45 9SB
Brewery: Unit 2, Wervil Grange Farm, Pentregat, Ceredigion, SA44 6HW
Tel/Fax (01545) 561417
Tel (01239) 654888
Email brian@ceredigionbrewery.fs.business.co.uk
Website www.bestofruralwales.co.uk
Tours by arrangement

Bragdy Ceredigion (Cardigan Brewery) is situated on the coastal belt of West Wales and housed in a converted barn on Wervil Grange

Farm. A family-run craft brewery established in 1997 by Brian and Julia Tilby, it produces bottle-conditioned and cask-conditioned ales. No chemical additives are used and the bottle-conditioned beers are suitable for vegans. An organic beer with certified pale malt and organic hops was added in 2001 and a range of organic fruit beers is planned. Bottle-conditioned beers: as for cask beers, save for the Spirit of the Forest.

Ysbryd O'r Goeden/Spirit of the Forest (OG 1036, ABV 3.8%)

Gwrach Ddu/Black Witch (OG 1038, ABV 4%)

Draig Aur/Gold Dragon (OG 1039, ABV 4.2%)

Barcud Coch/Red Kite (OG 1040, ABV 4.3%)

Blodeuwedd/Flowerface organic beer (OG 1043, ABV 4.5%)
Golden beer with a citrus hop and juicy malt aroma. Peppery hops dominate the palate, balanced by creamy malt, while the finish is hoppy and bitter with a continuing citrus fruit note.

Cwrw 2000/Ale 2000 (OG 1049, ABV 5%)

Yr Hen Darw Du/Old Black Bull (OG 1058, ABV 6.2%)

Chalk Hill

Chalk Hill Brewery, Rosary Road, Norwich, Norfolk, NR1 4DA
Tel/Fax (01603) 477078

⊗ Run by former Reindeer brew-pub owner Bill Thomas and his partners Tiny Little and Dave Blake, Chalk Hill began production with a 15-barrel plant in 1993. It is developing plans for expansion and new brews, and supplies its own pub. The beers are also available nationwide via beer agencies. Occasional beer: IPA (ABV 5.3%).

Tap Bitter (OG 1036, ABV 3.6%) ◆
A pale brown brew with a gentle fruity nose. Lightly flavoured with swirling apple notes among a malty support. Steeply fading finish with a hint of bitterness.

CHB (OG 1042, ABV 4.2%) ◆
A singular malty aroma introduces a full-bodied plummy ale. Fruit vies with malt for domination in this filling, copper-coloured extravaganza. Fruitiness rolls on to overshadow fading bitterness.

Dreadnought (OG 1049, ABV 4.9%) ◆
A heavy malt-based, mid-brown beer with a slight hoppiness providing balance to the roast and caramel undertones. A subtle change in the ending creates a deeper roast finish.

Flintknapper's Mild (OG 1052, ABV 5%) ◆
Chocolate, stewed fruits, liquorice, hops and malt can all be found in this rich red-coloured brew. The light malt nose belies the variety of flavours. Rich and sticky.

Old Tackle (OG 1056, ABV 5.6%) ◆
Red hued with a matching blackcurrant bouquet, this rich malty brew slowly subsides to a long dryish end. Roast notes remain consistent as initial caramel declines to an echo.

Cheriton SIBA

Cheriton Brewhouse, Cheriton, Alresford, Hampshire, SO24 0QQ
Tel (01962) 771166
Fax (01962) 771595
Email bestbeer1@aol.com
Tours by arrangement

⊗ The brewery was founded in 1993 by the owners of the adjacent Flower Pots pub and two working partners, Ray Page and Martin Roberts. With an emphasis on quality rather than quantity, the beers soon gained an appreciative audience in local pubs. Full capacity has been achieved. 50 outlets are supplied direct. Seasonal beers: Green Light (ABV 3.3%, winter & spring), Russet (ABV 4%, autumn), Beltane (ABV 4.5%, spring), Flower Power (ABV 5.2%, summer), Turkey's Delight (ABV 5.9%, Christmas).

Pots Ale (OG 1036.5, ABV 3.8%) ◆
A clean-tasting, pale brown bitter, characterised by a citrus aroma, floral hoppiness and a pleasing bitterness that lingers in the mouth. Hops dominate throughout but with a background maltiness to add balance. A long-lasting dry, bitter finish.

Village Elder (OG 1038, ABV 3.8%) ◆
A straw-coloured session bitter brewed with elderflowers that provide a light fruity flavour balanced by a noticeable hoppiness and a bitter-sweet finish. Champion Beer of Hampshire 2004.

Amber Gambler (OG 1040, ABV 3.9%)

Best Bitter (OG 1043, ABV 4.2%) ◆
A malty and fruity taste continues into the aftertaste. A dark brown beer with a malty and fruity nose.

Diggers Gold (OG 1044.5, ABV 4.6%)
A full-bodied, well-balanced golden best bitter. A glorious hoppy, grapefruit aroma leads to a strong hoppy bite in the flavour. A dry finish. Bitter and hoppy in all respects.

Chiltern SIBA

Chiltern Brewery, Nash Lee Road, Terrick, Aylesbury, Buckinghamshire, HP17 0TQ
Tel (01296) 613647
Fax (01296) 612419
Email info@chilternbrewery.co.uk
Website www.chilternbrewery.co.uk
Shop 9-5 Mon-Sat
Tours every Saturday at noon (by arrangement) and weekdays for groups (by arrangement)

⊗ The Chiltern Brewery is a second generation independent family brewery run by the Jenkinsons. Founded in 1980, the brewery produces a broad range of beers, both draught and bottled, using traditional methods with English ingredients. The spring of 2004 saw the culmination of 18 months of investment in the brewery, with a new brewhouse and brew-plant, a temperature-controlled cool room for conditioning and storing the beer, and improvements to the fermenting room. Seasonal beers: Golden Sovereign (ABV 3.7%, summer), Glad Tidings (ABV 4.6%, winter). Bottle-conditioned beers: Glad Tidings (Christmas), Bodgers Barley Wine (ABV 8.5%).

Ale (OG 1037, ABV 3.7%) ◈
A refreshing session bitter, amber in colour, with a predominantly malty character. The aroma is of pale malt with a hint of grape, with some sweetness in the mouth and a short finish.

Beechwood Bitter (OG 1043, ABV 4.3%) ◈
A pale brown, refreshing beer with a rich butter-toffee aroma, lots of pale malt and fruit in the mouth and a finish that is more sweet and fruity than bitter.

Three Hundreds Old Ale (OG 1049, ABV 4.9%) ◈
A strong old ale with some crystal malt and roast character plus hints of liquorice. Deceptively strong. It is not brewed during the summer.

Church End SIBA

Church End Brewery Ltd, 109 Ridge Lane, Nuneaton, Warwickshire, CV10 0RD
Tel (01827) 713080
Fax (01827) 717328
Shop during tap opening hours
Tours by arrangement

⊗ Founded by Stewart Elliott in 1994 with a four-barrel plant. Growth and the need for a retail outlet led to a move to Ridge Lane in 2001 to a purpose-built 10-barrel plant in a former social club. The brewery is visible from the adjoining Brewery Tap, which opened in 2002. Many unusual beers are produced throughout the year (e.g. damson, coffee, green hop). Some 250 outlets are supplied. Seasonal beer: Rest in Peace (ABV 7%, winter). Bottle-conditioned beers: Nuns Ale (ABV 4.5%), Rugby Ale (ABV 5%), Arthur's Wilt (ABV 6%).

Poachers Pocket (OG 1036, ABV 3.5%)

Cuthberts (OG 1038, ABV 3.8%) ◈
A refreshing, hoppy beer, with hints of malt, fruit and caramel taste. Lingering bitter aftertaste.

Goat's Milk (OG 1038, ABV 3.8%)

Gravediggers (OG 1038, ABV 3.8%) ◈
A premium mild. Black and red in colour, with a complex mix of chocolate and roast flavours, it is almost a light porter.

Hop Gun (OG 1041, ABV 4.1%)

Without-a-Bix (OG 1042, ABV 4.2%) ◈
A wheat beer; clear, malty and pale, combining German hops and English wheat.

What the Fox's Hat (OG 1043, ABV 4.2%) ◈
A beer with a malty aroma, and a hoppy and malty taste with some caramel flavour.

Pooh Beer (OG 1044, ABV 4.3%) ◈
A bright golden beer brewed with honey. Sweet, yet hoppy.

Vicar's Ruin (OG 1044, ABV 4.4%) ◈
A straw-coloured best bitter with an initially hoppy, bitter flavour, softening to a delicate malt finish.

Stout Coffin (OG 1046, ABV 4.6%)

Fallen Angel (OG 1050, ABV 5%)

City of Cambridge EAB

City of Cambridge Brewery Co Ltd, Ely Road, Chittering, Cambridge, CB5 9PH
Tel (01223) 864864
Email sales@cambridge-brewery.co.uk
Website www.cambridge-brewery.co.uk

⊗ City of Cambridge opened in 1997 and moved to its present site in 2002. It is recognised for the quality of its products and its concern for the environment. In addition to prizes for its cask beers, the brewery holds a conservation award for the introduction of native reed beds at its site to naturally treat its brewery water. Seasonal ales (subject to availability): Jet Black (ABV 3.7%), Bramling Traditional (ABV 5.5%), Drummer St Stout (ABV 4.5%), Mich'aelmas (ABV 4.6%), Holly Heaven (ABV 5.2%). All beers are available in bottle-conditioned form.

Boathouse Bitter (ABV 3.8%) ◈
Copper-brown and full-bodied session bitter, starting with impressive citrus and floral hop; grassy fruit notes are present with finally a fading, gentle bitterness.

Rutherford IPA (ABV 3.8%) ◈
Satisfying session bitter with a soft hoppy, bitter-sweet balance and a light sulphury character after a fruity, malty start. This amber brew ends dry and bitter with a light balance of malt and hops.

Hobson's Choice (ABV 4.1%) 🗍 ◈
A highly drinkable, golden brew with a pronounced hop aroma and taste, and a fruity, bitter balance in the mouth, finishing gently dry.

Sunset Square (ABV 4.4%)
A blend of two best-selling beers to create a unique smooth flavour. A pleasing, golden colour, with a refreshing aftertaste.

Atom Splitter (ABV 4.7%) ◈
Robust copper-coloured strong bitter with a hop aroma and taste, and a distinct sulphury edge.

Darwin's Downfall (ABV 5%)
A blended, ruby golden coloured beer. Hoppy with a fruity character and a refreshing citrus aftertaste.

Parkers Porter (ABV 5.3%) ◈
Impressive reddish brew with a defined roast character throughout, and a short, fruity, bitter-sweet palate.

Bramling Traditional (ABV 5.5%)
Made with Bramling Cross hops, fruity and delicious.

City of Stirling

City of Stirling Brewery, Unit 70, Bandeath Industrial Estate, Stirling, FK7 7NP
Tel (01786) 834555
Fax (01786) 833426

Email brewery@ cityofstirlingbrewery.com
Tours by arrangement

A custom-built, 20-barrel brewery based in a former torpedo factory. It started brewing in 2004 in the historic Royal Burgh of Stirling, Scotland's newest city. A range of traditional ales is planned, including regular seasonals.

Ale (OG 1052, ABV 4.8%)

Clark's SIBA

HB Clark & Co (Successors) Ltd, Westgate Brewery, Wakefield, West Yorkshire, WF2 9SW
Tel (01924) 373328
Fax (01924) 372306
Email clarksbrewery@hbclark.co.uk
Website www.hbclark.co.uk
Shop 9-5pm
Tours by arrangement

◎ Founded in 1905, Clark's ceased brewing during the 1960s and 1970s. It resumed cask ale production in 1982 and now delivers to more than 100 outlets. Clark's owns four pubs, all serving cask ale. Clark's is a micro-brewery but is often thought of as a regional due to its substantial wholesale business. Seasonal beers can be found on the website.

Classic Blonde (OG 1039, ABV 3.9%)
A light blond ale with a citrus and hoppy flavour, a distinctive grapefruit aroma and a dry finish.

No Angel (OG 1040, ABV 4%)

Classic Brunette (ABV 4.2%)

Rams Revenge (OG 1046, ABV 4.6%) ◆
A rich, ruby-coloured premium ale, well-balanced with malt and hops, with a deep fruity taste and a dry hoppy aftertaste, with a pleasant hoppy aroma.

Golden Hornet (OG 1050, ABV 5%) ◆
A crisp golden premium beer with a full fruity taste, with full hop aroma and dry hop aftertaste.

Mulberry Tree (OG 1050, ABV 5%)

Clarke's Organic*

Clarke's Organic Brewery Ltd, Thornhill Hall Farm, Hall Lane, Dewsbury, West Yorkshire, WF12 0QL
Tel (01924) 489222

The brewery was launched in 2004 with the sole purpose of brewing a small range of organic bottled beers, although beer may be available to festivals in cask form. A 3.5-barrel plant is used.

Clearwater SIBA

Clearwater Brewery, 2 Devon Units, Hatchmoor Industrial Estate, Torrington, Devon, EX38 7HP
Tel (01805) 625242
Tours by arrangement

⊗ Clearwater took on the closed St Giles in the Wood brewery in 1999 and has steadily grown since. The brewery has a 10-12 barrel capacity and the owners plan to bottle their beers. Around 80 outlets are supplied. Seasonal beer: Ebony & Ivory (ABV 4.2%, winter).

Bottle-conditioned beers: Cavalier Ale (ABV 4%), 1646 (ABV 4.8%), Oliver's Nectar (ABV 5.2%).

Culley Village Pride (ABV 3.7%)

Cavalier (OG 1041, ABV 4%) ◆
Mid-brown, full-bodied best bitter with a burnt, rich malt aroma and taste, leading to a bitter, well-rounded finish.

Torridge Best (OG 1044, ABV 4.4%)

1646 (OG 1047, ABV 4.8%)

Oliver's Nectar (OG 1051, ABV 5.2%)

Clockwork

🍺 Clockwork Beer Co, 1153-55 Cathcart Road, Glasgow, G42 9HB
Tel/Fax (0141) 649 0184
Email rhg@talk21.com
Tours by arrangement

Clockwork is a micro-brewery in the middle of a bar. A wide range of beers, including fruit beers, wheat beers and lagers, is produced. Most are cold-conditioned and pressurised but strong ales of more than 5% are cask conditioned.

Oregon IPA (ABV 5.5%)

Thunder and Lightning (ABV 6%)

Coach House SIBA

Coach House Brewing Company Ltd, Wharf Street, Warrington, Cheshire, WA1 2DQ
Tel (01925) 232800
Fax (01925) 232700
Email info@coach-house-brewing.co.uk
Website www.coach-house-brewing.co.uk
Tours by arrangement for CAMRA groups

◎ The brewery was founded in 1991 by four ex-Greenall Whitley employees. In 1995 Coach House increased its brewing capacity to cope with growing demand and it now delivers to some 250 outlets throughout England, Wales and Scotland, either from the brewery or via wholesalers. The brewery also brews a large number of one-off and special beers. Seasonal beers: Ostlers Summer Pale Ale (ABV 4%, summer), Squires Gold (ABV 4.2%, spring), Summer Sizzler (ABV 4.2%, summer), Countdown (ABV 4.7%, 6 December onwards), Taverners Autumn Ale (ABV 5%, autumn), Blunderbus Old Porter (ABV 5.5%, winter).

Coachman's Best Bitter (OG 1037, ABV 3.7%) ◆
A well-hopped, malty bitter, moderately fruity with a hint of sweetness and a peppery nose.

Gunpowder Mild (OG 1037, ABV 3.8%) ◆
Dark brown, lightly hopped, malty mild with faint roast undertones. Easy drinking but not as characterful as it once was.

Honeypot Bitter (OG 1037, ABV 3.8%)

Farrier's Best Bitter (OG 1038, ABV 3.9%)

Dick Turpin (OG 1042, ABV 4.2%) ◆
Malty, hoppy pale brown beer with some initial sweetish flavours leading to a short, bitter aftertaste. Also sold under other names as a pub house beer.

Flintlock Pale Ale (OG 1044, ABV 4.4%)

Innkeeper's Special Reserve (OG 1044, ABV 4.5%) ♦
A darkish, full-flavoured bitter. Quite fruity, with a strong, bitter aftertaste.

Postlethwaite (OG 1045, ABV 4.6%)

Gingernut Premium (OG 1049, ABV 5%)

Posthorn Premium (OG 1049, ABV 5%) ♦
Well-hopped and fruity, with bitterness and malt also prominent. Hoppy aroma and fruity aftertaste.

For John Joule of Stone

Old Knotty (ABV 3.6%)

Old Priory (ABV 4.4%)

Victory (ABV 5.2%)

Coles

Coles Family Brewery, White Hart Thatched Inn & Brewery, Llanddarog, Carmarthen, SA32 8NT
Tel (01267) 275395
Tours by arrangement

Coles is based in an ancient inn built in 1371. Centuries ago beer was brewed on site, but brewing only started again in 1999. The brewery has its own water supply 320 feet below ground, free from pollution. Coles makes a large selection of cask ales due to a system that allows small-batch production. Two pubs are owned. Seasonal beers: Cwrw Nadolig (ABV 3%, Christmas), Summer Harvest (ABV 3.8%).

Nettle Ale (OG 1039, ABV 3.8%)

Amber Ale (OG 1042, ABV 4%)

Black Stag (OG 1042, ABV 4%)

Cwrw Betys Beetroot Ale (OG 1042, ABV 4%)

Liquorice Stout (OG 1042, ABV 4%)

Oaten Barley Stout (OG 1042, ABV 4%)

Roasted Barley Stout (OG 1042, ABV 4%)

Cwrw Llanddarog (OG 1043, ABV 4.1%)

Cwrw Blasus (OG 1044, ABV 4.3%)

Dewi Sant (OG 1045, ABV 4.4%)

Concertina SIBA

Concertina Brewery, 9A Dolcliffe Road, Mexborough, South Yorkshire, S64 9AZ
Tel (01709) 580841
Tours by arrangement

The brewery started in 1992 in the cellar of a club once famous as the home of a long-gone concertina band. The plant produces up to eight barrels a week for the club and other occasional outlets. Other beers are brewed on a seasonal basis. 25 outlets are supplied.

Club Bitter (ABV 3.9%) ♦
A fruity session bitter with a good bitter flavour.

Old Dark Attic (OG 1038, ABV 3.9%)
A dark brown beer with a fairly sweet, fruity taste.

Bengal Tiger (OG 1043, ABV 4.6%) ♦
Light amber ale with an aromatic hoppy nose followed by a wonderful combination of fruit and bitterness. A very smooth finish.

Coniston SIBA

Coniston Brewing Co Ltd, Coppermines Road, Coniston, Cumbria, LA21 8HL
Tel (01539) 441133
Fax (01539) 441177
Email info@conistonbrewery.com
Website www.conistonbrewery.com
Shop 10-11. Tours by arrangement.

A 10-barrel brewery set up in 1995 behind the Black Bull inn, Coniston, it achieved national fame when it won the Champion Beer of Britain competition in 1998 for Bluebird Bitter. This was followed by SIBA North first prize in 2003. It is now brewing 30 barrels a week and supplies 30 local outlets while the beers are distributed nationally by wholesalers. One pub is owned. Bottle-conditioned Coniston beers are brewed by Ridgeway (qv) using Hepworth's Horsham plant (qv): Bluebird in bottle is ABV 4.2%, Old Man Ale ABV 4.8%. Seasonal beer: Blacksmith's Ale (ABV 5%, Dec-March).

Bluebird Bitter (OG 1036, ABV 3.6%) ♦
A yellow-gold, predominantly hoppy and fruity beer, well-balanced with some sweetness and a rising bitter finish.

Opium (OG 1039, ABV 4%) ♦
Copper-coloured with distinctly fruity, hoppy aromas; a well-balanced flavour with malt, hops and fruit, and more bitter and astringent in the aftertaste.

Bluebird XB (OG 1042, ABV 4.2%) ♦
Well-balanced, hoppy and fruity golden bitter. Bitter-sweet in the mouth with dryness building.

Old Man Ale (OG 1042, ABV 4.2%) ♦
Delicious fruity, winey beer with a complex, well-balanced richness.

Conwy

Conwy Brewing Ltd, Unit 17, Ffordd Sam Pari, Conwy Morfe Business Park, Conwy, LL32 8HB
Tel (01492) 585287
Email enquiries@conwybrewery.co.uk
Website www.conwybrewery.co.uk
Tours by arrangement

Conwy started brewing in an industrial unit in 2003 with help from a Welsh Assembly investment grant. All the cask beers are now available in bottle-conditioned form. Seasonal ales were introduced in 2004 with beers planned for spring, summer, autumn, winter and a mild ale in May. A brewery shop is planned. All the beers are available with Welsh and/or English language names. 30 outlets are supplied direct. Seasonal beer: Fireside Ale (ABV 5%, winter). Bottle-conditioned beer: Celebration Ale.

Castle Bitter/Cwrw Castell (OG 1037, ABV 3.8%)

Celebration Ale/Cwrw Gwledd (OG 1040, ABV 4.2%)

Honey Fayre/Cwrw Mêl (ABV 4.5%)

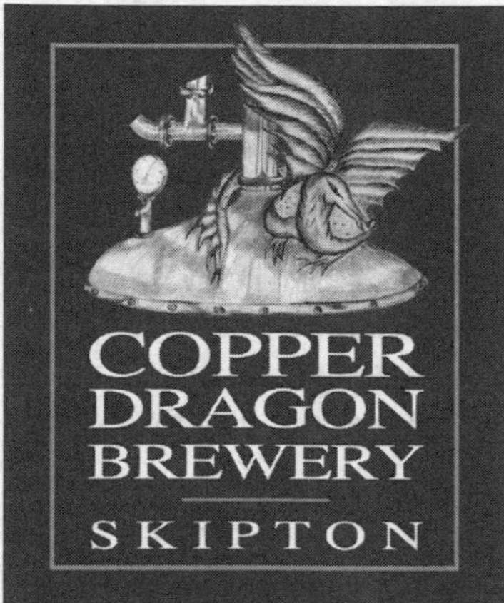

Copper Dragon SIBA

Copper Dragon Brewery Ltd, Snaygill Industrial Estate, Keighley Road, Skipton, North Yorkshire, BD23 2QR
Tel (01756) 702130
Fax (01756) 702136
Email post@copperdragon.uk.com
Website www.copperdragon.uk.com
Shop Mon-Fri 9-5. Tours by arrangement

Copper Dragon began brewing in 2003 and now brews 160 barrels a week. There are 18 employees and beer is produced on a German plant. The company supplies free trade within an 80-mile radius of Skipton. The brewery is acquiring its own outlets in Lancashire and Yorkshire with plans to expand production. Some 600 outlets are supplied.

Black Gold (OG 1036, ABV 3.7%) ◆
A dark ale with subtle fruit and dark malts on the nose. Quite bitter with roast coffee flavours throughout and a long burnt finish.

Best Bitter (OG 1036, ABV 3.8%) ◆
A delicate hoppy aroma leads to an aggressively bitter and hoppy taste, with a bitter finish.

Golden Pippin (OG 1037, ABV 3.9%) ◆
This straw-coloured beer has an intense citrus aroma and flavour, characteristic of American Cascade hops. The dry, bitter astringency increases in the aftertaste.

Scotts 1816 (OG 1041, ABV 4.1%) ◆
A well-balanced, full-bodied, copper-coloured premium bitter with a fruity, hoppy and slightly nutty character. Bitterness increases in the finish to leave a dry, hoppy fruitiness.

Challenger IPA (OG 1042, ABV 4.4%) ◆
Amber coloured, this is a best bitter in the traditional style. Initial maltiness gives way to hops and a growing bitter, dry finish.

Corvedale SIBA

⌂ Corvedale Brewery, Sun Inn, Corfton, Craven Arms, Shropshire, SY7 9DF
Tel (01584) 861239
Email norman@suninncorfton.co.uk
Website www.suninncorfton.co.uk
Tours by arrangement

◎ Brewing started in 1999 in a building behind the pub. Landlord Norman Pearce is also the brewer and he uses only British malt and hops, with water from a local borehole. Corvedale swaps its beer with those of other small craft breweries, making them available in many parts of the country. One pub is owned and 10 outlets are supplied. Seasonal beer: Teresa's Pride (ABV 4.3%, January). All beers are on sale in the pub in bottle-conditioned form and not fined, making them suitable for vegetarians and vegans.

Katie's Pride (OG 1040, ABV 4%)

Norman's Pride (OG 1043, ABV 4.3%)
A golden amber beer with a refreshing, slightly hoppy taste and a bitter finish.

Secret Hop (OG 1045, ABV 4.5%)
A clear, ruby bitter with a smooth malty taste. Customers are invited to guess the hop!

Dark and Delicious (OG 1045, ABV 4.6%)
A dark ruby beer with hops on the aroma and palate, and a sweet aftertaste.

Cotleigh SIBA

Cotleigh Brewery, Ford Road, Wiveliscombe, Somerset, TA4 2RE
Tel (01984) 624086
Fax (01984) 624365
Email info@cotleighbrewery.com
Website www.cotleighbrewery.co.uk
Tours Yes, to select CAMRA groups

⊗ Situated in the historic brewing town of Wiveliscombe, Cotleigh Brewery is one of the oldest and most successful small breweries in the West Country. The brewery, which started trading in 1979, is housed in specially converted premises with a modern plant capable of producing 140 barrels a week. 150 pubs, mostly in Devon and Somerset, are supplied from the brewery; the beers are also widely available across the country via selected wholesalers. The business was sold in 2003 to Stephen Heptinstall and Fred Domellof. Seasonal beers: Buzzard (ABV 4.8%, Oct-April), Kookaburra (ABV 4.4%, August), New Harvest (ABV 4%, September), Red Nose Reinbeer (ABV 5%, Nov-Dec). Bottle-conditioned beer: Red Nose Reinbeer (Nov-Dec only).

Tawny Bitter (OG 1038, ABV 3.8%) ◆
Well-balanced, tawny-coloured bitter with plenty of malt and fruitiness on the nose, and malt to the fore in the taste, followed by hop fruit, developing to a satisfying bitter finish.

Golden Eagle (OG 1042, ABV 4.2%) ◆
A gold, well-hopped premium bitter with a flowery hop aroma and fruity hop flavour, clean mouthfeel, leading to a dry, hoppy finish.

Barn Owl Bitter (OG 1045, ABV 4.5%) ◆
A pale to mid-brown beer with a good balance of malt and hops on the nose; a smooth, full-bodied taste where hops dominate, but balanced by malt, following through to the finish.

Cotswold Spring*

Cotswold Spring Brewery, Springs Farm, Dodington Ash, Chipping Sodbury, Bristol, BS37 6RX

Tel (01454) 323088
Fax (01454) 323089
Email sales@cotswoldbrewery.com
Website www.cotswoldbrewery.com

A brewery launched in 2005 using a 10-barrel refurbished plant installed in a new building on the site of the Cotswold Spring mineral water company, although operated as a separate company. The natural spring water is used for brewing.

Olde English Rose (ABV 3.8%)

Codrington Codger (ABV 4.2%)

Codrington Royal (ABV 4.5%)

Cottage SIBA

Cottage Brewing Co, The Old Cheese Dairy, Brue Farm, Lovington, Castle Cary, Somerset, BA7 7PP
Tel (01963) 240551
Fax (01963) 240383
Tours by arrangement

⊗ The brewery, which celebrated its 10th anniversary in 2003, was founded in West Lydford in 1993 and upgraded to a 10-barrel plant in 1994. Owned by former airline pilot Chris Norman and his wife Helen, the company got off to a flying start when Norman's Conquest won the Champion Beer of Britain title at the 1995 Great British Beer Festival. The brewery moved to larger premises in 1996, doubling the brewing capacity at the same time. In 2001, Cottage installed a 30-barrel plant. 1,500 outlets are supplied. The malt used is Maris Otter and hops come mainly from Kent. No pubs are owned but the beers are supplied as far away as Liverpool and Yorkshire. The names of beers mostly follow a railway theme. Seasonal beers: Goldrush (ABV 5%), Santa's Steaming Ale (ABV 5.5%, Christmas). Norman's Conquest is also available in bottle-conditioned form.

Southern Bitter (OG 1039, ABV 3.7%) ◆
Gold-coloured beer with malt and fruity hops on the nose. Malt and hops in the mouth with a long fruity, bitter finish.

Champflower Ale (OG 1041, ABV 4.2%) ◆
Amber beer with a fruity hop aroma, full hop taste and powerful bitter finish.

Somerset & Dorset Ale (OG 1044, ABV 4.4%)
A well-hopped, malty brew, with a deep red colour.

Golden Arrow (OG 1043, ABV 4.5%) ◆
A hoppy golden bitter with a powerful floral bouquet, a fruity, full-bodied taste and a lingering dry, bitter finish.

Norman's Conquest (OG 1066, ABV 7%) ◆
A dark strong ale, with plenty of fruit in the aroma and taste; rounded vinous, hoppy finish.

Countrylife SIBA

Countrylife Brewery, The Big Sheep, Abbotsham, Bideford, North Devon, EX39 5AP
Tel (01237) 420808/07971 267790
Tel (01237) 420808
Shop open 7 days a week
Tours by arrangement

⊗ Since moving to the Big Sheep tourist attraction, the brewery welcomes some 1,000 visitors in the summer, tasting and buying beer. A major expansion is planned, including a bottling line. 30-40 outlets are supplied. Seasonal beer: Lacey's Lager (ABV 5%, winter). Bottle-conditioned beers: all cask beers; the ABV of Old Appledore is increased to 4.2%.

Old Appledore (OG 1037, ABV 3.7%)

Wallop (OG 1044, ABV 4.4%)

Golden Pig (OG 1046, ABV 4.7%)

Country Bumpkin (OG 1058, ABV 6%)

Cox & Holbrook EAB

Cox & Holbrook, Manor Farm, Brettenham Road, Buxhall, Suffolk, IP14 3DY
Tel/Fax (01449) 736323
Tours by arrangement

The five-barrel brewery was set up in 1992 by David Cox. It moved to Buxhall in 2002. Investment in new bottling equipment and expansion of the range are planned. 12 outlets are supplied.

Crown Dark Mild (OG 1034, ABV 3.6%)

Shelley Dark Mild (OG 1035, ABV 3.6%)

Bux Hill Old Mill (OG 1035, ABV 3.8%)

Beyton Bitter (OG 1037, ABV 3.8%)

Bridge Road Bitter (OG 1040, ABV 4%)

Rattles Den Best Bitter (OG 1040, ABV 4%)

Remus (OG 1044, ABV 4.5%)

Goodcock's Winner (OG 1047, ABV 5%)

Stormwatch (OG 1048, ABV 5%)

Stowmarket Porter (OG 1050, ABV 5%)

East Anglian Pale Ale (OG 1060, ABV 6%)

Crondall*

Crondall Brewing Co Ltd, Lower Old Park Farm, Dora's Green Lane, Crondall, near Farnham, Surrey, GU10 5DX
Tel (01252) 319000

David and Chrissy Taraszek have converted an old granary barn into an eight-barrel micro-brewery. The second-hand equipment came from Roosters Brewery (qv). Brewing started in May 2005 and the beer can be found in local pubs and beer festivals close to the brewery. New beers were planned for later in 2005.

Mr T's Wedding Ale (ABV 3.8%)

Cropton SIBA

⊕ Cropton Brewery, Cropton, near Pickering, North Yorkshire, YO18 8HH
Tel (01751) 417330
Fax (01751) 417582
Email info@croptonbrewery.co.uk
Website www.croptonbrewery.co.uk
Shop merchandise available all year round at the New Inn
Tours by arrangement

⊕ Brewing returned to Cropton in 1984 when the cellars of the pub were converted to accommodate a five-barrel plant. The plant was extended in 1988, but by 1994 it had outgrown the cellar and a purpose-built brewery was installed in the grounds of Woolcroft Farm behind the pub. Production fluctuates between 35 and 50 barrels a week according to season. Cropton's additive-free beers are supplied to more than 100 independent outlets from the brewery and nationwide through wholesalers. One pub, the New Inn, is owned. All the beers, with the exception of Balmy Mild and Haunting Hanks, are available bottle conditioned and can be purchased from the visitor centre attached to the pub. All bottled beers are available all year round, regardless of the cask-conditioned version being permanent or seasonal, and are suitable for vegetarians and vegans. Seasonal beers: Haunting Hanks (ABV 4.9%), Rudolph's Revenge (ABV 4.6%), Balmy Mild (ABV 4.4%), Uncle Sam's (ABV 4.4%), Scoresby Stout (ABV 4.2% G).

King Billy **(OG 1036, ABV 3.6%)** ◈
A refreshing, straw-coloured bitter, quite hoppy, with a strong but pleasant bitter finish that leaves a clean, dry taste on the palate.

Endeavour Ale **(OG 1038, ABV 3.6%)**
A light session ale, made with the best quality hops, providing a refreshing drink with a delicate fruity aftertaste.

Two Pints **(OG 1040, ABV 4%)** ◈
A good, full-bodied bitter. Malt flavours initially dominate, with a touch of caramel, but the balancing hoppiness and residual sweetness come through.

Honey Gold **(OG 1042, ABV 4.2%)** ◈
A medium-bodied beer, ideal for summer drinking. Honey is apparent in both aroma and taste but does not overwhelm. Clean finish with a hint of hops.

Yorkshire Moors Bitter **(OG 1046, ABV 4.6%)**
A fine ruby beer brewed with Fuggles and Progress hops. A unique hoppy beer with a fruity aftertaste.

Monkmans Slaughter **(OG 1060, ABV 6%)** ◈
Rich tasting and warming; fruit and malt in the aroma and taste, with dark chocolate, caramel and autumn fruit notes. Subtle bitterness continues into the aftertaste.

Crouch Vale SIBA

Crouch Vale Brewery Ltd, 12 Redhills Road, South Woodham Ferrers, Chelmsford, Essex, CM3 5UP
Tel (01245) 322744
Fax (01245) 329082
Email info@crouch-vale.co.uk
Website www.crouch-vale.co.uk
Tours by arrangement

⊗ Founded over 20 years ago by two CAMRA enthusiasts, Crouch Vale is now well established as a major craft brewer in Essex, still brewing in its original premises. The company is also a major wholesaler of cask ale from other independent breweries, which they supply to more than 250 outlets as well as beer festivals throughout the region. One tied house, the

Queen's Head in Chelmsford, is owned, serving a range of Crouch Vale beers with additional guest ales. Seasonal beers: two beers are available each month, details on website.

Essex Boys Bitter **(OG 1035, ABV 3.5%)** ◈
Amber light bitter with a spicy, citrus aroma and a building dry bitterness.

Blackwater Mild **(OG 1037, ABV 3.7%)** ◈
A dark, roasty bitter ale. Fruity but not sweet with a base of malt and hops, and a subsiding dryness.

Brewers Gold **(OG 1040, ABV 4%)** ◼ ◻ ◈
Honey-toned golden ale, with grapefruit sharpness offset by suggestions of melon and pineapple. Lacks the subtle maltiness found in previous years; a little unbalanced as a result.

Crouch Best **(OG 1040, ABV 4%)** ◈
Clean, copper-coloured bitter with a light balance of hops and malt, and a strong developing dryness.

Anchor Street Porter **(OG 1049, ABV 4.9%)** ◻ ◈
Full-bodied, dark red beer with a pleasing balance of roast grain and fruity sweetness.

Crown

Crown Brewery, Sheffield: see Edale and Wellington

Cuillin*

Cuillin Brewery Ltd, Sligachan Hotel, Sligachan, Carbost, Isle of Skye, IV47 8SW
Tel (01478) 650204
Fax (01478) 650207
Email info@cuillinbrewery.co.uk
Website www.cuillinbrewery.co.uk

Cuillin started brewing in 2004 in a hotel complex, using a five-barrel former Firkin plant. A stout, Black Face, was being tested as the guide went to press.

Eagle Ale **(ABV 3.8%)**

Sky Ale **(ABV 4.1%)**

Custom*

Custom Beers Ltd, Little Burchetts Farm, Isaacs Lane, Haywards Heath, TH16 4RZ
Tel (01273) 504988

Peter Skinner brewed at Dark Star in Brighton several years ago. He launched his new, five-barrel brewery in 2005 in converted bullock-rearing sheds on a farm, using a combination of new and refurbished plant. The four regular beers are complemented by seasonal and special brews.

Goldings Pale Ale (ABV 3.7%)

Chinook Best Bitter (ABV 4.2%)

Cascade Special Bitter (ABV 4.8%)

Dark Roast Porter (ABV 5.5%)

Cwmbran SIBA

Cwmbran Brewery, Gorse Cottage, Graig Road, Upper Cwmbran, Torfaen, NP44 5AS
Tel/Fax (01633) 485233
Email cwmbran.brewery@btopenworld.com
Website www.cwmbranbrewery.co.uk

◎ Cwmbran Brewery is a craft brewery on the slopes of Mynydd Maen in Upper Cwmbran in Gwent's eastern valley. It is sited alongside the brewer's cottage home. A mountain spring supplies the water used for brewing liquor. The brewery produces a range of cask beers, some with fruit flavours, using traditional methods and ingredients. An extension to the brewery has increased both capacity and flexibility. Seasonal beers: Drayman's Gold (ABV 4.5%), Golden Wheat (ABV 4.5%), Pink Panther (ABV 4.8%) in summer; Santa's Tipple (ABV 4.8%, Christmas).

Drayman's Choice (OG 1039, ABV 3.8%)

Double Hop (OG 1039, ABV 4%)

Blackcurrant Stout (OG 1040, ABV 4%)

Crow Valley Bitter (OG 1042, ABV 4.2%) ◆
Gentle malt and hop aroma followed by a crisp, clean mix of malt, hop and fruit flavours. Moderate bitterness builds, leaving a lasting finish.

Crow Valley Stout/Deryn Du
(OG 1042, ABV 4.2%)

Nut Brown Premium Ale
(OG 1045, ABV 4.5%)

Four Seasons (OG 1048, ABV 4.8%)

Full Malty (OG 1048, ABV 4.8%)

Gorse Porter (OG 1048, ABV 4.8%)

Daleside

Daleside Brewery Ltd, Camwal Road, Harrogate, North Yorkshire, HG1 4PT
Tel (01423) 880022
Fax 01423 541717
Email dalesidebrewery@aol.com

◎ Founder Bill Witty opened the brewery in 1991 in Harrogate with a 20-barrel plant. The brewery has grown over the years and today can produce more than 175 barrels a week. The ownership of the brewery changed in 2005 with Alan Barker becoming chairman and Bill's son, Craig, in charge of brewing. The beers are available in 500 pubs regionally and nationally through wholesale and pub chain customers. Seasonal beers: Santa's Progress (ABV 4.2%), St George's Ale (ABV 4.1%), Starbeck Stout (ABV 4.2%).

Bitter (OG 1039, ABV 3.7%) ◆
Pale brown in colour, this well-balanced, hoppy beer is pleasantly complemented by fruity bitterness and a hint of sweetness, leading to a moderately long, bitter finish.

Blonde (OG 1041, ABV 3.9%) ◆
A pale golden beer with a predominantly hoppy aroma and taste, leading to a refreshing hoppy, bitter but short finish.

Old Lubrication (OG 1043, ABV 4.1%)

Old Legover (OG 1043, ABV 4.1%) ◆
A well-balanced, mid-brown, refreshing beer that leads to an equally well-balanced, fruity and bitter aftertaste.

Pride of England (OG 1042, ABV 4.3%)

Old Rogue Ale (OG 1046, ABV 4.5%) ◆
Well-balanced, full-bodied amber bitter with strong hop and fruit overtones. The fruitiness carries through to the aftertaste, which has a long, dry, bitter finish.

Monkey Wrench (OG 1055, ABV 5.3%) ◆
A powerful strong ale, mid-brown to ruby in hue. Aromas of fruit, hops, malt and roast malt give way to well-balanced fruit, malt and hoppiness on the tongue, with some sweetness throughout.

For AVS Kent

Shrimpers (OG 1043, ABV 4.1%)
A mid-amber bitter with a malty nose and a hint of fruitiness. Hops and malt carry over to leave a clean, hoppy aftertaste.

Danelaw*

Danelaw Brewery Ltd, 9 St Peter's Road, Chellaston, Derby, DE73 6UU
Tel (07799) 607253
Email steve@danelawbrewery.co.uk
Website www.danelawbrewery.co.uk

The owners and equal partners of Danelaw are Paul Martin and Steve Twells. Both are full-time professional engineers and long-term CAMRA members who run the brewery as a part-time venture. Brewing started in April 2005 on a former Leadmill 2.5-barrel plant to serve local free trade outlets and beer festivals. The brewery is named after the Viking occupation of the region, and the beer names also carry this theme

Geld (OG 1040, ABV 4%)

Cnut (OG 1045, ABV 4.5%)

Valhalla (OG 1050, ABV 5%)

Rape & Pillage (OG 1057, ABV 5.7%)

Dark Star SIBA

Dark Star Brewing Co Ltd, Moonhill Farm, Ansty, Haywards Heath, West Sussex, RH17 5AH
Tel/Fax (01444) 412311
Email info@darkstarbrewing.co.uk
Website www.darkstarbrewing.co.uk
Tours by arrangement

⊗ The brewery was started in 1994 in the cellar of the Evening Star pub in Brighton. The tiny plant was built by Rob Jones, former brewer and partner at Pitfield Brewery. Rob joined the brewery a year later, bringing with him his experience and recipes, including Dark Star, his Champion Beer of Britain in 1987, now renamed Original. In 2001 the brewery moved to larger premises at Ansty with a 15-barrel plant. It supplies some 40 free trade outlets throughout East and West Sussex. The brewery has a strategy of producing a permanent range of ales, seasonal beers and monthly specials. The 6.2% IPA was a special in 2004, which won its class in the Beauty of Hops competition. One pub is owned. Seasonal beers: Sunburst (ABV 4.8%, summer), Porter (ABV 5.5%, winter), Golden Gate (ABV 4.5%, winter). Bottle-conditioned beers: Porter (ABV 5.5%), Critical Mass (ABV 7.4%).

Hophead **(OG 1040, ABV 3.8%)**
A light, hoppy, refreshing bitter.

Over the Moon **(OG 1040, ABV 3.8%)**

Landlords Wit **(OG 1041, ABV 4.1%)**

Espresso Stout **(OG 1043, ABV 4.2%)**

Best Bitter **(OG 1044, ABV 4%)**

Original **(OG 1053, ABV 5%)**
Dark, full-bodied ale with a roast malt aroma and a dry, bitter stout-like finish.

Festival **(OG 1053, ABV 5%)**

DarkTribe

DarkTribe Brewery, Dog & Gun, High Street, East Butterwick, Lincolnshire, DN17 3AJ
Tel (01724) 782324
Fax (01724) 782324
Email dixie@darktribe.co.uk
Website www.darktribe.co.uk

The small brewery was built during the summer of 1996 in a workshop at the bottom of the garden by Dave 'Dixie' Dean. In May 2005 Dixie bought the Dog & Gun pub and moved the 2.5-barrel brewing equipment there. The beers generally follow a marine theme, recalling Dixie's days as an engineer in the Merchant Navy and his enthusiasm for sailing. DarkTribe has merged with Duffield of Harmston, Lincs. Twelve outlets are supplied. Seasonal beers: Dixie's Midnight Runner (ABV 6.5%, Dec-Jan), Dark Destroyer (ABV 9.7%, August onwards).

Dixie's Mild **(ABV 3.6%)**

Honey Mild **(ABV 3.6%)**

Albacore **(ABV 3.8%)**

Full Ahead **(ABV 4%)**
A malty smoothness is backed by a slightly fruity hop that gives a good bitterness to this amber-brown bitter.

Red Duster **(ABV 4%)**

Red Rock **(ABV 4.2%)**

Sternwheeler **(ABV 4.2%)**

Bucket Hitch **(ABV 4.4%)**

Dixie's Bollards **(ABV 4.5%)**

Dr Griffin's Mermaid **(ABV 4.5%)**

Old Gaffer **(ABV 4.5%)**

Galleon **(ABV 4.7%)**
A tasty, golden, smooth, full-bodied ale with fruity hops and consistent malt. The thirst-quenching bitterness lingers into a well-balanced finish.

Twin Screw **(ABV 5.1%)**
A fruity, rose-hip tasting beer, red in colour. Good malt presence with a dry, hoppy bitterness coming through in the finish.

Darwin SIBA

Darwin Brewery Ltd, 63 Back Tatham Street, Sunderland, Tyne & Wear, SR1 2QE
Tel (0191) 514 4746
Fax (0191) 515 2531
Email info@darwinbrewery.com
Website www.darwinbrewery.com
Tours by arrangement (including tasting at local venue)

The Darwin Brewery first brewed in 1994 and expanded with the construction of its Wearside brewery in central Sunderland in 2002 after a move from the Hodges brewhouse in Crook, Co Durham. The current brewery uses the plant from the former Butterknowle Brewery and produces a range of beers with the strong individual character of the North-east region. Darwin specialises in recreations of past beers such as Flag Porter, a beer produced with yeast rescued from a shipwreck in the English Channel. The brewery also produces trial beers from the Brewlab training and research unit at the University of Sunderland, and experiments in the production of novel and overseas styles for occasional production. The brewery also produces the beers of the closed High Force Brewery in Teesdale. Seasonal beers: Richmond Ale (ABV 4.5%, summer/autumn), Saints Sinner (ABV 5%, autumn/winter). Bottle-conditioned beers: Richmond Ale (ABV 4.5%), Hammond's Porter (ABV 4.7%), Extinction Ale (ABV 8.2%), Hammond's Stingo (ABV 10%), Cauldron Snout, Forest XB.

Sunderland Best **(OG 1041, ABV 3.9%)**

Evolution Ale **(OG 1041, ABV 4%)**
A dark amber, full-bodied bitter with a malty flavour and a clean, bitter aftertaste.

Durham Light Ale **(OG 1042, ABV 4%)**

Ghost Ale **(OG 1041, ABV 4.1%)**

Killer Bee **(OG 1054, ABV 6%)**

Extinction Ale **(OG 1084, ABV 8.3%)**

For High Force Hotel

Forest XB **(OG 1044, ABV 4.2%)**

Cauldron Snout **(OG 1056, ABV 5.6%)**

De Koninck

See final entry in Independents section

Dent SIBA

Dent Brewery Ltd, Hollins, Cowgill, Sedbergh, Cumbria, LA10 5TQ
Tel (015396) 25326
Email paul@dentbrewery.co.uk
Website www.dentbrewery.co.uk

A brewery set up in a converted barn in the picturesque Yorkshire dales. Originally it brewed to supply the Sun Inn in Dent but, by popular demand, expansion has allowed the beer to be supplied throughout the country to some 50 free trade outlets. Monthly specials are produced, all at ABV 4.5%.

Bitter (OG 1035, ABV 3.7%)
Fruity throughout and lightly hopped. This beer has a pervading earthiness that is evident to a lesser extent in other Dent beers. A short, bitter finish.

Aviator (OG 1039, ABV 4%)
This medium-bodied amber ale is characterised by strong citrus and hoppy flavours that develop into a long bitter finish.

Rambrau (OG 1042, ABV 4.5%)
A cask-conditioned lager.

Ramsbottom Strong Ale (OG 1042, ABV 4.5%)
This complex, mid-brown beer has a warming, dry, bitter finish to follow its unusual combination of roast, bitter, fruity and sweet flavours.

Kamikaze (OG 1047, ABV 5%)
Hops and fruit dominate this full-bodied, golden, strong bitter, with a dry bitterness growing in the aftertaste.

T'Owd Tup (OG 1056, ABV 6%)
A rich, fully-flavoured, strong stout with a coffee aroma. The dominant roast character is balanced by a warming sweetness and a raisiny, fruitcake taste that linger on into the finish.

Derby*

Derby Brewing Co Ltd, Masons Place, Nottingham Road, Derby DE21 6AQ
Tel 07887 556788
Fax (01322) 242888
Email sales@derbybrewing.co.uk
Website www.derbybrewing.co.uk

The first beers left the brewery in October 2004. It is owned by Trevor Harris, former brewer at the Brunswick Tavern in Derby.

Triple Hop (ABV 4.1%)

Dark Delight (ABV 4.3%)

Business As Usual (ABV 4.4%)

Awesome (ABV 4.6%)

Over The Hill (ABV 4.8%)

Nectar (ABV 5%)

Old Intentional (ABV 5%)

Derwent

Derwent Brewery Co, Units 2A/2B Station Road Industrial Estate, Silloth, Cumbria CA7 4AG
Tel (016973) 31522
Fax (016973) 31523
Tours by arrangement

Derwent was set up in 1996 in Cockermouth by Hans Kruger and Frank Smith, both former Jenning's employees, and moved to Silloth in 1998. It supplies beers throughout the North of England, with outlets in Cheshire, Cumbria, Lancashire, Yorkshire and the North-east. It organises the Silloth Beer Festival every September. It has supplied Carlisle State Bitter to the House of Commons, a beer that recreates one produced by the former state-owned Carlisle Brewery. Seasonal beers: Derwent Summer Rose (ABV 4.2%), Derwent Spring Time (ABV 4.3%), Harvesters Ale (ABV 4.3%), Bill Monk (ABV 4.5%), Auld Kendal (ABV 5.7%, winter).

Carlisle State Bitter (OG 1037, ABV 3.7%)
A light hoppy beer with underlying malt and fruit and a dry, yeasty finish.

Parsons Pledge (OG 1040, ABV 4%)

Winters Gold (ABV 4.1%)

Hofbrau (ABV 4.2%)

W&M Kendal Pale Ale (OG 1044, ABV 4.4%)
A sweet, fruity, hoppy beer with a bitter finish.

Derwent Rose

Derwent Rose Brewery, Grey Horse, 115 Sherburn Terrace, Consett, Co Durham, DH8 6NE
Tel (01207) 502585
Email paul@thegreyhorse.co.uk
Website www.thegreyhorse.co.uk

A micro-brewery based in Consett's oldest surviving pub, 158 years old. It produced its first brew in a former stable block behind the pub in 1997. Seasonal beer: St Patricks.

3 Giants (ABV 3.2%)

Mutton Clog (ABV 3.8%)

Steel Town (ABV 3.8%)

Target Ale (ABV 4%)

Conroy's Stout (ABV 4.1%)

Potts' Clock (ABV 4.2%)

Red Dust (ABV 4.2%)

Swordmaker (ABV 4.5%)

Angel Ale (ABV 5%)

Coast 2 Coast (ABV 5%)

Derwent Deep (ABV 5%)

Devon

Devon Ales Ltd, Mansfield Arms, 7 Main Street, Sauchie, Clackmannanshire, FK10 3JR
Tel (01259) 722020
Email john.gibson@btinternet.com
Tours by arrangement

Devon opened in 1992 and is still producing hand-crafted beer. Two pubs are owned and two outlets are supplied direct.

Original **(OG 1038, ABV 3.8%)**

Thick Black **(OG 1042, ABV 4.2%)**

Pride **(OG 1046, ABV 4.8%)**

Doghouse SIBA

Doghouse Brewery, Scorrier, Redruth, Cornwall, TR16 5BN
Tel/Fax (01209) 822022
Email starhawk@dsl.pipex.com
Tours by arrangement

⊗ Established in 2001, this five-barrel brewery continues to brew in a former dog rescue kennel at Startrax Pets Hotel. The second-hand equipment was originally from the Fly and Firkin in Middlesbrough. All the beers have a dog theme and test brews appear at the one tied house a few miles away in Zelah. Some 60 outlets are supplied. Seasonal beers: Staffi Stout (ABV 4.7%, Feb-March), Dingo Lager (ABV 5%, May-Oct), Christmas Tail/Winter's Tail (ABV 5.8%, Dec-Jan). Bottle-conditioned beers: all seasonal ales plus Biter, Dozey Dawg, Cornish Corgi and Bow Wow.

Wet Nose **(OG 1038, ABV 3.8%)**
A gold-coloured, quaffing bitter with plenty of hoppy bite in the aftertaste.

Retriever **(OG 1039, ABV 3.9%)**
A golden-coloured, easy-drinking beer.

Biter **(OG 1040, ABV 4%)**
A standard mid-brown bitter.

Snoozy Suzy **(OG 1043, ABV 4.3%)**

Dozey Dawg **(OG 1044, ABV 4.4%)**
A light golden, refreshing beer.

Cornish Corgi **(OG 1045, ABV 4.5%)**
A golden premium ale brewed with Pilot hedgerow hops.

Bow Wow **(OG 1050, ABV 5%)**
Dark ruby-coloured premium ale; well rounded maltiness gives way to a more bitter aftertaste.

Dolphin

Dolphin Bar & Brewery, 48 St Michael's Street, Shrewsbury, Shropshire, SY1 2EZ
Tel (01743) 350419
Email brewers@thedolphinbrewery.co.uk

⊗ Dolphin was launched in 2000 by Peter Buy and Nigel Morton and was upgraded to 4.5 barrels in 2001. There are further plans to expand the plant and install a small bottling line. One pub is owned. Porter is suitable for vegetarians and vegans.

Best Bitter **(OG 1043, ABV 4.2%)**

Gold **(OG 1044, ABV 4.5%)**

Porter **(OG 1045, ABV 4.6%)**

Brew **(OG 1046, ABV 4.8%)**

Donnington IFBB

Donnington Brewery, Stow-on-the-Wold, Cheltenham, Gloucestershire, GL54 1EP
Tel (01451) 830603

⊛ Thomas Arkell bought a 13th-century watermill in idyllic countryside in 1827 and he began brewing on the site in 1865. Today, it is owned and run by a direct family descendant, Claude Arkell, and the millwheel is still used to drive small pumps and machinery. Donnington supplies its own 15 tied houses and a number of free trade outlets. XXX is brewed in small quantities, mainly for beer festivals and the free trade.

XXX **(OG 1035, ABV 3.6%)** ◆
Dark mild, thin in aroma but very flavoursome. More subtle than others in its class, it has some hops and traces of chocolate and liquorice in the taste and a notably malty finish.

BB **(OG 1035, ABV 3.6%)** ◆
A pleasant amber bitter with a slight hop aroma, a good balance of malt and hops in the mouth and a bitter aftertaste.

SBA **(OG 1045, ABV 4.4%)** ◆
Malt dominates over bitterness in the subtle flavour of this premium bitter, which has a hint of fruit and a dry malty finish.

Dorset SIBA

Dorset Brewing Co, Hope Square, Weymouth, Dorset, DT4 8TR
Tel/Fax (01305) 777515
Email giles@quaybrewery.com
Website www.fineale.com
Shop at Brewers Quay 10-5.30 daily
Tours by arrangement via Timewalk at Brewers Quay

⊗ The Dorset Brewing Company, formerly the Quay Brewery, is the most recent in a long succession of distinguished breweries in one of the oldest sites in England, Hope Square, Weymouth. Brewing first started there in 1256 but in more recent times it was famous for being the home of the Devenish and Groves breweries. Brewing stopped in 1986 but restarted in 1996, when Giles Smeath set up Quay in part of the old brewery buildings. All the award-winning beers are brewed in the traditional manner with no artificial additives. They are available in local Weymouth pubs and selected outlets throughout the South-west. Giles hopes to move to a new site as Hope Square is cramped and there is no room for expansion. Seasonal beers: Summer Knight (ABV 3.8%), Silent Knight (ABV 5.9%).

Weymouth Harbour Master (OG 1036, ABV 3.6%) ◆
Well-balanced, mid-brown session beer, slightly nutty with blackcurrant background. May be rebadged by pubs as a house beer.

Weymouth Best Bitter (OG 1038, ABV 3.9%) ◆
Light, sweetish session bitter; amber with a fruity aroma.

Weymouth JD 1742 (OG 1040, ABV 4.2%) ◆
Clean-tasting, easy-drinking bitter. Well balanced with lingering bitterness after moderate sweetness.

Steam Beer (OG 1043, ABV 4.5%) ◆
Complex old ale with roast malt predominating from the nose to the long bitter finish.

Jurassic (OG 1045, ABV 4.7%)
An organic premium bitter, pale golden colour; smooth with suggestions of honey underlying a complex hop palate.

Durdle Door (ABV 5%)
A full-bodied, clean-tasting, strong ale. Vanilla/citrus aroma; hints of marmalade on the palate.

Dow Bridge

Dow Bridge Brewery, 2-3 Rugby Road, Catthorpe, Leicestershire, LE17 6DA.
Tel/Fax (01788) 869121
Email dowbridge.brewery@virgin.net
Tours By prior arrangement

Since commercial operations started in 2002, additional fermenters have been installed to increase capacity to five barrels. Emphasis remains on traditional brewing without the use of added sugars, adjuncts or additives. The brewery is currently being extended to enable capacity to be increased. Beers are supplied to some 87 outlets and are now also available through selected specialist independent wholesalers.

Bonum Mild (OG 1035, ABV 3.5%) ◆
Reddish/brown in colour, very complex, full-flavoured mild with a strong roast taste to the fore. Flavours develope in the aftertaste leading to a long, satisfying finish.

Acris (OG 1037, ABV 3.8%)

Ratae'd (OG 1042, ABV 4.3%) ◆
Tawny-coloured, very bitter beer in which bitter and hop flavours dominate, leading to a long, bitter and astringent aftertaste.

Fosse (OG 1046, ABV 4.8%)

For Castle Brewing Co

Morgan's Delight (ABV 3.8%)

Morgan's Special (ABV 4%)

Olde Codger (ABV 4.4%)

Bishops Revenge (ABV 5%)

Downton

Downton Brewery Co Ltd, Unit 11, Batten Road, Downton Business Centre, Downton, Salisbury, Wiltshire, SP5 3HU
Tel (01722) 322890
Tours by arrangement

The brewery was set up in 2003 with equipment leased from Hop Back (qv) on the same industrial estate, with a 20-barrel copper and two 20-barrel fermenters. Seasonal beer: Chimera Dark Delight (ABV 5.5%, winter). Bottle-conditioned beer: Dark Delight (ABV 6%). The bottle-conditioned Firebrand (OG 1050, ABV 5%) is brewed for Threshers and bottled at Hop Back

Chimera Gold (OG 1043, ABV 4.3%)

Chimera Wheat Porter (OG 1044, ABV 4.4%)

Chimera Red (OG 1046, ABV 4.6%)

Chimera Wheat (OG 1047, ABV 4.7%)

Chimera India Pale Ale (OG 1068, ABV 6.8%)

Driftwood

🍺 Driftwood Brewery, Driftwood Spars Hotel, Trevaunance Cove, St Agnes, Cornwall, TR5 0RT
Tel (01872) 552428/553323
Fax (01872) 553701
Email driftwoodspars@hotmail.com
Website www.driftwoodspars.com
Tours by arrangement

Gordon Treleaven started brewing in 2000 in this famous Cornish pub and hotel that dates back to 1660. The brewery is based in the former Flying Dutchman café across the road. The Old Horsebridge one-barrel plant has been replaced by a customised, five-barrel kit. Pale malt comes from Tuckers of Newton Abbot and the hops are Fuggles.

Cuckoo Ale (OG 1045, ABV 4.5%)

Dunn Plowman SIBA

Dunn Plowman Brewery, Unit 1A, Arrow Court Industrial Estate, Hergest Road, Kington, Herefordshire, HR5 3ER
Tel (01544) 231993
Fax (01544) 231985
Email dunnplowman.brewery@talk21.com
Tours by arrangement

⊗ The brewery was established in 1987 as a brew-pub, moved to Leominster in 1992 and then to its present site in 2002, when Dunn Plowman bought SP Sporting Ales. The brewery supplies the Old Tavern, its brewery tap, and 30 other outlets within a 50-mile radius. It is run by husband and wife team Steve and Gaye Dunn. Seasonal beers: Santa's Porter Call (ABV 5.7%). Bottle-conditioned beers: Old Jake Stout, Kyneton Ale (ABV 5%), Golden Haze Wheat Beer (ABV 5%), Crooked Furrow.

Brewhouse Bitter (OG 1037, ABV 3.8%)

Emerald Ale (OG 1038, ABV 3.9%)

Early Riser (OG 1039, ABV 4%)

Sting (OG 1040, ABV 4.2%)

Kingdom Bitter (OG 1043, ABV 4.5%)

Old Jake Stout (OG 1046, ABV 4.8%)

Shirehorse Ale (OG 1053, ABV 5.5%)

Crooked Furrow (OG 1063, ABV 6.5%)

Durham SIBA

Durham Brewery Ltd, Unit 5A, Bowburn North Industrial Estate, Bowburn, Co Durham, DH6 5PF
Tel (0191) 3771991
Fax (0191) 3770768
Email gibbs@durham-brewery.co.uk
Website www.durham-brewery.co.uk
Shop open during business hours
Tours by arrangement

Established in 1994, Durham now has a portfolio of around 20 beers plus a bottle-conditioned range. Bottles can be purchased via the online shop and an own label/special message service is available. News from the brewery is delivered by email newsletter via free subscription on the website. Seasonal beers: Sunstroke (ABV 3.6%, summer), Frostbite (ABV 3.6%, winter).

Gold (ABV 3.7%)

Green Goddess (ABV 3.8%)
English Goldings hops give a spicy, bitter flavour.

Magus (ABV 3.8%)
Golden, refreshing dry bitter. An excellent session and summer ale, with a medium fruity/dry aftertaste.

Bonny Lass (ABV 3.9%)
Ruby coloured but with the flavour of a wheat beer.

White Gem (ABV 3.9%)

White Herald (ABV 3.9%)

Black Velvet (ABV 4%)
Black like a stout but with the strength of a porter. Traditional English hops balance rich liquorice and roast flavours.

White Gold (ABV 4%)
Pale and aromatic, mouth-filling and thirst-quenching with citrus aromas and flavours.

Scimitar (ABV 4.1%)

White Amarillo (ABV 4.1%)
Named after the predominant hop (Amarillo is a light and floral American variety). The addition of Goldings hops add a little more spice. The result is a deliciously fragrant, light session beer.

Bede's Gold (ABV 4.2%)

Keltic (ABV 4.2%)

White Velvet (ABV 4.2%)
Smooth, golden bitter with a tangy hop and fruit taste. The aftertaste lingers with a pleasant fruitiness.

Canny Lad (ABV 4.3%)
Rich, malty Scotch-type beer. Six malts make a complex body and ruby colour.

Dark Secret (ABV 4.3%)

White Crystal (ABV 4.3%)
Crystal is an aromatic American hop. The flavour is clean, spicy and refreshing.

County (ABV 4.4%)

White Bullet (ABV 4.4%)

Prior's Gold (ABV 4.5%)

White Friar (ABV 4.5%)
A strong version of White Gold. All the aroma and rich grapefruit bitterness with a fuller body.

White Sapphire (ABV 4.5%)
Light and easy, aromatic and refreshing.

Bishop's Gold (ABV 4.6%)

Cuthberts Cross (ABV 4.7%)
Pale gold in colour but rich with grapefruit notes. This bitter is strong in alcohol and flavour, yet is thirst quenching. Named after St Cuthbert's Cross in Durham Cathedral.

White Bishop (ABV 4.8%)
A premium ale using lager malt. American fruity hops make this strong beer easy going and satisfying.

Evensong (ABV 5%)

Black Abbot (ABV 5.3%)

Magnificat (ABV 6.5%)

E&S Elland SIBA

E&S Elland, Eastwood & Sanders (Fine Ales Ltd), Units 3-5 Heathfield Industrial Estate, Heathfield Street, Elland, West Yorkshire, HX5 9AE
Tel (01422) 377677
Fax (01422) 370922
Email admin@eastwood-sanders.fsnet.co.uk
Shop in brewery office. Normal office hours
Tours by prior arrangement

Eastwood & Sanders was formed in 2002 as a result of the amalgamation of the Barge & Barrel Brewery and West Yorkshire Brewery. While the official company name remains Eastwood & Sanders, it now trades as E&S Elland. E&S has invested in additional vessels and equipment to meet increased demand with more than 100 outlets regularly supplied. One pub is owned. As well as the core brands, there is a rolling programme of seasonal beers. Seasonal beers: Living in the Cask (ABV 3.6%), Born to be Mild (ABV 3.7%), Yorkshireman (ABV 4.1%), Maximum Darkness (ABV 4.3%), Night Porter (ABV 4.3%), Stocking Top (ABV 4.4%), Halifax Bomber (ABV 4.8%), Sam's Revenge (ABV 5%), Bark at the Moon (ABV 5.6%), True Leveller (ABV 5.7%), IPA (ABV 6.5%). Bottle-conditioned beers: Beyond the Pale, 1872 Porter.

First Light (OG 1037, ABV 3.5%)
Light, crisp, refreshing Pennine mild. Pale with a clean aftertaste.

Bargee (OG 1038, ABV 3.8%)
Amber gold session bitter with a well-balanced bitter flavour, balanced with fruit, finishing with a pronounced bitter aftertaste.

Best Bitter (OG 1041, ABV 4%)
Made with a single malt and English and American hops, this is a straw-coloured bitter with a strong hoppy aroma and taste. Fruity and malty in character, the dry citrus, bitter flavour lingers to the end.

Beyond the Pale (OG 1042, ABV 4.2%) ◆
Amber-coloured best bitter. Light fruit and hop aroma with a predominant bitter, hoppy flavour balanced with citrus fruit. Strong bitter aftertaste.

Fireball (OG 1042, ABV 4.2%)
A copper-coloured bitter with crystal malt flavours and a long, hoppy finish.

Nettlethrasher (OG 1042, ABV 4.4%)
A premium bitter brewed with three different malts, and English and American hops.

Elland Back (OG 1047, ABV 4.6%)
A pale premium bitter with grapefruit and citrus top notes in the nose, and a bitter yet fruity palate from the use of all American hops.

1872 Porter (OG 1065, ABV 6.5%) ◆
Prime, full-flavoured porter. Rich liquorice flavours with a hint of coffee from the roast malt. Slightly sweet with surprising bitter aftertaste coming from the malt.

Eagles Bush*

Eagles Bush Brewery, Borough Arms, 2 New Henry Street, Neath, SA11 1PH
Tel (01639) 644902

◇ A brew-pub that opened in 2004 with a one-barrel plant. All the equipment is self-made. Two barrels a week are produced only for the pub.

Osprey Dark (OG 1040, ABV 3.9%)

Golden Eagle IPA (OG 1044, ABV 4.2%)

Old Buzzard Best (OG 1046, ABV 4.5%)

Earl Soham SIBA

Earl Soham Brewery, The Street, Earl Soham, Woodbridge, Suffolk, IP13 7RT
Tel/Fax (01728) 684097
Email thebrewer@bjornson.fsnet.co.uk
Website www.earlsohambrewery.co.uk
Shop Village store Tastebuds next to brewery
Tours by previous arrangement

⊗ Earl Soham was set up behind the Victoria pub in 1984 and continued there until 2001 when the brewery moved 200 metres down the road. The Victoria and the Station in Framlingham both keep the beers on a regular basis and, when there is spare stock, they are supplied to local free houses and as many beer festivals as possible. Ten outlets are supplied and two pubs are owned. Seasonal beer: Jolabrugg (ABV 5%, December until finished). Most of the beers are bottle-conditioned for Tastebuds next door and are only available there.

Gannet Mild (OG 1034, ABV 3.3%)
An unusual, full-tasting mild with a bitter finish and roast flavours that compete with underlying maltiness.

Victoria Bitter (OG 1037, ABV 3.6%)
A characterful, well-hopped, malty beer with a tangy, hoppy aftertaste.

Pale Ale (OG 1040, ABV 4%)

Sir Roger's Porter (OG 1040, ABV 4%)
Full-flavoured dark brown malty beer with bitter overtones, and a fruity aftertaste.

Albert Ale (OG 1045, ABV 4.4%)
Hops dominate every aspect of this beer, but especially the finish. A fruity, astringent beer.

Empress of India Pale Ale (OG 1048, ABV 4.7%)

Eastwood

Eastwood the Brewer, Barge & Barrel, 10-20 Park Road, Elland, West Yorkshire, HX5 9AP
Tel 07732 374216
Tours by arrangement

A new brewery set up at the end of 2002 by John Eastwood following his departure from Eastwood & Sanders (qv). John has moved the brewery from Huddersfield to the Barge & Barrel pub. Some 12 to 15 outlets are supplied.

Sterling (ABV 3.8%)
Copper-coloured session beer with a pleasant, long-lasting finish.

Best Bitter (ABV 4%)
Straw-coloured single malt beer, strong on both aroma and flavour.

Gold Award (ABV 4.4%)
Five different malts and English and American hops are used.

Mosquito (ABV 4.7%)
A strong tasting bitter with four types of malt and three hops.

Black Prince (ABV 5%)
Distinctive strong black porter, with a blend of pale and chocolate malts and roasted barley.

EPA (ABV 5%)
The big brother to Best Bitter.

Lilburne (ABV 5.7%)
Copper-coloured beer bursting with malt and hops.

Myrtle's Temper (ABV 7%)

Eccleshall SIBA

Eccleshall Brewing Co Ltd, Castle Street, Eccleshall, Staffordshire, ST21 6DF
Tel (01785) 850300
Fax (01785) 851452
Email information@thegeorgeinn.freeserve.co.uk
Website www.thegeorgeinn.freeserve.co.uk
Tours by arrangement

⊗ The brewery was opened in 1995, has been extended twice and has plans for a move to new premises. It has won numerous awards from CAMRA and currently supplies 600 outlets direct throughout the country. One pub is owned. Seasonal beers are available.

Slaters Monkey Magic Mild (OG 1034, ABV 3.4%)
Dark brown mild ale with distinct liquorice aroma. Roast taste and aftertaste with a sweet and fruity finish.

Slaters Bitter (OG 1036, ABV 3.6%)
Golden bitter with a hop and fruit aroma. Hoppiness develops to a good bitter finish.

Slaters Original (OG 1040, ABV 4%)
Amber looks with a creamy head. Hoppy aroma with hints of caramel. Fruity tastes with hops developing a long, bitter finish.

Slaters Top Totty (OG 1040, ABV 4%)
A light, straw-coloured bitter with a big hoppy aroma. The hops with fruit produce a full, bitter finish.

Slaters Premium (OG 1044, ABV 4.4%)
Pale brown with a caramel, malt and hop aroma. Complex hop and fruit with hints of roast develop into a bitter finish with a malty background.

Slaters Shining Knight (OG 1045, ABV 4.5%)
No dominant flavours but hops and fruit combine in the bitter finish. A good session beer for its strength.

Slaters Supreme (OG 1047, ABV 4.7%)
Copper-coloured bitter with a fresh fruity and hoppy aroma; sweet start and a dry, bitter finish.

Edale SIBA

Edale Brewery Co, t/a Ruskin Villa, Hope Road, Edale, Derbyshire, S33 7ZE
Tel (01433) 670289
Fax (01433) 670134
Email info@edalebrewery.co.uk
Website www.edalebrewery.co.uk
Tours by arrangement

Edale has a 2.5-barrel plant in Derbyshire as well as a five-barrel plant in its pub in Sheffield (where the Crown and Wellington brewery operates: see entry for Wellington). The company operates as a collective and is more interested in quality than profit. It started brewing in 2001 and expanded by buying the Hillsborough Hotel in 2004. One pub is owned and some 20 outlets are supplied. Bottle-conditioned beers: Downfall (ABV 5%), Ringing Roger (ABV 6%). It is planned to produce organic beers.

Kinder Right to Roam (OG 1039, ABV 3.9%)

Kinder Trespass (OG 1040, ABV 4%)

Kinder Cross (OG 1043, ABV 4.3%)

Kinder Stout (OG 1046, ABV 4.6%)

Kinder Downfall (OG 1050, ABV 5%)

Ringing Roger (OG 1060, ABV 6%)

Eglesbrech

Crispnew Ltd, 14 Melville Street, Falkirk, FK1 1HZ
Tel (01324) 633338
Fax (01324) 613258
Email info@behindthewall.co.uk
Website www.behindthewall.co.uk
Tours by prior arrangement

The brewery is part of an extension to the Ale House in Falkirk. Eglesbrech brews only for its own customers. Occasional special beers are made and a Falkirk Wheel Ale is planned to tie in with the area's newest tourist attraction, the Canal Boat Lift. Three pubs are owned, one of which serves cask beer.

Falkirk 400 (ABV 3.8%)

Golden Nectar (ABV 3.8%)

Antonine (ABV 3.9%)

Cascade (ABV 4.1%)

Stones Ginger Beer (ABV 4.2%)

Alt Bier (ABV 4.4%)

Egyptian

The Egyptian Sand & Gravel Co Ltd, t/a Leggers Inn, Stable Buildings, Saville Town Wharf, Mill Street East, Dewsbury, West Yorkshire, WF12 9BD
Tel (01924) 502846
Tours by arrangement

Egyptian started brewing in a cellar in 1999 to supply beer to its own bar. The brewery has a capacity of one barrel and underwent a refit in 2004.

Prospect Road Bitter (OG 1040, ABV 4%)

Marriots Ale (OG 1042, ABV 4%)

Golden Eye 700 (OG 1044, ABV 4.2%)
Pale golden bitter, lightly hopped, with a well-balanced fruity and malty character, and a smooth finish.

Pharaoh's Curse (OG 1048, ABV 4.6%)

Elgood's IFBB SIBA

Elgood & Sons Ltd, North Brink Brewery, Wisbech, Cambridgeshire, PE13 1LN
Tel (01945) 583160
Fax (01945) 587711
Email info@elgoods-brewery.co.uk
Website www.elgoods-brewery.co.uk
Shop May-Sept, Tue-Thur, 11.30-4.30pm
Tours as above at 2pm, by arrangement

⊗ The North Brink Brewery was established in 1795 and was one of the first classic Georgian breweries to be built outside London. In 1878 it came under the control of the Elgood family and is still run today as one of the few remaining independent family breweries, with the fifth generation of the family now helping to run the company. The beers go to 43 Elgood's public houses within a 50-mile radius of Wisbech and free-trade outlets throughout East Anglia, while wholesalers distribute nationally. Elgood's has a visitor centre, offering the opportunity to combine a tour of the brewery and the magnificent gardens. Seasonal beers: see website.

Black Dog (OG 1036, ABV 3.6%) ◆
Full-flavoured, black-red, bitter-sweet mild with gentle roast malt on the nose, building in the mouth with a balance of liquorice and caramel and ending with a persistent dryness.

Cambridge Bitter (OG 1038, ABV 3.8%) ◆
Deep amber session bitter with a light malty aroma. A bitter, malty palate with underlying hops ending increasingly dry and bitter.

Golden Newt (ABV 4.1%) ◆
Aromatic golden ale with citrus hop aroma and a bitter-sweet, hoppy palate with underlying malt.

Pageant Ale (OG 1043, ABV 4.3%)
A premium beer, with a good aroma of hops and malt, giving a well-balanced bitter-sweet flavour and a satisfying finish.

Thin Ice (OG 1047, ABV 4.7%)
Fragrant hops and orange fruit aromas introduce this golden bitter. Citrus fruit and resiny hop fill the mouth, and the finish is delightfully bitter, with hops and fruit persisting.

North Brink Porter (ABV 5%)
Dark in colour resembling a dry stout, although less creamy and lighter in body with a coffeeish dryness.

Greyhound Strong Bitter (OG 1052, ABV 5.2%) ◆
Full-bodied, copper-coloured brew with a fruity aroma, a malty, fruity palate complemented by a bitter edge and a strong, developing dry, bitter finish.

Elveden* EAB

Elveden Ales, The Courtyard, Elveden Estate, Elveden, Thetford, Norfolk, IP24 3TA
Tel (01842) 878922

Elveden is a five-barrel brewery based on the estate of Lord Iveagh, a member of the ennobled branch of the Guinness family. The brewery is run by Frances Moore, daughter of Brendan Moore at Iceni Brewery (qv). Frances is a student and brews once a month. In the winter of 2004 she brewed Charter Ale (ABV 10%) to mark the celebrations for the award of a Royal Charter for Harwich in 1604. The beer is based on a 19th-century style known as Arctic Ale first brewed by Allsopps of Burton-on-Trent for Arctic explorers. The beer was available in cask and bottle-conditioned versions. The phone number listed above is shared with Iceni. Bottle-conditioned beers: Stout (ABV 5%), Elveden Ale (ABV 5.2%).

Empire*

Empire Brewing, 219 Quarmby Road, Quarmby, Huddersfield, West Yorkshire, HD3 4FB
Tel (01484) 460188 (m) 07966 592276
Tours by arrangement

Empire has a five-barrel plant, set up in a garage by Russell Beverley. The first beer, Strikes Back, was launched in 2004 at the Huddersfield Beer Festival when it won Beer of the Festival. Two new beers, both pale hoppy bitters, have been produced since then. Beers are supplied to local free houses and CAMRA festivals.

Golden Warrior (ABV 3.8%)

Strikes Back (ABV 4%)

Crusader (ABV 5%)

Enville SIBA

Enville Ales Ltd, Enville Brewery, Cox Green, Enville, Stourbridge, West Midlands, DY7 5LG
Tel (01384) 873728
Fax (01384) 873770
Email info@envilleales.com
Website www.envilleales.com
Tours by arrangement for small groups only

⊛ Enville is based on a picturesque Victorian farm complex. Using the same water source as the original Village Brewery (closed in 1919), the beers also incorporate more than three tons of honey annually, and originally used recipes passed down from the proprietor's great-great aunt. Six outlets are supplied. Seasonal beer: Gothic (ABV 5.2%, Oct-March).

Chainmaker Mild (OG 1037, ABV 3.6%)

Nailmaker Mild (OG 1041, ABV 4%)

White (OG 1041, ABV 4.2%) ◆
A clean, well-balanced, golden, sweet bitter, light in flavour. An appealing beer.

Saaz (OG 1042, ABV 4.2%) ◆
Golden lager-style beer. Lager bite but with more taste and lasting bitterness. The malty aroma is late arriving but the bitter finish, balanced by fruit and hops, compensates.

Ale (OG 1044, ABV 4.5%) ◆
Pale gold to yellow. Very sweet start but with a bite. Heathery almost whisky hints give way to a thirst-quenching hoppiness and pleasing end.

Porter (OG 1044, ABV 4.5%)

Ginger (OG 1045, ABV 4.6%)

Evan Evans*

Wm. Evan Evans, The New Brewery, 1 Rhosmaen Street, Llandeilo, Carmarthenshire, SA14 6LU
Tel (01558) 824455
Fax (01558) 824400
Email info@evan-evans.com
Website www.evan-evans.com
Shop Opens May 2005
Tours by arrangement

The brewery opened in 2004, owned by Simon Buckley, a member of the Welsh brewing family. The company has built a modern, purpose-built brewery, with a 20-barrel brew length and integrated fermenting room. Ten pubs are owned and 60 outlets are supplied. Seasonal beer: Cwrw Cadno (ABV 4.2%, November), Cwrw Santa (ABV 4.5%, Christmas).

BB (OG 1038, ABV 3.8%)

Cwrw (OG 1043, ABV 4.2%)

SBA (OG 1045, ABV 4.5%)

Everards IFBB

Everards Brewery Ltd, Castle Acres, Enderby, near Narborough, Leicestershire, LE19 1BY
Tel (0116) 201 4100
Fax (0116) 281 4199
Email mail@everards.co.uk
Website www.everards.co.uk
Shop may be added to the Cash & Carry soon
Tours by arrangement

⊗ An independent, family-owned brewery run by the great-great grandson of the founder. The regular beers were re-branded with new pump clips in 2004 to underscore the company's commitment to cask. Based at Narborough on the outskirts of Leicester, Everards celebrated its 150th anniversary in 1999. A tenanted estate of approximately 140 pubs is based largely in Leicestershire and surrounding counties. Nearly all the pubs serve a full range of cask-conditioned beers and many serve guest ales. Everards ales are all brewed to individual recipes using only the finest English hops and barley. The principal beers are all dry-hopped and conditioned for a week prior to dispatch from the brewery. Daytime weekday tours can be arranged for CAMRA branches. Some 500 outlets are supplied. Seasonal beers: Terra Firma organic (ABV 4.5%, Jan-March). Perfick, Sunchaser and Equinox are brewed during the course of the year, and Sleighbell over Christmas.

Beacon Bitter (OG 1036, ABV 3.8%) ◆
Light, refreshing, well-balanced pale amber bitter in the Burton style.

Tiger Best Bitter (OG 1041, ABV 4.2%) ◆
A mid-brown, well-balanced best bitter crafted for broad appeal, benefiting from a long, bitter-sweet finish.

Original (OG 1050, ABV 5.2%) ◆
Full-bodied, this mid-brown strong bitter is smooth and well-balanced. The malted bitterness continues into a long finish.

Evesham

S M Murphy Associates Ltd, t/a Evesham Brewery, rear of Blue Maze, Oat Street, Evesham, Worcestershire, WR11 4PJ
Tel (01386) 443462
Fax (01386) 443628
Email asumgold@aol.com

The brewery opened in 1993 in the old bottle store at the Green Dragon pub (now the Blue Maze). The adjacent Gordon Hart pub was purchased in 2003 and incorporated with the Green Dragon to form the Blue Maze nightclub (Thursday to Sunday), pub, beer garden and function venue. The brewery supplies four other outlets locally and the Fish & Anchor, Offenham. Asum in the beer names is the local pronunciation of Evesham. Seasonal beer: Santa's Nightmare (ABV 5%, Christmas).

Asum (OG 1038, ABV 3.8%) ◆
Dry, sharp tawny bitter with an interplay of malt, hops and fruit in the aroma and taste. Fruit fades as a dry, almost harsh, finale develops.

Asum Gold (OG 1052, ABV 5.2%) ◆
A well-balanced premium ale that has all the range of tastes from malt to a fruity hoppiness that make it a very satisfying drink.

For Fish & Anchor:

Britain's Best (OG 1038, ABV 3.8%)

Exe Valley SIBA

Exe Valley Brewery, Silverton, Exeter, Devon, EX5 4HF
Tel (01392) 860406
Fax (01392) 861001
Email exevalley@supanet.com
Website www.siba-southwest.co.uk/breweries/exevalley
Brewery tours not available except to pre-arranged groups – charge made

⊗ Exe Valley was established as Barron's Brewery in 1984. Guy Sheppard, who joined the business in 1991, continues to run the company. The beers are all brewed traditionally, using spring water, Devon malt and English hops. Direct deliveries are made to some 60 pubs within a 40-mile radius of the brewery; the beers are also available nationally via wholesalers. Seasonal beers: Devon Summer (ABV 3.9%, June-Aug), Spring Beer (ABV 4.3%, March-May), Autumn Glory (ABV 4.5%, Sept-Nov), Devon Dawn (ABV 4.5%, Dec-New Year), Winter Glow (ABV 6%, Dec-Feb). Bottle-conditioned beer: Devon Glory (ABV 4.7%).

Bitter (OG 1036, ABV 3.7%) ◆
Mid-brown bitter, pleasantly fruity with underlying malt through the aroma, taste and finish.

Barron's Hopsit (OG 1040, ABV 4.1%) ◆
Straw-coloured beer with strong hop aroma, hop and fruit flavour and a bitter hop finish.

Dob's Best Bitter (OG 1040, ABV 4.1%) ◆
Light brown bitter. Malt and fruit predominate in the aroma and taste with a dry, bitter, fruity finish.

Devon Glory (OG 1046, ABV 4.7%)
Mid-brown, fruity-tasting pint with a sweet, fruity finish.

Mr Sheppard's Crook (OG 1046, ABV 4.7%) ◆
Smooth, full-bodied, mid-brown beer with a malty-fruit nose and a sweetish palate leading to a bitter, dry finish.

Exeter Old Bitter (OG 1046, ABV 4.8%) ◆
Mid-brown old ale with a rich fruity taste and slightly earthy aroma and bitter finish.

Exmoor SIBA

Exmoor Ales Ltd, Golden Hill Brewery, Wiveliscombe, Somerset, TA4 2NY
Tel (01984) 623798
Fax (01984) 624572
Email info@exmoorales.co.uk
Website www.exmoorales.co.uk
Tours by arrangement

⊗ Somerset's largest brewery was founded in 1980 in the old Hancock's plant, which had been closed since 1959. It quickly won national acclaim, as its Exmoor Ale took the Best Bitter award at CAMRA's Great British Beer Festival that year, the first of many prizes. The brewery has enjoyed many years of continuous expansion and steadily increasing demand. Around 250 pubs in the South-west are supplied and others nationwide via wholesalers and pub chains. Seasonal beers: Hound Dog (ABV 4%, March-May), Wild Cat (ABV 4.4%, Sept-Nov), Beast (ABV 6.6%, Oct-April), Exmas (ABV 5%, Nov-Dec).

Ale (OG 1039, ABV 3.8%) ◆
A pale to mid-brown, medium-bodied session bitter. A mixture of malt and hops in the aroma and taste lead to a hoppy, bitter aftertaste.

Fox (OG 1043, ABV 4.2%)
Crafted from a blend of several malts and hops to produce a mid-brown beer of unusual subtlety and taste. The slight maltiness on the tongue is followed by a burst of hops with a lingering bitter-sweet aftertaste.

Gold (OG 1045, ABV 4.5%) ◆
A yellow/golden best bitter with a good balance of malt and fruity hop on the nose and the palate. The sweetness follows through an ultimately more bitter finish.

Hart (OG 1049, ABV 4.8%) ◆
A mid-to-dark brown beer with a mixture of malt and hops in the aroma. A rich, full-bodied malt and fruit flavour follows through to a clean, hoppy aftertaste.

Stag (OG 1050, ABV 5.2%) ◆
A pale brown beer, with a malty taste and aroma, and a bitter finish.

Facer's SIBA

Facer's Brewery, 6 Knoll Street Industrial Park, Knoll Street, The Cliff, Salford, Greater Manchester, M7 2BL
Tel/Fax (0161) 792 7755
Email facers@tiscali.co.uk
Tours for CAMRA groups by arrangement

Established in 2003, the plant is shared with Bazens' Brewery (qv), with the joint venture known as the Salford Brewery Syndicate (SBS). In 2004, the SBS expanded the brewhouse from a five-barrel plant to nine-barrel brew length. The five regular Facer's brews are supplemented by special beers inspired by Greats of English Literature. They change every two months, but the ABV is always 3.9%. Some 60 outlets are supplied.

Twin City (OG 1035, ABV 3.3%) ◆
Red/brown in colour with a fruity nose. Quite complex with a warm spiciness adding to the roast, caramel and fruit flavours. Fairly short malty aftertaste.

Northern County (OG 1037, ABV 3.8%)

Crabtree (OG 1041, ABV 4.3%)

Dave's Happy Beer/DHB (OG 1041, ABV 4.3%)

Landslide 1927 (OG 1047, ABV 4.9%)

Falstaff

Falstaff Brewery, 24 Society Place, Normanton, Derby, DE23 6UH
Tel (01332) 342902
Email info@thefalstaffbrewery.co.uk
Website www.falstaffbrewery.co.uk
Tours by arrangement

⊗ The brewery has been in operation for more than four years and in that time it has produced two milds, a complete range of high-quality beers and a themed Spaghetti Western range, as well as a commemorative special for the Rugby World Cup. One pub is owned. A house beer is produced for the Babington Arms, Derby. Seasonal beers vary from year to year: see website. Bottle-conditioned beer: Wilko (ABV 8.5%).

3 Faze (OG 1038, ABV 3.8%) ◆
A smooth, golden light session ale with fruit and hop throughout, ending in a lasting clean, bitter aftertaste.

Phoenix (OG 1045, ABV 4.7%) ◆
A smooth, tawny ale with fruit and hop, joined by plenty of malt in the mouth. A subtle sweetness produces a drinkable ale.

Smiling Assassin (OG 1050, ABV 5.2%)
A warm copper-coloured beer.

Fantasy*

Fantasy Brewery, Lloyds Bar, 10 Bond Street, Nuneaton, Warwickshire, CV11 4BX
Tel (02476) 373343
Fax (02476) 372156
Email fantasybrewery@fantasybrewery.co.uk
Website www.fantasybrewery.com

When brewing ceased at the Rat & Ratchet, Huddersfield, the equipment was purchased and installed at the rear of Lloyds Bar, Nuneaton. Fantasy Brewery was launched at an in-house beer festival in 2004 that included the first six brews. Plans are to have occasional brews and one-off specials as well take-away polypins and bottle-conditioned beers. Just the one pub is owned. There are no regular beers at present.

Far North SIBA

🍺 Far North Brewery, Melvich Hotel, Melvich, Thurso, Caithness, KW14 7YJ
Tel (01641) 531206
Fax (01641) 531347
Email farnorthbrewery@aol.com
Website www.smoothhound.co.uk/hotels/melvich
Tours for hotel residents

⊗ The most northerly brew-pub in Britain. It originally brewed just one cask a week for hotel guests working at Dounray power station. Far North now has a two-barrel plant from Dark Star's original brewery in Brighton. Owner Peter Martin plans to add a bottle-conditioned John O'Groats Ale for summer tourist outlets. One pub is owned and one outlet is supplied direct.

John O'Groats Ale (OG 1038, ABV 3.8%)

Real Mackay (OG 1038, ABV 3.8%)

Special (OG 1040, ABV 4.2%)

Split Stone Pale Ale (OG 1042, ABV 4.2%)

Fast Reactor (OG 1048, ABV 4.8%)

Porter (OG 1048, ABV 4.8%)

Edge of Darkness (OG 1065, ABV 7%)

Fat Cat*

See Norfolk Cottage

Federation

Northern Clubs Federation Brewery, Lancaster Road, Dunston Industrial Estate, Gateshead, Tyne & Wear, NE11 9HR

The brewery was bought by Scottish & Newcastle (qv Global Giants) in 2004. S&N closed its Newcastle brewery and transferred production of keg and bottled beers to Gateshead.

Felinfoel IFBB

Felinfoel Brewery Co Ltd, Farmers Row, Felinfoel, Llanelli, Carmarthenshire, SA14 8LB
Tel (01554) 773357
Fax (01554) 752452
Email enquiries@felinfoel-brewery.com
Website www.felinfoel-brewery.com
Shop 9-5 Mon-Fri; 10-12 Sat

☺ Founded in 1830 by David John, the company is still family-owned and is now the oldest brewery in Wales. The present buildings are Grade II* listed and were built in the 1870s. Felinfoel was the first brewery in Europe to can beer in the 1930s. It supplies cask ale to half its 84 houses, though some use top pressure, and to approximately 350 free trade outlets.

Dragon Bitter Ale (OG 1034, ABV 3.4%)

Best Bitter (OG 1038, ABV 3.8%) ◆
A balanced beer, with a low aroma. Bitter-sweet initially with an increasing moderate bitterness.

Double Dragon Ale (OG 1042, ABV 4.2%) ◆
This pale brown beer has a malty, fruity aroma. The taste is also malt and fruit with a background hop presence throughout. A malty and fruity finish.

Fellows, Morton & Clayton

Fellows, Morton & Clayton Brewhouse Company, 54 Canal Street, Nottingham, NG1 7EH
Tel (0115) 950 6795
Fax (0115) 9838
Email fellowsgalley@aol.co.uk
Website www.galleyrestaurant.co.uk

A brewpub previously owned by Interbrew but sold in 2004 to Enterprise Inns (qv).

Fellows (OG 1039, ABV 3.8%)

Post Haste (OG 1048, ABV 4.5%)

Felstar EAB

Felstar Brewery, Felsted Vineyards, Crix Green, Felsted, Essex, CM6 3JT
Tel (01245) 361504/(07973) 315503
Fax (01245) 361504
Email felstarbrewery@supanet.com
Shop 10-dusk 7 days/week
Tours by arrangement

⊗ The Felstar Brewery opened in 2001 and the five-barrel plant is based in the old bonded warehouse of the Felsted Vineyard. A small number of outlets are supplied. Seasonal beer: Howlin' Hen (ABV 6.5%). Bottle-conditioned beers: all the cask beers plus Pecking Order (ABV 5%), Lord Kulmbach (ABV 4.4%) and Dark Wheat (ABV 5.4%).

Essex Knight (OG 1039, ABV 3.8%)

Crix Gold (OG 1041, ABV 4%)

Hop-Hop-Hurray (OG 1042, ABV 4%)

Chick-Chat (OG 1043, ABV 4.1%)

Hopsin (OG 1048, ABV 4.6%)

Wheat (OG 1048, ABV 4.8%)

Good Knight (OG 1050, ABV 5%)

Lord Essex (OG 1056, ABV 5.4%)

Haunted Hen (OG 1062, ABV 6%)

Fenland SIBA

Fenland Brewery Ltd, Unit 2, Fieldview, Cowbridge Hall Road, Little Downham, Cambridgeshire, CB6 2UQ
Tel (01353) 699966
Fax (01353) 699967
Email enquiries@elybeer.co.uk
Website www.elybeer.co.uk
Tours by arrangement

⊗ The brewery was set up in 1997 by Dr Rob Thomas and his wife, Liz, and was originally based in Chatteris, but moved to new premises on the Isle of Ely. In 2003, the company was bought by David Griffiths. Beers are supplied to more than 100 outlets throughout Bedfordshire, Cambridgeshire, Lincolnshire, Norfolk, and Northamptonshire. Seasonal beers: Doctors Orders (ABV 5%), Winter Warmer (ABV 5.5%).

St Audreys Ale (ABV 3.9%)

Amber Solstice (ABV 4.1%)

Babylon Banks (ABV 4.1%)

Osier Cutter (ABV 4.2%)

Hereward's Wake (ABV 4.4%)

Sparkling Wit (ABV 4.5%)

Fernandes SIBA

Fernandes Brewery, 5 Avison Yard, Kirkgate, Wakefield, West Yorkshire, WF1 1UA
Tel (01924) 291709/369547
Website www.fernandes-brewery.gowyld.com
Tours by arrangement

☺ The brewery opened in 1997 and is housed in a 19th-century malthouse. It incorporates a home-brew shop and a brewery tap. It has won Wakefield CAMRA's Pub of the Year every year since 1999 and has been awarded Yorkshire Regional Pub of the Year 2001 and 2002. One pub is owned and 10-15 outlets are supplied. Seasonal beer: 12 monthly special beers, named after the months, are brewed.

Malt Shovel Mild (OG 1038, ABV 3.8%)
A dark, full-bodied, malty mild with an abundance of roast malt and chocolate flavours, leading to a lingering, dry, malty finish.

Triple O (ABV 3.9%)

Ale to the Tsar (OG 1042, ABV 4.1%)
A pale, smooth, well-balanced beer with some sweetness leading to a nutty, malty and satisfying aftertaste.

Wakefield Pride (OG 1045, ABV 4.5%)
A light-coloured and full-bodied, clean-tasting malty beer with a good hop character leading to a dry, bitter finish.

Empress of India (OG 1058, ABV 6%)
A strong, light-coloured, malty beer with a complex bitter palate. Fruit and malt dominate the aftertaste.

Double Six (OG 1062, ABV 6%)
A powerful, dark and rich strong beer with an array of malt, roast malt and chocolate flavours and a strong, lasting malty finish, with some hoppiness.

FILO SIBA

FILO Brewing Co Ltd, First In Last Out, 14-15 High Street, Hastings, East Sussex, TN34 3EY
Tel (01424) 425079 Fax (01424) 420802
Email mike@thefilo.co.uk
Website www.thefilo.co.uk
Tours by arrangement

⊗ FILO Brewery was first installed in 1985, using old milk tanks. The current owner, Mike Bigg, took over in 1988 and remains in control of the pub and brewery business. In 2000, the

brewery went through a complete overhaul, although it remains a small, five-barrel capacity craft brewery with the First In Last Out pub as the only outlet plus occasional beer festivals.

Crofters (ABV 4%)

Ginger Tom (ABV 4.4%)

Cardinal (ABV 4.4%)

Gold (ABV 4.8%)

Font Valley*

Font Valley Brewery, Selby House, Stanton, Morpeth, Northumberland, NE65 8PR
Tel (01670) 772235

The first beer from this farm-based brewery was launched in November 2004. Michael Hegarty worked as an electrician at the Federation Brewery in Gateshead before joining the biochemistry industry where he specialised in fermentation. He used both his skills to build a brewery with his partner Selby Potts, who owns the farm where the brewery is sited. The plant is five-barrels in length and has been 'cobbled together' from second-hand equipment. Second Brew takes its name from the fact that it won a bronze award at the Newcastle beer festival even though it was only the second brew Michael and Selby had put through the plant.

Milk of Amnesia (ABV 4.5%)

SB/Second Brew (ABV 5%)

Four Alls

Four Alls Brewery, Ovington, Richmond, Co Durham, DL11 7BP
Tel (01833) 627302
Tours by arrangement

The one-barrel brewery was launched in 2003 by John Stroud, one of the founders of Ales of Kent, using that name. In 2004 it became Four Alls, named after the pub where it is based, the only outlet except for two beers supplied twice yearly to Darlington beer festivals. Phone first to check if beer is available.

Bitter (OG 1035, ABV 3.6%)

Iggy Pop (OG 1036, ABV 3.6%)
A honey-coloured beer, made from pale, crystal and wheat malts and hopped with First Gold and Goldings.

30 Shilling (OG 1039, ABV 3.8%)
A dark session ale made from pale, crystal and chocolate malts with First Gold and Fuggles hops.

Red Admiral (OG 1041, ABV 3.9%)

Fowler's

Fowler's Ales (Prestoungrange) Ltd, The Prestoungrange Gothenburg, 227-229 High Street, Prestonpans, East Lothian, EH32 9BE
Tel (01875) 819922
Fax (01875) 819911
Email info@prestoungrange.org
Website www.prestoungrange.org
Tours by arrangement

Fowler's opened in 2004. A new brewer, Craig Allan, joined in February 2005 to brew beers for the Gothenburg pub and the surrounding area. Brewing courses and brew-your-own beer facilities are available by arrangement. One pub, the Gothenburg, is owned.

70/- (OG 1038, ABV 3.9%)

80/- (OG 1041, ABV 4.2%)

IPA (OG 1043, ABV 4.5%)

Fox EAB

Fox Brewery, 22 Station Road, Heacham, Norfolk, PE31 7EX
Tel (01485) 570345 Fax (01485) 579492
Email info@foxbrewery.co.uk
Website www.foxbrewery.co.uk
Shop Fox and Hounds noon-11pm
Tours by arrangement

The brewery produces a range of beers in a 2002 conversion of an outbuilding at the Fox & Hounds pub. One pub is owned and 30 outlets are supplied. Bottle-conditioned beers: all cask ales listed below. England Expects (ABV 3.8%) is a bottle-conditioned beer brewed for the Lord Nelson in Burham Thorpe, Nelson's home village. The Branthill beer range is brewed with malted barley grown on Granthill Farm, Wells-next-the-Sea, home of the Real Ale Shop, and malted at Crisps of Great Ryburgh. Seasonal beers: Perfick (ABV 3.7%, summer), Wootton Wild (ABV 4.9%, autumn-winter).

Branthill Best (OG 1037, ABV 3.8%)
Old fashioned best bitter.

Heacham Gold (OG 1037, ABV 3.9%)
Light, fruity, crisp bitter.

LJB (OG 1040, ABV 4%)
Fruity, well-balanced, moderately bitter.

Red Knocker (OG 1043, ABV 4.2%)
Copper coloured and malty.

Branthill Norfolk Nectar (OG 1043, ABV 4.3%)
Slightly sweet. Brewed only with Maris Otter pale malt.

Cerebus Norfolk Stout (OG 1046, ABV 4.5%)
Dark, fruity and easy drinking.

Branthill Pioneer (OG 1050, ABV 5%)
Malty, fresh aroma. Hops are present in the background.

IPA (OG 1051, ABV 5.2%)
Based on a 19th-century recipe. Easy drinking for its strength.

Punt Gun (OG 1056, ABV 5.9%)
Full bodied, dark brown beer with liquorice flavour.

Foxfield

Foxfield Brewery, Prince of Wales, Foxfield, Broughton in Furness, Cumbria, LA20 6BX
Tel (01229) 716238
Email drink@princeofwalesfoxfield.co.uk
Website www.princeofwalesfoxfield.co.uk
Tours by arrangement

Foxfield is a three-barrel plant run by Stuart and Lynda Johnson in old stables attached to the Prince of Wales inn, across the road from the railway station. A few other outlets are supplied. The Johnsons also own Tigertops in Wakefield (qv). The beer range constantly changes, as Stuart tends to brew as the fancy takes him. The beers listed here may not necessarily be available. There are many occasional and seasonal beers. Dark Mild is suitable for vegetarians and vegans.

Sands (OG 1038, ABV 3.4%)
A pale, light, aromatic quaffing ale.

Fleur-de-Lys (OG 1038, ABV 3.6%)

Dark Mild (OG 1040, ABV 3.7%)

Brief Encounter (OG 1040, ABV 3.8%)
A fruity beer with a long, bitter finish.

Franklin's

Franklin's Brewery, Bilton Lane, Bilton, Harrogate, North Yorkshire, HG1 4DH
Tel/Fax (01423) 322345
Email tim@franklinsbrewery.co.uk
Website www.franklinsbrewery.co.uk

A brewery set up in 1980 by Sean Franklin of Roosters (qv) and run by Leeds CAMRA founder-member Tommy Thomas and stepson Tim Osborne. Seasonal beer: Blotto (ABV 4.7%, winter).

Bitter (OG 1038, ABV 3.8%)
A tremendous hop aroma precedes a flowery hop flavour, combined with malt. Long, hoppy, bitter finish. A fine, unusual amber bitter.

Frankton Bagby

Frankton Bagby Brewery, The Old Stables, Green Lane, Church Lawford, Rugby, Warwickshire, CV23 9EF
Tel (02476) 540770
Tours by arrangement

Frankton Bagby was set up in 1999 by three local families. The five-barrel plant is housed in a small, 18th-century stable block that has been carefully renovated by Warwickshire craftsmen. More than 150 outlets are supplied direct. Seasonal beers: Crackerjack (ABV 5%, Christmas), Dizzy Blonde (ABV 4%, summer), Rugby Special (ABV 4.5%, rugby season).

Red Oak (ABV 3.9%)

Old Chestnut (OG 1040, ABV 4%)

A chestnut-coloured bitter brewed using a combination of Green Bullet and Fuggles hops that give the beer a distinctive mellow flavour; the late addition of Styrian Goldings adds a fruity nose.

Squires Brew **(OG 1042, ABV 4.2%)**
A straw-coloured best bitter, smooth on the palate with a good, hoppy aftertaste. A mix of Challenger and Fuggles hops is used in the main brew and Styrian Goldings are added for late hopping.

Freedom

Freedom Brewing Co, 11 Galena Road, Hammersmith, London, W6 0LT
Tel (020) 8870 9700
Email info@freedombrewery.com
Website www.freedombrewery.com

⊗ Founded in 1995 to specialise in unpasteurised lagers, brewed to the German Beer Purity Law, the Reinheitsgebot. It disposed of its brew cafes in 2003 and has added one cask-conditioned beer.

Soho Red **(ABV 4.7%)**

Freeminer SIBA

Freeminer Brewery Ltd, Whimsey Road, Steam Mills, Cinderford, Gloucestershire, GL14 3JA
Tel (01594) 827989
Fax (01594) 829464
Email sales@freeminer.com
Website www.freeminer.com
Tours by arrangement

⊗ Founded in 1992 by Don Burgess, the brewery is based in the Royal Forest of Dean. In 1999 the brewery moved and expanded from a five-barrel to a 40-barrel brew plant to cope with an increase in cask and bottle sales at home and abroad. Distribution outside the local rural area is made via a number of independent wholesalers, while some 40 pubs are supplied by the brewery. Beer names are linked to the local mining history of the area with names such as Pot Lid, Stay and Drink and Resolution (all ABV 4.5%) being added to the regular seasonal beers such as Strip and At It (ABV 4%, summer) and Iron Brew (ABV 4.2%, spring). Bottle-conditioned beers: Trafalgar (ABV 6%), Speculation (ABV 4.8%), Gold Miner (ABV 5%: exclusive to the Co-op).

Bitter **(OG 1039, ABV 4%)** ◆
A light, hoppy session bitter with an intense hop aroma and a dry, hoppy finish.

Speculation **(OG 1047, ABV 4.8%)** ◆
An aromatic, chestnut-brown, full-bodied beer with a smooth, well-balanced mix of malt and hops, and a predominately hoppy aftertaste.

Back Street Heroes **(OG 1047, ABV 4.8%)**
A brown ale packed with malt flavour and Worcestershire-grown English hops.

Frog & Parrot

Frog & Parrot Brewhouse, Division Street, Sheffield, South Yorkshire, S1 4GF
Tel (0114) 272 1280

A brew-pub that opened in 1982. Ownership passed to Interbrew, who transferred it to the Laurel Pub Co (qv). The beers are brewed from malt extact. Brewing is suspended during long students' vacations. There are occasional/one-off brews.

Roger & Out **(ABV 12.5%)**

Frog Island SIBA

Frog Island Brewery, The Maltings, Westbridge, St James' Road, Northampton, NN5 5HS
Tel (01604) 587772
Fax (01604) 750754
Email beer@frogislandbrewery.co.uk
Website www.frogislandbrewery.co.uk
Shop by arrangement
Tours to licensed trade only, by arrangement

⊗ Started in 1994 by home-brewer Bruce Littler and business partner Graham Cherry in a malt house built by the long-defunct brewery Thomas Manning & Co, Frog Island expanded by doubling its brew length to 10 barrels in 1998. It specialises in beers with personalised bottle labels, available by mail order. Some 40 free trade outlets are supplied, with the beer occasionally available through other micro-brewers. Seasonal beers: Fuggled Frog (ABV 3.5%, May), Head in the Clouds (ABV 4.5%, August). Bottle-conditioned beers: Natterjack, Fire Bellied Toad, Croak & Stagger. Bottled beers are available for sale in a shop on the brewery forecourt.

Best Bitter **(OG 1040, ABV 3.8%)** ◆
Blackcurrant and gooseberry enhance the full malty aroma with pineapple and papaya joining on the tongue. Bitterness develops in the fairly long Target/Fuggles finish.

Shoemaker **(OG 1043, ABV 4.2%)** ◆
An orangey aroma of fruity Cascade hops is balanced by malt. Citrus and hoppy bitterness lasts into a long, dry finish. Amber colour

That Old Chestnut **(OG 1044, ABV 4.4%)**
A malty, chestnut-brown ale brewed with Maris Otter pale malt, with a hint of crystal and malted wheat, and coloured with roast barley. Target is the bittering hop with Cascade as a late addition for aroma.

Natterjack **(OG 1048, ABV 4.8%)** ◆
Deceptively robust, golden and smooth. Fruit and hop aromas fight for dominance before the grainy astringency and floral palate give way to a long, dry aftertaste with a hint of lingering malt.

Fire Bellied Toad **(OG 1050, ABV 5%)** ◆
Amber-gold brew with an extraordinary long bitter/fruity finish. Huge malt and Phoenix hop flavours have a hint of apples. The pink grapefruit nose belies its punchy overall hit.

Croak & Stagger **(OG 1056, ABV 5.8%)** ◆
The initial honey/fruit aroma is quickly overpowered by roast malt then bitter chocolate and pale malt sweetness on the tongue. Gentle, bitter-sweet finish. A dark winter brew.

Fugelestou

Fugelestou Ales, Fulstow Brewery, 6 North Way, Fulstow, Louth, Lincolnshire, LN11 0XH

Tel: (01507) 363642
Email Fulstow.brewery.virgin.net
Tours by arrangement

Fugelestou is a 2.5-barrel plant bought from Brown Cow brewery in North Yorkshire. Some 20 outlets are supplied. Seasonal ales: Sumerheade (ABV 4.7%), Autumn Gold (ABV 4.4%), Christmas Spirit (ABV 5%) and White Christmas (ABV 4.2%).

Fulstow Common (OG 1038, ABV 3.8%)

Schizophrenia (OG 1041, ABV 4.2%)

Wat Pasture (OG 1042, ABV 4.3%)

Sweating Sickness (OG 1055, ABV 6.1%)

Fuller's IFBB

Fuller, Smith and Turner plc, Griffin Brewery, Chiswick Lane South, London, W4 2QB
Tel (020) 8996 2000
Fax (020) 8995 0230
Email fullers@fullers.co.uk
Website www.fullers.co.uk
Shop 10-6 Mon-Fri, 10-5 Sat
Tours by arrangement

⊗ Fuller, Smith & Turner's Griffin Brewery in Chiswick has stood on the same site for more than 350 years and direct descendants of the founding families are still involved in running the company. Fuller's has won the Champion Beer of Britain award five times in the 25 years the competition has been staged. The beers have been Best in Class no less than nine times and ESB has been voted Best Strong Ale an unprecedented seven times. Sales of London Pride have grown from 80,000 barrels a year in 2001 to 130,000 in 2004. Almost all Fuller's 240 pubs, bars and hotels serve cask ales. Fuller's also supplies close to 600 free trade accounts. Fuller's Organic Honey Dew (cask and bottle) is the world's first honey-flavoured organic ale and its winter ale, Jack Frost, is made with the addition of blackberries. Fuller's continues to invest in brewing capacity and has bought land adjacent to the brewery that will increase the site area by 11%. Seasonal beers: London Porter (5.4%), India Pale Ale (ABV 4.8%), Organic Honey Dew (ABV 4.3%,), Jack Frost (ABV 4.5%). Bottle-conditioned beers: 1845 (ABV 6.3%), Vintage Ale (ABV 8.5%).

Chiswick Bitter
(OG 1034.5, ABV 3.5%)
A pale brown beer with malt and some citrus hops throughout, leading to a short, clean, bitter finish.

Discovery (ABV 3.9%)
Launched in May 2005, Discovery is Fuller's first new permanent cask beer for 20 years. It is brewed with malted wheat as well as barley malt plus carapils, and is hopped with Czech Saaz for bitterness and American Liberty for aroma. It is a blond beer served cooler than the other beers in the range.

London Pride
(OG 1040.5, ABV 4.1%)
Tawny brown with golden hues, the beer has flavours of fruity bitter orange balanced with hops and malt on nose and palate, lingering in the aftertaste and leaving a pleasant dry bitterness.

ESB (OG 1054, ABV 5.5%)
Tawny coloured; marmalade, hops and malt combine to produce a rich, complex, full-bodied quality that is previewed in the enticing aroma and remains to the close, complemented by some roast bitterness.

Full Mash

Full Mash Brewery, 17 Lower Park Street, Stapleford, Nottinghamshire, NG9 8EW
Tel (0115) 9499262
Email karlwaring@yahoo.com

Full Mash started brewing in 2003 after Karl Waring had spent some years as an enthusiastic home brewer and thought he could make a commercial success if he went full time. The brewery has now expanded to a 2.25-barrel plant and plans are in hand to acquire premises to accommodate a five-barrel plant and brewery tap. Trade is buoyant with two regular beers and a number of seasonal ales plus special one-off brews.

Whistlin' Dixie (OG 1038, ABV 3.9%)

Apparition (OG 1044, ABV 4.5%)

Funfair

Funfair Brewing Co, 34 Spinney Road, Ilkeston, Derbyshire, DE7 4LH
Tel (07971) 540186
Email sales@funfairbrewingcompany.com
Website www.funfairbrewingcompany.com
Tours by arrangement

David Tizard launched Funfair in 2004 at the Wheel Inn in Holbrook, Derbyshire. The brewhouse, a 2.5-barrel plant, was situated behind the pub in a small out-building. The brewing kit came from the Parish Brewery in Leicestershire. Modifications were made to the plant in 2004 to raise capacity to five barrels. In December 2004, the pub was sold to Punch Taverns and the brewing equipment was removed and relocated to its new site in Ilkeston. The brewery will continue to supply Funfair beers to the Wheel Inn. Seasonal beer: Roller Ghoster (ABV 4.5%, Halloween).

The Big Wheel (OG 1039, ABV 3.9%)

Speedway (OG 1041, ABV 4.1%)

Waltzer (OG 1045, ABV 4.5%)

Dodgem (OG 1047, ABV 4.7%)

Ghost Train (OG 1050, ABV 5%)

Fyfe SIBA

Fyfe Brewing Co, 469 High Street, Kirkcaldy, Fife, KY1 2SN
Tel (01592) 646211/264270
Fax (01592) 646211
Email fyfebrew@blueyonder.co.uk
Website www.fyfebrewery.co.uk
Tours by arrangement

Established in 1995 behind the Harbour Bar, Fyfe was the town's first brew-pub in the 20th century. Most of the output is taken by the pub, the remainder being sold direct to 10 local outlets and to the free trade via wholesalers. One pub is owned and 50-plus outlets are supplied. Seasonal beer: Cauld Turkey (ABV 6%, winter).

Rope of Sand (OG 1037, ABV 3.7%)
A quenching bitter. Malt and fruit throughout, with a hoppy, bitter aftertaste.

Greengo (OG 1038, ABV 3.8%)

Torque Ale (OG 1039. ABV 3.9%)

Auld Alliance (OG 1040, ABV 4%)
A very bitter beer with a lingering, dry, hoppy finish. Malt and hop, with fruit, are present throughout, fading in the finish.

Hedge Your Best (OG 1042, ABV 4.2%)

Lion Slayer (OG 1042, ABV 4.2%)

First Lyte (OG 1043, ABV 4.3%)

Lino Richie (OG 1045, ABV 4.5%)

Weiss Squad (OG 1045, ABV 4.5%)
Wheat beer

Fyre (OG 1048, ABV 4.8%)

J.P.S. Pilsner (OG 1050, ABV 5%)

Fyne SIBA

Fyne Ales, Achadunan, Cairndow, Argyll, PA26 8BJ
Tel/Fax (01499) 600238
Email jonny@fyneales.com
Website www.fyneales.com
Tours by arrangement

Fyne Ales brewed for the first time on St Andrew's Day 2001. The 10-barrel plant was installed in a redundant milking parlour on a farm in Argyll. The brewery has an enthusiastic following in the central belt and the Highlands. A number of regular wholesalers also helped to build trade south of the border. Seasonal beers: Summerled (ABV 4%), Holly Daze (ABV 5%).

Piper's Gold (OG 1037.5, ABV 3.8%)
An easy-drinking, golden session ale. Bitter-sweet taste with a hoppy finish.

Maverick (OG 1040.5, ABV 4.2%)
Smooth, nutty session beer with a sweet, fruity finish.

Vital Spark (OG 1042.5, ABV 4.4%)
A rich, dark beer that shows glints of red. The taste is clean and slightly sharp with a hint of blackcurrant.

Highlander (OG 1045.5, ABV 4.8%)
A strong traditional ale with intense malt flavours and a citrus hop aroma.

Gale's IFBB

George Gale & Co Ltd, The Hampshire Brewery, Horndean, Hampshire, PO8 0DA
Tel (02392) 571212
Fax (02392) 598641
Email thebrewery@galesales.co.uk
Website www.gales.co.uk
Shop 10-5 Mon-Fri; 10-2 Sat
Tours by arrangement

Richard Gale bought the Ship & Bell pub with its brewery in 1847. The brewhouse was rebuilt after a fire in 1869. The Bowyer family bought the company in 1896 and still control the company. The brewery was re-equipped in the 1920s. A major development in the brewhouse was opened in 1984 and there has been a gradual modernisation of the plant over the past 20 years. 110 pubs are owned and 480 free trade outlets are supplied. Seasonal beers: Summer Hog (ABV 3.8%, Jul-Aug), Trafalgar Ale (ABV 4.2%, Oct-Nov), Winter Brew (ABV 4.2%, Nov-Feb), Swing Low (ABV 4.1%, Feb-March), Robin's Revenge (ABV 4%, Nov-Dec). Bottle-conditioned beers: GB Export Strength (ABV 4.5%), Festival Mild Ale, HSB, Christmas Ale (ABV 8.5%), Prize Old Ale (ABV 9%), Trafalgar Ale (ABV 10%)

Butser Bitter (OG 1034, ABV 3.4%)
A mid-brown chestnut session beer. A slightly malty and fruity aroma precedes a sweet taste, with some fruit and malt. The aftertaste is sweet and fruity with a little bitterness.

Best (OG 1040, ABV 3.9%)
A replacement for GB with the same gravity but a lower ABV. This pale brown beer is hoppier than other Gale's brews. Bitter-sweet, with a balance of malt and hops in the taste. Somewhat lacking in body with a dry, bitter aftertaste.

HSB (OG 1050, ABV 4.8%)
A mid-brown beer with a malty and fruity aroma. The full-bodied, sweet and fruity taste, with noticeable maltiness, follows through to the aftertaste. For those with a sweet tooth.

Festival Mild (OG 1052, ABV 4.8%)
Black in colour, with a red tinge. The aroma is of fruit and caramel. A sweet, fruity and malty taste, with some toffee, carries through to the aftertaste, but where there is more bitterness.

Garton SIBA

Garton Brewery, Station House, Station Road, Garton on the Wolds, Driffield, East Yorkshire, YO25 3EX
Tel (01377) 252340
Email gartonbrewery@aol.com
Tours by arrangement

Garton was launched in 2001 by Richard Heptinstall with the aim of resurrecting some of the powerful beers of Dickensian times. Beers of a lesser magnitude are also brewed, but the big beers are the driving force of the brewery. Liquid Lobotomy is available in five-litre mini-casks. Seasonal beers: Goodnight Vienna (ABV 8%), Chocolate Frog (ABV 8%).

Woldsman Bitter (OG 1048, ABV 4.5%)
This refreshing bitter is gold in colour. The full-

bodied beer has a mix of hops and fruit balancing the sweetness. A dry, crisp finish.

Old Buffer (OG 1050, ABV 4.5%)
A dark mild of a type brewed around the time of the First World War.

Stunned Mullet (OG 1053, ABV 5%)
A premium quality bitter with a deep red hue.

Liquid Lobotomy Stout (OG 1080, ABV 8%)
Garston's flagship beer, its strength derived from grain without the aid of extracts and sugars.

George and Dragon*

George and Dragon, Church End, Foulness Island, Southend-on-Sea, Essex, SS3 9XQ
Tel (01702) 219460
Email fred.fara@gandpub.fsnet.co.uk
Website www.georgeanddragonpub.co.uk

A pub-brewery that came on stream in December 2004 in the cellar of the George & Dragon. Nine gallons can be produced at a time. An occasional mild is brewed.

Beaters Best Bitter (ABV 5%)

Glastonbury SIBA

Glastonbury Ales, Unit 10, Wessex Park, Somerton Business Park, Somerton, Somerset, TA11 6SB
Tel (01458) 272244
Email glastonburyales@ukonline.co.uk
Tours by prior arrangement

⊗ Glastonbury Ales was established in 2002 by Greig Nicholls, after many years as a home brewer. Production has increased to 15 barrels a week and is still rising. The five-barrel plant uses malt from Tuckers of Newton Abbot and hops from Charles Faram in Worcestershire. 60 outlets are supplied. Seasonal beers: Ley Line (ABV 4.2%, Jan-March), Pomparles Porter (ABV 4.5%, Feb-March), Spring Loaded (ABV 4.4%, Feb-June), Pilton Pop (ABV 4.2%, May-June), Brue (ABV 4%, May-Nov), Black As Yer 'At (ABV 4.3%, Sept-Nov), FMB (ABV 5%, Sept-Dec), Holy Thorn (ABV 4.2%, Oct-Dec), Excalibur (ABV 4%, Nov-May). Bottle-conditioned beers: Mystery Tor, Lady of the Lake, Golden Chalice, FMB (ABV 5%).

Mystery Tor (OG 1040, ABV 3.8%)
A golden bitter with plenty of floral hop and fruit on the nose and palate, the sweetness giving way to a bitter hop finish. Full-bodied for a session bitter.

Lady of the Lake (OG 1042, ABV 4.2%)
A full-bodied amber best bitter with plenty of hops to the forefront balanced by a fruity malt flavour and a subtle hint of vanilla, leading to a clean, bitter hop aftertaste.

Hedgemonkey (OG 1048, ABV 4.6%)
A ruby bitter with toffee/coffee undertones that give way to a medium hopped, spicy finish.

Golden Chalice (OG 1048, ABV 4.8%)
Light and golden best bitter with a robust malt character. Strong bitterness provided by Challenger hops gives way to a light floral aftertaste, due to the late addition of American Mount Hood hops.

Glentworth SIBA

Glentworth Brewery, Glentworth House, Crossfield Lane, Skellow, Doncaster, South Yorkshire, DN6 8PL
Tel (01302) 725555
Fax (01302) 724133
Email glentworthbrewery@btconnect.com

☺ The brewery was formed in 1996 and is housed in dairy buildings. The five-barrel plant supplies more than 80 pubs. Production is concentrated on mainly light-coloured, hoppy ales. Due to demand, a second cold room has been added, doubling storage capacity. Seasonal beers (brewed to order): Oasis (ABV 4.1%), Happy Hooker (ABV 4.3%), North Star (ABV 4.3%), Perle (ABV 4.4%), Dizzy Blonde (ABV 4.5%), Whispers (ABV 4.5%).

Lightyear (OG 1037, ABV 3.9%)

Goacher's

P&DJ Goacher, Unit 8, Tovil Green Business Park, Burial Ground Lane, Tovil, Maidstone, Kent, ME15 6TA
Tel (01622) 682112
Tours by arrangement

⊗ A traditional brewery that uses only malt and Kentish hops for all its beers. Goacher's celebrated 21 years in the business in 2004. Phil and Debbie Goacher have concentrated on brewing good wholesome beers without gimmicks. Two tied houses and around 30 free trade outlets in the mid-Kent area are supplied. Special, a mix of Light and Dark ales, is also available to pubs for sale under house names. Seasonal beer: Old 1066 (ABV 6.7%).

Real Mild Ale (OG 1033, ABV 3.4%)
A full-flavoured malty ale with background bitterness.

Fine Light Ale (OG 1036, ABV 3.7%)
A pale, golden brown bitter with a strong, floral, hoppy aroma and aftertaste. A hoppy and moderately malty session beer.

Special/House Beer (OG 1037, ABV 3.8%)

Best Dark Ale (OG 1040, ABV 4.1%)
An intensely bitter beer, balanced by a moderate maltiness, with a complex aftertaste.

Crown Imperial Stout (OG 1044, ABV 4.5%)
A classic Irish-style stout with a clean palate and satisfying aftertaste from Kent Fuggles hops.

Gold Star Strong Ale (OG 1050, ABV 5.1%) ◆
A strong pale ale brewed from 100% Maris Otter malt and all Kent hops.

Old/Maidstone Old Ale (OG 1066, ABV 6.7%)

Goddards SIBA

Goddards Brewery Ltd, Barnsley Farm, Bullen Road, Ryde, Isle of Wight, PO33 1QF
Tel (01983) 611011
Fax (01983) 611012
Email office@goddards-brewery.co.uk
Website www.goddards-brewery.co.uk

⊗ Housed in a converted 18th-century barn on a farm near Ryde, the brewery went into production in 1993. Sales of its award-winning beers have been rising steadily. Around 40 outlets are supplied. Seasonal beers: Ale of Wight (ABV 4%, spring), Duck's Folly (ABV 5%, early autumn), Iron Horse (ABV 4.8%, late autumn), Inspiration (ABV 5.2%), Winter Warmer (ABV 5.2%).

Special Bitter (OG 1038.5, ABV 4%) ◆
Well-balanced session beer that maintains its flavour and bite with compelling drinkability.

Fuggle-Dee-Dum (OG 1048.5, ABV 4.8%) ◆
Brown-coloured strong ale with bags of malt and hops.

Goff's SIBA

Goff's Brewery Ltd, 9 Isbourne Way, Winchcombe, Cheltenham, Gloucestershire, GL54 5NS
Tel (01242) 603383
Fax (01242) 603959
Email brewery@goffs.biz
Website www.goffs.biz
Tours by arrangement

⊗ Goff's is a family concern that celebrated its 10th anniversary in 2004. Its ales are available regionally in more than 200 outlets and nationally through wholesalers. The addition of the seasonal Ales of the Round Table provides a range of 12 beers of which four or five are always available. Two pubs are leased, in Cheltenham and Gretton. Seasonal beers: Mordred (ABV 4.2%, Jan-Feb), Launcelot (ABV 4.5%, March-April), Guinevere (ABV 4.1%, May), Galahad (ABV 4.3%, June), Excalibur (ABV 3.8%, July), Lamorak (ABV 5%, August), Merlin (ABV 4.3%, Sept-Oct), Camelot (ABV 4.4%, Nov-Dec).

Tournament (OG 1038, ABV 4%) ◆
Dark golden in colour, with a pleasant hop aroma. A clean, light and refreshing session bitter with a pleasant hop aftertaste.

Jouster (OG 1040, ABV 4%) ◆
A drinkable, tawny-coloured ale, with a light hoppiness in the aroma. It has a good balance of malt and bitterness in the mouth, underscored by fruitiness, with a clean, hoppy aftertaste.

White Knight (OG 1046, ABV 4.7%) ◆
A well-hopped bitter with a light colour and full-bodied taste. Bitterness predominates in the mouth and leads to a dry, hoppy aftertaste.

Black Knight (OG 1053, ABV 5.3%) ◆
A dark, ruby-red tinted beer with a strong chocolate malt aroma. It has a smooth, dry, malty taste, with a subtle hoppiness, leading to a dry finish.

Golcar SIBA

Golcar Brewery, Swallow Lane, Golcar, Huddersfield, West Yorkshire, HD7 4HT
Tel (01484) 644241 (m) 0797 026 7555
Email golcarbrewery@btconnect.com
Tours by arrangement

◎ Golcar started brewing in 2001 and production has increased from 2.4 barrels to five barrels a week. The brewery owns one pub, the Rose and Crown at Golcar, and supplies four other outlets in the local area.

Dark Mild (OG 1033, ABV 3.2%) ◆
Dark mild with a light roasted malt and liquorice taste. Smooth and satisfying.

Pennine Gold (OG 1038, ABV 3.8%)
A hoppy and fruity session beer.

Bitter (OG 1039, ABV 3.9%) ◆
Amber bitter with a hoppy, citrus taste, with fruity overtones and a bitter finish.

Weavers Delight (OG 1042, ABV 4.4%)
Malty best bitter with fruity overtones.

Winkle Warmer Porter (OG 1047, ABV 5%)
A robust all grain and malty working man's porter.

Goldfinch

Goldfinch Brewery, 47 High East Street, Dorchester, Dorset, DT1 1HU
Tel (01305) 264020

Alan Finch, the owner of the brewery, died in January 2005 and the future of the company had not been decided when the guide went to press.

Goodmanham

Goodmanham Brewery, Goodmanham Arms, Main Street, Goodmanham, East Yorkshire, YO43 3JA
Tel (01430) 873849
Email info@goodmanhamarms.co.uk
Website www.goodmanhamarms.co.uk
Tours by arrangement

Geoff Cawthray founded the brewery in 2002 and subsequently sold it to the present owner, Peter Southcott, in 2003. Peter started brewing again that year. The brewery is housed in an out-building, adjacent to the Goodmanham Arms. One pub is owned and three or four outlets are supplied direct. Recent brews include a seasonal beer, Choirboy's Dread (ABV 3.8%) and a carbonated lager, Heavenly Body (ABV 4.3%).

Pale Mild (ABV 3.2%)

Randy Monk (OG 1044, ABV 4.2%)

Filthy Habit (ABV 5.7%)

Goose Eye SIBA

Goose Eye Brewery Ltd, Ingrow Bridge, South Street, Keighley, West Yorkshire, BD21 5AX

Tel/Fax (01535) 605807
Email enquiries@goose-eye-brewery
Website www.goose-eye.co.uk

Goose Eye has been run by Jack and David Atkinson for the past 13 years at Ingrow Bridge. They are brewing to capacity and are looking for bigger premises. The brewery supplies 60-70 regular outlets, mainly in West and North Yorkshire, and Lancashire. The beers are also available through national wholesalers and pub chains. It produces an ever-expanding range of occasional beers, sometimes brewed to order, and is diversifying into wholesaling and bottled beers (filtered but not pasteurised). No-Eye Deer is often re-badged under house names.

Barm Pot Bitter (OG 1038, ABV 3.8%)
The hop and citrus flavours that dominate this amber session bitter are balanced by a malty base. The finish is increasingly dry and bitter.

Bronte Bitter (OG 1040, ABV 4%)
A malty amber best bitter with bitterness increasing to give a lingering dry finish.

No-Eye Deer (OG 1040, ABV 4%)
A faint fruity and malty aroma. Strong hoppy flavours and a long, bitter finish characterise this refreshing, copper-coloured bitter.

Golden Goose (OG 1045, ABV 4.5%)
A straw-coloured beer light on the palate with a smooth and refreshing hoppy finish.

Wharfedale (OG 1045, ABV 4.5%)
Malt and hops dominate the taste of this copper-coloured premium bitter. Bitterness comes through into the finish.

Over and Out (OG 1052, ABV 5.2%)

Pommies Revenge (OG 1052, ABV 5.2%)
An extra strong, single malt bitter.

Grainstore SIBA

Davis'es Brewing Co Ltd (Grainstore), Grainstore Brewery, Station Approach, Oakham, Rutland, LE15 6RE
Tel (01572) 770065
Fax (01572) 770068
Email grainstorebry@aol.com
Website www.rutnet.co.uk/customers/grainstore
Shop Grainstore serves as shop
Tours by arrangement

Grainstore, the smallest county's largest brewery, has been in production since 1995. The brewery's curious name comes from the fact that it was founded by Tony Davis and Mike Davies. After 30 years in the industry, latterly with Ruddles, Tony decided to set up his own business after finding a derelict Victorian railway grainstore building. The brewery is designed traditionally, relying on whole hops and Maris Otter barley malt. 60 outlets are supplied. In 2004 the brewery started a bottling line for Ten Fifty and it has also taken over two existing pubs, which have been renovated and reopened. They both serve real ale. Ten Fifty won the East Midlands SIBA award for best beer and the bottled version came second in its class. Seasonal beers: Springtime (ABV 4.5%, March-May), Gold (ABV 4.5%, May-Oct), Tupping Ale (ABV 4.5%, Sept-Oct), Three Kings (ABV 4.5%, Nov-Dec), Winter Nip (ABV 7.3%, Nov-Dec). Bottle-conditioned beer: Ten Fifty.

Rutland Panther (OG 1034, ABV 3.4%)
Black brew with the drinkability of a mild or light bitter, combined with the roast flavours associated with a stout.

Cooking Bitter (OG 1036, ABV 3.6%)
A smooth, copper-coloured beer, full-bodied for its gravity. Malt and hops on the nose; malt and fruit to taste, with a malty aftertaste.

Triple B (OG 1042, ABV 4.2%)
Initially hops dominate over malt in both the aroma and taste, but fruit is there, too. All three linger in varying degrees in the sweetish aftertaste of this tawny brew.

Steamin' Billy Bitter (OG 1043, ABV 4.3%)
Brewed for the Steaming Billy Brewing Co of Leicester (qv).

Ten Fifty (OG 1050, ABV 5%)
This full-bodied, tawny beer is hoppy and fruity right into the aftertaste. A little malt on the nose and in the initial taste, with an underlying sweetness and an increasing bitterness.

Grand Union SIBA

Grand Union Brewery Co, 10 Abenglen Industrial Estate, Betam Road, Hayes, Middlesex, UB3 1SS
Tel (0208) 573 9888
Fax (0208) 573 8885
Email info@gubrewery.co.uk
Website www.gubrewery.co.uk
Tours groups by prior arrangement

Grand Union Brewery started brewing in 2002 with a 10-barrel plant that came from Mash and Air in Manchester. The kit is able to produce both traditional ales and continental-style lagers that are properly aged. Direct deliveries are made to Greater London and surrounding counties and the beers are available through selected wholesalers. The single varietal One Hop series of beers uses hop varieties from around the world. Some 200 outlets are supplied. Seasonal beers: Mild (ABV 3.6%, April-June), English Wheat Beer (ABV 4.4%, May-July), Autumn Ale (ABV 4.4%, Sept-Nov), Old Ale (ABV 6-8.5%, autumn-winter), Brass Monkeys (ABV 4.1%, Nov-Jan).

Bitter (OG 1036, ABV 3.7%) ◆
A dark gold, light-drinking beer with some lemon citrus notes throughout and an increasing bitter dryness.

Gold (OG 1040, ABV 4.2%) ◆
A floral hop fragrance changes to a citrus hop character on the palate, followed with a bitter-sweet finish.

Special (OG 1044, ABV 4.5%) ◆
A copper-coloured beer with a sweet fruit aroma and a drinkable hoppy bitterness.

Kolsch Style (OG 1043, ABV 4.8%) ◆
A refreshing blonde beer with a hoppy fruitiness and a bitter dryness.

Stout (OG 1050, ABV 4.8%) ◆
A dry, well-balanced stout with a roasted malt finish.

Honey Porter (OG 1050, ABV 4.9%) ◆
Chocolate and fruit dominate the aroma of this black beer. The flavour is sweet and fruity with some caramel notes leaving a warm afterglow.

Great Gable

🍺 Great Gable Brewing Co Ltd, Wasdale Head Inn, Gosforth, Cumbria, CA20 1EX
Tel (019467) 26229 Inn 26333
Fax (019467) 26334
Email info@greatgablebrewing.com
Website www.greatgablebrewing.com
Tours by arrangement

☺ Great Gable brewery is situated at the famous Wasdale Head Inn, birthplace of British climbing. The inn is at the head of remote and unspoiled Wasdale, at the foot of Great Gable, one of England's highest mountains and near its deepest lake. The brewery was the brain-child of Giles Holiday and Howard Christie, co-workers at the Wasdale Head Inn for many years and now brewmaster and director respectively. The Wasdale Head is the main outlet for the beers. Bottle-conditioned beer: Yewbarrow. All the beers are fined with isinglass; in addition, Yewbarrow contains a little honey.

Liar (OG 1037, ABV 3.4%)

Great Gable (OG 1035, ABV 3.7%)
Made from Thomas Fawcett's pale malt with a little dark crystal malt. High alpha Challenger hops for bittering and another hop for aroma.

Wry 'Nose (OG 1039, ABV 4%)

Burnmoor Pale (OG 1040, ABV 4.2%)

Wasd'ale (OG 1042, ABV 4.4%)
Ruby in colour with a fine aftertaste.

Scawfell (OG 1046, ABV 4.8%)
Reminiscent of an old-fashioned ale, brewed with pale malt and a small amount of pale crystal. The hops are Bramling Cross.

Illgill IPA (OG 1048, ABV 5%)
A blend of pale malts, highly hopped with only aroma varieties.

Yewbarrow (OG 1054, ABV 5.5%)
A rich, dark, mellow, strong dark mild (some say stout) with an unusual fruit flavour.

Great Oakley*

Great Oakley Brewery, Bridge Farm, 11 Brooke Road, Great Oakley, Corby, Northamptonshire, NN18 8HG
Tel (01536) 742460
Email mikevans2001@yahoo.co.uk

Great Oakley is a five-barrel plant installed in stables behind the home of one of the owners of the Malt Shovel pub in Northampton. Brewing started in May 2005.

Whot's Occurring (ABV 3.9%)

Harpers (ABV 4.3%)

Tailshaker (ABV 5%)

Gobble (ABV 6%)

Great Orme*

Great Orme Brewery/Bragdy y Gogarth, Nant y Cywarch Farm, Glan Conwy, Colwyn Bay, Conwy, LL28 5PP
Tel (01492) 596465
Email info@greatormebrewery.co.uk
Website www.greatormebrewery.co.uk

Great Orme started brewing in May 2005. It is based on a hillside halfway up the Conwy Valley between Deganwy and Betws-y-Coed, with views of Liverpool Bay and Great Orme. Jonathan Hughes has based his brewery in a former cow shed on the family farm. A spring in the grounds provides pure Welsh water from the hills.

Best (ABV 3.8%)

Extravaganza Ale (ABV 4.4%)

Green Dragon

🍺 Green Dragon, 29 Broad Street, Bungay, Suffolk, NR35 1EE
Tel/Fax (01986) 892681
Tours by arrangement

⊗ The Green Dragon pub was purchased from Brent Walker in 1991 and the buildings at the rear converted to a brewery. In 1994 the plant was expanded and moved into a converted barn across the car park. The doubling of capacity allowed the production of a larger range of ales, including seasonal and occasional brews. The beers are available at the pub and beer festivals. Seasonal beers: Mild (ABV 5%, autumn/winter), Wynnter Warmer (ABV 6.5%).

Chaucer Ale (OG 1037, ABV 3.7%)

Gold (OG 1045, ABV 4.4%)

Bridge Street Bitter (OG 1046, ABV 4.5%)

Greene King

See New Nationals section

Greenfield

Greenfield Real Ale Brewery Ltd, Unit 8, Tanners Business Centre, Waterside Mill, Chew Valley Road, Greenfield, Saddleworth, Greater Manchester, OL3 7PF
Tel (01457) 879789
Email percivalbrewer@hotmail.com
Tours by prior arrangement: contact 07813 176121

Greenfield was launched in 2002 by Peter Percival, former brewer at Saddleworth. Tony Hart joined Peter in 2005 as a partner. They plan to expand the delivery area and look into the possibility of producing bottled beer. Some 40-50 outlets are supplied.

Ammons Ale **(OG 1040, ABV 4%)**

Celebration **(OG 1040, ABV 4%)**

Dovestones Bitter **(OG 1040, ABV 4%)**

Tanners Ale **(OG 1040. ABV 4%)**

Delph Donkey **(OG 1041, ABV 4.1%)**

Evening Glory **(OG 1041, ABV 4.2%)**

Ice Breaker **(OG 1041, ABV 4.2%)**

Jabeths **(OG 1041, ABV 4.2%)**

Pride of England **(OG 1041, ABV 4.2%)**

Uppermill Ale **(OG 1041, ABV 4.2%)**

Brassed Off **(OG 1044, ABV 4.4%)**

Friezeland Ale **(OG 1044, ABV 4.4%)**

Longwood Thump **(OG 1050, ABV 4.5%)**

Rudolph's Tipple **(OG 1050, ABV 5%)**

Green Jack

Green Jack Brewery, Triangle Tavern, 29 St Peters Street, Lowestoft, Suffolk, NR32 1QA
Tel (01502) 582711
Tours by arrangement

Green Jack started brewing again in 2003. It plans to double production at the brewery. 20 outlets are supplied and two pubs are owned. Seasonal ales: Summer Dream (ABV 4%), Cherry Popper (ABV 6%).

Canary **(OG 1038, ABV 3.8%)**

Orange Wheat **(OG 1042, ABV 4.2%)** ◆
Citrus notes dominate the introduction to this deceptively interesting beer. Gold coloured with equal hints of hop and mandarin in the first impression. A dry bitterness develops as the fruit slowly melts away.

Grasshopper **(OG 1045, ABV 4.6%)**

Gone Fishing **(OG 1052, ABV 5.5%)**

Ripper **(OG 1074, ABV 8.5%)**

Green Tye EAB

Green Tye Brewery, Green Tye, Much Hadham, Hertfordshire, SG10 6JP
Tel (01279) 841041
Fax (01279) 842956
Email info@gtbrewery.co.uk
Website www.gtbrewery.co.uk
Shop No, but bottled beer & branded clothing may be bought from brewery
Tours by arrangement

Green Tye was established in 1999 by William Compton. It uses traditionally malted, Hertfordshire grown Maris Otter barley. The brewery produces eight barrels a week and plans to expand to meet demand. One pub is owned and 25 outlets are supplied. All cask ales are also bottle-conditioned. Seasonal beers: Snowdrop (ABV 3.9%, spring), Mad Morris (ABV 4.2%, summer), Autumn Rose (ABV 4.2%, late autumn), Conkerer (ABV 4.7%, early autumn), Coal Porter (ABV 4.5%, winter). Bottle-conditioned beers: Boy Stout (ABV 3.1%), Shot in the Dark (ABV 3.6%), Mustang Mild (ABV 3.7%), Uncle Jon's Ferret (ABV 3.8%), Ditch Diver (ABV 4.2%), Coal Ported (ABV 4.7%), Merry Maker (ABV 4.6%), Citrus Sin (ABV 4.8%), Tumbledown Dick (ABV 5.3%).

Union Jack **(OG 1036, ABV 3.6%)**
A copper-coloured bitter, fruity with a citrus taste and a hoppy, citrus aroma, with a balanced, bitter finish.

Smile for the Camera **(OG 1040, ABV 4%)**

Field Marshall **(OG 1040, ABV 4%)**

Good Elf **(OG 1042, ABV 4.2%)**

Green Tiger **(OG 1042, ABV 4.2%)**

XBF **(OG 1042, ABV 4%)**

Wheelbarrow **(OG 1044, ABV 4.3%)**
Amber-coloured beer with a soft, fruity nose and taste. Gentle malt, with underlying hop bitterness, with a fruity and slightly dry finish.

Greenwood*

William Greenwood Brewing Co Ltd, Unit 4, Fireclay Business Park, Thornton Road, Thornton, Bradford, BD13 3NW
Tel (01274) 830441
Email beer@williamgreenwood.com
Website www.williamgreenwood.com
Tours by arrangement

William Greenwood was set up on an industrial estate in late 2004 with the old West Yorkshire Brewery's four-barrel plant. Three Rugby League fans from the Keighley area – John Williams, Peter Fell and Rick Greenwood – produce beers with names based on the game. Rick brewed previously with the now closed Moorland Brewery at Oxenhope and uses malt from Yorkshire, pure Pennine water and hops from many countries. In May 2005 the partners bought the Cock & Bottle pub in Bradford, which has a Grade II-listed interior and is on CAMRA's National Inventory. The pub was due to reopen at the end of June 2005 and will sell Greenwood's beer and guest ales, and the brewery will move there during 2005.

Flying Winger **(ABV 3.6%)**

Blind Ref **(ABV 3.8%)**

Drop Kick **(ABV 4.4%)**

Red Card (ABV 4.6%)

Fat Prop (ABV 5%)

Jock Strap Stout (ABV 6%)

Gribble

Gribble Brewery Ltd, Gribble Inn, Oving, West Sussex, PO20 6BP
Tel 07813321795
Email gribblebeers@hotmail.co.uk
Website www.gribblebrewery.co.uk

⊗ The Gribble Brewery is 25 years old. Until February 2005 it was run as a managed house operation by Badger (qv) but it is now an independent micro-brewery owned by Brian Olderfield, the previous manager. Brian and brewer Rob Cooper still brew K&B Mild for Badger and will continue to brew and sell the full range of Gribble beers for the free trade. Eight outlets are supplied direct, but more are in the offing. Seasonal beer: Wobbler (ABV 7.2%).

Slurping Stoat (ABV 3.8%)

Ale (ABV 4.1%)

Reg's Tipple (ABV 5%)
Reg's Tipple was named after a customer from the early days of the brewery. It has a smooth nutty flavour with a pleasant afterbite.

Plucking Pheasant (ABV 5.2%)

Pig's Ear (ABV 5.8%)
A full-bodied old ale with a rich ruby-brown colour.

For Badger

K&B Mild Ale (ABV 3.5%)
A truly dark mild with a toffee, roast malt character that is present throughout. Short aftertaste. Nothing like the old K&B Mild, but pleasant nonetheless.

Gwynant*

Bragdy Gwynant, Tynllidiart Arms, Capel Bangor, Aberystwyth, Ceredigion, SY23 3LR
Tel (01970) 880248
Tours by arrangement

Brewing started in 2004 in a building at the front of the pub, measuring just 4ft 6ins by 4ft, with a brew length of nine gallons. Beer is sold only in the pub and there are no plans for expansion. An application has been made to the Guinness Book of Records for Bragdy Gwynant to be officially recognised as the world's smallest commercial brewery.

Cwrw Gwynant (OG 1044, ABV 4.2%)

Hadrian & Border SIBA

Alnwick Ales Ltd, t/a Hadrian & Border Brewery, Unit 11, Hawick Crescent Industrial Estate, Newcastle upon Tyne, Tyne & Wear, NE6 1AS
Tel (0191) 276 5302
Fax (0191) 265 5312
Email border@rampart.freeserve.co.uk
Tours by arrangement

Hadrian & Border is the result of a merger between Border Brewery of Berwick-on-Tweed and Four Rivers of Newcastle. The company is based at the ex-Four Rivers 20-barrel site in Newcastle. There are plans to move to a new site. The company's brands are available from Glasgow to Yorkshire, and nationally through wholesalers. They are hard to find on Tyneside, though the Sir John Fitzgerald group (qv) stocks them from time to time. Approximately 100 outlets are supplied.

Vallum Bitter (OG 1034, ABV 3.6%)
A well-hopped, amber-coloured bitter with a distinctive dry, refreshing taste.

Gladiator (OG 1036, ABV 3.8%)
Tawny-coloured bitter with plenty of malt in the aroma and palate, leading to a strong bitter finish.

Farne Island Pale Ale (OG 1038, ABV 4%)
A copper-coloured, dry bitter with a refreshing malt/hop balance.

Flotsam (OG 1038, ABV 4%)
Bronze coloured with a citrus bitterness and a distinctive floral aroma.

Legion Ale (OG 1040, ABV 4.2%)
Well-balanced, amber-coloured beer, full bodied with good malt flavours. Well hopped with a long bitter finish.

Secret Kingdom (OG 1042, ABV 4.3%)
Dark, rich and full-bodied, slightly roasted with a malty palate ending with a pleasant bitterness.

Reiver's IPA (OG 1042, ABV 4.4%)
Dark golden bitter with a clean citrus palate and aroma with subtle malt flavours breaking through at the end.

Centurion Best Bitter (OG 1043, ABV 4.5%)
Smooth, clean-tasting bitter with a distinct hop palate leading to a good bitter finish.

Halifax Steam

Halifax Steam Brewing Co Ltd, Southedge Works, Hipperholme, Halifax, West Yorkshire, HX3 8EF
Tel (07967) 802488
Fax (01484) 715074 (phone first)
Email davidearnshaw@blueyonder.co.uk

David Earnshaw started brewing in 2001 in a converted garage, inspired by CAMRA's series of home-brewing books. He bought his five-barrel plant from the Fox & Firkin in Lewisham, south London, which he collected and installed himself in new premises. In addition to brewing, David supplies temporary bars for events and beer festivals. His beers are supplied to approximately 50 pubs locally and further afield via brewery swaps and the Flying Firkin wholesaler. The beers are based loosely on old Whitakers of Halifax brands and one of Ramsden's beers.

Morning Glory (ABV 3.8%)
Light mild.

Lilly Fogg (ABV 4%)
Straw-coloured best bitter.

Mostly Organic (ABV 4%)

Pickel Hut Imposter (ABV 4%)
Cask lager.

Probably Organic (ABV 4%)

Bantam (OG 1043, ABV 4.1%)
Best bitter.

Rhode Island Red (ABV 4.5%)

Golden Glory (ABV 4.6%)
Fruity, honey-coloured strong bitter.

Golden Rain (ABV 4.6%) ◆
Distinctive best bitter at a different end of the taste spectrum to other steam beers. Predominant exotic fruit flavour.

Luftkissenfahrzeug (ABV 4.6) ◆
Pale beer brewed with a lager recipe, with a good balance of flavours and slight bitter aftertaste.

Cock of the North (OG 1048, ABV 4.9%)
Strong bitter.

Shirley Crabtree (ABV 4.9%)
Strong bitter.

Hambleton SIBA

Nick Stafford Hambleton Ales, Holme-on-Swale, Thirsk, North Yorkshire, YO7 4JE
Tel (01845) 567460
Email sales@hambletonales.co.uk
Website www.hambletonales.co.uk
Shop 9-4 Mon-Fri
Tours by arrangement

⊛ Hambleton was established in 1991 by Nick Stafford on the banks of the River Swale in the heart of the Vale of York. New brewing equipment was installed in 2000, doubling capacity to 100 barrels a week while a bottling line caters for micros and larger brewers, handling more than 20 brands. A mail-order service for all bottled brands is available from the brewery or its website. 100 outlets are supplied. Hambleton brews beers under contract for the Village Brewer wholesale company (01325) 374887 and Black Dog of Whitby (qv). The brewery also produces an additional special beer, ABV 4%, which changes monthly.

Bitter (OG 1037.5, ABV 3.6%) ◻ ◆
Rich, hoppy flavour rides through this light and drinkable beer. Taste is bitter with citrus and marmalade character and a solid body. Ends dry with a spicy mouthfeel.

Goldfield (OG 1041, ABV 4.2%) ◆
A light amber bitter with good hop character and increasing dryness. A fine blend of malts gives a smooth overall impression.

Stallion (OG 1041, ABV 4.2%) ◆
A premium bitter, moderately hoppy throughout and richly balanced in malt and fruit, developing a sound and robust bitterness, with earthy hops drying the aftertaste.

Stud (OG 1042.5, ABV 4.2%) ◆
A strongly bitter beer, with rich hop and fruit. It ends dry and spicy.

Nightmare (OG 1050, ABV 5%) ◆
Fully deserving its acclaim, this impressively flavoured beer satisfies all parts of the palate. Strong roast malts dominate, but hoppiness rears out of this complex blend.

For Village Brewer

White Boar (OG 1037.5, ABV 3.8%) ◆
A light, flowery and fruity ale; crisp, clean and refreshing, with a dry-hopped, powerful but not aggressive, bitter finish.

Bull (OG 1039, ABV 4%) ◆
A pale, full, fruity bitter, well hopped to give a lingering bitterness.

Old Raby (OG 1045, ABV 4.6%) ◆
A full-bodied, smooth, rich-tasting dark ale. A complex balance of malt, fruit character and creamy caramel sweetness offsets the bitterness. A classic old ale.

For Malton Brewery:

Double Chance (ABV 3.8%)

Golden Chance (ABV 4.2%)

Auld Bob (ABV 4.5%)

Hampshire SIBA

Hampshire Brewery Ltd, 6 Romsey Industrial Estate, Greatbridge Road, Romsey, Hampshire, SO51 0HR
Tel (01794) 830529
Fax (01794) 830528
Email online@hampshirebrewery.com
Website www.hampshirebrewery.com
Shop 9-4 Mon-Fri.
Tours for parties of 10-18 by arrangement

⊗ Hampshire was founded in 1992 and merged with the Millennium Bottling Company in 2002. All the beers are also available in bottle-conditioned form from the company's new bottling plant. The brewery produces four core beers, 24 monthly specials at two per month, and three other seasonal beers over longer three-four month periods: see website for full details. Some 300 outlets are supplied. Seasonal ales: Lionheart (ABV 4.5%), Pendragon (ABV 4.8%), King's Ransom (ABV 4.8%, June-Aug), 1066 (ABV 6%).

King Alfred's (OG 1037, ABV 3.8%) ◆
A pale brown beer featuring a malty aroma with some hops and fruit. Well-balanced citrus taste with plenty of malt and a dry, bitter finish.

Strong's Best Bitter (OG 1037, ABV 3.8%) ◆
Named after the original Romsey Brewery, this tawny-coloured bitter is predominantly malty. An initially hoppy aroma gives way to an increasingly bitter finish.

Ironside (OG 1041, ABV 4.2%) ◻ ◆
A clean-tasting, flavoursome best bitter with a gorgeous fruit and hops aroma. Hops are predominant throughout but balanced by malt and fruit and some sweetness. The finish is long and dry.

Pride of Romsey (OG 1050, ABV 5%) ◆
A strong citrus aroma leads to a beautifully-balanced mix of fruit and hops that continues to build in the aftertaste.

Hanby SIBA

Hanby Ales Ltd, Aston Park, Soulton Road, Wem, Shropshire, SY4 5SD
Tel/Fax (01939) 232432
Email info@hanbyales.co.uk
Website www.hanbyales.co.uk
Tours by arrangement

⊗ Hanby was set up in 1988 by Jack Hanby following the closure of the Shrewsbury & Wem Brewery. The aim was to continue the 200 year-old tradition of brewing in the area. In 1990 the brewery moved to its present home, and has recently upgraded to 130-barrel production runs. Hanby supplies 300 outlets. Seasonal beer: Green Admiral (ABV 4.5%, Sept-Oct). Bottle-conditioned beers: Rainbow Chaser, Shropshire Stout, Golden Honey, Premium Bitter, Cherry Bomb.

Drawwell Bitter (OG 1039, ABV 3.9%) ◆
A hoppy beer with excellent bitterness, both in taste and aftertaste. Beautiful amber colour.

Black Magic Mild (OG 1040, ABV 4%) ◆
A dark, reddish-brown mild, which is dry and bitter with a roast malt taste.

All Seasons (OG 1042, ABV 4.2%)
A light, hoppy bitter, well balanced and thirst quenching, brewed with a fine blend of Fuggles and Cascade hops.

Rainbow Chaser (OG 1043, ABV 4.3%)
A pale beer brewed with Pioneer hops.

Cascade (OG 1045, ABV 4.4%)
A very pale beer, brewed with Cascade hops, producing a clean crisp flavour and a hoppy finish.

Wem Special (OG 1044, ABV 4.4%)
A pale, smooth, hoppy bitter.

Golden Honey (OG 1045, ABV 4.5%)
A beer made with the addition of Australian honey.

Scorpio Porter (OG 1045, ABV 4.5%)
A dark porter with an interesting and complex palate introducing hints of coffee and chocolate, contrasting and complementing the background hoppiness.

Shropshire Stout (OG 1044, ABV 4.5%)
A full-bodied, rich ruby/black coloured stout. A blend of four malts produces a distinct chocolate malt dry flavour, with a mushroom-coloured head.

Premium (OG 1046, ABV 4.6%)
A pale brown beer that is sweeter and fruitier than most of the beers above. Slight malt and hop taste.

Old Wemian (OG 1049, ABV 4.9%)
Golden-brown colour with an aroma of malt and hops and a soft, malty palate.

Taverners (OG 1053, ABV 5.3%)
A smooth and fruity beer full of body.

Cherry Bomb (OG 1060, ABV 6%)
Beer made with the addition of cherries.

Joy Bringer (OG 1060, ABV 6%)

Nutcracker (OG 1060, ABV 6%) ■
Very full tawny beer, a fine blend of malt and hops.

Hardys & Hansons IFBB

Hardys & Hansons plc, The Brewery, Kimberley, Nottingham, NG16 2NS
Tel (0115) 938 3611
Fax (0115) 945 9055
Email info@hardysandhansons.plc.uk
Website www.hardysandhansons.plc.uk
Tours by arrangement

◎ Established in 1832 and 1847 respectively, Hardys and Hansons were two competitive breweries until a merger in 1930 produced the present company. The brewery is still run by descendants of the original families. The majority of its 252 tied houses take its award-winning real ales, mostly drawn by handpump, although some metered dispense is still found. 2003 saw the re-branding of beers and pubs, with the renaming of regular beers and the introduction of Olde Trip as a new premium beer: the name reflects the brewery's ownership of the Olde Trip to Jerusalem in Nottingham, the country's oldest tavern. As well as tied trade, around 75 other outlets are also supplied. A range of seasonal ales, with a rotation or new beer every month under the Cellarman's Cask banner, has been extended: see website.

Kimberley Mild (OG 1035, ABV 3.1%) ◆
A deep ruby mild dominated by chocolate malt. The fruitiness and caramel sweetness are well balanced in the taste, with a faintly hoppy finish.

Kimberley Bitter (OG 1038, ABV 3.9%) ◆
A beer with a flowery, hoppy and fruity nose, although malt is never far away. Fruity hop is evident in the taste and there is a consistent bitterness.

Olde Trip (OG 1043, ABV 4.3%)

HART
Brewery

Hart

Hart Brewery Ltd, Cartford Hotel, Cartford Lane, Little Eccleston, Preston, Lancashire, PR3 0YP
Tel (01995) 670166
Fax (01772) 797069
Tours by arrangement Tue-Thur evenings

◎ The brewery was founded in 1994 in a small private garage in Preston. It moved to its present site at the rear of the Cartford Hotel in 1995. With a 10-barrel plant, Hart now supplies around 150 outlets nationwide and does swaps with other breweries. Seasonal beers: Gold Beach (ABV 3.8%, summer), Lord of the Glen (ABV 4%, summer), Snowella (ABV 4.3%, winter), Bat Out of Hell (ABV 4.5%, Halloween), Val Addiction (ABV 4.8%, winter).

Dishie Debbie **(OG 1040, ABV 4%)**

Ice Maiden **(OG 1040, ABV 4%)**

Squirrels Hoard **(OG 1040, ABV 4%)**

Nemesis **(OG 1045, ABV 4.5%)**

Harveys IFBB

Harvey & Son (Lewes) Ltd, The Bridge Wharf Brewery, 6 Cliffe High Street, Lewes, East Sussex, BN7 2AH
Tel (01273) 480209
Fax (01273) 486074
Email maj@harveys.org.uk
Website www.harveys.org.uk
Shop 9.30-4.45 Mon-Sat
Tours by arrangement (currently two-year waiting list)

Established in 1790, this independent family brewery operates from the banks of the River Ouse in Lewes. A major development in 1985 doubled the brewhouse capacity and subsequent additional fermenting capacity has seen production rise to in excess of 37,000 barrels a year. Harveys supplies real ale to all its 46 pubs and 450 free trade outlets in Sussex and Kent. Seasonal beers: Kiss (ABV 4.8%, February), 1859 Porter (ABV 4.8%, March), Knots of May Light Mild (ABV 3%, May), Copperwheat Beer (ABV 4.8%, June), Tom Paine (ABV 5.5%, July), Southdown Harvest Ale (ABV 5%, September), Star of Eastbourne (ABV 5.5%, October), Sussex XXXX Old Ale (ABV 4.3%, Oct-May), Bonfire Boy (ABV 5.8%, November), Christmas Ale (ABV 8.1%, December). Bottle-conditioned beer: Le Coq's Imperial Extra Double Stout (ABV 9%).

Sussex XX Mild Ale **(OG 1030, ABV 3%)**
A dark copper-brown colour. Roast malt dominates the aroma and palate leading to a sweet, caramel finish.

Sussex Pale Ale **(OG 1033, ABV 3.5%)**

Sussex Best Bitter **(OG 1040, ABV 4%)**
Full-bodied brown bitter. A hoppy aroma leads to a good malt and hop balance, and a dry aftertaste.

Armada Ale **(OG 1045, ABV 4.5%)**
Hoppy amber best bitter. Well-balanced fruit and hops dominate throughout with a fruity palate.

Harviestoun SIBA

Harviestoun Brewery Ltd, Alva Industrial Estate, Alva, Clackmannanshire, FK12 5DQ
Tel (01259) 769100
Fax (01259) 763003
Email harviestoun@talk21.com
Shop Mon-Fri 9-4.30

Harviestoun, winner of Champion Beer of Britain 2003, started in a barn in the village of Dollar in 1985 with a five-barrel brew plant. Winning awards has helped the company achieve great success: Champion Beer of Scotland twice; Tesco Beer Challenge Winner three times; Schiehallion three Golds and four Silver awards at GBBF since its launch eight years ago. Harviestoun has built a state-of-the-art 50-barrel brewery seven miles from the original site and has nationwide supermarket sales of bottled Bitter & Twisted, which won Supreme Champion Bottled Beer 2004 at the Brewing Industry International awards. The brewery supplies local outlets itself and nationwide through wholesalers. Seasonal beers: Jack the Lad (ABV 4.1%, wheat beer, January), Ice Maiden (ABV 4.2%, February), Belgian White (ABV 4.3%, lager malt, wheat and malted oats, March), Spring Fever (ABV 3.8%, April), Navigator (ABV 4.3%, Mount Hood hops, May), Dragonfly (ABV 3.6%, Amarillo hops, June), Natural Blonde (ABV 4%, Pilot hops, July), Gold Rush (ABV 3.9%, Brewers Gold hops, August), Late Harvest (ABV 3.8%, Cascade and EKG hops, September), Gremlin (ABV 4.3%, First Gold hops, October), Old Manor (ABV 4.6%, winter brew, November), Good King Legless (ABV 4.5%, December).

Bitter & Twisted **(OG 1036, ABV 3.8%)**
Refreshingly hoppy beer with fruit throughout. A bitter-sweet taste with a long bitter finish. A golden session beer.

Indian Summer IPA **(OG 1044, ABV 4.1%)**

Ptarmigan **(OG 1047, ABV 4.5%)**
A well-balanced, bitter-sweet beer in which hops and malt dominate. The blend of malt, hops and fruit produces a clean, hoppy aftertaste.

Schiehallion **(OG 1048, ABV 4.8%)**
A Scottish cask lager, brewed using a lager yeast and Hersbrucker hops. A hoppy aroma, with fruit and malt, leads to a malty, bitter taste with floral hoppiness and a bitter finish.

Hawkshead SIBA

Hawkshead Brewery Co, Town End, Hawkshead, Cumbria, LA22 0JU
Tel/Fax (015394) 36111
Email info@hawksheadbrewery.co.uk
Website www.hawksheadbrewery.co.uk
Tours occasionally by arrangement

Hawkshead Brewery was established in 2002 in a disused dairy farm at the head of Esthwaite Water, in the heart of the Lake District, just outside the picturesque village of Hawkshead. The brewery, which is owned by former BBC foreign correspondent Alex Brodie, is housed in a restored 17th-century listed barn. In partnership with The Head of Steam pub company (qv), Hawkshead acquired its first pub in 2004, the Swan Inn, Ulverston. Hawkshead beers are sold in some 60 outlets in and around the Cumbrian hills and in others across the North-west. The main outlet for bottled beers is Booths supermarkets. There are plans to increase capacity. The bottled version of Hawkshead Gold won SIBA North first prize in 2004 and the cask Hawkshead Gold won first place in the Best Bitter category at the SIBA Championship in 2005. All Hawkshead beers are brewed with Maris Otter malted barley. Damson Beer is an occasional brew.

Bitter (OG 1037, ABV 3.7%)
A pale, hoppy and bitter session beer. It has a distinct fruity aroma and a dry and bitter finish.

Ulverston Pale Ale (OG 1041, ABV 4.1%)

Best Bitter (OG 1042, ABV 4.2%)
A reddish, malty, yet bitter, fuller-bodied English ale. It has a definite malty and spicy aroma and initial taste, but is not sweet as the maltiness suggests; rather it finishes dry and bitter.

Gold (OG 1043, ABV 4.4%)

Red (OG 1045, ABV 4.6%)

Premium (OG 1046, ABV 4.8%)

Haywood

Haywood Brewery, Callow Top Holiday Park, Sandybrook, Ashbourne, Derbyshire, DE6 2AQ
Tel (01335) 344884, m 07974 948427
Fax (01335) 343726, (01335) 344884
Email acphaywood@aol.com
Website www.callowtop.co.uk
Shop 9-5pm seasonal
Tours by arrangement

The brewery is situated in a barn at Callow Top Holiday Park, adjacent to Haywood Farm. It started brewing with Dr Samuel Johnson Ale, which won a gold award at the 2003 Peterborough Beer Festival for best new brewery. One pub is owned and four outlets are supplied. Bottle-conditioned beer: Dr Samuel Johnson (ABV 4.5%). An organic beer is planned.

Dr Samuel Johnson (ABV 4.5%)

Bad Ram (ABV 5%)

Woggle Dance (ABV 5%)

Callow Top IPA (ABV 5.2%)

Hebridean SIBA

Hebridean Brewing Co, 18A Bells Road, Stornoway, Isle of Lewis, HS1 2RA
Tel (01851) 700123
Fax (01851) 700234
Email info@hebridean-brewery.co.uk
Website www.hebridean-brewery.co.uk
Shop Yes, in summer months
Tours by arrangement

⊚ The company was set up in 2001 by Andy Ribbens, whose family came from Lewis. The plant is steam powered with a 14-barrel brew length. An off-licence is attached to the brewery and the beers are now being bottled (not bottle conditioned). The company has bought its first pub in Uig, Skye. Seasonal beers are produced for Mods, Gaelic festivals that are the Scottish equivalent of the Welsh Eisteddfod.

Celtic Black Ale (OG 1036, ABV 3.9%)
A dark ale full of flavour, balancing an aromatic hop combined with a subtle bite and a pleasantly smooth caramel aftertaste.

Clansman Ale (OG 1036, ABV 3.9%)
A light Hebridean beer, brewed with Scottish malts and lightly hopped to give a subtle bittering.

Seaforth Ale (ABV 4.2%)
A golden beer in the continental style.

Islander Strong Premium Ale (OG 1044, ABV 4.8%)
A deep ruby in colour, the beer is predominantly malty with a robust hopping to match. SIBA Bronze Medal and Beer of Scotland 2003, Premium Cask Ale category.

Berserker Export Pale Ale (OG 1068, ABV 7.5%)
Brewed using traditional methods and based on 19th-century recipes. Matured to develop a smooth, intricate flavour.

Hepworth SIBA

Hepworth & Co (Brewers) Ltd, The Beer Station, The Railway Yard, Horsham, West Sussex, RH12 2NW
Tel (01403) 269696
Fax (01403) 269690
Email mail@thebeerstation.co.uk
Website www.thebeerstation.co.uk
Shop 9am-6pm
Tours by arrangement

⊗ Four workers from King & Barnes started the brewery in 2001, bottling beer only. In 2003 draught beer brewing was started with Sussex malt and hops. In 2004, an organic lager was introduced in bottle and draught. 20 outlets are supplied direct. Seasonal beer: Old Ale (ABV 4.8%, Nov-Jan). Bottle-conditioned beer: Christmas Ale (ABV 7.5%).

Traditional Sussex Bitter (OG 1035, ABV 3.6%) ◆
A fine, clean-tasting amber session beer. A bitter beer with a pleasant fruity and hoppy aroma that leads to a crisp, tangy taste that belies the beer's strength. A long, dry finish.

Pullman First Class Ale (OG 1041, ABV 4.2%) ◆
A sweet, nutty maltiness and fruitiness are balanced by hops and bitterness in this easy-drinking, pale brown best bitter. There is little aroma but a subtle bitter aftertaste.

Iron Horse (OG 1048, ABV 4.8%) ◆
There's a fruity, toffee aroma to this light brown, full-bodied bitter. A citrus flavour balanced by caramel and malt leads to a clean, dry finish.

Hereward

Hereward Brewery, 50 Fleetwood, Ely, Cambridgeshire, CB6 1BH
Tel (01353) 666441
Email Michael.Czarnobaj@ntlworld.com

A small home-based brewery launched in 2003 by Michael Czarnobaj who had brewed for several years before going on a Brewlab course in Sunderland. He has 10-gallon kit and brews two or three times a month in his garage. He mainly supplies beer festivals. Seasonal beer: Uncle Joe's Winter Ale (ABV 5%).

Bitter (ABV 3.8%)

St Ethelreda's Golden Bitter (ABV 4%)

Porta Porter (ABV 4.2%)

Oatmeal Stout (ABV 4.5%)

Hesket Newmarket SIBA

Hesket Newmarket Brewery Ltd, Old Crown Barn, Back Green, Hesket Newmarket, Cumbria, CA7 8JG
Tel/Fax (016974) 78066
Email brewer@hesketbrewery.co.uk
Website www.hesketbrewery.co.uk
Tours via The Old Crown Inn (016974) 78288

☺ The brewery was established in 1988 by Jim Fearnley. In 1999 it was bought by a co-operative of villagers, anxious to preserve a community resource when Jim retired. It is now managed on their behalf by Mike Parker, ex-Stones head brewer. Most of Jim's recipes have been retained, all named after local fells except for the famous Doris's 90th Birthday Ale. A 10-barrel plant was installed in 2004 followed by bottling on a small scale in late 2005. Some 30 regular outlets are supplied. Seasonal beer: Autumn Chestnut (ABV 4.7%).

Great Cockup Porter (OG 1035, ABV 3%)
A refreshing, dark and chocolatey porter with a dry finish.

Blencathra Bitter
(OG 1035, ABV 3.2%) ◆
A malty, tawny ale, mild and mellow for a bitter, with a dominant caramel flavour.

Skiddaw Special Bitter (OG 1035, ABV 3.6%)
An amber session beer, malty throughout, thin with a dryish finish.

Doris's 90th Birthday Ale
(OG 1045, ABV 4.3%) ◆
A full-bodied, nicely balanced malty beer with an increasing hop finish and butterscotch in the mouth.

Sea Fell Blonde (OG 1047, ABV 4.5%)

Catbells Pale Ale (OG 1050, ABV 5%) ◆
A powerful golden ale with a well-balanced malty bitterness, ending with a bitter and decidedly dry aftertaste.

Old Carrock Strong Ale
(OG 1060, ABV 6%)
A dark red, powerful ale.

Hexhamshire SIBA

Hexhamshire Brewery, Leafields, Ordley, Hexham, Northumberland, NE46 1SX
Tel (01434) 606577
Fax (01434) 600973
Email ghb@hexhamshire.co.uk

⊗ Hexhamshire was founded in 1992 in a converted cattle shed. The brewery has been operated by one of the founding partners and his family since 1997. Five beers are brewed regularly for the Dipton Mill pub and to some 20 other outlets. One pub is owned.

Devil's Elbow (OG 1036, ABV 3.6%) ◆
Amber brew full of hops and fruit, leading to a bitter finish.

Shire Bitter (OG 1037, ABV 3.8%) ◆
A good balance of hops with fruity overtones, this amber beer makes an easy-drinking session bitter.

Devil's Water (OG 1041, ABV 4.1%) ◆
Copper-coloured best bitter, well-balanced with a slightly fruity, hoppy finish.

Whapweasel (OG 1048, ABV 4.8%) ◻ ◆
An interesting smooth, hoppy beer with a fruity flavour. Amber in colour, the bitter finish brings out the fruit and hops.

Old Humbug (OG 1055, ABV 5.5%)

Hidden SIBA

Hidden Brewery Ltd, Unit 1, Oakley Industrial Estate, Wylye Road, Dinton, Salisbury, Wiltshire, SP3 5EU
Tel/Fax (01722) 716440
Email sales@thehiddenbrewery.co.uk
Shop Mon-Sat 10-4pm
Tours by arrangement

Hidden was founded in 2003. Head brewer Gary Lumber was previously at Oakhill. The brewery is named after its location, hidden away in the Wiltshire countryside. Capacity is being increased to include a bottling line. Between 150 and 200 outlets are supplied. A range of beers under the general title of Froth & Nonsense is targeted at a younger market. Seasonal beers: Hidden Spring (ABV 4.5%), Hidden Fantasy (ABV 4.6%), Hidden Pleasure (ABV 4.8%), Hidden Depths (ABV 4.6%), Hidden Treasure (ABV 4.8%).

Pint (OG 1039, ABV 3.8%)
A clean-tasting, tangy, mid-brown beer with a good hop content, and a citrus fruit and malt balance.

Old Sarum (OG 1042, ABV 4.1%)
A well-balanced bitter with a complex combination of malts and hops. The aroma is floral and spicy, full-flavoured with a dry bitterness. The colour is dark ruby-brown.

Quest (OG 1042, ABV 4.2%)
An amber-coloured bitter with a malt background, with a fruity aroma and a dry finish.

Highgate SIBA

Highgate Brewery Ltd, Sandymount Road, Walsall, West Midlands, WS1 3AP
Tel (01922) 644453
Fax (01922) 644471

Email info@highgatebrewery.com
Website www.highgatebrewery.com
Tours by arrangement

☺ Built in 1898, Highgate was an independent brewery until 1938 when it was taken over by Mitchells & Butlers and subsequently became the smallest brewery in the Bass group. It was brought back into the independent sector in 1995 as the result of a management buy-out and was subsequently bought by Aston Manor (qv) in 2000. Some of the original equipment in the traditional Victorian brewery is still in use, but a new racking line and laboratory have been added along with a visitor facility. Highgate has now acquired 10 tied houses towards a target of 50, including the City Tavern, a restored Victorian ale house off Broad Street in Birmingham. Five of the tied houses serve cask-conditioned beer. Around 200 outlets are supplied. The company also has a major contract to supply Mitchells & Butlers pubs. Seasonal beer: Old Ale (ABV 5.3%, winter).

Dark Mild **(OG 1036.8, ABV 3.6%)**
A dark brown Black Country mild with a good balance of malt and hops, and traces of roast flavour following a malty aroma.

Special Bitter **(OG 1037.8, ABV 3.8%)**

Davenports Bitter **(OG 1040.8, ABV 4%)**

Saddlers Best Bitter
(OG 1043.8, ABV 4.3%)
A fruity, pale yellow bitter with a strong hop flavour and a light, refreshing bitter aftertaste.

Davenports Premium **(OG 1046.8, ABV 4.6%)**

For Coors

M&B Mild **(OG 1034.8, ABV 3.2%)**

High House SIBA

High House Farm Brewery, Matfen, Northumberland, NE20 0RG
Tel (01661) 886192
Fax (01661) 886394
Email info@highhousefarmbrewery.co.uk
Website www.highhousefarmbrewery.co.uk
Shop planned for 2006
Tours by arrangement

The brewery was established in 2003 by Steven Urwin on the family farm. Located in a converted grain store, the brewery and offices provide a modern and efficient business base with its roots grounded in history and tradition. A bottling plant has recently been added and the beers are available locally.

Auld Hemp **(OG 1038, ABV 3.8%)**
Tawny-coloured ale with malt and fruit flavours and a good bitter finish.

Nel's Best **(OG 1041, ABV 4.2%)**
Golden hoppy ale full of flavour with a clean bitter finish.

Matfen Magic **(OG 1046.5, ABV 4.8%)**

Highland*

Highland Brewing Co Ltd, Swannay Brewery, Birsay, Orkney, KW17 2NP
Tel (01856) 761111
Email sales@highlandbrewingcompany.co.uk
Website www.highlandbrewingcompany.co.uk
Shop Yes, ring to check
Tours by arrangement

Set up in 2005 in an old cheese factory by Rob Hill (ex Moorhouse's) and the Orkney Brewery. It is a traditional, 40-barrel plant on an impressive, historic farmstead set amid rolling countryside. Future plans include a visitor centre, café and children's play area. Four outlets are supplied direct.

Best **(OG 1042, ABV 4.2%)**

Scapa Special **(OG 1044, ABV 4.4%)**

St Magnus Ale **(OG 1050, ABV 5%)**

Highlands and Islands

See Atlas and Orkney

Highwood

See Tom Wood

Hilden

Hilden Brewing Co, Hilden House, Hilden, Lisburn, County Antrim, BT27 4TY
Tel (028 92) 663863
Fax (028 92) 603511
Email hilden.brewery@uk.gateway.net
Shop 10-5 Mon-Sat
Tours by arrangement

☺ Hilden Brewery was established by Ann and Seamus Scullion in 1981 and is now the oldest independent brewery in Ireland. It's looking forward, in conjunction with the latest wave of small breweries on the island, to meet a growing demand for choice in a market dominated by a beer monopoly. Bottle-conditioned beer: Original (ABV 4.6%).

Ale **(OG 1038, ABV 4%)**
An amber-coloured beer with an aroma of malt, hops and fruit. The balanced taste is slightly slanted towards hops, and hops are also prominent in the full, malty finish. Bitter and refreshing.

Molly Malone's Porter **(OG 1048, ABV 4.6%)**
Dark ruby-red porter with complex flavours of hop bitterness and chocolate malt.

Scullion's Irish **(OG 1048, ABV 4.6%)**
Initially smooth on the palate, it finishes with a clean, hoppy aftertaste.

Hill Island

Michael Griffin t/a Hill Island Brewery, Unit 7, Fowlers Yard, Back Silver Street, Durham City, DH1 3RA
Tel (07740) 932584
Email mike@hillisland.freeserve.co.uk
Shop Most weekdays 10am-2pm.
Bulk purchasing only. Ring before visit.
Tours by arrangement for groups of 10 or more. Ring for details.

☺ Hill Island is a literal translation of Dunhdme from which Durham is derived. The brewery began trading in 2002 and stands by the banks of the Wear in the heart of Durham City. Many of the beers produced have names reflecting local history and heritage. The brewer, Michael Griffin, produces a core range of six beers along with seasonal and occasional beers. Brews are also made exclusively for individual outlets, such as Silly Steps for the New Board Inn in Esh, near Durham. Some 40 outlets are supplied. Seasonal beers: Priory Summer Ale (ABV 3.5%), Festive Ale (ABV 4%), St Oswald's Xmas Ale (ABV 4.5%).

Peninsula Pint **(OG 1036.5, ABV 3.7%)**

Bitter **(OG 1038, ABV 3.9%)**

Dun Cow Bitter **(OG 1039, ABV 4%)**

Fulling Mill Bitter **(OG 1040.5, ABV 4.1%)**

Cathedral Ale **(OG 1042, ABV 4.3%)**

Griffin's Irish Stout **(OG 1045, ABV 4.5%)**

Hobden's

See Wessex

Hobsons SIBA

Hobsons Brewery & Co Ltd, Newhouse Farm, Cleobury Mortimer, Kidderminster, Worcestershire, DY14 8RD
Tel (01299) 270837
Fax (01299) 270260
Email beer@hobsons-brewery.co.uk
Website www.hobsons-brewery.co.uk

⊗ Established in 1993, Hobsons moved to its present site in 1996. Production was developed further in 2002, including the installation of a bottling plant. Approx 100 outlets are supplied. Bottle-conditioned beers: Old Henry, Town Crier, Manor Ale (ABV 4.2%).

Mild **(OG 1034, ABV 3.2%)** ◆
A classic mild. Complex layers of taste come from roasted malts that predominate and give lots of flavour.

Best Bitter **(OG 1038.5, ABV 3.8%)** ◆
A pale brown to amber, medium-bodied beer with strong hop character throughout. It is consequently bitter, but with malt discernible in the taste.

Town Crier **(OG 1044, ABV 4.5%)** 🗍
An elegant straw-coloured bitter. The hint of sweetness is complemented by subtle hop flavours, leading to a dry finish.

Old Henry **(OG 1051, ABV 5.2%)**
Complex malty flavours give a richness that is balanced by the clean, hoppy finish.

Hoggleys SIBA

Hoggleys Brewery, 30 Mill Lane, Kislingbury, Northampton, NN7 4BD
Tel (01604) 831762 (m) 07717 078402
Email enquiries@hoggleys.co.uk
Website www.hoggleys.co.uk
Tours occasionally for organisations

Hoggleys opened in 2003 and is now consolidating and building the business. The brewhouse has a one-barrel run but will soon expand to two barrels. Future plans are to expand to the limits of the present site and equipment, then to enlarge and become a full-time brewery. In the meantime, new markets are being developed while sustaining present outlets. Approximately 15 outlets are supplied. Bottle-conditioned beers: all cask beers are available in bottle. Solstice Stout and Mill Lane Mild are suitable for vegetarians.

Mill Lane Mild **(OG 1040, ABV 4%)**
Brewed from pale, black and crystal malts and hopped with Fuggles and Goldings.

Northamptonshire Bitter **(OG 1040, ABV 4%)**
A straw-coloured bitter brewed with pale malt only. The hops are Fuggles and Northdown and the beer is late hopped with Goldings for aroma.

Kislingbury Bitter **(OG 1041, ABV 4%)**

Solstice Stout **(OG 1044, ABV 5%)**

Hogs Back SIBA

Hogs Back Brewery Ltd, Manor Farm, The Street, Tongham, Surrey, GU10 1DE
Tel (01252) 783000
Fax (01252) 782328
Email info@hogsback.co.uk
Website www.hogsback.co.uk
Shop Yes, see website
Tours by arrangement see website

⊗ The traditional-style, purpose-built brewery has occupied a range of 18th-century farm building since 1992. The popularity of its ales; the award-winning TEA in particular, has necessitated an expansion over the years. Seasonal and commemorative ales are brewed throughout the year, from milds and porters to strong winter ales and barley wines. The brewery shop and visitor centre now sell more than 400 different bottled beers from around the world plus Hogs Back draught and bottled beers, along with brewery merchandise, either direct from the brewery or via mail order and e-commerce. There are regular, fully-guided tours and tastings by arrangement; consult the website. Seasonal beers: Dark Mild (ABV 3.4%), Spring Call (ABV 4%), Summer This (ABV 4.2%), Easter Teaser (ABV 4.2%), Blackwater Porter (ABV 4.4%), Advent Ale (ABV 4.4%), X-Hibition Stout (ABV 4.5%), Autumn Seer (ABV 4.8%), Rip Snorter (ABV 5%). Bottle-conditioned beers: TEA, BSA (ABV 4.5%), OTT (ABV 6%), Brewster's Bundle (ABV 7.4%), Wobble in a Bottle (ABV 7.5%), A over T (ABV 9%).

Hair of the Hog (OG 1036, ABV 3.5%) ◆
A smooth, pale brown session bitter. Malty but balanced by some bitterness, fruit and a light hop character. A bitter-sweet finish.

Legend (OG 1040, ABV 4%) ◆
Complex and drinkable, this golden-coloured beer contains both wheat and lager malts, and has a dry, malty and bitter taste that lingers.

TEA or Traditional English Ale (OG 1044, ABV 4.2%) ◆
A pale brown best bitter with both malt and hops prominent in the nose. These carry through into a well-rounded bitter flavour, balanced by fruit and some sweetness. Hoppy bitterness grows in the aftertaste.

Hop Garden Gold (OG 1048, ABV 4.6%) ◆
Pale golden best bitter, full bodied and well balanced with an aroma of malt, hops and fruit. Delicate flowery-citrus hop flavours are balanced by malt and fruit. Hoppy bitterness grows in an increasingly dry aftertaste.

Holden's IFBB

Holden's Brewery Ltd, George Street, Woodsetton, Dudley, West Midlands, DY1 4LW
Tel (01902) 880051
Fax (01902) 665473
Email holdens.brewery@virgin.net
Website www.holdensbrewery.co.uk
Shop at Reception Mon-Fri 9-5 (beers & merchandise)
Tours by arrangement

A family brewery going back four generations, Holden's began life as a brew-pub when Edwin and Lucy took over the Park Inn (the brewery tap) in the 1920s; the inn has now been restored to its former Victorian heritage. Holden's also renovated a Grade II listed railway building in Codsall. The latest addition to the Holden's estate is the Waterfall in Blackheath. Holden's continues to grow with 21 tied pubs. It supplies some 60 other outlets.

Black Country Mild (OG 1037, ABV 3.7%) ◆
A good, red/brown mild; a refreshing, light blend of roast malt, hops and fruit, dominated by malt throughout.

Black Country Bitter (OG 1039, ABV 3.9%) ◆
A medium-bodied, golden ale; a light, well-balanced bitter with a subtle, dry, hoppy finish.

XB (OG 1042, ABV 4.1%) ◆
A sweeter, slightly fuller version of the Bitter. Sold in a number of outlets under different names.

Golden Glow (OG 1045, ABV 4.4%)
A pale golden beer, with a subtle hop aroma plus gentle sweetness and a light hoppiness.

Special (OG 1052, ABV 5.1%) ◆
A sweet, malty, full-bodied amber ale with hops to balance in the taste and in the good, bitter-sweet finish.

Holland

Holland Brewery, 5 Browns Flats, Kimberley, Nottinghamshire, NG16 2JU
Tel (0115) 938 2685
Email hollandbrew@btopenworld.com

Len Holland, a keen home-brewer for 30 years, went commercial in 2000, in the shadow of Hardys & Hansons. His nine-gallon capacity brewery is in his shed. Seasonal beers: Holly Hop Gold (ABV 4.7%, Xmas), Dutch Courage (ABV 5%, winter), Glamour Puss (ABV 4.2%, spring), Blonde Belter (ABV 4.5%, summer).

Chocolate Clog (OG 1038, ABV 3.8%)

Golden Blond (OG 1040, ABV 4%)

Lip Smacker (OG 1040, ABV 4%)

Cloghopper (OG 1042, ABV 4.2%)

Double Dutch (OG 1045, ABV 4.5%)

Mad Jack Stout (OG 1045, ABV 4.5%)

Holme Valley

See Upper Agbrigg

Holt IFBB

Joseph Holt Ltd, Derby Brewery, Empire Street, Cheetham, Manchester, M3 1JD
Tel (0161) 834 3285
Fax (0161) 834 6458
Website www.joseph-holt.com
Shop brewery reception
Tours Saturday mornings, £10 per head (donated to Christie Hospital), 10-15 clients

Joseph Holt's was established in 1849 and remains popular with the drinking public for the low cost of its beers: in 2004-5 bitter was £1.40 a pint. Bitter is often delivered to pubs in 54-gallon hogsheads. A new 30-barrel brewing plant caters for seasonal beers. In 2004 a contract was won to supply Tesco stores with bottled Humdinger (ABV 3.5%). 128 pubs are owned, all serving cask-conditioned beer and approximately 75 outlets are supplied. Seasonal ales: Nuts & Holts (ABV 4.1%, Sept-Nov), Nearly Holt Upright (ABV 4.4%, Dec), Thunder Holt (ABV 4.5%, March-May), Lightning Holt (ABV 4.3%, June-Aug).

Mild Ale (OG 1033, ABV 3.2%) ◆
A dark brown beer with a fruity, malty nose. Roast, malt and some fruit in the taste, with strong bitterness for a mild, and a dry malt and hops finish.

Bitter (OG 1040, ABV 4%) ◆
Copper-coloured beer with malt and hops in the aroma and taste. Uncompromisingly bitter.

Home County

Home County Brewers, The Old Brewery, Wickwar Trading Estate, Station Road,

Wickwar, Gloucestershire, GL12 8NB
Tel 07813 535252
Shop call brewery
Tours call brewery

⊗ The brewery has currently stopped brewing, but plans to increase capacity and re-launch.

Hook Norton IFBB

Hook Norton Brewery Co Ltd, The Brewery, Hook Norton, Banbury, Oxfordshire, OX15 5NY
Tel (01608) 737210 (brewery), (01608) 730384 (visitor centre)
Fax (01608) 730294
Email info@hook-norton-brewery.co.uk
Website www.hook-norton-brewery.co.uk
Shop Mon-Fri 9-5
Tours by arrangement: visitor centre open 9am-5pm Mon-Fri

⊗ Hook Norton was founded in 1849 by John Harris, a farmer and maltster. The current premises were built in 1900 and Hook Norton is one of the finest examples of a Victorian tower brewery, with a 25hp steam engine for most of its motive power. The brewhouse is currently expanding, with new fermenters, copper, mash tun and racking plant. Hook Norton owns 45 pubs and supplies approximately 400 free trade accounts. All Hook Norton draught beers are cask conditioned and dry hopped. All the beers use water drawn from wells beneath the brewery, Maris Otter malt and English Challenger, Fuggles and Goldings hops. Seasonal beers: First Light (ABV 4.3%, May-June), Steaming On (ABV 4.4%, Sept-Oct), Copper Ale (ABV 4.8%, March-April), Double Stout (ABV 4.8%, Jan-Feb), Haymaker (ABV 5%, July-Aug), Twelve Days (ABV 5.5%, Nov-Dec).

Hooky Dark (OG 1033, ABV 3.2%) ◆
A new name for Dark Mild: dark, red/brown mild with a malty aroma and a malty, sweetish taste, tinged with a faint hoppy balance. Malty in the aftertaste.

Best Bitter (OG 1035, ABV 3.4%) ◆
A fruity and hoppy aroma introduces this complex, well-crafted amber bitter. Moderate maltiness underpins the hops, leading to a long, bitter-sweet finish.

303AD (OG 1041, ABV 4%) ◆
A pale brown best bitter, predominantly hoppy but balanced with moderate malt and banana fruit. The fruit and malt decline to a relatively short, hoppy finish.

Old Hooky (OG 1048, ABV 4.6%) ◆
A well-balanced and full-bodied pale copper beer that is fruity with pale and crystal malt and hops on the aroma and taste. The hoppy character gives way to a sweet and fruity finish.

Hop Back SIBA

Hop Back Brewery plc, Unit 22 Downton Business Centre, Downton, Salisbury, Wiltshire, SP5 3HU
Tel (01725) 510986
Fax (01725) 513116
Email info@hopback.co.uk
Website www.hopback.co.uk
Tours by arrangement

⊗ Started by John Gilbert in 1987 at the Wyndham Arms in Salisbury, the new 20-barrel brewery has expanded steadily ever since. It went public via a Business Expansion Scheme in 1993 and has enjoyed rapid continued growth. Summer Lightning has won many awards. The brewery has 11 tied houses and also sells to more than 200 other outlets. Seasonal beers are produced on a monthly basis. Bottle-conditioned beers: Summer Lightning, Taiphoon (ABV 4.2%), Crop Circle (ABV 4.2%), Entire Stout.

GFB/Gilbert's First Brew (OG 1035, ABV 3.5%) ◆
A golden beer, with the sort of light, clean quality that makes it an ideal session ale. A hoppy aroma and taste lead to a good, dry finish. Refreshing.

Odyssey (OG 1040, ABV 4%)
A new, darker beer with a blend of four malts.

Crop Circle (OG 1041, ABV 4.2%) ◆
A refreshingly sharp and hoppy summer beer. Gold coloured with a slight citrus taste. The crisp, dry aftertaste lingers.

Entire Stout (OG 1043, ABV 4.5%) ◆
A rich, dark stout with a strong roasted malt flavour and a long, sweet and malty aftertaste. A beer suitable for vegans. Also produced with ginger.

Summer Lightning (OG 1049, ABV 5%) ◆
A pleasurable pale bitter with a good, fresh, hoppy aroma and a malty, hoppy flavour. Finely balanced, it has an intense bitterness leading to a long, dry finish. Though strong, it tastes like a session ale.

Hopdaemon

Hopdaemon Brewery Co Ltd, Unit 1, Parsonage Farm, Seed Road, Newnham, Sittingbourne, Kent, ME9 0NA
Tel (01795) 892078
Email hopdaemon@supanet.com

Tonie Prins opened a 12-barrel plant in 2001 in Canterbury and within six months was supplying more than 30 pubs in the area, as well as exclusive bottle-conditioned, own-label beers for London's British Museum, Southwark Cathedral and Science Museum and more recently for the Barbican and National Gallery. In 2005, the brewery moved a few miles to Newnham to bigger premises and some 100 outlets are now supplied. Bottle-conditioned beers: National Gallery Beer (ABV 4.5%), Skrimshander IPA, Green Daemon Natural (ABV 5%), Barbican Beer (ABV 5%), British Museum Beer (ABV 5%), Science Museum Beer Deep Blue (ABV 5%), Southwark Cathedral Beer Pilgrims Pleasure (ABV 5%), National Gallery Beer (ABV 4%), Barbican Beer (5%) and Leviathan. Green Daemon Natural, brewed with organic ingredients and no finings, is suitable for vegetarians and vegans.

Golden Braid (OG 1039, ABV 3.7%)

Incubus (OG 1041, ABV 4%)

Skrimshander IPA (OG 1045, ABV 4.5%)

Leviathan (OG 1057, ABV 6%)

Hopstar*

Hopstar Brewery, c/o The Black Horse, 72 Redearth Street, Darwen, Lancashire, BB3 2AF
Email hopstar@theblackun.co.uk

Hopstar first brewed in 2004 using a 2.5-barrel plant supplied by Porter Brewery. A second five-barrel plant previously installed at Red Rose Brewery is also used. The brewery is in a local private garage and the only way to contact it is via email.

Hoskins Brothers

Hoskins Brothers Ales, The Ale Wagon, 27 Rutland Street, Leicester, LE1 1RE
Tel (0116) 262 3330
Email mail@alewagon.com
Website www.alewagon.co.uk

Stephen and Philip Hoskins founded Hoskins and Oldfield in Leicester in 1984. This ceased operation in 2001 and the beers were contract brewed, most recently by Tower, and the name was changed to Hoskins Brothers. A seven-barrel plant is currently in the process of being installed at their pub, the Ale Wagon in Leicester. It is intended to use this to brew the full range of the former Hoskins and Oldfield beers. Two outlets are supplied direct.

Hob Best Mild (ABV 3.5%)

Hob Bitter (ABV 4%)

White Dolphin (ABV 4%)
Wheat beer.

Tom Kelly's Stout (ABV 4.2%)

EXS (ABV 5%)

Ginger Tom (ABV 5.2%)
Ginger Ale

Old Navigation Ale (ABV 7%)

Houston SIBA

Houston Brewing Co, South Street, Houston, Renfrewshire, PA6 7EN
Tel (01505) 614528
Fax (01505) 614133
Email ale@houston-brewing.co.uk
Website www.houston-brewing.co.uk
Shop open pub hours, every day
Tours by arrangement

⊗ A well-established brewery attached to the Fox and Hounds pub and restaurant. Brewery tours include dinner and tastings. Gift packs and bottles are also available. 200 outlets are supplied. There is a rolling programme of seasonal beers: see website.

Killellan (OG 1037, ABV 3.7%)
A light session ale, with a floral hop and fruity taste. The finish of this amber beer is dry and quenching.

Blonde Bombshell (OG 1040, ABV 4%)
A gold-coloured ale with a fresh hop aroma and rounded maltiness.

Barochan (OG 1041, ABV 4.1%)
A red, malty beer, in which fruit is balanced by roast and hop overtones; dry, bitter-sweet finish.

Peter's Well (OG 1042, ABV 4.2%)
Well-balanced fruity taste with sweet hop, leading to an increasingly bitter-sweet finish.

Warlock Stout (ABV 4.7%)

Howard Town*

Howard Town Brewery Ltd, Unit 10, Howard Town Mill, Mill Street, Glossop, Derbyshire, SK13 8PT
Tel (01457) 8699800
Email enquiries@howardtownbrewery.co.uk
Website www.howardtownbreweery.co.uk

Howard Town was set up in the summer of 2005 by partners Tony Hulme and Les Dove with their wives. It is an eight-barrel plant installed by Porter Brewing. The beer list had not been finalised when the guide went to press.

Sarah Hughes

Sarah Hughes Brewery, 129 Bilston Street, Sedgley, West Midlands, DY3 1JE
Tel (01902) 883381
Fax (01902) 884020
Tours by prior arrangement

A traditional Black Country tower brewery, established in 1921. The original grist case and rare open-topped copper add to the ambience of the Victorian brewhouse and give a unique character to the brews. Future plans involve additional seasonal beers, expanding fermenting space to cope with demand and adding a full range of bottle-conditioned beers. One pub, the Beacon Hotel, is owned. Seasonal beer: Snow Flake (ABV 8%). Bottle-conditioned beer: Dark Ruby.

Pale Amber (OG 1038, ABV 4%)
A well-balanced beer, initially slightly sweet but with hops close behind.

Surprise Bitter (OG 1048, ABV 5%)
A bitter-sweet, medium-bodied, hoppy ale with some malt.

Dark Ruby (OG 1058, ABV 6%)
A dark ruby strong ale with a good balance of fruit and hops, leading to a pleasant, lingering hops and malt finish.

Humpty Dumpty

Humpty Dumpty Brewery, Church Road, Reedham, Norfolk, NR13 3TZ
Tel (01493) 701818
Fax (01493) 700727
Email mick@humptydumptybrewery.co.uk
Website www.humptydumptybrewery.co.uk
Shop 9-6 daily
Tours by arrangement

⊗ Humpty Dumpty was opened in 1998 by Mick Cottrell and moved to its present site in 2001. Brewing capacity expanded from five to 11 barrels and the brewery is currently producing 25 to 35 barrels a week. The brewery shop sells a wide range of bottle-conditioned beers (their own and other breweries), and home-brew kits, and has a full off-licence. Buildings on the site have now been developed for retail and Mick has taken on the Reed Cutter pub in Cantley. He sells to the Railway Tavern in Reedham and some 150 pubs nationwide. There is a full range of bottle-conditioned ales.

Little Sharpie (ABV 3.8%) ◆
A delicate hoppy aroma is a forerunner to a sweet hoppy, lagerish flavour. A clean golden yellow bitter with a finish in which bitterness grows.

Ferryman (ABV 3.8%)
A light, hoppy beer.

Lemon and Ginger (ABV 4%)

Humpty Dumpty (ABV 4.1%) ◆
Amber coloured with an overtly hoppy nose and grainy feel. The balance of this brew is definitely on the bitter side. Underlying sweetness fades to leave a long, dry finish.

Claud Hamilton (ABV 4.1%) ◆
A well-rounded, red-brown beer with a distinct hickory stick aroma. The solid roast malt base lingers as the bitter-sweet beginning fades into a light hoppy dryness.

Reed Cutter (ABV 4.2%) ◆
Light hoppy airs introduce this golden ale. An initial cloying sweetness quickly fades to leave an increasingly bitter finish.

Cheltenham Flyer (ABV 4.6%)
A medium pale ale.

Butt Jumper (ABV 4.8%) ◆
Toffee and malt dominate the aroma of this tawny-hued ale. Full-flavoured, with malt vying with a fruity bitterness for dominance. The long, lingering finish does not fade as a nutty bitterness becomes prevalent.

Spark Arrester (ABV 4.8%)
A dark beer.

Railway Sleeper (ABV 5%) ◆
Full-bodied tawny brew with a rich, fruity nature. Slight malt bouquet belies the strong plummy character where sweetness and malt counterbalance the background bitterness. A quick, spicy, bitter finish.

Peto's Porter (ABV 5%)

Hydes IFBB

Hydes' Brewery Ltd, 46 Moss Lane West, Manchester, M15 5PH
Tel (0161) 226 1317
Fax (0161) 227 9593
Email mail@hydesbrewery.com
Website www.hydesbrewery.com
Tours by arrangement

Hydes' dramatic expansion continues. The past 12 months have seen significant growth in the brewery, contract brewing and the number of free trade accounts. Hydes is now the biggest volume producer of cask ales in the North-west with further expansion planned. The contract to brew cask Boddingtons has now been sealed despite objections from CAMRA and the trade unions at the closure of Strangeways Brewery. Hydes has expanded its warehousing and packaging operations on to the site adjoining the brewery and has also doubled the maximum brewing capacity from 100,000 barrels to 200,000 barrels. This additional capacity has allowed Hydes to produce more experimental and occasional beers. The future of XXXX is in some doubt due to disappointing sales. Hydes owns 74 tied houses, supplying cask ale to all but two of these outlets. Seasonal beers: Perfection (ABV 4.8%, Jan-Feb), Satisfaction (ABV 4.2%, March-April), Elevation (ABV 4.4%, May-June), Celebration (ABV 4%, July-Aug), Inspiration (ABV 4.5%, Sept-Oct), Insulation (ABV 5%, Nov-Dec).

Light Mild (OG 1033.5, ABV 3.5%)

Traditional Mild (OG 1033.5, ABV 3.5%)

Dark Mild (OG 1033.5, ABV 3.5%) ◆
Dark brown/red in colour with a fruit and malt nose. Complex taste, including berry fruits, malt and a hint of chocolate. Satisfying aftertaste.

Traditional Bitter
(OG 1036.5, ABV 3.8%) ◆
Pale brown beer with a malty nose, malt and an earthy hoppiness in the taste, and a good bitterness through to the finish.

Jekyll's Gold Premium
(OG 1042, ABV 4.3%) ◆
Pale gold in colour, with a fruity nose. A well-balanced beer with hops, fruit and malt all in evidence, and a bitter, hoppy finish.

XXXX (OG 1070, ABV 6.8%)

For Interbrew UK

Boddingtons Bitter (OG 1038, ABV 4.1%)

Iceni SIBA EAB

Iceni Brewery, 3 Foulden Road, Ickburgh, near Mundford, Norfolk, IP26 5BJ
Tel (01842) 878922
Fax (01842) 879216
Email icenibrewe@aol.com
Website www.icenibrewery.co.uk
Shop 8.30-5, Mon-Fri, 9-3 Sat
Tours by arrangement

Brendan Moore launched Iceni in 1995 and is now at the forefront of local brewing as a member of SIBA and a founder member of the East Anglian Brewers' Co-operative. Iceni was launched after Redundancy Plus help from a Rural Enterprise Grant. Equipment is ex-dairy/milk farm stock. The brewery has its own hop garden and barley plot aimed at amusing the many visitors that flock to the shop to buy the 28 different ales, stout and lagers bottled on-site. Beer as a gift is an increasingly important trend at Iceni. 40 outlets are supplied and Brendan also targets local farmers' markets and the tourist shop in nearby Thetford Forest. Special beers are brewed for festivals. Seasonal: Winter Lightning (ABV 5%). All cask ales are also bottle conditioned; there are many additional bottle-conditioned beers: see website.

Fine Soft Day (OG 1038, ABV 4%) ◆
Full-bodied and hoppy amber ale with a lingering aftertaste of hops and malt.

Celtic Queen **(OG 1038, ABV 4%)**
A light summer ale, packed with flavour.

Fen Tiger **(OG 1040, ABV 4.2%)**

It's A Grand Day **(OG 1044, ABV 4.5%)**

Raspberry Wheat **(OG 1048, ABV 5%)**

Men of Norfolk **(OG 1060, ABV 6.2%)**

Innis & Gunn

Innis & Gunn Brewing Co Ltd, PO Box 17246, Edinburgh, EH11 1YR
Tel (0131) 337 4420
Email dougal.sharp@innisandgunn.com
Website www.innisandgunn.com

Innis & Gunn was launched in 2003 by Dougal Sharp, former head brewer at Caledonian, and his father, Russell Sharp, who led the management buy-out of Caledonian when it was threatened with closure in the 1980s. They produce one regular bottled (not bottle-conditioned) product, Oak Aged Beer (ABV 6.6%), which has a 77-day production cycle, including maturation in oak whisky casks supplied by William Grant. The beer is brewed for the Sharps by an unnamed Scottish brewery. The beer was named Supreme Champion in the International Beer Competition in 2004 as well as the Safeway Consumers' Beer of the Year.

Inveralmond SIBA

Inveralmond Brewery Ltd, 1 Inveralmond Way, Inveralmond, Perth, PH1 3UQ
Tel/Fax (01738) 449448
Email info@inveralmond-brewery.co.uk
Website www.inveralmond-brewery.co.uk

☺ Established in 1997, Inveralmond was the first brewery in Perth for more than 30 years. The brewery has gone from strength to strength, with some 150 outlets supplied and wholesalers taking beers nationwide. The intention is to expand into premises next door to the existing brewery in 2005, more than doubling the floor space. Seasonal ales: Inkie Pinkie (ABV 3.7%), Amber Bead (ABV 4.1%), Pint Stowp (ABV 4.2%), Pundie (ABV 5%), Special (ABV 3.7%, May-June), IPA (ABV 3.8%, Sept-Oct), XXX (ABV 4.4%, July-Aug), Brown Ale (ABV 4.6%, Nov-Dec), Lager (ABV 4.8%, Jan-Feb), Export Pale Ale (ABV 5.6%, March-April).

Independence **(OG 1040, ABV 3.8%)** ◆
A well-balanced Scottish ale with fruit and malt tones. Hop provides an increasing bitterness in the finish.

Ossian's Ale **(OG 1042, ABV 4.1%)** 🗍 ◆
Well-balanced best bitter with a dry finish. This full-bodied amber ale is dominated by fruit and hop with a bitter-sweet character, although excessive caramel can distract from this.

Thrappledouser **(OG 1043, ABV 4.3%)** ◆
A refreshing amber beer with reddish hues. The crisp, hoppy aroma is finely balanced with a tangy but quenching taste.

Lia Fail **(OG 1048, ABV 4.7%)** ◆
The name is the Gaelic title for the Stone of Destiny. A dark, robust, full-bodied beer with a deep malty taste. Smooth texture and balanced finish.

Islay

Islay Ales Co Ltd, The Brewery, Islay House Square, Bridgend, Isle of Islay, Argyll, PA44 7NZ
Tel/Fax (01496) 810014
Email info@islayales.com
Website www.islayales.com

The brewery was founded in 2003 by two Englishmen and a German; Paul Hathaway worked for Rolls Royce, Paul Capper is a retired fireman and the German is Walter Schobert, a retired museum curator. Their aim is to bring quality real ale to Islay, Jura and Colonsay for the enjoyment of both locals and visitors alike. Their first brew was in 2004. The brewery can be found in the outbuilding of Islay House in a former tractor shed. It is a two-room operation – shop and sample room and the brewhouse. The brewery has a four-barrel plant and there are three brews a week. Seasonal beer: Saligo Ale (ABV 4.4%). Bottle-conditioned beers: all cask ales.

Finlaggan Ale **(OG 1039, ABV 3.7%)**

Black Rock Ale **(OG 1040, ABV 4.2%)**

Dun Hogs Head Ale **(OG 1045, ABV 4.4%)**

Isle of Mull*

Isle of Mull Brewing Co Ltd, Ledaig, Tobermory, Isle of Mull, Argyll, PA75 6NR
Tel (01688) 302821
Email isleofmullbrewing@btinternet.com

Brewing started in May 2005, using a five-barrel plant supplied by Brewing Solutions. The beer is available at macGochans Bar in Tobermory as well as other local outlets. Seasonal and bottle-conditioned beers are planned.

MacCaig's Folly **(ABV 4.2%)**

Galleon Gold **(ABV 5%)**

Isle of Purbeck

⌂ Isle of Purbeck Brewery, Manor Road, Studland, Dorset, BH19 3AU
Tel (01929) 450225
Fax (01929) 450307
Tours by arrangement

The 10-barrel brewing equipment from the former Poole Brewery has been installed in the grounds of the Bankes Arms Hotel that overlooks the sweep of Studland Bay. There are plans to add new brews and the size of the plant will enable the brands to be sold to other pubs. 20 outlets are supplied. Seasonal beer: Thermal Cheer (ABV 4.8%, winter).

Fossil Fuel (OG 1040, ABV 4.1%)

Solar Power (OG 1043, ABV 4.3%)

Studland Bay Wrecked (OG 1044, ABV 4.5%)

Ale (OG 1047, ABV 4.8%)

Isle of Skye

Isle of Skye Brewing Co (Leann an Eilein) Ltd, The Pier, Uig, Isle of Skye, IV51 9XP
Tel (01470) 542477
Fax (01470) 542488
Email info@skyebrewery.co.uk
Website www.skyebrewery.co.uk
Shop Apr-Oct 10-6 Mon-Sat; 12-4.30 Sun
Tours by arrangement

Established in 1995 with a 10-barrel plant, the Isle of Skye was first upgraded to a 20-barrel plant to meet rising demand, with a new 22-barrel copper added in 2004 and fermenting capacity increased to 80 barrels. Conditioning capacity now stands at 100 barrels. Once a real ale desert, the island now boasts some 21 outlets serving cask ale although many are seasonal. The brewery is owned by ex-teacher Angus MacRuary. Some 100 outlets are supplied. Seasonal beers: Misty Isle wheat beer (ABV 4 .3%, summer) Oyster Stout (4.6%). Bottle-conditioned beer: Misty Isle, suitable for vegetarians/vegans.

Young Pretender (OG 1039, ABV 4%)
Predominantly hoppy and fruity, this golden amber ale has hops and fruit on the nose. The bitter taste is also dominated by fruit and hop, with the hops lingering in to the long, bitter finish.

Red Cuillin (OG 1041, ABV 4.2%)
This tawny-reddish beer has a light fruity, malty nose that leads to a deliciously bitter-sweet palate and a long, dry aftertaste.

Hebridean Gold (OG 1041.5, ABV 4.3%)
Oats are used to produce this golden beer. Nicely balanced, it has a refreshing, bitter, fruity flavour. Thirst-quenching and drinkable.

Black Cuillin (OG 1044, ABV 4.5%)
A complex, tasty brew worthy of its many awards. Full-bodied, malts hold sway but there are plenty of hops and fruit to be discovered in its varied character. A truly delicious Scottish old ale.

Blaven (OG 1047, ABV 5%)
Sweetish amber ale with orange fruit notes. There is plenty of hop bitterness to balance the fruitiness. The malty aroma gives way to a bitter-sweet finish.

Cuillin Beast (OG 1061.5, ABV 7%)
Sweet and fruity, and much more drinkable than the strength would suggest. Plenty of caramel throughout with a creamy, dry mouthfeel.

For Devanha Brewery

XXX (OG 1043, ABV 4.4%)

Itchen Valley SIBA

Itchen Valley Brewery Ltd, Unit 4, Shelf House, New Farm Road, Alresford, Hampshire, SO24 9QE
Tel (01962) 735111
Fax (01962) 735678
Email info@itchenvalley.com
Website www.itchenvalley.com
Shop 9-5 Mon-Fri
Tours by arrangement

The brewery, founded in 1997, has enlarged its range of beers, which are sold in more than 150 pubs in Berkshire, Hampshire, London, Surrey and Sussex. It is now exchanging beers with other micro-breweries to increase the range available to local customers and allow the beers to be supplied throughout the country. The brewery also offers bottle-conditioned ales in supermarkets and independent off-licences, and direct to the public online as well through farmers' markets and agricultural shows. There is an extensive seasonal programme featuring at least 15 different cask ales each year. Seasonal beers: Hambledon Bitter (ABV 4%), Watercress Line (ABV 4.2%), Treacle Stout (ABV 4.4%), Green Jackets (ABV 4.5%); see also website.

Godfathers (OG 1038, ABV 3.8%)
An earthy hop character with a malty taste leading to an increasingly bitter finish. Pale brown colour.

Fagin's (OG 1041, ABV 4.1%)
Enjoyable copper-coloured best bitter with a hint of crystal malt and a pleasant bitter aftertaste.

Hampshire Rose (OG 1042, ABV 4.2%)
An elegant, golden amber ale. Fruit and hops dominate the taste throughout, with a good mouth feel.

Pure Gold (OG 1048, ABV 4.8%)
An aromatic, hoppy, golden bitter. Initial grapefruit flavours lead to a dry, bitter finish that leaves you wanting more.

Wat Tyler (OG 1050, ABV 5%)

Jarrow SIBA

Jarrow Brewery, The Robin Hood, Primrose Hill, Jarrow, Tyne & Wear, NE32 5UB
Tel/Fax (0191) 4836792
Email jarrowbrewery@btconnect.com
Tours by arrangement

◎ Brewing started in 2002 and during the first year the brewery won five champion and supreme beer awards. Owners and brewers Jess and Alison McConnell own three pubs on South Tyneside: the Albion Inn, Bill Quay; the Robin Hood, Jarrow; and the recently acquired Maltings, South Shields, a former Co-op dairy. They supply 120 outlets, mainly on Tyneside. Seasonal beers: Riley's Army (ABV 4.3%, Jan-March), Red Ellen (ABV 4.4%, July-Sept), Venerable Bede (ABV 4.5%, April-June), Old Cornelius (ABV 4.8%, Oct-Dec).

Bitter (OG 1037.5, ABV 3.8%)
A light golden session bitter with a delicate hop aroma and a lingering fruity finish.

Palmers Resolution (OG 1037.5, ABV 3.8%)

Rivet Catcher (OG 1039, ABV 4%) ■
A light, smooth, satisfying gold bitter. Subtle fruity hops give the taste profile on the tongue and nose.

Joblings Swinging Gibbet (OG 1041, ABV 4.1%)
A copper-coloured, evenly balanced beer with a good hop aroma and a fruity finish.

McConnell's Irish Stout (OG 1045, ABV 4.6%)

Jennings

See Wolverhampton & Dudley in New Nationals

Jersey SIBA

Ann Street Brewery Co Ltd, t/a Jersey Brewery, Tregear House, Longueville, St Saviour, JE2 7WF
Tel (01534) 834377
Fax (01534) 834360
Tours by arrangement

Jersey, better known as Ann Street, phased out cask ale after a brief flirtation in the 1980s and '90s. It has 56 tied houses, of which six take real ale from other suppliers. It has closed its subsidiary, Guernsey Brewery. Jersey Brewery also owns the Tipsy Toad brew-pub (qv), which brews the award-winning Jersey Bitter.

Jolly Brewer*

Jolly Brewer, 1 College Street, Wrexham, LL13 8LU
Tel (01978) 263338
Email pene@jollybrewer.co.uk
Website www.jollybrewer.co.uk
Shop open Mon-Sat, 10am-5pm

Penelope Coles has been brewing for the past 25 years. Some 10 years ago, she decided to open a craft brewing shop and five years later added a real ale off-licence, the Jolly Brewer in College Street, Wrexham. She then decided to become a registered brewer in order to sell her beer in the shop. The brewing plant, based in Penelope's home, can produce between five and 15 gallons a time. She now supplies one pub – the Ffrwd, Ffrwd Road, Wrexham, which sells dark lager on a regular basis, and another shop in Birmingham. Bottle-conditioned beer: Taids Garden, Pleasure Beach (ABV 4.5%), Bah Humbug (ABV 6%), Dark Lager.

Taids Garden (OG 1040, ABV 4%)

Dark Lager (OG 1060, ABV 6.4%)

Jollyboat

Jollyboat Brewery (Bideford) Ltd, The Coach House, Buttgarden Street, Bideford, Devon, EX39 2AU
Tel (01237) 424343

⊗ The brewery was established in 1995 by Hugh Parry and his son, Simon. The brewery went into receivership in 2000 and was re-established in 2000. In 2004, Contraband became Reserve Champion Beer at the SIBA South-west Festival at Tucker's Maltings, Newton Abbot. In-house bottling was due to come on line in 2005. Jollyboat currently supplies some 16 outlets. A Jollyboat is a sailors' leave boat that brings them ashore. All the beer names have nautical connections. Bottle-conditioned beers: Privateer (ABV 4.8%), Plunder (ABV 4.8%), Contraband (ABV 5.8%).

Grenville's Renown (ABV 3.8%)

Freebooter (OG 1040, ABV 4%)

Mainbrace (OG 1041, ABV 4.2%) ◆
Pale brown brew with a rich fruity aroma and a bitter taste and aftertaste.

Kelburn SIBA

Kelburn Brewing Co Ltd, 10 Muriel Lane, Barrhead, East Renfrewshire, G78 1QB
Tel (0141) 881 2138
Fax (0141) 881 2145
Email info@kelburnbrewery.com
Website www.kelburnbrewery.com
Tours by arrangement

⊗ A family business run by Derek Moore who brewing started in 2002. In the first three years of business, Kelburn beers have won 15 awards. Goldihops was voted Best Beer of Glasgow 2002 and Cart Blanche SIBA Best Strong Beer of Scotland 2004. Beers are available in bottle and take-away polypins. Five brews are available year-round and there is currently one seasonal ale Ca'Canny (ABV 5.2%, winter only).

Goldihops (OG 1038, ABV 3.8%) ■
Well-hopped session ale with a fruity taste and a bitter-sweet finish.

Misty Law (ABV 4%)

Red Smiddy (OG 1040, ABV 4.1%)
A smooth ale with a reddish hue and a citrus, fruity aftertaste.

Dark Moor (OG 1044, ABV 4.5%)
A dark, fruity ale with undertones of liquorice and blackcurrant.

Cart Blanche (OG 1048, ABV 5%)
A golden, full-bodied ale with a dry aftertaste.

Kelham Island SIBA

Kelham Island Brewery Ltd, Alma Street, Sheffield, South Yorkshire, S3 8SA
Tel (0114) 249 4804
Fax (0114) 249 4803
Email info@kelhambrewery.co.uk
Website www.kelhambrewery.co.uk
Tours by arrangement

Home of Pale Rider, the Supreme Champion Beer of Britain 2004. The brewery was established in 1990 in the Kelham Island area of Sheffield. A key ingredient is pure water from the foothills of the Pennines. There is a full range of seasonal ales including Golden Eagle (ABV 4.2%), Bete Noire (ABV 5.5%) and Grande Pale (ABV 6.6%). The demand for Pale Rider forced the company to seek a brewing partner and the beer, named Pale Island to avoid any suggestion it is the original, is now also brewed by Ridley's (qv).

Bitter (OG 1038.8, ABV 3.8%)
A clean, characterful, crisp, pale brown beer. The nose and palate are dominated by refreshing hoppiness and fruitiness, which, with a good bitter dryness, lasts in the aftertaste.

Gold (OG 1038.8, ABV 3.8%)
A light golden ale, a hoppy nose and finish, a smooth drinking bitter.

Easy Rider (OG 1041.8, ABV 4.3%)
A pale, straw-coloured beer with a sweetish flavour and delicate hints of citrus fruits. A beer with hints of flavour rather than full-bodied.

Pale Rider (OG 1050.8, ABV 5.2%)
A full-bodied, straw pale ale, with a good fruity aroma and a strong fruit and hop taste. Its well-balanced sweetness and bitterness continue in the finish.

Keltek SIBA

Keltek Brewing Co Ltd, Unit 3A, Restormel Industrial Estate, Liddicoat Road, Lostwithiel, Cornwall, PL22 0HG
Tel/Fax (01208) 871199
Tours by arrangement

Keltek Brewery moved to Lostwithiel in 1999 and started brewing again in that year. Monthly specials and house beers for pubs are brewed. 50 outlets in Cornwall and north Devon are supplied. Seasonal beers: Olde Smugglers Ale (ABV 4.2%, September), Olde Pirates Ale (ABV 4.8%, March). Bottle-conditioned beers: King, Revenge.

4K Mild (OG 1038, ABV 3.8%)
Dark and fruity.

Golden Lance (OG 1038, ABV 3.8%)
Light golden, refreshing brew.

Magik (OG 1042, ABV 4.2%)
A rounded, well-balanced and complex beer.

King (OG 1051, ABV 5.1%)
Complex but well-balanced beer with fruit and malt in the taste and a dry finish.

Revenge (OG 1066, ABV 7%)
Dark ruby in colour; sweetish with a bitter edge.

Kemptown SIBA

Kemptown Brewery Co Ltd, Hand in Hand, 33 Upper St James's Street, Kemptown, Brighton, East Sussex, BN2 1JN
Tel/Fax (01273) 693070
Email bev@kemptownbreweryltc.co.uk
Tours by arrangement

A brewery established in 1989 and built in the tower tradition behind the Hand in Hand, which is possibly the smallest pub in England with its own brewery. It takes its name and logo from the former Charrington's Kemptown Brewery 500 yards away, which closed in 1964. Six free trade outlets are supplied. Seasonal beer: Old Grumpy (winter). Bottle-conditioned beers: Old Trout Ale, Dragons Blood.

Black Moggy Mild (ABV 3.6%)

Dolphin (ABV 3.8%)

Bitter (ABV 4%)

Old Trout Ale (OG 1045, ABV 4.5%)

Dragons Blood (ABV 5%)

Khean

See Woodlands

King SIBA

W J King & Co (Brewers), 3-5 Jubilee Estate, Foundry Lane, Horsham, West Sussex, RH13 5UE
Tel (01403) 272102
Fax (01403) 754455
Email office@kingfamilybrewers.co.uk
Website www.kingfamilybrewers.co.uk
Shop Sat 10-2pm
Tours by arrangement, limited to 15

Launched in 2001 by former King & Barnes managing director Bill King, with a 20-barrels-a week ex-Firkin plant, the brewery had expanded to a capacity of 50 barrels a week by mid-2004. In 2004 the lease of premises next door was taken over to give more cellar space and to enable room to stock more bottle-conditioned beers. One pub is owned and approximately 200 regular and occasional outlets are supplied. Seasonal beers: Kings Old Ale, (ABV 4.5%, winter), Summer Ale (ABV 4%, summer), Merry Ale (ABV 6.5%, Christmas). Bottle-conditioned beers: Red River (ABV 5%), Kings Old Ale (ABV 4.5%), Cereal Thriller (ABV 6.3%), Five Generation (ABV 4.4%), Merry Ale (ABV 6.5%). All the bottled beers are suitable for vegetarians as no isinglass finings are used.

Horsham Best Bitter (OG 1038, ABV 3.8%)
A predominantly malty best bitter, brown in colour. The nutty flavours have some sweetness with a little bitterness that grows in the aftertaste. Crystal malt and three different hops are used.

Red River (OG 1048, ABV 4.8%) ◆
A full-flavoured, mid-brown beer with a red tinge. Using the same ingredients as Horsham Best Bitter, this is very malty with some berry fruitiness in the aroma and taste. The finish is reasonably balanced with a sharp bitterness increasingly coming through.

Kings Head

Kings Head Brewery, Kings Head, 132 High Street, Bildeston, Ipswich, Suffolk, IP7 7ED
Tel (01449) 741434
Email enquiries@bildestonkingshead.co.uk
Website www.bildestonkingshead.co.uk
Shop Open pub hours
Tours By prior arrangement

Kings Head has been brewing since 1996 in the old stables at the back of the pub. The plant has approximately five barrels' capacity and brewing takes place twice a week. The brewery stages a beer festival in May (Late Spring Bank Holiday) every year where most of the 40 beers on offer are from other micros around the country. Six other pubs and many beer festivals are supplied. Seasonal beer: Dark Vader (ABV 5.4%, winter). Bottle-conditioned beers: Blondie, Apache, Crowdie and Dark Vader.

Not Strong Beer/NSB (OG 1030, ABV 2.8%)

Best Bitter (OG 1040, ABV 3.8%)

Blondie (OG 1041, ABV 4%)

First Gold (OG 1044, ABV 4.3%)

Apache (OG 1046, ABV 4.5%)

Crowdie (OG 1050, ABV 5%)

Kinver*

Kinver Brewery, 2 Fairfield Drive, Kinver, Staffordshire, DX7 6EW
Tel (07715) 842679
Email info@kinverbrewery.co.uk
Website www.kinverbrewery.co.uk
Tours by arrangement

The brewery was founded in 2004 by two CAMRA members. The five-barrel plant produces three regular beers in a small plant behind the Plough and Harrow pub, which is a separate business. There are plans for a variety of seasonal ales, including a Maibock, a Mild and a summer ale. Seasonal beer: Over the Edge (ABV 7.6%, winter).

Edge Best Bitter (ABV 4.2%)

Caveman Strong Bitter (ABV 5.2%) ◆
Pale brown with a caramel start, sweet and fruity middle, fruity finish going bitter with satisfying astringency.

Lancaster*

Lancaster Brewery Co Ltd, Unit 19, Lansil Walk, Lansil Industrial Estate, Lancaster, LA1 3PQ.
Tel (01524) 844610
Email info@lancasterbrewery.co.uk
Website www.lancasterbrewery.co.uk

Trial brews were being carried out in June 2005. The beer list had not been finalised when the guide went to press.

Langton

Langton Brewery, Grange Farm, Welham Road, Thorpe Langton, Market Harborough, Leicestershire, LE16 7TU
Tel (07840) 532826
Website www.thebellinn.co.uk
Tours by arrangement

Langton Brewery is run by three partners, Alistair Chapman, Dave Dyson and Derek Hewitt. Using a four-barrel plant in a barn that has been converted to industrial use, they brew Caudle Bitter (named after the range of local hills) and Bowler, which marks the nearby Bell Inn's long association with Langton Cricket Club; the Bell was the brewery's first home. Boxer Heavyweight is named after Jack Gardner, British Heavyweight champion, who was resident in the Langtons. The beers are available for take-away. Seasonal beers: Buzz Light Beer (ABV 4.2%), Bankers Draught (ABV 4.2%), Langton Belle (ABV 4.5%) and Boxer Heavyweight Porter (ABV 5.2%).

Caudle Bitter (OG 1039, ABV 3.9%)
A session bitter, close to pale ale in style.

House Special (ABV 4%)

Bowler Strong Ale (ABV 4.4%)
A strong traditional ale with a deep red colour and a hoppy nose.

Larkins SIBA

Larkins Brewery, Chiddingstone, Edenbridge, Kent, TN8 7BB
Tel (01892) 870328
Fax (01892) 871141
Tours by arrangement Nov-Feb

Larkins Brewery was founded in 1986 by the Dockerty family, farmers and hop growers, who bought the Royal Tunbridge Wells Brewery. The company moved to Larkins Farm in 1987. Since then the production of three regular brews and a Porter in the winter months has steadily increased. Brews are made using only Kentish hops, yeast and malt; no sugars or brewing adjuncts are added to the beers. Larkins owns one pub, the Rock at Chiddingstone Hoath, and supplies around 70 free houses within a radius of 20 miles.

Traditional Ale (OG 1035, ABV 3.4%)
Tawny in colour, a full-tasting hoppy ale with plenty of character for its strength.

Chiddingstone (OG 1040, ABV 4%)
Named after the village where the brewery is based, Chiddingstone is a mid-strength, hoppy, fruity ale with a long, bitter-sweet aftertaste.

Best (OG 1045, ABV 4.4%) ◆
Full-bodied, slightly fruity and unusually bitter for its gravity.

Porter (OG 1052, ABV 5.2%) ◆
Each taste and smell of this potent black winter beer (Nov-April) reveals another facet of its character. An explosion of roasted malt, bitter and fruity flavours leaves a bitter-sweet aftertaste.

Lass O'Gowrie

Lass O'Gowrie Brewhouse, 36 Charles Street, Manchester, M1 7DB
Tel (0161) 273 6932
Tours by arrangement

Victorian pub that was revamped and reopened as a malt extract brew-pub in 1983. Ownership passed from Whitbread to Interbrew in 2000 and in 2004 it was transferred to the L:aurel Pub company (qv). The brewery in the cellar is visible from the bar and the beer is stored in casks. Occasional/one-off brews: Lass Ale (ABV 4.1%), Mukka (ABV 4.4%).

Leadmill

Leadmill Brewery, Unit 1, Park Hall, Park Hall Road, Denby, Derbyshire, DE5 8PX
Tel (01332) 883577
Email tlc@leadmill.fsnet.co.uk
Website www.leadmillbrewery.co.uk
Tours by arrangement

⊗ Originally set up in a pig sty in Selston, Leadmill moved to Denby in 2001-02 and now has a four-barrel plant. The company has bought the Old Oak pub in Horsley Woodhouse. The Old Stables Bar at the brewery functions as a visitor centre and offers up to 12 Leadmill beers and guest ales. The brewery has increased its brewing capacity to a four-barrel plant. Leadmill is in the process of finalising the purchase of its latest pub, the William IV at Milford. Three pubs are owned and some 20 outlets are supplied. Seasonal beers: Jersey City (ABV 5%, autumn), Ginger Spice (ABV 5%, summer). New Leadmill beers regularly appear.

Old Oak Bitter (OG 1037, ABV 3.8%)

UXB (OG 1041, ABV 4.1%)

Old Mottled Cock (OG 1041, ABV 4.2%)

Charisma Bypass (OG 1041, ABV 4.3%)

Strawberry Blonde (OG 1043, ABV 4.4%)

Derby Festival Stout (OG 1045, ABV 4.7%)

Snakeyes (OG 1046, ABV 4.8%)

William IV ESM (OG 1057, ABV 6%)

Weapon of Mass Destruction/WMD (OG 1062, ABV 6.7%)

Leatherbritches SIBA

Leatherbritches Brewery, Bentley Brook Inn, Fenny Bentley, Ashbourne, Derbyshire, DE6 1LF
Tel (01335) 350278
Fax (01335) 350422
Email all@bentleybrookinn.co.uk
Website www.bentleybrookinn.co.uk
Shop 7 days a week, 7am-12pm
Tours by arrangement

The brewery was started by Steamin' Billy Allingham in the 1990s and is now owned and run by his brother Edward, who has expanded the site from two barrel capacity to 14 barrels. Bottled beers are now exported worldwide. The Bentley Brook Inn that fronts the brewery is also run by the Allingham family. Some 100 outlets are supplied. Seasonal beer: Raspberry Belter (ABV 4.4%, summer). Bottle-conditioned beers: Hairy Helmet (ABV 4.9%), Bespoke (ABV 5.2%), Porter (ABV 5.5%), Blue (ABV 9%).

Goldings (OG 1036, ABV 3.6%)
A light golden beer with a flowery hoppy aroma and a bitter finish.

Ginger Spice (OG 1036, ABV 3.8%)
A light, highly-hopped bitter.

Ashbourne Ale (OG 1040, ABV 4%)
A pale bitter brewed with Goldings hops for a crisp lasting taste.

Belter (OG 1040, ABV 4.4%)
Maris Otter malt produces a pale but interesting beer.

Belt-n-Braces (OG 1040, ABV 4.4%)

Dovedale (OG 1044, ABV 4.4%)

Hairy Helmet (OG 1047, ABV 4.7%)
Pale bitter.

Ginger Helmet (OG 1047, ABV 4.7%)

Bespoke (OG 1050, ABV 5%)

Bentley Brook Bitter (OG 1050, ABV 5.2%)

Leek

Leek Brewing Co Ltd, t/a Leek Brewers Co, Units 11 & 12, Churnet Side, Cheddleton, nr Leek, Staffordshire, ST13 7EF
Tel (01538) 361919
Email leekbrewery@hotmail.com
Tours by arrangement

The brewery has moved to an industrial unit outside Leek. The plan in 2005 was to install a new brewery to increase capacity. All the beers are available in bottle-conditioned form and all are suitable for vegetarians. 25 outlets are supplied and one pub is owned. Seasonal beer: Leek Abbey Ale (ABV 5.5%).

Staffordshire Gold (ABV 3.8%) ◆
Hoppy aroma and dominant hop taste. Dry finish with hops lingering.

Danebridge IPA (ABV 4.1%)

Staffordshire Bitter (ABV 4.2%)
Amber with a fruity aroma. Malty and hoppy start with the hoppy finish diminishing quickly.

Black Grouse (ABV 4.5%)

Hen Cloud (ABV 4.5%)

St Edwards (ABV 4.7%)

Rudyard Ruby (ABV 4.8%)

Double Sunset (ABV 5.2%)

Danebridge XXX (ABV 5.5%)

Cheddleton Steamer (ABV 6%)

Tittesworth Tipple (ABV 6.5%)

Lees IFBB

J W Lees & Co (Brewers) Ltd, Greengate Brewery, Middleton Junction, Manchester, M24 2AX
Tel (0161) 643 2487
Fax (0161) 655 3731
Email mail@jwlees.co.uk
Website www.jwlees.co.uk
Tours by arrangement

Lees is a family-owned brewery founded in 1828 by John Lees and run by the sixth generation of the family. Brewing takes place in the 1876 brewhouse designed and built by John Willie Lees, the grandson of the founder. All 170 pubs (most in north Manchester) serve cask beer. Seasonal beers: Two-faced Janus (ABV 4.2%, Jan-Feb), Brooklyn Best (ABV 5%, March-April), 1828 Anniversary Ale (ABV 4.6%, May-June), Scorcher (July-Aug), Razzmatazz (ABV 4.4%, Sept-Oct), Plum Pudding (ABV 4.8%, Nov-Dec).

GB Mild (OG 1032, ABV 3.5%)
Red-brown beer with malt and roast aroma. Creamy mouthfeel with roast and chocolate malt flavours. Fairly bitter, malty finish.

Bitter (OG 1037, ABV 4%)
Copper-coloured beer with a malty, hoppy aroma. Distinctive malty, dry flavour and aftertaste.

Moonraker (OG 1073, ABV 7.5%)
A reddish-brown beer with a strong, malty, fruity aroma. The flavour is rich and sweet, with roast malt, and the finish is fruity yet dry. Available only in a handful of outlets.

Leith Hill

Leith Hill Brewery, c/o Plough Inn, Coldharbour Lane, Coldharbour, Dorking, Surrey, RH5 6HD
Tel (01306) 711793
Fax (01306) 710055
Email theploughinn@btinternet.com
Website www.ploughinn.com
Tours by arrangement

Leith Hill was formed in 1996 using home-made equipment to produce nine-gallon brews in a room in part of the pub. A purpose-built, two-barrel plant was installed in 2001 in converted store rooms.

Crooked Furrow (OG 1040, ABV 4%)
A tangy, particularly bitter beer, with strong malt and some balancing hop flavours. Pale brown in colour with a long, dry and bitter aftertaste.

Tallywhacker (OG 1056, ABV 5.6%)
A dark, full-bodied old ale, with a strong aroma of malt and toffee. An initial burst of blackcurrant fades into a vinous flavour with malt and caramel, and an underlying sweetness. A sweet finish but a noticeable lack of bitterness throughout.

Leyden SIBA

Leyden Brewing Ltd, Lord Raglan, Nangreaves, Bury, Greater Manchester, BL9 6SP
Tel/Fax (0161) 764 6680
Email info@leydenbrewery.com
Website www.leydenbrewery.com
Tours by arrangement

A brewery built by Brian Farnworth that started production in 1999. Additional fermenting vessels have been installed, allowing a maximum production of 12 barrels a week. One pub is owned and 30 outlets are supplied. Raglan Sleeve and Forever Bury are available in filtered bottled form.

Balaclava (ABV 3.8%)

Black Pudding (ABV 3.8%)
A dark brown, creamy mild with a malty flavour, followed by a faint, balanced finish.

Nanny Flyer (OG 1040, ABV 3.8%)
A drinkable session bitter with an initial dryness, and a hint of citrus, followed by a strong, malty finish.

Light Brigade (OG 1043, ABV 4.2%)
Copper in colour with a citrus aroma. The flavour is a balance of malt, hops and fruit, with a bitter finish.

Forever Bury (ABV 4.5%)

Raglan Sleeve (OG 1047, ABV 4.6%)
Dark red/brown beer with a hoppy aroma and a dry, roasty, hoppy taste and finish.

Crowning Glory (OG 1069, ABV 6.8%)
A surprisingly smooth-tasting beer for its strength, ideal for cold winter nights.

Lidstones

See Wensleydale

Linfit

Linfit Brewery, Sair Inn, 139 Lane Top, Linthwaite, Huddersfield, West Yorkshire, HD7 5SG
Tel (01484) 842370

A 19th-century brew-pub that started brewing again in 1982, producing an impressive range of ales for sale at the pub. New plant installed in 1994 has almost doubled capacity. Beer can only be bought from the brewery. Seasonal beer: Xmas Ale (ABV 8%). Dark Mild and English Guineas Stout are suitable for vegetarians and vegans as isinglass finings are not used.

Dark Mild (OG 1032, ABV 3%) ◆
Roast grain dominates this straightforward dark mild, which has some hops in the aroma and a slightly dry flavour. Malty finish.

Bitter (OG 1035, ABV 3.7%) ◆
A refreshing session beer. A dry-hopped aroma leads to a clean-tasting, hoppy bitterness, then a long, bitter finish with a hint of malt.

Gold Medal (OG 1040, ABV 4.2%)
Very pale and hoppy. Use of the new dwarf variety of English hops, First Gold, gives an aromatic and fruity character.

Special (OG 1041, ABV 4.3%) ◆
Dry-hopping provides the aroma for this rich and mellow bitter, which has a very soft profile and character: it fills the mouth with texture rather than taste. Clean, rounded finish.

Autumn Gold (OG 1045, ABV 4.7%) ◆
Straw-coloured best bitter with hop and fruit aromas, then the bitter-sweetness of autumn fruit in the taste and the finish.

English Guineas Stout (OG 1050, ABV 5.3%) ◆
A fruity, roast aroma preludes a smooth, roasted barley, chocolaty flavour that is bitter but not too dry. Excellent appearance; good, bitter finish.

Old Eli (OG 1050, ABV 5.3%)
A well-balanced premium bitter with a dry-hopped aroma and a fruity, bitter finish.

Leadboiler (OG 1060, ABV 6.6%) ◆
Powerful malt, hop and fruit in good balance on the tongue, with a well-rounded bitter sweet finish.

Enoch's Hammer (OG 1075, ABV 8%) ◆
A straw-coloured beer with malt, hop and fruit aromas. Mouth-filling, smooth malt, hop and fruit flavours with a long, hoppy bitter finish. Dangerously drinkable.

Little Valley*

Little Valley Brewery Ltd, Turkey Lodge Farm, New Road, Cragg Vale, Hebden Bridge, West Yorkshire, HX7 5TT
Tel (01422) 883888 Fax (01422) 883222
Email info@littlevalleybrewery.co.uk
Website www.littlevalleybrewery.co.uk

The brewery, which opened in May 2005, is based in the Upper Calder Valley high above Cragg Vale. The 10-barrel plant was installed by Porter Brewing in a converted pig shed. The brewery has fulfilled a lifetime's ambition for brewer Wim van der Spek. His passion for brewing started at the age of 15 years with his first home brew. Since qualifying as a master brewer he has developed award-winning beers in his native Netherlands, in Germany and the Scottish Highlands. Season beer: Moor Ale (ABV 5.5%, autumn/winter). All the cask beers are also available in bottle-conditioned form.

Withens IPA (ABV 3.9%)
Refreshing floral hops and hints of spice, orange and citrus, with a smooth finish.

Cragg Vale Bitter (ABV 4.2%)
Rich red-brown colour with a full rounded body and a crisp and fruity character with spices and lemon.

Hebden's Wheat (ABV 4.5%)
A hazy white beer with aromas of coriander and lemon.

Stoodley Stout (ABV 4.8%)
A rich, black stout containing chocolate malt blended with oats and wheat. It has a rich and creamy roasted flavours with aromas of orange, citrus and berry.

Tod's Blonde (ABV 5%)
A bright, yellow beer with a mellow character that's lightly fruity and spicy.

Litton

Litton Ale Brewery, Queens Arms, Litton, Skipton, North Yorkshire, DB23 5QJ
Tel 07834 622632
Email queensarmslitton@amserve.net
Website www.yorkshirenet.co.uk/stayat/queensarms
Tours by arrangement

Brewing started in 2003 in a purpose-built, stone extension at the rear of the pub. Brewing liquor is sourced from a spring that provides the pub with its own water supply. The brew length is three barrels and all production is in cask form. Some 40 outlets are supplied, mainly in Yorkshire. Seasonal beer: Dark Star (ABV 4%). There are plans to produce beer in bottle-conditioned form.

Ale (OG 1038, ABV 3.8%)

Leading Light (OG 1038, ABV 3.8%)

Potts Beck (OG 1042, ABV 4.3%)

Lizard*

Lizard Ales Ltd, Unit 2A, Treskewes Industrial Estate, St Keverne, Helston, Cornwall, TR12 6PE
Tel (01326) 281135

Lizard Ales was launched by Mike Nattrass in autumn 2004. Mike – a relative of the famous 1970s Newcastle United footballer named Nattrass – was a litigation lawyer who 'wanted to switch to a more respectable profession' and spent four years assembling new and second-hand equipment. He had also been a keen home brewer. Lizard is based on a small industrial estate and has four to five regular outlets for the beer and several more on a guest beer basis.

Kernow Gold (ABV 3.7%)

Bitter (ABV 4.2%)

Loddon SIBA

Loddon Brewery Ltd, Dunsden Green Farm, Church Lane, Dunsden, Reading, Berkshire, RG4 9QD
Tel (01189) 481111
Fax (01189) 481010
Email loddonbrewery@aol.com
Website www.loddonbrewery.co.uk
Shop 8-5pm Mon-Fri, 9-1 Sat
Tours by arrangement

Loddon was established in 2003 by Chris and Vanessa Hearn between Reading and Henley-on-Thames in Oxfordshire despite the postal address. Extensive rebuilding work on a 240 year-old brick and flint barn was required in order to house the 90-barrel brewery that produces beers made with Maris Otter barley and whole hops. Chris has been in the brewing industry since 1976 and head brewer Steve Brown has 21 years' experience, most recently at Brakspear (qv). Some 172 accounts are supplied including 12 Wetherspoons and 10 Unique/Enterprise pubs. There are monthly special beers in a range of styles: see website. Seasonal beers: Bloomin' Eck (ABV 4%, Feb-March), Flight of Fancy (ABV 4.2%, April-Aug), Russet (ABV 4.5%, autumn), Hocus Pocus (ABV 4.6%, winter). Bottle-conditioned beers: Hullabaloo, Ferrymans Gold.

Kite Mild (OG 1032.8, ABV 3.2%)
A traditional medium dark mild with an aroma of roast malt.

Hoppit (OG 1035.5, ABV 3.5%)
Moderate in strength but packed with flavour. Smooth, malty body, quite bitter with the aroma and taste of East Kent Goldings.

Hullabaloo (OG 1043.8, ABV 4.2%)
A copper-coloured best bitter with rich, nutty malt balanced by the dry, herbal flavour of English Fuggles hops.

Ferrymans Gold (OG 1044.8, ABV 4.4%)
Golden, smooth body with masses of zesty, aromatic Styrian Goldings.

Bamboozle (OG 1048.8, ABV 4.8%)
A straw-coloured strong pale ale with a pure malty body and a smack of refreshing hops.

Lowes Arms

Lowes Arms Brewery, Lowes Arms, 301 Hyde Road, Denton, Manchester, M34 3FF
Tel (0161) 336 3064
Fax (0161) 285 9015
Email info@lowesarms.co.uk
Website www.lowesarms.co.uk
Shop during pub opening hours
Tours by arrangement

The brewery, known as The Lab, was set up by Peter Wood, landlord of the Lowes, who had brewed as a student, and Anthony Firmin, a keen home-brewer. The brewery is located in the cellars of the pub. It produces a range of five beers named after local landmarks and sites of interest. The brewery is a 2.5-barrel system, but two new fermenting vessels have been added to enable The Lab to brew four times a week. There are plans to wholesale the beer.

Jet Amber (OG 1040, ABV 3.5%)
Brewed for the Stockport and Manchester Mild Challenge.

IPA (ABV 3.8%)

Frog Bog (OG 1040, ABV 3.9%)
A light, easy-drinking bitter with an orange aroma and a light hoppy taste.

Sweaty Clog (ABV 4%)

Wild Wood (OG 1043, ABV 4.1%)
A spicy session bitter with a malty and fruity aroma, and spicy hop taste.

Broomstairs (OG 1043, ABV 4.3%)
A dark best bitter with distinct roast flavours and a hoppy aftertaste.

Haughton Weave (OG 1043, ABV 4.5%)
Distinct tangerine aromas in this light-coloured beer are followed by lots of bitterness and hoppy tastes in the mouth.

Loweswater

Loweswater Brewery, Kirkstile Inn, Loweswater, Cumbria, CA13 0RU
Tel (01900) 85219
Fax (01900) 85239
Email info@kirkstile.com
Website www.kirkstile.com
Tours by arrangement

The Loweswater Brewery was set up at the Kirkstile Inn in 2003 by head brewer Matt Webster. Situated in an outbuilding, the 2.5-barrel equipment came from the Tirril Brewery (qv). Brewing has re-established a tradition at the inn, which brewed 180 years ago. A second fermenting vessel has been purchased to double capacity and five barrels a week are now being produced.

Melbreak Bitter (OG 1038, ABV 3.7%)
Pale bronze with a tangy fruit and hop resins aroma, and a long, bitter finish.

Rannerdale (OG 1042, ABV 4.2%)
A fruity beer made with Goldings hops.

Grasmoor Dark Ale (OG 1043, ABV 4.3%)
Deep ruby red beer with pronounced chocolate malt on the aroma, and hop resins, roast malt and raisin fruit on the palate.

Maclay

See Belhaven

McCowans

McCowans Brewhouse, 134 Dundee Street, Edinburgh, EH11 1AF
Tel (0131) 228 8198
Fax (0131) 228 8201
Email mikelangan@hotmail.com

Opened in 1998 by Scottish & Newcastle, McCowans brewed until 2003 and was then sold to the Spirit Group. After a long fight, the pub management convinced Spirit that brewing should start again and it recommenced in 2004 with a range of Domnhul – pronounced Donnel – ales.

Domnhul Ban (ABV 3.8%)

Domnhul (ABV 4.5%)

Domnhul Dubh (ABV 4.5%)

McGuinness SIBA

Thomas McGuinness Brewing Co, Cask & Feather, 1 Oldham Road, Rochdale, Greater Manchester, OL16 1UA
Tel (01706) 711476
Fax (01706) 669654
Email tonycask@hotmail.com

Website www.mcguinnessbrewery.com
Tours by arrangement

⊗ McGuinness opened in 1991 and now averages 15-20 barrels a week. It supplies beer to its own pub and several other outlets. There are seasonal beers at ABV 3.8-4.2% plus Tommy Todd's Porter (ABV 5% ⊟) in winter.

Feather Pluckers Mild (ABV 3.4%) ◆
A dark brown beer, with roast malt dominant in the aroma and taste, with hints of chocolate. Satisfying bitter and roast finish.

Best Bitter (ABV 3.8%) ◆
Gold in colour with a hoppy aroma: a clean, refreshing beer with hop and fruit tastes and a hint of sweetness. Bitter aftertaste.

Utter Nutter (ABV 3.8%)

Special Reserve Bitter/SRB (ABV 4%) ◆
A tawny beer, sweet and malty, with underlying fruit and bitterness, and a bitter-sweet aftertaste.

Junction Bitter (ABV 4.2%) ◆
Mid-brown in colour, with a malty aroma. Maltiness is predominant throughout, with some hops and fruit in the taste and bitterness coming through in the finish.

McMullen IFBB

McMullen & Sons Ltd, 26 Old Cross, Hertford, SG14 1RD
Tel (01992) 584911
Fax (01992) 500729
Email fjmcmullen@aol.com
Website www.mcmullens.co.uk

⊗ McMullen, Hertfordshire's oldest independent brewer, founded in 1827, continues to recover from the dispute that seriously threatened the future of the company in 2003. It remains controlled by a series of trusts and the future, as an integrated brewery and pub business, appears assured. Contract brewing has now ceased and McMullen is able to benefit from reductions in duty under the government's Progressive Beer Duty scheme. In 2004 the company announced it planned to build a new brewhouse that would give it greater flexibility to produce its regular cask beers and small-volume special brews. Cask ale is served in every one of McMullen's 135 pubs in Hertfordshire, Essex and London, although all managed houses use cask breathers on all their cask beers, as do many of the tenanted pubs. McMullen also delivers to more than 50 free trade outlets. Seven or eight seasonal beers are produced each year, though these are not always available in all pubs. When not available, these beers are interspersed with cask beers from other companies.

AK (OG 1036, ABV 3.7%) ◆
A pleasant mix of malt and hops leads to a distinctive, dry aftertaste that isn't always as pronounced as it used to be.

Country Best Bitter (OG 1042, ABV 4.3%) ◆
A full-bodied beer with a well-balanced mix of malt, hops and fruit throughout.

Maldon

Maldon Brewing Co. Ltd, (also trading as Farmers Ales), The Stable Brewery, Silver Street, Maldon, Essex, CM9 4QE
Tel (01621) 840925
Email maldonbrewingco@aol.com
Website www.maldonbrewing.co.uk
Shop open for beer sales at the brewery
Tours by arrangement for small parties only

Situated in a restored stable block behind the ancient Blue Boar Hotel, the brewery started brewing in 2002 and has enjoyed considerable success, including awards at the Maldon Beer Festival. Initially a 2.5-barrel plant, this was upgraded to a five-barrel unit in 2004. Bottled beers are now available in a number of local outlets as well as direct from the brewery and this is seen as an important growth area for the future. Bottle-conditioned beers: all cask beers listed below.

A Drop of Nelson's Blood (OG 1038, ABV 3.8%) ◆
Red-hued, full-bodied beer, initially sweet, with hops and malt but, becoming very bitter in the long, complex aftertaste.

Blue Boar Bitter (OG 1040, ABV 4%) ◆
Fruity bitter whose palate packs more punch than the strength would suggest. Earthy hop tones comes through in the full, malty taste and are more dominant in the finish.

Hotel Porter (OG 1041, ABV 4.1%) ◆
An oatmeal stout rather than a porter with some sweetness to balance the roast character.

Pucks Folly (OG 1042, ABV 4.2%) ◆
Modern pale ale, brewed with Goldings rather than American hops. A vanilla/plum aroma introduces a refreshing beer in which honey and fresh peppermint are underpinned by delicate biscuity malt.

Edward Bright's Stout (OG 1048, ABV 4.8%)

Mallard SIBA

Mallard Brewery, 15 Hartington Avenue, Carlton, Nottingham, NG4 3NR
Tel/Fax (0115) 952 1289
Email phil@mallard-brewery.co.uk
Website www.mallard-brewery.co.uk
Tours by arrangement

⊗ Phil Mallard built and installed a two-barrel plant in a shed at his home and started brewing in 1995. The brewery is a mere nine square metres and contains a hot liquor tank, mash tun, copper, and three fermenters. Since 1995 production has risen from one barrel a week to between six or eight barrels, which is the plant's maximum. Phil has no plans at present to expand and now supplies around 14 outlets, of which seven are on a regular weekly basis. He has also launched a small-scale bottling enterprise and plans to produce bottled beers as limited editions supplied direct from the brewery by mail order. Seasonal beer: Waddlers Mild (ABV 3.7%, spring), DA (ABV 5.8%, Jan-March), Quismas Quacker (ABV 6%, December).

Duck 'n' Dive (OG 1039, ABV 3.7%)
A light, single-hopped beer made from the hedgerow hop, First Gold. A bitter beer with a hoppy nose, good bitterness on the palate and a dry finish.

Quacker Jack (OG 1040, ABV 4%)

Feather Light (OG 1040, ABV 4.1%)
A very pale lager-style bitter with a floral bouquet and sweetness on the palate. A light, hoppy session beer.

Duckling (OG 1041, ABV 4.2%)
A crisp refreshing bitter with a hint of honey and citrus flavour. Dry hopped.

Spittin' Feathers (OG 1044, ABV 4.4%)
A mellow, ruby bitter with a complex malt flavour of chocolate, toffee and coffee, complemented with a full and fruity/hoppy aftertaste.

Drake (OG 1045, ABV 4.5%)
A full-bodied premium bitter, with malt and hops on the palate, and a fruity finish.

Owd Duck (OG 1048, ABV 4.8%)
A dark ruby bitter with a smooth mellow smoky flavour and fruity finish.

Friar Duck (OG 1050, ABV 5%)
A pale, full malt beer, hoppy with a hint of blackcurrant flavour.

Duck 'n' Disorderly (OG 1050, ABV 5%)

Malton SIBA

Malton Brewery t/a Suddabys (Malton) Ltd, Crown Hotel, 12 Wheelgate, Malton, North Yorkshire, YO17 7HP
Tel (01653) 697580
Fax (01653) 691812
Email enquiries@suddabys.co.uk
Website www.suddabys.com

⊗ Malton is not currently brewing while a bigger site is sought. The main beers are brewed at Hambleton (qv) while Brown Cow (qv) brews short run and speciality beers.

Malvern Hills SIBA

Malvern Hills Brewery Ltd, 15 West Malvern Road, Great Malvern, Worcestershire, WR14 4ND
Tel (01684) 560165
Fax (01684) 577336
Email mhb.ales@tiscali.co.uk
Website www.malvernhillsbrewery.co.uk
Tours by arrangement

⊗ The brewery was founded in 1997 in an old dynamite store on the northern slopes of the Malvern Hills. The business now has some 40 regular outlets and is an established presence at many beer festivals. Almost all sales are made direct to pubs, with little use made of wholesalers. Beer names commemorate landmarks on the Malvern Hills or local people. Mr Phoebus, the latest addition to the range, is named after Edward Elgar's bicycle. Moel Bryn (Welsh for Bare Hill) is the new name for Malvern Hills Bitter. Seasonal beer: Dr Gully's Winter Ale (ABV 5.2%).

Red Earl (OG 1037, ABV 3.7%) ◆
A very light beer that does not overpower the senses. With a hint of apple fruit, it is ideal for slaking the thirst.

Moel Bryn (OG 1039, ABV 3.9%)

Swedish Nightingale (OG 1040, ABV 4%)

Worcestershire Whym (OG 1042, ABV 4.2%)

Black Pear (OG 1044, ABV 4.4%) ◆
A sharp citrus hoppiness is the main constituent of this golden brew that has a long, dry aftertaste.

Black Country Wobble (OG 1045, ABV 4.5%) ◆
A sharp, clean-tasting golden beer with an aroma of hops challenged by fruit and malt, which hold up well in the mouth. A bitter dryness grows as the contrasting sweetness subsides.

Mr Phoebus (OG 1047, ABV 4.7%)

Mansfield

See Wolverhampton & Dudley in New Nationals section

Marble SIBA

Marble Beers Ltd, 73 Rochdale Road, Manchester, M4 4HY
Tel/Fax (0161) 819 2694
Email enquiries@marblebeers.co.uk
Website www.marblebeers.co.uk
Tours by arrangement

The Marble Brewery was designed by brewmaster Brendan Dobbin and opened in the Marble Arch inn in 1997. As a result of the success of the brewery and a request to brew an organic beer for the Manchester Food Festival, the brewery has now gone totally organic and vegan, and is registered with the Soil Association and the Vegetarian Society. The five-barrel plant operates at full capacity, producing five regular beers plus seasonal brews. Two pubs are owned and four outlets are supplied. Seasonal beers: Chorlton-cum-Hazy (ABV 3.8%), Cloudy Marble (ABV 4%), Uncut Amber (ABV 4.7%), Port Stout (ABV 4.7%), Chocolate (ABV 5.5%).

Bitter (OG 1039.5, ABV 3.9%) ◆
Dark yellow in colour, with a hoppy, fruity nose. Citrus fruit and bitter hop in the mouth and finish.

Cloudy Marble (OG 1040, ABV 4%) ◆
Amber in colour, with a hoppy/fruity nose. Hops, fruit and bitterness in the mouth, with quite a strong bitter finish.

Manchester Bitter (OG 1042, ABV 4.2%) ◆
Yellow beer with a hoppy aroma. A balance of malt, hops and fruit on the palate, with a hoppy and bitter aftertaste.

Ginger Marble (OG 1045, ABV 4.5%)

Lagonda IPA (OG 1048, ABV 5%)
A classic pale ale with immense citrus and floral hop notes balanced against a dry bitter finish.

Marches

Marches Brewing Co, The Old Hop Kiln, Claston, Dormington, Herefordshire, HR1 4EA
Tel (01584) 878999

⊗ Brewing restarted at Marches in 2004 at the new Herefordshire Food & Drink Centre. The brewery is now housed in two converted hop kilns. Beer is mostly brewed for owner Paul Harris's two shops (one in Ludlow and one next to the new brewery) although he does supply some 20 local pubs. Paul works closely with hop growers to develop traditional beer styles and produces single-varietal beers using new varieties of hops; he is also involved with the tourism and information aspects of the new Food & Drink Centre, including promoting beer with food. A new bottling line is to be installed.

Dormington Gold (OG 1044, ABV 4.5%)
A light golden bitter brewed using First Gold hedgerow hops. It has an intense bitterness with a citrus zest.

Marston Moor

Marston Moor Brewery Ltd, PO Box 9, York, YO26 7XW
Tel (01423) 359641
email info@marstonmoor.breweryco.uk

◎ A small brewery established in 1983 by Peter Smith. The business was purchased by Rudgate Brewery in 2005 enabling Peter to devote more time to building brewing plant and associated equipment. The current range of beers will be retained with the development of further seasonal/special beers. There are 100-plus outlets currently served.

Cromwell Bitter (ABV 3.8%) ◆
A golden beer with hops and fruit in strong evidence on the nose. Bitterness as well as fruit and hops dominate the taste and long aftertaste.

Mongrel (ABV 4%)

Brewers Pride (OG 1041, ABV 4.2%) ◆
A light but somewhat thin, fruity beer, with a hoppy, bitter aftertaste.

Merrie Maker (OG 1044, ABV 4.5%)

Brewers Droop (OG 1048, ABV 5%)
A pale, robust ale with hops and fruit notes in prominence. A long, bitter aftertaste.

Marston's

See Wolverhampton & Dudley in New Nationals section

Mash SIBA

⌂ Mash Ltd, 19-21 Great Portland Street, London, W1W 8QB
Tel (0207) 637 5555
Fax (0207) 637 7333
Tours by arrangement

The micro-brewery is the centrepiece of the Mash bar and restaurant. The American-style brewery can be toured to inspect the process at close hand and the restaurant provides a tutored lunch or dinner where the beers are matched to food. The beers are not cask conditioned but are stored in cellar tanks using a CO2 system. Regular beer: Mash Wheat (ABV 5.2%). Other beers include a Blackcurrant Porter, Scotch, IPA, Peach, Extra Stout and Pils.

Mauldons SIBA EAB

Mauldons Ltd, The Black Adder Brewery, 13 Churchfield Road, Sudbury, Suffolk, CO10 2YA
Tel (01787) 311055
Fax (01787) 379538
Email sims@mauldons.co.uk
Website www.mauldons.co.uk
Shop Mon-Fri 9.30-4pm
Tours by arrangement

⊗ The Mauldon family started brewing in Sudbury in 1795. The brewery with 26 pubs was bought by Greene King in the 1960s. The current business, established in 1982, was bought by Steve and Alison Sims – both former employees of Adnams – in 2000. They relocated to a new brewery in January 2005, with a 30-barrel plant that has doubled production. There is also a brewery shop. Some 200 outlets are supplied. There is a rolling programme of seasonal beers: see website. Bottle-conditioned beers: Suffolk Pride, Bah Humbug (ABV 4.9%), Black Adder.

Mild (OG 1035, ABV 3.5%)
Malt, liquorice, chocolate and molasses dominate the aroma and palate but there is a strong hop presence.

Bitter (OG 1036, ABV 3.6%)
A traditional session bitter with a strong floral nose and lingering, bitter finish.

Moletrap Bitter (OG 1038, ABV 3.8%) ◆
A well-balanced session beer with a crisp, hoppy bitterness balancing sweet malt.

Pickwick (OG 1042, ABV 4.2%)
A best bitter with a rich, rounded malt flavour with ripe aromas of hops and fruit. A bitter-sweet finish.

Suffolk Pride (OG 1048, ABV 4.8%) ◆
A full-bodied strong bitter. The malt and fruit in the aroma are reflected in the taste, and there is some hop character in the finish. Deep tawny/red in colour.

Black Adder (OG 1053, ABV 5.3%) ◆
A dark stout. Roast malt is strong in the aroma and taste, but malt, hop and bitterness provide an excellent balance and a lingering finish.

White Adder (OG 1053, ABV 5.3%) ◆
A pale brown, almost golden, strong ale. A warming, fruity flavour dominates and lingers into a dry, hoppy finish.

Suffolk Comfort (OG 1066, ABV 6.6%)
A powerful peppery Goldings aroma with malt

notes. There is a rich balance of crystal malt and hops in the mouth with a long, malty finish.

Mayfields*

Mayfields Brewery, Mayfields, Bishop Frome, Worcestershire, WR6 5AS
Tel (01531) 640015
Email themayfieldsbrewery@yahoo.co.uk

Brothers James and Tom Lewis started brewing in May 2005 on a five-barrel plant in an 18th-century hop kiln. The site was previously used by Frome Valley Brewery. James learnt the brewing skills at Teignworthy. The brothers use hops grown on their own farm.

Pioneer (ABV 3.9%)

Drovers Delight (ABV 4.3%)

Mayflower

Mayflower Brewery, Mayflower House, 15 Longendale Road, Standish, Wigan, Greater Manchester, WN6 0UE
Tel (01257) 400605
Email info@mayflowerbrewery.co.uk
Website www.mayflowerbrewery.co.uk

Mayflower was established in 2000 at the Worthington Lake industrial estate in Standish. Due to the demolition of the original site, the brewery has been relocated to the Royal Oak in Wigan. The premises are much smaller but the original vessels and casks are still used. The Royal Oak is supplied as well as a number of other outlets in and around Wigan. Seasonal beers: Oakey Cokey (ABV 8%, winter), A Winter's Ale (ABV 5.5%, winter), Cuckoo Spit (ABV 4.4%, spring).

Black Diamond (OG 1033.5, ABV 3.4%)

Dark Oak (OG 1034, ABV 3.5%)

Myles Best Bitter (OG 1036, ABV 3.7%)

Best Bitter (OG 1037, ABV 3.8%)

Light Oak (OG 1038, ABV 4%)

Special Branch (OG 1038, ABV 4%)

Wigan Bier (OG 1039.5, ABV 4.2%)

Maypole SIBA

Maypole Brewery, North Laithes Farm, Wellow Road, Eakring, Newark, Nottinghamshire, NG22 0AN
Tel (07971) 277598/07947 242683
Tours by arrangement

⊗ The brewery was founded in 1995 in a converted 18th-century farm building. After changing hands in 2001 it was bought in 2005 by the former head brewer and the owner of the Eight Jolly Brewers pub in Gainsborough, Lincolnshire. Maypole beers are always available at the Eight Jolly Brewers and the Beehive, Maplebeck. Some 50 other outlets are supplied on an occasional basis. A range of seasonal and occasional beers is produced. The beer range is likely to grow.

May Day Mild (ABV 3.5%)

May Fly Bitter (ABV 3.8%)

Mayfair (ABV 4.1%)

Maybee (ABV 4.3%)

Wellow Gold/Mae West (ABV 4.6%)
A blond, Belgian-style wheat beer where citrus flavours dominate the nose and palate. A deceptively drinkable beer for its strength. It sells under the Mae West name in some outlets.

Ghost Train (ABV 4.7%)
A smooth black porter, with a slight sweetness to begin with, giving way to a bitter finish.

Mayhem (ABV 5%)

Meantime SIBA

Meantime Brewing Co Ltd, 2 Penhall Road, Greenwich, London, SE7 8RX
Tel (020) 8293 1111
Fax (020) 8293 4004
Email sales@meantimebrewing.co.uk
Website www.meantimebrewing.com
Tours by arrangement

⊗ Brewing started in 2000 and has been at full capacity ever since, despite trebling its output. It was the only British brewery to win any medals at the World Beer Cup in 2004. Meantime specialises in properly matured beers and produces traditional Continental styles as well as innovative new flavours. One pub is owned in Greenwich with further additions to come. Meantime launched its first cask ale in 2003. Bottle-conditioned beers: Bavarian-style Wheat Beer (ABV 5%), Raspberry Beer (ABV 5%), Strawberry (ABV 5%). Sainsbury's Organic Lager is suitable for vegetarians and vegans.

Late Hopped Blonde Ale (ABV 4.5%)

Meesons*

⚲ **Meesons Brewery, Masons Arms, 2 Quarry School Place, Headington, Oxford, OX3 8LH**
Tel (01865) 764579

A pub-brewery with a one-barrel plant that was previously at Bitter End. Trial brews were taking place during the summer of 2005 and the beer range had not been formulated as the guide went to press.

Melbourn

Melbourn Bros Brewery, 22 All Saints Street, Stamford, Lincolnshire, PE9 2PA
Tel (01780) 752186
Email info@melbournbrothers.co.uk
Website www.melbournbrothers.co.uk

A famous Stamford brewery that opened in 1825 and closed in 1974. It re-opened in 1994 and is owned by Samuel Smith of Tadcaster (qv). Melbourn brews spontaneously fermented fruit beers primarily for the American market but which can be ordered by the case in Britain by mail order. The beers are Apricot, Cherry and Strawberry (all ABV 3.4%). The brewery is open for tours Wednesday to Sunday 10am-4pm and there are open evenings for brewery tours, and beer and food tastings: prior booking essential.

Merlin*

Merlin Brewery Ltd, Unit 12, Victoria Street Industrial Estate, Victoria Street, Leigh, Greater Manchester, WN7 5SE
Tel (01942) 262950

Merlin first brewed in December 2004. The brewery is run by Don and Ann Wyatt who had brewed beer and wine at home for some years. They have a 2.5-barrel plant.

Astley Gold (ABV 3.8%)

King's Ransom (ABV 4%)

Three Rivers (ABV 4%)

Vision (ABV 4.2%)

Cannonball (ABV 5%)

Legacy (ABV 5%)

Mersea Island*

Mersea Island Brewery, Mersea Island Vineyard, Rewsalls Lane, East Mersea, Colchester, Essex, CO5 8SX
Tel (01206) 385900
Fax (01206) 383600
Email beer@merseawine.com
Website www.merseawine.com
Shop 11-5pm daily, closed Tuesday
Tours by arrangement

A new brewery that started production in January 2005, producing cask- and bottle-conditioned beers. The beers are available from an on-site shop and also served in a café.

Mud Mild (OG 1035, ABV 3.6%)

Yo Boy Bitter (OG 1038, ABV 3.8%)

Skippers Bitter (OG 1047, ABV 4.8%)

Mighty Oak SIBA

Mighty Oak Brewing Co Ltd, 14B, West Station Yard, Spital Road, Maldon, Essex, CM9 7TW
Tel (01621) 843713
Fax (01621) 840914
Email info@mightyoakbrewery.co.uk
Website www.mightyoakbrewery.co.uk
Shop 8.30-5pm
Tours by arrangement

⊗ Founded in 1996 by former Ind Coope Romford employee John Boyce and his partner Ruth O'Neill, a management accountant, Mighty Oak continues to grow. The beers are delivered to around 200 pubs in Essex and the surrounding counties of Bedfordshire, Hertfordshire and Kent, plus North and East London. Mighty Oak Ales are available from other breweries around the country through beer swaps and an increasing number of wholesalers. Each year the brewery produces a range of monthly ales based on a theme; the theme for 2005 was sport and included Maiden Over and Load of Old Bails.

IPA (OG 1036.1, ABV 3.6%)
Delicate honey and vanilla tones complement a moderate bitterness in this well-balanced, amber session beer.

Oscar Wilde (OG 1039.5, ABV 3.7%)
Flavoursome dark red mild, with hints of blackberry and coconut on the nose, and liquorice and coffee balancing the malty taste. The finish displays more bitterness but fruit and caramel persist. (In Cockney rhyming slang, Oscar Wilde means Mild.)

Maldon Gold (OG 1039.5, ABV 3.8%)
Honey and bubblegum dominate the aroma of this fruity golden ale. Sweet pineapple in the taste yields to a drier finish in which malt and hops are well balanced.

Burntwood Bitter (OG 1040.9, ABV 4%)
Full-bodied tawny beer with more roast character than many bitters. A spicy hop character complements the suggestions of fresh coffee and robust maltiness.

Simply The Best (OG 1044.1, ABV 4.4%)
Complex and fruity best bitter with a solid, meaty taste.

English Oak (OG 1047.9, ABV 4.8%)
Copper-coloured strong bitter with a full body dominated by malt and a reasonable level of bitterness. The hoppy aroma also has a trace of vanilla.

Saxon Strong Ale (OG 1063.6, ABV 6.5%)

Milestone*

Milestone Brewing Co, Old Great North Road, Cromwell, Newark, Nottinghamshire, NG23 6JE
Tel (01636) 822255
Fax (01636) 822200
Email info@milestonebrewery.co.uk
Website www.milestonebrewery.co.uk
Tours by arrangement

Milestone was established by the owners of Maypole Brewery, which has since been sold. Production started in January 2005 using brewing equipment purchased from the Tipperary Brewing Company. A new range of beers will be developed, while production of two former Maypole beers, Lions Pride and Loxley Ale, has been switched to Milestone. Some 50 outlets are supplied.

Hoptimism (ABV 3.6%)

Lions Pride (ABV 3.8%)
Copper-coloured session beer.

Loxley Ale (ABV 4.2%)
A light golden ale.

Black Pearl (ABV 4.3%)
Irish-style stout

Crusader (ABV 4.4%)
Belgian-style blond beer.

Rich Ruby (ABV 4.5%)
A ruby-red beer.

Imperial Pale Ale (ABV 4.8%)

Milk Street SIBA

Milk Street Brewery, The Griffin, 25 Milk Street, Frome, Somerset, BA11 3DB
Tel (01373) 467766
Tours by arrangement

The brewery was commissioned in 1999 and has a capacity of 20 barrels a week. Four beers are brewed, with seasonal brands every two months. Milk Street owns three pubs and plans to expand. 50 other outlets are supplied. (NB The Griffin, home to the brewery, is not open until 5pm.) Seasonal beer: Zig-Zag Stout (ABV 4.5% (Oct-Feb).

Gulp (OG 1036, ABV 3.5%)
An amber beer that is fresh and lively on the palate. The aroma is reminiscent of grapefruit peel and freshly-picked hawthorn leaves.

Funky Monkey (OG 1041, ABV 4%)

Mermaid (OG 1042, ABV 4.1%)

Amarillo (OG 1044, ABV 4.3%)

Nick's (OG 1045, ABV 4.4%)
A clean-drinking bitter, refreshing with an excellent balance of malt flavours.

Beer (OG 1051, ABV 5%)

Elderfizz (OG 1051, ABV 5%)

Millis

Millis Brewing Co Ltd, St Margaret's Farm, St Margaret's Road, South Darenth, Dartford, Kent, DA4 9LB
Tel/Fax (01474) 566903
Email john@millis-brewing.com
Website www.millis-brewing.co.uk

⊗ John Millis started with a half-barrel brew-length plant in a specially designed brewery at his home in Gravesend. Demand outstripped the facility and Millis moved in 2003 to a new site – a former World War II cold store – with a 10-barrel plant. He now regularly supplies some 35-40 clubs and pubs within a 50-mile radius. Seasonal beers Gravesend Guzzler (ABV 3.7, April-Sept), Winter Witch (ABV 4.8%, Oct-March).

Tuggies Dark Mild (ABV 3.5%)
A traditional dark mild with chocolate and roasted notes.

Oast Shovellers Bitter (ABV 3.9%)
A copper-coloured ale with a pale and crystal malt base, ending with a distinctive, clean finish.

Dartford Wobbler (ABV 4.3%)
A tawny-coloured, full-bodied best bitter with complex malt and hop flavours and a long, clean, slightly roasted finish.

Ginger Freak (ABV 4.3%)

Golden Export Ale (ABV 4.3%)
A full-bodied, straw-coloured premium beer.

Kentish Red Ale (ABV 4.3%)
A traditional red ale with complex malt, hops and fruit notes.

Raspberry Rumpus (ABV 4.3%)

Thieves and Fakirs (ABV 4.3%)
A full-bodied beer with fruit, hops and malt notes, with a long, clean finish.

Millstone SIBA

Millstone Brewery Ltd, Unit 4, Vale Mill, Micklehurst Road, Mossley, Greater Manchester, OL5 9JL
Tel/Fax (01457) 835835
Email info@millstonebrewery.co.uk
Website www.millstonebrewery.co.uk
Tours by arrangement

Established in 2003 by Nick Boughton and Jon Hunt, the brewery is located in an 18th-century textile mill. The range has been extended to include six regular and three seasonal beers; most are available in bottles. Some 100 plus outlets are supplied. Seasonal beers: Summer Daze (ABV 4.1%), Autumn Leaves (ABV 4.3%), Christmas Ruby (ABV 4.7%). Bottle-conditioned beers: Three Shires Bitter, Windy Miller, Grain Storm, Millstone Edge, Autumn Leaves, Christmas Ruby.

A Millers Ale (OG 1039, ABV 3.8%)

Three Shires Bitter (OG 1040, ABV 4%)
A pale, hoppy beer, with fruity aromas derived from three hop varieties.

Windy Miller (OG 1042, ABV 4.1%)

Grain Storm (OG 1043, ABV 4.2%)

Millstone Edge (OG 1044, ABV 4.4%)
A copper-coloured, traditional best bitter.

True Grit (OG 1050, ABV 5%)

Milton SIBA EAB

Milton Brewery Cambridge Ltd, 111 Norman Industrial Estate, Cambridge Road, Milton, Cambridgeshire, CB4 6AT
Tel (01223) 226198
Fax (01223) 226199
Email enquiries@miltonbrewery.co.uk
Website www.miltonbrewery.co.uk
Tours by arrangement

⊗ The brewery has grown steadily since it was founded in 1999. More than 100 outlets are supplied, usually within one hour of Cambridge. The flagship beer, Pegasus, was a CAMRA Beer of the Year for 2003. Now with three tied houses (Peterborough and London), further expansion is being carried out to cope with demand. Seasonal beer: Mammon (ABV 7%, from December) ■.

Minotaur (OG 1035, ABV 3.3%)
Rich and very full-bodied for its strength, a malty chocolatyness predominates, but vanilla and liquorice flavours also surface.

Jupiter (OG 1037, ABV 3.5%)
A light malty aroma and a delicate hoppy palate lead to a bitter finish. A light barley sugar aroma and taste underpin this amber session bitter

Neptune (OG 1039, ABV 3.8%)
Delicious hop aromas introduce this well-balanced, nutty and refreshing copper-coloured ale. Good hoppy finish.

Pegasus (OG 1043, ABV 4.1%)
Clean-tasting amber best bitter with a malty, fruity and slightly sulphury start, augmented by a gentle mix of hops and toffee in the mouth that persists in the sustained bitter ending.

Electra (OG 1046, ABV 4.5%)
A restrained bitter and hoppy backbone with short, sweet, fruity undertones and a light malt flavour after a gentle, fruity aroma. This full-bodied amber premium bitter ends with a persistent hop bitterness.

Cyclops (OG 1055, ABV 5.3%)
Deep copper-coloured ale, with a rich hoppy aroma and full body; fruit and malt notes develop in the finish.

Moles SIBA

Moles Brewery, Merlin Way, Bowerhill Trading Estate, Melksham, Wiltshire, SN12 6TJ
Tel (01225) 704734/708842
Fax (01225) 790770
Email salesdesk@molesbrewery.com
Website www.molesbrewery.com
Shop 9-5 Mon-Fri. Tours by arrangement

Moles has been brewing at Bowerhill since 1982 and has bought two pubs in its home town of Melksham. The traditionally brewed, all Wiltshire malt beers, balanced with bitterness from Kent hops, can now be drunk within shouting distance of the brewery, as well as nationwide. 14 pubs are owned, all serving cask beer. 150 outlets are supplied. Seasonal beers: Barleymole (ABV 4.2%, summer), Molegrip (ABV 4.3%, autumn), Holy Moley (ABV 4.7%, spring), Moel Moel (ABV 6%, winter).

Tap Bitter (OG 1035, ABV 3.5%)
A session bitter with a smooth, malty flavour and clean bitter finish.

Best Bitter (OG 1040, ABV 4%)
A well-balanced, amber-coloured bitter, clean, dry and malty with some bitterness, and delicate floral hop flavour.

Landlords Choice (OG 1045, ABV 4.5%)
A dark, strong, smooth porter beer, with a rich fruity palate and malty finish.

Molennium (OG 1045, ABV 4.5%)
There are fruit, caramel and malty overtones in the aroma of this deep amber-coloured ale, balanced by a pleasant bitterness in the taste.

Rucking Mole (OG 1045, ABV 4.5%)

Molecatcher (OG 1050, ABV 5%)
A copper-coloured ale with a delightfully spicy hop aroma and taste, and a long bitter finish.

Moonstone

Moonstone Brewery (Gem Taverns Ltd), The Ministry of Ale, 9 Trafalgar Street, Burnley, Lancashire, BB11 1TQ
Tel (01282) 830909
Email meet@ministryofale.co.uk
Website www.moonstonebrewery.co.uk
Tours by arrangement

A small, 2.5-barrel brewery, based in the Ministry of Ale pub. Brewing started in 2001 and beer is only generally available in the pub. Owner Mick Jaques occasionally brews other beers. Seasonal: Red Jasper (ABV 6%, winter).

Black Star (OG 1037, ABV 3.4%)

Tigers Eye (OG 1037, ABV 3.8%)

Dark (OG 1040, ABV 4.2%)

Moor SIBA

Moor Beer Co, Whitley Farm, Ashcott, Bridgwater, Somerset, TA7 9QW
Tel/Fax (01458) 210050
Email arthur@moorbeer.co.uk
Website www.moorbeer.co.uk
Tours by arrangement

Moor has been brewing since 1996 when farmer Arthur Frampton and his wife Annette swapped beef for beer and set up a brewery on their former dairy farm. It is now a 10-barrel operation with Arthur's daughter Holly doing the brewing. The brewery also runs a successful beer wholesaling business. The brewery triumphed in the CAMRA Winter Beer of Britain competition in 2004 with Old Freddy Walker; it was also named CAMRA Somerset's Beer of the Festival at Minehead in 2004. Seasonal beers: Santa Moors (ABV 4%). There are many monthly specials with a rail theme. Bottle-conditioned beers: Old Freddy Walker, Peat Porter, Merlin's Magic.

Withy Cutter (OG 1040, ABV 3.8%)
A lightly malty, pale brown beer with a moderately bitter finish.

Avalon (OG 1041, ABV 4%)

Merlin's Magic (OG 1044, ABV 4.3%)
Dark amber-coloured, complex, full-bodied beer, with fruity notes.

Peat Porter (OG 1045, ABV 4.5%)
Dark brown/black beer with an initially fruity taste leading to roast malt with a little bitterness. A slightly sweet malty finish.

Somerland Gold (OG 1052, ABV 5%)

Old Freddy Walker (OG 1074, ABV 7.3%)
Rich, dark, strong ale with a fruity complex taste, leaving a fruitcake finish. Champion Winter Beer of Britain 2004.

Moorcock*

Moorcock Brewing Co, Hawes Rural Workshop Estate, Brunt Acres Road, Hawes, Cumbria, DL8 3UZ
Tel (01969) 666188
Email info@moorcockinn.com
Website www.moorcockinn.com

The brewery was launched in January 2005. The plant was originally located at the Moorcock inn in Garsdale, but has been moved five miles away to an industrial unit in Hawes. Mark Owens was the landlord of the Moorcock for three years and was always keen to brew. He opened with a 2.5-barrel kit from Moss Brew but within five months had to upgrade to five barrels. He currently supplies only the Moorcock.

Garsdale (ABV 3.2%)

OPA (ABV 3.8%)

Mescan's Porter (ABV 4.3%)

Hail Ale (ABV 4.8%)

1888 (ABV 5%)

Moorhouses SIBA

Moorhouses Brewery (Burnley) Ltd, The Brewery, Moorhouse Street, Burnley, Lancashire, BB11 5EN
Tel (01282) 422864/416004
Fax (01282) 838493
Email info@moorhouses.co.uk
Website www.moorhouses.co.uk
Tours by arrangement

Established in 1865 as a drinks manufacturer, the brewery started brewing cask-conditioned ale in 1978 and has achieved recognition by winning more international and CAMRA awards than any other brewery of its size. Two new additional 30-barrel fermenters were installed in 2004, taking production to 320 barrels a week maximum. The company owns six pubs, all serving cask-conditioned beer, and supplies some 250 free trade outlets. There is a selection of seasonal ales throughout the year: see website. The brewery celebrated 140 years of brewing in June 2005 with a steam train extravaganza.

Black Cat (OG 1036, ABV 3.4%)
A dark, complex ale with a faint roast coffee aroma. Roast, liquorice and fruit flavours predominate over a malty base. The finish is quite bitter with the roast flavour lingering on.

Premier Bitter (OG 1036, ABV 3.7%)
A clean and satisfying bitter aftertaste rounds off this well-balanced hoppy, amber session bitter.

Pride of Pendle (OG 1040, ABV 4.1%)
A fine balance of malt and hops gives this copper-coloured beer a long, dry and extremely satisfying finish.

Blond Witch (OG 1045, ABV 4.5%)

Pendle Witches Brew (OG 1050, ABV 5.1%)
A distinctive amber-coloured strong bitter with a faint malt and hop aroma. The taste is full-bodied and malty with honey-sweet overtones. The finish is increasingly hoppy, dry and bitter.

Mordue SIBA

Mordue Brewery, Units D1 and D2, Narvic Way, Tyne Tunnel Estate, North Shields, Tyne & Wear, NE29 7XJ
Tel/Fax (0191) 2961879
Email enquiries@morduebrewery.com
Website www.morduebrewery.com
Shop Please telephone
Tours by arrangement

The original Mordue Brewery closed in 1879 and the name was revived in 1995 by two brothers, Garry and Matthew Fawson. Workie Ticket won the Champion Beer of Britain competition in 1997. In 1998, a 20-barrel plant and a move to bigger premises allowed production to keep pace with demand. By 2005 the business had expanded to the point where another move became necessary. Mordue is now located on a large estate that will enable the brewery to realise its potential. The full range of Mordue beers is distributed nationally and 150 outlets are supplied by the brewery. An export market in Denmark is opening up. Seasonal beers: Summer Tyne (ABV 3.6%), Millennium Bridge Ale (ABV 3.8%), Spring Tyne (ABV 4%), Autumn Tyne (ABV 4%), A'l Wheat Pet (ABV 4.1%), Headmasters Xmas Sermon (ABV 5.2%), Zehn Dunkel (ABV 5.8%).

Five Bridge Bitter (OG 1038, ABV 3.8%)
Crisp, golden beer with a good hint of hops. The bitterness carries on in the finish. A good session bitter.

Geordie Pride (OG 1042, ABV 4.2%)
Well-balanced and hoppy with a long, bitter finish.

Workie Ticket (OG 1045, ABV 4.5%)
Complex, tasty bitter with plenty of malt and hops and a long, satisfying, bitter finish.

Radgie Gadgie (OG 1048, ABV 4.8%)
Strong, easy-drinking bitter with plenty of fruit and hops.

IPA (OG 1051, ABV 5.1%)
Easy-drinking, golden ale with plenty of hops. The bitterness carries on into the finish.

Morrells

See Burtonwood

Moulin

Moulin Brewery, Baledmund Road, Pitlochry, Perthshire, PH16 5EW
Tel (01796) 472196
Fax (01796) 474098
Email enquiries@moulinhotel.co.uk

Website www.moulinhotel.co.uk
Shop 12-3 daily. Tours by arrangement
Tours by prior arrangement

☺ The brewery opened in 1995 to celebrate the Moulin Hotel's 300th anniversary. Two pubs are owned and four outlets are supplied. Bottle-conditioned beer: Ale of Atholl.

Light (OG 1036, ABV 3.7%) ◆
Thirst-quenching, straw-coloured session beer, with a light, hoppy, fruity balance, ending with a gentle, hoppy sweetness.

Braveheart (OG 1039, ABV 4%) ◆
An amber bitter, with a delicate balance of malt and fruit and a Scottish-style sweetness.

Ale of Atholl (OG 1043.5, ABV 4.5%) ◆
A reddish, quaffable, malty ale, with a solid body and a mellow finish.

Old Remedial
(OG 1050.5, ABV 5.2%) ◆
A distinctive and satisfying dark brown old ale, with roast malt to the fore and tannin in a robust taste.

Nags Head

Nags Head Inn, Abercych, Boncath, Pembrokeshire, SA37 0HJ
Tel (01239) 841200

Pub-brewery producing just one beer for its own customers and two other outlets.

Old Emrys (OG 1038-40, ABV 3.8-4%)

Naylors*

Naylor's Brewery, c/o Old White Bear, 6 Keighley Road, Crosshills, Keighley, West Yorkshire, BD20 7RN
Tel (01535) 632115
Fax (01535) 634875
Email naylorsbrewery@oldwhitebear.go-legend.net

After selling their business interest in the Old Bear Brewery, the Naylor brothers set up their own plant with a Porter Brewing Company bespoke eight-barrel plant. Beer is initially only on sale at the Old White Bear. It is a tied house and part of Enterprise Inns that has an old Whitbread lease with the guest ale provision.

Best Bitter (OG 1038, ABV 3.8%)

Nelson

Nelson Brewing Co Ltd, Unit 2, Building 64, Historic Dockyard, Chatham, Kent, ME4 4TE
Tel (01634) 832828
Fax (01634) 832278
Email enquiries@nelsonbrewingcompanyltd.com
Shop 8-5pm
Tours by arrangement

⊗ Located in Chatham's preserved Georgian dockyard, Nelson – originally Flagship – distributes to 150 regular outlets with further supplies available via wholesalers and other breweries. Seasonal beers: Spring Pride (ABV 4.4%, Powder Monkey (ABV 4.4%), Moby Dick (ABV 4.4%, Frigging Yuletide (ABV 5.5%.

Victory Mild (OG 1036, ABV 3.5%)

Rochester Bitter (OG 1038, ABV 3.7%)

Admiral's Bitter (OG 1037, ABV 3.8%)

Trafalgar Bitter (OG 1039, ABV 4.1%)

Ensign (OG 1040, ABV 4.2%)

Spanker (OG 1040, ABV 4.2%)

Friggin in the Riggin (OG 1048, ABV 4.7%)
A premium bitter with a smooth malt flavour and a bitter-sweet aftertaste.

Crow's Nest (OG 1047, ABV 4.8%)
A straw-coloured, sweet and fruity ale with a hoppy aroma.

Futtock (OG 1055, ABV 5.2%)
A fruity, ruby-coloured ale, with a roast malt aftertaste.

Nelson's Blood (OG 1062, ABV 6%)

Nelson's Blood Extra (OG 1070, ABV 7.1%)

Nethergate SIBA EAB

Nethergate Brewery Co Ltd, The Street Brewery and Wine Cellars, Pentlow, Cavendish, Suffolk, CO10 7JJ
Tel (01787) 283220
Fax (01787) 283221
Email orders@nethergate.co.uk
Website www.nethergatebrewery.co.uk
Tours by arrangement

⊗ Nethergate Brewery was established at Clare, in Suffolk. Production tripled in the 1990s, but the brewery was unable to meet demand and in February 2005 moved four miles away to a new site to enable production to double. Some 380 outlets are supplied. Seasonal beers: Brewers Drop (ABV 4.6%, January), Wild Fox (ABV 4.3%, February), Hares Breadth (ABV 4.4%, March), Mad Bob (ABV 4.1%, April), Painted Lady (ABV 4.2%, May), Dr John's Panacea (ABV 4.3%, June), Old Chap (ABV 4.2%, July), Crossborder (ABV 4.1%, August), Azzarat (ABV 4.4%, September), Monks Habit (ABV 4.2%, October), Greedy Pike (ABV 4.2%, November), Dirty Dick (ABV 5.2%, December).

IPA (OG 1036, ABV 3.5%) ◆
This amber-coloured session bitter is clean, crisp and very drinkable. Plenty of malt and hoppy bitterness together with some fruit are pleasing to the palate. Bitterness lingers in a long dry aftertaste.

Priory Mild (OG 1036, ABV 3.5%) ◆
Distinctive, full-flavoured, very dark mild. Pronounced lingering roast and dry hop aftertaste.

Umbel Ale (OG 1039, ABV 3.8%) ◆
Wort is percolated through coriander seeds to give a wonderful, warming, spicy fruit tang to both the taste and aroma. The hops are strong enough to make themselves known and a strong, bitter malt finish hits late.

Suffolk County Best Bitter (OG 1041, ABV 4%) ◆
Dry tasting, red-brown beer, dominated by increasing bitterness and roast grain astringency.

Augustinian Ale (OG 1046, ABV 4.5%) ◆
A pale, refreshing, complex best bitter. A fruity aroma leads to a bitter-sweet flavour and aftertaste with a predominance of citrus tones.

Old Growler (OG 1052, ABV 5%) 🍾 ◆
A complex and satisfying porter, smooth and distinctive. Sweetness, roast malt and fruit feature in the palate, with bitter chocolate lingering. The finish is powerfully hoppy.

Umbel Magna (OG 1052, ABV 5%) 🍾
The addition of coriander to the Old Growler wort completes the original 1750s recipe for this distinctive dark beer. The powerful spiciness only adds to this porter's appeal.

Newby Wyke SIBA

Newby Wyke Brewery, Willoughby Arms Cottages, Station Road, Little Bytham, Lincolnshire, NG33 4RA
Tel (01780) 411119
Fax (01780) 411240
Email newbywyke.brewery@btopenworld.com
Website www.newbywyke.co.uk
Tours by arrangement

⊗ The brewery is named after a Hull trawler that was skippered by brewer Rob March's grandfather. After starting as a 2.5-barrel brewery in 1998, growth has been steady, resulting in a move to purpose-built premises behind the Willoughby Arms. Two new fermenters were installed in 2004, bringing brewing capacity up to 50 barrels a week. 100 outlets are supplied direct. Stamford Gold (ABV 4.4%) is brewed for the Greenman, Stamford, while Grantham Gold (ABV 4.2%) is brewed for the Nobody Inn, Grantham. England Expects (ABV 4.6%) is brewed for Trafalgar Day and when an England sports team is playing in a tournament such as Euro 2004, Six-Nations and The Ashes.

Sidewinder (ABV 3.8%)

Kingston Topaz (ABV 4.2%)

Bear Island (ABV 4.6%)

White Squall (ABV 4.8%)

Chesapeake (ABV 5.5%)

Newmans SIBA

Newmans Brewery, Meadow Court, Wolvershill Road, Banwell, Somerset, BS29 6DJ
Tel (01934) 520746
Email sales@newmansbrewery.com
Website www.newmansbrewery.com

Newman's Brewery has developed new branding for all of its beers as part of a drive to spread sales further afield. Tom Newman has also started to buy nearby freehold property to convert into new brewing premises. The company also owns a bar/bistro, the Castle Tavern, at Kewstoke, Weston-Super-Mare. 100 outlets are supplied. The brewery will move to new premises during the lifetime of this edition of the guide.

Red Stag Bitter (ABV 3.6%)

Cave Bear Stout (ABV 4%)

Wolvers Ale (ABV 4.1%) ◆
Well-rounded best bitter with good body for its strength. Initial sweetness with a fine malt flavour is balanced by a slightly astringent, hoppy finish.

Woolly Mammoth Weis (ABV 4.5%)

Bite IPA (ABV 4.6%)

Nobby's*

Nobby's Brewery, 3 Pageant Court, Kettering, Northants, NN15 6GR
Tel (01536) 521868
Email info@nobbysbrewery.co.uk
Website www.nobbysbrewery.co.uk

Keen home brewer Paul Mulliner, known to friends as Nobby, started brewing commercially in 2004 on a half-barrel plant in his garage. A new 2.5 barrel plant, ex-Newby Wyke, was due to be installed in the cellar of the Alexandra Arms, Kettering, in July 2005. Seasonal beers: Santa's Secret (ABV 5%, Xmas) and Merlin's Magic (ABV 3.4%, winter).

Alexandra Best (OG 1039, ABV 3.8%)

Tressler XXX Mild (OG 1039, ABV 3.8%)

Monster Mash (OG 1044, ABV 4.2%)

Landlords Own (OG 1049, ABV 5%)

Norfolk Cottage*

Norfolk Cottage Brewing, The Shed, 98-100 Lawson Road, Norwich, Norfolk, NR3 4LF
Tel (01603) 270520/ 07775 668520
Fax (01603) 270349
Email norfolkcottagebrewing@ntlworld.com

Founded in 2004 by Ray Ashworth, founder of Woodforde's, Norfolk Cottage undertakes consultancy brewing and pilot brews for the Fat Cat Brewing Company at the same address. One standard bitter is available to the trade plus bespoke ales in small quantities to order. Three outlets are supplied direct.

Bitter (OG 1039, ABV 3.8%)

North Cotswold

North Cotswold Brewery, Ditchford Farm, Stretton-on-Fosse, Gloucestershire, GL56 9RD
Tel/Fax (01608) 663947
Email jon@pillingweb.co.uk

☺ North Cotswold is a 10-barrel brewery taken over in 2005 by former Cox's Yard brewer Jon Pilling from brothers David and Roger Tilbrook. The brewery is on the estate of Lord Willoughby de Broke. Twenty outlets are supplied. Seasonal beers: Mayfair Mild (ABV 4.1%, May), Summer Solstice (ABV 4.5%, summer), Winter Solstice (ABV 4.6%, winter), Stour Stout (ABV 5%, March-April), Blitzen (ABV 6.5%, Nov-Dec), Hung-Drawn-n-Portered (ABV 5%, Jan-Feb). All regular and seasonal beers are also produced in bottle-conditioned form.

Pig Brook (OG 1038, ABV 3.8%)

Genesis (OG 1038, ABV 4%)

Northern SIBA

Northern Brewing Ltd, Unit 1, Cormorant Centre, Cormorant Drive, Runcorn, Cheshire, WA7 4NQ
Tel (01928) 566222
Fax (01928) 590777
Email sales@norbrew.co.uk
Website www.norbrew.co.uk

Northern first brewed in 2003. The five-barrel plant was formerly located at Orchard Brewery Bar, Barnsley.

All-Niter (ABV 3.8%)
Three types of English malted barley and three varieties of English hops combine to produce a refreshing session beer.

Spellbinder (ABV 4.1%)

Dancer (ABV 4.2%)

Star (ABV 4.3%)

One-Der-Ful Wheat (ABV 4.7%)

North Yorkshire

North Yorkshire Brewing Co, Pinchinthorpe Hall, Pinchinthorpe, Guisborough, North Yorkshire, TS14 8HG
Tel/Fax (01287) 630200
Email nyb@pinchinthorpe.freeserve.co.uk
Website www.pinchinthorpehall.co.uk
Shop through hotel or bistro
Tours by arrangement

The brewery was founded in Middlesbrough in 1989 and moved in 1998 to Pinchinthorpe Hall, a moated and listed medieval estate near Guisborough that has its own spring water. The site also includes a hotel, restaurant and bistro. More than 100 free trade outlets are currently supplied. A special monthly beer is produced together with three beers in the Cosmic range. All beers are organic including the following bottle-conditioned beers: Cereal Killer, Dizzy Dick, Crystal Tips, Flying Herbert, Honey Bunny, Fools Gold, Boro Best, Best Bitter, Love Muscle, Priors Ale, Lord Lee's, Gold Ale, Ruby Ale.

Best Bitter (OG 1036, ABV 3.6%)
Clean tasting, well hopped, pale-coloured traditional bitter.

Prior's Ale (OG 1036, ABV 3.6%)
Light, refreshing and surprisingly full-flavoured for a pale, low gravity beer, with a complex, bitter-sweet mixture of malt, hops and fruit carrying through into the aftertaste.

Boro Best (OG 1040, ABV 4%)
Northern-style, full-bodied beer.

Ruby Ale (OG 1040, ABV 4%)
A full-bodied beer with a malty aroma and a balanced malt and hops taste, with vanilla notes.

Fools Gold (OG 1046, ABV 4.6%)
Hoppy, pale-coloured premium beer.

Golden Ale (OG 1046, ABV 4.6%)
A well-hopped, lightly-malted, golden premium bitter, using Styrian Goldings and Goldings hops.

Flying Herbert (OG 1047, ABV 4.7%)
Full-flavoured premium bitter, smooth and well balanced.

Lord Lee's (OG 1047, ABV 4.7%)
A refreshing, red/brown beer with a hoppy aroma. The flavour is a pleasant balance of roast malt and sweetness that predominates over hops. The malty, bitter finish develops slowly.

Northumberland

Northumberland Brewery Ltd, Earth Balance, West Sleekburn Farm, Bedlington, Northumberland, NE22 7AD
Tel/Fax (01670) 822112
Email dave@northumberlandbrewery.co.uk
Website www.northumberlandbrewery.co.uk
Shop yes. Tours by arrangement

The brewery has been operating for nine years on the Earth Balance organic farm and visitor centre. It has a 10-barrel brew-length. Some 150 outlets are supplied. The brewery tap, the Lake Shore Inn, is an integral part of the Earth Balance project. The beers are not fined with isinglass and are suitable for vegetarians and vegans.

Castles (ABV 3.8%)
A golden, full-flavoured beer with a hoppy aftertaste.

Reivers (ABV 3.9%)
A light hoppy session bitter with a fruity aftertaste.

County (ABV 4%)

Kitty Brewster (ABV 4%)

Bedlington Terrier (ABV 4.2%)

GNC (ABV 4.3%)

Original Northumberland Ale (ABV 4.3%)
Formerly Secret Kingdom, a lager-coloured ale.

Best Bitter (ABV 4.5%)
A traditional, smooth and quaffable best bitter with a dry finish.

Sheep Dog (ABV 4.7%)
An old-fashioned tawny beer, with fruit and malt throughout and a hoppy finish.

Bomar Bitter (ABV 5%)
A pale, robust ale, fruity with a lingering dry finish.

Premium (ABV 5%)
A dark, strong-tasting ale with a delicate, fruity aftertaste.

Nottingham SIBA

Nottingham Brewing Co Ltd, The Plough Inn, 17 St Peter's Street, Radford, Nottingham, NG7 3EN
Tel (0115) 9422649/ 0781 5073447
Fax (0115) 9422649
Email philip.darby@nottinghambrewery.com
Website www.nottinghambrewery.com
Tours by arrangement

Founded in 2001, the brewery produces classic beers in the style of the original historic Nottingham Brewery that closed in 1960.

Successful awards have included gold, silver and bronze in the SIBA East Midlands Championship and a bronze medal at the 2004 GBBF for Extra Pale Ale. Owners Niven Balfour and Philip and Peter Darby are planning expansion to the brewing plant and are entering into a bottling enterprise. There are also plans to widen the customer base in the Midlands. Fifty-seven outlets are supplied and one pub is owned.

Rock Ale Bitter Beer (OG 1038, ABV 3.8%)

Rock Ale Mild Beer (OG 1038, ABV 3.8%)

Legend (OG 1040, ABV 4%)

Extra Pale Ale (OG 1042, ABV 4.2%)

Dreadnought (OG 1046, ABV 4.5%)

Bullion (OG 1048, ABV 4.7%)

Sooty Stout (OG 1050, ABV 4.8%)

Supreme Bitter (OG 1055, ABV 5.2%)

O'Hanlon's SIBA

O'Hanlon's Brewing Co Ltd, Great Barton Farm, Whimple, Devon, EX5 2NY
Tel (01404) 822412
Fax (01404) 823700
Email info@ohanlons.co.uk
Website www.ohanlons.co.uk

⊗ Since moving to Whimple in Devon in 2000, O'Hanlon's has gone from strength to strength, winning the SIBA Wheat Beer of Britain award for the second time and gaining a silver medal in the World Beer Cup with Port Stout. A recent export contract to America yielded a surprise dividend when the brewery was offered the rights to brew the former Eldridge Pope brands Thomas Hardy's Ale, Royal Oak and Country Bitter, for both the bottle and cask market. The plant is being expanded in order to cope with these new products without detriment to the existing range of ales, and to include a new bottling line. Export sales also now include Canada, Denmark, Germany, Ireland and New Zealand. Some 80 outlets are supplied. Bottle-conditioned beers: Port Stout, Royal Oak, Double Champion Wheat, Thomas Hardy's Ale (ABV 11.7%).

Firefly (OG 1035, ABV 3.7%)
Malty and fruity light bitter. Hints of orange in the taste.

Double Champion Wheat (OG 1037, ABV 4%)
1999 and 2002 SIBA Champion Wheat Beer of Britain has a fine citrus taste.

Dry Stout (OG 1041, ABV 4.2%)
A dark malty, well-balanced stout with a dry, bitter finish and plenty of roast and fruit flavours up front.

Yellowhammer (ABV 4%)
A well-balanced, smooth pale yellow beer with a predominant hop and fruit nose and taste, leading to a dry, bitter finish.

Port Stout (OG 1041, ABV 4.8%)
A black beer with roast malt in the aroma that remains in the taste but gives way to hoppy bitterness in the aftertaste.

Royal Oak (OG 1048, ABV 5%)
Well-balanced copper-coloured beer with a strong fruit and malt aroma; a malty, fruity and sweet taste; and bitter aftertaste.

Oakham SIBA EAB

Oakham Ales, 80 Westgate, Peterborough, Cambridgeshire, PE1 2AA
Tel (01733) 358300
Fax (01733) 892658
Email oakhamales@aol.com
Website www.Oakham-ales.co.uk
Tours by arrangement

⊗ Oakham was commissioning a bigger plant on a new site as the guide went to press, so a move is imminent from Europe's biggest brew-pub in Peterborough. The company also plans to find new pubs with character to slowly build a tied estate. Currently, three pubs are owned, each tied and selling cask ale. Between 60 and 100 outlets are supplied. Seasonal beers: Tsunami (ABV 4%), JHB Extra (ABV 4.2%), 5 Leaves Left (ABV 4.5%), Kaleidoscope (ABV 4.7%), Harlequin (ABV 4.9%), Mompessons Gold (ABV 5%), Helter Skelter (ABV 5%), Old Tosspot (ABV 5.2%), Black Hole Porter (ABV 5.5%), Cold Turkey (ABV 6.3%).

Jeffrey Hudson Bitter or JHB (OG 1038, ABV 3.8%)
Popular, straw-coloured, light-bodied bitter with a strong aromatic hoppy signature, hints of grapefruit marmalade, and a strong bitter and drying finish.

White Dwarf Wheat Beer (OG 1043, ABV 4.3%)
Full-bodied yellow-golden beer with a well-defined citrus hop, and a gentle underlying malty sweetness in the mouth but ending bone-dry with hops holding up well.

Bishops Farewell (OG 1046, ABV 4.6%)
Intensely hoppy and full-bodied golden best bitter. Tropical fruit flavours provide a counterpoint to the grapefruit hoppy character. An abiding dryness develops.

Oakleaf SIBA

Oakleaf Brewing Co Ltd, Unit 7, Clarence Wharf Industrial Estate, Mumby Road, Gosport, Hampshire, PO12 1AJ
Tel (023) 9251 3222

Fax (023) 9251 0148
Email info@oakleafbrewing.co.uk
Website www.oakleafbrewing.co.uk
Tours by arrangement

⊗ Ed Anderson, a former Firkin brewer, set up Oakleaf with his father in law Dave Pickersgill in 2000. The brewery stands on the side of Gosport Harbour but there are plans to move to the former munitions buildings around the bay in the near future. Bottled beers are sold in the Victory Shop at the historic dockyard, Portsmouth. Some 75 outlets are supplied. Seasonal beers: Green Gold (ABV 4.3%, September), Reindeer's Delight (ABV 4.5%, Christmas), Piston Porter (ABV 4.6%, Oct-Nov), I Can't Believe It's Not Bitter (ABV 4.9%, May-Sept), Stoker's Stout (ABV 5%, Jan-Feb), IPA (ABV 5.5%, on demand), Blake's Heaven (ABV 7%, Dec-Jan). Bottle-conditioned beer: Blake's Gosport Bitter, Hole Hearted, Heart of Oak, Bitter.

Farmhouse Ale (OG 1036, ABV 3.5%) ◆
A full-flavoured session beer that belies its strength. Predominantly bitter and quite sharp, but with some maltiness and a long, dry finish.

Bitter (OG 1038, ABV 3.8%) ◆
A pale brown beer with a hoppy and malty aroma that leads to an intensely hoppy and bitter flavour, with some balancing lemon and grapefruit and a long, dry finish.

Maypole Mild (OG 1040, ABV 3.8%) ◆
This dark mild has a gorgeous full aroma. A lasting mix of flavours, roast and toffee lead to a slightly unexpected hoppiness. A roast, bitter finish.

Nuptu'ale (OG 1042, ABV 4.2%) ◆
A full-bodied pale ale, strongly hopped with an uncompromising bitterness. Well balanced with malts and citrus flavours that make for a very refreshing bitter.

Heart of Oak (OG 1044, ABV 4.5%)

Hole Hearted (OG 1048, ABV 4.7%) ◆
An amber-coloured strong bitter with strong floral hop and citrus notes in the aroma. These continue to dominate the flavour and lead to a long, bitter-sweet finish.

Blake's Gosport Bitter (OG 1053, ABV 5.2%) ◆
Packed with berry fruits and roastiness, this old ale is almost Belgian in style with a superb hoppy bitterness. Roast and caramel are prevalent as sweetness builds to an uncompromising, vinous finish. Warming, well balanced and delicious.

For Suthwyk Ales:

Bloomfields Bitter (ABV 3.8%)

Skew Sunshine Ale (ABV 4.8%)

Liberation (ABV 4.2%)

Oakwell

Oakwell Brewery, PO Box 87, Pontefract Road, Barnsley, South Yorkshire, ST1 1EZ
Tel (01226) 296161
Fax (01226) 771457

⊛ Brewing started in 1997 and there are plans for expansion. Oakwell supplies some 30 outlets.

Old Tom Mild (ABV 3.4%)

Barnsley Bitter (OG 1036, ABV 3.8%)

Okells SIBA

Okell & Son Ltd, Kewaigue, Douglas, Isle of Man, IM2 1QG
Tel (01624) 661120 Fax (01624) 625234
Email mac@okells.co.uk
Website www.okells.co.uk
Tours by arrangement

⊛ Founded in 1874 by Dr Okell and formerly trading as Isle of Man Breweries, this is the main brewery on the island, having taken over and closed the rival Castletown Brewery in 1986. The brewery moved in 1994 to a new, purpose-built plant at Kewaigue to replace the Falcon Brewery in Douglas. All the beers are produced under the Manx Brewers' Act 1874 (permitted ingredients: water, malt, sugar and hops only). All of the company's 56 IoM pubs and four on the mainland sell cask beer and some 70 free trade outlets are also supplied. Seasonal beers: Spring Ram (ABV 4.2%), Autumn Dawn (ABV 4.2%), Summer Storm (ABV 4.2%), St Nick (ABV 4.5%).

Mild (OG 1034, ABV 3.4%) ◆
A genuine, well-brewed mild ale, with a fine aroma of hops and crystal malt. Reddish-brown in colour, this beer has a full malt flavour with surprising bitter hop notes and a hint of blackcurrants and oranges. Full, malty finish.

Bitter (OG 1035, ABV 3.7%) ◆
A golden beer, malty and superbly hoppy in aroma, with a hint of honey. Rich and malty on the tongue, it has a wonderful, dry, malt and hop finish. A complex but rewarding beer.

Maclir (OG 1042, ABV 4.4%)
Beer with resiny hops and lemon fruit on the aroma, banana and lemon in the mouth and a big, bitter finish, dominated by hops, juicy malt and citrus fruit.

Dr Okells IPA (OG 1044, ABV 4.5%)
An extremely light-coloured beer with a surprising full-bodied taste. The sweetness is offset by a strong hopping rate that gives the beer an overall roundness with spicy lemony notes and a fine dry finish to counteract the initial sweetness.

Old Bear

Old Bear Brewery, Unit 4B, Atlas Works, Pitt Street, Keighley, West Yorkshire, BD21 4YL
Tel/Fax (01535) 601222
Email sales@oldbearbrewery.com
Website www.oldbearbrewery.com
Tours by arrangement

⊛ The brewery was founded in 1993 and has moved to custom-designed premises in Keighley. Ian Cowling is now the sole proprietor and is responsible for brewing. The range of beers brewed has been expanded to include a Porter and a Yorkshire lager. Old Bear Hibernator was awarded second place in the Strong Bitter category at the 26th Norwich Beer Festival. 60 outlets are supplied. The cask beers are also available in bottle-conditioned form and all are suitable for vegetarians.

Original (OG 1038, ABV 3.9%) ◆
A refreshing and easy-to-drink bitter. The balance of malt and hops gives way to a short, dry, bitter aftertaste.

Honeypot (OG 1046, ABV 4.4%)
Honey beer.

Goldilocks (OG 1048, ABV 4.5%)

Hibernator (OG 1055, ABV 5%)
Strong bitter.

Old Cannon

Old Cannon Brewery Ltd, 86 Cannon Street, Bury St Edmunds, Suffolk, IP33 1JR
Tel (01284) 768769
Fax (01284) 701137
Website www.oldcannon.co.uk
Tours by arrangement

⊗ St Edmunds Head pub opened in 1845 with its own brewery. Brewing ceased in 1917, and Greene King closed the pub in 1995. It re-opened in 1999 complete with a unique state-of-the-art brewery housed in the bar area. There are plans for bottling, further off-sales, more seasonal beers and the acquisition of a further pub. Ten outlets are supplied. Seasonal beers: Blonde Bombshell (ABV 4.2%), Old Chestnut (ABV 4.2%), Grapeshot (ABV 4.4%), Black Pig (ABV 4.8%).

Best Bitter (OG 1037, ABV 3.8%) ◆
An excellent session bitter brewed using Styrian Goldings, giving a crisp grapefruit aroma and taste. Very refreshing and full of flavour.

Gunner's Daughter (OG 1052, ABV 5.5%) ◆
A well-balanced strong ale with a complexity of hop, fruit, sweetness and bitterness in the flavour, and a lingering, pleasant, hoppy, bitter aftertaste.

Old Chimneys

Old Chimneys Brewery, The Street, Market Weston, Diss, Norfolk, IP22 2NZ (office), Hopton End Farm, Market Weston, Diss, Norfolk, IP22 2NX (brewery).
Tel Office (01359) 221411, Brewery (01359) 221013
Fax (01359) 221843
Shop Open Fri 2-7pm, Sat 11am-2pm
Tours by arrangement

⊗ A craft brewery opened in 1995 by former Vaux/Greene King/Broughton brewer Alan Thomson. In 2001 the brewery moved to larger premises in a converted farm building in the same village. Despite the postal address, the brewery is in Suffolk. The beers produced are mostly named after endangered local species. Old Chimneys currently supplies 30 outlets. Seasonal beers: Corncleavers Ale (ABV 4.3%, summer), Golden Pheasant (ABV 4.5%, summer), Winter Cloving (ABV 6%, winter). Bottle-conditioned beers: all cask ales listed below, plus IPA (ABV 5.6%), Brimstone Lager (ABV 6.5%), Greenshank (ABV 7%), Redshank (ABV 8.7%). In bottled form, Military Mild is known as Meadow Brown. All bottle-conditioned beers are suitable for vegetarians and all except Black Rat are suitable for vegans. Greenshank is organic.

Military Mild (OG 1035, ABV 3.3%) ◆
A rich, dark mild with good body for its gravity. Sweetish toffee and light roast bitterness dominate, leading to a dry aftertaste.

Great Raft Bitter (OG 1040, ABV 4%)
Pale copper bitter bursting with fruit. Malt and hops add to the sweetish fruity flavour, which is nicely rounded off with hoppy bitterness in the aftertaste.

Polecat Porter (OG 1043, ABV 4.2%)

Black Rat Stout (OG 1046, ABV 4.4%)

Natterjack (OG 1050, ABV 5%)

Good King Henry (OG 1107, ABV 9%)

Old Cottage

Burton Old Cottage Beer Co, Unit 10, Eccleshall Business Park, Hawkins Lane, Burton upon Trent, Staffordshire, DE14 1PT
Tel (07780) 900006
Email kevinjs@tesco.net
Tours by arrangement

⊗ Old Cottage was installed in the old Heritage Brewery, once Everards production plant in Burton. When the site was taken over, Kevin Slater was evicted and set up in a modern industrial unit. Due to growth in sales, he has now moved to a larger unit in the same yard. He purchased his first pub in 2001. Eight other outlets are supplied.

Oak Ale (OG 1044, ABV 4%) ◆
Tawny, full-bodied bitter. A sweet start gives way to a slight roast taste with some caramel. A dry, hoppy finish.

Chariot Ale (OG 1045, ABV 4.5%)

Stout (OG 1047, ABV 4.7%) ◆
Dense black but not heavy. Sweet with lots of caramel, hints of liquorice and a roast and bitter finish.

Halcyon Daze (OG 1050, ABV 5.3%) ◆
Tawny and creamy with touches of hop, fruit and malt aroma. Fruity taste and finish.

Old Laxey

Old Laxey Brewing Co Ltd, Shore Hotel Brew Pub, Old Laxey, Isle of Man, IM4 7DA

Tel (01624) 861509
Email shore@mcb.net
Tours by arrangement

Beer brewed in the Isle of Man is brewed to a strict Beer Purity Act. Additives are not permitted to extend its shelf life, nor are chemicals allowed to assist with head retention. Most of Old Laxey's beer is sold through the bar attached to the brewery.

Bosun Bitter (OG 1038, ABV 3.8%)
Crisp and fresh with a hoppy aftertaste.

Old Luxters SIBA

Old Luxters Brewery, Hambleden, Henley-on-Thames, Oxfordshire, RG9 6JW
Tel (01491) 638330
Fax (01491) 638645
Email david@oldluxters.co.uk
Website www.oldluxters.co.uk
Shop Mon-Fri 9-6, Sat/Sun 11-6, winter 9-5 & 11-5
Tours by arrangement

⊗ A traditional, full-mash, independent farm brewery was established in 1990 in a 17th-century barn alongside the Chiltern Valley vineyard. The craft brewery continues to supply its cask beers through the brewery shop. The brewery is in Buckinghamshire, despite the postal address. Bottle-conditioned beers: Barn Ale (ABV 5.4%), Dark Roast Ale (ABV 5%), Luxters Gold (ABV 5%), Winter Warmer (ABV 5%), Damson Ale (ABV 7%). Old Windsor Gold (ABV 4.5%) is brewed for the Royal Household Farm shops.

Barn Ale Bitter (OG 1038, ABV 4%)
A fruity, aromatic, fairly hoppy, bitter beer.

Barn Ale Special (OG 1042.5, ABV 4.5%) ◆
Predominantly malty, fruity and hoppy in taste and nose, and tawny/amber in colour. Fairly strong in flavour: the initial, sharp, malty and fruity taste leaves a dry, bitter-sweet, fruity aftertaste. It can be slightly sulphurous.

Dark Roast Ale (OG 1048, ABV 5%)

Old Mill

Old Mill Brewery, Mill Street, Snaith, East Yorkshire, DN14 9HU
Tel (01405) 861813
Fax (01405) 862789
Email mail@oldmillbrewery.co.uk
Website www.oldmillbrewery.co.uk
Tours by arrangement to organisations and customers only

◎ Old Mill is a craft brewery opened in 1983 in a 200-year-old former malt kiln and corn mill. The brew-length is 60 barrels. The brewery is building a tied estate, now standing at 17 houses. The innovation of selling beer in plastic, non-returnable handicasks has meant that the beer can now be found nationwide. Around 80 free-trade outlets are supplied by the brewery. There is a rolling programme of seasonal beers (see website) and monthly specials.

Mild (OG 1034, ABV 3.4%) ◆
A satisfying roast malt flavour dominates this easy-drinking, quality dark mild.

Bitter (OG 1038.5, ABV 3.9%) ◆
A malty nose is carried through to the initial flavour. Bitterness runs throughout.

Old Curiosity (OG 1044.5, ABV 4.5%) ◆
Slightly sweet amber brew, malty to start with. Malt flavours all the way through.

Bullion (OG 1047.5, ABV 4.7%) ◆
The malty and hoppy aroma is followed by a neat mix of hop and fruit tastes within an enveloping maltiness. Dark brown/amber in colour.

Old Stables SIBA

Old Stables Brewing Co, 38 The Avenue, Sandy, Bedfordshire, SG19 1ER
Tel (Pub) (01767) 680607
(Office/Fax) (01767) 692151
Tours by arrangement

⊗ The brewery is situated in an old stable block at the rear of the Sir William Peel pub, which is also the brewery tap. There are now five regular beers produced along with seasonal and special occasion brews. Although still only a 2.5-barrel plant, production has increased and the brewery supplies some 10 local free houses and beer festivals. Bottle-conditioned beers: Black Beauty, Hoppy Dayz.

Palomino Pale Ale (OG 1041, ABV 4.2%)

Stable Ale (OG 1041, ABV 4.2%)

Bright Bay Best (OG 1042, ABV 4.3%)

Black Beauty (OG 1044, ABV 4.4%)

Hoppy Dayz (OG 1044, ABV 4.5%)

Olde Swan

Olde Swan Brewery, 87-89 Halesowen Road, Netherton, Dudley, West Midlands, DY2 9PY
Tel (01384) 253075
Tours by arrangement

◎ A famous and much-loved brew-pub, best known in the old days as 'Ma Pardoe's', after the matriarch who ruled it for years. The pub has been licensed since 1835 and the present brewery and pub were built in 1863. Brewing continued until 1988 and restarted in 2001. The plant brews primarily for the on-site pub with some beer available to the trade. Some 20 outlets are supplied. Seasonal beer: Black Widow (ABV 6.7%, winter).

Original (OG 1034, ABV 3.5%) ◆
Straw-coloured light mild, smooth but tangy, and sweetly refreshing with a faint hoppiness.

Dark Swan (OG 1041, ABV 4.2%) ◆
Smooth, sweet dark mild with very late roast malt in the finish.

Entire (OG 1043, ABV 4.4%) ◆
Faintly hoppy, amber premium bitter with sweetness persistent throughout.

Bumble Hole Bitter (OG 1052, ABV 5.2%) ◆
Sweet, smooth amber ale with hints of astringency in the finish.

Old Wheelton

See Pictish

Oldershaw SIBA

Oldershaw Brewery, 12 Harrowby Hall Estate, Grantham, Lincolnshire, NG31 9HB
Tel (01476) 572135
Fax (01476) 572193
Email oldershawbrewery@btconnect.com
Website www.oldershawbrewery.com
Tours by arrangement

⊗ Experienced home-brewer Gary Oldershaw and his wife Diane set up the brewery at their home in 1997. Grantham's first brewery for 30 years, Oldershaw now supplies 60 local free houses. It concentrates on delivering direct to outlets and is enjoying steady growth. The Oldershaws plan to introduce some small-scale bottling, to include Old Boy, Yuletide, Royal Blonde and Grantham Stout. Seasonal beers: Sunnydaze (ABV 4%, summer wheat beer, May-Aug), Topers Tipple (ABV 4.5%, Nov-Feb), Yuletide (ABV 5.2%, Nov-Dec).

Mowbrays Mash (OG 1037, ABV 3.7%)

High Dyke (OG 1039, ABV 3.9%)
Golden and moderately bitter. A predominantly hoppy session beer.

Newton's Drop (OG 1041, ABV 4.1%) ◆
Balanced malt and hops but with a strong bitter, lingering taste in this mid-brown beer.

Caskade (OG 1042, ABV 4.2%)
Pale, golden beer brewed with American Cascade hops to give a distinctive floral, hoppy flavour and aroma, and a clean lasting finish.

Ermine Ale (OG 1042, ABV 4.2%)
Golden brown with a fruity hop the dominant feature on nose and taste giving a bitterness that lasts; malt plays a supporting role.

Ahtanum Gold (OG 1043, ABV 4.3%)
A gold-coloured, fruity, hoppy beer balanced with some maltiness. Moderately bitter.

Grantham Stout (OG 1043, ABV 4.3%) ▯
Dark brown and smooth with rich roast malt flavour, supported by some fruit and bitterness. A long, moderately dry finish.

Regal Blonde (OG 1043, ABV 4.4%) ◆
Straw-coloured, lager-style beer with a good malt/hop balance throughout; strong bitterness on the taste lingers.

Isaac's Gold (OG 1044, ABV 4.5%)

Old Boy (OG 1047, ABV 4.8%) ◆
A full-bodied amber ale, fruity and bitter with a hop/fruit aroma. The malt that backs the taste dies in the long finish.

Organic SIBA

Organic Brewhouse, Unit 1, Higher Bochym Workshops, Cury Cross Lanes, Helston, Cornwall, TR12 7AZ
Tel (01326) 241555
Fax (01326) 241188
Email a.hamer@btclick.com
Tours by arrangement

⊗ Laid out as a mini 'tower' system, Organic's production has increased to five regular beers. It was established by Andy Hamer in 2000 and is dedicated to supplying exclusively organic beer, using its own source of natural mineral water. Some 20 local outlets are supplied regularly and the beers occasionally head north with wholesalers. All the beers are also available bottle-conditioned and all are suitable for vegetarians.

Halzephron Gold (OG 1033, ABV 3.6%)

Lizard Point (OG 1038, ABV 4%)

Serpentine Dark Ale (OG 1042, ABV 4.5%)

Black Rock Stout (OG 1044, ABV 4.7%) ◆
Hop and apple aroma masked by complex roast overtones.

Wolf Rock (OG 1047, ABV 5%)

Orkney SIBA

Orkney Brewery, Highlands & Islands Breweries Ltd, Quoyloo, Stromness, Orkney, KW16 3LT
Tel (01856) 841802
Fax (01856) 841754
Email info@orkneybrewery.com
Website www.orkneybrewery.com and www.hibreweries.com

⊕ Set up in 1988 in an old school building in the remote Orkney hamlet of Quayloo, the brewery was completely modernised in 1995 with new buildings and brewing equipment. Capacity is now 120 barrels a week, all brewed along strict ecological lines from its own water supply. All waste water is treated through two lakes on the brewery's land, which in turn support fish and several dozen mallard ducks. There are plans for additional fermenting capacity and a visitors' centre by the end of 2006. Along with Atlas (qv), Orkney is part of Highlands & Islands Breweries; the combined business distributes to some 350 outlets across Scotland and via wholesalers to the rest of Britain. The extra distribution has improved chances of finding Orkney's more specialist beers such as Dragonhead and Skullsplitter. Seasonal beer: White Christmas (ABV 5%, December).

Raven Ale (OG 1038, ABV 3.8%) ◆
A well-balanced, quaffable bitter. Malty fruitiness and bitter hoppiness last through to the long, dry aftertaste.

Dragonhead Stout **(OG 1040, ABV 4%)**
A strong, dark malt aroma flows into the taste in this superb Scottish stout. The roast malt continues to dominate the aftertaste, and blends with chocolate to develop a strong, dry finish. Hard to find.

Northern Light **(OG 1040, ABV 4%)**
A straw-coloured beer, hoppy and refreshing. Fruity hop notes can develop a true lager nose. A late copper hop is intense without being cloying.

Red MacGregor **(OG 1040, ABV 4%)**
Generally a well-balanced bitter, this tawny red ale has a powerful smack of fruit and a clean, fresh mouthfeel. A thoroughbred from a successful stable.

Dark Island **(OG 1045, ABV 4.6%)**
An excellent brew with many accolades and awards. The amount of roast and chocolate malt character varies, making it hard to categorise this beer as a stout or an old ale. Generally a sweetish roast malt taste leads to a long-lasting roasted, slightly bitter finish.

Skullsplitter **(OG 1080, ABV 8.5%)**
An intense velvet malt nose with hints of apple, nutmeg and spice. Hops to the fore are balanced by satiny smooth malt with fruity, spicy edges leading to a long dry finish with a hint of nut.

Ossett SIBA

Ossett Brewing Co. Ltd, t/a Ossett Brewery, Kings Yard, Low Mill Road, Ossett, West Yorkshire, WF5 8ND
Tel (01924) 261333
Fax (01924) 261356
Email brewery@ossett.co.uk
Website www.ossett-brewery.co.uk
Shop opens late 2005
Tours by arrangement

Established in 1998, Ossett Brewery now has breweries on two sites. The original plant at the rear of the Brewers Pride pub brews specials and occasional beers and the new larger plant produces all the mainstream beers. The new brewery opened in March 2005 and is capable of producing more than 250 barrels a week. Awards for its beers include Supreme National Champion 2003 for Excelsior and National Champion 2002 for Silver King in the SIBA Beer Competitions. It makes direct deliveries to some 130 outlets and many others through selected wholesalers. The brewery now operates four tied outlets with another soon to open, including the Black Bull, Liversedge, and the Rat and Ratchet, Huddersfield. Its range of bottled beers are exported to Japan and Hong Kong and are available from the brewery. Seasonal Beers: Silver Fox (ABV 4.1%, spring), Silver Link (ABV 4.6%, summer), Oregon Pale (ABV 4.7%, autumn).

Pale Gold **(OG 1038, ABV 3.8%)**
A light, refreshing pale ale with a floral/spicy aroma derived from American hops.

Silver King **(OG 1041, ABV 4.3%)**
A lager-style beer with a crisp, dry flavour and citrus fruity aroma.

Dazzler **(OG 1044, ABV 4.5%)**
A delicately-flavoured pale ale. The smooth, slightly spicy aroma is derived from use of classic English Goldings hops.

Fine Fettle **(OG 1048, ABV 4.8%)**
A strong yet refreshing pale ale with a crisp clean flavour and citrus fruity aroma.

Excelsior **(OG 1051, ABV 5.2%)**
A mellow yet full flavour that develops into fruity dryness on the palate. A fresh, hoppy aroma with citrus, toffee and floral characteristics.

Otter SIBA

Otter Brewery Ltd, Mathayes, Luppitt, Honiton, Devon, EX14 4SA
Tel (01404) 891285
Fax (01404) 891124
Email info@otterbrewery.com
Website www.otterbrewery.com
Tours by arrangement

David and Mary Ann McCaig (both with Whitbread connections) set up Otter Brewery in 1990 and it has grown into one of the West Country's major producers of beers. The brewery is located in the Blackdown Hills, between Taunton and Honiton. An 80-barrel plant, built in exactly the same style as the old brewery, was commissioned in 2004 and has proved invaluable in supplying demand. The beers are made with local spring water. Otter Beers are delivered to 300 outlets.

Bitter **(OG 1036, ABV 3.6%)**
Well-balanced amber session bitter with a fruity nose and bitter taste and aftertaste.

Bright **(OG 1039, ABV 4.3%)**
Fruit and hop aroma in a straw-coloured bitter with a strong bitter finish.

Ale **(OG 1043, ABV 4.5%)**
A full-bodied best bitter. A malty aroma predominates with a fruity taste and finish.

Head **(OG 1054, ABV 5.8%)**
Fruity aroma and taste with a pleasant bitter finish. Dark brown and full-bodied.

Oulton

Oulton Ales Ltd, Lake Lothing Brewery, Harbour Road, Oulton Broad, Lowestoft, Suffolk, NR32 3LZ
Tel (01502) 587905
Fax (01502) 583387
Email wayne@oultonales.co.uk
Website www.oultonales.co.uk
Tours by arrangement

Several new names have been added to the range to reflect the nautical history of Oulton Broad and Lowestoft. Plans for the future are to enlarge the brewery plant and increase availability of bottles. 20 outlets are supplied as well as its own three pubs. Bottle-conditioned beers: Nautilus, Gone Fishing, Roaring Boy.

Bitter **(OG 1037, ABV 3.5%)**

Nutford Mild **(OG 1038, ABV 3.7%)**

Bedazzled **(OG 1040, ABV 4%)**

Sunrise **(OG 1040, ABV 4%)**

Nautilus (OG 1042, ABV 4.2%)

Sunset (OG 1041, ABV 4.2%)

Wet and Windy (OG 1044, ABV 4.3%)

Windswept (OG 1044, ABV 4.5%)

Excelsior (OG 1045, ABV 4.6%)

Gone Fishing (OG 1049, ABV 5%)

Keelhaul (OG 1060, ABV 6.5%)

Roaring Boy (OG 1075, ABV 8.5%)

Outlaw

See Roosters

Owl*

Owl Brewing Co Ltd, Hope Inn, 32 Greenacres Road, Oldham, Greater Manchester, OL4 1HB
Tel/Fax (01706) 840356
Email gordon@owlbrew.co.uk
Website www.owlbrew.co.uk

Owl was set up in autumn 2004 by Gordon Potts, who had spent 20 years designing pubs and breweries and thought it was time to brew some beer himself. He had also been a keen home brewer. He can produce eight barrels per brew.

Greenacres Gold (ABV 3.8%)

Night Owl (ABV 3.8%)

OB Bitter (ABV 4.1%)

Russet Owl (ABV 4.2%)

Oxfordshire Ales*

Bicester Beers & Minerals Ltd, 12 Pear Tree Farm Industrial Units, Bicester Road, Marsh Gibbon, Bicester, Oxon, OX27 0GB
Tel (01869) 278765 Fax (01869) 278768
Email bicesterbeers@tiscali.co.uk

The company first brewed in February 2005. The five-barrel plant was previously at Picks Brewery.

Triple B (ABV 3.7%)
An 'autumn leaf' brown bitter, well hopped with English and Styrian Goldings.

IPA (ABV 4.1%)
A full-flavoured, well-balanced, chestnut-coloured IPA.

Marshmellow (ABV 4.7%)
A deep amber beer with a generous, warming flavour, fruity and malty with a lingering bitter taste.

Oyster*

Oyster Bar & Brewery, Ellenabeich, Easdale, Oban, Argyll & Bute, PA34 4RQ
Tel (01852) 300121
Email gascoignea@tiscali.co.uk
Website www.oysterbrewery.com

The brewery was built in November 2004 and came on stream in the spring of 2005. Head brewer Andy Gascoigne brought the state-of-the-art brewery north after first installing it in his pub in West Yorkshire.

Easd'ale (ABV 3.8%)
Golden smooth bitter with a dry aftertaste.

Thistle Tickler (ABV 4%)
Amber, fruity session bitter using Fuggles hops and Vienna malt.

Red Pearl (ABV 4.5%)
Traditional red-hued Scottish ale brewed with a blend of malts and roasted barley with First Gold hops. Toffeish aftertaste.

Old Tosser (ABV 5%)
Strong dark ale brewed with roasted barley and American Cascade hops to give a rich, full-bodied character.

Palmer IFBB SIBA

JC & RH Palmer Ltd, The Old Brewery, West Bay Road, Bridport, Dorset, DT6 4JA
Tel (01308) 422396
Fax (01308) 421149
Email enquiries@palmersbrewery.com
Website www.palmersbrewery.com
Shop Mon-Sat 9-6pm
Tours by arrangement (01308) 427500

⊗ Palmers is Britain's only thatched brewery and dates from 1794. It is based in an idyllic location by the sea in west Dorset. The company is run by John and Cleeves Palmer, great-grandsons of Robert Henry and John Cleeves Palmer, who bought the brewery in 1896. Palmers enjoys sustained growth in real ale sales. Heavy investment is made in free trade ale dispense. Some 55 pubs are owned and a further 240 outlets are supplied.

Copper Ale (OG 1036, ABV 3.7%) ◆
Well-balanced session ale. Gentle fruit and caramel on the nose lead through a sweetish taste with hop bitterness developing.

Best Bitter IPA
(OG 1040, ABV 4.2%) ◆
A deep copper beer that is hoppy and bitter throughout. Fruit and malt undertones give some balance in the aroma and taste, and there is a lingering bitter aftertaste.

Dorset Gold (OG 1046, ABV 4.5%)
A golden premium ale, refreshing and thirst-quenching, full and fruity.

200 (OG 1052, ABV 5%) ◆
Full-bodied: caramel sweetness and fruity aroma are balanced with a dry finish; not excessively bitter; a deep-copper ale. First brewed to mark the brewery's 200th anniversary.

Tally Ho! (OG 1057, ABV 5.5%)
A strong, nutty, full-strength dark beer with a distinctive and long-lasting taste.

Paradise SIBA

Paradise Brewing Co, Unit 2, The Old Creamery, Station Road, Wrenbury, Nantwich, Cheshire, CW5 8EX
Tel/Fax (01270) 780916
Email john@gillmorgan.go-plus.net
Shop Fri/Sat/Sun noon-4pm
Tours by arrangement

In 2003 the brewery came under the sole ownership of John Wood, one of its founders. Two annual beer festivals are held, featuring local micro breweries. One is held in July to coincide with the local Scarecrow Trail, the other between Christmas and New Year. The brewery is located at the side of Wrenbury Railway Station. Ten outlets are supplied, varying with the season. 50% of beer is now in bottle-conditioned form, sold at local farmers' markets.

Mild (OG 1036, ABV 3.6%)

Farmers Favourite (ABV 4%)

Dabbers Wheat (OG 1048, ABV 5%)

Nantwich Ale (ABV 5.6%)

Parish

♀ Parish Brewery, 6 Main Street, Burrough-on-the-Hill, Leicestershire, LE14 2JQ
Tel/Fax (01664) 454801
Tours by arrangement

◎ Parish is a fully-refurbished, 20-barrel brewery, housed in a 400 year-old building where it originally started in 1983. The brewery moved to Somerby in 1990 and returned to Burrough-on-the-Hill in 2003. 20 local outlets are supplied. Bottle-conditioned beer: Baz's Bonce Blower.

Special Bitter or PSB (OG 1039, ABV 3.9%)

Somerby Premium (OG 1041, ABV 4.2%)

Farm Gold (OG 1042, ABV 4.2%)

Bitter (OG 1048, ABV 4.7%)

Poachers Ale (OG 1050, ABV 5%)

Baz's Bonce Blower (OG 1110, ABV 11.5%)

Peak Ales*

Peak Ales, Barn Brewery, Cunnery Barn, Chatsworth, Bakewell, Derbyshire, DE45 1EX
Tel (01246) 583737

Proprietor and brewer Rob Evans started production in February 2005 in a converted barn on the Chatsworth Estate. A 10-barrel plant was supplied by a German manufacturer.

Swift Nick (ABV 3.8%)

Bakewell Best Bitter (ABV 4.2%)

Peakstones Rock*

Peakstones Rock Brewery, Peakstones Farm, Cheadle Road, Alton, Stoke-on-Trent, Staffordshire, ST10 4DH.
Tel 07891 350908
Email dfedwards@fwi.co.uk

David Edwards, a keen CAMRA member, started brewing in May 2005 on a purpose-built, five-barrel plant on a dairy farm.

Nemesis (ABV 3.8%)

Best Bitter (ABV 4.8%)

Peelwall*

Peelwall Brewery, Peelwalls Farmhouse, Ayton, Borders, TD15 5RL
Tel (01289) 332047
Email peelwallbrewery@aol.com

A new brewery based on a farm that came on stream in the summer of 2005.

Smugglers (ABV 4%)

Emperor (ABV 4.8%)

Broon Bruin Brew (ABV 5.4%)

Borders Heavy (ABV 6.2%)

Penlon Cottage*

Penlon Cottage Brewery, Pencae, Llanarth, Ceredigion, SA47 0QN
Tel (01545) 580022
Email penlon@onetel.com

The latest brewery in Ceredigion – formerly Cardiganshire – started operation in 2004 and is located on a working farm run by Stefan and Penny Samociuk. Currently only bottle-conditioned beers are brewed but future cask ale is not being ruled out. Bottling is by hand. Bottle-conditioned beers: Harvest Gold (ABV 3.2%), Ewes Frolic Lager (ABV 3.6%), Tipsy Tup Pale Ale (ABV 3.6%), Stock Ram Stout (ABV 3.6%), Twin Ram IPA (ABV 4.6%).

Phoenix

Phoenix Brewery, Green Lane, Heywood, Greater Manchester, OL10 2EP
Tel (01706) 627009
Fax (01706) 623235
Email tony@phoenixbrewery.fsnet.co.uk

◎ A company established as Oak Brewery in 1982 at Ellesmere Port. It moved in 1991 to Heywood and changed its name in 1992 to Phoenix (after the original name of the brewery it occupies). It now supplies 400 to 500 free trade outlets mostly in the North-west of England as well as several national pubcos and suppliers. A vast range of seasonal beers is brewed; for details, contact the brewery via email.

Bantam (ABV 3.5%) ◆
Light brown beer with a fruity aroma. Balance of malt, citrus fruit and hop in taste. Hoppy, bitter finish.

Navvy (ABV 3.8%) ◻ ◆

Amber beer with a citrus fruit and malt nose. Good balance of citrus fruit, malt and hops with bitterness coming through in the aftertaste.

Best Bitter (ABV 3.9%)

Monkeytown Mild (ABV 3.9%)

Arizona (ABV 4.1%) ◆
Yellow in colour with a fruity and hoppy aroma. A refreshing beer with citrus, hop and good bitterness, and a shortish dry aftertaste.

Pale Moonlight (ABV 4.2%)

Black Bee (ABV 4.5%)

Old Oak Ale (ABV 4.5%) ◆
A well-balanced, brown beer with a multitude of mellow fruit flavours. Malt and hops balance the strong fruitiness in the aroma and taste, and the finish is malty, fruity and dry.

White Monk (ABV 4.5%) ◆
Yellow beer with a citrus fruit aroma, plenty of fruit, hop and bitterness in the taste, and a hoppy bitter finish.

Thirsty Moon (ABV 4.6%) ◆
Tawny beer with a fresh citrus aroma. Hoppy, fruity and malty with a dry, hoppy finish.

West Coast IPA (ABV 4.6%)

Double Dagger (ABV 5%) ◆
A pale brown, malty brew, more pleasantly dry and light than its gravity would suggest. Moderately fruity throughout; a hoppy bitterness in the mouth balances the strong graininess.

Double Gold (ABV 5%)

Wobbly Bob (ABV 6%) ◆
A red/brown beer with a malty, fruity aroma. Strongly malty and fruity in flavour and quite hoppy, with the sweetness yielding to a dryness in the aftertaste.

Pictish

Pictish Brewing Co. Ltd, Unit 9, Canalside Industrial Estate, Rochdale, Greater Manchester, OL16 5LB
Tel/fax (01706) 522227
Email mail@pictish-brewing.co.uk
Website www.pictish-brewing.co.uk

The brewery was established in 2000 by Richard Sutton, formerly senior brewer for the north with the Firkin Brewery group. The brewery supplies 60 free trade outlets in the North-west and West Yorkshire. Seasonal beers: Northern Dawn (ABV 4.3%, Jan-Feb), Claymore (ABV 4.5%, Feb-March), Dolmen (ABV 4%, March-April), Maelstrom (ABV 5%, April-May), Black Diamond (ABV 3.5%, May-June), Summer Solstice (ABV 4.7%, May-Aug), Ginger Ale (ABV 3.9%, June-July), Siren (ABV 4.1%, July-Aug), Corn Dolly (ABV 5%, Aug-Sept), Staddle Stone (ABV 4.5%, Sept-Oct), Z-Rod (ABV 4.8%, Nov-Dec), Porter (ABV 4%, Nov-March), Winter Solstice (ABV 4.7%, Dec-Jan).

Brewers Gold (OG 1038, ABV 3.8%) ◆
Yellow in colour, with a hoppy, fruity nose. Soft maltiness and a strong hop/citrus flavour lead to a dry, bitter finish.

Celtic Warrior (OG 1042, ABV 4.2%) ◆
Tawny beer with malt and hops dominant in aroma and taste. Good bitter finish.

Alchemists Ale (OG 1043, ABV 4.3%)

For Crown Inn, Bacup

Bare Arts (OG 1035, ABV 3.5%)

IBA (OG 1050, ABV 5%)

Pilgrim SIBA

Pilgrim Ales, The Old Brewery, West Street, Reigate, Surrey, RH2 9BL
Tel (01737) 222651
Fax (01737) 225785
Email david@pilgrim.co.uk
Website www.pilgrim.co.uk

⊗ Set up by David Roberts in 1982 and based in Reigate since 1985, Pilgrim has gradually increased its capacity and its beers have won both local and national awards, although sales are mostly concentrated in the Surrey area (around 60 outlets). Pilgrim owns one tied house, the Rising Sun, Epsom. Seasonal beers: Autumnal (ABV 4.5%, Sept-Oct), Excalibur (ABV 4.5%, March-May), Pudding (ABV 7.3%, Nov-Jan).

Surrey Bitter (OG 1037, ABV 3.7%) ◆
There are grapefruit and spicy aromas in this well-balanced quaffing beer. Initial biscuity maltiness with a hint of vanilla gives way to bitterness that becomes more pronounced in a refreshing, bitter-sweet finish.

Porter (OG 1040, ABV 4%) ◆
Black beer with a good balance of dark malts and hints of berry fruit. Roast character is present throughout; bitter-sweet finish.

Progress (OG 1040, ABV 4%) ◆
A well-rounded, tawny-coloured bitter, predominantly fruity, with an underlying maltiness. The flavour is well balanced overall with a subdued bitterness. The aftertaste dissipates quickly.

Crusader (OG 1049, ABV 4.9%)

Talisman (OG 1049, ABV 5%) ◆
A strong ale with a tawny red colour. Gentle aroma and a subsiding sweet malty flavour, with a noticeably short-lived bitterness.

Pitfield

Pitfield Brewery, London Beer Co, 14 Pitfield Street, London, N1 6EY
Tel (020) 7739 3701
Email sales@pitfieldbeershop.co.uk
Website www.pitfieldbeershop.co.uk
Shop 11-7 Tue-Fri; 10-4 Sat
Tours by arrangement

⊗ Pitfield Brewery was established in 1982, two years after its sister business, the Beer Shop. To celebrate its 21st birthday, a range of historical, non-organic beers have been brewed under the banner of the London Beer Co, to distinguish them from the organic Pitfield range. The organic bottled range is now exported to Denmark and cask ale may be distributed nationally by a wholesaler. Pitfield's beer can be found on draught at the Wenlock Arms, London N1, where the beers are fined. Vegetarians are directed to the Duke of Cambridge London N1, or to the bottled versions at the beer shop. Four outlets are supplied. Bottle-conditioned beers: Organic Original, Shoreditch Stout, East Kent Goldings, Eco Warrior, Hoxton Best Bitter, Black Eagle. Non-organic: 1850 London Porter (ABV 5%), 1830 Amber Ale (ABV 6%), 1824 Mild Ale (ABV 6.5%), 1837 India Pale Ale (ABV 7%), 1792 Imperial Stout (ABV 9.3%), 1896 XXXX Stock Ale (ABV 10%). All the bottled beers are suitable for vegans.

Original (ABV 3.7%)

Singhboulton/Pitfield Special (ABV 3.7%)
Brewed for the Singboulton organic pubs in London.

Shoreditch Stout (OG 1040, ABV 4%) ◆
Chocolate and a raisin fruitiness on the nose lead to a fruity roast flavour and a sweetish finish with a little bitterness.

East Kent Goldings (ABV 4.2%) ◆
A dry, yellow beer with bitter notes throughout and a faint hint of honey on the palate.

Eco Warrior (ABV 4.5%) ◆
This pale golden beer has a hoppy citrus aroma and flavour that is balanced by some sweetness and a bitterness that builds on drinking.

Hoxton Best Bitter (ABV 4.8%) ◆
A well-balanced beer with a malty sweetness that lingers in the bitter, dry aftertaste.

Black Eagle (ABV 5%) ◆
A light-drinking strong old ale, black with red hues, with a lasting roast malt flavour and a malty, dryish aftertaste.

Plassey SIBA

Plassey Brewery, Eyton, Wrexham, LL13 0SP
Tel (01978) 781111/07050 327127
Fax (01978) 781219
Email plassey@globalnet.co.uk
Website www.plasseybrewery.co.uk
Shop open office hours
Tours by arrangement

The brewery was founded in 1985 on the 250-acre Plassey Estate, which also incorporates a touring caravan park, craft centres, a golf course, three licensed outlets for Plassey's ales, and a brewery shop. Some 30 free trade outlets also take the beer. Seasonal beers: Ruddy Rudolph (ABV 4.5%, Christmas), Lager (ABV 4%). Bottle-conditioned beer: Fusilier.

Welsh Border Exhibition Ale
(OG 1036, ABV 3.5%)

Bitter (OG 1041, ABV 4%) ◆
Full-bodied and distinctive best bitter. Good balance of hops and fruit flavours with a lasting dry bitter aftertaste.

Fusilier (OG 1046, ABV 4.5%) ▢

Cwrw Tudno (OG 1048, ABV 5%) ▢ ◆
A mellow, sweetish premium beer with classic Plassey flavours of fruit and hops.

Dragon's Breath (OG 1060, ABV 6%)
A fruity, strong bitter, smooth and quite sweet, though not cloying, with an intense, fruity aroma. A dangerously drinkable winter warmer.

Poachers

Poachers Brewery, Unit 4, Camp Road, Witham St Hughs, Lincoln, LN6 9TW
Tel (01522) 868889
Email george@poachersbrewery.co.uk
Website www.poachersbrewery.co.uk
Tours by arrangement

The Poachers Brewery, opened in 2001, is a five-barrel plant situated on the former site of RAF Swinderby, a wartime Bomber Command Station. The brewery is owned and operated by George Batterbee, a former RAF man with 25 years' service who has come full circle as he spent his first five years of RAF service working 200 yards from where the brewery now stands. Regular outlets are supplied throughout Lincolnshire and surrounding counties; outlets further afield are supplied via wholesalers. All the beers are also available in bottle-conditioned form with bottling done on-site. Seasonal beer: Santa's Come (ABV 6.5%, Christmas).

Trembling Rabbit
(OG 1034, ABV 3.4%)
Rich, dark mild with a smooth malty flavour and a slightly bitter finish.

Shy Talk (OG 1037, ABV 3.7%)
Clean-tasting session beer, pale gold in colour; slightly bitter finish, dry hopped.

Pride (OG 1040, ABV 4%)
Amber bitter brewed using Cascade hops that produce a wonderful flavour and aroma that lingers.

Trail (OG 1042, ABV 4.2%) ◆
A flowery hop-nosed, mid-brown beer with a well-balanced but bitter taste that stays with the malt, becoming more apparent in the drying finish.

Den (OG 1042, ABV 4.2%) ◆
Pale amber with a fruit hop aroma that gives way to a citrus hoppiness in the taste, and moderate bitterness that leads to a pleasant malty aftertaste.

Dick (OG 1045, ABV 4.5%)
Ruby-red bitter, smooth fruity flavour balanced by the bitterness of Goldings hops.

Black Crow (OG 1045, ABV 4.5%)
Dry stout with burnt toffee and caramel flavour.

Gold (OG 1049, ABV 5%)
Cask-conditioned lager brewed in the Czech style using Saaz hops and caramalt.

Jock's Trap (OG 1050, ABV 5%)

Trout Tickler (OG 1055, ABV 5.5%)

For the Bluebell Inn, Tattershall Thorpe, Lincolnshire

Pathfinders Ale (ABV 4.4%)

For the Dovecote, Swinderby, Lincolnshire

Fant Ale (ABV 4%)

Port Mahon SIBA

Port Mahon Brewery, c/o Cask and Cutler, 1 Henry Street, Sheffield, South Yorkshire, S3 7EQ
Tel (0114) 2492295

Brewing started in 2001 in a purpose-built brewery behind the Cask and Cutler, using a one-barrel plant. There are plans to install a four-barrel kit. The brewery produces one-off beers mainly for festivals and special occasions. It is planned to brew a permanent house bitter and a range of beer styles that will alternate with the other guest ales in the pub. The beer range is yet to be established.

Porter

Porter Brewing Co Ltd, Rossendale Brewery, Griffin Inn, 84 Hud Rake, Haslingden, Lancashire, BB4 5AF
Tel/Fax (01706) 214021
Email dporter@porterbrewing.fsnet.co.uk
Website www.pbcbreweryinstallations.com
Tours by arrangement

The company has three tied pubs and all sell a minimum of five real ales. All beers sold in the tied pubs are vegan products (ask managers for confirmation). Seasonal beers: Timmy's Ginger Beer (ABV 4.2%, March and Aug), Stout (ABV 5.5%, Sept-Oct), Sleighed (ABV 6.5%, Dec-Jan), Celebration Ale (ABV 7.1%, July-Aug).

Dark Mild (OG 1033, ABV 3.3%)
A plain, well-made dark mild with a faint fruity aroma and a hint of roast in the finish.

Floral Dance (OG 1035, ABV 3.6%)
Pale and fruity.

Bitter (OG 1037, ABV 3.8%)
Unusually dark for a standard bitter, this beer has a dry and assertively bitter character that develops in the finish.

Railway Sleeper (OG 1040, ABV 4.2%)
Intensely bitter and hoppy.

Rossendale Ale (OG 1041, ABV 4.2%)
A malty aroma leads to a complex, malt-dominated flavour supported by a dry, increasingly bitter finish.

Porter (OG 1050, ABV 5%)
A rich beer with a slightly sweet, malty start, counter-balanced with sharp bitterness and a noticeable roast barley dominance.

Sunshine (OG 1050, ABV 5.3%)
A hoppy and bitter golden beer with a citrus character. The lingering finish is dry and spicy.

Potbelly*

Potbelly Brewery, c/o Corium Leather Co Ltd, 25-31 Durban Road, Kettering, Northants, NN16 0JA
Tel (01536) 410818
Fax (01536) 411135
Email toni@potbelly-brewery.co.uk
Tours by arrangement

Potbelly started brewing in February 2005 in a purpose-built building behind a leather fashion accessories manufacturer. The 10-barrel plant was manufactured by Abbott and Co of Newark. The beers are regularly available at the Cock Inn at Denford and can also be found in other local outlets.

Aisling (ABV 4%)

Redwing (ABV 4.8%)

Potton SIBA

Potton Brewery Co Ltd, 10 Shannon Place, Potton, Sandy, Bedfordshire, SG19 2SP
Tel (01767) 261042
Fax (01767) 631693
Email info@potton-brewery.co.uk
Website www.potton-brewery.co.uk
Shop 8.30-5pm
Tours by arrangement

Set up by Clive Towner and Bob Hearson in 1998, both former managers at Greene King's now closed Biggleswade Brewery, they resumed brewing in Potton for the first time since 1922. They expanded from 20 barrels a week to 50 in 2004. Some 150 outlets are supplied direct. Seasonal beers: Bunny Hops (ABV 4.1%, March-April), No-Ale (ABV 4.8%, Nov-Dec). Bottle-conditioned beers: Butlers Ale (ABV 4.3%;) for the National Trust, Wimpole Hall, Shambles Bitter.

Shannon IPA (OG 1035, ABV 3.6%)
A well-balanced session bitter with good bitterness and fruity late-hop character. SIBA Eastern Region class winner 2003.

Gold (OG 1040, ABV 4.1%)
Golden-coloured, refreshing beer with a spicy/citrus late-hop character.

Village Bike (OG 1042, ABV 4.3%)
Classic English premium bitter, amber in colour, heavily late-hopped. CAMRA Bedfordshire champion beer 2003.

Shambles Bitter (OG 1043, ABV 4.3%)
A robust pale, heavily hopped beer with a subtle dry hop character imparted by Styrian Golding hops.

Pride of Potton (OG 1057, ABV 6%)
Impressive, robust amber ale with a malty aroma, malt and ripe fruit in the mouth, and a fading sweetness.

Princetown SIBA

Princetown Breweries Ltd, Tavistock Road, Princetown, Yelverton, Devon, PL20 6QF
Tel (01822) 890719
Fax (01822) 890798
Tours by arrangement

A brewery that is claimed to be the highest in England at 1,400 feet above sea level has moved to a new building and German-built plant. The site and plant has meant an investment of £1 million. The new brew-length is 30 barrels with scope to produce 60 barrels a day. Bottle-conditioned beer: Jail Ale.

Dartmoor IPA (OG 1039.5, ABV 4%)
There is a flowery hop aroma and taste with a bitter aftertaste to this full-bodied, amber-coloured beer.

Jail Ale (OG 1047.5, ABV 4.8%) ◆
Hops and fruit predominate in the flavour of this mid-brown beer, which has a slightly sweet aftertaste.

Purple Moose*

Bragdy Mws Piws Cyf/Purple Moose Brewery Ltd, Madoc Street, Porthmadog, Gwynedd, LL49 9DB
Tel/Fax (01766) 515571
Email beer@purplemoose.co.uk
Website www.purplemoose.co.uk
Shop Planned opening soon
Tours by arrangement

A 10-barrel plant opened in 2005 by Lawrence Washington in a former saw mill and farmers' warehouse in the coastal town of Porthmadog, famous for the Ffestiniog Railway and the adjoining harbour. The names of the beers reflect local history and the nearby mountains of Snowdonia.

Cwrw Madog/Madog's Ale (OG 1037, ABV 3.7%)

Cwrw Glaslyn/Glaslyn Ale (OG 1041, ABV 4.2%)

Ochr Tywyll y Mws/Dark Side of the Moose (OG 1044, ABV 4.6%)

Quartz*

Quartz Brewing Ltd, Archers, Archers Road, Kings Bromley, Staffordshire, DE13 7HW
Tel (01543) 473965
Email info@quartzbrewing.co.uk
Website www.quartzbrewing.co.uk

Brewing equipment was installed in May 2005 with trial brews due to take place in the summer. The brewery is run by Scott Barnett, a brewing engineer previously with Bass, and his wife Julia, a master brewer from Carlsberg-Tetley. The beer range had not been finalised when the guide went to press. See website.

Quay

See Dorset

Railway Tavern

♀ Famous Railway Tavern Brewing Co, 58 Station Road, Brightlingsea, Colchester, Essex, CO7 0DT
Tel (01206) 302581
Email famousrailway@yahoo.co.uk
Website www.geocities.com/famousrailway
Tours by arrangement

⊗ The brewery started life as a kitchen-sink affair, with Crab & Winkle Mild the staple brew. Crouch Vale Brewery obtained two fermenters from Vaux for the pub and now two barrels are brewed weekly, from September to the end of June. The future is likely to involve a bitter being added to the existing range of dark ales. Seasonal beers: Old Ale (ABV 4.7%, autumn), Fireside Porter (ABV 4.3%,winter/spring), Historic Nettle Ale (ABV 4.5%, May-June). Note that Crab & Winkle is made without any finings.

Crab & Winkle Mild (OG 1040, ABV 3.7%)

Bladderwrack Stout (OG 1050, ABV 4.3%)

Rainbow

♀ Rainbow Inn & Brewery, 73 Birmingham Road, Allesley Village, Coventry, West Midlands, CV5 9GT
Tel (024) 76402888
Tours by arrangement

⊕ Rainbow was set up in 1994 by Terry Rotherham. Since Unique Pub Co (now part of Enterprise Inns) took over the lease in 1999, only one guest ale is allowed.

Piddlebrook (OG 1035, ABV 3.8%)

Ramsbottom

Ramsbottom Brewery, Back Square Street, Ramsbottom, Bury, Greater Manchester, BL0 9BE
Tel (07739) 507416
Fax (0161) 761 1776
Email paulrammybrew@ontel.net.uk
Tours by arrangement

⊕ The brewery opened in 2002 with a five-barrel plant in the basement of an old Co-op. Beers are supplied nationwide by an agreement with Boggart Hole (qv). 25 outlets are supplied by the brewery. Seasonal beers: Santa Special (ABV 6%), Wind Farmer (ABV 6%).

Free Fall (OG 1042, ABV 3.8%)

Old Ground Mild (OG 1042, ABV 3.8%)
A traditional dark mild.

Ramsons (OG 1043, ABV 3.8%)
Amber session beer with a crisp, bitter aftertaste.

Tower Bitter (OG 1044, ABV 4%)
A straw-coloured beer with a complex mixture of fruit flavours.

Provident (OG 1048, ABV 4.5%)
Similar straw colour to Tower, but this is a very different beer. Herbal/spice aromas lead to strong fruit flavours with a bitter finish.

Ramsbury*

Ramsbury Brewery, Priory Farm, Axford, Marlborough, Wiltshire, SN8 2HA
Tel (01672) 541407
Fax (01672) 520753

A new brewery formed in the autumn of 2004, based on a farm high on the Marlborough Downs, using a 10-barrel plant in a refurbished building.

Bitter (ABV 3.6%)
Amber-coloured beer using traditional malted Optic spring barley from the farm. Goldings hops are used to give a smooth, delicate aroma and flavour.

Kennet Valley (ABV 4.1%)
A light amber, hoppy bitter with a distinctive Goldings aroma, using a blend of malted spring barley and a small amount of crystal malt. A complex beer with a long, dry finish.

Flintknapper (ABV 4.2%)

A blend of Optic and chocolate malts give a rich amber colour and malty taste. Goldings hops produce a smooth hoppy character.

Gold (ABV 4.5%)
A rich golden-coloured beer produced by blending Optic malt, crystal malt and a small amount of torrefied wheat. Goldings and Styrian Goldings hops give a light hoppy aroma and taste.

Ramsgate SIBA

Ramsgate Brewery Ltd, 98 Harbour Parade, Ramsgate, Kent, CT11 8LP
Tel (trade) (01843) 580037
Email info@ramsgatebrewery.co.uk
Website ramsgatebrewery.co.uk
Tours by arrangement

Ramsgate was established in 2002 by Lois and Eddie Gadd in a derelict restaurant on the sea front. The beers are brewed with Kentish hops and English malts only. Capacity was doubled in 2004 and there were plans to start bottling during 2005. Some 12 outlets are supplied. Seasonal beers: Doctor Sunshine's Special Friendly English Wheat Ale (ABV 4.2% summer), Gadds Dogbolter Winter Porter (ABV 5.6%, winter), Gadds Old Pig Ramsgate Brown Ale (ABV 4.8%, autumn).

Gadds No. 7 Ramsgate Bitter (OG 1037, ABV 3.8%)
Satisfying session bitter using local Fuggles hops.

Gadds Dark Mild (OG 1041, ABV 4%)

Gadds No. 5 Ramsgate Best (OG 1043, ABV 4.4%)
Complex, easy-drinking best bitter using East Kent Goldings and Fuggles hops.

Gadds No. 3 Ramsgate Pale Ale (OG 1048, ABV 5%)
A light and refreshing, full-strength pale ale, brewed with locally-grown East Kent Goldings hops.

Randalls SIBA

RW Randall Ltd, Vauxlaurens Brewery, St Julian's Avenue, St Peter Port, Guernsey, GY1 3JG
Tel (01481) 720134
Fax (01481) 713233
Shop 9-5
Tours by arrangement

Founded five generations ago, Randalls is the last independent, family-owned brewery in the islands. Seventeen pubs are owned (10 serving cask-conditioned beer) and 18 outlets are supplied. Seasonal beer: Island Gold (ABV 3.8%, spring/summer), Stout (ABV 5.5%, winter).

Mild (OG 1034, ABV 3.4%)

Cynful (OG 1035, ABV 3.5%)

Island Gold (ABV 3.8%)

Pale Ale (OG 1038, ABV 3.8%)

Patois (OG 1048, ABV 4.8%)
Amber in colour, with a hoppy aroma. Bitter and hoppy both in the palate and finish.

For the Cock & Bull, Guernsey

Sipping Bull (OG 1042, ABV 4.2%)
Medium-strong mild.

RCH SIBA

RCH Brewery, West Hewish, Weston-Super-Mare, Somerset, BS24 6RR
Tel (01934) 834447
Fax (01934) 834167
Email rchbrew@aol.com
Website www.rchbrewery.com
Shop. Mon-Fri 8.30-4

The brewery was originally installed in the early 1980s behind the Royal Clarence Hotel at Burnham-on-Sea. Since 1993 brewing has taken place on a commercial basis in a former cider mill at West Hewish. A new 30-barrel plant was installed in 2000. RCH now supplies 75 outlets and the award-winning beers are available nationwide through its own wholesaling company, which also distributes beers from other small independent breweries. Seasonal beers: see website. Bottle-conditioned beers: Pitchfork, Old Slug Porter, Double Header, Firebox, Ale Mary (ABV 6%).

Hewish IPA (OG 1036, ABV 3.6%)
Light, hoppy bitter with some malt and fruit, though slightly less fruit in the finish. Floral citrus hop aroma; pale/brown amber colour.

PG Steam (OG 1039, ABV 3.9%)
Amber-coloured, medium-bodied with a floral hop aroma with some fruit. Hoppy and bitter to taste, with some malt, fruit and subtle sweetness. The finish is similar.

Pitchfork (OG 1043, ABV 4.3%)
Floral citrus hop aroma with pale malt. Yellow/gold in colour, hops predominate in a full-bodied taste, which is slightly sweet. Long finish – a class act.

Old Slug Porter (OG 1046, ABV 4.5%)
Chocolate, coffee, roast malt and hops with lots of body and dark fruits. A complex, rich beer, dark brown in colour.

East Street Cream (OG 1050, ABV 5%)
A superb premium ale, pale brown in colour, it tastes malty with chocolate hints, hoppy, fruity and bitter-sweet. All flavours vie for dominance in what is a notable and well-crafted ale.

Double Header (OG 1053, ABV 5.3%)
Light brown, full-bodied strong bitter. Beautifully balanced flavours of malt, hops and tropical fruits are followed by a long, bitter-sweet finish. Very refreshing and easy drinking for its strength.

Firebox (OG 1060, ABV 6%) ◆
An aroma and taste of citrus hops and pale crystal malt are followed by a strong, complex, full-bodied, mid-brown beer with a well-balanced flavour of malt and hops.

Rebellion SIBA

Rebellion Beer Co, Marlow Brewery, Bencombe Farm, Marlow Bottom, Buckinghamshire, SL7 3LT
Tel (01628) 476594
Fax (01628) 476617
Email info@rebellionbeer.co.uk
Website www.rebellionbeer.co.uk
Shop 8-5.30 Mon-Fri; 9-5 Sat
Tours by arrangement 1st Tuesday every month at 7.30pm (£8)

⊗ The launch of the Rebellion Beer Company in 1993 marked the revival of Marlow's illustrious brewing tradition, dating back over 200 years. Rebellion filled the gap left in Marlow when Whitbread closed Wethereds in 1988. Since the brewery's relocation in 1999, Rebellion has had a steady growth, with several expansion projects underway in 2005. The Three Horseshoes pub is the brewery tap. 200 outlets are supplied. Rebellion Mild (ABV 3.5%) is supplied exclusively to the pub. Seasonal beers: Overdraft (ABV 4.3%, Jan-Feb), Zebedee (ABV 4.7%, spring), Blonde (ABV 4.3%, summer), Red (ABV 4.7%, autumn), Roasted Nuts (ABV 4.6%, winter). Bottle-conditioned beer: White (ABV 4.5%).

IPA (OG 1039, ABV 3.7%) ◆
Copper-coloured bitter, sweet and malty, with resinous and red apple flavours. Caramel and fruit decline to leave a dry, bitter and malty finish.

Smuggler (OG 1042, ABV 4.1%) ◆
A red-brown beer, well-bodied and bitter with an uncompromisingly dry, bitter finish.

Mutiny (OG 1046, ABV 4.5%) ◆
Tawny in colour, this full-bodied best bitter is predominantly fruity and moderately bitter with crystal malt continuing to a dry finish.

Rectory SIBA

Rectory Ales Ltd, Streat Hill Farm Barn, Streat Hill Farm, Streat Hill, Streat, East Sussex, BN6 8RP
Tel/Fax (01273) 890570
Email sales@rectory-ales.co.uk
Tours by arrangement

⊗ Rectory was founded in 1995 by the Rector of Plumpton, the Rev Godfrey Broster, to generate funds for the maintenance of his three parish churches. 107 parishioners are shareholders. The brewing capacity is now 20 barrels a week. All outlets are supplied from the brewery. Seasonal beer: Christmas Cheer (ABV 3.8%, December). Bottle-conditioned beer: Rector's Revenge.

The Rector's Ale (OG 1038, ABV 3.8%)

Rector's Revenge (OG 1054, ABV 5.4%)
Copper-brown strong bitter with a complex aroma, becoming more hoppy in the mouth with a dry, bitter finish.

Redburn

Redburn Brewery, Roselea, Redburn, Hexham, Northumberland, NE47 7EA
Tel/Fax (01434) 344656
Email redburnbrewery@btinternet.com

Redburn Brewery, in the heart of Roman Wall country, marks the resurrection of the Black Bull Brewery at Haltwhistle, with the plant removed to Redburn. There are some occasional beers. Seasonal beers: Mitis Mild (ABV 3.5%), Solis Pale Ale (ABV 4.1%), Bishop Ridley Ale (ABV 4.8%), Viscum (ABV 5%). Bottle-conditioned beers: Haltwhistle Pride (ABV 4.3%), Fortis Stout, Bishop Ridley Ale, Twice Brewed IPA (ABV 5.2%), Redburn Special (ABV 6%), Optimus (ABV 7%).

Ebrius Bitter (ABV 3.7%)

1555 (ABV 4.1%)

Fortis Stout (ABV 4.3%)

Summus Best Bitter (ABV 4.4%)

Optimus Ale (ABV 5%)

Red Rose SIBA

Red Rose Brewery, Unit 4, Stanley Court, Alan Ramsbottom Way, Great Harwood, Blackburn, Lancashire, BB6 7UR
Tel (01254) 877373
Fax (01254) 877375
Email beer@redrosebrewery.co.uk
Tours by arrangement

☺ Red Rose Brewery was launched in 2002 by micro-electronic design engineer Peter Booth to supply the Royal Hotel, Great Harwood. A 2.5-barrel capacity plant was installed to replace the pilot 0.75 kit and to allow for sales to other pubs. Demand for the ales outstripped capacity and the brewery expanded to four fermenting vessels, bringing production up to more than 10 barrels a week. Further expansion in to a new unit in 2005 has allowed production to grow further and as a result the beers are now available nationwide. Red Rose uses English malted barley and English hops. No extracts or adjuncts are used. Seasonal beers: Cold Turkey Festive Ale (ABV 3.8%), Blackpool Belle Golden Age Ale (ABV 4%), Pissed Over Pendle Halloween Ale (ABV 4.4%), 34th Street Miracle Beer (ABV 4.9%). Special beers are available throughout the year.

Bowley Best (ABV 3.7%)
Darkish northern bitter. Malty, yet sharp with hoppy citrus finish.

Quaffing Ale (ABV 3.8%)

Treacle Miners Tipple (ABV 3.9%)

Blackpool Belle (OG 1040, ABV 4%)
Golden bitter with robust taste, soft, slightly sweet and malty.

Felix (ABV 4.2%)
Dry, pale and remarkably hoppy with a keen nose, yet rounded and smooth with a lingering finish.

Old Ben (ABV 4.3%)
Pale, clean-tasting, crisp beer with a strong hop presence and no sweetness.

Lancashire and Yorkshire Aleway/Steaming (ABV 4.5%)
Copper-coloured, strong beer. Initially sweet and malty, though with a good hop aroma. Full and fruity.

Older Empire (ABV 5.5%)

Care Taker of History (ABV 6%)
A dark, strong ale with a roast malt aroma. The taste is complex, rich and warming. Well-balanced and drinkable.

Red Shoot

Red Shoot Inn Brewery, Toms Lane, Linwood, Ringwood, Hampshire, BH24 3QT
Tel (01425) 475792

The brewery, owned by Wadworth, was commissioned in 1998 with Forest Gold as the first brew. Tom's Tipple was introduced in 1998 as a winter brew and is now a permanent brand. Red Shoot would like to expand but the size of plant (2.5 barrels) makes this difficult, though some occasional beers are produced.

Forest Gold (ABV 3.8%)

Tom's Tipple (ABV 4.8%)

Red Squirrel*

Red Squirrel Brewery, 14B Mimram Road, Hertford, SG14 1NN
Tel (01992) 501100
Fax (01992) 500660
Email gary@redsquirrelbrewery.co.uk
Website www.redsquirrelbrewery.co.uk
Tours by arrangement

Red Squirrel started brewing in 2004 with a 10-barrel plant. There are plans to expand the brewery and product range, including adding bottled beers and speciality American beers. 40 outlets are supplied.

Dark Ruby Mild (OG 1036, ABV 3.7%)

RSB (OG 1036, ABV 3.7%)

Conservation Bitter (OG 1040, ABV 4.1%)

IPA (OG 1040, ABV 4.1%)

Gold (OG 1041, ABV 4.2%)

Scottish Ale (OG 1042, ABV 4.2%)

Wheat Beer (OG 1044, ABV 4.5%)

Stout (OG 1047, ABV 4.9%)

Hertfordshire Honey Porter (OG 1048, ABV 5%)

Reepham

Reepham Brewery, Unit 1, Collers Way, Reepham, Norwich, Norfolk, NR10 4SW
Tel (01603) 871091

Reepham has completed 21 years of continuous brewing on the same premises. A beer in the style of Newcastle Brown Ale was introduced (Tyne Brown), to show support for the Tynesiders' brewery. Some 20 outlets are supplied. Bottle-conditioned beer: Rapier Pale Ale (ABV 4.2%).

Granary Bitter (OG 1038, ABV 3.5%)
A gold-coloured beer with a light hoppy aroma followed by a malty sweetish flavour with some smoke notes. A well-balanced beer with a long, moderately hoppy aftertaste.

Rapier Pale Ale (OG 1043, ABV 4.2%)
Pale brown beer with a swirling citrus and malt nose. A complex mix of bitter hoppiness and lemon bolstered by a smoky malt background. The long-lasting finish becomes refreshingly dry.

Velvet Sweet Stout (OG 1044, ABV 4.5%)
There is a heavy roast influence in aroma and taste. A smoky malt feel to the taste produces an interesting combination that is both creamy and well-defined. Initial fruit and hop contributions indicate a subtle sweetness that soon fades to leave a growing dry bitterness.

Tyne Brown (OG 1046, ABV 4.6%)

St Agnes (OG 1047, ABV 4.8%)
Fund-raising brew for a local church. Smooth and creamy with bananas to the fore in aroma and taste. Smoky malt overtones subside as increasing bitterness dominates a gently receding finish.

Rhymney*

Rhymney Brewery Ltd, Unit A2 Valley Enterprise Centre, Pant Industrial Estate, Dowlais, Merthyr Tydfil, CF48 2SR
Tel (01685) 722253
Email enquiries@rhymneybreweryltd.com
Website www.rhymneybreweryltd.com

Rhymney first brewed in January 2005. The 50-hl plant, sourced from Canada, is capable of producing both cask and keg beers.

Centenary Ale (ABV 3.9%)

Bevans Bitter (ABV 4.2%)

Bitter (ABV 4.5%)

Ridgeway SIBA

Ridgeway Brewing, Beer Counter Ltd, South Stoke, Oxfordshire, RG8 0JW
Tel (01491) 873474
Email peter.scholey@beercounter.co.uk

Ridgeway was set up by ex-Brakspear head brewer Peter Scholey, who also acts as an adviser at the new Brakspear plant at Witney (qv). At present the cask and bottle-conditioned beers are brewed by Peter using Hepworth of Horsham's equipment (qv). Bottle-conditioned beers: Ridgeway Bitter, Bad Elf (ABV 6%, mainly for US market).

Bitter (OG 1040, ABV 4%)
Uses Challenger and the new Boadicea hop.

Iron Man (OG 1045, ABV 4.5%)
Goldings and German Hallertauer hops.

For Coniston Brewing (bottle conditioned):

Coniston Bluebird (ABV 4.2%)

Coniston Old Man (ABV 4.8%)

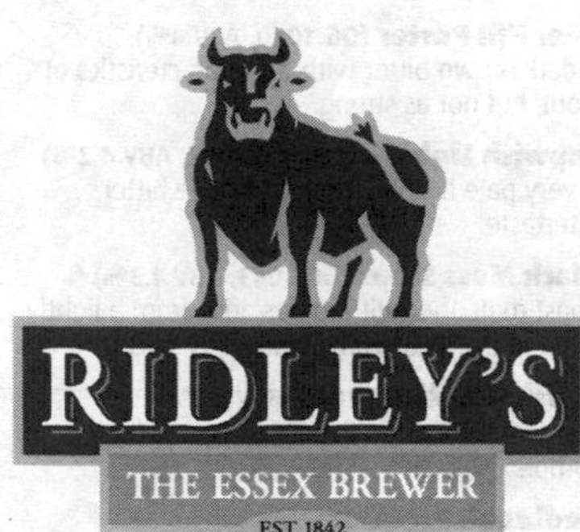

Ridleys IFBB SIBA

**T D Ridley & Sons Ltd,
Hartford End Brewery, Hartford End,
Chelmsford, Essex, CM3 1JZ
Tel (01371) 820316
Fax (01371) 821216
Email info@ridleys.co.uk
Website www.ridleys.co.uk**
Shop open via reception Mon-Fri 9-4
Due to close Autumn 2005

⊗ Ridleys was established by Thomas Dixon Ridley in 1842 and is still a family-owned company. It has an estate of 75 pubs and also supplies 500-600 other outlets. In 2002, Ridleys purchased Tolly Cobbold and closed the Ipswich brewery. Only Tolly Original survives, Mild and Old Strong having been withdrawn. Ridley's now brews XX Mild under contract for Greene King. In order to help Kelham Island (qv) cope with the demand for Pale Rider, Ridley's brews a carefully-matched version of the beer called Pale Island. Seasonal beers: Rumpus (ABV 4.5%, Jan-March) ■, Prospect (ABV 4.1%, April-June), Spectacular (ABV 4.6%, July-Sept), Witchfinder Porter (ABV 4.3%, Oct-Nov) Winter Royale (ABV 4.6%, Dec-Jan).

IPA (OG 1034, ABV 3.5%) ◆
Pleasant session bitter with a good balance of malt and hops, and a light aroma that hints at greater complexity.

Tolly Original (OG 1038, ABV 3.8%) ◆
A fruity aroma with suggestions of toffee precedes a taste dominated by liquorice and malt. Bitter hops are more prominent in the finish.

Old Bob (OG 1055, ABV 5.1%) ◻ ◆
Sweetish strong bitter with a warming maltiness offset by hints of liquorice and fennel.

For Greene King

XX Mild (OG 1035, ABV 3%) ◆
Biscuity mild with a roast coffee character. Chocolate tones come through in the finish; malt persists throughout. A good copy of the original Greene King brew.

For Kelham Island

Pale Island (OG 1050, ABV 5.2%) ◆
Initially a soft, fruity golden ale, with an aroma redolent of honey and melon. Bitterness increases in the finish. A faithful copy of Kelham Island Pale Rider (qv).

Ring O' Bells SIBA

**Ring O' Bells Brewery Ltd, Pennygillam Way, Pennygillam Industrial Estate, Launceston, Cornwall, PL15 7ED
Tel/Fax (01566) 777787
Email enquiries@ringobellsbrewery.co.uk
Website www.ringobellsbrewery.co.uk**
Shop Mon-Fri 9-4pm
Tours by arrangement

⊗ Ring O'Bells started trading in the 13th century as a cider farm-cum-alehouse for the stonemasons of St Torney Church, North Hill. It closed in 1918 and after 79 years of neglect new owners set about restoring the old ale house and rebuilding the cider press and vat. Intensive research with the help of micro-biologists re-cultured the original yeast strain that was trapped within the walls of the old vat. The culture is now used to ferment today's ales, some 600 years later. The success of the beers when launched in 1999 led to the brewery moving to new premises in Launceston in 2001. Some 300 outlets are supplied.

Porkers Pride (OG 1036, ABV 3.8%)
A light, refreshing ale that is well-balanced with a hoppy, malty, clean, finish.

Surf Boar (OG 1038, ABV 4%)
A golden-coloured ale with a pronounced hoppy aroma and taste with a clean bitter finish.

Bodmin Boar (OG 1041.5, ABV 4.3%) ◆
Apple and aromatic nose, heavy and fruity in the mouth with a long bitter finish.

One & All (OG 1042, ABV 4.4%)
A light, clean ale with a good hoppy aroma and dry finish. Proceeds go to the Pirate Trust.

Farmer Dray (OG 1043, ABV 4.5%)
Light, ruby-coloured ale with a good flowery aroma.

Dreckly (OG 1046, ABV 4.8%)
A warm, ruby-coloured, strong ale fortified with gorse and heather. Rich in malt with a spicy aroma and good malty aftertaste.

Tipsy Trotters (OG 1048.3, ABV 5.1%)
A strong, dark ale with a good malty taste, a wheaty aroma, clean finish and a pleasant bite.

Sozzled Swine (OG 1051.8, ABV 5.5%)
A rich, ruby-coloured strong ale with a good flowery aroma, well balanced with a malty aftertaste.

Ringwood IFBB SIBA

Ringwood Brewery Ltd, Christchurch Road, Ringwood, Hampshire, BH24 3AP
Tel (01425) 471177
Fax (01425) 480273
Email enquiries@ringwoodbrewery.co.uk
Website www.ringwoodbrewery.co.uk
Shop 9.30-5 Mon-Fri; 9.30-12 Sat
Tours by arrangement

⊗ Ringwood opened in 1978 as a tiny micro and moved in 1986 to the former Tunks Brewery site in Ringwood. A new brewhouse and fermenters have been installed, boosting production to 30,000 barrels a year. Some 600 outlets are supplied from the brewery. Seven pubs are owned. A major new development in 2004-05 has been the sourcing of local Maris Otter barley – for use mainly in seasonal beers – from Hampshire growers, which is then malted at Warminster Maltings. Seasonal beers: Boondoggle (ABV 4%, summer), Bold Forester (ABV 4.2%, spring), Huffkin (ABV 4.4%, autumn), XXXX Porter (ABV 4.7%, winter). All seasonal beers are now being bottled, with the exception of Boondoggle. Bottle-conditioned beers: Fortyniner ■, XXXX Porter, Bold Forester, Huffkin.

Best Bitter **(OG 1038, ABV 3.8%)** ◆
Easy-drinking, well-balanced session bitter. A malty and hoppy aroma leads to a malty taste with some hops and sweetness. A malty and bitter finish.

Fortyniner **(OG 1049, ABV 4.9%)** ◆
A mid-brown beer. A fruity aroma with some malt leads to a well-balanced taste with malt, fruit and hop flavours all present. The finish is bitter-sweet with some fruit.

Old Thumper **(OG 1055, ABV 5.6%)** ◆
A powerful mid-brown beer. A fruity aroma preludes a sweet, malty taste with some fruit. Surprisingly bitter aftertaste, with malt and hops.

Riverhead

⚲ Riverhead Brewery Ltd, 2 Peel Street, Marsden, Huddersfield, West Yorkshire, HD7 6BR
Tel (01484) 841270
Email info@riverheadbrewery.co.uk
Website www.riverheadbrewery.co.uk
Tours by arrangement

Riverhead is a brew-pub that opened in 1995 after conversion from an old grocery store. The seven beers are named after local reservoirs, with the height of the reservoir relating to the strength of the beer. Occasional specials such as Jazz Bitter (ABV 4%, for Marsden Jazz Festival), and Ruffled Feathers Bitter (ABV 4.2%, for Marsden Cuckoo Day) are brewed. The brewery also supplies three local outlets on an occasional basis. Black Moss Stout is suitable for vegans and vegetarians.

Sparth Mild **(OG 1038, ABV 3.6%)** ◻ ◆
A light-bodied, dry mild, with a dark ruby colour. Fruity aroma with roasted flavour and a dry finish.

Butterley Bitter **(OG 1038, ABV 3.8%)** ◆
A dry, amber-coloured, hoppy session beer.

Deer Hill Porter **(OG 1040, ABV 4%)**
A dark brown bitter with the characteristics of stout, but not as strong.

Cupwith Light Bitter **(OG 1042, ABV 4.2%)**
A very pale bitter with a distinctive bitter aftertaste.

Black Moss Stout **(OG 1043, ABV 4.3%)** ◆
Roast malt and fruit aromas arise from a lightly hopped dry stout with a chocolaty finish.

March Haigh **(OG 1046, ABV 4.6%)**
A smooth, rounded flavour is created by the complex selection of hops.

Redbrook Premium
(OG 1055, ABV 5.5%) ◆
A rich and malty strong beer, with malt and fruit in the taste, and a sweet, fruity finish.

Riverside

Riverside Brewery, Unit 1, Church Lane, Wainfleet All Saints, Lincolnshire, PE24 4BY.
Tel (01754) 881288
Website
www.wainfleet.info/shops/brewery-riverside
Tours by arrangement

Riverside started brewing in 2003 almost across the road from Bateman's, using a five-barrel plant supplied by Rob Jones of Dark Star. Owner John Dixon had not previously brewed but he was assisted by his father Ken, who had been head brewer at several breweries, including Bateman's and Castletown. Eight barrels a week are produced for local trade, with some 15 outlets supplied.

Dixon's Major Bitter **(OG 1038, ABV 3.9%)**

Light Brigade **(OG 1038, ABV 3.9%)**

Dixon's Desert Rat **(OG 1048, ABV 4.8%)**

John Roberts SIBA

John Roberts Brewing Co Ltd, 16 Market Square, Bishops Castle, Shropshire, SY9 5BW
Tel/Fax (01588) 638392
Email tunsbrewery@aol.co.uk
Website under construction
Tours by prior arrangement

⊗ Following a long period of renovation and investment in new plant, the famous old brewery is now in full production under head brewer Bill Bainbridge, who has a passion for producing old-fashioned ales. Some 60 outlets are supplied. Seasonal beer: Old Scrooge (ABV 6%, winter/Christmas).

Three 8 **(ABV 3.8%)**

XXX **(ABV 4.3%)** ◆
A pale, sweetish bitter with a light hop aftertaste that has a honey finish. Very drinkable.

Castle Steamer **(ABV 4.4%)** ◆
A very dark and well-roasted porter/stout with coffee tastes and a hop finish.

Cleric's Cure **(ABV 5%)**
A pale beer with strong hopping to resemble old IPAs.

Robinson's IFBB

Frederic Robinson Ltd, Unicorn Brewery, Stockport, Cheshire, SK1 1JJ
Tel (0161) 612 4061
Fax (0161) 476 6011
Email brewery@frederic-robinson.co.uk
Website www.frederic-robinson.co.uk
Shop – visitors' shop only
Tours by arrangement

⊗ Established in 1838, the brewery is now run by the fifth and sixth generation of the Robinson family. With an estate of more than 400 pubs in the North-west and an ever increasing free trade presence, Robinson beers are now available nationally through wholesalers. As a result of the takeover of Jennings (qv) by Wolverhampton & Dudley, Robinson's no longer owns shares in the Cockermouth brewery. Seasonal beers: Enigma (ABV 4.7%), English Champion, Coopers Bell, Sunny Jim (all ABV 3.8%), Kick Off (ABV 4.2%), Robin (ABV 4.5%).

Hatters (OG 1032, ABV 3.3%)
A light mild with a fruity aroma, and biscuity malt and a fresh fruitiness in the taste and finish. A darkened version is available in a handful of outlets and badged Dark Mild.

Old Stockport (OG 1034, ABV 3.5%)
A beer with a refreshing taste of malt, hops and citrus fruit, a fruity aroma, and a short, dry finish.

XB (OG 1040, ABV 4%)
An overly sweet and malty bitter with a bitter citrus peel fruitiness and a hint of liquorice in the finish.

Cumbria Way (OG 1040, ABV 4.1%)
A pronounced malt aroma with rich fruit notes. Rounded malt and hops in the mouth, long dry finish with citrus fruit notes. Brewed for the Hartley's estate in Cumbria.

Unicorn (OG 1041.5, ABV 4.2%)
Amber beer with a fruity aroma. Hoppy, bitter and quite fruity to taste, with a bitter finish.

Double Hop (OG 1050, ABV 5%)
Pale brown beer with malt and fruit on the nose. Full hoppy taste with malt and fruit, leading to a hoppy, bitter finish.

Old Tom (OG 1079.4, ABV 8.5%)
A full-bodied, dark beer with malt, fruit and chocolate in the aroma. A delightfully complex range of flavours includes dark chocolate; full maltiness, port and fruits lead to a long, bitter-sweet aftertaste.

Rockingham SIBA

Rockingham Ales, c/o 25 Wansford Road, Elton, Cambridgeshire, PE8 6RZ
Tel (01832) 280722
Email brian@rockinghamales.co.uk
Website www.rockinghamales.co.uk

⊗ A part-time brewery established in 1997 that operates from a converted farm building near Blatherwycke, Northamptonshire (business address as above). The two-barrel plant produces a prolific range of beers and supplies half a dozen local outlets. The regular beers are brewed on a rota basis, with special beers brewed to order. Seasonal beers: Fineshade (ABV 3.8%, autumn), Sanity Clause (ABV 4.3%, December), Old Herbaceous (ABV 4.5%, winter).

Forest Gold (OG 1040, ABV 3.9%)
A hoppy blonde ale with citrus flavours. Well-balanced and clean finishing.

Hop Devil (OG 1040, ABV 3.9%)
Six hop varieties give this light amber ale a bitter start and spicy finish.

A1 Amber Ale (OG 1041, ABV 4%)
A hoppy session beer with fruit and blackcurrant undertones.

Saxon Cross (OG 1041, ABV 4.1%)
A golden-red ale with nut and coffee aromas. Citrus hop flavours predominate.

Fruits of the Forest (OG 1043, ABV 4.2%)
A multi-layered beer in which summer fruits and several spices compete with a big hop presence.

Dark Forest (OG 1050, ABV 5%)
A dark and complex beer, similar to a Belgian dubbel, with numerous malty/smoky flavours that give way to a fruity bitter finish.

Rodham's*

Rodham's Brewery, 74 Albion Street, Otley, West Yorkshire, LS21 1BZ
Tel (01943) 464530

Michael Rodham has put 25 years of home-brewing to use by going commercial with a one-barrel plant in the cellar of his house.

Bitter (ABV 3.5%)

Old Albion (ABV 4.6%)

Rooster's SIBA

Rooster's Brewing Co Ltd, Unit 3, Grimbald Park, Wetherby Road, Knaresborough, North Yorkshire, HG5 8LJ
Tel/Fax (01423) 865959
Email sean@roosters.co.uk
Website www.roosters.co.uk

⊛ Rooster's Brewery was opened in 1993 by Sean and Alison Franklin. Its sister company, Outlaw Brewery Co, started in 1996. In 2001 the brewery relocated to larger premises at Knaresborough. Production is close to 80 barrels a week. Under the Rooster's label, Sean and Alison make seven regular beers while Outlaw produces experimental beers. They change materials or process or both to make a new beer every two months. Sean Franklin is a devotee of hops and uses many varieties, including North American, in his brews. 500 outlets are supplied.

Special (OG 1038, ABV 3.9%)
Yellow in colour, a full-bodied, floral bitter with fruit and hop notes being carried over in to the long aftertaste. Hops and bitterness tend to increase in the finish.

YPA (OG 1042, ABV 4.3%)

Yankee (OG 1042, ABV 4.3%)
A straw-coloured beer with a delicate, fruity aroma leading to a well-balanced taste of malt and hops with a slight evidence of sweetness, followed by a refreshing, fruity/bitter finish.

Hooligan (OG 1042, ABV 4.3%)

Pale and aromatic bitter, with a citrus fruit aroma with hints of tangerine. The palate has pronounced fruit and hops with a hint of sweetness. Bitterness and hops linger in the aftertaste, accompanied by a background of fruit flavours.

Cream (OG 1045, ABV 4.7%) ◆
A pale-coloured beer with a complex, floral bouquet leading to a well-balanced, refreshing taste. Fruit lasts throughout and into the aftertaste.

Rother Valley SIBA

Rother Valley Brewing Co, Gate Court Farm, Station Road, Northiam, East Sussex, TN31 6QT
Tel (01797) 252922
Fax (01797) 253550
Tours by arrangement

⊗ Rother Valley was established in Northiam in 1993 on a hop farm overlooking the river that marks the boundary between Kent and Sussex. Brewing capacity increased in 2005 and some 60 outlets are supplied. Special monthly beers are brewed to complement the range. Seasonal beers: Golden Valley Wheat Beer (ABV 4.2%, summer), Blues (ABV 5%, autumn-winter), Holly Daze (ABV varies, Christmas).

Wealden Bitter (OG 1038, ABV 3.7%)

Smild (OG 1038, ABV 3.8%)
Dark, chocolaty mild.

Level Best (OG 1040, ABV 4%) ◆
Full-bodied tawny session bitter with a malt and fruit aroma, malty taste and a dry, hoppy finish.

Hoppers Ale (OG 1044, ABV 4.4%)

Boadicea (OG 1046, ABV 4.6%)

Rudgate SIBA

Rudgate Brewery Ltd, 2 Centre Park, Marston Moor Business Park, Tockwith, York, North Yorkshire, YO26 7QF
Tel/Fax (01423) 358382
Email sales@rudgate-beers.co.uk
Website www.rudgate-beers.co.uk
Shop Mail-order available

⊛ Rudgate Brewery was founded in 1992 and is located in an old armoury building on the edge of a disused World War II airfield. It has a 15-barrel plant and four open fermenting vessels, producing more than 30 barrels a week. Rudgate uses only Yorkshire malts from Fawcetts and mainly English whole hops. The brewery now supplies more than 250 outlets. Christmas beers include Rudolph's Ruin (ABV 4.6%) and Crimble Ale (ABV 4.2%). Other seasonal beers are produced on a monthly basis.

Viking Bitter (OG 1038, ABV 3.8%) ▢ ◆
An initially warming and malty, full-bodied beer, with hops and fruit lingering into the aftertaste.

Battleaxe (OG 1041, ABV 4.2%) ◆
A well-hopped bitter with slightly sweet initial taste and light bitterness. Complex fruit character gives a memorable aftertaste.

Ruby Mild (OG 1044, ABV 4.4%) ▢
Nutty, rich ruby ale, stronger than usual for a mild.

Special (OG 1042, ABV 4.5%)

Well Blathered (OG 1045.5, ABV 5%)

Rugby*

Rugby Brewing Company Ltd, Units 2-6, Upton Road, Rugby, Warwickshire, CV22 7DL
Tel (0845) 0091626

Rugby started brewing in 2005 and is owned by the Pig Pub Company. All the beer names are connected to the town or Rugby Union football. The brewery supplies beer to a number of local outlets, including a night club, the White Rooms.

1823 (ABV 3.5%)
A chocolate mild.

Webb Ellis (ABV 3.8%)
A light ale.

Victory (ABV 4.2%)
A reddish-coloured bitter.

Union (ABV 4.4%)
A hoppy, light-coloured beer.

No 8 (ABV 5%)

Ryburn SIBA

Ryburn Brewery, 26 Wakefield Road, Sowerby Bridge, Halifax, West Yorkshire, HX6 2AZ
Tel (01422) 835413 Fax (01422) 836488
Email ryburnbrewery@talk21.com
Tours by arrangement

⊛ The brewery was established in 1989 at Mill House, Sowerby Bridge, but has since been relocated to the company's sole tied house, the Rams Head. Some business is done with the local free trade but the chief market for the brewery's products is via wholesalers.

Best Mild (OG 1033, ABV 3.3%)

Best Bitter (OG 1038, ABV 3.8%) ◆
Light-coloured, easy-drinking standard Northern bitter. Lightly flavoured with a bitter aftertaste.

Numpty Bitter (OG 1044, ABV 4.2%) ◆
Amber-coloured best bitter with a sweeter, fruitier flavour than Best Bitter.

Rydale Bitter (OG 1044, ABV 4.2%)

Light Ale (OG 1044, ABV 4.4%)

Luddite (OG 1048, ABV 5%) ◆
Complex flavoured black beer with a liquorice undertone and a well-balanced sweetness. Sustained malty finish.

Stabbers Bitter (OG 1052, ABV 5.2%) ◆
Copper-coloured fruity bitter. Its drinkability belies its strength.

Saddleworth

Church Inn & Saddleworth Brewery, Church Lane, Uppermill, Oldham, Greater Manchester, OL3 6LW
Tel (01457) 820902/872415
Tours by arrangement

⊛ Saddleworth started brewing in 1997 in a brewhouse that had been closed for around 120 years. The first brew, Saddleworth More, sold for £1 per pint; it now sells at £1.10. Brewery and inn are set in an historic location at the top of a valley overlooking Saddleworth and next to St Chads Church, which dates from 1215. Seasonal beers: Ayrton's Ale (ABV 4.1%, April-May), Robyn's Bitter (ABV 4.6%, Nov-Dec), Christmas Carol (ABV 7.5%, Dec-Jan), Harvest Moon (ABV 4.1%, Aug-Sept).

More (ABV 3.8%)

Bert Corner (ABV 4%)

St George's Bitter (ABV 4%)

Hop Smacker (ABV 4.1%)
A golden, refreshing bitter, brewed with five different varieties of hops.

Indian Z Pale Ale (ABV 4.1%)

Shaftbender (ABV 5.4%)
A black porter/stout bitter.

St Austell IFBB SIBA

St Austell Brewery Co Ltd, 63 Trevarthian Road, St Austell, Cornwall, PL25 4BY
Tel (01726) 74444
Fax (01726) 68965
Email info@staustellbrewery.co.uk
Website www.staustellbrewery.co.uk
Shop 9-5 Mon-Fri
Visitor centre and tours (01726) 66022

St Austell Brewery celebrated 150 years of brewing in 2001. Founded by Walter Hicks in 1851, the company is still family owned and run, with Walter Hicks's great-great-grandson, James Staughton, at the helm as managing director since 2000. He leads a young team, with head brewer Roger Ryman, and there is a powerful commitment to cask beer. The beer range has been overhauled, with new branding and pump clips in pubs. Cask beer is available in all 150 licensed houses, as well as in the free trade throughout Cornwall, Devon and Somerset. An attractive visitor centre offers guided tours and souvenirs from the brewery. The brewery hosts its own Celtic Beer Festival late in the year (see website). Bottle-conditioned beers: Admiral's Ale (ABV 5%), Clouded Yellow (ABV 5%).

IPA (OG 1034, ABV 3.4%)
Copper/bronze in colour, the nose blossoms with fresh hops. The palate is clean and full bodied with a hint of toffee caramel. The finish is short and crisp.

Tinners Ale (OG 1038, ABV 3.7%)
A deservedly popular, golden beer with an appetising malt aroma and a good balance of malt and hops in the flavour. Lasting finish.

Dartmoor Best Bitter (OG 1039, ABV 3.9%)
A delicately hopped, golden bitter. Originally brewed at the now-closed Ferguson Brewery in Plymouth, DBB was brewed by St Austell for Carlsberg, but it is now owned by St Austell and is spearheading the company's increased presence in Devon.

Black Prince (OG 1041, ABV 4%)
Little aroma, but a strong, malty character. A caramel-sweetish flavour is followed by a good, lingering aftertaste that is sweet but with a fruity dryness.

Tribute (OG 1043, ABV 4.2%)
Pale brown ale capable of a tight, persistent head. The aroma is of malt and fruity Oregon hops, with a balance of malt and hoppy bitterness in the mouth. The finish is moderately dry with malt. A refreshing best bitter aimed to expand beyond Cornwall.

Hicks Special Draught/HSD (OG 1051, ABV 5%)
An aromatic, fruity, hoppy bitter that is initially sweet and has an aftertaste of pronounced bitterness, but whose flavour is fully rounded. A good premium beer.

St George's

St George's Brewing Co Ltd, Bush Lane, Callow End, Worcester, WR2 4TF
Tel/Fax (01905) 831316
Email info@stgeorgesbrewery.com
Tours by arrangement

The brewery was established in 1998 and is now owned by Brian McCluskie and managed by Andrew Sankey. They have a strong commitment to traditional brewing. The five-barrel plant produces a range of monthly specials, as well as bespoke beers on request. St George's supplies some 100 outlets and uses wholesalers for wider distribution.

Maiden's Saviour (ABV 3.9%)
Light and refreshing, brewed using traditional English barley and hops.

Paragon Steam (ABV 4%)
Styled on California steam beer, this amber thirst-quencher features a marked maize and hop character.

War Drum (ABV 4.1%)
A sharp, bitter taste with a hint of sweetness. Afterwards the memory is of bitter hops.

Premium (ABV 4.3%)
Straw-coloured and medium-bodied with a gentle fruity nose and a combination of bitterness with malt on the palate and finish.

Nimrod (ABV 4.5%)
Robust tawny ale with a rich maltiness evident throughout, complemented by fruity hops and slight roast undertones on the tongue, which then continue to the end.

St Peter's SIBA EAB

St Peter's Brewery Co. Ltd, St Peter's Hall, St Peter South Elmham, Bungay, Suffolk, NR35 1NQ
Tel (01986) 782322

Fax (01986) 782505
Email beers@stpetersbrewery.co.uk
Website www.stpetersbrewery.co.uk
Shop Weekdays 9-5, Sat-Sun 11-5
Tours by arrangement

⊗ St Peter's was launched in 1996 by marketing expert John Murphy. The brewery concentrates in the main on bottled beer (80% of capacity) but has a rapidly increasing cask market. Recent brewery developments include an in-house rotary bottling line and an increase in brewing capacity from 100 barrels a week to 175 barrels. Two pubs are owned and 30 outlets are supplied. Seasonal beers: Ruby Red (ABV 4.3%), Wheat Beer (ABV 4.7%), Summer Ale (ABV 6.5%), Winter Ale (ABV 6.5%), Spiced Ale (ABV 6.5%), Cream Stout (ABV 6.5%).

Mild (OG 1037, ABV 3.7%)

Best Bitter (OG 1038, ABV 3.7%) ◆
A complex but well-balanced hoppy brew. A gentle hop nose introduces a singular hoppiness with supporting malt notes and underlying bitterness. Other flavours fade to leave a long, dry, hoppy finish.

Organic Best (OG 1041, ABV 4.1%)
Soil Association accredited, organically-grown Chariot malted barley is used to make the mash for this beer, which is hopped with organic Hallertauer hops.

Organic Ale (OG 1045, ABV 4.5%)
Soil Association standard, light malted barley from Scotland, with organic Target hops create a refreshing ale with a delicate character.

Golden Ale (OG 1047, ABV 4.7%) ◆
Amber-coloured, full-bodied, robust ale. A strong hop bouquet leads to a mix of malt and hops combined with a dry, fruity hoppiness. The malt quickly subsides, leaving creamy bitterness.

Grapefruit Beer (OG 1047, ABV 4.7%)
Wheat Beer is the base for this refreshing, zesty/pithy beer.

Lemon and Ginger Spiced Ale (OG 1047, ABV 4.7%)
A traditional English ale with a light citrus aroma and a delicate ginger aftertaste.

Salamander

Salamander Brewing Co Ltd, 22 Harry Street, Bradford, West Yorkshire, BD4 9PH
Tel (01274) 652323
Fax (01274) 680101
Email salamanderbrewing@fsmail.net
Website www.salamanderbrewing.com
Tours by arrangement

⊗ Salamander first brewed in 2000 in a former pork pie factory. It is mainly composed of ex-dairy plant with some equipment from Mitchells of Lancaster. Further expansion during 2004 took the brewery to 40-barrel capacity. There are direct deliveries to more widespread areas such as Cumbria, East Yorkshire and Lancashire in addition to the established trade of about 100 outlets throughout Lancashire, Manchester, North Yorkshire and Derbyshire.

Mudpuppy (OG 1042, ABV 4.2%) ◆
A well-balanced, copper-coloured best bitter with a fruity, hoppy nose and a bitter finish.

Golden Salamander (OG 1045, ABV 4.5%) ◆
Citrus hops characterise the aroma and taste of this golden premium bitter, which has malt undertones throughout. The aftertaste is dry, hoppy and bitter.

Stout (OG 1045, ABV 4.5%) ◆
Rich roast malts dominate the smooth, rich coffee and chocolate flavour. Nicely balanced. A dry, roast, bitter finish develops over time.

Salopian SIBA

Salopian Brewing Co Ltd, 67 Mytton Oak Road, Shrewsbury, Shropshire, SY3 8UQ
Tel (01743) 248414
Tours by arrangement

◎ The brewery was opened in 1995 in an old dairy on the outskirts of Shrewsbury. Owner Wilf Nelson has developed cask sales locally and nationally through wholesalers. Capacity has increased to 65 barrels. The brewery has acquired its first brewery tap, the Star at Market Drayton. Fifty-five outlets are supplied.

Shropshire Gold (OG 1037, ABV 3.8%)

Icon (OG 1041, ABV 4.2%)

Heaven Sent (OG 1044, ABV 4.5%)

Lemon Dream (OG 1043, ABV 4.5%)

Proud Salopian (OG 1044, ABV 4.5%)

Golden Thread (OG 1048, ABV 5%)

Sawbridgeworth

Sawbridgeworth Brewery, 81 London Road, Sawbridgeworth, Hertfordshire, CM21 9JJ
Tel (01279) 722313
Email the.gate.pub@dial.pipex.com
Website www.the-gate-pub.co.uk
Tours by arrangement

⊗ The brewery was set up in 2000 by Tom and Gary Barnett with equipment from the Alford Arms, Frithsden, at the back of the Gate pub. One pub is owned. There is a rolling programme of monthly special beers. Tom is a former professional footballer whose clubs included Crystal Palace.

Selhurst Park Flyer (ABV 3.7%)

Is It Yourself (ABV 4.2%)

Stout (ABV 4.3%)

Brooklands Express (ABV 4.6%)

Piledriver (ABV 5.3%)

Scarecrow

Scarecrow Brewery Ltd, Arreton Craft Village, Arreton, Isle of Wight, PO30 3AA
Tel (01983) 856161
Shop Open daily 10am-8pm

Scarecrow Brewery, owned by Ventnor Brewery (qv) is located at Arreton Craft Village alongside the Dairyman's Daughter Inn. Brewing takes place once a week and four pubs and beer festivals are supplied. Brewing can be viewed from the Beer Emporium, which specialises in bottled beers from all over the country as well as breweriana. The beer shop has a full range of Ventnor Brewery products and merchandise and a wide range of beers from all over Britain. Bottle-conditioned beer: Best.

Best (OG 1042, ABV 4.2%)

Scattor Rock

Scattor Rock Brewery Ltd, Unit 5 Gidley's Meadow, Christow, Exeter, Devon, EX6 7QB
Tel (01647) 252120
Email inquiries@scattorrockbrewery.com
Website www.scattorrockbrewery.com
Tours by arrangement

The brewery was set up in 1998 on Dartmoor National Park and is named after a well-known local landmark. More than 60 outlets are supplied on a permanent or regular basis. There is a seasonal beer available every month and branded as part of the Tor Collection.

Scatty Bitter (OG 1040, ABV 3.8%)

Teign Valley Tipple (OG 1042, ABV 4%)
A well-balanced, tawny-coloured beer with a hoppy aroma.

Skylark (OG 1043, ABV 4.2%)
A refreshing, light brown session ale.

Devonian (OG 1045, ABV 4.5%)
A strong, fruity, light-coloured ale.

Golden Valley (OG 1046, ABV 4.6%)
A golden refreshing ale.

Valley Stomper (OG 1051, ABV 5%)
Light brown and deceptively drinkable.

Selby

Selby (Middlebrough) Brewery Ltd, 131 Millgate, Selby, North Yorkshire, YO8 3LL
Tel (01757) 702826
Shop 10-12 and 6-10 Mon-Sat

Selby is an old family brewery that resumed production in 1972 after a gap of 18 years but which is now mostly involved in wholesaling. Its beers, which are brewed on an occasional basis, are available, while stocks last (only in bulk) at the shop and not at the company's single pub. They are also sold as guest beers in the local free trade.

No.1 (OG 1040, ABV 4%)

No.3 (OG 1040, ABV 4%)

Old Tom (OG 1065, ABV 6.5%)

Shakespeare's*

Shakespeare's Brewery, Smallbrook Business Centre, Bidford-on-Avon, Warwickshire, B50 4JE
Tel (0845) 838 1564
Email info@shakesbrew.co.uk
Website www.shakesbrew.co.uk

The brewery, with a 2.5-barrel plant, opened in May 2005. As well as selling to local pubs, there are plans to produce bottle-conditioned beers as well.

Noble Fool (ABV 3.6%)
Light, fruity and aromatic.

The Scottish Ale/Macbeth (ABV 4.6%)
Malty, bold, traditional Scottish-style ale.

Tempest (ABV 5.5%)
Dark, intensely hopped storm in a glass.

Shardlow

Shardlow Brewing Co Ltd, The Old Brewery Stables, British Waterways Yard, Cavendish Bridge, Shardlow, Leicestershire, DE72 2HL
Tel (01332) 799188
Tours by arrangement

Brewing on a site associated with brewing since 1819, Shardlow delivers to outlets throughout the East Midlands. It deals with other craft brewers and as a result its beers are sold in East Anglia, the West Midlands and Yorkshire. Reverend Eaton's Ale is named after a scion of the Eaton brewing family, Rector of Shardlow for 40 years. The brewery tap is the Blue Bell Inn at Melbourne, Derbyshire, where four cask ales including a mild are regularly available, together with other guests. Seasonal beers are produced, including strong winter beers up to ABV 7%. Bottle-conditioned beers: Special Bitter, Golden Hop, Narrow Boat, Reverend Eaton's Ale, Five Bells, Whistle Stop.

Chancellors Revenge (OG 1036, ABV 3.6%)
A light-coloured, refreshing, full-flavoured and well-hopped session bitter.

Cavendish Dark (OG 1037, ABV 3.7%)

Special Bitter (OG 1039, ABV 3.9%)
A well-balanced, amber-coloured, quaffable bitter.

Golden Hop (OG 1041, ABV 4.1%)

Narrowboat (OG 1043, ABV 4.3%)
A pale amber bitter, with a short, crisp hoppy aftertaste.

Reverend Eaton's Ale (OG 1045, ABV 4.5%)
A smooth, medium-strong bitter, full of malt and hop flavours with a sweet aftertaste.

Five Bells (OG 1050, ABV 5.2%)

Whistle Stop (OG 1050, ABV 5.2%)
Maris Otter pale malt and two hops produce this smooth and surprisingly strong pale beer.

Sharp's SIBA

Sharp's Brewery Ltd, Pityme Industrial Estate, St Minver, Wadebridge, Cornwall, PL27 6NU
Tel (01208) 862121

Fax (01208) 863727
Email enquiries@sharpsbrewery.co.uk
Website www.sharpsbrewery.co.uk
Shop 9-4pm weekdays
Tours by arrangement

⊗ Sharp's Brewery was founded in 1994. The success and growth of the brewery has been phenomenal and it is now a major brewer of cask-conditioned beer in the South-west. The quality of the beer has enabled rapid progress from micro to regional brewery status in less than a decade. Sharp supplies some 650 free trade accounts in Devon and Cornwall, and the beers are also widely available via wholesalers. The brewery is upgrading its equipment to cope with continued demand for the beers. Eden Ale is now bottled (not bottle conditioned), with other beers from the range to follow.

Cornish Coaster (OG 1035, ABV 3.6%) ◆
A smooth, easy-drinking beer, golden in colour, with a fresh hop aroma and dry malt and hops in the mouth. The finish starts malty but becomes dry and hoppy.

Cornish Jack (OG 1037, ABV 3.8%)

Doom Bar Bitter (OG 1038.5, ABV 4%) ◼ ◻ ◆
Smooth, quaffable bitter with a persistent and pleasant bitter aftertaste.

Eden Ale (OG 1042.5, ABV 4.4%)
Brewed in celebration of Cornwall's Eden Project, it boasts a full and rounded flavour with a distinctively crisp and refreshing, dry hop finish.

Own (OG 1042.5, ABV 4.4%) ◆
A deep golden brown beer with a delicate hops and malt aroma, and dry malt and hops in the mouth. Like the other beers, its finish starts malty but turns dry and hoppy.

Will's Resolve (OG 1045, ABV 4.6%)
A rich golden brown beer with a fresh hop aroma and with dry malt and hops in the mouth.

Special (OG 1048.5, ABV 5.2%) ◆
Deep golden brown with a fresh hop aroma. Dry malt and hops in the mouth; the finish is malty but becomes dry and hoppy.

Shaws

Shaws Brewery, The Old Stables, Park Road, Dukinfield, Greater Manchester, SK16 5LX
Tel (0161) 330 5471
Fax (0161) 343 1879

⊛ The brewery is housed in the stables of William Shaws Brewery, established in 1856 and closed by John Smiths in 1941. Brewing re-started in 2002 with a five-barrel plant, designed and commissioned by brewers Neil Hay and Phillip Windsor. Beer is supplied to more than 30 local free trade outlets and beer festivals. Monthly guest beers are produced.

Best Bitter (OG 1038, ABV 4%)

Golden Globe (OG 1040, ABV 4.3%)

IPA (OG 1044, ABV 4.8%)

Shepherd Neame IFBB

Shepherd Neame Ltd, 17 Court Street, Faversham, Kent, ME13 7AX
Tel (01795) 532206
Fax (01795) 538907
Email company@shepherd-neame.co.uk
Website www.shepherd-neame.co.uk
Shop 11-3 Mon-Fri
Tours by arrangement

⊗ Kent's major independent brewery is believed to be the oldest continuous brewer in the country (since 1698), but records show brewing began on the site as far back as the 12th century. The same water source is still used today and steam engines are still usable. A visitors' reception hall is housed in a restored medieval hall (tours by arrangement). In 2000, Shepherd Neame invested £2.2 million in a new brewhouse that boosted production to 200,000 barrels a year. The company has 372 tied houses in the South-east, nearly all selling cask ale, but tenants are encouraged to keep beers under blanket pressure if the cask is likely to be on sale for more than three days. More than 2,000 other outlets are also supplied. Seasonal beers: Early Bird (ABV 4.5%, spring), Late Red (ABV 4.5%, autumn), Goldings (ABV 4.7%, summer), Original Porter (ABV 4.8%, winter ◻). Bottle-conditioned beer: 1698 (ABV 6.5%).

Master Brew Bitter (OG 1032, ABV 3.7%) ◆
A distinctive bitter, mid-brown in colour, with a hoppy aroma. Well-balanced, with a nicely aggressive bitter taste from its hops, it leaves a hoppy/bitter finish, tinged with sweetness.

Master Brew Best Bitter (OG 1036, ABV 4.1%) ◆
Mid-brown, with less marked characteristics than the bitter. However, the nose is very well balanced and the taste enjoys a malty, bitter smokiness. Malty, well-rounded finish. It also appears under the name Canterbury Jack.

Spitfire (OG 1039, ABV 4.5%)
A commemorative Battle of Britain brew for the RAF Benevolent Fund's appeal, now a permanent feature.

Bishops Finger (OG 1046, ABV 5%)
A cask-conditioned version of a famous bottled beer.

Shoes SIBA

♀ Shoes Brewery, Three Horseshoes Inn, Norton Canon, Hereford, HR4 7BH
Tel/Fax (01544) 318375
Tours by arrangement

Landlord Frank Goodwin was a keen home brewer who decided in 1994 to brew on a commercial basis for his pub. The beers are brewed from malt extract, stored in casks and dispensed under a blanket of mixed gas. Bottle-conditioned beer: Farriers Beer (ABV 15.1%).

Norton Ale (OG 1038, ABV 3.6%)

Canon Bitter (OG 1040, ABV 4.1%)

Shugborough*

Shugborough Brewery, Shugborough Estate, Shugborough, Milford, near Stafford, ST17 0XB
Tel (01782) 823447
Fax (01782) 812349
Tours by arrangement

Brewing in the original brewhouse at Shugborough, home to Lord Lichfield, re-commenced in 1990 but a lack of expertise led to the brewery being a static museum piece until Titanic Brewery of Stoke-on-Trent began helping in 1996. Since then, the brewery has produced many one-off brews under Titanic's guidance. Plans are now being prepared to brew more regularly with Keith Bott of Titanic as head brewer. Ten outlets are supplied.

Miladys Fancy (OG 1048, ABV 4.6%)

Coachmans Tipple (OG 1049, ABV 4.7%)

Gardeners Retreat (OG 1049, ABV 4.7%)

Farmers Half (OG 1049, ABV 4.8%)

Butlers Revenge (OG 1053, ABV 4.9%)

Lordships Own (OG 1054, ABV 5%)

Six Bells SIBA

Six Bells Brewery, Church Street, Bishop's Castle, Shropshire, SY9 5AA
Tel (01588) 638930
Fax (01588) 630132
Website www.bishops-castle.co.uk/SixBells/brewery/htm
Tours by arrangement

⊗ Neville Richards – 'Big Nev' – started brewing in 1997 with a five-barrel plant and two fermenters. Alterations in 1999 included two more fermenters, a new grain store and mashing equipment, and some automation. He currently supplies a number of customers both within the county and over the border in Wales. Seasonal beers: Old Recumbent (ABV 5.2%, Oct-spring), Spring Forward (ABV 4.6%, March-May), Seven Bells (ABV 5.5%, Christmas), Festival Pale (ABV 5.2%, June-July for town's annual beer festival).

Big Nev's (OG 1037, ABV 3.8%)
A pale, fairly hoppy bitter.

Roo Brew (OG 1038, ABV 3.8%)
Brewed exclusively for the Kangaroo Inn, Aston on Clun, to the publican's recipe. Copper-coloured, hoppy and heavily late hopped with Goldings.

Marathon Ale (OG 1040, ABV 4%)
Dark ruby-coloured and malty.

Cloud Nine (OG 1042, ABV 4.2%)
Pale amber-colour with a slight citrus finish.

Duck & Dive (OG 1044, ABV 4.6%)
Pale and hoppy.

Brew 101 (OG 1048, ABV 4.8%)
A dark, fruity beer.

Skinner's SIBA

Skinner's Brewing Co Ltd, Riverside, Newham Road, Truro, Cornwall, TR1 2SU
Tel (01872) 271885
Fax (01872) 271886
Email info@skinnersbrewery.com
Website www.skinnersbrewery.com
Shop 10-5pm Mon-Sat
Tours by arrangement

⊗ Skinner's brewery was founded in the cathedral city of Truro by Steve and Sarah Skinner in July 1997.The brewery moved to bigger premises in 2004 and now employs 22 people. A brewery shop opened in 2003 and a visitor's centre and brewery tours were added in 2005. Seasonal beers: Pennycomequick (ABV 4.5%), Skilliwidden (ABV 5.1%), Jingle Knocker (ABV 5.5%).

Spriggan Ale (OG 1038, ABV 3.8%)
A light golden, hoppy bitter. Well-balanced with a smooth bitter finish.

Betty Stogs (OG 1040, ABV 4%)
Pleasant session beer with well-balanced hop and fruit in the taste, and a lasting, bitter finish.

Heligan Honey (OG 1040, ABV 4%)
A slightly sweet amber bitter, brewed with West Country malt and Heligan Gardens honey.

Keel Over (OG 1041, ABV 4.2%)
A classic Cornish bitter, amber in colour, beautifully balanced with a smooth finish.

Cornish Knocker Ale (OG 1044, ABV 4.5%)
Complex beer with flowery, fruity overtones and malt undertone, easily mistaken for a session beer.

Figgy's Brew (OG 1044, ABV 4.5%)
A classic, dark, premium-strength bitter. Full-flavoured with a smooth finish.

Cornish Blonde (OG 1048, ABV 5%)
A combination of wheat malt and English and American hops makes this light-coloured wheat beer deceptively easy to drink.

Slaughterhouse SIBA

Slaughterhouse Brewery Ltd, Bridge Street, Warwick, CV34 5PD
Tel/Fax (01926) 490986
Email Stephen@ridgway171.freeserve.co.uk
Tours by arrangement

Production began in 2003 in an old slaughterhouse. The four-barrel plant is the original Church End equipment. Future plans include producing bottle-conditioned beers. 50-plus outlets are supplied. Arkwright's Special Bitter (ABV 3.8%) is brewed as the house beer for the Waterman at Hatton, near Warwick. Seasonal beer: Wild Boar (ABV 5.2%, winter).

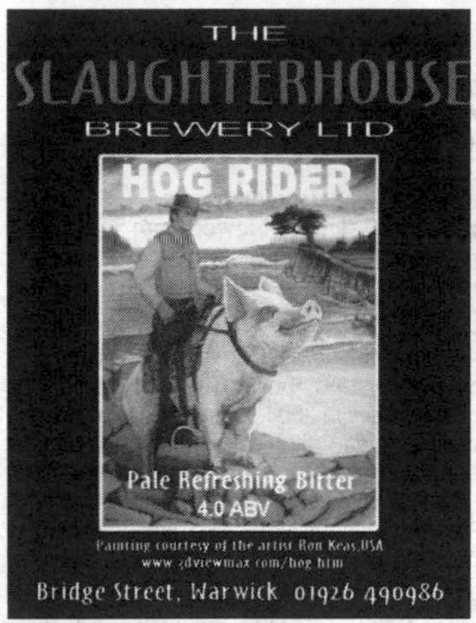

Hog Rider (OG 1039, ABV 4%)

Swillmore Original (OG 1041, ABV 4.2%)
A traditional, medium-bodied, bronze-red bitter. It has a fruity/hoppy character with Challenger hop bitterness coming through, especially in the finish.

Swillmore Pale Ale (OG 1042, ABV 4.5%)
A pale dry hoppy bitter. A lighter, less malty version of Original.

Hog Goblin (OG 1045, ABV 4.6%)

Samuel Smith

Samuel Smith Old Brewery (Tadcaster), High Street, Tadcaster, North Yorkshire, LS24 9SB
Tel (01937) 832225
Fax (01937) 834673
Tours by arrangement

Although related to the nearby John Smith's, this fiercely independent, family-owned company is radically different. Tradition, quality and value are important, resulting in traditional brewing without adjuncts, with real ale supplied in wooden casks. Sadly, nitro-keg beer has crept in, especially in London. A fine range of bottled beers is produced, though they are not bottle conditioned. A filtered draught wheat beer is a recent addition. Some 200 pubs are owned.

Old Brewery Bitter/OBB
(OG 1040, ABV 4%)
Malt dominates the aroma, with an initial burst of malt, hops and fruit in the taste, which is sustained in the aftertaste.

Snowdonia SIBA

Snowdonia Brewery,
Snowdonia Parc Brewpub & Campsite, Waunfawr, Caernarfon, Gwynedd, LL55 4AQ
Tel (01286) 650218
Fax (01286) 650409 (phone first)
Email info@snowdonia-park.co.uk
Website www.snowdonia-park.co.uk

Snowdonia started brewing in 1998 in a two-barrel brewhouse. Brewing is carried out by Karen Humphreys and Carmen Pierce. Two pubs are owned.

Gold (OG 1048, ABV 5%)

Welsh Highland Bitter (OG 1048, ABV 5%)

Somerset (Electric) SIBA

Somerset (Electric) Brewery, New Inn, Halse, Taunton, Somerset, TA4 3AF
Tel (01823) 432352
Fax (01823) 432363
Email mark@newinnhalse.co.uk
Website www.newinnhalse.co.uk

The brewery was established in 2003 in the cellar of the New Inn, Halse, CAMRA 2004-5 South West and 2004 Somerset Branch Pub of the Year. All the beers are brewed by landlord Mark Leadeham to his own recipes. Mark I was runner-up in the standard bitter class of the SIBA 2004 Tuckers Maltings beer festival. Many beer festivals are supplied and the West Somerset Railway regularly serves them in its dining carriages. All the beers are brewed using West Country floor-malted barley and whole cone hops. Many occasional beers are brewed, including beers suitable for vegans. Seasonal beers: Golden Age of Steam (ABV 4.2%, summer), Magwitch (ABV 6%, winter).

Mark I (OG 1039, ABV 3.9%)
Light mahogany in colour, full-bodied, easy drinking and refreshing. The aroma and flavour are well balanced by malt, followed by a subtle yet long-lasting bitterness.

British Somerset Time/BST
(OG 1043, ABV 4.3%)
A copper-coloured, dry-hopped beer brewed using Maris Otter pale malt and Fuggles and Goldings hops. A well-balanced ale with a fine hoppy aroma.

Somerset Sunrise (OG 1047, ABV 4.8%)
A good hop aroma introduces this premium golden bitter. Citrus hop flavours abound and blend with a pleasant malty sweetness. This leads to an intensely bitter finish.

South Hams SIBA

South Hams Brewery Co Ltd, Stokeley Barton, Stokenham, Kingsbridge, Devon, TQ7 2SE
Tel/Fax (01548) 581151
Fax (01548) 581010
Email info@southhamsbrewery.co.uk
Website www.southhamsbrewery.co.uk
Tours by arrangement

The brewery, formerly Sutton Brewing, moved to its present site in 2003, with a 10-barrel plant and plenty of room to expand. It supplies more than 60 outlets in Plymouth and south Devon. Wholesalers are used to distribute to other areas. Two pubs are owned. Seasonal beers: spring and summer – Wild Blonde (ABV 4.4%) and Hopnosis (ABV 4.5%); autumn and winter: Porter (ABV 5%) and Knickadroppa Glory (ABV 5%).

Devon Pride (OG 1039, ABV 3.8%)

XSB (OG 1043, ABV 4.2%)
Amber nectar with a fruity nose and a bitter finish.

Sutton Comfort (OG 1045, ABV 4.5%)

Hoppy-tasting, mid-brown beer with a bitter hop finish underscored by malt and fruit.

Eddystone (OG 1050, ABV 4.8%)

Pandemonium (OG 1050, ABV 4.8%)

Southport

Southport Brewery, Unit 3, Enterprise Business Park, Russell Road, Southport, Merseyside, PR9 7RF
Tel (07748) 387652

The Southport brewery was opened by Paul Bardsley in 2004 with a 2.5-barrel plant. It supplies five town centre pubs on a regular basis and the free trade via Boggart Hole Clough Brewery (qv). Seasonal beers: Carousel Best Bitter (ABV 4%, summer), Old Shrimper (ABV 6%, winter), Tower Mild (ABV 3.7%, May and Sept).

Sandgrounder Bitter (OG 1039.5, ABV 3.8%)
A light-coloured, hoppy bitter.

Bothy Beer (OG 1040.5, ABV 3.9%)
Amber-coloured bitter with a hint of citrus lemon flavour.

Natterjack Premium Bitter (OG 1043.5, ABV 4.3%)
A darker, malty brew.

Spectrum SIBA EAB

Spectrum Brewery, c/o 23 Briton Way, Wymondham, Norfolk, NR18 0TT
Tel (07949) 254383
Email andy@spectrumbrewery.co.uk
Website www.spectrumbrewery.co.uk

⊗ After escaping from the IT industry, proprietor and founder Andy Mitchell gained experience working for a number of East Anglian brewers, as well as gaining an MSc in brewing and distilling, before establishing Spectrum Brewery in 2002. It's the only East Anglian brewery to brew exclusively from organic malt and hops. The brewery shares plant and premises with Blue Moon Brewery and supplies some 40 outlets. Seasonal beers: Light Fantastic (ABV 3.7%, spring-autumn). An additional 'red beer' is produced mid-Sept-Nov. Black Buffle and Old Stoatwobbler are suitable for vegans.

Light Fantastic (OG 1035, ABV 3.7%)
Thirst-quenching light bitter.

Bezants (OG 1039.5, ABV 4%) ◆
A well-hopped, clean-tasting bitter. Although some maltiness can be detected in both the aroma and taste, it is hops that dominate. A residual bitterness adds to a long aftertaste that ends in a lingering dryness.

42 (OG 1042, ABV4.2%)
Hoppy and easy-drinking best bitter.

Black Buffle (OG 1046, ABV 4.5%)
A stout, named after the brewer's cat.

Wizzard (OG 1047.5, ABV 4.9%) ◆
A pungent sultana and malt aroma introduces this well-balanced mid-brown beer. Sweet dried fruit flavours dominate the taste through to the long, sustained finish. A dryish hop feel can be detected in the background.

Trip Hazard (OG 1062.5, ABV 6.5%) ◆
Exceptionally malty but easy-drinking for its strength. Rich fruity flavours dominate throughout, date and sultana to the fore. A growing bitterness in the finish.

Old Stoatwobbler (OG 1064.5, ABV 6%) ◆
Wonderfully complex brew with dark chocolate, morello cherry, raisin and banana vying for dominance alongside hops and malt. A black-coloured brew with a solid fruity nose, and a well-balanced, smooth but soft finish.

Spinning Dog SIBA

Spinning Dog Brewery, 88 St Owen's Street, Hereford, HR1 2QD
Tel (01432) 274998
Tel/Fax (01432) 342125
Email jfkenyon@aol.com
Website www.spinningdogbrewery.co.uk
Tours by arrangement

The brewery was built in a room of the Victory in 2000 by Jim Kenyon, following the purchase of the pub. Initially the brewery served only the pub but is now supplying some 500 other outlets. As a result of the closure of Flannery's of Aberystwyth, Jim has taken on its beers. In 2002, the brewery expanded from its four-barrel plant to a 10-barrel one and extensive work was carried out on the brewhouse. There is a programme of monthly beers.

Chase Your Tail (OG 1036, ABV 3.6%)
A good session beer with an abundance of hops and bitterness. Dry, with citrus aftertaste.

Herefordshire Owd Bull (ABV 3.9%)

Mutleys Mongrel (OG 1039, ABV 3.9%)
Brewed with a blend of three different hops to create a very hoppy ale.

Hereford Cathedral Bitter (OG 1040, ABV 4%)
A crisp amber beer made with local hops, producing a well-rounded malt/hop bitterness throughout and a pleasing, lingering aftertaste.

Mutleys Dark (OG 1040, ABV 4%)
A dark, malty mild with a hint of bitterness and a touch of roast caramel. A smooth drinkable ale.

Herefordshire Light Ale (ABV 4%)

Top Dog (OG 1042, ABV 4.2%)
A hoppy beer with both malt and fruit flavours.

SPINNING DOG BREWERY
CHASE YOUR TAIL
HEREFORD
OG. 1036°

Mutleys Oatmeal Stout (OG 1044, ABV 4.4%)
Robust, full-bodied and satisfying.

Celtic Gold (OG 1045, ABV 4.5%)

Harvest Moon (OG 1045, ABV 4.5%)
Pale in colour with a malty, bitter, lingering aftertaste.

Mutleys Revenge (OG 1048, ABV 4.8%)
A strong, smooth, hoppy beer, amber in colour. Full-bodied with a dry, citrus aftertaste.

Mutts Nuts (OG 1050, ABV 5%)
A dark, strong ale, full bodied with a hint of a chocolate aftertaste.

Springhead SIBA

Springhead Fine Ales, Unit 3, Sutton Workshops, Old Great North Road, Sutton-on-Trent, Newark, Nottinghamshire, NG23 6QS
Tel (01636) 821000
Fax (01636) 821150
Email info@springhead.co.uk
Website www.springhead.co.uk
Tours by arrangement

◎ Springhead continues to go from strength to strength since the appointment of head brewer Shirley Reynolds in 2001. A new 50-barrel plant was commissioned in 2004 to meet demand. Cask ales are supplied throughout the Midlands and Yorkshire areas and nationally via leading wholesalers. Two pubs are owned and 400 outlets are supplied. Bottle-conditioned beers: Roundheads Gold, The Leveller, Roaring Meg, Cromwells Hat. Puritans Porter is suitable for vegetarians and vegans.

Surrender 1646 (OG 1038, ABV 3.6%)
A burnished, copper-coloured bitter with a good combination of malt and hops. Long dry finish.

Bitter (OG 1041, ABV 4%)
A clean-tasting, easy-drinking, hoppy beer.

Puritans Porter (OG 1041, ABV 4%)
A porter, dark but not heavy. Smooth with a lingering finish of roasted barley.

Roundhead's Gold (OG 1042, ABV 4.2%)
Golden beer made with wild flower honey. Refreshing but not too sweet with the glorious aroma of Saaz hops.

Rupert's Ruin (OG 1042, ABV 4.2%)
A coppery, complex beer with a fruity aroma and a long, malty aftertaste.

Goodrich Castle (OG 1044, ABV 4.4%)
Brewed following a 17th-century recipe using rosemary: a pale ale, light on the palate with a bitter finish and a delicate flavour.

Oliver's Army (OG 1044, ABV 4.4%)

Charlie's Angel (OG 1045, ABV 4.5%)

Sweet Lips (OG 1046, ABV 4.6%)
A light, smooth and refreshing beer with some grapefruit notes from American Cascade hops.

Bare Bones (OG 1046, ABV 4.7%)

The Leveller (OG 1047, ABV 4.8%)

Newark Castle Brown (OG 1049, ABV 5%)

Willy's Wheatbeer (OG 1051, ABV 5.3%)

Roaring Meg (OG 1052, ABV 5.5%)
Smooth and sweet with a dry finish and citrus honey aroma.

Cromwell's Hat (OG 1056, ABV 6%)

Stanway

Stanway Brewery, Stanway, Cheltenham, Gloucestershire, GL54 5PQ
Tel (01386) 584320
Website www.stanwaybrewery.co.uk

⊗ Stanway is a small brewery founded in 1993 with a five-barrel plant that confines its sales to the Cotswolds area (15 to 20 outlets). The brewery is the only known plant in the country to use wood-fired coppers for all its production. Seasonal beers: Lords-a-Leaping (ABV 4.5%, Christmas), Cotteswold Gold (ABV 3.9%, summer).

Stanney Bitter (OG 1042, ABV 4.5%) ➘
A light, refreshing, amber-coloured beer, dominated by hops in the aroma, with a bitter taste and a hoppy, bitter finish.

Station House*

Station House Brewery, Unit 1, Meadow Lane Industrial Park, Ellesmere Port, Cheshire, CH65 4TY
Tel/Fax (0151) 356 3000
Email enquiries@stationhousebrewery.co.uk

Station House opened in April 2005. Barry Davidson was a keen home brewer who worked for a local authority and went on a Brewlab course in Sunderland to perfect his brewing skills. He wanted to lease a disused railway station house but the deal fell through. He kept the name as he is close to Ellesmere Port station, on an industrial unit. Barry's plant can produce between five and seven barrels at a time.

1'st Lite (ABV 3.8%)

Ode 2 Joy (ABV 4.1%)

Hazel I's (ABV 4.3%)

Lady o'the Stream (ABV 4.4%)

3 Score (ABV 4.5%)

Steamin' Billy

Steamin' Billy Brewing Co Ltd, 5 The Oval, Oadby, Leicestershire, LE2 5JB
Tel (0116) 271 2616
Email enquiries@steaminbilly.co.uk
Website www.steaminbilly.co.uk

A company formed in 1995 to brew and supply its three pubs. In 1999 a re-organisation saw the Steamin Billy beers, named after the owner's Jack Russell dog, contracted to Grainstore (qv) in Oakham where the beers are still brewed under licence. Six outlets are supplied and two pubs are owned. Seasonal beers: Lazy Summer (ABV 4.5%), Spring Goldings (ABV 4.5%), Knock Out (ABV 7.1%). Bottle-conditioned beer: Skydiver.

Country Bitter (OG 1036, ABV 3.6%)
A full-bodied, copper-coloured beer.

Grand Prix Mild (OG 1036, ABV 3.6%)

Robert Catesby (OG 1042, ABV 4.2%)

Bitter (OG 1043, ABV 4.3%)
The floral flavour and aroma are derived from dry hopping with Goldings.

Skydiver (OG 1050, ABV 5%)
A strong, rich, mahogany-coloured beer with malty sweetness and pronounced hop bitterness.

Stewart

Stewart Brewing Ltd, 42 Dryden Road, Bilston Glen Industrial Estate, Loanhead, Lothian. EH20 9LZ
Tel (07808) 095020 Fax (0131) 667 0242
Email steve.stewart@stewartbrewing.co.uk
Website www.stewartbrewing.co.uk

Steve Stewart, a qualified master brewer with the Institute of Brewing, worked for 10 years in the brewing industry worldwide and returned to Edinburgh to launch his own company. The brewery specialises in the production of high-quality international beer styles and premium cask ales.

Pentland IPA (OG 1041, ABV 4.1%)
A golden dry ale with slight fruit tones and a complex but refreshing character as a result of hops being added in four stages.

Copper Cascade (OG 1042, ABV 4.2%)
Deep red colour, full bodied and rounded with a generous addition of American Cascade hops.

Edinburgh No.3 Premium Scotch Ale (OG 1043, ABV 4.3%)
A rich, dark, malty beer based on a style that 100 years ago made Edinburgh famous for its many breweries and excellent beers.

Stonehenge SIBA

Stonehenge Ales Ltd, The Old Mill, Mill Road, Netheravon, Salisbury, Wiltshire, SP4 9QB
Tel (01980) 670631
Fax (01980) 671187
Email website@bigfoot.com
Website www.stonehengeales.co.uk
Tours by arrangement

⊗ The beers are brewed in a mill built in 1914 to generate electricity for the new airfield nearby, using the water power of the River Avon. It was put to a variety of other uses after generating ceased and was sold by the Ministry of Defence in 1983. The site was converted for brewing in 1984 and in 1993 Danish master brewer Stig Anker Andersen bought the company and took up the challenge of making English beer. Cask-conditioned beers are delivered to some 100 free trade outlets within a radius of 50 miles and a number of wholesalers are also supplied. Seasonal beers: Sign of Spring (ABV 4.6%), Old Smokey (ABV 5%, autumn), Rudolph (ABV 5%, Christmas).

Spire Ale (OG 1037, ABV 3.8%)

Pigswill (OG 1040, ABV 4%)
A full-bodied beer, rich in hop aroma, with a warm amber colour.

Body Line (OG 1042, ABV 4.3%)

Heel Stone (OG 1042, ABV 4.3%)
A crisp, clean, refreshing bitter, deep amber in colour, well balanced with a fruity blackcurrant nose.

Second to None (ABV 4.6)

Great Bustard (OG 1046, ABV 4.8%)

Danish Dynamite (OG 1048, ABV 5%)
A light golden, dry strong ale, slightly fruity with a well-balanced hop flavour and bitterness.

Old Smokey (OG 1050, ABV 5%) ◆
A delightful, warming, dark bitter ale, with a roasted malt taste and a hint of liquorice surrounding a developing bitter flavour.

Storm

Storm Brewing Co, 2 Waterside, Macclesfield, Cheshire, SK11 7HJ
Tel/Fax (01625) 431234
Email thompsonhugh@talk21.com

Storm Brewing was founded in 1998 by Hugh Thompson and David Stebbings. They operated from an old ICI boiler room until 2001 when the brewing operation moved to the current location, which until 1937, was a public house known as the Mechanics Arms. Storm supplies more than 60 outlets in Cheshire, Manchester and the Peak District. Seasonal beer: Looks Like Rain Dear (ABV 4.8%, Christmas). Bottle-conditioned beer: as for all cask beers.

Beauforts Ale (OG 1038, ABV 3.8%)
Golden brown, full-flavoured session bitter with a lingering hoppy taste.

Bitter Experience (OG 1040, ABV 4%)
A distinctive hop aroma draws you into this amber-coloured bitter. The palate has a mineral dryness that accentuates the crisp hop flavour and clean bitter finish.

Desert Storm (OG 1040, ABV 4%)
Amber-coloured beer with a smoky flavour of fruit and malt.

Twister (OG 1041, ABV 4%)
A light golden bitter with a smooth fruity hop aroma complemented by a subtle bitter aftertaste.

Bosley Cloud (OG 1041, ABV 4.1%)
Golden-coloured ale with an aromatic explosion of fruity flavours.

Brainstorm (OG 1041, ABV 4.1%)
Light gold in colour and strong in citrus fruit flavours.

Ale Force (OG 1042, ABV 4.2%)
Amber, smooth-tasting, complex beer that balances malt, hop and fruit on the taste, leading to a roasty, slightly sweet aftertaste.

Tornado (OG 1044, ABV 4.4%)

Hurricane Hubert (OG 1045, ABV 4.5%)
A dark beer with a refreshing full, fruity hop aroma and a subtle bitter aftertaste.

Windgather (OG 1045, ABV 4.5%)
A gold-coloured beer with a distinctive crisp, fruity flavour right through to the aftertaste.

Damage (OG 1047, ABV 4.7%)
A light-coloured, well-hopped and fruity beer balanced by a clean bitterness and smooth full palate.

Silk of Amnesia (OG 1047, ABV 4.7%)
A full-flavoured dark beer with a hoppy aroma and rich chocolate palate following through to a clean bitter finish.

Typhoon (OG 1050, ABV 5%)

Strangford Lough*

Strangford Lough Brewing Co, 22 Shore Road, Killyleagh, Downpatrick, Northern Ireland, BT30 9UE
Tel (028) 4482 1461 Fax (028) 4482 1273
Email contact@slbc.ie
Website www.slbc.ie

Beers for this company are contract-brewed by an unnamed English brewery, though there are plans to build a plant in Northern Ireland. Bottle-conditioned beers: St Patrick's (ABV 3.8%), St Patrick's Ale (ABV 6%), Barelegs Brew (ABV 4.5%), Legbiter (ABV 4.8%)

Stumpy's

Stumpy's Brewery, Unit 5, Lycroft Farm, Park Lane, Upper Swanmore, Southampton, Hampshire, SO32 2QQ
Tel (01329) 664902/ 07771 557378
Fax (01329) 664902
Email lewisw556@aol.com
Tours by arrangement

⊗ A five-barrel brewery opened in 2004 in a converted hen house on a farm so remote than an Ordnance Survey map and reference (SU 588185) are essential to find it. The owner and brewer is CAMRA member Brian 'Stumpy' Lewis. Brian brewed for several months at Yates' on the Isle of Wight and the acclaim for his brews there encouraged him to set up on his own. New beers were in the pipeline during 2005. Twelve outlets are served. Bottled beers: as for all cask ales. Seasonal beer: Silent Night (ABV 5%, autumn-winter).

Dog Daze (OG 1040, ABV 3.8%)
Light, quaffable summer brew.

Hop a Doodle Doo (OG 1040, ABV 4%)

Old Stumpy (OG 1045, ABV 4.5%)
Grassy best bitter with a strong hoppy and fruity aroma. Some malt and bitterness in the flavour lead to a sharp, dry finish.

Haven (OG 1050, ABV 5%)
Creamy and deceptively strong.

Sulwath SIBA

Sulwath Brewers Ltd, The Brewery, 209 King Street, Castle Douglas, Dumfries & Galloway, DG7 1DT
Tel/Fax (01556) 504525
Email allen@scottdavid98.freeserve.co.uk
Website www.sulwathbrewers.co.uk
Shop Fully licensed visitor centre & off-sales Mon-Sat 10-4
Tours Mon-Sat

⊕ Sulwath is a small, privately-owned company that started brewing in 1995. Maris Otter malts are used in each full mash brew, with the addition of whole hop flowers from the Hereford area. The beers are now supplied to markets as far away as Devon in the south and Aberdeen in the north. Cask ales are sold direct to some 100 outlets and three wholesalers.

Cuil Hill (OG 1039, ABV 3.6%)
Distinctively fruity session ale with malt and hop undertones. The taste is bitter-sweet with a long-lasting dry finish.

Black Galloway (OG 1046, ABV 4.4%)
A robust porter/stout that derives its colour from the abundance of Maris Otter barley and chocolate malts used in the brewing process.

Criffel (OG 1044, ABV 4.6%)
Full-bodied beer with a distinctive bitterness. Fruit is to the fore of the taste with hop becoming increasingly dominant in the taste and finish.

Galloway Gold (OG 1049, ABV 5%)
A cask-conditioned lager that will be too sweet for many despite being heavily hopped.

Knockendoch (OG 1047, ABV 5%)
Dark, copper-coloured, reflecting a roast malt content, with bitterness from Challenger hops.

Summerskills SIBA

Summerskills Brewery, 15 Pomphlett Farm Industrial Estate, Broxton Drive, Plymouth, Devon, PL4 7BG
Tel/Fax (01752) 481283
Email info@summerskills.co.uk
Website www.summerskill.co.uk

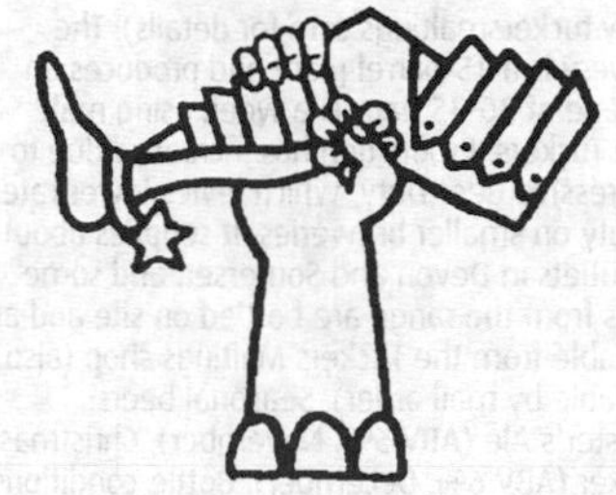

⊗ Originally established in a vineyard in 1983 at Bigbury-on-Sea, Summerskills moved to its present site in 1985 and has expanded since then. National distribution is carried out by experienced wholesalers. Twenty outlets are supplied by the brewery.

Cellar Vee (OG 1037, ABV 3.7%)

Hopscotch (OG 1042, ABV 4.1%)

Best Bitter (OG 1043, ABV 4.3%) ◆
A mid-brown beer, with plenty of malt and hops through the aroma, taste and finish. A good session beer.

Tamar (OG 1037, ABV 4.3%)
A tawny-coloured bitter with a fruity aroma and a hop taste and finish.

Menacing Dennis (OG 1045, ABV 4.5%)

Whistle Belly Vengeance (OG 1046, ABV 4.7%) ◆
A red/brown beer with a beautiful malt and fruit taste and a pleasant, malty aftertaste.

Surrey Hills*

Surrey Hills Brewery Ltd, Old Scotland Farm, Staple Lane, Shere, Guildford, Surrey, GU5 9TE
Tel (01483) 212812
Email info@surreyhills.co.uk
Website www.surreyhills.co.uk

Surrey Hills is based in an old milking parlour and produced its first commercial beers in May 2005. Seasonal beers: Albury Ruby (ABV 4.6%, winter), Gilt Complex (ABV 4.6%, summer).

Ranmore Drop (ABV 3.8%)
A light session bitter, full of flavour.

Shere Drop (ABV 4.2%)
Pale, hoppy and fruity.

Suthwyk*

Suthwyk Ales, Offwell Farm, Southwick, Fareham, Hampshire, PO17 6DX.
Tel/Fax (023) 9232 5252
Email mjbazeley@suthwykales.com
Website www.suthwykales.com

Barley farmer Martin Bazeley does not brew himself. The beers are produced by Oakleaf Brewing (qv) in Gosport, using Martin's Optic malt. The beers listed are also available in bottle-conditioned form and can be bought by mail order: see website.

Bloomfields (ABV 3.8%)

Liberation (ABV 4.2%)

Skew Sunshine Ale (ABV 4.6%)

Sutton

See South Hams

Swan

⊕ Gimbal Trading Ltd, Swan on the Green, West Peckham, Maidstone, ME18 5JW
Tel (01622) 812271
Fax (01622) 814977, (0870) 0560556
Email info@swan-on-the-green.co.uk
Website www.swan-on-the-green.co.uk
Tours by arrangement

⊗ The brewery was established in 2000 to produce hand-crafted beers. Major developments have taken place to include lager production and standard British bitters. The beers are not filtered and no artificial ingredients are used. There are plans to expand the plant. One pub is owned and other outlets and beer festivals are occasionally supplied.

Fuggles Pale (OG 1037, ABV 3.6%)
A session bitter, traditionally hoppy, using local Fuggles hops.

Whooper (OG 1037, ABV 3.6%)
Straw coloured and lightly hopped with American Cascade for a subtle fruity aroma.

Trumpeter Best (OG 1041, ABV 4%)
A copper-coloured ale hopped with First Gold and Target.

Porter (OG 1045, ABV 4.5%)

Bewick (OG 1051-1054, ABV 5.3%)
A heavyweight premium bitter hopped with Target for bite and softened with Kentish Goldings for aroma.

Swansea SIBA

⊕ Swansea Brewing Co, Joiners Arms, 50 Bishopston Road, Bishopston, Swansea, SA3 3EJ
Office: 74 Hawthorne Avenue, Uplands, Swansea, SA2 0LY
Tel (01792) 232658 brewery, (01792) 290197 office
Email rorygowland@fsbdial.co.uk
Tours by arrangement

◎ Opened in 1996, Swansea was the first commercial brewery in the area for almost 30 years and is the city's only brew-pub. It doubled its capacity within the first year and now produces four regular beers and occasional experimental ones. The founder, Rory Gowland, learnt his trade working in the chemistry department of Swansea University. Four regular outlets are supplied along with other pubs in the South Wales area. Seasonal beers: St Teilo's Tipple (ABV 5.5%), Barland Strong (ABV 6%), Pwll Du XXXX (ABV 4.9%).

Deep Slade Dark (OG 1034, ABV 4%)

Bishopswood Bitter (OG 1038, ABV 4.3%) ☐ ◆
A delicate aroma of hops and malt in this pale brown colour. The taste is a balanced mix of hops and malt with a growing hoppy bitterness ending in a lasting bitter finish.

Three Cliffs Gold (OG 1042, ABV 4.7%) ◆
A golden beer with a hoppy and fruity aroma, a hoppy taste with fruit and malt, and a quenching bitterness. The pleasant finish has a good hop flavour and bitterness.

Original Wood (OG 1046, ABV 5.2%) ◆
A full-bodied, pale brown beer with an aroma of hops, fruit and malt. A complex blend of these flavours with a firm bitterness ends with increasing bitterness.

Timothy Taylor IFBB

Timothy Taylor & Co Ltd, Knowle Spring Brewery, Keighley, West Yorkshire, BD21 1AW
Tel (01535) 603139
Fax (01535) 691167
Website www.timothy-taylor.co.uk

☺ One of the classic brewers of pale ale, Timothy Taylor is an independent family-owned company established in 1858. It moved to the site of the Knowle Spring in 1863. Its prize-winning ales, which use Pennine spring water, are served in all 23 of the brewery's pubs as well as 300-plus other outlets. In 2003 the brewery was given planning permission for a £1 million expansion programme that included a new brewhouse. Draught beer uses isinglass finings but bottled beers are suitable for vegans and vegetarians. Seasonal beer: Ram Tam (ABV 4.3%, winter).

Golden Best (OG 1033, ABV 3.5%) ◆
A clean-tasting and refreshing traditional Pennine light mild. A little fruit in the nose increases to complement the delicate hoppy taste. Background malt throughout. A good session beer.

Dark Mild (OG 1034, ABV 3.5%) ◆
Malt and caramel dominate with hints of fruit, hops and bitterness, leading to a dry finish.

Porter (OG 1041, ABV 3.8%) ◆
Sweetness and caramel can dominate this beer if it is served too young. However, when mature, the sweetness is balanced by fruity flavours and bitterness in the finish.

Best Bitter (OG 1038, ABV 4%) ◆
Hops and citrus fruit combine well with a nutty malt character in this drinkable bitter. Bitterness increases down the glass and lingers in the aftertaste.

Landlord (OG 1042, ABV 4.3%) ◆
An increasingly dry, hoppy, bitter finish complements the spicy, citrus character of this full-flavoured and well-balanced amber beer.

Teignworthy SIBA

Teignworthy Brewery, The Maltings, Teign Road, Newton Abbot, Devon, TQ12 4AA
Tel/Fax (01626) 332066
Email john@teignworthy.freeserve.co.uk
Shop 10-5 weekdays at Tuckers Maltings
Tours to Trade customers only

⊗ Teignworthy Brewery was established in 1994 by John and Rachel Lawton and is located in part of the historic Tuckers Maltings. There are regular tours of the maltings from Easter to the end of October, which includes the brewery and a sample of beer (tel 01626 334734 or www.tuckersmaltings.com for details). The brewery is a 15-barrel plant and produces an average of 30-35 barrels a week using malt from Tuckers. Production has increased due to Progressive Beer Duty, which levies lower rates of duty on smaller breweries. It supplies about 75 outlets in Devon and Somerset, and some beers from the range are bottled on site and are available from the Tuckers Maltings shop (also available by mail order). Seasonal beers: Maltster's Ale (ABV 5%, November), Christmas Cracker (ABV 6%, December). Bottle-conditioned beers (all suitable for vegans): Reel Ale, Springtide, Old Moggie, Beachcomber, Harvey's Ale (ABV 4.6%, April and Oct), Amy's Ale (ABV 4.8%, April and Oct), Maltster's Ale (ABV 5%, November), Martha's Mild (ABV 5.3%, April and Oct), Christmas Cracker (ABV 6%, December).

Reel Ale (OG 1039.5, ABV 4%) ◆
Clean, sharp-tasting bitter with lasting hoppiness; predominantly malty aroma.

Springtide (OG 1043.5, ABV 4.3%) ◆
An excellent, full and well-rounded, mid-brown beer with a dry, bitter taste and aftertaste.

Old Moggie (OG 1044.5, ABV 4.4%)
A golden, hoppy and fruity ale.

Beachcomber (OG 1045.5, ABV 4.5%) ◆
A pale brown beer with a light, refreshing fruit and hop nose, grapefruit taste and a dry, hoppy finish.

Teme Valley SIBA

Teme Valley Brewery, The Talbot, Bromyard Road, Knightwick, Worcester, WR6 5PH
Tel (01886) 821235
Fax (01886) 821060
Email enquiries@temevalleybrewery.co.uk
Website www.temevalleybrewery.co.uk
Tours by arrangement

☺ Teme Valley Brewery opened in 1997. In 2005, new investment enabled the brewery to expand to a 10-barrel brew-length. It maintains strong ties with local hop farming, using only Worcestershire-grown hops. Some 30 outlets are supplied. Seasonal beers: Talbot Porter (ABV 4.4%, Nov-Jan), Heartwarmer (ABV 6%, December), The Hops Nouvelle (ABV 4.1%, Sept-Oct), Spring's First (ABV 4.7%, Feb-Mar), Dark Stranger (ABV 4.4%, June-July), 3 Pears (ABV 3.9%, July-Aug). Bottle-conditioned beers: This, That, The Hop Nouvelle, Wotever Next? (ABV 5%).

T'Other (OG 1035, ABV 3.5%) ◆
Easy-drinking, golden hoppy beer with a dry, bitter aftertaste.

This (OG 1037, ABV 3.7%) ◆
A refreshing quaffing beer with a pungent hoppy aroma and a balanced flavour.

That (OG 1041, ABV 4.1%) ◆
Copper-coloured bitter with a gentle aroma and a refreshing balance of hops and malt.

Theakston

T&R Theakston Ltd, The Brewery, Wellgarth, Masham, Ripon, North Yorkshire, HG4 4YD
Tel (01765) 680000
Fax (01765) 689921

Email simon.theakston@theakstons.co.uk
Website www.theakstons.co.uk

After almost 20 years under the control of first Matthew Brown and then Scottish & Newcastle, Theakstons returned to the independent sector in 2003 when S&N sold the company back to the family. It is run by three Theakston brothers. The brewery is one of the oldest in Yorkshire, built in 1875 by the brothers' great-grandfather, Thomas Theakston, the son of the company's founder. The Theakston's range, with the exception of Best Bitter, is brewed at Masham but as a result of restraints on capacity the company has contracted Scottish Courage to brew Best Bitter at John Smith's in Tadcaster. Seasonal beers: Lightfoot Bitter (ABV 4.3%), Hogshead Bitter (ABV 4%), Coopers Butt (ABV 4.4%). Lightfoot and Hogshead are suitable for vegans and vegetarians.

Mild Ale (OG 1035, ABV 3.6%) ◆
A rich and smooth mild ale with a creamy body and a rounded liquorice taste. Dark ruby/amber in colour, with a mix of malt and fruit on the nose, and a dry, hoppy aftertaste.

Black Bull Bitter (OG 1037, ABV 3.9%) ◆
A distinctively hoppy aroma leads to a bitter, hoppy taste with some fruitiness and a short bitter finish. Rather thin.

Cool Cask (OG 1042, ABV 4.2%)
A beer served through special cooling equipment at 10 degrees C.

XB (OG 1044, ABV 4.6%)
A sweet-tasting bitter with background fruit and spicy hop. Some caramel character gives this ale a malty dominance.

Old Peculier (OG 1057, ABV 5.7%) ◆
A full-bodied, dark brown, strong ale. Slightly malty but with hints of roast coffee and liquorice. A smooth caramel overlay and a complex fruitiness leads to a bitter chocolate finish.

Masham Ale (OG 1065, ABV 6.5%)

Abraham Thompson

Abraham Thompson's Brewing Co, Flass Lane, Barrow-in-Furness, Cumbria, LA13 0AD
Tel 07708 191437
Email abraham.thompson@btinternet.com

Abraham Thompson was set up in 2004 by John Mulholland, a long-standing CAMRA member, with a mission to return Barrow-brewed beers to local pubs. This was achieved in April 2005 after an absence of more than 30 years following the demise of Case's Brewery in 1972. With a half-barrel plant, Abe's nano-brewery has concentrated almost exclusively on dark beers, reflecting the tastes of the brewer. As a result of the small output, finding the beers outside the Low Furness area is difficult. The only frequent stockist is the Black Dog Inn between Dalton and Ireleth.

Dark Mild (ABV 3.5%)

Lickerish Stout (ABV 4%)
A black, full-bodied stout with heavy roast flavours and good bitterness.

Porter (ABV 4.1%)
A deep, dark porter with good body and a smooth chocolate finish.

Letargion (ABV 9%)
Black, bitter and heavily roast but still very drinkable. A meal in a glass.

John Thompson

John Thompson Inn and Brewery, Ingleby, Derbyshire, DE73 1HW
Tel (01332) 852469
Fax (01332) 865647
Email nick-w-thompson@yahoo.co.uk
Tours by arrangement

John Thompson set up the brewery in the 1970s. Pub and brewery are now run by his son, Nick. Seasonal beer: Summer Gold (ABV 4.5%).

JTS Bitter (OG 1041, ABV 4.1%)

Porter (OG 1045, ABV 4.5%)

Thornbridge*

Thornbridge Hall Country House Brewing Co, Thornbridge Hall, Ashford in the Water, Bakewell, Derbyshire, DE45 1NZ
Tel (01629) 640617
Fax (01629) 640039
Email jim@thornbridgehall.co.uk
Website www.thornbridgehall.co.uk
Tours by arrangement

Brewing started in 2004 with a 10-barrel plant based in a former barn on the estate of Thornbridge Hall, a stately home in Derbyshire, with advice from Kelham Island in Sheffield (qv), for whom occasional brewing is carried out. Two full-time brewers are assisted on a part-time basis by experienced consultant brewer Dave Corby.

Lord Marples (ABV 4%)

Blackthorn Ale (ABV 4.4%)

Three B's

Three B's Brewery, Unit 5, Laneside Works, Stockclough Lane, Feniscowles, Blackburn, Lancashire, BB2 5JR
Tel/Fax (01254) 207686
Email info@threebsbrewery.co.uk
Website www.threebsbrewery.co.uk
Tours by arrangement

Robert Bell designed and began building his two-barrel brewery in 1997 and in 1998 he obtained premises in Hamilton Street, Blackburn, to set up the equipment and complete the project. It is now a 10-barrel brewery. 20 outlets are supplied. Bottle-conditioned beers: Knocker Up, Tackler's Tipple.

Stoker's Slake (ABV 3.6%)
A traditional dark mild with roast malt aromas and creamy chocolate notes.

Bobbin's Bitter (ABV 3.8%)
Warm aromas of malt, Goldings hops and nuts; a full, fruity flavour with a light dry finish.

Tackler's Tipple (ABV 4.3%)
A best bitter with full hop flavour, biscuit tones on the tongue and a deep, dry finish. A darker coloured ale with a fascinating blend of hops and dark malt.

Doff Cocker (ABV 4.5%) ◆
Clean-tasting, well-balanced, yellow-coloured beer with a predominance of hops and fruit. A long, tangy aftertaste.

Pinch Noggin' (ABV 4.6%)
A luscious balance of malt, hops and fruit, with a lively, colourful spicy aroma of citrus fruit. A quenching golden beer.

Knocker Up (ABV 4.8%) ◆
A smooth, rich, creamy porter. The roast flavour is foremost without dominating and is balanced by fruit and hop notes.

Shuttle Ale (ABV 5.2%)
A strong pale ale, light in colour with a balanced malt and hop flavour, a Goldings hops aroma, a long dry finish and delicate fruit notes.

Three Rivers SIBA

Three Rivers Brewing Co, Unit 12, Vauxhall Industrial Estate, South Reddish, Greater Manchester, SK5 7BR
Tel (0161) 477 3333
Email threerivers@acedial.co.uk

Mike Hitchen, previously at Beecham's Bar in St Helens, launched Three Rivers in 2004. Seasonal beer: Summer Rays (ABV 4%)

GMT (ABV 3.8%)
Named after the three rivers Goyt, Mersey and Tame.

Manchester IPA (ABV 4.2%)

Oxbow (ABV 4.5%)

Delta Dark Mild (ABV 4.8%)

Old Disreputable (ABV 5.2%)

Thwaites IFBB

Daniel Thwaites Brewery, Star Brewery, Blackburn, Lancashire, BB1 5BU
Tel (01254) 686868
Fax (01254) 681439
Email info@thwaites.co.uk
Website www.thwaites.co.uk/www.thwaitesbeers.co.uk
Tours by arrangement

☺ Thwaites will celebrate its 200th anniversary in 2007 and is still controlled by the founder's descendants, the Yerburgh family. The company has expressed its intention to refocus on cask beer, largely by promoting Lancaster Bomber and Original. Cask beer is available in around two-thirds of Thwaites' 432 pubs but Dark Mild is hard to find. Seasonal beers: Bloomin' Ale (ABV 3.9%, spring), Good Elf (ABV 4.9%, Xmas), Liberation (ABV 4.5%), Craftsman (ABV 4.2%). Dates had not been set for the availability of the last two seasonal beers but this information will be found in due course on the second of the websites listed above.

Dark Mild (OG 1036, ABV 3.3%) ◆
A tasty traditional dark mild presenting a malty flavour with caramel notes and a slightly bitter finish.

Original (OG 1035, ABV 3.6%) ■ ◆
A pale brown session bitter with a faint malt and hop aroma. The taste is well balanced between malt and hops. The hop character has increased and continues through in to the finish.

Thoroughbred (OG 1038, ABV 4%) ◆
A copper-coloured best bitter with a dry hop aroma. It has a balanced taste with no distinctive characteristics. The finish is rather thin.

Lancaster Bomber (OG 1044, ABV 4.4%) ◆
Toasted malt and hops feature in the aroma of this mid-brown premium bitter. Fine-balanced flavour with a pronounced fruity finish.

Tigertops SIBA

Tigertops Brewery, c/o 35a Church Road, Altofts, Normanton, West Yorkshire, WF6 2NN
Tel (01229) 716238/(01924) 897728
Tours by arrangement

☺ Tigertops was established in 1995 by Stuart Johnson, a former chairman of the Wakefield branch of CAMRA, and his wife Lynda and they still own the brewery as well as running the Foxfield brew-pub in Cumbria (qv). Tigertops is run on their behalf by Barry Smith. In the past 12 months the brewery has exhibited at three Belgian beer festivals. Many one-off beers, including fruit ones, are produced.

Charles Town Bitter (ABV 3%)

Axetown Block (OG 1036, ABV 3.6%)
A malty beer with a good hop finish.

Dark Mild Wheat (OG 1036, ABV 3.6%)
An unusual mild made primarily with wheat malt.

Charles Town Best Bitter (ABV 4%)

Blanche de Newland (OG 1044, ABV 4.5%)
A Belgian-style wheat beer.

Ginger Fix (ABV 4.6%)

White Max (ABV 4.6%)

Tindall EAB

Tindall Ales Brewery, Toad Lane, Seething, Norwich, Norfolk, NR35 2EQ
Tel (01508) 483844/07795 113163
Fax (01508) 483844
Email greenangela5@aol.com
Shop Off licence by prior appointment
Tours by arrangement

⊗ Tindall Ales opened in 1998 and is a family-run business with the main objective of producing good quality ale made from local malt and Kentish hops. Various outlets are supplied. Seasonal beers: Summer Loving (ABV 3.6%), Autumn Brew (ABV 4%), Lovers Ale (ABV 4%, Valentines), Christmas Cheers (ABV 4%). All the beers listed below, except IPA, are available in bottle-conditioned form.

IPA (OG 1036, ABV 3.6%)
A smooth tasting pale ale. The Goldings hops lead to a delicate, refreshing finish, without lacking in flavour.

Best Bitter (OG 1037, ABV 3.7%) ◆
Hoppiness and bitterness dominate to produce a dry, almost astringent bitter with a grainy mouthfeel. Copper coloured with little aroma and a sharp decline in flavour as any remaining fruitiness disappears,

Fuggled Up! (ABV 3.7%)

Mild (OG 1037, ABV 3.7%)
A good dark mild.

Liberator (OG 1038, ABV 3.8%) ◆
Named after the warplanes that flew from the former airfield that now houses the brewery. A jaunty, undemanding bitter with a hoppy citrus nose and tumbling mix of hop, citrus, malt and sweetness.

Alltime (OG 1040, ABV 4%) ◆
A well-balanced, traditional English bitter. The blend of hop and malt is reflected in both the bouquet and taste. The residual bitterness increases towards the end of a long, sustained finish.

Mundham Mild (ABV 4%)

Ditchingham Dam (OG 1042, ABV 4.2%) ◆
Strong ginger and malt notes fight for supremacy in the swirling bouquet of this mid-brown brew. The flavours linger on the tongue to produce a refreshingly clean finish. As the malt slowly wanes, the ginger notes continue in full flow.

Seething Pint (ABV 4.3%)

Norfolk 'n' Good (OG 1046, ABV 4.6%) ◆
A golden-hued brew with light lemonade airs. There is a good balance of hops and malt that gives a refreshing citrus-like sensation. Some bitterness creeps in to a lingering finish that maintains its complexity to the end.

Norwich Dragon (ABV 4.6%)

Honeydo (OG 1050, ABV 5%)
A lighter ale full of flavour. Laced with Norfolk honey for a distinctive taste.

Tipples* EAB

Tipples Brewery, Unit 6, Damgate Lane Industrial Estate, Acle, Norwich, Norfolk, NR13 3DJ
Tel/Fax (01493) 741007
Email brewery@tipplesbrewery.com
Website www.tipplesbrewery.com

The owner's name really is Tipple, Jason Tipple in full. He worked in the financial services and the food industry but was clearly destined to get involved in brewing. Jason has a six-barrel plant built by Porter Brewing Company and his first beer came on stream in autumn 2004.

Longshore (ABV 3.6%)

Ginger (ABV 3.8%)

Redhead (ABV 4.2%)

Battle (ABV 4.3%)

Topper (ABV 4.5%)

Moon Rocket (ABV 5%)

Jacks' Revenge (ABV 5.9%)

Tipsy Toad

Tregear House, Longueville, St Saviour, Jersey, JE2 7WF
Tel (01534) 834376
Email paul.hurley@annstreet.co.uk
Tours by arrangement

⊗ In 2004 the former 40-barrel Jersey Brewery plant (previously known as Ann Street) was relocated to Tregear House alongside the eight-barrel Tipsy Toad plant from the Star brew-pub in St Peter. Most cask beers are produced on the smaller plant, although the bigger one, which usually produces keg beers, can also be used for cask production. Seasonal beers are produced.

Ale (OG 1038, ABV 3.8%)

Guernsey Sunbeam (OG 1042, ABV 4.2%)

Jimmy's Bitter (OG 1042, ABV 4.2%)

Horny Toad (ABV 1050, ABV 5%)

Tirril SIBA

Tirril Brewery Ltd, c/o Red House, Long Marton, Appleby-in-Westmorland, Cumbria, CA16 6BN
Tel (017683) 61846
Fax (017683) 61841
Email chris@tirrilbrewery.co.uk
Website www.tirrilbrewery.co.uk
Tours by arrangement

Tirril started brewing for the award-winning Queens Head at Tirril in 1999, 100 years after Siddle's Brewery had been bought and closed in 1899. The brewery moved after the 2001 foot-and-mouth epidemic to Brougham Hall, to the original 1823 brewing rooms. Plans have been submitted to expand to a 20-barrel plant to keep up with demand. One pub is owned and 50-plus outlets are supplied.

Bewsher's Best Bitter (OG 1038.5, ABV 3.8%)
A lightly-hopped, golden brown session beer, named after the landlord and brewer at the Queen's Head in the 1830s.

Brougham Ale (OG 1039, ABV 3.9%)
A gently hopped, amber bitter.

Old Faithful (OG 1040, ABV 4%)
Pale gold, aromatic and well-hopped.

1823 (OG 1041, ABV 4.1%)

Academy Ale (OG 1041.5, ABV 4.2%)
A dark, full-bodied, traditional rich and malty ale.

Titanic SIBA

Titanic Brewery Co Ltd, Unit 5, Callender Place, Burslem, Stoke-on-Trent, Staffordshire, ST6 1JL
Tel (01782) 823447
Fax (01782) 812349
Email titanic@titanicbrewery.co.uk
Website www.titanicbrewery.co.uk
Shop No, but merchandise available
Tours by arrangement

⊛ Founded in 1985, the brewery is named in honour of Captain Smith who hailed from the Potteries and had the misfortune to captain the Titanic. A monthly seasonal beer provides the opportunity to offer distinctive beers of many styles, each with a link to the once proud liner. Now supplying 300 free trade outlets, Titanic beers are available throughout the country. One pub is owned. Bottle-conditioned beer: Titanic Stout ◼ ◻.

Best Bitter (OG 1036, ABV 3.5%) ◆
Straw-coloured bitter with a sulphurous nose, a fruity start, a well-hopped middle and a dry finish.

Mild (OG 1036, ABV 3.5%) ◆
Roast and malt aroma in this red-brown ale. Hops give a dry finish after a smooth, sweet body.

Fullkiln Ale (OG 1040, ABV 4%)

Lifeboat (OG 1040, ABV 4%) ◆
A fruity and malty, dark red with a fruity finish.

Iceberg (OG 1042, ABV 4.1%) ◼ ◻ ◆
Gold coloured, with a hoppy and fruity aroma leading to a fruity and hoppy taste with tones of honey and grass. Bitterness develops in the long finish.

Premium Bitter (OG 1042, ABV 4.1%) ◆
Copper-coloured with a sulphurous aroma parting to reveal fruit and hops. A robust bitterness relaxes in to a long, dry, hoppy finish.

Stout (OG 1046, ABV 4.5%) ◆
Full roast aroma from this ultra-black stout. It has a roast taste with fruit and hops, and a mouth-watering, dry roast finish with touches of smoke or charcoal.

White Star (OG 1050, ABV 4.8%) ◆
Golden bitter with some hop and fruit aromas. Touches of honey and citrus begin the taste. Malty sweetness arrives but quickly gives way to a bitterness that lingers to perfection.

Captain Smith's Strong Ale
(OG 1054, ABV 5.2%) ◆
A full-bodied, dark red/brown beer, hoppy and bitter with malt and roast malt flavours, and a long, bitter-sweet finish.

Toll End*

Toll End Brewery, Waggon & Horses, 131 Toll End Road, Tipton, Derbyshire, DY4 0ET
Tel (0121) 502 6453

A two-barrel brewery was installed at the pub in November 2004. With the exception of Phoebe's Ale, which is named after the publican's daughter, the beers commemorate local landmarks.

Lost City Mild (ABV 4%)

PA/Phoebe's Ale (ABV 4.6%)

Black Bridge (ABV 4.8%)

Tom Wood SIBA

Highwood Brewery Ltd, Melton Highwood, Barnetby, Lincolnshire, DN38 6AA
Tel (01472) 255500
Fax (01472) 255501
Email tomwood@tom-wood.com
Website www.tom-wood.com
Shop Wholesale business open Mon-Fri 8-5pm, Sat 8-1pm

⊗ Highwood, best known under the Tom Wood brand name, started brewing in a converted Victorian granary on the family farm in 1995. The brew-length was increased from 10 barrels to 30 in 2001, using plant from Ash Vine brewery. In 2002, Highwood bought Conway's Licensed Trade Wholesalers. It now distributes most regional and national cask ales throughout Lincolnshire and Nottinghamshire. More than 200 outlets are supplied. Seasonal beers: see website. All products are suitable for vegetarians and vegans.

Dark Mild (OG 1034, ABV 3.5%)

Best Bitter (OG 1034, ABV 3.5%) ◻ ◆
A good citrus, passion fruit hop dominates the nose and taste, with background malt. A lingering hoppy and bitter finish makes this amber bitter very drinkable.

Shepherd's Delight
(OG 1040, ABV 4%) ◆
Malt is the dominant taste in this amber brew, although the fruity hop bitterness complements it all the way.

Harvest Bitter (OG 1042, ABV 4.3%)
A well-balanced amber beer where the hops and bitterness just about outdo the malt.

Old Timber (OG 1043, ABV 4.5%) ◆
Hoppy on the nose, but featuring well-balanced malt and hops otherwise. A slight, lingering roast/coffee flavour develops, but this is generally a bitter, darkish brown beer.

Bomber County (OG 1046, ABV 4.8%) ◆
An earthy malt aroma but with a complex underlying mix of coffee, hops, caramel and apple fruit. The beer starts bitter and intensifies to the end.

Topsham and Exminster

Topsham and Exminster Brewery, Lions Rest Industrial Estate, Exminster, Exeter, Devon, EX6 8DZ
Tel (01392) 823013

The brewery was launched in 2003 with the plant installed by the proprietor, Lawrence Wetherston, in a former welding shop. It comprises a new five-barrel plant with a recycled dairy milk plant forming the fermenting vessel. The beers are only available in a few selected local pubs and clubs.

Avocet (OG 1036, ABV 3.8%)

Ferryman (OG 1041, ABV 4.4%)

Tower SIBA

Tower Brewery, The Old Water Tower, Walsitch Maltings, Glensyl Way, Burton upon Trent, Staffordshire, DE14 1LX
Tel/Fax (01283) 530695
Email towerbrewery@aol.com
Tours by arrangement

⊗ Established in 2001 by John Mills, previously the brewer at Burton Bridge, in a converted derelict water tower of Thomas Salt's Maltings. The conversion was given a Civic Society award for the restoration of a Historic Industrial Building in 2001. Tower has 20 regular outlets. Seasonal beers: Sundowner (ABV 4%, May-Aug), Spring Equinox (ABV 4.6%, March-May), Autumn Equinox (ABV 4.6%, Sept-Nov), Winter Spirit (ABV 5%).

Thomas Salt's Bitter (OG 1038, ABV 3.8%)

Bitter (OG 1042, ABV 4.2%) ◆
Gold coloured with a malty, caramel and hoppy aroma. A full hop and fruit taste with the fruit lingering. A bitter and astringent finish.

Malty Towers (OG 1044, ABV 4.4%) ◆
Yellow with a malty aroma as named, with a hint of tobacco. Strong hops give a long, dry, bitter finish with pleasant astringency.

Pale Ale (OG 1048, ABV 4.8%)

Tower of Strength (OG 1076, ABV 7.6%)

Townes SIBA

Townes Brewery, Speedwell Inn, Lowgates, Staveley, Chesterfield, Derbyshire, S43 3TT
Tel (01246) 472252
Email woodcurly@aol.com
Tours by arrangement

⊗ Townes Brewery started in 1994 in an old bakery on the outskirts of Chesterfield using a five-barrel plant. It was the first brewery in the town for more than 40 years. After a period of steady progress, the Speedwell Inn at Staveley was bought and the plant was moved to the rear of the pub. Brewing at Staveley started in 1997 and, after a period of renovation, the pub opened a year later. It was the first brew-pub in north Derbyshire in the 20th century. Bottling is now established and there are plans to extend this part of the operation. More than 40 outlets are supplied on an occasional basis. Seasonal beers: Stargazer (ABV 5.5%, winter), Sunshine (ABV 3.7%, summer). A monthly special is available under the Real Gone motif. Two seasonal milds are produced to increase interest in the style: Golden Bud (ABV 3.8%, summer) and Muffin Man (ABV 4.6%, winter). Staveley Cross, IPA, Oatmeal Stout and Staveleyan are also available in bottle-conditioned form and are suitable for vegetarians and vegans.

Speedwell Bitter (OG 1039, ABV 3.9%)

Lockoford Best Bitter (ABV 4%)

Lowgate Light (OG 1041, ABV 4.1%)

Staveley Cross (OG 1043, ABV 4.3%)

IPA (OG 1045, ABV 4.5%)

Oatmeal Stout (OG 1047, ABV 4.7%)

Staveleyan (OG 1049, ABV 4.9%)

Town House

Town House Brewery Ltd, No. 2 Town House Studios, Town House Farm, Alsager Road, Audley, Staffordshire, ST7 8JQ
Tel (07976) 209437

Town House was set up by Tony Nixon in Audley in 2002 with a 2.5-barrel plant. It mainly supplied the Plough at Bignall End and a few other local outlets within a short distance. In 2004 the brewery began an expansion to a five-barrel plant. As Tony Nixon's previous occupation was as a welder/fabricator, he designed and built the plant. The new brewery has been in production since 2004 and supplies an ever-greater number of outlets. Mark Nixon, Tony's son, is now responsible for sales and delivery, as well as being assistant brewer. Ten outlets are supplied.

Audley Bitter (OG 1038, ABV 3.8%)
A pale, well-balanced session bitter.

Dark Horse (OG 1042, ABV 4.3%)
Ruby ale with dark malt character and late hoppy finish.

Audley Gold (OG 1043, ABV 4.5%)
Pale, golden bitter with malt and fruity character.

Parker's Pride (OG 1044, ABV 4.6%)
A copper-coloured bitter, malty with a balanced hoppy taste.

Special Bitter (OG 1048, ABV 5%)
A balanced best bitter with floral hop palate and fruity, dry, bitter finish.

Traquair SIBA

Traquair House Brewery, Traquair House, Innerleithen, Peeblesshire, EH44 6PW
Tel (01896) 830323
Fax (01896) 830639
Email enquiries@traquair.co.uk
Website www.traquair.co.uk
Shop and Brewery Museum 12-5 daily April-Sept, 10.30-5.30 daily June-Aug, 11-4 Oct
Tours by arrangement April-Sept

The 18th-century brewhouse is based in one of the wings of the 1,000-year-old Traquair House, Scotland's oldest inhabited house, visited by Mary Queen of Scots and Prince Charles Edward Stuart. The brewhouse was rediscovered by the 20th Laird, the late Peter Maxwell Stuart, in 1965. He began brewing again using all the original equipment, which remained intact, despite having lain idle for more than 100 years. The brewery has been run by Peter's daughter, Catherine Maxwell Stuart, since his death in 1990. The Maxwell Stuarts are members of the Stuart clan, and the main Bear Gates will remain shut until a Stuart returns to the throne. All the beers are oak-fermented and 60 per cent of production is exported, mostly bottled Traquair House Ale and Jacobite Ale. Some five outlets take the cask beer. Seasonal beers: Stuart Ale (ABV 4.5%, summer), Bear Ale (ABV 5%, winter).

House Ale (ABV 7%)

Tring SIBA

Tring Brewery Co Ltd, 81-82 Akeman Street, Tring, Hertfordshire, HP23 6AF
Tel (01442) 890721
Fax (01442) 890740
Email info@tringbrewery.com
Website www.tringbrewery.com
Tours by arrangement in the evenings

⊗ Tring is an eight-barrel plant on a small industrial estate founded in 1992 by Richard Shardlow. Many of the ales are named after local myths and legends and are easily identified by their inverted triangular pump clips. In addition to regular ales, a new range of seasonal ales and a range of specials are produced, including the limited winter special, Death or Glory (ABV 7.2%). Polypins and mini-casks are available for collection by arrangement and the brewery may produce some bottled beers in the future. The brewery supplies 120 outlets.

Side Pocket for a Toad (OG 1035, ABV 3.6%)
Citrus notes from American Cascade hops balanced with a floral aroma and a crisp, dry finish in a straw-coloured ale.

Ridgeway (OG 1039, ABV 4%)

Jack O'Legs (OG 1041, ABV 4.2%)
A combination of four types of malt and two types of aroma hops provide a copper-coloured premium ale with full fruit and a distinctive hoppy bitterness.

Colley's Dog (OG 1051, ABV 5.2%)
Dark but not over-rich, strong yet drinkable, this premium ale has a long dry finish with overtones of malt and walnuts.

Triple fff SIBA

Triple fff Brewing Ltd, Unit 3, Old Magpie Works, Four Marks, Alton, Hampshire, GU34 5HN
Tel (01420) 561422 Fax (01420) 560159
Email triplefffbrewing@aol.com
Website www.triplefff.com
Tours by arrangement

⊗ Opened in 1997 with a five-barrel plant, Triple fff is now in the sole ownership of Graham Trott, who also owns the Railway Arms in Alton. There has been a steady expansion of output, which is now produced on an 18-barrel plant. One pub is owned and some 100 outlets are supplied direct. Graham has installed a bottling plant with a capacity of 4,000 bottles a day. Seasonal beers: Afterglow (ABV 4%), Snow Blind (ABV 4.2%), Apache Rose Peacock (ABV 4.2%), Trotneys Red Barrel (ABV 4.2%), Little Red Rooster (ABV 5%), Witches Promise (ABV 6%), I Can't Remember (ABV 6.8%).

Alton's Pride (ABV 3.8%)
Excellent, clean-tasting, golden brown session bitter, full-bodied for its strength. It has a delicious aroma of malt and hops. The malty flavour fades as citrus notes and hoppiness take over, leading to a lasting hoppy, bitter finish.

Pressed Rat & Warthog (ABV 3.8%)
Complex hoppy and bitter mild; not in the classic style but nevertheless delicious. Ruby in colour, a roast malt aroma with hints of blackcurrant and chocolate leads to a well-balanced flavour with roast, toffee and malt vying with the hoppy bitterness and a dry bitter finish.

After Glow (ABV 4%)
Golden best bitter with malt and hop flavours throughout. Well balanced with a citrus hoppiness that builds with bitterness into a long, dry finish.

Moondance (ABV 4.2%)
An amber-coloured best bitter, wonderfully hopped, with a huge aromatic, citrus hop nose, balanced by a biting bitterness and dryness in the mouth. Bitterness increases in the finish as the fruit declines.

Dazed and Confused (ABV 4.6%)
A strongish bitter, pale yellow in colour, with pale lager malts and a suggestion of elderflower. Refreshing, hoppy and increasingly bitter. Full of flavour.

Stairway to Heaven (ABV 4.6%)
An aroma of pale and crystal malts introduces this pale brown beer with a flavour of summer fruits. Well-balanced, with a dry, strong, hoppy finish. Predominantly bitter with some malt.

Comfortably Numb (ABV 5%)

I Can't Remember (ABV 6.8%)

Trossachs Craft

🍺 Trossachs Craft Brewery, c/o Lade Inn, Kilmahog, Callender, FK17 8HD
Tel (07789) 403384
Fax (01786) 833426
Email brewery@trossachscraftbrewery.com
Website www.theladeinn.com
Tours by arrangement

Trossach started brewing in an outbuilding of the Lade Inn in 2003. The brewery only brews organic ales and the beers listed are brewed exclusively for the Lade Inn. The brewery is set in a beautiful rural setting in the Trossach National Park, where the beers are brewed with pure Scottish mountain water.

Waylade (OG 1040, ABV 3.9%)
A good flavoured bitter with a malty, fruity nose and lightly hopped aftertaste.

Ladeback (OG 1048, ABV 4.5%)
A rounded, creamy, refreshing, well-balanced ale with a hop-dominated dry finish.

Lade Out (OG 1055, ABV 5.1%)
A robust, satisfying ale with a complex flavour.

Tryst

Tryst Brewery, Lorne Road, Larbert, Stirlingshire, FK5 4AT
Tel (01324) 554000
Email johnmcgarva@tinyworld.co.uk

John McGarva, a member of Scottish Craft Brewers, started brewing in 2003 in an industrial unit near Larbert station. Some 35 outlets are supplied direct.

Brockville Dark (OG 1039, ABV 3.8%)

Brockville Pale (OG 1040, ABV 3.8%)

Buckled Wheel (OG 1042, ABV 4.1%)

Carronade IPA (OG 1042, ABV 4.1%)

Tunnel*

Tunnel Brewery Ltd, Lord Nelson Inn, Birmingham Road, Ansley, Nuneaton, Warwickshire, CV10 9PQ
Tel (024 7639) 4888

Bob Yates and Mike Walsh started brewing in April 2005, taking the name from the half-mile long rail tunnel that passes under the village. The five-barrel plant was installed by Porter Brewing in an out-building of the Lord Nelson. Maris Otter malts and Worcestershire First Gold hops are used. Pub and brewery are independent of one another but the beers are available in the pub as well as the free trade. The pub sells a special cheese made with Tunnel beer. Commemorative beers are planned at intervals throughout the year.

Late Ott (ABV 4%)
Dark golden session bitter with a fruity nose and perfumed hop edge. The finish is dry and bitter.

Trade Winds (ABV 4.6%)
An aromatic, copper-coloured beer with an aroma of Cascade hops and a clean, crisp hint of citrus, followed by fruity malts and a dry finish full of scented hops.

Sweet Parish Ale (ABV 4.7%)
A reddish-amber, malty ale with a slight chocolate aroma enhanced by citrus notes on the nose. It becomes increasingly fruity as the English hops kick in. Smooth, gentle hop bitterness in the finish.

Turkey

🍺 Turkey Inn, Goose Eye, Oakworth, Keighley, West Yorkshire, BD22 0PD
Tel (01535) 681339
Tours by arrangement

⊛ Turkey is a purpose-built brewery with walls four feet thick, built into the hillside at the back of the pub. Some of the beers are named after local caves. Brewery trips are free, with a small donation to Upper Wharfdale Fell Rescue. Beer festivals are staged every May Bank Holiday.

Bitter (ABV 3.9%)

Black Shiver (ABV 4.3%)

Twickenham*

Twickenham Fine Ales Ltd, The Crane Brewery, Ryecroft Works, Edwin Road, Twickenham, Middlesex, TW2 6SP
Tel (0208) 241 1825
Fax (0208) 241 2815
Email stevebrown@twickenham-fine-ales.co.uk
Website www.twickenham-fine-ales.co.uk
Tours by arrangement

This is the first brewery in the town for nearly a century. Brandon's, previously Cole's, which had been brewing since before 1635, closed in 1927. The new brewery was launched by Steve Brown with many small investors providing the start-up capital. Equipment came from Springhead Brewery. In January 2005 former Whim brewer Don Weir joined, bringing new ideas and a passion for the job. The brewery currently supplies pubs and clubs in west and south-west London and the surrounding counties. Bottling was due to start in 2005. Some 60 outlets are supplied. Seasonal beer: Strong and Dark (ABV 5.2%, winter).

Crane Sundancer (OG 1038, ABV 3.7%)

Original (OG 1043, ABV 4.2%)

IPA (OG 1046, ABV 4.5%)

Ufford*

Ufford Ales, Ye Olde White Hart, Main Street, Ufford, Stamford, Cambridgeshire, PE9 3BH
Tel (01780) 740250/07763 767673

Ufford opened in February 2005. The five-barrel plant was set up with the assistance of the Parish Brewery in Leicestershire (qv). The beers will initially only be available in the four pubs related to owner Mick Thurlby: Smiths of Bourne, Crown Hotel of Stamford, Periwig of Stamford and White Hart of Ufford. Regular seasonal specials are produced.

Idle Hour (ABV 3.9%)

Offspring (ABV 4.5%)

Uley

Uley Brewery Ltd, The Old Brewery, 31 The Street, Uley, Gloucestershire, GL11 5TB
Tel (01453) 860120
Email chas@uleybrewery.com
Website www.uleybrewery.com
Shop Saturday morning
Tours by arrangement

⊗ Brewing at Uley began in 1833 at Price's Brewery. After a long gap, the premises were restored and Uley Brewery opened in 1985. It has its own spring water, which is used to mash with Tuckers Maris Otter malt and boiled with Hereford hops. No sugar or additives are used. Uley serves 40-50 free trade outlets in the Cotswold area and is brewing to capacity. Expansion is not an option as the brewery is a listed building. Seasonal ales: Harping Hog (ABV 5%).

Hogshead PA (OG 1038, ABV 3.8%) ◆
A pale-coloured, hoppy session bitter with a good hop aroma and a full flavour for its strength, ending in a bitter-sweet aftertaste.

Bitter (OG 1040, ABV 4%) ◆
A copper-coloured beer with hops and fruit in the aroma and a malty, fruity taste, underscored by a hoppy bitterness. The finish is dry, with a balance of hops and malt.

Laurie Lee's Bitter (OG 1045, ABV 4.5%)

Old Ric (OG 1045, ABV 4.5%) ◆
A full-flavoured, hoppy bitter with some fruitiness and a smooth, balanced finish. Distinctively copper-coloured, this is the house beer, solely for the Old Spot Inn, Dursley.

Old Spot Prize Ale (OG 1050, ABV 5%) ◆
A distinctive full-bodied, red/brown ale with a fruity aroma, a malty, fruity taste, with a hoppy bitterness, and a strong, balanced aftertaste.

Pig's Ear Strong Beer (OG 1050, ABV 5%) ◆
A pale-coloured beer, deceptively strong. Notably bitter in flavour, with a hoppy, fruity aroma and a bitter finish.

Uncle Stuarts EAB

Uncle Stuarts Brewery, Antoma, Pack Lane, Lingwood, Norwich, Norfolk, NR13 4PD
Tel (01603) 211833/07732 012112
Email stuartsbrewery@aol.com
Website www.unclestuartsbrewery.com
Tours by arrangement

⊗ The brewery started in 2002, selling bottle-conditioned beers and polypins direct to customers and by mail order. Since 2003, all the beers are available in nine-gallon casks. Seasonal beer: Xmas (ABV 7%).

Pack Lane (OG 1038, ABV 4%)

Excelsior (OG 1042, ABV 4.5%)

Church View (OG 1050, ABV 4.7%)

Buckenham Woods (OG 1051, ABV 5.6%)

Upper Agbrigg

Holme Valley Ales, Upper Agbrigg Brewery, Unit 12, Honley Business Centre, New Mill Road, Honley, Holmfirth, West Yorkshire, HD9 6QB
Tel (01484) 660008
Fax (01484) 663359
Email info@homevalleyales.co.uk

☺ Upper Agbrigg Brewery was founded in 2001 by Andrew Balmforth in the cellar of his house with a three-barrel brew length. The popularity of his beer was such that Andrew has now teamed up with Clive Donald of Brupaks, a leading supplier of brewing equipment and ingredients, and installed a brand new brewery in Brupaks' warehouse in Honley. The beers listed are the result of the new partnership. A bottling line is due to be installed. Fifteen outlets are supplied. Seasonal beers: Kellerbier (ABV 4.8%), Oatmeal Stout (ABV 4.8%), Rauchbier (ABV 4.8%), Winterfest (ABV 5.4%).

Holme Valley Bitter (ABV 3.8%)
Maris Otter pale malt gives this beer a great depth of sweet malt flavour, which is balanced by a subtle bitterness from East Kent Goldings hops. Hop aroma is provided by Styrian Goldings.

Holme Valley Special (ABV 4.4%)
A golden bitter ale with a malty profile but balanced with a pronounced hop character.

India Pale Ale (ABV 5.5%)
Deep copper in colour with a full malt flavour balanced by a massive Cascade hop character.

Ushers

See Wadworth and Wychwood

Vale SIBA

Vale Brewery Co, Thame Road, Haddenham, Buckinghamshire, HP17 8BY
Tel (01844) 290008
Fax (01844) 292505
Email valebrewery@yahoo.co.uk
Website www.valebrewery.co.uk
Tours by arrangement

⊗ After many years working for large regional breweries and allied industries, brothers Mark and Phil Stevens opened a small, purpose-built brewery in Haddenham. This revived brewing in a village where the last brewery closed at the end of World War II. The plant was expanded in 1996 and 1999, and now has a capacity of 50 barrels. All the beer is traditionally brewed without adjuncts, chemicals, or preservatives. A bottling line was added in 1997, which produces a range of 10 different ales plus own label beers in short runs. In 2003 the brewery took over an additional unit on the estate to give it larger storage for conditioning beer, a reception area and a brewery shop. Vale now runs five pubs and around 200 local outlets take the beers. Seasonal beers: Hadda's Spring Gold (ABV 4.6%), Hadda's Summer Glory (ABV 4%), Hadda's Autumn Ale (ABV 4.5%), Hadda's Winter Solstice (ABV 4.1%), Good King Senseless (ABV 5.2%). Bottle-conditioned beers: all regular cask beers except Notley Ale. All are suitable for vegetarians and vegans.

Black Swan Dark Mild (OG 1033, ABV 3.3%)

Notley Ale (OG 1033, ABV 3.3%) ◆
A refreshing, copper-coloured session bitter with some malt in the aroma and taste, and an uncompromisingly dry finish.

Best Bitter (OG 1036, ABV 3.7%)

Wychert Ale (OG 1038, ABV 3.9%)
A full-flavoured beer with nutty overtones.

Black Beauty Porter (OG 1043, ABV 4.3%)

Edgar's Golden Ale (OG 1043, ABV 4.3%) ◆
A golden, hoppy best bitter with some sweetness and a dry, bitter-sweet finish. An unpretentious and well-crafted beer.

Special (OG 1046, ABV 4.5%)
Deep brown-coloured premium ale brewed with Maris Otter, crystal and chocolate malts blended with choicest hops.

Grumpling Premium Ale (OG 1046, ABV 4.6%)

Hadda's Headbanger (OG 1050, ABV 5%)

Valhalla

Valhalla Brewery, Shetland Refreshments Ltd, Baltasound, Unst, Shetland, ZE2 9DX
Tel/Fax (01957) 711658
Email sonnyandsylvia@valhallabrewery.co.uk
Website www.valhallabrewery.co.uk
Tours by arrangement

The brewery started production in 1997, set up by husband and wife team Sonny and Sylvia Priest. A bottling plant was installed in 1999. The Priests plan a new brewery/visitor centre within the next two years. One outlet is supplied.

White Wife (OG 1038, ABV 3.8%) ◆
Predominantly malty aroma with hop and fruit, which remain on the palate. The aftertaste is increasingly bitter.

Simmer Dim (OG 1039, ABV 4%) ◆
A light golden bitter, named after the long Shetland twilight. The sulphur features do not mask the fruits and hops of this well-balanced beer.

Auld Rock (OG 1043, ABV 4.5%) ◆
A full-bodied, dark Scottish-style best bitter, it has a rich malty nose but does not lack bitterness in the long dry finish.

Sjolmet Stout (OG 1048, ABV 5%) ◆
Full of malt and roast barley, especially in the taste. Smooth, creamy, fruity finish, not as dry as some stouts.

Ventnor SIBA

Ventnor Brewery Ltd, 119 High Street, Ventnor, Isle of Wight, PO38 1LY
Tel (01983) 856161
Fax (01983) 530960
Email ventnorbrewery@onetel.com
Website www.ventnorbrewery.co.uk
Shop on line at www.ventnorbrewery.co.uk

☺ The brewery is situated on the south of the island in the old Victorian town of Ventnor. Beer has been brewed on the site since 1840. The beers today are still brewed with St Boniface natural spring water that flows through the brewery. The 10-barrel plant produces a range of six beers and seasonal beers in both cask and bottles. Ventnor supplies pub chains, wholesalers and supermarkets nationwide. Some 90 outlets are supplied direct. Seasonal beer: Antifreeze (ABV 5.2%, Sept-Feb). Bottle-conditioned beer: Old Ruby Ale (ABV 4.7%). Hygena Organic Ale is suitable for vegetarians and vegans.

Golden (OG 1040, ABV 4%) ◆
Creamy, light bitter with hints of honey and gorse persisting through to the aftertaste.

Sunfire (OG 1043, ABV 4.3%) ◆
A generously and distinctively bittered amber beer that could be toned down if pulled through a sparkler.

Pistol Night (OG 1043, ABV 4.4%) ◆
Deceptive light, flowery, professionally-crafted hoppy bitter with scents and flavours of early spring that continue through to a pleasant and satisfying finish.

Oyster Stout (OG 1045, ABV 4.5%) ◆
Rich, sugary, malty but watery dark brown beer.

Hygena Organic Ale (OG 1046, ABV 4.6%) ◆
A malty beer but refreshing beer.

Wight Spirit (OG 1050, ABV 5%) ◆
Predominantly bitter, hoppy and fruity strong and very pale ale.

Sandrock Smoked Ale (OG 1056, ABV 5.6%)

Verulam SIBA

Verulam Brewery, Farmers Boy, 134 London Road, St Albans, Hertfordshire, AL1 1PQ
Tel (01727) 766702
Tours by arrangement

A brewery housed behind the Farmers Boy pub run by Viv and Tina Davies. There are monthly specials.

Best (OG 1037, ABV 3.8%)

Clipper IPA (OG 1039, ABV 4%)
Impressive straw-coloured, very hoppy beer.

Farmers Joy (OG 1043, ABV 4.5%)
A malty beer with overtones of sweetness.

Village Brewer

See Hambleton

Wadworth IFBB

Wadworth & Co Ltd, Northgate Brewery, Devizes, Wiltshire, SN10 1JW
Tel (01380) 723361
Fax (01380) 724342
Email sales@wadworth.co.uk
Website www.wadworth.co.uk
Shop (reception) Mon-Fri. 9-5. Stables open weekday afternoons
Tours Trade April-Oct. Public September (by prior arrangement)

A market town brewery set up in 1885 by Henry Wadworth. It is one of few remaining breweries to sell beer locally in oak casks; the brewery still employs a cooper. Though solidly traditional, with its own dray horses, it continues to invest in the future and to expand, producing up to 2,000 barrels a week to supply a wide-ranging free trade, round 300 outlets in the south of England, as well as its own 256 pubs. All tied houses serve cask beer. Wadworth 6X is still handmade in Devizes and sold nationally through wholesalers, pubcos and regional brewers. 6X has had considerable marketing investment in recent years, with spending in excess of £1 million a year in the national press, poster sites and trade support. Seasonal beers: Old Father Timer (ABV 5.8%, Nov-Dec), Malt n' Hops (ABV 4.5%, Oct-Nov), Summersault (ABV 4%, May-Sept).

Henry's IPA (OG 1035, ABV 3.6%)
A booming sulphurous nose introduces this lively, well-balanced bitter. Smoky hop notes aid the well-defined maltiness that is a counterpoint to the continued sulphurous presence. The long finish retains flavours.

6X (OG 1041, ABV 4.3%)
Copper-coloured ale with a malty and fruity nose, and some balancing hop character. The flavour is similar, with some bitterness and a lingering malty, but bitter finish. Full-bodied and distinctive.

JCB (OG 1046 ABV 4.7%)
A deep amber, robust but perfectly balanced, traditional English ale with a rich, malty body, complex hop character and a hint of tropical fruit in the aroma and taste. A gentle barley sugar sweetness blends wonderfully with smooth nutty malt and rounded hop bitterness before a dry, biscuity, bitter finish.

For Refresh UK

Ushers Best Bitter (ABV 3.8%)

The Bishop's Tipple (ABV 6.5%, winter)

Walsh's Bakehouse SIBA

Walsh's Bakehouse Brewery Ltd, Scar Bank, Millers Road, Warwick, CV34 5DB
Tel (01926) 492574
Fax (01926) 400796
Email sales@bakehouseales.co.uk
Website www.bakehouseales.co.uk

The brewery is a five-barrel plant originally commissioned in 1996 in the Flyer and Firkin, Reading. The first brews took place in 2003. The brewery has been set up in a previously unused part of the family bakery. The brewery is able to offer a range of cakes and bar snacks alongside the beers. Some 30-plus outlets are supplied. Flying Top won the silver award in the brewers' category at the 2003 Peterborough beer festival and was voted Beer of the Festival at Harbury in the same year. Beer of the Festival (Harbury 2004) was won for Two Llocks. Seasonal beers: Bun in the Oven (ABV 3.8%, Jun-Aug), Fired Up (ABV 4.1%, Sept-Nov), Walsh's Warmer (ABV 5%, Dec-Jan).

Bakehouse Bitter (OG 1038, ABV 3.8%)

Two Llocks (OG 1040, ABV 4%)

Rock 'n' Roll (OG 1042, ABV 4.2%)

Flying Top (OG 1044, ABV 4.4%)

Old Gridlap (OG 1048, ABV 5%)

Wapping

Wapping Beers Ltd, Baltic Fleet, 33A Wapping, Liverpool, Merseyside, L1 8DQ
Tel/Fax (0151) 707 2242
Website www.wappingbeers.com

Established in 2002 using the former Passageway plant, Wapping has expanded by installing another two fermenting vessels, increasing capacity by half. The brewery delivers to trade in the local area. Seasonal beer: see website plus Winter Ale (ABV 6.5%, mid-Nov to mid-Feb).

Bitter (OG 1036, ABV 3.6%)
Light, easy-drinking session beer with a good, bitter finish.

Bow Sprit (OG 1036, ABV 3.6%)

Summer Ale (OG 1042, ABV 4.2%)
Golden/straw coloured, thirst-quenching with a bite in the finish.

Stout (OG 1050, ABV 5%)
Dark with hints of roasted coffee.

Warcop

Warcop Country Ales, 9 Nellive Park, St Brides Wentlooge, South Wales, NP10 8SE
Tel/Fax (01633) 680058
Email williampicton@compuserve.com

A small brewery based in a converted milking parlour, serving 30 outlets and others supplied by two wholesalers. Seasonal beers brewed normally at Christmas: Red Hot Furnace (ABV 9%), Furnace Fire (ABV 7.2%), Oil Fire (ABV 6 or 6.7%). All the cask ales are also bottle-conditioned.

Pit Shaft (ABV 3.4%)
Dark mild.

Pitside (ABV 3.7%)
A malty beer with a delicate taste..

Arc (ABV 3.8%)
Light session beer with a dry, hoppy taste.

Pit Prop (ABV 3.8%) ◆
Fruit and roast aroma, dark brown in colour. A mixture of roast, malt, caramel and fruit in taste and aftertaste. The bitterness builds, adding to the character.

Black and Amber (ABV 4%)
A traditional pale ruby bitter, lightly hopped and full of flavour.

Casnewydd (ABV 4%)
Light, easy-drinking beer.

Drillers (ABV 4%)
A lightly hopped, golden-yellow ale.

Hackers (ABV 4%)
Pale yellow, lightly-hopped bitter.

Hilston Premier (ABV 4%)
Rustic coloured, medium dry, autumnal beer.

Steelers (ABV 4.2%)
Light red, malty-tasting brew.

Raiders (ABV 4.3%)
A lightly hopped, strong yellow ale.

Zen (ABV 4.4%)
A light yellow ale with a dry finish.

Refuge (ABV 4.5%)
A well hopped, golden-yellow strong ale using Fuggles hops.

Riggers (ABV 4.5%)
A strongly hopped golden beer with body.

Rollers (ABV 4.5%)
A light ruby-coloured, well-hopped bitter.

Printers (ABV 4.6%)
Pale yellow strong ale.

Rockers (ABV 4.8%)
A pale yellow, refreshing strong ale.

Deep Pit (ABV 5%)
Ruby, full-bodied beer with distinctive taste.

Dockers (ABV 5%)
Golden, fruity, full-bodied beer with real taste.

Painters (ABV 5%)
Pale yellow, full-bodied strong ale.

QE2 (ABV 6%)
A pale yellow, full-bodied, strong ale.

Warrior*

Warrior Brewing Co, Matford House, Old Matford Lane, Matford, Exeter, Devon, EX2 8XS
Tel (01392) 221451
Email warrior@warrior.go-plus.net

James Warrior started brewing in November 2004. He is a professional actor (Coronation Street, Casualty and many other TV shows) and established his five-barrel brewery with his wife Jude. They were advised by Philip Darby and Niven Balfour of Nottingham Brewery (qv).

Best Bitter (ABV 4%)
A hoppy, refreshing, amber bitter.

Geronimo (ABV 4.9%)
Full-bodied with a good hoppy aftertaste.

Warwickshire

Warwickshire Beer Co Ltd, The Brewery, Queen Street, Cubbington, Leamington Spa, Warwickshire, CV32 7NA
Tel (01926) 450747
Fax (01926) 450763
Email info@warwickshirebeer.co.uk
Website www.warwickshirebeerco.co.uk
Shop 8-12 Sat (ring first)
Tours by arrangement

Warwickshire is a seven-barrel brewery operating in a former village bakery since 1998. Brewing takes place four times a week and, in addition, some beer is produced under licence by Highgate Brewery. The cask beers are available in approximately 80 outlets as well as the brewery's two pubs, the Market Tavern in Atherstone and the Market Tavern in Southam. Polypins and bottles are available from the brewery shop. Seasonal beers: Xmas Bare (ABV 4.9%), Thunderbolt (ABV 8.5%). Bottle-conditioned beers: Best Bitter, Lady Godiva, Churchyard Bob (ABV 4.9%), King Maker (ABV 5.5%).

Best Bitter (OG 1039, ABV 3.9%)
A golden brown session bitter flavoured with First Gold hops.

Lady Godiva (OG 1042, ABV 4.2%)
Blond, gentle, and full-bodied.

Falstaff (OG 1044, ABV 4.4%)
A mahogany-coloured bitter flavoured with Cascade and First Gold hops.

Golden Bear (OG 1049, ABV 4.9%)
Golden in colour with well-balanced bitterness and spicy/fruity notes.

Tomos Watkin SIBA

Hurns Brewing Co Ltd, Tomos Watkin Brewery, Unit 3, Century Park, Valley Way, Swansea Enterprise Park, Swansea, SA6 8RP
Tel (01792) 797300
Fax (01792) 797281
Email beer@hurns.co.uk
Website www.hurnsbeer.co.uk
Tours by arrangement

⊛ Brewing started in 1995 in Llandeilo using a 10-barrel plant in converted garages. Tomos Watkin moved to larger premises in Swansea in 2000 and the plant increased to a 50-barrel capacity. HBC Ltd was formed in 2002 when the Swansea Brewery was purchased from Tomos Watkin. The addition of bottled beers has allowed successful entry into several major national supermarket chains. Plans are under way to build a state-of-the-art, interactive visitor centre with shop and brewery tap. Some 100 outlets are supplied. Seasonal beers: Cwrw Ceridwen (ABV 4.2%, spring), Cwrw Haf (ABV 4.2%, summer), Owain Glyndwr (ABV 4.2%, autumn), Cwrw Santa (ABV 4.6%, winter).

Cwrw Braf (OG 1037, ABV 3.7%)

Brewery Bitter (OG 1041, ABV 4%)
Pale brown with a hop and malt nose. A moderate bitterness with a rounded flavour of hops, malt and fruit. The building bitterness adds to a pleasing finish.

Merlin Stout (OG 1043, ABV 4.2%)
A satisfying blend of roast, malt, caramel and hop flavours. A malty, roast aroma and moderate bitterness in the finish. Dark brown in colour.

Old Style Bitter/OSB
(OG 1046, ABV 4.5%)
Deep amber with an inviting aroma of hops and malt. A full-bodied mouthfeel, good bitterness and a blend of hops, malt and fruit flavours with a clean, lasting finish.

Waveney

Waveney Brewing Co,
Queen's Head, Station Road,
Earsham, Norfolk, NR35 2TS
Tel (01986) 892623
Email lyndahamps@aol.com

Established at the Queens Head in 2004 by landlord and landlady John and Lynda Hamps with the aid of Tom Knox, head brewer at Nethergate (qv), the five-barrel brewery produces three beers, regularly available at the pub along with free trade outlets. Occasional beers are brewed and there are plans to bottle beers in the near future. Seasonal beer: Raging Bullace (ABV 5.1%, Dec-Jan).

East Coast Mild (OG 1037, ABV 3.8%)
A traditional East Anglian mild with distinctive roast malt aroma and red-brown colouring. A sweet, plummy malt beginning quickly fades as a dry roasted bitterness begins to make its presence felt.

Lightweight (OG 1039, ABV 3.9%)
A gentle concoction with a light but well-balanced hop and malt character. A light body is reflected in the quick, bitter finish. Golden hued with a distinctive strawberry and cream nose.

Great White Hope (OG 1047, ABV 4.8%)

Weatheroak

Weatheroak Brewery, Coach & Horses Inn,
Weatheroak Hill, Alvechurch,
Birmingham, B48 7EA
Tel (07798) 773894 (day)/(0121) 445 4411 (eve)
Email dave@weatheroakales.co.uk
Website www.weatheroakales.co.uk
Shop Real Ale Off-Licence, Alvechurch,
Thur, Fri & Sat 5.30-8.30pm
Tours by arrangement

The brewery was set up in 1997 in an outhouse at the Coach & Horses by Dave and Pat Smith by arrangement with pub owners Phil and Sheila Meads. The first brew was produced in 1998. A real ale off-licence has been opened in nearby Alvechurch. Weatheroak supplies 40 outlets.

Light Oak (ABV 3.6%)
Refreshing amber beer with malt and citrus hops evident on the nose as well as the tongue.

Ale (ABV 4.1%)
A fruity aroma leads to a sweet bitter balance on the palate of this amber session beer.

Redwood (ABV 4.7%)
This ruby-brown beer has a fruity roast aroma that gives way to a complex mixture of tastes and so gives a satisfyingly rounded aftertaste.

Keystone Hops (ABV 5%)
Strong pale ale made with American hops.

Weetwood

Weetwood Ales Ltd, Weetwood Grange,
Weetwood, Tarporley, Cheshire, CW6 0NQ
Tel (01829) 752377
Email sales@weetwoodales.co.uk
Website www.weetwoodales.co.uk

The brewery was set up at an equestrian centre in 1993. In 1998, the five-barrel plant was replaced by a 10-barrel kit. Around 200 regular customers are now supplied.

Best Bitter (OG 1038.5, ABV 3.8%)
A clean, dry and malty bitter with little aroma. Bitterness dominates the finish.

Eastgate Ale (OG 1043.5, ABV 4.2%)
Well-balanced, pale, refreshing beer with malty, fruity taste and short, dry finish.

Old Dog Bitter (OG 1045, ABV 4.5%)
A fuller-bodied version of the bitter: fruitier, with a hint of sweetness.

Ambush Ale (OG 1047.5, ABV 4.8%)
Smooth, dark, amber-coloured beer with the fruity flavour balanced by the addition of Styrian Goldings hops.

Oasthouse Gold (OG 1050, ABV 5%)
Sweet, golden beer with some light malt and hop flavours. Typical Weetwood sharp aftertaste. It is deceptively drinkable for a beer of this strength.

Wellington

Edale Brewery Co, Hillsborough Hotel,
54-58 Langsett Road, Sheffield,
South Yorkshire, S6 2UB
Tel (0114) 2322100

Fax (0114) 2500200
Email info@edalebrewery.co.uk
Website www.edalebrewry.co.uk
Tours by arrangement

The Hillsborough Hotel, where the Crown and Wellington beers are brewed, was purchased in 2004. The company also has a 2.5-barrel plant in Edale (qv), which brews Edale Brewery beers. Some 20 outlets are supplied and one pub is owned. Bottle-conditioned beers: Loxley Gold, Stannington Stout, Sam Berry's IPA, Volenti. An organic beer is planned.

Conviction (OG 1038, ABV 3.8%)

HPA (OG 1039, ABV 3.9%)

Mitigation (OG 1043, ABV 4.3%)

Loxley Gold (OG 1045, ABV 4.5%)

Sam Berry 's IPA (OG 1050, ABV 5%)

Stannington Stout (OG 1050, ABV 5%)

Volenti (OG 1052, ABV 5.2%)

Beyond the Call (OG 1060, ABV 6%)

Wells IFBB

Charles Wells Ltd, Eagle Brewery,
Havelock Street, Bedford, MK40 4LU
Tel (01234) 272766
Fax (01234) 279000
Email postmaster@charleswells.co.uk
Website www.charleswells.co.uk
Shop Mon-Thu 7.30-10pm
Tours Groups by prior arrangement

The largest independent, family-owned brewery in the country, established in 1876 and still run by descendants of the founder. The brewery has been on the current site since 1976 and owns 255 pubs, of which 230 serve cask beer. Wells also supplies a large number of other outlets, while wholesalers distribute the beers nationally. Bombardier is now one Britain's biggest-selling premium cask beers. In 2001 it launched cask-conditioned Bombardier in vented cans for supermarket sales. Seasonal beers: Summer Solstice (ABV 4.1%, June), Lock, Stock and Barrel (ABV 4.3%, September), Banana Bread Beer (ABV 4.5%, Jan/June), Winter Cheer (ABV 5.5%, Nov-Dec).

Eagle IPA (OG 1035, ABV 3.6%)
A refreshing, amber session bitter with pronounced citrus hop aroma and palate, faint malt in the mouth, and a lasting dry, bitter finish.

Bombardier (OG 1042, ABV 4.3%)
Gentle citrus hop is balanced by traces of malt in the mouth, and this pale brown best bitter ends with a lasting dryness. Sulphur often dominates the aroma, particularly with younger casks.

Welton SIBA

Welton's Brewery Ltd,
1 Mulberry Trading Estate, Foundry Lane,
Horsham, West Sussex, RH13 5PX
Tel (01403) 242901/251873
Email sales@weltons.co.uk
Website www.weltons.co.uk
Tours by arrangement

Ray Welton moved his brewery a factory unit in Horsham in 2003, which has given him space to expand. A bottling facility was due to be installed in 2005. Some 350 outlets are supplied. Seasonal beer: Horsham Old (ABV 4.5%, Oct-March).

Pride 'n' Joy (ABV 2.8%)
A light brown bitter with a slight malty and hoppy aroma. Fruity with a pleasant hoppiness and some sweetness in the flavour, leading to a short malty finish. Well balanced and drinks well for its strength.

Kid & Bard (OG 1036, ABV 3.5%)
Mid-brown session beer. Some fruit and hops in the aroma lead to a well-balanced beer with hops dominating, but malt and fruit prevalent. Bitterness grows in to a pleasant hoppy, bitter finish.

Horsham Bitter (ABV 3.8%)

Sussex Pride (ABV 4%)

Old Cocky (OG 1043, ABV 4.3%)

Horsham Old (OG 1046, ABV 4.5%)
Roast and toffee flavours predominate with some bitterness in this traditional old ale. Bitter-sweet with plenty of caramel and roast in a rather short finish.

Old Harry (OG 1051, ABV 5.2%)

Wensleydale

Wensleydale Brewery, Foresters Arms,
Carlton-in-Coverdale, Leyburn,
North Yorkshire, DL8 4BB
Tel (01969) 640272
Email peter@wensleydalebrewery.com
Website www.wensleydalebrewery.com
Tours by arrangement

Lidstones, which relocated to the Foresters Arms in the North Yorkshire Dales National Park, started brewing again in 2003, and changed the name to Wensleydale. The company contract-brews the house beers for the owner of the Foresters Arms. The beers are also distributed throughout the country. One pub is owned and about 30 outlets are supplied.

Rowley Mild (OG 1037, ABV 3.2%)
Chocolate and toffee aromas lead into what, for its strength, is an impressively rich and flavoursome ale. The finish is pleasantly bitter-sweet.

Session Bitter
(OG 1038, ABV 3.7%)
Intensely aromatic, straw-coloured ale offering a superb balance of malt and hops on the tongue; an ideal session beer by any standards.

Foresters Ale (OG 1039, ABV 3.8%)

Keepers Ale (OG 1041, ABV 4.1%)

Lucky Punter (OG 1041, ABV 4.1%)
Golden ale with a hint of banana on the nose. The taste is clean, crisp and hoppy, with grapefruit flavours also present.

Oat Stout (OG 1044, ABV 4.4%)
Black beer brimming with a roasted chocolate aroma.

Black Dub (OG 1048, ABV 4.7%)

Rawalpindi IPA **(OG 1049, ABV 5%)** ◆
Citrus flavours dominate both aroma and taste in this pale, smooth, refreshing beer; the aftertaste is quite dry.

Wentworth SIBA

Wentworth Brewery Ltd, The Powerhouse, Gun Park, Wentworth, Rotherham, South Yorkshire, S62 7TF
Tel (01226) 747070
Fax (01226) 747050
Email info@wentworth-brewery.com
Website www.wentworth-brewery.com
Tours by arrangement

Wentworth was built during the summer of 1999, using equipment from two defunct Sheffield breweries, Stones and Wards. Brewing started in 1999 and the first brew, WPA, won Best Beer of the Festival at CAMRA's Sheffield festival. Wentworth has installed three 15-barrel fermenters, boosting production to 70 barrels. One pub is owned and the owners plan to create a small tied estate. Approximately 300 outlets are supplied. A bottling plant is being built. Bottle-conditioned beers: WPA, Oatmeal Stout, Rampant Gryphon.

Needles Eye **(OG 1035, ABV 3.5%)**
A session bitter with a rather bitter taste that dominates the aftertaste.

WPA **(OG 1039.5, ABV 4%)** ◆
An extremely well hopped IPA-style beer that leads to some astringency. A very bitter beer.

Best Bitter **(OG 1040, ABV 4.1%)** ◆
A hoppy, bitter beer with hints of citrus fruits. A bitter taste dominates the aftertaste.

Premium Bitter **(OG 1044, ABV 4.4%)**

Rock Spalt **(OG 1045, ABV 4.5%)**
Straw-coloured, aromatic, dry and drinkable. Spalt is the German variety of hop used.

Black Zac **(OG 1046, ABV 4.6%)**
A mellow, dark ruby-red ale with chocolate and pale malts leading to a bitter taste, with a coffee finish.

Oatmeal Stout **(OG 1050, ABV 4.8%)** ◆
Black, smooth, with roast and chocolate malt and coffee overtones.

Rampant Gryphon **(OG 1062, ABV 6.2%)** ◆
A strong, well-balanced golden ale with hints of fruit and sweetness but which retains a hoppy character.

Whistle Jacket **(ABV 8.4%)**
A dark, extremely strong ale with sweet overtones.

Wessex SIBA

Wessex Brewery, Rye Hill Farm, Longbridge Deverill, Warminster, Wiltshire, BA12 7DE
Tel/Fax (01985) 844532
Email wessexbrewery@tinyworld.co.uk
Tours by arrangement

The brewery went into production in 2001 as Hobden's Wessex Brewery and moved to a more easily maintained building in 2004 at which time the name Wessex Brewery was adopted. Seven outlets are supplied by the brewery with further distribution via wholesalers.

Burlington Bertie **(OG 1033, ABV 3.3%)**

Naughty Ferret **(OG 1035, ABV 3.5%)**
A session bitter with full flavour. Tawny colour, spicy bitterness and citrus hop aroma.

Crockerton Classic **(OG 1041, ABV 4.1%)**
Full bodied, tawny, full flavoured; bitter, fruity and malty.

Kilmington Best **(OG 1041, ABV 4.2%)**

Old Deverill Valley Pale **(OG 1042, ABV 4.2%)**

Beast of Zeals **(OG 1064, ABV 6.6%)**

Russian Stoat **(OG 1080, ABV 9%)**

West Berkshire SIBA

West Berkshire Brewery Co Ltd, The Old Bakery, Yattendon, Thatcham, Berkshire, RG18 0UE
Tel/Fax (01635) 202968
Email davemaggs@wbbrew.co.uk
Website www.wbbrew.co.uk
Shop Craft shop on site. Opening hours vary. Telephone in advance. Tours by arrangement

The brewery quickly outgrew its five-gallon plant when it started business in 1995 in outbuildings attached to the Pot Kiln pub, Frilsham, and the owners converted an old bakery into an additional 25-barrel brewery in nearby Yattendon. With a staff of six, weekly production in both sites now regularly exceeds 50 barrels, supplying the free trade throughout Berkshire and Oxfordshire. At least one different additional beer is brewed every month, usually in the range of 4.2 to 4.8% ABV, and including stouts and porters as well as bitters. Beers are often brewed as one-off commissions for festivals and other special events. Full Circle gained a silver award for Best Bitter at GBBF 2003. Brick Kiln Bitter (ABV 4%) is brewed solely for the Pot Kiln pub. Bottle-conditioned beer: Full Circle (various ABVs).

Old Father Thames **(OG 1038, ABV 3.4%)**

Mr Chubb's Lunchtime Bitter **(OG 1040, ABV 3.7%)**
A traditional beer with all English hops and a good bitterness balanced by Maris Otter malts. The beer is named after the brewer's father who was the lock-keeper at Whitchurch-on-Thames and was nicknamed Mr Chubb.

Maggs Mild **(OG 1041, ABV 3.8%)** ◆
An easy-to-drink southern mild with a good balance of malt and hops for the style. This dark red-brown beer has a short, dry finish.

Good Old Boy **(OG 1043, ABV 4%)** ◆
A well-balanced, fruity and hoppy beer with some sweetness in the finish.

Dr Hexter's Wedding Ale **(OG 1044, ABV 4.1%)**
There are hints of grapefruit in this pale-coloured beer, with strong hop aromas and a long, bitter finish.

Full Circle **(OG 1047, ABV 4.5%)**

Dr Hexter's Healer **(OG 1052, ABV 5%)** ◆
A full-bodied, vinous and sweet, end-of-the evening beer that tastes stronger than it is. Tawny in colour, fruity and warming, with masses of malt and roast character.

Westbury*

Westbury Ales, Horse & Groom, Alfred Street, Westbury, Wiltshire, BA13 3DY
Tel 07771 976865
Email brewing@westburyales.com
Website www.westburyales.com
Brewery tours available

Brewing started in autumn 2004, using a 2.5-barrel plant and expanded a few months later to 10-barrel production. The brewery supplies some 40 outlets, including its own pub, the Horse & Groom. Seasonal beers: Faith, Hop & Charity (ABV 3.7%), Holly Daize (ABV 4.2%), Pale Storm (ABV 4.3%), Dark Horse (ABV 3.7%), PSZ (ABV 4%).

Amber Daize (ABV 4.1%)

Early Daize (ABV 4.1%)

Bitham Blonde (ABV 4.5%)

Midnight Mash (5.1%)

Westerham SIBA

Westerham Brewery Co Ltd, Grange Farm, Pootings Road, Crockham Hill, Edenbridge, Kent, TN8 6SA
Head office Little Redwood, Bratsed Chart, Westerham, Kent, TN16 1LX
Tel (01959) 565837
Email info@westerhambrewery.co.uk
Website www.westerhambrewery.co.uk
Tours by arrangement

Robert Wicks set up the brewery in 2004, trading in a top job in the City of London to brew on modern copper and stainless steel equipment imported from Canada and the US. He has restored brewing in Westerham that was lost when the Black Eagle Brewery was taken over by Ind Coope of Burton and Romford in 1959 and closed in 1965. Black Eagle's beers were enjoyed by Sir Winston Churchill, who lived close by at Chartwell, and by airmen at RAF Biggin Hill during World War II. Two of Black Eagle's yeast strains were deposited at the National Collection of Yeast Cultures and are being used to recreate the true flavour of Westerham beers. The new brewery is based at the National Trust's Grange Farm in a former dairy and uses the same water supply as Black Eagle. More than 60 free trade outlets are supplied in Kent, Surrey and Sussex. Seasonal beers: General Wolfe Maple Ale (ABV 4.5%), God's Wallop Christmas Ale (ABV 4.5%), Puddledock Porter (ABV 4.5%). Bottle-conditioned beer: British Bulldog.

Grasshopper Kentish Bitter (OG 1039, ABV 3.8%)

Black Eagle Special Pale Ale (OG 1039, ABV 3.8%)

British Bulldog (OG 1042, ABV 4.3%)

Sevenoaks 7X (OG 1046, ABV 4.8%)

Special Bitter Ale 1965 (OG 1048, ABV 5%)

WF6*

WF6 Brewing Co, c/o 21 Rose Farm Approach, Normanton, West Yorkshire, WF6 2RZ
Tel 07876 141336
Email info@wf6brewingcompany.co.uk
Website www.wf6brewingcompany.co.uk

WF6 started brewing in 2004 with a five-barrel plant based in a converted barn on a farm. Seasonal beers: Birkwoods Festive Fuel (ABV 4.4%), Birkwoods January Ale (ABV 4.2%), Birkwoods Advent Ale (ABV 3.6%)

Birkwoods Reflection (ABV 3.6%)

Birkwoods Retreat (ABV 3.6%)

Birkwoods BST (ABV 3.8%)

Birkwoods Squares (ABV 3.8%)

Birkwoods Walkabout (ABV 3.8%)

Birkwoods Introduction (ABV 4%)

Birkwoods Circles (ABV 4.5%)

Birkwoods Original (4.6%)

Birkwoods Brewers Storm (ABV 5%)

Whalebone

Whalebone Brewery, 163 Wincolmlee, Hull, East Yorkshire, HU2 0PA
Tel (01482) 327980
Tours by arrangement

The Whalebone pub, which dates from 1796, was bought by Hull CAMRA founding member Alex Craig in 2002. He opened the brewery the following year and his beer have names connected with the former whaling industry on the adjoining River Hull. Two or three outlets are supplied as well as the pub. Seasonal beers: Truelove Porter (ABV 4.7%), Joseph Allen (ABV 5%), Moby Dick (ABV 8%), Full Ship (ABV 8.4%).

Diana Mild (ABV 3.6%)

Neckoil Bitter (OG 1036, ABV 3.9%)

Wharfedale SIBA

Wharfedale Brewery Ltd, Coonlands Laithe, Hetton, Skipton, North Yorkshire, BD23 6LY
Tel/Fax (01756) 730555
Email nigel@follyale.com
Website www.follyale.com
Tours by arrangement

Opened in 2003 by the Duke of Kent, the brewery is based in an old hay barn within the Yorkshire Dales National Park. Water comes from its own 56 metres-deep borehole. Three beers are permanently available, plus one special each month. Supply is direct to free houses and distributors throughout Yorkshire, Lancashire and the West Midlands. All permanent beers are also available in bottle.

Folly Ale (OG 1038, ABV 3.8%) ◆
A pale brown bitter with hops coming through in the taste and biscuity malt throughout.

Executioner (OG 1046, ABV 4.5%) ◆
A complex reddish brown best bitter. Dark malts and fruit flavours predominate.

Folly Gold (OG 1051, ABV 5%) ◆
A full-bodied pale golden premium strong bitter with a bitter, hoppy and malty palate. The dry character extends into the finish.

Wheal Ale

Wheal Ale Brewery, Paradise Park, Trelissick Road, Hayle, Cornwall, TR27 4HY
Tel (01736) 753974

Founded in 1980 as Paradise Brewery, the small brewhouse is behind a large pub, the Bird in Hand, at the entrance to the Paradise Park bird sanctuary. The six-barrel plant has been run by George Miller for the past 13 years. He brews twice a month and more regularly in the summer as demand increases. Seasonal beers: Millers Ale (ABV 4.2%, summer), Pickled Parrot (ABV 6.6%, winter). Old Speckled Parrot is also available in bottle-conditioned form.

Old Speckled Parrot (OG 1052, ABV 5.5%)
Strong, dark and a little on the sweet side.

Whim SIBA

Whim Ales Ltd, Whim Farm, Hartington, near Buxton, Derbyshire, SK17 0AX
Tel/Fax (01298) 84991

⊗ A brewery opened in 1993 in outbuildings at Whim Farm by Giles Litchfield who bought Broughton Brewery (qv) in 1995. Whim's beers are available in 50-70 outlets and the brewery's tied house, the Wilkes Head in Leek, Staffs. Some one-off brews are produced. Occasional/seasonal beers: Kaskade (ABV 4.3%, a lager), Snow White (ABV 4.5%, a wheat beer), Easter Special (ABV 4.8%), Stout Jenny (ABV 4.7%), Black Christmas (ABV 6.5%).

Arbor Light (OG 1035, ABV 3.6%)
Light-coloured bitter, sharp and clean with lots of hop character and a delicate light aroma.

Hartington Bitter (OG 1039, ABV 4%)
A light, golden-coloured, well-hopped session beer. A dry finish with a spicy, floral aroma.

Hartington IPA (OG 1045, ABV 4.5%)
Pale and light-coloured, smooth on the palate allowing malt to predominate. Slightly sweet finish combined with distinctive light hop bitterness. Well rounded.

White

White Brewing Co, 1066 Country Brewery, Pebsham Farm Industrial Estate, Pebsham Lane, Bexhill-on-Sea, East Sussex, TN40 2RZ
Tel (01424) 731066
Fax (01424) 732995
Email whitebrewing@fsbdial.co.uk
Tours by arrangement

The brewery was founded in 1995 by husband and-wife team David and Lesley White to serve local free trade outlets and some wholesalers. White has expanded production threefold with the addition of seasonal and occasional ales. Some 25 to 30 outlets are supplied. Seasonal beers: White Gold (ABV 4.9%, summer), Chilly Willy (ABV 5.1%, winter), Old White Christmas (ABV 4%), Heart of Rother (spring).

1066 Country Bitter (OG 1040, ABV 4%)
Amber-gold in colour, a light, sweetish beer with good malt and hop balance, and a bitter, refreshing finish.

Dark (OG 1040, ABV 4%)

White Horse*

White Horse Brewery, 3 Ware Road, White Horse Business Park, Stanford in the Vale, Oxfordshire, SN7 8NY
Tel (01367) 718700
Website www.whitehorsebrewery.com

White Horse Brewery was founded on a modern industrial estate in 2004 by Andy Wilson and Stuart Wastie, both previously employed by Wychwood Brewery (qv). The second-hand brewing plant was manufactured in Belgium and has a brew-length of 7.5 barrels. The beers are mainly available in plastic nine-gallon firkins, but some 18-gallon kilderkins are also used. Oxfordshire Bitter won SIBA Midlands and CAMRA festival awards in 2004. Some 100 outlets are supplied.

Oxfordshire Bitter (OG 1039, ABV 3.7%)

Wayland Smithy (OG 1049, ABV 4.4%)

White Star SIBA

White Star Brewery Ltd, 5 Radcliffe Court, Radcliffe Road, Northam, Southampton, Hampshire, SO14 0PH
Tel (023) 8023 2480
Fax (023) 80 23 2580
Email info@whitestarbrewery.com
Website www.whitestarbrewery.com
Tours by arrangement

⊗ The 10-barrel plant was set up in 2003 by brothers Andy and Chris Ingram on a small industrial estate next to the main railway line and close to Southampton FC's St Mary's Stadium. The name comes from the White Star Shipping Line of Southampton, whose most famous liner was the Titanic. It is the first brewery in Southampton for 53 years. The brewing equipment came from the closed Woodhampton Brewery. Bottling started in 2004. There are half-a-dozen regular brews with distribution throughout the country. 60 outlets are supplied by the brewery. Seasonal beers: Black Panther Stout (ABV 4.4%), Royal Standard (ABV 4.3%), Battleaxe (ABV 4.6%), Steamer (ABV 5%), Frostbite (ABV 4.5%), Crafty Shag (ABV 4.1%). The full range of beers is also available in bottle-conditioned form.

Best Bitter (ABV 3.5%)
Copper-coloured session bitter, thirst-quenching and well hopped with a malty finish.

U-X-B (ABV 3.8%) ◆
Session bitter with a gentle aroma and some hops and malt in the flavour and finish. Rather sulphurous throughout.

Majestic (ABV 4.2%) ◆
A Burton-style best bitter, characteristically sulphurous and sharp but with some hop and malt balance. Quite hoppy and slightly sweet in the finish.

Dark Destroyer (ABV 4.7%)
Roasted malts produce a rich, dark ale blended with English hops. A good thirst quencher.

Starlight (ABV 5%) ◆
Little aroma in this hoppy strong bitter, with hints of toffee and fruit. A light body and a sharp finish.

Capstan Full Strength (ABV 6%) ◆
A smooth, dark ale, with a spicy aroma of blackberries and blackcurrants. Strong fruit flavours dominate but with hops and malt providing some balance. The finish is bitter-sweet and fruity.

Whitewater

Whitewater Brewing Co, 40 Tullyframe Road, Kilkeel, Co Down, Northern Ireland, BT34 4RZ
Tel/Fax (028) 4176 9449
Email kerrysloan@hotmail.co.uk
Website www.whitewaterbrewing.co.uk
Tours by arrangement

◎ Set up in 1996 and nestling in the idyllic setting of the heart of the Mourne Mountains, Whitewater is now the largest micro-brewery in Northern Ireland. It produces 11 different cask-conditioned ales. The plant was designed and built by Kerry and Bernard Sloan, and, with an expansion in 2000, it now boasts a 15-barrel brew-length. With its stainless-steel construction, the plant has a fermenting capacity of 2,000 gallons a week. The brewery is currently supplying 18 outlets in Northern Ireland and owns one pub. Seasonal beers: see website.

Mill Ale (OG 1038, ABV 3.7%)

White Gold (ABV 3.9%)

Blonde Lager (ABV 4%)

Belfast Ale (OG 1046, ABV 4.5%)

Whitley Bridge

Whitley Bridge Brewing Co, 11 Silver Street, Newton Hill, Wakefield, West Yorkshire, WF1 2HZ
Tel (07818) 407086
Email big1neil@aol.com
Tours by arrangement, up to 14 people

Neil Land was a professional brewer for 14 years with Tetleys. His brewery started in an unused stables at Whitley Bridge but moved to Wakefield in 2004 where production has more than trebled, brewing twice a week on a four-barrel plant. Some 30 outlets are supplied.

Emberzale (OG 1043, ABV 4.3%)

Gunslingers (OG 1043, ABV 4.3%)

Nelly's Ale (OG 1043, ABV 4.3%)

Newton Bar Bitter (OG 1043, ABV 4.3%)

Kudos (OG 1050, ABV 5%)

Whitstable

Whitstable Brewery, Little Telpits Farm, Woodcock Lane, Grafty Green, Kent, ME17 2AY
Tel (01622) 851007
Fax (01622) 859993
Website www.whitstablebrewery.info
Tours by arrangement

⊗ Whitstable Brewery was created when the Swale and North Weald Brewery was sold in 2003 to the Green family who initially produced beer for their own outlets in Whitstable (a hotel and two restaurants) and beer festivals. The company has now decided to supply beer further afield and is looking for potential outlets. They also plan a brew-pub next to the East Quay restaurant in Whitstable. The seven-barrel plant will be visible to customers and was due to come on stream in 2005. Brewing will continue on both sites. Three pubs are owned and eight outlets are supplied.

Bitter (ABV 3.7%)

East India Pale Ale (OG 1044, ABV 4.1%)
A light, refreshing pale ale with floral hop aroma and bitterness gives a well-balanced flavour.

Oyster Stout (OG 1047, ABV 4.5%)
Rich and dry with deep chocolate and mocha flavours great served with oysters.

Raspberry Wheat (OG 1049, ABV 5.2%)

Wheat Beer (OG 1049, ABV 5.2%)

Whittington's SIBA

Whittington's Brewery, Three Choirs Vineyard Ltd, Welsh House Lane, Castle Tump, Newent, Gloucestershire, GL18 1LS
Tel (01531) 890223
Fax (01531) 890877
Email info@whittingtonsbrewery.co.uk
Website www.whittingtonsbrewery.co.uk
Shop daily 10-5pm
Tours Brewery open 10-5pm

The five-barrel brewing plant is purpose built and is located within the vineyard buildings. Production started in 2003. Dick Whittington was born nearby, hence the name and feline theme. Cats Whiskers is available as a bottle-conditioned ale. Some 30 outlets are supplied.

Nine Lives (OG 1036, ABV 3.6%)

Cats Whiskers (OG 1038, ABV 4.2%)
Gloucestershire Beer of the Year 2004.

Wicked Hathern

Wicked Hathern Brewery Ltd, The Willows, 46 Derby Road, Hathern, Loughborough, Leicestershire, LE12 5LD
Tel (01509) 842585
Email beer@hathern.com
Website www.wicked-hathern.co.uk
Tours by arrangement, £3 charge (includes beer tasting)

⊛ Opened in the first month of the new millennium, the 2.5-barrel brewery is owned and operated by John and Marc Bagley, John Worsfold and Sean O'Neill, in their spare time. They generally supply beer on a guest basis to many local pubs and beer festivals, and brew commissioned beers for special occasions, such as beer festivals. Since 2002 they have bottled their beers to supply mainly their local shop, as the policies of owners of the pubs in Hathern preclude the brewery having a regular village outlet. Seasonal beers: Gladstone Tidings (ABV 5.1%, Christmas). All beers are available in bottles from selected off-licences (see website) and from Hathern Village shop. Bottled beers are brewed exclusively for Alexander Wines off-licence in Earlsdon, Coventry, namely Restoration Ale, Lazy Bones and Barking Mad.

WHB/Wicked Hathern Bitter
(OG 1038, ABV 3.8%)
A light-tasting session bitter with a dry palate and good hop aroma.

Cockfighter (OG 1043, ABV 4.2%)
A pale bitter with a pronounced maltiness offset by a delicate hop flavour.

Hawthorn Gold (OG 1045, ABV 4.5%)

Derby Porter (OG 1048, ABV 4.8%)

Soar Head (OG 1048, ABV 4.8%)
A dark ruby bitter with a complex rich fruit taste and a mellow aroma.

For the Albion pub, Loughborough:

Albion Special (OG 1041, ABV 4%)
A light, copper-coloured bitter with a nutty aroma and smoky malt taste, hops leading through.

Wickwar SIBA

Wickwar Brewing Co Ltd,
The Old Brewery, Station Road, Wickwar, Gloucestershire, GL12 8NB
Tel/Fax (01454) 294168
Email bob@wickwarbrewing.co.uk
Website www.wickwarbrewing.co.uk
Shop 9.30-4.30 Mon-Fri, 10-12 Sat
Tours by arrangement

⊗ Since setting up Wickwar in 1990 in the cooper's shed of the old Arnold, Perrett & Co Brewery, Ray Penny's ambition has been to move into the main brewery building across the road. This was achieved in 2004 with the installation of a 50-barrel plant. A new beer was introduced, IKB (Isambard Kingdom Brunel), to mark the fact that Brunel built the railway tunnel that runs at the rear of the old brewery. The original brewery was built around 1840 but spent most of the 20th century as a cider factory and latterly as a bonded warehouse. Wickwar Brewery supplies some 350 outlets and is considering further expansion of its pub estate. Seasonal beers: Premium Spring Ale (ABV 3.8%, April-May), Sunny Daze (ABV 4.2%, June-Aug), Christmas Cracker (ABV 4.3%, December), Autumnale (ABV 4.5%, Sept-Nov). Rite Flanker (ABV 4.4%) is brewed during all major rugby competitions. Bottle-conditioned beers: Cotswold Way, Old Arnold, Station Porter, Brand Oak Bitter, Mr Perretts Traditional Stout ◫.

Coopers WPA (OG 1036.5, ABV 3.5%) ◫ ◆
Golden-coloured, this well-balanced beer is light and refreshing, with hops, citrus fruit, apple/pear flavour and notable pale malt character. Bitter, dry finish. A crisp and quenching ale.

Brand Oak Bitter (BOB)
(OG 1039, ABV 4%) ◆
Amber-coloured, this has a distinctive blend of hop, malt and apple/pear citrus fruits. The slightly sweet taste turns into a fine, dry bitterness, with a similar malty-lasting finish.

Cotswold Way (OG 1043, ABV 4.2%) ◼ ◆
Amber-coloured, it has a pleasant aroma of pale malt, hop and fruit. Good dry bitterness in the taste with some sweetness. Similar though less sweet in the finish, with good hop content.

IKB (OG 1045, ABV 4.5%)
A ruby-red ale with a complex hop aroma and flavour derived from the use of three hop varieties. Flowery but well balanced.

Old Arnold (OG 1045.5, ABV 4.6%)
Named after the founder of the original brewery, this is a ruby-red ale, sweetish with malt and bitter overtones, and Challenger hops providing rich fruitiness.

Old Merryford Ale (OG 1049, ABV 4.8%) ◆
Full-flavoured and well-balanced ale, with malt, hops and cherry fruit throughout. Amber/pale brown, it is slightly sweet, with a long-lasting, malty, dry, fruity and increasingly bitter finish.

Mr Perretts Traditional Stout
(OG 1059, ABV 5.9%) ◫ ◆
Aroma and taste of smoky chocolate malts and peppery hops. Dark fruits of black cherry and blackcurrant give hints of sweetness to the dry, quite bitter, slightly spicy, well-balanced taste.

Station Porter (OG 1062, ABV 6.1%) ◆
This is a rich, smooth, dark ruby-brown ale. Starts with roast malt; coffee, chocolate and dark fruit then develops a complex, spicy, bitter-sweet taste and a long roast finish.

Wild's*

Wild's Brewery Ltd, White Hill Park, Weobley, Herefordshire, HR4 8QE
Tel/Fax (01544) 319333
Tours by arrangement

After an eight-year break, Pete and Wendy Wild returned to brewing in 2005 after many months of taste-testing.

One (OG 1041, ABV 4.1%)

Six (OG 1042, ABV 4.2%)

Blonde (OG 1045, ABV 4.5%)

Night (OG 1045, ABV 4.5%)

Williams SIBA

Williams Brothers Brewing Company, New Alloa Brewery, Kelliebank, Alloa, FK10 1NT
Tel (01259) 725511
Fax (01259) 725522
Tours occasionally

The Williams brothers, Bruce and Scott, took over the Forth Brewery. Some 200 outlets are supplied. Seasonal beers: Kelpie (ABV 4.4%, May-July), Grozet (ABV 4.5%, Aug-Oct), Ebulum (ABV 5.8%, Nov-Jan), Alba (ABV 6%, Feb-April).

Gold (ABV 3.9%)

Fraoch (OG 1043, ABV 4.1%)
The unique taste of heather flowers is very noticeable in this beer. A fine floral aroma and spicy taste give character to this drinkable speciality beer.

Black (ABV 4.2%)

Joker (ABV 4.3%)

Red (ABV 4.5%)

Willy's SIBA

Willy's Brewery Ltd, 17 High Cliff Road, Cleethorpes, Lincolnshire, DN35 8RQ
Tel (01472) 602145 Fax (01472) 603578
Tours by arrangement

The brewery opened in 1989 to provide beer for two outlets in Grimsby and Cleethorpes. It has a five-barrel plant with maximum capacity of 15 barrels a week. The brewery can be viewed at any time from pub or street.

Original Bitter (OG 1038, ABV 3.8%)
A light brown 'sea air' beer with a fruity, tangy hop on the nose and taste, giving a strong bitterness tempered by the underlying malt.

Burcom Bitter (OG 1044, ABV 4.2%)
Sometimes known as Mariner's Gold, although the beer is dark ruby in colour. It is a smooth and creamy brew with a sweet chocolate-bar maltiness, giving way to an increasingly bitter finish.

Last Resort (OG 1044, ABV 4.3%)

Weiss Buoy (OG 1045, ABV 4.5%)
A cloudy wheat beer.

Coxswains Special (OG 1050, ABV 4.9%)

Old Groyne (OG 1060, ABV 6.2%)
An initial sweet banana fruitiness blends with malt to give a vanilla quality to the taste and slightly bitter aftertaste. A copper-coloured beer reminiscent of a Belgian ale.

Winchester*

Winchester Brewery Ltd, Unit 19, Longbridge Industrial Park, Floating Bridge Road, Southampton, Hampshire, SO14 3FL
Tel (023) 8071 0131
Email info@winchesterbrewery.com
Website www.winchesterbrewery.com

The brewery was launched in January 2005 by David Wealleans and Phil Ambrose. As the name suggests, it was intended to brew in Winchester but technical problems led to it being installed in its current location with a five-barrel plant.

Best Bitter (ABV 3.7%)
Flavoursome mix of hops and special malt gives a distinct character.

Summer of '76 (ABV 3.7%)

Windsor Castle*

Windsor Castle Brewery Ltd, t/a Sadler's Ales, 7 Stourbridge Road, Lye, Stourbridge, West Midlands, DY9 7DG
Tel (01384) 897809
Fax (01384) 893666
Email johnsadler@windsorcastlebrewery.com
Website www.windsorcastlebrewery.com
Shop 5-10pm daily (not Sun or Mon)
Tours by arrangement

Nathaniel Sadler opened the original brewery in 1900 adjacent to the Windsor Castle Inn, Oldbury. Although brewing ceased in 1927, his son John Caleb Nathaniel Sadler, who was brought up in the brewery, passed on all he knew to the current John Sadler. John and his son Chris have reopened the brewery in its new location, continuing the brewing tradition of the Sadler family. There is an off-licence on site.

Jack's Ale (ABV 3.8%)
Light, hoppy beer with a crisp and zesty lemon undertone.

Bitter Ale (ABV 4.3%)
Smooth, refreshing session bitter with underlying flavours of honey and caramel, with a complex hop character.

Worcester Sorcerer (ABV 4.3%)
Pale beer, light and refreshing yet smooth and fruity with hints of mint and lemon. Floral aroma and crisp bitterness combine to make a balanced and clean-tasting beer.

1900 Original (ABV 4.5%)
Dark malty bitter with a light hoppy aroma and a dry, lingering finish.

IPA (ABV 4.8%)
Classic India Pale Ale, light, tangy and bitter with a distinctive refreshing aftertaste.

Winter's SIBA

Winter's Brewery, 8 Keelan Close, Norwich, Norfolk, NR6 6QZ
Tel/Fax (01603) 787820
Email sales@wintersbrewery.com
Website www.wintersbrewery.com

⊗ David Winter, who had previous award winning success as brewer for both Woodforde's and Chalk Hill breweries, decided to set up on his own in 2001. He purchased the brewing plant from the now defunct Scott's Brewery in Lowestoft. He produces five ales at present, and delivers to the local free trade.

Mild (OG 1036.5, ABV 3.6%) ◆
A gentle roast aroma introduces this dark brown, softly-flavoured mild. The gentle blend of hops and roast lingers to a long finish and a dry, fruity background.

Bitter (OG 1039.5, ABV 3.8%) ◆
A copper-coloured bitter with a light hop aroma. A gentle mix of hop, malt and bitterness produces a smooth, uncomplicated but well-balanced bitter. Initial flavours subside quickly.

Golden (ABV 4.1%) ◻ ◆
Grapefruit astringency adds depth to the hop framework of this golden-hued ale. Light and airy with a sustained dry, almost lager-like finish.

Revenge (OG 1047, ABV 4.7%) ◆
Blackcurrant notes give depth to the inherent maltiness of this pale brown beer. A bitter-sweet background becomes more pronounced as the fruitiness gently wanes.

Storm Force (OG 1053, ABV 5.3%) ◻ ◆
Superbly balanced mix of plum pudding richness and a booming malt base. A supporting mix of bitterness and hop augments a faint vinous background that just goes on and on.

Tempest (OG 1062, ABV 6.2%)

Wissey Valley

Wissey Valley Brewery, Grey House, Lynn Road, Stoke Ferry, Norfolk, PE33 9SW
Tel (01366) 500767
Email info@wisseyvalleybrewery.co.uk
Website www.wisseyvalleybrewery.co.uk

The brewery was launched in 2002 as Captain Grumpy at the Ship in Downham Market and moved to new premises in 2003. The brewery supplies the Ship and CAMRA festivals. The brewer is concentrating on bottle-conditioned beers sold at farmers' markets.

Best Bitter (ABV 3.9%)

Busted Flush (ABV 4.5%)

Golden Rivet (ABV 5.1%)

Wizard SIBA

Wizard Ales, The Hops, Whichford, Shipston-on-Stour, Warwickshire, CV36 5PE
Tel (01608) 684355
Email brewery@thenormanknight.co.uk
Website www.thenormanknight.co.uk/wizard_brewery
Tours by prior arrangement

⊗ Brewing started in 2003 on a 1.25-barrel plant, previously used by Swaled Ale Brewery in Gunnerside. A new five-barrel plant is now fully operational. One pub is owned and more than 20 local outlets are regularly supplied. Seasonal beer: Bah Humbug (ABV 5.8%, Christmas). Bottle-conditioned beer: Druids Fluid.

Apprentice (OG 1038, ABV 3.6%)
Amber-coloured session beer with a dry finish.

Whichford Best (OG 1038, ABV 3.6%)
A pale-coloured session beer.

One For The Toad (OG 1041, ABV 4%)
A light-coloured beer with a good hop flavour.

Mother in Law (OG 1043, ABV 4.2%)
A rich, darkish beer with strong hop flavour.

Black Magic (OG 1044, ABV 4.3%)
A pale beer with crystal and lots of chocolate malt, wheat, Fuggles and Northdown whole hops.

Sorcerer (OG 1044, ABV 4.3%)
Pale and crystal malts, wheat, Fuggles and Goldings hops.

White Witch (OG 1045, ABV 4.5%)
A pale beer using lager malt, wheat, Challenger, Green Bullet and Northdown whole hops.

Bullfrog (OG 1047, ABV 4.8%)
Pale, wheat and Fuggles hops.

Druid's Fluid (OG 1048, ABV 5%)

Wold Top SIBA

Wold Top Brewery, Hunmanby Grange, Wold Newton, Driffield, East Yorkshire,YO25 3HS
Tel (01723) 892222
Fax (01723) 892229
Email enquiries@woldtopbrewery.co.uk
Website www.woldtopbrewery.co.uk
Tours by arrangement in summer only

Wold Top started brewing in 2002 in a converted granary on a farm. The brewery grows its own barley, uses its own water and would like to grow its own hops. A 10-barrel plant is used. One pub, the Falling Stone in Thwing, is owned. 120 outlets are served. Seasonal beer: Mars Magic Premium Ale (ABV 4.6%, Nov-March), Wold Gold Light Summer Beer (ABV 4.8%, April-Oct). A bottling plant was installed in 2003 and all beers are now available in bottled form from off-licences and via mail order.

Bitter (OG 1037, ABV 3.7%)
Maris Otter pale and a small amount of crystal malt form the basis of the beer, with Northdown hops for aroma and bitterness.

Falling Stone (OG 1042, ABV 4.2%)
A full-bodied and well-rounded beer. The rich colour is produced by adding a small amount of chocolate malt to the mash, which is based around Maris Otter pale malt. Progress hops are used for aroma.

Wolf SIBA

Wolf Brewery Ltd, 10 Maurice Gaymer Road, Attleborough, Norfolk, NR17 2QZ
Tel (01953) 457775
Fax (01953) 457776
Email info@wolf-ales.co.uk

Website www.wolf-brewery.ltd.uk
Tours by arrangement

⊗ The brewery was founded by Wolfe Witham, the former owner of the Reindeer Brewery, in 1996, using a 20-barrel plant housed on the site of the old Gaymer's cider orchard. 200 outlets are supplied. All the beers are also sold in bottle-conditioned form. In the 2005 SIBA national cask beer championships Wolf won the supreme championship with Granny Wouldn't Like It, a silver for Golden Jackal and a bronze for Woild Moild. Seasonal beer: Timber Wolf (ABV 5.8%, winter).

Golden Jackal (OG 1039, ABV 3.7%)
Refreshingly hoppy, with a lemony aroma and a distinct grapefruit character. A well-balanced pale brown beer with a sweet maltiness countering the fruity hop backbone. A long, dry finish.

Wolf In Sheep's Clothing (OG 1039, ABV 3.7%)
A malty aroma with fruity undertones introduces this reddish-hued mild. Malt, with a bitter background that remains throughout, is the dominant flavour of this clean-tasting beer.

Bitter (OG 1041, ABV 3.9%)
Malt and hops mix well throughout this copper-coloured brew. A consistent mix in both aroma and taste is overshadowed by a growing bitterness in the aftertaste. Some dryness develops at the end.

Coyote Bitter (OG 1044, ABV 4.3%)
Citrus notes introduce this amber-coloured bitter. The first impression is of a distinctive mix of malt and bitterness side by side with a dry hoppiness. The flavours are distinctive but none is initially dominant. Bitterness holds up well as the other flavours quickly fade.

Newshound 2001 (ABV 4.5%)
Copper coloured with a light hop and malt nose. Malt takes the edge off the bitter backbone of this solid tasting beer. Vanilla and citrus hints can be detected as the long finish grows into a dry hoppiness.

Woild Moild (OG 1048, ABV 4.8%)
A big roast coffee bean aroma leads into a distinctively roasted barley base. A good balance of malt with a liquorice bitterness aids this dark red mild towards a smoky, dark and long-lasting rich finish.

Granny Wouldn't Like It (OG 1049, ABV 4.8%)
Dark red, rich and filling, the swirling mix of flavours produces a complex but satisfying experience. Both the nose and taste have a fruity blend of malt and bitter-sweet hoppiness with smoky overtones.

Lupus Lupus (ABV 5%)
A soft blackcurrant nose introduces this red coloured brew. Hops vie with bitterness in the initial taste. Fruity malt notes soon fade to leave a long bitter finish with just a hint of blackcurrant fruitiness.

Wolverhampton & Dudley

See Banks's, Jennings and Marston's in the New Nationals section

Wood SIBA

Wood Brewery Ltd, Wistanstow, Craven Arms, Shropshire, SY7 8DG
Tel (01588) 672523
Fax (01588) 673939
Email mail@woodbrewery.co.uk
Website www.woodbrewery.co.uk
Shop. Goods available at brewery, working hours and by mail
Tours by arrangement

⊗ The brewery opened in 1980 in buildings next to the Plough Inn, still the brewery's only tied house. Steady growth over the years included the acquisition of the Sam Powell Brewery and its beers in 1991. Building extension was completed in 2003 to enlarge fermentation, storage and office space. 2005 marked the brewery's silver anniversary. Production averages 60 barrels a week. 200 outlets are supplied. Seasonal beers: Summer That! (ABV 3.9%, June-Aug), Woodcutter (ABV 4.2%, Sept-Nov), Hopping Mad (ABV 4.7%, March-May), Christmas Cracker (ABV 6%, Nov-Dec). A monthly beer is also brewed.

Quaff (ABV 3.7%)
A pale and refreshing light bitter with a clean, hoppy finish.

Craven Ale (ABV 3.8%)
An attractively coloured beer with a pleasant hop aroma and a refreshing taste.

Parish Bitter (OG 1040, ABV 4%)
A blend of malt and hops with a bitter aftertaste. Pale brown in colour.

Special Bitter (OG 1042, ABV 4.2%)
A tawny brown bitter with malt, hops and some fruitiness.

Shropshire Lad (OG 1045, ABV 4.5%)
A strong, well-rounded bitter, drawing flavour from a fine blend of selected English malted barley and traditional English Fuggles and Golding hops.

Old Sam (OG 1047, ABV 4.6%)
A dark copper ale with a ripe, rounded flavour and hop bitterness.

Wonderful (OG 1048, ABV 4.8%)
A mid-brown, fruity beer, with a roast and malt taste.

Wooden Hand

Wooden Hand Brewery, Unit 2B, Grampound Road Industrial Estate, Grampound Road, Truro, Cornwall, TR2 4TB
Tel/fax (01726) 884596

Wooden Hand took over the plant from the former Ventonwyn Brewery. The company is run by Anglo-Swedish businessman Rolf Munding, who also owns the Zatec Brewery in the Czech Republic. 30 outlets are served direct.

Smugglers Gold (OG 1036, ABV 3.6%)

Black Pearl (OG 1039, ABV 4%)

Cornish Mutiny (OG 1048, ABV 4.8%)

Woodforde's SIBA

**Woodforde's Norfolk Ales,
Broadland Brewery, Woodbastwick,
Norwich, Norfolk, NR13 6SW
Tel (01603) 720353
Fax (01603) 721806
Email info@woodfordes.co.uk
Website www.woodfordes.co.uk**
Shop 10.30-4.30 Mon-Fri; 1130-430 weekends & Bank Holidays
Tours Tuesday and Thursday evenings

⊗ Founded in 1981 in Drayton near Norwich, Woodforde's moved to Erpingham near Aylsham in 1982, and then moved again to a converted farm complex, with greatly increased production capacity, in the picturesque Broadland village of Woodbastwick in 1989. A major expansion of Broadland Brewery took place in 2001-2002 to more than double production capacity and included a new brewery shop and visitor centre. Woodforde's brews an extensive range of beers and runs three tied houses with some 500 other outlets supplied on a regular basis. Bottle-conditioned beers: Wherry Bitter, Great Eastern, Nelson's Revenge, Admiral's Reserve, Norfolk Nog, Headcracker, Norfolk Nip. Admiral's Reserve was added to the range in 2002 to celebrate Woodforde's 21st anniversary.

Mardler's (OG 1035, ABV 3.5%)
A traditional Norfolk dark mild. A somewhat light blend of roast malt and chocolate sweetness with little body. Roast notes heighten as other flavours fade.

Kett's Rebellion
(OG 1034.4, ABV 3.6%)
Brewed to celebrate the 450th anniversary of Kett's land workers' rebellion, this moderately bitter session beer retains a hoppiness to the finish. Sweet caramel notes fade in the finish.

Wherry Best Bitter
(OG 1037.4, ABV 3.8%)
A complex explosion of aroma and flavour in this amber brew. Hops dominate throughout with fresh citrus support. Low key malt gives balance and counters a long, dryish finish.

Great Eastern (OG 1039.8, ABV 4.3%)
A light citrus bouquet introduces this gentle blend of toffee sweetness and dry hoppiness. Hop flavours fade quickly to leave a heavy, sweet fruitiness.

Nelson's Revenge
(OG 1042.7, ABV 4.5%)
Richly flavoured pale brown brew. Both taste and aroma are heavy with blackcurrant fruitiness and a bitter-sweet hoppiness. The finish sustains itself with a luxurious sherry-like dryness.

Norfolk Nog
(OG 1046.8, ABV 4.6%)
Dark red, with a deep roast character. Little bitterness in the dominant roast body. Liquorice appears in both flavour and nose. Lingering finish dominated by dried fruit.

Admiral's Reserve (OG 1050, ABV 5%)
A kaleidoscope of flavours. Malt and hops mix with strawberry jam and dark roast components. No dominant character but something for everyone. Increasing bitterness in flowing, sustained finish.

Headcracker (OG 1065.7, ABV 7%)
Surprisingly clean-tasting for a barley wine. A booming, plummy aroma buttressed with malt continues through to become the dominant taste throughout. A pleasant winey bitterness provides a counterpoint. A dry sultana plumminess provides a fitting finale.

Norfolk Nip (OG 1076, ABV 8.5%)
Dark mahogany in colour, this intensely flavoured beer has a stunning range of malts and hops enveloped by a warming balanced bitterness. This traditional dark barley wine is matured in the cask to develop the rich and robust flavours that give it a personality of its own. This beer benefits from long storage.

Woodlands*

**Woodlands Brewing Co, Unit 5 Creamery Industrial Estate, Station Road, Wrenbury, Nantwich, Cheshire, CW5 8EX
Tel (01270) 780730
Email woodlandsbrewery@aol.com**

A new brewery that opened in autumn 2004 with a five-barrel plant from the former Khean Brewery. The beers are brewed using water from a spring that comes to the surface of a peat field on nearby Woodlands Farm. Consideration is being given to moving the plant closer to the water source and possibly to add a still to enable the production of spirits. Seasonal beers: Summer Festival (ABV 4.2%), Autumn Gold (ABV 4.2%), Woodlands Winterland (ABV 5%).

Drummer Bitter (ABV 3.9%)

Full Boddied (ABV 4.2%)

Oak Beauty (ABV 4.2%)

IPA (ABV 4.3%)

Bitter (ABV 4.4%)

Midnight Stout (ABV 4.4%)

Special (ABV 4.8%)

Worfield

**Worfield Brewing Co, All Nations Brewhouse, Coalport Road, Madeley, Shropshire, TF7 6DP
Tel (01952) 585747**

Worfield started brewing in 1994 at the Davenport Arms and moved to Bridgnorth in 1998. Following the reopening of the All Nations in Madeley, the brewery produced Dabley Ale for the pub and subsequently brewer Mike

Handley moved his plant to the All Nations in 2004. 200 outlets are supplied. Seasonal beers: Hopstone Bitter (OG 1040, ABV 4%), Winter Classic (ABV 4.5%, January), Spring Classic (ABV 4.5%, March), Summer Classic (ABV 4.5%, June), Autumn Classic (ABV 4.5%).

OBJ (OG 1043, ABV 4.2%) ◆
A light and sweet bitter; delicate flavour belies the strength.

Shropshire Pride (OG 1045, ABV 4.5%)

For All Nations

Dabley Ale (OG 1039, ABV 3.8%)

George Wright

George Wright Brewing Co, Unit 11, Diamond Business Park, Sandwash Close, Rainford, St Helens, Merseyside, WA11 8LY
Tel (01744) 886686
Fax (01744) 752311
Email sales@georgewrightbrewing.co.uk
Website www.georgewrightbrewing.co.uk
Tours by arrangement

The George Wright Brewery started production in 2003. The original plant consisted of a 2.5-barrel system, but it soon became apparent that this was too small and a five-barrel brewing plant was installed. This has now been upgraded to 25 barrels and is fully computer controlled.

Long Boat (ABV 3.9%)

Wounded Goose (ABV 3.9%)

Winter Sun (ABV 4.2%)

Pipe Dream (ABV 4.3%)

IPA (ABV 4.5%)

Kings Shillin' (ABV 4.5%)

Cheeky Pheasant (ABV 4.7%)

Blackbeard Stout (ABV 5%)

Wychwood SIBA

Wychwood Brewery Ltd, Eagle Maltings, The Crofts, Witney, Oxfordshire, OX28 4DP
Tel (01993) 890800
Fax (01993) 772553
Email info@wychwood.co.uk
Website www.wychwood.co.uk
Shop Merchandise available on-line as above
Tours by arrangement

⊗ Wychwood Brewery is located in the Oxford Cotswolds on the fringes of the ancient medieval forest, The Wychwood. The brewery was founded in 1983 by two local characters, Paddy Glenny and Chris Moss, on a site dating back to the 1800s, which was once the original maltings for the town's brewery. The brewery, now owned by Refresh UK, has recently been renovated and expanded, and the site also includes the Brakspear Brewery (qv). The beers contain local water from the river Windrush and no additives are used. A range of seasonal beers is also produced, including the infamous Dog's Bollocks.

Shires Bitter (OG 1035, ABV 3.7%) ◆
A copper-coloured session beer with a fruity and malty aroma and admirable hop character. Good body for its strength. Fruit declines to a dry finish.

Fiddler's Elbow Bitter (OG 1042, ABV 4.5%) ◆
A spicy amber beer, complex, with a spicy hop aroma and a suggestion of cinnamon. Easy to drink, with a crisp and refreshing finish.

Hobgoblin (OG 1050, ABV 5%) ◆
Powerful, full-bodied, copper-red, well-balanced brew. Strong in roasted malt, with a moderate bitterness and a slight fruity character.

For Ushers pubs owned by InnSpired (qv)

Autumn Frenzy (OG 1038, ABV 4%)

Spring Fever (OG 1038, ABV 4%)

Summer Madness (OG 1038, ABV 4%)

Winter Storm (OG 1038, ABV 4%)

Wye Valley SIBA

Wye Valley Brewery, Stoke Lacy, Herefordshire, HR7 4HG
Tel 01885 490505
Fax 01885 490595
Email enquiries@wyevalleybrewery.co.uk
Website www.wyevalleybrewery.co.uk
Shop Mon-Fri 10-4pm
Tours by arrangement

⊗ Wye Valley Brewery was founded in 1985 in Canon Pyon, Herefordshire. The following year it moved to the old stable block of the Barrels pub in Hereford and 2002 saw another move to Stoke Lacy in the north of the county. During this move, the plant was expanded and upgraded and has a capacity to brew 80 barrels a day. There are plans for a bottling line. Two pubs are owned, with plans for more over the next few years. Some 350 outlets are supplied. Seasonal beers: DG Springtime Ale (ABV 4%, Feb-April), DG Summertime Ale (ABV 4.2%, May-July), DG Autumn Ale (ABV 4.4%, Aug-Oct), DG Winter Tipple (ABV 4.7%, Nov-Jan). Bottle-conditioned beers: DG Golden Ale, Butty Bach, DG Wholesome Stout ◼, Country Ale (ABV 6%).

Bitter (OG 1037, ABV 3.7%) ◆
A beer whose aroma gives little hint of the bitter hoppiness that follows right through to the aftertaste.

Hereford Pale Ale (OG 1040, ABV 4%) ◆
A pale, hoppy, malty brew with a hint of sweetness before a dry finish.

Dorothy Goodbody's Golden Ale (OG 1042, ABV 4.2%)
A light, gold-coloured, refreshing ale with a hint of malty sweetness from the pale crystal malt, balancing well with the aroma and flavour of the classic English hop varieties used.

Butty Bach (OG 1046, ABV 4.5%)
A burnished gold, full-bodied premium ale.

Dorothy Goodbody's Wholesome Stout (OG 1046, ABV 4.6%) ◻ ◆
A smooth and satisfying stout with a bitter edge to its roast flavours. The finish combines roast grain and malt.

Wylam SIBA

Wylam Brewery Ltd, South Houghton Farm, Heddon on the Wall, Northumberland, NE15 0EZ
Tel/Fax (01661) 853377
Email admin@wylambrew.co.uk
Website www.wylambrew.co.uk
Tours by arrangement

⊗ Built by John Boyle and Robin Leighton in 2000, Wylam started with a 4.5-barrel plant, which increased to nine barrels in 2002. Output has doubled every year. A new brewing hall was due to be built in 2005. The brewery delivers to more than 200 local outlets. Seasonal beer: Spring Thing (ABV 3.4%, spring), Hopping Mad (ABV 4.2%, autumn).

Hedonist (OG 1038, ABV 3.8%)

Bitter (OG 1039, ABV 3.8%) ◆
A refreshing, copper-coloured, hoppy bitter with a clean, bitter finish.

Gold Tankard (OG 1040, ABV 4%) ◆
Fresh, clean flavour, full of hops. This golden ale has a hint of citrus in the finish.

Magic (OG 1042, ABV 4.2%)

Whistle Stop (OG 1046, ABV 4.4%)

Bohemia (OG 1046, ABV 4.6%) ☐ ◆
Tawny in colour with a heady bouquet of malt and hops, and a deep finish of fruit.

Haugh (OG 1046, ABV 4.6%) ◆
A smooth velvet porter packed with flavour. Roast malt and a slight fruitiness provide a satisfying pint with a smooth finish.

Landlords Choice (OG 1046, ABV 4.6%)

Silver Ghost (OG 1050, ABV 5%)

Wyre Piddle

Wyre Piddle Brewery, Highgrove Farm, Peopleton, near Pershore, Worcestershire, WR10 2LF
Tel/Fax (01905) 841853

⊗ A brewery established in a converted stable by a former publican and master builder in 1992. Some 200 pubs in the Midlands take the beer. The brewery relocated and upgraded its equipment in 1997 and has now moved again to Highgrove Farm. It also brews for Green Dragon, Malvern: Dragon's Downfall (ABV 3.9%), Dragon's Revenge (ABV 4%). For Severn Valley Railway: Royal Piddle (ABV 4.2%). Seasonal beers: Piddle in the Sun (ABV 5.2%, summer), Yule Piddle (ABV 4.5%, Christmas).

Piddle in the Hole
(OG 1039, ABV 3.9%) ◆
Copper-coloured and quite dry, with lots of hops and fruitiness throughout.

Piddle in the Dark (ABV 4.5%)
A rich ruby-red bitter with a smooth flavour.

Piddle in the Wind (ABV 4.5%) ◆
This drink has a superb mix of flavours. A hoppy nose continues through to a lasting aftertaste, making it a good, all-round beer.

Piddle in the Snow (ABV 5.2%) ◆
A dry, strong taste all the way through draws your attention to the balance between malt and hops in the brew. A glorious way to end an evening's drinking.

Yates

Yates Brewery Ltd, Ghyll Farm, Westnewton, Wigton, Cumbria, CA7 3NX
Tel (016973) 21081
Email enquiry@yatesbrewery.freeserve.co.uk
Website www.yatesbrewery.co.uk
Tours by arrangement

◎ Established in 1986 in a range of outbuildings at Ghyll Farm, Westnewton, the brewery was bought in 1998 by Graeme and Caroline Baxter, who had previously owned High Force Brewery in Teesdale. More beers have been added to the range and direct distribution now includes Tyneside and Wearside, in addition to the traditional stronghold of the Lake District. 40 outlets are supplied. The brewery now bottles the beers on the premises.

Bitter (OG 1035, ABV 3.7%) ◆
A balanced beer with a sweet start that leads to hops and a long bitter finish.

Fever Pitch (OG 1039, ABV 3.9%)

No. 3 (OG 1040, ABV 4.2%)

Sun Goddess (OG 1042, ABV 4.2%)

Best Cellar (OG 1058, ABV 5.8%)

Yates' SIBA

Yates' Brewery, The Inn at St Lawrence, Undercliff Drive, St Lawrence, Ventnor, Isle of Wight, PO38 1XG
Tel (01983) 731731/07855 621599
Fax (01983) 731731
Email info@yates-brewery.fsnet.co.uk
Website www.yates-brewery.co.uk
Tours by arrangement

NEW BREWERIES

The following new breweries have been notified to the Guide and should come on stream during 2005/2006:

Allgate, Wigan
Atomic, Rugby
Barnwell, Yorkshire
Battledown, Cheltenham
Birnbeck, Somerset
Charlbury, Oxon
Chequers Inn, Norfolk
Cwrwraig, Cardiff
Dunkery, Somerset
Enfield, London
Leeming Waters, Yorkshire
Old Poets Corner, Ashover
Old Spot, Yorkshire
Purity, Warwickshire
Saltair, Yorkshire
Sherbourne, Dorset
Union, Devon
Vale of Glamorgan, Barry
Vinopolis, London
Watermill, Cumbria
Wear Valley, Bishop Auckland

David Yates previously worked for the original Burts Brewery in Ventnor, which went into receivership in 1992. He started brewing for Hartridge at the Island Brewery before installing his own five-barrel plant at St Lawrence. Brewing started in 2000 and he now supplies about 40 outlets. Seasonal beers: Little Bitter Spring (ABV 4.5%), Little Bitter Summer (ABV 4.5%), Little Bitter Autumn (ABV 4.5%), Wight Christmas (ABV 5.2%). Bottle-conditioned beers: as for all cask beers.

Bugle Best (OG 1039, ABV 3.8%)

Undercliff Experience (OG 1040, ABV 4.1%)
Traditional brown bitter

Holy Joe (OG 1050, ABV 4.9%)
Strongly bittered golden ale with pronounced spice and citrus character, and underlying light hint of malt.

Wight Winter (OG 1050, ABV 5%)

Special Bitter (YSD)
(OG 1056, ABV 5.5%)
Easy-drinking strong, amber ale with pronounced tart bitterness and a refreshing bite in the aftertaste.

Yetman's *

Yetman's Brewery, c/o Yetman's Restaurant, 37 Norwich Road, Holt, Norfolk, NR25 6SA
Tel (01263) 713320

A 2.5-barrel plant built by Moss Brew was installed in restored medieval barns in March 2005. The brewery supplies the restaurant and other local free trade outlets.

Yellow (ABV 3.5%)

Red (ABV 3.8%)

Orange (ABV 4.2%)

Green (ABV 4.6%)

Ynys Môn SIBA

Bragdy Ynys Mon/Isle of Anglesey Brewery, Cae Cwta Mawr, Talwrn, Anglesey, LL77 7SD
Tel/Fax (01248) 723801
Email martyn@angleseyale.co.uk
Website www.angleseyale.co.uk
Shop available when brewery open. Please ring
Tours by arrangement

Martyn Lewis started brewing in 1999 in a converted outbuilding of a farmhouse that faces the mountains of Snowdonia. A bottling plant has been added in a former stable. All the cask beers are available in bottle-conditioned form. Organic Sosban Fach and all bottled beers are made without finings, and are suitable for vegetarians and vegans.

Medra (OG 1039, ABV 4%)
Attractive-looking, copper-coloured, soft, malty bitter with hints of berries in the short, dry finish.

Wennol (OG 1040, ABV 4.1%)
The name means Swallow. Golden toned fruity beer with a lingering bitter finish.

Seuruik (OG 1042, ABV 4.2%)

Sosban Fach (OG 1043, ABV 4.3%)

Tarw Du (OG 1045, ABV 4.5%)
The name means Black Bull. Inviting black porter-style beer that has an earthy flavour with some chocolate/coffee notes and a long, dry aftertaste.

Amnesia (OG 1048, ABV 4.9%)
Full-bodied, rich hop and malt character throughout with a delectable aftertaste.

R.I.P.

The following breweries have closed, gone out of business, suspended operations or merged with another company since the 2005 Guide was published:

Alewife
Bodicote
Boston Experience
Breadalbane
Brysons
Featherstone
Garden Barber
Glossop
Haggards
John O'Gaunt
MacBride
Points West
Portchester
Smiles
Sweet William
Travellers Inn

York SIBA

York Brewery Co Ltd, 12 Toft Green, York, YO1 6JT
Tel (01904) 621162 Fax (01904) 621216
Email info@yorkbrew.co.uk
Website www.yorkbrew.co.uk
Shop Mon-Sat 12-6 daily
Tours Mon-Sun 12.30, 2.00, 3.30, 5.00 daily (Sun May-Sept)

York started production in 1996, the first brewery in the city for 40 years. It has a visitor centre with bar and gift shop. It is designed as a show brewery, with a gallery above the 20-barrel plant and viewing panels to fermentation and conditioning rooms. The brewery opened a pub on Stonegate in 2004, fronted by its own gift shop. In 2000, York, in partnership with the Tynemill pub company (qv), set up the Mildly Mad Pub Co and opened the Last Drop Inn in Colliergate, the Three Legged Mare in High Petergate and the Rook and Gaskill, Lawrence Street, which was voted the local CAMRA Pub of the Year for 2005. More than 400 pubs take the beers. Four pubs are owned and 200-plus outlets are supplied. Seasonal beers: see website.

Guzzler (OG 1036, ABV 3.6%)

Stonewall (OG 1037, ABV 3.7%)
A light amber bitter with little maltiness but strong hop and fruit aromas and flavours.

Yorkshire Terrier (OG 1041, ABV 4.2%)
Refreshing and distinctive, well-balanced fruit and hops on the aroma and taste, with a background of malt. Hoppy bitterness remains assertive in the aftertaste of this amber-gold brew.

Centurion's Ghost Ale
(OG 1051, ABV 5.4%) ◆
Dark ruby in colour, full-tasting with mellow roast malt character balanced by bitterness that lingers into the aftertaste.

Young's IFBB

Young & Co's Brewery plc, Ram Brewery, High Street, Wandsworth, London, SW18 4JT
Tel (020) 8875 7000
Fax (020) 875 7100
Email sales@youngs.co.uk
Website www.youngs.co.uk
Shop 11-6, Mon-Fri
Tours by prior arrangement

⊗ Beer has been brewed continuously alongside the River Wandle since 1581, making it the oldest site in Britain for continuous beer production. The brewery was bought by Charles Allen Young and Anthony Fothergill Bainbridge in 1831; the business was continued by the Young family and, while it's a public company, it remains very much a family affair. The company brews award-winning beers in the traditional manner and also produces up to four seasonal beers. 500-600 free-trade outlets are supplied. Young's tied estate stands at 206 pubs. The brewery has entered into talks with Wandsworth Council concerning the redevelopment of the town centre. The brewery is keen to emphasise there are no immediate plans to relocate the brewery and a feasibility study may take years to complete. Young's Bitter is available at most central London railway stations.
Bottle-conditioned beers: Special London Ale (ABV 6.4% ◼ ◻), Champion Live Ale (ABV 5%).

Bitter (OG 1036, ABV 3.7%) ◻ ◆
A light brown bitter beer that is well balanced by fruity citrus hop notes and some malt, finishing with a refreshing dryness.

Special (OG 1044, ABV 4.5%) ◆
Sweet citrus on the nose follows through into a malty, hoppy flavour with a dry bitter aftertaste and a touch of toffee.

Waggledance (OG 1052, ABV 5%) ◼ ◻ ◆
An amber beer with some honey on the nose and palate, but the sweetness is well balanced by hops, leaving a rich, fruity finish.

Winter Warmer (OG 1055, ABV 5%) ◼ ◻ ◆
A full-flavoured, ruby-black-brown beer with raisins, caramel and dark roast notes throughout, giving way to a typical Young's pleasant dry finish.

Zerodegrees SIBA

⌂ Zerodegrees Micro-brewery, 29-31 Montpelier Vale, Blackheath, London, SE3 0TJ
Tel (020) 8852 5619
Fax (020) 8852 4463
Email info@zerodegrees-microbrewery.co.uk
Website www.zerodegrees-microbrewery.co.uk

⊗ Brewing started in 2000 and incorporates a state-of-the-art, computer-controlled German plant, producing unfiltered and unfined ales and lagers, served from tanks using air pressure (not CO2). Five pubs are owned and a further five outlets are supplied. All beers are suitable for vegetarians and vegans.

Fruit Beer (OG 1042, ABV 4%)
The type of fruit used varies during the year.

Wheat Ale (OG 1042, ABV 4.2%)

Pale Ale (OG 1045, ABV 4.6%) ◆
A copper-coloured beer with a high level of bitterness tempered by some sweet fruit notes that linger in to a dry finish.

Pilsner (OG 1048, ABV 4.8%) ◆
Dry hoppy bitterness is overlaid with hints of grapefruit to produce a clean-tasting, refreshing beer that is served cold, hiding much of the aroma.

Black Lager (OG 1052, ABV 4.8%) ◆
A creamy, ruby-black beer with chocolate/coffee roast notes, with a dry finish balanced by a little sweetness.

Zerodegrees

⌂ Zerodegrees Micro-brewery, 58 Colston Street, Bristol, BS1 5BA
Tel (0117) 9252 706
Email info@zerodegrees-microbrewry.co.uk
Website www.zerodegrees-bristol.co.uk

⊗ A branch of Zerodegrees run along similar lines to the London brew-pub. There are regular monthly special beers, including fruit beers.

Wheat Beer (OG 1042, ABV 4.2%)

Pale Ale (OG 1045, ABV 4.6%)

Pilsner (OG 1048, ABV 4.8%)

Black Lager (OG 1052, ABV 4.8%)

FROM OVERSEAS

De Koninck

Brouwerij De Koninck NV, 291 Mechelsesteenweg, 2018 Antwerp, Belgium
Tel (0032) 3 218 4048
Email info@dekoninck.com
Website: www.dekoninck.be

Legendary Belgian brewer of a classic pale ale, founded in 1833. In its home territory the beer is served under pressure but a cask-conditioned version is now available in Wetherspoon's pubs in Britain. The beer is sent in tankers to Shepherd Neame in Faversham (qv) where it is fined and racked into casks. It is called Ambrée in Britain but is known simply as De Koninck in Belgium.

Ambrée (ABV 5%)

New nationals

Greene King and Wolverhampton & Dudley Breweries have been called 'super regionals' for some years as a result of their size and market share. But now their growth gives them the new status of national breweries. They do not match the size of the global brewers but they do reach most areas of Britain as a result of both their tied and free trade activities. Unlike the global producers or the old national brewers who disappeared in the 1990s, Greene King and W&D are committed to cask beer production. Greene King IPA, winner of the Bitter class in the 2004 Champion Beer of Britain competition, is the biggest-selling standard cask beer in the country while Marston's Pedigree now outsells Draught Bass in the premium sector. There is a down-side to this progress: in some parts of the country, the choice of real ale is often confined to the products of the two groups, and their continued expansion is cause for concern for drinkers who cherish choice and diversity.

Greene King

Greene King plc, Westgate Brewery, Bury St Edmunds, Suffolk, IP33 1QT
Tel (01284) 763222
Fax (01284) 706502
Email solutions@greeneking.co.uk
Website www.greeneking.co.uk
Shop Mon-Sat 10-5, Sun 12-4
Tours 11am, 2pm and evening by arrangements

⊠ Greene King has been brewing in the market town of Bury St Edmunds in the heart of rural Suffolk since 1799. It closed its Biggleswade brewery in Cambridgeshire in the late 1990s, where it brewed only lager, in order to concentrate on cask beer production. In the 1990s it bought the brands of the former Morland and Ruddles breweries and promotes them with some fervour, Old Speckled Hen in particular; the Ruddles beers bear little relationship to the former brews, either in taste or strength. As a result of buying the former Morland pub estate, the company acquired a major presence in the Thames Valley region. But it has not confined itself to East Anglia or the Home Counties. Its tenanted and managed pubs, which include Old English Inns and Hungry Horse, total more than 2,100 while the assiduous development of its free trade sales, totalling more than 3,000 outlets, means its beers can be found as far away from its home base as Wales and the north of England. City of London speculation in the early summer of 2005 linked Greene King with a possible bid for Belhaven of Dunbar in Scotland (qv). Belhaven, unusually for a Scottish brewer, has a large pub estate that would enable Greene King to build sales north of the border. In June 2004, Belhaven posted impressive annual profits that would not have gone unnoticed in Bury St Edmunds.
Bottle-conditioned beer: Hen's Tooth (ABV 6.5%).

IPA (OG 1036, ABV 3.6%) 🗍 ◆
A light, uncomplicated session bitter. Copper coloured with a subtle malty nose and just as hint of hops. A light bitter introduction with a sweetish, malty undertone give a refreshing, lemonade-type feel. A long, tapering finish turns drier and increases bitterness.

Ruddles Best Bitter (OG 1037, ABV 3.7%) ◆
An amber/brown beer, strong on bitterness but with some initial sweetness, fruit and subtle, distinctive Bramling Cross hop. Dryness lingers in the aftertaste.

Morland Original Bitter (OG 1039, ABV 4%)

Ruddles County (OG 1048, ABV 4.3%) ◆
Richer and slightly darker than Ruddles Best, this premium ale shares similar characteristics. Sweetness and fruit on the palate give way to bitterness and a distinctly hoppy, dry finish. Good body for its strength.

Abbot Ale (OG 1049, ABV 5%)
A full-bodied, very distinctive beer with a bitter-sweet aftertaste.

Old Speckled Hen (OG 1050, ABV 5.2%) ◆
Rich and cloying in both nose and taste, with an intense malty nose and plummy overtones. The flavour spectrum matches this with rich spicy maltiness overwhelming the latent bitterness. A solid mouthfeel helps retain the fruity sweetness as the heavy malt framework slowly turns to a light dryness.

Brewed by Ridleys (qv) for Greene King:

XX Mild (OG 1035, ABV 3%)

Wolverhampton & Dudley

Wolverhampton & Dudley Breweries plc, PO Box 26, Park Brewery, Wolverhampton, West Midlands, WV1 4NY
Tel (01902) 711811
Fax (01902) 429136
Website www.wdb.co.uk

Wolverhampton & Dudley has grown with spectacular speed in recent years. It became a 'super regional' in 1999 when it bought both Mansfield and Marston's breweries, though it quickly closed Mansfield. In May 2005 it bought Jennings of Cockermouth; despite opposition from CAMRA, which wrote to all Jenning's shareholders, the bid was accepted by the board. There was speculation that W&D would close the Jenning's site and transfer production to the Burtonwood Brewery, but in June 2005 the group announced it would invest £250,000 at Cockermouth to expand fermenting and cask racking capacity. However, drinkers can expect to find Marston's Pedigree on Jenning's bars in the near future. In total, W&D owns some 2,200 pubs and supplies some 3,000 free trade pubs and clubs throughout the country.

Banks's and Hanson's

Banks's Brewery, Park Brewery, Wolverhampton, West Midlands, WV1 4NY
Contact details as above.

Banks's was formed in 1890 by the amalgamation of three local companies. Hanson's was acquired in 1943 but its Dudley brewery was closed in 1991. Hanson's beers are now brewed in Wolverhampton, though its pubs retain the Hanson's livery. Banks's Original, the biggest-selling brand, is a fine example of West Midlands mild ale but the name was changed to give it a more 'modern' image. Beers from the closed Mansfield Brewery are now brewed at Wolverhampton.

Hanson's Mild Ale (OG 1035, ABV 3.3%)
A mid-to-dark brown mild with a malty roast flavour and aftertaste.

Mansfield Dark Mild (OG 1035, ABV 3.5%)

Riding Bitter (OG 1035, ABV 3.6%)

Banks's Original (OG 1036, ABV 3.5%)
An amber-coloured, well-balanced, refreshing session beer.

Bank's Bitter (OG 1038, ABV 3.8%)
A pale brown bitter with a pleasant balance of hops and malt. Hops continue from the taste through to a bitter-sweet aftertaste.

Mansfield Cask Ale (OG 1038, ABV 3.9%)

Burtonwood

Burtonwood Brewery, Burtonwood, Warrington: see also Thomas Hardy Burtonwood in Independents section.

The brewing equipment is owned by Thomas Hardy Burtonwood but the bricks and mortar of the site are now owned by W&D, which also controls the Burtonwood pub estate. THB brews beer for the pubs.

Jennings IFBB

Jennings Bros plc, Castle Brewery, Cockermouth, Cumbria, CA13 9NE
Tel 0845 1297185 Fax 0845 1297186
Website www.jenningsbrewery.co.uk
Shop 9-5 Mon-Fri, 10-4 Sat, 10-4 Sun (July & aug)
Tours by arrangement

Jennings Brewery was established as a family concern in 1828 in the village of Larton. The company moved to its present location in 1874, in the historic market town of Cockermouth, in the shadow of Cockermouth Castle, at the point where the rivers Cocker and Derwent meet. Pure Lakeland water is still used for brewing, drawn from the brewery's own well, along with Maris Otter barley malt and Fuggles and Goldings hops. A distribution centre in Workington services the brewery's estate of 127 pubs and 350 free trade houses. Seasonal beers: Wards (ABV 4%, Jan-Feb), Crag Rat (ABV 4.3%, March-April), Golden Host (ABV 4.3%, March-April), Redbreast (ABV 4.5%, Oct-Jan).

Dark Mild (OG 1031, ABV 3.1%)
A well-balanced, dark brown mild with a malty aroma, strong roast taste, not over-sweet, with some hops and a slightly bitter finish.

Bitter (OG 1035, ABV 3.5%)
A malty beer with a good mouthfeel that combines with roast flavour and a hoppy finish.

Cumberland Ale (OG 1039, ABV 4%)
A light, creamy, hoppy beer with a dry aftertaste.

Cocker Hoop (OG 1044, ABV 4.6%)
A rich, creamy, copper-coloured beer with raisiny maltiness balanced with a resiny hoppiness, with a developing bitterness towards the end.

Sneck Lifter (OG 1051, ABV 5.1%)
A strong, dark brown ale with a complex balance of fruit, malt and roast flavours through to the finish.

Marston's

Marston, Thompson & Evershed, Marston's Brewery, Shobnall Road, Burton upon Trent, Staffordshire, DE14 2BW
Tel (01283) 531131 Fax (01283) 510378
Website www.wdb.co.uk

Marston's has been brewing cask beer in Burton since 1834 and the current site is the home of the only working 'Burton Union' fermenters, housed in rooms known collectively as the 'Cathedral of Brewing'. Burton Unions were developed in the 19th century to cleanse the new pale ales of yeast. Fermentation takes place in giant oak casks linked by troughs and pipes. Fermenting wort and yeast rise up swan-necked pipes into the troughs above. The wort runs back into the casks but the yeast is trapped in the troughs. Only Pedigree is fermented in the unions but yeast from the system is used to ferment the other beers.

Burton Bitter (OG 1037, ABV 3.8%)
A light, fruity beer with a touch of roast. There is some bitterness later, but little aroma.

Pedigree (OG 1043, ABV 4.5%)
A hint of sulphur on the aroma leads to a hoppy and fruity taste and follows with a dry, bitter finish.

Old Empire (OG 1057, ABV 5.7%)
Sulphur dominates the aroma over malt. Stylish, copper-coloured beer, malty and sweet to start but developing bitterness with fruit and a touch of sweetness. A balanced aftertaste of hops and fruit leads to a lingering bitterness.

For Interbrew UK:

Draught Bass (OG 1043, ABV 4.4%)
An amber-coloured beer with a malt, hops and fruit aroma. A malty sweet and fruity start gives way to a hoppy/caramel mix followed by bitterness.

Global giants

Eight out of ten pints of beer brewed in Britain come from the international groups listed below. Most of these huge companies have little or no interest in cask beer. Increasingly, their real ale brands are produced for them by smaller regional brewers

Anheuser-Busch UK

Anheuser-Busch UK, Thames Link House, 1 Church Road, Richmond, Surrey, TW9 2QW. Tel (020) 8332 2302

The company brews 'American' Budweiser at the Stag Brewery, Lower Richmond Road, Mortlake, London SW14 7ET, the former Watneys plant. Budweiser, bottle, can and keg, is brewed from rice (listed first on the label), malt and hops, with planks of wood – the famous beechwood chips – used to clarify the beer. Not to be confused with the classic Czech lager, Budweiser Budvar.

Carlsberg UK

Carlsberg Brewing Ltd, PO Box 142, The Brewery, Leeds, West Yorkshire, LS1 1QG
Tel (0113) 259 4594
Fax (0113) 259 4000
E-mail via website
Website www.carlsberg.co.uk/carlsberg.com

Tetley, the historic Leeds brewery with its open Yorkshire Square fermenters, now answers to the name of Carlsberg UK: Carlsberg-Tetley was unceremoniously dumped in 2004. A wholly-owned subsidiary of Carlsberg Breweries of Copenhagen, Denmark, Carlsberg is an international giant best known for its pale lagers, though in Denmark it brews a large range of beers, including brown lagers and a porter-stout, all made by cold fermentation. In Britain its lagers are brewed at a dedicated plant in Northampton, while Tetley in Leeds produces ales and some Carlsberg products. Some 250,000 barrels are produced annually. Tetley's cask brands receive little or no promotional support, advertising being reserved for the nitro-keg version of Tetley's Bitter.

Tetley's Dark Mild (OG 1031, ABV 3.2%)
A reddish, mid-brown beer with a light malt and caramel aroma. A well-balanced taste of malt and caramel follows, with good bitterness and a satisfying finish.

Tetley's Mild (OG 1034, ABV 3.3%)
A mid-brown beer with a light malt and caramel aroma. A well-balanced taste of malt and caramel follows, with good bitterness and a satisfying finish.

Ansells Mild (OG 1035, ABV 3.4%)

Ansells Best Bitter (OG 1035, ABV 3.7%)

Tetley's Cask Bitter (OG 1035, ABV 3.7%)
A variable, amber-coloured light, dry bitter with a slight malt and hop aroma, leading to a moderate bitterness with a hint of fruit, ending with a dry and bitter finish.

Tetley's Imperial (ABV 4.3%)

Burton Ale (OG 1047, ABV 4.8%)
A beer with hops, fruit and malt present throughout, and a lingering complex aftertaste, but lacking some hoppiness compared to its Burton original.

Carlsberg also brews Greenalls Bitter (ABV 3.8%) for former Greenalls pubs supplied by wholesalers. Greenalls Mild has been discontinued.

Coors

Coors Brewers Ltd, 137 High Street, Burton upon Trent, Staffs, DE14 1JZ.
Tel (01283) 511000
Fax (01283) 513873
Website www.coorsbrewers.com

Coors of Colorado established itself in Europe in 2002 by buying part of the former Bass brewing empire, when Interbrew was instructed by the British government to divest itself of some of its interests in Bass. Coors owns several cask ale brands. It brews 110,000 barrels of cask beer a year (mainly under licensing arrangements with other brewers) and also provides a further 50,000 barrels of cask beer from other breweries. Coors closed the Mitchells & Butlers brewery in Birmingham in 2002. It has discontinued the premium Worthington's 1744, launched as a competitor to Draught Bass.

M&B Mild (OG 1034, ABV 3.2%)
Brewed under licence by Highgate Brewery, Walsall

Stones Bitter (OG 1037, ABV 3.7%)
Brewed for Coors by Everards

Hancock's HB (OG 1038, ABV 3.6%)
A pale brown, slightly malty beer whose initial sweetness is balanced by bitterness but lacks a noticeable finish. A consistent if inoffensive Welsh beer brewed for Coors by Brains.

Worthington's Bitter (OG 1038, ABV 3.6%)
A pale brown bitter of thin and unremarkable character.

M&B Brew XI (OG 1039.5, ABV 3.8%)
A sweet, malty beer with a hoppy, bitter aftertaste, brewed under licence by Brains of Cardiff.

Worthington's White Shield
(ABV 5.6%)
Brewed virtually unchanged since 1829. A bottle-conditioned IPA with a clean fruit aroma and a fruity/nutty taste.

White Shield Brewery

Horninglow Street, Burton upon Trent, Staffs, DE14 1YQ
Tel (0845) 6000598
Fax (01283) 513509
E-mail via website
Website www.coorsvisitorcentre.com
Shop (in Museum of Brewing) 9.30-4.30
Tours by arrangement

The White Shield Brewery – formerly the Museum Brewing Co – based in the Museum of Brewing, is part of Coors. Confusingly, while it brews White Shield, the beer is now a Coors brand (see above). The brewery opened in 1994 and recreates some of the older Bass beers that had been discontinued. The range has been drastically reduced in the past year, giving rise to fears about the future of the enterprise. The brewery dates from 1920 with some equipment going back to 1840. It has a maximum capacity of 60 barrels a week. Production is divided 50:50 between cask and bottled beers. P2 Imperial Stout and No 1 Barley Wine are now brewed on an occasional basis and in bottle only, though draught versions are supplied to CAMRA festivals when supplies are available.

St Modwen (OG 1037.5, ABV 4.2%)

Worthington E (OG 1043, ABV 4.8%)
Cask version of Bass's 1970s keg beer.

P2 Imperial Stout (ABV 8%)
Christmas pudding aroma, sweet and full bodied, with a dry liquorice finish that is dry, hoppy, mouth-watering and astringent.

No 1 Barley Wine (ABV 10.5%)
Unbelievably fruity! Thick and chewy, with fruit and sugar going in to an amazing complex of bitter, fruity tastes. Brewed in summer and fermented in casks for 12 months.

Guinness

Guinness Brewing GB, Park Royal Brewery, London, NW10 7RR

An Anglo-Irish giant, part of the Diageo drinks group, with world-wide brewing operations and distribution. It closed its London brewery in 2005 and the site will be demolished. All Guinness keg and bottled products on sale in Britain are now brewed in Dublin.

Interbrew

Interbrew UK Ltd, Porter Tun House, 500 Capability Green, Luton, Beds, LU1 3LS
A wholly-owned subsidiary of InBev of Belgium and Brazil
Tel (01582) 391166
Fax (01582) 397397
E-mail name.surname@interbrew.co.uk
Website www.interbrew.com

Interbrew of Belgium became the world's biggest brewer in 2004 when it bought Brazil's leading producer, Ambev, leapfrogging Anheuser-Busch in the production stakes. Its international name is now InBev. InBev is a major player in the European market with such lager brands as Stella Artois and Jupiler, and internationally with Labatt and Molson of Canada. It has some interest in ale brewing with the cask- and bottle-conditioned wheat beer, Hoegaarden, and the Abbey beer Leffe. It has a ruthless track record of closing plants and disposing of brands. In the summer of 2000 it bought both Bass's and Whitbread's brewing operations, giving it a 32 per cent market share. The British government told Interbrew to dispose of parts of the Bass brewing group, which were bought by Coors (qv). Draught Bass has declined to around 100,000 barrels a year: it once sold more than two million barrels a year, but was sidelined by the Bass empire. It is now brewed under licence by Marston's (see W&MD in New Nationals section). Only 30 per cent of draught Boddingtons is now in cask form and this is brewed under licence by Hydes of Manchester (qv Independents section). Interbrew has closed the Boddingtons plant despite stiff resistance from the trade unions and CAMRA.

Scottish Courage

2-4 Broadway Park, South Gyle Broadway, Edinburgh, EH12 9JZ
Tel (0131) 528 1000

A subsidiary of Scottish & Newcastle

Scottish Courage – the brewing arm of Scottish & Newcastle [S&N] – is Britain's biggest brewing group with close to 30 per cent of the market. S&N joined the ranks of the global brewers in 2000 when it bought Brasseries Kronenbourg and Alken Maes from the French group Danone; Kronenbourg is the biggest French beer brand and is exported internationally. Alken Maes is a major Belgian group that produces lagers and the Grimbergen abbey beer range. The group also has extensive brewing interests in Russia and the Baltic States through a consortium, BBH, formed with Carlsberg. BBH owns the biggest brewery in Russia, Baltika. S&N also has brewing interests in China, India and Portugal. The group has focused on Kronenbourg and its Baltic operations to such an extent that a major rationalisation of its brewing operations in Britain was announced in 2004, with the closure of both the Fountain and Tyne breweries. Scottish & Newcastle was formed in 1960, a merger between Scottish Brewers (Younger and McEwan) and Newcastle Breweries. In 1995 it bought Courage from its Australian owners, Foster's. Since the merger that formed Scottish Courage, the group has rationalised by closing its breweries in Nottingham, Halifax and the historic Courage [George's] Brewery in Bristol. The remaining beers were transferred to John Smith's in Tadcaster. In 2003 Scottish Courage announced it planned to sell its entire retail estate of 1,400 outlets in order to concentrate on brewing. It also bought the financially stricken Bulmer's Cider group, which included the Beer Seller wholesalers, now part of Waverley TBS. In 2003, S&N sold the Theakston's Brewery in Yorkshire back to the original family (see Theakston's entry in Independents section) but still brews some of the beer at John Smith's. In February 2004, S&N entered into an arrangement with the Caledonian Brewery in Edinburgh that gave S&N a 30% stake in Caledonian and 100% control of the brewery's assets (see Caledonian in the Independents). ScotCo's sole Scottish cask beer, McEwan's 80/-, is now brewed at Caledonian.

John Smith's

Scottish Courage Brewing Ltd, John Smith's Brewery, Tadcaster, North Yorkshire, LS24 9SA
Tel (01937) 832091
Fax (01937) 833766
Tours by arrangement.

The brewery was built in 1879 by a relative of Samuel Smith (qv). John Smith's became part of the Courage group in 1970. Major expansion has taken place since the formation of Scottish Courage, with 11 new fermenting vessels installed. Traditional Yorkshire Square fermenters have been replaced by conical vessels.

John Smith's Bitter
(OG 1035.8, ABV 3.8%) ◆
A copper-coloured beer, well-balanced but with no dominating features. It has a short hoppy finish.

Courage Best Bitter (OG 1038.3, ABV 4%) ◆
Pale brown beer with hops throughout and a bitter aftertaste.

Courage Directors Bitter
(OG 1045.5, ABV 4.8%) ◆
Fruity, medium-bodied, pale brown beer with hoppy and yeasty notes throughout.

For Theakston's of Masham (qv)

Theakston Best Bitter (OG 1038, ABV 3.8%)
A dry and metallic bitter with light hop character when fresh. Older samples lose character and end watery and pale.

Brewery organisations

There are three organisations mentioned in the Breweries section to which breweries can belong.

The Independent Family Brewers of Britain (IFBB) represents around 35 regional companies still owned by families. As many regional breweries closed in the 1990s, the IFBB represents the interests of the survivors, staging events such as the annual Cask Beer Week to emphasise the important role played by the independent sector.

The Society of Independent Brewers (SIBA) represents the growing number of small craft or micro brewers: some smaller regionals are also members. SIBA is an effective lobbying organisation and played a leading role in persuading the government to introduce Progressive Beer Duty. It has also campaigned to get large pub companies to take beers from small breweries and has had considerable success with Enterprise Inns, the biggest pubco.

The East Anglian Brewers' Co-operative (EAB) was the brainchild of Brendan Moore at Iceni Brewery. Finding it impossible to get their beers into pub companies and faced by the giant power of Greene King in the region, the co-op makes bulk deliveries to the genuine free trade and also sells beer at farmers' markets and specialist beer shops.

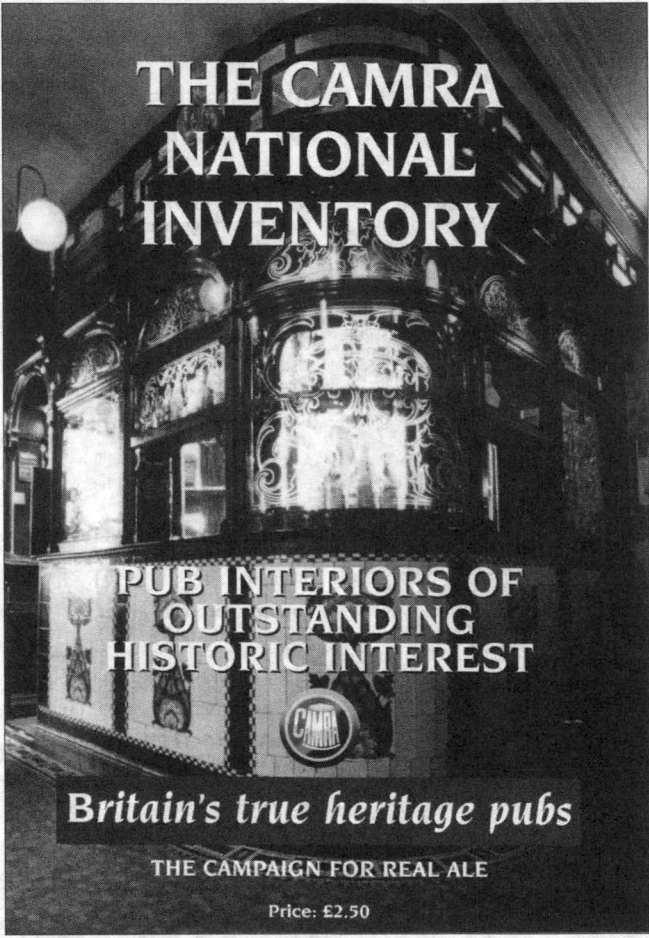

Pub Groups

Pubs groups or 'pubcos' [pub companies] dominate beer retailing in Britain but, with the exception of Wetherspoon, tend not to brand their outlets. The national brewers have disengaged from running pubs, preferring to sell beer to the pub groups. As a result of the deep discounts demanded by the pubcos, most sell beers mainly from the nationals, thus restricting drinkers' choice, and forming a barrier to regional and micro-breweries. The market is dominated by three giant pub companies: Enterprise, which acquired the Unique chain, Mitchells & Butlers (the former Bass managed pubs), and Punch, which merged with Pubmaster. These groups act like supermarkets: buying heavily-discounted national brands in large volumes and selling them at inflated prices, though, due to lobbying by the Society of Independent Brewers, Enterprise does now stock beers from smaller breweries in selected outlets. There are some independent companies that are committed to cask beer: * after a company's name indicates it's an independent pub group that focuses on cask.

Avebury

Avebury Taverns Ltd, Sterling House, 20 Station Road, Gerrards Cross, Bucks, SL9 8EL
Tel (01753) 482600
Fax (01753) 482601
Website www.averburypubs.co.uk

Avebury operates 800 tenanted and leased pubs throughout England and Wales. All pubs trade as independent free houses with tenants able to choose 'market-leading brands' supplied by national, regional and local brewers. Its main suppliers are Coors, Carlsberg, Interbrew, and Scottish Courage. Cask beers include Marston's Pedigree. Bought by Punch (qv) in July 2005.

Barracuda

Barracuda Group Ltd, Henley Road, Medmenham, Marlow, Bucks, SL7 2ER
Tel (0845) 345 2528
Fax (0845) 345 2527
Email makeadifference@barracudagroup.co.uk
Website www.barracudagroup.co.uk

Barracuda was formed in 2000. It runs 135 managed outlets. The main pub brands in Barracuda are the 20-strong Smith & Jones chain and Varsity student bars. It takes its main cask beers from Adnams, Coors, Interbrew, Greene King, and Scottish Courage.

Barter

Barter Inns, 132 Gypsy Hill, London, SE19 1PW
Tel/fax (020) 8670 7001.
Email barterinns@aol.com

Barter has 28 managed pubs in the South-east. It takes ales from Interbrew and Scottish Courage, but its best-selling beer is Fuller's London Pride.

Botanic Inns

Botanic Inns Ltd, 261-263 Ormeau Road, Belfast, North Ireland, BT7 3GG
Tel (0289) 0509 700

Botanic runs nine bars, two hotels and two off-licences. It takes extremely limited amounts of cask beer from unspecified suppliers.

Brakspear

W H Brakspear & Sons plc, The Bull Courtyard, Bell Street, Henley-on-Thames, Oxon, RG9 2BA.
Tel (01491) 570200
Fax (01491) 570201
E-mail information@brakspear.co.uk
Website www.brakspear.co.uk

A pub company that emerged from the ashes of a much-loved Henley brewery. The directors quit brewing in 2002, selling the prime site in Henley for £10 million to make way for luxury apartments overlooking the Thames. It sold the brands to Refresh UK: see Brakspear in Independent Breweries section. The company runs 100 pubs. The only cask beers sold are the Brakspear brands now brewed at Witney.

Brunning & Price*

Brunning & Price, Yew Tree Farm Buildings, Saighton, Chester, CH3 6EG.
Tel (01244) 333100 Fax (01244) 333110
Website www.brunningandprice.co.uk

Runs 12 managed pubs in the North-west. The company is committed to cask beer; its managers and tenants are free to choose their beers but are encouraged to support independents and micros. Customers may find Hydes, Ossett, Robinsons, Rooster and Phoenix. See website for the company's beer page.

Bulldog

Bulldog Pubs Co, 6-8 Bridge Street, Boston, Lincolnshire, PE21 8QF
Tel (01205) 355522
Fax (01205) 355534
Email kevin.charity@bpcgroup.co.uk
Website www.bpcgroup.com

Formed in 1996, Bulldog runs 16 pubs in the Midlands and East Anglia.

Burtonwood

Burtonwood plc, Bold Lane, Burtonwood, Warrington, WA5 4PJ
Tel (01925) 225131 Fax (01925) 229033
Email seyles@burtonwood.co.uk
Website www.burtonwood.co.uk

Burtonwood's 400 pubs, the majority of which are traditional tenancies, were sold to Wolverhampton & Dudley Breweries in 2005. The brewery is owned by Thomas Hardy Burtonwood, which brews Burtonwood brands for the pub estate (qv Independent breweries sections). Fewer than half the Burtonwood pubs stock cask beer but the number is expected to increase under the new owner.

Caledonian Heritable

Caledonian Heritable, 4 Hope Street, Edinburgh, EH2 4DB.
Tel (0131) 220 5511
Fax (0131) 225 6546
Email ga@caleyheritable.co.uk

A group with 290 pubs, all in Scotland. Beers come mainly from Scottish Courage, but the best-selling ale is Caledonian Deuchars IPA.

Camelot

Camelot Inns & Taverns, 22 Bancroft, Hitchin, Hertfordshire, SG5 1JS
Tel (01462) 455188
Fax (01462) 455099
Email mikek@camelotinns.fsnet.co.uk

Formed in 1993, Camelot runs 12 managed pubs in Hertfordshire and North-east London.

Capital*

Capital Pub Co, 131 Waterloo Road, London SE1 8UR
Tel (020) 7401 9876 Fax (020) 7928 1880
Email enquiries@capitalpubcompany.com
Website www.capitalpubcompany.com

Formed in 2000 by veteran pub owner David Bruce of Firkin brew-pub fame. It runs 10 managed pubs in London.

Cascade

Cascade Public House Management, 5 Merlin Way, Bowerhill, Melksham, Wiltshire, SN12 6TJ
Tel (01225) 704734) Fax (01255) 790770
Email cascade@blueyonder.co.uk

Formed in 1993, it runs 14 managed pubs in South-west England.

Catmere

Catmere Group, Bridge House, Station Road, Scunthorpe, Lincolnshire, DN15 6PY
Tel (01724) 861703
Fax (01724) 861708

Catmere owns 10 pubs in Leicestershire and Lincolnshire. Five serve cask beer from both national and regional brewers.

CCT Group

CCT Group/Jack Beard, 76 Mitcham Road, Tooting, London, SW17 9NG.
Tel (020) 8767 8967
Fax (020) 8767 3675
Email admin@jackbeards.co.uk

A South-east based company with 34 managed pubs operating under the Jack Beards name. Beer is supplied by Scottish Courage and Greene King.

Celtic*

Celtic Inns, c/o TradeTeam, Nutsey Lane, Calmore Industrial Estate, Totton, Hampshire, SO40 3NB.
Tel (02380) 666111
Fax (02380) 865472
Email mail@celticinns.co.uk
Website www.celticinns.co.uk

Formed in 2002, Celtic runs 52 pubs in Wales and has a strong commitment to cask beer.

Chapman

Chapman Group, Syon House, High Street, Angmering, West Sussex, BN16 4AG.
Tel (01903) 856744 Fax (01903) 856816)
Email vicki@thechapmansgroup.co.uk
Website www.thechapmansgroup.co.uk

Formed in 1978, Chapman runs 24 pubs in southern England and Gloucestershire.

Churchill

Churchill Taverns Group, Avon House, Tithe Barn Road, Wellingborough, Northamptonshire, NN8 1DH
Tel (01933) 222110
Fax (01933) 277006
Email frwpjm@churchilltaverns.freeserve.co.uk

Formed in 1997, Churchill runs 17 managed pubs in Northamptonshire.

Clark

Clark Pub Co, 6a Western Corner, Edinburgh, EH12 5PY
Tel (0131) 466 7190 Fax (0131) 466 7074
Email info@clarkpubco.co.uk
Website www.clarkpubs.com

Formed in 1997, Clark runs four pubs in Scotland. It sold eight outlets to London & Edinburgh in 2003.

Tom Cobleigh

Tom Cobleigh, Spencer House, Cliftonville Road, Northampton, NN1 5BU
Tel (01604) 745000
Fax (01604) 745001

Established in 1992 with just two pubs, the estate grew to 75 across England. The company was taken over by the Rank Group in 1996 but was bought back by its management. It was then sold to Spirit Group (qv) for £106 million

Conquest Inns

14 Theobald Steet, Borehamwood, Hertfordshire, WD6 4SE

A company owned by CI Traders (formerly Ann Street Brewery of Jersey) with 66 pubs in London, the South-east and East Anglia, it was bought by Punch for £261 million.

county estate management

County Estate

County Estate Management, 9 Harley Street, London W1G 9QF
Tel (020) 7436 2080 Fax (020) 7436 1040
Email mail@countyestate.co.uk
Website www.countyestate.co.uk

County Estate runs 650 pubs nationwide. It takes beers mainly from Coors and has its own supply company. Many houses serve cask beer.

JT Davies

JT Davies & Sons Ltd, 7 Aberdeen Road, Croydon, Surrey, CR0 1EQ
Tel (020) 8681 3222 Fax (020) 8760 0390
Email postbox@jtdavies.co.uk
Website www.jtdavies.co.uk

Wine merchants now controlling 46 tenancies and leased houses in the South-east. Its main suppliers are Interbrew and Scottish Courage, with some beers from Fuller's and Harveys. In June 2002, the company bought a 28% share in Henley pub company W H Brakspear.

Davy

Davy & Co, 59-63 Bermondsey Street, London, SE1 3XF
Tel (020) 7407 9670 Fax (020) 7407 5844
Email info@davy.co.uk
Website www.davy.co.uk

Wine merchants and shippers since 1870, Davy has been opening wine bars and restaurants in the London area since 1965, taking previously unlicensed properties and creating a Dickensian, sawdust, nooks-and-crannies type of establishment. Its Davy's Old Wallop (ABV 4.8%) is a re-badged brew of undeclared origin (though Courage Directors fits the bill). This is usually served in pewter tankards or copper jugs. The company currently runs around 45 outlets, including a few pubs.

Dorbiere

Dorbiere Public Houses, Patricroft, Eccles, Manchester, M30 0RJ
Tel (0161) 707 7787 Fax (0161) 789 6713
Email enquiries@lwc-drinks.co.uk

Dorbiere runs 29 pubs in the North of England.

Dukedom

Durkedom Leisure, Victoria House, Pearson Court, Pearson Way, Teesside Park, Thornaby, TS17 6PT
Tel (01642) 808500 Fax (01642) 808511
Email enquiries@dukedom.co.uk

Dukedom runs 27 managed pubs in the Midlands and North-east England.

Eldridge Pope

Eldridge Pope & Co plc, Weymouth Avenue, Dorchester, ST1 1QT
Tel (01305) 251251 Fax (01305) 258300
Email enquiries@eldridge-pope.co.uk
Website www.eldridge-pope.co.uk

Founded as the Green Dragon Brewery in 1837, Eldridge Pope divorced itself from brewing in 1996 when it split into two wings, the brewing side becoming known as Thomas Hardy Burtonwood, with breweries in Burtonwood and Dorchester; Dorchester closed in 2003. The pub company, with 182 outlets, was bought in 2004 by Michael Cannon. Cannon has a long track record in the industry of buying groups of pubs and eventually selling them on. EP has supply agreements with Coors, Interbrew and Scottish Courage.

Elizabeth Holdings

Elizabeth Holdings, Merchant House, 33 Fore Street, Ipswich, Suffolk, IP4 1JL
Tel (01473) 217458 Fax (01473) 258237
Email info@elizabethholdings.co.uk

Formerly Ryan Elizabeth Holdings, the company runs 63 pubs in East Anglia, many bought from national brewers. Some pubs are tied to Interbrew. Other suppliers are Adnams, Greene King and Nethergate.

English Inns*

English Inns, 5 Mill Meadow, Langford, Bedfordshire, SG18 9UR
Tel (01462) 701750
Email burlisoninns@aol.com

Formely Burlison Inns, English owns seven pubs in Bedfordshire, Cambridgeshire, Hertfordshire and Warwickshire. Its main cask beer supplier is Everards and it also takes beers from B&T, City of Cambridge, Nethergate, and Tring.

Enterprise Inns

Enterprise Inns plc, 3 Monkspath Hall Road, Solihull, West Midlands, B90 4SJ
Tel (0121) 733 7700 Fax (0121) 733 6447

Formed in 1991 with an initial acquisition of 372 pubs from Bass, the company has grown rapidly and is now Britain's biggest pub group. In 2002 it bought the former Whitbread tenanted pub estate known as Laurel Inns, and it has consolidated its position by adding the Unique pub estate from Nomura. Enterprise previously purchased pubs from John Labatt Retail, Discovery Inns, Gibbs Mew, Mayfair Taverns,

Century Inns (Tap & Spile), and Swallow Inns. Enterprise added to this number by buying 439 former Whitbread pubs, and then in 2001 bought 432 managed houses from Scottish & Newcastle. Its current estate numbers 9,400. A range of cask beers from all the major brewers, as well as many of the regionals, is available through the Enterprise central distribution network.

Fitzgerald*

Sir John Fitzgerald Ltd, Cafe Royal Buildings, 8 Nelson Street, Newcastle upon Tyne, NE1 5AW
Tel (0191) 232 0664
Fax (0194) 261 4509
Website www.sjf.co.uk

Long-established, family-owned property and pubs company. Its pubs convey a free house image, most offering a good choice of cask beers, including guest ales from smaller craft breweries. The 28 pubs are mainly in the North-east but there are also outlets in Edinburgh, Harrogate and London.

G1

G1 Group, 62 Virginia Street, Glasgow, G1 1DA.
Tel (0141) 552 4494.
Fax (0141) 552 3730.
Website www.g1group.co.uk

G1 owns 22 managed pubs in Scotland.

Gray*

Gray & Sons (Chelmsford) Ltd, Rignals Lane, Galleywood, Chelmsford, Essex, CM2 8RE
Tel (01245) 475181 Fax (01245) 475182

Former Chelmsford brewery that ceased production in 1974 and which now supplies its 49 tied houses in Essex with a choice of cask beers from Adnams, Greene King and Mighty Oak. The tenants are also free to choose from a monthly guest list that features at least 10 different ales.

Great British Pub Co

Great British Pub Company, Redhill House, Hope Street, Salthey, Cheshire, CH4 8BU
Tel (01244) 678780
Fax (01244) 682667
Email info@gbpubco.co.uk

Formed in 1998, the company runs an estate of 35 managed pubs in Yorkshire. It sold 25 pubs in 2003.

Head of Steam*

Head of Steam Ltd, Manesty, Leazes Lane, Hexham, Northumberland, NE46 3AE.
Tel/Fax (01434) 607393
Email tony@theheadofsteam.co.uk
Website www.theheadofsteam.com

Founded by CAMRA activist Tony Brookes, Head of Steam has pubs based on railway station concourses at London Euston, Huddersfield, Newcastle-on-Tyne, and Liverpool. All the outlets serve a wide range of cask beers.

Heavitree

Heavitree Brewery plc, Trood Lane, Matford, Exeter, EX2 8YP
Tel (01392) 217733
Fax (01392) 229939

A West Country brewery, established in 1790, which gave up production in 1970 to concentrate on running pubs. The current estate, which is mainly confined to Devon, stands at 103. The pubs are tied to beers from Interbrew.

Heritage

Heritage Pub Co, Donnington House, Riverside Road, Pride Park, Derby, DE24 8HY
Tel (01332) 384808
Fax (01332) 384818
Email firstname@heritagepubs.com

Heritage runs 231 tenanted pubs in the East Midlands. Its main suppliers are Hardy's & Hansons and Interbrew. Its best-selling cask beer is Marston's Pedigree. The company was bought in July 2005 by Robert Tchenguiz of Laurel and Yates.

Honeycombe*

Honeycombe Leisure, Marian House, Beech Grove, Preston, Lancashire, PR2 1DU
Tel (01772) 723764
Fax (01772) 722470
Email firstname.surname@honeycombe.co.uk
Website www.honeycombe.co.uk

Formed in 1976, Honeycombe bought the Devonshire Pub Co in 2000 and now has 95 houses. Beers are supplied by the nationals plus Burton Bridge, Eccleshall, Moorhouses, Phoenix and Timothy Taylor, and most micro-brewers in the North-west. It is one of the biggest sellers of Black Sheep.

Inns & Leisure

Inns & Leisure, 20-24 Leicester Road, Preston, Lancashire, PR1 1PP.
Tel (01772) 252917 Fax (01772) 204543
Email inns@dial.pipex.com

Inns & Leisure, formed in 1970, runs 30 pubs in Cumbria, Lancashire and Yorkshire.

InnSpired

InnSpired Pubs & Taverns, Wiltshire Drive, Trowbridge, Wiltshire, BA14 0TT
Tel (01225) 763171
Fax (01225) 715120
Email ploader@innspired.co.uk
Website www.innspired.co.uk

InnSpired represents the remains of Ushers of Trowbridge, a famous West Country brewery founded in 1824. It has an estate of 1,022 pubs. InnSpired's landlords can offer a wide range of beers, often from local breweries.

Interpub

Interpub, c/o the Stag, Hawthorn Lane, Burnham Beeches, Buckinghamshire, SL2 3TA.
Tel (01753) 647603 Fax (01753) 647604
Email office@interpub.co.uk
Website www.interpub.co.uk

Formed in 1996, Interpub runs 14 pubs in London, Cornwall and Scotland.

Inventive

Inventive Leisure, 21 Old Street, Ashton-under-Lyne, Lancashire, OL6 6LA
Tel (0161) 330 3876 Fax (0161) 343 7144
Email neil@revolution-bars.co.uk
Website www.revolution-bars.co.uk

Formed in 1990, Inventive runs 36 managed pubs nationwide.

Kingdom

Kingdom Taverns, Dean House, 191 Nicol Street, Kirkcaldy, Fife, KY1 1PF
Tel (01592) 200033 Fax (01592) 200044

Formed in 1972, Kingdom has a pub estate of 36 in Scotland.

Laurel

Laurel Pub Co, Porter Tun House, 500 Capability Green, Luton, Bedfordshire, LU1 3LS
Tel 07002 528735 Fax (01582) 540698
Email communications@laurelpubco
Website www.laurelpubco.com

Laurel was created in 2001 by Morgan Grenfell/Deutsche Bank, who bought the Whitbread pub estate. Laurel sold the tenanted pubs to Enterprise Inns (qv) a year later, but kept the managed houses, including the Hogshead chain. They are being re-branded as Hogs Head and no longer specialise in cask beer. The company was bought in 2005 by Robert Tchenguiz who then added the Yates's estate of 149 pubs for £202 million. Christopher Hutt, who ran CAMRA's pubs in the 1970s and more recently Wizard Inns, is now chairman of Laurel.

Lionheart

Lionheart Inns, Porter Black Holdings, 7 Market Street, Newton Abbot, Devon, TQ12 2RJ
Tel (01626) 882000 Fax (01626) 882001
Email admin@lionheartinns.co.uk
Website www.lionheartinns.co.uk

Lionheart runs 33 managed pubs throughout the country.

London & Edinburgh

London & Edinburgh Group, 4 Clarendon Place, King Street, Maidstone, Kent, ME14 1BQ
Tel (01622) 685200 Fax (01622) 687555
Email name@londoninns.com

Formed in 1996, London & Edinburgh has an estate of 712 pubs nationwide.

Luminar

Luminar, 41 King Street, Luton, Bedfordshire, LU1 2DW
Tel (01582) 589400 Fax (01582) 589401
Email firstname.lastname@luminar.co.uk
Website www.luminar.co.uk

Formed in 1987, Luminar's pubs and bar were on the market as the guide went to press.

Maclay*

Maclay Group plc, The e-Centre, Cooperage Wat Business Village, Alloa, FK10 3LP{
Tel (01259) 272087 Fax (01259) 272088
Email mail@maclay.co.uk

Maclay, founded in 1830, stopped brewing in 1999. It owns 17 managed pubs and supplies them with cask ales under the Maclay name brewed by Belhaven (qv).

McManus

McManus Taverns, Kingsthorpe Road, Northampton, NN2 6HT
Tel (01604) 713601 Fax (01604) 7902209
Email enquiry@mcmanuspub.co.uk
Website www.mcmanuspub.co.uk

Company formed in 1970 with 22 pubs in the East Midlands. Half serve cask beer mainly from ScotCo and Wadworth.

Market Town Taverns*

Market Town Taverns, 6 Green Dragon Yard, Knaresborough, North Yorkshire, HG5 8AU.
Tel (01423) 866100
Email office@markettaverns.co.uk
Website www.markettowntaverns.co.uk

Run by CAMRA member Ian Fozard, the group owns eight pubs in North and West Yorkshire. It concentrates on beers from independent and micro-breweries, including Black Sheep and Timothy Taylor.

massiveunbranded*

Massive

Massive Pub Co, Central House, 124 High Street, Hampton Hill, Middlesex, TW12 1NS
Tel (020) 8977 0633 Fax (020) 8288 1502
Email peter@massivepub.com
Website www.massivepub.com

Formed in 1993, Massive owns 39 pubs in London, Surrey and Hampshire.

Mercury

Mercury Management (UK) Ltd, Mercury House, 19-20 Amber Business Village, Amington, Tamworth, Staffordshire, B77 4RP
Tel (01827) 62345 Fax (01827) 64166
E-mail headoffice@mercurymanagement.co.uk
Website www.mercurymanagement.co.uk

Mercury Management is the result of a 1999 buy-out of Mercury Taverns. It has slimmed down its estate from 45 pubs to 16.

Mill House

Mill House Inns, Berkeley House, Fallon Close, Quedgeley, Gloucestershire, GL2 4LY
Tel (01452) 887222
Fax (01452) 887333
Website www.millhouseiins.co.uk

Mill House has 60 managed pubs nationwide, ranging from town bars to country pubs and family pub-diners. Its main supply agreement is with Interbrew.

Mitchells & Butlers

Mitchells & Butlers plc, 27 Fleet Street, Birmingham, B3 1JP
Tel 0870 609 3000
fax (0121) 233 2246
Email communications@mbplc.com
Website www.mbplc.com

M&B is the new name for Six Continents, the former Bass pub estate. When the Bass empire was sold off, Coors closed the giant M&B Brewery in Birmingham but a year later the name resurfaced as a pub company. M&B owns more than 2,000 pubs, bars and restaurants. Its brands include Vintage Inns, Ember Inns, and Goose. All these pubs serve cask beer and Ember also holds mini-beer festivals. Most pubs stock Draught Bass and also offer a choice of cask beers from Coors and some regional breweries.

Morrells

Morrells of Oxford Ltd, Ferry Hinskey Road, Osney Mead Industrial Estate, Oxford, OX2 0ES
Tel (01865) 263000
Fax (01865) 791868

Morrells of Oxford was bought by Greene King in June 2002 for £60 million, from Michael Cannon, who bought the 132 pubs from Morrells. The pubs are all that remain of the once much-loved Oxford brewery that closed in 1998 following a boardroom split and the eviction of two members of the Morrell family. Morrells beers are brewed by Burtonwood (qv).

New Century

New Century Inns, Belasis Business Centre, Coxwold Way, Billingham, TS23 4EA
Tel (01642) 343415 Fax (01642) 345729
Email NCI@newcenturyinns.co.uk
Website www.newcentury inns.co.uk

Formed in 1999, New Century owns 40 pubs in Yorkshire and the North-east.

Noble House

Noble House Pub Co, Alma Road, Windsor, Berkshire, SL4 3HD
Tel (01753 483800 Fax (01753) 624660
Email mail@noblehouseleisure.com

A subsidiary of Noble House Leisure. The group is run by Robert Breare, who masterminded the exit from brewing by Ushers of Trowbridge to become the pub company InnSpired (qv). Noble House owns 90 managed pubs.

Old English

Old English Inns was bought by Greene King in 2001.

Pub Estate

Pub Estate Co Ltd, Blenheim House, Foxhole Road, Ackhurst Park, Chorley, Lancashire, PR7 1NY
Tel (01257) 238800 Fax (01257) 238801
Email info@pub-estate.co.uk
Website www.pub-estate.co.uk

A company established with the purchase of 230 pubs from Scottish & Newcastle, it currently has 510 pubs nationwide. The pubs offer beers from Coors, Interbrew, Carlsberg and Scottish Courage.

Pubs 'n' Bars

Pubs 'n' Bars, Sandwood House, 10-12 Weir Road, London, SW12 0NA
Tel (020) 8228 4800 Fax (020) 8675 1950

Formed in 1990, the group owns 66 pubs within the M25, Wales and the West Country.

Pubmaster

See Punch

Punch Group

Punch Taverns, Jubilee House, Second Avenue, Burton upon Trent, Staffordshire, DE14 2WF
Tel (01283) 501600 Fax (01283) 501601
Email firstname.lastname@punchpubs.co.uk
Website www.punchtaverns.com

Punch was formed in 1998 by a team led by Hugh Osmond, founder of Pizza Express, with the purchase of the Bass leased pub estate. In 1999, Punch, with the backing of Bass, bought Allied Domecq's pub estate. It sold 550 former managed houses to Bass, now Mitchells & Butlers (qv). In 2004, Punch merged with Pubmaster, creating an estate of more than 8,000 pubs. Punch claims its lessees are free to take guest beers, but brewers who supply the group are closely monitored and have to offer substantial discounts to be accepted. The main cask ales sold by Punch are Tetley and Worthington, with guest ales from a number of regionals.

Pyramid

Pyramid Pub Co Ltd, Suite H3, Steam Mill Business Centre, Steam Mill Street, Chester, CH3 5AN
Tel (01244) 321171
Fax (01244) 317665
Email amandab@pyramidpub.co.uk
Website www.pyramidpub.co.uk

Pyramid manages 433 pubs. It was formerly known as Paramount and bought its estate from Royal Bank of Scotland. The pub estate is widely spread, mainly in towns and cities. Beers are supplied by Burtonwood, Interbrew, Scottish Courage and Wolverhampton & Dudley. Banks's is the leading cask ale.

Randall Vautier

Randall Vautier Ltd, PO Box 43, Clare Street, St Helier, Jersey, JE4 8NZ
Tel (01534) 887788
Fax (01534) 888350
Email firstname.lastname@randalls.je

A brewery that ceased production in 1992. It now runs 30 pubs on Jersey selling beers from Interbrew, Scottish Courage, and Marston's. Not to be confused with Randalls of Guernsey (see Independents).

Regent Inns

Regent Inns plc, 77 Muswell Hill, London, N10 3PJ
Tel (020) 8375 3000
Fax (020) 8375 3001
Email firstname.lastname@regent-inns.plc.uk
Website www.regentinns.co.uk

Founded in 1980, Regent owns 70 managed pubs in London and the Home Counties. Most of the pubs are unbranded, are allowed to retain their own identities, and are not tied to any supplier. Most pubs feature a wide range of national, local and seasonal cask ales chosen by managers. The company has contracts with Coors, Interbrew and Scottish Courage plus half a dozen regional breweries, but licensees can also take beer from the Beer Seller wholesaler. Branded pubs include Walkabout Inns and Jongleurs.

Scorpio Inns

Scorpio Inns Ltd, Commerce House, Abbey Road, Torquay, TQ2 5PJ
Tel (01803) 296111
Fax (01803) 296202

Formed in 1991, it ran 111 pubs (nearly all tenanted). It was bought by Punch in 2002.

SFI

SFI Group plc, SFI House, 165 Church Street East, Woking, Surrey, GU21 1HJ
Tel (01483) 227900
Fax (01483) 227903
Website www.sfigroup.co.uk

Established in 1986, the SFI Group, formerly Surrey Free Inns, runs 146 pubs and café bars in England, Scotland and Wales. Beers come from national brewers and a range of smaller regional brewers. Cask ale is a feature of the Litten Trees outlets. Not all the pubs are branded: around 20, such as the historic Ostrich Inn, at Colnbrook, near Heathrow, have kept their own identity. The company went into liquidation in 2005 and Laurel (qv) bought 98 of the pubs.

Spirit

Spirit Group, 107 Station Road, Burton upon Trent, Staffordshire, DE14 1BZ
Tel (01283) 545320 Fax (01283) 502357
Email info@thespiritgroup.com
Website www.thespiritgroup.com

The new name (previously Punch Retail) for the managed pubs of the Punch Group. It's based in the former offices of Allied Domecq and operates 1,046 pubs. There was speculation in summer 2005 that Punch or M&B might buy the group.

Tadcaster Pub Company

Tadcaster Pub Co, Commer Group Ltd, Commer House, Station Road, Tadcaster, North Yorkshire, LS24 9JF
Tel (01937) 833311
Fax (01937) 834236
E-mail commer@commer.co.uk
Website www.commer.co.uk

The company has scaled down its pub operation from 75 to just five outlets but plans to buy a further 20.

Taverna Inns

Taverna Inns, Marquis of Granby, Main Street, Hoveringham, Nottinghamshire, NG14 7JR
Tel (0115) 966 5566
Email tavernainns@freuk.com

Formed in 1990, Taverna owns 30 in the Midlands, Lincolnshire and NE England.

Thorley Taverns

Thorley Taverns, 60 Gladstone Road, Broadstairs, Kent, CT10 2HZ
Tel (01843 602010 Fax (01843) 866333
Email ho@thorleytaverns.com
Website www.thorleytaverns.com

Founded in 1971, Thorley operates 40 managed pubs in Kent and London.

Tynemill*

Tynemill Ltd, 2nd Floor, Victoria Hotel, Dovecote Lane, Beeston, Nottingham, NG9 1JG
Tel (0115) 925 3333 Fax (0115) 922 6741

Founded by former CAMRA chairman Chris Holmes, Tynemill has been established in the East Midlands for more than 20 years, and now owns 17 pubs. It has a 'pubs for everyone' philosophy, avoiding trends and gimmicks, and concentrating on quality cask ales and food in good surroundings, including public bars where space permits. It sold more than 1,500 different cask ales during 2000, thought to be more than anyone else in the industry. Managers have complete autonomy on guest beers they sell. During 2000, Tynemill entered into two joint ventures: the Mildly Mad Pub Co with York Brewery, to develop an estate in the York region, and with Breakthroughpoint in Nottingham. Tynemill is now the sole owner of the Castle Rock Brewery in Nottingham (qv).

Wellington

Wellington Pub Co,
c/o Criterion Asset Management Ltd,
Beechwood Place,
Thames Business Park, Wenman Road,
Thame, Oxfordshire, OX9 3XA
Tel (01844) 262200
Fax (01844) 262208
Email tim.crouch@criterionasset.co.uk
Website www.criterionasset.co.uk

A private company running 840 leased pubs nationwide. It is chaired by Hugh Osmond, founder of Pizza Express, who also formed the Punch Group.

Wessex Taverns

Wessex Taverns, 6 Telford Court, Morpeth,
Northumberland, NE61 2DB
Tel (01670) 503333
Fax (01670) 503344
Email pam@wessextaverns.co.uk
Website www.wessextaverns.co.uk

Formed in 1990, Wessex operates 40 managed pubs in NE England, East Anglia and southern England.

Wetherspoon*

JD Wetherspoon plc,
Wetherspoon House, Central Park,
Reeds Crescent,
Watford, Hertfordshire, WD24 4QL
Tel (01923) 477777
Fax (01923) 219810
Website www.jdwetherspoon.co.uk

Wetherspoon is a vigorous and independent pub retailer that currently owns more than 600 managed pubs. No music is played in any of the pubs, all offer no-smoking areas – some are completely non-smoking – and food is served all day. Each pub stocks regional ales from the likes of Cains, Fuller's, Greene King and Wolverhampton & Dudley, plus at least two guest beers. There are usually two beer festivals a year, one in the spring, the other in the autumn, at which up to 30 micro-brewery beers are stocked over a four-day period. Wetherspoon joined the Cask Marque scheme in 2000 and now enjoys CM accreditation in more than 435 pubs. The group also owns the Lloyds No 1 chain.

Wharfedale

Wharfedale Taverns Ltd,
Highcliffe Court, Greenfold Lane,
Wetherby,
West Yorkshire, LS22 6RG
Tel (01937) 580805
Fax (01937) 580806
E-mail
wharfedale_taverns@compuserve.com
Website www.wharfdaletaverns.co.uk

A company set up in 1993 by former Tetley employees to lease 90 pubs from that company, it currently owns 32 pubs, mainly in the north. The main beers come from Carlsberg; guest beers are from the Tapster's Choice range.

Wizard Inns

The company and its 63 pubs were sold in 2004 to Wolverhampton & Dudley for £89.9 million.

Yates's

Company founded in Oldham in 1884 by wine merchant Peter Yates, was sold in 2005 to Laurel Inns (qv).

Zelgrain

Zelgrain, The Five Ways Rooms,
146 Springfield Road, Brighton,
East Sussex, BN1 6BZ
Tel (01273) 550000
Fax (01273) 550123
Website www.zelnet.com

Zelgrain was formed in 1995 and operates 33 pubs in South-east England.

Real bottled beer

In August 2004 CAMRA launched an accreditation scheme for bottle-conditioned beers. Brewers who have joined the scheme can use the logo shown here as a sign that their beers contain live yeast. See the CAMRA website: www.camra.org.uk

The beers index

Over 2,500 beers are listed. They refer to beers in bold type in the breweries section

C

D

G

H

I

J

K

L

M

N

O

P

Q

R

S

T

U

V

W

X

Crown Liquor Saloon, Belfast

Readers' recommendations

Suggestions for pubs to be included or excluded

All pubs are surveyed by local branches of the Campaign for Real Ale. If you would like to comment on a pub already featured, or any you think should be featured, please fill in the form below (or copy it), and send it to the address indicated. Your views will be passed on to the branch concerned. Please mark your envelope with the county where the pub is, which will help us to sort the suggestion efficiently.

Pub name:

Address:

Reason for recommendation/criticism:

Pub name:

Address:

Reason for recommendation/criticism:

Pub name:

Address:

Reason for recommendation/criticism:

Your name and address:

Pub name:

Address:

Reason for recommendation/criticism:

Pub name:

Address:

Reason for recommendation/criticism:

Pub name:

Address:

Reason for recommendation/criticism:

Pub name:

Address:

Reason for recommendation/criticism:

Your name and address:

Please send to: [Name of county] Section, Good Beer Guide,
230 Hatfield Road, St Albans, Hertfordshire AL1 4LW

Support the Campaign. Purchase official CAMRA merchandise and clothing!

Mousemat
£3.00

CAMRA Embroidere
T-shirt
£9.50
Sizes M-XXL
blue, black or red

Cuddly Toy
£8.95

Rugby Shirt
£27.50
Sizes M-XXL
black or red

Full range displayed on the CAMRA website:
www.camra.org.uk/shop

Life is Simple
Black T-shirt
£8.50
Sizes M-XXL

Carry Keg
£4.95

Order Form

Quantity	Item	Size/Colour	Price	Total
		Postage		
		Total		

Card Number	
Expiry Date	
Issue Number	
Name	
Date	
Signature	
Membership Number	
Address	
Postcode	
Telephone Number	

- Postage is included in all prices for UK customers
- Please add £2 per item in the European Union
- Please add £4 per item Rest of the World

- Please return this form with your card details or a cheque made payable to CAMRA to: CAMRA, 230 Hatfield Road St Albans, Herts, AL1 4LW.

- Orders can also be placed over the phone on 01727 867201, or via our website www.camra.org.uk/shop where you can see the full range of clothing and merchandise.

- We deliver your order as soon as possible. We will normally send your order within 10 business days. This could extend to 15 days in peak periods.

An offer for CAMRA members
GOOD BEER GUIDE
Annual Subscription

Being a CAMRA member brings many benefits, not least the big discount on the Good Beer Guide. Now you can take advantage of an even bigger discount on the Guide by taking out an annual subscription.

Simply fill in the form below and the Direct Debit form opposite (photocopies will do if you don't want to spoil your book), and send them to CAMRA at the usual St Albans address.

You will then receive the *Good Beer Guide* automatically every year. It will be posted to you before the official publication date and before any other postal sales are processed.

You won't have to bother with filling in cheques every year and you will receive the book at a lower price than other CAMRA members (for instance, the 2005 Guide was sold to annual subscribers at only £8.50).

So sign up now and be sure of receiving your copy early every year.

Note: This offer is open only to CAMRA members and is only available through using a Direct Debit instruction to a UK bank (use the form opposite, or copy it if you do not want to spoil your book). This offer applies to the 2007 *Guide* onwards.

Name

CAMRA Membership No.

Address and Post code

I wish to purchase the *Good Beer Guide* annually by Direct Debit and I have completed the Direct Debit instructions to my bank which are enclosed.

Signature Date

Instruction to your Bank or Building Society to pay by Direct Debit

Please fill in the form and send to: Campaign for Real Ale Ltd. 230 Hatfield Road, St. Albans, Herts. AL1 4LW

Name and full postal address of your Bank or Building Society

To The Manager — Bank or Building Society

Address

Postcode

Name (s) of Account Holder (s)

Bank or Building Society account number

Branch Sort Code

Reference Number

Originator's Identification Number

9	2	6	1	2	9

FOR CAMRA OFFICIAL USE ONLY
This is not part of the instruction to your Bank or Building Society

Membership Number

Name

Postcode

Instruction to your Bank or Building Society

Please pay CAMRA Direct Debits from the account detailed on this Instruction subject to the safeguards assured by the Direct Debit Guarantee. I understand that this instruction may remain with CAMRA and, if so, will be passed electronically to my Bank/Building Society

Signature(s)

Date

Banks and Building Societies may not accept Direct Debit Instructions for some types of account

detached and retained this section

This Guarantee should be detached and retained by the payer.

The Direct Debit Guarantee

- This Guarantee is offered by all Banks and Building Societies that take part in the Direct Debit Scheme. The efficiency and security of the Scheme is monitored and protected by your own Bank or Building Society.
- If the amounts to be paid or the payment dates change CAMRA will notify you 7 working days in advance of your account being debited or as otherwise agreed.
- If an error is made by CAMRA or your Bank or Building Society, you are guaranteed a full and immediate refund from your branch of the amount paid.
- You can cancel a Direct Debit at any time by writing to your Bank or Building Society. Please also send a copy of your letter to us.

It takes all sorts to campaign for real ale

Join by Direct Debit and get three months' membership FREE!

CAMRA, the Campaign for Real Ale, is an independent, not-for-profit, volunteer-led consumer organisation. We actively campaign for full pints and longer licensing hours as well as protecting the local pub and lobbying government to champion pub-goers' rights.

CAMRA has 77,000 members from all ages and backgrounds, brought together by a common belief in the issues that CAMRA deals with and their love of good quality British beer. For just £18 a year, that's less than a pint a month, you can join CAMRA and enjoy the following benefits:

- A monthly newspaper informing you about beer and pub news and detailing events and beer festivals around the country.
- Free or reduced entry to over 140 national, regional and local beer festivals.
- Money off many of our publications including the Good Beer Guide.
- Access to a members' only section of our national website, www.camra.org.uk, which gives up-to-the-minute news stories and includes a special offer section with regular features saving money on beer and trips away.
- The opportunity to campaign to save pubs under threat of closure, for pubs to be open when people want to drink and a reduction in beer duty that will help Britain's brewing industry survive.

Do you feel passionately about your pint? Then why not join CAMRA?

Just fill in the application form (or a photocopy of it) and the Direct Debit form on the previous page to receive three months' membership FREE! If you wish to join but do not want to pay by Direct Debit, please fill in the application form below and send a cheque, payable to CAMRA, to: CAMRA, 230 Hatfield Road, St Albans, Hertfordshire AL1 4LW.

Please tick appropriate box

Single Membership (UK &EU)	**£18**	☐
Under 26 membership	**£10**	☐
Over 60 membership	**£10**	☐

■ For joint membership add £3 (For concessionary rates both members must be eligible for the membership rate). ■ Life membership information is available on request.

If you join by Direct Debit you will receive three months' membership extra free!

Title ______ Surname ______

Forename (s) ______

Address ______

______ Post Code ______

Date of Birth ______ E-mail address ______

Signature ______

Partners details if required

Title ______ Surname ______

Date of Birth ______ E-mail address ______

☐ Please tick here if you would like to receive occasional e-mails from CAMRA, (at no point will your details be released to a third party).

Find out more about CAMRA at www.camra.org.uk